AMERICAN PUBLIC SCHOOL LAW

FIFTH EDITION

Kern Alexander

M. David Alexander

WEST

THOMSON LEARNING ™

Australia • Canada • Mexico • Singapore • Spain • United Kingdom • United States

WEST

THOMSON LEARNING

Education Editor: Dan Alpert
Associate Development Editor: Tangelique Williams
Editorial Assistant: Alex Orr
Marketing Manager: Becky Tollerson
Marketing Assistant: Ingrid Hernandez
Project Editor: Trudy Brown
Print Buyer: Mary Noel

Permissions Editor: Bob Kauser
Production Service: Lachina Publishing Services
Copy Editor: Lachina Publishing Services
Compositor: Lachina Publishing Services
Text and Cover Printer: R.R. Donnelley and Sons,
    Willard

Library of Congress Cataloging-in-Publication Data

Alexander, Kern.
    American public school law / Kern Alexander,
    M. David Alexander.--5th ed.
        p. cm.
    Includes index.
    ISBN 0-534-57744-X (hardcover)
    1. Educational law and legislation--United States.
    I. Alexander, M. David. II. Title.

KF4118 .A39 2001
344.73'071--dc21   00-049949

Wadsworth/Thomson Learning
10 Davis Drive
Belmont, CA 94002-3098
USA

For more information about our products, contact us:
Thomson Learning Academic Resource Center
1-800-423-0563
http://www.wadsworth.com

International Headquarters
Thomson Learning
International Division
290 Harbor Drive, 2nd Floor
Stamford, CT 06902-7477
USA

UK/Europe/Middle East/South Africa
Thomson Learning
Berkshire House
168-173 High Holborn
London WC1V 7AA
United Kingdom

Asia
Thomson Learning
60 Albert Street, #15-01
Albert Complex
Singapore 189969

Canada
Nelson Thomson Learning
1120 Birchmount Road
Toronto, Ontario M1K 5G4
Canada

To our wives, Elizabeth and Nancy

ABOUT THE AUTHORS

Kern Alexander was the lead author of this text when it was first published in 1969 under the title of *Public School Law* and he has either authored or co-authored all subsequent editions. Dr. Alexander is a widely published author in the fields of education law and finance. During his career he has served as Professor of Educational Administration at the University of Florida for two decades, and later as University Distinguished Professor at Virginia Tech. He has also been President of Western Kentucky University and is currently President of Murray State University, Kentucky. He takes an active role throughout the United States in litigation involving equity in school finance.

M. David Alexander is Professor and Chair of the Department of Educational Leadership and Policy Studies, Virginia Tech. Dr. Alexander has authored or co-authored several books and many chapters and articles in the area of education law. He has taught public school law and college and university law for nearly thirty years and is widely consulted on issues pertaining to education law and arbitration.

CONTENTS IN BRIEF

CONTENTS

TABLE OF CASES

The principle cases are in bold type. Cases cited or discussed in the text
are roman type. References are to pages. Cases cited in principal cases and
within other quoted materials are not included.

PREFACE

THIS FIFTH EDITION of *American Public School Law*, dated 2001, marks over three decades that this book has been published, the first publication being dated 1969. The book is intended for graduate students studying education or students in law schools who desire a comprehensive view of the law that governs the public school system of America. The legal precedents presented and discussed herein deal with the multitude of issues occurring in a country that has developed an extraordinary reliance on the public schools as a mechanism for social and economic justice and improvement. The desire to educate the nation's masses to a high degree of competency has resulted in the emergence of public schools as the common ground of learning for all backgrounds and persuasions. An undertaking of the pervasive magnitude of public schools, involving such an amalgam of people, is naturally fertile ground for conflicting human differences and perceptions. This book is about those conflicts that were not resolvable through the normal political processes and ultimately required judicial resolution. What the courts have said in enunciating legal precedents is valuable information for all those involved with the public schools.

The public education system in America is large, diverse, and, unlike most European systems, federalistic in nature, with all fifty states having unique origins that add strength and vitality to the whole. Because of the decentralized nature of our educational structure, it is often difficult to identify any single rule of law

that prevails in all states. Even with the great sweep of constitutional precedents that have developed under the hand of the Supreme Court of the United States, the law governing our schools can frequently be difficult to accurately assess and summarize. Beyond constitutional law, which is more focused because the Supreme Court can give the final word, we have a large mass of law pertaining to contracts, property, torts, general administrative law, and so on, which all bear on the administration of the schools. Also, substantial variation may be found from state to state, not merely because of the differing statutory bases, but also because of widely varying perspectives and philosophies of education that the judges themselves may have in viewing particular school litigation; and, of course, the social contexts of the cases may have strong influences on the outcome of particular disputes.

Therefore, the reader of this book should keep in mind that the authors have had to select cases from among the hundreds of jurisdictions in this country that appear to best exemplify the prevailing view of the courts in the various areas of law. The precedents identified by the authors may not neatly fit the numerous situations and conditions that can exist in all the local school districts across the nation. For this reason, the reader is well advised to carefully compare the precedents in the book with the rule of law in his or her own locality before drawing conclusions. Also, as explained in the first chapter of the text, the reader should, at all times, realize that the facts of the case are of utmost importance, and small variations in facts may result in very large differences in the rule of law.

This book employs the "case" or "discussion" method of teaching the law. Over the years, this approach to instruction has been largely used in business schools and law schools and has been found to be a very effective instructional device for immersing the student in the learning process. This method enables the instructor to depart from merely lecturing or "telling" about the law and instead employ a more Socratic method to facilitate classroom discussion. Using this approach, the instructor, assisted by the text, encourages a classroom dialectic, invoking discussion to discover and expose the reasoning of the law. Here, the instructor can circumscribe the issue for the students and then, by questioning, probing, and challenging, bring forth the rules of law. This technique allows each student to relate a rule of law to a particular set of facts that will clarify or distinguish the educational dispute in question. By relating concrete factual situations to the law, students will be better able to recognize similar experiences when they encounter them as practicing teachers or school administrators. For the fledgling educator, the study of actual cases may well substitute for actual experience and prevent costly repetition. In some instances, a more comprehensive knowledge of both education and the law may prevent resorting to the courts for redress. Employment of the case approach gives the student the opportunity to study the law in a setting where the consequences of misjudgment are not so great. Learning by discussing and examining the experiences of others is of course not new; in 1570, Roger Ascham observed in his dissertation entitled *The Schoolmaster* that "learning teacheth more in one year than experience in twenty; and learning teacheth safely, when experience maketh more miserable than wise. He hasardeth sore that waxeth wise by experience. . . . It is costly wisdom that is brought by experience." The case method in conveying not only the rule of law but also the litigious factual experiences of earlier educators provides an inexpensive method of learning valuable lessons.

An effort is made herein to present an encompassing book, ranging across civil, criminal, and constitutional laws as they touch the student, teacher, and administrator. Several chapters in the book may be of primary interest to teachers who are directly concerned with such matters as curriculum, tenure, contracts, student rights, and collective bargaining. These aspects of the law are also essential information for the school administrator, though the administrator may also have a vital interest in the law of finance, property, desegregation, and intergovernmental relations. It is with cognizance of the needs of all educators that additional and separate chapters are included on various topics. Because of the profusion of litigation that has emanated from federal statutes in recent years, separate chapters are provided for issues concerning the education of the handicapped and employment discrimination. In total, the book represents an attempt to convey to the educator a fully comprehensive treatment of the law, regardless of whether it emerges from common law, statute, or constitutional law.

This fifth edition evidences the inexorable march of new precedents that continue to form the law of education. The evolution of the law gives new shape to the public schools that emerge from the social forces that prescribe and portend the direction of the law. Contained therein is a discernible pattern of the ebb and flow of student and teacher rights and freedoms that ultimately define the nature and context of the public schools. It would be redundant to discuss here all the text modifications from the earlier editions that reveal these changes, yet a few are particularly noteworthy. This edition reflects an apparent general pattern of a growing reticence of today's increasingly conservative judiciary to resist expansion of the latitude of student and teachers in the exercise of their rights and freedoms. One can distinguish a hesitancy on the part of courts to add new meaning of constitutional rights and freedoms while expending increased energy on the interpretation of the extensive array of federal statutes that affect education policy. Also, as observed in the last edition, there appears to be a greater tendency for the courts to revert to the logic of common law precedents for their rationale. From this discussion one can see the redefinition of students' constitutional rights as the federal courts in the last decade appeared to grasp for rationale found in earlier common law concepts to address constitutional law issues. For example, the freedom of the press provisions applicable to student newspapers now appear to have sought stability by substantial reliance on earlier common law precedents. Additional precedents regarding students' security against illegal search and seizure and drug testing, as well as the various applications of substantive and procedural due process, find solid ground in the earlier rationale of common law. This book devotes extensive discussion to the considerations of the rights of disabled children as delineated by Congress through the Individuals with Disabilities Education Act (IDEA), including the amendments of 1997. What constitutes the definition of a least-restrictive environment in the context of school placement, the attendant ramifications for the extended school year, and the restraints on discipline of handicapped children are all subjects of new and expanded treatment in the text. Of particular concern, too, is, of course, the modern plague, acquired immunodeficiency syndrome (AIDS), and the application of the law to those children affected by this dread disease.

The employment of teachers and its multifaceted ramifications is addressed in this new edition. In this context, the book deals with the nature of the teacher/school board employment relationship as affected by Title VII. Moreover, the Supreme Court's decision in *Connick* leads to a dissection of freedom of speech in schools into public and private contexts that has led to a plethora of new litigation, with the predictable result of more narrowly circumscribing exercise of teachers' rights of speech.

Also, this new edition elucidates the emerging perspective of the Supreme Court on church/state relations. As observed in the fourth edition, recent precedents suggest a movement toward diminishing the uniquely American "wall of separation." The Rehnquist Court's interpretation of the establishment clause of the First Amendment clearly indicates a new doctrine that would allow for expanded use of public tax dollars for parochial schools. The emergent theory maintains that the founding fathers intended that the state could aid religious institutions so long as it did not prefer one over another. This means, of course, state tax money

could conceivably flow to parochial schools as it does to public schools so long as one religion is not favored nor given advantage over another. This interpretation of the establishment clause is far afield from earlier Supreme Court precedents.

Further, this new edition reveals that the courts are tending to be more restrained in their view of curricular and instructional matters, exhibiting a reemerging reluctance of less activist courts to intervene in school board decisions. This judicial deference to school boards concerning curricular matters suggests the possibility of newfound strength of school boards establishing and implementing school policy.

Finally, developments in several other areas of the law have stimulated additions of new sections of the book, including discussions of the Supremacy Clause, the Eleventh Amendment, sovereign powers of states, charter schools, and the refinement of the legal definition of free public schools, as well as questions surrounding the equality of financial resources among local school districts. Extensive expansion of law is found in sections of the book concerning federal civil rights statutes that prohibit racial, sexual, religious, and age discrimination in public school employment. Additional discussion is devoted to sexual harassment and Title IX issues, as indicated by prevailing precedents that affect students, teachers, and administrators. Sexual harassment, in its many shapes and forms, is shown to be an area of the law that is expanding very rapidly, and new precedents are continually creating new law.

In acknowledging those most helpful and responsible for the completion of this fifth edition, the authors are, of course, more aware than ever of the generous support of our wives, who with faithful understanding have persevered with good humor, thoughtful encouragement, and an abiding faith that the project would at some point actually be completed.

The authors are furthermore most appreciative of the good and able assistance of the fine staff at Wadsworth/Thomson Learning. In particular we wish to acknowledge thoughtful attention given to this project by editors Dianne Lindsay and Dan Alpert, who worked closely with the authors in the overall conduct and direction of the project. Special thanks is also extended to Trudy Brown, Tangelique Williams, and Becky Tollerson, who provided prompt and thoughtful advice and counsel in all aspects of the revision process. Too, the highly competent copyediting and proofreading by the production house, Lachina Publishing Services, was without peer as to accuracy in both the technical aspects and the substantive considerations of the text. The authors also wish to acknowledge the excellent work of Elaine Clark, project manager at Lachina Publishing Services, who carried the project with such a high degree of professional efficiency, as she had also done earlier with the fourth edition. The assistance of Elizabeth Degenhard is also gratefully recognized for her intervention and assistance in serving as complementary project manager for Lachina Publishing Services to bring the book to press.

Projects of this magnitude always require the unremitting dedication of a central figure who coordinates the entire endeavor from the authors' side of the process. In this instance that principal player was Bridgette Garrison, to whom the authors owe a great debt of gratitude. Her work in bearing much of the technical burden of legal research, information retrieval, copyediting, verification of endnotes, and other essential details was indeed critical throughout the many months of revision. Again, we would like to acknowledge and thank Shenette Campbell for her earlier work on the fourth edition and for her general advice and support of the current edition. Too, as with the last edition, Pat Bryant, Virginia Tech, provided ready assistance in all phases of the manuscript preparation as she had previously done with two earlier editions of the book, and we are most appreciative to her for her good services. Others who played important roles include Sandra Dika and Mike Perry of Virginia Tech, to whom we wish to extend our many thanks.

Finally, we wish to recognize several of our colleagues at other universities who have over the years reviewed and have, therefore, significantly contributed to the book as it stands today. As in all endeavors in our lives and institutions, we stand on the achievements of those who have gone before us, and this book is no exception. The comments, counsel, and advice of these thoughtful professors regarding various aspects of both the third and fourth editions of the book have enabled the authors to produce a much improved fifth edition. For this result and to this end we are especially grateful to the following professors: Jerry Austin, Eastern Kentucky University; Carol Baker, Northwest Missouri State University; David Bowick, Pepperdine University; Frank Brown, University of North Carolina at Chapel Hill; Martha Bruckner, University of Nebraska at Omaha; Donald V. Cairns, Montana State University; Paul F. Caraher, Tennessee State University; Mary Jane Connelly, University of Tennessee; John Cook, Governors State University; Gayle Ecton, Western Kentucky University; Richard Flynn, Murray State University; Richard Fossey, Louisiana State University; Gene Gallegos, California State University at Bakersfield; George Garrett, Governors State University; Dean Grant, DeKalb County Board of Education; Warren Hodge, University of North Florida; Robert B. Lowe, Angelo State University; John McLaughlin, St. Cloud State University; Richard Middleton III, Jackson State University; Kenneth T. Murray, University of Central Florida; Earl Ogletree, Chicago State University; Joyce Pigge, Bethany College; William T. Rebore, St. Louis University; Steve Ross, North Georgia College and State University; Tanya L. Ryskind, Western Michigan University; William Sharp, University of Akron; John Skehan, University of Maine; Jacqueline A. Stefkovich, Pennsylvania State University; and Rodney E. Wells, St. Bonaventure University.

Kern Alexander
M. David Alexander

CHAPTER 1

THE LEGAL SYSTEM

We must not expect a good constitution because those who make it are moral men.
Rather it is because of a good constitution that we may expect a society composed
of moral men.

—Immanuel Kant

CHAPTER OUTLINE

- POWERS AND FUNCTIONS OF COURTS
- THE PURPOSE OF LAW
- STARE DECISIS
- UNDERSTANDING JUDICIAL DECISIONS
- CASE OR CONTROVERSY
- THE AMERICAN COURT SYSTEM

THE LAW OF THE SCHOOL includes all those areas of jurisprudence that bear on the operation of public elementary and secondary schools in the United States. "School law" as a field of study is a generic term covering a wide range of legal subject matter including the basic fields of contracts, property, torts, constitutional law, and other areas of law that directly affect the educational and administrative processes of the educational system. Due to the breadth of the subject matter involved, it is necessary for the school law student to be versed in certain fundamental concepts of the American legal system and to be able to apply this knowledge to situations that daily affect school operation.

Because a public school is a governmental agency, its conduct is circumscribed by prece-

dents of public administrative law supplemented by those legal and historical traditions surrounding an educational organization that is state established, yet locally administered. In this setting, legal and educational structural issues must be considered that define the powers to operate, control, and manage the schools. In analyzing the American educational system and comparing it to central state systems of education in foreign countries, one is struck by the diversity of authority under which the American public schools are governed. As a federal and not a national system, the government of the United States comprises a union of states united under one central government. The particular form of American federalism creates a unique educational system, which is governed

1

by laws of fifty states with component parts amounting to several thousand local school district operating units. Through all of this organizational multiformity, and indeed complexity, runs the legal basis on which the entire system is founded.

The fundamental principles of legal control are those generally prescribed by our constitutional system, from which the basic organic law of the land emanates: the written constitutions of the fifty states and the federal government. Constitutions at both levels of government are basic because the positive power to create public educational systems is assumed by state constitutions, and provisions of both the state and federal constitutions serve as restraints to protect the people from unwarranted denial of basic constitutional rights and freedoms.

The power of operation of the public educational system, therefore, originates with a constitutional delegation to the legislature to provide for a system of education. With legislative enactments providing the basis for public school law, it then becomes the role of the courts, through litigation, to interpret the will of the legislature. The combination of constitutions, statutes, and court (or case) law forms the primary legal foundation on which the public schools are based.

CONSTITUTIONS

A constitution is a body of precepts that provides a framework of law within which orderly governmental processes can operate. The constitutions of this country are characterized by their provisions for securing fundamental liberty, property, and political rights. One of the basic principles embodied in a constitution is the provision for authorized modification of the document. Experience in human and governmental relations teaches that to be effective a constitution must be flexible and provide for systematic change processes. The Constitution of the United States expressly provides in Article V a process for proposing amendments by a two-thirds vote of each house of Congress or by a convention that shall be called by Congress upon application by two-thirds of the state legislatures. Amendments must be ratified by the legislatures of three-fourths of the states or by conventions in three-fourths of the states.

Another precept reflected in the state and federal constitutions of this country is the importance of a government of separated powers. Although all state constitutions do not expressly provide for a separation of all legislative, executive, and judicial departments, in actual practice, all states have governments of separated powers. There is no requirement in the federal constitution that the states have constitutions that require a separation of powers. Theoretically, if a state so desired, it could clothe an officer or an agency with not only executive but plenary judicial and legislative powers. However, as indicated previously, this is not the case, and all states have governments with separate branches, each of which exercises checks and balances on the powers of other branches.

All state constitutions make provision for a system of free public schools. Such provisions range from very specific educational provisions to broad mandates that the legislature of the state shall provide funds for the support of a public school system.

STATUTES

A statute is an act of government expressing legislative will and constituting a law of the state. "Statute" is a word derived from the Latin term *statutum*, which means "it is decided." Statutes, in our American form of government, are the most viable and effective means of making new law or changing old law. Statutes enacted at the state or federal level may either follow custom or forge ahead and establish new laws that shape the future.

Statutes in this country are subject to review by the judiciary to determine their constitutionality. This procedure is different from that used in England, where the legislature has ultimate authority and there are no means by which the courts can hold legislation unconstitutional. This is true primarily because in England the constitution, for the most part, is unwritten and the legislature, Parliament, may amend the constitution when it so desires.

The public schools of the United States are governed by statutes enacted by state legislatures. The schools have no inherent powers, and the authority to operate them must be found in either express or implied terms of statute. The specificity of statutes governing the operation of public schools varies from state to state and from subject to subject. As an example, one state may generally require appropriate measures to be followed in budgeting and accounting for public funds, while in another state the legislature may actually specify each line item of the budget for school systems and prescribe intricate details for fund accounting.

Rules and regulations of both state and local boards of education fall within the category of statutory sources of school law. As a general rule, the legislature cannot delegate its legislative powers to govern the schools to a subordinate agency or official. Boards of education must, in devising rules and regulations for the administration of the schools, do so within the limits defined by the legislature and cannot exercise legislative authority. However, the legislature may expressly or impliedly confer administrative duties upon an agency or official through statute. These administrative powers must be well defined and "canalized" within definitely circumscribed channels.

COURT, OR CASE, LAW

The third source of school law is judge-made or case law, sometimes called common law. The terms "case law" or "common law" are used to distinguish rules of law that are enunciated by the courts from those that have originated in legislative bodies. The term "common law," in its broadest sense, may sometimes be used to contrast the entire system of Anglo-American law with the law of non-English-speaking countries sometimes referred to as having systems of civil law. Civil law is a system of statutes in which there is no reliance on precedent. Common law originated in England, where precedents of various parts of the country became common to the entire country. These customs became crystallized into legal principles that were applied and used as precedent throughout England.

COMMON LAW

"The common law is a body of general rules prescribing social conduct."[1] The common law has five recognizable attributes. First, it is general, overarching precedent that applies throughout the state or country. Second, the general rules are applied and enforced by the courts without

necessarily involving either the executive or legislative branches of government. Third, the common law enunciates principles derived from actual legal controversies. Fourth, the common law emanates from use of the jury system to ascertain the facts to which the law is applicable. Fifth, the common law is premised upon the rule of law or doctrine of supremacy of law—that is, the rule of law and not of man, the rule of established principles and not acts of caprice or arbitrariness.[2]

Hogue says that these five principles prescribe a positive definition, to wit: "the common law is a body of general rules prescribing social conduct, enforced by ordinary . . . courts, and characterized by the development of its own principles in actual legal controversies, by the procedure of trial by jury, and by the doctrine of the supremacy of law."[3]

■ POWERS AND FUNCTIONS OF COURTS

The question of what powers may be exercised by the judiciary in reviewing decisions or enactments by the other two branches of government is essential to our system of government. The courts have traditionally maintained and enforced the concept of "separation of powers" when confronted with cases involving education. They do not usually question the judgment of either the administrative agencies of the executive branch or the legislative branch. This is true at the federal level as well as the state level.

One court, in describing the hesitancy of the courts to interfere with the other two branches of government, said:

> This reluctance is due, in part, to an awareness of the sometimes awesome responsibility of having to circumscribe the limits of their authority. Even more persuasive is an appreciation of the importance in our system of the concept of separation of powers so that each division of government may function freely within the area of its responsibility. This safeguarding of the separate powers is essential to preserve the balance which has always been regarded as one of the advantages of our system.[4]

In accordance with this reasoning, the courts presume that legislative or administrative actions were enacted conscientiously with due deliberation and are not arbitrary or capricious.[5] When the courts do intervene, they perform three types of judicial functions: (1) settle controversies by applying principles of law to a specific set of facts, (2) construe or interpret enactments of the legislature, and (3) determine the constitutionality of legislative or administrative actions.

APPLYING PRINCIPLES

In applying principles of law to factual situations, the court may find the disputants to be either school districts, individuals, or both. Although school law cases generally involve the school district itself, they may, in some instances, concern litigation between individuals, for example, a teacher and a student. In many cases, the principles of law governing the situation are vague, and statutory and constitutional guidance are difficult to find. In such instances, the judges must look to judicial precedent for guidance. Cardoza related the process in this manner:

> Where does the judge find the law he embodies in his judgment? There are times when the source is obvious. The rule that fits the case may be supplied by the constitution or by statute. If that is so, the judge looks no further. The correspondence ascertained, his duty is to obey. The constitution overrides a statute, but a statute, if consistent with the constitution, overrides the law of judges. In this sense, judge-made law is secondary and subordinate to the law that is made by legislators. . . . We reach the land of mystery when constitution and statute are silent, and the judge must look to the common law for the rule that fits the case. He is the "living oracle of the law" in Blackstone's vivid phrase.[6]

INTERPRETING STATUTES

The second function of the courts, the task of construing and interpreting statutes, is the most common litigation involving public school operation. Because statutes are merely words, to which many definitions and interpretations may be applied, courts may actually affect the meaning of the legislation. Pound conceives of four ways with which legislation may be dealt by the courts once litigation arises:

1. They might receive it fully into the body of the law as affording not only a rule to be applied but a principle from which to reason, and hold it, as a later and more direct expression of the general will, of superior authority to judge-made rules on the same general subject; and so reason from it by analogy in preference to them.

2. They might receive it fully into the body of the law to be reasoned from by analogy the same as any other rule of law, regarding it, however, as of equal or coordinate authority in this respect with judge-made rules upon the same general subject.

3. They might refuse to receive it fully into the body of the law and give effect to it directly only; refusing to reason from it by analogy but giving it, nevertheless, a liberal interpretation to cover the whole field it was intended to cover.

4. They might not only refuse to reason from it by analogy and apply it directly only, but also give to it a strict and narrow interpretation, holding it down rigidly to those cases which it covers expressly.[7]

The last hypothesis is probably the orthodox, traditional approach; however, the courts today, in interpreting statutes, tend to adhere more and more to the second and third hypotheses.

The philosophy of the courts toward statutory interpretation varies not only among judges and courts but also in the content of the legislation being interpreted. The courts are generally more willing to grant implied authority to perform educational programs where large sums of public monies are not involved. For cases in which taxing authority is in question or in which large capital outlay programs are at issue, the courts tend to require very specific and express statutory authority in order for a school board to perform.[8]

Another, and possibly clearer, explanation of how courts construe statutes may be found in rules of law laid down by several judicial precedents. These rules—the Mischief Rule, the Golden Rule, the Literal Rule, and the Plain Meaning Rule—are useful in delineating the judiciary's options in dealing with statutory construction.[9]

The Mischief Rule [F]or the sure and true interpretation of all statutes in general (be they penal or beneficial, restrictive or enlarging of the common law) four things are to be discerned and considered:

1. What was the common law before the making of the Act?
2. What was the mischief and defect for which the common law did not provide?
3. What remedy the Parliament hath resolved and appointed to cure the disease of the commonwealth?
4. The true reason of the remedy; and then the office of all the Judges is always to make sure construction as shall suppress the mischief, and advance the remedy, and to suppress subtle inventions and evasions for continuance of the mischief, and *pro privato commodo,* and to add force and life to the cure and remedy, according to the true intent of the makers of the Act, *pro bono publico.*[10]

The "Golden" Rule   But it is to be borne in mind that the office of the judges is not to legislate, but to declare the expressed intention of the Legislature, even if that intention appears to the court injudicious; and I believe that it is not disputed that what Lord Wensleydale used to say is right, namely that we are to take the whole statute together, and construe it all together, giving the words their ordinary signification, unless when so applied they produce an inconsistency, or an absurdity or inconvenience so great as to convince the court that the intention could not have been to use them in their ordinary signification, and to justify the court in putting on them some other signification, which, though less proper, is one which the court thinks the words will bear.[11]

The Literal Rule   If the language of a statute be plain, admitting of only one meaning, the Legislature must be taken to have meant and intended what it has plainly expressed, and whatever it has in clear terms enacted must be enforced though it should lead to absurd or mischievous results. If the language of this subsection be not controlled by some of the other provisions of the statute, it must, since its language is plain and unambiguous, be enforced, and your lordships' House sitting judicially is not concerned with the question whether the policy it embodies is wise or unwise, or whether it leads to consequences just or unjust, beneficial or mischievous.[12]

I should like to have a good definition of what is such an absurdity that you are to disregard the plain words of an Act of Parliament. It is to be remembered that what seems absurd to one man does not seem absurd to another. . . . I think it is infinitely better, although an absurdity or an injustice or other objectionable result may be evolved as the consequence of your construction, to adhere to the words of an Act of Parliament and leave the legislature to set it right than to alter those words according to one's notion of an absurdity.[13]

The Plain Meaning Rule   It is elementary that the meaning of a statute must, in the first instance, be sought in the language in which the act is framed, and if that is plain, and if the law is within the constitutional authority of the lawmaking body which passed it, the sole function of the courts is to enforce it according to its terms. . . .

Where the language is plain and admits of no more than one meaning the duty of interpretation does not arise and the rules which are to aid doubtful meanings need no discussion. . . . Statutory words are uniformly presumed, unless the contrary appears to be used in their ordinary and usual sense, and with the meaning commonly attributed to them.[14]

The general rule is perfectly well settled that, where a statute is of doubtful meaning and susceptible upon its face of two constructions, the court may look into prior and contemporaneous acts, the reasons which induced the act in question, the mischiefs intended to be remedied, the extraneous circumstances, and the purpose intended to be accomplished by it to determine its proper construction. But when the act is clear upon its face, and when standing alone it is fairly susceptible of but one construction, that construction must be given to it. . . .

The whole doctrine applicable to the subject may be summed up in the single observation that prior acts may be resorted to, to *solve,* but not to *create* an ambiguity.[15]

DETERMINING CONSTITUTIONALITY

The functions and responsibility of the judiciary in determining the constitutionality of legislation were set out early in *Marbury v. Madison*[16] in prescribing the power of the United States Supreme Court. This case shaped the American view of the role of the judiciary. Chief Justice Marshall's landmark opinion stated:

It is emphatically the province and duty of the judicial department to say what the law is. Those who apply the rule to particular cases, must of necessity expound and interpret that rule. If two laws conflict with each other, the courts must decide on the operation of each. So, if a law be in opposition to the constitution; if both the law and the constitution apply to a particular case, so that the court must either decide that case, conformably to the law, disregarding the constitution; or conformably to the constitution, disregarding the law; the court must determine which of these conflicting rules governs the case. This is of the very essence of judicial duty. If then the courts are to regard the constitution, and the constitution is superior to any ordinary act of the legislature; the constitution, and not such ordinary act, must govern the case to which they both apply.

In determining the constitutionality of statutes, the courts first presume the act to be constitutional and anyone maintaining the contrary must bear the burden of proof. The Florida Supreme Court has related the principle in this manner: "We have held that acts of the legislature carry such a strong presumption of validity that they should be held constitutional if there is any reasonable theory to that end. . . . Moreover, unconstitutionality must appear beyond all reasonable doubt before an Act is condemned. . . ."[17] If a statute can be interpreted in two different ways, one by which it will be constitutional, the courts will adopt the constitutional interpretation.[18]

With specific regard to the United States Supreme Court's review of legislation, either state or federal, the judicial duty in the eyes of Justice Brandeis was that "[i]t must be evident that the power to declare legislative enactment void is one which the judge, conscious of the fallibility of human judgment, will shrink from exercising in any case where he can conscientiously and with due regard to duty and official oath decline the responsibility."[19] Using this basic philosophy, Justice Brandeis, in 1936, set out certain criteria for judicial review that are still generally referred to today in considering the standing of litigants before the Supreme Court.

1. The Court will not pass upon the constitutionality of legislation in a friendly, nonadversary proceeding, declining because to decide such questions is legitimate only in the last resort, and as a necessity in the determination of real, earnest, and vital controversy between individuals.
2. The Court will not anticipate a question of constitutional law in advance of the necessity of deciding it. It is not the habit of the Court to decide questions of a constitutional nature unless absolutely necessary to a decision of the case.
3. The Court will not formulate a rule of constitutional law broader than is required by the precise facts to which it is to be applied.

4. The Court will not pass upon a constitutional question although properly presented by the record, if there is also present some other ground upon which the case may be disposed of. This rule has found most varied application. Thus, if a case can be decided on either of two grounds, one involving a constitutional question, the other a question of statutory construction or general law, the Court will decide only the latter.
5. The Court will not pass upon the validity of a statute upon complaint of one who fails to show that he or she is injured by its operation. Among the many applications of this rule, none is more striking than the denial of the right of challenge to one who lacks a personal or property right. Thus, the challenge by public officials interested only in the performance of their official duty will not be entertained.
6. The Court will not pass upon the constitutionality of a statute at the instance of one who has availed himself or herself of its benefits.
7. When the validity of an act of Congress is drawn in question, and even if a serious doubt of constitutionality is raised, it is a cardinal principle that this Court will first ascertain whether the construction of the statute is fairly possible by which the question may be avoided.[20]

■ THE PURPOSE OF LAW

An Invitation to Jurisprudence, Harry W. Jones

Reprinted with permission, Colum.L.Rev. 1023, 1031–32 (1974).

[F]ive of law's most viable ends-in-view [are]: Preservation of the public peace and safety, the settlement of individual disputes, the maintenance of security of expectations, the resolution of conflicting social interests, and the channeling of social change. This is no complete inventory of law's tasks, nor is it a neat set of mutually exclusive teleological pigeon holes. There are manifest overlappings—for example, the resolution of conflicting social interests is one of the ways in which law helps to channel the forces of social change—and some of the law's ends-in-view can come into collision with others, as when law's adjustment to social change involves some unavoidable impairment of the security of individual expectations. In law as in ethics, the hardest task is often not the identification of values, but the assignment of priorities when, in a specific problem context, one value cannot be fully served without some sacrifice of another. But even and particularly when values cut across one another, disinterested and informed judgement on legal and social problems requires that each of the competing ends-in-view be understood in its full claim as an aspect or dimension of what law is *for*: the creation or preservation of a social environment in which, to the degree manageable in a complex and imperfect world, the quality of human life can be spirited, improving and impaired.

■ STARE DECISIS

Implicit in the concept of common or case law is the reliance on past court decisions that reflect the historical development of legal controversies. Precedents established in past cases form the groundwork for decisions in the future. In the United States, the doctrine of precedent or the rule of *stare decisis*, "let the decision stand," prevails, and past decisions are generally considered to be binding on subsequent cases that have the same or substantially the same factual situations. The rule of *stare decisis* is rigidly adhered to by lower courts when following decisions by higher courts in the same jurisdiction. Courts can limit the impact of the doctrine of precedent by carefully distinguishing the facts of the case from those of the previous case that established the rule of law. Aside from distinguishing factual situations, courts of last resort can reverse their own previous decisions and change a rule of law that they themselves established.

Stare decisis in American law does not constitute the strict adherence to older decisions that is found in English courts. The American rule of today is probably best stated by Justice Brandeis when he said that "stare decisis is usually the wise policy . . . "[21] and by Justice Cardozo, who observed that "I think adherence to precedent should be the rule and not the exception."[22]

The Historical Development of the Doctrine of Precedent, Harold J. Berman and William R. Greiner

Reprinted with permission, The Nature and Functions of Law *(The Foundation Press, 1966, pp. 491–94).*

If we go back to the early history of modern English law, we find that by the end of the twelfth century, virtually as soon as records of court proceedings were kept, there developed an interest in judicial decisions as guides to what the law is. Bracton in his treatise on English law, written in the middle of the thirteenth century, referred to about 500 decided cases; he also wrote a Notebook containing digests of 2000 cases. The word "precedent," however, is entirely absent from Bracton's vocabulary; cases for him and for his contemporaries were not binding authorities but merely illustrations of legal principles.

In the fourteenth, fifteenth, and early sixteenth centuries law students kept notes of oral arguments in court cases. These notes, preserved in the so-called Yearbooks, show that not only the students but also the courts were concerned with analogizing and distinguishing cases. Again, however, the decisions were not treated as authorities in any sense, and if a judge did not approve of a decision he would just say it was wrong.

In the sixteenth and seventeenth centuries we get the first systematic reports of cases and the first mention of precedent. Judges then began to say that they are bound by precedents in matters of procedure, and especially in matters of pleading, and the practice of citing previous cases became firmly established. It is interesting to note, however, that in the first known use of the word "precedent," in 1557, it is stated that a decision was given "notwithstanding two precedents." Indeed, the doctrine of precedent which developed in those centuries did not provide that a single decision was binding but rather that a line of decisions would not be overturned. Lord Mansfield could still say, in the latter part of the eighteenth century, "The reason and spirit of cases make law; not the letter of particular precedents."

Nevertheless, with the development in the seventeenth century of the distinction between dictum and holding, the way was paved for the modern doctrine. It should be noted that the seventeenth century in England was a time when analogical reasoning also became prevalent in fields other than law.

In the later nineteenth century for the first time there developed the rule that a holding by a court in a previous case is binding on the same court (or on an inferior court) in a similar case. The doctrine was called *stare decisis*—"to stand by the decisions." It was never absolute. The court is only bound "in the absence of weighty reasons.". . .

In the heyday of the doctrine of *stare decisis*, that is, in the last quarter of the nineteenth and the first quarter of the twentieth century, belief was prevalent that certainty in law could be obtained by a scientific use of precedent. The legislature alone was thought to have the function of changing the law; the court's function was "merely" to apply the law, and to apply it in accordance with the holdings of previous decisions. The common law as an organically growing body of experience and doctrine was supposed, in effect, to have been superseded by a body of fixed rules which could be mechanically applied.

The idea that the common law is a body of fixed rules vanished in the second quarter of the twentieth century, and perhaps earlier, in the face of overwhelming changes in social, economic, and political life. The mathematical or mechanical jurisprudence of the late nineteenth century which denied that there is an ethical element in the analogizing and distinguishing of cases can seldom be found today among leaders of legal thought, at least in the United States. This does not mean, however, that the doctrine of precedent has been repudiated. It means, rather, that there has been a return to an older concept of precedent. Precedent is seen as a means of marshalling past experience, of providing a historical context, for making the choice at hand. While condemning the hocuspocus aspects of the strict nineteenth century doctrine, many American thinkers about law would agree with Lord Mansfield that "the common law works itself pure."

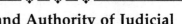

Nature and Authority of Judicial Precedents, Henry Campbell Black

The Law of Judicial Precedents 10–11 (1912).

Not as a classification, but as exhibiting the chief aspects or applications of the doctrine of precedents, the subject might be broadly divided into five branches, in each of which there is to be noted one general rule or governing principle, as follows:

First. Inferior courts are absolutely bound to follow the decisions of the courts having appellate or revisory jurisdiction over them. In this aspect, precedents set by the higher courts are imperative in the strictest sense. They are conclusive on the lower courts, and leave to the latter no scope for independent judgment or discretion.

Second. The judgments of the highest court in any judicial system—state or national—are binding on all other courts when they deal with matters committed to the peculiar or exclusive jurisdiction of the court making the precedent. Thus, when the Supreme Court of the United States renders a decision construing the federal constitution or an act of Congress, that decision must be accepted by all state courts, as well as the inferior federal courts, as not merely persuasive, but of absolutely conclusive authority. In the same way, when the supreme court of a state pronounces judgment upon the interpretation of a statute of the state, its decision has imperative force in the courts of the United States, as well as in the courts of another state.

Third. It is the duty of a court of last resort to abide by its own former decisions, and not to depart from or vary them unless entirely satisfied, in the first place, that they were wrongly decided, and, in the second place, that less mischief will result from their overthrow than from their perpetuation. This is the proper application of the maxim, "stare decisis."

Fourth. When a case is presented to any court for which there is no precedent, either in its own former decisions or in the decisions of any court whose rulings, in the particular matter, it is bound to follow, it may consult and be guided by the applicable decisions by any other court, domestic or foreign. In this case, such decisions possess no constraining force, but should be accorded such a measure of weight and influence as they may be intrinsically entitled to receive, the duty of the court being to conform its decision to what is called the "general current of authority" or the "preponderance of authority," if such a standard can be ascertained to exist with reference to the particular question involved.

Fifth. On the principle of judicial comity, a court which is entirely free to exercise its independent judgment upon the matter at issue, and under no legal obligation to follow the decision of another court on the same question, will nevertheless accept and conform to that decision, as a correct statement of the law, when such a course is necessary to secure the harmonious and consistent administration of the law or to avoid unseemly conflicts of judicial authority. But comity does not require any court to do violence to its own settled convictions as to what the law is.

❖ — ❖ — ❖

Commentaries

*1 W. Blackstone, Commentaries *69–70.*

For it is an established rule to abide by former precedents, where the same points come again in litigation: as well to keep the scale of justice even and steady, and not liable to waver with every new judge's opinion; as also because the law in that case being solemnly declared and determined, what before was uncertain, and perhaps indifferent, is now become a permanent rule, which it is not in the breast of any subsequent judge to alter or vary from according to his private sentiments: he being sworn to determine, not according to his own private judgment; but according to the known laws and customs of the land; not delegated to pronounce a new law, but to maintain and expound the old one. Yet this rule admits of exception, where the

former determination is most evidently contrary to reason; much more if it be clearly contrary to the divine law. But even in such cases the subsequent judges do not pretend to make a new law, but to vindicate the old one from misrepresentation. For if it be found that the former decision is manifestly absurd or unjust, it is declared, not that such a sentence was *bad law,* but that it was *not law;* that is, that it is not the established custom of the realm, as has been erroneously determined. And hence it is that our lawyers are with justice so copious in their encomiums on the reason of the common law; that they tell us, that the law is the perfection of reason, that it always intends to conform thereto, and that what is not reason is not law. Not that the particular reason of every rule in the law can at this distance of time be always precisely assigned; but it is sufficient that there be nothing in the rule flatly contradictory to reason, and then the law will presume it to be well founded.

❖ — ❖ — ❖

The Role of Precedent in Judicial Decision, John Hanna

Reprinted with permission from Villanova Law Review Vol. 2, No. 3, pp. 367–68. Copyright 1957 by Villanova University.

Stare decisis or, in its complete form, *stare decisis et non quieta movere* is usually translated "to stand by (or adhere to) decisions and not to disturb what is settled." The classic English version is by Coke: "They said that those things which have been so often adjudged ought to rest in peace." Blackstone says: "The doctrine of the law then is this: that precedents and rules be followed, unless flatly absurd or unjust; for though their reason be not obvious at first view, yet we owe such a deference to former times as not to suppose that they acted wholly without consideration." The general American doctrine as applied to courts of last resort is that a court is not inexorably bound by its own precedents but will follow the rule of law which it has established in earlier cases, unless clearly convinced that the rule was originally erroneous or is no longer sound because of changing conditions and that more good than harm will come by departing from precedent. The alternative to stare decisis as popularly defined would be (1) absolute discretion on the part of a court to decide each case without reference to any precedent; or (2) complete codification of our law, with a requirement that each court look independently to the code for a basis of decision. A more limited reform would be to bar the courts from following precedents of decisions on statutory and constitutional law. None of these alternatives is a matter of much contemporary debate in America. If we define stare decisis in terms of its proper limitations, it should always be applied. We shall stay closer to the points of controversy if we appreciate that our real subject is the theory of judicial precedent.

■ UNDERSTANDING JUDICIAL DECISIONS

In order to determine the rule of a case, it is necessary to find the *ratio decidendi*, or the point on which the judgment balances. This is done primarily by carefully analyzing the facts of the case that are treated as material by the judge. Only the material facts are relevant to the identification of the *ratio decidendi* of a case. Conclusions of a judge departing from the *ratio* are not binding as precedent and are considered to be *obiter dicta*. Essentially there are two types of *obiter dicta*. First, a statement of law is *obiter* if it is based on facts that are immaterial or that are found not to exist. Second, it may also be a statement of a law that, although based on established facts of the case, does not form the rationale for the decision. A statement of law supporting a dissenting opinion is one example. Another instance of the second type of *obiter* may be when a court makes a statement of law leading to one conclusion but then reaches a contrary decision on the facts for a different reason.[23]

Karl N. Llewellyn,[24] late professor of law, University of Chicago, in his work *The Bramble Bush*, probably offers the best and most concise explanation of what to look for when reading case law. Since the case method is employed in presenting most of the materials in this book, it seems appropriate to quote a portion of Llewellyn's comments on reading and analyzing judicial opinions.

The first thing to do with an opinion, then, is read it. The next thing is to get clear the actual decision, the judgment rendered. Who won, the plaintiff or defendant? And watch your step here. You are after in first instance the plaintiff and defendant below, in the trial court. In order to follow through what happened you must therefore first know the outcome below; else you do not see what was appealed from, nor by whom. You now follow through in order to see exactly what further judgment has been rendered on appeal. The stage is then cleared of form—although of course you do not yet know all that these forms mean, that they imply. You can turn now to what you peculiarly do know. Given the actual judgments below and above as your indispensable framework—what has the case decided, and what can you derive from it as to what will be decided later?

You will be looking, in the opinion, or in the preliminary matter plus the opinion, for the following: a statement of the facts the court assumes; a statement of the precise way the question has come before the court—which includes what the plaintiff wanted below, and what the defendant did about it, the judgment below, and what the trial court did that is complained of; then the outcome on appeal, the judgment; and finally the reasons this court gives for doing what it did. This does not look so bad. But it is much worse than it looks. For all our cases are decided, all our opinions are written, all our predictions, all our arguments are made, on certain four assumptions. . . . (1) *The court must decide the dispute that is before it.* It cannot refuse because the job is hard, or dubious, or dangerous. (2) *The court can decide only the particular dispute which is before it.* When it speaks to that question it speaks *ex cathedra*, with authority, with finality, with an almost magic power. When it speaks to the question before it, it announces law, and if what it announces is new, it legislates, it makes the law. But when it speaks to any other question at all, it says mere words, which no man needs to follow. Are such words worthless? They are not. We know them as judicial *dicta*; when they are wholly off the point at issue we call them *obiter dicta*—words dropped along the road, wayside remarks. Yet even wayside remarks shed light on the remarker. They may be very useful in the future to him, or to us. But he will not feel bound to them, as to his *ex cathedra* utterance. They came not hallowed by a Delphic frenzy. He may be slow to change them; but not so slow as in the other case. (3) *The court can decide the particular dispute only according to a general rule which covers a whole class of like disputes.* Our legal theory does not admit of single decisions standing on their own. If judges are free, are indeed forced, to decide new cases for which there is no rule, they must at least make a new rule as they decide. So far, good. But how wide or how narrow, is the general rule in this particular case? That is a troublesome matter. The practice of our case-law, however, is I think, fairly stated thus: It pays to be suspicious of general rules which look too wide; it pays to go slow in feeling certain that a wide rule has been laid down at all, or that, if seemingly laid down, it will be followed. For there is a fourth accepted canon: (4) *Everything, everything, everything, big or small, a judge may say in an opinion, is to be read with primary reference to the particular dispute, the particular question before him.* You are not to think that the words mean what they might if they stood alone. You are to have your eye on the case in hand, and to learn how to interpret all that has been said merely as a reason for deciding that case that way. . . .

■ CASE OR CONTROVERSY

Article III of the Constitution of the United States limits the power of the judiciary to "decide and pronounce a judgment and carry it into effect between persons and parties who bring a case before it for decision."[25] The judicial branch may settle conflicts that involve only actual "cases" and "controversies."[26] The determination of what constitutes a case and controversy is left to the judgment of the Supreme Court.

The courts of the United States do not sit to decide questions of law presented in a vacuum, but only to decide such questions as arise in a case or controversy.[27] The two terms can be used interchangeably for we are authoritatively told that a controversy, if distinguishable at all from a case, is distinguishable only in that it is a less comprehensive term and includes only suits of a civil nature.[28]

That which is a case or controversy—justiciable in the federal courts—was defined by Chief Justice Hughes in a classic and cryptic statement. He said: "A 'controversy' in this sense must be one that is appropriate for judicial determination. A justiciable controversy is thus distinguished from a difference or dispute of a hypothetical character; from one that is academic or moot. The controversy must be definite and concrete, touching the legal relations of parties having adverse legal interests. It must be a real and substantial controversy admitting of specific relief through a decree of a conclusive character, as distinguished from an opinion advising what the law would be upon a hypothetical state of facts."[29]

Later, Chief Justice Warren said of the case or controversy requirement that "those two words have an iceberg quality, containing beneath their surface simplicity submerged complexities which go to the very heart of our constitutional form of government. Embodied in the words 'cases' and 'controversies' are two complementary but somewhat different limitations. In part those words limit the business of federal courts to questions presented in an adversary context and in a form historically viewed as capable of resolution through the judicial process. And in part those words define the role assigned to the judiciary in a tripartite allocation of power to assure that the federal courts will not intrude into areas committed to the other branches of government. Justiciability is the term of art employed to give expression to this dual limitation placed upon federal courts by the case and controversy doctrine."[30]

It should also be noted that the limitation to "case or controversy" is intimately related to the doctrine of judicial review. In *Marbury v. Madison*[31] it was central to Marshall's argument that a court has power to declare a statute unconstitutional only as a consequence of the power of the court to decide a case properly before it. There may be unconstitutional statutes, but unless they are involved in a case properly susceptible of judicial determination, the courts have no power to pronounce that they are unconstitutional. The reluctance of courts to pass on constitutional issues unless absolutely necessary has led to a rigorous set of rules as to what constitutes a justiciable case or controversy.

A LEGITIMATE CONTROVERSY

The U.S. Supreme Court will not consider disputes that do not constitute a legitimate case or controversy. For such to exist, the plaintiff must have sufficient bases and conditions to bring the matter before the Court. Such considerations may be summarized into four (4) categories:

1. *Advisory opinions.* The separation of powers between the branches of government prevents the federal judiciary from rendering advisory opinions to the executive or legislative branches. In primary precedent, Chief Justice Jay concluded in correspondence with President George Washington and Secretary of State Thomas Jefferson that the federal

judiciary may not constitutionally give advisory opinions.[32] Objections to advisory opinions are summarized by Nowak and others as follows: (a) "Advisory opinions may not be binding on the parties, in that advice given need not be accepted. The power of the Court is then eroded. . . . (b) Advisory opinions also undermine the basic theory behind the adversary system. . . . (c) With a real controversy before it, the Court might be able to avoid a constitutional issue entirely and decide the case on narrower grounds. Advisory opinions unnecessarily force the Court to reach and decide complex, if not impossible, constitutional issues. . . . (d) The power to render such an advisory opinion is really a greater power than the reluctant judicial review justified by [Justice] Marshall because it increases the situations where the court can exercise this significant power of judicial review."[33]

2. *Mootness.* Under Article III of the U.S. Constitution, the federal courts cannot decide moot questions. If a question is moot, then "there is no subject matter on which the judgment of the court's order can operate."[34] A case may be found to be moot and therefore non-justicible for several reasons: facts did not hold at all stages of the appellate process; the law has changed; the defendant no longer wishes to appeal; the wrongful behavior has passed and cannot reasonably be expected to recur; a statutory age limit no longer applies because of lapse of time; or a party to the suit has died.[35]

3. *Ripeness and prematurity.* Just as a case may be brought too late and is thereby moot, it may also be mooted if raised before an offense has occurred. For example, where a federal law prohibited officers or employees of the federal government from participating in political campaigns, but no one had been offended by the law because of its enforcement, the Court said: "A hypothetical threat is not enough. We can only speculate as to the kinds of political activity the appellants desire to engage in. . . ."[36]

4. *Standing.* According to Freund, defining the problem of standing is "among the most amorphous in the entire public domain." In order for standing to exist, the plaintiff must

have a definitive interest in the controversy. For example, a case where a taxpayer challenged a federal statute merely because she paid federal income taxes was found to be too remote and insubstantial to maintain standing.[37] The Supreme Court said that a federal taxpayer's interest is too "minute and indeterminable to support standing."[38] The Court has stated the standing test as follows: "The party who invokes the power (of judicial review) must be able to show not only that the statute is invalid but that he has sustained or is immediately in danger of sustaining some direct injury as a result of its enforcement, and not merely that he suffers in some indefinite way in common with people generally."[39]

The requisite and necessary standing requirements were found to exist in *Flast v. Cohen*, a case where taxpayers challenged the expenditure of federal funds under the Elementary and Secondary Education Act of 1965 to finance reading, arithmetic, and other programs in parochial schools. The Court found in this case that the taxpayers did have standing and asserted an important principle: "[I]n ruling on standing, it is both appropriate and necessary to look to the substantive issues . . . to determine whether there is a logical nexus between the status asserted and the claim sought to be adjudicated."[40]

The nexus required had two aspects. First, the taxpayer must establish a logical link between the grievance, the taxpayer's status, and the challenged legislature enactment. Second, the taxpayer must establish a nexus between his or her status and the exact nature of the constitutional alleged fringement.[41]

The rules enunciated above apply only to the federal courts. Individual states have their own jurisdictional requirements for their respective state courts. The state supreme courts in several states will render advisory opinions to the executive or the legislative branches of government.

■ THE AMERICAN COURT SYSTEM

In our federal form of government, it is necessary to have a dual judicial system: state and federal. Cases involving public schools may be litigated at either level, and while most actions involve nonfederal questions and are decided by state courts, recent years have brought on a substantial increase in the number of school cases handed down by federal courts.

STATE COURTS

State constitutions generally prescribe the powers and the jurisdiction of the primary or main state courts. The legislature, through power granted in the constitution, provides for the specific operation of the constitutional courts, and it may create new and additional courts if so authorized by the constitution.

State courts can be classified into four categories: courts of last resort, intermediate appellate courts, courts of general jurisdiction, and courts of limited jurisdiction.

Courts of Last Resort

These courts are found at the top of the judicial hierarchy in each state and are established by the state constitution. In forty-three states the official name of this highest court is the Supreme Court. The exceptions are Maryland (Court of Appeals), Maine (Supreme Judicial Court sitting as Law Court), Massachusetts (Supreme Judicial Court), New York (Court of Appeals), and West Virginia (Supreme Court of Appeals). Oklahoma and Texas are unique because they have dual-headed systems that have, respectively, a Supreme Court and a Court of Criminal Appeals as the courts of last resort. Except for Texas and Oklahoma, where civil and criminal cases are separated, all of the courts of last resort have mandatory and discretionary jurisdiction for civil, criminal, and administrative cases. State statute prescribes where types of cases must be taken and which ones may be heard at the discretion of the highest court. A mandatory case refers to an "appeal of right," which the court must hear and decide on the merits.[42] Mandatory appeals make up about 70 percent of the caseloads of the courts of last resort, with discretionary cases constituting the remainder. Discretionary jurisdiction of appellate courts refers to cases in which a party must file a petition to seek redress of the court. The court, then, must exercise its discretion in accepting or rejecting the case.[43]

Intermediate Appellate Courts

These courts have been established in thirty-eight states to hear appeals from trial courts and administrative agencies as specified by state statute.[44] The role of these appellate courts is to review specific trial court proceedings to correct errors in the application of law and procedure[45] and to serve to extend and expand the law for the good of the community. Both of these generic purposes are held in common by both the intermediate appellate courts and the courts of last resort. The intermediate appellate courts hear both mandatory and discretionary cases. In the two-tier appellate state systems, a pattern exists that indicates that the highest court, the court of last resort, tends to control the docket by accepting more discretionary appeals than the intermediate appellate court.[46] Today, as appellate caseloads increase, there is a trend toward creation of new intermediate appellate courts. During the last thirty years, twenty-five states created two-tier systems establishing intermediate appellate courts.[47]

Courts of General Jurisdiction

These courts are major courts of record from which there exists a right of appeal to the intermediate appellate court or, in some cases, to the court of last resort. The jurisdiction of these courts covers all cases except those reserved for limited or special jurisdiction. Courts of general jurisdiction have court filings in broad areas of civil (31 percent), criminal (13 percent), juvenile (4 percent), and traffic (52 percent) cases, and these are heard by nearly 9,000 judges in the state court systems throughout the country.[48] These courts hold a variety of names, including common circuit, chancery, district, superior, and juvenile.

Courts of Limited Jurisdiction

These courts are lower trial courts with specified jurisdiction. These courts are variously named municipal, district justice, justice of the peace, small claims, traffic, and probate. About three-fourths of all the cases in these courts have to do with traffic offenses. Presently, there are over 13,000 courts of limited jurisdiction in the fifty states.

FEDERAL COURTS

Article III of the Constitution of the United States provides in part that: "The judicial power of the United States, shall be vested in one supreme court, and in such inferior courts as the Congress may from time to time ordain and establish."[49] Pursuant to this provision, Congress has created a network of courts. Today, the federal court system in the United States includes district courts, courts of appeals, special federal courts, and the Supreme Court.

There is at least one district court in each state and usually more than two; California, Texas, and New York have four each. Cases litigated before federal district courts may largely be classified into two types: (1) cases between citizens of different states and (2) cases involving litigation of federal statutes of the federal constitution. Cases before district courts are usually presided over by one judge. However, in limited situations involving challenges to apportionment of statewide legislative bodies or apportionment of congressional districts or otherwise required by Congress, a three-judge court made up of a circuit judge and two district judges may be appointed to hear a case.

Decisions of district courts may be appealed to the federal courts of appeals and, in some instances, directly to the Supreme Court of the United States. There are thirteen courts of appeals, one for the District of Columbia, one for all federal districts, and eleven for numbered circuits. (See Figures 1.1, 1.2, and 1.3.)

In addition, federal courts have been established by the Congress to handle special problems or to cover special jurisdictions. These courts are the courts of the District of Columbia, the Court of Claims, the Tax Court, the Customs Courts, the Courts of Customs and Patent Appeals, the Emergency Court of Appeals, and the territorial courts.

The Supreme Court of the United States is the highest court in the land, beyond which there is no redress. Cases may be brought before the Supreme Court by appeal, *writ of certiorari*, or through the original jurisdiction of the Court. Most school cases that go to the Supreme Court are taken on *writs of certiorari*, certiorari being an original action whereby a case is removed from an inferior to a superior court for trial. Cases may be taken to the Supreme Court from state courts by *writ of certiorari* where a state statute

FIGURE 1.1   *The United States Court System*

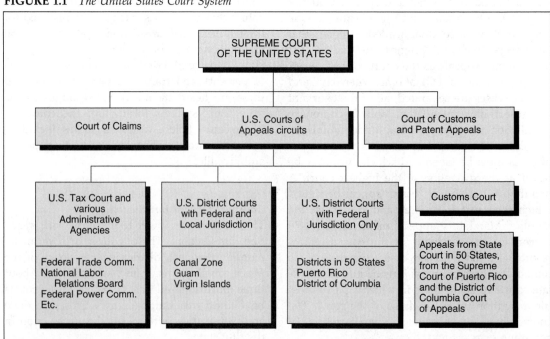

FIGURE 1.2 *General Structure of State Court Systems*

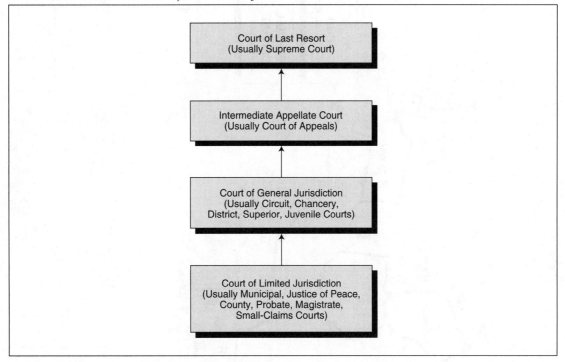

or federal statute is questioned as to its validity under the federal Constitution or where any title, right, privilege, or immunity is claimed under the Constitution. Since most school law cases fall within this category, the *writ of certiorari* is the most common means of getting a case before the Supreme Court.

❖ — ❖ — ❖

The Role of the Supreme Court in American Society, Archibald Cox

Reprinted with permission, 50 Marq.L.Rev. 575, 582–84 (1967).

The task of protecting the individual against the aggressions of government, which under our system usually means aggressions willed by representatives of a majority of the people, often conflicts with the Court's special duty of maintaining the frame of government, which includes the separation of legislative and judicial power. Judicial review calls upon the Court to go over the very social, political and economic questions committed to the Congress and State legisla-tures, yet it can scarcely do so without usurping in some degree the legislative function of weighing and balancing competing interests. . . .

The conventional escape from this dilemma is to say that the conclusions of Congress will stand unless they are so wrong, upon any state of facts that might rationally be supposed to exist, as to be irrational, arbitrary or capricious, fundamentally unfair or shocking to the conscience of a free people. The formula has substance to command it but the difference between saying that an important law is foolish and saying that it is arbitrary or violates fundamental rights lies chiefly in the strength of the speaker's conviction. Any weighing and balancing of the very same interests appraised by the legislature inescapably evokes personal judgments upon the relative importance of imponderable elements.

Whatever the answer to these questions, the Court's responsibility for the framework of government does less to check the Court's reviewing of laws affecting personal liberty than its scrutiny of statutes regulating business and economic practices. This position has strong roots

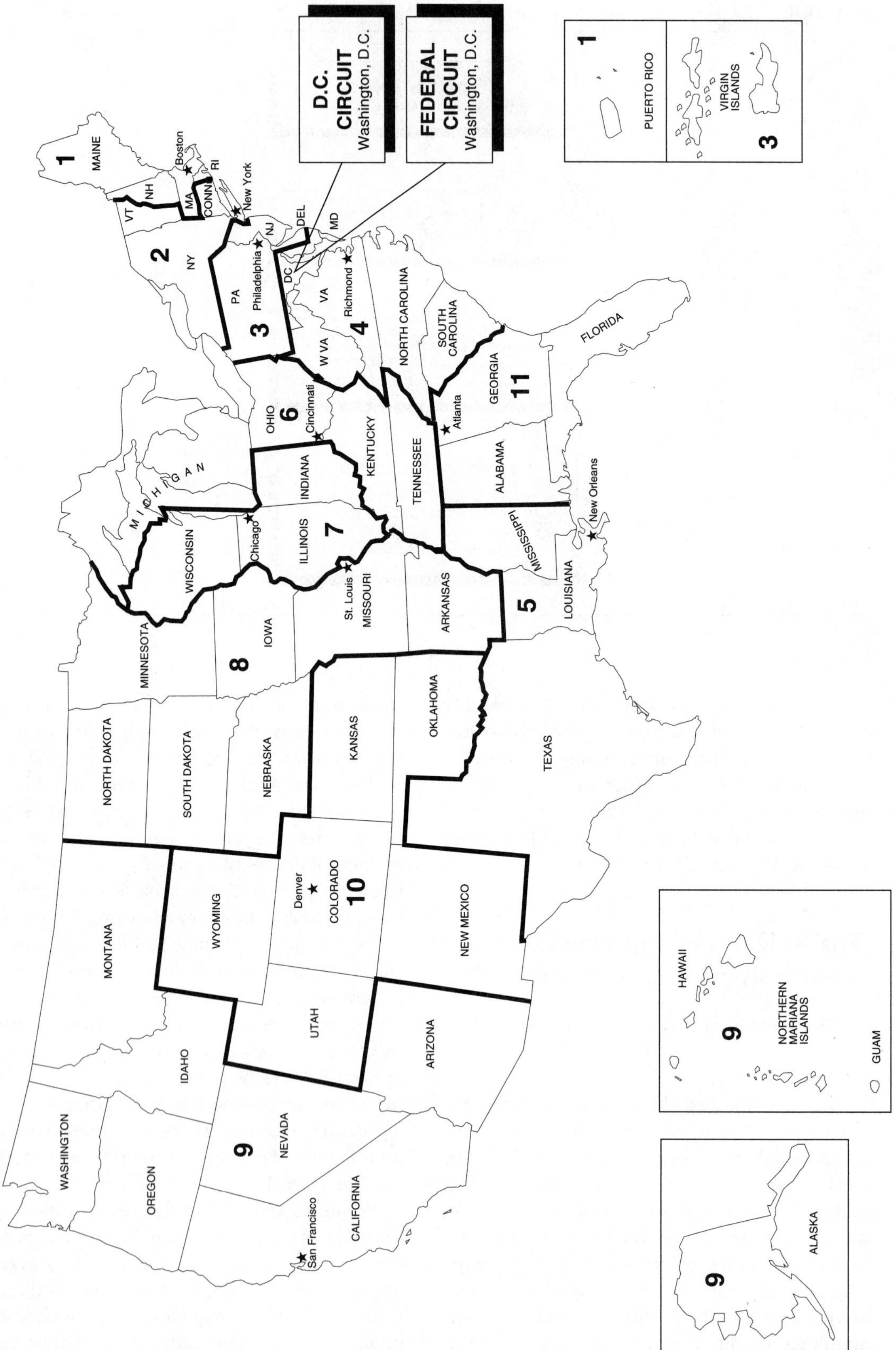

FIGURE 1.3 *The Thirteen Federal Judicial Circuits*

in constitutional history. The Bill of Rights is the chief express constitutional limitation upon legislative power. It is concerned not with the physical safety of society, jobs or economic activity and security—the bricks and mortar of the community—but with the realm of the spirit. The Framers dreamed that if their hopes for civil liberty were codified, man's energies of mind and spirit, released from fear, would flourish. They also knew that society's respect for the freedom of a man to grow and choose the best he can discern must be founded upon the protection of privacy and just and humane criminal procedure.

—————————— ❖ — ❖ — ❖ ——————————

Vertical Judicial Federalism: The Legal Context

Reprinted with permission: G. Alan Tarr and Mary Cornelia Aldis Porter, State Supreme Courts in State and Nation *(New Haven and London: Yale University Press, 1988), pp. 5–13.*

Federal law is extremely influential in structuring the relations between state supreme courts and federal courts. First of all, it defines the jurisdiction of the federal courts. For although Article III of the United States Constitution grants the federal judicial power to the national government, it does not create a separate system of federal courts (save for the U.S. Supreme Court), leaving Congress free to establish inferior federal courts to assign them the jurisdiction it deems appropriate. Historically Congress has not vested in the courts it created the full range of judicial power that might be assigned to them. Prior to 1875, for example, the federal district courts did not have general original jurisdiction in cases raising federal questions, that is, cases arising under the Constitution, laws, and treaties of the United States. And although the federal judicial power extends to all civil cases between citizens of different states (the so-called diversity-of-citizenship jurisdiction), the Judiciary Act of 1789 permitted initiation of such suits in federal courts only when the amount in dispute exceeded $500, in order to prevent citizens from being summoned long distances to defend small claims. (With the passage of time and the effects of inflation, the min-

imum amount has been raised to $10,000.) Furthermore, in conferring diversity jurisdiction on federal courts, Congress has also determined what restrictions shall be placed on the removal of a suit from a state court to a federal district court. Lastly, it is Congress alone that decides whether federal jurisdiction is to be exclusive, thereby precluding initiation of actions in state court, or concurrent.

By determining what sorts of cases may be initiated in federal courts and what sorts may not be initiated in state courts, federal law does more than affect the business of federal and state trial courts. Since state supreme courts serve as appellate tribunals within state judicial systems, the mix of cases they receive is vitally affected by the mix of cases at the trial level. Perhaps not surprisingly, then, comparative analysis of the dockets of federal courts of appeals and state supreme courts reveals major differences in the sorts of issues each addresses. Generally speaking, state supreme courts are much more likely to address issues of state law, and federal courts to address issues of federal law, especially federal statutory law. In more substantive terms, state supreme courts issue many more rulings involving tort law, family law and estates, and real property than do federal courts of appeals. On the other hand, federal appellate courts confront public law issues much more frequently—indeed, they compose the single largest category of business for those courts.

Despite these differences, each system of courts may have occasion to rule on issues of both federal and state law. And since federal constitutional or statutory claims may be advanced in a state proceeding, a state court may need to resolve issues of both state and federal law in reaching its decisions. Three legal principles govern the exposition and interrelation of these two bodies of law. First is the supremacy of federal law. Under the Supremacy Clause of the United States Constitution, all inconsistencies between federal and state law are to be resolved in favor of the federal law. Indeed, the Constitution expressly mandates that "the Judges in every State" are bound by this principle and requires that they take an oath to support the Constitution. Second is the authority of each system of courts to expound its own body of law: state courts must not only give precedence to federal law over state law but also interpret that law in line with the current rulings of the U.S. Supreme Court. As the Mississippi Supreme Court put it in striking down a state law prohibiting the teaching of evolution in public schools, "In determining this question we are *constrained* to follow the decisions of the Supreme Court of the United States wherein that court has construed similar statutes involving the First Amendment to the Constitution of the United States."[50] Conversely, in interpreting state law, the federal courts are obliged to accept as authoritative the interpretation of the highest court of the state. Third is the so-called autonomy principle; that is, when a case raises issues of both federal and state law, the U.S. Supreme Court will not review a ruling grounded in state law unless the ruling is inconsistent with federal law. . . . [W]hen a state ruling rests on an "independent state ground," it is immune from review by the U.S. Supreme Court.

As this reference to review by the Supreme Court implies, Congress has established mechanisms to ensure the accuracy and faithfulness of state interpretations of federal law. Foremost among these is the provision for review by the Supreme Court of state rulings that present issues of federal constitutional or statutory law. The result, as the Supreme Court has recently noted, is that "a State [court] may not impose greater restrictions [on state powers] as a matter of *federal constitutional law* when this Court specially refrains from imposing them."[51] This augmentation of the Supreme Court's authority to supervise the development of federal constitutional law by state courts has become increasingly important in recent years. According to one account, between 1972 and 1980, the Court reversed twenty state supreme court decisions that ruled in favor of the individual on federal constitutional grounds.[52]

Rulings by state supreme courts in criminal cases are subject not only to direct review on appeal but also to collateral review when state prisoners petition federal courts for a writ of habeas corpus. Although institutional means have long been available for ensuring that state courts faithfully apply federal law, until recently there were no comparable procedures for ensuring that federal courts properly interpreted state law. In 1967 Florida took the lead in attempt-

ing to remedy this situation, authorizing its supreme court to rule on questions of state law certified to it by either the United States Supreme Court or federal courts of appeals. During the next decade and a half, twenty-three other states followed Florida's example by permitting certification of questions of state law to their supreme courts, and in 1983 the American Bar Association adopted a resolution urging that all states adopt certification procedures. Federal judges have lauded this procedure as a means of securing authoritative pronouncements on previously unconsidered issues of state law and building "a sense of proper relationship and respect between federal and state courts."[53] Yet despite this praise, certification is not widely used, and in its absence, state high courts have no means for reviewing federal courts' interpretations of state law. On the other hand, they are not bound by federal interpretations of state law that they consider erroneous, and by their rulings in subsequent cases they may seek to correct these errors.

Several observations can be made on the legal context of state supreme courts' relations with federal courts.

First, it is emphatically federal law rather than state law that structures these relationships.

Second, whereas the legal principles governing these relationships have not changed over time, the institutional arrangements and procedures designed to vindicate those principles clearly have, affecting both the division of responsibilities between state and federal courts and the avenues for interaction between them.

Third, although some changes in the applicable federal statutory law have resulted from a concern for more efficient or rational judicial administration, more frequently they have reflected substantive policy concerns, in particular a dissatisfaction with or suspicion of rulings by state courts. Efforts during the 1980s to limit the power of federal courts to hear abortion and school prayer cases likewise reflected the injection of policy concerns into jurisdictional issues, although these proposals were of course premised on the assumption that state courts would be more likely to rule in line with their sponsors' wishes.[54]

Fourth, despite these recent proposals, the trend has been toward an increased availability of federal forums, which—when combined with decisional and statutory limitations on the powers of state courts—has affected the sorts of cases brought to state supreme courts and the finality of their rulings. Thus congressional expansion of the types of issues that can be litigated in federal court, as exemplified by the extension of the courts' jurisdiction over federal questions in 1875, has in effect diverted some types of cases to federal forums that might otherwise have been brought to state supreme courts on review. And the expansion of habeas corpus has transformed federal review of state supreme courts' criminal justice rulings from occasional intervention to a more regularized and consistent oversight.

NOTE

United States Circuit Court of Appeals, 42 U.S.C.A. § 41. (Number and composition of circuits.) The thirteen judicial circuits of the United States are constituted as follows:

Circuits	Composition
District of Columbia	District of Columbia
First	Maine, Massachusetts, New Hampshire, Puerto Rico, Rhode Island
Second	Connecticut, New York, Vermont
Third	Delaware, New Jersey, Pennsylvania, Virgin Islands
Fourth	Maryland, North Carolina, South Carolina, Virginia, West Virginia
Fifth	District of the Canal Zone, Louisiana, Mississippi, Texas
Sixth	Kentucky, Michigan, Ohio, Tennessee
Seventh	Illinois, Indiana, Wisconsin
Eighth	Arkansas, Iowa, Minnesota, Missouri, Nebraska, North Dakota, South Dakota
Ninth	Alaska, Arizona, California, Idaho, Montana, Nevada, Oregon, Washington, Guam, Hawaii
Tenth	Colorado, Kansas, New Mexico, Oklahoma, Utah, Wyoming
Eleventh	Alabama, Florida, Georgia
Federal	All federal judicial districts

■ ENDNOTES

1. Arthur R. Hogue, *Origins of the Common Law* (Bloomington: Indiana University Press, 1966), p. 178.
2. Ibid.
3. Ibid.
4. Ricker v. Board of Education of Millard County School District, 16 Utah 2d 106, 396 P.2d 416 (1964).
5. Latham v. Board of Education of City of Chicago, 31 Ill.2d 178, 201 N.E.2d 111 (1964).
6. Benjamin N. Cardoza, *The Nature of the Judicial Process* (New Haven and London: Yale University Press, 1962), pp. 18–19.
7. Roscoe Pound, "Common Law and Legislation," 21 *Harvard Law Review*, pp. 383, 385 (1908). Copyright © 1908 by The Harvard Law Review Association.
8. Marion & McPherson Railway Co. v. Alexander, 63 Kan. 72, 64 P. 978 (1901).
9. See H. Hart and A. Sacks, *The Legal Process: Basic Problems in the Making and Application of Law* (Cambridge, 10th ed. 1958), pp. 1144–46. Reprinted by permission of Dan Albert M. Sacks.
10. T. Heydon's Case, Exchequer, 30 Co. 7a, 76 Eng.Rep. 637 (1584).
11. Lord Blackburn in River Wear Commissioners v. Adamson, 2 App.Cas. 742, 746 (House of Lords, 1877).
12. Lord Atkinson, in Vacher & Sons, Limited v. London Society of Compositors, 107 L.T.Rep. 722 (House of Lords, 1913).
13. Lord Bramwell, in Hill v. East and West India Dock Co., 9 A.C. 448, 464–65 (House of Lords, 1884).
14. Mr. Justice Day, in Caminetti v. United States, 242 U.S. 470, 485–86, 37 S.Ct. 192, 194 (1917).
15. Mr. Justice Brown, in Hamilton v. Rathbone, 175 U.S. 414, 419, 421, 20 S.Ct. 155, 157 (1899).
16. 5 U.S. (1 Cranch) 137 (1803).

17. Bonvento v. Board of Public Instruction of Palm Beach County, 194 So.2d 605 (Fla.1967).

18. Hobbs v. County of Moore, 267 N.C. 665, 149 S.E.2d 1 (1966).

19. Ashwander v. Tennessee Valley Authority, 297 U.S. 288, 56 S.Ct. 466 (1936).

20. Ibid.

21. Burnet v. Coronado Oil & Gas Co., 285 U.S. 393, 52 S.Ct. 443 (1932).

22. Ibid., p. 449.

23. R. J. Walker & M. G. Walker, *The English Legal System* (London: Butterworths, 1972), p. 124.

24. K. N. Llewellyn, *The Bramble Bush, On Our Law and Its Study* (New York: Oceana Publications, 1960), pp. 41–43.

25. Muskrat v. United States, 219 U.S. 346, 31 S.Ct. 250 (1911).

26. Constitution of the United States, Art. III, § 2.

27. Charles Alan Wright, *Law of Federal Courts* (St. Paul, Minn.: West Publishing Co., 1970).

28. Aetna Life Insurance Co. v. Haworth, 300 U.S. 227, 57 S.Ct. 461, 463, 108 A.L.R. 1000 (1937), quoting from In re Pacific Railway Commission, 32 Fed. 241, 255 (N.D.Cal. 1887).

29. Ibid.

30. Flast v. Cohen, 392 U.S. 83, 94–95, 88 S.Ct. 1942, 1949–50 (1968).

31. 5 U.S. (1 Cranch) 137 (1803).

32. John E. Nowak, Ronald D. Rotunda, J. Nelson Young, *Constitutional Law* (St. Paul, Minn.: West Publishing Co., 1986), p. 56.

33. Ibid., pp. 58–59.

34. *Ex parte* Boez, 177 U.S. 378, 390, 20 S.Ct. 673 (1900).

35. Nowak, op cit., pp. 59–60.

36. United Public Workers v. Mitchell, 330 U.S. 75, 67 S.Ct. 556 (1947).

37. Frothingham v. Mellon, 262 U.S. 447, 43 S.Ct. 597 (1923). See Paul A. Freund, *Constitutional Law* (Boston: Little, Brown and Company, 1961), pp. 46–63.

38. Ibid.

39. 262 U.S. at 488, 43 S.Ct. at 601.

40. 392 U.S. at 101, 88 S.Ct. at 1953 (1968).

41. Nowak, op cit., pp. 72, 73.

42. *State Court Caseload Statistics: Annual Report 1988* (The National Center for State Courts, February 1990), p. 39.

43. Ibid, pp. 38–45.

44. Ibid, p. 18.

45. Ibid.

46. Ibid, pp. 19–20.

47. Ibid.

48. Ibid, p. 5.

49. Constitution of the United States, Art. III, § 1.

50. *Smith v. State*, 242 So.2d 692, 696 (Miss. 1970).

51. *Oregon v. Hass*, 420 U.S. 714, 719, 95 S.Ct. 1215, 1219 (1975).

52. Hans A. Linde, "First Things First: Rediscovering the States' Bill of Rights," *University of Baltimore Law Review* 9 (Spring 1980): 389, n. 42. See also, more generally, Spaeth, "Burger Court Review."

53. See e.g., S. 26, 98th Cong., 1st Sess. (1983), which would have deprived lower federal courts of jurisdiction in cases involving state or local abortion laws, and S. 88, 98th Cong., 1st Sess. (1983), which would have deprived all federal courts, including the U.S. Supreme Court, of jurisdiction in cases involving voluntary prayer in the public schools.

54. Ibid.

CHAPTER 2

HISTORICAL PERSPECTIVE OF PUBLIC SCHOOLS

Public education is a duty that society owes to all its citizens.

—Condorcet

I consider knowledge to be the soul of a Republic, and as the weak and the wicked are generally in alliance, as much care should be taken to diminish the number of the former as of the latter. Education is the way to do this, and nothing should be left undone to afford all ranks of people the means of obtaining a proper degree of it at a cheap and easy rate.

—John Jay, first Chief Justice of the United States

CHAPTER OUTLINE

- AMERICA'S FIRST SCHOOL LAWS
- THE PURITAN INFLUENCE
- A SYSTEM OF EDUCATION
- EDUCATION AS A RIGHT
- COMMON SCHOOL IDEAL IMPLEMENTED
- EDUCATION PROVISIONS OF STATE CONSTITUTIONS

- EDUCATION PROVISION AS LIMITATION ON LEGISLATURE
- JUDICIAL APPROVAL OF COMMON SCHOOLS
- EXPANSION OF PUBLIC SCHOOLS
- CHARTER SCHOOLS
- TUITION AND FEES IN PUBLIC SCHOOLS

PUBLIC EDUCATION is shaped by the political philosophy of particular governments and the social and cultural traditions of the country in which those governments are found. There is an unavoidable reciprocity that transpires by which the educated people sustain and transform the government. Public school law is an essential manifestation of the peoples' conceptu-

alization of the various forms of government and how the governments work.

The traditions of the United States clearly enunciate the desire and necessity for maintaining a republican form of government. To this end, universal public education is required. Political philosophy supporting the American form of government leaves no doubt as to the foundational nature of public education. Montesquieu in his famous *The Spirit of Laws* published in 1748 observed that among the various types of government, a democracy ensures the greatest virtue and that to sustain it, the people must be imbued with a selflessness, benevolence of attitude to others, and a devotion to country. According to Montesquieu, "This virtue may be defined, as the love of the laws and of our country. As this love requires a constant preference of public to private interest, it is the source of all particular virtues. . . . Everything therefore depends on establishing this love in a republic, and to inspire it ought to be the principal business of education. . . . It is in a republican government that the whole power of education is required. . . ." [1]

Rousseau in 1755 wrote that the exercise of citizenship was dependent on education and that "public education . . . is one of the fundamental rules of popular or legitimate government. . . ." [2] Of course, Thomas Jefferson, James Madison, and John Adams had read these and other works of the era of the Enlightenment and were influenced by them. [3]

■ AMERICA'S FIRST SCHOOL LAWS

In the early years, though, predating the founding the United States, the American colonies had to overcome the accepted pattern of the class-oriented English educational system in which free and universal education was beyond the eye of the most progressive governmental leaders. Children of poor and lower-class families received no education at all or were attached as apprentices to learn a trade and develop manual skills.

Even though there was some governmental recognition of the benefits of education, as evidenced by a 1642 statute in Massachusetts in which all parents were charged with seeing to the education of their children and later by a 1647 statute in which the legislature required certain towns to appoint a teacher and permitted taxes for education, by and large early colonial legislatures tended to ignore education. The law of 1647 was promulgated to teach all to read the Scriptures in order to avoid falling prey to "the old deluder, Satan."

According to Horace Mann, it was at the Massachusetts Bay Colony in the seventeenth century that the concept of public universal education was born. Mann said that "it was reserved for 'the Fathers' to engraft that great principle in the laws of a country, as a maxim of government, *that all the people of a State should be educated by the State.*" [4]

Thus, it would not be accurate to say that the Massachusetts legislation of 1642 and 1647 was solely intended for religious purposes. At this time, there was an emerging feeling that education of youth was essential to the well-being of the state and that a stable social environment could best be facilitated if all persons were literate. In 1650, Connecticut followed Massachusetts by enacting its own school law following the "old deluder, Satan, law" in full and adding new elements whereby failure of "masters of families" to educate their "children and servants" could lead to compulsory removal to other masters until ages twenty-one for boys and eighteen for girls. These new masters would "more strictly look unto and force them to submit unto government, according to the rules of this order, if by fair means and former instructions they will not be drawn unto it." [5]

■ THE PURITAN INFLUENCE

The revolution in England that saw the rise to power of Oliver Cromwell and the Puritans introduced a charitable and humanitarian outlook that was found wanting under the Tudor and Stuart monarchies. There were, during this era, meaningful debates about the value of education and the necessity for governmental involvement in education. Francis Bacon had contributed greatly to this dialogue by urging the scientific scholasticism of the church. In 1641, Jan Amos Comenius, the Moravian exile of Czechoslovakia, internationally known as a preeminent educational thinker, urged that children be taught on realistic lines. Comenius visited England at the invitation of the Puritans to explore the reformation and extension of education. Comenius also called for universal books and universal schools to be implemented by the creation of a system of graded schools in all towns and villages. Even the great John Milton contributed to the interchange regarding education with his *Of Education,* wherein he advanced the idea that the "reforming of education . . . be one of the greatest and noblest designs that can be thought on and for want where of this nation perishes."[6] Unfortunately, Comenius's idea did not come to fruition, as the conflict between Charles I and Parliament escalated and civil war broke out. The influence of the newfound Puritan interest in education nevertheless had a direct effect on America. In 1656, James Harrison argued that the provision of schools was one of the state's primary responsibilities.[7] Unfortunately, with the restoration of Charles II to the throne after the death of Cromwell, the free flow of ideas regarding universal education subsided and lay virtually dormant for another 200 years.

The emphasis on learning in England and the colonies was, however, feeble compared to the continent, where elementary education was made universal and compulsory for both sexes in the duchy of Wurttemberg in 1565, in the Dutch Republic in 1618, and in the duchy of Weimar in 1619. In 1722, Frederick I of Prussia decreed universal public education whereby every parish was required to maintain a school; by 1750 under Frederick II, the Great, Prussia led all of Europe in primary and secondary education.[8] England itself did not have any provision of governmental education until two centuries later, in 1870. England began to break free of the control of the privileged, who sent their children to the English "public" schools (exclusive private schools), which were operated primarily by the Church of England. It was not until 1880 that local attendance bylaws became compulsory. Even Scotland and France were more egalitarian in their perspective toward education, founding systems of universal education in 1696 and 1698 respectively, even though the French system did not provide for secondary education except in Jesuit schools.

The strongest influences of the English system on colonial efforts were mostly negative ones, causing pauper school laws to be created. These laws provided that if indigent parents would declare themselves paupers, their children could be sent to specified private or pay schools for a free education.[9] Another vestige of the English system that was used in some colonies was the "rate bill," which required the parent to pay an amount for each child to supplement inadequate school revenues. The amount assessed was collected from the parents through ordinary tax bills. Such rate bills were still in effect in New York State as late as 1867.[10]

It was not until the eighteenth-century Enlightenment that a new political philosophy fully developed that conceived of education as essential to the welfare of the state. Until then, the benefits of education were viewed as largely personal; the external value of education to society had not yet been realized. As the colonies began to struggle for independence from England, the concept of free public education gained momentum. Americans became obsessed with freedom, and schools were viewed as the primary means by which freedom could be obtained and maintained.

■ A SYSTEM OF EDUCATION

During the 1760s and 1770s the idea developed that there should be a free system of education that would provide for a general diffusion of knowledge, cultivate new learning, and nurture the democratic ideals of government. A "system" of education implied at least three attributes. First, there should be some uniformity of access so that the general population would have the opportunity to acquire some appropriate level of learning. Second, there should be some method by which one could pursue a particular curriculum. Third, there should be some institutional organization whereby a person could progress from primary to secondary to college or university.[11] This view was especially well enunciated by Benjamin Rush, who called for the state to be "tied together by one system of education." "The university," he said, "will in time furnish masters for the colleges, and colleges will furnish masters for the free schools, while the free schools, in their turns, will supply the colleges and universities with scholars, students and pupils. The same systems of grammar, oratory and philosophy, will be taught in every part of the state, and the literary features of Pennsylvania will thus designate one great, and equally enlightened family."[12]

Rush emphasized the need to have a free and uniform system of education that would "render the mass of the people more homogeneous, and thereby fit them more easily for uniform and peaceable government."[13]

As Butts observed, "the really important reason for believing in the value of education is that it can be the foundation of freedom. In the first place, a truly democratic society must rest upon the knowledge, intelligence, and wisdom of all people."[14] John Adams observed that nothing is more effective in countering political oppression than the general diffusion of knowledge. Adams wrote that "wherever a general knowledge and sensibility have prevailed among the people, arbitrary government and every kind of oppression have lessened and disappeared in proportion."[15] Americans generally embraced the words of Jefferson, that "a people who mean to be their own Governors must arm themselves with the power which knowledge gives." More than any other's, Jefferson's words redounded the public or common school philosophy that was to sweep the young nation in generations to come. Typical of Jefferson's position was his letter from Paris in 1786 to his former professor George Wythe, written in support of a bill for general education:

> I think by far the most important bill in our whole code is that for the diffusion of knowledge among the people. No other sure foundation can be devised for the preservation of freedom and happiness. . . . Preach, my dear sir, a crusade against ignorance; establish and improve the law for educating the common people. Let our countrymen know . . . that the tax which will be paid for this purpose is not more than the thousandth part of what will be paid to kings, priests, and nobles who will rise up among us if we leave the people in ignorance."[16]

In this new era, universal education was in greater demand, and a discernible shift toward more practical studies was in evidence. The old Latin grammar school began to deteriorate as the major source of learning. After 1750 the enthusiasm for schools based on religious motivations began to die down, and the European traditions for both types and methods of education no longer satisfied the American appetite for knowledge.[17] A concept of public education evolved that was uniquely American. During this period, general school laws in older states led the progression of public education, requiring maintenance of schools by towns for a definite term each year, imposing taxation, and generally statutorily sanctioning the public school movement that had evolved over a century and a half.[18]

A clearly defined role of the state in education, however, had not emerged by 1796 when George Washington, in his farewell address, called for the American people to

> [p]romote, then, as an object of primary importance, institutions for the general diffusion of knowledge. In proportion as the structure of a government gives force of public opinion, it is essential that public opinion be enlightened.[19]

To progress from the sporadic and inadequate early general school laws to uniform state systems of free public education was a laborious journey with battles over tax support and sectarianism marking the way. By 1825, it had become commonly recognized that a state system of education would require general and direct taxation of a major source of revenue, such as real property. A broad base of taxation became the watchword: "The wealth of the State must educate the children of the State" aptly described the principle of taxation for education that was eventually to emerge.[20]

Established traditions were not easily overcome, and it was difficult to convince many of the citizens that pauper schools were not the appropriate educational concept, since it was believed the poor and poverty-stricken would benefit from free public schools.

A major impetus for education had come from the churches that sought to advance Christianity through knowledge of the Bible. Early states generally recognized and supported these efforts, and several states set aside lands to help church schools. As the new philosophy of public education became entrenched and people started to grasp its benefits, new advocates for state education emerged, and conflict with church leaders developed. The inherent discord between sectarian education and free state education was soon manifested in bitter struggles in several states, the story of which is more fully developed in a later chapter of this book.

■ EDUCATION AS A RIGHT

Public school advocates, led by Horace Mann of Massachusetts,[21] preached an educational awakening that was ultimately to form the basis for state systems of public education as we know them today—free secular public schools supported by both local and state general taxation. Mann's idea of free, public, common, universal education was based on natural law, or the external principles of natural ethics, which requires that "the obligation of the predecessors, and the right of the successors, extend to and embrace the means of such an amount of education as will prepare each individual to perform all the duties which devolve upon him [or her] as a man [or woman] and a citizen."[22]

Mann saw education as an "absolute right" or a "natural right." He said, "We can cite no attributes or purpose of the divine nature, for giving birth to any human being, and then inflicting upon that being the curse of ignorance, of poverty and of vice, with all their attendant calamities."[23]

Thus, natural ethics requires the creation and maintenance of public common schools in fulfillment of the state's obligation to pass on to the succeeding generation all the wealth (knowledge) of the preceding generation. The paramount law of nature requires that children should come into possession of all knowledge of the earlier generation.[24]

Mann's view of knowledge as property or wealth was not new. Madison, in the Federalist Papers, had broadly defined property to include "everything to which a man may attach a value and have a right. . . ."[25] According to Madison, man has an "equal property in the free use of his facilities," and his facilities encompass knowledge and learning.[26] Similarly to Mann, Madison thought that knowledge was the most important property that man possesses, and each generation has the obligation through education to pass all that property on to succeeding generations. Public schools are the means by which the state ensures the efficient and just transfer of knowledge: "[T]he claim of a child, then, to a portion of the preexistent property begins with the first breath he draws. . . . He is to receive this, not in the form of lands, or of gold and silver, but in the form of knowledge and a training to good habits."[27]

Thus, according to Mann in reliance on his conception of natural ethics, the state has an obligation to every child to enact a code of laws establishing free public schools. These laws governing education become "the fundamental law of the State."

These laws of the public common school system are based on three propositions:

1. The successive generations of men taken collectively, constitute one great commonwealth.
2. The property of this Commonwealth is pledged for the education of all its youth, up to such a point as will save them from poverty and vice, and prepare them for the adequate performance of their social and civil duties.
3. The successive holders of this property are trustees, bound to the faithful execution of their trust, by the most sacred obligations. . . .[28]

The obligation under these inviolate propositions that form the philosophical foundation for the intergenerational transfer of knowledge require the establishment of a system of public common schools.

Aligned with Mann in the early nineteenth century was an extraordinary group of dedicated and effective leaders who as "public school men" emerged in several states. They argued against tuition in any shape or form and most importantly they maintained that the term "free school" should no longer mean merely a place where the poor were given a free education and all others paid tuition. Class distinctions, they argued, would be reduced if all children could be given a free education financed with revenues from taxes levied on everyone.[29]

This view was reflected in an 1822 report to the Kentucky legislature that advocated free common schools and specifically rejected the pauper school approach:

To be separated from the rest of the community as a distinct and inferior caste, and held out to the world as the objects of public charity, is a degradation too humiliating for the pride of freemen.[30]

■ COMMON SCHOOL IDEAL IMPLEMENTED

In Kentucky in 1819, the governor, in an eloquent plea to the legislature for creation of a system of common schools, asserted both the value of education for the welfare of the state and for the equality and livelihood of the people. Although his message fell on deaf legislative ears at that time, his statement is worth repeating because this is the philosophy on which the free common schools of the United States were founded:

Our government depends for its perpetuity upon the virtue and wisdom of the people; virtue is the offspring of wisdom. To be virtuous, the people must be wise. But how shall they be wise, unless the appropriate means are employed? And how shall the appropriate means be extended to the bereaved and destitute, otherwise than by legislative provision? Education is more vitally important in a republican than in any other form of government; for there the right to administer the government is common to all, and when they have the opportunity of administering the government, the means of obtaining the wisdom requisite for its administration should be accessible to all. The wealthy are never without the means of obtaining education; the poor never, or rarely possess them. But the capacity for the acquisition of knowledge, and the display of virtue, is not confined to the wealthy. It is often, and perhaps more frequently found amongst the poor. Instances are not rare in which genius has emerged from poverty, surmounted the difficulties and privations inseparable from that condition, and like the sun burst through a cloud, illumined the social and political horizon by its benignant irradiations. The ornaments and benefactors of society have not unfrequently arisen when but very slight helps were afforded, from the humblest walks of life.[31]

During this period, struggles over public schools were fought with conviction by those on both sides. Cubberley described this era when public, free, nonsectarian, tax-supported schools were first given serious consideration and there was much public debate between church and private school advocates and public school proponents:

> The second quarter of the nineteenth century may be said to have witnessed the battle for tax-supported, publicly controlled and directed, and nonsectarian common schools. In 1825 such schools were the distant hope of statesmen and reformers; in 1850 they were becoming an actuality in almost every Northern State. The twenty-five years intervening marked a period of public agitation and educational propaganda; of many hard legislative fights; of a struggle to secure desired legislation, and then to hold what had been secured; of many bitter contests with church and private-school interests, which felt that their "vested rights" were being taken from them; and of occasional referenda in which the people were asked, at the next election, to advise the legislature as to what to do. Excepting the battle for the abolition of slavery, perhaps no question has ever been before the American people for settlement which caused so

much feeling or aroused such bitter antagonisms. Old friends and business associates parted company over the question, lodges were forced to taboo the subject to avoid disruption, ministers and their congregations often quarreled over the question of free schools, and politicians avoided the issue. The friends of free schools were at first commonly regarded as fanatics, dangerous to the State, and the opponents of free schools were considered by them as old-time conservatives or as selfish members of society. . . .

> Many thought that tax-supported schools would be dangerous for the State, harmful to individual good, and thoroughly undemocratic. There was danger, too, of making education too common. Schools of any kind were, or should be, for the few, and chiefly for those who could afford private instruction. It was argued that education demands a leisure class and that the poor do not have the necessary leisure, that it was not possible for the government to provide a general educational system, and that all such proposals represented the deliberate confiscation of the property of one class in society for the benefit of another class. These and other arguments were well answered some years later by Horace Mann when he stated, at some length, the political and economic "Ground of the Free School System." Others were afraid that free schools were only a bait, the real purpose being to "religiously traditionalize the children," and then later unite Church and State. Many did not see the need for schools at all, and many more were in the frame of mind of the practical New England farmer who declared that "the Bible and figgers is all I want my boys to know." Strangely enough, the most vigorous opposition often came from the ignorant, improvident, hand-to-mouth laborers, who most needed schools, and free schools at that. Often those in favor of taxation were bitterly assailed, and even at times threatened with personal violence. Henry Barnard, who rendered such useful service in awakening Connecticut and Rhode Island, between 1837 and 1845, to the need for better schools, tells us that a member of the Rhode Island legislature told him that a bill providing a small state tax for schools, which he was then advocating, even if passed by the legislature, could not be enforced in Rhode Island at the point of the bayonet.[32]

Legislatures gradually accepted the idea of free or common schools for all and by statute began to require local school districts to tax themselves to support the public schools. In this early period, it became clear that the states must require rather than permit localities to establish free schools. Local control of education gradually became limited by state constitutions and by actions of state legislatures. Uniformity of education across states, it was decided, would be better brought to fruition by a degree of central state planning rather than through completely decentralized local school control.[33]

By 1852, when Massachusetts enacted the first compulsory attendance law, the responsibility for public education was firmly lodged at the state level. The idea of free common schools was well established, but the implementation of the concept developed slowly. It remained for succeeding generations to deal with the pervasive issues of "uniformity" and "equality," which have grown to be as vital to the public school movement as the word "freedom" was originally.

As a major governmental enterprise, the development of the public school system was accompanied by a continuous string of legal controversies in every state in the nation. As a result, court decisions have, to a great extent, given form and substance to the philosophical base on which the public schools are founded. The courts have made it quite clear that "[p]ublic education is not merely a function of government; it is of government."[34] In legal theory, public schools exist not only to confer benefits on the individual but also, just as importantly, to advance civil society, for which they are necessary, indeed essential.[35] Of such importance is the public education function that the state can, under certain conditions, limit parental control in order to advance the common weal.[36]

The rationale for the creation of a system of free public schools has been reiterated many times by the courts, expounding the importance of an educated citizenry for the general welfare of the people and for the protection of the state.[37]

Recognition of the role and importance of public schools to the well-being of the people and the state was expressed by the Supreme Court of Illinois in 1914. This court declared that public schools were created

> not out of philanthropic motives, but out of a consideration of the essentials of good government. The conduct and maintenance of schools . . . is no less an "exercise of the functions vested in those charged with the conduct of government," is no less a part of "the science and art of government," and deals no less with the "organization, regula-

tion and administration of a State" in its internal affairs, than the construction and maintenance of roads by the commissioners of highways; the conduct and maintenance of the charitable institutions of the state by the board of administration; the inspection of factories, and the enforcement of the laws for the protection of workers and in regard to the employment of women and children by the factory inspectors; the performance of the industrial board of the duties imposed upon it by law, and the performance of many other duties by public officials that, however beneficial to individuals, are not undertaken from philanthropic or charitable motives, but for the protection, safety, and welfare of the citizens of the state in the interest of good government.[38]

Similarly, it was said by the Supreme Court of New Hampshire:

> The primary purpose of the maintenance of the common school system is the promotion of the general intelligence of the people constituting the body politic and thereby to increase the usefulness and efficiency of the citizens, upon which the government of society depends. Free schooling furnished by the state is not so much a right granted to pupils as a duty imposed upon them for the public good. If they do not voluntarily attend the schools provided for them, they may be compelled to do so. While most people regard the public schools as the means of great personal advantage to the pupils, the fact is too often overlooked that they are governmental means of protecting the state from the consequences of an ignorant and incompetent citizenship.[39]

This judicial philosophy is stated in various ways by the decisions in other state supreme courts. The high court for Tennessee, for example, saw a need for a uniform system of public schools to promote the general welfare "by educating the people, and thus, by providing and securing a higher state of intelligence and morals, conserve the peace, good order, and well-being of society."[40]

❖ — ❖ — ❖

The Massachusetts Law of 1647

From "Records of the Governor and Company of the Massachusetts Bay in New England," vol. 2 (Boston, 1853), cited in Ellwood P. Cubberley, Readings in Public Education in the United States (Boston: Houghton Mifflin Company, 1934), pp. 18–19.

This historical act, often referred to as "the old deluder, Satan, Act," was enacted on November 11, 1647, and reads as follows.

It being one cheife proiect of ye ould deluder, Satan, to keepe men from the knowledge of ye Scriptures, as in form^r times by keeping y^m in an unknowne tongue, so in these latt^r times by perswading from ye use of tongues, y^t so at least ye true sence & meaning of ye originall might be clouded by false glosses of saint seeming deceivers, y^t learning may not be buried in ye grave of o^r fath^{rs} in ye church and commonwealth, the Lord assisting o^r endeavo^{r}s,—

It is therefore ord^{r}ed, y^t ev^{r}y towneship in this iurisdiction, aft^r ye Lord hath increased y^m number to 50 houshold^{rs,} shall then forthwth appoint one wthin their towne to teach all such children as shall resort to him to write & reade, whose wages shall be paid eith^r by ye parents or mast^{rs} of such children, or by ye inhabitants in gen^{r}all, by way of supply, as ye maior part of those yet ord^r ye prudentials of ye towne shall appoint; provided, those y^t send their children be not oppressed by paying much more y^n they can have y^m taught for in oth^r townes; & it is furth^r ordered, y^t where any towne shall increase to ye numb^r of 100 families or household^{rs,} they shall set up a grammar schoole, ye m^r thereof being able to instruct youth so farr as they shall be fited for ye university, provided, y^t if any towne neglect ye peformance hereof above one yeare, y^t every such towne shall pay 5 £ to ye next schoole till they shall performe this order.

❖ — ❖ — ❖

Preamble to a Bill for the More General Diffusion of Knowledge (1779)

From The Works of Thomas Jefferson, *collected and edited by Paul Leicester Ford, vol. 2, Federal Edition (New York: G.P. Putnam's Sons, 1904), pp. 414–26, abridged.*

Whereas it appeareth that however certain forms of government are better calculated than others to protect individuals in the free exercise of their natural rights, and are at the same time themselves better guarded against degeneracy, yet experience hath shown, that even under the

best forms, those entrusted with power have, in time, and by slow operations, perverted it into tyranny; and it is believed that the most effectual means of preventing this would be, to illuminate, as far as practicable, the minds of the people at large, and more especially to give them knowledge of those facts, which history exhibiteth, that, possessed thereby of the experience of other ages and countries, they may be enabled to know ambition under all its shapes, and prompt to exert their natural powers to defeat its purposes. And whereas, it is generally true that people will be happiest whose laws are best, and are best administered, and that laws will be wisely formed, and honestly administered, in proportion as those who form and administer them are wise and honest; whence it becomes expedient for promoting the publick happiness that those persons, whom nature hath endowed with genius and virtue, should be rendered by liberal education worthy to receive, and able to guard the sacred deposit of the rights and liberties of their fellow citizens, and that they should be called to that charge without regard to wealth, birth or other accidental condition or circumstance; but the indigence of the greater number disabling them from so educating, at their own expense, those of their children whom nature hath fitly formed and disposed to become useful instruments for the public, it is better that such should be sought for and educated at the common expence of all, than that the happiness of all should be confided to the weak or wicked. . . .

❖ — ❖ — ❖

Education as an Absolute Right, Horace Mann's Tenth Report (1846)

I believe in the existence of a great, immutable principle of natural law, or natural ethics, a principle antecedent to all human institutions and incapable of being abrogated by any ordinances of man, a principle of divine origin, clearly legible in the ways of Providence as those ways are manifested in the order of nature and in the history of the race, which proves the *absolute right* of every human being that comes into the world to an education; and which, of course, proves the correlative duty of every government to see that the means of that education are provided for all.

In regard to the application of this principle of natural law, that is, in regard to the extent of the education to be provided for all, at the public expense, some differences of opinion may fairly exist, under different political organizations; but under a republican government, it seems clear that the minimum of this education can never be less than such as is sufficient to qualify each citizen for the civil and social duties he will be called to discharge; such an education as teaches the individual the great laws of bodily health; as qualifies for the fulfillment of parental duties; as is indispensable for the civil functions of a witness or a juror; as is necessary for the voter in municipal affairs; and finally, for the faithful and conscientious discharge of all those duties which devolve upon the inheritor of a portion of the sovereignty of this great republic.

❖ — ❖ — ❖

Education, the Balance-Wheel of Social Machinery, Horace Mann's Twelfth Report (1848)

The Capacities of Our Present School System to Improve the Pecuniary Condition and to Elevate the Intellectual and Moral Character of the Commonwealth

Under the Providence of God, our means of education are the grand machinery by which the "raw material" of human nature can be worked up into inventors and discoverers, into skilled artisans and scientific farmers, into scholars and jurists, into the founders of benevolent institutions, and the great expounders of ethical and theological science. By means of early education, those embryos of talent may be quickened, which will solve the difficult problems of political and economical law; and by them, too, the genius may be kindled which will blaze forth in the Poets of Humanity. Our schools, far more than they have done, may supply the Presidents and Professors of Colleges, and Superintendents of Public Instruction, all over the land; and send, not only into our sister states, but across the Atlantic, the man of practical science, to superintend the construc-

tion of the great works of art. Here, too, may those judicial powers be developed and invigorated, which will make legal principles so clear and convincing as to prevent appeals to force; and, should the clouds of war ever lower over our country, some hero may be found, the nursing of our schools, and ready to become the leader of our armies, the best of all heroes, who will secure the glories of a peace, unstained by the magnificent murders of the battlefield. . . .

Without undervaluing any other human agency, it may be safely affirmed that the Common School, improved and energized, as it can easily be, may become the most effective and benignant of all the forces of civilization. Two reasons sustain this position. In the first place, there is a universality in its operation, which can be affirmed of no other institution whatever. If administered in the spirit of justice and conciliation, all the rising generation may be brought within the circle of its reformatory and elevating influences. And, in the second place, the materials upon which it operates are so pliant and ductile as to be susceptible of assuming a greater variety of forms than any other earthly work of the Creator. . . .

I proceed, then, in endeavoring to show how the true business of the schoolroom connects itself, and becomes identical, with the great interests of society. The former is the infant, immature state of those interests; the latter, their developed, adult state. As "the child is father to the man," so may the training of the schoolroom expand into the institutions and fortunes of the State.

According to the European theory, men are divided into classes—some to toil and earn, others to seize and enjoy. According to the Massachusetts theory, all are to have an equal chance for earning, and equal security in the enjoyment of what they earn. The latter tends to equality of condition; the former to the grossest inequalities. Tried by any Christian standard of morals, or even by any of the better sort of heathen standards, can any one hesitate, for a moment, in declaring which of the two will produce the greater amount of human welfare, and which, therefore, is the more conformable to the Divine will? . . .

I suppose it to be the universal sentiment of all those who mingle any ingredient of benevolence with their notions on Political Economy, that vast and overshadowing private fortunes are among the greatest dangers to which the happiness of the people in a republic can be subjected. Such fortunes would create a feudalism of a new kind; but one more oppressive and unrelenting than that of the Middle Ages. The feudal lords in England, and on the continent, never held their retainers in a more abject condition of servitude, than the great majority of foreign manufacturers and capitalists hold their operatives and laborers at the present day. The means employed are different, but the similarity in results is striking. What force did then, money does now. . . . The baron prescribed his own terms to his retainers; those terms were peremptory, and the serf must submit or perish. . . .

Now, surely, nothing but Universal Education can counter-work this tendency to the domination of capital and the servility of labor. If one class possesses all the wealth and the education, while the residue of society is ignorant and poor, it matters not by what name the relation between them may be called; the latter, in fact and in truth, will be the servile dependents and subjects of the former. But if education be equally diffused, it will draw property after it, by the strongest of all attractions; for such a thing never did happen, and never can happen, as that an intelligent and practical body of men should be permanently poor. . . .

Education, then, beyond all other devices of human origin, is the great equalizer of the conditions of men—the balance-wheel of the social machinery. I do not here mean that it so elevates the moral nature as to make men disdain and abhor the oppression of their fellow-men. This idea pertains to another of its attributes. But I mean that it gives each man the independence and the means, by which he can resist the selfishness of other men. . . .

For the creation of wealth, then—for the existence of a wealthy people and a wealthy nation—intelligence is the grand condition. The number of improvers will increase, as the intellectual constituency, if I may so call it, increases. In former times, and in most parts of the world even at the present day, not one man in a million has ever had such a development of mind, as made it possible for him to become a contributor

to art or science. Let this development precede, and contributions, numberless, and of inestimable value, will be sure to follow. That Political Economy, therefore, which busies itself about capital and labor, supply and demand, interest and rents, favorable and unfavorable balances of trade; but leaves out of account the element of a wide-spread mental development, is nought but stupendous folly. The greatest of all the arts in political economy is to change a consumer into a producer; and the next greatest is to increase the producing power—an end to be directly attained, by increasing his intelligence. . . .

■ EDUCATION PROVISIONS OF STATE CONSTITUTIONS

Some state constitutions have very general provisions for education, requiring that a system of education be established and maintained, while others are more specific, including adjectives such as "free," "thorough and efficient," "uniform," "suitable," or "adequate." Such words are "terms of art" that, when interpreted by the courts, circumscribe the basis to which the legislature must conform in establishing a public school system. While legislatures are given general authority to govern the schools and may go beyond the minimal constitutional mandates, the constitutional prescription must be satisfied. Where legislators fail to fulfill the constitutional requirements, their acts may be invalidated by the courts. The fact that education is specifically set out in state constitutions as a required state function gives education a preferential position relative to other state governmental functions that are not so mentioned.

Provisions for the establishment and maintenance of public schools are enunciated differently in the various state constitutions, yet there exist certain underlying principles that are generally common to all. These may be summarized as follows:

1. *The legislature is required to bear the responsibility for enactment of laws to govern the public or common schools.* This obligation cannot be averted or delegated to other state or local agencies. Legislatures may provide for local discretion but must ultimately bear the responsibility for the maintenance of a public

school system within the context of the wording and meaning of the education provision of the state constitution.

2. *The public schools, by and large, are considered to be a cohesive unit: one organization or organic whole whose particular organizational pattern and subparts are within the prerogative of the legislature.* The word "system," which is used in most constitutions, requires a measure of orderliness and uniformity regardless of the number of local school districts, implies a unitary cohesiveness, and is not intended to create merely a conglomeration of locally independent school agencies.

3. *The schools as public entities are to be of the body politic of the state, controlled by the public and governed by the people.* Early American experiments, ranging from church and private schools to pauper, rate-bill, and academy schools, quasi-private or semipublic in nature, were rejected as constitutional alternatives to public schools. The various devices to foster control by private interests, reducing public participation and preventing full access by the people, run counter to the ideal of a public school.

4. *The nature of the public school is that it be free and common to all, with no charges to limit access.* Early attempts to create public schools were hindered by the reluctance of legislatures to tax at a level of sufficiency to operate a completely public system. The idea that education is a family or private concern and should be paid for out of private resources has resulted in imposition of various fees levied on the child's family; such fees can potentially harm access and are contrary to the philosophical foundation on which public schools are premised. To sustain full participation and access by all the people requires that the schools be financed by all the people through common taxation.

5. *The concept of public common schools as a state governmental enterprise requires that tax resources be allocated throughout the state in a manner that will ensure that the quality of a child's education will not be dependent on private or personal influence or wealth nor on the financial capabilities of the locality or political subdivision of the state.* State constitutions do not envisage a system of schools with widely variant educational opportunity brought about by either political vicissitude or the vagaries of local fiscal fortune.

Each of these principles, to varying degrees, has been emphasized by judicial interpretation of the education provisions in state constitutions. The nomenclature in state constitutions requiring the creation and maintenance of public schools is terminology of art, most of which has a long historical and legal tradition as to usage and intent.

These general principles establishing public schools are implicit in the meaning of words such as to "maintain a general, suitable and efficient system of free schools," as is found in Article XIV of the Arkansas Constitution, or "a general uniform and thorough system," as is included in the Montana Constitution, Article XII, §1. Such wording of education provisions is replete with significant implications for the conduct of education. For example, the Supreme Court of New Jersey held that the words "thorough and efficient" defining "system" demanded that the state provide equal educational opportunity for all children of the state."[41]

These constitutional provisions can be classified in different ways, but one convenient categorization suggests a minimum of three types.[42] The first of these can be called the adjective or gloss group, wherein the constitution employs words of amplification such as "efficient," "uniform," or "thorough" to specify the qualities of the system required. The second category can simply be called the system group. Here, the state constitution mandates the establishment and maintenance of a system but does not prescribe the type of system other than that it be free, public, or common. An example of this type is the California Constitution, which requires that the state provide for a "system of common schools." A third category is what Mize calls the cherish group, or the New England category. A better term may be "virtue," because in this type of provision the virtues of education are lauded and commended, but there is no positive requirement mandating any particular action by the legislature. In this category the New Hampshire Constitution is one of the most descriptive, stating that "[i]t shall be the duty of the legislators and magistrates in all future periods of the government, to cherish the interests of literature and the sciences, and all seminaries and public schools." Including New Hampshire, there are at least four states with virtue provisions: Massachusetts, Rhode Island, and Virginia. Three other states that can be classified as both system and virtue states are California, Vermont, and Connecticut. Virginia rests comfortably in all three categories by reason of some rather unique wording in its bill of rights[43] that is separate from the education provision of its constitution.[44] This provision, Section 15 of the Virginia Bill of Rights, enacted in 1971, taken from Jefferson's Bill for the More General Diffusion of Knowledge, 1779, states:

> That free government rests, as does all progress, upon the broadest possible diffusion of knowledge, and that the Commonwealth should avail itself of those talents which nature has sown so liberally among its people by assuring the opportunity for their fullest development by an effective system of education throughout the Commonwealth.[45]

This admonishment to the Virginia legislature of the value of widespread knowledge in concert with the requirement that the people be given "opportunity for their fullest development" combines the rationale of the virtue provisions with the qualitative standards of the adjectival provisions.

───────── ❖ — ❖ — ❖ ─────────

Duty of the Legislature to Cherish Public Schools

Jami McDuffy et al. v. Secretary of the Executive Office of Education et al.

Supreme Judicial Court of Massachusetts, 1993.
415 Mass. 545, 615 N.E.2d 516.

In this case, sixteen students of the Commonwealth's public schools in sixteen different towns and cities of the Commonwealth sued the Board of Education, the Commissioner of Education, the Secretary of the Executive Office of Education, and the Treasurer and Receiver General, seeking a declaration of rights under G. L. c. 231A (1990 ed.) that the Commonwealth has failed to fulfil its duty to provide them an education as mandated by the Constitution. The plaintiffs claim that the State's school-financing system effectively denies them the opportunity to receive an adequate education in the public schools in their communities. This denial of the opportunity for an adequate education, the plaintiffs claim, violates both Part II, c. 5, §2, and arts. 1 and 10 of the Declaration of Rights of the Massachusetts Constitution.

. . . [W]e shall restrict ourselves to a determination whether the constitutional language of Part II, c. 5, §2, is merely hortatory, or aspirational, or imposes instead a constitutional duty on the Commonwealth to ensure the education of its children in the public schools.

We conclude that a duty exists. Second, we shall attempt to describe the nature of that duty and where it lies. Third, we shall consider whether on this record such a duty is shown to be violated. . . .

We turn now to an examination of Part II, c. 5, §2, of the Massachusetts Constitution to determine whether, as the plaintiffs claim, its provisions impose on the State an enforceable obligation to provide to each young person in the Commonwealth the opportunity for an education.

The Constitution of Massachusetts is a frame of government for a sovereign power. It was designed by its framers and accepted by the people as an enduring instrument, so comprehensive and general in its terms that a free, intelligent and moral body of citizens might govern themselves under its beneficent provisions through radical changes in social, economic and industrial conditions. It declares only fundamental principles as to the form of government and the mode in which it shall be exercised. . . .

Part II, c. 5, §2, of the Massachusetts Constitution was adopted as part of the Constitution of the Commonwealth in 1780. We repeat the part relevant to this case.

> *Wisdom and knowledge,* as well as virtue, diffused generally among the body of the people, *being necessary for the preservation of their rights and liberties; and as these depend on spreading the opportunities and advantages of education* in the various parts of the

country, and among the different orders of the people, *it shall be the duty of legislatures and magistrates,* in all future periods of this Commonwealth, *to cherish the interests of literature and the sciences,* and all seminaries of them; *especially the* university at Cambridge, *public schools and grammar schools in the towns* . . . (emphasis supplied).

The plaintiffs agree that "the duty of legislatures and magistrates, in all future periods of this Commonwealth, to cherish . . . public schools and grammar schools in the towns" includes the duty to provide an adequate education to the young people of the State, and that this duty is "an enforceable obligation" of the Commonwealth. The defendant education officials argue that the language of the entire section is "aspirational" and a "noble expression of the high esteem in which the framers held education," but that it is not "mandatory."

. . . Part II, c. 5, §2, opens with two declarations, or statements, and then proceeds to establish the "duty . . . to cherish the . . . public schools." First, it declares that "[w]isdom and knowledge, as well as virtue, diffused generally among the body of the people" are "necessary for the preservation of [the people's] rights and liberties." Second, it states that the diffusion of wisdom, knowledge, and virtue among the body of the people "depend[s] on spreading the opportunities and advantages of education in the various parts of the country, and among the different orders of the people." Following these two declarations, the section provides that "it shall be the duty of legislatures and magistrates, in all future periods of this Commonwealth, to cherish the interests of literature and the sciences, and all seminaries of them; especially . . . public schools and grammar schools in the towns."

The two statements at the beginning of Part II, c. 5, §2, state plainly the premises on which the duty is established: First, the protection of rights and liberties requires the diffusion of wisdom, knowledge, and virtue throughout the people. Second, the means of diffusing these qualities and attributes among the people is to spread the opportunities and advantages of education throughout the Commonwealth. In the statement of these two premises for which the duty is established it is revealed that: The duty is established so that the rights and liber-

ties of the people will be preserved. The immediate purpose of the establishment of the duty is the spreading of the opportunities and advantages of education throughout the people; the ultimate end is the preservation of rights and liberties. Put otherwise, an educated people is viewed as essential to the preservation of the entire constitutional plan: a free, sovereign, constitutional democratic state.

The language of the section makes clear the connection between the opening declarations and the duty which follows: "[A]s these [wisdom, knowledge, and virtue, diffused among the people] *depend on* spreading the opportunities and advantages of education . . . it *shall be* the duty of legislatures and magistrates . . . to *cherish* . . . public schools" (emphasis added). From the context, it is clear that "as" is used to mean "because," and that there is a clear causal chain connecting the two statements and the establishment of the duty. The language of Part II, c. 5, §2, thus leaves little doubt about the reasons for which the duty to cherish is established.

The duty established is, inter alia, placed on the "legislatures and magistrates, in all future periods of this Commonwealth." . . . The common meaning of "duty" in 1780, according to a dictionary of the English language published that year, was "that to which a man is by any natural or legal obligation bound." T. Sheridan, A General Dictionary of the English Language 1780 (Scholar Press 1967). "[I]n the sense most obvious to the common intelligence," *Buckley v. Secretary of the Commonwealth,* . . . both then and now, a duty is that to which one is bound, or an "obligation."

Most importantly, that distinctive meaning can be seen from works of the framers themselves. John Adams, in Dissertation on the Canon and Feudal Law (1765), reprinted in 3 Works of John Adams 447 (C.F. Adams ed. 1851), described an "aspiring, noble principle founded in benevolence, and *cherished* by knowledge" (*id.* at 448); declared that "none of the means of information are more sacred, or have been *cherished* with more tenderness and care by the settlers of America, than the press" (id. at 457); and proclaimed that "[t]his spirit [of liberty], however, without knowledge, would be little better than a brutal rage. Let us tenderly and kindly *cherish,* therefore, the means of knowledge. Let us dare to read, think, speak, and write" (*id.* at 462) (emphasis supplied). In 1789, John Hancock, then Governor of the Commonwealth, spoke to the Massachusetts Legislature about the "commencement and operation" of the new Federal government, pronouncing that "[t]he early laws of the Union must *cherish* commerce" (emphasis supplied).

Thus, according to common usage in the late eighteenth century, a duty to cherish was an obligation to support or nurture. Hence, the "duty . . . to cherish the interests of literature and the sciences, and all seminaries of them; especially . . . public schools and grammar schools in the towns" is an obligation to support or nurture these interests and institutions. The breadth of the meaning of these terms ("duty . . . to cherish"), together with the articulated ends for which this duty to cherish is established, strongly support the plaintiffs' argument that the "duty . . . to cherish . . . the public schools" encompasses the duty to provide an education to the people of the Commonwealth. Part II, c. 5, §2, states plainly that the duty to "cherish"—support—public schools arises out of the need to educate the people of the Commonwealth; it is reasonable therefore to understand the duty to "cherish" public schools as a duty to ensure that the public schools achieve their object and educate the people.

Constitutional structure, as well as constitutional language, supports the plaintiffs' argument that Part II, c. 5, §2, imposes a duty on "legislatures and magistrates" to provide for the education of the populace. . . . Part II, c. 5, §2, is distinctively and prominently placed in the Constitution.

The framers' decision to dedicate an entire chapter—one of six—to the topic of education signals that it was to them a central concern. Their decision to treat education differently from other objects of government by devoting a separate chapter to education rather than listing it as a matter within the powers of the legislative or executive branches indicates structurally what is said explicitly by words: that education is a "duty" of government, and not merely an object within the power of government. Lastly, the framers' decision to place the provisions concerning education in "The Frame of Government"—rather than in the "Declaration of Rights"—demonstrates that the framers conceived of education as fundamentally related to the very existence of government.

This last point illustrates an instance where structure echoes language. The preservation of rights and liberties was one of the principal reasons for the formation of the Commonwealth and the adoption of a republican form of government. The Preamble to the Constitution states that the "end of the institution, maintenance and administration of government, is to secure the existence of the body politic, to protect it, and to furnish the individuals who compose it, with the power of enjoying in safety and tranquility their natural rights and the blessings of life." Education, which Part II, c. 5, §2, states is the means of diffusing wisdom, knowledge, and virtue, is, therefore, a prerequisite for the existence and survival of the Commonwealth.

. . . [In] the past, the founders of the Massachusetts Bay Colony, and later of the Province of Massachusetts Bay, "appreciated the importance and necessity of providing for the universal education of the people, at a very early period," and "laid the foundation of a system of common schools," *Jenkins v. Andover,* 103 Mass. 94, 96–97 (1869). See *Cushing v. Newburyport,* 10 Met. 508, 511 (1845). . . .

A public commitment to education was evidenced from the first days of the colonial period. The Massachusetts Bay Colony was founded in 1630. Five years later, in 1635, the people of Boston agreed that "our brother Philemon Purmont shall be intreated to become scholemaster for the teaching and nourtering of children with us." The next year, in 1636, the General Court made a public grant of 400 English pounds to found a college. 1 Massachusetts Bay Records 183 (October 28, 1636). In 1642 the General Court enjoined the selectmen of every town to keep "a vigilant eye over their brethren and neighbours" to see "that none of them shall suffer so much Barbarism in any of their families, as not to endeavour to teach, by themselves or others, their Children and Apprentices," and prescribed a twenty-shilling fine for such neglect.

In 1647, in a law which is credited with beginning the history of public education in America, the General Court required the towns to maintain a system of public schools. . . .

Educational concerns are evidenced in the poor laws of the provincial government. The overseers of the poor in the towns (or the selectmen of the towns where there were no overseers) were authorized by the General Court to "bind out" for work "all such children whose parents shall . . . be thought . . . unable to maintain them," with the proviso, however, that provision was "to be made for the instruction of children so bound out, to read and write, as they may be capable." . . .

By 1780, a system of public schools had been in existence for over 130 years in Massachusetts, a college had been in existence for over 140 years, and the values of public education had been expressed and supported in a wide variety of ways. It was against this background and with this experience that the delegates to the Constitutional Convention of 1779–1780 framed, and the people of Massachusetts adopted, the Constitution of the Commonwealth, including Part II, c. 5, §2.

We now examine the history of the adoption of Part II, c. 5, §2, of the Constitution. Part II, c. 5, §2, was drafted by a drafting committee charged by the delegates to the 1779–1780 Constitutional Convention with the task of preparing the initial draft of a Constitution. John Adams is generally regarded as the principal author of the draft Constitution produced by this committee, including the section which became Part II, c. 5, §2. At the convention, the delegates accepted Part II, c. 5, §2, as drafted, and included it without change in the proposed Constitution. The delegates then sent the proposed Constitution to the towns for review by the people. When the town returns were in, the delegates determined that the people had approved the proposed Constitution as written, and declared the Constitution ratified, including Part II, c. 5, §2, as originally drafted.

. . . We believe that the people of those other towns, who voted for the provision without objection, and whose affirmative vote carried the day, endorsed the provision with the understanding that it would require the Legislature to mandate universal public education.

It seems plain that this is what the framers of the Constitution of 1780 intended. There is substantial evidence that John Adams believed that widespread public education was integral to the very existence of a republican government. In an early and influential essay, Adams described the strong alliances between ignorance and oppression, and between knowledge and liberty. He praised the early English settlers of the colony as deeply learned and deeply committed to liberty. They knew, he said, that nothing countered political oppression more than "knowledge diffused generally through the whole body of the people" and so they set out to "propagate and perpetuate knowledge." Under their efforts, "the education of all ranks of people was made the care and expense of the public," and the result was that a "native of America who cannot read and write is as rare an appearance as . . . a comet or an earthquake." There were, he claimed, however, some persons in Massachusetts "who affect to censure this provision for the education of our youth as a needless expense, and an imposition upon the rich in favor of the poor"; this attitude, Adams continued, was calculated to foster ignorance and, with it, servility. Ignorance and servility were not the lot of the people of Massachusetts, however, because people have natural rights to liberty and to knowledge (they have "a right, from the frame of their nature, to knowledge"). In Massachusetts, the right to liberty was not only a natural right but also the inheritance bequeathed by "our fathers [who] have earned and bought it for us, at the expense of their ease, their estates, their pleasure, and their blood." Dissertation on the Canon and Feudal Law, in 3 Works of John Adams 456 (C.F. Adams ed. 1851). To Adams, these rights were interdependent; the former could not be maintained without the latter: "[L]iberty cannot be preserved without a general knowledge among the people." *Id.* For this reason, he argued, "the preservation of the means of knowledge among the lowest ranks, is of more importance to the public than all the property of all the rich men in the country." *Id.* at 457.

In 1776, three years before drafting the Constitution of the Commonwealth, Adams wrote and published a pamphlet entitled Thoughts on Government, in which he endeavored to answer the question "what plan I would advise a colony to pursue, in order to get out of the old government and into a new one." He offered that "there is no good government but what is republican." Thoughts on Government, in 4 Works of John Adams 194 (C. F. Adams ed. 1851). He described the requirements of a Constitution for a republican government. He prescribed a tripartite system of government in which the executive, legislative, and judicial branches are independent of one another, a "militia law," and provisions for widely dispersed public education: "Laws for the liberal education of youth, especially of the lower class of people, are so extremely wise and useful, that, to a humane and generous mind, no expense for this purpose would be thought extravagant." In a subsequent version of this plan, he wrote that "two things are indispensably to be adhered to,—one is, some regulation for securing forever an equitable choice of representatives; another is, the education of youth, both in literature and morals."

Samuel Adams, the second member of the drafting subcommittee of three, also took pride in and instruction from the commitment of the early settlers to public education. In 1775, he wrote to James Warren: "Our Ancestors in the most early Times laid an excellent Foundation for the security of Liberty by setting up in a few years after their Arrival a publick Seminary of Learning; and by their Laws they obligd every Town consisting of a certain Number of Families to keep and maintain a Grammar School." He wrote also of his regret that the "extraordinary Expence" of waging the Revolution was taking resources away from the public schools and asked whether, if this "Inattention" were to continue, "would not the leading Gentlemen do eminent Service to the Publick, by impressing upon the Minds of the People, the Necessity & Importance of encouraging that System of Education, which in my opinion is so well calculated to diffuse among the Individuals of the Community the Principles of Morality, so essentially necessary to the Preservation of publick Liberty."

This examination of the views of those who framed and those who adopted our Constitution provides compelling support for the argument that Part II, c. 5, §2, was intended to impose on Legislatures and magistrates the duty to provide for the education of the people. . . .

Throughout the early years of the Commonwealth, legislators and magistrates—several of whom had been delegates to the constitutional convention—publicly articulated their views of the responsibilities imposed on them by Part II, c. 5, §2. In speeches and other public messages, they stressed several points repeatedly: They described Part II, c. 5, §2, of the Constitution as imposing on them a duty or injunction. They stated emphatically that public education was integral to the republican form of government newly adopted in the Commonwealth. They characterized and extolled public education as education for the rich and the poor alike. Lastly, they stated, in numerous different ways, that ensuring the education of the population was a matter of State-wide responsibility. . . .

In 1793, Governor Hancock requested the Legislature to turn its attention to the entire system of public schools in the Commonwealth: "Amongst the means by which our government has been raised to its present height of prosperity, that of education has been the most efficient; you will therefore encourage and support our Colleges and Academies, but more watchfully the Grammar and other town schools. These offer equal advantages to poor and rich; should the support of such institutions be neglected, the kind of education which a free government requires to maintain its force, would soon be forgotten."

In 1794, Samuel Adams, assuming the office of Governor on the death of Governor Hancock, addressed the General Court on the "great and important" subject of "the education of our children and youth." Samuel Adams declared that the security of the State depended on the education of youth; one reason, among others, was that education "qualif[ies] them [youth] to discover any error, if there should be such, in the forms and administration of Governments, and point out the method of correcting them." Address to the Massachusetts Legislature, Jan. 17, 1794, reprinted in 4 Writings of Samuel Adams 359–360 (H. A. Cushing ed. 1968). "But," Governor Adams continued, "I need not press this subject, being persuaded, that this Legislature from the inclination of their minds, as well as in regard to the duty enjoined by the Constitution, will cherish the interest of Literature, the Sciences, and all their Seminaries." *Id.* at 360. The next year, Governor Adams, like Governor Hancock just two years before, warned the legislative body of the dangers to the public schools of the growing phenomenon of private "Academies." While praising the "patriotic exertions of worthy citizens" to establish the private academies, he continued: "[P]erhaps it may be justly apprehended, that multiplying them, may have a tendency to injure the ancient and beneficial mode of Education in Town Grammar Schools. The peculiar advantage of such schools is that the poor and the rich may derive equal benefit from them; but none excepting the more wealthy, generally speaking, can avail themselves of the benefits of the Academies. Should these institutions detach the attention and influence of the wealthy, from the generous support of town Schools, is it not to be feared that useful learning, instruction and social feelings in the early parts of life, may cease to be so equally and universally disseminated, as it has heretofore been." Address to the Legislature of Massachusetts, June 3, 1795, in 4 Writings of Samuel Adams, *supra* at 375, 378–379. . . .

We have reviewed at great length the history of public education in Massachusetts so that we might glean an understanding of the meaning of c. 5, §2. In doing so, we have considered the history of the colony, the province, the condition and concepts relating to education underlying the drafting of the Constitution of the Commonwealth, and, in particular, c. 5, §2. We have examined the intention of the framers, the language and the structure of the Constitution, the ratification process by the towns and also the words, acts, and deeds of contemporaries of that time, and especially the views, addresses, and statutes of early Governors (magistrates) and the Legislatures. In this light, we have considered the proper meaning of the words "duty" and "cherish" found in c. 5, §2. What emerges from this review is that the words are not merely aspirational or hortatory, but obligatory. What emerges also is that the Commonwealth has a duty to provide an education for *all* its children, rich and poor, in every city and town of the Commonwealth at the public school level, and that this duty is designed not only to serve the interests of the children, but, more fundamentally, to prepare them to participate as free citizens of a free State to meet the needs and interests of a republican government, namely the Commonwealth of Massachusetts.

This duty lies squarely on the executive (magistrates) and legislative (Legislatures) branches of this Commonwealth. That local control and fiscal support have been placed in greater or lesser measure through our history on local governments does not dilute the validity of this conclusion. While it is clearly within the power of the Commonwealth to delegate some of the implementation of the duty to local governments, such power does not include a right to abdicate the obligation imposed on magistrates and Legislatures placed on them by the Constitution.

. . . As Horace Mann, the first secretary of the Board of Education, stated many years ago: "In regard to the application of this principle of natural law,—that is, in regard to the extent of the education to be provided for all, at the public expense,—some differences of opinion may fairly exist, under different political organizations; but under our republican government, it seems clear that the minimum of this education can never be less than such as is sufficient to qualify each citizen for the civil and social duties he will be called to discharge;—such an education as teaches the individual the great laws of bodily health; as qualifies for the fulfillment of parental duties; as is indispensable for the civil functions of a school or a juror; as is necessary for the voter in municipal and in national affairs; and finally, as is requisite for the faithful and conscientious discharge of all those duties which devolve upon the inheritor of a portion of the sovereignty of this great republic." The Massachusetts System of Common Schools: Tenth Annual Report of the Massachusetts Board of Education 17 (1849).

The content of the duty to educate which the Constitution places on the Commonwealth necessarily will evolve together with our society. Our Constitution, and its education clause, must be interpreted "in accordance with the demands of modern society or it will be in constant danger of becoming atrophied and, in fact, may even lose its original meaning." *Seattle Sch. Dist. No. 1 v. State*, 90 Wash. 2d 476, 516 (1978). Justice Holmes aptly captured this principle of constitutional jurisprudence:

[W]hen we are dealing with words that also are a constituent act, like the Constitution of the United States, we must realize that they have called into life a being the development of which could not have been foreseen completely by the most gifted of its begetters. . . .

Thus, we leave it to the magistrates and the Legislatures to define the precise nature of the task which they face in fulfilling their constitutional duty to educate our children today, and in the future.

These cases are remanded to the county court for entry of a judgment declaring that the provisions of Part II, C. 5, §2, of the Massachusetts Constitution impose an enforceable duty on the magistrates and Legislatures of this Commonwealth to provide education in the public schools for the children there enrolled, whether they be rich or poor and without regard to the fiscal capacity of the community or district in which such children live.

■ EDUCATION PROVISION AS LIMITATION ON LEGISLATURE

Historically, state courts have seldom intervened to limit legislative prerogative in interpreting the intent of "education provisions" of state constitutions. Education provisions are typically those that place an affirmative Constitutional obligation on the legislature to create a school system. The courts have most often followed the philosophy expressed by an Illinois court that refused to substitute its judgment for the legislature's, saying that "[t]he efficiency and fairness of a state system is for the determination of the legislature."[46] Typically, the courts have not viewed the education provisions of state constitutions as limitations on the legislature. The education provisions were not considered to be limitations, but merely elaborations on enabling provisions to be used and defined as the legislature thought necessary. This attitude is expressed by a 1926 Virginia court that said, "While the Constitution of the state provides, in mandatory terms, that the Legislature shall establish and maintain public free schools, there is neither mandate nor inhibition in the provisions as to the regulation thereof. The Legislature, therefore, has the power to enact any legislation in regard to the conduct, control, and regulation of the public free schools, which does not deny to the citizen the Constitutional right

to enjoy life and liberty, to pursue happiness and to acquire property."[47] Thus, words in a state constitution defining the type of education the people required were not to be interpreted by the courts as limitations on legislative prerogative. The power of the legislature would not generally be questioned unless the legislation transgressed on the more important freedom provisions such as the right to life, liberty, happiness, and property.

Lately, however, this view has changed. The courts have become more assertive and have begun to more carefully scrutinize legislation in light of the education provisions. In several instances the courts have held state methods of financing the schools to be unconstitutional as violative of these provisions (see Chapter 18 on school finance). Such cases are beginning to establish an imposing array of precedents, which give definition to terms such as "thorough," "efficient," "throughout," "uniform," and a host of other terms.

A judgment of this type was rendered by the Supreme Court of Kentucky in 1989, invoking the term "efficient" to invalidate the entire system of public schools. The broad sweep of this opinion in enforcing the education provision of a state constitution makes it a particularly significant precedent.

———————— ❖ — ❖ — ❖ ————————

Legislature Fails Constitutional Requirement to Establish an Efficient System of Common Schools

Rose v. The Council for Better Education, Inc.

Supreme Court of Kentucky, 1989.
790 S.W.2d 186.

STEPHENS, Chief Justice. The issue we decide on this appeal is whether the Kentucky General Assembly has complied with its constitutional mandate to "provide an efficient system of common schools throughout the state."

In deciding that it has not, we intend no criticism of the substantial efforts made by the present General Assembly and by its predecessors, nor do we intend to substitute our judicial authority for the authority and discretion of the General Assembly. We are, rather, exercising our constitutional duty in declaring that, when we consider the evidence in the record, and when we apply the constitutional requirement of Section 183 to that evidence, it is crystal clear that the General Assembly has fallen short of its duty to enact legislation to provide for an efficient system of common schools throughout the state. In a word, the present system of common schools in Kentucky is not an "efficient" one in our view of the clear mandate of Section 183. The common school system in Kentucky is constitutionally deficient.

In reaching this decision, we are ever mindful of the immeasurable worth of education to our state and its citizens, especially to its young people. The framers of our constitution intended that each and every child in this state should receive a proper and an adequate education, *to be provided for by the General Assembly.* This opinion dutifully applies the constitutional test of Section 183 to the existing system of common schools. We do no more, nor may we do any less.

. . . The overall effect of appellants' evidence is a virtual concession that Kentucky's system of common schools is underfunded and inadequate; is fraught with inequalities and inequities throughout the 168 local school districts; is ranked nationally in the lower 20–25% in virtually every category that is used to evaluate educational performance; and is not uniform among the districts in educational opportunities. When one considers the evidence presented by the appellants, there is little or no evidence to even begin to negate that of the appellees. The tidal wave of the appellees' evidence literally engulfs that of the appellants.

In spite of the Minimum Foundation Program and the Power Equalization Program, there are wide variations in financial resources and dispositions thereof which result in unequal educational opportunities throughout Kentucky. The local districts have large variances in taxable property per student. Even a total elimination of all mismanagement and waste in local school districts would not correct the situation as it now exists. A substantial difference in the curricula offered in the poorer districts contrasts

with that of the richer districts, particularly in the areas of foreign language, science, mathematics, music and art.

The achievement test scores in the poorer districts are lower than those in the richer districts and expert opinion clearly established that there is a correlation between those scores and the wealth of the district. Student-teacher ratios are higher in the poorer districts. Moreover, although Kentucky's per capita income is low, it makes an even lower per capita effort to support the common schools.

Students in property poor districts receive inadequate and inferior educational opportunities as compared to those offered to those students in the more affluent districts. . . .

In a few simple, but direct words, the framers of our present Constitution set forth the will of the people with regard to the importance of providing public education in the Commonwealth.

> The General Assembly shall, by appropriate legislation, provide for an efficient system of common schools throughout the State. Ky. Const. Sec. 183.

Several conclusions readily appear from a reading of this section. First, it is the obligation, the sole obligation, of the General Assembly to provide for a system of common schools in Kentucky. The obligation to so provide is clear and unequivocal and is, in effect, a constitutional mandate. Next, the school system must be provided throughout the entire state, with no area (or its children) being omitted. The creation, implementation and maintenance of the school system must be achieved by appropriate legislation. Finally, the system must be an efficient one.

It is, of course, the last 'conclusion' that gives us pause and requires study and analysis. What, indeed, is the meaning of the word "efficient" as used in Section 183?

. . . In language which brings together and re-emphasizes earlier decisions, we said,

> The fundamental mandate of the Constitution and Statutes of Kentucky is that there shall be equality and that all public schools shall be nonpartisan and nonsectarian.
>
> Uniformity does not require equal classification but it does demand that there shall be a substantially uniform system and equal school facilities

without discrimination as between different sections of a district or a county.

The lack of uniformity and the unequal educational opportunity existing in the county was said to constitute "a violation of both the spirit and intent of Section 183 of our State Constitution." That reasoning therein applies, *a fortiori*, to the entire state system of common schools. Public schools must be efficient, equal and substantially uniform.

As can be seen, this Court, since the adoption of the present Constitution, has, in reflecting on Section 183, drawn several conclusions:

1. The General Assembly is mandated, is duty bound, to create and maintain a system of common schools—throughout the state.
2. The expressed purpose of providing such service is vital and critical to the well being of the state.
3. The system of common schools must be efficient.
4. The system of common schools must be free.
5. The system of common schools must provide equal educational opportunities for all students in the Commonwealth.
6. The state must control and administer the system.
7. The system must be, if not uniform, 'substantially uniform' with respect to the state as a whole.
8. The system must be equal to and for all students.

Numerous well-qualified experts testified in this case. They were all well educated, experienced teachers, educators, or administrators; and all were familiar with the Kentucky system of common schools and with other states' and national school issues.

Dr. Richard Salmon testified that the concept of efficiency was a three-part concept. First, the system should impose no financial hardship or advantage on any group of citizens. Further, local school districts must make comparable tax efforts. Second, resources provided by the system must be adequate and uniform throughout the state. Third, the system must not waste resources.

Dr. Kern Alexander opined that an efficient system is one which is unitary. It is one in which

there is uniformity throughout the state. It is one in which equality is a hallmark and one in which students must be given equal educational opportunities, regardless of economic status, or place of residence. He also testified that "efficient" involves pay and training of teachers, school buildings, other teaching staff, materials, and adequacy of all educational resources. Moreover, he, like Dr. Salmon, believed that "efficient" also applies to the quality of management of schools. Summarizing Dr. Alexander's opinion, an efficient system is unitary, uniform, adequate and properly managed.

The definitions of "efficient" were documented and supported by numerous national and local studies, prepared and authorized by many of the giants of the education profession.

The primary expert for the appellees was a local school superintendent who felt that an efficient system is one which is operated as best as can be with the money that was provided. We reject such a definition, which could result in a system of common schools, efficient only in the uniformly deplorable conditions it provides throughout the state.

In summary, the experts in this case believed that an "efficient" system of common schools should have several elements:

1. The system is the sole responsibility of the General Assembly.
2. The tax effort should be evenly spread.
3. The system must provide the necessary resources throughout the state—they must be uniform.
4. The system must provide an adequate education.
5. The system must be properly managed.

We now hone in on the heart of this litigation. In defining "efficient," we use all the tools that are made available to us. In spite of any protestations to the contrary, we do not engage in judicial legislating. We do not make policy. We do not substitute our judgment for that of the General Assembly. We simply take the plain directive of the Constitution, and, armed with its purpose, we decide what our General Assembly must achieve in complying with its solemn constitutional duty.

Any system of common schools must be created and maintained with the premise that education is absolutely vital to the present and to the future of our Commonwealth . . .

The sole responsibility for providing the system of common schools is that of our General Assembly. It is a duty—it is a constitutional mandate placed by the people on the 138 members of that body who represent those selfsame people.

The General Assembly must not only establish the system, but it must monitor it on a continuing basis so that it will always be maintained in a constitutional manner. The state must carefully supervise it, so that there is no waste, no duplication, no mismanagement, at any level.

The system of common schools must be adequately funded to achieve its goals. The system of common schools must be substantially uniform throughout the state. Each child, *every child*, in this Commonwealth must be provided with an equal opportunity to have an adequate education. Equality is the key word here. The children of the poor and the children of the rich, the children who live in the poor districts and the children who live in the rich districts must be given the same opportunity and access to an adequate education. This obligation cannot be shifted to local counties and local school districts.

. . .

A child's right to an adequate education is a fundamental one under our Constitution. The General Assembly must protect and advance that right. We concur with the trial court that an efficient system of education must have as its goal to provide each and every child with at least the seven following capacities: (i) sufficient oral and written communication skills to enable students to function in a complex and rapidly changing civilization; (ii) sufficient knowledge of economic, social, and political systems to enable the student to make informed choices; (iii) sufficient understanding of governmental processes to enable the student to understand the issues that affect his or her community, state, and nation; (iv) sufficient self-knowledge and knowledge of his or her mental and physical wellness; (v) sufficient grounding in the arts to enable each student to appreciate his or her cultural and historical heritage; (vi) sufficient training or preparation for advanced training in

either academic or vocational fields so as to enable each child to choose and pursue life work intelligently; and (vii) sufficient levels of academic or vocational skills to enable public school students to compete favorably with their counterparts in surrounding states, in academics or in the job market.

The essential, and minimal, characteristics of an "efficient" system of common schools may be summarized as follows:

1. The establishment, maintenance and funding of common schools in Kentucky is the sole responsibility of the General Assembly.
2. Common schools shall be free to all.
3. Common schools shall be available to all Kentucky children.
4. Common schools shall be substantially uniform throughout the state.
5. Common schools shall provide equal educational opportunities to all Kentucky children, regardless of place of residence or economic circumstances.
6. Common schools shall be monitored by the General Assembly to assure that they are operated with no waste, no duplication, no mismanagement, and with no political influence.
7. The premise for the existence of common schools is that all children in Kentucky have a constitutional right to an adequate education.
8. The General Assembly shall provide funding which is sufficient to provide each child in Kentucky an adequate education.
9. An adequate education is one which has as its goal the development of the seven capacities recited previously.

We have described, infra, in some detail, the present system of common schools. We have noted the overall inadequacy of our system of education, when compared to national standards and to the standards of our adjacent states. We have recognized the great disparity that exists in educational opportunities throughout the state. We have noted the great disparity and inadequacy of financial effort throughout the state.

In spite of the past and present efforts of the General Assembly, Kentucky's present system of common schools falls short of the mark of the constitutional mandate of "efficient." When one juxtaposes the standards of efficiency as derived from our Constitution, the cases decided thereunder, the persuasive authority from our sister states and the opinion of experts, with the virtually unchallenged evidence in the record, no other decision is possible.

We have decided this case solely on the basis of our Kentucky Constitution, Section 183. We find it unnecessary to inject any issues raised under the United States Constitution or the United States Bill of Rights in this matter. We decline to issue any injunctions, restraining orders, writs of prohibition or writs of mandamus.

We have decided one legal issue—and one legal issue only—viz., that the General Assembly of the Commonwealth has failed to establish an efficient system of common schools throughout the Commonwealth.

Lest there by any doubt, the result of our decision is that Kentucky's *entire system* of common schools is unconstitutional. There is no allegation that only part of the common school system is invalid, and we find no such circumstance. This decision applies to the entire sweep of the system—all its parts and parcels. This decision applies to the statutes creating, implementing and financing the *system* and to all regulations, etc., pertaining thereto. . . .

Since we have, by this decision, declared the system of common schools in Kentucky to be unconstitutional, Section 183 places an absolute duty on the General Assembly to recreate, reestablish a new system of common schools in the Commonwealth. As we have said, the premise of this opinion is that education is a basic, fundamental constitutional right that is available to all children within this Commonwealth. The General Assembly should begin with the same premise as it goes about its duty. The system, as we have said, must be efficient, and the criteria we have set out are binding on the General Assembly as it develops Kentucky's new system of common schools. . . .

■ JUDICIAL APPROVAL OF COMMON SCHOOLS

The egalitarian motivation for the common school necessitated the enrollment of all children of all social and economic backgrounds.

To enlarge public schools from a system of limited free education for poor children—pauper schools—to common schools at the elementary and high school levels required an ever-increasing commitment of public funds.[48]

The transformation to truly *common* schools required that the public schools be of such quality that they could attract the children of the more affluent in addition to the children of the poor. Ravitch points out that this movement toward common schools was a logical extension of the Jacksonian philosophy of 1828 that heralded the frontier philosophy of equality and the decline of social class based on wealth and position. "Political equality forced the emergence of new political patterns, and the schools, like other social institutions, began to adjust to the demands of the rising middle class."[49]

Opposition to this movement was expressed both politically and in the courts. An early example of such litigation is found in the *Hartman*[50] case in Pennsylvania (decided in 1851), wherein school directors refused to comply with a statute requiring them to create a system of common schools for all children, not just the poor. The school directors defended their position by maintaining that the Pennsylvania Constitution did not permit the legislature to expand the public schools from pauper schools to common schools. The court disagreed.

❖ — ❖ — ❖

Legislature Is Not Prohibited from Creating a System of Common Schools by Expanding on the Pauper School Provision in State Constitution

Commonwealth v. Hartman

Supreme Court of Pennsylvania, 1851.
17 Pa. 118.

The appellants, Hartman and five others, had been elected school directors of Lowhill township, Lehigh county. They organized by electing the officers required by the common school law, and made provision for the education of the poor children in that township, but refused to comply with the provisions of the Acts of Assembly of 1848 and 1849, requiring them to provide for the establishment of common schools in that township: and they refused to resign. A petition was presented to the Court of Quarter Sessions, on April 30, 1849, praying the court to declare their offices vacant, and to appoint substitutes. The court granted a rule upon them to appear and answer; and on May 5, 1849, JONES, J., vacated their office and appointed others in their stead to act until the next annual election for directors. The objection made on the part of Hartman and others was that the school laws of 1848 and 1849 *were unconstitutional*, as being at variance with the provision in the first section of the 7th article of the Constitution of Pennsylvania, which is as follows: Sect. 1. "The legislature shall, as soon as conveniently may be, provide by law for the establishment of schools throughout the state, in such manner that the poor may be taught *gratis*." It was provided in the Act of Assembly of 11th April, 1848, "That the common school system, from and after the passage of this Act, shall be deemed, held, and taken to be adopted by the several school districts in this Commonwealth" . . . .

In the Act of 7th April 1849, it is provided, "That a system of common school education be and the same is hereby deemed, held, and taken to be adopted, according to the provisions of this Act, in all the counties in this Commonwealth" . . . .

The Act points out the mode of electing directors, and defines their "general powers and duties." It provided that "They shall establish a sufficient number of *common schools* for the education of every individual between the ages of five and twenty-one years, in the districts, who may apply for admission and instruction, either in person, or by parent, guardian, or next friend [italics added]."

The opinion of the court was delivered Dec. 29, 1851, by BLACK, C.J. The only ground on which this court has been urged to reverse the order of the Quarter Sessions, is, that the school law is unconstitutional. We are of opinion that there is nothing in that law, certainly nothing in that part of it to which our attention has been particularly called, which, in the slightest

degree, contravenes the constitution. It is to be remembered, that the rule of interpretation for the state constitution differs totally from that which is applicable to the constitution of the United States. The latter instrument must have a strict construction; the former a liberal one. Congress can pass no laws but those which the constitution authorizes either expressly or by clear implication; while the Assembly has jurisdiction of all subjects on which its legislation is not prohibited. The powers, not granted to the government of the Union, are withheld; but the state retains every attribute of sovereignty which is not taken away. In applying this principle to the present case, it is enough to say, that there is no syllable in the constitution which forbids the legislature to provide for a system of general education in any way which they, in their own wisdom, may think best. But it is argued, that for the purpose of promoting education, and carrying out the system of common schools, laws may be passed which will work intolerable wrong, and produce grievous hardship. The answer to this is, that a decent respect for a coordinate branch of the government, compels us to deny that any such danger can ever exist. But if a law, unjust in its operation, and nevertheless not forbidden by the constitution, should be enacted, the remedy lies, not in an appeal to the judiciary, but to the people, who must apply the corrective themselves, since they have not intrusted the power to us.

The constitution, in sect. 1 of article VII, provides that "the legislature shall, as soon as conveniently may be, provide by law for the establishment of schools throughout the state *in such manner that the poor may be taught gratis*." It seems to be believed that the last clause of this section is a limitation to the power of the legislature, and that no law can be constitutional which looks to any other object than that of teaching the poor gratis. The error consists in supposing this to define the *maximum* of the legislative power, while in truth it only fixes the minimum. It enjoins them to do thus much, but does not forbid them to do more. If they stop short of that point, they fail in their duty; but it does not result from this that they have no authority to go beyond it.

Order affirmed.

■ EXPANSION OF PUBLIC SCHOOLS

Earlier, education above the elementary school level had to be acquired at private academies for which a tuition fee was charged and few, if any, poor children attended. Common schools were generally looked upon as being for the elementary grades only. Yet, free public high schools soon became a democratic necessity. Cubberley observed that "the rising democracy of the second quarter of the nineteenth century now demanded and obtained the democratic high school."[51] Gradually the high school became an integral part of the free public school system.

The academy had succeeded the old Latin schools with a more practical curriculum designed to more adequately meet the needs of the older youths beyond preparation for college. These academies spread rapidly and were variously known as institutes, seminaries, collegiate institutes, and sometimes colleges. By the early 1800s, Massachusetts had thirty-six academies, New York nineteen, Georgia ten, and some states, including Kentucky and Indiana, by the early 1800s had systems of county academies.[52] The greatest growth of the academies was during the period from 1820 to 1840. Most of these academies were residential schools that charged fees for room and board as well as for tuition. Some were financed by local taxation, and a few even had state assistance. The academies, however, were inadequate to meet the burgeoning need for extended educational opportunity. The tuition and fees made accessibility difficult for the poor, and even though their numbers were substantial, they were not numerous enough to be within reasonable walking, wagon, or horseback distance from rural homes to be nonresidential.

The solution was the genesis of the American high school. The American high school had no forerunners and was distinguished from previous European models by its close relationship to the common schools. The high school was an extension of the common elementary school, making it, from the beginning, a higher common school.

The first American high school was established in Boston in 1821, and the increase in the number of high schools was slow, but methodical, for the next thirty years. Skepticism as to the viability of the high school was expressed by many who were imbued with the tradition of the academy. As late as 1874, President Porter of Yale University observed that "the expenditure of money for high schools to prepare boys and girls for college was a doubtful experiment." By 1872, 70 percent of the students entering colleges in the east were graduates of academies, but by 1920, 90 percent of the entering freshmen were graduates of high schools.

Opposition to the high school as an extension of the common school generally came from taxpayers who did not want to bear the increased financial burden, as well as from those advocates of the academies and private sectarian schools who thought that creation of high schools would further diminish the public's reliance on their respective schools.

The court decision generally credited with opening the doors to the public high school as we know it today was the famous *Kalamazoo* case in 1872.[53] No constitutional or legislative provisions in Michigan had previously explicitly established a system of high schools. The legal basis for education was found in legislation in 1817, which contained a provision for public academies, and in the constitution of 1835, which provided for free primary schooling, but neither established a pathway between the primary schooling and the university. Local students aspiring to a university education had entered the preparatory department of the private Kalamazoo College (chartered in 1855). No public accommodation had been made for students' preparation for college until 1858, when the local school superintendent created the union high school at a time when several of these union high schools had been created elsewhere in Michigan. This particular school thrived amid local controversy created by both taxpayers, who objected to paying for the school, and the proprietors of Kalamazoo College, who had lost students to the union high school. Finally, in 1873 a group of prominent citizens filed suit to restrain the school board from expending public funds to support the high school. Ultimately, the case was appealed to the Supreme Court of Michigan, where Judge Thomas M. Cooley rendered a landmark decision.

Even though there was other litigation of this nature during this period, this case was particularly important because of the stature of the court and the judicial rationale by which the high school was justified. Courts are generally reticent, in the absence of express statutory language, to imply authority to perform some public function if the expenditure of funds is involved, but here the court did not hesitate to do so.

This judicial recognition of the importance of public schools provided a philosophical basis for both legislatures and courts to broaden educational opportunity by extending the school system not only upward, but also downward to kindergartens, as well as to expand the scope of education to areas such as vocational education, special education for the handicapped, and compensatory education.

■ CHARTER SCHOOLS

Charter schools became increasingly popular among state legislatures during the 1990s. By the end of the decade about two-thirds of the states had legislated some provision permitting the establishment of charter schools.

The charter school in its most favorable light seeks to increase choice of educational programs, without fueling private self-interests that separate and segregate children of the community. It places great store in the importance of competition in improving the quality of schools. As Minow observes, charter schools are "anchored in faith in consumer sovereignty"[54] and "confidence in market-style mechanisms,"[55] and that by such means of competition, the freedom of an educational marketplace will make schools more efficient and productive.

Parents, of course, now have choice among private schools, but their choosings are not supported by public funds. Private schools are now chartered or incorporated as private entities in their respective states, and any institution, religious organization, or group of parents can easily obtain a charter to incorporate as a private school. The sanctity of such charters was guaranteed as a constitutionally protected interest under the Obligation of Contracts provision of the U.S. Constitution as defined by the U.S. Supreme Court in the famous *Dartmouth College*

case in 1819.[56] Moreover, the right to establish and keep such private schools is protected by the Due Process Clause of Fourteenth Amendment as interpreted by the U.S. Supreme Court in *Pierce v. Society of Sisters* in 1925.[57]

The "charter school" was first proposed as a definitional mirage that would redefine the term "public schools" to include private and parochial schools. The idea was advanced to circumvent constitutional prohibitions to the giving of public funds to private and parochial schools. The approach as it originated was to permit all private and parochial schools to become chartered in their respective states by meeting minimal state established criteria. These minimal criteria "roughly corresponding to the criteria many states now employed in accrediting private schools" would then allow a private school to be "chartered as a public school and granted the right to accept students and receive public money."[58] By this means any and all private and parochial schools participating would *ipso facto* become "public schools" as defined by the new system.[59] Such newly defined "public schools" would retain their independence while avoiding constitutional restrictions that normally apply to the public sector and would, as well, retain their religious affiliations. This "definitional reshuffling," as Henig called it, was earlier proposed by Jencks, who advocated the use of charter schools as a means to achieve the intent of public funding of private and parochial schools without actually resorting to tuition vouchers or tuition tax credits. Jencks, said that "a lot of our thinking about the voucher system is based on an attempt to rethink the question of where the line between the public and private should be drawn."[60]

The idea of the charter school as a vehicle to circumvent the constitutional proscription against the use of public monies to support religious schools apparently originated in the concept advanced by Justice White in the *Allen* case rendered by the U.S. Supreme Court in 1968.[61] (See Chapter 5 of this book). In that case Justice White observed that parochial schools do an "acceptable job of providing secular education to their students,"[62] in addition to their sectarian instruction. In other words the nonsectarian aspects of parochial school instruction served a public purpose in keeping with the purpose of the public school. From there it took only a small leap of logic to suggest that the presence of secular aspects of the educational programs in parochial schools was so substantial that it merited them the status of a kind of quasi-public school, justifying their receiving public funds.

This attempt to redefine public schools was advanced by President Bush in 1992 when he explained that, "Whether a school is organized by privately financed educators or town councils or religious orders or denominations any school that serves the public and is held accountable by public authority provides public education."[63] Henig points out that such an indiscriminate stretch of the label "public" to "cover largely deregulated, market-based systems of educational choice is possible only because the term public has been so devalued."

In its ungarnished form the "charter school" is designed to remain private, *sans* public control and accountability. As described by Minow, "these independent schools are intended to operate with public funds, but outside the regulations of the public system."[64]

The thrust of the charter school concept changed dramatically when President Clinton advocated school choice that could be exercised only in public schools and not in private or parochial schools. As charter schools have developed, however, they have taken on various permutations in state legislation. Moving away from the base form of a private sectarian institution, in keeping with the Clinton Administration's definition, the charter school has evolved in most jurisdictions as a form of public nonsectarian school that requires diversity of racial, economic, and social mix of students. Federal charter school legislation[65] passed in 1994 and bearing President Clinton's imprint defines such schools as having the following features. They are exempted from state and local regulations that inhibit flexible management, yet they are operated under general public supervision and direction, designed with specific educational objectives as their purpose; they are nonsectarian in their programs, admissions, policies, and employment practices and are not affiliated with a sectarian school or religious institution; they are free of tuition and fees; they must be in compliance with federal civil rights legislation; they must provide for admission of students by

lottery; they must comply with federal and state financial audit requirements as do other elementary and secondary schools; they must meet required federal, state, and local health and safety requirements; and they are required to operate in accordance with state law.[66] This law makes it clear that the concept of the "charter school" adopted by the federal government is a school operating under public auspices and control. It is not a private school defined as public. Yet, these requirements apply only if a state desires to receive federal funding for the planning, design, and initial implementation of charter schools.

Thus, the set of suggested features or principles in the federal law reflects just one philosophical view of the nature and characteristics of charter schools. In actuality, state laws vary widely, indicating the diversity of social, economic, religious, and political forces that define and influence state education policy. In practice, some state laws permit such an extent of private discretion and so little state or local control that the charter school leans far more toward being a private, or sectarian, school than a public school. Too, state laws differ in that some may limit the number of charter schools or the number of students permitted to enroll in such schools. Others designate various agencies that can sponsor charter schools, such as state boards of education, local school boards, chief state school officers, boards of community colleges, boards of public universities, state boards of regents, or special state charter boards. In some states, charters may be granted to schools that were previously public schools, or to schools that were previously private. The exact legal status of charter schools may also vary among states. Charter schools may be independent entities, corporate entities, or nonprofit organizations, or may remain legally attached to the local school district. A range of conditions may govern employment of personnel, including independent employment with the charter school as the employer or as public employees remaining within the personnel system of the local school district. In several states, charter schools are subject to public collective bargaining laws, and in other states the statutes are silent on the subject.

Therefore, state charter school legislation ranges from sincere attempts to improve the public schools by providing greater parental choice and involvement in the educational processes to the more extreme efforts by religious conservatives to capture public funds for their own religious schools. The Michigan case presented below deals with the two most visible legal aspects of the charter school issue, the redefinition of public schools and the use of public funds for sectarian purposes. The court in this case approves a Michigan statute that broadens the definition of public schools to encompass charter schools, bringing them within the public system, and further holds that such a publicly controlled school does not violate the Michigan constitutional prohibition of the use of public monies to support sectarian schools.

❖ — ❖ — ❖

*Definition of Public School Includes
Charter School and Does Not Constitute
Parochiaid to Religious Schools*

Council of Organizations of Others for Education about Parochiaid v. Governor

Supreme Court of Michigan, 1997.
455 Mich. 557, 566 N.W. 2d 208

Opinion

BRICKLEY, Justice.

This case concerns 1993 P.A. 362, the statute commonly known as the charter schools act, which authorized the creation of public school academies. The plaintiffs brought this suit to enjoin the distribution of public funds by challenging the constitutionality of the statute. . . .

On December 24, 1993, the Michigan Legislature passed enrolled SB 896. On January 14, 1994, Governor John Engler signed the bill into law (1993 P.A. 362). . . .

The issue in this case is whether the charter schools act is constitutional under art. 8 §2 of the Michigan Constitution as amended in 1970 that prohibits public aid to parochial schools by means of direct payments, credits, tax benefits, tuition vouchers, or under art. 8, §3, that requires leadership and general supervision over all public education to be vested in the state board of education.

During the spring of 1994, Noah Webster Academy submitted an application to charter a public school academy to School District No. 3 Fractional of the townships of Berlin and Orange. The application was accepted by the townships and the charter was authorized by the school district. During July and August of the same year, Ronald Helmer's application to start Northlane Math and Science Academy was considered and approved by Central Michigan University. Noah Webster Academy and Northlane Math and Science Academy applied to the state for funding.

The Department of Education made a formal decision on October 17, 1994, to approve Northlane Math and Science Academy and seven other public school academies for state funding. Noah Webster was the only applicant that was denied funding by the Department of Education because it did not meet the requirements of Act 362, as it was essentially a home-study school. Noah Webster has been operating since 1994 without funding. . . .

On November 1, 1994, the trial court determined that Act 362 was unconstitutional, finding that public school academies were not under the "immediate, exclusive control of the state . . . ." The court further held that public school academies were not governed by publicly elected bodies; therefore, public school academies were not "public schools" under art. 8, §2 of the Michigan Constitution.

Additionally, the trial court held that Act 362 divested the State Board of Education of its constitutional authority to provide "[l]eadership and general supervision" over public education as required by Const. 1963, art. 8, §3, a finding that was based on a comparison of 1993 P.A. 284 and 1993 P.A. 362. Consequently, a permanent injunction was issued, prohibiting the dispersion of any state school funding.

. . . The Court of Appeals, in a two-to-one decision by Judge Marilyn Kelly, affirmed the trial court's finding that Act 362 was unconstitutional. . . .

On December 13, 1994, the Legislature passed Act 416, which amended Act 362 by amending part 6A and establishing part 6B. The public school academies currently operating in the state do so under part 6B. . . .

In order to determine the constitutionality of the statute, a review of its provisions is necessary. Under Act 362, a public school academy is organized as a nonprofit corporation under the Nonprofit Corporation Act. M.C.L. §450.2101 *et seq.*; M.S.A. §21.197(101) *et seq.* Subsection 502(1). A public school academy is administered under the direction of a board of directors in accordance with Act 362 and the nonprofit corporation bylaws contained in the public school academy's contract.

To organize a public school academy, an applicant, either a person or an entity, must submit an application to an authorizing body. . . .

Act 362 specifies four types of authorizing bodies: (1) the board of a school district, (2) intermediate school board, (3) the board of a community college, and (4) the governing board of a state public university. . . . An authorizing body is not required to issue any public school academy contracts, but if it does, it must issue the contracts "on a competitive basis taking into consideration the resources available for the proposed public school academy, the population to be served by the proposed public school academy, and the educational goals to be achieved by the proposed public school academy.". . . Before granting a contract to operate a public school academy, an authorizing body is required to adopt a resolution establishing the method of selection, length of term, and number of members of the public school academy's board of directors.

The authorizing body for a public school academy is the fiscal agent for the public school academy, and its aid payments are paid to the authorizing body. The authorizing body is responsible for the public school academy's compliance with the contract and all applicable law. Further, the contract may be revoked at any time the public school academy fails to abide by the statute.

Subsection 501(1) states that "[a] public school academy is a public school under section 2 of Article VII of the state constitution of 1963, and is considered to be a school district for the purposes of section 11 of article IX of the state constitution of 1963." Act 362 does not expressly limit the power of a board of education. In fact, Act 362 states that "[a] public school academy shall comply with all applicable law. . . ." Sub-

section 503(5). Moreover, the law states that a church or other religious organization cannot organize a public school academy and that a public school academy is prohibited from having organizational or contractual affiliations with churches or other religious organizations to the extent such agreements are prohibited by the state or federal constitutions. . . .

Furthermore, Act 362 specifically provides that a public school academy is prohibited from charging tuition and is required to abide by the pupil admission policies set forth in the statute. Section 504. If the public school academy has more applicants than space, it is required to hold a random selection process for the enrollment of the students. *Id.* . . .

The 1963 Michigan Constitution does not define the term "public schools." However, it does state that the Legislature has the responsibility for maintain[ing] and support[ing] a system of free public education. . . ." Art. 8, §2. The Legislature has had the task of defining the form and the institutional structure through which public education is delivered in Michigan since the time Michigan became a state. See Const. 1835, art. 10, §3.

The appellees assert that the system established by our Legislature violates art. 8, §2 because public school academies are not public, 1) in that they are not under the ultimate and immediate, or exclusive, control of the state and 2) because the academy's board of directors is not publicly elected or appointed by a public body. . . .

Our constitution does not mandate exclusive control, it requires that "[t]he legislature shall maintain and support a system of free public elementary and secondary schools. . . ." Art. 8, §2. Therefore, plaintiff's first assertion fails because there is no requirement in our constitution that the state must have exclusive control of the school system. . . .

The plaintiffs further argue that because a public school academy is run by a private board of directors and because the authorizing body has no means for selecting members of the board, the public school academies are not public schools.

The Court has stated:

> The authority granted by the Constitution to the Legislature to establish a common or primary

school system carried with it the authority to prescribe what officers should be chosen to conduct
the affairs of the school districts, to define their
powers and duties, their term of office, *and how
and by whom they should be chosen.* . . .

Subsection 503(3) of 1993 P.A. 362 provides:

An authorizing body shall adopt a resolution
establishing the method of selection, length of
term, and number of members of the board of
directors of each public school academy subject to
its jurisdiction.

Therefore, the Legislature has mandated the
board of director's selection process. The Legislature has this control, and it can change this
process at any time.

Additionally, the board of the authorizing
bodies is publicly elected or appointed by public bodies. While the boards of the public school
academies may or may not be elected, the public maintains control of the schools through the
authorizing bodies.

Further, if we examine the common understanding of what a "public school" is, as
adopted by the 1961 Constitutional Convention,
for the first paragraph of §2, and if we inquire
into the common understanding of "private,
denominational or other nonpublic" school, as
adopted by the voters in 1970 for the second
paragraph of §2, we find that public school
academies are "public schools." . . .

However, we do not have a requirement in
our state constitution that mandates that the
school is under the control of the voters of the
school district. In fact, a review of our constitutional history shows that our forefathers envisioned public education to be under the control
of the Legislature, which is under the command
of the entire state electorate. . . .

The parochiaid amendment does not limit
the definition of public schools to exclude public school academies. Article 8, §2 was amended
by the electorate in 1970 by what is commonly
known as the parochiaid amendment. . . .

. . . [T]he common understanding of the voters in 1970 was that no monies would be spent
to run a parochial school. However, public
school academies are not parochial schools. The
statute specifically prohibits religious organization from organizing a public school academy
and further prohibits any organizational or con-

tractual affiliations with churches or other religious organizations. Subsection 502(1). Additionally, a public school academy is not a
parochial school in that the charging of tuition
is prohibited, as is any restriction on admission
other than a random selection process if the
school has more applicants than space.

The plaintiffs argue that the act violates
Const. 1963, art. 8, §3 because it allegedly
divests the State Board of Education of the duty
to lead and exercise general supervision over
public education.

Article 8, §3 provides in relevant part that the
"Leadership and general supervision over all
public education . . . is vested in a state board of
education. . . .

Because the Legislature declared that public
school academies are public schools, subsection
501(1), they are necessarily subject to the leadership and general supervision of the State Board
of Education to the same extent as are all the
other public schools. Further, subsection 503(5)
provides that a "public school academy shall
comply with all applicable law," a requirement
that incorporates the constitutional provision in
issue. . . .

Thus, it is clear that the board retains its constitutional authority over public school academies. . . .This is evidenced by the power of the
board to deny funding, as it did to Noah Webster. It should be noted that public school academy board members are public officials and are
subject to all applicable law pertaining to public
officials. . . .

We hold that 1993 P.A. 362 does not violate
art. 8, §2 or art. 8, §3 of the Michigan Constitution of 1963. . . . We remand this case to the trial
court for it to vacate its injunction and order the
Department of Treasury to make payments to
the public school academies that were operating
under 1993 P.A. 362.

CASE NOTES

In a challenge contesting the decision of a local
school board to close a neighborhood elementary school and open a charter school, Hispanic
parents claimed that the impact was discriminatory in violation of the Equal Protection Clause
of the Fourteenth Amendment and the Civil
Rights Act of 1964. The U.S. Court of Appeals,

Tenth Circuit, held that the parents had failed to show that action discriminated against Hispanic students. The court found that the State of Colorado had a legitimate interest in enacting a Charter Schools Act designed to increase educational opportunities for at-risk students, as this school was designed to do. Moreover, the court found that under the Act, the charter school must admit all children on an equal basis who are not classified as at risk. *Villanueva v. Carere,* 85 F.3d 481 (10th Cir., 1996).

■ TUITION AND FEES IN PUBLIC SCHOOLS

Courts have generally held that tuition fees, "matriculation" or "registration" fees, and fees for materials, activities, or privileges cannot be levied in public schools.[67] In most cases invalidating fees, the courts have reasoned that the fee was charged as a condition of attendance, which violated the state's constitutional or statutory provisions establishing "free" public schools.

In deciding whether school districts in California could charge a fee for participation in extracurricular activities such as dramatic productions, music groups, and cheerleading, fees were imposed by school districts without the benefit of a statutory authorization. The Court determined that extracurricular activities constitute "an integral component of public education" and are a "fundamental ingredient of the educational process."[68] Therefore, no fee for these activities may be charged because of the constitutional free school guarantee. Later, a California legislature authorized local districts to charge a transportation fee to nonindigent parents and guardians. This fee was also challenged under the free school guarantee of the constitution as in the *Hartzell* case. The California Supreme Court ruled that transportation is not an educational activity, therefore was not protected by the reasoning in *Hartzell.* The free school provision of the state constitution applies to educational activities, and noneducational activities such as transportation are not required to be free.[69]

Another reason often given by the courts for invalidating fees is the lack of statutory author-

ity to exact the fee. Courts have usually held fees invalid when the fees have been charged for an essential element of a school's activity. When fees have been upheld, the courts have found that there was statutory authorization for the fee, that the purpose for the fee was a reasonable one, or that the term "free schools" did not include the item, such as textbooks, for which the school was charging.[70]

Courts have, on occasion, distinguished tuition fees from incidental fees, and, in at least one jurisdiction, a court has upheld an incidental fee of twenty-five cents per pupil per month to be used for raising funds to pay for fuel to heat the schoolroom, for brooms to sweep the schoolroom, and for water buckets to contain water.[71] In the same jurisdiction, an incidental fee for improvement of grounds, insurance, and other incidental expenses did not violate the state constitution.[72]

However, in other jurisdictions, incidental fees have been held invalid. In Georgia,[73] a very early decision held that a state statute requiring each child upon entering municipal public schools to pay the board of education an "incidental fee" was "clearly unconstitutional." However, a court in Illinois ruled that the state constitutional provision requiring the establishment of a thorough and efficient system of free schools did not prevent the state legislature from authorizing school boards to purchase textbooks and rent them to pupils.[74]

In most cases, fees for activities, materials, or privileges have been held invalid.[75] A $25 annual fee required by one school district as a condition to furnishing each high school student a transcript of courses studied and grades achieved was held to be unconstitutional in Idaho.[76] The fee consisted of $12.50 for school activity fees and $12.50 for textbook fees, and it had to be paid before a student could receive a transcript. Responding to each of these separately, the court reasoned that the student activity fee was imposed on all students whether they participated in extracurricular activities or not. Therefore the fee was on attendance, not on activity, and as such contravened the state constitutional mandate that public schools be free. The court did note that since social and extracurricular activities were not necessarily principal elements of a high school career, the state constitution did not prohibit the school district from setting activity fees for students who voluntarily participated. With regard to the textbook fee, the court observed that since textbooks were necessary to the school, they were indistinguishable from other fixed educational expense items, such as building maintenance and teachers' salaries, for all of which fees could not be charged.[77]

The requirement that pupils purchase textbooks and school supplies has been held invalid in Michigan.[78] In this case, the school district maintained that the word "free" in the state constitution did not include textbooks and supplies. The Supreme Court of Michigan held that books and supplies were necessary elements of any school's activity and an integral and fundamental part of elementary and secondary education.

———————— ❖ — ❖ — ❖ ————————

Fee for Textbooks and Materials Violates the Free Public Schools Provision of the State Constitution.

Randolph County Board of Education v. Adams

Supreme Court of Appeals of West Virginia, 1995.
467 S.E.2d 150.

CLECKLEY, Justice:

The plaintiff below and appellant herein, Randolph County Board of Education (Board), appeals from an order of the Circuit Court of Randolph County, which held in a declaratory judgment action that it was unconstitutional for the Board to charge parents of non-needy school children a book user fee for school books and materials necessary for the completion of the "required school curriculum. . . ."

According to the defendants below and appellees herein, the Board's book user fee essentially amounted to tuition because the fee was mandatory on a non-needy basis regardless of what type of books and materials was given to the child and regardless of whether the parents purchased textbooks through private vendors.

The Board claims, and there is no evidence to the contrary, that no student was deprived of a textbook or restricted from school based on non-payment of the book user fee. The Board created a standard for classifying students by economic need by relying on a list of children actually receiving reduced cost or free meals through a school lunch program. . . .

In this appeal, we are asked to clarify, if not define, what is meant in the West Virginia Constitution by "free schools." . . . The textbook user fee system at issue was adopted by the Board in response to an unfortunate reality: the rejection of a school levy by the citizens of Randolph County that, if passed, would have avoided the necessity for the adoption of such a fee. Nevertheless, we now determine that the "free schools" clause prevents local school authorities from charging students and their parents a fee for the use of necessary textbooks. In voiding the fee under the West Virginia Constitution, we attempt to avoid engrafting upon this constitutional provision a judicial gloss so protean, elusive, or arbitrary as to prevent the political branches from performing their mandatory constitutional function of providing "for a thorough and efficient system of free schools." Our cautious approach in construing Section 1, therefore, is intended not to excessively encroach on the powers which the Constitution has reserved for the Legislature. . . .

The "free schools" clause contained in Section 1 of Article XII of the West Virginia Constitution provides: "The Legislature shall provide, by general law, for a thorough and efficient system of free schools." Its central mandate is to require equal and quality educational opportunities for all West Virginians. Though the application of this imperative raises difficult choices and questions, the framers of our Constitution enacted Section 1 to facilitate public access to education. Premised on the belief that an educated electorate is vital to the proper operation of a democracy, Section 1 is intended to create an expedient for achieving this end while at the same time making the Legislature responsible for raising funds for that purpose. We, therefore, proceed to the basic interpretive question aware that we are interpreting a constitutional provision that seeks broadly to overcome all hostility to quality public education. . . .

Section 1 of Article XII of the West Virginia Constitution creates a strong presumption in favor of making everything that is deemed a necessary component to public education cost-free. When a board of education seeks to charge parents for their children's participation in public education, the board bears a heavy burden in rebutting this constitutionally based presumption. To provide otherwise would render the constitutional guarantee of a free public education an empty and cruel illusion.

With this background we turn to the central issue in this case: Whether a county board of education may charge a book user fee to nonneedy school children. The Board points to various statutes, case law, the West Virginia Constitution, and its financial problems to justify charging the book user fee to non-needy students. The defendants argue, on the other hand, that the book user fee is unconstitutional and ultra vires. More specifically, the parties focus on whether the phrase "free school" includes the distribution of textbooks to all students without charge. . . .

At first glance, the "free schools" language of Section 1 of Article XII seems clear and unambiguous. However, the word "free" can be a word of many meanings and its construction is often influenced by its context. When used as an adjective, the word takes on many different connotations. Because the word "free" is open to divergent interpretations, we must examine the word in the context of this constitutional provision. Without doubt, the drafters of the Constitution intended to create a system of free public schools. . . .

> "Our basic law makes education's funding second in priority only to payment of State debt, and ahead of every other State function. Our Constitution manifests, throughout, the people's clear mandate to the Legislature, that public education is a prime function of our State government. [Therefore, w]e must not allow that command to be unheeded." *Pauley v. Kelley,* 162 W.Va. 672, 719, 255 S.E.2d 859, 884 (1979). . . .

In . . . State ex rel. *Board of Education for County of Grant v. Manchin,* 179 W. Va. 235, 366 S.E.2d 743 (1988), we stated:

> The mandatory requirements of "a thorough and efficient system of free schools" found in Article XII, Section 1 of the West Virginia Constitution, make education a fundamental, constitutional right in this State. . . .

[I]t is clear that the Constitution provides a clear entitlement to a basic education. Although we have never interpreted the "free schools" portion of Section 1 of Article XII, we have considered what the "thorough and efficient" portion of this section and article means in relation to a school system. We define a "thorough and efficient" system of schools as: "It develops, as best the state of education expertise allows, the minds, bodies and social morality of its charges to prepare them for useful and happy occupations, recreation and citizenship, and does so economically.". . .

". . . We recognize that part of the goal of the school system is to instruct students so they might become well-rounded, academically talented, and productive citizens. How one goes about this task and what materials are used are key. For this reason, we find that whatever items are deemed necessary to accomplish the goals of a school system and are in fact an 'integral fundamental part of the elementary and secondary education' must be provided free of charge to all students in order to comply with the constitutional mandate of a "free school" system. . . .

Are the textbooks and materials at issue in this case such an "integral fundamental part of the elementary and secondary education" that they must be provided free? We find that the answer to this question is "yes." Of course, providing a place of instruction and qualified teachers are extremely important; however, hindering access to necessary materials would make the educational process nearly meaningless. . . .

Throughout the history of this State, we have taken great strides to ensure that each child has an equal opportunity to receive a quality education. . . . Specifically, textbooks have always been an important issue in the great educational debate. Moreover, there generally has been a "push" to equalize education and providing "free textbooks followed as a matter of course.". . .

Various legislative enactments and case law have solidified the concept that free textbooks are a fundamental part of the learning experience. Even in the general authorization of power to the State Board of Education, the Legislature indicated that the supervision over the distribution of free textbooks was one of the duties of the State Board.

. . . [T]he Board [argues] that never in the history of this State has it been required to provide textbooks free of charge for all students. By narrowly focusing on the failure to provide textbooks in the past, the Board fails to embrace the full history surrounding the educational system in this State. Although Section 1 of Article XII provides textual support for the right to a free education, it is clear the framers intended and the populace continues to support the notion that all students are entitled to a basic level of education free of budgetary concerns. History is indeed very important, but it alone cannot be permitted to overwhelm or replace the constitutional provision in question. . . . What may have been fundamental for a quality education in the past does not make it necessarily so now. Textbooks for modern students are a fundamental part of the learning experience. To find otherwise would ignore reality and, moreover, constitutional mandates. . . .

Balancing constitutional mandates with fiscal constraints while still maintaining quality educational programs has placed a tremendous burden on school systems to make difficult choices. We understand and sympathize with the Board concerning its dire financial straits. However, its extreme need is still no justification for a violation of rights of constitutional magnitude. . . .

The dilemma faced by the Board is indistinguishable from any number of difficult choices that governmental agencies must make under our constitutional system. Section 1 necessarily exerts pressure on our Legislature and boards of education to make hard—and sometimes undesirable—decisions while staying within constitutional limitations. Thus, we are compelled to underscore that financial hardship is an insufficient basis for ignoring the West Virginia Constitution. The imposition of these difficult choices is an inevitable and unavoidable attribute that emanates from our Constitution.

Although we find our interpretive choice difficult, we believe that our interpretation is most faithful to the Constitution. Concededly, our interpretation limits the Legislature's and the Board's authority to carry out their mandate of providing "for a thorough and efficient system of free schools." The history of Section 1, to the extent informative, indicates that the framers saw the word "free" as part of a guarantee that education in West Virginia would remain user

friendly and that the financial burden to achieve this purpose would be shared generally by the taxpayers of West Virginia. The context of Section 1 confirms this understanding of the framers' intent. . . .

Accordingly, for the reasons discussed above, we affirm the judgment of the Circuit Court of Randolph County.

Affirmed.

❖ — ❖ — ❖

Textbook Fee in Elementary Grades
Violates State Constitution

Cardiff v. Bismarck Public School District

Supreme Court of North Dakota, 1978.
263 N.W.2d 105.

SAND, Justice. . . . Gary Cardiff and other parents of school children attending elementary schools in the Bismarck Public School District brought an action in Burleigh County district court challenging the authority of the school district to charge rental fees for the use of necessary school textbooks. . . .

The basic issue for our resolution is whether or not §148 of the North Dakota Constitution provides for free textbooks and prohibits the Legislature from authorizing school districts to charge for textbooks. The parents contend the constitutional provision prohibits charging for textbooks, and the school district contends it merely prohibits charging tuition. . . .

To resolve the first issue we must examine and construe the provisions of §148 of the North Dakota Constitution, which provides as follows:

> The legislative assembly shall provide at their first session after the adoption of this constitution, for a uniform system of free public schools throughout the state, beginning with the primary and extending through all grades up to and including the normal and collegiate course.

In 1968 this section was amended, as follows:

> The legislative assembly shall provide for a uniform system of free public schools throughout the state, beginning with the primary and extending

through all grades up to and including schools of higher education, except that the legislative assembly may authorize tuition, fees and service charges to assist in the financing of public schools of higher education.

In construing a written constitution we must make every effort to determine the intent of the people adopting it. . . .

We must examine the whole instrument in order to determine the true intention of every part so as to give effect to each section and clause. If different portions seem to be in conflict, we must make a true effort to harmonize them if practicable.

In interpreting clauses in a constitution we must presume that words have been employed in their natural and ordinary meaning.

Both parties contended that contemporaneous construction, as an aid in construction and interpretation of the constitution, . . . favored its point of view on the construction of §148 of the North Dakota Constitution. . . .

From this examination we are left with a firm conviction that the legislative acts referred to do not lend any significant comfort or aid to the resolution of the basic question under consideration, namely, what does the term "uniform system of free public schools" mean? Contemporaneous construction in this instance is not helpful to either party. The Journal entries of the constitutional convention are not very helpful in determining the meaning of the language "free public schools."

The first item relating to public schools introduced at the North Dakota Constitutional Convention, as found in the Journal, was File No. 47, §2, which provided, in part:

It shall be the duty of the Legislature to establish and maintain a system of free public schools, adequate for education of all children in the state, between the ages of six and eighteen years, inclusive, in the common branches of knowledge, and in virtue and christian morality. . . .

From this brief review it is clear that the framers consistently had in mind a free public school.

. . . [W]e have concluded that the courts have consistently construed the language "without payment of tuition" or "wherein tuition shall be without charge" or such similar language to mean that a school is prohibited from charging a fee for a pupil attending school. This language has also been construed as not prohibiting the charging of fees for textbooks.

However, as to constitutions containing language such as "free public schools" or "free common schools" or similar language, the courts have generally held, with a few exceptions, that this language contemplates furnishing textbooks free of charge, at least to the elementary schools. The exceptions have generally relied upon extrinsic material such as contemporary construction, history, or practices, as well as the language itself. Although the cases involving language similar to that contained in the North Dakota Constitution are not in themselves conclusive, they nevertheless are helpful, if not persuasive.

A comparison of the key constitutional provisions and existing case law of states which entered the Union at the same time and under similar conditions as North Dakota will be very helpful and valuable in determining the intent of the people of North Dakota in adopting §148 of the North Dakota Constitution.

At the time North Dakota formulated and adopted its Constitution, three other States—Montana, South Dakota, and Washington—were going through a similar process. All four States were included in the same Enabling Act, Chapter 180, 25 Statutes at Large, 676, and were required to meet the conditions in §4, which provided

[t]hat provision shall be made for the establishment and maintenance of systems of public schools, which shall be open to all the children of said states, and free from sectarian control.

The key language in the constitutional provisions of the four States is as follows:

Montana: . . . thorough system of public, free common schools.

South Dakota: . . . uniform system of public schools wherein tuition shall be without charge.

North Dakota: . . . uniform system of free public schools throughout the state. . . .

Washington: . . . uniform system of public schools.
. . .

We are impressed with the different language employed in the constitutions of the four states,

Montana, South Dakota, North Dakota, and Washington, which came into the Union at the same time and under the same Enabling Act. We must assume that each state had available the same information as the other states and was free to choose its constitutional provisions, provided they met the requirements of the Enabling Act. It is significant to note that Montana and North Dakota adopted the "free common schools" and the "free public schools" concept, whereas South Dakota adopted the "public schools wherein tuition shall be without charge" concept, and Washington merely provided for a "uniform system of public schools."

We also note that the Washington Supreme Court, in the *Bryan* case, School District #20, Spokane County v. Bryan, 51 Wash. 498, 99 P.28 (1909) supra, under the Washington Constitution held that a common school district is free for all children of proper age even though its Constitution merely required a uniform system of public schools. Therefore, if the term "common schools" implies a school for which no tuition may be charged, then the expression "free public schools" should mean something more than merely not permitting the charging of tuition. This position becomes persuasive when we recognize that other states specifically provided that no charge for "tuition" would be allowed.

If the framers of the North Dakota Constitution and the people of North Dakota had in mind only to provide public schools without charging tuition, they could have, and probably would have, used the language "without payment of tuition" or "wherein tuition shall be without charge," rather than the language "free public schools." We must assume that the framers of the constitution made a deliberate choice of words which reflected or expressed their thoughts. The term "free public schools" without any other modification must necessarily mean and include those items which are essential to education.

It is difficult to envision a meaningful educational system without textbooks. No education of any value is possible without school books....

We cannot overlook the fact that attendance at school between certain ages was compulsory from the very beginning under penalty of law. This lends support to the contention that textbooks were to be included in the phrase "free public schools." . . .

The word "free" takes on its true and full meaning from the context in which it is used. There can be no doubt that the term means "without charge or cost." In the absence of any other showing we must conclude that the term was commonly understood by the people to mean "without charge or cost." Books and school supplies are a part of the education system. This is true whether we apply the necessary elements of the school's activities test or the integral part of the educational system test.

After a review of the case law and constitutional provisions of other states, and after a careful analysis of the key language of the four states which were admitted under the same Enabling Act, we have come to the conclusion that the term "free public schools" means and includes textbooks, and not merely "free from tuition."

However, our conclusion must necessarily apply only to the elementary schools, as they are the only ones covered in this action. The action in district court was not a class action and factually involved only students enrolled in the elementary schools. . . . This opinion therefore is limited to textbooks used in elementary schools in the required subjects, as set out in [statute]. . . .

[T]o the extent that they apply to elementary textbooks [they] are in conflict with §148 of the North Dakota Constitution and are therefore invalid and unconstitutional as to elementary school textbooks. . . .

The judgment and order of the district court are both affirmed.

CASE NOTE

The definition of the word "free" in state constitutions requiring free public schools has been the subject of considerable litigation. The Supreme Court of North Dakota in Cardiff v. Bismarck Public School District, above, cited precedents from several other states. The question before the court was whether the term "free" merely prohibits the charging of tuition or also prohibits the charging for textbooks. The court reviewed the language of several state constitutions and the rulings of the courts in the respective states.

Arizona: In *Carpio v. Tucson High School District No. 1 of Pima County*, 111 Ariz. 127, 524 P.2d 948 (1974), cert. denied 420 U.S. 932, 95 S.Ct. 1412, 43 L.Ed.2d 664, the court had under consideration Article XI, §6, of the Arizona Constitution. The court held that textbooks were not required to be furnished to high school students. However, the court referred to an earlier decision, *Shoftstall v. Hollins,* 110 Ariz. 88, 515 P.2d 590 (1973), where the court held that the constitution had been satisfied when the legislature provided for the means of establishing required courses, qualifications of teachers, textbooks to be used in common schools, etc. Considering this statement and the statement in *Carpio* that "textbooks have not been provided free in high schools as they have been in the common schools" leaves the impression that under the constitutional provisions of Arizona, textbooks in common schools were provided free of charge.

Colorado: In *Marshall v. School District RE #3 Morgan County,* 553 P.2d 784 (Colo. 1976), the court held that the school district was not required to furnish books free of charge to all students.

Indiana: In *Chandler v. South Bend Community School Corporation,* 160 Ind.App. 593, 312 N.E.2d 915 (1974), the court held that the constitution did not require textbooks to be provided free, but merely to provide a system of common schools where tuition would be without charge.

Illinois: In *Beck v. Board of Education of Harlem Consolidated School District No. 122,* 63 Ill.2d 10, 344 N.E.2d 440 (1976), the court held that workbooks, and other educational material, were not textbooks so as to come within the statutory provision of free textbooks, and as such it did not preclude the school board from charging the parents a fee for supplying the students with such material.

Wisconsin: The court, in *Board of Education v. Sinclair,* 65 Wis.2d 179, 222 N.W.2d 143 (1974), held that the schools may charge a fee for the use of textbooks and items of similar nature authorized by statute and that such did not violate the constitution commanding that schools shall be free without charge for tuition for all children. It basically held that the term "free" referred to school buildings and equipment and what is normally understood by the term "tuition."

Idaho: In *Paulson v. Minidoka County School District No. 331,* 93 Idaho 469, 463 P.2d 935 (1970), the court held that school districts could not charge students for textbooks under the state constitutional provision. It also held that public high schools in Idaho are "common schools."

Michigan: The Michigan court, in *Bond v. Public Schools of Ann Arbor School District,* 383 Mich. 693, 178 N.W.2d 484 (1970), held that the 1963 constitution meant that books and school supplies were an essential part of the system of free public elementary and secondary schools and that the schools should not charge for such items. The 1908 Constitution provided "without charge for tuition," whereas the 1963 Constitution provides for a system of "free public elementary and secondary schools."

New Mexico: The court, in *Norton v. Board of Education of School District No. 16,* 89 N.M. 470, 553 P.2d 1277 (1976), held that under this state's constitution courses required of every student shall be without charge to the student. However, reasonable fees may be charged for elective courses.

Missouri: The court held, in *Concerned Parents v. Caruthersville School District No. 18,* 548 S.W.2d 554 (Mo.1977), that under that state's constitution school districts were prohibited from charging registration fees or course fees in connection with courses for which academic credit was given.

State Constitutional Provision for Free Public Schooling Prohibits Fees for Either Regular or Extracurricular Programs

Hartzell v. Connell

Supreme Court of California, In Bank, 1984.
35 Cal.3d 899, 201 Cal.Rptr. 601, 679 P.2d 35.

BIRD, Chief Justice. May a public high school district charge fees for educational programs simply because they have been denominated "extracurricular"?

The Santa Barbara High School District (District) offers a wide variety of extracurricular activities, ranging from cheerleading to madrigal singing, and from archery to football. Many of these activities are of relatively recent origin. For example, in 1956, Santa Barbara High School fielded six athletic teams while today there are thirty-eight.

Prior to the 1980–1981 school year, any student could participate in these activities free of charge. The programs were financed by a combination of District contributions (mostly state aid and local tax revenues), ticket sales, and fundraising activities conducted by the constituent high schools.

In the spring of 1980, the District school board (Board) decided to cut its budget by $1.1 million. This decision reflected a drop in revenues due to the combined effects of inflation, declining enrollment, and the adoption of Proposition 13. Among the items to be reduced was the District's contribution to the high school extracurricular programs.

The Board considered two plans for adapting the programs to fit its reduced budget. The first plan called for a major cut in interscholastic athletic competition, including the reduction of the high school program from over thirty teams to only eight and the elimination of interscholastic competition at the ninth-grade level. Under this plan, the surviving programs were to remain open to all students free of charge.

The second plan provided for a less extensive cut in athletic competition—elimination of the ninth-grade program only. To make up the difference, it proposed to raise money by charging students fees for participation in dramatic productions, musical performances, and athletic competition.

The Board chose the second option. Under the plan finally adopted, students are required to pay $25 for *each* athletic team in which they wish to participate, and $25 per category for any or all activities in *each* of the following four categories: (1) dramatic productions (e.g., plays, dance performances, and musicals); (2) vocal music groups (e.g., choir and madrigal groups); (3) instrumental groups (e.g., orchestra, marching band, and related groups such as the drill team and flag twirlers); and (4) cheerleading groups.

Thus, a student who desires to play football in the fall and tennis in the spring, in addition to participating in a dramatic production, must pay $75. A more musically inclined student, who plays an instrument, sings in a group, and performs in a musical, also pays $75.

None of the affected activities yield any credit toward graduation. . . .

The teachers of the credit courses also supervise the noncredit performances. . . .

In an attempt to ensure that the fees would not prevent any students from participating, the District has implemented a fee-waiver program. Upon a showing of financial need, a student may obtain a "scholarship" to participate without paying the fee. The standard of need is similar to that of the free lunch program. . . .

The District's three high schools granted a total of seventy-seven waivers. . . .

Shortly before the start of the 1980–1981 school year, Barbara Hartzell, a taxpayer with two children in the public schools, and the Coalition Opposing Student Fees, a grouping of community organizations, filed this taxpayers' action against the District, various school officials, and the members of the Board. . . .

The California Constitution requires the Legislature to "provide for a system of common schools by which a *free school* shall be kept up and supported in each district. . . ." (Cal. Const., art. IX, §5, emphasis added.) This provision entitled "the youth of the State . . . to be educated at the public expense." (*Ward v. Flood* (1874) 48 Cal. 36, 51.)

Plaintiffs assert that the imposition of fees for educational extracurricular activities violates the free school guarantee. They are correct.

The first question raised by plaintiffs' challenge is whether extracurricular activities fall within the free education guaranteed by section 5. California courts have not yet addressed this issue. The reported decisions from other jurisdictions reveal two distinct approaches.

One approach restricts the free school guarantee to programs that are "essential to the prescribed curriculum." . . . Under this view, the right to an education does not extend to activities that are "outside of or in addition to the regular academic courses or curriculum of a school." . . . Accordingly, it has been held that students have no right to participate in extracurricular activities. . . .

The second approach holds that the free school guarantee extends to all activities which constitute an "integral fundamental part of the elementary and secondary education" or which amount to "necessary elements of any school's activity." . . . Courts applying this approach have held that "the right to attend school includes the right to participate in extracurricular activities." In particular, courts have struck down extracurricular activities fees as unconstitutional. . . .

To determine which, if either, of these approaches is consistent with California's free school guarantee, this court must examine the role played by education in the overall constitutional scheme. Because the nature of the free school concept has rarely been addressed by the courts, it will be necessary to explore its underpinnings in some depth.

The free school guarantee was enacted at the Constitutional Convention of 1878–1879. Also adopted was article IX, §1, which proclaims that "[a] general diffusion of knowledge and intelligence [is] essential *to the preservation of the rights and liberties of the people.* . . ." [Emphasis added.] Joseph W. Winans, chairperson for the convention's Committee on Education, elaborated: "Public education forms the basis of self-government and constitutes the very corner stone of republican institutions." (Debates and Proceedings, Cal. Const. Convention 1878–1879, p. 1087 [hereafter Proceedings].) In support of section 1, delegate John T. Wickes argued that "a liberal education . . . breaks down aristocratic caste; for the man who has a liberal education, if he has no money, if he has no wealth, he can stand in the presence of his fellow-men with the stamp of divinity upon his brow, and shape the laws of the people. . . ." (Proceedings, at p. 1088.)

This theme runs like a unifying thread through the writings of our forefathers. In 1786, Thomas Jefferson wrote from France, then a monarchy: "I think by far the most important bill in our whole code is that for the diffusion of knowledge among the people. No other sure foundation can be devised for the preservation of freedom, and happiness. . . ." (Jefferson, *Letter to George Wythe,* in The Portable Thomas Jefferson (Peterson edit. 1979) pp. 399–400.)

John Swett, California's most prominent free school advocate at the time section 5 was adopted, warned: "Our destruction, should it come at all, will be . . . [f]rom the inattention of the people to the concerns of their government. . . . I fear that they may place too implicit confidence in their public servants and fail properly to scrutinize their conduct. . . . Make them intelligent, and they will be vigilant; give them the means of detecting the wrong, and they will apply the remedy." (Quoted in Cloud, The Story of California's Schools (194–), p. 20.) Without education for all, a majority of the people would be—in the words of Horace Mann—"the vassals of as severe a tyranny, in the form of capital, as the lower classes of Europe are bound to in the form of brute force." (Mann, *Twelfth Annual Report,* in Educational Ideas in America: A Documentary History (Rippa edit. 1969) p. 199.)

Perhaps the most eloquent expression of the free school idea came not from a political leader or educator, but from the poet Ralph Waldo Emerson: "We have already taken, at the planting of the Colonies, . . . the initial step, which for its importance, might have been resisted as the most radical of revolutions, thus deciding at the start of the destiny of this country,—this, namely, that the poor man, whom the law does not allow to take an ear of corn when starving, nor a pair of shoes for his freezing feet, is allowed to put his hand into the pocket of the rich, and say, You shall educate me, not as you will, but as I will: not alone in the elements, but, by further provisions, in the languages, in sciences, in the useful and in elegant arts." (Emerson, *Education,* in Educational Ideas in America: A Documentary History, supra, at p. 176.)

The contribution of education to democracy has a political, an economic, and a social dimension.

As this court has previously noted, education prepares students for active involvement in political affairs. . . . Education stimulates an interest in the political process and provides the intellectual and practical tools necessary for political action. Indeed, education may well be "the dominant factor in influencing political participation and awareness." . . . Without high quality education, the populace will lack the knowledge, self-confidence, and critical skills to evaluate independently the pronouncements of pundits and political leaders. . . .

Not only does education provide skills useful in political activity, it also prepares individuals to participate in the institutional structures—such as labor unions and business enterprises—that distribute economic opportunities and exercise economic power. Education holds out a "bright hope" for the "poor and oppressed" to participate fully in the economic life of American society. . . .

Finally, education serves as a "unifying social force" among our varied population, promoting cohesion based upon democratic values. . . . The public schools bring together members of different racial and cultural groups and, hopefully, help them to live together "in harmony and mutual respect." . . .

Viewed in light of these constitutionally recognized purposes, the first of the two tests described above is insufficient to ensure compliance with California's free school guarantee. That approach determines whether a given program falls within the guarantee not by assessing its actual educational value, but by deferring to a school board's decision on whether or not to offer it for formal, academic credit. Under this test, a for-credit program would fall within the guarantee, while a noncredit program with identical content—and equal value in fulfilling the constitutionally recognized purposes of education—could be offered for a fee.

The second approach, on the other hand, does not sever the concept of education from its purposes. It focuses not upon the formalities of credit, but upon the educational character of the activities in question.

It can no longer be denied that extracurricular activities constitute an integral component of public education. Such activities are "generally recognized as a fundamental ingredient of the educational process." . . . They are "[no] less fitted for the ultimate purpose of our public schools, to wit, the making of good citizens physically, mentally, and morally, than the study of algebra and Latin. . . ."

In a variety of legal contexts, courts have emphasized the vital importance of student participation in educational extracurricular programs. . . .

In addition to the particular skills taught, group activities encourage active participation in community affairs, promote the development of leadership qualities, and instill a spirit of collective endeavor. These results are directly linked to the constitutional role of education in preserving democracy, as set forth in article IX, section 1, and elaborated in *Serrano I*, 96 Cal.Rptr. 601, 487 P.2d 1241.

Accordingly, this court holds that all educational activities—curricular or "extracurricular"—offered to students by school districts fall within the free school guarantee of article IX, section 5. Since it is not disputed that the programs involved in this case are "educational" in character, they fall within that guarantee.

Defendants argue, however, that the fee-waiver policy for needy students satisfies the requirements of the free school guarantee. They suggest that the right "to be educated at the public expense" . . . amounts merely to a right *not to be financially prevented* from enjoying educational opportunities. This argument contradicts the plain language of the Constitution.

In guaranteeing "free" public schools, article IX, section 5 fixes the precise extent of the financial burden which may be imposed on the right to an education—none. . . . A school which conditions a student's participation in educational activities upon the payment of a fee clearly is *not* a "free school."

The free school guarantee reflects the people's judgment that a child's public education is too important to be left to the budgetary circumstances and decisions of individual families. It makes no distinction between needy and non-needy families. Individual families, needy or not, may value education more or less depending upon conflicting budget priorities. As John Swett, the "father of the California public school system," recognized in 1863, "[i]f left to their own unaided efforts, a great majority of the people will fail through want of means to properly educate their children; *another class, with means at command, will fail through want of interest.* The people then, can be educated only by a system of Free Schools, supported by taxation, and controlled directly by the people." (Swett, *Duties of the State to Public Schools*, reprinted in Swett, History of the Public School System of California (1876) p. 110, emphasis added.)

The free school guarantee lifts budgetary decisions concerning public education out of the individual family setting and requires that such decisions be made by the community as a whole. Once the community has decided that a particular educational program is important enough to be offered by its public schools, a student's participation in that program cannot be made to depend upon his or her family's decision whether to pay a fee or buy a toaster.

Nor may a student's participation be conditioned upon application for a special waiver. The stigma that results from recording some students as needy was recognized early in the struggle for free schools. Thaddeus Stevens once declared, in response to an 1835 proposal that teachers keep a list of "poor scholars": "Sir, hereditary distinctions of rank are sufficiently odious; but that which is founded on poverty is infinitely more so. Such a law should be entitled 'an act for branding and marking the poor, so that they may be known from the rich and proud.'" (Stevens, *A Plea for Free Schools*, in Educational Ideas in America: A Documentary History, supra, at p. 188.) Defendants' extracurricular programs are not truly "free" even to those students who are eligible for waivers. "[T]o a child or his parents financially unable to pay the additional fees and charges imposed by a *free, public school system*, any waiver procedure is a degrading experience." . . .

Finally, defendants warn that, if the fees are invalidated, many school districts may be forced to drop some extracurricular activities. They argue that invalidation would—in the name of the free school guarantee—produce the anomalous result of reducing the number of educational opportunities available to students.

This court recognizes that, due to legal limitations on taxation and spending, school districts do indeed operate under difficult financial constraints. However, financial hardship is no defense to a violation of the free school guarantee. . . .

Perhaps, in view of some, public education could be more efficiently financed by peddling it on the open market. Under the California Constitution, however, access to public education is a right enjoyed by all—not a commodity for sale. Educational opportunities must be provided to all students without regard to their families' ability or willingness to pay fees or request special waivers. This fundamental feature of public education is not contingent upon the inevitably fluctuating financial health of local school districts. A solution to those financial difficulties must be found elsewhere—for example, through the political process.

In conclusion, this court holds that the imposition of fees for educational activities offered by public high school districts violates the free school guarantee. The constitutional defect in such fees can neither be corrected by providing waivers to indigent students, nor justified by pleading financial hardship. . . .

In conclusion, the imposition of fees as a precondition for participation in educational programs offered by public high schools on a noncredit basis violates the free school guarantee of the California Constitution and the prohibition against school fees contained in title 5, section 350 of the California Administrative Code.

The judgment is reversed.

(The lower court decided for the school district and the Supreme Court of California reversed.)

CASE NOTE

Whether a user fee for school bus transportation is constitutionally invalid must rest with state courts in interpreting state constitutional intent. Such fees do not violate the Equal Protection Clause of the Fourteenth Amendment of the U.S. Constitution. In *Kadrmas*, in 1988, the U.S. Supreme Court emphasized that education is not a fundamental right under the Equal Protection Clause; thus, a state's enactment of a law allowing for permissible local user fees for school transportation was not prohibited by the U.S. Constitution. *Kadrmas v. Dickinson Public Schools*, 487 U.S. 450, 108 S.Ct. 2481 (1988).

■ ENDNOTES

1. Montesquieu, *The Spirit of Laws* (1748), trans. and ed. David Wallace Carrithers (Berkeley, Calif.: University of California Press, 1977), p. 130.

2. Jean-Jacques Rousseau, *A Discourse on Political Economy* (1758), trans. G. D. H. Cole (London: J. M. Dent and Sons, 1973), p. 149.

3. In 1760, John Adams noted in his diary that he had begun to read *The Spirit of Laws*. About fifteen years later, Thomas Jefferson devoted twenty-eight pages in his *Commonplace Book* to extracts from Montesquieu, and James Madison, in 1792, in his essay on "Spirit of Governments," compared Montesquieu's contributions to political philosophy to those of Francis Bacon in natural philosophy. See the Introduction to Montesquieu's *The Spirit of Laws* (1748), trans. and ed. David Wallace Carrithers, p. xiii.

4. Horace Mann, *Tenth Annual Report of the Board of Education* (Boston: Dutton and Wentworth Printers, 1847), p. 14.

5. "The Connecticut Law of 1650, Codification of 1650," in Barnard's *American Journal of Education*, vol. 4, p. 660. Cited in Ellwood P. Cubberley, *Readings in Public Education in the United States* (Boston: Houghton Mifflin Company, 1934), pp. 19–20.

6. See John Lawson and Harold Silver, *A Social History of Education in England* (London: Methicen & Co., 1973), p. 154.

7. Ibid., p. 155.

8. Will and Ariel Durant, *The Age of Voltaire*, Vol. 9 (New York: MJF Books, 1965), p. 438.

9. Ellwood P. Cubberley, *A Brief History of Education* (Boston: Houghton Mifflin Company, 1922), p. 374.

10. Ibid., p. 376.

11. Lawrence A. Cremin, *American Education: The National Experience 1783–1876* (New York: Harper & Row Publishers, 1980), p. 125.

12. Benjamin Rush, *Essays, Moral and Philosophical*, 2nd ed. (Thomas and William Bradford, 1806), pp. 4, 6–7.

13. Ibid., pp. 7–8.

14. R. Freeman Butts, "Search for Freedom: The Story of American Education," *NEA Journal* (March 1960): pp. 33–48.

15. John Adams, "Dissertation on the Canon and Feudal Law," in *3 Works of John Adams*, ed. C. F. Adams (1851), pp. 447, 448, cited in McDuffy v. Secretary of the Executive Office of Education, 415 Mass. 545, 615 N.E.2d 516 (1993).

16. Letter from Thomas Jefferson to George Wythe, Paris, August 14, 1786; Bernard Mayo, *Jefferson Himself* (Charlottesville: University Press of Virginia, 1942), p. 89.

17. Cubberley, *A Brief History of Education*, p. 286.

18. Ibid. General school laws were enacted in Connecticut in 1700, 1712, and 1714; Vermont in 1782, in addition to earlier statutes in Massachusetts (1647); and New Hampshire (1680). Georgia created a state system of academies in 1783. In 1795, New York provided for a state system of elementary education. Delaware established a state school fund in 1796, and Virginia enacted an optional school law in 1796.

19. Ibid., p. 288.

20. Ibid., p. 371.

21. Cremin, *American Education*, pp. 133–42.

22. Ibid., p. 127.

23. Ibid., p. 125.

24. Ibid., p. 123.

25. Marvie Meyers, ed., *Sources of the Political Thought of James Madison* (Hanover and London: Brandeis University Press, 1973), p. 186.

26. Ibid.

27. Mann, *Tenth Annual Report*, pp. 124–25.

28. Ibid.

29. Butts, "Search for Freedom."

30. *House Journal* 1822, Commonwealth of Kentucky, p. 236.

31. *House Journal* 1818–1819, Commonwealth of Kentucky, p. 13.

32. Ellwood P. Cubberley, *Public Education in the United States*, pp. 164–66. Copyright 1934, renewed 1962 by Ira S. Lillick, adapted by permission of Houghton Mifflin Company.

33. Butts, "Search for Freedom."

34. Newton Edwards, *The Courts and the Public Schools* (The University of Chicago Press, 1955), p. 23.

35. Ibid., p. 24.

36. Meyer v. State of Nebraska, 262 U.S. 390, 43 S.Ct. 625 (1923).

37. Fogg v. Board of Education, 76 N.H. 296, 82 A. 173 (1912).

38. Scown v. Czarnecki, 264 Ill. 305, 106 N.E. 276 (1914).

39. Fogg v. Board of Education, 76 N.H. 296, 82 A. 173, 174–75 (1912).

40. Leeper v. State, 103 Tenn. 500, 53 S.W. 962 (1899).

41. Robinson v. Cahill, 62 N.J. 473, 303 A.2d 273 (1973).

42. This classification is a slight modification of that suggested by James M. Mize in his article entitled "San Antonio Independent School District v. Rodriguez: A Study of Alternatives Open to State Courts," *University of San Francisco Law Review*, vol. 8 (1973–74): pp. 105–11.

43. The Constitution of Virginia, 1971, Art. I, §15.

44. Ibid., Art. VIII, §§1 and 2.

45. Ibid., Art. I, §15.

46. McLain v. Phelps, 409 Ill. 393, 100 N.E.2d 753 (1951).

47. Flory v. Smith, 145 Va. 164, 134 S.E. 360 (1926).

48. Cubberley, *Public Education in the United States*, p. 260.

49. Diane Ravitch, *The Great School Wars, New York City, 1805–1973* (New York: Basic Books, 1974), p. 23.

50. Commonwealth v. Hartman, 17 Pa. 118 (1851).

51. Cubberley, *Public Education in the United States*, p. 386.

52. Ibid., p. 247.

53. Stuart v. School District No. 1 of Village of Kalamazoo, 30 Mich. 69 (1874).

54. Martha Minow, "Reforming School Reform," 68 *Fordham L. Rev.* 257 (1999).

55. Ibid.

56. Dartmouth College v. Woodward, 4 Wheat 518 (1819).

57. Pierce v. Society of Sisters, 268 U.S. 355 (1925).

58. John E. Chubb and Terry M. Moe, *Politics, Markets and America's Schools* (Washington, D.C. : Brookings Institution, 1989), p. 219.

59. Ibid.

60. James A. Mecklenburger and Richard W. Hostrop, *Education Vouchers: From Theory to Alum Rock* (Homewood, Ill.: ETC Publishers, 1972), pp. 112–13.

61. Board of Education of Central School District No. 1 v. Allen, 392 U.S. 236, 88 S.Ct. 1923 (1968).

62. Ibid.

63. See Jeffrey R. Henig, *Rethinking School Choice, Limits of the Market Metaphor* (Princeton, N.J.: Princeton University Press, 1994), p. 94.

64. Minow, "Reforming School Reform."

65. 20 U.S.C.A. § 8061 to § 8066.

66. Ibid.

67. 41 A.L.R.3rd 755.

68. Hartzell v. Connell, 35 Cal.3d 899, 679 P.2d 35 (1984).

69. Arcadia Unified School District v. State Dept. of Education, 825 P.2d 438 (Cal. 1992).

70. 41 A.L.R.3rd 755.

71. Kennedy v. County Board of Education, 214 Ala. 349, 107 So. 907 (1926).

72. Vincent v. County Board of Education, 222 Ala. 216, 131 So. 893 (1931).

73. Irvin v. Gregory, 86 Ga. 605, 13 S.E. 120 (1891).

74. Hamer v. Board of Education, 47 Ill.2d 480, 265 N.E.2d 616 (1970).

75. Mathis v. Gordy, 119 Ga. 817, 47 S.E. 171 (1904).

76. Paulson v. Minidoka County School District, 93 Idaho 469, 463 P.2d 935 (1970).

77. Ibid.

78. Bond v. Public Schools of Ann Arbor School District, 383 Mich. 693, 178 N.W.2d 484 (1970).

CHAPTER 3

ROLE OF THE
FEDERAL GOVERNMENT

The question of the relation of the States to the federal government is the cardinal question of our constitutional system. At every turn of our national development we have been brought face to face with it, and no definition either of statesmen or of judges has ever quieted or decided it. It cannot, indeed, be settled by the opinion of any one generation, because it is a question of growth, and every successive stage of our political and economic development gives it a new aspect, makes it a new question.

—Woodrow Wilson, *Constitutional Government
in the United States*, 173 (1908)

CHAPTER OUTLINE

HISTORICALLY, the federal government has exhibited an active interest in education. Education was much on the minds of the founding fathers, who believed that public virtue and the welfare of the state were dependent on the ability of the people to properly exercise their democratic prerogatives. The founders of the American republic, influenced by John Locke, believed that the citizens were neither innately wise nor foolish, good nor bad, but were products of

their learning and exhibited civic responsibilities accordingly. From this assumption, it was imminently reasonable to conclude that "mankind could be greatly improved by education."[1]

Moreover, no lesser light than Kant, the great German philosopher, in the decade of the adoption of the American Constitution, had maintained that man had a duty to raise himself "from his crude state of nature" and to "diminish his ignorance by instruction," and by education attain his own moral perfection.[2] And, of course, Montesquieu, whom the American founding fathers had read so thoroughly, had stoutly maintained that education is a prime necessity of a republican form of government: "It is in a republican government that the whole power of education is required."[3]

There existed an implicit desire to guarantee the perpetuation of the democratic form of government by educating and "remaking the whole people . . . to conform the principles, morals and manners of our citizens to our republican forms of government."[4] In this light, many statesmen of the new nation believed that education was the best preservative of freedom, and most republicans tied general education and dissemination of knowledge to the success of the new republic.[5]

In the Constitutional Convention of 1787, the matter of education and a national university was advanced by several delegates, including Madison, but to no avail. The problem lay not in the delegates' general belief in the importance of education, but in the pressing concern that the sovereign states and not the federal government should be the proper repository of such power. The hesitancy to vest the power over education in the central government prevailed, and the state orientation of education became the pattern in the United States. Nevertheless, the interest in education at the federal level continued and stimulated educational progress throughout the states.

■ THE LAND ORDINANCES

Even before the adoption of the Constitution, the Continental Congress enacted the Land Ordinances of 1785 and 1787, which provided impetus for creation of educational systems in all the states joining the union. Initially, the original colonies had claimed almost unlimited territory extending west beyond the Alleghenies. For purposes of mutual accord, the matter was settled in the Continental Congress in 1780, when the existing states ceded their claims to the federal government, creating a national domain. This "common estate" created a common interest and bond among the first states of the new nation, and it was from this national

domain that new states were to be carved for westward expansion.

Although the primary motivation of Congress was to raise revenues for the debt-ridden nation that had just emerged from the War of Independence with England, the provision for education in the ordinances caused the new states to address the issue of education at the very beginning of their statehood. The Land Ordinance of 1785 included a provision reserving the sixteenth section of every township "for the maintenance of public schools within the said township." The purpose of this provision was to make the purchase of land more attractive to persons with families who might venture west. Regardless of the profit motive, however, the effect was a very positive force in the expansion of education. The survey plan of 1785 laid out square townships, six miles by six miles, containing a total of thirty-six sections. The sixteenth section, one mile by one mile (640 acres), was dedicated for schools (see Figure 3.1).

Within two years after the enactment of the Ordinance Survey of 1785 in mid-July of 1787, the Continental Congress met and enacted the Ordinance of 1787, known as the Northwest Ordinance. This ordinance is included in Article III, the now-famous provision, which stated that

> [r]eligion, morality, and knowledge being necessary to good government and the happiness of mankind, schools and the means of education shall be forever encouraged.

The Northwest Ordinance set out the requirements necessary for territorial areas to become states. Provisions for education, *habeas corpus*, due process, and religious freedom were all to be provided for in the compact, which was required by the central government as a condition for a territory to become a state.

The legislatures of the new states were thus required, in accordance with the Ordinance of 1785, to oversee the sixteenth-section lands, or to account for the funds if sold; the Northwest Ordinance of 1787 required that each state have an education provision in its basic law.

Later, when Ohio became a state in 1802, the problem arose as to whether states could tax federal property within their boundaries. A compromise was reached that provided that states would receive "5-percent" of the sale of

FIGURE 3.1   *A Congressional Township*

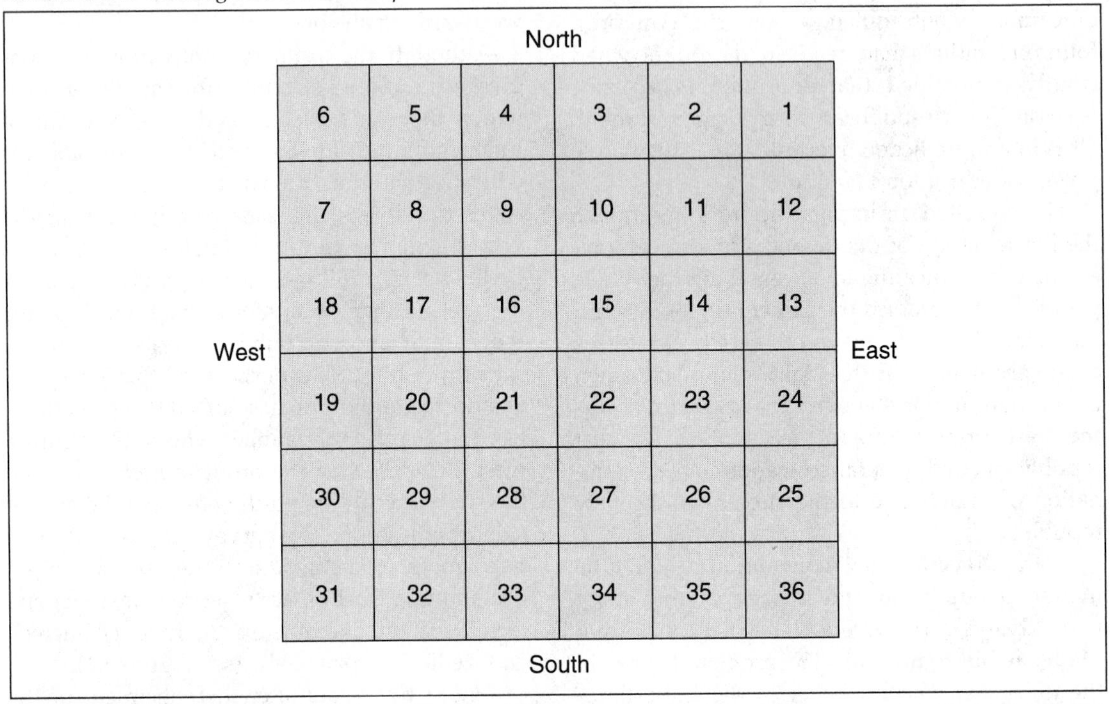

			North		
6	5	4	3	2	1
7	8	9	10	11	12
18	17	16	15	14	13
19	20	21	22	23	24
30	29	28	27	26	25
31	32	33	34	35	36

West — East (labels at sides), South (label at bottom)

Showing sections, quarter sections, plan of numbering, and the location of section 16, required for public schools. The township is six miles on a side, containing thirty-six square miles. It is subdivided into thirty-six sections containing one square mile, or 640 acres.

Source: Ira W. Harvey, *A History of Educational Finance in Alabama, 1819–1986* (Auburn, Ala.: The Truman Pierce Institute for the Advancement of Teacher Education, Auburn University, 1989), p. 17. Reprinted with permission.

public lands, if in turn federal property would be exempt from state taxation. These "5-percent" funds, along with income from salt lands and swamp lands, added to the revenues available for the public schools. Later, as a result of Jackson's decentralization efforts, the Surplus Revenue Deposit Act of 1836 distributed $28 million in federal funds back to state governments, much of which was devoted to school purposes.

These federal initiatives, in combination, provided an important stimulus for the states to assume responsibility for education. When the use and the sale of the land grant and the surplus revenues became inadequate to support state funding of education, the state legislatures began to move slowly toward appropriation of supplemental funds. One can only speculate as to what might have happened had the federal government not ended the inertia that retarded the creation of public schools. Perhaps some states would not have assumed the responsibility at all and would have allowed education to languish as an entirely local function or even, possibly, have allowed education to remain almost entirely in the hands of individuals or charitable and religious groups.

■ **INDIRECT FEDERAL ROLE**

The early method of federal land grants for education was most notable for two particular aspects. First, the grants were made for the purpose of creating and aiding public schools directly, thus espousing a federal interest in mass general common school education for everyone; second, the federal government exercised no control over education as a condition for receiving the grants.[6] From these beginnings, it was established that the federal government was to play an indirect role in the development of public education, to serve a stimulus function without direct control of educational policy and operation.

Over the years, the federal government's role has remained one of indirect support of education. Never directly controlling education, but generally in a positive and affirmative manner, the Congress has, from time to time, fashioned educational policy to address certain perceived national interests. The first Morrill Act, passed by Congress in 1862, like the early land grants, shaped American educational policy by providing a grant of land to each state; the land was to be sold, with the proceeds to be used for the "endowment, maintenance and support of at least one college where the leading object shall be, without excluding other scientific and classical studies and including military tactics, to teach such branches of learning as are related to agriculture and mechanic arts in such manner as the legislatures of the states may respectively prescribe."[7] In relying on this act, the great land-grant colleges were established and supported. Herein, Congress advanced a role of higher education that transcended the traditional, narrow, European model by expanding and giving credibility to the study of agriculture and engineering, disciplines that a new and developing nation so badly needed. Subsequent legislation—the second Morrill Act of 1890 and the Hatch Act of 1887, the Adams Act of 1906, and other provisions—expanded the activities of the land-grant colleges and introduced grants-in-aid as another type of federal support.

Following these initial steps, the federal government has continued to provide assistance to various phases of education. Categorical grants that were geared toward bringing about a particular educational emphasis became the method of allocation most relied upon. Federal grants of particular importance have been the Smith-Lever Act of 1914, which was quite specific in purpose, prescribing the expenditure of grant funds for, among other things, extension services by county agents for agriculture and homemaking and for training of teachers in these areas; the Smith-Hughes Act of 1917, which provided for funds for vocational education below college level; the National Defense Education Act of 1958 (the response to Sputnik I), which instituted several types of programs at the elementary, secondary, and higher education levels to give impetus to scientific training and research; the Higher Education Facilities Act of 1963, which created financial assistance for construction at all levels of higher education; the Vocational Education Act of 1963, which substantially increased federal appropriations for vocational education; and the Elementary and Secondary Education Act of 1965, the most important elementary and secondary program ever enacted by Congress, which provided funding primarily for the education of culturally disadvantaged children.[8]

In 1982, Congress passed the Education Consolidation and Improvement Act (ECIA), which replaced the Elementary and Secondary Education Act with block grants, eliminating several categorical grant programs. The purpose as officially espoused was to allow administration at the state level "with a minimum of paperwork."[9] This legislation includes three parts, called chapters, with Chapter 1, the largest, being directed to expansion of educational opportunities for educationally deprived children. Those to be aided under this provision are children of low-income families and children with special educational needs, and of migrant parents, Indian children, and disabled, neglected, and delinquent children. Chapter 1 funds are allocated under two types of grants: basic and concentration grants. Basic grants are allocated to counties according to a formula that uses two factors: the number of formula-eligible children in each county and the average expenditure per pupil in the state. This is the largest and most important part of Chapter 1 funds, amounting to nearly 90 percent of the Chapter 1 funds distributed. The other type of grant, concentration grants, provides funds for local educational agencies in counties with high numbers or high percentages of poor children.

Chapter 2 of the Elementary and Secondary Education Act has several titles. Title II provides funds for children falling behind, encompassing several smaller grants and consolidating twenty-nine original federal categorical programs for educational partnerships, innovation, improvement, and for library and instructional support in critical skills in mathematics and science. This part is known as the Dwight D. Eisenhower Mathematics and Science Education Act. Other parts of Chapter 2 provide presidential awards for teaching excellence; assistance for magnet schools; funds for women's educational equity and for gifted and talented programs; and grants for drug prevention, dropout reduction, bilingual education programs, and various initiatives.

The second-most important federal assistance, in terms of the magnitude of funding, is the Individuals with Disabilities Education Act enacted in October 1990, successor to the 1975 law entitled the All Handicapped Children Act of 1975. This act provides for funding as well as an elaborate set of procedures for the identification and education of disabled children. More about this act is given in a later chapter of this book.

All of the federal programs combined, however, constitute a small portion of all the revenues necessary for elementary and secondary schools. In each of these acts, the role of the federal government is conveyed by Congress to be one of supplementary assistance to the state systems of education. The Congress has sought to shape educational policy through the indirect means of categorical grants, giving direction to certain educational programs once states accept the funds. In each instance, the states have the option of accepting or rejecting the funds, but once they are accepted, the states must abide by the federal guidelines for use of the resources. As states have accepted the conditions of these categorical grants over the years, the role of the federal government in guiding educational choices has become more predominant, and some commentators have maintained that too much control is today vested in the federal government. As a result, even though the federal government's role in education is said to be indirect and secondary, myriad regulations and conditions bear down quite heavily on the public schools and have led some to question the legal scope of federal powers. Unfortunately, legal definition of the role of the federal government in education is as hazy and uncertain as the legal parameters of our federal system of government itself. Courts continue today to ponder the nature of the states' relationship to the central government not only in education, but in all areas of domestic activity.

■ STATE SOVEREIGNTY AND THE TENTH AMENDMENT

The powers of the federal government are circumscribed by delegation within the Constitu-
tion and are specifically limited by the Tenth Amendment, which provides that "[t]he powers not delegated to the United States by the Constitution, nor prohibited by it to the States, are reserved to the States respectively or to the people." Education is not mentioned in the Constitution and is, therefore, presumably reserved to the states or to the people. The Tenth Amendment was intended to reconfirm the implicit understanding at the time of the Constitution's adoption that powers not granted to the central government were reserved.[10] James Madison, at the urging of Jefferson, sponsored the Tenth Amendment. In the course of debate that took place while the amendment was still pending, Madison declared: "Interference with the power of the States was no constitutional criterion of the power of Congress. If the power was not given, Congress could not exercise it; if given, they might exercise it, although it should interfere with the laws, or even the Constitutions of the States."[11]

A discrete boundary line between federal and state power was not to evolve, however, in spite of Madison's apparently clear conception of the doctrine. Chief Justice Marshall, in the famous case of *McCulloch v. Maryland*,[12] added ambiguity by noting that the word "expressly" was not included in the Tenth Amendment as it had been in the Articles of Confederation, effectively leaving the issue of "whether the particular power which may become the subject of contest has been delegated to the one government, or prohibited to the other," to depend upon a fair construction of the whole instrument.[13] Justice Marshall's view of the Tenth Amendment was merely a restatement of the already presumed and established relationship that is delineated in other parts of the Constitution. In *United States v. Darby*, the Court said:

The Amendment states but a truism that all is retained which has not been surrendered. There is nothing in the history of its adoption to suggest that it was more than declaratory of the relationship between the national and state governments as it had been established by the Constitution before the amendment or that its purpose was other than to allay fears that the new national government might seek to exercise powers not granted, and that the states might not be able to exercise fully their reserved powers.[14]

Standing alone, the Tenth Amendment bears witness that our system of government assures separation of powers and prevents federal activity without express or implied constitutional authority. As such, there is a presumption of state power, which effectively places the burden on the federal government to justify in court its involvement in affairs that may have been presumed to be left to the states. As Justice Cardozo declared, the Tenth Amendment voices an assumption of "quasi-sovereignty . . . which the state is privileged to redress as a suitor in the courts."[15]

The U.S. Supreme Court now sitting has enunciated a very strong opinion and, indeed, a constitutional philosophy, that emphasizes the sovereignty of states in the constitutional design of our federal system. The Supreme Court emphatically maintains that states do not derive their powers from the U.S. Constitution, but, rather, are possessed of certain inherent and sovereign powers of independent governmental entities, some of which were ceded or delegated to the central government by the U.S. Constitution. This view is not without controversy, and the extent of this ceding of powers is the source of substantial disagreement. The present balance reflects the opinion of five justices of the U.S. Supreme Court who are generally viewed as the conservative majority of the Court. This Court has said that "the founding document (the U.S. Constitution) 'specifically recognizes the States as sovereign entities,'"[16] and by so concluding implicitly expands the concept of state sovereignty from the more limited "quasi-sovereigns," or limited sovereign philosophy as espoused as by Justice Cardoza, that is contrary to the current more full-blown idea that states have a pronounced and weighty inherent and original constitutional sovereignty. The concern over the balance between the powers of the central government and state government was, of course, the principal issue that animated the debates in the thirteen states when their conventions were held to ratify the U.S. Constitution. At that time the Anti-Federalists argued that a Bill of Rights and, in particular, a Tenth Amendment, was necessary to assert clearly and positively that states retained all those preexisting, sovereign rights that were not specifically delegated to the new central government. Moreover,

the Anti-Federalists were concerned that the Supremacy Clause, when implemented by the federal courts, would "sweep aside all prior claims of states' rights and authority."[17]

The importance of this structural issue in the formation of the U.S. Constitution cannot be overstated; in this regard the Supreme Court has said: "The Constitution never would have been ratified if the States and their courts were to be stripped of their sovereign authority except as expressly provided by the Constitution itself."[18] Thus, the Anti-Federalists' arguments that supported the passage of the Bill of Rights were primarily concerned with unstated rights and prerogatives of the states and of the people and to whether these rights could ever be preserved if they were not specifically designated.

The Supreme Court said in *Hall* that:

[I]n view of the Tenth Amendment's reminder that powers not delegated to the Federal Government nor prohibited to the States are reserved to the States or to the people, the existence of express limitations on state sovereignty may equally imply that caution should be exercised before concluding that unstated limitations on state power were intended by the Framers.[19]

Thus, the Supreme Court makes it clear that: First, states retain inherent sovereign powers that were not ceded or given up to the federal government in the Constitution; second, the federal government has only those powers delegated; third, the Tenth Amendment is a positive expression that verifies the existence of the inherent state sovereignty, as well as a formal declaration of the preservation of the rights of the people.[20]

Accordingly, it is the position of the current Supreme Court that the inherent sovereign powers of the states are to be found and preserved in the design of the "federative"[21] system in the Constitution where "The Federal Government, by contrast, 'can claim no powers which are not granted to it by the constitution, and the powers actually granted must be such as are expressly given, or given by necessary implication.'"[22]

This presumption, on behalf of the states, provides a constitutional basis through which a state can seek legal redress in challenging a federal statute. Without the Tenth Amendment, no such action would be possible. In the face of such challenges, the federal government has been forced, on several occasions, to identify other constitutional provisions that justify its activity in regulation of functions that states have assumed to be within their prerogative. In this light, the federal government does not possess general police powers, as such, and in justifying its many educational activities it must assert implied powers of the general welfare and commerce clauses of the Constitution.

■ FEDERAL INVOLVEMENT IN EDUCATION

By virtue of the Tenth Amendment, federal control over education is secondary to the power exercised by the states. While a state can create, organize, and reorganize school districts, employ and dismiss personnel, prescribe curriculum, establish and enforce accreditation standards, and govern all management and operation functions of the public schools directly, the federal government can intervene only in a peripheral and oblique way. Federal authority to enter the education arena emanates from three sources: (1) acquiescence by states in accepting federal grants that are provided under the authority given the Congress by the general welfare clause; (2) standards or regulations that the Congress has authorized within the commerce clause; and (3) constrained actions by courts enforcing federal constitutional provisions protecting individual rights and freedoms.

EDUCATION AND GENERAL WELFARE

Two major questions concern education and general welfare: first, does education come under the definition of general welfare? Second, how can Congress provide for education if it does come within the definition? Section 8 of Article I gives Congress the power to tax and spend: "The Congress shall have Power to lay and collect Taxes, Duties, Imports and Excises, to pay the Debts and provide for the common Defense and General Welfare of the United States. . . ."[23]

The interpretation of the general welfare clause has been the subject of much debate and controversy. James Madison contended that the clause "amounted to no more than a reference to other powers enumerated in subsequent clauses of the same section; that, as the United States is a government of limited and enumerated powers, the grant of power to tax and spend for the general welfare must be confined to the enumerated legislative fields committed to the Congress."[24] Madison pointed out that the framers of the Constitution borrowed the phrase from the Articles of Confederation, and it was not looked upon as a phrase to extend the parameters of federal authority. In taking an opposing point of view, Hamilton maintained that this article conferred upon the Congress a substantive power to tax and spend for purposes that would provide for the general welfare of the United States.

The Supreme Court adopted the Hamiltonian philosophy in a 1936 case that tested the constitutionality of the Agriculture Adjustment Act.[25] The Court stated that Congress was not limited in the expenditure of public monies to the direct or express grants of legislative power found in the Constitution.

In a later case, *Helvering v. Davis*,[26] the Supreme Court upheld the Social Security Act and in so doing ruled conclusively that Congress can tax and spend under the general welfare clause. In this case, the Court said that the general welfare concept is not static but flexible, and Congress may tax and expend public money for general welfare purposes so long as it does not demonstrate a display of arbitrary power. With this elastic definition of general welfare, the Congress is free to define education as general welfare and to tax and appropriate funds for educational purposes.

With the prerogative to broadly define general welfare as inclusive of education, Congress then looks to the taxing power of the clause for the instrumentality to "provide" for education. Jefferson explained the power and purpose of the clause in this manner: "[T]he laying of taxes is the *power* and the general welfare the *purpose* for which the power is to be exercised. They [Congress] are not to lay taxes *ad libitum for any purpose they please*, but only *to pay the debts or provide for the welfare of the Union*. In like manner, they are not *to do anything they please* to provide for the general welfare, but only *to lay taxes* for that purpose [italics added]."[27] This clause therefore expresses not an unlimited power but only a qualified one. Congress has never acted to assert an unlimited power to tax, and the Court has therefore never been compelled to decide the point.[28]

The last sentence in Jefferson's statement raises the point quite clearly that Congress cannot provide for the general welfare in any manner other than through its taxing and appropriation power. With regard to education, this means that Congress can involve itself in educational matters only through the indirect means of appropriation of funds and does not have the power to directly legislate changes in education. It is for this reason that Congress has so consistently used the categorical aid approach to bring about change in education. Constitutionally, regulation of educational functions can be acquired only through conditional grants.

The federal government cannot, therefore, affirmatively and directly require that states alter educational policy; this would be an affront to state autonomy. Constitutionally, the issue is really one of inducement versus compulsion, as one commentator has observed:

> The Constitution counts upon the necessary participation of the states . . . not by direct command but by incentive of not losing the opportunity of participation.[29]

In matters of education, then, the Congress can effect change only through persuasion or by giving the states an option that allows a state to act of its own volition. Welch says:

> The volitional nature of the state's acquiescence to conditional spending programs touches the very core of political autonomy. . . . Undoubtedly, economic necessity often forces states to alter governmental operations to qualify for federal funds; yet, the conditioning of needed funds does not preempt the state's decision-making process. Although the distinction may often be one of form rather than substance, the Court treats it as a critically important question of form. Such observance of form is more than a ritualistic bow to the founders' respect for the states. Apparently, the Court considers the sanctity of a state's decision-making process a necessary component of the Constitution's structure which endows the states with at least a degree of autonomous, volitional control.[30]

A choice of accepting the grant and the conditions attached thereto must be provided the state. Under the general welfare clause, then, a state may elect not to participate in a federal program if the conditions are educationally, financially, or legally offensive.[31]

EDUCATION AND COMMERCE

Congress has relied on the commerce clause to require certain actions by states. Quite beyond the limitations governing general welfare, the Congress has power under this clause to "regulate Commerce with foreign Nations, and among the several States, and with the Indian Tribes."[32] Education can be affected by congressional action pursuant to this clause in many different ways, but most notably safety, transportation, and labor regulations have touched education. While one would naturally assume that the term "commerce" included commercial activity—buying, selling, and trading goods to and fro among states—the definition, as applied by the Supreme Court, has been given broader meaning. In Gibbons v. Ogden,[33] Chief Justice Marshall rejected the narrow "trading" definition and maintained that it was "something more—intercourse." Commerce, as intercourse, was defined in Gibbons not merely as an exchange of goods but also as a means for "advancement of society, labor, transportation, *intelligence*, care, and various mediums of exchange [italics added]. . . ." That education is the foundation of commerce is not a new idea. The importance of literacy as a necessity, and indeed a right, of every human being began its ascendancy with the great innovation of movable type for printing by Gutenberg. Later, according to Condorcet, writing in 1793, "knowledge became the subject of a brisk and universal trade."[34] Condorcet attributed the rapid advancement of scientific discoveries to this "universal trade,"[35] citing the prodigious expansion of scientific knowledge by Bacon, Boyle, Newton, Halley, Huygens, Mercator, Kepler, Franklin, and others who fueled the advances in architecture, mathematics, medicine, astronomy, chemistry, and physics. Thus, the rationale required to support a constitutional assertion of education and knowledge as an aspect of commerce is neither new nor difficult to maintain.

As a mere limitation on states to prevent interference with interstate commerce, such a definition has little practical effect on education, but when read in its larger context in relation to the "necessary and proper clause,"[36] then Congress may act to improve commerce in an affirmative way rather than merely act to prevent state impediments. This, coupled with the fact that commerce regulation is not limited to interstate but may also, under certain conditions, include intrastate activities, brings public education within the purview of the clause.[37] In this broad context, education could conceivably be brought within the scope of commerce in that the movement of an intelligent citizenry among the states is vital to the growth and prosperity of the nation.

With this definition the courts are presented with a difficult dilemma of weighing the state powers under the Tenth Amendment against the apparent boundless scope of "commerce." Few decisions have been rendered in favor of state prerogative. In expounding the philosophy of the "political process," in which each state has representation in the Congress and this representation will protect state interests, the Supreme Court largely exhibited a hands-off attitude toward the expansion of the federal role through the commerce clause.[38]

The expansive view of the commerce clause was expounded by the Supreme Court in 1941 in upholding Congress' Fair Labor Standards Act of 1938, which established a national minimum wage and prohibited the shipment in interstate commerce of goods produced by child labor. The Court said:

> The power of Congress over interstate commerce is not confined to the regulation of commerce among the states. It extends to those activities intrastate which so affect interstate commerce or the exercise of the power of Congress as to make regulation of them appropriate means to the attainment of a legitimate end, the exercise of the granted power of Congress to regulate interstate commerce . . .[39]

By 1942, Congress's economic regulatory power was viewed by the Supreme Court as being virtually unlimited. In that year, Justice Jackson, Roosevelt's latest appointee, delivered the opinion of the Court:

> Whether the subject of the regulation in question was "production," "consumption," or "marketing" is . . . not material for purposes of deciding the

question of federal power before us. That an activity is of a local character may help in a doubtful case to determine whether Congress intended to reach it. The same consideration might help in determining whether in the absence of Congressional action it would be permissible for the state to exert its power on the subject matter, even though in so doing it to some degree affected interstate commerce. But even if appellee's activity be local and though it may not be regarded as commerce, it may still, whatever its nature, be reached by Congress if it exerts a substantial economic effect on interstate commerce, and this irrespective of whether such effect is what might at some earlier time have been defined as "direct" or "indirect."[40]

Later, in 1946, the Court said that the commerce power is "as broad as the economic needs of the nation."[41] At that time the national prerogative, through the commerce clause, attained its broadest scope.

This expansive view, though, was apparently changed, if not reversed, in *National League of Cities v. Usery,*[42] handed down by the Supreme Court in 1976. Under litigation were the 1974 amendments to the Fair Labor Standards Act, which extended wage and hour standards to almost all public employment, including local school districts. In this case, the Court, while admitting that the amendments were within the scope of the commerce clause, nevertheless held that the Tenth Amendment was violated. The decision enunciated a more restricted view of the commerce clause and interpreted the Tenth Amendment as an affirmative limitation upon the power of Congress to regulate activities of state and local governments.[43] Justice Rehnquist, writing for the majority, maintained that the state's power to determine wages of its own employees is an "undoubted attribute of state sovereignty" and that the functions performed by the affected state employees were "essential to the separate and independent existence" of the state.[44]

Usery, however, was reversed by the Supreme Court on February 19, 1985, in *Garcia v. San Antonio Metropolitan Transit Authority.*[45] In this 5–4 decision, Justice Blackmun, writing for the majority, said that judicial restraint in assuring state sovereignty is unnecessary in our federal system. Blackmun said that the *Usery* test "inevitably invites an unelected federal judiciary to make decisions about state policies it favors and those it dislikes." Blackmun was of the opinion that the balance in the federal system is sufficiently ensured by the political processes, and constant intervention by the courts is unnecessary. He further stated, "[S]tate sovereign interests, then, are more properly protected by procedural safeguards inherent in the structure of the federal system than by judicially created limitations on federal power."

Therefore, in *Garcia*, Blackmun was willing to rely on the legislative and executive branches of the central government to define the limits of federalism. In this conclusion, he cited James Madison's discussion in the Federalist Papers, Number 39, wherein Madison wrestled with determining whether the U.S. Constitution established a federal or a national government, and the nature and attributes of a federal system. Blackmun pointed out that Madison had interpreted the Constitution to clearly mean that the states had "residuary and inviolable sovereignty" over those matters of government not delegated specifically to the central government, but where delegation of power had been made to the central government, as in the case of the commerce clause, the Constitution gave no further guidance as to the limits on the central government in the exercise of those enumerated powers. It was Blackmun's contention in *Garcia* that any commerce clause limitations on the powers of the central government could not derive from the judiciary but rather must come from self-imposed restraints that the legislative and executive branches would place on themselves. Blackmun observed that

> [i]n short, the Framers chose to rely on a federal system in which special restraints on federal power over the States inhered principally in the workings of the National Government itself, rather than in discrete limitations on the objects of federal authority.[46]

Blackmun, therefore, entrusted the Congress and the president in their respective powers to prescribe the limits of the commerce clause. The difficulty with Blackmun's determination in *Garcia* is inherent in the nature of the U.S. Constitution as to whether it is, in fact, a federal or a national system of government. Perhaps this is a strength in that the issue is not cut-and-dried, and the political winds that periodically evolve are free, to some extent, to define the limits of federalism without impairing the foundation of the entire system. Madison himself had concluded, nebulously, that the new Constitution could not be discretely classified as either federal or national. Madison said:

> The proposed Constitution therefore is in strictness neither a national nor a federal constitution; but a composition of both. In its foundation, it is federal, not national; in the sources from which the ordinary powers of Government are drawn, it is partly federal [the Senate] and partly national [the House of Representatives and the president]: in the operation of these powers, it is national, not federal: In the extent of them again, it is federal, not national: And finally, in the authoritative mode of introducing amendments, it is neither wholly federal, nor wholly national.[47]

The difficulty in defining the nature of our form of government is, therefore, manifested in the inability of the Supreme Court to lay down a rule of law that defines the boundaries between the powers of the central government and the sovereignty of the states.

The Supreme Court took another turn at circumscribing Congress' powers in 1995 in *United States v. Lopez*,[48] in which the power of Congress to create gun-free school zones came into question. In this case a man named Garcia was arrested and convicted of possessing a firearm in a gun-free zone, as established by Congress in the Gun-Free School Zones Act, 1990. Garcia challenged the constitutionality of the act, claiming Congress had exceeded its authority. The congressional act was defended by asserting that commerce clause powers gave Congress the authority to make such laws regulating commerce. The Supreme Court held the law unconstitutional, finding that Congress had exceeded its powers because it could not be reasonably maintained that possession of a gun in a local school zone was an economic activity affecting interstate commerce.

By this ruling the Supreme Court effectively overruled Justice Blackmun's position in *Garcia* that gave virtually unlimited authority to Congress to statutorily prescribe the limits of its own powers with regard to the commerce clause. The Court quoted Chief Justice Marshall's 1819 decision in *McCulloch v. Maryland*[49] explaining the uncertainty of the extent of Congress' powers. Marshall said:

The [federal] government is acknowledged by all to be one of enumerated powers. The principle that it can exercise only the powers granted to it ... is now universally admitted. But the question respecting the extent of the powers actually granted, is perpetually arising, and will probably continue to arise, as long as our system shall exist.

As the cases of *Usery, Garcia,* and *Lopez* indicate, the precise balance inherent in the commerce clause has not been clearly and finally decided. The Supreme Court in *Lopez* attempts to define those boundaries.

❖ — ❖ — ❖

Congress' Gun-Free School Zones Act violates the Commerce Clause

United States v. Lopez

Supreme Court of the United States, 1995.
131 L.Ed.2d 626, 115 S.Ct. 1624.

Chief Justice REHNQUIST delivered the opinion of the Court.

In the Gun-Free School Zones Act of 1990, Congress made it a federal offense "for any individual knowingly to possess a firearm at a place that the individual knows, or has reasonable cause to believe, is a school zone." 18 U.S.C. §922(q)(1)(A) (1988 ed., Supp. V). The Act neither regulates a commercial activity nor contains a requirement that the possession be connected in any way to interstate commerce. We hold that the Act exceeds the authority of Congress "[t]o regulate Commerce . . . among the several States. . . ." U.S. Const., Art. I, §8, cl. 3.

On March 10, 1992, respondent, who was then a 12th-grade student, arrived at Edison High School in San Antonio, Texas, carrying a concealed .38 caliber handgun and five bullets. Acting upon an anonymous tip, school authorities confronted respondent, who admitted that he was carrying the weapon. He was arrested and charged under Texas law with firearm possession on school premises.

The next day, the state charges were dismissed after federal agents charged respondent by complaint with violating the Gun-Free

School Zones Act of 1990. 18 U.S.C. §992(q)(1)(A) (1988 ed., Supp. V).

A federal grand jury indicted respondent on one count of knowing possession of a firearm at a school zone, in violation of §922(q). Respondent moved to dismiss his federal indictment on the ground that §922(q) "is unconstitutional as it is beyond the power of Congress to legislate control over our public schools." The District Court denied the motion, concluding that §922(q) "is a constitutional exercise of Congress' well-defined power to regulate activities in and affecting commerce, and the 'business' of elementary, middle and high schools . . . affects interstate commerce."

Respondent waived his right to a jury trial. The District Court conducted a bench trial, found him guilty of violating §922(q), and sentenced him to six months' imprisonment and two years' supervised release.

On appeal, respondent challenged his conviction based on his claim that §922(q) exceeded Congress' power to legislate under the Commerce Clause. The Court of Appeals for the Fifth Circuit agreed and reversed respondent's conviction.

We start with first principles. The Constitution creates a Federal Government of enumerated powers. See U.S. Const., Art. I, §8. As James Madison wrote, "[t]he powers delegated by the proposed Constitution to the federal government are few and defined. Those which are to remain in the State governments are numerous and indefinite." The Federalist No. 45, pp. 292–293 (C. Rossiter ed. 1961).

The Constitution delegates to Congress the power "[t]o regulate Commerce with foreign Nations, and among the several States, and with the Indian Tribes." U.S. Const., Art. I, §8, cl. 3. The Court, through Chief Justice Marshall, first defined the nature of Congress' commerce power in *Gibbons v. Ogden,* 9 Wheat. 1, 189–190, 6 L.Ed. 23 (1824):

> Commerce, undoubtedly, is traffic, but it is something more: it is intercourse. It describes the commercial intercourse between nations, and parts of nations, in all its branches, and is regulated by prescribing rules for carrying on that intercourse.

The commerce power "is the power to regulate; that is, to prescribe the rule by which commerce is to be governed. . . ."

In 1887, Congress enacted the Interstate Commerce Act, 24 Stat. 379, and in 1890, Congress enacted the Sherman Antitrust Act, 26 Stat. 209, as amended, 15 U.S.C. §1 *et seq.* These laws ushered in a new era of federal regulation under the commerce power. When cases involving these laws first reached this Court, we imported from our negative Commerce Clause cases the approach that Congress could not regulate activities such as "production," "manufacturing," "mining." . . .

. . . [W]e have identified three broad categories of activity that Congress may regulate under its commerce power. . . . First, Congress may regulate the use of the channels of interstate commerce. . . . "[T]he authority of Congress to keep the channels of interstate commerce free from immoral and injurious uses has been frequently sustained, and is no longer open to question." Quoting Caminetti v. U.S., 242 U.S. 270, 491, 37 S.Ct. 192, 197, 61 L.Ed. 442 (1917) . . .

. . . Second, Congress is empowered to regulate and protect the instrumentalities of interstate commerce, or persons or things in interstate commerce, even though the threat may come only from intrastate activities. . . .

Finally, Congress' commerce authority includes the power to regulate those activities having a substantial relation to interstate commerce, i.e. those activities that substantially affect interstate commerce. . . .

Within this final category, admittedly, our case law has not been clear whether an activity must "affect" or "substantially affect" interstate commerce in order to be within Congress' power to regulate it under the Commerce Clause. . . .

. . . We conclude, consistent with the great weight of our case law, that the proper test requires an analysis of whether the regulated activity "substantially affects" interstate commerce.

We now turn to consider the power of Congress, in the light of this framework, to enact §922(q). The first two categories of authority may be quickly disposed of: §922(q) is not a regulation of the use of the channels of interstate commerce, nor is it an attempt to prohibit the interstate transportation of a commodity through the channels of commerce; nor can §922(q) be justified as a regulation by which Congress has sought to protect an instrumentality of interstate commerce or a thing in interstate commerce. Thus, if §922(q) is to be sustained, it must be under the third category as a regulation of an activity that substantially affects interstate commerce.

First, we have upheld a wide variety of congressional Acts regulating intrastate economic activity where we have concluded that the activity substantially affected interstate commerce. . . .

Section 922(q) is a criminal statute that by its terms has nothing to do with "commerce" or any sort of economic enterprise, however broadly one might define those terms. Section 922(q) is not an essential part of a larger regulation of economic activity, in which the regulatory scheme could be undercut unless the interstate activity were regulated. It cannot, therefore, be sustained under our cases upholding regulations of activities that arise out of or are connected with a commercial transaction, which viewed in the aggregate, substantially affects interstate commerce.

Second, §922(q) contains no jurisdictional element which would ensure, through case-by-case inquiry, that the firearm possession in question affects interstate commerce. . . .

The Government's essential contention, *in fine,* is that we may determine here that §922(q) is valid because possession of a firearm in a local school zone does indeed substantially affect interstate commerce. . . . The Government argues that possession of a firearm in a school zone may result in violent crime and that violent crime can be expected to affect the functioning of the national economy in two ways. First, the costs of violent crime are substantial, and, through the mechanism of insurance, those costs are spread throughout the population. . . . Second, violent crime reduces the willingness of individuals to travel to areas within the country that are perceived to be unsafe.

The Government also argues that the presence of guns in schools poses a substantial threat to the educational process by threatening the learning environment. A handicapped educational process, in turn, will result in a less productive citizenry. That, in turn, would have an adverse effect on the Nation's economic well-being. As a result, the Government argues that Congress could rationally have concluded that §922(q) substantially affects interstate commerce.

We pause to consider the implications of the Government's arguments. The Government admits, under its "costs of crime" reasoning, that Congress could regulate not only all violent crime, but all activities that might lead to violent crime, regardless of how tenuously they relate to interstate commerce. . . . Similarly, under the Government's "national productivity" reasoning, Congress could regulate any activity that it found was related to the economic productivity of individual citizens: family law (including marriage, divorce, and child custody), for example. Under the theories that the Government presents in support of §922(q), it is difficult to perceive any limitation on federal power, even in areas such as criminal law enforcement or education where States historically have been sovereign. Thus, if we were to accept the Government's arguments, we are hard-pressed to posit any activity by an individual that Congress is without power to regulate.

Although Justice BREYER argues that acceptance of the Government's rationales would not authorize a general federal police power, he is unable to identify any activity that the States may regulate but Congress may not. Justice BREYER posits that there might be some limitations on Congress' commerce power such as family law or certain aspects of education. *Post,* at 1661–1662. These suggested limitations, when viewed in light of the dissent's expansive analysis, are devoid of substance.

Justice BREYER focuses, for the most part, on the threat that firearm possession in and near schools poses to the educational process and the potential economic consequences flowing from that threat. *Post,* at 1659–1661. Specifically, the dissent reasons that (1) gun-related violence is a serious problem; (2) that problem, in turn, has an adverse effect on classroom learning; and (3) that adverse effect on classroom learning, in turn, represents a substantial threat to trade and commerce. *Post,* at 1661. This analysis would be equally applicable, if not more so, to subjects such as family law and direct regulation of education.

For instance, if Congress can, pursuant to its Commerce Clause power, regulate activities that adversely affect the learning environment, then, *a fortiori,* it also can regulate the educational process directly. Congress could determine that a school's curriculum has a "significant" effect on the extent of classroom learning. As a result, Congress could mandate a federal curriculum for local elementary and secondary schools because what is taught in local schools has a significant "effect on classroom learning," cf. *post,* at 1661, and that, in turn, has a substantial effect on interstate commerce.

These are not precise formulations, and in the nature of things they cannot be. But we think they point the way to a correct decision of this case. The possession of a gun in a local school zone is in no sense an economic activity that might, through repetition elsewhere, substantially affect any sort of interstate commerce. Respondent was a local student at a local school; there is no indication that he had recently moved in interstate commerce, and there is no requirement that his possession of the firearm have any concrete tie to interstate commerce.

To uphold the Government's contentions here, we would have to pile inference upon inference in a manner that would bid fair to convert congressional authority under the Commerce Clause to a general police power of the sort retained by the States. Admittedly, some of our prior cases have taken long steps down that road, giving great deference to congressional action. The broad language in these opinions has suggested the possibility of additional expansion, but we decline here to proceed any further. To do so would require us to conclude that the Constitution's enumeration of powers does not presuppose something not enumerated, . . . and that there never will be a distinction between what is truly national and what is truly local. . . . This we are unwilling to do.

For the foregoing reasons the judgment of the Court of Appeals is

Affirmed.

CASE NOTES

1. Even though the Supreme Court struck down the Agricultural Adjustment Act in 1936, in *United States v. Butler,* 297 U.S. 1, 56 S.Ct. 312 (1936), the Court interpreted the general welfare clause as giving Congress broad powers. In so doing, the Court adopted the Hamilton expansive viewpoint and rejected Madison's more restrictive view. The Court said, "Congress is expressly empowered to lay taxes to provide for the general welfare. Funds in the Treasury, as a result of taxation, may be expended only

through appropriation, Article 1, §9, cl. 7. They can never accomplish the objects for which they were collected, unless the power to appropriate is as broad as the power to tax. The necessary implication is that public funds may be appropriated 'to provide for the general welfare of the United States.'"

2. In the case of *Helvering v. Davis*, 301 U.S. 619, 57 S.Ct. 904 (1937), the Supreme Court of the United States was called upon to determine the constitutionality of the Social Security Act of 1935. Although this case does not directly involve education, it provides precedent for interpreting the meaning of the "general welfare clause." In this case, the Court makes two especially important determinations: (1) In drawing the line between what is "general" welfare and what is "particular," the determination of Congress must be respected by the courts, unless it be plainly arbitrary; (2) The concept of "general welfare" is not static but adapts itself to the crises and necessities of the times. The Court said:

> Congress may spend money in aid of the "general welfare". . . . There have been great statesmen in our history who have stood for other views. We will not resurrect the contest. It is now settled by decision. . . . The conception of the spending power advocated by Hamilton and strongly reinforced by Story has prevailed over that of Madison, which has not been lacking in adherents. Yet difficulties are left when the power is conceded. The line must still be drawn between one welfare and another, between particular and general. Where this shall be placed cannot be shown through a formula in advance of the event. There is a middle ground or certainly a penumbra in which discretion is at large. The discretion, however, is not confined to the courts. The discretion belongs to Congress, unless the choice is clearly wrong, a display of arbitrary power, not an exercise of judgment. This is now familiar law. . . .
>
> When such a contention comes here we naturally require a showing that by no reasonable possibility can the challenged legislation fall within the wide range of discretion permitted to the Congress. . . . Nor is the concept of the general welfare static. Needs that were narrow or parochial a century ago may be interwoven in our day with the well-being of the Nation. What is critical or urgent changes with the times.

3. Powers not expressly or impliedly conferred by the Constitution on the federal government are reserved to the "States respectively or to the people." (Amendment X, Constitution of the United States of America.) James Madison, in debate concerning the pending Tenth Amendment, declared that "[i]nterference with the power of the States was no constitutional criterion of the power of Congress. If the power was not given, Congress could not exercise it; if given, they might exercise it, although it should interfere with the laws, or even the constitutions of the States." (Annals of Congress, 1897, 1791.)

4. It is interesting to note that in 1788, before the Tenth Amendment was enacted, Madison described the federal government relationship to the states in the new Constitution thusly:

> The powers delegated by the proposed Constitution to the Federal Government, are few and defined. Those which are to remain in the State Governments are numerous and indefinite. The former will be exercised principally on external objects, as war, peace, negotiation, and foreign commerce; with which the power of taxation will for the most part be connected. The powers reserved to the several States will extend to all the objects, which, in the ordinary course of affairs, concern the lives, liberties and properties of the people; and the internal order, improvement, and prosperity of the State. (The Federalist, No. 45, January 26, 1788.)

5. The United States Supreme Court has summarily rejected doctrines of nullification and interposition. The doctrine of interposition being a

> concept based on the proposition that the United States is a compact of States, any one of which may interpose its sovereignty against the enforcement within its borders of any decision of the Supreme Court or act of Congress, irrespective of the fact that the constitutionality of the act has been established by decision of the Supreme Court. . . . [I]nterposition is not a constitutional doctrine . . . [and] if taken seriously, it is illegal defiance of constitutional authority. (*United States v. State of Louisiana*, 364 U.S. 500, 81 S.Ct. 260 (1960).)

The Supreme Court had this to say about interposition as it concerns education: although "the responsibility of public education is primarily the concern of the States . . . such responsibilities . . . must be exercised consistently with federal constitutional requirements as they apply to state action." (*Cooper v. Aaron*, 358 U.S. 1, 78 S.Ct. 1401 (1958).)

6. In an early case, the Kentucky Court of Appeals described the relationship of the federal government to the states: "The power of the states to establish and maintain systems of common schools, to raise money for that purpose by taxation, and to govern, control, and regulate such schools when established, is one of 'the powers not delegated to the United States by the Constitution, nor prohibited by it to the states,' and consequently it is reserved to the states respectively or to their people." (*Marshall v. Donovan*, 73 Ky. (10 Bush) 681 (1874).)

■ SUPREMACY CLAUSE

Occasionally in the field of education a state statute will come in direct conflict with a federal statute. If such occurs, the state law must give way and accede primacy to the federal law. This, of course, assumes that the federal law in question is enacted within the scope of appropriate constitutional authority. In anticipation of such occurrences, the founding fathers in 1787 included in the new Constitution a provision that became known as the "supremacy clause" whereby the central government of delegated powers could have a preeminent counterbalance against the strong sovereign powers of the states.

Article I, Section 8 of the Constitution grants to Congress broad power to enact legislation in several delegated areas of national concern. This power is buttressed by the supremacy clause that elevates the authority of congressional legislation above that of state legislation in areas in which Congress possesses constitutionally delegated authority. This preeminence of congressional power, however, must conform to the overall governance structure of the United States as contemplated by the Constitution.

Article VI, Clause 2 of the U.S. Constitution contains the "supremacy clause." This clause states; "This Constitution, and the Laws of the United States which shall be made in Pursuance thereof; . . . , shall be the supreme Law of the Land; and the Judges in every State shall be bound thereby; any Thing in the Constitution or Laws of any State to the Contrary notwithstanding."

The rationale for the supremacy of the laws of the central government is to be found in Madison's explanation in the *Federalist Papers*, Number 33, wherein he points out that "the laws of the Union are to be the *supreme law* of the land."[50] Madison observes that "If a number of political societies enter into a larger political society, . . . the laws of the latter must necessarily be supreme over those societies and the individuals of whom they are composed. It would otherwise be a mere treaty . . . , and not a government. . . . "[51] Yet, Madison goes on to note in a point that is cited by the U.S. Supreme Court in *Alden*, in 1999, that it does not, however, follow "from this doctrine that acts of the larger society which are not pursuant to its constitutional powers, but which are invasions of the residuary authorities of the smaller societies, will become the supreme law of the land."[52] The smaller societies in the case of the American system are, of course, the states that retain residual powers of their sovereignty.

The adoption of the supremacy clause provoked what was perhaps the most contentious of all the debates of the delegates to the Constitutional Convention at Philadelphia in 1787. The basis for the clause is to be found in James Madison's proposal in the Virginia Plan that gave the national legislature a "dominance" over state laws that conflicted with laws or articles of the Union.[53] The debate over this provision and the power of the judiciary in the separation of powers dominated the convention from May 29 until August 23, 1787. The prevailing view finally accepted, leading to the inclusion of the supremacy clause, was advanced by delegate William Paterson of New Jersey, who proposed that "all acts" of Congress "shall be the supreme law of the respective states" and that "the judiciary of the several states shall be bound thereby in their decisions, anything in the respective laws of the individual states to the contrary notwithstanding."[54] The Committee on Detail of the Constitutional Convention adopted Paterson's language and terminology, "supreme law," with little change, and reported it to the convention, whereby the supremacy clause was approved in a final vote on the Constitution on September 12, 1787. Peter Irons, in his seminal work on the Supreme Court, observes that Paterson, in his choice of words, "gave the advocates of a strong national government the design of a judicial battering ram that would knock down hundreds of state laws over the next two centuries."[55]

Yet, the issue was never clearly decided in the minds of the delegates at the Constitutional Convention. In *The Federalist Papers*, Number 39, Madison, after analyzing aspects of the powers of the central government as bestowed by the new Constitution, was inconclusive as to whether the new government was either federal, national, or something in between. He summarized that: "The proposed Constitution, therefore, even when tested by the rules laid down by its antagonists, is, in strictness, neither a national nor a federal Constitution, but a composition of both."[56]

According to Rakove, it was Madison's favored image that "the new federal system was to occupy a middle ground between a confederation of sovereign states and a consolidated nation."[57] Because the new system was not well defined and never really understood or agreed upon by the delegates at Philadelphia, great reliance was placed on the federal judiciary. The judiciary was to interpret the supremacy clause in actual cases and controversies and thereby develop an accepted balance between states and the central government. Implicitly, then, the supremacy clause attempted to incorporate a principle of judicial review to create the appropriate equilibrium that would establish limits on state sovereignty while advancing the necessary cohesion of the central government. Rakove says that "[t]he supremacy clause held out the more hopeful prospect that conflicts between national and state law could be channeled into a forum where the rules and forms of adjudication would mute the overt clash of political wills."[58] Rakove notes, "It seems evident, . . . that the framers believed the ultimate judicial power to resolve conflicts between national and state laws would reside in the Supreme Court,"[59] through its interpretation of actual cases and controversies and that from there would evolve an appropriate and desirable balance. The supremacy clause as interpreted by the Supreme Court was, therefore, to provide the legal nexus on which the American brand of federalism would ultimately be determined. Thus, under the supremacy clause, the federal courts must decide whether the state law in question is compatible with the policy as

enunciated by the federal statute. If the state law is in conflict with the federal statute and policy, the state law must yield.[60]

As anticipated by Madison, the balance between the powers of the "union" government and the residual powers of the state would be more fully defined by the judiciary as it interpreted cases and controversies over the succeeding years and decades. The balance has tended to reflect the political philosophy of the members of the U.S. Supreme Court and as a result the lines drawn do not remain static, tending to shift with the political climate of the times. Nowhere is the expression "the living constitution" more readily apparent than in the Supreme Court's interpretations as to the evolving balance of power between the central and state governments.

Today, the U.S. Supreme Court decisions have taken on a gloss and tone of decentralization as opposed to the centrist view of a few decades ago. The Supreme Court in 1999, in *Alden v. Maine*, devotes considerable attention to the explanation of what the U.S. Constitution intended for the design of our government as viewed through the lenses of today's more conservative Court. Interestingly the Court in *Alden* speaks of a "National Government" and "States as sovereign entities" operating in a "Federal system." Thus, to this Court the system seems to be federal rather than national even though the word "National" is used for the central government. Yet, it would appear, as measured by Madison, that the system is probably neither national nor federal, "neither wholly federal nor wholly national."[61]

The view of the current U.S. Supreme Court is explicated by Justice Kennedy writing for the majority in *Alden*.

> The federal system established by our Constitution preserves the sovereign status of the States in two ways. First, it reserves to them a substantial portion of the Nation's primary sovereignty, together with the dignity and essential attributes inhering in that status. The States "form distinct and independent portions of the supremacy, no more subject, within their respective spheres, to the general authority than the general authority is subject to them, within its own sphere." (*The Federalist, No.* 39).
>
> Second, even as to matters within the competence of the National Government, the constitu-

tional design secures the founding generation's rejection of "the concept of a central government that would act upon and through the States" in favor of "a system in which the State and Federal Governments would exercise concurrent authority over the people—who were, in Hamilton's words, 'the only proper objects of government.'" (quoting *The Federalist,* No. 15).

The States thus retain "a residuary and inviolable sovereignty." (*The Federalist,* No. 39). They are not relegated to the role of mere provinces or political corporations, but retain the dignity, though not the full authority, of sovereignty.[62]

Thus, according to Justice Kennedy, "the Supremacy Clause enshrines as 'the supreme law of the land' only those federal acts that accord with the constitutional design";[63] therefore the supremacy clause sits as the test and raises the eternal question of the constitutional design as to whether a law enacted by the Congress is "a valid exercise of national power."[64]

State Statute Impeding Intent of Federal Statute Violates Supremacy Clause

Shepheard v. Godwin

United States District Court of Eastern Virginia, 1968.
280 F.Supp. 869.

ALBERT V. BRYAN, Circuit Judge. . . . "Impacted" school areas are those whose school populations have been substantially enlarged by the attendance of Federal employees' children, but at the same time are losing school tax revenues because of the United States government's immunity from land taxes, both factors arising from increased Federal activities in the area. These conditions prompted Congress to provide financial aid for operation of the local educational facilities, P.L. 874.

In applying a State formula for State assistance to local school districts, Virginia has deducted from the share otherwise allocable to the district a sum equal to a substantial percentage of any Federal "impact" funds receivable by the district.

Residents, real estate owners and taxpayers of the City of Norfolk, later joined by those of the County of Fairfax, Virginia, in behalf of themselves and others similarly situated, here attack this deduction . . . as violative of the purpose and intent of the act of Congress and as transgressing the Fourteenth Amendment. We uphold their contention. . . .

The theory of the deduction in toto was that the Federal moneys were substituting for the taxes lost to the district by reason of the immunity of the Government property, and hence should be charged to the locality, just as the taxes would have been, in fixing the State supplementary aid. . . .

The grievance of the plaintiffs is obvious: any deduction whatsoever of the Federal supplement in apportioning State aid, pro tanto burdens them as taxpayers, for they and the other property owners in Norfolk and Fairfax have to make up the unindemnified portion of the impact costs. They contend that any deduction is prohibited by the purpose and plan of the Federal act.

The rejoinder of the defendant officials is, first, that the impact pupils are counted by the State in computing the minimum program cost in the district, and in accounting with the district for the State's supplementary aid it is not inequitable to insist upon a deduction of a commensurate amount of the impact moneys. At first appealing, this argument ignores the fact that the Federal children are to a large extent paying their own way so far as the *State* is concerned. Quite soundly, the Congressional Committee on Education and Labor, in recommending passage of P.L. 874, observed that the influx of Federal employees, and the withdrawal of real estate from taxes, did not diminish the tax sources of the State or otherwise burden the State. . . .

Our conclusion is that the State formula wrenches from the impacted localities the very benefaction the act was intended to bestow. The State plan must fall as violative of the supremacy clause of the Constitution. Our decision rests entirely on the terms, pattern and policy of the act.

The act makes these propositions clear: (1) the Federal funds are exclusively for supplementation of the local sources of revenues for school purposes; and (2) the act was not intended to

</br>
</br>

lessen the efforts of the State. Those postulates are manifested in the statute by these provisions, especially: that the Federal contribution be paid directly to the local school agency on reports of the local agency, and that the contribution be computed by reference to the expenditures "made from revenues derived from local sources" in comparable school districts.

But the State formula at once sets these precepts at naught. It uses the impact funds to account in part for fulfillment of the State's pledge of supplementary aid to the community; and the State moneys thus saved are available for State retention or such use as Virginia determines. Without the inclusion of the Federal sums, the State's annual payments towards supplementary aid would be increased, it is estimated, by more than $10,000,000.

This commandeering of credit for the Federal moneys severely injures both the community and the pupil. First and foremost, it does not relieve the local taxpayers to the extent Congress contemplated. Next, without the exclusive application of the funds to the areas where the need arose and remains, the result may be to lower the standard of education provided in an impacted district. Instead of maintaining the previous standards for the additional pupils, the impact money when thinned by the State would obviously be inadequate to continue that level for the increased school attendance, a result certainly thwarting the aim of the Federal law.

The construction and the implications we put upon the act find confirmation in its legislative history. . . . The exposition underscores the Congressional mandate that the impact payments are for local use and are not to be applied to compensate the State in any respect. Thus, at p. 13, it is stated:

> The effect of the payments provided for in this section is to compensate the local educational agency for loss in its local revenues. *There is no compensation for any loss in States revenues* [italics added]. . . .

Since its explanation in 1950 when P.L. 874 was passed that no compensation was intended for the State, Congress has reiterated this intention. In this repetition it definitely disapproves the accounting use Virginia's formula makes of the impact moneys. The House of Representatives Committee Report No. 1814, dated August 5, 1966, in proposing an amendment to P.L. 874, stated:

> Fifteen States offset the amount of Public Law 874 funds received by their school districts by reducing part of their State aid to those districts. *This is in direct contravention to congressional intent.* Impact aid funds are intended to compensate districts for loss of tax revenues due to Federal connection, not to substitute for State funds the districts would otherwise receive.

The committee report and the amendment are cited merely as evidence of Congressional intendment. The amendment provides only an administrative remedy of the Government and does not deprive the plaintiffs of standing to prevent future State infringement of their Constitutional right to the benefits of the aid proposed by Congress. Necessarily, then, the upshot is that the defendants must be enjoined from hereafter in any way denying to the impacted area the exclusive use and enjoyment of the impact funds. . . .

An order implementing this opinion is filed herewith. . . .

———————— ❖ — ❖ — ❖ ————————

State Is Not Obligated to Expend Federal Funds for Purposes That Violate the State Constitution

Wheeler v. Barrera

Supreme Court of the United States, 1974.
417 U.S. 402, 94 S.Ct. 2274, *modified and remanded,*
422 U.S. 1004, 95 S.Ct. 2625 (1975).

Mr. Justice BLACKMUN delivered the opinion of the Court. Title I of the Elementary and Secondary Education Act of 1965, as amended, 20 U.S.C.A. §241a et seq., provides for federal funding of special programs for educationally deprived children in both public and private schools.

This suit was instituted on behalf of parochial school students who were eligible for Title I benefits and who claimed that the public school authorities in their area, in violation of the Act, failed to provide adequate Title I programs for private school children as compared with those programs provided for public school children. The defendants answered that the extensive aid sought by the plaintiffs exceeded the requirements of Title I and contravened the State's Constitution and state law and public policy. First Amendment rights were also raised by the parties. The District Court, concluding that the State had fulfilled its Title I obligations, denied relief. The United States Court of Appeals for the Eighth Circuit, by a divided vote, reversed. We granted certiorari to examine serious questions that appeared to be present as to the scope and constitutionality of Title I. . . .

The questions that arise in this case concern the scope of the State's duty to insure that a program submitted by a local agency under Title I provides "comparable" services for eligible private school children.

Plaintiff-respondents are parents of minor children attending elementary and secondary nonpublic schools in the inner city area of Kansas City, Missouri. They instituted this class action in the United States District Court for the Western District of Missouri on behalf of themselves and their children, and others similarly situated, alleging that the defendant-petitioners, the then State Commissioner of Education and the members of the Missouri Board of Education, arbitrarily and illegally were approving Title I programs that deprived eligible nonpublic school children of services comparable to those offered eligible public school children. The complaint sought an injunction restraining continued violations of the Act and an accounting and restoration of some $13,000,000 in Title I funds allegedly misapplied from 1966 to 1969. . . .

In what perhaps may be described as something less than full cooperation by both sides, the possibility of providing "comparable" services was apparently frustrated by the fact that many parochial schools would accept only services in the form of assignment of federally funded Title I teachers to teach in those schools during regular school hours. At the same time, the petitioners refused to approve any program providing for on-the-premises instruction on the grounds that it was forbidden under both Missouri law and the First Amendment and, furthermore, that Title I did not require it. Since the larger portion (over 65%) of Title I funds allocated to Missouri has been used to provide per-

sonnel for remedial instruction, the effect of this stalemate is that substantially less money per pupil has been expended for eligible students in private schools, and that the services provided in those schools in no sense can be considered "comparable." . . .

In response to petitioners' argument that Missouri law forbids sending public school teachers into private schools, the court held that the state constitutional provision barring use of "public" school funds in private schools had no application to Title I funds. The court reasoned that although the Act was generally to be accommodated to state law, the question whether Title I funds were "public," within the meaning of the Missouri Constitution, must necessarily be decided by federal law. . . .

In this Court the parties are at odds over two issues: First, whether on this record Title I requires the assignment of publicly employed teachers to provide remedial instruction during regular school hours on the premises of private schools attended by Title I eligible students, and, second, whether that requirement, if it exists, contravenes the First Amendment. We conclude that we cannot reach and decide either issue at this stage of the proceedings.

As the case was presented to the District Court, petitioners clearly had failed to meet their statutory commitment to provide comparable services to children in nonpublic schools. The services provided to the class of children represented by respondents were plainly inferior, both qualitatively and quantitatively, and the Court of Appeals was correct in ruling that the District Court erred in refusing to order relief. But the opinion of the Court of Appeals is not to be read to the effect that petitioners *must* submit and approve plans that employ the use of Title I teachers on private school premises during regular school hours.

The legislative history, the language of the Act, and the regulations clearly reveal the intent of Congress to place plenary responsibility in local and state agencies for the formulation of suitable programs under the Act. There was a pronounced aversion in Congress to "federalization" of local educational decisions. . . . Although this concern was directed primarily at the possibility of HEW's assuming the role of a national school board, it has equal application to the possibility of a federal court's playing an overly active role in supervising the manner of Title I expenditures.

At the outset, we believe that the Court of Appeals erred in holding that federal law governed the question whether on-the-premises private school instruction is permissible under Missouri law. Whatever the case might be if there were no expression of specific congressional intent, Title I evinces a clear intention that state constitutional spending prescriptions not be preempted as a condition of accepting federal funds. The key issue, namely, whether federal aid is money "donated to any state fund for public school purposes," within the meaning of the Missouri Constitution, Art. 9, §5, is purely a question of state and not federal law. By characterizing the problem as one involving "federal" and not "state" funds, and then concluding that federal law governs, the Court of Appeals, we feel, in effect nullified the Act's policy of accommodating state law. The correct rule is that the "federal law" under Title I is to the effect that state law should not be disturbed. If it is determined, ultimately, that the petitioners' position is a correct exposition of Missouri law, Title I requires, not that the law be preempted, but, rather, that it be accommodated by the use of services not proscribed under state law. The question whether Missouri law prohibits the use of Title I funds for on-the-premises private school instruction is still unresolved.

Furthermore, in the present posture of this case, it was unnecessary for the federal court even to reach the issue whether on-the-premises parochial school instruction is permissible under state law. The state-law question appeared in the case by way of petitioners' defense that it could not provide on-the-premises services because it was prohibited by the State's Constitution. But, as is discussed more fully below, the State is not obligated by Title I to provide on-the-premises instruction. The mandate is to provide "comparable" services. Assuming, *arguendo*, that state law does prohibit on-the-premises instruction, this would not provide a defense to respondents' complaint that comparable services are not being provided. The choice of programs is left to the State, with the proviso that comparable (not identical) programs are also made available to eligible private school children. If one form of services to parochial school children is rendered unavailable because of state constitu-

tional proscriptions, the solution is to employ an acceptable alternative form. In short, since the illegality under state law of on-the-premises instruction would not provide a defense to respondents' charge of noncompliance with Title I, there was no reason for the Court of Appeals to reach this issue. By deciding that on-the-premises instruction was not barred by state law, the court in effect issued an advisory opinion. Even apart from traditional policies of abstention and comity, it was unnecessary to decide this question in the current posture of the case.

The Court of Appeals properly recognized, as we have noted, that petitioners failed to meet their broad obligation and commitment under the Act to provide comparable programs. "Comparable," however, does not mean "identical," and, contrary to the assertions of both sides, we do not read the Court of Appeals' opinion or, for that matter, the Act itself, as ever requiring that identical services be provided in nonpublic schools. Congress recognized that the needs of educationally deprived children attending nonpublic schools might be different from those of similar children in public schools; it was also recognized that in some States certain programs for private and parochial schools would be legally impossible because of state constitutional restrictions, most notably in the church-state area. Title I was not intended to override these individualized state restrictions. Rather, there was a clear intention that the assistance programs be designed on local levels so as to accommodate the restrictions.

Inasmuch as comparable, and not identical, services are required, the mere fact that public school children are provided on-the-premises Title I instruction does not necessarily create an obligation to make identical provision for private school children. Congress expressly recognized that different and unique problems and needs might make it appropriate to utilize different programs in the private schools. A requirement of identity would run directly counter to this recognition. It was anticipated, to be sure, that one of the options open to the local agency in designing a suitable program for private school children was the provision of on-the-premises instruction, and on remand this is an option open to these petitioners and the local agency. If, however, petitioners choose not to pursue this method, or if it turns out that state law prevents its use, three broad options still remain:

First, the State may approve plans that do not utilize on-the-premises private school Title I instruction but, nonetheless, still measure up to the requirement of comparability. . . . In essence, respondents are asking this Court to hold, as a matter of federal law, that one mode of delivering remedial Title I services is superior to others. To place on this Court, or on any federal court, the responsibility of ruling on the relative merits of various possible Title I programs seriously misreads the clear intent of Congress to leave decisions of that kind to the local and state agencies. It is unthinkable, both in terms of the legislative history and the basic structure of the federal judiciary, that the courts be given the function of measuring the comparative desirability of various pedagogical methods contemplated by the Act.

In light of the uncontested statutory proscription in Missouri against dual enrollment, it may well be a significant challenge to these petitioners and the local agencies in their State to devise plans that utilize on-the-premises public school instruction and, at the same time, forgo on-the-premises private school instruction. . . .

Of course, the cooperation and assistance of the officials of the private school are obviously expected and required in order to design a program that is suitable for the private school. It is clear, however, that the Act places ultimate responsibility and control with the public agency, and the overall program is not to be defeated simply because the private school refuses to participate unless the aid is offered in the particular form it requests. The private school may refuse to participate if the local program does not meet with its approval. But the result of this would then be that the private school's eligible children, the direct and intended beneficiaries of the Act, would lose. The act, however, does not give the private school a veto power over the program selected by the local agency.

In sum, although it may be difficult, it is not impossible under the Act to devise and implement a legal local Title I program with comparable services despite the use of on-the-premises instruction in the public schools but not in the private schools. On the facts of this case, peti-

tioners have been approving plans that do not meet this requirement, and certainly, if public school children continue to receive on-the-premises Title I instruction, petitioners should not approve plans that fail to make a genuine effort to employ comparable alternative programs that make up for the lack of on-the-premises instruction for the nonpublic school children. A program which provides instruction and equipment to the public school children and the same equipment but no instruction to the private school children cannot, on its face, be comparable. In order to equalize the level and quality of services offered, something must be substituted for the private school children. The alternatives are numerous. Providing nothing to fill the gap, however, is not among the acceptable alternatives.

Second, if the State is unwilling or unable to develop a plan which is comparable while using Title I teachers in public but not in private schools, it may develop and submit an acceptable plan which eliminates the use of on-the-premises instruction in the public schools and, instead, resorts to other means, such as neutral sites or summer programs that are less likely to give rise to the gross disparity present in this case.

Third, and undoubtedly least attractive for the educationally deprived children, is nonparticipation in the program. Indeed, under the Act, the Commissioner, subject to judicial review, 20 U.S.C.A. §241k, may refuse to provide funds if the State does not make a bona fide effort to formulate programs with comparable services. 20 U.S.C.A. §241j.

The second major issue is whether the Establishment Clause of the First Amendment prohibits Missouri from sending public school teachers paid with Title I funds into parochial schools to teach remedial courses. The Court of Appeals declined to pass on this significant issue, noting that since no order had been entered requiring on-the-premises parochial school instruction, the matter was not ripe for review. We agree. As has been pointed out above, it is possible for the petitioners to comply with Title I without utilizing on-the-premises parochial school instruction. Moreover, even if, on remand, the state and local agencies do exercise their discretion in favor of such instruction, the range of possibilities is a broad one and the First Amendment implications may vary according to the precise contours of the plan that is formulated. . . .

It would be wholly inappropriate for us to attempt to render an opinion on the First Amendment issue when no specific plan is before us. A federal court does not sit to render a decision on hypothetical facts, and the Court of Appeals was correct in so concluding.

. . . The comparability mandate is a broad one, and in order to implement the overriding concern with localized control of Title I programs, the District Court should make every effort to defer to the judgment of the petitioners and of the local agency. Under the Act, respondents are entitled to comparable services, and they are, therefore, entitled to relief. As we have stated repeatedly herein, they are not entitled to any particular form of service, and it is the role of the state and local agencies, and not the federal courts, at least at this stage, to formulate a suitable plan.

On this basis, the judgment of the Court of Appeals is affirmed.

CASE NOTE

Wheeler v. Barrera was later modified and remanded, 422 U.S. 1004, 95 S.Ct. 2625 (1975), but the substance of the original decision was not changed.

■ ELEVENTH AMENDMENT IMMUNITY OF THE STATES

One of the most important changes in constitutional law in decades is the series of recent U.S. Supreme Court precedents that create a "new balance" of federalism. In reversing a trend of several decades that vested greater authority in the Congress to enact laws and to impose liability on state governments and their state entities for noncompliance with those laws, the Court has now begun to test federal laws from a new perspective that places greater importance on state sovereignty. The principal constitutional provision that is being elevated and reinterpreted by the Court is the Eleventh Amend-

ment. The new balance directly affects several federal laws that impact state education policy. The results are having a marked effect on state education policy, as we have seen recently the U.S. Supreme Court strike down Congress' attempts to hold states liable under the Religious Freedom Restoration Act (RFRA),[65] Fair Labor Standards Act (FLSA),[66] the Patent Remedy Act (PRA),[67] and the Age Discrimination in Employment Act (ADEA),[68] and may place in jeopardy the enforcement of the Americans with Disabilities Act (ADA).[69]

The question of whether the federal courts and the Congress can impose liability for damages on state governments is integral to the balance of our system of government and, indeed, has great importance to the conduct of the state public school systems. The U.S. Supreme Court said in 1999 that "the States' immunity from suit is a fundamental aspect of the sovereignty which States enjoyed before the ratification of the Constitution."[70] The Eleventh Amendment to the U.S. Constitution bars a private party from recovery of funds from a state treasury for a liability judgment against the state. It does not bar such judgments against public officials or local entities not considered to be state entities. To date, the prevailing view is that local school districts are not state entities for purposes of the Eleventh Amendment. The Eleventh Amendment provides that:

> . . . the judicial power of the United States shall not be construed to extend to any suit in law or equity, commenced or prosecuted against one of the United States by Citizens of another state, or by Citizens or Subjects of any Foreign State.

The Eleventh Amendment is therefore an explicit limitation on the power of the judiciary to hold states liable, and is, thereby, a reinforcement of the sovereign power of the states.[71] The Eleventh Amendment was ratified in 1798 in response to a public outcry emanating from two early cases, one in 1791 and another in 1793. The first case, *Vanstophorst*, permitted a group of Dutch bankers, as creditors to the state of Maryland, to sue the state for recovery of debts;[72] the second case involved an action by two citizens of South Carolina, *Chisholm*, against the state of Georgia.[73] The thought of the consequences of having foreign nationals and citizens of other states invade the sovereignty of the various states "literally shocked the nation."[74] Sentiment to prevent such actions quickly gained momentum, and five years later, during John Adams' presidency, the Eleventh Amendment was ratified.

The idea that states as sovereign entities should be immune from liability was supported by both Madison and Hamilton. Madison said, "I do not conceive that any controversy can ever be decided, in these courts, between an American state and a foreign state, without consent of the parties."[75] Hamilton observed in *The Federalist*, Number 81, that "[i]t is inherent in the nature of sovereignty not to be amenable to the suit of an individual *without its* [the state's] *consent*." Such invasion on state legislative prerogative, it was thought, would hinder the operation of states and unduly restrain the exercise of their sovereignty. The Supreme Court has held that the amendment, by implication, also bars suits against the state by any and all citizens, including the state's own citizenry.[76] The Supreme Court has thus stated the general rule" of law as follows: "[A] suit by private parties seeking to impose a liability which must be paid from public funds in the state treasury is barred by the Eleventh Amendment."[77]

The Supreme Court has explained that the Eleventh Amendment's explicit reference to the immunity of states from suits that are "commenced or prosecuted" against one of the states by citizens or subjects of any foreign nation[78] is a "convenient shorthand but somewhat of a misnomer, for the sovereign immunity of the States neither derives from nor is limited by the terms of the Eleventh Amendment."[79] Thus, sovereign immunity of independent states predated the admission of the states to the union of the United States under the Constitution, and such immunity is retained by the states.

The immunity from suit is a prerogative enjoyed as an absolute right for centuries throughout the world by independent states or nations. Under English common law, the state could not be sued without the sovereign's own consent and according to the U.S. Supreme Court, this principle of English law was retained in American jurisprudence. The Supreme Court has said that:

Although the American people had rejected other aspects of English political theory, the doctrine that the sovereign could not be sued without its consent was universal in the State when the Constitution was drafted and ratified.[80]

Because of the delicate balance between central versus state powers, sovereign immunity was of utmost importance to the states in their decision to ratify the Constitution. This issue strikes at the core of the concept of a union of states.

As noted above in the discussion of the Supremacy Clause, the U.S. Supreme Court, of late, has adopted the philosophy that holds that "a more perfect union" is devised of separate sovereign states that "clearly preceded the Union in point of time. . . ."[81] This is the current view of the Supreme Court as expounded in *Kimel*, 2000, in *Alden*, 1999, *Florida Prepaid*, 1999, and *Seminole Tribe*, 1996.[82] According to the Supreme Court,[83] the Eleventh Amendment confirms a presupposition that may be expressed in two parts: "first, that each State is a sovereign entity in our federal system";[84] and "second, that 'it is inherent in the nature of sovereignty not to be amenable to suit of an individual without its consent.'"[85] Thus, the Eleventh Amendment is founded on the idea, indeed, "rooted in a recognition that the States, although a union, maintain certain attributes of sovereignty, including sovereign immunity."[86] Immunity of the state as derived from the concept of sovereignty antedates the U.S. Constitution, and the Eleventh Amendment is, therefore, merely a restatement, a renunciation, an assertion of positive law regarding the fact of sovereignty.

The immunity of states is, however, not without limits. The Supreme Court, in *Alden*, pointed out that "the constitutional privilege of a state to assert its sovereign immunity . . . does not confer upon the State a concomitant right to disregard either the Constitution or valid federal law. The states and their agencies are bound by obligations imposed by the Constitution and by federal statutes that comport with the constitutional design."[87] Thus, even though state sovereignty predated the formation of the Nation, where conflicts arise and a state violates a substantive aspect of the Constitution, then state sovereign immunity may be overridden, and liability may be imposed on the state by the state itself, by Congress, or by the federal courts. There are basically two ways that state sovereign immunity can be abrogated. The first is "if a State waives its immunity and consents to suit in Federal court."[88] Concerning this waiver, the Supreme Court has held that "a State will be deemed to have waived its immunity only where stated by the most express language or by such overwhelming implication from the text as to leave no room for any other reasonable construction."[89] The second is for Congress to unilaterally abrogate state immunity by its own legislative act. For Congress to abrogate state sovereign immunity, two questions must be answered, and both must be answered in the affirmative. The first is whether Congress has "unequivocally expresse[d] its intent to abrogate the immunity,"[90] and the second is whether Congress has acted "pursuant to a valid exercise of power."[91]

Where Congress abrogates, there must be unambiguous intent to abolish the immunity of the states, and such must be set forth in "a clear legislative statement."[92] A general authorization for a suit in federal court is insufficient to abrogate immunity.[93] Such authority to deny state sovereign immunity by Congress has not been taken lightly by the Supreme Court and is narrowly circumscribed. The Supreme Court has said that "the Eleventh Amendment immunity may not be lifted by Congress unilaterally deciding that it will be replaced by grant of some other authority."[94] Therefore, the mere fact that a state has agreed to receive federal funds does not in and of itself establish that the state has consented to waive its immunity and be sued in federal court.[95] As to whether Congress has such power, the Supreme Court will ask whether the law enacted by Congress was "passed pursuant to a constitutional provision granting Congress the power to abrogate?"[96]

Importantly, the Supreme Court has made it quite clear that the fact that Congress has authority under the Constitution in Article I to establish the supreme law of the land does not foreclose a state from asserting its sovereign immunity from liability claims arising from federal law. Therefore, for example, while the

enactment of Fair Labor Standards Act is a valid exercise of Congressional power, the federal statute cannot subject a state to liability without contravening the Eleventh Amendment.[97] With regard to enforcement of such federal laws, the Supreme Court has said that: "We reject any contention that substantive federal law by its own force necessarily overrides the sovereign immunity of the States."[98]

The Supreme Court in *Seminole Tribe* held that Congress cannot abrogate state sovereignty based on its constitutional powers under Article I alone, the constitutional provision from which Congress receives its delegated powers.[99] In the final analysis, therefore, any federal statute that attempts to abrogate state sovereign immunity must find its justification in the substance and enforcement of the Fourteenth Amendment. Congress must "identify conduct transgressing the Fourteenth Amendment's substance provisions in Section 1, and enforce the substance under Section 5. Congress must tailor its legislative scheme to remedying or preventing undesirable conduct."[100] Using this rationale the Supreme Court, in the *City of Boerne* case, found that Congress' attempt to abrogate state immunity under the Religious Freedom Restoration Act was not valid because it did not specifically identify the state conduct that transgressed the substantive provisions of the Fourteenth Amendment. In short, according to the Court, in order for Congress to tie legislation to the Fourteenth Amendment in an effort to validate abrogation of state sovereign immunity, the Congress must identify the "evil" or "wrong" that Congress intends to remedy, and the propriety of enforcement under Section 5 must be "judged with reference to historical experience . . . it reflects."[101] More recently, the U.S. Supreme Court held in *Kimel v. Florida Board of Regents*[102] that Congress could not invoke Section 5 of the Fourteenth Amendment to impose liability on states in enforcing the Age Discrimination in Employment Act of 1967 (ADEA). In *Kimel*, Justice O'Connor, writing for the majority, concluded that "ADEA does not contain a clear statement of Congress' intent to abrogate the States' immunity" and that Congress had exceeded its authority in justifying its actions under Section 5 of the Fourteenth Amendment;

the Act was, therefore, unconstitutional. Thus, the Supreme Court has demonstrated that it will be very restrictive in its interpretations of Congressional Acts that attempt to pierce state sovereign immunity, even if Congress attaches its rationale to the Fourteenth Amendment.[103]

Even when liability is permitted, it is not to be retroactive but must apply to prospective redress only. In *ex parte Young*,[104] the Supreme Court required the state to conform only its future conduct to the requirements of the Fourteenth Amendment. In *Edelman*, the Supreme Court forbade the payment of retroactive "equitable restitution" from state funds.[105] However, if a state agrees to be sued, by so consenting, the state forgoes its Eleventh Amendment immunity and agrees to pay damages if found to be liable. Consent by a state cannot be implied or be mere constructive acquiescence; rather, it must be an express denial of its own immunity. The fact that a state participates in a federal program does not implicitly waive the state's immunity from suit.[106]

> [W]hen we are dealing with the sovereign exemption from judicial interference in the vital field of financial administration, a clear declaration of the state's intention to submit its fiscal problems to other courts than those of its own creation must be found.[107]

It makes no difference whether the state had abrogated its common law sovereign immunity;[108] the waiving of common law immunity does not affect Eleventh Amendment immunity.

Finally, and very importantly, the reader should again be reminded that these Eleventh Amendment precedents apply only to "state" liability and not to individual liability. It should therefore be noted that Eleventh Amendment immunity protection does not extend to suits against public officials as individuals;[109] the fact that the state is immune from damages claimed by an aggrieved party does not necessarily mean that an individual will avoid liability. Too, the foregoing discussion does not address the potential liability of local school districts as governmental entities apart from state government. Liability of local school districts is discussed in Chapter 13. The predominant view of the courts is that local school districts may be held liable and are not provided immunity by the Eleventh Amendment. Moreover, the above material does not consider liability under the specific Congressional legislation for Individuals with Disabilities Education Act (IDEA), which is fully discussed in Chapters 9 and 17.

ENDNOTES

1. Forrest McDonald, *Novus Ordo Seclorum* (Lawrence, Kan.: University Press of Kansas, 1985), p. 53.

2. Immanuel Kant, *The Metaphysics of Morals* (1797), trans. Mary Gregor (Cambridge: Cambridge University Press, 1991), pp. 190–92.

3. Montesquieu, *The Spirit of Laws* (1748), trans. and ed. David Wallace Carrithers (Berkeley, Calif.: University of California Press, 1977), p. 130.

4. Ibid., pp. 190–91.

5. Ibid., p. 191.

6. Roe L. Johns, Edgar L. Morphet, and Kern Alexander, *The Economics and Financing of Education*, 4th ed. (Upper Saddle River, N.J.: Prentice Hall, 1983), p. 332.

7. U.S.C.A., Title 20, Education 81 to 1686.

8. Ibid.

9. Federal Register 47, no. 22 (November 19, 1982), *Rules and Regulations* (Washington, D.C.: U.S. Government Printing Office, 1982), p. 1.

10. United States v. Sprague, 282 U.S. 716, 51 S.Ct. 220 (1931).

11. Annals of Congress, 1897 (1791). See Edward S. Corwin, ed., *The Constitution of the United States of America* (U.S. Government Printing Office, Washington, D.C., 1964), pp. 1035–36.

12. 17 U.S. (4 Wheat) 316 (1819).

13. Ibid., p. 406.

14. United States v. Darby, 312 U.S. 100, 124, 61 S.Ct. 451, 453 (1941).

15. Hopkins Federal Sav. and Loan Ass'n v. Cleary, 296 U.S. 315, 56 S.Ct. 235 (1935).

16. Seminole Tribe of Florida v. Florida, 517 U.S. 44, 116 S.Ct. 1114 (1996).

17. Jack N. Rakove, *Original Meanings: Politics and Ideas in the Making of the Constitution* (New York: Vintage Books, 1997), pp. 324–25.

18. Atascadero State Hospital v. Scanlon, 473 U.S. 234, 105 S.Ct. 3142 (1985); See also Edelman v. Jordan, 415 U.S. 651, 94 S.Ct. 1347 (1974).

19. Nevada v. Hall, 440 U.S. 418, 99 S.Ct. 1182 (1979).

20. Rakove, *Original Meanings*, pp. 324–25.

21. John Locke used the term "federative power" in describing aspects of a government concerned with relations among several states. See Rakove, *Original Meanings*, p. 167.

22. Alden v. Maine, 527 U.S. 706, 119 S.Ct. 2240 (1999). See Martin v. Hunter's Lessee, 1 Wheat 304 (1816); City of Boerne v. Flores, 521 U.S. 507, 117 S.Ct. 2157 (1997); United States v. Lopez, 514 U.S. 549, 115 S.Ct. 1624 (1995).

23. Article I, §8, cl. 1.

24. United States v. Butler, 297 U.S. 1, 56 S.Ct. 312 (1936).

25. Ibid.

26. 301 U.S. 619, 57 S.Ct. 904 (1937).

27. 3 *Writings of Thomas Jefferson* (Library Edition, 1904), pp. 147–49.

28. Edward S. Corwin, *The Constitution*, rev. Harold W. Chose and Craig R. Ducet (Princeton University Press, 1978), pp. 139–44.

29. Henry Hart, "The Relations Between State and Federal Law," *Columbia Law Review*, vol. 54 (1954): p. 489.

30. Richard E. Welch III, "At Federalism's Crossroads: National League of Cities v. Usery," *Boston University Law Review* (1977): p. 178.

31. Wheeler v. Barrera, 417 U.S. 402, 94 S.Ct. 2274 (1974), modified 422 U.S. 1004, 95 S.Ct. 2625 (1975).

32. Article I, §8, cl. 3.

33. 22 U.S. (9 Wheat) 1 (1824).

34. Edward Goodell, *The Nobel Philosopher, Condorcet and The Enlightenment* (Buffalo, N.Y.: Prometheus Books, 1994), p. 215.

35. Ibid.

36. The power of Congress "[t]o make all Laws which shall be necessary and proper for carrying into Execution the foregoing Powers. . . . " Article I, §8, cl. 18.

37. Justice Marshall in Gibbons stated: "[T]he power of Congress does not stop at the jurisdictional lines of the several States," but "must be exercised whenever [and wherever] the subject exists. . . . Commerce among the States must, of necessity, be commerce [within] the States." Gibbons v. Ogden, 22 U.S. (9 Wheat) 1 (1824).

38. "[T]he power over commerce . . . is vested in Congress as absolutely as it would be in a single government, having in its constitution the same restrictions on the exercise of the power as are found in the constitution of the United States. The wisdom and the discretion of Congress, their identity with the people, and the influence which their constituents possess at elections, are . . . the sole restraints on which they have relied, to secure them from its abuse. They are the restraints on which the people must often rely solely, in all representative governments." Gibbons v. Ogden, 22 U.S. (9 Wheat) 1 (1824).

39. United States v. Darby, 312 U.S. 100, 61 S.Ct. 451 (1941).

40. Wickard v. Filburn, 317 U.S. 111, 63 S.Ct. 82 (1942).

41. American Power and Light Co. v. Securities and Exchange Commission, 329 U.S. 90, 67 S.Ct. 133 (1946).

42. 426 U.S. 833, 96 S.Ct. 2465 (1976).

43. Welch, "At Federalism's Crossroads," pp. 178–79.

44. National League of Cities v. Usery, 426 U.S. 833, 96 S.Ct. 2465 (1976).

45. Garcia v. San Antonio Metro Transit Auth., 469 U.S. 528, 105 S.Ct. 1005 (1985).

46. Garcia, *supra*.

47. James Madison, *The Federalist*, no. 39, in *The Origins of the American Constitution: A Documentary History*, ed. Michael Kammen (New York: Penguin Books, 1986), pp. 180–86.

48. 63 U.S. 4343, 115 S.Ct. 1624 (1995).

49. 17 U.S. (4 Wheat) 316 (1819).

50. James Madison, Alexander Hamilton, and John Jay, *The Federalist Papers*, ed. Issac Krammick, first published in 1788 (Hammondsworth, England: Penguin Books, 1987), p. 225.

51. Ibid.

52. Ibid.; See also Alden v. Maine, 527 U.S. 706, 119 S. Ct. 2240 (1999) and Printz v. United States, 521 U.S. 898, 117 S.Ct. 2365 (1997).

53. See Peter Irons, *A People's History of the Supreme Court* (New York: Viking, 1999), pp. 44–45.

54. Ibid.

55. Ibid., p. 46.

56. *The Federalist Papers*, op. cit., p. 259.

57. Jack N. Rakove, *Original Meanings* (New York: Vintage Books, Random House, 1997), p. 168.

58. Ibid., p. 175.

59. Ibid., pp. 175–76.

60. Ibid., pp. 808–9.

61. Madison, op. cit.

62. Alden v. Maine, op. cit.

63. Alden v. Maine, op. cit.

64. Ibid.

65. City of Boerne v. Flores, 521 U.S. 507, 117 S.Ct. 2157 (1997). See also Seminole Tribe of Florida v. Florida, 517 U.S. 44, 116 S.Ct. 1114 (1996).

66. Alden v. Maine, op. cit.

67. Florida Prepaid Postsecondary Education Expense Board v. College Savings Bank, 527 U.S. ____, 119 S.Ct. 2199 (1999).

68. Kimel v. Florida Board of Regents, 528 U.S. _____, 120 S.Ct. 631 (2000).

69. See Alsbrook v. City of Maumelle, 184 F.3d 999 (8th Cir. 1999).

70. Alden v. Maine, op. cit.

71. Missouri v. Fiske, 290 U.S. 18, 54 S. Ct. 18, 20 (1933).

72. Vanstophorst v. Maryland, 2 U.S. (2 Dall.) 401 (1791).

73. Chisholm v. Georgia, 2 U.S. (2 Dall.) 419 (1792).

74. Edelman v. Jordan, 415 U.S. 651, 94 S.Ct. 1347 (1974).

75. 3 Elliott's Debates, 553.

76. Hans v. Louisiana, 134 U.S. 1, 10 S.Ct. 504 (1890); Employees v. Department of Public Health and Welfare, 411 U.S. 279, 93 S.Ct. 1614 (1973).

77. Great Northern Life Insurance Co. v. Read, 322 U.S. 47, 64 S.Ct. 873 (1944).

78. Alden v. Maine, op. cit.

79. Ibid.

80. Ibid.

81. Rakove, op. cit., p. 163.

82. See Kimel v. Florida Board of Regents, op. cit. Alden v. Maine, op. cit.; Florida Prepaid Postsecondary Education Expense Board v. College Savings Bank and United States, 527 U.S. 627, 119 S.Ct. 2199 (1999); Seminole Tribe of Florida v. Florida, op. cit.

83. Seminole Tribe of Florida v. Florida, op. cit.

84. Blatchford v. Native Village of Noatak, 501 U.S. 775, 111 S.Ct. 2578 (1991); Hans v. Louisiana, 134 U.S. 1, 10 S.Ct. 504 (1890).

85. *The Federalist Papers* Number 81, op. cit.

86. See Seminole Tribe of Florida v. Florida, op cit., citing, Puerto Rico Aqueduct and Sewer Authority v. Metcalf & Eddy, 506 U.S. 139, 113 S.Ct. 684 (1993).

87. Alden v. Maine, op. cit.

88. Atascadero State Hospital v. Scanlon, 473 U.S. 234, 105 S.Ct. 3142 (1985).

89. Edelman, op. cit., p. 673, 94 S.Ct. at 1360.

90. Green v. Mansour, 474 U.S. 64, 106 S.Ct. 423 (1985).

91. Ibid.

92. Blatchford v. Native Village of Noatak, op. cit.

93. Atascadero State Hospital v. Scanlon, op. cit.

94. Seminole Tribe of Florida v. Florida, op. cit.

95. See Atascadero State Hospital v. Scanlon, op. cit.

96. Seminole Tribe of Florida v. Florida, op. cit.; See also Fitzpatrick v. Bitzer, 427 U.S. 445, 96 S.Ct. 2666 (1976).

97. Employees of Department of Public Health and Welfare of Missouri v. Department of Public Health and Welfare of Missouri, 411 U.S. 279, 9 S.Ct. 1614 (1973).

98. Ibid.

99. Seminole Tribe of Florida v. Florida, op. cit.

100. Ibid.

101. City of Boerne v. Flores, op. cit.

102. Kimel v. Florida Board of Regents, op. cit.

103. Florida Prepaid Postsecondary Education Expense Board v. College Savings Bank and United States, op. cit.

104. 209 U.S. 123, 28 S.Ct. 441 (1908).

105. Edelman, op. cit.

106. Edelman v. Jordan, op. cit. See also Atascadero State Hospital v. Scanlon, op. cit.; Fitzpatrick v. Bitzer, op. cit.; and Quern v. Jordan, 440 U.S. 332, 342, 99 S.Ct. 1139, 1140 (1979).

107. Ibid.

108. See Molitor v. Kaneland Community Unit District No. 302, 18 Ill. 2d 11, 163 N.E. 2d 89 (1959).

109. Ibid.

CHAPTER 4

GOVERNANCE OF PUBLIC SCHOOLS

The powers delegated by the proposed Constitution to the federal government are few and defined. Those which are to remain in the state governments are numerous and indefinite. The former will be exercised principally on external objects, as war, peace, negotiation, and foreign commerce; with which last the power of taxation will, for the most part, be connected. The powers reserved to the several states will extend to all the objects, which, in the ordinary course of affairs, concern the lives, liberties, and properties of the people, and the internal order, improvement, and prosperity of the State.

—James Madison, *The Federalist*, no. 45, 2:82 (1788).

CHAPTER OUTLINE

- EDUCATION AS A STATE FUNCTION
- LIMITS OF STATE CONTROL
- STATE AND LOCAL EDUCATIONAL AGENCIES
- EXECUTIVE FUNCTIONS

- SCHOOL OFFICERS
- SCHOOL ELECTIONS
- SCHOOL BOARD MEETINGS
- OPEN MEETINGS AND PUBLIC RECORDS LAWS

IT IS THROUGH THE STATE and by its governance that the people collectively act for the good of society and themselves. Every state is an association,[1] and each is formed to achieve a societal good that is not attainable by individuals acting in their own separate interest. The formation and governance of the public schools probably constitute the most important aspect of government used to improve the condition of humankind.

The state, as a community, is a form of "unifying relationship between human beings" in which "practical reasonableness" is achieved from collective and cooperative judgment.[2] It is surmised that the common good will be best identified and achieved through action of the state in carrying out the will of the people. Public reason requires that public schools be created by political society as the principal vehicle to advance the common good. "This public reason" emanates from the intellectual and moral power that is rooted in the ideals and aspirations of society.[3]

Thus, "public reason" to obtain the common good is an attribute of a democratic society, and the creation of public schools is a direct manifestation of that public reason.[4] Public reason is the foundation of the state educational systems. According to Rawls,[5] public schools are a product of that philosophy in at least three ways: (1) it is the reason of citizens as such, it is the reason of the public (not nonpublic); (2) it is subject to the good of the public and matters of fundamental justice; and (3) it is public in its nature and content, "being given by the ideals and principles expressed by society's conception of political justice. . . ."[6] In the exercise of that public reason, the state creates public schools to ensure fundamental political justice.

■ EDUCATION AS A STATE FUNCTION

The courts have consistently held that the power over education is an essential attribute of state sovereignty of the same order as the power to tax, to exercise police power, and to provide for the welfare of the citizenry. In the exercise of this pervasive function, states have established systems of public schools that are operated as administrative arms of the state government.

The broad power of the state extends to provision for education generally within its boundaries and not merely to the public schools alone. Education, in this broader context, encompasses educational purposes and pursuits of the populace and the schools, both public and private. The interest in an educated citizenry is such an important part of state sovereignty that a certain minimal quality of education for all children is required, whether their education is acquired in public or private schools.

Court decisions abundantly support the preeminence of the state in control of education. Interestingly, most precedents indicate that the legislature has the prerogative to govern education, when actually education is governed by the democratic legislative process, which requires action by both the legislative and executive branches of government. The legal principles controlling education have been stated many times in different ways by state courts; for example, the legislature has plenary power to set up public schools,[7] the maintenance of common schools is a concern of the state and legislature,[8] or a uniform system of public schools is exclusively within the province of the legislature.[9] The pervasiveness of this power is adequately illustrated by a Michigan decision, which states that "[t]he legislature has entire control over the schools of the state. . . . The division of the territory of the state into districts, the conduct of the schools, the qualifications of teachers, the subjects to be taught therein, are all within its (the state's) control."[10]

An Ohio court has briefly encapsulated this power as follows:

> [T]hat the control of schools, be they public or private, providing elementary and secondary education for the youth of Ohio, reposes in the Legislature of our state. When the General Assembly speaks on matters concerning education it is exercising *plenary* power and its action is subject only to the limitations contained in the Constitution. . . . We can, therefore, indulge in generalities and make a broad statement to the effect that the Legislature of Ohio, in passing laws concerning elementary and secondary schools, is restrained only by its own conscience, [and] fear of the electorate. . . .[11]

The power of the state to control education has sometimes been characterized as emanating from the state's police power.[12] Although "police power" has not been fully defined by the courts, it is clear that the term encompasses all the elements vested in state sovereignty, including those powers necessary to preserve the peace, morals, good order, and well-being of society.[13] It embraces the broad prerogatives of general welfare. The U.S. Supreme Court has said: "The police power of a state extends to the protection of the lives, limbs, health, comfort, and quiet of all persons, and to the protection of all property, within the state, and hence to the making of all regulations promotive of domestic order, morals, health, and safety."[14] Within this framework is the power of the state to protect the individual and society through provision for a system of education.

In holding that education is a state function, the courts maintain that the state's authority over education is not a distributive one to be exercised by local government, but is a central power residing in the state. The legislature has the prerogative to prescribe the methods of education, and the courts will not intervene unless the legislature is contrary to constitutional provisions.

The state legislature has both the power and the responsibility to enact laws to govern education. These laws prescribe the nature and number of local school districts and define their powers. The legislature may, if it so decides, create, alter, or do away with local school districts.[15] A Nebraska court has observed:

> [T]he state may change or repeal all powers of a school district, take without compensation its property, expand or restrict its territorial area, unite the whole or part of it with another subdivision or agency of the state, or destroy the district with or without the consent of the citizens.[16]

In matters of education, as in all other functions of state government, the state constitution is fundamental and is determinative of the broad scope within which the legislature can operate. The fact that the legislature is created by the constitution and given lawmaking authority, in conjunction with the executive branch, is in and of itself a pervasive and general delegation that is not limited to special conditions or situations. By way of explaining this prerogative, the Court of Appeals of New York has said: "The people, in framing the constitution, committed to the legislature the whole law making power of the state, which they did not expressly or impliedly withhold. Plenary power in the legislature of all purposes of civil government is the rule."[17] Unlike the Congress of the United States, which has only those powers delegated to it by the Constitution, state legislatures have plenary power and may pass any act that is not expressly or impliedly forbidden by the state constitution.[18] According to Edwards, "The legislature must do so much; it may do more."[19]

■ LIMITS OF STATE CONTROL

Strictly speaking, the term "plenary," meaning complete, absolute, and unqualified, should be used with proper qualification. Even though the courts have frequently used the term in defining the legislature's prerogative, in actuality, legislative power is subject to definite limits imposed on it by both the federal and state constitutions, as well as by federal statutes—which are supreme and take precedence over state

statutes. This limitation must be recognized as of major significance. The term "plenary" can be a particularly poor choice of words in view of recent trends in which courts have not only invoked the general constitutional restraints of equal protection, liberty, property, and so forth, but also have begun to directly circumscribe legislative action within the limits of education clauses of state constitutions. As indicated in Chapter 2 of this book, terms such as "efficient," "thorough," "effective," "uniform," and "system" as used in education clauses have increasingly been invoked by the courts to strike down statutes governing the financing of public schools. Several recent decisions[20] have revitalized the education clauses, and their interpretations may, in the future, represent important precedents and, as a consequence, important limitations on legislative power. Thro observes that prior to the 1989 cases, the "education clauses (in state constitutions) were largely useless as tools for school finance reform," but today legislatures are subject to a new duty and responsibility to provide for public schools.[21] The imposition by the courts of this new duty on the state legislatures creates an increased standard to which legislative action must adhere. This standard, emanating from more assertive interpretation of education clauses, is seen by some courts as creating

> a "duty" that is supreme, preeminent and dominant. Flowing from this constitutionally imposed "duty" is its jural correlative, a correspondent "right" permitting control of another's conduct. Therefore, all children residing within the borders of the state possess a "right," arising from a constitutionally imposed "duty" of the State, that the State make ample provision for their education. Further, since the "duty" is characterized as paramount, the correlative "right" has equal stature. . . . Consequently, all children residing within the State's borders have a "right" to be amply provided with an education.[22]

■ STATE AND LOCAL EDUCATIONAL AGENCIES

All states and the federal government have networks of administrative agencies (usually called boards, commissions, bureaus, or offices) that have been created to implement and administer statutes. State legislatures and the U.S. Congress have not seen fit historically to actually administer legislative enactments themselves, even though the legislative branch of government could conceivably assume the role of program administration. Traditionally, the view has been that the legislature should not perform the multiduties of enacting legislation, appropriating funds, and then administering the funds, thereby invading the gray area of executive responsibility. In education, for example, it would be tedious and legislatively cumbersome for a state legislature to attempt to establish by statute rules and regulations governing specific certification requirements for teachers.

In this regard, an Illinois court has said that delegation of public school responsibilities from the general assembly to subordinate agencies—duly elected school boards—is of practical necessity because the legislature could not itself conveniently or efficiently attend to the details of establishing, maintaining, and operating the public schools.[23]

Jaffe has suggested the reasoning for such delegation of regulatory power by saying:

> Power should be delegated where there is agreement that a task must be performed and it cannot be effectively performed by the legislature without the assistance of a delegate or without an expenditure of time so great as to lead to the neglect of equally important business.[24]

The result has been for the state legislature to create agencies that handle the administrative functions necessary to properly implement legislation. In most states, this delegation by the legislature manifests itself in a state board of education, which may be either elected or appointed and has authority to perform administrative and supervisory functions. An alternative to this approach is to vest officials of the executive branch with regulatory and attendant authority to administer the school system of the state; such officers are generally referred to as chief state school officers. Legislatures may also delegate powers to local school districts.

It is well established that the local school district is a state agency that simply operates at the local level. The Supreme Court of Michigan has said the school district is a legislative creation. "It is true that it was provided for in obedience to a constitutional requirement; and whatever

we may think . . . we cannot doubt that such management must be in conformity to the provisions of such laws of a general character as may from time to time be passed, and that the property of the district is in no sense private property, but is public property devoted to the purposes of the state for the general good, just as almshouses and courthouses are, although confined to local management, and applied to uses which are in a sense local, though in another sense general."[25]

Another Michigan decision described the legal relationship between the state and local school districts in this way:

> Fundamentally, provision for and control of our public school system is a state matter, delegated and lodged in the state legislature by the Constitution in a separate article entirely distinct from that relating to local government. The general policy of the state has been to retain control of its school system, to be administered throughout the state under state laws by local state agencies organized with plenary powers independent of the local government with which, by location and geographical boundaries, they are necessarily closely associated and to a greater or lesser extent authorized to cooperate. "Education belongs to the state."[26]

Because local school boards are state bodies, it follows that school board members are state, not local, officials.[27] Local school boards are vested with a portion of the sovereignty of the state through delegation, by which they acquire certain administrative functions having attributes of all three branches of government: executive, quasi-judicial, and regulatory (or quasi-legislative). As creatures of the legislature or constitution, local school districts abide within their legal prerogatives and cannot give away or redelegate their judgmental powers to other agencies or individuals.

The courts commonly divide the administrative functions of the local school board into two categories, discretionary and ministerial. The meaning of discretionary powers here is those acts that require judgment on the part of the board. Examples of such responsibilities could be the location of a school building site, the employment of a particular teacher, or the purchase of a certain type of school bus. The greatest portion of a board's powers may be classified as discretionary. In exercising these discretionary powers, a board of education is limited only by the requirements and restrictions of the law. As has been pointed out in the case of state educational agencies, the courts will not interfere with a board's exercise of discretion even though the judgment is unwise except where the board's action violates the law, abuses authority, or is *ultra vires*.

The operation of school districts is based upon the express or implied authority of statute. The courts in circumscribing the authority of school boards from statutory implication have held that in the absence of statute, travel expenses can be paid for the recruitment of teachers outside the state,[28] a school district can establish a cafeteria,[29] and a school board can establish a school health inspection department made up of doctors, dentists, and nurses.[30] On the other hand, authority has been denied for a school district to pay for surgical and dental operations for pupils,[31] for medical care for pupils injured in athletic contests,[32] and for purchases of basketball uniforms to be used on land not under school control.[33]

FUNCTIONS OF EDUCATIONAL AGENCIES

Functions of public agencies can generally be classified as (1) legislative, (2) executive, and (3) judicial (or quasi-judicial). As agencies of government, both state and local educational authorities have these basic powers.

Administration encompasses the rule-making and adjudication processes and incidental powers, such as coordinating, supervising, investigating, prosecuting, advising, and declaring.[34] The exercise of administrative functions may be reviewed by the courts to determine if duties have been carried forth within the scope of law and whether proper procedures have been followed.

DELEGATION OF LEGISLATIVE POWERS

Legislative functions of the state agency include the promulgation of rules and regulations made pursuant to and within the scope of statute. The legislative function performed by state agencies has been justified on the grounds that the agency was merely "filling in the details" within the meaning of general statute.[35] In the public

interest, it is said the state agency should not have legislative powers, since agency officials are not direct representatives of the people with constitutionally sanctioned lawmaking prerogative. This is a basic tenet of representative government recognized early by John Locke. In his treatises on civil government, he said:

> The legislature cannot transfer the power of making laws to any other hands, for it being but a delegated power from the people, they who have it cannot pass it over to others. . . . [N]obody else can say other men shall make laws for them; nor can they be bound by any laws but such as are enacted by those whom they have chosen and authorized to make laws for them.[36]

Exclusive powers of the legislature should not therefore be delegated to subordinate agencies. In clarification of this theory of government, a Michigan court has said:

> This is not to say, however, that a subordinate body or official may not be clothed with authority to say when the law shall operate, or to whom, or upon what occasion, provided, however, that the standards prescribed for guidance are as reasonably precise as the subject matter requires or permits.[37]

Davis maintains, though, that formulations by state courts that attempt to circumscribe the legislative function of subordinate agencies are largely without substance.[38] While generally it appears that most courts seek to restrain too broad a delegation in order to prevent arbitrary use of uncontrolled power by subordinate officials, the actual legal theory and its implementation by the courts is sometimes difficult to follow. Basically, the theory of delegation appears to have been justified on the grounds of "adequacy of standards."

Does the statute provide sufficient delineation of the particular requirement or prohibition so that in light of the surrounding facts and circumstances the agency can ascertain, interpret, and implement the true purpose of the act? The legislature must prescribe a "reasonably adequate standard."[39] Some courts maintain that "definite standards are indispensable, not only to avoid a delegation of the essential legislative power, but to guard against an arbitrary use of the delegated administrative authority."[40] Limitations on legislative delegation to subordinate agencies may have been best described by a Washington court that said:

> The legislature may delegate these legislative controls to an administrative agency of the state; provided, in so doing, it defines what is to be done; the instrumentality which is to accomplish it; and the scope of the instrumentality's authority in so doing, by prescribing reasonable administrative standards.[41]

This statement probably represents the prevailing view of the courts, but the doctrine of delegation is one that must be treated as highly flexible. Courts, for example, tend to restrict agency prerogatives in the area of taxation, property rights, or individual civil rights. On the other hand, state educational agencies may have broad latitude in dealing with regulation of purely educational matters, such as school district organization. For example, a Wisconsin statute was contested as being unconstitutional because it authorized the state school superintendent to merge certain school districts of low assessed valuation with contiguous school districts. The Wisconsin Supreme Court said that "the power to exercise discretion in determining whether such districts shall be altered ... may be delegated without any standard whatsoever to guide in the exercise of the power delegated."[42]

The tendency in recent years has been for the courts to follow a much more lenient policy toward delegation of legislative power.[43] Changes in the nature of modern government and the increasing complexity of society necessitate that public agencies have more general authority to assume broader prerogatives. As it now stands, the delegation principle is still applicable to the state educational process, and it remains in use to prevent unconstitutional usurpation of unauthorized powers, but it is much less pervasive than before. The rule today as expounded by state courts is best exemplified by a New York court[44] that quoted with approval the standard established by the U.S. Supreme Court, which said that a legislative body

> does not abdicate its functions when it describes what job must be done, who must do it, and what is the scope of his authority. In our complex economy that indeed is frequently the only way in which the legislative process can go forward.[45]

Although the rationale of the courts continues to follow the delegation doctrine, it should be observed that proper delegation and guarantee against arbitrary action by agencies cannot be assured through the specification of standards in legislative declarations. Protection against inappropriate action and injustice in education are to be found more in procedural safeguards and various checks and balances, the most effective of which is, of course, justification of the action to the voters and taxpayers.

■ EXECUTIVE FUNCTIONS

Although functions of educational agencies are difficult to compartmentalize, it is possible to identify certain ones that may be more readily described as executive rather than legislative or judicial. In fact, the organizational structures of state educational agencies tend to adhere to such definition in that the legislative functions are usually vested in a state board of education, the executive functions in a chief state school officer and his or her staff (the state department of education), and the quasi-judicial functions within the authority of either or both. A similar situation exists at the local level, where the board makes policy and the superintendent implements it, with both sometimes exercising quasi-judicial functions.

The distinction between legislative and executive acts can be expressed as the difference between the general and the particular:

> A legislative act is the creation and promulgation of a general rule of conduct without reference to particular cases; an administrative act cannot be exactly defined, but it includes the adoption of policy, the making and issue of specific direction, and the application of a general rule to a particular case in accordance with the requirements of policy and expediency of administrative practice.[46]

Activities of the educational agency that may be classified as purely executive are declaring and enforcing policy as well as advising and supervising implementation of policy. One can easily identify such activities as they are performed daily in state agencies; for example, when a policy is established, it must be properly interpreted and conveyed to the local school district administrators, then advice may be given and certain supervisory activities may be followed to assist in implementation. Should problems arise, steps must be taken to ensure enforcement of the particular policy.

Executive actions can also be viewed in the more commonly used legislative categories of ministerial and discretionary functions. "Ministerial" refers to those required duties performed by the administrator for which no exercise of judgment is permitted. "Discretionary" functions, as noted above, are judgmental and represent exercise of substantial administrative prerogative. An official can pass on to a subordinate ministerial functions, but cannot delegate duties that are discretionary in nature. Discretionary functions, of course, represent an area of major overlap with the broader quasi-judicial functions of agencies. The maxim *delegatus non potest delegare* has, on the whole, been more strictly enforced when applied to subdelegation than at the primary or legislative level of delegation. In other words, courts tend to examine more critically the internal delegation of a discretionary function from the state superintendent down to an assistant than from the legislature to the agency itself. For example, where statute vests a specific discretionary power in a state board, the board cannot subdelegate to one board member or to some other officer, such as the state superintendent. Similarly, statutory discretion vested in the state superintendent cannot be redelegated to a deputy or assistant. Ministerial functions, on the other hand, can be subdelegated.

As is true at the state level, a local school board cannot delegate discretionary functions, but it may delegate ministerial functions. The exact definition between discretionary powers that cannot be delegated and ministerial powers that can be delegated, is, however, indistinct. A good illustration is provided by a 1987 Colorado case in which the power to dismiss personnel was delegated. Normally, personnel matters involving hiring and firing of employees are considered to be discretionary or quasi-judicial powers that cannot be delegated; yet the high court of Colorado upheld the dismissal of a school bus driver by the school district's director of business services, because the court found that such discharges were administrative matters and did not constitute action "significantly related to the policy-making duties" of the school district.[47]

Will has pointed out that there is a discernible trend toward the separation of the legislative function and the executive powers in state educational administration. He describes the pattern in this way:

> Students of state educational administration commonly hold that the central education agency should consist of a state board of education, a chief state school officer, and the necessary staff. The state board of education is looked upon as the agency's legislative policy-making body, the chief state school officer as the agency's executive officer, and the organized staff as the agency's work force. A virtually complete separation of legislative and executive powers at the administrative level is intended under this pattern.[48]

The powers and duties of the state board of education, the chief state school officer, and the state department of education vary from state to state; however, general rules governing the delegation of legislative powers, the exercises of discretionary authority, and the quasi-judicial role of central state agencies are carefully circumscribed by court decisions.

QUASI-JUDICIAL FUNCTIONS

In their tripartite capacity, administrative agencies hand down many more decisions affecting individuals than do the formal courts of this country. Decisions by educational tribunals form an important source of law under which education operates. Authority for decisions by educational tribunals may be found at federal, state, and local levels. At the federal level, statutes often vest the United States Commissioner of Education with quasi-judicial authority to render decisions in disputes over federal grant processes and procedures that may have direct impact on individuals or states. At the state level, quasi-judicial authority may be given to state boards of education, to state superintendents, or, in some cases, to other legislatively authorized bodies. New Jersey and New York are good examples of states in which such powers are vested in the chief state school officer.

The state commissioner of education in New Jersey has the authority to decide cases involving internal administrative operations of the public schools of that state. A New Jersey court has said that a statute providing that the state commissioner shall decide all controversies under the school laws of the state is evidence of legislative purpose to set up a comprehensive system of internal appeals with broad powers. Such an authority invested in administrative tribunals ensures that controversies are justly disposed of in accordance with the law.[49]

In another New Jersey case illustrating the judicial function of the state commissioner of education, the court said that the commissioner must enforce all rules and regulations prescribed by the state board and decide all questions arising under rules and regulations of the state board.[50]

Determinations by these tribunals are binding on the parties involved and serve additionally to establish a type of quasi-judicial *stare decisis* within the agencies' jurisdiction. Agencies, in exercise of their judicial powers, are required generally to merely provide fair treatment to the parties involved. Some states, through administrative procedure acts, may provide specific definition of the requirements of fairness, and, when administrative tribunals are dealing with disputes involving constitutional interests, more elaborate procedures are necessary. In the absence of statutory or constitutional restraints, however, the courts have been very liberal in allowing educational tribunals to establish their own procedures. In so doing, courts more or less adhere to a requirement similar to the English doctrine of *audi alteram partem* of natural justice that requires tribunals to adjudicate fairly. Fairness is not always easily defined, but may be roughly equated to reasonableness and good faith. These two standards are not the same, but may be viewed as complementary. It has been said that "some of the most honest people are the most unreasonable; and some excesses may be sincerely believed in but yet be quite beyond the limits of reasonableness."[51] It is true, however, that the actions of one conducting a hearing could be so unreasonable as to be arbitrary and capricious and as such appear to be taken in bad faith.

The objective is for justice to be rendered by tribunals, whether they are courts of law or administrative agencies. When persons stand before tribunals, there is an implicit assumption that the tribunal will act "neutrally in a principled way" because there is a natural right of justice for requiring that tribunals not help nor hinder one side more than the other.[52]

Fairness of a hearing may also be explained in terms of equality before the law. It is expected that persons coming before a tribunal will be treated equally, and the determination favorable or unfavorable toward one or the other will be described on the merits of the case. Equality, as an aspect of fairness, requires that "rules of law shall be applied according to their terms without regard to the person(s) involved. . . ." This equal application of laws is guaranteed not only by common law, but also by constitutional provisions guaranteeing due process.[53]

A particularly perplexing problem is presented when the tribunal is itself a party to the action that comes before it. Because school boards have tripartite jurisdiction—legislative, executive, and quasi-judicial—it is not uncommon for a board to sit in judgment in its own cause. Because of the nature of our governmental system, however, this problem cannot be avoided.

This particular issue, whether a school board can sit in judgment when it is a party in the dispute, has been litigated before the U.S. Supreme Court. The Court held that the mere fact that a public agency is, as a body, a party to a dispute before it is not alone an indication of bias sufficient to violate due process.[54]

In the Absence of Bias, a School Board May Sit in Its Quasi-Judicial Capacity in Judgment of a Case to Which It Is a Party

Hortonville Joint School District No. 1 v. Hortonville Education Association

Supreme Court of the United States, 1976.
426 U.S. 482, 96 S.Ct. 2308.

Mr. Chief Justice BURGER delivered the opinion of the Court. We granted certiorari in this case to determine whether School Board members, vested by state law with the power to employ and dismiss teachers, could, consistent with the Due Process Clause of the Fourteenth Amendment, dismiss teachers engaged in a strike prohibited by state law.

The petitioners are a Wisconsin school district, the seven members of its School Board, and three administrative employees of the district. Respondents are teachers suing on behalf of all teachers in the district and the Hortonville Education Association (HEA), the collective-bargaining agent for the district's teachers.

During the 1972–1973 school year Hortonville teachers worked under a master collective-bargaining agreement; negotiations were conducted for renewal of the contract, but no agreement was reached for the 1973–1974 school year. The teachers continued to work while negotiations proceeded during the year without reaching agreement. On March 18, 1974, the members of the teachers' union went on strike, in direct violation of Wisconsin law. . . .

On April 1, most of the striking teachers appeared before the Board with counsel. Their attorney indicated that the teachers did not want individual hearings, but preferred to be treated as a group. Although counsel agreed that the teachers were on strike, he raised several procedural objections to the hearings. He also argued that the Board was not sufficiently impartial to exercise discipline over the striking teachers and that the Due Process Clause of the Fourteenth Amendment required an independent, unbiased decisionmaker. . . .

The sole issue in this case is whether the Due Process Clause of the Fourteenth Amendment prohibits this School Board from making the decision to dismiss teachers admittedly engaged in a strike and persistently refusing to return to their duties.

Respondents' argument rests in part on doctrines that have no application to this case. They seem to argue that the Board members had some personal or official stake in the decision whether the teachers should be dismissed . . . and that the Board has manifested some personal bitterness toward the teachers, aroused by teacher criticism of the Board. . . .

[T]he teachers did not show, and the Wisconsin courts did not find, that the Board members had the kind of personal or financial stake in the decision that might create a conflict of interest, and there is nothing in the record to support charges of personal animosity. . . .

The only other factor suggested to support the claim of bias is that the School Board was involved in the negotiations that preceded and precipitated the striking teachers' discharge. Participation in those negotiations was a statutory duty of the Board. The Wisconsin Supreme Court held that this involvement, without more, disqualified the Board from deciding whether the teachers should be dismissed:

> The board was the collective bargaining agent for the school district and thus was engaged in the collective bargaining process with the teachers' representative, the HEA. It is not difficult to imagine the frustration on the part of the board members when negotiations broke down, agreement could not be reached and the employees resorted to concerted activity. . . . They were . . . not uninvolved in the events which precipitated decisions they were required to make. . . .

Mere familiarity with the facts of a case gained by an agency in the performance of its statutory role does not, however, disqualify a decisionmaker. . . . Nor is a decisionmaker disqualified simply because he has taken a position, even in public, on a policy issue related to the dispute, in the absence of a showing that he is not "capable of judging a particular controversy fairly on the basis of its own circumstances." . . .

Due process, as this Court has repeatedly held, is a term that "negates any concept of inflexible procedures universally applicable to every imaginable situation." . . .

Determining what process is due in a given setting requires the Court to take into account the individual's stake in the decision at issue as well as the State's interest in a particular procedure for making it. . . . Our assessment of the interests of the parties in this case leads to the conclusion that . . . the public interest in maintaining uninterrupted classroom work required that teachers striking in violation of state law be discharged.

The teachers' interest in these proceedings is, of course, self-evident. They wished to avoid termination of their employment, obviously an important interest, but one that must be examined in light of several factors. Since the teachers admitted that they were engaged in a work stoppage, there was no possibility of an erroneous factual determination on this critical threshold issue. . . . The Board's decision whether to dismiss striking teachers involves broad considerations, and does not in the main turn on the Board's view of the "seriousness" of the teachers' conduct or the factors they urge mitigated their violation of state law. It was not an adjudicative decision, for the Board had an obligation to make a decision based on its own answer to an important question of policy: What choice among the alternative responses to the teachers' strike will best serve the interests of the school system, the interests of the parents and children who depend on the system, and the interests of the citizens whose taxes support it? . . .

State law vests the governmental, or policymaking, function exclusively in the School Board, and the State has two interests in keeping it there. First, the Board is the body with overall responsibility for the governance of the school district; it must cope with the myriad day-to-day problems of a modern public school system including the severe consequences of a teachers' strike; by virtue of electing them the constituents have declared the Board members qualified to deal with these problems, and they are accountable to the voters for the manner in which they perform. Second, the state legislature has given to the Board the power to employ and dismiss teachers, as a part of the balance it has struck in the area of municipal labor relations; altering those statutory powers as a matter of federal due process clearly changes that balance. Permitting the Board to make the decision at issue here preserves its control over school district affairs, leaves the balance of power in labor relations where the state legislature struck it, and assures that the decision whether to dismiss the teachers will be made by the body responsible for that decision under state law.

Respondents have failed to demonstrate that the decision to terminate their employment was infected by the sort of bias that we have held to disqualify other decisionmakers as a matter of federal due process. A showing that the Board was "involved" in the events preceding this decision, in light of the important interest in leaving with the Board the power given by the

state legislature, is not enough to overcome the presumption of honesty and integrity in policymakers with decisionmaking power. . . . Accordingly, we hold that the Due Process Clause of the Fourteenth Amendment did not guarantee respondents that the decision to terminate their employment would be made or reviewed by a body other than the School Board.

The judgment of the Wisconsin Supreme Court is reversed, and the case is remanded for further proceedings not inconsistent with this opinion.

Reversed and remanded.

❖ — ❖ — ❖

Delegation of Authority Must Be Accompanied by Specific Standards

Fremont RE-1 School District v. Jacobs

Supreme Court of Colorado, 1987.
737 P.2d 816.

ROVIRA, Justice. Respondent Joyce Jacobs, a bus driver for the Fremont RE-1 School District, filed suit in May 1983 after she was fired by Norman Lemons, the school district's director of business services, in February 1983. She alleged that her firing was unlawful because the school board could not delegate to the director of business services the power to discharge her. . . . We now conclude that the school board could lawfully delegate to its agents the task of firing bus drivers and that the standards set forth by the Fremont School Board in this case were adequate as a matter of law. . . .

Undisputed facts in the record show that prior to the firing of Jacobs the Fremont Board of Education had adopted a policy for the discharge of "classified personnel"—which included bus drivers like Jacobs and also secretaries, office clerks, bookkeepers, and maintenance employees. The policy, which was published in an employee handbook, provided that:

The Board of Education delegates to the Superintendent of Schools the authority to dismiss classified personnel. Further, the Superintendent of Schools may delegate this authority to the Director of Business Services and/or the Director of Personnel. Classified employees shall be employed for such time as the District is in need of, or desirous of, the services of such employees. The duration of employment is unspecified and solely rests at the discretion of the District. . . .

[D]ismissal of classified employees shall be unaffected by the employee's religious beliefs, marital status, racial or ethnic background, sex, or participation in community affairs.

In February 1983, following a disagreement between Jacobs and her superiors stemming from a disciplinary action Jacobs had taken on her bus, she was discharged by Lemons. Later, after Jacobs filed suit, the school board ratified her discharge.

The sole question presented for review here is whether the board of education could lawfully delegate to the superintendent of schools and, through him, to Lemons the authority to dismiss Jacobs. An examination of the relevant statutes discloses that the legislature has imposed upon school boards certain "duties". . . , and has granted them certain "powers". . . . The Fremont school board points out that the legislature has granted school boards the "power" to discharge personnel . . . , but has not made employee discharge a "duty" of school boards. . . . It argues, therefore, that the school board was authorized to delegate the responsibility for discharging employees.

We disagree with this line of argument. As we read the statutes, section 22-32-109 sets forth mandatory "duties" of school boards and section 22-32-110 sets forth discretionary "powers." The listing of employee discharge as a "power" under section 22-32-110 indicates only that a school board may, but need not, exercise its authority to fire employees. The statutes, as we read them, do not specify the scope of a school board's authority to delegate its duties and powers—they merely indicate which powers a school board *may* exercise and which duties it *must* perform. . . .

We turn, therefore, to the rule of construction we adopted in *Big Sandy School District No. 100-J v. Carroll*, 164 Colo. 173, 433 P.2d 325 (1967), a case which presented us with a similar issue. In that case, members of a school board informally

authorized the superintendent to hire a principal-teacher and provided him with a signed, blank contract. Thereafter, the superintendent apparently hired one Barney Carroll for the post, but discharged him ten days later. Carroll sued for breach of contract. The issue, as a result, was whether the superintendent had authority to hire a principal-teacher without the school board's explicit approval of the job applicant and his rate of pay. In examining the Colorado statute then in effect, we initially noted that it was the school board's "duty" to employ teachers. We then discussed and applied the established rule of construction applicable to quasi-municipal corporations like the school district:

[T]he general rule is that . . . a quasi-municipal corporation . . . may delegate to subordinate officers and boards powers and functions which are ministerial or administrative in nature, where there is a fixed and certain standard or rule which leaves little or nothing to the judgment or discretion of the subordinate. However, legislative or judicial powers, involving judgment and discretion on the part of the municipal body, which have been vested by statute in a municipal corporation may *not* be delegated unless such has been expressly authorized by the legislature.

. . . Analyzing the facts under this standard, we concluded that the power to employ teachers and fix their wages is a nondelegable statutory power which the legislature has conferred solely on the school board. It was thus not subject to delegation without explicit legislative authorization.

The principle announced in *Big Sandy* serves several salutary purposes. By placing limits on the delegation of power by school boards, it assures the public that school board members—who are subject to public election—must take responsibility for significant policy decisions associated with management of the school district. . . . Further, the rule protects school districts from incurring significant liabilities based on actions taken by school administrators without the full considered approval of the school board. Lastly, by limiting delegation as a rule of statutory construction, questions concerning the constitutionality of delegation of legislative powers are avoided. . . .

However, we are convinced that the *Big Sandy* rule should not be extended beyond the limited purposes it serves. As a practical matter, school districts require a significant degree of administrative flexibility in order to function smoothly on a day-to-day basis between meetings of their school boards. As school organizations have grown in size and their functions have become more diverse and complex, the need for administrative delegation has become all the more imperative. If the law were to insist on strict limitations on delegation of authority, school board members might tend to become mired in the details of routine operations, and the effectiveness and usefulness of school administrators might be hampered. As a result, the trend in this area of the law has been to allow greater flexibility and away from the insistence on detailed and definite standards. . . . In this vein, we have said:

> The modern tendency of the courts is toward greater liberality in permitting grants of discretion to administrative officials in order to facilitate the administration of the laws as the complexity of governmental and economic conditions increases.

. . . In a somewhat different context, we have held that

> [t]he [School] Board can select reasonable means to carry out its duties and responsibilities incidental to the sound development of employer-employee relations, as long as the means selected are not prohibited by law or against public policy.

. . . Analyzing the question before us with these principles in mind, we conclude that the discharge of a bus driver is an administrative function subject to delegation by the school board. In our view, this action was not significantly related to the policy-making duties of the Fremont school board. . . . In reaching this conclusion, we note that the character of this action— the discharge of a bus driver—is collateral to the school board's educational mission, and the significance of this action is not so great that the law should demand the formal accountability of school board members before recognizing the validity of the action. . . .

We recognize that in the past we have held that the power to hire teachers and fix their wages and the power to dismiss them are nondelegable powers. . . . However, the hiring and firing of teachers directly affect the educational mission of the school district, and a central purpose for the election of school board members is .

to obtain their judgment on such matters. Actions that do not have a significant impact on institutional policy, on the other hand, are properly characterized as administrative in character and therefore are delegable. . . . We do not believe the discharge of a bus driver significantly affects the Fremont school board's institutional policy; therefore, we agree with the court of appeals that the power to discharge Jacobs was properly delegable.

However, we disagree with the holding of the court of appeals that further investigation of the adequacy of the standards limiting the discretion of the school administrators is required in this case. In our view, the standards set forth by the Fremont school board were adequate as a matter of law. Under the school board's employee handbook, "classified employees" served at the will of the district except that they could not be dismissed on account of their religious beliefs, marital status, racial or ethnic background, sex or participation in community affairs.

Ordinarily, a delegation of discretion this broad might run afoul of even the liberalized rules that have been applied to administrative delegation in recent cases. The requirement of standards to limit administrative discretion is designed to assure that administrative action will be rational and consistent and that subsequent judicial review will be available and effective. . . . However, the law has traditionally accorded employers—including government agencies—broad discretion in the discharge of employees who are terminable at will. The general rule is that, absent a violation of constitutional rights, judicial review is not available to review the firing of an employee who is terminable at will. . . . Such an employee may be dismissed without any justifying cause whatever. . . .

Further, the traditional rule with respect to local government employees has been that

> local government employees hold their posts at the pleasure of the proper local government authorities and can be dismissed without cause, in the absence of restrictions or limitations provided by law.

. . . Here, no additional restrictions or limitations relevant to this case have been provided by law. To the contrary, the Colorado legislature has explicitly provided tenure for specified teachers but has adopted no comparable protections for "classified employees" like Jacobs. . . . Furthermore, the Fremont school board has explicitly categorized classified employees as terminable at will with a few limitations not pertinent here. As a result, we are not convinced the rule of construction applied in *Big Sandy* should operate to override the considered policy choices of the legislature and the school board.

The court of appeals' insistence on specific standards for dismissal, however, might indirectly convert Fremont's terminable at will employees to employees terminable only for cause—unless the school board were willing to decide itself every case involving the discharge of a "classified employee." Further, the adoption of more specific standards for dismissal could well create "property" rights for classified employees that would entitle them to a panoply of procedural due process protections. . . . Additionally, the adoption of specific dismissal standards might convert what is now an administrative function into a judicial function, which is not subject to delegation under the *Big Sandy* rule absent explicit legislative authorization. . . . Consequently, it may be meaningless to hold that the discharge power may be delegated if more specific standards are adopted; if more specific standards are adopted, the power may no longer be delegable. We decline to overrule the policy decisions of the Colorado legislature and the Fremont school board in such a roundabout fashion. In our view, the standards adopted by the school board are sufficient as a matter of law.

Accordingly, the judgment of the court of appeals is affirmed in part and reversed in part, and we remand to the court with instructions that it reinstate summary judgment on behalf of the petitioners [school board].

Case Notes

1. The decision of the Commissioner of Education of New York in interpreting a statute is to be given great weight by the courts and unless irrational or unreasonable it will be upheld. *Board of Education of Roslyn Union Free School District v. Nyquist*, 90 Misc.2d 955, 396 N.Y.S.2d 567 (1977).

2. Administrative agencies in quasi-judicial hearings have traditionally not been held to the intricate procedural requirement of the courts. However, there are fundamental requirements of fairness which must be observed. A West Virginia court had this to say concerning the conduct of hearings by administrative agencies:

> An administrative body, clothed by law with quasi-judicial powers, must never depart from those elemental principles of discreetness and circumspection which our system of law requires in all tribunals which purport to conduct trials. . . . There was a time in the history of English jurisprudence when a felon was not entitled to have the assistance of an attorney at law, but in America, the very word "hearing," both in common and legal parlance, implies some kind of trial, formal or informal, and presupposes permission to have legal aid if desired. *State ex rel. Rogers v. Board of Education of Lewis County*, 125 W.Va. 579, 25 S.E.2d 537 (1943).

3. Legislation in Texas has been interpreted to mean that all administrative steps should be taken to resolve a dispute before appeal can be taken to the courts. Exception to this rule is only found where an action involves a question of taxation, *City of Dallas v. Mosely*, 286 S.W. 497 (Tex. Civ. App. 1926), if the facts are undisputed and the issue is one purely of law and not of education; in such instances, direct access to the courts is available. *Alvin Independent School District v. Cooper*, 404 S.W.2d 76 (Tex.Civ.App.1966).

4. A Maryland court has held that the state board of education has the last word on any matter concerning educational policy or administration of the system of public instruction; however, it cannot finally decide pure questions of law nor exercise its visitatorial power fraudulently, in bad faith, or in breach of trust. Where the State Board of Education of Maryland set a rule of a county board of education requiring fingerprint cards of all employees to be submitted to local police, the court upheld the action of the state board as being a valid exercise of its authority. *Wilson v. Board of Education of Montgomery County*, 234 Md. 561, 200 A.2d 67 (1964).

5. A Missouri court has held that, where four local school districts were unable to reorganize because of refusal of one to discuss the matter, the state board of education was vested with exclusive jurisdiction to make the decision for the board, and once this decision by the state board was approved by the voters, the school district became officially and legally organized.

State ex inf. Eagleton ex rel. *Reorganized School District R-I of Miller County v. Van Landuyt*, 359 S.W.2d 773 (Mo. 1962).

———————— ❖ ————————

JUDICIAL REVIEW OF EDUCATIONAL AGENCY ACTIONS

Whether the administrative actions be legislative, executive, or judicial, the courts agree that school boards or officials may exercise those powers expressly granted by statute, and those fairly and necessarily implied:

> The rule respecting such powers is that, in addition to the powers expressly given by statute to an officer or board of officers, he or it has by implication such additional powers as are necessary for the due and efficient exercise of the powers expressly granted or which may be fairly implied from the statute granting the express powers.[55]

While some flexibility in discretion is necessary, indeed indispensable, for the schools to operate efficiently, the courts cannot usurp the legislative function by too broad an interpretation of administrative powers.[56]

In challenging the exercise of administrative powers by an educational agency, be they express or implied, the aggrieved parties are required by the courts to exhaust their administrative remedies before they are allowed to bring an action before the courts. Such a rule assures the courts that issues have been properly treated at lower levels, within the realm of administrative authority, thus preventing continuous involvement of the courts in educational disputes where legitimate legal controversy is not present. Examples of the hesitancy of courts to intervene until administrative remedies are exhausted may be found in many instances.[57]

In New York, the state administrative decisions are considered to have substantial weight owing largely to a statute that provides that decisions of the commissioner of education "shall be final and conclusive, and not subject to question or review in any place or court whatsoever." While this provision on its face would appear to preclude any judicial intervention, the true "intent" has been interpreted to mean that the decisions of the commissioner would stand so long as they were not arbitrary.[58]

The general rule of law is probably best expounded by an Illinois court, which stated:

A court of review cannot substitute its judgment for the judgment of the administrative tribunal. The question is not simply whether the court of review agrees or disagrees with the finding. . . . It has been said that courts should not disturb administrative findings unless such findings are arbitrary, or constitute an abuse of discretion, or are without substantial foundation in evidence, or are obviously and clearly wrong, or unless an opposite conclusion is clearly evident.[59]

While this rule governing judicial review of administrative actions is generally followed by courts across the country, the individual interpretations of the rule are widely variant, ranging from rather strict adherence to what some would consider to be relative disregard. As a matter of fact, courts may exercise their prerogatives to intervene and alter administrative action with several different legal bases. Ministerial actions of government agencies have been successfully challenged under the ancient legal doctrines of nonfeasance, misfeasance, or malfeasance. Failure to perform properly may be remedied by the courts by use of the common law remedy, *writ of mandamus*. If the aggrieved party is seeking to prevent an inappropriate action, then an *injunction* may be the appropriate legal remedy.

On the other hand, if discretionary actions are in question, then the person challenging the action may proceed from a broader legal basis. As mentioned above, fairness and reasonableness of action are requisite to appropriate use of the quasi-judicial authority of an agency. More directly, discretionary powers may be viewed quite broadly, and if an agency acts beyond the scope of its powers, it may well be *ultra vires*. A discretionary power may be abused in either good faith or in bad faith, but in both instances the action may be voided by the courts.[60] Beyond inquiry into *vires*, judicial intervention may be justifiable in the following situations:

1. A power granted to an agency is not properly applied. Here the courts will seek to determine whether the agency had either express or implied statutory power to perform as it did, and if the statute was broad enough, with possibly a plurality of purposes sufficient to support the action. The court will generally apply certain tests, including seeking to ascertain: (a) the true purpose for the

action, (b) the dominant purpose, and (c) if there was an unauthorized or illicit purpose,[61] or if the action was taken in bad faith.

2. The agency, official, or tribunal was influenced by considerations that could not have been lawfully taken into account, or it ignored obviously relevant considerations. Plaintiff, though, must show that irrelevant considerations were actually relied upon in the decision. Certainly if extraneous or irrelevant matters are set out as reasons in support of the decision, then courts may consider the result to be invalid.

3. Prescription of law is not followed in effecting administrative actions. While most instances that come to mind here involve ministerial functions (e.g., following election procedures or budgetary submission processes), the educational agency's action may also be challenged if it fails to recognize or appreciate the amplitude of its discretion.[62] For example, a state authority may have the statutory power to grant salary increases or increase fringe benefits, but misconstrues and through misunderstanding fails to recognize the discretion. Here it is not the reasonableness of the decision made by the agency, but the failure of the agency to recognize its power, that is judicially questionable.

4. A public education board binds itself through its own regulation in such a way as to constrict or disable itself from fulfilling the primary purposes for which it was created. Where a public body is entrusted by the legislature with certain powers and duties either express or implied for public purposes, the body cannot divest itself of such powers and duties. Regulations or bylaws that effectively thwart statutory intent, for example, by contracting away a power or requiring the exercise of a broad power in a restrictive way, may be unreasonable and incompatible with public purpose.

Courts do not penalize a state agency for possible error in the exercise of discretion where judgment or opinion of the public officials is in contest. If there are reasonable grounds, the judge has no further duty to inquire. The criterion of reasonableness is not subjective, but objective in the sense that it must be weighed in light of surrounding facts and circumstances.

This rule applies to actions of local school agencies as well as to state educational agencies. The Supreme Court of Virginia has refused to intervene and question a school division action even if the court would quite probably not have agreed with the result of the decision. The Court said:

> [W]here there is rational, legal and factual basis for a school board's administrative determination, the Court will not overturn such decision and substitute its own judgment even if it would have reached a contrary conclusion.[63]

The Court is concerned with whether the judgment rendered by the board is founded on "rational, legal and factual" information, not whether the Court, viewing the same situation and evidence, would have reached a contrary decision. The party who assails a school board's decision must prove that the board acted arbitrarily and without regard for the evidence, and thus illegally, before a court will upset a board's decision.[64]

❖ — ❖ — ❖

Regulation of Common Schools Is within the Power of the Legislature

State ex rel. Clark v. Haworth

Supreme Court of Indiana, 1890.
122 Ind. 462, 23 N.E. 946.

ELLIOTT, J. . . . It is sufficient, to bring the question clearly enough before the mind for investigation and consideration, to say that the relator petitioned for a writ of mandate to compel the appellee, as school trustee of Monroe township, in the county of Howard, to certify to the county superintendent of schools the number of textbooks required by the children of the township for use in the public schools, and to procure and furnish such books as the law requires . . . Elliott's Supp. §1289 (Acts 1889, p. 74).

The act assailed does not impinge in the slightest degree upon the right of local self-government. The right of local self-government is an inherent, and not a derivative, one. Individualized, it is the right which a man possesses in virtue of his character as a free man. It is not bestowed by legislatures, nor derived from statutes. But the courts which have carried to its utmost extent the doctrine of local self-government have never so much as intimated that it exists as to a matter over which the constitution has given the law-making power supreme control; nor have they gone beyond the line which separates matters of purely local concern from those of state control. Essentially and intrinsically, the schools in which are educated and trained the children who are to become the rulers of the commonwealth are matters of state, and not of local, jurisdiction. In such matters the state is a unit, and the legislature the source of power. The authority over schools and school affairs is not necessarily a distributive one, to be exercised by local instrumentalities; but, on the contrary, it is a central power, residing in the legislature of the state. It is for the law-making power to determine whether the authority shall be exercised by a state board of education, or distributed to county, township, or city organizations throughout the state. With that determination the judiciary can no more rightfully interfere than can the legislature with a decree or judgment pronounced by a judicial tribunal. The decision is as conclusive and inviolable in the one case as in the other; and an interference with the legislative judgment would be a breach of the constitution which no principle would justify, nor any precedent excuse.

. . . Judge Cooley has examined the question with care, and discussed it with ability; and he declares that the legislature has plenary power over the subject of the public schools. He says, in the course of his discussion, that "to what degree the legislature shall provide for the education of the people at the cost of the state, or of its municipalities, is a question which, except as regulated by the constitution, addresses itself to the legislative judgment exclusively." Again, he says, "The governing school boards derive all their authority from the statute, and can exercise no powers except those expressly granted, and those which result by necessary implication from the grant." Const.Lim. (5th Ed.) p. 225, note 1. No case has been cited by counsel, and none has been discovered by us,—although we have searched the reports with care,—which

denies the doctrine that the regulation of the public schools is a state matter, exclusively within the dominion of the legislature. . . .

As the power over schools is a legislative one, it is not exhausted by exercise. The legislature, having tried one plan, is not precluded from trying another. It has a choice of methods, and may change its plans as often as it deems necessary or expedient; and for mistakes or abuses it is answerable to the people, but not to the courts. It is clear, therefore, that, even if it were true that the legislature had uniformly entrusted the management of school affairs to local organizations, it would not authorize the conclusion that it might not change the system. To deny the power to change, is to affirm that progress is impossible, and that we must move forever "in the dim footsteps of antiquity." But the legislative power moves in a constant stream, and is not exhausted by its exercise in any number of instances, however great. It is not true, however, that the authority over schools was originally regarded as a local one. On the contrary, the earlier cases asserted that the legislature could not delegate the power to levy taxes for school purposes to local organizations, but must itself directly exercise the power; thus denying, in the strongest possible form, the theory of local control. . . . All the public schools have been established under legislative enactments, and all rules and regulations have been made pursuant to statutory authority. Every school that has been established owes its existence to legislation, and every school officer owes his authority to the statute.

It is impossible to conceive of the existence of a uniform system of common schools without power lodged somewhere to make it uniform; and, even in the absence of express constitutional provisions, that power must necessarily reside in the legislature. If it does reside there, then that body must have, as an incident of the principal power, the authority to prescribe the course of study, and the system of instruction, that shall be pursued and adopted, as well as the books which shall be used. Having this authority, the legislature may not only prescribe regulations for using such books, but it may also declare how the books shall be obtained and distributed. If it may do this, then it may provide that they shall be obtained through the medium of a contract awarded to the best or lowest bidder, since, if it be true, as it unquestionably is, that the power is legislative, it must also be true that the legislature has an unrestricted discretion, and an unfettered choice of methods. It cannot be possible that the courts can interfere with this legislative power, and adjudge that the legislature shall not adopt this method or that method; for, if the question is at all legislative, it is so in its whole length and breadth. . . .

Either the state has power to regulate and control the schools it owns, or it has not. That it does not have the power, we venture to say, no one will affirm. If it does have the power, it must reside in the law-making department, for it is impossible for it to exist elsewhere. If the power does reside in the law-making department, then that department must exercise its discretion, and adopt such measures as it deems best; and, if the measures adopted lead to the exclusion of some book-owners, it is an incident that no ingenuity can escape, nor any system avoid. The denial of the right to select the books is the denial of the right of regulation and control, and we cannot conceive it possible to deny this right. If the right of regulation and control exists, then the fact that the exercise of the right does not exclude some publisher is an inseparable and unavoidable condition of the exercise of the right. Without it, the right is annihilated. If a clear and manifest legislative right cannot be exercised without conferring privileges in the nature of a monopoly, then, as the authorities all agree, a monopoly may be created; for a denial of the right will not be suffered. This doctrine is discussed by Judge Cooley in his work on Torts, and by Mr. Tiedeman in his work on the Police Power, to which we refer without comment. Cooley, Torts, 277; Tied.Lim. 315 *et seq.* But we need not enter the field traveled by those authors, for here there is no denial of a right to sell books to a community. All that is here done is to provide that the person who receives, after fair and open competition, the contract for supplying books to the school children, shall enjoy an exclusive privilege for the period prescribed by the statute. Judge Cooley says that "it is held competent for the state to contract with a publisher to supply all the schools of the state with textbooks of a uniform character and price." Const.Lim. (5th Ed.) p. 225, note 1. . . .

Judgment reversed, with instructions to proceed in accordance with this opinion. . . .

CASE NOTES

1. The broad extent of legislative power over local school districts is shown in a statement by a Texas court:

> The Legislature has the power to create school districts at will without any kind of notice. It also has the power to change the boundaries of or to abolish school districts, to consolidate them, to group them for high school purposes, to annex school districts to other school districts and to provide the mode and agencies for effecting such action. *Neill v. Cook*, 365 S.W.2d 824 (Tex.1963).

2. The Supreme Court of New York has held that the requirement of the New York Constitution stating that "the legislature shall provide for the maintenance and support of a system of free common schools, wherein all the children of this state may be educated" gave the legislature power to govern the educational system of the state, *Cohen v. State*, 52 Misc.2d 324, 275 N.Y.S.2d 719 (1966). Such power allows the legislature to create school districts and to establish different types and structures of school boards to govern and regulate the local school districts.

3. The Supreme Court of Tennessee early explained the role of the legislature in exercising police power over public education:

> We are of the opinion that the legislature, under the constitutional provision, may as well establish a uniform system of schools and a uniform administration of them, as it may establish a uniform system of criminal laws and of courts to execute them. The object of the criminal laws is, by punishment, to deter others from the commission of crimes, and thus preserve the peace, morals, good order and well-being of society; and the object of the public-school system is to prevent crime, by educating the people, and thus, by providing and securing a higher state of intelligence and morals, conserve the peace, good order, and well-being of society. The prevention of crime, and preservation of good order and peace, is the highest exercise of the police power of the state, whether done by punishing offenders or educating the children. What is the scope and meaning of the term "police power" has never been defined. The supreme court of the United States has expressly declined to define its limits. *Stone v. Mississippi*, 101 U.S.

814, 25 L.Ed. 1079 (1879). In *Mayor, etc., v. Miln,* [36 U.S. 102,] 11 Pet. 139, 9 L.Ed. 648 (1835), it is said: "It embraces every law which concerns the welfare of the whole people, of the state or any individual within it, whether it relates to their rights or duties, whether it respects them as men or citizens of the state, whether in their public or private relations, whether it relates to the rights of persons or property of the whole people of the state or of any individual within it." In *Railroad Co. v. Husen,* 95 U.S. 465, 24 L.Ed. 527 (1877), it is said: "The police power of a state extends to the protection of the lives, limbs, health, comfort, and quiet of all persons, and to the protection of all property, within the state, and hence to the making of all regulations promotive of domestic order, morals, health, and safety." In *Smith v. State,* 100 Tenn. 494, 46 S.W. 566, it is said, in substance, that it extends to all questions of health, morals, safety, order, comfort, and well-being of the public, and that this enumeration does not make the list complete. Similar language has but recently been used in the case of *Harbison v. Iron Co.,* [103 Tenn. 421] 53 S.W. 955, and this is no new doctrine, either in this state or in the United States. *Leeper v. State,* 103 Tenn. 500, 53 S.W. 962 (1899).

❖ — ❖ — ❖

School Districts Can Exercise Only Those Powers Fairly Implied or Expressly Granted by Statute

McGilvra v. Seattle School District No. 1

Supreme Court of Washington, 1921.
113 Wash. 619, 194 P. 817.

PARKER, J. The plaintiffs, McGilvra and others, residents and taxpayers of Seattle school district No. 1, of King county, suing for themselves and in behalf of all others similarly situated, commenced this action in the superior court for that county, seeking an injunction to restrain the school district and its officers from maintaining in one of its school buildings and expending funds of the school district for the maintenance therein of a so-called clinic, which, as we proceed we think it will appear would be more properly designated as a "hospital," for the medical, surgical, and dental treatment of the physical ailments of pupils of the schools of the district, whose parents or guardians are financially unable to furnish such treatment. Trial in the superior court upon the merits resulted in findings and judgment denying the relief prayed for, from which the plaintiffs have appealed to this court. . . .

The question to be here answered is: Have the school district and its officers legal authority for so furnishing the use of, and equipping rooms in its buildings and the maintenance therein of such clinic, by the expenditure of the taxpayers' funds collected and placed at their disposal, for the sole purpose of maintaining the public schools of the district? At the outset let us be reminded in the language of Judge Dillon, in his work on Municipal Corporations, quoted with approval by this court in *State ex rel. Winsor v. Mayor and Council,* 10 Wash. 4, 37 Pac. 761, that

[i]t is a general and undisputed proposition of law that a municipal corporation possesses and can exercise the following powers, and no others: First, those granted in express words; second, those necessarily or fairly implied in or incident to the powers expressly granted; third, those essential to the declared objects and purposes of the corporation—not simply convenient but indispensable. Any fair or reasonable doubt concerning the existence of power is resolved by the courts against the corporation, and the power is denied.

This view of the law is of added weight when applied to school districts, because they are municipal corporations with powers of a much more limited character than are cities, or towns, or even than counties. . . .

We are quite unable to find in . . . statutory provisions any power given to the school district officers, other than the power to cause inspection of the buildings and premises of the district to be made with a view to making them sanitary and healthful, and to cause inspection of persons with a view to the exclusion from the school premises of all persons afflicted with contagious diseases, to the end that such diseases shall not obtain a foothold among the pupils and other persons whose duties require them to be upon the school premises.

Counsel for the school district officers call our attention to, and rely upon, our decision in *State ex rel. School District No. 56 v. Superior Court*, 69 Wash. 189, 124 Pac. 484, and *Sorenson v. Perkins & Co.*, 72 Wash. 16, 129 Pac. 577, commonly known as the "playground" and "gymnasium" cases, wherein it was held that a school district has the power to acquire, by expenditure of the funds of the district, additional land for playgrounds for the pupils, and also at the expense of the district to construct and equip gymnasiums. We do not think these cases are of any controlling force touching the present inquiry. Playgrounds in connection with public schools have for generations been so common that it must be presumed that the Legislature by giving the general power to maintain public schools incidentally intended to also give the authority to provide such playgrounds in connection therewith; and, while gymnasiums in connection with public schools have not been so common, the work and exercise of the students carried on therein is manifestly so intimately connected with the education of the pupil as to warrant the assumption that the Legislature intended the school districts and their officers to possess the power of providing the same as a proper public school equipment. The rendering of medical, surgical, and dental services to the pupils, however, is, and always has been, we think, so foreign to the powers to be exercised by a school district or its officers, that such power cannot be held to exist in the absence of express legislative language so providing. . . .

The specific legislative enumeration of these powers which it seems could with much sounder reason be considered as implied powers in the absence of express language in the statute than the claimed powers here in question, argues, in the light of well-settled rules of statutory construction, that the Legislature has not intended that here should be an exercise of such claimed powers. We see no argument lending any substantial support, in a legal way, to the view that a school district and its officers possess the powers they are seeking to exercise and threatening to continue to exercise. There is much in the argument of counsel for the school officers which might be considered as lending support to the view that such powers ought to be possessed by the school district and its officers, and it is probable that counsel has many well meaning people upon his side of that question. The Legislature may give heed to such arguments, but the courts cannot do so.

The judgment of the trial court is reversed, and the case remanded to that court, with directions to render a judgment enjoining the school district and its officers from furnishing or equipping upon the school premises, or elsewhere, appliances for the medical, surgical, or dental treatment of the physical ailments of the pupils of the schools at the expense of the district, and from employing physicians, dentists, or nurses for the rendering of such medical, surgical, or dental treatment; it being understood, however, that such injunction shall not restrain the school district or its officers from the doing of these things at the expense of the district in connection with, and as may be necessary in, the maintenance of the parental schools of the district and the proper care of the pupils committed to such schools.

Case Notes

1. In the few instances where the state constitution gives local school boards specific authority separating state control functions from local ones, the general rule that the state legislative has plenary power over the public schools may be mitigated. For example, in Colorado the state constitution gives the state board of education general supervisory authority and vests in local school boards the authority for "control of instruction." In this instance the Supreme Court of Colorado has held that the court must strike a balance between state and local control. The balance that is maintained must not have the effect of usurping the local board's decision making authority to implement, guide, or manage educational programs. *Denver Board of Education v. Booth*, 984 P.2d 639 (Colo. 1999).

2. Boards of education are creatures of statute and, as such, have only those powers that are expressly granted by statute or are necessarily implied therefrom. *Schwing v. McClure*, 120 Ohio St. 335, 166 N.E. 230 (1929); See also: *Tax Deferred Annuities Corp. v. Cleveland Board of Education*, 24 Ohio App. 3d 105, 493 N.E.2d 305 (1985).

❖ — ❖ — ❖

*School Council's Delegated Powers under
School-Based Decision-Making Statute Can
Bypass Local District School Board*

Board of Education of Boone County v. Bushee

Supreme Court of Kentucky, 1994.
889 S.W.2d 809, 96 Ed. 839.

STEPHENS, Chief Justice.

This appeal concerns the intent of the legislature when it delegated decision-making authority to both local school boards and individual school councils in enacting the Kentucky Educational Reform Act [hereinafter "KERA"]. The parties question the scope of each group's delegated authority. To be more specific, the parties ask to what extent can the school council operate as an autonomous decision-making body?

The appellees, who include officers of the Boone County Education Association and a teacher in the Boone County School system [hereinafter "the Council"], filed a declaratory judgment action against appellant, the Boone County Board of Education [hereinafter "the Board"], challenging a portion of the Board's policy created to meet statutory requirements. KRS 160.345 requires that each "local board of education shall adopt a policy for implementing school-based decision making" that addresses and complies with the additional requirement that each school form a council that has "the responsibility to set school policy consistent with district board policy. . . ." KRS 160.345.

The specific provision of the Board's policy in question reads:

> By each September Board of Education meeting, each council shall submit in writing for Board review and *approval* the following:
>
> 1. Measurable goals and objectives for the school year. The goals shall be related to the goals listed in HB 940, Part 1, Section 2 and 3.
> 2. Implementation plan for achieving its goals and objectives.

> 3. Method of evaluating the effectiveness of the implementation plan.

(Emphasis added.)

The Council contends this provision of the Board's policy invades the province of the school councils as envisioned by the legislature when pursuing the broad educational reforms of KERA. The Council argues that the required Board approval of these enumerated responsibilities essentially usurps the Council of the authority delegated to it by the legislature to act as an independent decision-making body. The trial court held that the Board's policy did not overstep its statutory authority. The Court of Appeals reversed. We affirm the result reached by the Court of Appeals but believe our understanding of KERA to be different than that expressed by that Court. This opinion will attempt to clarify the designated participatory roles for each contributor to the public education system.

. . . The essential strategic point of KERA is the decentralization of decision-making authority so as to involve all participants in the school system, affording each the opportunity to contribute actively to the educational process. The language of KRS 158.645 overwhelmingly reflects this intention:

> The General Assembly recognizes that public education involves *shared responsibilities*. State government, local communities, parents, students, and school employees must work together to create an efficient public school system. . . . The cooperation of all involved is necessary to assure that desired outcomes are achieved. (Emphasis added.)

The remaining statutory provisions set out the structural framework by which this decentralization of decision-making authority is to occur. These statutory provisions instruct all participating groups—state government, local communities, parents, students and school employees—as to their delegated responsibilities and how they are to interface with the other participating groups.

While the question before this court does not address the division of responsibility that exists between the state and local levels, the principles inherent to this division continue throughout the remaining statutory framework. The concept of decentralized decision-making ability continues down to the individual local school councils and their relationships to the local school board. This is the question before this Court. We will directly address that issue now.

The third participant to whom the General Assembly has delegated responsibility is the local school board, whose general powers and duties are found at KRS 160.290. "Each board of education shall have general control and management of the public schools in its district." KRS 160.290. Later language of the provision clearly identifies what is meant by "general control and management" including "control and management of all school funds and all public school property," "appoint[ment of] the superintendent," and "fix[ing] the compensation of employees." *Id. See also, Chapman*, at 235–6.

Conspicuously absent from these listed powers is any suggestion that the District School board is responsible for setting school policy at individual schools within the district. Rather, the nature of the duties enumerated suggests that the powers delegated to the local board of education are reflective of those with which a district-wide body should be concerned. The General Assembly has reasonably determined that the management of funds that are distributed at a district level is most effectively addressed by a body consisting of representatives from the entire district. The hiring of a Superintendent of Schools for the district should be managed at the district level, so the legislature put the responsibility there. Fixing the compensation of employees within the same locality also most effectively rests at the district-wide level. The point is clear that the legislature delegated to the district-wide school boards the authority to handle the matters most relevant to its representative body, primarily managing funds, property, and district-wide personnel decisions.

Keeping in mind that decentralization of authority and the development of school-based decision making are two primary objectives of KERA, the statutory delegation of authority to the school councils completes the requisite framework. The school councils are the focal point of decision making for the individual schools within the district. The council's body consists of members of that representative group only. Therefore, these people are charged with focusing on issues relevant to that school alone.

KRS 160.345 continues this part of the framework. The local board of education is mandated to adopt a policy for "implementing *school-based decision making* [that] . . . allow[s] the professional staff members of a school to be involved in the decision-making process as they work to meet educational goals established" pursuant to KRS 158.645 and 158.6451. KRS 160.345 (2). The obvious intent here is to have the decisions affecting the individual schools within the district to be made by persons most affected by what occurs at that school; this is what "school-based *decision making*" means.

The statute provides the mechanism by which this is to occur, the school council. KRS 160.345 reads "[e]ach participating school *shall* form a school council." (Emphasis added.) "The school council *shall have the responsibility* to set school policy . . . : which shall provide an environment to enhance the students' achievement and help the school meet the goals established by KRS 158.645 and 158.6451." *Id.* (Emphasis added.) This delegation of authority by the General Assembly to the School Council is clear.

. . . KRS 160.345(2)(G) further defines the authority of the school council as follows:

The school council shall determine which textbooks, instructional materials, and student support services shall be provided in the school. Subject to available resources, the local board shall allocate an appropriation to each school that is adequate to meet the school's needs related to instructional materials and school-based student support services, *as determined by the school council.* (Emphasis added.)

This statutory language is helpful in understanding the interaction intended between the school council and the school board. KRS 160.345(2)(G) clearly indicates that it is the responsibility of the council to determine the textbooks, materials, and student services that will be provided in that particular school. The local board is *directed* to allocate funds that will enable the school to provide the materials and services determined necessary by the council. The primary limitation on the council's ability to determine what is to be acquired is the availability of resources. The resources that are available would be determined by district policy. . . .

. . . Further, if the council believes additional funding would be necessary, the ability to request a waiver enables the needed flexibility. This is one area where approval by the Board would be necessary, and it is statutorily based in KRS 160.345(3)(g).

KRS 160.345(3)(f) further illustrates this interaction between the two groups. The statute directs that after the school council has received notification of available funds from the school board, the school council is able to determine the personnel it finds necessary within the school. The limitations on the council, however, are found in KRS 160.290, which reflects the delegated authority of the Board. As previously noted, the statute indicates that the Board shall "fix the compensation of employees." Therefore, while the council can determine the number of persons to be employed in each classification, it cannot determine the compensation of these employees. Once again, however, this is a situation where a waiver request may be useful in enabling flexibility.

CONCLUSION

The above examination of these statutes clearly convinces this court that each participating group in the common school system has been delegated its own independent sphere of responsibility. State government is held accountable for providing adequate funding and for the overall success of the common school system. The local boards are responsible for the administrative functions of allocating funding, managing school property, appointing the superintendent, and fixing the compensation of employees. The councils are responsible for the site-based issues, including, but not limited to, determining curriculum, planning instructional practices, selecting and implementing discipline techniques, determining the composition of the staff at the school, and choosing textbooks and instructional materials. . . .

We, therefore, uphold the ruling of the Court of Appeals in result only. The legislature did not delegate the authority to the local boards of education to require approval of council actions.

❖ — ❖ — ❖

County Board of Education Has Implied Authority to Establish Day Care Centers

Clark v. Jefferson County Board of Education

Supreme Court of Alabama, 1982.
410 So.2d 23.

MADDOX, Justice. Does a county board of education have legal authority to operate a child care center? That is the sole question presented by this appeal.

The Jefferson County Board of Education offers child care services as an adjunct to its regular academic program. . . .

Participation in these programs is voluntary and on a fee basis. The community education program of the Board and the child care program, in particular, are "self-sufficient" in that all expenses are met by fees generated from the programs. All programs are conducted within existing school facilities.

Appellant Clara Clark owns two day care centers in Jefferson County and one in Shelby County under the name of Happy House Day Care Center, Inc. The Jefferson County facilities owned and operated by Clark are in Irondale and Hoover. Clark identified several facilities which she contends are in competition with her Irondale facility, including at least one child care program operated by the Jefferson County Board of Education. . . .

The trial judge held that the operation of a child care center was an activity within the broad powers granted to county boards of education. . . . .

We first state, in summary form, Clark's argument that the Board has no authority to operate a child care program. She says that county boards of education, creatures of statute, can exercise only those powers which are expressly conferred upon them, that the powers granted to county boards by Code 1975, §§16-8-8 and 16-8-9, to administer and supervise is limited to *public schools,* and that a day care program is not a part of a *public school* because "public schools" are those established and maintained for persons between the ages of 7 and 21. . . . Clark's position is aptly stated by this quote from her brief: "No statute authorizes the education of children between one day and 5 years old."

The County Board contends that "the curricular and extracurricular offerings of the public school systems within this state, as in all states, are established by local boards of education in the exercise of their broad discretionary authority conferred by statute" and that in Alabama, this grant of authority is manifested throughout Chapter 8 of Title 16 of the Alabama Code. . . .

The Board, therefore, says that where there is a broad grant of statutory authority, no specific grant of authority to operate a child care program is required. . . .

The Board also calls our attention to evidence introduced during the trial which shows that the State Board of Education has actively and officially supported the implementation and development of Community Education in local school systems. Illustrative of this evidence is a position statement adopted by the Alabama State Board of Education on March 23, 1977, which reads as follows:

> The State Board of Education in its efforts to provide the highest quality education for the citizens of Alabama recognizes the components of community education as a most positive influence on the lifelong learning process and the democratic way of life. . . .

Other exhibits included a publication which showed that the Alabama State Department of Education defines "community education" as follows:

> WHAT IS COMMUNITY EDUCATION?
> Community education is a concept that stresses an expanded role for public education and provides a dynamic approach to individual and community improvement. . . .

The publication includes a page which shows that "day care" is one of the activities under the umbrella of "people of all ages together using a community school and community resources."

The concept of community education is probably best expressed in a publication entitled "Community Education: A Position Statement," which was adopted by the Alabama State Board of Education in March, 1977, and which is included in the record. . . . The publication

states that "the State Board of Education, recognizing the importance of and supporting the concepts involved in Community Education, adopted a resolution in March, 1975, urging all local school systems 'to actively pursue the community education concept.'" . . .

Based on the foregoing facts, and applying the law to those facts, we conclude that the judgment of the trial court is due to be affirmed.

The legislature has made broad grants of authority to the Alabama State Board of Education, the Alabama State Department of Education and to the individual county boards of education to administer and supervise the public schools. It is apparent that the Alabama State Board of Education, pursuant to authority granted it by law, has encouraged the development of "community education," of which "day care" is a part, and has determined that community education is in the best interest of the public schools in Alabama. . . .

We have carefully considered Clark's argument that a public body, without statutory authority, is encroaching upon an area of private enterprise.

Upon consideration of the facts and the law, we hold that while there is no specific statutory grant of authority to local boards of education to operate day care centers, there is authority for such activity under the broad grants of power which we have evaluated and discussed in this opinion. We, therefore, affirm the judgment of the trial court.

Affirmed.

CASE NOTES

1. Where the legislature empowers local school boards to perform certain functions, the courts will not interfere with the exercise of those powers unless the school board's actions are found to be "palpably arbitrary, unreasonable or capricious." *Tyska By Tyska v. Board of Education of Township High School District 214, Cook County*, 117 Ill.App.3d 917, 73 Ill.Dec. 209, 453 N.E.2d 1344 (1983).

2. The Supreme Court of Nebraska has defined the Legislature's power to delegate authority as follows:

> The law appears to be well settled that the Legislature may properly delegate authority to an

executive or administrative agency to formulate rules and regulations to carry out the expressed legislative purpose, or to implement such expressed purpose in order to provide for the complete operation and enforcement of the statute. The purpose of the delegation of authority ordinarily must be limited by express standards which have the effect of restricting the actions of the agency to the expressed legislative intent. In *State ex rel. Martin v. Howard*, 96 Neb. 278, 147 N.W. 689, this court approved the following: "In order to justify the courts in declaring invalid as a delegation of legislative power a statute conferring particular duties or authority upon administrative officers, it must clearly appear beyond a reasonable doubt that the duty or authority so conferred is a power that appertains exclusively to the legislative department, and the conferring of it is not warranted by the provisions of the Constitution. . . . Authority to make rules and regulations to carry out an expressed legislative purpose, or for the complete operation and enforcement of a law within designated limitations, is not an exclusively legislative power. Such authority is administrative in its nature and its use by administrative officers is essential to the complete exercise of the powers of all the departments." . . .

The difference between a delegation of legislative power and the delegation of authority to an administrative agency to carry out the expressed intent of the Legislature and the details involved has long been a difficult and important question. Increased complexity of our social order, and the multitude of details that necessarily follow, has led to a relaxation of the specific standards in the delegating statute in favor of more general ones where a specialized state agency is concerned. It is almost impossible for a legislature to prescribe all the rules and regulations necessary for a specialized agency to accomplish the legislative purpose. The delegation of authority to a specialized department under more generalized standards has been the natural trend as the need for regulation has become more evident and complex. . . . *School District No. 8 of Sherman County v. State Board of Education*, 176 Neb. 722, 127 N.W.2d 458 (1964).

3. The courts have held that discretionary administrative powers may be delegated while legislative powers cannot. In this regard, the Supreme Court of Nebraska has said:

The legislature cannot delegate legislative authority to an individual. It can prescribe the terms and conditions which may bring into operation a dissolution or consolidation of school dis-

tricts. This is the legislative act. It then can authorize the county superintendent to determine if the facts exist which call the law into operation. *Bierman v. Campbell*, 175 Neb. 877, 124 N.W.2d 918 (1963).

An Illinois court has said that the legislature may not delegate legislative authority but it may "give an administrative body discretionary powers to decide an issue if it establishes standards under which that discretion may be exercised." *People ex rel. Community Unit School District No. 1 v. Decatur School District No. 61*, 45 Ill.App.2d 33, 194 N.E.2d 659 (1963).

4. The courts have held that the Superintendent of Public Instruction of Illinois is the head of the public school system of that state and has been vested by the General Assembly with the duty of establishing standards in education, along the lines delineated by statute. *Games v. County Board of School Trustees of McDonough County*, 13 Ill.2d 78, 147 N.E.2d 306 (1958).

5. A Massachusetts court has held that the state Commissioner of Education has the power to compel local school officials to produce information by racial census. The court said that the Commissioner had the implied authority to do in an ordinary and reasonable manner those things required for the efficient exercise of powers and satisfactory performance of duties. *School Committee of New Bedford v. Commissioner of Education*, 349 Mass. 410, 208 N.E.2d 814 (1965).

6. In a Kentucky case concerning the constitutionality of delegation of legislative power to agencies in general and county boards of education in particular, the court said:

It has been suggested that the statute in this respect . . . is unconstitutional as being a delegation of legislative power to the several county boards of education. Such bodies may and do have conferred upon them legislative authority in a degree, for rules and regulations partake of that function. But delegation of legislative power in relation to constitutional limitations means delegation of discretion as to what the law shall be, and does not mean that the legislature may not confer discretion in the administration of the law itself. . . . Many are the instances where powers more nearly approaching the legislative prerogative than this have been vested in executive or administrative agencies and sustained as valid. This authority given the school boards is administrative and not legislative, and the act does not offend the Constitution in this regard. *Board of Education of Bath County v. Goodpaster*, 260 Ky. 198, 84 S.W.2d 55 (1935).

■ SCHOOL OFFICERS

A school officer, as distinguished from an employee, is one who possesses a delegation of sovereign power of the state. An Indiana court[65] has defined a public office as "a position to which a portion of the sovereignty of the state attaches for the time being, and which is exercised for the benefit of the public." The most important characteristic that may be said to distinguish an office from an employment is that the duties of an office must involve an exercise of some part of the sovereignty; there are powers and duties conferred by the legislature or the constitution. The duties must be performed independently, without the control of a superior power, unless statute provides for a subordinate office. Other characteristics that typically identify the office are a permanency or continuity of office, a required oath of office, and a procedure for removal that is usually fixed by statute. In addition, employees may exercise only ministerial powers and have no authority to exercise discretionary powers.

A superintendent of a local school district is, in most states, considered an employee. A case in point is that of a local superintendent in California who was discharged by the board of education and claimed he could be discharged only by the grand jury since he was a school officer. The school code provided that the school board shall "elect" a superintendent for a four-year term. Other provisions of the code said the school board may "employ" a superintendent. The superintendent in this case asserted that the term "elect" was indicative of public office. The court, however, held that the terms "elect" and "employ" in this case meant the same thing. The court further pointed out that the position of superintendent did not exercise a sovereign power, was not created by the constitution or statute, and that statutes did not impose independent police power duties upon the individual.[66]

Public officers are not allowed to hold two offices that are in conflict. Offices may be incompatible when one exercises control over the other, one office is subordinate to another, or the offices are held in more than one branch of the government at the same time. For example, a judge cannot also be a prosecuting attorney, a legislator cannot also be a school board member, and a governor cannot also be a legislator. Extending this principle further, it has been held that teachers, even though they are only employees, cannot also serve as board members in the same school district.[67]

Some state constitutions may say that a person cannot hold two lucrative offices regardless of whether one is subordinate to the other. The Indiana Constitution provides, "No person holding a lucrative office or appointment under the United States or under this State, shall be eligible to a seat in the General Assembly; nor shall any person hold more than one lucrative office at the same time, except as in this Constitution expressly prohibited. . . ."[68] Such "lucrative offices" have been held to prevent a person from serving both as a justice of the peace and a school board member, or to be sheriff while serving as a school board member.

Nearly all states have statutes that prevent public officers from having an interest in contracts made with the agencies they administer. A case illustrating a conflict of interest occurred when a board member with an interest in an insurance company wrote a policy for his own school district. The court held that this board member could be removed because he had wrongfully gained advantage through his public position.[69]

A conflict of interest may be in the form of nepotism. Nepotism can be prohibited by common law, statute, or state constitutional provision. Nepotism is defined by the courts as the "bestowal of patronage by public officers in appointing others to positions by reason of blood or marital relationship to the authority."[70] Thus, violation may occur where a school board appoints the blood kin or spouse of a board member to a position with the schools.

A public office, theoretically, is a public duty; an officer must have the consent of the governing power before he or she can resign. In other words, a public office is held at the will of both parties, and the public has a right to the services of its citizens. Therefore, to be valid, a resignation must be accepted. Without acceptance, the resignation is of no effect, and the officer remains in office.[71] Although this is one theory of vacation of a public office, some states provide for an "absolute" right to resign.[72] In states in which the officer has an "absolute" right to resign, if he or she tenders a resignation, he or she cannot withdraw it. There is immediate unconditional acceptance. In states that follow the "public duty" theory, a resignation probably can be withdrawn prior to acceptance or prior to an effective date if resignation specifies such a date. An Illinois court has held that resignations in advance are not legal. In a case in which a mayor required board members to put resignations in writing at the time of appointment, and the mayor later accepted them, the court said that such resignations were invalid because they were not contemplated by the law.[73]

Statutes provide the procedure to be used for the removal of public officers. In the absence of statute, removal is an incidental power of the appointing agency. For removal for cause, only a notice and a hearing are generally required. Cause may be malfeasance; improper or illegal performance of duties; or breach of good faith, inefficiency, and incapacity. A public officer cannot be removed during a term of office when the term is fixed by statute, unless for cause. In a case in which school board members took "kickbacks" from a contractor for violation of competitive bid law, the court removed the board. The court held that even in the absence of statute, the board members could be punished under common law for willful misconduct in office.[74]

------------------ ❖ — ❖ — ❖ ------------------

Constitutional Prohibition of Nepotism
Is Violated Where School Board Enters into
Teaching Contract with Spouse of Board Member

Smith v. Dorsey

Supreme Court of Mississippi, 1988.
530 So.2d 5.

EN BANC. On Petition for Rehearing Griffin, Justice, for the Court.

In this appeal this Court is asked to construe Section 109 as applied to contracts of teachers whose spouses are school board members. Stated differently, may a local school board contract with spouses of its members?

Proceedings in the lower court were held on October 9, 1986. Testimony at trial and stipulated exhibits include documents issued to defendants by the Secretary of State certifying them as Claiborne County School Board members; contracts for employment for their spouses—Jo Anne Collins Smith, Mary Jennings, Ernestine Williams and Catherine Knox—as teachers in the Claiborne County School District, at the time defendants served as board members; the teachers' payroll records from 1980–1986; and minutes of the Claiborne County School Board from 1980–1986.

On October 10, 1986, the chancellor entered an order finding all defendants to be in violation of Section 109. He further adjudicated the defendants' spouses' contracts to be null and void, and that each defendant had an indirect interest in these contracts as he had been a Trustee of the Claiborne County Board of Education when said Board approved one or more contracts for the employment of the defendants' spouses.

Finally, the chancellor ordered claims of restitution be made against the spouses of the defendants because of the Section 109 violations. The Court found that these violations as to all defendants and their spouses had existed for several years up to and including the present date.

This appeal followed.

Article 4, Section 109, of the Mississippi Constitution of 1890 provides:

> No public officer or member of the legislature shall be interested, directly or indirectly, in any contract with the state, or any district, county, city or town thereof, authorized by any law passed or order made by any board of which he may be or may have been a member, during the term for which he shall have been chosen, or within one year after the expiration of such term.

In *Frazier, supra* [514 So.2d 675 (Miss.1987)] at 693, we said that this section prohibits any officer from:

(a) having any direct or indirect interest in any contract

(b) with the state or any political subdivision

(c) executed during his term of office or one year thereafter, and

(d) authorized by any law, or order of any board of which he was a member.

The chancellor found that each defendant had an indirect interest in his spouse's contract as prohibited by Section 109. We would agree. . . .

However, without hesitation we find that logic dictates some manifest interest by appellants herein in the public school employment contracts of their wives. Appellants are directly responsible for the hiring and firing of their spouses. Additionally, the record indicates that these school board members share fully in the process behind which the salaries are awarded to public school teachers in their district. This is not to say that we question the integrity or fairness of these board members in any way; we simply recognize that each has an indirect interest in his wife's contract, which violates the constitutional provision.

Next, we address the question of restitution ordered by the lower court and brought up on appeal.

In the trial below plaintiffs and appellees herein neither plead nor raised the question of any bad faith committed by appellants for their role in the employment of their spouses. Nor did the chancellor make any finding of such.

In our review of the record, we can see no allegation by these Claiborne County taxpayers that they did not receive value for services performed by the teachers, whose time of employment ranged from two (2) to thirty-three (33) years. Further, in at least one instance the record shows that a spouse of one board member had been teaching long before his election to that body.

We have no doubt that such circumstances involving husband and wife teams in which one teaches and the other serves as a member of the school board are commonplace across this state, with no thought to any wrongdoing by the parties involved.

The record reflects that the conduct of the defendants here had been the general practice in Claiborne County for many years, and we would concede that a similar case could be made in many other counties of the state. The claim for restitution, however, should be denied on other grounds. There is no way the parties can be put back in their original position before the teaching contracts were entered. For restitution to be equitable, there would have to be some way of restoring to the teachers the value of the services they have rendered to the schools. Obviously, this cannot be done. To require restitution under the facts of this case would place these school teachers in a position where they would have served as public school teachers without pay, and in several instances for a number of years. The equitable remedy of restitution should not be enforced in such an inequitable way.

We hold that the above premise, coupled with the fact that there is no allegation or finding of bad faith on the part of the appellants, would make it grossly inequitable to require restitution on the peculiar facts presented here. . . .

We, therefore, uphold the chancellor's order finding appellants herein have been and are in violation of Sec. 109; declaring the contracts of appellants' spouses to be null and void; and enjoining any further payment of salaries, etc., to said spouses while appellants remain as members of the Board of the Claiborne County School District and for a period of one year after the defendants shall leave their official capacities. . . .

Case Notes

1. A state criminal statute prohibiting "self-dealing and nepotism" is violated by a county school superintendent who nominates his wife for a central administration position. *West Virginia Education Association v. Preston County Board of Education,* 171 W.Va. 38, 297 S.E.2d 444 (1982).

2. An anti-nepotism statute precluding relatives of school employees from serving as members of a school board does not inflict significant injury on the First Amendment rights of voters or school board candidates, restricting the voters' choice of candidates or a candidate's right to run in school board election. Neither does the statute deny equal protection of the law, because it is rationally related to a legitimate state interest in avoiding conflicts of interest. Moreover, the statute does not operate to deny either procedural or substantive due process of law. School board members were allowed to serve out their elected terms, thus there was no deprivation of any perceived property interest. *Chapman v. Gorman,* 839 S.W.2d 232 (Ky.1992).

--- ❖ — ❖ — ❖ ---

Conflict of Interest Statutes Are Designed to Engender Confidence in Public Bodies

Williams v. Augusta County School Board

Supreme Court of Virginia, 1994.
445 S.E.2d 118.

LACY, Justice.

In this appeal, we construe Code §2.1-639.16 of the State and Local Government Conflict of Interests Act, Code §§2.1-639.1 through -639.24 (the Act), as it applies to a school board's employment of the sister-in-law of a member of the school board.

The Augusta County School Board (the Board) employed Rebecca C. Williams as a full-time teacher from August 1969 until she left teaching in May 1975. Thirteen years later, in the summer of 1988, Williams applied for a teaching position in Augusta County, but the Board refused to consider her application. The Board maintained that Williams was ineligible because she was the sister-in-law of the Chairman of the Board, George P. Williams, and Code §2.1-639.16 prohibits the employment of a person with that relationship to a member of a board. Although Williams obtained contrary interpretations from both the Augusta County Attorney and the Attorney General, the Board declined to change its position.

Williams sued the Board, seeking a declaration that Code §2.1-639.16 does not preclude the Board from considering her for employment. After an *ore tenus* hearing, the trial court entered judgment in favor of the Board. We awarded Williams an appeal.

Since 1928, the General Assembly has restricted the authority of a school board to employ relatives of its members. Initially, a father, mother, brother, sister, wife, son, or daughter of a school board member could not be hired as a teacher in the board member's school district. Code §660 (1924 & Supp. 1928). No exceptions were allowed. From that time until the present,

this hiring restriction has been expanded, modified, and recodified. In its present form, Code §2.1-639.16 provides that a person who is a father, mother, brother, sister, spouse, son, daughter, son-in-law, daughter-in-law, sister-in-law, or brother-in-law of a member of the school board may not be employed by the school board. The section includes an exception to this prohibition which provides, in relevant part:

> This section shall not apply to any person within such relationship who has been (i) regularly employed . . . by any school board prior to the taking of office of any member of such board.

Williams contends that qualification for this exception requires only that the applicant have been regularly employed by a school board at some point prior to the time the relative becomes a member of the school board. Consequently, she concludes that she is entitled to the exception because she was regularly employed as full-time teacher from 1969 to 1975, prior to 1983 when her brother-in-law was appointed to the Board.

The Board construes the language of the exemption to apply only if the individual was regularly employed at the time the employee's relative became a member of the Board. Because Williams was not regularly employed by the Board in 1983 when her brother-in-law became a member of the Board, the Board argues that she does not qualify for the exception.

With this background, we begin with an examination of the language in the exemption. The exemption applies to one who "has been employed" prior to a relative becoming a member of the school board. The verb form used is the present perfect tense, which denotes an action beginning in the past and continuing to the present. Applying the principle of grammar, "has been employed" means that a person be employed by a school board both before and at the time the conflict arises. Williams's interpretation of the exemption, employment at any time before the conflict arose, would require use of a verb form in the past perfect tense—"had been employed," *i.e.*, an event beginning and ending in the past.

Furthermore, in contrast to the narrowed exemption which results from the use of the present perfect verb tense, Williams's interpretation results in a very broad construction of the exemption, covering all persons who were ever employed by any school board at any time prior to the inception of a conflict. Adoption of such a broad interpretation is inconsistent with the legislative directive that exemptions from the Act's provisions be narrowly construed.

The legislative intent of the Act is to engender confidence in public bodies and to eliminate situations in which preference or undue influence could come to bear in the operation of government. . . . Construction of the exemption in a way that specifically allows situations in which preference or undue influence in hiring decisions based on a familial relationship could occur is directly contrary to the Act's goals. Accordingly, we hold that the exemption contained in Code §2.1-639.16 is not applicable to Williams because she was not regularly employed by the Board at the time her brother-in-law was appointed to the Board. Accordingly, we will affirm the judgment of the trial court.

Affirmed.

CASE NOTES

1. A conflict of interest still exists even though a school board member cast a negative vote against his wife's employment as a teacher in the school district. The board member's attempt to "insulate" himself by voting against his wife was insufficient to protect him from constitutional and statutory prohibitions against any direct or indirect personal interest in a public contract. The board member and his wife were required to make restitution to the school board for money paid to the wife. *Waller v. Moore ex rel. Quitman County School District*, 604 So.2d 265 (Miss. 1992).

2. A chief state school officer may, in exercise of statutory power, remove a local school board member from office for conflict of interest where a due process hearing found substantial evidence to that effect. In this case, a school board member who operated a building and a home supply store received credits from a paint manufacturer for assisting in acquiring paint sales to the school district. *State Board of Elementary and Secondary Education v. Ball*, 847 S.W.2d 743 (Ky. 1993).

3. No conflict of interest exists where the husband of a public school teacher serves in the state legislature. The fact that the spouse while serving in the legislature votes on general public school laws and educational appropriations does not create a constitutional conflict. *Frazier v. State by and through Pittman*, 504 So.2d 675 (Miss.1987).

■ SCHOOL ELECTIONS

Legal issues relating to school elections are nearly as diverse as the general election laws of the state. No attempt is made here to fully encompass this wide body of law, but it is necessary to generally examine election law with regard to reapportionment precedents and to those legal requirements pertaining to compliance with election statutes.

Until 1962, the view of the courts prevailed that legislative representation and how it was apportioned throughout a state was a matter for only the legislature to determine. Malapportionment and rotten boroughs were of grave concern to many, and the problems became more acute as population mobility left some voters with very little legislative power while others reaped disproportionately great political muscle. Judicial precedent, which permitted this to transpire, was found in *Colegrove v. Green*,[75] in which case Justice Frankfurter, writing for the Supreme Court, opted to keep the courts out of the "political thicket." Frankfurter said:

> To maintain this action would cut very deep into the very being of Congress. Courts ought not to enter this political thicket. The remedy for unfairness in distributing is to secure state legislatures that will apportion properly, or to invoke the ample powers of Congress. . . . The Constitution has left the performance of many duties in our governmental scheme to depend on the fidelity of the executive and legislative action and, ultimately, in the vigilance of the people in exercising their political rights.[76]

After this decision, it soon became clear that the problems of apportionment would not be corrected by the legislators themselves, and the people were powerless to fully exercise their political rights. In reevaluation of its position, the Supreme Court handed down a new precedent in *Baker v. Carr*[77] in 1962. In so doing, the court found that the equal protection clause was violated by the resulting discrimination against some voters, which was not reasonable or rational, but instead was arbitrary and capricious.

This case has had bearing on school district elections in the same manner as it has influenced statewide elections; if officials are elected by popular vote, then the Constitution ensures "that each person's vote counts as much, insofar as it is practicable, as any other person's."[78]

— ❖ — ❖ — ❖ —

Equality of Voting Power Is Required in Local District Elections

Hadley v. Junior College District of Metropolitan Kansas City, Mo.

Supreme Court of the United States, 1970.
397 U.S. 50, 90 S.Ct. 791.

Mr. Justice BLACK delivered the opinion of the Court. This case involves the extent to which the Fourteenth Amendment and the "one man, one vote" principle apply in the election of local governmental officials. Appellants are residents and taxpayers of the Kansas City School District, one of eight separate school districts that have combined to form the Junior College District of Metropolitan Kansas City. Under Missouri law separate school districts may vote by referendum to establish a consolidated junior college district and elect six trustees to conduct and manage the necessary affairs of that district. The state law also provides that these trustees shall be apportioned among the separate school districts on the basis of "school enumeration," defined as the number of persons between the ages of six and twenty years, who reside in each district. In the case of the Kansas City School District this apportionment plan results in the election of three trustees, or 50 percent of the total number from that district. Since that district contains approximately 60 percent of the total school enumeration in the junior college district, appellants brought suit claiming that their right to vote for trustees was being unconstitutionally diluted in violation of the Equal

Protection Clause of the Fourteenth Amendment. The Missouri Supreme Court upheld the trial court's dismissal of the suit, stating that the "one man, one vote" principle was not applicable in this case. . . . [F]or the reasons set forth below we reverse and hold that the Fourteenth Amendment requires that the trustees of this junior college district be apportioned in a manner that does not deprive any voter of his right to have his own vote given as much weight, as far as is practicable, as that of any other voter in the junior college district. . . .

This Court has consistently held in a long series of cases that in situations involving elections, the States are required to insure that each person's vote counts as much, in so far as it is practicable, as any other person's. We have applied this principle in congressional elections, state legislative elections, and local elections. The consistent theme of those decisions is that the right to vote in an election is protected by the United States Constitution against dilution or debasement. While the particular offices involved in these cases have varied, in each case a constant factor is the decision of the government to have citizens participate individually by ballot in the selection of certain people who carry out governmental functions. Thus in the case now before us, while the office of junior college trustee differs in certain respects from those offices considered in prior cases, it is exactly the same in the one crucial factor—these officials are elected by popular vote. . . . While there are differences in the powers of different officials, the crucial consideration is the right of each qualified voter to participate on an equal footing in the election process. It should be remembered that in cases like this one we are asked by voters to insure that they are given equal treatment, and from their perspective the harm from unequal treatment is the same in any election, regardless of the officials selected. . . .

It has also been urged that we distinguish for apportionment purposes between elections for "legislative" officials and those for "administrative" officers. Such a suggestion would leave courts with an . . . unmanageable principle since governmental activities "cannot easily be classified in the neat categories favored by civics texts," . . . and it must also be rejected. We therefore hold today that as a general rule, whenever a state or local government decides to select persons by popular election to perform governmental functions, the Equal Protection Clause of the Fourteenth Amendment requires that each qualified voter must be given an equal opportunity to participate in that election, and when members of an elected body are chosen from separate districts, each district must be established on a basis that will insure, as far as is practicable, that equal numbers of voters can vote for proportionally equal numbers of officials. . . .

Although the statutory scheme reflects to some extent a principle of equal voting power, it does so in a way that does not comport with constitutional requirements. This is so because the Act necessarily results in a systematic discrimination against voters in the more populous school districts. This discrimination occurs because whenever a large district's percentage of the total enumeration falls within a certain percentage range it is always allocated the number of trustees corresponding to the bottom of that range. Unless a particularly large district has exactly 33-1/3 percent, 50 percent or 66-2/3 percent of the total enumeration it will always have proportionally fewer trustees than the small districts. As has been pointed out, in the case of the Kansas City School District, approximately 60 percent of the total enumeration entitles that district to only 50 percent of the trustees. Thus while voters in large school districts may frequently have less effective voting power than residents of small districts, they can never have more. Such built-in discrimination against voters in large districts cannot be sustained as a sufficient compliance with the constitutional mandate that each person's vote count as much as another's, as far as is practicable. . . . We have said before that mathematical exactitude is not required . . . but a plan that does not automatically discriminate in favor of certain districts is.

In holding that the guarantee of equal voting strength for each voter applies in all elections of governmental officials, we do not feel that the States will be inhibited in finding ways to insure that legitimate political goals of representation are achieved. We have previously upheld against constitutional challenge an election scheme that required that candidates be residents of certain districts that did not contain equal numbers of people. . . . Since all the officials in that case were elected at large, the right

of each voter was given equal treatment. We have also held that where a State chooses to select members of an official body by appointment rather than election, and that choice does not itself offend the Constitution, the fact that each official does not "represent" the same number of people does not deny those people equal protection of the laws. . . . And a State may, in certain cases, limit the right to vote to a particular group or class of people. . . . But once a State has decided to use the process of popular election and "once the class of voters is chosen and their qualifications specified, we see no constitutional way by which equality of voting power may be evaded." . . .

CASE NOTES

1. The Federal Voting Rights Act of 1965 was enacted to eradicate discriminatory voting practices. Under Section Two of the Act States and their political subdivisions are barred from maintaining discriminatory voting practices or standards and procedures. This section may be violated if the electoral system is not open to equal participation based on race. Section five of the Act identifies particular states and their political subdivisions as covered jurisdictions. In these covered jurisdictions new election laws cannot be passed unless they are shown to be nondiscriminatory. Section five of the Act establishes preclearance procedures requiring federal district court approval. Preclearance requires, among other things, that any new electoral system must not have a "dilutive impact" that will reduce or deny voting power of African-American voters. See: *Reno v. Bossier Parish School Board*, 520 U.S. 471, 117 S.Ct. 1491 (1997).

2. A statute limiting the franchise in school elections to parents of children enrolled in the public schools and owners and leasees of taxable real property denies equal protection. *Kramer v. Union Free School District No. 15*, 395 U.S. 621, 89 S.Ct. 1886 (1969).

Similarly, the Supreme Court has held unconstitutional a statute that limited electors in a public utility bond election to only "property taxpayers." *Cipriano v. City of Houma*, 395 U.S. 701, 89 S.Ct. 1897 (1969).

3. The Civil Rights Acts of 1957 and 1960 protect voters in federal elections from intimidation and interference and require State elec-

tion officials to preserve federal election records. 42 U.S.C.A. §§1971(b), 1974–1974(b). Also, state laws requiring literacy to vote cannot be ambiguous and vague, violating the Fifteenth Amendment. *Smith v. Allwright*, 321 U.S. 649, 64 S.Ct. 757 (1944).

4. The one-person, one-vote standard is not applicable to appointive boards. *Sailors v. Board of Education of Kent County*, 387 U.S. 105, 87 S.Ct. 1549 (1967).

5. Where there is no fraud, bad faith, or misleading of the voters, it is a well-settled rule that statutory provisions that are treated as mandatory before an election will be construed as directory after the election. *Lindahl v. Independent School District No. 306*, 270 Minn. 164, 133 N.W.2d 23 (1965).

6. A Minnesota court, in *Bakken v. Schroeder*, 269 Minn. 381, 130 N.W.2d 579 (1964), stated that challenges to consolidation proceedings will not serve to invalidate the election unless there is proof of prejudice and that statutory requirements are treated as directory rather than mandatory when election proceedings are contested following the election. In a case involving a challenge, the court quoted an earlier decision, *Erickson v. Sammons*, 242 Minn. 345, 65 N.W.2d 198 (1954), and said:

> It is the general rule that, before an election is held, statutory provisions regulating the conduct of the election will usually be treated as mandatory and their observance may be insisted upon and enforced. After an election has been held, the statutory regulations are generally construed as directory and such rule of construction is in accord with the policy of this state, which from its beginning has been that, in the absence of fraud or bad faith or constitutional violation, an election which has resulted in a fair and free expression of the will of the legal voters upon the merits will not be invalidated because of a departure from the statutory regulations governing the conduct of the election except in those cases where the legislature has clearly and unequivocally expressed an intent that a specific statutory provision is an essential jurisdictional prerequisite and that a departure therefrom shall have the drastic consequence of invalidity. . . .

7. The Supreme Court of Texas, in *McKinney v. O'Conner*, 26 Tex. 5 (1861), has stated the rule for elections as

rules prescribing the manner in which the qualified electors shall hold the election, at the time and place designated, and those prescribing the manner in which their act, when done, shall be authenticated, so as to import verity on its face, are directory. Irregularities in their observance will not vitiate an election, unless they be such that the true result of the ballot cannot be arrived at with reasonable certainty. The ultimate test of the validity of an election is involved in the questions: *Did the qualified electors, at the time and place designated, acting in concert, either actively or by acquiescence, hold an election and cast their votes in the ballot box; and has it been done in a manner sufficiently conformable to the directions of the law, as that the true result can be arrived at with reasonable certainty?* [Emphasis supplied.]

8. In a case contending a lack of sufficiency of notice for a special election, a Missouri court said that "[g]enerally, statutory provisions as to notice of special elections are mandatory, must be strictly followed, the failure to properly call a special election will invalidate it. . . . A special election, however, will not be vitiated by failure to comply strictly with the statutory requirements with respect to the giving of notice where the electors were in fact informed of the time, place, and purpose of the election and generally voted on the question submitted; where it is not shown that the electors did not participate in the election because of lack of notice or knowledge or that a different result would have obtained if the full statutory notice had been given. *State v. Whittle*, 401 S.W.2d 401 (Mo. 1966).

■ SCHOOL BOARD MEETINGS

A fundamental rule of school board meetings is that the meeting must be held within the geographic boundaries of the school district. A Missouri court has explained the reasons for this requirement in this manner:

> [I]t is obvious that considerations of public policy demand that the official meetings of public bodies be held within the limits of their territorial jurisdictions; otherwise, public servants might do in secret that which they would not attempt to do under public scrutiny, and thereby much injury might be done the public welfare. . . . It would be just as proper for the state legislature to hold its

sessions outside the state or for a county court to transact business in another county. . . .

The courts have traditionally been rather lenient concerning the procedure used by boards of education in meetings. Unless the rules of procedure are prescribed by statute, a board of education may establish its own rules of procedure. Where neither statutes nor adopted board procedures are used, the generally accepted rules of parliamentary procedure will control. As indicated, the courts are indulgent concerning procedure and will not insist on a specific set of rules. The court is primarily concerned that every board member has been given a right to be heard and to vote.

The actual board meeting is an important prerequisite to an action by a board of education. Action taken separately or individually, by board members outside a board meeting, has no validity. Likewise, promises made by individual board members outside official meetings have no legal validity. However, a board of education, if it chooses, may ratify a previous individual commitment made by a board member. Official action at a later meeting is necessary for ratification.

------------------ ❖ — ❖ — ❖ ------------------

Allegation That Board Had Made Decision Prior to Official Meeting Not Sustained by Facts

Aldridge v. School District of North Platte

Supreme Court of Nebraska, 1987.
225 Neb. 580, 407 N.W.2d 495.

WHITE, Justice. Gary R. Aldridge appeals from an order of the district court for Lincoln County, Nebraska, granting summary judgment in favor of the appellees, the school district of North Platte and six members of its board of education. . . .

The petition in this case attacked decisions made by the board in regard to the employment status of the superintendent of schools. On

August 31, 1984, the superintendent was found guilty of third degree sexual assault. The board called a meeting on September 5, 1984, a week before the next scheduled meeting. The meeting was largely attended, and when the matter concerning the superintendent's conviction arose, board member Linda L. Gale requested that there be no discussion on the subject. Dallas F. Darland, a board member, announced that he had been tendered a resignation by the superintendent and read aloud the letter, which stated that the superintendent would resign voluntarily in December. Darland moved to accept the offer to resign; the motion was seconded and passed. Board member Myra Satterfield then made a motion to suspend the superintendent from his duties with pay until his resignation was effective. The motion also was seconded and passed. There was no discussion of these motions except for the reading of the letter and the making of the motions.

Aldridge's petition alleges two causes of action: first, that a quorum of the board met with the attorney for the school district and discussed and made policy in violation of the public meetings law; and second, that the motion by Satterfield to suspend the superintendent with pay passed without public discussion based on the prior nonpublic briefing and meeting alleged in the first count.

In his deposition Aldridge stated he based his allegations that the public meetings law was violated on two facts: that a major motion passed without discussion and that a witness saw a quorum (four of six) of the board members at the school board attorney's office earlier in the day of the September 5 meeting. The witness, Kathy Seacrest, testified on deposition that she saw four board members in the "entryway" of the attorney's office and that two of them were leaving as she left. She heard no discussion or comments made by the members.

A reading of the depositions of the board members exposes no discrepancies in their stories. The four members met with the attorney to discuss the legal ramifications of various options to remove the superintendent from office. Each feared a long legal battle and was informed that the superintendent had due process and contractual rights in his employment. Each was aware that certain of the benefits would vest in December and that the superintendent knew this. They specifically denied that a quorum ever met to decide policy and testified that they left the office having made no decision in the matter. . . .

At oral argument counsel for Aldridge argued that Gale's statement limiting discussion on the issue was a violation of the public meetings law. The petition shows two causes of action: that an illegal meeting of a quorum of the board took place prior to the public meeting and that, without public discussion, the board passed a motion based on the previous illegal deliberations. The petition does not maintain that public discussion may not be limited or prohibited by the board at its meetings. See Neb.Rev.Stat. §84-1412(2) (Cum.Supp. 1984). . . .

Appellant's counsel conceded at argument that the attorney for the board could advise members two at a time without violating the public meetings law. However, he still argues that the lack of discussion at the meeting implies that the real decision was made illegally prior to the meeting.

The appellant based his case on Seacrest's statements that she saw four board members in the attorney's office. She corroborated their statements that two were leaving as two were waiting. Obviously, no meeting of the board members in which a quorum was present occurred. . . .

The appellees' testimony establishes that no improper meeting occurred. The appellant then had the burden to introduce evidence in opposition to the motion for summary judgment that would tend to prove that a meeting did occur. . . . He could not produce such evidence. Since no issue of fact existed, the motion for summary judgment was properly granted in favor of the appellees.

Affirmed.

CASE NOTES

1. A teachers' association can videotape proceedings of a school board meeting. A court in New Jersey, in upholding videotaping of a board meeting, reasoned that video cameras and recorders are so commonplace today that one would have great difficulty showing that their use would in some manner impede the deliberations or harm the public interest. On the school board's behalf, the court did say that the videotaping equipment could not be used in such a manner as to disrupt the meeting. The court, though, was not sympathetic with school board members who wanted to ban the cameras merely because the cameras' presence made the members feel uncomfortable or inhibited. *Maurice River Board of Education v. Maurice River To. Teachers Ass'n*, 193 N.J.Super. 488, 475 A.2d 59 (App.Div. 1984). See also *Sony Corp. of America v. Universal City Studios, Inc.*, 464 U.S. 417, 104 S.Ct. 774 (1984).

2. *Procedure.* As pointed out earlier, courts are rather flexible as to the procedure used by local school boards.

In 1960, a New Hampshire court upheld action by a school board when there was considerable irregularity in parliamentary procedure. The court said that a board's action could not be voided so long as no statutes were violated. If the machinery of government were not allowed a little play in its joints, it would not work. *Lamb v. Danville School Board*, 102 N.H. 569, 162 A.2d 614 (1960).

However, the courts will not go too far in upholding flimsy procedure. In a Missouri case, two board members, without notifying a third, got together informally at home and decided to call a special school election. No minutes were kept. The court said that school elections called as a result of the meeting were invalid. The board meeting was not a legal one: "While there is no question but that the motives of the [board members] . . . were of the highest, we think their manner of getting together had no more dignity than any ordinary fence-row conference."

3. *Executive Sessions.* Executive sessions, where the board retires to privacy, may be used for discussion, but not for action. Where a board met in open session, adjourned for an hour or so, reconvened in executive session, and then met again in open session, and teachers' contracts were terminated in the open session after discussion in the executive session, the teachers sued, questioning the validity of the action. The court said the meeting was a legal one, despite the fact that the contracts were discussed in the executive session. The requirements of the law

were met when the official action of the board was taken in open session. *Alva v. Sequoia Union High School District*, 98 Cal.App.2d 656, 220 P.2d 788 (1950); *Dryden v. Marcellus Community Schools*, 401 Mich. 76, 257 N.W.2d 79 (1977).

In a later case, in Illinois, the board of education voted in an executive session to condemn land. The action was challenged, and the court held that the action in the executive session was "not an effective exercise of the power of the board to commence condemnation." However, since the board had later ratified the action in an official meeting, the condemnation proceedings were legal. *Goldman v. Moore*, 35 Ill.2d 450, 220 N.E.2d 466 (1966). *State ex rel. Stewart v. Consolidated School District*, 281 S.W.2d 511 (Mo.App.1955).

Boards of education should adopt rules of procedure. However, when they do, they are bound by their own rules. In an early Kentucky case illustrating the binding force of a board rule, a board made a rule that purchases of supplies and materials of $500 or less could be made without bid. Pianos were purchased in an amount of $2,500 without bids. The membership of the board changed, and the new board refused to pay for the pianos. The vendor sued. The action of the vendor was unsuccessful. The court held that the school board rules had the force of law upon the board itself, which the board could not disregard. *Montenegro-Riehm Music Co. v. Board of Education of Louisville*, 147 Ky. 720, 145 S.W. 740 (1912).

An Ohio school board passed a rule that provided that bus drivers involved in five accidents causing police investigation shall be dismissed. A bus driver arrived home from a vacation trip at three in the morning and arose four hours later to drive a school bus. The bus left the road and struck an embankment seventeen feet from the highway. No one was injured. The board dismissed the driver, and the driver sued. The court held for the driver, saying that the board's rule of five accidents was "unfortunate." Since there was evidence of only one accident and even though the discharge of the driver was desirable, the board could not discharge him because of its own regulation. *State ex rel. Edmundson v. Board of Education*, 2 Ohio Misc. 137, 201 N.E.2d 729 (Com.Pl. 1964).

4. *Quorum*. A quorum under common law is a simple majority of the total membership. In the absence of statute, the common law rule will be applied. *Gunnip v. Lautenklos*, 33 Del.Ch. 415, 94 A.2d 712 (1953). See also *Matawan Regional Teachers Association v. Matawan-Aberdeen Regional Board of Education*, 223 N.J.Super. 504, 538 A.2d 1331 (1988).

A Kentucky court has held that where there was one vacancy on a five-member board, the four remaining members represented a quorum. *Trustees v. Brooks*, 163 Ky. 200, 173 S.W. 305 (1915). The number required for a quorum is not reduced by a reduction in the membership due to vacancies. This means that in the case of a five-member board that has three vacancies, the two remaining board members cannot take action.

5. *Voting*. Boards, in the absence of statute, may establish voting procedures (voice vote, show of hands, secret ballot). There is no authority for a board member to allow someone else to vote for him or her.

When a board member refuses to vote, the general rule is that this vote is considered as an assent to the will of the majority. *Mullins v. Eveland*, 234 S.W.2d 639 (Mo.App.1950). In a Tennessee case in which a board of seven members considered a motion to execute a contract, three voted in favor, two opposed, and two did not vote. The court said the motion carried by a vote of five to two. Those not voting were considered as assenting to the majority. *Collins v. Janey*, 147 Tenn. 477, 249 S.W. 801 (1923).

Common law does not require that individual votes be recorded in the board minutes so long as the totals are made a part of the record. *Diefenderfer v. Budd*, 563 P.2d 1355 (Wyo.1977).

6. *Minutes and Records*. Courts hold that the school board can act only through their minutes. The minutes of a board member are the only legal evidence of what has transpired during the meeting. An Illinois court has said that "[p]roper minutes and records should be kept by a board of education to the end that the persons who are carrying the tax load may make reference thereto and the future boards may be advised of the manner of disposition of questions that have arisen." *Hankenson v. Board of Education*, 10 Ill.App.2d 79, 134 N.E.2d 356

(1956). *Reversed* on different issue, 10 Ill.2d 560, 141 N.E.2d 5 (1957).

A board secretary may record minutes after the meeting has adjourned. *Kent v. School District*, 106 Okl. 30, 233 P. 431 (1925).

Memoranda kept by the board secretary cannot be examined by the public prior to transcribing the minutes. In a 1954 case, on the day after a board meeting, citizens requested permission to examine the minutes. The school board secretary had not as yet transcribed his notes and refused permission to the group. The court upheld the board and said "the clerk's untranscribed notes reasonably are not classifiable as a public writing . . . whereas the transcribed minutes, in final form, but awaiting only approval and placement in the journal, are a public writing. . . ." *Conover v. Board of Education*, 1 Utah 2d 375, 267 P.2d 768 (1954).

The form and wordage used in school board minutes are looked upon with indulgence by the court. "Although they may be unskillfully drawn, if by fair and reasonable interpretation their meaning can be ascertained, they will be sufficient to answer the requirements of law." *Noxubee County v. Long*, 141 Miss. 72, 106 So. 83 (1925).

A public records law may require that names of applicants screened for a superintendent's position be released to the press. *Attorney General v. School Committee of Northampton*, 375 Mass. 127, 375 N.E.2d 1188 (1978).

7. *Notice of Meetings.* In order for a board meeting to be legal, proper notice must be given and all members must be notified in time to be given an opportunity to participate. A reasonable time in advance of a meeting for notice to be given is "sufficient time to the party notified for preparation and attendance at the time and place of such meeting." *Green v. Jones*, 144 W.Va. 276, 108 S.E.2d 1 (1959).

When a board meeting was called with a few minutes' notice, making the chairman unable to attend, and the board employed a teacher, the court held the employment invalid. "[The chairman] was hardly bound to quit the work he had started to do and rush over to attend a suddenly called meeting of the board. The notice should have given him reasonable opportunity to attend. It did not." *Wood v. School District*, 137 Minn. 138, 162 N.W. 1081 (1917).

Notice should include the time and the place of the meeting. Members should be notified of any changes.

When a meeting is held without notice, and all members are present and consent to act, the requirement of notice is waived.

Notice is not required for regular board meetings because members have constructive notice. For example, boards usually establish a regular meeting date each month for which special notice is not required. Notice is only required for special board meetings.

8. *Bylaws.* In the absence of statute to the contrary, a board's bylaws are binding on the board. School boards cannot set aside or render nugatory a bylaw by suspension of a mere rule of order for the convenience of transacting business.

A bylaw must be changed using appropriate procedures, with notice, and following proper regulatory processes. See *Matawan Regional Teachers Association v. Matawan-Aberdeen Regional School District Board of Education*, 223 N.J.Super. 504, 538 A.2d 1331 (App.Div.1988).

■ OPEN MEETINGS AND PUBLIC RECORDS LAWS

In recent years, state legislatures have sought to make public board meetings more open and public records more accessible to the public. Even though there has always been a general common law right of the citizenry to be informed through openness of public meetings and public records, actual implementation of the ideal often fell short of the mark. Technicalities regarding when meetings were open, the justification for executive sessions, notice, and the logistics of access to public records have presented problems that legislatures have attempted to resolve by enactment of statutes specifically governing meetings and records. As a result of this legislation, much new litigation has transpired that endeavors to interpret the meaning of the statutes.

The most important difference between the traditional common law covering public meetings and the new statutes is that public school boards could adjourn to executive session to discuss virtually any matter bearing on operation of the schools, while the new laws narrowly define the purposes and procedures for the conduct of closed or executive sessions. Most sunshine laws require both deliberations and actions to be taken in public, the exception being only for a limited number of sensitive matters that would, if aired in public, be personally detrimental to some party or would harm the public interest. The underlying purpose of both open meeting and public records laws is to display to the public marketplace and subject to public scrutiny the truth about official acts of public servants.[79]

Most sunshine laws closely track the common law by permitting executive sessions of school boards for information and strategy concerning collective negotiations or bargaining, purchase or lease of real property, consultation with an attorney in connection with litigation, business pertaining to lawful privilege, or confidentiality regarding investigations of possible law violations. Yet the actual official actions of boards taken by vote of the membership must be conducted in public.

In this regard, a Pennsylvania court permitted a school board to take a "straw vote" in executive session in order to reduce the number of applicants, from five to three, for the position of school superintendent in the district. The court said that "[j]ust because a vote is taken in executive session does not mean that it is an 'official action.' . . ."[80] To be a vote constituting official actions as defined [in] . . . the Sunshine Act, it must be a matter that commits the agency to a course of conduct." A "straw vote," according to this court, came within the definition of "discussion and deliberation" not constituting "official action."[81]

In determining whether a meeting of a school board violates a state sunshine law, the court will look at the decision making as a whole to determine if the citizenry has been deprived of a meaningful opportunity to respond or to hold officials accountable for their actions. A West Virginia court has pointed out that courts will normally look for certain indicators of an illegal meeting, to wit. First. The content of the discussion is crucial to a policy decision. School board members can gather in complete privacy at will, and the meeting will not violate the law if matters discussed are entirely unrelated to school business. Second. The number attending a meet-

ing is important. If only two of ten board members attend a meeting, it is far less suspect than if eight of ten attend, thus, the percentage of the public body present is important. Third. The significance of the identity of those not attending, those absent in opposition to an issue before the board. Fourth. The intentions of members. Fifth. The nature and degree of planning for the meeting by those involved. If the meeting is by happenstance, legal objection to the meeting is reduced. Sixth. Duration of the meeting is of importance; longer meetings are more suspect. Seventh. The setting and opportunity for private discussion. Eighth. The possible effects on decision making of having the meeting in private. Does the situation inhibit meaningful opportunity to respond or does it lessen public accountability of the officials? In enumerating this list of considerations, the West Virginia court concluded that while they are all relevant, none of the criteria are individually controlling.

Using these criteria, this court invalidated a vote taken as a result of a private meeting held by several members of a school board when evidence indicated that (a) a quorum of the board was present; (b) the gathering addressed the highly controversial matter of merger of schools; (c) information was conveyed that was of great importance and sensitivity to the decision; and (d) the meeting was prearranged, took place in school board offices, was a two-hour meeting, and was on the day before a crucial board vote. Thus, the actual board vote taken in a public meeting a day later was found to be legally defective.[82]

PUBLIC RECORDS

In determining the public nature of meetings and records, the courts must weigh the extent of the public interest involved. A case in point involved the investigation by an Atlanta television station that sought the release of personnel records of bus drivers who transported schoolchildren. The drivers worked for a private bus company that had contracted to transport school children to and from school in buses owned by the school district. The private company refused to release the personnel files, claiming it was a private entity.

The television station claimed that the transportation of pupils was a "legitimate function" of the school board and that the private company was merely a "management tool" used by the board to carry out public responsibilities. The court agreed, saying that "without question, then, operation of school buses or arranging for their operation, is 'a legitimate function' of the Board,"[83] and, therefore, the public should be entitled to inspect the records. The court found it important to note that there is a significant public interest in the safe transportation of children and that the board's public duty to ensure safety required that the personnel records of the private company be held open to public scrutiny.

One of the most controversial aspects of open meetings laws is determining what actually constitutes a meeting. Is it a meeting if a quorum of board members meet to play a round of golf, have dinner together, or play cards? Some state statutes provide that a public meeting shall not include an informal gathering.[84] Even though the precise wording of the statute will prevail, it may be generally concluded that the actual intent of the meeting must be the true test. If the intent of a meeting is purely social and informal, then by definition no public business is conducted. If no public business is conducted, then the meeting is not subject to open meeting requirements. A Missouri court has defined public business as "those matters over which the public governmental body has supervision, control, jurisdiction or advisory power."[85] A workshop at a mountain retreat to improve the personal relations and foster social interaction among board members who had a history of divisive behavior is not a matter of public business.[86] In this particular case, the court said that

> [a]s a matter of law, it was not public business for the Board to discuss the betterment of interpersonal relationships in the context of a workshop when the discussions of interpersonal relationships did not include reference to any business matters which would come before the Board for consideration and action.[87]

In another interesting case, a statute defined "meeting" as constituting "any deliberation between a quorum of members" at which "public business" is discussed, the court found that at a meeting that was held by a quorum of board members who merely sat and listened to a consultant's report—a briefing session—and at which no members indulged in verbal exchange or discussion, the open meetings law was not violated. The court in this case said explicitly that

> a meeting such as that held by the Board . . . , does not violate the Act so long as a quorum of the Board does not conduct a verbal exchange between themselves or with any other person about any issue within the jurisdiction of the government body or any public business.[88]

This court did not speculate as to what the result would have been if board members had communicated with each other in sign language, body language, or writing.

OPEN RECORDS

A threshold issue in all these cases involves the definition of a public body or a public agency to which the sunshine meeting or public records requirements are applied. Of course, private meetings, or purely private records, are not subject to openness requirements. Some public boards have sought to limit possible overbreadth of sunshine statutes by employing private entities to perform certain sensitive functions. For example, job searches for school superintendents have, at times, been delegated to private firms in order to shield the identity of applicants who would not want their names revealed for fear of jeopardizing their current employment. Litigation over the permissible latitude of public boards in this regard has been relatively frequent, with newspapers as the usual plaintiffs. General legal rules that determine whether an entity is the functional equivalent of a public body are applied in such cases. If an entity is the functional equivalent of the public body for which it performs a task, then its meetings and records must be open to scrutiny of the press and the citizenry. The criteria are as follows:

1. Whether the entity performs a governmental function
2. The level of governmental funding supporting the entity
3. The extent of governmental involvement and regulation
4. Whether the agency was related by the government[89]

The following cases clearly define the matter.

------------ ❖ — ❖ — ❖ ------------

*School Committee's Closed-Session Discussion
and Approval of Drug Search Was Exempt
from Open Meetings Law*

Rhode Island Affiliate, American Civil Liberties Union, Inc. v. Bernasconi

Supreme Court of Rhode Island, 1989.
447 A.2d 1232.

FAY, Chief Justice. This case comes before us on appeal from a Superior Court order granting the defendants' motion to dismiss pursuant to Rule 12(b)(6) of the Superior Court Rules of Civil Procedure. The plaintiffs, Rhode Island Affiliate, American Civil Liberties Union (ACLU), and Steven Brown, Executive Director, contend that the trial justice erred in granting that motion....

On January 26 and February 12, 1987, the Chariho school committee (school committee) held regularly scheduled public meetings. During the meetings, the school committee voted unanimously to enter into closed executive session pursuant to G.L. 1956 (1984 Reenactment) §42-46-5(a)(1) and (2). These provisions allow a public body to hold a closed meeting, in limited circumstances, following an affirmative vote of the majority of its members.

On April 8, 1987, plaintiffs filed an action to impose civil fines against defendants, in their individual capacities and in their capacities as members of the school committee, for violations of the Rhode Island Open Meetings Law. Chapter 46 of title 42. The plaintiffs alleged, on information and belief, that the school committee discussed and approved a plan to search student lockers at the Chariho Regional Junior-Senior High School. Thereafter, state and local police conducted a search of approximately 800 lockers at the school. The plaintiffs maintained that these closed sessions of the school commit-

tee violated multiple provisions of the open-meetings law....

... [P]laintiffs aver that the school committee's closed-session discussion and approval of a drug search is not a matter exempted from the requirement that meetings of a public body remain open to the public. Assuming, as required, that all allegations in the complaint are true, we find that the topic of a drug search falls within the statutory guidelines enunciated in §§42-46-4 and 42-46-5. This topic clearly implicates security matters as contemplated by §42-46-5(a)(3). Additionally, these closed sessions may involve or lead to investigative proceedings concerning allegations of civil or criminal misconduct. *See* §42-46-5(a)(4). We believe that the sale and use of drugs in a school system represents a serious threat to the security, health, and welfare of a student body. It would be inconceivable for this court to find that the topic is not a legitimate concern for a closed session. Therefore, we hold that the discussion and approval of a drug search is exempted by §§42-46-4 and 42-46-5....

The plaintiffs further argue that the school committee violated §42-46-6(b), as amended by P.L.1984, ch. 372, §1, which requires notice of agenda topics. In the present case, defendants did not include the matter of the drug search on the agenda for the January and/or February meetings. We may infer, however, that defendants provided adequate notice of the meetings pursuant to §42-46-6(a) and (c). We note that any announcement of this subject matter would be self-defeating and hold that defendants' action does not operate to their detriment....

For the reasons stated, the plaintiffs' appeal is denied and dismissed. The judgment appealed from is affirmed, and the case is remanded to the Superior Court for further proceedings consistent with this opinion.

CASE NOTES

1. *Open Meetings.* The gathering of school board members on occasion at various restaurants, sometimes before and sometimes after official board meetings, did not violate the Oregon Open Meetings Law even though, at times, a quorum was present. The court held that there was not a "convening of the body" of the board

for the purpose of making "a decision or to deliberate toward a decision." *Harris v. Nordquist,* 96 Or.App. 19, 771 P.2d 637 (1989).

A student suspension hearing before a school board must be open to the public if such is requested by the student or parent. Meetings may not be closed unless they are intended to evaluate the professional competency of an employee or to consider employment actions such as for hiring or dismissal. No exception is contained in the Iowa law for students. *Schumacher v. Lisbon School Board,* 582 N.W. 2d 183 (Iowa 1998).

Where a quorum of school board members attended a meeting of another school board in an adjacent town where the topic discussed was possible merger, the court ruled that the open meetings law was not violated because the board members were not "meeting for the purpose of exercising the school board's responsibilities, powers or duties." *Paulton v. Volkmann,* 141 Wis.2d 370, 415 N.W.2d 528 (App.1987).

A Wisconsin court has held that failure to announce with specificity the reason for going into closed session did not violate the state's open meetings law. *State v. Van Lare,* 125 Wis.2d 40, 370 N.W.2d 271 (App.1985).

The Open Meetings Act of Illinois has been held not to require notice in the school board agenda of topics to be considered in closed session. In so holding, the court expanded on the rationale for openness of public boards as that which provides the greatest "public advantage":

> While we keep in mind that the purpose of the Act is to promote the openness of public business, we must not overlook the larger, overriding purposes of the Act within which the promotion of openness is subsumed and made a constituent part—aiding the conduct of the people's business, or, in other words, securing public advantage. (*People ex rel. Hopf v. Barger* (1975), 30 Ill.App.3d 525, 332 N.E.2d 649.) In promoting the ultimate goal of requiring public bodies to carry out their business in the manner most beneficial to the public they represent, there are occasions in which it is not to the public's advantage that a public body carry on its business in a meeting open to the public. Therefore, it is not always possible for both of the above-stated purposes of the Act to be promoted in harmony. It is our belief that where the purposes of the Act cannot be promoted in harmony, priority should be given to the more dominant or overriding purpose.

This is particularly true in the instant case where the purpose of promoting openness is not separate and distinct from the overriding purpose of promoting the ultimate goal of public advantage. Openness is in most circumstances an element fundamental in furthering public advantage; however, in some instances openness simply prevents or defeats public advantage.

For example, consideration of topics concerning matters such as personal information, bargaining position, and negotiating strategy makes it necessary that a public body meet in private, lest it run the risk that the business undertakings will be rendered, for all practical purposes, ineffective and meaningless. Public knowledge of their officials' intentions and actions resulting from compulsory public deliberative sessions when considering matters such as the purchase of real estate would destroy any advantage to be gained from negotiation and work a severe detriment upon the officers and the public they represent. (*Collinsville Community Unit School District Number 10 v. Witte* (1972), 5 Ill.App.3d 600, 603, 283 N.E.2d 718, 720–21.) Likewise, forcing public officers to discuss sensitive issues in meetings open to the public may result in these topics being intentionally overlooked, at the public's expense. Premised by a familiarity with the common use of discretion that results in many sensitive issues being better left alone, especially when the audience is large and confidence is wanting, consider the negative effects resulting from open discussion of personal problems that might impede upon the workplace of a public office, such as alcohol abuse, tardiness, poor hygiene, or cigarette smoking. While these problems might be resolved if the appropriate public body were able to discuss the matter freely, it is unlikely that this will occur when such matters cannot be discussed in confidence. As a result, work quality continues to wane, at the public's expense. *Gosnell v. Hogan,* 179 Ill.App.3d 161, 128 Ill.Dec. 252, 534 N.E.2d 434 (5th Dist.1989).

2. Attorney-client privilege is normally an exception to open meetings requirements. When such a privilege would come into play is expressed by a Minnesota court:

> When a public body can show that litigation is imminent or threatened, or when a public body needs advice above the level of general legal advice, i.e., regarding specific acts and their legal consequences, then the attorney-client exception applies.

Star Tribune v. Board of Education, Special School District No. 1, 507 N.W.2d 869 (Minn.App.1993).

3. The Michigan Open Meetings Act has been interpreted to permit "straw polls" in closed sessions where members did not actually vote or make a decision as defined by law. *Moore v. Fennville Public Schools Board of Education*, 566 N.W. 2d 31. (Mich. App. 1997).

❖ — ❖ — ❖

Citizen May Review Teacher's Personnel File under Authority of State Public Record Law

Hovet v. Hebron Public School District

Supreme Court of North Dakota, 1988.
419 N.W.2d 189.

VANDE WALLE, Justice. Meredith Hovet appealed from a judgment of dismissal declaring his personnel file to be a public record open for inspection by the public under the provisions of Sections 44-04-18 and 15-29-10, N.D.C.C., and Article XI, Section 6, of the North Dakota Constitution. We affirm.

Hovet was employed by the Hebron Public School District (School District) as a teacher of business education and physical education during the 1986–1987 school year and had been so employed for the previous three school years. During the course of this employment a personnel file was maintained by the School District.

By a letter dated May 21, 1987, Madonna Tibor requested that the School District allow her to review Hovet's personnel file. Subsequently the superintendent for the School District agreed to provide a review of Hovet's personnel file on June 2, 1987.

Hovet then filed a complaint seeking a permanent injunction enjoining the School District from allowing the review of his personnel file by anyone other than a legal representative of the School District. At this time Hovet also sought a temporary restraining order prohibiting the review. A hearing was held and a temporary restraining order was granted. . . .

Hovet and the School District each argued that the personnel file was confidential. Tibor argued that the personnel file was a public record open to inspection. Thereafter the trial court determined that Hovet's personnel file was a public record open for inspection under Sections 44-04-18 and 15-29-10, N.D.C.C., and Article XI, Section 6, of the North Dakota Constitution. The trial court issued a judgment of dismissal. It is from this judgment that Hovet appealed. We note that the School District has aligned itself with Hovet and against Tibor on appeal.

Hovet and the School District concede that the personnel file is a governmental record, but argue that it is a record not open to public inspection because certain statutes protect a teacher's personnel file from inspection under the open-records law. The concession that the personnel file is a governmental record is based upon this court's decisions. . . .

Open governmental records in North Dakota are required by our Constitution and our statutes. Article XI, Section 6, of the North Dakota constitution provides:

> Unless otherwise provided by law, all records of public or governmental bodies, boards, bureaus, commissions, or agencies of the state or any political subdivision of the state, or organizations or agencies supported in whole or in part by public funds, or expending public funds, shall be public records, open and accessible for inspection during reasonable office hours.

Section 44-04-18, N.D.C.C., tracks and implements Article XI, Section 6. It provides:

> 1. Except as otherwise specifically provided by law, all records of public or governmental bodies, boards, bureaus, commissions or agencies of the state or any political subdivision of the state, or organizations or agencies supported in whole or in part by public funds, or expending public funds, shall be public records, open and accessible for inspection during reasonable office hours.
> 2. Violations of this section shall be punishable as an infraction.

The first argument of Hovet and the School District is that Section 15-47-38, N.D.C.C., provides an implied exception to the open-records law. Section 15-47-38 specifies the procedures to be utilized when a school board discharges a teacher or decides to not renew a teacher's contract. Among these procedures are the following: For a nonrenewal decision the reasons for nonrenewal must be drawn from specific and documented findings arising from formal reviews conducted by the board with respect to the teacher's overall performance; that such proceedings must be held in an executive session unless both parties agree to open them to the public; that no action for libel or slander shall lie for statements expressed orally or in writing at the executive sessions. Hovet and the School District argue that these procedures are designed to facilitate openness in the proceedings and to protect the teacher's reputation. They reason that opening to the public a teacher's personnel file—which would be reviewed at these proceedings—harms the above-stated goals. Thus, they conclude, an exception for teachers' personnel files from the open-records law must be implied.

This argument, however, ignores the language of the open-records law. Section 44-04-18(1), N.D.C.C., provides that all governmental records are open to the public "Except as otherwise *specifically* provided by law. . . ." (Emphasis added.) Our Code provides that "Words used in any statute are to be understood in their ordinary sense, unless a contrary intention plainly appears. . . ." The word "specific" usually is defined to mean "explicitly set forth; particular, definite." . . . This definition is opposite to the meaning of "implied," which is defined to mean "suggested, involved, or understood although not clearly or openly expressed." . . . Thus, because the open-records law provides that governmental records are to be open to the public "Except as otherwise specifically provided by law," an exception to the open-records law may not be implied. In order that a record may be excerpted from the open-records law, the Legislature must specifically address the status of that type of record—*e.g.,* statements that a certain type of record is confidential or that it is not open to the public. . . .

Thus, for an exception to the open-records law to exist under our constitutional and statutory provisions, it must be specific, i.e., the Legislature must directly address the status of the record in question, for a specific exception, by the plain terms of those provisions, may not be implied. Therefore, the contention that an exception to the open-records law for teacher personnel files should be implied from Section 15-47-38, N.D.C.C., must fail.

Hovet next alleges that he has a right to privacy guaranteed to him by the United States Constitution and the North Dakota Constitution, which will be violated if the public is allowed to inspect his personnel file. Teachers, like students, do not "shed their constitutional rights . . . at the schoolhouse gate." *Tinker v. Des Moines Community School Dist.* . . . But we rejected the claim that a governmental employee's personnel file is protected by a constitutional right to privacy in *City of Grand Forks v. Grand Forks Herald.* . . . Our position has not changed.

In *Grand Forks Herald* we decided that personnel records are not protected by the right to privacy arising under the Federal Constitution because personnel records do not concern a subject to which the Federal right to privacy has been recognized as applying. As we noted, the Federal right to privacy is limited to "cases involving governmental intrusions into matters relating to marriage, procreation, contraception, family relationships, child rearing, and education." . . .

In *Grand Forks Herald* we also refused to find that a governmental employee's personnel record was protected by a right to privacy arising from the North Dakota Constitution. We noted that there is no explicit right to privacy under our Constitution, and we declined to consider whether such a right to privacy could be inferred under our Constitution. Even if a right to privacy existed under our Constitution, there would be no right of privacy "in a personnel record of a person employed by a public agency. . . ." 307 N.W.2d at 580. [VandeWalle, J., concurring specially.] A teacher's personnel file has not been shown to be different from the personnel files of other governmental employees. Therefore, we reject Hovet's argument.

We recognize that Hovet and the School District have raised some strong public-policy arguments for the exception of teacher personnel records from the open-records law. However, as the trial court noted, "such policy considerations are for the legislature, and the courts must apply the law as it exists." . . .

The judgment is affirmed. . . .

CASE NOTES

1. *Public Records.* Florida statute defines public records as

all documents, papers, letters, maps, books, tapes, photographs, films, sound recordings or other material, regardless of physical form or characteristics, made or received pursuant to law or ordinance or in connection with the transaction of official business by any agency. Section 119.011 (1), West's Florida Statutes Annotated.

In holding that the transcript of a dismissal proceeding, held by a school board to determine the fitness of a school administrator, must be released on request of a newspaper, the Supreme Court of Iowa said that, as a method of public policy, "Disclosure is favored over non-disclosure, and exemptions from disclosure are to be strictly construed and granted sparingly." *Board of Directors of Davenport Community School District v. Quad City Times,* 382 N.W.2d 80 (Iowa 1986).

2. Where a public records statute provided that "records of any executive session may remain secret as long as publication may defeat purposes of the executive session, but no longer," the court held that closed-session minutes of a hearing charging sexual harassment of an employee must be released on request to the newspaper after the employee had resigned. The court said:

> The lawful purposes of the executive sessions called by the school committee were to discuss the litigation that the school committee was engaged in with the director. By the time this case was filed, the director had resigned, and the litigation was terminated. Thus, the lawful purposes, . . . for which the executive sessions were held were no longer extant.

One is likely to be perplexed with this result because the minutes may have continuing harmful effects on the employee. In this case, however, the trial judge concluded that the purpose of the executive session was not to discuss or preserve the employee's reputation, but rather to consider complaints or charges brought against the employee. *Foudy v. Amherst-Pelham Regional School Committee,* 402 Mass. 179, 521 N.E.2d 391 (1988).

3. A request was made to review a teacher's personnel file, in particular the college transcript of the teacher. The court ruled that the Family Educational Rights and Privacy Act did not protect the transcript. Also the teacher's right to privacy under the federal Constitution was rejected, and the Texas open records law

required disclosure of the transcript. *Klein Independent School District v. Mattox,* 830 F.2d 576 (5th Cir.1987).

ENDNOTES

1. Aristotle, *The Politics,* trans. T. A. Sinclair, revised and re-presented by Trevor J. Saunders (London: Penguin Books, 1981), p. 54.

2. John Finnis, *Natural Law and Natural Rights* (Oxford: Clarendon Press, 1980), p. 138.

3. John Rawls, *Political Liberalism* (New York: Columbia University Press, 1993), p. 212.

4. Ibid., p. 213.

5. Ibid.

6. Ibid.

7. State Tax Commission v. Board of Education of Jefferson County, 235 Ala. 388, 179 So. 197 (1938).

8. Board of Education v. Stoddard, 294 N.Y. 667, 60 N.E.2d 757 (1945).

9. Moore v. Board of Education, 212 N.C. 499, 193 S.E. 732 (1937).

10. Child Welfare Society of Flint v. Kennedy School District, 220 Mich. 290, 189 N.W. 1002 (1922).

11. Board of Education of Aberdeen-Huntington Local School District v. State Board of Education, 116 Ohio App. 515, 189 N.E.2d 81 (1962).

12. Campbell v. Aldrich, 159 Or. 208, 79 P.2d 257 (1938), appeal dismissed 305 U.S. 559, 59 S.Ct. 87 (1938).

13. Leeper v. State, 103 Tenn. 500, 53 S.W. 962 (1899).

14. Hannibal and St. J. Railroad Co. v. Husen, 95 U.S. (5 Otto) 465 (1877).

15. Leroy J. Peteron, Richard A. Rossmiller, and Marlin M. Volz, *The Law and Public School Operation* (New York: Harper & Row Publishers, 1978), p. 90.

16. *Halstead v. Rozmiarek,* 167 Neb. 652, 94 N.W.2d 37 (1959).

17. People v. Draper, 15 N.Y. 532 (1857).

18. See Newton Edwards, *The Courts and the Public Schools* (University of Chicago Press, 1955), p. 27; also, Commonwealth v. Hartman, 17 Pa. 118 (1851); Moseley v. Welch, 209 S.C. 19, 39 S.E.2d 133 (1946); Board of Education of Chicago v. Upham, 357 Ill. 263, 191 N.E. 876 (1934); Board of Education v. State Board of Education, 116 Ohio App. 515, 189 N.E.2d 81 (1962); Associated Schools of Independent District No. 63 v. School District No. 83 of Renville County, 122 Minn. 254, 142 N.W. 325 (1913).

19. Edwards, *The Courts and the Public Schools,* p. 28.

20. See Helena Elementary School District No. 1 v. State, 236 Mont. 44, 769 P.2d 684 (1989); Rose v. Council for Better Education, Inc., 790 S.W.2d 186 (Ky.1989); Edgewood Independent School District v. Kirby, 777 S.W.2d 391 (Tex.1989). These school finance cases are discussed in more detail in Chapter 18 in this book; Affirmed as modified, 236 Mont. 44, 784 P.2d 412.

21. William E. Thro, "The Third Wave: The Impact of the Montana, Kentucky and Texas Decisions on the Future of Public School Finance Reform Litigation," *Journal of Law and Education* 19, no. 2 (Spring 1990): p. 240.

22. Seattle School Dist. No. 1 v. State, 90 Wn.2d 476, 511–513, 514, 585 P.2d 71, 91–92 (1978).

23. Tyska by Tyska v. Board of Education, 117 Ill.App.3d 917, 73 Ill.Dec. 209, 453 N.E.2d 1344 (1983).

24. Louis L. Jaffe, Essay on Delegation of Legislative Power 47 *Col.L.Rev.* 359, 361 (1947).

25. Attorney General v. Lowrey, 131 Mich. 639, 92 N.W. 289 (1902).

26. MacQueen v. City Com'n of City of Port Huron, 194 Mich. 328, 160 N.W. 627 (1916).

27. Board of Educ. Louisville v. Society of Alumni of Louisville Male High School, 239 S.W.2d 931 (Ky.1951).

28. School District No. 1, Multnomah County v. Bruck, 225 Or. 496, 358 P.2d 283 (1960).

29. Goodman v. School District No. 1, 32 F.2d 586 (8th Cir. 1929).

30. Hallett v. Post Printing & Publishing Co., 68 Colo. 573, 192 P. 658 (1920).

31. McGilvra v. Seattle School District No. 1, 113 Wash. 619, 194 P. 817 (1921).

32. Jarrett v. Goodall, 113 W.Va. 478, 168 S.E. 763 (1933).

33. Brine v. City of Cambridge, 265 Mass. 452, 164 N.E. 619 (1929).

34. Kenneth Culp Davis, *Administrative Law Treatise*, vol. 1 (St. Paul, Minn.: West Publishing Company, 1958), p. 5.

35. Ibid. p. 102.

36. John Locke, *Two Treatises of Civil Government*, Book 2, Ch. 11, Sec. 141.

37. Osius v. City of St. Clair Shores, 344 Mich. 693, 75 N.W.2d 25 (1956).

38. Davis, *Administrative Law Treatise*, p. 103.

39. Ward v. Scott, 11 N.J. 117, 93 A.2d 385 (1952).

40. Ibid.

41. State v. Kinnear, 70 Wn.2d 482, 423 P.2d 937 (1967).

42. School District No. 3 of Town of Adams v. Callahan, 237 Wis. 560, 297 N.W. 407 (1941).

43. Schinck v. Board of Education of Westwood Consolidated School Dist., 60 N.J.Super. 448, 159 A.2d 396 (1960).

44. Jokinen v. Allen, 15 Misc.2d 124, 182 N.Y.S.2d 166 (1958).

45. Bowles v. Willingham, 321 U.S. 503, 64 S.Ct. 641 (1944).

46. S.A. de Smith, *Judicial Review of Administrative Action* (London: Stevens & Sons, 1973), p. 60.

47. Fremont RE-1 School District v. Jacobs, 737 P.2d 816 (Colo.1987).

48. Robert F. Will, *State Education, Structure and Organization* (United States Department of Health, Education and Welfare, United States Office of Education, 1964), pp. 8–10.

49. Laba v. Board of Education of Newark, 23 N.J. 364, 129 A.2d 273 (1957).

50. In re Masiello, 25 N.J. 590, 138 A.2d 393 (1958).

51. R. v. Roberts, 2 K.B. 695 (1924). See also Kern Alexander, "Administrative Prerogative: Restraints of Natural Justice on Student Discipline," *Journal of Law and Education* 7, no. 3 (July 1978): pp. 331–58.

52. Joseph Raz, *The Morality of Freedom* (Oxford: Clarendon Press, 1986), p. 113.

53. Lloyd L. Weinreb, *Natural Law and Justice* (Cambridge, Mass.: Harvard University Press, 1987), p. 166.

54. Hortonville Joint School District No. 1 v. Hortonville Education Association, 426 U.S. 482, 96 S.Ct. 2308 (1976).

55. A. H. Andrews Co. v. Delight Special School District, 95 Ark. 26, 128 S.W. 361 (1910).

56. Edwards, *The Courts and the Public Schools*, p. 147.

57. Knox County Board of Education v. Fultz, 241 Ky. 265, 43 S.W.2d 707 (1931); Lyerley v. Manila School District 15, 214 Ark. 245, 215 S.W.2d 733 (1948); Board of Education v. County Board of School Trustees, 25 Ill.App.2d 390, 166 N.E.2d 472 (1960); Detroit Edison Co. v. East China Township School District No. 3, 366 Mich. 638, 115 N.W.2d 298 (1962); School District No. 12, Phillips County v. Hughes, 170 Mont. 267, 552 P.2d 328 (1976).

58. Board of Education of City of New York v. Allen, 6 N.Y.2d 127, 188 N.Y.S.2d 515, 160 N.E.2d 60 (1959).

59. Board of Education v. County Board of School Trustees, 32 Ill.App.2d 1, 176 N.E.2d 633 (1961).

60. de Smith, *Judicial Review of Administrative Action*, p. 283.

61. Ibid., pp. 288, 289.

62. Ibid., p. 279.

63. Bristol Virginia School Board v. Quarles, 235 Va. 108, 119–20, 366 S.E.2d 82, 89 (1988).

64. Wood v. Board of Supervisors of Halifax County, 236 Va. 104, 372 S.E.2d 611 (1988).

65. Shelmadine v. City of Elkhart, 75 Ind.App. 493, 129 N.E. 878 (1921).

66. Main v. Claremont Unified School District, 161 Cal.App.2d 189, 326 P.2d 573 (1958).

67. Maddox v. State, 220 Ark. 762, 249 S.W.2d 972 (1952).

68. Constitution of Indiana, Art. 2, §9.

69. People v. Becker, 112 Cal.App.2d 324, 246 P.2d 103 (1952).

70. State ex rel. Robinson v. Keefe, 111 Fla. 701, 149 So. 638 (1933).

71. Green v. Jones, 144 W.Va. 276, 108 S.E.2d 1 (1959).

72. Leech v. State, 78 Ind. 570 (1881).

73. People v. Reinberg, 263 Ill. 536, 105 N.E. 715 (1914).

74. Commonwealth v. Fahey, 156 Pa.Super. 254, 40 A.2d 167 (1944).

75. 328 U.S. 549, 66 S.Ct. 1198 (1946).

76. Ibid.

77. 369 U.S. 186, 82 S.Ct. 691 (1962).

78. Hadley v. Junior College District of Metropolitan Kansas City, Mo., 397 U.S. 50, 90 S.Ct. 791 (1970).

79. Conover v. Board of Education, 1 Utah 2d 375, 267 P.2d 768 (1954).

80. Morning Call v. Board of School Directors, 164 Pa. Cmwlth. 263, 642 A.2d 619 (1994).

81. Ibid.

82. McCemas v. Board of Educ. of Fayette Co., 475 S.E. 2d 280 (W.Va. 1996).

83. Hackworth v. Board of Education for the City of Atlanta, 214 Ga.App.17, 447 S.E.2d 78 (1994).

84. Kansas City Star Co. v. Fulson, 859 S.W.2d 934 (Mo.App.W.D. 1993).

85. Ibid., p. 940.

86. Ibid.

87. Ibid.

88. Dallas Morning News Company v. Board of Trustees of Dallas Independent School District, 861 S.W.2d 532 (Tex.App.1993).

89. Board of Trustees v. Freedom of Information Commission, 181 Conn. 544, 436 A.2d 266 (1980).

CHAPTER 5

CHURCH AND STATE

Believing with you that religion is a matter which lies solely between man and his God, that he owes account to none other for his faith or his worship, that the legislative powers of government reach actions only, and not opinions, I contemplate with sovereign reverence that act of the whole American people which declared that their legislature should "make no law respecting an establishment of religion, or prohibiting the free exercise thereof," thus building a wall of separation between church and State.

—Thomas Jefferson, reply to
Danbury Baptists, Connecticut, January 1, 1802

CHAPTER OUTLINE

- WALL OF SEPARATION
- RELIGIOUS INTOLERANCE
- COLONIAL ESTABLISHMENTS
- RELIGIOUS ASSESSMENTS
- CHURCH OPPOSITION TO SCHOOLS OF THE REPUBLIC
- THE PUBLIC SCHOOL AND RELIGION
- PUBLIC TAXATION TO SUPPORT RELIGIOUS SCHOOLS
- THE ESTABLISHMENT CLAUSE AND THE *LEMON* TEST

- ANTIESTABLISHMENT PROVISIONS IN STATE CONSTITUTIONS
- RELEASED TIME FOR RELIGIOUS INSTRUCTION
- SECULARIZATION OF PUBLIC SCHOOLS: PRAYER AND BIBLE READING
- STUDENT-INITIATED RELIGIOUS SPEECH
- EQUAL ACCESS ACT
- FACILITIES
- FLAG SALUTE

REPORTS OF RELIGIOUS CONFLICTS worldwide are emblazoned across the front pages and covers of major newspapers and magazines in virtually every edition. Religious and ethnic cleansing, genocide, and the expulsion of peoples in the name of religion are today standard fare in daily news accounts. Palestine, Ireland, Armenia, Bosnia, Indonesia, Pakistan, Iran, Turkey, and Egypt—the list of trouble spots is virtually endless. Religious discord is the most volatile and historically the most insoluble issue facing world peace. The magnitude and frequency of religious strife are so great that those who are not directly involved tend to be desensitized to the consequences, most of which are brutal violations of moral standards and human rights. *The Economist* magazine has called this increasing religious militancy "a Crisis of Conscience,"[1] with primary reference to Bosnia, Croatia, and Serbia, but with generalized implications for religious strife in many lands.

Nor is this religious intolerance restricted to foreign and remote lands. As we have seen lately, religious fanaticism has bred dire and sorrowful problems in our own country, as witnessed by the debacle at Waco and the bombing of the World Trade Center in New York. In the United States, there has been a recent and dramatic shift by large and prominent religious groups toward the view that "religiously trained professionals should exert spiritual influence over the secular matters of government."[2] Cox, a professor of religion at Harvard, has explained, in an article entitled "The Warring Visions of the Religious Right," the theological bases for the emergence of this new wave of Christian fundamentalism and its political implications at both the state and the federal levels. This fundamentalism argues that those with "Judeo-Christian" values are best qualified "to rule" and should be given their "rightful place of leadership at the top of the world" before world peace can or should be restored. This doctrine has been given increasing credence in legislative halls.[3] All of this is not new, but with new momentum religious fundamentalism has recently reached out in efforts to control both state legislatures and the U.S. Congress, materially affecting the nature and structure of public schools in America. The court cases bearing on efforts by various religious groups to use tax monies to enhance religious schools, coupled with efforts to introduce sectarianism into the activities of public schools, reflect the multiplication and magnification of this religious discord surrounding public schools.

This chapter is about the struggle for liberty of conscience and the requirements on the public schools in maintaining neutrality in matters of religion.

■ WALL OF SEPARATION

In 1879, the Supreme Court in *Reynolds v. United States*[4] first invoked Jefferson's famous dictum, calling for the erection of a "wall of separation between church and state." More than a century

of judicial struggle has resulted in precious little resolution of the church and state conflict. In fact, it appears that the plethora of litigation over the years has merely tended to obscure the boundaries of separation envisaged by Jefferson. Indeed, lately it seems that the vision of separation, the foundational premise[5] of religious freedom, may be becoming so obscure as to have undiscernible contours and boundaries. Indeed, the newer members of the Supreme Court will most likely reflect the position of Chief Justice Rehnquist, who in dissent in *Wallace v. Jaffree* roundly condemned the idea and desirability of a "wall of separation," saying that it is "a metaphor based on bad history, a metaphor which has proved useless as a guide to judging," and that it "should be frankly and explicitly abandoned."[6]

Thus, the issue of separation and the interrelationship between religion and government retains its characteristic preeminence as a divisive issue in American society. To better understand the problem requires a brief look backward to the antecedents of the church-state issues touching the schools of this country. Centuries of religious strife in Europe left an indelible mark on the minds of the fathers of the American Constitution. Controversy over religion has not abated and today causes as much international and domestic discord as it did a thousand years ago. The diversity of religious backgrounds among the American colonies was so great, and religious sentiments so deep, that representatives at the Constitutional Convention in Philadelphia in 1787 were loath to address the issue lest the convention founder on the shoals of religious dissension. Avoidance was implicitly agreed upon by all, and everyone more or less adopted the position of John Adams, who assumed that if the issue was not mentioned, both the state and religion would be best served. Adams expressed the hope that "Congress will never meddle with religion further than to say their own prayers, and to fast and to give thanks once a year."[7]

Some believed that simple omission was not the appropriate solution to the religious dilemma, and although it was not acted upon by the convention, Pinckney of South Carolina sought to make the absence of congressional power in religion explicit by proposing that the new constitution provide that "the legislature of the United

States shall pass no law on the subject of religion."[8] Even though no general religious provision was acted upon, there is little doubt that the failure resulted from the delegates' firm belief that such a provision was not necessary to preserve religious liberty. While no general religious separation provision was thought to be needed, the convention did decide to specifically prohibit states from imposing religious tests for federal office. Madison explained that it might be implied that "without [an] exception, a power would have been given to impose an oath involving religious test as a qualification for office."[9] Obviously, it was in the interest of the central government to prevent states with different religious ties from requiring religious tests for federal office. With cognizance of this, the convention adopted Pinckney's motion that "no religious test shall ever be required as a qualification to any office or public trust under the United States"; this became the last clause of Article VI in the Constitution.

Thus, when the Constitution was ratified by the states, only the "religious test" of office provision was included, and no other reference was made regarding religious toleration. This omission was not taken lightly when the states were called upon to ratify the document. Six states ratified but proposed amendments guaranteeing religious liberty, and two other states, North Carolina and Rhode Island, refused to ratify until a bill of rights including religious freedom was promulgated.[10] Although Madison defended the omission, saying that "the government has no jurisdiction over [religion],"[11] it was argued by others that there was no security for the rights of conscience. Jefferson ultimately convinced Madison that a religious provision in a bill of rights was necessary. Commenting on the proposed constitution in a letter to Madison from Paris, where Jefferson was serving as ambassador, he said:

> I will now add what I do not like. First, the omission of a bill of rights providing clearly and without the aid of sophisms for freedom of religion, freedom of the press, protection against monopolies, the external and unremitting force of the habeas corpus laws, and trials by juries. . . . [A] bill of rights is what the people are entitled to against every government on earth, general or particular, and what no just government should refuse or rest on inference.[12]

The very uncertainty itself of whether such rights were implied in the Constitution was evidence enough that a bill of rights protecting religious freedom and ensuring disestablishment was necessary. Madison, with Jefferson's urging and his own experience in persuading the states to ratify only after promising amendments as specific affirmation of individual rights and freedoms, stated that he now favored amendments to provide for "all essential rights, particularly the rights of Conscience in the fullest latitude, the freedom of the press, trial by jury, etc."[13] In accordance with this position, Madison introduced to the House of Representatives, in 1789, a compilation of proposals for amendments that he maintained would prevent encroachments by the sovereign power into individual rights and liberties. Madison's proposals before the House were to finally become the Bill of Rights, which was approved by the requisite number of states in 1791. Prominent among these rights was the separation of church and state provision, which guaranteed religious freedom and prohibited establishment of religion by government. The First Amendment states:

Congress shall make no law respecting an establishment of religion, or prohibiting the free exercise thereof; or abridging the freedom of speech, or of the press; or the right of the people peaceably to assemble and to petition the Government for a redress of grievances.

■ RELIGIOUS INTOLERANCE

Much of the history of Western civilization has had its basis in religious controversy. Disputes between tribal chiefs and priests were fertile ground for discord that materially affected both church and state. In more primitive eras, the state did not attempt to delineate religious and secular activities, with some polytheistic societies merely cataloging and assigning gods to a particular divine hierarchy, as in the Code of Hammurabi.[14] In most instances, the state and religion were entwined in the interests and affairs of the day, but it was very clear that of the two forces, the state was supreme. In ancient Greece, the head of state was also chief priest and served as the supreme guardian of the religion. As the Athenian republic became well established, the unity of religion with state continued.[15]

Rome, too, was originally a state of many gods, with the innovation that great heads of state, upon death, were placed among the ranks of the gods.[16] So long as there were many gods to worship and everyone recognized the state was supreme, little conflict developed; however, with the advent of Christianity, full-fledged discord became apparent. Christians subscribed to a dogmatic exclusiveness that was not tolerated by the Romans. Religious persecution of Christians began with Nero, with the justification that they were "enemies of mankind" and "arsonists," conveniently serving as scapegoats for the burning of Rome.[17] Persecution continued until 312 or 313 A.D., when Constantine issued the Edict of Milan, a document of great importance in religious history, providing "that liberty of worship shall not be denied to any, but that the mind and will of every individual shall be free to manage divine affairs according to his own choice."[18] From this point on, the Christian religion became dominant, as Constantine adopted it as a primary means of consolidating his empire.[19]

In the centuries that followed, the Christian church gained power and authority, to the point that it became quite clear that the church was supreme over any head of state. The strength of the church was demonstrated by Pope Gelasius I in 496, when he proclaimed to the emperor:

> There are two things, most august emperor, by which this world is chiefly ruled: the sacred authority of the priesthood and the royal power. Of these two the priests carry the greater weight, because they will have to render account in the divine judgment even for the kings of men.[20]

Although Christianity had, under the Romans, been the oppressed, when it gained dominion, it became the oppressor, and little tolerance was exhibited. Augustine strongly advanced the conviction that the civil power of the state should be used to suppress dissidents of the church. Compulsion was the watchword, and Augustine espoused the belief that "freedom to err" was the worst killer of the soul. In keeping with that philosophy, "the Medieval Church was intolerant, was the source and author of persecution, justified and defended the most violent measures which could be taken against those who differed from it."[21]

From this basis, the development of medieval Europe was a continual struggle between church and state, with kings rebelling against the church and the sword of the state being readily put to use to stamp out heretics and nonconformists.

While most people are aware of the centuries of intolerance on the European continent, the most extreme example of which is probably the Spanish Inquisition, our more direct church-state antecedents derive from English origins. With the Reformation, problems of church and state were compounded as new religious doctrines were advanced and various ideologies began to emerge as separate and viable religions. Intolerance prevailed, whether Catholics or Protestants were in power. Henry VIII's conflict with Rome blossomed into bloody internal strife as Edward VI, Mary, and Elizabeth took the throne and in succession persecuted religious opponents. For her deeds, Mary is remembered in history as Bloody Mary. During Elizabeth's long reign, the Church of England was firmly established as the state religion, and the supremacy of the state over the church was complete. Ecclesiastical offices were regulated by her proclamations, and opposing religious viewpoints were not tolerated. From this point in England, there existed a church that was Protestant in nature and entirely subject to state authority and control. Intra-Protestant struggles developed, and internal Protestant religious peace was not actually achieved in England until 1689 with the Act of Toleration.

Even though the great religious wars of Europe were not of the same era as the formation of the Constitution of the United States, the strife of the Old World was still much in our forefathers' minds. The Supreme Court of the United States has best expressed the situation:

> The centuries immediately before and contemporaneous with the colonization of America had been filled with turmoil, civil strife, and persecution, generated in large part by established sects determined to maintain their absolute political and religious supremacy. With the power of government to support them, at various times and places, Catholics had persecuted Protestants, Protestants had persecuted Catholics, Protestant sects had persecuted other Protestant sects, Catholics of one shade of belief had persecuted Catholics of another shade of belief, and all of these had from time to time persecuted Jews.[22]

When the matter of religion was to be considered in 1787, there were essentially three rationalizations for church-state relationships that had arisen out of the Reformation: the Erastian (named after the German philosopher Erastus), the theocratic, and the separatist. Dominant among these was the Erastian view, which assumed state superiority over ecclesiastical affairs and used religion to further the interests of the state. It was during the Elizabethan era in England that the Erastian philosophy was fully implemented. The second, the theocratic, was founded in the idea that the church is supreme and the state should be used to further ecclesiastical policy. Third, complete separation was advanced as the proper course by minority dissident groups in Europe, but it did not find full expression until 1791 in America.[23] It was, however, John Locke on whom both Madison and Jefferson relied for their basic philosophical ideas concerning separation. In his *Letter Concerning Toleration*, Locke maintained that "[t]he care of souls cannot belong to the civil magistrate because his power consists only in outward force, but true and saving religion consists in the inward persuasion of the mind."[24]

Locke's ideas were developed and expanded under fire in the great dispute in Virginia over the established religion that had been carefully protected by statutes promulgated by the Anglican Church until the Revolution. These laws provided for religious services according to the laws and orders of the Church of England: compulsory attendance at religious services, regulation of nonconformists, glebe lands for support of the clergy, and a system of governmentally sanctioned vestries empowered to levy tithes for upkeep of the church and ministers' salaries.

■ COLONIAL ESTABLISHMENTS

The colonies during the seventeenth and eighteenth centuries reflected the precedent of single-church establishments of Europe. While the intensity of the force of the preferred church varied among the colonies, there nevertheless existed strong and unquestioned establishments of the Congregational Church in New England—Massachusetts, Connecticut, and New Hampshire—and of the Anglican Church in the South—Virginia, North Carolina, and South Carolina. Another group of colonies—New York, New Jersey, Maryland, and Georgia—evolved through periods of preference for different churches, and tax support for Protestant churches, as the population changed. In New York, for example, the Dutch Reformed Church was initially established, but as the colony grew, a heterogeneous group of other believers entered, including Calvinists, Lutherans, Mennonites, Quakers, Catholics, and Jews. When the English took over New Netherland and it became New York, the inclinations of the Stuarts toward Catholicism forced more toleration for all religious groups. The ultimate effect was that, by 1693, New York, while Anglican, was reasonably tolerant toward Catholics and generally provided tax support for all Protestant ministries.[25] Because the religious preference of New York was largely unclear, a battle raged for years between the royal governors and the Anglican clergy, who demanded the clear and certain establishment of the Church of England. The policy ultimately became one of multiple establishment, whereby a variety of churches were provided funding by the state.

A fourth group of colonies—Pennsylvania, Delaware, and Rhode Island—had a large measure of religious freedom, which generally prevailed from their origins. Pennsylvania advanced a toleration that generally followed William Penn's philosophy as expounded in his *Frame of Government*, promoting freedom of religion.[26] Delaware broke off from Pennsylvania in 1702 and continued this policy of religious freedom and the prohibition of use of public funds for church purposes.

But Rhode Island, under Roger Williams, was the prototype of religious tolerance that came ultimately to prevail. From the time that Williams landed in Massachusetts in 1631, conflict developed with the Puritan establishment. Because of his insistence on separation of civil and ecclesiastical aspects of society, Williams was banished in 1635. In 1636, he formed a plantation in Rhode Island territory, and in 1643, a patent was obtained from Charles I to form a new colony. Williams's ideas regarding the separation of church and state were predominant in Rhode Island, evolving from four basic theses: (1) attempts by the state to enforce religious orthodoxy produce persecution and religious wars and pervert God's plan for the regeneration of souls; (2) God has not blessed a particular form of government, and governments will vary with the nature of the people governed; (3) political and religious diversity cannot be avoided; and (4) the human conscience must be totally free, through religious freedom and the separation of church and state.[27] These ideas were elaborated in Williams's *Bloudy Tenet of Persecution* in 1644.

Williams's ideas undoubtedly influenced the American attitude toward disestablishment that became prevalent after the war for independence, but Williams's legacy apparently had little carryover on those who formed the new federal Constitution in 1787 and the subsequent First Amendment.[28]

■ RELIGIOUS ASSESSMENTS

Jefferson, more than any other person, led in enunciating and implementing the separation principle. In 1776, while he was in Philadelphia writing the Declaration of Independence, he drafted a proposed constitution for Virginia that stated: "All persons shall have full and free liberty of religious opinion; nor shall any be compelled to frequent or maintain any religious institution."[29] Although this particular measure was not passed, it nevertheless set the tone for religious freedom for Virginia in the era to come. In spite of Jefferson's position, however, in 1779 a bill was introduced in the Virginia legislature declaring that "the Christian Religion shall in all times coming be deemed and held to be the established Religion of the Commonwealth."[30] It required every person to enroll his or her name with the county clerk and designate the society that he or she intended to support, whereupon the clerk would present the roll for the appropriate religious group to determine assessment rates; these were then collected by the sheriff, and the proceeds were turned over to the church. Persons failing to enroll in a religious society had their payments spread across all religious groups.[31]

In 1784, the bill was called up for a vote. Entitled a Bill Establishing a Provision for Teachers of the Christian Religion, it was sponsored by Patrick Henry. Although the bill was defeated, from the preceding and ensuing

debate, two of the most important documents in religious freedom were written, Jefferson's Bill for Establishing Religious Freedom and Madison's *Memorial and Remonstrance against Religious Assessments.* Jefferson's bill was written and introduced in the Virginia General Assembly in 1779 but was not enacted into law until January 1786.

Madison's *Memorial,* in opposition to Henry's bill for religious assessments, was of great historical significance. The philosophy stated therein has often been referred to by the U.S. Supreme Court in support of its opinions. The *Memorial* presents several arguments against the religious assessment bill, but more important, it conveys a philosophy of separation that, along with Jefferson's, provided the logic and rationale for the "wall of separation" provisions of the First Amendment in 1791.

An Act for Establishing Religious Freedom, Thomas Jefferson

Written and introduced in 1779, enacted in 1786.

Well aware that Almighty God hath created the mind free; that all attempts to influence it by temporal punishments or burdens, or by civil incapacitations, tend only to beget habits of hypocrisy and meanness, and are a departure from the plan of the Holy Author of our religion, who being Lord both of body and mind, yet chose not to propagate it by coercions on either, as was in his Almighty power to do;

That the impious presumption of legislators and rulers, civil as well as ecclesiastical, who, being themselves but fallible and uninspired men, have assumed dominion over the faith of others, setting up their own opinions and modes of thinking as the only true and infallible, and as such endeavoring to impose them on others, hath established and maintained false religions over the greatest part of the world, and through all time;

That to compel a man to furnish contributions of money for the propagation of opinions which he disbelieves, is sinful and tyrannical; that even the forcing him to support this or that teacher of his own religious persuasion, is depriving him of the comfortable liberty of giving his contributions to the particular pastor whose morals he would make his pattern, and whose power he feels most persuasive to righteousness, and is withdrawing from the ministry those temporal rewards, which proceeding from an approbation of their personal conduct, are an additional incitement to earnest and unremitting labors for the instruction of mankind;

That our civil rights have no dependence on our religious opinions, any more than our opinions in physics or geometry; that, therefore, the proscribing any citizen as unworthy of the public confidence by laying upon him an incapacity of being called to the offices of trust and emolument, unless he profess or renounce this or that religious opinion, is depriving him injuriously of those privileges and advantages to which in common with his fellow citizens he has a natural right;

That it tends also to corrupt the principles of that very religion it is meant to encourage, by bribing, with a monopoly of worldly honors and emoluments, those who will externally profess and conform to it; that though indeed these are criminal who do not withstand such temptation, yet neither are those innocent who lay the bait in their way;

That to suffer the civil magistrate to intrude his powers into the field of opinion and to restrain the profession or propagation of principles, on the supposition of their ill tendency, is a dangerous fallacy, which at once destroys all religious liberty, because he being of course judge of that tendency, will make his opinions the rule of judgment, and approve or condemn the sentiments of others only as they shall square with or differ from his own;

That it is time enough for the rightful purposes of civil government, for its officers to interfere when principles break out into overt acts against peace and good order;

And finally, that truth is great and will prevail if left to herself, that she is the proper and sufficient antagonist to error, and has nothing to fear from the conflict, unless by human interposition disarmed of her natural weapons, free argument and debate, errors ceasing to be dangerous when it is permitted freely to contradict them.

Be it therefore enacted by the General Assembly, That no man shall be compelled to frequent or support any religious worship, place or ministry whatsoever, nor shall be enforced, restrained, molested, or burthened in his body or goods, nor shall otherwise suffer on account of his religious opinions or belief; but that all men shall be free to profess, and by argument to maintain, their opinions in matters of religion, and that the same shall in nowise diminish, enlarge, or affect their civil capacities.

And though we well know this Assembly, elected by the people for the ordinary purposes of legislation only, have no power to restrain the acts of succeeding assemblies, constituted with the powers equal to our own, and that therefore to declare this act irrevocable, would be of no effect in law, yet we are free to declare, and do declare, that their rights hereby asserted are of the natural rights of mankind, and that if any act shall be hereafter passed to repeal the present or to narrow its operation, such act will be an infringement of natural right.

Memorial and Remonstrance against Religious Assessments, James Madison

1785.

To the Honorable General Assembly of the Commonwealth of Virginia. A Memorial and Remonstrance.

We, the subscribers, citizens of the said Commonwealth, having taken into serious consideration, a Bill printed by order of the last Session of General Assembly, entitled "A Bill establishing a provision for teachers of the Christian Religion," and conceiving that the same, if finally armed with the sanctions of a law, will be a dangerous abuse of power, are bound as faithful members of a free State, to remonstrate against it, and to declare the reasons by which we are determined. We remonstrate against the said Bill,

Because we hold it for a fundamental and undeniable truth, "that religion, or the duty which we owe to our Creator, and the manner of discharging it, can be directed only by reason and conviction, not by force or violence."[32] The Religion then of every man must be left to the conviction and conscience of every man; and it is the right of every man to exercise it as these may dictate. This right is in its nature an unalienable right. . . .

Because, it is proper to take alarm at the first experiment on our liberties. We hold this prudent jealousy to be the first duty of citizens, and one of [the] noblest characteristics of the late Revolution. The freemen of America did not wait till usurped power had strengthened itself by exercise, and entangled the question in precedents. They saw all the consequences in the principle, and they avoided the consequences by denying the principle. We reverse this lesson too much, soon to forget it. Who does not see that the same authority which can establish Christianity, in exclusion of all other Religions, may establish with the same ease any particular sect of Christians, in exclusion of all other Sects? That the same authority which can force a citizen to contribute three pence only of his property for the support of any one establishment, may force him to conform to any other establishment in all cases whatsoever?

Because, the bill violates that equality which ought to be the basis of every law, and which is more indispensable, in proportion as the validity or expediency of any law is more liable to be impeached. If "all men are by nature equally free and independent,"[33] all men are to be considered as entering into Society on equal conditions; as relinquishing no more, and therefore retaining no less, one than another, of their natural rights. Above all are they to be considered as retaining an "equal title to the free exercise of Religion according to the dictates of conscience."[34] Whilst we assert for ourselves a freedom to embrace, to profess and to observe the Religion which we believe to be of divine origin, we cannot deny an equal freedom to those whose minds have not yet yielded to the evidence which has convinced us. If this freedom be abused, it is an offense, against God, not against man: To God, therefore, not to men, must an account of it be rendered. As the Bill violates equality by subjecting some to peculiar burdens; so it violates the same principle, by granting to others peculiar exemptions. Are the Quakers and Menonists the only sects who think a compulsive support of their religions unnecessary and unwarrantable? Can their piety alone be entrusted with the care of public worship? Ought their Religions to be endowed above all others, with extraordinary privileges, by which proselytes may be enticed from all others? We think too favorably of the justice and good sense of these denominations, to believe that they either covet preeminencies over their fellow citizens, or that they will be seduced by them, from the common opposition to the measure. . . .

What influence in fact have ecclesiastical establishments had on Civil Society? In some instances they have been seen to erect a spiritual tyranny on the ruins of Civil authority; in many instances they have been seen upholding the thrones of political tyranny; in no instance have they been seen the guardians of the liberties of the people. Rulers who wished to subvert the public liberties, may have found an established clergy convenient auxiliaries. A just government, instituted to secure and perpetuate it, needs them not. Such a government will be best supported by protecting every citizen in the enjoyment of his Religion with the same equal hand which protects his person and his property; by neither invading the equal rights by any Sect, nor suffering any Sect to invade those of another.

Because the proposed establishment is a departure from that generous policy, which offering an asylum to the persecuted and oppressed of every Nation and Religion, promised a lustre to our country, an accession to the number of its citizens. What a melancholy mark is the Bill of sudden degeneracy? Instead of holding forth an asylum to the persecuted, it is itself a signal of persecution. It degrades from the equal rank of citizens all those whose opinions in Religion do not bend to those of the Legislative authority. Distant as it may be, in its present form, from the Inquisition it differs from it only in degree. The one is the first step, the other the last in the career of intolerance. . . .

Because, it will destroy that moderation and harmony which the forbearance of our laws to intermeddle with Religion, has produced amongst its several sects. Torrents of blood have been spilt in the old World, by vain attempts of the secular arm to extinguish Religious discord, by proscribing all difference in Religious opinions. Time has at length revealed the true remedy. Every relaxation of narrow and rigorous policy, wherever it has been tried, has been found to assuage the disease. The American Theatre has exhibited proofs, that equal and complete liberty, if it does not wholly eradicate it, sufficiently destroys its malignant influence on the health and prosperity of the State. If with the salutary effects of this system under our own eyes, we begin to contract the bonds of Religious freedom, we know no name that will too severely reproach our folly. At least let warning be taken at the first fruit of the threatened innovation. The very appearance of the Bill has transformed that "Christian forbearance,[35] love and charity," which of late mutually prevailed, into animosities and jealousies, which may not soon be appeased. What mischiefs may not be dreaded should this enemy to the public quiet be armed with the force of a law? . . .

Because, finally, "the equal right of every citizen to the free exercise of his Religion according to the dictates of conscience" is held by the same tenure with all our other rights. If we recur to its origin, it is equally the gift of nature; if we weigh its importance, it cannot be less dear to us; if we consult the Declaration of those rights which pertain to the good people of Virginia, as the "basis and foundation of Government,"[36] it is enumerated with equal solemnity, or rather studied emphasis. Either then, we must say, that the will of the Legislature is the only measure of their authority; and that in the plentitude of this authority, they may sweep away all our fundamental rights; or, that they are bound to leave this particular right untouched and sacred: Either we must say, that they may control the freedom of the press, may abolish the trial by jury, may swallow up the Executive and Judiciary powers of the State; nay that they may despoil us of our very right of suffrage, and erect themselves into an independent and hereditary assembly: or we must say, that they have no authority to enact into law the Bill under consideration. We, the subscribers, say, that the General Assembly of the Commonwealth have no such authority: And that no effort may be omitted in our part against so dangerous an usurpation, we oppose to it, this remonstrance; earnestly praying, as we are in duty bound, that the Supreme Lawgiver of the Universe, by illuminating those to whom it is addressed, may on the one hand turn their councils from every act which would affront his holy prerogative, or violate the trust committed to them: and on the other, guide them into every measure which may be worthy of his [blessing, may re]dound to their own praise, and may establish more firmly the liberties, the prosperity, and the Happiness of the Commonwealth.

■ CHURCH OPPOSITION TO SCHOOLS OF THE REPUBLIC

The idea of "schools of the republic," or public schools, arose in the era of Enlightenment from about 1740 to 1800 in Germany, France, and America, the time of revolution and the forming of new republics. Earlier, universal education was far from the most progressive contemplation, and ignorance and prejudice retarded the human condition on both sides of the Atlantic.[37] With the breadth of change emanating from the Enlightenment, a new secular and utilitarian spirit found the old system of religious education to be not only inadequate, but also a primary reason for the vast social ills that restrained the human spirit, manifested inequality, and resulted in a general denial of prospects in life for the poor and ignorant. Ultimately, the American and French revolutionaries of the 1790s, versed in the philosophy of the Enlightenment, moved to fill the educational vacuum that had long existed.[38] Universal primary schooling became the ideal of a progressive nation. Essential to that ideal was the assumption that "children belonged to the nation as well as their families."[39] As Danton, the great French revolutionary, declared, "I too am a father, but my son does not belong to me, he belongs to the Republic."[40] In short, the education of the children was too important to be left to the parents and the Church. The theory of public secular schools that emerged from the Enlightenment philosophy was advanced by the founding fathers of the American Constitution: the best education was to be thorough and common to all children in public schools, and schools were to be nonsectarian and religiously neutral. As one commissioner of the Directory in the French Revolution in Paris stated, predating Jefferson's reference to a wall, "it is necessary to erect a wall of separation between education and religion."[41]

For a brief time in the 1790s, it appeared that public nonsectarian schools created during the Revolution might gain a foothold and succeed in France, but there soon emerged a great deterrent that one French historian called the "imperious demands for instruction in religious doctrines."[42] The Catholic Church was convinced that education not conducted by the Church itself could lead only to a general perversion of morals and the degeneration of the condition of society.[43] In France, intense competition developed between the Catholic Church and the public schools.[44] Accordingly, the Church fathers imposed "religious works" into the public school classrooms.[45] The competition between the newly created public and parochial schools intensified and was manifested in various ways, including community discord among teachers, parents, and pupils, even deteriorating into physical strife and pitched street fights. Moreover, the social and religious pressures resulted in the public schools drawing a poorer and smaller clientele of students than did the parochial schools. In the end, the new experiment of public schools in France was eclipsed as the government no longer sought to preserve a secular atmosphere in the public schools. The public school classrooms returned to the use of "religious texts, served as sacristans to the clergy and conformed to the religious 'prejudices' of the parents."[46] By 1811, virtually "all primary education had religious coloration";[47] thus, the public secular school ideal, fostered and given philosophical sustenance by the rationale and reasoning of the Enlightenment, never really obtained reality in revolutionary and postrevolutionary France.

Public common schools, schools of the republic, fared better in America, where religious divisiveness and discord were not indigenous and well entrenched. In the early 1800s, various states set about creating public school systems that would not offend the diverse religious beliefs of those who populated the new nation. Commager's cogent phrase, "How Europe Imagined and America Realized the Enlightenment," was nowhere more evident than in the creation of American public schools.[48] In the new republic, unlike in France and England, secularization and rationalism had made "inroads on the claims of the clergy to pre-eminence in the public arena," and in particular with regard to public education.[49] The early experience of England and the colonies taught that investing authority of the state in a privileged church had produced very little except "resentment and acrimony"[50] and that "a broad text of toleration and equality" should be the goal of society and its schools.[51] In America, there emerged, after much discord, an understanding that the separation of church and state would not impair morals or weaken any religion, but rather would strengthen both the state and the church.[52]

Yet America was not destined to cleanly escape the problems of the age-old religious strife of Europe that had prevented the successful establishment of a system of public schools in France and England. Each state in America had its own instances of religious opposition to the creation of public schools intertwined with attempts by various religious groups to encroach on the school curriculum and to obtain public tax funds to support their own sectarian schools. Such conflict was particularly evident in New England and other original colonies, where church and state had not been separated prior to the American Revolution.

As observed in Chapter 2 of this book, much opposition to public schools was manifested by Protestant churches in Massachusetts, developing into what Cubberley would later call "The Battle for Free State Schools."[53] Not only was this battle joined by people who simply did not want to pay taxes for public schools, but also the opposition largely emanated from the ranks of conservative Protestant ministers who argued that public schools would injure religious schools' attendance, thereby reducing their influence and thus retarding the progress and welfare of the churches. More intense objection came from more extreme Protestant sects, which feared that there was an ulterior motive of the state, "priestcraft," the purpose of which was to create a state school that would then evolve into a state church.[54]

Such opposition was not new, as was the experience during the Enlightenment in France, where Catholic theologians had militated against schools of the new republic and the entire concept of secular public education. In Massachusetts, Mann was roundly castigated as being antireligious and the principal exponent of "Godless public schools."[55] Cubberley, in writing about New England Puritan opposition to the creation of public schools, observed: "Those who believed in the old system of religious instruction, . . . those who desired to . . . stop the development of the public schools, united their forces in this first big attack (in America) against secular education."[56] Thus, a substantial segment of the Protestants opposed public schools and vigorously denounced them because they were nonsectarian and did not espouse particular religious beliefs. In 1838, Massachusetts public schools were assailed as being incapable of teaching moral values if they remained nonsectarian. It was said that "[t]he Bible . . . the need of a Redeemer . . . the holy employments of the redeemed in heaven—should be daily and thoroughly taught in the schools."[57] Later, in 1846, a great hue and cry arose in Massachusetts, where Protestant fundamentalist groups charged that the increase in "intemperance, crime, and juvenile depravity in the state was due to the 'Godless schools.'"[58]

Possibly the greatest early discord occurred in New York City, where Catholic immigrants from Europe, who constituted a large percentage of the total population, launched a determined resistance to the establishment of public schools. This episode was the principal event in the establishment of the parochial schools in America. In New York, Catholic clergy in the late 1830s and 1840s objected to the creation of public schools for the same reasons that were advanced by the Church in France during and after the French Revolution. The Catholic argument was basically twofold: first, by excluding sectarianism, positive Christianity was banished from public schools, and, second, if the public schools were to be sectarian, they could only be of the Catholic faith.[59] If the public schools were not to teach Catholic doctrine as the only brand of religion, then the public schools would be promoting infidelity to Christianity; therefore, if the public common schools did not convey the Catholic theology, then Catholic children would not be permitted to attend.[60] The Catholic Church defined religion as being inseparable from specific denominational doctrines and denied that any school could teach moral principles in the absence of the Catholic catechism.[61]

This reasoning therefore effectively foreclosed the possibility that the Catholic Church could ever support public common schools.

The only condition under which an accord could be reached with the Catholic Church to participate in a system of education was for the state to pay for a "Catholic Public School System." Any type of a public school system that did not inculcate Catholic doctrine and that was nonsectarian and nondenominational was unacceptable. Thus, the permanent and insoluble problem was set, wherein fundamentalist Protestant groups and the Catholic Church could never agree with the principles and philosophy that form the foundation of public schools. As had been the case in France, the Catholic Church and fringe fundamentalist Protestant groups opposed the creation of secular public schools in America. This struggle remains alive and in force today. The U.S. Supreme Court decisions in *Agostini*[62] and *Helms*[63] indicate that this church opposition to the idea of public common schools has now been accepted by the Court and that the religion provisions of the First Amendment will no longer be interpreted to prevent tax funds going to church schools.

Thus, the ideal of public schools, envisaged as perhaps the most important aspect of a republic—a system of universal, secular common schools supported by general taxation—is an Enlightenment idea that confronted severe opposition at its birth and as an institution appears to perhaps be waning in its political strength relative to the political power of ecclesiastical schools. The public school as "imagined" in Europe but brought to reality in the United States has functioned well for about 150 years. The opinions of the members of the U.S. Supreme Court today, however, clearly reflect the weight and political prominence of conservative religion's antipathy toward secular public schools. At this writing, there are bills in over one-half of the state legislatures that propose various voucher schemes to utilize public tax revenues to fund private and religious schools. Perhaps this trend in reducing the wall of separation may foretell the slowly engulfing twilight for the public school experiment in America. The following pages of this chapter present the issues pertaining to the establishment of religion and the progression of Supreme Court decisions allowing state and federal laws to channel public tax funds to sectarian schools.

■ THE PUBLIC SCHOOL AND RELIGION

The public school is founded on three fundamental assumptions that relate either directly or indirectly to the issue of church and state. First, education is a benefit to the entire society, and the legislature has the power to tax all for support. Essential to this concept is that general taxation is used for support and that taxation is not levied merely on those who use the public schools—the childless and those who send their children to private schools must all pay their fair share. Thaddeus Stevens in 1835, in dramatically defeating a legislative proposal to repeal general taxation for education, enunciated the principle of universal responsibility for universal education in Pennsylvania. Opponents of public schools claimed that it was unjust to tax people to educate the children of others; Stevens responded thusly:

> It is for their own benefit, inasmuch as it perpetrates the government and ensures the due administration of the laws under which they live, and by which their lives and property are protected. Why do they not urge the same objection against all other taxes? The industrious, thrifty, rich farmer pays a heavy county tax to support criminal courts, build jails, and pay sheriffs and jail keepers, and yet probably he never has had and probably never will have any direct personal use for them. . . . He cheerfully pays burdensome taxes which are necessarily levied to support and punish convicts, but loudly complains of that which goes to prevent his fellowbeing from becoming a criminal and to obviate the necessity of those humiliating institutions.[64]

To Stevens, education was a public obligation that must be nurtured to develop the entire civic intelligence to better govern through an elective republic. Those who do not directly benefit from public education certainly gain indirectly through association with an enlightened citizenry.

Second, education provided by the state must be secular, and individual religious beliefs should not be inhibited. An important element of the secular state envisioned by Jefferson was a system of public schools that could convey all necessary temporal knowledge and yet not impede religious freedom. The power of the state could not be used to inculcate religious beliefs, nor could the authority of the state to tax be used to assist religious training.

The First Amendment has two religious clauses that protect the individual's religious liberty, the establishment clause and the free exercise clause. These two clauses prevent the use of public schools to proselytize and, correspondingly, forbid the expenditure of public tax funds to support religion.

One of the basic tenets in creating schools of the republic, or public schools, as envisioned by Jefferson, Madison, and other founding fathers, was that the power of the government to tax the citizenry should not be employed to provide funding for religious establishments. Jefferson clearly admonishes in his Act for Establishing Religious Freedom (partially quoted above) that "to compel a man to furnish contributions of money for the propagation of opinions which he disbelieves, is sinful and tyrannical; that even the forcing him to support this or that teacher of his own religious persuasion, is depriving him of the comfortable liberty. . . .'

Tax support of religious establishments in Europe and in the American colonies was a precedent not easily overcome in creating a new republic that could operate independent of church control. Madison's *Remonstrance* against general taxation assessments in Virginia "for support of teachers of the Christian religion" was probably the most comprehensive and compelling statement regarding the establishment of religion since John Locke's *Letter Concerning Toleration* a century earlier.

An extract from an opinion by the Supreme Court of Iowa forcefully expresses the idea that public tax funds should not be used for religious instruction and, further, should not be used by religious groups to proselytize:

> If there is any one thing which is well settled in the policies and purposes of the American people as a whole, it is the fixed and unalterable determination that there shall be an absolute and unequivocal separation of church and state, and that our public school system, supported by the taxation of the property of all alike—Catholic, Protestant, Jew, Gentile, believer and infidel—shall not be used directly or indirectly for religious instruction, and

above all that it shall not be made an instrumentality of proselyting influence, in favor of any religious organization, sect, creed, or belief.[65]

Third, the state can compel all parents to provide their children with a minimum secular education. This assumption is essential to the concept of general mass education. Every government has as a goal its own continuation and preservation, and in a republic, an educated electorate is fundamental. As such, the state must be conceived as *parens patriae* in enforcing minimum educational and welfare requirements. The validity of the state's interest was established years ago in *Prince v. Massachusetts*.[66]

The primary issue emanates from placing the force and power of the state, whether it be through taxation or other public policy decision, in a position to either enhance or inhibit religion. This was one of the most obstinate problems that Horace Mann was forced to overcome in his great crusade to found free common schools in Massachusetts. Mann vigorously maintained that the only purpose of religious education in the schools was to convey to each child the idea and respect of religious liberty. According to him, the child should be able

> to judge for himself according to the dictates of his own reason and conscience, what his religious obligations are and whither they lead. But if a man is taxed to support a school where religious doctrines are inculcated which he believes to be false, and which he believes that God condemns, then he is excluded from the school by the divine law, at the same time that he is compelled to support it by the human law. This is a double wrong.[67]

The public schools of America are secular and not merely nonsectarian; this is necessary if separation of church and state is to be complete. The important position of education in the governmental process is the key to maintaining religious liberty. Pfeffer observes that to be secular does not mean to be "Godless"; it is merely a guarantee that the state will not dictate or encroach on religious beliefs of the individual. He says:

> A secular state requires a secular state school; but the secularization of the state does not mean the secularization of society. Only by accepting a totalitarian philosophy, either in religion or politics or both, can be equated with society. We are a reli-

gious people even though our government is secular. Our democratic state must be secular, for it does not purport or seek to pre-empt all of societal life. Similarly the public school need not and should not be the totality of the education process.[68]

In this regard, the public school ideal in America precludes religious indoctrination in the public schools, and it proscribes the state from pre-empting all the child's time, thereby allowing substantial opportunity for religious training outside the school by parents and churches.[69] Whether the U.S. Supreme Court will continue to disallow the providing of public funds to parochial schools is a continuing saga, the outcome of which is still uncertain.

■ PUBLIC TAXATION TO SUPPORT RELIGIOUS SCHOOLS

The U.S. Supreme Court, in the case of *Cochran v. Louisiana State Board of Education,* ruled that a state plan to provide textbooks to parochial school students does not violate the Fourteenth Amendment.[70] The Court in this case was not asked to determine whether the First Amendment was violated. The decision in the *Cochran* case was rendered in 1930, ten years before the Court decided in the *Cantwell* case that the religious liberties of the First Amendment not only provided protection against actions by the Congress, but also, when applied through the Fourteenth Amendment, protected the individual from arbitrary acts of the states.[71] However, the Court in this case did identify and adopt the "child benefit" concept, which has subsequently been used in many instances to defend the appropriation of public funds for private and parochial school use.

The Supreme Court in *Everson v. Board of Education,* a 1947 decision, held that the use of public funds for transportation of parochial school children does not violate the First Amendment. However, many state constitutions impose stricter regulations concerning separation of church and state than does the U.S. Constitution, and as a result, the highest courts in several states have ruled that their state constitutions would be violated if public funds were used to provide transportation for parochial school pupils.

In the *Everson* case, the legislature of New Jersey enacted a law that allowed boards of education to provide transportation for parochial school children at public expense. A school board, acting under this statute, authorized reimbursement of parents for bus fares spent in sending their children to parochial schools. The plaintiff attacked the statute on the grounds that it violated the First and Fourteenth Amendments of the federal Constitution. The Court, in a five-to-four decision, ruled that the statute did not violate the Constitution. The Court adopted the "child benefit" doctrine and reasoned that the funds were expended for the benefit of the individual child and not for religious purposes. The transportation law was a general program that provided assistance in getting children safely to and from school, regardless of their religion.

In 1968, the Supreme Court in *Board of Education of Central School District v. Allen* applied the reasoning of the *Cochran* and *Everson* cases in upholding as constitutional a New York statute that provided for distribution of textbooks free of charge to students attending parochial schools. The Court stated that there was no indication that the books were being used to teach religion and that, since private schools serve a public purpose and perform a secular as well as a sectarian function, such an expenditure of public funds is not unconstitutional.[72]

*Establishment Clause Does Not Prohibit
Spending Tax Funds to Pay Bus Fares for
Parochial School Students*

Everson v. Board of Education

Supreme Court of the United States, 1947.
330 U.S. 1, 67 S.Ct. 504.

Mr. Justice BLACK delivered the opinion of the Court. A New Jersey statute authorizes its local school districts to make rules and contracts for the transportation of children to and from schools. The appellee, a township board of edu-

cation acting pursuant to this statute authorized reimbursement to parents of money expended by them for the bus transportation of their children on regular buses operated by the public transportation system. Part of this money was for the payment of transportation of some children in the community to Catholic parochial schools. These church schools give their students, in addition to secular education, regular religious instruction conforming to the religious tenets and modes of worship of the Catholic Faith. The superintendent of these schools is a Catholic priest.

The appellant, in his capacity as a district taxpayer, filed suit in a State court challenging the right of the Board to reimburse parents of parochial school students. He contended that the statute and the resolution passed pursuant to it violated both the State and the Federal Constitutions. That court held that the legislature was without power to authorize such payment under the State constitution. . . .

The only contention here is that the State statute and the resolution, in so far as they authorized reimbursement to parents of children attending parochial schools, violate the Federal Constitution in these two respects, which to some extent, overlap. First. They authorize the State to take by taxation the private property of some and bestow it upon others, to be used for their own private purposes. This, it is alleged, violates the due process clause of the Fourteenth Amendment. Second. The statute and the resolution forced inhabitants to pay taxes to help support and maintain schools which are dedicated to, and which regularly teach, the Catholic Faith. This is alleged to be a use of State power to support church schools contrary to the prohibition of the First Amendment, which the Fourteenth Amendment made applicable to the states.

First. The due process argument that the State law taxes some people to help others carry out their private purposes is framed in two phases. The first phase is that a state cannot tax A to reimburse B for the cost of transporting his children to church schools. This is said to violate the due process clause because the children are sent to these church schools to satisfy the personal desires of their parents, rather than the public's interest in the general education of all children. This argument, if valid, would apply equally to prohibit state payment for the transportation of children to any nonpublic school, whether operated by a church, or any other nongovernment individual or group. But, the New Jersey legislature has decided that a public purpose will be served by using tax-raised funds to pay the bus fares of all school children, including those who attend parochial schools. The New Jersey Court of Errors and Appeals has reached the same conclusion. The fact that a state law, passed to satisfy a public need, coincides with the personal desires of the individuals most directly affected is certainly an inadequate reason for us to say that a legislature has erroneously appraised the public need. . . .

It is much too late to argue that legislation intended to facilitate the opportunity of children to get a secular education serves no public purpose. *Cochran v. Louisiana State Board of Education*, 281 U.S. 370, 50 S.Ct. 335, 74 L.Ed. 913. . . . The same thing is no less true of legislation to reimburse needy parents, or all parents, for payment of the fares of their children so that they can ride in public buses to and from schools rather than run the risk of traffic and other hazards incident to walking or "hitchhiking." . . . Nor does it follow that a law has a private rather than a public purpose because it provides that tax-raised funds will be paid to reimburse individuals on account of money spent by them in a way which furthers a public program. . . . Subsidies and loans to individuals such as farmers and home owners, and to privately owned transportation systems, as well as many other kinds of businesses, have been commonplace practices in our state and national history.

Insofar as the second phase of the due process argument may differ from the first, it is by suggesting that taxation for transportation of children to church schools constitutes support of a religion by the State. But if the law is invalid for this reason, it is because it violates the First Amendment's prohibition against the establishment of religion by law. This is the exact question raised by appellant's second contention, to consideration of which we now turn.

Second. The New Jersey statute is challenged as a "law respecting an establishment of religion." The First Amendment, as made applicable to the states by the Fourteenth, . . . commands that a state "shall make no law respecting an establishment of religion, or prohibiting the free exercise thereof." These words of the First Amendment reflected in the minds of early Americans a vivid mental picture of conditions and practices which they fervently wished to stamp out in order to preserve liberty for themselves and for their posterity. Doubtless their goal has not been entirely reached; but so far has the Nation moved toward it that the expression "law respecting an establishment of religion" probably does not so vividly remind present-day Americans of the evils, fears, and political problems that caused that expression to be written into our Bill of Rights. . . .

The "establishment of religion" clause of the First Amendment means at least this: Neither a state nor the Federal Government can set up a church. Neither can pass laws which aid one religion, aid all religions, or prefer one religion over another. Neither can force nor influence a person to go to or to remain away from church against his will or force him to profess a belief or disbelief in any religion. No person can be punished for entertaining or professing religious beliefs or disbeliefs, for church attendance or nonattendance. No tax in any amount, large or small, can be levied to support any religious activities or institutions, whatever they may be called, or whatever form they may adopt to teach or practice religion. Neither a state nor the Federal Government can, openly or secretly, participate in the affairs of any religious organizations or groups and vice versa. In the words of Jefferson, the clause against establishment of religion by law was intended to erect "a wall of separation between Church and State." *Reynolds v. United States*, 98 U.S. at page 164, 25 L.Ed. 244.

We must consider the New Jersey statute in accordance with the foregoing limitations imposed by the First Amendment. But we must not strike that state statute down if it is within the state's constitutional power even though it approaches the verge of that power. . . . New Jersey cannot consistently with the "establishment of religion" clause of the First Amendment contribute tax-raised funds to the support of an institution which teaches the tenets and faith of any church. On the other hand, other language of the amendment commands that New Jersey cannot hamper its citizens in the free exercise of their own religion. Consequently, it cannot exclude individual Catholics, Lutherans, Mohammedans, Baptists, Jews, Methodists, Nonbelievers, Presbyterians, or the members of any other faith, *because of their faith, or lack of it,* from receiving the benefits of public welfare legislation. While we do not mean to intimate that a state could not provide transportation only to children attending public schools, we must be careful, in protecting the citizens of New Jersey against state-established churches, to be sure that we do not inadvertently prohibit New Jersey from extending its general State law benefits to all its citizens without regard to their religious belief.

Measured by these standards, we cannot say that the First Amendment prohibits New Jersey from spending tax-raised funds to pay the bus fares of parochial school pupils as a part of a general program under which it pays the fares of pupils attending public and other schools. It is undoubtedly true that children are helped to get to church schools. There is even a possibility that some of the children might not be sent to the church schools if the parents were compelled to pay their children's bus fares out of their own pockets when transportation to a public school would have been paid for by the State. The same possibility exists where the state requires a local transit company to provide reduced fares to school children including those attending parochial schools, or where a municipally owned transportation system undertakes to carry all school children free of charge. Moreover, state-paid policemen, detailed to protect children going to and from church schools from the very real hazards of traffic, would serve much the same purpose and accomplish much the same result as state provisions intended to guarantee free transportation of a kind which the state deems to be best for the school children's welfare. And parents might refuse to risk their children to the serious danger of traffic accidents going to and from parochial schools, the approaches to which were not protected by policemen. Similarly, parents might be reluctant to permit their children to attend schools which

the state had cut off from such general government services as ordinary police and fire protection, connections for sewage disposal, public highways and sidewalks. Of course, cutting off church schools from these services, so separate and so indisputably marked off from the religious function, would make it far more difficult for the schools to operate. But such is obviously not the purpose of the First Amendment. That Amendment requires the state to be neutral in its relations with groups of religious believers and non-believers; it does not require the state to be their adversary. State power is no more to be used so as to handicap religions, than it is to favor them. . . .

The First Amendment has erected a wall between church and state. That wall must be kept high and impregnable. We could not approve the slightest breach. New Jersey has not breached it here.

Affirmed.

CASE NOTES

1. A Pennsylvania statute that allowed the transportation of private school children beyond school district boundary lines was ruled constitutional. *School District of Pittsburgh v. Commonwealth Department of Education*, 33 Pa.Cmwlth. 535, 382 A.2d 772 (1978), appeal dismissed, 443 U.S. 901, 99 S.Ct. 3091 (1979). See also *Springfield School District v. Department of Education*, 483 Pa. 539, 397 A.2d 1154 (1979), appeal dismissed, 443 U.S. 901, 99 S.Ct. 3091 (1979).

2. Relate the historical background and rationale of Jefferson's Bill for Establishing Religious Freedom and Madison's *Memorial and Remonstrance against Religious Assessments* to *Everson*.

3. In the *Everson* case, is the state's contribution under the New Jersey law in defraying the cost of conveying pupils to a place where they will receive primarily religious instruction in fact a substitution of resources for parents and an encouragement to aid religion?

4. Statutes that authorize public transportation for parochial school children to travel to and from the private schools do not constitute mandatory authority for the public schools to

also transport such children for educational field trips. *Cook v. Griffin,* 47 A.D.2d 23, 364 N.Y.S.2d 632 (1975). See also *Wolman v. Walter,* 433 U.S. 229, 97 S.Ct. 2593 (1977).

———————— ❖ — ❖ — ❖ ————————

Loan of Textbooks to Parochial School Students Does Not Violate Establishment Clause

Board of Education of Central School District No. 1 v. Allen

Supreme Court of the United States, 1968.
392 U.S. 236, 88 S.Ct. 1923.

Mr. Justice WHITE delivered the opinion of the Court. A law of the State of New York requires local public school authorities to lend textbooks free of charge to all students in grades seven through twelve; students attending private schools are included. This case presents the question whether this statute is a "law respecting an establishment of religion, or prohibiting the free exercise thereof," and so in conflict with the First and Fourteenth Amendments to the Constitution, because it authorizes the loan of textbooks to students attending parochial schools. We hold that the law is not in violation of the Constitution. . . .

Beginning with the 1966–1967 school year, local school boards were required to purchase textbooks and lend them without charge "to all children residing in such district who are enrolled in grades seven to twelve of a public or private school which complies with the compulsory education law."[73] The books now loaned are "text-books which are designated for use in any public, elementary or secondary schools of the state or are approved by any boards of education," and which—according to a 1966 amendment—"a pupil is required to use as a text for a semester or more in a particular class in the school he legally attends."

Appellant Board of Education of Central School District No. 1 in Rensselaer and Columbia Counties brought suit in the New York

courts against appellee James Allen. The complaint alleged that §701 violated both the State and Federal Constitutions; that if appellants, in reliance on their interpretation of the Constitution, failed to lend books to parochial school students within their counties, appellee Allen would remove appellants from office; and that to prevent this, appellants were complying with the law and submitting to their constituents a school budget including funds for books to be lent to parochial school pupils. Appellants therefore sought a declaration that §701 was invalid, an order barring appellee Allen from removing appellants from office for failing to comply with it, and another order restraining him from apportioning state funds to school districts for the purchase of textbooks to be lent to parochial students. . . .

Everson and later cases have shown that the line between state neutrality to religion and state support of religion is not easy to locate. "The constitutional standard is the separation of Church and State. The problem, like many problems in constitutional law, is one of degree." *Zorach v. Clauson,* 343 U.S. 306, 314, 72 S.Ct. 679, 684, 96 L.Ed. 954 (1952). . . . Based on *Everson, Zorach, McGowan,* and other cases, *Abington Tp. School District v. Schempp,* 374 U.S. 203, 83 S.Ct. 1560, 10 L.Ed.2d 844 (1963), fashioned a test subscribed to by eight Justices for distinguishing between forbidden involvements of the State with religion and those contacts which the Establishment Clause permits:

> The test may be stated as follows: what are the purpose and the primary effect of the enactment? If either is the advancement or inhibition of religion then the enactment exceeds the scope of legislative power as circumscribed by the Constitution. That is to say that to withstand the strictures of the Establishment Clause there must be a secular legislative purpose and a primary effect that neither advances nor inhibits religion. *Everson v. Board of Education.* . . . 374 U.S. at 222, 83 S.Ct., at 1571.

This test is not easy to apply, but the citation of *Everson* by the *Schempp* Court to support its general standard made clear how the *Schempp* rule would be applied to the facts of *Everson*. The statute upheld in *Everson* would be considered a law having "a secular legislative purpose and a primary effect that neither advances nor inhibits religion." We reach the same result with respect to the New York law requiring school books to be loaned free of charge to all students in specified grades. The express purpose of §701 was stated by the New York Legislature to be furtherance of the educational opportunities available to the young. Appellants have shown us nothing about the necessary effects of the statute that is contrary to its stated purpose. The law merely makes available to all children the benefits of a general program to lend school books free of charge. Books are furnished at the request of the pupil and ownership remains, at least technically, in the State. Thus no funds or books are furnished to parochial schools, and the financial benefit is to parents and children, not to schools. Perhaps free books make it more likely that some children choose to attend a sectarian school, but that was true of the state-paid bus fares in *Everson* and does not alone demonstrate an unconstitutional degree of support for a religious institution. . . .

The major reason offered by appellants for distinguishing free textbooks from free bus fares is that books, but not buses, are critical to the teaching process, and in a sectarian school that process is employed to teach religion. However, this Court has long recognized that religious schools pursue two goals, religious instruction and secular education. In the leading case of *Pierce v. Society of Sisters*, 268 U.S. 510, 45 S.Ct. 571, 69 L.Ed. 1070 (1925), the Court held that although it would not question Oregon's power to compel school attendance or require that the attendance be at an institution meeting State-imposed requirements as to quality and nature of curriculum, Oregon had not shown that its interest in secular education required that all children attend publicly operated schools. A premise of this holding was the view that the State's interest in education would be served sufficiently by reliance on the secular teaching that accompanied religious training in the schools maintained by the Society of Sisters. Since *Pierce*, a substantial body of case law has confirmed the power of the States to insist that attendance at private schools, if it is to satisfy state compulsory-attendance laws, be at institutions which provide minimum hours of instruction, employ teachers of specified training, and cover prescribed subjects of instruction. Indeed,

the State's interest in assuring that these standards are being met has been considered a sufficient reason for refusing to accept instruction at home as compliance with compulsory education statutes. These cases were a sensible corollary of *Pierce v. Society of Sisters:* if the State must satisfy its interest in secular education through the instrument of private schools, it has a proper interest in the manner in which those schools perform their secular educational function. Another corollary was *Cochran v. Louisiana State Board of Education,* 281 U.S. 370, 50 S.Ct. 335, 74 L.Ed. 913 (1930), where appellants said that a statute requiring school books to be furnished without charge to all students, whether they attend public or private schools, did not serve a "public purpose," and so offended the Fourteenth Amendment. Speaking through Chief Justice Hughes, the Court summarized as follows its conclusion that Louisiana's interest in the secular education being provided by private schools made provision of textbooks to students in those schools a properly public concern: "[The State's] interest is education, broadly; its method, comprehensive. Individual interests are aided only as the common interest is safeguarded." 281 U.S., at 375, 50 S.Ct., at 336.

Underlying these cases, and underlying also the legislative judgments that have preceded the court decisions, has been a recognition that private education has played and is playing a significant and valuable role in raising national levels of knowledge, competence, and experience. Americans care about the quality of the secular education available to their children. They have considered high quality education to be an indispensable ingredient for achieving the kind of nation, and the kind of citizenry, that they have desired to create. Considering this attitude, the continued willingness to rely on private school systems, including parochial systems, strongly suggests that a wide segment of informed opinion, legislative and otherwise, has found that those schools do an acceptable job of providing secular education to their students. This judgment is further evidence that parochial schools are performing, in addition to their sectarian function, the task of secular education.

Against this background of judgment and experience, unchallenged in the meager record before us in this case, we cannot agree with appellants either that all teaching in a sectarian school is religious or that the processes of secular and religious training are so intertwined that secular textbooks furnished to students by the public are in fact instrumental in the teaching of religion. This case comes to us after summary judgment entered on the pleadings. Nothing in this record supports the proposition that all textbooks, whether they deal with mathematics, physics, foreign languages, history, or literature, are used by the parochial schools to teach religion. No evidence has been offered about particular schools, particular courses, particular teachers, or particular books. We are unable to hold, based solely on judicial notice, that this statute results in unconstitutional involvement of the State with religious instruction or that §701, for this or the other reasons urged, is a law respecting the establishment of religion within the meaning of the First Amendment. . . .

Mr. Justice BLACK, dissenting. . . . I believe the New York law held valid is a flat, flagrant, open violation of the First and Fourteenth Amendments which together forbid Congress or state legislatures to enact any law "respecting an establishment of religion." For that reason I would reverse the New York Court of Appeals' judgment. . . .

The *Everson* and *McCollum* cases plainly interpret the First and Fourteenth Amendments as protecting the taxpayers of a State from being compelled to pay taxes to their government to support the agencies of private religious organizations the taxpayers oppose. To authorize a State to tax its residents for such church purposes is to put the State squarely in the religious activities of certain religious groups that happen to be strong enough politically to write their own religious preferences and prejudices into the laws. This links state and churches together in controlling the lives and destinies of our citizenship—a citizenship composed of people of myriad religious faiths, some of them bitterly hostile to and completely intolerant of the others. It was to escape laws precisely like this that a large part of the Nation's early immigrants fled to this country. It was also to escape such laws and such consequences that the First Amendment was written in language strong and clear barring passage of any law "respecting an establishment of religion." . . .

I know of no prior opinion of this Court upon which the majority here can rightfully rely to support its holding this New York law constitutional. In saying this, I am not unmindful of the fact that the New York Court of Appeals purported to follow *Everson v. Board of Education,* in which this Court, in an opinion written by me, upheld a New Jersey law authorizing reimbursement to parents for the transportation of children attending sectarian schools. That law did not attempt to deny the benefit of its general terms to children of any faith going to any legally authorized school. Thus, it was treated in the same way as a general law paying the streetcar fare *of all school children,* or a law providing midday lunches for all children, or a law to provide police protection for children going to and from school, or general laws to provide police and fire protection for buildings, including, of course, churches and church school buildings as well as others. . . .

This New York law, it may be said by some, makes but a small inroad and does not amount to complete state establishment of religion. But that is no excuse for upholding it. It requires no prophet to foresee that on the argument used to support this law others could be upheld providing for state or federal government funds to buy property on which to erect religious school buildings or to erect the buildings themselves, to pay the salaries of the religious school teachers, and finally to have the sectarian religious groups cease to rely on voluntary contributions of members of their sects while waiting for the Government to pick up all the bills for the religious schools. Arguments made in favor of this New York law point squarely in this direction, namely, that the fact that government has not heretofore aided religious schools with tax-raised funds amounts to a discrimination against those schools and against religion. And that there are already efforts to have government supply the money to erect buildings for sectarian religious schools is shown by a recent Act of Congress which apparently allows for precisely that. See Higher Education Facilities Act of 1963, 77 Stat. 363, 20 U.S.C.A. §701 et seq.

I still subscribe to the belief that tax-raised funds cannot constitutionally be used to support religious schools, buy their school books, erect their buildings, pay their teachers, or pay any other of their maintenance expenses, even to the extent of one penny. The First Amendment's prohibition against governmental establishment of religion was written on the assumption that state aid to religion and religious schools generates discord, disharmony, hatred, and strife among our people, and that any government that supplies such aids is to that extent a tyranny. And I still believe that the only way to protect minority religious groups from majority groups in this country is to keep the wall of separation between church and state high and impregnable as the First and Fourteenth Amendments provide. The Court's affirmance here bodes nothing but evil to religious peace in this country. . . .

CASE NOTES

1. Observe that Justice Black wrote the majority opinion in *Everson* and dissented in *Allen*. This is particularly interesting, since the majority opinion by Justice White relied heavily on the interpretation and meaning of the majority in *Everson*.

2. The *Cochran* case in Louisiana was preceded by *Borden v. Louisiana State Board of Education*, 168 La. 1005, 123 So. 655 (1929), which held that the Acts of 1928, Nos. 100 and 143, the same acts contested in *Cochran*, were not violative of constitutional provisions prohibiting public funds for private or benevolent purposes and were not adverse to due process requirements.

3. Appellants in *Allen* argued that transportation of parochial pupils may be constitutional, whereas providing textbooks is not. How does the Court react to this argument? Compare the Court's opinion to the dissenting opinion of Justice Jackson in the *Everson* case. In *Everson*, Justice Jackson said:

I find myself, contrary to first impressions, unable to join in this decision. I have a sympathy, though it is not ideological, with Catholic citizens who are compelled by law to pay taxes for public schools, and also feel constrained by conscience and discipline to support other schools for their own children. Such relief to them as this case involves is not in itself a serious burden to taxpayers and I had assumed it to be as little serious in principle. Study of this case convinces me otherwise. The Court's opinion marshals every argument in favor of state aid and puts the case in its most favorable light, but much of its reasoning confirms my conclusions that there are no good grounds upon which to support the present legislation. In fact, the undertones of the opinion, advocating complete and uncompromising separation of Church from State, seem utterly discordant with its conclusion yielding support to their commingling in educational matters. The case which irresistibly comes to mind as the most fitting precedent is that of Julia who, according to Byron's reports, "whispering 'I will ne'er consent,'—consented."

4. What is the implication of Justice White's statement that "parochial schools are performing, in addition to their sectarian function, the task of secular education"?

5. How does Justice Black, in dissent in *Allen*, distinguish textbooks from transportation in *Everson*, in which he wrote the majority opinion?

■ THE ESTABLISHMENT CLAUSE AND THE *LEMON* TEST

The decision by the Supreme Court in the *Allen* case[74] created many questions on the part of both public and parochial school leaders throughout the country. The language of Justice White, speaking for the majority, was unclear, failing to delineate First Amendment restrictions in providing state aid to parochial schools. White applied the public purpose theory and reasoned that the state could give assistance to religious schools so long as the aid was provided for only secular services in the operation of parochial schools. He said that

a wide segment of informed opinion, legislative and otherwise, has found that [parochial] schools do an acceptable job of providing secular education to their students. *This judgment is further evidence that parochial schools are performing, in addition to their sectarian function, the task of secular education.* [Italics added.]

This statement was taken by many parochial school educators to mean that a state could permissibly provide funds to parochial schools for such things as teachers' salaries, operations, buildings, and so on, so long as the funds were used by the parochial schools only for "public secular purposes." State legislatures were suddenly flooded with hundreds of bills to provide state support to parochial schools; some were passed and others, for various reasons, failed.[75]

THE *LEMON* TEST

It was into this fertile area of conjecture that the U.S. Supreme Court walked in 1971, when it was asked to rule on the constitutionality of two such state acts from Pennsylvania and Rhode Island. This was the now famous *Lemon v. Kurtzman* case, which first enunciated the three-part test of constitutionality of state acts pertaining to the establishment of religion. Both states, capitalizing on the vagueness of *Allen*, were attempting to give public funds to parochial schools. The Supreme Court struck down the statutes of both states. The Court found the "secular purpose" standard alone to be inadequate and then added another standard, that of "excessive entanglement." This standard seeks to prevent the state from infringing on the separate rights of religion by becoming too intermingled with the process of religion. The Supreme Court enunciated a three-part test for determining whether a state statute is constitutional under the establishment clause of the First Amendment: (1) the statute must have a secular legislative purpose, (2) its principal or primary effect must be one that neither advances nor inhibits religion, and (3) it must not foster excessive government entanglement with religion.

❖ — ❖ — ❖

State Aid to Parochial Schools through Salary Supplements and Purchase of Services Constitutes Impermissible Entanglement between Church and State

Lemon v. Kurtzman

Supreme Court of the United States, 1971.
403 U.S. 602, 91 S.Ct. 2105.

Mr. Chief Justice BURGER delivered the opinion of the Court. These two appeals raise questions as to Pennsylvania and Rhode Island statutes providing state aid to church-related elementary and secondary schools. Both statutes are challenged as violative of the Establishment and Free Exercise Clauses of the First Amendment and the Due Process Clause of the Fourteenth Amendment.

Pennsylvania has adopted a statutory program that provides financial support to nonpublic elementary and secondary schools by way of reimbursement for the cost of teachers' salaries, textbooks, and instructional materials in specified secular subjects. Rhode Island has adopted a statute under which the State pays directly to teachers in nonpublic elementary schools a supplement of 15 percent of their annual salary. Under each statute state aid has been given to church-related educational institutions. We hold that both statutes are unconstitutional.

The Rhode Island Salary Supplement Act[76] was enacted in 1969. It rests on the legislative finding that the quality of education available in nonpublic elementary schools has been jeopardized by the rapidly rising salaries needed to attract competent and dedicated teachers. The Act authorizes state officials to supplement the salaries of teachers of secular subjects in nonpublic elementary schools by paying directly to a teacher an amount not in excess of 15 percent of his current annual salary. As supplemented, however, a nonpublic school teacher's salary cannot exceed the maximum paid to teachers in the State's public schools, and the recipient must be certified by the state board of education in substantially the same manner as public school teachers.

In order to be eligible for the Rhode Island salary supplement, the recipient must teach in a nonpublic school at which the average per-pupil expenditure on secular education is less than the average in the State's public schools during a specified period. Appellant State Commissioner of Education also requires eligible schools to submit financial data. If this information indicates a per-pupil expenditure in excess of the statutory limitation, the records of the school in question must be examined in order to assess how much of the expenditure is attributable to secular education and how much to religious activity.

The Act also requires that teachers eligible for salary supplements must teach only those subjects that are offered in the State's public school.

They must use "only teaching materials which are used in the public schools." Finally, any teacher applying for a salary supplement must first agree in writing "not to teach a course in religion for so long as or during such time as he or she receives any salary supplements" under the Act.

Appellees are citizens and taxpayers of Rhode Island. . . . Appellants are state officials charged with administration of the Act, teachers eligible for salary supplements under the Act, and parents of children in church-related elementary schools whose teachers would receive state salary assistance.

A three-judge federal court was convened pursuant to 28 U.S.C.A. §§2281, 2284. It found that Rhode Island's nonpublic elementary schools accommodated approximately 25 percent of the State's pupils. About 95 percent of these pupils attended schools affiliated with the Roman Catholic church. To date some 250 teachers have applied for benefits under the Act. All of them are employed by Roman Catholic schools.

The court held a hearing at which extensive evidence was introduced concerning the nature of the secular instruction offered in the Roman Catholic schools whose teachers would be eligible for salary assistance under the Act. Although the court found that concern for religious values does not necessarily affect the content of secular subjects, it also found that the parochial school system was "an integral part of the religious mission of the Catholic Church."

The District Court concluded that the Act violated the Establishment Clause, holding that it fostered "excessive entanglement" between government and religion. In addition two judges thought that the Act had the impermissible effect of giving "significant aid to a religious enterprise." . . . We affirm.

Pennsylvania has adopted a program that has some but not all of the features of the Rhode Island program. The Pennsylvania Nonpublic Elementary and Secondary Education Act[77] was passed in 1968 in response to a crisis that the Pennsylvania Legislature found existed in the State's nonpublic schools due to rapidly rising costs. The statute affirmatively reflects the legislative conclusion that the State's educational goals could appropriately be fulfilled by government support of "those purely secular educational objectives achieved through nonpublic education. . . . "

The statute authorizes appellee state Superintendent of Public Instruction to "purchase" specified "secular educational services" from nonpublic schools. Under the "contracts" authorized by the statute, the State directly reimburses nonpublic schools solely for their actual expenditures for teachers' salaries, textbooks, and instructional materials. A school seeking reimbursement must maintain prescribed accounting procedures that identify the "separate" cost of the "secular educational service." These accounts are subject to state audit. The funds for this program were originally derived from a new tax on horse and harness racing, but the Act is now financed by a portion of the state tax on cigarettes.

There are several significant statutory restrictions on state aid. Reimbursement is limited to courses "presented in the curricula of the public schools." It is further limited "solely" to courses in the following "secular" subjects: mathematics, modern foreign languages,[78] physical science, and physical education. Textbooks and instructional materials included in the program must be approved by the state Superintendent of Public Instruction. Finally, the statute prohibits reimbursement for any course that contains "any subject matter expressing religious teaching, or the morals or forms of worship of any sect."

The Act went into effect on July 1, 1968, and the first reimbursement payments to schools were made on September 2, 1969. It appears that some $5 million has been expended annually under the Act. The State has now entered into contracts with some 1,181 nonpublic elementary and secondary schools with a student population of some 535,215 pupils—more than 20 percent of the total number of students in the State. More than 96 percent of these pupils attend church-related schools, and most of these schools are affiliated with the Roman Catholic church.

Appellants brought this action in the District Court to challenge the constitutionality of the Pennsylvania statute. The organizational plaintiffs-appellants are associations of persons resident in Pennsylvania declaring belief in the separation of church and state; individual plaintiffs-appellants are citizens and taxpayers of Pennsylvania. Appellant Lemon, in addition to being a citizen and a taxpayer, is a parent of a child attending public school in Pennsylvania. Lemon also alleges that he purchased a ticket at a race track and thus had paid the specific tax that supports the expenditures under the Act.... The District Court held that the individual plaintiffs-appellants had standing to challenge the Act. . . .

The court granted appellees' motion to dismiss the complaint for failure to state a claim for relief. . . . It held that the Act violated neither the Establishment nor the Free Exercise Clause. . . . We reverse. . . .

The language of the Religion Clauses of the First Amendment is at best opaque, particularly when compared with other portions of the Amendment. Its authors did not simply prohibit the establishment of a state church or a state religion, an area history shows they regarded as very important and fraught with great dangers. Instead they commanded that there should be "no law *respecting* an establishment of religion." A law may be one "respecting" the forbidden objective while falling short of its total realization. A law "respecting" the proscribed result, that is, the establishment of religion, is not always easily identifiable as one violative of the Clause. A given law might not *establish* a state religion but nevertheless be one "respecting" that end in the sense of being a step that could lead to such establishment and hence offend the First Amendment.

In the absence of precisely stated constitutional prohibitions, we must draw lines with reference to the three main evils against which the Establishment Clause was intended to afford protection: "sponsorship, financial support, and active involvement of the sovereign in religious activity." *Walz v. Tax Commission*, 397 U.S. 664, 668, 90 S.Ct. 1409, 1411, 25 L.Ed.2d 697 (1970).

Every analysis in this area must begin with consideration of the cumulative criteria developed by the Court over many years. Three such tests may be gleaned from our cases. First, the statute must have a secular legislative purpose;

second, its principal or primary effect must be one that neither advances nor inhibits religion, *Board of Education v. Allen*, 392 U.S. 236, 243, 88 S.Ct. 1923, 1926, 20 L.Ed.2d 1060 (1968); finally, the statute must not foster "an excessive government entanglement with religion." *Walz*, supra, at 674, 90 S.Ct. at 1414.

Inquiry into the legislative purposes of the Pennsylvania and Rhode Island statutes affords no basis for a conclusion that the legislative intent was to advance religion. On the contrary, the statutes themselves clearly state that they are intended to enhance the quality of the secular education in all schools covered by the compulsory attendance laws. There is no reason to believe the legislatures meant anything else. A State always has a legitimate concern for maintaining minimum standards in all schools it allows to operate. As in *Allen*, we find nothing here that undermines the stated legislative intent; it must therefore be accorded appropriate deference.

In *Allen* the Court acknowledged that secular and religious teachings were not necessarily so intertwined that secular textbooks furnished to students by the State were in fact instrumental in the teaching of religion. . . . The legislatures of Rhode Island and Pennsylvania have concluded that secular and religious education are identifiable and separable. In the abstract we have no quarrel with this conclusion.

The two legislatures, however, have also recognized that church-related elementary and secondary schools have a significant religious mission and that a substantial portion of their activities is religiously oriented. They have therefore sought to create statutory restrictions designed to guarantee the separation between secular and religious educational functions and to ensure that State financial aid supports only the former. All these provisions are precautions taken in candid recognition that these programs approached, even if they did not intrude upon, the forbidden areas under the Religion Clauses. We need not decide whether these legislative precautions restrict the principal or primary effect of the programs to the point where they do not offend the Religion Clauses, for we conclude that the cumulative impact of the entire relationship arising under the statutes in each

State involves excessive entanglement between government and religion. . . .

RHODE ISLAND PROGRAM

The District Court made extensive findings on the grave potential for excessive entanglement that inheres in the religious character and purpose of the Roman Catholic elementary schools of Rhode Island, to date the sole beneficiaries of the Rhode Island Salary Supplement Act.

The church schools involved in the program are located close to parish churches. This understandably permits convenient access for religious exercises since instruction in faith and morals is part of the total educational process. The school buildings contain identifying religious symbols such as crosses on the exterior and crucifixes, and religious paintings and statues either in the classrooms or hallways. Although only approximately thirty minutes a day are devoted to direct religious instruction, there are religiously oriented extracurricular activities. Approximately two-thirds of the teachers in these schools are nuns of various religious orders. Their dedicated efforts provide an atmosphere in which religious instruction and religious vocations are natural and proper parts of life in such schools. Indeed, as the District Court found, the role of teaching nuns in enhancing the religious atmosphere has led the parochial school authorities to attempt to maintain a one-to-one ratio between nuns and lay teachers in all schools rather than to permit some to be staffed almost entirely by lay teachers.

On the basis of these findings the District Court concluded that the parochial schools constituted "an integral part of the religious mission of the Catholic Church." The various characteristics of the schools make them "a powerful vehicle for transmitting the Catholic faith to the next generation." This process of inculcating religious doctrine is, of course, enhanced by the impressionable age of the pupils, in primary schools particularly. In short, parochial schools involve substantial religious activity and purpose.

The substantial religious character of these church-related schools gives rise to entangling church-state relationships of the kind the Religion Clauses sought to avoid. Although the District Court found that concern for religious values did not inevitably or necessarily intrude into the content of secular subjects, the considerable religious activities of these schools led the legislature to provide for careful governmental controls and surveillance by state authorities in order to ensure that state aid supports only secular education. . . .

The Rhode Island Legislature has not, and could not, provide state aid on the basis of a mere assumption that secular teachers under religious discipline can avoid conflicts. The State must be certain, given the Religion Clauses, that subsidized teachers do not inculcate religion— indeed the State here has undertaken to do so. To ensure that no trespass occurs, the State has therefore carefully conditioned its aid with pervasive restrictions. An eligible recipient must teach only those courses that are offered in the public schools and use only those texts and materials that are found in the public schools. In addition the teacher must not engage in teaching any course in religion.

A comprehensive, discriminating, and continuing state surveillance will inevitably be required to ensure that these restrictions are obeyed and the First Amendment otherwise respected. Unlike a book, a teacher cannot be inspected once so as to determine the extent and intent of his or her personal beliefs and subjective acceptance of the limitations imposed by the First Amendment. These prophylactic contacts will involve excessive and enduring entanglement between state and church.

There is another area of entanglement in the Rhode Island program that gives concern. The statute excludes teachers employed by nonpublic schools whose average per-pupil expenditures on secular education equal or exceed the comparable figures for public schools. In the event that the total expenditures of an otherwise eligible school exceed this norm, the program requires the government to examine the school's records in order to determine how much of the total expenditures is attributable to secular education and how much to religious activity. This kind of state inspection and evaluation of the religious content of a religious organization is fraught with the sort of entanglement that the Constitution forbids. It is a relationship pregnant with dangers of excessive government direction of church schools and hence of churches. . . .

PENNSYLVANIA PROGRAM

The Pennsylvania statute also provides state aid to church-related schools for teachers' salaries. The complaint describes an educational system that is very similar to the one existing in Rhode Island. According to the allegations, the church-related elementary and secondary schools are controlled by religious organizations, have the purpose of propagating and promoting a particular religious faith, and conduct their operations to fulfill that purpose. Since this complaint was dismissed for failure to state a claim for relief, we must accept these allegations as true for purposes of our review.

As we noted earlier, the very restrictions and surveillance necessary to ensure that teachers play a strictly nonideological role give rise to entanglements between church and state. The Pennsylvania statute, like that of Rhode Island, fosters this kind of relationship. Reimbursement is not only limited to courses offered in the public schools and materials approved by state officials, but the statute excludes "any subject matter expressing religious teaching, or the morals or forms of worship of any sect." In addition, schools seeking reimbursement must maintain accounting procedures that require the State to establish the cost of the secular as distinguished from the religious instruction.

The Pennsylvania statute, moreover, has the further defect of providing state financial aid directly to the church-related schools. This factor distinguishes both *Everson* and *Allen,* for in both those cases the Court was careful to point out that state aid was provided to the student and his parents—not to the church-related school.... In *Walz v. Tax Commission, . . .* the Court warned of the dangers of direct payments to religious organizations:

> Obviously a direct money subsidy would be a relationship pregnant with involvement and, as with most governmental grant programs, could encompass sustained and detailed administrative relationships for enforcement of statutory or administrative standards. . . .

The history of government grants of a continuing cash subsidy indicates that such programs have almost always been accompanied by varying measures of control and surveillance. The government cash grants before us now provide no basis for predicting that comprehensive measures of surveillance and controls will not follow. In particular the government's post-audit power to inspect and evaluate a church-related school's financial records and to determine which expenditures are religious and which are secular creates an intimate and continuing relationship between church and state.

A broader base of entanglement of yet a different character is presented by the divisive political potential of these state programs. In a community where such a large number of pupils are served by church-related schools, it can be assumed that state assistance will entail considerable political activity. Partisans of parochial schools, understandably concerned with rising costs and sincerely dedicated to both the religious and secular educational missions of their schools, will inevitably champion this cause and promote political action to achieve their goals. Those who oppose state aid, whether for constitutional, religious, or fiscal reasons, will inevitably respond and employ all of the usual political campaign techniques to prevail. Candidates will be forced to declare and voters to choose. It would be unrealistic to ignore the fact that many people confronted with issues of this kind will find their votes aligned with their faith.

Ordinarily political debate and division, however vigorous or even partisan, are normal and healthy manifestations of our democratic system of government, but political division along religious lines was one of the principal evils against which the First Amendment was intended to protect. . . . The potential divisiveness of such conflict is a threat to the normal political process. . . .

The potential for political divisiveness related to religious belief and practice is aggravated in these two statutory programs by the need for continuing annual appropriations and the likelihood of larger and larger demands as costs and populations grow. . . .

In *Walz* it was argued that a tax exemption for places of religious worship would prove to be the first step in an inevitable progression leading to the establishment of state churches and state religion. That claim could not stand up against more than 200 years of virtually universal practice embedded in our colonial experience and continuing into the present.

The progression argument, however, is more persuasive here. We have no long history of state aid to church-related educational institutions comparable to 200 years of tax exemption for churches. Indeed, the state programs before us today represent something of an innovation. We have already noted that modern governmental programs have self-perpetuating and self-expanding propensities. These internal pressures are only enhanced when the schemes involve institutions whose legitimate needs are growing and whose interests have substantial political support. Nor can we fail to see that in constitutional adjudication some steps, which when taken were thought to approach "the verge," have become the platform for yet further steps. A certain momentum develops in constitutional theory and it can be a "downhill thrust" easily set in motion but difficult to retard or stop. Development by momentum is not invariably bad; indeed, it is the way the common law has grown, but it is a force to be recognized and reckoned with. The dangers are increased by the difficulty of perceiving in advance exactly where the "verge" of the precipice lies. As well as constituting an independent evil against which the Religion Clauses were intended to protect, involvement or entanglement between government and religion serves as a warning signal. . . .

The judgment of the Rhode Island District Court in No. 569 and No. 570 is affirmed. The judgment of the Pennsylvania District Court in No. 89 is reversed, and the case is remanded for further proceedings consistent with this opinion. . . .

CASE NOTE

In a case where a school in Michigan displayed a portrait of Jesus Christ in a hallway near the school gymnasium for at least thirty years, a student claimed that such a display by the school constituted proselytizing for Christianity, offending non-Christians. The court held that the display of the portrait violated all three parts of the *Lemon* test. *Washegesic v. Bloomingdale Public Schools*, 33 F.3d 679 (6th Cir.1994), cert. denied, 514 U.S. 1095, 115 S.Ct. 1822 (1995).

PRECEDENTS SHORTLY AFTER *LEMON*

The Supreme Court, on June 25, 1973, delivered three opinions regarding financial aid to private schools. The first case was *Levitt v. Committee for Public Education and Religious Liberty*, involving an appropriation of funds by the New York legislature in 1970 to reimburse nonpublic school expenses for various services performed by the nonpublic schools. These services included

> administration, grading and the compiling and reporting of the results of tests and examinations, maintenance of records of pupils' enrollment and reporting hereon, maintenance of pupil health records, recording of personnel qualifications and characteristics and the preparation and submission to the state of various other reports as provided for or required by law or regulation.[79]

The most expensive of these services was the administration, grading, compiling, and reporting of tests, which included both state-prepared examinations and teacher-prepared tests. The New York statute made no provision for auditing[80] the expenditures to determine the private schools' expenditures. The Supreme Court ruled that the funds impermissibly aided religion, violating the establishment clause.

Almost immediately after the *Levitt* case was rendered, the New York legislature sought to remedy the defects by enacting a revised statute unencumbered by the unconstitutional aspects. The new statute was to pay the actual cost incurred by the nonpublic schools in complying with state reporting mandates, which included a pupil evaluation program, basic educational data system, regent examinations, and other state-prepared examinations, as well as several reporting requirements designed to confirm school performance of the other functions. Payments were to be audited by the state, a requirement that had not been included in the earlier law. With these changes, the statute was litigated before the Supreme Court in the case of *Committee for Public Education and Religious Liberty v. Regan*.[81] The law, this time, passed constitutional muster. The legislature had been successful in skillfully paring and shaping the law to skirt the edges of unconstitutionality to permit aid to parochial schools.

In a second case, *Committee for Public Education and Religious Liberty v. Nyquist*,[82] the challenge was based on a New York statute designed to aid nonpublic schools. The New York legislature had amended the education and tax laws to provide financial aid to nonpublic elementary and secondary schools by way of (1) grants to nonpublic schools for "maintenance and repair" of facilities and equipment,[83] (2) a tuition reimbursement plan for nonpublic school parents whose children were enrolled in elementary and secondary schools,[84] and (3) tax relief for parents who did not qualify for the tuition reimbursement plan. The U.S. Supreme Court ruled that each of the three provisions violated the establishment clause because each one subsidized, and thereby advanced, religion.

The third case, decided in 1973, brought down a Pennsylvania law entitled the Parent Reimbursement Act for Nonpublic Education, which compensated parochial school parents for a portion of their private school tuition expenses.[85] The Court found that there was no constitutionally significant difference between the Pennsylvania and the New York statutes, both being in violation of the establishment clause.

By the mid-1970s, the Supreme Court was again faced with an even more complex and circuitous Pennsylvania effort to aid nonpublic schools.[86] One part of the law, Act 194, provided auxiliary services to children enrolled in nonpublic schools, including counseling, testing, psychological services, speech and hearing therapy, and services for disadvantaged and exceptional children. The Court ruled that because the services were provided in predominantly church-related schools, excessive entanglement existed. The second part, Act 195, extended a direct loan of textbooks and instructional materials and equipment to parochial schools. The law defined instructional materials and equipment as photographs, maps, charts, globes, films, projection equipment, recording equipment, and so forth. The Court ruled that because the textbooks were secular and were the same as those used in the public schools, their benefits accrued only to the parents or students and not to the parochial school. The Court refused to bring instructional materials under the constitutional umbrella that had been fashioned by *Cochran* and *Allen*. Even though the

instructional materials and equipment were merely loaned to the parochial school, the Court ruled that the primary effect of the law was to advance religion.

Still more litigation ensued in 1977 from Ohio, a state aggressively persistent in its efforts to provide public funds to aid private schools. In this case, Justice Blackmun commented, "This is still another case presenting the recurrent issue of the limitations imposed by the Establishment Clause of the First Amendment . . . on state aid to pupils in church-related elementary and secondary schools."[87] Here the Ohio law provided funds to nonpublic schools for (1) textbooks, (2) testing and scoring of standardized tests, (3) diagnostic services, (4) therapeutic services, (5) instructional materials and equipment, and (6) field trips by nonpublic school children. The law required that the textbooks purchased by private schools with state funds be the same as those used in the public schools. The books were to be loaned to the pupils in nonpublic schools. The Supreme Court dissected the issues and concluded that based on its decisions in *Allen* and *Meek*, the textbook provision was constitutional, as were the state payments for testing and scoring. Similarly, the Court upheld the payment for diagnostic services as distinguishable from teaching or counseling, reasoning that such services encompassed no educational content and were not closely associated with the educational mission of the nonpublic school.[88] Concerning the therapeutic, guidance, and remedial services to be provided in public schools, public centers, or mobile units located off the nonpublic school premises, the Supreme Court held that because the locus of the service was not on parochial school property, there was no excessive entanglement. Finally, the Court ruled that the loan of instructional materials and equipment to parochial schools was unconstitutional because there was no way of ensuring their secular use.[89] The field trip scheme met the same fate of unconstitutionality.

These cases, when combined, bear witness to the political pressure that is today exerted on state legislatures to aid parochial schools and show the intensified efforts to use public tax funds to support private and parochial schools.

THE WALL BEGINS TO CRUMBLE

The issue of aid to nonpublic schools in the form of tax credits or tax deductions is not a new idea. In 1972, a lower federal district court invalidated Ohio's Parental Reimbursement Grant, which provided a tax credit[90] to nonpublic school parents, a decision that was summarily affirmed by the U.S. Supreme Court in 1973.[91] As described earlier, the Supreme Court addressed the tax benefit in *Nyquist* and found a New York statute for nonpublic school parents was unconstitutional.[92] Again, in 1979, the Supreme Court confronted the tax benefit issue, at which time it summarily affirmed the decision[93] of the Third Circuit Court of Appeals invalidating a tax benefit program for nonpublic school parents in New Jersey. This program allowed nonpublic school parents a $100 tax deduction for each dependent child's attendance at a tuition-charging nonpublic school. In yet another case, the U.S. Court of Appeals, First Circuit, ruled in 1980 in *Norberg*, a Rhode Island case, that a statute allowing parents of nonpublic school students a state income tax deduction for tuition, textbooks, and transportation expenses was unconstitutional as violative of the establishment clause.[94]

The leading case on the subject of tax credits resulted from a Minnesota statute that allowed all parent taxpayers to deduct from their income taxes a legislatively specified amount. In approving this scheme of aid to private schools, the U.S. Supreme Court[95] appeared to chart a new direction of even greater leniency in provision of public monies for parochial schools. In validating the Minnesota plan, the Court distinguished its rejection of the earlier tax deduction or credit plans by noting that each of those limited tax benefits was available only to parents of private school children, while the Minnesota deduction was available to parents of *all* children in both private and public schools. The Court did not seem to be concerned that tax deduction benefits to public school parents would be minimal because public schools do not charge tuition or transportation fees and textbooks are, by and large, free. The primary benefits would then, of course, accrue largely to the advantage of parochial school parents. Justice Rehnquist, in applying the three-part test for the five-to-four majority, found that the statute had a secular purpose, that it did not advance or promote religion, and that governmental entanglement with the church was minimal and unimportant.

Importantly, Rehnquist, in justifying the decision, expressed a view of the Court to the effect that parochial schools are a viable and important alternative to public schools, fostering "wholesome competition," and that states are justified in giving them tax support.[96] This same view is a slightly different version of that expressed by Justice White in 1968 in *Board of Education of Central School District v. Allen.*[97] There the Court justified the loan of textbooks on the grounds that parochial schools were performing an important secular function that was of sufficient public importance to merit public financial assistance.

Buchanan has said that the present situation of condoning aid to private schools supports a "total subsidy" position.[98] He maintains that any aid will be constitutional if the aid has a secular purpose and if the aid is offered to religious and nonreligious entities, as in Minnesota, where the tax deduction or credit is available to *all* parents.[99]

In *School District of the City of Grand Rapids v. Ball,*[100] in 1985, the Supreme Court, under the hand of Justice Brennan, momentarily returned to a more strict adherence to separation. In this case, a Grand Rapids plan offered benefits to parochial schools through shared time and community education programs financed by the public school system. Justice Brennan, writing for the majority, found that the plan had the primary effect of advancing religion.

Justice Brennan again prevailed in the 1985 *Aguilar v. Felton* decision,[101] in which he formed a majority coalition of justices, enabling the Court to strike down a New York City plan that provided funds under Title I of the federal Elementary and Secondary Education Act of 1965 to pay for the education of eligible parochial school students on parochial school premises. The Supreme Court found that such a benefit to the parochial schools offended the establishment clause. Justice Brennan went to great length to explain why this particular plan, which involved the use of public school teachers in parochial schools as well as an elaborate monitoring system, violated the excessive entanglement test.

Historically, the Court has kept religion out of public schools and has generally prevented public tax funds from flowing to parochial schools. Today, however, there has been a dramatic change toward a judicially sanctioned permissiveness in giving public dollars to religious schools. The courts have been forced to respond to a consistent and seemingly endless array of attempts by legislatures in states with large percentages of parochial school students to circumvent separation barriers in efforts to allow tax funds to flow to religious schools. The repeated attempts to override or change the precedents, making them more favorable to private schools, have apparently now been successful. These legislative blows at a crumbling wall of separation have given credence to the arguments of those who have traditionally asserted that the creation of a wall of separation of church and state is an inappropriate and impractical pursuit.

The continuing erosion of the wall as far as aid to parochial schools is concerned is premised on the philosophical rationale enunciated by Chief Justice Rehnquist in his dissent in *Wallace v. Jaffree* in 1985,[102] where he maintained that the true intent of the establishment clause is merely to prohibit a "national religion" or the "official designation of any church as a national one," as well as to discourage the preference of any particular religious sect over another. It did not intend, according to Rehnquist, to create "government neutrality between religion and irreligion, nor did it prohibit the federal government from providing nondiscriminating aid to religion."[103] This nonpreferential philosophy would therefore allow state and federal tax funds to go to religious schools so long as one or a few religious sects were not preferred over others. The fact that the Catholic Church may control 80 percent of America's private schools would apparently make no difference in the application of this nonpreferential philosophy.[104] This position is, of course, diametrically opposed to the intent enunciated in Madison's *Memorial and Remonstrance*, which declared that government should not aid one religion or *all* religions. Rehnquist's nonpreferential stance, however, now represents the view of the Supreme Court and will undoubtedly rule in the foreseeable future.

THE MARGINALIZING OF *LEMON*

As indicated, the *Lemon* test was used in all school cases in the 1980s and for all but two non-school cases: *Marsh v. Chambers*[105] (here the so-called historical analysis was used) and *Larson v. Valente*.[106] In a number of decisions, the Supreme Court has downgraded the importance of the *Lemon* test. The test was described as only a "guideline" in *Committee for Public Education and Religious Liberty v. Nyquist*[107] and then as "no more than [a] useful 'guideline'" in *Mueller v. Allen*.[108] Later, in *Lynch v. Donnelly*,[109] the Court stated that the *Lemon* test has never been binding on the Court. There was speculation that the Supreme Court would overturn *Lemon* or establish a new test when *Lee v. Weisman*[110] was argued before the Court in 1992. But Justice Kennedy, writing for the majority, averted the issue, stating that "the court will not reconsider its decision in *Lemon*."[111] The Court thereby did not use the tripartite *Lemon* test in *Weisman*, but, rather, it applied a new standard—the coercion test. The Court stated: "The principle that government may accommodate the free exercise of religion does not supersede the fundamental limitation imposed by the Establishment Clause, which guarantees at a minimum that a government may not coerce anyone to support or participate in religion or its exercise, or otherwise act in a way which 'establishes a [state] religion or religious faith, or tends to do so.'"[112]

The Supreme Court judge most critical of *Lemon* has been Justice Scalia. Scalia, a proponent of parochial schools, in his dissent in *Lamb's Chapel*,[113] attacked the *Lemon* test, stating:

> As to the Court's invocation of the *Lemon* Test: Like some ghoul in a late-night horror movie that repeatedly sits up in its grave and shuffles abroad, after being repeatedly killed and buried, *Lemon* stalks our Establishment Clause jurisprudence once again, frightening the little children. . . .[114]

Justice Scalia's efforts to overturn the *Lemon* test and demolish Jefferson's wall of separation have now apparently come to fruition.

The Court did not use the *Lemon* test in deciding *Board of Education of Kiryas Joel Village School District v. Grumet*;[115] rather, it applied a "neutrality" standard, saying, "A proper respect for both the Free Exercise and the Establishment Clauses compels the State to pursue a course of 'neutrality' toward religion."[116] In this case, the state legislature created a separate special education school district for a religious educational enclave:

> The New York Village of Kiryas Joel is a religious enclave of Satmar Hasidim, practitioners of a strict form of Judaism. Its local incorporation intentionally drew its boundaries under the state's general village incorporation law to exclude all but Satmars.[117]

This state statute specifically carved out the special school district exclusively for the Satmar Hasidic sect. In declaring the act unconstitutional, the Supreme Court stated: "Because this unusual act is tantamount to an allocation of political power on a religious criterion and neither presupposes nor requires governmental impartiality toward religion, we hold that it violates the prohibition against establishment."[118]

THE ESTABLISHMENT CLAUSE REDUCED

Earlier Supreme Court precedents confirming the establishment clause as a strong deterrent against state aid to parochial or religious schools have now been largely repudiated by rulings of the Reagan-Bush appointees to the U.S. Supreme Court. Justices Rehnquist, O'Connor, Kennedy, Scalia, and Thomas now form the majority of a Supreme Court that has modified First Amendment precedent to reduce its reach in preventing the flow of public tax funds to parochial schools. In the 1997 case of *Agostini v. Felton*,[119] the Supreme Court, with Justice O'Connor writing for a five-to-four majority, announced what it labeled a "significant change in Establishment Clause law." In this decision, the Court repeatedly referred to its "current understanding of the Establishment Clause." This "current understanding" is based on this Supreme Court's recent precedents in *Witters v. Washington Department of Services for the Blind*,[120] *Zobrest v. Catalina Foothills School District*,[121] *Rosenberger v. Rector and Visitors of the University of Virginia*,[122] and *Board of Education of Kiryas Joel Village School District v. Grumet*.[123] In these cases, the Court established a chain of rationale leading to what probably amounts to a negation of the effects of the establishment clause as it applies to public funding of parochial schools.

The Court's reasoning was synthesized and enunciated as new precedent in *Agostini v. Felton*, in which it overruled the earlier precedents of *Aguilar v. Felton*[124] and *School District of the City of Grand Rapids v. Ball*.[125] As pointed out earlier in this chapter, the original *Aguilar* case, with former Justice Brennan writing for the majority, had held that the use of federal Title I funds to pay for educational services in parochial schools was unconstitutional. The same Court in the *Grand Rapids* case had reinforced the establishment clause principle of separation of church and state by invalidating a state plan to provide public funds for shared time and ommunity education programs in parochial schools. Subsequently, however, Justices Brennan and Marshall retired, and the philosophy of the Court shifted dramatically. The new appointees to the Court have now gained a majority, and in *Agostini*, they annulled *Aguilar* and *Grand Rapids*. The Supreme Court, while not directly overruling *Lemon* and its three-prong test, did nevertheless reinterpret *Lemon* in such a way as to greatly reduce its strength in preventing public aid to parochial schools.

In addressing the *Lemon* standards, the Court observed that its new ruling in *Agostini* had not materially changed the first prong of *Lemon*, the purpose test. The fact that the Court let this part stand without reinterpretation did not, however, change current jurisprudence. For some time now, the Court's precedents have indicated that the purpose test does not prevent government from providing tax funds to parochial schools.[126] The real and pervasive shift in the new establishment clause judicial philosophy emanated from this Court's virtual obliteration of the second prong, the effect test, and the third prong, the excessive entanglement test. The majority in *Agostini* pointed out that the Court's ruling in *Zobrest* (see Chapter 9 of this text) was controlling in the application of the effect test; in *Zobrest*, the Court held that the use of public funds to pay for a special education employee in a Roman Catholic high school did not have the impermissible effect of advancing religion. The Court's ruling in *Agostini* cited its own decision in *Witters* as precedent and pointed out that its new establishment clause jurisprudence did not prevent direct grants to students in religious schools even though the money would be used to obtain a religious education. *Zobrest* and *Witters* directly repudiate the previously held assumptions in *Aguilar* and *Grand Rapids* that a publicly funded employee in a religious school creates the unacceptable effect of advancing religion. Thus, *Zobrest*, *Witters*, and *Agostini*, in concert, apparently largely nullify the effect test as a deterrent to government funding for parochial schools.

The Court in *Agostini* most clearly indicated its negation of the separation criteria of earlier Supreme Court decisions when it examined the federal Title I program in light of the third prong of *Lemon*, excessive entanglement. The Court observed that monitoring by public officials of parochial school programs, administrative interaction between public school boards and the parochial schools, and possible "political divisiveness" created by aid to parochial schools cannot be construed to be excessive entanglement. Thus, in view of this Court's treatment of the excessive entanglement standard, it is difficult to conjure a scenario where excessive entanglement could be adjudged so intrusive as to be violative of this third *Lemon* test.

In June 2000, the U.S. Supreme Court handed down *Mitchell v. Helms*,[127] a decision that appears to nullify the remaining establishment clause deterrence to public funding of sectarian schools. The opinion, rendered by a plurality of four justices, consolidates and reinforces the Court's position encapsulated in *Agostini*,[128] wherein it flatly broke from previous Supreme Court decisions that had prohibited providing sectarian schools with public funds. The Supreme Court observed in *Agostini*, noted above, that "stare decisis is not an inexorable command"; therefore, earlier precedents did not bind this court to the earlier Supreme Court ruling that held that the establishment clause prohibited public funding of ecclesiastical schools. *Agostini* and *Helms* gave birth to a so-called new establishment clause jurisprudence because of its departure from the historical American separation of church and state philosophy. Justice Clarence Thomas, writing for the plurality of justices, explained that the new establishment jurisprudence hinges primarily on an "effect" test that has only two considerations: neutrality of the governmental funding and whether the aid subsidizes a selected religious group. In

reality, there is little, if any, difference between the two. According to Justice Thomas, if the government funds have no strings attached and do not require that the sectarian schools teach a particular brand of religion, then use of public funds by the church schools is permissible. If in the use of the public funds the sectarian school chooses to inculcate its own religious doctrine, and such cannot be attributed to governmental action, then there is no violation of the establishment clause. Therefore, according to the Court, public funds can be used for religious indoctrination so long as it is the choice made by the particular religious sect that conducts the school and does not constitute a religious doctrine prescribed by the government as a condition for receiving the funds. This reasoning the Court calls the neutrality principle. In short, what the Court is apparently saying is that if the public funds are not used to impose a "state religion" upon the sectarian schools or are not given to only one particular type of religious school, then the governmental funding comports with the establishment clause.

Even though the Court in *Helms* was not required by the appeal to address the "purpose test" or the "excessive entanglement test" of *Lemon*, the implication is clear that neither will be recognized as effective deterrents to the channeling of public dollars to religious schools. The new criteria of Justice Thomas's effect test appear to subsume the original "purpose" test of *Lemon*, indicating that there is no constitutional violation if the state aid is allocated on a neutral and secular basis, neither favoring nor disfavoring any particular religious sect.

Further, regardless of the fact that the excessive entanglement test was not directly raised in *Helms*, the Court indicated that it would probably give this test rather short shrift in the future due to its "pared down" judicial concern for potential divisiveness that might accrue from financial aid to religion. Too, the Court suggested foreclosure of entanglement considerations in its elongated dismissal of the issue of diversion of funds. The plaintiffs in *Helms* had complained that governmental funds provided to sectarian schools could be easily diverted for religious indoctrination, regardless of their original secular purpose. *Lemon* had held that the act of monitoring the use of public funds by government to prevent their diversion within the sectarian school to religious purposes created excessive entanglements. The Court in *Helms* responded that all this is obviated if the diversion comes about as a result of the choices made by the clergy controlling the schools or the parents of children attending the religious schools. Church and family choices justify such diverting of funds. Moreover, the Court indicated it would simply disregard any concern of political divisiveness as an entanglement issue.

Finally, the *Helms* Court apparently cleared the way for the approval of tuition vouchers by pointing out that the direct versus indirect distinction between methods of distributing public dollars to sectarian schools was a distinction without meaning and that such formalisms are irrelevant to the establishment clause. The implication apparently is that it matters little whether the public funds are used to directly buy educational materials and equipment or flow more generally and indirectly through the means of vouchers or some other such schemes. The result is the same: each is constitutionally permissible. The Court did point out, however, in passing that a straight governmental appropriation to church schools in the same manner as state funds are distributed through state foundation programs for public schools could possibly raise an unresolved constitutional question that was not presented in the facts of the *Helms* case.[129]

Therefore, the *Helms* case constitutes one more major step in the Court's systematic disassembling of the judicial precedents that had earlier in American history forbidden tax support for the benefit of sectarian schools. The new jurisprudence of the establishment clause, as propounded by the current Supreme Court, has now apparently dismantled the principal constitutional barriers that earlier in American history prevented general taxation for the support of ecclesiastical schools.

Therefore, in summary, the current Supreme Court in *Agostini* and *Helms* leaves little of *Lemon* to prevent public aid to parochial schools. When the precedents of the Reagan-Bush Court are combined and considered as the new jurisprudence of the establishment clause, the *Lemon* limitations restraining government

aid to religious schools appear to be largely nullified and the separation precedents of earlier Supreme Court decisions, in most relevant parts, rescinded.

Tax Deductions Benefiting Parents of Parochial School Children Do Not Violate the Establishment Clause

Mueller v. Allen

Supreme Court of the United States, 1983.
463 U.S. 388, 103 S.Ct. 3062.

Justice REHNQUIST delivered the opinion of the Court. Minnesota allows taxpayers, in computing their state income tax, to deduct certain expenses incurred in providing for education of their children. . . .

Minnesota, like every other state, provides its citizens with free elementary and secondary schooling. It seems to be agreed that about 820,000 students attended this school system in the most recent school year. During the same year, approximately 91,000 elementary and secondary students attended some 500 privately supported schools located in Minnesota, and about 95% of these students attended schools considering themselves to be sectarian.

Minnesota, by a law originally enacted in 1955 and revised in 1976 and again in 1978, permits state taxpayers to claim a deduction from gross income for certain expenses incurred in educating their children. The deduction is limited to actual expenses incurred for the "tuition, textbooks and transportation" of dependents attending elementary or secondary schools. A deduction may not exceed $500 per dependent in grades K through six and $700 per dependent in grades seven through twelve. . . .

Today's case is no exception to our oft-repeated statement that the Establishment Clause presents especially difficult questions of interpretation and application. It is easy enough to quote the few words comprising that clause— "Congress shall make no law respecting an establishment of religion." It is not at all easy, however, to apply this Court's various decisions construing the Clause to governmental programs of financial assistance to sectarian schools and the parents of children attending those schools. Indeed, in many of these decisions "we have expressly or implicitly acknowledged that 'we can only dimly perceive the lines of demarcation in this extraordinarily sensitive area of constitutional law.'" *Lemon v. Kurtzman,* 403 U.S. 602, 609, 612, 91 S.Ct. 2105, 2109, 2111, 29 L.Ed.2d 745 (1971), quoted with approval in *Nyquist,* 413 U.S., at 761, 93 S.Ct., at 2959.

One fixed principle in this field is our consistent rejection of the argument that "any program which in some manner aids an institution with a religious affiliation" violates the Establishment Clause. . . .

Petitioners place particular reliance on our decision in *Committee for Public Education v. Nyquist,* . . . where we held invalid a New York statute providing public funds for the maintenance and repair of the physical facilities of private schools and granting thinly disguised "tax benefits," actually amounting to tuition grants, to the parents of children attending private schools. As explained below, we conclude that §290.09(22) bears less resemblance to the arrangement struck down in *Nyquist* than it does to assistance programs upheld in our prior decisions and those discussed with approval in *Nyquist.*

The general nature of our inquiry in this area has been guided, since the decision in *Lemon v. Kurtzman,* 403 U.S. 602, 91 S.Ct. 2105, 29 L.Ed.2d 745 (1971), by the "three-part" test laid down in that case:

> First, the statute must have a secular legislative purpose; second, its principal or primary effect must be one that neither advances nor inhibits religion . . . ; finally, the statute must not foster "an excessive government entanglement with religion." Ibid., at 612–613, 91 S.Ct., at 2111.

While this principle is well settled, our cases have also emphasized that it provides "no more than [a] helpful signpost" in dealing with Establishment Clause challenges. *Hunt v. McNair,* 413 U.S., at 741, 93 S.Ct., at 2873. With this caveat in mind, we turn to the specific challenges raised against §290.09(22) under the *Lemon* framework.

Little time need be spent on the question of whether the Minnesota tax deduction has a secular purpose. Under our prior decisions, governmental assistance programs have consistently survived this inquiry even when they have run afoul of other aspects of the *Lemon* framework. This reflects, at least in part, our reluctance to attribute unconstitutional motives to the states, particularly when a plausible secular purpose for the state's program may be discerned from the face of the statute.

A state's decision to defray the cost of educational expenses incurred by parents—regardless of the type of schools their children attend—evidences a purpose that is both secular and understandable. . . .

We turn therefore to the more difficult but related question whether the Minnesota statute has "the primary effect of advancing the sectarian aims of the nonpublic schools." In concluding that it does not, we find several features of the Minnesota tax deduction particularly significant. First, an essential feature of Minnesota's arrangement is the fact that §290.09(22) is only one among many deductions—such as those for medical expenses, Minn.Stat. §290.09(10), and charitable contributions, Minn.Stat. §290.21—available under the Minnesota tax laws. . . . Under our prior decisions, the Minnesota legislature's judgment that a deduction for educational expenses fairly equalizes the tax burden of its citizens and encourages desirable expenditures for educational purposes is entitled to substantial deference.

Other characteristics of §290.09(22) argue equally strongly for the provision's constitutionality. Most importantly, the deduction is available for educational expenses incurred by *all* parents, including those whose children attend public schools and those whose children attend nonsectarian private schools or sectarian private schools. . . .

In this respect, as well as others, this case is vitally different from the scheme struck down in *Nyquist.* There, public assistance amounting to tuition grants was provided only to parents of children in *nonpublic* schools. This fact had considerable bearing on our decision striking down the New York statute at issue; we explicitly distinguished both *Allen* and *Everson* on the grounds that "[i]n both cases the class of beneficiaries included *all* schoolchildren, those in public as well as those in private schools." Moreover, we intimated that "public assistance (e.g., scholarships) made available generally without regard to the sectarian-nonsectarian or public-nonpublic nature of the institution benefited" might not offend the Establishment Clause. We think the tax deduction adopted by Minnesota is more similar to this latter type of program than it is to the arrangement struck down in *Nyquist*. . . .

We also agree with the Court of Appeals that, by channeling whatever assistance it may provide to parochial schools through individual parents, Minnesota has reduced the Establishment Clause objections to which its action is subject. It is true, of course, that financial assistance provided to parents ultimately has an economic effect comparable to that of aid given directly to the schools attended by their children. It is also true, however, that under Minnesota's arrangement public funds become available only as a result of numerous, private choices of individual parents of school-age children. For these reasons, we recognized in *Nyquist* that the means by which state assistance flows to private schools is of some importance: we said that "the fact that aid is disbursed to parents rather than to . . . schools" is a material consideration in Establishment Clause analysis, albeit "only one among many to be considered." . . .

We find it useful, in the light of the foregoing characteristics of §290.09(22), to compare the attenuated financial benefits flowing to parochial schools from the section to the evils against which the Establishment Clause was designed to protect. These dangers are well-described by our statement that "what is at stake as a matter of policy [in Establishment Clause cases] is preventing that kind and degree of government involvement in religious life that, as history teaches us, is apt to lead to strife and frequently strain a political system to the breaking point." It is important, however, to "keep these issues in perspective."

At this point in the 20th century we are quite far removed from the dangers that prompted the Framers to include the Establishment Clause in the Bill of Rights. The risk of significant religious or denominational control over our democratic processes—or even of deep political division along religious lines—is remote, and when viewed against the positive contributions of sectarian schools, such risk seems entirely tolerable in light of the continuing oversight of this Court. *Wolman*, 433 U.S., at 263, 97 S.Ct., at 2613.

The Establishment Clause of course extends beyond prohibition of a state church or payment of state funds to one or more churches. We do not think, however, that its prohibition extends to the type of tax deduction established by Minnesota. The historic purposes of the clause simply do not encompass the sort of attenuated financial benefit, ultimately controlled by the private choices of individual parents, that eventually flows to parochial schools from the neutrally available tax benefit at issue in this case.

Petitioners argue that, notwithstanding the facial neutrality of §290.09(22), in application the statute primarily benefits religious institutions. Petitioners rely, as they did below, on a statistical analysis of the type of persons claiming the tax deduction. They contend that most parents of public school children incur no tuition expenses, and that other expenses deductible under §290.09(22) are negligible in value; moreover, they claim that 96% of the children in private schools in 1978–1979 attended religiously affiliated institutions. Because of all this, they reason, the bulk of deductions taken under §290.09(22) will be claimed by parents of children in sectarian schools. Respondents reply that petitioners have failed to consider the impact of deductions for items such as transportation, summer school tuition, tuition paid by parents whose children attended schools outside the school districts in which they resided, rental or purchase costs for a variety of equipment, and tuition for certain types of instruction not ordinarily provided in public schools.

We need not consider these contentions in detail. We would be loath to adopt a rule grounding the constitutionality of a facially neutral law on annual reports reciting the extent to which various classes of private citizens claimed benefits under the law. Such an approach would scarcely provide the certainty that this field stands in need of, nor can we perceive principled standards by which such statistical evidence might be evaluated. Moreover, the fact that private persons fail in a particular year to claim the tax relief to which they are entitled—under a facially neutral statute—should be of little importance in determining the constitutionality of the statute permitting such relief. . . .

Thus, we hold that the Minnesota tax deduction for educational expenses satisfies the primary effect inquiry of our Establishment Clause cases.

Turning to the third part of the *Lemon* inquiry, we have no difficulty in concluding that the Minnesota statute does not "excessively entangle" the state in religion. The only plausible source of the "comprehensive, discriminating and continuing state surveillance" necessary to run afoul of this standard would lie in the fact that state officials must determine whether particular textbooks qualify for a deduction. In making this decision, state officials must disallow deductions taken from "instructional books and materials used in the teaching of religious tenets, doctrines or worship, the purpose of which is to inculcate such tenets, doctrines or worship." Making decisions such as this does not differ substantially from making the types of decisions approved in earlier opinions of this Court. In *Board of Education v. Allen*, 392 U.S. 236, 88 S.Ct. 1923, 20 L.Ed.2d 1060 (1968), for example, the Court upheld the loan of secular textbooks to parents or children attending nonpublic schools; though state officials were required to determine whether particular books were or were not secular, the system was held not to violate the Establishment Clause. See also *Wolman v. Walter; Meek v. Pittenger.* The same result follows in this case.

For the foregoing reasons, the judgment of the Court of Appeals is Affirmed.

CASE NOTE

In 1992, a federal district court in Iowa held that Iowa's income tax laws that allowed a taxpayer to claim an income tax deduction or credit for payment of elementary or secondary school tuition or for textbooks did not violate the establishment or free exercise clause of the First Amendment. The court relied on *Mueller v.*

Allen, discussed above. *Luthens v. Bair,* 788 F.Supp. 1032, 74 Educ.L.Rep. 1140 (S.D.Iowa 1992).

Statute Creating Special School District as a Religious Enclave Violates the Establishment Clause

Board of Education of Kiryas Joel Village School District v. Grumet

Supreme Court of the United States, 1994.
62 U.S. 4665, 114 S.Ct. 2481.

Justice SOUTER delivered the opinion of the Court.

The Village of Kiryas Joel in Orange County, New York, is a religious enclave of Satmar Hasidim, practitioners of a strict form of Judaism. The village fell within the Monroe-Woodbury Central School District until a special state statute passed in 1989 carved out a separate district, following village lines, to serve this distinctive population. 1989 N.Y.Laws, ch. 748. The question is whether the Act creating the separate school district violates the Establishment Clause of the First Amendment, binding on the States through the Fourteenth Amendment. Because this unusual act is tantamount to an allocation of political power on a religious criterion and neither presupposes nor requires governmental impartiality toward religion, we hold that it violates the prohibition against establishment.

The Satmar Hasidic sect takes its name from the town near the Hungarian and Romanian border where, in the early years of this century, Grand Rebbe Joel Teitelbaum molded the group into a distinct community. After World War II and the destruction of much of European Jewry, the Grand Rebbe and most of his surviving followers moved to the Williamsburg section of Brooklyn, New York. Then, 20 years ago, the Satmars purchased an approved but undeveloped subdivision in the town of Monroe and began assembling the community that has since become the Village of Kiryas Joel. When a zoning dispute arose in the course of settlement, the Satmars presented the Town Board of Monroe with a petition to form a new village within the town, a right that New York's Village Law gives almost any group of residents who satisfy certain procedural niceties. . . . Neighbors who did not wish to secede with the Satmars objected strenuously, and after arduous negotiations the proposed boundaries of the Village of Kiryas Joel were drawn to include just the 320 acres owned and inhabited entirely by Satmars. The village, incorporated in 1977, has a population of about 8,500 today. . . .

The residents of Kiryas Joel are vigorously religious people who make few concessions to the modern world and go to great lengths to avoid assimilation into it. They interpret the Torah strictly; segregate the sexes outside the home; speak Yiddish as their primary language; eschew television, radio, and English-language publications; and dress in distinctive ways that include headcoverings and special garments for boys and modest dresses for girls. Children are educated in private religious schools, most boys at the United Talmudic Academy where they receive a thorough grounding in the Torah and limited exposure to secular subjects, and most girls at Bais Rochel, an affiliated school with a curriculum designed to prepare girls for their roles as wives and mothers. . . .

These schools do not, however, offer any distinctive services to handicapped children, who are entitled under state and federal law to special education services even when enrolled in private schools. . . . Starting in 1984 the Monroe-Woodbury Central School District provided such services for the children of Kiryas Joel at an annex to Bais Rochel, but a year later ended that arrangement in response to our decisions in *Aguilar v. Felton*, 473 U.S. 402, 105 S.Ct. 3232, 87 L.Ed.2d 290 (1985), and *School Dist. of Grand Rapids v. Ball*, 473 U.S. 373, 105 S.Ct. 3216, 87 L.Ed.2d 267 (1985). Children from Kiryas Joel who needed special education (including the deaf, the mentally retarded, and others suffering from a range of physical, mental, or emotional disorders) were then forced to attend public schools outside the village, which their families

found highly unsatisfactory. Parents of most of these children withdrew them from the Monroe-Woodbury secular schools, citing "the panic, fear and trauma [the children] suffered in leaving their own community and being with people whose ways were so different," and some sought administrative review of the public-school placements. . . .

Monroe-Woodbury, for its part, sought a declaratory judgment in state court that New York law barred the district from providing special education services outside the district's regular public schools. . . . The New York Court of Appeals disagreed, holding that state law left Monroe-Woodbury free to establish a separate school in the village because it gives educational authorities broad discretion in fashioning an appropriate program. . . . The court added, however, that the Satmars' constitutional right to exercise their religion freely did not require a separate school, since the parents had alleged emotional trauma, not inconsistency with religious practice or doctrine, as the reason for seeking separate treatment. . . .

By 1989, only one child from Kiryas Joel was attending Monroe-Woodbury's public schools; the village's other handicapped children received privately funded special services or went without. It was then that the New York Legislature passed the statute at issue in this litigation, which provided that the Village of Kiryas Joel "is constituted a separate school district, . . . and shall have and enjoy all the powers and duties of a union free school district. . . ." 1989 N.Y.Laws, ch. 748. The statute thus empowered a locally elected board of education to take such action as opening schools and closing them, hiring teachers, prescribing textbooks, establishing disciplinary rules, and raising property taxes to fund operations. . . . In signing the bill into law, Governor Cuomo recognized that the residents of the new school district were "all members of the same religious sect," but said that the bill was "a good faith effort to solve th[e] unique problem" associated with providing special education services to handicapped children in the village. . . .

Although it enjoys plenary legal authority over the elementary and secondary education of all school-aged children in the village, . . . the Kiryas Joel Village School District currently runs only a special education program for handicapped children. The other village children have stayed in their parochial schools, relying on the new school district only for transportation, remedial education, and health and welfare services. If any child without handicap in Kiryas Joel were to seek a public-school education, the district would pay tuition to send the child into Monroe-Woodbury or another school district nearby. Under like arrangements, several of the neighboring districts send their handicapped Hasidic children into Kiryas Joel, so that two thirds of the full-time students in the village's public school come from outside. In all, the new district serves just over 40 full-time students, and two or three times that many parochial school students on a part-time basis. . . .

We . . . granted certiorari. . . .

"A proper respect for both the Free Exercise and the Establishment Clauses compels the State to pursue a course of 'neutrality' toward religion," . . . favoring neither one religion over others nor religious adherents collectively over nonadherents. . . . Chapter 748, the statute creating the Kiryas Joel Village School District, departs from this constitutional command by delegating the State's discretionary authority over public schools to a group defined by its character as a religious community, in a legal and historical context that gives no assurance that governmental power has been or will be exercised neutrally. . . .

. . . [A] State may not delegate its civic authority to a group chosen according to a religious criterion. Authority over public schools belongs to the State, N.Y. Const., Art. XI, §1 (McKinney 1987), and cannot be delegated to a local school district defined by the State in order to grant political control to a religious group. . . .

It is undisputed that those who negotiated the village boundaries when applying the general village incorporation statute drew them so as to exclude all but Satmars, and that the New York Legislature was well aware that the village remained exclusively Satmar in 1989 when it adopted Chapter 748. . . . The significance of this fact to the state legislature is indicated by the further fact that carving out the village school district ran counter to customary districting practices in the State. Indeed, the trend in New York is not toward dividing school districts but toward consolidating them. The thousands of small common school districts laid out in the early 19th century have been combined and recombined, first into union free school districts and then into larger central school districts, until only a tenth as many remain today. . . . Most of these cover several towns, many of them cross county boundaries, and only one remains precisely coterminous with an incorporated village. . . . The object of the State's practice of consolidation is the creation of districts large enough to provide a comprehensive education at affordable cost, which is thought to require at least 500 pupils for a combined junior-senior high school. . . . The Kiryas Joel Village School District, in contrast, has only 13 local, full-time students in all (even including out-of-area and part-time students leaves the number under 200), and in offering only special education and remedial programs it makes no pretense to be a full-service district.

The origin of the district in a special act of the legislature, rather than the State's general laws governing school district reorganization, is likewise anomalous. Although the legislature has established some 20 existing school districts by special act, all but one of these are districts in name only, having been designed to be run by private organizations serving institutionalized children. They have neither tax bases nor student populations of their own but serve children placed by other school districts or public agencies. . . . The one school district petitioners point to that was formed by special act of the legislature to serve a whole community, as this one was, is a district formed for a new town, much larger and more heterogeneous than this village, being built on land that straddled two existing districts. . . . Thus the Kiryas Joel Village School District is exceptional to the point of singularity, as the only district coming to our notice that the legislature carved from a single existing district to serve local residents. . . .

Because the district's creation ran uniquely counter to state practice, following the lines of a religious community where the customary and neutral principles would not have dictated the same result, we have good reasons to treat this district as the reflection of a religious criterion for identifying the recipients of civil authority. Not even the special needs of the children in this community can explain the legislature's unusual Act, for the State could have responded to the concerns of the Satmar parents without implicating the Establishment Clause. . . . We therefore find the legislature's Act to be substantially equivalent to defining a political subdivision and hence the qualification for its franchise by a religious test, resulting in a purposeful and forbidden "fusion of governmental and religious functions." . . .

The fact that this school district was created by a special and unusual Act of the legislature also gives reason for concern whether the benefit received by the Satmar community is one that the legislature will provide equally to other religious (and nonreligious) groups. . . .

The fundamental source of constitutional concern here is that the legislature itself may fail to exercise governmental authority in a religiously neutral way. The anomalously case-specific nature of the legislature's exercise of state authority in creating this district for a religious community leaves the Court without any direct way to review such state action for the purpose of safeguarding a principle at the heart of the Establishment Clause, that government should not prefer one religion to another, or religion to irreligion. . . . Because the religious community of Kiryas Joel did not receive its new governmental authority simply as one of the many communities eligible for equal treatment under a general law, we have no assurance that the next similarly situated group seeking a school district of its own will receive one; unlike an administrative agency's denial of an exemption from a generally applicable law, which "would be entitled to a judicial audience," . . . a legislature's failure to enact a special law is itself unreviewable. Nor can the historical context in this case furnish us with any reason to suppose that the Satmars are merely one in a series of communities receiving the benefit of special school district laws. Early on in the development of public education in New York, the State rejected highly localized school districts for New York City when they were promoted as a way to allow separate schooling for Roman Catholic children. . . .

The general principle [is] that civil power must be exercised in a manner neutral to religion. . . .

In finding that Chapter 748 violates the requirement of governmental neutrality by extending benefit of a special franchise, we do not deny that the Constitution allows the state to accommodate religious needs by alleviating special burdens. Our cases leave no doubt that in commanding neutrality the Religion Clauses do not require the government to be oblivious to impositions that legitimate exercises of state power may place on religious belief and practice. Rather, there is "ample room under the Establishment Clause for benevolent neutrality which will permit the religious exercise to exist without sponsorship and without interference." . . . The fact that Chapter 748 facilitates the practice of religion is not what renders it an unconstitutional establishment. . . .

But accommodation is not a principle without limits, and what petitioners seek is an adjustment to the Satmars' religiously grounded preferences that our cases do not countenance. Prior decisions have allowed religious communities and institutions to pursue their own interests free from governmental interference, . . . but we have never hinted that an otherwise unconstitutional delegation of political power to a religious group could be saved as a religious accommodation. Petitioners' proposed accommodation singles out a particular religious sect for special treatment, and whatever the limits of permissible legislative accommodations may be, . . . it is clear that neutrality as among religions must be honored. . . .

In this case we are clearly constrained to conclude that the statute before us fails the test of neutrality. It delegates a power this Court has said "ranks at the very apex of the function of a State," . . . to an electorate defined by common religious belief and practice, in a manner that fails to foreclose religious favoritism. It therefore crosses the line from permissible accommodation to impermissible establishment. . . .

Affirmed.

CASE NOTE

After the U.S. Supreme Court rendered its *Kiryas Joel Village* decision, the New York legislature repealed the law and passed new legislation allowing municipalities to establish their own school districts if they met certain criteria.

Taxpayers challenged the new law, arguing that the criteria were designed to allow the restoration of the Hasidic school district. The New York Supreme Court, Appellate Division, agreed with the taxpayers that the new law merely created the same result that was earlier held to be unconstitutional. The criteria were educationally meaningless and served only as a subterfuge to avoid the prior U.S. Supreme Court decision. *Grumet v. Cuomo,* 647 N.Y. 5. 2d (A.D.3d Dept.1996).

In an appeal of the state appellate court's decision, the higher court found that despite the apparently neutral statutory criteria in the amended law, the Hasidic village was the only municipality that could ever avail itself of the new law; therefore, the court found that a law that accommodates one sect alone cannot be neutral and was thus unconstitutional. A further appeal to the New York Court of Appeals produced the same result. The court said that even though the law was facially neutral with regard to religion, it nevertheless had the effect of benefiting only Kiryas Joel residents of one religion. By its design, the law could not benefit any religious group other than the Satmar sect of Kiryas Joel and thereby violated the establishment clause of the First Amendment. *Grumet v. Pataki,* 1999 WL 289458 (N.Y.1999).

Payment of Title I Teachers in Parochial Schools Does Not Violate the Establishment Clause

Agostini v. Felton

Supreme Court of the United States, 1997.
521 U.S. 203, 117 S.Ct. 1997.

Justice O'CONNOR delivered the opinion of the Court.

In *Aguilar v. Felton,* 473 U.S. 402, 105 S.Ct. 3232, 87 L.Ed.2d 290 (1985), this Court held that the Establishment Clause of the First Amendment barred the city of New York from sending public school teachers into parochial schools to provide remedial education to disadvantaged

children pursuant to a congressionally mandated program. On remand, the District Court for the Eastern District of New York entered a permanent injunction reflecting our ruling. Twelve years later, petitioners—the parties bound by that injunction—seek relief from its operation. Petitioners maintain that *Aguilar* cannot be squared with our intervening Establishment Clause jurisprudence and ask that we explicitly recognize what our more recent cases already dictate: *Aguilar* is no longer good law. . . .

In 1965, Congress enacted Title I of the Elementary and Secondary Education Act of 1965, 79 Stat. 27, as modified, 20 U.S.C. §6301 et seq., to "provid[e] full educational opportunity to every child regardless of economic background." . . . Toward that end, Title I channels federal funds, through the States, to "local educational agencies" . . . . The LEA's spend these funds to provide remedial education, guidance, and job counseling to eligible students. . . . Title I funds must be made available to all eligible children, regardless of whether they attend public schools. . . .

An LEA providing services to children enrolled in private schools is subject to a number of constraints that are not imposed when it provides aid to public schools. Title I services may be provided only to those private school students eligible for aid, and cannot be used to provide services on a "school-wide" basis. . . . In addition, the LEA must retain complete control over Title I funds; retain title to all materials used to provide Title I services; and provide those services through public employees or other persons independent of the private school and any religious institution. . . . The Title I services themselves must be "secular, neutral, and nonideological," . . . and must "supplement, and in no case supplant, the level of services" already provided by the private school....

Petitioner Board of Education of the City of New York (Board), an LEA, first applied for Title I funds in 1966 and has grappled ever since with how to provide Title I services to the private school students within its jurisdiction. Approximately 10% of the total number of students eligible for Title I services are private school students. Recognizing that more than 90% of the private schools within the Board's jurisdiction are sectarian, *Felton v. Secretary, United States*

Dept. of Ed., 739 F.2d 48, 51 (C.A.2 1984), the Board initially arranged to transport children to public schools for after-school Title I instruction. But this enterprise was largely unsuccessful. Attendance was poor, teachers and children were tired, and parents were concerned for the safety of their children. . . . After this program also yielded mixed results, the Board implemented the plan we evaluated in *Aguilar v. Felton*, 473 U.S. 402, 105 S.Ct. 3232, 87 L.Ed.2d 290 (1985).

That plan called for the provision of Title I services on private school premises during school hours. Under the plan, only public employees could serve as Title I instructors and counselors. Assignments to private schools were made on a voluntary basis and without regard to the religious affiliation of the employee or the wishes of the private school. . . . The vast majority of Title I teachers also moved among the private schools, spending fewer than five days a week at the same school.

Before any public employee could provide Title I instruction at a private school, she would be given a detailed set of written and oral instructions emphasizing the secular purpose of Title I and setting out the rules to be followed to ensure that this purpose was not compromised. . . .

In 1978, in *Aguilar*, six federal taxpayers—respondents here—sued the Board in the District Court for the Eastern District of New York. . . . In a 5–4 decision, this Court affirmed on the ground that the Board's Title I program necessitated an "excessive entanglement of church and state in the administration of [Title I] benefits." 473 U.S., at 414, 105 S.Ct., at 3239. . . .

The Board, like other LEA's across the United States, modified its Title I program so it could continue serving those students who attended private religious schools. Rather than offer Title I instruction to parochial school students at their schools, the Board reverted to its prior practice of providing instruction at public school sites, at leased sites, and in mobile instructional units (essentially vans converted into classrooms) parked near the sectarian school. The Board also offered computer-aided instruction, which could be provided "on premises" because it did not require public employees to be physically present on the premises of a religious school.

It is not disputed that the additional costs of complying with *Aguilar*'s mandate are significant. . . .

In order to evaluate whether *Aguilar* has been eroded by our subsequent Establishment Clause cases, it is necessary to understand the rationale upon which *Aguilar*, as well as its companion case, *School Dist. of Grand Rapids v. Ball*, 473 U.S. 373, 105 S.Ct. 3216, 87 L.Ed.2d 267 (1985), rested.

In *Ball*, the Court evaluated two programs implemented by the School District of Grand Rapids, Michigan. The district's Shared Time program, the one most analogous to Title I, provided remedial and "enrichment" classes, at public expense, to students attending nonpublic schools. The classes were taught during regular school hours by publicly employed teachers, using materials purchased with public funds, on the premises of nonpublic schools. . . . Accordingly, a majority found a "'substantial risk'" that teachers—even those who were not employed by the private schools—might "subtly (or overtly) conform their instruction to the [pervasively sectarian] environment in which they [taught]."

The presence of public teachers on parochial school grounds had a second, related impermissible effect: It created a "graphic symbol of the 'concert or union or dependency' of church and state". . . .

Third, the Court found that the Shared Time program impermissibly financed religious indoctrination by subsidizing "the primary religious mission of the institutions affected." . . .

Distilled to essentials, the Court's conclusion that the Shared Time program in *Ball* had the impermissible effect of advancing religion rested on three assumptions: (i) any public employee who works on the premises of a religious school is presumed to inculcate religion in her work; (ii) the presence of public employees on private school premises creates a symbolic union between church and state; and (iii) any and all public aid that directly aids the educational function of religious schools impermissibly finances religious indoctrination, even if the aid reaches such schools as a consequence of private decisionmaking. Additionally, in *Aguilar* there was a fourth assumption: that New York City's Title I program necessitated an excessive government entanglement with religion because public employees who teach on the premises of religious schools must be closely monitored to ensure that they do not inculcate religion.

Our more recent cases have undermined the assumptions upon which *Ball* and *Aguilar* relied. To be sure, the general principles we use to evaluate whether government aid violates the Establishment Clause have not changed since *Aguilar* was decided. For example, we continue to ask whether the government acted with the purpose of advancing or inhibiting religion, and the nature of that inquiry has remained largely unchanged. . . .

As we have repeatedly recognized, government inculcation of religious beliefs has the impermissible effect of advancing religion. Our cases subsequent to *Aguilar* have, however, modified in two significant respects the approach we use to assess indoctrination. First, we have abandoned the presumption erected in *Meek* and *Ball* that the placement of public employees on parochial school grounds inevitably results in the impermissible effect of state-sponsored indoctrination or constitutes a symbolic union between government and religion. In *Zobrest v. Catalina Foothills School Dist.,* 509 U.S. 1, 113 S.Ct. 2462, 125 L.Ed.2d 1 (1993), we examined whether the IDEA, 20 U.S.C. §1400 et seq., was constitutional as applied to a deaf student who sought to bring his state-employed sign-language interpreter with him to his Roman Catholic high school. We held that this was permissible, expressly disavowing the notion that "the Establishment Clause [laid] down [an] absolute bar to the placing of a public employee in a sectarian school." . . . *Zobrest* therefore expressly rejected the notion—relied on in *Ball* and *Aguilar*—that, solely because of her presence on private school property, a public employee will be presumed to inculcate religion in the students. *Zobrest* also implicitly repudiated another assumption on which *Ball* and *Aguilar* turned: that the presence of a public employee on private school property creates an impermissible "symbolic link" between government and religion. . . .

Second, we have departed from the rule relied on in *Ball* that all government aid that directly aids the educational function of religious schools is invalid. In *Witters v. Washington Dept.*

of Servs. for Blind, 474 U.S. 481, 106 S.Ct. 748, 88 L.Ed.2d 846 (1986), we held that the Establishment Clause did not bar a State from issuing a vocational tuition grant to a blind person who wished to use the grant to attend a Christian college and become a pastor, missionary, or youth director. Even though the grant recipient clearly would use the money to obtain religious education, we observed that the tuition grants were "'made available generally without regard to the sectarian-nonsectarian, or public-nonpublic nature of the institution benefited.'". . . The grants were disbursed directly to students, who then used the money to pay for tuition at the educational institution of their choice. In our view, this transaction was no different from a State's issuing a paycheck to one of its employees, knowing that the employee would donate part or all of the check to a religious institution. In both situations, any money that ultimately went to religious institutions did so "only as a result of the genuinely independent and private choices of" individuals. The same logic applied in *Zobrest,* where we allowed the State to provide an interpreter, even though she would be a mouthpiece for religious instruction, because the IDEA's neutral eligibility criteria ensured that the interpreter's presence in a sectarian school was a "result of the private decision of individual parents" and "[could] not be attributed to state decisionmaking." 509 U.S., at 10, 113 S.Ct., at 2467 (emphasis added). Because the private school would not have provided an interpreter on its own, we also concluded that the aid in *Zobrest* did not indirectly finance religious education by "reliev[ing] the sectarian schoo[l] of costs [it] otherwise could have borne in educating [its]students." . . .

Zobrest and *Witters* make clear that, under current law, the Shared Time program in Ball and New York City's Title I program in *Aguilar* will not, as a matter of law, be deemed to have the effect of advancing religion through indoctrination. Indeed, each of the premises upon which we relied in *Ball* to reach a contrary conclusion is no longer valid. First, there is no reason to presume that, simply because she enters a parochial school classroom, a full-time public employee such as a Title I teacher will depart from her assigned duties and instructions and embark on religious indoctrination, any more than there was a reason in *Zobrest* to think an interpreter would inculcate religion by altering her translation of classroom lectures. Certainly, no evidence has ever shown that any New York City Title I instructor teaching on parochial school premises attempted to inculcate religion in students. . . . Thus, both our precedent and our experience require us to reject respondents' remarkable argument that we must presume Title I instructors to be "uncontrollable and sometimes very unprofessional." . . .

Nor under current law can we conclude that a program placing full-time public employees on parochial campuses to provide Title I instruction would impermissibly finance religious indoctrination. In all relevant respects, the provision of instructional services under Title I is indistinguishable from the provision of sign-language interpreters under the IDEA. Both programs make aid available only to eligible recipients. That aid is provided to students at whatever school they choose to attend. . . .

Although we examined in *Witters* and *Zobrest* the criteria by which an aid program identifies its beneficiaries, we did so solely to assess whether any use of that aid to indoctrinate religion could be attributed to the State. A number of our Establishment Clause cases have found that the criteria used for identifying beneficiaries are relevant in a second respect, apart from enabling a court to evaluate whether the program subsidizes religion. Specifically, the criteria might themselves have the effect of advancing religion by creating a financial incentive to undertake religious indoctrination. . . . This incentive is not present, however, where the aid is allocated on the basis of neutral, secular criteria that neither favor nor disfavor religion, and is made available to both religious and secular beneficiaries on a nondiscriminatory basis. Under such circumstances, the aid is less likely to have the effect of advancing religion. . . .

In *Ball* and *Aguilar*, the Court gave this consideration no weight. Before and since those decisions, we have sustained programs that provided aid to all eligible children regardless of where they attended school. . . .

Applying this reasoning to New York City's Title I program, it is clear that Title I services are allocated on the basis of criteria that neither favor nor disfavor religion. The services are available to all children who meet the Act's eligibility requirements, no matter what their religious beliefs or where they go to school, 20 U.S.C. §6312(c)(1)(F). The Board's program does not, therefore, give aid recipients any incentive to modify their religious beliefs or practices in order to obtain those services.

We turn now to *Aguilar*'s conclusion that New York City's Title I program resulted in an excessive entanglement between church and state. Whether a government aid program results in such an entanglement has consistently been an aspect of our Establishment Clause analysis. We have considered entanglement both in the course of assessing whether an aid program has an impermissible effect of advancing religion, *Walz v. Tax Comm'n of City of New York*, 397 U.S. 664, 674, 90 S.Ct. 1409, 1414, 25 L.Ed.2d 697 (1970), and as a factor separate and apart from "effect," *Lemon v. Kurtzman*, 403 U.S., at 612–613, 91 S.Ct., at 2111. . . .

Not all entanglements, of course, have the effect of advancing or inhibiting religion. Interaction between church and state is inevitable, and we have always tolerated some level of involvement between the two. Entanglement must be "excessive" before it runs afoul of the Establishment Clause. . . .

The pre-*Aguilar* Title I program does not result in an "excessive" entanglement that advances or inhibits religion. As discussed previously, the Court's finding of "excessive" entanglement in *Aguilar* rested on three grounds: (i) the program would require "pervasive monitoring by public authorities" to ensure that Title I employees did not inculcate religion; (ii) the program required "administrative cooperation" between the Board and parochial schools; and (iii) the program might increase the dangers of "political divisiveness." . . . Under our current understanding of the Establishment Clause, the last two considerations are insufficient by themselves to create an "excessive" entanglement. They are present no matter where Title I services are offered, and no court has held that Title I services cannot be offered off-campus. . . . Further, the assumption underlying the first consideration has been undermined. In *Aguilar*, the Court presumed that full-time public employees on parochial school grounds would be tempted to inculcate religion, despite the ethical standards they were required to uphold. Because of this risk pervasive monitoring would be required. But after *Zobrest* we no longer presume that public employees will inculcate religion simply because they happen to be in a sectarian environment. Since we have abandoned the assumption that properly instructed public employees will fail to discharge their duties faithfully, we must also discard the assumption that pervasive monitoring of Title I teachers is required. There is no suggestion in the record before us that unannounced monthly visits of public supervisors are insufficient to prevent or to detect inculcation of religion by public employees. Moreover, we have not found excessive entanglement in cases in which States imposed far more onerous burdens on religious institutions than the monitoring system at issue here. . . .

To summarize, New York City's Title I program does not run afoul of any of three primary criteria we currently use to evaluate whether government aid has the effect of advancing religion: it does not result in governmental indoctrination; define its recipients by reference to religion; or create an excessive entanglement. We therefore hold that a federally funded program providing supplemental, remedial instruction to disadvantaged children on a neutral basis is not invalid under the Establishment Clause when such instruction is given on the premises of sectarian schools by government employees pursuant to a program containing safeguards such as those present here. The same considerations that justify this holding require us to conclude that this carefully constrained program also cannot reasonably be viewed as an endorsement of religion. . . . Accordingly, we must acknowledge that *Aguilar*, as well as the portion of *Ball* addressing *Grand Rapids'* Shared Time program, are no longer good law.

The doctrine of stare decisis does not preclude us from recognizing the change in our law and overruling *Aguilar* and those portions of *Ball* inconsistent with our more recent decisions. As we have often noted, "[s]tare decisis is not an inexorable command," but instead reflects a policy judgment that "in most matters it is more

important that the applicable rule of law be settled than that it be settled right". . . . As discussed above, our Establishment Clause jurisprudence has changed significantly since we decided *Ball* and *Aguilar*, so our decision to overturn those cases rests on far more than "a present doctrinal disposition to come out differently from the Court of [1985]." . . . We therefore overrule *Ball* and *Aguilar* to the extent those decisions are inconsistent with our current understanding of the Establishment Clause. . . .

We therefore conclude that our Establishment Clause law has "significant[ly] change[d]" since we decided *Aguilar*. . . .

For these reasons, we reverse the judgment of the Court of Appeals and remand to the District Court with instructions to vacate its September 26, 1985, order.

It is so ordered.

❖ — ❖ — ❖

Federal Funds to Sectarian Schools for Acquisition of Instructional and Educational Materials Does Not Violate the Establishment Clause

Mitchell v. Helms

Supreme Court of the United States, 2000.
____ U.S. ___, 120 S.Ct. 2530, 2000 WL 826256.

Justice Thomas announced the judgment of the Court and delivered an opinion, in which the Chief Justice, Justice Scalia, and Justice Kennedy join.

As part of a longstanding school aid program known as Chapter 2, the Federal Government distributes funds to state and local governmental agencies, which in turn lend educational materials and equipment to public and private schools, with the enrollment of each participating school determining the amount of aid that it receives. The question is whether Chapter 2, as applied in Jefferson Parish, Louisiana, is a law respecting an establishment of religion, because many of the private schools receiving Chapter 2 aid in that parish are religiously affiliated. We hold that Chapter 2 is not such a law. . . .

Chapter 2 of the Education Consolidation and Improvement Act of 1981, Pub.L. 97-35, 95 Stat. 469, as amended, 20 U.S.C. §§7301–7373, has its origins in the Elementary and Secondary Education Act of 1965 (ESEA), and is a close cousin of the provision of the ESEA that we recently considered in *Agostini v. Felton*, 521 U.S. 203 (1997). Like the provision at issue in *Agostini*, Chapter 2 channels federal funds to local educational agencies (LEA's), which are usually public school districts, via state educational agencies (SEA's), to implement programs to assist children in elementary and secondary schools. Among other things, Chapter 2 provides aid "for the acquisition and use of instructional and educational materials, including library services and materials (including media materials), assessments, reference materials, computer software and hardware for instructional use, and other curricular materials." . . . LEA's and SEA's must offer assistance to both public and private schools (although any private school must be nonprofit). Participating private schools receive Chapter 2 aid based on the number of children enrolled in each school, and allocations of Chapter 2 funds for those schools must generally be "equal (consistent with the number of children to be served) to expenditures for programs . . . for children enrolled in the public schools of the [LEA]." LEA's just in all cases "assure equitable participation" of the children of private schools "in the purposes and benefits" of Chapter 2. Further, Chapter 2 funds may only "supplement and, to the extent practical, increase the level of funds that would . . . be made available from non-Federal sources." LEA's and SEA's may not operate their programs "so as to supplant funds from non-Federal sources."

Several restrictions apply to aid to private schools. Most significantly, the "services, materials, and equipment" provided to private schools must be "secular, neutral, and nonideological." In addition, private schools may not acquire control of Chapter 2 funds or title to Chapter 2 materials, equipment, or property. A private school receives the materials and equipment listed . . . by submitting to the LEA an application detailing which items the school seeks and how it will use them; the LEA, if it approves the application, purchases those items from the school's allocation of funds, and then lends them to that school.

In Jefferson Parish (the Louisiana governmental unit at issue in this case) , as in Louisiana as a whole, private schools have primarily used their allocations for nonrecurring expenses, usually materials and equipment. In the 1986–1987 fiscal year, for example, 44% of the money budgeted for private schools in Jefferson Parish was spent by LEA's for acquiring library and media materials, and 48% for instructional equipment. Among the materials and equipment provided have been library books, computers, and computer software, and also slide and movie projectors, overhead projectors, television sets, tape recorders, VCR's, projection screens, laboratory equipment, maps, globes, filmstrips, slides, and cassette recordings.

It appears that, in an average year, about 30% of Chapter 2 funds spent in Jefferson Parish are allocated for private schools. For the 1985–1986 fiscal year, 41 private schools participated in Chapter 2. For the following year, 46 participated, and the participation level has remained relatively constant since then. Of these 46, 34 were Roman Catholic; 7 were otherwise religiously affiliated; and 5 were not religiously affiliated. . . .

Respondents filed suit in December 1985, alleging, among other things, that Chapter 2, as applied in Jefferson Parish, violated the Establishment Clause of the First Amendment of the Federal Constitution. . . .

The Establishment Clause of the First Amendment dictates that "Congress shall make no law respecting an establishment of religion." In the over 50 years since Everson, we have consistently struggled to apply these simple words in the context of governmental aid to religious schools. . . .

In *Agostini*, however, we brought some clarity to our case law, by overruling two anomalous precedents (*Meek and Wolman*, one in whole, the other in part) and by consolidating some of our previously disparate considerations under a revised test. Whereas in *Lemon* we had considered whether a statute (1) has a secular purpose, (2) has a primary effect of advancing or inhibiting religion, or (3) creates an excessive entanglement between government and religion, . . . in *Agostini* we modified *Lemon* for purposes of evaluating aid to schools and examined only the first and second factors. . . . We acknowledged that our cases discussing excessive entanglement had applied many of the same considerations as had our cases discussing primary effect, and we therefore recast *Lemon's* entanglement inquiry as simply one criterion relevant to determining a statute's effect. . . . We also acknowledged that our cases had pared somewhat the factors that could justify a finding of excessive entanglement. . . . We then set out revised criteria for determining the effect of a statute:

> To summarize, New York City's Title I program does not run afoul of any of three primary criteria we currently use to evaluate whether government aid has the effect of advancing religion: It does not result in governmental indoctrination; define its recipients by reference to religion; or create an excessive entanglement. . . .

In this case, our inquiry under *Agostini's* purpose and effect test is a narrow one. Because respondents do not challenge the District Court's holding that Chapter 2 has a secular purpose, and because the Fifth Circuit also did not question that holding, . . . we will consider only the first two *Agostini* criteria, since neither respondents nor the Fifth Circuit has questioned the District Court's holding, . . . that Chapter 2 does not create an excessive entanglement. Considering Chapter 2 in light of our more recent case law, we conclude that it neither results in religious indoctrination by the government nor defines its recipients by reference to religion. We therefore hold that Chapter 2 is not a "law respecting an establishment of religion." In so holding, we acknowledge what both the Ninth and Fifth Circuits saw was inescapable—*Meek* and *Wolman* are anomalies in our case law. We therefore conclude that they are no longer good law. . . .

As we indicated in *Agostini,* and have indicated elsewhere, the question whether governmental aid to religious schools results in governmental indoctrination is ultimately a question whether any religious indoctrination that occurs in those schools could reasonably be attributed to governmental action. . . . We have also indicated that the answer to the question of indoctrination will resolve the question whether a program of educational aid "subsidizes" religion, as our religion cases use that term. . . .

In distinguishing between indoctrination that is attributable to the State and indoctrination that is not, we have consistently turned to the principle of neutrality, upholding aid that is offered to a broad range of groups or persons without regard to their religion. If the religious, irreligious, and areligious are all alike eligible for governmental aid, no one would conclude that any indoctrination that any particular recipient conducts has been done at the behest of the government. For attribution of indoctrination is a relative question. If the government is offering assistance to recipients who provide, so to speak, a broad range of indoctrination, the government itself is not thought responsible for any particular indoctrination. To put the point differently, if the government, seeking to further some legitimate secular purpose, offers aid on the same terms, without regard to religion, to all who adequately further that purpose, . . . then it is fair to say that any aid going to a religious recipient only has the effect of furthering that secular purpose. The government, in crafting such an aid program, has had to conclude that a given level of aid is necessary to further that purpose among secular recipients and has provided no more than the same level to religious recipients.

As a way of assuring neutrality, we have repeatedly considered whether any governmental aid that goes to a religious institution does so "only as a result of the genuinely independent and private choices of individuals." . . . We have viewed as significant whether the "private choices of individual parents," as opposed to the "unmediated" will of government, . . . determine what schools ultimately benefit from the governmental aid, and how much. For if numerous private choices, rather than the single choice of a government, determine the distribution of aid pursuant to neutral eligibility criteria, then a government cannot, or at least cannot easily, grant special favors that might lead to a religious establishment. Private choice also helps guarantee neutrality by mitigating the preference for pre-existing recipients that is arguably inherent in any governmental aid program. . . . and that could lead to a program inadvertently favoring one religion or favoring religious private schools in general over nonreligious ones.

The principles of neutrality and private choice, and their relationship to each other, were prominent not only in *Agostini*, . . . but also in *Zobrest, Witters,* and *Mueller.* The heart of our reasoning in *Zobrest,* upholding governmental provision of a sign-language interpreter to a deaf student at his Catholic high school, was as follows:

> The service at issue in this case is part of a general government program that distributes benefits neutrally to any child qualifying as "disabled" under the [statute], without regard to the "sectarian-nonsectarian, or public-nonpublic nature" of the school the child attends. By according parents freedom to select a school of their choice, the statute ensures that a government-paid interpreter will be present in a sectarian school only as a result of the private decision of individual parents. In other words, because the [statute] creates no financial incentive for parents to choose a sectarian school, an interpreter's presence there cannot be attributed to state decisionmaking. . . .

As this passage indicates, the private choices helped to ensure neutrality, and neutrality and private choices together eliminated any possible attribution to the government even when the interpreter translated classes on Catholic doctrine. . . .

The tax deduction for educational expenses that we upheld in *Mueller* was, in these respects, the same as the tuition grant in *Witters.* We upheld it chiefly because it "neutrally provides state assistance to a broad spectrum of citizens," . . . and because "numerous, private choices of individual parents of school-age children," determined which schools would benefit from the deductions. We explained that "[w]here, as here, aid to parochial schools is available only as a result of decisions of individual parents no "imprimatur of state approval" can be deemed to have been conferred on any particular religion, or on religion generally."

Agostini's second primary criterion for determining the effect of governmental aid is closely related to the first. The second criterion requires a court to consider whether an aid program "define[s] its recipients by reference to religion." As we briefly explained in *Agostini*, this second criterion looks to the same set of facts as does our focus, under the first criterion, on neutrality, but the second criterion uses those facts to answer a somewhat different question—whether the criteria for allocating the aid "creat[e] a financial incentive to undertake religious indoctrination." In *Agostini* we set out the following rule for answering this question:

> This incentive is not present, however, where the aid is allocated on the basis of neutral, secular criteria that neither favor nor disfavor religion, and is made available to both religious and secular beneficiaries on a nondiscriminatory basis. Under such circumstances, the aid is less likely to have the effect of advancing religion. . . .

The cases on which *Agostini* relied for this rule, and *Agostini* itself, make clear the close relationship between this rule, incentives, and private choice. For to say that a program does not create an incentive to choose religious schools is to say that the private choice is truly "independent," . . . When such an incentive does exist, there is a greater risk that one could attribute to the government any indoctrination by the religious schools. . . .

We hasten to add, what should be obvious from the rule itself, that simply because an aid program offers private schools, and thus religious schools, a benefit that they did not previously receive does not mean that the program, by reducing the cost of securing a religious education, creates, under *Agostini*'s second criterion, an "incentive" for parents to choose such an education for their children. For any aid will have some such effect. . . .

Respondents inexplicably make no effort to address Chapter 2 under the *Agostini* test. Instead, dismissing *Agostini* as factually distinguishable, they offer two rules that they contend should govern our determination of whether Chapter 2 has the effect of advancing religion. They argue first, and chiefly, that "direct, nonincidental" aid to the primary educational mission of religious schools is always impermissible. Second, they argue that provision to religious schools of aid that is divertible to religious use is similarly impermissible. Respondents" arguments are inconsistent with our more recent case law, in particular *Agostini* and *Zobrest,* and we therefore reject them. . . .

Although some of our earlier cases, particularly *Ball,* . . . did emphasize the distinction between direct and indirect aid, the purpose of this distinction was merely to prevent "subsidization" of religion. . . . As even the dissent all but admits, . . . our more recent cases address this purpose not through the direct/indirect distinction but rather through the principle of private choice, as incorporated in the first *Agostini* criterion (i.e., whether any indoctrination could be attributed to the government). If aid to schools, even "direct aid," is neutrally available and, before reaching or benefiting any religious school, first passes through the hands (literally or figuratively) of numerous private citizens who are free to direct the aid elsewhere, the government has not provided any "support of religion," . . . . Although the presence of private choice is easier to see when aid literally passes through the hands of individuals—which is why we have mentioned directness in the same breath with private choice, . . . there is no reason why the Establishment Clause requires such a form. . . .

As *Agostini* explained, the same reasoning was at work in *Zobrest*, where we allowed the government-funded interpreter to provide assistance at a Catholic school, "even though she would be a mouthpiece for religious instruction," because the interpreter was provided according to neutral eligibility criteria and private choice. . . . Therefore, the religious messages interpreted by the interpreter could not be attributed to the government. (We saw no difference in *Zobrest* between the government hiring the interpreter directly and the government providing funds to the parents who then would hire the interpreter. . . .) We rejected the dissent's objection that we had never before allowed "a public employee to participate directly in religious indoctrination." . . . Finally, in *Agostini* itself, we used the reasoning of *Witters* and *Zobrest* to conclude that remedial classes provided under Title I of the ESEA by public employees did not impermissibly finance religious indoctrination. . . . We found it insignificant that students did not have to directly apply for Title I services, that Title I instruction was provided to students in groups rather than individually, and that instruction was provided in the facilities of the private schools. . . .

Respondents also contend that the Establishment Clause requires that aid to religious schools not be impermissibly religious in nature

or be divertible to religious use. We agree with the first part of this argument but not the second. Respondents" "no divertibility" rule is inconsistent with our more recent case law and is unworkable. So long as the governmental aid is not itself "unsuitable for use in the public schools because of religious content," . . . and eligibility for aid is determined in a constitutionally permissible manner, any use of that aid to indoctrinate cannot be attributed to the government and is thus not of constitutional concern. And, of course, the use to which the aid is put does not affect the criteria governing the aid's allocation and thus does not create any impermissible incentive under *Agostini*'s second criterion. Our recent precedents, particularly *Zobrest*, require us to reject respondents' argument. For *Zobrest* gave no consideration to divertibility or even to actual diversion. Had such things mattered to the Court in *Zobrest*, we would have found the case to be quite easy—for striking down rather than, as we did, upholding the program. . . . Quite clearly, then, we did not, as respondents do, think that the use of governmental aid to further religious indoctrination was synonymous with religious indoctrination by the government or that such use of aid created any improper incentives.

Similarly, had we, in *Witters*, been concerned with divertibility or diversion, we would have unhesitatingly, perhaps summarily, struck down the tuition-reimbursement program, because it was certain that *Witters* sought to participate in it to acquire an education in a religious career from a sectarian institution. Diversion was guaranteed. *Mueller* took the same view as *Zobrest* and *Witters*, for we did not in *Mueller* require the State to show that the tax deductions were only for the costs of education in secular subjects. . . .

The issue is not divertibility of aid but rather whether the aid itself has an impermissible content. Where the aid would be suitable for use in a public school, it is also suitable for use in any private school. Similarly, the prohibition against the government providing impermissible content resolves the Establishment Clause concerns that exist if aid is actually diverted to religious uses. . . .

In *Agostini* itself, we approved the provision of public employees to teach secular remedial classes in private schools partly because we concluded that there was no reason to suspect that indoctrinating content could be part of such governmental aid. . . . Relying on *Zobrest*, we refused to presume that the public teachers would "inject religious content" into their classes, . . . especially given certain safeguards that existed; we also saw no evidence that they had done so. . . .

A concern for divertibility, as opposed to improper content, is misplaced not only because it fails to explain why the sort of aid that we have allowed is permissible, but also because it is boundless—enveloping all aid, no matter how trivial—and thus has only the most attenuated (if any) link to any realistic concern for preventing an "establishment of religion." Presumably, for example, government-provided lecterns, chalk, crayons, pens, paper, and paintbrushes would have to be excluded from religious schools under respondents' proposed rule. But we fail to see how indoctrination by means of (i.e., diversion of) such aid could be attributed to the government. In fact, the risk of improper attribution is less when the aid lacks content, for there is no risk (as there is with books), of the government inadvertently providing improper content. . . .

Finally, any aid, with or without content, is "divertible" in the sense that it allows schools to "divert" resources. Yet we have "not accepted the recurrent argument that all aid is forbidden because aid to one aspect of an institution frees it to spend its other resources on religious ends." . . .

It is perhaps conceivable that courts could take upon themselves the task of distinguishing among the myriad kinds of possible aid based on the ease of diverting each kind. But it escapes us how a court might coherently draw any such line. It not only is far more workable, but also is actually related to real concerns about preventing advancement of religion by government, simply to require, as did *Zobrest, Agostini,* and *Allen,* that a program of aid to schools not provide improper content and that it determine eligibility and allocate the aid on a permissible basis. . . .

The dissent serves up a smorgasbord of 11 factors that, depending on the facts of each case "in all its particularity," post, at 11, could be relevant to the constitutionality of a school-aid program. And those 11 are a bare minimum. We are reassured that there are likely more. Pre-

sumably they will be revealed in future cases, as needed, but at least one additional factor is evident from the dissent itself: The dissent resurrects the concern for political divisiveness that once occupied the Court but that post-*Aguilar* cases have rightly disregarded. . . . As Justice O'Connor explained in dissent in *Aguilar*: "It is curious indeed to base our interpretation of the Constitution on speculation as to the likelihood of a phenomenon which the parties may create merely by prosecuting a lawsuit." While the dissent delights in the perverse chaos that all these factors produce, . . . the Constitution becomes unnecessarily clouded, and legislators, litigants, and lower courts groan, as the history of this case amply demonstrates. . . .

One of the dissent's factors deserves special mention: whether a school that receives aid (or whose students receive aid) is pervasively sectarian. The dissent is correct that there was a period when this factor mattered, particularly if the pervasively sectarian school was a primary or secondary school. . . . But that period is one that the Court should regret, and it is thankfully long past.

There are numerous reasons to formally dispense with this factor. First, its relevance in our precedents is in sharp decline. Although our case law has consistently mentioned it even in recent years, we have not struck down an aid program in reliance on this factor since 1985, in *Aguilar* and *Ball*. *Agostini* of course overruled *Aguilar* in full and *Ball* in part. . . [I]n *Zobrest* and *Agostini*, we upheld aid programs to children who attended schools that were not only pervasively sectarian but also were primary or secondary. *Zobrest*, in turning away a challenge based on the pervasively sectarian nature of Salpointe Catholic High School, emphasized the presence of private choice and the absence of government-provided sectarian content. . . . *Agostini*, in explaining why the aid program was constitutional, did not bother to mention that pervasively sectarian schools were at issue. . . . In disregarding the nature of the school, *Zobrest* and *Agostini* were merely returning to the approach of *Everson* and *Allen,* in which the Court upheld aid programs to students at pervasively sectarian schools. . . .

Second, the religious nature of a recipient should not matter to the constitutional analysis, so long as the recipient adequately furthers the government's secular purpose. . . . If a program offers permissible aid to the religious (including the pervasively sectarian), the areligious, and the irreligious, it is a mystery which view of religion the government has established, and thus a mystery what the constitutional violation would be. The pervasively sectarian recipient has not received any special favor, and it is most bizarre that the Court would, as the dissent seemingly does, reserve special hostility for those who take their religion seriously, who think that their religion should affect the whole of their lives, or who make the mistake of being effective in transmitting their views to children.

Third, the inquiry into the recipient's religious views required by a focus on whether a school is pervasively sectarian is not only unnecessary but also offensive. It is well established, in numerous other contexts, that courts should refrain from trolling through a person's or institution's religious beliefs. . . .). Yet that is just what this factor requires, as was evident before the District Court, . . . In addition, and related, the application of the "pervasively sectarian" factor collides with our decisions that have prohibited governments from discriminating in the distribution of public benefits based upon religious status or sincerity. See *Rosenberger v. Rector and Visitors of Univ. of Va.*, 515 U.S. 819 (1995); *Lamb's Chapel v. Center Moriches Union Free School Dist.*, 508 U.S. 384 (1993); *Widmar v. Vincent*, 454 U.S. 263 (1981).

Finally, hostility to aid to pervasively sectarian schools has a shameful pedigree that we do not hesitate to disavow. . . . Although the dissent professes concern for "the implied exclusion of the less favored." . . . [T]he exclusion of pervasively sectarian schools from government-aid programs is just that, particularly given the history of such exclusion. Opposition to aid to "sectarian" schools acquired prominence in the 1870's with Congress's consideration (and near passage) of the Blaine Amendment, which would have amended the Constitution to bar any aid to sectarian institutions. Consideration of the amendment arose at a time of pervasive hostility to the Catholic Church and to Catholics in general, and it was an open secret that "sectarian" was code for "Catholic." . . . Notwithstanding its history, of course, "sectarian" could,

on its face, describe the school of any religious sect, but the Court eliminated this possibility of confusion when, in *Hunt v. McNair*, 413 U.S., at 743, it coined the term "pervasively sectarian"— a term which, at that time, could be applied almost exclusively to Catholic parochial schools and which even today's dissent exemplifies chiefly by reference to such schools. . . . In short, nothing in the Establishment Clause requires the exclusion of pervasively sectarian schools from otherwise permissible aid programs, and other doctrines of this Court bar it. This doctrine, born of bigotry, should be buried now.

Applying the two relevant *Agostini* criteria, we see no basis for concluding that Jefferson Parish's Chapter 2 program "has the effect of advancing religion." . . . Chapter 2 does not result in governmental indoctrination, because it determines eligibility for aid neutrally, allocates that aid based on the private choices of the parents of schoolchildren, and does not provide aid that has an impermissible content. Nor does Chapter 2 define its recipients by reference to religion.

Taking the second criterion first, it is clear that Chapter 2 aid "is allocated on the basis of neutral, secular criteria that neither favor nor disfavor religion, and is made available to both religious and secular beneficiaries on a nondiscriminatory basis." . . . Aid is allocated based on enrollment: "Private schools receive Chapter 2 materials and equipment based on the per capita number of students at each school," . . . and allocations to private schools must "be equal (consistent with the number of children to be served) to expenditures for programs under this subchapter for children enrolled in the public schools of the [LEA]." . . . LEA's must provide Chapter 2 materials and equipment for the benefit of children in private schools "[t]o the extent consistent with the number of children in the school district of [an LEA] . . . who are enrolled in private nonprofit elementary and secondary schools." . . . The allocation criteria therefore create no improper incentive. Chapter 2 does, by statute, deviate from a pure per capita basis for allocating aid to LEA's, increasing the per-pupil allocation based on the number of children within an LEA who are from poor families, reside in poor areas, or reside in rural areas. But respondents have not contended, nor do we have any reason to think, that this deviation in the allocation to the LEA's leads to deviation in the allocation among schools within each LEA, . . . and, even if it did, we would not presume that such a deviation created any incentive one way or the other with regard to religion.

Chapter 2 also satisfies the first *Agostini* criterion. The program makes a broad array of schools eligible for aid without regard to their religious affiliations or lack thereof. . . . We therefore have no difficulty concluding that Chapter 2 is neutral with regard to religion. . . . Chapter 2 aid also, like the aid in *Agostini, Zobrest,* and *Witters,* reaches participating schools only "as a consequence of private decisionmaking." . . . Private decisionmaking controls because of the per capita allocation scheme, and those decisions are independent because of the program's neutrality. . . . It is the students and their parents—not the government—who, through their choice of school, determine who receives Chapter 2 funds. The aid follows the child.

Because Chapter 2 aid is provided pursuant to private choices, it is not problematic that one could fairly describe Chapter 2 as providing "direct" aid. The materials and equipment provided under Chapter 2 are presumably used from time to time by entire classes rather than by individual students (although individual students are likely the chief consumers of library books and, perhaps, of computers and computer software), and students themselves do not need to apply for Chapter 2 aid in order for their schools to receive it, but, as we explained in Agostini, these traits are not constitutionally significant or meaningful. . . . Nor, for reasons we have already explained, is it of constitutional significance that the schools themselves, rather than the students, are the bailees of the Chapter 2 aid. The ultimate beneficiaries of Chapter 2 aid are the students who attend the schools that receive that aid, and this is so regardless of whether individual students lug computers to school each day or, as Jefferson Parish has more sensibly provided, the schools receive the computers. Like the Ninth Circuit, . . . we "see little difference in loaning science kits to students who then bring the kits to school as opposed to loaning science kits to the school directly." . . .

Finally, Chapter 2 satisfies the first *Agostini* criterion because it does not provide to religious

schools aid that has an impermissible content. The statute explicitly bars anything of the sort, providing that all Chapter 2 aid for the benefit of children in private schools shall be "secular, neutral, and nonideological," . . . and the record indicates that the Louisiana SEA and the Jefferson Parish LEA have faithfully enforced this requirement insofar as relevant to this case. The chief aid at issue is computers, computer software, and library books. The computers presumably have no pre-existing content, or at least none that would be impermissible for use in public schools. Respondents do not contend otherwise. Respondents also offer no evidence that religious schools have received software from the government that has an impermissible content.

There is evidence that equipment has been, or at least easily could be, diverted for use in religious classes. . . . Justice O'Connor, however, finds the safeguards against diversion adequate to prevent and detect actual diversion. . . . The safeguards on which she relies reduce to three: (1) signed assurances that Chapter 2 aid will be used only for secular, neutral, and nonideological purposes, (2) monitoring visits, and (3) the requirement that equipment be labeled as belonging to Chapter 2. As to the first, Justice O'Connor rightly places little reliance on it. As to the second, monitoring by SEA and LEA officials is highly unlikely to prevent or catch diversion. As to the third, compliance with the labeling requirement is haphazard, . . . and, even if the requirement were followed, we fail to see how a label prevents diversion. In addition, we agree with the dissent that there is evidence of actual diversion and that, were the safeguards anything other than anemic, there would almost certainly be more such evidence. . . . In any event, for reasons we discussed in Part II-B-2, supra, the evidence of actual diversion and the weakness of the safeguards against actual diversion are not relevant to the constitutional inquiry, whatever relevance they may have under the statute and regulations.

Respondents do, however, point to some religious books that the LEA improperly allowed to be loaned to several religious schools, and they contend that the monitoring programs of the SEA and the Jefferson Parish LEA are insufficient to prevent such errors. The evidence, however, establishes just the opposite, for the improper lending of library books occurred—and was discovered and remedied—before this litigation began almost 15 years ago. In other words, the monitoring system worked. . . .

Further, the violation by the LEA and the private schools was minor and, in the view of the SEA's coordinator, inadvertent. There were approximately 191 improper book requests over three years (the 1982–1983 through 1984–1985 school years); these requests came from fewer than half of the 40 private schools then participating; and the cost of the 191 books amounted to "less than one percent of the total allocation over all those years."

The District Court found that prescreening by the LEA coordinator of requested library books was sufficient to prevent statutory violations, . . . and the Fifth Circuit did not disagree. Further, as noted, the monitoring system appears adequate to catch those errors that do occur. We are unwilling to elevate scattered de minimis statutory violations, discovered and remedied by the relevant authorities themselves prior to any litigation, to such a level as to convert an otherwise unobjectionable parishwide program into a law that has the effect of advancing religion. . . .

In short, Chapter 2 satisfies both the first and second primary criteria of *Agostini*. It therefore does not have the effect of advancing religion. For the same reason, Chapter 2 also "cannot reasonably be viewed as an endorsement of religion," . . . Accordingly, we hold that Chapter 2 is not a law respecting an establishment of religion. Jefferson Parish need not exclude religious schools from its Chapter 2 program. To the extent that *Meek* and *Wolman* conflict with this holding, we overrule them.

The judgment of the Fifth Circuit is reversed. It is so ordered.

CASE NOTE

The Supreme Court of Arizona, sitting en banc, has held that an Arizona statute allowing a state tax credit for donations to a school tuition organization (STO) does not violate the establishment clause of the federal Constitution. The court concluded that the primary beneficiaries of the tax credit, which capped tax credits at $200 for public school extracurricular activities and tax credits for tuition at private schools at $500, were the parent taxpayers and not the religious schools. Further, the court held that neither did the statute violate the Arizona Constitution, which forbids the creation of a state church or religion. *Kotterman v. Killian*, 193 Ariz. 273, 972 P.2d 606 (1999).

■ ANTIESTABLISHMENT PROVISIONS IN STATE CONSTITUTIONS

The ideals of toleration and freedom of conscience are reflected in the state constitutions as well as in the First Amendment of the U.S. Constitution. A state law that is constitutional under the First Amendment of the U.S. Constitution may not be constitutional under the state constitution. Some of the state provisions establish strong and effective barriers preventing the mixing of affairs of state with those of religion. The history, tradition, and religious influence of both Protestant and Catholic churches in the various states, though, have led to judicial interpretations that have, in many instances, weakened the separation of church and state. As political pressure for use of tax funds for support of religious schools has intensified, primarily in states with greater numbers of parochial schools, the establishment principles of those state constitutions have been interpreted by state courts to be less restrictive. For example, even though the states of Rhode Island, New York, Pennsylvania, Ohio, and Illinois have strongly worded constitutional prohibitions against establishment of religion, lenient judicial interpretations have given the legislatures substantial latitude in aiding parochial schools. In these states, the courts have generally ruled that the state constitutional restraints are no more, and probably less, restrictive than the First Amendment of the U.S. Constitution.

As an example, the various pressures for aid to parochial schools in Rhode Island, ironically the state of Roger Williams, have caused the courts to negate the meaning of the strong disestablishment language of the Rhode Island Constitution, which says, "[W]e, therefore, declare that no man shall be compelled to frequent or to *support* any religious worship, place, or ministry whatever" (italics added).[130] The Supreme Court of Rhode Island, in considering the constitutionality of textbook aid to parochial schools, noted that the allegedly offending statute was less vulnerable to attack under the Rhode Island Constitution than under the First Amendment. This court held that the Rhode Island Constitution erected a lower wall of separation than did the First Amendment:

> Nor can we agree with appellees that the language of the constitution of this state prohibiting establishment of religion or the interference with the free exercise thereof is more restrictive than the language of the federal constitution as interpreted in *Allen*. . . .[131]

Similarly, an apparently strong and definitive prohibition in the Illinois Constitution, forbidding state aid to church schools by stating that neither the state nor any school district or public corporation "shall ever make any appropriation or pay from any public fund whatever, anything in aid of any church or sectarian purpose, or to help support or sustain any school . . . controlled by any church or sectarian denomination whatever,"[132] has been substantially weakened by state court interpretation. The Supreme Court of Illinois has held that the Illinois Constitution is no more restrictive than the First Amendment.[133]

This view of the Illinois court appears to reflect a prevailing pattern of precedents of state courts in interpreting their own constitutions, closely adhering to the constitutional tests that the U.S. Supreme Court applied to the First Amendment case in *Lemon v. Kurtzman*.[134]

In Connecticut, the state supreme court followed the *Everson* precedent and upheld a state statute that provided public funds for transportation of parochial school students.[135] The "public purpose" theory used by the U.S. Supreme Court in *Everson* was cited as the controlling rationale for the Connecticut Constitution. The Connecticut court said:

> It cannot be said that their transportation does not serve the purpose of education, and [e]ducation in itself serves a public purpose. . . .[136]

Similarly, the Indiana Constitution has been held to be no more forceful in the separation of church and state than is the First Amend-

ment.[137] Moreover, most states, including Iowa,[138] Kansas,[139] Maine,[140] Michigan,[141] Minnesota,[142] New Jersey,[143] and Wisconsin,[144] have applied the U.S. Supreme Court's First Amendment rationale to the church-state provisions of their own constitutions. The judicial precedents of many of these states explicitly follow the establishment of religion tests used by the U.S. Supreme Court.

It remains to be seen whether a lessening of the strictures by the U.S. Supreme Court in interpreting the establishment clause of the First Amendment—a distinct possibility, as indicated by the decision in *Agostini v. Felton*[145] and by the current makeup of the membership of the Court—will in turn elicit a corresponding lowering of the establishment standards of state constitutions, as decided by the respective state supreme courts. It is possible, of course, that state supreme courts will choose instead to maintain a higher standard in the protection of religious liberties. There is precedent for greater assertiveness on the part of state courts in the protection of individual rights and freedoms.[146]

The history and legal precedents of some states do indicate that there may be substantial resistance to reinterpretation that would diminish present religious liberty protections in state constitutions. Several states, including Alaska, Colorado, Hawaii, Idaho, Iowa, Kentucky, Missouri, Montana, Washington, and Wyoming, have constitutional provisions that would suggest strong and definite opposition to legislative action to use public monies to aid parochial schools. For example, the Alaska Supreme Court in *Matthews v. Quinton*[147] found "unpersuasive" the U.S. Supreme Court's rationale in *Everson* that the transportation of school children to parochial schools was for the benefit of the children only. Rather, the Alaska court concluded that furnishing transportation to nonpublic school students at public expense was a direct benefit to the school, just as would be the payment of teachers' salaries or building and equipment costs.[148] Reasoning thusly, the court in *Matthews* held that furnishing transportation to parochial school students violated the provision in the Alaska Constitution that forbade the use of "public funds for the direct benefit of any religious or other private educational foundation."[149]

The Colorado Constitution, too, appears to contain a stronger church-state provision than that of the First Amendment. Article V, §34 of the Colorado Constitution forbids state appropriation for educational purposes to any person or corporation not under absolute control of the state or to any denominational or sectarian institution.[150] Moreover, Article IX, §7 of the Colorado Constitution provides that

> [n]either the general assembly, nor any county, city, town, township, school district or other public corporation, shall ever make any appropriation, or pay from any public fund or moneys whatever, anything in aid of any church or sectarian society, or for any sectarian purpose, or to help support or sustain any school, academy, seminary, college, university or other literary or scientific institution, controlled by any church or sectarian denomination whatsoever . . . .[151]

Similarly, the Hawaii Constitution is quite specific in banning the use of public money for aid to parochial schools. In Spears v. Honda,[152] a 1968 case, the Supreme Court of Hawaii refused the permissive interpretation advanced by the U.S. Supreme Court in *Everson*, saying,

> We find that the framers did not open the door one bit. The language of the Constitution itself is unequivocal. It explicitly states, "Nor shall public funds be appropriated for the support or benefit of any sectarian or private educational institution."[153]

In the same vein, the Idaho Supreme Court has said:

> The Idaho Constitution places much greater restriction upon the power of state government to aid activities undertaken by religious sects than does the First Amendment to the Constitution of the United States.[154]

The 1918 Iowa case of *Knowlton v. Baumhover*[155] enunciates a stronger state separation requirement than does the federal First Amendment. In this case, the Iowa Supreme Court rejected the idea that a religious school could be publicly funded because it had both secular and sectarian purposes. In dismissing the reasoning that was later given currency by the U.S. Supreme Court in *Allen*,[156] the Iowa court denied the constitutionality of an act that provided state funds to parochial schools for aspects of the secular school program. In 1969, the attorney general of

Iowa[157] relied on *Knowlton*,[158] saying that "[t]he case held that every church or other organization upholding or promoting any form of religion or religious faith or practice is a "sect" and that the right to use public school funds for the advancement of religious or sectarian teaching is denied to each and all. The Court found that to constitute a sectarian school or sectarian instruction which may not lawfully be maintained at public expense, it is not necessary to show that the school is wholly devoted to religious or sectarian teaching." The reasoning by the Iowa court in *Knowlton* appears to reject both the child benefit and the public purpose rationales used to justify aid to parochial schools.

The Supreme Court of Missouri has made it quite clear that the Missouri constitutional restraint is more restrictive than the federal First Amendment.[159] The Missouri Supreme Court has said that "[t]he constitutional policy of our state has decreed the absolute separation of church and state, not only in governmental matters, but in educational ones as well."[160] This court has further stated that

> it is the unqualified policy of the State of Missouri that no public funds or properties, either directly or indirectly, be used to support or sustain any school affected by religious influences or teachings or by any sectarian or religious beliefs . . . .[161]

In comparing the Missouri establishment standard to the establishment clause of the First Amendment, the Missouri Court said:

> [I]t becomes readily apparent that the provisions of the Missouri Constitution declaring that there shall be a separation of church and state are not only more explicit but [also] more *restrictive than the Establishment Clause of the United States Constitution.*[162]

There is little doubt that the Missouri Constitution is a definitive obstacle to legislation designed to provide public funds for parochial schools.

Both Montana and Wyoming have religious liberty protections that are stronger than those of the First Amendment. The Montana Supreme Court in 1971,[163] in barring the employment of public school teachers in parochial schools, noted that the practice would probably have violated the First Amendment as interpreted by the *Lemon v. Kurtzman*[164] tripartite test, but the Montana court made it clear that the Montana Constitution was actually more pervasive than the federal Constitution. The Montana Constitution of 1972 maintained the strict separation language of the old 1889 constitution, which prohibited appropriations "for religious, charitable, industrial, educational or benevolent purposes to any private corporation not under the control of the state."[165] It is unlikely that such strong language could be watered down to the point that it would permit the use of state funds for parochial schools, whether the aid was extended through direct or indirect funding devices. In support of this supposition, Howard has noted that "Montana's Constitution appears to establish stricter barriers to denominational schools and colleges than does the First Amendment to the United States Constitution."[166]

There are several other examples of such strong constitutional restraints. A notable provision is Article 1, §19 of the Wyoming Constitution, which simply states that "[n]o money of the state shall ever be given or appropriated to any sectarian or religious society or institution." The conclusiveness of this provision imposes "strong bars to any state funding for private or sectarian schools."[167]

The Oregon Constitution, like that of Missouri, has an antiestablishment provision that has been held to constitute a more restrictive barrier than the First Amendment in preventing the flow of public funds to church schools. Article I, §5 of the Oregon Constitution states in part: "No money shall be drawn from the Treasury for the benefit of any religious or theological institution. . . ."

The Supreme Court of Oregon has interpreted this provision as precluding the use of public funds to provide textbooks to students in parochial schools.[168] In so holding, the court rejected the "child benefit" theory and found that textbooks, being essential to the educational process and not an incidental, were an asset to the religious institution. In 1991, proponents of parochiaid in Oregon placed on the ballot a proposed amendment to Article I, §5 that would have allowed tax credits for parents sending their children to parochial schools. The plan called for tax credits of up to $2,500 per child

for tuition and costs incurred for private schools or for home school education. This effort was roundly defeated by the Oregon voters in the spring of 1991.

The state of Washington has perhaps one of the strongest provisions for guaranteeing religious liberty and separation of church and state. The Supreme Court of Washington rejected the reasoning of the U.S. Supreme Court in *Everson* as to a precedent applicable to the provisions of the Washington Constitution. The "independent vitality" of that state's constitution appears to more strictly adhere to more basic principles of religious freedom than does the First Amendment. For example, in *Visser v. Nooksack Valley School District*,[169] the Washington Supreme Court rejected the *Cochran* and *Everson* logic, which used the "child benefit" theory to justify the use of public funds for textbooks and transportation for parochial schools. The court in *Visser*[170] said that the conclusion is inescapable that free transportation of pupils serves to aid and build up the parochial school itself and it is therefore immaterial that the children and parents might derive a benefit from it. This court quoted with approval an earlier Washington case that concluded that the use of tax funds to support transportation of nonpublic school children constitutes a "direct, substantial, and continuing public subsidy" to the schools themselves.[171]

In *Weiss v. Bruno*, 82 Wash.2d 199, 509 P.2d 973 (1973), the Supreme Court of Washington expanded on its reasoning in *Visser* beyond transportation programs. In *Weiss*, the court held that a statute providing financial assistance to needy and disadvantaged students in grades one through twelve in parochial schools violated Article 9, §4 of the state constitution, which prohibits the use of public funds for support of sectarian schools. The evidence indicated that a substantial amount of the state funds would flow to the Catholic Schools of the Spokane Diocese, which is owned and under the control of the Catholic Bishop of Spokane. The fact that a full curriculum of secular subjects was taught in the parochial schools was not determinative of the issue; regardless, such schools were under sectarian influence.

Therefore, the antiestablishment provisions of state constitutions may be strong or weak, effectual or ineffectual, depending on their wording and the interpretations of the state supreme courts. Some state supreme courts, such as the one in Illinois, have emasculated relatively strong constitutional provisions, while other state courts have given weaker statements even stronger meaning.

Whether the state supreme courts, though, will follow new U.S. Supreme Court precedents such as *Agostini v. Felton* in a diminution of religious liberty and an erosion of the wall of separation remains to be seen.

———————— ❖ — ❖ — ❖ ————————

Oregon Law Providing Textbooks to Parochial Schools Cannot Be Justified on Child Benefit Theory

Dickman v. School District No. 62 C

Supreme Court of Oregon, 1961.
232 Or. 238, 366 P.2d 533, cert. denied,
371 U.S. 823, 83 S.Ct. 41 (1962).

O'Connell, J. This is a suit in equity brought by plaintiff taxpayers against School District No. 62 C, its board and clerk, to enjoin defendants from supplying textbooks without charge for the use of pupils enrolled in St. John's The Apostle School, a parochial school maintained and operated by the Catholic church. Plaintiffs also seek a judicial declaration that the so-called free textbook statute (ORS 337.150), under which distribution was made to the St. John's school and other parochial schools, does not authorize defendants to supply textbooks free of charge to church or parochial schools, or if the statute is so construed that it be declared unconstitutional....

For a period of several years the defendant district has furnished free textbooks for the use of the pupils of St. John's school. In a period of three school years these books have cost the district approximately $4,000. The books were purchased by the district from money in its General Fund, a part of which was derived from taxes levied upon real property in the district, including real property owned by plaintiffs. . . . The district retains title to the books, a matter of little practical significance however, because the books are not ordinarily retrieved by the district. Textbooks furnished for the use of parochial school students do not differ from those delivered to public schools. A school is not entitled to receive free textbooks unless it complies with standards established by the Oregon statutes as implemented by administrative regulation. The St. John's school met these standards.

The evidence establishes, and the trial judge found, that the purpose of the Catholic church in operating in the St. John's school and other similar schools under this supervision is to permeate the entire educational process with the precepts of the Catholic religion. . . .

. . . The principal issue presented to us is whether the expenditure of public funds by the defendant school district for the purpose of furnishing textbooks free of charge to pupils of a parochial school is within these constitutional prohibitions.

We have concluded that the expenditure authorized by ORS 337.150 is within the proscription of Article I, §5 of the Oregon Constitution. . . . [T]he statute violates also the First or Fourteenth Amendments to the United States Constitution. Nor is it necessary to consider whether Article VIII, §2 of the Oregon Constitution has been violated.

Article I, §5 prohibiting the use of public moneys "for the benefit of any religious or theological institution," was designed to keep separate the functions of state and church and to prevent the influence of one upon the other. In this respect our constitution follows the general pattern of other state constitutions and may be regarded as expressing, in more specific terms, the policy of the First Amendment as it has been explained in the *Everson* case.

The historical setting in which constitutional provisions such as Article I, §5 were written and the factors which prompted their adoption have been thoroughly explained elsewhere; it is not necessary, therefore, to restate those observations here. We need only say that we regard the separation of church and state no less important today than it was at the time Article I, §5 and its counterpart in other constitutions were adopted.

The general policy is clear. Our problem is to determine whether that policy is violated by the distribution of free textbooks to parochial schools under ORS 337.150. . . .

Defendants' principal argument in support of the statute is that the expenditure of public funds for the purpose of furnishing books to pupils of parochial and public schools benefits the pupils who receive these books and not the schools themselves. . . .

This so-called "child benefit theory" has been applied in other cases in which the expenditure of public funds is made for the purpose of meeting the educational needs of pupils, including those attending parochial schools. The difficulty with this theory is, however, that unless it is qualified in some way, it can be used to justify the expenditure of public funds for every educational purpose, because all educational aids are of benefit to the pupil. . . .

It is argued that the aid to school children is for a public purpose because the compulsory school law compels all children to attend school and that the state may, therefore, make expenditures to further compliance. But this begs the basic question—the state may not compel compliance through the device of furnishing aid to religious schools if that aid is in violation of the constitution. Moreover, the state does not compel pupils to attend *parochial* schools. . . .

We recognize that whether an expenditure is an aid to a religious institution in its religious function or in some other capacity is a question of degree. But it seems clear that the line must be drawn to include within the constitutional proscription the furnishing of textbooks to pupils of parochial schools. This conclusion is compelled because such books are an integral part of the educational process. As we have already pointed out, the teaching of the precepts of Catholicism is an inseparable part of the educational process in the St. John's school. Considering the purpose of Article I, §5, we are unable to see any substantial distinction between the furnishing of textbooks and the furnishing of blackboards, desks, laboratory instruments, or other equipment clearly necessary to the operation of the school. In comparing these various essential tools we agree with the dissenting opinion in *Everson v. Board of Education of Ewing Twp.*, 133 NJL 350, 359, 44 A2d 333 (1945), that there is no way of "satisfactorily distinguishing one item of expense from another in the long process of child education."

It is argued that the strict notions of separation in vogue at the time of the adoption of our constitutional provisions no longer exist and that these provisions should be interpreted to reflect this change in attitude. Conceding that such change has occurred, there are still important considerations warranting the resolve that the wall of separation between church and state "must be kept high and impregnable." *Everson v. Board of Education*, supra, 330 US at p. 18, 67 S Ct at p. 513, 91 L ed at 725, 168 ALR at 1406. . . . These considerations convince us that the wall of separation in this state must also be kept "high and impregnable" to meet the demands of Article I, §5. . . .

The trial judge was of the opinion that the expenditures in question constituted a violation of the constitutional principle of separation of church and state, but he concluded that he was bound by *Everson v. Board of Education*, 330 US 1, 67 S Ct 504, 91 L ed 711, 168 ALR 1392 (1946). A decision of the Supreme Court of the United States holding that certain legislation is not in violation of the federal constitution is not an adjudication of the constitutionality of the legislation under a state constitution. In such a case it is not only within the power of the state courts, it is their duty to decide whether the state constitution has been violated. Our views on the policy or interpretation of a particular constitutional provision do not always coincide with those of the Supreme Court of the United States. As we have indicated, *Everson v. Board of Education*, supra, is distinguishable from the case at bar. Even if it were not, our conclusion would be the same.

The judgment is reversed. The trial court is directed to enter a decree in accordance with the prayer in plaintiffs' complaint.

CASE NOTE

The Supreme Court of Oklahoma has held that Article II, § 5 of that state's constitution prevents use of public funds to transport parochial school students to school. *Gurney v. Ferguson,*

190 Okl. 254, 122 P.2d 1002 (1941); *Board of Education v. Antone,* 384 P.2d 911 (Okl.1963).

In *Antone,* the court wrote:

> The law leaves to every man the right to entertain such religious views as appeal to his individual conscience, and to provide for the religious instruction and training of his own children to the extent and in the manner he deems essential or desirable. When he chooses to seek for them educational facilities which combine secular and religious instruction, he is faced with the necessity of assuming the financial burden which that choice entails.

In specifically rejecting the *Everson* precedent as applicable to Oklahoma, the Oklahoma Supreme Court pointed out that *Everson* is merely an interpretation of federal law and does not negate the more restrictive provisions of the Oklahoma Constitution.

The Oklahoma Supreme Court said further:

> As we pointed out in *Gurney v. Ferguson* . . . , if the cost of school buses and the operation and maintenance thereof is in aid of the public schools, then it would seem to necessarily follow that when pupils of parochial schools are transported by them, such service is in aid of that school. Any such aid or benefit, either directly or indirectly, is expressly prohibited by the above quoted provision of the constitution of Oklahoma.

Antone, 384 P.2d 911 (Okl. 1963); the provision referred to is Article II, §5 of the Oklahoma Constitution.

■ RELEASED TIME FOR RELIGIOUS INSTRUCTION

The practice of releasing public school children during regular school hours for religious instruction first began in the United States in Gary, Indiana, in 1914. Since then, the Supreme Court has had before it two cases involving release time. The first was the *McCollum* case in 1948,[172] in which pupils were released to attend religious instruction in the classrooms of the public school building. Students who did not want to participate were not released but were required to leave their classrooms and go to another part of the building to pursue their secular studies. The Supreme Court held that this "release time" program violated the First Amendment of the Constitution.

In 1952, the Supreme Court was once again called upon to test the constitutionality of "release time." In this case, a New York statute permitted pupils to leave the school building and grounds to attend religious centers for religious instruction.[173] Students who did not wish to participate in such services stayed in their classrooms, and no supervision or approval of their activities was required. The Supreme Court found that this statute did not violate the doctrine of separation of church and state. The Court pointed out that while the Constitution forbids the government to finance religious groups and promote religious instruction, the First Amendment does not require governmental hostility toward religion. From this decision, it is clear that the Supreme Court does not prohibit some cooperation between schools and churches, but the nature and degree of the cooperation are important; if they exceed certain reasonable limitations, the relationship will violate the Constitution.

❖ — ❖ — ❖

Released Time for Religious Instruction on Public School Premises Is Unconstitutional

Illinois ex rel. McCollum v. Board of Education of School District No. 71, Champaign County, Illinois

Supreme Court of the United States, 1948.
333 U.S. 203, 68 S.Ct. 461.

Mr. Justice BLACK delivered the opinion of the Court. This case related to the power of a state to utilize its tax-supported public school system in aid of religious instruction insofar as that power may be restricted by the First and Fourteenth Amendments to the Federal Constitution. . . .

Appellant's petition for mandamus alleged that religious teachers, employed by private religious groups, were permitted to come weekly into the school buildings during the regular hours set apart for secular teaching, and then and there for a period of thirty minutes substitute their religious teaching for the secular education provided under the compulsory education law. The petitioner charged that this joint public-school religious-group program violated the First and Fourteenth Amendments to the United States Constitution. The prayer of her petition was that the Board of Education be ordered to "adopt and enforce rules and regulations prohibiting all instruction in and teaching of all religious education in all public schools in Champaign District Number 71 . . . and in all public school houses and buildings in said district when occupied by public schools." . . .

Although there are disputes between the parties as to various inferences that may or may not properly be drawn from the evidence concerning the religious program, the following facts are shown by the record without dispute. In 1940 interested members of the Jewish, Roman Catholic, and a few of the Protestant faiths formed a voluntary association called the Champaign Council on Religious Education. They obtained permission from the Board of Education to offer classes in religious instruction to public school pupils in grades four to nine inclusive. Classes were made up of pupils whose parents signed printed cards requesting that their children be permitted to attend; they were held weekly, thirty minutes for the lower grades, forty-five minutes for the higher. The council employed the religious teachers at no expense to the school authorities, but the instructors were subject to the approval and supervision of the superintendent of schools. The classes were taught in three separate religious groups by Protestant teachers, Catholic priests, and a Jewish rabbi, although for the past several years there have apparently been no classes instructed in the Jewish religion. Classes were conducted in the regular classrooms of the school building. Students who did not choose to take the religious instruction were not released from public school duties; they were required to leave their classrooms and go to some other place in the school building for pursuit of their secular studies. On the other hand, students who were released from secular study for the religious instructions were required to be present at the religious classes. Reports of their presence or absence were to be made to their secular teachers.

The foregoing facts, without reference to others that appear in the record, show the use of tax-supported property for religious instruction and the close cooperation between the school authorities and the religious council in promoting religious education. The operation of the state's compulsory education system thus assists and is integrated with the program of religious instruction carried on by separate religious sects. Pupils compelled by law to go to school for secular education are released in part from their legal duty upon the condition that they attend the religious classes. This is beyond all question a utilization of the tax-established and tax-supported public school system to aid religious groups to spread their faith. And it falls squarely under the ban of the First Amendment (made applicable to the States by the Fourteenth) as we interpreted it in *Everson v. Board of Education*, 330 U.S. 1, 67 S.Ct. 504. . . .

To hold that a state cannot consistently with the First and Fourteenth Amendments utilize its public school system to aid any or all religious faiths or sects in the dissemination of their doctrines and ideals does not, as counsel urge, manifest a governmental hostility to religion or religious teachings. A manifestation of such hostility would be at war with our national tradition as embodied in the First Amendment's guaranty of the free exercise of religion. For the First Amendment rests upon the premise that both religion and government can best work to achieve their lofty aims if each is left free from the other within its respective sphere. Or, as we said in the *Everson* case, the First Amendment has erected a wall between Church and State which must be kept high and impregnable.

Here not only are the state's tax supported public school buildings used for the dissemination of religious doctrines. The State also affords sectarian groups an invaluable aid in that it helps to provide pupils for their religious classes through the use of the state's compulsory public school machinery. This is not separation of Church and State.

The cause is reversed and remanded to the State Supreme Court for proceedings not inconsistent with this opinion.

Reversed and remanded.

CASE NOTES

1. *Released Time.* Courts upholding the discretionary power of boards of education to provide released time programs: *People ex rel. Lewis v. Graves,* 245 N.Y. 195, 156 N.E. 663 (1927); *People ex rel. Latimer v. Board of Education of City of Chicago,* 394 Ill. 228, 68 N.E.2d 305 (1946); *Dilger v. School District 24 CJ,* 222 Or. 108, 352 P.2d 564 (1960). Some decisions indicated parents had the right to have children excused or released from school for religious purposes: *Lewis v. Spaulding,* 193 Misc. 66, 85 N.Y.S.2d 682 (1948), appeal dismissed 299 N.Y. 564, 85 N.E.2d 791 (1949); *Gordon v. Board of Education of City of Los Angeles,* 78 Cal.App.2d 464, 178 P.2d 488 (1947); *Perry v. School District No. 81,* Spokane, 54 Wash.2d 886, 344 P.2d 1036 (1959).

2. In a similar modern adaptation of *McCollum,* a Texas school district adopted a program requiring the district to recruit area clergy representatives to serve as counselors for students. The clergy volunteers were given written guidelines advising them not to discuss religion or provide information regarding their religious affiliation. Students that met with the clergy were selected by school principals and counselors without parental notification or consent. Plaintiff parents claimed that the practice violated their children's rights of religious liberty, specifically offending the establishment clause. The federal court in striking down the practice reasoned that students who were taken from classes to participate could not refuse for fear of being stigmatized as atheists or nonconformists by their teachers and classmates. According to the court, the program promoted and endorsed religion and afforded clergy volunteers preferential access to students. Moreover, the program conveyed a message that religion was to be promoted over other belief systems. *Doe v. Beaumont Independent School District,* 173 F. 3d 274 (5th Cir. 1999).

❖ — ❖ — ❖

Released Time for Public School Students to Attend Religious Classes Off Public School Grounds Is Constitutional

Zorach v. Clauson

Supreme Court of the United States, 1952.
343 U.S. 306, 72 S.Ct. 679.

Mr. Justice DOUGLAS delivered the opinion of the Court. New York City has a program which permits its public schools to release students during the school day so that they may leave the school buildings and school grounds and go to religious centers for religious instruction or devotional exercises. A student is released on written request of his parents. Those not released stay in the classrooms. The churches make weekly reports to the schools, sending a list of children who have been released from public school but who have not reported for religious instruction.

This "released time" program involves neither religious instruction in public school classrooms nor the expenditure of public funds. All costs, including the application blanks, are paid for by the religious organizations. The case is therefore unlike *McCollum v. Board of Education.* . . .

Appellants, who are taxpayers and residents of New York City and whose children attend its public schools, challenge the present law, contending it is in essence not different from the one involved in the *McCollum* case. . . . The New York Court of Appeals sustained the law against this claim of unconstitutionality. . . .

It takes obtuse reasoning to inject any issue of the "free exercise" of religion into the present case. No one is forced to go to the religious classroom and no religious exercise or instruction is brought to the classrooms of the public schools. A student need not take religious instruction. He is left to his own desires as to the manner or time of his religious devotions, if any.

There is a suggestion that the system involves the use of coercion to get public school students into religious classrooms. There is no evidence in the record before us that supports that conclusion. The present record indeed tells us that the school authorities are neutral in this regard and do no more than release students whose parents so request. If in fact coercion were used, if it were established that any one or more teachers were using their office to persuade or force students to take the religious instruction, a wholly different case would be presented. Hence we put aside that claim of coercion both as respects the "free exercise" of religion and "an establishment of religion" within the meaning of the first Amendment. . . .

We would have to press the concept of separation of Church and State to these extremes to condemn the present law on constitutional grounds. . . .

We are a religious people whose institutions presuppose a Supreme Being. We guarantee the freedom to worship as one chooses. We make room for as wide a variety of beliefs and creeds as the spiritual needs of man deem necessary. We sponsor an attitude on the part of government that shows no partiality to any one group and that lets each flourish according to the zeal of its adherents and the appeal of its dogma. When the state encourages religious instruction or cooperates with religious authorities by adjusting the schedule of public events to sectarian needs, it follows the best of our traditions. For it then respects the religious nature of our people and accommodates the public service to their spiritual needs. To hold that it may not would be to find in the Constitution a requirement that the government show a callous indifference to religious groups. That would be preferring those who believe in no religion over those who do believe. Government may not finance religious groups nor undertake religious instruction nor blend secular and sectarian education nor use secular institutions to force one or some religion on any person. But we find no constitutional requirement which makes it necessary for government to be hostile to religion and to throw its weight against efforts to widen the effective scope of religious influence. The government must be neutral when it comes to competition between sects. It may not thrust any sect on any person. It may not make a reli-

gious observance compulsory. It may not coerce anyone to attend church, to observe a religious holiday, or to take religious instruction. But it can close its doors or suspend its operations as to those who want to repair to their religious sanctuary for worship or instruction. No more than that is undertaken here. . . .

In the *McCollum* case the classrooms were used for religious instruction and the force of the public school was used to promote that instruction. Here, as we have said, the public schools do no more than accommodate their schedules to a program of outside religious instruction. We follow the *McCollum* case. But we cannot expand it to cover the present released time program unless separation of Church and State means that public institutions can make no adjustments of their schedules to accommodate the religious needs of the people. We cannot read into the Bill of Rights such a philosophy of hostility to religion.

Affirmed.

CASE NOTES

1. *Shared Time.* "Dual enrollment," or "shared time," is an arrangement between a public school and a private school by which the shared use of the public school facilities is provided for public school teachers or students. A pupil may be a part-time student in a public school while attending a nonpublic school part-time.

2. The U.S. Court of Appeals, Tenth Circuit, has held that provisions in a released-time program in which students attended church-related seminaries and received public school credit for classes that were "mainly denominational" in content were unconstitutional. Also unconstitutional was a procedure whereby the public school bore the burden of gathering the seminary's attendance slips. *Lanner v. Wimmer*, 662 F.2d 1349 (10th Cir.1981).

3. In a case involving "shared time," the Supreme Court of Missouri held that use of public monies to send speech teachers of a school district into parochial schools for speech therapy was not for the purpose of maintaining free public schools and was therefore unconstitutional (Section 5 of Article IX, Missouri Constitution). Also, when the school district provided speech therapy for parochial school

children in buildings maintained by the school district and parochial children who desired such therapy were released from school for part of their regular six-hour day, such practice violated compulsory attendance laws that required each school child to attend school regularly for six hours a school day. *Special District for the Education and Training of Handicapped Children of St. Louis County v. Wheeler,* 408 S.W.2d 60 (Mo.1966).

4. An Illinois court reached a conclusion different from that of the Missouri court concerning shared time. Plaintiffs in this case sought to enjoin the board of education from maintaining a dual-enrollment program where children were enrolled part-time in a public school and part-time in a nonpublic school on the grounds that the program violated statutory and constitutional provisions. The court held that the dual-enrollment program did not violate either statutory or constitutional provisions:

> The object of compulsory attendance law is that all children be educated and not that they be educated in any particular manner or place, and part-time enrollment in a public school and part-time enrollment in a nonpublic school under a dual enrollment program is permitted so long as the child receives a complete education.

Morton v. Board of Education of City of Chicago, 69 Ill.App.2d 38, 216 N.E.2d 305 (1966).

5. How does the released-time program of the *Zorach* case differ from the program in the *McCollum* case?

6. What does the Court say about the relationship between church and state? What is the role of the state in dealing with religion?

7. Relate the reasoning in the decisions by the Supreme Court in *McCollum* and *Zorach* to the concept of dual enrollment. What legal principles of the cases may be applied in a case involving dual enrollment?

8. In regard to a shared-time program where the school district leased parochial school facilities and public school teachers taught classes therein, the court held that neither the state nor the federal constitution was violated. This was true even in light of the fact that classes were conducted in the same building. *Citizens to Advance Public Education v. Porter,* 65 Mich.App. 168, 237 N.W.2d 232 (1975).

9. In a case where parents of a nonpublic school student filed suit to compel a public school district to enroll their child in a band class, the Supreme Court of Michigan held that (1) nonessential elective courses offered to public school students must be offered to resident nonpublic school students on a shared-time basis and (2) provision of nonessential elective courses to resident nonpublic school students on a shared-time basis does not violate the establishment clause where shared-time instruction is conducted on public school premises. *Snyder v. Charlotte Public School District,* Eaton County, 421 Mich. 517, 365 N.W.2d 151 (1984).

■ SECULARIZATION OF PUBLIC SCHOOLS: PRAYER AND BIBLE READING

As is apparent from the earlier discussions in this chapter, there are really two major thrusts to the question of separation of church and state in the field of education. The first concerns the use of public funds to support sectarian or parochial schools. The question, succinctly put, is whether the public should be taxed to support schools where the mission is to inculcate a particular religion. The second is the issue of secularizing the public schools, the continuing historical struggle to keep the schools of the republic apart and above sectarian strife and influences. Regarding the first, state aid to religious schools, the series of U.S. Supreme Court cases after *Lemon,* beginning with *Mueller,*[174] and then *Zobrest,*[175] *Agostini,*[176] and *Helms,*[177] indicates that schools controlled by religious groups will have little constitutional deterrence to their access to public tax funds. The Supreme Court has created a very low or no threshold of constitutional restraint in allowing tax credits, vouchers, and, possibly, direct aid to parochial or sectarian schools. On the other hand, regarding the question of secularization of the public schools, the Supreme Court has taken a strict separationist view of the First Amendment, whereby its decisions absolutely deny religious activities in public schools. This is true in spite of the persistent efforts in states and local school districts by many religious sects to interject their beliefs into public school functions.

A BIFURCATED STANDARD

Thus, the Supreme Court appears to have established a bifurcated standard of separation by which one branch of cases, represented by *Weisman*[178] and *Santa Fe*,[179] are strong in secularizing the public schools, while another branch of cases, represented by *Mueller*,[180] *Zobrest*,[181] *Agostini*,[182] and *Helms*[183] allow almost unlimited constitutional leeway for legislatures to provide public funds to sectarian schools.

The effort to secularize the public schools is a long-running melodrama that has produced much antipathy toward the public schools. As a plethora of Supreme Court decisions indicate, from *McCollum* in 1948 through *Weisman* in 1992 and *Santa Fe* in 2000, attempts at incursions into public schools by religious groups are an unceasing phenomenon. The struggle to prevent public schools from being controlled by any church or religious sect has been the most difficult issue to face public schools since the idea of public schools was conceived in Europe in the eighteenth century and came to fruition in the United States in the nineteenth century.

The material in the following pages discusses the many and continuing attempts by religious sects to conduct activities in the public schools in an effort to inculcate their own religious beliefs. The list of attempts to reduce the public schools to sectarian educational enclaves reflecting the majority beliefs of a locality or state is virtually endless, and many of the episodes have been memorialized in U.S. Supreme Court precedents. The discussion and cases following seek to capture the essence of the many and multifaceted innovations used by religious sects to enter the public schools and to inculcate religion. Many of the cases address the conduct of prayer and Bible reading and various issues regarding the protection of religious liberty in the public schools.

More than half the states have, at some point, permitted or required prayer and Bible reading in public schools. Prior to 1962, at least twelve states and the District of Columbia required Bible reading. The typical attitude of the courts was that the Bible and general prayer were not sectarian in nature and their use did not violate constitutional religious guarantees.[184] That the Bible was not sectarian was even reflected in

statute; the North Dakota legislature had observed that

> [t]he Bible shall not be deemed a sectarian book. It shall not be excluded from any public school. It may be the option of the teacher to read in school without sectarian comment, not to exceed ten minutes daily. No pupil shall be required to read it nor be present in the schoolroom during the reading thereof contrary to the wishes of his parents or guardian or other person having him in charge.[185]

VOLITIONAL EXERCISES

The voluntariness of the exercise, whether it was Bible reading or prayer, was thought to be an important factor, as evidenced by this type of legislation. Proponents of religious exercise generally relied upon voluntariness, tradition, and the nonsectarian nature of the Bible as the primary defenses of the practice. In 1962, however, the U.S. Supreme Court in *Engel v. Vitale*[186] found a New York Regents prayer unconstitutional and a year later held both prayer and Bible reading offensive to the First Amendment even though the defendants claimed that the exercises were voluntary and the Bible was nondenominational. This result could probably have been anticipated, since the position established by the Court in *McCollum* in 1948 indicated that neither the nature of the religious instruction nor the voluntariness of the exercise was a valid defense. In *McCollum*, Justice Frankfurter stated:

> That a child is offered an alternative may reduce the constraint; it does not eliminate the operation of influence by the school in matters sacred to conscience and outside the school's domain. The law of imitation operates, and nonconformity is not an outstanding characteristic of children. The result is an obvious pressure upon children to attend. . . .[187]

Likewise, the nondenominational nature of a prayer was found to be no defense when the issue was raised in *Engel*. The Court explained that neither the fact that a prayer is denominationally neutral nor the fact that it is voluntary can serve to free it from the limitations of the establishment clause of the First Amendment. According to the Court:

> The Establishment Clause, unlike the Free Exercise Clause, does not depend upon any showing of

direct governmental compulsion and is violated by the enactment of laws which establish an official religion whether those laws operate directly to coerce non-observing individuals or not. . . .[188]

SECULAR PURPOSE

The result of *Engle, Schempp,* and their companion case, *Murray,*[189] in 1963 was that religious exercises in the public schools are clearly unconstitutional. Neither state, nor school, nor teacher can hold religious services of any type in the public schools. The Court did point out, however, that the study of the Bible as part of a secular program of education for its literary and historic values would not be unconstitutional.

In 1980, the Supreme Court in *Stone v. Graham*[190] followed the precedents of *Schempp* and *Murray* in holding unconstitutional a Kentucky statute that required the posting of the Ten Commandments in each public school classroom. In spite of an avowal by the state that the posting was premised on a secular legislative purpose, the High Court said that no legislative recitation of a supposed secular purpose could deny that the Ten Commandments are a sacred text of the Jewish and Christian faiths.

SILENT MEDITATION

During the past few years, a plethora of school prayer cases has been decided by the courts. Legislatures have passed statutes permitting voluntary prayer in public schools,[191] state constitutions have been changed,[192] challenges have been made to prayers at football games [193] and graduation exercises, and there have been cases in which teachers have maintained that the free exercise clause of the First Amendment permits them to conduct prayers in the classroom.[194]

The U.S. Supreme Court in 1985 held in *Wallace v. Jaffree*[195] that a period of silence for meditation or voluntary prayer in the public schools is unconstitutional. The Court ruled that the purpose of the legislative enactment was not secular and therefore violated the establishment clause.

In 1984, the people of West Virginia voted to amend the state constitution, permitting public schools to designate time at the beginning of the day for student contemplation, meditation, or prayer. A federal court ruled that the "prayer amendment" failed all three aspects of the *Lemon* test and therefore violated the establishment clause of the First Amendment. The court, in referring to the "Prayer Amendment," said it was "a hoax conceived in political expediency . . . perpetrated upon those sincere citizens of West Virginia who voted for this amendment to the West Virginia Constitution in belief that even if it violated the United States Constitution, "majority rule" would prevail."[196]

■ STUDENT-INITIATED RELIGIOUS SPEECH

Religious speech in public schools is not banned by any constitutional provision, and no federal or state court has ever prohibited religious speech unless the exercise of such speech results in the use of the school as a sectarian forum to inculcate religion. Students may speak about religion and engage in religious activities so long as religion is not advanced or sponsored by the public school.[197] "What is crucial is that a government practice not have the effect of communicating a message of government endorsement or disapproval of religion."[198] State employees cannot prescribe prayer, conduct Bible reading, or lead, participate in, or endorse prayer or religious exercises during curricular or extracurricular events.[199] Nothing in the Constitution implies that the public schools should be "cleansed" of all religious expression;[200] only state-promulgated or -endorsed religious expression must be excluded. The government cannot prefer disbelief over belief, or belief over disbelief. "The First Amendment requires only that the State tolerate both, while establishing neither."[201]

Genuinely student-initiated religious speech or prayer is valid and must be permitted.[202] Religious speech is protected speech, and, of course, the public schools cannot censor its content.[203] Yet even genuinely student-initiated prayer or religious speech may constitute state action and thereby be unconstitutional if the state participates in or supervises, encourages, suggests, or requires the speech.[204]

Teacher participation in religious speech brings the state into play because teachers are employees and thereby constitute arms of the state. In *Mergens*[205] and *Edwards*,[206] the Supreme Court observed that the Equal Access Act expressly prohibits teacher participation in religious exercises for the very good reason that it avoids the problems of the "students" emulation of teachers as role models."[207] Thus, religion is not foreclosed from schools; students can pray, read the Bible, and conduct whatever religious rites, rituals, or ceremonies, no matter how conventional, heretical, or pagan, so long as the activity or event is not under the supervision and oversight of the school and it is held at a reasonable time, place, and manner, as pertains to all other student speech in school.[208] Supervision or oversight that is merely custodial is not constitutionally objectionable; however, if school supervision or oversight crosses the line and becomes endorsement, encouragement, or participation, then the boundaries of constitutionality have been exceeded.[209]

The right to engage in student-initiated prayer or religious rites is not, however, without limit. Of course, as aforementioned, reasonable restrictions, in keeping with freedom of speech conditions as to time, place, and manner, can be placed on the student's religious activities, but importantly a student cannot use the school as a pulpit to conduct missionary work or use the "machinery of the state as a vehicle for converting his audience."[210] Public schools are not required to permit religious proselytizing. As observed in *Lee v. Weisman*, proselytizing speech is inherently coercive.[211]

PRAYER AT GRADUATION AND EXTRACURRICULAR ACTIVITIES

Insistence by various groups that religious exercises be included in the public schools has assumed many shapes and definitions over the years. Those advocating more religious exercises in the schools maintain that the prohibitions of the free exercise clause apply only to the classroom and do not prevent religious exercises in ancillary activities, such as commencement exercises, baccalaureate services, and related school events. The U.S. Supreme Court has, however, not drawn definitive lines between curricular and extracurricular activities. The Supreme Court in *Lee v. Weisman*[212] invalidated prayer at high school graduation ceremonies conducted by clergy. In this case, the school principal had invited a rabbi to offer prayers at high school graduation. The principal had as a precaution provided the rabbi with guidelines to ensure that the prayer was nonsectarian and could be defended as a "public prayer." The Court rejected the argument that the prayer was a kind of "nonsectarian prayer" legitimately conveyed by the state to advance a "civic religion." The Court said that while some common ground of moral and ethical behavior is highly desirable for any society, for the state to advance a Judeo-Christian religious doctrine under the mantle of some preconceived civic religious motivation is clearly in conflict with the religion clauses. The Court explained the intent of the religion clauses of the First Amendment to mean that "religious beliefs and religious expression are too precious to be either proscribed or prescribed by the state." The Court gave substantial weight to what it called "coercive" pressure, which, though subtle, nevertheless can create great discomfort for students who do not believe in the particular brand of religion that is being visited upon them.

Less than a year after *Weisman*, the U.S. Supreme Court remanded a student-initiated prayer case, *Jones v. Clear Creek Independent School District*,[213] to the Fifth Circuit. The Fifth Circuit distinguished *Jones* from *Weisman* because the prayer in *Jones* was student initiated and student led; therefore, the Fifth Circuit concluded that there was no violation of the establishment clause. The rationale is, of course, that voluntary, student-initiated prayers do not imply government endorsement of religion and are therefore not unconstitutional.

As a result of conflicting lower court interpretations, the U.S. Supreme Court took up the issue of student-led, student-initiated prayer at public school extracurricular events in the case of *Santa Fe Independent School District v. Doe*,[214] and in following the rationale in *Lee v. Weisman*, the Court concluded that such practices were unconstitutional as violative of the establishment clause.

The Santa Fe school district had tried various devices to circumvent the Supreme Court precedents that eliminate sectarian religious influences in the public schools. The Supreme Court held that a carefully contrived procedure whereby a student elected as the high school student council chaplain would deliver a prayer over the public address system at football games was a veiled attempt to advance the religious beliefs of a heavily conservative Baptist community that controlled the school board policy. The school board policy was challenged by a Catholic and a Mormon student, both alumni, and their mothers. The Court in reinforcing the secularization of the public schools held unequivocally that the school's defense, maintaining that the policy constituted a secular activity, and not a sectarian one, was a "sham" whose true intent was to perpetuate a previously invalidated school prayer policy. Justice Stevens, writing for the majority of the Court, held that the district's claim that the invocation was private student speech, and not public speech, belied the fact that the message was religious in nature and was conducted under the auspices of the public school itself. Thus, *Santa Fe* joins a rather consistent array of precedents that enforce the secularization of the public schools.

This no-nonsense position taken by the Court in secularizing the public schools is dramatized by the contrast with the Court's position in *Agostini* and *Helms*, where the establishment clause is loosely interpreted to permit public funds to be channeled to sectarian schools, which in turn may use those funds to advance particular spiritual beliefs. The establishment clause appears to be solid on one front but amazingly porous on the other.

———————— ❖ — ❖ — ❖ ————————

State-Enforced Bible Reading and Prayer in the Public Schools Are Unconstitutional

School District of Abington Township v. Schempp and Murray v. Curlett

Supreme Court of the United States, 1963.
374 U.S. 203, 83 S.Ct. 1560.

Mr. Justice CLARK delivered the opinion of the Court. Once again we are called upon to consider the scope of the provision of the First Amendment to the United States Constitution which declares that "Congress shall make no law respecting an establishment of religion, or prohibiting the free exercise thereof. . . ." These companion cases present the issues in the context of state action requiring that schools begin each day with readings from the Bible. While raising the basic questions under slightly different factual situations, the cases permit of joint treatment. In light of the history of the First Amendment and of our cases interpreting and applying its requirements, we hold that the practices at issue and the laws requiring them are unconstitutional under the Establishment Clause, as applied to the States through the Fourteenth Amendment.

The Facts in Each Case: No. 142. The Commonwealth of Pennsylvania by law, 24 Pa.Stat. §15-1516, as amended, Pub.Law 1928 (Supp.1960) Dec. 17, 1959, requires that "At least ten verses from the Holy Bible shall be read, without comment, at the opening of each public school on each school day. Any child shall be excused from such Bible reading, or attending such Bible reading, upon the written request of his parent or guardian." The Schempp family, husband and wife and two of their three children, brought suit to enjoin enforcement of the statute, contending that their rights under the Fourteenth Amendment to the Constitution of the United States are, have been, and will continue to be violated unless this statute be declared unconstitutional as violative of these provisions of the First Amendment. They sought to enjoin the appellant school district, wherein the Schempp children attend school, and its officers and the Superintendent of Public Instruction of the Commonwealth from continuing to conduct such readings and recitation of the Lord's Prayer in the public schools of the district pursuant to the statute. . . .

No. 119. In 1905 the Board of School Commissioners of Baltimore City adopted a rule pursuant to Art. 77, §202 of the Annotated Code of Maryland. The rule provided for the holding of opening exercises in the schools of the city, consisting primarily of the "reading, without comment, of a chapter in the Holy Bible and/or the use of the Lord's Prayer." The petitioners, Mrs. Madalyn Murray and her son, William J. Murray III, are both professed atheists. Following unsuccessful attempts to have the respondent school board rescind the rule, this suit was filed for mandamus to compel its rescission and cancellation. It was alleged that William was a student in a public school of the city and Mrs. Murray, his mother, was a taxpayer therein; that it was the practice under the rule to have a reading on each school morning from the King James version of the Bible; that at petitioners' insistence the rule was amended[215] to permit children to be excused from the exercise on request of the parent and that William had been excused pursuant thereto; that nevertheless the rule as amended was in violation of the petitioners' rights "to freedom of religion under the First and Fourteenth Amendments" and in violation of "the principle of separation between church and state, contained therein."

Applying the Establishment Clause principles to the cases at bar we find that the States are requiring the selection and reading at the opening of the school day of verses from the Holy Bible and the recitation of the Lord's Prayer by the students in unison. These exercises are prescribed as part of the curricular activities of students who are required by law to attend school. They are held in the school buildings under the supervision and with the participation of teachers employed in those schools. None of these factors, other than compulsory school attendance, was present in the program upheld in *Zorach v. Clauson*. The trial court in No. 142 has found that such an opening exercise is a religious ceremony and was intended by the State to be so. We agree with the trial court's finding as to the religious character of the exercises. Given that finding, the exercises and the law requiring them are in violation of the Establishment Clause.

There is no such specific finding as to the religious character of the exercises in No. 119, and the State contends (as does the State in No. 142) that the program is an effort to extend its benefits to all public school children without regard to their religious belief. Included within its secular purposes, it says, are the promotion of moral values, the contradiction to the materialistic trends of our times, the perpetuation of our institutions and the teaching of literature. The case came up on demurrer, of course, to a petition which alleged that the uniform practice

under the rule had been to read from the King James version of the Bible and that the exercise was sectarian. The short answer, therefore, is that the religious character of the exercise was admitted by the State. But even if its purpose is not strictly religious, it is sought to be accomplished through readings, without comment, from the Bible. Surely the place of the Bible as an instrument of religion cannot be gainsaid, and the State's recognition of the pervading religious character of the ceremony is evident from the rule's specific permission of the alternative uses of the Catholic Douay version as well as the recent amendment permitting nonattendance at the exercises. None of these factors is consistent with the contention that the Bible is here used either as an instrument for nonreligious moral inspiration or as a reference for the teaching of secular subjects.

The conclusion follows that in both cases the laws require religious exercises and such exercises are being conducted in direct violation of the rights of the appellees and petitioners. Nor are these required exercises mitigated by the fact that individual students may absent themselves upon parental request, for that fact furnishes no defense to a claim of unconstitutionality under the Establishment Clause. . . . Further, it is no defense to urge that the religious practices here may be relatively minor encroachments on the First Amendment. The breach of neutrality that is today a trickling stream may all too soon become a raging torrent and, in the words of Madison, "it is proper to take alarm at the first experiment on our liberties." *Memorial and Remonstrance against Religious Assessments.* . . .

It is insisted that unless these religious exercises are permitted a "religion of secularism" is established in the schools. We agree of course that the State may not establish a "religion of secularism" in the sense of affirmatively opposing or showing hostility to religion, thus "preferring those who believe in no religion over those who do believe." *Zorach v. Clauson*, 343 U.S., at 314, 72 S.Ct., at 684, 96 L.Ed. 954. We do not agree, however, that this decision in any sense has that effect. In addition, it might well be said that one's education is not complete without a study of comparative religion or the history of religion and its relationship to the advancement of civilization. It certainly may be said that the Bible is worthy of study for its literary and historic qualities. Nothing we have said here indicates that such study of the Bible or of religion, when presented objectively, as part of a secular program of education, may not be effected consistently with the First Amendment. But the exercises here do not fall into those categories. They are religious exercises, required by the States in violation of the command of the First Amendment that the Government maintain strict neutrality, neither aiding nor opposing religion.

Finally, we cannot accept that the concept of neutrality, which does not permit a State to require a religious exercise even with the consent of the majority of those affected, collides with the majority's right to free exercise of religion. While the Free Exercise Clause clearly prohibits the use of state action to deny the rights of free exercise to *anyone*, it has never meant that a majority could use the machinery of the State to practice its beliefs. Such a contention was effectively answered by Mr. Justice Jackson for the Court in *West Virginia Board of Education v. Barnette*, 319 U.S. 624, 638, 63 S.Ct. 1178, 1185, 87 L.Ed. 1628 (1943):

> The very purpose of a Bill of Rights was to withdraw certain subjects from the vicissitudes of political controversy, to place them beyond the reach of majorities and officials and to establish them as legal principles to be applied by the courts. One's right to . . . freedom of worship . . . and other fundamental rights may not be submitted to vote; they depend on the outcome of no elections.

The place of religion in our society is an exalted one, achieved through a long tradition of reliance on the home, the church and the inviolable citadel of the individual heart and mind. We have come to recognize through bitter experience that it is not within the power of government to invade that citadel, whether its purpose or effect be to aid or oppose, to advance or retard. In the relationship between man and religion, the State is firmly committed to a position of neutrality. Though the application of that rule requires interpretation of a delicate sort, the rule itself is clearly and concisely stated in the words of the First Amendment. Applying that rule to the facts of these cases, we affirm the judgment in No. 142. In No. 119, the judgment is reversed and the cause remanded to the Maryland Court of Appeals for further proceedings consistent with this opinion.

It is so ordered.

Judgment in No. 142 affirmed; judgment in No. 119 reversed and cause remanded with directions.

❖ — ❖ — ❖

State Statute Authorizing a Period for Meditation or Voluntary Prayer Violates the Establishment Clause

Wallace v. Jaffree

Supreme Court of the United States, 1985.
472 U.S. 38, 105 S.Ct. 2479.

Justice STEVENS delivered the opinion of the Court. At an early stage of this litigation, the constitutionality of three Alabama statutes was questioned: (1) §16-1-20, enacted in 1978, which authorized a one-minute period of silence in all public schools "for meditation"; (2) §16-1-20.1, enacted in 1981, which authorized a period of silence "for meditation or voluntary prayer"; and (3) §16-1-20.2, enacted in 1982, which authorized teachers to lead "willing students" in a prescribed prayer to "Almighty God . . . the Creator and Supreme Judge of the world."

At the preliminary-injunction stage of this case, the District Court distinguished §16-1-20 from the other two statutes. It then held that there was "nothing wrong" with §16-1-20, but that §§16-1-20.1 and 16-1-20.2 were both invalid because the sole purpose of both was "an effort on the part of the State of Alabama to encourage a religious activity." After the trial on the merits, the District Court did not change its interpretation of these two statutes, but held that they were constitutional because, in its opinion, Alabama has the power to establish a state religion if it chooses to do so.

The Court of Appeals agreed with the District Court's initial interpretation of the purpose of both §§16-1-20.1 and 16-1-20.2, and held them both unconstitutional. We have already affirmed the Court of Appeals' holding with respect to

§16-1-20.2. Moreover, appellees have not questioned the holding that §16-1-20 is valid. Thus, the narrow question for decision is whether §16-1-20.1, which authorizes a period of silence for "meditation or voluntary prayer," is a law respecting the establishment of religion within the meaning of the First Amendment. . . .

On August 2, 1982, the District Court held an evidentiary hearing on appellees' motion for a preliminary injunction. At that hearing, State Senator Donald G. Holmes testified that he was the "prime sponsor" of the bill that was enacted in 1981 as §16-1-20.1. He explained that the bill was an "effort to return voluntary prayer to our public schools . . . it is a beginning and a step in the right direction." Apart from the purpose to return voluntary prayer to public schools, Senator Holmes unequivocally testified that he had "no other purpose in mind." A week after the hearing, the District Court entered a preliminary injunction. The court held that appellees were likely to prevail on the merits because the enaction of §§16-1-20.1 and 16-1-20.2 did not reflect a clearly secular purpose.

In November 1982, the District Court held a four-day trial on the merits. The evidence related primarily to the 1981–1982 academic year—the year after the enactment of §16-1-20.1 and prior to the enactment of §16-1-20.2. The District Court found that during that academic year each of the minor plaintiffs' teachers had led classes in prayer activities, even after being informed of appellees' objections to these activities.

In its lengthy conclusions of law, the District Court reviewed a number of opinions of this Court interpreting the Establishment Clause of the First Amendment, and then embarked on a fresh examination of the question whether the First Amendment imposes any barrier to the establishment of an official religion by the State of Alabama. After reviewing at length what it perceived to be newly discovered historical evidence, the District Court concluded that "the establishment clause of the first amendment to the United States Constitution does not prohibit the state from establishing a religion." In a separate opinion, the District Court dismissed appellees' challenge to the three Alabama statutes because of a failure to state any claim for which relief could be granted. The court's dismissal of this challenge was also based on its conclusion that the Establishment Clause did not bar the States from establishing a religion.

The Court of Appeals consolidated the two cases; not surprisingly, it reversed. The Court of Appeals noted that this Court had considered and had rejected the historical arguments that the District Court found persuasive, and that the District Court had misapplied the doctrine of *stare decisis*. The Court of Appeals then held that the teachers' religious activities violated the Establishment Clause of the First Amendment. With respect to §16-1-20.1 and §16-1-20.2, the Court of Appeals stated that "both statutes advance and encourage religious activities." The Court of Appeals then quoted with approval the District Court's finding that §16-1-20.1 and §16-1-20.2 were efforts "to encourage a religious activity. Even though these statutes are permissive in form, it is nevertheless state involvement respecting an establishment of religion." Thus, the Court of Appeals concluded that both statutes were "specifically the type which the Supreme Court addressed in *Engel*. . . ."

Our unanimous affirmance of the Court of Appeals' judgment concerning §16-1-20.2 makes it unnecessary to comment at length on the District Court's remarkable conclusion that the Federal Constitution imposes no obstacle to Alabama's establishment of a state religion. Before analyzing the precise issue that is presented to us, it is nevertheless appropriate to recall how firmly embedded in our constitutional jurisprudence is the proposition that the several States have no greater power to restrain the individual freedoms protected by the First Amendment than does the Congress of the United States.

As is plain from its text, the First Amendment was adopted to curtail the power of Congress to interfere with the individual's freedom to believe, to worship, and to express himself in accordance with the dictates of his own conscience. Until the Fourteenth Amendment was added to the Constitution, the First Amendment's restraints on the exercise of federal power simply did not apply to the States. But when the Constitution was amended to prohibit any State from depriving any person of liberty without due process of law, that Amendment imposed the same substantive limitations on the States' power to legislate that the First Amendment had always imposed on the Congress' power. This Court has confirmed and endorsed this elementary proposition of law time and time again. . . .

Just as the right to speak and the right to refrain from speaking are complementary components of a broader concept of individual freedom of mind, so also the individual's freedom to choose his own creed is the counterpart of his right to refrain from accepting the creed established by the majority. At one time it was thought that this right merely proscribed the preference of one Christian sect over another, but would not require equal respect for the conscience of the infidel, the atheist, or the adherent of a non-Christian faith such as Mohammedism or Judaism. But when the underlying principle has been examined in the crucible of litigation, the Court has unambiguously concluded that the individual freedom of conscience protected by the First Amendment embraces the right to select any religious faith or none at all. This conclusion derives support not only from the interest in respecting the individual's freedom of conscience, but also from the conviction that religious beliefs worthy of respect are the product of free and voluntary choice by the faithful, and from recognition of the fact that the political interest in forestalling intolerance extends beyond intolerance among Christian sects—or even intolerance among "religions"—to encompass intolerance of the disbeliever and the uncertain. As Justice Jackson eloquently stated in *Board of Education v. Barnette*, 319 U.S. 624, 642, 63 S.Ct. 1178, 1187, 87 L.Ed. 1628 (1943):

> If there is any fixed star in our constitutional constellation, it is that no official, high or petty, can prescribe what shall be orthodox in politics, nationalism, religion, or other matters of opinion or force citizens to confess by word or act their faith therein.

The state of Alabama, no less than the Congress of the United States, must respect that basic truth.

When the Court has been called upon to construe the breadth of the Establishment Clause, it has examined the criteria developed over a period of many years. Thus, in *Lemon v. Kurtzman*, . . . we wrote:

> Every analysis in this area must begin with consideration of the cumulative criteria developed by the Court over many years. Three such tests may

be gleaned from our cases. First, the statute must have a secular legislative purpose; second, its principal or primary effect must be one that neither advances nor inhibits religion, *Board of Education v. Allen*, . . . finally, the statute must not foster "an excessive government entanglement with religion.". . .

It is the first of these three criteria that is most plainly implicated by this case. As the District Court correctly recognized, no consideration of the second or third criteria is necessary if a statute does not have a clearly secular purpose. For even though a statute that is motivated in part by a religious purpose may satisfy the first criterion, . . . the First Amendment requires that a statute must be invalidated if it is entirely motivated by a purpose to advance religion.

In applying the purpose test, it is appropriate to ask "whether government's actual purpose is to endorse or disapprove of religion." In this case, the answer to that question is dispositive. For the record not only provides us with an unambiguous affirmative answer, but it also reveals that the enactment of §16-1-20.1 was not motivated by any clearly secular purpose—indeed, the statute had no secular purpose.

The sponsor of the bill that became §16-1-20.1, Senator Donald Holmes, inserted into the legislative record—apparently without dissent—a statement indicating that the legislation was an "effort to return voluntary prayer" to the public schools. Later Senator Holmes confirmed this purpose before the District Court. In response to the question whether he had any purpose for the legislation other than returning voluntary prayer to public schools, he stated, "No, I did not have no other purpose in mind." The State did not present evidence of *any* secular purpose. . . .

The legislative intent to return prayer to the public schools is, of course, quite different from merely protecting every student's right to engage in voluntary prayer during an appropriate moment of silence during the school day. The 1978 statute already protected that right, containing nothing that prevented any student from engaging in voluntary prayer during a silent minute of meditation. Appellants have not identified any secular purpose that was not fully served by §16-1-20 before the enactment of §16-1-20.1. Thus, only two conclusions are consistent with the text of §16-1-20.1: (1) the statute was enacted to convey a message of State endorsement and promotion of prayer; or (2) the statute was enacted for no purpose. No one suggests that the statute was nothing but a meaningless or irrational act. . . .

The Legislature enacted §16-1-20.1 despite the existence of §16-1-20 for the sole purpose of expressing the State's endorsement of prayer activities for one minute at the beginning of each school day. The addition of "or voluntary prayer" indicates that the State intended to characterize prayer as a favored practice. Such an endorsement is not consistent with the established principle that the Government must pursue a course of complete neutrality toward religion.

The importance of that principle does not permit us to treat this as an inconsequential case involving nothing more than a few words of symbolic speech on behalf of the political majority. For whenever the State itself speaks on a religious subject, one of the questions that we must ask is "whether the Government intends to convey a message of endorsement or disapproval of religion." The well-supported concurrent findings of the District Court and the Court of Appeals—that §16-1-20.1 was intended to convey a message of State-approval of prayer activities in the public schools—make it unnecessary, and indeed inappropriate, to evaluate the practical significance of the addition of the words "or voluntary prayer" to the statute. Keeping in mind, as we must, "both the fundamental place held by the Establishment Clause in our constitutional scheme and the myriad, subtle ways in which Establishment Clause values can be eroded," we conclude that §16-1-20.1 violates the First Amendment.

The judgment of the Court of Appeals is affirmed.

It is so ordered.

❖ — ❖ — ❖

Nonsectarian Prayer at High School Graduation Is Unconstitutional

Lee v. Weisman

Supreme Court of the United States, 1992.
505 U.S. 577, 112 S.Ct. 2649

Justice KENNEDY delivered the opinion of the Court.

School principals in the public school system of the city of Providence, Rhode Island, are permitted to invite members of the clergy to offer invocation and benediction prayers as part of the formal graduation ceremonies for middle schools and for high schools. The question before us is whether including clerical members who offer prayers as part of the official school graduation ceremony is consistent with the Religion Clauses of the First Amendment, provisions the Fourteenth Amendment makes applicable with full force to the States and their school districts. . . .

Deborah Weisman graduated from Nathan Bishop Middle School, a public school in Providence, at a formal ceremony in June 1989. She was about 14 years old. . . . Acting for himself and his daughter, Deborah's father, Daniel Weisman, objected to any prayers at Deborah's middle school graduation, but to no avail. The school principal, petitioner Robert E. Lee, invited a rabbi to deliver prayers at the graduation exercises for Deborah's class. . . .

It has been the custom of Providence school officials to provide invited clergy with a pamphlet entitled "Guidelines for Civic Occasions," prepared by the National Conference of Christians and Jews. The Guidelines recommend that public prayers at nonsectarian civic ceremonies be composed with "inclusiveness and sensitivity," though they acknowledge that "[p]rayer of any kind may be inappropriate on some civic occasions." The principal gave Rabbi Gutterman the pamphlet before the graduation and advised him the invocation and benediction should be nonsectarian. . . .

The principle that government may accommodate the free exercise of religion does not supersede the fundamental limitations imposed by the Establishment Clause. It is beyond dispute that, at a minimum, the Constitution guarantees that government may not coerce anyone to support or participate in religion or its exercise, or otherwise act in a way which "establishes a [state] religion or religious faith, or tends to do so." . . . The State's involvement in the school prayers challenged today violates these central principles.

That involvement is as troubling as it is undenied. A school official, the principal, decided that an invocation and a benediction should be given; this is a choice attributable to the State, and from a constitutional perspective it is as if a state statute decreed that the prayers must occur. The principal chose the religious participant, here a rabbi, and that choice of a rabbi is not disclosed by the record, but the potential for divisiveness over the choice of a particular member of the clergy to conduct the ceremony is apparent.

. . . The potential for divisiveness is of particular relevance here though, because it centers around an overt religious exercise in a secondary school environment where, as we discuss below, subtle coercive pressures exist and where the student had no real alternative which would have allowed her to avoid the fact or appearance of participation.

The State's role did not end with the decision to include a prayer and with the choice of clergyman. Principal Lee provided Rabbi Gutterman with a copy of the "Guidelines for Civic Occasions," and advised him that his prayers should be nonsectarian. Through these means the principal directed and controlled the content of the prayer. . . . It is a cornerstone principle of our Establishment Clause jurisprudence that "it is no part of the business of government to compose official prayers for any group of the American people to recite as a part of a religious program carried on by government," . . . and that is what the school officials attempted to do.

Petitioners argue, and we find nothing in the case to refute it, that the directions for the content of the prayers were a good-faith attempt by the school to ensure that the sectarianism which is so often the flashpoint for religious animosity be removed from the graduation ceremony. The concern is understandable, as a prayer which uses ideas or images identified with a particular religion may foster a different sort of sectarian rivalry than an invocation or benediction in terms more neutral. The school's explanation, however, does not resolve the dilemma caused by its participation. The question is not the good faith of the school in attempting to make the prayer acceptable to most persons, but the legitimacy of its undertaking that enterprise at all

when the object is to produce a prayer to be used in a formal religious exercise which students, for all practical purposes, are obligated to attend. . . .

The First Amendment's Religious Clauses mean that religious beliefs and religious expression are too precious to be either proscribed or prescribed by the State. The design of the Constitution is that preservation and transmission of religious beliefs and worship is a responsibility and a choice committed to the private sphere, which itself is promised freedom to pursue that mission. . . .

These concerns have particular application in the case of school officials, whose effort to monitor prayer will be perceived by the students as inducing a participation they might otherwise reject. Though the efforts of the school officials in this case to find common ground appear to have been a good-faith attempt to recognize the common aspects of religions and not the divisive ones, our precedents do not permit school officials to assist in composing prayers as an incident to a formal exercise for their students. . . . And these same precedents caution us to measure the idea of a civic religion against the central meaning of the Religious Clauses of the First Amendment, which is that all creeds must be tolerated and none favored. The suggestion that government may establish an official or civic religion as a means of avoiding the establishment of a religion with more specific creeds strikes us as a contradiction that cannot be accepted.

The degree of school involvement here made it clear that the graduation prayers bore the imprint of the State and thus put school-age children who objected in an untenable position. We turn our attention now to consider the position of the students, both those who desired the prayer and she who did not.

To endure the speech of false ideas or offensive content and then to counter it is part of learning how to live in a pluralistic society, a society which insists upon open discourse toward the end of a tolerant citizenry. And tolerance presupposes some mutuality of obligation. It is argued that our constitutional vision of a free society requires confidence in our own ability to accept or reject ideas of which we do not approve, and that prayer at a high school graduation does nothing more than offer a choice. . . . This argument cannot prevail, however. It overlooks a fundamental dynamic of the Constitution.

The First Amendment protects speech and religion by quite different mechanisms. Speech is protected by insuring its full expression even when the government participates, for the very object of some of our most important speech is to persuade the government to adopt an idea as its own. . . . The method for protecting freedom of worship and freedom of conscience in religious matters is quite the reverse. In religious debate or expression the government is not a prime participant, for the Framers deemed religious establishment antithetical to the freedom of all. The Free Exercise Clause embraces a freedom of conscience and worship that has close parallels in the speech provisions of the First Amendment, but the Establishment Clause is a specific prohibition on forms of state intervention in religious affairs with no precise counterpart in the speech provisions. . . . The explanation lies in the lesson of history that was and is the inspiration of the Establishment Clause, the lesson that in the hands of government what might begin as a tolerant expression of religious views may end in a policy to indoctrinate and coerce. A state-created orthodoxy puts at grave risk that freedom of belief and conscience which are the sole assurance that religious faith is real, not imposed. . . .

As we have observed before, there are heightened concerns with protecting freedom of conscience from subtle coercive pressure in the elementary and secondary public schools. . . . We recognize, among other things, that prayer exercises in public school carry a particular risk of indirect coercion. The concern may not be limited to the context of schools, but it is most pronounced there. . . . What to most believers may seem nothing more than a reasonable request that the nonbeliever respect their religious practices, in a school context may appear to the nonbeliever or dissenter to be an attempt to employ the machinery of the State to enforce a religious orthodoxy.

We need not look beyond the circumstances of this case to see the phenomenon at work. The undeniable fact is that the school district's supervision and control of a high school gradua-

tion ceremony places public pressure, as well as peer pressure, on attending students to stand as a group or, at least, maintain respectful silence during the Invocation and Benediction. This pressure, though subtle and indirect, can be as real as any overt compulsion. . . . It is of little comfort to a dissenter, then, to be told that for her the act of standing or remaining in silence signifies mere respect, rather than participation. What matters is that, given our social conventions, a reasonable dissenter in this milieu could believe that the group exercise signified her own participation or approval of it. . . .

The injury caused by the government's action, and the reason why Daniel and Deborah Weisman object to it, is that the State, in a school setting, in effect required participation in a religious exercise. It is, we concede, a brief exercise during which the individual can concentrate on joining its message, meditate on her own religion, or let her mind wander. But the embarrassment and the intrusion of the religious exercise cannot be refuted by arguing that these prayers, and similar ones to be said in the future, are of a *de minimis* character. . . .

There was a stipulation in the District Court that attendance at graduation and promotional ceremonies is voluntary. Petitioners and the United States, as *amicus*, made this a center point of the case, arguing that the option of not attending the graduation excuses any inducement or coercion in the ceremony itself. The argument lacks all persuasion. Law reaches past formalism. And to say a teenage student has a real choice not to attend her high school graduation is formalistic in the extreme. True, Deborah could elect not to attend commencement without renouncing her diploma; but we shall not allow the case to turn on this point. Attendance may not be required by official decree, yet it is apparent that a student is not free to absent herself from the graduation exercise in any real sense of the term "voluntary," for absence would require forfeiture of those intangible benefits which have motivated the student through youth and all her high school years. Graduation is a time for family and those closest to the student to celebrate success and express mutual wishes of gratitude and respect, all to the end of impressing upon the young person the role that it is his or her right and duty to assume in the community and all of its diverse parts.

The importance of the event is the point the school district and the United States rely upon to argue that a formal prayer ought to be permitted, but it becomes one of the principal reasons why their argument must fail. Their contention, one of considerable force were it not for the constitutional constraints applied to state action, is that the prayers are an essential part of these ceremonies because for many persons an occasion of this significance lacks meaning if there is no recognition, however brief, that human achievements cannot be understood apart from their spiritual essence. We think the Government's position that this interest suffices to force students to choose between compliance or forfeiture demonstrates fundamental inconsistency in its argumentation. It fails to acknowledge that what for many of Deborah's classmates and their parents was a spiritual imperative was for Daniel and Deborah Weisman religious conformation compelled by the State. While in some societies the wishes of the majority might prevail, the Establishment Clause of the First Amendment is addressed to this contingency and rejects the balance urged upon us. The Constitution forbids the State to exact religious conformity from a student as the price of attending her own high school graduation. This is the calculus the Constitution commands.

The Government's argument gives insufficient recognition to the real conflict of conscience faced by the young student. The essence of the Government's position is that with regard to a civic, social occasion of this importance it is the objector, not the majority, who must take unilateral and private action to avoid compromising religious scruples, here by electing to miss the graduation exercise. This turns conventional First Amendment analysis on its head. It is a tenet of the First Amendment that the State cannot require one of its citizens to forfeit his or her rights and benefits as the price of resisting conformance to state-sponsored religious practice. To say that a student must remain apart from the ceremony at the opening invocation and closing benediction is to risk compelling conformity in an environment analogous to the classroom setting, where we have said the risk of compulsion is especially high. Just as in *Engel v. Vitale*, 370

U.S., at 430, 82 S.Ct., at 1266, and *School District of Abington Township v. Schempp*, 374 U.S., at 224–225, 88 S.Ct., at 1572–1573, where we found that provisions within the challenged legislation permitting a student to be voluntarily excused from attendance or participation in the daily prayers did not shield those practices from invalidation, the fact that attendance at the graduation ceremonies is voluntary in a legal sense does not save the religious exercise. . . .

We do not hold that every state action implicating religion is invalid if one or a few citizens find it offensive. People may take offense at all manner of religious as well as nonreligious messages, but offense alone does not in every case show a violation. We know too that sometimes to endure social isolation or even anger may be the price of conscience or nonconformity. But, by any reading of our cases, the conformity required of the student in this case was too high an exaction to withstand the test of the Establishment Clause. The prayer exercises in this case are especially improper because the State has in every practical sense compelled attendance and participation in an explicit religious exercise at an event of singular importance to every student, one the objecting student had no real alternative to avoid. . . .

For reasons we have stated, the judgment of the Court of Appeals is Affirmed.

❖ — ❖ — ❖

School District's Policy Permitting Student-Led, Student-Initiated Prayer at Football Games Violates the Establishment Clause

Santa Fe Independent School District v. Doe

Supreme Court of the United States, 2000
____ U.S. ____, 120 S.Ct. 2266, 2000 WL 775587

JUSTICE STEVENS delivered the opinion of the Court.

Prior to 1995, the Santa Fe High School student who occupied the school's elective office of student council chaplain delivered a prayer over the public address system before each varsity football game for the entire season. This practice, along with others, was challenged in District Court as a violation of the Establishment Clause of the First Amendment. While these proceedings were pending in the District Court, the school district adopted a different policy that permits, but does not require, prayer initiated and led by a student at all home games. The District Court entered an order modifying that policy to permit only nonsectarian, nonproselytizing prayer. The Court of Appeals held that, even as modified by the District Court, the football prayer policy was invalid. We granted the school district's petition for certiorari to review that holding.

. . . Respondents are two sets of current or former students and their respective mothers. One family is Mormon and the other is Catholic. The District Court permitted respondents (Does) to litigate anonymously to protect them from intimidation or harassment.

Respondents commenced this action in April 1995 and moved for a temporary restraining order to prevent the District from violating the Establishment Clause at the imminent graduation exercises. In their complaint the Does alleged that the District had engaged in several proselytizing practices, such as promoting attendance at a Baptist revival meeting, encouraging membership in religious clubs, chastising children who held minority religious beliefs, and distributing Gideon Bibles on school premises. They also alleged that the District allowed students to read Christian invocations and benedictions from the stage at graduation ceremonies, and to deliver overtly Christian prayers over the public address system at home football games.

On May 10, 1995, the District Court entered an interim order addressing a number of different issues. With respect to the impending graduation, the order provided that "nondenominational prayer" consisting of "an invocation and/or benediction" could be presented by a senior student or students selected by members of the graduating class. The text of the prayer was to be determined by the students, without scrutiny or preapproval by school officials. References to particular religious figures "such as Mohammed, Jesus, Buddha, or the like"

would be permitted "as long as the general thrust of the prayer is non-proselytizing." . . .

In response to that portion of the order, the District adopted a series of policies over several months dealing with prayer at school functions. The policies enacted in May and July for graduation ceremonies provided the format for the August and October policies for football games. The May policy provided:

> The board has chosen to permit the graduating senior class, with the advice and counsel of the senior class principal or designee, to elect by secret ballot to choose whether an invocation and benediction shall be part of the graduation exercise. If so chosen the class shall elect by secret ballot, from a list of student volunteers, students to deliver nonsectarian, nonproselytizing invocations and benedictions for the purpose of solemnizing their graduation ceremonies. (emphasis deleted).

The parties stipulated that after this policy was adopted, "the senior class held an election to determine whether to have an invocation and benediction at the commencement [and that the] class voted, by secret ballot, to include prayer at the high school graduation." . . . In a second vote the class elected two seniors to deliver the invocation and benediction.

In July, the District enacted another policy eliminating the requirement that invocations and benedictions be "nonsectarian and nonproselytising," but also providing that if the District were to be enjoined from enforcing that policy, the May policy would automatically become effective.

The August policy, which was titled "Prayer at Football Games," was similar to the July policy for graduations. It also authorized two student elections, the first to determine whether "invocations" should be delivered, and the second to select the spokesperson to deliver them. Like the July policy, it contained two parts, an initial statement that omitted any requirement that the content of the invocation be "nonsectarian and nonproselytising," and a fallback provision that automatically added that limitation if the preferred policy should be enjoined. On August 31, 1995, according to the parties' stipulation, "the district's high school students voted to determine whether a student would deliver prayer at varsity football games. . . . The students chose to allow a student to say a prayer at football games." . . . A week later, in a separate election, they selected a student "to deliver the prayer at varsity football games." . . .

The final policy (October policy) is essentially the same as the August policy, though it omits the word "prayer" from its title, and refers to "messages" and "statements" as well as "invocations." It is the validity of that policy that is before us. . . .

We granted the District's petition for certiorari, limited to the following question: "Whether petitioner's policy permitting student-led, student-initiated prayer at football games violates the Establishment Clause." . . . We conclude, as did the Court of Appeals, that it does. . . .

The first Clause in the First Amendment to the Federal Constitution provides that "Congress shall make no law respecting an establishment of religion, or prohibiting the free exercise thereof." The Fourteenth Amendment imposes those substantive limitations on the legislative power of the States and their political subdivisions. *Wallace v. Jaffree*, 472 U.S. 38, 49–50 (1985). In *Lee v. Weisman*, 505 U.S. 577 (1992), we held that a prayer delivered by a rabbi at a middle school graduation ceremony violated that Clause. Although this case involves student prayer at a different type of school function, our analysis is properly guided by the principles that we endorsed in *Lee*. . . .

These invocations are authorized by a government policy and take place on government property at government-sponsored school-related events. Of course, not every message delivered under such circumstances is the government's own. We have held, for example, that an individual's contribution to a government-created forum was not government speech. . . . Although the District relies heavily on *Rosenberger* and similar causes involving such forums, it is clear that the pregame ceremony is not the type of forum discussed in those cases. The Santa Fe school officials simply do not "evince either "by policy or by practice," any intent to open the [pregame ceremony] to "indiscriminate use," . . . by the student body generally." *Hazelwood School Dist. v. Kuhlmeier*, 484 U.S. 260, 270 (1988). . . . Rather, the school allows only

one student, the same student for the entire season, to give the invocation. The statement or invocation, moreover, is subject to particular regulations that confine the content and topic of the student's message. . . .

Granting only one student access to the stage at a time does not, of course, necessarily preclude a finding that a school has created a limited public forum. Here, however, Santa Fe's student election system ensures that only those messages deemed "appropriate" under the District's policy may be delivered. That is, the majoritarian process implemented by the District guarantees, by definition, that minority candidates will never prevail and that their views will be effectively silenced. . . .

In *Lee*, the school district made the related argument that its policy of endorsing only "civic or nonsectarian" prayer was acceptable because it minimized the intrusion on the audience as a whole. We rejected that claim by explaining that such a majoritarian policy "does not lessen the offense or isolation to the objectors. At best it narrows their number, at worst increases their sense of isolation and affront." . . . Similarly, while Santa Fe's majoritarian election might ensure that most of the students are represented, it does nothing to protect the minority; indeed, it likely serves to intensify their offense.

Moreover, the District has failed to divorce itself from the religious content in the invocations. It has not succeeded in doing so, either by claiming that its policy is "one of neutrality rather than endorsement" or by characterizing the individual student as the "circuit-breaker" in the process. Contrary to the District's repeated assertions that it has adopted a "hands-off" approach to the pregame invocation, the realities of the situation plainly reveal that its policy involves both perceived and actual endorsement of religion. In this case, as we found in *Lee*, the "degree of school involvement" makes it clear that the pregame prayers bear "the imprint of the State and thus put school-age children who objected in an untenable position." . . .

The District has attempted to disentangle itself from the religious messages by developing the two-step student election process. The text of the October policy, however, exposes the extent of the school's entanglement. The elections take place at all only because the school "board has chosen to permit students to deliver a brief invocation and/or message." . . . The elections thus "shall" be conducted "by the high school student council" and "[u]pon advice and direction of the high school principal." Id., at 104–105. The decision whether to deliver a message is first made by majority vote of the entire student body, followed by a choice of the speaker in a separate, similar majority election. Even though the particular words used by the speaker are not determined by those votes, the policy mandates that the "statement or invocation" be "consistent with the goals and purposes of this policy," which are "to solemnize the event, to promote good sportsmanship and student safety, and to establish the appropriate environment for the competition." . . .

In addition to involving the school in the selection of the speaker, the policy, by its terms, invites and encourages religious messages. The policy itself states that the purpose of the message is "to solemnize the event." A religious message is the most obvious method of solemnizing an event. Moreover, the requirements that the message "promote good citizenship" and "establish the appropriate environment for competition" further narrow the types of message deemed appropriate, suggesting that a solemn, yet nonreligious, message, such as commentary on United States foreign policy, would be prohibited. Indeed, the only type of message that is expressly endorsed in the text is an "invocation"—a term that primarily describes an appeal for divine assistance. In fact, as used in the past at Santa Fe High School, an "invocation" has always entailed a focused religious message. Thus, the expressed purposes of the policy encourage the selection of a religious message, and that is precisely how the students understand the policy. The results of the elections described in the parties' stipulation make it clear that the students understood that the central question before them was whether prayer should be a part of the pregame ceremony. We recognize the important role that public worship plays in many communities, as well as the sincere desire to include public prayer as a part of various occasions so as to mark those occasions' significance. But such

religious activity in public schools, as elsewhere, must comport with the First Amendment.

The actual or perceived endorsement of the message, moreover, is established by factors beyond just the text of the policy. Once the student speaker is selected and the message composed, the invocation is then delivered to a large audience assembled as part of a regularly scheduled, school-sponsored function conducted on school property. . . .

In this context the members of the listening audience must perceive the pregame message as a public expression of the views of the majority of the student body delivered with the approval of the school administration. . . . Regardless of the listener's support for, or objection to, the message, an objective Santa Fe High School student will unquestionably perceive the inevitable pregame prayer as stamped with her school's seal of approval. . .

Most striking to us is the evolution of the current policy from the long-sanctioned office of "Student Chaplain" to the candidly titled "Prayer at Football Games" regulation. This history indicates that the District intended to preserve the practice of prayer before football games. The conclusion that the District viewed the October policy simply as a continuation of the previous policies is dramatically illustrated by the fact that the school did not conduct a new election, pursuant to the current policy, to replace the results of the previous election, which occurred under the former policy. Given these observations, and in light of the school's history of regular delivery of a student-led prayer at athletic events, it is reasonable to infer that the specific purpose of the policy was to preserve a popular "state-sponsored religious practice." . . .

School sponsorship of a religious message is impermissible because it sends the ancillary message to members of the audience who are nonadherants "that they are outsiders, not full members of the political community, and an accompanying message to adherants that they are insiders, favored members of the political community." Lynch v. Donnelly, 465 U.S., at 688 (1984) (O'CONNOR, J., concurring). The delivery of such a message—over the school's public address system, by a speaker representing the student body, under the supervision of school faculty, and pursuant to a school policy that explicitly and implicitly encourages public prayer—is not properly characterized as "private" speech. . . .

The District next argues that its football policy is distinguishable from the graduation prayer in *Lee* because it does not coerce students to participate in religious observances. . . .

One of the purposes served by the Establishment Clause is to remove debate over this kind of issue from governmental supervision or control. We explained in *Lee* that the "preservation and transmission of religious beliefs and worship is a responsibility and a choice committed to the private sphere." . . . The two student elections authorized by the policy, coupled with the debates that presumably must precede each, impermissibly invade that private sphere. The election mechanism, when considered in light of the history in which the policy in question evolved, reflects a device the District put in place that determines whether religious messages will be delivered at home football games. The mechanism encourages divisiveness along religious lines in a public school setting, a result at odds with the Establishment Clause. Although it is true that the ultimate choice of student speaker is "attributable to the students," . . . the District's decision to hold the constitutionally problematic election is clearly "a choice attributable to the State." . . .

The District further argues that attendance at the commencement ceremonies at issue in *Lee* "differs dramatically" from attendance at high school football games, which it contends "are of no more than passing interest to many students" and are "decidedly extracurricular," thus dissipating any coercion. . . . Attendance at a high school football game, unlike showing up for class, is certainly not required in order to receive a diploma. . . .

There are some students, however, such as cheerleaders, members of the band, and, of course, the team members themselves, for whom seasonal commitments mandate their attendance, sometimes for class credit. The District also minimizes the importance to many students of attending and participating in extracurricular activities as part of a complete educational experience. As we noted in *Lee*, "[l]aw reaches past formalism." 505 U.S., at 595.

To assert that high school students do not feel immense social pressure, or have a truly genuine desire, to be involved in the extracurricular event that is American high school football is "formalistic in the extreme." . . . The constitution, moreover, demands that the school may not force this difficult choice upon these students for "[I]t is a tenet of the First Amendment that the State cannot require one of its citizens to forfeit his or her rights and benefits as the price of resisting conformance to state-sponsored religious practice." Id., at 596.

Even if we regard every high school student's decision to attend a home football game as purely voluntary, we are nevertheless persuaded that the delivery of a pregame prayer has the improper effect of coercing those present to participate in an act of religious worship. For "the government may no more use social pressure to enforce orthodoxy than it may use more direct means." . . . The constitutional command will not permit the District "to exact religious conformity from a student as the price" of joining her classmates at a varsity football game. . . .

The narrow question before us is whether implementation of the October policy insulates the continuation of such prayers from constitutional scrutiny. It does not. . . .

The District, nevertheless, asks us to pretend that we do not recognize what every Santa Fe High School student understands clearly—that this policy is about prayer. The District further asks us to accept what is obviously untrue: that these messages are necessary to "solemnize" a football game and that this single-student, year-long position is essential to the protection of student speech. We refuse to turn a blind eye to the context in which this policy arose, and that context quells any doubt that this policy was implemented with the purpose of endorsing school prayer. . . .

This policy likewise does not survive a facial challenge because it impermissibly imposes upon the student body a majoritarian election on the issue of prayer. Through its election scheme, the District has established a governmental electoral mechanism that turns the school into a forum for religious debate. It further empowers the student body majority with the authority to subject students of minority views to constitutionally improper messages.

The award of that power alone, regardless of the students' ultimate use of it, is not acceptable. . . . Such a system encourages divisiveness along religious lines and threatens the imposition of coercion upon those students not desiring to participate in a religious exercise. Simply by establishing this school-related procedure, which entrusts the inherently nongovernmental subject of religion to a majoritarian vote, a constitutional violation has occurred. . . .

. . . The policy is invalid on its face because it establishes an improper majoritarian election on religion, and unquestionably has the purpose and creates the perception of encouraging the delivery of prayer at a series of important school events.

The judgment of the Court of Appeals is, accordingly, affirmed.

It is so ordered.

CASE NOTES

1. *Prayers.* The U.S. Supreme Court in *Marsh v. Chambers*, 463 U.S. 783, 103 S.Ct. 3330 (1983), upheld the validity of opening prayers at legislative sessions. The Eleventh Circuit, though, refused to apply *Marsh* to schools and held that *Lemon* controlled. *Jager v. Douglas County School District*, 862 F.2d 824 (11th Cir.1989).

2. Prayers conducted by the Cleveland, Ohio, school board more closely resemble the school prayers in *Lee v. Weisman* than the legislative prayers in *Marsh v. Chambers*. In holding the Cleveland prayers unconstitutional for violating the establishment clause, the U.S. Court of Appeals, Sixth Circuit, said that the board-conducted prayers violated all three *Lemon* tests. As to violating the purpose test, the court said that the purpose was religious because the board meetings could have been conducted without resort to prayers. Concerning the primary effect of endorsing religion, the court found the prayers were clearly sectarian, having repeating references to Jesus and the Bible and conducted by a Christian minister. Moreover, the school board's practice of choosing a member from the local community to give the prayers and the fact that the school board president composed and delivered some of the prayers created an excessive entanglement. Thus, the school board prayers failed on all

three counts. *Coles v. Cleveland Board of Education*, 171 F.3d 369 (6th Cir. 1999).

3. The U.S. Court of Appeals for the Fifth Circuit has held unconstitutional the conduct of a prayer by a coach at athletic games and practices. This court ruled that it does not violate the establishment clause to permit the choir to adopt the theme of Christian religious songs. The choir had a legitimate secular purpose in teaching students to sight read and sing *a capella*. Moreover, the court observed that given the dominance of religious music in the choral music, to forbid religious songs would constitute hostility toward religion. *Doe v. Duncanville Independent School District*, 70 F.3d 402, 104 Educ.L.Rep. 1032 (5th Cir.1995). See also *Bauchman v. West High School*, 900 F.Supp. 254, 104 Educ.L.Rep. 292 (D.Utah 1995).

4. The U.S. Court of Appeals for the Sixth Circuit has ruled that the use of a "Blue Devil" as the school athletic mascot does not violate the establishment clause. *Kunselman v. Western Reserve Local School District*, 70 F.3d 931, 105 Educ.L.Rep. 43 (6th Cir.1995).

5. In a case, cited above, students sued to have a portrait of Christ removed from the school's hallway, the court ruled the presence of the portrait violated the establishment clause. *Washegesic v. Bloomingdale Public Schools*, 33 F.3d 679, 94 Educ.L.Rep. 32 (6th Cir.1994), cert. denied, 514 U.S. 1095, 115 S.Ct. 1822 (1995).

6. A Georgia statute requiring a period of quiet reflection was held to be constitutional by a federal district court in that state. *Brown v. Gwinnett County School District*, 895 F.Supp. 1564, 103 Educ.L.Rep. 207 (D.Ga.1995).

7. Where a school district allowed morning prayer to be broadcast over the school intercom and allowed student-led prayer in the classrooms during school hours, the court enjoined the school's action on the likelihood that the plaintiff would be successful on the merits in showing that the functions violated the establishment clause. *Herdahl v. Pontotoc County School District*, 887 F.Supp. 902, 101 Educ.L.Rep. 190 (D.Miss.1995).

8. *Dancing.* Whether dancing is a religious activity has been ruled upon by the courts. In a case where a local school board policy prohibited dancing on school property, the students and parents filed suit, claiming the policy vio-

lated the establishment clause. Religious groups of the small rural community opposed dancing and spoke out in support of the school policy. The court ruled that dancing was not religious but that it was not unconstitutional for a school board to have a rule that is compatible with the belief of a large, vocal segment of the community. The court, in holding for the board, stated that the plaintiff's remedy is to be found at the ballot box and not in the Constitution. *Clayton by Clayton v. Place*, 884 F.2d 376 (8th Cir.1989).

9. Before the *Engel* and *Schempp* cases, many decisions were rendered by state courts that found that morning religious activities did not violate constitutional or statutory provisions. Some of these were *Hackett v. Brooksville Graded School District*, 120 Ky. 608, 87 S.W. 792 (1905); *Donahoe v. Richards*, 38 Me. 379, 61 Am.Dec. 256 (1854); *Moore v. Monroe*, 64 Iowa 367, 20 N.W. 475 (1884); *Billard v. Board of Education of City of Topeka*, 69 Kan. 53, 76 P. 422 (1904); *Knowlton v. Baumhover*, 182 Iowa 691, 166 N.W. 202 (1918); and *McCormick v. Burt*, 95 Ill. 263 (1880).

The following state courts held that religious exercises offended their constitutions: *State ex rel. Weiss v. District Board*, 76 Wis. 177, 44 N.W. 967 (1890); *State ex rel. Freeman v. Scheve*, 65 Neb. 853, 91 N.W. 846 (1902); *People ex rel. Ring v. Board of Education of District 24*, 245 Ill. 334, 92 N.E. 251 (1910); *Herold v. Parish Board of School Directors*, 136 La. 1034, 68 So. 116 (1915); *State ex rel. Finger v. Weedman*, 55 S.D. 343, 226 N.W. 348 (1929).

10. *Religious Garb in Public Schools.* Whether public school teachers can wear religious garb of any particular religious order or society has been litigated on several occasions. While there is no precise definition of what constitutes religious garments, some states have sought to prohibit any apparel showing the person belongs to a particular sect, denomination, or order. See Donald E. Boles, *The Two Swords* (Ames: Iowa State University Press, 1967), p. 222. (See Chapter 15 on teacher rights and freedoms.)

In 1894, the Supreme Court of Pennsylvania held that the wearing by nuns of garb and insignia of the Sisterhood of St. Joseph while teaching in the public schools did not constitute sectarian teaching. *Hysong v. School District of Gallitzin Borough*, 164 Pa. 629, 30 A. 482 (1894). The court reasoned that to prohibit the wearing of such apparel would violate the teachers' religious liberty. Later, the legislature of Pennsylvania prohibited the wearing of garb by public school teachers while in performance of their duties. This statute was subsequently upheld by the Pennsylvania Supreme Court. This time the court maintained that the act was a reasonable exercise of state power in regulating the educational system to prevent sectarian control. The court found that the legislation "is directed against acts, not beliefs, and only against acts of the teacher while engaged in the performance of his or her duties as such teacher." *Commonwealth v. Hert*, 229 Pa. 132, 78 A. 68 (1910).

11. Bibles can be distributed on the sidewalk in front of a public school. In a case where an individual was barred from distributing Gideon Bibles on the sidewalk in front of a high school, the plaintiff claimed that the sidewalk was used for teachers to picket, pass out leaflets, and other activities and was therefore a "public forum." The court held that the school district's policy violated the individual's First Amendment and equal protection rights. *Bacon v. Bradley-Bourbonnais High School District No. 307*, 707 F.Supp. 1005 (C.D.Ill.1989).

12. *Clergy in Schools.* A program where a school district invited individual members of the local clergy into the schools to provide volunteer counseling during school hours violated the establishment clause. The program did not have a secular purpose and had the primary effect of advancing religion. The program lacked neutrality because it invited only clergymen and no laymen. The court observed that a governmental measure advances religion if it gives preferential benefit to religion and does not extend the same to anything else. As conducted, the program violated the "coercion test" of *Lee v. Weisman* because the students were selected for participation by administrators without notifying parents or obtaining parental consent, placing the students in the untenable position of having to attend a session or to decline an invitation and thus risk "opprobrium and ostracism" from administrators. Too, the court held that the program violated the third prong of the *Lemon* test, excessive entanglement, because school officials were intimately and continuously involved in an overt and intrusive way in administering the program, recruiting the clergy, providing ongo-

ing training for the clergy, disseminating counseling guidelines, selecting students, monitoring, and facilitating the clergy/student dialogue at the counseling sessions. *Doe v. Beaumont Independent School District*, 173 F.3d 274 (5th Cir.1999).

In considering this case note, one should remember the facts in *Illinois ex rel. McCollum v. Board of Education*, 333 U.S. 203, 68 S.Ct. 461 (1948), where Protestant, Catholic, and Jewish clergy were brought into the schools for religious instruction. In *McCollum*, parents signed printed cards requesting that their children be permitted to attend. Students who did not want to attend were required to go elsewhere in the building. The fact that parental permission was obtained was irrelevant. The U.S. Supreme Court in *McCollum* held that the activity violated the First Amendment in that the state's tax-supported public school buildings were used for dissemination of religious doctrines and that the public schools' compulsory attendance machinery provided an invaluable aid to religion.

Beaumont raises the same issue that was decided with finality in *McCollum*, a fifty-one-year-old precedent. The *Beaumont* case reflects a revived and rather aggressive attempt by the more fundamentalist Protestant sects to abrogate the basic principles of nonsectarianism of the public common schools and to refashion them as institutions that inculcate religion.

13. At the request of President Clinton, U.S. Secretary of Education Richard W. Riley issued a statement of principles, gleaned from the precedents of the various court decisions, explaining the extent to which religious expression and activity are permitted in the public schools. The document, entitled *Religious Expression in Public Schools*, was published in August 1995 and amended and republished in 1998.

■ EQUAL ACCESS ACT

The Equal Access Act, passed by the U.S. Congress in 1984, was based on the free speech determination of *Widmar v. Vincent*.[216] In *Widmar*, the University of Missouri had refused to allow a religious group the use of university facilities because of the possible violation of the establishment clause. The Court ruled that to refuse religious groups access to facilities, while allowing other groups to use the same facilities, violated the students' right of free speech. The Reagan administration, using this case as a rationale, applied the equal access concept to noncurricular high school activities in order to allow religious functions in public schools. The Equal Access Act provides that if a school district receives federal money and allows noncurricular activities and club meetings, then it is unlawful to deny students the right to meet for religious activities. Therefore, if a public high school has noncurricular meetings, such as a photography club, and this activity is not directly related to a specific class or a class requirement, then the school has created a "limited open forum." If a limited open forum exists, then all groups, regardless of their religious, political, or philosophical beliefs, are allowed to form and hold meetings and activities in the public high school. Such groups must be student initiated and not sponsored by the school.

The Supreme Court on June 4, 1990, upheld the constitutionality of the Equal Access Act. In *Board of Education of Westside Community Schools v. Mergens*,[217] the Court ruled that if a school allows any noncurricular groups to meet, then a limited open forum is created, and any student-initiated group has a right to assemble. These groups would be allowed to convene during noninstructional time when other groups, such as the chess club, meet.

Students Have a Right to Organize Their Own Groups in Public Schools, Whether These Groups Be Religious, Political, or Philosophical

Board of Education of the Westside Community Schools v. Mergens

Supreme Court of the United States, 1990.
496 U.S. 226, 110 S.Ct. 2356.

Justice O'Connor delivered the opinion of the Court except as to Part III. This case requires us to decide whether the Equal Access Act, 98 Stat. 1302, 20 U.S.C. §§4071–4074, prohibits Westside High School from denying a student religious group permission to meet on school premises during noninstructional time, and if so, whether the Act, so construed, violates the Establishment Clause of the First Amendment.

Respondents are current and former students at Westside High School, a public secondary school in Omaha, Nebraska. At the time this suit was filed, the school enrolled about 1,450 students and included grades 10 to 12; in the 1987–1988 school year, ninth graders were added. Westside High School is part of the Westside Community School system, an independent public school district. . . .

Students at Westside High School are permitted to join various student groups and clubs, all of which meet after school hours on school premises. The students may choose from approximately 30 recognized groups on a voluntary basis. . . .

School Board Policy 5610 concerning "Student Clubs and Organizations" recognizes these student clubs as a "vital part of the total education program as a means of developing citizenship, wholesome attitudes, good human relations, knowledge and skills." . . . Board Policy 5610 also provides that each club shall have faculty sponsorship and that "clubs and organizations shall not be sponsored by any political or religious organization, or by any organization which denies membership on the basis of race, color, creed, sex or political belief." Board Policy 6180 on "Recognition of Religious Beliefs and Customs" requires that "[s]tudents adhering to a specific set of religious beliefs or holding to little or no belief shall be alike respected." In addition, Board Policy 5450 recognizes its students' "Freedom of Expression," consistent with the authority of the Board.

There is no written school board policy concerning the formation of student clubs. Rather, students wishing to form a club present their request to a school official who determines whether the proposed club's goals and objectives are consistent with school board policies and with the school district's "Mission and Goals"—a broadly worded "blueprint" that expresses the district's commitment to teaching academic, physical, civic, and personal skills and values.

In January 1985, respondent Bridget Mergens met with Westside's principal, Dr. Findley, and requested permission to form a Christian club at the school. . . .

Findley denied the request, as did associate superintendent Tangdell. In February 1985, Findley and Tangdell informed Mergens that they had discussed the matter with superintendent Hanson and that he had agreed that her request should be denied. The school officials explained that school policy required all student clubs to have a faculty sponsor, which the proposed religious club would not or could not have, and that a religious club at the school would violate the Establishment Clause. In March 1985, Mergens appealed the denial of her request to the Board of Education, but the Board voted to uphold the denial. . . .

Respondents . . . then brought this suit in the United States District Court for the District of Nebraska seeking declaratory and injunctive relief. They alleged that petitioners' refusal to permit the proposed club to meet at Westside violated the Equal Access Act, 20 U.S.C. §§4071–4074, which prohibits public secondary schools that receive federal financial assistance and that maintain a "limited open forum" from denying "equal access" to students who wish to meet within the forum on the basis of the content of the speech at such meetings . . . . Respondents further alleged that petitioners' actions denied them their First and Fourteenth Amendment rights to freedom of speech, association, and the free exercise of religion. Petitioners responded that the Equal Access Act did not apply to Westside and that, if the Act did apply, it violated the Establishment Clause of the First Amendment and was therefore unconstitutional. . . .

In *Widmar v. Vincent*, 454 U.S. 263 (1981), we invalidated, on free speech grounds, a state university regulation that prohibited student use of school facilities "for purposes of religious worship or religious teaching." In doing so, we held that an "equal access" policy would not violate the Establishment Clause under our decision in *Lemon v. Kurtzman*. . . . In particular, we held that such a policy would have a secular purpose, would not have the primary effect of advancing religion, and would not result in excessive entanglement between government and religion. . . . We noted, however, that "[u]niversity students are, of course, young adults. They are less impressionable than younger students and should be able to appreciate that the University's policy is one of neutrality toward religion."

In 1984, Congress extended the reasoning of *Widmar* to public secondary schools. Under the Equal Access Act, a public secondary school with a "limited open forum" is prohibited from discriminating against students who wish to conduct a meeting within that forum on the basis of the "religious, political, philosophical, or other content of the speech at such meetings." . . . Specifically, the Act provides:

> It shall be unlawful for any public secondary school which receives Federal financial assistance and which has a limited open forum to deny equal access or a fair opportunity to, or discriminate against, any students who wish to conduct a meeting within that limited open forum on the basis of the religious, political, philosophical, or other content of the speech at such meetings. 20 U.S.C. §4071(a).

A "limited open forum" exists whenever a public secondary school "grants an offering to or opportunity for one or more noncurriculum related student groups to meet on school premises during noninstructional time." "Meeting" is defined to include "those activities of student groups which are permitted under a school's limited open forum and are not directly related to the school curriculum." "Noninstructional time" is defined to mean "time set aside by the school before actual classroom instruction begins or after actual classroom instruction ends." Thus, even if a public secondary school allows only one "noncurriculum related student group" to meet, the Act's obligations are triggered and the school may not deny other clubs, on the basis of the content of their speech, equal access to meet on school premises during noninstructional time.

The Act further specifies that "[s]chools shall be deemed to offer a fair opportunity to students who wish to conduct a meeting within its limited open forum" if the school uniformly provides that the meetings are voluntary and

student initiated; are not sponsored by the school, the government, or its agents or employees; do not materially and substantially interfere with the orderly conduct of educational activities within the school; and are not directed, controlled, conducted, or regularly attended by "nonschool persons." . . . "Sponsorship" is defined to mean "the act of promoting, leading, or participating in a meeting. The assignment of a teacher, administrator, or other school employee to a meeting for custodial purposes does not constitute sponsorship of the meeting." If the meetings are religious, employees or agents of the school or government may attend only in a "nonparticipatory capacity." Moreover, a State may not influence the form of any religious activity, require any person to participate in such activity, or compel any school agent or employee to attend a meeting if the content of the speech at the meeting is contrary to that person's beliefs. . . .

Finally, the Act does not "authorize the United States to deny or withhold Federal financial assistance to any school," . . . or "limit the authority of the school, its agents or employees, to maintain order and discipline on school premises, to protect the well-being of students and faculty, and to assure that attendance of students at the meetings is voluntary" . . . .

The parties agree that Westside High School receives federal financial assistance and is a public secondary school within the meaning of the Act. . . . The Act's obligation to grant equal access to student groups is therefore triggered if Westside maintains a "limited open forum"— *i.e.*, if it permits one or more "noncurriculum related student groups" to meet on campus before or after classes.

Unfortunately, the Act does not define the crucial phrase "noncurriculum related student group." Our immediate task is therefore one of statutory interpretation. We begin, of course, with the language of the statute. . . . The common meaning of the term "curriculum" is "the whole body of courses offered by an educational institution or one of its branches." *Webster's Third New International Dictionary* 557 (1976); see also *Black's Law Dictionary* 345 (5th ed. 1979) ("The set of studies or courses for a particular period, designated by a school or branch of a school"). . . . Any sensible interpretation of "noncurriculum related student group" must therefore be anchored in the notion that such student groups are those that are not related to the body of courses offered by the school. The difficult question is the degree of "unrelatedness to the curriculum" required for a group to be considered "noncurriculum related."

The Act's definition of the sort of "meeting[s]" that must be accommodated under the statute . . . sheds some light on this question. "[T]he term "meeting" includes those activities of student groups which are . . . not *directly related* to the school curriculum." . . . Congress' use of the phrase "directly related" implies that student groups directly related to the subject matter of courses offered by the school do not fall within the "noncurriculum related" category and would therefore be considered "curriculum related."

The logic of the Act also supports this view, namely, that a curriculum-related student group is one that has more than just a tangential or attenuated relationship to courses offered by the school. Because the purpose of granting equal access is to prohibit discrimination between religious or political clubs on the one hand and other noncurriculum-related student groups on the other, the Act is premised on the notion that a religious or political club is itself likely to be a noncurriculum-related student group. It follows, then, that a student group that is "curriculum related" must at least have a more direct relationship to the curriculum than a religious or political club would have.

Although the phrase "noncurriculum related student group" nevertheless remains sufficiently ambiguous that we might normally resort to legislative history, . . . we find the legislative history on this issue less than helpful. Because the bill that led to the Act was extensively rewritten in a series of multilateral negotiations after it was passed by the House and reported out of committee by the Senate, the committee reports shed no light on the language actually adopted. During congressional debate on the subject, legislators referred to a number of different definitions, and thus both petitioners and respondents can cite to legislative history favoring their interpretation of the phrase. . . .

We think it significant, however, that the Act, which was passed by wide, bipartisan majorities in both the House and the Senate, reflects at least some consensus on a broad legislative purpose. The committee reports indicate that the Act was intended to address perceived widespread discrimination against religious speech in public schools. . . . The committee reports also show that the Act was enacted in part in response to two federal appellate court decisions holding that student religious groups could not, consistent with the Establishment Clause, meet on school premises during noninstructional time. . . . A broad reading of the Act would be consistent with the views of those who sought to end discrimination by allowing students to meet and discuss religion before and after classes.

In light of this legislative purpose, we think that the term "noncurriculum related student group" is best interpreted broadly to mean any student group that does not *directly* relate to the body of courses offered by the school. In our view, a student group directly relates to a school's curriculum if the subject matter of the group is actually taught, or will soon be taught, in a regularly offered course; if the subject matter of the group concerns the body of courses as a whole; if participation in the group is required for a particular course; or if participation in the group results in academic credit. We think this limited definition of groups that directly relate to the curriculum is a commonsense interpretation of the Act that is consistent with Congress' intent to provide a low threshold for triggering the Act's requirements.

For example, a French club would directly relate to the curriculum if a school taught French in a regularly offered course or planned to teach the subject in the near future. A school's student government would generally relate directly to the curriculum to the extent that it addresses concerns, solicits opinions, and formulates proposals pertaining to the body of courses offered by the school. If participation in a school's band or orchestra were required for the band or orchestra classes, or resulted in academic credit, then those groups would also directly relate to the curriculum. The existence of such groups at a school would not trigger the Act's obligations.

On the other hand, unless a school could show that groups such as a chess club, a stamp-collecting club, or a community service club fell within our description of groups that directly relate to the curriculum, such groups would be "noncurriculum related student groups" for purposes of the Act. The existence of such groups would create a "limited open forum" under the Act and would prohibit the school from denying equal access to any other student group on the basis of the content of the group's speech. Whether a specific student group is a "noncurriculum related student group" will therefore depend on a particular school's curriculum, but such determinations would be subject to factual findings well within the competence of trial courts to make.

Petitioners contend that our reading of the Act unduly hinders local control over schools and school activities, but we think the schools and school districts nevertheless retain a significant measure of authority over the type of officially recognized activities in which their students participate. . . . First, schools and school districts maintain their traditional latitude to determine appropriate subjects of instruction. To the extent that a school chooses to structure its course offerings and existing student groups to avoid the Act's obligations, that result is not prohibited by the Act. . . . Second, the Act expressly does not limit a school's authority to prohibit meetings that would "materially and substantially interfere with the orderly conduct of educational activities within the school." . . . The Act also preserves "the authority of the school, its agents or employees, to maintain order and discipline on school premises, to protect the well-being of students and faculty, and to assure that attendance of students at meetings is voluntary." . . . Finally, because the Act applies only to public secondary schools that receive federal financial assistance, . . . a school district seeking to escape the statute's obligations could simply forgo federal funding. Although we do not doubt that in some cases this may be an unrealistic option, Congress clearly sought to prohibit schools from discriminating on the basis of the content of a student group's speech, and that obligation is the price a federally funded school must pay if it opens its facilities to noncurriculum-related student groups. . . .

The parties in this case focus their dispute on 10 of Westside's approximately 30 voluntary student clubs: Interact (a service club related to Rotary International); Chess; Subsurfers (a club for students interested in scuba diving); National Honor Society; Photography; Welcome to Westside (a club to introduce new students to the school); Future Business Leaders of America; Zonta (the female counterpart to Interact); Student Advisory Board (student government); and Student Forum (student government). . . . Petitioners contend that all of these student activities are curriculum-related because they further the goals of particular aspects of the school's curriculum. Welcome to Westside, for example, helps "further the School's overall goal of developing effective citizens by requiring student members to contribute to their fellow students." . . . The student government clubs "advance the goals of the School's political science classes by providing an understanding and appreciation of government processes." Subsurfers furthers "one of the essential goals of the Physical Education Department—enabling students to develop lifelong recreational interests." Chess "supplement[s] math and science courses because it enhances students' ability to engage in critical thought processes." Participation in Interact and Zonta "promotes effective citizenship, a critical goal of the WHS curriculum, specifically the Social Studies Department."

To the extent that petitioners contend that "curriculum related" means anything remotely related to abstract educational goals, however, we reject that argument. To define "curriculum related" in a way that results in almost no schools having limited open fora, or in a way that permits schools to evade the Act by strategically describing existing student groups, would render the Act merely hortatory. . . . ("[A] limited open forum should be triggered by what a school does, not by what it says.") As the court below explained:

> Allowing such a broad interpretation of "curriculum-related" would make the [Act] meaningless. A school's administration could simply declare that it maintains a closed forum and choose which student clubs it wanted to allow by tying the purposes of those clubs to some broadly defined educational goal. At the same time the administration could arbitrarily deny access to school facilities to

any unfavored student club on the basis of its speech content. This is exactly the result that Congress sought to prohibit by enacting the [Act]. A public secondary school cannot simply declare that it maintains a closed forum and then discriminate against a particular student group on the basis of the content of the speech of that group. . . .

Rather, we think it clear that Westside's existing student groups include one or more "noncurriculum related student groups." Although Westside's physical education classes apparently include swimming, . . . counsel stated at oral argument that scuba diving is not taught in any regularly offered course at the school. . . . Based on Westside's own description of the group, Subsurfers does not directly relate to the curriculum as a whole in the same way that a student government or similar group might. . . . Moreover, participation in Subsurfers is not required by any course at the school and does not result in extra academic credit. Thus, Subsurfers is a "noncurriculum related student group" for purposes of the Act. Similarly, although math teachers at Westside have encouraged their students to play chess, chess is not taught in any regularly offered course at the school, . . . and participation in the chess club is not required for any class and does not result in extra credit for any class. . . . The chess club is therefore another "noncurriculum related student group" at Westside. Moreover, Westside's principal acknowledged at trial that the Peer Advocates program—a service group that works with special education classes—does not directly relate to any courses offered by the school. . . . Peer Advocates would therefore also fit within our description of a "noncurriculum related student group." The record therefore supports a finding that Westside has maintained a limited open forum under the Act.

Although our definition of "noncurriculum related student activities" looks to a school's actual practice rather than its stated policy, we note that our conclusion is also supported by the school's own description of its student activities. . . . [T]he school states that Band "is included in our regular curriculum"; Choir "is a course offered as part of the curriculum"; Distributive Education "is an extension of the Distributive Education class"; International Club is "developed through our foreign language classes"; Latin Club is "designed for those students who are taking Latin as a foreign language"; Student Publications "includes classes offered in preparation of the yearbook (Shield) and the student newspaper (Lance)"; Dramatics "is an extension of a regular academic class"; and Orchestra "is an extension of our regular curriculum." These descriptions constitute persuasive evidence that these student clubs directly relate to the curriculum. By inference, however, the fact that the descriptions of student activities such as Subsurfers and chess do not include such references strongly suggests that those clubs do not, by the school's own admission, directly relate to the curriculum. We therefore conclude that Westside permits "one or more noncurriculum related student groups to meet on school premises during noninstructional time" . . . . Because Westside maintains a "limited open forum" under the Act, it is prohibited from discriminating, based on the content of the students' speech, against students who wish to meet on school premises during noninstructional time.

The remaining statutory question is whether petitioners' denial of respondents' request to form a religious group constitutes a denial of "equal access" to the school's limited open forum. Although the school apparently permits respondents to meet informally after school, . . . respondents seek equal access in the form of official recognition by the school. Official recognition allows student clubs to be part of the student activities program and carries with it access to the school newspaper, bulletin boards, the public address system, and the annual Club Fair. Given that the Act explicitly prohibits denial of "equal access . . . to . . . any students who wish to conduct a meeting within [the school's] limited open forum" on the basis of the religious content of the speech at such meetings, . . . we hold that Westside's denial of respondents' request to form a Christian club denies them "equal access" under the Act.

Because we rest our conclusion on statutory grounds, we need not decide—and therefore express no opinion on—whether the First Amendment requires the same result.

Petitioners contend that even if Westside has created a limited open forum within the meaning of the Act, its denial of official recognition to the proposed Christian club must nevertheless stand because the Act violates the Establishment Clause of the First Amendment, as applied to the States through the Fourteenth Amendment. Specifically, petitioners maintain that because the school's recognized student activities are an integral part of its educational mission, official recognition of respondents' proposed club would effectively incorporate religious activities into the school's official program, endorse participation in the religious club, and provide the club with an official platform to proselytize other students.

We disagree. In *Widmar,* we applied the three-part *Lemon* test to hold that an "equal access" policy, at the university level, does not violate the Establishment Clause. . . . We concluded that "an open-forum policy, including nondiscrimination against religious speech, would have a secular purpose," . . . and would in fact *avoid* entanglement with religion. . . . We also found that although incidental benefits accrued to religious groups who used university facilities, this result did not amount to an establishment of religion. First, we stated that a university's forum does not "confer any imprimatur of state approval on religious sects or practices." Indeed, the message is one of neutrality rather than endorsement; if a State refused to let religious groups use facilities open to others, then it would demonstrate not neutrality but hostility toward religion. "The Establishment Clause does not license government to treat religion and those who teach or practice it, simply by virtue of their status as such, as subversive of American ideals and therefore subject to unique disabilities." . . . Second, we noted that "[t]he [University's] provision of benefits to [a] broad . . . spectrum of groups"—both nonreligious and religious speakers—was "an important index of secular effect." . . .

We think the logic of *Widmar* applies with equal force to the Equal Access Act. As an initial matter, the Act's prohibition of discrimination on the basis of "political, philosophical, or other" speech as well as religious speech is a sufficient basis for meeting the secular purpose prong of the *Lemon* test. . . . Congress' avowed purpose—to prevent discrimination against religious and other types of speech—is undeniably secular. Even if some legislators were motivated

by a conviction that religious speech in particular was valuable and worthy of protection, that alone would not invalidate the Act, because what is relevant is the legislative *purpose* of the statute, not the possibly religious *motives* of the legislators who enacted the law. Because the Act on its face grants equal access to both secular and religious speech, we think it clear that the Act's purpose was not to ""endorse or disapprove of religion'". . . .

Petitioners' principal contention is that the Act has the primary effect of advancing religion. Specifically, petitioners urge that, because the student religious meetings are held under school aegis, and because the state's compulsory attendance laws bring the students together (and thereby provide a ready-made audience for student evangelists), an objective observer in the position of a secondary school student will perceive official school support for such religious meetings. . . .

We disagree. First, although we have invalidated the use of public funds to pay for teaching state-required subjects at parochial schools, in part because of the risk of creating "a crucial symbolic link between government and religion, thereby enlisting—at least in the eyes of impressionable youngsters—the powers of government to the support of the religious denomination operating the school," . . . there is a crucial difference between *government* speech endorsing religion, which the Establishment Clause forbids, and *private* speech endorsing religion, which the Free Speech and Free Exercise Clauses protect. We think that secondary school students are mature enough and are likely to understand that a school does not endorse or support student speech that it merely permits on a nondiscriminatory basis. . . . The proposition that schools do not endorse everything they fail to censor is not complicated. "[P]articularly in this age of massive media information . . . the few years difference in age between high school and college students [does not] justif[y] departing from *Widmar*." . . .

Indeed, we note that Congress specifically rejected the argument that high school students are likely to confuse an equal access policy with state sponsorship of religion. . . . Given the deference due "the duly enacted and carefully considered decision of a coequal and representative branch of our Government," . . . we do not lightly second-guess such legislative judgments, particularly where the judgments are based in part on empirical determinations.

Second, we note that the Act expressly limits participation by school officials at meetings of student religious groups, §§4071(c)(2) and (3), and that any such meetings must be held during "noninstructional time" . . . . The Act therefore avoids the problems of "the students'" emulation of teachers as role models" and "mandatory attendance requirements" . . . . To be sure, the possibility of *student* peer pressure remains, but there is little if any risk of official state endorsement or coercion where no formal classroom activities are involved and no school officials actively participate. Moreover, petitioners' fear of a mistaken inference of endorsement is largely self-imposed, because the school itself has control over any impressions it gives its students. To the extent a school makes clear that its recognition of respondents' proposed club is not an endorsement of the views of the club's participants, . . . students will reasonably understand that the school's official recognition of the club evinces neutrality toward, rather than endorsement of, religious speech.

Third, . . . [a]lthough a school may not itself lead or direct a religious club, a school that permits a student-initiated and student-led religious club to meet after school, just as it permits any other student group to do, does not convey a message of state approval or endorsement of the particular religion. Under the Act, a school with a limited open forum may not lawfully deny access to a Jewish students' club, a Young Democrats club, or a philosophy club devoted to the study of Nietzsche. To the extent that a religious club is merely one of many different student-initiated voluntary clubs, students should perceive no message of government endorsement of religion. Thus, we conclude that the Act does not, at least on its face and as applied to Westside, have the primary effect of advancing religion. . . .

Petitioners' final argument is that by complying with the Act's requirement, the school risks excessive entanglement between government and religion. The proposed club, petitioners urge, would be required to have a faculty sponsor who would be charged with actively directing the activities of the group, guiding its leaders, and ensuring balance in the presentation of controversial ideas. Petitioners claim that this influence over the club's religious program would entangle the government in day-to-day surveillance of religion of the type forbidden by the Establishment Clause.

Under the Act, however, faculty monitors may not participate in any religious meetings, and nonschool persons may not direct, control, or regularly attend activities of student groups. . . . Moreover, the Act prohibits school "sponsorship" of any religious meetings, . . . which means that school officials may not promote, lead, or participate in any such meeting. . . . Although the Act permits "[t]he assignment of a teacher, administrator, or other school employee to the meeting for custodial purposes," . . . such custodial oversight of the student-initiated religious group, merely to ensure order and good behavior, does not impermissibly entangle government in the day-to-day surveillance or administration of religious activities. . . . Indeed, as the Court noted in *Widmar*, a denial of equal access to religious speech might well create greater entanglement problems in the form of invasive monitoring to prevent religious speech at meetings at which such speech might occur. . . .

Accordingly, we hold that the Equal Access Act does not on its face contravene the Establishment Clause. Because we hold that petitioners have violated the Act, we do not decide respondents' claims under the Free Speech and Free Exercise Clauses. For the foregoing reasons, the judgment of the Court of Appeals is affirmed.

It is so ordered.

CASE NOTES

1. Interpretation of the Equal Access Act after *Mergens* has become an interesting amalgamation of the statute and various provisions of the U.S. Constitution, including the establishment, free exercise, freedom of speech, and equal protection clauses. In *HSU v. Roslyn Union Free School District No. 3*, the U.S. Court of Appeals, Second Circuit, addressed the issue of whether a Bible club could operate in a public high school if the club charter stated that only Christians could be club officers. The school refused the

club charter for this reason, and the students sued. The court in a complicated web of reasoning concluded that the club's Christian officers requirement is essential to the expressive content of the meetings and to the club's preservation of its purpose and identity and is therefore protected by the Equal Access Act. The leadership provision of the club's constitution applied only to the president, vice-president, and music coordinator. The court concluded that unconditioned recognition of the club would not violate the establishment clause or the equal protection clause of the U.S. Constitution. Moreover, in spite of the club's exclusionary requirements, to deny the club recognition as an after-school Bible group would constitute irreparable injury to the Bible club students and violate their rights under the Equal Access Act. *HSU v. Roslyn Union Free School District No. 3*, 85 F.3d 839 (2nd Cir. 1996).

2. The Equal Access Act was passed, at least partially, with religious motivation as a remonstrance against public school secularism, which effectively prevented sectarian activities on school grounds and during the school day. The words of the act requiring schools to provide for a "limited open forum on the basis of religious, political philosophy and other content" were carefully fashioned but are now having some effects that were not fully anticipated. The act in effect removes the discretion and autonomy in deciding what school activities will be permitted from the hands of school boards and vests them in the courts. Moreover, for the Equal Access Act itself to be constitutional, it had to be broader than simply a subterfuge to assure that religious clubs had access to school buildings and school time. As it turns out, as *Mergens* indicates, the only meetings that schools can prohibit are those that would materially and substantially interfere with the orderly conduct of the school. Thus, we have begun to see considerable waffling by school boards and courts as they experience some discomfort as a result of less convential club meetings. A good example is a recent lower federal court case in California where the court found that a school district had violated the Equal Access Act when the school board voted to deny the application for club status of the Gay Straight Alliance Club.

The court observed that the school board would likely be able to show that groups of students discussing homophobia and acceptance of homosexuals would not disrupt the school. Thus, because the board had created a "limited open forum," with several other clubs being recognized, the gay students group had to be given the same rights and privileges as the other student groups. *Colin v. Orange Unified School District*, 83 F.Supp. 1135 (C.D.Cal.2000).

3. In 1995, the U.S. Court of Appeals for the Ninth Circuit ruled the Equal Access Act was violated when students were not permitted to have a religious club meeting during lunchtime. The school had previously allowed other, nonreligious clubs to hold such meetings. The court noted that the lunch period was noninstructional time within the meaning of the Equal Access Act and that to hold voluntary religious meetings during that time did not violate the establishment clause. *Ceniceros v. Board of Trustees of the San Diego Unified School District*, 66 F.3d 1535, 103 Educ.L.Rep. 934 (9th Cir.1995).

4. If a school recognizes a nonreligious club, it must not deny recognition to a religious one. Where a school board recognized the school Key Club but refused recognition to the Bible Club, the court ruled that because the Key Club was not curriculum related, the school had created a "limited open forum" under the Equal Access Act and must therefore recognize religious clubs such as the Bible Club as well. Not to do so would violate the Equal Access Act. *Pope by Pope v. East Brunswick Board of Education*, 12 F.3d 1244, 88 Educ.L.Rep. 552 (3d Cir.1993).

5. *Bibles.* In a case where a school board in West Virginia allowed a group to distribute Bibles from tables located in the school hallways, the evidence presented by the school board indicated that students were not coerced to accept the Bibles. The federal court held that the Constitution did not require the withholding of access to the Bible group. According to the court, if such access were withheld, it would create the impression that religious speech was disfavored. While upholding the practice as a valid exercise of freedom of speech in high schools, the court nevertheless held that such a practice could not be permitted in elementary schools because of the possibility of coercing

younger and more impressionable children. *Peck v. Upshur County Board of Education,* 155 F.3d 274 (4th Cir.1998).

6. *Equal Access Act.* The statement of principles entitled *Religious Expression in Public Schools* issued by the U.S. Department of Education also included a statement explaining the meaning of the Equal Access Act as interpreted by the courts.

■ FACILITIES

After *Widmar* and *Mergens,* the courts began to rely on the free speech test more frequently when dealing with church-state issues. They reasoned that if religious groups were denied the use of school facilities, while other groups, such as civic organizations, scouts, and so forth, were permitted use of them, then the religious groups' free speech rights would be denied. To hold otherwise would violate the requirement of neutrality. The free speech test, sometimes called the public forum test, has been applied to the use of school facilities. In earlier cases, the courts ruled that school boards could adopt policies that allowed groups to use school facilities based on the type of organization and the nature of its activities. For example, a school board could allow school facilities to be used by the Boy Scouts and Girl Scouts but could deny access to religious groups.

When the free speech/public forum rationale is applied to the use of school facilities, the school must show that the decision as to facility use is "viewpoint neutral." The viewpoint neutrality analysis was used by the U.S. Supreme Court in *Lamb's Chapel v. Center Moriches Union Free School District.*[218] In this case, Center Moriches school district in New York denied Lamb's Chapel Church the after-hours use of school facilities for showing a series of "family values" films.

The Supreme Court ruled that such exclusion effectively violated the religious group's freedom of speech because evidence was presented showing that the school district had created a "limited public forum" by opening the school premises for "social, civic, and recreational" purposes, such as the Salvation Army Band,

Center Moriches Quilting Bee, Center Moriches Drama Club, Girl Scouts, Boy Scouts, and Center Moriches Music Awards Association, among others. According to the court, to open school premises for other groups but to close them to religious groups is not to remain viewpoint neutral.

A result similar to *Lamb's Chapel* was rendered by the U.S. Court of Appeals, First Circuit, in 1991, two years before *Lamb's Chapel.*[219] Here the court determined that the school district had created a public forum and that subsequent denial of use of the high school cafeteria for a Christmas dinner violated the free speech rights of members of the organization. Additionally, the court found the religious clauses of the First Amendment did not bar such religious accommodation by the school district.[220] If a school board allows any group to use school facilities, then it cannot exclude another simply because it disagrees with the group's philosophy.

❖ — ❖ — ❖

School District Violated Free Speech Clause of First Amendment by Denying Church Access to School Premises Solely because Film Dealt with Subject from a Religious Standpoint

Lamb's Chapel v. Center Moriches Union Free School District

Supreme Court of the United States, 1993.
508 U.S. 384, 113 S.Ct. 2141.

Justice WHITE delivered the opinion of the Court.

Section 414 of the New York Education Law (McKinney 1988 and Supp.1993) authorizes local school boards to adopt reasonable regulations for the use of school property for 10 specified purposes when the property is not in use for school purposes. Among the permitted uses is the holding of "social, civic and recreational meetings and entertainments, and other uses pertaining to the welfare of the community; but such meetings, entertainment and uses shall be non-exclusive and open to the general public." The list of permitted uses does not include meetings for religious purposes. . . .

Pursuant to §414's empowerment of local school districts, the Board of Center Moriches Union Free School District (District) has issued rules and regulations with respect to the use of school property when not in use for school purposes. The rules allow only 2 of the 10 purposes authorized by §414: social, civic, or recreational uses (Rule 10) and use by political organizations if secured in compliance with §414 (Rule 8). Rule 7, however, consistent with the judicial interpretation of state law, provides that "[t]he school premises shall not be used by any group for religious purposes." App. to Pet. for Cert. 57a.

The issue in this case is whether, against this background of state law, it violates the Free Speech Clause of the First Amendment, made applicable to the States by the Fourteenth Amendment, to deny a church access to school premises to exhibit for public viewing and for assertedly religious purposes, a film dealing with family and child-rearing issues faced by parents today.

Petitioners (Church) are Lamb's Chapel, an evangelical church in the community of Center Moriches, and its pastor John Steigerwald. Twice the Church applied to the District for permission to use school facilities to show a six-part film series containing lectures by Doctor James Dobson. . . . [T]he film series would discuss Dr. Dobson's views on the undermining influences of the media that could only be counterbalanced by returning to traditional, Christian family values instilled at an early stage. The brochure went on to describe the contents of each of the six parts of the series. The District denied the first application, saying that "[t]his film does appear to be church related and therefore your request must be refused." The second application for permission to use school premises for showing the film, which described it as a "[f]amily oriented movie—from the Christian perspective," was denied using identical language.

The Church brought suit in District Court. . . . The District Court granted summary judgment

for respondents, rejecting all of the Church's claims. . . .

The Court of Appeals affirmed the judgment of the District Court "in all respects." . . . It held that the school property, when not in use for school purposes, was neither a traditional nor a designated public forum; rather, it was a limited public forum open only for designated purposes, a classification that "allows it to remain non-public except as to specified uses." . . . Because the holding below was questionable under our decisions [Supreme Court], we granted the petition for certiorari, which in principal part challenged the holding below as contrary to the Free Speech Clause of the First Amendment.

There is no question that the District, like the private owner of property, may legally preserve the property under its control for the use to which it is dedicated. . . . It is also common ground that the District need not have permitted after-hours use of its property for any of the uses permitted by §414 of the state education law. The District, however, did open its property for 2 of the 10 uses permitted by §414. The Church argued below that because under Rule 10 of the rules issued by the District, school property could be used for "social, civic, and recreational" purposes, the District had opened its property for such a wide variety of communicative purposes that restrictions on communicative uses of the property were subject to the same constitutional limitations as restrictions in traditional public fora such as parks and sidewalks. Hence, its view was that subject-matter or speaker exclusions on District property were required to be justified by a compelling state interest and to be narrowly drawn to achieve that end. . . . The argument has considerable force, for the District's property is heavily used by a wide variety of private organizations. . . .

With respect to public property that is not a designated public forum open for indiscriminant public use for communicative purposes, we have said that "[c]ontrol over access to a nonpublic forum can be based on subject matter and speaker identity so long as the distinctions drawn are reasonable in light of the purpose served by the forum and are viewpoint neutral." . . . The Court of Appeals appeared to recognize that the total ban on using District property for religious purposes could survive First Amendment challenge only if excluding this category of speech was reasonable and viewpoint neutral. The court's conclusion in this case was that Rule 7 met this test. We cannot agree with this holding, for Rule 7 was unconstitutionally applied in this case.

The Court of Appeals thought that the application of Rule 7 in this case was viewpoint neutral because it had been and would be applied in the same way to all uses of school property for religious purposes. That all religions and all uses for religious purposes are treated alike under Rule 7, however, does not answer the critical question whether it discriminates on the basis of viewpoint to permit school property to be used for the presentation of all views about family issues and child-rearing except those dealing with the subject matter from a religious standpoint.

There is no suggestion from the courts below or from the District or the State that a lecture or film about child-rearing and family values would not be a use for social or civic purposes otherwise permitted by Rule 10. That subject matter is not one that the District has placed off-limits to any and all speakers. Nor is there any indication in the record before us that the application to exhibit the particular film involved here was or would have been denied for any reason other than the fact that the presentation would have been from a religious perspective. In our view, denial on that basis was plainly invalid. . . . The film involved here no doubt dealt with a subject otherwise permissible under Rule 10, and its exhibition was denied solely because the film dealt with the subject from a religious standpoint. The principle that has emerged from our cases "is that the First Amendment forbids the government to regulate speech in ways that favor some viewpoints or ideas at the expense of others." . . . That principle applies in the circumstances of this case. . . .

The District, as a respondent, would save its judgment below on the ground that to permit its property to be used for religious purposes would be an establishment of religion forbidden by the First Amendment. This Court suggested in *Widmar v. Vincent* that the interest of the State

in avoiding the Establishment Clause violation "may be [a] compelling" one justifying an abridgment of free speech otherwise protected by the First Amendment; but the Court went on to hold that permitting use of University property for religious purposes under the open access policy involved there would not be incompatible with the Court's Establishment Clause cases.

We have no more trouble than did the *Widmar* Court in disposing of the claimed defense on the ground that the posited fears of an Establishment Clause violation are unfounded. The showing of this film would not have been during school hours, would not have been sponsored by the school, and would have been open to the public, not just to church members. The District property had repeatedly been used by a wide variety of private organizations. Under these circumstances, as in *Widmar*, there would have been no realistic danger that the community would think that the District was endorsing religion or any particular creed, and any benefit to religion or to the Church would have been no more than incidental. As in *Widmar*, permitting District property to be used to exhibit the film involved in this case would not have been an establishment of religion under the three-part test articulated in *Lemon v. Kurtzman*. The challenged governmental action has a secular purpose, does not have the principal or primary effect of advancing or inhibiting religion, and does not foster an excessive entanglement with religion. [Footnote: "[T]here is a proper way to inter an established decision and *Lemon*, however frightening it might be to some, has not been overruled."]

For the reasons stated in this opinion, the judgment of the Court of Appeals is Reversed.

CASE NOTES

1. Where a school board charged churches higher rental fees for school facilities than it charged other nonprofit organizations, the court ruled that the practice violated the free speech clause and interfered with and/or burdened the church's right to speak and practice religion as protected by the free exercise clause. *Fairfax*

Covenant Church v. Fairfax County School Board,
17 F.3d 703 (4th Cir. 1994). See also *Shumway v.
Albany County School District No. 1 Board of Education,* 826 F.Supp. 1320, 84 Educ.L.Rep. 989
(D.Wyo.1993); *Trinity United Methodist Parish
v. Board of Education of the City School District of
the City of Newburgh,* 907 F.Supp. 707, 105
Educ.L.Rep. 943 (D.N.Y.1995).

2. Another federal court ruled that a school's
use-of-premises policy discriminated against a
religious club in violation of the free speech
clause of the First Amendment. *Good News/Good
Sports Club v. School District,* 28 F.3d 1501, 92
Educ.L.Rep. 1148 (8th Cir.1994), cert. denied, 515
U.S. 1173, 115 S.Ct. 2640 (1995).

3. In another federal court case, a school district was found not to violate the establishment
clause when it allowed Boy Scouts to distribute
literature during school hours and hang posters
on school property. *Sherman v. Community Consolidated School District 21 of Wheeling Township,* 8
F.3d 1160, 87 Educ.L.Rep. 57 (7th Cir.1993), cert.
denied, 114 S.Ct. 201 (1994).

■ FLAG SALUTE

The flag-salute ceremony in the United States
originated in 1892 after a substantial rise in
national sentiment to stimulate patriotism in the
schools. In 1898, New York passed the first flag-salute statute only one day after the United
States declared war on Spain.[221] By 1940, eighteen states had statutes making provision for
"some sort of teaching regarding the flag."[222]
Even though the statutes did not specifically
require individual recitation, the reality of the
classroom regimentation tended to make such
statutory pronouncement unnecessary.[223] Opposition sprang up on sporadic bases from certain
religious groups, the most persistent of which
was Jehovah's Witnesses. In early litigation, the
Georgia Supreme Court held that the Witnesses'
religious freedom was not violated, since the
flag salute was merely an exercise in patriotism
and not a religious rite.[224] The plaintiffs received
other unfavorable rulings, the most intolerant of
which stated that "[t]hose who do not desire to
conform with the demands of the statute can
seek their school elsewhere."[225] In California,
the state's high court upheld the expulsion of

pupils for refusing to salute the flag.[226] Similarly, a New York court in 1939 held that "[t]he
flag has nothing to do with religion"; therefore,
religious freedoms could not be offended.[227]

Nationalistic fervor just before World War II
brought on more heated controversy, and the
Supreme Court, in 1940, rendered a decision. In
this case, Justice Frankfurter, speaking for an
eight-to-one majority, held that freedom of religion guaranteed by the First Amendment was
not violated by a Pennsylvania statute that
required a flag salute and pledge of allegiance.
Significantly, the *Gobitis* opinion concluded that

> [c]onscientious scruples have not, in the course of
> the long struggle for religious toleration, relieved
> the individual from obedience to a general law not
> aimed at the promotion or restriction of religious
> beliefs. The mere possession of religious convictions which contradict the relevant concerns of a
> political society does not relieve the citizen from
> the discharge of political responsibilities.[228]

This decision engendered substantial controversy, and the legal and academic community
generally disapproved of the decision as an infringement on individual constitutional rights.[229]
Some state courts tended to ignore the federal
constitutional implications and held that flag-salute requirements violated their own state constitutions.[230] Other state courts followed the
decision.[231] Disenchantment with the *Gobitis* decision was so great and the constitutional foundation so weak that the case was officially overruled in *West Virginia State Board of Education
v. Barnette* in 1943.[232] In reconsideration of the
issues, Justice Jackson, writing for a six-person
majority, held that a state may require pupils to
attend educational exercises based on American
history and civics to teach patriotism but that
ceremonies involving compulsory rituals, such
as the flag salute, were unconstitutional. Justices
Black, Douglas, and Murphy had changed their
minds, and even though Justice Frankfurter remained steadfast, the precedent of *Gobitis* was
overturned. The swing vote of the three justices
was predictable; a year earlier, in 1942, in *Jones v.
Opelika*[233] the court announced that "[s]ince we
joined in the opinion in the *Gobitis* case, we think
this is an appropriate occasion to state that we
now believe that it was . . . wrongly decided."

❖ — ❖ — ❖

*Required Participation in Flag
Salute Is Unconstitutional*

West Virginia State Board of Education v. Barnette

Supreme Court of the United States, 1943.
319 U.S. 624, 63 S.Ct. 1178.

Mr. Justice JACKSON delivered the opinion of the Court. Following the decision by this Court on June 3, 1940, in *Minersville School District v. Gobitis*, 310 U.S. 586, 60 S.Ct. 1010, 84 L.Ed. 1375, 127 A.L.R. 1493, the West Virginia legislature amended its statutes to require all schools therein to conduct courses of instruction in history, civics, and in the Constitutions of the United States and of the State "for the purpose of teaching, fostering and perpetuating the ideals, principles and spirit of Americanism, and increasing the knowledge of the organization and machinery of the government." Appellant Board of Education was directed, with advice of the State Superintendent of Schools, to "prescribe the courses of study covering these subjects" for public schools. The Act made it the duty of private, parochial and denominational schools to prescribe courses of study "similar to those required for the public schools."

The Board of Education on January 9, 1942, adopted a resolution containing recitals taken largely from the Court's *Gobitis* opinion and ordering that the salute to the flag become "a regular part of the program of activities in the public schools," that all teachers and pupils "shall be required to participate in the salute honoring the Nation represented by the Flag; provided, however, that refusal to salute the Flag be regarded as an Act of insubordination, and shall be dealt with accordingly." . . .

Appellees, citizens of the United States and of West Virginia, brought suit in the United States District Court for themselves and others similarly situated asking its injunction to restrain enforcement of these laws and regulations against Jehovah's Witnesses. The Witnesses are an unincorporated body teaching that the obligation imposed by law of God is superior to that of laws enacted by temporal government. Their religious beliefs include a literal version of Exodus, Chapter 20, verses 4 and 5, which says: "Thou shalt not make unto thee any graven image, or any likeness of anything that is in heaven above, or that is in the earth beneath, or that is in the water under the earth; thou shalt not bow down thyself to them nor serve them." They consider that the flag is an "image" within this command. For this reason they refuse to salute it. . . .

This case calls upon us to reconsider a precedent decision, as the Court throughout its history often has been required to do. Before turning to the *Gobitis* case, however, it is desirable to notice certain characteristics by which this controversy is distinguished.

The freedom asserted by these appellees does not bring them into collision with rights asserted by any other individual. It is such conflicts which most frequently require intervention of the State to determine where the rights of one end and those of another begin. But the refusal of these persons to participate in the ceremony does not interfere with or deny rights of others to do so. Nor is there any question in this case that their behavior is peaceable and orderly. The sole conflict is between authority and rights of the individual. The State asserts power to condition access to public education on making a prescribed sign and profession and at the same time to coerce attendance by punishing both parent and child. The latter stand on a right of self-determination in matters that touch individual opinion and personal attitude. . . .

Nor does the issue as we see it turn on one's possession of particular religious views or the sincerity with which they are held. While religion supplies appellees' motive for enduring the discomforts of making the issue in this case, many citizens who do not share these religious views hold such a compulsory rite to infringe constitutional liberty of the individual. It is not necessary to inquire whether non-conformist beliefs will exempt from the duty to salute unless we first find power to make the salute a legal duty.

The *Gobitis* decision, however, *assumed*, as did the argument in that case and in this, that power exists in the State to impose the flag salute discipline upon school children in general. The Court only examined and rejected a claim based on religious beliefs of immunity from an unquestioned general rule. The question which underlies the flag salute controversy is whether such a ceremony so touching matters of opinion and political attitude may be imposed upon the individual by official authority under powers committed to any political organization under our Constitution. . . .

The Fourteenth Amendment, as now applied to the States, protects the citizen against the State itself and all of its creatures—Boards of Education not excepted. These have, of course, important, delicate, and highly discretionary functions, but none that they may not perform within the limits of the Bill of Rights. That they are educating the young for citizenship is reason for scrupulous protection of Constitutional freedoms of the individual, if we are not to strangle the free mind at its source and teach youth to discount important principles of our government as mere platitudes. . . .

The very purpose of a Bill of Rights was to withdraw certain subjects from the vicissitudes of political controversy, to place them beyond the reach of majorities and officials and to establish them as legal principles to be applied by the courts. One's right to life, liberty, and property, to free speech, a free press, freedom of worship and assembly, and other fundamental rights may not be submitted to vote; they depend on the outcome of no elections. . . .

National unity as an end which officials may foster by persuasion and example is not in question. The problem is whether under our Constitution compulsion as here employed is a permissible means for its achievement. . . .

If there is any fixed star in our constitutional constellation, it is that no official, high or petty, can prescribe what shall be orthodox in politics, nationalism, religion, or other matters of opinion or force citizens to confess by word or act their faith therein. If there are any circumstances which permit an exception, they do not now occur to us.

We think the action of the local authorities in compelling the flag salute and pledge transcends constitutional limitations on their power and invades the sphere of intellect and spirit which it is the purpose of the First Amendment to our Constitution to reserve from all official control.

The decision of this Court in *Minersville School District v. Gobitis* and the holding of those few per curiam decisions which preceded and foreshadowed it are overruled, and the judgment enjoining enforcement of the West Virginia Regulation is affirmed. . . .

CASE NOTES

1. When a student was offered the option of either leaving the classroom or standing silently during the pledge of allegiance, the court held that to leave the classroom is a benign type of punishment for nonparticipation, while to compel the student to stand in silence was to compel an act of acceptance of the pledge over the student's deeply held contrary convictions. The requirement of the school was therefore unconstitutional, regardless of option. *Goetz v. Ansell*, 477 F.2d 636 (2d Cir.1973).

2. It is clear under *Barnette* that the state cannot compel a student to recite the pledge of allegiance, but can a student who objects to the content of the pledge prevent the teacher and other students from reciting it in his or her presence? The U.S. Court of Appeals, Seventh Circuit, has answered this question in the negative. This court said: "By remaining neutral on religious issues, the state satisfies its duties under the free exercise clause. All that remains is *Barnette* itself, and so long as the school does not compel pupils to espouse the content of the Pledge as their own belief, it may carry on with patriotic exercises. Objection by the few does not reduce to silence the many who want to pledge allegiance to the flag "and to the Republic for which it stands.'"

According to this court, the reference "under God," because of its "history and ubiquity," is not understood to convey approval of any particular religious belief. *Sherman v. Community Consolidated School District 21*, 980 F.2d 437 (7th Cir.1992).

■ ENDNOTES

1. *The Economist,* July 22–28, 1995, pp. 15–16.
2. *The Economist,* October 7–13, 1995, p. 58.
3. Harvey Cox, "The Warring Visions of the Religious Right," *Atlantic Monthly,* November 1995, pp. 59–69.
4. 98 U.S. (8 Otto) 145 (1879).
5. Everson v. Board of Education, 330 U.S. 1, 67 S.Ct. 504 (1947).
6. 472 U.S. 38, 107, 105 S.Ct. 2517.
7. Evarts B. Green, *Religion and the State in America* (New York: New York University Press, 1941), p. 83.
8. Jonathan Elliot, *The Debates in the Several State Conventions on the Adoption of the Federal Constitution,* 2d ed. (Philadelphia: J. B. Lippincott & Co., 1988), p. 131.
9. Leo Pfeffer, *Church, State and Freedom* (Boston: Beacon Press, 1967), p. 123.
10. R. Freeman Butts, *The American Tradition in Religion and Education* (Boston: Beacon Press, 1950), p. 72.
11. Pfeffer, *Church, State and Freedom,* p. 125.
12. Ibid.
13. Ibid., p. 126.
14. Ibid., p. 4.
15. Ibid.
16. Ibid.
17. Williston Walker, *A History of the Christian Church* (New York: Charles Scribner's Sons, 1929), p. 464.
18. *History of Christianity in the Light of Modern Knowledge* (London: Blackie and Son, 1929), p. 464.
19. Pfeffer, *Church, State and Freedom,* p. 14.
20. M. Searle Bates, *Religious Liberty: An Inquiry* (New York and London: International Missionary Council, 1945), p. 134.
21. Alexander J. Carlyle, *The Christian Church and Liberty* (London: J. Clark, 1924), p. 96.
22. Everson v. Board of Education, 330 U.S. 1, 67 S.Ct. 504 (1947).
23. Pfeffer, *Church, State and Freedom,* p. 26.
24. John Locke, *A Letter Concerning Toleration* (Liberal Arts Press, 1955), pp. 17–18.
25. R. Freeman Butts and Lawrence A. Cremin, *A History of Education in American Culture* (New York: Henry Holt and Company, 1953), p. 15.
26. Ibid., p. 22.
27. Ibid., p. 21.
28. Ibid.
29. Saul K. Padover, *The Complete Jefferson* (New York: Duell, Sloan & Pearce, 1943).
30. Ibid.
31. Pfeffer, *Church, State and Freedom,* p. 109.
32. Decl. Rights, Art. 16. [Note in the original.]
33. Decl. Rights, Art. 1. [Note in the original.]
34. Art. 16. [Note in the original.]
35. Art. 16. [Note in the original.]
36. Decl. Rights-title. [Note in the original.]
37. Daniel Roche, *France in the Enlightenment,* translated by Arthur Goldhammer (Cambridge: Harvard University Press, 1998), p. 339.

38. Isser Woloch, *The New Regime: Transformations of the French Civic Order, 1789–1820's* (New York: W. W. Norton, 1994), p. 174.
39. Ibid.
40. Ibid.
41. Ibid.
42. Ibid., p. 195.
43. Ibid.
44. Ibid.
45. Ibid.
46. Ibid.
47. Ibid.
48. Henry Steele Commager, *The Empire of Reason: How Europe Imagined and America Ralized the Enlightenment* (Garden City, N.Y.: Anchor Press/Doubleday, 1978).
49. Ibid., p. 250.
50. Ibid., p. 229.
51. Ibid.
52. Ibid., p. 230.
53. Ellwood P. Cubberley, *Public Education in the United States* (Boston: Houghton Mifflin, 1934), p. 163.
54. Ibid., p. 166.
55. Ibid., p. 234.
56. Ibid.
57. Ibid.
58. Ibid.
59. Vincent P. Lannie, *Public Money and Parochial Education* (Cleveland, Ohio: Press of Case Western Reserve University, 1968), p. 62.
60. Ibid., p. 88.
61. Ibid., p. 90.
62. Agostini v. Felton, 521 U.S. 203, 117 S.Ct.1997 (1997).
63. Mitchell v. Helms, 2000 WL 826256.
64. V. T. Thayer, *The Attack upon the American Secular School* (Boston: Beacon Press, 1951), pp. 26–27.
65. Knowlton v. Baumhover, 182 Iowa 691, 166 N.W. 202 (1918).
66. 321 U.S. 158, 64 S.Ct. 438 (1944).
67. Joseph L. Blow, *Cornerstones of Religious Freedom in America* (Boston: Beacon Press, 1949), pp. 179–82.
68. Pfeffer, *Church, State and Freedom,* p. 338.
69. Wisconsin v. Yoder, 406 U.S. 205, 92 S.Ct. 1526 (1972).
70. 281 U.S. 270, 50 S.Ct. 335 (1930).
71. Cantwell v. Connecticut, 310 U.S. 296, 60 S.Ct. 900 (1940).
72. 392 U.S. 236, 88 S.Ct. 1923 (1968).
73. New York Education Law, §701 (Supp. 1967).
74. Board of Education of Central School District No. 1 v. Allen, 392 U.S. 236, 88 S.Ct. 1923 (1968).
75. Sloan v. Lemon, 413 U.S. 825, 93 S.Ct. 2982, rehearing denied, 414 U.S. 881, 94 S.Ct. 30 (1973); Committee for Public Education and Religious Liberty v. Nyquist, 413 U.S. 756, 93 S.Ct. 2955 (1973).
76. R.I.Gen.Laws §16-51-1 et seq.
77. 24 Pa.Stat. §§5601–9.
78. Latin, Hebrew, and classical Greek are excluded.
79. 413 U.S. 472, 474, 93 S.Ct. 2814, 2816 (1973).

80. Payments were $27 for each pupil in average daily attendance (ADA) in grades 1 to 6 and $45 for each pupil in ADA in grades 7 to 12, in two installments during the year.

81. 444 U.S. 646, 650, 100 S.Ct. 840, 845 (1980).

82. 413 U.S. 756, 93 S.Ct. 2955 (1973).

83. The school had to qualify by having a high concentration of low-income families; the amount of the grant was $30 per pupil, or $40 per pupil if the facility was more than twenty-five years old. The grant could not exceed 50 percent of the average per-pupil cost for equivalent services in the public schools. Nyquist, 413 U.S. at 761, 93 S.Ct. at 2959.

84. A parent had to have a taxable income of less than $5,000 and would be reimbursed $50 per grade school child and $100 per high school child so long as these amounts did not exceed 50 percent of the tuition.

85. Sloan v. Lemon, 413 U.S. 825, 93 S.Ct. 2982 (1973).

86. Meek v. Pittenger, 421 U.S. 349, 363, 95 S.Ct. 1753, 1762 (1975).

87. Wolman v. Walter, 433 U.S. 229, 232, 97 S.Ct. 2593, 2597 (1977).

88. Ibid., 97 S.Ct. at 2603.

89. Ibid., 97 S.Ct. at 2606.

90. Kosydar v. Wolman, 353 F.Supp. 744 (S.D.Ohio 1972).

91. Ibid., affirmed sub nom. Grit v. Wolman, 413 U.S. 901, 93 S.Ct. 3062 (1973).

92. Committee for Public Education and Religious Liberty v. Nyquist, op. cit.

93. Byrne v. Public Funds for Public Schools, 442 U.S. 907, 99 S.Ct. 2818 (1979), affirming 590 F.2d 514 (3d Cir.1979).

94. Rhode Island Federation of Teachers, AFL-CIO v. Norberg, 630 F.2d 855 (1st Cir.1980).

95. Mueller v. Allen, 463 U.S. 388, 103 S.Ct. 3062 (1983).

96. Ibid.

97. 392 U.S. 236, 88 S.Ct. 1923 (1968).

98. G. Sidney Buchanan, "Governmental Aid to Religious Entities: The Total Subsidy Position Prevails," *Fordham Law Review* 58 (October 1989): p. 53.

99. Ibid.

100. 473 U.S. 373, 105 S.Ct. 3216 (1985).

101. 473 U.S. 402, 105 S.Ct. 3232 (1985).

102. 472 U.S. 38, 107, 114, 105 S.Ct. 2479, 2516, 2519 (1985).

103. Ibid.

104. Leonard Levy, *The Establishment Clause, Religion and the First Amendment* (New York: Macmillan Publishing Company, 1986), p. 92.

105. 463 U.S. 783, 103 S.Ct. 3330 (1983).

106. 456 U.S. 228, 102 S.Ct. 1673 (1982).

107. 413 U.S. 756, 93 S.Ct. 2955 (1973).

108. 463 U.S. 388, 103 S.Ct. 3062 (1983).

109. 465 U.S. 668, 104 S.Ct. 1355 (1984).

110. 505 U.S. 577, 112 S.Ct. 2649 (1992).

111. Ibid., 112 S.Ct. at 2650.

112. Ibid., 112 S.Ct. at 2655.

113. Lamb's Chapel v. Center Moriches Union Free School District, 508 U.S. 384, 113 S.Ct. 2141 (1993).

114. Ibid., 113 S.Ct. at 2149–50.

115. Board of Education of Kiryas Joel Village School District v. Grumet, 62 U.S. 4665, 114 S.Ct. 2481 (1994).

116. Ibid., 114 S.Ct. at 2487.

117. Ibid., 114 S.Ct. at 2483.

118. Ibid., 114 S.Ct. at 2484.

119. 1997 WL 338583 (U.S.), June 23, 1997, 97 Cal.Daily Op.Serv. 4765, Daily Journal D.A.K. 7843.

120. 474 U.S. 481, 106 S.Ct. 748 (1986).

121. 509 U.S. 1, 113 S.Ct. 2462 (1993).

122. 515 U.S. 819, 115 S.Ct. 2510 (1995).

123. 512 U.S. 687, 114 S.Ct. 2481 (1994).

124. 473 U.S. 402, 105 S.Ct. 3232 (1985).

125. 473 U.S. 373, 105 S.Ct. 3216 (1985).

126. See Witters v. Washington Department of Services for the Blind, 474 U.S. 481, 485, 106 S.Ct. at 750 (1986); Bowen v. Kendrick, 487 U.S. 589, 108 S.Ct. 2562 (1988); Board of Education of Westside Community Schools v. Mergens, 496 U.S. 226, 115 S.Ct. 2356 (1990).

127. Mitchell v. Helms, _____ U.S. _____, 120 S.Ct. 2530, 2000 WL 826256 (2000).

128. Agostini v. Felton, 521 U.S. 203, 117 S.Ct. 1997 (1997).

129. The Court cited Rosenberger v. Rector and Visitors of the University of Virginia, 515 U.S. 819, 842, as a possible distinguishing situation.

130. Rhode Island Constitution, Article 1, §3.

131. Bowerman v. O'Connor, 104 R.I. 519, 247 A.2d 82 (1968).

132. Constitution of Illinois, Article 1, §3.

133. Board of Education v. Bakalis, 54 Ill.2d 448, 299 N.E.2d 737 (1973). See A. E. Dick Howard, *State Aid to Private Higher Education* (Charlottesville, Va.: Michie, 1977), p. 254.

134. 403 U.S. 602, 91 S.Ct. 2105 (1971).

135. Snyder v. Town of Newton, 147 Conn. 374, 161 A.2d 770 (1960), appeal dismissed, 365 U.S. 299, 81 S.Ct. 692 (1961).

136. Ibid., 161 A.2d at 774–75.

137. State ex rel. Johnson v. Boyd, 217 Ind. 348, 28 N.E.2d 256 (1940); Burford v. Southeast Dubois County School Corp., 472 F.2d 890 (7th Cir.), cert. denied, 411 U.S. 967, 93 S.Ct. 2151 (1973); Opinion of Attorney General 241 (1967).

138. Article I, §3 Constitution of Iowa; Knowlton v. Baumhover, 166 N.W. 202 (Iowa 1918). Howard, *State Aid*, p. 303. Howard states that Article I, Section 3 of the Iowa Constitution has the same meaning as the United States Supreme Court's interpretation of the First Amendment.

139. Howard, *State Aid*, p. 314; see Wright v. School District, 151 Kan. 485, 99 P.2d 737 (1940).

140. Squires v. City of Augusta, 155 Me. 151, 153 A.2d 80 (1959); Opinion of the Justices, 261 A.2d 58 (Me.1970).

141. In re Opinion on the Constitutionality of Amendatory Act. No. 100 in the Public Acts of 1970, 384 Mich. 82, 180 N.W.2d 265 (1970).

142. Americans United Inc. v. Independent School District No. 622, 288 Minn. 196, 179 N.W.2d 146 (1970).

143. Everson v. Board of Education, 330 U.S. 1, 67 S.Ct. 504 (1947).

144. State ex rel. Warren v. Nusbaum (III), 64 Wis.2d 314, 219 N.W.2d 577 (1974).

145. 463 U.S. 388, 103 S.Ct. 3062 (1983).

146. San Antonio Independent School District v. Rodriguez, 411 U.S. 1, 93 S.Ct. 1278, rehearing denied, 411 U.S. 959, 93 S.Ct. 1919 (1973). See Chapter 19 of this book.

147. 362 P.2d 932 (Alaska 1961), cert. denied and appeal dismissed, 368 U.S. 517, 82 S.Ct. 530 (1961).

148. Ibid.

149. Alaska Constitution, Article VII, § 1. See Howard *State Aid*, pp. 98–99. It should be noted that the Alaska legislature apparently violated this constitutional provision when in 1972 it enacted a law that provided aid for transportation of nonpublic school children.

150. People ex rel. Vollmar v. Stanley, 81 Colo. 276, 255 P. 610 (1927); Howard, State Aid, pp. 154–57.

151. West's Colorado R.S.A. Constitution, Article IX, §7.

152. 51 Haw. 1, 449 P.2d 130 (1968).

153. Ibid.

154. Board of County Commissioners v. Idaho Health Facilities Authority, 96 Idaho 498, 531 P.2d 588 (1974).

155. 182 Iowa 691, 166 N.W. 202 (1918).

156. Board of Education of Central School District No. 1 v. Allen, 392 U.S. 236, 88 S.Ct. 1923 (1968).

157. See Howard, *State Aid*, p. 300.

158. Knowlton v. Baumhover, op. cit.

159. Paster v. Tussey, 512 S.W.2d 97 (Mo.1974), cert. denied, 419 U.S. 1111, 95 S.Ct. 785 (1975).

160. Harfst v. Hoegen, 349 Mo. 808, 163 S.W.2d 609, 614 (1941).

161. Berghorn v. Reorganized School District No. 8, 364 Mo. 121, 260 S.W.2d 573, 582–83 (1953).

162. Paster v. Tussey, 512 S.W.2d at 101–2 (italics added).

163. State ex rel. Chambers v. School District No. 10, 155 Mont. 422, 472 P.2d 1013 (1970).

164. 403 U.S. 602, 91 S.Ct. 2105 (1971).

165. Article V, §II(5).

166. Howard, *State Aid*, p. 250.

167. Ibid., p. 987.

168. Dickman v. School District, 232 Or. 238, 366 P.2d 533 (1961), cert. denied, 371 U.S. 823, 83 S.Ct. 41 (1962); see also Fisher v. Clackamas County School, 13 Or.App. 56, 507 P.2d 839 (1973).

169. 33 Wash.2d 699, 207 P.2d 198 (1949).

170. Ibid.

171. Ibid.

172. Illinois ex rel. McCollum v. Board of Education of School District No. 71, 333 U.S. 203, 68 S.Ct. 461 (1948).

173. Zorach v. Clauson, 343 U.S. 306, 72 S.Ct. 679 (1952).

174. *Mueller*, op. cit.

175. *Zobrest*, op. cit.

176. *Agostini*, op. cit.

177. Mitchell v. Helms, ____ U.S. ____, 120 S.Ct. 2530, 2000 WL 826256 (2000).

178. *Weisman*, op. cit.

179. Santa Fe Independent School District v. Doe, ____ U.S. ____, 120 S.Ct. 2266, 2000 WL 775587 (2000).

180. *Mueller*, op. cit.

181. *Zobrest*, op. cit.

182. *Agostini*, op. cit.

183. Mitchell v. Helms, op. cit.

184. Hackett v. Brooksville Graded School District, 120 Ky. 608, 87 S.W. 792 (1905).

185. North Dakota Compiled Laws, § 1388 (1913).

186. 370 U.S. 421, 82 S.Ct. 1261 (1962).

187. Illinois ex rel. McCollum v. Board of Education, 333 U.S. 203, 68 S.Ct. 461 (1948).

188. Engel v. Vitale, op. cit.

189. School District of Abington Township v. Schempp and Murray v. Curlett, 374 U.S. 203, 83 S.Ct. 1560 (1963).

190. 449 U.S. 39, 101 S.Ct. 192 (1980).

191. Wallace v. Jaffree, 472 U.S. 38, 105 S.Ct. 2479 (1985); Duffy v. Las Cruces Public Schools, 557 F.Supp. 1013 (D.N.M.1983).

192. Walter v. West Virginia Board of Education, 610 F.Supp. 1169 (S.D.W.Va.1985).

193. Jager v. Douglas County School District, 862 F.2d 824 (11th Cir.1989).

194. Breen v. Runkel, 614 F.Supp. 355 (W.D.Mich.1985); May v. Evansville-Vanderburgh School Corp., 787 F.2d 1105 (7th Cir.1986).

195. Wallace v. Jaffree, op. cit.

196. Walter v. West Virginia Board of Education, op. cit.

197. Chandler v. Jones, 180 F.3d 1254 (1999).

198. Lynch v. Donnelly, 465 U.S. 668, 104 S.Ct. 1355 (1984).

199. Lee v. Weisman, 505 U.S. 577, 112 S.Ct. 2649 (1992); County of Alleghany v. ACLU, 492 U.S. 573, 109 S.Ct. 3086 (1989); Doe v. Duncanville, 70 F.3d 402 (th Cir.1995).

200. Lynch v. Donnelly, 465 U.S. 668, 104 S.Ct. 1355 (1984).

201. Ibid.

202. Mergens, op. cit.

203. Lamb's Chapel v. Center Moriches Union Free School District, 508 U.S. 384, 113 S.Ct. 2141 (1993).

204. *Duncanville*, 70 F.3d at 406–7.

205. *Mergens*, 496 U.S. at 251, 110 S.Ct. 2356.

206. Edwards v. Aguillard, 482 U.S. 578, 107 S.Ct. 2573 (1987).

207. Ibid.

208. *Mergens*, op. cit.

209. Ibid.

210. School District of Abington Township v. Schempp, 374 U.S. 203, 83 S.Ct. 1560 (1963).

211. 505 U.S. 577, 112 S.Ct. 2649 (1992).

212. 505 U.S. 577, 112 S.Ct. 2649 (1992).

213. 977 F.2d 963 (5th Cir.), rehearing denied, 983 F.2d 234 (5th Cir.1992), cert. denied, 508 U.S. 967, 113 S.Ct. 2950 (1993).

214. ____ U.S. ____, 120 S.Ct. 2266, 2000 WL 775587 (2000).

215. The rules as amended provide as follows:
Opening Exercises. Each school, either collectively or in classes, shall be opened by the reading, without comment, of a chapter in the Holy Bible and/or the use of the Lord's Prayer. The Douay version may be used by those pupils who prefer it. Appropriate patriotic exercises should be held as a part of the general opening exercise of the school or class. Any child shall be excused from participating in the opening exercises or from attending

the opening exercises upon the written request of his parent or guardian.

216. 454 U.S. 263, 102 S.Ct. 269 (1981).

217. 496 U.S. 226, 110 S.Ct. 2356 (1990).

218. 508 U.S. 384, 113 S.Ct. 2141 (1993).

219. Grace Bible Fellowship v. Maine School Administration #5, 941 F.2d 45 (1st Cir.1991).

220. Shumway v. Albany County School District No. 1 Board of Education, 826 F.Supp. 1320 (D.Wyo.1993).

221. Boles, *The Two Swords*, p. 139.

222. D. R. Manwaring, *Render unto Caesar: The Flag-Salute Controversy* (Chicago: University of Chicago Press, 1962).

223. Ibid.

224. Leoles v. Landers, 184 Ga. 580, 192 S.E. 218, appeal dismissed, 302 U.S. 656, 58 S.Ct. 364 (1937).

225. Hering v. State Board of Education, 117 N.J.L. 455, 189 A. 629 (1937).

226. Gabrielli v. Knickerbocker, 12 Cal.2d 85, 82 P.2d 391 (1938).

227. People ex rel. Fish v. Sandstrom, 279 N.Y. 523, 18 N.E.2d 840 (1939).

228. Minersville School District v. Gobitis, 310 U.S. 586, 60 S.Ct. 1010 (1940).

229. Boles, *The Two Swords*, p. 148.

230. State v. Smith, 155 Kan. 588, 127 P.2d 518 (1942); Bolling v. Superior Court, 16 Wash.2d 373, 133 P.2d 803 (1943).

231. In re Latrecchia, 128 N.J.L. 472, 26 A.2d 881 (1942); State v. Davis, 58 Ariz. 444, 120 P.2d 808 (1942).

232. 319 U.S. 624, 63 S.Ct. 1178 (1943).

233. 316 U.S. 584, 62 S.Ct. 1231 (1942); see Bates, *Religious Liberty*, pp. 151–52.

CHAPTER 6

SCHOOL ATTENDANCE

The primary social fact which blocks and hinders the success of our experiment in self-government is that our citizens are not educated for self-government. We are terrified by ideas, rather than challenged and stimulated by them. Our dominant mood is not the courage of people who dare to think. It is the timidity of those who fear and hate whenever conventions are questioned.

—Alexander Meiklejohn, "The First Amendment Is an Absolute," 1961 Supreme Court Review 245, 263

CHAPTER OUTLINE

- STATE PREROGATIVE
- COMPULSORY SCHOOL ATTENDANCE
- RELIGION: THE AMISH EXCEPTION
- HOME INSTRUCTION
- OTHER REASONS FOR NONATTENDANCE
- VACCINATION

KNOWLEDGE is the most important prerequisite to the exercise of liberty and freedom. Only through knowledge can persons expect to raise themselves from their crude state of nature to a higher level of humanity.[1] A person without education cannot expect to attain what Kant has called "moral perfection."[2] It follows, then, that the general happiness of all is promoted, and liberty acquired, only if human beings are adequately educated. Both practical and moral reasoning therefore suggest that it is the duty of the state to see to the education of the entire citizenry.[3] This logic did not escape the notice of the early leaders in all the states of the United States when they developed systems of public education and required school attendance of all youth.

The state's prerogative to educate all youth is premised on the idea that all persons have a duty to educate others, if for no other reason than to protect themselves. The interests of all are promoted by a rising level of education of the entire community. States and nations, therefore, have not only the discretion but the right to require education. Throughout history, persons who do not understand that their own welfare is dependent on the educational level of those around them have challenged the right of government to provide universal education and to require school attendance. These persons have typically campaigned against universal education and compulsory attendance as being, in some manner, subversive to their individual liberties or freedoms. Such reasoning has usually called for forms of private education that would be beneficial to only a select group of a particular racial, religious, social, or economic orientation. This philosophy runs directly counter to the ideal that maintains that universal education is the ultimate solution to separation and ethnic division in society. Butts has summarized the rationale for compulsory universal education, saying:

> If education alone could provide the intelligent electorate and leadership necessary for republican government, if education alone could prevent crime, provide for the general happiness, and secure the rights of persons and property, then the state had the right to compel it for the general welfare. Moreover, a government which had already established the power to tax for public education certainly had the right to enforce school attendance.[4]

The responsibility of the state to require education to protect and elevate society, to promote happiness, and to protect liberties implies a corollary right of the child to have equal opportunity to acquire education. School attendance is therefore justified on the dual grounds of both governmental and individual interests. The state has an undeniable interest in sustaining an educated citizenry that will engender morality among the people and will foster virtue in government.

■ STATE PREROGATIVE

In keeping with ideals and with a faith in the value of education, state legislatures have prescribed the admission and residence requirements for attendance in the public schools. Where state constitutions have established the age span within which all have a right to attend public schools, legislatures must provide at least the specified minimum education, but are not restricted from creating additional educational opportunities. For example, the constitutional requirement that a state provide schools for all children between the ages of five and twenty years does not prevent the legislature from establishing a nursery school for four-year-olds. Neither does such a provision prohibit the establishment of institutions for higher education.

When a state establishes a system of public education, it cannot arbitrarily withhold services from a particular class of persons. While a state is not required by the federal constitution to provide public education at all, when it does so provide, it must be open and available to all.[5] In this regard, children whose parents are illegal aliens are entitled to attend public schools so long as they reside in the United States. The U.S. Supreme Court has said that if a state is to deny the child of illegal alien parents a free public education, then the state must demonstrate that the denial advances a substantial state interest. It is insufficient for the state to claim the denial of a free education is justified on the grounds that the presence of undocumented children requires the state to spread scarce fiscal resources among greater numbers of children.[6]

States, though, can impose restrictions on school attendance provided they are reasonably related to a valid state purpose. Reasonableness may relate to the health, safety, and welfare of other children or may have to do with the orderly organization and administration of school systems. Residence requirements based on geographical boundaries drawn within and between school districts have been upheld provided there is no intent to invidiously discriminate against a certain class of students. Indeed, the drawing of attendance zones has been upheld as a valid exercise of state prerogative where boundaries were drawn to effectuate integration.

Most state laws require that children be residents of the school district in which they attend school. A school district has the legal authority to challenge the residence of a student. A student who changes guardianship solely for the purposes of attending a particular school may be denied attendance.[7] The United States Supreme Court has held that an appropriately defined and uniformly applied residence law is constitutionally valid. The state's interest in ensuring appropriate educational services to be enjoyed by the residents is rationale enough to support such a requirement.[8]

To establish residence, one must be physically present and intend to remain at that location. The Supreme Court of Maine, in an early decision, held that residence was established "when a person takes up his abode in a given place, without any present intention to remove therefrom. . . ."[9]

❖ — ❖ — ❖

*Undocumented Children of Alien Parents
Cannot Be Denied a Public Education*

Plyler v. Doe

Supreme Court of the United States, 1982.
457 U.S. 202, 102 S.Ct. 2382.

Mr. Justice BRENNAN delivered the opinion of the Court. The question presented by these cases is whether, consistent with the Equal Protection Clause of the Fourteenth Amendment, Texas may deny to undocumented school-age children the free public education that it provides to children who are citizens of the United States or legally admitted aliens.

Since the late nineteenth century, the United States has restricted immigration into this country. Unsanctioned entry into the United States is a crime, 8 U.S.C. §1325, and those who have entered unlawfully are subject to deportation, 8 U.S.C. §§1251–1252. But despite the existence of these legal restrictions, a substantial number of persons have succeeded in unlawfully entering the United States, and now live within various States, including the State of Texas.

In May 1975, the Texas legislature revised its education laws to withhold from local school districts any state funds for the education of children who were not "legally admitted" into the United States. The 1975 revision also authorized local school districts to deny enrollment in their public schools to children not "legally admitted" to the country. Tex.Educ.Code Ann. §21.031 (Vernon Cum.Supp.1981). These cases involve constitutional challenges to those provisions. . . .

The Fourteenth Amendment provides that "No State shall. . . deprive any person of life, liberty, or property, without due process of law; nor deny to *any person within its jurisdiction* the equal protection of the laws." Appellants argue at the outset that undocumented aliens, because of their immigration status, are not "persons within the jurisdiction" of the State of Texas, and that they therefore have no right to the equal protection of Texas law. We reject this argument. Whatever his status under the immigration laws, an alien is surely a "person" in any ordinary sense of that term. Aliens, even aliens whose presence in this country is unlawful, have long been recognized as "persons" guaranteed due process of law by the Fifth and Fourteenth Amendments. Indeed, we have clearly held that the Fifth Amendment protects aliens whose presence in this country is unlawful from invidious discrimination by the Federal Government.

Appellants seek to distinguish our prior cases, emphasizing that the Equal Protection Clause directs a State to afford its protection to persons *within its jurisdiction* while the Due Process Clauses of the Fifth and Fourteenth Amendments contain no such assertedly limiting phrase. In appellants' view, persons who have entered the United States illegally are not "within the jurisdiction" of a State even if they are present within a State's boundaries and subject to its laws. Neither our cases nor the logic of the Fourteenth Amendment supports that constricting construction of the phrase "within its jurisdiction." We have never suggested that the class of persons who might avail themselves of the equal protection guarantee is less than coextensive with that entitled to due process. To the contrary, we have recognized that both provisions were fashioned to protect an identical class of persons, and to reach every exercise of State authority.

> The Fourteenth Amendment to the Constitution is not confined to the protection of citizens. It says: "Nor shall any state deprive any person of life, liberty or property without due process of law; nor deny to any person within its jurisdiction the equal protection of the laws." *These provisions are universal in their application, to all persons within the territorial jurisdiction,* without regard to any differences of race, color, or of nationality; and the protection of the laws is a pledge of the protection of equal laws. (Emphasis added.)

In concluding that "all persons within the territory of the United States," including aliens unlawfully present, may invoke the Fifth and Sixth Amendment to challenge actions of the Federal Government, we reasoned from the understanding that the Fourteenth Amendment was designed to afford its protection to all within the boundaries of a State. . . .

There is simply no support for appellants' suggestion that "due process" is somehow of greater stature than "equal protection" and therefore available to a larger class of persons. To the contrary, each aspect of the Fourteenth Amendment reflects an elementary limitation on state power. To permit a State to employ the phrase "within its jurisdiction" in order to identify subclasses of persons whom it would define as beyond its jurisdiction, thereby relieving itself of the obligation to assure that its laws are designed and applied equally to those persons, would undermine the principal purpose for which the Equal Protection Clause was incorporated in the Fourteenth Amendment. The Equal Protection Clause was intended to work nothing less than the abolition of all caste and invidious class-based legislation. That objective is fundamentally at odds with the power the State asserts here to classify persons subject to its laws as nonetheless excepted from its protection. . . .

Use of the phrase "within its jurisdiction" thus does not detract from, but rather confirms, the understanding that the protection of the Fourteenth Amendment extends to anyone, citizen or stranger, who is subject to the laws of a State, and reaches into every corner of a State's territory. That a person's initial entry into a State, or into the United States, was unlawful, and that he may for that reason be expelled, cannot negate the simple fact of his presence within the State's territorial perimeter. Given such presence, he is subject to the full range of obligations imposed by the State's civil and criminal laws. And until he leaves the jurisdiction—either voluntarily, or involuntarily in accordance with the Constitution and laws of the United States—he is entitled to the equal protection of the laws that a State may choose to establish.

Our conclusion that the illegal aliens who are plaintiffs in these cases may claim the benefit of the Fourteenth Amendment's guarantee of equal protection only begins the inquiry. The more difficult question is whether the Equal Protection Clause has been violated by the refusal of the State of Texas to reimburse local school boards for the education of children who cannot demonstrate that their presence within the United States is lawful, or by the imposition by those school boards of the burden of tuition on those children. . . .

The Equal Protection Clause directs that "all persons similarly circumstanced shall be treated alike." But so too, "The Constitution does not require things which are different in fact or opinion to be treated in law as though they were the same." The initial discretion to determine what is "different" and what is "the same" resides in the legislatures of the States. A legislature must have substantial latitude to establish classifications that roughly approximate the nature of the problem perceived, that accommodate competing concerns both public and private, and that account for limitations on the practical ability of the State to remedy every ill. In applying the Equal Protection Clause to most forms of state action, we thus seek only the assurance that the classification at issue bears some fair relationship to a legitimate public purpose.

But we would not be faithful to our obligations under the Fourteenth Amendment if we applied so deferential a standard to every classification. The Equal Protection Clause was intended as a restriction on state legislative action inconsistent with elemental constitutional premises. Thus we have treated as presumptively invidious those classifications that disadvantage a "suspect class," or that impinge upon the exercise of a "fundamental right." With respect to such classifications, it is appropriate to enforce the mandate of equal protection by requiring the State to demonstrate that its classification has been precisely tailored to serve a compelling governmental interest. In addition, we have recognized that certain forms of legislative classification, while not facially invidious, nonetheless give rise to recurring constitutional difficulties; in these limited circumstances we have sought the assurance that the classification reflects a reasoned judgment consistent with the ideal of equal protection by inquiring whether it may fairly be viewed as furthering a substantial interest of the State. We turn to a consideration of the standard appropriate for the evaluation of §21.031.

Sheer incapability or lax enforcement of the laws barring entry into this country, coupled with the failure to establish an effective bar to the employment of undocumented aliens, has resulted in the creation of a substantial "shadow population" of illegal migrants—numbering in the millions—within our borders. This situation raises the specter of a permanent caste of undocumented resident aliens, encouraged by some to remain here as a source of cheap labor, but nevertheless denied the benefits that our society makes available to citizens and lawful residents. The existence of such an underclass presents most difficult problems for a Nation that prides itself on adherence to principles of equality under law.

The children who are plaintiffs in these cases are special members of this underclass. Persuasive arguments support the view that a State may withhold its beneficence from those whose very presence within the United States is the product of their own unlawful conduct. These arguments do not apply with the same force to classifications imposing disabilities on the minor *children* of such illegal entrants. At the least, those who elect to enter our territory by stealth and in violation of our law should be prepared to bear the consequences, including, but not limited to, deportation. But the children of those illegal entrants are not comparably situated. Their "parents have the ability to conform their conduct to societal norms," and presumably the ability to remove themselves from the State's jurisdiction; but the children who are plaintiffs in these cases "can affect neither their parents' conduct nor their own status." Even if the State found it expedient to control the conduct of adults by acting against their children, legislation directing the onus of a parent's misconduct against his children does not comport with fundamental conceptions of justice. . . .

Of course, undocumented status is not irrelevant to any proper legislative goal. Nor is undocumented status an absolutely immutable characteristic since it is the product of conscious, indeed unlawful, action. But §21.031 is directed against children, and imposes its discriminatory burden on the basis of a legal characteristic over which children can have little control. It is thus difficult to conceive of a rational justification for penalizing these children for their presence within the United States. Yet that appears to be precisely the effect of §21.031.

Public education is not a "right" granted to individuals by the Constitution. But neither is it merely some governmental "benefit" indistinguishable from other forms of social welfare legislation. Both the importance of education in maintaining our basic institutions, and the lasting impact of its deprivation on the life of the child, mark the distinction. . . .

In sum, education has a fundamental role in maintaining the fabric of our society. We cannot ignore the significant social costs borne by our Nation when select groups are denied the means to absorb the values and skills upon which our social order rests. . . .

Paradoxically, by depriving the children of any disfavored group of an education, we foreclose the means by which that group might raise the level of esteem in which it is held by the majority. But more directly, "education prepares individuals to be self-reliant and self-sufficient participants in society." Illiteracy is an enduring disability. The inability to read and write will handicap the individual deprived of a basic education each and every day of his life. The inestimable toll of that deprivation on the social, economic, intellectual, and psychological well-being of the individual, and the obstacle it poses to individual achievement, makes it most difficult to reconcile the cost or the principle of a status-based denial of basic education with the framework of equality embodied in the Equal Protection Clause. . . .

These well-settled principles allow us to determine the proper level of deference to be afforded §21.031. Undocumented aliens cannot be treated as a suspect class because their presence in this country in violation of federal law is not a "constitutional irrelevancy." Nor is education a fundamental right; a State need not justify by compelling necessity every variation in the manner in which education is provided to its population. But more is involved in this case than the abstract question whether §21.031 discriminates against a suspect class, or whether education is a fundamental right. Section 21.031 imposes a lifetime hardship on a discrete class of children not accountable for their disabling status. The stigma of illiteracy will mark them for the rest of their lives. By denying these children a basic education, we deny them the ability to live within the structure of our civic institutions, and foreclose any realistic possibility that they will contribute in even the smallest way to the progress of our Nation. In determining the rationality of §21.031, we may appropriately take into account its costs to the Nation and to the innocent children who are its victims. In light of these countervailing costs, the discrimination contained in §21.031 can hardly be considered rational unless it furthers some substantial goal of the State. . . .

To be sure, like all persons who have entered the United States unlawfully, these children are subject to deportation. 8 U.S.C. §§1251–1252. But there is no assurance that a child subject to deportation will ever be deported. An illegal entrant might be granted federal permission to continue to reside in this country, or even to become a citizen. See, e.g., 8 U.S.C. §§1252, 1253(h), 1254. In light of the discretionary federal power to grant relief from deportation, a State cannot realistically determine that any particular undocumented child will in fact be deported until after deportation proceedings have been completed. It would of course be most difficult for the State to justify a denial of education to a child enjoying an inchoate federal permission to remain. . . .

Appellants argue that the classification at issue furthers an interest in the "preservation of the state's limited resources for the education of its lawful residents." . . . Apart from the asserted state prerogative to act against undocumented children solely on the basis of their undocumented status—an asserted prerogative that carries only minimal force in the circumstances of this case—we discern three colorable state interests that might support §21.031.

First, appellants appear to suggest that the State may seek to protect the State from an influx of illegal immigrants. While a State might have an interest in mitigating the potentially harsh economic effects of sudden shifts in population, §21.031 hardly offers an effective method of dealing with an urgent demographic or economic problem. There is no evidence in the record suggesting that illegal entrants impose any significant burden on the State's economy. . . .

Second, while it is apparent that a state may "not . . . reduce expenditures for education by barring [some arbitrarily chosen class of] children from its schools," appellants suggest that undocumented children are appropriately singled out for exclusion because of the special burdens they impose on the State's ability to provide high quality public education. But the record in no way supports the claim that exclusion of undocumented children is likely to improve the overall quality of education in the State. . . . In terms of educational cost and need, however, undocumented children are "basically indistinguishable" from legally resident alien children.

Finally, appellants suggest that undocumented children are appropriately singled out because their unlawful presence within the United States renders them less likely than other children to remain within the boundaries of the State, and to put their education to productive social or political use within the State. Even assuming that such an interest is legitimate, it is an interest that is most difficult to quantify. The State has no assurance that any child, citizen or not, will employ the education provided by the State within the confines of the State's borders. In any event, the record is clear that many of the undocumented children disabled by this classification will remain in this country indefinitely, and that some will become lawful residents or citizens of the United States. It is difficult to understand precisely what the State hopes to achieve by promoting the creation and perpetuation of a subclass of illiterates within our boundaries, surely adding to the problems and costs of unemployment, welfare, and crime. It is thus clear that whatever savings might be achieved by denying these children an education, they are wholly insubstantial in light of the costs involved to these children, the State, and the Nation.

If the State is to deny a discrete group of innocent children the free public education that it offers to other children residing within its borders, that denial must be justified by a showing that it furthers some substantial state interest. No such showing was made here. Accordingly, the judgment of the Court of Appeals in each of these cases is Affirmed.

CASE NOTES

1. A Texas school district policy requiring students to reside in the district with parent or

legal guardian, regardless of the "primary purpose" of living in the school district, violated the equal protection clause. The school district's policy did not further a state interest of preventing overcrowding that was allegedly caused by "white flight," since the school district's interest was adequately addressed by its policy requiring that the primary purpose for residing in the school district must not be school attendance. *Major v. Nederland Independent School District*, 772 F.Supp. 944 (E.D.Tex.1991).

2. Physical presence and intent to remain in the school district is sufficient to establish residency in a school district, even though parents or legal guardians lived elsewhere. *Byrd v. Livingston Independent School District*, 674 F.Supp. 225 (E.D.Tex.1987). See also *Orozco by Arroyo v. Sobol*, 674 F.Supp. 125 (S.D.N.Y.1987).

3. *Homeless Children.* A lower New York state court has ruled that children who live in a shelter for the homeless in a school district were entitled to be educated in the schools of that district regardless of whether their residency would be short or long, temporary or permanent, and regardless of whether their mother expressed a desire to have the children registered in the district where they previously attended school. *Delgado v. Freeport Public School District*, 131 Misc.2d 102, 499 N.Y.S.2d 606 (1986).

A federal district court in New York held that New York school authorities had denied due process of law to "homeless" children when they were excluded from school without proper notice on grounds of nonresidency. The homeless mother and her children were entitled to nominal damages of $1 for violation of their procedural due process rights. *Harrison v. Sobol*, 705 F.Supp. 870 (S.D.N.Y.1988).

———— ❖ — ❖ — ❖ ————

Bona Fide Residence Requirement That Furthers State Interest Is Constitutional

Martinez v. Bynum

Supreme Court of the United States, 1983.
461 U.S. 321, 103 S.Ct. 1838.

Justice POWELL delivered the opinion of the Court. This case involves a facial challenge to the constitutionality of the Texas residency requirement governing minors who wish to attend public free schools while living apart from their parents or guardians.

Roberto Morales was born in 1969 in McAllen, Texas, and is thus a United States citizen by birth. His parents are Mexican citizens who reside in Reynosa, Mexico. He left Reynosa in 1977 and returned to McAllen to live with his sister, petitioner Oralia Martinez, for the primary purpose of attending school in the McAllen Independent School District. Although Martinez is now Morales's custodian, she is not—and does not desire to become—his guardian. As a result, Morales is not entitled to tuition-free admission to the McAllen schools. Section 21.031(b) and (c) of the Texas Education Code would require the local school authorities to admit him if he or "his parent, guardian, or the person having lawful control of him" resided in the school district, Tex.Educ.Code Ann. §21.031(b) and (c) (Supp. 1982), but §21.031(d) denies tuition-free admission for a minor who lives apart from a "parent, guardian, or other person having lawful control of him under an order of a court" if his presence in the school district is "for the primary purpose of attending the public free schools." Respondent McAllen Independent School District therefore denied Morales's application for admission in the fall of 1977. . . .

This Court frequently has considered constitutional challenges to residence requirements. On several occasions the Court has invalidated requirements that condition receipt of a benefit on a minimum period of residence within a jurisdiction, but it always has been careful to distinguish such durational residence requirements from bona fide residence requirements. . . .

We specifically have approved bona fide residence requirements in the field of public education. The Connecticut statute before us in *Vlandis v. Kline*, 412 U.S. 441, 93 S.Ct. 2230, 37 L.Ed.2d 63 (1973), for example, was unconstitutional because it created an irrebuttable presumption of nonresidency for state university students whose legal addresses were outside of the State before they applied for admission. The statute violated the Due Process Clause because it in effect classified some bona fide state residents as nonresidents for tuition purposes. But we "fully recognize[d] that a State has a legitimate interest in protecting and preserving . . . the right of its own bona fide residents to attend [its colleges and universities] on a preferential tuition basis." This "legitimate interest" permits a "State [to] establish such reasonable criteria for in-state status as to make virtually certain that students who are not, in fact, bona fide residents of the State, but who have come there solely for educational purposes, cannot take advantage of the in-state rates." Last Term, in *Plyler v. Doe*, 457 U.S. 202, 102 S.Ct. 2382, 72 L.Ed.2d 786 (1982), we reviewed an aspect of Tex.Educ.Code Ann. §21.031—the statute at issue in this case. Although we invalidated the portion of the statute that excluded undocumented alien children from the public free schools, we recognized the school districts' right "to apply . . . established criteria for determining residence." . . .

A bona fide residence requirement, appropriately defined and uniformly applied, furthers the substantial state interest in assuring that services provided for its residents are enjoyed only by residents. Such a requirement with respect to attendance in public free schools does not violate the Equal Protection Clause of the Fourteenth Amendment. It does not burden or penalize the constitutional right of interstate travel, for any person is free to move to a State and to establish residence there. A bona fide residence requirement simply requires that the person *does* establish residence before demanding the services that are restricted to residents. . . .

The provision of primary and secondary education, of course, is one of the most important functions of local government. Absent residence requirements, there can be little doubt that the proper planning and operation of the schools would suffer significantly. The State thus has a substantial interest in imposing bona fide residence requirements to maintain the quality of local public schools.

The central question we must decide here is whether §21.031(d) is a bona fide residence requirement. Although the meaning may vary according to context, "residence" generally requires both physical presence and an intention to remain. As the Supreme Court of Maine explained over a century ago,

when . . . a person voluntarily takes up his abode in a given place, with intention to remain permanently, or for an indefinite period of time; or, to speak more accurately, when a person takes up his abode in a given place, without any present intention to remove therefrom, such place of abode becomes his residence. . . . *Inhabitants of Warren v. Inhabitants of Thomaston*, 43 Me. 406, 418 (1857).

This classic two-part definition of residence has been recognized as a minimum standard in a wide range of contexts time and time again. . . . But at the very least, a school district generally would be justified in requiring school-age children or their parents to satisfy the traditional, basic residence criteria—i.e., to live in the district with a bona fide intention of remaining there—before it treated them as residents.

Section 21.031 is far more generous than this traditional standard. It compels a school district to permit a child such as Morales to attend school without paying tuition if he has a bona fide intention to remain in the school district indefinitely, for he then would have a reason for being there other than his desire to attend school: his intention to make his home in the district. Thus §21.031 grants the benefits of residency to all who satisfy the traditional requirements. The statute goes further and extends these benefits to many children even if they (or their families) do not intend to remain in the district indefinitely. As long as the child is not living in the district for the sole purpose of attending school, he satisfies the statutory test. . . .

The Constitution permits a State to restrict eligibility for tuition-free education to its bona fide residents. We hold that §21.031 is a bona fide residence requirement that satisfies constitutional standards. The judgment of the Court of Appeals accordingly is

Affirmed.

CASE NOTES

1. School districts may inquire as to the reason for the change in the custody of a child and can deny admission if the parent's purpose is to circumvent the school district's zoning requirements. *Matter of Curry*, 113 Mich.App. 821, 318 N.W.2d 567 (1982).

2. A change in student residence simply to participate in an athletic program may be de-

nied by athletic association rules without violating a student's property rights. *Pennsylvania Interscholastic Athletic Association, Inc. v. Greater Johnstown School District*, 76 Pa.Cmwlth. 65, 463 A.2d 1198 (1983).

3. The Supreme Court of Arkansas has held that children residing in one school district could pay tuition and attend school in another school district, but only if both school districts agree to the arrangement. *Delta Special School District No. 5 v. McGehee Special School District No. 17*, 280 Ark. 489, 659 S.W.2d 508 (1983).

4. The word "domicile" is derived from the Latin "domus" meaning home or dwelling house. The word may be defined, by law, as the true place of habitation. A Washington statute was upheld as constitutional by the United States Supreme Court when it defined "domicile" as "a person's true, fixed and permanent home and place of habitation. It is the place where he intends to remain, and to which he expects to return when he leaves without intending to establish a new domicile elsewhere." *Sturgis v. Washington*, 414 U.S. 1057, 94 S.Ct. 563 (1973). A bona fide residence requirement may have the same legal connotation as "domicile." "Domicile" and "residence" are usually in the same place, but the terms are not identical. A person may have two residences, but can have only one domicile. Whether the term "residence" or "domicile" is used, the key is the "intention to remain."

5. *Constellation of Interests.* The physical location of a child's home is not necessarily dispositive in determining residency. In a case where the home actually sat astride the boundary line between two municipalities (though a larger portion of the dwelling was in one of the municipalities), the court held that residency for purposes of attending school should not be determined by the physical location of the home but rather at the locus of the "full constellation of interests" of the family. The ruling in this case was supported by the court's citation of 1 Restatement (second), Conflict of Laws §18, comment (h) (1971), wherein precedent was summarized as follows:

A person's domicile of choice should be in the place to which he is most closely related. In the normal situation, a person's domicile of choice is in the political division where his dwelling place is situated. When the dwelling place is situated upon a dividing line between political divisions, it may be difficult to determine in which of these divisions this domicile is. Usually, the domicile will be in that political division where the major portion of the dwelling place is located, particularly if only an uninhabitable part lies in the other. On rare occasions, however, the preponderant portion of the person's dwelling place may be in one political division, while the bulk of his interests and activities, and also those of his family, are in the other. One such case might be that of a farmer, all of whose tillable land, barn and out-buildings are situated in one political division but the major portion of whose dwelling place is situated in another. A second case may be that of a man who votes and holds public office, attends church, sends his children to school and follows a gainful employment in the political division which contains only a lesser part of his dwelling place. In these cases, it may well be that the person is more closely related to the political division which is the center of his interests and activities than to that which contains the major part of his dwelling place. If this is the case, his domicile of choice should be in the former division. When the boundary line cuts the dwelling place in half, or nearly so, primary weight should be given to the interests and activities of the person and his family, and the domicile placed in the political division where most of these interests and activities are centered.

This Connecticut court further concluded:

[A]n approach based on the whole constellation of interests including both geography and the community orientation of the plaintiff and his family is congruent with the Connecticut statutory scheme pertaining to education and consistent with relevant Connecticut case law. A fact-based "constellation of interests" approach, which takes into account not only the physical property, but the other factors associated with the plaintiff and his family, finds persuasive support, not only in 1 Restatement (Second), supra, comment (h), but also in many well-reasoned cases. See *Board of Education of Golf School District No. 67 v. Regional Board of School Trustees*, 89 Ill.2d 392, 60 Ill.Dec. 443, 433 N.E.2d 240 (1982); *Dresner v. Regional Board of School Trustees of Kane County*, 150 Ill.App.3d 765, 103 Ill.Dec. 666, 501 N.E.2d 983 (1986); *Granfield v. Regional Board of School Trustees of Bureau County*, 108 Ill.App.3d 703, 64 Ill.Dec. 246, 439 N.E.2d 497 (1982); *Fowler v. Clayton School District*, 528 S.W.2d 955, 958 (Mo.App.1975). *Baerst v. State Board of Education*, 34 Conn.App. 567, 642 A.2d 76 (1994).

■ COMPULSORY SCHOOL ATTENDANCE

While the benefits of universal education were recognized at an early stage of our national development, the idea that all youth should be compelled to attend school came later. Even though the first compulsory attendance law was enacted in Massachusetts in 1853 and in New York one year later, the idea was not firmly established until the turn of the century, by which time thirty-two states had enacted such laws.

That the state's interests should take precedence over parental rights to govern the activities of the child is the basis for both compulsory attendance and child labor laws. The employment records of the nineteenth century and early twentieth century indicate that it took both types of legislation to take children out of the workforce and put them in school.

In large cities children were virtually enslaved—in factories and shops, from daylight until dark—working for abysmally low wages. In the South, public school advocates and the labor unions crusaded against the abuse of child labor. In 1900 three out of ten workers in mills of the South were children under sixteen years of age, and 57.5 percent of those children were between ten and thirteen. Those under ten were not enumerated for statistical purposes. It was estimated that 75 percent of the spinners in the cotton mills of North Carolina were fourteen or younger. The number of children under sixteen working in the mills increased sixfold between 1880 and 1900. In 1894, the only child labor law that was on the books of a leading textile state was in Alabama. The law was enacted in 1887 and repealed in 1895, on demand of a large Massachusetts company that opened a mill in Alabama in 1895.[10]

The *Manufacturers Record*[11] attacked child labor laws as "radical," "unreasonable," and "inflammatory"; others charged that taking away child labor would cripple the economy of the South. Fortunately, by 1912 all southern states had adopted an age-and-hour limit and some prohibition against night work of children, yet in most states the age limit for employment was only twelve and the work week was sixty hours.

Thus, a combination of industrial exploitation and the inability of parents to make decisions in the best interest of their own children greatly retarded educational progress for many years. It was not until compulsory attendance laws and child labor laws were enforced, in concert, that the public school became a viable social phenomenon.

Even today, there are some who maintain that compulsory attendance should be abolished and all children should be given the option and opportunity to attend school, but not be compelled to do so. Milton Friedman, the Nobel laureate in economics, argues that compulsory attendance laws are unnecessary and should be abolished. In his national bestseller of 1980, *Free to Choose*, he observed:

> But it is far from clear that there is any justification for the compulsory attendance laws themselves.... Like most laws, compulsory attendance laws have costs as well as benefits. We no longer believe the benefits justify the costs.[12]

Friedman's primary objection to compulsory attendance laws seems to be that such laws are merely an unwarranted justification for governmental control over parents. This argument is, of course, not a new one. It is of the nineteenth century, during which era a great outcry was raised by opponents of public schools, who saw compulsory attendance as an unnecessary governmental device that would deny parental authority and weaken private schools. Though the logical connection is relatively difficult to rationalize, it was basically argued that society had no right to force anyone to be educated, and if they were educated, they should do so of their own volition using their own resources.

It was argued that the child and parent should be given freedom to choose or not choose education. "What right," it was exclaimed, "has society to force me to learn reading, if I do not want to? or writing, if I can get along without it? or numbering, if I will know enough of it by the practical schooling of hard life? or geography, if I can make my way through life without maps?"[13] It was further argued that those who advocated compulsory attendance implicitly assumed that "a man cannot be honest and industrious without having passed through a primary school...."[14] Finally, it was maintained that the general welfare of the people did not justify the government's requirement that all attend school.[15]

The argument against compulsory attendance also played a role in the struggle to desegregate the public schools of the South during the 1950s and 1960s. The desegregation movement both prior to and subsequent to *Brown v. Board of Education*[16] led several southern states to abolish their compulsory attendance laws, apparently on the theory that equal protection of the laws would not apply if one were not required to attend school, or possibly on the more perverse notion that if black children were truant from school, there was no legal obligation on the part of the state to see that they were educated. The legislature of Virginia, for example, repealed its compulsory attendance laws in 1959 and adopted the general policy of massive resistance to desegregation.[17] Without compulsory attendance the "freedom of choice" program, coupled with the tuition vouchers for whites to attend private schools, combined to create formidable desegregation problems.[18] Alabama went a step further, amending its constitution in 1956 to prevent any challenge to legislative discretion in the matter of control of public education attendance policy or rights pertaining thereto.

In short, the issue of compulsory school attendance has been and continues to be a volatile area of dispute between those who argue for broader and universal education and those who seek a more limited use of education for particularized purposes and interests. The argument is a historical one, with the basic motivations changing little over the years. The courts have generally resolved the dilemma by maintaining that education is vital to the welfare of the state, and that the requirement that all persons be exposed to schooling is not an unreasonable or arbitrary exercise of state power. On the other hand, the courts do not compel the state legislatures to require attendance in a school, so those states that have little interest in universal education or for some reason seek to limit educational opportunity by either rescinding attendance laws or by greatly expanding the reasons for exemptions are free to do so at their own volition.

PARENS PATRIAE

Legal authority for the state to require school attendance is found in the common law doctrine of *parens patriae*, which maintains, essentially, that as a parent to all persons, the state has the inherent prerogative to provide for the commonwealth and individual welfare. It can through the exercise of the police power of the legislature establish reasonable laws, not repugnant to the constitution, as it may judge for the good of the state. As guardian over everyone, the state has the authority to protect those who are not legally competent to act in their own behalf, *non sui juris* (literally, "not his own master"). This protection was quite naturally interpreted to apply to minor children, who because of their age, were unable to take care of themselves. Unavoidably, the state's interest in the child was to collide with parental interest, and this, today, still forms the framework on which most compulsory education and curriculum controversies are litigated. It is well established, going back into English law, that the state's or the King's prerogative is superior to that of the parent when the parent's natural right is improperly exercised. Authority for the power of the state was clearly stated in English precedent, and parens patriae was adopted throughout the United States "to the end that the health, patriotism, morality, efficiency, industry, and integrity of its citizenship may be preserved and protected, looking to the preservation and stability of the state."[19] In this country, the desirability of the doctrine as a rudiment of governmental responsibility was well expressed in an 1882 Illinois case, wherein the court said:

> It is the unquestioned right and imperative duty of every enlightened government, in its character of *parens patriae*, to protect and provide for the comfort and well-being of such of its citizens as by reason of infancy . . . were unable to take care of themselves. The performance of these duties is justly regarded as one of the most important of governmental functions, and all constitutional limitations must be so understood and construed as not to interfere with its proper and legitimate exercise.[20]

A child has a right to be protected not only from the patent abuses of his or her parents but also against the ignorance of his or her parents. The state has recognized more truth than fiction in the adage "There are no delinquent children, only delinquent parents." In support of this view, juvenile courts and welfare agencies of the state have traditionally intervened between parent and child in cases of parental abuse. Public education may thus serve as a mechanism to free the child from the shackles of unfit parents.

To protect the child from the parent requires affirmative state action. A child has no constitutional protection from the parent; such protection must come in the form of statutory action by the state to protect the child, examples of which are compulsory attendance laws and requirements that children be exposed to certain kinds of educational curricula. On the other hand, the state's action must be supported by a compelling or, at least, a rational state interest before either the child's or the parent's rights can be restricted or infringed upon.

In the United States today, a dual set of precedents has emerged. One tends to limit *parens patriae*, as is evidenced by court-imposed limitations on state handling of juvenile cases.[21] This precedent was illustrated by the exception from the state compulsory attendance laws in *Yoder*.[22] The second precedent is judicial authorization for legislatures to protect the infant from parental abuse, as was reflected by the United States Supreme Court in *Ford v. Ford* in 1962:

Unfortunately, experience has shown that the question of custody, so vital to a child's happiness and well-being, frequently cannot be left to the discretion of the parents. This is particularly true where, as here, the estrangement of husband and wife beclouds parental judgment with emotion and prejudices.[23]

The language of the Supreme Court in *Pierce v. Society of Sisters*[24] indicated that only limited tolerance would be given the state in interfering with the parent's control of the child:

In this day and under our civilization, the child of man is his parent's child and not the state's. . . . It is not seriously debatable that the parental right to guide one's child intellectually and religiously is the most substantial part of the liberty and freedom of the parent.

This does not mean that parental rights fully preempt those of the state. On the contrary, it would appear that a parent may forfeit his or her right to control his or her child by either omission or commission. In such case, the parent has no immunity from state intervention.

Nearly twenty years after *Pierce*, in 1943, the Supreme Court more clearly defined its position toward state intervention in *Prince v. Massachu-*

setts.[25] Here, a legal guardian was found guilty of contributing to the delinquency of a minor by permitting her nine-year-old ward to sell Jehovah's Witnesses publications on a public street. The act was found to be in violation of Massachusetts's child labor laws. The Supreme Court addressed the conflicting claims of parent and state, saying:

[T]he family itself is not beyond regulation in the public interest. . . . [A]cting to guard the general interest in youth's well being, the state as parens patriae may restrict the parent's control by requiring school attendance, regulating or prohibiting the child's labor and in many other ways.

In *Yoder*, the court said that the power of the parent, even when linked to free exercise of religion, may be subject to limitation if it appears that parental decisions will jeopardize the health or safety of the children or have "potential for significant social burdens."

A common thread running through these precedents is a renewed judicial concern for the child, with the parental interest and the state interest secondary. However, the general welfare is always a concern of the state, and the maxim *salus populi suprema lex esto*, "let the welfare of the people be the supreme law," is sufficient justification for the exercise of the *parens patriae* doctrine.

State intervention to compel attendance includes distinguishable premises: the state may provide education for all who cannot appropriately educate themselves, protect infants from those who would deny them education, and compel all citizens to act in ways most beneficial to the child and society.[26] Reflecting state concern in these areas, compulsory attendance laws require schooling and provide enforcement to protect the child from undesirable parental conduct.[27]

Cases involving challenges to compulsory attendance laws generally emanate from disputes between parents and officials. This may be due, in part, to the old notion that "the basic right of a juvenile is not to liberty but to custody."[28] It may also result directly from enforcement provisions in compulsory attendance laws that penalize the parent, rather than the child.

Confrontation between state and parent instead of between state and child is probably the result of two subtle theories suggested by

Kleinfeld.[29] One is that parents have a duty to a child to educate him or her, and the state may compel fulfillment of this duty. The other is that parents have a duty to the state to educate their children, which the state may compel them to perform.

Whether the judgment of the parent should prevail over the collective judgment of the state in educational matters is a much broader question, however, than may be evidenced by simple challenges to compulsory attendance laws. In a dispute between parent and state regarding an educational matter, parents may be pictured as intelligent, well meaning, and motivated for the betterment of the child. This is not always the case. The invocation of the doctrine of *parens patriae* in matters of education may result from broken homes where parents will not assist or support the child in obtaining an education. Where children have sought financial assistance from parents toward a common school education, the courts have uniformly termed such education as "necessary" and granted the support. Common school education is a "necessary," as are food, lodging, clothing, and medicine.[30]

In the courts' view, education has traditionally been of such importance that even items assisting school attendance have been considered necessary for child support purposes. For example, one early Texas court held that a buggy may be a "necessary" if it is needed to convey a child to and from school.[31] In some states, the courts have given alimony in divorce decrees that consider education to be a "necessary" over and beyond the normal public school education.[32]

Exercise of *parens patriae* by the state may result in more severe action than that of requiring a child to attend school or mandating that a parent furnish resources for attendance in school or college. The child-parent relationship can be partly or totally severed by judicial enforcement of divorce, neglect,[33] or child abuse statutes.[34] The concept of *parens patriae* extends to compulsory medical care over the objection of parents. Some states have explicit statutory language declaring a parent neglectful if he or she fails to provide medical care for his or her child. Under a finding of neglect, the court is empowered to provide the necessary medical care.[35] Courts, acting as *parens patriae*, have made children wards of the state and required medical care in the absence of statute, under common law.[36]

It should be noted that the invocation of *parens patriae* by the state does not restrict parental authority in all cases. In some instances, such action may even strengthen it. In cases in which parents are unable to control their own children, the child's action produces not only disharmony within the family but sometimes becomes a nuisance to the public generally. For such situations, some states have enacted "stubborn child laws"[37] that protect the public from children who are "runaways, night walkers, common railers and brawlers."

INSTRUCTION IN PRIVATE SCHOOLS

When compulsory attendance laws are mentioned, one usually thinks of children being compelled to attend only public schools. However, many alternatives and exceptions exist. A child may attend a private, profit, nonprofit, sectarian, or secular school or, with state statutory permission, be permitted to have home instruction. A child may also be exempt from required attendance because of religion, marriage, physical or mental incapacity, distance of travel, and so on. Courts have established many precedents that even today are in a state of transition.

Few cases have defined "private school" as used in compulsory attendance laws.[38] Precise definition is lacking, because in several jurisdictions children are not required to attend either public or private schools but must obtain "equivalent instruction."[39]

The state cannot, however, impose too many regulations on private schools. In holding Ohio's regulation of private schools overly restrictive, tending to make private schools the images of public schools, the court said that the overregulation of the private schools emanated from state educational agency regulations. These regulations governed "the content of the curriculum that [was] taught, the manner in which it [was] taught, the person or persons who [taught] it, the physical layout of the building in which the students [were] taught, the hours of instruction, and the educational policies intended to be achieved through the instruction offered."[40]

Most courts have held that to be "recognized," a private school must provide instruction equivalent to the free instruction furnished in public schools. To have equivalent instruction, it is also necessary for the private school to comply with the statutory period of attendance.[41]

EQUIVALENT INSTRUCTION

The state has the prerogative to define what constitutes equivalent instruction, and the private school must accommodate the state. Although vaguely defining the term "equivalent" as meaning "equal," the courts generally refer to the qualifications of the instructor and the available teaching materials as the primary criteria for determining equivalency of instruction. Should the state require that students be tested, it makes no difference that the private school would rather opt for some other measure of equivalency.[42] The court will uphold the state standards so long as they are reasonable and are not too vague for proper implementation. State equivalency regulations may require that children (1) be taught by a certified teacher; (2) be taught a minimum specified, listed curriculum; (3) fulfill specified minimum attendance standards that are appropriate and will be upheld by the courts; or (4) pass tests as specified by the state.[43]

However, in Missouri, where the state compulsory attendance law provided that home instruction be permitted as an alternative to compulsory attendance if the instructional program is "substantially equivalent" to that of a public or private school, a U.S. district court ruled that the provision was unconstitutionally vague because nowhere in the statute were the terms defined. No guidelines were issued to interpret, and both parents and school officials could only guess at its meaning.[44]

Thus, as with all laws touching on individual freedoms, appropriate governmental restraints must be specifically and properly defined or they will be invalidated by the courts as too vague to be enforceable.[45]

Courts may thus continue to find that tests, certification of teachers, and other measures constitute a reasonable exercise of state power.[46]

Although the state can require instruction equivalent to that of a public school, it cannot deny the parent the right to send his or her child to a private school. In a 1925 case, *Pierce v. Society of Sisters*, a private school itself, as a cor-

poration, claimed denial of due process of law because an Oregon compulsory attendance statute required all children ages eight to sixteen to attend public schools.[47] The appellees in the case were the Roman Catholic order of the Society of Sisters and Hill Military Academy, both private, profit-making corporations. The schools claimed that enforcement of the compulsory attendance law would deprive them of students, destroy the profitable features of their businesses, and diminish the value of their property.

The compulsory education controversy had been raised by those who were concerned that private schools created religious hostility and prejudice, and that American government and loyalty to democratic ideals could best be taught in public schools. Further, the law was enacted at the time when there was a great worldwide fear of the spread of Bolshevists, syndicalists, and Communists; there was concern that private schools could be started and fostered by such groups. In 1922, the Oregon voters adopted an initiative—by a margin of 115,000 to 103,000—requiring that all children between the ages of eight and sixteen years attend a public school or be exempted by permission of the county school superintendent.

In ruling in the plaintiffs' favor in *Pierce*, the United States Supreme Court decided the case on the grounds that the state cannot, through improper regulation, deprive a business corporation of its patrons or customers. The law deprived the corporations of a liberty protected by the Fourteenth Amendment. In this regard, the Court commented on the rights of both parent and child:

> The fundamental theory of liberty upon which all governments in this union repose excludes any general power of the state to standardize its children by forcing them to accept instruction from public teachers only. The child is not the mere creature of the state; those who nurture him and direct his destiny have the right, coupled with the high duty, to recognize and prepare him for additional obligations.[48]

Religious interests may be used as rationale by private school operators to maintain that their schools should remain open regardless of adherence to state curriculum regulations. Courts will weigh religious interests against state interests, and the result may hang in balance on the facts involved. For example, even a church itself may be closed if worship services are held in a residential area of a city and the religious chanting during worship services disturbs the neighborhood.[49] With private religious schools, though, the facts and the interests involved may concern more esoteric questions, such as whether accommodation of minimal state educational requirements is, in and of itself, an encroachment on religious interests. In Nebraska, a lengthy and highly publicized conflict developed when the state closed a private religious school because it did not adhere to state requirements for private schools. The Supreme Court of Nebraska held that the state interests prevailed over the religious interests of the private school proprietors and parents.[50] Religious convictions do not exempt operators of private schools from compliance with reasonable state school laws.[51] In this regard an appeals court in Michigan has held that parochial schools can be required to submit to the state the records of enrollment of pupils attending the schools and the qualifications of teachers. Similarly, the state can enforce curriculum and teacher certification requirements.[52]

--- ❖ — ❖ — ❖ ---

Compulsory Education Law Requiring All Children to Attend Public Schools Violates Due Process Clause

Pierce v. Society of the Sisters of the Holy Names of Jesus and Mary

Supreme Court of the United States, 1925.
268 U.S. 510, 45 S.Ct. 571.

Mr. Justice McREYNOLDS delivered the opinion of the Court. These appeals are from decrees, based upon undenied allegations, which granted preliminary orders restraining appellants from threatening or attempting to enforce the Compulsory Education Act adopted November 7, 1922 (Laws Or.1923, p. 9), under the initiative provision of her Constitution by the voters of Oregon. Judicial Code, §266 (Comp.St. §1243). . . .

The challenged act, effective September 1, 1926, requires every parent, guardian, or other person having control or charge or custody of a child between eight and sixteen years to send him "to a public school for the period of time a public school shall be held during the current year" in the district where the child resides; and failure so to do is declared a misdemeanor. There are exemptions—not specially important here—for children who are not normal, or who have completed the eighth grade, or whose parents or private teachers reside at considerable distances from any public school, or who hold special permits from the county superintendent. The manifest purpose is to compel general attendance at public schools by normal children, between eight and sixteen, who have not completed the eighth grade. And without doubt enforcement of the statute would seriously impair, perhaps destroy, the profitable features of appellees' business and greatly diminish the value of their property.

Appellee the Society of Sisters is an Oregon corporation, organized in 1880, with power to care for orphans, educate and instruct the youth, establish and maintain academies or schools, and acquire necessary real and personal property. It has long devoted its property and effort to the secular and religious education and care of children, and has acquired the valuable good will of many parents and guardians. . . . It owns valuable buildings, especially constructed and equipped for school purposes. The business is remunerative—the annual income from primary schools exceeds $30,000—and the successful conduct of this requires long time contracts with teachers and parents. The Compulsory Education Act of 1922 has already caused the withdrawal from its schools of children who would otherwise continue, and their income has steadily declined. The appellants, public officers, have proclaimed their purpose strictly to enforce the statute.

After setting out the above facts, the Society's bill alleges that the enactment conflicts with the right of parents to choose schools where their children will receive appropriate mental and religious training, the right of the child to influence the parents' choice of a school, the right of schools and teachers therein to engage in a useful business or profession, and is accordingly repugnant to the Constitution and void. And, further, that unless enforcement of the measure is enjoined the corporation's business and property will suffer irreparable injury.

Appellee Hill Military Academy is a private corporation organized in 1908 under the laws of Oregon, engaged in owning, operating, and conducting for profit an elementary, college preparatory, and military training school for boys between the ages of five and twenty-one years. . . . It owns considerable real and personal property, some useful only for school purposes. The business and incident good will are very valuable. . . .

The Academy's bill states the foregoing facts and then alleges that the challenged act contravenes the corporation's rights guaranteed by the Fourteenth Amendment and that unless appellants are restrained from proclaiming its validity and threatening to enforce it irreparable injury will result. The prayer is for an appropriate injunction. . . .

The court ruled that the Fourteenth Amendment guaranteed appellees against the deprivation of their property without due process of law consequent upon the unlawful interference by appellants with the free choice of patrons, present and prospective. It declared the right to conduct schools was property and that parents and guardians, as a part of their liberty, might direct the education of children by selecting reputable teachers and places. . . .

No question is raised concerning the power of the state reasonably to regulate all schools, to inspect, supervise and examine them, their teachers and pupils; to require that all children of proper age attend some school, that teachers shall be of good moral character and patriotic disposition, that certain studies plainly essential to good citizenship must be taught, and that nothing be taught which is manifestly inimical to the public welfare.

The inevitable practical result of enforcing the act under consideration would be destruction of appellees' primary schools, and perhaps all other private primary schools for normal children within the state of Oregon. Appellees are engaged in a kind of undertaking not inherently harmful, but long regarded as useful and meritorious. Certainly there is nothing in the present records to indicate that they have failed to discharge their obligations to patrons, students or the state. And there are no peculiar circumstances or present emergencies which demand extraordinary measures relative to primary education.

Under the doctrine of *Meyer v. Nebraska*, we think it entirely plain that the Act of 1922 unreasonably interferes with the liberty of parents and guardians to direct the upbringing and education of children under their control. As often heretofore pointed out, rights guaranteed by the Constitution may not be abridged by legislation which has no reasonable relation to some purpose within the competency of the state. The fundamental theory of liberty upon which all governments in this Union repose excludes any general power of the state to standardize its children by forcing them to accept instruction from public teachers only. The child is not the mere creature of the state; those who nurture him and direct his destiny have the right, coupled with the high duty, to recognize and prepare him for additional obligations.

Appellees are corporations, and therefore, it is said, they cannot claim for themselves the liberty which the Fourteenth Amendment guarantees. Accepted in the proper sense, this is true. . . . But they have business and property for which they claim protection. These are threatened with destruction through the unwarranted compulsion which appellants are exercising over present and prospective patrons of their schools. And this court has gone very far to protect against loss threatened by such action. . . .

Generally, it is entirely true, as urged by counsel, that no person in any business has such an interest in possible customers as to enable him to restrain exercise of proper power of the state upon the ground that he will be deprived of patronage. But the injunctions here sought are not against the exercise of any proper power. Appellees asked protection against arbitrary, unreasonable, and unlawful interference with their patrons and the consequent destruction of their business and property. Their interest is clear and immediate. . . .

The decrees below are affirmed.

■ RELIGION: THE AMISH EXCEPTION

After *Pierce v. Society of Sisters*,[53] it was uniformly assumed that children could be compelled to attend a public, private, or parochial school, but that no child had a right *not* to attend school at all.

Early cases established that the child's and the parents' rights of religious freedom, as protected by the First Amendment of the United States Constitution, were not sufficient to diminish the state's power to compel compulsory attendance. Justice Cardozo, in a concurring opinion in *Hamilton v. Regents*[54] (a case dealing with the rights of a conscientious objector), maintained that undesirable results may evolve where religious scruples predominate over reasonable state laws. In delivering the opinion Cardozo said:

> Manifestly a different doctrine would carry us to lengths that have never yet been dreamed of. The conscientious objector, if his liberties were to be thus extended, might refuse to contribute taxes in furtherance of any other end condemned by his conscience as irreligious or immoral. The right of private judgment has never yet been so exalted above the powers and the compulsion of the agencies of government. One who is a martyr to a principle—which may turn out in the end to be a delusion or an error—does not prove by his martyrdom that he has kept within the law.[55]

Following this rationale, other courts have concluded that the individual cannot be permitted, on religious grounds, to be the judge of his duty to obey reasonable civil requirements enacted in the interest of public welfare.

In a 1945 Virginia case, the parents of three families sought to prevent the enforcement of compulsory attendance laws on religious grounds. These parents interpreted the Bible as commanding parents to teach and train their own children. They believed that sending their children to public schools was incompatible with the primary religious obligation they felt they owed their Maker. Their willful intent to violate the law was solely because of sincere religious convictions. Yet the court decided against the parents, and declared:

> No amount of religious fervor he [parent] may entertain in opposition to adequate instruction should be allowed to work a lifelong injury to his child. Nor should he, for this religious reason, be suffered to inflict another illiterate citizen on his community or his state.[56]

Although the religious issue was the *ratio decidendi* in this case, the court ruled that the parents were not capable of adequately educating the children themselves.

Religious grounds have been ruled insufficient to limit the number of days a child attends school. A Muslim parent claimed that his religion prevented him from sending his children to school on Fridays. Regardless of the validity of his religious motives, the court said the state allowed parental choice among public, private, and parochial schools. The parent and child did not, however, have the option of nonattendance on Fridays.[57]

Thus, the prevailing view of the courts was that religious beliefs cannot impair achievement of the state's objective—universal compulsory education. The precedent-setting case that has altered this view is *Wisconsin v. Yoder*.[58] This case contested the power of the state to require the school attendance of Amish children after the eighth grade. Although the issue in this case is limited to the compulsory attendance of Amish children between the time they complete the eighth grade and the time they reach sixteen years of age, it nevertheless has profound implications for all future cases involving compulsory attendance.

The decision of the Court in this case can be summarized in three points. First, although the state has power to impose reasonable regulation, this power must be balanced against fundamental rights and interests of individuals. Second, beliefs that are philosophical rather than personal are not sufficient to invoke free exercise of religion. Third, where parents show that enforcement of compulsory education will endanger their religious beliefs, the *parens patriae* power of the state must give way to the free exercise clause of the First Amendment.

Two dramatic limitations on the general applicability of *Yoder* are the objection of the Amish to only post-eighth-grade compulsory attendance of fourteen- and fifteen-year-olds and the well-established Amish customs of living near the soil and shunning modern society generally. These features of the case tend to diminish the compelling interest of the state; they eliminate the possibility of illiteracy by providing at least eight years of schooling and negate the chance of these children becoming unproductive members of society.

The ultimate question of who will determine the child's destiny is not answered by *Yoder*. The court is content, instead, to speak rather vaguely of balancing the fundamental religious freedom of the parents against the interest of the state.

Litigation following *Yoder* indicates that the courts will tend to circumscribe the "Amish exception" very narrowly, and that in most instances requests to have other churches, religions, or religious views added to the list of valid exemptions from compulsory attendance are not likely to be granted. Actions by fundamentalist Baptists seeking to convince the courts that the Amish exemption should extend to their religion have been to no avail.[59] Where the Amish exception is applied to one religious group and not to another,[60] the courts have held that equal protection is not violated.

❖ — ❖ — ❖

State Cannot Compel Amish Children to Attend Public High School

State of Wisconsin v. Yoder

Supreme Court of the United States, 1972.
406 U.S. 205, 92 S.Ct. 1526.

. . . Respondents Jonas Yoder and Wallace Miller are members of the Old Order Amish religion, and respondent Adin Yutzy is a member of the Conservative Amish Mennonite Church. They and their families are residents of Green County, Wisconsin. Wisconsin's compulsory school-attendance law required them to cause their children to attend public or private school until reaching age sixteen but the respondents declined to send their children, ages fourteen and fifteen, to public school after they completed the

eighth grade. The children were not enrolled in any private school, or within any recognized exception to the compulsory-attendance law, and they are conceded to be subject to the Wisconsin statute.

On complaint of the school district administrator for the public schools, respondents were charged, tried, and convicted of violating the compulsory-attendance law in Green County Court and were fined the sum of $5 each. Respondents defended on the ground that the application of the compulsory-attendance law violated their rights under the First and Fourteenth Amendments. . . .

The history of the Amish sect was given in some detail, beginning with the Swiss Anabaptists of the sixteenth century who rejected institutionalized churches and sought to return to the early, simple, Christian life deemphasizing material success, rejecting the competitive spirit, and seeking to insulate themselves from the modern world. As a result of their common heritage, Old Order Amish communities today are characterized by a fundamental belief that salvation requires life in a church community separate and apart from the world and worldly influence. This concept of life aloof from the world and its values is central to their faith. . . .

Formal high school education beyond the eighth grade is contrary to Amish beliefs, not only because it places Amish children in an environment hostile to Amish beliefs, with increasing emphasis on competition in class work and sports and with pressure to conform to the styles, manners, and ways of the peer group, but also because it takes them away from their community, physically and emotionally, during the crucial and formative adolescent period of life. . . .

The Amish do not object to elementary education through the first eight grades as a general proposition because they agree that their children must have basic skills in the "three R's" in order to read the Bible, to be good farmers and citizens, and to be able to deal with non-Amish people when necessary in the course of daily affairs. They view such a basic education as acceptable because it does not significantly expose their children to worldly values or interfere with their development in the Amish community during the crucial adolescent period.

While Amish accept compulsory elementary education generally, wherever possible they have established their own elementary schools in many respects like the small local schools of the past. In the Amish belief higher learning tends to develop values they reject as influences that alienate man from God. . . .

There is no doubt as to the power of a State, having a high responsibility for education of its citizens, to impose reasonable regulations for the control and duration of basic education. See, e.g., *Pierce v. Society of Sisters*, 268 U.S. 510, 534, 45 S.Ct. 571, 573, 69 L.Ed. 1070 (1925). Providing public schools ranks at the very apex of the function of a State. Yet even this paramount responsibility was, in *Pierce*, made to yield to the right of parents to provide an equivalent education in a privately operated system. There the Court held that Oregon's statute compelling attendance in a public school from age eight to age sixteen unreasonably interfered with the interest of parents in directing the rearing of their offspring, including their education in church-operated schools. As that case suggests, the values of parental direction of the religious upbringing and education of their children in their early and formative years have a high place in our society. . . . Thus a State's interest in universal education, however highly we rank it, is not totally free from a balancing process when it impinges on fundamental rights and interests, such as those specifically protected by the Free Exercise Clause of the First Amendment, and the traditional interest of parents with respect to the religious upbringing of their children so long as they, in the words of *Pierce*, "prepare [them] for additional obligations." 268 U.S., at 535, 45 S.Ct., at 573.

It follows that in order for Wisconsin to compel school attendance beyond the eighth grade against a claim that such attendance interferes with the practice of a legitimate religious belief, it must appear either that the State does not deny the free exercise of religious belief by its requirement, or that there is a state interest of sufficient magnitude to override the interest claiming protection under the Free Exercise Clause. . . .

The essence of all that has been said and written on the subject is that only those interests of the highest order and those not otherwise served can overbalance legitimate claims to the free exercise of religion. We can accept it as settled, therefore, that, however strong the State's interest in universal compulsory education, it is by no means absolute to the exclusion or subordination of all other interests. . . .

We come then to the quality of the claims of the respondents concerning the alleged encroachment of Wisconsin's compulsory school-attendance statute on their rights and the rights of their children to the free exercise of the religious beliefs they and their forbears have adhered to for almost three centuries. In evaluating those claims we must be careful to determine whether the Amish religious faith and their mode of life are, as they claim, inseparable and interdependent. A way of life, however virtuous and admirable, may not be interposed as a barrier to reasonable state regulation of education if it is based on purely secular considerations; to have the protection of the Religion Clauses, the claims must be rooted in religious belief. Although a determination of what is a "religious" belief or practice entitled to constitutional protection may present a most delicate question, the very concept of ordered liberty precludes allowing every person to make his own standards on matters of conduct in which society as a whole has important interests. Thus, if the Amish asserted their claims because of their subjective evaluation and rejection of the contemporary secular values accepted by the majority, much as Thoreau rejected the social values of his time and isolated himself at Walden Pond, their claims would not rest on a religious basis. Thoreau's choice was philosophical and personal rather than religious, and such belief does not rise to the demands of the Religion Clauses.

Giving no weight to such secular considerations, however, we see that the record in this case abundantly supports the claim that the traditional way of life of the Amish is not merely a matter of personal preference, but one of deep religious conviction, shared by an organized group, and intimately related to daily living. . . .

As the society around the Amish has become more populous, urban, industrialized, and complex, particularly in this century, government regulation of human affairs has correspondingly become more detailed and pervasive. The Amish mode of life has thus come into conflict increasingly with requirements of contemporary society exerting a hydraulic insistence on conformity to majoritarian standards. So long as compulsory education laws were confined to eight grades of elementary basic education imparted in a nearby rural schoolhouse, with a large proportion of students of the Amish faith, the Old Order Amish had little basis to fear that school attendance would expose their children to the worldly influence they reject. But modern compulsory secondary education in rural areas is now largely carried on in a consolidated school, often remote from the student's home and alien to his daily home life. As the record so strongly shows, the values and programs of the modern secondary school are in sharp conflict with the fundamental mode of life mandated by the Amish religion; modern laws requiring compulsory secondary education have accordingly engendered great concern and conflict. The conclusion is inescapable that secondary schooling, by exposing Amish children to worldly influences in terms of attitudes, goals, and values contrary to beliefs, and by substantially interfering with the religious development of the Amish child and his integration into the way of life of the Amish faith community at the crucial adolescent stage of development, contravenes the basic religious tenets and practice of the Amish faith, both as to the parent and the child.

The impact of the compulsory-attendance law on respondents' practice of the Amish religion is not only severe, but inescapable, for the Wisconsin law affirmatively compels them, under threat of criminal sanction, to perform acts undeniably at odds with fundamental tenets of their religious beliefs. . . .

In sum, the unchallenged testimony of acknowledged experts in education and religious history, almost 300 years of consistent practice, and strong evidence of a sustained faith pervading and regulating respondents' entire mode of life support the claim that enforcement of the State's requirement of compulsory formal education after the eighth grade would gravely endanger if not destroy the free exercise of respondents' religious beliefs. . . .

The State advances two primary arguments in support of its system of compulsory education. It notes, as Thomas Jefferson pointed out early in our history, that some degree of education is necessary to prepare citizens to participate effectively and intelligently in our open political system if we are to preserve freedom and independence. Further, education prepares individuals to be self-reliant and self-sufficient participants in society. We accept these propositions.

However, the evidence adduced by the Amish in this case is persuasively to the effect that an additional one or two years of formal high school for Amish children in place of their long-established program of informal vocational education would do little to serve those interests. Respondents' experts testified at trial, without challenge, that the value of all education must be assessed in terms of its capacity to prepare the child for life. It is one thing to say that compulsory education for a year or two beyond the eighth grade may be necessary when its goal is the preparation of the child for life in modern society as the majority live, but it is quite another if the goal of education be viewed as the preparation of the child for life in the separated agrarian community that is the keystone of the Amish faith. . . .

The State attacks respondents' position as one fostering "ignorance" from which the child must be protected by the State. No one can question the State's duty to protect children from ignorance but this argument does not square with the facts disclosed in the record. Whatever their idiosyncrasies as seen by the majority, this record strongly shows that the Amish community has been a highly successful social unit within our society, even if apart from the conventional "mainstream." Its members are productive and very law-abiding members of society; they reject public welfare in any of its usual modern forms. The Congress itself recognized their self-sufficiency by authorizing exemption of such groups as the Amish from the obligation to pay social security taxes. . . .

Insofar as the State's claim rests on the view that a brief additional period of formal education is imperative to enable the Amish to participate effectively and intelligently in our democratic process, it must fall. The Amish alternative to formal secondary school education has enabled them to function effectively in their day-to-day life under self-imposed limitations on relations with the world, and to survive and prosper in contemporary society as a separate, sharply identifiable and highly self-sufficient community for more than 200 years in this country. In itself this is strong evidence that they are capable of fulfilling the social and political responsibilities of citizenship without compelled attendance beyond the eighth grade at the price of jeopardizing their free exercise of religious belief. When Thomas Jefferson emphasized the need for education as a bulwark of a free people against tyranny, there is nothing to indicate he had in mind compulsory education through any fixed age beyond a basic education. Indeed, the Amish communities singularly parallel and reflect many of the virtues of Jefferson's ideal of the "sturdy yeoman" who would form the basis of what he considered as the ideal of a democratic society. Even their idiosyncratic separateness exemplifies the diversity we profess to admire and encourage. . . .

There is no intimation that the Amish employment of their children on family farms is in any way deleterious to their health or that Amish parents exploit children at tender years. Any such inference would be contrary to the record before us. Moreover, employment of Amish children on the family farm does not present the undesirable economic aspects of eliminating jobs that might otherwise be held by adults.

Finally, the State, on authority of *Prince v. Massachusetts,* argues that a decision exempting Amish children from the State's requirement fails to recognize the substantive right of the Amish child to a secondary education, and fails to give due regard to the power of the State as *parens patriae* to extend the benefit of secondary education to children regardless of the wishes of their parents. Taken at its broadest sweep, the Court's language in *Prince* might be read to give support to the State's position. However, the Court was not confronted in *Prince* with a situation comparable to that of the Amish as revealed in this record; this is shown by the Court's severe characterization of the evils that it thought the legislature could legitimately associate with child labor, even when performed in the company of an adult. . . .

This case, of course, is not one in which any harm to the physical or mental health of the child or to the public safety, peace, order, or welfare has been demonstrated or may be properly inferred. The record is to the contrary, and any reliance on that theory would find no support in the evidence. . . .

For the reasons stated we hold, with the Supreme Court of Wisconsin, that the First and Fourteenth Amendments prevent the State from compelling respondents to cause their children to attend formal high school to age sixteen. . . . It cannot be overemphasized that we are not dealing with a way of life and mode of education by a group claiming to have recently discovered some "progressive" or more enlightened process for rearing children for modern life.

Aided by a history of three centuries as an identifiable religious sect and a long history as a successful and self-sufficient segment of American society, the Amish in this case have convincingly demonstrated the sincerity of their religious beliefs, the interrelationship of belief with their mode of life, the vital role that belief and daily conduct play in the continued survival of Old Order Amish communities and their religious organization, and the hazards presented by the State's enforcement of a statute generally valid as to others. Beyond this, they have carried the even more difficult burden of demonstrating the adequacy of their alternative mode of continuing informal vocational education in terms of precisely those overall interests that the State advances in support of its program of compulsory high school education. In light of this convincing showing, one that probably few other religious groups or sects could make, and weighing the minimal difference between what the State would require and what the Amish already accept, it was incumbent on the State to show with more particularity how its admittedly strong interest in compulsory education would be adversely affected by granting an exemption to the Amish. . . .

Nothing we hold is intended to undermine the general applicability of the State's compulsory school-attendance statutes or to limit the power of the State to promulgate reasonable standards that, while not impairing the free exercise of religion, provide for continuing agricultural vocational education under parental and church guidance by the Old Order Amish or others similarly situated. The States have had a long history of amicable and effective relationships with church-sponsored schools, and there is no basis for assuming that, in this related context, reasonable standards cannot be established concerning the content of the continuing vocational education of Amish children under parental guidance, provided always that state regulations are not inconsistent with what we have said in this opinion.

Affirmed.

❖ — ❖ — ❖

State Justified in Denial of "Amish Exception" to Baptist School

Johnson v. Charles City Community Schools Board of Education

Supreme Court of Iowa, 1985.
368 N.W.2d 74.

Considered en banc.

HARRIS, Justice. Plaintiffs are the pastor and certain members of a fundamentalist Baptist church in Charles City. The controversy arose following their organization of a parochial school. The parents were charged with violating Iowa's compulsory attendance law, Iowa Code section 299.1 (1983). The section is quite typical in that it places the sanction for failure to attend on the parent rather than on the child. The parents here responded by bringing two separate proceedings. One was a declaratory judgment action which challenged our statutory education requirements, not only the compulsory attendance statute but also certain reporting requirements in chapter 299. The second response was to apply to the state board of public instruction for relief under section 299.24, popularly called the Amish exception. . . .

The district court denied declaratory relief and affirmed on the administrative appeal. We agree with plaintiffs' contention that the religious freedoms guaranteed them under the first amendment entitle them to educate their children at the private religious school they have established. The same guarantees accord them

the right to operate the school with minimal necessary supervision by the state. . . .

Both challenges are rooted in the plaintiffs' deeply held religious beliefs. They perceive their school, which they describe as their "week day educational ministry," to be an integral part of the exercise of their religion. It is named Calvary Baptist Christian Academy.

When it was set up in the fall of 1980 the school was not incorporated separately from the church. The curriculum chosen, the Accelerated Christian Education Program, has not as yet been challenged as inadequate by any state authorities. At the bottom of this litigation is the fact that plaintiffs are unwilling to submit to any state inquiry on the matter. In their view, the educational content and process of their school, because it is so central to their religion, is not properly subject to state oversight. . . .

According to the trial court's findings, beginning in the 19th century, there has been growing concern among Christian "fundamentalist" churches with what they consider to be the calamitous threat of secular humanism. The trial court pointed out in its findings. . . .

Iowa law does not require that all children attend public schools, reflecting a long tradition of friendly coexistence between private and public schools. . . . This accommodation, dating from the first years of our statehood, was reached at least three quarters of a century before the United States Supreme Court ruled that a state cannot compel all students to be educated in public schools. *Pierce v. Society of Sisters*, 268 U.S. 510, 45 S.Ct. 571, 69 L.Ed. 1070 (1925). . . .

While the state authority to intrude into private religious schools is, as we shall point out, confined to a necessary minimum, a clear authority, even a duty, does exist. . . .

Under *Pierce*, parents are free, notwithstanding compulsory education statutes, to provide for a private education in a religious forum of their own choosing. This fundamental right would be hollow to the point of nonexistence if the state were to so closely superintend the school as to compromise its religious independence. . . .

In their appellate brief and upon oral submission of their appeal the plaintiffs, as mentioned, suggest that their position of absolute and total rejection of any public regulation can and should be accommodated by Iowa's educational scheme. Yet they concede the general right of the public to demand education for all its children. Plaintiffs suggest that the public could satisfy its rightful role while at the same time protecting plaintiffs' first amendment rights by merely testing the children.

We reject the suggestion because it does not do enough for the children. To merely test the children, as we shall explain in a later division, does not satisfy the state's rightful role. Whatever limitations are imposed on the state's general right and duty to see to the education of its youth, the right extends beyond occasional testing. It plainly extends to such matters as basic parameters for curriculum and teacher qualifications. . . .

A principal difficulty in plaintiffs' assertion is that anyone can make it, not only high-minded and sincere people, but also a host of others whose childrens' educations also are at stake.

The state has a clear right to set minimum educational standards for all its children and a corresponding responsibility to see to it that those standards are honored. When such standards are set in place, compliance with them falls within the ambit of the fundamental contract between the citizen and society. It need scarcely be said that each of us, in order to enjoy membership in an organized social order, is pledged to adhere to a number of minimum norms. Of these, one of the most central is society's duty to educate its children.

The nature and extent of education remain largely a matter of personal choice. But there are basic minimums and, this being true, it is up to the people as a whole to set them. One way they have done this is to enact compulsory education statutes. A citizen must submit to them, persuade society to change them, or join a society without them. . . .

It is enough here to reject the challenge plaintiffs do raise. We reject it because the state can reasonably regulate the basic educational requirements of all children within its borders. The state can inquire into private educational institutions in order to see this is done. . . .

It remains for us to consider plaintiffs' appeal from the district court decision on judicial review. . . .

This was the proceeding in which plaintiffs sought a determination that their school should escape state control under section 299.24, the Amish exception.

This provision was noted in *Wisconsin v. Yoder,* 406 U.S. at 208, 92 S.Ct. at 1529, 32 L.Ed.2d at 21 n. 3, as Iowa's resolution of the conflict between compulsory education and the uniquely isolated Amish culture in our midst. Under section 299.24 certain religious societies can apply to the state superintendent for an exemption from the compulsory attendance laws. Upon being satisfied the requirements of the statute are met, the superintendent, subject to the approval of the state board of public instruction, may, but is not required to, grant the exemption.

The district court quoted the material parts of section 299.24 as follows:

> When members or representatives of a local congregation of a reorganized church . . . established for ten years or more within the State of Iowa prior to July 1, 1967, which professes principles or tenets that differ substantially from the objectives, goals, and philosophy of education embodied in the standards set forth in section 257.25, and rules adopted in implementation thereof. . . .

The board of education denied the application in the belief there was no essential conflict between plaintiffs' legitimate educational goals and those specified in section 257.25. Section 257.25 specifies in considerable detail the educational standards for public schools in Iowa. The district court held there was nothing unreasonable, arbitrary, or capricious in the denial. It also held the denial did not render section 299.24 unconstitutional as applied to the plaintiffs.

Plaintiffs' administrative appeal challenges both of these determinations. Plaintiffs contend they fall within the ambit of the statute's language and hence qualify for the exemption. They also contend it is unconstitutional to deny them the exemption. Our scope of review differs from the two contentions. . . .

In view of the historical background for section 299.24 (the plaintiffs themselves call it the "Amish exception") we do not think the legislature intended the exemption to be available to any and all church groups who seek to provide for a religiously oriented education. If this had been the legislative goal a much broader statute would have been required. . . . [P]lainly, all parochial schools in the state are not intended for the exemption. The statute calls, not for a religious evaluation by the superintendent, but for an analysis of the educational goals of the group applying for exemptions and a comparison of those goals with those set up for public school children. Because of the conviction that religion is the basis for education, held by these plaintiffs and by all who support parochial education, the superintendent faces a mixed and somewhat complex question.

To obtain an exemption under section 299.24, plaintiffs had to prove their church "professes principles or tenets that differ substantially from the objectives, goals, and philosophy of education embodied in standards set forth in section 257.25, and rules adopted in implementation thereof. . . . " . . .

Plaintiffs offered no evidence that any principle or tenet of their church is in conflict with teaching the subjects listed in the statute. Rather, they insisted only that their church be able to teach those subjects in its own way with books and teachers of its own exclusive choice. Nothing in section 257.25, as interpreted and applied here, would deny them that opportunity. Thus the state board cannot be said to have acted unreasonably, arbitrarily or capriciously in rejecting their exemption request.

What prevents plaintiffs from having their way is not any objective, goal or philosophy of education embodied in section 257.25, but the requirement in section 299.1 that their church employ only certified teachers. Their church's opposition to that requirement, however, is not made a basis for obtaining an exemption under section 299.24. They must look to section 257.25, not section 299.1, to establish their right to exemption.

We conclude, giving due and required deference to the administrative findings of the superintendent, that the plaintiffs have not established any substantial dissimilarity between their educational goals and those specified for public schools, certainly none which sets them apart from all the many other parochial schools in the state. . . .

We next consider the first of two constitutional facets of plaintiffs' challenge to the administrative denial of their application for an Amish exemption. They first argue it was a violation of their first amendment rights to deny them the exemption.

Section 299.24 was our legislature's response to precisely the same concerns later involved in *Wisconsin v. Yoder.* The statute, its subject, purpose, meaning, and application are fully explained in the *Yoder* opinion.

The United States Supreme Court employed a balancing test to weigh the acknowledged and valid public interest in imposing reasonable regulations and minimum educational standards against the fundamental right of the Amish to direct the religious upbringing of their children. A number of factors were considered in the weighing:

1. The sincerity of their commitment to a long established religion;
2. An intricate and crucial interrelationship between those beliefs and their mode of life;
3. The vital role their beliefs and life mode play in the survival of Amish culture;
4. The hazards of enforcing compulsory education laws against them; and
5. The adequacy, in terms of their peculiar needs, of the informal vocational education provided to their youth past the eighth grade.

The court found that the state failed to show how, on balance, its legitimate interest in assuring educated and self-reliant citizens justified a requirement that Amish children attend school for two additional years (past eighth grade) in contravention of their religious beliefs. The state moreover failed to prove that exempting the Amish from two additional years of education would seriously curtail the efficient operation of their school laws.

When the same factors are placed in balance on this record the opposite conclusion asserts itself. Sincerity of belief is the only factor wholly common to both the Amish and these plaintiffs. The beliefs of the plaintiffs are greatly less interwoven with their daily mode of life. The Amish culture is greatly more isolated from mainstream American life. Plaintiffs' children, for all the distinctive religious convictions they will be given, will live, compete for jobs, work, and move about in a diverse and complex society. Their educational needs are plainly not as circumscribed as those of Amish children. Neither does exposure to the more general American culture pose such an immediate threat to plaintiffs' mode of living as is the case with the Amish.

Whatever they may feel about their children's religious needs, the plaintiffs have not established that their children's educational needs are significantly different from those of other children. The superintendent's determination not to grant plaintiffs an Amish exception did not infringe upon their religious rights under the first amendment.

Plaintiffs also ground their appeal from the decision on judicial review upon an equal protection claim. . . .

On an equal protection challenge the first question is whether some fundamental right is involved. The answer determines the burden to be borne by the challenger. . . . Without doubt, and plaintiffs agree, the state has a compelling interest in educating its youth. . . .

For reasons we have already explained we think this vital state interest is served by the classification. Education is of transcendent importance to all children. . . .

The educational needs of the children involved here are, as we have said, much different and much greater than the needs of Amish children. Even at school age there is much greater mixing by these children in general society. Some church members send their children to other schools, a matter which would ostracize children from Amish culture. . . .

The principal difference is to consider the world for which the children here will have to be prepared. They will have to compete with well-educated children, will associate with them in a society very different from the simple, rural and largely isolated one that lies ahead for Amish children. The state was fully justified in the classification. The equal protection challenge is rejected. . . .

Affirmed.

CASE NOTES

1. *Religious Exemption.* The Virginia compulsory attendance statute provides that "[a] school board . . . [s]hall excuse from attendance at school any pupil who, together with his parents, by reason of *bona fide* religious training or belief, is conscientiously opposed to attendance at

school." This statutory provision also states, "The term *bona fide* religious training or belief does not include essentially political, sociological, or philosophical views or merely a personal moral code." The Virginia Supreme Court ruled a school board did not need to state the reasons for denying a religious exemption. *Johnson v. Prince William County School Board,* 241 Va. 383, 404 S.E.2d 209 (1991).

2. *Truancy.* Under compulsory attendance laws, the state may define what constitutes truancy. The language defining "truancy" of a Wisconsin statute reads as follows:

> "Truancy" means *any absence* of *part or all of one or more days* from school during which the school attendance officer, principal or teacher has not been notified of the legal cause of such absence by the parent or guardian of the absent pupil, and also means intermittent attendance carried on for the purpose of defeating the intent of s. 188.15. (Emphasis added.)

A Wisconsin court, in interpreting this statute, said:

> The standard is clear. Attendance without statutory excuse or excuse by the school board is compulsory. Failure to attend even a period of the day not excused is considered truancy. . . . A person in control [of the child] must see to it that the child attends unless there is a statutory excuse. If the child does not attend, the child is truant.

The court said that a person of ordinary intelligence would deduce from this statute that any unexcused absence of part of a day or all of one day is a deviation from the constant and uniform. It is a *truancy.* Five such occasions out of ten consecutive days or part of all of ten or more days in a semester means that the child is termed a "habitual truant." Sections 118.16(1)(a)1.2. Less than that is nonetheless a truancy. This is further notice that any absence is considered irregular. (Emphasis added.) *State of Wisconsin v. White,* 509 N.W.2d 434 (Wis.App.1993).

■ HOME INSTRUCTION

In recent years state legislatures have increasingly amended state compulsory attendance laws to permit home schooling. Gordon et al., in studying developments in this particular area of education legislation, have observed that in

1982 only two states, Nevada (1956) and Utah (1957), had statutes that specifically provided for home schooling. By 1993, this number had increased to thirty-two, with, in addition, Maryland and New York permitting home instruction by state regulation.[61]

Litigation has correspondingly greatly increased in this area, usually involving three issues: (1) statutory interpretation of exemptions, (2) complaints regarding state requirements for home instructors' qualifications, and (3) state evaluations of the home instruction programs.

Denial of home instruction and compulsion to attend school do not violate the religious freedom of the parent. A U.S. district court has held that parents have no fundamental right to maintain home instruction for their children and that parental rights of free exercise of religion are not abridged by the state's denial of home instruction.[62]

The state may compel all children to attend a school, public or private, and home instruction will not suffice as an exemption from compulsory attendance requirements unless state statute so specifies. The rationale for subordinating a parent's desire to keep his or her child at home to the state's interest in compelling the child to attend a school is best summarized by Butts and Cremin:

> Clearly, the child has a right to education. If governments are instituted among men to secure to all enjoyment of their rights, then what objection could be raised to the government compelling parents and guardians to send their children to school?[63]

To allow parents, at will, to nullify the effects of compulsory attendance laws would have not only a detrimental effect on society as a whole, but importantly, would allow the parent to limit and restrict the ultimate development and future prospects of the child. In this regard parents find themselves in the difficult position of arguing that less opportunity is preferable to more opportunity.

Assuming that parents could provide as thoroughly comprehensive and varied a curriculum at home as at school, courts still may hold that having the child physically in school with other children is a valuable socialization process, the fostering of which is in the state's interest and for which home instruction cannot be an adequate substitute.

Several states refuse to allow home instruction because it is believed that the sequestration of children in the home, insulated from society and other children, will inhibit social consciousness and prevent the child from living a normal and productive life. A New Jersey court has said that "[c]loister and shelter have their place but not in the everyday give and take of life."[64]

Moreover, a legislature's denial of home instruction does not violate equal protection of the Fourteenth Amendment. A New Mexico court has held that the state need only to show that such denial is rationally related to a legitimate state purpose. The state's desire to have children attend school with other children of their age is an appropriate and defensible state interest. This court said, "By bringing children into contact with some person, other than those in the excluded group, those children are exposed to at least one other set of attitudes, values, morals, lifestyles and intellectual abilities."[65]

An Oregon appellate court has held that the state does not violate equal protection when it distinguishes between children taught by parents or a private teacher in home instruction, and those taught in a private school. The state may clearly have a rational basis for such distinctions.[66]

Courts will uphold reasonable state criteria to qualify for exemption from compulsory attendance. Where a statute provided that parents show a "manifest educational hardship," it was not sufficient that parents show merely the one criterion of manifest educational hardship to qualify validly for exemption from compulsory attendance. A state board of education may require adherence to one or more of the criteria, such as the competency of parents to teach, the scope of the subject matter, the child's potential for interaction with peers and adults, and the teaching methods to be employed, before the exemption is considered valid.[67]

An early Washington case rejected the home as a private school. In that case, the parent claimed his home instruction was authorized by a statute providing that children must attend "the public school of the district in which the child resides, for the full time such school may be in session, or. . . attend a private school for the same time." The parent further claimed that he was a qualified and competent teacher giving home instruction within the definition to the statute. This claim was rejected by the court, which explained:

> We do not think that the giving of instruction by a parent to a child, conceding the competency of the parent to fully instruct the child in all that is taught in the public schools, is within the meaning of the law "to attend a private school." Such a requirement means more than home instruction; it means that the same character of school as the public school, a regular, organized and existing institution making a business of instructing children of school age in the required studies and for the full time required by the laws of this state. . . . There may be a difference in institution and government, but the purpose and end of both public and private schools must be the same—the education of children of school age. The parent who teaches his children at home, whatever be his reason for desiring to do so, does not maintain such a school.[68]

Home instruction has been rejected because of difficulty of supervision. The state bears the responsibility of reasonable supervision to guarantee that students obtain an adequate education. If home instruction imposes an unreasonable burden on the state's performance of its duties, the instruction is not allowed. For example, a situation may exist where parents use education units so small or facilities of such doubtful quality that supervision creates an unusual expense for the state. The state requires that proper educational facilities be provided for the child and supplied in a way that the state can ascertain facts about the instructional program and maintain proper direction without undue cost.[69]

Critics have charged that home instruction does not comply with statutory requirements that a child attend a public, private, denominational, or parochial school and be taught by a competent instructor. In Kansas, the legislature reenacted a compulsory attendance law, leaving out a former provision for home instruction as a valid exemption from compulsory attendance. The court said that exclusion of home instruction, while including private, denominational,

and parochial school instruction as valid, indicated legislative intent to disallow home instruction as an excuse for nonattendance.[70]

Another Kansas case distinguished between a "private school" and "scheduled home instruction." Here parents operated a "school," serving as tutors themselves, with only their own children in attendance. The only grades taught were those in which their own children were enrolled. The court interpreted this as falling short of the definition of a private school, and it ruled that the instruction given did not meet statutory requirements. In the view of the court, the program was nothing more than "home instruction."[71]

Where reference to home instruction was excluded from the statute, a California court refused to officially regard home instruction programs as qualified "private schools."[72]

Other cases, however, have established that home instruction may constitute "private school" instruction in contemplation of the law. For example, a parent who employs a competent, noncertified school teacher to instruct his or her child in the same curriculum and for the same period of time as the public schools is complying with the law that requires instruction in a public, private, or parochial school.[73] In commenting on this situation, the court said:

> The law was made for the parent who does not educate his child, and not for the parent who employs a teacher and pays him out of his private purse, and so places within the reach of the child the opportunity and means of acquiring an education equal to that obtainable in the public schools of the State.

In summary, if a state statute allows for home instruction as an alternative to compulsory attendance, the burden falls on the state to show that the parent is not, in fact, providing such instruction. If the state has set out few standards governing home instruction, the inadequacy of such instruction may be difficult to prove. The state must produce evidence documenting the parent's failure to furnish adequate home instruction, and the parent must respond to such evidence.[74] However, the final burden of proof rests on the state to show that the instruction failed to meet state requirements.[75]

❖ — ❖ — ❖

School Board Rule Denying Part-Time Attendance of Home-Schooled Child Does Not Violate Free Exercise Clause of Hybrid-Rights of Child and Parents

Swanson v. Guthrie Independent School District I-L

United States Court of Appeals, Tenth Circuit, 1998
135 F.3d 694

Annie Swanson and her parents as next friends (Plaintiffs) appeal the district court's grant of summary judgment to Defendants. Annie had filed suit claiming that Defendants' refusal to allow her to attend public school on a part-time basis violated her rights under the Free Exercise Clause of the United States Constitution, her parents' constitutional right to direct her education, and her rights under Oklahoma state law. We affirm the judgment of the district court.

Annie has been home-schooled by her parents since she started school. The purpose behind the home-schooling is religious—Annie's parents wish to be able to teach her Christian principles that are excluded from the public-school curriculum. When Annie reached the seventh grade, her parents decided that she would benefit by taking a few classes at the public school. Annie's parents believed the public school's ability to teach certain classes (particularly foreign-language classes, vocal music, and some science classes) was superior to their instructional capability in those areas, and that attending some classes at the public school would better prepare Annie for college.

Annie's parents spoke to the then-superintendent of schools and received permission for her to attend two seventh-grade classes for the last nine weeks of the school year. She attended those classes, performed very well in them, and caused no disruption to the school system. Annie then pre-registered for two classes for the eighth grade. Before she began school, however, Defendant Bowman was hired as the new

superintendent. He refused to allow Annie to attend the eighth grade on a part-time basis, and told her parents they would need permission from the school board. He also made some statements that Mrs. Swanson interpreted as criticism of Christian home-schoolers. . . .

At the September meeting of the school board the board voted to adopt the following part-time-attendance policy:

> It is the policy of the Guthrie Board of Education that all students enrolling in Guthrie Public Schools must do so on a full-time basis. Full-time basis shall be defined as attending classes for the full instructional day within the public school system or in conjunction with another state accredited institution such as vocational-technical school or a college or university for concurrent enrollment. The only exceptions to this policy shall be for fifth-year seniors and special education students whose IEP's require variations of student schedules. . . .

The Board feared that Annie's request, if granted, could set a precedent allowing other home-schooled children as well as private-school students to use the public school's facilities on an as-wanted basis, without a corresponding increase in state financial aid. Pursuant to the board's policy, Annie was not allowed to take classes of her choice from the public school during the 1994–95 school year, or to otherwise attend the public school on a part-time basis. . . .

FREE-EXERCISE CLAIM

The question at issue in this case is the validity of the rule or regulation enacted by the school board, as it impacts on Plaintiffs' right to the free exercise of their religion. Plaintiffs maintain that the part-time-attendance policy is a burden, albeit indirect, on the full and free exercise of their religious beliefs concerning the way in which children should be raised and educated. Therefore, they argue, the policy should be subjected to a type of strict scrutiny, requiring that it be justified by a compelling governmental interest and that it be narrowly tailored to meet that interest. . . . Defendants, on the other hand, contend that the policy is a neutral policy of general applicability that need not satisfy the compelling-governmental-interest requirement. In the alternative, they claim there were compelling governmental interests at stake in the adoption of the part-time-attendance policy.

As a general proposition, a law (or policy) that is neutral and of general applicability need not be justified by a compelling governmental interest even if that law incidentally burdens a particular religious practice or belief. . . . On its face, the policy enacted by the school board in this case is neutral and of general application— it applies to all persons who might wish to attend public school on a part-time basis, and prohibits such part-time attendance (with certain specific exceptions, such as fifth-year seniors and special-education students). It applies to students who are home-schooled for secular reasons as well as those home-schooled for religious reasons, and it applies to students attending private schools whether or not those private schools are religious or secular in orientation. . . .

We are therefore left with the fact that the board's policy is a neutral policy of general applicability. Plaintiffs do not attempt to argue that the policy directly burdens their right to free expression, nor could they. The policy does not prohibit them from home-schooling Annie in accordance with their religious beliefs, and does not force them to do anything that is contrary to those beliefs. . . . The board's policy therefore does not violate traditional free-exercise principles. . . .

Plaintiffs point out that parents have a constitutional right to raise and educate their children, and that the part-time-attendance policy infringes on this right as well as on the free-exercise right discussed above. Therefore, according to Plaintiffs, the compelling interest/ closely-tailored analysis must be applied to determine the validity of the policy. . . .

It is difficult to delineate the exact contours of the hybrid-rights theory. . . . As we discuss below, however, we believe that simply raising such a claim is not a talisman that automatically leads to the application of the compelling-interest test. We must examine the claimed infringements on the party's claimed rights to determine whether either the claimed rights or the claimed infringements are genuine. We will begin with Plaintiffs' parental-rights claim.

We have no quarrel with Plaintiffs' assertion that Annie's parents have a constitutional right to direct her education, up to a point. For example, they have a right to send her to a private school, whether that school is religious or secular. Numerous cases, however, have made it clear that this constitutional right is limited in scope. Federal courts addressing the issue have held that parents have no right to exempt their children from certain reading programs the parents found objectionable, or from a school's community-service requirement, or from an assembly program that included sexually explicit topics. . . . The case law in this area establishes that parents simply do not have a constitutional right to control each and every aspect of their children's education and oust the state's authority over that subject. . . .

The claimed constitutional right Plaintiffs wish to establish in this case is the right of parents to send their children to public school on a part-time basis, and to pick and choose which courses their children will take from the public school. Plaintiffs would have this right override the local school board's explicit decision to disallow such part-time attendance (except where the school would receive state funding for the part-time attendee). However, decisions as to how to allocate scarce resources, as well as what curriculum to offer or require, are uniquely committed to the discretion of local school authorities, as well as the cases above demonstrate. . . .

The above discussion establishes that Plaintiffs have shown no colorable claim of infringement on the constitutional right to direct a child's education. Accordingly, we hold that this is not a hybrid-rights case. . . . Based on the foregoing, we hold that Defendants were not required to show a compelling state interest in this case, despite Plaintiffs' attempt to invoke the hybrid-rights doctrine.

Relying on a series of Supreme Court cases decided in the unemployment context . . . , Plaintiffs make the following argument: (1) they have been denied a benefit that has been conferred on other students who are allowed to attend public school part-time; (2) they have been denied that benefit because their religious beliefs require that Annie be educated at home part-time; and (3) therefore, an exception must be made to accommodate their beliefs and allow Annie to attend part-time. . . .

Plaintiffs' religious reasons for wanting Annie to attend public school only part-time must be given credence.

. . . Put simply, Plaintiffs argue (as they explicitly acknowledged at oral argument) that if anyone is allowed to attend the public school part-time, Annie must be allowed to do so also, because her motivation for wanting to do so is religious. According to Plaintiffs' argument, if a governmental entity offers a benefit such as part-time attendance under limited qualifying conditions, and a claimant's religious beliefs or practices prevent him or her from meeting those conditions, the benefit must be awarded to the claimant despite the failure to meet the conditions.

The difficulty we have with this argument is that it would elevate Plaintiffs to a higher status than other home-schoolers who educate their children at home (or, for that matter, in a private school) for secular rather than religious reasons. That is, the part-time attendance policy, which at present precludes Annie and all other home-schooled or private-schooled children from taking a few selected classes from the public school, would be rendered inapplicable to religious home-schooling families but not to secular home-schooling or private-schooling families. The Free Exercise Clause does not extend so far. It is designed to prevent the government from impermissibly burdening an individual's free exercise of religion, not to allow an individual to exact special treatment from the government. . . . Nothing in the Free Exercise Clause requires that such special treatment be provided. . . .

CONCLUSION

Plaintiffs have attempted to portray this case as one involving religious discrimination against Christian home-schoolers. The record provided to the district court and this court, however, indicates that it involves only financial distinctions between certain part-time students and all home-schoolers, secular or religious, as well as private-school students. Since this case involved only a neutral rule of general applicability, it was sufficient for Defendants to prove a reasonable relationship between the part-time-attendance policy and a legitimate purpose of the school board. Plaintiffs have not argued that Defendants failed to meet this low threshold, and it is clear that Defendants have satisfied it.

Therefore, the district court's decision dismissing all of Plaintiffs' claims is AFFIRMED.

State's Use of Achievement Tests to Monitor Home Instruction Is Constitutionally Valid

Murphy v. State of Arkansas

United States Court of Appeals,
Eighth Circuit, 1988.
852 F.2d 1039.

HEANEY, Circuit Judge. Appellants challenge the decision of the district court upholding the constitutionality of the Arkansas Home School Act, Ark. Code Ann. §§6-15-501–6-15-507. We affirm the decision of the district court.

Doty and Phyllis Murphy are evangelical Christians who believe that "Christian Scriptures require parents to take personal responsibility for every aspect of their children's training and education." They have six children, ages four through eighteen. The Murphys educate their children at home, providing an "education that is pervasively religious in nature and which does not conflict with the religious beliefs they hold, based upon their understanding of the scriptures."

Under Arkansas law, a parent must educate her children through the age of sixteen. This requirement may be satisfied by sending the child to public, private, or parochial school or by educating the child at home. The Arkansas Home School Act, Ark. Code Ann. §§6-15-501–6-15-507, requires parents intending to school their children at home to notify in writing the superintendent of their local school district prior to the commencement of each school year. The notice must provide information concerning the name, age, and grade of each student, the core curriculum to be offered, the schedule of instruction and the qualifications of the person teaching. The parent must also agree to submit the children to standardized achievement tests each year and, when the children reach the age of fourteen, to a minimum performance test. All of these tests are administered, interpreted, and acted upon by the Arkansas Department of Education. Finally, the parent must provide any information to the superintendent which might indicate the need for special educational services for the children.

The achievement test administered to a student schooled at home is chosen by the parent from a list of nationally recognized tests provided by the director of the State Department of Education or the director's designee. The parent may be present when the standardized test is administered, but both parent and student are under the supervision of a test administrator. The results of the standardized tests are used for several purposes. Most significantly, if a home school student does not achieve a composite score within eight months of grade level in designated subjects, the student must be placed in a public, private, or parochial school. No such annual testing is required for students in public, private, or parochial schools. If children not schooled at home are, for some reason, tested, no remedial placement is required for those who do not achieve certain scores.

The Murphys allege that the Arkansas statutory scheme deprives them of the right to free exercise of religion, the right of due process of law, the right of equal protection of the laws, and the right of privacy and parental liberty in violation of the United States Constitution. The Murphys brought an action for a declaratory judgment in federal district court. That court awarded judgment to the state.

The Murphys assert that Ark.Code Ann. §6-15-504, requiring that a standardized test be given to their children under the supervision of a test administrator, deprives them of the right to free exercise of religion as guaranteed by the first amendment. They argue that their religious beliefs require they must be *completely* responsible for *every* aspect of their children's education. In contrast, the Arkansas Home School Act places responsibility for testing and interpreting test results with the State of Arkansas, rather than with the parents.

To determine whether governmental conduct infringes upon an individual's first amendment free exercise rights, a court must first inquire whether the challenged governmental action interferes with the claimant's "sincerely held religious beliefs." Second, if such a belief is interfered with, the court must determine whether the governmental action is the least restrictive means of achieving some compelling governmental interest. . . .

In the case before us, the parties have stipulated that the testing requirements of the Arkansas law interfere with the Murphys' sincerely held religious beliefs. Thus, we will go no further in examining the subtleties of the Murphys' beliefs. Consequently, the resolution of the free exercise claim involves answering two related questions: First, does the state have a compelling interest in the education of all children? Second, if so, is the Arkansas statutory scheme the least restrictive means of achieving that objective? We believe that the answer to both of these questions is yes.

The government has a compelling interest in educating all of its citizens. Education of the citizenry is and always has been a preeminent goal of American society. Reaching back through the collective memory of the Republic, the fundamental importance of education in the design of our system of government rapidly becomes clear. Article III of the Northwest Ordinance states in part: "Religion, morality, and knowledge being necessary to good government and the happiness of mankind, schools and the means of education shall forever be encouraged." . . .

The fundamental importance of education in terms of access and achievement in American society was further underscored by the Court in *Brown v. Board of Education.* . . .

It is the very foundation of good citizenship. Today it is a principal instrument in awakening the child to cultural values, in preparing him for later professional training, and in helping him to adjust normally to his environment. In these days, it is doubtful that any child may reasonably be expected to succeed in life if he is denied the opportunity of an education. . . .

Thus, as the district court correctly noted, it is "settled beyond dispute, as a legal matter, that the state has a compelling interest in ensuring that all its citizens are being adequately educated."

Given the existence of a compelling governmental interest, we must next inquire whether Arkansas' home testing system is the least restrictive means to achieve that purpose. In doing so, we recognize that the state must have a mechanism by which it can confidently and objectively be assured that its citizens are being adequately educated.

Upon examination, it would appear that Arkansas has created the least restrictive system possible to assure its goal. By providing the option of home schooling, Arkansas allows parents vast responsibility and accountability in terms of their children's education—control far in excess of limitations on religious rights that have been previously upheld. . . . Arkansas requires neither that the parent instructing the home-schooled child be a certified teacher nor that the parent follow a mandated curriculum. The state's only safeguard to ensure adequate training of the home-schooled student is the standardized achievement test. Even regarding this test, the state allows wide latitude to the parents. The parent may choose a test administered from a list of nationally recognized standard achievement tests and may be present while the test is administered.

Finally, the Murphys make no showing, as made by the Amish in *Yoder*, that the state can be assured its interest will be attained if appellants' religious beliefs are accommodated. We reject the Murphys' argument that parental "testing" of children provides a sufficient safeguard to assure the state's interest in education is protected. Likewise, parental affidavits concerning the children's progress would also be insufficient. In the end, we believe that the state has no means less restrictive than its administration of achievement tests to ensure that its citizens are being properly educated.

The Murphys argue that the Arkansas Home School Act violates the equal protection clause of the fourteenth amendment. Specifically, they claim that those who school their children at home for religious reasons are a suspect class or that parental control over a child's education involves a fundamental right. . . . Thus, the Murphys contend that the state appears irrationally to allow parents to educate their children in religious private schools without any regulatory supervision but subjects children schooled at home to the various requirements of the Home School Act.

While home school families impelled by deep-seated religious convictions might be the type of "discrete and insular minorit[y]" . . . , the broad secular category of individuals who prefer to school their children at home is not. Clearly, the statute is aimed at this second category of individuals.

It could be argued that the statute, while superficially neutral, has a discriminatory impact on the category of deeply religious individuals impelled by their convictions to school their children at home. Yet, even if such discriminatory impact were shown—which it has not been—this would not be sufficient to invoke strict scrutiny. The Murphys would still bear the burden of proving discriminatory purpose or intent. . . . Because no such showing of either discriminatory impact or discriminatory intent has been made, strict scrutiny analysis is inappropriate here. . . .

Given that strict scrutiny analysis does not apply, we move to the question of whether Arkansas has a rational reason to subject home schooling to regulatory requirements, while at the same time freeing private schools from virtually any regulation. . . . In this area of the law, the Supreme Court has declared its willingness to uphold any classification based "upon [any] state of facts that reasonably can be conceived to constitute a distinction, or difference in state policy. . . . "

We believe that such a state of facts exists here. First, it could be argued that the notion of an actual independent school, away from home, implies more formality and structure than a home school. This could lead the state to believe that more serious instruction would be occurring there than in the relaxed atmosphere of a child and parents in their own home. Second, the notion that more than one family is likely to be sending their children to the private school may provide an additional objective indication of the private school's quality that is not present in the context of individual home schools. Finally, unlike a home school, parents sending a child to a private school have to pay money for education, and, hence, would be more likely to demand their money's worth of instructional quality from the private school. All these possibilities together could provide Arkansas with a passable reason for the challenged distinction under the minimum rationality standards of the equal protection clause.

The Murphys argue that the right of privacy should be extended to protect parental decisions concerning the direction of a child's education from state interference. . . .

> The Court has repeatedly stressed that while parents have a constitutional right to send their children to private schools and a constitutional right to select private schools that offer specialized instruction, they have no constitutional right to provide their children with private school education unfettered by reasonable government regulation. . . . Indeed, the Court in *Pierce* expressly acknowledged "the power of the State reasonably to regulate all schools, to inspect, supervise and examine them, their teachers and pupils."

427 U.S. at 178, 96 S.Ct. at 2598 (citations omitted).

The Supreme Court has spoken clearly on this issue, and we are bound by its decision. Moreover, we agree with the Court's reasoning and its conclusion. We thus decline to extend the right of privacy to this situation.

For the foregoing reasons, the decision of the district court is affirmed.

CASE NOTES

1. In most states today, public schools have academic standards and performance requirements that must be applied to students who wish to transfer from home schooling or private schools into public schools. Evaluations of students to determine their levels of academic achievement, however, have experienced some resistance from parents when their home-schooled or private-schooled children seek to transfer credits and enroll in public schools. In a recent Texas case a student who attended a non-accredited private Christian academy sought to transfer during the eleventh grade. Not only was the private school she attended not accredited, but, further, teachers were not required to be certified, students were "self directed" with few standards for class work or grades, and credit was sometimes awarded without testing. School board policy in the district to which the student aspired required that students who had taken courses in institutions, other than fully accredited public or private schools, must be tested and achieve a specified score. If a student from a nonaccredited school wished to avoid the tests, options were provided by which a student could complete correspondence courses or take an additional year in the public school. The student refused to take the tests, rejected both other options, and sued, claiming denial of Free Exercise of Religion and Equal Protection. The court rejected both claims. With regard to Free Exercise, the court said that because the policy applied to all students who wished to transfer the testing policy was religion-neutral.

With regard to Equal Protection the court concluded that the policy was rationally related to a legitimate state interest, and was therefore constitutional. *Hubbard by Hubbard v. Buffalo Ind. School District*, 20 F.Supp. 1012 (N.W. Texas, 1998).

2. The state statutory requirement that a child being educated at home be taught by a person who is legally certified does not offend a parent's religious beliefs. The court held that the state had a compelling interest in the education of children, and the requirement of teacher certification was among the least personally intrusive methods available to satisfy that interest. *State v. Merlin*, 428 N.W.2d 227 (N.D.1988).

This same court had earlier held the requirement of teacher certification did constitute a burden on the parents' religious freedom, but in balancing the parents' religious interests against the compelling interest of the state, certification was among the least-intrusive means of satisfying that interest in education. *State v. Patzer*, 382 N.W.2d 631 (N.D.1986).

3. Parents of children enrolled in a home instruction program in Indiana showed unusual vehemence against public school authority when filing an action for monetary damages against a school superintendent for his attempts to gain information from the parents to verify compliance with a home instruction law. The court held in denying the damages that the parents had frustrated attempts to verify their compliance and that the superintendent exhibited no hostility toward the parents in seeking to obtain adherence to the law. *Mazanec v. North Judson-San Pierre School Corporation*, 798 F.2d 230 (7th Cir.1986).

❖ — ❖ — ❖

Under State Statute, Families Educating Their Children at Home Are Free to Choose between Private School Exception and Home School Exception to Compulsory Attendance Law

Birst v. Sanstead

Supreme Court of North Dakota, 1992.
493 N.W.2d 690 (N.D.1992).

ERICKSTAD, Chief Justice.

Clinton Birst and Judith Birst (the Birsts) appeal from an order and declaratory judgment entered by the District Court for Morton County. The Birsts appeal from a part of the district court's decision requiring them to make their home, also used to educate their children, comply with all municipal and state health, fire, and safety laws applicable to private school buildings. . . . The part the school officials appeal from allows parents educating their children at home to elect either the private school exception or the home-based instruction exception to the compulsory school attendance laws, Chapter 15-34.1, N.D.C.C. We affirm in part and reverse in part.

Until 1989, there was no specific home-based instruction exception to the compulsory school attendance laws in North Dakota. Therefore, parents educating their children at home had to adhere to the private school exception.

Although this Court has never addressed the issue directly, it has acquiesced in the notion that allowing parents to educate their children at home under the private school exception is a legal method of avoiding prosecution for violation of the compulsory school attendance laws of Section 15-34.1-01. N.D.C.C. . . .

The Birsts have educated their children at home since 1983. During the time period within which the Birsts have utilized their home school, they contend that they have met all requirements of the private school exception. More importantly, the North Dakota Department of Public Instruction informed the Birsts on different occasions during the period from 1983 to 1989 that it approved of their home school as a private school.

On July 6, 1989, an amendment to Chapter 15-34.1, N.D.C.C., took effect which specifically addresses situations where school-aged children receive their education at home. The amendment adds a home-based instruction exception to Section 15-34.1-03, N.D.C.C. This amendment provoked the school officials to send the Birsts correspondence directing them to comply with the home-based instruction amendment rather than the private school exception they abided by for over six years. . . . The Birsts contended that because the legislature has not expressly stated that all home schools must comply with the requirements of the new amendment, nor specifically repealed or amended their privilege to continue as before, they are free to elect either the home-based instruction exception or the private school exception to the compulsory school attendance laws. In the district court action, the school officials countered the Birsts' argument by asserting that the Birsts, as well as all other families practicing home education, have to comply with the home-based instruction exception. In the alternative, the school officials contended that, if the Birsts and others like them are allowed to utilize the private school exception, then they must satisfy all of the municipal and state health, fire, and safety laws applicable to private school buildings.

We will consider the issue of election of exceptions first. As the Birsts assert, the home-based instruction exception does not refer to or conflict with the private school exception. The statute as amended does not specifically say that the home-based instruction exception is the exclusive method by which families with home schools may proceed to avoid the compulsory school attendance laws. Nor does it expressly limit the options which a family educating children at home may utilize. The amendment did not alter or limit the use of the subsection concerning private schools. Additionally, the private school exception and the home-based instruction exception are not repugnant when read together, nor do they facially conflict. . . .

In essence, the school officials are asking us to give new meaning to a part of this statute, when the part they ask us to give new meaning to was not explicitly amended. If we were to do as requested, we would be confronted with the well-established rule that precludes us from amending or repealing legislation by implication. . . .

Nothing contained within the language of the home-based instruction exception and the private school exception indicates to us that the presumption against implied amendment or repeal has been overcome. The two provisions do not conflict with or refer to each other. Neither explains that it is the exclusive exception to compulsory school attendance laws for a family with a home school. In harmonizing the two provisions, we must give them both full effect. In light of the above principles, we conclude that families educating their children at home are free to elect between the private school exception and the new home-based instruction exception to the compulsory school attendance laws. The new exception is not the exclusive method available for home school families. We affirm the district court's order and declaratory judgment on this issue.

The second issue on appeal is whether or not home schools using the private school exception must comply with all municipal and state health, fire, and safety laws applicable to private school buildings. We hold that they do not, and reverse the district court on this issue.

In oral argument, the Birsts informed us that they educate only their own children in their home, and that they have four children. This was not disputed by the school officials. . . . The primary use of their (the Birsts) dwelling house is as a home, not a school. Because they live in their home, they educate their children there and not vice versa. The instruction of their children is incidental to the primary purpose of the occupancy of the dwelling house, which is the utilization of it as a home. The part of the N.F.P.A. (National Fire Protection Association) Code regulating private school buildings does not apply to them. Instead, they must comply with regulations for a one-family dwelling.

For the foregoing reasons, we affirm that part of the district court's order and declaratory judgment which permitted the Birsts to elect to comply with the private school exception to the compulsory school attendance laws; we reverse that part of the district court's order and declaratory judgment which required the Birsts

to comply with private school health, fire, and safety laws and regulations. The Birsts are entitled on remand to the ordinary costs on appeal.

CASE NOTES

1. *Certification of Home Instruction in North Dakota.* North Dakota has been a hotbed of home instruction enthusiasts, and the result has been a plethora of litigation in that state on the subject. The following gives the status of the various precedents that affirm the validity of requiring home school instructors to be certified:

■ Children taught in the home must be taught by an individual with a valid teacher's certificate, and this requirement does not infringe upon the parents' right of free exercise of religion. *State v. Merlin*, 428 N.W.2d 227 (N.D.1988), cert. denied 488 U.S. 942, 109 S.Ct. 367 (1988).

■ Requiring the teacher of children in a home school to have a teacher's certificate does not violate the establishment clause. *State v. Anderson*, 427 N.W.2d 316 (N.D.1988) cert. denied 488 U.S. 965, 109 S.Ct. 491 (1988).

■ A teacher certification requirement for home schools is among the least-intrusive methods available to satisfy the government's interest and does not violate the parent's right to free exercise of religion. *State v. Patzer*, 382 N.W.2d 631 (N.D.1986), cert. denied 479 U.S. 825, 107 S.Ct. 99 (1986).

See also *State v. Brewer*, 444 N.W.2d 923 (N.D.1989); and *State v. Toman*, 436 N.W.2d 10 (N.D.1989).

2. *State Approval of Home Instruction.* A state's prior approval of home instruction does not violate parents' rights of free exercise of religion. See *Blount v. Department of Educational and Cultural Services et al.*, 551 A.2d 1377 (Maine, 1988).

3. *Home Visit.* School district inspection visits to the home instruction site are a part of some evaluation processes. Some home instruction parents have objected to such visits on various constitutional grounds, including restraint of liberty, invasion of privacy, inhibition of religion, and illegal search. The court responses are not clearly definitive as to the limits of state

power or to the limitless liberty of parents in physical exclusion of the state from their homes. The United States Court of Appeals, First Circuit, declined to rule on the precise question of whether home visits are necessary in ensuring that all children "shall be educated." In this case, parents had objected to even prearranged, infrequent visits. The federal court referred the case back to a state court to determine first whether the state law did, in fact, require or permit such home visits of the local school committee. Thus, in Massachusetts, the issue is not yet decided. *Pustell v. Lynn Public Schools*, 18 F.3d 50 (1st Cir.1994).

Once a state decides to permit the home-schooling exemption from compulsory attendance, a further decision must be made as to whether the home instruction should be subject to state-mandated quality standards. Most states do have some such requirements, although the enforcement of these standards may be rather lax in many circumstances. In Massachusetts, the quality of the home instruction is subject to a home instruction plan developed by the local school committee. The plan is enforced by periodic observation and evaluation by the local school superintendent or designee. A Massachusetts court has upheld the validity of this process but has held that "the approval of a home school proposal must not be conditioned on requirements that are not essential to the state interest in ensuring that 'all the children shall be educated.'"[76] This court observed that periodic standardized testing or periodic progress reports conducted in lieu of formal testing were acceptable methods to evaluate the educational progress of home-schooled children.

■ OTHER REASONS FOR NONATTENDANCE

Litigation regarding exceptions from school attendance are usually of two types. The first involves the aforementioned cases in which parents seek exemption for their children from school attendance in favor of private school or home instruction or, perhaps, no formal education at all. The second common source of litigation emanates from simple truancy wherein chil-dren merely fail to attend school without offering or claiming alternative forms of education.

EXCESSIVE ABSENCES

Excused absences from school must be authorized by statute or regulation and usually allow for a reasonable number of days of nonattendance for illness, family emergency, educational travel, medical appointments, or approved school activities. To violate such rules may result in an action against parents for failure to see that the child is attending school. A situation illustrative of such a case emanated from an action in a Maryland case where two women, each with two children, allowed the children to miss a total of seventy school days. The state sought conviction of the women for violation of the compulsory attendance laws. The women defended, claiming their constitutional rights of due process were violated because the law imposed "strict liability" by prosecuting parents for actions of their children. The court held that the law, on the contrary, did not prosecute parents for the failure of their children, but prosecuted them for their own failure to see that their children attended school. Performance of such an affirmative duty as imposed by the law is offended by "passive acquiescence (by the parent) in the child's nonattendance of school."[77]

TRAVEL

Parental insistency on taking their children from school for no authorized purpose may be grounds for conviction under attendance laws. In one such case, school board policy limited excused absences for educational trips to one trip per year not to exceed five days. The parents of four children had already expended leave time on a trip to Washington, D.C., and later requested additional time to travel to Europe. The school refused permission; the parents took the children and departed for Europe anyway. Upon the family's return, the school filed a truancy action against the parents that led to conviction. The appellate court upheld the lower court, concluding that the discretionary authority over such matters rested with the local school board.[78]

Students themselves cannot be punished for truancy if the state law only imposes penalties against parents. In a Washington case, the court reversed a truancy fine against students because the state statute provided that "parents, guardians, and the persons in this state having custody . . . shall cause such child to attend . . . school." Under such a law, which is typical of most states, failure of the students to attend school may result in orders, fines, and contempt citations against the parents of truants, but not against the truants themselves.[79]

ILLNESS

Parents who claim that their child is ill and cannot attend school must show valid medical proof of illness. An Illinois case illustrates how a claim of illness may well result in a charge of truancy. Under Illinois law, a child is considered to be truant if absent without "valid cause," which is defined as illness, death in the immediate family, family emergency, or other circumstances that cause concern to the parent for the child's health or safety. In this case, the student was absent from school for 339 1/2 days during a two-year period. Testimony from the student's doctor indicated that he had conducted tests and found that the child had certain allergies, but that these were not of such magnitude to warrant absences from school. Having no other proof of illness to justify the noncompliance with the law, the parents' conviction was upheld.[80]

MARRIAGE

Exemption from compulsory attendance is a dubious benefit of marriage, yet courts have agreed that when a minor of less than sixteen years (otherwise required to attend school) is married, he or she is usually exempt from further compulsory attendance.

One of the precedents in this area was rendered by the Supreme Court of Louisiana. A fifteen-year-old girl and her husband sought to set aside a judgment of a lower court committing her to the State Industrial School for Girls as a result of her truancy and alleged juvenile delinquency.[81] The girl did not deny truancy but claimed that her legal marriage exempted her from attendance. Although marriage of a female under sixteen years of age was prohibited by law, the court ruled that once a girl is married,

she enjoys the status of wife and has a right to live as such, emancipated from both school and parents. The court stated:

> The marriage relationship, regardless of the age of the persons involved, creates conditions and imposes obligations upon the parties that are obviously inconsistent with compulsory school attendance or with either the husband or wife remaining under the legal control of parents or other persons.

In another Louisiana case, a truant, neglected girl of fourteen, was married only a few days after the truant officer had taken her into custody.[82] The lower court committed the girl to a state girls' school for an indefinite period of time. The judge, exercising *parens patriae*, was of the opinion that the girl needed the care and protection of the state. The Supreme Court of Louisiana, while sympathetically viewing the judge's concern for the girl's welfare, held that the lower juvenile court could not commit her to the girls' school or prevent her from assuming the responsibilities of a married woman. The court stated that the power of such public policy determinations rested with the legislature and not the court.

A New York court followed the rationale of these two cases. In one of the cases a girl resisted attempts to force her to attend school because she was married and wanted to be a housewife and homemaker.[83] The court, while recognizing the state's sovereignty concerning compulsory attendance, decided for the girl, observing that times and mores had changed since the compulsory attendance law was passed. The court expressed doubt that the legislature had anticipated the question of such youthful marriage in passing the law.

In the eyes of the law, then, youthful marriage is a valid exemption from compulsory attendance laws. Effectively, marriage removes both state and parental control over minors. Consequently, married minors have the choice and the right to decide on their own further education.

■ VACCINATION

To protect the health and welfare of citizens, states have required school children to be vaccinated. Courts have generally held that if a parent violates a statute requiring vaccination, the parent is subject to arrest or fine, even if he or she claims religious, conscientious, or scientific objections.

In 1905, the United States Supreme Court held that a board of health requirement that all persons in Cambridge, Massachusetts, be vaccinated did not violate personal liberties found under the Fourteenth Amendment. In this case, the Court noted that "the liberty secured by the Constitution of the United States to every person within its jurisdiction does not impart an absolute right on each person to be, at all times and in all circumstances, wholly freed from restraint. There are manifold restraints to which every person is necessarily subject for the common good."[84]

Although this particular decision directly challenged the vaccination regulation rather than compulsory attendance, the Supreme Court,[85] nevertheless, cited several state court decisions approving state statutes and making vaccination of children a condition of the right to attend public schools.[86]

In *Viemeister v. White*,[87] a turn-of-the-century New York decision, the appellant argued that vaccination not only did not prevent smallpox but tended instead to bring on other harmful diseases. The court, while not ruling that vaccination was a smallpox preventive, nevertheless maintained that laypersons and physicians alike commonly believed that it did prevent smallpox. The court concluded that, even if it could not be conclusively proved that the vaccination was a preventive, in our republican form of government the legislature has the right to pass laws based on common belief and the will of the people to promote health and welfare.

Is a parent guilty of violating the compulsory attendance law, then, if he or she sends his or her child to school without vaccination and the child is sent home by school authorities? Answering this question in the affirmative, a New York court said that attendance at a public school imposes certain conditions on a child. These requirements must be met in order for the child to attend. However, the court went on to say that under the public health law, vaccination was required only for children attending public schools, not private schools. The parent could

offer private equivalent education to the child and avoid vaccination. Here, however, the parent had not provided equivalent education and was, therefore, subject to penalty under the compulsory attendance law.[88]

In an earlier New York case, little tolerance was evidenced for parents who used vaccination as an excuse to prevent their children's attendance in public schools:

It is obvious that a parent should not be allowed to escape his duty to send his children to school as provided by law on any excuse which is not an ample justification for such course. Our public school system has been developed with great pains and solicitude, and its maintenance and support have been recognized as so important for the welfare of the state that they have been provided for and safeguarded in the Constitution itself. As a part of this system a statute has been passed requiring attendance at school of children within certain limits. If indifferent or selfish parents, for ulterior purposes, such as the desire to place young children at labor, instead of school, or from capricious or recalcitrant motives, may be allowed to manufacture easy excuses for not sending their children to school, a ready method will have been developed for evading the statute compelling such attendance, and, if the statute requires parents to see to it that their children attend and take advantage of this school system may be lightly and easily evaded, the purposes of the state in providing and insisting on education will be frustrated and impaired. Failure to comply with the statute ought not to be excused, except for some good reason.[89]

The earlier cases concerning school vaccinations were not generally related to First Amendment religious protections. As observed above, the Supreme Court did not clarify the application of the "no state" provision of the Fourteenth Amendment until 1940, in *Cantwell v. Connecticut*.[90] The precedent of religious exemption from compulsory attendance, established in *Yoder*,[91] holds implications for cases involving religious freedom from vaccination. At this time, though, the precedents indicate that statutes requiring vaccination do not violate the free exercise of religion.

Parents in *State v. Drew* refused to have their child vaccinated, giving reasons as "partly religious and partly because they did not want that poison injected into their child." The Supreme Court of New Hampshire upheld the parents' conviction for violating the compulsory attendance law and said:

> The defendant's individual ideas, whether "conscientious," "religious," or "scientific," do not appear to be more than opinions. . . . The defendant's views cannot affect the validity of the statute or entitle him to be excepted from its provisions. . . . It is for the Legislature, not for him or for us, to determine the question of policy involved in public health regulations.[92]

Where an epidemic is imminent, there is no question concerning the state's power to protect the citizenry by requiring vaccination. However, when there is no evidence of the imminence of an epidemic, how do the courts view the issue? Can the state's requirement of vaccination be a reasonable and permissible restraint on constitutional rights in the absence of epidemic?

In *Maas*,[93] the defendant argued that compulsory vaccination and immunization were not needed because there had been no smallpox or diphtheria for almost a decade. The court disagreed and ruled that the absence of an emergency does not warrant a denial of the exercise of preventive means. The court said, "A local board of education need not await an epidemic, or even a single sickness or death, before it decides to protect the public. To hold otherwise would be to destroy prevention as a means of combating the spread of disease."

Likewise, in *Stull v. Reber*,[94] the fact that there had been no smallpox in the borough for forty years did not prevent enforcement of the compulsory vaccination regulation. Health authorities were not required to wait for an epidemic before acting.[95] Neither does the fact that an epidemic has already started prevent enforcement of compulsory vaccination.[96]

If the state board of health enacts a compulsory vaccination regulation made pursuant to statute, the general statutory requirements requiring all pupils to comply with law are sufficient grounds for the board of education to enforce the statute.[97]

All the aforementioned cases contested duly promulgated board rules that were enacted pursuant to state statutes. However, where no statute exists to empower school or health boards to pass compulsory vaccination regulations, the issues shift quite drastically. A board cannot enact regulations unless they are based on existing statutes. Where the board acts regardless of statute, the act is *ultra vires* (in excess of legal authority). Further, a board rule restricting school attendance cannot prevail over a legislative act granting free unlimited admittance to public schools.

Accordingly, two Illinois courts have decided that in the absence of a compulsory vaccination statute, an unvaccinated child cannot be denied a public education.[98] In both of these cases, however, it appeared that the school boards made little effort to draw enabling implications from health or education statutes.

In summary, one can reasonably draw several conclusions regarding compulsory attendance and vaccination: (1) the legislature has power to enact a statute providing for vaccination and including a penalty for noncompliance. (2) Neither the parent nor the child has a constitutional right to schooling without complying with the statutory requirement of vaccination. (3) A parent cannot escape conviction for failing to have his or her child vaccinated by demanding that the child be admitted to school unvaccinated. (4) Religious objection has not generally prevented enforcement of compulsory vaccination and attendance requirements.

❖ — ❖ — ❖

*School Board Action to Exclude Unimmunized
Children from School Does Not Violate
Equal Protection Rights*

Maack v. School District of Lincoln

Supreme Court of Nebraska, 1992.
241 Neb. 847, 491 N.W.2d 341.

SHANAHAN, Justice.

Jessica Maack and Melissa Maack, students enrolled at Lincoln East Junior-Senior High School, were not immunized against rubeola (measles). During an outbreak of measles in Lincoln during May 1989, Jessica and Melissa Maack were excluded from attending classes at

Lincoln East for the period from May 10, 1989, until May 20, 1989. Lincoln East is under the jurisdiction of the board of education of School District No. 1 of Lancaster County, Nebraska (Lincoln Public Schools). After a series of administrative appeals within the school system, in which the exclusion was affirmed, Jessica and Melissa Maack, with their parents, Linda Maack and Timothy J. Maack, on June 29, 1989, appealed to the district court for Lancaster County, which affirmed the board of education's exclusionary order.

Jessica and Melissa Maack enrolled and attended classes at Lincoln East under a parental waiver of student immunization against certain diseases, including measles. Such waiver is authorized by Neb.Rev.Stat. §79-444.01 (Reissue 1987), which provides:

> Each board of education and the governing authority of each school in this state shall require each student to be protected against measles, mumps, rubella, poliomyelitis, diphtheria, pertussis, and tetanus by immunization . . . unless a parent or guardian of such student presents a written statement that he or she does not wish to have such student so immunized.

While the Maack children were enrolled at Lincoln East, §79-4,177(1) provided in pertinent part:

> (1) Any student may be excluded from school in the following circumstances[:]
> (a) If the student has a dangerous communicable disease transmissible through normal school contacts and poses an imminent threat to the health and safety of the school community; or
> (b) If the student's conduct presents a clear threat to the physical safety of himself, herself, or others, or is so extremely disruptive as to make temporary removal necessary to preserve the rights of other students to pursue an education.

Since 1981, there had been no reported cases of measles in Lincoln. However, in the spring of 1989, a measles "outbreak" occurred in the Lincoln area. Between April 20 and May 12, 1989, there were 24 confirmed cases of measles in the area. On May 5, a student at Lincoln East was found with a clinically confirmed case of measles. Jane Ford, director of the Lincoln-Lancaster County Department of Health, consulted with Dr. Richard A. Morin, a physician who is a board-certified internist with a subspe-

cialty in the field of infectious diseases. After her conference with Dr. Morin, Ford contacted the administration of Lincoln Public Schools on May 6 and "directed that all unimmunized children be excluded from Lincoln East Junior-Senior High effective 8:30 a.m. Monday, May 8, 1989, for a period of not less than 2 weeks or until they are properly immunized or their immune status confirmed." At Lincoln East there were 79 students, including Jessica and Melissa Maack, who had not been immunized against measles. Also, among the Lincoln East students were some whose physical condition was the basis for special education.

Parents of the 79 unimmunized students were informed that a clinically confirmed case of measles had been found at Lincoln East and that unimmunized children could not attend school "until there are no new cases of measles or until proof of immunization is provided." After Timothy Maack received the message about measles at Lincoln East, he called the school nurse, Janet Zenner, and requested more information. Zenner told Timothy Maack about the clinically confirmed case of measles and that health officials were concerned about the safety of children at Lincoln East, including the Maack children. Timothy Maack told Zenner that his daughters were not, and would not be, immunized against measles. Linda and Timothy Maacks' rejection of immunization for their children was based on personal preference and was not based on religious or medical reasons.

Since the measles virus locates in a persons's "air way," exposure to measles results from an infected person's coughing or sneezing in the air, spreading the "virus contained in the mucous that has been sprayed in the air." The sprayed virus is "viable for several hours." Measles is especially dangerous, because an infected person may be "relatively asymptomatic," but can communicate the disease several days before and after the manifested symptoms of measles. Measles is especially dangerous in a community where there has been a long period without reported cases of measles, such as the time during which the Lincoln area had no reported cases of measles, and is "particularly dangerous in those situations in which there are multi-handicapped individuals such as those who attend [Lincoln] East Junior-Senior High School."

Dr. Morin concluded that in view of the "community-wide outbreak" of measles and the clinically confirmed case of measles at Lincoln East Junior-Senior High School, without immunization against measles Jessica and Melissa Maack were "a clear threat to the physical safety of themselves and others" at the junior-senior high school. Also, in Dr. Morin's opinion, as previously related to Ford, director of the Lincoln-Lancaster County Department of Health, the clinically confirmed case of measles at Lincoln East required that all unimmunized children be excluded from Lincoln East for a period of 2 weeks or until they were properly immunized or their immune status was confirmed.

First, Maacks contend that §79-4,177(1)(b) does not authorize a student's exclusion from school when the student is not infected with a dangerous communicable disease. Therefore, Maacks argue, since Jessica and Melissa Maack were not shown to have measles, the Maack children could not be excluded from school under §79-4,177(1). However a student's "conduct [that] presents a clear threat to the physical safety" of the student or other students may be found in a situation involving a student who is unimmunized against a dangerous and communicable disease and who, nevertheless, attends a school where presence of the disease is confirmed. In that situation, the unimmunized student's presence in school, exposing the student to the contagious disease, poses a clear threat to the student's health, that is, the student's physical safety, especially if there is a strong likelihood that the unimmunized student will contract the dangerous and communicable disease. Therefore, we hold that pursuant to §79-4,177(1)(b), attendance by a public school student at a school where presence of a dangerous and communicable disease is confirmed, when the student is unimmunized against the disease, is conduct that presents a clear threat to the physical safety of the unimmunized student and other students and allows the unimmunized student's exclusion from school. In Maacks' case, according to Dr. Morin, there was a "practically 100 percent infection rate" for the unimmunized Maack children, once they were exposed to measles. We need not further reiterate the remainder of Dr. Morin's testimony concerning the dire consequences of measles, condi-

tions, and complications that certainly and clearly constitute a serious threat to one unimmunized against the extremely contagious disease. For that reason, §79-4,177(1)(b) supplies authority for the Maack children's exclusion from school under the circumstances.

Next, Maacks argue, in substance, that §79-444.01, the immunization waiver statute, operates in absolute isolation from §79-4,177(1), the exclusionary statute, so that a child unimmunized against measles may attend school even during an outbreak of measles if there has been the appropriate waiver of immunization. The school district argues that the emergency situation of a measles epidemic authorizes exclusion of an unimmunized student pursuant to §79-4,177(1)(b) notwithstanding the immunization waiver provision of §79-444.01. . . .

In the present case, it is difficult to imagine, if not inconceivable, that the Legislature would intend to withhold, withdraw, or shackle a school district's authority to prevent a dangerous and communicable disease from endangering unimmunized students and spreading through classrooms. Consequently, we hold that pursuant to §§79-444.01 and 79-4,177(1) taken together, a school board may exclude an unimmunized student from school during presence of a disease specified by §79-444.01, despite a waiver of immunization in conformity with §79-444.01. Thus, an unimmunized student's right to attend school on presentation of a properly signed immunization waiver pursuant to §79-444.01 is limited by a school board's authority, under §79-4,177(1), to exclude the unimmunized student from school during presence of a disease specified by §79-444.01. The board of education of Lincoln Public Schools, that is, the board of education of School District No. 1 of Lancaster County, Nebraska, was authorized by §79-4,177(1)(b) to exclude Jessica and Melissa Maack under the circumstances.

The Maacks argue that their right to equal protection, guaranteed by the 14th Amendment to the U.S. Constitution, was violated when Lincoln Public Schools excluded unimmunized students at Lincoln East, while students in the following categories were not simultaneously excluded: (1) students at Lincoln East who were insufficiently immunized, namely, those vaccinated between the ages of 12 months and 15 months, and (2) the unimmunized students at the University of Nebraska–Lincoln.

"The Equal Protection Clause [of the 14th Amendment to the U.S. Constitution] does not forbid classifications. It simply keeps governmental decisionmakers from treating differently persons who are in all relevant respects alike." . . .

Since the classifications about which Maacks complain do not thwart the exercise of fundamental right nor present categories based on a constitutionally suspect characteristic, the classifications in Maacks' case are examined in reference to a rational basis test. When considered under a rational basis test, the classifications of excluded students do not violate Maacks' equal protection rights. The students at Lincoln East who are insufficiently immunized are not in all relevant respects the same as Jessica and Melissa Maack, because the insufficiently immunized, if exposed, have only a 15 percent chance of contracting measles, while unimmunized students, such as the Maacks, have a 100 percent chance of catching the disease.

The unimmunized students at the University of Nebraska–Lincoln are not in the same category of students or classification as the Maack children. Students at University of Nebraska–Lincoln, unlike students at Lincoln East, are not under the control of the board of education of Lincoln Public Schools. Since only the school board is a party to this action, classifications created by other state officials are outside the scope of our review.

As far as we can glean from the record, Maacks are trying to raise an issue involving due process relative to notice in the exclusionary action, hearing, and reviews of Lincoln Public Schools. However, Maacks do not argue any due process question in their appellate brief. Therefore, for this reason we do not consider any due process issue in the exclusionary action by the board of education of Lincoln Public Schools.

For the foregoing reasons, we find that Jessica and Melissa Maack's conduct in attending school during a measles outbreak without being immunized against measles posed a clear threat to themselves and other students. Consequently, the board of education of Lincoln Public Schools

was statutorily authorized to temporarily exclude the Maack children during the measles outbreak, and such exclusion did not violate the equal protection rights of Jessica and Melissa Maack. Therefore, we affirm the judgment of the district court.

Affirmed.

CASE NOTE

A statutory provision allowing exemption to parents who oppose immunization of their children for religious grounds does not extend to exemptions for persons whose opposition to vaccination is based purely on moral, medical, or scientific considerations, nor is exemption permitted for personal secular or philosophical beliefs. *Berg v. Glen Cove City School District*, 853 F.Supp. 651 (E.D.N.Y.1994).

■ ENDNOTES

1. Immanuel Kant, *The Metaphysics of Morals*, trans. Mary Gregor (Cambridge: Cambridge University Press, 1993), pp. 191–92.

2. Roger J. Sullivan, *Immanuel Kant's Moral Theory* (Cambridge: Cambridge University Press, 1995), p. 287.

3. Ibid.

4. R. Freeman Butts and Lawrence A. Cremin, *A History of Education in American Culture* (New York: Henry Holt and Company, 1953), p. 357.

5. Griffin v. County School Board of Prince Edward County, 377 U.S. 218, 84 S.Ct. 1226 (1964).

6. Plyler v. Doe, 457 U.S. 202, 102 S.Ct. 2382 (1982).

7. In the Matter of Proios, 111 Misc.2d 252, 443 N.Y.S.2d 828 (Sur.1981).

8. Martinez v. Bynum, 461 U.S. 321, 103 S.Ct. 1838 (1983).

9. Inhabitants of Warren v. Inhabitants of Thomaston, 43 Me. 406 (1857).

10. C. Vann Woodward, *Origins of the New South, 1877–1913* (Baton Rouge, La.: Louisiana State University Press, 1971), pp. 416–17.

11. *Manufacturer's Record*, XLII (August 28, 1902), pp. 93–95.

12. Milton and Rose Friedman, *Free to Choose* (New York: Harcourt Brace Jovanovich, 1980), pp. 162–63.

13. S. G. Messmer, "Compulsory Education," *American Ecclesiastical Review* 6 (1892): 279–98.

14. Ibid.

15. R. Freeman Butts and Lawrence A. Cremin, *A History of Education in American Culture* (New York: Henry Holt and Company, 1953), pp. 357–58.

16. 347 U.S. 483, 74 S.Ct. 686 (1954).

17. Acts of Assembly, Chapter 2, p. 4 (1959), repealing Virginia Code 1950 §22.251 to 22-275.

18. See Chapter 10, "Desegregation," of this book for more detail on desegregation; see also A. E. Dick Howard, Commentaries on the Constitution of Virginia (Charlottesville, Va.: University Press of Virginia, 1974), vol. 2, p. 893.

19. Strangway v. Allen, 194 Ky. 681, 240 S.W. 384 (1922).

20. County of McLean v. Humphrey, 104 Ill. 378 (1882).

21. In re Gault, 387 U.S. 1, 87 S.Ct. 1428 (1967).

22. Wisconsin v. Yoder, 406 U.S. 205, 92 S.Ct. 1526 (1972).

23. 371 U.S. 187, 83 S.Ct. 273 (1962).

24. 268 U.S. 510, 45 S.Ct. 571 (1925).

25. 321 U.S. 158, 166, 64 S.Ct. 438, 442 (1944).

26. Andrew Jay Kleinfeld, "The Balance of Power Among Infants, Their Parents and the State," *ABA Family Law Quarterly* 5 (1971): 107.

27. Salem Community School Corp. v. Easterly, 150 Ind. App. 11, 275 N.E.2d 317 (1971).

28. Kleinfeld, "The Balance of Power," p. 92.

29. Ibid., p. 93.

30. Morris v. Morris, 92 Ind.App. 65, 171 N.E. 386 (1930); Sisson v. Schultz, 251 Mich. 553, 232 N.W. 253 (1930).

31. Heffington v. Jackson and Norton, 43 Tex.Civ.App. 560, 96 S.W. 108 (1906).

32. Luques v. Luques, 127 Me. 356, 143 A. 263 (1928).

33. Hiram D. Gordon, "Terminal Placements of Children and Permanent Termination of Parental Rights: The New York Permanent Neglect Statute," *St. Johns Law Review* 46 (1971): 215.

34. Harvey J. Eger and Anthony J. Popeck, "The Abused Child: Problems and Proposals," *Duquesne Law Review* 8 (1969–70): 136.

35. State v. Perricone, 37 N.J. 463, 181 A.2d 751 (1962); People v. Pierson, 176 N.Y. 201, 68 N.E. 243 (1903).

36. Morrison v. State, 252 S.W.2d 97 (Mo.App.1952).

37. Massachusetts Gen.Laws Ann., ch. 272, §53 (1958).

38. See Alexander v. Bartlett, 14 Mich.App. 177, 165 N.W.2d 445 (1968).

39. 14 A.L.R.2d 1369; Knox v. O'Brien, 7 N.J.Super. 608, 72 A.2d 389 (1950).

40. State v. Whisner, 47 Ohio St.2d 181, 351 N.E.2d 750 (1976).

41. State v. Garber, 197 Kan. 567, 419 P.2d 896 (1966).

42. Murphy v. State of Arkansas, 852 F.2d 1039 (1988).

43. Ibid.

44. Ellis v. O'Hara, 612 F.Supp. 379 (E.D.Mo.1985).

45. Murphy v. State of Arkansas, 852 F.2d 1039 (1988).

46. Ibid.

47. Pierce v. Society of the Sisters of the Holy Names of Jesus and Mary, 268 U.S. 510, 45 S.Ct. 571 (1925).

48. Morris, op. cit.

49. Grosz v. City of Miami Beach, Florida, 721 F.2d 729 (11th Cir.1983).

50. State ex rel. Douglas v. Faith Baptist Church, 207 Neb. 802, 301 N.W.2d 571 (1981), appeal dismissed 454 U.S. 803, 102 S.Ct. 75 (1981).

51. State ex rel. Douglas v. Calvary Academy, 217 Neb. 450, 348 N.W.2d 898 (1984). See also McCurry v. Tesch, 738 F.2d 271 (8th Cir.1984).

52. Sheridan Road Baptist Church v. Department of Education, 132 Mich.App. 1, 348 N.W.2d 263 (1984).

53. Pierce, op. cit.

54. 293 U.S. 245, 55 S.Ct. 197 (1934).

55. Rice v. Commonwealth, 188 Va. 224, 49 S.E.2d 342, 3 A.L.R.2d 1392 (1948).

56. Commonwealth v. Bey, 57 York Leg.Rec. (Pa.) 200, 92 Pitts.Leg.J. 84 (1944).

57. See also in re Currence, 42 Misc.2d 418, 248 N.Y.S.2d 251 (1963). Here religious observance was no defense for withdrawing a boy from school weekly on Wednesday afternoons and Thursday mornings.

58. 406 U.S. 205, 92 S.Ct. 1526 (1972).

59. Fellowship Baptist Church v. Benton, 815 F.2d 485 (8th Cir.1987).

60. Ibid.

61. William M. Gordon, Charles J. Russos and Albert S. Miles, *The Law of Home Schooling* (Topeka, Kan.: National Organization on Legal Problems of Education, 1994), p. 3.

62. Null v. Board of Education of County of Jackson, 815 F.Supp. 937 (S.D.W.Va.1993).

63. Butts and Cremin, *A History of Education in American Culture*, p. 357.

64. Knox v. O'Brien, 7 N.J.Super. 608, 72 A.2d 389 (1950).

65. State v. Edgington, 99 N.M. 715, 663 P.2d 374 (1983).

66. State v. Bowman, 60 Or. App. 184, 653 P.2d 254 (1982).

67. Appeal of Pierce, 122 N.H. 762, 451 A.2d 363 (1982).

68. State v. Counort, 69 Wash. 361, 124 P. 910 (1912).

69. State v. Hoyt, 84 N.H. 38, 146 A. 170 (1929).

70. State v. Will, 99 Kan. 167, 160 P. 1025 (1916).

71. State v. Lowry, 191 Kan. 701, 383 P.2d 962 (1963).

72. People v. Turner, 121 Cal.App.Supp.2d 861, 263 P.2d 685 (1953).

73. State v. Peterman, 32 Ind.App. 665, 70 N.E. 550 (1904).

74. Sheppard v. State, 306 P.2d 346 (Okl.Crim.App.1957).

75. State v. Massa, 95 N.J.Super. 382, 231 A.2d 252 (1967).

76. Care and Protection of Charles, 399 Mass. 324, 504 N.E.2d 592 (1987).

77. In re Jeannette L., 71 Md.App. 70, 523 A.2d 1048 (1987).

78. Commonwealth v. Hall, 309 Pa.Super. 407, 455 A.2d 674 (1983).

79. State v. Turner, 9 Wn.2d 731, 658 P.2d 658 (1983).

80. People v. Berger, 109 Ill.App.3d 1054, 65 Ill.Dec.600, 441 N.E.2d 915 (1982).

81. State v. Priest, 210 La. 389, 27 So.2d 173 (1946).

82. In re State, 214 La. 1062, 39 So.2d 731 (1949).

83. In re Rogers, 36 Misc.2d 680, 234 N.Y.S.2d 172 (1962).

84. Jacobson v. Commonwealth of Massachusetts, 197 U.S. 11, 25 S.Ct. 358 (1905).

85. Ibid., p. 364.

86. Blue v. Beach, 155 Ind. 121, 56 N.E. 89 (1900); Morris v. Columbus, 102 Ga. 792, 30 S.E. 850 (1898); State v. Hay, 126 N.C. 999, 35 S.E. 459 (1900); Abeel v. Clark, 84 Cal. 226, 24 P. 383 (1890); Bissell v. Davison, 65 Conn. 183, 32 A. 348 (1894); Hazen v. Strong, 2 Vt. 427 (1830); Duffield v. School Dist. of Williamsport, 162 Pa. 476, 29 A. 742 (1894).

87. 179 N.Y. 235, 72 N.E. 97 (1904).

88. People v. McIlwain, 151 N.Y.S. 366 (1915).

89. People v. Ekerold, 211 N.Y. 386, 105 N.E. 670 (1914).

90. 310 U.S. 296, 60 S.Ct. 900, 128 ALR 1352 (1940).

91. Yoder, op. cit.

92. State v. Drew, 89 N.H. 54, 192 A. 629 (1937).

93. Board of Education of Mountain Lakes v. Maas, 56 N.J. Super. 245, 152 A.2d 394 (App. Div. 1959).

94. 215 Pa. 156, 64 A. 419 (1906).

95. Hill v. Bickers, 171 Ky. 703, 188 S.W. 766 (1916).

96. Board of Trustees v. McMurtry, 169 Ky. 457, 184 S.W. 390 (1916).

97. Mosier v. Barren County Board of Health, 308 Ky. 829, 215 S.W.2d 967 (1948).

98. Potts v. Breen, 167 Ill. 67, 47 N.E. 81 (1897); People ex rel. Labaugh v. Board of Education of District No. 2, 177 Ill. 572, 52 N.E. 850 (1899).

CHAPTER 7

THE INSTRUCTIONAL PROGRAM

[There] is a close link between evolution of knowledge and moral progress. As we become more intelligent we become more moral.

—Owen Chadwick, *The Secularization of the European Mind in the Nineteenth Century,* 1975.

CHAPTER OUTLINE

- Robust Exchange of Ideas
- Judges Not Education Experts
- Curriculum and the Pall of Orthodoxy
- Obscenity and Sex
- Evolution versus Creationism
- Student Testing and Promotion
- Grading and Academic Requirements
- Bilingual Education Programs

As A GENERAL RULE, the precedents of the U.S. Supreme Court have fostered openness and expansiveness of knowledge preventing both the purveyors of knowledge as well as the recipients from limiting inquiry or restraining access to information. Students are possessed with fundamental rights that the state must protect, and the students themselves must respect their obligations to the state.[1] The Supreme Court in *Tinker* addressed this relationship between the state and the student, saying: "In our system, students may not be regarded as closed-circuit recipients of only that which the State chooses to communicate. They may not be confined to the expression of those sentiments that are officially approved."[2] On the other hand, it is within the prerogative of the State to determine what the school curriculum shall be. The state must ultimately decide what is being taught and the methodology for teaching so long as the freedoms of teachers and students are not offended.

This view was most succinctly expressed by one federal court when it said that "[t]he boundaries of expressive conduct have been particularly cabined when the conduct is associated with school curricula."[3] The state, as the sovereign, possesses the authority to prescribe the curriculum and prescribe the conditions under which the knowledge is to be conveyed.

Upon entering a public school, a child becomes subject to state and local administrative regulations, as well as to state laws governing public education. These regulations are an exercise of state police power, which is the inherent sovereign power allowing the state to provide for the health, safety, and well-being of its citizens. Such provisions establish the framework within which each child is afforded a free public education.

Education may be viewed differently by educators, parents, students, or various special interest groups, but few would argue that a public education program should not be expansive and broadening of one's perspective and knowledge. The public school has been quite accurately defined as a "marketplace of ideas."

■ ROBUST EXCHANGE OF IDEAS

The critical position of education in a democratic society is self-evident. Over the years the courts have come to conclude that society is best served by an educational system that teaches "through wide exposure to that robust exchange of ideas which discovers truth 'out of a multitude of tongues' [rather] than through any kind of authoritative selection."[4] Thus, because of the importance of the schools and because this "robust exchange of ideas" is so vital to the educational process, the perpetuation of that exchange is, at all levels of the educational system, "a special concern of the First Amendment."[5] No school can function as a marketplace of ideas unless both students and faculty enjoy an atmosphere conducive to debate and scholarly inquiry.[6] The First Amendment not only creates a marketplace of intellectual ideas for the students, but also benefits the teacher in the presentation of ideas.

Courts have, thus, generally given wide latitude to the state in matters involving the educational program. In one notable case in Michigan, parents sought a *writ of mandamus* to prevent using the novel *Slaughterhouse Five* as a part of the instructional program. The parents alleged that the material was obscene, profane, and repugnant to the religious provisions of the First Amendment.

The court, in an exposition on the law, first observed that, although there may have been religious references in the work, the book itself did not violate the students' and parents' religious freedom. To declare otherwise, the court concluded, would censor and prevent the public schools from making use of many great works of the past:

> If plaintiffs' contention was correct, then public school students could no longer marvel at Sir Galahad's saintly quest for the Holy Grail, nor be introduced to the dangers of Hitler's *Mein Kampf* nor read the mellifluous poetry of John Milton and John Donne. Unhappily, Robin Hood would be forced to forage without Friar Tuck and Shakespeare would have to delete Shylock from *The Merchant of Venice*. Is this to be the state of our law? Our Constitution does not command ignorance; on the contrary, it assures the people that the state may not relegate them to such a status and guarantees to all the precious and unfettered freedom of pursuing one's own intellectual pleasures in one's own personal way.[7]

■ JUDGES NOT EDUCATION EXPERTS

Even more to the point, the Michigan court in this case observed that the judges are not to be the experts in what educational programs are offered in the schools. Citing Justice Brennan's admonition in *Schempp*,[8] the court contended that curriculum determination should be entrusted to the experienced school officials of the nation's public schools and not to the judges. The appellate court reprimanded the lower trial court for imposing its judgment of "right" and "morality" over that of the school authorities. Such action by a court was forbidden by the state constitution and a matter for the lawfully elected school board to determine. The appellate court concluded that the judicial censor was *persona non grata* in the formation of public education curriculum policies.

Because the public school is a creature of the legislature,[9] and the local school board is the recipient of governance powers delegated by the legislature, the school board occupies a critical juncture in the free flow of ideas and information.[10]

The educational program of the public school has both academic and disciplinary aspects. Courts have been very hesitant to enter into the academic arena. The position of the courts is stated by the United States Supreme Court in a higher education case that has applicability for elementary and secondary school operation. In *Horowitz*, the Court said:

> Academic evaluations of a student, in contrast to disciplinary determinations, bear little resemblance to the judicial and administrative fact-finding proceedings to which we have traditionally attached a full learning requirement. . . . Like the decision of an individual professor as to the proper grade for a student in his course, the determination whether

to dismiss a student for academic reasons requires expert evaluation of cumulative information and is not readily adapted to the procedural tools of judicial or administrative decisionmaking. . . . Courts are particularly ill-equipped to evaluate academic performance.[11]

The courts have generally supported school boards when the schools have expanded the school program or introduced innovative curricula. Thus far, the courts have agreed that the school has the power to regulate and develop curricula for the well-being of the students. These cases also remind us that not all parental discontent is aimed at broadening student knowledge and choice. In many instances, parents seek to restrict or "contract the spectrum of knowledge." As a result, the courts will tend to weigh parental grievances very carefully, even when a parent feels that a constitutional right is being offended.

This judicial position has been demonstrated when a school board sought to reduce the length of the school day, thereby restricting the educational program. For lack of funds, the school board decided to hold one-half-day sessions and to teach certain subjects on a compressed schedule.[12] The Supreme Court of Michigan decided that in the absence of state board regulations limiting local school board authority in this area, the reduction in the school program was valid.

Although the content of the school program itself is an area of concern to parents, an even more direct concern is the placement of their children. Aside from the recent statutory emphasis and litigation dealing with handicapped children, much of the controversy between parent and school has arisen during the child's first few years of schooling. It is at this level of early childhood education that the parent and the child experience the separation of the child from the home, a particularly sensitive time for parents.

In one such New York State case, a mother petitioned the court for an order directing the board of education to admit her son to the first grade.[13] Previously, the boy had established an unenviable reputation as a "disciplinary problem." The school had demoted the boy from the first grade back to kindergarten, an action the parent maintained was arbitrary, capricious, unreasonable, and in violation of the Fourteenth

Amendment and the New York Constitution. The board defended itself by maintaining the school principal had made an "educational decision" based on the boy's inability to perform first-grade work, his test results, and his lack of self-control. The petitioner was unable to rebut the test results. The court held that the placement of the child was within the school's authority to provide rules and regulations for promotion from grade to grade, based not on age but on training, knowledge, and ability.[14]

In a similar New York State decision, the parents of a five-year-old child sought to compel the school board to accept the child into the first grade.[15] According to New York law, a five-year-old is entitled to attend public schools, and the boy's parents claimed that kindergarten was not the public schools. The court disagreed with the parents, holding that when a kindergarten is established it becomes a part of the public school system. Since the boy was already in public school, the court maintained, the parents had no right to insist that the boy be admitted to a particular grade or class in the public school.

Most precedents indicate that the courts, though sympathetic with the intentions of the parent, generally defer to authorized and trained educational experts in matters of school policy. In recent years, however, there has been a greater tendency by the courts to delve deeper into the justification and rationale supporting educational policy. School authorities, therefore, are well advised to document placement and curriculum decisions with solid educational rationale. However, the collective judgment of the school does hold substantial influence with the courts.

LIMITATION ON STATE POWER

Although the school has generally prevailed in curriculum and placement disputes with parents, the state's power is by no means absolute. Where legitimate constitutional concerns are present, the courts stand ready to invalidate the offending regulations, particularly if the action of the school, as a state agency, tends to contract rather than expand knowledge. Such judicial intervention is not uncommon and has been demonstrated in several notable U.S. Supreme Court cases.[16]

One such defining case was *Meyer v. Nebraska*, 1923, which emanated from a national response to World War I that saw several states enact anti-German legislation. The war created an unusual spirit of nationalism and an environment in which suspicion of foreign influence was of paramount concern. Even President Wilson declared in his 1917 war message to Congress that a war effort required "a firm hand of stern responsibility,"[17] to curtail domestic disloyalty. Strong words. At Wilson's request Congress imposed a military draft, enacted an Espionage Act that authorized the denaturalization and deportation of foreign-born radicals, and made it a criminal offense to obstruct recruitment of troops or to cause military insubordination. The federal Justice Department interpreted the Espionage Act to permit censorship of statements critical of the war effort, and the postal service revoked mailing privileges for publications that could "embarrass or hamper the government in conducting the war."[18]

As the intensity of anti-German feelings increased during the war, Congress responded in 1918 by expanding the Espionage Act to prohibit "disloyal" or "abusive" statements about the American form of government.[19] It was these events that led to the Supreme Court's famous precedent in 1919 upholding the conviction of the socialist leader Charles T. Schenck for encouraging draft-age men to resist conscription. In this era of war-induced extremes, education was naturally affected. State governments followed the national example of restriction on speech and liberty by enacting legislation designed to induce and enhance a greater nationalistic spirit of the citizenry. In *Schenck*, the great Supreme Court Justice Oliver Wendell Holmes said in a much-quoted passage, upholding the Act, that the question is whether the words uttered "are of such a nature to create a clear and present danger," if so the conviction will stand.[20]

Notable among these types of war statutes at the state level was prohibition of the teaching of German in all schools, both public and private. Yet, by the time such state legislation was challenged before the U.S. Supreme Court in 1923, the fear of war had subsided, the Treaty of Versailles had been signed, and the country had assumed a more balanced view of civil liberties and freedom of speech and expression. It was in this new and more tolerant postwar period that the Supreme Court examined the anti-German school legislation in *Meyer v. Nebraska* and found it to be impermissible as violative of the due process clause of the Fourteenth Amendment. Two other cases, *Bartels* from Iowa[21] and *Bohning* from Ohio,[22] raised essentially the same issues as were litigated in Nebraska, and the Supreme Court ruled accordingly. These cases were meaningful because they formed the constitutional rationale for invoking a substantive aspect of the due process clause to protect civil liberties and freedoms. (See Chapter 8 for a more complete explanation of substantive due process.) After *Meyer*, any state legislation that constricted the flow of information or knowledge became suspect as having the potential to offend due process.

❖ — ❖ — ❖

Board Has the Power to Enforce Reasonable Rules Prescribing Specific Curriculum

State ex rel. Andrews v. Webber

Supreme Court of Indiana, 1886.
108 Ind. 31, 8 N.E. 708.

HOWK, C.J. . . . The relator . . . said that he was the father and natural guardian of one Abram Andrew, who was a white male child, between the ages of six and twenty-one years, to-wit, of the age of twelve years. . . . The said Abram Andrew being sufficiently advanced in his studies, in accordance with the relator's desire and consent, and in compliance with his legal rights in the premises, was admitted as a pupil in such high school, to receive instruction therein, and thereafter, until his suspension, as hereinafter stated, was regular in his attendance and deportment, and was obedient and respectful to his teachers, and properly subordinate to the rules and regulations of such school; that among the exercises prescribed by such superintendent, with the sanction of such board of trustees, for the pupils of the high school, was a requirement that each of the pupils should, at stated intervals, employ a certain period of time in the study and practice of music, and that they should provide themselves with prescribed books for that purpose; that the relator, believing it was not for the best interest of said Abram Andrew, and not in accordance with the relator's wishes regarding the instruction of his said son, in a respectful manner asked of such superintendent that Abram Andrew might be excused from the study and practice of music at such exercises, and directed Abram Andrew not to participate therein, all in good faith, and in a respectful manner, and with no intention of in any manner interfering with the government, rules, and regulations of such schools, except in so far as he might legally control and direct the education of his said son, which purpose and desire were fully communicated by him to such superintendent.

But the relator said that, notwithstanding his said desire and request so communicated to such superintendent as aforesaid, the superintendent, on or about the fourteenth day of October, 1885, in disregard of the relator's wishes and request, required said Abram Andrew to participate in the practice and study of music, and upon the refusal of said Abram Andrew to participate in such exercises and study, which he did without disrespect to such superintendent, and entirely because of the relator's direction, which was so communicated to such superintendent as aforesaid, the superintendent suspended said Abram Andrew from such school, without assigning any cause therefore. . . .

This action is brought by the father and natural guardian of the suspended pupil, to compel, by mandate, the governing authorities of the school corporation to revoke such suspension, and to readmit such pupil to the high school.

The question for our decision in this case, as it seems to us, may be thus stated: Is the rule or regulation for the government of the pupils of the high school of the school city of La Porte, in relation to the study and practice of music, a valid and reasonable exercise of the discretionary power conferred by law upon the governing authorities of such school corporation? In section 4497, Rev.St.1881, in force since August 16, 1869, it is provided as follows: "The common schools of the state shall be taught in the English language; and the trustee shall provide to have

taught in them orthography, reading, writing, arithmetic, geography, English grammar, physiology, history of the United States, and good behavior, and such other branches of learning, and other languages, as the advancement of pupils may require, and the trustees from time to time direct." Under this statutory provision and others of similar purport and effect, to be found in our school laws, it was competent, we think, for the trustees of the school city of La Porte to enact necessary and reasonable rules for the government of the pupils of its high school, directing what branches of learning such pupils should pursue, and regulating the time to be given to any particular study, and prescribing what book or books should be used therein. Such trustees were and are required, by the express provisions of section 4444, Rev.St.1881, in force since March 8, 1873, to "take charge of the educational affairs" of such city of La Porte; "they may also establish graded schools, or such modifications of them as may be practicable, and provide for admitting into the higher departments of the graded school, from the primary schools of their townships, such pupils as are sufficiently advanced for such admission."

The power to establish graded schools carries with it, of course, the power to establish and enforce such reasonable rules as may seem necessary to the trustees, in their discretion, for the government and discipline of such schools, and prescribing the course of instruction therein. Confining our opinion strictly to the case in hand, we will consider and decide these two questions, in the order of their statement, namely: (1) Has the appellant's relator shown, by the averments of his verified complaint, that the rule or regulation for the government of the pupils of the high school, in the school city of La Porte, of which he complains, was or is an unreasonable exercise of the discretionary power conferred by law upon the trustees of such school corporation and the superintendent of its schools? (2) Conceding or assuming such rule or regulation to be reasonable and valid, has the relator shown, in his complaint herein, any sufficient or satisfactory excuse for the noncompliance therewith, and the disobedience thereof, of his son, Abram Andrew, a pupil of such high school, or any sufficient or legal ground for the revocation of the suspension of his son, or for his son's readmission, as a pupil in such high school?

As to the first of these questions . . . we think that the legislature has given the trustees of the public school corporations the discretionary power to direct, from time to time, what branches of learning, in addition to those specified in the statute, shall be taught in the public schools of their respective corporations. Where such trustees may have established a system of graded schools, or such modifications of them as may be practicable, within their respective corporations, they are clothed by law with the discretionary power to prescribe the course of instruction in the different grades of their public schools. We are of opinion that the rule or regulation of which the relator complains in the case under consideration was within the discretionary power conferred by law upon the governing authorities of the school city of La Porte; that it was not an unreasonable rule; but that it was such a one as each pupil of the high school, in the absence of sufficient excuse, might lawfully be required to obey and comply with. . . .

. . . The only cause or reason assigned by the relator for requiring his son to disobey such rule or regulation was that he did not believe it was for the best interest of his son to participate in the musical studies and exercises of the high school, and did not wish him to do so. The relator has assigned no cause or reason, and it may be fairly assumed that he had none, in support either of his belief or his wish. The important question arises, which should govern the public high school of the city of La Porte, as to the branches of learning to be taught and the course of instruction therein,—the school trustees of such city, to whom the law has confided the direction of these matters, or the mere arbitrary will of the relator, without cause or reason in its support? We are of opinion that only one answer can or ought to be given to this question. The arbitrary wishes of the relator in the premises must yield and be subordinated to the governing authorities of the school city of La Porte, and their reasonable rules and regulations for the government of the pupils of its high school. . . .

For the reasons given, our conclusion is that no error was committed by the court below in sustaining appellees' demurrer to the relator's complaint.

The judgment is affirmed, with costs.

<hr />

Denial of Promotion for Failure to Complete Requisite Reading Level Does Not Violate Constitutional Rights

Sandlin v. Johnson

United States Court of Appeals,
Fourth Circuit, 1981.
643 F.2d 1027.

MURNAGHAN, Circuit Judge. Four second-grade students filed the case as a class action on behalf of themselves and eighteen other similarly situated second graders against the principal of their school, and the superintendent of schools and school board of Pittsylvania County, Virginia. Plaintiffs attended the Whitmell Elementary School. Only one member of their class was promoted to the third grade at the end of the 1977–1978 school year. The stated and undisputed ground for denial of promotion was the students' failure to complete the requisite level of the Ginn Reading Series. While plaintiffs do not deny that they failed to demonstrate the required reading level, they argue that they are nevertheless capable of reading at the third-grade level. They sued pursuant to 42 U.S.C. §1983 claiming a denial of equal protection of the law because, as their Complaint had it:

> By either the defendants' negligent and careless supervision of the instruction of plaintiffs or by their arbitrary and negligent grading and classification of these plaintiffs, plaintiffs have been effectively denied third-grade educational opportunities commensurate with their abilities and in accord with educational opportunities provided other students similarly situated in the Pittsylvania County School System.

Plaintiffs contended that defendants' actions damaged them by delaying the completion of their education and their obtaining employment, by foreclosing "certain lucrative employment . . . because of a lack of education provided them commensurate with their abilities," and by burdening them with the stigma of failure. . . .

Defendants responded that they had provided equal opportunities to plaintiffs, that while plaintiffs' intelligence was such that they were capable of reading at the third-grade level, they had failed to progress to that level of mastery, and that promoting plaintiffs before they had mastered the requisite reading skills would be counterproductive and would increase plaintiffs' reading deficiencies. . . .

There is no allegation in the case that plaintiffs were classified on the basis of race or any other basis calling for heightened scrutiny, i.e., religious affiliation, alienage, illegitimacy, gender or wealth. Nor is public education a fundamental right which would trigger strict scrutiny of claims of denial of equal protection. Thus, in reviewing the equal protection claim, the only question, as recognized by all parties, is whether the classification by the governmental entity which is at issue here is rationally related to a permissible governmental end.

Defendants here classified plaintiffs according to their attained reading level. The stated purpose for the classification was to enable the school to provide students with the level of instruction most appropriate to their abilities and needs. The objective was to further the education, the preparation for life of the plaintiffs. The governmental end is a permissible one, and defendants' classification scheme is clearly rationally related to achieving it. Defendants, therefore, have not implicated any constitutional right of plaintiffs by classifying them according to their reading level.

Plaintiffs also claim that defendants or the teachers under their supervision negligently and carelessly failed to ensure that plaintiffs were properly and appropriately taught. What appellants denominate a denial of equal educational opportunity sounds rather in tort as a breach of some duty owed by teachers or school boards to their pupils to give them an education. If there is any such cause of action, it does not rise to the level of a constitutional claim and, therefore, is not cognizable in an action pursuant to 42 U.S.C. §1983. . . .

Decisions by educational authorities which turn on evaluation of the academic performance of a student as it relates to promotion are peculiarly within the expertise of educators and are particularly inappropriate for review in a judicial context. ("We decline to further enlarge the judicial presence in the academic community and thereby risk deterioration of many beneficial aspects of the faculty-student relationship.") We, therefore, affirm the district court's dismissal.

Affirmed. (Held for the school board.)

❖ — ❖ — ❖

Statute Prohibiting Teaching of Foreign Language Violates Substantive Due Process

Meyer v. Nebraska

Supreme Court of the United States, 1923.
262 U.S. 390, 43 S.Ct. 625.

Mr. Justice McREYNOLDS delivered the opinion of the Court. Plaintiff in error was tried and convicted in the district court for Hamilton county, Nebraska, under an information which charged that on May 25, 1920, while an instructor in Zion Parochial School he unlawfully taught the subject of reading in the German language to Raymond Parpart, a child of ten years, who had not attained and successfully passed the eighth grade. The information is based upon "An act relating to the teaching of foreign languages in the state of Nebraska," approved April 9, 1919 (Laws 1919, c. 249), which follows:

> Section 1. No person, individually or as a teacher, shall, in any private, denominational, parochial or public school, teach any subject to any person in any language than the English language.
> Sec. 2. Languages other than the English language, may be taught as languages only after a pupil shall have attained and successfully passed the eighth grade as evidenced by a certificate of graduation issued by the county superintendent of the county in which the child resides.

. . . The Supreme Court of the state affirmed the judgment of conviction. It declared the offense charged and established was "the direct and intentional teaching of the German language as a distinct subject to a child who had not passed the eighth grade," in the parochial school maintained by Zion Evangelical Lutheran Congregation, a collection of Biblical stories being used therefore. And it held that the statute forbidding this did not conflict with the Fourteenth Amendment, but was a valid exercise of the police power. The following excerpts from the opinion sufficiently indicate the reasons advanced to support the conclusion.

> The salutary purpose of the statute is clear. The Legislature had seen the baneful effects of permitting foreigners, who had taken residence in this country, to rear and educate their children in the language of their native land. The result of that condition was found to be inimical to our own safety. To allow the children of foreigners, who had emigrated here, to be taught from early childhood the language of the country of their parents was to rear them with that language as their mother tongue. It was to educate them so that they must always think in that language, and, as a consequence, naturally inculcate in them the ideas and sentiments foreign to the best interests of this country. The statute, therefore, was intended not only to require that the education of all children be conducted in the English language, but that, until they had grown into that language and until it had become a part of them, they should not in the schools be taught any other language. The obvious purpose of the statute was that the English language should be and become the mother tongue of all children reared in this state. The enactment of such a statute comes reasonably within the police power of the state. . . .

. . . The problem for our determination is whether the statute as construed and applied unreasonably infringes the liberty guaranteed to the plaintiff in error by the Fourteenth Amendment. "No state . . . shall deprive any person of life, liberty or property without due process of law."

While this court has not attempted to define with exactness the liberty thus guaranteed, the term has received much consideration and some of the included things have been definitely stated. Without doubt, it denotes not merely freedom from bodily restraint but also the right of the individual to contract, to engage in any of the common occupations of life, to acquire useful knowledge, to marry, establish a home and bring up children, to worship God according to the dictates of his own conscience, and generally to enjoy those privileges long recognized at common law as essential to the orderly pursuit of happiness by free men. . . . The established

doctrine is that this liberty may not be interfered with, under the guise of protecting the public interest, by legislative action which is arbitrary or without reasonable relation to some purpose within the competency of the state to effect. Determination by the Legislature of what constitutes proper exercise of police power is not final or conclusive but is subject to supervision by the courts. . . .

The American people have always regarded education and acquisition of knowledge as matters of supreme importance which should be diligently promoted. The Ordinance of 1787 declares: "Religion, morality and knowledge being necessary to good government and the happiness of mankind, schools and the means of education shall forever be encouraged." Corresponding to the right of control, it is the natural duty of the parent to give his children education suitable to their station in life; and nearly all the states, including Nebraska, enforce this obligation by compulsory laws.

Practically, education of the young is only possible in schools conducted by especially qualified persons who devote themselves thereto. The calling always has been regarded as useful and honorable, essential, indeed, to the public welfare. Mere knowledge of the German language cannot reasonably be regarded as harmful. Heretofore it has been commonly looked upon as helpful and desirable. Plaintiff in error taught this language in school as part of his occupation. His right thus to teach and the right of parents to engage him so to instruct their children, we think, are within the liberty of the amendment. . . .

That the state may do much, go very far, indeed, in order to improve the quality of its citizens, physically, mentally and morally, is clear; but the individual has certain fundamental rights which must be respected. The protection of the Constitution extends to all, to those who speak other languages as well as to those born with English on the tongue. Perhaps it would be highly advantageous if all had ready understanding of our ordinary speech, but this cannot be coerced by methods which conflict with the Constitution—a desirable end cannot be promoted by prohibited means. . . .

The power of the State to compel attendance at some school and to make reasonable regulations for all schools, including a requirement that they shall given instructions in English, is not questioned. Nor has challenge been made of the State's power to prescribe a curriculum for institutions which it supports. Those matters are not within the present controversy. Our concern is with the prohibition approved by the Supreme Court. *Adams v. Tanner*, 244 U.S. 594, 37 S.Ct. 662, 61 L.Ed. 1336, pointed out that mere abuse incident to an occupation ordinarily useful is not enough to justify its abolition, although regulation may be entirely proper. No emergency has arisen which renders knowledge by a child of some language other than English so clearly harmful as to justify its inhibition with the consequent infringement of rights long freely enjoyed. We are constrained to conclude that the statute as applied is arbitrary and without reasonable relation to any end within the competency of the State.

As the statute undertakes to interfere only with teaching which involves a modern language, leaving complete freedom as to other matters, there seems no adequate foundation for the suggestion that the purpose was to protect the child's health by limiting his mental activities. It is well known that proficiency in a foreign language seldom comes to one not instructed at an early age, and experience shows that this is not injurious to the health, morals or understanding of the ordinary child.

The judgment of the court below must be reversed and the cause remanded for further proceedings not inconsistent with this opinion.

Reversed.

CASE NOTE

Meyer, along with the *Pierce* case (Chapter 6 of this text), both indicate the primacy of the parents in "the custody, care and nurture" of their own children. But this right over the child does not give the parent a license to restrict or control what is offered in the public school curriculum to other children.

The U.S. Court of Appeals, First Circuit, in a 1995 decision explained the limits of parental rights in this way.

> The *Meyer* and *Pierce* cases, we think, evince the principle that the state cannot prevent parents from choosing a specific educational program—

whether it be religious instruction at a private school or instruction in a foreign language. That is, the state does not have the power to "standardize its children" or "foster a homogenous people" by completely foreclosing the opportunity of individuals and groups to choose a different path of education. We do not think, however, that this freedom encompasses a fundamental constitutional right to dictate the curriculum at the public school to which they have chosen to send their children. We think it is fundamentally different for the state to say to a parent, "You can't teach your child German or send him to a parochial school," than for the parent to say to the state, "You can't teach my child subjects that are morally offensive to me." The first instance involves the state proscribing parents from educating their children, while the second involves parents prescribing what the state shall teach their children. If all parents had a fundamental constitutional right to dictate individually what the schools teach their children, the schools would be forced to cater a curriculum for each student whose parents had genuine moral disagreements with the school's choice of subject matter. We cannot see that the Constitution imposes such a burden on state educational systems, and accordingly find that the rights of parents as described by *Meyer* and *Pierce* do not encompass a broad-based right to restrict the flow of information in the public schools.

Brown v. Hot, Sexy and Safer Productions, Inc., 68 F.3d 525, at 533 (1st Cir.1995).

Mandatory Community Service as a Graduation Requirement Does Not Violate Students' Constitutional Rights

Steirer by Steirer v. Bethlehem Area School District

United States Court of Appeals,
Third Circuit, 1993.
987 F.2d 989.

SLOVITER, Chief Judge.

May a public high school constitutionally require its students to complete sixty hours of community service before graduation? On this issue of first impression for an appellate court, plaintiffs, two high school students and their parents, argue that the mandatory community service program compels expression in violation of the First and Fourteenth Amendments and constitutes involuntary servitude in violation of the Thirteenth Amendment. The district court rejected both challenges. We have jurisdiction under 28 U.S.C. §1291 (1988).

The facts are not in dispute. On April 30, 1990, the Bethlehem Area School District, by a majority vote of its Board of Directors, adopted a graduation requirement that every public high school student, except those in special education classes, complete a total of sixty hours of community service during the student's four years of high school. These hours may be completed after school hours, on weekends, or during the summer. Students must complete this requirement through participation in a course entitled the "Community Service Program" (the Program), which requires them to "perform sixty (60) hours of unpaid service to organizations or experiential situations approved by the Bethlehem Area School District." . . .

The stated goal of the Program is to "help students acquire life skills and learn about the significance of rendering services to their communities . . . [and] gain a sense of worth and pride as they understand and appreciate the functions of community organizations." . . . The four objectives of the Program are described in the Curriculum Course Guide as:

1. Students will understand their responsibilities as citizens in dealing with community issues.
2. Students will know that their concern about people and events in the community can have positive effects.
3. Students will develop pride in assisting others.
4. Students will provide services to the community without receiving pay.

As an alternative to providing service to an approved community service organization, a student may choose to participate in an "experiential situation." . . . This option allows a student to "develop [his or her] own individual community service experience." . . . This alternative experience requires parental approval, the recommendation of the school counselor,

and verification by a responsible adult. . . . It may involve the arts, community special events, aid to the elderly, the handicapped or the homeless, emergency services, the environment, library/historical research, recreation activities, or tutoring. . . .

After completing the sixty hours of community service, the student must complete a written Experience Summary Form describing and evaluating his or her community service activity. Once the school counsel (i) certifies that the sixty hours of service were completed; and (ii) reviews and approves the student's Experience Summary Form, the student receives half a unit of course credit and a grade of Satisfactory (S). A student who does not satisfactorily complete the Program will not receive a high school diploma.

Barbara and Thomas Steirer and Thomas and Barbara Moralis, individually and as parents and guardians of Lynn Ann Steirer and David Stephen Moralis, respectively, and their two children brought suit in federal district court challenging the constitutionality of the Program and seeking a permanent injunction against its enforcement. Although both minor plaintiffs have performed and intend to continue performing volunteer work on their own time, they object to being forced to engage in community service as a graduation requirement. . . .

The district court granted summary judgment for defendants on plaintiffs' First Amendment claim on the ground that the community service required by the school district is nonexpressive conduct. Plaintiffs contend on appeal that performing mandatory community service is expressive conduct because it forces them to declare a belief in the value of altruism. Proceeding on this premise, plaintiffs argue that heightened scrutiny should be applied and that the school board's reasons for making the program mandatory are not sufficiently compelling to outweigh the infringement of the students' First Amendment right to refrain from expressing such a belief.

The freedom of speech protected by the First Amendment, though not absolute, "includes both the right to speak freely and the right to refrain from speaking at all." . . .

To support their position that the required community service is expressive of the school district's ideological viewpoint favoring altruism, plaintiffs point to statements made by individual members of the school board expressing a favorable view of altruism. Plaintiffs argue that the ideology of altruism is a matter of opinion not shared by all, and that "when a student goes out and works for others in his community, it is natural for an observer to assume that the student supports the idea that helping others and serving the community are desirable." . . . Thus, plaintiffs conclude, a student who participates in the community service program is being forced to engage in expressive conduct.

We may assume *arguendo* that the members of the school board who approved the mandatory community service program believed that there was a value in community service, and that this belief may be equated with what plaintiffs choose to call the philosophy of altruism. It does not follow that requiring students to engage in a limited period of community service as an experiential program that is part of the school curriculum is constitutionally invalid. The gamut of courses in a school's curriculum necessarily reflects the value judgments of those responsible for its development, yet requiring students to study course materials, write papers on the subjects, and take the examinations is not prohibited by the First Amendment.

The Supreme Court has noted that "[s]tates and local school boards are generally afforded considerable discretion in operating public schools," *Edwards v. Aguillard,* 482 U.S. 578, 583, 107 S.Ct. 2573, 2577, 96 L.Ed.2d 510 (1987), and it has discouraged judicial intervention in the day-to-day operation of public schools. . . .

On the other hand, we do not accept the suggestion made by defendants at oral argument that once the educational purpose of the Program is established, the Program is *ipso facto* constitutional. Even "teaching values" must conform to constitutional standards. The constitutional line is crossed when, instead of merely teaching, the educators demand that students express agreement with the educators' values. . . .

Thus, the question presented by this appeal is whether the performance of community service as a required school program carries with it the same "affirmation of a belief and an attitude of mind" that is a prerequisite for First Amendment protection. . . . Unlike the act of commu-

nity service, the activity involved in cases holding compelled conduct to be violative of the First Amendment included an obviously expressive element. . . .

Specifically, the actor must have "[a]n intent to convey a particularized message . . . and in the surrounding circumstances the likelihood [must be] great that the message would be understood by those who viewed it." . . . Thus, in deciding whether conduct is expressive, we must look to the nature of the activity in conjunction with the factual context and environment in which it is undertaken.

The significance for First Amendment purposes of the viewer's perception is readily apparent in the holdings of the Court that protected expressive conduct includes wearing a black arm band to protest the Vietnam war, . . . burning a draft card to protest the war, . . . demonstrating on the grounds of a state capitol, . . . a civil rights march, . . . leafletting, . . . and labor picketing. . . .

However, while acknowledging that the First Amendment protects more than "pure" speech, the Supreme Court has also consistently rejected the view that "an apparently limitless variety of conduct can be labeled 'speech' whenever the person engaging in the conduct intends thereby to express an idea." . . .

Nonetheless, we do not discount entirely the possibility that a school-imposed requirement of community service could, in some contexts, implicate First Amendment considerations. Arguably, a student who was required to provide community service to an organization whose message conflicted with the student's contrary view could make that claim. Plaintiffs in this case do not make that argument, and the record is to the contrary. The Program does not limit students to providing service to a particular type of community service organization. Students have a multitude of service options which allows them to provide services to organizations with a wide-range of political, religious, and moral views. Activities range from playing in a band to walking a dog for the SPCA. . . . The list of approved organizations is extensive and open to additions. Furthermore, students are free to design their own experiential situations. . . .

There is no basis in the record to support the argument that the students who participate in the program are obliged to express their belief, either orally or in writing, in the value of community service. Thus, they are not "confined to the expression of those sentiments that are officially approved." . . . To the contrary, as plaintiff Thomas Moralis admitted in his deposition, there is no indication that a student who criticized the Program would not receive a passing grade. Nothing in the record contradicts Moralis' understanding that the students who participate in the Program need not express their agreement with its objectives in order to receiving a passing grade.

Finally, plaintiffs have produced no evidence that people in the community who see these students performing community service are likely to perceive their actions as an intended expression of a particularized message of their belief in the value of community service and altruism. We cannot accept plaintiffs' *ipse dixit*. It is just as likely that students performing community service under the auspices of a highly publicized required school program will be viewed merely as students completing their high school graduation requirements.

Because we conclude that the act of performing community service in the context of the Bethlehem Area School District high school graduation requirement is not an expressive act that "directly and sharply implicate[s] constitutional values," . . . we think that it is not our role to say that a school system cannot seek to expose its students to community service by requiring them to perform it. To the extent that there is an implicit value judgment underlying the program it is not materially different from that underlying programs that seek to discourage drug use and premature sexual activity, encourage knowledge of civics and abiding in the rule of law, and even encourage exercise and good eating habits. Schools have traditionally undertaken to point students toward values generally shared by the community. In fact, the Supreme Court has stated that public schools have a long history and tradition of teaching values to their students, including those associated with community responsibility. Public schools are important "in the preparation of individuals for participation as citizens, [] in the preservation of the values on which our society

rests" and for "inculcating fundamental values necessary to the maintenance of a democratic political system." . . .

Having decided that the Program does not compel expression protected by the First Amendment, it is unnecessary to consider whether the state has a compelling interest in implementing a mandatory community service graduation requirement. Accordingly, we find that the district court properly granted summary judgment for defendants on plaintiffs' claim that the mandatory community service program violates the First and Fourteenth Amendments.

Plaintiffs' second contention is that a mandatory community service program in a public high school constitutes "involuntary servitude" in violation of the Thirteenth Amendment.

. . . As the Supreme Court has acknowledged, it is easier to comprehend the "general spirit" of the phrase "involuntary servitude" than it is to define the exact range of conditions it prohibits. . . .

Plaintiffs argue (i) that the program is servitude because the students provide unpaid service to the community for the benefit of others; and (ii) that participation in the program is involuntary because the threat of not receiving a diploma is *prima facie* coercion. . . . [W]e believe that it is a mistake to dissect the phrase "involuntary servitude" into two components: instead it is more appropriate to consider whether, taking as a whole the set of conditions existing in the imposition of a mandatory community service program in a public high school, the students providing the services are in a condition of involuntary servitude. . . .

The prohibition against involuntary servitude has always barred forced labor through physical coercion. . . . In addition, it may bar forced labor through legal coercion. . . . As the Supreme Court has pointed out, the critical factor in every case finding involuntary servitude is that the victim's only choice is between performing the labor on the one hand and physical and/or legal sanctions on the other. *See Kozminski*, 487 U.S. at 943, 108 S.Ct. at 2760.

Significantly, not even every situation in which an individual faces a choice between labor or legal sanction constitutes involuntary servitude. Governments may require individuals to perform certain well-established "civic duties," such as military service and jury duty, and impose legal sanctions for the failure to perform. . . .

Modern day examples of involuntary servitude have been limited to labor camps, isolated religious sects, or forced confinement. . . .

Outside of these contexts, courts have consistently rejected claims that "forced labor" amounted to involuntary servitude. For example, it is not involuntary servitude when the state requires attorneys to provide a fixed number of hours of legal representation without compensation as a condition of practicing law. . . . Similarly, it is not involuntary servitude for the government to collect liquidated damages from a participant in the National Health Service Corps scholarship program who, after accepting the scholarship money and completing his medical degree, declined to perform the required services. . . . Finally, it is not involuntary servitude to offer prisoners an option of participating in a work-release program, even though the consequence of not working and remaining in jail may be "painful." . . .

In each of these situations courts found no compulsion because the individuals had alternatives to performing the labor: a lawyer can choose not to practice law to avoid the mandatory service requirement; a doctor can refuse to provide the contracted-for services and instead pay the damages for breach of the contract; and a prisoner can choose to stay in jail rather than enter the work-release program. The fact that these choices may not be appealing does not make the required labor involuntary servitude. . . .

Thus, we follow the Supreme Court and other courts of appeals in taking a contextual approach to involuntary servitude by confining the Thirteenth Amendment to those situations that are truly "akin to African slavery." . . .

There is no basis in fact or logic which would support analogizing a mandatory community service program in a public high school to slavery. The record amply supports the defendants' claim that the community service program is primarily designed for the students' own benefit and education, notwithstanding some incidental benefit to the recipients of the services. An educational requirement does not become involuntary servitude merely because one of the stated objectives of the Program is that the students will work "without receiving pay." . . .

Accordingly, we hold that the mandatory community service program instituted in the Bethlehem Area School District as a high school graduation requirement does not constitute involuntary servitude prohibited by the Thirteenth Amendment.

For the foregoing reasons, we will affirm the district court's grant of summary judgment for defendants on plaintiffs' claims under the First and Thirteenth Amendments.

CASE NOTE

Involuntary Servitude. A federal district court in Hawaii ruled that a state regulation requiring children in public schools to work in the school cafeteria did not constitute involuntary servitude because "the public, and not private, interest and benefit are being served." *Bobilin v. Board of Education,* 403 F.Supp. 1095 (D.Haw. 1975).

■ CURRICULUM AND THE PALL OF ORTHODOXY

The Supreme Court has said that the courts should not intervene in conflicts that arise in the daily operation of the schools, so long as the conflicts do not involve basic constitutional values. However, the courts will not "tolerate laws which cast a pall of orthodoxy over the classroom."[23]

The Supreme Court stated in *Sweezy v. New Hampshire:*[24]

> Scholarship cannot flourish in an atmosphere of suspicion and distrust. Teachers and students must always remain free to inquire, to study and to evaluate. . . . [The state cannot] chill that free play of the spirit which all teachers ought especially to cultivate and practice.[25]

Since the beginnings of the public schools, the nature and content of the curriculum have been subject to continuing and perplexing debate. As observed elsewhere in this book, one of the primary obstacles that faced early public school reformers was the formulation of a commonly accepted curriculum that would not

unduly advance any particularized or specialized interest to the exclusion of others. Early
experience found that the most difficult of such
interests to overcome had to do with religious
sectarianism and the hundreds of beliefs that
touched on human values, morality, and ethics.
A public school system that did not advance the
cause of a particular group quickly encountered
discord and conflict as a result. Cognizant of
this problem, the early public school leaders
sought to build a nonsectarian common school
curriculum that would not be offensive to any
particular religious view or sectarian viewpoint.
In this pursuit, the public schools have been
condemned by conservative religious groups for
being ungodly or irreligious. Such groups, too,
have sought to impose their beliefs on the public schools in an attempt to make their particular
views the official policy of the state. This has
not materially changed over the years, for it was
this same issue that led to vigorous opposition
to public schools initially. Butts and Cremin
noted that what Horace Mann's "attackers were
urging was not that religion, ethics and morals
be taught in the schools, but that their particular
sectarian doctrines be taught."[26]

In his concurring opinion in *McCollum*, Justice Jackson observed that

> authorities list 256 separate and substantial reli-
> gious bodies to exist in the United States. Each of
> them . . . has as good a right (as any other) to
> demand that the courts compel the schools to sift
> out of their teaching everything that is objection-
> able to any of these warring sects or inconsistent
> with any of their doctrine. If we are to eliminate
> everything that is objectionable to any of these
> warring sects or inconsistent with any of their doc-
> trines, we will leave public education in shreds.[27]

To identify and avoid all such conflicts was
difficult, if not impossible. Fortunately, though,
the tenacity with which most sects imposed
their particular tenets on the public varied considerably, allowing for some considerable flexibility. Butts and Cremin have noted that

> so long as each religious sect held firmly and
> uncompromisingly to a set of specific religious
> doctrines in opposition to all other sects, the ten-
> dency would be to insist upon religious schools
> that taught those tenets and only those tenets. . . .

It is entirely possible that if some kind of nonsectarian outlook in religion had not appeared, the
rise of the public school open to all religious
groups alike would not have been possible.[28]

Over the years the intolerance for beliefs of
others has, however, subsided very little, and
the tendency for some sects to continue their
objections to public schools is commonplace.
There also has been a tendency for religious
fundamentalism to ebb and flow in popular
appeal over the years, making the imposition of
particular sectarian beliefs more politically
viable at certain times than at others. The attitudes of legislatures, school boards, and even
the courts have sometimes reflected these popu-
larized views. It is because of the great difficulty
in accommodating these divisive forces that the
public schools have sought to convey a general
attitude of secular impartiality to the views of
various sects. The courts have generally enforced the view that the public schools should
deal with temporal matters and remain apart
and separate from ecclesiastical affairs.

The legal controversies that normally arise in
this area generally involve some particular
group seeking to impose a particular belief by
restricting the school curriculum or demanding
that certain textbooks, films, courses, or programs be excluded from the instructional program. In response, the courts have traditionally
felt most comfortable in upholding the expansion rather than the contraction of knowledge.

In *Pico*,[29] the Supreme Court reinforced the
"pall of orthodoxy" rule by forbidding removal
of books by the local school board that was
responding to political pressure from a local
group of conservative parents. The court
observed that the expansion of information and
knowledge was the most desirable end to education policy and said that "the right to receive
ideas is a necessary predicate to the recipient's
meaningful exercise of his own rights of speech,
press, and political freedom."[30]

This general precedent, that expansion of information and knowledge is paramount, and
that even school boards' actions will be invalidated if they impair the flow of ideas, was
closely followed in 1982 by the U.S. Court of
Appeals, Eighth Circuit, in Pratt.[31] Here the

court ruled that the school board's removal of a film from the school library was constitutionally invalid because the "First Amendment precludes local authorities from imposing a 'pall of orthodoxy' on classroom instruction which implicates the state in propagation of a particular religious or ideological viewpoint."[32]

More recently, though, a new judicial pattern has emerged that may suggest a possible retreat from the "pall of orthodoxy" rule. The present U.S. Supreme Court has indicated that it is willing to allow the final decision regarding the curriculum and the availability of books, films, and materials to reside fully within the prerogative of the local school board, even though there may be a resulting constriction on the flow of information and a possible diminution of knowledge. This position was implied by the Supreme Court in *Hazelwood School District v. Kuhlmeier*,[33] in which excision of two pages from a student newspaper was upheld because, as the Court said, such regulation is permissible so long as it is "reasonably related to legitimate pedagogical concerns."[34] (See Chapter 8 of this book for details of *Hazelwood School District v. Kuhlmeier.*) Such a reasonableness standard is less definitive and gives the local school board greater flexibility in determining whether to restrict or expand the curriculum. In this case, the Supreme Court gave further justification for restriction of curriculum content by observing that "a school must be able to take into account the emotional maturity of the intended audience."[35]

In following this precedent of giving greater latitude to local school boards in controlling (and possibly limiting) curriculum, books, and materials, the U.S. Court of Appeals, Eleventh Circuit, followed *Kuhlmeier* and upheld a school board's action in removing material from the curriculum because the removal was related to "legitimate pedagogical concerns."[36]

The new trend of the courts appears to place less emphasis on a broadly conceived standard that secures the expansion of knowledge and prevents the "casting of a pall of orthodoxy." Instead, it allows more flexibility in allowing curriculum decisions to be made on the basis of local school board judgment and, possibly, local political pressure.

❖ — ❖ — ❖

Local School Board May Not Remove Books from School Libraries Simply Because It Dislikes the Ideas Contained in the Books

Board of Education, Island Trees Union Free School District No. 26 v. Pico

Supreme Court of the United States, 1982.
457 U.S. 853, 102 S.Ct. 2799.

Justice BRENNAN announced the judgment of the Court, and delivered an opinion in which Justice MARSHALL and Justice STEVENS joined, and in which Justice BLACKMUN joined except for Part II-A-(1). The principal question presented is whether the First Amendment imposes limitations upon the exercise by a local school board of its discretion to remove library books from high school and junior high school libraries.

Petitioners are the Board of Education of the Island Trees Union Free School District No. 26, in New York, and Richard Ahrens, Frank Martin, Christina Fasulo, Patrick Hughes, Richard Melchers, Richard Michaels, and Louis Nessim. When this suit was brought, Ahrens was the President of the Board, Martin was the Vice President, and the remaining petitioners were Board members. The Board is a state agency charged with responsibility for the operation and administration of the public schools within the Island Trees School District, including the Island Trees High School and Island Trees Memorial Junior High School. Respondents are Steven Pico, Jacqueline Gold, Glenn Yarris, Russell Rieger, and Paul Sochinski. When this suit was brought, Pico, Gold, Yarris, and Rieger were students at the High School, and Sochinski was a student at the Junior High School.

In September 1975, petitioners Ahrens, Martin, and Hughes attended a conference sponsored by Parents of New York United (PONYU), a politically conservative organization of parents concerned about education legislation in the

State of New York. At the conference these petitioners obtained lists of books described by Ahrens as "objectionable," and by Martin as "improper fare for school students." It was later determined that the High School library contained nine of the listed books, and that another listed book was in the Junior High School library. [The nine books in the high school library were *Slaughterhouse Five,* by Kurt Vonnegut, Jr.; *The Naked Ape,* by Desmond Morris; *Down These Mean Streets,* by Piri Thomas; *Best Short Stories of Negro Writers,* edited by Langston Hughes; *Go Ask Alice,* of anonymous authorship; *Laughing Boy,* by Oliver LaFarge; *Black Boy,* by Richard Wright; *A Hero Ain't Nothin' but a Sandwich,* by Alice Childress; and *Soul on Ice,* by Eldridge Cleaver. The book in the junior high school library was *A Reader for Writers,* edited by Jerome Archer. Still another listed book, *The Fixer,* by Bernard Malamud, was found to be included in the curriculum of a twelfth grade literature course.] In February 1976, at a meeting with the superintendent of schools and the principals of the High School and Junior High School, the Board gave an "unofficial direction" that the listed books be removed from the library shelves and delivered to the Board's offices, so that Board members could read them. When this directive was carried out, it became publicized, and the Board issued a press release justifying its action. It characterized the removed books as "anti-American, anti-Christian, anti-Semitic, and just plain filthy," and concluded that "It is our duty, our moral obligation, to protect the children in our schools from this moral danger as surely as from physical and medical dangers."

A short time later, the Board appointed a "Book Review Committee," consisting of four Island Trees parents and four members of the Island Trees schools staff, to read the listed books and to recommend to the Board whether the books should be retained, taking into account the books' "educational suitability," "good taste," "relevance," and "appropriateness to age and grade level." In July, the Committee made its final report to the Board, recommending that five of the listed books be retained [*The Fixer, Laughing Boy, Black Boy, Go Ask Alice,* and *Best Short Stories of Negro Writers*] and that two others be removed from the school libraries [*The Naked Ape* and *Down These Mean Streets*]. As for the remaining four books, the Committee could not agree on two [*Soul on Ice* and *A Hero Ain't Nothin' but a Sandwich*], took no position on one [*A Reader for Writers*]—the reason given for this disposition was that all members of the Committee had not been able to read the book, and recommended that the last book be made available to students only with parental approval [*Slaughterhouse Five*]. The Board substantially rejected the Committee's report later that month, deciding that only one book should be returned to the High School library without restriction [*Laughing Boy*], that another should be made available subject to parental approval [*Black Boy*], but that the remaining nine books should "be removed from elementary and secondary libraries and [from] use in the curriculum." [As a result, the nine removed books could not be assigned or suggested to students in connection with school work. However, teachers were not instructed to refrain from discussing the removed books or the ideas and positions expressed in them.] The Board gave no reasons for rejecting the recommendations of the Committee that it had appointed.

Respondents reacted to the Board's decision by bringing the present action. They alleged that petitioners had

> ordered the removal of the books from school libraries and proscribed their use in the curriculum because particular passages in the books offended their social, political and moral tastes and not because the books, taken as a whole, were lacking in educational value.

Respondents claimed that the Board's actions denied them their rights under the First Amendment. They asked the court for a declaration that the Board's actions were unconstitutional. . . .

We emphasize at the outset the limited nature of the substantive question presented by the case before us. Our precedents have long recognized certain constitutional limits upon the power of the State to control even the curriculum and classroom. For example, *Meyer v. Nebraska,* 262 U.S. 390, 43 S.Ct. 625, 67 L.Ed. 1042 (1923), struck down a state law that forbade the teaching of modern foreign languages in public and private schools, and *Epperson v. Arkansas,* 393 U.S. 97, 89 S.Ct. 266, 21 L.Ed.2d 228 (1968), declared unconstitutional a state law that prohibited the teaching of the Darwinian theory of evolution in any state-supported school. But the current action does not require us to re-enter this difficult terrain, which *Meyer* and *Epperson* traversed without apparent misgiving. For as this case is presented to us, it does not involve textbooks, or indeed any books that Island Trees students would be required to read. Respondents do not seek in this Court to impose limitations upon their school board's discretion to prescribe the curricula of the Island Trees schools. On the contrary, the only books at issue in this case are *library* books, books that by their nature are optional rather than required reading. Our adjudication of the present case thus does not intrude into the classroom, or into the compulsory courses taught there. Furthermore, even as to library books, the action before us does not involve the *acquisition* of books. Respondents have not sought to compel their school board to add to the school library shelves any books that students desire to read. Rather, the only action challenged in this case is the *removal* from school libraries of books originally placed there by the school authorities, or without objection from them. . . . [T]he issue before us in this case is a narrow one, both substantively and procedurally. . . . Does the First Amendment impose *any* limitations upon the discretion of petitioners to remove library books from the Island Trees High School and Junior High School? . . .

The Court has long recognized that local school boards have broad discretion in the management of school affairs. . . . [B]y and large, "public education in our Nation is committed to the control of state and local authorities," and . . . federal courts should not ordinarily "intervene in the resolution of conflicts which arise in the daily operation of school systems." *Tinker v. Des Moines School Dist.*, 393 U.S. 503, 507, 89 S.Ct. 733, 736, 21 L.Ed.2d 731 (1969), noted that we have "repeatedly emphasized . . . the comprehensive authority of the States and of school officials . . . to prescribe and control conduct in the schools." We have also acknowledged that public schools are vitally important "in the preparation of individuals for participation as citizens," and as vehicles for "inculcating fundamental values necessary to the maintenance of a democratic political system." We are therefore in full agreement with petitioners that local school boards must be permitted "to establish and apply their curriculum in such a way as to transmit community values," and that "there is a legitimate and substantial community interest in promoting respect for authority and traditional values, be they social, moral, or political."

At the same time, however, we have necessarily recognized that the discretion of the States and local school boards in matters of education must be exercised in a manner that comports with the transcendent imperatives of the First Amendment. . . .

In short, "First Amendment rights, applied in light of the special characteristics of the school environment, are available to . . . students."

Of course, courts should not "intervene in the resolution of conflicts which arise in the daily operations of school systems" unless "basic constitutional values" are "directly and sharply implicate[d]" in those conflicts. But we think that the First Amendment rights of students may be directly and sharply implicated by the removal of books from the shelves of a school library. Our precedents have focused "not only on the role of the First Amendment in fostering individual self-expression but also on its role in affording the public access to discussion, debate, and the dissemination of information and ideas." And we have recognized that "[t]he State may not, consistently with the spirit of the First Amendment, contract the spectrum of available knowledge." . . . This [the right to receive information and ideas] is an inherent corollary of the rights of free speech and press that are explicitly guaranteed by the Constitution, in two senses. First, the right to receive ideas follows ineluctably from the *sender's* First Amendment right to send them: "The right of freedom of speech and press . . . embraces the right to distribute literature, . . . and necessarily protects the right to receive it." "The dissemination of ideas can accomplish nothing if otherwise willing addressees are not free to receive and consider them. It would be a barren marketplace of ideas that had only sellers and no buyers."

More importantly, the right to receive ideas is a necessary predicate to the *recipient's* meaningful exercise of his own rights of speech, press, and political freedom. Madison admonished us that a popular Government, without popular information, or the means of acquiring it, is but a Prologue to a Farce or a Tragedy; or, perhaps both. Knowledge will forever govern ignorance: And a people who mean to be their own Governors, must arm themselves with the power which knowledge gives. . . .

In sum, just as access to ideas makes it possible for citizens generally to exercise their rights of free speech and press in a meaningful manner, such access prepares students for active and effective participation in the pluralistic, often contentious society in which they will soon be adult members. Of course all First Amendment rights accorded to students must be construed "in light of the special characteristics of the school environment." But the special characteristics of the school make that environment especially appropriate for the recognition of the First Amendment rights of students.

A school library, no less than any other public library, is "a place dedicated to quiet, to knowledge, and to beauty." . . . The school library is the principal locus of such freedom.

Petitioners emphasize the inculcative function of secondary education, and argue that they must be allowed *unfettered* discretion to "transmit community values" through the Island Trees schools. But that sweeping claim overlooks the unique role of the school library. It appears from the record that use of the Island Trees school libraries is completely voluntary on the part of students. Their selection of books from these libraries is entirely a matter of free choice; the libraries afford them an opportunity at self-education and individual enrichment that is wholly optional. Petitioners might well defend their claim of absolute discretion in matters of *curriculum* by reliance upon their duty to inculcate community values. But we think that petitioners' reliance upon that duty is misplaced where, as here, they attempt to extend their claim of absolute discretion beyond the compulsory environment of the classroom, into the school library and the regime of voluntary inquiry that there holds sway.

In rejecting petitioners' claim of absolute discretion to remove books from their school libraries, we do not deny that local school boards have a substantial legitimate role to play in the determination of school library content. . . .

Petitioners rightly possess significant discretion to determine the content of their school libraries. But that discretion may not be exercised in a narrowly partisan or political manner. If a Democratic school board, motivated by party affiliation, ordered the removal of all books written by or in favor of Republicans, few would doubt that the order violated the constitutional rights of the students denied access to those books. The same conclusion would surely apply if an all-white school board, motivated by racial animus, decided to remove all books authored by blacks or advocating racial equality and integration. Our Constitution does not permit the official suppression of *ideas.* Thus whether petitioners' removal of books from their school libraries denied respondents their First Amendment rights depends upon the motivation behind petitioners' actions. If petitioners *intended* by their removal decision to deny respondents access to ideas with which petitioners disagreed, and if this intent was the decisive factor in petitioners' decision, then petitioners have exercised their discretion in violation of the Constitution. To permit such intentions to control official actions would be to encourage the precise sort of officially prescribed orthodoxy unequivocally condemned in *Barnette.* On the other hand, respondents implicitly concede that an unconstitutional motivation would *not* be demonstrated if it were shown that petitioners had decided to remove the books at issue because those books were pervasively vulgar. And again, respondents concede that if it were demonstrated that the removal decision was based solely upon the "educational suitability" of the books in question, then their removal would be "perfectly permissible." In other words, in respondents' view such motivations, if decisive of petitioners' actions, would not carry the danger of an official suppression of ideas, and thus would not violate respondents' First Amendment rights.

As noted earlier, nothing in our decision today affects in any way the discretion of a local school board to choose books to *add* to the libraries of their schools. Because we are concerned in this case with the suppression of ideas, our holding today affects only the discretion to *remove* books. In brief, we hold that local school boards may not remove books from school library shelves simply because they dislike the ideas contained in those books and seek by their removal to "prescribe what shall be orthodox in politics, nationalism, religion, or other matters of opinion." . . .

CASE NOTE

The plurality decision in *Pico* in which no clear-cut majority logic is ascertainable prevents the case from standing as binding precedent. In *Muir v. Alabama Educational Television Commission*, the U.S. Court of Appeals, Fifth Circuit, Judge Hill writing, said "that the 'no-clear-majority' nature of *Pico* meant that its First Amendment analysis did not have precedential value." 688 F.2d 1033 (5th Cir.1982). Later, the Fifth Circuit observed that *Pico* provided guidance in such cases but was not a binding precedent. *Campbell v. St. Tammany Parish School Board*, 64 F.3d 184 (5th Cir., 1995). In the latter case the court reversed a summary judgment by a federal district court that held the removal of the book *Voodoo and Hoodoo* from library shelves of all district schools was unconstitutional. In reviewing this case, the Fifth Circuit summarized the U.S. Supreme Court's primary points in *Pico* for guidance in future cases.

a. The *Pico* plurality stressed the "unique role of the school library" as a place where students could engage in voluntary inquiry.

b. It also observed that "students must always remain free to inquire, to study and to evaluate, to gain new maturity and understanding" and that the school library served as "the principal locus of such freedom."

c. The *Pico* plurality recognized that the high degree of deference accorded to educators' decisions regarding curricular matters diminishes when the challenged decision involves a noncurricular matter.

d. Emphasizing the voluntary nature of public school library use, the plurality in *Pico* observed that school officials' decisions regarding public school library materials are properly viewed as decisions that do not involve the school curriculum and that are therefore subject to certain constitutional limitations.

e. In rejecting the school officials' claim of absolute discretion to remove books from their school libraries, the *Pico* plurality recognized that students have a First Amendment right to receive information and that school officials are prohibited from exercising their discretion to remove books from school library shelves "simply because they dislike the ideas contained in those books and seek by their removal to 'prescribe what shall be orthodox in politics, nationalism, religion, or other matters of opinion.'"

f. The *Pico* plurality observed that if school officials intended by their removal decision to deny students access to ideas with which the school officials disagreed, and this intent was the decisive factor in the removal decision, then the school officials had "exercised their discretion in violation of the Constitution."

g. The Court in its plurality opinion implicitly recognized, however, that an unconstitutional motivation would not be demonstrated if the school officials removed the books from the public school libraries based on a belief that the books were "pervasively vulgar" or on grounds of "educational suitability."

Campbell v. St. Tammany Parish School Board, 64 F.2d. 184, at 187, 188. (5th Cir., 1995).

❖ — ❖ — ❖

School Board's Removal of Works by Aristophanes and Chaucer from Curriculum Is Reasonably Related to Legitimate Pedagogical Concerns

Virgil v. School Board of Columbia County, Florida

United States Court of Appeals,
Eleventh Circuit, 1989.
862 F.2d 1517.

ANDERSON, Circuit Judge. This case presents the question of whether the first amendment prevents a school board from removing a previously approved textbook from an elective high school class because of objections to the material's vulgarity and sexual explicitness. We conclude that a school board may, without contravening constitutional limits, take such action where, as here, its methods are "reasonably related to legitimate pedagogical concerns." Accordingly, we affirm the judgment of the district court.

The essential facts were stipulated by the parties to this dispute. Since about 1975 the educational curriculum at Columbia High School has included a course entitled "Humanities to 1500" offered as part of a two-semester survey of Western thought, art and literature. In 1985 the school designed the course for eleventh- and twelfth-grade students and prescribed as a textbook Volume I of *The Humanities: Cultural Roots and Continuities*. This book contained both required and optional readings for the course.

Among the selections included in Volume I of *Humanities* which were neither required nor assigned are English translations of *Lysistrata*, written by the Greek dramatist Aristophanes in approximately 411 B.C., and *The Miller's Tale*, written by the English poet Geoffrey Chaucer around 1380–1390 A.D. During the fall semester of the 1985–86 school year, a portion of *Lysistrata* was read aloud in class during a session of the Humanities course.

In the spring of 1986, after the first semester had ended, the Reverend and Mrs. Fritz M. Fountain, the parents of a student who had taken the class in the fall of 1985, filed a formal complaint concerning Volume I of *Humanities* with the School Board of Columbia County. The Fountains also submitted a Request for Examination of School Media. Their objections centered upon *Lysistrata* and *The Miller's Tale*.

In response to this parental complaint, the School Board on April 8, 1986, adopted a Policy on Challenged State Adopted Textbooks to address any complaints regarding books in use in the curriculum. Pursuant to the new policy, the School Board appointed an advisory committee to review Volume I of *Humanities*. Upon examination, the committee recommended that the textbook be retained in the curriculum, but that *Lysistrata* and *The Miller's Tale* not be assigned as required reading.

At its April 22, 1986, meeting the School Board considered the advisory committee's report. Silas Pittman, Superintendent of the Columbia County School System, offered his disagreement with the committee's conclusion, and recommended that the two disputed selections be deleted from Volume I or that use of the book in the curriculum be terminated. Adopting the latter proposal, the School Board voted to discontinue any future use of Volume I in the curriculum.

Pursuant to the Board decision, Volume I of *Humanities* was placed in locked storage and has been kept there ever since. . . .

On November 24, 1986, parents of students at Columbia High School filed an action against the School Board and the Superintendent seeking an injunction against the textbook removal and a declaration that such action violated their first amendment rights. . . .

It has long been clear that public school students do not "shed their constitutional rights to freedom of speech or expression at the schoolhouse gate." . . . At the same time, the Supreme Court has held that the rights of students in public schools are not automatically coextensive with the rights of adults, . . . and has recognized the central role of public schools in transmitting values necessary to the development of an informed citizenry. . . .

In matters pertaining to the curriculum, educators have been accorded greater control over expression than they may enjoy in other spheres of activity. . . .

[C]ourts that have addressed the issue have failed to achieve a consensus on the degree of discretion to be accorded school boards to restrict access to curricular materials. . . .

The most direct guidance from the Supreme Court is found in the recent case of *Hazelwood School District v. Kuhlmeier*, 484 U.S. 260, 108 S.Ct. 562, 98 L.Ed.2d 592 (1988). In *Hazelwood* the Court upheld the authority of a high school principal to excise two pages from a school-sponsored student newspaper on the grounds that articles concerning teenage pregnancy and divorce were inappropriate for the level of maturity of the intended readers, the privacy interests of the articles' subjects were insufficiently protected, and the controversial views contained therein might erroneously be attributed to the school. *Hazelwood* established a relatively lenient test for regulation of expression which "may fairly be characterized as part of the school curriculum." Such regulation is permissible so long as it is "reasonably related to legitimate pedagogical concerns." . . .

In applying that test the Supreme Court identified one such legitimate concern which is relevant to this case: "a school must be able to take into account the emotional maturity of the intended audience in determining whether to disseminate student speech on potentially sensitive topics . . . , [e.g.,] the particulars of teenage sexual activity." . . .

In applying the *Hazelwood* standard to the instant case, two considerations are particularly significant. First, we conclude that the Board decisions at issue were curricular decisions. The materials removed were part of the textbook used in a regularly scheduled course of study in the school. Plaintiffs argue that this particular course was an elective course, and not a required course. However, common sense indicates that the overall curriculum offered by a school includes not only the core curriculum (i.e., required courses) but also such additional, elective courses of study that school officials design and offer. Each student is expected to select from the several elective courses which school officials deem appropriate in order to fashion a curriculum tailored to his individual needs.

One factor identified in *Hazelwood* as relevant to the determination of whether an activity could fairly be characterized as part of the curriculum is whether "the public might reasonably perceive [the activity] to bear the imprimatur of the school." . . . It is clear that elective courses designed and offered by the school would be so perceived.

Plaintiffs further point out that the materials removed in this case not only were part of an elective course, but were optional, not required readings. For the reasons just mentioned, we conclude that the optional readings removed in this case were part of the school curriculum. Just as elective courses are designed by school officials to supplement required courses, optional readings in a particular class are carefully selected by the teacher as relevant and appropriate to supplement required readings in order to further the educational goals of the course. This is especially true in the instant circumstances, where the optional readings were included within the text itself, and thus had to accompany the student every time the text was taken home. Such materials would obviously carry the imprimatur of school approval.

The second consideration that is significant in applying the *Hazelwood* standard to this case is the fact that the motivation for the Board's removal of the readings has been stipulated to be related to the explicit sexuality and excessively vulgar language in the selections. It is clear from *Hazelwood* and other cases that this is a legitimate concern. School officials can "take into account the emotional maturity of the intended audience in determining . . . [the appropriateness of] potentially sensitive topics" such as sex and vulgarity. . . .

Since the stipulated motivation of the School Board relates to legitimate concerns, we need only determine whether the Board action was *reasonably* related thereto. It is of course true, as plaintiffs so forcefully point out, that *Lysistrata* and *The Miller's Tale* are widely acclaimed masterpieces of Western literature. However, after careful consideration, we cannot conclude that the school's actions were not reasonably related to its legitimate concerns regarding the appropriateness (for this high school audience) of the sexuality and vulgarity in these works. Notwithstanding their status as literary classics, *Lysistrata* and *The Miller's Tale* contain passages of exceptional sexual explicitness, as numerous commentators have noted. In assessing the reasonableness of the Board's action, we also take into consideration the fact that most of the high school students involved ranged in age from fifteen to just over eighteen, and a substantial number had not yet reached the age of majority. We also note that the disputed materials have not been banned from the school. The *Humanities* textbook and other adaptations of *Lysistrata* and *The Miller's Tale* are available in the school library. No student or teacher is prohibited from assigning or reading these works or discussing the themes contained therein in class or on school property. . . . Under all the circumstances of this case, we cannot conclude that the Board's action was not reasonably related to the stated legitimate concern.

We decide today only that the Board's removal of these works from the curriculum did not violate the Constitution. Of course, we do not endorse the Board's decision. Like the district court, we seriously question how young persons just below the age of majority can be harmed by these masterpieces of Western literature. However, having concluded that there is no constitutional violation, our role is not to second guess the wisdom of the Board's action.

The judgment of the district court is affirmed.

CASE NOTE

Chilling Effect: In denying a parent's complaint, under the Equal Protection Clause of the Fourteenth Amendment and Title VI of the Civil Rights Act of 1964, to compel a school board to remove from the required reading in an English class the two classic literary works, *The Adventures of Huckleberry Finn,* by Mark Twain, and the short story *A Rose for Emily,* by William Faulkner, federal court pointed out the potential quagmire of judicial literary censorship that could result if courts began to substitute their judgments for those of school boards in the selection of curricular materials. Further, the court noted that the effect of such selective judicial approvals and disapprovals would create a "chilling effect" on local school boards that could restrict generally the expansion and conveyance of knowledge. The court said:

> There is, of course, an extremely wide—if not unlimited—range of literary products that might be considered injurious or offensive, particularly when one considers that high school students frequently take Advanced Placement courses that are equivalent to college-level courses. White plaintiffs could seek to remove books by Toni Morrison, Maya Angelou, and other prominent Black authors on the ground that they portray Caucasians in a derogatory fashion; Jews might try to impose civil liability for the teachings of Shakespeare and of more modern English poets where writings exhibit a similar anti-Semitic strain. Female students could attempt to make a case for damages for the assignment of some of the works of Tennessee Williams, Hemingway, or Freud, and male students for the writings of Andrea Dworkin or Margaret Atwood. The number of potential lawsuits that could arise

from the highly varied educational curricula throughout the nation might well be unlimited and unpredictable. Many school districts would undoubtedly prefer to "steer far" from any controversial book and instead substitute "safe" ones in order to reduce the possibility of civil liability and the expensive and time-consuming burdens of a lawsuit—even one having but a slight chance of success. In short, permitting lawsuits against school districts on the basis of the content of literary works to proceed past the complaint stage could have a significant chilling effect on a school district's willingness to assign books with themes, characters, snippets of dialogue, or words that might offend the sensibilities of any number of persons or groups.

Monteiro v. The Tempe Union High School Dist., 158 F.3d 1022 (9th Cir.1998)

According to this court such a "chilling effect" could well deny First Amendment rights of other students who were denied the information and ideas. This decision is consistent with *Virgil* to the extent that it rejects judicial encroachment into curricular decisions of school boards.

❖ — ❖ — ❖

Requirements That Students Study Basic Reader Series Is Not Unconstitutional as Violative of Students' Religious Beliefs

Mozert v. Hawkins County Board of Education

United States Court of Appeals, Sixth Circuit, 1987. 827 F.2d 1058.

LIVELY, Chief Judge. This case arose under the Free Exercise Clause of the First Amendment, made applicable to the states by the Fourteenth Amendment. The district court held that a public school requirement that all students in grades one through eight use a prescribed set of reading textbooks violated the constitutional rights of objecting parents and students. . . .

Early in 1983 the Hawkins County, Tennessee, Board of Education adopted the Holt,

Rinehart and Winston basic reading series (the Holt series) for use in grades 1–8 of the public schools of the county. . . .

Like many school systems, Hawkins County schools teach "critical reading" as opposed to reading exercises that teach only word and sound recognition. "Critical reading" requires the development of higher order cognitive skills that enable students to evaluate the material they read, to contrast the ideas presented, and to understand complex characters that appear in reading material. . . .

The plaintiff Vicki Frost is the mother of four children, three of whom were students in Hawkins County public schools in 1983. At the beginning of the 1983–84 school year Mrs. Frost read a story in a daughter's sixth grade reader that involved mental telepathy. Mrs. Frost, who describes herself as a "born again Christian," has a religious objection to any teaching about mental telepathy. Reading further, she found additional themes in the reader to which she had religious objections. After discussing her objections with other parents, Mrs. Frost talked with the principal of Church Hill Middle School and obtained an agreement for an alternative reading program for students whose parents objected to the assigned Holt reader. The students who elected the alternative program left their classrooms during the reading sessions and worked on assignments from an older textbook series in available office or library areas. Other students in two elementary schools were excused from reading the Holt books.

In November 1983 the Hawkins County School Board voted unanimously to eliminate all alternative reading programs and require every student in the public schools to attend classes using the Holt series. Thereafter the plaintiff students refused to read the Holt series or attend reading classes where the series was being used.

On December 2, 1983, the plaintiffs, consisting of seven families—14 parents and 17 children—filed this action pursuant to 42 U.S.C. §1983. In their complaint the plaintiffs asserted that they have sincere religious beliefs which are contrary to the values taught or inculcated by the reading textbooks and that it is a violation of the religious beliefs and convictions of the plaintiff students to be required to read the books and a violation of the religious beliefs of the plaintiff parents to permit their children to read the books. The plaintiffs sought to hold the defendants liable because "forcing the student-plaintiffs to read school books which teach or inculcate values in violation of their religious beliefs and convictions is a clear violation of their rights to the free exercise of religion protected by the First and Fourteenth Amendments to the United States Constitution." . . .

Vicki Frost was the first witness for the plaintiffs and she presented the most complete explanation of the plaintiffs' position. The plaintiffs do not belong to a single church or denomination, but all consider themselves born again Christians. Mrs. Frost testified that the word of God as found in the Christian Bible "is the totality of my beliefs." There was evidence that other members of their churches, and even their pastors, do not agree with their position in this case.

Mrs. Frost testified that she had spent more than 200 hours reviewing the Holt series and had found numerous passages that offended her religious beliefs. She stated that the offending materials fell into seventeen categories which she listed. These ranged from such familiar concerns of fundamentalist Christians as evolution and "secular humanism" to less familiar themes such as "futuristic supernaturalism," pacifism, magic, and false views of death.

In her lengthy testimony Mrs. Frost identified passages from stories and poems used in the Holt series that fell into each category. Illustrative is her first category, futuristic supernaturalism, which she defined as teaching "Man as God." Passages that she found offensive described Leonardo da Vinci as the human with a creative mind that "came closest to the divine touch." Mrs. Frost testified that it is an "occult practice" for children to use imagination beyond the limitation of scriptural authority. She testified that the story that alerted her to the problem with the reading series fell into the category of futuristic supernaturalism. Entitled "A Visit to Mars," the story portrays thought transfer and telepathy in such a way that "it could be considered a scientific concept," according to this witness. This theme appears in the testimony of several witnesses, *i.e.*, the materials objected to "could" be interpreted in a manner repugnant to their religious beliefs.

Mrs. Frost described objectionable passages from other categories in much the same way. Describing evolution as a teaching that there is no God, she identified 24 passages that she considered to have evolution as a theme. . . .

Another witness for the plaintiffs was Bob Mozert, father of a middle school and an elementary school student in the Hawkins County system. His testimony echoed that of Vicki Frost in large part, though his answers to questions tended to be much less expansive. . . .

The first question to be decided is whether a governmental requirement that a person be exposed to ideas he or she finds objectionable on religious grounds constitutes a burden on the free exercise of that person's religion as forbidden by the First Amendment. . . .

It is also clear that exposure to objectionable material is what the plaintiffs objected to, albeit they emphasize the repeated nature of the exposure. The complaint mentioned only the textbooks that the students were required to read. It did not seek relief from any method of teaching the material and did not mention the teachers' editions. The plaintiffs did not produce a single student or teacher to testify that any student was ever required to affirm his or her belief or disbelief in any idea or practice mentioned in the various stories and passages contained in the Holt series. However, the plaintiffs appeared to assume that materials clearly presented as poetry, fiction and even "make-believe" in the Holt series were presented as facts which the students were required to believe. Nothing in the record supports this assumption. . . .

. . . Proof that an objecting student was *required* to participate beyond reading and discussing assigned materials, or was disciplined for disputing assigned materials, might well implicate the Free Exercise Clause because the element of compulsion would then be present. But this was not the case either as pled or proved. The record leaves no doubt that the district court correctly viewed this case as one involving exposure to repugnant ideas and themes as presented by the Holt series.

Vicki Frost testified that an occasional reference to role reversal, pacifism, rebellion against parents, one-world government and other objectionable concepts would be acceptable, but she

felt it was the repeated references to such subjects that created the burden. . . .

. . . Mrs. Frost testified that it would be acceptable for the schools to teach her children about other philosophies and religions, but if the practices of other religions were described in detail, or if the philosophy was "profound" in that it expressed a world view that deeply undermined her religious beliefs, then her children "would have to be instructed to [the] error [of the other philosophy]." It is clear that to the plaintiffs there is but one acceptable view—the Biblical view, as they interpret the Bible. Furthermore, the plaintiffs view every human situation and decision, whether related to personal belief and conduct or to public policy and programs, from a theological or religious perspective. . . .

The Supreme Court has recently affirmed that public schools serve the purpose of teaching fundamental values "essential to a democratic society." These values "include tolerance of divergent political and religious views" while taking into account "consideration of the sensibilities of others." . . . The Court has noted with apparent approval the view of some educators who see public schools as an "assimilative force" that brings together "diverse and conflicting elements" in our society "on a broad but common ground." . . . The critical reading approach furthers these goals. Mrs. Frost stated specifically that she objected to stories that develop "a religious tolerance that all religions are merely different roads to God." Stating that the plaintiffs reject this concept, presented as a recipe for an ideal world citizen, Mrs. Frost said, "We cannot be tolerant in that we accept other religious views on an equal basis with ours." While probably not an uncommon view of true believers in any religion, this statement graphically illustrates what is lacking in the plaintiffs' case.

The "tolerance of divergent . . . religious views" referred to by the Supreme Court is a civil tolerance, not a religious one. It does not require a person to accept any other religion as the equal of the one to which that person adheres. It merely requires a recognition that in a pluralistic society we must "live and let live." If the Hawkins County schools had required the plaintiff students either to believe or say they believe that "all religions are merely different roads to God," this would be a different case. No instrument of government can, consistent with the Free Exercise Clause, require such a belief or affirmation. However, there was absolutely no showing that the defendant school board sought to do this; indeed, the school board agreed at oral argument that it could not constitutionally do so. Instead, the record in this case discloses an effort by the school board to offer a reading curriculum designed to acquaint students with a multitude of ideas and concepts, though not in proportions the plaintiffs would like. While many of the passages deal with ethical issues, on the surface at least, they appear to us to contain no religious or anti-religious messages. Because the plaintiffs perceive every teaching that goes beyond the "three Rs" as inculcating religious ideas, they admit that any value-laden reading curriculum that did not affirm the truth of their beliefs would offend their religious convictions.

Although it is not clear that the plaintiffs object to all critical reading, Mrs. Frost did testify that she did not want her children to make critical judgments and exercise choices in areas where the Bible provides the answer. There is no evidence that any child in the Hawkins County schools was required to make such judgments. It was a goal of the school system to encourage this exercise, but nowhere was it shown that it was required. When asked to comment on a reading assignment, a student would be free to give the Biblical interpretation of the material or to interpret it from a different value base. The only conduct compelled by the defendants was reading and discussing the material in the Holt series, and hearing other students' interpretations of those materials. This is the exposure to which the plaintiffs objected. What is absent from this case is the critical element of compulsion to affirm or deny a religious belief or to engage or refrain from engaging in a practice forbidden or required in the exercise of a plaintiff's religion. . . .

Since we have found none of the prohibited forms of governmental compulsion in this case, we conclude that the plaintiffs failed to establish the existence of an unconstitutional burden. Having determined that no burden was shown,

we do not reach the issue of the defendants' compelling interest in requiring a uniform reading series or the question, raised by the defendant, of whether awarding damages violated the Establishment Clause. . . .

. . . There was no evidence that the conduct required of the students was forbidden by their religion. Rather, the witnesses testified that reading the Holt series "could" or "might" lead the students to come to conclusions that were contrary to teachings of their and their parents' religious beliefs. This is not sufficient to establish an unconstitutional burden. . . .

The judgment of the district court granting injunctive relief and damages is reversed, and the case is remanded with directions to dismiss the complaint. No costs are allowed. The parties will bear their own costs on appeal.

Case Notes

1. *Sequel to Mozert.* Following the determination in the Hawkins County case, Vicki Frost, a "born again Christian," was arrested for failure to leave school grounds after being told on several occasions by the principal that her repeated removal of her child from reading class and her conducting of reading lessons in the school parking lot, in the family car, was in violation of school policy. Frost sued, claiming denial of freedom of expression and due process because she was denied custody of her child during the school day. The court held that the school board had not deprived Frost of her freedom of expression nor had she been deprived of custody of her child without due process. Further, the court held that the city police were not liable for arresting her on school grounds. Her presence on school grounds and repeated refusal to leave was in violation of state statute forbidding trespass on school property. *Frost v. Hawkins County Board of Education,* 851 F.2d 822 (6th Cir.1988).

2. *Secular Humanism and Textbooks.* Plaintiffs in an Alabama case, *Smith v. Board of School Commissioners of Mobile County,* 827 F.2d 684 (11th Cir.1987), claimed that use of certain home economics textbooks required students to accept tenets of humanistic psychology, a term that the lower court found to be a "manifestation of

humanism." Humanism or secular humanism, it was maintained, was a religion advanced by the public schools through the use of home economics, history, and social studies textbooks that "implied that a person uses the same process in deciding a moral issue that he uses in choosing one pair of shoes over another." It was contended that these home economics, history, and social studies textbooks inferred that "the student must determine right and wrong based only on his own experience, feelings and [internal] values" and that such "moral choice is only to be decided by the student." The plaintiffs further asserted that the textbooks assumed that "self-actualization is the goal of every human being, and that man has no supernatural attributes. . . , that there are only temporal and physical consequences for man's actions, and that these results, alone, determine the morality of an action." This "belief strikes at the heart of many theistic religious beliefs that certain actions are in and of themselves immoral, whatever the consequences." By not seeking ecclesiastical answers in resolving human decisions, the schools, it was claimed, denied or inhibited religion and advanced secularism. In support of the charge that the schools were purely temporal, the plaintiffs cited a recommended decision-making process cited by the textbooks. This process called for resolving problems by (1) defining the problem, (2) establishing goals, (3) listing goals in priority order, (4) looking for resources, (5) studying the alternatives, (6) making a decision, (7) carrying out the decision, and (8) evaluating the results. Because this process did not invoke divine guidance or include a step for spiritual involvement, the plaintiffs and the lower court concluded that the textbooks advanced secular humanism as a religion and denied theistic religious views. The appeals court found for the School Board and in so doing, concluded:

> . . . Examination of the contents of these textbooks, including the passages pointed out by Appellees as particularly offensive, in the context of the books as a whole and the undisputedly nonreligious purpose sought to be achieved by their use, reveals that the message conveyed is not one of endorsement of secular humanism or any religion. Rather, the message conveyed is one of a governmental attempt to instill in Alabama public school

children such values as independent thought, tolerance of diverse views, self-respect, maturity, self-reliance and logical decision-making. This is an entirely appropriate secular effect. Indeed, one of the major objectives of public education is the "inculca[tion of] fundamental values necessary to the maintenance of a democratic political system." . . . Nor do these textbooks evidence an attitude antagonistic to theistic belief. The message conveyed by these textbooks with regard to theistic religion is one of neutrality: the textbooks neither endorse theistic religion as a system of belief, nor discredit it. . . . There is no doubt that these textbooks were chosen for the secular purpose of education in the areas of history and social studies, and we find that the primary effect of the use of these textbooks is consistent with that stated purpose. We do not believe that an objective observer could conclude from the mere omission of certain historical facts regarding religion or the absence of a more thorough discussion of its place in modern American society that the State of Alabama was conveying a message of approval of the religion of secular humanism. . . . There simply is nothing in this record to indicate that omission of certain facts regarding religion from these textbooks of itself constituted an advancement of secular humanism or an active hostility towards theistic religion prohibited by the establishment clause.

———————— ❖ — ❖ — ❖ ————————

Curriculum Discussing Witchcraft and
Sorcerers Does Not Violate Establishment Clause

Brown v. Woodland Joint Unified School District

United States Court of Appeals,
Ninth Circuit, 1994.
27 F.3d 1373.

O'SCANNLAIN, Circuit Judge:

We must decide whether classroom activities in a California public school district require children to practice the "religion" of witchcraft in violation of the federal Establishment Clause and the California Constitution.

Douglas E. Brown and Katherine E. Brown, parents of two students formerly enrolled in the

Woodland Joint Unified School District (the "School District"), seek injunctive and declaratory relief under 42 U.S.C. §1983, alleging that the School District had violated their children's rights under the United States and California Constitutions. The Browns and their children are part of the Christian Assembly of God denomination.

The Browns object to the School District's use of portions of *Impressions*, a teaching aid, in the first through sixth grades. *Impressions* is a series of 59 books containing approximately 10,000 literary selections and suggested classroom activities. It implements a "whole language" approach to reading instruction that has the goal of inducing children to read more quickly and with greater enthusiasm through the use of high quality literary selections. Literary selections are followed by suggested learning activities, such as having children compose rhymes and chants, act out the selections, and discuss the selections' characters and themes. The selections reflect a broad range of North American cultures and traditions.

The Browns challenge 32 of the *Impressions* selections (the "Challenged Selections"). They contend that these selections promote the practice of witchcraft, which they assert is a religion called "Wicca." Most of the Challenged Selections ask children to discuss witches or to create poetic chants. Some selections also ask students to pretend that they are witches or sorcerers and ask them to role-play these characters in certain situations.

The Browns have provided evidence indicating that practitioners of the witchcraft religion are known as sorcerers and witches and that spells and charms are sacred rituals of this occult religion. The Browns contend that, because the Challenged Selections resemble witchcraft rituals, the School District's use of the selections violates the federal and state Constitutions. . . .

The School District does not contest the Browns' assertion that witchcraft ("Wicca") is a religion under the California and federal Constitutions, and we will assume, without deciding, that it is a religion for the purpose of this appeal. We thus apply the *Lemon* test to the Browns' claim, which requires a challenged government practice (1) to have a secular purpose, (2) to have a primary effect that neither ad-

vances nor inhibits religion, and (3) not to foster excessive state entanglement with religion. . . .

The Browns concede that the author-editors of *Impressions* chose the Challenged Selections for a secular purpose and that the School District adopted *Impressions* for a secular purpose. They also do not assert that any School District teachers are using the Challenged Selections for the purpose of advancing witchcraft. Use of the Challenged Selections thus does not violate the purpose prong of the *Lemon* test.

The Browns contend that the use of the Challenged Selections violates the second prong of the *Lemon* test, which bars any government practice that has the "primary" effect of advancing or disapproving of religion, even if that effect is not intended. The concept of a "primary" effect encompasses even nominally "secondary" effects of government action that directly and immediately advance, or disapprove of, religion. . . .

The parties dispute the standard for judging whether a government action "conveys a message" of endorsement or disapproval of religion. The Browns assert that this inquiry must be made from the subjective perspective of an "impressionable child." The School District counters that the correct perspective is that of a reasonable observer. The district court took a middle ground between these approaches, concluding that "[t]he effect analysis is influenced to some degree by the audience to whom the message is conveyed. . . ."

We agree with the district court that the primary effect of a challenged practice generally is considered under the reasonable observer standard. . . . "This hypothetical observer is informed as well as reasonable; we assume that he or she is familiar with the history of the government practice at issue." . . . However, these assumptions are less valid for elementary school children, who are less informed, more impressionable and more subject to peer pressure than average adults. . . . Courts thus have considered the more vulnerable nature of school-age children when analyzing the primary effect of state actions in the elementary school environment.

The Browns contend that this perspective demands a *subjective* standard for determining whether a challenged practice appears to children as endorsing or disapproving of a religion.

We disagree. Rather than consider what effect a challenged government practice has had on a particular public school student, the Supreme Court and this circuit consistently have applied an objective standard for public school Establishment Clause inquiries. . . . Use of this standard makes good sense. "People may take offense at all manner of religious as well as nonreligious messages." . . . If an Establishment Clause violation arose each time a student believed that a school practice either advanced or disapproved of a religion, school curricula would be reduced to the lowest common denominator, permitting each student to become a "curriculum review committee" unto himself or herself. . . .

Thus we will analyze whether an objective observer in the position of an elementary school student would perceive a message of endorsement of witchcraft, or of disapproval of Christianity, in the Challenged Selections.

The Browns assert that a message of endorsement is communicated because the Challenged Selections engage children in witchcraft rituals and cause them to pretend that they are witchcraft practitioners. The closest case in this circuit to the instant controversy is *Grove v. Mead School District No. 354*, 753 F.2d 1528 (9th Cir.1985). In *Grove*, the plaintiffs alleged that a book entitled *The Learning Tree*, which was part of the defendant school's sophomore curriculum, advanced the religion of secular humanism in violation of the federal Establishment Clause. The court rejected their claim. Observing that the "Supreme Court has stated clearly that literary or historic study of the Bible *is not* prohibited religious activity," the court concluded that the reading of the book was "not a ritual" but a study of the "expectations and orientations of Black Americans." . . . It further concluded that the book was "included in a group of religiously neutral books in a review of English literature, as a comment on an American subculture."

To the extent that the Challenged Selections involve no more than merely reading, discussing or contemplating witches, their behavior, or witchcraft, they fall squarely within the holding of *Grove*. *See Grove*, 753 F.2d at 1540 (Canby, J. concurring) ("Luther's 'Ninety-Nine [sic] Theses' are hardly balanced or objective, yet their pronounced and even vehement bias does not prevent their study in a history class' exploration of the Protestant Reformation, nor is Protestantism itself 'advanced' thereby"). Such selections thus are not reasonably viewed as communicating a message of endorsement. . . .

The Browns then argue that the resemblance of the Challenged Selections to the practices of witchcraft causes children reasonably to believe that they are engaging in witchcraft ritual. However, a practice's mere consistency with or coincidental resemblance to a religious practice does not have the primary effect of advancing religion. . . .

The fact that the Challenged Selections constitute only a minute part of the *Impressions* curriculum further ensures that an objective observer in the position of an elementary school student would not view them as religious rituals endorsing witchcraft. . . .

The Browns assert that the context in which the Challenged Selections appear cannot neutralize their religious content. They argue that context is irrelevant where a person is required to participate in a religious ritual. . . . This position is untenable, however, because the Challenged Selections are not formal religious rituals; at best, the Browns can prove only that children may perceive them as such. The context in which Challenged Selections exist is relevant to determining whether children will have such a perception. . . .

The Browns assert that use of the Challenged Selections was not necessary to accomplish the School District's pedagogical goals and conclude that the unnecessary use of practices resembling religious ritual endorses religion. However, once the state is free to use a secular means of attaining a goal, it is not required to use an alternative secular means that is less likely to be associated with religion. . . . As we have established, the Challenged Selections are secular, not sectarian. Consequently, the School District's decision not to use alternative educational tools did not endorse witchcraft. . . .

The Browns argue that a failure by this panel to find that the Challenged Selections endorse witchcraft would discriminate against Christianity and other popular religions. Their argument rests on their observation that it would "obviously" violate the Establishment Clause if *Impressions* selections were to require children intentionally to perform, for example, a baptism, to take communion or to chant a rosary.

These hypothetical examples are distinguishable from the Challenged Selections. Baptism, communion, and the rosary *are* "overt religious exercises," performed for sectarian purposes. . . . Mimicry of them by public school children thus more likely, though perhaps not necessarily, . . . would give the appearance of an endorsement of religion. In contrast, the activities in the Challenged Selections are fantasy activities, drawn from a secular source and used for a secular purpose, that happen to resemble religious practices. They are *not* "overt religious exercises" that raise Establishment Clause concerns. Consequently, we do not believe that affirmance of the district court's judgment will lead to disparate adverse treatment of popular religions.

Finally, the Browns argue that the School District's use of the Challenged Selections denigrates Christianity and makes Christians feel like outsiders. Their argument relies on their assertion that the alleged witchcraft activities in the Challenged Selections are repugnant to their religious beliefs.

For the reasons expressed above, a child's subjective perception that a state action disapproves of or is hostile toward his or her religion is not, by itself, sufficient to establish an Establishment Clause violation. A party must show that an objective observer in the position of an elementary school student would have this view. The purported state hostility toward or disapproval of Christianity consists of the alleged coincidental resemblance of the Challenged Selections to rituals and practitioners of witchcraft. For the same reasons that the use of these selections does not endorse witchcraft, it does not evince hostility toward or otherwise disapprove of Christianity.

The Browns have not persuaded us that the second, "effects," prong of *Lemon* has been violated here.

The third prong of the *Lemon* test prohibits a practice that fosters an excessive entanglement of the state with religion. . . . The Browns assert that *Impressions* fosters excessive entanglement by generating political divisiveness "along religious lines" and requiring undue state surveillance of the purportedly religious-oriented aspects of the curriculum. . . .

. . . The political divisiveness doctrine generally is applied only in cases involving direct government subsidies to sectarian institutions. . . . Unlike those cases, the School District's use of the Challenged Selections is not an intentional effort to aid overtly religious exercises and issues. The district court's decision not to apply the political divisiveness doctrine thus was proper. . . .

The Browns have failed to persuade us that any of the three prongs of the *Lemon* test has been breached here. We conclude, therefore, that the School District has not violated the federal Establishment Clause in its use of the *Impressions* series.

The Browns also bring pendant claims under the California Constitution. . . .

The Establishment Clause of the California Constitution states that "[t]he Legislature shall make no law respecting the establishment of religion." Cal. Const. art. I, §4. As under the federal Establishment Clause, the California Establishment Clause generally prohibits public schools from requiring their students to engage in religious ritual. . . . No California decision suggests, however, that the California Establishment Clause goes beyond its federal counterpart to prohibit school exercises that coincidentally resemble religious rituals. We thus believe that, if confronted with this question, California courts would uphold the use of the Challenged Selections from state constitutional attack.

California's No Preference Clause reads: "Free exercise and enjoyment of religion without discrimination or preference are guaranteed." Cal. Const. art I, §4. . . . These facts, in addition to the fact that the Challenged Selections are among a wide variety of other cultural selections, indicate that the use of these selections will not evince a preference for witchcraft. . . . There is no violation of the No Preference Clause.

Article IX, section 8 of the California Constitution provides that no "sectarian or denominational doctrine [shall] be taught, or instruction thereon be permitted, directly or indirectly, in any of the common schools of this State." Cal. Const. art. IX, §8. The Challenged Selections were chosen for reasons unrelated to the religion of witchcraft, and the use of the Challenged Selections does not appear to endorse religion. The use of exercises that coincidentally resemble practices of witchcraft therefore does not teach the religion of witchcraft even indirectly. There is no violation of article IX, section 8.

The Browns do not raise a genuine issue of material fact that a violation of the United States or California Constitutions has occurred. Summary judgment in favor of the School District is therefore

AFFIRMED.

CASE NOTE

In another case involving the *Impressions* reading series, parents claimed similarly that the series violated the establishment clause and free exercise clause of the First Amendment.

The parents alleged that the series fostered "a religious belief in the existence of superior beings exercising power over human beings" and focused on supernatural powers of wizards, sorcerers, and giants, indoctrinating children in values contrary to Christian beliefs. First, the court applied the *Lemon* test in rejecting the parents' claims, saying that a "few stories about witches and goblins" do not violate the secular purpose test. Second, the stories that were offensive to the plaintiff parents were only a small portion of all the readings in the series, and other stories touched on and were consistent with Protestant and Catholic beliefs about Christmas and so forth. Simply because the stories "coincide or harmonize with tenets of some or all religions" does not endorse or enhance a religion but is merely designed to improve the children's reading skills.

Concerning the third leg of the *Lemon* test, the court found no entanglement simply because a curriculum review committee of the school district had reviewed the series before it was purchased. Further, the court concluded that no coercion existed so as to deprive children of the free exercise of religion. *Fleischfresser v. Directors of School District 200*, 15 F.3d 680 (1994).

■ OBSCENITY AND SEX

Freedom of speech and expression ensure that public schools will be open and expansive in acquisition and purveyance of knowledge. Yet, the type and content of information that may be provided to school children is not without limitation. Society at large has the right and the obligation to protect children from harmful influences, and the public schools have the power and prerogative to make and enforce judgments about those things that are beneficial or deleterious to the development of youth. Even John Stuart Mill, the great expositor of individual liberty, maintained that liberties that were the rights of adults could not necessarily be indiscriminately assumed to vest in minors. In his essay *On Liberty*, Mill observed:

It is, perhaps, hardly necessary to say that this doctrine is meant to apply only to human beings in the maturity of their faculties. We are not speaking of children or of young persons below the age which the law may fix as that of manhood or womanhood. Those who are still in a state to require being taken care of by others must be protected against their own actions as well as against external injury.[37]

The school district can select the substance to be taught and can proscribe inappropriate books, films, or other materials. Sexually explicit books or films can be prohibited by the school district by valid regulation. Such regulation cannot be unconstitutionally vague nor so overly broad that a reasonable person could not determine what is, in fact, denied.

Such regulatory proscriptions may be bedeviled by imprecision of definition. With proper definition, though, the use of obscene books, films, or other materials can be prohibited. Yet the school can also prohibit materials that are not necessarily obscene but are otherwise inappropriate. In other words, schools may exclude materials that are, in the judgment of school officials, unsuitable whether they are technically obscene or not. If materials are merely vulgar but have no pedagogical value, they can be proscribed as well.

Obscenity is not constitutionally protected under either the speech or press provisions of the First Amendment.[38] Because obscenity is not constitutionally protected, the U.S. Supreme Court has been diligent in its attempts to define the term so as not to permit regulatory overreach that could conceivably encroach on constitutional liberties of speech and press. The difficulty that the Supreme Court has experienced in conceptualizing a workable definition of obscenity is illustrated by Justice William Brennan's frustrations with the issue; he said:

> I put sixteen years into that damn obscenity thing. I tried and I tried, and I waffled back and forth, and finally gave up. If you can't define it, you can't prosecute people for it.[39]

Yet, over the years, the Supreme Court has defined obscenity in a series of cases,[40] and it thereby provides a legal context in which our society must operate. It was in the *Beauharnais* case[41] in 1952 that Justice Frankfurter wrote for the Court that obscenity is without constitutional protection, that by definition obscenity is not entitled to protection. In this case the Court drew the distinction between sex and obscenity, saying that "obscene material is material which deals with sex in a manner appealing to the prurient interest,"[42] while the mere portrayal of sex in art, literature, scientific works, and similar forums "is not itself sufficient reason to deny material the constitutional protection of freedom of speech and press."

Later, the Supreme Court in *Roth* established the formula to identify obscenity as follows:

> Material may be determined to be obscene and, thus, beyond constitutional protection, if it (a) appeals to a prurient interest in sex; (b) has no serious literary, artistic, political, or scientific merit; and (c) is on the whole offensive to the average person under contemporary community standards.[43]

The word "prurient" has caused definitional problems since its inception. The Court has sought to clarify its meaning by defining it as material that has "a tendency to excite lustful thoughts."[44] Some justices, however, early expressed the view that even this definition was too imprecise, and that such imprecision of terminology would give "the censor free range over a vast domain."[45] Not long after *Roth*, it was generally concluded that the Court intended to require that offensive material, taken as a whole, must be determined by how the average person reflecting the attitudes of a common community standard would adjudge the material. Further, because "prurient" could be understood differently in different circumstances, it was concluded that the terminology

was so subjective that it could be applied only in a relative sense.[46] This "variable obscenity" standard manifested such uncertainty that Justice Potter Stewart was led to conclude in despair that he could not define it, but that "I know it when I see it."[47]

Finally, the definitional problem forced a modification of definitional precedent that was set forth in *Miller v. California*, prescribing a new test for obscenity. The basic guidelines are as follows:

> (a) [W]hether "the average person, applying contemporary community standards," would find that the work, taken as a whole, appeals to the prurient interest, (b) whether the work depicts or describes, in a patently offensive way, sexual conduct specifically defined by the applicable state law, and (c) whether the work, taken as a whole, lacks serious literary, artistic, political, or scientific value.[48]

The first part of the test adopted a community standards test and implicitly rejected a national standards test for obscenity. The Supreme Court in *Miller* stated explicitly that "[i]n resolving the inevitable sensitive questions of fact and law, we must continue to rely on the jury system, accompanied by safeguards that judges, rules of evidence, presumption of innocence, and other protective features provide."[49] Such issues cannot all be decided under perceptions of the judges at the U.S. Supreme Court or national level. The Court concluded that the trier of fact should not be required to guess at some hypothetical "medium" standard for the nation.

Part two of the test allows the state to prohibit patently offensive "representations or descriptions of ultimate sexual acts, normal or perverted, actual or simulated."[50]

The third part of the test replaced the earlier test standard of "utterly without redeeming social value."[51] The *Miller* standard appears to be better defined and a bit more restrictive than earlier versions. The word "serious" replaces "utterly," and "social value" is replaced by the increased specification of "literary, artistic, political, or scientific value." Later, in 1987, in an elaboration on *Miller*, the Supreme Court held that the third prong of the *Miller* test is not to be determined by a jury applying "local contemporary community standards" but rather by a jury being instructed to decide whether a reasonable person would find serious literary, artistic, political, or scientific value in the material taken as a whole: "The value of a work, unlike its prurient appeal or patent offensiveness [that is, unlike the first two elements of *Miller*] does not vary from community to community based on the degree of local acceptance it has won."[52]

This definition of obscenity is the view of the U.S. Supreme Court as it prevails today. Public schools, however, are a more restricted legal environment, with an educational purpose and a clientele of youth who are subject to curricular prescription as devised by the state. Obscenity is, of course, proscribed in schools, but school officials can go even further in preventing the use or distribution of offensive materials in schools, regardless of whether such materials fall within the definition of obscenity.

The primary precedent covering such situations is *Hazelwood School District v. Kuhlmeier*,[53] in which the U.S. Supreme Court vested educators with substantial discretion in control of speech and press in the school. The Court pointedly held that "[e]ducators do not offend the First Amendment by exercising editorial control over the style and content of student speech in school-sponsored expressive activities so long as their actions are reasonably related to legitimate pedagogical concerns."[54]

Educators can, in legitimate exercise of their prerogatives, prescribe the content of the curriculum and censor inappropriate materials. The *Hazelwood* court said further:

> It is only when the decision to censor a school-sponsored publication, theatrical production, or other vehicle of student expression has no valid educational purpose that the First Amendment is so directly and sharply implicated as to require judicial intervention to protect students' constitutional rights.[55]

The *Hazelwood* precedent has been followed by lower courts in giving school boards broad discretion in banning the use of certain books, films, and other materials. One such example of the reach of such broad authority was illustrated in *Virgil v. School Board of Columbia County, Florida*,[56] in which the U.S. Court of Appeals, Eleventh Circuit, upheld a school board's removal of Aristophanes' *Lysistrata* and Chaucer's *The Miller's Tale* from use in school, based on the school board's opinion that the

books were "excessively vulgar" and too expressive of sexuality. It was not necessary for the school board to show that the books were obscene in order to ban them. This court, citing *Hazelwood*, said that "*Hazelwood* established a relatively lenient test for regulation of expression which may fairly be characterized as part of the school curriculum. Such regulation is permissible so long as it is 'reasonably related to legitimate pedagogical concerns.'"[57]

FILMS

The use of films as teaching aids in classrooms has become increasingly more common, and the choice of some films and their use have led to litigation. In one such case, where a nontenured teacher showed an R-rated film, the federal district court ruled that failure to renew the teacher's contract for showing the film in class was not violative of her First Amendment rights. Whether the decision to show the film was reasonable depended on whether it offended legitimate pedagogical concerns, given the school's right to establish curriculum content. This court identified two types of cases that were applicable to the showing of films as constitutional expression in the classroom: first, those cases involving the curriculum and the school rules that prescribe curricular content, and second, those cases where a teacher is disciplined for exercise of classroom expression beyond the prescribed curriculum and in which no particular school rule is violated. Regarding the former, the courts have established as a general rule that "a school administration may establish the curricular contents of a course."[58]

Moreover, the courts have reasoned that in a public school system, where the state pays the costs of education, it is appropriate for the curriculum to reflect the value system and collective will of the children being educated.[59] "Consequently, the cases involving challenges to school-imposed restrictions of the content of courses can be characterized as being deferential to the judgment of school administrators."

In applying the precedents pertaining to curriculum content, the *Krizek* court observed that "the school has a 'legitimate concern' over the display of vulgarity and sexual scenes to students in a public school system."[60] Though not binding on either the court or the school, the fact that a film is R-rated is an indication that reasonable people could determine whether a film was inappropriate for students of younger than seventeen years of age.

Regarding the second type of situation, the court, in *Krizek,* after reviewing the applicable precedents of cases in which teachers were disciplined for expression that violated no specific rule, concluded that the standard established in *Mailloux v. Kiley*[61]—"[A] school may never fire a teacher 'after the fact' for poor judgment in choice of teaching material,"—was bad precedent, being too restrictive on school administrators. The court rejected the *Mailloux* standard for two reasons. First, because "it would be impossible for a school to proscribe every imaginable inappropriate material." Second, schools may not be encouraged to attempt to enact regulations against every conceivable act of bad judgment or indiscretion of teachers. The court reasoned that the resulting maze of restrictive regulations would have chilling effect on classroom activities. After reviewing precedents relevant to the second type of dismissal, the *Krizek* court found no clear standard and therefore concluded that it must set its own standard of review, to wit: Was the school action "reasonable" in view of the circumstances?

For some obscure reason, Louisiana had an unusual amount of litigation regarding the use of objectionable films in schools. Perhaps the teachers subject students to an extraordinarily heavy diet of films, or parents and citizenry are excessively sensitive to improprieties exercised by some filmmakers. Regardless of the reason, several cases have been rendered that suggest an emerging list of film precedents that are important to public schools. The reasonableness standard discussed above was applied by a state appellate court in Louisiana in upholding the decision of a school board in suspending a teacher for a semester for showing a PG-rated film to a special education class. The film contained the word "nigger." The teacher's stated intent for showing the film was to illustrate the obnoxiousness of the word and by its exposure to curtail the use of the word among the schoolchildren. The court said, "We fail to understand how such an offensive movie could, without thorough discussion, effectively curtail the use of the word 'Nigger' amongst learning-hampered

black students."[62] Thus the teacher's reasoning was rejected, and the school board prevailed.

As these precedents indicate, a school board has substantial discretion in regulation of the content of the curriculum. The strength of the school board's authority emanates from the constitutional interpretation of the Supreme Court in *Hazelwood.* Educational purpose and reasonableness appear to be reliable to ensure validity of school board actions in establishing and implementing such regulatory control.

❖ — ❖ — ❖

State Can Validly Require a Course in Sex Education for All Students

Cornwell v. State Board of Education

United States District Court, Maryland, 1969. 314 F.Supp. 340 (D.Md.1969), affirmed 428 F.2d 471 (4th Cir.1970), cert. denied 400 U.S. 942, 91 S.Ct. 240 (1970).

HARVEY, District Judge. In this civil action, Baltimore County taxpayers are suing the Maryland State Board of Education seeking to prevent the implementation in the Baltimore County Schools of a program of sex education. In particular, the plaintiffs, who are school children and their parents, seek to have this Court declare unconstitutional a bylaw duly adopted by the State Board. The provision in question is By-Law 720, Section 3, Subsection 4, which provides as follows:

> It is the responsibility of the local school system to provide a comprehensive program of family life and sex education in every elementary and secondary school for all students as an integral part of the curriculum including a planned and sequential program of health education.

. . . In determining whether there is here a substantial question of constitutionality, this Court concludes initially that no question whatsoever arises under the Fourteenth Amendment. There is first no denial of substantive due process to the plaintiffs. Under Section 6 of Article 77 of the Maryland Code (as amended and re-codified by Chapter 405 of the Acts of 1969), The State Board is directed to determine the educational policies of the state and to enact bylaws for the administration of the public school system, which when enacted and published shall have the force of law. Assuredly it cannot be said that the bylaw here is an arbitrary or unreasonable exercise of the authority vested in the State Board to determine a teaching curriculum, nor that there is no basis in fact for the legislative policy expressed in the bylaw. Furthermore, it does not appear that the bylaw denies equal protection of the laws, as on its face it applies to all pupils equally.

Plaintiffs allege that the enactment of this bylaw was based on a study made in reference to pregnant pupils. But whatever the genesis of the bylaw, it is not the study that is being attacked here but the bylaw itself, and it is being attacked on its face. It is the provisions of the bylaw then that must be examined in the light of the United States Constitution. The plaintiffs' argument that the bylaw is defective because it applies to nonpregnant as well as to pregnant pupils is difficult to follow. There would appear to be just as much reason for the State Board to provide sex education for the nonpregnant (and, incidentally, for the nonimpregnating) as for those students who, because of a lack of information on the subject (or for other reasons), have become pregnant or who have caused pregnancy.

The plaintiffs further assert that they have the exclusive constitutional right to teach their children about sexual matters in their own homes, and that such exclusive right would prohibit the teaching of sex in the schools. No authority is cited in support of this novel proposition, and this Court knows of no such constitutional right. This Court, then, is satisfied that the claims asserted in this complaint under the Fourteenth Amendment are so insubstantial that they do not confer jurisdiction here.

In support of their First Amendment claim, the plaintiffs assert that they have been denied the free exercise of their religious concepts and that the teaching of sex in the Baltimore County Schools will in fact establish religious concepts. . . .

Applying the principles that have been established by the various cases, it is quite clear to this Court that the purpose and primary effect of the bylaw here is not to establish any particular religious dogma or precept, and that the bylaw does not directly or substantially involve the state in religious exercises or in the favoring of religion or any particular religion. The bylaw may be considered quite simply as a public health measure. As the Supreme Court indicated in *Prince v. Massachusetts,* 321 U.S. 158, 64 S.Ct. 438, 88 L.Ed. 645 (1944), the State's interest in the health of its children outweighs claims based upon religious freedom and the right of parental control. The Court in that particular case said this (at pages 168–169):

> A democratic society rests . . . upon the healthy, well-rounded growth of young people into full maturity as citizens. . . . It is too late now to doubt that legislation appropriately designed to reach such evils is within the state's police power, whether against the parent's claim to control of the child or one that religious scruples dictate contrary action.

In summary, then, the Court concludes that the federal question here is plainly insubstantial. Construing the allegations in a light most favorable to the plaintiffs, as the Court must do on these motions to dismiss, this Court finds that the constitutional questions relied upon are obviously without merit. The unsoundness and insubstantiality of the plaintiffs' position is clearly indicated by the various decisions of the Supreme Court to which I have alluded.

For these reasons then, the two motions to dismiss are granted.

CASE NOTES

1. Sex education does not invade the privacy of school children or parents. *Medeiros v. Kiyosaki,* 52 Hawaii 436, 478 P.2d 314 (1970).

2. The Supreme Court of New Jersey has upheld a state board of education regulation that requires each school district to develop and implement a family life education program in the public elementary and secondary school curricula. The focus of the program was to be on teaching about human sexuality. The regulation included an "excusal clause" establishing procedures by which a parent could withdraw

his or her child if the course conflicted with religious belief or conscience. The court held that the regulation did not violate either the free exercise or establishment clause of the First Amendment. Concerning free exercise, the court placed emphasis on the fact that the regulation contained an "excusal" provision. In applying the establishment clause, the court pointed out that the regulation does not enhance any particular religious viewpoint, nor does it favor a "secular" view over a "religious" one. *Smith v. Ricci,* 89 N.J. 514, 466 A.2d 501 (1982).

3. The federal circuit court in *Cornwell* dismissed parents' free exercise argument even though there was no provision for the student to be excused. In *Medeiros* (note 1) and *Smith* (note 2), however, the courts relied on "excusal" provisions in the regulations to offset the free exercise issue.

Academic Freedom Extends to Protect Teacher in Use of "Dirty" Word If Conveyed for Demonstrated Educational Purpose

Keefe v. Geanakos

United States Court of Appeals,
First Circuit, 1969.
418 F.2d 359.

ALDRICH, Chief Judge. . . . Reduced to fundamentals, the substance of plaintiff's position is that as a matter of law his conduct which forms the basis of the charge did not warrant discipline. Accordingly, he argues, there is no ground for any hearing. He divides this position into two parts. The principal one is that his conduct was within his competence as a teacher, as a matter of academic freedom, whether the defendants approved of it or not. The second is that he had been given inadequate prior warning by such regulations as were in force, particularly in the light of the totality of the circumstances known to him, that his actions would be considered improper, so that an ex post facto ruling would, itself, unsettle academic freedom.

The defendants, essentially, deny plaintiff's contentions. They accept the existence of a principle of academic freedom to teach, but state that it is limited to proper classroom materials as reasonably determined by the school committee in the light of pertinent conditions, of which they cite in particular the age of the students. Asked by the court whether a teacher has a right to say to the school committee that it is wrong if, in fact, its decision was arbitrary, counsel candidly and commendably (and correctly) responded in the affirmative. This we consider to be the present issue. . . .

On the opening day of school in September 1969 the plaintiff gave to each member of his senior English class a copy of the September 1969 *Atlantic Monthly* magazine, a publication of high reputation, and stated that the reading assignment for that night was the first article therein. September was the educational number, so-called, of the *Atlantic,* and some seventy-five copies had been supplied by the school department. Plaintiff discussed the article, and a particular word that was used therein, and explained the word's origin and context, and the reasons the author had included it. The word, admittedly highly offensive, is a vulgar term for an incestuous son. Plaintiff stated that any student who felt the assignment personally distasteful could have an alternative one.

The next evening the plaintiff was called to a meeting of the school committee and asked to defend his use of the offending word. Following his explanation, a majority of the members of the committee asked him informally if he would agree not to use it again in the classroom. Plaintiff replied that he could not, in good conscience, agree. His counsel states, however, without contradiction, that in point of fact plaintiff has not used it again. No formal action was taken at this meeting. Thereafter plaintiff was suspended, as a matter of discipline, and it is now proposed that he should be discharged.

The Lifton article, which we have read in its entirety, has been described as a valuable discussion of "dissent, protest, radicalism, and revolt." It is in no sense pornographic. We need no supporting affidavits to find it scholarly, thoughtful and thought-provoking. The single offending word, although repeated a number of times, is not artificially introduced, but, on the contrary, is important to the development of the thesis and the conclusions of the author. Indeed, we would find it difficult to disagree with plaintiff's assertion that no proper study of the article could avoid consideration of this word. It is not possible to read the article, either in whole or in part, as an incitement to libidinous conduct, or even thoughts. If it raised the concept of incest, it was not to suggest it, but to condemn it; the word was used, by the persons described, as a superlative of opprobrium. We believe not only that the article negatived any other concept, but that an understanding of it would reject, rather than suggest the word's use. . . .

Hence the question in this case is whether a teacher may, for demonstrated educational purposes, quote a "dirty" word currently used in order to give special offense, or whether the shock is too great for high school seniors to stand. If the answer were that the students must be protected from such exposure, we would fear for their future. We do not question the good faith of the defendants in believing that some parents have been offended. With the greatest of respect to such parents, their sensibilities are not the full measure of what is proper education.

We of course agree with defendants that what is to be said or read to students is not to be determined by obscenity standards for adult consumption. . . . At the same time, the issue must be one of degree. A high school senior is not devoid of all discrimination or resistance. Furthermore, as in all other instances, the offensiveness of language and the particular propriety or impropriety is dependent on the circumstances of the utterance. . . . We accept the conclusion of the court below that "some measure of public regulation of classroom speech is inherent in every provision of public education." But when we consider the facts at bar as we have elaborated them, we find it difficult not to think that its application to the present case demeans any proper concept of education. The general chilling effect of permitting such rigorous censorship is even more serious.

We believe it equally probable that the plaintiff will prevail on the issue of lack of any notice that a discussion of this article with the senior class was forbidden conduct. The school regulation upon which defendants rely, although un-questionably worthy, is not apposite. It does not follow that a teacher may not be on notice of impropriety from the circumstances of a case without the necessity of a regulation. In the present case, however, the circumstances would have disclosed that no less than five books, by as many authors, containing the word in question were to be found in the school library. It is hard to think that any student could walk into the library and receive a book, but that his teacher could not subject the content to serious discussion in class.

Such inconsistency on the part of the school has been regarded as fatal. . . . We, too, would probably so regard it. At the same time, we prefer not to place our decision on this ground alone, lest our doing so diminish our principal holding, or lead to a bowdlerization of the school library.

Finally, we are not persuaded by the district court's conclusion that no irreparable injury is involved because the plaintiff, if successful, may recover money damages. Academic freedom is not preserved by compulsory retirement, even at full pay.

The immediate question before us is whether we should grant interlocutory relief pending appeal. This question, as defendants point out, raises the ultimate issue of the appeal itself. The matter has been extensively briefed and argued by both sides. We see no purpose in taking two bites, and believe this a case for action under Local Rule 5. The order of the district court denying an interlocutory injunction pending a decision on the merits is reversed and the case is remanded for further proceedings consistent herewith.

CASE NOTES

1. In *Zykan*, the United States Court of Appeals, Seventh Circuit, has held that courts will not intervene in school matters unless there is shown to be a "flagrant abuse of discretion" on the part of school officials. This court said:

> [C]omplaints filed by secondary school students to contest the educational decision of local authorities are sometimes cognizable but generally must cross a relatively high threshold before entering upon the field of a constitutional claim. . . . [N]othing in

the Constitution permits the courts to interfere with local discretion until local authorities begin to substitute rigid and exclusive indoctrination for the right to make pedagogic choices regarding matters of legitimate dispute.

The court went on to deny the plaintiffs' claim because they failed to prove a "flagrant abuse of discretion on the part of the defendants." Thus, the Seventh Circuit has established and articulated what may be called a "flagrant abuse of discretion" standard of review. *Zykan v. Warsaw Community School Corp.,* 631 F.2d 1300, 1306 (7th Cir.1980).

2. In a case in which a secondary school teacher wrote on the blackboard using a four-letter word to illustrate changes in standards of morality, the court held that the teacher must be able to show that the instructional method used is in keeping with the preponderant opinion of the teaching profession. The court said:

> While secondary schools are not rigid disciplinary institutions, neither are they open forums in which mature adults, already habituated to social restraints, exchange ideas on a level of parity. Moreover, it cannot be accepted as a premise that the student is voluntarily in the classroom and willing to be exposed to a teaching method which, though reasonable, is not approved by the school authorities or by the weight of professional opinion. A secondary school student, unlike most college students, is usually required to attend school classes, and may have no choice as to his teacher.
>
> Bearing in mind these competing considerations, this court rules that when a secondary school teacher uses a teaching method which he does not prove has the support of the preponderant opinion of the teaching profession or of the part of it to which he belongs, but which he merely proves is relevant to his subject and students, is regarded by experts of significant standing as serving a serious educational purpose, and was used by him in good faith, the state may suspend or discharge a teacher for using that method but it may not resort to such drastic sanctions unless the state proves he was put on notice either by a regulation or otherwise that he should not use that method. *Mailloux v. Kiley,* 323 F.Supp. 1387 (D.Mass 1971).

On appeal of this case, the higher court cast some doubt on the feasibility of the rule measuring the validity of a teaching method on the preponderant opinion of other educators and noted that each case must be examined on an independent basis, the court considering that "the propriety of regulations or sanctions must depend on such circumstances as the age and sophistication of the students, the closeness of the relation to the specific [teaching] technique used and some concededly valid educational objective, and the context and manner of presentation." *Mailloux v. Kiley,* 448 F.2d 1242 (1st Cir.1971).

3. In 1973, a group of teachers requested a pilot program, Global Studies, as an alternative to the conventional history course. Students were given a choice between Global Studies and the conventional course, and most chose the conventional one. Two teachers filed a grievance regarding the student registration procedure because of the decline in students in Global Studies and the fact that they had to teach the traditional class. When they lost the grievance at all levels they filed suit claiming, *inter alia,* that their academic freedom had been violated, and they asserted the right of a teacher to select teaching methods and materials. The Supreme Court of Washington ruled that

> if Global Studies detracts from the scope of a conventional history course—because it emphasizes small groups, independent reading and writing, and inquiry-discovery techniques—[the teachers] may be compelled to abandon their own preferred techniques and to teach history in a more conventional manner. While teachers should have some measure of freedom in teaching techniques employed, they may not ignore or omit essential course material or disregard the course calendar. *Millikan v. Board of Directors of Everett School Dist. No. 2,* 93 Wn.2d 522, 611 P.2d 414 (1980).

4. The United States Court of Appeals, Sixth Circuit, has held that academic freedom

> does not encompass the right of a nontenured teacher to have her teaching style insulated from review by her superiors . . . just because her methods and philosophy are considered acceptable within the teaching profession. *Hetrick v. Martin,* 480 F.2d 705, 709 (6th Cir.1973), cert. denied 414 U.S. 1075, 94 S.Ct 592 (1973). See also *Adams v. Campbell County School District, Campbell County, Wyoming,* 511 F.2d 1242 (10th Cir.1975); *Saunders v. Reorganized School District No. 2,* 520 S.W.2d 29 (Mo.1975); *Clark v. Holmes,* 474 F.2d 928 (7th Cir.1972), cert. denied, 411 U.S. 972, 93 S.Ct. 2148 (1973); *Parducci v. Rutland,* 316 F.Supp. 352 (M.D.Ala.1970).

❖ — ❖ — ❖

*Teacher's Dismissal Upheld for Objectionable
Film That under Circumstances Was Not
Expressive nor Communicative*

Fowler v. Board of Education of Lincoln County, Kentucky

United States Court of Appeals,
Sixth Circuit, 1987.
819 F.2d 657.

MILBURN, Circuit Judge. . . . Plaintiff Jacqueline Fowler was a tenured teacher employed by the Lincoln County, Kentucky, school system for fourteen years. She was discharged in July, 1984 for insubordination and conduct unbecoming a teacher. The basis for this action was that she had an "R" rated movie, *Pink Floyd—The Wall,* shown to her high school students on the last day of the 1983–84 school year. The students in Fowler's classes were in grades nine through eleven and were of the ages fourteen through seventeen.

The day on which the movie was shown, May 31, 1984, was a noninstructional day used by teachers for completing grade cards. A group of students requested that Fowler allow the movie to be shown while she was completing the grade cards. Fowler was unfamiliar with the movie and asked the students whether it was appropriate for viewing at school. Charles Bailey, age fifteen, who had seen the movie on prior occasions, indicated that the movie had "one bad place in it." . . .

When Fowler had the movie shown on the morning of May 31, 1984, she instructed Charles Bailey, the fifteen-year-old student who had seen the movie, to edit out any parts that were unsuitable for viewing at school. He did so by attempting to cover the 25" screen with an 8-1/2" by 11" letter-sized file folder. . . .

There is conflicting testimony as to whether, or how much, nudity was seen by the students. At the administrative hearing, several students testified that they saw no nudity. . . . One student testified that she saw "glimpses" of nudity, but "nothing really offending." . . .

There is also conflicting testimony regarding the amount of sexual innuendo existing in the "unedited" version of the film. Because some parts of the film are animated, they are susceptible to varying interpretations. One particularly controversial segment of scenes is animated in which flowers appear on the screen, are transformed into the shape of male and female sex organs and then engage in an act of intercourse. . . .

Once again, there is conflicting testimony concerning the effectiveness of the editing attempt. . . .

In addition to the sexual aspects of the movie, there is a great deal of violence. One scene involves a bloody battlefield. . . . Another scene shows children being fed into a giant sausage machine. . . .

On the afternoon of May 31, 1984, Principal Jack Portwood asked Fowler to give him the video tape, and she did so. After the movie was viewed by the superintendent and members of the Lincoln County Board of Education, proceedings were instituted to terminate Fowler's contract.

Plaintiff Fowler received her termination notice on or about June 19, 1984. The notice advised her that a hearing would be held on July 10, 1984, and she subsequently advised the board of her intention to appear at the hearing and contest the charges.

On July 10, 1984, plaintiff Fowler appeared with counsel at the administrative hearing. She testified that, despite the fact that she had never seen the movie before having it shown to her students, and despite the fact that she was posting grades on report cards and left the room several times while the movie was being shown, she believed it had significant value. She believed the movie portrayed the dangers of alienation between people and of repressive educational systems. She testified that she would show an edited version of the movie again if given the opportunity to explain it. She stated that she did not at any time discuss the movie with her students because she did not have enough time.

The board viewed the movie once in its entirety and once as it had been edited in the classroom. The board then retired into executive session. Following this executive session, the board returned to open session and voted unanimously to terminate plaintiff's employment for insubordination and conduct unbecoming a teacher. . . .

The district court concluded that Fowler's conduct was protected by the First Amendment, and that she was discharged for exercising her constitutionally protected rights. . . .

In the present case the district court concluded that Mrs. Fowler was entitled to the protection of the First Amendment *while acting as a teacher.* That a teacher does have First Amendment protection under certain circumstances cannot be denied. . . . Likewise, a motion picture is a form of expression which may be entitled to the protection of the First Amendment. . . .

However, I conclude that Fowler's conduct in having the movie shown under the circumstances present here did not constitute expression protected by the First Amendment. It is undisputed that Fowler was discharged for the showing of the movie, *Pink Floyd—The Wall.* Such conduct, under the circumstances involved, clearly is not "speech" in the traditional sense of the expression of ideas through use of the spoken or written word. . . .

However, not every form of conduct is protected by the First Amendment right of free speech. . . .

In the present case, it is undisputed that Fowler did not see the movie before she had it shown to her class on the morning of May 31, 1984, a noninstructional day. Fowler agreed to allow the movie to be shown, at the students' request, because May 31 was "their treat type of day." . . . It is also undisputed that she left the room on several occasions while the film was being shown. Under circumstances such as these, I cannot conclude that Fowler possessed "[a]n intent to convey a particularized message" to her students. . . . The mere fact that at some point she may have developed an approval of the content of the movie is not, standing alone, a sufficient basis for the conclusion that her conduct in having the movie shown was a form of expression entitled to protection under the First Amendment.

If any sort of conduct that people wish to engage in is to be considered "speech" simply because those who engage in conduct are, in one sense,

necessarily expressing their approval of it, the line between "speech" protected by the First Amendment and conduct not so protected will be destroyed. . . .

Moreover, the surrounding circumstances in the present case indicate that there was little likelihood "that the message would be understood by those who viewed it." . . . As we have noted, the "R" rated movie was shown on a noninstructional day to students in Fowler's classes in grades nine through eleven who were of ages ranging from fourteen through seventeen. Furthermore, Fowler never at any time made an attempt to explain any message that the students might derive from viewing the movie. . . .

. . . [C]onduct is protected by the First Amendment *only* when it is expressive or communicative in nature. In the present case, because plaintiff's conduct in having the movie shown cannot be considered expressive or communicative, under the circumstances presented, the protection of the First Amendment is not implicated. . . .

Plaintiff argues that Ky.Rev.Stat. §161.790 (1)(b), which proscribes "conduct unbecoming a teacher," is unconstitutionally vague as applied to her because the statute failed to give notice that her conduct would result in discipline. We find this argument to be without merit. . . .

In the present case, plaintiff Fowler had a fifteen-year-old student show a controversial, highly suggestive and somewhat sexually explicit movie to a group of high school students aged fourteen to seventeen. She did not preview the movie, despite the fact that she had been warned that portions were unsuitable for viewing in this context. She made no attempt at any time to explain the meaning of the movie or to use it as an educational tool. Rather, she had it shown for the purpose of keeping her students occupied during a noninstructional day while she was involved in posting grades on report cards. We conclude that the statute proscribing "conduct unbecoming a teacher" gave her adequate notice that such conduct would subject her to discipline. Accordingly, we conclude that the statute is not unconstitutionally vague as applied to Fowler's conduct. . . .

In the present case, we conclude that plaintiff's conduct, although not illegal, constituted serious misconduct. Moreover, there was a direct connection between this misconduct and Fowler's work as a teacher. She introduced a controversial and sexually explicit movie into a classroom of adolescents without preview, preparation or discussion. In the process, she abdicated her function as an educator. Her having the movie shown under the circumstances involved demonstrates a blatant lack of judgment. Having considered the entire record, including the viewing of the movie, which we describe as gross and bizarre and containing material completely unsuitable for viewing by a classroom of students aged fourteen to seventeen, we conclude that such conduct falls within the concept of conduct unbecoming a teacher under Kentucky law.

Accordingly, for the reasons stated, the judgment of the district court is vacated and this cause is dismissed.

■ EVOLUTION VERSUS CREATIONISM

Tennyson once remarked while looking through a microscope, "Strange that these wonders should draw some men to God and repel others."[63] The ageless, inevitable, and, perhaps, the most human debates of humankind, those pitting science against theology, observation against belief, knowledge against superstition, have persisted down through the centuries and remain today almost uninterrupted. Due to advancements in learning, the world is today less reliant on augurs and oracles to exorcise the influence of witches, demons, and goblins. As science advances and the unknown becomes known, the field of debate narrows, but the intensity and vehemence of the proponents abide. The poor and less educated are usually more susceptible to "the intellectual miasma"[64] that confuses and blights the pursuit of worthwhile knowledge.[65]

All are aware of the Galileo incident, perhaps the most frequently cited example of religion dampening the scientific quest and stifling the ardour for new knowledge. Galileo, of course, proved that Copernicus's heliocentric theories condemned by the Catholic Church were correct and was branded as a heretic for his efforts about a century after Copernicus. In 1633 Galileo

stood trial in Rome for heresy and was convicted by the Holy Office of the Inquisition for "having held and believed the doctrine which is false and contrary to the Sacred and Devine Scriptures, that the sun is the center of the world and does not move from east to west and that the Earth moves and is not the center of the world." The tribunal sentenced Galileo to formal "imprisonment in this Holy Office at our pleasure."[66] Subsequently, Galileo remained under house arrest in his own home for the remainder of his life. It was not until 1992 that the Catholic Church acknowledged that Galileo was right after all, that the sun really does not revolve around the earth, little consolation for poor Galileo. A grand mosaic of such events could be constructed from similar, but less famous, events throughout history where religious revelation substituted for verifiable facts and knowledge. Indeed, the preemption of quantifiable physical proofs by religiously revealed truths, contrived answers for complex questions regarding natural phenomenon, undoubtedly was a principal contributor to the paucity and even the retrogression of learning that caused the Dark Ages and stagnated human progress for a thousand years.

To our generation, the controversy over Darwin's theory of evolution and the publication of his *The Origin of Species* is nearly as current as was Galileo's verification of Copernicus's theories. The potential for escalated controversy between scientists and religious fundamentalism was already in play before Darwin published *Origin*. In fact, Darwin's due concern for an anticipated widespread negative reaction to his research by the religious community led him to solicit advice from various learned persons of the day, one of whom, fearing the impending uproar, responded with the politically sage, but scientifically questionable advice, to "scrap the *Origin* and write instead about pigeons."[67] Yet, as a scientist, Darwin, himself, clearly understood the restrictive effects on the advancement of human knowledge that resulted from non-scientific solutions conjured by religious dogma to explain everything in nature. In the *Origin*, Darwin said: "Great is the power of steady misinterpretation; but the history of science shows that fortunately this power does not long endure."[68]

Actually, for two centuries before Darwin's *Origin* the certainty of scripture had been under stress with the steady increase of scientific inquiry. As scientific research became more sophisticated, the struggle between science and religion intensified, even in light of the fact that two of the greatest intellectual lights of the seventeenth century, Robert Boyle and Isaac Newton, had resolved the conflict to their own satisfaction in a way that was well summarized much earlier in a poignant observation by a Catholic Church official, who in sympathy with Galileo observed that "the Bible was a book about how one goes to Heaven, not how Heaven goes."[69] Boyle, of Boyle's Law fame, maintaining throughout his life a great personal piety, justified his own extensive scientific research, some of which tended to refute scripture, by pointing out that God permitted scientific inquiry. Boyle said, "If the omniscient author of nature knew that the study of his works tends to make men disbelieve his Being or Attributes, he would not have given them so many invitations to study and contemplate Nature."[70] Newton, who died in 1727, saw no conflict between religion and his research into gravity and light, arguing that God "governs all things, not as the soul of the world; but as Lord over all." God to Newton was a "powerful, ever-living Agent" who by his magnificence prevents stars from falling and by "miraculous means regulates the solar system."[71] According to Newton the laws of nature, themselves, are the creation of God.[72]

Later, in 1730, Voltaire commented that he had not seen a Newtonian scientist yet "who is not a theist in the strictest sense of the word."[73] While some philosophers disagreed with Newton, most scientists of the pre-Enlightenment and Enlightenment era, the eighteenth century, tended to agree with Boyle and Newton.[74] Yet, during that period, there was a growing secularization that gained momentum with new research and knowledge. Increasingly it was thought that Christian dogma was contrary to reason and rationality and that the physical world and the spiritual world could not be reconciled. From this point in history, science became the central ingredient of a more progressive and enlightened world.

Darwin sailed from Plymouth on the *Beagle* on December 7, 1831, and returned to Falmouth on October 2, 1836. The publication date of *Origin* was November 24, 1859. The repercussions were readily apparent when only one year later Thomas Huxley, an ardent defender of Darwin, wrote that "There is not the slightest doubt that, if a general council of the Church scientific had been held at that time, we should have been condemned by an overwhelming majority."[75] The years immediately following the publication saw a plethora of books and debates on the subject of evolution, religion, and morality, so much so that, according to Himmelfarb, "Even Darwin's own opinions on religious and social subjects became apart of the public realm of Darwinism."[76] Later, unanticipated by Darwin, the idea of biological Darwinism was stretched to justify *laissez faire* capitalism, the antiegalitarian idea of survival of the fittest, and was more generally used to rationalize the political theory that became known as "social Darwinism."[77] Throughout the generations Darwinism was perverted to every extreme that suited any scheme, from justifying Napoleon's conquering of Europe to the "every cheating tradesman."[78] Darwin would undoubtedly have been appalled by the misappropriation of his ideas.

We remain in a period of absorption and emerging proofs of evolution. The famous John Scopes "monkey trial" in Dayton, Tennessee, in 1925 was probably a high point in America in the rancor that followed the *Origin*.[79] In the Scopes trial a technical victory was won by William Jennings Bryan for the state, but Clarence Darrow, the great Chicago trial lawyer, gained a popular victory in his devastating cross-examination of Bryan. Although the statute that made the teaching of evolution in public schools in Tennessee a criminal offense was not overturned, it was largely ignored and went unenforced after John Scopes was convicted in the trial. Seven decades after the Scopes trial, the Tennessee legislature continues in its attempts to suppress the teaching of evolution. Books are published[80] and vigorous battles are waged in many other state legislative halls and school board rooms over restraint of the teaching of the theory of evolution along with reassertion of Biblical creationism into the curriculum of public schools.

Conservative Christians apparently believe that the acceptance of the theory of evolution by its very nature denies the literal truth of the Bible and augurs against religious faith that human beings were divinely created in God's image.[81] Creationism is based on an absolutist interpretation of the Bible, that the Bible cannot be errant, fallible, deviating, wandering, or straying aside from the literal truth. There are apparently two general classes of creationist, the "young-earth creationists," who believe in a very young creation based on the "begats" and other related Biblical passages, that the earth is about 6,000 years old, and the "old-earth creationists," who accept the evidence of nuclear physics and radiometric dating, thereby conceding that the earth could be four to five billion years old. Both positions hold that God suddenly created everything, and both reject the idea of evolution.[82] The case for creationism is largely couched in various attempts to show gaps in scientific evidence authenticating evolution. As Pennock observes, no creationist has come up with anything other than "if I can show that evolution is false, then my Genesis-based story must be true."[83] Eldredge notes in this regard that the march of science in modern anthropology, psychology, biology, geology, chemistry, and physics, all works in progress, combine to make the task of disproving evolution an exceedingly difficult undertaking.[84]

An upsurge of creationism in some southern and midwestern states was reflected in the decision of the state board of education in Kansas, in the summer of 1999, to remove evolution from the list of subjects required to be taught in public high schools of Kansas. Later the state board of education of Kentucky voted to discontinue the use of the word "evolution" from course materials in that state's high schools.

Actually, though, the percentage of all Americans who believe that evolution should not be taught in the public schools is probably quite small. In a national survey taken in the spring of 2000, it was found that the vast majority of Americans, 83 percent, believe evolution should be taught in public schools.[85] Survey responses to the evolution versus creationism issue usually draw the qualification that most Americans believe, as did Newton and Boyle, that "God created evolution."[86] The fact that most Americans do not support the conservative Protestant view that calls for the exclusion of evolution from the public schools is pointed out by Stephen Jay Gould, the eminent Harvard paleontologist, who has observed that "Creationism is not an issue given serious consideration in the international, scientific or religious communities, but rather is "a home-grown phenomenon of American sociocultural history—a splinter movement of Protestant fundamentalists who believe that every word of the Bible must be literally true, . . . "[87] Gould further notes that among the mainline Protestants, Catholics, and Jewish faiths there is apparently the prevailing view that there is no conflict between science and religion, or evolution and religion, in that there is general agreement that there is a lack of sufficient overlap between the two to cause a conflict.[88] This view was probably best enunciated by Pope John Paul II in a 1996 statement to the Pontifical Academy of Sciences, in a document entitled "Truth Cannot Contradict Truth," wherein he concluded that the evidence of evolution is not inconsistent with Catholic religious doctrine.[89] In this vein of separating the realm of the spiritual from the realm of the physical world, the majority of both the religious and scientific communities appear to find common ground and agree that there is no necessary disjunction between the "net of science" covering the empirical, natural, and physical realm and the "net of religion," encompassing questions of theology, the soul, religion, and conjecture about an afterlife.[90]

Quite apart from this position, the creationists of today attempt to elevate the Biblical story to the level of science while reducing evolution to the level of fable or allegory. Some legislatures and local school boards, mostly in the South, continue to try to circumvent earlier court decisions that prohibited the teaching of "creation science" as a counterpoint to evolution science.

In 1968, an antievolution statute in Arkansas was challenged as violative of the First Amendment.[91] The United States Supreme Court found in the statute implicit state support of the Christian doctrine of creation from the Book of Genesis, and the Court declared the law unconstitutional.

In a later version of the issue, the governor of Arkansas signed into law in 1981 a bill that required balanced treatment for creation science and evolution in the public schools. Proponents of the new statute maintained that not only was creationism a science, but that Darwin's theory of evolution actually constituted a kind of obverse religion, secular humanism, and, as such, its use in the classroom was tantamount to teaching an atheistic religion in public schools.

The statute was promptly challenged as violative of the religion provisions of the First Amendment. The State of Arkansas defended by maintaining, first, that a literal interpretation of Genesis did not necessarily mean that creation science was religious; second, that the state's reference to creation did not imply that the creation was caused by a supreme being or God; and, third, that to teach in public schools about the concept of a creator was not religious per se. The federal court in *McLean v. Arkansas Board of Education*[92] held against the state on all counts. The judge observed that creation science was not a science at all, but, instead, a religious doctrine. For the state to impose such a belief on the youth in public schools violated the First Amendment.

In January 1985, a federal district judge held a Louisiana creation statute, similar to Arkansas's, unconstitutional because it "promotes the beliefs of some theistic sects to the detriment of others." According to the judge, the so-called balanced treatment statute removed the state from a position of neutrality toward advancing a particular religious belief. This case, *Edwards v. Aguillard*,[93] was appealed to the U.S. Supreme Court, and the Louisiana statute was held to be unconstitutional. The Court observed that the true legislative intent was to impose into the public schools the teaching of creationism as a religious doctrine, and the statute was therefore unconstitutional.

Eldredge summarizes the issue in a pragmatic statement of political and economic realism when he observes that his opposition to attempts by creationists to obstruct the teaching of evolution is "not because I care what individuals believe, in either a religious or simply intellectual context, on the matter of who we humans are and how we happen to be here. . . . Rather the source of my animus . . . is itself purely political: like it or not, we live in a heavily science-dependent technological world—one which will depend for its future guidance on intelligent decisions made by the electorate. For this reason alone, neither the United States nor

any other nation can afford to have second rate science education—yet that is where the creationism debate has got us, . . . the tragic decision of the Kansas school board."[94]

In short, the unfortunate result of the conflict of beliefs over how man began and how he will end when left to the hands of creationists appears to lead to an unavoidable contracting of the spectrum of scientific knowledge. Stephen Hawking, the great Cambridge mathematician in a lecture at Oxford,[95] best captured the essence of the problem when he posed the question "How can our finite minds comprehend an infinite universe?" The danger, of course, lies in further restricting the reach of the limited human intellectual capacity with external beliefs that impose constraints on the human being already limited by a finite mind.

❖ — ❖ — ❖

Statute Forbidding the Teaching of Evolution Is Unconstitutional

Epperson v. State of Arkansas

Supreme Court of the United States, 1968.
393 U.S. 97, 89 S.Ct. 266.

Mr. Justice FORTAS delivered the opinion of the Court. This appeal challenges the constitutionality of the "anti-evolution" statute which the State of Arkansas adopted in 1928 to prohibit the teaching in its public schools and universities of the theory that man evolved from other species of life. . . .

The Arkansas law makes it unlawful for a teacher in any state-supported school or university "to teach the theory or doctrine that mankind ascended or descended from a lower order of animals," or "to adopt or use in any such institution a textbook that teaches" this theory. Violation is a misdemeanor and subjects the violator to dismissal from his position.

The present case concerns the teaching of biology in a high school in Little Rock. According to the testimony, until the events here in litigation, the official textbook furnished for the high school biology course did not have a section on the Darwinian Theory. Then, for the academic year 1965–1966, the school administration, on recommendation of the teachers of biology in the school system, adopted and prescribed a textbook which contained a chapter setting forth "the theory about the origin . . . of man from a lower form of animal."

Susan Epperson, a young woman who graduated from Arkansas' school system and then obtained her master's degree in zoology at the University of Illinois, was employed by the Little Rock school system in the fall of 1964 to teach tenth grade biology at Central High School. At the start of the next academic year, 1965, she was confronted by the new textbook (which one surmises from the record was not unwelcome to her). She faced at least a literal dilemma because she was supposed to use the new textbook for classroom instruction and presumably to teach the statutorily condemned chapter; but to do so would be a criminal offense and subject her to dismissal. . . . Only Arkansas and Mississippi have such "anti-evolution" or "monkey" laws on their books. There is no record of any prosecutions in Arkansas under its statute. It is possible that the statute is presently more of a curiosity than a vital fact of life in these States. Nevertheless, the present case was brought, the appeal as of right is properly here, and it is our duty to decide the issues presented.

At the outset, it is urged upon us that the challenged statute is vague and uncertain and therefore within the condemnation of the Due Process Clause of the Fourteenth Amendment. The contention that the Act is vague and uncertain is supported by language in the brief opinion of Arkansas' Supreme Court. That court, perhaps reflecting the discomfort which the statute's quixotic prohibition necessarily engenders in the modern mind, stated that it "expresses no opinion" as to whether the Act prohibits "explanation" of the theory of evolution or merely forbids "teaching that the theory is true." Regardless of this uncertainty, the court held that the statute is constitutional.

On the other hand, counsel for the State, in oral argument in this Court, candidly stated that, despite the State Supreme Court's equivocation Arkansas would interpret the statute "to mean that to make a student aware of the theory . . . just to teach that there was such a theory" would be grounds for dismissal and for prosecution under the statute, and he said "that the Supreme Court of Arkansas' opinion should be interpreted in that manner." He said: "If Mrs. Epperson would tell her students that 'Here is Darwin's theory, that man ascended or descended from a lower form of being,' then I think she would be under this statute liable for prosecution."

In any event, we do not rest our decision upon the asserted vagueness of the statute. On either interpretation of its language, Arkansas' statute cannot stand. It is of no moment whether the law is deemed to prohibit mention of Darwin's theory, or to forbid any or all of the infinite varieties of communication embraced within the term "teaching." Under either interpretation, the law must be stricken because of its conflict with the constitutional prohibition of state laws respecting an establishment of religion or prohibiting the free exercise thereof. The overriding fact is that Arkansas' law selects from the body of knowledge a particular segment which it proscribes for the sole reason that it is deemed to conflict with a particular religious doctrine; that is, with a particular interpretation of the Book of Genesis by a particular religious group. . . .

Judicial interposition in the operation of the public school system of the Nation raises problems requiring care and restraint. Our courts, however, have not failed to apply the First Amendment's mandate in our educational system where essential to safeguard the fundamental values of freedom of speech and inquiry and of belief. By and large, public education in our Nation is committed to the control of state and local authorities. Courts do not and cannot intervene in the resolution of conflicts which arise in the daily operation of school systems and which do not directly and sharply implicate basic constitutional values. On the other hand, "[t]he vigilant protection of constitutional freedoms is nowhere more vital than in the community of American schools," *Shelton v. Tucker*, 364 U.S. 479, 487, 81 S.Ct. 247, 251, 5 L.Ed.2d 231 (1960). As this Court said in *Keyishian v. Board of Regents*, the First Amendment "does not tolerate laws that cast a pall of orthodoxy over the classroom." 385 U.S. 589, 603, 87 S.Ct. 675, 683, 17 L.Ed.2d 629 (1967). . . .

There is and can be no doubt that the First Amendment does not permit the State to require that teaching and learning must be tailored to the principles or prohibitions of any religious sect or dogma. . . .

In the present case, there can be no doubt that Arkansas has sought to prevent its teachers from discussing the theory of evolution because it is contrary to the belief of some that the Book of Genesis must be the exclusive source of doctrine as to the origin of man. No suggestion has been made that Arkansas' law may be justified by considerations of state policy other than the religious views of some of its citizens. It is clear that fundamentalist sectarian conviction was and is the law's reason for existence. Its antecedent, Tennessee's "monkey law," candidly stated its purpose: to make it unlawful "to teach any theory that denies the story of the Divine Creation of man as taught in the Bible, and to teach instead that man has descended from a lower order of animals." Perhaps the sensational publicity attendant upon the *Scopes* trial induced Arkansas to adopt less explicit language. It eliminated Tennessee's reference to "the story of the Divine Creation of man" as taught in the Bible, but there is no doubt that the motivation for the law was the same: to suppress the teaching of the theory which it was thought "denied" the divine creation of man. . . .

The judgment of the Supreme Court of Arkansas is reversed.

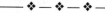

Louisiana Statute Requiring Balanced Treatment of Creation Science and Evolution Science Violates First Amendment

Edwards v. Aguillard

Supreme Court of the United States, 1987.
482 U.S. 578, 107 S.Ct. 2573.

Justice BRENNAN delivered the opinion of the Court. The question for decision is whether Louisiana's "Balanced Treatment for Creation-Science and Evolution-Science in Public School

Instruction" Act (Creationism Act), La.Rev. Stat.Ann. §§17:286.1–17:286.7 (West 1982), is facially invalid as violative of the Establishment Clause of the First Amendment.

The Creationism Act forbids the teaching of the theory of evolution in public schools unless accompanied by instruction in "creation science." §17:286.4A. No school is required to teach evolution or creation science. If either is taught, however, the other must also be taught. The theories of evolution and creation science are statutorily defined as "the scientific evidences for [creation or evolution] and inferences from those scientific evidences." . . .

Appellees, who include parents of children attending Louisiana public schools, Louisiana teachers, and religious leaders, challenged the constitutionality of the Act in District Court, seeking an injunction and declaratory relief. . . .

The Establishment Clause forbids the enactment of any law "respecting an establishment of religion." The Court has applied a three-pronged test to determine whether legislation comports with the Establishment Clause. First, the legislature must have adopted the law with a secular purpose. Second, the statute's principal or primary effect must be one that neither advances nor inhibits religion. Third, the statute must not result in an excessive entanglement of government with religion. . . . State action violates the Establishment Clause if it fails to satisfy any of these prongs.

In this case, the Court must determine whether the Establishment Clause was violated in the special context of the public elementary and secondary school system. States and local school boards are generally afforded considerable discretion in operating public schools. . . .

The Court has been particularly vigilant in monitoring compliance with the Establishment Clause in elementary and secondary schools. Families entrust public schools with the education of their children, but condition their trust on the understanding that the classroom will not purposely be used to advance religious views that may conflict with the private beliefs of the student and his or her family. Students in such institutions are impressionable and their attendance is involuntary. . . . The State exerts great authority and coercive power through mandatory attendance requirements, and because of the students' emulation of teachers as role models and the children's susceptibility to peer pressure. . . . Furthermore, "[t]he public school is at once the symbol of our democracy and the most pervasive means for promoting our common destiny. In no activity of the State is it more vital to keep out divisive forces than in its schools. . . .

Consequently, the Court has been required often to invalidate statutes which advance religion in public elementary and secondary schools. . . .

Therefore, in employing the three-pronged *Lemon* test, we must do so mindful of the particular concerns that arise in the context of public elementary and secondary schools. We now turn to the evaluation of the Act under the *Lemon* test.

Lemon's first prong focuses on the purpose that animated adoption of the Act. "The purpose prong of the *Lemon* test asks whether government's actual purpose is to endorse or disapprove of religion." . . . A governmental intention to promote religion is clear when the State enacts a law to serve a religious purpose. This intention may be evidenced by promotion of religion in general, . . . or by advancement of a particular religious belief. . . . If the law was enacted for the purpose of endorsing religion, "no consideration of the second or third criteria is necessary." . . . In this case, the petitioners have identified no clear secular purpose for the Louisiana Act.

True, the Act's stated purpose is to protect academic freedom. La.Rev.Stat.Ann. §17:286.2 (West 1982). This phrase might, in common parlance, be understood as referring to enhancing the freedom of teachers to teach what they will. The Court of Appeals, however, correctly concluded that the Act was not designed to further that goal. We find no merit in the State's argument that the "legislature may not [have] use[d] the terms 'academic freedom' in the correct legal sense. They might have [had] in mind, instead, a basic concept of fairness; teaching all of the evidence." . . . Even if "academic freedom" is read to mean "teaching all of the evidence" with respect to the origin of human beings, the Act does not further this purpose. The goal of providing a more comprehensive science curriculum is not furthered either by outlawing the teaching of evolution or by requiring the teaching of creation science.

While the Court is normally deferential to a State's articulation of a secular purpose, it is required that the statement of such purpose be sincere and not a sham. . . .

It is clear from the legislative history that the purpose of the legislative sponsor, Senator Bill Keith, was to narrow the science curriculum. During the legislative hearings, Senator Keith stated: "My preference would be that neither [creationism nor evolution] be taught." Such a ban on teaching does not promote—indeed, it undermines—the provision of a comprehensive scientific education.

It is equally clear that requiring schools to teach creation science with evolution does not advance academic freedom. The Act does not grant teachers a flexibility that they did not already possess to supplant the present science curriculum with the presentation of theories, besides evolution, about the origin of life. . . .

Furthermore, the goal of basic "fairness" is hardly furthered by the Act's discriminatory preference for the teaching of creation science and against the teaching of evolution. While requiring that curriculum guides be developed for creation science, the Act says nothing of comparable guides for evolution. . . . Similarly, research services are supplied for creation science but not for evolution. . . . Only "creation scientists" can serve on the panel that supplies the resource services. The Act forbids school boards to discriminate against anyone who "chooses to be a creation-scientist" or to teach "creationism," but fails to protect those who choose to teach evolution or any other noncreation science theory, or who refuse to teach creation science. . . .

If the Louisiana legislature's purpose was solely to maximize the comprehensiveness and effectiveness of science instruction, it would have encouraged the teaching of all scientific theories about the origins of humankind. But under the Act's requirements, teachers who were once free to teach any and all facets of this subject are now unable to do so. Moreover, the Act fails even to ensure that creation science will be taught, but instead requires the teaching of this theory only when the theory of evolution is taught. Thus we agree with the Court of

Appeals' conclusion that the Act does not serve to protect academic freedom, but has the distinctly different purpose of discrediting "evolution by counterbalancing its teaching at every turn with the teaching of creation science. . . ."

. . . There is a historic and contemporaneous link between the teachings of certain religious denominations and the teaching of evolution. It was this link that concerned the Court in *Epperson v. Arkansas*, 393 U.S. 97, 89 S.Ct. 266, 21 L.Ed.2d 228 (1968), which also involved a facial challenge to a statute regulating the teaching of evolution. . . . Although the Arkansas anti-evolution law did not explicitly state its predominant religious purpose, the Court could not ignore that "[t]he statute was a product of the upsurge of 'fundamentalist' religious fervor" that has long viewed this particular scientific theory as contradicting the literal interpretation of the Bible. . . .

These same historic and contemporaneous antagonisms between the teachings of certain religious denominations and the teaching of evolution are present in this case. The preeminent purpose of the Louisiana legislature was clearly to advance the religious viewpoint that a supernatural being created humankind. The term "creation science" was defined as embracing this particular religious doctrine by those responsible for the passage of the Creationism Act. Senator Keith's leading expert on creation science, Edward Boudreaux, testified at the legislative hearings that the theory of creation science included belief in the existence of a supernatural creator (noting that "creation scientists" point to high probability that life was "created by an intelligent mind"). Senator Keith also cited testimony from other experts to support the creation-science view that "a creator [was] responsible for the universe and everything in it." . . .

The legislative history therefore reveals that the term "creation science," as contemplated by the legislature that adopted this Act, embodies the religious belief that a supernatural creator was responsible for the creation of humankind.

Furthermore, it is not happenstance that the legislature required the teaching of a theory that coincided with this religious view. The legislative history documents that the Act's primary purpose was to change the science curriculum

of public schools in order to provide persuasive advantage to a particular religious doctrine that rejects the factual basis of evolution in its entirety. . . . The legislation therefore sought to alter the science curriculum to reflect endorsement of a religious view that is antagonistic to the theory of evolution.

In this case, the purpose of the Creationism Act was to restructure the science curriculum to conform with a particular religious viewpoint. Out of many possible science subjects taught in the public schools, the legislature chose to affect the teaching of the one scientific theory that historically has been opposed by certain religious sects. As in *Epperson*, the legislature passed the Act to give preference to those religious groups which have as one of their tenets the creation of humankind by a divine creator. . . . Because the primary purpose of the Creationism Act is to advance a particular religious belief, the Act endorses religion in violation of the First Amendment.

We do not imply that a legislature could never require that scientific critiques of prevailing scientific theories be taught. . . . But because the primary purpose of the Creationism Act is to endorse a particular religious doctrine, the Act furthers religion in violation of the Establishment Clause. . . .

We agree with the lower courts that these affidavits do not raise a genuine issue of material fact. The existence of "uncontroverted affidavits" does not bar summary judgment.

The Louisiana Creationism Act advances a religious doctrine by requiring either the banishment of the theory of evolution from public school classrooms or the presentation of a religious viewpoint that rejects evolution in its entirety. The Act violates the Establishment Clause of the First Amendment because it seeks to employ the symbolic and financial support of government to achieve a religious purpose. The judgment of the Court of Appeals therefore is

Affirmed.

CASE NOTE

The aggressive efforts by the Louisiana legislature and school parishes to intermingle church and state in education continues to create litigation. From *Cochran v. Louisiana* in 1930, 281 U.S.

270, 50 S.Ct. 335 (1930), to the most recent *Mitchell v. Helms,* in June 2000, 530 U.S. ____, ____ S.Ct. ____, 2000 WL 419832, the state of Louisiana has with great persistence sought to justify the use of public tax funds to support Catholic schools as discussed in Chapter 5 of this book. In keeping with the Louisiana history of efforts to erase the wall of separation between religion and public education, and to utilize the machinery of the state to advance religion, the school board in Tangipahoa Parish Public Schools passed a resolution requiring that a disclaimer be read immediately before the teaching of evolution in all elementary and secondary classes. The resolution followed a failed attempt by the Tangipahoa Parish school board to introduce creation science, the Biblical story of creation, into science curriculum of the school curriculum as a scientific alternative to teaching about evolution. Having been thwarted earlier by the courts in this effort the Tangipahoa board conjured a disclaimer scheme designed to distance the school curriculum from the theory of evolution. The board resolution said in fact that:

> It is hereby recognized by the Tangipahoa Board of Education, that the lesson to be presented, regarding the origin of life and matter, is known as the Scientific Theory of Evolution and should be presented to inform students of the scientific concept and not intended to influence or dissuade Biblical version of creation or any other concept.

The U.S. Court of Appeals, Fifth Circuit, held that the disclaimer violated the second prong of the *Lemon* test; it had the primary effect of protecting and maintaining a particular religious viewpoint as well as endorsing religion. The court in invalidating the resolution observed that the disclaimer cited the "Biblical version of Creation" as the only alternative theory explicitly referenced. The U.S. Supreme Court denied certiorari of this case on June 20, 2000. See: *Freiler v. Tangipahoa Board of Education,* 185 F.3d 337 (5th Cir.1999).

■ STUDENT TESTING AND PROMOTION

The state has the authority to establish standards for promotion and graduation. In recent years, states have begun to rely more and more on the standardized test as a criterion to determine students' competencies. So long as such measures of academic attainment are reasonable and nondiscriminatory, the courts will not intervene. Courts have traditionally given school officials and teachers wide latitude in deciding on appropriate academic requirements. The United States Supreme Court, in *Horowitz*, pointed out that "Courts are particularly ill-equipped to evaluate academic performance."[96] This judicial position of nonintervention was adopted early by the courts. In a 1913 case in Massachusetts, the court said that "[s]o long as the school committee acts in good faith, their conduct in formulating and applying standards and making decisions touching this matter is not subject to review by any other tribunal."[97]

Courts, of course, are not equipped to evaluate the academic standards of the myriad areas of subject matter and to review student performance. The courts confine themselves to determining whether due process is given, whether discrimination exists, or if a student suffers ill treatment from arbitrary or capricious action by the school. In *Gaspar v. Bruton*,[98] the United States Court of Appeals for the Tenth Circuit observed that "[t]he courts are not equipped to review academic records based upon academic standards within the particular knowledge, experience and expertise of academicians. . . . Thus, when presented with a challenge . . . for failure re academic standards, the court may grant relief, as a practical matter, only in those cases where the student presents positive evidence of ill will or bad motives."

DUE PROCESS AND TESTING

In recent years, states have moved to competency tests as minimal criteria for the awarding of high school diplomas. Because of society's great reliance on high school and college diplomas as measures of attainment, the diploma is of special interest to the student. The diploma, therefore, meets the criteria for a property interest under the due process clause of the Fourteenth Amendment, as enunciated in *Board of Regents v. Roth* by the United States Supreme Court. There the Court stated that "[t]o have a property interest in a benefit, a person clearly must have more than an abstract need or desire for it. He must have more than a unilateral expectation of it. He must, instead, have a legitimate claim of entitlement to it."[99] Certainly, a diploma is a benefit that everyone needs, and when a student progresses academically for twelve years, one may logically assume that the diploma will be forthcoming. The reasonableness of expectation of receipt of a diploma is, of course, contingent on the school standards and normal academic progress.

In requiring that students pass minimal competency tests in order to graduate, states have established new criteria to which a student must respond in order to have a reasonable expectation of graduation. The criteria for graduation, level of test scores, type of questions, and the difficulty of items are all issues requiring subjective academic judgment. Substantive due process, property, and liberty interests do not apply to such subjective standards. It is the objective standards over which the courts will exercise scrutiny. The United States Supreme Court in *Mathews v. Eldridge*[100] enunciated the rationale for invoking due process, saying that the dictates of due process are (1) the nature of the private interest denied by official action, (2) the risk of erroneous deprivation if appropriate procedures are not followed, and (3) the state's interest in imposing the particular requirements or denying the benefit.

Where tests are concerned, "risk of erroneous deprivation" may be caused by tests that do not measure the content that they are supposed to measure. If the tests do not measure the content, then they lack validity. A second test concept is reliability, which requires that the measure must yield consistent results.

These issues of validity and reliability became the foci of the court in the case of *Debra P. v. Turlington,* in which the Florida functional literacy examination was challenged. In the original litigation, the plaintiffs prevailed on the due process issues because the state could not show that the school curriculum prepared the students for the items tested.[101] The United States Court of Appeals for the Fifth Circuit, in addressing test validity as a due process issue, remanded the case for further findings of fact to determine whether the literacy test covered "material actually taught in Florida's classrooms." To provide this information, the Florida

Department of Education went through an elaborate process of surveying teachers to determine the content of courses they were teaching in order to verify that the questions on the literacy test were addressed in the classroom. On rehearing of the case, the federal district court accepted the evidence submitted by the state, indicating validity of the questions, and ruled for the state.

Debra P. is an important due process precedent because it expands the judicial view of objective criteria to the extent that test questions come under the scrutiny of the court. This case tends to narrow the state's prerogative in interpreting what has traditionally been a subjective consideration. By more carefully circumscribing objective criteria in terms of statistical measures of validity and reliability, the court effectively extends the realm of judicial scrutiny into student evaluation processes. In so doing, the court shifts the burden of proof and forces the state to demonstrate that the test was a fair assessment of what was taught.

Debra P. has subsequently been used as precedent by other courts. In *Anderson v. Banks,* a federal district court in Georgia required the school district to show that the questions on the California Achievement Test (CAT) had actually been covered in the high school curriculum before the court would allow the test to be used for an exit examination. The school district sustained this burden by conducting a study that matched objectives measured by the CAT with the school curriculum. The study also showed that the textbook content closely paralleled the types of items used and the content measured on the CAT. This was sufficient to meet the court's due process requirements. The court, in quoting *Debra P.,* said that "[t]o require school officials to produce testimony that every teacher finished every lesson and assigned every problem in the curriculum would impose a paralyzing burden on school authorities. . . . "[102]

EQUAL PROTECTION AND TESTING

Courts are very much aware of the potential for use of tests as a means to justify racial discrimination in violation of equal protection. In 1967, a federal district judge in Washington, D.C., held that the use of tests for tracking students was unconstitutional. The court found that the effect of the tests was to categorize students according to race, and that little opportunity was afforded to move from one track to another. Similarly, the use of IQ tests to evaluate students for placement in classes for the mentally retarded was invalidated by a federal court in California because the state could not show how the IQ tests were related to the intellectual capabilities of the students.[103] The effect of these tests was to place an inordinate number of black children in the mentally retarded category.[104]

The "effect" standard required that school officials show a compelling interest to administer such tests if the result was to effectively separate the races in the schools. School officials were uniformly unable to sustain this compelling interest burden and were, thus, virtually foreclosed from using standardized tests for placement or promotion.

Then the United States Supreme Court, in *Washington v. Davis*,[105] set down a new precedent that required plaintiffs to show not merely that the "effect" of the tests was to racially discriminate, but that the state in adopting the tests had the "intent" to discriminate. In this case, the Court found that to use tests producing racially disparate results was not a violation of equal protection unless it could be shown that there was official intent to discriminate.

Since the *Davis* decision, lower courts have refined the intent standard with a moderating criterion called "institutional intent." This standard requires that officials show a substantial nonracial objective, not a compelling interest, if discriminatory results can be reasonably foreseen. This compromise test has been defined this way: "Where the school board adopts policies that foreseeably further an illegitimate objective, and it cannot justify or adequately explain such policies in terms of legitimate educational objectives, one must presume that the school board would not have adopted such a policy but for an illegitimate purpose. Consistent with this perspective, 'institutional segregative intent' may be said to exist where a school board adopts a more, rather than a less, segregative policy and cannot justify its choice in terms of legitimate educational objectives."[106]

The important issue is to determine what is a "compelling" state interest as opposed to what is merely a "reasonable" state interest. There is

little doubt that tests can be used as diagnostic instruments even though classifications fall along racial lines. But there may be some legitimate question as to whether such tests can be used as a culling device to weed out those who are not as academically able as others, especially where no opportunity for academic redress is offered the student. Most importantly, though, the "institutional intent" standard shifts the burden of proof to the school district, whereas with the simple "intent" test the plaintiff must show evidence that the state had the purpose and intent to discriminate.

Functional Literacy Test May Be Required as Prerequisite for High School Diploma, but Test Must Be a Valid Measure of Instruction

Debra P. v. Turlington

United States District Court,
Middle District of Florida, 1983.
564 F.Supp. 177, affirmed 730 F.2d
1405 (11th Cir.1984).

GEORGE C. CARR, District Judge. In 1978, the Florida Legislature approved an amendment to the Educational Accountability Act of 1976, Fla.Stat. §229.55 et seq., which required public school students in the State of Florida to pass a functional literacy examination in order to receive a state high school diploma. Fla.Stat. §232.246(1)(b). Shortly after its enactment, Florida high school students filed a class action challenging the constitutionality of the literacy test requirement. This Court found that the test violated both the equal protection and due process clauses of the Constitution and enjoined its use as a diploma sanction until the 1982–83 school year. *Debra P. v. Turlington*, 474 F.Supp. 244 (M.D.Fla.1979). On appeal, the Fifth Circuit Court of Appeals affirmed many of this Court's findings. *Debra P. v. Turlington*, 644 F.2d 397 (5th Cir.1981). However, the appellate court remanded the case for further factual findings on two key issues. Specifically, this Court was directed to make further findings on whether or not the functional literacy test, the Florida Student State Assessment Test, Part II (SSAT-II), covers material actually taught in Florida's classrooms. In addition, the Court of Appeals requested this Court to reexamine the "role and effect of the 'vestiges' of past discrimination" upon twelfth-grade black students.

The SSAT-II is a test of a student's ability to successfully apply basic communications and mathematics skill to everyday life situations. . . . The test covers twenty-four basic skills. Of these, eleven are designated as communications skills and thirteen are designated as mathematics skills. . . .

The Court of Appeals has upheld the denial of a diploma to these students so long as the "test is a fair test of that which was taught." The Court reasoned that "[i]f the test is not fair, it cannot be said to be rationally related to a state interest" and therefore it would be violative of the Equal Protection Clause. In other words, the SSAT-II is only constitutional if it is instructionally valid. . . .

Put simply, the task assigned to this Court by the Court of Appeals was to find out if Florida is teaching what it is testing. Unfortunately, the answer to this apparently easy question is quite complex.

In an effort to carry its burden of proving that the test is instructionally valid, the defendants commissioned . . . a private consultant firm, to develop a study. . . . The survey asked teachers whether they had provided instruction relating to the twenty-four skills tested on the SSAT-II. If they had, the teachers were then asked if they had provided sufficient instruction for a student to master the skills. The teachers were required to answer separately for each individual skill. In addition, although the survey was anonymous, the teachers were asked to identify whether they were an elementary or secondary teacher and, if a secondary teacher, they were to identify their major field of emphasis.

The second part of the study . . . was a survey sent to the sixty-seven school districts and four university laboratory schools in Florida. . . .

The third component of the . . . study consisted of a series of site visits to verify the accuracy of the district reports. . . .

The fourth component of the . . . study was a student survey administered by the site visitors to one or two eleventh-grade social studies and English classes. The survey asked the students to state whether or not they had been taught in school how to answer the types of questions found on the SSAT-II. The sample questions provided to the students included questions on all twenty-four SSAT-II skills.

At trial, the defendant offered three expert witnesses who opined, based on the array of data outlined above, that Florida was teaching what it was testing. . . .

. . . [E]vidence suggests [that] the resolution of the instructional validity issue depends both on whose experts are believed and on what sort of proof is required. With regard to the former, it is important to understand that the instructional validity issue, and the related concept of minimum competency testing, are relatively new and highly controversial subjects which seem to have polarized the educational community. Thus, in large part, this Court has been called upon to settle not only a legal argument but also a professional dispute. . . .

But, what does the Constitution require in this instance? It may not be fair to expect students with differing interests and abilities to learn the same material at the same rate, but is it unconstitutional? Similarly, it may be inequitable that some students, through random selection, are assigned to mediocre teachers while others are given excellent instructors, but does this inequity rise to the level of a constitutional violation?

These questions lead to other issues concerning the appropriate burden of proof. The plaintiffs argue that the defendants have not carried their burden because they have not attempted to follow students throughout their entire careers. They also assert that there is insufficient evidence of what actually goes on in the classrooms. But, absent viewing a videotape of every student's school career, how can we know what really happened to each child? Even assuming that such videotapes were available, how could this Court decide, in constitutional terms, which students received appropriate instruction and which did not? Suppose that there is one student who never encountered a teacher who taught the SSAT-II skills, or a teacher who taught the skills well, should the entire test be declared invalid? What if the number of students were 3,000 rather than one?

It is necessary to consider these questions in order to appreciate the dilemma confronted by this Court. Instructional validity is an elusive concept. Moreover, unlike some of the other claims made by the plaintiffs at the first trial, the instructional validity issue strikes at the heart of the learning and teaching process. It also lends itself to individualized determinations rather than objective treatment.

Instructional validity is a subpart of content validity which together with curricular validity, insures that a test covers matters actually taught. As the Court of Appeals noted, and as this Court previously found, the SSAT-II is a "good test of what the students *should* know.". . . That is, the subjects tested parallel the curricular goals of the State. To this end, the Department of Education publishes minimum performance standards and also "periodically examine[s] and evaluate[s] procedures, records, and programs in each district to determine compliance with laws and rules established by the state board." Thus, although the individual districts are still somewhat autonomous, they no longer have the authority to decide that they will not teach certain minimum skills. In the same vein, the Department of Education, the individual districts, and the separate schools are required to submit annual reports of how well school instructional programs are helping students acquire minimum performance skills. In sum, since at least 1979, school administrators and teachers have been well aware of the minimum performance standards imposed by the State and their duty to teach these skills. . . .

The districts also receive funding from the State to remediate students who need special educational assistance in order to master the basic skills. . . . Each district school board is also required to establish pupil progression plans to insure that students are not promoted without consideration of each student's mastery of basic skills. The State has also established uniform testing standards for grades three, five, eight and eleven to monitor the acquisition of basic skills by students statewide.

These legislative requirements bolster the conclusion that the SSAT-II is, at least, curricularly valid. They lend support to the opinions of

the defendants' experts that the SSAT-II is instructionally valid. It is clear from the survey results that the terms of the Educational Accountability Act are not just hollow words found in a statute book. Rather, the district reports, teacher surveys, and site visit audits, as interpreted by the defendants' experts, all indicate that the directives of the Act are a driving force in all of Florida's public schools.

Nevertheless, it is the plaintiffs' position that the instructional validity of the test cannot be established by showing that the skills tested are included in a recognized curriculum. To the contrary, they believe that the only touchstone of the test's validity is proof of what graduating seniors were actually, not theoretically, taught. Without such proof, the plaintiffs posit that no one can tell whether the students had a "fair" opportunity to learn. . . .

As noted above, it is impossible to prove conclusively the degree to which every one of the more than 100,000 graduating seniors were exposed to the SSAT-II skills. What is known, is that the districts have reported that these skills are included in their curriculum and that a substantial number of public school teachers have stated that they adhere to this curriculum by including these skills in their course of instruction. In addition, and of even greater significance in determining the constitutionality of the test, it is known that students are given five chances to pass the SSAT-II between the tenth and twelfth grades of school and that, if they fail, they are offered remedial help. They also have the option of staying in school for an additional year in order to "receive special instruction designed to remedy [their] identified deficiencies." Certainly, some remedial programs and teachers will be more effective than others. However, this disparity cannot be said to be unfair in a constitutional sense. While it might be preferable from an educator's standpoint to insure that students learn the requisite skills during their regular courses rather than in remedial sessions, the Constitution clearly does not mandate such a result. What is required is that the skills be included in the official curriculum and that the majority of the teachers recognize them as being something they should teach. Once these basic facts are proven, as they have been in this case, the only logical inference is that the teachers are doing the job they are paid to do and are teaching these skills. It strains credibility to hypothesize that teachers, especially remedial teachers, are uniformly avoiding their responsibilities at the expense of their pupils. . . .

For the reasons stated above, and based on a review of the evidence presented by both sides, the Court finds that the defendants have carried their burden of proving by a preponderance of the evidence that the SSAT-II is instructionally valid and therefore constitutional. Although the instruction offered in all the classrooms of all the districts might not be ideal, students are nevertheless afforded an adequate opportunity to learn the skills tested on the SSAT-II before it is used as a diploma sanction.

As noted earlier, deciding that the SSAT-II is a fair test of that which is taught in the Florida public schools does not end this Court's inquiry. The Court must still decide whether or not the State should be enjoined from imposing the diploma sanction because the vestiges of past purposeful discrimination have an unconstitutional impact on black high school students.

No one disputes the fact that the SSAT-II failure rate among black students is disproportionately high. Of the three thousand twelfth-grade students who have not passed the test, about 57 percent are black even though blacks only constitute about 20 percent of the entire student body. While these statistics are alarming, they do not, standing alone, answer the constitutional question this Court must confront.

In order for this Court to continue to prohibit the State from using the SSAT-II as a diploma sanction, the disproportionate failure rate among today's high school seniors must be found to have been caused by past purposeful segregation or its lingering effects. If the disparate failure of blacks is not due to the present effects of past intentional segregation or if the test is necessary to remedy those effects, then the four-year injunction entered in 1979 cannot be extended. . . .

. . . [T]he plaintiffs seem to argue that the SSAT-II will be invalid as long as any vestiges of discrimination exist.

In the 1979 trial, this Court found, "the most significant burden which accompanied black children into the integrated schools was the existence of years of inferior education." This burden is not shouldered by the Class of 1983.

Unlike the Class of 1979, black and white members of the Class of 1983 have had the same textbooks, curricula, libraries and attendance requirements throughout their public school years. Thus, while no two students can have an identical academic experience, their educational opportunities have nonetheless been equal in a constitutional sense. Moreover, to the extent that insidious racism is a problem in the schools, it would seem that a test like the SSAT-II, with objective standards and goals, would lead to its eradication. . . .

Twelve years have passed since the Florida public schools became physically unitary. Since that time, the State of Florida has undertaken massive efforts to improve the education of all of its school children. The SSAT-II is an important part of those efforts. Its use can be enjoined only if it perpetuates the effects of past school segregation or if it is not needed to remedy those effects. Applying this standard to the facts presented at both the 1979 and 1983 trials, the Court finds that the injunction should not be extended. The State of Florida may deny diplomas to the members of the Class of 1983 who have not passed the SSAT-II.

CASE NOTE

Achievement or Ability Grouping. Where plaintiff black children alleged that a school district's use of achievement tests for ability grouping violated their rights under the equal protection clause and the Civil Rights Act of 1964, the court ruled that the former was not violated because the evidence indicated that achievement grouping was a sound educational practice, and that disadvantaged children, including black students, had made significant academic progress since the inception of the achievement-grouping program. Regarding the charge of discrimination under the Civil Rights Act, the court said that the "disparate impact" test of the act required that the plaintiffs show by a preponderance of evidence that a racially neutral practice, such as achievement tests, have a racially disproportionate impact. If the plaintiffs are able to sustain such evidence, then the burden of proof shifts to the defendant to prove substantial legitimate justification for its action. In this case the defendants bore the burden and were able to show that the school district's achievement-grouping practices had a manifest, demonstrable relationship to classroom education and, thus, did not violate Title VI of the Civil Rights Act of 1964. *Georgia State Conference of Branches of NAACP v. State of Georgia*, 775 F.2d 1403 (11th Cir.1985).

■ GRADING AND ACADEMIC REQUIREMENTS

Educational processes of public schools are generally systematic and incremental in nature. Student progress is normally measured and evaluated accordingly. The school fits the conceptual bases discussed early by Benjamin Rush and Jefferson in their correspondence, wherein they called for a uniform system of education that would provide essential curriculum for the masses and an orderly means of incremental learning—elementary, secondary, higher education, and so on.[107] The organization of the graded class system in which students build on the knowledge gained from previous schooling assumes, implicitly, some evaluation process to determine knowledge gained.

Because such evaluations are so important to the individual's future, it is inevitable that litigation should arise regarding grading, testing, and sanction of a student's educational progress.

The courts have been reluctant to intervene in the internal academic affairs of schools, preferring to defer to the judgment of professional educators where issues of student evaluation are concerned. This reticence was illustrated by the U.S. Supreme Court in a 1978 higher education case, where a fine line was drawn distinguishing academic penalties from disciplinary actions. The Court observed that academic considerations are by their "nature more subjective and evaluative than the typical factual questions presented in the average disciplinary decision" and that such academic judgments should be left to educators.[108] More recently, the Supreme Court upheld faculty judgment in denying a student the opportunity to retake an examination that was a prerequisite to obtaining a degree because the student had a poor overall academic standing and had failed to score at an acceptable level on a particular examination. The Court upheld the school's action, even though some other students had been allowed

to retake the examination.[109] The Court said that "when judges are asked to review the substance of a genuinely academic decision. . . , they should show great respect for the faculty's professional judgment."[110]

WITHHOLDING DIPLOMA

It is within the sound judgment of school authorities to determine if and when a pupil has completed the prescribed courses entitling him or her to a diploma. However, there is no direct relationship between participation in a graduation exercise and the issuance of a diploma. Once the pupil has completed successfully all of the required courses, the issuance of a diploma is a ministerial act that the school officials must perform. Refusal of a pupil to perform some act that is not a part of curriculum nor is required by school regulation prior to graduation will not justify withholding of the diploma. Thus, school authorities may deny a student participation in graduation ceremonies as a disciplinary measure but may not withhold the diploma unless the student is academically deficient.[111]

In a 1921 case in which a student's refusal to wear a cap and gown to graduation resulted in the board's withholding the pupil's diploma, the court mandated that the diploma be granted and stated:

> A diploma, therefore is *prima facie* evidence of educational worth, and is the goal of the matriculate. . . . The issuance of a diploma by the school board to a pupil who satisfactorily completes the prescribed course of study and who is otherwise qualified is mandatory, and, although such duty is not expressly enjoined upon the board by statute, it does arise by necessary and reasonable implication. . . . This Plaintiff . . . having complied with all the rules and regulations precedent to graduation, may not be denied her diploma by the arbitrary action of the school board subsequent to her being made the recipient of the honors of graduation. *Valentine v. Independent School Dist. of Casey*, 191 Iowa 1100, 183 N.W. 434 (1921).[112]

GRADE REDUCTION

Challenges to school grading policies have usually been couched in due process of law. In response to such an allegation, a court in Michigan held that a student has no vested property interest in a particular grade, and that a school board has the implied authority to set grading policies even though state statute does not expressly grant such authority.[113]

Courts have generally held that grades cannot be reduced as a disciplinary measure for violation of school rules. Where a student, while on a school field trip, drank a glass of wine in violation of school rules, the school suspended her for five days, expelled her from the cheerleading squad and the National Honor Society, prohibited her participation in school activities during the days she was expelled from school, and imposed a further penalty of grade reduction. The school policy called for the reduction of grades in all classes by two percentage points for each day of suspension. Upon challenge, the court held for the student and ruled that a school board may not impose a grade reduction sanction for infractions that are not related to education. To do so, the court maintained, was to misrepresent the student's true scholastic achievement for college entrance and other purposes.[114]

Yet, attendance at school and academic performance may be reasonably connected, and failure to attend school may affect the overall educational process. If a school board decides that attendance is essential to fulfill academic requirements, and if rules are so promulgated, then the courts are not likely to intervene.[115]

Thus, while school authorities have broad authority in the evaluation of students, the exercise of the authority cannot be so broad and indiscriminate as to permit unreasonable or improper exercise of discretion. What constitutes appropriate use of discretion largely depends on how well the school documents its rationale and how closely that rationale relates to the desirable educational end that the rule is designed to achieve.

GRADE STANDARDS FOR EXTRACURRICULAR ACTIVITIES

Lately, much has been written about the relationship between the regular and the extracurricular activities of the school and the importance of requiring reasonable minimum academic standards as conditions precedent to participation. Minimal participation standards have been imposed in several states, and in some instances litigation has resulted. The Montana Supreme

Court has held that a school district requirement that a student maintain a 2.0, or C, grade average for the preceding nine weeks in order to participate in extracurricular activities was a valid exercise of school board authority.[116] The court reasoned that participation in extracurricular activities is not a fundamental right under either the Montana or federal constitutions, and that therefore, the board need show only that its rule was reasonable and rational. The reasonableness of the board's action was found in its desire to develop the full educational potential of each person in providing a basic quality education and providing incentive for those students who wish to participate in extracurricular activities. In a similar case, a Louisiana court held that requiring a 1.6 grade average to participate in cheerleading tryouts was rationally related to promotion of academic excellence and was not violative of equal protection.[117]

In such cases the rule will be upheld if its purpose is rationally related to the educational objective of the school. Because courts have generally held that participation in extracurricular activities and interscholastic athletics does not rise to the level of a constitutionally protected right, there is no entitlement of procedural due process protections, and the school board does not need to bear the more severe equal protection burden of showing that it has a compelling reason to invoke such a rule.[118]

❖ — ❖ — ❖

School Board Policy Imposing Academic Sanctions for Nonattendance Is Not Ultra Vires, nor Does It Violate Due Process or Equal Protection Guarantees

Campbell v. Board of Education of Town of New Milford

Supreme Court of Connecticut, 1984.
193 Conn. 93, 475 A.2d 289.

PETERS, Associate Justice. This case concerns the validity of the policy of a local school board that imposes academic sanctions for nonattendance upon high school students. . . . The plaintiff claimed that the defendants' policy was ultra vires in light of governing state statutes, and unconstitutional in light of operative provisions of the Connecticut constitution and the United States constitution. The trial court rendered judgment for the defendants and the plaintiff has appealed.

The underlying facts are undisputed. The New Milford attendance policy, set out in an annually distributed student handbook, provides two sets of academic sanctions for students who are absent from school. Course credit is withheld from any student who, without receiving an administrative waiver, is absent from any year-long course for more than twenty-four class periods. In the calculation of the twenty-four maximum absences, all class absences are included except absences on school-sponsored activities or essential administrative business. In addition to the twenty-four absence limit, the course grade of any student whose absence from school is unapproved is subject to a five-point reduction for each unapproved absence after the first. In any one marking period, the grade may not, however, be reduced to a grade lower than 50, which is a failing grade. The grade reduction for unexcused absences is, like the twenty-four maximum absence policy, subject to administrative waiver. The policy of the school board entails extensive opportunities for counseling after a student's first confirmed unapproved absence from a class and thereafter.

The stated purpose of the attendance policy is educational rather than disciplinary. A student's disciplinary suspension from school, for reasons unrelated to attendance, is considered an approved rather than an unapproved absence. Such an absence cannot result in the diminution of a class grade although it may be counted, unless waived, as part of the twenty-four maximum absences for class credit. A student's absence from school, whether approved or unapproved, is not a ground for suspension or expulsion.

A student's report card lists, for each course, grades for each marking period, a final examination grade, a final grade, the amount of credit awarded, and the number of approved and unapproved absences. The report card conspicuously bears the following legend: "A circled grade indicates that the grade was reduced due to unapproved absences." In the case of the named plaintiff, his report card indicated grade reductions by the circling of grades in each of his academic courses, with the result that in three of the courses his final grade was lowered from passing to failing. In the fourth course, Architectural Drafting II, where the plaintiff's final grade was passing despite an indicated reduction for unapproved absences, the report card assigned him no credit because of a total of thirty-eight absences, thirty-one of which were approved and seven of which were unapproved. Any report card thus discloses, on its face, those grades which are affected by the enforcement of the attendance policy.

The plaintiff's appeal argues that the trial court erred in ruling that the defendants' attendance policy: (1) was not ultra vires or preempted by governing state statutes; (2) did not violate the rights of the plaintiff class to substantive due process under the Connecticut and the United States constitutions; (3) did not deprive the plaintiff class of procedural due process under the Connecticut and the United States constitutions; (4) did not deny the rights of the plaintiff class to equal protection of the law under the Connecticut and the United States constitutions. We find no error.

The plaintiff's first argument on appeal is that the defendant school board's policy is invalid because it conflicts with a number of state statutes. This argument is twofold, that the attendance policy is ultra vires because it exceeds the authority conferred upon local school boards by state law and that the policy is preempted by state statutes with which it is inconsistent. We find neither argument persuasive.

The authority of local boards of education derives from their role as agents of the state. "[T]he furnishing of education for the general public, required by article eighth, §1, of the Connecticut constitution, is by its very nature a state function and duty." . . . This responsibility has been delegated to local boards which, as "agencies of the state in charge of education in the town . . . possess only such powers as are granted to them by the General Statutes expressly or by necessary implication." . . .

The trial court found authority for the defendant school board's attendance policy in General Statutes §§10-220 and 10-221.

The first of these statutes, §10-220, requires a local school board to "implement the educational interests of the state" and to "provide such other educational activities as in its judgment will best serve the interests of the school district." The second statute, §10-221, instructs local boards of education to "prescribe rules for the management, studies, classification and discipline of the public schools." In addition, the trial court noted that General Statutes §§10-184 and 10-199 permit local school boards to investigate and to regulate "the irregular attendance of pupils at school."

The plaintiff contends that these statutes do not furnish support for the defendant school board's policy because its policy is properly to be characterized not as an academic regulation assigning a uniform grading value to classroom presence but rather as unauthorized punishment for nonattendance. . . .

We do not read the school board's authority in so limited a fashion. The authority to adopt uniform rules concerning irregularity of attendance is necessarily implied in the conjunction of statutory provisions authorizing local implementation of the educational mission of the state. Significantly, §10-220 expressly charges local boards with responsibility for the oversight of the school attendance of children from the ages of seven to sixteen made mandatory by §10-184. Furthermore, the plaintiff's concession that school teachers, upon the instruction of local school boards, may properly consider class participation in the assignment of grades, logically implies the existence of an educational nexus between classroom presence and grading. If local school boards can delegate to others the authority to impose academic sanctions for nonattendance, the decision to adopt uniform school-wide rules for such sanctions can hardly be deemed ultra vires.

None of the out-of-state cases upon which the plaintiff relies compels the conclusion that school-wide academic sanctions for nonattendance should generally be adjudged to be ultra vires. It may well be improper to reduce a student's grade for nonattendance as an additional punishment for unrelated conduct leading to a suspension from class . . . , but this school board's program does not permit such double punishment. It would indubitably be unlawful to apply a nonattendance program in an unreasonable, capricious, arbitrary or inequitable manner . . . , but no such allegation has been factually demonstrated. It would finally be troublesome to bar a truant student from further class attendance and from taking a final examination . . . , but the defendant board's program neither removes such a student from class nor excuses further compliance with the state's compulsory education law. In short, the plaintiff has cited no authority for his claim that attendance rules promulgated by local school boards, if carefully drafted and fairly applied, are to be deemed per se ultra vires. Our own research has likewise revealed no such case-law. We agree that such regulations fall within the authority granted to local school boards by the statutes of this state. . . .

. . . [T]he plaintiff urges that the state statutes governing academic discipline, which require that a suspended or expelled student be afforded alternate educational opportunities; General Statutes §§10-233c and 10-233d; be read as a mandate that any student be given full academic credit for completion of academic work, and as a prohibition of locally imposed academic sanctions for nonattendance.

The defendant school board's reply to these arguments calls upon us to recognize a distinction between sanctions which are disciplinary in nature and sanctions which relate to academic requirements. The question is not whether we concur in the judgment of the defendant board of education that "[l]earning experiences that occur in the classroom are . . . essential components of the learning process" or that "[t]ime lost from class tends to be irretrievable in terms of opportunity for instructional interaction." The policy decision that academic credentials should reflect more than the product of quizzes, examinations, papers and classroom participation nonetheless constitutes an academic judgment about academic requirements. We agree with the defendants' characterization of their policy. . . .

Even if the defendant school board's attendance policy is authorized by the relevant state statutes, the plaintiff class asserts that the policy cannot pass constitutional muster. The plaintiff relies on provisions of our state and federal constitutions to raise three different constitutional claims: a right to substantive due process, a right to procedural due process, and a right to equal protection of the laws. The trial court, upon consideration of these claims, found no infringement of the plaintiff's constitutional rights. We agree.

The plaintiff's challenge to the New Milford attendance policy as violative of the requirements of substantive due process claims infringement of students' fundamental rights to public education, of students' liberty interests in their academic reputation and of students' property interests in grades reflecting academic achievement. The first of these claims is based on article eighth, §1, of the Connecticut constitution; the others rely on article first, §§8 and 10, of the Connecticut constitution and the fourteenth amendment of the United States constitution.

Of these substantive due process claims, the most serious is the charge of impairment of a fundamental right, because, if such an impairment were properly before us, the validity of the questioned governmental regulation would require strict scrutiny to determine whether the regulation was compellingly justified and narrowly drafted. . . . We must therefore decide the applicability of the fundamental rights guaranteed by article eighth, §1, to the school board's policy of imposing uniform school-wide academic sanctions for nonattendance. In *Horton v. Meskill*, 172 Conn. 615, 648–49, 376 A.2d 359 (1977), we held, in the context of state-wide disparities in the financing of public school education, that "elementary and secondary education is a fundamental right, [and] that pupils in the public schools are entitled to the equal enjoyment of that right." The plaintiff argues that *Horton v. Meskill* implies that strict scrutiny must be the test for any and all governmental regulations affecting public school education. We disagree. The underlying issue in *Horton v. Meskill* was the provision of "a substantially equal educational opportunity" for Connecticut students in the state's "free public elementary and secondary schools." . . .

This school board policy, which is neither disciplinary . . . nor an infringement of equal educational opportunity, does not jeopardize any fundamental rights under our state constitution.

The standard by which the plaintiff's remaining substantive due process claims must be measured is therefore the more usual rational basis test. . . . In order to succeed on these claims, the plaintiff bears the heavy burden of proving that the challenged policy has no reasonable relationship to any legitimate state purpose . . . and that the plaintiff class has suffered a specific injury as a result of the policy's enforcement. . . . The plaintiff has established neither the legal nor the factual predicate for meeting this burden of proof.

The plaintiff argues that it is unconstitutionally arbitrary and capricious for the defendant school board to require student grades to reflect more than academic achievement. With respect to the plaintiff's liberty interest, we can find no factual impairment of whatever rights the plaintiff might possibly assert. Inspection of the report card of the named plaintiff discloses the relationship between his academic performance and the reduction in his grades and class credit that resulted from application of the attendance policy. The plaintiff has failed to show how a student's reputation could be injured by a report card in this form. With respect to the plaintiff's property interest, we find it difficult to understand how a uniform school-wide policy that links class grades with attendance can be on its face more arbitrary, as a constitutional matter, than are similar judgments by individual teachers who may justifiably, according to the plaintiff, adjust classroom grades to reflect classroom participation. . . . On this record, the plaintiff class has not proven infringement of its liberty or property interest in a fair grading system. . . .

The plaintiff's final constitutional claim invokes the equal protection provisions of article first, §20, of the Connecticut constitution and the fourteenth amendment to the United States constitution. . . . It is irrational, and a violation of equal protection, according to the plaintiff, to waive grade reduction for students who do "outstanding" work and to impose such sanctions on students whose work is, because of academic difficulties unrelated to class absence, only average.

The defendants offer several answers to this argument. Factually, they deny the premise that the waiver provision favors students on account of their ability rather than on account of their effort, since work may be considered "outstanding" in light of a particular student's past performance. Legally, they note that the waiver provision imports a reasonable element of flexibility into the assessment of a student's total classroom performance. Finally, they remind us that a district-wide policy is more likely to assure equality of treatment for all students than is a policy administered on an ad-hoc basis by individual classroom teachers. We find the defendants' arguments persuasive and therefore reject the plaintiff's equal protection claim.

There is no error.

In this opinion the other Judges concurred.

CASE NOTES

1. A member of the National Honor Society cheated on a calculus examination by etching the formulas on his calculator. The court upheld the student's dismissal from the society. *Jacob v. School Board of Lee County*, 419 S.2d 1002 (Fla.App.1987).

2. Denial of membership in the National Honor Society does not give rise to a property interest. *Price v. Young*, 580 F.Supp. 1 (E.D.Ark. 1983). See also *Karnstein v. Pewaukee School Board*, 557 F.Supp. 565 (E.D.Wis.1983).

■ BILINGUAL EDUCATION PROGRAMS

A school's curriculum must provide special instructional services for limited-English-proficiency students. As to the nature and method of instruction required, the courts have left substantial school board discretion. In 1974 the U.S. Supreme Court held, in *Lau v. Nichols*, that the failure of the San Francisco public school system to provide for the lingual needs of non–English-speaking Chinese students violated Section 601 of the Civil Rights Act of 1964.[119] The Court said that

> there is no equality of treatment merely by providing students the same facilities, textbooks, teachers, and curriculum; for students who do not understand English are effectively foreclosed from any meaningful education.

Later, in 1978, the Ninth Circuit Court of Appeals held that neither the federal Constitution nor the civil rights laws required that all courses, instructional materials, instructors, and testing procedures be bicultural or bilingual.[120] The Court indicated that compensatory education programs for non–English-speaking children were sufficient to satisfy the Court's mandate in *Lau v. Nichols*.

In 1974, the U.S. Congress enacted the Equal Educational Opportunities Act (EEOA), which requires that school systems develop appropriate programs for limited-English-proficiency students. The act states in pertinent part that

> no state shall deny educational opportunity to an individual on account of his or her race, color, sex, or national origin, by . . . the failure by an educational agency to take appropriate action to overcome language barriers that impede equal participation by its students in its instructional programs.[121]

In applying this law the Fifth Circuit Court of Appeals, in 1981, in *Castaneda I*, observed that Congress, while requiring appropriate remedial programs, gave local school districts "a substantial amount of latitude" in meeting these obligations.[122] In this case the court found that the challenged bilingual programs were nondiscriminatory. Later, in 1986, in a sequel to *Castaneda I*, the fifth circuit *upheld* the school district's ability-grouping and classroom assignment system as not being racially and ethnically discriminatory. The court said:

> We by no means imply, however, that a state must provide a program of bilingual education to all limited English speaking students in order to satisfy §1703(f) of the EEOA. We hold fast to our conviction, voiced in *Castaneda I*, that in enacting §1703(f) Congress intended to leave state and local educational authorities a substantial amount of latitude in choosing the programs and techniques they would use. (See *Castaneda I*, 648 F.2d at 1009.)[123]

Of significance in this court's validation of the school district's bilingual program was the fact that a majority of the teachers were native speakers of the Spanish language and the remainder were "proficient in Spanish." Further, the court was satisfied that adequate steps had been taken to ensure that these teachers had appropriate in-service teacher training to "develop and hone the skills necessary to be an adequate bilingual teacher."[124]

Guidelines emerging from the *Castaneda* cases may be summarized from the court's conclusion in *Castaneda I*, that the appropriateness of remediation programs in satisfying the EEOA may be evaluated with three queries: (1) Is the school district's program based upon reorganized, sound educational theory or principles? (2) Is the school district's program or practice designed to implement the adopted theory? (3) Has the program produced satisfactory results?[125]

Concerning the pertinent federal legislation, Congress had passed a Bilingual Education Act in 1968[126] and, as discussed above, revised it in the Bilingual Education Act in 1974.[127] In the former, supplemental funding was provided for school districts to address the educational needs of low-income students with limited English proficiency. The Bilingual Education Act of 1974 expanded coverage to include children other than those from low-income families. The act also provided a more precise definition of the bilingual education program required in English and in the child's native language to the extent needed for the child to make effective progress.

———————— ❖ — ❖ — ❖ ————————

School System's Failure to Provide English-Language Instruction to Chinese-Speaking Children Violates the Civil Rights Act of 1964

Lau v. Nichols

Supreme Court of the United States, 1974.
414 U.S. 563, 94 S.Ct. 786.

Mr. Justice DOUGLAS delivered the opinion of the Court. . . . This class suit brought by non-English-speaking Chinese students against officials responsible for the operation of the San Francisco Unified School District seeks relief against the unequal educational opportunities, which are alleged to violate the Fourteenth Amendment. No specific remedy is urged upon us. Teaching English to the students of Chinese ancestry who do not speak the language is one choice. Giving instructions to this group in Chinese is another. There may be others. Petitioners ask only that the Board of Education be directed to apply its expertise to the problem and rectify the situation. . . .

The Court of Appeals reasoned that "every student brings to the starting line of his educational career different advantages and disadvantages caused in part by social, economic and cultural background, created and continued completely apart from any contribution by the school system." Yet in our view the case may not be so easily decided. This is a public school system of California and §71 of the California Education Code states that "English shall be the basic language of instruction in all schools." That section permits a school district to determine "when and under what circumstances instruction may be given bilingually." That section also states as "the policy of the state" to insure "the mastery of English by all pupils in the schools." And bilingual instruction is authorized "to the extent that it does not interfere with the systematic, sequential, and regular instruction of all pupils in the English language."

Moreover, §8573 of the Education Code provides that no pupil shall receive a diploma of graduation from grade twelve who has not met the standards of proficiency in "English," as well as other prescribed subjects. Moreover, by §12101 of the Education Code children between the ages of six and sixteen years are (with exceptions not material here) "subject to compulsory full-time education."

Under these state-imposed standards there is no equality of treatment merely by providing students with the same facilities, textbooks, teachers, and curriculum; for students who do not understand English are effectively foreclosed from any meaningful education.

Basic English skills are at the very core of what these public schools teach. Imposition of a requirement that, before a child can effectively participate in the educational program, he must already have acquired those basic skills is to make a mockery of public education. We know that those who do not understand English are certain to find their classroom experiences wholly incomprehensible and in no way meaningful.

We do not reach the Equal Protection Clause argument which has been advanced but rely solely on §601 of the Civil Rights Act of 1964, 42 U.S.C.A. §2000d, to reverse the Court of Appeals.

That section bans discrimination based "on the ground of race, color, or national origin," in "any program or activity receiving Federal financial assistance." The school district involved in this litigation receives large amounts of federal financial assistance. HEW, which has authority to promulgate regulations prohibiting discrimination in federally assisted school systems, 42 U.S.C.A. §2000d-1, in 1968 issued one guideline that "school systems are responsible for assuring that students of a particular race, color, or national origin are not denied the opportunity to obtain the education generally obtained by other students in the system." 33 CFR 4955. In 1970 HEW made the guidelines more specific, requiring school districts that were federally funded "to rectify the language deficiency in order to open" the instruction to students who had "linguistic deficiencies," 35 Fed.Reg. 11595.

By §602 of the Act HEW is authorized to issue rules, regulations, and orders to make sure that recipients of federal aid under its jurisdiction conduct any federally financed projects consistently with §601. HEW's regulations, 45 CFR §80.3(b)(1), specify that the recipients may not

provide any service, financial aid, or other benefit to an individual which is different, or is provided in a different manner, from that provided to others under the program. . . .

Restrict an individual in any way in the enjoyment of any advantage or privilege enjoyed by others receiving any service, financial aid, or other benefit under the program.

Discrimination among students on account of race or national origin that is prohibited includes "discrimination . . . in the availability or use of any academic . . . or other facilities of the grantee or other recipient." Id., §80.5(b).

Discrimination is barred which has that *effect* even though no purposeful design is present: a recipient "may not . . . utilize criteria or methods of administration which have the effect of subjecting individuals to discrimination" or have "the effect of defeating or substantially impairing accomplishment of the objectives of the program as respect individuals of a particular race, color or national origin." Id., §80.3(b)(2).

It seems obvious that the Chinese-speaking minority receive fewer benefits than the English-speaking majority from respondents' school system, which denies them a meaningful opportunity to participate in the educational program—all earmarks of the discrimination banned by the regulations. In 1970 HEW issued clarifying guidelines (35 Fed.Reg. 11595) which include the following:

Where inability to speak and understand the English language excludes national origin–minority group children from effective participation in the educational program offered by a school district, the district must take affirmative steps to rectify the language deficiency in order to open its instructional program to these students (Pet.Br.App. 1a).

Any ability grouping or tracking system employed by the school system to deal with the special language skill needs of national origin–minority group children must be designed to meet such language skill needs as soon as possible and must not operate as an educational deadend or permanent track (Pet.Br. p. 2a).

Respondent school district contractually agreed to "comply with title VI of the Civil Rights Act of 1964 . . . and all requirements imposed by or pursuant to the Regulation" of HEW (45 CFR pt. 80) which are "issued pursuant to that title . . . " and also immediately to "take any measures necessary to effectuate this agreement." The Federal Government has power to fix the terms on which its money allotments to the States shall be disbursed. . . . Whatever may be the limits of that power . . . they have not been reached here. Senator Humphrey, during the floor debates on the Civil Rights Act of 1964, said:

Simple justice requires that public funds, to which all taxpayers of all races contribute, not be spent in any fashion which encourages, entrenches, subsidizes, or results in racial discrimination.

We accordingly reverse the judgment of the Court of Appeals and remand the case for the fashioning of appropriate relief.

Reversed.

CASE NOTES

1. A school district may admit students who achieve in the top 15 percent to a preferred, college-preparatory high school without violating the Civil Rights Act or the Fourteenth Amendment, even though the percentage of black and Spanish-American students is dispro-

portionately low. The court found that the school district's legitimate interest outweighed any harm imagined or suffered by students whose achievement had not qualified them for admission. *Berkelman v. San Francisco Unified School District*, 501 F.2d 1264 (9th Cir.1974).

2. A federal district court has within its inherent legal prerogative the equitable power to fashion a bilingual-bicultural program that will ensure that Spanish-surnamed children receive meaningful education. *Serna v. Portales Municipal Schools*, 499 F.2d 1147 (10th Cir.1974).

■ ENDNOTES

1. Tinker v. Des Moines Independent Community School District, 393 U.S. 503, 89 S.Ct. 733 (1969).

2. Ibid., at 511, 89 S.Ct. at 739.

3. Steirer by Steirer v. Bethlehem Area School District, 987 F.2d 989 (3d Cir.1993).

4. Keyishian v. Board of Regents, 385 U.S. 589, 603, 87 S.Ct. 675, 683, 684 (1967), quoting United States v. Associated Press, 52 F.Supp. 362, 372 (S.D.N.Y.1943), affirmed 326 U.S. 1, 65 S.Ct. 1416 (1945); see Weiman v. Updegraff, 344 U.S. 183, 197–98, 73 S.Ct. 215, 221–22 (1952) (Frankfurter, J., concurring).

5. Keyishian v. Board of Regents, 385 U.S. 589, 603, 87 S.Ct. 675, 683, 684 (1967).

6. "Academic Freedom in the Public Schools: The Right to Teach," *New York University Law Review* 48 (Dec. 1973): 1183.

7. Todd v. Rochester Community Schools, 41 Mich.App. 320, 200 N.W.2d 90 (1972).

8. School District of Abington Township v. Schempp, 374 U.S. 203, 300, 83 S.Ct. 1560, 1612 (1963).

9. Sturgis v. County of Allegan, 343 Mich. 209, 72 N.W.2d 56 (1955).

10. Kelly v. Dickson County School District, 64 Lack.Jur. 13 (Pa.Com.Pl.1962).

11. Board of Curators of University of Missouri v. Horowitz, 435 U.S. 78, 98 S.Ct. 948 (1978).

12. Welling v. Board of Education, 382 Mich. 620, 171 N.W.2d 545 (1969).

13. Pittman v. Board of Education of Glen Cove, 56 Misc.2d 51, 287 N.Y.S.2d 551 (1967).

14. Ibid.

15. Isquith v. Levitt, 285 App. Div. 833, 137 N.Y.S.2d 497 (1955).

16. Meyer v. State of Nebraska, 262 U.S. 390, 43 S.Ct. 625 (1923).

17. Edward J. Larson, *Summer for the Gods, The Scopes Trial and America's Continuing Debate Over Science and Religion* (Cambridge, Mass., Harvard University Press, 1997), p. 61. See: Woodrow Wilson, "War Message, April 2, 1997," in Papers of Woodrow Wilson Vol. 41 (Princeton: N.J.: Princeton University Press, 1983), pp. 519–527.

18. Larson, *Ibid*, See: Postmaster General Albert S. Burleson, quoted in Paul L. Murphy, *World War I and the Origin of Civil Liberties in the United States* (New York: Norton, 1979), p. 98.

19. Larson, Ibid.

20. Schenck v. United States, 249 U.S. 47, 39 S.Ct. 247 (1919).

21. Bartels v. Iowa, 262 U.S. 404, 43 S.Ct. 628 (1923).

22. Bohning v. Ohio, 262 U.S. 404, 43 S.Ct. 628 (1923).

23. Keyishian v. Board of Regents, 385 U.S. 589, 87 S.Ct. 675 (1967).

24. 354 U.S. 234, 77 S.Ct. 1203 (1957).

25. Ibid., at 250, 77 S.Ct. at 1212.

26. R. Freeman Butts and Lawrence A. Cremin, *A History of Education in American Culture* (New York: Henry Holt and Company, 1953), p. 273.

27. People ex rel. McCollum v. Board of Education, 333 U.S. 203, 68 S.Ct. 461 (1948).

28. Butts and Cremin, *A History of Education,* p. 165.

29. Board of Education, Island Trees Union Free School District No. 26 v. Pico, 457 U.S. 853, 102 S.Ct. 2799 (1982).

30. Ibid.

31. Pratt v. Independent School District No. 831, Forest Lake, Minnesota, 670 F.2d 771 (8th Cir.1982).

32. Ibid.

33. 484 U.S. 260, 108 S.Ct. 562 (1988). This case is more fully discussed in Chapter 8 of this book.

34. Ibid.

35. Ibid., at 273, 108 S.Ct. at 571.

36. Virgil v. School Board of Columbia County, Florida, 862 F.2d 1517 (11th Cir.1989).

37. John Stuart Mill, *On Liberty* (Indianapolis: Bobbs-Merrill, 1956), pp. 13–14.

38. *Roth v. United States,* 354 U.S. 476, 77 S.Ct. 1304 (1957), rehearing denied 355 U.S. 852, 78 S.Ct. 8 (1957).

39. William J. Brennan, Jr., quoted in Nat Hentoff, "Profiles: The Constitutionalist," *The New Yorker,* March 12, 1990, pp. 45, 56.

40. *Chaplinsky v. New Hampshire,* 315 U.S. 568, 62 S.Ct. 766 (1942); *Beauharnais v. Illinois,* 343 U.S. 250, 72 S.Ct. 725 (1952); *Roth v. United States,* op cit.; A Book Named "John Cleland's Memoirs of a Woman of Pleasure" v. Attorney General of Massachusetts, 383 U.S. 413, 86 S.Ct. 975 (1966); *Miller v. California,* 413 U.S. 15, 93 S.Ct. 2607 (1973).

41. Beauharnais v. Illinois, op. cit.

42. Roth, 354 U.S. at 487, 77 S.Ct. at 1310.

43. Ibid.

44. 354 U.S. at 487 n. 20, 77 S.Ct. at 1310 n. 20.

45. 354 U.S. at 509, 77 S.Ct. at 1322 (dissenting opinion).

46. W. Lockhart and R. McClure, "Censorship of Obscenity: The Developing Constitutional Standards," *Minnesota Law Review* 45 (1960): p. 5; W. Lockhart and R. McClure, "Obscenity Censorship: The Core Constitutional Issue—What Is Obscene?" *Utah Law Review* 7 (1961): p. 289.

47. Jacobellis v. Ohio, 378 U.S. 184, 84 S.Ct. 1676 (1964).

48. Miller v. California, 413 U.S. 15, 93 S.Ct. 2607 (1973), rehearing denied 414 U.S. 881, 94 S.Ct. 26 (1973).

49. Ibid.

50. Ibid.

51. Ibid.

52. Pope v. Illinois, 481 U.S. 497, 107 S.Ct. 1918 (1987), on remand 162 Ill.App.3d 299, 113 Dec. 547, 515 N.E.2d 356 (1987).

53. 484 U.S. 260, 108 S.Ct. 562 (1988).

54. Ibid.

55. Ibid.

56. Virgil v. School Board of Columbia County, Florida, 862 F.2d 1517 (11th Cir.1989).

57. Ibid.

58. Krizek v. Cicero-Stickney Twp. High School District No. 201, 713 F.Supp. 1131 (N.D.Ill.1989).

59. Cary v. Board of Education, 598 F.2d 535, 543 (10th Cir.1979).

60. Krizek, op. cit.

61. Mailloux v. Kiley, 323 F.Supp. 1387 (D.Mass.1971), affirmed 448 F.2d 1242 (1st Cir.1971).

62. Spurger v. Rapides Parish School Board, 628 So.2d 1317 (La.App.3d Cir.1993).

63. Gertrude Himmelfarb, *Darwin and the Darwinian Revolution* (Chicago: Elephant Paperbacks, Ivan R. Dee Publisher, 1996), p. 390.

64. Will and Ariel Durant, *The Age of Reason* (New York: Simon and Schuster, 1961), p. 162.

65. Ibid.

66. Dava Sobel, *Galileo's Daughter* (New York: Walker & Company, 1999), p. 274.

67. Gertrude Himmelfarb, op cit., p. 355.

68. Charles Darwin, *The Origin of Species* (New York: Penguin Books, Inc., 1958), p. 452, first published in 1859.

69. Dava Sobel, op cit., p. 65. Sobel quotes the Vatican Librarian Cesare Cardinal Baronio; this view was adopted by Galileo himself.

70. "Some Considerations Touching the Usefulness of Experimental Philosophy" (1663), quoted in Martha Ornstein, *The Role of Scientific Societies in the Seventeenth Century* (3rd ed. 1938), p. 58–59; cited above in Peter Gay, *The Enlightenment; The Science of Freedom* (New York: W.W. Norton & Company, 1969), p. 140.

71. Gay, ibid., p. 141.

72. Ibid.

73. Quoting Voltaire, in *Éléments de la philosophie de Newton, in Éuvres XXII*, p. 403–404, cited in Gay, op cit, p. 142.

74. See Peter Gay, op cit., p. 144.

75. Thomas Huxley, *Life and Letters, II*, p. 186, cited in Himmelfarb, op cit. p. 286.

76. Himmelfarb, op cit., p. 380.

77. Ibid., pp. 412–413.

78. Ibid.

79. Darwin's *The Origin of Species* was published by Murray publishing house in London on November 24, 1859.

80. See Carl Sagan, *The Demon-Haunted World: Science as a Candle in the Dark* (New York: Random House, 1996).

81. Niles Eldredge, "History of Science, More Corn from Kansas," in *Times Literary Supplement* (TLS), February 18, 2000, p. 9, review of book by Robert T. Pennock, *Tower of Babel* (Boston: MIT Press, 2000), p. 429.

82. Ibid.

83. Ibid.

84. Ibid.

85. Dan Yankelovich, DYG, Inc.; See Ellen Goodman, "Are Americans too Tolerant?" *Washington Post* editorial, March 19, 2000.

86. See Ralph Neas, *People for the United Way*, in Ellen Goodman, op cit.

87. Stephen Jay Gould, *Leonardo's Mountain of Clams and The Diet of Worms* (New York: Three Rivers Press, 1999), p. 270.

88. Gould, op cit., p. 271.

89. Ibid., p. 272.

90. Ibid., p. 274.

91. Epperson v. State of Arkansas, 393 U.S. 97, 89 S.Ct. 266 (1968).

92. 529 F.Supp. 1255 (E.D.Ark.1982).

93. Edwards v. Aguillard, 482 U.S. 578, 107 S.Ct. 2573 (1987).

94. Eldredge, Ibid.

95. Stephen Hawking, "Builders of the Millennium Lecture," University College Oxford University as reported in *Oxford Today, The University Magazine*, Volume 12, No. 2 (Hilary Issue, 2000): 2.

96. Board of Curators of University of Missouri v. Horowitz, 435 U.S. 78, 98 S.Ct. 948 (1978).

97. Barnard v. Inhabitants of Shelburne, 216 Mass. 19, 102 N.E. 1095 (1913).

98. 513 F.2d 843, 851 (10th Cir.1975).

99. 408 U.S. 564, 92 S.Ct. 2701 (1972).

100. 424 U.S. 319, 96 S.Ct. 893 (1976).

101. Debra P. v. Turlington, 474 F.Supp. 244 (M.D. Fla. 1979), affirmed 644 F.2d 397 (5th Cir.1981).

102. Anderson v. Banks, 540 F.Supp. 761, 765 (S.D.Ga. 1982).

103. Hobson v. Hansen, 269 F.Supp. 401 (D.D.C.1967), affirmed sub nom Smuck v. Hobson, 408 F.2d 175 (D.C.Cir.1969).

104. P. v. Riles, 343 F.Supp. 1306 (N.D.Cal.1972), affirmed 502 F.2d 963 (9th Cir.1974).

105. 426 U.S. 229, 96 S.Ct. 2040 (1976).

106. "Reading the Mind of the School Board: Segregative Intent and the De Facto/De Jure Distinction." *Yale Law Journal* 86 (1976): pp. 317, 335.

107. Lawrence A. Cremin, *American Education, The National Experience, 1783–1876* (New York: Harper and Row, 1980), p. 117.

108. Board of Curators of the University of Missouri v. Horowitz, 435 U.S. 78, 98 S.Ct. 948 (1978).

109. Regents of the University of Michigan v. Ewing, 474 U.S. 214, 106 S.Ct. 507 (1985).

110. Ibid.

111. Swany v. San Ramon Valley Unified School District, 720 F.Supp. 764 (N.C.Cal.1989).

112. Valentine v. Independent School District of Casey, 191 Iowa 1100, 183 N.W. 434 (1921).

113. Slocum v. Holton Board of Education, 171 Mich. App. 92, 429 N.W.2d 607 (1988).

114. Katzman v. Cumberland Valley School District, 84 Pa. Cmwlth. 474, 479 A.2d 671 (1984).

115. Campbell v. Board of Education of Town of New Milford, 193 Conn. 93, 475 A.2d 289 (1984).

116. State v. Board of Trustees of School Dist. No. 1, 223 Mont. 269, 726 P.2d 801 (1986).

117. Rousselle v. Plaquemines Parish School Board, 527 So.2d 376 (La.App.1988).

118. Truby v. Broadwater, 175 W.Va. 270, 332 S.E.2d 284 (1985).

119. 414 U.S. 563, 94 S.Ct. 786 (1974).

120. Guadalupe Organization, Inc. v. Tempe Elementary School District No. 3, 587 F.2d 1022 (9th Cir.1978).

121. 20 U.S.C.A. §1703(f).

122. Castaneda v. Pickard, 648 F.2d 989 (5th Cir.1981).

123. Casteneda v. Pickard, 781 F.2d 456 (5th Cir.1986).

124. Ibid.

125. Castaneda v. Pickard, 648 F.2d at 1009–1010; see also Martha McCarthy and Nelda H. Cambron-McCabe, Public School Law, 2d ed. (Boston: Allyn and Bacon, 1987), pp. 186–87.

126. 20 U.S.C.A. §880b et seq.

127. 20 U.S.C.A. §880b-1(a)(4)(A).

CHAPTER 8

STUDENT RIGHTS

The attainment of freedom of expression is not the sole aim of the good society. As the private right of the individual, freedom of expression is an end of itself, but it is not the only end of man as an individual. . . . Any theory of freedom of expression must therefore take into account other values, such as public order, justice, equality and moral progress, and the need for substantive measures designed to promote those ideals. Hence there is a real problem of reconciling freedom of expression with the other values and objectives sought by the good society.

—Thomas I. Emerson

CHAPTER OUTLINE

SCHOOL AUTHORITIES are vested with broad powers for the establishment and conduct of the education program. This prerogative, however, is by no means absolute, and the school officials must act within the scope of reasonable regulations. Rules are usually held to be reasonable if they materially contribute to the maintenance and advancement of the educational process. Court decisions in recent years indicate the judiciary is ever diligent in the requirement of reasonableness and fairness in protecting the constitutional rights of the students. The courts, though, even under the weight of a great quantum of challenges to school board authority, continue to give school boards wide discretion in

promulgating and interpreting regulations governing student conduct. In a 1982 case, the U.S. Supreme Court reversed a circuit court decision in which the court substituted its own interpretation of a school board rule for that of the school board,[1] and in 1992, the Court reiterated the importance of having state and local authorities control the operation of their own schools with as little external judicial control as possible.[2]

Too, earlier, in *Wood v. Strickland*, the Supreme Court stated that a lower federal court erred "in substituting its own notions for a school board's definition of its rules."[3] The Court said, "The Court of Appeals was ill advised to supplant the interpretation of the regulation of those officers who adopted it and are entrusted with its enforcement."[4]

A school board rule, however, cannot be so broad or vague as to allow arbitrary interpretation and application. Such overbreadth can result in a violation of a student's right of due process. In acknowledging such eventuality, the Supreme Court has said in *dictum* that "[a] case may be hypothesized in which a school board's interpretation of its rules is so extreme as to be in violation of due process."[5] School regulations are generally held to be sufficiently definitive if they provide students with adequate information as to what is expected of them and are so stated that persons of common intelligence are not required to guess at their meaning. Reasonable certainty of interpretation requires only the use of ordinary and commonly used terminology. Reasonableness, however, is not predicated on formal adoption and publication of rules before they can have effect, and the absence of a preexisting rule on the books does not prohibit official action. Absence of such formality, though, may make it much more difficult to convince a court that a rule was necessary and that its enforcement was not capricious.

This chapter discusses the power of school boards in promulgation of rules of student conduct and the reasonableness of the application by school administrators and teachers. Much of the chapter is devoted to limitations that the courts may impose to protect students where governmental actions have been unreasonable, vague, arbitrary, or contrary to constitutional rights or freedoms.

■ COMMON LAW AND THE STUDENT

Court decisions throughout the years have established a common law of the school, under which the teacher and the student have mutual responsibilities and obligations. The mutuality of the relationship is predicated on society's expectations of the school in the advancement of the common good of the community. The teacher's responsibility is diverse and multifaceted, owing both to the community and to the student. The courts have recognized that in order for teachers to address the diversity of ex-

pectations placed upon them, they must be given sufficient latitude in the control of the conduct of the school for an appropriate decorum and learning atmosphere to prevail. In keeping with this objective, the courts have allowed teachers general control over students in the school setting. Edwards has summarized the view of the courts with regard to the teacher's authority by observing, "There is inherent in his position the authority to govern the school in a reasonable and humane way. . . ."[6]

The reference to "inherent" authority means that the teacher does not derive all of his or her authority from direct enunciations of statute or regulation but, in addition, holds by virtue of the special teacher/student relationship a built-in obligation to promote the harmony of the school by requiring discipline, while protecting and advancing the interest of the child. As such, the teacher has much unprescribed discretion to advance learning and to prohibit those disharmonies inimical to learning. Within this scope is constituted the common law of the school. The Wisconsin Supreme Court has perhaps best explained the common law with regard to the teacher's power and authority:

> While the principal or teacher in charge of a public school is subordinate to the school board or board of education of his district or city, and must enforce rules and regulations adopted by the board for the government of the school, and execute all its lawful orders in that behalf, he does not derive all his power and authority in the school and over his pupils from the affirmative action of the board. He stands for the time being *in loco parentis* to his pupils, and because of that relation, he must necessarily exercise authority over them in many things concerning which the board may have remained silent.[7]

On the other hand, the student has a corresponding and reciprocal obligation to the school not only to partake of its benefits, but also, by action and deed, to assist in the advancement of its purposes and causes. The student fulfills this obligation by respecting school decorum, by exhibiting the conduct and manners appropriate to the situation. This behavior requires a degree of subordination of the student's individual freedom for the general good and lawful purposes of the school. The student's responsibility has been clearly defined by the aforementioned Wisconsin court:

> In the school, as in the family, there exist on the part of the pupils the obligations of obedience to lawful commands, subordination, civil deportment, respect for the rights of other pupils and fidelity to duty. These obligations are inherent in any proper school system, and constitute, so to speak, the common law of the school, and every student is subject thereto, whether or not such laws have been reenacted by the district board in the form of written rules and regulations. Indeed it would seem impossible to frame rules which would cover all cases of insubordination and all acts of vicious tendency which the teacher is likely to encounter daily and hourly.[8]

The situation of the student in school is not significantly different from that of the citizen in society; some reduction in individual freedom is necessary throughout society. In fact, a commonwealth, or Latin *civitas*, is formed by individuals consenting to submit their wills for unity of the whole or common good. Hobbes, in *Leviathan*, spoke of a covenant in which a *quid pro quo* was given between the protector and the protected, a contract for mutual benefit. He described it this way:

> [I]t is a real unity of them all, in one and the same person, made by covenant of every man, in such a manner, as if every man should say to every man, I authorize and give up my right of governing myself, to this condition, that thou give up the right to him, and authorize all his actions in like manner. This done, the multitude united in one person, is called a commonwealth. . . . [9]

In a less severe conceptualization, Rousseau defined the common interest in forming society and government, to the effect that each individual must "acquire his rights by discharging his duties,"[10] and this forms a social compact wherein

> [e]ach of us puts his person and all his power in common under the supreme direction of the general will, and, in our corporate capacity, we receive each member as an indivisible part of the whole.

At once, in place of the individual personality of each contrasting party, this act of association creates a corporate and collective body . . . ,

receiving from this act its unity, its common identity, its life, and its will.[11]

It is this commonality of the social purpose of public schools that creates the obligations and responsibilities on the part of the school, the teacher, and the student. The exchange of autonomy for benefits as defined by philosophers as diverse as Hobbes and Rousseau can easily be translated into the circumstances of the public school. The common good is advanced by the common law of the school, which prescribes acceptable social conditions and standards for the operation of the schools. Again, Rousseau makes the critical connection:

> Public education, therefore, under regulation prescribed by the Sovereign, is one of the fundamental rules of popular or legitimate government. If children are brought up in common in the bosom of equality; if they are imbued with the laws of the State and precepts of general will; if they are surrounded by examples and objects which constantly remind them of the tender mother who nourishes them, . . . we cannot doubt that they will learn to cherish one another mutually as brothers, to will nothing contrary to the will of society . . . , and to become, in time, defenders and fathers of the country of which they will have been so long children.[12]

Thus, the common law of the school, as prescribed by extensive judicial precedent, reflects a synthesis, characterized by the school, wherein the highest interest of the individual and the preeminent interest of the community coincide.[13] The individual, the student, "[i]n pursuing his own interest, . . . pursues that of the community, and in promoting the interest of the community, he promotes his own."[14] This "harmony of interests"[15] is defined and furthered by the common law of the public school.

Therefore, we may understand in the context of both law and philosophy the reasoning of the common law, which conveys to the teacher the authority to maintain an orderly atmosphere of learning, a benefit to both the students and the community. The rule of law as enunciated by an early Missouri court is thus clearly understood:

> The teacher of a school as to the children of his school, while under his care, occupies, for the time being, the position of parent or guardian, and it is

his right and duty not only to enforce discipline to preserve order and to teach, but also to look after the morals, the health and the safety of his pupils; to do and require his pupils to do whatever is reasonably necessary to preserve and conserve all these interests. . . . [16]

REASONABLENESS

Reasonableness of a school rule in the control of students has at least two aspects—the jurisdictional reach of the school's authority beyond the school grounds and the nature and degree of the discipline visited upon the student. Reasonableness is the common law watchword of the teacher/student relationship. To act reasonably is the primary test of tort law and is a favorite definition of proper and expected conduct in society generally.

The meaning of reasonableness in the abstract is difficult to determine, but when coupled with facts found in scholastic circumstances, the term usually takes on greater lucidity. In its detached sense, though, it means that which is proper, rational, and fair; it precludes conduct that can be characterized as immoderate, excessive, and unsuitable to the particular conditions or circumstances. Because the authority of the teacher cannot be completely circumscribed by state law or by school regulations and because every eventuality in school cannot be anticipated by applicable rules, considerable judicial flexibility must be allowed in determining reasonable behavior of the teacher. Further, the reciprocal responsibilities of the students must also be viewed in the context of reasonableness.

IN LOCO PARENTIS

Though the term *in loco parentis* translated to English means "in the place of a parent," the courts have never intended that school authorities or teachers stand fully in the place of parents in control of their children. School officials' and teachers' prerogatives are circumscribed by and limited to school functions and activities. The concept emanated from English law that governed the private schools of that country, usually giving schoolmasters extraordinary, and sometimes unconscionable, powers over pupil conduct. Even though common law approves of the concept, the boundaries of the teacher's

authority are marked by requirements of reasonableness and restraint. Blackstone himself, in his *Commentaries*, observed that the teacher has only that portion of parental powers necessary for the conduct of the school.[17] In *Lander v. Seaver*,[18] the Supreme Court of Vermont made the very important point that the power of the teacher over the child is not coextensive with that of the parent.[19] Importantly, this court observed that because the teacher does not have the natural affection of the parent for the child, his or her acts of discipline must be viewed circumspectly by the courts. Because the teacher has no innate natural parental concern for the child, "he may not be trusted with all a parent's authority. . . ."[20]

Nevertheless, even with its limitations, the doctrine of *in loco parentis*, as a vestige of common law, is viable and operates to help define the relationship between school and student in the public schools today. Its justification is found in the necessity for an orderly and well-behaved student in keeping with an agreeable learning environment. The doctrine is probably best defined by a Nebraska court as follows:

[G]eneral education and control of pupils who attend public schools are in the hands of school boards, superintendents, principals, and teachers. This control extends to health, proper surroundings, necessary discipline, promotion of morality and other wholesome influences, while parental authority is temporarily superseded.[21]

Recent trends in constitutional law that bear on the interests of the student in the context of public school operation have more sharply defined the legal concept but have not replaced it. In *New Jersey v. T. L. O.*, the U.S. Supreme Court held that although the *in loco parentis* doctrine did not exempt school officials from Fourth Amendment search and seizure restrictions, the doctrine "retains vitality in appropriate circumstances."[22] Other Supreme Court cases have also recognized the continuing viability of the doctrine.[23] Significantly, the Supreme Court, in *Bethel School District No. 403 v. Fraser*, reiterated the importance of the *in loco parentis* doctrine in protecting children "especially in a captive audience from exposure to sexually explicit, indecent, or lewd speech."[24]

Thus, not only does *in loco parentis* appear to be an active legal concept, but also in recent years it has taken on new and more definitive meaning.

❖ — ❖ — ❖

School District Policy on "Loitering" Is Not Unconstitutionally Vague or in Violation of First Amendment

Wiemerslage v. Maine Township High School District 207

United States Court of Appeals,
Seventh Circuit, 1994.
29 F.3d 1149.

BAUER, Circuit Judge.

Kurt Wiemerslage, a student at Maine Township High School South ("Maine South") in Park Ridge, Illinois, was given a three-day suspension from school for violating the school's anti-loitering rule. Alleging that the rule violated his constitutional rights under the First and Fourteenth Amendments, he filed suit under 42 U.S.C. §1983. The district court dismissed his complaint for failure to state a claim. . . . We affirm.

The Maine Township High School District 207 ("School District") publishes a manual outlining its disciplinary procedures. That manual authorizes school administrators to designate certain areas as off-limits to students. In a letter dated August, 1992, Thomas J. Cachur, principal of Maine South, notified parents and students that the area adjacent to the school's east side gate, referred to as the Hamlin Gate Area, continued to be off-limits to students. "While students can use this area to enter or leave the school campus before and after school, loitering is not permitted in this area." Cachur's letter informed parents and students that violation of this rule would result in a three-day suspension. The policy was apparently the result of com-plaints made by residents in the vicinity concerning the students' disregard for neighborhood property and traffic safety.

On September 23, 1992, shortly after school had ended for the day, Wiemerslage, a Maine South freshman, was standing with some friends outside of the Hamlin Gate on Gillick Street between Hamlin and Home Avenues. The students were discussing their plans for that afternoon when they were approached by Thomas Swoboda, a security officer retained by the School District. Swoboda took their names and cited them for violating the school's rule against loitering.

Judy Bovenmyer, Dean of Students at Maine South, informed Wiemerslage and his parents that he had been found in violation of the disciplinary rule and that he was suspended from school for three days. After meeting with Bovenmyer, Wiemerslage's parents asked to meet with Cachur. Dissatisfied with the results of this meeting, the Wiemerslages then requested, as was their right, a formal hearing before an officer of the School District. Upon completion of the hearing, the School District upheld the school's decision to suspend Wiemerslage. . . .

Wiemerslage argues that the disciplinary rule is rendered unconstitutionally vague by its use of the term "loitering" to define the prohibited conduct. Laws declared unconstitutional on vagueness grounds may offend due process in different ways. By failing to articulate with any specificity the conduct to be proscribed, vague laws might not provide fair warning. . . . Moreover, vague laws inevitably confer on law enforcement and judicial officers an inordinate amount of discretion which easily translates into arbitrary or even discriminatory application. . . .

Worth noting, however, is that flexibility or breadth should not necessarily be confused for vagueness. "There is little doubt that imagination can conjure up hypothetical cases in which the meaning of [disputed] terms will be in nice question." . . . A vagueness challenge must be considered in the context of the rule at issue. As framed by the Supreme Court, the inquiry is whether the law defines the proscribed conduct "with sufficient definiteness that ordinary people can understand what conduct is prohibited and in a manner that does not encourage arbitrary and discriminatory enforcement." . . . Given the peculiar issues facing school administrators, a school's disciplinary rules need not be drafted as narrowly or with the same precision as criminal statutes. . . .

In this instance, Maine South students entering and leaving school through Hamlin Gate presented school officials with two problems. First, there was a concern for the students' own safety because of the traffic in the area. Second, residents in the vicinity reported damage to their properties as a result of students milling about the area. To address these twin concerns, school officials prohibited students from congregating in a specific area as a means of inducing them to proceed wherever it was they were going.

Maine South's response to these problems was appropriate. Personal safety and damage to property are two legitimate reasons to regulate speech and assembly. . . . The rule drafted by Maine South was narrowly tailored in that it was limited to a confined space and proscribed conduct regardless of its expressive content.

Wiemerslage fails to allege facts which render these restrictions constitutionally unreasonable. Maine South's anti-loitering rule was not designed to prevent student speech or assembly. Wiemerslage does not articulate why the school's concerns for safety and property damage were somehow outweighed by his need to exercise his rights of free speech and assembly in the Hamlin Gate area. Nor does he explain why the rule was overly broad. Consequently, his claim alleging violations of the First Amendment was properly dismissed.

Because Wiemerslage's complaint fails to state a claim upon which relief can be granted, the trial court's decision to dismiss the complaint is

AFFIRMED.

CASE NOTES

1. *Behavior off School Premises.* Students are not deprived of constitutional rights of free speech and property interests when disciplined for behavior that is detrimental to the school, regardless of whether the incident transpired on or off school property. The applicable rule of law may be summarized as follows: "A reasonable school regulation is one which is essential in maintaining order and discipline on school property and which measurably contributes to the maintenance of order and decorum within the educational system." 68 Am.Jur.2d §254. See also *Blackwell v. Issaquena County Board of Education,* 363 F.2d 749 (5th Cir.1966).

For example, a federal court in Pennsylvania held that lewd comments made about a teacher on Sunday, off school premises, were sufficiently detrimental to the school to warrant disciplinary action. In this case, the facts indicated that as a teacher passed by an automobile in a shopping center on a Sunday evening, a student shouted, "There's Stear," and a second student in another automobile loudly responded, "He's a prick." On Monday morning, the teacher explained the facts to the vice-principal. The vice-principal confronted the second student, who admitted calling Mr. Stear a prick, whereupon the student was given an in-school suspension, was not allowed to participate in the senior trip, was not permitted to attend any extracurricular activities, and was placed on other restrictions while at school, such as being required to sit at the restricted table in the cafeteria.

The student challenged the disciplinary action as a violation of his freedom of speech and denial of a property right to an education. The court stated, "It is the opinion of the court that the First Amendment rights of the plaintiff were not violated. His conduct involved an invasion of the right of teacher Stear to be free from being loudly insulted in a public place by 'lewd, lascivious or indecent words or language.'" The court went on to say, "It is our opinion that when a high school student refers to a high school teacher in a public place on a Sunday by a lewd and obscene name in such a loud voice that the teacher and others hear the insult, it may be deemed a matter for discipline in the discretion of the school authorities. To countenance such student conduct even in a public place without imposing sanctions could lead to devastating consequences in the school." Furthermore, since the student continued his education while serving the in-school suspension, he was not deprived of any property right. *Fenton v. Stear,* 423 F.Supp. 767 (W.D.Pa.1976).

2. School discipline extends to activities beyond school grounds, particularly where safety of students may be compromised. A case illustrating the point occurred where two students, one in a jeep and the other in a pickup truck, impeded the progress of a school bus loaded with children traveling to school. The driver of the jeep positioned his vehicle in front of the bus, while the pickup truck was behind, and by alternatively slowing and speeding up, they obstructed the operation of the bus. Upon arriving at the school, the students, who had been positively identified, were cited by the Wyoming highway patrol and suspended by the school. They challenged the disciplinary action by the school authorities. The court states, "It matters little that the proscribed conduct occurred on a public highway. It is generally accepted that school authorities may discipline pupils for out-of-school conduct having a direct and immediate effect on the discipline or general welfare of the school. This is particularly true where the discipline is reasonably necessary for the student's physical or emotional safety and well-being of other students." *Clements v. Board of Trustees of Sheridan County School District No. 2,* 585 P.2d 197 (Wyo.1978); see also 53 A.L.R.3d 1124; 68 Am.Jur.2d, Schools §§256, 266.

3. In a case where a student was expelled from school for committing a battery on another student on a public street after school, the student challenged the school's authority to discipline him for off-school-grounds behavior. The court upheld the school's action, observing that imposing discipline off school grounds is not arbitrary or capricious. *Nicholas B. v. School Committee,* 412 Mass. 20, 587 N.E.2d 211 (1992).

4. The safety and welfare of students are, of course, tied to the contagion of drugs in our society. Drug dealing off school grounds naturally affects the schools. In a case where a student sold cocaine to an undercover state police officer on three occasions, none on the school property, the student was arrested at the high school, suspended by the principal, and subsequently expelled by the school board. The student challenged the expulsion, claiming the school board lacked authority to expel him for a nonschool activity off school grounds. The court upheld the school board, where the board said

the student was a threat to the safety and welfare of other students even if he was an off-campus drug dealer. *Howard v. Colonial School District,* 621 A.2d 362 (Del.Super.1992).

■ CONSTITUTIONAL DUE PROCESS

As pointed out elsewhere in this book, the Fourteenth Amendment to the federal Constitution provides that no state shall deprive a person of life, liberty, or property without due process of law. Stated positively, a state may deprive a person of life, liberty, or property so long as the individual is given due process.

There are two types of due process. One is called "procedural due process." This means that if a person is to be deprived of life, liberty, or property, a prescribed constitutional procedure must be followed. The U.S. Supreme Court has said that in order to give an individual procedural due process as required by the federal Constitution, three basic factors must be present. The person must have proper notice that he or she is about to be deprived of life, liberty, or property; he or she must be given an opportunity to be heard; and the hearing must be conducted fairly.

A second type of due process is called "substantive due process." To satisfy this constitutional requirement, if a state is going to deprive a person of life, liberty, or property, the state must have a valid objective, and the means used must be reasonably calculated to achieve that objective. Early interpretations by the U.S. Supreme Court recognized only the procedural aspects of due process of law.[25] It was not until 1923 in *Meyer v. Nebraska* (see Chapter 7) that the Supreme Court arrived at a reasonably clear definition that due process of law is an aspect of the law that possesses "substantive" protections.[26] Substantive due process was defined by one court as follows:

> The phrase "due process of law," when applied to substantive rights, as distinguished from procedural rights, means that the state is without power to deprive a person of life, liberty or property by an act having no reasonable relation to any proper governmental purpose, or which is so far beyond the necessity of case as to be an arbitrary exercise of governmental power.[27]

■ SUBSTANTIVE DUE PROCESS

As early as 1798, the justices of the U.S. Supreme Court debated whether there were implicit natural law protections, beyond the explicit wording of the U.S. Constitution, that extended the rights of individuals and limited the powers of government.[28] At that time, the issue was argued as to whether the justices had authority to interject unwritten standards of justice into the meaning of the Constitution in order to protect the rights of the people from heavy-handed government. Advocates for extension of constitutional intent maintained that there is a moral law beyond the words specified in the Constitution, a substantive aspect that protects individual rights of liberty, equality, and justice.[29] Various legal philosophers, including Locke, had earlier posited that the state is created to protect natural rights and to guarantee justice and that social compacts that bind the people into a government should be a restraint on governmental excesses and should not be so strictly construed as to prevent recognition of a broader array of individual rights and freedoms.[30] Accordingly, proponents of natural law have argued that there is an implicit meaning in the Constitution that individual rights are not those merely established within the text of the document itself, but also include all those natural and moral rights that pertain to fairness, equity, and the pursuit of happiness.[31] Justice therefore requires that the courts look not simply to the explicit content of the Constitution, but also to the "substance" of the Constitution that is implicit in human rights of transcending moral consequence.

Therefore, judges of the natural law persuasion believe that substantive due process should be open ended and expanded as the courts deem necessary to protect individual rights, regardless of whether the protection can be premised on some explicit constitutional provision. In this view, the Supreme Court should "invalidate legislation if the justices [believe] that it [interferes] with rights that the natural law [has] vested in the people."[32] The constitutional vehicle for inclusion of the natural law concept is "substantive due process." Those who oppose the expansion of substantive due process and the theory of natural law maintain that the courts should exercise judicial restraint and that even if natural law is an acceptable theory, there is no valid power of the courts to enforce such a standard over the will of the people as expressed by governmental statute. In essence, those who oppose the idea of substantive due process contend that "the courts have no role in enforcing natural law principles because enforcement of such principles would result in the subservience of the people to the individual views of the justices."[33]

Between these two extremes, the constitutional law had developed, not fully adopting either position. A string of constitutional law precedents over two hundred years, coupled with the enactment of the Fourteenth Amendment in 1868, has led the Supreme Court to adopt a modified natural law approach that incorporates implicit meaning into due process. The evolution of precedents has resulted in a judicial philosophical compromise that holds that laws should be invalidated only if there exists some reasonable linkage to specific constitutional provisions. For example, even though the equal protection clause of the Fourteenth Amendment was enacted as a "protective shield" to blacks against laws that unfairly discriminated against them, the Court has expanded the substantive meaning to protect certain economic groups and other individuals as well.[34]

Substantive due process was given important impetus by subsequent interpretations of the Fourteenth Amendment that expanded on the idea of due process and its relationship to equal protection.[35] Today, the Supreme Court strictly reviews statutes and regulations that affect essential and fundamental rights even though the precise wording referring to those rights is not specifically used in the Constitution. For example, there is a fundamental "right to privacy" even though the terminology is not used anywhere in the Constitution.[36] In *Griswold v. Connecticut*,[37] Justice Douglas noted that such a right, while not explicit, is found in the "penumbras" of several guarantees of the Bill of Rights.[38] In *Griswold*, Justice Harlan specifically justified a right of privacy based on natural law theory, which permitted the judiciary to select values that were of such philosophical and historical importance that they could be regarded as fundamental.[39] In the same case, Justice Black dissented, objecting to the natural law approach in defining due process, and he concluded that there was no substantive right of privacy in the Constitution.[40]

Today, the U.S. Supreme Court is only lukewarm to any expansion of substantive due process. Justice White, writing for the majority in *Bowers v. Hardwick*,[41] inveighed against too broad an expansion of substantive due process and, by so doing, probably best reflected the current view of the Court toward the concept:

> [T]here should be, therefore, great resistance to expand the substantive reach of those clauses [the due process clauses of the Fifth and Fourteenth Amendments], particularly if it requires redefining the category of rights deemed to be fundamental. Otherwise, the judiciary necessarily takes to itself further authority to govern the country without expressed constitutional authority.[42]

More-Specific-Provision Rule

While acknowledging the continuing importance of substantive due process as a guard against arbitrary governmental action, the Supreme Court has more narrowly defined the circumstances in which it is to be utilized. In *Graham v. Connor*,[43] the Supreme Court set out what it called the "more-specific-provision" rule. This rule forecloses the use of substantive due process as grounds for a constitutional claim if the claim can be couched in another more specific provision of the Constitution.

For example, if a question of a valid exercise of free speech is at issue, then the governmental action must be challenged under the First Amendment, not the substantive aspect of the due process clause of the Fourteenth Amendment. In a 1998 case, *County of Sacramento v. Lewis*,[44] Justice Souter noted that the Supreme Court has "always been reluctant to expand the concept of substantive due process"[45] and that plaintiffs could not invoke it in every case: "[W]here a particular amendment provides an explicit textual source of constitutional protection against a particular sort of governmental behavior, that Amendment, not the more generalized notion of substantive due process, must be a guide for analyzing these claims."[46] More directly, Justice Souter explained that the Supreme

Court's rule "simply requires that if a constitutional claim is covered by a specific constitutional provision, such as the Fourth and Eighth Amendment, the claim must be analyzed under the standard appropriate to that specific provision, not under the rubric of substantive due process."[47]

Justice Souter further explains that constitutional provisions requiring due process of law were intended to "secure the individual from the arbitrary exercise of the powers of government, unrestrained by the established principles of private right and distributive justice."[48] Due process protects against governmental arbitrariness whether it has to do with taking of property, denial of a governmental benefit, imprisonment, or any other exercise of governmental power without any reasonable justification.[49]

Conscience Shocking

Recent Supreme Court decisions indicate that the "substantive component of the Due Process Clause is violated by executive action only when it 'can properly be characterized as arbitrary', or conscience shocking, in a constitutional sense."[50] Whether a governmental action is "conscience shocking" must be determined based on the facts of each circumstance and the context of the events in question. The Supreme Court has said that "[r]ules of due process are not, however, subject to mechanical application in unfamiliar territory. Deliberate indifference that shocks in one environment may not be as patently egregious in another."[51] That which constitutes a denial of fundamental fairness in one circumstance may fall short of a denial of due process in other circumstances.

Thus, the Supreme Court, today, in taking a more restrictive posture toward substantive due process has concluded that a plaintiff's successful reliance on a constitutional challenge to governmental action requires that (1) there be no other "more-specific provision" in the Constitution under which the claim can be brought; (2) the allegations be sufficient to state a substantive violation through governmental abuse of power; (3) the governmental action be properly characterized as arbitrary, or conscience shocking, in a constitutional sense; and (4) the standard for arbitrary, or conscience-shocking, action be determined only by conditions and circumstances of the particular case because no general rule applies.

The concept of substantive due process remains rather tentative even today. According to Nowak et al., "All that can be said with certainty is that the justices have selected a group of individual rights which do not have a specific textual basis in the Constitution or its amendments and deemed them to be 'fundamental.'"[52] Those substantive rights that have been advanced by Supreme Court interpretations fall into at least six categories of fundamental guarantees. *Nowak et al.* set these out as follows:[53]

1. The freedom of association has been found to be a fundamental substantive right implicit in the First Amendment even though there is no direct textual reference to it.[54]
2. The right to vote and to participate in the electoral process has been deemed a form of substantive liberty under the due process clauses of both the Fifth and the Fourteenth Amendments.[55]
3. The right of mobility and interstate travel has been given the status of a fundamental value and is considered to be a substantive right deriving from several provisions of the Constitution.[56]
4. The right of fairness in criminal process is a substantive due process right. This particular right overlaps the natural justice right of procedural due process as guaranteed by the Fifth and Fourteenth Amendments.[57]
5. The right to fairness in recognition of individual rights emanating from deprivations of life, liberty, or property is recognized as a substantive right. Here, too, substantive and procedural due process tend to converge in that the due process clauses intertwine the procedural rights of natural justice with the substantive rights of natural law. The nexus of the two elements of due process can be seen later in this text in discussions of student expulsion,[58] school finance,[59] and teacher rights.[60] The specific substantive aspects of liberty and property as they apply to teachers will also be discussed later in this text.
6. The right to privacy, as mentioned above, is a substantive aspect of due process and includes various forms of freedoms and choices

pertaining to the individual's personal life. The right of privacy has been found in a person's choice of marital decisions[61] and childbearing.[62] The Supreme Court has ruled that the right of privacy "implicit in the concept of ordered liberty" does not extend to a "claimed constitutional right of homosexuals to engage in acts of sodomy."[63]

As noted earlier in this text, the Supreme Court in *Pierce v. Society of Sisters*[64] found a substantive right in due process with regard to the property of a private school. Later, however, the Court in *Prince v. Massachusetts*[65] refused to expand substantive parental rights in child rearing to limit the state's interest in establishing child labor and compulsory attendance laws.

In *Meyer v. Nebraska*,[66] in 1923, the Supreme Court related substantive protection of the due process clause of the Fourteenth Amendment to education when it held unconstitutional a Nebraska statute forbidding the teaching in public or private schools of foreign languages to pupils below the eighth grade. Since the U.S. Constitution provided no express relief for offending the statute, the Court extended the due process clause to protect the teacher. The Court related the teacher's right to teach to an expanded substantive interpretation of "liberty" and said:

> The problem for our determination is whether the statute as construed and applied unreasonably infringes the liberty guaranteed to the Plaintiff . . . by the Fourteenth Amendment. "No state shall . . . deprive any person of life, liberty, or property, without due process of law."
>
> While this court has not attempted to define with exactness the liberty thus guaranteed, the term has received much consideration and some of the included things have been definitely stated. Without doubt, it denotes not merely freedom from bodily restraint but also the right of the individual to contract, to engage in any of the common occupations of life, to acquire useful knowledge, to marry, establish a home and bring up children, to worship God according to the dictates of his own conscience, and generally to enjoy those privileges long recognized at common law as essential to the orderly pursuit of happiness by free men. . . . The established doctrine is that this liberty may not be interfered with, under the guise of protecting the

public interest, by legislative action which is arbitrary or without reasonable relation to some purpose within the competency of the State to effect. . . . [The teacher's] right thus to teach and the right of parents to engage him so to instruct their children, we think, are within the liberty of the Amendment.[67]

With this decision, the Supreme Court not only acknowledged the substantive protections of due process covering life, liberty, and property, but also clearly extended them to protect a person's right of education.[68]

From 1923 to 1961, there was no further development of education as a substantive due process interest. Generally during that period, the *Meyer* precedent was construed very narrowly, having little implication for education rights. An important case, however, emerged in 1961 which indicated that education is a substantive interest of such magnitude as to invoke procedural due process if it is to be denied. In *Dixon v. Alabama State Board of Education*,[69] a federal court held that attendance at a college is so essential that it cannot be taken away without a hearing and attendant due process procedures. Without specifically saying so, this court implied that education is of such importance that it may be implied within the substance of the term "liberty" or "property" under the due process clause.

Then, in *Tinker v. Des Moines Independent Community School District*,[70] the Supreme Court explicitly recognized the substantive nature of due process rights of students: "First Amendment rights, applied in light of the special characteristics of the school environment, are available to teachers and students. It can hardly be argued that either students or teachers shed their constitutional rights to freedom of speech or expression at the schoolhouse gate. This has been the unmistakable holding of this court for almost fifty years."[71]

In spite of the impact of *Dixon* and *Tinker,* the relationship between education and due process was not clearly defined until 1975 in *Goss v. Lopez*,[72] where the Supreme Court pointed out that denial of education for even a short period of time could not be construed as inconsequential. In explaining that the individual's interest in education falls within the substantive scope of "liberty and property," the Court said: "[N]ei-

ther the property interest in education benefits temporarily denied nor the liberty interest in reputation, which is also implicated, is so insubstantial that suspensions may constitutionally be imposed by any procedure one school chooses, no matter how arbitrary."[73]

The Supreme Court has explained the property interest in this way: "Property interests . . . are not created by the Constitution. Rather they are created and their dimensions are defined by existing rules or understandings that stem from an independent source such as state law—rules or understandings that secure certain benefits and that support claims of entitlement to those benefits."[74] In this regard, the federal Constitution does not create education as a fundamental right, but rather education becomes a "property" interest when state law establishes a public educational system, which all children have a right to attend. Where the right of attendance in public school is extended to all children throughout a state, the state then cannot selectively deny education without procedural due process. Thus, when the state creates a public educational system, education is effectively established as a property right or interest for all pupils.

As observed above, due process also forbids arbitrary deprivation of "liberty" or denial of those interests that are implied by that term. A person's liberty includes his or her "good name, reputation, honor, or integrity." The Supreme Court in *Meyer*[75] said that the Court would not attempt to give an exact definition for liberty, and in *Roth,* the Court said:

> Liberty and property are broad and majestic terms. They are among the great constitutional concepts. Purposely left to gather meaning from experience . . . , they relate to the whole domain of social and economic fact, and the statesmen who founded this Nation knew too well that only a stagnant society remains unchanged.[76]

In *Goss v. Lopez*,[77] where it was found that procedural due process had not been afforded, the Supreme Court ruled that the recording of suspensions in student permanent files effectively attached a stigma infringing on the students' liberty interests. The Court said: "If sustained and recorded, those charges could seriously damage the students' standing with their fellow pupils and their teachers as well as interfere with later opportunities for higher education and employment."[78]

————————— —————————

Giving Students "F" for Violating School Rules
Does Not Violate Substantive Due Process
Where Action Does Not Shock the Conscience

Dunn v. Fairfield Community High School District No. 225

United States Court of Appeals, Seventh Circuit, 1998.
158 F. 3d 962

DIANE P. WOOD, Circuit Judge.

Shaun Dunn and Bill McCullough were both budding musicians who participated as guitar players in the high school band program at Fairfield Community High School, operated by the defendant Fairfield Community High School District No. 225. (We refer to them both as "Fairfield," as there is no distinction important to this appeal.) Fairfield prohibited its band members from departing from the planned musical program during band performances, and it specifically forbade guitar solos during the performances. In direct defiance of those rules and their teacher's explicit orders, Dunn and McCullough (along with two other students) played two unauthorized guitar pieces (instrumentals, with no words) at a February 10, 1995, band program. In due course, the discipline they received for this infraction caused them both to receive an "F" for the band course, and that "F" prevented McCullough from graduating with honors. . . . Dunn and McCullough have now appealed from the district court's decision to grant summary judgment for Fairfield. While as a practical matter the school may have overreacted to the spectacle of two young musicians playing the "wrong" pieces, we conclude that its actions violated no right cognizable under the federal civil rights statutes, and we therefore affirm the district court. . . .

There is little more to the underlying story than the facts we have just outlined.

The students' complaint alleged that Fairfield had violated their constitutional rights . . . , that it violated their "right to substantive due process . . . by imposing disciplinary measures unrelated to academic conduct and . . . outside the parameters and intent of the Illinois School Code and [Fairfield's] disciplinary policy,". . . . The disciplinary action in question, the court concluded, bore a rational relation to the school's interest in maintaining order and providing an education. The court also commented in a footnote that if the plaintiffs were to prevail, "[a]lmost every disciplinary action could become a federal case." . . .

Even though the students are entitled to this court's de novo review of the summary judgment for Fairfield, this generous standard cannot salvage their case. The fundamental flaw in their theory of the case arises from their failure to appreciate the difference between the procedural protections afforded by the Fourteenth Amendment against state deprivations and the far more limited substantive standards that Amendment imposes on state actors. If this had been a case (as it is not) in which Dunn and McCullough had complained that Fairfield threw them out of Band class and effectively condemned them to an "F" in the course without giving them some kind of notice and a hearing, we would delve into the nature of the property interest Illinois law creates in a public education. . . .

But that is not the students' claim. Instead, they assert that the federal Constitution places substantive restrictions on the type of disciplinary measures public school districts may use for conceded violations of rules of student conduct. At some extreme, that is certainly true; the question here is where the outer boundaries lie. The students seem to think that federal constitutional protection is co-extensive with the right recognized under Illinois law to a free public education through the end of high school. The Supreme Court's recent decision in *County of Sacramento v. Lewis*, __U.S.__, 118 S.Ct. 1708 (1998), definitively shows that they are wrong....

The Supreme Court . . . emphasized once again how limited the scope of the substantive due process doctrine is. . . . In so doing, it relied on two independent grounds: first, that substantive due process does not apply when a particular part of the Constitution "provides an explicit textual source of constitutional protection against a particular sort of government behavior," . . . and second, that "in any event the allegations are insufficient to state a substantive due process violation through executive abuse of power." . . . We turn to the latter part of the Court's opinion, because no one claims that Fairfield's actions should be judged under a more specific part of the federal Constitution.

The touchstone of due process, the Court explained, is "protection of the individual against arbitrary action of government," . . . whether the problem is the denial of fundamental procedural fairness or the exercise of governmental power without any reasonable justification. The criteria that govern what is fatally arbitrary . . . depend upon whether legislation or a specific act of a governmental officer is at issue. . . . [T]he court has looked for an abuse of power that "shocks the conscience". . . . Looked at from the opposite point of view, the Court reiterated that "the due process guarantee does not entail a body of constitutional law imposing liability whenever someone cloaked with state authority causes harm." . . . Negligent conduct can virtually never meet the constitutional threshold. Instead, the Court said, "conduct intended to injure in some way unjustifiable by any governmental interest" would be most likely to rise to the conscience-shocking level....

. . . [I]t would be nearly absurd to say that a school principal's decision effectively to give two students an "F" in Band class did. It may be worth acknowledging that this in no way necessarily implies approval of the state official's action; . . . and [in hindsight] we may have similar doubts about the wisdom of the severity of Fairfield's sanctions against the rebel musicians here.

Although the briefs are not entirely clear on this point, we understand from oral argument that Dunn and McCullough are also asserting a legislative violation of substantive due process rights, insofar as they are attacking Fairfield's written disciplinary classifications and penalty structure. . . . [T]he [Supreme] Court [has stated] that "[t]he Due Process Clause guarantees more than fair process, and the 'liberty' it protects includes more than the absence of physical restraint." . . . The substantive component of the clause, the [Supreme] Court explained, "pro-

vides heightened protection against governmental interference with certain fundamental rights and liberty interests," including things like the right to marry, to have children, to direct the education and upbringing of one's children, to marital privacy, to use contraception, to bodily integrity, and to choose an abortion. Id. (giving examples of each). Once again, measured by that standard the school policy that the students attack comes nowhere close to a constitutional violation. Although students may have some substantive due process rights while they are in school, . . . education itself is not a fundamental right. . . . That means that Fairfield's decision to stack the deck so that these students would fail Band must be sustained unless it is wholly arbitrary. Here, however, Dunn and McCullough freely conceded that they had violated a school rule, that the rule was designed to preserve discipline in the classroom and to punish student insubordination, and that these were legitimate interests on the part of the school district. That alone is enough to show that their claim cannot possibly succeed. The Constitution does not guarantee these or any other students the right not to receive an "F" in a course from which they were excluded because of misbehavior.

. . . On a practical level, we share the district court's concern about transforming the federal courts into an appellate arm of the schools throughout the country, but this is not a "floodgates" inspired decision. Our conclusion that Dunn and McCullough have not stated a claim under the substantive component of the due process clause of the Fourteenth Amendment rests exclusively on our understanding of the scope of that doctrine as it has been explicated by the Supreme Court.

For these reasons, we AFFIRM the judgment of the district court.

CASE NOTE

Interscholastic Athletics as a Substantive Due Process Interest. "A clear majority of the courts" has held that students do not have a substantive constitutional entitlement to participate in interscholastic athletics. *Brands v. Sheldon Community School,* 671 F.Supp. 627 (N.D.Iowa 1987). See *Colorado Seminary v. NCAA,* 570 F.2d 320 (10th Cir.1978); *Hamilton v. Tennessee Secondary School*

Athletic Association, 552 F.2d 681 (6th Cir.1976); *Mitchell v. Louisiana High School Athletic Association*, 430 F.2d 1155 (5th Cir.1970). In a case from the U.S. Court of Appeals, Eighth Circuit, the court stated that "a student's interest in participating in a single year of interscholastic athletics amounts to a mere expectation rather than a constitutionally protected claim of entitlement." *In re United States ex rel. Missouri State High School Activities Association*, 682 F.2d 147 (8th Cir.1982), quoting *Walsh v. Louisiana High School Athletic Association*, 616 F.2d 152 (5th Cir.1980), cert. denied, 449 U.S. 1124, 101 S.Ct. 939 (1981).

In *Brands*, the court noted that "once awarded, a college scholarship may give rise to a property interest in its continuation," citing *Hall v. University of Minnesota*, 530 F.Supp. 104 (D.Minn.1982).

The court in *Brands* further elaborated,

> [w]hen scholarships are awarded at the discretion of a college coach, and such discretion has not yet been exercised, no property interest in the receipt of a scholarship can exist, and the plaintiff can not invoke his expectation that he would earn a scholarship at the state tournament in order to claim a property interest.

❖

CORPORAL PUNISHMENT, THE EIGHTH AMENDMENT, AND SUBSTANTIVE DUE PROCESS

The courts have upheld the right of school authorities to physically punish children in order to preserve school propriety and discipline. Cases have generally dealt with the degree and reasonableness of the discipline and not with whether corporal punishment could be administered at all.

A teacher's right to discipline students is subject to the reasonableness that is applicable to parents in disciplining their own children. Courts have advanced two standards governing a teacher's corporal punishment of a child: (1) the reasonableness standard, that it "must be exerted within bounds of reason and humanity"; and (2) the good-faith standard. With regard to the first standard, the authority of a teacher over the pupil is considered a delegation by the state to the teacher of at least a portion of parental authority. As such, there is a presumption in favor of the correctness of the teacher's actions. Concerning the second standard, the teacher must not have been activated by malice or have inflicted the punishment wantonly or excessively. The teacher may not be liable for error in judgment, even though the punishment is too severe, if the punishment is not of a nature to cause injury and he or she acts in good faith.

The legality of corporal punishment in the public schools has been drawn into question in recent years as numerous state legislatures have statutorily abolished physical punishment as a means of discipline. A recent study indicated that nineteen states have abolished corporal punishment in the public schools, and ten of these laws have been enacted since 1988. Yet, under common law and constitutional law precedents, corporal punishment remains permissible.

Eighth Amendment

In *Ingraham v. Wright*,[79] the U.S. Supreme Court ruled flatly that corporal punishment, as administered in the schools, could not be construed to violate the Eighth Amendment. The Court said the amendment's prohibition against cruel and unusual punishment does not apply to paddling in the schools; rather, it was designed to protect those convicted of crimes from punishment that is inhumane, vicious, or barbarous. The amendment's intent is threefold: to limit the kinds of punishment that can be imposed on those convicted of crimes, to proscribe punishment grossly disproportionate to the severity of the crime, and to impose substantive limits on what can be made criminal and punished as such. In this light, the Court concluded that it is difficult to conceive of corporal punishment as being within the scope of the Eighth Amendment. According to the Court, the amendment was not so intended.

Liberty Interest

At present, the courts are in conflict over whether at some level of severity corporal punishment may be so excessive as to deny a student's substantive liberty interests. The Supreme Court, in *Ingraham*, declared that "corporal punishment in public schools implicates a constitutionally protected liberty interest."[80] The Court noted that "among the liberty interests 'long recognized at common law as essential to the orderly pursuit of happiness of free men'" is the "right to be free from, and obtain judicial relief for, unjustified intrusions on personal security," including "bodily restraint and punishment."[81]

Yet, the Supreme Court noted that ordinary corporal punishment does not violate substantive rights. Further, if the Supreme Court did believe that substantive due process interests come into play at a certain level of severity, it apparently did not feel that the severe beating that the students suffered in *Ingraham* was of sufficient magnitude to invoke such substantive interests. Therefore, the Supreme Court left the issue hanging. The Fifth Circuit Court of Appeals, in dealing with *Ingraham* at the lower court level, had observed that substantive rights could not be reduced to a review of the severity of corporal punishment in each case, an untenable position in which the courts would find themselves counting the weight and number of paddle licks.[82]

The U.S. Courts of Appeals for the Fourth[83] and Tenth[84] Circuits have, however, sought more definitive standards with regard to punishment. Both have maintained that punishment may be so severe as to constitute denial of a substantive due process interest. The Appeals Court for the Fourth Circuit in *Hall v. Tawney*[85] said that the scope and magnitude were of a different level than commonly considered in tort law, whether "ten licks rather than five licks" is excessive; rather, the court observed that "substantive due process is concerned with violation of personal rights of privacy and bodily security of so different an order of magnitude" that an overly simplistic application, such as counting of licks, is not necessarily appropriate.

The U.S. Court of Appeals for the Tenth Circuit in *Garcia v. Miera*[86] followed the rationale of *Hall v. Tawney* and disagreed with the fifth circuit's conclusion in *Ingraham*. This court concluded "that grossly excessive corporal punishment may indeed constitute a violation of substantive due process rights."[87]

The views expressed in *Hall* and *Garcia* have been followed and reinforced by precedents from the third and eighth circuits. The third circuit has said that

[a] decision to discipline a student, if accomplished through excessive force and appreciable physical pain, may constitute an invasion of the child's Fifth Amendment liberty interest in his personal security and a violation of substantive due process prohibited by the Fourteenth Amendment.[88]

The eighth circuit has agreed that "at some point the administration of corporal punishment may violate a student's liberty interest in his personal security and substantive due process rights."[89]

Even though the nebulous nature of the U.S. Supreme Court's decision in *Ingraham* leaves the question in doubt and the U.S. courts of appeals are not in agreement, it appears that the view enunciated in *Hall* and *Garcia* may portend the prevailing precedent whereby a substantive due process interest is implicated if corporal punishment is excessively immoderate, "inhumane or brutal."[90]

❖ — ❖ — ❖

Cruel and Unusual Punishment Clause of Eighth Amendment Does Not Apply to Corporal Punishment in Schools

Ingraham v. Wright

Supreme Court of the United States, 1977.
430 U.S. 651, 97 S.Ct. 1401.

Mr. Justice POWELL delivered the opinion of the Court. This case presents questions concerning the use of corporal punishment in public schools: first, whether the paddling of students as a means of maintaining school discipline constitutes cruel and unusual punishment in violation of the Eighth Amendment; and second, to the extent that paddling is constitutionally permissible, whether the Due Process Clause of the Fourteenth Amendment requires prior notice and an opportunity to be heard. . . .

. . . In the 1970–1971 school year many of the 237 schools in Dade County used corporal punishment as a means of maintaining discipline pursuant to Florida legislation and a local school board regulation. The statute then in effect authorized limited corporal punishment by negative inference, proscribing punishment which was "degrading or unduly severe" or which was inflicted without prior consultation with the principal or the teacher in charge of the school. The regulation . . . contained explicit directions and limitations. . . .

The use of corporal punishment in this country as a means of disciplining school children dates back to the colonial period. It has survived the transformation of primary and secondary education from the colonials' reliance on optional private arrangements to our present system of compulsory education and dependence on public schools. Despite the general abandonment of corporal punishment as a means of punishing criminal offenders, the practice continues to play a role in the public education of school children in most parts of the country. Professional and public opinion is sharply divided on the practice, and has been for more than a century. Yet we can discern no trend toward its elimination.

At common law a single principle has governed the use of corporal punishment since before the American Revolution: teachers may impose reasonable but not excessive force to discipline a child. . . . The basic doctrine has not changed. The prevalent rule in this country today privileges such force as a teacher or administrator "reasonably believes to be necessary for [the child's] proper control, training, or education." . . . To the extent that the force is excessive or unreasonable, the educator in virtually all States is subject to possible civil and criminal liability.

. . . All of the circumstances are to be taken into account in determining whether the punishment is reasonable in a particular case. Among the most important considerations are the seriousness of the offense, the attitude and past behavior of the child, the nature and severity of the punishment, the age and strength of the child, and the availability of less severe but equally effective means of discipline. . . .

. . . Against this background of historical and contemporary approval of reasonable corporal punishment, we turn to the constitutional questions before us.

The Eighth Amendment provides, "Excessive bail shall not be required, nor excessive fines imposed, nor cruel and unusual punishments inflicted." Bail, fines and punishment traditionally have been associated with the criminal process, and by subjecting the three to parallel limitations the text of the Amendment suggests an intention to limit the power of those entrusted with the criminal law function of government. An examination of the history of the Amendment and the decisions of this Court construing the proscription against cruel and unusual punishment confirms that it was designed to protect those convicted of crimes. We adhere to this longstanding limitation and hold that the Eighth Amendment does not apply to the paddling of children as a means of maintaining discipline in public schools. . . .

Petitioners acknowledge that the original design of the Cruel and Unusual Punishments Clause was to limit criminal punishments, but urge nonetheless that the prohibition should be extended to ban the paddling of school children. . . .

The prisoner and the schoolchild stand in wholly different circumstances, separated by the harsh facts of criminal conviction and incarceration. . . .

The schoolchild has little need for the protection of the Eighth Amendment. Though attendance may not always be voluntary, the public school remains an open institution. Except perhaps when very young, the child is not physically restrained from leaving school during school hours; and at the end of the school day, the child is invariably free to return home. Even while at school, the child brings with him the support of family and friends and is rarely apart from teachers and other pupils who may witness and protest any instances of mistreatment.

The openness of the public school and its supervision by the community afford significant safeguards against the kinds of abuses from which the Eighth Amendment protects the prisoner. In virtually every community where corporal punishment is permitted in the schools, these safeguards are reinforced by the legal constraints of the common law. Public school teachers and administrators are privileged at common law to inflict only such corporal punishment as is reasonably necessary for the proper education and discipline of the child; any punishment going beyond the privilege may result in both civil and criminal liability. . . . As long as the schools are open to public scrutiny, there is no reason to believe that the common law constraints will not effectively remedy and deter excesses such as those alleged in this case.

We conclude that when public school teachers or administrators impose disciplinary corporal punishment, the Eighth Amendment is inapplicable. The pertinent constitutional question is whether the imposition is consonant with the requirements of due process.

The Fourteenth Amendment prohibits any State deprivation of life, liberty or property without due process of law. Application of this prohibition requires the familiar two-stage analysis: we must first ask whether the asserted individual interests are encompassed within the Fourteenth Amendment's protection of "life, liberty or property"; if protected interests are implicated, we then must decide what procedures constitute "due process of law." . . . Following that analysis here, we find that corporal punishment in public school implicates a constitutionally protected liberty interest, but we hold that the traditional common law remedies are fully adequate to afford due process.

"[T]he range of interests protected by procedural due process is not infinite." . . . Among the historic liberties so protected was a right to be free from and to obtain judicial relief, for unjustified intrusions on personal security.

While the contours of this historic liberty interest in the context of our federal system of government have not been defined precisely, they always have been thought to encompass freedom from bodily restraint and punishment. . . . It is fundamental that the state cannot hold and physically punish an individual except in accordance with due process of law.

This constitutionally protected liberty interest is at stake in this case. There is, of course, a *de minimis* level of imposition with which the Constitution is not concerned. But at least where school authorities, acting under color of state law, deliberately decide to punish a child for misconduct by restraining the child and inflicting appreciable physical pain, we hold that Fourteenth Amendment liberty interests are implicated.

"[T]he question remains what process is due." . . . Were it not for the common law privilege permitting teachers to inflict reasonable corporal punishment on children in their care, and the availability of the traditional remedies for abuse, the case for requiring advance procedural safeguards would be strong indeed. But here we deal with a punishment—paddling—within that tradition, and the question is whether the common law remedies are adequate to afford due process. . . . Whether in this case the common law remedies for excessive corporal punishment constitute due process of law must turn on an analysis of the competing interests at stake, viewed against the background of "history, reason, [and] the past course of decisions." The analysis requires consideration of three distinct factors: "first, the private interest that will be affected . . . ; second, the risk of an erroneous deprivation of such interest . . . and the probable value, if any, of additional or substitute procedural safeguards; and, finally, the [state] interest, including the function involved and the fiscal and administrative burdens that the additional or substitute procedural requirement would entail." . . .

Because it is rooted in history, the child's liberty interest in avoiding corporal punishment while in the care of public school authorities is subject to historical limitations. . . .

The concept that reasonable corporal punishment in school is justifiable continues to be recognized in the laws of most States. . . . It represents "the balance struck by this country" . . . between the child's interest in personal security and the traditional view that some limited corporal punishment may be necessary in the course of a child's education. Under that long-standing accommodation of interests, there can be no deprivation of substantive rights as long as disciplinary corporal punishment is within the limits of the common law privilege.

This is not to say that the child's interest in procedural safeguards is insubstantial. The school disciplinary process is not "a totally accurate, unerring process, never mistaken and never unfair. . . . " . . . In any deliberate infliction of corporal punishment on a child who is restrained for that purpose, there is some risk that the intrusion on the child's liberty will be unjustified and therefore unlawful. In these circumstances the child has a strong interest in procedural safeguards that minimize the risk of wrongful punishment and provide for the resolution of disputed questions of justification.

We turn now to a consideration of the safeguards that are available under applicable Florida law.

Florida has continued to recognize, and indeed has strengthened by statute, the common law right of a child not to be subjected to excessive corporal punishment in school. Under Florida law the teacher and principal of the school decide in the first instance whether corporal punishment is reasonably necessary under the circumstances in order to discipline a child who has misbehaved. But they must exercise prudence and restraint. For Florida has preserved the traditional judicial proceedings for determining whether the punishment was justified. If the punishment inflicted is later found to have been excessive—not reasonably believed at the time to be necessary for the child's discipline or training—the school authorities inflicting it may be held liable in damages to the child and, if malice is shown, they may be subject to criminal penalties. . . .

. . . In view of the low incidence of abuse, the openness of our schools, and the common law safeguards that already exist, the risk of error that may result in violation of a schoolchild's substantive rights can only be regarded as minimal. Imposing additional administrative safeguards as a constitutional requirement might reduce that risk marginally, but would also entail a significant intrusion into an area of primary educational responsibility. We conclude that the Due Process Clause does not require notice and a hearing prior to the imposition of corporal punishment in the public schools as that practice is authorized and limited by the common law. . . .

CASE NOTES

1. The U.S. Court of Appeals, Eighth Circuit, has held that the paddling of a pupil leaving bruises on the buttocks does not constitute a violation of substantive due process. *Wise v. Pea Ridge School District*, 855 F.2d 560 (8th Cir.1988).

2. The eighth circuit has been rather consistent in its restrictive interpretation of substantive due process. In 1999, this court held that an altercation between teacher and student, in which the student "slammed" the teacher against a table and the teacher banged the stu-dent's head against a metal pole, was insufficient to hold that the student's substantive due process rights were violated. *London v. Directors of the DeWitt Public Schools*, 194 F.3d 873 (8th Cir.1999).

3. The U.S. Court of Appeals for the Fifth Circuit in *Woodard v. Los Fresnos Independent School District*, 732 F.2d 1243 (5th Cir.1984), has pointed out that "if the state affords the student adequate post punishment remedies to deter unjustified or excessive punishment and to redress that which may nevertheless occur, the student receives all the process that is constitutionally due," even though "the infliction of punishment may transgress constitutionally protected liberty interests."

4. In following its own precedent in *Cunningham v. Beavers*, 858 F.2d 269 (5th Cir.1988), the fifth circuit ruled in a Texas case that severe spankings, leaving black-and-blue marks on two girls, for the offense of snickering did not implicate substantive due process and that relief, if any existed, was to be found in Texas common law.

5. *Arbitrary and Capricious Action*. If a school board's actions are arbitrary and capricious, then a substantive due process denial may be shown by the student. *Brands v. Sheldon Community School*, 671 F.Supp. 627 (N.D.Iowa 1987).

6. *Rule of Privileged Force*. A teacher may claim that use of force in controlling or disciplining a student is privileged and as such is a defense against a civil assault charge. Such a privilege emanates from the concept of *in loco parentis* but is couched in different terminology. This rule has been defined as follows:

> [A]ny force used must be that which the teacher reasonably believes necessary (1) to enforce compliance with a proper command issued for the purpose of controlling, training or educating the child, or (2) to punish the child for prohibited conduct; and in either case, the force or physical contact must be reasonable and not disproportionate to the activity or the offense.

Hogenson v. Williams 542 S.W.2d 456 (Tex.Civ. App.Texarkana 1976).

7. *Mandatory Punishment*. The Supreme Court of Mississippi has held that a rule with prescribed mandatory punishment is valid. The court explained:

As a matter of state substantive due process, a school board's disciplinary rule or scheme is enforceable when fairly viewed it furthers a substantial legitimate interest of the school.

Mandatory school disciplinary rules are not unconstitutional simply because they are mandatory.

The fact that a school rule may be worded in mandatory language does not deprive school boards and their subordinates of the authority to administer the rule with flexibility and leniency. *Clinton Municipal Separate School District v. Byrd,* 477 So.2d 237 (Miss.1985).

8. Reasonable physical force by the teacher to restore order to the classroom or school does not implicate due process or the Fourth Amendment. In a case where a teacher grasped the elbow and wrist of a student to remove her from the classroom because the student was fighting with another female student, the student claimed a violation of her Fourth Amendment and due process rights, allegedly including the excessive use of corporal punishment. The Seventh Circuit Court of Appeals held for the teacher and said that

> public school students have protection of their liberty rights under the Fourth Amendment, but we ought not countenance the degradation of this historic shield into a device by which ill-informed or inventive litigants attempt to undermine the necessary authority that teachers and school administrators exert over students. Public school teachers and administrators must have considerable latitude in performing their educational responsibilities, including maintaining order and discipline by reasonably restraining the liberty of students.
>
> Here, a teacher was confronted in his classroom with two teenage girls shouting obscenities and a fight about to break out; he separated the girls and ordered one out of the classroom—briefly seizing her in the process. This most emphatically is not a matter rising to the level of a constitutional violation. This type of §1983 litigation denigrates the Constitution and is a disservice to school systems, the federal courts, and the public they serve.

Wallace by Wallace v. Batavia School District 101, 68 F.3d 1010 (7th Cir.1995).

9. Detention of students, if reasonable, does not violate their substantive due process rights. In a case where sixth grade students were taken on a school-sponsored jail tour at the County Youth Center, one student was cautioned about being disrespectful and was subsequently placed in a holding cell for fifty minutes. The other students continued the tour. The parents claimed a violation of rights under the Fourth, Eighth, and Fourteenth Amendments. The circuit court ruled that the student had suffered no violation of his constitutional rights. *Hassan v. Lubbock Independent School District,* 55 F.3d 1075 (5th Cir.1995). In a similar case in North Carolina, a student was locked up for seven minutes because she was disruptive during a jail tour; the parents sued, but the court ruled that there was no violation of substantive constitutional rights. *Harris v. County of Forsyth,* 921 F.Supp. 325 (M.D.N.C.1996).

10. In the absence of state statutes to the contrary, teachers may paddle students in spite of parental opposition. One federal district court upheld the spanking of a child over the parents' protest and said that even though parents generally have control of their children's discipline, "the state has a countervailing interest in the maintenance of order in the school sufficient to sustain the right of teachers and school officials to administer reasonable corporal punishment" over a parent's objections. *Baker v. Owen,* 395 F.Supp. 294 (M.D.N.C.1975), affirmed without opinion, 423 U.S. 907, 96 S.Ct. 210 (1975).

11. In a Texas case, a teacher whipped a pupil with a switch for fighting after school; the court held that the fact that the fighting occurred after school did not deprive the teacher of his legal right to punish the pupil. *Hutton v. State,* 23 Tex.App. 386, 5 S.W. 122 (1887). The court stated:

> The authority of the teacher is not confined to the school room or grounds, but he may prohibit and punish all acts of his pupils which are detrimental to the good order and best interests of the school, whether such acts are committed in school hours or while the pupil is on his way to or from school or after he has returned home.

12. An example of excessive and unreasonable punishment by a teacher is illustrated in an 1872 Kentucky case. In this case, a teacher was taking part in a playground activity with the pupils, and one pupil differed with the opinion of the teacher on a trivial matter. The teacher in turn beat the boy. The court said: "The authority of a teacher to hold his pupil to strict accountability in school for disorderly behavior did not

justify him in assaulting and beating the pupil on the playground." *Hardy v. James*, 5 Ky. Op 36. (1872).

———————————— ❖ ————————————

PROCEDURAL DUE PROCESS

The requirement of procedural due process is neither novel nor new to the law. As discussed elsewhere in this book, Article 39 of the Magna Carta required due process, and the common law has long required a fair hearing by an impartial tribunal as a fundamental staple of justice.

Procedural due process, or natural justice, encompasses two basic or elemental standards of fairness:

1. The rule against bias: No person shall be a judge in his or her own case, or *nemo judex in causa sua.*
2. The right to a hearing: No person shall be condemned unheard, or *audi alteram partem.*

The right to a hearing requires that the accused know the case against him or her and have an opportunity to state his or her own case. Each party must have the chance to present his or her version of the facts and to make submissions relevant to the case. Fairness is the hallmark of this process, and though the extent of process required is sometimes in question, the principle that "no one should be condemned unheard" prevails.

The Fifth and Fourteenth Amendments of the U.S. Constitution provide that neither the federal government nor a state shall "deprive any person of life, liberty or property, without due process of law." Originally, these provisions were interpreted to apply to judicial proceedings only and not to quasi-judicial proceedings conducted by educational agencies. Because school officials stood *in loco parentis*, in a privileged relationship to students, particular legal standards of fair play were not required. It was not until the landmark case of *Dixon v. Alabama State Board of Education*[91] in 1961 that this changed. *Dixon* established that procedural due process does manifestly apply to schools and other governmental agencies and that deviations from minimal fairness in disciplinary ac-

tion, depending on the magnitude and severity, may well deny the student a constitutional interest.

Later, in *Soglin v. Kauffman*,[92] the court said the point at which disciplinary actions should be subject to constitutional scrutiny is when the action involves suspension "for any period of time substantial enough to prevent one from obtaining credit for a particular term."

The circumstances and the interests of the parties involved are paramount in prescribing the standards of procedural due process.[93] The U.S. Supreme Court has said:

> Due process unlike some legal rules is not a technical conception with a fixed content, unrelated to time, place and circumstances. . . . It is a delicate process of adjustment inescapably involving the exercise of judgment by those to whom the Constitution entrusted the unfolding of its process.[94]

In providing procedural due process, the courts are not uniform in their requirements, but all insist that fundamental fairness must be afforded and that "both sides must be given an opportunity to present their sides of the story in detail."[95]

In *Due v. Florida Agricultural and Mechanical University*, the court outlined three minimal due process requirements:

> First, the student should be given adequate notice in writing of the specific ground or grounds and the nature of the evidence on which the disciplinary proceedings are based. Second, the student should be given an opportunity for a hearing in which the disciplinary authority provides a fair opportunity for hearing of the student's position, explanations and evidence. The third requirement is that no disciplinary action be taken on grounds which are not supported by any substantial evidence.[96]

Fundamental fairness prescribed in these early cases for long suspension or expulsion of students has been extended to temporary, short-term suspensions by the U.S. Supreme Court in *Goss v. Lopez*.[97] The formality and intensity, though, of the procedural process are not fixed, the requirement being only that the process be commensurate with the length of suspension or the detriment that may be imposed on the student.

❖ — ❖ — ❖

*Procedural Due Process Required for
Students When Expelled*

Dixon v. Alabama State Board of Education

United States Court of Appeals,
Fifth Circuit, 1961.
294 F.2d 150, cert. denied,
368 U.S. 930, 82 S.Ct. 368 (1961).

RIVES, Circuit Judge. The question presented by the pleadings and evidence, and decisive of this appeal, is whether due process requires notice and some opportunity for hearing before students at a tax-supported college are expelled for misconduct. We answer that question in the affirmative.

The misconduct for which the students were expelled has never been definitely specified. Defendant Trenholm, the President of the College, testified that he did not know why the plaintiffs and three additional students were expelled and twenty other students were placed on probation. The notice of expulsion which Dr. Trenholm mailed to each of the plaintiffs assigned no specific ground for expulsion, but referred in general terms to "this problem of Alabama State College." . . .

As shown by the findings of the district court . . . the only demonstration which the evidence showed that *all* of the expelled students took part in was that in the lunch grill located in the basement of the Montgomery County Courthouse. . . .

The evidence clearly shows that the question for decision does not concern the sufficiency of the notice or the adequacy of the hearing, but is whether the students had a right to any notice or hearing whatever before being expelled. . . . After careful study and consideration, we find ourselves unable to agree with the conclusion of the district court that no notice or opportunity for any kind of hearing was required before these students were expelled.

It is true, as the district court said, that "there is no statute or rule that requires formal charges and/or a hearing . . . ," but the evidence is without dispute that the usual practice at Alabama State College had been to give a hearing and opportunity to offer defenses before expelling a student. . . .

Whenever a governmental body acts so as to injure an individual, the Constitution requires that the act be consonant with due process of law. The minimum procedural requirements necessary to satisfy due process depend upon the circumstances and the interests of the parties involved. . . .

The precise nature of the private interest involved in this case is the right to remain at a public institution of higher learning in which the plaintiffs were students in good standing. It requires no argument to demonstrate that education is vital and, indeed, basic to civilized society. Without sufficient education the plaintiffs would not be able to earn an adequate livelihood, to enjoy life to the fullest, or to fulfill as completely as possible the duties and responsibilities of good citizens. . . .

. . . Turning then to the nature of the governmental power to expel the plaintiffs, it must be conceded, as was held by the district court, that that power is not unlimited and cannot be arbitrarily exercised. Admittedly, there must be some reasonable and constitutional ground for expulsion or the courts would have a duty to require reinstatement. The possibility of arbitrary action is not excluded by the existence of reasonable regulations. There may be arbitrary application of the rule to the facts of a particular case. Indeed, that result is well nigh inevitable when the Board hears only one side of the issue. In the disciplining of college students there are no considerations of immediate danger to the public, or of peril to the national security, which should prevent the Board from exercising at least the fundamental principles of fairness by giving the accused students notice of the charges and an opportunity to be heard in their own defense. . . .

For the guidance of the parties in the event of further proceedings, we state our views on the nature of the notice and hearing required by due process prior to expulsion from a state college or university. They should, we think, comply with the following standards. The notice should contain a statement of the specific charges and grounds which, if proven, would justify expulsion under the regulations of the Board of Education. The nature of the hearing should vary depending upon the circumstances of the particular case. The case before us requires something more than an informal interview with an administrative authority of the college. By its nature, a charge of misconduct, as opposed to a failure to meet the scholastic standards of the college, depends upon a collection of the facts concerning the charged misconduct, easily colored by the point of view of the witnesses. In such circumstances, a hearing which gives the Board or the administrative authorities of the college an opportunity to hear both sides in considerable detail is best suited to protect the rights of all involved. This is not to imply that a full-dress judicial hearing, with the right to cross-examine witnesses, is required. Such a hearing, with the attending publicity and disturbance of college activities, might be detrimental to the college's educational atmosphere and impractical to carry out. Nevertheless, the rudiments of an adversary proceeding may be preserved without encroaching upon the interests of the college. In the instant case, the student should be given the names of the witnesses against him and an oral or written report on the facts to which each witness testifies. He should also be given the opportunity to present to the Board, or at least to an administrative official of the college, his own defense against the charges and to produce either oral testimony or written affidavits of witnesses in his behalf. If the hearing is not before the Board directly, the results and findings of the hearing should be presented in a report open to the student's inspection. If these rudimentary elements of fair play are followed in a case of misconduct of this particular type, we feel that the requirements of due process of law will have been fulfilled.

The judgment of the district court is reversed and the cause is remanded for further proceedings consistent with this opinion.

Reversed and remanded.

---

*Temporary Suspension Requires
Procedural Due Process*

Goss v. Lopez

Supreme Court of the United States, 1975.
419 U.S. 565, 95 S.Ct. 729.

Mr. Justice WHITE delivered the opinion of the Court. This appeal by various administrators of the Columbus, Ohio, Public School System (CPSS) challenges the judgment of a three-judge federal court, declaring that appellees—various high school students in the CPSS—were denied due process of law contrary to the command of the Fourteenth Amendment in that they were temporarily suspended from their high schools without a hearing either prior to suspension or within a reasonable time thereafter, and enjoining the administrators to remove all references to such suspensions from the students' records.

Ohio law, Rev.Code Ann. §3313.64 (1972), provides for free education to all children between the ages of six and twenty-one. Section 3313.66 of the Code empowers the principal of an Ohio public school to suspend a pupil for misconduct for up to ten days or to expel him. In either case, he must notify the student's parents within twenty-four hours and state the reasons for his action. A pupil who is expelled, or his parents, may appeal the decision to the Board of Education and in connection therewith shall be permitted to be heard at the board meeting. The Board may reinstate the pupil following the hearing. No similar procedure is provided in §3313.66 or any other provision of state law for a suspended student. Aside from a regulation tracking the statute, at the time of the imposition of the suspensions in this case the CPSS itself had not issued any written procedure applicable to suspensions. Nor, so far as the record reflects, had any of the individual high schools involved in this case. Each, however, had formally or informally described the conduct for which suspension could be imposed.

The nine named appellees, each of whom alleged that he or she had been suspended from public high school in Columbus for up to ten days without a hearing pursuant to §3313.66, filed an action under 42 U.S.C.A. §1983 against the Columbus Board of Education and various administrators of the CPSS. The complaint sought a declaration that §3313.66 was unconstitutional in that it permitted public school administrators to deprive plaintiffs of their rights to an education without a hearing of any kind, in violation of the procedural due process component of the Fourteenth Amendment. It also sought to enjoin the public school officials from issuing future suspensions pursuant to §3313.66 and to require them to remove references to the past suspensions from the records of the students in question.

The proof below established that the suspensions arose out of a period of widespread student unrest in the CPSS during February and March 1971. Six of the named plaintiffs . . . were each suspended for ten days on account of disruptive or disobedient conduct committed in the presence of the school administrator who ordered the suspension. . . . The other four Marion-Franklin students were suspended for similar conduct. None was given a hearing to determine the operative facts underlying the suspension, but each, together with his or her parents, was offered the opportunity to attend a conference, subsequent to the effective date of the suspension, to discuss the student's future. . . .

. . . On the basis of this evidence, the three-judge court declared that plaintiffs were denied due process of law because they were "suspended without hearing prior to suspension or within a reasonable time thereafter," and that Ohio Rev.Code Ann. §3313.66 (1972) and regulations issued pursuant thereto were unconstitutional in permitting such suspensions. It was ordered that all references to plaintiffs' suspensions be removed from school files.

Although not imposing upon the Ohio school administrators any particular disciplinary procedures and leaving them "free to adopt regulations providing for fair suspension procedures which are consonant with the educational goals of their schools and reflective of the characteristics of their school and locality," the District Court declared that there were "minimum requirements of notice and a hearing prior to suspension, except in emergency situations." In explication, the court stated that relevant case authority would (1) permit "[i]mmediate removal of a student whose conduct disrupts the academic atmosphere of the school, endangers fellow students, teachers or school officials, or damages property"; (2) require notice of suspension proceedings to be sent to the students' parents within twenty-four hours of the decision to conduct them; and (3) require a hearing to be held, with the student present, within seventy-two hours of his removal. Finally, the court stated that, with respect to the nature of the hearing, the relevant cases required that statements in support of the charge be produced, that the student and others be permitted to make statements in defense or mitigation, and that the school need not permit attendance by counsel.

The defendant school administrators have appealed the three-judge court's decision. Because the order below granted plaintiffs' request for an injunction—ordering defendants to expunge their records—this Court has jurisdiction of the appeal pursuant to 28 U.S.C.A. §1253. We affirm.

At the outset, appellants contend that because there is no constitutional right to an education at public expense, the Due Process Clause does not protect against expulsions from the public school system. . . .

Appellants . . . argue that even if there is a right to a public education protected by the Due Process Clause generally, the Clause comes into play only when the State subjects a student to a "severe detriment or grievous loss." The loss of ten days, it is said, is neither severe nor grievous and the Due Process Clause is therefore of no relevance. Appellants' argument is again refuted by our prior decisions; for in determining "whether due process requirements apply in the first place, we must look not to the 'weight' but to the nature of the interest at stake." . . . Appellees were excluded from school only temporarily, it is true, but the length and consequent severity of a deprivation, while another factor to weigh in determining the appropriate form of hearing, "is not decisive of the basic right" to a hearing of some kind. . . . The Court's view has been that as long as a property deprivation is not *de minimis,* its gravity is irrelevant to the question whether account must be taken of the Due Process Clause. . . . A ten-day suspension from school is not *de minimis* in our view and may not be imposed in complete disregard of the Due Process Clause.

A short suspension is, of course, a far milder deprivation than expulsion. But, "education is perhaps the most important function of state and local governments," . . . and the total exclusion from the educational process for more than a trivial period, and certainly if the suspension is for ten days, is a serious event in the life of the suspended child. Neither the property interest in educational benefits temporarily denied nor the liberty interest in reputation, which is also implicated, is so insubstantial that suspensions may constitutionally be imposed by any procedure the school chooses, no matter how arbitrary. . . .

There are certain bench marks to guide us, however. . . . "The fundamental requisite of due process of law is the opportunity to be heard," . . . a right that "has little reality or worth unless one is informed that the matter is pending and can choose for himself whether to . . . contest." . . . At the very minimum, therefore, students facing suspensions and the consequent interference with a protected property interest must be given some kind of notice and afforded some kind of hearing. "Parties whose rights are to be affected are entitled to be heard; and in order that they may enjoy that right they must first be notified." . . .

It also appears from our cases that the timing and content of the notice and the nature of the hearing will depend on appropriate accommodation of the competing interests involved. . . . The student's interest is to avoid unfair or mistaken exclusion from the educational process, with all of its unfortunate consequences. The Due Process Clause will not shield him from suspensions properly imposed, but it disserves both his interest and the interest of the State if his suspension is in fact unwarranted. The concern would be mostly academic if the disciplinary process were a totally accurate, unerring process, never mistaken and never unfair. Unfor-

tunately, that is not the case, and no one suggests that it is. Disciplinarians, although proceeding in utmost good faith, frequently act on the reports and advice of others; and the controlling facts and the nature of the conduct under challenge are often disputed. The risk of error is not at all trivial, and it should be guarded against if that may be done without prohibitive cost or interference with the educational process.

The difficulty is that our schools are vast and complex. Some modicum of discipline and order is essential if the educational function is to be performed. Events calling for discipline are frequent occurrences and sometimes require immediate, effective action. Suspension is considered not only to be a necessary tool to maintain order but a valuable educational device. The prospect of imposing elaborate hearing requirements in every suspension case is viewed with great concern, and many school authorities may well prefer the untrammeled power to act unilaterally, unhampered by rules about notice and hearing. But it would be a strange disciplinary system in an educational institution if no communication was sought by the disciplinarian with the student in an effort to inform him of his dereliction and to let him tell his side of the story in order to make sure that an injustice is not done. "[F]airness can rarely be obtained by secret, one-sided determination of facts decisive of rights. . . . " "Secrecy is not congenial to truth-seeking and self-righteousness gives too slender an assurance of rightness. No better instrument has been devised for arriving at truth than to give a person in jeopardy of serious loss notice of the case against him and opportunity to meet it." . . .

We do not believe that school authorities must be totally free from notice and hearing requirements if their schools are to operate with acceptable efficiency. Students facing temporary suspension have interests qualifying for protection of the Due Process Clause, and due process requires, in connection with a suspension of ten days or less, that the student be given oral or written notice of the charges against him and, if he denies them, an explanation of the evidence the authorities have and an opportunity to present his side of the story. The Clause requires at least these rudimentary precautions against unfair or mistaken findings of misconduct and arbitrary exclusion from school.

There need be no delay between the time "notice" is given and the time of the hearing. In the great majority of cases the disciplinarian may informally discuss the alleged misconduct with the student minutes after it has occurred. We hold only that, in being given an opportunity to explain his version of the facts at this discussion, the student first be told what he is accused of doing and what the basis of the accusation is. . . . Since the hearing may occur almost immediately following the misconduct, it follows that as a general rule notice and hearing should precede removal of the student from school. We agree with the District Court, however, that there are recurring situations in which prior notice and hearing cannot be insisted upon. Students whose presence poses a continuing danger to persons or property or an ongoing threat of disrupting the academic process may be immediately removed from school. In such cases, the necessary notice and rudimentary hearing should follow as soon as practicable, as the District Court indicated.

In holding as we do, we do not believe that we have imposed procedures on school disciplinarians which are inappropriate in a classroom setting. Instead we have imposed requirements which are, if anything, less than a fair-minded school principal would impose upon himself in order to avoid unfair suspensions. . . .

We stop short of construing the Due Process Clause to require, countrywide, that hearings in connection with short suspensions must afford the student the opportunity to secure counsel, to confront and cross-examine witnesses supporting the charge, or to call his own witnesses to verify his version of the incident. Brief disciplinary suspensions are almost countless. To impose in each such case even truncated trial-type procedures might well overwhelm administrative facilities in many places and, by diverting resources, cost more than it would save in educational effectiveness. Moreover, further formalizing the suspension process and escalating its formality and adversary nature may not only make it too costly as a regular disciplinary tool but also destroy its effectiveness as part of the teaching process.

On the other hand, requiring effective notice and informal hearing permitting the student to give his version of the events will provide a meaningful hedge against erroneous action. At least the disciplinarian will be alerted to the existence of disputes about facts and arguments about cause and effect. He may then determine himself to summon the accuser, permit cross-examination, and allow the student to present his own witnesses. In more difficult cases, he may permit counsel. In any event, his discretion will be more informed and we think the risk of error substantially reduced.

Requiring that there be at least an informal give-and-take between student and disciplinarian, preferably prior to the suspension, will add little to the factfinding function where the disciplinarian himself has witnessed the conduct forming the basis for the charge. But things are not always as they seem to be, and the student will at least have the opportunity to characterize his conduct and put it in what he deems the proper context.

We should also make it clear that we have addressed ourselves solely to the short suspension, not exceeding ten days. Longer suspensions or expulsions for the remainder of the school term, or permanently, may require more formal procedures. Nor do we put aside the possibility that in unusual situations, although involving only a short suspension, something more than the rudimentary procedures will be required.

The District Court found each of the suspensions involved here to have occurred without a hearing, either before or after the suspension, and that each suspension was therefore invalid and the statute unconstitutional insofar as it permits such suspensions without notice or hearing. Accordingly, the judgment is

Affirmed.

--------------- ❖ — ❖ — ❖ ---------------

Procedural Due Process Is a Flexible Concept

McClain v. Lafayette County Board of Education

United States Court of Appeals, Fifth Circuit, 1982.
673 F.2d 106, rehearing denied, 687 F.2d 121 (1982).

COLEMAN, Circuit Judge. On September 23, 1980, Michael carried a switchblade knife to school. The physical education teacher saw the knife in the student's possession and took him forthwith to the principal's office where . . . Michael admitted that he had the knife. He also admitted that he knew that it was against the rule. His explanation was that he had found the knife, forgot that he had it in his pocket, and unintentionally had brought it to school.

The principal sent Michael back to class and later the same day directed him to appear in his office the following morning with his mother.

On September 24, 1980, Michael and his mother met with Mr. Bigham in his office, where they were informed that Michael would be indefinitely suspended for his possession of the knife. At that time the principal gave Mrs. McClain a letter informing her that Michael was "indefinitely suspended" because of his possession and display of a switchblade knife and that she had a right to attend the Lafayette County School Board meeting which was to be held on September 30, 1980, to "request re-admittance" for Michael.

Mrs. McClain arranged an appointment in accordance with the third paragraph of the letter. She, along with Michael, attended the meeting of the Lafayette County School Board on the night of September 30, 1980. The principal and the physical education teacher attended the meeting and related their accounts of the switchblade knife event leading to Michael's suspension. Tape recordings of statements taken from other students during the course of the investigation which followed Michael's September 24 suspension were played. Mrs. McClain and Michael were given the opportunity to question anyone present, and they were also afforded the opportunity to explain any facts or circumstances which might have a bearing on the Board's decision regarding Michael's reinstatement.

Lafayette County High School provides each of its students with a *Student Handbook* at the start of the school year. . . . [T]he *Student Handbook* was read aloud to Michael and other members of his class on the first day of classes. In addition, Mrs. McClain testified that she had read the *Handbook*.

The School Board voted to change Michael's indefinite suspension to a suspension for the remainder of the school year. Mrs. McClain was notified later on the night of the meeting of the Board's actions.

This suit for injunctive relief soon followed and the District Court held an evidentiary hearing, filed findings of fact, and denied injunctive relief.

On appeal, the McClains contend that Michael's procedural due process rights were violated when he was suspended for an indefinite period of time from the high school without first being given a hearing. They argue that this indefinite suspension was in fact a long-range suspension, which should have been preceded by a fair, impartial and meaningful hearing on both the charges and the appropriate punishment. Furthermore, they contend even if the suspension by Mr. Bigham were viewed as a short-range suspension, Michael's procedural due process rights were violated during the School Board meeting because he was not given adequate notice of the type of hearing and the charges, the names of his accusers and a summary of their expected testimonies, the right to retain and to be represented by counsel, nor the right to confront and cross-examine the witnesses.

[T]he State is constrained to recognize a student's legitimate entitlement to a public education is a property interest which is protected by the Due Process Clause and which may not be taken away for misconduct without adherence to the minimum procedures required by the Clause. . . .

Once it is determined that due process applies, the question remains what process is due. . . .

At the very minimum . . . students facing suspension and the consequent interference with a protected property interest must be given *some* kind of notice and afforded *some* kind of hearing....

[D]ue process requires, in connection with a suspension of ten days or less, that the student be given oral or written notice of the charges against him and, if he denies them, an explanation of the evidence the authorities have and an opportunity to present his side of the story. . . . There need be no delay between the time "notice" is given and the time of the hearing. In the great majority of the cases the disciplinarian may informally discuss the alleged misconduct with the student minutes after it has occurred. We hold only that, in being given an opportunity to explain his version of the facts at this discussion, the student first be told what he is accused of doing and what the basis of the accusation is. . . .

The Supreme Court has cautioned that "suspensions or expulsions for the remainder of the school term, or permanently, may require more formal procedures." . . .

The District Court held that the standards of *Goss v. Lopez* . . . were met. Michael admitted the possession of the knife when first taken to the principal. Indeed, he could hardly have done otherwise because the physical education teacher saw him in possession of it and took it from him. Never at any time or place, including the hearing in the District Court, did Michael deny it. He did say that he forgot about having this large jackknife, and a switchblade at that, in his pocket. This is not the kind of defense to carrying a deadly weapon that a jury or other factfinder must accept.

Relying upon *Dixon v. Alabama State Board of Education,* . . . plaintiff argues that he should have been given the names of the witnesses against him and an oral or written report of their testimonies. Plaintiff contends that the taped testimony denied him a right of confrontation. Though the *Dixon* Court did find that the students in that case should have been given a list of witnesses against them, the Court noted, "The nature of the hearing should vary depending upon the circumstances of the particular case."...

We can conceive of situations in which the playing of the tapes as done here might be a denial of due process. Not in this instance, however. The issue was whether Michael had carried a switchblade knife to school. There is no representation that the tapes presented any untruths or dealt with any other issue. Therefore, they were merely cumulative on an issue in which Michael had conceded his guilt and has never afterward denied it.

The nub of the matter is that the student was given an opportunity to present his side of the case, including anything by way of denial or mitigation. He and his mother appeared and participated. There has never been any doubt of Michael's guilt in carrying this deadly weapon to school. There was nothing fundamentally unfair or legally prejudicial in the proceedings.

The judgment of the District Court denying injunctive relief is

Affirmed.

CASE NOTES

1. *Procedural Technicality and Hearsay.* When a high school principal read statements made by teachers in an expulsion hearing, the students challenged, claiming that hearsay evidence could not be used in such school hearings. The United States Court of Appeals, Fifth Circuit, stated:

> There is a seductive quality to the argument—advanced here to justify the importation of technical rules of evidence into administrative hearings conducted by laymen—that, since a free public education is a thing of great value, comparable to that of welfare sustenance or the curtailed liberty of a parolee, the safeguards applicable to these should apply to it. . . . In this view we stand but a step away from the application of the *strictissimi juris* due process requirements of criminal trials to high school disciplinary processes. And if to high school, why not to elementary school? It will not do. Basic fairness and integrity of the fact-finding process are the guiding stars. Important as they are, the rights at stake in a school disciplinary hearing may be fairly determined upon the "hearsay" evidence of school administrators charged with the duty of investigating the incidents. We decline to place upon a board of laymen the duty of observing and applying the common-law rules of evidence.

Boykins v. Fairfield Board of Education, 492 F.2d 697 (5th Cir.1974), cert. denied, 420 U.S. 962, 92 S.Ct. 1350 (1975).

Although *Boykins* predates *Goss v. Lopez*, the hearsay principle was reaffirmed by the fifth circuit in *Tasby v. Estes*, 643 F.2d 1103 (5th Cir.1981). Other courts' opinions have been somewhat mixed concerning hearsay evidence. *Tasby v. Estes* (hearsay may be allowed in hearings for serious student offenses); *Linwood v. Board of Education*, 463 F.2d 763 (7th Cir.1972), cert. denied, 409 U.S. 1027, 93 S.Ct. 475 (1972) (hearsay may be allowed by implication in expulsion hearing); *Whiteside v. Kay*, 446 F.Supp. 716 (W.D.La.1978) (hearsay may be allowed by implication at expulsion hearing); *Racine Unified School District v. Thompson*, 107 Wis.2d 657, 321 N.W.2d 334 (1982) (hearsay evidence may be allowed from school teachers or staff); *Fielder v. Board of Education*, 346 F.Supp. 722 (D.Neb.1972) (hearsay may not be allowed by implication at expulsion hearing); *DeJesus v. Penberthy*, 344 F.Supp. 70 (D.Conn.1972) (hearsay may not be allowed in hearing for thirty-day suspension).

2. *Double Jeopardy.* When faced with both criminal and school disciplinary punishments, students have claimed that the constitutional prohibition against double jeopardy comes into play. In *Paine v. Board of Regents of University of Texas System*, 355 F.Supp. 199 (W.D.Tex.1972), affirmed, 474 F.2d 1397 (5th Cir.1973), a group of students faced criminal prosecution for drug use and suspension from the university. The court rejected their double jeopardy claims:

> Through two separate governmental organs, the *legislative branch* and the *Board of Regents,* the State does indeed impose two successive sanctions for the same offense: judicially imposed punishment and automatic suspension from the University of Texas System. However, the state laws defining criminal conduct and authorizing its punishment are intended to vindicate public justice in regard to the individual offender while . . . the Regents' Rule mandating . . . suspension of student drug or narcotic offenders is intended to protect the university community and the educational goals of the institution from such adverse influence as the offender may wield if he is allowed to remain a student. Thus the two sanctions imposed by the state upon plaintiffs have *sufficiently different underlying purposes* to permit characterization of the first as "criminal" or "punitive" and the second as "civil," "remedial" or "administrative." Since the Double Jeopardy Clause operates only upon sanctions of the first type successively imposed for the same offense, plaintiffs may not avail themselves of its protection here.

See also *Clement v. Board of Trustees of Sheridan County School District No. 2*, 585 P.2d 197 (Wyo.1978).

3. *Miranda Warning.* A student is not entitled to a Miranda warning prior to being questioned by school authorities. *Boynton v. Casey*, 543 F.Supp. 995 (D.Me.1982); see *Baxter v. Palmigiano*, 425 U.S. 308, 96 S.Ct. 1551 (1976). In another case, the principal was not required to give a juvenile a Miranda warning. *In the Matter of Appeal in Navajo Juvenile No. JV91000058*, 901 P.2d 1247 (Div.1 Dept.E 1995). See also *S. A. v. State of Indiana*, 654 N.E.2d 791 (Ind. App.1995); *State of New Jersey v. Biancamano*, 666 A.2d 199 (N.J.App.Div.1995).

4. *Charges and Evidence.* An informal discussion of the student's offense and the circumstances of the incident may be sufficient to inform the student of the evidence against him or her. *Lamb v. Panhandle Community School District No. 2*, 826 F.2d 526 (7th Cir.1987).

5. *Cross-Examination.* While acknowledging that "the value of cross-examination to the discovery of truth cannot be overemphasized," *Davis v. Alaska*, 415 U.S. 308, 94 S.Ct. 1105 (1974), the U.S. Court of Appeals for the Sixth Circuit held in 1988 that protecting student witnesses in testifying against fellow students is of paramount importance if order and discipline are to be maintained in the school. This court of appeals has discussed in some detail the rationale for differing standards of cross-examination between the criminal courts and public schools. The court states:

> The value of cross-examining student witnesses in school disciplinary cases, however, is somewhat muted by the fact that the veracity of a student account of misconduct by another student is initially assessed by a school administrator—in this case, the school principal—who has, or has available to him, a particularized knowledge of the student's trustworthiness. The school administrator generally knows firsthand (or has access to school records which disclose) the accusing student's disciplinary history, which can serve as a valuable gauge in evaluating the believability of the student's account. Additionally, the school administrator often knows, or can readily discover, whether the student witness and the accused have had an amicable relationship in the past. Consequently, the process of cross-examining the student witness may often be merely duplicative of the evaluation process undertaken by the investigating school administrator.
>
> The value of cross-examining student witnesses in pre-expulsion proceedings must be set against the burden that such a practice would place upon school administration. Today's public schools face severe challenges in maintaining the order and discipline necessary for the impartation of knowledge. A recent study conducted by the Fullerton, California, Police Department and the California Department of Education, for instance, shows that, while schoolteachers in the 1940's listed talking, chewing gum, and running in the hallways as the primary disciplinary problems they encountered, today's schoolteachers are more concerned with drug abuse, rape, robbery, assault, burglary, arson,

and bombings. Bowen, *Getting Tough*, TIME, Feb. 1, 1988, at 54. Indeed, in a recent Supreme Court decision involving the fourth amendment restraints on school administrators, the Court noted that "drug use and violent crime in the schools have become major social problems." . . . (citing 1 NIE, U.S. Dept. of Health, Education and Welfare, Violent Schools—Safe Schools: The Safe School Study Report to the Congress (1978)).

In this turbulent, sometimes violent, school atmosphere, it is critically important that we protect the anonymity of students who "blow the whistle" on their classmates who engage in drug trafficking and other serious offenses. Without the cloak of anonymity, students who witness criminal activity on school property will be much less likely to notify school authorities, and those who do will be faced with ostracism at best and perhaps physical reprisals. Giving due weight to the important interest a student accused of serious misconduct has in his public education, we conclude that the necessity of protecting student witnesses from ostracism and reprisal outweighs the value to the truth-determining process of allowing the accused student to cross-examine his accusers.

Newsome v. Batavia Local School District, 842 F.2d 920 (6th Cir.1988).

6. *Bias.* One of the primary elements of ancient natural justice and modern procedural due process is the requirement that the hearing officer or the tribunal sitting in judgment over an offender be impartial and not be motivated by bias. The question, therefore, arises as to whether a school administrator can be both the accuser and an impartial dispenser of justice.

In *Brewer v. Austin Independent School District*, 779 F.2d 260 (5th Cir.1985), the U.S. Court of Appeals, Fifth Circuit, said:

> A school administrator involved in the initiation and investigation of charges is not thereby disqualified from conducting a hearing on the charges, although the facts of an occasional case may demonstrate that a school official's involvement in an incident created a bias "such as to preclude his affording the student an impartial hearing."

Where a student claimed that a principal or other administrator was biased and unable to be impartial, the court said that school administrators cannot be disqualified from hearings unless the plaintiff student can show that administrators "possessed either a pre-existing animus towards him, or had developed a bias because

of their involvement in the incident, [such that] they would not have been able to act as decisionmakers." *Newsome v. Batavia Local School District*, 842 F.2d 920 (6th Cir.1988).

7. *New Evidence.* New evidence cannot be introduced against a student before a closed session with the school board if the student is not aware of the information and it was not originally brought to the student's attention in the notice of the hearing or in the preliminary hearing. Minimal due process requires that students have notice of the charges against them and an explanation of the evidence the authorities intend to use in the disciplinary action. See *Goss v. Lopez*, 419 U.S. 565, 95 S.Ct. 729 (1975); *Newsome v. Batavia Local School District*, 842 F.2d 920 (6th Cir.1988).

8. *Admissibility of Evidence.* Procedural due process has been held denied where the accuser sent an affidavit based on a photo of the student and did not personally appear at the hearing. *Smith v. Miller*, 213 Kan. 1, 514 P.2d 377 (1973). Similarly, a student's expulsion was invalidated by a court where the accusing teacher was not called and did not come to the hearing. *Dillon v. Pulaski County Special School District*, 594 F.2d 699 (8th Cir.1979).

9. *In-School Suspension.* Is procedural due process required? Temporary isolation using in-school "timeout" has been held to be a *de minimis* punishment not interfering with property or liberty interests. *Dickens by Dickens v. Johnson County Board of Education*, 661 F.Supp. 155 (E.D.Tenn.1987).

In *Fenton v. Stear*, 423 F.Supp. 767 (W.D.Pa. 1976), school officials required a student to attend a detention hall instead of joining the class sight-seeing trip. While so confined to his small "prison," as he called it, the student was required to do schoolwork. The court held that such punishment is *de minimis* and procedural due process is not required.

An informal "give-and-take" session between a school principal and students prior to a ten-day suspension may satisfy procedural due process requirements. *Keough v. Tate County Board of Education*, 748 F.2d 1077 (5th Cir.1984).

10. *Admission of Offense.* If a student admits the offensive conduct, then there is no issue with regard to procedural errors except those errors that may pertain to the school's determi-

nation of appropriateness of punishment. *Brewer v. Austin Independent School District,* 779 F.2d 260 (5th Cir.1985).

■ SEXUAL HARASSMENT OF STUDENTS

Title IX of the Education Amendments of 1972 and Title VII of the Civil Rights Act of 1964 are the two important federal statutes that may be used to deter sexual harassment in education programs. Title VII was designed to prevent discrimination in the workplace on the basis of race, sex, religion, color, and national origin. Title VII is, therefore, directed to employment discrimination (discussed more fully in Chapter 17 of this text). Title IX, on the other hand, was enacted to rid educational institutions of sex discrimination. The Office for Civil Rights (OCR) of the U.S. Department of Education is the administrative agency empowered to enforce Title IX. Title VII is enforced by the Equal Employment Opportunity Commission (EEOC).

Defining sexual harassment is difficult, but basically it constitutes "the unwanted imposition of sexual requirements in the context of a relationship of unequal power."[98] This characterization of sexual harassment is applicable to the teacher/student relationship, wherein there exists an exploitation of a power relationship to gain sexual favors. A teacher quite obviously holds power over a student by being in a position to affect the student's grades, academic attainments, and career choices. Title IX, therefore, seeks to prohibit unwelcome sexual behavior by any party who is in an inherently unequal position in relation to another.

Two basic categories of behavior constitute sexual harassment under Title IX. The first is *quid pro quo* harassment, by which the teacher, administrator, or other person in power attempts to compel submission to sexual demands by conditioning rewards or punishment upon the student's acquiescence or lack thereof. This is sometimes called "bargain" harassment, whereby the person in power implicitly or explicitly coerces the student into being receptive to the advances. The second category, hostile environment, encompasses behavior that causes the educational environment to become hostile, offensive, or intimidating to the student as a result of the harassment, and it may be manifested in the teacher's mistreatment of the student solely due to gender.

Originally, the implementation of Title IX was retarded by statutory language that limited its application to programs within an educational institution and not to the entire institution itself. Controversy over the application of Title IX occurred as a result of the federal government's requirement that a private college, Grove City College, supply assurance of compliance.[99] The college refused, and the U.S. Department of Education cut off the students' federal financial assistance. The U.S. Supreme Court, in 1984, held that Title IX applied only to "programs" receiving federal assistance and not to the entire institution. Under a narrow interpretation of the statute, the Court held that the college was obliged to submit assurance of compliance for the office responsible for administration of student federal financial aid, and not for the college as a whole.

This decision was the impetus for Congress to amend Title IX with the Civil Rights Restoration Act of 1988,[100] correcting the loophole identified in the *Grove City* case. Effectively, *Grove City* narrowed the coverage not only of Title IX, but also of Title VI of the Civil Rights Act of 1964, Section 504 of the Rehabilitation Act of 1973, and the Age Discrimination Act of 1975. The Civil Rights Restoration Act of 1988 restored institutionwide application of these laws. The 1988 law added no new language to the coverage or fund termination provisions of the four acts, but it amended each of the affected statutes by adding a section defining the terms "program or activity" and "program" to make it clear that discrimination is prohibited throughout the entire institution or agency if any part is the recipient of federal financial assistance.

The 1988 act provides that the entire institution or system is covered, not just the program receiving federal assistance. If federal aid is distributed to any part of a public school district, the entire school system is subject to compliance requirements. Thus, violation of Title IX may result in the loss of federal funds to the entire school district. Private education corporations are also covered if they receive federal funding.

Yet, even with the amendments of 1988, relatively few legal actions resulted until the U.S. Supreme Court held in *Franklin v. Gwinnett County Public Schools* that plaintiffs could recover compensatory and punitive damages under Title IX.

With the possibility of damages as established in *Franklin*—as opposed to the more limited remedy of loss of federal funds to the government entity—the number of judicial actions increased dramatically. Shortly after the *Franklin* litigation, substantial numbers of cases began to appear involving peer-to-peer sexual harassment in the schools. In these cases, plaintiffs claim that the schools are liable for damages when students sexually harass other students. The theory supporting such allegations is premised on the plaintiffs proving that a hostile environment exists. These hostile environment cases are modeled after the Title VII hostile environment litigation. Whereas Title VII involves employee-to-employee workplace harassment, Title IX addresses employee-to-employee, employee-to-student, and student-to-student harassment.

Within the context of this litigation, it is clear that a school district is obligated to take reasonable steps to prevent sexual harassment by school employees. However, the extent and nature of the preventive actions required are less certain. Such actions have been litigated primarily under Title IX following the *Franklin* decision.

———————— ❖ — ❖ — ❖ ————————

A Damage Remedy Is Available from
Action to Enforce Title IX

Franklin v. Gwinnett County Public Schools

Supreme Court of the United States, 1992.
503 U.S. 60, 112 S.Ct. 1028.

Justice WHITE delivered the Opinion of the Court.

This case presents the question whether the implied right of action under Title IX of the Education Amendments of 1972, 20 U.S.C. §§1681–1688 (Title IX), which this Court recognized in *Cannon v. University of Chicago*, . . . supports a claim for monetary damages.

Petitioner Christine Franklin was a student at North Gwinnett High School in Gwinnett County, Georgia, between September 1985 and August 1989. Respondent Gwinnett County School District operates the high school and receives federal funds. According to the complaint filed on December 29, 1988, in the United States District Court for the Northern District of Georgia, Franklin was subjected to continual sexual harassment beginning in the autumn of her tenth grade year (1986) from Andrew Hill, a sports coach and teacher employed by the district. Among other allegations, Franklin avers that Hill engaged her in sexually oriented conversations in which he asked about her sexual experiences with her boyfriend and whether she would consider having sexual intercourse with an older man, . . . that Hill forcibly kissed her on the mouth in the school parking lot, . . . that he telephoned her at her home and asked if she would meet him socially, . . . and that, on three occasions in her junior year, Hill interrupted a class, requested that the teacher excuse Franklin, and took her to a private office where he subjected her to coercive intercourse. The complaint further alleges that though they became aware of and investigated Hill's sexual harassment of Franklin and other female students, teachers and administrators took no action to halt it and discouraged Franklin from pressing charges against Hill. On April 14, 1988, Hill resigned on the condition that all matters pending against him be dropped. The school thereupon closed its investigation.

In this action, the District Court dismissed the complaint on the ground that Title IX does not authorize an award of damages. The Court of Appeals affirmed. . . .

. . . We reverse.

In *Cannon v. University of Chicago*, . . . the Court held that Title IX is enforceable through an implied right of action. We have no occasion here to reconsider that decision. Rather, in this case we must decide what remedies are available in a suit brought pursuant to this implied right. As we have often stated, the question of what remedies are available under a statute that provides a private right of action is "analytically distinct" from the issue of whether such a right exists in the first place. . . . Thus, although we examine the text and history of a statute to determine whether Congress intended to create a right of action, . . . we presume the availability of all appropriate remedies unless Congress has expressly indicated otherwise. . . . This principle has deep roots in our jurisprudence. . . .

"[W]here legal rights have been invaded, and a federal statute provides for a general right to sue for such invasion, federal courts may use any available remedy to make good the wrong done." *Bell v. Hood.* . . . The Court explained this longstanding rule as jurisdictional, and upheld the exercise of the federal courts' power to award appropriate relief so long as a cause of action existed under the Constitution or laws of the United States.

The *Bell* Court's reliance on this rule was hardly revolutionary. From the earliest years of the Republic, the Court has recognized the power of the judiciary to award appropriate remedies to redress injuries actionable in federal court, although it did not always distinguish clearly between a right to bring suit and a remedy available under such a right. In *Marbury v. Madison,* 5 U.S. (1 Cranch) 137, 163, 2 L.Ed. 60 (1803), for example, Chief Justice Marshall observed that our government "has been emphatically termed a government of laws, and not of men. It will certainly cease to deserve this high appellation, if the laws furnish no remedy for the violation of a vested legal right." This principle originated in the English common law, and Blackstone described "it as a general and indisputable rule, that where there is a legal right, there is also a legal remedy, by suit or action at law, whenever that right is invaded." 3 W. Blackstone, Commentaries 23 (1783). . . .

Respondents and the United States as *amicus curiae,* however, maintain that whatever the traditional presumption may have been when the Court decided *Bell v. Hood,* it had disappeared in succeeding decades. We do not agree. . . .

. . . The general rule . . . is that absent clear direction to the contrary by Congress, the federal courts have the power to award any appropriate relief in a cognizable cause of action brought pursuant to a federal statute. . . .

We now address whether Congress intended to limit application of this general principle in the enforcement of Title IX. . . . Because the cause of action was inferred by the Court in *Cannon,* the usual recourse to statutory text and legislative history in the period prior to that decision necessarily will not enlighten our analysis. Respondents and the United States fundamentally misunderstand the nature of the inquiry, therefore, by needlessly dedicating large portions of their briefs to discussions of how the text and legislative intent behind Title IX are "silent" on the issue of available remedies. Since the Court in *Cannon* concluded that this statute supported no express right of action, it is hardly surprising that Congress also said nothing about the applicable remedies for an implied right of action.

During the period prior to the decision in *Cannon,* the inquiry in any event is *not* "'basically a matter of statutory construction,'" as the United States asserts. . . . Rather, in determining Congress's intent to limit application of the traditional presumption in favor of all appropriate relief, we evaluate the state of the law when the legislature passed Title IX. . . . In the years before and after Congress enacted this statute, the Court "follow[ed] a common-law tradition [and] regarded the denial of a remedy as the exception rather than the rule." . . . [T]his has been the prevailing presumption in our federal courts since at least the early nineteenth century. In *Cannon,* the majority upheld an implied right of action in part because in the decade immediately preceding enactment of Title IX in 1972, this Court had found implied rights of action in six cases. In three of those cases, the Court had approved a damages remedy. . . . Wholly apart from the wisdom of the *Cannon* holding, therefore, the same contextual approach used to justify an implied right of action more than amply demonstrates the lack of any legislative intent to abandon the traditional presumption in favor of all available remedies.

In the years *after* the announcement of *Cannon,* on the other hand, a more traditional method of statutory analysis is possible, because Congress was legislating with full cognizance of that decision. Our reading of the two amendments to Title IX enacted after *Cannon* leads us to conclude that Congress did not intend to limit the remedies available in a suit brought under Title IX. In the Civil Rights Remedies Equalization Amendment of 1986, 42 U.S.C. §2000d-7, Congress abrogated the States' Eleventh Amendment immunity under Title IX, Title VI, §504 of the Rehabilitation Act of 1973, and the Age Discrimination Act of 1975. This statute cannot be read except as a validation of *Cannon*'s holding. A subsection of the 1986 law provides that in a suit against a State, "remedies (including remedies both at law and inequity) are available for such a violation to the same extent as such remedies are available for such a violation in the suit against any public or private entity other than a State." 42 U.S.C. §2000d-7(a)(2). While it is true that this savings clause says nothing about the nature of those other available remedies, . . . absent any contrary indication in the text or history of the statute, we presume Congress enacted this statute with the prevailing traditional rule in mind.

In addition to the Civil Rights Remedies Equalization Amendment of 1986, Congress also enacted the Civil Rights Restoration Act of 1987, Pub.L. 100-259, 102 Stat. 28 (1988). Without in any way altering the existing rights of action and the corresponding remedies permissible under Title IX, Title VI, §504 of the Rehabilitation Act, and the Age Discrimination Act, Congress broadened the coverage of these antidiscrimination provisions in this legislation. In seeking to correct what it considered to be an unacceptable decision on our part in *Grove City College v. Bell*, . . . Congress made no effort to restrict the right of action recognized in *Cannon* and ratified in the 1986 act or to alter the traditional presumption in favor of any appropriate relief for violation of a federal right. We cannot say, therefore, that Congress has limited the remedies available to a complainant in a suit brought under Title IX. . . .

In sum, we conclude that a damages remedy is available for an action brought to enforce Title IX. The judgment of the Court of Appeals, therefore, is reversed and the case is remanded for further proceedings consistent with this opinion.

So ordered.

Deliberate Indifference

The legal standard regarding sexual harassment in schools was set forth by the U.S. Supreme Court in 1998 in *Gebser v. Lago Vista Independent School District*,[101] wherein the Court concluded that a school district may not be liable in damages unless a school official who had knowledge of the situation and the authority to take corrective action was "deliberately indifferent" to the misconduct. The Court pointed out that while *Franklin* had determined that a school district could be liable in damages for a teacher's sexual harassment of a student, the case had not prescribed the parameters of that liability. In defining the "contour" of liability of a school district under Title IX for an employee's harassment of another person, whether a co-worker or a student, it must be determined under what circumstances the district itself is culpable. The Court concluded that Congress in fashioning Title IX did not intend that the aggrieved should recover damages against a school district that was unaware of the inappropriate behavior. The Court rejected the argument by the plaintiffs that the school district should be automatically liable for the acts of its employees, and it further rejected the alternative argument that the school district should be liable if it only "should have known" of the offensive act. The Court felt that either of these options would open the floodgates to litigation against school districts, making them liable for unwarranted and unknown acts of employees that were beyond the districts' ability to control. The Court feared that such circumstances could frustrate the purposes of Title IX by diverting public funds from educational purposes to damages and legal fees.

The Court said that "it does not appear that Congress contemplated unlimited recovery of damages against a funding recipient where the recipient is unaware of discrimination in its program."[102] Rather, the Court decided neither to permit sexual harassment to be imputed to a school district nor to assume that the district had constructive notice of the teacher's harassment when, in fact, the school district had no knowledge whatsoever of the teacher's misconduct.

Thus, the Court found that a school district could be liable only for its own official actions and not for an employee's independent actions.

The standard adopted by the Court, therefore, requires that for a school district to be liable "an appropriate person, at a minimum, an official"[103] of the school district with authority to take corrective action, have actual knowledge of the sexual harassment and fail to adequately respond. In this regard, the Court said specifically, "We think, moreover, that the response must amount to deliberate indifference to discrimination."[104]

❖ — ❖ — ❖

Individual Misconduct by a Teacher in the Sexual Harassment of a Student Does Not Render the School District Liable under Title IX unless a School Official Had Knowledge of the Situation and Responded with Deliberate Indifference

Gebser v. Lago Vista Independent School District

Supreme Court of the United States, 1998.
524 U.S. 274, 118 S.Ct. 1989.

Justice O'CONNOR delivered the opinion of the Court.

The question in this case is when a school district may be held liable in damages in an implied right of action under Title IX of the Education Amendments of 1972 . . . for the sexual harassment of a student by one of the district's teachers. We conclude that damages may not be recovered in those circumstances unless an official of the school district who at a minimum has authority to institute corrective measures on the district's behalf has actual notice of, and is deliberately indifferent to, the teacher's misconduct. . . .

In the spring of 1991, when petitioner Alida Star Gebser was an eighth-grade student at a middle school in respondent Lago Vista Independent School District (Lago Vista), she joined a high school book discussion group led by Frank Waldrop, a teacher at Lago Vista's high school. . . . During the book discussion sessions,

Waldrop often made sexually suggestive comments to the students. Gebser entered high school in the fall and was assigned to classes taught by Waldrop in both semesters. Waldrop continued to make inappropriate remarks to the students, and he began to direct more of his suggestive comments toward Gebser. . . . He initiated sexual contact with Gebser in the spring, when, while visiting her home ostensibly to give her a book, he kissed and fondled her. The two had sexual intercourse on a number of occasions during the remainder of the school year. Their relationship continued through the summer and into the following school year, and they often had intercourse during class time, although never on school property.

Gebser did not report the relationship to school officials, testifying that while she realized Waldrop's conduct was improper, she was uncertain how to react and she wanted to continue having him as a teacher. In October 1992, the parents of two other students complained to the high school principal about Waldrop's comments in class. The principal arranged a meeting, at which, according to the principal, Waldrop indicated that he did not believe he had made offensive remarks but apologized to the parents and said it would not happen again. The principal also advised Waldrop to be careful about his classroom comments and told the school guidance counselor about the meeting, but he did not report the parents' complaint to Lago Vista's superintendent, who was the district's Title IX coordinator. A couple of months later, in January 1993, a police officer discovered Waldrop and Gebser engaging in sexual intercourse and arrested Waldrop. Lago Vista terminated his employment, and subsequently, the Texas Education Agency revoked his teaching license. During this time, the district had not promulgated or distributed an official grievance procedure for lodging sexual harassment complaints; nor had it issued a formal anti-harassment policy. . . .

Title IX provides in pertinent part that, "[n]o person . . . shall, on the basis of sex, be excluded from participation in, be denied the benefits of, or be subjected to discrimination under any education program or activity receiving Federal financial assistance." 20 U.S.C. §1681(a). The express statutory means of enforcement is administrative: The statute directs federal agencies who distribute education funding to establish requirements to effectuate the nondiscrimination mandate, and permits the agencies to enforce those requirements through "any . . . means authorized by law," including ultimately the termination of federal funding. . . . The Court held in *Cannon v. University of Chicago* . . . that Title IX is also enforceable through an implied private right of action, a conclusion we do not revisit here. We subsequently established in *Franklin v. Gwinnett County Public Schools* . . . that monetary damages are available in the implied private action.

In *Franklin*, a high school student alleged that a teacher had sexually abused her on repeated occasions and that teachers and school administrators knew about the harassment but took no action, even to the point of dissuading her from initiating charges. . . . We [concluded] that Title IX supports a private action for damages, at least "in a case such as this, in which intentional discrimination is alleged." . . . *Franklin* thereby establishes that a school district can be held liable in damages in cases involving a teacher's sexual harassment of a student; the decision, however, does not purport to define the contours of that liability. . . .

Because the private right of action under Title IX is judicially implied, we have a measure of latitude to shape a sensible remedial scheme that best comports with the statute. . . . That endeavor inherently entails a degree of speculation, since it addresses an issue on which Congress has not specifically spoken. . . . To guide the analysis, we generally examine the relevant statute to ensure that we do not fashion the parameters of an implied right in a manner at odds with the statutory structure and purpose. . . .

As a general matter, it does not appear that Congress contemplated unlimited recovery in damages against a funding recipient where the recipient is unaware of discrimination in its programs. When Title IX was enacted in 1972, the principal civil rights statutes containing an express right of action did not provide for recovery of monetary damages at all, instead allowing only injunctive and equitable relief. . . . It was not until 1991 that Congress made damages available under Title VII, and even then, Congress carefully limited the amount recover-

able in any individual case, calibrating the maximum recovery to the size of the employer. . . . Adopting petitioners' position would amount, then, to allowing unlimited recovery of damages under Title IX where Congress has not spoken on the subject of either the right or the remedy, and in the face of evidence that when Congress expressly considered both in Title VII it restricted the amount of damages available.

Congress enacted Title IX in 1972 with two principal objectives in mind: "to avoid the use of federal resources to support discriminatory practices" and "to provide individual citizens effective protection against those practices." . . . The statute was modeled after Title VI of the Civil Rights Act of 1964, . . . which is parallel to Title IX except that it prohibits race discrimination, not sex discrimination, and applies in all programs receiving federal funds, not only in education programs. . . . The two statutes operate in the same manner, conditioning an offer of federal funding on a promise by the recipient not to discriminate, in what amounts essentially to a contract between the Government and the recipient of funds. . . .

That contractual framework distinguishes Title IX from Title VII, which is framed in terms not of a condition but of an outright prohibition. Title VII applies to all employers without regard to federal funding and aims broadly to "eradicat[e] discrimination throughout the economy." . . . Title VII, moreover, seeks to "make persons whole for injuries suffered through past discrimination." . . . Thus, whereas Title VII aims centrally to compensate victims of discrimination, Title IX focuses more on "protecting" individuals from discriminatory practices carried out by recipients of federal funds. . . .

Title IX's contractual nature has implications for our construction of the scope of available remedies. When Congress attaches conditions to the award of federal funds under its spending power, . . . as it has in Title IX and Title VI, we examine closely the propriety of private actions holding the recipient liable in monetary damages for noncompliance with the condition. . . . Our central concern in that regard is with ensuring "that the receiving entity of federal funds [has] notice that it will be liable for a monetary award." . . . If a school district's liability for a teacher's sexual harassment rests on principles of constructive notice or *respondeat superior,* it will likewise be the case that the recipient of funds was unaware of the discrimination. It is sensible to assume that Congress did not envision a recipient's liability in damages in that situation. . . .

Most significantly, Title IX contains important clues that Congress did not intend to allow recovery in damages where liability rests solely on principles of vicarious liability or constructive notice. Title IX's express means of enforcement—by administrative agencies—operates on an assumption of actual notice to officials of the funding recipient. . . .

In the event of a violation, a funding recipient may be required to take "such remedial action as [is] deem[ed] necessary to overcome the effects of [the] discrimination." . . . While agencies have conditioned continued funding on providing equitable relief to the victim, . . . the regulations do not appear to contemplate a condition ordering payment of monetary damages, and there is no indication that payment of damages has been demanded as a condition of finding a recipient to be in compliance with the statute. . . .

Presumably, a central purpose of requiring notice of the violation "to the appropriate person" and an opportunity for voluntary compliance before administrative enforcement proceedings can commence is to avoid diverting education funding from beneficial uses where a recipient was unaware of discrimination in its programs and is willing to institute prompt corrective measures. The scope of private damages relief proposed by petitioners is at odds with that basic objective. When a teacher's sexual harassment is imputed to a school district or when a school district is deemed to have "constructively" known of the teacher's harassment, by assumption the district had no actual knowledge of the teacher's conduct. Nor, of course, did the district have an opportunity to take action to end the harassment or to limit further harassment.

It would be unsound, we think, for a statute's *express* system of enforcement to require notice to the recipient and an opportunity to come into voluntary compliance while a judicially *implied* system of enforcement permits substantial liability without regard to the recipient's knowl-

edge or its corrective actions upon receiving notice. . . . Moreover, an award of damages in a particular case might well exceed a recipient's level of federal funding. . . . (Lago Vista's federal funding for 1992–1993 was roughly $120,000). Where a statute's express enforcement scheme hinges its most severe sanction on notice and unsuccessful efforts to obtain compliance, we cannot attribute to Congress the intention to have implied an enforcement scheme that allows imposition of greater liability without comparable conditions. . . .

Because the express remedial scheme under Title IX is predicated upon notice to an "appropriate person" and an opportunity to rectify any violation, . . . we conclude, in the absence of further direction from Congress, that the implied damages remedy should be fashioned along the same lines. An "appropriate person" . . . is, at a minimum, an official of the recipient entity with authority to take corrective action to end the discrimination. Consequently, in cases like this one that do not involve official policy of the recipient entity, we hold that the damages remedy will not lie under Title IX unless an official who at a minimum has authority to address the alleged discrimination and to institute corrective measures on the recipient's behalf has actual knowledge of discrimination in the recipient's programs and fails adequately to respond.

We think, moreover, that the response must amount to deliberate indifference to discrimination. The administrative enforcement scheme presupposes that an official who is advised of a Title IX violation refuses to take action to bring the recipient into compliance. The premise, in other words, is an official decision by the recipient not to remedy the violation. That framework finds a rough parallel in the standard of deliberate indifference. Under a lower standard, there would be a risk that the recipient would be liable in damages not for its own official decision but instead for its employees' independent actions. . . .

Applying the framework to this case is fairly straightforward, as petitioners do not contend they can prevail under an actual notice standard. The only official alleged to have had information about Waldrop's misconduct is the high school principal. That information, however, consisted of a complaint from parents of other students charging only that Waldrop had made inappropriate comments during class, which was plainly insufficient to alert the principal to the possibility that Waldrop was involved in a sexual relationship with a student. Lago Vista, moreover, terminated Waldrop's employment upon learning of his relationship with Gebser....

The number of reported cases involving sexual harassment of students in schools confirms that harassment unfortunately is an all too common aspect of the education experience. No one questions that a student suffers extraordinary harm when subjected to sexual harassment and abuse by a teacher, and that the teacher's conduct is reprehensible and undermines the basic purposes of the educational system. The issue in this case, however, is whether the independent misconduct of a teacher is attributable to the school district that employs him under a specific federal statute designed primarily to prevent recipients of federal financial assistance from using the funds in a discriminatory manner. Our decision does not affect any right of recovery that an individual may have against a school district as a matter of state law or against the teacher in his individual capacity under state law or under 42 U.S.C. §1983. Until Congress speaks directly on the subject, however, we will not hold a school district liable in damages under Title IX for a teacher's sexual harassment of a student absent actual notice and deliberate indifference. We therefore affirm the judgment of the Court of Appeals.

It is so ordered.

❖ — ❖ — ❖

School Board May Be Liable for Student-to-Student Sexual Harassment but Only When Acting with "Deliberate Indifference"

Davis v. Monroe County Board of Education

Supreme Court of the United States, 1999.
526 U.S. 629, 119 S.Ct. 1662.

Justice O'CONNOR delivered the opinion of the Court.

Petitioner brought suit against the Monroe County Board of Education and other defendants, alleging that her fifth-grade daughter had been the victim of sexual harassment by another student in her class. Among petitioner's claims was a claim for monetary and injunctive relief under Title IX of the Education Amendments of 1972 (Title IX). . . . The District Court dismissed petitioner's Title IX claim on the ground that "student-on-student," or peer, harassment provides no ground for a private cause of action under the statute. The Court of Appeals for the Eleventh Circuit, sitting en banc, affirmed. We consider here whether a private damages action may lie against the school board in cases of student-on-student harassment. We conclude that it may, but only where the funding recipient acts with deliberate indifference to known acts of harassment in its programs or activities. Moreover, we conclude that such an action will lie only for harassment that is so severe, pervasive, and objectively offensive that it effectively bars the victim's access to an educational opportunity or benefit. . . .

Petitioner's minor daughter, LaShonda, was allegedly the victim of a prolonged pattern of sexual harassment by one of her fifth-grade classmates at Hubbard Elementary School, a public school in Monroe County, Georgia. According to petitioner's complaint, the harassment began in December 1992, when the classmate, G. F., attempted to touch LaShonda's breasts and genital area and made vulgar statements such as "'I want to get in bed with you'" and "'I want to feel your boobs.'" . . . Similar conduct allegedly occurred on or about January 4 and January 20, 1993. . . . LaShonda reported each of these incidents to her mother and to her classroom teacher. . . . Petitioner, in turn, also contacted [the teacher], who allegedly assured petitioner that the school principal . . . had been informed of the incidents. Petitioner contends that, notwithstanding these reports, no disciplinary action was taken against G. F. . . .

G. F.'s conduct allegedly continued for many months. In early February, G. F. purportedly placed a door stop in his pants and proceeded to act in a sexually suggestive manner toward LaShonda during physical education class. . . .

LaShonda reported G. F.'s behavior to her physical education teacher. . . . Approximately one week later, G. F. again allegedly engaged in harassing behavior, this time while under the supervision of another classroom teacher. . . . Again, LaShonda allegedly reported the incident to the teacher, and again petitioner contacted the teacher to follow up. . . .

The string of incidents finally ended in mid-May, when G. F. was charged with, and pleaded guilty to, sexual battery for his misconduct. . . . The complaint alleges that LaShonda had suffered during the months of harassment, however; specifically, her previously high grades allegedly dropped as she became unable to concentrate on her studies, . . . and, in April 1993, her father discovered that she had written a suicide note. . . . The complaint further alleges that, at one point, LaShonda told petitioner that she "'didn't know how much longer she could keep [G. F.] off her.'" . . .

Nor was LaShonda G. F.'s only victim; it is alleged that other girls in the class fell prey to G. F.'s conduct. . . . At one point, in fact, a group composed of LaShonda and other female students tried to speak with Principal Querry about G. F.'s behavior. . . . According to the complaint, however, a teacher denied the students' request with the statement, "'If [Querry] wants you, he'll call you.'" . . .

Petitioner alleges that no disciplinary action was taken in response to G. F.'s behavior toward LaShonda. . . . When petitioner inquired as to what action the school intended to take against G. F., [the principal] simply stated, "'I guess I'll have to threaten him a little bit harder.'" . . . Yet, petitioner alleges, at no point during the many months of his reported misconduct was G. F. disciplined for harassment. . . .

Nor, according to the complaint, was any effort made to separate G. F. and LaShonda. . . . On the contrary, notwithstanding LaShonda's frequent complaints, only after more than three months of reported harassment was she even permitted to change her classroom seat so that she was no longer seated next to G. F. . . . Moreover, petitioner alleges that, at the time of the events in question, the Monroe County Board of Education (Board) had not instructed its personnel on how to respond to peer sexual harassment and had not established a policy on the issue. . . .

Petitioner urges that Title IX's plain language compels the conclusion that the statute is intended to bar recipients of federal funding from permitting this form of discrimination in their programs or activities. She emphasizes that the statute prohibits a student from being "*subjected to discrimination* under any education program or activity receiving Federal financial assistance." . . . It is Title IX's "unmistakable focus on the benefited class," . . . rather than the perpetrator, that, in petitioner's view, compels the conclusion that the statute works to protect students from the discriminatory misconduct of their peers.

Here, however, we are asked to do more than define the scope of the behavior that Title IX proscribes. We must determine whether a district's failure to respond to student-on-student harassment in its schools can support a private suit for money damages. . . . This Court has indeed recognized an implied private right of action under Title IX, . . . and we have held that money damages are available in such suits. . . .

. . . Respondents contend, specifically, that the statute only proscribes misconduct by grant recipients, not third parties. Respondents argue, moreover, that it would be contrary to the very purpose of Spending Clause legislation to impose liability on a funding recipient for the misconduct of third parties, over whom recipients exercise little control. . . .

We agree with respondents that a recipient of federal funds may be liable in damages under Title IX only for its own misconduct. The recipient itself must "exclud[e] [persons] from participation in, . . . den[y] [persons] the benefits of, or . . . subject[t] [persons] to discrimination under" its "program[s] or activit[ies]" in order to be liable under Title IX. The Government's enforcement power may only be exercised against the funding recipient, . . . and we have not extended damages liability under Title IX to parties outside the scope of this power. . . .

We disagree with respondents' assertion, however, that petitioner seeks to hold the Board liable for G. F.'s actions instead of its own. Here, petitioner attempts to hold the Board liable for its *own* decision to remain idle in the face of known student-on-student harassment in its schools. In *Gebser* [*v. Lago Vista Independent*

School District, 524 U.S. 274, 118 S. Ct 1989 (1998)], we concluded that a recipient of federal education funds may be liable in damages under Title IX where it is deliberately indifferent to known acts of sexual harassment by a teacher. . . .

. . . [W]e concluded in *Gebser* that recipients could be liable in damages only where their own deliberate indifference effectively "cause[d]" the discrimination. . . . The high standard imposed in *Gebser* sought to eliminate any "risk that the recipient would be liable in damages not for its own official decision but instead for its employees' independent actions." . . .

Gebser thus established that a recipient intentionally violates Title IX, and is subject to a private damages action, where the recipient is deliberately indifferent to known acts of teacher-student discrimination. Indeed, whether viewed as "discrimination" or "subject[ing]" students to discrimination, Title IX "[u]nquestionably . . . placed on [the Board] the duty not" to permit teacher-student harassment in its schools, . . . and recipients violate Title IX's plain terms when they remain deliberately indifferent to this form of misconduct.

We consider here whether the misconduct identified in *Gebser*—deliberate indifference to known acts of harassment—amounts to an intentional violation of Title IX, capable of supporting a private damages action, when the harasser is a student rather than a teacher. We conclude that, in certain limited circumstances, it does. . . .

The common law, too, has put schools on notice that they may be held responsible under state law for their failure to protect students from the tortious acts of third parties. . . . In fact, state courts routinely uphold claims alleging that schools have been negligent in failing to protect their students from the torts of their peers. . . .

This is not to say that the identity of the harasser is irrelevant. On the contrary, both the "deliberate indifference" standard and the language of Title IX narrowly circumscribe the set of parties whose known acts of sexual harassment can trigger some duty to respond on the part of funding recipients. Deliberate indifference makes sense as a theory of direct liability under Title IX only where the funding recipient has some control over the alleged harassment. A

recipient cannot be directly liable for its indifference where it lacks the authority to take remedial action.

The language of Title IX itself—particularly when viewed in conjunction with the requirement that the recipient have notice of Title IX's prohibitions to be liable for damages—also cabins the range of misconduct that the statute proscribes. The statute's plain language confines the scope of prohibited conduct based on the recipient's degree of control over the harasser and the environment in which the harassment occurs. If a funding recipient does not engage in harassment directly, it may not be liable for damages unless its deliberate indifference "subject[s]" its students to harassment. . . . Moreover, because the harassment must occur "under" "the operations of" a funding recipient, . . . the harassment must take place on a context subject to the school district's control. . . .

Where, as here, the misconduct occurs during school hours and on school grounds—the bulk of G. F.'s misconduct, in fact, took place in the classroom—the misconduct is taking place "under" an "operation" of the funding recipient. . . . In these circumstances, the recipient retains substantial control over the context in which the harassment occurs. More importantly, however, in this setting the Board exercises significant control over the harasser. We have observed, for example, "that the nature of [the State's] power [over public schoolchildren] is custodial and tutelary, permitting a degree of supervision and control that could not be exercised over free adults." . . . On more than one occasion, this Court has recognized the importance of school officials' "comprehensive authority . . . , consistent with fundamental constitutional safeguards, to prescribe and control conduct in the schools." . . . The common law, too, recognizes the school's disciplinary authority. See Restatement (Second) of Torts §152 (1965). We thus conclude that recipients of federal funding may be liable for "subject[ing]" their students to discrimination where the recipient is deliberately indifferent to known acts of student-on-student sexual harassment and the harasser is under the school's disciplinary authority. . . .

We stress that our conclusion here—that recipients may be liable for their deliberate indifference to known acts of peer sexual harassment—does not mean that recipients can avoid liability only by purging their schools of actionable peer harassment or that administrators must engage in particular disciplinary action. . . .

. . . We . . . conclude that funding recipients are properly held liable in damages only where they are deliberately indifferent to sexual harassment, of which they have actual knowledge, that is so severe, pervasive, and objectively offensive that it can be said to deprive the victims of access to the educational opportunities or benefits provided by the school. . . .

Whether gender-oriented conduct rises to the level of actionable "harassment" thus "depends on a constellation of surrounding circumstances, expectations, and relationships," . . . including, but not limited to, the ages of the harasser and the victim and the number of individuals involved. . . . Courts, moreover, must bear in mind that schools are unlike the adult workplace and that children may regularly interact in a manner that would be unacceptable among adults. . . . Indeed, at least early on, students are still learning how to interact appropriately with their peers. It is thus understandable that, in the school setting, students often engage in insults, banter, teasing, shoving, pushing, and gender-specific conduct that is upsetting to the students subjected to it. Damages are not available for simple acts of teasing and name-calling among school children, however, even where these comments target differences in gender. Rather, in the context of student-on-student harassment, damages are available only where the behavior is so severe, pervasive, and objectively offensive that it denies its victims the equal access to education that Title IX is designed to protect. . . .

The fact that it was a teacher who engaged in harassment in *Franklin* and *Gebser* is relevant. The relationship between the harasser and the victim necessarily affects the extent to which the misconduct can be said to breach Title IX's guarantee of equal access to educational benefits and to have a systemic effect on a program or activity. Peer harassment, in particular, is less likely to satisfy these requirements than is teacher-student harassment. . . .

Applying this standard to the facts at issue here, we conclude that the Eleventh Circuit erred in dismissing petitioner's complaint. Peti-

tioner alleges that her daughter was the victim of repeated acts of sexual harassment by G. F. over a 5-month period, and there are allegations in support of the conclusion that G. F.'s misconduct was severe, pervasive, and objectively offensive. The harassment was not only verbal; it included numerous acts of objectively offensive touching, and, indeed, G. F. ultimately pleaded guilty to criminal sexual misconduct. Moreover, the complaint alleges that there were multiple victims who were sufficiently disturbed by G. F.'s misconduct to seek an audience with the school principal. Further, petitioner contends that the harassment had a concrete, negative effect on her daughter's ability to receive an education. The complaint also suggests that petitioner may be able to show both actual knowledge and deliberate indifference on the part of the Board, which made no effort whatsoever either to investigate or to put an end to the harassment.

On this complaint, we cannot say "beyond doubt that [petitioner] can prove no set of facts in support of [her] claim which would entitle [her] to relief." . . . Accordingly, the judgment of the United States Court of Appeals for the Eleventh Circuit is reversed, and the case is remanded for further proceedings consistent with this opinion.

It is so ordered.

■ CHILD ABUSE*

While child abuse and neglect are ageless, only recently have they been given national attention.[105] Commencing in 1962, state legislatures began enacting legislation designed to deal with problems of child abuse and neglect, and in 1974 a federal statute, the Child Abuse Prevention and Treatment Act, was enacted.[106] The purpose of this legislation was to provide federal financial assistance to the states that had implemented programs for identification, prevention, and treatment of instances of child abuse and neglect.[107] Currently, all fifty states plus the District of Columbia, Puerto Rico, and

---

*Reprinted with permission, Richard G. Salmon and M. David Alexander, "Child Abuse and Neglect: Implications for Educators," *West's Education Law Reporter* 28 (1986): pp. 9–19.

the Virgin Islands have enacted various forms of child abuse and neglect statutes.[108] A component of the 1974 act was the National Center on Child Abuse and Neglect, which developed the Model Child Protection Act (Model Act).[109] The Model Act has been used extensively throughout the nation for development of individual state child abuse legislation.[110]

DEFINITION

The Model Act included the following succinct definition of child abuse and neglect:

> [C]hild abuse and neglect means the physical or mental injury, sexual abuse, negligent treatment, or maltreatment of a child under the age of eighteen by a person who is responsible for the child's welfare under circumstances which indicate that the child's health or welfare is harmed or threatened thereby, as determined in accordance with regulations prescribed by the Secretary.[111]

Commonly contained within state child abuse and neglect statutes is a purpose statement that outlines the intent of the legislation. Typically, the primary purpose of child abuse and neglect statutes is to identify children who are being abused or neglected so that state protection may be provided.[112] Often, as in the case of Virginia, the state desires to preserve "the family life of the parents and children, where possible, by enhancing parental capacity for adequate child care."[113]

In contrast with the rather general federal definition of child abuse and neglect, state definitions tend to be more specific, as typified by the Virginia definition:

> *Abused or neglected child* shall mean any child less than eighteen years of age whose parents or other person responsible for his care:
>
> 1. Creates or inflicts, threatens to create or inflict, or allows to be created or inflicted upon such a child a physical or mental injury by other than accidental means, or creates a substantial risk of death, disfigurement, impairment of bodily or mental functions;
> 2. Neglects or refuses to provide care necessary for his health; provided, however, that no child who in good faith is under treatment solely by spiritual means through prayer in accordance with tenets and practices of a recognized

> church or religious denomination shall for that reason alone be considered to be an abused or neglected child; or
>
> 3. Abandons such child; or
> 4. Commits or allows to be committed any sexual act upon a child in violation of the law.[114]

Nearly all states have accepted the federal definition of "child" as a person under the age of eighteen, but they vary widely in regard to definitions of abuse and neglect.[115] Some states provide separate definitions of what constitutes child abuse and neglect, while other states have not attempted to distinguish between them.[116] In a recent survey of state child abuse statutes, child abuse and neglect were defined as follows:

> Implicit in most definitions of abuse is that the injury is deliberately inflicted. Abuse includes bodily violence (beating, squeezing, poisoning, burning, cutting, and exposing to heat or cold); sexual molestation (ranging from inappropriate fondling to intercourse); and psychological or mental injury (insults and accusations, prevention of sleep, and sensory overload relating to light, sound, pain, itching, stench, and aversive taste).
>
> Neglect is generally an omission—a failure to provide for a child's physical or emotional needs or both. Neglect includes deprivation of physiological necessities such as drink, nourishment, clothing, shelter, and sanitation. In addition, neglect encompasses the failure to fulfill psychological needs for sensory stimulation and social communication. These parental failures do not amount to neglect, however, if they are beyond the parents' control.[117]

REPORTING

An integral component of state child abuse and neglect statutes is the mandated reporting of suspected instances of child abuse and neglect by certain professionals. During initial legislation, child abuse and neglect legislation required only physicians to report instances of suspected child abuse and neglect.[118] Currently, in addition to medical personnel such as nurses, surgeons, medical examiners or coroners, dentists, osteopaths, optometrists, chiropractors, and podiatrists, other professionals including school teachers and officials, police, peace or law enforcement officers, social workers, and day-care personnel often are required to report instances of child abuse and neglect.[119] Forty-nine states have mandated that teachers report to certain authorities suspected instances of child abuse and neglect.[120] . . .

If the reports of suspected child abuse and neglect are determined to be unfounded, teachers are said to fear possible liability suits for slander, libel, defamation of character, invasion of privacy, and breach of confidence. However, all states have enacted legislation which grants immunity to reporters of child abuse and neglect from criminal and civil liability if the report *is made in good faith*. For example, the Virginia immunity statute states: "A person making a report . . . shall be immune from any civil or criminal liability in connection therewith unless it is proven that such person acted with malicious intent."[121] . . .

A 1985 Oregon case, *McDonald v. State, by and through CSD*[122] serves to illustrate the statutory immunity granted reporters of child abuse and neglect. In this case, a teacher observed scratches on the neck of one of her pupils and had him examined by a child development specialist. When questioned about how he had acquired the scratches, the child told two stories. One version attributed the scratches to his kitten, and the second version suggested that the child's mother had made the scratches by choking him, as the child said she had done on several occasions. The principal was informed, who in turn instructed the child development specialist to report the incident to the state Children's Services Division. The child was removed from parental custody and placed in a foster home. Subsequently, the parents appeared in court, where the allegations of child abuse were ruled groundless and the child reinstated with his parents. The parents brought suit against the Children's Services Division, principal, teacher, and others. The court dismissed the parents' complaint and indicated that, even though two versions of the derivation of scratches were told and the principal relied upon the opinion of the child development specialist only, both the principal and teacher had acted in good faith and had reasonable grounds to report suspected child abuse.

PENALTY FOR FAILURE TO REPORT

In order to gain compliance from those persons required to report instances of child abuse and neglect, most states permit the assessment of penalties for knowing and willful failure to report.[123] Most states have enacted criminal penalties for those persons guilty of not reporting suspected cases of child abuse and neglect.[124] Some states have legislated both criminal and civil penalties, and a few states provide only for civil remedies.[125]

Those states that have established criminal penalties for persons found guilty of not reporting instances of child abuse and neglect commonly classify such an offense as a misdemeanor.[126] Punishments normally include fines up to $1,000, jail sentences up to one year, or both.[127]

The threat of criminal prosecution, possibly due to inaction by persons responsible for initiating criminal proceedings, has not resulted in high levels of reporting compliance by teachers. As a result, some interest is being given to initiation of civil suits against teachers for their failure to report instances of child abuse and neglect.

Civil liability may be imposed against teachers who fail to report instances of child abuse and neglect in states that either have not specified penalties for nonreporters or have established criminal sanctions. In *Landeros v. Flood*,[128] the court ruled that a physician could be held civilly liable for injuries sustained by a child if he had negligently failed to diagnose and report suspected child abuse. However, teachers failing to report instances of child abuse and neglect are much more vulnerable to civil suits in states that have legislatively established provisions of civil liability for mandatory reporters.[129]

DEFENSES FOR FAILURE TO REPORT

Included within child abuse and neglect statutes for most states that provide criminal penalties for failure of mandatory reporters to report instances of child abuse and neglect are statements such as "reasonable cause to believe," "cause to believe,"[130] or, as in the case of Oklahoma, "reason to believe."[131] Such statements are considered to provide an objective standard on which to determine compliance.[132] Less rigorous statements, such as "knows or suspects," are considered to provide a subjective standard and one that may permit mandatory reporters to shield their own poor judgments.[133] Regardless of whether the standard is objective or subjective, a teacher charged with failure to report suspected child abuse and neglect under the criminal code of a state likely will attempt to show that there was no "reasonable cause to believe" that child abuse and neglect had occurred.[134]

In regard to civil liability for failure to report instances of suspected child abuse and neglect, the teacher will have to defeat allegations of negligence.[135]

❖ — ❖ — ❖

Reasonable Force in Paddling a Student
Does Not Constitute Child Abuse

Arkansas Department of Human Services v. Caldwell

Court of Appeals of Arkansas, Division II, 1992.
39 Ark.App. 14, 832 S.W.2d 510.

ROGERS, Judge.

The Department of Human Services appeals from the decision of the Baxter County Circuit Court reversing the agency's finding of some credible evidence of abuse, as allegedly perpetrated by appellee, Pat Caldwell, and thereby directing the removal of appellee's name from the State Central Registry. . . .

On Thursday, September 22, 1988, appellee, who is an assistant principal at the Guy Berry Middle School in Mountain Home, paddled three fifth grade students who had been caught smoking on the playground. . . . In the presence of another teacher as a witness, the child in question received three licks with a wooden paddle, as did another one of the girls, while the third child only received one lick, as she did not actually smoke the cigarette. The girls were also instructed to write a report on smoking. The following afternoon, the child's mother noticed bruises on her daughter's buttocks. Feeling that the bruises had resulted from the spanking, the mother contacted school officials and then reported the paddling to the Baxter County Division of Children and Family Ser-

vices as an incident of suspected child abuse. The assigned caseworker met with the child and her mother the next morning and took pictures of the child's buttocks. Upon completing the investigation, which included interviews with appellee and school personnel, and after consulting with her area manager, the caseworker "substantiated" the allegation of child abuse and forwarded a written report of the investigation for recordation in the State Central Registry, as is required pursuant to Ark.Code Ann. §12-12-508 (1987). Appellee then requested administrative review of this determination, seeking to expunge her name from the registry. A hearing was held on May 31, 1989, after which the hearing officer issued an order in which she found "some credible evidence" to substantiate the occurrence of abuse. Appellee appealed to the circuit court, which reversed the agency's decision and directed that appellee's name be stricken from the registry. This appeal followed.

As its first issue, appellant contends that the trial court erred in determining that the hearing officer's findings were not supported by some credible evidence. We disagree.

Under the School Discipline Act, it is stated that any teacher or school principal may use corporal punishment in a reasonable manner against any pupil for good cause in order to maintain discipline and order within the public schools. Ark.Code Ann. §6-18-505(c) (1987). For our purposes here, "abuse" is defined as any nonaccidental physical injury inflicted on a child by anyone legally responsible for the care and maintenance of the child, or an injury which is at variance with the history given. . . . The question upon review in the circuit court is whether there is some credible evidence of alleged abuse to support the maintenance of the alleged abuser's name in the State Central Registry. . . .

At the administrative hearing, appellee testified that she was in charge of the school that day because the principal was absent. She said that she learned of the infraction from another teacher, and that, before deciding to paddle the children, she called another administrator for advice as to the appropriate punishment, stating that it was a difficult decision since this was the first incident of smoking she had confronted involving children in that age group. Appellee questioned the girls both separately and together. . . . Appellee testified that she followed the normal routine in administering the paddling, which included obtaining another teacher as a witness. The children were first made to tell the witness what they had done wrong, and when paddled, each were told to bend over and touch their knees, so that the buttocks would be easily hit, and to look forward, rather than at her, to hopefully prevent them from moving. She said that the child remained still while she was being paddled, and that she gave her three "average" swats. She denied that she paddled the child in anger, and said that she would not have expected the child to have bruised from the paddling that she gave. She felt that she had spanked her appropriately and had not abused her, and that the only thing she could think of was that the child was wearing a thin dress that day.

The witness, Patricia Wallace, a fourth grade teacher, testified that she was positioned in front of the children as they were being paddled, and that the child displayed little reaction to the paddling. She said that she witnesses about half of the paddlings that occur at the school, and remarked that the licks in this instance were not out of the ordinary or excessive, but that they were rather light. She stated that appellee was calm, and not angry when she spanked these children. Michelle Ervin, the school nurse, saw the child on Monday, September 26th, four days after the paddling. In her report, she stated that she observed four very faint bruises which were each about three quarters of an inch in diameter. She said that there was no swelling or other abrasions in the area. In her testimony, she said that she had to kneel and get about eight inches away before the bruises could be seen.

The child also testified at the hearing. She related that her behind was sore after the paddling, particularly when she sat down, and she felt that she was being hit hard when she was spanked. She said that she cried both before and after the paddling. She further testified that appellee was disappointed in her for smoking, but not angry.

The child's mother testified that she learned of the spanking the next day when appellee directed the child to telephone her from school because the child had someone else sign her name to the note which was sent home to inform her of the paddling. She said that, when her daughter got home that afternoon, she looked at the child's buttocks and observed bruises after the child had explained to her how badly the spanking had hurt and that it hurt to sit down. The mother agreed that the child deserved a spanking for what she had done, but she felt that the paddling was excessive, stating that "it was just too hard." She said that her daughter bruised often, but "normal" in comparison to other children.

Jennifer Baker, the caseworker who investigated the report, testified that after she had completed the interviews she did not feel that appellee had been abusive. In substantiating the allegation, she said that the deciding factor was that marks were left from the paddling. She related that according to the department's policy she must substantiate an allegation of abuse if bruises remain after a twenty-four hour period. Because of this policy, she stated that she was compelled to substantiate the allegation in this case since bruises had resulted from the paddling. John Hangen, Ms. Baker's supervisor, who advised her in reaching a decision on this matter, testified it was the agency's position that, "if there is bruising, it is abusive and with bruising, we substantiate abuse." He said that his staff is directed to consider that discipline which results in bruising is excessive and physically abusive. He explained that the department needed to have a guideline, and that the guideline was that bruising is abusive.

Based on our review of the testimony and the photographs that were taken, we must agree with the decision of the circuit court reversing the agency's determination. In so holding, we are impressed with the caseworker's testimony that she did not feel that the paddling was abusive, and that substantiation was based solely on the evidence of bruising. We do not believe that one factor, standing alone and applied as a litmus test, without consideration of all the attendant circumstances, is an appropriate measure to be used in all cases for determining whether an allegation of abuse is to be substantiated. There must be some exercise of judgment, as this is an area which does not lend itself to facile determination. On this record, we uphold the circuit court's finding of no credible evidence to support the allegation of abuse, and its finding that the punishment was not excessive or abusive. . . .

CASE NOTES

1. In another Arkansas case, a report was made that a middle school principal hit a student three times on the buttocks with a wooden paddle. The Department of Human Services investigated and concluded there was "some credible evidence of child abuse." The principal appealed to the circuit court, which found the allegations unsubstantiated, but the law required even unsubstantiated charges to be retained on the central registry for three years. The principal challenged this as a violation of due process and equal protection. The court ruled there was no violation to retain "unsubstantiated" charges in the central registry for three years, and it therefore refused to direct registry expurgation of the charges. *Arkansas Department of Human Services v. Heath,* 312 Ark. 206, 848 S.W.2d 927 (1993).

2. In another case where a teacher was placed on the state register for suspected child abuse, the court ruled placement on the state register implicates a federal liberty interest and invades the due process interest of the teacher. *Cavarretta v. Department of Children and Family Services,* 277 Ill.App.3d 16, 214 Ill.Dec. 59, 660 N.E.2d 250 (2 Dist.1996).

3. The Alabama Supreme Court has held that the Alabama Child Abuse Reporting Act imposes a duty on an individual to make a report, but there was no intent to impose civil liability for failure to report. The act provides that the failure to report constitutes a misdemeanor with a punishment of no more than six months' imprisonment or a fine of no more than $500. *C. B. v. Bobo,* 659 So.2d 98 (Ala.1995).

4. Where a teacher grabbed a student and left a "mark," the court found no "abuse." Moreover, the act did not constitute excessive corporal punishment. *Korunka v. Department of Children and Family Services,* 259 Ill.App.3d 527, 197 Ill.Dec. 537, 631 N.E.2d 759 (4 Dist.1994).

■ FREEDOM OF SPEECH AND EXPRESSION

Few areas of the law are more misunderstood by laypeople than those connected with First Amendment rights, especially as they relate to freedom of speech and expression. While it is true that the right to speak one's mind carries with it at least the moral obligation to mind one's speech, this rule of thumb is not the prevailing yardstick or standard used by the courts in resolving issues in this area.

The Supreme Court has relied primarily on two tests to determine whether the state can control freedom of speech or expression: (1) clear and present danger and (2) material and substantial disruption. In 1919, the Court[136] said that the question to be asked is whether the words used are used in such circumstances and are of such a nature as to create a "clear and present danger" that they will bring about substantial evils that may harm the state. In subsequent decisions,[137] the Court further defined the concept. Justice Brandeis said that

> no danger flowing from speech can be deemed clear and present, unless the incidence of the evil apprehended is so imminent that it may befall before there is opportunity for full discussion. If there be time to expose through discussion the falsehood and fallacies, to avert the evil by the processes of education, the remedy to be applied is more speech, not enforced silence.[138]

Government cannot limit speech where the dangers are merely perceived or are not "present" or "imminent." Justice Black observed that "[w]hat finally emerges from the 'clear and present danger' cases is a working principle that the substantive evil must be extremely serious and the degree of imminence extremely high before utterances can be punished."[139]

MATERIAL AND SUBSTANTIAL DISRUPTION

The second rationale, "material and substantial disruption," is the standard applied to public education by the Supreme Court in the famous *Tinker* case. The Court in this case made it clear that school authorities are not permitted to deny a student the fundamental right of freedom of expression simply because of "a mere desire to avoid discomfort and unpleasantness that always accompany an unpopular viewpoint."[140]

The material and substantial disruption standard is, however, so broad that proper interpretation of specific school incidents is sometimes difficult. It is important to note that the precedent set in *Tinker* was based on facts relating to the intense political controversy surrounding the Vietnam War. Therefore, the curtailment of expression at this level of political concern is of significant constitutional magnitude. The Supreme Court, though, acknowledges that even expression at this level of importance can be limited if the school officials can reasonably forecast material and substantial disruption. As to when and how such restraint can take place, the Court in *Tinker* is rather nebulous. The interpretation and application of the standard are left to later court decisions in which it is applied to other factual situations.

One such decision that provides good guidance for school officials is *Guzick v. Drebus*,[141] a federal circuit court decision in which *Tinker* was applied to a situation in Shaw High School in Cleveland. Here the school forbade the wearing of buttons in an antiwar protest because the history of school disturbance and the wearing of insignia of various kinds strongly suggested to school officials that disruption would ensue. This fear was so pronounced that the court agreed that the officials could reasonably forecast substantial disruption. Thus, in a particular setting where disruptive antecedents can be documented and long-standing uniform rules can be applied, even political expression can be restrained.

TINKER REDEFINED

More recently, the U.S. Supreme Court has provided additional clarification to the *Tinker* standard.[142] In one case, the Court drew a line between the "political message" of the armbands of *Tinker* and other content that is a less compelling subject in terms of First Amendment protection. In this case, *Bethel School District No. 403 v. Fraser*,[143] a student made a lewd speech full of sexual innuendos, and the school responded by suspending him. The Court observed that *Tinker* cannot be interpreted to mean that public schools had to tolerate indecent speech that offended both the teachers and other students of the school. The Court observed that in *Tinker*, the expression did not intrude "upon the work of the schools or the rights of other students." The Court further noted, "Surely it is a highly appropriate function of public school education to prohibit the use of vulgar and offensive terms in public discourse."[144]

STUDENT APPEARANCE

The great weight of judicial authority supports the proposition that a board of education possesses the authority to regulate pupil dress and personal appearance if they become so extreme as to interfere with a school's favorable learning atmosphere. An illustration of this judicial position was provided many years ago when the Arkansas Appellate Court[145] upheld a school regulation that forbade the wearing of low-necked dresses, any immodest dress, or the use of face paints or cosmetics. An application of somewhat more recent vintage is the right of a school district to require pupils to participate in physical education programs and to wear clothing suitable for these occasions. The majority rule in these instances is that the pupils must participate in physical education programs, but they may not be required to wear "immodest" attire.[146]

Students and parents have relied on several legal issues in contesting student appearance regulations, including freedom of speech, guaranteed by the First Amendment; the due process and equal protection clauses of the Fourteenth Amendment; the Ninth Amendment, which provides for retention of rights by the people; and even the civil rights acts. The cases convey a lack of agreement by the courts in the application of these rights to students in public schools.

HAIR LENGTH

As an indication of this lack of a clear precedent, the courts appear to be about evenly split on the constitutional status of haircuts. The courts have been unable to agree and enunciate any consistent constitutional guideline for schools to follow in dealing with the issue of personal appearance generally and haircuts specifically. While the precedents generally follow *Tinker*, it is difficult to see precisely how untidy hair can rise to the level of a constitutional concern for either the student or the school. From the student's viewpoint, it is difficult to convincingly show that a haircut will in some fashion harm a constitutionally protected interest—that is, of course, providing that the school officials had in mind clipping the hair and not pulling it out. On the other hand, school officials are hard-pressed to show that untidy hair is of much educational significance and, certainly, that unkempt or long hair would substantially disrupt the school. The U.S. Supreme Court has rejected the entire question by pointing out that the issue is *de minimis*.

Nevertheless, much litigation has enveloped this problem. The federal circuit courts of appeals are divided as to whether and under what conditions schools may regulate student hairstyles. The third, fifth, sixth, ninth, tenth, and eleventh circuits have upheld school regulation of haircuts, while the first, second, fourth, seventh, and eighth have ruled that grooming has attendant constitutional rights. In *King v. Saddleback Junior College District*,[147] the ninth circuit ruled that long hair is not protected by the constitutional rights of privacy. The sixth circuit ruled that hair that is a distracting influence could be regulated.[148] In the same year, the first circuit found that students' hair is protected by the due process clause of the Fourteenth Amendment (establishing "a sphere of personal liberty").[149]

In the case of *Ferrell v. Dallas Independent School District*,[150] a suit was brought to enjoin school officials from refusing to enroll male pupils who had failed to comply with a school regulation banning long hair. The U.S. District Court for the Northern District of Texas denied any injunctive relief, and the pupils appealed. The court of appeals held that the regulation promulgated by the principal was valid.

In another case, the fifth circuit ruled against three male pupils who refused to shave in compliance with a good-grooming rule of their school. This court noted, with approval, the sentiment of the district court that "the Court felt somewhat put upon by having to fit a controversy over shaving into an inordinately busy schedule. It was viewed as a problem for school administrators. . . . The entire problem seems minuscule in light of other matters involving the school system."[151]

The fourth circuit,[152] in reviewing all the relevant appellate haircut decisions, concluded that the state interest may overcome the student's constitutional interest if the evidence indicates that the health and safety of the student are jeopardized. In so holding, this court, though, did acknowledge that hairstyle is a constitutionally protected right, "to be secure in one's person" as guaranteed by substantive due process.

Thus, buried in the haircut cases is a full panoply of constitutional provisions including freedom of expression, substantive due process, and equal protection. Whether these constitutional standards apply to restrict the authority of school officials depends more on the jurisdiction than on the constitutional concept invoked by the plaintiff. The impact of *Bethel* on these cases is yet to be determined, but if current judicial trends continue to vest more discretion in school officials, it is likely that lower courts will increasingly allow for less student latitude.

SCHOOL UNIFORMS

Public schools are the foremost institutions in society created to elevate humanity and to instill a heightened level of civility among the citizenry. This is done by engendering values of community and restraining the more primitive and negative natural impulses of youth. Those impulses have at least two aspects with which the school must deal. First, young persons tend to be more susceptible to discord and passion than adults, a circumstance that is exacerbated by less education and experience. Each person, adult and youth alike, as Thomas Hobbes explained in 1658, is possessed of a self-interest and, "supposing himself above others, will have license to do what he lists, and challenges respect and honour, as due him before others; which is an argument of a fiery spirit."[153] Fiery spirit and combativeness are a trait of the young with which the schools must constantly contend if decorum is to be maintained and learning is to prevail. The second aspect is the natural human tendency to form into groups, tribes, states, or nations to better effectuate self-interests. Nations as large bodies of people are possessive and territorial, seeking hegemony over others, to advance their wills and designs by strength of numbers. In order to advance their nationalism, these large groups coalesce around flags, patriotic songs, ideology, myths, language, dress, and other means of identification. Too often these groups are mobilized to indulge in conflicts with tragic results. Youth gangs reflect these human characteristics in a microcosm, and schools are unfortunately the venue where these primitive but natural urges are most frequently exhibited. As *Guzick*[154] indicates, school administrators are well aware of the problems that can emanate from buttons, insignia, or dress that creates artificial barriers within the student body that have divisive effects for the conduct of the school. A recent popular method of masking differences in students is the requirement of the wearing of school uniforms. Supporters of uniforms in schools cite statistics that show that the incidence of gangs, violence, and crime in schools has dropped dramatically after compulsory uniform policies have been implemented.[155]

Yet, some students and parents oppose these requirements, maintaining that the compulsory wearing of uniforms denies freedom of expression and speech. An Arizona court[156] has held that a mandatory school policy requiring that all students wear plain white shirts and navy pants, shorts, or skirts is constitutional. The court said the rule was "content-neutral" and did not constitute an impermissible restriction on the students' religious or political beliefs or sentiments. According to this court, *Tinker*[157] did not control because the uniform policy was not "content-based" and because, based on the facts presented, the school was not a public forum. The court concluded that the policy was reasonable in that it increased campus safety and security and in that it related to a legitimate pedagogical purpose of the school. Yet, it should be noted that in this case the decision was apparently influenced by the fact that students who objected to the uniform policy could transfer to another school, either within or outside the school district.

In another state court case, the Superior Court of Connecticut in *Byars*[158] upheld a school uniform policy with an "opt-out" provision that permitted students, with parental permission, to be excluded from the requirement. The court said for openers that it agreed with the U.S. Supreme Court's assertion in *Belotti*[159] that minors do not have rights equal with those of adults, and consequently the state could exercise greater control over children than it could

over adults. The school district in *Byars* justified the school uniform policy in several ways, indicating that it maintained order and decorum in the educational environment, avoided disruptions in the classroom, promoted discipline, avoided distractions of other pupils, prevented disturbances, and promoted safety. Too, with regard to safety, evidence was presented to the court showing that the uniform dress policy prevented the wearing of baggy blue jeans in which weapons could be concealed.[160] Further, the court accepted the district's evidence that the uniformity of dress fosters school unity and pride, eliminates dress competition, ensures modest dress, simplifies dressing, and costs parents less.

The court further cited the Supreme Court in *O'Brien*[161] where it held that the wearing of a particular type or style of clothing usually is not seen as expression of speech in a constitutionally protected sense. The state court concluded that the school attire policy was rationally related to the school district's legitimate interest in protecting the health and safety of students.

Neither *Byars*[162] nor the Arizona case, *Green*,[163] decided directly whether an "opt-out" provision is essential to the constitutionality of a school uniform policy, If, however, such a policy is viewed as content-neutral, the school is considered as a nonpublic forum, then an opt-out provision may not be necessary; however, most school districts having school uniform policies do include such provisions.[164] The limited litigation thus far regarding uniforms suggests that later court decisions may not find *Tinker* or *Bethel* to be particularly applicable to these situations.

Denial of Freedom of Expression Must Be Justified by a Reasonable Forecast of Substantial Disruption

Tinker v. Des Moines Independent Community School District

Supreme Court of the United States, 1969.
393 U.S. 503, 89 S.Ct. 733.

Mr. Justice FORTAS delivered the opinion of the Court. Petitioner John F. Tinker, fifteen years old, and petitioner Christopher Eckhardt, sixteen years old, attended high schools in Des Moines, Iowa. Petitioner Mary Beth Tinker, John's sister, was a thirteen-year-old student in junior high school.

In December 1965, a group of adults and students in Des Moines held a meeting at the Eckhardt home. The group determined to publicize their objections to the hostilities in Vietnam and their support for a truce by wearing black armbands during the holiday season and by fasting on December 16 and New Year's Eve. Petitioners and their parents had previously engaged in similar activities, and they decided to participate in the program.

The principals of the Des Moines schools became aware of the plan to wear armbands. On December 14, 1965, they met and adopted a policy that any student wearing an armband to school would be asked to remove it, and if he refused he would be suspended until he returned without the armband. Petitioners were aware of the regulation that the school authorities adopted.

On December 16, Mary Beth and Christopher wore black armbands to their schools. John Tinker wore his armband the next day. They were all sent home and suspended from school until they would come back without their armbands. They did not return to school until after the planned period for wearing armbands had expired—that is, until after New Year's Day. . . .

. . . On appeal, the Court of Appeals for the Eighth Circuit considered the case *en banc*. The court was equally divided, and the District Court's decision was accordingly affirmed, without opinion. . . .

The District Court recognized that the wearing of an armband for the purpose of expressing certain views is the type of symbolic act that is within the Free Speech Clause of the First Amendment. . . . As we shall discuss, the wearing of armbands in the circumstances of this case was entirely divorced from actually or potentially disruptive conduct by those participating in it. It was closely akin to "pure speech" which, we have repeatedly held, is entitled to comprehensive protection under the First Amendment. . . .

First Amendment rights, applied in light of the special characteristics of the school environment, are available to teachers and students. It can hardly be argued that either students or teachers shed their constitutional rights to freedom of speech or expression at the schoolhouse gate. This has been the unmistakable holding of this Court for almost fifty years. . . .

The school officials banned and sought to punish petitioners for a silent, passive expression of opinion, unaccompanied by any disorder or disturbance on the part of petitioners. There is here no evidence whatever of petitioners' interference, actual or nascent, with the schools' work or of collision with the rights of other students to be secure and to be let alone. Accordingly, this case does not concern speech or action that intrudes upon the work of the schools or the rights of other students.

Only a few of the 18,000 students in the school system wore the black armbands. Only five students were suspended for wearing them. There is no indication that the work of the schools or any class was disrupted. Outside the classrooms, a few students made hostile remarks to the children wearing armbands, but there were no threats or acts of violence on school premises.

The District Court concluded that the action of the school authorities was reasonable because it was based upon their fear of a disturbance from the wearing of the armbands. But, in our system, undifferentiated fear or apprehension of disturbance is not enough to overcome the right to freedom of expression. Any departure from absolute regimentation may cause trouble. Any variation from the majority's opinion may inspire fear. Any word spoken, in class, in the lunchroom, or on the campus, that deviates from the views of another person may start an argument or cause a disturbance. But our Constitution says we must take this risk, . . . and our history says that it is this sort of hazardous freedom—this kind of openness—that is the basis of our national strength and of the independence and vigor of Americans who grow up and live in this relatively permissive, often disputatious, society.

In order for the State in the person of school officials to justify prohibition of a particular expression of opinion, it must be able to show that its action was caused by something more than a mere desire to avoid the discomfort and unpleasantness that always accompany an unpopular viewpoint. Certainly where there is no finding and no showing that engaging in the forbidden conduct would "materially and substantially interfere with the requirements of appropriate discipline in the operation of the school," the prohibition cannot be sustained. . . .

In the present case, the District Court made no such finding, and our independent examination of the record fails to yield evidence that the school authorities had reason to anticipate that the wearing of the armbands would substantially interfere with the work of the school or impinge upon the rights of other students. Even an official memorandum prepared after the suspension that listed the reasons for the ban on wearing the armbands made no reference to the anticipation of such disruption.

On the contrary, the action of the school authorities appears to have been based upon an urgent wish to avoid the controversy which might result from the expression, even by the silent symbol of armbands, of opposition to this Nation's part in the conflagration in Vietnam. It is revealing, in this respect, that the meeting at which the school principals decided to issue the contested regulation was called in response to a student's statement to the journalism teacher in one of the schools that he wanted to write an article on Vietnam and have it published in the school paper. (The student was dissuaded.)

It is also relevant that the school authorities did not purport to prohibit the wearing of all symbols of political or controversial significance. The record shows that students in some of the schools wore buttons relating to national political campaigns, and some even wore the Iron Cross, traditionally a symbol of Nazism. The order prohibiting the wearing of armbands did not extend to these. Instead, a particular symbol—black armbands worn to exhibit opposition to this Nation's involvement in Vietnam— was singled out for prohibition. Clearly, the prohibition of expression of one particular opinion, at least without evidence that it is necessary to avoid material and substantial interference with schoolwork or discipline, is not constitutionally permissible.

In our system, state-operated schools may not be enclaves of totalitarianism. School officials do not possess absolute authority over their students. Students in school as well as out of school are "persons" under our Constitution. They are possessed of fundamental rights which the State must respect, just as they themselves must respect their obligations to the State. In our system, students may not be regarded as closed-circuit recipients of only that which the State chooses to communicate. They may not be confined to the expression of those sentiments that are officially approved. In the absence of a specific showing of constitutionally valid reasons to regulate their speech, students are entitled to freedom of expression of their views. . . .

If a regulation were adopted by school officials forbidding discussion of the Vietnam conflict, or the expression by any student of opposition to it anywhere on school property except as part of a prescribed classroom exercise, it would be obvious that the regulation would violate the constitutional rights of students, at least if it could not be justified by a showing that the students' activities would materially and substantially disrupt the work and discipline of the school. . . . In the circumstances of the present case, the prohibition of the silent, passive "witness of the armbands," as one of the children called it, is no less offensive to the constitution's guarantees.

As we have discussed, the record does not demonstrate any facts which might reasonably have led school authorities to forecast substantial disruption of or material interference with school activities, and no disturbances or disorders on the school premises in fact occurred. These petitioners merely went about their ordained rounds in school. Their deviation consisted only in wearing on their sleeve a band of black cloth, not more than two inches wide. They wore it to exhibit their disapproval of the Vietnam hostilities and their advocacy of a truce, to make their views known, and, by their example, to influence others to adopt them. They neither interrupted school activities nor sought to intrude in the school affairs or the lives of others. They caused discussion outside of the classrooms, but no interference with work and no disorder. In the circumstances, our Constitution does not permit officials of the State to deny their form of expression.

We express no opinion as to the form of relief which should be granted, this being a matter for the lower courts to determine. We reverse and remand for further proceedings consistent with this opinion.

Reversed and remanded.

——————— ❖ — ❖ — ❖ ———————

Students' Lewd and Indecent Speech Is Not Protected by First Amendment

Bethel School District No. 403 v. Fraser

Supreme Court of the United States, 1986.
478 U.S. 675, 106 S.Ct. 3159.

Chief Justice BURGER delivered the opinion of the Court. We granted certiorari to decide whether the First Amendment prevents a school district from disciplining a high school student for giving a lewd speech at a school assembly.

On April 26, 1983, respondent Matthew N. Fraser, a student at Bethel High School in Bethel, Washington, delivered a speech nominating a fellow student for student elective office. Approximately 600 high student schools, many of whom were 14-year-olds, attended the assembly. Students were required to attend the assembly or to report to the study hall. The assembly was part of a school-sponsored educational program in self-government. Students who elected not to attend the assembly were required to report to study hall. During the entire speech, Fraser referred to his candidate in terms of an elaborate, graphic, and explicit sexual metaphor.

Two of Fraser's teachers, with whom he discussed the contents of his speech in advance, informed him that the speech was "inappropriate and that he probably should not deliver it," and that his delivery of the speech might have "severe consequences."

During Fraser's delivery of the speech, a school counselor observed the reaction of students to the speech. Some students hooted and yelled; some by gestures graphically simulated the sexual activities pointedly alluded to in respondent's speech. Other students appeared to be bewildered and embarrassed by the speech. One teacher reported that on the day following the speech, she found it necessary to forgo a portion of the scheduled class lesson in order to discuss the speech with the class.

A Bethel High School disciplinary rule prohibiting the use of obscene language in the school provides:

> Conduct which materially and substantially interferes with the educational process is prohibited, including the use of obscene, profane language or gestures.

The morning after the assembly, the Assistant Principal called Fraser into her office and notified him that the school considered his speech to have been a violation of this rule. Fraser was presented with copies of five letters submitted by teachers, describing his conduct at the assembly; he was given a chance to explain his conduct, and he admitted to having given the speech described and that he deliberately used sexual innuendo in the speech. Fraser was then informed that he would be suspended for three days, and that his name would be removed from the list of candidates for graduation speaker at the school's commencement exercises.

Fraser sought review of this disciplinary action through the School District's grievance procedures. . . . The examiner determined that the speech fell within the ordinary meaning of "obscene," as used in the disruptive-conduct rule, and affirmed the discipline in its entirety. Fraser served two days of his suspension, and was allowed to return to school on the third day.

Respondent, by his father as guardian *ad litem*, then brought this action [and] . . . alleged violation of his First Amendment right to freedom of speech and sought both injunctive relief and monetary damages under 42 U.S.C. §1983. . . .

The Court of Appeals for the Ninth Circuit affirmed the judgment of the District Court, 755 F.2d 1356 (1985), holding that respondent's speech was indistinguishable from the protest armband in *Tinker v. Des Moines Independent Community School Dist.* . . . The court explicitly rejected the School District's argument that the speech, unlike the passive conduct of wearing a black armband, had a disruptive effect on the educational process. The Court of Appeals also rejected the School District's argument that it had an interest in protecting an essentially captive audience of minors from lewd and indecent language in a setting sponsored by the school, reasoning that the school board's "unbridled discretion" to determine what discourse is "decent" would "increase the risk of cementing white, middle-class standards for determining what is acceptable and proper speech and behavior in our public schools." . . . Finally, the Court of Appeals rejected the School District's argument that, incident to its responsibility for the school curriculum, it had the power to control the language used to express ideas during a school-sponsored activity.

We granted certiorari. . . . We reverse.

This Court acknowledged in *Tinker v. Des Moines Independent Community School Dist.* . . . that students do not "shed their constitutional rights to freedom of speech or expression at the schoolhouse gate." . . . The Court of Appeals read that case as precluding any discipline of Fraser for indecent speech and lewd conduct in the school assembly. That court appears to have proceeded on the theory that the use of lewd and obscene speech in order to make what the speaker considered to be a point in a nominating speech for a fellow student was essentially the same as the wearing of an armband in *Tinker* as a form of protest or the expression of a political position.

The marked distinction between the political "message" of the armbands in *Tinker* and the sexual content of respondent's speech in this case seems to have been given little weight by the Court of Appeals. In upholding the students' right to engage in a nondisruptive, passive expression of a political viewpoint in *Tinker,* this Court was careful to note that the case did "not concern speech or action that intrudes upon the work of the schools or the rights of other students."

It is against this background that we turn to consider the level of First Amendment protection accorded to Fraser's utterances and actions before an official high school assembly attended by 600 students.

The role and purpose of the American public school system was well described by two historians, saying "public education must prepare pupils for citizenship in the Republic. . . . It must inculcate the habits and manners of civility as values in themselves conducive to happi-

ness and as indispensable to the practice of self-government in the community and the nation." C. Beard & M. Beard, New Basic History of the United States 228 (1968). . . .

These fundamental values of "habits and manners of civility" essential to a democratic society must, of course, include tolerance of divergent political and religious views, even when the views expressed may be unpopular. But these "fundamental values" must also take into account consideration of the sensibilities of others, and, in the case of a school, the sensibilities of fellow students. The undoubted freedom to advocate unpopular and controversial views in schools and classrooms must be balanced against the society's countervailing interest in teaching students the boundaries of socially appropriate behavior. Even the most heated political discourse in a democratic society requires consideration for the personal sensibilities of the other participants and audiences.

In our Nation's legislative halls, where some of the most vigorous political debates in our society are carried on, there are rules prohibiting the use of expressions offensive to other participants in the debate. . . . Can it be that what is proscribed in the halls of Congress is beyond the reach of school officials to regulate?

The First Amendment guarantees wide freedom in matters of adult public discourse. A sharply divided Court upheld the right to express an antidraft viewpoint in a public place, albeit in terms highly offensive to most citizens. . . . It does not follow, however, that simply because the use of an offensive form of expression may not be prohibited to adults making what the speaker considers a political point, that the same latitude must be permitted to children in a public school. . . .

Surely it is a highly appropriate function of public school education to prohibit the use of vulgar and offensive terms in public discourse. Indeed, the "fundamental values necessary to the maintenance of a democratic political system" disfavor the use of terms of debate highly offensive or highly threatening to others. Nothing in the Constitution prohibits the states from insisting that certain modes of expression are inappropriate and subject to sanctions. The inculcation of these values is truly the "work of the schools." . . . The determination of what manner of speech in the classroom or in school assembly is inappropriate properly rests with the school board.

The process of educating our youth for citizenship in public schools is not confined to books, the curriculum, and the civics class; schools must teach by example the shared values of a civilized social order. Consciously or otherwise, teachers—and indeed the older students—demonstrate the appropriate form of civil discourse and political expression by their conduct and deportment in and out of class. Inescapably, like parents, they are role models. The schools, as instruments of the state, may determine that the essential lessons of civil, mature conduct cannot be conveyed in a school that tolerates lewd, indecent, or offensive speech and conduct such as that indulged in by this confused boy.

The pervasive sexual innuendo in Fraser's speech was plainly offensive to both teachers and students—indeed to any mature person. By glorifying male sexuality, and in its verbal content, the speech was acutely insulting to teenage girl students. . . . The speech could well be seriously damaging to its less mature audience, many of whom were only 14 years old and on the threshold of awareness of human sexuality. Some students were reported as bewildered by the speech and the reaction of mimicry it provoked.

This Court's First Amendment jurisprudence has acknowledged limitations on the otherwise absolute interest of the speaker in reaching an unlimited audience where the speech is sexually explicit and the audience may include children. . . . These cases recognize the obvious concern on the part of parents, and school authorities acting *in loco parentis* to protect children—especially in a captive audience—from exposure to sexually explicit, indecent, or lewd speech.

We have also recognized an interest in protecting minors from exposure to vulgar and offensive spoken language. . . .

We hold that petitioner School District acted entirely within its permissible authority in imposing sanctions upon Fraser in response to his offensively lewd and indecent speech. Unlike the sanctions imposed on the students wearing armbands in *Tinker,* the penalties imposed in this case were unrelated to any political viewpoint. The First Amendment does not prevent the school officials from determining that to permit a vulgar and lewd speech such as respondent's would undermine the school's basic educational mission. A high school assembly or classroom is no place for a sexually explicit monologue directed towards an unsuspecting audience of teenage students. Accordingly, it was perfectly appropriate for the school to disassociate itself to make the point to the pupils that vulgar speech and lewd conduct is wholly inconsistent with the "fundamental values" of public school education. Justice Black, dissenting in *Tinker,* made a point that is especially relevant in this case:

> I wish therefore . . . to disclaim any purpose . . . to hold that the federal Constitution compels the teachers, parents and elected school officials to surrender control of the American public school system to public school students. 393 U.S., at 522, 526, 89 S.Ct., at 744, 746.

Respondent contends that the circumstances of his suspension violated due process because he had no way of knowing that the delivery of the speech in question would subject him to disciplinary sanctions. This argument is wholly without merit. We have recognized that "maintaining security and order in the schools requires a certain degree of flexibility in school disciplinary procedures, and we have respected the value of preserving the informality of the student-teacher relationship." . . . Given the school's need to be able to impose disciplinary sanctions for a wide range of unanticipated conduct disruptive of the educational process, the school disciplinary rules need not be as detailed as a criminal code which imposes criminal sanctions. . . . Two days' suspension from school does not rise to the level of a penal sanction calling for the full panoply of procedural due process protections applicable to a criminal prosecution. . . . The school disciplinary rule proscribing "obscene" language and the pre-speech admonitions of teachers gave adequate warning to Fraser that his lewd speech could subject him to sanctions.

The judgment of the Court of Appeals for the Ninth Circuit is

Reversed.

Justice BLACKMUN concurs in the result.

Justice BRENNAN, concurring in the judgment.

Respondent gave the following speech at a high school assembly in support of a candidate for student government office:

'I know a man who is firm—he's firm in his pants, he's firm in his shirt, his character is firm—but most . . . of all, his belief in you, the students of Bethel, is firm.

'Jeff Kuhlman is a man who takes his point and pounds it in. If necessary, he'll take an issue and nail it to the wall. He doesn't attack things in spurts—he drives hard, pushing and pushing until finally—he succeeds.

'Jeff is a man who will go to the very end—even the climax, for each and every one of you.

'So vote for Jeff for A.S.B. vice-president—he'll never come between you and the best our high school can be.'

The Court, referring to these remarks as "obscene," "vulgar," "lewd," and "offensively lewd," concludes that school officials properly punished respondent for uttering the speech. Having read the full text of respondent's remarks, I find it difficult to believe that it is the same speech the Court describes. To my mind, the most that can be said about respondent's speech—and all that need be said—is that in light of the discretion school officials have to teach high school students how to conduct civil and effective public discourse, and to prevent disruption of school educational activities, it was not unconstitutional for school officials to conclude, under the circumstances of this case, that respondent's remarks exceeded permissible limits. Thus, while I concur in the Court's judgment, I write separately to express my understanding of the breadth of the Court's holding.

Speech in the Form of Buttons Protesting Substitute Teachers as "Scabs" Evaluated in Light of the Tinker, Fraser (Bethel), *and* Hazelwood *Precedents*

Chandler v. McMinnville School District

United States Court of Appeals. Ninth Circuit, 1992.
978 F.2d 524.

WALLACE, Chief Judge. . . .

On February 8, 1990, the school teachers in McMinnville, Oregon, commenced a lawful strike. In response to the strike, the school district hired replacement teachers. Chandler and Depweg were students at McMinnville High School and their fathers were among the striking teachers. On February 9, 1990, Chandler and Depweg attended school wearing various buttons and stickers on their clothing. Two of the buttons displayed the slogans "I'm not listening scab" and "Do scabs bleed?" Chandler and Depweg distributed similar buttons to some of their classmates.

During a break in the morning classes, a temporary administrator saw Depweg aiming his camera in a hallway as if to take a photograph. The administrator asserted that Depweg had no right to take his photograph without permission and instructed Depweg to accompany him to the vice principal's office. Chandler witnessed the request and followed Depweg into the office, where they were met by vice principal Whitehead. Whitehead, upon noticing the buttons, asked both students to remove them because they were disruptive. Depweg told Whitehead that his morning classes had not been disrupted. A replacement teacher in one of Depweg's classes confirmed that there had been no disruption. Nonetheless, Whitehead ordered that the buttons be removed. Chandler and Depweg, in the belief that the buttons were protected as a lawful exercise of free speech, refused to comply. They also refused to be separated. Whitehead then suspended them for the remainder of the school day for willful disobedience.

Depweg and Chandler returned to school on February 13, 1990, the next regularly scheduled school day, with different buttons and stickers on their clothing. They each wore a button that read "Scabs" with a line drawn through it (i.e., "no Scabs"), and a sticker that read "Scab we will never forget." In addition, they displayed buttons with the slogans "Students united for fair settlement," and "We want our real teachers back." Approximately 1:45 p.m., assistant vice principal Hyder asked Chandler to remove those buttons and stickers containing the word "scab" because they were disruptive. Chandler, anticipating further disciplinary action, complied with the request.

Chandler and Depweg filed this action in district court, . . . alleging that the school officials' reasons for requesting the removal of the buttons were false and pretextual, and therefore violated their First Amendment rights to freedom of expression. They state that the buttons caused no classroom disruption. . . .

We start on agreed ground: students in public schools do not "shed their constitutional rights to freedom of speech or expression at the schoolhouse gate." *Tinker v. Des Moines Indep. Community School Dist.* . . . "They cannot be punished merely for expressing their personal views on the school premises . . . unless school authorities have reason to believe that such expression will 'substantially interfere with the work of the school or impinge upon the rights of other students.'" *Hazelwood School Dist. v. Kuhlmeier.* . . . The schoolroom prepares children for citizenship, and the proper exercise of the First Amendment is a hallmark of citizenship in our country. Nevertheless, this educational experience has its limitations. The First Amendment rights of public school students "are not automatically coextensive with the rights of adults in other settings." *Bethel School Dist. No. 403 v. Fraser.* . . .

Chandler and Depweg argue that the district court applied an incorrect standard when it dismissed the complaint as a matter of law. They contend that this case is governed by *Tinker.* . . .

Chandler and Depweg argue that *Fraser* (*Bethel*) is distinguishable from this case on three grounds. First, they contend that the buttons constituted a "silent, passive expression of opinion" "akin to 'pure speech.'" *Tinker,* 393 U.S. at 508, 89 S.Ct. at 737. They contrast the silent expression of the buttons with the sexually implicit speech in *Fraser.* Next, the students focus on the fact that the speech in *Fraser* was made at a school assembly, a sanctioned school event, whereas their display of the buttons was a passive expression of personal opinion. They cite language in *Hazelwood* that distinguishes between suppression of "a student's personal expression that happens to occur on the school premises," and "educators' authority over school-sponsored [activities] that students, parents, and members of the public might reasonably perceive to bear the imprimatur of the school." *Hazelwood,* 484 U.S. at 271, 108 S.Ct. at

570. Finally, Chandler and Depweg argue that because their buttons expressed a political viewpoint they are therefore accorded greater protection. They point out that the Court in *Fraser* distinguished between the lewd speech in *Fraser* and the political speech in *Tinker,* thereby implying that restrictions on political speech should be governed by the more exacting *Tinker* test. *Fraser,* 478 U.S. at 685, 106 S.Ct. at 3165.

We turn to *Hazelwood* for guidance in interpreting the meaning and scope of the earlier *Tinker* and *Fraser* cases. *Hazelwood* involved a dispute over the deletion of two pages of an issue of a school newspaper. The principal deleted the pages because they contained an article addressing students' experiences with pregnancy, and another article describing the impact of divorce on students at the school. The newspaper was written and edited by students in a journalism class as part of the school's curriculum. . . . The Court declined to apply *Tinker,* holding instead that "the standard articulated in *Tinker* for determining when a school may punish student expression need not also be the standard for determining when a school may refuse to lend its name and resources to the dissemination of student expression." . . . The Court then validated discretionary editorial control by school officials over the school-sponsored newspaper "so long as their actions are reasonably related to legitimate pedagogical concerns." . . .

Although *Hazelwood* is not directly on point, it is instructive because it interpreted *Tinker* and *Fraser* together. The Court pointed out that there is a

> difference between the First Amendment analysis applied in *Tinker* and that applied in *Fraser.* . . . The decision in *Fraser* rested on the "vulgar," "lewd," and "plainly offensive" character of a speech delivered at an official school assembly rather than on any propensity of the speech to "materially disrup[t] classwork or involv[e] substantial disorder or invasion of the rights of others." . . .

We have discerned three distinct areas of student speech from the Supreme Court's school precedents: (1) vulgar, lewd, obscene, and plainly offensive speech, (2) school-sponsored speech, and (3) speech that falls into neither of these categories. We conclude, as discussed below, that the standard for reviewing the suppression of vulgar, lewd, obscene, and plainly offensive speech is governed by *Fraser*, . . . school-sponsored speech by *Hazelwood*, . . . and all other speech by *Tinker*. . . .

We first address the question of whether school officials may suppress vulgar, lewd, obscene, and plainly offensive speech, even when it is expressed outside the context of an official school program or event. *Hazelwood* focused on two factors that distinguish *Fraser* from *Tinker*: (1) the speech was "'vulgar,' 'lewd,' and 'plainly offensive,'" and (2) it was given at an official school assembly. . . . Whereas both of these factors were present in *Fraser*, we believe the deferential *Fraser* standard applies when the first factor alone is present. "Surely it is a highly appropriate function of a public school education to prohibit the use of vulgar and offensive terms in public discourse." . . . "A school need not tolerate student speech that is inconsistent with its 'basic educational mission,' even though the government could not censor similar speech outside the school." . . . Therefore, school officials may suppress speech that is vulgar, lewd, obscene, or plainly offensive without a showing that such speech occurred during a school-sponsored event or threatened to "substantially interfere with [the school's] work." . . . Such language, by definition, may well "impinge[] upon the rights of other students," . . . and therefore its suppression is "reasonably related to legitimate pedagogical concerns." . . .

We turn next to the second category involving speech or speech-related activities that "students, parents, and members of the public might reasonably perceive to bear the imprimatur of the school." In such cases, school officials are entitled to "greater control" over student expression. . . . A school has the discretion to "disassociate itself" from an entire range of speech, including "speech that is, for example, ungrammatical, poorly written, inadequately researched, biased or prejudiced, vulgar or profane, or unsuitable for immature audiences." . . . According to *Hazelwood*, federal courts are to defer to the school's decision to suppress or punish vulgar, lewd, or plainly offensive speech, and to "disassociate itself" from speech that a reasonable person would view as bearing the imprimatur of the school, when the decision

is "reasonably related to legitimate pedagogical concerns." . . .

The third category involves speech that is neither vulgar, lewd, obscene, or plainly offensive, nor bears the imprimatur of the school. To suppress speech in this category, school officials must justify their decision by showing "facts which might reasonably have led school authorities to forecast substantial disruption of or material interference with school activities." . . . However, the "First Amendment does not require school officials to wait until disruption actually occurs. . . . In fact, they have a duty to prevent the occurrence of disturbances." . . .

We now turn to the facts alleged in this case. No effort was made by the school officials to suppress the buttons containing the statements "Students united for fair settlement" or "We want our real teachers back." Rather, the suppression only involved statements containing the word "scab." The word "scab," in the context most applicable to this case, is defined as "a worker who accepts employment or replaces a union worker during a strike." . . . Although a dictionary definition may not be determinative in all cases, it is helpful here. "To be sure, the word is most often used as an insult or epithet." . . . Given the requirement to construe the complaint in a light most favorable to Chandler and Depweg, we are satisfied that these buttons cannot be considered per se vulgar, lewd, obscene, or plainly offensive within the meaning of *Fraser*. At this stage in the litigation, the school officials have made no showing that the word "scab" reasonably could be so considered.

This brings us to the second category of school speech. There is nothing in the complaint alleging that Chandler and Depweg's buttons reasonably could have been viewed as bearing the imprimatur of the school. The buttons expressed the personal opinion of the students wearing them, and they were displayed in a manner commonly used to convey silently an idea, message, or political opinion to the community. . . . In addition, they expressed a position on a local political issue that was diametrically opposed to the school district's decision to hire replacement teachers. Therefore, the complaint does not show that a reasonable person could have viewed the buttons as bearing the imprimatur of the school.

We turn, therefore, to the third category of school speech and its standard: whether the "scab" buttons were properly suppressed because the school officials reasonably forecasted that they would substantially disrupt, or materially interfere with, school activities. . . . The district court held that the "scab" buttons were inherently disruptive, but nothing in the complaint or the analysis of the district court substantiates this conclusion. We conclude that the district court erred in holding, without more, that the "scab" buttons were inherently disruptive.

We express no opinion on the question whether, on remand, the school district may be able to meet the reasonable forecast test. . . . [W]e hold that the "scab" buttons were not inherently disruptive. Although some of the slogans employed by Chandler and Depweg could be interpreted as insulting, disrespectful or even threatening, we must consider the facts in the light most favorable to the students in reviewing the district court's dismissal of the complaint. . . .

In a case such as this one, where arguably political speech is directed against the very individuals who seek to suppress that speech, school officials do not have limitless discretion. "Courts have a First Amendment responsibility to insure that robust rhetoric . . . is not suppressed by prudish failures to distinguish the vigorous from the vulgar." . . . Subsequent proof may show that the word "scab" can reasonably be viewed as insulting, and may show that the slogans were directed at the replacement teachers. Such evidence would bear upon the issue of whether the buttons might reasonably have led school officials to forecast substantial disruption to school activities. Mere use of the word "scab," however, does not establish as a matter of law that the buttons could be suppressed absent the showing set forth above. Perhaps, after trial or summary judgment, the record might support the school officials' actions. On the basis of the naked complaint, however, this support is absent. The passive expression of a viewpoint in the form of a button worn on one's clothing "is certainly not in the class of those activities which inherently distract students and break down the regimentation of the classroom." . . . The district court erred in dismissing the complaint. . . .

REVERSED AND REMANDED. . . .

CASE NOTES

1. According to one federal district court, hair length of Native Americans has such constitutional overtones as to reach the issue of religious freedom as well as substantive due process and free speech. This court held that even though hair length does not constitute a fundamental tenet of Native American religious orthodoxy, long hair is nevertheless deeply rooted in traditional Indian religious beliefs, and regulation of hair length by the school intrudes on those beliefs. The school's interest in having a dress code that fostered respect for authority and projected a good public image is not so compelling as to overcome religious practice and belief. Further, the court found that both liberty and property interests of the Indian students were offended as well as freedom of speech. *Alabama & Coushatta Tribes v. Big Sandy School District,* 817 F.Supp. 1319 (E.D.Tex.1993).

2. Lower courts have begun to follow the *Bethel School District No. 403 v. Fraser* precedent in giving school officials greater discretion in regulating student conduct. A case in point is *Gano,* an Idaho case, in which a federal district court upheld the suspension of a student for drawing and having printed on T-shirts a caricature of the principal, vice-principal, and dean of men sitting against a fence, holding alcoholic beverages, and acting drunk. The plaintiff wore one of the T-shirts to school. The court in holding against the student said that in Idaho the schools are statutorily charged with teaching the "effects of alcohol." To depict the school administrators in a drunken stupor was not only to falsely accuse them of being drunk, but to do damage to the school's decorum as well. The court said:

> The administrators are role models, as stated by the United States Supreme Court, and their position would be severely compromised if this T-shirt was circulated among students.

Further, the court noted that "[t]his case appears to clearly fall within the *Bethel* precedent." *Gano v. School District No. 411 of Twin Falls County, State of Idaho,* 674 F.Supp. 796 (D.Idaho 1987).

3. In a case where students dressed as persons of the opposite sex and were escorted from the school prom by police at the request of school officials, the court held for the officials, saying that students were not denied First Amendment, due process, or equal protection rights. *Harper v. Edgewood Board of Education*, 655 F.Supp. 1353 (S.D.Ohio 1987). In so holding, the court cited *Gfell v. Rickelman*, 441 F.2d 444 (6th Cir.1971), wherein the sixth circuit upheld grooming codes regarding hair length as reasonably related to "the maintenance of discipline, promotion of safety . . . and the furtherance of valid educational purposes." In further quoting *Gfell*, the court said that

> regulations which deal generally with dress and the like are a part of the disciplinary process which is necessary in maintaining a balance as between the rights of individual students and the rights of the whole in the functioning of schools.

441 F.2d at 446.

4. In a 1987 case, a federal district court was able to relate the wearing of earrings to the buttons of *Guzick* and the armbands of *Tinker* and to square its ruling with *Bethel* as well. In this case, a student wanted to wear an earring because he believed it expressed his individuality and would possibly be attractive to young women at the school. Each time he wore the earring, on several occasions, he was suspended under a school board rule that forbade all gang symbols, including jewelry and emblems. The wearing of earrings by males was included in the ban, although girls could wear earrings. The board had earlier, in 1984, passed the rule because of gang problems between 1981 and 1985, when the board discovered that students had been intimidated by gang members and that the gangs had warring factions in and around the school. The rule did not, however, specifically ban the wearing of earrings. In upholding the board rule and its enforcement, the court, citing *Bethel*, said that the board of education

> has the responsibility to teach not only English and History, but the role of young men and women in our democratic society. They are taught to have individual rights and that those rights must be balanced with the rights of others. The

direction and manner of this instruction rests with the Board, not the federal court.

Concerning protection of political expression, the court noted that the student's "message" was one of "individuality" and not one of "politics"; thus, it was not within the scope of the First Amendment. *Olesen v. Board of Education of School Dist. No. 228*, 676 F.Supp. 820 (N.D.Ill.1987).

5. The influence of *Bethel* is further evidenced by a 1989 case from the fifth circuit, in which a student was disqualified from a school election because of "rude" and "discourteous" remarks he made about the school principal in a campaign speech in school assembly. The court upheld the school in declaring the student ineligible. In so doing, the court cited *Bethel*, saying that

> the determination of what manner of speech in the classroom or in school assembly is inappropriate properly rests with the school board. *Bethel School District No. 403 v. Fraser*, 478 U.S. 675, 683, 106 S.Ct. 3159, 3164 (1986).

The court further stated that, pursuant to *Bethel* logic, "[t]he art of stating one's views without unnecessarily hurting the feelings of others surely has a legitimate place in any high school curriculum, and we are not prepared to say that the lesson Unicoi High tried to teach Dean Poling [the student] and his captive audience was illegitimate." *Poling v. Murphy*, 872 F.2d 757 (6th Cir.1989).

6. The suspension of black students for disrupting a student assembly because the tune "Dixie" was played was upheld by the United States Court of Appeals, Eighth Circuit. The court said that "[o]n the record we cannot say that the tune 'Dixie' constitutes a badge of slavery or that the playing of the tune under the facts as presented constituted officially sanctioned racial abuse. Such a rule would lead to the prohibition of the playing of many of our most famous tunes." *Tate v. Board of Education of Jonesboro, Arkansas*, 453 F.2d 975 (8th Cir.1972).

7. The Fifth Circuit has held that symbols and insignia such as the Confederate flag, indicating the desire to maintain a segregated school, must be removed. *Smith v. St. Tammany Parish School Board*, 448 F.2d 414 (5th Cir.1971).

■ STUDENT PUBLICATIONS

Freedom of the press is a cornerstone of the basic freedoms of the Constitution. In settling the Pentagon papers dispute between the *New York Times* and the U.S. government, the Supreme Court said:

> In the First Amendment the Founding Fathers gave the free press the protection it must have to fulfill its essential role in our democracy. The press was to serve the governed, not the governors. The Government's power to censor the press was abolished so that the press would remain forever free to censure the Government.[165]

That a free press is essential to the proper functioning of a democratic government was well established among the framers of the U.S. Constitution. Blackstone, the great English jurist, reflected these sentiments when he observed that "[t]he liberty of the press is indeed essential to the nature of a free state."[166] By the time the First Amendment was written by Madison, "[f]reedom of the press had become part . . . of government and the protection of civil liberties."[167]

The press, though, does have some limitations that have been debated over the years. It was maintained by Alexander Hamilton in 1804 that freedom of the press "consists of the right to publish, with impunity, truth, with good motives, for justifiable ends, though reflecting on government, magistracy, or individuals."[168] The expectation that the press would endeavor to be truthful, publish with proper motivation, without malice, for appropriate ends is a standard that the press has had difficulty in maintaining. Because what constitutes proper motives, appropriate ends, and truth rests largely in the eye of the beholder, much litigation has ensued in defining the role that the press will play in society. Truth and proper motives, especially in the discussion of politics, have always been a nebulous and largely unenforceable standard. That the freedom of the press is to be defended on the basis of truth is thus an unsatisfactory condition. Thompson early observed that to maintain truth as a defense is like asking a jury to decide which is "the most palatable food, agreeable drink, or beautiful color."[169] In spite of the problems with proving truth

in defense of publication, this standard prevailed in 1964, when the U.S. Supreme Court in *New York Times v. Sullivan* held that public persons could not succeed in a libel action against the press by compelling the defense to show truth and good motives.[170] Today, an action for the publication of falsehoods can be maintained by private persons against the press, but public persons must prove that the newspaper published with malicious intent, a very difficult burden to sustain.

The courts have always been particularly suspicious of prior restraint; that is, when a publication is censored before it can reach the street. The historical view has been that the freedom of thought and enquiry should be subject not to previous restraints, but only to subsequent redress through civil or criminal action after publication. McKean, in 1797, observed that "[e]very free man has an undoubted right to lay what sentiments he pleases before the public . . . but take the consequences."[171]

The issue of prior restraint versus retrospective redress has been largely obviated by the Supreme Court decision in the Pentagon papers case.[172] Today, there is no question that government cannot exercise prior restraint, except possibly in the most extreme circumstance, when the governmental interest is so absolutely compelling that there is little doubt that the health and safety of the people will be harmed.

Freedom of press in the public schools, however, is governed by a different set of constitutional precedents. Regulation of student newspapers is subject to the Supreme Court decision in *Hazelwood School District v. Kuhlmeier*,[173] in which the Court distinguished government censorship of publications outside schools from that of student newspapers. Here the Court ruled that prior restraint was permissible because the student newspaper was not a "public forum" and the restraint was reasonably related to a valid educational purpose. The Court found that the "material and substantial disruption" standard of *Tinker* did not apply because in *Hazelwood* the student newspaper was school sponsored, whereas in *Tinker* free expression was exhibited by armbands that were not school sponsored, but instead were individual political expression. The Court said,

"[W]e conclude that the standard articulated in *Tinker* for determining when a school may punish student expression need not also be the standard for determining when a school may refuse to lend its name and resources to the dissemination of student expression."[174]

The Court thus removed the *Tinker* burden of proof from school officials with regard to regulation of student newspapers.

In spite of *Hazelwood*, however, school officials do not have an entirely free hand in censorship of student newspapers. School officials are not permitted to exercise powers of censorship merely as a matter of taste or fancy.[175] Rather, school determinations should be based on a school rule that advances an educational purpose and is uniformly enforced.[176] Without such rules, coupled with proper enforcement, substantive due process rights may be implicated.[177]

The Supreme Court has identified two "evils" of prior restraint provisions that must be avoided by school policies and practices. "First, a regulation that places 'unbridled discretion' in the hands of a government official constitutes a prior restraint and may result in censorship."[178] The courts have said that school officials must have valid reasons for rejecting an article, such as one that has potential for disruption or is obscene. Such evaluations by school officials must be content-neutral. A second evil that schools must avoid is to collect and hold materials indefinitely, thereby frustrating publication with an official nonresponse. With regard to this second evil, school policy must provide for reasonable time limits within which the school official must make a decision as to whether the proposed publication is allowable. Prior review must be done in an expeditious manner; to permit otherwise would allow the official to simply ice the process and hold the material indefinitely. Normally, prior restraint is not *per se* unconstitutional, yet at least one court has held prior restraint to be *per se* unconstitutional.[179] Other courts have found prior restraint to be constitutional only if accompanied by specific standards and procedural safeguards, such as expedited review and due process.[180]

Therefore, while it is essential to our democracy that government not have the authority to censor the press, school districts are viewed differently and are given particularized leeway to exercise limited controls over student publications. The districts' authority derives from the historical special legal relationships between schools and students. The Supreme Court in *Bethel* explained that the relationships between students and public schools must be viewed differently than those between private press and government generally. "[T]he First Amendment rights of students in the public schools are not automatically coextensive with the rights of adults in other settings and must be applied in light of the special characteristics of the school environment."[181]

FORUM ANALYSIS OF *HAZELWOOD*

Tinker v. Des Moines makes it quite clear that students have a constitutional right of freedom of political expression, speech, and press that cannot be encroached upon by the school unless the exercise of this right "materially and substantially" disrupts the school or is such that there can be a "reasonable forecast of material and substantial disruption." This *Tinker* test for the protection of speech and expression has, however, been more clearly circumscribed by subsequent Supreme Court decisions. The most important precedent in this regard is *Bethel v. Fraser* (discussed above),[182] in which the Court permitted restraint of speech and advanced what has become known as the "forum analysis" in determining the permissible limits of speech restraint in public schools.

The "public forum" precedent advanced by the Supreme Court in *Hague v. C. I. O.*[183] and later refined by other courts has enunciated three types of forums and has described the restrictions that can be imposed under each. The first type is a "'traditional public forum,' which [has] immemorially been held in trust for use of the public and . . . [has] been used for the purposes of assembly communicating thoughts between citizens, and discussing public questions."[184] This forum has generally been applied to areas such as sidewalks and parks. In this type of forum, a speaker's speech may be withdrawn only because of a compelling state interest. The reason for such restraint must be narrowly drawn and must pass muster under a strict scrutiny analysis.

The second type is a "limited public forum." Here the forum is created when the state opens its property for public use. A school is generally assumed not to be a limited public forum unless school officials purposely open the school for public use. A limited forum will not be found to exist in a public school unless (1) there is a governmental interest in creating such a forum or (2) outsiders seek access to the school and there is evidence that wide access has been otherwise granted. The state is not required to create this type of forum, but once created, it is subject to the same regulations as a public forum, and any restraint on speech must pass a strict scrutiny analysis.

The third forum is the "nonpublic forum," or "closed forum." This forum exists when the state does not open public property for indiscriminate public use. "Control over access to a nonpublic forum can be based on subject matter and speaker identity so long as the distinctions drawn are reasonable in light of the purpose served by the forum and are viewpoint neutral."[185] In a nonpublic forum, the regulations as to time, place, and manner may also be applicable. The governmental agency must apply the content-neutral standard; in other words, all content must be treated the same.[186]

Most recently, the courts have tended to dissect the speech and expression issue by determining the type of forum in which the speech and expression are exercised. The result has been a tendency for courts to increasingly bypass the *Tinker* "material and substantial disruption" test in favor of the forum analysis of free speech. With *Bethel,* the rights enunciated in *Tinker* were substantially clarified.[187]

In 1988, the Supreme Court further clarified the rights of student expression in *Hazelwood v. Kuhlmeier*[188] and applied the distinctions in the types of forums. The essential question in *Hazelwood* became then, according to the Supreme Court, What was "the forum for the public expression"? The Court ruled that educators do not offend student expression by exercising editorial control over school-sponsored newspapers as long as the educators or school board has a legitimate pedagogical reason to prohibit such expression. Should a school have educational concerns about curricular activities involving student expression, it need not lend its name or resources to these activities. Thus, freedom of expression in school study newspapers is not today controlled by the *Tinker* standard of "material and substantial disruption."

CATEGORIES OF PUBLICATIONS

In addition to the forum considerations, the courts will usually determine the permissible limits of restraint based on the type of publication affected. Litigation concerning student publications has fallen into four categories: (1) school-sponsored newspapers; (2) nonschool, or underground, newspapers written and distributed by students; (3) materials distributed by students at school but written and published by nonstudents; and (4) the Internet.

School-Sponsored Publications

The Supreme Court in *Hazelwood v. Kuhlmeier*[189] found that school-sponsored publications require a different test for prior restraint than nonschool publications. The *Hazelwood* decision permitted the school administration to control or censor a school-sponsored paper. Nonschool publications may be regulated only by time, place, and manner of distribution; they cannot be regulated as to content. The time, place, and manner restrictions of student publications are contingent upon the school having created a limited public forum as opposed to a nonpublic or closed forum.

In *Hazelwood,* plaintiffs challenged a high school principal's deletion of two articles written by students on the subjects of student pregnancy and divorce. The principal refused to allow the articles to be printed in the high school newspaper. The Court said the high school newspaper published by the journalism students could not be characterized as a "public forum"; therefore, school officials retained the right to exercise reasonable restraint upon what went into the newspaper. School newspapers, theatrical productions, and other expressions that are perceived to "bear the imprimatur" of the school are all considered nonpublic forums.[190]

Underground Publications

Hazelwood distinguished those publications that are not officially school connected and those that are school sponsored.

If a school permits nonschool materials to be distributed, then a limited public forum has been created. When such a forum has been established, the restrictions established by school officials must be content-neutral. The school may place appropriate time, place, and manner restrictions on access to school grounds, but it cannot control the content, as is permitted with school-sponsored publications.

A case in point is *Burch v. Barker*,[191] wherein students distributed a student-written four-page newspaper entitled *Bad Astra*. The paper was critical of the school administration but included no profanity, obscenity, or defamatory statements. School policy required that all nonschool publications be submitted to the principal for prior approval. Since this was not a school-sponsored publication, *Hazelwood* did not apply; therefore, the paper was "not within the purview of the school's exercise of reasonable editorial control."[192] Using *Tinker* as precedent, the court ruled that the prior approval aspect of the policy violated the Constitution by suppressing speech. The court said: "[S]uppressing speech before it is uttered, as opposed to punishment of individuals after expression has occurred, is prior restraint, which generally comes before a court bearing a 'heavy assumption' of unconstitutionality."[193]

Religious Publications

A number of recent cases have concerned the distribution of religious material on school campuses. In these cases, the students have attempted to distribute religious newsletters written by nonstudents. One court has ruled students may not distribute the Gideon Bible in school,[194] but other court decisions have not been uniform when it comes to distributing other religious materials, such as newsletters. These cases have juxtaposed free speech protections and establishment clause restrictions, with some uncertainty as to the prevailing precedent.

Some of the cases have been decided on the basis of the previously discussed limited public forum question. In these cases, the schools have been found to be closed forums. According to *Hazelwood*, if school officials have opened the school to "indiscriminate use," then the school becomes a public forum, and a "limited public forum" may be created.[195] If this is the situation, then denial of the right to distribute religious materials may be unconstitutional.[196]

School officials may exercise editorial control over school-sponsored publications if they have a legitimate pedagogical reason. If there are nonschool publications and the school has created a "limited public forum," then the school officials may control only the time, place, and manner of distribution, but not content. If a school policy requires that students submit materials before distribution, then strong due process procedures must be in place, or the policy is vulnerable to prior restraint challenge.

Internet and Free Speech

As yet, the law governing the use of the Internet by schools is in its infancy. Substantial uncertainty exists as to the degree to which a school can control Internet speech. We do know that the U.S. Supreme Court has held in *Reno*[197] that the Internet as a medium of communication is fully protected by the First Amendment and is more directly related to print than to broadcast. The Internet, however, because of its ubiquitous nature does not fit neatly into First Amendment precedents regarding freedom of speech and press. Internet instruction used as a part of the school education program may be regulated by the school in accordance with *Hazelwood*.[198] Yet, student use of the Internet outside the school instructional program may well be beyond the reach of school regulation. A student can be a content provider with electronic publication emanating from many sites—school, home, or any other location. Regardless of the originating site, however, the content conveyed may have an undesirable effect on the proper conduct of the school. One can easily see the nearly unlimited possibilities of Internet-conveyed insults and invective launched from remote locations that may denigrate and embarrass students, teachers, and school administrators, with the potential for harmful effects on the good conduct of the school.

Therefore, the nature of electronic conveyance of questionable content does not lend itself to the usual legal questions arising out of litigation regarding "prior restraint." With the Internet, the school would seldom be in a position to pre-empt or censor publication of undesirable material. Presumably, most Internet litigation will arise beyond the "purview of the school's exercise of reasonable editorial control," leaving the Internet to be classified under the *Hazelwood* criteria as a public forum or a limited public forum, as would be an underground publication. If the facts of a case indicate that Internet publication is not school sponsored and does not bear the imprimatur of the school, then the conveyance of information would not be subject to school control.

The public forum analysis of *Hazelwood* does not, however, answer several questions. The foremost issue is, of course, raised by the fact that the Internet user does not need the school's permission for nonschool materials to be distributed in order to establish a limited public forum. Students can access a website regardless of the school's acquiescence. Moreover, the school's authority to determine the appropriate "time, place, and manner" of distribution of a hard-copy publication on campus is hardly applicable where electronic communication is concerned.

Therefore, the uniqueness of electronic publication portends the emergence of new precedents not addressed by *Hazelwood*. In seeking more firm ground of precedent, the federal district court in Missouri in *Beussink*[199] reverted to *Tinker v. Des Moines*[200] in determining the constitutional appropriateness of a school's disciplinary action against a student who posted a homepage on the Internet that criticized the school and included "crude and vulgar language."[201] The *Tinker*[202] test, which requires the school to show that the exercise of free speech "would materially and substantially interfere" with the operation of the school, was applied in *Beussink.* Here the school principal made no claim and gave no testimony to indicate that the disciplinary measure was taken against the student out of fear of disruption or interference with school discipline.[203]

Without further guidance from higher federal courts to the contrary, the prevailing view appears to be that the courts will resolve Internet disputes between students and schools by relying on the *Tinker* rationale in preference to the *Hazelwood* reasoning.

❖ — ❖ — ❖

Schools May Regulate the Content of School-Sponsored Newspapers

Hazelwood School District v. Kuhlmeier

Supreme Court of the United States, 1988.
484 U.S. 260, 108 S.Ct. 562.

Justice WHITE delivered the opinion of the Court. This case concerns the extent to which educators may exercise editorial control over the contents of a high school newspaper produced as part of the school's journalism curriculum.

Petitioners are the Hazelwood School District in St. Louis County, Missouri, [and] various school officials. . . . Respondents are three former Hazelwood East students who were staff members of *Spectrum,* the school newspaper. They contend that school officials violated their First Amendment rights by deleting two pages of articles from the May 13, 1983, issue of *Spectrum.*

Spectrum was written and edited by the Journalism II class at Hazelwood East. The newspaper was published every three weeks or so during the 1982–1983 school year. More than 4,500 copies of the newspaper were distributed during that year to students, school personnel, and members of the community.

The Board of Education allocated funds from its annual budget for the printing of *Spectrum.* These funds were supplemented by proceeds from sales of the newspaper. The printing expenses during the 1982–1983 school year totaled $4,668.50; revenue from sales was $1,166.84. The other costs associated with the newspaper—such as supplies, textbooks, and a portion of the journalism teacher's salary—were borne entirely by the Board.

The Journalism II course was taught by Robert Stergos for most of the 1982–1983 academic year. Stergos left Hazelwood East to take a job in private industry on April 29, 1983, when the May 13 edition of *Spectrum* was nearing completion, and petitioner Emerson took his place as newspaper adviser for the remaining weeks of the term.

The practice at Hazelwood East during the spring 1983 semester was for the journalism teacher to submit page proofs of each *Spectrum* issue to Principal Reynolds for his review prior to publication. On May 10, Emerson delivered the proofs of the May 13 edition to Reynolds, who objected to two of the articles scheduled to appear in that edition. One of the stories described three Hazelwood East students' experiences with pregnancy; the other discussed the impact of divorce on students at the school.

Reynolds was concerned that, although the pregnancy story used false names "to keep the identity of these girls a secret," the pregnant students still might be identifiable from the text. He also believed that the article's references to sexual activity and birth control were inappropriate for some of the younger students at the school. In addition, Reynolds was concerned that a student identified by name in the divorce story had complained that her father "wasn't spending enough time with my mom, my sister and I" prior to the divorce, "was always out of town on business or out late playing cards with the guys," and "always argued about everything" with her mother. . . . Reynolds believed that the student's parents should have been given an opportunity to respond to these remarks or to consent to their publication. He was unaware that Emerson had deleted the student's name from the final version of the article.

Reynolds believed that there was no time to make the necessary changes in the stories before the scheduled press run and that the newspaper would not appear before the end of the school year if printing were delayed to any significant extent. He concluded that his only options under the circumstances were to publish a four-page newspaper instead of the planned six-page newspaper, eliminating the two pages on which the offending stories appeared, or to publish no newspaper at all. Accordingly, he directed Emerson to withhold from publication the two pages containing the stories on pregnancy and divorce. He informed his superiors of the decision, and they concurred.

Respondents subsequently commenced this action in the United States District Court. . . .

Students in the public schools do not "shed their constitutional rights to freedom of speech or expression at the schoolhouse gate." . . . They cannot be punished merely for expressing their personal views on the school premises— whether "in the cafeteria, or on the playing field, or on the campus during the authorized hours," . . . unless school authorities have reason to believe that such expression will "substantially interfere with the work of the school or impinge upon the rights of other students."

We have nonetheless recognized that the First Amendment rights of students in the public schools "are not automatically coextensive with the rights of adults in other settings," *Bethel School District No. 403 v. Fraser*, 478 U.S. 765, 106 S.Ct. 3159, 3164, 92 L.Ed.2d 549 (1986), and must be "applied in light of the special characteristics of the school environment." . . . A school need not tolerate student speech that is inconsistent with its "basic educational mission," . . . even though the government could not censor similar speech outside the school. Accordingly, we held in *Fraser* that a student could be disciplined for having delivered a speech that was "sexually explicit" but not legally obscene at an official school assembly, because the school was entitled to "disassociate itself" from the speech in a manner that would demonstrate to others that such vulgarity is "wholly inconsistent with the 'fundamental values' of public school education." We thus recognized that "[t]he determination of what manner of speech in the classroom or in school assembly is inappropriate properly rests with the school board," . . . rather than with the federal courts. It is in this context that respondents' First Amendment claims must be considered.

We deal first with the question whether *Spectrum* may appropriately be characterized as a forum for public expression. The public schools do not possess all of the attributes of streets, parks, and other traditional public forums that "time out of mind, have been used for purposes of assembly, communicating thoughts between citizens, and discussing public questions." . . . Hence, school facilities may be deemed to be public forums only if school authorities have "by policy or by practice" opened those facilities "for indiscriminate use by the general public," . . . or by some segment of the public, such as student organizations. . . . If the facilities have instead been reserved for other intended purposes, "communicative or otherwise," then no public forum has been created, and school officials may impose reasonable restrictions on the speech of students, teachers, and other members of the school community. "The government does not create a public forum by inaction or by permitting limited discourse, but only by intentionally opening a nontraditional forum for public discourse." . . .

The policy of school officials toward *Spectrum* was reflected in Hazelwood School Board Policy 348.51 and the Hazelwood East Curriculum Guide. Board Policy 348.51 provided that "[s]chool sponsored publications are developed within the adopted curriculum and its educational implications in regular classroom activities." . . . The Hazelwood East Curriculum Guide described the Journalism II course as a "laboratory situation in which the students publish the school newspaper applying skills they have learned in Journalism I." The lessons that were to be learned from the Journalism II course, according to the Curriculum Guide, included development of journalistic skills under deadline pressure, "the legal, moral, and ethical restrictions imposed upon journalists within the school community," and "responsibility and acceptance of criticism for articles of opinion." Journalism II was taught by a faculty member during regular class hours. Students received grades and academic credit for their performance in the course.

School officials did not deviate in practice from their policy that production of *Spectrum* was to be part of the educational curriculum and a "regular classroom activit[y]." The District Court found that Robert Stergos, the journalism teacher during most of the 1982–1983 school year, "both had the authority to exercise and in fact exercised a great deal of control over *Spectrum*." . . . For example, Stergos selected the editors of the newspaper, scheduled publication dates, decided the number of pages for each issue, assigned story ideas to class members, advised students on the development of their stories, reviewed the use of quotations, edited stories, selected and edited the letters to the editor, and dealt with the printing company. Many of these decisions were made without consultation with the Journalism II students. The District Court thus found it "clear that Mr. Stergos was the final authority with respect to almost every aspect of the production and publication of *Spectrum*, including its content." Moreover, after each *Spectrum* issue had been finally approved by Stergos or his successor, the issue still had to be reviewed by Principal Reynolds prior to publication. Respondents' assertion that they had believed that they could publish "practically anything" in *Spectrum* was therefore dismissed by the District Court as simply "not credible." These factual findings are amply supported by the record, and were not rejected as clearly erroneous by the Court of Appeals. . . .

School officials did not evince either "by policy or by practice" . . . any intent to open the pages of *Spectrum* to "indiscriminate use," by its student reporters and editors, or by the student body generally. Instead, they "reserve[d] the forum for its intended purpos[e]," . . . as a supervised learning experience for journalism students. Accordingly, school officials were entitled to regulate the contents of *Spectrum* in any reasonable manner. It is this standard, rather than our decision in *Tinker*, that governs this case.

The question whether the First Amendment requires a school to tolerate particular student speech—the question that we addressed in *Tinker*—is different from the question whether the First Amendment requires a school affirmatively to promote particular student speech. The former question addresses educators' ability to silence a student's personal expression that happens to occur on the school premises. The latter question concerns educators' authority over school-sponsored publications, theatrical productions, and other expressive activities that students, parents, and members of the public might reasonably perceive to bear the imprimatur of the school. These activities may fairly be characterized as part of the school curriculum, whether or not they occur in a traditional classroom setting, so long as they are supervised by faculty members and designed to impart particular knowledge or skills to student participants and audiences.

Educators are entitled to exercise greater control over this second form of student expression to assure that participants learn whatever lessons the activity is designed to teach, that readers or listeners are not exposed to material that may be inappropriate for their level of maturity, and that the views of the individual speaker are not erroneously attributed to the school. Hence, a school may in its capacity as publisher of a school newspaper or producer of a school play "disassociate itself," . . . not only from speech that would "substantially interfere with [its] work . . . or impinge upon the rights of other students," . . . but also from speech that is, for example, ungrammatical, poorly written, inadequately researched, biased or prejudiced, vulgar or profane, or unsuitable for immature audiences. A school must be able to set high standards for the student speech that is disseminated under its auspices—standards that may be higher than those demanded by some newspaper publishers or theatrical producers in the "real" world—and may refuse to disseminate student speech that does not meet those standards. In addition, a school must be able to take into account the emotional maturity of the intended audience in determining whether to disseminate student speech on potentially sensitive topics, which might range from the existence of Santa Claus in an elementary school setting to the particulars of teenage sexual activity in a high school setting. A school must also retain the authority to refuse to sponsor student speech that might reasonably be perceived to advocate drug or alcohol use, irresponsible sex, or conduct otherwise inconsistent with "the shared values of a civilized social order." . . . or to associate the school with any position other than neutrality on matters of political controversy. Otherwise, the schools would be unduly constrained from fulfilling their role as "a principal instrument in awakening the child to cultural values, in preparing him for later professional training, and in helping him to adjust normally to his environment." . . .

Accordingly, we conclude that the standard articulated in *Tinker* for determining when a school may punish student expression need not also be the standard for determining when a school may refuse to lend its name and resources to the dissemination of student expression. Instead, we hold that educators do not offend the First Amendment by exercising editorial control over the style and content of student speech in school-sponsored expressive activities so long as their actions are reasonably related to legitimate pedagogical concerns.

This standard is consistent with our oft-expressed view that the education of the Nation's youth is primarily the responsibility of parents, teachers, and state and local school officials, and not of federal judges. . . . It is only when the decision to censor a school-sponsored publication, theatrical production, or other vehicle of student expression has no valid educational purpose that the First Amendment is so "directly and sharply implicate[d]" as to require judicial intervention to protect students' constitutional rights.

We also conclude that Principal Reynolds acted reasonably in requiring the deletion from the May 13 issue of *Spectrum* of the pregnancy article, the divorce article, and the remaining articles that were to appear on the same pages of the newspaper.

The initial paragraph of the pregnancy article declared that "[a]ll names have been changed to keep the identity of these girls a secret." The principal concluded that the students' anonymity was not adequately protected, however, given the other identifying information in the article and the small number of pregnant students at the school. Indeed, a teacher at the school credibly testified that she could positively identify at least one of the girls and possibly all three. It is likely that many students at Hazelwood East would have been at least as successful in identifying the girls. Reynolds therefore could reasonably have feared that the article violated whatever pledge of anonymity had been given to the pregnant students. In addition, he could reasonably have been concerned that the article was not sufficiently sensitive to the privacy interests of the students' boyfriends and parents, who were discussed in the article but who were given no opportunity to consent to its publication or to offer a response. The article did not contain graphic accounts of sexual activity. The girls did comment in the article, however, concerning their sexual histories and their use or nonuse of birth control. It was not unreasonable for the principal to have concluded that such frank talk was inappropriate in a school-sponsored publication distributed to 14-year-old freshmen and presumably taken home to be read by students' even younger brothers and sisters.

The student who was quoted by name in the version of the divorce article seen by Principal Reynolds made comments sharply critical of her father. The principal could reasonably have concluded that an individual publicly identified as an inattentive parent—indeed, as one who chose "playing cards with the guys" over home and family—was entitled to an opportunity to defend himself as a matter of journalistic fairness. These concerns were shared by both of Spectrum's faculty advisers for the 1982–1983 school year, who testified that they would not have allowed the article to be printed without deletion of the student's name.

Principal Reynolds testified credibly at trial that, at the time that he reviewed the proofs of the May 13 issue during an extended telephone conversation with Emerson, he believed that there was no time to make any changes in the articles, and that the newspaper had to be printed immediately or not at all. It is true that Reynolds did not verify whether the necessary modifications could still have been made in the articles, and that Emerson did not volunteer the information that printing could be delayed until the changes were made. We nonetheless agree with the District Court that the decision to excise the two pages containing the problematic articles was reasonable given the particular circumstances of this case. These circumstances included the very recent replacement of Stergos by Emerson, who may not have been entirely familiar with Spectrum editorial and production procedures, and the pressure felt by Reynolds to make an immediate decision so that students would not be deprived of the newspaper altogether.

In sum, we cannot reject as unreasonable Principal Reynolds' conclusion that neither the pregnancy article nor the divorce article was suitable for publication in *Spectrum*. Reynolds could reasonably have concluded that the students who had written and edited these articles had not sufficiently mastered those portions of the Journalism II curriculum that pertained to the treatment of controversial issues and personal attacks, the need to protect the privacy of individuals whose most intimate concerns are to be revealed in the newspaper, and "the legal, moral, and ethical restrictions imposed upon journalists within [a] school community" that includes adolescent subjects and readers. Finally, we conclude that the principal's decision to delete two pages of *Spectrum*, rather than to delete only the offending articles or to require that they be modified, was reasonable under the circumstances as he understood them. Accordingly, no violation of First Amendment rights occurred.

The judgment of the Court of Appeals for the Eighth Circuit is therefore

Reversed.

CASE NOTES

1. *Religious Publications.* Once a school opens its doors to become a public forum, it is very difficult to justify exclusion of certain types of publications. In a case where school policy stated that the distribution of printed noncurricular materials was allowed subject to regulations and procedures unless material was "unacceptable" and where the policy further specified that "material that proselytizes a particular religious or political belief" was unacceptable, the court ruled the ban unlawful. The court found that the students had a right to engage in political and religious speech and that the school had no "compelling interest" in restricting such speech. *Rivera v. East Otero School District R-1*, 721 F.Supp. 1189 (D.Colo.1989). See also *Clark v. Dallas Independent School District*, 806 F.Supp. 116 (N.D.Tex.1992).

2. *Time, Place, and Manner.* In another case where the court used the public forum analysis, students wanted to distribute a newspaper, *Issues and Answers*, in the school hallways. The school policy, however, permitted distribution only outside the school building property. The court said the school hallways were nonpublic; therefore, the only applicable regulation was time, place, and manner. The students were, however, allowed to distribute outside the school building. The court observed: "Common sense dictates that the hallways would resemble a three ring circus" if distributions were allowed for all in the hallways. The court quoted Justice Black, who dissented in the famous *Tinker* case but was quoted in both *Bethel School District No.*

403 v. Fraser and *Hazelwood School District v. Kuhlmeier*: "I wish therefore, . . . to disclaim my purpose . . . to hold that the Federal Constitution compels the teachers, parents and elected officials to surrender control of the American public school system to public school students." *Hemry by Hemry v. School Board of Colorado Springs*, 760 F.Supp. 856 (D.Colo.1991).

In yet another case involving distribution of the newspaper *Issues and Answers*, the school policy on the distribution of nonschool materials was challenged. The court again used the free speech forum analysis in preference to the *Tinker* material and substantial disruption test. The court upheld the school policy that required that the materials first be approved by the principal. The court ruled the principal could determine time, place, and manner of distribution. The court also ruled that prior regulations prohibiting the distribution of political and religious literature violate the First Amendment's free speech clause. *Nelson v. Moline School District No. 40*, 725 F.Supp. 965 (C.D.Ill.1989). See also *Slotterback v. Interboro School District*, 766 F.Supp. 280 (E.D.Penn.1991), which used forum analysis.

3. *Underground Papers.* A school policy governing unofficial or underground newspapers and giving school officials the power to exercise prior review and restraint may be constitutionally valid. Thus, a school rule that prohibited publication of material that is pervasively indecent or vulgar was held permissible, though the terms were poorly defined and contained large elements of subjectivity to the extent that reasonable people might disagree as to the meaning. *Bystrom v. Fridley High School Independent School District No. 14*, 822 F.2d 747 (8th Cir.1987).

4. *Vagueness.* A school rule, though, may be too broad and so vague as to give school authorities unbridled discretion in exercising prior restraint. In *Burch v. Barker*, the ninth circuit held that a high school prior restraint policy was unconstitutional for lack of specificity on distribution and approval procedures, but, most important, the school policy was overly broad concerning the content-based requirements for the exercise of prior restraint. *Burch v. Barker*, 861 F.2d 1149 (9th Cir.1988).

❖ — ❖ — ❖

Homepage Created by Student at Home May Be Constitutionally Protected Speech

Beussink v. Woodland R-IV School District

U.S. District Court, Eastern District of Missouri, 1998.
30 F.Supp.2d 1175.

SIPPEL, District Judge.

This matter is before the Court on plaintiff's request for a preliminary injunction. A hearing on the request for a preliminary injunction was held on October 8, 1998.

Plaintiff, Brandon Beussink ("Beussink"), claims that the Woodland R-IV School District ("the Woodland School District") violated his rights under the First Amendment to the United States Constitution. Specifically, Beussink claims that the Woodland School District suspended him from school for ten days because he had posted a homepage on the Internet which was critical of Woodland High School. The homepage's criticism of the high school included crude and vulgar language.

The evidence presented at the hearing satisfies the standard for granting preliminary injunctive relief in Beussink's favor. The request for a preliminary injunction will be granted. . . .

Beussink is currently enrolled in the twelfth grade at Woodland High School. At the time of the events in the Complaint, he was a junior at the school. . . .

In early February 1998 Beussink created a homepage, which he posted on the Internet. The information in the homepage could be accessed by other Internet users.

There is no evidence that Beussink used school facilities or school resources to create his homepage. The homepage was created at home on Beussink's own computer. The homepage was not created during school hours. Beussink created the homepage using a program which he found on the Internet.

Beussink's homepage was highly critical of the administration at Woodland High School. Beussink used vulgar language to convey his opinion regarding the teachers, the principal and the school's own homepage. Beussink's homepage also invited readers to contact the school principal and communicate their opinions regarding Woodland High School. Beussink's homepage also contained a hyper-link that allowed a reader to access the school's homepage from Beussink's homepage.

Beussink testified that he did not intend the homepage to be accessed or viewed at Woodland High School. He just wanted to voice his opinion. There was no evidence presented at the hearing indicating that the homepage was accessed at Woodland High School prior to the events of February 17, 1998. . . .

Prior to February 17, 1998 Beussink allowed a friend, Amanda Brown, to use his home computer. While using Beussink's home computer, Ms. Brown saw Beussink's homepage. Ms. Brown testified that sometime after she first viewed Beussink's homepage, she had an argument with Beussink. Ms. Brown testified that she wanted to retaliate against Beussink because she was angry with him. On February 17, 1998 Amanda Brown, purposefully accessed Beussink's homepage during the second hour of school and showed it to Delma Ferrell, the computer teacher at Woodland High School.

Beussink was not with Brown when she accessed his homepage. Brown testified that she did not access the homepage at Beussink's request, with his authorization, or even with his knowledge. Beussink had not given the Internet address of his homepage to Amanda Brown.

At the time Brown accessed the homepage and showed it to Ms. Ferrell, there was only one other student in the room. That student did not view the screen and there was no evidence of a disturbance. . . .

Ms. Ferrell was upset by what she read on Beussink's homepage. Ms. Ferrell went directly to the school office to inform the principal, Mr. Yancy Poorman. Principal Poorman returned to the computer lab with Ms. Ferrell and viewed the homepage. Principal Poorman testified at the preliminary hearing that he and Ms. Ferrell were upset by the homepage. Principal Poorman further testified that he did not know at that time what the exact nature of the disciplinary measure would be, but he made the decision to discipline Beussink *immediately* upon viewing the homepage. Principal Poorman decided to discipline Beussink because he was upset that the homepage's message had been displayed in one of his classrooms. Principal Poorman made the decision to discipline Beussink before he knew whether any other students had seen or even had knowledge of the homepage. . . .

It is not clear how many times Beussink's homepage was seen at Woodland High School on that day. The testimony at the hearing indicated that Beussink's homepage was accessed as many as two other times that day. . . .

. . . [T]here was no evidence that Beussink showed the homepage to other students. Nor is there any evidence that there was a disturbance in the library on February 17, 1998.

Two class periods later, the computer teacher, Ms. Ferrell, apparently allowed some of the students in her fourth hour class to access the homepage. There is no evidence that Beussink was present in the classroom when this took place. There is no evidence that Beussink instigated the contact with his homepage in Ms. Ferrell's fourth hour class.

Ms. Ferrell testified that three of the students had located the homepage. Ms. Ferrell testified that the students accessed Beussink's homepage after she granted them permission to do so. Ms. Ferrell discussed the homepage with the students. Another group of students also found the homepage. Ms. Ferrell told them to exit the page. The students followed Ms. Ferrell's instructions. Ms. Ferrell was not aware of any other disruption to her classroom that day. . . .

Principal Poorman issued the first disciplinary notice to Beussink during the fourth period. This disciplinary notice suspended Beussink from school for five days. The notice was delivered to Beussink. . . .

. . . Principal Poorman issued a second disciplinary notice increasing Beussink's suspension period from 5 to 10 days. This second notice was delivered to Beussink during seventh hour. . . .

Beussink went to the school office to speak with Principal Poorman shortly after he received the second disciplinary notice. Principal Poorman did not reconsider the 10 day suspension. At this meeting, Principal Poorman told Beussink to "clean up" his home page or "clear it out". . . .

When he arrived home at the end of the school day, Beussink removed his homepage from the Internet. Beussink served the 10 day suspension. He returned to school after the suspension. Beussink has not reposted the homepage. . . .

The Woodland School District has an absenteeism policy which "drops" students' grades in each class by one letter grade for each unexcused absence in excess of ten days. Suspension days are considered unexcused absences. At the time of the suspension, Beussink had already accumulated 8.5 days of unexcused absence. The additional 10 days of suspension increased his number of unexcused absences to 18.5. Application of the absenteeism policy dropped Beussink's grades 8.5 grade levels.

Before applying the absenteeism policy, Beussink was failing two of his classes and passing four classes. Application of the absenteeism policy resulted in Beussink failing *all* of the classes in which he was enrolled for the second semester of his junior year.

The United States Supreme Court has made it clear that students do not shed their First Amendment rights at the schoolhouse gate. *Tinker v. Des Moines Indep. Community Sch. Dist.*, 393 U.S. 503, 506, 89 S.Ct. 733, 21 L.Ed.2d 731 (1969). It is equally clear, however, that a student's right to free speech is not without limitation. . . . Schools may limit student speech. But, any limitation on student speech is permissible only in narrowly defined circumstances.

> In order for the State in the person of school officials to justify prohibition of a particular expression of opinion, it must be able to show that its action was caused by something more than a mere desire to avoid the discomfort and unpleasantness that always accompany an unpopular viewpoint. Certainly where there is no finding and no showing that engaging in the forbidden conduct would 'materially and substantially interfere with the requirements of appropriate discipline in

the operation of the school,' the prohibition can not be sustained. . . .

While speech may be limited based upon a fear or projection of such disruption, that fear must be "reasonable" and not an "undifferentiated fear" of a disturbance. . . .

Principal Poorman testified at the preliminary injunction hearing that he made the determination to discipline Beussink *immediately* upon seeing the homepage. He was upset that the message had found its way into his school's classrooms. Principal Poorman's testimony does not indicate that he disciplined Beussink based on a fear of disruption or interference with school discipline (reasonable or otherwise.) Principal Poorman's own testimony indicates he disciplined Beussink because he was upset by the content of the homepage.

Disliking or being upset by the content of the student's speech is not an acceptable justification for limiting student speech under *Tinker*.

Beussink has demonstrated a likelihood for success on the merits of his First Amendment claim. . . .

Irreparable harm is established any time a movant's First Amendment rights are violated. . . . "The loss of First Amendment freedoms, for even minimal periods of time, unquestionably constitutes irreparable injury." . . . [I]t is likely that Beussink will be able to prove that his First Amendment rights were violated when he was disciplined by the Woodland School District. Additionally, Principal Poorman directed Beussink to "clean up" his homepage or remove it from the Internet. Beussink followed Principal Poorman's direction. As a result, any violation of Beussink's First Amendment rights is continuing.

Beussink also faces academic harm. Beussink's grades were dropped one grade level for each day his number of unexcused absences exceeded ten. The testimony at trial indicated that this resulted in Beussink failing four classes that he would not otherwise have failed. Beussink is currently a senior. The loss of these credits will potentially delay Beussink's graduation with his class at the end of this school year. . . .

Beussink's homepage did not materially and substantially interfere with school discipline. Further, there was no evidence to support a particularized reasonable fear of such interference. Beussink was disciplined for engaging in speech that this Court believes may be constitutionally protected speech.

The harm to Beussink if the injunction is not granted outweighs the harm to the Woodland School District if it is granted. . . .

When placed in the context . . . the evidence presented at the preliminary injunction hearing weighs in favor of issuing the preliminary injunctive relief sought by Beussink. Woodland School District will be enjoined from using the ten day suspension in its application of its absenteeism policy to Beussink's grades for the second semester of his junior year. Further the Woodland School District will be enjoined from enforcing any other sanction arising from Beussink's homepage which is the subject of this lawsuit. Finally, the Woodland School District will be enjoined from restricting Beussink's use of his home computer to repost that homepage. . . .

IT IS HEREBY ORDERED that plaintiff's request for preliminary injunctive relief is GRANTED. Defendant is hereby enjoined from using the ten day suspension, which is the subject of this lawsuit, in its application of the school's absenteeism policy to Beussink's grades for the second semester of Beussink's junior year. Further the Woodland School District will be enjoined from enforcing any other sanction arising from Beussink's homepage, which is the subject of this lawsuit. Finally, the Woodland School District is enjoined from restricting Beussink's use of his home computer to repost that homepage.

Case Note

The Internet and Free Speech. The regulation of telecommunications in preventing transmission of obscene or indecent communications to minors has become an important political issue at both the federal and the state levels. In an attempt to protect minors, persons under the age of eighteen, from undue exposure to offensive information, the U.S. Congress enacted the Communications Decency Act (CDA) in 1996. This act sought to control "cyberporn" and, thereby, to protect minors from harmful material on the Internet. The Congress, under CDA,

criminalized the "knowing" transmission of "obscene or indecent" messages to any recipient under eighteen years of age. The U.S. Supreme Court held the act to be unconstitutional because it was "facially overbroad" in violation of the First Amendment. The Court, while acknowledging that its own precedents in *Ginsberg v. New York*, 390 U.S. 629, 88 S.Ct. 1274 (1968), and *FCC v. Pacifica*, 438 U.S. 726, 98 S.Ct. 3026 (1978), permitted governmental restriction of certain materials to children, pointed out that this particular act (CDA) was too vague and ill-defined. The Supreme Court concluded that:

> [w]e are persuaded that the CDA lacks the precision that the First Amendment requires when a statute regulates the content of speech. In order to deny minors access to potentially harmful speech, the CDA effectively suppresses a large amount of speech that adults have a constitutional right to receive and to address to one another. That burden on adult speech is unacceptable if less restrictive alternatives would be at least as effective in achieving the legitimate purpose that the statute was enacted to serve.

The imprecision in the CDA statute came from the failure of the Congress to define "indecent" and "patently offensive" material. The Court observed that under the law as now written a parent could face a lengthy prison term for sending her seventeen-year-old college freshman daughter information about birth control by e-mail. *Reno v. American Civil Liberties Union*, 1997 WL 348012, 97 Cal. Daily Op.Serv. 4998 (1997).

■ Search and Seizure

The Fourth Amendment of the U.S. Constitution provides: "The right of people to be secure in their persons, houses, papers, and effects, against unreasonable searches and seizures shall not be violated, and no warrants shall issue, but upon probable cause. . . . "

To search or not to search a pupil's desk, locker, pockets, purse, book bag, coat, shoes and socks, and automobile is a question frequently confronting school administrators. Oftentimes, the issue must be decided forthwith because the gravity of the situation—bomb threats, dangerous weapons, illegal drugs—could result in serious injury to school pupils.[204]

The legality of search and seizure in the public schools balances primarily on whether the court views the school teacher or administrator as a parent or a police officer. To assume that the school administrator or teacher represents the state and seeks to obtain seized goods for purposes of criminal prosecution would require a warrant. A majority of the student search and seizure cases are initiated during criminal proceedings by students who are seeking suppression of evidence obtained through a search at school. The students are concerned that the contraband will be used against them in the criminal proceedings, but appear to be little concerned as to whether the items will be used for school administrative procedures, such as suspension or expulsion.

The Fourth Amendment has five important components. First, it enunciates and protects the *right* of people "to be secure in their persons, houses, papers and effects." Second, it protects persons from *unreasonable* searches and seizures. Third, it ensures that a search cannot be instituted without government showing *probable cause,* or giving evidence that a search is necessary. Fourth, it ensures that the search must be *specific,* describing the place to be searched and the articles to be seized. Last, it ensures that a *magistrate* or *judge* is interposed between the individual and the government, requiring that the government justify with evidence the necessity of the search.

Application of three of these five components is easily made to student searches in public schools. Students have a right of privacy—to be secure in their persons, papers, and effects—and this right protects them against unreasonable searches and seizures. Moreover, any search must be specific as to what is sought in the search and the location where it is secreted. The courts do not, however, require that school officials be able to provide evidence constituting probable cause or that they obtain a warrant from a judge justifying a search.

REASONABLE SUSPICION

School officials need have only "reasonable suspicion," a standard of proof less rigorous than the requirement of "probable cause, in order to conduct a legal search." Suspicion itself implies a belief or opinion based upon facts or circumstances that do not amount to proof.[205] Until James Madison composed the Fourth Amendment, the terms "reasonable suspicion," "reason to suspect," "sufficient foundation," and "probable cause" had been used more or less interchangeably. Virginia's recommendation for amendments to the proposed constitution, in 1788, used the words "legal and sufficient cause" for issuance of warrants.[206] "Probable cause," as used by Madison in the Fourth Amendment, "required more than mere suspicion or even reasonable suspicion."[207]

Although the standard of "reasonable suspicion" is a lower standard than that of "probable cause" (required for police to obtain a warrant), it is not so unrestrictive as to place no restraint on school personnel.[208] A New York court held that school personnel conducting a strip search of fifth-grade students after classroom thefts violated the children's Fourth Amendment rights because there were no acts that allowed school officials to particularize which student might have actually taken the money. The court maintained that there must be some available facts that together provide reasonable grounds to search, and the search must be conducted in order to further a legitimate school purpose, such as the maintenance of discipline in the school.

A student's freedom from unreasonable search and seizure must be balanced against the school officials' need to maintain order and discipline and to protect the health and welfare of all the students. Where an assistant principal threatened to call a student's parents, forcing the student to reluctantly, but voluntarily, empty his pockets, producing a pipe and marijuana, the court held that such a search was legitimate. Where the scope of intrusion is slight and there is no police involvement, school officials are held only to a "reasonable cause to believe" standard.[209]

The Supreme Court in *New Jersey v. T. L. O.* established the prevailing precedent regarding school searches and seizures. The Court in this case held that the Fourth Amendment does apply to schools and that in order for searches to be constitutionally valid, reasonableness must prevail. The Court stated that "the legality of a search of a student should depend on the reasonableness, under all circumstances, of the search."[210] According to the Court in *T. L. O.*, the constitutional validity of a search is to be determined at two levels. The first level involves consideration of whether the search is initially justified at its inception. The inception of the search is the point at which reasonable suspicion comes into play. Was the motivation for the search reasonable in light of the information obtained by the school official? The second level concerns the reasonableness of the search itself; the "measures adopted for the search must be reasonably related to the objectives of the search and not excessively intrusive in light of the age and sex of the student and the nature of the infraction."[211] A search is not reasonable if it lacks specificity or if it excessively intrudes on the student's privacy.

Inception of Search

The facts leading to the initiation of the search must indicate the suspicion was reasonable. In a case where a student was observed in an office where items had been stolen and was also found to have unauthorized objects concealed in his clothing, the court concluded that reasonable suspicion was established for a search of the student's locker.[212] In another case, reasonable suspicion was established where a school administrator had previously heard reports that a student was involved in drugs. A subsequent search of the student's locker and car revealed drugs and therefore was found reasonable and constitutional.[213]

In another drug case, a student's car was searched, revealing cocaine, after the assistant principal observed that the student had glassy eyes, a flushed face, and slurred speech; smelled of alcohol; and walked with an unsteady gait. The court found that this was ample evidence to support reasonable suspicion.[214]

Intrusiveness of Search

Whether a search is reasonable is a subjective determination, and the courts determine the standard on the individual facts of each case. It is clear, though, that excessively intrusive searches must be supported by a relatively strong degree of suspicion by the school officials. The courts will require a corresponding relationship between the extensiveness of grounds supporting reasonable suspicion and the degree to which a search intrudes on a student's privacy. Where money was missing from a schoolroom and a teacher searched the books of two students and then required them to remove their shoes, the court found that the fact that the two students had been alone in the room where the stolen money disappeared was sufficient to support reasonable suspicion to conduct a limited search.[215]

A more extensive and intrusive search, however, may require more evidence to establish reasonable suspicion. In a case where an assistant principal spied a boy carrying a small calculator case with an odd bulge, the principal searched the case and found marijuana. The court held that merely noticing a bulge was not sufficient to establish reasonable suspicion and pointed out that reasonable suspicion must be established by a clear articulation of facts, with rational inferences drawn from those facts, in order to warrant the conclusion of reasonable suspicion. This court noted that without having prior knowledge of the student's involvement in drug use, the mere observation of the calculator case was insufficient to establish a reason to suspect something illegal was hidden in the case.[216]

Where a girl was forced to remove her jeans and submit to visual inspection of her brassiere, the court held that the fact that she had ducked behind a car and had given a school security guard a false name was insufficient to establish reasonable suspicion. The court noted that without further specific information, the school had no more reason to believe that the girl was hiding drugs than to believe that she was skipping class, stealing hubcaps, or doing anything else, legal or illegal.[217]

Context of Search

Further, the courts have held that "what is reasonable depends on the context within which the search takes place."[218] A context indicating a loosely articulated factual background that is not necessarily related to a specific violation is too nebulous to support "reasonable suspicion." The lack of specificity in a wide search of large groups of students without specific knowledge of rule violations by any particular student is not reasonable.[219] Some individualized suspicion is essential as a prerequisite to a constitutional search. One court has cautioned that even though general searches are easier and may be more effective in finding illegal contraband, such searches will not survive the reasonableness test without individualized suspicion unless other safeguards are available to ensure respect for individual privacy.[220]

Guidelines for Searches

These precedents therefore suggest that even though school officials must adhere to the lesser standards of "reasonable suspicion" rather than "probable cause," the courts will nevertheless be vigilant in scrutinizing the conditions attendant to school searches. Certain conclusions can be drawn that provide guidelines governing school searches:

1. Students have a right to privacy of their persons, papers, and effects.
2. In determining whether a search is reasonable, the courts will consider the magnitude of the offense and extent of the intrusiveness on the student's privacy.
3. To establish reasonable suspicion justifying the inception of a search requires that the school official have some evidence regarding the particular situation, including possibly the background of the student, that would lead to the conclusion that something is hidden in violation of school rules.
4. A search must be supported by *specificity* as to the offense and by a particularized knowledge as to where the illegal contraband is located as well as to the identity of the offending student. This guideline is taken from the Fourth Amendment, which states that issuance of a warrant is dependent on particularity: "describing the place to be searched, and the persons or things to be seized."[221]

CANINE SEARCHES

It should be noted that canine search cases predate the U.S. Supreme Court case of *New Jersey v. T. L. O.* Using the standards in *T. L. O.*, it appears that individual suspicion or a very high risk to the health and safety of the student body would be required to justify a canine search. Even before *T. L. O.*, the courts viewed the canine search cases from differing legal perspectives, with mixed results as to what the Constitution required.

The Tenth Circuit Court of Appeals in *Zamora v. Pomeroy*[222] upheld the use of dogs in the exploratory sniffing of lockers. The court noted that since the schools gave notice at the beginning of the year that the lockers might be periodically opened, the lockers were jointly possessed by student and school. The court further stated that since the school officials have a duty to maintain a proper educational environment, it is necessary for them to inspect lockers and, even though there might be a slight Fourth Amendment infringement, it was not significant.

The seventh circuit in *Doe v. Renfrow*[223] held that school officials stand *in loco parentis* and have a right to use dogs to seek out drugs, especially because of the diminished expectations of privacy inherent in the public schools. School officials have a duty to maintain an educational environment that is conducive to learning. This decision may be contrary to *New Jersey v. T. L. O.*, in which the Supreme Court expressly limited the application of *in loco parentis*.

In the federal district court case of *Jones v. Latexo Independent School District*,[224] the decision was different from those in *Doe* and *Zamora*. The school district in *Jones* used dogs to sniff both students and automobiles. The court ruled that, in the absence of individual suspicion, the sniffing of the students is too intrusive and not reasonable. Because the students did not have access to their automobiles during the school day, the school's interest in sniffing the cars was minimal, and therefore also unreasonable.

In *Horton v. Goose Creek Independent School District*,[225] the court stated, "The problem presented in this case is convergence of two troubling questions. First, is the sniff of a drug-detecting dog a 'search' within the purview of the Fourth Amendment? Second, to what extent does the Fourth Amendment protect students against searches by school administrators seeking to maintain a safe environment conducive to education?"[226] In response to the first question, the court stated, "We accordingly hold that the sniff of the lockers and cars did not constitute a search and, therefore, we need make no inquiry into the reasonableness of the sniffing of the lockers and automobiles."[227] Concerning the second question, the court ruled that school officials may search students if they have "reasonable cause," but "the intrusion on dignity and personal security that goes with the type of canine inspection of the student's person involved in this case cannot be justified by the need to prevent abuse of drugs and alcohol when there is no individualized suspicion; and we hold it unconstitutional."[228]

One court pointed out how constitutionally invasive and educationally ludicrous it was for school officials to subject a young girl to a strip search simply because a dog had pinpointed her as the result of a sniff search. This court ruled that neither reasonable suspicion nor probable cause could be established based merely on the veracity of a dog's identification.

STRIP SEARCHES

School officials can search a student if they have reasonable suspicion that the student is in possession of some illegal contraband or is secreting something that may be harmful to other students. During the 1980s, the courts ruled in the majority of cases that strip searches are too intrusive and therefore violate the Fourth Amendment. The rule of law is that the more intrusive the search is, the more necessary it is to show probable cause rather than merely reasonable suspicion. In many cases, the strip searches were undertaken to recover stolen money or contraband of relatively minor significance. In *Bellnier v. Lund*,[229] a court ruled that a teacher's search for money was so intrusive as to exceed the reasonable suspicion standard, and thereby violated the Fourth Amendment. In 1995, in *Oliver v. McClung*,[230] a court ruled it unreasonable to strip-search a class of seventh-grade girls to recover four dollars and fifty cents. In both *Bellnier* and *Oliver,* the court noted that the relatively slight danger of the missing money has to be considered and, if something more dangerous were at stake, the result might be different. The court said: "It does not require a constitutional scholar to conclude that a nude search of a thirteen-year-old child is an invasion of constitutional rights of some magnitude. More than that; It is a violation of any known principle of human decency. Apart from any constitutional readings and rulings, simple common sense would be, in permitting such a nude

search, not only unlawful but outrageous under settled indisputable principles of law."[231]

On the other hand, the pervasiveness of drugs in American society and their deleterious effects on the schools have led some courts to give school officials increasing latitude in the conduct of searches.[232] Strip searches have been upheld where reasonable suspicion was established by word of mouth among school employees and students, bulges in clothes, and other indications of concealment of drugs.

METAL DETECTOR SEARCHES

In order to provide for an appropriate and safe educational environment, some schools have been forced to use metal detectors to discover knives, guns, and other weapons. When a weapon is detected, the student possessing the weapon may be arrested, and subsequent legal action by the student usually involves search-and-seizure constraints of the Fourth Amendment. To date, three cases have been reported concerning the constitutionality of metal detector screening in the public schools. All three cases have upheld the constitutionality of random metal detector searches based on the reasonable rationale that such is necessary for a safe school environment.

In one of the cases, *In re F. B.*,[233] a student in a Philadelphia school was found to be carrying a folding knife. After being arrested, he filed a motion to have the seized evidence suppressed, claiming the search was unreasonable in that there existed no reasonable individual suspicion at the inception of the search. In applying the reasonableness factors of the *T. L. O.* case, the court found the search was justified at the inception due to the high rate of violence in the Philadelphia schools. Moreover, the search was considered to be reasonable and constitutional because there was no way of knowing whether a student had a weapon prior to entering the building. In a similar case,[234] metal detector screening was conducted in a Chicago high school when the Chicago Police Department thought it was needed. In one such search, a student was found to have a loaded .38-caliber handgun in his pants, and he was arrested. The court upheld the validity of the search and said "we find . . . the screening satisfied the Fourth Amendment reasonableness test established in

T. L. O.: The action was justified at its inception by the reality of violence in the schools; the search as conducted was reasonably related in scope to the circumstances which justified the interference in the first place."[235]

In a third case, the New York City Board of Education established guidelines for the use of metal detectors in a high school that required a team of special police officers from a central task force. In implementing these guidelines, police officers set up a scanning post in a school's main lobby. All students entering the school were subject to the search, and the officers could choose to limit the search by any random formula if the waiting lines became too long. In the process of the search, a student was found to be carrying a switchblade knife. She was charged with criminal possession of a weapon, a Class A misdemeanor; the student filed an action to suppress the evidence. The court held that an administrative search is reasonable when the intrusion involved in the search is no greater than necessary to satisfy the governmental interest underlying the need for the search. In other words, in determining whether a search is reasonable, the courts balance the degree of intrusion, including the discretion given to the person conducting the search, against the severity of the damages posed. In this case, the court found the metal detector search satisfied the balancing test and was not unreasonable because the school had a compelling need for security.[236] Thus, as in other areas of the law, a balancing test of reasonableness will be the primary determinant of the constitutionality validity of such searches.

EXCLUSIONARY RULE

School officials should be primarily concerned with removing danger from the school environment and not with criminal prosecution of students *per se*. Because materials seized in public schools are frequently illegal and may be turned over to law enforcement officials, the exclusionary rule has been often raised. Can illegal materials seized by school officials be used in criminal prosecutions?

In 1914, in *Weeks v. United States*,[237] the Supreme Court established that evidence (in this instance, lottery tickets, private letters, and papers) seized without a warrant cannot be used in federal courts for federal prosecution. This doctrine, the *Weeks* doctrine, thereafter excluded evidence obtained illegally by federal officials from use in federal trials.

In *Wolf v. People of the State of Colorado* in 1949,[238] the question arose concerning the issue of whether materials illegally seized could be used in state courts. The question was:

> Does a conviction by a state court for a state offense deny the "due process of law" required by the Fourteenth Amendment, solely because evidence that was admitted at the trial was obtained under circumstances which would have rendered it inadmissible in a prosecution for violation of a federal law in a court of the United States because there deemed to be an infraction of the Fourth Amendment as applied in *Weeks v. United States*.[239]

The court reasoned that the *Weeks* doctrine did not apply to states because other remedies could be used to negate arbitrary police actions in conducting illegal searches.[240]

In *Mapp v. Ohio*, in 1961[241] the Supreme Court reversed the *Wolf* doctrine and expanded the *Weeks* doctrine, or exclusionary rule, to ban illegally seized evidence in state courts. This extension of the exclusionary rule has been litigated numerous times in public education cases. The courts generally have allowed materials seized by school officials to be used in a criminal prosecution. Therefore, the exclusionary rule has not been applied.

DRUG TESTING

The private business sector and state and federal governmental agencies are now resorting to mandatory testing as a means to deter drug use and to ensure job health and safety. The U.S. Supreme Court in 1989 ruled on two cases, one of which concerned the testing of railway employees and the other the testing of customs service employees. The Court ruled that a drug or alcohol test, whether it be a blood test, urine test, or breath test, constitutes a search. "The [Supreme] Court has long recognized that . . . intrusion into the body for blood to be tested for alcohol content and the ensuing chemical analysis constitutes searches."[242] Although the testing of rail workers and customs officials constitutes a search, the Court upheld the testing programs because of the government's compelling interest in protecting the public safety. With railway workers, the overriding factor is the government's interest in preventing accidents and casualties, and the major factor in the customs service case is that workers carry firearms.[243] In these cases, individualized suspicion is not required because of the government's compelling need to preserve the health and safety of the public.

In 1995, the U.S. Supreme Court added further clarification as to the privacy rights of students and to the schools' legitimate prerogatives with regard to drug testing in certain circumstances, such as athletics. In this case, *Acton*,[244] the Court found that a school district's drug policy of conducting random urinalysis for athletes engaged in interscholastic athletics does not impermissibly invade a student's constitutional rights. This case is presented in detail later in this chapter.

LIABILITY FOR ILLEGAL SEARCH

One may wonder what the consequences are of illegal search of students by teachers or school administrators. What redress is available for the student? If a search is conducted by school officials, the contraband may or may not be excluded from prosecution evidence presented in the court where the criminal trial of the student ensues. Beyond this, the student may conceivably bring an action under Section 1983 of Title 42 of the U.S. Code. A student may seek damages if school officials maliciously deny his or her constitutional rights. The U.S. Court of Appeals for the Sixth Circuit, in *Williams*,[245] noted that government officials performing discretionary functions are generally shielded from liability for civil damages insofar as their conduct does not violate clearly established statutory or constitutional rights of which a reasonable person would have known. It is important to observe that if school officials deny a student his or her constitutional rights but do so in the good-faith fulfillment of school responsibilities and not in ignorance of and disregard for established indisputable principles of law, no liability will occur. This immunity is accorded only within the bounds of reason. When school officials, in *Doe v. Renfrow*,[246] strip-searched a child "without any individualized suspicion and without reasonable cause," the court said, "We

suggest as strongly as possible that the conduct herein described exceeded the 'bounds of reason' by two and a half country miles. It is not enough for us to declare that the little girl involved was indeed deprived of her constitutional and basic human rights. We must also permit her to seek damages from those who caused this humiliation. . . . "

Search of Students by School Officials Is Constitutionally Permissible if Reasonable and Not Excessively Intrusive

New Jersey v. T. L. O.

Supreme Court of the United States, 1985.
469 U.S. 325, 105 S.Ct. 733.

JUSTICE WHITE delivered the opinion of the Court. We granted certiorari in this case to examine the appropriateness of the exclusionary rule as a remedy for searches carried out in violation of the Fourth Amendment by public school authorities. Our consideration of the proper application of the Fourth Amendment to the public schools, however, has led us to conclude that the search that gave rise to the case now before us did not violate the Fourth Amendment. Accordingly, we here address only the questions of the proper standard for assessing the legality of searches conducted by public school officials and the application of that standard to the facts of this case.

On March 7, 1980, a teacher at Piscataway High School in Middlesex County, N.J., discovered two girls smoking in a lavatory. One of the two girls was the respondent T. L. O., who at that time was a 14-year-old high school freshman. Because smoking in the lavatory was a violation of a school rule, the teacher took the two girls to the Principal's office, where they met with Assistant Vice Principal Theodore Choplick. In response to questioning by Mr. Choplick, T. L. O.'s companion admitted that she had violated the rule. T. L. O., however, denied that she had been smoking in the lavatory and claimed that she did not smoke at all.

Mr. Choplick asked T. L. O. to come into his private office and demanded to see her purse. Opening the purse, he found a pack of cigarettes, which he removed from the purse and held before T. L. O. as he accused her of having lied to him. As he reached into the purse for the cigarettes, Mr. Choplick also noticed a package of cigarette rolling papers. In his experience, possession of rolling papers by high school students was closely associated with the use of marihuana. Suspecting that a closer examination of the purse might yield further evidence of drug use, Mr. Choplick proceeded to search the purse thoroughly. The search revealed a small amount of marihuana, a pipe, a number of empty plastic bags, a substantial quantity of money in one-dollar bills, an index card that appeared to be a list of students who owed T. L. O. money, and two letters that implicated T. L. O. in marihuana dealing.

Mr. Choplick notified T. L. O.'s mother and the police, and turned the evidence of drug dealing over to the police. At the request of the police, T. L. O.'s mother took her daughter to police headquarters, where T. L. O. confessed that she had been selling marihuana at the high school. On the basis of the confession and the evidence seized by Mr. Choplick, the State brought delinquency charges against T. L. O. in the Juvenile and Domestic Relations Court of Middlesex County. Contending that Mr. Choplick's search of her purse violated the Fourth Amendment, T. L. O. moved to suppress the evidence found in her purse as well as her confession, which, she argued, was tainted by the allegedly unlawful search. . . .

The New Jersey Supreme Court agreed with the lower courts that the Fourth Amendment applies to searches conducted by school officials. The court also rejected the State of New Jersey's argument that the exclusionary rule should not be employed to prevent the use in juvenile proceedings of evidence unlawfully seized by school officials. Declining to consider whether applying the rule to the fruits of searches by school officials would have any deterrent value, the court held simply that the precedents of this Court establish that "if an official search violates constitutional rights, the evidence is not admissible in criminal proceedings." . . .

. . . In determining whether the search at issue in this case violated the Fourth Amendment, we are faced initially with the question whether that Amendment's prohibition on unreasonable searches and seizures applies to searches conducted by public school officials. We hold that it does.

It is now beyond dispute that "the Federal Constitution, by virtue of the Fourteenth Amendment, prohibits unreasonable searches and seizures by state officers." Equally indisputable is the proposition that the Fourteenth Amendment protects the rights of students against encroachment by public school officials:

> The Fourteenth Amendment, as now applied to the States, protects the citizen against the State itself and all of its creatures—Boards of Education not excepted. These have, of course, delicate, and highly discretionary functions, but none that they may not perform within the limits of the Bill of Rights. That they are educating the young for citizenship is reason for scrupulous protection of constitutional freedoms of the individual, if we are not to strangle the free mind at its source and teach youth to discount important principles of our government as mere platitudes. *West Virginia State Bd. of Ed. v. Barnette*, 319 U.S. 624, 637, 63 S.Ct. 1178, 1185, 87 L.Ed. 1628 (1943).

It may well be true that the evil toward which the Fourth Amendment was primarily directed was the resurrection of the pre-Revolutionary practice of using general warrants or "writs of assistance" to authorize searches for contraband by officers of the Crown. But this Court has never limited the Amendment's prohibition on unreasonable searches and seizures to operations conducted by the police. Rather, the Court has long spoken of the Fourth Amendment's strictures as restraints imposed upon "governmental action"—that is, "upon the activities of sovereign authority." . . .

Notwithstanding the general applicability of the Fourth Amendment to the activities of civil authorities, a few courts have concluded that school officials are exempt from the dictates of the Fourth Amendment by virtue of the special nature of their authority over schoolchildren. Teachers and school administrators, it is said, act *in loco parentis* in their dealings with students: their authority is that of the parent, not the State, and is therefore not subject to the limits of the Fourth Amendment.

Such reasoning is in tension with contemporary reality and the teachings of this Court. We have held school officials subject to the commands of the First Amendment, . . . and the Due Process Clause of the Fourteenth Amendment. . . . If school authorities are state actors for purposes of the constitutional guarantees of freedom of expression and due process, it is difficult to understand why they should be deemed to be exercising parental rather than public authority when conducting searches of their students. More generally, the Court has recognized that "the concept of parental delegation" as a source of school authority is not entirely "consonant with compulsory education laws." Today's public school officials do not merely exercise authority voluntarily conferred on them by individual parents; rather, they act in furtherance of publicly mandated educational and disciplinary policies. . . . In carrying out searches and other disciplinary functions pursuant to such policies, school officials act as representatives of the State, not merely as surrogates for the parents, and they cannot claim the parents' immunity from the strictures of the Fourth Amendment.

To hold that the Fourth Amendment applies to searches conducted by school authorities is only to begin the inquiry into the standards governing such searches. Although the underlying command of the Fourth Amendment is always that searches and seizures be reasonable, what is reasonable depends on the context within which a search takes place. The determination of the standard of reasonableness governing any specific class of searches requires "balancing the need to search against the invasion which the search entails." On one side of the balance are arrayed the individual's legitimate expectations of privacy and personal security; on the other, the government's need for effective methods to deal with breaches of public order. . . .

The State of New Jersey has argued that because of the pervasive supervision to which children in the schools are necessarily subject, a child has virtually no legitimate expectation of privacy in articles of personal property "unnecessarily" carried into a school. This argument has two factual premises: (1) the fundamental incompatibility of expectations of privacy with the maintenance of a sound educational environment; and (2) the minimal interest of the child in bringing any items of personal property into the school. Both premises are severely flawed.

Although this Court may take notice of the difficulty of maintaining discipline in the public schools today, the situation is not so dire that students in the schools may claim no legitimate expectations of privacy. We have recently recognized that the need to maintain order in a prison is such that prisoners retain no legitimate expectations of privacy in their cells, but it goes almost without saying that "[t]he prisoner and the schoolchild stand in wholly different circumstances, separated by the harsh fact of criminal conviction and incarceration." We are not yet ready to hold that the schools and the prisons need be equated for purposes of the Fourth Amendment.

Nor does the State's suggestion that children have no legitimate need to bring personal property into the schools seem well anchored in reality. Students at a minimum must bring to school not only the supplies needed for their studies, but also keys, money, and the necessaries of personal hygiene and grooming. In addition, students may carry on their persons or in purses or wallets such nondisruptive yet highly personal items as photographs, letters, and diaries. Finally, students may have perfectly legitimate reasons to carry with them articles of property needed in connection with extracurricular or recreational activities. In short, schoolchildren may find it necessary to carry with them a variety of legitimate, noncontraband items, and there is no reason to conclude that they have necessarily waived all rights to privacy in such items merely by bringing them onto school grounds.

Against the child's interest in privacy must be set the substantial interest of teachers and administrators in maintaining discipline in the classroom and on school grounds. Maintaining order in the classroom has never been easy, but in recent years, school disorder has often taken particularly ugly forms: drug use and violent crime in the schools have become major social problems. . . . Accordingly, we have recognized that maintaining security and order in the schools requires a certain degree of flexibility in school disciplinary procedures, and we have respected the value of preserving the informality of the student-teacher relationship.

How, then, should we strike the balance between the schoolchild's legitimate expectations of privacy and the school's equally legitimate need to maintain an environment in which learning can take place? It is evident that the school setting requires some easing of the restrictions to which searches by public authorities are ordinarily subject. The warrant requirement, in particular, is unsuited to the school environment: requiring a teacher to obtain a warrant before searching a child suspected of an infraction of school rules (or of the criminal law) would unduly interfere with the maintenance of the swift and informal disciplinary procedures needed in the schools. Just as we have in other cases dispensed with the warrant requirement when "the burden of obtaining a warrant is likely to frustrate the governmental purpose behind the search," we hold today that school officials need not obtain a warrant before searching a student who is under their authority.

The school setting also requires some modification of the level of suspicion of illicit activity needed to justify a search. Ordinarily, a search—even one that may permissibly be carried out without a warrant—must be based upon "probable cause" to believe that a violation of the law has occurred. However, "probable cause" is not an irreducible requirement of a valid search. The fundamental command of the Fourth Amendment is that searches and seizures be reasonable, and although "both the concept of probable cause and the requirement of a warrant bear on the reasonableness of a search, . . . in certain limited circumstances neither is required." . . .

We join the majority of courts that have examined this issue in concluding that the accommodation of the privacy interests of schoolchildren with the substantial need of teachers and administrators for freedom to maintain order in the schools does not require strict adherence to the requirement that searches be based on probable cause to believe that the subject of the search has violated or is violating the law. Rather, the legality of a search of a student should depend simply on the reasonableness, under all the circumstances, of the search. Determining the reasonableness of any search involves a twofold inquiry: first, one must consider "whether the . . . action was justified at its inception," second, one must determine whether the search as actually conducted "was reasonably related in scope to the circumstances which justified the interference in the first place." Under ordinary circumstances, a search of a student by a teacher or other school official will be "justified at its inception" when there are reasonable grounds for suspecting that the search will turn up evidence that the student has violated or is violating either the law or the rules of the school. Such a search will be permissible in its scope when the measures adopted are reasonably related to the objectives of the search and not excessively intrusive in light of the age and sex of the student and the nature of the infraction.

This standard will, we trust, neither unduly burden the efforts of school authorities to maintain order in their schools nor authorize unrestrained intrusions upon the privacy of schoolchildren. By focusing attention on the question of reasonableness, the standard will spare teachers and school administrators the necessity of schooling themselves in the niceties of probable cause and permit them to regulate their conduct according to the dictates of reason and common sense. At the same time, the reasonableness standard should ensure that the interests of students will be invaded no more than is necessary to achieve the legitimate end of preserving order in the schools.

There remains the question of the legality of the search in this case. We recognize that the "reasonable grounds" standard applied by the New Jersey Supreme Court in its consideration of this question is not substantially different from the standard that we have adopted today. Nonetheless, we believe that the New Jersey court's application of that standard to strike down the search of T. L. O.'s purse reflects a somewhat crabbed notion of reasonableness. Our review of the facts surrounding the search leads us to conclude that the search was in no sense unreasonable for Fourth Amendment purposes.

The incident that gave rise to this case actually involved two separate searches, with the first—the search for cigarettes—providing the suspicion that gave rise to the second—the search for marihuana. Although it is the fruits of the second search that are at issue here, the validity of the search for marihuana must depend on the reasonableness of the initial search for cigarettes, as there would have been no reason to suspect that T. L. O. possessed marihuana had the first search not taken place. Accordingly, it is to the search for cigarettes that we first turn our attention.

The New Jersey Supreme Court pointed to two grounds for its holding that the search for cigarettes was unreasonable. First, the court observed that possession of cigarettes was not in itself illegal or a violation of school rules. Because the contents of T. L. O.'s purse would therefore have "no direct bearing on the infraction" of which she was accused (smoking in a lavatory where smoking was prohibited), there was no reason to search her purse. Second, even assuming that a search of T. L. O.'s purse might under some circumstances be reasonable in light of the accusation made against T. L. O., the New Jersey court concluded that Mr. Choplick in this particular case had no reasonable grounds to suspect that T. L. O. had cigarettes in her purse. At best, according to the court, Mr. Choplick had "a good hunch."

Both these conclusions are implausible. T. L. O. had been accused of smoking, and had denied the accusation in the strongest possible terms when she stated that she did not smoke at all. Surely it cannot be said that under these circumstances, T. L. O.'s possession of cigarettes would be irrelevant to the charges against her or to her response to those charges. T. L. O.'s possession of cigarettes, once it was discovered, would both corroborate the report that she had been smoking and undermine the credibility of her defense to the charge of smoking. To be sure, the discovery of the cigarettes would not prove that T. L. O. had been smoking in the lavatory; nor would it, strictly speaking, necessarily be inconsistent with her claim that she did not smoke at all. But it is universally recognized that evidence, to be relevant to an inquiry, need not conclusively prove the ultimate fact in issue, but only have "any tendency to make the existence of any fact that is of consequence to the determination of the action more probable

or less probable than it would be without the evidence." The relevance of T. L. O.'s possession of cigarettes to the question whether she had been smoking and to the credibility of her denial that she smoked supplied the necessary "nexus" between the item searched for and the infraction under investigation. Thus, if Mr. Choplick in fact had a reasonable suspicion that T. L. O. had cigarettes in her purse, the search was justified despite the fact that the cigarettes, if found, would constitute "mere evidence" of a violation.

Of course, the New Jersey Supreme Court also held that Mr. Choplick had no reasonable suspicion that the purse would contain cigarettes. This conclusion is puzzling. A teacher had reported that T. L. O. was smoking in the lavatory. Certainly this report gave Mr. Choplick reason to suspect that T. L. O. was carrying cigarettes with her; and if she did have cigarettes, her purse was the obvious place in which to find them. Mr. Choplick's suspicion that there were cigarettes in the purse was not an "inchoate and unparticularized suspicion or 'hunch,'" rather, it was the sort of "common-sense conclusio[n] about human behavior" upon which "practical people"—including government officials—are entitled to rely. Of course, even if the teacher's report were true, T. L. O. *might* not have had a pack of cigarettes with her; she might have borrowed a cigarette from someone else or have been sharing a cigarette with another student. But the requirement of reasonable suspicion is not a requirement of absolute certainty: "sufficient probability, not certainty, is the touchstone of reasonableness under the Fourth Amendment. . . ." Because the hypothesis that T. L. O. was carrying cigarettes in her purse was itself not unreasonable, it is irrelevant that other hypotheses were also consistent with the teacher's accusation. Accordingly, it cannot be said that Mr. Choplick acted unreasonably when he examined T. L. O.'s purse to see if it contained cigarettes.

Our conclusion that Mr. Choplick's decision to open T. L. O.'s purse was reasonable brings us to the question of the further search for marihuana once the pack of cigarettes was located. The suspicion upon which the search for marihuana was founded was provided when Mr. Choplick observed a package of rolling papers in the purse as he removed the pack of cigarettes. Although T. L. O. does not dispute the reasonableness of Mr. Choplick's belief that the rolling papers indicated the presence of marihuana, she does contend that the scope of the search Mr. Choplick conducted exceeded permissible bounds when he seized and read certain letters that implicated T. L. O. in drug dealing. This argument, too, is unpersuasive. The discovery of the rolling papers concededly gave rise to a reasonable suspicion that T. L. O. was carrying marihuana as well as cigarettes in her purse. This suspicion justified further exploration of T. L. O.'s purse, which turned up more evidence of drug-related activities: a pipe, a number of plastic bags of the type commonly used to store marihuana, a small quantity of marihuana, and a fairly substantial amount of money. Under these circumstances, it was not unreasonable to extend the search to a separate zippered compartment of the purse; and when a search of that compartment revealed an index card containing a list of "people who owe me money" as well as to letters, the inference that T. L. O. was involved in marihuana trafficking was substantial enough to justify Mr. Choplick in examining the letters to determine whether they contained any further evidence. In short, we cannot conclude that the search for marihuana was unreasonable in any respect.

Because the search resulting in the discovery of the evidence of marihuana dealing by T. L. O. was reasonable, the New Jersey Supreme Court's decision to exclude that evidence from T. L. O.'s juvenile delinquency proceedings on Fourth Amendment grounds was erroneous. Accordingly, the judgment of the Supreme Court of New Jersey is

Reversed.

———————— ❖ — ❖ — ❖ ————————

School District's Drug Policy of Random Urinalysis
for Interscholastic Athletes Is Constitutional

Vernonia School District 47J v. Acton

Supreme Court of the United States, 1995.
515 U.S. 646, 115 S.Ct. 2386.

Justice SCALIA delivered the opinion of the Court.

The Student Athlete Drug Policy adopted by School District 47J in the town of Vernonia, Oregon, authorizes random urinalysis drug testing of students who participate in the District's school athletics programs. We granted certiorari to decide whether this violates the Fourth and Fourteenth Amendments to the United States Constitution.

Petitioner Vernonia School District 47J (District) operates one high school and three grade schools in the logging community of Vernonia, Oregon. As elsewhere in small-town America, school sports play a prominent role in the town's life, and student athletes are admired in their schools and in the community.

Drugs had not been a major problem in Vernonia schools. In the mid-to-late 1980's, however, teachers and administrators observed a sharp increase in drug use. Students began to speak out about their attraction to the drug culture, and to boast that there was nothing the school could do about it. Along with more drugs came more disciplinary problems. Between 1988 and 1989 the number of disciplinary referrals in Vernonia schools rose to more than twice the number reported in the early 1980's, and several students were suspended. Students became increasingly rude during class; outbursts of profane language became common.

Not only were student athletes included among the drug users but, as the District court found, athletes were the leaders of the drug culture. . . .

Initially, the District responded to the drug problem by offering special classes, speakers, and presentations designed to deter drug use. It even brought in a specially trained dog to detect drugs, but the drug problem persisted. . . . At that point, District officials began considering a drug-testing program. They held a parent "input night" to discuss the proposed Student Athlete Drug Policy (Policy), and the parents in attendance gave their unanimous approval. The school board approved the Policy for implementation in the fall of 1989. Its expressed purpose is to prevent student athletes from using drugs, to protect their health and safety, and to provide drug users with assistance programs.

The Policy applies to all students participating in interscholastic athletics. Students wishing to play sports must sign a form consenting to the testing and must obtain the written consent of their parents. Athletes are tested at the beginning of the season for their sport. In addition, once each week of the season the names of the athletes are placed in a "pool" from which a student, with the supervision of two adults, blindly draws the names of 10% of the athletes for random testing. Those selected are notified and tested that same day, if possible. . . .

If a sample tests positive, a second test is administered as soon as possible to confirm the result. If the second test is negative, no further action is taken. If the second test is positive, the athlete's parents are notified, and the school principal convenes a meeting with the student and his parents, at which the student is given the option of (1) participating for six weeks in an assistance program that includes weekly urinalysis, or (2) suffering suspension from athletics for the remainder of the current season and the next athletic season. The student is then retested prior to the start of the next athletic season for which he or she is eligible. The Policy states that a second offense results in automatic imposition of option (2); a third offense in suspension for the remainder of the current season and the next two athletic seasons.

In the fall of 1991, respondent James Acton, then a seventh-grader, signed up to play football at one of the District's grade schools. He was denied participation, however, because he and his parents refused to sign the testing consent forms. The Actons filed suit, seeking declaratory and injunctive relief from enforcement of the Policy on the grounds that it violated the Fourth and Fourteenth Amendments to the United States Constitution. . . . We granted certiorari. . . .

The Fourth Amendment to the United States Constitution provides that the Federal Government shall not violate "[t]he right of the people to be secure in their persons, houses, papers, and effects, against unreasonable searches and seizures. . . ." . . .

As the text of the Fourth Amendment indicates, the ultimate measure of the constitutionality of a governmental search is "reasonableness." At least in a case such as this, where there was no clear practice, either approving or disapproving the type of search at issue, at the time the constitutional provision was enacted,

whether a particular search meets the reasonableness standard "'is judged by balancing its intrusion on the individual's Fourth Amendment interests against its promotion of legitimate governmental interests.'" . . . Where a search is undertaken by law enforcement officials to discover evidence of criminal wrongdoing, this Court has said that reasonableness generally requires the obtaining of a judicial warrant. . . . Warrants cannot be issued, of course, without the showing of probable cause required by the Warrant Clause. But a warrant is not required to establish the reasonableness of *all* government searches; and when a warrant is not required (and the Warrant Clause therefore not applicable), probable cause is not invariably required either. A search unsupported by probable cause can be constitutional, we have said, "when special needs, beyond the normal need for law enforcement, make the warrant and probable-cause requirement impracticable." . . .

We have found such "special needs" to exist in the public-school context. There, the warrant requirement "would unduly interfere with the maintenance of the swift and informal disciplinary procedures [that are] needed," and "strict adherence to the requirement that searches be based upon probable cause" would undercut "the substantial need of teachers and administrators for freedom to maintain order in the schools." . . . The school search we approved in *T. L. O.*, while not based on probable cause, *was* based on individualized *suspicion* of wrongdoing. As we explicitly acknowledged, however, "'the Fourth Amendment imposes no irreducible requirement of such suspicion'". . . .

The first factor to be considered is the nature of the privacy interest upon which the search here at issue intrudes. The Fourth Amendment does not protect all subjective expectations of privacy, but only those that society recognizes as "legitimate." . . . What expectations are legitimate varies, of course, with context, . . . depending, for example, upon whether the individual asserting the privacy interest is at home, at work, in a car, or in a public park. In addition, the legitimacy of certain privacy expectations vis-à-vis the State may depend upon the individual's legal relationship with the State. . . . Central, in our view, to the present case is the fact that the subjects of the Policy are (1) children, who (2) have been committed to the temporary custody of the State as schoolmaster.

Traditionally at common law, and still today, unemancipated minors lack some of the most fundamental rights of self-determination—including even the right of liberty in its narrow sense, i.e., the right to come and go at will. They are subject, even as to their physical freedom, to the control of their parents or guardians. . . .

In *T. L. O.* we rejected the notion that public schools . . . exercise only parental power over their students, which of course is not subject to constitutional constraints. . . . Such a view of things, we said, "is not entirely 'consonant with compulsory education laws,'" . . . and is inconsistent with our prior decisions treating school officials as state actors for purposes of the Due Process and Free Speech Clauses. . . . But while denying that the State's power over schoolchildren is formally no more than the delegated power of their parents, *T. L. O.* did not deny, but indeed emphasized, that the nature of that power is custodial and tutelary, permitting a degree of supervision and control that could not be exercised over free adults. "[A] proper educational environment requires close supervision of schoolchildren, as well as the enforcement of rules against conduct that would be perfectly permissible if undertaken by an adult." . . . While we do not, of course, suggest that public schools as a general matter have such a degree of control over children as to give rise to a constitutional "duty to protect," . . . we have acknowledged that for many purposes "school authorities ac[t] *in loco parentis*," . . . with the power and indeed the duty to "inculcate the habits and manners of civility". . . . Thus, while children assuredly do not "shed their constitutional rights . . . at the schoolhouse gate," . . . the nature of those rights is what is appropriate for children in school. . . .

Fourth Amendment rights, no less than First and Fourteenth Amendment rights, are different in public schools than elsewhere; the "reasonableness" inquiry cannot disregard the schools' custodial and tutelary responsibility for children. . . .

Legitimate privacy expectations are even less with regard to student athletes. School sports are not for the bashful. They require "suiting up" before each practice or event, and showering and changing afterwards. Public school locker rooms, the usual sites for these activities, are not notable for the privacy they afford. . . .

There is an additional respect in which school athletes have a reduced expectation of privacy. By choosing to "go out for the team," they voluntarily subject themselves to a degree of regulation even higher than that imposed on students generally. In Vernonia's public schools, they must submit to a preseason physical exam . . . , they must acquire adequate insurance coverage or sign an insurance waiver, maintain a minimum grade point average, and comply with any "rules of conduct, dress, training hours and related matters as may be established for each sport by the head coach and athletic director with the principal's approval." . . . Somewhat like adults who choose to participate in a "closely regulated industry," students who voluntarily participate in school athletics have reason to expect intrusions upon normal rights and privileges, including privacy. . . .

Having considered the scope of the legitimate expectation of privacy at issue here, we turn next to the character of the intrusion that is complained of. We recognize[] . . . that collecting the samples for urinalysis intrudes upon "an excretory function traditionally shielded by great privacy." . . . We noted, however, that the degree of intrusion depends upon the manner in which production of the urine sample is monitored. . . . Under the District's Policy, male students produce samples at a urinal along the wall. They remain fully clothed and are only observed from behind, if at all. Female students produce samples in an enclosed stall, with a female monitor standing outside listening only for sounds of tampering. These conditions are nearly identical to those typically encountered in public restrooms, which men, women, and especially school children use daily. Under such conditions, the privacy interests compromised by the process of obtaining the urine sample are in our view negligible.

The other privacy-invasive aspect of urinalysis is, of course, the information it discloses concerning the state of the subject's body, and the materials he has ingested. In this regard it is significant that the tests at issue here look only for drugs, and not for whether the student is, for example, epileptic, pregnant, or diabetic. . . . Moreover, the drugs for which the samples are screened are standard, and do not vary according to the identity of the student. And finally, the results of the tests are disclosed only to a limited class of school personnel who have a need to know; and they are not turned over to law enforcement authorities or used for any internal disciplinary function. . . .

Finally, we turn to consider the nature and immediacy of the governmental concern at issue here, and the efficacy of this means for meeting it. . . .

That the nature of the concern is important—indeed, perhaps compelling—can hardly be doubted. Deterring drug use by our Nation's schoolchildren is at least as important as enhancing efficient enforcement of the Nation's laws against the importation of drugs. . . .

As for the immediacy of the District's concerns: We are not inclined to question—indeed, we could not possibly find clearly erroneous—that "a large segment of the student body, particularly those involved in interscholastic athletics, was in a state of rebellion," that "[d]isciplinary actions had reached 'epidemic proportions,'" and that "the rebellion was being fueled by alcohol and drug abuse as well as by the student's misperceptions about the drug culture." . . .

As to the efficacy of this means for addressing the problem: It seems to us self-evident that a drug problem largely fueled by the "role model" effect of athletes' drug use, and of particular danger to athletes, is effectively addressed by making sure the athletes do not use drugs. Respondents argue that a "less intrusive means to the same end" was available, namely, "drug testing on suspicion of drug use." . . .

Taking into account all the factors we have considered above—the decreased expectation of privacy, the relative unobtrusiveness of the search, and the severity of the need met by the search—we conclude Vernonia's Policy is reasonable and hence constitutional.

We caution against the assumption that suspicionless drug testing will readily pass constitutional muster in other contexts. The most significant element in this case is the first we discussed: that the Policy was undertaken in furtherance of the government's responsibilities, under a public school system, as guardian and tutor of children entrusted to its care. . . . [W]hen the government acts as guardian and tutor the relevant question is whether the search is one that a reasonable guardian and tutor

might undertake. . . . [W]e conclude that in the present case it is.

We may note that the primary guardians of Vernonia's schoolchildren appear to agree. The record shows no objection to this districtwide program by any parents other than the couple before us here—even though, as we have described, a public meeting was held to obtain parents' views. We find insufficient basis to contradict the judgment of Vernonia's parents, its school board, and the District Court, as to what was reasonably in the interest of these children under the circumstances. . . .

It is so ordered. . . .

CASE NOTES

1. Following *Vernonia*, the U.S. Court of Appeals, Seventh Circuit, held that students can be required to undergo random suspicionless drug testing as a condition of their participation in extracurricular activities. This court followed the reasoning of *Vernonia* with regard to random urinalysis as a condition for participation in interscholastic athletes and expanded on *Vernonia*'s application to approve random testing for all students who volunteer to participate in extracurricular activities. According to the seventh circuit, "[s]tudents in other extracurricular activities, like athletes, 'can take leadership roles in the school community and serve as an example to others,' . . . carrying enhanced prestige and status," and, therefore, it is not unreasonable to couple such benefits with a corresponding obligation to undergo drug testing. *Todd v. Rush County Schools*, 133 F.3d 984 (7th Cir.1988), cert. denied, 525 U.S. 824, 119 S.Ct. 68 (1998). See also *Schaill v. Tippecanoe County School Corp.*, 864 F.2d 1309 (7th Cir.1988).

2. In a more restrictive application of the *Vernonia* rationale, the Supreme Court of Colorado held unconstitutional a school district's requirement of drug testing of members of the school's marching band. The school offered two elective regular band classes, and a student enrolling in either or both of the classes was required to participate in the marching band. On the other hand, a student wishing to march in the band was required to enroll in one or both of the classes. Thus, the effect of the drug testing policy was that students in order to enroll in these classes must provide urine samples for drug

testing. The Colorado court further noted that marching band members, unlike students who volunteer to participate in athletics, do not expect intrusions into their privacy as is normal among athletes. According to this court, band members are different from athletes because they do not "suit up" and shower together after each practice session and game. Moreover, students who sign up for the required credit courses and march in the band do not voluntarily subject themselves to the degree of regulation and the intrusions upon rights and privileges as is expected in athletics.

Finally, in distinguishing the facts in this case from those in *Vernonia*, the Colorado court concluded that (1) the marching band does not undergo the same type of public undressing and communal showers as student athletes, and (2) the type of voluntariness in athletics referred to in *Vernonia* is very much dissimilar from students who want to enroll in a for-credit class as a part of the school curriculum. Thus, "[t]he Policy's actual scope extended vastly beyond the policy upheld in Vernonia." *Trinidad School District No. 1 v. Lopez*, 963 P.2d 1095 (Colo.1998).

3. The reach of permissibility of drug testing under *Vernonia* has also been found to have further limits. Where a school corporation in Indiana sought to compel drug testing of a student who had engaged in fighting at school, the U.S. Court of Appeals, Seventh Circuit, found that the "causal nexus" between "fighting and illegal substance use is not strong enough to support a conclusive presumption of reasonable suspicion." Even though the school corporation presented certain data and studies suggesting fighting and drugs were closely related, the court pointed out that the list of possible signs of substance abuse "could be endless," and, therefore, if all were considered valid, justifications for "reasonable suspicion" could also presumably be endless. Therefore, the court concluded that the mere fact that a student was suspended for fighting was not sufficient to establish reasonable suspicion of substance abuse. The court said that the privacy interest here is different from that in *Vernonia* in at least two important respects: First, athletes' participation assumes less privacy in that there is "communal undress" in locker rooms; and, second, the privacy interest at issue in *Vernonia* applied only to

students who had voluntarily chosen to participate in an athletic activity. Even though the school corporation attempted to encompass *Vernonia* reasoning by claiming that the student in this case had voluntarily engaged in fighting, the court was unconvinced by this tenuous logic. *Willis v. Anderson Community School Corp.*, 158 F.3d 415 (7th Cir.1998).

❖ — ❖ — ❖

*Strip Search of Student Was Reasonable;
No Violation of Fourth Amendment*

Cornfield v. Consolidated High School District No. 230

U.S. Court of Appeals, Seventh Circuit, 1993.
991 F.2d 1316.

FLAUM, Circuit Judge.

Brian Cornfield was enrolled in a behavioral disorder program at Carl Sandburg High School. Kathy Stacy, a teacher's aide in that program, found him outside the school building in violation of school rules on March 7, 1991. When she reported the infraction to Richard Spencer, Cornfield's teacher, and Dean Richard Frye, Stacy also alerted them to her suspicion that Cornfield appeared "too well-endowed." Another teacher, Joyce Lawler, and teacher's aide Lori Walsh corroborated Stacy's observation of an unusual bulge in Cornfield's crotch area. Neither defendant took any action at that time. The following day Cornfield was boarding the bus home when Spencer and Frye took him aside. Spencer himself had observed the unusual bulge in the crotch area of Cornfield's sweatpants. Believing the sixteen-year-old Cornfield was "crotching" drugs, Spencer and Frye asked him to accompany them to Frye's office to investigate further. When confronted with their suspicion, Cornfield grew agitated and began yelling obscenities. At Cornfield's request, Frye telephoned the minor's mother Janet Lewis to seek consent for a search. She refused.

Spencer and Frye nevertheless proceeded with the search. Believing a pat down to be excessively intrusive and ineffective at detecting drugs, they escorted Cornfield to the boys' locker room to conduct a strip search. After making certain that no one else was present in the locker room, they locked the door. Spencer then stood about fifteen feet from Cornfield, and Frye was standing on the opposite side, approximately ten to twelve feet away, while they had him remove his street clothes and put on a gym uniform. Spencer and Frye visually inspected his naked body and physically inspected his clothes. Neither man performed a body cavity search. They found no evidence of drugs or any other contraband. Afterwards the school bus was recalled, and it took Cornfield home.

Alleging that the search violated his Fourth, Fifth, and Fourteenth Amendment rights, Cornfield brought an action . . . against Consolidated High School District No. 230 ("District 230"), the parent organization of Carl Sandburg High School, and against Spencer and Frye in their professional and individual capacities.

After the filing of affidavits, the district court granted summary judgment in favor of Spencer and Frye in their individual capacities, a decision that we review *de novo*. . . .

The first question we address on review is whether the strip search of Cornfield was consistent with the Fourth Amendment. The Supreme Court established in *New Jersey v. T. L. O.* that reconciling the privacy interests of children with the needs of schools to maintain order does not require strict adherence to a probable cause standard for Fourth Amendment purposes. By its express language, the Fourth Amendment prohibits only unreasonable searches:

> . . . The determination of the standard of reasonableness governing any specific class of searches requires "balancing the need to search against the invasions which the search entails." On one side of the balance are arrayed the individual's legitimate expectations of privacy and personal security; on the other, the government's need for effective methods to deal with breaches of public order.

. . . To strike a balance, the Supreme Court fashioned a two-prong test for evaluating whether a search of a student is constitutional. First, the search must be "justified at its inception." . . . Second, the search must be permissi-

ble in scope: "[T]he measures adopted are reasonably related to the objectives of the search and not excessively intrusive in light of the age and sex of the student and the nature of the infraction." . . .

Therefore, whether a search is "reasonable" in the constitutional sense will vary according to the context of the search. In this regard, a couple of points should be immediately apparent. A nude search of a student by an administrator or teacher of the opposite sex would obviously violate this standard. Moreover, a highly intrusive search in response to a minor infraction would similarly not comport with the sliding scale advocated by the Supreme Court in *T. L. O.* To elaborate, "[a] search of a child's person or of a closed purse or other bag carried on her person, no less than a similar search carried out on an adult, is undoubtedly a severe violation of subjective expectations of privacy." . . . Accordingly, . . . "[s]ubjecting a student to a nude search is more than just the mild inconvenience of a pocket search, rather it is an intrusion into an individual's basic justifiable expectation of privacy." . . . What may constitute reasonable suspicion for a search of a locker or even a pocket or pocketbook may fall well short of reasonableness for a nude search.

Thus, this flexible standard allows a school administrator or court to weigh the interest of a school in maintaining order against the substantial privacy interests of students in their bodies. In this regard, no one would seriously dispute that a nude search of a child is traumatic. . . .

Whether the search of Cornfield comports with the two-prong *T. L. O.* standard requires careful scrutiny of the circumstances surrounding the search. One fact is not in dispute: Cornfield was in a behavioral disorder program at the high school. In this regard, Cornfield contends that his problems are exclusively behavioral, which would be too thin a reed to support reasonable suspicion for a strip search: The fact that students in such a program exhibit inconsistent behavior and that drug users behave erratically does not lead inevitably to a conclusion that a student in a behavioral disorder program is a drug user. Spencer and Frye, however, have attested to a number of other independent factors to support the reasonableness of their suspicions of drug possession by Cornfield.

Spencer, one of Cornfield's teachers, had more direct contact with the appellant than Frye and alleged in his affidavit several incidents on which to ground his suspicions. According to Spencer, Cornfield once stated that prior to December 1990 he was dealing drugs and that in February 1991, he would test positive for marijuana. Spencer also believed that Cornfield did not successfully complete a drug rehabilitation program in December of 1990. And on January 29, 1991, Cornfield was found in possession of a live bullet at school. The remaining incidents giving rise to Spencer's suspicion occurred at some unspecified time prior to the date of the strip search: Cornfield's bus driver had reported the smell of marijuana from where Cornfield was sitting on the bus, one student reported having observed Cornfield smoking marijuana on one occasion on the bus, another student had advised Spencer of Cornfield's possession of drugs while on school grounds, Cornfield himself had related to Spencer that he was constantly thinking about drugs, and teacher's aide Kathy Stacy had informed Spencer that Cornfield claimed he had "crotched" drugs during a police raid at his mother's house. Spencer also attested to the fact that he had the opportunity to view Cornfield throughout the year; and March 7, 1991, was the first time he had observed the unusual bulge in Cornfield's crotch area.

According to Frye's affidavit, Spencer shared with Frye any information or incidents involving Cornfield. In addition, Palos Park police officer William Jackson communicated to Carl Sandburg's Head Dean Sutor that on October 24, 1990, he had received information that Cornfield was selling marijuana to other students. Head Dean Sutor conveyed this to Frye. Cornfield also acknowledged at some point to Sutor, in the presence of Kathy Stacy, that he failed a urine analysis for cocaine. Sutor advised Spencer and Frye of this as well. . . .

Cornfield's case does differ from other student search cases in that Spencer and Frye based their decision on evidence or events that had occurred over some period of time. . . . This aspect of the case evokes some concern because school teachers and administrators can marshal negative incidents and perceptions while discounting any contrary evidence that may accumulate over the course of a number of months, or longer. As the facts of this case stand, however, Spencer and Frye relied on a number of relatively recent incidents reported by various teachers and aides as well as their personal observations, the cumulative effect of which is sufficient to create a reasonable suspicion that Cornfield was crotching drugs.

The second prong of our inquiry concerns whether the search was permissible in scope. On the one hand, the sixteen-year-old Cornfield was of an age at which children are extremely self-conscious about their bodies; thus, the potential impact of a strip search was substantial. However, given Spencer and Frye's suspicion that Cornfield was crotching drugs, their conclusion that a strip search was the least intrusive way to confirm or deny their suspicions was not unreasonable. As administered, two male school personnel performed the search and did so in the privacy of the boys' locker room. . . . As Cornfield changed, Spencer and Frye observed from a certain distance away to ensure Cornfield could not conceal any drugs or other contraband he was suspected of carrying. In addition, Spencer and Frye did not physically touch him or subject him to a body cavity search, nor did they have him suffer the indignity of standing naked before them but allowed him to put on a gym uniform while they searched his street clothes. Finally, the fact that Spencer and Frye found no drugs or other contraband does not allow us to conclude retrospectively that the search was unreasonable in scope. . . .

. . . Of course, no school searches can be administered without reasonable suspicion; and clearly, a highly intrusive search necessarily requires more compelling evidence to reach the floor of reasonableness, as this case reflects. This determination is inevitably committed to the sound discretion of school personnel. . . .

For the foregoing reasons, the decision of the district court is AFFIRMED. . . .

CASE NOTES

1. *Metal Detector Searches.* In *In re F. B.*, a student was found to be carrying a Swiss-type folding knife, and after being arrested, he filed motion to have the seized evidence suppressed. He claimed the search was unreasonable because

there was not reasonable individual suspicion at the inception of the search. In applying the reasonableness factors of *T. L. O.*, the court found the search was justified. This justification was due to the high rate of violence in the Philadelphia schools; there was no way of knowing whether a student had a weapon prior to entering the school building. The search therefore met the *T. L. O.* reasonableness standard. *In re F. B.*, 442 Pa.Super. 216, 658 A.2d 1378 (1995).

When a student was found to have a loaded .38-caliber handgun in his pants and was arrested, the court said, "[W]e find . . . the screening satisfied the Fourth Amendment reasonableness test established in *T. L. O.*; the action was justified at its inception by the reality of violence in the schools, thus, the search as conducted was reasonably related in scope to the circumstances which justified the interference in the first place." *People v. Pruitt*, 278 Ill.App.3d 194, 214 Ill.Dec. 974, 662 N.E.2d 540 (1 Dist. 1996).

The Board of Education of New York City established guidelines for the use of metal detectors in high schools; the detectors required a team of special police officers from the Central Task Force for School Safety to set up a scanning post in the school's main lobby. All students entering the school were subject to the search, although the officers could choose to limit the search by any random formula if the waiting lines became too long. A student was searched with a metal detector, and a four- to five-inch switchblade knife was found. She was charged with criminal possession of a weapon, a misdemeanor. The student filed an action to suppress the evidence. The court ruled that an administrative search is reasonable when the intrusion involved in the search is no greater than necessary to satisfy the governmental interest underlying the need for the search. In determining whether the search is reasonable, the courts will balance the degree of intrusion, including the discretion given to the person conducting the search, against the severity of the damages imposed. This court found the metal detector search satisfied the balancing test and was not unreasonable; the school had a compelling need for security. *People v. Dukes*, 151 Misc.2d 295, 580 N.Y.S.2d 850 (N.Y.City Crim.Ct.1992). See also 75 Op.Cal. Att'y Gen. 155, 1992 WL 469726.

2. *Field Trip Search.* Some schools have established procedures for searching student baggage before departing on field trips. These searches have been challenged, and currently the courts are split, with one pre–*T. L. O.* decision finding the searches unreasonable because they were not "particularized with respect to each individual searched." In this case, the court believed such procedures to be "fishing expeditions" with no reasonable suspicion as a basis for the searches. *Kuehn v. Renton School District No. 403*, 103 Wash.2d 594, 694 P.2d 1078 (1985). The other case, a post–*T. L. O.* ruling, found that the search of hand luggage prior to a field trip was justified under the Fourth Amendment. This court held that there is a legitimate interest of school administrators in deterring students from taking contraband on field trips: "[T]he deterrent effect of the board's search policy advances a legitimate interest . . . in preventing students from taking contraband. . . ." The fact that this deterrence is not perfect because students can hide some contraband (e.g., small quantities of drugs) does not render the search unconstitutional. *Desilets v. Clearview Regional Board of Education*, 265 N.J.Super. 370, 627 A.2d 667 (1993).

❖ — ❖ — ❖

School Had Reasonable Suspicion to Search
Student's Backpack for Stolen Tennis Shoes

DesRoches v. Caprio and School Board of the City of Norfolk

United States Court of Appeals,
Fourth Circuit, 1998.
156 F.3d 571, 129 Educ.L.Rep. 628

MURNAGHAN, Circuit Judge: . . .

On May 2, 1997, James DesRoches was a ninth-grade student at Granby High School, a public high school in Norfolk, Virginia. On that day, he attended his fourth period art class, which met for half an hour before and after lunch. During the first half of class, one of the nineteen students in the class, Shamra Hursey (Hursey), placed her girls' tennis shoes on top of her desk. While the students went to lunch, Hursey left her shoes unattended in the classroom.

During lunch, the art classroom was unlocked, and the teacher remained in the classroom. For a "very short" portion of the time, however, the teacher was in a closet in the classroom cutting paper. The teacher could not see out of the closet into the classroom, but she stated that while she was in the classroom she never saw any students whom she did not know. One student in the classroom during the lunch period, however, testified that a student who was not enrolled in the fourth period art class was in the classroom during lunch. A few other students who were enrolled in the class returned to the classroom for a few minutes during lunch.

Upon Hursey's return from class, she noticed her shoes were missing. DesRoches and others assisted Hursey in looking for the shoes. When the shoes were not found, Hursey reported the shoes as stolen to the school's Dean of Students, James Lee, whose responsibilities include attending to matters of school security. Lee was aware that a ring had been reported missing in the same class the day before.

Upon arriving at the classroom, Lee spoke in the hallway with the class's teacher, Ms. Ratliffe, who informed him that, to her knowledge, only three students had remained in the classroom during lunch. When interviewed, those students informed Lee that Hursey had placed the shoes on her desk before the lunch period and that they were unaware of what might have happened to the shoes during lunch.

From his talks with these people, it was Lee's understanding that there had been students in the art classroom at all times during lunch, that the teacher knew all these students, that none of the students had been left alone in the classroom, and that the teacher was in the classroom at all times. It is also clear from the record that, although a student testified at trial to (1) seeing DesRoches in the cafeteria or courtyard during the lunch break; (2) seeing DesRoches with his backpack during lunch; and (3) whether DesRoches returned to the classroom after Shamra, no one told Lee anything about this at or before the time of the search.

On the basis of what he had learned during his investigation, Lee determined that it was necessary to conduct a search of the personal belongings of all nineteen students in the class. He announced his intention to search, asking whether anyone objected. At that point, Des Roches and another student raised their hands. When Lee reminded them that school policy authorized a ten-day suspension for a student's refusal to consent, the other student provided his consent but DesRoches continued to refuse. Lee told DesRoches "that he could just sit there and [they] would talk about it later," and then proceeded to search the bags and backpacks of the consenting students. Because those searches were unfruitful, Lee escorted DesRoches to the principal's office where the school's principal, Michael Caprio, renewed Lee's request to search Des Roches's backpack. When DesRoches refused, Caprio allowed him to call his parents in the unrealized hope that they would convince him to change his mind. DesRoches was then suspended for ten days, commencing immediately. . . .

The sole issue presented on appeal is whether the district court erred in concluding that the proposed search of DesRoches was unreasonable under the Fourth Amendment. Appellants answer that question in the affirmative, arguing that Lee's demand to search DesRoches was reasonable under the circumstances.

The Fourth Amendment provides that "[t]he right of the people to be secure in their persons, houses, papers, and effects, against unreasonable searches and seizures, shall not be violated. . . ." U.S. Const. amend. IV. Although it was once open to debate whether that protection extends to school children, the Supreme Court held for the first time in *New Jersey v. T.L.O.* . . . that searches and seizures conducted on school premises by school officials are governed by the limits of the Fourth Amendment. . . . In reaching that conclusion, the Court rejected the notion that school officials act purely *in loco parentis* over school children. . . .

The Supreme Court has held that the existence of Fourth Amendment protections depends on whether the individual has a legitimate expectation of privacy in the thing or place to be searched. . . . Like members of the public generally, schoolchildren enjoy a legitimate expectation of privacy in their persons and effects. . . . In *T.L.O.*, the Court emphasized that, in the adult world, "even a limited search of the person . . . [or] of closed items of personal luggage" is a "substantial invasion of privacy." . . . The same is equally true, the Court held, with similar searches conducted on school children, since "[a] search of a child's person or of a closed purse or other bag carried on her person, no less than a similar search carried out on an adult, is undoubtedly a severe violation of subjective expectations of privacy," . . . which expectations society recognizes as "legitimate," . . . . Therefore, in the present case, there is no question but that DesRoches enjoyed a legitimate expectation of privacy in his backpack so as to trigger the protections of the Fourth Amendment.

The next question, then, is whether the proposed search of the backpack was reasonable under the circumstances. Consistent with our discussion above, we begin by determining whether the search was supported by individualized suspicion. Our analysis of that question is guided by *T.L.O.* There, the Court explained that the first step in the reasonableness inquiry is to determine whether the search was "justified at its inception," which requires us to determine whether there were "reasonable grounds for suspecting that the search will turn up evidence that the student has violated or is violating either the law or the rules of the school." . . .

In the present case, where consent to search was requested and the individual was later punished for refusing consent, we are faced with the threshold issue of what constitutes the "inception" of the search. Not surprisingly, the parties offer competing views of the matter. DesRoches argues that the inception of the search occurred when school officials first announced their intention to search the class. He maintains, therefore, that the reasonableness of the school's actions must be judged by the circumstances known to school officials prior to their search of the first student. Appellants, on the other hand, argue that the inception of the search occurred not at the moment DesRoches was threatened with suspension, but at the

moment he was actually suspended for refusing to consent. Therefore, while Appellants concede that individualized suspicion was lacking with respect to DesRoches when the search was first announced to the class, they maintain that such suspicion had arisen by the time DesRoches was punished for refusing to consent to the search.

The district court agreed with DesRoches. In the court's opinion, "allowing [DesRoches] to be searched after the fruitless search of the consenting students compromises the principle that a search's reasonableness must be judged at its inception." As the court saw it, "[a] bifurcated search (first of the consenters, then of the nonconsenters) guarantees that the search of the non-consenting students would be judged . . . after the inception of the search of all the other students." Such an arrangement, the district court believed, would allow "[o]ne's constitutional rights . . . [to] wax and wane according to whether others stand upon their . . . rights."

We respectfully disagree. Underlying the district court's reasoning is the premise that school officials conducted but one search of nineteen students, such that the reasonableness of the school's actions must be judged in the aggregate. We believe that premise is flawed, since school officials conducted not one but nineteen individual searches, each of which must be independently assessed for its reasonableness. Therefore, whether any given search was justified at its inception must be adjudged according to the circumstances existing at the moment that particular search began, rather than, as the district court believed, the circumstances existing when the first student in the class was searched.

DesRoches argues that the inception of the search, as directed against him, occurred when school officials threatened him with suspension after he refused their request to search his backpack, because at that point he was required to choose between the proposed search and the possibility of suspension. We believe that argument misses the mark. For DesRoches to maintain a Fourth Amendment claim, there must have been an infringement on a protected Fourth Amendment interest. While we agree, of course, that actual suspension for refusal to consent constitutes such an infringement when the proposed search is unreasonable, we cannot agree that the

Fourth Amendment is implicated merely by a demand to search coupled with threats of punishment, where the threats are unsuccessful in bringing about the individual's consent.

DesRoches contends that his punishment became final when he refused, for the second time, to consent to the requested search, after being warned that his refusal to do so would result in a ten-day suspension. He argues, in essence, that his punishment was automatically imposed when he refused to provide his consent. Yet, the facts do not support such a contention. Far from automatically punishing DesRoches for refusing to consent, school officials told DesRoches "that he could just sit there, and [they] would talk about it later." In fact, following the threat of suspension, DesRoches was provided with at least two more opportunities to consent to the search before his suspension was actually imposed.

In light of the discussion thus far, it is apparent that the inception of the school's actions with respect to DesRoches occurred not when the search was first announced to the class, nor when DesRoches was threatened the first or second time with suspension, but when DesRoches was actually punished for refusing to provide his consent. So viewing the inception of the search, we agree with Appellants that, while school officials initially lacked individualized suspicion with respect to Des Roches, they developed such suspicion by virtue of their unsuccessful search of the classroom and the other eighteen students. As the facts demonstrate, those who remained in the classroom during lunch informed school officials that, to the best of their knowledge, only one student from outside the art class had entered the classroom during lunch. Therefore, once the classroom and the other eighteen students had been searched, school officials had certainly developed individualized suspicion with respect to DesRoches and the unnamed nonclassmember, not by way of any particular information suggesting that one of those two was the thief, but simply by the process of elimination. We therefore cannot fault school officials for renewing their request to search once individualized suspicion had arisen, or for suspending DesRoches when he refused to consent to the search. . . .

In summary, we hold that the proposed search of DesRoches's backpack was reasonable under the Fourth Amendment. The judgment of the district court is, therefore, REVERSED.

❖ — ❖ — ❖

Student Does Not Have Reasonable Expectation of Privacy When Storing Personal Items in School Locker

Isiah B. v. State of Wisconsin

Supreme Court of Wisconsin, 1993.
176 Wis.2d 639, 500 N.W.2d 637.

STEINMETZ, Justice.

Isiah B. appeals contending that the random search of his school locker was unconstitutional under the Fourth Amendment to the United States Constitution and Article I, sec. 11, of the Wisconsin Constitution. At the time of the search, there was a significant risk of imminent, serious personal harm to students and staff. We conclude that under the circumstances present at Madison High School, Milwaukee, Wisconsin, on November 19, 1990, the random search of the locker was permissible under the United States and Wisconsin Constitutions. Accordingly, we affirm the judgment of the circuit court.

The problems at Madison High School began in the fall of 1990 when the school administration was confronted with a series of gun-involved complaints and/or incidents in and around the school. In total, between October 23, 1990, and November 17, 1990, the Madison High School administration investigated five or six incidents where guns were said to have been used or were present on the school's premises. . . . As to these five or six incidents, the circuit court concluded that "[w]hile they were all cause for serious concern, . . . incidents appeared to be escalating in terms of the immediate threat of harm to students and staff at Madison High School."

On the weekend of November 16, 1990, the weekend before the search at issue, two incidents occurred which involved gunfire on school premises. First, on Friday night students reported that they were fired at as they left the school following a basketball game. Second, on Saturday night following a school dance a near riot occurred on school grounds when the departing students and security personnel for the school heard multiple gunshots. . . .

The circuit court found that on the following Monday morning, November 19, 1990, "an atmosphere of tension and fear dominated" Madison High School. The school staff and security personnel received reports of guns present in the school, gun sightings on school buses, and rumors that a shootout at the school on that date was, in effect, inevitable. As to these reports, the circuit court noted that "[t]he identities of those reporting such rumors/sightings were either genuinely unknown to witnesses or they feigned ignorance out of apparent concern for the safety of those students." Despite announcements by Principal Willie Lee Jude regarding the administration's ongoing investigation into the incidents and administration's efforts to address the situation, some staff members and students requested to leave the school out of fear for their safety. The efforts to resolve the atmosphere of fear in the school included staff meetings to gather the facts and identify students who might have information as to the perpetrators of the incident on Saturday and/or those who might have weapons in school on that morning. The circuit court found that the administration's efforts were met with little success.

Due to the heightened fear and tension and the significant risk of imminent, serious personal harm to students and staff, Principal Jude ordered school security personnel to begin a "random" search of student lockers as a preventative measure while he continued investigatory interviews. . . . The circuit court . . . indicated that evidence was introduced, including a Milwaukee Public School Handbook, to indicate that "it is announced school policy that lockers are the property of the school system and subject to inspection as determined necessary or appropriate." Students and parents are apprised of this policy. In addition, the school administration has pass keys for the lockers, and students

are prohibited from putting private locks on their lockers. Nathan Shoate, a Madison High School security aide, conducted the individual locker searches at the direction of Principal Jude. . . . The school officials had no particularized or individualized suspicion that Isiah B.'s locker would contain evidence of law or school rule violations. Isiah B. did not have a history of prior weapon violations, nor did the school officials suspect his involvement in the recent gun incidents.

At Isiah B.'s locker, Shoate opened the locker, removed a coat and immediately believed it to be unusually heavy. He then patted the exterior of the coat and felt a hard object, which he believed to be a gun, in an interior pocket. Shoate immediately notified the principal. Before the principal arrived, Shoate observed the handle of a gun in the coat by pulling open the pocket. The circuit court concluded that the coat was then brought to the principal's office where Isiah B. was confronted with it, whereupon he admitted that cocaine was also in the coat. Testimony in the trial transcript indicates that the cocaine was discovered prior to the time Isiah B. came to the office. . . .

Subsequently, a delinquency petition was filed against Isiah B. alleging possession of a dangerous weapon on school property and possession of cocaine with intent to deliver. Isiah B. moved the circuit court for an order suppressing the gun and cocaine as products of an illegal search. The circuit court denied Isiah B.'s motion to suppress the evidence gathered in the search and adjudicated Isiah B. a delinquent child. . . . We accepted the certification of this case from the court of appeals.

The Fourth Amendment to the United States Constitution and Article I, sec. 11, of the Wisconsin Constitution proscribe unreasonable searches and seizures. . . .

Unlike many cases involving the constitutionality of a search, the search at issue in this case was not conducted by law enforcement officials. Rather, Madison High School officials conducted the search of Isiah B.'s locker. The law concerning the legality of searches conducted by public school officials was quite unsettled until 1985. In 1985, the United States Supreme Court decided *New Jersey v. T. L. O.* . . .

At issue in *T. L. O.* was the constitutionality of a search of a student's purse. . . . The Court in *T. L. O.* began its analysis of the Fourth Amendment issue by addressing whether the Fourth Amendment's provisions apply to searches conducted by public school officials. . . . The Supreme Court [concluded] that:

> . . . In carrying out searches and other disciplinary functions pursuant to such policies, school officials act as representatives of the State, not merely as surrogates for the parents, and they cannot claim the parents' immunity from the strictures of the Fourth Amendment.

. . . We are bound by the Supreme Court's conclusion that public school officials are state agents for purposes of Fourth Amendment search and seizure analysis and as such must conform their conduct to the strictures of that amendment. Thus, applying the dictates of the Fourth Amendment, the question in this case is whether the search of Isiah B.'s locker was one done subject to the Fourth Amendment.

As to determining the reasonableness of a search, the Supreme Court in *T. L. O.* stated:

> What is reasonable depends on the context within which a search takes place. The determination of the standard of reasonableness governing any specific class of searches requires "balancing the need to search against the invasion which the search entails." On one side of the balance are arrayed the individual's legitimate expectations of privacy and personal security; on the other, the government's need for effective methods to deal with breaches of public order.

. . . Recognizing that before a balancing of interest can take place a court must first conclude that a reasonable expectation of privacy exists on the student's side of the balance, the Supreme Court concluded that a student has a legitimate reasonable expectation of privacy in a purse. . . . However, the court specifically declined to express any opinion on whether a student has a legitimate reasonable expectation of privacy in a school locker. . . . The state of Wisconsin urges this court to conclude that Isiah B. had no reasonable expectation of privacy in his locker and thus no search for Fourth Amendment purposes took place.

We agree with the state and hold that when the Milwaukee Public School System (M.P.S.), as here, has a written policy retaining ownership and possessory control of school lockers (hereinafter referred to as a locker policy), and notice of the locker policy is given to students, then students have no reasonable expectation of privacy in those lockers. Consequently, the circuit court properly denied his motion to suppress.

If school authorities do not have a locker policy like the one in this case, students might have a lowered reasonable expectation of privacy in their lockers. With respect to a public school student's reasonable expectation of privacy, the Supreme Court stated the following in *T. L. O.*:

> To receive the protection of the Fourth Amendment, an expectation of privacy must be one that society is "prepared to recognize as legitimate." . . .
>
> Although this Court may take notice of the difficulty of maintaining discipline in the public schools today, the situation is not so dire that students in the schools may claim no legitimate expectations of privacy. . . . [S]choolchildren may find it necessary to carry with them a variety of legitimate, noncontraband items, and there is no reason to conclude that they have necessarily waived all rights to privacy in such items merely by bringing them onto school grounds.

School administrations may adopt a locker policy retaining ownership and possessory control of school lockers and give notice of that policy to students.

Because Isiah B. had no reasonable expectation of privacy in his locker, there was no Fourth Amendment violation, and the circuit court properly denied Isiah B.'s motion to suppress. We affirm the judgment of the circuit court.* . . .

The judgment of the Milwaukee county circuit court is affirmed. . . .

---

*Isiah B. argues that a valid Fourth Amendment search of a student's locker by public school officials requires said officials to promulgate and conform to written guidelines governing locker searches. Isiah B. also argues that public school officials must possess an individualized suspicion that a student's locker contains evidence of a crime or school rule violation before said locker can be searched in accord with the Fourth Amendment. Because we conclude that Isiah B. did not have a reasonable expectation of privacy in his locker, we do not reach these issues.

CASE NOTES

1. *Police Search Lockers with School Permission.* A school may give the police permission to search lockers. In a case where detectives presented a search warrant to the school principal, searched students, found nothing, and then, in a subsequent search of the students' lockers, found four marijuana cigarettes, the court rejected a motion to suppress. The court stated:

> Indeed, it is doubtful if a school would be properly discharging its duty of supervision over the students, if it failed to retain control over the lockers. Not only have the school authorities a right to inspect, but this right becomes a duty when suspicion arises that something of an illegal nature may be secreted there. When Dr. Panitz [the principal] learned of the detectives' suspicion, he was obligated to inspect the locker. This interest, together with the nonexclusive nature of the locker, empowered him to consent to the search by the officers.

People v. Overton, 20 N.Y.2d 360, 283 N.Y.S.2d 22, 229 N.E.2d 596 (1969), affirmed on reargument, 24 N.Y.2d 522, 301 N.Y.S.2d 479, 249 N.E.2d 366 (1969).

2. The law is well decided that a school search instigated by a police officer must be accompanied by a search warrant to be valid. However, gray areas of fact exist where proof must be adduced as to who actually initiated the search and for what reason. The validity of a school-initiated search, not requiring a search warrant, rests on whether evidence can be produced by the defendant to show that the search "activities were at *the behest* of a law enforcement agency." Where a vice-principal of a school requested that a police liaison officer accompany her in the search of a locker of a particular student and the police officer, pursuant thereto, conducted a limited pat-down search of the student, the court upheld the search as valid and said:

> The imposition of a probable cause warrant requirement based on the limited involvement of . . . (the police officer) would not serve the interest of preserving swift and informal disciplinary procedures in schools.

This court further noted that the pat-down search was justified and was conducted with "reasonable suspicion" based on evidence obtained earlier by the vice-principal, and was therefore valid. *Carson v. Cook,* 810 F.2d 188 (8th Cir.1987).

3. *Qualified Immunity for Search.* School principals, assistant principals, superintendents, and individual board members are qualifiedly immune from Section 1983 (42 U.S.C.A. §1983; U.S. Const. Amend. 4) suits for damages. In a case where a student was subjected to a warrantless strip search by school officials following a confidential tip by a fellow student that the student was using drugs and after parents had expressed a concern about drugs, the court said the search was justified at its inception and the student's production of a vial of drugs warranted further search. *Williams by Williams v. Ellington,* 936 F.2d 881 (6th Cir.1991).

4. *Identity of Informant.* The school principal need not reveal the identity of the informant whose information led to his reasonable suspicion. The court said that the informant "was neither an essential witness on a basic issue in the case nor was he or she apparently an active participant in the crime for which defendant is prosecuted." *State v. Biancamano,* 284 N.J.Super. 654, 666 A.2d 199 (1995).

5. *Establishing Reasonable Suspicion.* A school resource officer paid by the sheriff's office searched students on request from the principal. The officer had no independent information, did not conduct an investigation, and searched solely on the principal's request. No evidence was given by the principal as to why he thought the student should be searched. The court could not uphold either probable cause or reasonable suspicion. *A. J. M. v. State,* 617 So.2d 1137 (Fla.App.1 Dist.1993).

6. *Anonymous Call to Establish Reasonable Suspicion.* Where a school administrator received an anonymous phone call indicating that a student "would be carrying a substantial amount of drugs including LSD with him at school that day" and the administration and teachers had previously expressed concern and suspicion that the pupil was distributing drugs, the pupil was searched, revealing marijuana, a semiautomatic pistol, and 121 "hits" of LSD. The court said, "The telephone call informing [the administrator] that the [pupil] would be carrying drugs to school that day, taken in light of exist-

ing suspicions of the defendant's drug involvement, was more than enough to justify the inception of the search." *State v. Drake*, 139 N.H. 662, 662 A.2d 265 (1995).

■ ENDNOTES

1. Board of Education of Rogers, Arkansas v. McCluskey, 458 U.S. 966, 102 S.Ct. 3469 (1982).

2. Freeman v. Pitts, 503 U.S. 467, 112 S.Ct. 1430 (1992).

3. 420 U.S. 308, 95 S.Ct. 992 (1975).

4. Ibid.

5. Board of Education of Rogers, Arkansas v. McCluskey, 488 U.S. at 970, 102 S.Ct. at 3471.

6. Newton Edwards, *The Courts and the Public Schools* (Chicago: University of Chicago Press, 1955), p. 604.

7. State ex rel. Burpee v. Burton, 45 Wis. 150, 30 Am.Rep. 706 (1878).

8. Ibid.

9. Thomas Hobbes, *Leviathan* (New York: Collier, Macmillan, 1962), p. 132. Hobbes conveyed the newly published *Leviathan* to Mr. Francis Godolphin, Paris, April 15–25, 1651.

10. Jean-Jacques Rousseau, *The Social Contract and Discourses,* trans. G. D. H. Cole (London: J. M. Dent & Sons, Everyman's Library); *A Discourse on Political Economy,* first published in 1758, p. 149.

11. Rousseau, *A Discourse,* p. 192.

12. Ibid.

13. Edward Hallett Carr, *The Twenty Years' Crisis, 1919–1939* (New York: Harper Torchbooks, Harper & Row Company, 1964; originally published in 1939), p. 42.

14. Ibid.

15. Ibid.

16. State v. Randall, 79 Mo.App. 226 (1899).

17. See Lander v. Seaver, 32 Vt. 114, 76 Am.Dec. 156 (1859).

18. Ibid.

19. Ibid.

20. Ibid.

21. Richardson v. Braham, 125 Neb. 142, 249 N.W. 557 (1933).

22. 469 U.S. 325, 105 S.Ct. 733 (1985).

23. Ginsberg v. New York, 390 U.S. 629, 88 S.Ct. 1274 (1968); Board of Education of Island Trees v. Pico, 457 U.S. 853, 102 S.Ct. 2799 (1982).

24. 478 U.S. 675, 106 S.Ct. 3159 (1986).

25. Hurtado v. California, 110 U.S. 516, 4 S.Ct. 111 (1884).

26. Meyer v. Nebraska, 262 U.S. 390, 43 S.Ct. 625 (1923). See also Adkins v. Children's Hospital, 261 U.S. 525, 43 S.Ct. 394 (1923).

27. Valley National Bank of Phoenix v. Glover, 62 Ariz. 538, 159 P.2d 292 (1945).

28. Calder v. Bull, 3 U.S. (3 Dall.) 386 (1798). In *Calder,* the Court engaged in a debate over whether it had the authority under natural law to overrule the legislation of the Connecticut legislature.

29. See Lloyd L. Weinreb, *Natural Law and Justice* (Cambridge: Harvard University Press, 1987), pp. 224–65.

30. Parenthetically, it should be observed that England has an unwritten constitution that has the force of law but is simply a collection of conventions, traditions, judicial legal precedents, and parliamentary acts.

31. See D. D. Raphael, *Problems of Political Philosophy* (London: Macmillan, 1989), pp. 102–3.

32. John E. Nowak, Ronald D. Rotunda, and J. Nelson Young, *Constitutional Law* (St. Paul, Minn.: West, 1986), p. 332.

33. Ibid.

34. Ibid.

35. Ibid.

36. Griswold v. Connecticut, 381 U.S. 479, 85 S.Ct. 1678 (1965).

37. Ibid.

38. Ibid.

39. Ibid.

40. Ibid.

41. 478 U.S. 186, 106 S.Ct. 2841, rehearing denied, 478 U.S. 1039, 107 S.Ct. 29 (1986) (homosexual rights).

42. Ibid.

43. 490 U.S. 386, 109 S.Ct. 1865 (1989).

44. 523 U.S. 833, 118 S.Ct.1708 (1998).

45. Ibid.

46. Ibid.

47. Graham v. Connor, op. cit.

48. See Bank of Columbia v. Okely, (4 Wheat.) 235 (1819); Hurtado v. California, 110 U.S. 516, 4 S.Ct. 111 (1884).

49. County of Sacramento v. Lewis, op. cit.

50. Ibid.

51. Ibid.

52. Nowak et al., *Constitutional Law,* p. 369.

53. Ibid., p. 370.

54. NAACP v. Alabama ex rel. Patterson, 357 U.S. 449, 78 S.Ct. 1163 (1958); Bates v. Little Rock, 361 U.S. 516, 80 S.Ct. 412 (1960).

55. Harper v. Virginia State Board of Elections, 383 U.S. 663, 86 S.Ct. 1079 (1966); Carrington v. Rash, 380 U.S. 89, 85 S.Ct. 775 (1965).

56. Shapiro v. Thompson, 394 U.S. 618, 89 S.Ct. 1322 (1969).

57. See Douglas v. California, 372 U.S. 353, 83 S.Ct. 814 (1963) (right to counsel); Mayer v. Chicago, 404 U.S. 189, 92 S.Ct. 410 (1971) (right to transcript); Bounds v. Smith, 430 U.S. 817, 97 S.Ct. 1491 (1977) (right to legal materials and access to courts).

58. Goss v. Lopez, 419 U.S. 565, 95 S.Ct. 729 (1975).

59. San Antonio Independent School District v. Rodriguez, 411 U.S. 1, 93 S.Ct. 1278, rehearing denied, 411 U.S. 959, 93 S.Ct. 1919 (1973): Papasan v. Allain, 478 U.S. 265, 106 S.Ct. 2932 (1986).

60. Board of Regents v. Roth, 408 U.S. 564, 92 S.Ct. 2701 (1972); Perry v. Sindermann, 408 U.S. 593, 92 S.Ct. 2694 (1972).

61. Boddie v. Connecticut, 401 U.S. 371, 91 S.Ct. 780 (1971); Loving v. Virginia, 388 U.S. 1, 87 S.Ct. 1817 (1967).

62. Roe v. Wade, 410 U.S. 113, 93 S.Ct. 705, rehearing denied, 410 U.S. 959, 93 S.Ct. 1407 (1973); Skinner v.

Oklahoma, 316 U.S. 535, 62 S.Ct. 1110 (1942) (reproductive ability—sterilization). See also Bowers v. Hardwick, 478 U.S. 186, 106 S.Ct. 2841 rehearing denied, 478 U.S. 1039, 107 S.Ct. 29 (1986) (homosexual rights).

63. Bowers, op. cit.

64. 268 U.S. 510, 45 S.Ct. 571 (1925).

65. 321 U.S. 158, 64 S.Ct. 438 (1944).

66. 262 U.S. 390, 43 S.Ct. 625 (1923); see Pierce v. Society of Sisters, 268 U.S. 510, 45 S.Ct. 571 (1925).

67. Meyer v. Nebraska, op. cit.

68. Ibid.; Pierce v. Society of Sisters, op. cit.

69. 294 F.2d 150 (5th Cir.), cert. denied, 368 U.S. 930, 82 S.Ct. 368 (1961).

70. 393 U.S. 503, 89 S.Ct. 733 (1969).

71. Ibid., 393 U.S. at 505, 89 S.Ct. at 735. See also Meyer v. Nebraska, op. cit.; Bartels v. Iowa, 262 U.S. 404, 43 S.Ct. 628 (1923); Pierce v. Society of Sisters, op. cit.; West Virginia Board of Education v. Barnette, 319 U.S. 624, 63 S.Ct. 1178 (1943).

72. 419 U.S. 565, 95 S.Ct. 729 (1975).

73. Ibid., 419 U.S. at 565, 95 S.Ct. at 732 (1975).

74. Board of Regents v. Roth, 408 U.S. at 577, 92 S.Ct. at 2709.

75. Meyer v. Nebraska, op. cit.

76. Board of Regents v. Roth, 408 U.S. at 571, 92 S.Ct. 2706.

77. Goss, op. cit.

78. Ibid.

79. 430 U.S. 651, 97 S.Ct. 1401 (1977).

80. Ibid.

81. Ibid.

82. Ibid.

83. Hall v. Tawney, 621 F.2d 607 (4th Cir.1980).

84. Garcia v. Miera, 817 F.2d 650 (10th Cir.1987).

85. Hall v. Tawney, op. cit.

86. Garcia v. Miera, op. cit.

87. Ibid.

88. Metzger v. Osbeck, 841 F.2d 518 (3d Cir.1988).

89. Wise v. Pea Ridge School District, 855 F.2d 560 (8th Cir.1988).

90. Hall v. Tawney, op. cit.

91. 294 F.2d 150, cert. denied, 368 U.S. 930, 82 S.Ct. 368 (1961).

92. 295 F.Supp. 978 (W.D.Wis.1968), affirmed, 418 F.2d 163 (7th Cir.1969).

93. Hobson v. Bailey, 309 F.Supp. 1393 (W.D.Tenn.1970); Zanders v. Louisiana State Board of Education, 281 F.Supp. 747 (W.D.La.1968).

94. Joint Anti-Fascist Refugee Committee v. McGrath, 341 U.S. 123, 71 S.Ct. 624 (1951) (concurring opinion of Justice Frankfurter).

95. Dixon v. Alabama State Board of Education, 294 F.2d 150 (5th Cir.), cert. denied, 368 U.S. 930, 82 S.Ct. 368 (1961). For an excellent discussion of procedural due process, see William G. Buss, "Procedural Due Process for School Discipline: Probing the Constitutional Outline," *University of Pennsylvania Law Review* 119 (1971): pp. 545–641.

96. 233 F.Supp. 396 (N.D.Fla.1963).

97. 419 U.S. 565, 95 S.Ct. 729 (1975).

98. C. MacKinnon, "Sexual Harassment of Working Women; A Hidden Issue," as cited in Donna Greff Schneider, "Sexual Harassment and Higher Education," *Texas Law Review* 65 (1987): pp. 25 and 46.

99. Grove City College v. Bell, 465 U.S. 555, 104 S.Ct. 1211 (1984).

100. Public Law 100-259.

101. 524 U.S. 274, 118 S.Ct. 1989 (1998).

102. Ibid.

103. Ibid.

104. Ibid.

105. Marjorie R. Freiman, "Unequal and Inadequate Protection under the Law: State Child Abuse Statutes," *George Washington Law Review* 50, no. 2 (January 1982): pp. 243–44.

106. Ibid., p. 252.

107. Public Law 93-247, 88 Stat. 4 (1974) [codified as amended at 42 U.S.C.A. §§5101–5107].

108. Freiman, "Unequal and Inadequate Protection."

109. 42 U.S.C.A. §5112.

110. Freiman, "Unequal and Inadequate Protection," pp. 253–54.

111. 42 U.S.C.A. §5102.

112. Freiman, "Unequal and Inadequate Protection," p. 254.

113. Virginia Code 1950, Chapter 12.1, §63.1-248.1.

114. Ibid., §63.1-248.2.

115. Freiman, "Unequal and Inadequate Protection," pp. 252–69.

116. Arthur Schwartz and Harold Hirsh, "Child Abuse and Neglect: A Survey of the Law," *Medical Trial Technique Quarterly* 28 (Winter 1982): pp. 298–302.

117. Freiman, "Unequal and Inadequate Protection," p. 247.

118. Jody Aaron, "Civil Liability for Teachers' Negligent Failure to Report Suspected Child Abuse," *Wayne Law Review* 28 (1981): p. 187.

119. Sanford N. Katz et al., "Legal Research on Child Abuse and Neglect: Past and Future," *Family Law Quarterly* XI, no. 2 (Summer 1977): p. 151.

120. Freiman, "Unequal and Inadequate Protection," p. 259 (footnote).

121. Virginia, Code 1950, §63.1-248.5.

122. 71 Or.App. 751, 694 P.2d 569, 22 Educ.L.Rep. 1001 (1985).

123. Freiman, "Unequal and Inadequate Protection," p. 263.

124. Ibid.

125. Ibid.

126. Schwartz and Hirsh, "Child Abuse and Neglect," p. 311.

127. Ibid.

128. 17 Cal.3d 399, 131 Cal.Rptr. 69, 551 P.2d 389 (1976).

129. Aaron, "Civil Liability."

130. Schwartz and Hirsh, "Child Abuse and Neglect," p. 304.

131. *Oklahoma Statutes Annotated*, Title 21, §846.

132. Freiman, "Unequal and Inadequate Protection," pp. 260–61.

133. Ibid.

134. Schwartz and Hirsh, "Child Abuse and Neglect," pp. 304–5.

135. Aaron, "Civil Liability," p. 191. See also Chapter 11 on tort liability of this book for further discussions of a teacher's potential liability.

136. Schenck v. United States, 249 U.S. 47, 39 S.Ct. 247 (1919).

137. Whitney v. California, 274 U.S. 357, 47 S.Ct. 641 (1927); Bridges v. California, 314 U.S. 252, 62 S.Ct. 190 (1941).

138. Whitney v. California, op. cit.

139. Bridges v. California, op. cit.

140. Tinker v. Des Moines Independent Community School District, 393 U.S. 503, 89 S.Ct. 733 (1969).

141. 431 F.2d 594 (6th Cir.1970).

142. Tinker, 89 S.Ct. at 737.

143. 478 U.S. 675, 106 S.Ct. 3159 (1986).

144. Ibid.

145. Pugsley v. Sellmeyer, 158 Ark. 247, 250 S.W. 538 (1923).

146. Mitchell v. McCall, 273 Ala. 604, 143 So.2d 629 (1962).

147. 445 F.2d 932 (9th Cir.1971).

148. Jackson v. Dorrier, 424 F.2d 213 (6th Cir.), cert. denied, 400 U.S. 850, 91 S.Ct. 55 (1970).

149. Richards v. Thurston, 424 F.2d 1281 (1st Cir.1970). See also Breen v. Kahl, 419 F.2d 1034 (7th Cir.1969), holding regulation unconstitutional.

150. 392 F.2d 697 (5th Cir.1968).

151. Stevenson v. Board of Education of Wheeler County, Georgia, 426 F.2d 1154 (5th Cir.1970).

152. Massie v. Henry, 455 F.2d 779 (4th Cir.1972). See also Humphries v. Lincoln Parish School Board, 467 So.2d 870 (La.App.1985); Dominco v. Rapids Parish School Board, 675 F.2d 100 (5th Cir.1982).

153. Thomas Hobbes, *Man and Citizen,* June 24, 1658, ed. Bernard Gert (Indianapolis: Hackett Publishing Co., 1991), p. 114.

154. 431 F.2d 594 (6th Cir.1970).

155. See Jennifer Starr, "School Violence and Its Effect on the Constitutionality of Public School Uniform Policies," *Journal of Law and Education* 29 (January 2000): p. 113.

156. Phoenix Elementary School District No. 1 v. Green, 943 P.2d 836 (Ariz.Ct.App.1997).

157. Tinker v. Des Moines Independent Community School District, 393 U.S. 503, 89 S.Ct. 733 (1969).

158. Byars v. City of Waterbury, 1999 WL 391033 (Conn. Super., June 4, 1999).

159. Belotti v. Baird, 443 U.S. 622, 99 S.Ct. 3035 (1979).

160. The Court relied on Bivens v. Albuquerque Public Schools, 899 F.Supp.556 (D.N.M.1995).

161. United States v. O'Brien, 391 U.S. 367, 88 S.Ct. 1673 (1968).

162. Byars v. City of Waterbury, op. cit.

163. Phoenix Elementary School District No. 1 v. Green, op. cit.

164. See Joseph R. McKinney, "A New Look at Student Uniform Policies," 140 Educ.L.Rep. 791 (March 2000).

165. New York Times Co. v. United States, 403 U.S. 713, 91 S.Ct. 2140 (1971).

166. William Blackstone, *Commentaries on the Laws of England,* book 4, chapter II (London, 1765–1769), p. 153.

167. Leonard W. Levy, *Original Intent and the Framers' Constitution* (New York: MacMillan Publishing Co. 1988) p. 213.

168. People v. Crosswell, 3 John.Cas. 337 (N.Y.Supp.1804).

169. John Thompson, *An Enquiry, Concerning the Liberty, and Licentiousness of the Press* (New York, 1801), 84 pp., reprinted by DeCapo Press, 1970.

170. 376 U.S. 254, 84 S.Ct. 710 (1964).

171. "Trial of William Cobbett," Nov. 1797, in Francis Wharten, ed., *State Trials of the United States during the Administration of Washington and Adams* (Philadelphia, 1849), pp. 323–24. See also Levy, op. cit., p. 197.

172. New York Times v. United States, op. cit.

173. 484 U.S. 260, 108 S.Ct. 562 (1988).

174. Ibid., 108 S.Ct. at 570.

175. Tinker v. Des Moines Independent Community School District, 393 U.S. 503, 513, 89 S.Ct. 733, 740 (1969).

176. Leeb v. DeLong, 198 Cal.App.3d 47, 243 Cal.Rptr. 494 (4 Dist.1988). See Trachtman v. Anker, 563 F.2d 512 (2d Cir.1977), cert. denied, 435 U.S. 925, 98 S.Ct. 1491 (1978).

177. Baughman v. Freienmuth, 478 F.2d 1345 (4th Cir.1973).

178. City of Lakewood v. Plain Dealer Publishing Co., 486 U.S. 750, 756, 108 S.Ct. 2138, 2143 (1988).

179. Burch v. Barker, 861 F.2d 1149 (9th Cir.1988).

180. Bystrom v. Fridley High School, 822 F.2d 747 (8th Cir.1987); see also Quarterman v. Byrd, 453 F.2d 54 (4th Cir.1971).

181. Bethel School District No. 403 v. Fraser, 478 U.S. 675, 106 S.Ct. 3159 (1986).

182. Ibid.

183. 307 U.S. 496, 59 S.Ct. 954 (1939).

184. Ibid., 307 U.S. at 515, 59 S.Ct. at 964.

185. Slotterback v. Interboro School District, 766 F.Supp. 280, 291 (E.D.Pa.1991).

186. Ibid., p. 291; see also Gregorie v. Centennial School District, 907 F.2d 1366 (3d Cir.1990).

187. Bethel, 478 U.S. at 683, 103 S.Ct. at 3164.

188. 484 U.S. 260, 108 S.Ct. 562 (1988).

189. Ibid.

190. Ibid., 484 U.S. at 270, 108 S.Ct. at 569.

191. 861 F.2d 1149 (9th Cir.1988).

192. Burch, 861 F.2d at 1159.

193. Ibid., p. 1154.

194. Berger v. Rensselaer Central School Corp., 982 F.2d 1160 (7th Cir.1993).

195. Hazelwood, 484 U.S. at 260–61, 108 S.Ct. at 564.

196. Hedges v. Wauconda Community School District No. 118, 9 F.3d 1295 (7th Cir.1993).

197. Reno v. American Civil Liberties Union, 521 U.S. 844, 117 S.Ct. 2329 (1997).

198. Hazelwood School District v. Kuhlmeier, 484 U.S. 260, 108 S.Ct. 562 (1988).

199. Beussink v. Woodland R-IV School District, 30 F.Supp.2d 1175 (E.D.Mo.1998).

200. 393 U.S. 503, 89 S.Ct. 733 (1969).

201. Ibid.

202. Tinker, op. cit.

203. Beussink, op. cit.

204. See Mary Jane Connelly, "Search and Seizure in Education," Ph.D. diss., Virginia Tech University, 1982.

205. *Black's Law Dictionary* (St. Paul, Minn.: West, 1968), p. 1616.

206. Levy, op. cit., p. 242.

207. Ibid.

208. Bellnier v. Lund, 438 F.Supp. 47 (N.D.N.Y.1977).

209. State v. Stein, 203 Kan. 638, 456 P.2d 1 (1969), cert. denied, 397 U.S. 947, 90 S.Ct. 966 (1970).

210. New Jersey v. T. L. O., 469 U.S. 325, 105 S.Ct. 733 (1985).

211. Ibid.

212. R. D. L. v. State, 499 So.2d 31 (Fla.App. 2 Dist.1986).

213. State v. Slattery, 56 Wash.App. 820, 787 P.2d 932 (1990).

214. Shamberg v. State, 762 P.2d 488 (Alaska App.1988). See also Coffman v. State, 782 S.W.2d 249 (Tex.App.1989).

215. Wynn v. Board of Education of Vestavia Hills, 508 So.2d 1170 (Ala.1987).

216. Shamberg v. State, op. cit.

217. Cales v. Howell Public Schools, 635 F.Supp. 454 (E.D.Mich.1985).

218. T. L. O., op. cit.

219. Kuehn v. Reston School District No. 403, 103 Wash.2d 594, 694 P.2d 1078 (1985).

220. Burnham v. West, 681 F.Supp. 1169 (E.D.Va.1988).

221. Levy, op. cit., p. 244.

222. 639 F.2d 662 (10th Cir.1981).

223. 475 F.Supp. 1012 (N.D.Ind.1979), opinion adopted on this issue and reversed on another issue, 631 F.2d 91 (7th Cir.1980), rehearing denied, 635 F.2d 582, cert. denied, 451 U.S. 1022, 101 S.Ct. 3015 (1981).

224. 499 F.Supp. 223 (E.D.Tex.1980).

225. 690 F.2d 470 (5th Cir.1982).

226. Ibid., p. 475.

227. Ibid., p. 477.

228. Ibid., pp. 481–82.

229. 438 F.Supp. 47 (N.D.N.Y.1977).

230. 919 F.Supp. 1206 (N.D.Ind.1995).

231. Doe v. Renfrow, 631 F.2d 91 (7th Cir.1980), cert. denied, 451 U.S. 1022, 101 S.Ct. 3015 (1981).

232. Ibid., pp. 92–93.

233. 658 A.2d 1378 (Pa.Super.1993).

234. People v. Pruit, 662 N.E.2d 540 (Ill.App.1 Dist.1996).

235. Ibid., p. 547.

236. People v. Dukes, 580 N.Y.S.2d 850 (N.Y.City Crim. Ct.1992). See also 75 Op. Cal. Att'y Gen. 155, 1992 WL 469726.

237. 232 U.S. 383, 34 S.Ct. 341 (1914).

238. 338 U.S. 25, 69 S.Ct. 1359 (1949).

239. 232 U.S. 383, 34 S.Ct. 341 (1914).

240. Ibid.

241. 367 U.S. 643, 81 S.Ct. 1684 (1961).

242. Skinner v. Railway Labor Executives' Association, 489 U.S. 602, 109 S.Ct. 1402 (1989).

243. National Treasury Employees Union v. Von Raab, 489 U.S. 656, 109 S.Ct. 1384 (1989).

244. Vernonia School District 47J v. Acton, 515 U.S. 646, 115 S.Ct. 2386 (1995).

245. Williams by Williams v. Ellington, 936 F.2d 881 (6th Cir.1991).

246. 631 F.2d 91 (7th Cir.1980).

CHAPTER 9

RIGHTS OF DISABLED CHILDREN

Without care and compassion, there can be no justice.

—Robert C. Solomon

CHAPTER OUTLINE

- A History of Neglect
- The Turning Point
- Congressional Action
- Interpretation of the IDEA (EAHCA)
- Acquired Immunodeficiency Syndrome (AIDS)

PROGRAMS FOR DISABLED CHILDREN developed slowly in public schools. Meager financial resources and public apathy combined to prevent significant efforts to extend an equal educational opportunity to disabled persons until relatively recently.

During the 1940s through the 1960s, several states distributed categorical funds to local school districts for handicapped programs. A few states required local school districts to establish programs for disabled children to receive state foundation program allocations, but such efforts were not comprehensive and failed to address the special needs of most disabled children, particularly those who were severely disabled.

It was not until the latter part of the 1960s and early 1970s that pervasive concern for the equality of educational opportunity swept the nation. During the Johnson presidency, that concern had expanded to touch the disabled. The watershed in the development of these programs in public schools, however, came with a few key court decisions and the federal government's landmark legislation in 1975 entitled the Education for All Handicapped Children Act (EAHCA).[1] The original Education for All Handicapped Children Act, signed on November 29, 1975, by President Gerald R. Ford, was amended in 1978 and 1986 and, in 1990, was finally incorporated into a new law, the Individuals with Disabilities Education Act (IDEA) (20 U.S.C.A. §§1400–1485).

In 1997, Congress reauthorized and amended the IDEA[2] reaffirming the intent of the law and seeking to address several of the issues that have emerged in litigation since 1975. These amendments of 1997 also expanded the purpose of the law beyond that of merely requiring access to, further, require an emphasis on the measurement of outcomes for preparing disabled children for employment and independent living.[3]

To better understand the recent court cases interpreting this federal legislation, it is instructive to briefly review the antecedents of the provision of educational opportunity for disabled children.

■ A HISTORY OF NEGLECT*

Special education programs in the United States originated during the early nineteenth century, when isolated advocates of disabled children established educational programs for specific handicaps or pressured state legislatures to pass legislation to achieve this purpose. The earliest known school for disabled students was established in Hartford, Connecticut, in 1817. Thomas Hopkins Gallaudet founded the American Asylum for the Education of the Deaf and Dumb (now the American School for the Deaf) two years after returning from France, where he was newly trained in the French method of manual communication for the deaf. Gallaudet brought with him a deaf teacher, Laurent Clerc, and together the two men traveled to various American cities, soliciting money from private sources to establish their school.[4]

The Connecticut legislature appropriated $5,000 for the school in 1816, and by April 15, 1817, the school opened its doors to seven students. In 1819, the school's future was ensured when the federal government turned over 23,000 acres of land to the school, which the school in turn sold, accruing more than $300,000. During the same year, other states began providing the tuition moneys necessary to send deaf children to the American School.[5]

A second school, the New York Institution for the Education of the Deaf and Dumb, was opened in New York in 1818. This school was funded by private donations, but in 1821, the state of New York appropriated funds for its support. The New York school was the first day school for deaf students, but it soon evolved into a residential school program.

Pennsylvania was the site of the third school founded for deaf students in this country. Initially established in 1820, also as a private school, the state began supporting it in 1821 with funds to provide an education for fifty students. From 1823 to 1844, three new state schools were built for deaf students in Kentucky, Ohio, and Virginia. From 1844 to 1860, seventeen new schools for deaf students were established, and in 1864, the National Deaf Mute College was founded in Washington, D.C. The name later was changed to Gallaudet College in honor of the man who first began deaf education in the United States.

The need for educational services for other handicaps was not ignored. In 1830, due to the tireless efforts of Horace Mann, the Massachusetts state legislature passed into law a Resolve for Erecting a Lunatic Hospital,[6] and the first state hospital for the mentally ill was founded in the city of Worcester, Massachusetts. Mann, of course, was best known for his labors in establishing free compulsory public education for all children.

Elected in 1827 by the town of Dedham, Massachusetts, to the Massachusetts state legislature, Mann sought legislative support in improving the deplorable living conditions of the insane.[7] Forming a committee to study the plight of the insane, Mann toured poorhouses and jails throughout Massachusetts, gathering evidence to encourage legislative action. In 1830, Mann's bill was passed by the Massachusetts house and senate.

In 1832, New York established a school for blind students, and by 1852, New York, Pennsylvania, and Massachusetts all had appropriated money for programs for mentally retarded children.[8] In 1869, day programs for deaf students were started in Boston, and in 1896, programs for mentally retarded students were started in Providence, Rhode Island. Public school classes for physically disabled and blind

*The authors wish to express sincere appreciation to Patricia Anthony, Ph.D., for preparation of this portion of the chapter.

students were begun in Chicago in 1900. Consequently, by the early twentieth century, disabled children had gained entry into the public schools in several states.

Severely disabled students had a difficult time conforming to the structure and expectations of public school systems. Schools were ill-equipped to handle students who exhibited aberrant characteristics. In 1893, a Massachusetts court ruled that student behavior resulting from "imbecility" was grounds for expulsion, thereby barring many mentally retarded students from public schools.[9] In a later decision,[10] a Wisconsin Court ruled that a disabled student, although academically capable, could be excluded from regular public school classes because his disability had "a depressing and nauseating effect on the teachers and school children."[11]

This ruling prevented severely disabled children suffering from cerebral palsy or poliomyelitis from attending regular public school day classes. Since special classes for these severely disabled students had not yet been created in many cities, parents of such children had to resort to residential schools or private tutors, or they had to forgo formal education completely.

■ THE TURNING POINT

Despite these earlier judicial setbacks, social conditions of the twentieth century impacted favorably upon the growth of educational services for the disabled. The return home of disabled World War I veterans focused national attention upon the need for disabled educational programs for persons with disabilities.

In 1918, the Soldiers' Rehabilitation Act was passed by Congress, followed in 1920 by the Smith-Bankhead Act.[12] Both pieces of legislation offered vocational rehabilitation services in the form of job training and counseling. By 1944, these acts were amended to include services for mentally ill and mentally retarded individuals, as well as to provide additional funds for research and training programs.[13]

Another condition significantly affecting disabled children's quest for equal educational opportunity was the court-ordered desegregation of the public schools.[14] While specifically referring to the rights of black children, the legal mandate of *Brown v. Board of Education* set a precedent for the extension of educational access to all children, including those with disabilities.[15]

A significant turning point for disabled children's rights occurred in 1971, when a federal district court ruled that retarded children in Pennsylvania are entitled to a free public education.[16] The ruling stipulated that whenever possible, retarded children must be educated in regular classrooms rather than being segregated from the normal school population. The court said that a retarded child should receive a

> free, public program of education and training appropriate to the child's capacity, within the context of a presumption that, among the alternative programs of education and training required by statute to be available, placement in a regular public school class is preferable to placement in a special public school class [i.e., a class for "handicapped" children] and placement in a special public school class is preferable to placement in any other type of program of education and training. . . . [17]

Procedural due process and periodic reevaluations of retarded children were also part of the court's consent agreement.

THE *MILLS* CASE

In 1972, *Mills v. Board of Education of District of Columbia*[18] expanded the *Pennsylvania Association of Retarded Children (PARC)* decision to include all disabled children. Emphasizing the need for appropriate educational services in the District of Columbia, the court pointed out that the plaintiffs estimated that there are "22,000 retarded, emotionally disturbed, blind, deaf, and speech or learning disabled children, and perhaps as many as 18,000 of these children are not being furnished with programs of specialized education."[19] In granting summary judgment in favor of the plaintiffs, the court adopted a comprehensive plan that had been formulated by the District of Columbia Board of Education. Included in the plan were provisions for (1) a free appropriate education, (2) an individualized education program (IEP), and (3) due process procedures. The groundwork for future federal legislation in the area of disabled children's rights to an education had been laid.

❖ — ❖ — ❖

Procedural Due Process Is Required to
Reassign Disabled Children

Mills v. Board of Education of District of Columbia

United States District Court,
District of Columbia, 1972.
348 F.Supp. 866.

WADDY, District Judge. This is a civil action brought on behalf of seven children of school age by their next friends in which they seek a declaration of rights and to enjoin the defendants from excluding them from the District of Columbia Public Schools and/or denying them publicly supported education and to compel the defendants to provide them with immediate and adequate education and educational facilities in the public schools or alternative placement at public expense. . . . They allege that although they can profit from an education either in regular classrooms with supportive services or in special classes adapted to their needs, they have been labeled as behavioral problems, mentally retarded, emotionally disturbed or hyperactive, and denied admission to the public schools or excluded therefrom after admission, with no provision for alternative educational placement or periodic review. . . .

The genesis of this case is found (1) in the failure of the District of Columbia to provide publicly supported education and training to plaintiffs and other "exceptional" children, members of their class, and (2) the excluding, suspending, expelling, reassigning and transferring of "exceptional" children from regular public school classes without affording them due process of law.

The problem of providing special education for "exceptional" children (mentally retarded, emotionally disturbed, physically handicapped, hyperactive and other children with behavioral problems) is one of major proportions in the District of Columbia. The precise number of such children cannot be stated because the District has continuously failed to comply with Section 31-208 of the District of Columbia Code which requires a census of all children aged three to eighteen in the District to be taken. Plaintiffs estimate that there are "22,000 retarded, emotionally disturbed, blind, deaf, and speech or learning disabled children, and perhaps as many as 18,000 of these children are not being furnished with programs of specialized education." . . .

Each of the minor plaintiffs in this case qualifies as an "exceptional" child. . . .

Although all of the named minor plaintiffs are identified as Negroes the class they represent is not limited by their race. They sue on behalf of and represent all other District of Columbia residents of school age who are eligible for a free public education and who have been, or may be, excluded from such education or otherwise deprived by defendants of access to publicly supported education. . . .

Plaintiffs' entitlement to relief in this case is clear. The applicable statutes and regulations and the Constitution of the United States require it.

Section 31-201 of the District of Columbia Code requires that:

> Every parent, guardian, or other person residing [permanently or temporarily] in the District of Columbia who has custody or control of a child between the ages of seven and sixteen years shall cause said child to be regularly instructed in a public school or in a private or parochial school or instructed privately during the period of each year in which the public schools of the District of Columbia are in session. . . .

Under Section 31-203, a child may be "excused" from attendance only when

> upon examination ordered by . . . [the Board of Education of the District of Columbia, the child] is found to be unable mentally or physically to profit from attendance at school: Provided, however, That if such examination shows that such child may benefit from specialized instruction adapted to his needs, he shall attend upon such instruction.

Failure of a parent to comply with Section 31-201 constitutes a criminal offense. D.C. Code 31-207. The Court need not belabor the fact that requiring parents to see that their children attend school under pain of criminal penalties presupposes that an educational opportunity will be made available to the children. The Board of Education is required to make such opportunity available. . . .

A fortiori, the defendants' conduct here, denying plaintiffs and their class not just an equal publicly supported education but all publicly supported education while providing such education to other children, is violative of the Due Process Clause.

Not only are plaintiffs and their class denied the publicly supported education to which they are entitled, many are suspended or expelled from regular schooling or specialized instruction or reassigned without any prior hearing and are given no periodic review thereafter. Due process of law requires a hearing prior to exclusion, termination of classification into a special program. . . .

The defendants are required by the Constitution of the United States, the District of Columbia Code, and their own regulations to provide a publicly supported education for these "exceptional" children. Their failure to fulfill this clear duty to include and retain these children in the public school system, or otherwise provide them with publicly supported education, and their failure to afford them due process hearing and periodic review, cannot be excused by the claim that there are insufficient funds. In *Goldberg v. Kelly*, . . . the Supreme Court, in a case that involved the right of a welfare recipient to a hearing before termination of his benefits, held that constitutional rights must be afforded citizens despite the greater expense involved. The Court stated . . . "the State's interest that this [welfare recipient's] payments not be erroneously terminated, clearly outweighs the State's competing concern to prevent any increase in its fiscal and administrative burdens." Similarly the District of Columbia's interest in educating the excluded children clearly must outweigh its interest in preserving its financial resources. If sufficient funds are not available to finance all of the services and programs that are needed and desirable in the system then the available funds must be expended equitably in such a manner that no child is entirely excluded from a publicly supported

education consistent with his needs and ability to benefit therefrom. The inadequacies of the District of Columbia Public School System whether occasioned by insufficient funding or administrative inefficiency, certainly cannot be permitted to bear more heavily on the "exceptional" or handicapped child than on the normal child. . . .

Inasmuch as the Board of Education has presented for adoption by the Court a proposed "Order and Decree" embodying its present plans for the identification of "exceptional" children and providing for their publicly supported education, including a time table, and further requiring the Board to formulate and file with the Court a more comprehensive plan, the Court will not now appoint a special master as was requested by plaintiffs. . . .

. . . [I]t is hereby ordered, adjudged and decreed that summary judgment in favor of plaintiffs and against defendants be, and hereby is, granted, and judgment is entered in this action as follows:

1. That no child eligible for a publicly supported education in the District of Columbia public schools shall be excluded from a regular public school assignment by a rule, policy, or practice of the Board of Education of the District of Columbia or its agents unless such child is provided (a) adequate alternative educational services suited to the child's needs, which may include special education or tuition grants, and (b) a constitutionally adequate prior hearing and periodic review of the child's status, progress and the adequacy of any educational alternative.

2. The defendants, their officers, agents, servants, employees, and attorneys and all those in active concert or participation with them are hereby enjoined from maintaining, enforcing or otherwise continuing in effect any and all rules, policies and practices which exclude plaintiffs and the members of the class they represent from a regular public school assignment without providing them at public expense (a) adequate and immediate alternative education or tuition grants, consistent with their needs, and (b) a constitutionally adequate prior

hearing and periodic review of their status, progress and the adequacy of any educational alternatives; and it is further ORDERED that:

3. The District of Columbia shall provide to each child of school age a free and suitable publicly supported education regardless of the degree of the child's mental, physical or emotional disability or impairment. Furthermore, defendants shall not exclude any child resident in the District of Columbia from such publicly supported education on the basis of a claim of insufficient resources.

4. Defendants shall not suspend a child from the public schools for disciplinary reasons for any period in excess of two days without affording him a hearing pursuant to the provisions of Paragraph 13.f., below, and without providing for his education during the period of any such suspension.

5. Defendants shall provide each identified member of plaintiff class with a publicly supported education suited to his needs within thirty (30) days of the entry of this order. . . .

9. Defendants shall utilize public or private agencies to evaluate the educational needs of all identified "exceptional" children and, within twenty (20) days of the entry of this order, shall file with the Clerk of this Court their proposal for each individual placement in a suitable educational program, including the provision of compensatory educational services where required. . . .

10. Within forty-five (45) days of the entry of this order, defendants shall file with the Clerk of the Court, with copy to plaintiffs' counsel, a comprehensive plan which provides for the identification, notification, assessment, and placement of class members. Such plan shall state the nature and extent of efforts which defendants have undertaken or propose to undertake to

    a. describe the curriculum, educational objectives, teacher qualifications, and ancillary services for the publicly supported educational programs to be provided to class members; and,

    b. formulate general plans of compensatory education suitable to class members in order to overcome the present effects of prior educational deprivations. . . .

12. Within forty-five (45) days of the entry of this order, defendants shall file with this Court a report showing the expunction from or correction of all official records of any plaintiff with regard to past expulsions, suspensions, or exclusions effected in violation of the procedural rights. . . .

13. Hearing Procedures.

    a. Each member of the plaintiff class is to be provided with a publicly supported educational program suited to his needs, within the context of a presumption that among the alternative programs of education, placement in a regular public school class with appropriate ancillary services is preferable to placement in a special school class.

    b. Before placing a member of the class in such a program, defendants shall notify his parent or guardian of the proposed educational placement, the reasons therefore, and the right to a hearing before a Hearing Officer if there is an objection to the placement proposed. . . .

    e. Whenever defendants take action regarding a child's placement, denial of placement, or transfer . . . the following procedures shall be followed.

        1. Notice required hereinbefore shall be given in writing by registered mail to the parent or guardian of the child.

        2. Such notice shall:

            a. describe the proposed action in detail;

            b. clearly state the specific and complete reasons for the proposed action, including the specification of any tests or reports upon which such action is proposed;

            c. describe any alternative educational opportunities available on a permanent or temporary basis;

            d. inform the parent or guardian of the right to object to the proposed action at a hearing before the Hearing Officer;

            e. inform the parent or guardian that the child is eligible to receive, at no charge, the services of a federally or locally funded diagnostic center for an independent medical, psychological and educational evaluation and shall specify the name, address and telephone number of an appropriate local diagnostic center;

f. inform the parent or guardian of the right to be represented at the hearing by legal counsel; to examine the child's school records before the hearing, including any tests or reports upon which the proposed action may be based; to present evidence, including expert medical, psychological and educational testimony; and to confront and cross-examine any school official, employee, or agent of the school district or public department who may have evidence upon which the proposed action was based.

3. The hearing shall be at a time and place reasonably convenient to such parent or guardian. . . .

5. The hearing shall be a closed hearing unless the parent or guardian requests an open hearing.

6. The child shall have the right to a representative of his own choosing, including legal counsel.

7. The decision of the Hearing Officer shall be based solely upon the evidence presented at the hearing.

8. Defendants shall bear the burden of proof as to all facts and as to the appropriateness of any placement, denial of placement or transfer.

9. A tape recording or other record of the hearing shall be made and transcribed and, upon request, made available to the parent or guardian or his representative.

10. At a reasonable time prior to the hearing, the parent or guardian, or his counsel, shall be given access to all public school system and other public office records pertaining to the child, including any tests or reports upon which the proposed action may be based.

11. The independent Hearing Officer shall be an employee of the District of Columbia, but shall not be an officer, employee or agent of the Public School System. . . .

13. The parent or guardian, or his representative, shall have the right to present evidence and testimony, including expert medical, psychological or educational testimony.

14. Within thirty (30) days after the hearing, the Hearing Officer shall render a decision in writing. . . .

■ CONGRESSIONAL ACTION

The reasoned treatment of the disability question by the courts in the *PARC* and *Mills* cases initiated an enhanced level of public consciousness of the plight of disabled children. A near dormant humanitarian impulse of the public was awakened by these legal actions and presently spilled over to the legislative bodies of the country. An important, and indeed momentous, occasion was the concerted efforts by the U.S. Congress to redress the problem. Immediately following the *PARC* and *Mills* decisions, federal legislation was introduced in both chambers of Congress seeking to eliminate discrimination against the disabled in both the world of work and the public educational system of the country. This legislative action eventually culminated in the passage of two laws—the Rehabilitation Act of 1973[20] and the EAHCA in 1975.

REHABILITATION ACT OF 1973

Section 504 of the Rehabilitation Act states:

No otherwise qualified handicapped individual in the United States . . . shall, solely by reason of his handicap, be excluded from the participation in, be denied the benefits of, or be subjected to discrimination under any program or activity receiving Federal financial assistance.[21]

Section 504 applies to all agencies receiving federal funds for any purpose, and such funds may be forfeited if charges of agency discrimination against disabled persons are sustained.

Although Section 504 is concerned with discrimination against disabled individuals in work situations, it also addresses the problems encountered by disabled children in seeking equal educational opportunity. Five mandates included in Section 504 pertain directly to the educational needs of disabled children:

(a) location and notification, (b) free appropriate public education, (c) educational setting, (d) evaluation and placement, and (e) procedural safeguards.[22]

These provisions of Section 504 have been used successfully in obtaining desirable school programs and services for individual disabled students. Specifically, the provisions for a free appropriate public education and educational setting[23] enabled a child with cystic fibrosis to attend regular classes while receiving supportive services for a daily suctioning procedure[24] and later were instrumental in assisting children with acquired immunodeficiency syndrome (AIDS) to remain in school.[25]

The strength of this act was dealt a substantial, if temporary, blow by the U.S. Supreme Court in *Grove City College v. Bell.*[26] The Court held that Title IX,[27] a statute prohibiting sex discrimination, did not apply comprehensively to all aspects of an educational institution but covered only those parts of the educational institution receiving federal assistance. Because the wording of Title IX was similar to that of Section 504, the Supreme Court decision severely crippled the latter act's effectiveness. This Supreme Court precedent led to at least one lower court ruling in which the Sixth Circuit Court of Appeals, in 1986, held that because a student had not attempted to be included in a particular program receiving federal funding, he could not obtain redress under Section 504.[28]

The Supreme Court itself was not completely definitive as to whether *Grove City* applied to Section 504 because in 1987 it allowed, in *School Board of Nassau County v. Arline,*[29] relief for a disabled teacher who claimed Section 504 relief, ignoring the possible application of the *Grove City* restraint to Section 504. The teacher in *Arline* was not required to show that the specific program in which she was endeavoring to participate was a federally funded program.

The questions surrounding this constricted view of Section 504 were, however, obviated by congressional action that corrected the defect by enacting the Civil Rights Restoration Act in 1988.[30] This act amended Section 504 of the Rehabilitation Act by clarifying the language to remove all doubt that the law applies to all operations of public educational institutions.

EDUCATION FOR ALL HANDICAPPED CHILDREN ACT (EAHCA)

In 1975, federal legislation in the form of the EAHCA, Public Law 94-142 [formerly the Education of the Handicapped Act (EHA)], was enacted. Incorporating many provisions of earlier litigation and legislation, Public Law 94-142 ensured the right of all disabled children to a public school education.

The need for this law was expressed by Congress:

1. there are more than eight million handicapped children in the United States today;
2. the special educational needs of such children are not being fully met;
3. more than half of the handicapped children in the United States do not receive appropriate educational services which would enable them to have full equality of opportunity;
4. one million of the handicapped children in the United States are excluded entirely from the public school system and will not go through the educational process with their peers;
5. there are many handicapped children throughout the United States participating in regular school programs whose handicaps prevent them from having a successful educational experience because their handicaps are undetected.[31]

To ensure disabled children basic educational rights, Public Law 94-142 incorporated certain tenets: (1) a free appropriate public education, (2) an individualized education program, (3) special education services, (4) related services, (5) due process procedures, and (6) the least-restrictive environment (LRE) in which to learn.[32]

Congress authorized immediate implementation of all sections of the EAHCA on a priority basis, first addressing the needs of disabled children who were currently receiving no educational services at all and second upgrading the services to the most severely disabled children whose needs were inadequately served. The act further required that all disabled children between the ages of three and eighteen receive appropriate educational services by September 1, 1978; by September 1, 1980, all disabled children from age three to age twenty-one were to receive appropriate educational services.[33]

AMENDMENTS TO THE EAHCA

Since its enactment in 1975, the EAHCA has been amended numerous times;[34] each time, Congress has reaffirmed the original intent. A 1978 amendment stressed the importance of applied research and related activities to improve the educational opportunities of the disabled, and it reiterated the state's responsibility to refine and improve existing programs. In 1983, the law was amended to clarify the term "special education" as services designated "to meet the unique 'educational' needs of the handicapped child" and to specifically expand services for deaf-blind children. The committee report supporting the legislation emphasized the need to improve education for the severely disabled.[35] This legislation further reinforced Section 624, which sought to augment research, innovation, training, and dissemination activities in connection with centers and services for the disabled.[36]

The amendments in 1986 extended the age groups covered, mandating that all preschool disabled children aged three to five years be entitled to public education and establishing a new federal education program for disabled babies from birth through age two. The Senate committee report supporting the law stated that the provision was now made "for universal access to services for all handicapped children beginning at birth."[37] The 1986 amendments, however, focused in particular on the needs of deaf-blind children and those with multiple disabilities, extending provisions for specialized, intensive professional and allied services, methods, and aids that are found to be most effective.[38] In addition, the 1986 act, called the Handicapped Children's Protection Act (HCPA), enables disabled children, parents, or guardians to receive attorney's fees if they are successful in litigation against state or local agencies.[39]

In 1990, the statute was renamed the Individuals with Disabilities Education Act (IDEA).[40] Little of substance was added in the 1990 legislation except for expanding the definition of disabilities to include head trauma and autism and adding a provision to prevent states from using the Eleventh Amendment as a shield against liability in actions by disabled children. Also, the 1990 law required the development of services for disabled students to ease their transition into the adult world. Provisions for such transitional services must be included in the IEPs of all students sixteen years of age and older.

The 1997 amendments to the IDEA affected eligibility, evaluation, programming, private school placements, discipline, funding, attorney's fees, dispute resolution, and procedural safeguards.[41] The amendments did not change the general definition of a disabled child, but they did relax the requirement of the previous law in specifying the particular disability.[42] Under the earlier law, the school district was required to identify the particular disability for children before five years of age. Because of the difficulty in pinpointing the specific disability in young children, the amendments give school districts discretion to extend the identification period to include ages five through nine. This new flexibility permits school districts to have additional time in evaluating children for a particular disability. The effect of this change is to allow the child's disability at this age to be generalized to that of "child with a disability," who is "experiencing developmental delays" in any of the areas of physical, cognitive, communicative, social or emotional, or adaptive development.[43] The amendments further provide that "nothing in this Act requires that children be classified by their disability" so long as a student meets the definition of a child with a disability.[44] Thus, the amended law attempted to respond to a running disagreement among experts and advocates, some of whom believe that decategorization would reduce stereotyping of placement decisions and possible stigmatizing of students.[45]

The IDEA defines disabled children as those who are mentally retarded, hard of hearing, deaf, speech and language impaired, visually handicapped (including blindness), seriously emotionally disturbed, orthopedically impaired, or otherwise health impaired. In addition, the definition includes children with specific learning disabilities who require special education and related services.

As amended in 1997, the law clarifies the right to a free appropriate public education (FAPE) by extending coverage to all resident children with disabilities between the ages of three and twenty-one, inclusive, to the age of twenty-two. An exception is permitted for children who are convicted of felonies as adults. Dependent on state law that may provide otherwise, FAPE does not apply to students between the ages of eighteen through twenty-one who were not identified as disabled and did not have an individualized education program (IEP) "prior to their incarceration in an adult correction facility."[46] If, though, a student had been identified as having a disability or had been provided an IEP in his or her last educational placement, then the student is still entitled to IDEA benefits even if he or she had dropped out of school.[47]

A disability not specifically listed under the IDEA is attention deficit hyperactivity disorder (ADHD). Although not specifically listed, ADHD children may be covered under the IDEA, Section 504 of the Rehabilitation Act of 1973, and the Americans with Disabilities Act of 1990 (ADA). An ADHD child may be eligible for IDEA services under one of three categories: (1) other health impaired, (2) specific learning disability, and (3) seriously emotionally disturbed. The exact definition and identification of disabilities in many cases tend to be subjective, and both educational and medical experts can readily disagree in a particular situation. For example, the federal regulation promulgated to implement the IDEA attempts to define disabilities such as "serious emotional disturbance" as qualifying disabilities for special education services.[48] One court stated, "[E]vidence that a student's bad behavior was primarily caused by attention deficit disorder was sufficient to establish that the student was entitled to benefits under IDEA."[49]

The federal regulation defining "serious emotional disturbance" pointedly excludes "social maladjustment" as a disability. The differences are, however, still unclear, as litigants in *Springer v. Fairfax County School Board*, 1998, experienced.[50] After extensive evidentiary submissions and litigation, the U.S. Court of Appeals, Fourth Circuit, gave controlling weight to the testimony of three psychologists who, as experts in

the case, concluded that the plaintiff child did not show the signs of pervasive depression characteristic of serious emotional disturbance and that, too, there was not established a causal link between the characteristics of the child and the alleged educational difficulties. Thus, identification of such disabilities promises to be a continuing source of litigation, as experts conflict in each case. Moreover, the requirement of a causal link between the disability and educational attainment promises to be fertile ground for further differences of opinion among experts in each case.

Further, concerning application of Section 504, the ADHD child qualifies for protection because a major life activity, education, is implicated. Section 504 requires the schools to reasonably accommodate the child but is far less prescriptive than the IDEA. An ADHD child could also qualify under the Americans with Disabilities Act of 1990,[52] which prohibits discrimination against individuals with disabilities at work, at school, and in public accommodations. The ADA is not limited to those organizations and programs that receive federal funds. The schools, under the ADA, must make reasonable accommodations for disabled people.

■ INTERPRETATION OF THE IDEA (EAHCA)

The federal legislation beginning with Public Law 94-142 (EAHCA, formerly the EHA) has resulted in many court judicial decisions that interpret the statute's intent. In Chapter 1 of this book, we observed that a primary function of the courts is to interpret statutes to determine their true intent. This has been the primary function of the courts in dealing with disabled children's issues since the enactment of the federal laws. Since 1975, the pervasive nature of the EAHCA (and now the IDEA) tends to obviate the need for constitutional inquiry. The disabled children cases are devoted almost entirely to judicial responses to conflicts between school districts and parents of disabled children seeking definition of provisions of the federal disabled children legislation. These cases can be classified in several different ways, but they primarily fall into groups wherein the courts define the meanings of the following statutory provisions:

- Free appropriate public education
- Procedural safeguards
- Individualized education program (IEP)
- Least-restrictive environment
- Separate school placement
- Related services
- Discipline and "stay-put" provision
- Attorney's fees
- Tuition reimbursement

Judicial opinions interpreting these portions of the disability legislation are discussed in the following paragraphs.

FREE APPROPRIATE PUBLIC EDUCATION

To qualify for federal funds under the IDEA, a state must adopt a policy "that assures all handicapped children the right to a free appropriate public education." The act defines "free appropriate education." The term "free appropriate education" means special education and related services that (A) have been provided at public expense, under public supervision and direction, and without charge, (B) meet the standards of the state education agency, (C) include an appropriate preschool, elementary, or secondary education in the state involved, and (D) are provided in conformity with the individualized education program required under Section 1414 (a) (5) of this title.[53]

The act bestows upon disabled children the substantive right to a free appropriate public education (FAPE) and provides the procedural safeguards to effectuate that end.[54] Yet, beyond this declaration of substantive right, Congress does not define specifically what constitutes an "appropriate" education, opting instead to delegate latitude to public schools to make this determination in accordance with the procedural process as enunciated in the law.

The Supreme Court in *Rowley* noted the wisdom in Congress's decision not to give specific statutory definition to "appropriate education," observing that such statutory specification of educational programs would likely result in an "entirely unworkable standard requiring impossible measures and comparisons."[55]

Clearly seeing the virtue in its own reasoning, Congress in its 1997 amendments did not tamper with the flexible and broad definition of FAPE.[56] The end result therefore is that Congress seeks to expand education of disabled children by asserting an unmistakable overarching substantive right to an appropriate education guaranteed by the IDEA's structured procedural requirements, but leaves the educational decisions to the states and the local school districts.

A free appropriate public education must be specifically designed to meet the unique needs of the child. The federal program is designed for the child "to benefit." The act, as currently interpreted by the Supreme Court, requires no substantive measures regarding the level of education; therefore, the state does not have to maximize the potential of the child, only provide a program that benefits the child. In *Rowley*, the Supreme Court stated, "We therefore conclude that the 'basic floor of opportunity' provided by the Act consists of access to specialized instruction and related services which are individually designed to provide education benefit to the handicapped child."[57]

The educational methods to be used are the responsibility of the state, and the courts may review them to determine compliance with the act. The legal concerns are primarily twofold: "First, has the state complied with procedures set forth in the Act. And, second, is the individualized educational program developed pursuant to the Act's procedures reasonably calculated to enable the child to receive educational benefits."[58]

What constitutes a "benefit," though, is not easily discerned or readily agreed upon. In a vigorous dissent in *Rowley*, Justice White took issue with the use of the term "benefit," pointing out that in the case of a deaf student, instruction by "a teacher with a loud voice" could be viewed as an educational placement providing some benefit.[59]

"Benefit" itself, and whether it is required at all, was treated at length in *Timothy W. v. Rochester, New Hampshire, School District*.[60] Here the U.S. Court of Appeals for the First Circuit concluded that the EAHCA did not require that a child prove that he or she could benefit from the educational services before participation. The court said that the act was intended for *all* disabled children and that the most severely disabled children were to be given priority, not to be excluded. For a child to be compelled to show potential benefit as a condition precedent was neither intended nor contemplated by Congress in enacting the initial law.

Yet, as the *Timothy W.* case indicates, the extent of "benefit" to which a child is entitled remains an issue for the courts. In *Rowley,* the Supreme Court used the term "meaningful benefit" and further observed that "it would do no good for Congress to spend millions of dollars in providing access to public education only to have the . . . child receive no benefit from that education."[61] Most federal courts[62] have strictly applied *Rowley* and have only infrequently held that an IEP is insufficient for lack of "benefit" or "meaningful benefit." The prevailing view is indicated by the eighth circuit, in *Fort Zumwalt School District v. Clynes,* upholding the school district's IEP as likely to extend to the child an educational benefit.[63] The evidence of the benefit received in *Clynes* was passing grades, improvement in reading skills, and promotion to the next grade level.

On the other hand, some federal courts have argued that *Rowley* requires a higher standard of benefit, and quoting the Supreme Court, these courts have asserted that "Congress did not intend that a school system should discharge its duty . . . by providing a program that produces some minimal academic advancement, no matter how trivial."[64] This school of thought maintains that the IDEA is intended to provide progress beyond the "trivial." The "meaningful benefit" of *Rowley,* it is argued, was actually intended to be an uplifted basic floor of opportunity or an elevated threshold of educational benefit.[65] In this vein, the sixth circuit in *Doe v. Smith* pointed out that the "benefit must be more than *de minimis,*"[66] and the tenth circuit has held that *Rowley* requires more than *de minimis* benefit in the case of a severely disabled child.[67] Similarly, the Fifth Circuit has observed that the educational benefit cannot be "mere modicum or *de minimis.*"[68]

These views of the legislative intent of the IDEA and the *Rowley* decision are fertile ground for continuing litigation, and presumably the new 1997 amendments will do little to abate the rising tide of litigation.[69]

Extended School Year

Whether a disabled child is entitled to an extended school year depends on the individual child's IEP, which determines an appropriate ed-

ucation for each child. In *Battle v. Commonwealth of Pennsylvania,*[70] a federal circuit court ruled that a state could be required to provide educational programs beyond the regular school year. The court stated, "At the center of the controversy . . . is the definition of 'free appropriate public education.'"[71] The state of Pennsylvania through administrative policy set a limit of 180 days of instruction per year for all children, disabled or not. The case was brought by children who were profoundly impaired (PI) or emotionally disturbed (ED), claiming that the administrative policy denied them a free appropriate education as required by the EAHCA. The court found that during the summer break, all children regressed in their learning process. Although all children regressed, disabled children regressed more and required longer to recoup skills than did nondisabled children. The state claimed that the regression was caused by a multitude of factors, such as teacher incompetency, parental failure, and lack of functionality of skills taught. The court agreed that all of the factors attributed to the regression, but it thought that the program break was a major factor. The court said that no clear legislative guidance was provided, and the issues were convoluted:

> Where as in this case, the handicap in question profoundly affects the child's learning abilities, this comparison reaches a level of difficulty, which, in the absence of legislative guidance, approaches the perimeter of judicial competence.[72]

The *Battle* court, though, reasoned that because the federal statute requires special education programs to be individualized to "meet the unique needs" of each child, a fixed term of 180 days is contrary to the federal intent. The court said:

> Rather than ascertaining the reasonable educational needs of each child in light of reasonable education goals and establishing a reasonable program to attain those goals, the 180 day rule imposes with rigid certainty a program restriction which may be wholly inappropriate to the child's educational objectives.[73]

The fifth circuit in *Crawford v. Pittman*[74] found that a similar limited school year policy was in violation of the EAHCA; this court concluded

> that Mississippi's policy of refusing to consider or provide special education of a duration longer than 180 days is inconsistent with its obligations

under the Act. Rigid rules like the 180 day limitation violate not only the Act's procedural command that each child receive individual consideration but also its substantive requirements that each child receive some benefit and that lack of funds not bear more heavily on handicapped than non-handicapped children.

The eighth circuit, too, ruled that a Missouri policy limiting the education of disabled children violated the EAHCA; the Eleventh Circuit[75] made a similar ruling in invalidating a Georgia policy. After the cases of *Battle*,[76] *Yaris*,[77] *Crawford*,[78] and *Georgia Association of Retarded Citizens*,[79] the issue is no longer in doubt as to whether a disabled child can legally have available an extended school year as part of a free appropriate public education; the only question is what standards should be used to determine which child receives the extended school year services. The aforementioned cases all used as a criterion the fact that a child would regress during the summer break and concluded that if the learning regression is substantial enough to preclude rapid recoupment at the beginning of the next school year, then an extended school program is required.

Regression-Recoupment Dilemma

The regression-recoupment analysis has been commonly supported by expert testimony, but conflicts are apparent. One court noted:

> The school district's employees and consultants were unanimous in that they observed no significant regression, while doctors, therapists, and former teachers testified on behalf of [the student] that a continuous structural program . . . was required to prevent significant regression.[80]

In *Alamo Heights*,[81] a more multifaceted standard emerged that uses regression-recoupment as a factor but also employs other factors. Here, the standard maintains that

> if a child will experience severe or substantial regression during the summer months in the absence of a summer program, the handicapped child may be entitled to year round services. The issue is whether the benefits accrued to the child during the regular school year will be significantly jeopardized if he is not provided an educational program during the summer months. This is, of course, a general standard, but it must be applied

to the individual by the ARD [Admission, Review and Dismissal] Committee in the same way that juries apply other general legal standards such as negligence and reasonableness.[82]

In 1990, in *Johnson v. Independent School District No. 4 of Bixby*,[83] the court agreed with the *Alamo* analysis, saying that the use of the regression-recoupment analysis as the only test violated the right of the child to have his or her program individualized. This argument basically assumes that any fixed standard, such as the 180-day rule, must fall because it is static and negates the individualization that the act requires. The third circuit in *Polk*[84] also rejected the regression argument as the sole factor in determining the child's need for extended services. *Johnson* cited *Rowley* as providing a rationale for using many factors, pointing out that the Supreme Court in *Rowley* said that "[w]e do not attempt today to establish any one test for determining the adequacy of educational benefits conferred upon all children covered by the Act."[85] *Johnson* further concluded:

> In addition to degree of regression and the time necessary for recoupment, courts have considered many factors important in their discussions of what constitutes an "appropriate" educational program under the Act.[86]

In yet another case, *Cordrey*, the sixth circuit followed the twofold test from *Rowley* to determine what constituted an appropriate education: (1) whether the state had complied with all procedures set forth in the act and (2) whether the individualized education program was reasonably calculated to enable the child to receive educational benefits.[87] In this case, the court found that "hard empirical proof" of regression-recoupment is clearer and simpler, but the regression standard should not be interpreted to require absolutely that a child demonstrate regression in order to prove need for a summer program.[88] The court said that "the ESY [extended school year] standard should be open to developments in special education science, but not bound to any particular one."[89]

Thus, according to *Rowley*, a "free appropriate" education is defined in rather "general and somewhat imprecise" language, but if procedural guidelines are followed and a specialized program is developed for the child's needs, then the requirements of the act are met. The specialized program may or may not include extended school year services. This is a question that must be resolved based on the individual needs of each child.

PROCEDURAL SAFEGUARDS

As indicated in the *Mills* and *Rowley*[90] cases, proper procedures are a vital aspect in ensuring that appropriate educational services are extended to disabled children. The necessary due process specifications delineated in *Mills* were followed and embellished by the EAHCA in 1975. Section 1415 of that act contains procedures that are mandatory. Most important, the procedures specify that parents must be given notice and an opportunity to participate in the development of a child's education program. Inclusive is the requirement that parents be informed of all methods and procedures by which conflicts and grievances may be appealed and resolved. Implicit therein is the assurance that hearings regarding the child's placement will be impartial and unbiased. The law, Section 1415, emphasizes this standard of fairness by giving the parent a right to have the hearing conducted by a person who is an employee neither of the school district nor of the state department of education.[91]

As stated in *Rowley*, a reviewing court must make sure that procedures are followed by the district. A school district making a placement decision without reference to the IEP violates the requirements of the law and free appropriate public education.[92] On the other hand, if an insignificant procedural error is made but does not result in the child's loss of educational opportunity,[93] the court will decline to "exalt form over substance" by enforcing a technical infraction from the act's procedural standards.[94]

If the results of the hearing are not to the satisfaction of the parent or the school district, then appeal can be made to the state department of education.[95] During the time in which appeals are taken, the child must remain, or "stay put," in his or her "then current" program.[96] As discussed later in this chapter, indefinite suspension during pendency of appeal violates this section of the law.[97] Appeal to either state or federal courts may be taken after a decision has been rendered by the state department of education.[98]

INDIVIDUALIZED EDUCATION PROGRAM (IEP)

The purpose, of course, of all these procedural safeguards is to ensure to the parent and child that an appropriate individualized education program will be provided. The IEP goes beyond merely providing a place for the child in the public schools; more extensively, it must design and reduce to writing an educational plan that takes into account the identification of the child's educational needs, the annual instructional goals and objectives, the specific educational programs and services to be provided, and the evaluation procedures necessary to monitor the child's progress. An IEP is "more than a mere exercise in Public Relations";[99] indeed, it is the "centerpiece of the statute's education delivery system for disabled children":

> The term "individualized education program" means a written statement for each child with a disability developed in any meeting by a representative of the local educational agency or an intermediate educational unit who shall be qualified to provide, or supervise the provision of, specially designed instruction to meet the unique needs of children with disabilities. . . . [100]

This statement describing the child's educational goals and specifying required services is developed by a multidisciplinary team. For initial evaluation and placement, the IEP team must have as members a school official, the child's teacher(s), the parents, and a person or persons qualified to interpret evaluation results. Because the IEP must be jointly prepared by school officials and parents and reviewed annually, a condition of possible contention is created. Contests between parents and school districts over the nature of the IEP have resulted in a plethora of disabled-children litigation in recent years, all of which has begun to form a formidable body of case law.

The 1997 amendments, in creating a more pronounced outcome orientation, expect that greater expectations and results are to be achieved.[101] Some of the new IDEA requirements will surely require further judicial interpretation and possibly a reevaluation of *Rowley* by the Supreme Court. A critical part of future litigation will almost certainly interpret and reinterpret the congressional intent of the following 1997 requirements for the child's IEP statement.

1. The child's present level of performance must be stated, requiring the school district to specifically indicate "how the child's disability affects the child's involvement and progress in the general curriculum."[102]
2. The annual goals must be "measurable," and the child must "progress in the general curriculum."[103]
3. Program modifications must be provided that will enable the child to "advance appropriately" toward attaining annual goals.[104]
4. Provision must be made for the child to participate in state or school district student achievement assessments.[105]
5. Evaluation procedures must relate to IEP objectives and measure the child's progress toward annual goals.[106]
6. Parents must receive periodic report cards indicating the child's progress and the extent to which the progress is sufficient to achieve annual goals.[107]

Such definitive outcome requirements of the 1997 amendments will undoubtedly have important implications for measuring the "benefit" received by the disabled child. The requirement of "measurable annual goals"[108] alone will take the benefit discussion to a new level of judicial inquiry and explanation.

❖ — ❖ — ❖

The "Free Appropriate Public Education" Clause of the Education of the Handicapped Act Does Not Require a State to Maximize the Potential of Each Handicapped Child

Board of Education of Hendrick Hudson Central School District v. Rowley

Supreme Court of the United States, 1982.
458 U.S. 176, 102 S.Ct. 3034.

JUSTICE REHNQUIST delivered the opinion of the Court. This case presents a question of statutory interpretation. Petitioners contend that the Court of Appeals and the District Court misconstrued the requirements imposed by Congress upon States which receive federal funds under the Education of the Handicapped Act. We agree and reverse the judgment of the Court of Appeals.

The Education of the Handicapped Act provides federal money to assist state and local agencies in educating handicapped children, and conditions such funding upon a State's compliance with extensive goals and procedures. . . .

This case arose in connection with the education of Amy Rowley, a deaf student at the Furnace Woods School in the Hendrick Hudson Central School District, Peekskill, N.Y. Amy has minimal residual hearing and is an excellent lipreader. During the year before she began attending Furnace Woods, a meeting between her parents and school administrators resulted in a decision to place her in a regular kindergarten class in order to determine what supplemental services would be necessary to her education. Several members of the school administration prepared for Amy's arrival by attending a course in sign-language interpretation, and a teletype machine was installed in the principal's office to facilitate communication with her parents, who are also deaf. At the end of the trial period it was determined that Amy should remain in the kindergarten class, but that she should be provided with an FM hearing aid which would amplify words spoken into a wireless receiver by the teacher or fellow students during certain classroom activities. Amy successfully completed her kindergarten year.

As required by the Act, an IEP was prepared for Amy during the fall of her first-grade year. The IEP provided that Amy should be educated in a regular classroom at Furnace Woods, should continue to use the FM hearing aid, and should receive instruction from a tutor for the deaf for one hour each day and from a speech therapist for three hours each week. The Rowleys agreed with parts of the IEP but insisted that Amy also be provided a qualified sign-language interpreter in all her academic classes in lieu of the assistance proposed in other parts of the IEP. Such an interpreter had been placed in Amy's kindergarten class for a two-week experimental period, but the interpreter had reported that Amy did not need his services at that time. The school administrators likewise concluded that Amy did not need such an interpreter in her first-grade classroom. They reached this conclusion after consulting the school district's Committee on the Handicapped, which had received expert evidence from Amy's parents on the importance of a sign-language interpreter, received testimony from Amy's teacher and other persons familiar with her academic and social progress, and visited a class for the deaf.

When their request for an interpreter was denied, the Rowleys demanded and received a hearing before an independent examiner. After receiving evidence from both sides, the examiner agreed with the administrators' determination that an interpreter was not necessary because "Amy was achieving educationally, academically, and socially" without such assistance. The examiner's decision was affirmed on appeal by the New York Commissioner of Education on the basis of substantial evidence in the record. Pursuant to the Act's provision for judicial review, the Rowleys then brought an action in the United States District Court for the Southern District of New York, claiming that the administrators' denial of the sign-language interpreter constituted a denial of the "free appropriate public education" guaranteed by the Act. . . .

We granted certiorari to review. . . . Such review requires us to consider two questions: What is meant by the Act's requirement of a "free appropriate public education"? And what is the role of state and federal courts in exercising the review granted by 20 U.S.C. §1415? We consider these questions separately.

This is the first case in which this Court has been called upon to interpret any provision of the Act. . . . "[T]he Act itself does not define 'appropriate education,'" but leaves "to the courts and the hearing officers" the responsibility of "giv(ing) content to the requirement of an 'appropriate education.'" Petitioners contend that the definition of the phrase "free appropriate public education" used by the courts below overlooks the definition of that phrase actually found in the Act. Respondents agree that the Act defines "free appropriate public education,"

but contend that the statutory definition is not "functional" and thus "offers judges no guidance in their consideration of controversies involving 'the identification, evaluation, or educational placement of the child or the provision of a free appropriate public education.'" . . .

We are loath to conclude that Congress failed to offer any assistance in defining the meaning of the principal substantive phrase used in the Act. It is beyond dispute that, contrary to the conclusions of the courts below, the Act does expressly define "free appropriate public education":

> The term "free appropriate public education" means *special education* and *related services* which (A) have been provided at public expense, under public supervision and direction, and without charge, (B) meet the standards of the State educational agency, (C) include an appropriate preschool, elementary, or secondary school education in the State involved, and (D) are provided in conformity with the individualized education program required under section 1414(a)(5) of this title. §1401(18) (emphasis added).

"Special education," as referred to in this definition, means "specially designed instruction, at no cost to parents or guardians, to meet the unique needs of a handicapped child, including classroom instruction, instruction in physical education, home instruction, and instruction in hospitals and institutions." §1410(16). "Related services" are defined as "transportation, and such developmental, corrective, and other supportive services . . . as may be required to assist a handicapped child to benefit from special education." §1401(17).

Like many statutory definitions, this one tends toward the cryptic rather than the comprehensive, but that is scarcely a reason for abandoning the quest for legislative intent. . . .

According to the definitions contained in the Act, a "free appropriate public education" consists of educational instruction specially designed to meet the unique needs of the handicapped child, supported by such services as are necessary to permit the child "to benefit" from the instruction. . . .

Noticeably absent from the language of the statute is any substantive standard prescribing the level of education to be accorded handicapped children. Certainly the language of the statute contains no requirement like the one imposed by the lower courts—that States maximize the potential of handicapped children "commensurate with the opportunity provided to other children." That standard was expounded by the District Court without reference to the statutory definitions or even to the legislative history of the Act. Although we find the statutory definition of "free appropriate public education" to be helpful in our interpretation of the Act, there remains the question of whether the legislative history indicates a congressional intent that such education meet some additional substantive standard. For an answer, we turn to that history. . . .

. . . It is evident from the legislative history that the characterization of handicapped children as "served" referred to children who were receiving some form of specialized educational services from the States, and that the characterization of children as "unserved" referred to those who were receiving no specialized educational services. . . .

Respondents contend that "the goal of the Act is to provide each handicapped child with an equal educational opportunity." We think, however, that the requirement that a State provide specialized educational services to handicapped children generates no additional requirement that the services so provided be sufficient to maximize each child's potential "commensurate with the opportunity provided other children." Respondents and the United States correctly note that Congress sought "to provide assistance to the States in carrying out their responsibilities under . . . the Constitution of the United States to provide equal protection of the laws." But we do not think that such statements imply a congressional intent to achieve strict equality of opportunity or services. . . .

. . . In explaining the need for federal legislation, the House Report noted that "no congressional legislation has required a precise guarantee for handicapped children, i.e., a basic floor of opportunity that would bring into compliance all school districts with the constitutional right of equal protection with respect to handicapped children."

Assuming that the Act was designed to fill the need identified in the House Report—that is, to provide a "basic floor of opportunity" consistent with equal protection—neither the Act nor its history persuasively demonstrates that Congress thought that equal protection required anything more than equal access. Therefore, Congress' desire to provide specialized educational services, even in furtherance of "equality," cannot be read as imposing any particular substantive educational standard upon the States.

The District Court and the Court of Appeals thus erred when they held that the Act requires New York to maximize the potential of each handicapped child commensurate with the opportunity provided nonhandicapped children. Desirable though that goal might be, it is not the standard that Congress imposed upon States which receive funding under the Act. Rather, Congress sought primarily to identify and evaluate handicapped children, and to provide them with access to a free public education.

Implicit in the congressional purpose of providing access to a "free appropriate public education" is the requirement that the education to which access is provided be sufficient to confer some educational benefit upon the handicapped child. It would do little good for Congress to spend millions of dollars in providing access to a public education only to have the handicapped child receive no benefit from that education. The statutory definition of "free appropriate public education," in addition to requiring that States provide each child with "specially designed instruction," expressly requires the provision of "such . . . supportive services . . . as may be required to assist a handicapped child *to benefit* from special education." (Emphasis added.) We therefore conclude that the "basic floor of opportunity" provided by the Act consists of access to specialized instruction and related services which are individually designed to provide educational benefit to the handicapped child.

The determination of when handicapped children are receiving sufficient educational benefits to satisfy the requirement of the Act presents a more difficult problem. The Act requires participating States to educate a wide spectrum of handicapped children, from the marginally hearing-impaired to the profoundly retarded and palsied. . . . We do not attempt today to establish any one test for determining the adequacy of educational benefits conferred upon all children covered by the Act. Because in this case we are presented with a handicapped child who is receiving substantial specialized instruction and related services, and who is performing above average in the regular classrooms of a public school system, we confine our analysis to that situation.

The Act requires participating States to educate handicapped children with non-handicapped children whenever possible. When that "mainstreaming" preference of the Act has been met and a child is being educated in the regular classrooms of a public school system, the system itself monitors the educational progress of the child. Regular examinations are administered, grades are awarded, and yearly advancement to higher grade levels is permitted for those children who attain an adequate knowledge of the course material. The grading and advancement system thus constitutes an important factor in determining educational benefit. Children who graduate from our public school systems are considered by our society to have been "educated" at least to the grade level they have completed, and access to an "education" for handicapped children is precisely what Congress sought to provide in the Act.

When the language of the Act and its legislative history are considered together, the requirements imposed by Congress become tolerably clear. Insofar as a State is required to provide a handicapped child with a "free appropriate public education," we hold that it satisfies this requirement by providing personalized instruction with sufficient support services to permit the child to benefit educationally from that instruction. Such instruction and services must be provided at public expense, must meet the State's educational standards, must approximate the grade levels used in the State's regular education, and must comport with the child's IEP. In addition, the IEP, and therefore the personalized instruction, should be formulated in accordance with the requirements of the Act and, if the child is being educated in the regular classrooms of the public education system, should be reasonably calculated to enable the child to achieve passing marks and advance from grade to grade. . . .

In assuring that the requirements of the Act have been met, courts must be careful to avoid imposing their view of preferable educational methods upon the States. The primary responsibility for formulating the education to be accorded a handicapped child, and for choosing the educational method most suitable to the child's needs, was left by the Act to state and local educational agencies in cooperation with the parents or guardian of the child. The Act expressly charges States with the responsibility of "acquiring and disseminating to teachers and administrators of programs for handicapped children significant information derived from educational research, demonstration, and similar projects, and [of] adopting, where appropriate, promising educational practices and materials." §1413(a)(3). In the face of such a clear statutory directive, it seems highly unlikely that Congress intended courts to overturn a State's choice of appropriate educational theories in a proceeding conducted pursuant to §1415(e)(2). . . .

. . . [W]e conclude that the Court of Appeals erred in affirming the decision of the District Court. Neither the District Court nor the Court of Appeals found that petitioners had failed to comply with the procedures of the Act, and the findings of neither court would support a conclusion that Amy's educational program failed to comply with the substantive requirements of the Act. On the contrary, the District Court found that the "evidence firmly establishes that Amy is receiving an 'adequate' education, since she performs better than the average child in her class and is advancing easily from grade to grade." In light of this finding, and of the fact that Amy was receiving personalized instruction and related services calculated by the Furnace Woods school administrators to meet her educational needs, the lower courts should not have concluded that the Act requires the provision of a sign-language interpreter. Accordingly, the decision of the Court of Appeals is reversed, and the case is remanded for further proceedings consistent with this opinion.

So ordered.

———————— ❖ — ❖ — ❖ ————————

*The EAHCA Mandates the Education of
All Handicapped Children and Does Not
Require a Child to Demonstrate a Benefit as
a Condition Precedent to Participation*

Timothy W. v. Rochester, New Hampshire, School District

United States Court of Appeals,
First Circuit, 1989. 875 F.2d 954.

BOWNES, Circuit Judge. Plaintiff-appellant Timothy W. appeals an order of the district court which held that under the Education for All Handicapped Children Act, a handicapped child is not eligible for special education if he cannot benefit from that education, and that Timothy W., a severely retarded and multiply handicapped child, was not eligible under that standard. We reverse.

Timothy W. was born two months prematurely on December 8, 1975, with severe respiratory problems, and shortly thereafter experienced an intracranial hemorrhage, subdural effusions, seizures, hydrocephalus, and meningitis. As a result, Timothy is multiply handicapped and profoundly mentally retarded. He suffers from complex developmental disabilities, spastic quadriplegia, cerebral palsy, seizure disorder and cortical blindness. His mother attempted to obtain appropriate services for him, and while he did receive some services from the Rochester Child Development Center, he did not receive any educational program from the Rochester School District when he became of school age.

On February 19, 1980, the Rochester School District convened a meeting to decide if Timothy was considered educationally handicapped under the state and federal statutes, thereby entitling him to special education and related services. . . . In a meeting on March 7, 1980, the school district decided that Timothy was not educationally handicapped—that since his handicap was so severe he was not "capable of benefiting" from an education, and therefore was not entitled to one. During 1981 and 1982, the school district did not provide Timothy with any educational program. . . .

In response to a letter from Timothy's attorney, on January 17, 1984, the school district's placement team met. . . . The placement team recommended that Timothy be placed at the Child Development Center so that he could be provided with a special education program. The Rochester School Board, however, refused to authorize the placement team's recommendation to provide educational services for Timothy, contending that it still needed more information. The school district's request to have Timothy be given a neurological evaluation, including a CAT Scan, was refused by his mother. . . .

On November 17, 1984, Timothy filed a complaint in the United States District Court, pursuant to 42 U.S.C. §1983, alleging that his rights under the Education for All Handicapped Children Act (20 U.S.C. §1400 *et seq.*), the corresponding New Hampshire state law (RSA 186-C), §504 of the Rehabilitation Act of 1973 (29 U.S.C. §794), and the equal protection and due process clauses of the United States and New Hampshire Constitutions, had been violated by the Rochester School District. The complaint sought preliminary and permanent injunctions directing the school district to provide him with special education, and $175,000 in damages. . . .

Hearings were held on June 16 and 27, 1988, pursuant to Fed.R.Civ.P. 65(a)(2), relating "solely to the issue of whether or not Timothy W. qualifie[d] as an educationally handicapped individual." . . .

. . . On July 15, 1988, the district court rendered its opinion entitled "Order on Motion for Judgment on the Pleadings or in the Alternative, Summary Judgment." . . . The court then reviewed the materials, reports and testimony and found that "Timothy W. is not capable of benefiting from special education. . . . As a result, the defendant [school district] is not obligated to provide special education under either EAHCA [the federal statute] or RSA 186-C [the New Hampshire statute]." Timothy W. has appealed this order. Neither party objected to the procedure followed by the court.

The primary issue is whether the district court erred in its rulings of law. Since we find that it did, we do not review its findings of fact. . . .

. . . The language of the Act could not be more unequivocal. The statute is permeated with the words "*all* handicapped children" whenever it refers to the target population. It never speaks of any exceptions for severely handicapped children. Indeed, as indicated *supra,* the Act gives priority to the most severely handicapped. Nor is there any language whatsoever which requires as a prerequisite to being covered by the Act, that a handicapped child must demonstrate that he or she will "benefit" from the educational program. Rather, the Act speaks of the *state's* responsibility to design a special education and related services program that will meet the unique "needs" of all handicapped children. The language of the Act in its entirety makes clear that a "zero-reject" policy is at the core of the Act, and that no child, regardless of the severity of his or her handicap, is to ever again be subjected to the deplorable state of affairs which existed at the time of the Act's passage, in which millions of handicapped children received inadequate education or none at all. In summary, the Act mandates an appropriate public education for all handicapped children, regardless of the level of achievement that such children might attain. . . .

Given that the Act's language mandates that all handicapped children are entitled to a free appropriate education, we must next inquire if Timothy W. is a handicapped child, and if he is, what constitutes an appropriate education to meet his unique needs. . . .

There is no question that Timothy W. fits within the Act's definition of a handicapped child: he is multiply handicapped and profoundly mentally retarded. He has been described as suffering from severe spasticity, cerebral palsy, brain damage, joint contractures, cortical blindness, is not ambulatory, and is quadriplegic.

Appropriate Public Education. The Act and the implementing regulations define a "free appropriate public education" to mean "special education and related services which are provided at public expense . . . [and] are provided in con-

formity with an individualized education program." 34 C.F.R. §300.4; 20 U.S.C. §1401(a)(18).

(a) *"Special education"* means "specially designed instruction, at no cost to the parent, to meet the unique needs of a handicapped child, including classroom instruction, instruction in *physical education,* home instruction, and instruction in hospitals and institutions." 34 C.F.R. §300.14(a)(1); 20 U.S.C. §1401(a)(16) (emphasis added). It is of significance that the Act explicitly provides for education of children who are so severely handicapped as to require hospitalization or institutionalization. Timothy W.'s handicaps do not require such extreme measures, as he can be educated at home. . . .

. . . We conclude that the Act's language dictates the holding that Timothy W. is a handicapped child who is in need of special education and related services because of his handicaps. He must, therefore, according to the Act, be provided with such an educational program. There is nothing in the Act's language which even remotely supports the district court's conclusion that "under [the Act], an initial determination as to a child's ability to benefit from special education, must be made in order for a handicapped child to qualify for education under the Act." The language of the Act is directly to the contrary: a school district has a duty to provide an educational program for every handicapped child in the district, regardless of the severity of the handicap. . . .

. . . Moreover, the legislative history is unambiguous that the primary purpose of the Act was to remedy the then current state of affairs, and provide a public education for *all* handicapped children. . . .

Not only did Congress intend that all handicapped children be educated, it expressly indicated its intent that the most severely handicapped be given priority. This resolve was reiterated over and over again in the floor debates and congressional reports, as well as in the final legislation. . . .

In mandating a public education for all handicapped children, Congress explicitly faced the issue of the possibility of the non-educability of the most severely handicapped. The Senate Report stated, "The Committee recognizes that in many instances the process of providing special education and related services to handicapped children is *not guaranteed to produce any particular outcome.*" Senate Report at 11 (1975), 1975 U.S.Code Cong. & Admin.News, 1435, (emphasis added). . . .

Thus, the district court's major holding, that proof of an educational benefit is a prerequisite before a handicapped child is entitled to a public education, is specifically belied, not only by the statutory language, but by the legislative history as well. We have not found in the Act's voluminous legislative history, nor has the school district directed our attention to, a single affirmative averment to support a benefit/eligibility requirement. But there is explicit evidence of a contrary congressional intent, that *no* guarantee of any particular educational outcome is required for a child to be eligible for public education.

We sum up. In the more than three years of legislative history leading to passage of the 1975 Act, covering House and Senate floor debates, hearings, and Congressional reports, the Congressional intention is unequivocal: Public education is to be provided to all handicapped children, unconditionally and without exception. It encompasses a universal right, and is not predicated upon any type of guarantees that the child will benefit from the special education and services before he or she is considered eligible to receive such education. Congress explicitly recognized the particular plight and special needs of the severely handicapped, and rather than excluding them from the Act's coverage, gave them priority status. The district court's holding is directly contradicted by the Act's legislative history, as well as the statutory language. . . .

The statutory language of the Act, its legislative history, and the case law construing it, mandate that all handicapped children, regardless of the severity of their handicap, are entitled to a public education. The district court erred in requiring a benefit/eligibility test as a prerequisite to implicating the Act. . . .

The judgment of the district court is reversed, judgment shall issue for Timothy W. The case is remanded to the district court which shall retain jurisdiction until a suitable individualized education program (IEP) for Timothy W. is effectuated by the school district. Timothy W. is entitled to an interim special educational placement until a final IEP is developed and agreed upon by the parties. The district court shall also determine the question of damages.

Costs are assessed against the school district.

Case Notes

1. In a case where a disabled student's IEP lacked a specific statement of transitional services, did not designate a specific outcome, and lacked specificity, and where the child did receive transitional services, the court ruled that these constituted a procedural defect but upheld the IEP and found that it complied with other requirements of the IDEA. The child was therefore not denied a free appropriate education. *Urban by Urban v. Jefferson County School District,* 89 F.3d 720 (10th Cir.1996).

2. If the IEP does not confer some educational benefit, then the right to compensatory education begins at the time the school knows or should have known the IEP was deficient. The burden of determining whether the IEP is appropriate rests not with the parents but with the teachers, therapists, administrators, and multidisciplinary team that evaluates the student's progress. *M. C. on behalf of J. C. v. Central Regional School,* 81 F.3d 389 (3d Cir.1996).

3. In a case where a student repeated two grades in elementary school before being tested by the school to determine his need for special education assistance and, as a result of the delay, was too old by his senior year to compete in interscholastic baseball under the rules of the Missouri State High School Activities Association, the court upheld the athletic association's application of its age rule. The student had filed suit under Section 504 of the Rehabilitation Act of 1973, Title II of the Americans with Disabilities Act, and 42 U.S.C. §1983. The Missouri athletic association established that the age requirement was essential because it helped reduce competitive advantage, protected younger athletes from harm, prevented coaches from redshirting to gain a competitive edge, and also prevented athletes from delaying their education to play longer. The court ruled that the student was not an "otherwise qualified individual" under the Rehabilitation Act, the ADA, or Section 1983. *Pottgen v. Missouri State High School Activities Association,* 40 F.3d 926 (8th Cir.1994).

❖

LEAST-RESTRICTIVE ENVIRONMENT

The IDEA advances the general philosophy that disabled children should be educated with regular children in the normal educational setting whenever possible. The objective is to give the disabled child the opportunity to socialize and interact with other nondisabled children and, further, to reduce as much as possible any formal educational processes that would tend to stigmatize or differentiate the disabled child. This objective is clearly set out in the statute, which provides:

> To the maximum extent appropriate, children with disabilities, including children in public or private institutions or other care facilities, are educated with children who are not disabled, and special classes, separate schooling, or other removal of children with disabilities from the regular educational environment occurs only when the nature or severity of the disability of a child is such that education in regular classes with the use of supplementary aids and services cannot be achieved satisfactorily.[109]

This regulation requires that the broadest opportunity should be afforded to the student on a "continuum of alternative placements" and that when "selecting the *least restrictive environment*, consideration [must be] given to any potential harmful effect on the child."[110]

What precisely the "least restrictive environment" requirement means operationally has been fertile ground for speculation, frequently leading to court action. The regulation promulgated pursuant to the IDEA provides for a "continuum of alternative placements."[111] At one end of this continuum is the regular classroom, as the least-restrictive environment, and at the other end is the hospital, as the most restrictive.[112] Though mainstreaming is not specifically referred to by statute, it is generally considered to be an action that places the child in the least-restrictive environment. Numerous courts have recognized that the IDEA gave strong congressional preference to integrating children with disabilities into regular classrooms.[113] Although the basic concept of integrating disabled students into the regular classroom has been established by the courts, the standard used to evaluate mainstreaming has been interpreted differently in various cases.

The third, fifth, and eleventh circuits use what is known as the *Daniel R. R.* test, from a case of that name.[114] This test has a two-part inquiry: "First, we ask whether education in the regular classroom, with the use of supplemental aids and services, can be achieved satisfactorily for a given child. . . . If it cannot and the school intends to provide special education or to remove the child from regular education, we ask, second, whether the school has mainstreamed the child to the maximum extent appropriate."[115]

The court in the *Daniel R. R.* case referred to several factors that should be considered in deciding whether the regular classroom constitutes the proper placement. These are the disabled child's ability to profit from the regular curriculum, the nonacademic benefits such as social interaction, and the impact on the regular education student in the class. In determining the appropriateness of the placement, teachers need not devote all or the majority of their time to the disabled child or modify beyond recognition the regular curriculum to provide for the one disabled child.

The fourth, sixth, and eighth circuits have applied the test enunciated in *Roncker v. Walter*.[116] The *Roncker* court also recognized the strong congressional preference for mainstreaming but pointed out that it is not required in every case. For a child not to be mainstreamed, the *Roncker* test requires that the school show that a segregated facility would offer superior educational services. It cannot be assumed *ipso facto* that a segregated education is superior merely because it is more costly or because it is separate.[117] If a separate facility is considered to be superior to mainstreaming, it must be determined exactly why it is better and whether it is possible for the same services to be offered in a nonsegregated mainstream setting. If such additional and commensurate services can be offered in the regular classroom, then a separate and segregated placement is inappropriate. If, though, the "marginal benefits received from mainstreaming are far outweighed by the benefits gained from services which could not be feasibly provided in the nonsegregated setting," then the courts will hold that mainstreaming is not the appropriate placement.[118] The *Daniel R. R.* court stated, "[T]he factors that we consider today do not constitute an exhaustive list of factors relevant to the mainstreaming issue. Moreover, no single factor is depositive in all cases. Rather, our analysis is an individualized, fact-specific inquiry that requires us to examine carefully the nature and severity of the child's handicapping condition, his needs and abilities, and the schools' response to the child's needs."[119]

The ninth circuit, in the case of *Rachel H.*, combined elements from the *Daniel R. R.* and *Roncker* cases to determine whether a child should be mainstreamed. This four-factor analysis considered (1) the educational benefits of full-time placement in a regular class, (2) the nonacademic benefits of the placement, (3) the effect the student had on the teacher and other children in the class, and (4) the cost of mainstreaming the disabled student.[120] The *Rachel H.* court used cost as a factor, asking whether the cost was reasonable in relation to the progress of the disabled child. Several courts have ruled that "[c]ost is a proper factor to consider since excessive spending on one handicapped child deprives other handicapped children."[121]

What constitutes the least-restrictive environment is yet so uncertain that litigation continues to proliferate. The courts have generally held that where disputes arise over appropriate educational methodology, the courts will defer to the judgment of school officials: "The primary responsibility for formulating the education to be accorded a handicapped child, and for choosing the educational program most suitable to the child's needs, was left by the Act to state and local educational agencies in cooperation with the parents or guardians of the child and is determined by the fact-specific inquiry required by each case. The severity of the child's disability, his needs and abilities, and the school response are all important elements."[122]

As to whether the parents' choice will prevail over the school's, the court in *Lachman* concluded that parental discretion in the matter of placement must defer to the judgment of the professional educators of the public school district. This court said, "[P]arents, no matter how well-motivated, do not have a right under EAHCA (IDEA) to compel a school district to provide a specific program or employ a specific methodology in providing for education of their handicapped child."[123]

Inclusion

The terms "inclusion," "full inclusion," and "integrated services" are not found in Public Law 94-142 (EAHCA, 1975), Public Law 101-476 (IDEA, 1990), or their implementing regulations. The inclusion movement came out of the U.S. Department of Education in the early 1980s under the "regular education initiative." Regular education advocates criticized the system of special and regular education because disabled children were not being placed in regular education frequently enough. Although not defined in the statute or regulation, these terms are now being used by the courts when addressing the child's least-restrictive environment.[124] In *Mavis v. Sobol*, the court stated, "[I]n recent years use of the term mainstreaming has not been favored by some educators, and instead use of the term 'inclusion' is now preferred in some educational circles. Despite that, the court will continue to use the term mainstreaming in this case."[125] In *Oberti*, the court also preferred to use "mainstreaming" rather than "inclusion." The court said:

> Integrating children with disabilities in regular classrooms is commonly known as "mainstreaming." The Obertis [parents] point out that some educators and public school authorities have come to disfavor use of the term "mainstreaming" because it suggests, in their view, the shuttling of a child with disabilities in and out of a regular classroom without altering the classroom to accommodate the child. They prefer the term "inclusion" because of its great emphasis on the use of supplementary aids and support services within the regular classroom to facilitate inclusion of children with disabilities. While "inclusion" may be a more precise term, we will nonetheless use the term "mainstreaming" because it is currently the common parlance. Moreover, . . . "mainstreaming" as required under IDEA does not mean simply the placement of a child with disabilities in a regular classroom or school program.[126]

Thus, even though the terminology continues to evolve, there appears to be sustaining general agreement that disabled children should be placed in regular classrooms whenever possible. The congressional desire for disabled children to attend school in the regular classroom is given substantial new support in the 1997 amendments. The statutory language now requires that the IEP include "an explanation of the extent, if any, to which the child will not participate with nondisabled children in the regular class. . . ."[127] This is different from the earlier IDEA regulations, which required the child's IEP to state "the extent that the child will be able to participate in regular educational programs."[128] This change effectively shifts the burden to the school district to show why the disabled student should not participate in a regular classroom, not why he or she should. Implicit in this placement objective is the overriding and most important concern that all children benefit from the socialization processes that are inherent in being educated with one's peers. It is this attribute of commonality and neutral participation, so important to the learning process, that advances the time-honored idea of public schools—all should attend school in common, rubbing shoulders with the nondisabled and the disabled—and that best expresses the abiding spirit of public education.

❖ — ❖ — ❖

Burden of Proving Compliance with Mainstreaming Requirement Is Borne by the School District

Oberti v. Board of Education

United States Court of Appeals,
Third Circuit, 1993. 995 F.2d 1204.

BECKER, Circuit Judge.

Plaintiff-appellee Rafael Oberti is an eight year old child with Down's syndrome who was removed from the regular classroom by defendant-appellant Clementon School District Board of Education (the "School District") and placed in a segregated special education class. In this appeal, we are asked by the School District to review the district court's decision in favor of Rafael and his co-plaintiff parents Carlos and Jeanne Oberti concerning Rafael's right under IDEA to be educated in a regular classroom with nondisabled classmates. This court has not previously had occasion to interpret

or apply the "mainstreaming" requirement of IDEA.

We construe IDEA's mainstreaming requirement to prohibit a school from placing a child with disabilities outside of a regular classroom if educating the child in the regular classroom, with supplementary aids and support services, can be achieved satisfactorily. In addition, if placement outside of a regular classroom is necessary for the child to receive educational benefit, the school may still be violating IDEA if it has not made sufficient efforts to include the child in school programs with nondisabled children whenever possible. We also hold that the school bears the burden of proving compliance with the mainstreaming requirement of IDEA....

Although our interpretation of IDEA's mainstreaming requirement differs somewhat from that of the district court, we will affirm the decision of the district court that the School District has failed to comply with IDEA. More precisely, we will affirm the district court's order that the School District design an appropriate education plan for Rafael Oberti in accordance with IDEA, and we will remand for further proceedings consistent with this opinion. . . .

Rafael is an eight year old child with Down's syndrome, a genetic defect that severely impairs his intellectual functioning and his ability to communicate. . . . Prior to his entry into kindergarten, Rafael was evaluated in accordance with federal and state law by the School District's Child Study Team (the "Team"). . . . Based on its evaluation, the Team recommended to Rafael's parents that he be placed in a segregated special education class located in another school district for the 1989–90 school year. The Obertis visited a number of special classes recommended by the School District and found them all unacceptable. Thereafter the Obertis and the School District came to an agreement that Rafael would attend a "developmental" kindergarten class (for children not fully ready for kindergarten) at the Clementon Elementary School (Rafael's neighborhood school) in the mornings, and a special education class in another school district in the afternoons.

The Individualized Education Plan (IEP) developed by the School District for Rafael for the 1989–90 school year . . . assigned all of

Rafael's academic goals to the afternoon special education class. In contrast, the only goals for Rafael in the morning kindergarten class were to observe, model and socialize with nondisabled children.

While Rafael's progress reports for the developmental kindergarten class show that he made academic and social progress in that class during the year, Rafael experienced a number of serious behavioral problems there, including repeated toileting accidents, temper tantrums, crawling and hiding under furniture, and touching, hitting and spitting on other children. On several occasions Rafael struck at and hit the teacher and the teacher's aide.

These problems disrupted the class and frustrated the teacher. . . . The teacher made some attempts to modify the curriculum for Rafael, but Rafael's IEP provided no plan for addressing Rafael's behavior problems. Neither did the IEP provide for special education consultation for the kindergarten teacher, or for communication between the kindergarten teacher and the special education teacher. In March of 1990, the School District finally obtained the assistance of an additional aide, . . . but the presence of the extra aide in the kindergarten class did little to resolve the behavior problems. According to Rafael's progress reports for the afternoon special education class, and as the district court found, Rafael did not experience similar behavior problems in that class.

At the end of the 1989–90 school year, the Child Study Team proposed to place Rafael for the following year in a segregated special education class for children classified as "educable mentally retarded." . . . The Team's decision was based both on the behavioral problems Rafael experienced during the 1989–90 school year in the developmental kindergarten class and on the Team's belief that Rafael's disabilities precluded him from benefiting from education in a regular classroom at that time.

The Obertis objected to a segregated placement and requested that Rafael be placed in the regular kindergarten class in the Clementon Elementary School. The School District refused, and the Obertis sought relief by filing a request for a due process hearing. . . .

In January of 1991, the Obertis brought another due process complaint, renewing their re-

quest under IDEA that Rafael be placed in a regular class in his neighborhood elementary school. A . . . hearing was held . . . before an Administrative Law Judge (ALJ). . . . On March 15, 1991, the ALJ affirmed the School District's decision that the segregated special education class in Winslow was the "least restrictive environment" for Rafael.

. . . The ALJ thus concluded that the Winslow placement was in compliance with IDEA. . . .

Seeking independent review of the ALJ's decision . . . , the Obertis filed this civil action in the United States District Court. . . .

In August of 1992, . . . the district court issued its decision, finding that the School District had failed to establish by a preponderance of the evidence that Rafael could not at that time be educated in a regular classroom with supplementary aids and services. The court therefore concluded that the School District had violated IDEA. . . .

One of our principal tasks in this case is to provide standards for determining when a school's decision to remove a child with disabilities from the regular classroom and to place the child in a segregated environment violates IDEA's presumption in favor of mainstreaming. This issue is particularly difficult in light of the apparent tension within the Act between the strong preferences for mainstreaming . . . and the requirement that schools provide individualized programs tailored to the specific needs of each disabled child. . . .

The key to resolving this tension appears to lie in the school's proper use of "supplementary aids and services," . . . which may enable the school to educate a child with disabilities for a majority of the time within the regular classroom, while at the same time addressing that child's unique educational needs. We recognize, however, that "[r]egular classes . . . will not provide an education that accounts for each child's particular needs in every case." . . .

In *Daniel R. R.*, the Fifth Circuit derived . . . a two-part test for determining whether a school is in compliance with IDEA's mainstreaming requirement. First, the court must determine "whether education in the regular classroom, with the use of supplementary aids and services, can be achieved satisfactorily." . . . Second, if the court finds that placement outside of a regular classroom is necessary for the child to benefit educationally, then the court must decide "whether the school has mainstreamed the child to the maximum extent appropriate," i.e., whether the school has made efforts to include the child in school programs with nondisabled children whenever possible. We think this two-part test, which closely tracks the language of §1412(5)(B), is faithful to IDEA's directive that children with disabilities be educated with nondisabled children "to the maximum extent appropriate," . . . and to the Act's requirement that schools provide individualized programs to account for each child's specific needs. . . .

The district court in this case adopted the somewhat different test set forth by the Sixth Circuit in *Roncker v. Walter*, . . . the first federal court of appeals case to interpret IDEA's mainstreaming requirement. . . . In *Roncker*, the court stated:

> In a case where the segregated facility is considered superior [academically], the court should determine whether the services which make that placement superior could be feasibly provided in a non-segregated setting. If they can, the placement in the segregated school would be inappropriate under the Act.

. . . We believe, however, that the two-part *Daniel R. R.* test is the better standard because the *Roncker* test fails to make clear that even if placement in the regular classroom cannot be achieved satisfactorily for the major portion of a particular child's education program, the school is still required to include that child in school programs with nondisabled children (specific academic classes, other classes such as music and art, lunch, recess, etc.) whenever possible. We therefore adopt the two-part *Daniel R. R.* test rather than the standard espoused in *Roncker*.

In applying the first part of the *Daniel R. R.* test, i.e., whether the child can be educated satisfactorily in a regular classroom with supplementary aids and services, the court should consider several factors. First, the court should look at the steps that the school has taken to try to include the child in a regular classroom. . . . As we have explained, the Act and its regulations require schools to provide supplementary aids and services to enable children with disabilities to learn whenever possible in a regular classroom. . . . The regulations specifically require school dis-

tricts to provide "a continuum of placements . . . to meet the needs of handicapped children." The continuum must "[m]ake provision for supplementary services (such as resource room or itinerant instruction) to be provided in conjunction with regular class placement." . . .

Accordingly, the school "must consider the whole range of supplemental aids and services, including resource rooms and itinerant instruction," . . . speech and language therapy, special education training for the regular teacher, behavior modification programs, or any other available aids or services appropriate to the child's particular disabilities. The school must also make efforts to modify the regular education program to accommodate a disabled child. . . . If the school has given no serious consideration to including the child in a regular class with such supplementary aids and services and to modifying the regular curriculum to accommodate the child, then it has most likely violated the Act's mainstreaming directive. "The Act does not permit states to make mere token gestures to accommodate handicapped students: its requirement for modifying and supplementing regular education is broad." . . .

A second factor courts should consider in determining whether a child with disabilities can be included in a regular classroom is the comparison between the educational benefits the child will receive in a regular classroom (with supplementary aids and services) and the benefits the child will receive in the segregated, special education classroom. The court will have to rely heavily in this regard on the testimony of educational experts. Nevertheless, in making this comparison the court must pay special attention to those unique benefits the child may obtain from integration in a regular classroom which cannot be achieved in a segregated environment, i.e., the development of social and communication skills from interaction with nondisabled peers. . . . As IDEA's mainstreaming directive makes clear, Congress understood that a fundamental value of the right to public education for children with disabilities is the right to associate with nondisabled peers.

Thus, a determination that a child with disabilities might make greater *academic* progress in a segregated, special education class may not warrant excluding that child from a regular classroom environment. We emphasize that the Act does *not* require states to offer *the same* educational experience to a child with disabilities as is generally provided for nondisabled children. . . . To the contrary, states must address the unique needs of a disabled child, recognizing that that child may benefit differently from education in the regular classroom than other students. . . . In short, the fact that a child with disabilities will learn differently from his or her education within a regular classroom does not justify exclusion from that environment.

A third factor the court should consider in determining whether a child with disabilities can be educated satisfactorily in a regular classroom is the possible negative effect the child's inclusion may have on the education of the other children in the regular classroom. While inclusion of children with disabilities in regular classrooms may benefit the class as a whole, . . . a child with disabilities may be "so disruptive in a regular classroom that the education of other students is significantly impaired." . . . Moreover, if a child is causing excessive disruption of the class, the child may not be benefiting educationally in that environment. Accordingly, if the child has behavioral problems, the court should consider the degree to which these problems may disrupt the class. In addition, the court should consider whether the child's disabilities will demand so much of the teacher's attention that the teacher will be required to ignore the other students. . . .

In sum, in determining whether a child with disabilities can be educated satisfactorily in a regular class with supplemental aids and services (the first prong of the two-part mainstreaming test we adopt today), the court should consider several factors, including: (1) whether the school district has made reasonable efforts to accommodate the child in a regular classroom; (2) the educational benefits available to the child in a regular class, with appropriate supplementary aids and services, as compared to the benefits provided in a special education class; and (3) the possible negative effects of the inclusion of the child on the education of the other students in the class.*

---

*Additional factors may be relevant depending on the circumstances of the specific case. For example, other courts have considered cost as a relevant factor in determining compliance with the Act's mainstreaming requirement.

If, after considering these factors, the court determines that the school district was justified in removing the child from the regular classroom and providing education in a segregated, special education class, the court must consider the second prong of the mainstreaming test—whether the school has included the child in school programs with nondisabled children to the maximum extent appropriate. . . . IDEA and its regulations "do not contemplate an all-or-nothing educational system in which handicapped children attend either regular or special education." The regulations under IDEA require schools to provide a "continuum of alternative placements . . . to meet the needs of handicapped children." . . .

. . . [E]ven if a child with disabilities cannot be educated satisfactorily in a regular classroom, that child must still be included in school programs with nondisabled students wherever possible. . . .

. . . [W]e . . . address the School District's argument that the district court improperly placed the burden of proof under the Act on it. In the School District's view, while it may have had the initial burden at the state administrative level of justifying its educational placement, once the agency decided in its favor, the burden should have shifted to the parents who challenged the agency decision in the district court. Courts must place the burden on the party seeking to reverse the agency decision, the School District argues, in order to effectuate IDEA's requirements that "due weight shall be given to [the state administrative] proceedings." . . . We disagree. . . .

In light of the statutory purpose of IDEA and . . . practical considerations, we believe that when IDEA's mainstreaming requirement is specifically at issue, it is appropriate to place the burden of providing compliance with IDEA on the school. Indeed, the Act's strong presumption in favor of mainstreaming, 20 U.S.C. §1422(5)(B), would be turned on its head if parents had to prove that their child was worthy of being included, rather than the school district having to justify a decision to exclude the child from the regular classroom. . . . We therefore hold that the district court correctly placed the burden on the School District to prove that the segregated placement proposed for Rafael was in compliance with the mainstreaming requirement of IDEA. . . .

After evaluating the evidence on both sides, the district court found that "[t]here is nothing in the record which would suggest that *at this point in time* Rafael would present similar behavior problems if provided with an adequate level of supplementary aids and related services within the matrix of a regular education class. In fact, the record supports the opposite conclusion." . . . The court found that the behavioral problems Rafael experienced during the 1989–90 school year in the developmental kindergarten class "were exacerbated and remained uncontained due to the inadequate level of services provided there," that Rafael's behavior problems were diminished in settings where an adequate level of supplementary aids and services were provided, and that both the School District and the ALJ "improperly justified Rafael's exclusion from less restrictive placements in subsequent years based upon those behavior problems."

Although the School District presented ample evidence of Rafael's disruptive behavior in the 1989–90 kindergarten class, the Obertis' evidence supports the district court's finding that Rafael would not have had such severe behavior problems had he been provided with adequate supplementary aids and services in that kindergarten class, and that Rafael (who at the time of the district court trial was two years older than when he attended the kindergarten class) would most likely not present such problems if he were included in a regular class at that time. We therefore conclude that the district court's findings on this issue are not clearly erroneous, and, accordingly, that consideration of the possible negative effects of Rafael's presence on the regular classroom environment does not support the School District's decision to exclude him from the regular classroom. . . .

For all of these reasons, we agree with the district court's conclusion that the School District did not meet its burden of proving by a preponderance of the evidence that Rafael could not be educated satisfactorily in a regular classroom with supplementary aids and services. We will therefore affirm the district court's decision that the School District has violated the mainstreaming requirement of IDEA. . . .

The order of the district court will be affirmed.

Case Note

In *Clevenger v. Oak Ridge School Board*, 744 F.2d 514 (6th Cir.1984), the U.S. Court of Appeals stated:

> [C]ost can be a legitimate consideration when devising an appropriate program. . . . Nevertheless, cost considerations are only relevant when choosing between several options, all of which offer an appropriate education.

SEPARATE SCHOOL PLACEMENT

Disabled Children in Private Schools

The IDEA and its accompanying regulation addresses the issue of special education services provided to children in private schools. The statute requires that each state plan set forth policies and procedures regarding disabled children in private schools. The state must ensure the following:

> (A) That, to the extent consistent with the number and location of children with disabilities in the state who are enrolled in private elementary and secondary schools, provision is made for participation of such children in the program assisted or carried out under this subchapter by providing for such children special education and related services.[129]

The IDEA regulation requires the local educational agency to "provide special education and related services designed to meet the needs of private school children with disabilities residing in the jurisdiction of the agency."[130] The local school district must provide a genuine opportunity for equitable participation in the program. The local school district has discretion in determining the participation, but such must be related to the number of eligible private school students.[131] The regulation also specifies that service to private schools, while not required to be equal, should be comparable.

The federal statute refers to three categories of disabled students, two of which relate to private schools. The three categories are (1) disabled children attending public schools, (2) disabled children attending approved private schools in accordance with an IEP developed by the public schools, and (3) disabled children attending private schools voluntarily. Of course, those attending public schools must receive a free appropriate education. The second category refers to those disabled children placed in private schools following the appropriate IEP determination. These children are in private school programs specifically designed to meet their educational needs. The private facilities where these children are placed must be state approved, and the state must pay the cost.

The third category is made up of those students who are voluntarily placed in private schools. The law requires only that provision be made for participation for such children in the local special education programs. The participation should be "to the extent consistent with the number and location of children with disabilities." Congress intended to differentiate between public and private but also intended to distinguish between those children placed in private school by the local educational agency and those children whose parents voluntarily enrolled them in private schools. Children who are voluntarily enrolled in private schools have "a lesser entitlement"[132] than children in the other two categories. Although the state is responsible for providing "genuine opportunities" for children voluntarily placed in private schools, these opportunities are not as extensive as those of public school children.

The Burlington Test

The U.S. Supreme Court in 1985 in the case of *School Committee of Town of Burlington v. Department of Education, Massachusetts*[133] held that the language in the IDEA authorizes federal courts to "grant such relief as the court determines is appropriate,"[134] and, therefore, a court has the power to order school authorities to reimburse parents for expenditures on private special education if the court finds that the public school district's IEP is inappropriate. The Supreme Court in *Burlington* established a two-part test that the lower federal court should apply to determine whether the parents are entitled to reimbursement from the public school: (1) whether the school district's placement pursuant to its IEP is inappropriate and (2) whether the private placement desired by the parents is

appropriate. The *Burlington* test was used by the U.S. Court of Appeals, Second Circuit,[135] in holding that parents are entitled to reimbursement where a school district erroneously attributes a child's learning difficulties to a "mere conduct disorder" rather than the appropriate diagnosis of a "serious emotional disorder."

Later in 1993, the U.S. Supreme Court in *Florence County School District v. Carter*[136] used the *Burlington* rationale and concluded that if a court finds the educational placement to be inappropriate, then the public school can be ordered by the court to reimburse the parents for costs. In the *Florence County* case, the educational authorities found that the IEP developed for a child was adequate, but the parents disagreed and enrolled the child in a private academy. Later, the parents filed suit seeking reimbursement for tuition and other costs. The district court ruled that the public school's proposed IEP and educational goals "were wholly inadequate" and failed to meet the IDEA requirements. The Supreme Court stated: "This case presents the question whether a court may order reimbursement for parents who unilaterally withdraw their child from a public school that provides an inappropriate education under IDEA and put the child in a private school that provides an education that is otherwise proper under IDEA. . . . We hold that the court may order such reimbursement, and therefore affirm the judgment of the Court of Appeals."[137]

With cognizance of the *Florence County* case, Congress more clearly enunciated in the 1997 amendments what parents must do when they place a child in a private setting if they are to be reimbursed. The failure of parents to adhere to the following requirements may result in the reimbursement being reduced or denied if (1) the parents did not inform the school district at the most recent IEP meeting that they were rejecting the child's IEP, (2) the parents did not inform the school district that they intended to place the child in a private setting at public expense, (3) the parents did not give written notice of the impending removal ten business days prior to the actual removal, (4) the parents refused to make the child available for a sought-after evaluation by the school district, or (5) a court finds that the parents acted unreasonably.[138] The first three items are designed to give courts guidance in constraining unilateral parental action that deprives the school district of the opportunity to attempt to resolve the disagreement before the parent arbitrarily removes the student from the public school setting.[139] The last two items indicate arbitrary action on the part of the parents, for which federal courts have denied reimbursement to the parents.[140]

Disabled Children in Sectarian Schools

Another issue regarding the use of public funds for education of the disabled is whether public funding can be used for the education of disabled children in religious schools. In *Zobrest v. Catalina Foothills School District*,[141] the U.S. Supreme Court ruled that a public school district does not violate the establishment clause of the First Amendment by paying for a sign-language interpreter to accompany a student to classes at a Roman Catholic high school. In *Zobrest*, the student was provided an interpreter while enrolled in a public school, and then, when he enrolled of his own volition in sectarian schools, he requested the same services. The public school board refused to pay for the interpreter on the grounds that such assistance constituted aid to religion. The Supreme Court held that "the Establishment Clause does not prevent [the school board] from furnishing a disabled child enrolled in a sectarian school with a sign-language interpreter in order to facilitate his education. Government programs that neutrally provide benefits to a broad class of citizens defined without reference to religion are not readily subject to an Establishment Clause challenge just because sectarian institutions may also receive an attenuated financial benefit."[142]

Although the Supreme Court ruled that a school board may pay for services in a sectarian school, it did not rule that the school board is required to pay for these services. Recently, lower courts[143] have addressed this issue and have held that local schools are not required to pay for the private sectarian education of a disabled child.

The Supreme Court could not reconcile the logic of both *Zobrest* and *Aguilar*,[144] and finally simply overruled *Aguilar* (see Chapter 5). As discussed earlier in this text, in *Aguilar* the Supreme Court held that the use of public funds to pay for employees in sectarian schools vio-

lates the establishment clause. Now, however, the law appears to permit special education-related services and other services to be delivered in the sectarian school with little or no constitutional constraint.

Court May Order School District to Reimburse Parents Who Unilaterally Placed Child in Private School

Florence County School District Four v. Carter

Supreme Court of the United States, 1993.
510 U.S. 7, 114 S.Ct. 361.

Justice O'CONNOR delivered the opinion of the Court.

The Individuals with Disabilities Education Act (IDEA) . . . requires States to provide disabled children with a "free appropriate public education." . . . This case presents the question whether a court may order reimbursement for parents who unilaterally withdraw their child from a public school that provides an inappropriate education under IDEA and put the child in a private school that provides an education that is otherwise proper under IDEA, but does not meet all the requirements of §1401(a)(18). We hold that the court may order such reimbursement, and therefore affirm the judgment of the Court of Appeals.

Respondent Shannon Carter was classified as learning disabled in 1985, while a ninth grade student in a school operated by petitioner Florence County School District Four. School officials met with Shannon's parents to formulate an individualized education program (IEP) for Shannon, as required under IDEA. . . . The IEP provided that Shannon would stay in regular classes except for three periods of individualized instruction per week, and established specific goals in reading and mathematics of four months' progress for the entire school year. Shannon's parents were dissatisfied, and requested a hearing to challenge the appropriateness of the IEP. . . . Both the local educational officer and the state educational agency hearing officer rejected Shannon's parents' claim and concluded that the IEP was adequate. In the meantime, Shannon's parents had placed her in Trident Academy, a private school specializing in educating children with disabilities. Shannon began at Trident in September 1985 and graduated in the spring of 1988.

Shannon's parents filed this suit in July 1986, claiming that the school district had breached its duty under IDEA to provide Shannon with a "free appropriate public education," . . . and seeking reimbursement for tuition and other costs incurred at Trident. After a bench trial, the District Court ruled in the parents' favor. The court held that the school district's proposed educational program and the achievement goals of the IEP "were wholly inadequate" and failed to satisfy the requirements of the Act. . . . The court further held that "[a]lthough [Trident Academy] did not comply with all of the procedures outlined in [IDEA]," the school "provided Shannon an excellent education in substantial compliance with all the substantive requirements" of the statute. . . . The court found that Trident "evaluated Shannon quarterly, not yearly as mandated in [IDEA], it provided Shannon with low teacher-student ratios, and it developed a plan which allowed Shannon to receive passing marks and progress from grade to grade." . . . The court also credited the findings of its own expert, who determined that Shannon had made "significant progress" at Trident and that her reading comprehension had risen three grade levels in her three years at the school. . . . The District Court concluded that Shannon's education was "appropriate" under IDEA, and that Shannon's parents were entitled to reimbursement of tuition and other costs. . . .

The Court of Appeals for the Fourth Circuit affirmed. . . .

. . . We granted certiorari. . . .

In *School Comm. of Burlington v. Department of Ed. of Mass.,* . . . we held that IDEA's grant of equitable authority empowers a court "to order school authorities to reimburse parents for their expenditures on private special education for a child if the court ultimately determines that such placement, rather than a proposed IEP, is proper

under the Act." Congress intended that IDEA's promise of a "free appropriate public education" for disabled children would normally be met by an IEP's provision for education in the regular public schools or in private schools chosen jointly by school officials and parents. In cases where cooperation fails, however, "parents who disagree with the proposed IEP are faced with a choice: go along with the IEP to the detriment of their child if it turns out to be inappropriate or pay for what they consider to be the appropriate placement." . . . For parents willing and able to make the latter choice, "it would be an empty victory to have a court tell them several years later that they were right but that these expenditures could not in a proper case be reimbursed by the school officials." . . . Because such a result would be contrary to IDEA's guarantee of a "free appropriate public education," we held that "Congress meant to include retroactive reimbursement to parents as an available remedy in a proper case." . . .

As this case comes to us, two issues are settled: 1) the school district's proposed IEP was inappropriate under IDEA, and 2) although Trident did not meet the §1401(a)(18) requirements, it provided an education otherwise proper under IDEA. This case presents the narrow question whether Shannon's parents are barred from reimbursement because the private school in which Shannon enrolled did not meet the §1401(a)(18) definition of a "free appropriate public education."* We hold that they are not, because §1401(a)(18)'s requirements cannot be read as applying to parental placements.

Section 1401(a)(18)(A) requires that the education be "provided at public expense, under public supervision and direction." Similarly, §1401(a)(18)(D) requires schools to provide an IEP, which must be designed by "a representative of the local educational agency," . . . and

---

*Section 1401(a)(18) defines "free appropriate public education" as, "special education and related services that
(A) have been provided at public expense, under public supervision and direction, and without charge,
(B) meet the standards of the State educational agency,
(C) include an appropriate preschool, elementary, or secondary school education in the State involved, and
(D) are provided in conformity with the individualized education program. . . . "

must be "establish[ed]," "revise[d]," and "review[ed]" by the agency. . . . These requirements do not make sense in the context of a parental placement. In this case, as in all *Burlington* reimbursement cases, the parents' rejection of the school district's proposed IEP is the very reason for the parents' decision to put their child in a private school. In such cases, where the private placement has necessarily been made over the school district's objection, the private school education will not be under "public supervision and direction." Accordingly, to read the §1401(a)(18) requirements as applying to parental placements would effectively eliminate the right of unilateral withdrawal recognized in *Burlington*. Moreover, IDEA was intended to ensure that children with disabilities receive an education that is both appropriate and free. . . . To read the provisions of §1401(a)(18) to bar reimbursement in the circumstances of this case would defeat this statutory purpose.

Nor do we believe that reimbursement is necessarily barred by a private school's failure to meet state education standards. Trident's deficiencies, according to the school district, were that it employed at least two faculty members who were not state-certified and that it did not develop IEPs. As we have noted, however, the §1401(a)(18) requirements—including the requirement that the school meet the standards of the state educational agency, §1401(a)(18)(B)—do not apply to private parental placements. Indeed, the school district's emphasis on state standards is somewhat ironic. As the Court of Appeals noted, "it hardly seems consistent with the Act's goals to forbid parents from educating their child at a school that provides an appropriate education simply because that school lacks the stamp of approval of the same public school system that failed to meet the child's needs in the first place." . . .

Furthermore, although the absence of an approved list of private schools is not essential to our holding, we note that parents in the position of Shannon's have no way of knowing at the time they select a private school whether the school meets state standards. South Carolina keeps no publicly available list of approved private schools, but instead approves private school placements on a case-by-case basis. In fact, although public school officials had previously placed three children with disabilities at Trident, . . . Trident had not received blanket approval from the State. South Carolina's case-by-case approval system meant that Shannon's parents needed the cooperation of state officials before they could know whether Trident was state-approved. As we recognized in *Burlington*, such cooperation is unlikely in cases where the school officials disagree with the need for the private placement. . . .

The school district also claims that allowing reimbursement for parents such as Shannon's puts an unreasonable burden on financially strapped local educational authorities. The school district argues that requiring parents to choose a state-approved private school if they want reimbursement is the only meaningful way to allow States to control costs; otherwise States will have to reimburse dissatisfied parents for any private school that provides an education that is proper under the Act, no matter how expensive it may be.

There is no doubt that Congress has imposed a significant financial burden on States and school districts that participate in IDEA. Yet public educational authorities who want to avoid reimbursing parents for the private education of a disabled child can do one of two things: give the child a free appropriate public education in a public setting, or place the child in an appropriate private setting of the State's choice. This is IDEA's mandate, and school officials who conform to it need not worry about reimbursement claims.

Moreover, parents who, like Shannon's, "unilaterally change their child's placement during the pendency of review proceedings, without the consent of the state or local school officials, do so at their own financial risk." . . . They are entitled to reimbursement *only* if a federal court concludes both that the public placement violated IDEA, and that the private school placement was proper under the Act. . . .

Accordingly, we affirm the judgment of the Court of Appeals.

So ordered.

CASE NOTES

1. A private school's failure to comply with the state's licensure requirements or the state's

educational standards has been held not to bar tuition reimbursement to parents under the IDEA where a hearing panel found the private school to be a proper placement. *Warren G. v. Cumberland County School District*, 190 F.3d 80 (3d Cir.1999).

2. The cost of reimbursement was found appropriate for parents who placed their child with Down's syndrome in a private preschool where the public school was not shown to comport with the IDEA. *Board of Education v. LaGrange School District No. 105 v. Illinois State Board of Education*, 184 F.3d 912 (7th Cir. 1999).

3. The U.S. Court of Appeals, Fifth Circuit, has followed the *Burlington* test in holding that reimbursement for a disabled child's cost in attending private school may be ordered by the courts only if the parents or guardians establish that both prongs of the test have been met. If the reviewing court concludes that the first prong is satisfied, that the school district's IEP is appropriate, it need not reach the second prong, the appropriateness of the private school placement by parents. *Cypress-Fairbank Independent School District v. Michael*, 118 F.3d 245 (5th Cir.1997).

4. A school district is not required by the IDEA to "maximize a student's potential" or provide the "best possible education." The statute requires only that the public school provide sufficient specialized services in order for the student to benefit from the education. *Fort Zumwalt School District v. Clynes*, 119 F.3d 607 (8th Cir.1997).

5. Parents are not entitled to reimbursement for the time that a child is placed in a private school without permission of public school district if it is ultimately determined that the proposed IEP met IDEA requirements. *Fort Zumwalt School District v. Clynes*, 119 F.3d 607 (8th Cir.1997).

6. Where parents unilaterally enrolled a child in a private school before an IEP was developed by the school district and then sought to compel the district to pay for the costs, the court ruled for the school district, saying that "case law is clear that [parents] are not entitled to dictate educational methodology or to compel a school district to supply a specific program for their disabled child." *Tucker v. Calloway County Board of Education*, 136 F.3d 495 (6th Cir.1998).

Providing Services under the IDEA to Student Attending Catholic High School Does Not Violate the Establishment Clause

Zobrest v. Catalina Foothills School District

Supreme Court of the United States, 1993.
509 U.S. 1, 113 S.Ct. 2462.

Chief Justice REHNQUIST delivered the opinion of the Court.

Petitioner James Zobrest, who has been deaf since birth, asked respondent school district to provide a sign-language interpreter to accompany him to classes at a Roman Catholic high school in Tucson, Arizona, pursuant to the Individuals with Disabilities Education Act (IDEA). . . . The United States Court of Appeals for the Ninth Circuit decided, however, that provision of such a publicly employed interpreter would violate the Establishment Clause of the First Amendment. We hold that the Establishment Clause does not bar the school district from providing the requested interpreter.

James Zobrest attended grades one through five in a school for the deaf, and grades six through eight in a public school operated by respondent. While he attended public school, respondent furnished him with a sign-language interpreter. For religious reasons, James' parents . . . enrolled him for the ninth grade in Salpointe Catholic High School, a sectarian institution. When petitioners requested that respondent supply James with an interpreter at Salpointe, respondent referred the matter to the County Attorney, who concluded that providing an interpreter on the school's premises would violate the United States Constitution. . . . [T]he question next was referred to the Arizona Attorney General, who concurred in the County Attorney's opinion. Respondent accordingly declined to provide the requested interpreter.

Petitioners then instituted this action in the United States District Court. . . . Petitioners asserted that the IDEA and the Free Exercise

Clause of the First Amendment require respondent to provide James with an interpreter at Salpointe, and that the Establishment Clause does not bar such relief. . . . The District Court denied petitioners' request for a preliminary injunction, finding that the provision of an interpreter at Salpointe would likely offend the Establishment Clause. . . . The court thereafter granted respondent summary judgment, on the ground that "[t]he interpreter would act as a conduit for the religious inculcation of James—thereby, promoting James' religious development at government expense." . . .

The Court of Appeals affirmed by a divided vote, . . . applying the three-part test announced in *Lemon v. Kurtzman*. . . . We granted certiorari, . . . and now reverse. . . .

We have never said that "religious institutions are disabled by the First Amendment from participating in publicly sponsored social welfare programs." . . . For if the Establishment Clause did bar religious groups from receiving general government benefits, then "a church could not be protected by the police and fire departments, or its public sidewalk kept in repair." . . . Given that a contrary rule would lead to such absurd results, we have consistently held that government programs that neutrally provide benefits to a broad class of citizens defined without reference to religion are not readily subject to an Establishment Clause challenge just because sectarian institutions may also receive an attenuated financial benefit. Nowhere have we stated this principle more clearly than in *Mueller v. Allen* . . . and *Witters v. Washington Dept. of Services for Blind*, . . . two cases dealing specifically with government programs offering general educational assistance.

In *Mueller*, we rejected an Establishment Clause challenge to a Minnesota law allowing taxpayers to deduct certain educational expenses in computing their state income tax, even though the vast majority of those deductions (perhaps over 90%) went to parents whose children attended sectarian schools. . . . Two factors, aside from States' traditionally broad taxing authority, informed our decision. . . . We noted that the law "permits *all* parents—whether their children attend public school or private—to deduct their children's educational expenses." . . . We also pointed out that under

Minnesota's scheme, public funds became available to sectarian schools "only as a result of numerous private choices of individual parents of school-age children," thus distinguishing *Mueller* from our other cases involving "the direct transmission of assistance from the State to the schools themselves." . . .

Witters was premised on virtually identical reasoning. In that case, we upheld against an Establishment Clause challenge the State of Washington's extension of vocational assistance, as part of a general state program, to a blind person studying at a private Christian college to become a pastor, missionary, or youth director. Looking at the statute as a whole, we observed that "[a]ny aid provided under Washington's program that ultimately flows to religious institutions does so only as a result of the genuinely independent and private choices of aid recipients." . . . The program, we said, "creates no financial incentive for students to undertake sectarian education." . . . We also remarked that, much like the law in *Mueller*, "Washington's program is 'made available generally without regard to the sectarian-nonsectarian, or public-nonpublic nature of the institution benefited.'" . . . In light of these factors, we held that Washington's program—even as applied to a student who sought state assistance so that he could become a pastor—would not advance religion in a manner inconsistent with the Establishment Clause. . . .

That same reasoning applies with equal force here. The service at issue in this case is part of a general government program that distributes benefits neutrally to any child qualifying as "handicapped" under the IDEA, without regard to the "sectarian-nonsectarian, or public-nonpublic nature" of the school the child attends. By according parents freedom to select a school of their choice, the statute ensures that a government-paid interpreter will be present in a sectarian school only as a result of the private decision of individual parents. In other words, because the IDEA creates no financial incentive for parents to choose a sectarian school, an interpreter's presence there cannot be attributed to state decisionmaking. Viewed against the backdrop of *Mueller* and *Witters*, then, the Court of Appeals erred in its decision. When the government offers a neutral service on the premises of a sectarian school as part of a general program that "is in no way skewed towards religion," . . . it follows under our prior decisions that provision of that service does not offend the Establishment Clause. . . . Indeed, this is an even easier case than *Mueller* and *Witters* in the sense that, under the IDEA, no funds traceable to the government ever find their way into sectarian schools' coffers. The only indirect economic benefit a sectarian school might receive by dint of the IDEA is the handicapped child's tuition—and that is, of course, assuming that the school makes a profit on each student; that, without an IDEA interpreter, the child would have gone to school elsewhere; and that the school, then, would have been unable to fill that child's spot. . . .

. . . Salpointe is not relieved of an expense that it otherwise would have assumed in educating its students. And, . . . any attenuated financial benefit that parochial schools do ultimately receive from the IDEA is attributable to "the private choices of individual parents." . . . Handicapped children, not sectarian schools, are the primary beneficiaries of the IDEA; to the extent sectarian schools benefit at all from the IDEA, they are only incidental beneficiaries. Thus, the function of the IDEA is hardly "'to provide desired financial support for nonpublic, sectarian institutions.'" . . .

. . . [T]he task of a sign-language interpreter seems to us quite different from that of a teacher or guidance counselor. Notwithstanding the Court of Appeals' intimations to the contrary, . . . the Establishment Clause lays down no absolute bar to the placing of a public employee in a sectarian school. Such a flat rule, smacking of antiquated notions of "taint," would indeed exalt form over substance. Nothing in this record suggests that a sign-language interpreter would do more than accurately interpret whatever material is presented to the class as a whole. In fact, ethical guidelines require interpreters to "transmit everything that is said in exactly the same way it was intended." . . . James' parents have chosen of their own free will to place him in a pervasively sectarian environment. The sign-language interpreter they have requested will neither add to nor subtract from that environment, and hence the provision of such assistance is not barred by the Establishment Clause.

The IDEA creates a neutral government program dispensing aid not to schools but to individual handicapped children. If a handicapped child chooses to enroll in a sectarian school, we hold that the Establishment Clause does not prevent the school district from furnishing him with a sign-language interpreter there in order to facilitate his education. The judgment of the Court of Appeals is therefore

Reversed.

❖ — ❖ — ❖

Under 1997 Amendments, a Disabled Child Voluntarily Placed by Parents in Parochial School Has No Individual Right to Special Education Services

Foley v. Special School District of St. Louis County

United States Court of Appeals.
Eighth Circuit, 1998.
153 F.3d 863.

LOKEN, Circuit Judge.

This is an appeal from the denial of equitable relief compelling the Special School District of St. Louis County (SSD) to provide special education and related services to a child at the private religious school where she was voluntarily placed by her parents, rather than at a public school one mile away. We conclude the child has no individual right to such services under the 1997 amendments to the Individuals with Disabilities Education Act, 20 U.S.C. §§1400–1419 (IDEA). Accordingly, we affirm.

Clare Foley is an eleven year-old girl who is mildly mentally retarded. Her parents, Daniel and Margaret Foley, placed Clare in St. Peter's Catholic School but requested special education services from SSD. An evaluation team determined that Clare should have one hour of occupational therapy, one-half hour of physical therapy, and one hour of language services per week. The Foleys demanded those services in Clare's classroom at St. Peter's but SSD refused, construing state law as precluding public school educators from providing special education services on the premises of parochial schools. SSD offered the Foleys a dual enrollment alternative under which Clare would travel from St. Peter's to a nearby public school to receive the special education services. The Foleys accepted this arrangement under protest and requested an IDEA due process hearing. . . . Prior to the hearing, SSD and the Foleys stipulated that the Foleys voluntarily placed Clare at St. Peter's after SSD offered Clare a free appropriate public education at Keysor public elementary school. Thus, the issue is whether Clare has a right to special education services at her private school. . . .

One month after the Foleys commenced this appeal, Congress enacted the Individuals with Disabilities Education Act Amendments of 1997, Pub.L. No. 105-17, 111 Stat. 37 (1997) (the "1997 Amendments"). Courts previously construed IDEA as granting children with disabilities who voluntarily attend private school a right to special education and related services. This led to litigation, such as this case, over where such services must be provided. . . . The 1997 Amendments addressed this problem in detail by amending 20 U.S.C. §1412(a)—the section setting forth conditions States must meet to be eligible for federal education assistance—to include a new subsection (10), which provides in relevant part:

(A) Children enrolled in private schools by their parents
> **(i) In general.** To the extent consistent with the number and location of children with disabilities in the State who are enrolled by their parents in private elementary and secondary schools, provision is made for the participation of those children in the program assisted or carried out under this subchapter by providing for such children special education and related services in accordance with the following requirements . . . :
>> (I) Amounts expended for the provision of those services by a local educational agency shall be equal to a proportionate amount of Federal funds made available under this subchapter.
>> (II) Such services may be provided to children with disabilities on the premises of private, including parochial, schools, to the extent consistent with law. . . .

(C) Payment for education of children enrolled in private schools without consent of or referral by the public agency
> **(i) In general.** Subject to subparagraph (A), this subchapter does not require a local educational agency to pay for the cost of education, including special education and related services, of a child with a disability at a private school or facility if that agency made a free appropriate public education available to the child and the parents elected to place the child in such private school or facility.

. . . .

The Foleys argue that new §1412(a)(10)(A) gives Clare a right to special education services at St. Peter's because that location is more beneficial educationally and no more costly than providing the services at a public school. Relying on §1412(a)(10)(C)(i), SSD argues that the Foleys' claim must be rejected because SSD is not "require[d] . . . To pay for the cost of . . . special education . . . At [Clare's] private school." . . .

The 1997 Amendments expressly provide that public school agencies are not required to pay the costs of special education services for a particular child; States are required only to spend proportionate amounts on special education services for this class of students as a whole. 20 U.S.C. §§1412(a)(10)(A)(i)(I), 1412(a)(10)(C)(i). Thus whatever their rights under prior law, Clare and her parents now have no individual right under IDEA to the special education and related services in question, so they have no right to a federal court decree mandating that those services be provided at a particular location. This change in prior law compels us to conclude that the Foleys have no statutory right to the relief they seek.

Alternatively, even if we construed the 1997 Amendments as granting private school children a right to some level of special education services, we cannot read §1412(a)(10)(A)(i)(II)—which provides that such services "*may* be provided" on the premises of private schools "to the extent consistent with law"—as *mandating* that such services be provided on private school premises when that is *in*consistent with Missouri law. Missouri's refusal to allow public school educators on private school premises may not be mandated by the First Amendment, *see Agostini v. Felton*, 521 U.S. 203, 117 S.Ct. 1997, 138 L.Ed.2d 391 (1997), and it may even be unfortunate education policy. But we find nothing in the 1997 Amendments authorizing federal courts to override such a state policy. Rather, the 1997 Amendments provide a less intrusive remedy by authorizing the Secretary of Education to invoke the "by-pass" provisions of §1412(f) whenever state law frustrates the provision of services under §1412(a)(10)(A). . . .

For the foregoing reasons, the judgment of the district court is affirmed.

--------------- ❖ — ❖ — ❖ ---------------

A Public School Is Not Required to Provide Special Education and Related Services on Site of Private Religious School

KDM v. Reedsport School District

United States Court of Appeals.
Ninth Circuit, 1999.
196 F.3d 1046.

SCHWARZER, Senior District Judge:

WJM's son, KDM, is a minor who is legally blind and has cerebral palsy. As such, KDM is a "child with disabilities" entitled to special education and related services under the Individuals with Disabilities Education Act ("IDEA"). Oregon provides such services to children enrolled in public schools. The Oregon administrative regulation leaves it to the discretion of individual school districts whether to provide such services to children enrolled in private school but specifically provides that "such special education and related services shall be provided in a religiously-neutral setting."

Defendant Reedsport School District ("District") is willing to provide such services to KDM, but not at KDM's parochial school. We must decide whether the District's refusal to provide services at the school violates the IDEA or KDM's rights under the Free Exercise, Establishment, or Equal Protection Clauses of the Constitution. . . .

While attending public school, KDM received from the District the services of a vision specialist, physical therapy and special equipment at his school. Motivated by sincerely-held religious beliefs, KDM's parents transferred him to Har-

bor Baptist Church School ("Harbor Baptist"), a sectarian school. After the transfer, the District continued to supply him with special equipment (braillers, computers and other special equipment) at his new school. However, viewing the Harbor School setting as not religiously-neutral, it no longer supplied the vision specialist at the school. Instead, it provided that service at a fire hall down the street from Harbor Baptist. The adequacy of the service is not in dispute nor is it disputed that it is safe for KDM to travel to and from the fire hall, transportation being provided by the District. The service is provided for approximately ninety minutes twice a week. If this service were provided at Harbor Baptist, it would be provided in a room separate from the classroom because providing it in class could be disruptive to the instruction both of KDM and the other students in the classroom.

KDM brought this action through his father, WJM, against the District and Norma Paulus, Oregon's Superintendent for Public Instruction, for declaratory and injunctive relief requiring the defendants to place a vision specialist at Harbor Baptist. Plaintiff, in substance, made three claims: First, that defendants' refusal to provide a vision specialist at School violates the IDEA; second, that it violates the Free Exercise and Establishment clauses of the First Amendment; and, third, that it denies plaintiff the equal protection of the laws. Following a bench trial on stipulated facts, the district court entered judgment holding that the IDEA did not require the district to provide services at a private school, but that the Oregon regulation which permits services to be offered private school students only in a religiously-neutral setting violated the Free Exercise, Establishment and Equal Protection Clauses and enjoined its enforcement. . . . We now reverse the judgment. . . .

Plaintiff cross-appealed, contending that the IDEA requires the District to provide KDM with services on site at Harbor Baptist. While the IDEA requires states to provide some measure of special education and related services to disabled children in private schools, . . . since its amendment in 1997, the act has specifically provided that "[s]uch services may be provided to children with disabilities on the premises of private, including parochial, schools, to the extent consistent with law." Every circuit that has considered whether the IDEA as amended in 1997 requires services to be provided on site at a private school has concluded it does not. . . .

The narrow question before us is whether the free exercise rights of KDM and his parents were impermissibly burdened by the application of Oregon's regulation, which precludes the District from providing special education services to KDM at the sectarian school he attended. In deciding that question we are guided by the distinction the Supreme Court has recognized in the Establishment Clause context between a statute's invalidity on its face and its invalidity in particular applications. . . . Whatever the impact of the regulation might be in other factually distinct situations, . . . This is not a case in which the regulation impinges on plaintiffs' free exercise rights. The parties stipulated that the service provided to KDM at the fire hall down the street from the school twice a week for ninety minutes is in compliance with KDM's statutory individualized education plan, the adequacy of which is not in dispute, and that he could safely travel there—indeed, the vision specialist comes to KDM's school, picks him up and then returns him to his school. Moreover, plaintiffs have stipulated that the vision specialist's services would not be provided in-class at Harbor Baptist but in a separate room. Thus, there is no support for the district court's finding that the regulation forces KDM and his parents to choose between enrolling at Harbor Baptist and receiving special education at the fire hall or enrolling at a nonreligious school and receiving in-class services. In sum, there is no showing that application of the regulation to KDM's case burdens KDM's or his parents' free exercise of their religion. . . .

While the Oregon regulation is not "neutral" because it restricts the provision of services to "religiously-neutral settings," . . . as applied here it does not have "the object or purpose . . . [of] suppression of religion or religious conduct." . . . KDM is not subjected to "[o]fficial action that targets religious conduct for distinctive treatment." . . .

That the regulation, standing alone, "discriminates" against students in religious schools, i.e., treats them differently by denying them state

services on the school grounds, does not result in a burden on the free exercise of religion by someone in the position of KDM or his parents. . . . Here, the District's solicitousness in accommodating KDM could hardly be said to reflect a purpose to "suppress[ ] religion or religious conduct." The mere fact that the District makes its service to KDM available in the fire hall down the street from his school does not amount to suppression of religion or religious conduct.

We conclude that Oregon's regulation as applied to KDM and his parents does not impose an impermissible burden on their free exercise of religion. . . .

The district court also found that the Oregon regulation violates the Establishment Clause because it requires the State Superintendent of Education to decide on a case-by-case basis whether particular settings are religious. Since *Zobrest*, the mere presence of a public employee on religious premises clearly is not enough to invoke the Establishment Clause. . . . ("[A]fter *Zobrest* we no longer presume that public employees will inculcate religion simply because they happen to be in a sectarian environment.").

In *Agostini*, the Supreme Court held that monthly visits by supervisors to parochial school classrooms to ensure that remedial education provided by public school teachers remained secular did not result in excessive entanglement under the test of *Lemon v. Kurtzman*. . . . *Agostini* is merely the latest in a line of cases rejecting an entanglement claim when applied to the making of judgments by officials overseeing regulatory schemes concerning the religious character of activities. . . .

We conclude that the regulation does not offend the entanglement prong of the *Lemon* test. We need go no further because the district court did not determine that it offended the first (secular purpose), or second (primary effect to advance or inhibit religion), prong of the test. . . .

The district court held that the regulation violates the Equal Protection Clause because it "has the effect of allowing in-class services to disabled students at non-religious schools while prohibiting in-class services to disabled students at religious schools, both public and private. . . . Absent an anti-establishment interest, however, such a distinction lacks a rational, let alone compelling, justification." Because parochial school students are not a suspect class, scrutiny of their treatment by the state is under the rational basis test. . . . While under *Zobrest* the federal Establishment Clause raises no bar to providing on-site services to disabled students at sectarian schools, for purposes of equal protection analysis, Oregon's interpretation of its constitutional separation requirement remains a legitimate state interest. The parties stipulated that "[t]he State of Oregon interprets Article I, §5, of its constitution to require the provision of special education and related services in a religiously-neutral setting." . . .

The judgment is REVERSED.

CASE NOTES

1. The 1997 amendments do not require services to be provided to a student who is voluntarily enrolled in a private school. *Russman v. Board of Education*, 150 F.3d 219, 221–22 (2d Cir.1998) ("[S]tates are required to provide to children voluntarily enrolled in private schools only those services that can be purchased with a proportionate amount of the federal funds received under the program. . . . [The] statute does not require a school district to provide on-site services to a disabled child who is voluntarily enrolled in private school."); *Fowler v. Unified School District No. 259*, 128 F.3d 1431, 1436–37 (10th Cir.1997) ("[T]he [school district's] sole obligation is to spend on such students . . . 'a proportionate amount of Federal funds,' . . . "); *Cefalu v. East Baton Rouge Parish School Board*, 117 F.3d 231, 233 (5th Cir.1997) ("We therefore hold unambiguously that the defendants were not legally obligated to provide an on-site sign language interpreter to the plaintiff at the private school."). We agree with those courts and conclude that the district court properly declined to grant plaintiff relief under the IDEA.

2. The IDEA does not require a school district to provide special education services at a private parochial school where the child has been unilaterally placed by the parents so long as the services are made available at a public school. *Foley v. Special School District of St. Louis County*, 927 F.Supp. 1214 (E.D.Mo.1996).

3. If a pupil's individualized education program (IEP) was reasonably calculated to provide educational benefit, then the parents are not entitled to reimbursement for the cost of their son's placement at a private residential facility. *Hall v. Shawnee Mission School District (USD No. 512)*, 856 F.Supp. 1521 (D.Kan.1994).

4. The Individuals with Disabilities Education Act and Section 504 of the Rehabilitation Act of 1973 apply to disabled youths who are in correctional facilities. A new IEP need not be developed for those incarcerated at reception and evaluation centers, but a new IEP must be developed when the juvenile is sent to a long-term facility. *Alexander v. Boyd*, 876 F.Supp. 773 (D.S.C.1995). See also *Donnell v. Illinois State Board of Education*, 829 F.Supp. 1016 (N.D.Ill.1993); 20 U.S.C. §1412(6); 34 C.F.R. §300.600.

--------------------------- ❖ ---------------------------

RELATED SERVICES

Under Public Law 94-142, supportive services that enable disabled children to benefit from special education must be made available without cost to the parents. The act defines "related services":

> The term "related services" means transportation, and such developmental, corrective, and other supportive services (including speech pathology and audiology, psychological services, physical and occupational therapy, recreation, and medical and counseling services, except that such medical services shall be for diagnostic and evaluative purposes only) as may be required to assist a handicapped child to benefit from special education.[145]

The federal regulation promulgated pursuant to the act further defines "psychological services" as "planning and managing a program of psychological services, including psychological counseling for children and parents" (34 C.F.R. §300.13(b)(8)), and "counseling services" are defined as "services provided by qualified social workers, psychologists, guidance counselors, or other qualified personnel" (34 C.F.R. §300.13(b)(2)).

Confusion has arisen regarding which medical services fall within the domain of Public Law 94-142. In *Irving Independent School District v. Tatro*,[146] clean intermittent catheterization (CIC) was required by the Supreme Court in spite of the fact that the school district had claimed the service was not required under Public Law 94-142,[147] which exempt medical services except those for diagnostic and evaluation purposes.[148] The Court in *Tatro* stated, "Only those services necessary to aid a handicapped child to benefit from special education must be provided" under the act.[149]

Further, a federal district court has ruled that psychotherapy is a related service, although not specifically mentioned in either the act or the regulations.[150] Also, a federal circuit court has required out-of-district transportation, stating that "unless the transportation request is shown to be unreasonable, the EAHCA requires that such transportation be provided as a related service."[151]

When a child is placed in a facility for medical purposes and not for educational placement, then the child is not within the purview of the act. Where a child was placed in a hospital for psychiatric care, the court stated, "Although 'related services' may include medical services, the Act does not require a school system to provide services by a physician except those necessary for diagnostic and evaluation purposes."[152] Residential placement, however, is a related service in which social and emotional issues are intertwined with educational problems.[153]

❖ — ❖ — ❖

Catheterization Falls within Definition of Related Services

Irving Independent School District v. Tatro

Supreme Court of the United States, 1984.
468 U.S. 883, 104 S.Ct. 3371.

CHIEF JUSTICE BURGER delivered the opinion of the Court. We granted certiorari to determine whether the Education of the Handicapped Act or the Rehabilitation Act of 1973 requires a school district to provide a handicapped child with clean intermittent catheterization during school hours.

Amber Tatro is an eight-year-old girl born with a defect known as spina bifida. As a result, she suffers from orthopedic and speech impairments and a neurogenic bladder, which prevents her from emptying her bladder voluntarily. Consequently, she must be catheterized every three or four hours to avoid injury to her kidneys. In accordance with accepted medical practice, clean intermittent catheterization (CIC), a procedure involving the insertion of a catheter into the urethra to drain the bladder, has been prescribed. The procedure is a simple one that may be performed in a few minutes by a layperson with less than an hour's training. Amber's parents, babysitter, and teenage brother are all qualified to administer CIC, and Amber soon will be able to perform this procedure herself.

In 1979 petitioner Irving Independent School District agreed to provide special education for Amber, who was then three and one-half years old. In consultation with her parents, who are respondents here, petitioner developed an individualized education program for Amber under the requirements of the Education of the Handicapped Act, 84 Stat. 175, as amended significantly by the Education for All Handicapped Children Act of 1975, 89 Stat. 773, 20 U.S.C. §§1401(19), 1414(a)(5). The individualized education program provided that Amber would attend early childhood development classes and receive special services such as physical and occupational therapy. That program, however, made no provision for school personnel to administer CIC. . . .

This case poses two separate issues. The first is whether the Education of the Handicapped Act requires petitioner to provide CIC services to Amber. The second is whether §504 of the Rehabilitation Act creates such an obligation. We first turn to the claim presented under the Education of the Handicapped Act.

States receiving funds under the Act are obliged to satisfy certain conditions. A primary condition is that the state implement a policy "that assures all handicapped children the right to a free appropriate public education." 20 U.S.C. §1412(1). Each educational agency applying to a state for funding must provide assurances in turn that its program aims to provide "a free appropriate public education to all handicapped children." §1414(a)(1)(C)(ii).

A "free appropriate public education" is explicitly defined as "special education and related services." §1401(18). The term "special education" means

> specially designed instruction, at no cost to parents or guardians, to meet the unique needs of a handicapped child, including classroom instruction, instruction in physical education, home instruction, and instruction in hospitals and institutions, §1401(16).

"Related services" are defined as

> transportation, and such developmental, corrective, and other *supportive services* (*including* speech pathology and audiology, psychological services, physical and occupational therapy, recreation, and *medical* and counseling *services, except that such medical services shall be for diagnostic and evaluation purposes only) as may be required to assist a handicapped child to benefit from special education,* and includes the early identification and assessment of handicapping conditions in children. §1401(17) (emphasis added).

The issue in this case is whether CIC is a "related service" that petitioner is obliged to provide to Amber. We must answer two questions: first, whether CIC is a "supportive servic[e] . . . required to assist a handicapped child to benefit from special education"; and second, whether CIC is excluded from this definition as a "medical servic[e]" serving purposes other than diagnosis or evaluation.

The Court of Appeals was clearly correct in holding that CIC is a "supportive servic[e] . . . required to assist a handicapped child to benefit from special education." It is clear on this record that, without having CIC services available during the school day, Amber cannot attend school and thereby "benefit from special education." CIC services therefore fall squarely within the definition of a "supportive service."

As we have stated before, "Congress sought primarily to make public education available to handicapped children" and "to make such access meaningful." *Board of Education of Hendrick Hudson Central School District v. Rowley,* 458 U.S. 176, 192, 102 S.Ct. 3034, 3043, 73 L.Ed.2d 690 (1982). A service that enables a handicapped child to remain at school during the day is an important means of providing the child with the meaningful access to education that Congress

envisioned. The Act makes specific provision for services, like transportation, for example, that do no more than enable a child to be physically present in class, see 20 U.S.C. §1401(17); and the Act specifically authorizes grants for schools to alter buildings and equipment to make them accessible to the handicapped, §1406; see S.Rep.No. 94-168, p.38 (1975); 121 Cong. Rec. 19483–19484 (1975) (remarks of Sen. Stafford). Services like CIC that permit a child to remain at school during the day are no less related to the effort to educate than are services that enable the child to reach, enter, or exit the school.

We hold that CIC services in this case qualify as a "supportive servic[e] . . . required to assist a handicapped child to benefit from special education."

We also agree with the Court of Appeals that provision of CIC is not a "medical servic[e]," which a school is required to provide only for purposes of diagnosis or evaluation. See 20 U.S.C. §1401(17). We begin with the regulations of the Department of Education, which are entitled to deference. See, e.g., *Blum v. Bacon,* 457 U.S. 132, 141, 102 S.Ct. 2355, 2361, 72 L.Ed. 2d 728 (1982). The regulations define "related services" for handicapped children to include "school health services," 34 CFR §300.13(a) (1983), which are defined in turn as "services provided by a qualified school nurse or other qualified person," §300.13(b)(10). "Medical services" are defined as "services provided by a licensed physician." §300.13(b)(4). Thus, the Secretary has determined that the services of a school nurse otherwise qualifying as a "related service" are not subject to exclusion as a "medical service," but that the services of a physician are excludable as such.

This definition of "medical services" is a reasonable interpretation of congressional intent. Although Congress devoted little discussion to the "medical services" exclusion, the Secretary could reasonably have concluded that it was designed to spare schools from an obligation to provide a service that might well prove unduly expensive and beyond the range of their competence. From this understanding of congressional purpose, the Secretary could reasonably have concluded that Congress intended to impose the obligation to provide school nursing services.

Congress plainly required schools to hire various specially trained personnel to help handicapped children, such as "trained occupational therapists, speech therapists, psychologists, social workers and other appropriately trained personnel." S.Rep.No. 94-168, supra, at 33. School nurses have long been a part of the educational system, and the Secretary could therefore reasonably conclude that school nursing services are not the sort of burden that Congress intended to exclude as a "medical service." By limiting the "medical services" exclusion to the services of a physician or hospital, both far more expensive, the Secretary has given a permissible construction to the provision. . . .

To keep in perspective the obligation to provide services that relate to both the health and educational needs of handicapped students, we note several limitations that should minimize the burden petitioner fears. First, to be entitled to related services, a child must be handicapped so as to require special education. See 20 U.S.C. §1041(1); 34 CFR §300.5 (1983). In the absence of a handicap that requires special education, the need for what otherwise might qualify as a related service does not create an obligation under the Act. See 34 CFR §300.14, Comment (1) (1983).

Second, only those services necessary to aid a handicapped child to benefit from special education must be provided, regardless of how easily a school nurse or layperson could furnish them. For example, if a particular medication or treatment may appropriately be administered to a handicapped child other than during the school day, a school is not required to provide nursing services to administer it.

Third, the regulations state that school nursing services must be provided only if they can be performed by a nurse or other qualified person, not if they must be performed by a physician. See 34 CFR §§300.13(a), (b)(4), (b)(10) (1983). It bears mentioning that here not even the services of a nurse are required; as is conceded, a layperson with minimal training is qualified to provide CIC. . . .

Finally, we note that respondents are not asking petitioner to provide *equipment* that Amber needs for CIC. Tr. of Oral Arg. 18–19. They seek only the *services* of a qualified person at the school.

We conclude that provision of CIC to Amber is not subject to exclusion as a "medical ser-

vice," and we affirm the Court of Appeals' holding that CIC is a "related service" under the Education of the Handicapped Act.

Respondents sought relief not only under the Education of the Handicapped Act but under §504 of the Rehabilitation Act as well. . . . We hold today, in *Smith v. Robinson*, 468 U.S. 992, 104 S.Ct. 3457, 80 L.Ed.2d (1984), that §504 is inapplicable when relief is available under the Education of the Handicapped Act to remedy a denial of educational services. Respondents are therefore not entitled to relief under §504, and we reverse the Court of Appeals' holding that respondents are entitled to recover attorney's fees. In all other respects, the judgment of the Court of Appeals is affirmed.

It is so ordered.

❖ — ❖ — ❖

Continuous Nursing Service Is "Related Service" That School District Must Provide under IDEA

Cedar Rapids Community School District v. Garret F.

Supreme Court of the United States, 1999.
526 U.S. 66, 119 S.Ct. 992.

Justice STEVENS delivered the opinion of the Court.

The Individuals with Disabilities Education Act (IDEA), 84 Stat. 175, as amended, was enacted, in part, "to assure that all children with disabilities have available to them . . . a free appropriate public education which emphasizes special education and related services designed to meet their unique needs." Consistent with this purpose, the IDEA authorizes federal financial assistance to States that agree to provide disabled children with special education and "related services." See §§1401(a)(18), 1412(1). The question presented in this case is whether the definition of "related services" in §1401(a)(17) requires a public school district in a participating State to provide a ventilator-dependent student with certain nursing services during school hours.

Respondent Garret F. is a friendly, creative, and intelligent young man. When Garret was four years old, his spinal column was severed in a motorcycle accident. Though paralyzed from the neck down, his mental capacities were unaffected. He is able to speak, to control his motorized wheelchair through use of a puff and suck straw, and to operate a computer with a device that responds to head movements. Garret is currently a student in the Cedar Rapids Community School District (District), he attends regular classes in a typical school program, and his academic performance has been a success. Garret is, however, ventilator dependent, and therefore requires a responsible individual nearby to attend to certain physical needs while he is in school.

During Garret's early years at school his family provided for his physical care during the school day. When he was in kindergarten, his 18-year-old aunt attended him; in the next four years, his family used settlement proceeds they received after the accident, their insurance, and other resources to employ a licensed practical nurse. In 1993, Garret's mother requested the District to accept financial responsibility for the health care services that Garret requires during the school day. The District denied the request, believing that it was not legally obligated to provide continuous one-on-one nursing services. . . .

The District contends that §1401(a)(17) does not require it to provide Garret with "continuous one-on-one nursing services" during the school day, even though Garret cannot remain in school without such care. . . . However, the IDEA's definition of "related services," our decision in Irving Independent School Dist. v. Tatro, 468 U.S. 883, 104 S.Ct. 3371, 82 L.Ed.2d 664 (1984), and the overall statutory scheme all support the decision of the Court of Appeals.

The text of the "related services" definition, . . . broadly encompasses those supportive services that "may be required to assist a child with a disability to benefit from special education." As we have already noted, the District does not challenge the Court of Appeals' conclusion that the in-school services at issue are within the covered category of "supportive services." As a general matter, services that enable a disabled child to remain in school during the day provide the student with "the meaningful access to education that Congress envisioned." . . .

This general definition of "related services" is illuminated by a parenthetical phrase listing examples of particular services that are included within the statute's coverage. §1401(a)(17). "Medical services" are enumerated in this list, but such services are limited to those that are "for diagnostic and evaluation purposes." The statute does not contain a more specific definition of the "medical services" that are excepted from the coverage of §1401(a)(17).

The scope of the "medical services" exclusion is not a matter of first impression in this Court. In *Tatro* we concluded that the Secretary of Education had reasonably determined that the term "medical services" refer only to services that must be performed by a physician, and not to school health services. . . . Accordingly, we held that a specific form of health care (clean intermittent catheterization) that is often, though not always, performed by a nurse is not an excluded medical service. We referenced the likely cost of the services and the competence of school staff as justifications for drawing a line between physician and other services, but our endorsement of that line was unmistakable. It is thus settled that the phrase "medical services" in §1401(a)(17) does not embrace all forms of care that might loosely be described as "medical" in other contexts, such as a claim for an income tax deduction. . . .

The District does not ask us to define the term so broadly. Indeed, the District does not argue that any of the items of care that Garret needs, considered individually, could be excluded from the scope of §1401(a)(17). It could not make such an argument, considering that one of the services Garret needs (catheterization) was at issue in *Tatro*, and the others may be provided competently by a school nurse or other trained personnel. . . . [M]ost of the requested services are already provided by the District to other students, and the in-school care necessitated by Garret's ventilator dependency does not demand the training, knowledge, and judgment of a licensed physician. . . . While more extensive, the in-school services Garret needs are no more "medical" than was the care sought in *Tatro*.

Instead, the District points to the combined and continuous character of the required care, and proposed a test under which the outcome in any particular case would "depend upon a series of factors, such as [1] whether the care is continuous or intermittent, [2] whether existing school health personnel can provide the service, [3] the cost of the service, and [4] the potential consequences if the service is not properly performed."

The District's multi-factor test is not supported by any recognized source of legal authority. The proposed factors can be found in neither the text of the statute nor the regulations that we upheld in *Tatro*. Moreover, the District offers no explanation why these characteristics make one service any more "medical" than another. The continuous character of certain services associated with Garret's ventilator dependency has no apparent relationship to "medical" services, much less a relationship of equivalence. Continuous services may be more costly and may require additional school personnel, but they are not thereby more "medical." Whatever its imperfections, a rule that limits the medical services exemption to physician services is unquestionably a reasonable and generally workable interpretation of the statute. Absent an elaboration of the statutory terms plainly more convincing than that which we reviewed in *Tatro,* there is no good reason to depart from settled law.

Finally, the District raises broader concerns about the financial burden that it must bear to provide the services that Garret needs to stay in school. The problem for the District in providing these services is not that its staff cannot be trained to deliver them; the problem, the District contends, is that the existing school health staff cannot meet all of their responsibilities and provide for Garret at the same time. Through its multi-factor test, the District seeks to establish a kind of undue-burden exemption primarily based on the cost of the requested services. The first two factors can be seen as examples of cost-based distinctions: intermittent care is often less expensive than continuous care, and the use of existing personnel is cheaper than hiring additional employees. The third factor—the cost of the service—would then encompass the first

two. The relevance of the fourth factor is likewise related to cost because extra care may be necessary if potential consequences are especially serious.

The District may have legitimate financial concerns, but our role in this dispute is to interpret existing law. Defining "related services" in a manner that accommodates the cost concerns Congress may have had . . . is altogether different from using cost itself as the definition. Given that §1401(a)(17) does not employ cost in its definition of "related services" or excluded "medical services," accepting the District's cost-based standard as the sole test for determining the scope of the provision would require us to engage in judicial lawmaking without any guidance from Congress. It would also create some tension with the purposes of the IDEA. The statute may not require public schools to maximize the potential of disabled students commensurate with the opportunities provided to other children . . . ; and the potential financial burdens imposed on participating States may be relevant to arriving at a sensible construction of the IDEA. . . . But Congress intended "to open the door of public education" to all qualified children and "require[d] participating States to educate handicapped children with nonhandicapped children whenever possible." . . .

This case is about whether meaningful access to the public schools will be assured, not the level of education that a school must finance once access is attained. It is undisputed that the services at issue must be provided if Garret is to remain in school. Under the statute, our precedent, and the purposes of the IDEA, the District must fund such "related services" in order to help guarantee that students like Garret are integrated into the public schools.

The judgment of the Court of Appeals is accordingly affirmed.

CASE NOTES

1. *In-School Nurse.* The requirement for related services does not extend to providing an in-school nurse needed to attend to a child's daily medical needs. A child in a physical condition so severe as to require constant nursing care is beyond the requirements of "related services"

and falls in the realm of "medical services." *Detsel v. Board of Education,* 637 F.Supp. 1022 (N.D.N.Y.1986), affirmed, 820 F.2d 587 (2d Cir.), cert. denied, 484 U.S. 981, 108 S.Ct. 495 (1987).

2. *Treatment for Emotional Problems.* The dividing line between related services and medical services is most difficult to define when a child has an emotional disability. In addressing this issue, a federal district court was called upon to apportion expenses used between related and medical services in this nebulous area of mental and psychological treatment. The district court concluded that counseling, psychological services, and periodic psychiatric evaluations for medication purposes are "related services when provided by a psychologist, social worker, or other professional." Even though this decision was reversed on procedural grounds, this broad view of related services is likely to prevail. *Antkowiak v. Ambach,* 838 F.2d 635 (2d Cir.1988).

3. *Provision of Extracurricular Activities.* The EAHCA does not require that school districts provide extracurricular activities for disabled children. *Rettig v. Kent City School District,* 788 F.2d 328 (6th Cir.1986).

------------------- ❖ -------------------

DISCIPLINE AND THE STAY-PUT PROVISION

The mainstreaming of disabled children has underscored the need for guidelines governing the disciplining of disabled students. Neither Section 504 nor Public Law 94-142 addresses this issue, leaving it to the courts to decipher the legal ramifications involved.

Two provisions of IDEA must be considered when disciplinary action is taken with a disabled student: appropriate education and least-restrictive environment. Public Law 94-142 mandates that a disabled student be provided a free appropriate public education in the least-restrictive environment. Acceptable environments for the placement of a disabled child range from least restrictive (a regular classroom) to highly restrictive (an institution). However, each environment can be termed "least restrictive" depending on the seriousness of a particular disability and on the student's ability to cope within a specific environment.

Courts have consistently ruled that disabled students must be given special consideration in disciplinary proceedings.[154] Earlier court decisions prohibited expulsion, noting that, under Public Law 94-142, services must be provided through alternative placement in one of the other educational environments offered.[155]

In 1981, expulsion again surfaced as an issue when nine mentally disabled students in the state of Florida sued local districts and the state, claiming that they had been denied an appropriate education due to expulsion.[156] The court in *S-1 v. Turlington*[157] upheld expulsion as a viable form of discipline to be used with disabled students. The court, however, pointed out that cessation of all educational programs violated the rights of disabled students; consequently, even after expelling a student, services must be provided.

Suspension, on the other hand, has been viewed favorably by the courts as an appropriate disciplinary action for disabled students when it has been determined that misconduct is not related to the student's disability. If it is related to the disabling condition, an alternative or more-restrictive placement should be considered rather than suspension or expulsion.[158]

The "Stay-Put" Provision

The Education of the Handicapped Act contains a pendency-of-review provision that prohibits school authorities from unilaterally excluding a disabled child from school during review proceedings to determine the placement of the student. Section 1415(e)(3) of the act states that "the child shall remain in the then current educational placement" until proper placement can be determined. This so-called stay-put provision raises the question as to whether a child can be excluded from school for an indefinite period of time for dangerous or disruptive conduct growing out of a disability. *S-1 v. Turlington*[159] and other cases[160] left doubt as to whether there was, in fact, a "dangerousness" exclusion implied by the act. In *Honig v. Doe,* the U.S. Supreme Court resolved the issue by making it clear that the EAHCA (1) confers a substantive right to education on disabled students, (2) prohibits school officials from unilaterally excluding a disabled student from the classroom for dangerous or disruptive conduct for an indeterminate period of time where conduct grows out of a disability, and (3) permits school officials to temporarily suspend a student for up to ten days to protect the safety of others and to provide a "cooling down." During this time, an IEP meeting can be initiated to review the child's placement.

When Congress amended the IDEA in 1997, a major concern, and one of the most contentious of topics, was the disciplining of disabled students. The discipline issue is frequently given as the reason that the final IDEA regulation, which was due to be released in May 1998, was delayed until March 1999. The 1997 amendments and the IDEA regulation allow school personnel to order a change of placement of special needs children in certain situations. The change of placement may be made if the child brings a weapon to school or a school function or if the child possesses or uses illegal drugs. Under these conditions, the placement can be changed 1) "to an appropriate interim alternative setting, another setting, or suspension, for not more than 10 school days (to the extent such alternatives would be applied to children without disabilities); and 2) to an appropriate interim alternative educational setting for the same amount of time that a child without disability would be subject to discipline, but not more than 45 days. . . . "[161]

The hearing officer who orders the interim alternative educational placement must have determined that maintaining the current placement would cause harm to the student or others, that the current placement is inappropriate, and that the school has made an effort to minimize the risk with supplementary aids and other services.

When a disciplinary action is required, a manifestation determination review is also required. This review is to decide if the inappropriate behavior of the child is related to his or her disability. If after the review "the behavior of the child with a disability was not a manifestation of the child's disability, the relevant disciplinary procedures applicable to children without disabilities may be applied to the [disabled] child in the same manner in which they would be applied to children without disabilities."[162] Even if the child's inappropriate behavior is not a manifestation of his or her disability, the child must receive a free appropriate education. Therefore, when an IDEA child is suspended or expelled, services may not be terminated.[163]

❖ — ❖ — ❖

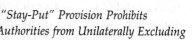

"Stay-Put" Provision Prohibits School Authorities from Unilaterally Excluding Disabled Students from Classroom for Dangerous Conduct Growing Out of Disability

Honig v. Doe

Supreme Court of the United States, 1988.
484 U.S. 305, 108 S.Ct. 592.

Justice BRENNAN delivered the opinion of the Court. As a condition of federal financial assistance, the Education of the Handicapped Act requires States to ensure a "free appropriate public education" for all disabled children within their jurisdictions. In aid of this goal, the Act establishes a comprehensive system of procedural safeguards designed to ensure parental participation in decisions concerning the education of their disabled children and to provide administrative and judicial review of any decisions with which those parents disagree. Among these safeguards is the so-called "stay-put" provision, which directs that a disabled child "shall remain in [his or her] then current educational placement" pending completion of any review proceedings, unless the parents and state or local educational agencies otherwise agree. 20 U.S.C. §1415(e)(3). Today we must decide whether, in the face of this statutory proscription, state or local school authorities may nevertheless unilaterally exclude disabled children from the classroom for dangerous or disruptive conduct growing out of their disabilities. In addition, we are called upon to decide whether a district court may, in the exercise of its equitable powers, order a State to provide educational services directly to a disabled child when the local agency fails to do so. . . .

The present dispute grows out of the efforts of certain officials of the San Francisco Unified School District (SFUSD) to expel two emotionally disturbed children from school indefinitely for violent and disruptive conduct related to their disabilities. In November 1980, respondent John Doe assaulted another student at the

Louise Lombard School, a developmental center for disabled children. Doe's April 1980 IEP identified him as a socially and physically awkward 17 year old who experienced considerable difficulty controlling his impulses and anger. Among the goals set out in his IEP was "[i]mprovement in [his] ability to relate to [his] peers [and to] cope with frustrating situations without resorting to aggressive acts." Frustrating situations, however, were an unfortunately prominent feature of Doe's school career: physical abnormalities, speech difficulties, and poor grooming habits had made him the target of teasing and ridicule as early as the first grade; his 1980 IEP reflected his continuing difficulties with peers, noting that his social skills had deteriorated and that he could tolerate only minor frustration before exploding.

On November 6, 1980, Doe responded to the taunts of a fellow student in precisely the explosive manner anticipated by his IEP: he choked the student with sufficient force to leave abrasions on the child's neck, and kicked out a school window while being escorted to the principal's office afterwards. Doe admitted his misconduct and the school subsequently suspended him for five days. Thereafter, his principal referred the matter to the SFUSD Student Placement Committee (SPC or Committee) with the recommendation that Doe be expelled. . . .

After unsuccessfully protesting these actions by letter, Doe brought this suit against a host of local school officials and the state superintendent of public education. Alleging that the suspension and proposed expulsion violated the EHA, he sought a temporary restraining order cancelling the SPC hearing and requiring school officials to convene an IEP meeting. The District Judge granted the requested injunctive relief and further ordered defendants to provide home tutoring for Doe on an interim basis; shortly thereafter, she issued a preliminary injunction directing defendants to return Doe to his then current educational placement at Louise Lombard School pending completion of the IEP review process. Doe re-entered school on December 15, 5 1/2 weeks, and 24 school days, after his initial suspension.

Respondent Jack Smith was identified as an emotionally disturbed child by the time he entered the second grade in 1976. School records prepared that year indicated that he was unable "to control verbal or physical outburst[s]" and exhibited a "[s]evere disturbance in relationships with peers and adults." Further evaluations subsequently revealed that he had been physically and emotionally abused as an infant and young child and that, despite above average intelligence, he experienced academic and social difficulties as a result of extreme hyperactivity and low self esteem. Of particular concern was Smith's propensity for verbal hostility; one evaluator noted that the child reacted to stress by "attempt[ing] to cover his feelings of low self worth through aggressive behavior[,] . . . primarily verbal provocations."

Based on these evaluations, SFUSD placed Smith in a learning center for emotionally disturbed children. . . .

At the beginning of the next school year, Smith was assigned to a full-day program; almost immediately thereafter he began misbehaving. School officials met twice with his grandparents in October 1980 to discuss returning him to a half-day program; although the grandparents agreed to the reduction, they apparently were never apprised of their right to challenge the decision through EHA procedures. The school officials also warned them that if the child continued his disruptive behavior—which included stealing, extorting money from fellow students, and making sexual comments to female classmates—they would seek to expel him. On November 14, they made good on this threat, suspending Smith for five days after he made further lewd comments. His principal referred the matter to the SPC, which recommended exclusion from SFUSD. . . .

After learning of Doe's action, Smith sought and obtained leave to intervene in the suit. The District Court subsequently entered summary judgment in favor of respondents on their EHA claims and issued a permanent injunction. In a series of decisions, the District Judge found that the proposed expulsions and indefinite suspensions of respondents for conduct attributable to their disabilities deprived them of their congressionally mandated right to a free appropriate public education, as well as their right to have that education provided in accordance with the procedures set out in the EHA. The District Judge therefore permanently enjoined the school district from taking any disciplinary action other than a two- or five-day suspension against any disabled child for disability-related misconduct, or from effecting any other change in the educational placement of any such child without parental consent pending completion of any EHA proceedings. In addition, the judge barred the State from authorizing unilateral placement changes and directed it to establish an EHA compliance-monitoring system or, alternatively, to enact guidelines governing local school responses to disability-related misconduct. Finally, the judge ordered the State to provide services directly to disabled children when, in any individual case, the State determined that the local educational agency was unable or unwilling to do so.

On appeal, the Court of Appeals for the Ninth Circuit affirmed the orders with slight modifications. . . .

Petitioner Bill Honig, California Superintendent of Public Instruction, sought review in this Court, claiming that the Court of Appeals' construction of the stay-put provision conflicted with that of several other courts of appeals which had recognized a dangerousness exception, . . . and that the direct services ruling placed an intolerable burden on the State. We granted certiorari to resolve these questions, . . . and now affirm. . . .

The language of §1415(e)(3) is unequivocal. It states plainly that during the pendency of any proceedings initiated under the Act, unless the state or local educational agency and the parents or guardian of a disabled child otherwise agree, "the child *shall* remain in the then current educational placement." §1415(e)(3) (emphasis added). Faced with this clear directive, petitioner asks us to read a "dangerousness" exception into the stay-put provision on the basis of either of two essentially inconsistent assumptions: first, that Congress thought the residual authority of school officials to exclude dangerous students from the classroom too obvious for comment; or second, that Congress inadvertently failed to provide such authority and this Court must therefore remedy the oversight. Because we cannot accept either premise, we

decline petitioner's invitation to re-write the statute.

Petitioner's arguments proceed, he suggests, from a simple, common-sense proposition: Congress could not have intended the stay-put provision to be read literally, for such a construction leads to the clearly unintended, and untenable, result that school districts must return violent and dangerous students to school while the often lengthy EHA proceedings run their course. We think it clear, however, that Congress very much meant to strip schools of the *unilateral* authority they had traditionally employed to exclude disabled students, particularly emotionally disturbed students, from school. In so doing, Congress did not leave school administrators powerless to deal with dangerous students; it did, however, deny school officials their former right to "self-help," and directed that in the future the removal of disabled students could be accomplished only with the permission of the parents or, as a last resort, the courts.

As noted above, Congress passed the EHA after finding that school systems across the country had excluded one out of every eight disabled children from classes. . . .

Congress attacked such exclusionary practices in a variety of ways. It required participating States to educate *all* disabled children, regardless of the severity of their disabilities, 20 U.S.C. §1412(2)(C), and included within the definition of "handicapped" those children with serious emotional disturbances. §1401(1). It further provided for meaningful parental participation in all aspects of a child's educational placement, and barred schools, through the stay-put provision, from changing that placement over the parent's objection until all review proceedings were completed. Recognizing that those proceedings might prove long and tedious, the Act's drafters did not intend §1415(e)(3) to operate inflexibly, see 121 Cong.Rec. 37412 (1975) (remarks of Sen. Stafford), and they therefore allowed for interim placements where parents and school officials are able to agree on one. Conspicuously absent from §1415(e)(3), however, is any emergency exception for dangerous students. This absence is all the more telling in light of the injunctive decree issued in *PARC*, which permitted school officials unilaterally to remove students in "'extraordinary circumstances.'" 343 F.Supp., at 301. Given the lack of any similar exception in *Mills*, and the close attention Congress devoted to these "landmark" decisions, see S.Rep., at 6, U.S.Code Cong. & Admin.News p. 1430, we can only conclude that the omission was intentional; we are therefore not at liberty to engraft onto the statute an exception Congress chose not to create.

Our conclusion that §1415(e)(3) means what it says does not leave educators hamstrung. The Department of Education has observed that, "[w]hile the [child's] placement may not be changed [during any complaint proceeding], this does not preclude the agency from using its normal procedures for dealing with children who are endangering themselves or others." Comment following 34 CFR §300.513 (1987). Such procedures may include the use of study carrels, timeouts, detention, or the restriction of privileges. More drastically, where a student poses an immediate threat to the safety of others, officials may temporarily suspend him or her for up to 10 school days. This authority, which respondent in no way disputes, not only ensures that school administrators can protect the safety of others by promptly removing the most dangerous of students, it also provides a "cooling down" period during which officials can initiate IEP review and seek to persuade the child's parents to agree to an interim placement. And in those cases in which the parents of a truly dangerous child adamantly refuse to permit any change in placement, the 10-day respite gives school officials an opportunity to invoke the aid of the courts under §1415(e)(2), which empowers courts to grant any appropriate relief. . . . As the EHA's legislative history makes clear, one of the evils Congress sought to remedy was the unilateral exclusion of disabled children by *schools*, not courts, and one of the purposes of §1415(e)(3), therefore, was "to prevent *school* officials from removing a child from the regular public school classroom over the parents' objection pending completion of the review proceedings." . . . The stay-put provision in no way purports to limit or pre-empt the authority conferred on courts by §1415(e)(2), . . . indeed, it says nothing whatever about judicial power.

In short, then, we believe that school officials are entitled to seek injunctive relief under §1415(e)(2) in appropriate cases. In any such action, §1415(e)(3) effectively creates a presumption in favor of the child's current educational placement which school officials can overcome only by showing that maintaining the child in his or her current placement is substantially likely to result in injury either to himself or herself, or to others. In the present case, we are satisfied that the District Court, in enjoining the state and local defendants from indefinitely suspending respondent or otherwise unilaterally altering his then current placement, properly balanced respondent's interest in receiving a free appropriate public education in accordance with the procedures and requirements of the EHA against the interests of the state and local school officials in maintaining a safe learning environment for all their students.

We believe the courts below properly construed and applied §1415(e)(3), except insofar as the Court of Appeals held that a suspension in excess of 10 school days does not constitute a "change in placement." We therefore affirm the Court of Appeals' judgment on this issue as modified herein. Because we are equally divided on the question whether a court may order a State to provide services directly to a disabled child where the local agency has failed to do so, we affirm the Court of Appeals' judgment on this issue as well.

Affirmed.

Case Notes

1. In *Honig v. Doe*, the Supreme Court stated that a school district may suspend a child who is dangerous to himself or herself, or to others, for up to ten days without violating the stay-put provision. If the school district needs more than ten days to develop a new IEP with a more-restrictive environment or if the parents do not agree with the new placement, then the school district may request that the courts issue an injunction to either keep the child out of school or temporarily place the child until an appropriate placement may be formulated.

In post-*Honig* litigation, school districts have requested injunctions because of the dangerous propensities of a child. One school district obtained an injunction to keep a seventeen-year-old autistic and behavior-disordered student out of school pending a new placement. The student became overtly sexually and physically aggressive, posing a danger to himself, fellow students, and the faculty and staff. Before issuing an injunction, the federal district court stated that four factors must be considered:

> (1) [W]hether the plaintiff is reasonably likely to succeed on the merits of the action; (2) whether the plaintiff will be irreparably harmed absent the injunction or will have an adequate remedy at law; (3) whether the prospective injury to the plaintiff outweighs the injury the injunction may impose upon the defendant; (4) whether a preliminary injunction will deserve the public interest. *Board of Education of Township High School District No. 211, Cook County, Illinois v. Corral,* 1989 WL 57041 (N.D.Ill.1989).

In another case, the school district recommended limiting the student's participation to a behavioral management class or home care because the child was a danger to himself and other students. The parents disagreed with this new placement. The child's behaviors included striking other students and staff, tearing off wooden door jambs, tearing up carpet, threatening to jump out a second-floor window, and so on. When the parents refused placement in a behavioral class or home instruction, the school sought and received an injunction from the court. The court said the child was "an ongoing major threat to others, as well as to himself." *Texas City Independent School District v. Jorstad,* 752 F.Supp. 231 (S.D.Tex.1990).

2. In a 1997 decision, the U.S. Court of Appeals, Tenth Circuit, held that the discontinuation of a particular type of occupational therapy did not violate the stay-put provision of the IDEA or state regulations in New Mexico. *Erickson v. Albuquerque Public Schools,* 193 F.3d 1116 (10th Cir.1999).

3. A number of courts have described the stay-put provision of the IDEA as an "automatic injunction." The seventh circuit states that the "stay-put order is sufficiently clear and definite to be enforceable by the usual sanction for violating an injunction—civil or criminal contempt—so that the order has not only the form of an injunction but also the bite that a real

injunction has." *Board of Education of Oak Park v. Illinois State Board of Education,* 79 F.3d 654, 657 (7th Cir.1996); see also *Rodiriecus v. Waukegan School District No. 60,* 90 F.3d 249 (7th Cir.1996).

4. Before a "stay-put" placement is invoked, it must be demonstrated that school officials knew, or should have known, that the student might be disabled, as assessed by his or her school performance. In a case where a juvenile enrolled at a middle school committed a robbery and was placed under the guardianship of the Illinois Department of Children, the principal recommended expulsion, and the student filed suit asserting the school was prohibited from expelling him while he was being evaluated as a disabled student. The question is whether the stay-put provision applies to a child not yet diagnosed as disabled. This student performed in an "average" manner, and the prospect of disability did not surface until he was going to be expelled. The court said, "The IDEA was intended to provide individualized public education for disabled children. The Act was not designated to act as a shield to protect a disruptive child from routine and appropriate school discipline." *Rodiriecus v. Waukegan School District No. 60,* 90 F.3d 249 (7th Cir.1996).

❖

COMPENSATORY EDUCATION

The entitlement of a free appropriate public education under the IDEA extends to students until they reach the age of twenty-one.[164] Yet, if a disabled student has suffered from earlier deprivation of a free appropriate public education, then a court may require compensatory education to continue beyond age twenty-one.[165] The courts, while not establishing a precise standard for awarding compensatory education, have generally concluded that a school district's flagrant failure to comply with the IDEA or egregious conduct by a school district detrimental to a disabled student is sufficient rationale for the awarding of compensatory education.[166] In *M. C. v. Central Regional School District,* the U.S. Court of Appeals, Third Circuit, helped clarify the standard, stating that "the right to compensatory education accrues when the school knows or should know that its IEP is not providing an appropriate education."[167] This court further ruled that the awarding of compensatory education to a disabled student does not require that the school district's behavior rise to a level of "slothfulness or bad faith"[168]; nor does it require that egregious disregard of the student's rights be proved.

The question, of course, thus arises as to whether the right to compensatory education is justified merely by the denial of an appropriate IEP or only if the child is denied an appropriate education. The court in *M. C.* held that "[a] school district that knows or should know that a child has an inappropriate [IEP] or is not receiving more than a *de minimis* benefit must, of course, correct the situation. We hold that . . . a disabled child is entitled to compensatory education for a period equal to the deprivation."[169] Following this rationale, the Third Circuit in *Ridgewood Board of Education v. N.E.*[170] rejected the idea that compensatory education could hinge on distinguishing the difference between the denial of an appropriate education and the denial of an appropriate IEP. This court said that "IDEA's central goal is that disabled students receive an appropriate education, not merely an appropriate IEP. Therefore, a disabled student's right to a compensatory education accrues when the school knows or should know that the student is receiving an inappropriate education."

Because compensatory education is provided to compensate for lost education opportunity, it becomes important to determine when and for how long the deficiency occurred. In answering this question, the Third Circuit has determined that the right of compensatory education accrues "when the school knows or should know that its IEP is not providing an appropriate education.[171]

ATTORNEY'S FEES

Attorney's fees may be awarded by the courts to parents who win lawsuits against school districts (§1415(e)(4)(B)). Attorney's fees were permitted by a 1986 amendment entitled the Handicapped Children's Protection Act (HCPA). The IDEA amendment provides that a "prevailing party" may be awarded attorney's fees and costs: "In any action or proceeding brought under this subsection, the court, in its discretion, may award reasonable attorneys' fees as

part of the costs to the parents or guardian of a child or youth with a disability who is the prevailing party." This amendment was considered necessary because Congress observed that the weight of heavy attorney's fees could conceivably make parents reluctant to raise valid complaints challenging school district actions. The amendment was initiated following a Supreme Court decision in 1984, in *Smith v. Robinson*,[172] in which the Court found that parents, in bringing EAHCA actions, could not claim attorney's fees under either Section 1983 of the Civil Rights Act of 1871 or Section 504 of the Rehabilitation Act.

Those who opposed the amendment maintained that an undefined right to attorney's fees was tantamount to giving a blank check for lawyer's fees not only for judicial action, but also for due process hearings and preliminary reviews in extrajudicial settings. Congress finally resolved the issue for purposes of the amendment by including specifications and limitations for courts to follow in awarding attorney's fees. The amendment, the Handicapped Children's Protection Act of 1986 (HCPA) (Public Law 99-372), further provided that, in addition to recovery under the IDEA, recovery could be sustained under the Rehabilitation Act and the Civil Rights Act. The only restriction to invoking the last two acts is that the disabled student must have exhausted IDEA procedures.

Under IDEA, the "prevailing party" can be awarded attorney's fees by the court. Thus, the law regarding the awarding of attorney's fees has developed into an entire subcategory of IDEA law. The primary issue, however, becomes the determination of the "prevailing party." For example, parents have been found not to be the prevailing party where they did not make the request for attorney's fees prior to the due process hearing,[173] and, too, parents have been held not to be the prevailing party where the school district's compliance was apparently voluntary and not the result of a judicially enforceable settlement.[174] Too, the "prevailing party" determination may depend on whether the court resolves the matter under state or federal law. In a 1999 Iowa case, the U.S. Court of Appeals, Eighth Circuit, decided that a disabled child was not a "prevailing party" under IDEA provisions for attorney's fees, even though he obtained the relief he sought, because the federal district court had couched its decision in favor of the child based on Iowa law, rather than the IDEA. Iowa law, unlike federal IDEA law, does not provide for attorney's fees for the prevailing party.[175]

Eligibility for Fees

Statutory provisions for attorney's fees do not extend to special education lay advocates who are not lawyers. To permit such fees would in the court's opinion allow a plethora of unlicensed legal practitioners to have access to public resources, which would not be in the public's best interest.[176]

The apparent majority view of the courts is that a parent-attorney who represents his or her own children in an IDEA action is not eligible to receive attorney's fees even if he or she prevails in the litigation.[177]

Private or Publicly Funded Attorneys

Section 1988 of the HCPA states that "reasonable fees are to be calculated according to the prevailing market rates in the relevant community, regardless of whether plaintiff is represented by private or non-profit counsel."[178]

LIABILITY FOR REIMBURSEMENT OF PARENTS

Local school districts may be liable for reimbursement of parents for tuition associated with alternative placement in private schools. As the Supreme Court has made clear in *Florence County School District v. Carter*[179] (page 466), parents of disabled children are entitled to reimbursement only if the public school placement violated the IDEA and the placement in a private school was proper.[180]

The liability of state governments, as opposed to local school districts, is a more complicated issue, however, since the Supreme Court has reasserted a rather rigorous application of the Eleventh Amendment immunity for state government.[181] (See Chapter 3, "Role of the Federal Government.") The Supreme Court has implicitly assumed that local school districts are not state government, and while Eleventh Amendment immunity from liability may pro-

tect the state, it does not similarly extend to local school districts.[182] (See Chapter 13, "Governmental Immunity.")

In *Dellmuth v. Muth* in 1989, the Supreme Court ruled that "[t]he Education of the Handicapped Act does not abrogate the state's Eleventh Amendment immunity" because that intention by Congress was not "unmistakably clear in the language of the statute." In the newly enacted IDEA, Congress attempted to make clear its intent to waive the Eleventh Amendment: Section 1403 of the act is titled "Abrogation of State Sovereign Immunity" and states as follows:

(a) A State shall not be immune under the Eleventh Amendment to the Constitution of the United States from suit in Federal court for a violation of this Act.

(b) In a suit against a State for a violation of this Act, remedies (including remedies both at law and in equity) are available for such a violation to the same extent as remedies are available for such a violation in the suit against any public entity other than a State.

(c) The provisions of subsections (a) and (b) of this section shall take effect with respect to violations that occur in whole or part after October 30, 1990.

Therefore, Congress sought to leave no doubt in waiving the Eleventh Amendment immunity of the state with regard to the Individuals with Disabilities Education Act. Yet, in spite of Congress's corrective action, there still remains some doubt as to whether state sovereign immunity prevails, particularly in view of the strong language of the U.S. Supreme Court in 1999 asserting the strength and intent of Eleventh Amendment immunity as a protective shield for state governments.[183]

Following what it believed to be the view of the Supreme Court, the U.S. Court of Appeals for the Eighth Circuit ruled in 1999 that Congress's attempt to abrogate state sovereign immunity in Title II of Americans with Disabilities Act (ADA), as amended, by means of attachment to Section 5, the enforcement provision of the equal protection clause of the Fourteenth Amendment, could not prevail.[184] This court reasoned that Congress's rationale for Title II assumed erroneously that most state programs and services discriminated arbitrarily against the disabled, an assumption that, if true, would justify the invoking of the equal protection clause of the Fourteenth Amendment. The eighth circuit maintained that the legislative record of the ADA does not support the proposition that most states discriminate, and, therefore, Congress's justification for abrogation of the states' Eleventh Amendment immunity from private suit could not be sustained.

On the other hand, the prevailing view of other U.S. Courts of Appeals[185] appears to be that Congress's justification under the amended version of the ADA is sufficient to abrogate the states' Eleventh Amendment immunity, permitting ADA suits for liability against state governments. The first circuit has stated in *dicta* that "we have considered the issue of Congress's authority sufficiently to conclude that, were we to confront the question head-on, we almost certainly would join the majority of the courts upholding the [abrogation] provision" of the ADA.[186] Similarly, the fourth circuit has ruled that the application of Title II of the ADA to state prisons, abrogating state immunity, is a constitutional exercise of Congress's power under Section 5 of the Fourteenth Amendment.[187] Thus, though there are exceptions, the majority of the federal circuits appear to agree that Congress's language in the ADA has validly abrogated the sovereign immunity of state governments and that state governments as well as local school districts are subject to liability for reimbursement to parents of tuition and costs under the ADA.

■ ACQUIRED IMMUNODEFICIENCY SYNDROME (AIDS)

A major problem facing society and public schools is the dreaded and lethal acquired immunodeficiency syndrome (AIDS). The first known case of this contagious disease was reported by the Centers for Disease Control (CDC) in 1981.[188]

AIDS is a disease believed to be caused by a retrovirus that destroys the immune system: "A retrovirus is a class of viruses with special genetic material which allows them to produce copies of themselves inside the cells they infect,

killing the host cells in the process."[189] A person may test positive for the virus and transmit the virus to others, but himself or herself be asymptomatic. The person who tests seropositive and displays a number of symptoms characteristic of the disease may not be considered to have AIDS. It is estimated, depending on the source, that 30 to 90 percent of those who are seropositive "healthy carriers"[190] will develop AIDS. When a person exhibits symptoms of a weakened immune system, he or she is no longer a carrier of the virus but has been attacked by the virus, and he or she has AIDS-related complex (ARC). At this stage, the individual is susceptible to disease because of the weakened immune system. There are no known cures for AIDS, and the disease is fatal.

Because of the finality of this disease, there has been widespread concern and fear within society. One court stated:

> While we wait for medical science to save us from what many think may be such a raging, indiscriminate inferno, it is the task of this court to deal with the here and now of this lethal, inevitability fatal disease, for which there is currently no inoculation and no cure. The mystery of the virus and its communicability challenges jurists legally to be assured our decisions do not lead us to allow proliferation of this disease by our ignorance.[191]

A number of cases have arisen in the public schools where children who have AIDS or children who have tested positive have been excluded from the regular classroom. The school districts have attempted to continue the child's education with homebound instruction or by other means. Numerous legal questions have arisen relating to AIDS, but the most prominent has been whether a school district can exclude a child who has AIDS or tests positive for the AIDS virus.

AIDS cases involving public school children have been litigated under the Rehabilitation Act of 1973, Section 504 (29 U.S.C.A. §794); the Education for All Handicapped Children Act (20 U.S.C.A. §1415(e)(2)); the due process and equal protection clauses of the U.S. Constitution; and various state statutes. The two major areas of contention have been the Rehabilitation Act of 1973 and the Education for All Handicapped Children Act.

REHABILITATION ACT OF 1973

The Rehabilitation Act of 1973 states:

> No otherwise qualified handicapped individual in the United States, as defined in section 705(7) of this title, shall, solely by reason of his handicap, be excluded from the participation in, be denied the benefits of, or be subjected to discrimination under any program or activity receiving Federal financial assistance. . . .

Therefore, for an AIDS child to successfully litigate under Section 504, the student must be a "handicapped individual" and must be "otherwise qualified" to attend a regular classroom under Section 504.

The law defines "handicapped individual" as a person who "(i) has a physical . . . impairment which substantially limits one or more of [his or her] major life activities, (ii) has a record of impairment, or (iii) is regarded as having such impairment" (29 U.S.C.A. §706(7)(B)). In *Doe*,[192] the court used the third standard of physical impairment as the basis for declaring an AIDS child handicapped under Section 504. This rationale was based on the Supreme Court decision in *School Board of Nassau County, Fla. v. Arline*, in which the court stated:

> [The] basic purpose of §504 . . . is to ensure that handicapped individuals are not denied jobs or other benefits because of the prejudiced attitudes or the ignorance of others. By amending the definition of "handicapped individual" to include not only those who are actually physically impaired but also those who are regarded as impaired and who, as a result, are substantially limited in a major life activity, Congress acknowledged that society's accumulated myths and fears about disability and disease are as handicapping as are the physical limitations that flow from actual impairment. Few aspects of a handicap give rise to the same level of public fear and misapprehension as contagiousness. . . . The Act is carefully structured to replace such reflexive reactions to actual or perceived handicaps with actions based on reasoned and medically sound judgments. . . .

Because of the seriousness of the AIDS disease, a student is likely to prevail also on the standard of "impairment of a major life activity." Several courts have ruled that a person is covered under Section 504 while he or she is seropositive and has not developed AIDS; simply having the virus has been considered a disabling condition. In *Thomas*, the court said, "[A]ny person infected with AIDS virus, even an asymptomatic carrier, is handicapped due to impairment of the hemic and reproductive systems, which makes procreation and childbirth dangerous to others." The majority of courts have determined that seropositive and AIDS students are covered by Section 504 as disabled.

The next question arising after determining that a child is disabled is whether he or she is "otherwise qualified" to attend a regular classroom. A person who presents a significant risk to others in the workplace or classroom will not be otherwise qualified if the risk cannot be eliminated through reasonable accommodation. The courts have used four factors when addressing the issue of "otherwise qualified":

> (a) the nature of the risk (how the disease is transmitted), (b) the duration of the risk (how long is the carrier infectious), (c) the severity of the risk (what is the potential harm to third parties), and (d) the probabilities the disease will be transmitted and will cause varying degrees of harm.[193]

Relying on the majority of medical evidence, the courts have decided that an AIDS child does not present a risk to other children in the classroom. A number of courts have cited the surgeon general of the United States, who has said:

> There is no known risk of non-sexual infection in most of the situations we encounter in our daily lives. We know that family members living with individuals who have the AIDS virus do not become infected except through sexual contact. There is no evidence of transmission (spread) of the AIDS virus by everyday contact even though these family members shared food, towels, cups, razors, even toothbrushes, and kissed each other.

When speaking specifically to the classroom environment, the surgeon general said:

> None of the identified cases of AIDS in the United States are known or are suspected to have been transmitted from one child to another in school, day care or foster care settings. Transmission would necessitate exposure of open cuts to the blood or other body fluids of the infected child, a highly unlikely occurrence. Even then, routine safety procedures for handling blood or other body fluids . . . would be effective in preventing transmission from children with AIDS to other

children in school. . . . Casual social contact between children and persons infected with AIDS virus is not dangerous.[194]

The U.S. Centers for Disease Control and the American Medical Association and other organizations have also maintained that a child with AIDS does not constitute a risk in a public school classroom. Therefore, based on Section 504, a child is disabled if he or she has AIDS and is otherwise qualified to attend a public school classroom, and he or she cannot be excluded from school.

IDEA AND AIDS

Another issue with AIDS students is whether they are covered by the Individuals with Disabilities Act. The IDEA defines "handicapped children" as

> mentally retarded, hard of hearing, deaf, speech or language impaired, visually handicapped, seriously emotionally disturbed, orthopedically impaired, *or other health impaired children,* or children with specific learning disabilities *who by reason thereof require special education and related services.*[195]

In the case of AIDS students, the category that would most closely fit is "other health impaired children." This phrase is defined as

> [l]imited strength, vitality or alertness due to chronic or acute health problems such as a heart condition, tuberculosis, rheumatic fever, nephritis, asthma, sickle-cell anemia, *hemophilia,* epilepsy, lead poisoning, leukemia, or diabetes, *which adversely affects a child's educational performance.*[196]

AIDS is not listed as an example of an acute or chronic health problem by the IDEA. In October of 1984, the Department of Education addressed the applicability of the IDEA to AIDS victims. The department stated that an AIDS child is not considered to be "handicapped" as defined in IDEA unless the child needs special education. The policy states:

> Children with AIDS could be eligible for special education programs under the category of "other health impaired," if they have chronic or acute health problems which adversely affect their educational performance.[197]

The IDEA applies to AIDS victims only if the virus adversely affects their educational performance. If a child is seropositive or a "healthy carrier," then he or she is not covered under the IDEA, but if the child becomes an AIDS victim and this diminishes his or her educational performance, then the IDEA must be enforced to meet the needs of the child.

———— ❖ — ❖ — ❖ ————

Is a Child with AIDS a Significant Risk, and If So, Could the Child Be Reasonably Accommodated? Case Remanded to Determine Risk

Martinez v. School Board of Hillsborough County, Florida

United States Court of Appeals,
Eleventh Circuit, 1988.
861 F.2d 1502.

VANCE, Circuit Judge: This case involves the appropriate educational placement of a mentally retarded child infected with the human immunodeficiency virus, the virus that causes Acquired Immunodeficiency Syndrome (AIDS). Appellant, Eliana Martinez, is seven years old and has an I.Q. of 41. This classifies her as a trainably mentally handicapped child. Eliana was born prematurely and received thirty-nine blood transfusions in the first four months of life. In April 1985 Eliana was diagnosed as suffering from AIDS Related Complex. She now is in the late stages of AIDS but her condition has been stabilized for several months. The court below found that Eliana is not toilet trained and suffers from thrush, a disease that can produce blood in the saliva. Eliana sucks her thumb and forefinger frequently, resulting in saliva on her fingers. In the past Eliana has suffered from skin lesions. When these occurred, Mrs. Rosa Martinez, her adoptive mother, has kept her at home. . . .

Two overlapping federal statutes establish the framework for determining appropriate educational placement for handicapped children—the Education of the Handicapped Act (the "EHA") [EHA is the same as EAHCA], and section 504 of the Rehabilitation Act of 1973 ("section 504"). . . .

When the EHA and section 504 are read together, a complementary set of standards emerges to determine the appropriate educational setting for a handicapped child. The EHA requires participating states to provide a "free appropriate public education" to handicapped children. 20 U.S.C. §1412(2)(B) (1982). Educational authorities must develop an individualized educational program stating the educational program and setting forth specific goals for each handicapped child. . . .

Section 504 of the Rehabilitation Act more broadly provides:

> No otherwise qualified handicapped individual . . . shall, solely by reason of his handicap, be excluded from the participation in, be denied the benefits of, or be subjected to discrimination under any program or activity receiving Federal financial assistance or under any program or activity conducted by any Executive agency or by the United States Postal Service.

29 U.S.C. §794 (1982). In considering whether an exclusion is prohibited by section 504, a trial judge must first determine whether the individual is "otherwise qualified." When a person is handicapped with a contagious disease this task requires the judge to conduct an individualized inquiry and to make appropriate findings of fact, "based on reasonable medical judgments . . . about (a) the nature of the risk (how the disease is transmitted), (b) the duration of the risk (how long is the carrier infectious), (c) the severity of the risk (what is the potential harm to third parties) and (d) the probabilities the disease will be transmitted and will cause varying degrees of harm." . . . As a second step the court must evaluate whether reasonable accommodations would make the handicapped individual otherwise qualified.

When a child with an infectious disease seeks relief under both the EHA and section 504 of the Rehabilitation Act, the relationship between these two statutory frameworks is particularly intricate. The trial judge must first determine the most appropriate educational placement for the handicapped child under EHA procedures. Next, the court must determine whether the child is otherwise qualified within the meaning of section 504 to be educated in this setting, despite the communicable disease. . . . If not, the court must consider whether reasonable accommodations could reduce the risk of transmission so as to make the child otherwise qualified to be educated in that setting. In considering accommodations that would make the child "otherwise qualified," the court must bear in mind the requirement that to the maximum extent appropriate, the child is to be educated in the least restrictive environment.

Eliana is entitled to a free appropriate public education under the EHA. She suffers from two handicaps under section 504 of the Rehabilitation Act: she is mentally retarded and has AIDS; each condition results in a "physical or mental impairment which substantially limits one or more major life activities." . . . Applying the standards under these two statutes to the facts of this case, the trial court first had to determine the most appropriate educational placement for Eliana under the EHA. Next, it had to consider whether Eliana was otherwise qualified to be educated in this setting. If the trial court found that Eliana was not otherwise qualified, it then had to consider whether reasonable accommodations would make her so. If, after reasonable accommodations, a significant risk of transmission would still exist, Eliana would not be otherwise qualified. *See Arline,* 107 S.Ct. at 1131 n.16.

As the parties agreed, the appropriate educational placement for Eliana under the EHA would be the regular TMH classroom if she did not suffer from AIDS. This presented the question whether the exclusion of Eliana from that setting is unlawful under section 504. In conducting this inquiry, the trial court had to determine whether Eliana was otherwise qualified to be educated in the regular TMH classroom. The trial court found a "remote theoretical possibility" of transmission with respect to tears, saliva and urine. This does not rise to the "significant" risk level that is required for Eliana to be excluded from the regular TMH classroom. . . . The court below made no findings with respect to the overall risk of transmission from all bodily substances, including blood in the saliva, to which other children might be exposed in the TMH classroom. Accordingly, we remand with directions that the trial court make findings as to the overall risk of transmission so that it can determine whether Eliana is otherwise qualified to attend classes in the TMH classroom.

If the risk of transmission supports a finding that Eliana is not "otherwise qualified" to attend classes with the other children in the TMH classroom, the court must consider whether reasonable accommodations would make her so. In evaluating possible accommodations, a trial court must consider the effect of each proposed accommodation on the handicapped child and the institution. . . . The court must be guided by the requirement that, to the maximum extent appropriate, these accommodations place the child in the least restrictive environment that would make the child otherwise qualified. Additionally, the court must consider the financial burden the accommodation would impose on the institution. . . .

We vacate the judgment of the district court and remand the case so that the district court may make the further required findings. The district court should receive such additional evidence as it deems necessary in light of such requirements. It should thereafter enter such judgment as is appropriate.

Vacated and remanded with instructions.

CASE NOTE

The Eleventh Circuit Court of Appeals remanded *Martinez* to the federal district court, and the court ruled:

The Court has seriously considered the allegations now being raised that the risk to Eliana far outweighs any benefit to her from attending school with other children. . . . The decision must balance the risk to the child versus the benefit which flows from the attendance at school. Keeping this child out of school does not guarantee her safety and long life; death if it seeks and takes Eliana may come from various sources which are available to her without restriction: the park, the mall, or her home. Upon conscientious consideration of the issue from all sides, the Court cannot find that the risk is significant enough to counterbalance the benefit and rights to this child inherent in attending school with other children. . . .

[The court concluded:]

1. The appropriate educational placement for Eliana Martinez under the Education for All Handicapped Children Act would be the regular Trainable Mentally Handicapped classroom if she did not suffer from AIDS.

2. The possibility of transmission with respect to tears, saliva, and urine is remote and theoretical and does not rise to the "significant" risk level that is required to bar Eliana Martinez from the regular Trainable Mentally Handicapped classroom.

3. The evidence does not support a finding that the overall risk of transmission from all bodily substances, including blood in the saliva, rises to the "significant" risk level of requiring this child's exclusion from the classroom.

4. The Court finds that Eliana Martinez is "otherwise qualified" to attend the Trainable Mentally Handicapped classroom at Manhattan Elementary School, which is the most appropriate educational setting for this child pursuant to the EHA.

5. Since the Court finds Eliana Martinez "otherwise qualified" to attend this classroom, it is unnecessary for the Court to consider the effect of any accommodation.

6. The Court readopts its previous conclusion of law stating that if there is a question of the advisability of Eliana being in the classroom on a certain day, the school nurse should be consulted for an evaluation of either Eliana, or another child, if the danger may be an infection from another child to Eliana. It is not necessary for Eliana, nor the rest of the TMH students, to be seen by the nurse or other health practitioner on a daily basis to determine if Eliana should be in the integrated classroom that day.

7. The Court will require that the Hillsborough County School Board provide educational programs to the school parent population, and student population as far as is practicable, that will be associated with Eliana Martinez in the classroom, with the aim of educating and informing them regarding the realities of AIDS, and the proper procedures in order to deal with the situation and minimize the risk of transmission to others. In addition a copy of this Order is to be made available to the public at the Office of Manhattan Elementary School. Accordingly, it is Ordered that Defendant, The School Board of Hillsborough County, Florida, admit Plaintiff Eliana Martinez to the Trainable Mentally Handicapped classroom of Manhattan Elementary School within the parameters of this order. Done and ordered.

Martinez v. School Board of Hillsborough County, Florida, 711 F.Supp. 1066 (M.D.Fla.1989).

■ ENDNOTES

1. Public Law 101-46, 104 Stat. 1103 (1975).
2. Public Law 105-17, 111 Stat. 37 (20 U.S.C. §1400 et seq.) (1997).
3. 20 U.S.C. §1401(d).
4. Donald F. Moores, *Educating the Deaf: Psychology, Principles and Practices* (Boston: Houghton Mifflin, 1978).
5. Moores, *Educating the Deaf*.
6. Resolve for Erecting a Lunatic Hospital (1831), Resolves of the General Court of the Commonwealth of Massachusetts.
7. Jonathan Messerli, *Horace Mann* (New York: Alfred A. Knopf, 1972).
8. Samuel A. Kirk and James J. Gallagher, *Educating Exceptional Children*, 4th ed. (Boston: Houghton Mifflin, 1983).
9. Watson v. City of Cambridge, 157 Mass. 561, 32 N.E. 864 (1893).
10. State ex rel. Beattie v. Board of Education, 169 Wis. 231, 172 N.W. 153 (1919).
11. Ibid., 172 N.W. at 154.
12. Ralph B. Kimbrough and Michael Y. Nunnery, *Educational Administration* (New York: Macmillan, 1976).
13. Ibid.
14. Brown v. Board of Education, 347 U.S. 483, 74 S.Ct. 686 (1954).
15. Ibid.
16. Pennsylvania Association for Retarded Children v. Commonwealth, 334 F.Supp. 1257 (E.D.Pa.1971), 343 F.Supp. 279 (E.D.Pa.1972).
17. Ibid.
18. 348 F.Supp. 866 (D.D.C.1972).
19. Ibid.
20. Section 504, Vocational Rehabilitation Act of 1973.
21. Ibid.
22. Ibid.
23. Ibid., §§84.33, 84.34.
24. Doe, State of Hawaii v. Katherine D., 531 F.Supp. 517 (D.Haw. 1982), affirmed in part and reversed in part as to attorney's fees, 727 F.2d 809 (9th Cir.1983).
25. Doe v. Dolton Elementary School District No. 148, 694 F.Supp. 440 (N.D.Ill.1988).
26. 465 U.S. 555, 104 S.Ct. 1211 (1984).
27. 20 U.S.C.A. §1681(a).
28. Gallagher v. Pontiac School District, 807 F.2d 75 (6th Cir.1986).
29. 480 U.S. 273, 107 S.Ct. 1123 (1987).
30. Civil Rights Reformation Act Public Law 100-259 (1988). See also Laura F. Rothstein, *Special Education Law* (New York: Longman, 1990), pp. 26–28.
31. Education for All Handicapped Children Act, 20 U.S.C.A. §1400(b).
32. Ibid., §1401.
33. Ibid.
34. Public Law 95-561, 92 Stat. 2364 (1978); Public Law 98-199, 97 Stat. 1357 (1983); Public Law 99-372, 100 Stat. 796 (1986); Public Law 99-457, 100 Stat. 1145 (1986).
35. Education of the Handicapped Act Amendments of 1983: Report of Mr. Hatch to Accompany S. 1341, Comm.

on Labor and Human Resources, S.Rep.No. 191, 98th Cong., 1st Sess. 7 (1983).
36. Ibid.
37. S.Rep.No. 315, 99th Cong., 2d Sess. 3, 5 (1986). See also H.Rep.No. 860, 99th Cong., 2d Sess., reprinted in 1986 U.S.Code Cong. & Admin.News 2401.
38. 20 U.S.C.A. §1422.
39. 20 U.S.C.A. §1415.
40. 20 U.S.C.A. §§1401–1491.
41. See Dixie Snow Huefner, "The Individuals with Disabilities Education Act Amendments of 1997," 122 Educ.L.Rep. 1103 (March 5, 1998).
42. Ibid., p. 1104.
43. 20 U.S.C. §1402(3).
44. 20 U.S.C. §1412(a)(3)(B).
45. Huefner, "IDEA Amendments," p. 1104.
46. 20 U.S.C. §1412(a)(1)(B)(ii).
47. Huefner, "IDEA Amendments."
48. See 34 C.F.R. §300.7(a) (1).
49. Capistrano Unified School District v. Wartenberg, 59 F.3d 884 (9th Cir.1995).
50. 134 F.3d 659 (4th Cir.1998).
51. 20 U.S.C. §794 (§504).
52. Public Law 101-336, 42 U.S.C. §12101 (1990).
53. §1401(18).
54. 20 U.S.C.A. §1415 (West Supp. 1997).
55. Board of Education v. Rowley, 458 U.S. 176, 102 S.Ct. 3034 (1982).
56. See Tara L. Eyer, "Greater Expectations: How the 1997 IDEA Amendments Raise the Basic Floor of Opportunity for Children with Disabilities," 126 Educ.L.Rep. 1 (August 6, 1998).
57. Board of Education of Hendrick Hudson Central School District v. Rowley, 458 U.S. 176, 201, 102 S.Ct. 3034, 3048 (1982).
58. Ibid., 485 U.S. at 206, 102 S.Ct. at 3051.
59. Ibid., 485 U.S. at 212, 102 S.Ct. at 3054.
60. 875 F.2d 954 (1st Cir.1989).
61. Rowley, op cit.
62. Timothy W. v. Rochester, New Hampshire School District, 875 F.2d 954 (1st Cir.1989); Fort Zumwalt School District v. Clynes, 119 F.3d 607 (8th Cir.1997). See Mark C. Weber, "The Transformation of Education of the Handicapped Act: A Study in the Interpretation of Radical Statutes," University of California at Davis Law Review 24 (Winter, 1990): p. 349.
63. 119 F.3d 607 (8th Cir.1997).
64. Rowley, op. cit. See Eyer, "Greater Expectations," p. 1.
65. Board of Education v. Diamond, 808 F.2d 987 (3rd Cir.1986); Hall v. Vance Co. Board of Education, 774 F.2d 629 (4th Cir.1985).
66. 879 F.2d 1340 (6th Cir.1989).
67. Urban v. Jefferson County School District, 89 F.3d 720 (10th Cir. 1996).
68. Cypress-Fairbanks Independent School District v. Michael F., 118 F.3d 245 (5th Cir.1997).
69. Perry A. Zirkel, "Special Education Law Update VI," 133 Educ.L.Rep. 323 (May 27, 1999).
70. 629 F.2d 269 (3d Cir. 1980).
71. Ibid., p. 272.

72. Ibid., p. 277.

73. Ibid., p. 280.

74. 708 F.2d 1028, 1035 (5th Cir.1983).

75. Georgia Association of Retarded Citizens v. McDaniel, 716 F.2d 1565 (11th Cir.1983).

76. Battle v. Commonwealth of Pennsylvania, op. cit.

77. Yaris v. Special School District of St. Louis, 558 F.Supp. 545 (E.D.Mo.1983), affirmed, 728 F.2d 1055 (8th Cir.1986).

78. Crawford v. Pittman, op. cit.

79. Georgia Association of Retarded Citizens v. McDaniel, 511 F.Supp. 1263 (N.D.Ga.1981), affirmed, 716 F.2d 1565 (11th Cir.1983).

80. Alamo Heights Independent School District v. State Board of Education, 790 F.2d 1153, 1159 (5th Cir.1986).

81. Ibid.

82. Ibid., p. 1158.

83. 921 F.2d 1022 (10th Cir.1990).

84. Polk v. Central Susquehanna Intermediate Unit 16, 853 F.2d 171 (3d Cir.1988).

85. Board of Education of Hendrick Hudson v. Rowley, supra at 3049.

86. Johnson v. Independent School District No. 4 of Bixby, 921 F.2d 1022 (10th Cir.1990).

87. Cordrey v. Euckert, 917 F.2d 1460, 1464 (6th Cir.1990).

88. Ibid., p. 1471.

89. Ibid., p. 1472.

90. Board of Education of Hendrick Hudson Central School District v. Rowley, op. cit.

91. 20 U.S.C.A. §1415; see also IDEA Regulation, 34 C.F.R. §§300.500–517.

92. Speilberg v. Henrico County Public Schools, 853 F.2d 256 (4th Cir.1988).

93. Burke County Board of Education v. Denton, 895 F.2d 973 (4th Cir.1990).

94. Doe v. Defendant I, 898 F.2d 1186, 1190 (6th Cir.1990).

95. 20 U.S.C.A. §1415(c).

96. 20 U.S.C.A. §1415(e)(3).

97. Honig v. Doe, 484 U.S. 305, 108 S.Ct. 592 (1988).

98. 20 U.S.C.A. §1415(e)(2).

99. Georgia Association of Retarded Citizens v. McDaniel, 716 F.2d 1565 (11th Cir.1983), vacated on other grounds, 468 U.S. 1213, 104 S.Ct. 3581 (1984), on remand, 740 F.2d 902 (11th Cir.1984).

100. 20 U.S.C.A. §1400. See also Honig v. Doe, op. cit.

101. See Eyer, "Greater Expectations."

102. 20 U.S.C.A. §1414 (d)(1)(A).

103. Ibid.

104. Ibid.

105. Ibid.

106. 20 U.S.C.A. §1414(d)(1)(A) (West Supp. 1997).

107. Ibid.

108. 20 U.S.C.A. §1414(d)(1)(A)(ii).

109. 20 U.S.C. §1412(a)(5)(A); see also 34 C.F.R. §300.551.

110. 34 C.F.R. §§300.551, 300.552(d).

111. 34 C.F.R. §300.551.

112. Rothstein, *Special Education Law*, p. 112.

113. Devries v. Fairfax County School Board, 882 F.2d 876, 878 (4th Cir.1989); Daniel R. R. v. State Board of Education, 874 F.2d 1036, 1044 (5th Cir.1989); A. W. v. Northwest R-1 School District, 813 F.2d 158, 162 (8th Cir.1987); Roncker v. Walter, 700 F.2d 1058, 1063 (6th Cir.1983), cert. denied, 464 U.S. 864, 104 S.Ct. 196 (1983).

114. Daniel R. R. v. State Board of Education, 874 F.2d 1036 (5th Cir.1989).

115. Ibid., p. 1048.

116. 700 F.2d 1058 (6th Cir.1983).

117. Ibid., p. 1062.

118. Ibid., p. 1063.

119. Sacramento City School District v. Rachel H., 14 F.3d 1398 (9th Cir.1994).

120. Daniel R. R., 874 F.2d at 1048.

121. Age v. Bullitt County Schools, 673 F.2d 141, 145 (6th Cir.1982); Roncker, 700 F.2d at 1063.

122. Lachman v. Illinois State Board of Education, 852 F.2d 290, 296 (7th Cir.1988), cert. denied, 488 U.S. 925, 109 S.Ct. 308 (1988); Board of Education of Hendrick Hudson Central School District v. Rowley, 458 U.S. 176, 207, 102 S.Ct. 3034, 3051 (1982).

123. Lachman, 852 F.2d at 297.

124. Public Law 101-476 20 U.S.C. §1422(5)(b) (IDEA 1990).

125. 839 F.Supp. 968, 971 (N.D.N.Y. 1993).

126. Oberti by Oberti v. Board of Education of Borough of Clementon School District, 995 F.2d 1204, 1207 (3d Cir.1993); see also Sacramento City School District v. Rachel H., 14 F.3d 1398 (9th Cir.1994).

127. 20 U.S.C.A. §1414(d)(1)(A)(vi).

128. 34 C.F.R. §300.346 (a)(3) (1996).

129. 20 U.S.C. §1413(a)(4).

130. 34 C.F.R. §300.452.

131. 34 C.F.R. §76.651(a)(1)(2).

132. K. R. v. Anderson Community School Corp., 81 F.3d 653 (7th Cir.1996).

133. 471 U.S. 359, 105 S.Ct. 1996 (1985).

134. 20 U.S.C. §1415(e)(2).

135. Muller v. Committee on Special Education of the East Islip Union Free School District, 145 F.3d 95 (2nd Cir.1998).

136. 510 U.S. 7, 114 S.Ct. 361 (1993).

137. Ibid., 114 S.Ct. at 363.

138. 20 U.S.C.A. §1412(a)(10)(C).

139. See Huefner, "IDEA Amendments," p. 1119.

140. Holland v. District of Columbia, 71 F.3d 417 (D.C.Cir.1995); Florence County School District Four v. Carter, 510 U.S. 7, 114 S.Ct. 361 (1993).

141. 509 U.S. 1, 113 S.Ct. 2462 (1993).

142. Ibid., 113 S.Ct. at 2463.

143. Goodall by Goodall v. Stafford County School Board, 60 F.3d 168 (4th Cir.1995), cert. denied, 64 U.S. 2092, 116 S.Ct. 706 (1996).

144. 473 U.S. 402, 105 S.Ct. 3232 (1985).

145. 20 U.S.C.A. §1401(17).

146. 468 U.S. 883, 104 S.Ct. 3371 (1984).

147. Public Law 94-142, 20 U.S.C. §1401(17).

148. Irving Independent School District v. Tatro, op. cit.

149. Ibid., 468 U.S. at 894, 104 S.Ct. at 3378.
150. T. G. v. Board of Education of Piscataway, 576 F.Supp. 420 (D.N.J.1983).
151. Alamo Heights Independent School District v. State Board of Education, op. cit.
152. Metropolitan Government v. Tennessee Department of Education, 771 S.W.2d 427, 429 (Tenn.App.1989).
153. Corbett v. Regional Center for the East Bay, Inc., 676 F.Supp. 964 (N.D.Cal.1988), injunction modified, 699 F.Supp. 230 (N.D.Cal.1988).
154. Stuart v. Nappi, 443 F.Supp. 1235 (D.Conn.1978); Doe v. Koger, 480 F.Supp. 225 (N.D.Ind.1979).
155. Stuart v. Nappi, op. cit.
156. S-1 v. Turlington, 635 F.2d 342 (5th Cir.), cert. denied, 454 U.S. 1030, 102 S.Ct. 566 (1981).
157. Ibid.
158. Doe v. Koger, 480 F.Supp. 225 (N.D.Ind.1979).
159. S-1 v. Turlington, op. cit. See also School Board of Prince William County, Virginia v. Malone, 662 F.Supp. 978 (E.D.Va.1984), affirmed, 762 F.2d 1210 (4th Cir.1985).
160. Jackson v. Franklin County School Board, 765 F.2d 535 (5th Cir.1985); Victoria L. v. District School Board of Lee County, Florida, 741 F.2d 369 (11th Cir.1984).
161. Anne Proffitt Dupre, "A Study in Double Standards, Discipline, and the Disabled Student," Washington Law Review 75 (January 2000): p. 1.
162. 20 U.S.C.A. §1415.
163. 20 U.S.C.A. §1412 (1) (A).
164. 20 U.S.C.A. §1412(2)(B).
165. M. C. v. Central Regional School District, 81 F.3d 389 (3d Cir.1996).
166. Carlisle Area School District v. Scott, 62 F.3d 520 (3d Cir.1995).
167. 81 F.3d 839 (3d Cir.1996).
168. Ibid.
169. Ibid.
170. 172 F.3d 238 (3d Cir.1999).
171. M. C. v. Central Regional School District, op. cit.
172. 468 U.S. 992, 104 S.Ct. 3457 (1984).
173. Soroko v. Gosling, 26 IDELR 1135 (4th Cir.1997). See Zirkel, "Special Education Law Update VI," p. 330.
174. Correa v. Vance, 950 F.Supp. 118 (D.Md.1996).
175. John T. v. Marion Independent School District, 173 F.3d 684 (8th Cir.1999).
176. Arons v. New Jersey State Board of Education, 842 F.2d 58 (3d Cir.1988).
177. Erickson v. Board of Education, 162 F.3d 289 (4th Cir.1998); Wenger v. Canastota Central School District, 146 F.3d 123 (2d Cir.1998).
178. Eggers v. Bullitt County School District, 854 F.2d 892 (6th Cir.1988).
179. 510 U.S. 7, 114 S.Ct. 361 (1993).
180. Ibid.
181. City of Boerne v. Flores, 521 U.S. 507, 117 S.Ct. 2157 (1997); Seminole Tribe of Florida v. Florida, 517 U.S. 44, 116 S.Ct. 1114 (1996); Florida Prepaid Postsecondary Education Expense Board v. College Savings Bank and United States, 527 U.S. 627, 119 S.Ct. 2199 (1999); Alden v. Maine, 527 U.S. 706, 119 S.Ct. 2240 (1999).
182. Mt. Healthy City School District Board of Education v. Doyle, 429 U.S. 274, 95 S.Ct. 568 (1977).
183. See Florida Prepaid Postsecondary Education Expense Board, op. cit.; Alden, op. cit.
184. Alsbrook v. City of Maumelle, 184 F.3d 999 (8th Cir.1999).
185. Coolbaugh v. Louisiana, 136 F.3d 1426 (11th Cir.1998); cert. denied, 525 U.S. 819, 119 S.Ct. 58 (1998); Clark v. California, 123 F.3d 1267 (9th Cir.1997), cert. denied sub. nom. Crawford v. Indiana Department of Corrections, 115 F.3d 481 (7th Cir.1997).
186. Torres v. Puerto Rico Tourism Co., 175 F.3d 1 (1st Cir.1999).
187. Amos v. Maryland Department of Public Safety and Correctional Services, 178 F.3d 212 (4th Cir. 1999); but see Brown v. North Carolina Division of Motor Vehicles, 166 F.3d 698 (4th Cir.1999), where the court found that Congress exceeded its powers under Title II of the ADA.
188. Ray v. School District of Desoto County, 666 F.Supp. 1524, 1529 (M.D.Fla.1987).
189. Doe v. Dolton Elementary School District No. 148, 694 F.Supp. 440, 441 (N.D.Ill.1988).
190. Ray v. School District of Desoto County, 666 F.Supp. 1524, 1529 (M.D.Fla.1987).
191. Ibid.
192. Doe v. Dolton Elementary School District No. 148, op. cit.
193. *School Board of Nassau County, Fla. v. Arline*, 480 U.S. at 288, 107 S.Ct. at 1131 (1987); rehearing denied, 481 U.S. 1024, 107 S.Ct. 1993 (1987).
194. U.S. Public Health Service, *Surgeon General's Report on Acquired Immune Deficiency* (Washington, D.C., Government Printing Office, 1986), p. 13.
195. 20 U.S.C.A. §1401(a)(1) (italics added).
196. 34 C.F.R. §300.5(b)(7) (italics added).
197. Doe v. Belleville Public School District No. 118, 672 F.Supp. 342, 344–45 (S.D.Ill.1987).

CHAPTER 10

DESEGREGATION

The Constitution of the United States does not, I think, permit any public authority to know the race of those entitled to be protected in the enjoyment of such rights. Every true man has pride of race, and under appropriate circumstances when the rights of others, his equals before the law, are not to be affected, it is his privilege to express such pride and to take such action based upon it as to him seems proper. But I deny that any legislative body or judicial tribunal may have regard to the race of citizens when the civil rights of those citizens are involved.

—John M. Harlan

CHAPTER OUTLINE

- HISTORICAL BACKGROUND
- EROSION OF SEPARATE-BUT-EQUAL
- *BROWN* AND THE DEMISE OF SEGREGATED SCHOOLS
- INTERPRETING *BROWN*
- *DE FACTO* SEGREGATION
- QUOTAS AND BUSING

- UNITARINESS
- REMEDIAL AND COMPENSATORY REMEDIES
- DIVERSITY AND RACIAL CLASSIFICATIONS
- INTERDISTRICT DESEGREGATION
- TITLE VI AND *BAKKE*

IN HIS FAMOUS solitary dissent in *Plessy v. Ferguson*, Justice John M. Harlan enunciated the principle of law that best describes both the intent of the Constitution and the desirable moral standard for the nation when he said, "[I]n view of the Constitution, in the eye of the law, there is in this country no superior, dominant, ruling class of citizens. . . . Our constitution is color-blind, and neither knows nor tolerates classes among its citizens."[1] The route taken by the American judiciary over an uncharted course in

elevating this principle of racial equality from a minority dissenting opinion to a majority view is indelibly linked with the history of public education. Because education is one of the most elemental and foundational aspects of any society, the problems inherent in racial inequality were most visible in the schools. Those who sought to maintain white racial superiority infected the schools with legally contrived discriminating measures designed to bring about segregation. Equality, though, demands that government be neutral and uniform in its treatment of all persons: "Equality is a synonym for uniformity" among guaranteed rights.[2] Enunciating the principle of equality, however, is much easier than implementing it, particularly where racial prejudice permeates the social fabric. Because the race issue is integral to American history—"The American Dilemma," as Mydral called it—and prejudice is endemic to all societies, its elimination became a most profound challenge for the judiciary of the United States. To eradicate racial prejudice required that the courts not only redress state-created segregation, but also intervene in institutionalized forms of private and social discrimination over which states may have had indirect influence. To do this, both federal constitutional and statutory law has been employed to overcome the vestiges of past discrimination. In protecting African-American school children, the courts have broadly endorsed congressional civil rights legislation designed to prevent the use of government policy to aid and enforce personal and individual prejudices in the educational system.

This chapter describes the judicial progression from its formal recognition and later prohibition of blatant statutory segregation, in both state and federal law, to the more subtle prejudicial mistreatment of African-Americans that has resulted in inferior educational opportunity. Presented herein is the evolution of judicial thinking in overcoming discrimination, while preserving individual rights and freedoms. The law presented in this chapter progresses through the stages of precedents from *Plessy* in 1898, to the famous *Brown* case in 1954, to the era of freedom of choice and unitariness, and to more recent and various remedial actions that have been generically referred to as affirmative action.

■ HISTORICAL BACKGROUND

No one could have predicted that the pre-1850 education of a five-year-old child by the name of Sarah Roberts would have such a profound effect on the historical development of the public schools. Sarah left home each day and walked through the streets of the city of Boston past five elementary schools for white children to reach the Smith Grammar School, which had been established in 1820 for blacks.

Not only was the school remote from the child's home, but also an evaluation committee had reported that the school was in poor condition—"The school rooms are too small, the paint is much defaced," and the equipment needed repair. Sarah's father tried repeatedly to place her in the better nearby schools for whites, but each time his efforts failed. After persistent rebuffs, Mr. Roberts sought a most able lawyer, civil rights enthusiast, and later U.S. senator, Charles Sumner, to represent his child and challenge the unequal treatment. From the ensuing legal conflict, the now infamous doctrine of "separate-but-equal" was born.

Citing the Massachusetts Constitution in passages that would later be likened to the equal protection clause of the Fourteenth Amendment, Sumner maintained that compelling black children to attend separate schools was to effectively "brand a whole race with the stigma of inferiority and degradation."[3] Eloquently, Sumner pointed out that segregated schools could not be considered equivalent to white schools because of the stigma of caste that mandatory attendance attached thereto. Sumner effectively expounded the same constitutional position that was to be the heart of the plaintiff's successful contention over one hundred years later in *Brown v. Board of Education*—that a separate school "exclusively devoted to one class must differ essentially, in its spirit and character, from that public school known to the law, where all classes meet together in equality."[4]

Justice Shaw of the Massachusetts court was, however, unconvinced and in his historic opinion set forth the separate-but-equal doctrine that was to prevail for so long. In theory, he agreed with "the great principle" advanced by Sumner that all persons ought to stand equal before the law, but he went on to conclude contrarily that the standard of equality implied not that all men and women were legally clothed with the same civil and political powers, but that all were merely entitled to equal consideration and protection for their maintenance and security. What exactly the protected rights were was dependent on the laws adapted to their "respective relations and conditions." As one of these conditions, race was seen to be a legitimate rationale for classification. Judge Shaw failed to show, however, that there was any reasonable relationship between racial classification and legitimate objectives of the school system; he merely asserted that school segregation was for the good of both races. With this decision, separate-but-equal was born into education, and it would not die for over one hundred years. During the intervening years, the Civil War would be fought, civil rights laws would be enacted by the U.S. Congress to little or no avail, and the U.S. Supreme Court itself would transplant the unfortunate standard from the Massachusetts Constitution to the Constitution of the United States.

In 1868, the Fourteenth Amendment was ratified to ensure the constitutionality of Reconstruction statutes that had been enacted to proscribe racial discrimination. The third clause of the critical second sentence of the amendment stated: "Nor shall any State . . . deny to any person within its jurisdiction the equal protection of the laws." In spite of the strength of the wording, the amendment was to have little immediate effect, as was evidenced by the *Civil Rights Cases* wherein the Supreme Court held that no application could be made to private enterprise discrimination, such as occurred in inns, conveyances, restaurants, and places of entertainment.[5]

The move from private discrimination to state-sanctioned discrimination came about through an educationally irrelevant decision concerning interstate commerce, in which a Mississippi statute requiring segregated train cars was upheld because it pertained solely to transportation within the state.[6] The equal protection clause was thereby circumvented, and state-enforced classification of citizens by race was made possible. In the South, state action began transforming the private custom of discrimination into state law. Jim Crow laws began in Florida in 1887 and soon engulfed the South.[7] Justice Powell, commenting much later, said: "[T]he Equal Protection Clause was virtually strangled in its infancy by post–Civil War judicial reactionism."[8]

The capstone of segregation, though, came in 1896 with *Plessy v. Ferguson*,[9] in which the separate-but-equal rationale of the *Roberts* court was implanted as a national standard applying to the Fourteenth Amendment. In *Plessy*, the Supreme Court maintained that an 1890 Louisiana law entitled "An Act to Promote the Comfort of Passengers," providing that "all railway companies carrying passengers in their coaches in this State, shall provide equal but separate accommodations for the white and colored races, by providing two or more passenger coaches for each passenger train, or by dividing the passenger coaches by a partition so as to secure accommodations," was not unconstitutional because state legislatures have wide discretion in promoting public peace and good order, and such actions will be upheld so long as they are reasonable. In a now-infamous passage, Justice Brown said:

> In determining the question of reasonableness, [the legislature] is at liberty to act with reference to the established usages, customs, and traditions of the people, and with a view to the promotion of their comfort, and the preservation of the public peace and good order. Gauged by this standard, we cannot say that a law which authorizes or even requires the separation of the two races in public conveyances is unreasonable. . . . [10]

In essence, the Court made the equal protection clause subject to custom and tradition in accordance with legislative interpretation, no matter how blatantly and objectionably the law affected a particular classification of people.

In his lonely dissent in *Plessy*, Justice Harlan attacked the majority opinion and enunciated the law that would eventually become the prevailing view over fifty years later. He maintained, "Our constitution is color-blind, and neither knows nor tolerates classes among its citizens. In respect to civil rights, all citizens are equal before the law."[11] He maintained that separation of the races was a "badge of servitude."

After *Plessy*, the precedent of separation of the races was quickly transferred to education and further extended. In the case of *Cumming v. Board of Education of Richmond County, Georgia*, the school board, discovering that it needed more facilities at the grade-school level to accommodate black children, discontinued the black high school and turned the building into a black elementary school.[12] The board advised the black high school students to seek their education in church-affiliated schools. Upon challenge, the U.S. Supreme Court held that in this matter the only interest of the federal judiciary was to see that all citizens share equitably in the tax burden, but that the matter of education and how it was conducted, supported by that taxation, was solely a state concern.

Further expansion of segregation in education was justified in 1908 in *Berea College v. Kentucky*,[13] wherein the Supreme Court upheld a state law that forbade any institution as a corporation to provide instruction to both races at the same time unless the classes were conducted at least twenty-five miles apart. The law, the Day Law as it was named after its author,[14] was enacted specifically to prohibit integration at Berea College, a small private college that had been founded in 1859 to provide nondiscriminatory education for needy students, both black and white. In upholding the law and sidestepping the direct issue of state-enforced racial discrimination in the private sector, the Court simply asserted that the college, as a corporation of Kentucky, was subject to state regulation and was not entitled to all the immunities to which individuals were entitled. Since the college, not black students, was the plaintiff, the Court was free to say that "a state may withhold from its corporations privileges and powers of which it cannot constitutionally deprive individuals."[15]

The *Plessy, Cumming,* and *Berea College* decisions fully established not only that the state could constitutionally maintain a separate system of education for blacks and whites, but also that the arm of the state could reach into private education and require that it be segregated as well. Beyond this, *Cumming* laid the groundwork for almost unlimited state discretion in defining what constituted separate-but-equal. In *Cumming,* the Richmond, Georgia, school board had decided that due to a shortage of money it would discontinue the black high school and convert the facility to a black primary school. The federal courts would not intervene. Separation of the races in education was subsequently expanded to include not only black and white, but also yellow, brown, and red. In *Gong Lum v. Rice*,[16] in 1927, the Supreme Court held that states could segregate a Mongolian child from the Caucasian schools and compel her to attend a school for black children. Segregation of the *Gong Lum* type was practiced in many states, in both the North and the South.

■ EROSION OF SEPARATE-BUT-EQUAL

As long as state legislatures had plenary power to define the limits of separate-but-equal, the concept was accepted with little or no argument. By the 1930s, however, the National Association for the Advancement of Colored People (NAACP) initiated a movement that was to pursue racial abuse and seek judicial clarification of the limits of separate-but-equal as a legal basis for segregation. At first, the intention was to attack segregation where equal facilities were obviously inadequate or nonexistent. As a result of these efforts, in 1938 a landmark desegregation decision, *Missouri ex rel. Gaines v. Canada,* was handed down by the Supreme Court.[17] By a vote of seven to one, the Supreme Court held a Missouri law prohibiting blacks from entering the University of Missouri Law School unconstitutional because there were no other public law schools in the state to which blacks could go as an alternative. The ruling was singularly important not only because it placed some outward boundaries on implementation of separate-but-equal, but also more significantly because it represented a reassertion of judicial authority in construing the equal protection clause as a limitation on previously unfettered state action in education.

With the World War II years intervening, little was accomplished during the next decade, but slowly a public attitude against separate-but-equal began to materialize, and this set the stage for more direct judicial action. The foundation of separate-but-equal was shaken by the Supreme Court in 1950, in another case involving a law school, this time that of the University of Texas.[18] Law schools were good targets for desegregation attorneys because judges and lawyers could more readily see the disparate condition in the legal field. In this case, a black Houston mail carrier by the name of Sweatt sought admission to the University of Texas Law School. Since the state had no law school for blacks, under the precedent of *Gaines* a lower Texas court ordered that the state set up a law school for blacks. The school that was established was woefully inadequate, and Sweatt further challenged, reasserting his claim to be admitted to the University of Texas Law School. Here the Supreme Court was presented with a rather different dilemma of comparing two schools and rendering a judgment as to their comparability. Thus, the high court found itself in the uneasy role of a superaccreditation agency. In ordering Sweatt admitted to the all-white law school, Chief Justice Fred Vinson pointed out that the new law school "could never hope to be equal in reputation of the faculty, experience of the administration, position and influence of the alumni, standing in the community, tradition and prestige."[19]

Vinson virtually eliminated the use of separate law schools for blacks by further observing that

> the law school to which Texas is willing to admit [Sweatt] excludes from its student body members of the racial groups which number 85 percent of the population of the State and include most of the lawyers, witnesses, jurors, judges, and other officials with whom [he] will inevitably be dealing when he becomes a member of the Texas Bar. With such a substantial and significant segment of society excluded, we cannot conclude that the education offered [Sweatt] is substantially equal to that which he would receive if admitted to the University of Texas Law School.[20]

The obvious educational infirmity of the separate-but-equal doctrine emerged with litigation in this case. Limitations on curriculum, faculty, educational atmosphere, and professional development combined to draw into serious constitutional question the further maintenance of separate higher-education facilities for blacks and whites. On the same day that *Sweatt* was handed down, the Supreme Court ruled that if a state chose not to establish separate and substantially equal facilities for blacks, it could not segregate them within the white school.[21] McLaurin, a black doctoral student in the College of Education at the University of Oklahoma, was allowed to enroll in the white school but was compelled to sit and study in designated sections for blacks while in the classrooms, library, and dining hall. The Court held this treatment unconstitutional as well.

Even though these cases served to expound the frailties of separate-but-equal, they did little to help the black elementary and secondary school children who were denied equal opportunity with no relief in sight. With *Cumming* as the precedent, the black child attended school in ramshackle facilities, had poor instructors, and in most cases attended schools that were in session for only a minor portion of the year. This circumstance could not be corrected so long as the separate-but-equal doctrine stood.

■ *BROWN* AND THE DEMISE OF SEGREGATED SCHOOLS

Several cases began making their way through the lower courts, each case holding potential for challenging the separate-but-equal doctrine head-on. Eventually, five cases, from Kansas, South Carolina, Virginia, Delaware, and Washington, D.C., reached the Supreme Court[22] and were first argued in December 1952.

Lower courts in each case, with the exception of the Delaware case, had denied relief to black children. In Delaware, a decision by the Delaware Court of Chancery, holding for the plaintiffs and requiring that black children be admitted to schools previously attended only by white children, was affirmed by the Supreme Court of Delaware. The defendants in this case applied for *certiorari* to the U.S. Supreme Court, challenging the immediate admission of black children to the white schools. In *Brown v. Board of Education,* the plaintiffs were black children of elementary age residing in Topeka. They brought action to enjoin a state statute that permitted, but did not require, cities in Kansas of more than 15,000 population to maintain separate facilities for black and white students. Under that authority, the Topeka Board of Education chose to establish segregated elementary schools. The lower federal court held that segregation in public education had a detrimental effect on black children but denied plaintiffs relief because the facilities were substantially equal. In both the South Carolina and Virginia cases, the lower courts had found the black schools to be inferior and had ordered improvements for equalization, but they had not required admission of the black children to the schools for white children during the transition period. In the Washington, D.C., case, black children directly challenged school segregation in the nation's capital, alleging that segregation deprived them of due process of law under the Fifth Amendment. It was necessary to couch this claim in the Fifth Amendment, since the Fourteenth Amendment did not apply to Congress.

These cases, combined, presented a range of situations by which the Supreme Court could comprehensively view the segregation issue. The Kansas case involved permissive segregation legislation for elementary children in a northern state; in the Virginia case, a compulsory segregation law was used to segregate high school students in an upper southern state; South Carolina represented the Deep South, and Delaware a border state.[23] The District of Columbia case drew due process and congressional power into question. The differing circumstances and the wide geographical distribution gave the decision more importance and imbued it with a national flavor and aura.

The importance of the case was reflected in the Court's hesitancy to rush to judgment. Though the case was first argued on December 9, 1952, the Court reached no decision, and on June 8, 1953, the Court issued an order setting the case for reargument that fall and submitted a series of questions for litigants to address. In the first question, the Court asked what evidence there was to indicate that Congress and the states contemplated that the Fourteenth Amendment, when ratified, was intended to abolish school segregation. Second, the Court asked whether Congress had the power to abolish school segregation and what the limits of the Court's own powers were. Third, the Court sought opinions on the extent of its own powers to resolve the issue, should the answer to the first two question be inconclusive. Fourth, the Court asked whether, in the event of a decision in favor of plaintiffs, desegregation should be immediate or gradual and whether the plaintiff children's grievance was personal and present. Fifth, the Court was concerned with the procedural form the final decree should take.[24]

Within the parameters of these issues, several alternatives were open to the Court. Ashmore listed those that appeared to be within the realm of possibility:[25]

1. That there was no need to rule on the constitutionality of segregation *per se,* since each case might be disposed of on other grounds. (The Supreme Court had repeatedly declared that it would not rule on questions of a constitutional nature if a case could be decided by any other means.)

2. That the separate-but-equal doctrine was still the law, and when the separate facilities were unequal, the Court would allow a reasonable period for the facilities to be made equal in fact.

3. That the separate-but-equal doctrine was still the law, but when the separate facilities were unequal, the Court would require immediate admission of blacks to the white schools, pending the achievement of actual equality of facilities.

4. That the separate-but-equal doctrine was still the law, but the Court might require nonsegregation in certain phases of public education that it deemed impossible of equality within the separate framework. (In other words, the Court might conceivably hold that a particular course of activity could not be provided equally under segregation, as it had at least implied in the higher education cases.)

5. That whether segregation in a given case was a denial of equal protection of the laws was a question of fact, to be decided, as are other questions of fact, in the lower trial court.

6. That segregation was unconstitutional; the Court recognized the need for orderly progress of transition to nonsegregation, but the Court would limit itself to minimum personal relief of the plaintiffs, leaving to Congress the job of legislating detailed rules for implementing desegregation in the schools generally. (This would be in keeping with the idea that the administration of local school systems involves a political question.)

7. That separate-but-equal was a clear denial of equal protection of the laws and thus unconstitutional, but the Court would permit a gradual changeover to a nonsegregated system under the supervision of the district courts or under the direction of a person appointed by the Supreme Court itself.

8. That separate-but-equal was unconstitutional and must be ended immediately; black plaintiffs in the case before the Court must be admitted at once to the white schools.

Realistically, the major point of the case could have been decided only one way, that separate-but-equal was unconstitutional. When asked how the Court would decide, the solicitor general of the United States responded that the court "properly could find only one answer."[26] The final judgment came in a unanimous decision written by Chief Justice Earl Warren. The Court ruled: "We conclude that in the field of public education the doctrine of separate but equal has no place. Separate educational facilities are inherently unequal."[27] For directness and finality, the decision was a model. In overturning separate-but-equal, Warren did not dwell on other judicial precedents because the precise issue before the Court had not been presented before. The validity of separate-but-equal, since *Roberts,* had been assumed but had never been argued and validly established.

The case was not only a watershed in American education, but also one of the most important decisions ever rendered by the Supreme Court. For sheer impact on society, it undoubtedly had the most far-reaching impact. Pollak commented: "Except for waging and winning the Civil War and World Wars I and II, the decision in the *School Segregation Cases* was probably the most important American governmental act of any kind since the Emancipation Proclamation."[28]

———— ❖ — ❖ — ❖ ————

Separate-but-Equal Facilities Are Inherently Unequal

Brown v. Board of Education of Topeka

Supreme Court of the United States, 1954.
347 U.S. 483, 74 S.Ct. 686.

Mr. Chief Justice WARREN delivered the opinion of the Court. These cases come to us from the States of Kansas, South Carolina, Virginia, and Delaware. They are premised on different facts and different local conditions, but a common legal question justifies their consideration together in this consolidated opinion.

In each of the cases, minors of the Negro race, through their legal representatives, seek the aid of the courts in obtaining admission to the public schools of their community on a non-segregated basis. In each instance, they have been denied admission to schools attended by white children under laws requiring or permitting segregation according to race. This segregation was alleged to deprive the plaintiffs of the equal protection of the laws under the Fourteenth Amendment. In each of the cases other than the Delaware case, a three-judge federal district court denied relief to the plaintiffs on the so-called "separate but equal" doctrine announced by this Court in *Plessy v. Ferguson,* 163 U.S. 537, 16 S.Ct. 1138, 41 L.Ed. 256. Under that doctrine, equality of treatment is accorded when the races are provided substantially equal facilities, even though these facilities be separate. In the Delaware case, the Supreme Court of Delaware adhered to that doctrine, but ordered that the plaintiffs be admitted to the white schools because of their superiority to the Negro schools.

The plaintiffs contend that segregated public schools are not "equal" and cannot be made "equal," and that hence they are deprived of the equal protection of the laws. Because of the obvious importance of the question presented, the Court took jurisdiction. Argument was heard in the 1952 Term, and reargument was heard this Term on certain questions propounded by the Court. . . .

In the first cases in this Court construing the Fourteenth Amendment, decided shortly after its adoption, the Court interpreted it as proscribing all state-imposed discriminations against the Negro race. The doctrine of "separate but equal" did not make its appearance in this Court until 1896 in the case of *Plessy v. Ferguson,* supra, involving not education but transportation. American courts have since labored with the doctrine for over half a century. In this Court, there have been six cases involving the "separate but equal" doctrine in the field of public education. In *Cumming v. Board of Education of Richmond County,* 175 U.S. 528, 20 S.Ct. 197, 44 L.Ed. 262, and *Gong Lum v. Rice,* 275 U.S. 78, 48 S.Ct. 91, 72 L.Ed. 172, the validity of the doctrine itself was not challenged. In more recent cases, all on the graduate school level, inequality was found in that specific benefits enjoyed by white students were denied to Negro students of the same educational qualifications. . . . In none of these cases was it necessary to re-examine the doctrine to grant relief to the Negro plaintiff. And in *Sweatt v. Painter,* the Court expressly reserved decision on the question whether *Plessy v. Ferguson* should be held inapplicable to public education.

In the instant cases, that question is directly presented. Here, unlike *Sweatt v. Painter,* there are findings below that the Negro and white schools involved have been equalized, or are being equalized, with respect to buildings, curricula, qualifications and salaries of teachers, and other "tangible" factors. Our decision, therefore, cannot turn on merely a comparison of these tangible factors in the Negro and white schools involved in each of the cases. We must look instead to the effect of segregation itself on public education.

In approaching this problem, we cannot turn the clock back to 1868 when the Amendment was adopted, or even to 1896 when *Plessy v. Ferguson* was written. We must consider public education in the light of its full development and its present place in American life throughout the Nation. Only in this way can it be determined if segregation in public schools deprives these plaintiffs of the equal protection of the laws.

Today, education is perhaps the most important function of state and local governments. Compulsory school attendance laws and the great expenditures for education both demonstrate our recognition of the importance of education to our democratic society. It is required in the performance of our most basic public responsibilities, even service in the armed forces. It is the very foundation of good citizenship. Today it is a principal instrument in awakening the child to cultural values, in preparing him for later professional training, and in helping him to adjust normally to his environment. In these days, it is doubtful that any child may reasonably be expected to succeed in life if he is denied the opportunity of an education. Such an opportunity, where the state has undertaken to provide it, is a right which must be made available to all on equal terms.

We come then to the question presented: Does segregation of children in public schools solely on the basis of race, even though the physical facilities and other "tangible" factors

may be equal, deprive the children of the minority group of equal educational opportunities? We believe that it does.

In *Sweatt v. Painter,* in finding that a segregated law school for Negroes could not provide them equal educational opportunities, this Court relied in large part on "those qualities which are incapable of objective measurement but which make for greatness in a law school." In *McLaurin v. Oklahoma State Regents,* the Court, in requiring that a Negro admitted to a white graduate school be treated like all other students, again resorted to intangible considerations: "his ability to study, to engage in discussions and exchange views with other students, and, in general, to learn his profession." Such considerations apply with added force to children in grade and high schools. To separate them from others of similar age and qualifications solely because of their race generates a feeling of inferiority as to their status in the community that may affect their hearts and minds in a way unlikely ever to be undone. The effect of this separation on their educational opportunities was well stated by a finding in the Kansas case by a court which nevertheless felt compelled to rule against the Negro plaintiffs:

> Segregation of white and colored children in public schools has a detrimental effect upon the colored children. The impact is greater when it has the sanction of the law; for the policy of separating the races is usually interpreted as denoting the inferiority of the Negro group. A sense of inferiority affects the motivation of a child to learn. Segregation with the sanction of law, therefore, has a tendency to [retard] the educational and mental development of Negro children and to deprive them of some of the benefits they would receive in a racial[ly] integrated school system.

Whatever may have been the extent of psychological knowledge at the time of *Plessy v. Ferguson,* this finding is amply supported by modern authority. Any language in *Plessy v. Ferguson* contrary to this finding is rejected.

We conclude that in the field of public education the doctrine of "separate but equal" has no place. Separate educational facilities are inherently unequal. Therefore, we hold that the plaintiffs and others similarly situated for whom the actions have been brought are, by reason of the segregation complained of, deprived of the equal protection of the laws guaranteed by the Fourteenth Amendment. This disposition makes unnecessary any discussion whether such segregation also violates the Due Process Clause of the Fourteenth Amendment.

Because these are class actions, because of the wide applicability of this decision, and because of the great variety of local conditions, the formulation of decrees in these cases presents problems of considerable complexity. On reargument, the consideration of appropriate relief was necessarily subordinated to the primary question—the constitutionality of segregation in public education. We have now announced that such segregation is a denial of the equal protection of the laws. In order that we may have the full assistance of the parties in formulating decrees, the cases will be restored to the docket, and the parties are requested to present further argument on Questions 4 and 5 previously propounded by the Court for the reargument this Term. The Attorneys General of the United States is again invited to participate. The Attorneys General of the states requiring or permitting segregation of public education will also be permitted to appear as *amici curiae* upon request to do so by September 15, 1954, and submission of briefs by October 1, 1954.

It is so ordered.

CASE NOTES

1. On the same day as *Brown*, the Court also announced a decision stating that "racial segregation in the public schools of the District of Columbia is a denial of the due process of law guaranteed by the Fifth Amendment to the Constitution." The Fourteenth Amendment applies to the states, but not to the District of Columbia. The Court found racial segregation of the District schools a denial of due process under the Fifth Amendment. The Court stated: "Classifications based solely on race must be scrutinized with particular care, since they are contrary to our traditions and hence constitutionally suspect. . . . " *Bolling v. Sharpe*, 347 U.S. 497, 74 S.Ct. 693 (1954).

2. One commentator has written as follows about the second *Brown* decision:

> The admission of a few dozen children to a few dozen schools would have presented no very grave difficulties calling for a study of means of

gradual adjustment. Seen in its totality, however, as involving some 5,000 school districts, nearly nine million white children and nearly three million colored, the situation exhibited great variety and complexity. To begin with, a vast number of statutes and regulations incorporating centrally or marginally the rule of segregation, would require change in order to conform to the new principle. Bickel, A., *The Least Dangerous Branch* (Bobbs-Merrill, New York, 1962), p. 248.

■ INTERPRETING *BROWN*

Over a generation after *Brown*, judicial decisions are still required to settle social and legal issues emanating from the circumstances surrounding desegregation. Full realization of the complexities brought on by the decision were probably, to a degree, foreseen by the Supreme Court when it first rendered its decision in 1954. Because of this awareness, the Court delayed granting specific relief and invited the U.S. attorney general and the attorneys general of all the states to submit their views regarding the ultimate order of the Court.

After due consideration of courses of action for implementation, the Court, with Chief Justice Warren again delivering the opinion, said that consideration should be given to "the public interest" as well as the "personal interest of the plaintiffs." In viewing this dichotomy, the Court directed lower courts to fashion remedies that would permit desegregation "with all deliberate speed."[29] In retrospect, the wisdom of the decision in *Brown II* has been called into question. Today, some maintain that the implementation decision, *Brown II*, allowed too much flexibility; others claim not enough. But from the Supreme Court's perspective, the wisest course was to allow the local federal district courts to settle the individual complaints on a case-by-case basis with due regard for equity for all concerned, and during the periods of transition, the lower courts were to retain jurisdiction to see that desegregation was properly implemented. The Supreme Court sought to avoid unreasonable delays by requiring specifically that the lower courts "require that the defendants make a prompt and reasonable start toward full compliance with our May 17, 1954, ruling."[30]

Considerable conflict followed the *Brown* decisions. Perhaps one of the most dramatic episodes occurred in Little Rock, Arkansas, where at first the National Guard was used to prevent black children from entering school, and later federal troops and the National Guard were used to protect the entrance of black children into the formerly white public schools.[31] Ultimately, the Supreme Court was called on to render a judgment in the Little Rock case. The question of nullification and interposition, the Civil War question, was again raised by the governor and the legislature of Arkansas, who asserted that they had no duty to obey federal court orders directed to them to effectuate desegregation.[32] The Court's response was direct and unambiguous:

> In short, the constitutional rights of children not to be discriminated against in school admission on grounds of race or color declared by this Court in the *Brown* case can neither be nullified openly and directly by state legislators or state executive or judicial officers, nor nullified indirectly by them through evasive schemes for segregation whether attempted "ingeniously or ingenuously."[33]

During the years immediately after *Brown*, school districts experimented with various devices to avoid desegregation. Initially, some states sought to provide funding for private schools through tuition or voucher arrangements. The most blatant example of this transpired in Virginia, where in Prince Edward County the public schools were closed and private schools were operated with state and county assistance. In holding this scheme to be unconstitutional, the Supreme Court said that "the record in the present case could not be clearer than Prince Edward's public schools were closed and private schools operated in their place . . . for one reason, and one reason only: to ensure . . . that white and colored children in Prince Edward County would not, under any circumstances, go to the same school."[34]

Brown definitely proscribed governmental action that compelled or encouraged segregation, but did it require governmental intervention to integrate or mix the races in the schools?

When the *Briggs* case, a companion to *Brown*, was remanded to a federal district court in South Carolina, the lower court judge discussed desegregation versus integration and defined the situation thusly:

> [A]ll that is decided, is that a state may not deny to any person on account of race the right to attend any school that it maintains. . . . The Constitution, in other words, does not require integration. It merely forbids segregation.[35]

The difference between desegregation and integration was also emphasized later by northern courts, which held that

> there is no constitutional duty on the part of the board to bus Negro or white children out of their neighborhoods or to transfer classes for the sole purpose of alleviating racial imbalance.[36]

Contrarily, in another case in the South, the United States Court of Appeals for the Fifth Circuit held that there was indeed an affirmative duty on the part of government to integrate the schools where *de jure* segregation had existed prior to *Brown*.[37] This court distinguished *de facto* segregation, caused by housing patterns, from *de jure* segregation, governmentally promulgated and enforced discrimination in the South.

These cases taken together enunciated a rule of law that required affirmative action by school boards in southern states, *de jure* states, but did not compel school boards in northern states, *de facto* states, to act affirmatively to move children about to ensure that black children attended school with white children.

This issue was not treated by the U.S. Supreme Court until 1968, when it held that "freedom of choice" was an acceptable plan for desegregation only if it did, in fact, erase the vestiges of the past dual system of education. The Court said: "The school officials have the continuing duty to take whatever action may be necessary to create a unitary, nonracial system."[38] The constitutionality of an "open door" or "freedom of choice" policy could be judged only in light of its utility in bringing about desegregation. Effectively, the courts dismissed the distinction between integration and desegregation. The standard required that school districts be unitary and not dual. Where *de jure* segregation existed before, the state had an obligation to affirmatively assert itself to remove barriers to desegregation.

After waiting for fifteen years for the lower courts to effectuate the desegregation mandate of *Brown II*, the Supreme Court acted in 1969 to require that all school districts operating in states that had legal segregation in 1954 immediately become unitary.[39] The "with all deliberate speed" standard was replaced with an "immediately" standard. Whether this was accomplished through rezoning, busing, or other devices was not of concern to the Court; it simply required that all districts become unitary without further delay.

❖ — ❖ — ❖

State's Closing of Public Schools and Contributing to the Support of Private Segregated Schools Is Unconstitutional

Griffin v. County School Board of Prince Edward County

Supreme Court of the United States, 1964.
377 U.S. 218, 84 S.Ct. 1226.

Mr. Justice BLACK delivered the opinion of the Court. This litigation began in 1951 when a group of Negro school children living in Prince Edward County, Virginia, filed a complaint in the United States District Court for the Eastern District of Virginia alleging that they had been denied admission to public schools attended by white children and charging that Virginia laws requiring such school segregation denied complainants the equal protection of the laws in violation of the Fourteenth Amendment. On May 17, 1954, ten years ago, we held that the Virginia segregation laws did deny equal protection. *Brown v. Board of Education*, 347 U.S. 483, 74 S.Ct. 686, 98 L.Ed. 873 (1954). On May 31, 1955, after reargument on the nature of relief, we remanded this case, along with others heard with it, to the District Courts to enter such orders as "necessary and proper to admit [complainants] to public schools on a racially nondiscriminatory basis with all deliberate speed. . . ." *Brown v. Board of Education*, 349 U.S. 294, 301, 75 S.Ct. 753, 757, 99 L.Ed. 1083 (1955).

Efforts to desegregate Prince Edward County's schools met with resistance. In 1956, Section 141 of the Virginia Constitution was amended to authorize the General Assembly and local governing bodies to appropriate funds to assist students to go to public or to nonsec-

tarian private schools in addition to those owned by the State or by the locality. The General Assembly met in special session and enacted legislation to close any public schools where white and colored children were enrolled together, to cut off state funds to such schools, to pay tuition grants to children in nonsectarian private schools, and to extend state retirement benefits to teachers in newly created private schools. The legislation closing mixed schools and cutting off state funds was later invalidated by the Supreme Court of Appeals of Virginia, which held that these laws violated the Virginia Constitution. *Harrison v. Day*, 200 Va. 439, 106 S.E.2d 636 (1959). In April 1959, the General Assembly abandoned "massive resistance" to desegregation and turned instead to what was called a "freedom of choice" program. The Assembly repealed the rest of the 1956 legislation, as well as a tuition grant law of January 1959, and enacted a new tuition grant program. At the same time the Assembly repealed Virginia's compulsory attendance laws and instead made school attendance a matter of local option.

In June 1959, the United States Court of Appeals for the Fourth Circuit directed the Federal District Court (1) to enjoin discriminatory practices in Prince Edward County schools, (2) to require the County School Board to take "immediate steps" toward admitting students without regard to race to the white high school "in the school term beginning September 1959," and (3) to require the Board to make plans for admissions to elementary schools without regard to race. *Allen v. County School Board of Prince Edward County*, 266 F.2d 507, 511 (C.A.4th Cir.1959). Having as early as 1956 resolved that they would not operate public schools "wherein white and colored children are taught together," the Supervisors of Prince Edward County refused to levy any school taxes for the 1959–1960 school year, explaining that they were "confronted with a court decree which requires the admission of white and colored children to all the schools of the county without regard to race or color." As a result, the county's public schools did not reopen in the fall of 1959 and have remained closed ever since, although the public schools of every other county in Virginia have continued to operate under laws governing the State's public school system and to draw funds provided by the State for that purpose. A private group, the Prince Edward School Foundation, was formed to operate private schools for white children in Prince Edward County and, having built its own school plant, has been in operation ever since the closing of the public schools. An offer to set up private schools for colored children in the county was rejected, the Negroes of Prince Edward preferring to continue the legal battle for desegregated public schools, and colored children were without formal education from 1959 to 1963, when federal, state, and county authorities cooperated to have classes conducted for Negroes and whites in school buildings owned by the county. . . .

In 1961 petitioners here filed a supplemental complaint, adding new parties and seeking to enjoin the respondents from refusing to operate an efficient system of public free schools in Prince Edward County and to enjoin payment of public funds to help support private schools which excluded students on account of race. The District Court, finding that "the end result of every action taken by that body [Board of Supervisors] was designed to preserve separation of the races in the schools of Prince Edward County," enjoined the county from paying tuition grants or giving tax credits so long as public schools remained closed. . . . At this time the District Court did not pass on whether the public schools of the county could be closed but abstained pending determination by the Virginia courts of whether the constitution and laws of Virginia required the public schools to be kept open. Later, however, without waiting for the Virginia courts to decide the question the District Court held that "the public schools of Prince Edward County may not be closed to avoid the effect of the law of the land as interpreted by the Supreme Court, while the Commonwealth of Virginia permits other public schools to remain open at the expense of the taxpayers." . . . Soon thereafter, a declaratory judgment suit was brought by the County Board of Supervisors and the County School Board in a Virginia Circuit Court. Having done this, these parties asked the Federal District Court to abstain from further proceedings until the suit in the state courts had run its course, but the District Court declined; it repeated its order that Prince Edward's public schools might

not be closed to avoid desegregation while the other public schools in Virginia remained open. The Court of Appeals reversed, Judge Bell dissenting, holding that the District Court should have abstained to await state court determination of the validity of the tuition grants and the tax credits, as well as the validity of the closing of the public schools. *Griffin v. Board of Supervisors of Prince Edward County*, 322 F.2d 332 (C.A.4th Cir.1963). We granted *certiorari*, stating:

> In view of the long delay in the case since our decision in the *Brown* case and the importance of the questions presented, we grant *certiorari* and put the case down for argument March 30, 1964, on the merits, as we have done in other comparable situations without waiting for final action by the Court of Appeals. 375 U.S. 391.

For reasons to be stated, we agree with the District Court that, under the circumstances here, closing the Prince Edward County schools while public schools in all the other counties of Virginia were being maintained denied the petitioners and the class of Negro students they represent the equal protection of the laws guaranteed by the Fourteenth Amendment. . . . The case has been delayed since 1961 by resistance at the state and county level, by legislation, and by lawsuits. The original plaintiffs have doubtless all passed high school age. There has been entirely too much deliberation and not enough speed in enforcing the constitutional rights which we held in *Brown v. Board of Education,* supra, had been denied Prince Edward County Negro children. We accordingly reverse the Court of Appeals' judgment remanding the case to the District Court for abstention, and we proceed to the merits.

In *County School Board of Prince Edward County v. Griffin*, 204 Va. 650, 133 S.E.2d 565 (1963), the Supreme Court of Appeals of Virginia upheld as valid under state law the closing of the Prince Edward County public schools, the state and county tuition grants for children who attend private schools, and the county's tax concessions for those who make contributions to private schools. The same opinion also held that each county had "an option to operate or not to operate public schools," 204 Va., at 671, 133 S.E.2d, at 580. We accept this case as a definitive and authoritative holding of Virginia law, binding on us, but we cannot accept the Virginia court's further holding, based largely on the Court of Appeals' opinion in this case, 322 F.2d 332, that closing the county's public schools under the circumstances of the case did not deny the colored school children of Prince Edward County equal protection of the laws guaranteed by the Federal Constitution.

Since 1959, all Virginia counties have had the benefits of public schools but one: Prince Edward. However, there is no rule that counties, as counties, must be treated alike; the Equal Protection Clause relates to equal protection of the laws "between persons as such rather than between areas." *Salsburg v. Maryland,* 346 U.S. 545, 551, 74 S.Ct. 280, 283, 98 L.Ed. 281 (1954). Indeed, showing that different persons are treated differently is not enough, without more, to show a denial of equal protection. . . .

Virginia law, as here applied, unquestionably treats the school children of Prince Edward differently from the way it treats the school children of all other Virginia counties. Prince Edward children must go to a private school or none at all; all other Virginia children can go to public schools. Closing Prince Edward's schools bears more heavily on Negro children in Prince Edward County since white children there have accredited private schools which they can attend, while colored children until very recently have had no available private schools, and even the school they now attend is a temporary expedient. Apart from this expedient, the result is that Prince Edward County school children, if they go to school in their own county, must go to racially segregated schools which, although designated as private, are beneficiaries of county and state support.

A State, of course, has a wide discretion in deciding whether laws shall operate statewide or shall operate only in certain counties, the legislature "having in mind the needs and desires of each." *Salsburg v. Maryland,* supra, 346 U.S., at 552, 74 S.Ct., at 284. A State may wish to suggest, as Maryland did in *Salsburg,* that there are reasons why one county ought not to be treated like another. But the record in the present case could not be clearer that Prince Edward's public schools were closed and private schools operated in their place with state and county assis-

tance, for one reason, and one reason only: to ensure, through measures taken by the county and the State, that white and colored children in Prince Edward County would not, under any circumstances, go to the same school. Whatever nonracial grounds might support a State's allowing a county to abandon public schools, the object must be a constitutional one, and grounds of race and opposition to desegregation do not qualify as constitutional. . . .

Accordingly, we agree with the District Court that closing the Prince Edward schools and meanwhile contributing to the support of the private segregated white schools that took their place denied petitioners the equal protection of the laws. . . .

The District Court held that "the public schools of Prince Edward County may not be closed to avoid the effect of the law of the land as interpreted by the Supreme Court, while the Commonwealth of Virginia permits other public schools to remain open at the expense of the taxpayers." . . . At the same time the court gave notice that it would later consider an order to accomplish this purpose if the public schools were not reopened by September 7, 1962. That day has long passed, and the schools are still closed. On remand, therefore, the court may find it necessary to consider further such an order. An order of this kind is within the court's power if required to assure these petitioners that their constitutional rights will no longer be denied them. The time for mere "deliberate speed" has run out, and that phrase can no longer justify denying these Prince Edward County school children their constitutional rights to an education equal to that afforded by the public schools in the other parts of Virginia.

The judgment of the Court of Appeals is reversed, the judgment of the District Court is affirmed, and the cause is remanded to the District Court with directions to enter a decree which will guarantee that these petitioners will get the kind of education that is given in the State's public schools. And, if it becomes necessary to add new parties to accomplish this end, the District Court is free to do so. It is so ordered.

Judgment of Court of Appeals reversed, judgment of the District Court affirmed and cause remanded with directions.

Mr. Justice CLARK and Mr. Justice HARLAN disagree with the holding that the federal courts are empowered to order the reopening of the public schools in Prince Edward County, but otherwise join in the Court's opinion.

————————— ❖ — ❖ — ❖ —————————

*State Must Institute Affirmative Action Where
"Freedom of Choice" Fails to Create Unitary System*

Green v. County School Board of New Kent County, Virginia

Supreme Court of the United States, 1968.
391 U.S. 430, 88 S.Ct. 1689.

Mr. Justice BRENNAN delivered the opinion of the Court. The question for decision is whether, under all the circumstances here, respondent School Board's adoption of a "freedom-of-choice" plan which allows a pupil to choose his own public school constitutes adequate compliance with the Board's responsibility "to achieve a system of determining admission to the public schools on a nonracial basis. . . ." *Brown v. Board of Education of Topeka, Kan.*, 349 U.S. 294, 300–301, 75 S.Ct. 753, 756, 99 L.Ed. 1083 (*Brown II*).

Petitioners brought this action in March 1965 seeking injunctive relief against respondent's continued maintenance of an alleged racially segregated school system. . . .

School boards such as the respondent . . . [were] clearly charged with the affirmative duty to take whatever steps might be necessary to convert to a unitary system in which racial discrimination would be eliminated root and branch. . . . The constitutional rights of Negro school children articulated in *Brown I* permit no less than this; and it was to this end that *Brown II* commanded school boards to bend their efforts.

In determining whether respondent School Board met that command by adopting its "freedom-of-choice" plan, it is relevant that this first step did not come until some eleven years after *Brown I* was decided and ten years after *Brown II* directed the making of a "prompt and reasonable start." This deliberate perpetuation

of the unconstitutional dual system can only have compounded the harm of such a system. Such delays are no longer tolerable, for "the governing constitutional principles no longer bear the imprint of newly enunciated doctrine." . . . The burden on a school board today is to come forward with a plan that promises realistically to work, and promises realistically to work *now*.

The obligation of the district courts, as it always has been, is to assess the effectiveness of a proposed plan in achieving desegregation. There is no universal answer to complex problems of desegregation; there is obviously no one plan that will do the job in every case. The matter must be assessed in light of the circumstances present and the options available in each instance. It is incumbent upon the school board to establish that its proposed plan promises meaningful and immediate progress toward disestablishing state-imposed segregation. It is incumbent upon the district court to weigh that claim in light of the facts at hand and in light of any alternatives which may be shown as feasible and more promising in their effectiveness. Where the court finds the board to be acting in good faith and the proposed plan to have real prospects for dismantling the state-imposed dual system "at the earliest practicable date," then the plan may be said to provide effective relief. Of course, the availability to the board of other more promising courses of action may indicate a lack of good faith; and at the least it places a heavy burden upon the board to explain its preference for an apparently less effective method. Moreover, whatever plan is adopted will require evaluation in practice, and the court should retain jurisdiction until it is clear that state-imposed segregation has been completely removed. . . .

We do not hold that "freedom of choice" can have no place in such a plan. We do not hold that a "freedom-of-choice" plan might of itself be unconstitutional, although that argument has been urged upon us. Rather, all we decide today is that in desegregating a dual system a plan utilizing "freedom of choice" is not an end in itself. . . .

The New Kent School Board's "freedom-of-choice" plan cannot be accepted as a sufficient step to "effectuate a transition" to a unitary system. In three years of operation not a single white child has chosen to attend Watkins school and although 115 Negro children enrolled in New Kent school in 1967 (up from 35 in 1965 and 111 in 1966) 85 percent of the Negro children in the system still attend the all-Negro Watkins school. In other words, the school system remains a dual system. Rather than further the dismantling of the dual system, the plan has operated simply to burden children and their parents with a responsibility which *Brown II* placed squarely on the School Board. The Board must be required to formulate a new plan and, in light of other courses which appear open to the Board, such as zoning, fashion steps which promise realistically to convert promptly to a system without a "white" school and a "Negro" school, but just schools.

The judgment of the Court of Appeals is vacated insofar as it affirmed the District Court and the case is remanded to the District Court for further proceedings consistent with this opinion. It is so ordered.

Dual School Systems Are to Be Terminated at Once, and Unitary Systems Are to Begin Immediately

Alexander v. Holmes County Board of Education

Supreme Court of the United States, 1969.
396 U.S. 19, 90 S.Ct. 29, rehearing denied, 396 U.S.
976, 90 S.Ct. 437 (1969).

PER CURIAM. This case comes to the Court on a petition for *certiorari* to the Court of Appeals for the Fifth Circuit. The petition was granted on October 9, 1969, and the case set down for early argument. The question presented is one of paramount importance, involving as it does the denial of fundamental rights to many thousands of school children, who are presently attending Mississippi schools under segregated conditions contrary to the applicable decisions of this Court. Against this background the Court of Appeals should have denied all motions for

additional time because continued operation of segregated schools under a standard of allowing "all deliberate speed" for desegregation is no longer constitutionally permissible. Under explicit holdings of this Court the obligation of every school district is to terminate dual school systems at once and to operate now and hereafter only unitary schools. . . . It is hereby adjudged, ordered, and decreed:

The Court of Appeals' order of August 28, 1969, is vacated, and the case is remanded to that court to issue its decree and order, effective immediately, declaring that each of the school districts here involved may no longer operate a dual school system based on race or color, and directing that they begin immediately to operate as unitary school systems within which no person is to be effectively excluded from any school because of race or color. . . .

The Court of Appeals shall retain jurisdiction to insure prompt and faithful compliance with its order, and may modify or amend the same as may be deemed necessary or desirable for the operation of a unitary school system.

■ *DE FACTO* SEGREGATION

De facto segregation is not unconstitutional, whether it occurs in the South or in the North. President Nixon summarized the law in this regard in 1969. He said: "There is a fundamental distinction between so-called 'de jure' and 'de facto' segregation: *de jure* segregation arises by law or by the deliberate act of school officials and is unconstitutional; *de facto* segregation results from residential housing patterns and does not violate the Constitution."

This legal position concerning *de facto* segregation has been reiterated several times by the courts in various decisions. A notable early example was the *Bell* decision, in which the U.S. Court of Appeals for the Seventh Circuit said: "[T]here is no affirmative United States constitutional duty to change innocently arrived at school attendance districts by the mere fact that shifts in population either increase or decrease the percentage of either Negro or white pupils."[40] Similarly, the Court of Appeals for the Fifth Circuit held that boards of education have no constitutional obligation to relieve racial imbalance that they do not cause or create.

These are both decisions from northern states, but fundamentally the law is the same, whether the segregation occurs in the North or in the South. If segregation is created by law or official act, then an affirmative duty to integrate the schools is required. The Supreme Court summarized the constitutional standard in a Denver, Colorado, case:

> [W]e have held that where plaintiffs prove that a current condition of segregated schooling exists within a school district where a dual system was compelled or authorized by statute at the time of our decision in *Brown* . . . , the State automatically assumes an affirmative duty to "effectuate a transition to a racially nondiscriminatory school system."[41]

In this case, the Supreme Court emphasized that the differentiating factor between *de jure* segregation and so-called *de facto* segregation is *purpose* or *intent*.

If school authorities practice purposeful segregation, then a *de jure* condition exists, and the school district will be required to take affirmative measures to correct racial imbalance in the schools.

❖ — ❖ — ❖

School Board Actions May Have Effect of Creating Unconstitutional De Jure *Segregation*

Keyes v. School District No. 1, Denver

Supreme Court of the United States, 1973.
413 U.S. 189, 93 S.Ct. 2686.

Mr. Justice BRENNAN delivered the opinion of the Court. This school desegregation case concerns the Denver, Colorado, school system. That system has never been operated under a constitutional or statutory provision that mandated or permitted racial segregation in public education. Rather, the gravamen of this action, brought in June 1969 in the District Court of the District of Colorado by parents of Denver schoolchildren, is that respondent School Board alone, by use of various techniques such as the manipulation of student attendance zones, schoolsite selection and a neighborhood school policy, created or maintained racially or ethnically (or both racially and ethnically) segregated schools throughout the school district, entitling petitioners to a decree directing desegregation of the entire school district. . . .

Before turning to the primary question we decide today, a word must be said about the District Court's method of defining a "segregated" school. Denver is a tri-ethnic, as distinguished from a bi-racial, community. The overall racial and ethnic composition of the Denver public schools is 66 percent Anglo, 14 percent Negro, and 20 percent Hispano. . . . What is or is not a segregated school will necessarily depend on the facts of each particular case. In addition to the racial and ethnic composition of a school's student body, other factors, such as the racial and ethnic composition of faculty and staff and the community and administration attitudes toward the school, must be taken into consideration. . . .

. . . [T]hough of different origins, Negroes and Hispanos in Denver suffer identical discrimination in treatment when compared with the treatment afforded Anglo students. In that circumstance, we think petitioners are entitled to have schools with a combined predominance of Negroes and Hispanos included in the category of "segregated" schools.

In our view, the only other question that requires our decision at this time is . . . whether the District Court and the Court of Appeals applied an incorrect legal standard in addressing petitioners' contention that respondent School Board engaged in an unconstitutional policy of deliberate segregation in the core city schools. Our conclusion is that those courts did not apply the correct standard in addressing that contention.

Petitioners apparently concede for the purposes of this case that in the case of a school system like Denver's, where no statutory dual system has ever existed, plaintiffs must prove not only that segregated schooling exists but also that it was brought about or maintained by intentional state action. Petitioners proved that for almost a decade after 1960 respondent School Board had engaged in an unconstitutional policy of deliberate racial segregation in the Park Hill schools. . . . This finding did not relate to an insubstantial or trivial fragment of the school system. On the contrary, respondent School Board was found guilty of following a deliberate segregation policy at schools attended, in 1969, by 37.69 percent of Denver's total Negro school population. . . . Respondent argues, however, that a finding of state-imposed segregation as to a substantial portion of the school system can be viewed in isolation from the rest of the district, and that even if state-imposed segregation does exist in a substantial part of the Denver school system, it does not follow that the District Court could predicate on that fact a finding that the entire school system is a dual system. We do not agree. We have never suggested that plaintiffs in school desegregation cases must bear the burden of proving the elements of *de jure* segregation as to each and every school or each and every student within the school system. Rather, we have held that where plaintiffs prove that a current condition of segregated schooling exists within a school district where a dual system was compelled or authorized by statute at the time of our decision in *Brown v. Board of Education*, 347 U.S. 483, 74 S.Ct. 686, 98 L.Ed. 873 (1954) (*Brown I*), the State automatically assumes an affirmative duty "to effectuate a transition to a racially nondiscriminatory school system," *Brown v. Board of Education*, 349 U.S. 294, 301, 75 S.Ct. 753, 756, 99 L.Ed. 1083 (1955) (*Brown II*); that is, to eliminate from the public schools within their school system all "vestiges of state-imposed segregation."

This is not a case, however, where a statutory dual system has ever existed. Nevertheless, where plaintiffs prove that the school authorities have carried out a systematic program of segregation affecting a substantial portion of the students, schools, teachers, and facilities within the school system, it is only common sense to conclude that there exists a predicate for a finding of the existence of a dual school system. Several considerations support this conclusion. First, it is obvious that a practice of concentrating Negroes in certain schools by structuring attendance zones or designating "feeder" schools on the basis of race has the reciprocal effect of keeping other nearby schools predominantly white. Similarly, the practice of building a school—such as the Barrett Elementary School in this case—to a certain size and in a certain location, "with conscious knowledge that it would be a segregated school," 303 F.Supp., at 285, has a substantial reciprocal effect on the racial composition of other nearby schools. So also, the use of mobile classrooms, the drafting of student transfer policies, the transportation of students, and the assignment of faculty and staff on racially identifiable bases, have the clear effect of earmarking schools according to their racial composition, and thus, in turn, together with the elements of school assignment and school construction, may have a profound reciprocal effect on the racial composition of residential neighborhoods, within a metropolitan area, thereby causing further racial concentration within the schools. We recognized this in *Swann*. . . .

In short, common sense dictates the conclusion that racially inspired school board actions have an impact beyond the particular schools that are subjects of those actions. This is not to say, of course, that there can never be a case in which the geographical structure of, or the natural boundaries within, a school district may have the effect of dividing the district into separate, identifiable and unrelated units. Such a determination is essentially a question of fact to be resolved by the trial court in the first instance, but such cases must be rare. In the absence of such a determination, proof of state-imposed segregation in a substantial portion of the district will suffice to support a finding by the trial court of the existence of a dual system. . . .

Although petitioners had already proved the existence of intentional school segregation in the Park Hill schools, this crucial finding was totally ignored when attention turned to the core city schools. Plainly, a finding of intentional segregation as to a portion of the school system is not devoid of probative value in assessing the school authorities' intent with respect to other parts of the same school system. On the contrary where, as here, the case involves one school board, a finding of intentional segregation on its part in one portion of the school system is highly relevant to the issue of the board's intent with respect to the other segregated schools in the system. This is merely an application of the well-settled evidentiary principle that "the prior doing of other similar acts, whether clearly a part of a scheme or not, is useful as reducing the possibility that the act in question was done with innocent intent."

Applying these principles in the special context of school desegregation cases, we hold that a finding of intentionally segregative school board actions in a meaningful portion of a school system, as in this case, creates a presumption that other segregated schooling within the system is not adventitious. It establishes, in other words, a prima facie case of unlawful segregative design on the part of school authorities, and shifts to those authorities the burden of proving that other segregated schools within the system are not also the result of intentionally segregative actions. This is true even if it is determined that different areas of the school district should be viewed independently of each other because, even in that situation, there is high probability that where school authorities have effectuated an intentionally segregative policy in a meaningful portion of the school system, similar impermissible considerations have motivated their actions in other areas of the system. We emphasize that the differentiating factor between *de jure* segregation and so-called *de facto* segregation to which we referred in *Swann* is *purpose* or *intent* to segregate. Where school authorities have been found to have practiced purposeful segregation in part of a school system, they may be expected to oppose system-wide desegregation, as did the respondents in this case, on the ground that their purposefully segregative actions were isolated and individual events, thus leaving plaintiffs with the burden of proving otherwise. But at that point where an intentionally segregative policy is practiced in a meaningful or significant segment of a school system, as in this case, the school authorities cannot be heard to argue that plaintiffs have proved only "isolated and individual" unlawfully segregative actions. In that circumstance, it is both fair and reasonable to require that the school authorities bear the burden of showing that their actions as to other segregated schools within the system were not also motivated by segregative intent. . . .

. . . We reject any suggestion that remoteness in time has any relevance to the issue of intent. If the actions of school authorities were to any degree motivated by segregative intent and the segregation resulting from those actions continues to exist, the fact of remoteness in time certainly does not make those actions any less "intentional." . . .

The respondent School Board invoked at trial its "neighborhood school policy" as explaining racial and ethnic concentrations within the core city schools, arguing that since the core city area population had long been Negro and Hispano, the concentrations were necessarily the result of residential patterns and not of purposefully segregative policies. We have no occasion to consider in this case whether a "neighborhood school policy" of itself will justify racial or ethnic concentrations in the absence of a finding that school authorities have committed acts constituting *de jure* segregation. It is enough that we hold that the mere assertion of such a policy is not dispositive where, as in this case, the school authorities have been found to have practiced *de jure* segregation in a meaningful portion of the school system by techniques that indicate that the "neighborhood school" concept has not been maintained free of manipulation. . . .

In summary, the District Court on remand, *first,* will afford respondent School Board the opportunity to prove its contention that the Park Hill area is a separate, identifiable, and unrelated section of the school district that should be treated as isolated from the rest of the district. If respondent School Board fails to prove that contention, the District Court, *second,* will determine whether respondent School Board's conduct over almost a decade after 1960 in carrying out a policy of deliberate racial segregation in the Park Hill schools constitutes the entire school system a dual school system. If the District Court determines that the Denver school system is a dual school system, respondent School Board has the affirmative duty to desegregate the entire system "root and branch." *Green v. County School Board*, 391 U.S., at 438, 88 S.Ct. at 1694. If the District Court determines, however, that the Denver school system is not a dual school system by reason of the Board's actions in Park Hill, the court, *third,* will afford respondent School Board the opportunity to rebut petitioners' prima facie case of intentional segregation in the core city schools raised by the finding of intentional segregation in the Park Hill schools. There, the Board's burden is to show that its policies and practices with respect to schoolsite location, school size, school renovations and additions, student-attendance zones, student assignment and transfer options, mobile classroom units, transportation of students, assignment of faculty and staff, etc., considered together and premised on the Board's so-called "neighborhood school" concept, either were not taken in effectuation of a policy to create or maintain segregation in the core city schools, or, if unsuccessful in that effort, were not factors in causing the existing condition of segregation in these schools. Considerations of "fairness" and "policy" demand no less in light of the Board's intentionally segregative actions. If respondent Board fails to rebut petitioners' prima facie case, the District Court must, as in the case of Park Hill, decree all-out desegregation of the core city schools.

The judgment of the Court of Appeals is modified to vacate instead of reverse the parts of the Final Decree that concern the core city schools, and the case is remanded to the District Court for further proceedings consistent with this opinion. . . .

It is so ordered.

CASE NOTES

1. In one of its first cases construing the equal protection clause of the Fourteenth Amendment, *Virginia v. Rives*, 100 U.S. (10 Otto) 313 (1879), the Court held that a mere showing that blacks were not included in a particular jury was not enough; there must be a showing of actual discrimination because of race. Down through the years, this has been the law of the land:

> The purpose of the Equal Protection Clause of the Fourteenth Amendment is to secure every person within the State's jurisdiction against intentional and arbitrary discrimination, whether occasioned by express terms of a statute or by its improper execution through duly constituted agents.

Sunday Lake Iron Co. v. Township of Wakefield, 247 U.S. 350, 38 S.Ct. 495 (1918). No different purpose was attributed to the amendment by the Court either in *Brown* or any case since decided.

Charles J. Bloch, "Does the Fourteenth Amendment Forbid De Facto Segregation?" *Western Reserve Law Review* 16 (1965): p. 542. Permission to quote granted by Wm. S. Hein and Company, Inc., Buffalo, New York.

2. The equal protection clause protects minorities from the "tyranny of the majority." Laws passed with racial motivation by the majority are invalid. In 1978, the school board of the Seattle School District No. 1 enacted a desegregation plan that made use of extensive mandatory busing. Subsequently, in November 1978, a statewide initiative (Initiative 350) was passed that prohibited school boards from requiring, with certain exceptions, any student to attend a school other than the one geographically nearest to his or her home. The U.S. Supreme Court held that Initiative 350 violated equal protection because it directly and invidiously curtailed "the operation of political processes ordinarily to be relied upon to protect minorities." The Court concluded that such an initiative was no more permissible than a referendum by all the people to deny members of a racial minority the right to vote. *Washington v. Seattle School District No. 1,* 458 U.S. 457, 102 S.Ct. 3187 (1982).

3. The Court of Appeals for the Fifth Circuit said in *United States v. Jefferson County Board of Education,* 372 F.2d 836 (5th Cir.1966), that

> [t]he Constitution is both color blind and color conscious. To avoid a conflict with the equal protection clause, a classification that denies a benefit, causes harm, or imposes a burden must not be based on race. But the Constitution is color conscious to prevent discrimination being perpetuated and to undo the effects of past discrimination. The criterion is the relevancy of color to a legitimate governmental purpose.

■ QUOTAS AND BUSING

If the vestiges of past state-sanctioned segregation remain, then the courts may do whatever is reasonably necessary to desegregate the schools. What constitutes legitimate remedies to overcome past segregation to bring into effect a unitary school system has been the subject of controversy since the days of "freedom of choice." Beyond freedom of choice, though, the state is required to assert a positive policy of placement of either students or facilities to bring about integration.

The problem really has two aspects: the measurement of inequality and the physical process used by the courts to effectuate integration. In determining the degree of inequality, the lower courts have tended to rely on quotas as a primary yardstick. In this regard, the Supreme Court has held that racial percentages of each school do not have to reflect the racial composition of the school system as a whole.[42] A fixed mathematical racial balance is not required and according to the Court should not be the sole criterion to determine appropriate movement toward a unitary state. The Supreme Court is consistent in this position in higher education as well as in elementary and secondary. In the celebrated *Bakke* decision,[43] the Supreme Court rejected the University of California's quota system for admission to medical school; the system specified a percentage of the student body be set aside for selected classifications of persons. The Court said that

> it is evident that the *Davis* special admission program involves the use of an explicit racial classification never before countenanced by this court. It tells applicants who are not Negro, Asian, or "Chicano" that they are totally excluded from a specific percentage of the seats in an entering class. . . . The fatal flaw in petitioner's preferential program is its disregard of individual rights as guaranteed by the Fourteenth Amendment.[44]

In both higher education and the public schools, the Court has allowed the use of quotas or percentages as one criterion or as a starting point, but it has never required or permitted such a criterion to be used as the sole determinant.

Several alternatives have been approved by the Supreme Court in overcoming *de jure* racial imbalances, and transportation is one such acceptable remedy. Significantly, in *Swann v. Charlotte-Mecklenburg*, the Court observed, "Desegregation plans cannot be limited to walk-in schools."

❖ — ❖ — ❖

Busing to Overcome Racial Segregation Is a Judicially Acceptable Alternative Where De Jure *Segregation Has Existed*

Swann v. Charlotte-Mecklenburg Board of Education

Supreme Court of the United States, 1971.
402 U.S. 1, 91 S.Ct. 1267.

Mr. Chief Justice BURGER delivered the opinion of the Court. . . . This case and those argued with it arose in States having a long history of maintaining two sets of schools in a single school system deliberately operated to carry out a governmental policy to separate pupils in schools solely on the basis of race. That was what *Brown v. Board of Education* was all about. . . .

In April 1969 the District Court ordered the school board to come forward with a plan for both faculty and student desegregation. Proposed plans were accepted by the court in June and August 1969 on an interim basis only, and the board was ordered to file a third plan by November 1969. In November the board moved for an extension of time until February 1970, but when that was denied the board submitted a partially completed plan. In December 1969 the District Court held that the board's submission was unacceptable and appointed an expert in education administration, Dr. John Finger, to prepare a desegregation plan. Thereafter, in February 1970, the District Court was presented with two alternative pupil assignment plans—the finalized "board plan" and the "Finger plan." . . .

On February 5, 1970, the District Court adopted the board plan, as modified by Dr. Finger, for the junior and senior high schools. The court rejected the board elementary school plan and adopted the Finger plan as presented. Implementation was partially stayed by the Court of Appeals for the Fourth Circuit on March 5, and this Court declined to disturb the

Fourth Circuit's order, 397 U.S. 978, 90 S.Ct. 1099, 25 L.Ed.2d 389 (1970).

On appeal the Court of Appeals affirmed the District Court's order as to faculty desegregation and the secondary school plans, but vacated the order respecting elementary schools. . . .

. . . The central issue in this case is that of student assignment, and there are essentially four problem areas:

1. to what extent racial balance or racial quotas may be used as an implement in a remedial order to correct a previously segregated system;
2. whether every all-Negro and all-white school must be eliminated as an indispensable part of a remedial process of desegregation;
3. what the limits are, if any, on the rearrangement of school districts and attendance zones, as a remedial measure; and
4. what the limits are, if any, on the use of transportation facilities to correct state-enforced racial school segregation.

RACIAL BALANCES OR RACIAL QUOTAS

The constant theme and thrust of every holding from *Brown I* to date is that state-enforced separation of races in public schools is discrimination that violates the Equal Protection Clause. The remedy commanded was to dismantle dual school systems. . . .

Our objective in dealing with the issues presented by these cases is to see that school authorities exclude no pupil of a racial minority from any school, directly or indirectly, on account of race; it does not and cannot embrace all the problems of racial prejudice, even when those problems contribute to disproportionate racial concentrations in some schools.

In this case it is urged that the District Court has imposed a racial balance requirement of 71 percent–29 percent on individual schools. The fact that no such objective was actually achieved—and would appear to be impossible—tends to blunt that claim, yet in the opinion and order of the District Court of December 1, 1969, we find that court directing

> that efforts should be made to reach a 71–29 ratio in the various schools so that there will be no basis for contending that one school is racially different from the others . . . [t]hat no school [should] be

operated with an all-black or predominantly black student body, [and] [t]hat pupils of all grades [should] be assigned in such a way that as nearly as practicable the various schools at various grade levels have about the same proportion of black and white students.

. . . As the voluminous record in this case shows, the predicate for the District Court's use of the 71 percent–29 percent ratio was twofold: first, its express finding, approved by the Court of Appeals and not challenged here, that a dual school system had been maintained by the school authorities at least until 1969; second, its finding, also approved by the Court of Appeals, that the school board had totally defaulted in its acknowledged duty to come forward with an acceptable plan of its own, notwithstanding the patient efforts of the District Judge who, on at least three occasions, urged the board to submit plans. . . .

We see therefore that the use made of mathematical ratios was no more than a starting point in the process of shaping a remedy, rather than an inflexible requirement. From that starting point the District Court proceeded to frame a decree that was within its discretionary powers, as an equitable remedy for the particular circumstances. As we said in *Green*, a school authority's remedial plan or a district court's remedial decree is to be judged by its effectiveness. Awareness of the racial composition of the whole school system is likely to be a useful starting point in shaping a remedy to correct past constitutional violations. In sum, the very limited use made of mathematical ratios was within the equitable remedial discretion of the District Court.

ONE-RACE SCHOOLS

The record in this case reveals the familiar phenomenon that in metropolitan areas minority groups are often found concentrated in one part of the city. . . .

In light of the above, it should be clear that the existence of some small number of one-race, or virtually one-race, schools within a district is not in and of itself the mark of a system that still practices segregation by law. The district judge or school authorities should make every effort to achieve the greatest possible degree of actual desegregation and will thus necessarily be concerned with the elimination of one-race schools. . . . Where the school authority's proposed plan for conversion from a dual to a unitary system contemplates the continued existence of some schools that are all or predominately of one race, they have the burden of showing that such school assignments are genuinely nondiscriminatory. The court should scrutinize such schools, and the burden upon the school authorities will be to satisfy the court that their racial composition is not the result of present or past discriminatory action on their part.

An optional majority-to-minority transfer provision has long been recognized as a useful part of every desegregation plan. Provision for optional transfer of those in the majority racial group of a particular school to other schools where they will be in the minority is an indispensable remedy for those students willing to transfer to other schools in order to lessen the impact on them of the state-imposed stigma of segregation. In order to be effective, such a transfer arrangement must grant the transferring student free transportation and space must be made available in the school to which he desires to move. . . . The court orders in this and the companion *Davis* case now provide such an option.

REMEDIAL ALTERING OF ATTENDANCE ZONES

The maps submitted in these cases graphically demonstrate that one of the principal tools employed by school planners and by courts to break up the dual school system has been a frank—and sometimes drastic—gerrymandering of school districts and attendance zones. An additional step was pairing, "clustering," or "grouping" of schools with attendance assignments made deliberately to accomplish the transfer of Negro students out of formerly segregated Negro schools and transfer of white students to formerly all-Negro schools. . . .

We hold that the pairing and grouping of noncontiguous school zones is a permissible tool and such action is to be considered in light of the objectives sought. . . . Maps do not tell the whole story since noncontiguous school zones may be more accessible to each other in terms of the critical travel time, because of traffic patterns and good highways, than schools geographically closer together. Conditions in different localities will vary so widely that no rigid rules can be laid down to govern all situations.

TRANSPORTATION OF STUDENTS

The scope of permissible transportation of students as an implement of a remedial decree has never been defined by this Court and by the very nature of the problem it cannot be defined with precision. No rigid guidelines as to student transportation can be given for application to the infinite variety of problems presented in thousands of situations. Bus transportation has been an integral part of the public education system for years, and was perhaps the single most important factor in the transition from the one-room schoolhouse to the consolidated school. . . .

Thus the remedial techniques used in the District Court's order were within that court's power to provide equitable relief; implementation of the decree is well within the capacity of the school authority.

The decree provided that the buses used to implement the plan would operate on direct routes. Students would be picked up at schools near their homes and transported to the schools they were to attend. The trips for elementary school pupils average about seven miles and the District Court found that they would take "not over thirty-five minutes at the most." This system compares favorably with the transportation plan previously operated in Charlotte under which each day 23,600 students on all grade levels were transported an average of fifteen miles one way for an average trip requiring over an hour. In these circumstances, we find no basis for holding that the local school authorities may not be required to employ bus transportation as one tool of school desegregation. Desegregation plans cannot be limited to the walk-in school.

An objection to transportation of students may have validity when the time or distance of travel is so great as to either risk the health of the children or significantly impinge on the educational process. . . . It hardly needs stating that the limits on time of travel will vary with many factors, but probably with none more than the age of the students. The reconciliation of competing values in a desegregation case is, of course, a difficult task with many sensitive facets but fundamentally no more so than remedial measures courts of equity have traditionally employed.

The Court of Appeals, searching for a term to define the equitable remedial power of the district courts, used the term "reasonableness." In *Green,* this Court used the term "feasible" and by implication, "workable," "effective," and "realistic" in the mandate to develop "a plan that promises realistically to work, and . . . to work *now.*" On the facts of this case, we are unable to conclude that the order of the District Court is not reasonable, feasible, and workable. However, in seeking to define the scope of remedial power or the limits on remedial power of courts in an area as sensitive as we deal with here, words are poor instruments to convey the sense of basic fairness inherent in equity. Substance, not semantics, must govern, and we have sought to suggest the nature of limitations without frustrating the appropriate scope of equity.

At some point, these school authorities and others like them should have achieved full compliance with this Court's decision in *Brown I.* The systems would then be "unitary" in the sense required by our decisions in *Green* and *Alexander.*

It does not follow that the communities served by such systems will remain demographically stable, for in a growing, mobile society, few will do so. Neither school authorities nor district courts are constitutionally required to make year-by-year adjustments of the racial composition of school bodies once the affirmative duty to desegregate has been accomplished and racial discrimination through official action is eliminated from the system. This does not mean that federal courts are without power to deal with future problems; but in the absence of a showing that either the school authorities or some other agency of the State has deliberately attempted to fix or alter demographic patterns to affect the racial composition of the schools, further intervention by a district court should not be necessary.

For the reasons herein set forth, the judgment of the Court of Appeals is affirmed as to those parts in which it affirmed the judgment of the District Court. The order of the District Court, dated August 7, 1970, is also affirmed.

It is so ordered.

■ UNITARINESS

As indicated earlier, the central purpose of the equal protection clause is to prevent governmental discrimination against a minority.[45] Plaintiffs seeking redress bear an initial burden of showing that the school board has intentionally created and maintained a racially segregated "dual" school system.[46] If the court finds that plaintiffs' proof is sufficient, then the school board has an affirmative duty to change the "dual" system to a "unitary" one.[47]

The term "unitary" has been defined as the status a school system achieves "when it no longer discriminates between school children on the basis of race" or the status of a school system when it affirmatively removes all vestiges of race discrimination of the formerly dual system.[48] *Alexander v. Board of Education* defined a unitary system as one "within which no person is to be effectively excluded from any school because of race or color."[49]

As the desegregation cases have evolved, the term "unitary" has been inconsistently defined, and now courts tend to distinguish a "unitary system" from a system that has achieved "unitary status." The federal district court in *Capacchione v. Charlotte-Mecklenburg Schools,*[50] devotes much attention to the meaning of these terms and explains the difference by pointing out that the concept of becoming unitary was established in *Green,* wherein the U.S. Supreme Court stated that the goal of equitable relief in a desegregation case is "to convert [a dual system] to a unitary system in which racial discrimination would be eliminated root and branch."[51] Since *Green,* however, "unitary" has been variously defined.[52] At times, the term has been used to describe a school system that has been released from supervision after fully remedying all vestiges of past discrimination.[53] However, the term has also been employed to describe a school system that has implemented a desegregation plan but has not yet eliminated the vestiges of past discrimination.[54] This latter definition draws a distinction between a school system that is "unitary" and one that has achieved "unitary status" in that a court may have declared that a school system is "unitary," meaning that it no longer is a dual system, but the district may not have ridded itself of vestiges of discrimination and received the "unitary status" declaration of a federal district court. Thus, "unitary status" can be achieved only by judicial order declaring that the vestiges of past discrimination have been removed. In this light, for example, the Charlotte-Mecklenburg school district has been operating a unitary system since 1975, but it was not granted "unitary status" until the federal district court acted in 1999.[55]

In determining whether a school system has eliminated the vestiges of *de jure* segregation, qualifying it to be granted "unitary status," the court must determine what the school system has accomplished with respect to six "*Green* factors," as enunciated by the U.S. Supreme Court in *Green v. County School Board of New Kent County*.[56] These factors are: (1) student assignment, (2) faculty, (3) staff, (4) transportation, (5) extracurricular activities, and (6) facilities.[57]

The dilemma that has faced the courts is to decide whether unitariness can be achieved in incremental stages in satisfying the *Green* criteria or whether unitariness can be satisfied only by attainment of all six criteria of *Green*, in concert. To require that all six had to be achieved together effectively subjected school districts to control of the federal courts for much longer periods of time and in some cases, perhaps, interminably. The U.S. Supreme Court finally resolved this question in *Freeman v. Pitts*[58] in 1992, wherein the Court ruled that the incremental approach was constitutionally acceptable.

In so ruling, the Court observed that the objective, in all instances in which federal courts have required redress for past discrimination, is to restore state and local control in operation of the school district as quickly as possible. The Supreme Court pointedly observed that what had been initially intended to be a temporary measure of judicial supervision over desegregation efforts had many times turned into protracted control lasting many decades. According to the Court, the objective remains to return the school district to the control of local authorities. The Supreme Court vested the lower federal courts with the discretion to return control to the local school districts in incremental stages. Thus, in *Freeman*, the Supreme Court agreed that the federal district court could permit the school district in DeKalb County, Georgia, to re-

gain control after meeting four of the six *Green* criteria. The Supreme Court thereby affirmed the lower federal court's decision to allow the school district to assume control over student assignment, transportation, physical facilities, and extracurricular activities, while retaining court supervision over the areas of faculty and administrative assignments as well as an additional seventh standard that the court termed "quality of education." Moreover, the Supreme Court acknowledged that federal district courts have the authority to create additional criteria or requirements that the school districts have to meet in attaining unitary status. The seventh criterion, "quality of education," relating to financial resources, which the lower federal court had created in *Freeman*, was adjudged appropriate by the Supreme Court. Thus, "unitary status," while within the discretion of the federal district court, does not require full and complete compliance before elements of control can be returned to the school district, and the control that is allowed depends on the district's satisfying the *Green* criteria and any other equitable criteria the lower court may decide are necessary.

❖ — ❖ — ❖

Where Desegregation Plan Had Established a Racially Neutral System, District Court Exceeded Its Authority in Requiring Annual Readjustment of Attendance Zones

Pasadena City Board of Education v. Spangler

Supreme Court of the United States, 1976.
427 U.S. 424, 96 S.Ct. 2697.

Mr. Justice REHNQUIST delivered the opinion of the Court. In 1968, several students in the public schools of Pasadena, Cal., joined by their parents, instituted an action in the United States District Court for the Central District of California seeking injunctive relief from allegedly unconstitutional segregation of the high schools of the Pasadena City Board of Education, which operates the Pasadena Unified School District (PUSD). . . .

On January 23, 1970, the court entered a judgment in which it concluded that the defendants' educational policies and procedures were violative of the Fourteenth Amendment. The court ordered the defendants "enjoined from failing to prepare and adopt a plan to correct racial imbalance at all levels in the Pasadena Unified School District." The defendants were further ordered to submit to the District Court a plan for desegregating the Pasadena schools. . . .

The defendant school officials voted to comply with the District Court's decree and not to appeal. They thereupon set out to devise and submit the plan demanded by the District Court. In February the defendants submitted their proposed plan, the "Pasadena Plan," and on March 10, 1970, the District Court approved the plan, finding it "to be in conformance with the Judgment entered herein January 23, 1970." App. 96. The "Pasadena Plan" was implemented the following September, and the Pasadena schools have been under its terms ever since.

In January 1974, petitioners, successors to the original defendants in this action, filed a motion with the District Court seeking relief from the court's 1970 order. Petitioners sought four changes: to have the judgment modified so as to eliminate the requirement that there be "no school in the District, elementary or junior high or senior high school, with a majority of any minority students"; to have the District Court's injunction dissolved; to have the District Court terminate its "retained jurisdiction" over the actions of the Board; or, as an alternative, to obtain approval of petitioners' proposed modifications of the "Pasadena Plan."

The District Court held hearings on these motions and, on March 1, 1974, denied them in their entirety. . . .

Petitioners requested the District Court to dissolve its injunctive order requiring that there be no school in the PUSD with a majority of any minority students enrolled. The District Court refused this request, and ordered the injunction continued. The court apparently based this decision in large part upon its view that petitioners had failed properly to comply with its original order. This conclusion was in turn premised upon the fact that although the School Board had reorganized PUSD attendance patterns in conformity with the court-approved Pasadena Plan, literal compliance with the terms of the court's order had been obtained in only the initial year of the plan's operation. Following the 1970–1971 school year, black student enrollment at one Pasadena school exceeded 50% of that school's total enrollment. The next year, four Pasadena schools exceeded this 50% black enrollment figure; and at the time of the hearing on petitioners' motion some five schools, in a system of 32 regular schools, were ostensibly in violation of the District Court's "no majority of any minority" requirement. It was apparently the view of the majority of the Court of Appeals' panel that this failure to maintain literal compliance with the 1970 injunction indicated that the District Court had not abused its discretion in refusing to grant so much of petitioner's motion for modification as pertained to this aspect of the order. We think this view was wrong. . . .

When the District Court's order in this case, as interpreted and applied by that court, is measured against what this Court said in its intervening decision in *Swann v. Charlotte-Mecklenburg Board of Education*, 402 U.S. 1, 91 S.Ct. 1267, 28 L.Ed.2d 554 (1971), regarding the scope of the judicially created relief which might be available to remedy violations of the Fourteenth Amendment, we think the inconsistency between the two is clear. The District Court's interpretation of the order appears to contemplate the "substantive constitutional right [to a] particular degree of racial balance or mixing" which the Court in *Swann* expressly disapproved. . . . It became apparent, at least by the time of the 1974 hearing, that the District Court viewed this portion of its order not merely as a "starting point in the process of shaping a remedy," which *Swann* indicated would be appropriate . . . but instead as an "inflexible requirement," to be applied anew each year to the school population within the attendance zone of each school.

The District Court apparently believed it had authority to impose this requirement even though subsequent changes in the racial mix in the Pasadena schools might be caused by factors for which the defendants could not be considered responsible. Whatever may have been the basis for such a belief in 1970, in *Swann* the Court cautioned that "it must be recognized that there are limits" beyond which a court may not go in seeking to dismantle a dual school system. . . . These limits are in part tied to the necessity of establishing that school authorities have in some manner caused unconstitutional segregation, for "[a]bsent a constitutional violation there would be no basis for judicially ordering assignment of students on a racial basis." While the District Court found such a violation in 1970, and while this unappealed finding afforded a basis for its initial requirement that the defendants prepare a plan to remedy such racial segregation, its adoption of the Pasadena Plan in 1970 established a racially neutral system of student assignment in the PUSD. Having done that, we think that in enforcing its order so as to require annual readjustment of attendance zones so that there would not be a majority of any minority in any Pasadena public school, the District Court exceeded its authority.

In so concluding, we think it important to note what this case does not involve. The "no majority of any minority" requirement with respect to attendance zones did not call for defendants to submit "step at a time" plans by definition incomplete at inception. . . . Nor did it call for a plan embodying specific revisions of the attendance zones for particular schools, as well as provisions for later appraisal of whether such discrete individual modifications had achieved the "unitary system" required by *Brown v. Board of Education*, 349 U.S. 294, 300, 75 S.Ct. 753, 756, 99 L.Ed. 1083 (1955). The plan approved in this case applied in general terms to all Pasadena schools, and no one contests that its implementation did "achieve a system of determining admission to the public schools on a nonracial basis," *id.*, at 300–301, 75 S.Ct., at 756.

There was also no showing in this case that those post-1971 changes in the racial mix of some Pasadena schools which were focused upon by the lower courts were in any manner caused by segregative actions chargeable to the defendants. The District Court rejected petitioners' assertion that the movement was caused by so-called "white flight" traceable to the decree itself. It stated that the "trends evidenced in

Pasadena closely approximate the state-wide trends in California schools, both segregated and desegregated." 375 F.Supp., at 1306. The fact that black student enrollment at 5 out of 32 of the regular Pasadena schools came to exceed 50% during the 4-year period from 1970 to 1974 apparently resulted from people randomly moving into, out of, and around the PUSD area. This quite normal pattern of human migration resulted in some changes in the demographics of Pasadena's residential patterns, with resultant shifts in the racial makeup of some of the schools. But as these shifts were not attributed to any segregative actions on the part of the petitioners, we think this case comes squarely within the sort of situation foreseen in *Swann*:

> It does not follow that the communities served by [unitary] systems will remain demographically stable, for in a growing, mobile society, few will do so. Neither school authorities nor district courts are constitutionally required to make year-by-year adjustments of the racial composition of student bodies once the affirmative duty to desegregate has been accomplished and racial discrimination through official action is eliminated from the system. 402 U.S., at 31–32, 91 S.Ct. at 1283, 1284.

. . . In this case the District Court approved a plan designed to obtain racial neutrality in the attendance of students at Pasadena's public schools. No one disputes that the initial implementation of this plan accomplished *that* objective. That being the case, the District Court was not entitled to require the PUSD to rearrange its attendance zones each year so as to ensure that the racial mix desired by the court was maintained in perpetuity. For having once implemented a racially neutral attendance pattern in order to remedy the perceived constitutional violations on the part of the defendants, the District Court had fully performed its function of providing the appropriate remedy for previous racially discriminatory attendance patterns. . . .

Because the case is to be returned to the Court of Appeals, that court will have an opportunity to reconsider its decision in light of our observations regarding the appropriate scope of equitable relief in this case. . . . The record in this case reflects the situation in Pasadena as it was in 1974. . . . And while any determination of compliance or noncompliance must, of course, comport with our holding today, it must also depend on factual determinations which the Court of Appeals and the District Court are in a far better position than we are to make in the first instance. Accordingly the judgment of the Court of Appeals is vacated, and the case is remanded to that court for further proceedings not inconsistent with this opinion.

So ordered.

CASE NOTES

1. *Affirmative Action.* A school board cannot satisfy its duty to eliminate past segregation by merely abandoning its prior discriminatory purpose. Neither can it take any action that would subvert the process of conversion to a unitary system. Once a violation is found, "[t]he Board has . . . an affirmative responsibility to see that pupil [and faculty] assignment policies and school construction and abandonment practices 'are not used and do not serve to perpetuate or re-establish the dual school system.'" *Dayton Board of Education v. Brinkman,* 443 U.S. 526, 538, 99 S.Ct. 2971, 2979 (1979) (*Dayton II*) (quoting *Columbus Board of Education v. Penick,* 443 U.S. 449, 460, 99 S.Ct. 2941, 2948 (1979).

2. *White Flight.* School officials cannot use "white flight" as an excuse to justify failure to dismantle a dual school system or as a pretext to resist or evade a present duty to desegregate. *United States v. Scotland Neck Board of Education,* 407 U.S. 484, 92 S.Ct. 2214 (1972). On the other hand, once a school system has been declared unitary, white flight cannot be used by plaintiffs to establish discriminatory intent on the part of the school board. *Riddick by Riddick v. School Board of City of Norfolk,* 784 F.2d 521 (4th Cir.1986); *Pasadena City Board of Education v. Spangler,* 427 U.S. 424, 96 S.Ct. 2697 (1976).

3. *Desegregation.* Once a school district has been declared to have "unitary status" and resegregation occurs, plaintiffs bear the burden of proving that discriminatory intent of the school board caused resegregation. In *Riddick,* the U.S. Court of Appeals, Fourth Circuit, held that resegregation due to population mobility and white flight did not require the school board to adopt a policy of mandatory busing to avoid the presumption of discriminatory intent. *Riddick by*

Riddick v. School Board of City of Norfolk, 784 F.2d 521 (4th Cir.1986).

4. *Effects of Unitary Status.* Once a formerly *de jure* segregated school system is declared to have "unitary status," school boards are free to act without federal court supervision so long as they do not purposefully and intentionally discriminate. *United States v. Overton,* 834 F.2d 1171 (5th Cir.1987).

5. *Recision of Plan.* "Recision of a voluntary desegregation plan itself may be found to be an act of segregation for a school board which has been found to have practiced *de jure* segregation and has not completed the transition from a dual to a unitary school system." *NAACP v. Lansing Board of Education,* 559 F.2d 1042 (6th Cir.), cert. denied, 434 U.S. 997, 98 S.Ct. 635 (1977). See *Riddick by Riddick v. School Board of City of Norfolk,* 784 F.2d 521 (4th Cir.1986).

6. *Modification of Plan.* "In a school system that has not become unitary the school board is not barred from ever changing a desegregation plan. In such a situation, however, the board must show that the proposed changes are consistent with its continuing affirmative duty to eliminate discrimination." *Clark v. Board of Education of Little Rock School District,* 705 F.2d 265 (8th Cir.1983). See *Riddick,* op. cit.

7. *Clearly Erroneous Standard.* Under this standard, a federal circuit court is "not entitled to 'reverse the finding of the trier of fact simply because [the upper court] is convinced that [it] would have decided the case differently.'" The upper court cannot "duplicate the role of a lower court." Duplication would take place where there are two permissible views of the evidence; when a choice is made based on the facts, the result cannot be "clearly erroneous." *Anderson v. City of Bessemer City, North Carolina,* 470 U.S. 564, 105 S.Ct. 1504 (1985); *Jacksonville Branch, NAACP v. Duval County School Board,* 883 F.2d 945 (11th Cir.1989). Citing the "clearly erroneous" standard, the U.S. Court of Appeals, Eleventh Circuit, upheld a federal district court's granting of "unitary status" to a school district based upon the lower court's conclusions that racial imbalances in the district were caused by changes in housing patterns and demographic shifts and were not the result of school policy. *Lockett v. Board of Education of*

Muscogee County School District, Georgia, 111 F. 3d 839 (11th Cir. 1997).

───────── ❖ — ❖ — ❖ ─────────

Federal Court's Regulatory Control over Previously De Jure *Segregated School District Is Limited to the Time Necessary to Remedy the Effects of Past Intentional Discrimination*

Board of Education of Oklahoma City Public Schools, Independent School District No. 89 v. Dowell

Supreme Court of the United States, 1991.
498 U.S. 237, 111 S.Ct. 630.

CHIEF JUSTICE REHNQUIST delivered the opinion of the Court. . . .

This school desegregation litigation began almost 30 years ago. In 1961, respondents, black students and their parents, sued petitioners, the Board of Education of Oklahoma City (Board), to end *de jure* segregation in the public schools. In 1963, the District Court found that Oklahoma City had intentionally segregated both schools and housing in the past, and that Oklahoma City was operating a "dual" school system— one that was intentionally segregated by race.... In 1965, the District Court found that the School Board's attempt to desegregate by using neighborhood zoning failed to remedy past segregation because residential segregation resulted in one race schools. . . . Residential segregation had once been state imposed, and it lingered due to discrimination by some realtors and financial institutions. The District Court found that school segregation had caused some housing segregation. . . . In 1972, finding that previous efforts had not been successful at eliminating state imposed segregation, the District Court ordered the Board to adopt the "Finger Plan."...

In 1977, after complying with the desegregation decree for five years, the Board made a

"Motion to Close Case." The District Court held in its "Order Terminating Case":

> The Court has concluded that [the Finger Plan] worked and that substantial compliance with the constitutional requirements has been achieved. The School Board, under the oversight of the Court, has operated the Plan properly, and the Court does not foresee that the termination of its jurisdiction will result in the dismantlement of the Plan. . . .
>
> . . . The School Board, as now constituted, has manifested the desire and intent to follow the law. The court believes that the present members and their successors on the Board will now and in the future continue to follow the constitutional desegregation requirements.
>
> Now sensitized to the constitutional implications of its conduct and with a new awareness of its responsibility to citizens of all races, the Board is entitled to pursue in good faith its legitimate policies without the continuing constitutional supervision of this Court. . . .
>
> . . . Jurisdiction in this case is terminated ipso facto subject only to final disposition of any case now pending on appeal. No. Civ-9452 (WD Okla., Jan. 18, 1977). . . .

This unpublished order was not appealed.

In 1984, the School Board faced demographic changes that led to greater burdens on young black children. As more and more neighborhoods became integrated, more standalone schools were established, and young black students had to be bused further from their inner-city homes to outlying white areas. In an effort to alleviate this burden and to increase parental involvement, the Board adopted the Student Reassignment Plan (SRP). . . .

In 1985, respondents filed a "Motion to Reopen the Case," contending that the School District had not achieved "unitary" status and that the SRP was a return to segregation. . . . The District Court refused to reopen the case, holding that its 1977 finding of unitariness was res judicata as to those who were then parties to the action, and that the district remained unitary. . . . Because unitariness had been achieved, the District Court concluded that court ordered desegregation must end.

The Court of Appeals for the Tenth Circuit reversed. . . . It held that, while the 1977 order finding the district unitary was binding on the parties, nothing in that order indicated that the 1972 injunction itself was terminated. The court reasoned that the finding that the system was unitary merely needed the District Court's active supervision of the case, and because the school district was still subject to the desegregation decree, respondents could challenge the SRP. The case was remanded to determine whether the decree should be lifted or modified.

On remand, the District Court found that demographic changes made the Finger Plan unworkable, that the Board had done nothing for 25 years to promote residential segregation, and that the school district had bused students for more than a decade in good faith compliance with the court's orders. . . . The court concluded that the previous injunctive decree should be vacated and the school district returned to local control. . . .

The Court of Appeals again reversed . . . holding that "an injunction takes on a life of its own and becomes an edict quite independent of the law it is meant to effectuate." . . . That court approached the case "not so much as one dealing with desegregation, but as one dealing with the proper application of the federal law on injunctive remedies." . . .

We granted the Board's petition for *certiorari* to resolve a conflict between the standard laid down by the Court of Appeals in this case and that laid down in *Spangler v. Pasadena City Board of Education*, 611 F.2d 1239 (CA9 1979), and *Riddick v. School Bd. of City of Norfolk*, 784 F.2d 521 (CA4 1986). We now reverse the Court of Appeals. . . .

In *Milliken v. Bradley (Milliken II)*, 433 U.S. 267 (1977), we said: "[F]ederal court decrees must directly address and relate to the constitutional violation itself. Because of this inherent limitation upon federal judicial authority, federal court decrees exceed appropriate limits if they are aimed at eliminating a condition that does not violate the Constitution or does not flow from such a violation. . . ." . . .

From the very first, federal supervision of local school systems was intended as a temporary measure to remedy past discrimination. . . .

Considerations based on the allocation of powers within our federal system, support our view . . . [D]ecrees are not intended to operate in perpetuity. Local control over the education of children allows citizens to participate in decisionmaking, and allows innovation so that school programs can fit local needs. . . . The legal justification for displacement of local authority by an injunctive decree in a school desegregation case is a violation of the Constitution by the local authorities. Dissolving a desegregation decree after the local authorities have operated in compliance with it for a reasonable period of time properly recognizes that "necessary concern for the important values of local control of public school systems dictates that a federal court's regulatory control of such systems not extend beyond the time required to remedy the effects of past intentional discrimination." . . .

A district court need not accept at face value the profession of a school board which has intentionally discriminated that it will cease to do so in the future. But in deciding whether to modify or dissolve a desegregation decree, a school board's compliance with previous court orders is obviously relevant. In this case the original finding of *de jure* segregation was entered in 1961, the injunctive decree from which the Board seeks relief was entered in 1972, and the Board complied with the decree in good faith until 1985. Not only do the personnel of school boards change over time, but the same passage of time enables the District Court to observe the good faith of the school board in complying with the decree. The test espoused by the Court of Appeals would condemn a school district, once governed by a board which intentionally discriminated, to judicial tutelage for the indefinite future. Neither the principles governing the entry and dissolution of injunctive decrees, nor the commands of the Equal Protection Clause of the Fourteenth Amendment, require any such Draconian result.

Petitioners urge that we reinstate the decision of the District Court terminating the injunction, but we think that the preferable course is to remand the case to that court so that it may decide, in accordance with this opinion, whether the Board made a sufficient showing of constitutional compliance as of 1985, when the SRP was adopted, to allow the injunction to be dissolved. The District Court should address itself to whether the Board had complied in good faith with the desegregation decree since it was entered, and whether the vestiges of past discrimination had been eliminated to the extent practicable.

In considering whether the vestiges of *de jure* segregation had been eliminated as far as practicable, the District Court should look not only at student assignments, but "to every facet of school operations faculty, staff, transportation, extracurricular activities and facilities." *Green,* 391 U.S., at 435. See also *Swann,* 402 U.S., at 18 ("[E]xisting policy and practice with regard to faculty, staff, transportation, extracurricular activities, and facilities" are "among the most important indicia of a segregated system").

After the District Court decides whether the Board was entitled to have the decree terminated, it should proceed to decide respondent's challenge to the SRP. A school district which has been released from an injunction imposing a desegregation plan no longer requires court authorization for the promulgation of policies and rules regulating matters such as assignment of students and the like, but it of course remains subject to the mandate of the Equal Protection Clause of the Fourteenth Amendment. If the Board was entitled to have the decree terminated as of 1985, the District Court should then evaluate the Board's decision to implement the SRP under appropriate equal protection principles. . . .

The judgment of the Court of Appeals is reversed, and the case is remanded to the District Court for further proceedings consistent with this opinion.

It is so ordered.

❖ — ❖ — ❖

Federal District Court in School Desegregation Case Has the Discretion to Order Incremental or Partial Withdrawal of Its Supervision and Control

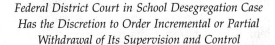

Freeman v. Pitts

Supreme Court of the United States, 1992.
503 U.S. 467, 112 S.Ct. 1430.

Justice KENNEDY delivered the opinion of the Court.

DeKalb County, Georgia, is a major suburban area of Atlanta. This case involves a court-ordered desegregation decree for the DeKalb County School System (DCSS). . . .

DCSS has been subject to the supervision and jurisdiction of the United States District Court for the Northern District of Georgia since 1969, when it was ordered to dismantle its dual school system. In 1986, petitioners filed a motion for final dismissal. The District Court ruled that DCSS had not achieved unitary status in all respects but had done so in student attendance and three other categories. In its order the District Court relinquished remedial control as to those aspects of the system in which unitary status had been achieved, and retained supervisory authority only for those aspects of the school system in which the district was not in full compliance. The Court of Appeals for the Eleventh Circuit reversed, 887 F.2d 1438 (1989), holding that a district court should retain full remedial authority over a school system until it achieves unitary status in six categories at the same time for several years. We now reverse the judgment of the Court of Appeals and remand, holding that a district court is permitted to withdraw judicial supervision with respect to discrete categories in which the school district has achieved compliance with a court-ordered desegregation plan. A district court need not retain active control over every aspect of school administration until a school district has demonstrated unitary status in all facets of its system. . . .

The District Court found the racial imbalance . . . was not a vestige of the prior *de jure* system. . . .

The District Court noted that DCSS had taken specific steps to combat the effects of demographics on the racial mix of the schools. . . .

In determining whether DCSS has achieved unitary status with respect to student assignment, the District Court saw its task as one of deciding if petitioners "have accomplished maximum practical desegregation of the DCSS or if the DCSS must still do more to fulfill their affirmative constitutional duty." . . .

Having found no constitutional violation with respect to student assignment, the District Court next considered the other *Green* factors, beginning with faculty and staff assignments. . . . The District Court also noted that DCSS has an "equally exemplary record" in retention of black teachers and administrators. . . . Nevertheless, the District Court found that DCSS had not achieved or maintained a ratio of black to white teachers and administrators in each school to approximate the ratio of black to white teachers and administrators throughout the system. In other words, a racial imbalance existed in the assignment of minority teachers and administrators. . . .

The court ordered DCSS to devise a plan to achieve compliance with *Singleton,* noting that "[i]t would appear that such compliance will necessitate reassignment of both teachers and principals." . . . With respect to faculty, the District Court noted that meeting *Singleton* would not be difficult, citing petitioners' own estimate that most schools' faculty could conform by moving, at most, two or three teachers. . . .

Despite its finding that there was no intentional violation, the District Court found that DCSS had not achieved unitary status with respect to quality of education because teachers in schools with disproportionately high percentages of white students tended to be better educated and have more experience than their counterparts in schools with disproportionately high percentages of black students, and because per-pupil expenditures in majority white schools exceeded per-pupil expenditures in majority black schools. From these findings, the District Court ordered DCSS to equalize spending and remedy the other problems.

The final *Green* factors considered by the District Court were: (1) physical facilities, (2) transportation, and (3) extracurricular activities. The District Court noted that although respondents expressed some concerns about the use of portable classrooms in schools in the southern portion of the county, they in effect conceded that DCSS has achieved unitary status with respect to physical facilities.

In accordance with its factfinding, the District Court held that it would order no further relief in the areas of student assignment, transportation, physical facilities, and extracurricular activities. The District Court, however, did order DCSS to establish a system to balance teacher and principal assignments and to equalize per-pupil expenditures throughout DCSS. . . .

Both parties appealed to the United States Court of Appeals for the Eleventh Circuit. The Court of Appeals affirmed the District Court's ultimate conclusion that DCSS has not yet achieved unitary status, but reversed the District Court's ruling that DCSS has no further duties in the area of student assignment. . . . The Court of Appeals held that the District Court erred by considering the six *Green* factors as separate categories. The Court of Appeals rejected the District Court's incremental approach, . . . and held that a school system achieves unitary status only after it has satisfied all six factors at the same time for several years. . . . We granted *certiorari,* 498 U.S. 1081, 111 S.Ct. 949, 112 L.Ed.2d 1038 (1991).

Two principal questions are presented. The first is whether a district court may relinquish its supervision and control over those aspects of a school system in which there has been compliance with a desegregation decree if other aspects of the system remain in noncompliance. As we answer this question in the affirmative, the second question is whether the Court of Appeals erred in reversing the District Court's order providing for incremental withdrawal of supervision in all the circumstances of this case.

The duty and responsibility of a school district once segregated by law is to take all steps necessary to eliminate the vestiges of the unconstitutional *de jure* system. This is required in order to ensure that the principal wrong of the *de jure* system, the injuries and stigma inflicted upon the race disfavored by the violation, is no longer present. . . .

The object of *Brown I* was made more specific by our holding in *Green* that the duty of a former *de jure* district is to "take whatever steps might be necessary to convert to a unitary system in which racial discrimination would be eliminated root and branch." . . . We also identified various parts of the school system which, in addition to student attendance patterns, must be free from racial discrimination before the mandate of *Brown* is met: faculty, staff, transportation, extracurricular activities, and facilities. . . . The *Green* factors are a measure of the racial identifiability of schools in a system that is not in compliance with *Brown,* and we instructed the District Courts to fashion remedies that address all these components of elementary and secondary school systems.

The concept of unitariness has been a helpful one in defining the scope of the district courts' authority, for it conveys the central idea that a school district that was once a dual system must be examined in all of its facets, both when a remedy is ordered and in the later phases of desegregation when the question is whether the district courts' remedial control ought to be modified, lessened, or withdrawn. . . .

We have said that the court's end purpose must be to remedy the violation and, in addition, to restore state and local authorities to the control of a school system that is operating in compliance with the Constitution. . . . A transition phase in which control is relinquished in a gradual way is an appropriate means to this end. . . . Returning schools to the control of local authorities at the earliest practicable date is essential to restore their true accountability in our governmental system.

We hold that, in the course of supervising desegregation plans, federal courts have the authority to relinquish supervision and control of school districts in incremental stages, before full compliance has been achieved in every area of school operations. While retaining jurisdiction over the case, the court may determine that it will not order further remedies in areas where the school district is in compliance with the decree. That is to say, upon a finding that a school system subject to a court-supervised desegregation plan is in compliance in some but not all areas, the court in appropriate cases may return control to the school system in those areas where compliance has been achieved, limiting further judicial supervision to operations that are not yet in full compliance with the court decree. In particular, the district court may determine that it will not order further remedies in the area of student assignments where racial imbalance is not traceable, in a proximate way, to constitutional violations.

A court's discretion to order the incremental withdrawal of its supervision in a school desegregation case must be exercised in a manner consistent with the purposes and objectives of its equitable power. Among the factors which must inform the sound discretion of the court in ordering partial withdrawal are the following: whether there has been full and satisfactory compliance with the decree in those aspects of the system where supervision is to be withdrawn; whether retention of judicial control is necessary or practicable to achieve compliance with the decree in other facets of the school system; and whether the school district has demonstrated, to the public and to the parents and students of the once disfavored race, its good-faith commitment to the whole of the court's decree and to those provisions of the law and the Constitution that were the predicate for judicial intervention in the first instance. . . .

We reach now the question whether the Court of Appeals erred in prohibiting the District Court from returning to DCSS partial control over some of its affairs. We decide that the Court of Appeals did err in holding that, as a matter of law, the District Court had no discretion to permit DCSS to regain control over student assignment, transportation, physical facilities, and extracurricular activities, while retaining court supervision over the areas of faculty and administrative assignments and the quality of education, where full compliance had not been demonstrated. It was an appropriate exercise of its discretion for the District Court to address the elements of a unitary system discussed in *Green,* to inquire whether other elements ought to be identified, and to determine whether minority students were being disadvantaged in ways that required the formulation of new and further remedies to ensure full compliance with the court's decree. . . .

The District Court's approach illustrates that the *Green* factors need not be a rigid framework. It illustrates also the uses of equitable discretion. By withdrawing control over areas where judicial supervision is no longer needed, a district court can concentrate both its own resources and those of the school district on the areas where the effects of *de jure* discrimination have not been eliminated and further action is necessary in order to provide real and tangible relief to minority students. . . .

In the case before us the District Court designed a comprehensive plan for desegregation of DCSS in 1969, one that included racial balance in student assignments. The desegregation decree was designed to achieve maximum practicable desegregation. Its central remedy was the closing of black schools and the reassignment of pupils to neighborhood schools, with attendance zones that achieved racial balance. The plan accomplished its objective in the first year of operation, before dramatic demographic changes altered residential patterns. For the entire 17-year period respondents raised no substantial objection to the basic student assignment system, as the parties and the District Court concentrated on other mechanisms to eliminate the *de jure* taint.

That there was racial imbalance in student attendance zones was not tantamount to a showing that the school district was in noncompliance with the decree or with its duties under the law. Racial balance is not to be achieved for its own sake. It is to be pursued when racial imbalance has been caused by a constitutional violation. Once the racial imbalance due to the *de jure* violation has been remedied, the school district is under no duty to remedy imbalance that is caused by demographic factors. . . .

The effect of changing residential patterns on the racial composition of schools, though not always fortunate, is somewhat predictable. Studies show a high correlation between residential segregation and school segregation. . . .

Where resegregation is a product not of state action but of private choices, it does not have constitutional implications. It is beyond the authority and beyond the practical ability of the federal courts to try to counteract these kinds of continuous and massive demographic shifts. To attempt such results would require ongoing and never-ending supervision by the courts of school districts simply because they were once *de jure* segregated. . . .

As the *de jure* violation becomes more remote in time and these demographic changes intervene, it becomes less likely that a current racial imbalance in a school district is a vestige of the prior *de jure* system. The causal link between current conditions and the prior violation is even more attenuated if the school district has demonstrated its good faith. In light of its finding that the demographic changes in DeKalb County are unrelated to the prior violation, the District Court was correct to entertain the suggestion that DCSS had no duty to achieve system-wide racial balance in the student population. It was appropriate for the District Court to examine the reasons for the racial imbalance before ordering an impractical, and no doubt massive, expenditure of funds to achieve racial balance after 17 years of efforts to implement the comprehensive plan in a district where there were fundamental changes in demographics, changes not attributable to the former *de jure* regime or any later actions by school officials. The District Court's determination to order instead the expenditure of scarce resources in areas such as the quality of education, where full compliance had not yet been achieved, underscores the uses of discretion in framing equitable remedies. . . .

We next consider whether retention of judicial control over student attendance is necessary or practicable to achieve compliance in other facets of the school system. Racial balancing in elementary and secondary school student assignments may be a legitimate remedial device to correct other fundamental inequities that were themselves caused by the constitutional violation. We have long recognized that the *Green* factors may be related or interdependent. Two or more *Green* factors may be intertwined or synergistic in their relation, so that a constitutional violation in one area cannot be eliminated unless the judicial remedy addresses other matters as well. We have observed, for example, that student segregation and faculty segregation are often related problems. . . .

There was no showing that racial balancing was an appropriate mechanism to cure other deficiencies in this case. It is true that the school district was not in compliance with respect to faculty assignments, but the record does not show that student reassignments would be a feasible or practicable way to remedy this defect. . . .

A history of good-faith compliance is evidence that any current racial imbalance is not the product of a new *de jure* violation, and enables the district court to accept the school board's representation that it has accepted the principle of racial equality and will not suffer intentional discrimination in the future. . . .

When a school district has not demonstrated good faith under a comprehensive plan to remedy ongoing violations, we have without hesitation approved comprehensive and continued district court supervision. . . . With respect to those areas where compliance had not been achieved, the District Court did not find that DCSS had acted in bad faith or engaged in further acts of discrimination since the desegregation plan went into effect. This, though, may not be the equivalent of a finding that the school district has an affirmative commitment to comply in good faith with the entirety of a desegregation plan, and further proceedings are appropriate for this purpose as well.

The judgment is reversed, and the case is remanded to the Court of Appeals. . . . Thereupon it should order further proceedings as necessary or order an appropriate remand to the District Court. Each party is to bear its own costs. It is so ordered.

CASE NOTE

Unitariness. The U.S. Court of Appeals, Tenth Circuit, has elaborated on its own view of unitariness and how it is to be determined, *Brown v. Board of Education of Topeka* (*Brown III*), 892 F.2d 851 (10th Cir.1989):

GENERAL PRINCIPLES OF UNITARINESS . . .

BURDEN OF PROOF To determine whether a school district has become unitary, . . . a court must consider what the school district has done or not done to fulfill its affirmative duty to desegregate, the current effects of those actions or inactions, and the extent to which further desegregation is feasible. After a plaintiff establishes intentional segregation at some point in the past and a current condition of segregation, a defendant then bears the burden of proving that its past acts have eliminated all traces of the past intentional segregation to the maximum feasible extent. . . .

CURRENT CONDITION OF SEGREGATION The actual condition of the school district at the time of trial is perhaps the most crucial consideration in a unitariness determination. The plaintiff bears the burden of showing the existence of a current condition of segregation. . . . In our view, a plaintiff must prove the existence of racially identifiable schools, broadly defined, to satisfy the burden of showing a current condition of segregation. Racially identifiable schools may be identifiable by student assignment alone, in the case of highly one-race schools, or by a combination of factors where the

school is not highly one-race in student assignment. . . .

Although virtual one-race schools "require close scrutiny," they are not always unconstitutional. *Swann,* 402 U.S. at 26, 91 S.Ct. at 1281. Their existence in a system with a history of *de jure* segregation, however, establishes a presumption that they exist as the result of discrimination and shifts the burden of proof to the school system. *Id.* The presence of essentially one-race schools is thus sufficient to satisfy a plaintiff's initial burden of showing a current condition of segregation. . . .

However, no particular degree of racial balance is required by the Constitution. A degree of imbalance is likely to be found in any heterogeneous school system. Therefore, the existence of some racial imbalance in schools will often not be conclusive in itself. . . .

THE PARTIES' BURDENS Once a plaintiff has proven the existence of a current condition of segregation, the school district bears the substantial burden of showing that that condition is not the result of its prior *de jure* segregation. Under the relevant Supreme Court decisions, mere absence of invidious intent on the part of the school district is not sufficient to satisfy its "heavy burden" of proof; the district's duty is to act affirmatively, not merely to act neutrally. . . .

The school district must show that no causal connection exists between past and present segregation, not merely that it did not intend to cause current segregation. The causal link between prior and current segregation is not snapped by the absence of discriminatory intent alone, or even by a firm commitment to desegregation, where it is not accompanied by action that in fact produces a unified school district. . . .

What the school district has done to integrate is crucial in determining whether the causal link between the prior segregation and the current disparities has been severed. The district may carry its burden by showing that it has acted affirmatively to desegregate. Absent such proof, the court must presume that current segregation is the result of prior intentional state action. A showing that the school district has not promoted segregation and has allowed desegregation to take place where neutral forces worked to that end is insufficient. . . .

The ultimate test of what the school district has done is its effectiveness, most significantly its effectiveness in eliminating the separation of white and minority children. While a district is not always required to choose the most desegregative alternative when it selects a particular option, the results of the sum of the choices made by the district must be to desegregate the system to the maximum possible extent. . . .

MAXIMUM PRACTICABLE DESEGREGATION What more can and should be done, if anything, is the final component in a determination of unitary status. Essentially, a defendant must demonstrate that it has done everything feasible. Courts must assess the school district's achievements with an eye to the possible and practical, but they must not let long-standing racism blur their ultimate focus on the ideal.

Where the school district has complied with the desegregation plan to the best of its ability, and has done what can be done in spite of the obstacles in its way, it is reasonable to conclude that no further desegregation is feasible.

In sum, when a school system was previously *de jure*, a plaintiff bears the burden of showing that there is a current condition of segregation. It may do so by proving the existence of racially identifiable schools. The school district must then show that such segregation has no causal connection with the prior *de jure* segregation, and that the district has in fact carried out the maximum desegregation practicable for that district.

■ REMEDIAL AND COMPENSATORY REMEDIES

Initial remedies in the early days of desegregation usually centered on movement of black and white students, teachers, and staff in an effort to make the racial makeup of the schools more homogeneous. More recently, though, the courts have allowed additional options as a part of the desegregation plans, to enrich the learning experiences of minority students. Rather than (or in addition to) the busing of students, various courts have approved programs for early childhood intervention, curriculum development, reduction in pupil-teacher ratios, counseling and career guidance, remedial reading, and staff development. *Milliken II* is perhaps the leading case extending relief for remediation of individual educational harms as a method of overcoming the vestiges of past discrimination. In *Milliken II*, the U.S. Supreme Court set out three principles that govern a lower court's options in providing such remedies. First, the remedy should be commensurate with the nature and scope of the constitutional violation. Second, the court's decree should be remedial in nature,

fashioned as nearly as possible "to restore the victims of discriminatory conduct to the position they would have occupied in the absence of such conduct." Third, in formulating a decree, the courts "must take into account the interest of state and local authorities in managing their own affairs, consistent with the Constitution."

In keeping with these guidelines, the Supreme Court recognized the need to justify the creation of new education programs to halt the ongoing effects of discrimination and to facilitate the process of desegregation. Moreover, *Milliken II* recognized that it may be necessary for a lower federal court to require remedies that will alleviate the individual learning effects and deficiencies caused by segregation. The Supreme Court justified programmatic remedies in observing that

> [c]hildren who have been thus educationally and culturally set apart from the larger community will inevitably acquire habits of speech, conduct, and attitudes reflecting their cultural isolation. They are likely to acquire speech habits, for example, which vary from the environment in which they must ultimately function and compete, if they are to enter and be a part of that community. . . .

Pupil assignment alone does not automatically remedy the impact of previous, unlawful educational isolation; the consequences linger and can be dealt with only by independent measures.[59]

Such remedies may be extensive and very costly, as was the case in *Missouri v. Jenkins I*. Here the U.S. Supreme Court upheld a lower court's mandate for increased revenues and the imposition of a tax increase by the school district in order to fund several remedial and compensatory programmatic initiatives, including an effective schools program, reduction in class size, summer school, full-day kindergarten, before- and after-school tutoring, early childhood education, magnet schools, and facilities improvements.[60] Even though the *Jenkins I* case caused anguished cries of "taxation without representation," the Supreme Court upheld the validity of both the education programs and the funding scheme as proper means to overcome the effects of state-created segregation.[61]

Special programs designed solely for remediation of educational deficiencies caused by past discrimination may be supplemented or replaced by other programs as well. Optional plans that make core city schools more attractive for whites may also be employed. For example, the creation of magnet programs in predominantly black schools and voluntary "majority to minority" transfers have been allowed.[62] In such an instance, the U.S. Court of Appeals, Eleventh Circuit, upheld the abandonment of mandatory busing, racial pairing of schools, and mandatory reassignment in favor of magnet programs, voluntary transfers, and revised attendance zones. In way of justification, the court observed: "The measure of the desegregation plan is its ultimate effectiveness. The type of plan employed is of little consequence so long as it effectively achieves the constitutionally required result that public schools be conducted on a unitary basis."[63]

However, a remedy required by the federal courts must not be disassociated with or unrelated to the cause of segregation. In other words, the desegregation orders of the federal courts must not be beyond the scope of the intradistrict *de jure* segregation violation. In *Missouri v. Jenkins II*,[64] the U.S. Supreme Court struck down a federal district court's remedy that required the state of Missouri to supplement local funds for salaries of Kansas City school district teachers and staff, raising them to a level greater than that in suburban school districts. The lower federal court sought to create "desegregative attractiveness" to draw students, teachers, and staff to the central city school system and from the suburbs. The U.S. Supreme Court held that such a remedy was "too far removed" from acceptable means of remedying previously legally mandated intradistrict segregation.

Moreover, in *Jenkins II*, the Supreme Court found that a mandated standard for a remedy of implementing "quality education" could not be premised on achievement levels based on national achievement test grade-level norms. Achievement tests as a "quality measure" can be used only to address the lower achievement of minority students that is directly attributable to prior *de jure* segregation. Use of interdistrict and national test norms as measures for redressing intradistrict legal segregation was found to be inappropriate; the Supreme Court admonished that such "remedial calculus" cannot

include factors external to the school districts.[65] This rejection by the Supreme Court of the use of interdistrict or national test standards obviously places an enormous burden on the lower federal district courts to justify the use of achievement test scores as a measure of "quality" supporting a particular remedy.

❖ — ❖ — ❖

Federal Courts Can Require School Districts to Levy Taxes in Excess of State Statutory Limits in Order to Fund Desegregation Remedies

Missouri v. Jenkins

Supreme Court of the United States, 1990.
495 U.S. 33, 110 S.Ct. 1651.

Justice WHITE delivered the opinion of the Court. The United States District Court for the Western District of Missouri imposed an increase in the property taxes levied by the Kansas City, Missouri, School District (KCMSD) to ensure funding for the desegregation of KCMSD's public schools. We granted *certiorari* to consider the State of Missouri's argument that the District Court lacked the power to raise local property taxes. For the reasons given below, we hold that the District Court abused its discretion in imposing the tax increase. We also hold, however, that the modifications of the District Court's order made by the Court of Appeals do satisfy equitable and constitutional principles governing the District court's power. . . .

The District Court . . . issued an order detailing the remedies necessary to eliminate the vestiges of segregation and the financing necessary to implement those remedies. . . . The District Court originally estimated the total cost of the desegregation remedy to be almost $88,000,000 over three years, of which it expected the State to pay $67,592,072 and KCMSD to pay $20,140,472. The court concluded, however, that several provisions of Missouri law would prevent KCMSD from being able to pay its share of the obligation. . . .

The District Court believed that it had the power to order a tax increase to ensure adequate funding of the desegregation plan, but it hesitated to take this step. It chose instead . . . to allow KCMSD to raise an additional $4,000,000 for the coming fiscal year. The court ordered KCMSD to submit to the voters a proposal for an increase in taxes sufficient to pay for its share of the desegregation remedy in following years. . . .

The Court of Appeals for the Eighth Circuit affirmed the District Court's findings of liability and remedial order in most respects. . . . The Court of Appeals agreed with the State, however, that the District Court had failed to explain adequately why it had imposed most of the cost of the desegregation plan on the State. The Eighth Circuit ordered the District Court to divide the cost equally between the State and KCMSD. *Id.*, at 685. We denied certiorari. *Kansas City, Missouri, School Dist. v. Missouri*, 484 U.S. 816, 108 S.Ct. 70, 98 L.Ed.2d 34 (1987).

Proceedings before the District Court continued during the appeal. In its original remedial order, the District Court had directed KCMSD to prepare a study addressing the usefulness of "magnet schools" to promote desegregation. . . . A year later, the District Court approved KCMSD's proposal to operate six magnet schools during the 1986–1987 school year. The court again faced the problem of funding, for KCMSD's efforts to persuade the voters to approve a tax increase had failed, as had its efforts to seek funds from the Kansas City Council and the state legislature. Again hesitating to impose a tax increase itself, the court continued its injunction against the Proposition C rollback to enable KCMSD to raise an additional $6,500,000. . . .

In November 1986, the District Court endorsed a marked expansion of the magnet school program. It adopted in substance a KCMSD proposal that every high school, every middle school, and half of the elementary schools in KCMSD become magnet schools by the 1991–1992 school year. It also approved the $142,736,025 budget proposed by KCMSD for implementation of the magnet school plan, as well as the expenditure of $52,858,301 for additional capital improvements. . . .

The District Court next considered, as the Court of Appeals had directed, how to shift the cost of desegregation to KCMSD. The District Court concluded that it would be "clearly inequitable" to require the population of KCMSD to pay half of the desegregation cost, and that "even with Court help it would be very difficult for the KCMSD to fund more than 25% of the costs of the entire remedial plan." The court reasoned that the State should pay for most of the desegregation cost. . . . The District Court then held that the State and KCMSD were 75% and 25% at fault, respectively, and ordered them to share the cost of the desegregation remedy in that proportion. To ensure complete funding of the remedy, the court also held the two tortfeasors jointly and severally liable for the cost of the plan. . . .

Three months later, the District Court adopted a plan requiring $187,450,334 in further capital improvements. By then it was clear that KCMSD would lack the resources to pay for its 25% share of the desegregation cost. KCMSD requested that the District Court order the State to pay for any amount that KCMSD could not meet. The District Court declined to impose a greater share of the cost on the State, but it accepted that KCMSD had "exhausted all available means of raising additional revenue." Finding itself with "no choice but to exercise its broad equitable powers and enter a judgment that will enable the KCMSD to raise its share of the cost of the plan," and believing that the "United States Supreme Court has stated that a tax may be increased if 'necessary to raise funds adequate to . . . operate and maintain without racial discrimination a public school system,'" . . . the court ordered the KCMSD property tax levy raised from $2.05 to $4.00 per $100 of assessed valuation through the 1991–1992 fiscal year. . . . KCMSD was also directed to issue $150,000,000 in capital improvement bonds. A subsequent order directed that the revenues generated by the property tax increase be used to retire the capital improvement bonds. . . .

The State appealed, challenging the scope of the desegregation remedy, the allocation of the cost between the State and KCMSD, and the tax increase. . . .

We turn to the tax increase imposed by the District Court. The State urges us to hold that the tax increase violated Article III, the Tenth

Amendment, and principles of federal/state comity. We find it unnecessary to reach the difficult constitutional issues, for we agree with the State that the tax increase contravened the principles of comity that must govern the exercise of the District Court's equitable discretion in this area.

It is accepted by all the parties, as it was by the courts below, that the imposition of a tax increase by a federal court was an extraordinary event. In assuming for itself the fundamental and delicate power of taxation the District Court not only intruded on local authority but circumvented it altogether. . . .

The District Court believed that it had no alternative to imposing a tax increase. But there was an alternative, the very one outlined by the Court of Appeals: it could have authorized or required KCMSD to levy property taxes at a rate adequate to fund the desegregation remedy and could have enjoined the operation of state laws that would have prevented KCMSD from exercising this power. . . . The difference between the two approaches is far more than a matter of form. Authorizing and directing local government institutions to devise and implement remedies not only protects the function of those institutions but, to the extent possible, also places the responsibility for solutions to the problems of segregation upon those who have themselves created the problems. . . .

The District Court therefore abused its discretion in imposing the tax itself. The Court of Appeals should not have allowed the tax increase to stand and should have reversed the District Court in this respect. . . .

We stand on different ground when we review the modifications to the District Court's order made by the Court of Appeals. As explained, . . . the Court of Appeals held that the District Court in the future should authorize KCMSD to submit a levy to the state tax collection authorities adequate to fund its budget and should enjoin the operation of state laws that would limit or reduce the levy below that amount. . . .

It is true that in *Milliken v. Bradley*, 433 U.S., at 291, 97 S.Ct., at 2763, we stated that the enforcement of a money judgment against the State did not violate principles of federalism be-cause "[t]he District Court . . . neither attempted to restructure local governmental entities nor . . . mandat[ed] a particular method or structure of state or local financing." But we did not there state that a District Court could never set aside state laws preventing local governments from raising funds sufficient to satisfy their constitutional obligations just because those funds could also be obtained from the States. To the contrary, 42 U.S.C. § 1983 (1982 ed.), on which respondents' complaint is based, is authority enough to require each tortfeasor to pay its share of the cost of the remedy if it can, and apportionment of the cost is part of the equitable power of the District Court. . . .

We turn to the constitutional issues. The modifications ordered by the Court of Appeals cannot be assailed as invalid under the Tenth Amendment. "The Tenth Amendment's reservation of nondelegated powers to the States is not implicated by a federal-court judgment enforcing the express prohibitions of unlawful state conduct enacted by the Fourteenth Amendment." . . .

Finally, the State argues that an order to increase taxes cannot be sustained under the judicial power of Article III. Whatever the merits of this argument when applied to the District Court's own order increasing taxes, a point we have not reached, . . . a court order directing a local government body to levy its own taxes is plainly a judicial act within the power of a federal court. . . .

The State maintains, however, . . . the federal judicial power can go no further than to require local governments to levy taxes *as authorized under state law*. In other words, the State argues that federal courts cannot set aside state-imposed limitations on local taxing authority because to do so is to do more than to require the local government "to exercise the power *that is theirs*." We disagree. . . .

It is therefore clear that a local government with taxing authority may be ordered to levy taxes in excess of the limit set by state statute where there is reason based in the Constitution for not observing the statutory limitation. . . . Here the KCMSD may be ordered to levy taxes despite the statutory limitations on its authority in order to compel the discharge of an obligation imposed on KCMSD by the Fourteenth Amendment. To hold otherwise would fail to take account of the obligations of local governments, under the Supremacy Clause, to fulfill the requirements that the Constitution imposes on them. However wide the discretion of local authorities in fashioning desegregation remedies may be, "if a state-imposed limitation on a school authority's discretion operates to inhibit or obstruct the operation of a unitary school system or impede the disestablishing of a dual school system, it must fall; state policy must give way when it operates to hinder vindication of federal constitutional guarantees." *North Carolina State Bd. of Education v. Swann,* 402 U.S. 43, 45, 91 S.Ct. 1284, 1286, 28 L.Ed.2d 586 (1971). Even though a particular remedy may not be required in every case to vindicate constitutional guarantees, where (as here) it has been found that a particular remedy is required, the State cannot hinder the process by preventing a local government from implementing that remedy.

Accordingly, the judgment of the Court of Appeals is affirmed insofar as it required the District Court to modify its funding order and reversed insofar as it allowed the tax increase imposed by the District Court to stand. The case is remanded for further proceedings consistent with this opinion.

It is so ordered.

Justice KENNEDY, with whom THE CHIEF JUSTICE, Justice O'CONNOR, and Justice SCALIA join, concurring in part and concurring in the judgment.

❖ — ❖ — ❖

Intradistrict De Jure *Segregation Does Not Justify Interdistrict Remedies*

Missouri v. Jenkins

Supreme Court of the United States, 1995.
515 U.S. 70, 115 S.Ct. 2038.

CHIEF JUSTICE REHNQUIST delivered the opinion of the Court. As this school desegregation litigation enters its 18th year, we are called upon again to review the decisions of the lower courts. In this case, the State of Missouri has challenged the District Court's order of salary increases for virtually all instructional and noninstructional staff within the Kansas City, Missouri, School District (KCMSD) and the District Court's order requiring the State to continue to fund remedial "quality education" programs because student achievement levels were still "at or below national norms at many grade levels."

. . . [W]e granted certiorari. This case has been before the same United States District Judge since 1977. . . . In June 1985, the District Court issued its first remedial order and established as its goal the "elimination of all vestiges of state imposed segregation." . . .

The District Court also ordered programs to expand educational opportunities for all KCMSD students: full-day kindergarten; expanded summer school; before- and after-school tutoring; and an early childhood development program. . . .

In November 1986, the District Court approved a comprehensive magnet school and capital improvements plan and held the State and the KCMSD jointly and severally liable for its funding. . . .

. . . The District Court's desegregation plan has been described as the most ambitious and expensive remedial program in the history of school desegregation. 19 F.3d, at 397 (Beam, J., dissenting from denial of rehearing en banc). The annual cost per pupil at the KCMSD far exceeds that of the neighboring SSD's or of any school district in Missouri. . . . Not surprisingly, the cost of this remedial plan has "far exceeded KCMSD's budget, or for that matter, its authority to tax." . . . The State, through the operation of joint-and-several liability, has borne the brunt of these costs. . . .

With this background, we turn to the present controversy. First, the State has challenged the District Court's requirement that it fund salary increases for KCMSD instructional and noninstructional staff. . . . The State claimed that funding for salaries was beyond the scope of the District Court's remedial authority. . . . Second, the State has challenged the District Court's order requiring it to continue to fund the remedial quality education programs for the 1992–1993 school year. . . . As a result, the State argued that the District Court should have relieved it of responsibility for funding those programs.

The District Court rejected the State's arguments. . . .

The Court of Appeals for the Eighth Circuit affirmed. . . .

Because of the importance of the issues, we granted *certiorari* to consider the following: (1) whether the District Court exceeded its constitutional authority when it granted salary increases to virtually all instructional and noninstructional employees of the KCMSD, and (2) whether the District Court properly relied upon the fact that student achievement test scores had failed to rise to some unspecified level when it declined to find that the State had achieved partial unitary status as to the quality education programs. . . .

The State argues that the order approving salary increases is beyond the District Court's authority because it was crafted to serve an "interdistrict goal," in spite of the fact that the constitutional violation in this case is "intradistrict" in nature. . . . "[T]he nature of the desegregation remedy is to be determined by the nature and scope of the constitutional violation." . . . Here, the District Court has found, and the Court of Appeals has affirmed, that this case involved no interdistrict constitutional violation that would support interdistrict relief. . . .

Thus, the proper response by the District Court should have been to eliminate to the extent practicable the vestiges of prior *de jure* segregation within the KCMSD: a system-wide reduction in student achievement and existence of 25 racially identifiable schools with a population of over 90% black students. . . . The District Court and Court of Appeals, however, have felt that because the KCMSD's enrollment remained 68.3% black, a purely intradistrict remedy would be insufficient. ("[V]oluntary interdistrict remedies may be used to make meaningful integration possible in a predominantly minority district.") But, as noted in *Milliken I*, supra, we have rejected the suggestion "that schools which have a majority of Negro students are not 'desegregated' whatever the racial makeup of the school district's population and however neutrally the district lines have been drawn and administered." . . .

Instead of seeking to remove the racial identity of the various schools within the KCMSD, the District Court has set out on a program to create a school district that was equal to or superior to the surrounding SSD's. Its remedy has focused on "desegregative attractiveness," coupled with "suburban comparability." . . . Examination of the District Court's reliance on "desegregative attractiveness" and "suburban comparability" is instructive for our ultimate resolution of the salary-order issue.

The purpose of desegregative attractiveness has been not only to remedy the system-wide reduction in student achievement, but also to attract nonminority students not presently enrolled in the KCMSD. This remedy has included an elaborate program of capital improvements, course enrichment, and extracurricular enhancement not simply in the formerly identifiable black schools, but in schools throughout the district. The District Court's remedial orders have converted every senior high school, every middle school, and one-half of the elementary schools in the KCMSD into "magnet" schools. The District Court's remedial order has all but made the KCMSD itself into a magnet district. . . .

In *Milliken I* we determined that a desegregation remedy that would require mandatory interdistrict reassignment of students throughout the Detroit metropolitan area was an impermissible interdistrict response to the intradistrict violation identified. . . . We held that before a district court could order an interdistrict remedy, there must be as showing that "racially discriminatory acts of the state or local school districts, or of a single school district have been a substantial cause of interdistrict segregation." . . . The District Court's pursuit of "desegregative attractiveness" is beyond the scope of its broad remedial authority. . . .

Respondents argue that the District Court's reliance upon desegregative attractiveness is justified in light of the District Court's statement that segregation has "led to white flight from the KCMSD to suburban districts." . . . The lower courts' "findings" as to "white flight" are both inconsistent internally, and inconsistent with the typical supposition, bolstered here by the record evidence, that "white flight" may result from desegregation, not *de jure* segregation. . . .

In *Freeman*, we stated that "[t]he vestiges of segregation that are the concern of the law in a school case may be subtle and intangible but nonetheless they must be so real that they have a causal link to the *de jure* violation being remedied." . . . The record here does not support the

District Court's reliance on "white flight" as a justification for a permissible expansion of its intradistrict remedial authority through its pursuit of desegregative attractiveness. . . .

The District Court's pursuit of "desegregative attractiveness" cannot be reconciled with our cases placing limitations on a district court's remedial authority. . . . This case provides numerous examples demonstrating the limitless authority of the District Court operating under this rationale. . . . In short, desegregative attractiveness has been used "as the hook on which to hang numerous policy choices about improving the quality of education in general within the KCMSD." . . .

Nor are there limits to the duration of the District Court's involvement. The expenditures per pupil in the KCMSD currently far exceed those in the neighboring SSD's. . . . Each additional program ordered by the District Court—and financed by the State—to increase the "desegregative attractiveness" of the school district makes the KCMSD more and more dependent on additional funding from the State; in turn, the greater the KCMSD's dependence on state funding, the greater its reliance on continued supervision by the District Court. But our cases recognize that local autonomy of school districts is a vital national tradition, . . . and that a district court must strive to restore state and local authorities to the control of a school system operating in compliance with the Constitution. . . . Although the District Court has determined that "[s]egregation has caused a system-wide reduction in achievement in the schools of KCMSD," . . . it never has identified the incremental effect that segregation has had on minority student achievement or the specific goals of the quality education programs. . . .

The District Court's pursuit of the goal of "desegregative attractiveness" results in so many imponderables and is so far removed from the task of eliminating the racial identifiability of the schools within the KCMSD that we believe it is beyond the admittedly broad discretion of the District Court. In this posture, we conclude that the District Court's order of salary increases, which was "grounded in remedying the vestiges of segregation by improving the desegregative attractiveness of the KCMSD," . . . is simply too far removed from an acceptable implementation of a permissible means to remedy previous legally mandated segregation. See *Milliken II, supra,* 433 U.S., 15 280, 97 S.Ct., at 2757. Similar considerations lead us to conclude that the District Court's order requiring the State to continue to fund the quality education programs because student achievement levels were still "at or below national norms at many grade levels" cannot be sustained. The State does not seek from this Court a declaration of partial unitary status with respect to the quality education programs. . . . It challenges the requirement of indefinite funding of a quality education program until national norms are met, based on the assumption that while a mandate for significant educational improvement, both in teaching and in facilities, may have been justified originally, its indefinite extension is not. . . .

In reconsidering this order, the District Court should apply our three-part test from *Freeman v. Pitts.* . . . As all the parties agree that improved achievement on test scores is not necessarily required for the State to achieve partial unitary status as to the quality education programs, the District Court should sharply limit, if not dispense with, its reliance on this factor. . . .

Just as demographic changes independent of *de jure* segregation will affect the racial composition of student assignments, *Freeman, supra,* 503 U.S., at 494–495, 112 S.Ct., at 1447–1448, so too will numerous external factors beyond the control of the KCMSD and the State affect minority student achievement. So long as these external factors are not the result of segregation, they do not figure in the remedial calculus. . . . Insistence upon academic goals unrelated to the effects of legal segregation unwarrantably postpones the day when the KCMSD will be able to operate on its own. The District Court also should consider that many goals of its quality education plan already have been attained. . . .

On remand, the District Court must bear in mind that its end purpose is not only "to remedy the violation" to the extent practicable, but also "to restore state and local authorities to the control of a school system that is operating in compliance with the Constitution." *Freeman, supra,* 503 U.S., at 489, 112 S.Ct., at 1445. The judgment of the Court of Appeals is reversed.

It is so ordered.

CASE NOTE

Test Scores. Recent cases indicate that courts are reluctant to accept statistical analyses that seek to prove that there is causal connection between previous discrimination and lower achievement test scores of black children. The U.S. Court of Appeals, Seventh Circuit, reversed a lower court decree that required a closing of one-half of the gap in achievement test scores between white and black students within a four-year period. The upper court rejected the use of test score evidence, implying that the statistical methodology used was not good science, and pointed out that the present size of the achievement test gap could not be attributable to past discrimination by the school district. *People Who Care v. Rockford Board of Education School District,* 111 F.3d 528 (7th Cir.1997).

■ DIVERSITY AND RACIAL CLASSIFICATIONS

States and school districts have in recent years increasingly sought to implement affirmative action racial policies by various means to create greater racial balance and diversity in schools. In so doing, some institutions have established policies based on racial distinctions that favor minority students.[66]

Yet, the U.S. Supreme Court has made it quite clear that racial classifications are highly suspect, to wit: "Distinctions between citizens solely because of their ancestry are by their very nature odious to free people whose institutions are founded upon the doctrine of equality."[67] Further, the Supreme Court has said that "preferring members of any one group for no reason other than race or ethnic origin is discrimination for its own sake."[68]

In light of the constitutional suspicion of distinctions based on race, racial classifications by a state agency can be justified only if they are shown to be for a compelling state interest. This means that the courts will subject the facts to strict judicial scrutiny and the state must in response bear the burden of proof in showing the necessity of the classification.[69]

The reasoning for application of strict scrutiny review to racial classifications is clearly enunciated by Justice O'Connor in *Croson,*

where she says that "the purpose of strict scrutiny is to 'smoke out' illegitimate uses of race by assuring that the legislative body is pursuing a goal important enough to warrant use of a highly suspect tool. The text also ensures that the means chosen 'fit' this compelling goal so closely that there is little or no possibility that the motive for the classification was illegitimate racial prejudice or stereotype."[70]

Under the strict scrutiny analysis, the Supreme Court will ask two questions: (1) Does the racial classification serve a compelling government interest, and (2) is it narrowly tailored to the achievement of that goal?[71] Strict scrutiny assures that the courts will give racial classifications careful attention and "detailed examination both as to ends and as to means."[72]

Racial classifications may be used by states and school districts to remediate the effects of past racial discrimination, and such is permitted and even required by the courts, as we have seen elsewhere in this chapter. On the other hand, racial classifications used for nonremedial purposes raise more complex questions. In *Freeman,*[73] the Supreme Court indicated that measures taken by school districts to create racial/ethnic balancing merely for its own sake and not for the purpose of erasing the vestiges of past discrimination are unconstitutional.[74]

NARROW TAILORING

If a school district has a policy of racial balancing for nonremedial reasons, then the federal courts in applying strict scrutiny review will require that the justification be *narrowly tailored* to address the specific circumstances if the policy is to be held constitutional. Narrow tailoring requires consideration of the following factors: "(1) the efficiency of alternative race-neutral policies, (2) the planned duration of the policy, (3) the relationship between the numerical goal and the percentage of minority group members in the relevant population or work force, (4) the flexibility of the policy, including the provision of waivers if the goal cannot be met, and (5) the burden of the policy on innocent third parties."[75] In applying these standards in *Tuttle*[76] and in *Eisenberg,*[77] the U.S. Court of Appeals, Fourth Circuit, held racial balancing policies to be deficient under these standards and therefore unconstitutional.

DIVERSITY

To maintain diversity is a frequently cited rationale for justifying racial balancing. The courts have not been decisive on ruling whether diversity is a compelling state interest. The fifth circuit in *Hopwood v. Texas*, the University of Texas Law School admission case, ruled that diversity is not a compelling state interest and therefore an affirmative action policy that balanced the races for the purpose of diversity was unconstitutional.[78] The court went on to conclude that the only compelling reason to justify racial classifications was to remedy past discrimination. The *Hopwood* court declined to follow the only applicable U.S. Supreme Court precedent on the subject, the concurring opinion in the California *Bakke* case, where Justice Powell wrote that diversity "furthers a compelling state interest."[79] This statement has been interpreted by some lower courts to mean that the state "is not absolutely barred from giving consideration to race" as a nonremedial action.[80] The statement, however, is not a strong enunciation of Supreme Court precedent, since no other Supreme Court Justice joined in the diversity portion of Justice Powell's concurrence. The Powell statement, though, clearly suggests that diversity may be a compelling interest in justifying racial balancing. Justice Powell's exact words are these: "[The attainment of a diverse student body] clearly is a constitutionally permissible goal for an institution of higher education."[81] The court in *Hopwood*, however, refused to accept Justice Powell's reasoning and ruled that diversity in a school's student body is not sufficient to justify racial classification. The *Hopwood* court pointed out that Justice Powell's argument in *Bakke* "garnered only his own vote and never represented the view of the majority" of the Supreme Court and is therefore not binding as precedent.[82] The *Hopwood* court concluded that diversity cannot be a compelling state interest to justify racial balancing; instead, "[d]iversity fosters, rather than minimizes the use of race. . . . It may further remedial purposes but, just as likely, may promote improper racial stereotypes, thus fueling racial hostility."[83]

Thus, even though the U.S. Supreme Court has not ruled directly on the issue, several precedents suggest that the purpose of maintaining a diverse student body cannot stand alone as a compelling state interest. For example, if racial and ethnic balance is used as a sole criterion to select students for a magnet school, then such racial balancing may be held unconstitutional.[84] The school district must prove that the justification is *narrowly tailored* to the special circumstances of the particular facts if the practice is to be permitted by a federal court.

■ INTERDISTRICT DESEGREGATION

Since school districts in the South are generally quite large geographically, most of the litigation has involved intradistrict desegregation. The courts found that much integration could be accomplished without going beyond the school district boundaries. Few instances are extant in which it has been necessary to question the boundaries of the basic school district unit in order to effectuate a unitary educational system. Some cases have, however, been initiated in the South when it appeared that the school district boundaries were actually being used to thwart effective desegregation.

In one such instance, a town in Virginia exercised its discretion under Virginia municipal law and withdrew from the county, forming an independent municipality.[85] At the time of withdrawal of municipal functions, the newly independent city decided to continue to operate the school system as a part of the overall county school system. Later, however, it was decided to also separate the independent city's school system from the countywide school district. This decision came about shortly after a federal district court had required a new desegregation plan for the entire county, replacing the older freedom-of-choice plan. The new reorganization resulted in an increase in the proportion of blacks in the county schools and a decrease in the city schools, although both systems retained a majority of blacks. The U.S. Supreme Court enjoined the reorganization, saying that the Court must look to the effect of such action on the segregation of the schools. When the effect is to exacerbate the problem of racial imbalance, the Court will frown on changing school district boundaries. The Supreme Court listed three factors supporting the conclusion under which such reorganizations may be judged constitutionally impermissible: (1) the likelihood of increased segregation, as white parents shifted their children to the new school district from private schools and the county system, was apparent; (2) the fact that the independent city schools in the state had traditionally been predominately white suggested that the same pattern might ensue here; and (3) the timing of the city's decision was psychologically poor, since it made it appear that the rationale for separating the school system was based on the lower court's prohibition of the use of a freedom-of-choice plan for the entire school system. Effectively, then, the Supreme Court said that where segregation is perpetuated as a result of *de jure* governmental action, the Court will not be deterred from intervening, even though the remedy goes beyond school district boundaries.[86]

In another decision rendered on the same day as the one just discussed, the Supreme Court refused to permit severance of Scotland Neck schools from those of surrounding Halifax County, North Carolina.[87] The Court reasoned that Scotland Neck's departure from the county school system was solely for purposes of segregation and that the effect of the action would be to weld the two systems into a segregated pattern, the new city district being predominately white and the county schools being basically black.

An entirely different situation was presented in the notable Richmond, Virginia, case.[88] Here a federal district court required the merger of three large and separate school districts to bring about desegregation. The Chesterfield County and Henrico County school districts are the suburban school districts surrounding Richmond, and as in most large urban areas, the city school district had become progressively segregated over the years as white families moved beyond the city limits. Effectively, the federal district judge's decision would have made one large administrative unit of the three systems, with a complex system of rezoning and busing among the school centers. On appeal, the U.S. Court of Appeals for the Fourth Circuit reversed the lower court decision, holding that there was no evidence to indicate that there was ever any state action taken to keep blacks confined to a particular school district. The court said:

This court believes that the root causes of the concentration of blacks in inner cities of America are simply not known and that the district court could not realistically place on the counties the responsibility for the effect that inner city decay has had on the public schools of Richmond. . . . The facts of this case do not show that state establishment and maintenance of school districts coterminous with the political subdivision of the city of Richmond and the counties of Chesterfield and Henrico have been intended to circumvent any federally protected right.[89]

In the review of this decision by the U.S. Supreme Court, eight justices were unable to render a decision, deadlocking four to four. Justice Powell had removed himself from the case because he had formerly been a member of the Richmond school board. Thus, the decision by the court of appeals stood.

A similar but more complicated situation arose in Michigan, where the school district pattern around Detroit was found by a lower federal district court to be so constituted as to create school segregation in the central city of Detroit.[90] Both the federal district court and the federal court of appeals concluded that desegregation of the Detroit schools was impossible unless the racial composition of the entire metropolitan area was taken into account. Dismantling of segregation therefore, according to these federal courts, required interdistrict busing between the Detroit core city and several suburban school districts. On appeal, the U.S. Supreme Court reversed the decision, holding that there was no evidence in the record to show that the original boundaries of the Detroit school district or any other school districts in Michigan were established for the purpose of segregation of the races.

Subsequent to the Supreme Court's decision in *Milliken*, the U.S. Court of Appeals for the Sixth Circuit upheld a federal district court decision that effectively merged the Louisville and Jefferson County, Kentucky, school districts.[91] The court did not depart from the *Milliken* rationale, but reached a different result because of the special circumstances that were attendant to the Louisville situation. The court found that there still remained vestiges of past *de jure* discrimination in the two large school districts, which was not true in *Milliken*. The court of appeals found the crucial difference between the Louisville and Detroit cases to lie in the fact that in the past, school district boundaries in Louisville had been ignored in order to segregate the schools. For example, it was shown that in pre-*Brown* days, black high school students in the Jefferson County school district were sent to Central High School, located in the Louisville school district. This was done because the Jefferson County system had no black high school. It was also shown that another city high school was actually located geographically in the county and students of both systems had attended school there. No such interplay was present or had ever transpired between the suburban school districts of Detroit and that of the central city. Further, school districts in Kentucky had been legally segregated in pre-*Brown* days and, as such, evinced a record of a segregated past that was not present in Michigan.

The Detroit and Louisville cases, although reaching different results, continued a consistent legal rationale enunciating a rule of law that states essentially that school district integration will be required, by busing or other means, either within or among school districts, where it can be shown that segregation is the result of governmental action that tends to create, maintain, or perpetuate segregation of the races. The rule applies to northern as well as to southern states. In the North, although schools were not segregated by statute before *Brown* in 1954, it is quite possible for subsequent governmental acts, whether patent or latent, to discriminate in such a way as to create patterns of racial imbalance in the schools. In such instances, the segregation will be viewed by the courts not as *de facto* but as *de jure* and therefore unconstitutional.

❖ — ❖ — ❖

Interdistrict Integration May Be an Improper Remedy to Overcome Single-District Segregation

Milliken v. Bradley

Supreme Court of the United States, 1974.
418 U.S. 717, 94 S.Ct. 3112.

Mr. Chief Justice BURGER delivered the opinion of the Court. We granted *certiorari* in these consolidated cases to determine whether a federal court may impose a multidistrict, areawide remedy to a single-district *de jure* segregation problem absent any finding that the other included school districts have failed to operate unitary school systems within their districts, absent any claim or finding that the boundary lines of any affected school district were established with the purpose of fostering racial segregation in public schools, absent any finding that the included districts committed acts which affected segregation within the other districts, and absent a meaningful opportunity for the included neighboring school districts to present evidence or be heard on the propriety of a multidistrict remedy or on the question of constitutional violations by those neighboring districts. . . . In *Brown v. Board of Education,* 349 U.S. 294, 75 S.Ct. 753, 99 L.Ed. 1083 (1955) (*Brown II*), the Court's first encounter with the problem of remedies in school desegregation cases, the Court noted:

> In fashioning and effectuating the decrees, the courts will be guided by equitable principles. Traditionally, equity has been characterized by a practical flexibility in shaping its remedies and by a facility for adjusting and reconciling public and private needs. Id., at 300, 75 S.Ct., at 756.

In further refining the remedial process, *Swann* held, the task is to correct, by a balancing of the individual and collective interests, "the condition that offends the Constitution." A federal remedial power may be exercised "only on the basis of a constitutional violation" and, "[a]s with any equity case, the nature of the violation determines the scope of the remedy." 402 U.S., at 16, 91 S.Ct., at 1276.

Proceeding from these basic principles, we first note that in the District Court the complainants sought a remedy aimed at the *condition* alleged to offend the Constitution—the segregation within the Detroit City School District. . . .

Viewing the record as a whole, it seems clear that the District Court and the Court of Appeals shifted the primary focus from a Detroit remedy to the metropolitan area only because of their conclusion that total desegregation of Detroit would not produce the racial balance which they perceived as desirable. Both courts proceeded on an assumption that the Detroit schools could not be truly desegregated—in their view of what constituted desegregation—unless the racial composition of the student body of each school substantially reflected the racial composition of the population of the metropolitan area as a whole. The metropolitan area was then defined as Detroit plus fifty-three of the outlying school districts. . . .

The Michigan educational structure involved in this case, in common with most States, provides for a large measure of local control, and a review of the scope and character of these local powers indicates the extent to which the interdistrict remedy approved by the two courts could disrupt and alter the structure of public education in Michigan. The metropolitan remedy would require, in effect, consolidation of fifty-four independent school districts historically administered as separate units into a vast new super school district. Entirely apart from the logistical and other serious problems attending large-scale transportation of students, the consolidation would give rise to an array of other problems in financing and operating this new school system. Some of the more obvious questions would be: What would be the status and authority of the present popularly elected school boards? Would the children of Detroit be within the jurisdiction and operating control of a school board elected by the parents and residents of other districts? What board or boards would levy taxes for school operations in these fifty-four districts constituting the consolidated metropolitan area? What provisions could be made for assuring substantial equality in tax levies among the fifty-four districts, if this were deemed requisite? What provisions would be made for financing? Would the validity of long-term bonds be jeopardized unless approved by all of the component districts as well as the State? What body would determine that portion of the curricula now left to the discretion of local school boards? Who would establish attendance zones, purchase school equipment, locate and construct new schools, and indeed attend to all the myriad day-to-day decisions that are necessary to school operations affecting potentially more than three-quarters of a million pupils?

It may be suggested that all of these vital operational problems are yet to be resolved by the District Court, and that this is the purpose of the Court of Appeals' proposed remand. But it is obvious from the scope of the interdistrict remedy itself that absent a complete restructuring of the laws of Michigan relating to school districts, the District Court will become first, a *de facto* "legislative authority" to resolve these complex questions, and then the "school superintendent" for the entire area. This is a task which few, if any, judges are qualified to perform and one which would deprive the people of control of schools through their elected representatives.

Of course, no state law is above the Constitution. School district lines and the present laws with respect to local control are not sacrosanct and if they conflict with the Fourteenth Amendment federal courts have a duty to prescribe appropriate remedies. . . . But our prior holdings have been confined to violations and remedies within a single school district. We therefore turn to address, for the first time, the validity of a remedy mandating cross-district or interdistrict consolidation to remedy a condition of segregation found to exist in only one district.

The controlling principle consistently expounded in our holdings is that the scope of the remedy is determined by the nature and extent of the constitutional violation. Before the boundaries of separate and autonomous school districts may be set aside by consolidating the separate units for remedial purposes or by imposing a cross-district remedy, it must first be shown that there has been a constitutional violation within one district that produces a significant segregative effect in another district. Specifically, it must be shown that racially discriminatory acts of the state or local school districts, or of a single school district, have been a substantial cause of interdistrict segregation. Thus an interdistrict remedy might be in order where the racially discriminatory acts of one or more school districts caused racial segregation in an adjacent district, or where district lines have been deliberately drawn on the basis of race. In such circumstances an interdistrict remedy would be appropriate to eliminate the interdistrict segregation directly caused by the constitutional violation. Conversely, without an interdistrict violation and interdistrict effect, there is no constitutional wrong calling for an interdistrict remedy.

The record before us, voluminous as it is, contains evidence of *de jure* segregated conditions only in the Detroit schools; indeed, that was the theory on which the litigation was initially based and on which the District Court took evidence. With no showing of significant violation by the fifty-three outlying school districts and no evidence of any interdistrict violation or effect, the court went beyond the original theory of the case as framed by the pleadings and mandated a metropolitan area remedy. To approve the remedy ordered by the court would impose on the outlying districts, not shown to have committed any constitutional violation, a wholly impermissible remedy based on a standard not hinted at in *Brown I* and *II* or any holding of this Court. . . .

The constitutional right of the Negro respondents residing in Detroit is to attend a unitary school system in that district. Unless petitioners drew the district lines in a discriminatory fashion, or arranged for white students residing in the Detroit district to attend schools in Oakland and Macomb Counties, they were under no constitutional duty to make provisions for Negro students to do so. . . .

. . . The boundaries of the Detroit School District, which are coterminous with the boundaries of the city of Detroit, were established over a century ago by neutral legislation when the city was incorporated; there is no evidence in the record, nor is there any suggestion by the respondents, that either the original boundaries of the Detroit School District, or any other school district in Michigan, were established for the purpose of creating, maintaining, or perpetuating segregation of races. There is no claim and there is no evidence hinting that petitioner outlying school districts and their predecessors, or the thirty-odd other school districts in the tri-county area—but outside the District Court's "desegregation area"—have ever maintained or operated anything but unitary school systems. Unitary school systems have been required for more than a century by the Michigan Constitution as implemented by state law. Where the schools of only one district have been affected,

there is no constitutional power in the courts to decree relief balancing the racial composition of that district's schools with those of the surrounding districts. . . .

We conclude that the relief ordered by the District Court and affirmed by the Court of Appeals was based upon an erroneous standard and was unsupported by record evidence that acts of the outlying districts effected the discrimination found to exist in the schools of Detroit. Accordingly, the judgment of the Court of Appeals is reversed and the case is remanded for further proceedings consistent with this opinion leading to prompt formulation of a decree directed to eliminating the segregation found to exist in Detroit city schools, a remedy which has been delayed since 1970.

Reversed and remanded.

CASE NOTE

In a suit seeking desegregation of the Indianapolis public schools, the litigation followed a course similar to that of *Milliken*. In its first opinion, the district court held that the Indianapolis city public schools were *de jure* segregated; the court of appeals affirmed, and the U.S. Supreme Court denied *certiorari*. *United States v. Board of School Commissioners*, 332 F.Supp. 655 (S.D.Ind.1971), affirmed, 474 F.2d 81 (7th Cir.), cert. denied, 413 U.S. 920, 93 S.Ct. 3066 (1973). In subsequent proceedings to select a remedy, the district court concluded that Indianapolis-only desegregation plans were inadequate and ordered the preparation of a metropolitan desegregation plan. 368 F.Supp. 1191 (S.D.Ind.1973). In 1969, after the filing of the suit, the Indiana legislature enacted a law consolidating the governments of Indianapolis and surrounding Marion County, but specifically excluding the area school districts from consolidation. The Court of Appeals for the Seventh Circuit vacated those portions of the district court's opinion ordering a metropolitan remedy, citing *Milliken*, 503 F.2d 68 (7th Cir.1974).

■ TITLE VI AND *BAKKE*

Title VI was passed in accordance with the constitutional authority vested in the Congress by Section 5 of the Fourteenth Amendment, which provides that Congress may pass legislation to enforce the Fourteenth Amendment. Although Title VI and Title VII of the Civil Rights Act of 1964 have the same prohibitory scope, they were enacted under different constitutional powers of Congress: Title VI under Section 5 of the Fourteenth Amendment and Title VII under the commerce clause. Title VI prohibits discrimination based on race, color, or national origin in federally assisted programs. Section 601 of Title VI of the Civil Rights Act reads as follows:

> No person in the United States shall, on the ground of race, color, or national origin, be excluded from participation in, be denied benefits of, or be subjected to discrimination under any program or activity receiving Federal financial assistance.

With Title VI, Congress provided a statutory remedy against discrimination apart from and beyond equal protection. The ultimate enforcement weapon given the federal agencies under this law is the denial of federal funds. It was under Title VI that *Adams v. Richardson*[92] originated, maintaining that the U.S. Department of Health, Education, and Welfare had been derelict in its enforcement responsibilities and that federal funds could be withheld from institutions of higher education that discriminated based on race. In that case, a federal court assumed responsibility for monitoring the enforcement of the federal regulation promulgated by the department pursuant to Title VI. The Title VI regulation requires desegregation of faculty, administration, and other personnel positions in public schools and universities.

The Supreme Court has exhibited some uncertainty as to the application of Title VI. The problem lies in whether officials are required to redress *de jure* segregation only or whether they have a corresponding statutory obligation to correct racial imbalance caused by *de facto* segregation as well. In the *Bakke* case, Justice Powell, writing for a splintered majority, said that Title VI requirements are coterminous with those of the equal protection clause and that neither requires school officials to correct unintended racial imbalances.[93] It is important to note that the Supreme Court in *Bakke* ruled only that Title VI was violated by discriminatory admissions policies. Justice Powell pointed out that the

precedents under equal protection from the school desegregation cases were not relevant to *Bakke* because they involved remedies designed to redress specific constitutional violations pertaining to race. Title VII of the Civil Rights Act did not apply because it covers employment discrimination and precedents pertaining to the employment of racial minorities in business and industry are not applicable to institutional admissions policies. Thus, equal protection, Title VI, and Title VII apply in different ways to protect against discriminatory educational and employment practices. On the other hand, four justices, while agreeing with Powell's general disposition of the case, disagreed with his interpretation of Title VI, maintaining that the congressional aim was to prohibit discrimination, regardless of intent. Writing for these four justices, Justice Stevens said that "the meaning of the Title VI ban on exclusion is crystal clear. Race cannot be the basis of excluding anyone from participation in a federally funded program." He further maintained that it was not necessary to liken Title VI to the equal protection clause, since Title VI emanated from its own legislative intent and history. But the Court in *Bakke* did clearly decide that a higher education institution's admissions policy that uses strict racial preferences violates Title VI, but that an admissions program that allows admissions officers to consider race as an affirmative factor without using quotas or clear racial preferences is not violative of either Title VI or the equal protection clause.

■ ENDNOTES

1. 163 U.S. 537, 16 S.Ct. 1138 (1896).
2. J. R. Pole, *The Pursuit of Equality in American History* (Berkeley: University of California Press, 1978), p. 287.
3. Roberts v. City of Boston, 59 Mass. (5 Cush.) 198 (1849).
4. Ibid.
5. See Jethro K. Lieberman, *Milestones, 200 Years of American Law* (New York: Oxford University Press; and St. Paul, Minn.: West, 1976), pp. 256–57; Richard Kluger, *Simple Justice* (New York: Vintage Books, 1977), pp. 77–78.
6. Louisville, New Orleans and Texas Railway Co. v. Mississippi, 133 U.S. 587, 10 S.Ct. 348 (1890).
7. Lieberman, *Milestones*, p. 260.
8. Regents of the University of California v. Bakke, 438 U.S. 265, 98 S.Ct. 2733 (1978).
9. 163 U.S. 537, 16 S.Ct. 1138 (1896).

10. Ibid.

11. Ibid.

12. 175 U.S. 528, 20 S.Ct. 197 (1899).

13. 211 U.S. 45, 29 S.Ct. 33 (1908).

14. See Kern Alexander and Erwin Solomon, *College and University Law* (Charlottesville, Va.: Michie Co., 1972), p. 518.

15. Berea College v. Kentucky, op. cit.

16. 275 U.S. 78, 48 S.Ct. 91 (1927).

17. 305 U.S. 337, 59 S.Ct. 232 (1938).

18. Sweatt v. Painter, 339 U.S. 629, 70 S.Ct. 848 (1950).

19. Ibid.

20. Ibid.

21. McLaurin v. Oklahoma State Regents for Higher Education, 339 U.S. 637, 70 S.Ct. 851 (1950).

22. Brown v. Board of Education, 98 F.Supp. 797 (D.Kan.1951), judgment reversed, 349 U.S. 294, 75 S.Ct. 753 (1955); Briggs v. Elliott, 98 F.Supp. 529 (E.D.S.C.1951); Davis v. County School Board, 103 F.Supp. 337 (E.D.Va.1952); Belton v. Gebhart, 32 Del.Ch. 343, 87 A.2d 862 (1952); Bolling v. Sharpe.

23. Loren Miller, "The Petitioners," in Harold W. Horowitz and Kenneth L. Karst, eds., *Law, Lawyers and Social Change* (Indianapolis, Ind.: Bobbs-Merrill, 1969), pp. 181–82.

24. Ibid.

25. Harry S. Ashmore, *The Negro and the Schools* (Chapel Hill: University of North Carolina Press, 1954), pp. 42–43.

26. Lieberman, *Milestones*, p. 276.

27. Brown v. Board of Education, 347 U.S. 483, 74 S.Ct. 686 (1954).

28. Louis H. Pollak, *The Constitution and the Supreme Court, A Documentary History*, vol. II (Cleveland: The World Publishing Company, 1966), p. 266.

29. Brown v. Board of Education of Topeka, 349 U.S. 294, 75 S.Ct. 753 (1955) (*Brown II*).

30. Ibid.

31. Cooper v. Aaron, 358 U.S. 1, 78 S.Ct. 1401 (1958).

32. Ibid.

33. Ibid.

34. Griffin v. County School Board of Prince Edward County, 377 U.S. 218, 84 S.Ct. 1226 (1964).

35. Briggs v. Elliott, 132 F.Supp. 776 (E.D.S.C.1955).

36. Bell v. School City of Gary, 324 F.2d 209 (7th Cir.1963), cert. denied, 377 U.S. 924, 84 S.Ct. 1223 (1964); Deal v. Cincinnati Board of Education, 369 F.2d 55 (6th Cir.1966), cert. denied, 389 U.S. 847, 88 S.Ct. 39 (1967).

37. United States v. Jefferson County Board of Education, 372 F.2d 836 (5th Cir.1966).

38. Green v. County School Board of New Kent County, Virginia, 391 U.S. 430, 88 S.Ct. 1689 (1968).

39. Alexander v. Holmes County Board of Education, 396 U.S. 19, 90 S.Ct. 29 (1969), rehearing denied, 396 U.S. 976, 90 S.Ct. 437 (1969).

40. Bell v. School City of Gary, *op cit.*

41. Keyes v. School District No. 1, Denver, 413 U.S. 189, 93 S.Ct. 2686 (1973).

42. Swann v. Charlotte-Mecklenberg Board of Education, 402 U.S. 1, 91 S.Ct. 1267 (1971).

43. Regents of the University of California v. Bakke, 438 U.S. 265, 98 S.Ct. 2733 (1978).

44. Ibid.

45. Washington v. Davis, 426 U.S. 229, 96 S.Ct. 2040 (1976).

46. Of course, in the original *de jure* cases, the burden shifted to the state automatically because the segregation was enforced by statute.

47. Green v. County School Board, op cit.

48. Columbus Board of Education v. Penick, 443 U.S. 449, 99 S.Ct. 2941 (1979).

49. Alexander v. Holmes County Board of Education, op. cit.

50. 57 F.Supp.2d 228 (W.D.N.C.1999).

51. Green v. County School Board, 391 U.S. at 437–38, 88 S.Ct. at 1694.

52. Board of Education v. Dowell, 498 U.S. 237, 111 S.Ct. 630 (1991).

53. United States v. Overton, 834 F.2d 1171 (5th Cir.1987); Riddick v. School Board, 784 F.2d 521 (4th Cir.1986); Vaughns v. Board of Education, 758 F.2d 983 (4th Cir.1985).

54. Georgia State Conference Branches of NAACP v. Georgia, 775 F.2d 1403 (11th Cir.1985).

55. Capacchione v. Charlotte-Mecklenburg Schools, op. cit.

56. Green v. County School Board, op. cit.

57. Ibid.

58. 503 U.S. 467, 112 S.Ct. 1430 (1992).

59. Milliken v. Bradley, 433 U.S. 267, 287–88 (1977).

60. Missouri v. Jenkins, 495 U.S. 33, 110 S.Ct. 1651 (1990).

61. See Charles J. Russo and Lawrence F. Rossow, "Missouri v. Jenkins: The Desegregation Battle Continues," 62 Educ.L.Rep. 399 (November 22, 1990).

62. Stell v. Savannah-Chatham County Board of Education, 888 F.2d 82 (11th Cir.1989).

63. Ibid.

64. 515 U.S. 70, 115 S.Ct. 2038 (1995).

65. Ibid.

66. Regents of the University of California v. Bakke, 438 U.S. 265, 98 S.Ct. 2733 (1978).

67. Hirabayashi v. United States, 320 U.S. 81, 63 S.Ct. 1375 (1943).

68. Regents of the University of California v. Bakke, op. cit.

69. Adarand Constructors, Inc. v. Pena, 515 U.S. 200, 115 S.Ct. 2097 (1995).

70. City of Richmond v. J. A. Croson Co., 488 U.S. 469, 109 S.Ct. 706 (1989).

71. Adarand Constructors, Inc. v. Pena, op. cit.

72. Ibid.

73. 503 U.S. 467, 112 S.Ct. 1430 (1992).

74. Tuttle v. Arlington County School Board, 195 F.3d 698 (4th Cir.1999).

75. United States v. Paradise, 480 U.S. 149, 107 S.Ct. 1053 (1987).

76. Tuttle v. Arlington County School Board, 195 F.3d 698 (4th Cir.1999).

77. Eisenberg v. Montgomery County Public Schools, 197 F.3d 123 (4th Cir.1999).

78. Hopwood v. Texas, 78 F.3d 932 (5th Cir.1996).

79. Regents of the University of California v. Bakke, 438 U.S. at 313, 98 S.Ct. at 2733.

80. Tuttle v. Arlington County School Board, op. cit.

81. Regents of the University of California v. Bakke, 438 U.S. at 311, 98 S.Ct. at 2759.

82. Hopwood v. Texas, 78 F.3d at 944.

83. Ibid., p. 945.

84. Eisenberg v. Montgomery County Public Schools, 197 F.3d 123 (4th Cir.1999).

85. Wright v. Council of the City of Emporia, 407 U.S. 451, 92 S.Ct. 2196 (1972).

86. See also Lee v. Macon County Board of Education, 448 F.2d 746 (5th Cir.1971); Stout v. Jefferson County Board of Education, 448 F.2d 403 (5th Cir.1971); Haney v. County Board of Education, 410 F.2d 920 (8th Cir.1969).

87. United States v. Scotland Neck City Board of Education, 407 U.S. 484, 92 S.Ct. 2214 (1972).

88. Bradley v. Richmond School Board, 456 F.2d 6 (4th Cir.1972); 416 U.S. 696, 94 S.Ct. 2006 (1974).

89. Bradley v. Richmond School Board, 456 F.2d 6 (4th Cir. 1972).

90. Milliken v. Bradley, 418 U.S. 717, 94 S.Ct. 3112 (1974).

91. Newburg Area Council, Inc. v. Gordon, 521 F.2d 578 (6th Cir.1975); Newburg Area Council, Inc. v. Board of Education, 510 F.2d 1358 (6th Cir.1974).

92. 480 F.2d 1159 (D.C.Cir.1973).

93. Regents of the University of California v. Bakke, 438 U.S. 265, 98 S.Ct. 2733 (1978).

CHAPTER 11

TORTS

What usually is done may be evidence of what ought to be done, but what ought to be done is fixed by a standard of reasonable prudence, whether it usually is complied with or not.

—Oliver Wendell Holmes Jr.

CHAPTER OUTLINE

- DEFINITION OF A TORT
- INTENTIONAL INTERFERENCE
- STRICT LIABILITY
- NEGLIGENCE

- ELEMENTS OF NEGLIGENCE
- DEFENSES FOR NEGLIGENCE
- EDUCATIONAL MALPRACTICE

HUMAN BEINGS bind themselves together in civil society for mutual advantage and protection that would not otherwise be afforded if they were left to fend for themselves in a state of nature. Seavey et al. have explained that "[a] primary purpose of primitive law was to preserve the peace and to prevent the use of force by one person against another or another's possession of property."[1] The law today prescribes a standard of conduct that has its foundations in acceptable tradition and custom that ensure personal rights against invasion by others, whether as individual groups or as governments. As our society has become more complex in this technological age with ever-increasing human and corporate interactions, the possibility of suffering injury at the hand of another has increased exponentially. Plucknett earlier observed these increasing social complexities and their impact on the law, noting that "the rapid prominence and growth of the law of torts in the last few generations is clearly associated with the sudden mechanism of contemporary life, and with the growth of large and wealthy businesses (necessarily carried on through fallible servants and agents) engaged in finance, insurance, transport and an endless variety of enterprises which are productive of torts and tort litigation."[2] To this list may be added education, the importance of which to society engenders increasing human interactions, some of which may result in various transgressions and injuries leading to litigious controversies.

Modern law acknowledges for each individual certain personal rights with regard to conduct that others must respect, and it prescribes a level of conduct by which each individual must in turn abide. Some of these rights arise through the execution of a contract between individuals, for breach of which financial liability may result. The law also grants to each individual certain personal rights not of a contractual nature, such as freedom from personal injury and security of life, liberty, and property. The law imposes corresponding duties and responsibilities on each individual to respect the rights of others. If, by speech, act, or other conduct, a person fails to respect these rights, thereby damaging another, a tort has been committed, and the offending party may be held liable.

■ DEFINITION OF A TORT

A tort is a civil wrong independent of contract. It may be malicious and intentional, or it may be the result of negligence and disregard for the rights of others.

Keeton et al. define a tort as a "civil wrong, other than for breach of contract, for which the court will provide a remedy in the form of an action for damages."[3] Perhaps the best and most concise definition is cited in Keeton et al.: "A tort is an act or omission which unlawfully violates a person's right created by the law, and for which the appropriate remedy is a common law action for damage by the injured person."[4] The central idea that best defines a tort is the standard of reasonableness in actions toward others; therefore, an unreasonable interference with the interests of others that causes injury is a tort.[5]

An action in tort compensates private individuals for harm caused to them by the unreasonable conduct of others. Social norms have provided the basis for legal precedent in the determination of that which is considered unacceptable or unreasonable conduct.

A legally proper relationship between two persons can be breached by injury caused by an act or an omission to act on the part of either party. The word "tort" is derived from the Latin word *tortus*, or "twisted."[6] In personal relationships, the term "twisted" is applied to activity that deviates from a normally acceptable pattern of behavior.

A tort is different from a crime and emanates from a separate and distinct body of law. A civil action for tort is initiated and maintained by the injured party for the purpose of obtaining compensation for the injury suffered, whereas in a criminal proceeding the action is brought by the state to protect the public from actions of a wrongdoer. In a criminal case, the state prosecutes not to compensate the injured person but rather to protect the public from further wrongful acts. Since criminal law does not, and was never intended to, compensate an injured individual, social justice demanded the birth of the action in tort.

Grounds for actions in tort can be divided into three categories: (1) intentional interference, (2) strict liability, and (3) negligence. Each of these can, at times, be applied to cases in public schools where pupils are injured.

■ INTENTIONAL INTERFERENCE

An intentional tort may result from an intended act, whether accompanied by enmity, antagonism, or maliciousness or by no more than a good-natured practical joke.[7] With this type of tort, it is not necessary for the wrongdoer to be hostile or desire to do harm to the injured party. Even when a person does not plan to injure another but proceeds intentionally to act in a way that invades the rights of another, he or she commits an intentional tort.

According to the *Restatement (Second) of Torts*, "intent" has reference to the consequences of an act rather than to the act itself.[8] Intent is, however, not limited to consequences that are desired. If the actor knows that the consequences are certain, or substantially certain, to result from an act and still goes ahead, he or she is treated by the law as if he or she had, in fact, desired to produce the result.[9] If the results are less certain or if what was originally intended becomes less direct, then intent is less certain and tends to be shaded toward recklessness. If the likelihood that the act will produce the intended result decreases even further, then the tort may emerge as one of ordinary negligence instead of one of intentional interference.[10]

The following statements illustrate the difference between an intentional interference and reckless or negligent conduct:

■ A throws a bomb into B's office for the purpose of killing B. A knows that C, B's stenographer, is in the office. A has no desire to injure C but knows that his act is substantially certain to do so. C is injured by the explosion. A is subject to liability to C for an intentional tort.

- On a curve in a narrow highway, A, without any desire to injure B or belief that he is substantially certain to do so, recklessly drives his automobile in an attempt to pass B's car. As a result of this recklessness, A crashes into B's car, injuring B. A is subject to liability to B for his reckless conduct but is not liable to B for an intentional tort.

Thus, for intent to exist, the activity of an individual must, with substantial certainty, be the result of his or her act. If one does not know with substantial certainty the result of an act and injury results, then it is negligence instead of an intentional tort.

ASSAULT

An intentional tort can be committed even if no physical "touching" takes place. Assault and battery are classified as intentional torts. Keeton et al. say that "[a]ssault and battery go together like ham and eggs." The difference between them is the difference between physical contact and the mere apprehension of it. One may exist without the other.[11] Assault, as distinguished from battery, constitutes essentially a mental rather than a physical violation. Assault may result in damages for fright, humiliation, emotional distress, and/or physical illness. Mental distress inflicted intentionally may be of such nature as to justify recovery of damages.[12]

To have assault, there must be an "overt act or an attempt, or the unequivocal appearance of an attempt, to do some immediate physical injury to the person of another." The overt act must be a display of force or menace of violence of such a nature as to cause reasonable apprehension of immediate bodily harm.[13] It is assault when a person stands within striking distance of another and with sword drawn says, "I intend to run you through." Such words and acts may be sufficient to put the plaintiff in immediate apprehension of imminent harm, and it is apparent that the offender has the present ability to effectuate the harm. Thus, an intentional tort can be consummated by an act that, while not involving physical contact, places a person in immediate fear that such action will transpire.

BATTERY

Technically, battery is an intentional tort that comes about through physical contact. It is a battery to injure a man in his sleep, even though he does not discover the injury until later, while it is an assault to shoot at him while he is awake and to frighten but miss him.[14] In both cases, a person's interests are invaded. If a wrongdoer swings a bottle, intending to strike the plaintiff, and the plaintiff sees the movement and is apprehensive for his own safety, there is assault; if the attack is consummated and the blow is actually landed, both assault and battery are present.

Teachers accused of assault and battery for administering corporal punishment are usually given considerable leeway as to the reasonableness of their action. In one case, the court explained the rule of law: "To be guilty of an assault and battery, the teacher must not only inflict on the child immoderate chastisement, but he must do so with legal malice or wicked motives or he must inflict some permanent injury."[15]

Cases involving assault and battery by a teacher usually result from a teacher's attempt to discipline a child. The courts generally allow wide latitude for teachers in chastisement of pupils, presuming that the teacher is innocent, has acted reasonably, and has done his or her duty until the contrary is proved.

The courts still uphold the ancient doctrine of *in loco parentis*, which holds that the teacher stands in place of the parent and in such capacity has the right to chastise a pupil. The teacher's prerogatives are, of course, limited to the jurisdiction of the school and are not unlimited. Within these boundaries, the teacher may require pupils to abide by all reasonable commands and may inflict reasonable corporal punishment to enforce compliance. One court stated the situation in this manner:

> In the school, as in the family, there exists on the part of the pupils the obligations of obedience to lawful commands, subordination, civil deportment, respect for the right of other pupils, and fidelity to duty. Those obligations are inherent in any proper school system, and constitute, so to speak, the common law of the school.[16]

Courts do, however, make it quite clear that a teacher may be guilty of assault and battery if chastisement is cruel, brutal,[17] or excessive[18] or is administered in anger or insolence.[19] In one interesting old case, the court said that a teacher was not justified in beating a scholar so severely as to wear out two whips, strike two blows to the head with fists, and kick the scholar in the face, all because he misspelled a word and refused to try again.[20]

Chastisement of a pupil may become assault and battery if the teacher does not administer the punishment reasonably.[21] Criteria used by courts to identify excessive punishment include

- proper and suitable weapon,
- part of the person to which it is applied,
- manner and extent of the chastisement,
- nature and gravity of the offense,
- age of the pupil,
- temper and deportment of the teacher,[22] and
- history of the pupil's previous conduct.

Both assault and battery may be criminal wrongs as well as torts where statutes so require. Criminal statutes usually define assault as attempted battery, requiring present ability. However, the reasoning pertaining to individual statutes may or may not have application to tort law.

INTERFERENCE WITH PEACE OF MIND

In keeping with the theory that every person who is injured should have recompense, modern courts have had a tendency to recognize, as a separate tort, interference with peace of mind, the infliction of mental or emotional anguish. In such cases, it is necessary and quite difficult to prove mental suffering. The courts have been unable to precisely delineate between actual tortious actions and what may be considered everyday rough language or immoderate personal behavior that hurts one's feelings yet is not so severe as to create an action in tort. One cannot recover damages simply because of hurt feelings.[23]

Courts have held that where an act is malicious, as distinguished from being merely negligent, there may be recovery for mental anguish, even though no physical injury results.[24] However, cases involving actions for mental anguish and suffering are easier to prove before a jury if the emotional distress has produced some visible or identifiable physical harm.

Another intentional tort is false imprisonment, sometimes called false arrest. Relatively few cases have occurred in this area, but the general rule is that an unauthorized person cannot detain or physically restrain the movements of another. This type of tort is not applicable to the situation in which a teacher confines a child in his or her classroom, since a teacher is charged with overseeing pupil activities in the school setting and is authorized to confine a pupil, if necessary, in order to discipline him or her.

❖ — ❖ — ❖

School District Liable in Damages for Intentional Act of Teacher Resulting in Emotional Harm to Child

Spears v. Jefferson Parish School Board

Court of Appeals of Louisiana,
Fifth Circuit, 1994.
646 So.2d 1104.

GOTHARD, Judge.

This appeal arises out of an action filed by the plaintiffs, Joyce and Samuel Spears individually and on behalf of their minor son, Justin, for injuries sustained while Justin was a kindergarten *Fact* student at Woodland West Elementary School, a part of the Jefferson Parish School System. Liability of the defendant was established by a joint stipulation of the parties, and the matter went to trial on the issue of quantum. In due course the trial court rendered judgment, accompanied by written reasons, in favor of the plaintiffs. *Holding*

On February 28, 1989, Justin Spears was a kindergarten student at Woodland West Elementary School. Because it was a rainy day, the students were seated on the floor of the Cafeteria watching a movie during their regularly scheduled Physical Education class under the supervision of Coach John Brooks and Coach Johnny *Fact* Peyton. Justin and two of his friends began to be slightly disruptive. At that time Coach Brooks called the boys over to sit near him. The boys began to play with his hair and his ears. Coach Brooks told the boys that if they did not stop annoying him he would "kill them." Because the coach was experiencing management problems with the three boys, he took two of them into an adjacent office with him while he did some paperwork, leaving the rest of the class to watch the movie. Justin stayed behind talking to Coach Peyton. The boys began asking Coach Brooks how he would kill them. Coach Brooks told them he would probably tie the jump rope around their neck and push them off a chair in the office. Because Justin was talking to Coach Peyton during this discussion, Coach Brooks asked the boys if they wanted to play a trick on Justin, and they agreed.

The testimony differs as to the events that followed, but it is clear that Coach Brooks led Justin to believe that his friends were dead. He told Justin he had hanged them by their neck with the jump rope, and at least one of the boys was lying on the floor pretending to be dead. When Justin saw the boy lying there he became upset and began to cry. Coach Brooks told Justin it was just a joke and that the boys were not really dead.

Plaintiffs introduced live testimony from Justin and both of his parents. They also introduced depositions from two psychologists who treated Justin. According to the evidence, Justin was a normal, well-adjusted five-year-old before the incident. However, in the weeks following the incident he began to exhibit infantile behavior. He refused to go to the bathroom alone and refused to wipe himself. He was afraid that Coach Brooks would come out of the mirror in the bathroom and harm him. Justin would no longer sleep in his own room. He became overly dependent on his mother and was not comfortable when she was out of sight.

Justin was treated by Dr. Lynne Shwery, a psychologist at Children's Hospital. Dr. Shwery testified at her deposition that she treated Justin from the time of the incident until he moved with his family to Virginia in June, 1991. She opined that Justin had "experienced an event that was outside the range of usual human experience and that would be markedly distressing to almost anyone." She diagnosed Justin as having Post-Traumatic Stress Disorder and explained that Justin was fearful and anxious. He had come to the realization that the

world was not a safe place and that all adults could not be trusted.

From the time of the family's relocation to Virginia in 1991, Justin was treated by Dr. Tonya Fridy; that treatment was still ongoing at the time of trial. Dr. Fridy's professional diagnosis concurred with that of Dr. Shwery. Additionally, Dr. Fridy stated that Justin had separation anxiety and social phobia disorder and would probably need three to five more years of therapy.

The defendant offered testimony from their own expert, Dr. Vincent Carbone. He conducted an evaluation of Justin and concluded that Justin was "a very anxious child who was very fearful of things in his environment," but Dr. Carbone did not agree that Justin was suffering from Post-Traumatic Stress Disorder.

After considering all of the evidence, the trial court rendered judgment in favor of plaintiff, accompanied by written reasons which included the finding that "this child has been effectively robbed of a normal, carefree childhood due to the careless actions of the coach."

In brief to this court the defendant assigns nine errors which can be placed into three arguments. First, it is argued that the trial court erred in its findings of fact concerning the magnitude of Justin's injuries, and thus the award of damages is excessive. Second, it is argued that the award of loss of consortium to the parents is incorrect. The final argument concerns an evidentiary ruling on the defendant's assertion that Justin's parents failed to mitigate the damages....

Given the circumstances of this case and the standard of review mandated by the Supreme Court, we do not find the trial court's award of general damages in the amount of $100,000.00 to Justin was an abuse of discretion. For the same reasons we cannot find that the award of $2,160.00 for future therapy was an abuse of discretion. Therefore, we will not overturn those portions of the judgment.

The defendant also complains of the award of $5,000.00 each to Justin's parents for loss of consortium....

Loss of consortium in the context of the parent/child relationship means loss of the aid, assistance and companionship of the child, or loss of affection, society and service.... It is clear from the record that the incident adversely affected the relationship between Justin and his parents. The child, who was developing normally before the incident, became a behavior problem as a direct result of defendant's actions. Injuries incurred by the child rendered the family life difficult afterward since Justin no longer wished to go on family outings. Consequently, we do not find error in the award on loss of consortium damages to the parents. . . .

For the foregoing reasons the judgment of the trial court is affirmed. Costs are assessed to the appellant.

AFFIRMED.

■ STRICT LIABILITY

Generally, liability for tort has been imposed with regard to "fault" on the part of the defendant. Both intentional interference and negligence are based on the supposition that someone was injured at the fault of another party. However, cases have arisen in which a person has been injured through no actual, identifiable fault of anyone. Such cases have forced some courts to hand down damage awards based on strict liability of the defendant. In these instances, a person may be liable even though he or she is not strictly at fault for the other party's injury. This rule was adopted in order to place the damages on the person best able to bear the burden. In these cases, the defendant's acts are not so important as the injury and suffering of the injured person. Underlying this type of decision is the older social justice reasoning requiring that "he who breaks must pay," regardless of whether the injury is knowingly or negligently caused.[25]

Therefore, strict liability is often referred to as liability without fault. Strict liability means "liability that is imposed on an actor apart from either (1) an intent to interfere with a legally protected interest without legal justification for doing so, or (2) a breach of a duty to exercise reasonable care, i.e., actionable negligence."[26] Strict liability arises as a result of the abnormal danger[27] of the activity itself and the risk that it creates to those in its vicinity.[28]

To determine whether an activity is ultrahazardous or "abnormally dangerous" requires asking "whether the risk created is so unusual, either because of its magnitude or because of the circumstances surrounding it, as to justify the imposition of strict liability for the harm that results from it, even though it is carried on with reasonable care."[29] The *Restatement (Second) of Torts* has set out six factors for determining whether an activity is abnormally dangerous: "a) existence of a high degree of risk of some harm to the person, land or chattels of others; b) likelihood that the harm that results from it will be great; c) inability to eliminate the risk by the exercise of reasonable care; d) extent to which the activity is not a matter of common usage; e) inappropriateness of the activity to the place where it is carried on; and f) extent to which its value to the community is outweighed by its dangerous attributes."[30] All of these factors are important in consideration, but not all are required, and one is not particularly more important than the others.[31]

The keeping of dangerous animals in domestic situations has historically been a source of strict liability litigation. Prosser observes that "[t]he keeper of a wild or abnormally dangerous domestic animal is subject to strict liability even in the absence of his negligence in its custody because by keeping it he introduces into the locality a danger that is not only uncommon but also unnecessary to satisfy any social purpose."[32] The prevailing view is that both licensees and invitees are entitled to recovery if in coming onto another property they are exposed to an abnormally dangerous animal.[33] The *Restatement (Second) of Torts* gives several illustrations of situations involving animals that could possibly be related to schools. Take the following situations as examples:

■ A keeps on his premises a tame bear so chained as to make it highly improbable that it will escape. A permits B, a student, to walk through his premises. While B is walking along a path in the vicinity of which the bear is chained, the bear is so infuriated by the teasing of other uninvolved students who have trespassed on A's land that it pulls up the stake by which it is confined and attacks B. A is subject to liability to B.[34]

■ A keeps in his home, effectively chained, a fighting pit bull dog which is extremely fierce. B, a student and a friend of A, unreasonably believing that the dog would not attack persons familiar to it, unchains it and takes it to school, whereupon the dog attacks C. A is subject to liability to C.[35]

An incident quite similar to the latter situation did occur, in an Ohio case in 1992, but the injured student sued the school district for negligence, claiming that the school district rather than the owner of the dog had breached its duty to protect the students. The court held that the school district was not liable because the school's common law duty of care did not require constant supervision of the school grounds, nor could the school officials have known that the dog was vicious and dangerous.[36] A showing that the animal was abnormally dangerous could possibly have permitted the plaintiff to prevail against the dog's owner in a strict liability action.

While strict liability cases reported by appellate courts involving activities in the public schools are scarce, the possibility of such actions nevertheless exists. For example, the hazards in schools caused by laboratory experiments, shop activities, or field trips present possibilities of actions involving strict liability. However, this area makes up only a small element of the total tort liability picture in schools.

———— ❖ — ❖ — ❖ ————

Trampoline Is Not Abnormally Dangerous for the Purpose of Imposing Strict Liability

Fallon v. Indiana Trail School

Appellate Court of Illinois, Second District, 1986.
148 Ill.App.3d 931, 102 Ill.Dec. 479,
500 N.E.2d 101.

Justice STROUSE delivered the opinion of the court. . . . The plaintiff's amended complaint sought to recover damages for spinal injuries suffered as a result of a trampoline accident which occurred on February 23, 1975. At that time the plaintiff was a sixth-grade student at

the school and the defendants, Roach and Roynan-Leo, were physical education teachers. The incident occurred when the plaintiff attempted a "front-drop" maneuver on the trampoline during her physical education class. In her attempt to perform the maneuver, the plaintiff sustained spinal injuries.

. . . Count I alleged that the school and school district were strictly liable for the consequences of exposing pupils to an "abnormally dangerous instrumentality," a trampoline, during the physical education program. Count II alleged that the school and school district were negligent in the selection and use of an "abnormally dangerous" apparatus, a trampoline. . . .

In count I, the plaintiff alleged that the trampoline was an abnormally dangerous instrumentality, and the school district should, therefore, be held accountable under strict tort liability for any injuries due to its use. In count II, the plaintiff charged the school and school district with negligence as a result of a violation of section 10.20.8 of the School Code (Ill.Rev.Stat.1985, ch. 122, par. 10-20.8) because the trampoline was an abnormally dangerous instrumentality. We must, therefore, decide whether the plaintiff has alleged sufficient facts to support the contention that the trampoline is an abnormally dangerous instrumentality and trampoline usage is an abnormally dangerous activity.

Illinois recognizes strict liability under two theories: unreasonably dangerous defective products . . . and the theory which plaintiff alleges is applicable to this case, ultrahazardous activities . . . . Sections 519 and 520 of the Restatement (Second) of Torts (1981) (Restatement) have formulated a definition of ultrahazardous activities. Under section 519(1) of the Restatement, "[o]ne who carries on an abnormally dangerous activity is subject to liability for harm to the person, land or chattels of another resulting from the activity, although he has exercised the utmost care to prevent the harm." (Restatement (Second) of Torts sec. 519(1) (1981).) Section 520 of the Restatement considers: "[E]xistence of a high degree of risk of some harm . . . ; likelihood that the harm that results from it will be great; inability to eliminate the risk by the exercise of reasonable care; extent to which the activity is not a matter of common usage. . . ." Restatement (Second) of Torts sec. 520 (1981).

Illinois has long recognized strict liability for damages caused by engaging in an ultrahazardous activity, although it has never explicitly relied upon the Restatement factors in determining whether a given activity is abnormally dangerous. In *City of Joliet v. Harwood* (1877), 86 Ill. 110, the Illinois Supreme Court held that blasting dynamite in a residential area was intrinsically dangerous and gave rise to strict liability for the blaster. . . .

The plaintiff concedes that there is no Illinois authority discussing either whether (1) trampoline usage of this sort is an ultrahazardous activity, or (2) the trampoline is an abnormally dangerous instrumentality. Indeed, the trial court, in its written disposition dismissing counts I and II, noted that most of the discussion which related to this subject had to do with such obviously dangerous instrumentalities and activities as blasting, transport of explosives, maintenance of high electrical current, large animals, and maintenance of water reservoirs. In support of her argument, the plaintiff attached Exhibit A, "Trampoline-Related Quadriplegia: Review of the Literature and Reflections on the American Academy of Pediatrics' Position Statement," a review documenting cervical spine injuries resulting from trampoline-related accidents.

After reviewing Exhibit A, the trial court's disposition, as well as the plaintiff's amended complaint, we believe the trial court was correct in finding that trampoline usage, as alleged in the present case, does not fall within the parameter of an abnormally dangerous activity. We also agree that the trampoline, as a matter of law, is not an abnormally dangerous instrumentality.

Trampolines are widely used in the school systems as well as other centers of gymnastic activity. The injuries that may be caused result not from the trampoline itself but rather from the manner of its use. The terms "ultrahazardous," "abnormally dangerous," or "intrinsically dangerous," as traditionally used, refer to that type of danger which is inherent in the instrumentality itself at all times and do not mean danger which arises from mere casual or collateral negligence of others with respect to it under the particular circumstances. More concisely, it means dangerous in its normal or non-

defective state. . . . We conclude that although its negligent use can be the basis for liability, neither the trampoline itself nor its ordinary use is abnormally dangerous or ultrahazardous. . . . Therefore, counts I and II were properly dismissed. . . . Accordingly, for the reasons set forth above, the decision of the trial court is affirmed.

Affirmed.

■ NEGLIGENCE

Negligence differs from an intentional tort in that negligent acts are neither expected nor intended, whereas an intentional tort can be both anticipated and intended. With negligence,[37] a reasonable person in the position of the actor could have anticipated the harmful results. A teacher, for example, could not have reasonably foreseen that a hidden can in an incinerator would explode and injure a child when the teacher had sent the child to empty the classroom wastebaskets.[38]

An accident that could not have been prevented by reasonable care does not constitute negligence. Many times what first appears to be an accident can be traced to someone's negligence; however, instances of pure accident, in which someone is injured and no one is actually at fault, do occur. For example, when a child closed a music room door, cutting off the tip of another student's finger, the court found no negligence, merely an accident.[39]

STANDARD OF CONDUCT

A negligent act in one situation may not be negligent under a different set of circumstances. No definite rules as to what constitutes negligence apply. The standard of conduct of the actor is the key. The conditions embracing a negligent act have been described in this fashion:

> It is fundamental that the standard of conduct which is the basis of the law of negligence is determined by balancing the risk, in the light of the social value of the interest threatened, and the probability and extent of the harm, against the value of the interest which the actor is seeking to protect, and the expedience of the course pursued.[40]

For the court to strike a balance between the threatened harm and the actor's conduct,[41] the court must establish a standard by which such activity can be measured. In attempting to set boundaries for negligent acts committed in different factual situations, the courts have developed the reasonableness theory. For negligence to be present, someone must sustain an injury resulting from an "unreasonable risk" taken by another person. To determine unreasonableness, the courts personify the test in terms of the "reasonable man."

THE REASONABLE PERSON

The reasonable man (more appropriately, the reasonable person) has been described by different courts as a prudent man, a man of average prudence, a man of ordinary sense using ordinary care[42] and skill, and a reasonably prudent man. He is an ideal, a model of conduct, and a community standard. The model for the reasonable man, although a community ideal, varies in every case. His characteristics are (1) the physical attributes of the defendant himself, (2) normal intelligence, (3) normal perception and memory with a minimum level of information and experience common to the community, and (4) such superior skill and knowledge as the actor has or holds himself out to the public as having.[43] While this standard of behavior provides a framework for the whole theory of negligence, the exact formula varies with the attributes of the persons involved and with the circumstances.

The reasonable man then has the same physical characteristics as the actor himself, and the acts in question are measured accordingly. Correspondingly, the person who is crippled is not held to the same standard as the person with no physical infirmities. The courts have also made allowances for the weaknesses or attributes connected with the gender[44] and age[45] of the individual.

The courts have not, however, been so lenient with individuals who have mental deficiencies. The courts have traditionally held that a person with less mental ability than an average person must adjust and conform to the rules of society. No allowance is given by the courts for subnormal mentality, but if a person is actually insane, a more convincing argument can be made for allowing for the particular incapacity.[46]

One such case illustrating this point of law occurred when a junior high school pupil entered the school and shot and killed the principal and wounded three other people, including a teacher and two students. The student was ruled criminally insane, but the wounded teacher and a student filed a civil action in tort. The court found that although a person is criminally insane, civil liability in damages is an appropriate remedy. The court said that "American courts have unanimously chosen to impose liability on an insane person rather than leaving the loss on the innocent victim."[47]

■ ELEMENTS OF NEGLIGENCE

To have a valid cause of action for negligence, certain prerequisites must exist and are frequently divided into four categories: (1) a *duty* to protect others; (2) a failure to exercise an appropriate *standard of care*; (3) the existence of a causal connection between the act and injury, called *proximate* or *legal cause*; and (4) an *injury*, damage or loss.

DUTY

The routine of everyday life creates situations in which persons constantly create risks and incur obligations for the safety of others. In negligence cases, a person has a duty to abide by a standard of reasonable conduct in the face of apparent risks.[48]

The courts generally hold that no duty exists when a defendant could not have reasonably foreseen the danger of risk involved. A duty owed by one person to another may well intensify as the risk increases. In other words, the duty to protect another is proportional to the risk or hazard of a particular activity. In certain school functions where risks are greater to children, a teacher has an increased level of obligation or duty to the children. For example, whenever children perform a dangerous experiment, the teacher has a greater obligation for the children's safety than when he or she is merely supervising a study hall. One judge has explained the duty requirement in this way:

Every person is negligent when, without intending any wrong, he does such an act or omits to take such a precaution that under the circumstances he, as an ordinary prudent person, ought reasonably to foresee that he will thereby expose the interest of another to an unreasonable risk of harm. A person is required to take into account such of the surrounding circumstances as would be taken into account by a reasonably prudent person and possess such knowledge as is possessed by an ordinary reasonable person and to use such judgment and discretion as is exercised by persons of reasonable intelligence under the same or similar circumstance.[49]

A school district generally has no duty to protect children who leave school grounds without permission and then are injured. However, a California court ruled that while a school district is not liable for injuries by a truant under all circumstances, a school district may be legally responsible if negligent supervision of the student while on school grounds was the proximate cause of the injuries that occurred off school premises.[50]

Generally, the law holds that a person is not liable for an omission to act when there is not some definite relationship between the parties; no general duty exists to aid a person in danger. For example, even though a moral duty may be present, no legal duty mandates that a mere bystander aid a drowning person. If, however, a person acts affirmatively to assist another in peril, he or she assumes a duty to the person, and all his or her subsequent acts must be performed reasonably. Because of this requirement, passersby in many situations will not assist victims of auto wrecks or other mishaps. Some states, in order to encourage more humanitarian responses and to protect well-meaning rescuers, have enacted laws that protect the "good Samaritan" from liability.

While a teacher has no more duty than anyone else to be a "good Samaritan" to the general public, he or she does have an obligation or duty to help a student under his or her jurisdiction when injured at school. Because of the teacher/student relationship, a teacher may be liable for an omission to act as well as for an affirmative act. In such a case, though, the teacher is required to provide only such assistance as a person with the same training and experience in similar circumstances could reasonably provide.

STANDARD OF CARE

A legally recognized duty requires the actor to conform to a certain standard of conduct or care. As the risk involved in an act increases, the standard of care required of the actor likewise increases.[51] The standard of care of a woodshop teacher is, of course, greater than that of a school librarian because the risk of being injured while handling power tools is much greater than the risk of being injured while reading a book. Similarly, chemistry classes require a high standard of care.[52]

The standard of care required by the courts is not uniform among all persons. Children and aged persons have generally been given substantially more leeway in their activities than is allowed a normal adult. While both children and aged persons are liable for their torts, they are not held to the same standard as others without impairments of age. Although it is difficult to pinpoint precise standards for determining the reasonableness of a child because of the great variations in age, maturity, and capacity, the courts have nevertheless established as a subjective test that which is "reasonable to expect of children of like age, intelligence, and experience."[53]

While most courts appear to follow the preceding criteria for determining negligence of children, some courts have applied criminal law standards that prescribe the following criteria:

- Children between one and seven years of age cannot be liable for negligence. They theoretically have no capacity for negligence.[54]
- Children between the ages of seven and fourteen have a *prima facie* case for incapacity, but it can be rebutted. In other words, children in this age group are presumed not to be capable of negligence until proved to the contrary.

Authorities generally agree that while arbitrary age limits for negligence have been established by some courts, it is not a generally acceptable rule of law, and that in the present-day circumstances, a child of six may well assume many responsibilities. With the assumption of responsibilities is a necesity for exercising some degree of care. Social cognizance of today's child stimulated by compulsory school attendance, the radio, television, Internet, and the movies, all tend to have this effect. The arbitrary cut-off rule ignores these factors and can permit a child who may be guilty of the most flagrant violation of duty to be precluded from any presumption of negligence.

With regard to teachers or others in the teaching profession, the generally accepted standard of care would be that of a reasonably prudent teacher, not that of a reasonably prudent layperson. A New York court has put it this way:

> The standard of care required of an officer or employee of a public school is that which a person of ordinary prudence charged with his duties would exercise under the same circumstances.[55]

A Vermont court has defined the "standard of care" owed to a pupil by a teacher in the following manner: A teacher's

> relationship to the pupils under his care and custody differs from that generally existing between a public employee and a member of the general public. In a limited sense the teacher stands in the parents' place in his relationship to a pupil . . . and has such a portion of the powers of the parent over the pupil as is necessary to carry out his employment. In such relationship, he owes his pupils the duty of supervision.[56]

While this is the prevailing view, some courts have held teachers to a lesser degree of care. These courts have said that a teacher can be charged only with reasonable care such as any person of ordinary prudence would exercise under comparable circumstances.

PROXIMATE OR LEGAL CAUSE

"Proximate cause," or "legal cause," is the connection between the act and the resultant injury. The question the court will ask is "Was the injury a natural and probable consequence of the wrongful act, and ought it to have been foreseen in light of the attendant circumstances?"[57] The *Restatement (Second) of Torts* explains the necessity of adequate causal relation in this way:

> In order that a negligent actor shall be liable for another's harm, it is necessary not only that the actor's conduct be negligent toward the other, but also that the negligence of the actor be a legal cause of the other's harm.[58]

To establish proximate cause, there must first be a duty or obligation on the part of the actor to maintain a reasonable standard of conduct. In most negligence cases, however, the courts do not refer to proximate cause but rely solely on the duty or obligation of the defendant and the standard of conduct required to avoid liability. Proximate cause as a criterion of liability has been used most often where some doubt exists as to whether the injured person was within the zone of obvious danger.[59]

In these cases, the courts require that the negligence of the defendant be the "substantial" cause of the harm to the plaintiff. In other words, the cause must be substantial enough to lead reasonable people to conclude it is indeed the cause of injury. If the negligence is not a substantial factor in producing the harm, then no liability follows.

The actor's negligent act must be in continuous and active force up to the actual harm, and the lapse of time must not be so great that contributing causes and intervening factors render the original negligent act to be an unsubstantial or insignificant force in the harm. Therefore, a teacher may be relieved of liability for negligent conduct if some intervening act is sufficient to break the causal connection between the act and a pupil's injury. For example, where a principal gave pupils permission to hold a race in a street and a "recklessly negligent" pupil ran into and injured a pedestrian, the court held that the causal relation was too remote to hold the principal liable.[60]

To break the chain of events causing injury, the intervening act must legally supersede the original negligent act. This rule is illustrated in a case in which a student was cleaning a power saw in shop class and another student turned on the switch, starting the machine in violation of safety rules. In this instance, the court held that the school board's negligence in not having a guard over the belt drive was not the proximate or legal cause of the injury.[61]

A different result might have been reached, however, if the intervening act had been foreseeable and could have been prevented by reasonable care on the part of the defendant. For example, if a teacher sends a child on an errand across a busy street and a motorist, while driving carelessly, injures the child, both the teacher and the motorist may be liable. Here the intervening negligent act is not substantial enough to entirely overcome the original act. In an actual case demonstrating this point, a school bus driver was negligent when a student was struck by an automobile after alighting from the bus. The driver of the automobile was also negligent; however, the court held that the negligent bus driver had a continuing obligation that was not ended by the negligence of the driver of the automobile. The automobile driver's negligence did not constitute a sufficient break in the causal connection to be a defense for the bus driver and was not a superseding or intervening cause.[62]

INJURY OR ACTUAL LOSS

A plaintiff, of course, cannot recover unless actual injury is suffered and the plaintiff is able to show actual loss or damages resulting from the defendant's act. If the harm suffered is caused by more than one person, then damages may be apportioned among the tortfeasors. Sometimes both school district and teacher are joined together by a plaintiff student in a case wherein it is claimed that the injury was caused by acts of both parties.

Breach of a Duty of Reasonable Care Imposes Liability on a School Board

Brown v. Tesack

Supreme Court of Louisiana, 1990.
566 So.2d 955.

Shortess, Justice, Pro Tem. On the afternoon of August 28, 1984, during summer recess, Leonard Kisack, age 13, and Gerald Preston (over 12) obtained four partially used cans of flammable duplicating fluid from a red metal garbage dumpster located in the rear of the Henderson H. Dunn Elementary School (Dunn School). . . . Dunn School has a significant history of break-ins and vandalism. . . .

Some time prior to August 28, 1984, an employee of the Dunn School disposed of a number of cans containing varying amounts of

duplicating fluid in the dumpster. Leonard and Gerald took four cans from the dumpster to a courtyard in the Desire Housing Project where they lived and began to play with the fluid by creating small fires. Plaintiff lived in the project but was not a party to these activities. Gerald returned to the dumpster for an additional can of fluid later that evening and began pouring fluid onto an already burning plastic milk carton. Plaintiff came around the corner and onto the scene, was struck in the chest by a "fireball," and was severely burned over an extensive portion of his face and body.

The trial court held that the Board had a duty to properly dispose of the duplicating fluid, citing its knowledge of the likelihood that children would play in and around the dumpster and that the Dunn School was commonly the target of vandals. Wilbert F. Dunn, principal of Dunn School, . . . testified that he took significant precautionary measures to keep the fluid secure, including storing the unused cans in a room to which only he, the assistant principal, and the chief custodian possessed keys; . . . and collecting partially used cans and storing them securely during school holidays. Dunn candidly explained the purpose of these safeguards:

> We were aware of the fact that Dunn School had a history of break-ins and vandalism and we did not want duplicating fluid to be used in setting fires. . . .

The duty to properly dispose of the duplicating fluid arose *because* the liquid is flammable and the risk of harm, *i.e.* physical injury resulting from its flammability, was specifically recognized by the Board. . . .

. . . The testimony is uncontroverted that a "fireball" was projected from the can of fluid. Moreover, the Board's policy manifests a self-imposed duty to properly *store* the substance. Clearly, these precautions were taken to ensure that the fluid did not fall into the hands of third parties—possibly children; the risk that it could were these precautions not taken, therefore, was not only foreseeable but *foreseen*. The operative risk of harm here, misuse of the fluid causing injury to persons or property from fire, was no less foreseeable. The record establishes that Board personnel were well aware that children played on the school grounds and rummaged in the dumpster. A duty was owed both to these children and to their potential victims. *See Brown*, 556 So.2d at 89. (Plotkin, J., dissenting) ("there is no difference between the recognizable risk of a minor's misuse of an inherently dangerous object and the likelihood that the minor will cause personal or property damages to others"). We agree . . . "children who possess a flammable substance can be expected to light it, to attract other children to join in the play and to commit criminal acts or engage in other misadventures."

We conclude that plaintiff's injuries were reasonably foreseeable. Additionally, the fact that the conduct (disposal of a flammable substance) was squarely within the duty and that the injuries were exactly those that the duty was imposed to prevent, is suggestive that the conduct fell short of that required by, *i.e.* was a breach of, the duty. . . . The recognition by the Board that this duplicating fluid was a dangerous substance, to be treated with special precautions, leads directly to the conclusion that it was not reasonable to dispose of several partially full cans in the Dunn School dumpster.

We must conclude that the evidence does show a breach of the duty to properly dispose of the duplicating fluid, irrespective of the length of time that the cans remained in the dumpster prior to the accident. Dunn testified the gates at the school remained open in the summer time as no attempt was made to stop children from playing on the grounds, and it would be futile to try. The dumpster was there and easily accessible to anyone on the grounds. Putting children and flammable mixtures together, unfortunately, more often than not, produces combustion. The risk of burn injuries resulting from children playing with the duplicating fluid was squarely within the scope of the duty to properly dispose of the fluid, and the Board must share responsibility for plaintiff's injuries.

. . . We note that the School Board was aware of the danger that children might obtain the flammable substance and create fires and that the risk was significant inasmuch as fires could have been started in or spread to the nearby housing project. There was no suggestion that the duplicating fluid was old or otherwise unusable, thus disposal of partially full cans would seem unnecessary; if disposal was necessary, some other method should have been

used. The Board occupied a superior position to the children; the duty to properly dispose of the fluid was imposed to prevent a situation where the conduct of third parties, possibly children, could cause injury. . . .

The judgments of the trial court and court of appeal dismissing plaintiff's suit against the School Board are reversed.

CASE NOTES

1. *Foreseeability.* The test of foreseeability was well stated in *McLeod v. Grant County School District No. 128*, 42 Wash.2d 316, 255 P.2d 360 (1953), a case that held the school district answerable in damages to a girl who was attacked in an unlighted room adjacent to the school gymnasium. The court said:

> Whether foreseeability is being considered from the standpoint of negligence or proximate cause, the pertinent inquiry is not whether the actual harm was of a particular kind which was expectable. Rather, the question is whether the actual harm fell within a general field of danger which should have been anticipated.

42 Wash.2d at 321, 255 P.2d at 363. The court further stated:

> The harm which came to appellant was not caused by the direct act of omission of the school district, but by the intervening act of third persons. The fact, that the danger stems from such an intervening act, however, does not of itself exonerate a defendant from negligence. If, under the assumed facts, such intervening force is reasonably foreseeable, a finding of negligence may be predicated thereon. 42 Wash.2d at 320, 255 P.2d at 362.

2. A school district will be held liable for foreseeable injuries proximately related to lack of supervision. Schools are under a duty to adequately supervise to prevent foreseeable injuries. A New York court has observed that obviously "school personnel cannot reasonably be expected to guard against all sudden, spontaneous acts that take place." It applied this principle where a female student was murdered by a male student in a wooded area on school property. The court held that the school district was not liable for negligence because the school

did not have "actual or constructive notice" or knowledge of the danger to the decedent. *Marshall v. Cortland Enlarged City School District*, 697 N.Y.S.2d 395 (S.Ct.App.3d N.Y.1999).

3. *Duty.* The establishment of a duty is necessary to determine the corresponding standard of care the defendant owes to the plaintiff. The Supreme Court of Oregon has explained: "Duty plays an affirmative role when an injured plaintiff invokes obligations arising from a defendant's particular status or relationships, or from legislation, beyond the generalized standards that the common law of negligence imposes on persons at large. In cases based solely on common law negligence, 'no duty' is a defensive argument asking a court to limit the reach of these generalized standards as a matter of law. Duty remains a formal element of the plaintiff's claim only in the sense that the plaintiff loses if the defendant persuades a court to phrase such a limit in terms of 'no duty.'" *Fazzolari v. Portland School District No. 1J*, 303 Or. 1, 734 P.2d 1326 (1987).

4. *Foreseeability and Duty.* Foreseeability is a judgment about a course of events, a factual judgment that one often makes outside any legal context. It therefore ordinarily depends on the facts of a concrete situation and, if disputed, is decided as an issue of fact. "Duty" expresses the formal link between factual conduct and legal liability; its content must be located in the law, not in facts or in morals, manners, or other values unless these are incorporated into law. When "duty" refers to legally obligatory conduct, it provides a person injured by noncompliance a premise to claim a legal remedy; at other times, the concept is invoked defensively to limit the reach of liability even though harm was caused by conduct falling short of a legal obligation. *Nylander v. State of Oregon*, 292 Or. 254, 257–58, 637 P.2d 1286, 1287–88 (1981).

5. *Care and Duty.* The care required of the school district must be commensurate with the duty owed. Dangerous conditions near or about a school may require that the school district exercise extra care in protecting students from injury. Where a student was injured on a construction site near a school, the court held that daily warnings to students about the dangerous conditions were insufficient and that the school was negligent because it did not post school employees to guard the construction site. *District of Columbia v. Royal*, 465 A.2d 367 (D.C.App.1983).

6. *Standard of Care Increases with Hazards.* The school district has a duty to maintain hazardfree conditions for students. A Massachusetts court held that glass panels, which were not shatterproof, constituted a dangerous condition rendering the city of Boston liable when a student lacerated tendons and injured nerves in his hand when he put his hand through a glass panel. *Johnson v. City of Boston*, 22 Mass.App.Ct. 24, 490 N.E.2d 1204 (1986).

7. *Adequate Supervision.* The adequacy of supervision is measured in terms of the required standard of care. To illustrate, a student was awarded damages for an injury occurring when the student slipped and cut his face on rocks or glass on the playground during a fight with another student. The court found that the playground had not been adequately supervised and that the school district had allowed a hazard to exist that could injure students. The presence of a hazard created a heightened standard of care. *Laneheart v. Orleans Parish School Board*, 524 So.2d 138 (La.App.4th Cir.1988).

8. *Adequate Supervision on a Field Trip.* In another example, a student on a field trip was hit by an automobile while crossing a street and sued two teachers for negligence. The court noted that the teachers had admonished the students to be careful in crossing the street, that the student was thirteen years old, and that the street was not unreasonably dangerous. The court concluded that the teachers had not acted unreasonably and had no duty to personally escort students across streets. *King v. Kartanson*, 720 S.W.2d 65 (Tenn.App.1986).

❖ — ❖ — ❖

School District Did Not Have Reason to Foresee a Gang-Related Shooting of a Student

Brownell v. Los Angeles Unified School District

Court of Appeal, Second District, Division 5, 1992.
4 Cal.App.4th 787, 5 Cal.Rptr.2d 756.

BOREN, Associate Justice.

The Los Angeles Unified School District (LAUSD) appeals following a $120,000 jury verdict arising from an incident in which a student, Ernest P. Brownell, III, was shot and wounded by gang members. The shooting occurred immediately after school hours and on a public street adjacent to school property. Brownell alleged negligent supervision in that LAUSD personnel had dismissed the students after school without first ascertaining if the street in front of the school was free of any gang members. . . . Among the group of people was another student, Keesha Pierson, who was herself waiting for some friends with whom she was going to walk home. At trial, Pierson testified as to the ensuing events.

After the school day ended on January 28, 1985, Brownell went out the main door of Johnson High School and stood in front of the school on the sidewalk along 42nd Street among a group of 15 to 20 people. . . . After Brownell had stood outside for approximately five minutes, several youths wearing red gang colors associated with the Bloods gang ran or walked quickly across the street and gathered around Brownell. One of the gang members swung at Brownell, causing him to go into the middle of the street where another gang member pulled out a gun and shot him.

The incident happened very fast. The gang members were not in front of the school when Pierson or Brownell first came out of the school. Pierson had no idea during that day at school that there was going to be an incident like that after school.

Brownell, who had never been a member of a gang, was apparently shot because he was mistaken by members of the Bloods for a member of a rival gang, the Crips. Johnson High School is located in an area known as a Crips neighborhood. Before Brownell was shot, a gym teacher at the high school told Brownell and other class members about an altercation at the school which had occurred at some unspecified time and involved one of Brownell's attackers, Lymus Ali, and another student. Ali had told the teacher that "he can't come to the school no more because there's some Crips here, and that he was a Blood." Ali had only been a student at Johnson High School for one or two days when

he was threatened and told the gym teacher he could no longer attend the school. The member of the Bloods who shot Brownell, Douglas Smith, was not a student at Johnson High School, and Brownell had never encountered Smith before Smith shot him.

At the time Brownell was shot, he and the other students had been dismissed from school for the day. Mary Maddox, dean and counselor at Johnson High School, and Wilma Manyweather, the principal of the school, were inside the school near the doors passing out bus tickets to the students. They normally gave out the tickets at the school gate, but they did so inside the building that day because it was raining. On the day Brownell was shot, neither Maddox nor Manyweather had heard any rumors or threats to any of the students or detected any other indications of trouble. As Maddox explained, "Usually when something was about to happen [in such a small school] you could feel it all day long, and the kids would be whispering and stuff like that. But I don't recall any of that happening on that day."

Johnson High School had a population of approximately 200 students. The students at Johnson High School were referred there from other high schools where they had had behavior problems, such as inability to get along with other students, truancy, destructiveness in the classroom, and involvement in gang-related activities. The school had no school police or security guards, but had campus aides who could contact the school administrators or school police by walkie-talkie. It was the policy of the school to prohibit the display on campus of gang colors and paraphernalia associated with gangs. During 1985, the year Brownell was shot, the school removed such gang-related items from students on almost a daily basis and also on occasion confiscated weapons from students. There had been no prior shootings at Johnson High School. . . .

LAUSD contends that it has no duty of care to students going to or from school regarding accidents which occur off school premises. Indeed, as a general principle, "school districts are not legally responsible for accidents that students may suffer once they have been released from school. . . . "

It is well settled that although a school district is not an insurer of its pupils' safety, school authorities have a duty to supervise the conduct of students on school grounds and to enforce rules and regulations necessary for their protection. (*Hoyem v. Manhattan Beach City Sch. Dist.,* *supra,* 22 Cal.3d at p. 513, 150 Cal.Rptr. 1, 585 P.2d 851.) The standard of due care imposed on school authorities in exercising their supervisorial responsibilities is that degree of care which a person of ordinary prudence, charged with comparable duties, would exercise under the same circumstances. . . . As the court explained in *Hoyem,* in the context of a student who claimed negligent supervision after he absented himself from the school grounds during school hours and was subsequently injured by a motorist, "We require ordinary care, not fortresses; schools must be reasonably supervised, not truant-proof." . . .

In the present case, we find that the school district exercised due care and, under any view of the evidence, satisfied its supervisorial responsibilities in regard to protecting students from potential gang-related violence. It is a tragic and sad commentary upon our society when an innocent student attending high school is assaulted and shot by gang members upon leaving school premises. Nonetheless, a school cannot and should not be an insurer of the safety of students, particularly after school and off school premises, when it has exercised ordinary prudence and due care appropriate to the circumstances. . . .

LAUSD exercised reasonable and ordinary care and satisfied its duty to supervise adequately students in view of (1) the general precautions the school always took to minimize gang-related problems (e.g., prohibiting wearing gang colors and confiscating weapons), and (2) the absence of any advance indication to school personnel of potential gang violence pertinent to the incident involving Brownell. . . .

Imposing . . . a duty of visual precaution is unwarranted and impractical, as indicated by the very sudden and unexpected nature of the attack upon Brownell. Even if school personnel happened to observe the mere presence of gang members near the school, it would apparently not constitute an unusual or alarming phenomenon, since gang members were present in the school and lived in the neighborhood of the school. We find that school personnel of ordi-

nary prudence under the circumstances described should not be required to engage in such visual precaution, absent either (1) any specific indication of a real and imminent gang-related threat at the particular time and place of the shooting, or (2) prior incidents reflecting not necessarily this identical type of assault but that "the possibility of this type of harm was foreseeable." . . . Here, LAUSD did not fail to take reasonable precautions against any foreseeable risk and fulfilled its duty of reasonable care.

The judgment is reversed, and the superior court is directed to dismiss the complaint. Each party is to bear its own costs on appeal.

CASE NOTES

1. *Duty.* A Florida court has provided a good explanation of the duty owed by the school to the student:

> To sustain a cause of action in negligence, a complaint must allege ultimate facts which establish a relationship between the parties giving rise to a legal duty on the part of the defendant to protect the plaintiff from the injury of which he complains. It must also show that the defendant negligently breached that duty, and that the plaintiff's injury was proximately caused by the defendant's negligence.

Ankers v. District School Board of Pasco County, 406 So.2d 72 (Fla.App.1981).

2. *Duty Owed on School Grounds.* A school district has a duty to supervise students while on the school premises during the school day, and the district may be held liable for a student's injuries that are proximately caused by the district's failure to exercise reasonable care under the circumstances. *Hoyem v. Manhattan Beach City School District,* 150 Cal.Rptr. 1, 585 P.2d 851 (1978). A California court has said that "[a] school district is under no duty to supervise, or provide for the protection of its pupils, *on their way home,* unless it has undertaken to provide transportation for them." *Kerwin v. County of San Mateo,* 176 Cal.App.2d 304, 1 Cal.Rptr. 437 (1959). See also *Girard v. Monrovia City School District,* 121 Cal.App.2d 737, 264 P.2d 115 (1953).

3. *Duty May Transcend Another's Act.* The school district's duty to a student is not absolved by mere wrongful conduct of a third party. The Supreme Court of California has held

that the fact that another student's misconduct was the immediate precipitating cause of injury does not compel a conclusion that negligent supervision by the teacher was not the proximate cause of a student's death. Neither the mere involvement of a third party nor the party's own wrongful conduct is sufficient in itself to absolve the defendants of liability, once a negligent failure to provide adequate supervision is shown. *Dailey v. Los Angeles Unified School District*, 2 Cal.3d 741, 87 Cal.Rptr. 376, 470 P.2d 360 (1970).

4. *Duty Owed Off School Grounds.* A school district's duty may extend off campus if negligent on-campus supervision is the proximate cause of off-campus injury. Thus, it is conceivable that a student who is injured while "playing hooky" may be able to recover damages against the school district if the school district could have (1) foreseen that the child would sneak away from school and did nothing about it and (2) foreseen that the surrounding circumstances—traffic, crime, etc.—could lead to injury. Whether such circumstances are present and foreseeable is a jury question. Thus, there is no precise dividing line between on-campus and off-campus liability of the school district. See *Dailey v. Los Angeles Unified School District*, 2 Cal.3d 741, 87 Cal.Rptr. 376, 470 P.2d 360 (1970).

❖ — ❖ — ❖

Reasonably Prudent Teacher Could Have Foreseen Possible Injury

Johnson v. School District of Millard

Supreme Court of Nebraska, 1998.
573 N.W. 2d 116.

WRIGHT, Justice.

The plaintiff commenced this negligence action pursuant to the Nebraska Political Subdivisions Tort Claims Act, alleging that the defendant, through its employee, was negligent in that the employee failed to properly supervise students who were under her care. The defen-

dant appeals from an award to the plaintiff in the amount of $21,226.10. . . .

On September 15, 1993, Robbie L. Johnson, a first grader at Willa Cather Elementary School, was injured while attending his music class. On this day, the teacher of the music class, Nancy Patton, taught her class the song and accompanying game of "London Bridge." London Bridge is a game in which two children, while singing a song, form a "bridge" by linking their arms. The children's linked arms are then lowered around the third child who is rocked back and forth. The children were taught how to sing the song, and then the teacher used two children to demonstrate how the accompanying game was played. The teacher picked two children at random and instructed them to link their arms together, explaining that they were to rock a third child within their linked arms. The teacher warned the children not to act silly and told them not to yell, scream, or swing their arms too much. After giving these instructions, the teacher allowed the children to play the game on their own. It was undisputed that this was the first time the students had played the game and that Johnson was the first child who was caught and rocked between the children's linked arms.

Johnson testified that he was swung "fast and hard" while caught in his classmates' arms. While swinging Johnson, the two children accidentally released their hands and threw Johnson into a bookcase at the end of the room, cutting his head above his right eyebrow. Johnson testified that he told the children swinging him to stop at least three times and asked for help twice before the accident occurred. He testified that he was trying to yell over the music, but everyone was talking, and some of the children were laughing and singing.

It is undisputed that the teacher was not watching Johnson when he was injured. Johnson testified that the teacher was writing on the blackboard, and he and another student testified that she had her back to the children when the accident occurred. The teacher testified that she saw Johnson caught within the children's arms but did not witness him being swung because she was aiding another child.

Johnson required 50 stitches to close the cut above his right eye. The cut extended to the bone and divided the muscle throughout its length. Johnson suffered blurred vision for a short period of time and continues to suffer headaches as a result of his injury.

The trial court held that the teacher's mere instruction to first grade children on how to play the game without direct supervision during at least the early portions of the game was negligent supervision. . . .

The proper standard of care regarding negligent supervision is whether the defendant acted as a reasonably prudent person would in a similar circumstance. . . . The trial court found that the teacher was negligent in not directly supervising the children during at least the early portions of the game. The question is whether the teacher had a duty to directly supervise her students at this time.

The school district argues that the trial court incorrectly required the teacher to provide direct supervision, which imposed a higher standard of care than that of a reasonably prudent person. The cases cited by the school district imply that constant supervision of students at all times is not required by a teacher acting as a reasonably prudent person and that direct supervision is needed only when children are engaged in dangerous activities. . . . By analogy, the school district argues that since London Bridge is not a dangerous activity, the court should not have required the teacher to provide constant and direct supervision.

We conclude that the trial court did not require the teacher to provide constant and direct supervision because the court's order states that the teacher needed to provide direct supervision to the children during only the "early portions of the game." The court did not hold the teacher to a higher standard of care than that of a reasonably prudent person. Instead, the court found that a reasonably prudent person would have given direct supervision to first graders during at least the early portions of a game which they were playing for the first time. We cannot say that the trial court was clearly wrong.

The school district claims that the teacher would not have had enough time to assist Johnson even if she had supervised him more closely and that, therefore, she is not responsible for Johnson's injury. We disagree. The trial court found that the teacher was in the blackboard area with her back to Johnson just prior to the injury and that Johnson did not trip and fall into the bookcase, but, rather, was propelled by the "fast and hard" swinging of the two children composing the bridge. The court found that Johnson told his classmates to stop and cried for help before the accident. The court found that the teacher was negligent in failing to stop the aggressive swinging by the two students making up the bridge and that this negligence was the proximate cause of Johnson's injury. As each of these findings is supported by the evidence, we cannot say that the trial court was clearly wrong.

We next address whether the school district's negligence was the proximate cause of Johnson's injury or whether the act of the other children constitutes an intervening cause which defeats causation. There are three basic requirements that must be met to establish causation: (1) that "but for" the defendant's negligence, the injury would not have occurred; (2) that the injury is the natural and probable result of the negligence; and (3) that there is no efficient intervening cause. . . . The school district argues that the act of Johnson's classmates, who released their hands and propelled Johnson into the bookcase, is an intervening cause which defeats causation.

In order for the children's accidentally releasing their hands to be an intervening cause, this court must find that the children's act was unforeseeable. . . . We conclude that it is reasonably foreseeable that children playing London Bridge might swing another child in such a manner that the sudden release of their hands could cause an accident. Therefore, the fact that the children released their hands and caused Johnson to hit his head is not an intervening cause. . . .

Finding all of the school district's assignments of error to be without merit, we affirm the judgment of the trial court.

Affirmed.

CASE NOTES

1. Following *Johnson v. School District of Millard*, the Supreme Court of Nebraska held that a school district has a duty to see that students wear protective clothing in a class where they are engaged in arc and acetylene welding projects. The court found that the standards of

the American Welding Society that had been adopted by the American National Standards Institute, saying that persons "should" wear special clothing to reduce combustibility, along with opinions of experts, are sufficient for the court to determine that the school is liable for injury sustained by a student who was badly burned when a loose-fitting cotton shirt he was wearing caught fire while he was operating a welding torch. The court concluded that the school should have foreseen such an occurrence and that the school's failure to require the protective clothing was the proximate cause of the injury. *Norman v. Ogallala Public School District*, 609 N.W.2d 338 (Neb.2000).

2. *The Doctrine of Proximate Cause*. In *Holler v. Lowery*, a Maryland case, the court said:

> There is no mystery in the doctrine of proximate cause. It rests upon common sense rather than legal formula. Expressed in the simplest terms it means that negligence is not actionable unless it, without the intervention of any independent factor, causes the harm complained of. It involves of course the idea of continuity, that the negligent act continuously extends through every event, fact, act and occurrence related to the tortious conduct of the defendant and is itself the logical and natural cause of the injury complained of. In the statement of the doctrine an intervening cause means not a concurrent and contributing cause, but a superseding cause, which is itself the natural and logical cause of the harm.

175 Md. 149, 161, 200 A. 353, 358 (1938).

3. *Proximate Cause and the* Palsgraf *Case*. Perhaps the most famous judicial consideration of proximate cause involved an injury sustained at a railroad station in New York. The case, *Palsgraf v. Long Island Railroad Co.*, 248 N.Y. 339, 162 N.E. 99 (1928), is important because of the uniqueness of the factual situation, the remoteness of causality, the detachment of the duty owed to the injured third party, and the fact that the great American jurist Benjamin Cardozo wrote the opinion. Although not a school case, the precedent of *Palsgraf* is important to most discussions of tort law. Keeton et al. discuss the *Palsgraf* case and its importance to tort law. They say:

> In 1928 something of a bombshell burst upon this field, when the New York Court of Appeals, forsaking "proximate cause," stated the issue of foreseeability in terms of duty. The case was Palsgraf v.

Long Island Railroad Co., which has become the most discussed and debated of all torts cases, and over which the argument still goes on. It involved what may be called, instead of unforeseeable consequences, the unforeseeable plaintiff. If the defendant's conduct threatens harm, which a reasonable person would foresee, to A, and A is in fact injured, we start with negligence toward A, and the problem is purely one of the extent of liability for consequences. But what if harm results instead to B, who was in no way threatened, stood outside of the zone of all apparent danger, and to whom no harm could reasonably be foreseen? Is the defendant's duty of care limited to A, toward whom the defendant has created a foreseeable risk, or does it extend also to the plaintiff whom the defendant has in fact injured, but could not reasonably foresee? We have seen the doctrine of "transferred intent," by which one shoots at A, and instead unexpectedly hits B, becomes liable to B. Is there such a thing as "transferred negligence," which will accomplish the same result? . . .

> . . . The factual hypothesis before the court was this: A passenger was running to catch one of the defendant's trains. The defendant's servants, trying to assist the passenger to board it, dislodged a package from the passenger's arms, and it fell upon the rails. The package contained fireworks, which exploded with some violence. The concussion overturned some scales, many feet away on the platform, and they fell upon the plaintiff and injured her. The defendant's servants, who were found by the jury to have been negligent in what they did, could have foreseen harm from their clumsiness to the package, or at most to the passenger boarding the train; but no harm to the plaintiff could possibly have been anticipated.

> In this situation Judge Cardozo, speaking for a majority of four, held that there was no liability, because there was no negligence toward the plaintiff. Negligence, he said, was a matter of relation between the parties, which must be founded upon the foreseeability of harm to the person in fact injured. The defendant's conduct was not a wrong toward her merely because it was negligence toward someone else. She must "sue in her own right for a wrong personal to her, and not as the vicarious beneficiary of a breach of duty to another."

Cardozo said:

> The conduct of the defendant's guard, if a wrong in its relation to the holder of the package, was not a wrong in its relation to the plaintiff, standing far away. Relatively to her it was not negligence at all. Nothing in the situation gave notice that the falling package had in it the potency of

peril to persons thus removed. Negligence is not actionable unless it involves the invasion of a legally protected interest, the violation of a right....

What the plaintiff must show is "a wrong" to herself, *i.e.,* a violation of her own right, and not merely a wrong to someone else, nor conduct "wrongful" because unsocial, but not "a wrong" to anyone.

4. *Proximate Cause.* A school district's responsibility does not extend off school grounds so as to incur liability unless a failure of reasonable care on the part of the school is the proximate cause of injury. Where a student was injured in an auto crash after he had obtained keys to a car, left school, and taken other students joyriding, the court ruled that the failure of the school to notify parents of the students' truancy was not the proximate cause of the injury. *Palella v. Ulmer,* 136 Misc.2d 34, 518 N.Y.S.2d 91 (1987).

5. The Supreme Court of Connecticut has defined proximate cause as "an actual cause that is a substantial factor in the resulting harm. This definition calls into play the "substantive factor" test. This test, the supreme court says, "reflects the inquiry fundamental to all proximate cause questions; that is, whether the harm which occurred was of the same general nature as the foreseeable risk created by the defendant's negligence." *Purzyski v. Town of Fairfield,* 708 A.2d 937 (Conn.1998); *Doe v. Manheimer* 563 A. 2d 699 (1989).

6. *Intervening Cause.* An intervening act, by definition, may intercede between the original act and the injury in such a way as to break the chain of causality. A California court has explained that

> where [an] injury was brought about by a later cause of independent origin . . . [the question of proximate cause] revolves around a determination of whether the later cause of independent origin, commonly referred to as an intervening cause, was foreseeable by the defendant or, if not foreseeable, whether it caused injury of a type which was foreseeable. If either of these questions is answered in the affirmative, then the defendant is not relieved of liability towards the plaintiff; if, however, it is determined that the intervening cause was not foreseeable and that the results which it caused were not foreseeable, then the intervening cause becomes a supervening cause and the defendant is relieved from liability for the plaintiff's injuries.

Akins v. County of Sonoma, 67 Cal.2d 185, 60 Cal.Rptr. 499, 430 P.2d 57 (1967).

The intervening act of a student throwing a bamboo high-jump crossbar, after school hours, and striking another student in the eye was the sole proximate cause of injury. High-jumping equipment is not an "inherently dangerous" instrumentality that imposes a duty on teacher or school to provide supervision during non-school hours. *Bush v. Smith,* 154 Ind.App. 382, 289 N.E.2d 800 (1972).

Intervening negligence of a third party does not break proximate cause, relieving the original tortfeasor of his or her negligence, if intervening negligence is foreseeable. *Leahy v. School Board of Hernando County,* 450 So.2d 883 (Fla.App.1984).

───────────── ❖ — ❖ — ❖ ─────────────

School Did Not Breach Its Duty to Maintain Premises in Reasonably Safe Condition

Richardson v. Corvallis Public School District No. 1

Supreme Court of Montana, 1997.
950 P.2d 748.

NELSON, Justice . . .

On the morning of December 17, 1992, Dan Rochester (Donna's boyfriend) drove Donna and her son, Lance Richardson, to the Corvallis High School. After parking their car, Donna walked with Lance into the School to explain his tardiness. Taking the straightest route from their parked car to the school building, Donna uneventfully walked over a path in the snow which crossed a grass area in front of the School. After remaining in the School for approximately five minutes, Donna returned by way of the same route toward her car. However, part way across the path in the snow which crossed the grass area, Donna slipped, fell and sustained injuries. Donna testified in her deposition that it was a cold morning, that the path consisted of packed, but not slippery snow, and that the path appeared to be safe.

On May 1, 1995, Donna filed a complaint against the School in the Twenty-First Judicial District Court, Ravialli County. . . .

Relying on Donna's undisputed version of the facts, the District Court granted the School summary judgment as a matter of law. The District Court ruled that the School had no duty to warn because the path where Donna fell contained no hidden or lurking dangers. Rather, the District Court concluded that the condition of the path was open and obvious. . . . Additionally, the District Court concluded that nothing in the record indicated that the School should have anticipated injury to Donna. Accordingly, the District Court held that the School used ordinary care to keep the premises reasonably safe. . . .

To prove negligence, a plaintiff must establish four elements: (1) duty; (2) breach of duty; (3) causation; and (4) damages. *Willey*, 900 P.2d at 312 (citation omitted). "[A]ctionable negligence arises only from breach of a legal duty. Therefore, in order for there to be a genuine issue of material fact in a negligence case there must be a duty imposed upon the defendant and allegations which, if proven, would support a finding of a breach of the duty." . . .

We have consistently held as a matter of law that "the owner of a premises has a duty to use ordinary care in maintaining his premises in a reasonably safe condition and to warn of any hidden or lurking dangers." . . . However, while we have consistently held that a property owner owes this general duty of care, we have not consistently articulated a standard by which the fact finder can determine whether a property owner has breached this duty. That is, we have not articulated a standard to determine what constitutes a "reasonably safe condition." . . . Consequently, we take this opportunity to set forth one consistent standard. . . .

. . . [W]e hold that the interests of both the possessors of premises and those persons foreseeably on the premises are better served by our adoption of the following standard of care:

> The possessor of the premises has a duty to use ordinary care in maintaining the premises in a reasonably safe condition and to warn of any hidden or lurking dangers. What constitutes a reasonably safe premises is generally considered to be a question of fact. Whether a premises is reasonably safe depends to a large extent on what use the property

is put to, its setting, location and other physical characteristics; the type of person who would foreseeably visit, use or occupy the premises; and the specific type of hazard or unsafe condition alleged. The possessor of the premises is not liable to persons foreseeably upon the premises for physical harm caused to them by any activity or condition on the premises whose danger is known or obvious to them, unless the possessor should anticipate the harm despite such knowledge or obviousness.

In other words, the possessor of the premises may no longer avoid liability simply because a dangerous activity or condition on the land is open and obvious; this includes avoiding liability for open and obvious natural accumulations of ice and snow. Rather, the possessor of the premises may only be absolved from liability for injuries resulting from open and obvious dangers if he should *not* have anticipated harm to occur. This does not mean that the possessor of the premises is an absolute insurer of the safety of the premises. . . . Instead, whether the possessor of the premises should have anticipated harm depends on "the degree of ordinary care which reasonable persons would use under the same or similar circumstances." . . .

We now turn to the case at bar. . . .

As a matter of law, the School had a duty to use ordinary care in maintaining the school grounds in a reasonably safe condition and to warn of any hidden or lurking dangers. However, whether the School breached this duty of ordinary care is a question of fact. In general, negligence actions involve questions of fact, and, therefore are not susceptible to summary judgment. . . . Yet, where reasonable minds cannot differ, questions of fact can be determined as a matter of law. . . . In this case, the District Court, relying upon Donna's undisputed version of the facts, determined that no material issues of fact existed and that the School did not breach its duty of ordinary care. Having reviewed the record, we conclude that the District Court was correct in granting the School summary judgment.

First, contrary to Donna's assertion, a material question of fact does not exist concerning whether the School created a hidden dangerous condition by allowing the appearance of walkway over uneven ground where no sidewalk actually existed. Donna asserts that a hidden dangerous condition existed based on the fact that at the time of her injury she did not know that the portion of the snow packed path on which she fell crossed an area of grass rather than a cement sidewalk. However, despite her claim that the path crossed uneven ground, Donna testified in her deposition that the path appeared plowed and described the path as snow packed and only "a little bumpy." Additionally, she testified in her deposition that the path was not slippery and that she had walked over it uneventfully only moments before she fell. Based on this testimony, reasonable minds could not differ in concluding that the condition of the path was not a hidden danger, but rather that the condition of the path was known and obvious to Donna.

Furthermore, we disagree with Donna's argument that even if the snow packed condition of the path was actually known or obvious, material questions of fact still exist concerning whether the School should have anticipated her injuries. As a parent of a student attending the School, Donna was a person foreseeably on the School's premises. Further, Donna was injured when she slipped and fell on a snow packed path that existed on the School's premises. However, because the snow packed path was known and obvious to her, the School will not be held liable for Donna's injuries unless the School should have anticipated Donna's injuries despite such knowledge or obviousness.

Donna testified that the snow packed path appeared to be the safest route into the School because it appeared plowed with snow berms several feet high on each side of the path and because it led directly from her parked car to one of the School's entrances. Donna also admitted in her deposition that she had walked across the path uneventfully on her way into the School and that it was not slippery. Furthermore, Donna presented no evidence contradicting the School's position that the sidewalks around the School were appropriately maintained and safe to walk on at the time of her fall. In fact, Donna testified that if she were presented with the same conditions again, she would have parked in the same location and walked toward the School along the same path. Under the circumstances of this case, reasonable minds could not differ in concluding that the School should not have anticipated Donna's injuries.

Once the School established that no material questions of fact existed, the burden shifted to Donna, as the person opposing summary judgment, to prove otherwise. . . . The District Court relied on Donna's undisputed version of the facts in granting the School summary judgment. On appeal, Donna has failed to set forth specific facts establishing that material questions of fact exist and instead merely sets forth her own interpretation of the facts. . . .

Because no material questions of fact exist in this case, we hold that the District Court properly granted summary judgment.

Affirmed.

■ DEFENSES FOR NEGLIGENCE

In all cases involving negligence, the defendant may attempt to show that he or she is not negligent because the injury was a mere accident; that his or her act was not the proximate, or legal, cause of injury; or that some other act intervened and was responsible for the injury. However, aside from these essentials of a tort claim, other rejoinders against negligence can be classified as defenses. The most common of these are (1) contributory negligence, (2) comparative negligence, (3) assumption of risk, and (4) immunity.

Of these defenses, contributory negligence and assumption of risk are most often used in school law cases. Immunity is a defense found in both common and statutory law that derives from the state's sovereignty. Each of these concepts is briefly explained in the following sections.

CONTRIBUTORY NEGLIGENCE
Contributory negligence involves some fault or breach of duty on the part of the injured person, or failure to exercise the required standard of care for his or her own safety. One court explained contributory negligence as conduct on the part of the injured party that caused or contributed to the injury and that would not have been done by a person exercising ordinary prudence under the circumstances.[63] The *Restate-*

ment (Second) of Torts defines contributory negligence in much the same manner:

> [c]onduct on the part of the plaintiff which falls below the standard to which he should conform for his own protection, and which is legally contributing cause cooperating with the negligence of the defendant in bringing about the plaintiff's harm.[64]

As previously pointed out, a child is capable of negligence, and his or her failure to conform to a required standard of conduct for a child of the same age, physical characteristics, gender, and training will result in the court assigning fault to his or her actions. Thus, if an injured child is negligent and his or her negligence contributes to the harm, then a defendant who is also negligent may be completely absolved from liability. If the student has superior knowledge that would be protective, the courts will take it into consideration in adjudging fault. In a case in which students knew that chemicals should not be held near a flame and the students intentionally set fire to the experiment and injury resulted, the court held the students were contributorily negligent because they should have known the consequences.[65]

However, since a child is not expected to act with the same standard of care as an adult, teachers have more difficulty in showing contributory negligence than they would if the plaintiff was an adult. A child is by nature careless and often negligent, and knowing this, a teacher should allow for an additional margin of safety. This is especially true with younger children. In fact, one court has said that where a child is concerned, the test to be employed is whether the child has committed a gross disregard of safety in the face of known, perceived, and understood dangers.[66]

In a case in which contributory negligence was found, a boy climbed on top of wire screening, fell through a hole, and was injured. The jury found the boy to be contributorily at fault because he did not exercise a reasonable degree of care for his own protection.[67]

Another court has held that a pupil who was injured when he mixed chemicals in a school laboratory was guilty of contributory negligence because he knew the chemicals were dangerous.[68]

If a plaintiff's negligence or fault contributes to the injury, the court will bar recovery of any damages at all. Some courts have held that the complete barring of any damages because of contributory fault is perhaps a little drastic and have therefore endeavored to prorate damages based on the degree of fault. This results in what is known as comparative negligence.

COMPARATIVE NEGLIGENCE

When contributory negligence on the part of the plaintiff is shown, the defendant is usually completely absolved from all liability. This, some courts and legislatures have felt, works a hardship on the negligent plaintiff, who suffers injury but can recover nothing from the negligent defendant. This concern for the injured party has led legislatures in some states to enact statutes to determine degree of negligence and to allow recovery based on the relative degree of fault. While the specific provisions of "comparative negligence" statutes vary from state to state, the concept works this way: If the plaintiff's fault is found to be about equal to the defendant's, the plaintiff will recover one-half the damages and must bear the remainder of the loss. If the plaintiff's negligence amounted to one-third the fault and the defendant's two-thirds, the plaintiff could recover two-thirds of the damages.

ASSUMPTION OF RISK

Assumption of risk is another defense against negligence. Here the plaintiff acts in a manner that effectively relieves the defendant of his or her duty or obligation of conduct. The plaintiff by expressed or implied agreement recognizes the danger and assumes the risk. The defendant is thereby under no legal duty to protect the plaintiff. With knowledge of the danger, the plaintiff voluntarily enters into a relationship with the defendant and, by so doing, agrees to take his or her chances.[69]

Plaintiff's knowledge and awareness of the danger are an important factor in this defense. For example, a boy playing basketball was injured when his arm went through a glass pane in a door immediately behind the basketball backboard. The court later said that the boy had not assumed the risk of such an injury. The boy did not know the glass in the door was not shatterproof.[70] However, another court held that a boy had assumed the risk when he suffered an injury by colliding with a doorjamb in a brick wall while playing as a voluntary member of a basketball team in a school gymnasium. The boy had played in the gym previously and knew the location of the basket, the door, and the wall and therefore was aware of the danger involved in voluntarily playing in this particular gymnasium.[71] In a case in which a batter in a softball game struck, with the bat, a classmate who was sitting on the third-base line, the court said the child who was struck either assumed the risk or was contributorily negligent.[72]

Courts have generally established that participants in athletic events, whether intramural or interscholastic, assume the risk of the normal hazards of the game. This rule also applies to spectators attending sports or amusement activities. Spectators assume all the obvious or normal risks of being hurt by flying balls,[73] fireworks,[74] or the struggles of combatants.[75]

Everyone has seen spectators knocked down along the sidelines of football games by players careening off the field. A high school girl was injured precisely in this fashion as she was standing by the sidelines and was run over by football players. The court found against the plaintiff in following prevailing precedent and said that a spectator at a sporting event assumes risks incident to the game. This is especially true when the spectator chooses to stay at an unsafe place despite the availability of protected seating.[76]

Essential to the doctrine of assumption of risk is that the plaintiff have knowledge of the risks; if she or he is ignorant of the conditions and dangers, she or he does not assume the risk. If reasonable precautions are not taken to determine the hazards involved, then she or he has not assumed the risk but may have been contributorily negligent instead. However, neither a participant nor a spectator assumes the risk for negligence or willful or wanton conduct of others. For example, a spectator at an athletic contest does not assume the risk of the stands falling at a football game, nor does she or he assume that when attending a baseball game, a player will intentionally throw a bat into the stands.

IMMUNITY

Immunity from tort liability is generally conferred on (1) national and state governments

unless abrogated by statute; (2) public officials performing quasi-judicial or discretionary functions; (3) charitable organizations, granted immunity in some states; (4) infants under certain conditions; and (5) insane persons in some cases.

Where public schools are concerned, the defense of immunity is usually employed to protect the public school district against liability.[77] This governmental, or sovereign, immunity is a historical and common law precedent that protects a state agency against liability for its torts. Because of the importance of this concept and its frequent applicability in public school tort cases, governmental, or sovereign, immunity is treated separately in Chapter 13.

❖ — ❖ — ❖

Brief Absence from Class Does Not Constitute Breach of Duty of Reasonable Supervision

Stevens v. Chesteen

Supreme Court of Alabama, 1990.
561 So.2d 1100.

Timothy Stevens was injured in a motorcycle accident on or about December 23, 1987. His injuries required that he undergo surgery to repair damage to his left knee. The doctor who performed the surgery allegedly told Timothy and the officials of the Geneva school system that Timothy was to be restricted from strenuous or hazardous activity that could result in further injury to his knee.

In his brief to this Court, Timothy Stevens argues that on or about February 11, 1988, he was instructed by Chesteen, his physical education teacher, to go to the Geneva High School football field with his physical education class. Timothy had been excused from participation in physical education classes and this fact was allegedly known to Chesteen. While at the football field, Timothy did not engage in the game of touch football that was being played, but stood on the sidelines and watched the action on the field. The evidence indicates that while Timothy was standing on the sidelines, his attention was diverted to some commotion in the stands, and he did not see the players that were coming toward him from the field of play. While chasing a ball carrier, one of the players ran into Timothy and severely reinjured his knee. This reinjury necessitated further treatment and surgery.

Timothy further alleges that after the class was sent to the football field, he did not see Chesteen. Chesteen, however, disputes this account and asserts that he was present when the injury occurred. In opposition to Chesteen's motion for summary judgment, Timothy produced the separate affidavits of two students who were present at the time of his injury. These two students stated that Chesteen was not present on the football field at the time of the injury, but was in a storage shed on the visitors' side of the field. One of the students stated that he went to the fence at the edge of the field and called to Chesteen, but that Chesteen did not hear him until he called a second time. Timothy was carried to the coach's office by several students. He waited there until his mother arrived and transported him to the hospital. . . .

Chesteen points to Timothy's deposition testimony and argues that that testimony itself contradicts any claim that Chesteen "ordered" Timothy to participate in physical education or that Timothy was "forced" to go to a dangerous area. Timothy's deposition testimony shows that he was aware that he was not to participate in physical education class and that Chesteen was also aware of that restriction and had excused Timothy from participation. Timothy, in fact, was not participating in the class at the time of his injury, but was standing off to one side of the football field looking up in the stands.

Timothy argues that his complaint alleged negligent supervision and, alternatively, that Timothy was "ordered" to participate in class and go to a hazardous area. . . .

The essence of the complaint is that Chesteen was guilty of negligence either in failing to provide proper supervision for the class or in ordering Timothy to participate. We must agree with the defendant's argument that Timothy's deposition negates any question of negligent supervision. The deposition testimony cited by the defendant shows that Chesteen did not force Timothy to participate in the physical education class at which he was injured. In fact, Timothy's deposition testimony indicates that he was excused from participation in the class and that he was not a participant at the time of the accident. Moreover, Timothy stated that he felt that he was a safe distance away from the action on the field before he was injured. . . .

The question whether certain conduct amounts to "reasonable supervision" and whether supervision would have prevented the injury complained of is, of course, a question that must be answered on a case-by-case basis. However, it must always be remembered that the reality of school life is such that a teacher cannot possibly be expected to personally supervise each student in his charge at every moment of the school day. Moreover, Timothy was engaged in a common practice in standing on the sidelines and watching the game progress. . . .

The affidavits and depositions in the record clearly indicate that Timothy was not participating in a physical education class and was not on the playing field either before or at the time the accident occurred. There is no evidence to indicate that Chesteen forced Timothy to go to the field or to the stadium. The affidavits produced by Chesteen, on the other hand, tend to indicate that Chesteen did not act negligently in his supervision of the class. Timothy did not produce any evidence that had Chesteen been present, if in fact he was not, the accident would not have occurred. . . . Even if Chesteen had been present, this accident could have occurred in the same manner.

On these facts, where there is no other evidence of negligence, we cannot hold that Chesteen's mere absence from class amounts to a breach of the duty of reasonable supervision. Teenagers like Timothy often engage in "pick-up" football games that are completely unsupervised. This case involved a "touch" football game, and not a tackle game, thus making violent collisions involving bystanders on the sidelines unlikely. Moreover, we note that Timothy was not a child of tender years and, as a reasonable person, had a duty to maintain a certain vigilance for his own safety and well being. . . .

Based upon the foregoing, we hold that the trial court properly entered the summary judgment for Chesteen. That judgment is affirmed.

❖ — ❖ — ❖

*Momentary Absence from Classroom
Does Not Constitute Negligence*

Simonetti v. School District of Philadelphia

Superior Court of Pennsylvania, 1982.
308 Pa.Super. 555, 454 A.2d 1038.

WIEAND, Judge. Richard Simonetti, a fifth-grade student, returned to the classroom from recess and was struck in the left eye by a pencil which had been propelled from the hand of a classmate when he tripped. The teacher, an employee of the School District of Philadelphia, was outside the classroom, standing at the door, when Simonetti was injured. There she was engaged in monitoring the return of her students from recess and talking with another teacher. The student who dropped or threw the pencil and two other students had been required to remain in the classroom during recess as punishment for misbehavior at breakfast. They had been talking with the teacher during the recess period and were instructed to take their seats when the teacher stepped outside the classroom to supervise the return of the students from recess.

In an action against the School District, it was contended by Simonetti that the teacher had been negligent in failing to provide adequate classroom supervision. . . . The teacher, it may confidently be observed, could not have been at two places at the same time. With equal confidence, it can be said that it was not negligence for the teacher to give priority to an entire class of approximately thirty students returning from recess rather than to remain in the classroom to supervise three students who had been required to stay in the classroom during the recess period.

It is common knowledge that children may indulge in horseplay. They may throw a pencil, shoot a paper clip or snap a rubber band when a teacher is absent or turns his or her back. In the instant case, the teacher attempted to guard against any horseplay by instructing the three students who were in the classroom to return to their seats and remain there. While these students were capable of free spirits and were even being punished for unrelated misconduct at breakfast, there is no evidence that they were hellions who required constant custody.

To require the teacher to anticipate the events which occurred while she was outside the classroom door would be to hold that a teacher is required to anticipate the myriad of unexpected acts which occur daily in classrooms in every school in the land. This is not the law, and we perceive no good reason for imposing such an absolute standard on teachers and school districts.

The judgment is reversed and is now entered for the appellant.

❖ — ❖ — ❖

*Injured Student with Knowledge of Risk
Involved Is Contributorily Negligent*

Hutchison v. Toews

Court of Appeals of Oregon, Department 2, 1970.
4 Or.App. 19, 476 P.2d 811.

LANGTRY, Judge. Plaintiff appeals from a judgment of involuntary nonsuit, entered on motion of both defendants at the conclusion of the plaintiff's case.

Plaintiff and his friend, Phillip Brown, both fifteen years old, attempted to shoot a homemade pipe cannon which exploded, injuring plaintiff's hands. They had made the explosive charge by mixing potassium chlorate and powdered sugar.

Brown, as plaintiff's witness, testified that he and the plaintiff had "badgered" defendant Toews, the chemistry teacher at Phoenix High School, for potassium chlorate to use in fireworks experimentation. He said they had asked Mr. Toews for the material about a dozen times. The plaintiff said five or six times. Finally, Mr. Toews had given them some powdered potassium chlorate, which they put in a baby food jar. A day or two later, when Mr. Toews left the separate chemical storage room unattended while he stepped into the adjoining chemistry classroom, Brown took, without Mr. Toews' knowledge or permission, some crystalline potassium chlorate also stored there. Brown positively identified this crystalline potassium chlorate as the substance used in the explosion. He was the one who mixed the ingredients. The plaintiff equivocated, first indicating that the powdered substance was what was used, but on cross-examination he said, "It looked like crystal." Brown waited approximately two years after the accident before he revealed to anyone that he had taken the crystalline substance and that it had caused the explosion. The plaintiff did not reveal that he knew the crystalline substance had been taken until after Brown's disclosure of the true facts. The injury occurred in November 1965. Plaintiff commenced this action for damages against defendant Toews only in June 1966, and filed an amended complaint in August 1967. In these complaints, plaintiff alleged that defendant Toews "supplied" the potassium chlorate to him. . . .

Prosser says:

[T]he kind of contributory negligence which consists of voluntary exposure to a known danger, and so amounts to assumption of risk, is ordinarily a defense. . . . Prosser, Torts 539, § 78 (3rd ed.1964).

We think the evidence construed in the light most favorable to plaintiff . . . justifies the judgment of the court. The boys had purchased from a mail order firm in Michigan a pamphlet which gave 100 formulas for explosives. Together, they built the cannon and conducted their experiments. They admitted that they had looked at the warnings in the pamphlet. They had shown the pamphlet to defendant Toews, and he had cautioned them, and told them they should have supervision. He had declined their invitation to supervise them because of another commitment. Among other things, the pamphlet warned:

Some of the formulas listed in this booklet are very dangerous to make. Therefore, it is strongly suggested that the making of fireworks be left in the hands of the experienced.

. . . They had previously experimented with homemade gunpowder in the cannon and in doing so had used up all of their fuses. When they mixed and placed the charge of potassium chlorate and powdered sugar in the cannon, they put the head of a paper match into the fuse hole and tried to light the paper end of the match in order to have time to take cover before the explosion. When Brown tried to light the paper match, wind impeded him. On Brown's request, plaintiff held his hands around the fuse hole to shield it from the wind. The charge exploded, and the closed pipe end "peeled like a banana." Plaintiff's hands were severely injured. The evidence is lengthy, but it is replete with statements from both of the boys that they knew the experiment conducted was dangerous. Plaintiff testified on cross-examination he knew "That you might get burned if you held onto it, or if you stood too close to it when it did shoot . . . that it might fly up or hit you in the face. . . . "

Plaintiff testified he knew that the pamphlet said the formula was very powerful. . . .

There are many cases involving tort liability of suppliers of explosives to children. No purpose is served by a detailed discussion of them here. We note that they usually turn on whether the plaintiff had or should have had knowledge and understanding so that he could have avoided the explosion. . . .

In the case at bar, the only reasonable conclusion from the evidence was that plaintiff had knowledge of the risk involved, and that he was contributorily negligent as a matter of law.

Affirmed.

CASE NOTES

1. *Proper Supervision.* If a rule can be developed from the teacher liability cases, it is this: A teacher's absence from the classroom, or failure to properly supervise students' activities, is not likely to give rise to a cause of action for injury to a student unless under all the circumstances the possibility of injury is reasonably foreseeable. In *Carroll v. Fitzsimmons,* 153 Colo. 1, 3, 384 P.2d 81, 82 (1963), the Supreme Court of Colorado had before it the question whether an allegation "that the plaintiff was struck in the eye by a rock thrown by a fellow student" and "that the defendant teacher permitted the rock

to be thrown" stated a cause of action. In affirming the dismissal of the complaint, the court quoted from *Nestor v. City of New York*, 28 Misc.2d 70, 71, 211 N.Y.S.2d 975, 977 (1961):

> There is no requirement that the teacher have under constant and unremitting scrutiny the precise spots wherein every phase of play activity is being pursued; nor is there compulsion that the general supervision be continuous and direct.

2. Requiring students to run to the dressing room when time between classes is short does not create an unreasonable risk. *Driscol v. Delphi Community School Corp.*, 155 Ind.App. 56, 290 N.E.2d 769 (1972).

3. In preparation of a project for a science fair, a girl was burned when students attempted to light a defective burner that had gone out and alcohol exploded after the teacher had set the experiment up, checked that it worked correctly, and returned to his regular class. The court, in holding the teacher liable for negligence, said: "[W]here one creates, deals in, handles or distributes an inherently dangerous object or substance . . . an extraordinary degree of care is required of those responsible. . . . The duty is particularly heavy where children are exposed to a dangerous condition which they may not appreciate." The duty was either to positively warn the students not to try to light the burner or to personally supervise; the teacher did neither. *Station v. Travelers Insurance Co.*, 292 So.2d 289 (La.App.1974).

4. A trade school welding student was not contributorily negligent when injured by an exploding freon cylinder. *Danos v. Foret*, 354 So.2d 667 (La.App.1977).

5. A chemistry experiment in an introductory high school course, requiring students to use materials that could explode, should be conducted under the strictest supervision and personal attention of the teacher. *Mastrangelo v. West Side Union High School District of Merced County*, 2 Cal.2d 540, 42 P.2d 634 (1935).

6. A coach is not liable for injury to a player on an opposing team, resulting from a rule violation of a player on his own team. The court said: "A coach cannot be held responsible for the wrongful acts of his players unless he teaches them to do the wrongful act or instructs them to commit the act." *Nydegger v. Don Bosco Preparatory High School*, 202 N.J.Super. 535, 495 A.2d 485 (1985).

7. *Liability of Teacher Aide for Pupil Injury.* When teacher aides are assigned tasks involving supervision, they are placed in a position of potential liability for pupil injury. In such a situation, liability is likely to arise out of negligence on the part of the aide. Any persons assigned such responsibilities are ignorant at their own peril. If they are not qualified to supervise playgrounds, they should not attempt to perform the task.

In cases involving pupil injury, the courts have traditionally held the teacher to a higher "standard of care" than that owed to the general public. Likewise, a teacher aide, when placed in a supervisory capacity, owes the pupils a greater "standard of care" than is normally required in other personal relationships.

8. *Liability of Administrator or Supervisor for Negligent Acts of Teacher Aide.* Where the administrator or supervisor appoints a well-qualified person to perform certain functions about the school and injury results, the administrator is not liable for negligence. The general rule of law is that in the public school situation the master is not liable for the commissions and omissions of his or her servant. In a Rhode Island case illustrating this principle, the court held that a school principal, who had authority over a school janitor, was not liable for injuries to a school teacher when the principal failed to warn her of a slippery floor in the school building. *Gray v. Wood*, 75 R.I. 123, 64 A.2d 191 (1949).

Therefore, a teacher or a principal is not liable for the negligent acts of a properly appointed and qualified teacher aide. On the other hand, if a teacher or a principal assigns duties for which the teacher aide is not qualified and the purposes of which do not fall within the scope of the aide's employment, the teacher or the principal may be liable for negligent acts by the aide.

9. An Illinois court, in relating tort liability to the *in loco parentis* standard, found that teachers are not subject to any greater liability than parents for injury to their children. Parents are liable only for willful and wanton misconduct, but not for mere negligence. *Montague v. School Board of the Thornton Fractional Township North High School District 215*, 57 Ill.App.3d 828, 15 Ill.Dec. 373, 373 N.E.2d 719 (1978).

10. *Suicide.* The Arkansas Supreme Court has said that a school cannot "shelter a growing child from every possible danger." Where a third-grade child hanged himself in a school bathroom by a length of nylon cord attached to a large plywood bathroom pass, the court said that the school had taken adequate safety measures and that it was "manifestly futile" to protect students from all possibilities of injury, self-inflicted or otherwise. *Gathright v. Lincoln Insurance Co.*, 286 Ark. 16, 688 S.W.2d 931 (1985).

11. *Damages.* The Supreme Court of Florida has attempted to set out an objective standard for review for damage awards. In the case of *Bould v. Touchette*, 349 So.2d 1181 (Fla.1977), the court stated:

> Where recovery is sought for a personal tort, or where punitive damages are allowed, we cannot apply fixed rules to a given set of facts and say that a verdict is for more than would be allowable under a correct computation. In tort cases damages are to be measured by the jury's discretion. The court should never declare a verdict excessive merely because it is above the amount which the court itself considers the jury should have allowed. The verdict should not be disturbed unless it is so inordinately large as obviously to exceed the maximum limit of a reasonable range within which the jury may properly operate.

❖ — ❖ — ❖

Female Student Assumed the Normal, Obvious Risks of Injury in Choosing to Play Tackle Football

Hammond v. Board of Education of Carroll County

Court of Special Appeals, Maryland, 1994.
100 Md.App. 60, 639 A.2d 223.

MOTZ, Judge.

On August 25, 1989, appellant, Tawana Hammond, the first female high school football player in Carroll County history, was injured in her team's initial scrimmage. Three years later, Tawana and her mother, appellant Peggy Hammond (collectively, the Hammonds), filed suit in the Circuit Court for Carroll County against appellee, the Board of Education of Carroll County (the Board), seeking $1.25 million in compensatory damages. The Hammonds asserted (1) that the high school authorities negligently failed to warn them of the potential risk of injury inherent in playing football and (2) that if they had been so warned Tawana would not have chosen to play football and her mother would not have permitted her to do so. After the parties conducted discovery, the Board moved for summary judgment, which the circuit court (Beck, J.) granted.

The record reveals that the underlying material facts are not disputed. Sixteen-year-old Tawana tried out for the Francis Scott Key High School varsity football team in the summer of 1989, prior to the beginning of her junior year in high school. Although Tawana had previously participated in a number of track events and played softball and soccer, she had never engaged in any contact sports. Tawana had watched football on television since she was six years old but did not become interested in football until her freshman year in high school; she had never observed any "really serious" injuries in these televised games, only a "twisted ankle or something." She saw a half dozen high school games during her freshman and sophomore years and saw no players hurt at those games. Tawana knew football was a "physical contact sport" and determined she wanted to play it because "[i]t was different."

In order for a student to play sports at Francis Scott Key High School, the student and the student's parent must sign a document entitled "Francis Scott Key High School Athletic Regulations and Permission Form." Both Tawana and her father, John Hammond (not a party herein), signed this form on June 18, 1989. The permission form states that the student has read the school handbook and regulations and agrees to abide by them and that the parent has read them and "consents" to the child's participation in the sport. One sentence in the permission form specifically states that "[w]e do our very best to avoid accidents, but we realize that in the normal course of events, some occur." In deposition, Tawana testified that she read the permission form and, in particular, this sentence before she started playing football and understood that she "could get a broken leg, [or] broken arm" as a result of playing varsity, tackle football. . . .

As practices continued, Tawana had no difficulty in keeping up physically with the other players on the team. On August 25, 1989, Tawana, along with the rest of the Francis Scott Key High School varsity football team, travelled to Anne Arundel County for the team's first practice scrimmage. Prior to the scrimmage, Tawana was interviewed by a television reporter and stated that "[p]laying football is a tough sport. I do have to admit that." During the scrimmage, while carrying the ball, Tawana was tackled by a rival player and sustained multiple internal injuries including a ruptured spleen. Her spleen and part of her pancreas were removed, and she was hospitalized for some time. On August 13, 1992, Tawana and her mother filed this suit. The circuit court granted summary judgment to the Board, concluding that (a) it had no duty to warn "of the risk of serious, disabling and catastrophic injury associated with playing on a high-school-varsity, tackle, football team"; (b) if there was a duty to warn the Hammonds it was satisfied; and (c) Tawana and her mother assumed the risk of injury as a matter of law. . . .

The central theory espoused by the Hammonds, that the school board had a duty to warn them of the severe injuries that might result from voluntarily participating on a varsity high school tackle football team, is one that, as far as we can determine, has never been adopted by any court in this country.

There are, to be sure, numerous cases in which minors injured while playing in school sporting events have sued school officials (or others similarly situated) asserting that the officials' negligence caused the participant's injuries. . . . In none of these cases, however, have the plaintiffs successfully asserted that the school officials were negligent because of some failure to warn the plaintiffs of the possible dangers involved in voluntarily participating in the contact sport. In the past, plaintiffs have made claims of negligence because of asserted inadequate or improper supervision, . . . instruction or training, . . . and inadequate equipment, . . . but the parties have not cited and we have not uncovered any case in which a plaintiff, in circumstances similar to the Hammonds', has successfully made a negligence claim based on a failure to warn of possible physical injury. Perhaps this is because permeating the sports injury cases is the recognition that "[p]hysical contact in . . . an athletic contest is foreseeable and expected." . . . The "general rule is that participants in an athletic contest accept the normal physical contact of the particular sport." Absent evidence of "mental deficiency," and there is no claim that Tawana is not at least of average intelligence, minors are held to "sufficiently appreciate[] the dangers inherent in the game of football," . . . to know that "football is a rough and hazardous game and that anyone playing or practicing such a game may be injured," . . . and that "[f]atigue, and unfortunately, injury are inherent in team competitive sports, especially football." . . .

Thus, it is "common knowledge that children participating in games . . . may injure themselves and . . . no amount of supervision . . . will avoid some such injuries, and the law does not make a school the insurer of the safety of pupils at play." . . .

As the Supreme Court of Oregon explained in rejecting a similar claim by a fifteen-year-old injured in a football game, the playing of football is a body-contact sport. The game demands that the players come into physical contact with each other constantly, frequently with great force. . . . [T]he ball-carrier . . . must be prepared to strike the ground violently. Body contacts, bruises, and clashes are inherent in the game. There is no other way to play it. No prospective player need be told that a participant in the game of football may sustain injury. That fact is self[-]evident. . . .

For these reasons, courts have been extremely inhospitable to claims that properly equipped, injured high school players should be able to recover from school officials for injuries sustained during an ordinary, voluntary contact sport game. Thus, in the vast majority of such cases, it has been held that those asserting such claims cannot recover as a matter of law. . . .

That principle is well established in Maryland. The Court of Appeals explained more than twenty-five years ago that when a pleading alleges a danger that is "ordinary and obvious," it has not sufficiently alleged "circumstances which would require the defendants to give a warning." . . . Here the hazard alleged—the possibility of injury to a voluntary participant in a varsity high school tackle football game—was "the normal, obvious and usual incident[]" of the activity. . . .

In light of our conclusion that the Board had no duty to warn the Hammonds, we need not reach the question of whether Tawana assumed the risk as a matter of law. . . .

Although she has not stated a cause of action against the Board, Tawana's injuries were serious, painful, and permanent. We regret them and sympathize with her. Our holding here, that school officials have no duty to warn a student or the student's parents that serious injury might result from the student's voluntary participation on a high school varsity tackle football team, does not mean that such a warning would not be a sound idea as a matter of public policy. Young men—and women—of the same age, who wish to participate in the same team contact sports, vary considerably in weight and size; unfortunately, the sport may occasionally pit the brawniest against the most slender. In view of the very serious injuries suffered by Tawana, school officials may well want to consider issuing a warning of the possibility of such injuries—even though there is no legal obligation to do so.

JUDGMENT AFFIRMED.

COSTS TO BE PAID BY APPELLANTS.

CASE NOTES

1. *Assumption of Risk.* A student assumes the normal "foreseeable consequences" of participation in a contact school sport. In a Florida case where some players were not issued football helmets for a nontackle, but contact, practice, plaintiff suffered a bad mouth injury, and the court found that neither the school district nor the coaches could defend by claiming the injured student assumed the risk. The court concluded that there was "no evidence that [the injured student] assumed the risk of participating in a training drill which was improperly supervised and for which he had improper and insufficient equipment." Moreover, the court found that an intervening cause that is foreseeable cannot insulate a defendant from liability. *Leahy v.*

School Board of Hernando County, 450 So.2d 883 (Fla.App.5 Dist.1984).

2. The student must voluntarily assume the risk of participation in the particular activity. Compulsion or "indirect compulsion" strong enough to compel participation overcomes the defense of assumption of risk. See *Benitez v. New York City Board of Education,* 73 N.Y.2d 650, 543 N.Y.S.2d 29, 541 N.E.2d 29 (1989).

3. With regard to assumption of risk, the Latin aphorism is applicable: "One who consents to an act does not suffer a compensable injury." *Benitez,* 541 N.Y.S.2d at 32.

Judge Benjamin Cardozo, referred to earlier in this chapter in the note regarding the *Palsgraf* case, best stated the assumption-of-risk theory in the "Flopper" amusement ride case. He said:

> One who takes part in such a sport accepts the dangers that inhere in it so far as they are obvious and necessary, just as a fencer accepts the risk of a thrust by the antagonist or a spectator at a ball game the chance of contact with the ball.

Murphy v. Steeplechase Amusement Co., 250 N.Y. 479, 482, 166 N.E. 173, 174 (1929).

4. Assumption of risk is integral to athletic competitions where participants are held to assume normal risks by their actual or implied consents to play the game. Normal risks are those "injury-causing events of reasonably foreseeable consequences of the participation." Participants do not consent to events that may transpire in the activity that are not assumed to be normal and certainly do not assume those risks that are reckless or intentional. *Turcotte v. Fell,* 68 N.Y.2d 432, 510 N.Y.S.2d 49, 502 N.E.2d 964 (1986).

Awareness of the risk assumed is "to be assessed against the background of the skill and experience of the particular plaintiff, and in that assessment a higher degree of awareness will be imputed to a professional than to one with less than professional experience in the particular sport." *Maddox v. City of New York,* 66 N.Y.2d 270, 278, 496 N.Y.S.2d 726, 729, 487 N.E.2d 553 (1985).

Players who voluntarily join in extracurricular interscholastic sports assume the risks to which their roles expose them but not the risks that are "unreasonably increased or concealed." *McGee v. Board of Education,* 16 A.D.2d 99, 102,

226 N.Y.S.2d 329, 332, leave denied, 13 N.Y.2d 596, 243 N.Y.S.2d 1025, 193 N.E.2d 644 (1963).

❖ — ❖ — ❖

Releases That Students or Parents Are Required to Sign as a Condition of Engaging in School Activities and That Exculpate School Districts from Liability for Negligence Are Invalid as Violative of Public Policy

Wagenblast v. Odessa School District No. 105-157-166J

Supreme Court of Washington (en banc), 1988.
110 Wash.2d 845, 758 P.2d 968.

ANDERSEN, Justice.

In these consolidated cases we consider an issue of first impression—the legality of public school districts requiring students and their parents to sign a release of all potential future claims as a condition to student participation in certain school-related activities.

The plaintiffs in these cases are public school children and their parents.

Odessa School District students Alexander and Charles Wagenblast and Ethan and Katie Herdrick all desired to participate in some form of interscholastic athletics. As a condition to such participation, the Odessa School District requires its students and their parents or guardians to sign a standardized form which releases the school district from "liability resulting from any ordinary negligence that may arise in connection with the school district's interscholastic activities programs." The releases are required by a group of small Eastern Washington school districts, including Odessa, which "pooled" together to purchase liability insurance.

The Seattle School District also requires students and their parents to sign standardized release forms as a condition to participation in interscholastic sports and cheerleading. When Richard and Paul Vulliet turned out for the Ballard High School wrestling team, they and their parents were required to sign release forms which released the Seattle School District, its employees and agents "from any liability result-ing from any negligence that may arise in connection with the School District's wrestling program." . . .

One issue is determinative of these appeals.

Can school districts require public school students and their parents to sign written releases which release the districts from the consequences of all future school district negligence, before the students will be allowed to engage in certain recognized school related activities, here interscholastic athletics?

We hold that the exculpatory releases from any future school district negligence are invalid because they violate public policy. . . .

Probably the best exposition of the test to be applied in determining whether exculpatory agreements violate public policy is that stated by the California Supreme Court. In writing for a unanimous court, the late Justice Tobriner outlined the factors . . . :

> Thus the attempted but invalid exemption involves a transaction which exhibits some or all of the following characteristics. It concerns a business of a type generally thought suitable for public regulation. The party seeking exculpation is engaged in performing a service of great importance to the public, which is often a matter of practical necessity for some members of the public. The party holds himself out as willing to perform this service for any member of the public who seeks it, or at least for any member coming within certain established standards. As a result of the essential nature of the service, in the economic setting of the transaction, the party invoking exculpation possesses a decisive advantage of bargaining strength against any member of the public who seeks his services. In exercising a superior bargaining power the party confronts the public with a standardized adhesion contract of exculpation, and makes no provision whereby a purchaser may pay additional reasonable fees and obtain protection against negligence. Finally, as a result of the transaction, the person or property of the purchaser is placed under the control of the seller, subject to the risk of carelessness by the seller or his agents.

. . . We agree.

Obviously, the more of the foregoing six characteristics that appear in a given exculpatory agreement case, the more likely the agreement is to be declared invalid on public policy grounds. In the consolidated cases before us, *all* of the characteristics are present in *each* case. We separately, then, examine each of these six characteristics as applied to the cases before us.

The agreement concerns an endeavor of a type generally thought suitable for public regulation.

Regulation of governmental entities usually means self-regulation. Thus, the Legislature has by statute granted to each school board the authority to control, supervise, and regulate the conduct of interscholastic athletics. In some situations, a school board is permitted, in turn, to delegate this authority to the Washington Interscholastic Activities Association (WIAA) or to another voluntary nonprofit entity. In the cases before us, both school boards look to the WIAA for regulation of interscholastic sports. . . .

Clearly then, interscholastic sports in Washington are extensively regulated, and are a fit subject for such regulation.

The party seeking exculpation is engaged in performing a service of great importance to the public, which is often a matter of practical necessity for some members of the public.

This court has held that public school students have no fundamental right to participate in interscholastic athletics. Nonetheless, the court also has observed that the justification advanced for interscholastic athletics is their educational and cultural value. . . . Given this emphasis on sports by the public and the school system, it would be unrealistic to expect students to view athletics as an activity entirely separate and apart from the remainder of their schooling. . . .

In sum, under any rational view of the subject, interscholastic sports in public schools are a matter of public importance in this jurisdiction.

Such party holds itself out as willing to perform this service for any member of the public who seeks it, or at least for any member coming within certain established standards.

Implicit in the nature of interscholastic sports is the notion that such programs are open to all students who meet certain skill and eligibility standards. . . .

Because of the essential nature of the service, in the economic setting of the transaction, the party invoking exculpation possesses a decisive advantage of bargaining strength against any member of the public who seeks the services.

Not only have interscholastic sports become of considerable importance to students and the general public alike, but in most instances there exists no alternative program of organized competition. . . . While outside alternatives exist for some activities, they possess little of the inherent allure of interscholastic competition. . . . In this regard, school districts have near-monopoly power. And, because such programs have become important to student participants, school districts possess a clear and disparate bargaining strength when they insist that students and their parents sign these releases.

In exercising a superior bargaining power, the party confronts the public with a standardized adhesion contract of exculpation, and makes no provision whereby a purchaser may pay additional reasonable fees and obtain protection against negligence.

Both school districts admit to an unwavering policy regarding these releases; no student athlete will be allowed to participate in any program without first signing the release form as written by the school district. In both of these cases, students and their parents unsuccessfully attempted to modify the forms by deleting the release language. In both cases, the school district rejected the attempted modifications. Student athletes and their parents or guardians have no alternative but to sign the standard release forms provided to them or have the student barred from the program.

The person or property of members of the public seeking such services must be placed under the control of the furnisher of the services, subject to the risk of carelessness on the part of the furnisher, its employees or agents.

A school district owes a duty to its students to employ ordinary care and to anticipate reasonably foreseeable dangers so as to take precautions for protecting the children in its custody from such dangers. This duty extends to students engaged in interscholastic sports. . . . The student is thus subject to the risk that the school district or its agent will breach this duty of care.

In sum, the attempted releases in the cases before us exhibit all six of the characteristics. . . . Because of this, and for the aforesaid reasons, we hold that the releases in these consolidated cases are invalid as against public policy. . . .

The remaining aspect of these appeals which merits discussion is the Legislature's role in deciding such matters of public policy. By act of the territorial Legislature of 1869, school districts were made liable for their acts of negligence. At the 1917 session of the State Legislature, a bill to absolutely immunize school districts from negligence passed the Senate, but the bill which was ultimately enacted that year was a compromise; that compromise barred actions against school districts for noncontractual acts or omissions relating to any park, playground, field house, athletic apparatus or appliance or manual training equipment. This compromise statute, in turn, was repealed some years later—by the 1967 Legislature. Thus, since territorial days, the State Legislature has generally followed a policy of holding school districts accountable for their negligence. Our decision today is in general accordance with that policy.

Legislative policies may, of course, change with changing conditions. This opinion is not to be construed as precluding school districts from attempting to convince the Legislature that their problems in this area require a legislative response of one kind or another. The Legislature through its hearing processes is well suited to making such inquiries and has tools and resources adequate to the task.

The decision of the trial court in the Odessa School District case is affirmed and the decision of the trial court in the Seattle School District case is reversed.

CASE NOTES

1. Exculpatory clauses purporting to contract away liability for intentional conduct, recklessness, or gross negligence are unenforceable. *Adams v. Roark*, 686 S.W.2d 73 (Tenn.1985).

2. A permission slip is not a valid exculpatory release.

3. A Mississippi court has held that minors cannot sign exculpatory releases and no one can sign for them. A court in that state has said: "Minors can waive nothing. In the law they are helpless, so much so that their representatives can waive nothing for them." *Khoury v. Saik*, 203 Miss. 155, 33 So.2d 616 (1948).

4. The Supreme Court of Connecticut has held that a parental release of liability is ineffec-

tive because a parent cannot release the child's action. *Doyle v. Bowdoin College*, 403 A.2d 1206 (Me.1979).

5. A Tennessee court has said that "[t]he law is clear that a guardian cannot, on behalf of an infant or incompetent, exculpate or indemnify against liability, those organizations which sponsor activities for children and the mentally disabled." *Childress v. Madison County*, 777 S.W.2d 1 (Tenn.App.1989).

■ EDUCATIONAL MALPRACTICE

Several courts in recent years have issued opinions on cases that fall under a general classification of educational malpractice. Such cases are not a separate area of law but instead represent an expansion of the traditional tort law concept as applied to the educational setting. Basically, educational malpractice is an attempt to apply tort law to educational outcomes in such a way as to redress a student for knowledge deficiencies allegedly created by some substandard treatment of the student during the educational process.

Evidence to support an allegation of intentional tort would seem to be very difficult to provide unless one could show that an educator, for some malicious purpose, set out to prevent a child from obtaining an education. The possibility of maintaining an action for intentional tort was recognized by a Maryland court when it stated: "It is our view that where an individual engaged in the education process is shown to have willfully and maliciously injured a child entrusted to his educational care, such outrageous conduct greatly outweighs any public policy considerations which would otherwise preclude liability so as to authorize recovery."[78]

The more common application of tort to redress a student's educational deficiencies is found in negligence. Here it is maintained that educators failed to act reasonably in meeting a student's educational needs. Such actions, though, have met with little or no success, as the courts have established an imposing array of precedents denying students damages. The courts have generally denied redress for three reasons: "the absence of a workable rule of care against which defendant's conduct may be measured, the inherent uncertainty in determining the cause and nature of any damages, and the extreme burden which would be imposed on the already strained resources of the public school system to say nothing of the judiciary."[79]

The first reason given is, of course, related directly to the negligence question. How can a court enunciate a standard of care without a clear determination of the actual duty owed to the student? Does the educator have a duty to fill the vessel of the student's mind with a given amount of knowledge, and if the vessel remains half full, does the educator, student, parent, or society bear the blame?

The problem of delineating an actionable duty was recognized by a California court in *Peter W.*[80] when it explained:

> The "injury" claimed here is plaintiff's inability to read and write. Substantial professional authority attests that the achievement of literacy in the schools, or its failure, is influenced by a host of factors which affect the pupil subjectively, from outside the formal teaching process, and beyond the control of its ministers. They may be physical, neurological, emotional, cultural, environmental; they may be present but not perceived, recognized but not identified.

In such a situation, the court could not find that the student had suffered injury within the meaning of negligence law, nor could it identify a workable "rule of care" that could be applied. Neither could the court find a causal relationship between any perceived injury and the alleged negligent commission or omission by the defendant. A New York court drew a conclusion similar to that in *Peter W.* and further maintained that judicial interference in this area would constitute a "blatant interference" with the administration of the public school system.[81] In agreement with these courts, the court in *Hunter* said that "to allow petitioners' asserted negligence claims to proceed would in effect position the courts of this state as overseers of both the day-to-day operation of our educational process as well as the formulation of its governing policies. This responsibility we are loath to impose on our courts."[82]

Other courts have likewise rejected plaintiffs' tort claims in negligence actions.[83]

❖ — ❖ — ❖

Educational Malpractice Is Not a Cognizable Cause of Action in Tort Law

Donohue v. Copiague Union Free School District

Court of Appeals of New York, 1979.
47 N.Y.2d 440, 418 N.Y.S.2d 375, 391 N.E.2d 1352.

JASEN, Judge. This appeal poses the question whether a complaint seeking monetary damages for "educational malpractice" states a cause of action cognizable in the courts.

Appellant entered Copiague Senior High School in September, 1972, and graduated in June, 1976. The thrust of appellant's claim is that notwithstanding his receipt of a certificate of graduation he lacks even the rudimentary ability to comprehend written English on a level sufficient to enable him to complete applications for employment. His complaint attributes this deficiency to the failure of respondent to perform its duties and obligations to educate appellant. To be more specific, appellant alleges in his complaint that respondent through its employees "gave to [appellant] passing grades and/or minimal or failing grades in various subjects; failed to evaluate [appellant's] mental ability and capacity to comprehend the subjects being taught to him at said school; failed to take proper means and precautions that they reasonably should have taken under the circumstances; failed to interview, discuss, evaluate and/or psychologically test [appellant] in order to ascertain his ability to comprehend and understand such matter; failed to provide adequate school facilities, teachers, administrators, psychologists, and other personnel trained to take the necessary steps in testing and evaluation processes insofar as [appellant] is concerned in order to ascertain the learning capacity, intelligence and intellectual absorption on the part of [appellant]."

Based upon these acts of commission and omission, appellant frames two causes of action, the first of which sounds in "educational malpractice" and the second of which alleges the negligent breach of a constitutionally imposed duty to educate. To redress his injury, appellant seeks the sum of $5,000,000. Upon respondent's motion, Special Term dismissed appellant's complaint for failure to state a cause of action. The Appellate Division affirmed, with one Justice dissenting. There should be an affirmance.

The second cause of action need not detain us long. The State Constitution (art. XI, § 1) commands that "[t]he legislature shall provide for the maintenance and support of a system of free common schools, wherein all the children of this state may be educated." Even a terse reading of this provision reveals that the Constitution places the obligation of *maintaining and supporting* a system of public schools upon the *Legislature*. To be sure, this general directive was never intended to impose a duty flowing directly from a local school district to individual pupils to ensure that each pupil receives a minimum level of education, the breach of which duty would entitle a pupil to compensatory damages. . . .

Appellant's first cause of action bears closer scrutiny. It may very well be that even within the strictures of a traditional negligence or malpractice action, a complaint sounding in "educational malpractice" may be formally pleaded. Thus, the imagination need not be overly taxed to envision allegations of a legal duty of care flowing from educators, if viewed as professionals, to their students. If doctors, lawyers, architects, engineers and other professionals are charged with a duty owing to the public whom they serve, it could be said that nothing in the law precludes similar treatment of professional educators. Nor would creation of a standard with which to judge an educator's performance of that duty necessarily pose an insurmountable obstacle. . . . As for proximate causation, while this element might indeed be difficult, if not impossible, to prove in view of the many collateral factors involved in the learning process, it perhaps assumes too much to conclude that it could never be established. This would leave only the element of injury and who can in good faith deny that a student who upon graduation from high school cannot comprehend simple English—a deficiency allegedly attributable to the negligence of his educators—has not in some fashion been "injured."

The fact that a complaint alleging "educational malpractice" might on the pleadings state a cause of action within traditional notions of tort law does not, however, require that it be sustained. The heart of the matter is whether, assuming that such a cause of action may be stated, the courts should, as a matter of public policy, entertain such claims. We believe they should not. . . .

To entertain a cause of action for "educational malpractice" would require the courts not merely to make judgments as to the validity of broad educational policies—a course we have unalteringly eschewed in the past—but, more importantly, to sit in review of the day-to-day implementation of these policies. Recognition in the courts of this cause of action would constitute blatant interference with the responsibility for the administration of the public school system lodged by Constitution and statute in school administrative agencies. . . . Of course, "[t]his is not to say that there may never be gross violations of defined public policy which the courts would be obliged to recognize and correct." . . .

Finally, not to be overlooked in today's holding is the right of students presently enrolled in public schools, and their parents, to take advantage of the administrative processes provided by statute to enlist the aid of the Commissioner of Education in ensuring that such students receive a proper education. The Education Law (§ 310, subd. 7) permits any person aggrieved by an "official act or decision of any officer, school authorities, or meetings concerning any other matter under this chapter, or any other act pertaining to common schools" to seek review of such act or decision by the commissioner.

Accordingly, the order of the Appellate Division should be affirmed, with costs.

WACHTLER, Judge (concurring).

I agree that complaints of "educational malpractice" are for school administrative agencies, rather than the courts, to resolve.

There is, however, another even more fundamental objection to entertaining plaintiff's cause of action alleging educational malpractice. It is a basic principle that the law does not provide a remedy for every injury. . . . As the majority notes, the decision of whether a new cause of action should be recognized at law is largely a question of policy. Critical to such a determination is whether the cause of action sought to be pleaded would be reasonably manageable within our legal system. The practical problems raised by a cause of action sounding in educational malpractice are so formidable that I would conclude that such a legal theory should not be cognizable in our courts. These problems, clearly articulated at the Appellate Division, include the practical impossibility of proving that the alleged malpractice of the teacher proximately caused the learning deficiency of the plaintiff student.

Factors such as the student's attitude, motivation, temperament, past experience and home environment may all play an essential and immeasurable role in learning. Indeed as the majority observes proximate cause might "be difficult, if not impossible, to prove."

I would, therefore, affirm the order of the Appellate Division on the ground that educational malpractice, as here pleaded, is not a cognizable cause of action. . . .

Order affirmed.

CASE NOTES

1. In a case with a slightly different perspective, the Montana Supreme Court, in a narrow four-to-three decision, held that misplacement of a child in a special education class constituted a kind of "malpractice." This court said the school owed a "duty of reasonable care in testing and placing the child in an appropriate special education program." In a concurring opinion, it was noted that the state's special education statutes created a "duty" that required "reasonable care." The court distinguished this situation from the *Peter W.* and *Donohue* cases.

In reality, this case becomes a special education statutory case that is quite different from the cause of action described as a common law tort for malpractice. It is a case of special education misplacement, not a case of tort based on negligence in the provision of basic academic skills. *B. M. v. State*, 200 Mont. 58, 649 P.2d 425 (1982). See Michael A. Magone, "Educational

Malpractice—Does the Cause of Action Exist?" *Montana Law Review* 49 (Winter 1988): p. 140.

2. A Maryland court agreed with regard to the educational malpractice determinations of the *Peter W.* and *Donohue* cases, pointing out:

> We find ourselves in substantial agreement with the reasoning employed by the courts in *Peter W.* and *Donohue,* for an award of money damages, in our view, represents a singularly inappropriate remedy for asserted errors in the educational process. The misgivings expressed in these cases concerning the establishment of legal cause and the inherent immeasurability of damages that is involved in such educational negligence actions against the school systems are indeed well founded. Moreover, to allow petitioners' asserted negligence claims to proceed would in effect position the courts of this State as overseers of both the day-to-day operation of our educational process as well as the formulation of its governing policies. This responsibility we are loathe to impose on our courts.

Hunter v. Board of Education of Montgomery County, 439 A.2d 582 (Md.1982).

3. A Pennsylvania court disagreed with the Montana court, saying that the misplacement of a handicapped student under special education law would support a common law action for educational malpractice. *Agostine v. School District of Philadelphia*, 106 Pa.Cmwlth. 492, 527 A.2d 193 (1987). The same result was reached in *Savino v. Board of Education of School District No. 1, West-bury N.Y.*, 123 A.D.2d 314, 506 N.Y.S.2d 210 (1986); and in *Doe v. Board of Education in Montgomery County*, 295 Md. 67, 453 A.2d 814 (1982). See also *D. S. W. v. Fairbanks North Star Borough School District*, 628 P.2d 554 (Alaska 1981).

4. In another special education diagnostic misplacement case in Maryland, the court held that an "educational malpractice" negligence case could not be sustained without a workable rule for measuring the school's conduct. Because such measures do not exist, the court ruled that damages for educational malpractice actions could not be justified. *Hunter v. Board of Education of Montgomery County*, 292 Md. 481, 439 A.2d 582 (1982).

5. A New York court held that a social services department could not be liable for negligence in plaintiffs' action for educational malpractice. The court said that public policy precluded an educa-

tional malpractice action against a public school or a child care agency. *Torres v. Little Flower Children's Services*, 64 N.Y.2d 119, 485 N.Y.S.2d 15, 474 N.E.2d 223 (1984).

■ ENDNOTES

1. Warren A. Seavey, Page Keeton, and Robert E. Keeton, *Law of Torts* (St. Paul, Minn.: West, 1957), p. 1.

2. Theodore F. T. Plucknett, *A Concise History of the Common Law*, 5th ed. (Boston: Little, Brown, 1956), p. 459.

3. W. Page Keeton, Dan B. Dobbs, Robert E. Keeton, and David G. Owen, *Prosser and Keeton on Torts*, 5th ed. (St. Paul, Minn.: West, 1984), p. 2.

4. Ibid.

5. Keeton et al., *Prosser and Keeton on Torts*, p. 6.

6. William L. Prosser, *Law of Torts* (St. Paul, Minn.: West, 1971), p. 1.

7. Reynolds v. Pierson, 29 Ind.App. 273, 64 N.E. 484 (1902); State v. Monroe, 121 N.C. 677, 28 S.E. 547 (1897).

8. *Restatement (Second) of Torts* (St. Paul, Minn.: American Law Institute Publishers, 1977), p. 15.

9. Ibid.

10. Ibid.

11. Keeton et al., *Prosser and Keeton on Torts*, p. 46.

12. Johnson v. Sampson, 167 Minn. 203, 208 N.W. 814 (1926).

13. State v. Ingram, 237 N.C. 197, 74 S.E.2d 532 (1953).

14. Prosser, *Law of Torts*, p. 37.

15. Suits v. Glover, 260 Ala. 449, 71 So.2d 49 (1954).

16. State ex rel. Burpee v. Burton, 45 Wis. 150 (1878).

17. Gardner v. State, 4 Ind. 632 (1853).

18. Vanvactor v. State, 113 Ind. 276, 15 N.E. 341 (1888).

19. Cooper v. McJunkin, 4 Ind. 290 (1853).

20. Gardner v. State, op. cit.

21. Frank v. Orleans Parish School Board, 195 So.2d 451 (La.App.1967).

22. Cooper v. McJunkin, 4 Ind. 290 (1853); Danenhoffer v. State, 69 Ind. 295 (1879).

23. Wallace v. Shoreham Hotel Corp., 49 A.2d 81 (D.C.Mun.App.1946).

24. Barnett v. Collection Service Co., 214 Iowa 1303, 242 N.W. 25 (1932).

25. Prosser, *Law of Torts*, p. 315.

26. *Restatement (Second) of Torts*, pp. 519–20.

27. Keeton et al., *Prosser and Keeton on Torts*, p. 534.

28. *Restatement (Second) of Torts*, § 519, p. 35.

29. Ibid., § 520, p. 37.

30. Ibid., § 520, p. 36.

31. Ibid., § 520, p. 37.

32. Keeton et al., *Prosser and Keeton on Torts*, § 79, p. 563.

33. *Restatement (Second) of Torts*, § 510, p. 20.

34. Ibid.

35. Ibid.

36. Nottingham v. Akron Board of Education, 81 Ohio App.3d 319, 610 N.E.2d 1096 (1992).

37. See Kern Alexander and Erwin Solomon, *College and University Law* (Charlottesville, Va.: Michie, 1972), pp. 590–602.

38. Prier v. Horace Mann Insurance Co., 351 So.2d 265 (La.App.1977).

39. Lewis v. St. Bernard Parish School Board, 350 So.2d 1256 (La.App.1977).

40. *Restatement (Second) of Torts*, pp. 291–93.

41. Prosser, *Law of Torts*, p. 123.

42. Ibid., p. 124.

43. Lehmuth v. Long Beach Unified School District, 53 Cal.2d 544, 2 Cal.Rptr. 279, 348 P.2d 887 (1960).

44. Michigan Central Railroad Co. v. Hasseneyer, 48 Mich. 205, 12 N.W. 155 (1882).

45. Johnson v. St. Paul City Railway Co., 67 Minn. 260, 69 N.W. 900 (1897); Kitsap County Transportation Co. v. Harvey, 15 F.2d 166 (9th Cir.1927).

46. In criminal law, the courts have applied the rule as established in *M'Naghten's Case*, 10 Ct. & F. 200, 8 E.R. 718 (1843), which holds the defense of insanity can be established only by showing that the accused was "laboring under such a defect of reason, from disease of the mind, as not to know the nature and quality of the act he was doing; or, if he did know it, that he did not know what he was doing was wrong."

47. Williams v. Kearbey, 13 Kan.App.2d 564, 775 P.2d 670, 672 (1989).

48. Morris v. Douglas County School District, No. 9, 241 Or. 23, 403 P.2d 775 (1965).

49. Osborne v. Montgomery, 203 Wis. 223, 234 N.W. 372 (1931).

50. Hoyem v. Manhattan Beach City School District, 150 Cal.Rptr. 1, 585 P.2d 851 (1978).

51. Circillo v. Milwaukee, 34 Wis.2d 705, 150 N.W.2d 460 (1967).

52. Connett v. Freemont County School District No. 6, 581 P.2d 1097 (Wyo.1978).

53. Prosser, *Law of Torts*, p. 127.

54. *The Restatement (Second) of Torts*, § 464, states that "[a]ge is only one of the elements to be considered, along with experience and judgment, the latter involving discretion and power of self-control, being predominant."

55. Ohman v. Board of Education of City of New York, 300 N.Y. 306, 90 N.E.2d 474 (1949), reargument denied, 301 N.Y. 662, 93 N.E.2d 927 (1950).

56. Eastman v. Williams, 124 Vt. 445, 207 A.2d 146 (1965).

57. Scott v. Greenville Pharmacy, 212 S.C. 485, 48 S.E.2d 324 (1948).

58. *Restatement (Second) of Torts*, § 430.

59. Prosser, *Law of Torts*, p. 252. See Woodsmall v. Mt. Diablo Unified School District, 188 Cal.App.2d 262, 10 Cal.Rptr. 447 (1961); Munson v. Board of Education, 17 A.D.2d 687, 230 N.Y.S.2d 919 (1962), affirmed, 13 N.Y.2d 854, 242 N.Y.S.2d 492, 192 N.E.2d 272 (1963).

60. McDonnell v. Brozo, 285 Mich. 38, 280 N.W. 100 (1938).

61. Meyer v. Board of Education, 9 N.J. 46, 86 A.2d 761 (1952).

62. Mikes v. Baumgartner, 277 Minn. 423, 152 N.W.2d 732 (1967).

63. Walsh v. West Coast Coal Mines, 31 Wash.2d 396, 197 P.2d 233 (1948).

64. *Restatement (Second) of Torts*, § 463.

65. Rixmann v. Somerset Public Schools, 83 Wis.2d 571, 266 N.W.2d 326 (1978). See also Lemelle v. State, Through

Board of Secondary and Elementary Education, 435 So.2d 1162 (La.App.3 Cir.1983).

66. Cormier v. Sinegal, 180 So.2d 567 (La.App.1965).

67. Basmajian v. Board of Education, 211 A.D. 347, 207 N.Y.S. 298 (1925).

68. Wilhelm v. Board of Education of City of New York, 16 A.D.2d 707, 227 N.Y.S.2d 791 (1962).

69. Prosser, *Law of Torts*, p. 303. See Passantino v. Board of Education of City of New York, 41 N.Y.2d 1022, 395 N.Y.S.2d 628, 363 N.E.2d 1373 (1977).

70. Stevens v. Central School District No. 1, 25 A.D.2d 871, 270 N.Y.S.2d 23 (1966).

71. Maltz v. Board of Education of New York City, 32 Misc.2d 492, 114 N.Y.S.2d 856 (1952).

72. Benedetto v. Travelers Insurance Co., 172 So.2d 354 (La.App.1965).

73. Brisson v. Minneapolis Baseball and Athletic Association, 185 Minn. 507, 240 N.W. 903 (1932).

74. Scanlon v. Wedger, 156 Mass. 462, 31 N.E. 642 (1891).

75. Dusckiewicz v. Carter, 115 Vt. 122, 52 A.2d 788 (1947).

76. Cadieux v. Board of Education of the City School District for the City of Schenectady, 25 A.D.2d 579, 266 N.Y.S.2d 895 (1966).

77. Barr v. Bernhard, 562 S.W.2d 844 (Tex.1978).

78. Hunter v. Board of Education of Montgomery County, 292 Md. 481, 439 A.2d 582 (1982).

79. Ibid.

80. Peter W. v. San Francisco Unified School District, 60 Cal.App.3d 814, 131 Cal.Rptr. 854 (1976).

81. Donohue v. Copiague Union Free School District, 47 N.Y.2d 440, 418 N.Y.S.2d 375, 391 N.E.2d 1352 (1979).

82. Hunter, 439 A.2d at 585.

83. See D. S. W. v. Fairbanks North Star Borough School District, 628 P.2d 554 (Alaska 1981); Smith v. Alameda County Social Services Agency, 90 Cal.App.3d 929, 153 Cal.Rptr. 712 (1979); Hoffman v. Board of Education of City of New York, 49 N.Y.2d 121, 424 N.Y.S.2d 376, 400 N.E.2d 317 (1979); Aubrey v. School District of Philadelphia, 63 Pa.Cmwlth. 330, 437 A.2d 1306 (1981).

CHAPTER 12

DEFAMATION AND
STUDENT RECORDS

Many things that are defamatory may be said with impunity through the medium of speech. Not so, however, when speech is caught upon the wing and transmuted into print. What gives the sting to the writing is its permanence of form. The spoken word dissolves, but the written one abides, and "perpetuates the scandal."

—Benjamin N. Cardozo

CHAPTER OUTLINE

- DEFAMATION DEFINED
- DEFAMATION IN PUBLIC SCHOOLS
- PUBLIC OFFICIALS AND FIGURES
- STUDENT RECORDS

THOUGH DEFAMATION is considered to be a tort, it descends from a different historical lineage than the common tort of negligence. The Anglo-Saxon law of defamation has traces of historical development in Germanic and Roman law.[1] In early Anglo-Saxon law, insulting words raised by one person against another were punished by penalties as severe as removing the offender's tongue[2] or as light as requiring the offender to hold his nose and call himself a liar.[3] The word "defamation" is a technical term derived from the Latin *diffamatus*, signifying a person of sufficiently notorious and evil reputation that the church was justified in accusing and placing him on trial. If the defendant was acquitted and his ill fame was determined to be unfounded, then his accusers could be tried for the calumny of committing a crime of false and hateful accusation.[4] In 1275, defamation became a criminal offense in the first of a long line of statutes that forbade insult of the king or his court.[5] This statute, known as *scandalum magnatum*, the slander of magnates, punished those who published false news producing discord between the king and his subjects. Because the nature of this offense was criminal and offenses were generally considered sedition, application did not extend beyond offenses against the crown.[6] Gradually, though, the common law courts developed defamation as a civil wrong, reasoning that "libelling calumniation is an offense against the law of God."[7]

The law of defamation was greatly abused by the Star Chamber and upon the abolition of that court in 1641, the law lay dormant for some years. In the latter part of the seventeenth century, the distinction between spoken and written defamation was established and became a permanent division in the law of defamation. The law of libel, written word, was developed as a supplement to the law of slander, spoken word. It was reasoned that spoken words imputing ill fame could be thoughtlessly conveyed in the heat of discussion and could, in many cases, be ignored; libel, however, because it was written, and presumably more carefully considered, suggested the presence of malice and was actionable for special damages.[8]

The elements of common law defamation were well established by the eighteenth century, and the American courts generally followed the rationale and precedents of the early English courts. Today, the most important changes have occurred in state statutes, expanding or redefining certain elements of the law.

■ DEFAMATION DEFINED

Defamation is the imputation of immorality, dishonesty, or dishonorable conduct to another by spoken or written word. Criticism is distinct from defamation in that it is addressed to public matters and does not follow a person into private or personal affairs. A true critic never resorts to personal denigration or ridicule but confines his or her commentary to the merits of the particular issue under consideration. A communication is defamatory if it "tends so to harm the reputation of another as to lower him in the estimation of the community or to deter third persons from associating or dealing with him."[9] Keeton et al. define defamation as that "which tends to injure 'reputation' in the popular sense; to diminish the esteem, respect, goodwill or confidence in which the plaintiff is held, or to excite adverse, derogatory or unpleasant feelings or opinions against him."[10]

The *Restatement (Second) of Torts* distinguishes libel and slander as follows:

(1) Libel consists of the publication of defamatory matter by written or printed words, by its embod-

iment in physical form or by any other form of communication that has the potentially harmful qualities characteristic of written or printed words.

(2) Slander consists of the publication of defamatory matter by spoken words, transitory gestures or by any form of communication other than those stated in Subsection (1).

(3) The area of dissemination, the deliberate and premeditated character of its publication and the persistence of the defamation are factors to be considered in determining whether a publication is a libel rather than a slander.[11]

On their faces, libel as written communication and slander as oral communication are easily distinguishable. However, other forms of communication, such as acts or gestures, motion pictures, and radio or television, complicate the dichotomy. Some courts simply maintain that defamation designed for visual perception is libel and defamation designed for all other forms of communication is slander.[12]

The courts are in agreement that "the broadcasting of defamatory matter by means of radio or television is libel."[13] Courts generally accept the following definitions: Libel is a malicious publication, expressed either in printing or writing or by signs and pictures, and slander is the speaking of base and false words, possibly emphasized by gestures, both of which tend to injure a party's situation in society.[14]

■ DEFAMATION IN PUBLIC SCHOOLS

Teachers and school administrators are particularly susceptible to actions in defamation because of the sensitivity of the personal information that they come into contact with each day. Teachers, as a matter of routine, process and communicate information that relates to pupil performance, the misuse of which could potentially harm the student's reputation and stigmatize his or her future. The problem of the administrator is even more complex in that he or she communicates information concerning teacher performance to other administrators or to school board members. Public interest in education, though, makes it essential that proper pupil and teacher evaluations be made and that public school officials and employees not be subjected to constant fear of personal liability.

PRIVILEGE

Because of this important public interest, the courts have generally recognized that statements regarding school matters are qualifiedly privileged if made by persons having a common duty or interest in the information and acting in good faith.[15] "In the absence of malice, a school official is not liable to a teacher for performing the duties of his office."[16] A teacher likewise has a qualified or conditional privilege when acting in good faith in school matters, but the qualified privilege is not unlimited, and no privilege attaches to a teacher's entry in a school register to the effect that a certain pupil "was ruined by tobacco and whiskey."[17] Absolute privileges are afforded only those individuals who perform vital governmental functions that the courts have defined as judicial proceedings, legislative proceedings, and certain executive proceedings. With the judiciary, absolute privilege extends only to the particular statements that are relevant or pertinent to the case at bar.[18] In the legislature, complete privilege extends to statements made in the course of debate, voting, or reports on work performed in committees.[19] Public officers holding executive positions also have absolute immunity for communications made in connection with the performance of their official duties.

While courts generally hold that school superintendents have a conditional or qualified privilege, some courts have maintained that public policy requires that superintendents be given an absolute privilege in evaluating teacher activities before a school board. Similarly, school board members have been held to have absolute privilege in imputing inefficiency and lack of qualification in evaluating a school superintendent's performance.[20]

The more common precedent to follow, though, is that officials, teachers, and others dealing in the public interest context have at least a qualified privilege. This conditional immunity can even extend to parents presenting a petition before a school board to the effect that a teacher is "incompetent."[21]

GOOD FAITH

A qualified privilege protects the teacher or school official when statements are made in good faith and without malice. One court explained such privileges in this way:

If a communication comes within the class denominated absolutely privileged or qualifiedly privileged, no recovery can be had. Privileged communications are divided and defined as follows: (1) that the communication was made by the defendant in good faith, without malice, not voluntarily but in answer to an inquiry, and in the reasonable protection of his own interest or performance of a duty to society; (2) that the defendant must honestly believe the communication to be true; (3) there must have been reasonable or probable grounds known to him for the suspicion; (4) that the communication, if made in answer to an inquiry, must not go further than to truly state the facts upon which the suspicion was founded, and to satisfy the inquirer that there were reasons for the suspicion.[22]

Under this definition, it is clear that the communication must be made in good faith, without malice, upon reasonable grounds, and in answer to inquiry, and, importantly, it must be made with regard to assisting or protecting the interests of either of the parties involved or in performing a duty to society. The school official's or employee's communication is qualifiedly privileged if it is prompted by a duty owed to either the public or a third party and is made in good faith and without malice.

DEFAMATION ACTIONABLE *PER SE* AND *PER QUOD*

Words that in and of themselves, without extrinsic proof, injure a person's reputation are actionable *per se*. With defamation *per se*, the plaintiff's cause of action is complete when he or she proves that the words have been articulated and conveyed. The words "actionable *per se*" mean that the publication is of such a nature as to make the publisher liable for defamation, regardless of whether special harm[23] is attributable to the publication, unless the information is true or the defamer is privileged. If such fault exists, the fact that the false and defamatory matter was published is actionable *per se*. A complaint by plaintiff that is actionable *per se* enables the aggrieved party to recover for actual harm. To support the complaint, the plaintiff is not required to prove actual injury or out-of-pocket monetary loss but rather must merely show that the words were of such kind as to impair his or her reputation or standing in the community or to cause personal anguish, suffering, or humiliation. The plaintiff need not prove that he or she suffered special harm or direct loss.

A Maine court has helped define defamation *per se*:

> We recognize that a good deal of confusion exists in the use of such terms as "libelous or slanderous *per se*" and "actionable *per se*." Courts and commentators often use these terms interchangeably, sometimes referring to technical common law pleading requirements that obviate the need to *allege* special damage and at other times referring to the nature of evidence at trial that obviates the need to *prove* special damages. . . . Specifically, the term slander *per se* refers to words that on their face without further proof or explanation injure the plaintiff in his business or occupation, i.e., are defamatory *per se*.[24]

Under American common law today, an action for defamation *per se* will lie without proof of special harm (damage) where (1) words impute (a) a criminal offense punishable by imprisonment or (b) that plaintiff is guilty of a crime involving moral turpitude; (2) words impute to the plaintiff an existing venereal or other loathsome or communicable disease; (3) words impute to the plaintiff conduct, characteristics, or a condition incompatible with proper conduct of his or her lawful business, trade, or profession, or a public or private offense; and (4) words impute unchastity to a woman.

If the plaintiff is unable to sustain the complaint under one of these categories, he or she must resort to proving special harm or actual damages by the communication[25] of defamation *per quod*.

Defamation *per quod* requires that the plaintiff's complaint show actual damage. The plaintiff must show that publication of the defamation was the legal cause of special harm. Special harm requires proof of actual economic or pecuniary loss.

The distinction between defamation *per se* and *per quod* may rest on whether a crime is imputed. For example, the law holds that it is defamation *per quod* and special damages must be proven if the words imputed to an offender appear to harm the teacher's reputation but do not relate to conduct of a crime, moral turpitude, or unchastity or do not damage the teacher in his or her profession. To say that a male teacher seduced a female student would, of course, be defamation *per se*. On the other hand, where a defendant had accused a headmaster of committing adultery with the school custodian's wife, the court found that the words had not been uttered in the context of the school or in reference to the plaintiff as schoolmaster; the charge could be defamation *per quod*, requiring a showing of special and actual damage, a burden that the plaintiff could not sustain. Since a teacher's reputation among students and the community is so vital to performance of his or her professional responsibilities, it is easy to see how, in the majority of cases, false imputations against a teacher could fall into the category of defamation *per se*.[26]

■ PUBLIC OFFICIALS AND FIGURES

Teachers, guidance counselors, principals, and other school officials who have an obligation as a part of their employment to obtain and dispense information on behalf of the school children are protected by a conditional privilege, meaning that an aggrieved plaintiff student would have to prove malice before liability could be determined and damages obtained. Conversely, the question arises, What is the protection of teachers or other school employees against imputations or defamation cast against them? If, for example, a newspaper article defames a teacher, what are the teacher's rights in maintaining an action for libel? Are school personnel viewed as private persons or as public personages when they themselves bring actions against newspapers, parents, or other publishers of defamatory information?

In answer, first it should be made clear that a private person may recover in an action for defamation where a public person cannot. Under common law, a private person's reputation is protected against false imputations by a publisher, and the publisher is strongly strictly liable without consideration of fault. Keeton et al. explain, with regard to defamation of private persons, that "the intentional publisher of defamatory matter (at common law) published at his own peril in assessing truth or falsity of the matter published. Moreover, the burden of proving the truth of the matter rested on the defendant-publisher."[27]

With regard to public persons, however, the situation is different. In the United States, the Supreme Court has interpreted the First Amendment to bestow a privilege on defendant-publishers for imputations made against public persons. A constitutional privilege is thereby extended to the defendant-publisher that effectively shifts the burden of proof to the defamed plaintiff to prove that the defendant intended harm to the plaintiff. The public person must prove that the published material was false and the defendant acted in reckless disregard for the truth or with malice.

The precedent that elaborated this "constitutional privilege to defame," as Keeton et al. put it, is *New York Times Co. v. Sullivan,* a highly significant decision.[28] Since *New York Times Co. v. Sullivan,*[29] a 1964 U.S. Supreme Court decision, the law of defamation as it pertains to freedom of speech and press has changed considerably. This and subsequent cases hold the interest of the publisher to be of vital importance to a free and informed society. The position of the press is elevated above the normal law of defamation, and special rules apply, as defined by *Sullivan.*

In *Sullivan,* a paid advertisement in the *New York Times* signed by a number of prominent individuals criticized the behavior of the Montgomery, Alabama, police in dealing with racial unrest. The police chief, Sullivan, claimed that the derogatory reference to police behavior amounted to defamation of him personally. The Alabama Supreme Court held that the publication was libel *per se* and that the *New York Times* was liable for half a million dollars without the plaintiff showing special damage or fault on the part of the *Times.*

The U.S. Supreme Court reversed the lower court, holding that the guarantee of free speech under the First Amendment prohibits a *public official* from recovering damages for a defamatory falsehood relating to his *official* conduct unless he or she proves that the statement was made with "actual malice" and that the statement was made with knowledge that it was false or in reckless disregard of whether it was false or not. This protection extended to both the newspaper and the private individuals who

paid for the advertisement and signed it. Plaintiff in the case was unable to show that the *New York Times* actually had knowledge of the falsity of portions of the statement.

Before *Sullivan,* the common law of libel established three rules that, taken together, effectively required a publisher to ensure the absolute accuracy of statements made in criticism of any person: (1) The burden of proof was always placed on the publisher because defamatory statements were presumed to be false; (2) false information was presumed to be published with malice regardless of whether it was merely a misstatement, a mistake, or bad luck; and (3) the aggrieved party did not need to prove actual harm to his or her reputation— damage to his or her reputation was presumed by the simple fact of publication. These common law rules of defamation applied to communications between private persons, and these common law standards still prevail where the press is not involved.[30]

Sullivan invoked "freedom of press" as a constitutional gloss on the common law and provided much more latitude for the press. Here the Supreme Court weighed the individual's interest in reputation against the public's interest in free speech and concluded that special consideration must be given the press when it criticizes public officials. *Sullivan* made two major changes in the law: It created the category of public official, and it shifted the burden of proof to the plaintiff to prove that an untruth was conveyed with malice.[31]

Cases following *Sullivan* have dealt primarily with two major questions: (1) What is the definition of *public official,* and how broad is the term? (2) What is the level of *privilege* of the press, and does it vary as the subject of the defamation becomes more remote from officialdom?[32]

In *Rosenblatt v. Baer,*[33] the Supreme Court further defined "public official," saying:

> It is clear, therefore, that the "public official" designation applies at the very least, to those among the hierarchy of government employees who have, or appear to have, substantial responsibility for or control over the conduct of governmental affairs.[34]

The definition of "public officials" in *Sullivan* was broadened in *Curtis Publishing Co. v. Butts*[35] to include "public figures":

The Supreme Court has characterized a "public figure" in the following manner: For the most part those who attain [the status of a public figure] have assumed roles of especial prominence in the affairs of society. Some occupy positions of such persuasive power and influence that they are deemed public figures for all purposes. More commonly, those classed as public figures have thrust themselves to the forefront of particular public controversies in order to influence the resolution of the issues involved. In either event, they invite attention and comment.[36]

The defendant-publisher's assertion of a privilege cannot be so broad as to include all public employees. The Supreme Court has said specifically that the status of "public official" cannot "be thought to include all public employees."[37] In order to be classed as a public official, the public employee must be found to have a "substantial responsibility for control over the conduct of the governmental affairs."[38]

In *Gertz v. Robert Welch, Inc.*, the Supreme Court in 1974 further clarified the meaning of "public figure" as one who assumes a role of importance in public affairs, that is, of general importance to the people.[39] The Supreme Court more specifically defined a public figure as being one of two types: (1) "those who are public figures for all purposes because they have achieved such a significant role in the resolution of issues of importance as to make most true and discreditable conduct and characteristics matters of legitimate public interest, relating as such information does to credibility, trustworthiness, and integrity"; and (2) those who are public figures only because they have voluntarily injected themselves into the resolution of particular controversies or issues of importance to the general public.[40]

Later cases appear to pinpoint three aspects of the public figure that are necessary to permit a defendant to exercise a constitutional privilege for a questionable communication. First, the plaintiff must have voluntarily entered into a public issue or controversy; second, the issue must have been one the resolution of which could affect the general public or a substantial portion of the public in a meaningful way; and third, the defamation must have grown out of or have been related to the particular issue. Thus, a mental health researcher who was the recipient of a government grant to conduct research, roundly condemned and ridiculed by U.S. Senator Proxmire in bestowing upon him the Golden Fleece Award, was found not to be a public figure.[41] The Golden Fleece Award was publicly announced as an example of the use of public funds for the conduct of "worthless" research. Because the researcher was not a public figure, the ridicule heaped upon him by Senator Proxmire was not privileged, and the public visibility created by the controversy, in itself, could not be the source of the researcher's being classified as a public figure. Moreover, with regard to this particular incident, the Court found that the legislative privilege that protects a member of Congress in the performance of his or her legislative functions is not extended to protect the legislator in private or public discussions outside the legislative functions.[42]

Unlike in the Proxmire situation, however, if a plaintiff is adjudged to be a public official or a public figure, the publisher of the defamation is protected by a privilege that requires a showing of malice to be overcome. The burden of proof is on the plaintiff to give evidence of malicious intent on the part of the defendant, a burden that has in most cases been very difficult to sustain.

Where a private individual is libeled by the press, liability of the press may be incurred by merely showing that the statement was untruthful. It is not necessary to show malice, nor is it required that the plaintiff show that the newspaper knew the publication was false. Whenever liability is imposed against the press for false publication, the damages must be limited to the actual injury sustained; general or punitive damages are not available.

Teachers are not usually considered to be public officials or public figures even though some jurisdictions have held that they are.[43] Thus, imputations against a teacher by the student press are actionable if the teacher shows the student publisher was at fault by directing the defamation toward the teacher. As with teachers, the precedents are mixed in determining whether school principals are public officials or public figures. It probably all depends on the specific situation in which the principal is involved. The classification of principals would therefore most readily be determined, as Justice Powell suggested in *Gertz*, on a case-by-case basis. He said that "it is preferable to reduce the public-figure question to a more meaningful context by looking to the nature and extent of an individual's participation in the particular controversy giving rise to the defamation."[44]

Board members and superintendents hold public positions, board members as officials and superintendents usually as employees. Both have substantial enough responsibility over conduct of public affairs, public taxation, and public services as to cast them into the class of public officials or public figures. Therefore, precedent suggests that both board members and superintendents would typically be classified as "public figures" because they have voluntarily injected themselves into issues that are of general importance to the public or into issues in which a large segment of the public has an interest.

MALICE

Malice in a legal sense characterizes all acts that are done with evil disposition and unlawful motive with intent to injure or cause harm to another. The law distinguishes at least two types of malice. The first is called "malice in law" or "implied malice" and is defamation *per se*. Here there is no excuse for the conveyance of hurtful information. Unsolicited, derogatory commentary, oral or written, may be of this form. Actual malice is the second form and is dependent on the defendant's motive for making the statement. Actual malice requires proof that the defendant's motives and interest were wrongful, ill-willed, and designed to harm the plaintiff's reputation.

A qualified privilege is an affirmative defense that must be pleaded and proved. Whether a privilege exists is a matter of law for the court to decide, not the jury. A qualified privilege can be overcome with a showing of malice. Punitive damages may not be available for malice in law, or implied malice, but they are generally assumed to be appropriate for actual malice.[45]

Parents have a qualified privilege to speak publicly before a school board regarding a teacher's instruction of their children. It is within the right of parents to oversee their children's education, to make statements pertaining to a teacher's competency or inefficiency in the classroom. A qualified privilege raises a presumption of good faith and places the burden on the plaintiff of proving express malice. In a Florida case, the court stated:

> Where a person speaks upon a privileged occasion, but the speaker is motivated more by a desire to harm the person defamed than by a purpose to protect the personal or social interest giving rise to the privilege, then it can be said that there was express malice and the privilege is destroyed. Strong, angry, or intemperate words do not alone show express malice; rather, there must be a showing that the speaker used his privileged position "to gratify his malevolence." . . . If the occasion of the communication is privileged because of a proper interest to be protected, and the defamer is motivated by a desire to protect that interest, he does not forfeit the privilege merely because he also in fact feels hostility or ill will toward the plaintiff. The incidental gratification of personal feelings of indignation is not sufficient to defeat the privilege where the primary motivation is within the scope of the privilege.[46]

As we shall see later, it is proof of actual malice that is required of public officials to overcome the privilege of the press, as enunciated in *New York Times Co. v. Sullivan*.[47] Thus, some courts refer to actual malice as "*New York Times* malice."[48] The standard of proof required of a public official to establish *New York Times* malice may be greater because of the newspapers' "constitutional" privilege. In such cases, the plaintiff public official must show "by clear and convincing evidence" a reckless disregard for truth. On the other hand, the "common" law qualified privilege of a teacher or a parent may be overcome by a lesser standard of proof, the intent to injure the plaintiff by a "preponderance of the evidence."

TRUTH

Falsity is the basic ingredient in the tort of defamation. Conveyance of truth is not defamation.

The *Restatement (Second) of Torts* states succinctly that

> [t]o create liability for defamation there must be publication of matter that is both defamatory and false. There can be no recovery in defamation for a statement of fact that is true, although the state-

ment is made for no good purpose and is inspired by ill will toward the person about whom it is published and is made solely for the purpose of harming him.[49]

Therefore, truth of a defamatory statement affords a complete defense to defamation regardless of whether ill will or malice is present.

Truth as an absolute defense against defamation emanated from the famous Peter Zenger case in 1735. Prior to this case, defamation of a public official was largely indefensible. One will recall that Zenger was indicted for printing an edition of the *New York Weekly Journal* that called the governor of New York a "rogue" and accused him of destroying the liberties of the citizenry. Zenger's lawyer argued that the charges were true and a jury agreed, acquitting Zenger. Although the Zenger affair was so imbued with politics that its importance was mitigated, the case nevertheless established that truth was a legitimate defense to libel and that truth was a matter of fact to be decided by a jury, not a matter of law to be decided by a judge. After the Zenger case, it was popularly maintained that "[t]ruth ought to govern the whole affair of libels."[50]

Under common law tort where the plaintiff is a private person, a defamatory statement is presumed to be false; the defendant must prove that the statement was true. The burden of proof is on the defendant, but as just noted, if the plaintiff is a "public official" or "public figure," the burden of proof shifts. The "public person" must present clear and convincing proof to the court that the defendant published false, defamatory information with knowledge of its falsity or with reckless disregard for the truth.

Thus, if a teacher has been the brunt of a defamatory statement, then the burden of proving truth is on the defendant because a teacher is generally a private person. If, for example, a parent or student published defamatory information about a teacher, the burden would be on the parent or student to prove the statement is true.

One could probably conceive of a situation in which a teacher could be a public figure if he or she had won fame for some reason, but this is generally not the case. So long as the teacher does not acquire the esteemed status of a public personage, then the burden of proving truth would be on the defendant if a publication harmed the teacher.

❖ — ❖ — ❖

Negative Recommendation Is Protected by a Conditional Privilege

Hett v. Ploetz

Supreme Court of Wisconsin, 1963.
20 Wis.2d 55, 121 N.W.2d 270.

GORDON, Justice. Hett brought this action to recover damages for injury to his professional reputation from an allegedly libelous publication by Ploetz. . . .

From 1956 to 1959 Hett had been employed as a speech therapist in the school system of the city of Cudahy, Wisconsin. His schedule required that he travel to six different schools and teach those pupils who were in need of his specialty....

Based upon their analysis of Hett's qualifications, the principals of the six schools in which Hett taught reported to Ploetz that they did not recommend renewal of Hett's contract for the 1959–1960 school year.

While the principals did not recommend Hett's retention for that year, Ploetz decided that because he had been the superintendent for only six months it would be unfair to Hett to recommend his dismissal.

Ploetz informed Hett that his contract was not going to be renewed and told him that it would be in his best interest to resign so that a dismissal would not appear on his record. Hett resigned. . . .

On November 9, 1959, Hett applied for a position as a speech therapist at the Southern Wisconsin Colony and Training School, Union Grove, Wisconsin. In his application he stated that the reason he left the Cudahy school system was that there was a lack of advancement opportunities. He listed Ploetz as a reference and gave permission to the Southern Colony officials to communicate with Ploetz. . . .

The plaintiff contends that he was libeled by the defendant's response to an inquiry from a prospective employer of the plaintiff. Hett had not only given Ploetz's name as a reference but had also given express permission to the prospective employer to communicate with Ploetz.

We must resolve two questions. The first is whether any privilege insulates the defendant's letter; the second is whether an issue of malice exists for trial.

It is clear that Ploetz's allegedly defamatory letter was entitled to a conditional privilege. Ploetz was privileged to give a critical appraisal concerning his former employee so long as such appraisal was made for the valid purpose of enabling a prospective employer to evaluate the employee's qualifications. The privilege is said to be "conditional" because of the requirements that the declaration be reasonably calculated to accomplish the privileged purpose and that it be made without malice. . . . Lord Blackburn has said:

> Where a person is so situated that it becomes right in the interests of society that he should tell to a third person facts, then, if he *bona fide* and without malice does tell them, it is a privileged communication.

The public school official who expresses an opinion as to the qualifications of a person who has submitted an application for employment as a school teacher should enjoy the benefits of a conditional privilege.

As previously noted, the employee had given Ploetz's name as a reference and had authorized that an inquiry be made of him. The letter contains certain factual matters as well as expressions of opinion. The factual portions are not contradicted by any pleading before this court. Thus, the following statement contained in the letter written by Ploetz stands unchallenged:

> Last year, our six Principals and Elementary Coordinator unanimously recommended that he be no longer retained in our system as a speech correctionist. He, therefore, was not offered a contract to return this year.

The expression of opinion of which Hett complains is contained in the following portion of the defendant's letter:

> We feel that Mr. Hett is not getting the results that we expected in this very important field. I, personally, feel that Mr. Hett does not belong in the teaching field. He has a rather odd personality, and it is rather difficult for him to gain the confidence of his fellow workers and the boys and girls with whom he works.

In our opinion, the record before us establishes that this expression of opinion is not founded in malice. The background of the relationship of Hett and Ploetz satisfactorily demonstrates that the latter's negative recommendation was grounded on the record and not upon malice. Ploetz was not an intermeddler; he had a proper interest in connection with the letter he wrote. . . .

The plaintiff has failed to recite any evidentiary facts which are sufficient to raise questions for trial. His allegations that the letter contains defamatory material are mere conclusions. No presumption of malice has arisen; no showing of express malice has been presented.

In *Otten v. Schutt* (1962), 15 Wis.2d 497, 503, 113 N.W.2d 152, 155, this court stated:

> The law relating to defamatory communications is based on public policy. The law will impute malice where a defamatory publication is made without sufficient cause or excuse, or where necessary to protect the interests of society and the security of character and reputation; but where the welfare of society is better promoted by a freedom of expression, malice will not be imputed. . . .

Public policy requires that malice not be imputed in cases such as this, for otherwise one who enjoys a conditional privilege might be reluctant to give a sincere, yet critical, response to a request for an appraisal of a prospective employee's qualifications.

. . . A thorough examination of the entire record compels our conclusion that the respondent is entitled to the benefit of a conditional privilege.

Judgment affirmed.

CASE NOTES

1. Per Quod *and* Per Se. To recover in an action for defamation, the plaintiff must establish the four basic elements of defamation: (1) a communication with a defamatory imputation, (2) malice, (3) publication, and (4) damages. Whether a communication is defamatory is a matter of law. Some words are not actionable in themselves yet may become actionable as "defamatory imputation" when they make

some allusion to some extrinsic fact or are understood to be used in a different sense from their normal meaning. Such words are deemed to be actionable *per quod*, acquiring a defamatory meaning when placed in context or connected with extrinsic facts or circumstances. If words are directly defamatory in nature without resort to extrinsic facts or circumstances, then they are said to be actionable *per se. McQueen v. Fayette County School Corp.,* 711 N.E.2d 62 (Ind.App.1999).

2. Libel cannot be proved where the published material was clearly understood as "parody, satire, humor or fantasy." In a case where a female teacher by the name of Salek was offended by a photograph in the school yearbook of a male teacher, holding his hand to his head, captioned "Not tonight Ms. Salek," Salek sued the school principal, claiming libel. Plaintiff's expert witness testified that the average reader of the yearbook would conclude that there was an ongoing sexual relationship between the plaintiff and the male teacher. The court denied relief, saying that the determination of "whether the photograph was defamatory must be made after consideration of the context in which it appeared in the yearbook." Here the court concluded the intent was obvious jest. *Salek v. Passaic Collegiate School,* 255 N.J.Super. 355, 605 A.2d 276 (1992).

3. If a statement is made by the defendant in response to an inquiry by the plaintiff, then a conditional privilege may be elevated to the status of an absolute privilege. An "absolute privilege is confined to relatively few situations. It is accorded judicial proceedings, legislative proceedings, proceedings of executive officers charged with responsibility of importance, publications made *with consent of the plaintiff* and communications between husband and wife." Prosser, *Law of Torts,* 2d ed. (St. Paul, Minn.: West, 1971); *Walker v. D'Alesandro,* 212 Md. 163, 129 A.2d 148 (1957).

The Supreme Court of Missouri invoked this rule when a superintendent responded to a question by a teacher in a hearing before the school board:

> When plaintiff asked the defendant at the board meeting why she was not going to be re-employed the following school year, the superintendent

should be at liberty to say to her, "Miss Williams, you have disobeyed school rules and regulations, you are insubordinate and are insufficient and inadequate with your students." In that situation [the superintendent] is absolutely protected in his explanation to plaintiff.

Williams v. School District of Springfield R-12, 447 S.W.2d 256 (Mo.1969).

4. A statement made by a school board member at a school board meeting referring to the fact that marijuana cigarettes had been found in a student's car was privileged, and the board member could not be found liable for defamation. The court reasoned that the board member held a conditional privilege that could not be overcome absent the showing of malice. The court said:

> Privileged communications are divided into two classes, namely, those which are absolutely privileged, and those which are qualifiedly or conditionally privileged. In cases where absolute privilege obtains there is no liability. Depending upon the circumstances of the case, there may or may not be liability with respect to qualifiedly or conditionally privileged communications. The distinction between the two classes is said to be that the protection of absolute privileged communications is not at all dependent upon their bona fides, while qualifiedly or conditionally privileged communications are merely freed from the legal imputation of malice, and become actionable only by virtue of the existence of express malice.

Morrison v. Mobile County Board of Education, 495 So.2d 1086 (Ala.1986).

5. The conditional privilege of a superintendent does not extend to negative and reckless commentary about a teacher who had not worked in the school district for two years. Where the superintendent, in a telephone conversation, stated that the former teacher was "more concerned with living up to the terms of his contract rather than going the extra mile" and that the teacher "did not turn students on," the evidence indicated, to the contrary, that the teacher had been a relatively good teacher, receiving affirmative evaluations and a complimentary letter from the superintendent. In light of such facts, the jury's conclusion that the superintendent's comments were made with "falsity" and "reckless disregard of their truth or

falsity" was affirmed by the appellate court. *True v. Ladner*, 513 A.2d 257 (Me.1986).

6. A New York court held that a school social worker has an absolute privilege for the social worker's report to the child protection agency. The same court ruled that a qualified privilege existed covering the information conveyed between the social worker and the school district committee to establish appropriate individualized education programs for disabled children. *Dunajewski v. Bellmore-Merrick Central High School District*, 138 A.D.2d 557, 526 N.Y.S.2d 139 (2 Dept. 1988).

7. In the case of *De Bolt v. McBrien*, 96 Neb. 237, 147 N.W. 462 (1914), the court applied the absolute privilege rule to a state superintendent of public instruction's statement to the county supervisor accusing the plaintiff of playing poker and being under the influence of liquor.

8. The Oklahoma Appellate Court found that defamatory statements about the school librarian made by the president and dean of the medical school at a session of the board of regents were absolutely privileged. See *Hughes v. Bizzell*, 189 Okla. 472, 117 P.2d 763 (1941).

9. Parents and patrons of the school have a qualified privilege in disclosing information at school board meetings. School patrons presented the school trustees with a letter charging that a teacher failed to keep proper order and discipline and allowed older boys to take improper privileges with her and female students. The court held that if the defendants believed the school was conducted as stated, then it was their right to complain to the trustees, since they were the only ones authorized to remedy it. According to the court, the central issue is whether the letter was presented with malicious intent. In reversing a judgment in favor of the teacher, the court remanded the case for jury determination of whether malice existed. According to the court, the jury should be instructed to find that malice was present if the publication by defendants was not made in good faith and had actually been intended to injure the teacher, not merely to correct the school situation. *Malone v. Carrico*, 16 Ky.L.Rptr. 155 (1894).

10. Residents and patrons of a school district were held to be protected by a qualified privilege when they presented a petition to the school board stating, "[W]e do not think she [plaintiff teacher] is a competent teacher and has but little control over the school." The court said that if the occasion, the motive, and the cause be proper, the publication or communication does not imply malice. To overcome a qualified privilege, malice must be proved by the person claiming to have been defamed, and the mere falsity of the alleged defamatory matter is not sufficient. *Hoover v. Jordan*, 27 Colo.App. 515, 150 P. 333 (1915); see also 40 A.L.R.3d 490.

11. A tenured teacher and assistant principal were responsible for investigating suspected drug involvement of students and for counseling students and their parents. Their communications to parents of a high school student concerning the sale of drugs in plaintiffs' place of business were qualifiedly privileged. Comments were made in good faith, on an occasion that properly served their duty, and under circumstances that were fairly warranted. The teacher and assistant principal were not liable to plaintiffs for defamation in the absence of express malice. The court defined "qualified privilege" in this way: "A communication, although it contains criminating matter, is privileged when made in good faith upon any subject in which the party communicating has an interest, or in reference to which he has a right or duty, if made to a person having a corresponding interest, right, or duty, and made upon an occasion to properly serve such right, interest, or duty, and in a manner and under circumstances fairly warranted by the occasion and the duty, right, or interest, and not so made as to unnecessarily or unduly injure another, or to show express malice." *Chapman v. Furlough*, 334 So.2d 293 (Fla.App.1976).

In defining "good faith," the court quoted an older Florida case, saying: "Good faith, a right, duty, or interest in a proper subject, a proper occasion, and a proper communication to those having a like right, duty, or interest, are all essential to constitute words spoken that are actionable *per se*, a privileged communication, so as to make the proof by the Plaintiff of express malice essential to liability. In determining whether or not a communication is privileged, the nature of the subject, the right, duty, or interest of the parties in such subject, the time, place, and circumstances of the occasion, and the manner, character, and extent of the communication should all be considered. When all these facts and circumstances are conceded, a court may decide whether a communication is a privileged one, so as to require the Plaintiff to prove express malice. . . . " *Abraham v. Baldwin*, 52 Fla. 151, 42 So. 591 (1906).

--------------- ❖ — ❖ — ❖ ---------------

Qualified Privilege Protects Parents Who Convey Information about Teachers

Desselle v. Guillory

Court of Appeals of Louisiana, Third Circuit, 1981.
407 So.2d 79.

SWIFT, Judge. . . . [In this consolidated case, teachers Kenneth Maillet, Maxwell Desselle, and Garland Desselle, plaintiff-appellants, appeal a defamation decision regarding a high school student's allegations of teachers' molesting students.] In July of 1979, Mrs. Jane Guillory was a counselor at a summer church camp for girls. She participated in a conversation with several of the girls who told her about incidents which they had heard or witnessed concerning certain teachers, including the plaintiffs, at Bordelonville High School. When Mrs. Guillory discussed with one of her church deacons the information, which included allegations that the teachers were fondling students, he advised her to inform the school principal.

The following month Mrs. Guillory took up the matter with Mr. Jimmy Bordelon, the principal of the high school, who assured her that he would observe the teachers' behavior.

On March 6, 1980, Mrs. Guillory visited with Mr. Bordelon to discuss a poor grade on a test given to her daughter by Maxwell Desselle. Mr. Desselle was called in to talk to Mrs. Guillory about it. They had a heated discussion concerning the test and the defendant also made a comment to the effect that she had something else on Desselle. After he returned to his classroom Mrs. Guillory told the principal that the teachers

had continued to molest the children. She testified that prior to this visit Abigail Farbes had informed her that it was still going on. The principal told Mrs. Guillory he did not believe such rumors and had not observed any such behavior. Mrs. Guillory then informed the principal she would take her information to the superintendent.

That same afternoon Mrs. Guillory had a conversation with Mrs. Jeannette Huffmaster. When Mrs. Guillory informed her of what she had heard, Mrs. Huffmaster told her that she had seen Maxwell Desselle pat a girl on the buttocks in the presence of Mr. Bordelon.

On March 7, 1980, Mr. Bordelon met with the plaintiffs and informed them of what Mrs. Guillory had said. The four then went to the Guillory home to discuss the matter. At this meeting an argument ensued and at least one of the plaintiffs threatened to sue the Guillorys for defamation.

Later that night Mrs. Guillory called her attorney who advised her to obtain written statements from the girls who had given her the information about the teachers. Mrs. Guillory went to the homes of Abigail Farbes, Joan Hess, Tammy Lemoine, Beverly Martin and Terry Bringold to obtain such statements. She said she explained the situation and alleged incidents to their parents and got their permission before asking the girls to write "letters" as to what they saw or heard about the matter. Three of these persons and her daughter did so.

On March 10, 1980, Mrs. Guillory and Mrs. Huffmaster drew up a petition calling for an investigation by the Evangeline Parish School Board into wrongdoings at Bordelonville High School. The petition did not contain the names of the plaintiffs or of any specific facts concerning the alleged wrongdoings. These ladies then visited five or six homes in an attempt to obtain signatures on the petition. The school board directed a representative to make an investigation. Upon his failure to obtain any testimony of wrongdoing, the board concluded there was no basis for action against any teacher and closed the case. The recorded statements taken by the representatives were destroyed and the interested parties were notified in writing of the board's decision. . . .

Beverly Martin testified she had told Mrs. Guillory that she had heard students say that some of the teachers played with the students. In particular, she had heard Kenneth Maillet would take girls in the bathroom after practice, but they wouldn't tell her what they did. She also told her that Garland Desselle was friendly with the girls and would allow them to sit in his lap and that he felt one girl during P.E. In addition she told Mrs. Guillory of an incident when Maxwell Desselle kissed her under the mistletoe. Abigail Farbes testified she had told Mrs. Guillory that Maxwell and Kenneth Maillet would flirt around with girls and that Beverly had told her that Maxwell Desselle once had grabbed Beverly and gave her a passionate kiss.

Joan Hess testified that before the Mardi Gras trip she had her majorette uniform on under her jeans and part of the uniform was showing. She stated Mr. Maillet tugged at the jeans and a button came undone from the jeans. Joan further testified she told Kaye Guillory, the defendant's daughter, that Kenneth Maillet tugged at her jeans pulling a button off.

Tammy Lemoine testified that in the written statement given Mrs. Guillory she said she heard that Kenneth Maillet and another girl "had something going on" and that Garland Desselle said "he was going to get some meat" from two girls "one of these days."

The testimony as to the content of the statements Mrs. Guillory made to the principal and the parents of high school students is in dispute. Mr. Bordelon, the principal, said Mrs. Guillory told him the teachers were fondling and molesting girls, although she never used the word "intercourse." Clara Laborde and Peggy Hess stated Mrs. Guillory had told them that one of the plaintiffs, Kenneth Maillet, had unzipped Mrs. Hess' daughter's pants before a Mardi Gras band trip and that the plaintiffs were molesting the girls. She also said some teachers were starting this in the elementary grades and taking them to bed by the time they reached the high school grades.

Mrs. Guillory testified that she did not accuse the plaintiffs of anything, but merely told Mrs. Hess and Mrs. Laborde what she had heard from the girls and said she felt the plaintiffs might be having sexual relations with the stu-

dents. Having heard things about these men, such as one girl having seen Kenneth Maillet with his pants down in the bathroom one night after basketball practice, she was trying to determine if they were true. She also stated at trial that she thought the parents had a right to know and she never intended to do any harm to the men allegedly involved.

The plaintiffs emphatically denied ever molesting or having intercourse with any high school students. Kenneth Maillet did not recall any incident where he unbuttoned a girl's jeans or did anything improper. Maxwell Desselle said he had harmlessly kissed Beverly Martin at a Christmas dinner. Mr. Bordelon and Maxwell Desselle denied the occurrence of Mr. Desselle patting a girl on the buttocks.

Concerning the statement Mr. Guillory made to James Armand, Mr. Armand stated Mr. Guillory told him certain teachers were molesting girls on a school trip and named the three plaintiffs. Mr. Guillory disputed this by saying he told him some of the girls had stated to his wife that some of the teachers were "messing around." He testified he did not intend any harm.

The issues presented by this appeal are: (1) whether or not the jury erred in rendering a verdict in favor of the defendants and (2) whether or not the jury erred in awarding the defendants attorney's fees under LSA-C.C. Article 2315.1.

In order to maintain an action in defamation, the plaintiff must establish the following elements: (1) defamatory words; (2) publication; (3) falsity; (4) malice, actual or implied; and (5) resulting injury.

The available defenses against an action in defamation are: (1) privilege and (2) truth.

The appellants argue that the evidence presented sufficiently proved the elements necessary for an action in defamation and the defendants failed to bear their burden of proving privilege or truth. Assuming the evidence was sufficient to prove the first three elements of defamation, we find that a qualified privilege existed between Mrs. Guillory and each person she discussed the rumors with.

A qualified privilege exists as to a communication, even if false, between parties sharing an interest or duty. However, to be a good defense such communication must be made in good faith and without malice.

In the present case Mrs. Guillory had discussions with the school principal and with several parents of girls attending Bordelonville High School concerning the alleged actions of certain teachers. The interests shared by each of these persons were to protect the welfare of their children at school and to provide good teachers in the public schools.

There was sufficient evidence for the jury to have found that Mrs. Guillory was in good faith and without malice in her communications to the principal and the parents. Several high school girls told her that certain teachers were playing with the female students. She had heard that one of the plaintiffs was taking girls into the bathroom after practice for an unmentioned purpose; that a teacher was allowing a girl to sit on his lap while he felt her body; that a teacher had unbuttoned the jeans of a girl; and that a teacher had kissed a student and he also had patted a girl on the buttocks. Hearing these things from the girls and a parent, it was not unreasonable for Mrs. Guillory to have believed that improprieties were occurring at the school. From these facts the jury could have concluded that Mrs. Guillory had reasonable grounds to believe her statements were true and were made in good faith and without malice. In such cases they were privileged. . . .

From our review of the record we are unable to say that the verdict of the jury favoring the defendants on the plaintiffs' demands is clearly wrong. . . .

We do not believe the filing of these suits was frivolous. Our decision is based on the defense of qualified privilege and the record contains no indication of any lack of sincerity on the part of plaintiffs as to their legal position. Therefore the jury award of $3,000 to the Guillorys for attorney's fees was in error and must be set aside. *Boyd v. Community Center Credit Corporation*, 359 So.2d 1048 (La.App.4 Cir.1978).

For these reasons the judgment of the district court is reversed and set aside insofar as it awarded $3,000.00 in attorney's fees to the plaintiffs-in-reconvention. Otherwise, it is affirmed. The costs of this appeal are assessed one-half to plaintiffs and one-half to the defendants.

Affirmed in part and reversed in part.

❖ — ❖ — ❖

Statements by Teachers about Student's Nickname Not a "False Light" Tort

Phillips v. Lincoln County School District

Court of Appeals of Oregon, 1998.
984 P.2d 947.

LANDAU, P.J.

The mother of a 12-year-old middle school student initiated this action for damages arising from the refusal of two employees of defendant school district to permit the student to use her nickname at school. The trial court entered summary judgment dismissing all claims. We affirm.

The relevant facts are not in dispute. Abby Phillips was a sixth-grade student at Waldport Middle School. Plaintiff Deborah Phillips is Abby's mother. To her friends and family, Abby always has been known by the nickname "Boo."

Briggs was a teacher at Waldport Middle School and taught the school's health curriculum. Alcohol and drug education is part of that curriculum. One lesson includes the identity of various drugs and requires students to list the street names for marijuana and other drugs. Every time Briggs taught that lesson, his students listed the word "boo" as a street name for marijuana.

At school, Abby turned in school assignments with her nickname, "Boo," at the top of the page. Briggs told her to use her full name on all assignments, as he required all other students to do. On at least one occasion, when another student referred to Abby by her nickname, Briggs told Abby and her classmates not to use the nickname, as it is the street name for marijuana. On another occasion, when a student referred to Abby by her nickname, another teacher, Kilduff, told the student not to use the nickname, because it is a synonym for "marijuana." When Abby objected, Kilduff told Abby to sit in the corner of the classroom. Following that, Abby was subjected to teasing by her peers, who called her "pot" and "marijuana."

Eventually, the teachers relented and permitted Abby to be called by her nickname in school.

Deborah Phillips, as guardian *ad litem* for Abby, filed a complaint against the school district of which Waldport Middle School is a part. The complaint alleged claims of negligence, false light invasion of privacy, and intentional inflection of emotional distress and requested damages for the emotional distress that Abby suffered as a result of her teachers' refusal to permit her to use her nickname in school. . . .

Plaintiff first challenges the trial court's ruling with respect to her negligence claim. According to plaintiff, the district's employees, Briggs and Kilduff, were negligent in failing to exercise reasonable care in making statements about Abby and the significance of her nickname when they knew or should have known of the harm to her that might result. Defendant contends that the trial court correctly dismissed plaintiff's negligence claim, because plaintiff neither alleged nor proved that Abby suffered any physical injury from the statements of Briggs and Kilduff. . . . Plaintiff acknowledges that Oregon courts follow the "physical impact" rule in negligence cases, but she insists that her claim falls within a recognized exception to the rule, which requires no physical impact or injury if a defendant "infringes on a legally protected interest or right." . . .

The independent basis of liability on which plaintiff relies in this case is the violation of the supposed common-law and constitutional right to be named in accordance with one's own wishes. Whatever the merits of plaintiff's contention that there is a common-law and constitutional right to be given a chosen name, such a right has no application to this case. What is at issue in this case is the asserted right to use a chosen nickname *at school* and the liability, if any, for violating that right. Plaintiff has cited no authority for the proposition that there lies an independent basis of liability for interfering with the ability of an individual to claim a nickname at school, and we are aware of none. *See Hazelwood School District v. Kuhlmeier*, 484 U.S. 260, 266, 108 S.Ct. 562, 98 L.Ed.2d 592 (1988) (constitutional rights of students at school "'are not automatically coextensive with the rights of adults in other settings'"). . . . It follows that plaintiff's negligence claim falls victim to the

"physical impact" rule and that the trial court correctly entered summary judgment in favor of defendant.

Plaintiff next challenges the trial court's ruling with respect to the false-light invasion of privacy claim. Plaintiff contends that, by telling other students that Abby's name was a synonym for marijuana, Briggs and Kilduff publicly suggested that Abby used illegal drugs such as marijuana or condoned the use of drugs such as marijuana. Defendant contends that the truth of Briggs's and Kilduff's statements—that "boo" is a street name for marijuana—defeats the claim. In any event, defendant argues, nothing that Briggs and Kilduff said suggested that Abby used or condoned the use of drugs or that they knew or acted in reckless disregard of the fact that what they said bore that implication.

In *Dean v. Guard Publishing Co.*, 73 Or.App. 656, 659, 699 P.2d 1158 (1985), we recognized an action for false light as a common-law tort and adopted the *Restatement (Second) Torts* §652 E as the proper description of the elements that must be proven to prevail in such an action:

> One who gives publicity to a matter concerning another that places the other before the public in a false light is subject to liability to the other for invasion of his privacy, if
> (a) the false light in which the other was placed would be highly offensive to a reasonable person, and
> (b) the actor has knowledge of or acted in reckless disregard as to the falsity of the publi[ci]zed matter and the false light in which the other would be placed.

The tort of false light is akin to the tort of defamation in that it is based on statements about a person that lead others to believe something about that person that is false. . . .

Defendant's argument that Briggs's and Kilduff's statements—that "boo" is a street name for marijuana—were not false is beside the point. The focus of the tort is not on the truth or falsity of a particular statement, but instead is whether what has been said leads others to believe something about *the plaintiff* that is false. . . . [I]n this case, the relevant issue is not whether "boo" refers to marijuana, but whether the teachers' association of the term with Abby falsely suggested that she used or condoned the use of the drug.

Defendant's other argument, however, is well taken. Briggs and Kilduff said only that Abby's nickname, "Boo," is a street name for marijuana and asked her not to use the name at school. Neither Briggs nor Kilduff told anyone that Abby used drugs or condoned the use of drugs. Even assuming for the sake of argument that what they did say somehow permitted others to infer that Abby must either use or condone the use of marijuana, the record still remains devoid of any suggestion that either Briggs or Kilduff knew of that inference or acted in reckless disregard of the likelihood that the inference would be made. We conclude therefore that plaintiff's false-light claim failed as a matter of law and that the trial court did not err in entering summary judgment in favor of defendant.

Finally, plaintiff contends that the trial court erred in ruling in favor of defendant on her claim for intentional infliction of emotional distress. She argues that defendant is liable because what Briggs and Kilduff said was "outrageous in the extreme" and caused Abby emotional distress. Defendant argues that the claim fails as a matter of law because what Briggs and Kilduff said does not rise to the level of actionable, outrageous conduct. . . .

Stripped of rhetoric, however, the facts boil down to Briggs and Kilduff telling Abby to use her given name in class. We fail to see how a reasonable juror could find that such conduct constitutes an extraordinary transgression of bounds of socially tolerable conduct. We conclude that the trial court did not err in entering summary judgment in favor of defendant on plaintiff's claim for intentional inflection of emotional distress.

Affirmed.

CASE NOTE

Where a Texas statute provided that a professional employee is not personally liable for any act that is within the scope of the duties of the employee or that involves judgement or discretion, a director of special education was found to be immune from liability for comments made on television about the reasons for dismissal of employees. The court held that, under the statute, the exercise of all discretionary functions is protected, and because the statute did not mention a requirement of good faith, or lack thereof, it is not required as a defense. The court examined the differences between discretionary and ministerial acts for purposes of defamation and concluded that

> [m]inisterial acts are those "where the law prescribes and defines the duties to be performed with such precision and certainty as to leave nothing to the exercise of discretion or judgement." On the other hand, discretionary acts involve "personal deliberation, decision, and judgement."

Enriquez v. Khouri, 13 S.W.3d 458 (Tex.2000). (See also Chapter 13 for further discussion of discretionary functions.)

❖ — ❖ — ❖

Newspaper Article Accusing Coach of Being a Liar Is Not Entitled to Separate Constitutional Privilege for "Opinion"

Milkovich v. Lorain Journal Co.

Supreme Court of the United States, 1990.
497 U.S. 1, 110 S.Ct. 2695.

Chief Justice REHNQUIST delivered the opinion of the Court. Respondent J. Theodore Diadiun authored an article in an Ohio newspaper implying that petitioner Michael Milkovich, a local high school wrestling coach, lied under oath in a judicial proceeding about an incident involving petitioner and his team which occurred at a wrestling match. Petitioner sued Diadiun and the newspaper for libel, and the Ohio Court of Appeals affirmed a lower court entry of summary judgment against petitioner. This judgment was based in part on the grounds that the article constituted an "opinion" protected from the reach of state defamation law by the First Amendment to the United States Constitution. We hold that the First Amendment does not prohibit the application of Ohio's libel laws to the alleged defamations contained in the article.

This case is before us for the third time in the odyssey of litigation spanning nearly 15 years. Petitioner Milkovich, now retired, was the wrestling coach at Maple Heights High School

in Maple Heights, Ohio. In 1974, his team was
involved in an altercation at a home wrestling
match with a team from Mentor High School.
Several people were injured. In response to the
incident, the Ohio High School Athletic Association (OHSAA) held a hearing at which Milkovich
and H. Don Scott, the Superintendent of Maple
Heights Public Schools, testified. Following the
hearing, OHSAA placed the Maple Heights
team on probation for a year and declared the
team ineligible for the 1975 state tournament.
OHSAA also censored Milkovich for his actions
during the altercation. Thereafter, several parents and wrestlers sued OHSAA in the Court
of Common Pleas of Franklin County, Ohio,
seeking a restraining order against OHSAA's
ruling on the grounds that they had been denied
due process in the OHSAA proceeding. Both
Milkovich and Scott testified in that proceeding.
The court overturned OHSAA's probation and
ineligibility orders on due process grounds.

The day after the court rendered its decision,
respondent Diadiun's column appeared in the
News-Herald, a newspaper which circulates in
Lake County, Ohio, and is owned by respondent
Lorain Journal Co. The column bore the heading
"Maple beat the law with the 'big lie,'" beneath
which appeared Diadiun's photograph and the
words "TD Says." The carryover page headline
announced ". . . Diadiun says Maple told a lie."
The column contained the following passages:

> A lesson was learned (or relearned) yesterday by
> the student body at Maple Heights High School,
> and by anyone who attended the Maple-Mentor
> wrestling meet of last Feb. 8.
>
> A lesson which, sadly, in view of the events of
> the past year, is well they learned early.
>
> It is simply this: If you get in a jam, lie your
> way out.
>
> If you're successful enough, and powerful
> enough, and can sound sincere enough, you stand
> an excellent chance of making the lie stand up,
> regardless of what really happened.
>
> The teachers responsible were mainly Maple
> wrestling coach, Mike Milkovich, and former
> superintendent of schools, H. Donald Scott. . . .
>
> Anyone who attended the meet, whether he be
> for Maple Heights, Mentor, or impartial observer,
> knows in his heart that Milkovich and Scott lied at
> the hearing after each having given his solemn
> oath to tell the truth.
>
> But they got away with it.

> Is that the kind of lesson we want our young
> people learning from their high school administra-
> tors and coaches?
>
> I think not. . . .

Petitioner commenced a defamation action
against respondents in the Court of Common
Pleas of Lake County, Ohio, alleging that the
headline of Diadiun's article and the 9 passages
quoted above "accused plaintiff of committing
the crime of perjury, an indictable offense in the
State of Ohio, and damaged plaintiff directly in
his life-time occupation of coach and teacher,
and constituted libel per se." . . .

Subsequently, . . . the Ohio Court of Appeals
in the instant proceedings affirmed a trial
court's grant of summary judgment in favor of
respondents, concluding that "it has been decided, as a matter of law, that the article in question was constitutionally protected opinion." . . .
We granted certiorari . . . to consider the important questions raised by the Ohio courts' recognition of a constitutionally required "opinion"
exception to the application of its defamation
laws. We now reverse.

Since the latter half of the 16th century, the
common law has afforded a cause of action for
damage to a person's reputation by the publication of false and defamatory statements. . . .

. . . Defamation law developed not only as a
means of allowing an individual to vindicate his
good name, but also for the purpose of obtaining
redress for harm caused by such statements. . . .
As the common law developed in this country,
apart from the issue of damages, one usually
needed only allege an unprivileged publication
of false and defamatory matter to state a cause
of action for defamation. See, *e.g.*, Restatement
of Torts §558 (1938); Gertz v. Robert Welch, Inc.,
418 U.S., at 370, 94 S.Ct., at 3022 (WHITE, J., dissenting) ("Under typical state defamation law,
the defamed private citizen had to prove only a
false publication that would subject him to hatred, contempt, or ridicule"). The common law
generally did not place any additional restrictions on the type of statement that could be actionable. Indeed, defamatory communications
were deemed actionable regardless of whether
they were deemed to be statements of fact or
opinion. See, *e.g.*, Restatement of Torts, *supra*,
§§565–567. As noted in the 1977 Restatement
(Second) of Torts §§566, Comment *a*:

Under the law of defamation, an expression of opinion could be defamatory if the expression was sufficiently derogatory of another as to cause harm to his reputation, so as to lower him in the estimation of the community or to deter third persons from associating or dealing with him. . . . The expression of opinion was also actionable in a suit for defamation, despite the normal requirement that the communication be false as well as defamatory. . . . This position was maintained even though the truth or falsity of an opinion—as distinguished from a statement of fact—is not a matter that can be objectively determined and truth is a complete defense to a suit for defamation.

However, due to concerns that unduly burdensome defamation laws could stifle valuable public debate, the privilege of "fair comment" was incorporated into the common law as an affirmative defense to an action for defamation. "The principle of 'fair comment' afford[ed] legal immunity for the honest expression of opinion on matters of legitimate public interest when based upon a true or privileged statement of fact." 1 F. Harper & F. James, Law of Torts §5.28, p. 456 (1956) (footnote omitted). As this statement implies, comment was generally privileged when it concerned a matter of public concern, was upon true or privileged facts, represented the actual opinion of the speaker, and was not made solely for the purpose of causing harm. See Restatement of Torts, *supra*, §606. "According to the majority rule, the privilege of fair comment applied only to an expression of opinion and not to a false statement of fact, whether it was expressly stated or implied from an expression of opinion." Restatement (Second) of Torts, supra, §566 Comment *a*. Thus under the common law, the privilege of "fair comment" was the device employed to strike the appropriate balance between the need for vigorous public discourse and the need to redress injury to citizens wrought by invidious or irresponsible speech.

In 1964, we decided in *New York Times Co. v. Sullivan*, 376 U.S. 254, 84 S.Ct. 710, 11 L.Ed.2d 686, that the First Amendment to the United States Constitution placed limits on the application of the state law of defamation. There the Court recognized the need for "a federal rule that prohibits a public official from recovering damages for a defamatory falsehood relating to his official conduct unless he proves that the statement was made with 'actual malice'—that is, with knowledge that it was false or with reckless disregard of whether it was false or not." . . . This rule was prompted by a concern that, with respect to the criticism of public officials in their conduct of governmental affairs, a state law " 'rule compelling the critic of official conduct to guarantee the truth of all his factual assertions' would deter protected speech." *Gertz v. Robert Welch, Inc.*, 418 U.S., at 334, 94 S.Ct., at 3004 (quoting *New York Times, supra,* 376 U.S., at 279, 84 S.Ct., at 725).

Three years later, in *Curtis Publishing Co. v. Butts*, 388 U.S. 130, 87 S.Ct. 1975, 18 L.Ed.2d 1094 (1967), a majority of the Court determined "that the *New York Times* test should apply to criticism of 'public figures' as well as 'public officials.' The Court extended the constitutional privilege announced in that case to protect defamatory criticism of nonpublic persons 'who are nevertheless intimately involved in the resolution of important public questions or, by reason of their fame, shape events in areas of concern to society at large.'" . . .

The next step in this constitutional evolution was the Court's consideration of a private individual's defamation actions involving statements of public concern. Although the issue was initially in doubt, . . . the Court ultimately concluded that the *New York Times* malice standard was inappropriate for a private person attempting to prove he was defamed on matters of public interest. . . . As we explained:

> Public officials and public figures usually enjoy significantly greater access to the channels of effective communication and hence have a more realistic opportunity to counteract false statements than private individuals normally enjoy. . . .
>
> [More important,] public officials and public figures have voluntarily exposed themselves to increased risk of injury from defamatory falsehood concerning them. No such assumption is justified with respect to a private individual. . . .

Nonetheless, the Court believed that certain significant constitutional protections were warranted in this area. First, we held that the States could not impose liability without requiring some showing of fault. . . . Second, we held that the States could not permit recovery of presumed or punitive damages on less than a showing of *New York Times* malice. . . .

Still later, in *Philadelphia Newspapers, Inc. v. Hepps,* . . . we held "that the common-law presumption that defamatory speech is false cannot stand when a plaintiff seeks damages against a media defendant for speech of public concern." . . . In other words, the Court fashioned "a constitutional requirement that the plaintiff bear the burden of showing falsity, as well as fault, before recovering damages." . . . Although recognizing that "requiring the plaintiff to show falsity will insulate from liability some speech that is false, but unprovably so," the Court believed that this result was justified on the grounds that "placement by state law of the burden of proving truth upon media defendants who publish speech of public concern deters from speech because of the fear that liability will unjustifiably result." . . .

Respondents would have us recognize, in addition to the established safeguards discussed above, still another First Amendment–based protection for defamatory statements which are categorized as "opinion" as opposed to "fact." For this proposition they rely principally on the following dictum from our opinion in *Gertz*:

> Under the First Amendment there is no such thing as a false idea. However pernicious an opinion may seem, we depend for its correction not on the conscience of judges and juries but on the competition of other ideas. But there is no constitutional value in false statements of fact. . . .

Read in context, though, the fair meaning of the passage is to equate the word "opinion" in the second sentence with the word "idea" in the first sentence. . . .

Thus we do not think this passage from *Gertz* was intended to create a wholesale defamation exemption for anything that might be labeled "opinion." . . . Not only would such an interpretation be contrary to the tenor and context of the passage, but it would also ignore the fact that expressions of "opinion" may often imply an assertion of objective fact.

If a speaker says, "In my opinion John Jones is a liar," he implies a knowledge of facts which lead to the conclusion that Jones told an untruth. Even if the speaker states the facts upon which he bases his opinion, if those facts are ei-

ther incorrect or incomplete, or if his assessment of them is erroneous, the statement may still imply a false assertion of fact. Simply couching such statements in terms of opinion does not dispel these implications; and the statement, "In my opinion Jones is a liar," can cause as much damage to reputation as the statement, "Jones is a liar." As Judge Friendly aptly stated: "[It] would be destructive of the law of libel if a writer could escape liability for accusations of [defamatory conduct] simply by using, explicitly or implicitly, the words 'I think.'" . . .

We are not persuaded that . . . an additional separate constitutional privilege for "opinion" is required to ensure the freedom of expression guaranteed by the First Amendment. The dispositive question in the present case then becomes whether or not a reasonable factfinder could conclude that the statements in the Diadiun column imply an assertion that petitioner Milkovich perjured himself in a judicial proceeding. We think this question must be answered in the affirmative. As the Ohio Supreme Court itself observed, "the clear impact in some nine sentences and a caption is that [Milkovich] 'lied at the hearing after . . . having given his solemn oath to tell the truth.'" . . . This is not the sort of loose, figurative or hyperbolic language which would negate the impression that the writer was seriously maintaining petitioner committed the crime of perjury. Nor does the general tenor of the article negate this impression.

We also think the connotation that petitioner committed perjury is sufficiently factual to be susceptible of being proved true or false. . . .

The numerous decisions discussed above establishing First Amendment protection for defendants in defamation actions surely demonstrate the Court's recognition of the Amendment's vital guarantee of free and uninhibited discussion of public issues. But there is also another side to the equation; we have regularly acknowledged the "important social values which underlie the law of defamation," and recognize that "[s]ociety has a pervasive and strong interest in preventing and redressing attacks upon reputation." . . . Justice Stewart put it with his customary clarity:

> The right of a man to the protection of his own reputation from unjustified invasion and wrongful

hurt reflects no more than our basic concept of the essential dignity and worth of every human being—a concept at the root of any decent system of ordered liberty. . . .

The destruction that defamatory falsehood can bring is, to be sure, often beyond the capacity of the law to redeem. Yet, imperfect though it is, an action for damages is the only hope for vindication or redress the law gives to a man whose reputation has been falsely dishonored. 86 S.Ct., at 679–680 (Stewart, J., concurring).

We believe our decision in the present case holds the balance true. The judgment of the Ohio Court of Appeals is reversed and the case remanded for further proceedings not inconsistent with this opinion.

Reversed.

CASE NOTES

1. A father's statement regarding the competency of a teacher of his child is protected by a qualified privilege. For the teacher to bring a successful action against the parent, it must be shown that the information conveyed by the parent was not only false, but also exhibited malice. The fact that the father communicated his complaint within the established channels of the school was insufficient to show malice. Here the parent wrote a letter to the school principal accusing the teacher of treating his child "most unfairly" and displaying a "remarkable insensitivity and behavior that was most unprofessional" and "inconsistent with good teaching practice." The court held for the parent, saying that "a qualified privilege extends to all communications made *bona fide* upon any subject matter in which the party communicating has an interest, or in reference to which he has a duty, to a person having a corresponding interest or duty, and embraces cases where the duty is not a legal one but is of a moral or social character of imperfect obligation." *Swenson-Davis v. Martel*, 135 Mich.App. 632, 354 N.W.2d 288 (1984), citing *Timmis v. Bennett*, 352 Mich. 355, 89 N.W.2d 748 (1958).

2. In a New York case, a high school football coach sued a reporter for defamation for an article that indicated that the coach "showed himself to be a big loser" and that he cursed, belittled, and verbally abused the players. Testimony from game officials, cheerleaders, players, and parents verified that the charge against the coach was false. The coach, however, conceded that he was a "public figure," invoking *New York Times* malice (actual malice) as the standard of proof against the reporter. The court explained that public figure status triggers three constitutionally based requirements that the plaintiff must meet in order to sustain a judgment against a newspaper:

- Plaintiff is required to prove defamatory statements were published with actual malice.
- Actual malice must be established by clear and convincing evidence.
- Appellate review must include an independent review of the evidence germane to the actual malice determination to ensure that the determination rests upon clear and convincing evidence.

The court further observed that falsity and actual malice are distinct concepts. "It is one thing to publish a false statement and quite another to do so knowingly and recklessly." Here the coach was unable to sustain the test of clear and convincing evidence of intentional and reckless disregard. *Mahoney v. Adirondack Publishing Co.*, 71 N.Y.2d 31, 523 N.Y.S.2d 480, 517 N.E.2d 1365 (1987).

Teacher Is Not a Public Official and Is Not Required to Prove Actual Malice to Recover Compensatory Damages for Libel

Richmond Newspapers, Inc., v. Lipscomb

Supreme Court of Virginia, 1987.
234 Va. 277, 362 S.E.2d 32.

WHITING, Justice. This action for defamation brought by a Richmond public school teacher, Vernelle M. Lipscomb (Lipscomb), against Richmond Newspapers, Inc. (the newspaper), a publisher, and its reporter, Charles E. Cox (Cox), arises out of the publication of a front-page article in the *Richmond Times Dispatch.* The trial judge sustained a jury's award of $45,000 in punitive damages against Cox, but required a remittitur of $900,000 of a $1,000,000 compensatory damage award against both defendants. We will affirm the reduced award of compensatory damages but reverse the award of punitive damages.

(1) Was Lipscomb, as a public school teacher, in that class of public officials which can only recover compensatory damages for defamation by establishing the constitutional malice described in *New York Times Co. v. Sullivan,* 376 U.S. 254, 84 S.Ct. 710, 11 L.Ed.2d 686 (1964)?

(2) If not, was negligent publication by Cox and the newspaper subsumed in the jury's finding of a publication with reckless disregard for the truth; and, if so, was the evidence in this case sufficient to support a finding of negligent publication?

(3) Was the evidence in this case sufficiently clear and convincing to support the jury's finding of publication by Cox with a reckless disregard for the truth, which Lipscomb must establish to recover punitive damages?

Collateral issues must also be resolved as to the admissibility of an expert's opinion on the standard of care, the obligation of a trial court to segregate potentially defamatory evidence from non-defamatory evidence in its instructions to the jury, and the size of the jury's verdict.

The news article was in the Sunday newspaper a few weeks prior to the opening of school in the fall of 1981. The article identified Lipscomb by name and said that certain parents and their children

> charge that a Thomas Jefferson High School teacher is disorganized, erratic, forgetful and unfair; that she returns graded papers weeks late and absents herself from the classroom for long periods; that she insists students stick to the rules, and flouts them herself. They say she demeans and humiliates students. The brighter they appear, the likelier they are to suffer at her hands, the parents protest.

One of Lipscomb's colleagues was quoted as saying that the teacher "might be out of her element in dealing with the students found in the honors course where most of the problems seem to have cropped up since the mid-1970's."

Dr. I. David Goldman, a physician and a teacher at the Medical College of Virginia and the father of one of the Lipscomb students, initiated the contact with Cox. Goldman allegedly told Cox that the school's principal "has had enough complaints about Ms. Lipscomb's performance over the years to know that there was trouble." . . .

The article quoted a student as saying, "She [Ms. Lipscomb] was patronizing, she was late for class, and she was missing from class a third of the time. When she was present she was so disorganized that few if any of [my] classmates understood what was expected of them. She didn't teach, I really learned nothing . . . , her verbal excesses . . . caused . . . pain, I cried in class, I cried outside her class." Another student was quoted as saying she was a victim of the teacher's harassment tactics, "[i]f I asked her a question, she would come back with something like, 'That's a stupid question.'" Dr. Goldman's daughter allegedly told the reporter that "[Ms. Lipscomb] seemed to hate what I represented, meaning middle-class, bright, articulate, assertive, questioning. . . . I questioned her grades, I questioned her before the others in the class. She really didn't like it [and] she was always chipping away at our self-confidence." . . .

Cox essentially confined his investigative activities to interviews with the complaining parents and students and to telephone conferences with Lipscomb's principal and two of Lipscomb's teaching colleagues. He obtained very little information from Lipscomb and the other school employees. The school board's attorney had advised Lipscomb and certain school administrative officials not to discuss the details of the Goldman complaints because of the law dealing with confidentiality of both student and individual teacher records and his fear of litigation over the Goldman issue with Lipscomb as a possible defendant.

We first consider whether the trial court correctly required Lipscomb to prove publication with a reckless disregard for the truth in her claim for compensatory damages. The answer to this question hinges upon whether the trial court properly classified Lipscomb as a "public official" under the *New York Times* malice rule.

New York Times prohibits "a public official from recovering damages for a defamatory falsehood relating to his official conduct unless he proves that the statement was made with 'actual malice'—that is, with knowledge that it was false or with reckless disregard of whether it was false or not." . . . "Actual malice" as described in *New York Times* might be confused with common law malice, which involves "motives of personal spite, or ill will." . . . Therefore, we will refer to such actual malice as *"New York Times"* malice.

The Supreme Court said in *New York Times v. Sullivan* "[w]e have no occasion here to determine how far down into the lower ranks of government employees the 'public official' designation would extend for purposes of this rule." . . . [T]he Supreme Court pointed out that it "has not provided precise boundaries for the category of 'public official'; it cannot be thought to include all public employees, however." Nevertheless, that Court has left little doubt that other courts are to determine who is a "public official" in accordance with "the purposes of a national constitutional protection," *Rosenblatt v. Baer*, 383 U.S. 75, 84, 86 S.Ct. 669, 675, 15 L.Ed.2d 597 (1966), and not by reference to state law standards. . . .

Cases construing the "public official" standards of *New York Times* are legion, but we have found no federal cases concerning school teachers. The state defamation cases are split on the issue of whether public school teachers are "public officials" subject to the *New York Times* malice rule.

There has been no showing that Lipscomb, who was not an elected official, either influenced or even appeared to influence or control any public affairs or school policy. On the contrary, the evidence shows her to have limited her activities to teaching and acting as a temporary department head of a small number of other English teachers. We also note there was no criticism of Lipscomb as an acting department head—it is all leveled at her teaching activities.

. . . When Cox and the newspaper chose to assist Dr. Goldman in going beyond his normal remedy by publicizing his dispute, they became subject to the same duty of due care to ascertain the accuracy of their charges that every citizen must assume when issuing statements, the substance of which makes substantial danger to reputation apparent.

The same reasoning applies to the defendants' contention that because the school system did not respond to Dr. Goldman's satisfaction, the conflict escalated into a public issue of evaluation of teacher competence in general and accountability of the school administration to the parents and students in particular. . . .

We find that the public had no independent interest in Lipscomb's qualifications and performance "beyond its general interest in the qualifications and performance of all government employees," and, therefore, conclude that Lipscomb was not a "public official" under *New York Times* but a private person. Accordingly, we decide that the trial court erred in requiring Lipscomb to prove *New York Times* malice before she could recover compensatory damages.

Because the jury found the plaintiff established *New York Times* malice, we must next consider whether we properly may enter a judgment for Lipscomb for compensatory damages or whether the case should be remanded for a new trial on that issue. . . . Two factors influence this determination; first, is a finding of negligence subsumed in a jury's finding of a reckless disregard for the truth? Second, if so, is the evidence sufficient to support a finding that Cox's investigation was negligent? . . .

. . . All parties, including Cox and his editors, recognized a substantial danger of injury to Lipscomb's reputation, raising a duty to investigate the accuracy of the statements made to Cox.

A number of supervisors, a fellow teacher, and students, including some classmates of the complaining students, testified as to Lipscomb's good qualities as a teacher and contradicted virtually all the negative statements made by the persons Cox interviewed. The students who contradicted the negative testimony were all shown to have been readily available for interview in the Richmond area. While the school authorities would not furnish Cox with the names or addresses of other students in Lipscomb's classes, the jury could have inferred from the evidence that Cox could have obtained this information from the students he interviewed but negligently failed to do so. In fact, one student gave Cox the names of the some of the other students, but Cox apparently did nothing with the information.

We find that the jury had ample evidence from which to conclude that a reasonably prudent news reporter writing this article could readily have contacted a number of other students to verify (or contradict) these accusations and should have done so. Moreover, because there is no issue as to Cox's agency, the newspaper company also is liable for his negligent performance under familiar principles of *respondeat superior.*

The jury awarded punitive damages against Cox. To sustain that award, Lipscomb, as a private person, is required to establish *New York Times* malice by clear and convincing proof. . . . To decide if that requirement has been met, we conduct an "independent examination of the whole record," . . . resolving disputed factual issues and inferences favorably to the plaintiff. Lipscomb maintains that Cox's reckless disregard for the truth is demonstrated by a consideration of the following six factors:

(1) Lipscomb says that the ill will Cox's sources bore Lipscomb was of such a character as to raise obvious doubts as to their veracity. . . .

Except for the bias suggested by their expressions of dissatisfaction with Lipscomb, there is nothing to impeach the credibility of the professor of medicine, the minister, the Richmond school teacher, and the state health department employee, who were the complaining parents, or of their four complaining children. We conclude that there was insufficient damaging evidence about the informants themselves to provide obvious reasons to doubt their veracity.

(2) Lipscomb claims Cox's testimony demonstrates a predetermination of the facts. The most persuasive testimony we can find to support this assertion is Cox's testimony that when Dr. Goldman first called him:

> He said that he had a story he wanted to talk to me about. And he told me in general about the thing. . . . He indicated enough to pique my interest about the thing. . . . [H]e had considerable documentation to present in this case, an extraordinary amount, obviously of documentation already built up in this case. There was a record there for the picking up. In other words . . . [h]e said that he thought it had a wide public interest. I thought so myself. I was impressed [by the long document Dr. Goldman had written the school board] and I

> made a lot of marks on this thing. . . . I'm cautious by nature and I considered this document and I considered Dr. Goldman rather carefully. I was interested in the story. I had been thinking about such a story for a long time. . . .

Lipscomb refers to three cases in support of her claim that Cox had "predetermined the facts" when he began writing the story and suppressed favorable evidence to achieve that end. A review of the facts in those cases illustrates the failure of Lipscomb's proof on this point. . . .

(3) Lipscomb argues that Cox not only resolved ambiguities in the story against her but actually omitted information that was favorable. Cox did fail to report that a substantial part of Lipscomb's extended absence from class was due to the death of her fiance, resulting in a leave of absence, which Lipscomb characterizes as a "brutal twisting of known facts." The omission of this favorable explanation for her absence may have been unfair, but we do not agree that it sufficiently evidenced either the "brutal twisting" claimed or a reckless disregard for the truth. . . .

Our review of the evidence convinces us that there is insufficient support for this claim.

(4) Lipscomb contends that the absence of deadline pressure "holds a libel defendant more accountable." While the cases cited by the plaintiff indicate that lack of a deadline is a factor to be considered, in each case there also was other evidence of conduct demonstrating a reckless disregard for truth. . . . Lipscomb cites no cases, however, where absence of deadline pressure, coupled with a biased source, was sufficient to establish *New York Times* malice.

. . . If the evidence available to Cox at the time of writing was legally insufficient to require a further investigation before publication, additional time to do such an investigation has no legal significance.

(5) Doubts of the newspaper staff members as to the accuracy of the story were said to be evidenced by their delay in publishing it until Cox returned from a vacation. Cox testified that upon his return his editors had fears and reservations because "[t]hey just wanted to be careful journalists. They wanted to be very, very sure of the sources on this. . . . they wanted their hands held, to be reassured I had done all my

work, as an employee, and I was able to tell them, I assume convincingly, that I had done my work, [they] wanted to be sure that what [I] had gotten was accurate and the sources were reliable." This is hardly "sufficient evidence to permit the conclusion that [either of] the defendant[s] in fact entertained serious [doubt] as to the truth of his publication." . . .

(6) The evidence is insufficient to support Lipscomb's final charge that Cox threatened and intimidated her, the school board's attorney, and the principal, the only favorable sources cited by her. On the contrary, the evidence shows that Cox was trying to persuade them to give Lipscomb's side of the controversy. . . .

Lipscomb, when asked if Cox had said, "You really ought to respond to the charges or words to that effect" replied, "Words to that effect, but it was more or less like an intimidating thing, like 'you'd better talk to me.' He didn't say, 'You ought to talk to me.' It was more or less an intimidation thing. . . . I just could detect something like a threat in his voice." Cox himself said, "I tried, I tried very hard to tell [Lipscomb] that these were serious charges. And it seemed to me that she ought to respond." . . .

We conclude that, even with the bias shown, no one of the six elements charged is legally sufficient to justify a jury's finding of a reckless disregard for the truth. We equally are convinced that a consideration of all these elements as a group demonstrates the same inadequacy. Although we are satisfied that the evidence was sufficient to create a factual issue of negligence, as stated above, we find it insufficient to establish *New York Times* malice by clear and convincing evidence. Accordingly, we will reverse the award of punitive damages against Cox. . . .

The defendants charge that the verdict for $1,000,000 in compensatory damages and $45,000 in punitive damages was the result of "passion, prejudice, or a misconception of the law" and that the verdict, therefore, should have been set aside in its entirety. . . .

. . . While we have found the evidence insufficient to show a reckless disregard for the truth by Cox, it is more than ample to justify a finding of negligence in his failure to interview other students and school officials before publishing manifestly damaging statements about Lipscomb. . . .

The defendants also complain that the size of the final awards—$100,000 in compensatory damages and $45,000 in punitive damages—was "so out of proportion to the damage sustained as to be excessive as a matter of law." We need not consider further the punitive damage award since we have set it aside.

. . . We believe an award of $1,000,000 clearly would have been excessive. However, the evidence does not demonstrate that the trial court abused its discretion in reducing the award to $100,000.

For the reasons assigned, we will affirm the judgment of $100,000 for compensatory damages against both defendants, will reverse the judgment of $45,000 for punitive damages against Cox, and will enter a final judgment of $100,000 against both defendants.

Affirmed in part, reversed in part, and final judgment.

❖ — ❖ — ❖

School Principal Is a Public Official within New Times Definition

Johnson v. Robbinsdale Independent School District No. 281

United States District Court,
District of Minnesota, 1993.
827 F.Supp. 1439.

DOTY, District Judge.

This matter is before the court on a motion for summary judgment brought by defendants Karen and Randy Forslund. Based on a review of the file, record and proceedings herein, and for the reasons stated below, the court grants defendants' motion. . . .

Shirley Johnson ("Johnson") is an African-American female. In 1990, Johnson was hired by

Robbinsdale Independent School District No. 281 ("the District") to serve as the principal of the Meadow Lake Elementary School ("Meadow Lake"). . . .

At the beginning of the school year, Johnson implemented a new lunch schedule that was unpopular with staff and parents. The Meadow Lake staff complained about Johnson's lack of communication and procedures being changed without their input. In October 1990, Johnson received an unfavorable evaluation concerning, primarily, her relationship with the staff and communication with parents. The District issued Johnson a notice of deficiency. The notice was revised and corrected in part in December 1990. Johnson filed a grievance challenging her performance appraisal.

On December 19, 1990, the District superintendent and forty staff members from Meadow Lake met to discuss concerns regarding Johnson's performance as principal. The staff alleged that Johnson gave preferential treatment to minority children. The staff accused Johnson of dismissing discipline problems concerning minority children as a "cultural thing," while punishing white children for similar behavior. After the meeting the District superintendent initiated an investigation.*

On December 21, 1990, a group of minority parents along with members of the news media asked to meet with Don Wagner ("Wagner"), director of elementary education for the District. After meeting with Wagner, the parents and media proceeded to Meadow Lake to meet with Johnson. The parents entered the school and disrupted some classrooms. The media interviewed Johnson and broadcast the segment on the evening news. Staff members and parents complained about how Johnson handled the

---

*In January 1991, the District suspended Johnson with pay and benefits pending the outcome of the investigation. Minority parents and others protested the suspension. On February 19, 1991, Johnson requested reinstatement and filed a charge with the Equal Employment Office Commission alleging racial discrimination. Johnson was reassigned as "principal on special assignment" with no change in pay or benefits. On May 21, 1991, Johnson was served with formal notice that the school board declined to renew her contract for the following year.

incident; some parents worried about the safety of their children.

Sometime in late December or early January, Karen and Randy Forslund wrote a letter to the superintendent and the school board voicing their concerns about Meadow Lake and Johnson. The letter said that the Forslund children "learned prejudice from Johnson" by watching "black children misbehave and having no consequences" while white children were punished for the same situation. The Forslund children apparently "saw black children return from the principal's office with candy while white children were given yellow slips." The Forslunds stated that black children had been assaulting white children on the bus. Although parents reported the problem, it continued for a month before Johnson took action by appearing on the bus and telling the students to stop. The Forslunds said they heard that Johnson called a certain teacher a racist during a confrontation with the faculty. The teacher was an acquaintance of the Forslunds and they defended her in the letter. The Forslunds also complained about the lunch schedule imposed for the first few weeks of the school year.

In summary, the Forslunds stated:

> All of these things show me that Shirley Johnson is not a good administrator. She cannot handle the job. In addition to not being able to do the job, she has introduced prejudice to the children and faculty. She should not be whining about her skin color. Her inability to be a principal has caused more harm to Meadow Lake school and its population than her skin color.

Johnson sued Karen and Randy Forslund based on the allegedly defamatory statements made in their letter.

The Forslunds move for summary judgment contending that Johnson is a public official within the meaning of *New York Times Co. v. Sullivan*, 376 U.S. 354, 84 S.Ct. 710, 11 L.Ed.2d 686 (1964), and has provided no evidence of actual malice. In the alternative, the Forslunds claim that Johnson is at least a public figure. Finally, the Forslunds urge this court to hold that the statements in the letter are shielded by a qualified privilege which has not been abused. Johnson contends that she is neither a public official nor a public figure. Johnson admits there is no evidence that the Forslunds acted with actual malice but requests that she be allowed more time to conduct discovery. . . .

In *New York Times*, the Supreme Court recognized that public policy supports a "profound national commitment to the principle that debate on public issues should be uninhibited, robust, and wide-open, and that it may include vehement, caustic, and sometimes unpleasantly sharp attacks on government and public officials." . . . To encourage open debate, the Court imposed a constitutional rule which bars a public official from recovering damages for defamatory publications unless the official proves the statements were made with actual malice.

The United States Supreme Court has not decided "how far down into the lower ranks of government employees the 'public official' designation would extend." . . . Not every public employee is a public official. . . .

The issue before the court is whether a public elementary school teacher is a public official within the meaning of *New York Times*. The question is one of first impression in Minnesota. The public or private status of a plaintiff in a defamation action is one of law. . . .

The Minnesota Supreme Court has evinced its intent to define "public official" broadly. The Court has held that government employees who "perform governmental duties, directly related to the public interest, are public officials and, as such, fall squarely within the 'actual malice' requirement set forth in *New York Times v. Sullivan*." *Hirman v. Rogers*, 257 N.W.2d 563, 566 (Minn.1977). The court uses three criteria in evaluating whether a plaintiff is a public official: (1) employees performing governmental duties directly related to the public interest; (2) employees holding a position to influence significantly the resolution of public issues; and (3) employees having, or appearing to the public to have, substantial responsibility for or control over the conduct of government affairs. . . .

While there are no Minnesota decisions directly on point, other jurisdictions have considered whether a school principal is a public official. Those courts are divided. See *Palmer v. Bennington School District, Inc.*, 615 A.2d 498, 501 (Vt.1992) (elementary school principal is a public official); *Kapiloff v. Dunn*, 27 Md.App.

514, 343 A.2d 251, 258 (1975) (high school principal is a public official), cert. denied, 426 U.S. 907, 96 S.Ct. 2228, 48 L.Ed.2d 832 (1976); . . . *Reaves v. Foster*, 200 So.2d 453, 456 (Miss.1967) (high school principal is a public official); *Junior-Spence v. Keenan*, 1990 WL 17241, *4 (Tenn.Ct.App.1990) (high school principal is a public official).* But see *Ellerbee v. Mills*, 262 Ga. 516, 422 S.E.2d 539, 540 (1992) (high school principal is not a public official), cert. denied, 507 U.S. 1025, 113 S.Ct. 1833, 123 L.Ed.2d 460 (1993); *McCutcheon v. Moran*, 99 Ill.App.3d 421, 54 Ill.Dec. 913, 914, 425 N.E.2d 1130, 1131 (1981) (public school principal's relationship to conduct of government is too remote to justify public official designation).

The division among courts appears to be based on differing perspectives concerning whether education is an important aspect of government and the responsibility for and control principals have over public education. Courts that have found public official status reason that the apparent importance of principals invokes an independent public interest in their qualifications and performance beyond the general public interest in all government employees. Courts that have not applied the heightened standard conclude that, under normal circumstances, a principal's relationship with government does not warrant public official status under *New York Times*.

Education of children is of vital importance to our society. . . . Education is an essential government function. . . . Minnesota's compulsory education statute reflects the centrality of public education. Principals are the persons who control, supervise and govern public schools. Minn.Stat. §123.34. While principals must adhere to rules set by the board of education and the school board, they have broad authority over the format of educational programs employed in public schools. . . . Thus, principals have significant governmental power over public education and the students they supervise.

The court concludes that Minnesota courts would hold that public school principals are

---

*The Tennessee appeals court relied on the decision in *Press, Inc. v. Verran*, 569 S.W.2d 435 (Tenn.1978), which is quoted favorably in *Britton*. See 470 N.W.2d 518, 523 (Minn.1991).

government employees who exercise significant authority in the performance of governmental duties. Thus, the court holds that public school principals criticized for their official conduct are public officials for purposes of defamation law. A contrary holding would stifle public debate about important local issues. . . .

It is undisputed that Johnson, as school principal, managed teachers and other school employees and at least appeared to the public to be the person in charge of operating the school. Johnson contends, however, that her job description does not present an accurate picture of her real authority. Johnson claims that her superiors, as well as disloyal subordinates, denied her the power she theoretically had as principal of Meadow Lake. It is clear that in the eyes of the public Johnson was the person in charge of Meadow Lake. The fact that Johnson appeared to have responsibility over the conduct of education at Meadow Lake is sufficient to trigger public official standards. . . . It is not crucial for Johnson to actually exercise the power the public perceived her to possess.

Because Johnson is a public official, an essential element of her defamation claim against the Forslunds is clear and convincing proof that the statements were made with actual malice. "Actual malice" means with knowledge that the statements were false or with reckless disregard of whether they were true or false. . . . "Reckless disregard" requires evidence that the defendants "in fact entertained serious doubts as to the truth of the publication." *St. Amant v. Thompson,* 390 U.S. 727, 731, 88 S.Ct. 1323, 1325, 20 L.Ed.2d 262 (1968). Whether the evidence in the record in a defamation case is sufficient to support a finding of actual malice is a question of law. . . .

The record reveals no evidence the Forslunds entertained any serious doubts as to the truth of their statements. Most of the information was provided to the Forslunds by their children. There is no evidence to suggest that the Forslunds had any reason to suspect their children's accounts were not credible. Johnson's reliance on *Hunt v. University of Minnesota,* 465 N.W.2d 88 (Minn.App.1911), is misplaced. . . . The court concludes that Johnson has failed to provide any evidence that the Forslunds made the statements with actual malice.

It is not necessary for the court to decide whether Johnson is a public figure or whether an important public issue is involved. If the court were to reach those issues, however, it would answer them affirmatively under the circumstances of this case. Likewise, the privilege issue raised in this case need not be decided. . . .

The court concludes that Johnson as a public school principal is a public official for purposes of applying the *New York Times v. Sullivan* defamation standard. Because Johnson is a public official, the Forslunds are liable for damages for criticizing her official conduct only if Johnson proves with convincing clarity that they made the statements with actual malice. This Johnson has failed to do.

Accordingly, IT IS HEREBY ORDERED that the motion of defendants Karen Forslund and Randy Forslund for summary judgment is granted. IT IS FURTHER ORDERED that the parties shall bear their own costs. The court, finding there is no just reason for delay, directs that JUDGMENT BE ENTERED as to defendants Karen Forslund and Randy Forslund.

CASE NOTES

1. *Teacher as Public Official or Public Figure.* The prevailing view of the courts is that teachers are not "public officials" or "public figures." See *Franklin v. Lodge 1108, Benevolent & Protective Order of Elks,* 97 Cal.App.3d 915, 159 Cal.Rptr. 131, 136–37 (1979); *Nodar v. Galbreath,* 462 So.2d 803, 808 (Fla. 1984); *McCutcheon v. Moran,* 99 Ill.App.3d 421, 54 Ill.Dec. 913, 916, 425 N.E.2d 1130, 1133 (1981); *Poe v. San Antonio Express-News Corp.,* 590 S.W.2d 537 (Tex.Civ.App.1979); *Richmond Newspapers, Inc. v. Lipscomb,* 234 Va. 277, 362 S.E.2d 32 (1987), cert. denied, 486 U.S. 1023, 108 S.Ct. 1997 (1988).

Yet courts in some jurisdictions have held public school teachers to be "public officials." *Sewell v. Brookbank,* 119 Ariz. 422, 581 P.2d 267 (Ct.App.1978); *Johnston v. Corinthian Television Corp.,* 583 P.2d 1101 (Okla.1978). Each of these decisions rested on the authority of *Basarich v. Rodeghero,* 23 Ill.App.3d 889, 321 N.E.2d 739, 742 (1974). This case held that public high school teachers are "public officials" or "public figures." Subsequent Illinois appellate cases have undermined the authority of *Basarich.* See *Mc-*

Cutcheon v. Moran, 99 Ill.App.3d 421, 54 Ill.Dec. 913, 425 N.E.2d 1130 (1981); *Johnson v. Board of Junior College No. 508*, 31 Ill.App.3d 270, 334 N.E.2d 442 (1975); *Kelley v. Bonney*, 221 Conn. 549, 606 A.2d 693 (1992); *Luper v. Black Dispatch Publishing Co.*, 675 P.2d 1028 (Okla.App.1983).

The rationale for not classifying teachers as public officials is given by a court in Maine:

We find too, that there are countervailing considerations that militate against stripping a public school teacher of the protection afforded by the common law tort of defamation. The Supreme Court noted in *Gertz v. Robert Welch, Inc.*, 418 U.S. 323, 94 S.Ct. 2997 (1974) that "[p]ublic officials and public figures usually enjoy significantly greater access to the channels of effective communication and hence have a more realistic opportunity to counteract false statements than private individuals normally enjoy." *Id.* at 344, 94 S.Ct. at 3009. We do not find that a public school teacher usually has this greater access. Like other private individuals, the teacher is vulnerable to injury from defamation, and the state interest in protecting the teacher is greater than the interest in protecting those with readier access to channels of communication. See *id.*; see also *Franklin*, 97 Cal.App.3d at 923, 159 Cal.Rptr. at 136 (application of the *New York Times* rule to a school teacher characterized as "a real and intolerable danger to the freedom of intellect and of expression which the teacher must have to teach effectively."). Moreover, we do not find any "assumption of the risk" by accepting a public teaching position, without more a private individual cannot be said to "have voluntarily exposed [himself] to increased risk of injury from defamatory falsehood."

True v. Ladner, 513 A.2d 257 (Me.1986).

2. *School Board Member as Public Official.* A New Mexico appellate court held that a member of a local school board is a "public official" and not merely an employee in a defamation action. According to this court, members of local school boards govern the public school system, a role of utmost importance in a community, and school board policies are subject to scrutiny of the entire community. Thus, this court found that such persons who are elected to make decisions for public education clearly "have, or appear to the public to have, substantial responsibility for or control over the conduct of gov-

ernmental affairs." Thus, the public interest in openness in public decisions requires that school board members be classified as public officials. *Garcia v. Board of Education*, 106 N.M. 757, 750 P.2d 118 (1988).

3. *School Superintendent as Public Official.* The superintendent of a municipal school system was held to be a "public official" in a libel action against a newspaper in Ohio. The court pointed out that the school superintendent is the executive officer for the school board and has substantial public responsibilities for operation of the public school system. The court felt that to hold that the school superintendent is not a "public official" could potentially stifle public debate about important local education issues. *Scott v. News-Herald*, 25 Ohio St.3d 243, 496 N.E.2d 699 (1986).

4. *School Principal as Public Official or Public Figure.* A school principal may be classified as a "public figure" under the definition of *New York Times Co. v. Sullivan*, 376 U.S. 254, 84 S.Ct. 710 (1964), further interpreted by the Supreme Court to the effect that "those who, by reason of the notoriety of their achievements or the vigor and success with which they seek the public's attention, are properly classed as public figures. . . ." *Gertz v. Robert Welch, Inc.*, 418 U.S. 323, 94 S.Ct. 2997 (1974). In following such rationale, a Maryland court found a school principal to be within the classification of a "public figure–public official." In this instance, the principal was unable to recover damages from a newspaper of general circulation that had published one article entitled "Rating of Principals," which had several negative opinions about the principal's job performance. The court concluded that comments, criticisms, and opinions concerning the involvement of public persons in matters of public interest are protected by a First Amendment privilege. To overcome the privilege, the plaintiff must prove a "reckless disregard" for the truth. An opinion regarding an evaluation of this nature cannot be construed as a defamation. *Kapiloff v. Dunn*, 27 Md.App. 514, 343 A.2d 251 (1975).

A Minnesota court in ruling that a school principal is a public official reviewed three criteria to determine if a person is a public official: (1) whether the person is employed in a position that performs governmental duties directly related to the public interest; (2) whether the person is employed in a position that can influence significantly the resolution of public issues; and (3) whether the person is employed in a position that has, or appears to the public to have, substantial responsibility for or control over the conduct of governmental affairs. In holding that school principals are public officials, this court said that education is an essential governmental function, that state compulsory attendance laws reflect the centrality of public education, and that principals are the persons who control, supervise, and govern the public schools; thus, principals are "public officials." *Britton v. Koep,* 470 N.W.2d 518 (Minn.1991). See also *Hirman v. Rogers,* 257 N.W.2d 563 (Minn.1977). A Mississippi court found that a principal of an attendance center for black students is a public official and could not prevail in a libel action against a newspaper without a showing of malice. *Reaves v. Foster,* 200 So.2d 453 (Miss.1967).

At least two court decisions in Tennessee have held that school principals are "public officials" within the *New York Times* definition. The fact that school principals are authority figures, represent government to the students and parents, and make decisions affecting taxpayers supports that conclusion. *Junior-Spence v. Keenan,* 190 Tenn.App. LEXIS 130 (1990); *Press, Inc. v. Verran,* 569 S.W.2d 435 (Tenn.1978).

In a widely publicized matter regarding a Vermont school district deficit and subsequent court action, a school principal alleged he had been defamed and sought damages against a newspaper. The court in ruling that the plaintiff school principal was a "public official" pointed out that he managed teachers and other employees, was in charge of the operation of the public school, disciplined pupils, and certified time cards for payment of employees from public tax funds. *Palmer v. Bennington School District,* 159 Vt. 31, 615 A.2d 498 (1992). The same conclusion was reached in another Vermont case even though the school principal claimed that he was not a public official, maintaining that he was merely a "small fish in a big pond" of the school district. The court observed that a contrary holding could possibly stifle public debate

about the conduct of schools and the use of taxpayer dollars. *Rosenblatt v. Baer,* 383 U.S. 75, 86 S.Ct. 669 (1966).

5. *Principal Not Public Official or Public Figure.* Defamation cases in some jurisdictions have held that school officials are not public officials. In Illinois, school principals appear not to be "public officials" within the *New York Times* rule. A white school principal sued, claiming that she had been defamed by public assertion that she was a racist, ran the school like a plantation, was insensitive to the community, was a dictator, and was destroying the children's minds. The court ruled that she was not a public official and therefore was not required to prove malice in order to prevail in the suit. *Stevens v. Tillman,* 568 F.Supp. 289 (N.D.Ill.1983), 661 F.Supp. 702 (N.D.Ill.1986), affirmed, 855 F.2d 394 (7th Cir.1988), cert denied, 489 U.S. 1065, 109 S.Ct. 1339 (1989); see also *McCutcheon v. Moran,* 99 Ill.App.3d 421, 425 N.E.2d 1130 (1981). In ruling that a school principal is not a "public official," a Georgia court pointed out that a principal is too far removed from governmental and public policy decision making to warrant such legal classification. *Ellerbee v. Mills,* 262 Ga. 516, 422 S.E.2d 539 (1992). The Ohio Supreme Court has held that a public school principal is not a public official for purposes of defamation law. *East Canton Education Assoc. v. McIntosh,* 709 N.E. 2d 468 (Ohio 1999).

6. *Coaches and Athletes as Public Officials or Public Figures.* A coach in a public university, a mere employee in a university department, subordinate to an athletic director, does not have the status of a "public official." Neither can the coach be classified as a "public figure" simply because of her or his success as a coach. In one case, *Moss v. Stockard,* the athletic director's allegations that the coach had misappropriated funds was slanderous, warranting a recovery of damages by the coach. The court found that public school coaches are not public officials or public figures. *Moss v. Stockard,* 580 A.2d 1011 (D.C.1990).

7. *Actual Malice.* A plaintiff who has been determined to be a public official must prove actual malice of a defendant-newspaper. To show that there was ill will or that the defendant failed to inquire more fully into the accu-

racy of a news article is insufficient to show malice. *Johnson v. Southwestern Newspaper Corp.*, 855 S.W.2d 182 (Tex.App.-Amarillo 1993); *St. Amant v. Thompson*, 390 U.S. 727, 88 S.Ct. 1323 (1968).

■ STUDENT RECORDS

Teachers, guidance counselors, and principals are generally involved in the release of student information and records to other teachers, professional personnel within the school, prospective employers outside the school, or other educational institutions to which students may be applying for entrance. Considering these areas of pupil information flow and the potential harm that can result, common law suggests certain practices to be appropriate.

PRACTICES SUGGESTED BY COMMON LAW

First, information should not be conveyed to other teachers or administrators unless the motive and purpose are to assist and enhance the educational opportunities of the pupil. Transmittal should be made in the proper channels and to persons assigned the responsibility for the relevant educational function. Gossip or careless talk among teachers, which is not calculated to help the student, may be shown to be malicious and not protected by the cloak of qualified privilege. Second, pupil information should be transmitted to prospective employers only upon request. This protects the teacher from the presumption that the transmittal was made with intent to defame the student with malicious intent.[51] A qualified privilege has been upheld when a communicator responded to a questionnaire and gave answers only to specific questions.[52] It is a good practice not to release information over a telephone unless the identity of the caller is absolutely certain. Third, records should be released to colleges and other institutions only if there is a statutory or regulatory requirement for the transmittals or if the pupil requests the conveyance. Most states have laws or regulations that require the transfer of elementary and secondary school pupils' records when they change schools. This,

of course, facilitates the transition for the pupil as well as for the school, and it provides needed data for placement and is therefore proper.

Beyond common law protection of student privacy, both state and federal statutes may intervene to provide additional safeguards. The Family Educational Rights and Privacy Act (FERPA) was passed in August 1974 as an amendment to the Omnibus Education Bill.[53] The act establishes standards to which school districts must adhere in handling student records. Failure to abide by the law can result in the withdrawal of federal education funds. Additionally, Congress included other privacy provisions in the 1978 General Education Provisions Act (GEPA)[54] and in the Education of All Handicapped Children Act of 1975.[55]

FAMILY EDUCATIONAL RIGHTS AND PRIVACY ACT (FERPA)

Under FERPA, every school district is required to publish a pupil records policy that includes annual notification to parents and to students over eighteen years of age.[56] Such a policy must adhere to certain requirements of the act, including the following:

■ Records of individual students containing "personally identifiable information" must be kept confidential and cannot be released by the school without written consent of the parent[57] or consent from the student if the student is eighteen or older.[58]

■ Parents and guardians of a student under age eighteen, as well as a student who is eighteen or older, have the right to inspect all school records concerning that student.[59]

■ The school district recordkeeping system must be described in sufficient detail for parents to locate their child's records.[60]

■ School district staff members with access to student records must be identified by title.[61]

■ Each child's file must include a record of access, which must be signed by each staff member whenever he or she withdraws that student's file.[62]

■ Parents have a right to appeal anything in a student's file that is considered incorrect, and if the school is not willing to delete the challenged material, the parents may request a hearing and/or provide a written statement to be attached to the challenged material.[63]

- The school policy must define what constitutes "directory information" and under what circumstances that information may be released without parental consent.[64] Treatment records "made or maintained by a physician, psychologist, or other recognized professional or paraprofessional acting in his or her professional capacity or assisting in a paraprofessional capacity" and used in the treatment of an eligible student, that is, a student over eighteen years of age or older or any student in an institution of postsecondary education, are excluded from the definition of "education records" in FERPA[65] and are not automatically accessible to the student.

An exception to FERPA is recognized for disclosures that were required by state statutes before enactment of the act.[66] Further, "personal notes" that are defined as "not education records"[67] are exempted from parental access. Personal notes that are not accessible to other school staff members are exempted from student or parental access. These personal notes are available to the substitutes of the original note writers.[68]

The FERPA regulation further provides that a school district may disclose personally identifiable information from an education record of a student without prior consent if the disclosure meets one or more of the following conditions: (1) Information is disclosed to other school officials, including teachers, who the school district has determined have a legitimate educational interest within the school district; (2) information is disclosed to another school, school system, or institution of postsecondary education where the student seeks to enroll; (3) information is disclosed to a representative of the comptroller general of the United States, the secretary of education of the United States, or state and local education authorities; (4) information is disclosed to agencies for student financial aid or agencies or institutions developing or validating tests, for health and safety emergency, and in response to judicial orders.[69]

Moreover, education records held by law enforcement units of a school district or institution retain their status as education records under FERPA and must be handled accordingly.[70] (See Appendix B.)

───────── ❖ — ❖ — ❖ ─────────

FERPA Alone Does Not Provide for Redress in Damages, But It May if Combined with Section 1983

Fay v. South Colonie Central School District

United States Court of Appeals,
Second Circuit, 1986.
802 F.2d 21.

MESKILL, Circuit Judge. This is an appeal and cross-appeal from a judgment of the United States District Court for the Northern District of New York, Miner, J. The plaintiffs below were Robert E. Fay (Fay) and his children, Theresa M. Fay and Thomas R. Fay. The defendants were the South Colonie Central School District, its superintendent (hereinafter the district and its superintendent are collectively described as "the school district") and the New York Commissioner of Education. The district court partially granted the plaintiffs' summary judgment motion, holding the school district liable under 42 U.S.C. §1983 (1982) for denying Robert Fay access to his children's education records, *see* 20 U.S.C. §1232g(a)(1)(A) (1982), awarding nominal damages for the denial of access to the records and granting injunctive relief on a pendent state law claim for violation of his rights as a parent with joint legal custody of his children. The court dismissed all of the plaintiff's claims against Commissioner Ambach. It also dismissed Fay's claim under section 1983 that the school district violated Fay's due process right to control the upbringing of his children and his right to equal protection of the laws. . . .

This suit involves an attempt to have the federal courts resolve a dispute that could be more appropriately resolved either by the state courts or by mediation.

Under a separation agreement Fay and his ex-wife have joint legal custody of their two children. The children live with Fay during the summer and live with their mother during the school year. The separation agreement further provides that the ex-wife

> must . . . consult with [Fay] concerning . . . schooling, relevant to which school [the children] should attend, whether public or private, matters concerning any special education courses which the children may pursue or desire to pursue and further, the [ex-]wife is to provide [Fay] with report cards of the children or photostatic copies thereof. . . .

. . . Fay alleges that his ex-wife has failed to comply fully with this provision.

Dissatisfied with the operation of this aspect of the separation agreement, Fay tried to get information regarding his children's activities and progress directly from the children's schools. In December 1980 Fay sent a letter to the superintendent of the school district demanding such information. Although Fay's original demand was inchoate, it later became clear that he sought information ranging from standardized test results and accident reports to notices about classroom parties and cafeteria menus. Instead of seeking to accommodate any of the demands, the superintendent responded that the school would "provide information to any person or organization whom the courts decide have a legal right to it." . . .

More letters were exchanged between Fay and the superintendent and in April 1981 the United States Department of Education advised the superintendent of Fay's rights under the Family Educational Rights and Privacy Act, 20 U.S.C. §1232g (1982) (FERPA). Thereafter, the school district began mailing copies of the Fay children's education records to Fay. The school district continued to refuse to mail to Fay duplicates of all school-related notices mailed to his ex-wife or carried home by his children.

In May or June 1981 Fay initiated an appeal of this continuing refusal to the New York Commissioner of Education, Gordon Ambach. . . . The Commissioner dismissed Fay's appeal. . . .

The Commissioner did not confine his observations to procedural matters, however. He also stated that Fay's request to receive copies of all communications sent by the school to his ex-wife would place "an unreasonable burden" on the school district. . . .

Fay brought an Article 78 proceeding to annul Commissioner Ambach's ruling. . . . The New York Supreme Court dismissed the proceeding. . . . In January 1983 the Appellate Division of the New York Supreme Court dismissed Fay's appeal.

In August 1983 Fay brought this action for damages and injunctive relief on behalf of himself and his children. The complaint alleged that the school district, the superintendent (in his official capacity) and Commissioner Ambach violated Fay's statutory rights under FERPA, his constitutional right to control the upbringing of his children and his constitutional right to equal protection of the laws. . . .

Fay appeals from the dismissal of the claims against Commissioner Ambach, the dismissal of his claim for the violation of his right to control his children's upbringing and the award of nominal damages. . . .

. . . We note, however, that Fay will have an opportunity on remand of his FERPA claim to prove damages similar to those sought under his due process claim. We now turn to the FERPA claim.

The school district argues that the district court erred in concluding that Fay could assert a cause of action under section 1983 for the school district's violation of FERPA between May 1980 and April 1981. This argument is without merit. Fay claims that the district court erred in awarding him only nominal damages for the FERPA violation. This claim has merit and we remand this portion of the complaint for further proceedings.

FERPA denies federal funds to a school "which has a policy of denying . . . the parents of students who are or have been in attendance at [the school] the right to inspect and review the education records of their children." 20 U.S.C. §1232g(a)(1)(A) (1982). *See also* id. at §(a)(4)(A) & (B) (definition of education records). The statute requires that the "Secretary . . . take appropriate actions to enforce" its provisions. Id. at §1232g(f).

FERPA itself does not give rise to a private cause of action. . . . Fay does not rely on a private cause of action under FERPA. Instead, he asserts the FERPA violation as the basis for a claim under section 1983. . . . The district court correctly determined that FERPA creates an interest that may be vindicated in a section 1983 action because Congress did not create so comprehensive a system of enforcing the statute as to demonstrate an intention to preclude a remedy under section 1983. . . . Although FERPA authorizes extensive enforcement procedures created by regulation, *see* 34 C.F.R. §§99.60–.67 (1985), these regulations do not demonstrate a congressional intent to preclude suits under section 1983 to remedy violations of FERPA. . . .

The school district "tacitly conceded liability" for violating FERPA for the eleven months between May 1980 and April 1981, . . . and it does not contest the entry of summary judgment on the issue of liability. Fay argues, however, that the district court erred in awarding him only nominal damages.

Where the amount of damages is not in dispute, a court may award damages on summary judgment. . . . In this case, however, the opposing arguments made in papers submitted in connection with Fay's motion to amend the judgment make it clear that there was no agreement among the parties as to what damages Fay suffered as a result of the violation of his right to inspect his children's education records.

A section 1983 violation is a species of tort liability in which the level of damages is determined by applying principles derived from tort law. . . . As a leading treatise notes, "even when plaintiff is successful . . . the grant is likely only to foreclose the issue of liability and leave any unliquidated claim for damages" for resolution by the factfinder. . . . Fay is entitled to present evidence to support his claim for compensatory damages and in light of the factual dispute the district court erred in awarding damages for the FERPA violation on summary judgment. We remand the action to the district court for further proceedings to determine the amount, if any, of Fay's damages. . . .

. . . His FERPA claim is remanded for further proceedings to determine the amount of compensatory damages. The parties shall bear their own costs.

CASE NOTES

1. *Remedy under FERPA.* FERPA does not create a "private cause of action" that could result in the award of damages to the plaintiff; rather, if the statute is violated, a school district may, after appropriate proceedings, be subject to loss of federal funds:

> In Plaintiff's Second Amended Complaint ("Complaint"), Plaintiff alleges that the actions of the defendants in denying access to Plaintiff's application constitute a violation of FERPA. FERPA was designed primarily to regulate the release of student records. A student's or parent's consent is required where personally identifiable information from the educational records of a student is to be disclosed. The Secretary of Education is empowered to enforce the various provisions of FERPA. 20 U.S.C. §1232g(f). An educational agency or institution that unlawfully releases a student's record may lose federal funding. 20 U.S.C. §1232g(b)(1). This is the only express remedy provided in the statute. The Fifth Circuit has found that FERPA does not explicitly provide for a private cause of action and that its legislative history does not indicate that the drafters of the legislation intended for there to be one. *Klein Independent School District v. Mattox,* 830 F.2d 576, 579 (5th Cir.1987), *cert. denied,* [485 U.S. 1008,] 108 S.Ct. 1473, [99 L.Ed.2d 702] (1988). Other circuits have found more definitively that no private cause of action, either explicitly or implicitly, was created or intended. . . . See *Girardier v. Webster College,* 563 F.2d 1267, 1277 (8th Cir.1977) (cited with approval in *Klein*). This Court finds therefore that a private cause of action does not exist under FERPA.

Tarka v. Franklin, 891 F.2d 102 (5th Cir.1989).

2. *Student Defined.* The U.S. Court of Appeals for the Fifth Circuit in *Tarka v. Franklin,* cited in the previous note, has explained the meaning of the term "student" under FERPA:

> The statute itself defines "student" with the following statement:
>
> > [T]he term "student" includes any person with respect to whom an educational agency or institution maintains education records or personally identifiable information, but does not include a person who has not been in attendance at such agency or institution.
>
> 20 U.S.C. §1232g(a)(6). Pursuant to the authority granted under subsection (c) of FERPA, the Secretary of Education has adopted regulations for implementing the Act. *See* [34] C.F.R. §99.1, *et seq.* These regulations further define the term "student" in the following provision:
>
> > "Student" (a) includes any individual with respect to whom an educational agency or institution maintains education records.

(b) The term does not include an individual who has not been in attendance at an educational agency or institution. A person who has applied for admission to, but has never been in attendance at a component unit of an institution of postsecondary education (such as the various colleges or schools which comprise a university), even if that individual is or has been in attendance at another component unit of that institution of postsecondary education, is not considered to be a student with respect to the component to which an application for admission has been made.

Tarka v. Franklin, 891 F.2d 102 (5th Cir.1989).

3. *Education Records Defined.* The lack of definition of "education records" initially caused much difficulty for school districts in interpreting and implementing FERPA. The act was later amended to provide greater clarity. A federal district court in New Hampshire explained the problem and the necessity of the amendment:

> When FERPA was initially enacted in August 1974, it did not define "education records" but provided a non-exclusive laundry list of records and documents which were to be made available to students and parents. "Juvenile records" were not included on this list. *See* Pub.L.No. 93-380, Title V, §513(a), 88 Stat. 571, 572 (Aug. 21, 1974).
>
> Recognizing that the statute as enacted was causing confusion in the educational community, Congress passed the Buckley/Pell Amendment (the "Amendment") in December 1974. The Amendment included the current definition of "education records."
>
> > The proposed amendments define "education records" in order to make clear what documents and other material parents and students will have access to. . . . [The] intent to be that, except as provided in the definition, *parents and students should have access to everything in institutional records maintained for each student in the normal course of business and used by the institution in making decisions that affect the life of the student.*
>
> 120 Cong.Rec. at 39858–39859 (emphasis added). In the Joint Statement the sponsors explained that
>
> > this definition is a key element in the amendment. An individual should be able to *know, review, and challenge all information*—with certain limited exceptions—that an institution keeps on him, particularly when the institution may make important decisions affecting his future....

> This is especially true when the individual is a minor. Parents need access to such information in order to protect the interest of their child.

120 Cong.Rec. 39858, 39862 (emphasis added). The sponsors further stated,

> The amendment . . . is intended . . . to open the bases on which decisions are made to more scrutiny by the students, or their parents about whom decisions are being made, and to give them the opportunity to challenge and to correct—or at least, enter an explanatory statement—inaccurate, misleading, or inappropriate information about them which may be in their files and which may contribute, or have contributed to, an important decision made about them by the institution.

Id. The change from the laundry list of items to the definition of "education records" as it appears today, along with the legislative history of the Amendment, lends support to the conclusion that the congressional intent was to fashion a broad definition.

Berlanger v. Nashua, New Hampshire, School District, 856 F.Supp. 40 (D.N.H.1994).

4. A New York court has held that FERPA (20 U.S.C.A. §1232g) implies that both parents have a right to inspect and review the education records of their children. The regulation implementing the act "allow[s] inspection by either parent, without regard to custody, unless such access is barred by state law, court order or legally binding instrument." Thus, a natural father, living apart from the child under terms of a separation agreement, has a right to inspect his child's records despite the fact that the mother had signed a statement indicating that she did not wish or authorize the school district to transmit school records to the father. The court said:

> It is beyond cavil that a non-custodial parent has not "abandoned" his child simply by reason of noncustody and, . . . while legal custody may be in one or both of the parents, the fact that it is placed in one does not necessarily terminate the role of the other as a psychological guardian and preceptor.

Matter of Unido R., 109 Misc.2d 1031, 441 N.Y.S.2d 325 (1981).

5. FERPA does not give a student the right to bring an action challenging a professor's grading process. Under the law, "[s]tudents' grades,

as reflected in educational records, can only be inaccurate or misleading if they do not reflect what the grader intended or if they are mathematically incorrect." The U.S. Court of Appeals, Fifth Circuit, has said that the provision in the act referring to "other rights of students," as amended, 20 U.S.C.A. §1232g(a)(2), cannot be construed as congressional intent to "afford students a federal right, enforced by federal regulations, to challenge their teachers' or educational institutions' grading process." *Tarka v. Cunningham*, 917 F.2d 890 (5th Cir.1990).

■ ENDNOTES

1. Theodore F. T. Plucknett, *A Concise History of the Common Law*, 5th ed. (Boston: Little, Brown, 1956).
2. III Edgar, 4 (C.946–C.961), cited in Plucknett, *A Concise History*, p. 983.
3. Borough Customs (Selden Society), i. 78; Plucknett, *A Concise History*, p. 483.
4. Plucknett, *A Concise History*, p. 484.
5. Ibid., p. 485.
6. Ibid., p. 486.
7. Ibid., p. 487.
8. King v. Lake, 1670; see Plucknett, *A Concise History*, p. 497.
9. *Restatement (Second) of Torts* (St. Paul, Minn.: American Law Institute Publishers, 1977), vol. 3, §558, p. 156.
10. W. Page Keeton, Dan B. Dobbs, Robert E. Keeton, and David G. Owen, *Prosser and Keeton on Torts*, 5th ed. (St. Paul, Minn.: West, 1984), p. 773.
11. *Restatement (Second) of Torts*, vol. 3, §568, pp. 177–78.
12. 50 *American Jurisprudence*, 2d, 516.
13. *Restatement (Second) of Torts*, §568A, p. 182.
14. Ibid.
15. *Restatement (Second) of Torts*, §596; 12 A.L.R. 147; 50 A.L.R. 339.
16. Barton v. Rogers, 21 Idaho 609, 123 P. 478 (1912).
17. Dawkins v. Billingsley, 69 Okla. 259, 172 P. 69 (1918).
18. William L. Prosser, *Law of Torts* (St. Paul, Minn.: West Publishing Company, 1971), p. 609.
19. Coffin v. Coffin, 4 Mass. 1, 3 Am.Dec. 189 (1808).
20. Smith v. Helbraun, 21 A.D.2d 830, 251 N.Y.S.2d 533 (1964).
21. Ottinger v. Ferrell, 171 Ark. 1085, 287 S.W. 391 (1926).
22. Baskett v. Crossfield, 190 Ky. 751, 228 S.W. 673 (1921).
23. *Restatement (Second) of Torts*, §§568–69, pp. 182–83.
24. Ramirez v. Rogers, 540 A.2d 475 (Me.1988).
25. Kern Alexander and M. David Alexander, *The Law of Schools, Students and Teachers in a Nutshell* (St. Paul, Minn.: West, 1984), p. 243.
26. Ibid., p. 244.
27. Keeton et al., *Prosser and Keeton on Torts*, p. 804.
28. 376 U.S. 254, 84 S.Ct. 710 (1964).
29. Ibid.
30. Harry Kalven Jr., *A Worthy Tradition: Freedom of Speech in America* (New York: Harper and Row, 1988), pp. 60–61.
31. Ibid., pp. 70–71.
32. Ibid.
33. 383 U.S. 75, 86 S.Ct. 669 (1966).
34. Ibid., 383 U.S. at 85, 86 S.Ct. at 676.
35. 388 U.S. 130, 87 S.Ct. 1975 (1967).
36. Hutchinson v. Proxmire, 443 U.S. 111, 99 S.Ct. 2675 (1979) (quoting Gertz v. Robert Welch, Inc., 418 U.S. 323, 94 S.Ct. 2997 (1974)); see also True v. Ladner, 513 A.2d 257 (Me.1986).
37. Hutchinson v. Proxmire, 443 U.S. 111, 99 S.Ct. 2675 (1979).
38. Rosenblatt v. Baer, 383 U.S. 75, 86 S.Ct. 669 (1966).
39. 418 U.S. 323, 94 S.Ct. 2997 (1974).
40. Keeton et al., *Prosser and Keeton on Torts*, p. 806.
41. Hutchinson v. Proxmire, 99 S.Ct. at p. 2675.
42. Ibid.
43. See Nodar v. Galbreath, 462 So.2d 803 (Fla.1984); True v. Ladner, 513 A.2d 257 (Me.1986).
44. Gertz v. Robert Welch, Inc., 418 U.S. 323, 94 S.Ct. 2997 (1974).
45. Vinson v. Linn-Mar Community School District, 360 N.W.2d 108 (Iowa 1984).
46. Nodar v. Galbreath, 462 So.2d 803, 811 (Fla.1984).
47. New York Times Co. v. Sullivan, op. cit.
48. E.g., Richmond Newspapers, Inc. v. Lipscomb, 234 Va. 277, 362 S.E.2d 32 (1987).
49. *Restatement (Second) of Torts*, vol. 3, §581A, p. 235.
50. Oscar Handlin and Lillian Handlin, *Liberty and Power 1600–1760* (New York: Harper and Row), vol. 1, p. 225.
51. Solow v. General Motors Truck Co., 64 F.2d 105 (2d Cir.1933).
52. Hoff v. Pure Oil Co., 147 Minn. 195, 179 N.W. 891 (1920).
53. Education Amendment of 1974, Public Law 93-380, 20 U.S.C.A. §1232g (sometimes referred to as the Buckley Amendment). See Appendix B.
54. 20 U.S.C.A. §1232h(1978).
55. 20 U.S.C.A. §1415(b)(1)(A) (1975).
56. 20 U.S.C.A. §1232g(e); 34 C.F.R. §99.7(a).
57. 20 U.S.C.A. §1232g(b)(1); 34 C.F.R. §99.30(a)(3).
58. 20 U.S.C.A. §1232g(d); 34 C.F.R. §99.5.
59. 20 U.S.C.A. §1232g(a)(1)(A); 34 C.F.R. §99.10.
60. 34 C.F.R. §99.6(a)(2)(iv).
61. 34 C.F.R. §99.6(a)(4).
62. 34 C.F.R. §§99.6(a)(5), 99.32.
63. 20 U.S.C.A. §1232g(a)(2); 34 C.F.R. §99.6(a)(7).
64. 20 U.S.C.A. §1232g(a)(5)(B); 34 C.F.R. §§99.3 (Directory Information), 99.6(a)(6), 99.37.
65. 34 C.F.R. §99.3 (Education Records) (6)(1).
66. 34 C.F.R. §99.31(a)(5).
67. 20 U.S.C.A. §1232g(a)(4)(B)(i); 34 C.F.R. §99.3 (Education Records).
68. See Mary H. B. Gelfman and Nadine Schwab, "School Health Services and Educational Records: Conflicts in the Law," *Educational Law Reports* 64 (January 31, 1991): p. 319.
69. 34 C.F.R. §99.31.
70. 34 C.F.R. §99.8.

CHAPTER 13

GOVERNMENTAL IMMUNITY

A sovereign is exempt from suit, not because of any formal conception or obsolete theory, but on the logical and practical ground that there can be no legal right as against the authority that makes the law on which the right depends.

—Oliver Wendell Holmes Jr.

CHAPTER OUTLINE

- SOVEREIGN IMMUNITY
- ABOLITION OF IMMUNITY
- DISCRETIONARY FUNCTIONS
- INSURANCE WAIVER OF IMMUNITY
- PROPRIETARY FUNCTIONS
- LICENSEE AND INVITEE

- NUISANCE
- SECTION 1983, CIVIL RIGHTS ACT OF 1871 LIABILITY
- ELEVENTH AMENDMENT AND LOCAL SCHOOL DISTRICTS

ALL SOVEREIGN GOVERNMENTS have the inherent prerogative to protect themselves from liability. This power has been exercised by differing means and in varying degrees, ranging from erecting virtually impenetrable shields to near total abrogation of immunity. While the common law defines the nature and extent of immunity generally, statutory law may change and modify it as legislatures see fit. The extent of the legal variations in this area is almost limitless, as evidenced by the precedents among the fifty states. Immunity is further complicated by the interaction of the states with the central government in our federal system. Because of the uncertainty of the prerogatives of government in the federal system, the Eleventh Amendment of the U.S. Constitution was enacted to define the limitations of federal power on states as

well as the boundaries of liability between citizens and states.

This chapter discusses both the common law and the statutory precedents regarding aspects of governmental immunity. Considerable attention is given to the Eleventh Amendment as it affects the state and local educational agencies.

■ SOVEREIGN IMMUNITY

Governmental agencies have historically been immune from tort liability. As a general rule, common law asserts that government is inherently immune unless the legislature specifically abrogates the privilege. The immunity concept evolved to this country from England, where the king could, theoretically, do no wrong. Various legal scholars maintain the concept was a product of the Dark Ages, when custom established that the lord of the fief was also the lawmaker and judge. As such, the lord was singly responsible for all laws and justice, and since he made and implemented the laws, he could not be sued without his permission.[1] As the feudal era drew to a close and fiefdoms became consolidated into larger governmental units, immunity became enmeshed with the "divine right of kings," placing the king in a superior and preferred legal position.[2] Sovereign immunity became formalized in English law at least as early as the thirteenth century, at which time the king could not be sued in his own courts.[3] Sovereign immunity apparently reached its zenith in fifteenth-century England, where it stabilized as a prerogative of the monarch. Judicial recognition of this power was taken when an English court held in 1607 that the king was not liable for damages to private property caused by the government's digging for saltpeter that was to be used in the manufacture of gunpowder.[4] In spite of his judicial sanction affirming sovereign immunity, the great jurist Coke held in the same year that the king could not sit as a judge in his own case.[5] Effectively, this began the whittling away of sovereign immunity; this process was not to culminate until over 250 years later, when the House of Lords held that a public entity is liable for the damages caused by acts of its employees.[6] Later, this rationale was applied to schools in England when a court held that if negligence occurred resulting in student injury, either the teacher or the school could be liable.[7]

The sovereign immunity doctrine may have been transported across the Atlantic to the United States directly under the precedent of *Russell v. The Men Dwelling in the County of Devon,*[8] as relied upon by a Massachusetts court in *Mower v. The Inhabitants of Leicester* in 1812.[9] It is unlikely, however, that the concept traversed the Atlantic through a single precedent, especially since the court in *Russell* attributed its holding of nonliability to (1) the lack of a public treasury, (2) general judicial apprehension that imposing liability would encourage a flow of such actions, (3) the belief that public inconvenience should be avoided, and (4) the fact that no legislation existed imposing such liability. No direct judicial notice was taken of the doctrine of Crown Prerogative, or the "king can do no wrong" doctrine. It seems more likely that sovereign immunity came to be commonly accepted in this country through the use by early lawyers and judges of English legal books and materials such as *Blackstone's Commentaries,* which were used as standard references. Also, of course, many of the notable jurists of early America received their legal training in the Inns of Court in London. Regardless of its origin, however, the U.S. Supreme Court and state courts adopted the principle that the sovereign could not be sued without its permission. The Supreme Court in 1869 commented that "[i]t is a familiar doctrine of the common law, that the sovereign cannot be sued in his own courts without his consent."[10] In the same year in another case, the Court stated that "[e]very government has an inherent right to protect itself against suits. . . . The principle is fundamental [and] applies to every sovereign power."[11] The federal government abrogated immunity to a statutorily prescribed extent in the Federal Tort Claims Act of 1946.

With regard to tort immunity of public schools themselves, some courts have enunciated the overriding reasoning that desirable public policy dictates immunity. The *American Law Reports* has summarized the public policy rationale as follows:

> The tort immunity of governmental agencies in their operation of schools has also been supported on public policy grounds, the courts having taken the position that public education is for the benefit of all, that the welfare of the few must be sacrificed in the public interest, and that school funds and property may not be diverted to pay private damages, since such diversion may impair public education.[12]

Beginning from the point of nearly universal adherence to the immunity doctrine, some state courts have moved away from the doctrine. Most significant is the *Molitor* case, which abolished immunity in Illinois and directly refuted the legal rationale that supported sovereign immunity.[13] In *Muskopf,* the California Supreme Court observed the trend away from immunity:

> Only the vestigial remains of such governmental immunity have survived; its requiem has long been foreshadowed. For years the process of erosion of governmental immunity has gone on unabated.

The Legislature has contributed mightily to that erosion. The courts, by distinction and extension, have removed much of the force of the rule. Thus, in holding that the doctrine of governmental immunity for torts for which its agents are liable has no place in our law, we make no startling break with the past but merely take the final step that carries to its conclusion an established legislative and judicial trend.[14]

Since *Molitor*, sovereign immunity has been in a state of considerable change. Some state courts have abrogated immunity only to have it reinstated by the legislatures, while other courts have approached the issue in a piecemeal way by creating exceptions for proprietary functions or nuisances, or different standards for licensees and invitees. Several courts have dissected the school program, abolishing immunity for transportation injuries, while maintaining it for the regular school program. Too, a trend exists for courts to sanction consensual waiver of immunity by school boards through the acquisition of liability insurance.

Yet, in spite of the many exceptions, for various reasons the general rule prevails that the state and its agencies are immune from tort liability, such immunity being grounded on the sovereign character of the state.[15] Thus, school districts, school boards, and other similar local governmental agencies whose responsibility it is to operate public schools have generally been held to be immune from tort liability, either for their own torts or for those of their agents, officers, or employees, while engaged in school functions of a governmental nature. This rule prevails in the absence of abrogation by a state legislative body or by a state court, as in *Molitor*.

❖ — ❖ — ❖

Sovereign Immunity May Be Abrogated by the Courts

Molitor v. Kaneland Community Unit District No. 302

Supreme Court of Illinois, 1959.
18 Ill.2d 11, 163 N.E.2d 89.

KLINGBIEL, Justice. Plaintiff, Thomas Molitor, a minor, by Peter his father and next friend, brought this action against Kaneland Community Unit School District for personal injuries sustained by plaintiff when the school bus in which he was riding left the road, allegedly as a result of the driver's negligence, hit a culvert, exploded and burned. . . .

In his brief, plaintiff recognizes the rule, established by this court in 1898, that a school district is immune from tort liability, and frankly asks this court to abolish the rule *in toto*. . . .

Thus we are squarely faced with the highly important question—in the light of modern developments—should a school district be immune from liability for tortiously inflicted personal injury to a pupil thereof arising out of the operation of a school bus owned and operated by said district?

Historically we find that the doctrine of the sovereign immunity of the state, the theory that "the King can do no wrong," was first extended to a subdivision of the state in 1788 in *Russell v. Men of Devon*, 2 Term Rep. 671, 100 Eng.Rep. 359. . . .

The immunity doctrine of *Russell v. Men of Devon* was adopted in Illinois with reference to towns and counties in 1870 in *Town of Waltham v. Kemper*, 55 Ill. 346. Then, in 1898, eight years after the English courts had refused to apply the *Russell* doctrine to schools, the Illinois court extended the immunity rule to school districts in the leading case of *Kinnare v. City of Chicago*, 171 Ill. 332, 49 N.E. 536, where it was held that the Chicago Board of Education was immune from liability for the death of a laborer resulting from a fall from the roof of a school building, allegedly due to the negligence of the Board in failing to provide scaffolding and safeguards. That opinion reasoned that since the State is not subject to suit nor liable for the torts or negligence of its agents, likewise a school district, as a governmental agency of the State, is also "exempted from the obligation to respond in damages, as master, for negligent acts of its servants to the same extent as is the State itself." Later decisions following the *Kinnare* doctrine have sought to advance additional explanations such as the protection of public funds and public property, and to prevent the diversion of tax moneys to the payment of damage claims. . . .

Of all of the anomalies that have resulted from legislative and judicial efforts to alleviate the injustice of the results that have flowed from the doctrine of sovereign immunity, the one most immediately pertinent to this case is the following provision of the Illinois School Code: "Any school district, including any non–high school district, which provides transportation for pupils may insure against any loss or liability of such district, its agents or employees, resulting from or incident to the ownership, maintenance or use of any school bus. Such insurance shall be carried only in companies duly licensed and authorized to write such coverage in this state. Every policy for such insurance coverage issued to a school district shall provide, or be endorsed to provide, that the company issuing such policy waives any right to refuse payment or to deny liability thereunder within the limits of said policy, by reason of the non-liability of the insured school district for the wrongful or negligent acts of its agents and employees, and its immunity from suit as an agency of the state performing governmental functions." Ill.Rev.Stat.1957, c. 122, §29-11a.

Thus, under this statute, a person injured by an insured school district bus may recover to the extent of such insurance, whereas, under the *Kinnare* doctrine, a person injured by an uninsured school district bus can recover nothing at all.

Defendant contends that the quoted provision of the School Code constitutes a legislative determination that the public policy of this State requires that school districts be immune from tort liability. We can read no such legislative intent into the statute. Rather, we interpret that section as expressing dissatisfaction with the court-created doctrine of governmental immunity and an attempt to cut down that immunity where insurance is involved. The difficulty with this legislative effort to curtail the judicial doctrine is that it allows each school district to determine for itself whether, and to what extent, it will be financially responsible for the wrongs inflicted by it. . . .

It is a basic concept underlying the whole law of torts today that liability follows negligence, and that individuals and corporations are responsible for the negligence of their agents and employees acting in the course of their employment. The doctrine of governmental immunity runs directly counter to that basic concept. What reasons, then, are so impelling as to allow a school district, as a quasimunicipal corporation, to commit wrongdoing without any responsibility to its victims, while any individual or private corporation would be called to task in court for such tortious conduct?

The original basis of the immunity rule has been called a "survival of the medieval idea that the sovereign can do no wrong," or that "the King can do no wrong." (38 Am.Jur., Mun. Corps., sec. 573, p. 266.) In *Kinnare v. City of Chicago*, 171 Ill. 332, 49 N.E. 536, 537, the first Illinois case announcing the tort immunity of school districts, the court said: "The state acts in its sovereign capacity, and does not submit its action to the judgment of courts, and is not liable for the torts or negligence of its agents, and a corporation created by the state as a mere agency for the more efficient exercise of governmental functions is likewise exempted from the obligation to respond in damages, as master, for negligent acts of its servants to the same extent as is the state itself, unless such liability is expressly provided by the statute creating such agency." This was nothing more nor less than an extension of the theory of sovereign immunity. Professor Borchard has said that how immunity ever came to be applied in the United States of America is one of the mysteries of legal evolution. (Borchard, Governmental Liability in Tort, 34 Yale L.J. 1, 6.) And how it was then infiltrated into the law controlling the liability of local governmental units has been described as one of the amazing chapters of American common-law jurisprudence. . . .

We are of the opinion that school district immunity cannot be justified on this theory. As was stated by one court, "The whole doctrine of governmental immunity from liability for tort rests upon a rotten foundation. It is almost incredible that in this modern age of comparative sociological enlightenment, and in a republic, the medieval absolutism supposed to be implicit in the maxim, 'the King can do no wrong,' should exempt the various branches of the government from liability for their torts, and that the entire burden of damage resulting from the wrongful acts of the government should be imposed upon the single individual who suffers the injury, rather than distributed among the entire community constituting the government, where it could be borne without hardship upon any individual, and where it justly belongs." *Barker v. City of Santa Fe*, 47 N.M. 85, 136 P.2d 480, 482. Likewise, we agree with the Supreme Court of Florida that in preserving the sovereign immunity theory, courts have overlooked the fact that the Revolutionary War was fought to abolish that "divine right of kings" on which the theory is based.

The other chief reason advanced in support of the immunity rule in the more recent cases is the protection of public funds and public property. This corresponds to the "no fund" or "trust fund" theory upon which charitable immunity is based. . . . This reasoning seems to follow the line that it is better for the individual to suffer than for the public to be inconvenienced. From it proceeds defendant's argument that school districts would be bankrupted and education impeded if said districts were called upon to compensate children tortiously injured by the negligence of those districts' agents and employees.

We do not believe that in this present day and age, when public education constitutes one of the biggest businesses in the country, that school immunity can be justified on the protection-of-public-funds theory.

In the first place, analysis of the theory shows that it is based on the idea that payment of damage claims is a diversion of educational funds to an improper purpose. As many writers have pointed out, the fallacy in this argument is that it assumes the very point which is sought to be proved, i.e., that payment of damage claims is not a proper purpose. "Logically, the 'No-fund' or 'trust fund' theory is without merit because it is of value only after a determination of what is a proper school expenditure. To predicate immunity upon the theory of a trust fund is merely to argue in a circle, since it assumes an answer to the very question at issue, to wit, what is an educational purpose? Many disagree with the 'no-fund' doctrine to the extent of ruling that the payment of funds for judgments resulting from accidents or injuries in schools is an educational purpose. Nor can it be properly argued that as a result of the abandonment of the common-law rule the district would be completely bankrupt. California, Tennessee, New

York, Washington and other states have not been compelled to shut down their schools." (Rosenfield, Governmental Immunity from Liability for Tort in School Accidents, 5 Legal Notes on Local Government, 376–377.) . . .

Neither are we impressed with defendant's plea that the abolition of immunity would create grave and unpredictable problems of school finance and administration. . . . While this factor may have had compulsion on some of the earlier courts, I seriously doubt that it has any great weight with the courts in recent years. In the first place, taxation is not the subject matter of judicial concern where justice to the individual citizen is involved. It is the business of other departments of government to provide the funds required to pay the damages assessed against them by the courts. . . . This argument is like so many of the horribles paraded in the early tort cases when courts were fashioning the boundaries of tort law. It has been thrown in simply because there was nothing better at hand. The public's willingness to stand up and pay the cost of its enterprises carried out through municipal corporations is no less than its insistence that individuals and groups pay the cost of their enterprises. "Tort liability is in fact a very small item in the budget of any well-organized enterprise." (Green, Freedom of Litigation, 38 Ill.L.Rev. 355, 378.)

We are of the opinion that none of the reasons advanced in support of school district immunity have any true validity today. Further, we believe that abolition of such immunity may tend to decrease the frequency of school bus accidents by coupling the power to transport pupils with the responsibility of exercising care in the selection and supervision of the drivers. As Dean Harno said: "A municipal corporation today is an active and virile creature capable of inflicting much harm. Its civil responsibility should be coextensive. The municipal corporation looms up definitely and emphatically in our law, and what is more, it can and does commit wrongs. This being so, it must assume the responsibilities of the position it occupies in society." (Harno, Tort Immunity of Municipal Corporations, 4 Ill.L.Q. 28, 42.) School districts will be encouraged to exercise greater care in the matter of transporting pupils and also to carry adequate insurance covering that transportation, thus spreading the risk of accident, just as the other costs of education are spread over the entire district. . . .

We conclude that the rule of school district tort immunity is unjust, unsupported by any valid reason, and has no rightful place in modern day society.

Defendant strongly urges that if said immunity is to be abolished, it should be done by the legislature, not by this court. With this contention we must disagree. The doctrine of school district immunity was created by this court alone. Having found that doctrine to be unsound and unjust under present conditions, we consider that we have not only the power, but the duty, to abolish that immunity.

CASE NOTE

After the *Molitor* case, the Illinois legislature restored immunity by enacting the Local Governmental and Governmental Employees Tort Immunity Act, protecting local government units and their employees from liability for failure to supervise an activity or for injuries arising from the use of public property. Under this law, school district officials or employees will not be held liable for torts unless they act willfully and wantonly and their act causes injury. See *Towner by Towner v. Board of Education of the City of Chicago*, 657 N.E.2d 28 (Ill.App.1st Dist.1995). See also *McGurk v. Lincolnway Community School District No. 210*, 679 N.E.2d 71 (Ill.App.3d Dist.1997).

——————— ❖ — ❖ — ❖ ———————

Where Legislature Has Statutorily Established Governmental Immunity, Court Will Refrain from Infringing on Legislative Policy-Making Authority

Richardson v. Rankin County School District

Supreme Court of Mississippi, 1989.
540 So.2d 5.

PRATHER, Justice, for the Court. This appeal revisits the doctrine of governmental immunity abandoned by this Court in *Pruett v. City of Rosedale,* 421 So.2d 1046 (Miss.1982), and seeks total and final abandonment of such doctrine again by this Court. Plaintiff Alma Jane Richardson suffered personal injury in an accident between her vehicle and a Rankin County school bus driven by Darlene Collier. . . .

Richardson filed her complaint alleging that on May 1, 1986, she was injured as a result of a collision involving her automobile and a school bus owned by the Rankin County School District and being operated by its employee, Darlene Collier. Richardson bases her theory of liability upon the statutory liability of the Rankin County School District, et al., as provided under Miss.Code Ann. §37-41-37, et seq. (1986 Supp.) and upon the theory of negligence. . . .

On March 31, 1987, all of the defendants filed their answer setting forth their defenses, including the defense that the defendants are immune from liability under the theory of sovereign or governmental immunity and denying all material allegations of the complaint and denying that Richardson is entitled to recover any sums whatsoever. . . .

The question of whether or not the doctrine of governmental or sovereign immunity should be totally abolished has come before this Court on a number of occasions. Finally, in *Pruett v. City of Rosedale,* 421 So.2d 1046 (Miss.1982), this Court recognized that the doctrine of sovereign immunity was a creature of the judiciary, and it was time for the judiciary to abolish it. The Court recognized, however, that it was the legislature, not the judiciary, that had the duty and responsibility of controlling and policing sovereign immunity.

> [T]he control and policing of sovereign immunity is a legislative responsibility and not that of the judiciary. The sovereign immunity doctrine is a creature of the judiciary. We are of the opinion that it should not be so; but that as said above, the details of handling the question is [sic] legislative rather than judicial. As has been said by many of the State's highest courts, the judicial branch is leaving the matter to the legislative branch. It was judicially created and necessarily should be judicially abrogated. [*Pruett* at page 1047.]

Pruett made clear that the immunity that was being abolished was the immunity of the sovereign, which means the state, the county, the municipality or any other local subdivision of the sovereign. This Court expressly noted that the abolition of sovereign immunity did not "apply to legislative, judicial and executive acts by individuals acting in their official capacity, or to similar capacities in local governments, either county or municipal." . . .

The legislature, in response to the *Pruett* decision, enacted what is now codified as Miss.Code Ann. §11-46-1, et seq. (1988 Supp.) (1984 Immunity Act). The intent of the legislature is clear. Section 11-46-3, Miss.Code Ann. (1988 Supp.) states:

> The Legislature of the State of Mississippi finds and determines as a matter of public policy and does hereby declare that from and after July 1, 1989, the "state" and, from and after October 1, 1989, its "political subdivisions," as such terms are defined in Section 11-46-1, shall not be liable and shall be immune from suit at law or in equity on account of any wrongful or tortious act or omission, including libel, slander or defamation, by the state or its political subdivisions, or any such act or omission by any employee of the state or its political subdivisions, notwithstanding that any such act or omission constitutes or may be considered as the exercise or failure to exercise any duty, obligation or function of a governmental, proprietary, discretionary or ministerial nature and notwithstanding that such act or omission may or may not arise out of any activity, transaction or service for which any fee, charge, cost or other consideration was received or expected to be received in exchange therefor.

The Immunity Act grants general legislative immunity to the State and its political subdivisions, including local school districts. It also waives such immunity of the State and its political subdivisions from claims for money damages arising out of the torts of such governmental entities and the torts of their employees while acting within the course and scope of their employment. Such immunity is waived only to the extent of the maximum amount of liability as provided under the provisions of the above quoted statutes. Miss.Code Ann. §11-46-15 (1988 Supp.) provides the limits of liability of a governmental entity of its employee. . . .

Thus, it is clear from the above statute that the Mississippi Legislature has, by appropriate legislation, given the state and its political subdivisions immunity from suit on account of any wrongful or tortious act or omission by any employee of the state or its political subdivisions, except as to the extent of liability permitted by statute.

There is no challenge to the constitutionality of the statute itself, only a request that this Court finally abolish governmental immunity. This request infringes upon the policy making authority of the legislature, and this Court refrains from infringing upon this legislative prerogative.

The trial court did not err in granting the Motion for Partial Summary Judgment below, and should, therefore, be affirmed.

Affirmed.

Case Note

"Within constitutional limitations, the legislature is empowered to control the liability to which the state and its agencies may be subjected for tort." *Bego v. Gordon*, 407 N.W.2d 801, 808 (S.D.1987).

❖ — ❖ — ❖

Doctrine of Sovereign Immunity is Constitutional

Dollar v. Dalton Public Schools

Court of Appeals of Georgia, 1999.
505 S.E.2d 789.

Anna Dollar's mother ("Dollar") sued the Dalton Public School District and two childcare workers after Anna fell from playground equipment and broke her arm while attending an after-school childcare program on Dalton Public School premises. The school district moved for summary judgment based on sovereign immunity and the childcare workers moved for summary judgment based on official immunity. Dollar also moved for partial summary judgment. The trial court granted the defendants' motions for summary judgment and denied Dollar's motion. Dollar appealed to the Supreme Court of Georgia, raising several constitutional issues.

The Supreme Court held that the constitutional issues raised involved application of well-settled principles and transferred the appeal to this Court. We affirm the judgment of the trial court.

. . . Dollar argues that sovereign immunity does not apply here because: (a) the after-school program is not a governmental function and is not covered by traditional notions of sovereign immunity; (b) sovereign immunity has been waived to the extent of insurance; (c) a special relationship exists between the school district and Dollar; (d) the school district maintained a nuisance; and (e) sovereign immunity does not prevent collection of damages from insurance proceeds.

(a) We disagree with Dollar's claim that the after-school program, for which she paid a fee, is not public education or a governmental activity and therefore the school district, like any private childcare provider, is not entitled to sovereign immunity.

Our legislature has specifically recognized that programs operated by boards of education which provide care and supervision of school-age children outside of normal school hours serve an educational purpose, are necessary or incidental to public education and can be an integral part of the total school program offered by public schools in this state. . . . The legislature has authorized boards of education to establish and operate such after-school programs. . . . An after-school program operated by a school district . . . is therefore clearly a governmental activity serving an educational purpose. This enumeration is without merit.

(b) The question of whether by having liability insurance the school district has waived sovereign immunity has been decided adversely to Dollar. See *Crisp County School System v. Brown*, 226 Ga.App. 800, 802(1), 487 S.E.2d 512 (1997) (school systems do not waive sovereign immunity merely by purchasing liability insurance); *Davis v. Dublin City Bd. of Ed.*, 219 Ga.App. 121, 123(3), 464 S.E.2d 251 (1995) (board of education entitled to summary judgment based on sovereign immunity despite existence of liability insurance coverage since no legislative act specifically provides that the board of education has waived sovereign immunity by purchasing liability insurance).

(c) [Dollar's] argument that the school district had a special duty of care toward her, is misplaced. The Supreme Court of Georgia has held that the public duty doctrine . . . does not apply outside of the police protection context. . . .

(d) Dollar argues that the playground equipment is a nuisance because it had insufficient padding beneath it, and that a municipality has no sovereign immunity where it maintains a nuisance. . . . The school district, however, is not a municipality. The immunity which protects school districts and their officials applies equally to claims in negligence and in nuisance. . . .

(e) We are not persuaded by Dollar's argument that the suit should proceed because she can always collect from the school district's insurer rather than from the school district itself. As discussed above, the school district is immune from suit despite the existence of insurance.

. . . Dollar claims official immunity does not apply to the childcare workers because their failure to supervise children as instructed was ministerial rather than discretionary; as after-school childcare providers they were engaged in non-governmental activity; and liability insurance was provided.

. . . [T]he latter two arguments are without merit. . . .

Dollar's argument that official immunity does not apply because the employees were engaged in ministerial acts is also without merit. The task imposed on teachers to monitor, supervise and control students is a discretionary action which is protected by the doctrine of sovereign immunity. . . .

. . . Dollar's constitutional arguments are without merit.

(a) In several enumerations, Dollar contends strict application of sovereign immunity is unconstitutional because it results in unfairness and irresponsible government. "Application of the doctrine of sovereign immunity has always involved the balancing of the interests of persons injured by government's wrongdoing and the interests of the taxpayers." . . . Indeed, in enacting the Georgia Tort Claims Act, . . . the General Assembly specifically "recognize[d] the inherently unfair and inequitable results which occur in the strict application of the traditional doctrine of sovereign immunity." . . . Accordingly, the Georgia Tort Claims Act does not provide blanket immunity from suit, but affords a plaintiff the benefit of a broad waiver of sovereign immunity. . . . Nonetheless, as noted in *Googe*, supra, the exposure of the state treasury to tort liability must be limited.

(b) Dollar claims sovereign immunity violates due process and equal protection clauses of the federal constitution because it constitutes deprivation with no remedy. "The bar of sovereign immunity neither results in a deprivation of property without just compensation nor constitutes a denial of equal protection or due process under the federal or state constitutions. The due process and equal protection clauses of the federal and state constitutions protect only rights, not mere privileges, and discrimination in the grant of privileges is not a denial of equal protection to those who are not favored. A waiver of sovereign immunity is a mere privilege, not a right, and the extension of that privilege is solely a matter of legislative grace." . . . We point out that, in this state [Georgia], sovereign immunity has constitutional status and cannot be abrogated by the judiciary. . . .

(c) The Georgia Tort Claims Act does not violate Art. I, Sec. II, Par. I of the Georgia Constitution of 1983, which article provides that government is founded on the will of the people and that public officers are trustees of and amenable to the people. "[A] majority of Georgia voters approved [the 1991 amendment] which provided for limited waiver of sovereign immunity through a legislative act. The language of that ballot amendment has received judicial approval. . . . " . . . The Georgia Tort Claims Act was enacted under the authority of the amendment. . . . Dollar's contention that the Act unconstitutionally violates the will of the people is therefore incorrect.

(d) The 1991 amendment (Art. I, Sec. II, Par. IX) to the Georgia Constitution of 1983 does not violate due process and equal protection guarantees for the reasons discussed in part (b) of this Division.

There being no genuine issues of material fact, the trial court did not err in granting summary judgment to the school district and its employees. . . .

Judgment affirmed.

❖ — ❖ — ❖

The Doctrine of Sovereign Immunity May Protect Teacher from Liability for Pupil Injury

Lentz v. Morris

Supreme Court of Virginia, 1988.
236 Va. 78, 372 S.E.2d 608.

COMPTON, Justice. The sole question presented in this appeal is whether the doctrine of sovereign immunity protects a high school teacher supervising a physical education class from a negligence action for damages brought by a student injured while a member of the class. . . .

The plaintiff asserts that on November 9, 1984, the day of the injury, he was a student and defendant was a teacher of health and physical education at Kellam High School in Virginia Beach. He alleges that he was assigned to a physical education class conducted "under the supervision and in the presence of Defendant." He further asserts that, while participating with the class in activities on school grounds, he and other students were "playing tackle football without wearing any protective equipment," which activity defendant knew or should have known posed danger to the participants. Plaintiff also alleges that as the result of the defendant's negligent supervision and control of the physical education activities, he was "tackled with great force and violence" which caused his injuries.

. . . [P]laintiff contends that the trial court erred in ruling that a school teacher is entitled to immunity "for his own acts of negligence." . . .

. . . [T]he plaintiff urges, "Insulation of this individual from responsibility for his own negligent acts does not achieve any of the purposes for which immunity is ordinarily extended to governmental employees." We do not agree.

Messina v. Burden [228 Va. 301, 321 S.E.2d 657 (1984)] was a watershed decision on the subject of sovereign immunity. In that case, we reviewed our prior decisions stemming from diverse factual settings and attempted to reconcile them. Reasserting the viability of the doctrine in the Commonwealth, we endeavored to explicate the circumstances under which "an employee of a governmental body is entitled to the protection of sovereign immunity," given the facts of the cases under consideration in *Messina*. . . .

Initially, we focused upon the purposes served by the doctrine. They include "protecting the public purse, providing for smooth operation of government, eliminating public inconvenience and danger that might spring from officials being fearful to act, assuring that citizens will be willing to take public jobs, and preventing citizens from improperly influencing the conduct of governmental affairs through the threat or use of vexatious litigation." . . . We then said that in order to fulfill those purposes, the reach of the doctrine could not be limited solely to the sovereign but must be extended to "some of the people who help run the government." . . . We noted that because the government acts only through individuals, it could be crippled in its operations if every government employee were subject to suit.

In *Messina*, against the background of the purposes of the doctrine, the general principles applicable to the concept, and the facts and circumstances of the cases at hand, we proceeded to engage in a necessary "line-drawing" exercise to determine which government employees were entitled to immunity. Thus, in one case, we held that a State supervisory employee who was charged with simple negligence while acting within the scope of his employment was immune, there being no charge of gross negligence or intentional misconduct. . . .

In the other *Messina* case, supra, we decided that an employee of a county, which shares the immunity of the State, was entitled to the benefits of sovereign immunity where his activities clearly involved the exercise of judgment and discretion. . . . In deciding that case, we outlined the test . . . to be used to determine entitlement to immunity. The factors to be considered include: (1) the nature of the function the employee performs; (2) the extent of the governmental entity's interest and involvement in the function; (3) the degree of control and direction exercised by the governmental entity over the employee; and (4) whether the alleged wrongful act involved the exercise of judgment and discretion. . . .

We hold the trial court correctly ruled that the health and physical education teacher in this case was immune from suit. The facts expressly alleged, and the inferences flowing from those facts, state the following case. The defendant, an employee of an immune governmental entity, was charged with simple negligence in the supervision and control of the class to which he was assigned. The facts do not support a charge of either gross negligence or intentional misconduct. In addition, and contrary to the contention of the plaintiff on brief, implicit in the facts alleged is the conclusion that the defendant was acting within the scope of his employment at the time of the injury.

Therefore, factors included in the *Messina* test for entitlement to immunity are present in this case. The employee is performing a vitally important public function as a school teacher. The governmental entity employing the teacher, the local school board, has official interest and direct involvement in the function of school instruction and supervision, and it exercises control and direction over the employee through the school principal. . . . And, a teacher's supervision and control of a physical education class, including the decision of what equipment and attire is to be worn by the student participants, clearly involves, at least in part, the exercise of judgment and discretion by the teacher.

Consequently, the *Messina* test, given the purposes served by the doctrine, mandates immunity for this defendant. If school teachers performing functions equivalent to this defendant are to be haled into court for the conduct set forth by these facts, fewer individuals will aspire to be teachers, those who have embarked on a teaching career will be reluctant to act, and the orderly administration of the school systems will suffer, all to the detriment of our youth and the public at large.

For these reasons, the judgment of the trial will be

Affirmed.

CASE NOTE

In a case involving a charge of negligent supervision against a teacher when a child fell from monkey bars in physical education class, breaking her arm, a Georgia court held that both the teacher and the school board were immune from liability and that the presumption of immunity could not be defeated without evidence of actual malice. *Crisp County School System v. Brown*, 487 S.E.2d 512 (Ga.App.1997).

■ ABOLITION OF IMMUNITY

As observed earlier, there has been a progression of statutory and judicial modifications of the original common law doctrine of sovereign immunity. State legislatures have, at times, acted to redefine the law at the impetus of the courts, and at other times, legislatures have responded to what they have perceived to be social necessities. Keeton et al. note that the great majority of the states have now consented to at least some liability for torts.[16] Only two states have retained what may be classified as total sovereign immunity,[17] while seven or eight other states technically retain immunity in the courts but have statutorily established administrative tribunals to hear and ascertain whether the state should be held liable.[18] Another group of states have waived tort immunity in certain classes of cases, usually those in which the state or locality has secured liability insurance that will pay for judgments against the governmental entity, or have adopted specified waivers of immunity for particular functions, such as injuries caused by motor vehicles or by negligence in upkeep or oversight of real property owned by the school.[19] Further, some states have drawn a distinction between governmental and proprietary functions performed by school districts.[20] Another group of states, about thirty—the largest group—has comprehensively abrogated immunity. In these states, governmental units at the state and local levels may be liable for both misfeasance and nonfeasance.[21] Even in these states, however, there may be a distinction between acts that are discretionary and those that are ministerial in nature.

The general rules that apply are given by the *Restatement (Second) of Torts* as follows:

(1) A State and its governmental agencies are not subject to suit without the consent of the State.

(2) Except to the extent that a State declines to give consent to tort liability, it and its governmental agencies are subject to the liability.

(3) Even when a State is subject to tort liability, it and its governmental agencies are immune to the liability for acts and omissions constituting

(a) the exercise of a judicial or legislative function, or

(b) the exercise of an administrative function involving the determination of fundamental governmental policy.

(4) Consent to suit and repudiation of general tort immunity do not establish liability for an act or omission that is otherwise privileged or is not tortious.[22]

■ DISCRETIONARY FUNCTIONS

Judicial and legislative functions of state government are typically immune from liability. Courts reaching an erroneous judicial decision cannot be held liable in damages. Neither can a legislature be held liable in damages in tort for an injury resulting from legislation. State and local agencies, such as state educational agencies and local school districts, do not necessarily retain immunity for all their acts and omissions, however.[23]

The U.S. Supreme Court has said that, "of course, it is not a tort for government to govern."[24] Thus, tort liability does not automatically arise from a failure of the state to act in providing a benefit or a service.[25] There is no liability for failure to provide police protection or for failure of the local government to enforce fire-safety codes or building codes or for issuance of a driver's license to one who drives a car unsafely.[26]

Most states draw a distinction between discretionary and ministerial acts in the application of immunity. Discretionary acts are afforded a qualified or conditional "malice-destructible" immunity, while no immunity at all is provided for "ministerial" acts. Discretionary and ministerial functions of public officials are discussed earlier in this text, but specificity as to liability is particularly important here. The *Restatement (Second) of Torts* says that there "is no single test" to distinguish between discretionary and ministerial acts.[27] The term "discretion," when applied to public functionaries, means "power or right conferred upon them by law of acting officially in certain circumstances according to the dictates of their own judgment or conscience, uncontrolled by the judgment or conscience of others."[28]

A ministerial act, on the other hand, is one that leaves nothing to judgment or discretion. It constitutes a simple and definite duty, imposed by law, involving only obedience to instructions.[29] The theory prescribes that if a public official is charged with exercising judgment, then no liability can accrue from error in that judgment. Liability may result, however, from not properly performing a ministerial function.

Because so many factors, in fact, interplay in most court decisions on the subject, the *Restatement (Second) of Torts* has concluded that liability will be determined by a series of considerations, not merely by strict adherence to the definitions of the two terms. The factors gleaned from various precedents revealing whether immunity will lie for discretionary acts are given by the *Restatement (Second) of Torts* as follows:

(1) The nature and importance of the function that the officer is performing. How important to the public is it that this function be performed? That it be performed correctly? That it be performed according to the best judgment of the officer, unimpaired by extraneous matters? . . .

(2) The extent to which passing judgment on the exercise of discretion by the officer will amount necessarily to passing judgment by the court on the conduct of a coordinate branch of government. . . . Is the action at the planning or the operational level? What is the level of the government? . . .

(3) The extent to which the imposition of liability would impair the free exercise of his discretion by the officer. Is this function peculiarly sensitive to the imposition of liability? . . . How far is the mere threat of vexatious suit, which the attendant publicity and the possible need of testifying as to the basis on which the decision was made, likely to affect the exercise of discretion? . . .

(4) The extent to which the ultimate financial responsibility will fall on the officer. . . .

(5) The likelihood that harm will result to members of the public if the action is taken. Is this action certain or substantially certain to impose damage on some people? . . .

(6) The nature and seriousness of the type of harm that may be produced. Is it a loss that can be easily borne by the injured party? . . . How far is the extent of the harm known or apparent to the officer? . . .

(7) The availability to the injured party of other remedies and other forms of relief. . . . Could he have insured against it? Can he obtain some other kind of judicial review of the correctness or validity of the officer's action? Is specific relief available?

Subsumed beneath all of these factors is the general attitude of the jurisdiction and of the court toward the subject of governmental tort liability. Does the court think first of the heavy responsibility and severe financial burden that may be imposed on the government, or does it regard first the harm to the injured party and assume that his loss should be spread among all the taxpayers? To spread the loss in this fashion, however, the officer's government must be willing to take it off the shoulders of the officer.[30]

❖ — ❖ — ❖

Statutory Immunity for Discretionary Acts
Absolves School District from Liability

Mosley v. Portland School District No. 1J

Supreme Court of Oregon, 1992.
315 Or. 85, 843 P.2d 415.

GILLETTE, Justice.

In this personal injury case, plaintiff brought an action against defendant school district for injuries sustained in a fight on school grounds during lunch period. A jury returned a verdict in favor of defendant on the ground that defendant was not negligent. . . .

On November 13, 1987, plaintiff was a student at one of defendant's high schools in Portland. She was cut by a knife during a fight with another student at her high school during lunch period. Plaintiff brought this action against defendant, alleging that defendant was liable for her injuries because it was negligent in: (1) failing to exercise proper supervision of students; (2) failing to provide proper security and sufficient security personnel for protection of students when defendant knew that students carried weapons at the school; (3) failing to prevent weapons from being carried into the school building; and (4) failing to stop the attack before the knife was used. Defendant asserted, among other things, the affirmative defense of discretionary immunity under the Oregon Tort Claims Act. ORS 30.265(3)(c). . . .

The only question before us concerns plaintiff's theories of negligence as to which the Court of Appeals held that defendant was not immune—allegations one and four. (The Court of Appeals held that defendant was immune as a matter of law with respect to plaintiff's other theories, and she has not sought review of that holding.) The parties present the same arguments that they did before the Court of Appeals. With respect to plaintiff's remaining theories, we turn to a consideration of whether defendant is immune as a matter of law under the "discretionary function or duty" provision of ORS 30.265(3)(c) from liability for plaintiff's injuries.

Because the defense that defendant claims under ORS 30.265(3)(c) is statutory, we must determine the statute's meaning. To be immune under ORS 30.265(3)(c), the decision at issue must be "a policy judgment by a person or body with governmental discretion." . . . The statute provides immunity "to decisions involving the making of policy, but not to routine decisions made by employees in the course of their day-to-day activities, even though the decision involves a choice among two or more courses of action." . . .

"[N]ot every exercise of judgment and choice is the exercise of discretion. It depends on the kind of judgments for which responsibility has been delegated to the particular officer. Discretion, as this court has noted in other contexts, involves 'room for policy judgment,' . . . or the responsibility for deciding 'the adaptation of means to an end, and discretion in determining how or whether the act shall be done or the course pursued'. . . ."

. . . A public body that owes a particular duty of care (such as that owed by a school district to its students who are required to be on school premises during school hours) has wide policy discretion in choosing the means by which to carry out that duty. . . . The range of permissible choices does not, however, include the choice of not exercising care. . . . Normally, a choice within the permissible range, in order to qualify for immunity, is one that has been made by a supervisor or policy-making body. . . . On the other hand, the choice to follow or not to follow a predetermined policy in the face of a particular set of facts involving the safety of a particular individual normally is not a discretionary policy choice entitled to immunity under ORS 30.265(3)(c). . . .

Under the foregoing principles, plaintiff's first allegation—that defendant failed to exercise proper supervision of students—concerns what is, on the face of it, a matter of discretion, *i.e.*, the location of security personnel to supervise the general student body at the school at any particular time. Thus, on its face, the first allegation should not have been submitted to the jury. . . . "'Discretion, as this court has noted in other contexts, involves "room for policy judgment" or the responsibility for deciding "the adaptation of means to an end, and discretion in determining how or whether the act shall be done or the course pursued."'" . . . The principal's decisions on the number and allocation of his security personnel were matters involving "room for policy judgment" and "the adaptation of means to an end." . . .

Plaintiff's fourth allegation—that defendant was negligent in failing to stop the fight before the knife was used—is not as clearly a policy judgment as are the facts asserted in plaintiff's first allegation. Nonetheless, we hold that, on this record, defendant's actions were immune. Plaintiff's fourth allegation can be read in two ways: (1) Defendant failed to anticipate that there would be a fight between students at the particular location within the school where this fight occurred, and to allocate security personnel accordingly; or (2) having observed the fight, defendant did nothing to break it up before the other student stabbed plaintiff. The first possible reading is simply an alternative way of criticizing the principal's policy choice in the way in which he allocated security and supervisory personnel within the high school building; it therefore adds nothing to the first allegation of negligence. Under such a reading, the allegation was insufficient for the reasons already discussed in connection with plaintiff's first allegation. The second possible reading, however, alleges knowledge of a kind that would remove defendant from the scope of the immunity afforded by ORS 30.265(3)(c), *i.e.,* it alleges *specific* knowledge concerning the incident involved in this case that, if acted on in a timely manner, would have enabled defendant to protect plaintiff.

That possible second reading does not aid plaintiff here, however. The evidence at trial, viewed in the light most favorable to plaintiff, would not permit a jury to find that defendant had specific knowledge that the fight was occurring or would occur and that defendant then failed to intervene in a timely way. In other words, there is no evidence that defendant acted negligently. Without such evidence, plaintiff could not prevail under her fourth allegation, even if it were read as extending to nondiscretionary acts.

Because plaintiff's claims and the record in this case related only to acts for which defendant either is immune for liability as a matter of law or as to which there was no evidence that defendant was negligent, we need not reach the issue whether the availability of the immunity defense under ORS 30.265(3)(c) may at times depend on factual questions that properly could be submitted to a jury. We hold that the trial court properly entered judgment in favor of defendant.

The decision of the Court of Appeals is affirmed in part and reversed in part. The judgment of the circuit court is affirmed.

CASE NOTE

Discretionary Function of Teacher. Supervision of students is considered to be a discretionary function of a teacher that is protected from liability by official immunity. Official immunity "protects individual public agents from personal liability for discretionary actions taken within the scope of their official authority, and done without willfulness, malice or corruption." A teacher's implementation of policies that relate to the monitoring, supervision, and control of students in and around school during school hours and during extracurricular activities is a discretionary and not a ministerial func-

tion. *Chamlee v. Henry County Board of Education,* 521 S.E.2d 78 (Ga.App.1999).

■ INSURANCE WAIVER OF IMMUNITY

Many states have waived immunity, by statute or case law, if the school district purchases liability insurance. If the school district does not purchase insurance, then the immunity remains in effect.[31]

The Supreme Court of Montana has explained the issue thus:

> We conclude that the Montana Legislature has reached the following conclusion: while a school district is granted immunity of various types, a school district still is granted authority to purchase insurance which may have the effect of waiver of immunity to the extent of the insurance proceeds. We do not find it necessary to imply a waiver, as the intention of the Legislature is clear. That intention is reemphasized by its authorization of tax levies sufficient to pay for insurance premiums. That intention is consistent with the legislative theory that a claim against a school district should be paid in a manner similar to payment required of a private party. We conclude that the Legislature has declared its intent to allow a school district to waive immunity to the extent of the insurance proceeds.[32]

Procedurally, where insurance is involved, it is assumed that a school district will attempt an administrative settlement before resorting to the courts.[33]

❖ — ❖ — ❖

Whether Sovereign Immunity Is Waived May Depend on the Specific Terms of Liability Insurance Policy

Dugger v. Sprouse

Supreme Court of Georgia, 1988.
257 Ga. 778, 364 S.E.2d 275.

SMITH, Justice. Appellee Anthony Plavich is an employee of Murray County school system. A suit was filed by a student, appellant Darin Dugger, for injuries he received when he was thrown from the back of a pickup truck while delivering wrestling mats from one county school to another. The appellee's motion for summary judgment, based upon the defense of sovereign immunity, was granted. We affirm.

If insurance coverage is obtained by a government entity, then the government entity (the county in this case) waives its sovereign immunity to the extent of such insurance coverage. . . . However, where the plain terms of the policy provide that there is no coverage for the particular claim, the policy does not create a waiver of sovereign immunity as to that claim. Here the trial court found that the policy did not provide coverage for the appellant's claim. Where there is no insurance coverage, there is no waiver of sovereign immunity.

Judgment affirmed.

All the Justices concur.

CASE NOTE

The Supreme Court of Oklahoma has held that sovereign immunity is still available as a common law defense. When a school district chooses to purchase liability insurance to cover a specified type of injury, then immunity is "waived to the extent of the insurance coverage only." *Lamont Independent School District v. Swanson*, 548 P.2d 215 (Okla. 1976); *Brewer v. Independent School District*, 848 P.2d 566 (Okla. 1993).

■ PROPRIETARY FUNCTIONS

Some courts, being reluctant to totally abrogate immunity, have sought ways to avoid direct confrontation with the issue. To sidestep the overall problem, courts have settled tort actions in several states on the basis of the activity or function that was being performed by the school district when the injury occurred. In this regard, we should note that school districts operate in a dual capacity: Performing functions that are strictly governmental the majority of the time, they also, on some occasions, perform proprietary functions, or functions that may be performed by a private corporation.

Proprietary functions have been defined as things not normally required by law or things

not governmental in nature. If a function is within the scope of the public school operation, as expressed or implied by statute, then the function is governmental and not proprietary. Courts have generally held that school athletic contests are governmental functions.[34] While the courts have rather consistently held that municipalities are liable for injuries arising out of functions for which admission is charged or some financial gain is realized, they have been reluctant to generally apply this standard to school districts.

Thus, if a spectator or participant is injured at an athletic contest, the courts do not usually impose liability on the school district, even when a fee is charged and the school has realized a profit. Of course, exceptions exist to all general rules, and in regard to this question, one court held that when a school district leased its football stadium to another for a fee, the lessor was held to have been engaged in a proprietary activity and was liable for injury to a spectator who was injured when a railing broke.

In following the rule that school districts are immune from liability for incidents arising during functions that charge fees, a Tennessee court said:

> The mere fact that an admission fee was charged by the high school does not make the transaction an enterprise for profit. . . . The duties of a County Board of Education are limited to the operation of the schools. This is a governmental function. Therefore, in legal contemplation, there is no such thing as such a Board acting in a proprietary capacity for private gain.[35]

A Kansas court[36] has said, *in dicta*, that if a school district can and does perform proprietary activities, then it must answer in damages when guilty in tort for injuries resulting from such functions. The Supreme Court of Oregon has laid down a test for distinguishing proprietary from governmental functions: "The underlying test is whether the act is for the common good of all without the element of special corporate benefit or pecuniary profit."[37]

The rule, therefore, may be summarized thus: As long as the purpose of the activity is educational and for the common good and the profit accrued is only incidental, the activity is governmental in nature.

This general rule is enunciated by a Michigan court in a 1984 decision:

> We therefore conclude that a governmental function is an activity which is expressly or impliedly mandated or authorized by constitution, statute, or other law. When a governmental agency engages in mandated or authorized activities, it is immune from tort liability, unless the activity is *proprietary* in nature.[38]

Not all courts agree with this rule, however. It is, of course, an entirely appropriate rejoinder to assert that because public schools have no legitimate function except as authorized by law, they cannot, in fact, legally perform proprietary functions. In this view, proprietary functions are *ultra vires* and, thereby, have no legal cognizance. This is precisely the position taken by an appellate court in Texas, which concludes simply that school districts cannot perform proprietary functions.[39] This court has stated:

> Since a school district is purely a governmental agency and exercises only such powers as are delegated to it by the state, it performs no proprietary functions that are separate from governmental functions.[40]

■ LICENSEE AND INVITEE

A school district owes a greater degree of care to an invitee than to a licensee. A licensee is one who steps beyond the limits of invitation, entering and using the premises by permission or by operation of law but without expressed or implied invitation.[41] A licensee does not commit trespass because he or she has passive permission to enter. Passive permission is not an implied invitation. On the other hand, an invitee is a person who enters the premises upon the invitation of the owner. Either the invitation may be "expressed," when the owner invites another to come and use the premises, or the invitation may be "implied," when the owner by his or her acts or conduct conveys the desire that the person enter the premises.

An owner of property normally does not owe a licensee particular duty and is therefore not responsible for exercising any particular standard of care to protect the licensee. Some courts, however, have held that an owner may be liable for willful or wanton disregard for the safety of the licensee. In this regard, the owner should not knowingly let the licensee run upon "hidden peril or wilfully cause him harm."[42] The standard of care owed an invitee is much higher, and the duty owed by the owner is substantially greater.

✧ — ✧ — ✧

Holder of a Free Pass to a Football Game Was an Invitee to Whom the School District Owed a Duty of Reasonable Care

Tanari v. School Directors of District No. 502

Supreme Court of Illinois, 1977.
69 Ill.2d 630, 14 Ill.Dec. 874, 373 N.E.2d 5.

UNDERWOOD, Justice. Plaintiff, Flora Tanari, brought an action . . . seeking damages for injuries she sustained when she allegedly was knocked to the ground by a group of children engaged in horseplay at a high school football game sponsored by defendant on its premises. The complaint alleged ordinary negligence on the part of defendant in failing to provide adequate supervision and control of children at the game. At the close of the evidence, the trial court granted the defendant's motion for a directed verdict on the ground that plaintiff was a licensee on defendant's premises; that defendant therefore only owed her the duty to refrain from wilful and wanton misconduct; and that breach of such duty had neither been alleged nor proved at trial. . . .

Plaintiff, age 64, was employed as a bus driver by an individual who had a contract with the defendant school district to transport students to and from school. She had been so employed for twenty-seven years and had attended all of the local high school football games for the last twenty-five years. On October 13, 1972, plaintiff attended the Hall Township High School homecoming football game with her daughter, son-in-law and grandchildren. The game was held on defendant's premises at a sports stadium under defendant's supervision and control. Plaintiff entered the stadium using a complimentary season pass issued by the defendant. As she was walking toward her seat, she noticed a crowd of boys and girls playing near the northwest end of the stadium, and the next thing she knew she had been knocked to the ground by a "big" boy who fell on top of her. The boy, who was never identified, got up, apologized and hurried away. . . .

The athletic director of Hall Township High School testified that he had hired off-duty policemen and teachers to keep order at all high school football games conducted by the defendant. . . . He responded in the affirmative when asked if he had seen boys and girls at almost every game "playing tag, or horseplaying and roughing it up" in the area in question. However, when he was later asked if there was "rowdiness and horseplaying by these kids in that area," he responded that he did not know whether it should be called rowdiness and horseplay, but the children were definitely there. He further testified that on previous occasions he had tried to "correct" the children but that, as soon as he left, they were back at it again. He knew from his personal observation that a policeman was in the area of the accident on the night in question.

The trial court allowed the defendant's motion for a directed verdict on the sole ground that plaintiff was a licensee on the defendant's premises and that there was no proof whatsoever that defendant had breached its duty to refrain from willful and wanton misconduct. . . . Considering the state of the record before us, we are unable to concur with the appellate court's conclusions regarding defendant's immunity. . . .

It is unnecessary to dwell at length on the common law distinctions between invitees and licensees which have evolved over the years. It suffices to observe that the general definition of an invitee is a visitor who comes upon premises at the invitation of the owner in connection with the owner's business or related activity. . . . Licensees are persons who have not been invited to enter upon the owner's premises and who come there for their own purposes and not those of the owner. . . . However, their presence is condoned by the owner, which distinguishes them from trespassers. The trial court concluded in the case at bar that since the plaintiff had not purchased a ticket but rather had attended the football game using a complimentary season pass, there was an absence of "commercial benefit" to the defendant school district, and she must therefore be considered a licensee. For the reasons hereafter stated, we must disagree with that conclusion.

In determining whether or not a person is an invitee or a licensee in a given situation, appellate courts in this State have often looked at the surrounding circumstances to determine whether, as between the visitor and the owner, there was a "mutuality of interest in the subject to which the visitor's business relates" . . . , "a mutually beneficial interest" . . . , a "mutuality of interest" . . . , [or] a "mutuality of benefit or a benefit to the owner" . . . , or whether the visitor had come to "transact business in which he and the owner have a mutual interest or to promote some real or fancied material, financial, or economic interest of the owner." . . . Such inquiries into the purpose and nature of the visit were deemed relevant, particularly in cases involving implied invitations, to ascertain whether the visitor was upon the owner's premises within the scope and purpose of the invitation or for some other reason.

That type of analysis is not necessary here. In our opinion, the complimentary pass issued to plaintiff was tantamount to an express invitation to attend Hall Township High School football games, and there can be no question about the fact that at the time of her injury, plaintiff was acting within the scope of that invitation. Unlike a person who comes upon an owner's premises for his own purposes rather than those of the owner and whose presence is merely condoned by the owner, plaintiff in this case was expressly invited and encouraged to come to the defendant's football stadium to swell the crowd in support of its team. In this type of situation, it would be entirely illogical to conclude that a person attending the game using a complimentary pass provided by the school district should be owed a lesser duty of care than a person otherwise similarly situated who had purchased a ticket. In our view, both persons should be owed the same duty of reasonable care, and we so hold.

Upon application of a reasonable care standard to the case at bar, we cannot conclude that all of the evidence, when viewed in its aspect most favorable to the plaintiff, so overwhelmingly favors the defendant that no verdict for the plaintiff could ever stand. . . . The question of whether defendant failed to exercise reasonable care in supervising children attending the football game and whether such failure, if found to exist, was the proximate cause of plaintiff's injuries, should have been submitted to the jury. . . .

Reversed and remanded.

CASE NOTES

1. The *Restatement (Second) of Torts* makes the following distinctions between an invitation and permission to enter a premises:

> An invitation differs from mere permission in this: an *invitation* is conduct which justifies others in believing that the possessor desires them to enter the land; permission is conduct justifying others in believing that the possessor is willing that they shall enter if they desire to do so. Any words or conduct of the possessor which lead or encourage the visitor to believe that his entry is desired may be sufficient for the invitation.

See *Howard County Board of Education v. Cheyne*, 99 Md.App. 150, 636 A.2d 22 (1994), quoting *Restatement (Second) of Torts*, §332.

2. The *Restatement (Second) of Torts* emphasizes the "purpose" element of the invitation. It is immaterial that the admission fee is not paid or that the landowner is not mindful of a business purpose or that the visitor's presence will lead to no possibility of benefit to the landowner, pecuniary or otherwise. It is essential, however, that the visitor is on the premises for the purpose for which the land is held open to the public. The *Restatement* illustrates the principle as follows: A visitor is an invitee at the free public library when she enters to read a book, but not when she enters to meet a friend or to get out of the rain. *Restatement (Second) of Torts*, §332(d), illustration 2.

In addition to purpose, the *Restatement (Second) of Torts*, §332(d), emphasizes the need for inducement or encouragement as in other instances of invitation. Thus, "the desire or willingness to receive that person which a reasonable man would understand as expressed by words or other conduct of the possessor" remains an important factor. See also *Restatement (Second) of Torts*, §332. *Howard County Board of Education v. Cheyne*, op. cit.

■ NUISANCE

Another device used by the courts to partially skirt the boundaries of immunity is the nuisance doctrine. A nuisance has been defined as "the existence or creation of a dangerous, unsafe, or offensive condition which is likely to cause injury, harm, or inconvenience to others." A more complete definition has been given by a Connecticut court:

> [T]o constitute a nuisance there must have arisen a condition, the natural tendency of which is to create danger or inflict injury upon person or property. . . . [T]here must be more than an act or failure to act on the part of the defendant. . . . [T]he danger created must have been a continuing one.[43]

A leading case in which a school district was held to have created a nuisance was one in which snow had fallen from the roof of a school building onto adjacent property, damaging the property. The owner was also injured when he fell on the ice. The court held that in this case there was both nuisance and trespass:

> The plaintiff had the right to the exclusive use and enjoyment of his property, and the defendant had no more right to erect a building in such a manner that the ice and snow would inevitably slide from the roof, and be precipitated upon the plaintiff's premises, than it would have to accumulate water upon its own premises, and then permit it to flow in a body upon his premises.[44]

In keeping with the legal definition, a dangerous condition must be created by the school district for nuisance to exist. In Kansas, an action was brought to recover damages for injury sustained by a nine-year-old pupil who slipped and fell on a wet lavatory floor. Pupils had made the floor wet and slippery by throwing wet paper towels and splashing water. The plaintiff claimed the district was maintaining a nuisance and was therefore liable. In response, the court held that the school did not create the nuisance, since pupils could be expected to splash water and throw wet towels on the floor while using the lavatory, and that wash basins were a necessary part of the school building equipment.[45]

The adequacy of supervision on the part of school personnel was another matter. Adequacy of supervision is not a question to be dealt with in a nuisance action, since to constitute nuisance there must be a continuing hazard and there must be more than a mere failure to act on the part of the defendant.[46]

It seems safe to conclude that while the "nuisance" theory is a viable method of averting direct confrontation with the governmental immunity issue, the courts in other jurisdictions will not plunge headlong toward its use as piecemeal abrogation. This, of course, does not mean courts will never employ the device, since it is an acceptable legal doctrine, but it does indicate a reluctance on the part of the courts to tamper with the doctrine of governmental immunity in this limited fashion.

Snow Pushed into Mounds on Playground Does Not Constitute Intentional Nuisance

Hendricks v. Southfield Public Schools

Court of Appeals of Michigan, 1989.
178 Mich.App. 672, 444 N.W.2d 143.

PER CURIAM. . . . On appeal, plaintiffs argue that the public building exception to governmental immunity applies to their case because piles of snow located on a school playground constitute a dangerous condition of a public building. M.C.L. §691.1406; M.S.A. §3.996(106). We disagree. . . .

The public building exception to governmental immunity has been interpreted to include items permanently affixed to a public building. . . . Our Supreme Court has indicated that the public building exception will not be so expansively interpreted as to extend to all public places. . . .

We do not believe that the Legislature intended its immunity exception to include the temporary condition of snow piles. Accepting as true all of plaintiffs' factual allegations contained in their pleadings and the conclusions to be reasonably drawn therefrom, plaintiffs' claim was so clearly unenforceable as a matter of law that no factual development could justify plaintiffs' right to recovery. Hence the trial court did not err in granting summary disposition on the basis that the piles of snow did not fall within the public building exception to the defense of governmental immunity. . . .

We are also unpersuaded by plaintiffs' argument that the mounds of snow should be deemed an intentional nuisance by which the claim of governmental immunity could be overcome.

To establish a claim of intentional nuisance against a governmental agency, a plaintiff must show that there is a condition which is a nuisance and that the agency intended to create that condition. . . .

Because the injury of which plaintiffs complain resulted from the school's failure to remove the mound of snow from the playground after clearing the parking lot, we conclude that the trial court in this case did not err in granting summary disposition to defendant on the basis that plaintiffs' well-pled facts involve circumstances showing the school's failure to act in removing the piles of snow.

Further, an intentionally created nuisance requires proof that the party creating or continuing the nuisance knew or must have known that harm to a plaintiff was substantially certain to follow. . . . Here, it cannot be said that harm was substantially certain to follow from the presence of the amount of snow at issue.

Accepting as true all of plaintiffs' factual allegations contained in the pleadings and conclusions to be reasonably drawn therefrom, plaintiffs could not have proved an intentionally created nuisance. Accordingly, the trial court did not err in granting summary disposition on the basis that the piles of snow did not constitute an intentional nuisance. . . .

Affirmed.

■ SECTION 1983, CIVIL RIGHTS ACT OF 1871 LIABILITY

"Section 1983 is the primary vehicle for obtaining damages and equitable relief against state and local officials who violate the constitutional rights of a person."[47] An individual's constitutional rights are protected through application of the Civil Rights Act of 1871, as codified in Section 1983 of Title 42 U.S.C.A. Thus, the "basic purpose" of the Section 1983 action for damages "is to compensate persons for injuries that are caused by deprivation of constitutional rights."[48] Under this statute, denial of an individual's constitutional or statutory rights can result in damages assessed by the court against the school board, individual school board member, administrator, or teacher, or against any government official or employee responsible for the denial. This act had been virtually dormant for almost a hundred years when it was revived in the early 1960s in the Supreme Court case of *Monroe v. Pape*,[49] at which time the Court applied the act to actions against public officials. The law itself states:

> Every person who, under color of any statute, ordinance, regulation, custom, or usage, of any State or Territory, subjects, or causes to be subjected, any citizen of the United States or other person within the jurisdiction thereof to the deprivation of any rights, privileges or immunities secured by the Constitution and laws, shall be liable to the party injured in an action at law, suit in equity, or other proper proceeding for redress.[50]

This law was enacted by Congress on April 20, 1871, after a month of debate, during which time it became clear that there was great sentiment toward providing legal redress against those southerners who repressed individual rights of southern blacks. The press at that time called the legislation the Southern-Outrage Repression Bill.[51]

PERSONS

As written, the law provides for both injunctive and monetary relief to be awarded by the federal courts. Offenders against whom action may be instituted are statutory persons—"persons" as the law is written.

A person acting "under color of" law is an individual acting in an official capacity of the state, clothed with the power of the state, or one who is the "repository of state power."[52] Accordingly, an official can act under color of law even when her actions are contrary to law, and

she can be held personally liable in damages for her violations of the Constitution.[53] The U.S. Supreme Court has had difficulty in deciding exactly who a "person" is, whether it is a public board or an individual official or employee. In *Monroe*, the Court first held that Congress did not intend the word "person" to include municipalities or agencies of the government. Therefore, suits seeking relief under the act were filed only against school officials and not against school districts as entities. The result was that from 1961 to 1978 school districts insured school officials against damages that may have been incurred by lawsuit in such cases, and the municipality was immune. On June 6, 1978, in *Monell v. Department of Social Services of City of New York*,[54] this all changed when the Supreme Court voted seven to two to overrule *Monroe* insofar as it provided immunity for municipalities. The Court, in so ruling, did not upset the interpretation of the *respondeat superior* doctrine that a public school district is not responsible for the wrongdoing of its employees, but it did say that the school district could be held liable under Section 1983 if it adopts an unconstitutional policy or acquiesces in an unconstitutional custom. Justice Brennan stated:

> We conclude, therefore, that a local government may not be sued for an injury inflicted solely by its employees or agents. Instead, it is when execution of a government's policy or custom, whether made by its lawmakers or by those whose edicts or acts may fairly be said to represent official policy, inflicts the injury that the government as an entity is responsible under Section 1983.

Monell therefore, taken in context with two other cases, *Wood v. Strickland*[55] and *Carey v. Piphus*,[56] clearly permits courts to assess damages against either a governmental agency or individual officials of government if it or they suppress one's civil rights, whether it be a student, teacher, or some other party. *Wood* established the potential liability of school board members for denial of students' due process rights, and *Carey* clarified the nature and extent of the damages that could be levied by the courts. In *Carey*, Justice Powell, writing for the Court, explained that there was a limitation to the damages that were possible under this kind of action. According to Powell, Section 1983 was not intended to provide purely punitive relief whereby the court would punish the wrongdoer for ill deeds, but instead the act was designed to compensate the victim for detriment and damage caused by the denial. Compensatory damages of this nature are quite difficult to prove, and the Supreme Court places this burden squarely on the shoulders of the plaintiff. In the absence of such proof, the individual is entitled to collect only nominal damages.

As discussed in Chapter 3 earlier in this text, in the *Seminole Tribe v. Florida* case,[57] the Eleventh Amendment prevents private parties from obtaining damages from a state government unless Congress clearly and unambiguously abrogates state sovereignty or the state itself waives immunity. Congress did not clearly abrogate state sovereign immunity when it enacted Section 1983 in 1871. Yet while Section 1983 itself, alone, does not abrogate state Eleventh Amendment immunity, such immunity can be waived by specific enactments by Congress that work in tandem with Section 1983 to provide a remedy to specified constitutional violations. Such abrogation, however, must be prescribed in the substance of the legislation that specifically redresses the violation of a constitutional right for which Congress has valid reason to be concerned, such as the Individuals with Disabilities Education Act. Remember, however, that sovereign immunity protects only the state, state agencies, and other arms of the state, including public institutions of higher education. Perversely, however, Eleventh Amendment immunity has not yet been extended to local school districts.

SCHOOL BOARD LIABILITY

As noted above, the Supreme Court in *Monell* held that municipalities cannot be liable under Section 1983 if the government itself does not cause the infliction of harm beyond the injury caused by one of the government's employees. According to the Supreme Court, governmental liability can be imposed only when the injury is caused by "the execution of a government's policy or custom, whether made by its lawmakers or by those whose edicts or acts may fairly be said to represent official policy."[58]

In *Pembaur v. Cincinnati*,[59] a 1986 case, the Supreme Court held that a school board cannot be held liable under Section 1983 unless there is

actual or constructive knowledge that an employee of the board has denied plaintiffs their constitutional rights.

The fifth circuit has further clarified by holding that a municipality must have an "underlying knowledge" of a custom or a policy that is violative of a citizen's constitutional rights.[60] The fifth circuit has explained:

> Actual knowledge must be shown by such means as discussions at council meetings or receipt of written information. Constructive knowledge may be attributed to the governing body on the ground that it would have known of the violations if it had properly exercised its responsibilities, as, for example, the violations were so persistent and widespread that they were the subject of prolonged public discussion and a high degree of publicity.[61]

OFFICIAL NEGLIGENCE

Even though the U.S. Supreme Court initially held that civil remedy under Section 1983 could be afforded for negligence,[62] the Court later reversed itself, holding that lack of due care by a state official could not be the basis for relief under Section 1983.[63] Mere negligence or an omission causing injury cannot be used as the basis to invoke the protections of the statute. Thus, the so-called constitutional tort founded under Section 1983 has the important constraint of being inapplicable to cases of official negligence. The Supreme Court, however, has left open the question of liability if there is a callous or reckless disregard for plaintiffs' rights and injury ensues.

In applying this principle, the U.S. Court of Appeals, Eighth Circuit, in *Rubek v. Barnhart*[64] found that parents seeking damages under Section 1983 could not prevail in an action for constitutional "negligence" against teachers and administrators for violation of due process in administering corporal punishment to the plaintiff children. The court required plaintiffs to show that the defendants, in administering the corporal punishment, had demonstrated "a reckless disregard or deliberate indifference to plaintiff's constitutional rights."[65]

Thus, the prevailing view appears to be that a governmental entity will not be liable unless there is shown a "deliberate indifference" for a child's rights. For a school board to be liable, the plaintiff must bear the difficult burden of proving that constitutional rights had been taken away as a result of overt official school district policy or custom. Moreover, the plaintiff must show that the board had knowledge of the policy or custom that caused the deprivation. The plaintiff must also show that the injury was caused by the board's "callous indifference" to the plaintiff's constitutional rights.[66]

INDIVIDUAL LIABILITY

Under certain circumstances, an employee or an official of a school district may be found to be individually liable even though a school board may not be. The individual employee or official cannot be liable unless the plaintiff shows that the action violated a clearly established law and that the individual exhibited a "callous indifference" for the rights of the plaintiff.[67]

In *Davis*, the U.S. Supreme Court held:

Officials are shielded from liability for civil damages insofar as their conduct does not violate the clearly established statutory or constitutional rights of which a reasonable person would have known at the time of the incident involved.[68]

Therefore, employees and officials, in their individual capacities, are immune from liability under Section 1983 unless they have exhibited a "callous indifference" to an individual's constitutional rights and have demonstrated "a lack of objective good faith."[69]

Horner has carefully summarized the law of liability as set forth in Section 1983 for both school boards and individuals:

Indeed courts generally look at two basic elements in determining whether Section 1983 should be imposed upon governmental entities and their employees. With respect to the liability of the entity, courts will impose liability only if a state official acts in a "callously indifferent" manner toward the rights of individuals pursuant to governmental policy or custom. In essence, a state official must not only perform an outrageous action, but such actions must also be common within that particular governmental entity. Individual liability revolves around the "callous indifference" standard. If an employee acts with "callous indifference" toward the rights of an individual, he or she may be subject to liability in his or her individual capacity.[70]

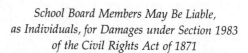

School Board Members May Be Liable, as Individuals, for Damages under Section 1983 of the Civil Rights Act of 1871

Wood v. Strickland

Supreme Court of the United States, 1975.
420 U.S. 308, 95 S.Ct. 992.

Mr. Justice WHITE delivered the opinion of the Court. Respondents Peggy Strickland and Virginia Crain brought this lawsuit against petitioners, who were members of the school board at the time in question, two school administrators, and the Special School District of Mena, Ark., purporting to assert a cause of action under 42 U.S.C.A. §1983, and claiming that their federal constitutional rights to due process were infringed under color of state law by their expulsion from the Mena Public High School on the grounds of their violation of a school regulation prohibiting the use or possession of intoxicating beverages at school or school activities. The complaint as amended prayed for compensatory and punitive damages against all petitioners, injunctive relief allowing respondents to resume attendance, preventing petitioners from imposing any sanctions as a result of the expulsion, and restraining enforcement of the challenged regulation, declaratory relief as to the constitutional invalidity of the regulation, and expunction of any record of their expulsion. . . .

The violation of the school regulation prohibiting the use or possession of intoxicating beverages at school or school activities with which respondents were charged concerned their "spiking" of the punch served at a meeting of an extracurricular school organization attended by parents and students. At the time in question, respondents were sixteen years old and were in the tenth grade. The relevant facts begin with their discovery that the punch had not been prepared for the meeting as previously planned. The girls then agreed to "spike" it. Since the county in which the school is located is "dry," respondents and a third girl drove across the state border into Oklahoma and purchased two twelve-ounce bottles of "Right Time," a malt liquor. They then bought six ten-ounce bottles of a soft drink, and after having mixed the contents of the eight bottles in an empty milk carton, returned to school. Prior to the meeting, the girls experienced second thoughts about the wisdom of their prank, but by then they were caught up in the force of events and the intervention of other girls prevented them from disposing of the illicit punch. The punch was served at the meeting, without apparent effect. . . . The board voted to expel the girls from school for the remainder of the semester, a period of approximately three months.

The board subsequently agreed to hold another meeting on the matter, and one was held approximately two weeks after the first meeting. The girls, their parents, and their counsel attended this session. The board began with a reading of a written statement of facts as it had found them. The girls admitted mixing the malt liquor into the punch with the intent of "spiking" it, but asked the board to forgo its rule punishing such violations by such substantial suspensions. . . . The board voted not to change its policy and, as before, to expel the girls for the remainder of the semester.

The District Court instructed the jury that a decision for respondents had to be premised upon a finding that petitioners acted with malice in expelling them and defined "malice" as meaning "ill will against a person—a wrongful act done intentionally without just cause or excuse." In ruling for petitioners after the jury had been unable to agree, the District Court found "as a matter of law" that there was no evidence from which malice could be inferred.

The Court of Appeals, however, viewed both the instruction and the decision of the District Court as being erroneous. Specific intent to harm wrongfully, it held, was not a requirement for the recovery of damages. Instead, "[i]t need only be established that the defendants did not, in the light of all the circumstances, act in good faith. The test is an objective, rather than a subjective one."

Petitioners as members of the school board assert here, as they did below, an absolute immunity from liability under §1983 and at the very least seek to reinstate the judgment of the

District Court. If they are correct and the District Court's dismissal should be sustained, we need go no further in this case. Moreover, the immunity question involves the construction of a federal statute, and our practice is to deal with possibly dispositive statutory issues before reaching questions turning on the construction of the Constitution. . . . We essentially sustain the position of the Court of Appeals with respect to the immunity issue.

The nature of the immunity from awards of damages under §1983 available to school administrators and school board members is not a question which the lower federal courts have answered with a single voice. There is general agreement on the existence of a "good faith" immunity, but the courts have either emphasized different factors as elements of good faith or have not given specific content to the good-faith standard. . . .

Common-law tradition, recognized in our prior decisions, and strong public-policy reasons also lead to a construction of §1983 extending a qualified good-faith immunity to school board members from liability for damages under that section. Although there have been differing emphases and formulations of the common-law immunity of public school officials in cases of student expulsion or suspension, state courts have generally recognized that such officers should be protected from tort liability under state law for all good-faith nonmalicious action taken to fulfill their official duties.

As the facts of this case reveal, school board members function at different times in the nature of legislators and adjudicators in the school disciplinary process. Each of these functions necessarily involves the exercise of discretion, the weighing of many factors, and the formulation of long-term policy. "Like legislators and judges, these officers are entitled to rely on traditional sources for the factual information on which they decide and act." . . . As with executive officers faced with instances of civil disorder, school officials, confronted with school behavior causing or threatening disruption, also have an "obvious need for prompt action, and decisions must be made in reliance on factual information supplied by others."

Liability for damages for every action which is found subsequently to have been violative of a school's constitutional rights and to have caused compensable injury would unfairly impose upon the school decision-maker the burden of mistakes made in good faith in the course of exercising his discretion within the scope of his official duties. School board members, among other duties, must judge whether there have been violations of school regulations and, if so, the appropriate sanctions for the violations. Denying any measure of immunity in these circumstances "would contribute not to principled and fearless decision-making but to intimidation." . . . The imposition of monetary costs for mistakes which were not unreasonable in the light of all the circumstances would undoubtedly deter even the most conscientious school decision-maker from exercising his judgment independently, forcefully, and in a manner best serving the long-term interest of the school and the students. The most capable candidates for school board positions might be deterred from seeking office if heavy burdens upon their private resources from monetary liability were a likely prospect during their tenure.

These considerations have undoubtedly played a prime role in the development by state courts of a qualified immunity protecting school officials from liability for damages in lawsuits claiming improper suspensions or expulsions. But at the same time, the judgment implicit in this common-law development is that absolute immunity would not be justified since it would not sufficiently increase the ability of school officials to exercise their discretion in a forthright manner to warrant the absence of a remedy for students subjected to intentional or otherwise inexcusable deprivations.

. . . We think there must be a degree of immunity if the work of the schools is to go forward; and, however worded, the immunity must be such that public school officials understand that action taken in the good-faith fulfillment of their responsibilities and within the bounds of reason under all the circumstances will not be punished and that they need not exercise their discretion with undue timidity. . . .

The disagreement between the Court of Appeals and the District Court over the immunity standard in this case has been put in terms of an "objective" versus a "subjective" test of good faith. As we see it, the appropriate standard necessarily contains elements of both. The official himself must be acting sincerely and with a belief that he is doing right, but an act violating a student's constitutional rights can be no more justified by ignorance or disregard of settled, indisputable law on the part of one entrusted with supervision of students' daily lives than by the presence of actual malice. To be entitled to a special exemption from the categorical remedial language of §1983 in a case in which his action violated a student's constitutional rights, a school board member, who has voluntarily undertaken the task of supervising the operation of the school and the activities of the students, must be held to a standard of conduct based not only on permissible intentions, but also on knowledge of the basic, unquestioned constitutional rights of his charges. Such a standard imposes neither an unfair burden upon a person assuming a responsible public office requiring a high degree of intelligence and judgment for the proper fulfillment of its duties, nor an unwarranted burden in light of the value which civil rights have in our legal system. Any lesser standard would deny much of the promise of §1983. Therefore, in the specific context of school discipline, we hold that a school board member is not immune from liability for damages under §1983 if he knew or reasonably should have known that the action he took within his sphere of official responsibility would violate the constitutional rights of the school affected, or if he took the action with the malicious intention to cause a deprivation of constitutional rights or other injury to the student. That is not to say that school board members are "charged with predicting the future course of constitutional law." . . . A compensatory award will be appropriate only if the school board member has acted with such an impermissible motivation or with such disregard of the student's clearly established constitutional rights that his action cannot reasonably be characterized as being in good faith.

The Court of Appeals based upon its review of the facts but without the benefit of the transcript of the testimony given at the four-day trial to the jury in the District Court, found that the board had made its decision to expel the girls on the basis of *no* evidence that the school regulation had been violated:

To justify the suspension, it was necessary for the Board to establish that the students possessed or used an "intoxicating" beverage at a school-sponsored activity. No evidence was presented at either meeting to establish the alcoholic content of the liquid brought to the campus. Moreover, the Board made no finding that the liquid was intoxicating. The only evidence as to the nature of the drink was that supplied by the girls, and it was clear that they did not know whether the beverage was intoxicating or not. 485 F.2d, at 190.

. . . In its statement of facts issued prior to the onset of this litigation, the school board expressed its construction of the regulation by finding that the girls had brought an "alcoholic beverage" onto school premises. The girls themselves admitted knowing at the time of the incident that they were doing something wrong which might be punished. In light of this evidence, the Court of Appeals was ill advised to supplant the interpretation of the regulation of those officers who adopted it and are entrusted with its enforcement. . . .

When the regulation is construed to prohibit the use and possession of beverages containing alcohol, there was no absence of evidence before the school board to prove the charge against respondents. The girls had admitted that they intended to "spike" the punch and that they had mixed malt liquor into the punch that was served. . . .

Given the fact that there was evidence supporting the charge against respondents, the contrary judgment of the Court of Appeals is improvident. It is not the role of the federal courts to set aside decisions of school administrators which the court may view as lacking a basis in wisdom and compassion. Public high school students do have substantive and procedural rights while at school. . . . But §1983 does not extend the right to relitigate in federal court evidentiary questions arising in school disciplinary proceedings or the proper construction of school regulations. The system of public education that has evolved in this Nation relies necessarily upon the discretion and judgment of school administrators and school board members, and §1983 was not intended to be a vehicle for federal-court correction of errors in the exercise of that discretion which do not rise to the level of violations of specific constitutional guarantees. . . .

Respondents have argued here that there was a procedural due process violation which also supports the result reached by the Court of Appeals. . . . But because the District Court did not discuss it, and the Court of Appeals did not decide it, it would be preferable to have the Court of Appeals consider the issue in the first instance.

The judgment of the Court of Appeals is vacated and the case remanded for further proceedings consistent with this opinion.

So ordered.

Case Notes

1. *Absolute Immunity.* The Supreme Court, in a series of cases, determined that absolute immunity is available as a defense for prosecutors in initiating and presenting the state's case, *Imbler v. Pachtman*, 424 U.S. 409, 96 S.Ct. 984 (1976), and for state legislators, *Tenney v. Brandhove*, 341 U.S. 367, 71 S.Ct. 783 (1951).

2. *Qualified or Conditional Immunity.* Prosecutors and legislators have absolute immunity. It may therefore appear that other state officials have absolute immunity; however, in *Scheuer v. Rhodes*, 416 U.S. 232, 94 S.Ct. 1683 (1974), the Supreme Court declared that the governor of Ohio and other state officials have only qualified or conditional immunity. Qualified or conditional immunity from civil liability means individuals are not liable as long as they are acting clearly within the scope of their authority for the betterment of those they serve. If they venture outside the scope of their authority and, in doing so, violate someone's rights, then they may be personally liable. Qualified immunity has been established by a Supreme Court decision for superintendents of state hospitals, *O'Connor v. Donaldson*, 422 U.S. 563, 95 S.Ct. 2486 (1975), and for local school board members, *Wood v. Strickland*, 420 U.S. 308, 95 S.Ct. 992 (1975).

3. *Good-Faith Immunity.* Although individuals may assert good faith as a defense in a constitutional tort action, a municipality has no immunity and may not assert a good-faith defense. *Owen v. City of Independence*, 445 U.S. 622, 100 S.Ct. 1398 (1980).

4. *Punitive Damages.* Individuals are entitled to recover only nominal damages unless they

can prove actual damages. The Supreme Court stated "that in the absence of proof of actual injury, the students are entitled to recover only nominal damages." *Carey v. Piphus*, 435 U.S. 247, 98 S.Ct. 1042 (1978). See also *Memphis Community School District v. Stachura*, 477 U.S. 299, 106 S.Ct. 2537 (1986).

A municipality is immune from punitive damages. The Supreme Court of the United States, in concluding that punitive damages should not be assessed against municipalities (or school districts), has said:

> Punitive damages by definition are not intended to compensate the injured party, but rather to punish the tortfeasor whose wrongful action was intentional or malicious, and to deter him and others from similar extreme conduct. . . . Regarding retribution, it remains true that an award of punitive damages against a municipality "punishes" only the taxpayers, who took no part in the commission of the tort. These damages are assessed over and above the amount necessary to compensate the injured party. Thus, there is no question here of equitably distributing the losses resulting from official misconduct. . . . Indeed, punitive damages imposed on a municipality are in effect a windfall to a fully compensated plaintiff, and are likely accompanied by an increase in taxes or a reduction of public services for the citizens footing the bill. Neither reason nor justice suggests that such retribution should be visited upon the shoulders of blameless or unknowing taxpayers.
>
> Under ordinary principles of retribution, it is the wrongdoer himself who is made to suffer for his unlawful conduct. If a government official acts knowingly and maliciously to deprive others of their civil rights, he may become the appropriate object of the community's vindictive sentiments.... A municipality, however, can have no malice independent of the malice of its officials. Damages awarded for *punitive* purposes, therefore, are not sensibly assessed against the governmental entity itself.

City of Newport v. Fact Concerts, Inc., 453 U.S. 247, 101 S.Ct. 2748 (1981).

■ ELEVENTH AMENDMENT AND LOCAL SCHOOL DISTRICTS

Does Eleventh Amendment immunity extend to local school districts? As observed earlier in this text (Chapter 4), local school districts are actually state agencies; local school board members are legally state officials; and locally derived funds are, in fact, state funds. Because this is true, it would seem logical that Eleventh Amendment immunity (see Chapters 3 and 9) should extend to local school districts as agencies of the state. This conclusion has, though, run afoul of the practical problems that would ensue if all education treasuries, state and local, were declared immune from suits by private citizens. The Supreme Court has therefore apparently concluded that the Eleventh Amendment requires a different test as to the state versus local school districts.

The Supreme Court held, in *Mt. Healthy*, that the Eleventh Amendment does not necessarily apply to "counties and similar corporations."[71] The Court has, though, concluded that the Eleventh Amendment bars suit against county officials if the resulting judgment would effectively constitute a judgment against the state's treasury itself.[72]

The question as to the local nature of school districts is, however, far from decided. The Supreme Court set a precedent in *Mt. Healthy* that has caused considerable confusion and is not likely to be resolved soon. In *Mt. Healthy*, the Court took the position that local school boards in Ohio are more like a "county or city" than they are like "an arm of the state." This conclusion is, of course, contrary to the prevailing view of state and federal precedents on the subject.

In maintaining that local school districts are not state agencies in Ohio, the Court perused the Ohio statutes and concluded that the "state" does not include "political subdivisions" and that local school districts fall within the category of "political subdivisions." The Court further noted that local school boards may levy taxes and issue bonds and are thereby local instead of state agencies. In so surmising, the Supreme Court ignored the Ohio Constitution, which clearly places the responsibility for provision of education in its entirety on the state legislature, not the locality.[73]

Regardless, the Supreme Court in *Mt. Healthy* held that a school board in Ohio is a local agency, distinct from a state agency, and is thereby not entitled to Eleventh Amendment immunity. This demarcation of immunity between state and local agencies is consistent with the Supreme Court's rulings in *Monell*[74] and *Pugh*,[75] which did not distinguish public schools from other local governmental agencies.

These precedents have left the lower courts with little guidance in attempting to determine whether school districts are state or local agencies for Eleventh Amendment pruposes. The lower courts are now split on the matter. For example, in applying the *Mt. Healthy* rationale to Louisiana, the U.S. Court of Appeals for the Fifth Circuit concluded that school parish boards in Louisiana are "local independent agents not shielded" by Eleventh Amendment immunity. On the other hand, the U.S. Court of Appeals for the Tenth Circuit has held that local school boards in New Mexico are arms of the state and therefore enjoy Eleventh Amendment immunity.[76]

Several conclusions can be drawn from this line of precedents. The foremost is that the Eleventh Amendment is a viable constitutional restraint on the judiciary, preserving immune status for state government unless Congress specifically and unequivocally abrogates it through the enforcement provision, Section 5, of the Fourteenth Amendment. Where relief is granted, it cannot be in the form of retroactive monetary damages taken from the state treasury.

Whether the treasuries of local school boards are similarly immune is a matter of application of the Supreme Court's criteria to determine immunity status. The *Mt. Healthy* criteria are[77]

- whether state statutes and case law characterize the local school district as an arm of the state;
- the source of funds to operate the schools;
- the degree of autonomy enjoyed by the school district;
- whether the school district is concerned primarily with local, rather than statewide, problems;
- whether the school district has authority to sue and be sued in its own name; and
- whether the school district has the right to hold and use property.[78]

These criteria will, of necessity, be applied by the courts in each case where Eleventh Amendment immunity is raised as a defense by local school districts.

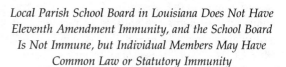

Local Parish School Board in Louisiana Does Not Have Eleventh Amendment Immunity, and the School Board Is Not Immune, but Individual Members May Have Common Law or Statutory Immunity

Minton v. St. Bernard Parish School Board

United States Court of Appeals,
Fifth Circuit, 1986.
803 F.2d 129.

ALVIN B. RUBIN, Circuit Judge. A Mississippi resident in whose favor a final tort judgment has been rendered by a Louisiana court against a Louisiana parish school district has been unable to collect her damages because the parish school board refuses to appropriate the funds necessary to satisfy her claim. . . .

In 1974, Connie Minton, a resident of Mississippi and a minor, was struck and injured by a school bus operated under the supervision of the Saint Bernard Parish School Board. Shortly thereafter, she and the administrator of her estate, Isaac D. Minton, brought an action to recover for her injuries in a Louisiana state court, and obtained judgment in her favor. . . . That judgment is now final.

Since then Minton and her administrator have tried unsuccessfully to obtain from the Saint Bernard Parish School Board an appropriation of funds to satisfy the judgment. . . .

. . . In their prayer for relief, the Mintons asked the district court for damages, including the unpaid portion of the judgment plus interest, attorney's fees, punitive damages, and any equitable relief the court deems appropriate.

The Saint Bernard Parish School Board relies first on the defenses that the Mintons' suit constitutes a suit against the state that is prohibited by the eleventh amendment to the United States Constitution. We must therefore determine whether the Saint Bernard Parish School Board is an arm of the state enjoying eleventh amendment immunity or whether it possesses an identity sufficiently distinct from that of the State of Louisiana to place it beyond that shield.

As Judge Garwood has recently stated in *Clark v. Tarrant County, Texas*, 798 F.2d 736 (1986), to draw that distinction "we 'must examine the particular entity in question and its powers and characteristics as created by state law. . . .'" The relevant factors include: (1) whether state statutes and case law characterize the agency as an arm of the state; (2) the source of funds for the entity; (3) the degree of local autonomy the entity enjoys; (4) whether the entity is concerned primarily with local, as opposed to statewide, problems; (5) whether the entity has authority to sue and be sued in its own name; and (6) whether the entity has the right to hold and use property.

These tests identify parish school boards as local independent agents not shielded by the state's eleventh amendment immunity. Although Louisiana courts have referred to school boards as "agencies" of the state, this characterization does not amount to an assertion that the boards are arms of the state within the meaning of the eleventh amendment. School boards generate funds for the operation of parish school districts through local ad valorem taxation, exercise a great deal of discretion in performing their functions and addressing their innately local concerns, have authority to sue or be sued in their own name, and can hold, use, or sell property as each local board determines necessary to fulfill its obligation to the public. In view of the inherently local nature of the interests of Louisiana school boards, the wide degree of local autonomy they are granted under state law, and the predominately local source of their funding, it cannot be said either that these entities are mere arms of the state or that monetary judgments against them would represent indirect impositions on the state treasury interfering with the state's fiscal autonomy. Louisiana school boards, therefore, are not entitled to eleventh amendment immunity to Section 1983 claims. . . .

. . . [T]he School Board asserts that the failure of its members to appropriate funds requested by the Mintons is a legislative action absolutely immune from federal court inquiry. . . . Qualified official immunity and absolute legislative immunity are doctrines that protect individuals acting within the bounds of their official duties, not the governing bodies on which they serve. Thus, even if the actions of the School Board members are legislative, rather than administra-

tive, the School Board itself as a separate entity is not entitled to immunity for violation of the Mintons' constitutional rights.

Whether the Board members' legislative immunity requires the complaint to be dismissed insofar as it seeks relief from them is a more complicated question. In *Tenney v. Brandhove** the Supreme Court held that state legislators who are acting within the scope of their legislative duty are, like their federal counterparts, absolutely immune to civil suits for damages, "not for their private indulgence but for the public good." This absolute immunity from suit under §1983 was extended to regional legislators . . . and to local legislators. . . . Thus, when acting in their legislative capacity, local legislators are granted even greater protection than the qualified immunity generally granted school officials for actions taken in "good faith fulfillment of their responsibilities and within the bounds of reason. . . . " If the School Board members are entitled to absolute immunity from the charges made by the Mintons, they are entitled not only to avoid "the consequences of litigation's results but also . . . the burden of defending themselves."

As the Supreme Court noted in *Scheuer v. Rhodes,*** official immunity "apparently rested, in its genesis, on two mutually dependent rationales: (1) the injustice, particularly in the absence of bad faith, of subjecting to liability an officer who is required, by the legal obligations of his position, to exercise discretion; (2) the danger that the threat of such liability would deter his willingness to execute his office with the decisiveness and the judgment required by the public good." Because, however, official immunity doctrines are premised upon the concern that the threat of personal liability may deter government officials from executing their offices with the decisiveness and good faith judgment required for the public good, the immunity does not protect officials when they are not threatened with personal liability. It does not, therefore, bar injunctive relief or suits in which officials are sued only in their official capacities and, therefore, cannot be held personally liable. . . .

---

*341 U.S. 367, 71 S.Ct. 783, 95 L.Ed. 1019 (1951).
**416 U.S. 232, 239–40, 94 S.Ct. 1683, 1688, 40 L.Ed.2d 90 (1974).

Local legislators who are acting within the scope of their legislative duty enjoy absolute immunity from personal liability under civil liability suits. Legislative absolute immunity, however, is actually only an extension of the qualified immunity granted other government officials, its objective being the implementation of additional safeguards that fulfill the mandate of the Speech or Debate Clause of art. I, §6 of the Constitution. Its protection, therefore, applies not only to legislators but to any other officials fulfilling legislative functions, including the President when exercising his authority to approve bills, justices of a state supreme court exercising legislative functions, and a city mayor vetoing a city ordinance. But even for legislators, the absolute immunity doctrine does not provide blanket protection from burdensome litigation. Not "everything a Member of Congress may regularly do is . . . a legislative act within the protection of the Speech or Debate Clause." It follows that not everything an official with legislative duties does is protected by absolute immunity. When an official possessing legislative responsibilities engages in official activities insufficiently connected with the legislative process to raise genuine concern that an inquiry into the motives underlying his actions will thwart his ability to perform his legislative duties vigorously, openly and forthrightly, he is not entitled to absolute immunity but only to the qualified immunity grounded in good faith that is bestowed upon other government officials. Although the School Board addressed this issue in cursory form in its brief, it would be inappropriate at this time for this court to attempt to resolve the issue. If absolute immunity is urged by the School Board members in the district court, that court must determine whether, under the statutory scheme in Louisiana, school board members' decisions whether to appropriate funds to pay a particular tort judgment involve the degree of discretion and public-policy-making traditionally associated with legislative functions or merely an administrative application of existing policies. . . .

. . . We conclude only that the Mintons have stated a claim for denial of equal protection for which some form of relief may be granted and that such claim is not barred by the eleventh amendment, abstention doctrines, or with regard to at least the School Board by legislative immunity.

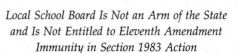

Local School Board Is Not an Arm of the State and Is Not Entitled to Eleventh Amendment Immunity in Section 1983 Action

Duke v. Grady Municipal Schools

United States Court of Appeals, Tenth Circuit, 1997.
127 F.3d 972.

STEPHEN H. ANDERSON, Circuit Judge.

. . . The sole issue presented in this appeal is whether local school boards and districts in New Mexico are arms of the state and therefore entitled to Eleventh Amendment immunity, or whether they are political subdivisions or some other form of local entity subject to liability under §1983. We hold that local school boards and districts in New Mexico are not arms of the state and are therefore not entitled to Eleventh Amendment immunity. We therefore reverse and remand. . . .

Ms. Duke commenced this §1983 action against the members of the Grady School Board in their individual capacities, alleging that they had deprived her of a protectable property interest in her employment without due process of law. While her action was pending in the district court, the New Mexico Supreme Court . . . held that a local school board is not an arm of the state entitled to Eleventh Amendment immunity and that such a board is a "person" under 42 U.S.C. §1983. . . .

The Eleventh Amendment provides that "[t]he Judicial power of the United States shall not be construed to extend to any suit in law or equity, commenced or prosecuted against one of the United States by Citizens of another State, or by Citizens or Subjects of any Foreign State."

U.S. Const. amend. XI. It thus "largely shields States from suit in federal court without their consent, leaving parties with claims against a State to present them, if the State permits, in the State's own tribunals." . . .

Eleventh Amendment immunity, however, "extends only to the states and governmental entities that are 'arms of the state.'" . . .

Whether a local entity is an arm of the state under the Eleventh Amendment "is a question of federal law." . . . However, "that federal question can be answered only after considering the provisions of state law that define the agency's character." . . . And while we have noted that most courts considering the issue since *Mount Healthy* have held that local school districts or boards are not entitled to Eleventh Amendment immunity, the question must nonetheless "be determined in each case on the basis of the individual state laws involved." . . .

. . . While we must view the issue of Eleventh Amendment immunity as a federal question, we cannot ignore the fact that the answer to the question requires a detailed analysis of New Mexico constitutional and statutory materials. And, "the State's highest court is the best authority on its own law." . . .

We conclude, after examining state statutes, the state constitution and state case law, that school districts and their governing boards in New Mexico are not arms of the state entitled to Eleventh Amendment immunity. . . .

The New Mexico constitution empowers the State Board to "determine public school policy" and to "have control, management and direction, including financial direction, distribution of school funds and financial accounting for all public schools." N.M. Const. Art. XII, §6; *see also* N.M. Stat. Ann. §22-2-1(A). By statute, the State Board has general authority over schools statewide, and authority, inter alia, to establish standards regarding curriculum, teacher accreditation and qualifications, and graduation requirements. As we acknowledged with respect to the Utah State Board of Education in *Ambus*, "[e]ach of these responsibilities relates to the management of the school system in the state as a whole." *Ambus*, 995 F.2d at 996.

Local school boards, however, have many other responsibilities and duties, which they perform without state control and supervision. For example, local board members are elected from residents of the district in which they live, N.M. Stat. Ann. §22-5-1.1; subject to state board regulations, they "supervise and control all public schools within the school district and all property belonging to or in the possession of the school district," §22-5-4(A); they approve or disapprove all employment decisions, §22-5-4(D); they "contract, lease, purchase and sell for the school district," §22-5-4(G); they "acquire and dispose of property," §22-5-4(H); they "have the capacity to sue and be sued," §22-5-4(I); they can "acquire property by eminent domain," §22-5-4(J); and they can "issue general obligation bonds of the school district," §22-5-4(K), although only for capital improvements. N.M. Const. Art. IX, §11; N.M. Stat. Ann. §22-18-1. As with Utah school districts, "significant autonomy is vested in the local boards." *Ambus*, 995 F.2d at 996. This factor therefore suggests such school boards should not receive Eleventh Amendment immunity. . . .

With respect to school districts' designation under state law, the New Mexico Constitution enumerates "State educational institutions," but local school districts are not among them. "School district" is defined in the Public School Code as "an area of land established as a political subdivision of the state," N.M. Stat. Ann. §22-1-2(K), of which the local board is its government body. §22-1-2(L). The Tort Claims Act defines a "local public body" as "all political subdivisions of the state and their agencies, instrumentalities and institutions." §41-4-3(C). It defines the "state" or "state agency" as "the state of New Mexico or any of its branches, agencies, departments, boards, instrumentalities or institutions." §41-4-3(H). The section concerning notice of claims suggests that school districts are classified as local public bodies. It states as follows:

> Every person who claims damages from the *state or any local public body* under the Tort Claims Act shall cause to be presented to the *risk management division for claims against the state*, the mayor of the municipality for claims against the municipality, *the superintendent of the school district for claims against the school district*, the county clerk of a county for claims against the county, *or to the*

administrative head of any other local public body for claims against such local public body . . . a written notice. . . .

N.M. Stat. Ann. §41-4-16(A) (emphasis added) (citations omitted). The section in the Tort Claims Act addressing the establishment of a public liability fund defines a school district by reference to the Public School Code, §22-1-2, which, as indicated, defines a school district as a political subdivision. Thus, while certainly not definitive, statutory definitions suggest the New Mexico legislature intended school districts or boards to be political subdivisions or local public bodies, not arms of the state. This factor therefore points away from Eleventh Amendment immunity for such entities. . . .

As all parties agree, New Mexico school districts statewide receive an average of approximately 95% of their funds from the state. The Grady Municipal School district receives 98% of its funds from the state. Moreover, New Mexico has adopted an equalizing formula to fund its schools, pursuant to which each school district's total budget is calculated by a formula which considers a number of factors. The state provides funding for the budget in the amount by which the budget exceeds local and federal revenues, less five percent. N.M. Stat. Ann. §22-8-25. As we have indicated, school districts or boards may levy taxes to pay for tort or workers' compensation judgments, but not for federal civil rights judgments. School districts may issue bonds, but only for capital improvements. Thus, school districts receive virtually all their money from the state, and they appear to have no independent fundraising ability. This factor therefore points in favor of Eleventh Amendment immunity. . . .

The final, but the most important, factor is whether the state treasury would be at risk of paying a judgment against a New Mexico school district or board, like defendant Grady Municipal Schools and its board. While the Supreme Court has indicated that this is the most "salient" factor, it is also among the most difficult to apply. This case, in particular, highlights the confusion in this area of Eleventh Amendment jurisprudence.

It appears that a civil rights judgment such as Ms. Duke's would be paid from the New Mexico Public Schools Insurance Authority or from a private insurance carrier. Premiums for participation in the Authority come from the school districts' budgets, which, in turn, are funded almost exclusively by the state. According to the affidavit of the Executive Director of the Authority, Dr. Eugene LeDoux, premiums "are collected [from school districts] based on such factors as district size and claim history." . . . Thus, as a *practical* matter, because virtually all of the operating funds of a school district in New Mexico, including the premiums which purchase the insurance from which a judgment would be satisfied, come from the state, the state treasury pays, at least indirectly, for a judgment against a school district and its governing board. . . .

The question is whether that practical impact analysis satisfies the Supreme Court's test for when a state's treasury is vulnerable for Eleventh Amendment immunity purposes, as set out in *Doe*. . . . In *Doe*, the Court appeared to give primacy to the legal liability of the state: "'The question is not who pays in the end; it is who is legally obligated to pay the judgment that is being sought.'" [*Regents of the Univ. Of Calif. v. Doe*, 519 U.S. at 428, 117 S.Ct. at 903 (1997)]. We interpret *Doe* to require us to focus on legal liability for a judgment, rather than practical, or indirect, impact a judgment would have on a state's treasury. As the Court specifically stated, "it is the entity's potential legal liability, rather than its ability or inability to require a third party to reimburse it, or to discharge the liability in the first instance, that is relevant." . . . And while such a focus in some ways ignores economic reality, it also provides a clear and workable test in this very confused area of the law. It directs courts away from having to make case-by-case fact-specific determinations of the practical impact on state treasuries. In this case, involving 98% state revenues, it may be relatively easy to determine to the practical effect on the state treasury, but determining when the impact is sufficient as the percentage of state revenues declines becomes increasingly difficult.

As applied to New Mexico's school districts and their boards, we must conclude that the factor relating to the liability of the state treasury points away from Eleventh Amendment immunity, for the simple reason that the state of New

Mexico is not *legally* liable for a judgment against a school district. Because this most important factor suggests there should be no Eleventh Amendment immunity, and because most of the other relevant factors point the same way, we hold that school districts and their governing boards in New Mexico are not arms of the state, and they are accordingly not shielded by the Eleventh Amendment from liability for a §1983 action in federal court. . . .

For the foregoing reasons, we REVERSE the judgment of the district court, and REMAND for further proceedings.

CASE NOTES

1. In *Duke v. Grady Municipal Schools,* above, the court relied heavily on *Daddow v. Carlsbad Municipal School District,* 120 N.M. 97, 898 P.2d 1235 (1995), wherein the Supreme Court of New Mexico held that a school district and a board of education and its members are not absolutely immune from suit under Section 1983. Significantly, this court found that a local school board is not an "arm of the state" entitled to Eleventh Amendment immunity and can be sued under Section 1983. The court reasoned that local boards do not benefit from state Eleventh Amendment immunity based on the facts that (a) local school boards are statutorily defined as local public bodies, (b) local school boards have significant political and financial autonomy, and (c) local school boards operate like other local political subdivisions of the state. The court further concluded in its "arm of the state" analysis, for purposes of Section 1983 actions, that local board members are elected by popular vote from counties and precincts and that school boards acquire and dispose of property and have capacity to sue and be sued. All of these aspects lead to the conclusion that local school boards are local and not state entities. The U.S. Court of Appeals in *Duke* found the reasoning of the New Mexico Supreme Court in *Daddow* to be compelling in its decision to hold that local school districts are not "arms of the state" and are not entitled to Eleventh Amendment immunity.

2. The Supreme Court of New Mexico in *Daddow* further explained the Section 1983 liability of localities and, in so doing, provided what is probably the best guide to the status of local school district liability in view of the Eleventh Amendment restrictions. As noted above, this court was unequivocal in holding that local school districts are not immune from liability under the Eleventh Amendment and may be held liable in damages under Section 1983. In drawing its conclusions, the New Mexico court explained the importance of *Monell* in this way:

[The] question before the [U.S. Supreme] Court in *Monell v. Department of Social Serv.,* 436 U.S. 658, 98 S.Ct. 2018, 56 L.Ed.2d 611 (1978), was "[w]hether local governmental officials and/or local independent school boards are 'persons' within the meaning of 42 U.S.C. §1983 when equitable relief in the nature of back pay is sought against them in their official capacities." In answering that question affirmatively, the [Supreme] Court examined the precursor to §1983, the Civil Rights Act of 1871. The Court first determined that the word "persons" covered more than natural persons, and was intended to cover legal persons as well. The Court also noted that he meaning of the word "persons" was applied "to bodies politic and corporate . . . unless the context shows that such words were intended to be used in a more limited sense," and that a municipality is a "body politic and corporate." In looking at the legislative history of the Civil Rights Act, the Court stated that the Act was "intended to give a broad remedy for violations of federally-protected civil rights." Therefore, the Court concluded, "since municipalities through their official acts could, equally with natural persons, create the harms intended to be remedied by [the Civil Rights Act], and, further, since Congress intended [the Act] to be broadly construed, there is no reason to suppose that municipal corporations would have been excluded from the sweep of [the Act]."

As explained further by the New Mexico court:

The [Supreme Court] in *Monell* also overruled *Monroe v. Pape,* 365 U.S. 167, 191–92, 81 S.Ct. 473, 486–87, 5 L.Ed.2d 492 (1961), in which the court had previously held that municipalities were not "persons" under §1983. *Monell,* 436 U.S. at 701, 98 S.Ct. at 2041. However, the [Supreme Court in] *Monell* pointed out that even under the more restrictive *Monroe* approach, school boards had always been "persons" for the purposes of §1983. The [Supreme] Court noted that both municipalities and school boards are "instrumentalities of state administration." *Monell,* 436 U.S. at 696, 98 S.Ct. at 2038. It also emphasized that Congress had "rejected efforts to strip the federal courts of jurisdiction over school boards." We interpret *Monell's* broad holding that *all* "local governing bodies" are subject to suit under §1983 to create a presumption that local school boards are included within the meaning of "person."

Daddow v. Carlsbad Municipal School District, 120 N.M. 97, 898 P.2d 1233 (1995).

3. "The Eleventh Amendment is an explicit limitation of the judicial power of the United States." *Missouri v. Fiske,* 290 U.S. 18, 25, 54 S.Ct. 18, 20 (1933). It deprives a federal court of power to decide certain claims against states that otherwise would be within the scope of Article III's grant of jurisdiction. For example, if a lawsuit against state officials under 42 U.S.C.A. §1983 alleges a constitutional claim, the federal court is barred from awarding damages against the state treasury, even though the claim arises under the Constitution. See *Quern v. Jordan,* 440 U.S. 332, 99 S.Ct. 1139 (1979). Similarly, if a Section 1983 action alleging a constitutional claim is brought directly against a state, the Eleventh Amendment bars a federal court from granting any relief on that claim. See *Alabama v. Pugh,* 438 U.S. 781, 98 S.Ct. 3057 (1978) (per curiam). The amendment thus is a specific constitutional bar against even hearing federal claims that otherwise would be within the jurisdiction of the federal courts. *Pennhurst State School & Hospital v. Halderman,* 465 U.S. 89, 104 S.Ct. 900 (1984).

4. The Eleventh Amendment does not bar suits for prospective injunctive relief from unconstitutional actions by state officials. Inferior governmental bodies such as local school districts do not share Eleventh Amendment immunity simply because they receive state funds. *Fay v. South Colonie Central School District,* 802 F.2d 21 (2d Cir.1986).

5. In *Will v. Michigan Department of State Police,* 491 U.S. 58, 109 S.Ct. 2304 (1989), the U.S. Supreme Court determined that a "[s]uit against a state official in his or her official capacity is a suit not against the official, but rather against the official's office; as such, it is a suit no different from one against the state itself" and therefore barred by the Eleventh Amendment. Later, the Court in *Hafer v. Melo,* 502 U.S. 21, 112 S.Ct. 258 (1991), determined that the same state official may be liable when acting in his or her personal capacity. The Court stated, "The Eleventh Amendment does not bar [42 U.S.C.A.] Section 1983 personal-capacity suits against state officials in federal court."

■ ENDNOTES

1. F. Pollock and F. W. Maitland, *The History of English Law before the Time of Edward I* (Boston: Little, Brown, 1905).
2. Eugene T. Conners, "Governmental Immunity: Legal Basis and Implications for Public Education," Ph.D. dissertation, University of Florida, 1977.
3. Ibid.
4. The Case of the King's Prerogative in Saltpeter, 12 Co.Rep. 12 (1607).
5. Prohibitions del Roy, 12 Rep. 63 (1607).
6. Mersey Trustees v. Gibbs, L.R. 1 H.L. 93 (1866).
7. Crisp v. Thomas, 63 LINS 756 (1890).
8. 100 Eng.Rep. 359, 2 T.R. 667 (1788).
9. 9 Mass. 247 (1812).
10. The Siren, 74 U.S. (7 Wall.) 152 (1869).
11. Nichols v. United States, 74 U.S. (7 Wall.) 122 (1869).
12. 33 A.L.R.3d 703 (1970).
13. Molitor v. Kaneland Community Unit District No. 302, 18 Ill.2d 11, 163 N.E.2d 89 (1959).
14. Muskopf v. Corning Hospital District, 55 Cal.2d 211, 11 Cal.Rptr. 89, 359 P.2d 457 (1961).
15. 33 A.L.R.3d 703 (1970).
16. W. Page Keeton, Dan B. Dobbs, Robert E. Keeton, and David G. Owen, *Prosser and Keeton on Torts,* 5th ed. (St. Paul, Minn.: West, 1984), p. 1044.
17. Maryland and Mississippi; Keeton et al., *Prosser and Keeton on Torts,* p. 1044.
18. Alabama, Arkansas, Georgia, Kentucky, North Carolina, Tennessee, West Virginia, and Wisconsin. Keeton et al. observe here that some states may retain immunity at the state level but waive immunity of political subdivisions at the local level. Keeton et al., *Prosser and Keeton on Torts,* p. 1044.
19. See Norwin School District v. Cortazzo, 625 A.2d 183 (1993).
20. Keeton et al., *Prosser and Keeton on Torts,* p. 1044.
21. Ibid., p. 1045.
22. *Restatement (Second) of Torts,* vol. 4, §895B, pp. 399–400.
23. Ibid., pp. 402–3.
24. Dalehite v. United States, 346 U.S. 15, 73 S.Ct. 956 (1953).
25. *Restatement (Second) of Torts,* vol. 4, §895B, p. 404.
26. Keeton et al., *Prosser and Keeton on Torts,* p. 1050.
27. *Restatement (Second) of Torts,* vol. 4, §895D, p. 415.
28. See *Black's Law Dictionary,* 7th ed. (St. Paul, Minn.: West Publishing Company, 1999), p. 553.
29. Ibid., p. 1148.
30. *Restatement (Second) of Torts,* vol. 4, §895D, pp. 416–17.
31. Keeton et al., *Prosser and Keeton on Torts,* p. 1045.

32. Crowell v. School District No. 7, 805 P.2d 552 (Mont.1991). See also *Hedges v. Swan Lake and Salmon Prairie School District No. 73,* 812 P.2d 334 (Mont.1991).

33. See Charles Gabus Ford, Inc. v. Iowa State Highway Commission, 224 N.W.2d 639 (Iowa 1974).

34. Sawaya v. Tucson High School District No. 1, 78 Ariz. 389, 281 P.2d 105 (1955).

35. Reed v. Rhea County, 189 Tenn. 247, 225 S.W.2d 49 (1949).

36. Koehn v. Board of Education of City of Newton, 193 Kan. 263, 392 P.2d 949 (1964).

37. Rankin v. School District No. 9, 143 Or. 449, 23 P.2d 132 (1933).

38. Ross v. Consumers Power Co., 420 Mich. 567, 363 N.W.2d 641 (1984) (italics added).

39. Stout v. Grand Prairie Independent School District, 733 S.W.2d 290 (Tex. App.–Dallas 1987).

40. Ibid., p. 296.

41. Boneau v. Swift & Co., 66 S.W.2d 172, 175 (Mo.App.1934).

42. Beehler v. Daniels, 18 R.I. 563, 29 A. 6 (1894).

43. Bush v. City of Norwalk, 122 Conn. 426, 189 A. 608 (1937).

44. Ferris v. Board of Education of Detroit, 122 Mich. 315, 81 N.W. 98 (1899).

45. Jones v. Kansas City, 176 Kan. 406, 271 P.2d 803 (1954).

46. Rose v. Board of Education, 184 Kan. 486, 337 P.2d 652 (1959).

47. Michael G. Collins, *Section 1983 Litigation in a Nutshell* (St. Paul, Minn.: West, 1997), p. 1.

48. Ibid., p. 151; Carey v. Piphus, 435 U.S. 247, 98 S.Ct. 1042 (1978).

49. 365 U.S. 167, 81 S.Ct. 473 (1961).

50. 42 U.S.C.A. §1983, enacted 1871.

51. Ernest W. Williams, "Liability of Public Schools and Public School Officials for Damages under 42 U.S.C. 1983," J.D. thesis, Harvard Law School, 1975, p. 1.

52. Home Tel. & Tel. Co. v. Los Angeles, 227 U.S. 278, 33 S.Ct. 312 (1913).

53. Collins, *Section 1983 Litigation,* p. 19.

54. 436 U.S. 658, 98 S.Ct. 2018 (1978).

55. 420 U.S. 308, 95 S.Ct. 992 (1975).

56. 435 U.S. 247, 98 S.Ct. 1042 (1978).

57. Seminole Tribe of Florida v. Florida, 517 U.S. 44, 116 S.Ct. 1114 (1996).

58. Monell v. Department of Social Services of City of New York, 436 U.S. 658, 98 S.Ct. 2018 (1978).

59. 475 U.S. 469, 106 S.Ct. 1292 (1986).

60. Bennett v. City of Slidell, 728 F.2d 762 (5th Cir.1984).

61. Ibid.

62. Parratt v. Taylor, 451 U.S. 527, 101 S.Ct. 1908 (1981).

63. Daniels v. Williams, 474 U.S. 327, 106 S.Ct. 662 (1986).

64. 814 F.2d 1283 (8th Cir.1987).

65. Ibid., p. 1284. See also Garcia v. Miera, 817 F.2d 650 (10th Cir.1987); Taylor v. Ledbetter, 818 F.2d 791 (11th Cir.1987).

66. Kibbe v. City of Springfield, 77 F.2d 801 (1st Cir.1985), cert. granted, 475 U.S. 1064, 106 S.Ct. 1374 (1986), cert. dismissed, 480 U.S. 257, 107 S.Ct. 1114 (1987).

67. Mitchell v. Forsyth, 472 U.S. 511, 105 S.Ct. 2806 (1985).

68. Davis v. Scherer, 468 U.S. 183, 104 S.Ct. 3012 (1984).

69. Harlow v. Fitzgerald, 457 U.S. 800, 102 S.Ct. 2727 (1982).

70. Jeffrey J. Horner, "The Anatomy of a Constitutional Tort," West's Educ. L. Rep. 47 (1988): p. 13.

71. Mt. Healthy City School District Board of Education v. Doyle, 429 U.S. 274, 97 S.Ct. 568 (1977).

72. Edelman v. Jordan, 415 U.S. 651, 94 S.Ct. 1347 (1974).

73. Article VI, §2, of the Ohio Constitution states, "The general assembly shall make such provision . . . as . . . will secure a thorough and efficient system of common schools throughout the state. . . . "

74. Monell v. Department of Social Services of City of New York, 436 U.S. 658, 98 S.Ct. 2018 (1978).

75. Alabama v. Pugh, 438 U.S. 781, 98 S.Ct. 3057 (1978).

76. Minton v. St. Bernard Parish School Board, 803 F.2d 129 (5th Cir.1986): Also, Duke v. Grady Municipal Schools, 127 F.3d 972 (1997).

77. Mt. Healthy, op. cit. See also Clark v. Tarrant County, Texas, 798 F.2d 736, 748 (5th Cir.1986).

78. Minton, 803 F.2d at 131.

CHAPTER 14

CERTIFICATION, CONTRACTS, AND TENURE

[I]t would be my aim again, to make better teachers, and especially better teachers for our common schools . . . teachers who would know more of the nature of children, of youthful development, more of the subjects to be taught, and more of the methods of teaching them. . . . In short, I was desirous of putting our schools in the hands of those who would make them places in which children could learn, not only to read and write and spell and cipher, but where they would have all their faculties trained in such harmony as would result in the highest formation of character.

—Cyrus Pierce, 1851

CHAPTER OUTLINE

- CERTIFICATION
- TEACHER CONTRACTS
- THE TENURE CONTRACT
- INCOMPETENCY
- INSUBORDINATION

- IMMORALITY
- CAUSE OR GOOD CAUSE
- REDUCTION IN FORCE
- CONSTITUTIONAL PROTECTION OF CONTRACTS

THE EMPLOYMENT CONDITIONS of public school teachers are governed by state statutory and regulatory policy. Because public education is exclusively a state function, the state may set the criteria for eligibility, qualification, and certification of teachers. The state in exercise of its sovereign power to provide for an efficient system of public schools for the enhancement of the welfare of the people can establish the conditions and requirements necessary to become a public school teacher:

A person has no constitutional right to be employed as a teacher in the public schools, as such employment is not an uninhibited privilege and he (or she) has no right to serve except on such terms as the state prescribes.[1]

A state at its option may have no certificate requirements, or it can establish complex conditions precedent to employment, with regard to experience, education, test scores, or any number of conditions that may be considered important to one's ability to teach. Too, the state may prescribe the contractual relationship between the teacher and the school board and, if it wishes, may create special contractual conditions pertaining to terms and conditions of employment. The actual contract between teacher and school board may be for any period of time but is usually annual, or there may be a statutorily created long-term arrangement of indefinite length known as a tenure or continuing contract. The conditions for such contracts, though, are prescribed by law, and teachers must agree to the legal conditions if they are to have and retain public school employment.

Common law precedents pertaining to contracts may be relied on by the courts when litigation arises regarding disputed statutory application or interpretation. Beyond specific statutory and regulatory provisions and relevant common law applications, the courts may, too, be called upon to determine the lawfulness of state restrictions or restraints on employment that may adversely affect teachers' constitutional rights.

Thus, the law pertaining to teacher employment in public schools derives from state statutory and regulatory prescriptions with a gloss of common law precedents where there is a lack of clarity. Too, the employment relationship is greatly affected by state and federal constitutional prohibitions that prevent government from arbitrarily and unilaterally denying a teacher a basic and fundamental constitutional right or interest.

This chapter is concerned with the eligibility and certification of teachers, their limited and tenure contractual relationships with school boards, and the conditions under which those relationships can be terminated. This chapter also deals with constitutional interests of teachers to the extent that they are affected by the obligation-of-contracts provision of the U.S. Constitution. Teachers' due process interests, their rights, and their freedoms under the U.S. Bill of Rights and Fourteenth Amendment, as well as their rights under federal antidiscrimination statutory provisions, are discussed in subsequent chapters.

■ CERTIFICATION

All state legislatures have enacted laws relating to the certification of teachers, and when such laws are properly promulgated with no intent to discriminate, and are not arbitrary, they will be upheld by the courts. These laws run the gamut from great particularity to gross generality. Thus, it is necessary to consider the specific laws of each state individually to determine specific certification requirements.

The general rule is that if a teacher satisfies all the requirements set forth in the statutes and regulations relative to the issuance of a certificate, the certifying body may not arbitrarily refuse to issue the certificate. However, in most cases, the certificate-issuing body is vested with discretionary authority. Also, the issuing agency may, in many instances, prescribe higher standards for certification than are contained in laws enacted by a state legislature.

BACKGROUND

Early schools in the United States were deficient for many reasons, but the most important reason was the lack of well-educated and -trained professional teachers. Few teachers were well versed in subject matter, and still fewer knew the techniques of teaching. Early schools were usually staffed by itinerant teachers, who were interviewed and hired by local school trustees, who themselves were ofttimes illiterate or only vaguely aware of the qualifications necessary to good teaching. Very little serious thought was given to the education and training of teachers in America until the mid–nineteenth century. The late beginnings of teacher education in this country tracked the general disinterest in public schools by parents who chose to send their children to private schools, where the teachers were equally poorly prepared, or who ignored formal education entirely, placing their children directly in the workforce at a very early age.

The Prussians had much earlier recognized the need for adequately trained teachers and had between 1750 and 1794 established dozens of seminaries for the special training of elementary school teachers. By 1808, the new French government under Napoleon had established the *École Normale Supérieure*, a higher-education normal school; between 1831 and 1833, France created thirty new normal schools for teacher training. It was not until 1839 that the first legislatively authorized normal school in America was established under the leadership of Horace

Mann in Lexington, Massachusetts.[2] Cubberley has commented on the trials and tribulations of this first teacher training school:

> The opening of this first school was not particularly auspicious. Ignorance, bigotry, and economy were arrayed against the undertaking. Few knew what such a school was to be. Many teachers regarded its creation as derogatory to them. Many academies did not especially welcome its completion. Not a note of congratulations welcomed its new principal to his post.[3]

Slowly, other states began to create normal schools in the realization that teachers should be especially trained in both subject matter and teaching methods. Most knowledgeable persons agreed that the study of didactics by teachers was essential if the public school was to be efficient and effective. Providing for well-trained personnel, however, addressed only part of the problem. The local orientation and control of public schools had produced the prevailing practice of lay certification through examination with little or no statewide coordination for quality control or continuity. It was said that even with the development of teacher training programs, many localities continued to indulge in "schoolkeeping," a system in which young, unmarried, and unqualified women taught while they were "anticipating marriage" or in which "traveling Ichabod Cranes *kept* school rather than professional teachers *teaching*" school.[4]

It was at this time proposed that the solution to the quality problem lay in "establishing a well-organized state system of examinations" managed at the local level by professional educators, superintendents, and professional teachers.[5] It was reasoned that certification should be granted to teachers by professional educators "for the same reason that only lawyers can legally examine law students applying for admission to the bar, that only physicians can legally examine medical students, and that only clergymen pass on the fitness of theological students to enter the ministry."[6] The nature of public schools as governmental agencies, however, prevented the implementation of such certification proposals. Eventually, a quasi-professional system was adopted whereby teacher training colleges would train and recommend certification of teachers to a state educational agency,

which would in turn issue teaching certificates. It was believed that this process was more effective than certification based upon lay examination or even statewide teacher tests for certification with little or no requisite education or training.

Partially because of the experiences of the past, the public today apparently believes that teachers should meet the rigors of certain prescribed academic attainment as evaluated by institutions of higher education as well as teacher tests in order to acquire a license to teach. This license itself is a certificate issued by the state, recognizing that a person is presumptively qualified to teach in the public schools. In this manner, the state extends some surety to the child and the taxpayer that the public schools are protected against "charlatans, ignoramuses, and humbugs"[7] masquerading as teachers.

REQUIREMENTS

Most states require that an applicant for a teaching certificate be of good moral character. To remain eligible for either continued certification or renewal of an existing certificate, the teacher must continue to evidence good moral character.

Besides good moral character, state law generally requires that applicants have successfully completed a predetermined number of college credits in the subject that the individual plans to teach (e.g., English). In 1980, only a few states required aspiring teachers to pass a test to become eligible for certification. By 1989–90, the number of states requiring state-prescribed standardized tests as a condition for entering the teaching profession numbered thirty-nine. All fifty states approve the content of teacher education programs conducted by colleges and universities.[8] States, too, generally require the individual to be of a specified age (usually eighteen or older) and a citizen of the United States. Some states require the pledging of loyalty to the state and/or federal constitution and, in recent years, have required the completion of an examination, such as the National Teacher Examination.

Teacher certification does not guarantee employment. State legislatures have delegated the authority for employment of teachers to local school boards. Local boards have been given wide latitude and may place additional requirements or restrictions on employment as long as these rules do not contradict or reduce the effect of state requirements. Neither can such rules violate one's constitutional or statutory rights. Local boards cannot impose requirements that are arbitrary, capricious, or enacted in bad faith.

Some additional requirements that have been upheld include mandating greater academic credentials than those established by the state and having employees take additional academic courses after employment.[9] School boards have been upheld in requiring teachers to establish residency within the boundaries of the school district,[10] restricting outside employment, adopting reasonable health and physical requirements (within federal and state provisions for the handicapped), assigning (within state statutes) teachers to teaching positions, and mandating the supervising of extracurricular activities.

Statute Forbidding Certification to Persons Who Are Not Citizens and Have Manifested No Intent to Become Citizens Is Not Violative of Equal Protection

Ambach v. Norwick

Supreme Court of the United States, 1979.
441 U.S. 68, 99 S.Ct. 1589.

Mr. Justice POWELL delivered the opinion of the Court. This case presents the question whether a State, consistently with the Equal Protection Clause of the Fourteenth Amendment, may refuse to employ as elementary and secondary school teachers aliens who are eligible for United States citizenship but who refuse to seek naturalization.

New York Education Law §3001(3) forbids certification as a public school teacher of any person who is not a citizen of the United States, unless that person has manifested an intention to apply for citizenship. The Commissioner of Education is authorized to create exemptions from this prohibition, and has done so with respect to aliens who are not yet eligible for cit-

izenship. Unless a teacher obtains certification, he may not work in a public elementary or secondary school in New York.

Appellee Norwick was born in Scotland and is a subject of Great Britain. She has resided in this country since 1965 and is married to a United States citizen. Appellee Dachinger is a Finnish subject who came to this country in 1966 and also is married to a United States citizen. Both Norwick and Dachinger currently meet all of the educational requirements New York has set for certification as a public school teacher, but they consistently have refused to seek citizenship in spite of their eligibility to do so. Norwick applied in 1973 for a teaching certificate covering nursery school through sixth grade, and Dachinger sought a certificate covering the same grades in 1975. Both applications were denied because of appellees' failure to meet the requirements of §3001(3). Norwick then filed this suit seeking to enjoin the enforcement of §3001(3), and Dachinger obtained leave to intervene as a plaintiff. . . .

Applying the rational basis standard, we held last term that New York could exclude aliens from the ranks of its police force. *Foley v. Connelie*, 435 U.S. 291, 98 S.Ct. 1067, 55 L.Ed.2d 287 (1978). Because the police function fulfilled "a most fundamental obligation of government to its constituency" and by necessity cloaked policemen with substantial discretionary powers, we viewed the police force as being one of those appropriately defined classes of positions for which a citizenship requirement could be imposed. Accordingly, the State was required to justify its classification only "by a showing of some rational relationship between the interest sought to be protected and the limiting classification."

The rule for governmental functions, which is an exception to the general standard applicable to classifications based on alienage, rests on important principles inherent in the Constitution. The distinction between citizens and aliens, though ordinarily irrelevant to private activity, is fundamental to the definition and government of a State. The Constitution itself refers to the distinction no less than eleven times, see *Sugarman v. Dougall* (Rehnquist, J., dissenting), indicating that the status of citizenship was meant to have significance in the structure of our government. The assumption of that status, whether by birth or naturalization, denotes an association with the polity which, in a democratic republic, exercises the powers of governance. The form of this association is important: an oath of allegiance or similar ceremony cannot substitute for the unequivocal legal bond citizenship represents. It is because of this special significance of citizenship that governmental entities, when exercising the functions of government, have wider latitude in limiting the participation of noncitizens.

In determining whether, for purposes of equal protection analysis, teaching in public schools constitutes a governmental function, we look to the role of public education and to the degree of responsibility and discretion teachers possess in fulfilling that role. Each of these considerations supports the conclusion that public school teachers may be regarded as performing a task "that go[es] to the heart of representative government."

Public education, like the police function, "fulfills a most fundamental obligation of government to its constituency." The importance of public schools in the preparation of individuals for participation as citizens, and in the preservation of the values on which our society rests, long has been recognized by our decisions:

> Today, education is perhaps the most important function of state and local governments. Compulsory school attendance laws and the great expenditures for education both demonstrate our recognition of the importance of education to our democratic society. It is required in the performance of our most basic public responsibilities, even service in the armed forces. It is the very foundation of good citizenship. Today it is a principal instrument in awakening the child to cultural values, in preparing him for later professional training, and in helping him to adjust normally to his environment. *Brown v. Board of Education*, 347 U.S. 483, 493, 74 S.Ct. 686, 691, 98 L.Ed. 873 (1954).

. . . Other authorities have perceived public schools as an "assimilative force" by which diverse and conflicting elements in our society are brought together on a broad but common ground. . . . These perceptions of the public schools as inculcating fundamental values necessary to the maintenance of a democratic political system have been confirmed by the observations of social scientists. . . .

Within the public school system, teachers play a critical part in developing students' attitude toward government and understanding the role of citizens in our society. Alone among employees of the system, teachers are in direct, day-to-day contact with students both in the classrooms and in the other varied activities of a modern school. In shaping the students' experience to achieve educational goals, teachers by necessity have wide discretion over the way the course material is communicated to students. They are responsible for presenting and explaining the subject matter in a way that is both comprehensible and inspiring. No amount of standardization of teaching materials or lesson plans can eliminate the personal qualities a teacher brings to bear in achieving these goals. Further, a teacher serves as a role model for his students, exerting a subtle but important influence over their perceptions and values. Thus, through both the presentation of course materials and the example he sets, a teacher has an opportunity to influence the attitudes of students toward government, the political process, and a citizen's social responsibilities. This influence is crucial to the continued good health of a democracy.

Furthermore, it is clear that all public school teachers, and not just those responsible for teaching the courses most directly related to government, history, and civic duties, should help fulfill the broader function of the public school system. Teachers, regardless of their specialty, may be called upon to teach other subjects, including those expressly dedicated to political and social subjects. More importantly, a State properly may regard all teachers as having an obligation to promote civic virtues and understanding in their classes, regardless of the subject taught. Certainly a State also may take account of a teacher's function as an example for students, which exists independently of particular classroom subjects. In light of the foregoing considerations, we think it clear that public school teachers come well within the "governmental function" principle recognized in *Sugarman* and *Foley*. Accordingly, the Constitution requires only that a citizenship requirement applicable to teaching in the public schools bears a rational relationship to a legitimate state interest. . . .

As the legitimacy of the State's interest in furthering the educational goals outlined above is undoubted, it remains only to consider whether §3001(3) bears a rational relationship to this interest. The restriction is carefully framed to serve its purpose, as it bars from teaching only those aliens who have demonstrated their unwillingness to obtain United States citizenship. Appellees, and aliens similarly situated, in effect have chosen to classify themselves. They prefer to retain citizenship in a foreign country with the obligations it entails of primary duty and loyalty. They have rejected the open invitation extended to qualify for eligibility to teach by applying for citizenship in this country. The people of New York, acting through their elected representatives, have made a judgment that citizenship should be a qualification for teaching the young of the State in the public schools, and §3001(3) furthers that judgment.

Reversed.

❖ — ❖ — ❖

Employee Residency Requirements Are Constitutional

Wardwell v. Board of Education of the City School District of the City of Cincinnati

United States Court of Appeals,
Sixth Circuit, 1976.
529 F.2d 625.

WILLIAM E. MILLER, Circuit Judge. In December, 1972, plaintiff, Terry Wardwell, was hired to teach in the Cincinnati schools. As a condition of employment he agreed to move into the city school district pursuant to a rule announced by the school superintendent in November, 1972, that all newly employed teachers must establish residence within the district within thirty days after employment. In January, 1973, the Board adopted the following resolution, essentially ratifying the superintendent's rule:

> RESOLVED, That any employee hired by the Cincinnati Schools after November 13, 1972, must either reside within the Cincinnati School District, or agree, as a condition of employment, to establish residency within the district within ninety days of employment. Employees who live in the district must continue to reside therein as long as they are so employed. This policy does not affect in any way personnel hired before the above date.

Plaintiff Wardwell lived outside the district but within the State of Ohio. Despite the requirement he failed to change his residence. He filed the present action in July, 1973, under 28 U.S.C. §1343 and 42 U.S.C. §1983, challenging the residency requirement on equal protection grounds and seeking injunctive relief and attorney's fees. . . .

The district court denied the request for an injunction and upheld the validity of the rule, relying heavily on the Fifth Circuit's reasoning in *Wright v. City of Jackson*, 506 F.2d 900 (5th Cir.1975).

Plaintiff argues that the Board's residency requirement infringes his constitutionally protected right to travel as defined in *Shapiro v. Thompson*, 394 U.S. 618, 89 S.Ct. 1322, 22, L.Ed.2d 600 (1969), and in *Dunn v. Blumstein*, 405 U.S. 330, 92 S.Ct. 995, 31 L.Ed.2d 274 (1972), extending the protection, as he contends, to both intrastate and interstate travel and embracing as a necessary corollary the right to remain in one place.

We find no support for plaintiff's theory that the right to intrastate travel has been afforded federal constitutional protection. An examination of *Shapiro*, supra, *Dunn*, supra, and the Supreme Court's more recent opinion in *Memorial Hospital v. Maricopa County*, 415 U.S. 250, 94 S.Ct. 1076, 39 L.Ed.2d 306 (1974), convinces us that the aspect of the right to travel with which the Court was concerned in those cases is not involved here. It is clear that the Court was dealing with the validity of durational residency requirements which penalized recent interstate travel. Such durational residency requirements or restrictions affecting the interstate aspect of travel will not pass constitutional muster "absent a compelling state interest." . . .

Our conclusion that *Shapiro* and the other right-to-travel cases are not applicable to intrastate travel and *continuing* employee residency requirements is supported by *Detroit Police Officers Association v. City of Detroit*, 405 U.S. 950, 92

S.Ct. 1173, 31 L.Ed.2d 227 (1972), on which the district court in this case and the Fifth Circuit in *Wright,* supra, relied. The case involved a Detroit residency requirement for policemen. The Michigan Supreme Court, applying the "rational basis test," determined that the classification bore a reasonable relationship to the object of the legislation and was therefore valid. *Detroit Police Officers Association v. City of Detroit,* 385 Mich. 519, 190 N.W.2d 97 (1971). The Supreme Court in a brief order dismissed the appeal "for want of a substantial federal question." . . . We conclude that the "compelling state interest" test is the applicable test in cases involving infringement of the right to interstate travel by *durational* residency requirements. On the other hand, where, as in the present case, a continuing employee residency requirement affecting at most the right of intrastate travel is involved, the "rational basis" test is the touchstone to determine its validity.

We find a number of rational bases for the residency requirement of the Cincinnati School Board. The Cincinnati school superintendent testified that promulgation of the rule was based on the following conclusions: (1) such a requirement aids in hiring teachers who are highly motivated and deeply committed to an urban educational system, (2) teachers who live in the district are more likely to vote for district taxes, less likely to engage in illegal strikes, and more likely to help obtain passage of school tax levies, (3) teachers living in the district are more likely to be involved in school and community activities bringing them in contact with parents and community leaders and are more likely to be committed to the future of the district and its schools, (4) teachers who live in the district are more likely to gain sympathy and understanding for the racial, social, economic, and urban problems of the children they teach and are thus less likely to be considered isolated from the communities in which they teach, (5) the requirement is in keeping with the goal of encouraging integration in society and in the schools. These conclusions appear to us clearly to establish rational bases for the residency requirement imposed by the Cincinnati Board. . . .

. . . [A]ppellant argues that the residency requirement is invalid because it requires newly hired teachers to move into and remain in the district and permits those already hired to remain or move outside the district. Appellee replies that distinguishing between new teachers and teachers with experience, who may have tenure and who did not know of the requirement when they accepted employment, is a reasonable distinction which the state is free to make. While we recognize that the limited applicability of the rule may be its most questionable feature, we do not believe that the residency requirement must fail because it does not apply to all teachers employed by the Cincinnati schools. The Supreme Court has pointed out that there is no constitutional requirement that regulations must cover every class to which they might be applied. It has further stated that "if the classification has some reasonable basis, it does not offend the constitution simply because the classification 'is not made with mathematical nicety or because in practice it results in some inequality.'"

Affirmed.

CASE NOTES

1. Where a school board policy required that certified personnel reside within the district or within a ten-mile driving distance of the limits of the school district and a teacher moved seventeen miles outside the district, her contract was not renewed. The court found that the policy had a rational basis, such as the necessity of community involvement. *McClelland v. Paris Public Schools,* 294 Ark. 292, 742 S.W.2d 907 (1988). See also *Mogle v. Sevier County School District,* 540 F.2d 478 (10th Cir.1976); *Simien v. City of San Antonio,* 809 F.2d 255 (5th Cir.1987).

2. Some states have passed legislation prohibiting municipalities from establishing residency requirements. The California Constitution states, "A city or county . . . may not require that its employees be residents of such city, county, or district; except that such employees may be required to reside within a reasonable and specific distance of their place of employment or other designated location."

3. City employees employed prior to the effective date of a residency requirement may be

exempt. *Providence Teachers Union Local No. 958 v. Napolitano*, 554 A.2d 641 (R.I.1989).

❖ — ❖ — ❖

Certificate May Be Denied When State Board Has Evidence to Question Good Moral Character of Applicant

Application of Bay

Supreme Court of Oregon, 1963.
233 Or. 601, 378 P.2d 558.

PERRY, Justice. Dean Norman Bay petitioned the circuit court of Union County for judicial review of the decision of appellant State Board of Education denying him issuance of a five-year elementary teacher's certificate. From the decree of the circuit court reversing the Board's decision for lack of competent evidence, appeal is made to this court.

In December of 1953, petitioner was tried and convicted in the state of Washington for his acts of breaking, entering, and grand larceny of several stores, the American Legion Club, and the local high school, committed while employed as a night policeman. At the time these acts were perpetrated, petitioner was twenty-four years old. After serving eighteen months of a two-year sentence, he was paroled. He moved to La Grande, Oregon, where, in the fall of 1956 he enrolled at the Eastern Oregon College of Education. In 1958 the state of Washington restored to him his full civil rights.

In 1960 petitioner was granted a one-year elementary teacher's emergency certificate by the Superintendent of Public Instruction, and taught elementary school while completing his fourth year at the college. Following graduation he applied for a five-year elementary teacher's certificate, but his application was denied on June 14, 1961.

On September 13, 1961, a hearing was conducted before the Board, the primary purpose of which was to determine whether petitioner had furnished the evidence of good moral character which ORS 342.060(2) authorizes the superintendent to require of an applicant. Whereas numerous witnesses appeared at the hearing to testify of petitioner's good character and overall reputation in the community, the sole evidence of bad character introduced was the record of the prior conviction. The Board concluded that petitioner had not met his burden of furnishing satisfactory evidence of good moral character and he thereupon petitioned the circuit court of Union County for review of the administrative order pursuant to ORS 183.480. The court held that evidence as to a prior conviction was irrelevant and immaterial in determining present character where not accompanied by other evidence which related the prior act to the present, and therefore adjudged there was no competent evidence to support the Board's findings. The Board was ordered to issue petitioner the certificate, from which order this appeal is taken. . . .

In order to properly discuss the issues presented it is first necessary to discuss the powers of the trial court in reviewing the Board's determination.

While the statute uses the language "as a suit in equity," it is quite clear that this language refers only to the fact that the review shall be made by the court, not a jury, and does not grant to a trial court the right on appeal to try the case de novo. That is, the reviewing court is not granted the power to weigh the evidence and substitute its judgment as to the preponderance thereof for that of the agency. The extent to which a reviewing court should review the action of an administrative agency has been expressed by this court as follows:

> Generally, they go no further than to determine whether the agency (1) acted impartially; (2) performed faithfully the duties delineated in the legislative acts which conferred jurisdiction upon it; (3) stayed within its jurisdiction; (4) committed no error of law; (5) exercised discretion judiciously and not capriciously; and (6) arrived at no conclusion which was clearly wrong. *Richardson v. Neuner*, 183 Or. 558, 564, 194 P.2d 989, 991.

The learned trial court recognized these guideposts and reached the conclusion that the finding of the Board as to lack of good moral character could not be sustained by the record. This conclusion of the court is based upon a finding that there was no evidence of bad moral character at the time of application and therefore the Board's conclusion was clearly wrong.

Whether or not the Board arrived at a conclusion which was clearly wrong depends upon whether a review of the entire record discloses any facts from which the conclusion drawn by the Board could be reached by reasonable minds. . . .

The Board made the following findings of fact which are pertinent to this appeal:

1. That the applicant on December 9, 1953, was convicted of grand larceny of four counts in the Superior Court for Klickitat County, State of Washington and received a one- to fifteen-year sentence by the said Court. That thereafter this sentence was fixed at a term of two years by the State Board of Terms and Parole of the State of Washington, and the applicant served an eighteen-month term at the Monroe Reformatory in the State of Washington.
2. Thereafter upon his release he was placed on parole for approximately a year and moved to the City of LaGrande, Oregon, and in the fall of 1956 entered the Eastern Oregon College of Education and enrolled in a teacher education course.
3. That by act of the Governor of the State of Washington full civil rights were restored to him on July 3, 1958. . . .
4. The Board further finds the offenses committed by Mr. Bay consisted of breaking and entering various stores in Goldendale, Washington, and grand larceny, and included safe burglaries at the American Legion Club, and Goldendale High School. That at the time he committed the offenses for which he was imprisoned he had reached the age of twenty-four years; that his offenses numbered not one but several; that he was a man of superior intelligence as evidenced by his scores on intelligence tests in his subsequent college record.
5. The Board further finds that at the time of the thefts he occupied a position of trust as a night policeman in the community and that

while so engaged he committed the acts resulting in his conviction.
6. That a teacher in a public school is the key factor in teaching by precept and example the subjects of honesty, morality, courtesy, obedience to law, and other lessons of a steadying influence which tend to promote and develop an upright and desirable citizenry, as required by ORS 336.240 and related statutes.
7. That there has been no evidence submitted to the Board of any violations of law or deviations from normally considered moral conduct from the time of his release from the Monroe Reformatory to the present time.

The Board then made the following conclusions of law:

1. That the applicant has not furnished evidence of good moral character deemed satisfactory and necessary by the Board to establish the applicant's fitness to serve as a teacher.

In resolving the question of moral character there must be kept in mind the distinction between character and reputation. "Character is what a man or woman is morally, while reputation is what he or she is reputed to be." *Leverich v. Frank,* 6 Or. 212; *State v. Charlie Sing,* 114 Or. 267, 229 P. 921.

> A person's "character" is usually thought to embrace all his qualities and deficiencies regarding traits of personality, behavior, integrity, temperament, consideration, sportsmanship, altruism, etc. which distinguish him as a human being from his fellow men. His disposition toward criminal acts is only one of the qualities which constitute his character.

Since the crux of the question before the Board was good moral character, the fact that he had been guilty of burglarizing properties while he held a position of trust was most pertinent. These actions of petitioner clearly evidenced a lack of the moral fiber to resist temptation. The trial court therefore erred in holding there was no evidence of lack of good moral character.

The petitioner offered numerous witnesses from which a conclusion might properly be reached that this lack of moral fiber no longer exists. However, this condition having been shown to have existed, it became a matter of judgment as to whether it had been overcome.

The power to decide such an issue was delegated by the legislature to the Board of Education, therefore, as previously pointed out, the courts are not permitted to substitute their judgment for that of the Board where there is substantial evidence to support the agency.

The judgment of the trial court is reversed with instructions to enter findings of fact and conclusions of law sustaining the action of the Board of Education.

CASE NOTES

1. One of the basic purposes of the certification laws is to provide a capable and competent instructor in every classroom. Consequently, not only is a teaching certificate a prerequisite to employment and reemployment, but also it is necessary for schools to qualify for state aid. It is a common practice in several states to permit student teachers to assume complete control of a class in the absence of the regular teacher. This violates not only the spirit, but also the letter of the law of many states because a student teacher is not a qualified teacher but is seeking to become a qualified teacher. If a teacher teaches without a certificate, she or he is considered to be a volunteer and is entitled to no compensation for services rendered. See *Floyd County Board of Education v. Slone*, 307 S.W.2d 912 (Ky.1957).

2. A teacher who had no certificate when entering into an employment contract with a school board could not recover salary for services rendered, even though he or she had obtained the license prior to actually beginning work. *McCloskey v. School District*, 134 Mich. 235, 96 N.W. 18 (1903); *O'Conner v. Francis*, 42 App.Div. 375, 59 N.Y.S. 28 (1899); *Lee v. Mitchell*, 108 Ark. 1, 156 S.W. 450 (1913).

3. "Our contention and the legislative enactments support [the teacher's] contention that the grant of a certificate from the State Board of Education inherently carries with it a presumption of competence, interest and training in the subjects designated." *Bauer v. Board of Education, Unified School District No. 452*, 244 Kan. 6, 765 P.2d 1129 (1988).

Teacher's Adultery Insufficient to Support Revocation of Certificate

Erb v. Iowa State Board of Public Instruction

Supreme Court of Iowa, 1974.
216 N.W.2d 339.

McCORMICK, Justice. In this appeal plaintiff Richard Arlan Erb challenges the revocation of his teaching certificate. The certificate was revoked by defendant Board of Educational Examiners after a hearing on July 16, 1971. Erb brought an action in certiorari alleging the board's action was illegal. After trial the writ of certiorari was annulled. Erb appealed. We reverse.

Under Code §260.1, the State Board of Public Instruction constitutes the Board of Educational Examiners. Code §260.2 empowers the examining board to issue teaching certificates "to applicants who are eighteen years of age or over, physically competent and morally fit to teach, and who have the [required] qualifications and training. . . . "

Erb, a native Iowan, military veteran, and holder of a master's degree in fine arts, received his Iowa teaching certificate in 1963. Since then he has taught art in the Nishna Valley Community School which serves an area including the towns of Strahn, Emerson, Hastings, and Stanton. He resides in Emerson, is married and has two young sons. In addition to teaching he has coached wrestling, assisted with football, and acted as senior class sponsor.

The complaint against Erb was made by Robert M. Johnson, a farmer whose wife Margaret taught home economics in the Nishna Valley School. Johnson told the board his goal was removal of Erb from the school and not revocation of his teaching certificate. He read an extensive statement in which he detailed his observations relating to an adulterous liaison between Erb and Johnson's wife which began and ended in spring 1970.

Margaret planned to quit teaching and open a boutique in Red Oak. Her association with Erb began in early spring when he agreed to assist her with design of the store. They saw each other often. By May, Johnson became suspicious of Margaret's frequent late-night absences from home. He suspected Margaret and Erb were meeting secretly and engaging in illicit activity in the Johnson automobile. One night in May he hid in the trunk of the car. Margaret drove the car to school, worked there for some time, and later drove to a secluded area in the country where she met Erb. Margaret and Erb had sexual intercourse in the back seat of the car while Johnson remained hidden in the trunk. Johnson did not disclose his presence or his knowledge of the incident.

Instead he consulted a lawyer with a view toward divorcing Margaret. He told the board he was advised his interests in a divorce action would be better served if he had other witnesses to his wife's misconduct. After several days of fruitless effort to catch Margaret and Erb in a compromising situation, he and his "raiding party" eventually located them one night in June parked in a remote area. Johnson and the others surrounded the car and took photographs of Margaret and Erb who were partially disrobed in the back seat. Johnson told Margaret not to come home and that further communication would be through lawyers. He told Erb to disclose the affair to his wife.

Erb did so. He and Margaret terminated their affair. Erb offered to resign his teaching position, but the local school board unanimously decided not to accept his resignation. The board president testified Erb's teaching was highly rated by his principal and superintendent, he had been forgiven by his wife and the student body, and he had maintained the respect of the community. Erb was retained for the ensuing school year and continued to teach in the Nishna Valley School.

Witnesses before the board included Erb's past and present high school principals, his minister, a parent of children in the school, and a substitute teacher. All vouched for his character and fitness to teach. His superintendent gave essentially the same testimony in district court. . . . Trial court ruled in its pretrial order that under the admitted record Erb's teacher-student relationship had not been impaired by his conduct.

The [state] board voted five to four to revoke Erb's teaching certificate and, without making any findings of fact or conclusions of law, ordered it revoked. Revocation was stayed by trial court and then by this court pending outcome of the certiorari action and appeal. Trial court held Erb's admitted adulterous conduct was sufficient basis for revocation of his certificate and annulled the writ. . . . In this appeal Erb contends the board acted illegally . . . in revoking his teaching certificate without substantial evidence that he is not morally fit to teach. . . .

Since the board made no findings there is no intelligible way to determine what interpretation the board gave to its statutory authorization to revoke the certificate of one not "morally fit to teach." But nothing prevents us from determining whether there is substantial evidence in the record which would have supported revocation if the proper standard had been applied. Erb contends there is not. We agree. We will first examine the standard and then the sufficiency of the evidence.

This court has not previously been called upon to decide what constitutes moral unfitness to teach. . . .

A teacher occupies a sensitive position. Since students are taught by example as well as lecture, the teacher's out-of-school conduct may affect his classroom fitness. . . .

> The private conduct of a man, who is also a teacher, is a proper concern to those who employ him only to the extent it mars him as a teacher, who is also a man. Where his professional achievement is unaffected, where the school community is placed in no jeopardy, his private acts are his own business and may not be the basis of discipline.

The board contends the fact Erb admitted adultery is sufficient in itself to establish his unfitness to teach. This assumes such conduct automatically and invariably makes a person unfit to teach. We are unwilling to make that assumption. It would vest the board with unfettered power to revoke the certificate of any teacher whose personal, private conduct incurred its disapproval regardless of its likely or actual effect upon his teaching. . . . ("Where the courts have been presented with the question whether or not specific conduct of a teacher constitutes moral unfitness which would justify revocation, they have apparently required that the conduct must adversely affect the teacher-student relationship before revocation will be approved.") . . .

> Surely incidents of extramarital heterosexual conduct against a background of years of satisfactory teaching would not constitute "immoral conduct" sufficient to justify revocation of a life diploma without any showing of an adverse effect on fitness to teach.

We emphasize the board's power to revoke teaching certificates is neither punitive nor intended to permit exercise of personal moral judgment by members of the board. Punishment is left to the criminal law, and the personal moral views of board members cannot be relevant. A subjective standard is impermissible and contrary to obvious legislative intent. . . .

In *Morrison* the California court discussed factors relevant to application of the standard:

> In determining whether the teacher's conduct thus indicates unfitness to teach the board may consider such matters as the likelihood that the conduct may have adversely affected students or fellow teachers, the degree of such adversity anticipated, the proximity or remoteness in time of the conduct, the type of teaching certificate held by the party involved, the extenuating or aggravating circumstances, if any, surrounding the conduct, the praiseworthiness or blameworthiness of the motives resulting in the conduct, the likelihood of the recurrence of the questioned conduct, and the extent to which disciplinary action may inflict an adverse impact or chilling effect upon the constitutional rights of the teacher involved or other teachers.

82 Cal.Rptr. at 186, 461 P.2d at 386.

These factors have relevance in deciding whether a teacher is morally fit to teach under Code §260.2. Since the same standard is applicable in determining whether a certificate should be revoked under Code §260.23, a certificate can be revoked only upon a showing before the board of a reasonable likelihood that the teacher's retention in the profession will adversely affect the school community.

There was no evidence of such adverse effect in the present case. No one even asserted such an effect. The complainant himself acknowledged his purpose was to remove Erb from the school rather than from teaching. The evidence showed Erb to be a teacher of exceptional merit. He is dedicated, hardworking and effective. There was no evidence to show his affair with Margaret Johnson had or is likely to have an adverse effect upon his relationship with the school administration, fellow teachers, the student body, or the community. Overwhelming and uncontroverted evidence of local regard and support for Erb is a remarkable testament to the ability of a community to understand, forgive and reconcile.

There was no evidence other than that Erb's misconduct was an isolated occurrence in an otherwise unblemished past and is not likely to recur. The conduct itself was not an open or public affront to community mores; it became public only because it was discovered by considerable effort and made public by others. Erb made no effort to justify it; instead he sought to show he regretted it, it did not reflect his true character, and it would not be repeated. . . .

The board acted illegally in revoking his certificate. Trial court erred in annulling the writ of certiorari.

Reversed.

CASE NOTE

Revocation of a teaching certificate for conviction of stealing drugs and money was valid. *Crumpler v. State Board of Education*, 71 Ohio App.3d 526, 594 N.E.2d 1071 (1991); 62 Ohio St.3d 1409, 577 N.E.2d 361 (table) (Sept. 18, 1991).

■ TEACHER CONTRACTS

A teacher's contract must satisfy the same requirements applicable to contracts in general. A school district is a legal entity, a corporate body with the power to sue and be sued; purchase, receive, hold, and sell real and personal property; make contracts and be contracted with; and do all other things necessary to accomplish the purposes for which it is created.

THE STANDARD CONTRACT

Contracts of school districts not only must conform to the requirements of general contract law, but also must satisfy other statutory and case law demands. A contract may be defined as an agreement between two or more competent persons for a legal consideration on a legal subject matter in the form required by law. This definition includes the five basic elements inherent in every valid contract, to wit: offer and acceptance, competent persons, consideration, legal subject matter, and proper form.

Offer and Acceptance

All contracts are agreements, but not all agreements are contracts. An agreement is an offer and an acceptance. Every valid contract contains an offer and acceptance. For example, a board of education offers a fifth-grade teaching position in a particular school to an individual. There is no agreement unless and until the individual accepts the offer.

Several significant factors concerning agreements should be kept in mind. An offer can be accepted only by the individual or individuals to whom it is made. Unless otherwise stated, an offer must be accepted within a reasonable time after it is made, or it will be terminated automatically. Newspaper advertisements are usually considered to be invitations for offers and not offers; that is, the board of education is soliciting offers. Also, an offer cannot be accepted unless, at the time the individual performed the act necessary to accept the offer, he or she knew of the existence of the offer. By way of illustration, let us assume that vandals have broken into a school building and that the board of education has offered a reward for information leading to the arrest and conviction of the vandals. The information is provided to the police by a man who is unaware of the reward offer. A majority of the states hold that the man is not entitled to the reward because he could not have accepted the offer, since he was unaware of its existence—there was no meeting of the minds.

Competent Persons

Each valid contract must be entered into between two or more competent persons—persons who have the legal capacity to contract. As already indicated, a board of education is considered a competent person under the law, with full capacity to enter into contracts. However, there are certain classes of people who have limited capacity to contract. These include minors,

married women, insane persons, drunken persons, and corporations.

A minor has the right to disaffirm his or her contract until a reasonable time after reaching his or her majority (i.e., becoming an adult). If a board of education contracts with a minor, the minor has the prerogative of electing to avoid the contract within a reasonable time after he or she becomes an adult, and no penalties for a contractual breach will be imposed against the minor. A board of education would have no right or option to avoid its contract with the minor.

If an individual is so insane or drunk at the time she or he enters into a contract that she or he does not know what she or he is doing, the person may have the contract set aside because there was no meeting of the minds, which is always essential in every valid contractual situation.

At the common law, married women did not possess the legal capacity to contract. This law was premised on the age-old concept that when a man and woman married, the two become one and the man was that one. This contractual limitation has been removed by statutes in all states, and women now possess the power to enter into contracts on the same basis as men.

Before entering into a contract with a corporation, a board of education should ascertain that the corporation has the power, by statute or under its articles of incorporation, to perform the services agreed upon.

Consideration

Valid contracts must be supported by consideration—something of value. Consideration is divided into three types. These are good, valuable, and a promise for an act.

Good consideration is love and affection. For example, a mother may convey property to a child for good consideration. This notion is seldom invoked by courts today.

Valuable consideration is cash or its equivalent. Most deeds will recite that the property is being conveyed for good and valuable consideration.

The third type of consideration is that found in a unilateral contract—a promise for an act. For example, a board of education promises a reward of $500 for information leading to the arrest and conviction of vandals who damaged school property. An individual, knowing of the offer, provides the information that leads to the arrest and conviction of the vandals; she is entitled to the reward. Her consideration was the doing of the act requested.

Legal Subject Matter

All contracts, to be valid, must involve a legal subject matter. Most, if not all, states prohibit the holding of various types of assemblies, such as rooster fighting. If a board of education entered into a contract to lease school premises for the purposes of staging a rooster-fighting conclave, such a contract would involve an illegal subject matter and would be declared void.

Proper Form

Contracts, to be enforceable, must in the form required by law. For example, all agreements with respect to the sale or leasing of real estate must be in writing to be enforceable. An oral agreement to sell real property, even if made in the town square before ten thousand people, is unenforceable in the courts. This is but one example of the requirement that contracts must be in the proper form to be enforceable. States require that teachers' contracts be in writing.

Beyond the technical statutory and common law requirements that govern the contractual relationships between teachers and school boards, there are the even more pervasive requirements of the state and federal constitutions, which sanctify the contract and protect the individual against arbitrary use of the contract by the state. This aspect of the contract is discussed later.

A Contract between a School Trustee and a Teacher to Pay "Good Wages" Is Too Indefinite to be Enforceable

Fairplay School Township v. O'Neal

Supreme Court of Indiana, 1891.
127 Ind. 95, 26 N.E. 686.

ELLIOTT, J. The complaint of the appellee alleges that she was duly licensed to teach school, and that her license was in force on the 31st day of March, 1888; that she entered into a verbal contract with the school trustee on that day, wherein she undertook to teach school for the term to be held in the school year 1888; that the school trustee promised in said oral contract to pay her "good wages"; that she has been ready and willing to teach, but the trustee refused to permit her to do so. The question presented is whether there was such a contract as bound the school township, and made it liable for damages for a breach. Our opinion is that there was no such contract. The trustee is an officer clothed with statutory power, and all who deal with him are bound to take notice of the nature and extent of his authority. . . . The authority of the trustee respecting schools is vested in him for a public purpose, in which all the citizens of the township have an interest, and upon many phases of which they have a right to be heard by petition or remonstrance. This is especially so with regard to the employment of teachers. It is necessary, for the information of the citizens, that contracts made with teachers should be certain and definite in their terms; otherwise the citizens cannot guard their interests, nor observe the conduct of their officer. It is necessary that the contract should be definite and certain, in order that when the time comes for the teacher to enter upon duty there may be no misunderstanding as to what his rights are. Any other rule would put in peril the school interests. Suppose, for illustration, that a contract providing for "good wages," "reasonable wages," "fair wages," or the like, is made, and when the time comes for opening the schools there arises a dispute as to what the compensation shall be. How shall it be determined, and in what mode can the teacher be compelled to go on with the duty he has agreed to perform? Until there is a definite contract, it can hardly be said that a teacher has been employed, and the public interest demands that there should be a definite agreement before the time arrives for the schools to open; otherwise the school corporation may be at the mercy of the teacher, or else there be no school. We think that a teacher cannot recover from the school corporation for the breach of an executory agreement, unless it is so full and definite as to be capable of specific enforcement. . . . There is much reason for scrutinizing with care contracts made so far in advance of the opening of the school year as was that here sued on, and sound policy requires that the terms should be definitely fixed and made known that all interested may have full and reliable information. It is, we may say in passing, not altogether clear that the statute does not require that all contracts shall be in writing and be recorded; but we do not deem it necessary to decide that question. Judgment reversed.

CASE NOTES

1. Teachers' general relationships with school boards are created by contract and governed by general principles of contract law. *Kirk v. Miller,* 83 Wash.2d 777, 522 P.2d 843 (1974).

2. Power to employ or discharge teachers is exclusively vested in the school board and cannot be delegated to any other body or official, such as a school superintendent. *Snider v. Kit Carson School District R-1, in Cheyenne County,* 166 Colo. 180, 442 P.2d 429 (1968).

3. In order to have a valid teacher employment contract, as in other discretionary matters, the school board must act as a board and not as individuals. *Landers v. Board of Education of Town of Hot Springs,* 45 N.M. 446, 116 P.2d 690 (1941).

❖ — ❖ — ❖

Teacher Who Did Not Obtain Necessary Credit Hours during Specified Period Was Not Entitled to Contract Renewal

Feldhusen v. Beach Public School District No. 3

Supreme Court of North Dakota, 1988.
423 N.W.2d 155.

VANDE WALLE, Justice. David Feldhusen appealed from a judgment dismissing his petition for a writ of mandamus. We affirm.

Feldhusen was employed by Beach Public School District No. 3 (Beach) as a teacher in the fall of 1981. His employment continued until his contract was nonrenewed in the spring of 1987.

Beach takes part in a voluntary "accreditation" program established by the State Department of Public Instruction. In order to be accredited a school district must establish and implement a policy for the professional growth of teachers. Beach implemented its policy through the following provision in its professional-negotiations agreement with the teachers in the school district:

> Summer school & extension course attendance shall be as follows to advance on the salary schedule:
>
> —a. All plus hours must be graduate hours.
> —b. *Teachers with degrees must acquire 8 semester or 12 quarter hours every five years.*
> —c. Teachers may substitute 16 hours of certified in-service training for 1 quarter hour. See attached policy on in-service hours.
> —d. All credits must be earned from an accredited college or university.
> —e. *All teachers must provide written proof each year by the second Monday in September that they meet above accreditation standards as required by North Dakota Department of Public Instruction. No salary increase will be granted the year accreditation standards are not met and no teacher contract will be offered the following year unless accreditation standards are met.* . . . [Emphasis added.]*

Beach established this policy in 1981. The 1985–1986 school year was the fifth year of the cycle for Feldhusen. At the end of that school year Feldhusen had completed only six of the requisite twelve quarter-hours.

In March of 1987 the Beach school board voted to contemplate nonrenewal of Feldhusen's teaching contract. A letter was sent to Feldhusen

---

*Schools are accredited and teachers are certified. Feldhusen was certified as a teacher. One of the standards required for accreditation of the school, a voluntary process, is that the school board establish and implement a policy of professional growth for each teacher and that it also locally establish the five-year period for each teacher who holds a life certificate. The language of the Beach policy requiring that teachers "meet . . . accreditation standards as required by North Dakota Department of Public Instruction" relates to the credits required of each teacher in order that the school meet the standards for accreditation.

informing him of the contemplated nonrenewal for the reason of "teacher qualifications" based upon Feldhusen's failure to meet the accreditation standards. . . .

After the end of the 1986–1987 school year Feldhusen performed coursework which would have given him the number of credits or quarter-hours required by the Beach accreditation policy. This work was completed in June of 1987. In July of 1987 Beach hired another teacher to fill the position which Feldhusen had held. Subsequently Feldhusen petitioned for a writ of mandamus requiring Beach to give him a contract. After a hearing was held, the trial court issued a judgment dismissing the petition. It is from that judgment that Feldhusen appeals.

The question before us is whether the trial court erred in dismissing Feldhusen's petition for a writ of mandamus. . . .

Feldhusen . . . argues that he has a clear legal right to a contract from Beach because there was no statutory basis for the Beach school board's nonrenewal decision. We disagree. The nonrenewal of teacher contracts is governed by Section 15-47-38(5), N.D.C.C. A portion of that statute provides:

> The reasons given by the board for not renewing a teacher's contract must be sufficient to justify the contemplated action of the board and may not be frivolous or arbitrary but must be related to the ability, competence, or qualifications of the teacher as a teacher, or the necessities of the district such as lack of funds calling for a reduction in the teaching staff.

Thus teachers' contracts can be nonrenewed for a lack of qualifications.

In this case Beach was voluntarily taking part in an accreditation program which required that it assure the professional growth of its teachers. In order to comply with the accreditation standards Beach, in tandem with its teachers, created a policy requiring its teachers to acquire a certain number of college credits in a five-year period. That policy became a part of the professional-negotiations agreement between the Beach school board and the teachers of Beach. It is readily apparent that one of the qualifications for a teacher in Beach was that the teacher abide by the contractual provision designed to retain Beach's accreditation. If a

teacher failed to abide by the provision regarding the acquisition of college credits, the negotiated policy specified that no teacher contract would be offered the following year, thus justifying nonrenewal under Section 15-47-38(5). Therefore, we cannot conclude that the trial court abused its discretion in denying the petition for a writ of mandamus which was predicated upon a claim that nonrenewal could not be grounded in a teacher's failure to abide by the Beach policy as formulated in the professional-negotiations agreement. . . .

The judgment is affirmed.

■ THE TENURE CONTRACT

Tenure is a statutory right to hold office or employment and to receive the benefits and emoluments of the position. Tenure in its general sense is a mode of holding or occupying a position or a job.[11] After meeting designated academic and teaching requirements in a school district for a prescribed number of years, a teacher, if recommended for reemployment, may acquire tenure. The benefit of tenure is that it bestows on the teacher a right of continued employment in the school district, and dismissal cannot occur without a hearing and presentation of proof of sufficient cause to meet the statutory requirements for removal.

Many court cases have arisen concerning the transferring of a tenured teacher from a particular class or school to another educational setting. Generally, a tenured teacher, like a teacher on a limited contract, may be assigned to any class or school in the district if she or he is qualified to teach in that position. The courts frown, however, upon any attempt of a school board or administrator to use "undesirable reassignment" as a means of retribution against a teacher who has achieved continuing contract status. If a teacher has committed an act for which her or his contract may be terminated, the proper legal procedure should be followed to terminate the contract rather than using subterfuges of questionable legality.

GROUNDS FOR TERMINATION
Tenure laws specify the grounds for and the manner by which a teacher's employment may be terminated. These laws may apply to the dis-

missal of teachers during the period of an annual contract or to the termination of teachers who have either continuing contracts or tenure. The most common grounds for dismissal are incompetency and insubordination.

Incompetency has been construed by the courts to mean any physical or mental condition that tends to incapacitate a teacher so he or she cannot perform effectively. This rather broad definition generally concerns a fitness to teach that contains a range of factors and has been used by many boards as a catchall for teacher dismissal. Insubordination, on the other hand, is of narrower meaning and imports a willful disregard for express or implied directions of the employer and/or repeated refusal to obey reasonable regulations.[12]

Other grounds for dismissal include immorality, misconduct, neglect of duty, and any other good or just cause. Every teacher is charged with the responsibility of setting a good example. Not only must teachers be of good moral character, but also their general reputation must attest to this fact. Teachers not only must be moral persons, but also must conduct themselves in such a manner that others will know of their virtue. Although court opinions are not uniform on the subject, it may generally be concluded that "misconduct" is a broader term than "immorality" and that different standards of proof are required for each.

❖ — ❖ — ❖

Teacher Did Not Acquire Tenure Rights by Working Fourth Year under Temporary Contract

Scheer v. Independent School District No. I-26 of Ottawa County

Supreme Court of Oklahoma, 1997.
948 P.2d 275 (1997).

SUMMERS, Vice Chief Justice.

A young teacher, near the end of her third and final year as a "probationary teacher,"

signed "a Temporary Certified Employee Contract" for her fourth year. When the school district did not rehire her after the fourth year she sued, claiming tenured or "career" status. This case gives us, for the first time, the chance to address the question of when does tenured (or career) status first take effect under Oklahoma's statutes for teachers. The District Court granted summary judgment to the school district. . . .

Connie Scheer was first employed by the Afton School District for the 1990–1991 school year. She was thereafter employed for each of the next two years. Each year she was given evaluations, the results of which were that she was asked to improve in several different areas. More than once she was given a plan for improvement written by her administrator.

On April 1, 1993, before Scheer had completed her third year of teaching, the school administration approached her and offered her a temporary contract for the following year. The school district was required by statute to make a decision as to her employment prior to April 10, or Scheer would have been entitled to continuing employment. . . . The school declined to offer her a permanent contract because of the many concerns about her teaching. Rather than terminating her, it offered the temporary contract as a "last chance" for improvement. After being given an opportunity to review the contract, Scheer signed it.

The contract stated clearly that it was a "TEMPORARY CERTIFIED EMPLOYEE CONTRACT." . . .

She worked as a teacher for the 1993–94 year under the temporary contract. When the School Board decided not to continue her employment beyond that year she brought suit in state court for breach of contract and loss of employment in violation of due process. The trial court granted summary judgment to the school district.

Essentially, Scheer urges that she was a tenured, or career, teacher. Recognizing that to be a tenured teacher she must have served as a teacher for three years, she claims tenure because she was employed under three one-year contracts, and the fourth contract—the temporary contract—was an invalid waiver of her rights to tenure. She finds it irrelevant that when she signed the temporary contract she had not yet completed her third year. In the alternative, she urges that by working the fourth year—albeit under a temporary contract—she attained career or tenured status.

The School District urges that Scheer was not a tenured teacher, and therefore the School District was not bound by the requirements accorded to tenured teachers at the time it offered the alternative contract in lieu of termination. It claims that realizing Scheer would soon be tenured, the District offered her a temporary contract rather than dismiss her altogether. In so doing, it did not intend to offer her tenure, but instead attempted to give her another chance for improvement. The School District also urges that according to state law her employment under a temporary contract did not count toward giving her career or tenured status.

There are two principal issues before us. First, was Scheer tenured, either before or after her performance under the temporary contract? If we answer this in the affirmative, we must next address whether a tenured teacher may waive tenure rights in a contract in exchange for continued employment for another year. We hold that under Oklahoma law she was not tenured either before or after the completion of the temporary contract. Because she had no tenure we need not address whether such rights may be waived by the teacher. . . .

. . . Clearly, she was not tenured at the time she signed the "temporary" teaching contact, because she had not completed her third consecutive year. The School District was required by statute to inform her prior to April 10 as to whether her contract would be renewed. In following its statutory obligation, the School District notified her that the most she would be offered was a temporary contract. This occurred before April 10, and before the completion of her third consecutive year of teaching. At the time she signed the contract she had no rights to tenure.

A narrow interpretation of the definition of "career teacher" might lead to the conclusion that she became tenured after this third year regardless of the school district's actions based on their dissatisfaction with her performance. But such an interpretation destroys the apparent intent of the statutory scheme created by the legislature. The legislature intended teachers to acquire tenure after their third year. At all times

prior to completion of the third year a teacher's status is probationary, as is expressly stated in the definition of "probationary teacher." 70 O.S. Supp.1991 §6-101.3(6). This permits a teacher to have three years to reach an acceptable level with regard to her or his teaching skills, and permits the school district three years to evaluate and perhaps seek improvement of a probationary teacher. . . .

If we were to follow Scheer's narrow interpretation, both the probationary teacher and the school district lose a year within which to improve and evaluate. If a probationary teacher in fact gains some expectancy of tenure after signing her third consecutive contract (which under statute must occur prior to April 10 of her second year), but before completing the performance required under the contract, a school district will be forced to allow a probationary teacher only two years within which to meet a particular teaching standard before being forced to decide whether the teacher should be re-employed or terminated. In essence, this interpretation would create a third class of teachers not contemplated by the legislature: probationary teachers with two years of experience who have signed a contract for the third year. Though still probationary under the statute they would be protected as tenured if they can just finish out the third year.

We decline to adopt the interpretation argued by Scheer. . . . To receive tenure a teacher must have completed a third successful year. At the time she signed the Temporary Contact (prior to April 10 of her third year) she was a probationary teacher, and the school district had the right to consider her as such. The school district could have simply non-renewed her contract prior to that April 10. The fact that she finished out the final month of school did not nullify or counteract the school's decision.

There is no legally protectible interest in tenure after two years. Both the school district and the probationary teacher are given three years to evaluate and meet standards. This interpretation not only complies with our statutory scheme, but also furthers one of the purposes of tenure by improving the level of teacher qualification. . . .

The second argument urged is that Scheer gained tenure by working her fourth year under the temporary contract. Our statutes require that we hold she did not. Title 70 O.S.Supp.1991, Section 6-101.23(A)(3) states that "teachers who are employed on temporary contracts" are exempt from the tenure laws. Scheer's employment was extended to a fourth year only by a temporary contract. Specifically, if she did not have tenure before signing the temporary contract, she was exempted under Section 6-101.23. The legislature did not intend for teachers under temporary contracts to have the due process rights afforded to career teachers working under permanent contracts. Scheer did not gain tenure by working a fourth year under a temporary contract. . . .

. . . The judgment of the District Court of Ottawa County is affirmed.

CASE NOTES

1. Tenure does not accrue until the statutory time has been completed. *Spiewak v. Board of Education*, 90 N.J. 63, 447 A.2d 140 (1982).

2. Tenure does not accrue until the anniversary date of first employment after a statutorily specified number of years. 126 Mich.App. 89, 342 N.W.2d 528 (1983).

3. A temporary contract does not apply toward time of employment for tenure purposes. The time of employment must be under a regular annual tenure-earning contract. *Cipu v. North Haven Board of Education*, 32 Conn.Supp. 264, 351 A.2d 76 (1974).

Reassignment of Teacher from Secondary Grade to Elementary Grade Is Not an Impermissible Demotion

Appeal of Santee

Supreme Court of Pennsylvania, 1959.
397 Pa. 601, 156 A.2d 830.

PER CURIAM. The decree appealed from is affirmed on the following opinion of Judge Flannery for the court en banc.

Miss Clara N. Santee has been a professional employee of the School District of the City of Hazleton where, since 1925, she has held the status of a teacher.

For the school year 1956–1957 she was assigned to the D.A. Harman, Jr. High School teaching English and Mathematics in the ninth grade.

On August 22, 1957, she was assigned to teach a sixth-grade class in the Arthur Street School, which assignment she regarded as a demotion and accepted under protest. Her salary was not affected by the transfer and is not here involved.

Exercising her rights under the School Code she demanded restoration of her previous status and requested a hearing before the School Board. That was granted and her petition was denied. She appealed to the Superintendent of Public Instruction of the Commonwealth of Pennsylvania who, by decision dated June 11, 1958, dismissed her appeal. From that decision she appealed to this court, and on October 3, 1958, we affirmed the decision and order of the Superintendent of Public Instruction. . . .

The question is narrow. Does an assignment from the ninth to the sixth grade constitute a demotion in type of position as contemplated by the Code? We believe it does not.

The statute provides:

> but there shall be no demotion of any professional employee either in salary or in type of position without the consent of the employee, or, if such consent is not received, then such demotion shall be subject to the right to a hearing before the board of school directors and an appeal in the same manner as hereinbefore provided in the case of the dismissal of a professional employee.

. . . There was a salary distinction between "elementary and secondary schools" under the Act of May 18, 1911, P.L. 309, as amended and revised. . . . But this distinction was swept away in the amendment of July 5, 1947, P.L. 1266, which provided for minimum salaries based on certification and academic qualifications and not on assignment and this system has been retained under the amendments to the Code. . . .

Thus the Legislature has abolished the legal distinction between elementary and secondary schools and unless we can find in the law some differences between the two in importance, dignity, responsibility, authority and/or prestige—some distinguishing difference—the appellant cannot prevail.

The definition of professional employee, as mandated in the Code, must be kept in mind. It provides:

> The term "professional employe" shall include teachers, supervisors, supervising principals, directors of vocational education, dental hygienists, visiting teachers, school secretaries the selection of whom is on the basis of merit as determined by eligibility lists, school nurses who are certified as teachers and any regular full-time employe of a school district who is duly certified as a teacher.

. . . We construe these to be the "type of position" referred to in Art. XI, Sec. 1151, which prohibits demotion of any professional employee either in salary or in type of position without the consent of the employee, as we have quoted above. Under this construction the appellant has not been demoted.

There is no less importance, dignity, responsibility, authority, prestige or compensation in the elementary grades than in secondary. Here the young student still pliant, still susceptible, still in the formative stage, receives his earlier impressions, his inspiration, his direction. Here personality traits are brought out and developed, tastes are instilled, habit patterns are established, character is formed. This is perhaps the most important period of life, the most crucial, the period which may determine a child's ultimate moral, ethical and intellectual stature. To be charged with the responsibility for children in this critical time of their lives is no demotion.

Decree affirmed at appellant's costs.

Case Notes

1. Tenure laws are enacted to provide job security for experienced teachers and to ensure that they are not discharged for insufficient and inadequate reasons. A system of tenure has as its objective the maintenance of an able teaching force whose members have undergone a period of probation, with the concomitant result that because of such protections, more talented personnel will be attracted to the teaching profession. *State v. Redman,* 491 P.2d 157 (Alaska 1971), appeal after remand, *Redman v. Department of Education,* 519 P.2d 760 (1974).

2. The broad purpose of teacher tenure is to protect worthy instructors from enforced yielding to political pressures and to guarantee employment, regardless of the vicissitudes of politics. *School District No. 8, Pinal County v. Superior Court of Pinal County,* 102 Ariz. 478, 433 P.2d 28 (1967).

3. A continuing contract has as one of its central purposes the elimination of uncertainty in the employment plans of both teacher and school district. *Peters v. South Kitsap School District No. 402,* 8 Wash.App. 809, 509 P.2d 67 (1973).

4. Tenure laws are not grants of power to school districts but rather constitute limitations on the power of school districts to freely contract with teachers. *Carlson v. School District No. 6 of Maricopa County,* 12 Ariz.App. 179, 468 P.2d 944 (1970).

■ INCOMPETENCY

Incompetency has been given broad interpretation by the courts. It is generally defined as "want of physical, intellectual, or moral ability; insufficiency; inadequacy; specific want of legal qualification or fitness."[13] Fitness to teach is essential and contains a broad range of factors. The courts have included in fitness to teach the lack of knowledge of subject matter, lack of discipline, unreasonable discipline, unprofessional conduct, and willful neglect of duty. Usually, when incompetency is alleged, other charges are also presented. In one case, the dismissal notification listed fourteen specific charges and included inadequate maintenance of discipline during class, excessive and ineffective use of films, ineffective classroom teaching, and failure to cooperate with school administrators. Here the school district presented a preponderance of evidence that children were disruptive, daydreamed in class, and left the room without permission. Incompetence was thereby proved, and the court upheld the dismissal.[14]

The manner of offering evidence in incompetency cases is generally through testimony. Both the quantity and the quality of evidence are important. The courts have liberally allowed opinions of principals, curriculum supervisors, and other supervisory personnel to stand as expert testimony. Other testimony by students and parents may be important, and actual observations of what transpired in the classroom are significant.

A teacher who has been certified by the state is assumed to be competent, and it is the responsibility of the school board to prove incompetency. As long as school boards are not arbitrary or capricious, the courts generally do not interfere. The Fifth Circuit Court of Appeals has said that "[f]or sound policy reasons, courts are loathe to intrude upon the internal affairs of local school authorities in such matters as teacher competency."[15] This court said, "The court, in absence of proof of an abuse of discretion, cannot substitute its opinion for the decision of the school board and of the district court where both of these tribunals were presented with substantial evidence upon which to base their decisions."

Unauthorized or excessive punishment of pupils may constitute incompetency. A New York court upheld the dismissal of a tenured teacher when the board gave evidence that the teacher administered excessive punishment on three separate occasions.[16] Incompetency may be evidenced by poor classroom decorum. In a case where a school district dismissed a tenured teacher on grounds of incompetency because she was unable to maintain order in her classroom—the classroom was littered with sunflower seeds, paper, and "junk"; the furniture and walls were covered with graffiti; and the teacher had not planned her lessons or given students proper directions—the court upheld the dismissal.[17] Moreover, of course, teacher ignorance may be a good and valid ground for dismissal. The dismissal of a tenured teacher who had been teaching for twenty-five years was upheld because the teacher used poor grammar and made spelling errors. The teacher also attempted to teach spelling before the children had mastered the alphabet.[18]

A teacher, though, cannot be dismissed for incompetency for nebulous and nondefinitive evaluations of competency.[19] Some state statutes require that teachers be given an opportunity to improve or to remediate themselves. If a statute

requires remediation, the school board must show that remediation has been attempted or that the situation was irremediable.[20]

❖ — ❖ — ❖

School Board's Termination of Teacher for Incompetence Stemming from Indiscreet Classroom Discussion of Homosexuality Was Arbitrary and Invalid

Collins v. Faith School District #46-2

Supreme Court of South Dakota, 1998.
574 N.W.2d 889.

AMUNDSON, Justice.

Richard Collins' contract with Faith School District was terminated on the basis of incompetency after he held a question and answer session with elementary school boys who had just seen a sex education video. In response to a question as to how two men could have sex, Collins described oral and anal sex to the boys. The school board's decision to terminate Collins' employment was upheld by the circuit court. We reverse and remand for reinstatement of Collins' employment and a determination of appropriate back pay.

Richard Collins was employed by the Faith School District for twenty-nine years prior to his termination. During most of those years he was a fifth-grade teacher. Although he was being reassigned to teach the fourth-grade class during the 1995–96 school year, Collins had a valid contract and was entitled to the protections of South Dakota's continuing contract law (SDCL 13-43-9.1 *et seq.*).

The Faith School Board (Board) had not established any formal sex education curriculum for its elementary school students. However, Board had made it a practice to contract with the community health nurse to provide sex education for elementary students for approximately fifteen years prior to 1995. The makeup of this program was basically set by the community health nurse without any prescreening by Board or administration.

A video chosen by the community health nurse covering the topics of puberty, maturation, and reproduction was shown to fourth, fifth, and sixth grade boys on April 24, 1995. This was the first time this particular video had been used by the nurse and this was the first time fourth grade students were included in the program. At the end of the video, the nurse went through a worksheet with the boys, addressing such topics as circumcision, nocturnal emissions, and semen. An opportunity for the boys to ask the nurse questions was then provided, but none were asked. The school nurse attributed this to the fact she was a woman and the boys were not comfortable discussing the subject with her.

As in past years, following the sex education presentation, the boys then went to Collins' classroom for a question and answer session. Before starting the session, Collins excused one student from the room because the student's parents did not wish to have the child involved in the sex education program. Collins then proceeded to ask if the boys had any questions. Collins undertook this duty because he had been asked by a previous health nurse to solicit questions after sex education programs from the boys because the female nurse realized that the boys would be uncomfortable asking her questions. Collins was instructed to answer the boys' questions as honestly as possible and he continued to carry out what had been an established practice for fifteen years. Questions were raised by the boys about circumcision, masturbation, nocturnal emissions and other topics from the film and worksheet. During the session, one of the boys also related that he had heard that two men could have sex and asked how this was possible. Collins preceded his explanation with the disclaimers that this type of conduct is frowned upon, most people do not believe in it, and the boys would find it gross. Collins then described oral and anal sexual intercourse in explicit language.

On April 25, 1995, complaints from parents were received by the superintendent which were critical of what the grade school boys had heard from Collins during school the previous day. In essence, the complaining parents were con-cerned about the effect Collins' answer to the question about homosexual intercourse would have on the boys. An informal meeting was conducted, involving one boy's parents, the superintendent, the principal, and Collins. At the conclusion of the meeting, Collins was advised by the superintendent that the matter was not resolved. Later that day, the superintendent took the matter to Board. Board directed the superintendent to send notice to Collins that a termination hearing would be scheduled before Board to consider his dismissal.

A notice of hearing and charges was provided to Collins on April 28, 1995, which referenced the parental complaint as well as warnings by Collins' evaluators in regard to lesson plans, instruction, maintenance of records and personal hygiene since 1985 that could be relevant as to his competence. On May 17, 1995, the hearing was held before Board, at which time witnesses and evidence were presented. . . .

The high school principal testified that it was inappropriate and immoral for a teacher to discuss homosexual activities with fourth and fifth grade boys. However, she indicated that she did not have any evidence that the children had been harmed in any way by the activity. She also testified that there had been no increased absenteeism or discipline problems of any kind. Nor were there any complaints from the children about feeling uncomfortable around Collins.

The superintendent testified without elaboration that the incident adversely affected Collins' ability to perform his teaching duties. However, the superintendent also testified that there was no evidence of any adverse impact on the students. In fact, the superintendent had not even been in Collins' classroom since the question and answer session to monitor for problems that may have developed because of the incident. Furthermore, he acknowledged that he had no evidence whatsoever that the children had lost confidence in Collins as a teacher and agreed that they evidently had some level of trust in Collins or they would not have been comfortable in asking the questions of him in the first place. The superintendent also indicated that he had no reason to question Collins' character.

At the conclusion of the hearing, Board voted to terminate Collins' contract on the basis of incompetency. . . .

Ignoring twenty-nine years of faithful service, the Board terminated Collins' teaching contract on the basis that he was incompetent. This determination rested purely on his indiscreet answer with regard to homosexual activity—a subject which invariably invokes intense debate and undoubtedly stirred emotions in this case.

It is undisputed that there is no evidence that the conduct of Collins complained of by Board violated any directive, regulation, rule, or order given to him by any administrator or Board. In fact, the evidence showed that the administration had abdicated total control over the sex education program to the health nurse. Neither the superintendent nor the Board took any steps to personally plan the program or place any limits on it. It is also undisputed that Collins had been asked by the previous health nurse to answer questions after sex education videos in the past, and had done so for the past fifteen years without incident. Even so, the Board terminated Collins' employment on the basis of incompetence for one moment of poor judgment.

"Incompetence" has been previously described by this court as "a relative term meaning lack of ability or fitness to discharge a required duty." *Hartpence v. Youth Forestry Camp*, 325 N.W.2d 292, 296 (S.D.1982) (quoting Black's Law Dictionary 688 (5th Ed. 1979)). Other courts have made it clear, however, that incompetence "does not invoke subjective analysis of standards of morality or professionalism which vary from individual to individual dependent on time, circumstances or custom." . . .

In *Hartpence*, we concluded that "the Commission's findings of fact address only the isolated instance of appellee's fall. Since incompetency arises from habitual and on-going actions, this finding does not support the Commission's conclusion of incompetency." 325 N.W.2d at 297. Similarly, the Faith School Board's decision to terminate its contract with Collins on the basis of one ill-advised answer, honestly given, was not the type of habitual and ongoing action that would support Board's conclusion that Collins was incompetent. . . .

Nevertheless, there are times when only one incident may be of such magnitude or of such far reaching consequences that a teacher's ability to perform his or her duties will be permanently impaired and a finding of "incompetence" would be proper. . . . However, there is no evidence that Collins' conduct rose to such a level. There has been no showing that Collins' teaching ability has been or will be impaired, or that any children have been detrimentally affected. . . . Nor has there been a showing that Collins is likely to exercise poor judgment in a similar situation in the future, since he has acknowledged that he used poor judgment in this case and regretted making the statement. . . .

. . . Collins' inappropriate explicitness on a single occasion can hardly amount to incompetence. . . .

The question must then be asked: Where is the relationship between Collins' ill-advised answer to the boys and the impairment of his capacity as a teacher? . . . While the superintendent makes the bare claim that the incident adversely affected Collins' ability to perform his teaching duties, he admits that he has not bothered to sit in on any of Collins' classes to actually note any problems. There have been no allegations that the students' education has suffered in any way. Absences have not increased. Discipline problems have not increased. Moreover, Board had the ability, pursuant to school policies, to suspend Collins prior to his termination. Instead, they chose to allow him to continue teaching from the April 24th incident to the May 17th board hearing, impliedly admitting they were not worried about Collins' ability to effectively teach his students after the incident. Furthermore, Board voted to extend Collins' contract for another year on the very same night that they discussed Brown's complaint that led to the hearing to determine if Collins should be dismissed. . . . The record contains no credible evidence that Collins' teaching ability has been impaired or even that the incident in question has any connection with his continued effectiveness as a teacher.

Accordingly, the decision of the circuit court is reversed and the case is remanded for reinstatement of Collins' teaching position and for a determination of the amount of back pay that Collins is entitled, less any offsets. . . .

Case Note

Numerous court decisions have made it clear that incompetence cannot be concluded from a single incident but rather must arise from a course of conduct or a series of incidents. *Tichenor v. Orleans Parish School Board*, 144 So.2d 603 (La.App.1962). Yet it is clear that incompetence hinges not on the number of incidents but rather on whether a single incident or a series of incidences was of such magnitude as to render a determination of unfitness to perform the duties of the job. Courts have commented, thusly: (a) Incompetency cannot be concluded from an isolated incident but rather arises from habitual and ongoing actions. *Hartpence v. Youth Forestry Camp*, 325 N.W.2d 292 (S.D.1982). (b) Incompetency does not invoke subjective analysis of standards of morality or professionalism, which vary from individual to individual dependent on time, circumstances, or custom. *Belcourt v. Fort Totten Public School District*, 454 N.W.2d 703 (N.D.1990). (c) Incompetency arises from habitual failure. *Collins v. Iowa Liquor Control Commission*, 252 Iowa 1359, 110 N.W.2d 548 (1961). This Iowa court explained incompetency in this manner: "A person who habitually fails to perform his work with the degree of skill or accuracy usually displayed by other persons regularly employed in such work is incompetent. And the same is true of one who usually performs substantially less than others regularly so employed." 110 N.W.2d at 550. (d) A Wyoming court held that "a single honest failure in the performance of one's duties does not without more amount to incompetency." *McCoy v. Thompson*, 677 P.2d 839 (Wyo.1984). (e) The Supreme Court of Nebraska has held that "evidence that a particular duty was not competently performed on certain occasions, or evidence of occasional neglect of some duty of performance, in itself, does not ordinarily establish incompetency or neglect of duty sufficient to constitute just cause for termination." *Sanders v. Board of Education*, 200 Neb. 282, 263 N.W.2d 461 (1978). (f) A California court has concluded that allowing students to repeat vulgar language in papers prepared for class does not constitute incompetence of the teacher unless further evidence could be produced to show that the incident warranted a conclusion that the teacher was unfit to teach. *Oakland Unified School District of Alameda County v. Olicker*, 25 Cal.App.3d 1098, 102 Cal.Rptr. 421 (1972). (g) Similarly, where a teacher of twenty years was arrested for three

misdemeanors arising out of driving while intoxicated, the court found that the school district was unable to produce evidence that rationally related the incident to the teacher's competence or turpitude or the proper performance of his duties as a classroom teacher; thus, the court ruled that the termination of the teacher's employment was arbitrary and capricious. *In the Matter of the Termination of Dwayne Kibbe v. Elida School District*, 996 P.2d 419 (N.M.2000).

■ INSUBORDINATION

Insubordination is a defiance of authority,[21] a disobedience to constituted authority; it is a refusal to obey some order that a superior officer is entitled to give and have obeyed.[22]

Courts have defined insubordination as "a willful disregard of express or implied directions of the employer and a refusal to obey reasonable orders."[23] Charges of insubordination are not supportable if (1) the alleged misconduct was not proved; (2) the existence of a pertinent school rule or a superior's order was not proved; (3) the pertinent rule or order was not violated; (4) the teacher tried, although unsuccessfully, to comply with the rule or order; (5) the teacher's motive for violating the rule or order was admirable; (6) no harm resulted from the violation; (7) the rule or order was unreasonable; (8) the rule or order was invalid as beyond the authority of its maker; (9) the enforcement of the rule or order revealed possible bias or discrimination against the teacher; or (10) the enforcement of the rule or order violated the First Amendment rights to free speech or academic freedom.[24]

Courts that require repetition and persistence of disobedience to establish insubordination[25] attach much importance to "willfulness" in violation of a reasonable rule. Evidence of willfulness and intent in refusing to obey a reasonable order is obviously established where the refusal is repeated.[26]

Some courts have held that a finding of insubordination does not necessarily hinge on whether it is a repeated refusal to obey reasonable rules or requirements. In some instances, refusal to obey school requirements is of such a nature that repetition is not necessary. Because the key to insubordination is willfulness, insubordination can be established by a single incident where there is evidence that a one-time occurrence clearly established that the teacher intended to break the school directive.[27] For example, where a teacher refused to leave an old school building and teach in a new one, the court found that the teacher's actions were willful and thus both insubordinate and neglectful of duty.[28]

In a case where a teacher was charged with insubordination for inappropriately punishing students and allowing card games to be played in study hall, the court ruled that there was no insubordination, even though the conduct was highly questionable, because the teacher ceased the activities after being admonished by the principal.[29]

In another insubordination case, a teacher was told not to use J. D. Salinger's *Catcher in the Rye* in his classroom and had agreed not to use the novel. Afterward, he began to use the novel again and was requested to meet with the principal concerning the issue. The teacher walked out of the meeting after five minutes and was charged with two counts of insubordination: (1) breaking the previous agreement and (2) walking out of a conference. The school board upheld the charges and dismissed the teacher. Upon appeal, the court determined the dismissal was too severe. Although the courts do not generally review administrative sanction, this court felt that the school board's punishment of the teacher was disproportionate to the offense and not fair, since students were not harmed and there was no indication of lack of fitness to teach.[30]

The requirements necessary to validate a teacher's dismissal for insubordination have been summarized by the *American Law Reports*[31] as follows:

> (1) Insubordination imports a wilful disregard of express or implied directions of the employer and a refusal to obey reasonable orders. (2) Insubordination is defined as a disobedience of orders, infraction of rules, or a generally disaffected attitude toward authority; it is generally synonymous with contumaciousness, which indicates persistent, wilful or overt defiance of, or contempt for, authority. (3) Insubordination is a constant or continuing intentional refusal to obey a direct or implied order, reasonable in nature, and given by and with proper authority.

In jurisdictions expressly requiring "willfulness" as an element to be proved to establish teacher insubordination, it has been held that the proof of willfulness required for insubordination may be satisfied by a single intentional act. In summary, in cases where insubordination was not upheld by the courts, one or more of the following were true in most instances: (1) The teacher's motive for violating the rule was not established, (2) no actual harm resulted from the violation, (3) the punishment was not proportional to the offense, (4) the rule or order that was broken was unreasonable, (5) the rule or order that was broken was beyond the authority of the maker, or (6) the rule or order that was broken violated a constitutional right of the teacher.[32]

Insubordination Can Be a Single Incident of Willful or Intentional Disobedience

Gaylord v. Board of Education, Unified District No. 218, Morton County

Court of Appeals of Kansas, 1990.
14 Kan.App.2d 462, 794 P.2d 307.

JOHN W. WHITE, District Judge, Assigned:

Steve Gaylord appeals from the district court's ruling affirming the termination of his teaching contract pursuant to K.S.A. 72-5436 *et seq.* by the Board of Education, Unified School District No. 218, Morton County, Kansas (Board). Gaylord argues that there was not substantial evidence to support the finding of insubordination and that the Board's decision to terminate the contract was, therefore, arbitrary and capricious. We affirm.

In April 1987, the Board voted to renew Gaylord's teaching contract for the 1987–88 school year. Gaylord decided to explore employment opportunities elsewhere and scheduled a job interview in Bovina, Texas, for May 21, 1987. Gaylord requested personal leave for that day, which fell during the last week of the school year. Principal Steve Barnes denied the request pursuant to the negotiated agreement, which forbade teacher absences the first or last week of any semester. Barnes told Gaylord that Superintendent Kenneth Fowler was the only one who could grant personal leave during that time period. Fowler also denied Gaylord's request.

Gaylord's wife called Barnes on the morning of May 21 and reported Gaylord was ill and would not be at work. Later that day, Fowler received a call from the high school principal in Bovina soliciting a recommendation for Gaylord. From that conversation, Fowler learned Gaylord had been in Bovina that morning.

The following day, Gaylord completed a sick leave form and attached a note from his physician. Fowler called Gaylord to his office, told him he knew about the Texas interview, requested his keys, and told him to leave school property. Gaylord was later notified of the Board's intent to terminate his contract. The reasons given for the Board's action were insubordination, failure to follow Board policy, and abusive treatment of students. . . .

The only issue to be considered for review by this court is the charge of insubordination. There is no contention that the Board acted outside the scope of its authority but only whether there was substantial evidence to support its finding. . . .

Insubordination is defined as "disobedience to constituted authority. Refusal to obey some order which a superior officer is entitled to give and have obeyed. Term imports a wilful or intentional disregard of the lawful and reasonable instructions of the employer." Black's Law Dictionary 720 (5th ed. rev. 1979). . . .

Although Kansas has not addressed insubordination in the context of teacher termination cases, in other jurisdictions insubordination has been found where the teacher refused to accept a teaching or school assignment, refused to admit a student to class, or has been absent without authorization. . . .

Some courts have found insubordination in a single incident. . . . Other courts have concluded insubordination can only occur when there is a constant or persistent course of conduct. . . .

In *Ware v. Morgan Cty. School D. No. RE-3,* 748 P.2d 1295, 1300 (Colo.1988), the court stated that, by interpreting insubordination

to include the willful or intentional disobedience of a reasonable order on a particular occasion, we provide the school board with the necessary latitude to determine whether, in light of community standards and subject to judicial review, the teacher's conduct on the occasion in question was sufficiently serious or aggravated to warrant an ultimate finding of insubordination and the serious sanction of dismissal. . . .

. . . The facts show Gaylord attempted to take, and was twice denied, a personal day during a time specifically prohibited by the negotiated agreement. Failing to secure permission, he had his wife call and report his illness on the day in question. He then drove to Texas to interview for a job and, upon his return, filled out an absence sheet claiming illness as the reason for his absence. Under the application of the community standards test articulated in *Ware,* substantial evidence exists to support the finding of insubordination warranting dismissal. . . .

The Board acted within the scope of its authority, there was substantial evidence to support its findings, and there is no evidence that the Board acted fraudulently, arbitrarily, or capriciously. The decision of the district court is affirmed.

❖ — ❖ — ❖

Insubordination and Inefficiency in Teaching Are
Grounds for Dismissal of Tenured Teacher

In re Termination of James E. Johnson

Court of Appeals of Minnesota, 1990.
451 N.W.2d 343.

GARDEBRING, Judge.

The school board passed a resolution terminating the employment of James Johnson, a tenured teacher, based upon the independent hearing examiner's findings of inefficiency in teaching and insubordination. Johnson appeals, contesting the sufficiency of the evidence to terminate his employment and the propriety of the procedures followed by the school in conducting its investigation. We affirm.

Prior to his termination, relator James Johnson was a tenured mathematics teacher employed by respondent Independent School District No. 709 (Duluth) since 1967. He taught seventh and ninth grade math at several schools within the school district. Beginning in 1970, he received intermittent performance evaluations, both formal and informal, some negative and some rating his teaching ability as satisfactory or better. In general, the evaluations noted four areas of concern: excessive failure rates, high volume of transfer requests, poor relationships with students and parents, and inappropriate teaching methods. In some instances, specific instructions were provided to Johnson as to required changes in classroom practice and teaching methodology.

On September 17, 1987, Johnson received a letter from Richard Wallin, Director of Secondary Education, outlining various directions Johnson must follow to improve his teaching performance. . . .

On January 13, 1988, Johnson was charged with inefficiency in teaching, conduct unbecoming a teacher, and insubordination, and was suspended without pay, effective immediately. The charges outlined the following deficiencies: (1) poor rapport with students; (2) insufficient communications with parents; (3) lack of student progress; (4) inappropriate use of class time; and (5) failure to follow the school's adopted mathematics curriculum. A hearing was conducted before an independent hearing examiner, a retired district court judge. The hearing lasted 29 days over a seven-week period in September and October 1988. On May 11, 1989, the hearing examiner issued his findings and concluded that while there were insufficient grounds for terminating on the basis of conduct unbecoming a teacher, there was substantial evidence to recommend termination for insubordination and inefficiency in teaching. On May 31, 1989, the school board adopted the examiner's recommendations and immediately terminated Johnson's employment.

Is the school board's decision to terminate Johnson supported by substantial evidence?

A school board's decision to terminate a teacher will not be set aside on appeal unless the decision is fraudulent, arbitrary, unreasonable, not supported by substantial evidence on the record, not within the school board's jurisdiction or is based on an erroneous theory of law. . . .

This matter was extensively heard by the hearing examiner. Eighty-three witnesses were called and 157 exhibits were received in evidence. The transcript of the proceedings consists of 29 volumes containing 6455 pages. . . .

Inefficiency in teaching and insubordination are two independent statutory grounds for termination. Minn.Stat. §125.17, subd. 4(1), (3) (1988). . . . We find that there is substantial evidence in the record to support the school board's decision to terminate Johnson's employment.

Evidence in the record demonstrates Johnson's poor rapport with students and insufficient communication with parents. The administration received numerous complaints from students and parents wherein the students describe feelings of frustration and confusion regarding Johnson's teaching methods and class assignments. Many of these complaints were accompanied by requests for transfer out of Johnson's class. Administrators observing Johnson's classes between 1977 and 1988 repeatedly noted the poor communication between Johnson and his students.

The record also contains evidence substantiating the charge of lack of student progress. Even judged by his own techniques, the evidence supports the finding that Johnson's students were not progressing satisfactorily. Although the test scores of highly motivated students improved, the scores of the other students remained the same or worsened. Many students failed his examinations. Testimony by the math teacher who took over Johnson's class after his suspension reveals that Johnson's students were behind in the curriculum. While evidence of requests by students and parents for transfer out of Johnson's classes are not indicative of poor teaching, it demonstrates a pattern of dissatisfaction with Johnson's teaching methods which is a proper area of concern for the school board to address.

Furthermore, the district's attention to Johnson's grading practices and failure rates was appropriate, and evidence on these issues supports the finding of teaching inefficiency. While Johnson has argued that he should not be evaluated on the attitudes of his students and their unwillingness to learn, evidence on grades, and in particular the large number of student failures, provides evidence of Johnson's inability to teach the mandated curriculum.

Although the assignment of a grade may be entitled to first amendment protection, academic freedom is not absolute. . . . Johnson was responsible for transmitting basic information to secondary school students. The district adopted a specific curriculum for achieving this objective. Johnson was terminated due to an inability to impart this basic knowledge, not because of the specific grades he assigned. We find no grounds to support Johnson's claim that his right to academic freedom was violated.

We note, however, that the school district's September 1987 directive to Johnson that his grade distribution not deviate by more than two percent from distributions in other similar classes was inappropriate. Such a rigid, numerical grading standard appears to us to potentially interfere with a teacher's legitimate need for classroom flexibility. School districts are cautioned in this area.

In reviewing the entire record, we conclude there is substantial evidence supporting the finding that Johnson was inefficient in teaching.

Insubordination is a "constant or continuing intentional refusal to obey a direct or implied order, reasonable in nature, and given by and with proper authority." . . . Johnson was specifically directed by Wallin and school principals to improve his relationship and rapport with students and parents. He was ordered to provide worksheets containing the assigned problems instead of having the students copy the problems off the blackboard. He was also directed to furnish each student with copies of tests and any material used to supplement the textbook.

In light of the numerous complaints received by the administrators, these orders are reasonable. Although Johnson participated in several teaching workshops, he continually refused to change his instructional methods. The record contains substantial evidence to support the finding of insubordination. . . .

Based upon the entire record, we find there is substantial evidence to support the school board's decision to terminate Johnson's employment.

Affirmed.

■ IMMORALITY

Teachers must be of good moral character, and statutory requirements pertaining to morality of teachers are constitutional.[33] Immorality has been interpreted to be such a "course of conduct as offends the morals of the community and is a bad example to the youth whose ideals a teacher is supposed to foster and elevate."[34]

Immorality is specified by tenure laws in a number of states as grounds for dismissal. Although the term "immorality" has been attacked as unconstitutionally vague,[35] it generally has been upheld by the courts, especially when it relates to fitness to teach and there is a rational nexus between the prohibited activity and the individual's conduct and decorum as a teacher. Immorality may include both heterosexual and homosexual activities, but it does not pertain to exclusively sexual activities:

> [W]e note that statutes from colonial days forward recognize the unique position of teachers as examples to our youth and charge them to "exert their best endeavors to impress on the minds of children and youth committed to their care and instruction" the values basic to our society . . . , requiring school committees to have full and satisfactory evidence of a teacher's moral character. This special role of teachers on impressionable and not fully tutored minds distinguished them from other public officials.[36]

Sexual involvement with students is, of course, looked upon with much concern and disdain by the courts. Because of the exemplary nature of teaching and the high community expectations of teachers, the courts have left little question about the seriousness of sexual involvement with students. Courts will uphold school boards in dismissing teachers even without absolute proof of sexual contact with students. In a case where a teacher enjoyed a reputation as a good teacher, with excellent rapport with students, but made sexual remarks and innuendos to female students as "good natured horse-play," the court found that there existed a nexus attaching to the teacher's classroom effectiveness and the questionable conduct, and the teacher was therefore unfit to teach.[37]

Sexual involvement with persons who are not students may have a logical nexus with the proper conduct of the school, and such activities may therefore be adjudged immoral. The courts, when dealing with cases of sexual activity of teachers with nonstudents, attempt to determine if there has been an impact on the teacher's fitness to teach and whether the activities were public or private. In a California case, a forty-eight-year-old elementary teacher had her life certificate revoked by the state board of education for immorality. The plaintiff was arrested at a private club by an undercover police officer after he watched her commit three separate acts of oral copulation, a violation of the penal code. After plea bargaining, the charges were reduced to the misdemeanor of "outraging public decency." The teacher and her husband had also appeared on television, in disguise, discussing nonconventional sexual lifestyles. Even though the teacher introduced into evidence her classroom evaluations, which were satisfactory, and a contract from the local board offering to rehire her, the court held that the state board was correct in revoking her certificate. The evidence showed that the sex acts were witnessed by several strangers in a semi-public atmosphere and "[p]laintiff's performance certainly reflected a total lack of concern for privacy, decorum or preservation of her dignity and reputation." The court said a teacher "in the public school system is regarded by the public and pupils in the light of an exemplar, whose words and actions are likely to be followed by children coming under her care and protection." Obviously, participation in sex orgies fell short of this standard.[38]

In order to dismiss a homosexual for immorality, the school district must demonstrate a rational nexus between the homosexual conduct of the teacher and fitness to teach. A showing of potential rather than actual harm to students will suffice. Factors such as adverse effect on students or fellow teachers, adversity anticipated within the school system, surrounding circumstances, and possible chilling effects on discipline may be used to establish unfitness.[39]

State statutes that prohibit public homosexual activity of a teacher—"crimes against nature"—have been upheld so long as they are not overly broad or vague.[40] Pursuant to such statutes, school districts may fire teachers for engaging in indiscreet public homosexual acts. However, a state statute that required the suspension or dismissal of teachers for "advocating . . . , encouraging or promoting public or private homosexual activity" has been held to be unconstitutional because it was too broad and vague. If such advocacy, however, materially or substantially interferes with the conduct of the school, then such speech could be prohibited.[41]

The ability of the school board to dismiss a teacher for homosexuality has presumably gained more strength from the U.S. Supreme Court's ruling in *Bowers v. Hardwick*,[42] where the justices by a five-to-four vote held that consenting adults had no fundamental right to engage in homosexual activity. The Court refused the plaintiff's contention that a Georgia statute prohibiting sexual activity between consenting adults of the same sex violated the constitutional right of privacy or equal protection. In so holding, the Court determined that it would defer to legislatures regarding the criminalization of such sexual activity. This case permits states to criminalize homosexual acts but does not extend to permitting states to impose punishment upon people for being homosexuals.[43]

Bowers indicates that school boards may validly dismiss teachers for homosexual activity, and it certainly allows for dismissal of tenured teachers for homosexual acts in states where homosexual acts are prohibited by criminal law. Such criminal activity would by its very nature invoke the nexus necessary to show harm to the public school.[44]

The case law would thus suggest that tenured teachers can be dismissed for sexual conduct that is detrimental to the school, whether that conduct is of a heterosexual or a homosexual nature. The nexus between the activity and the decorum of the school and integrity of the teaching process must be shown. If, however, the sexual activity is proscribed by state statute, as in the case of criminal laws against homosexual acts, then the need to establish such a nexus is obviated by the violation of state law. Guilt of criminal conduct has been held to constitute immorality *per se*. In this regard, dismissals of tenured teachers for immorality, based upon the fact that the teachers were convicted of crimes, are valid. A "guilty verdict of criminal conduct will support a finding of immorality."[45]

❖ — ❖ — ❖

Sexual Relationship with Student in Prior Teaching Employment Constitutes Immorality

Toney v. Fairbanks North Star Borough School District

Supreme Court of Alaska, 1994.
881 P.2d 1112.

MOORE, Chief Justice.

In March 1992, David Toney was fired from his position as a tenured teacher with the Fairbanks North Star Borough School District (the "District"). The termination was based on evidence establishing that Toney had engaged in a sexual relationship in 1980 with a 15 year old student while Toney was a teacher in Boise, Idaho. Toney appealed his termination to the superior court, which granted summary judgment in favor of the District. The court concluded that Toney's failure to disclose the relationship constituted a material misrepresentation and breach of the contractual covenant of good faith. The court also found that the relationship itself supported termination under AS 14.20.170(a). We affirm the superior court's grant of summary judgment in favor of the District on the latter ground.

In 1980, Toney was employed as a teacher at Capitol High School in Boise, Idaho. In December of that year, he entered into a sexual relationship with a 15 year old student, Traci F. At that time, Toney was in his early thirties. Shortly thereafter, Traci became pregnant with Toney's child. She then transferred to a school for pregnant teenagers. In November 1981, Traci gave birth and, with the consent of all parties, the child was adopted.

In October 1981, just prior to the birth of the child, Toney and Traci's father entered into a confidential written agreement concerning Traci's medical expenses and other costs relating to the child's birth. In the same document, Toney also agreed to "submit his resignation or take a leave of absence from the faculty of Capitol High School for the second semester of the 1981–82

school year and for the next school year in order to permit Traci to attend Capitol High School and to graduate therefrom." Pursuant to this agreement, Toney resigned from teaching in the Boise School District before the beginning of the 1982 spring semester.

Meanwhile, in the spring of 1981, Toney completed an application for employment with the Fairbanks North Star Borough School District. The application was dated February 3, 1981. However, it was not stamped as received by the District until April 28, 1981. Included in this application were Toney's assertions that he had not been asked to resign for any reason from a teaching position and that he had not been convicted of any offense involving moral turpitude.

In August 1982, Toney was contacted by Bill Rogers, a principal with the District, regarding his application. Toney reaffirmed his interest in a position with the District. Rogers then contacted Don Johnson, the principal of Capitol High School in Boise, who gave Toney a positive recommendation. Mr. Johnson did not reveal that Toney had resigned from Capitol High School at midyear during the 1981–82 school year.

Toney then came to Fairbanks to interview for a teaching position. During the interview, Toney did not disclose his relationship with Traci, nor did he disclose that he had not been employed as a teacher during the spring semester of the 1981–82 school year. Following the interview, Toney was recommended to fill a position with the District. Following this recommendation, Toney was asked to complete an "affidavit of teaching experience" and a "teacher's personal record" for the District's files. Toney incorrectly indicated on both documents that he held a full-time teaching position with the Boise School District for the entire 1981–82 school year. A non-tenured contract was executed on September 17, 1982.

In 1992, after learning that Toney was teaching in Fairbanks, Traci contacted District personnel and informed them of her prior relationship with Toney. After investigating the allegations, the District terminated Toney by letter dated March 26, 1992. The letter stated that Toney's firing was based on his failure to disclose to the District his relationship with Traci and his resignation pursuant to the agreement with Traci's father. In addition, the letter stated that Toney's conduct supported termination under AS 14.20.170(a)(2)–(3), on the grounds that it constituted "immorality and substantial noncompliance with the school laws of the state, the regulations or bylaws of the Department of Education, the bylaws of the District and the written rules of the superintendent."

Toney appealed his termination to the Borough's Board of Education. The Board upheld the dismissal by a vote of six to one. Toney then appealed to the superior court. Both parties filed motions for summary judgment. The superior court granted the District's motion in an Opinion and Order dated August 4, 1993. The court held that Toney's failure to reveal the relationship and the circumstances surrounding his resignation constituted misrepresentation and a breach of the contractual duty of good faith. The court further held that Toney's actions supported termination under AS 14.20.170(a)(2)–(3). Toney now appeals. . . .

Under AS 14.20.170(a)(2), a teacher, including a tenured teacher, may be dismissed for "immorality, which is defined as the commission of an act that, under the laws of the state, constitutes a crime involving moral turpitude." A criminal conviction is not necessary to support a teacher's dismissal under this provision. . . . In addition, it is well-established that there need not be a separate showing of a nexus between the act or acts of moral turpitude and the teacher's fitness or capacity to perform his duties. . . . As the court in *Brown* stated, "[i]f a teacher cannot abide by these standards his or her fitness as a teacher is necessarily called into question." . . . Thus, in the present case, so long as the District had sufficient evidence to conclude that Toney committed an act or acts which constituted a crime of moral turpitude, the dismissal is valid, even in the absence of a conviction. . . .

Toney acknowledges that he engaged in a sexual relationship with Traci when she was 15 years old and a student of his. This conduct satisfies the elements of the crimes of sexual abuse of a minor in the second and third degree under Alaska law as presently enacted. . . . Toney's conduct also constitutes a crime under Alaska law as it existed in 1981, under present Idaho law, and under Idaho law as it existed in 1981.

Toney does not dispute that his conduct with Traci was criminal, nor does he deny that his actions constituted crimes of moral turpitude. Instead, he argues that the statute authorizing dismissal for such acts does not reach conduct engaged in before a teacher is hired by a school district.

In addressing this argument, the superior court noted that the language of AS 14.20.170 (a)(2) "does not explicitly or implicitly limit the statute's application to . . . acts that occur only while a teacher is under contract with an Alaska school district." The court further found that the legislative history of the statute offered no support for Toney's argument. Finally, the court recognized that Toney's contention is contrary to sound public policy:

> As the Borough points out, the effect of such an interpretation would be contrary to public policy as it would allow an individual who commits an act of moral turpitude, and who successfully conceals his/her behavior from a school board, to be immune from dismissal upon subsequent discovery of the conduct.

Thus, the court concluded that Toney's conduct "establish[ed] immorality under AS 14.20.170(a)(2) and [was] sufficient grounds for his dismissal." . . .

Toney's sole argument is that AS 14.20.170 (a)(2) does not provide for the dismissal of a tenured teacher on the grounds of conduct occurring prior to the teacher's hiring. This argument is nonsensical. Nothing in the language of the statute or its legislative history suggests that such a limited interpretation is appropriate. In addition, as the superior court noted, such a construction would conflict with public policy, since it would immunize from dismissal a teacher who had engaged in illegal and immoral conduct prior to hiring, but who had successfully concealed such conduct. We therefore affirm the superior court's conclusion that Toney's actions were sufficient to support his dismissal under AS 14.20.170(a)(2).

Toney's criminal sexual relationship with a minor student is adequate grounds for his dismissal under AS 14.20.170(a)(2). The superior court's opinion and order upholding Toney's dismissal is therefore AFFIRMED.

CASE NOTES

1. *Moral Turpitude*. Moral turpitude is "[a]n act of baseness, vileness, or depravity in the private and social duties which a man owes to his fellow men, or to society in general, contrary to the accepted and customary rule of right and duty between man and man." *Black's Law Dictionary*, 7th ed. (St. Paul, Minn.: West, 1999), p. 1160. Moral turpitude is difficult to clearly define because it is premised on the moral standards of the community.

Revocation of the teaching certificates of two teachers for growing fifty-two marijuana plants in a greenhouse has been upheld by a Florida court because their actions violated the moral standards of the community. The court concluded that since teachers are in a leadership capacity and are obligated to maintain a high moral standard in the community, the possession of marijuana plants, and the ensuing publicity, seriously impaired their abilities to be effective teachers. *Adams v. State Professional Practices Council*, 406 So.2d 1170 (Fla.App.1981), petition denied, 412 So.2d 463 (Fla.1982). In an earlier decision, a teacher was found not to be guilty of moral turpitude where he was found to be cultivating only one marijuana plant out of curiosity. *Board of Trustees v. Judge*, 50 Cal.App.3d 920, 123 Cal.Rptr. 830 (1975).

Conviction for mail fraud constitutes moral turpitude justifying revocation of a teaching certificate. *Startzel v. Commonwealth of Pennsylvania, Department of Education*, 128 Pa.Cmwlth. 110, 562 A.2d 1005 (1989).

2. *Neglect of Duty*. A school board may properly dismiss for neglect of duty a teacher who while serving as cheerleader sponsor drank beer with the cheerleaders in violation of a school rule prohibiting the drinking of alcoholic beverages. The dismissal of the teacher was upheld by the court even though the hearing officer's recommendation to the board was that the teacher be retained. The court said, in relating "immorality" to "neglect of duty," that "neglect of duty is directly related to the teacher's fitness to teach"; "neglect of duty occurs when a teacher fails to carry out his or her obligations and responsibilities in connection with classroom or other school-sponsored activities." *Blaine v. Moffat County School District Region No. 1*, 748 P.2d 1280 (Colo.1988).

The duties required of a teacher by a board, when evaluating neglect of duty, were outlined in an Oregon case. The court said that the essential features are (1) the duty of a teacher to serve as a role model for students and community of good citizenship and law-abiding behavior; (2) the duty to maintain effective relationships with students, parents, and other staff of school; and (3) the duty to teach the approved school curriculum. *Jefferson County School District No. 509-J v. FDAB*, 311 Or. 389, 812 P.2d 1384 (1991).

Tenure Contract May Be Terminated for Off-Campus Immoral Conduct

Board of Education of Hopkins County v. Wood

Supreme Court of Kentucky, 1986.
717 S.W.2d 837.

WINTERSHEIMER, Justice. . . .

The issue is whether the contracts of tenured teachers may be terminated for immoral conduct or conduct unbecoming a teacher for off-campus activities involving students when no written records of such conduct are in the personnel file.

In 1983, a Hopkins County grand jury while investigating a murder received testimony from two 15-year-old girls that two days prior to the murder they had purchased 10 marijuana cigarettes and had taken the marijuana to the apartment of the Wood brothers where the girls and the Woods and others smoked some of the marijuana. The grand jury suggested that the matter be investigated further by the county attorney and subsequently the Woods were arrested in a misdemeanor charge of contributing to the delinquency of a minor. In district court, on September 20, 1983, the Woods both signed a statement pleading guilty to unlawful transaction with a minor in violation of KRS 530.070, a misdemeanor.

Officials of the Board of Education took the statements of the two girls on September 1, 1983, and on the basis of these statements, the Wood brothers were suspended from their teaching positions on September 6 for immoral character and conduct unbecoming a teacher. A hearing was conducted on September 28. At the hearing the Board presented the guilty plea filed in district court and the two girls as witnesses. The Woods denied smoking marijuana and three other witnesses testified that they did not see any marijuana smoking. Character witnesses also testified on behalf of the Woods. At the conclusion of the hearing the Board voted unanimously to terminate the Wood brothers. . . .

The Wood brothers argue that the Board has no right to terminate their teaching contracts by reason of acts committed during off-duty hours, during the summer months before the school year began and in the privacy of their own apartment.

. . . The evidence indicates that there was serious misconduct of an immoral and criminal nature and a direct connection between the misconduct and the teachers' work. The Wood brothers pled guilty in district court to an unlawful transaction with a minor after having entertained two 15-year-old female students in their home at a marijuana-smoking party. . . .

The purpose of teacher tenure laws is to promote good order in the school system by preventing the arbitrary removal of capable and experienced teachers by political or personal whim. It is not to protect those who violate the criminal law. A teacher is held to a standard of personal conduct which does not permit the commission of immoral or criminal acts because of the harmful impression made on the students. The school teacher has traditionally been regarded as a moral example for the students. . . .

Conduct unbecoming a teacher or immoral conduct, unless limited to behavior occurring on the school premises during school hours, could not possibly be documented by a record of school supervisory personnel in a manner that is probative or appropriate as contemplated by the statute. Such records relate to in-school professional performance, not off-school activities. Therefore to give the statute an absolutely literal interpretation leads to a patently absurd result. We must construe statutes of this nature in accordance with their purpose, which means making an exception to the literal language in the present statute to avoid an absurd and unworkable result. . . .

Great care must be taken to ensure that proof of conduct of an immoral nature or conduct unbecoming a teacher which is sufficient to merit discharge of a tenured teacher should be of the same quality as required by other subsections of the statute, that is, written documentation from impartial sources to substantiate the charges, as in the present case, or its substantial equivalent. In addition, the conduct, when it occurs in a context other than professional competency in the classroom, should have some nexus to the teacher's occupation, as was true in this case which involves smoking marijuana with two students. . . .

It was not the intention of the legislature to subject every teacher to discipline or dismissal for private shortcomings that might come to the attention of the Board of Education but have no relation to the teacher's involvement or example to the school community. The power of the Board to discipline teachers is not based on personal moral judgments by Board members. It exists only because of the legitimate interests of the government in protecting the school community and the students from harm. . . .

It is the holding of this Court that the contracts of tenured teachers may be terminated for conduct unbecoming a teacher or immoral conduct involving off-campus activities involving students notwithstanding written records indicating a satisfactory teacher performance.

The decision of the Court of Appeals is reversed and the judgment of the circuit court is reinstated.

All concur.

CASE NOTES

1. *Off-Campus Sex.* Consensual sexual conduct between a teacher and an adult of the opposite sex, committed off-campus, cannot without other extenuating circumstance constitute "good cause" for a school board's rejection of a superintendent's nomination of the teacher for reemployment. *Sherbourne v. School Board of Suwannee County*, 455 So.2d 1057 (Fla.App.1984).

2. *Commission of a Crime.* State statutes in a number of states provide that teachers may be dismissed for "a felony or crime of moral turpitude." A felony is "[a] crime of a graver or more atrocious nature than those designated as misdemeanors . . . , [g]enerally an offense punishable by death or imprisonment in the penitentiary." *Black's Law Dictionary*, 4th ed. (St. Paul, Minn.: West), p. 744.

Where a teacher was charged with theft, assault and battery, and fleeing a police officer, the court upheld his dismissal and stated, "[I]t cannot be said that a teacher's conduct outside the classroom bears no reasonable relation to his qualifications for employment." *Gary Teachers Union, Local 4, American Federation of Teachers v. School City of Gary*, 165 Ind.App. 314, 332 N.E.2d 256 (1975).

Dismissal for unfitness is not necessarily dependent on criminal conviction. A school board may dismiss a teacher for arrest for a felony, even though the trial does not result in conviction. In a case where a teacher was charged with a criminal act of engaging in oral copulation with another man and was acquitted of criminal charges, the school board dismissed the teacher for immorality and unfitness. The state code provided for school boards to dismiss teachers for sex offenses. The court held for the board and said that it was the responsibility of the board to determine the fitness of the employee even if acquitted of criminal charges. *Board of Education v. Calderon*, 35 Cal.App.3d 490, 110 Cal.Rptr. 916 (1973), cert. denied and appeal dismissed, 414 U.S. 807, 95 S.Ct. 19 (1974).

3. *Misdemeanor.* Included in the area of criminal convictions is the dismissal of a teacher for a misdemeanor. Misdemeanors are "[o]ffenses lower than felonies and generally those punishable by a fine, penalty, forfeiture, or imprisonment otherwise than in [a] penitentiary." *Black's Law Dictionary*, 7th ed. (St. Paul, Minn.: West, 1999), p. 1150.

In a case where a tenured teacher was arrested and charged with "disturbing the peace by being under the influence of intoxicants, attempting to fight, and display of a gun," his dismissal was upheld for good and just cause, and the board's action was held not to be arbitrary, irrational, or unreasonable. *Williams v. School District No. 40 of Gila County*, 4 Ariz.App. 5, 417 P.2d 376 (1966).

4. *Drugs and Immorality.* Teachers, in recent years, have been dismissed for possession and use of controlled substances. Since state statutes usually do not specify dismissal for drugs, teachers who have been involved with drugs have been dismissed under statutory provisions regarding fitness to teach, moral turpitude, immorality, and misdemeanor and felony convictions, plus other good and sufficient cause.

Such an example was found in Georgia, where a tenured teacher was arrested for possession of cocaine, glutethimide, and marijuana and pleaded guilty to violating that state's Controlled Substances Act. Since it was a first offense, the teacher was placed on probation. Because of the publicity, she was transferred to two other teaching positions during the remainder of the year. Finally, the board dismissed her for "immorality" and "other good and sufficient cause" based on her guilty plea. The court said, "[T]he proven fact of the teacher's possession of three dangerous drugs is evidence from which 'immorality' may be inferred, even in the absence of criminal purpose or intent." *Dominy v. Mays*, 150 Ga.App. 187, 257 S.E.2d 317 (1979). A similar result was reached in *Chicago Board of Education v. Payne*, 102 Ill.App.3d 741, 58 Ill.Dec. 368, 430 N.E.2d 310 (1981).

———— ❖ — ❖ — ❖ ————

A Teacher Who Had Sexual Relationship with Student of Another School Is Unfit to Teach

Elvin v. City of Waterville

Supreme Judicial Court of Maine, 1990.
573 A.2d 381.

McKUSICK, Chief Justice.

In January 1989 the City of Waterville discharged plaintiff Kathleen Elvin from her job as a fourth grade teacher on the findings of the Waterville Board of Education, pursuant to 20-A M.R.S.A. §13202 (1983), that she had proven "unfit" to teach and that her continued services were "unprofitable" to the school system. On her appeal, we find no reversible error in the

Board of Education's findings and so affirm, as did the Superior Court (Kennebec County, *Alexander, J.*).

Elvin, a divorcee, lives in Winslow with her two children. In the spring of 1987, Elvin engaged in sexual intercourse several times with a fifteen-year-old neighbor who occasionally babysat for her children and did errands for her. The boy, a public high school sophomore, turned sixteen in June some weeks after the first act of intercourse, and Elvin continued to maintain a sexual relationship with him for several months thereafter.

As a result of these acts, Elvin was indicted on two counts of sexual abuse of a minor on May 4, 1988. The sexual abuse charges were dropped in exchange for Elvin's *nolo contendere* plea to one count of assault stemming from the sexual contact. Shortly after being indicted, Elvin was suspended with pay from her teaching position. Pursuant to 20-A M.R.S.A. §13202, the Board held a hearing in January 1989 and voted to dismiss Elvin from her fourth grade teaching job. . . .

The employment of public school teachers in Maine is controlled by statute. "A school board, after investigation, due notice of hearing and hearing thereon, shall dismiss any teacher . . . who proves unfit to teach or whose services the board deems unprofitable to the school." 20-A M.R.S.A. §13202. The Board concluded that Elvin was unfit to teach and that her services were unprofitable to the school. . . . Based upon the evidence before the Board, we cannot say that its decision to dismiss Elvin was irrational or arbitrary.

The Board found as a fact that Elvin's "relationship [with the boy] was her own choice, fully consensual, and of long duration." It based its ultimate finding that Elvin had proven unfit to teach upon, *inter alia*, her poor judgment, her lack of concern for the emotional welfare of a public school student, and her impaired ability to deal with other sexually exploited students due to public awareness of her course of conduct. Each of these findings is supported by substantial evidence in the record. Elvin admitted that she exercised poor judgment. In the Rule 11 hearing at which Elvin pleaded *nolo contendere* to the assault charge, she agreed to pay part of the victim's cost of psychological counseling for the

reason that, as her counsel acknowledged, she was partly responsible for his current psychological problems. Elvin also admitted that she lied about her conduct when initially questioned by authorities and that she was aware of the boy's psychological problems prior to their sexual relationship. According to the Board, Elvin's actions "put more pressure on the victim" and "aggravated" the situation. Two school administrators testified that in their professional opinions, returning Elvin to the classroom "would be very detrimental to the schooling system," would adversely affect the system's credibility in dealing with sex abuse cases, would damage the school's reputation, and would cause the public to "los[e] respect and trust." Upon these findings the Board rationally concluded that Elvin was unfit to teach.

The Board further determined that continuation of Elvin's services would be unprofitable to the school system. In support of this conclusion, the Board found that "the publicity associated with this case certainly has made the public aware of the charges and the sexual relations that [Elvin] had with a young boy from a neighboring school" and that public awareness of her conduct will "undermine her ability and her reputation in dealing with . . . students and parents." The Board also found that her continued employment "will undermine the administration's program dealing with sexual abuse and exploitation of children." These findings are supported by substantial evidence in the record. Elvin's relationship with the boy attracted substantial media attention, and school administrators testified that at least one parent reported having a child who knew about the incident. The school administrators also testified about the deleterious consequences of returning Elvin to the classroom. Upon these findings, the Board rationally concluded that Elvin's continued employment would be unprofitable to the school system. . . .

The entry is:

Judgment affirmed.

All concurring.

Case Notes

1. Lying is considered to be immoral. Where a tenured teacher was denied permission to

attend a conference and she went anyway, and then upon her return she submitted a request for excused absences because of illness, the board dismissed her based on immorality. The court upheld the board and said: "[Q]uestions of morality are not limited to sexual conduct, but may include lying." *Bethel Park School District v. Krall*, 67 Pa.Cmwlth. 143, 445 A.2d 1377 (1982).

2. Some school boards have overreached the intent and meaning of the term "immorality" in tenure laws in their zeal to find legal grounds for suspension or dismissal of teachers. Such was the case in a Pennsylvania school district where two teachers were suspended for engaging in a water fight with students in which one of the students suffered minor skin irritation when a cleaning fluid was sprayed on the students by the teachers. The court said that such "horseplay" may have been outrageous and uncalled for, but it did not rise to the level of immorality. *Everett Area School District v. Ault*, 120 Pa.Cmwlth. 514, 548 A.2d 1341 (1988).

3. Being pregnant and unmarried does not constitute immorality. In a case where an unmarried pregnant teacher was dismissed for immorality, the school district argued that "unwed parenthood is *per se* proof of immorality and ... a parent of an illegitimate child is unfit role model," yet the school district could offer no support for such an assertion. The court said, "Therefore, we hold that [the teacher's] discharge was in violation of her rights under the equal protection clause of the Fourteenth Amendment." *Avery v. Homewood City Board of Education*, 674 F.2d 337 (5th Cir.1982).

❖ — ❖ — ❖

Homosexuality of Teacher Is
Immorality Justifying Dismissal

Gaylord v. Tacoma School District No. 10

Supreme Court of Washington, 1977.
88 Wash.2d 286, 559 P.2d 1340.

HOROWITZ, Associate Justice. Plaintiff-appellant, James Gaylord, appeals a judgment of the trial court upholding Gaylord's discharge from employment as a high school teacher by defendant school district. . . .

Defendant school district discharged Gaylord—who held a teacher's certificate—from his teaching position at the Wilson High School in Tacoma on the ground of "immorality" because he was a known homosexual. . . .

We need consider only the assignments of error which raise two basic issues: (1) whether substantial evidence supports the trial court's conclusion plaintiff-appellant Gaylord was guilty of immorality; (2) whether substantial evidence supports the findings, that as a known homosexual, Gaylord's fitness as a teacher was impaired to the injury of the Wilson High School, justifying his discharge by the defendant school district's board of directors. The relevant findings of the trial court may be summarized as follows.

Gaylord knew of his homosexuality for twenty years prior to his trial, actively sought homosexual company for the past several years, and participated in homosexual acts. He knew his status as a homosexual, if known, would jeopardize his employment, damage his reputation and hurt his parents.

Gaylord's school superior first became aware of his sexual status on October 24, 1972, when a former Wilson High student told the school's vice-principal he thought Gaylord was a homosexual. The vice-principal confronted Gaylord at his home that same day with a written copy of the student's statement. Gaylord admitted he was a homosexual and attempted unsuccessfully to have the vice-principal drop the matter.

On November 21, 1972, Gaylord was notified the board of directors of the Tacoma School Board had found probable cause for his discharge due to his status as a publicly known homosexual. This status was contrary to school district policy No. 4119(5), which provides for discharge of school employees for "immorality." After hearing, the defendant board of directors discharged Gaylord effective December 21, 1972.

The court found an admission of homosexuality connotes illegal as well as immoral acts, because "sexual gratification with a member of one's own sex is implicit in the term 'homosexual.'" These acts were proscribed by RCW 9.79.120 (lewdness) and RCW 9.79.100 (sodomy).

After Gaylord's homosexual status became publicly known, it would and did impair his teaching efficiency. A teacher's efficiency is determined by his relationship with his students, their parents, the school administration and fellow teachers. If Gaylord had not been discharged after he became known as a homosexual, the result would be fear, confusion, suspicion, parental concern and pressure on the administration by students, parents and other teachers.

The court concluded "appellant was properly discharged by respondent upon a charge of immorality upon his admission and disclosure that he was a homosexual" and that relief sought should be denied.

Was Gaylord guilty of immorality?

Our concern here is with the meaning of immorality in the sense intended by school board policy No. 4119(5). School boards have broad management powers. RCW 28A.58. Under RCW 28A.58.100(1) the school board may discharge teachers for "sufficient cause." Policy No. 4119(5) adopted by the school board and in effect during the term of Gaylord's teaching contract with defendant school district permits the Tacoma School Board of Directors to treat "immorality" as sufficient cause for discharge.

"Immorality" as used in policy No. 4119(5) does not stand alone. RCW 28A.67.110 makes it the duty of all teachers to "endeavor to impress on the minds of their pupils the principles of morality, truth, justice, temperance, humanity, and patriotism. . . . " RCW 28A.70.140 requires that an applicant for a teacher's certificate be "a person of good moral character." RCW 28A.70.160 makes "immorality" a ground for revoking a teacher's certificate. Other grounds include the commission of "crimes against the laws of the state." The moral conduct of a teacher is relevant to a consideration of that person's fitness or ability to function adequately as a teacher of the students he is expected to teach—in this case high school students. . . .

"Immorality" as a ground of teacher discharge would be unconstitutionally vague if not coupled with resulting actual or prospective adverse performance as a teacher. . . . The basic statute permitting discharge for "sufficient cause"

(RCW 28A.58.100(1)) has been construed to require the cause must adversely affect the teacher's performance before it can be invoked as a ground for discharge. . . .

The next question is whether the plaintiff's performance as a teacher was sufficiently impaired by his known homosexuality to be the basis for discharge. The court found that Gaylord, prior to his discharge on December 21, 1972, had been a teacher at the Wilson High School in the Tacoma School District No. 10 for over twelve years, and had received favorable evaluations of his teaching throughout this time. (Findings of fact Nos. 1 and 2.) The court further found that "while plaintiff's status as a homosexual [was] unknown to others in the school," his teaching efficiency was not affected nor did his status injure the school. When, however, it became publicly known that Gaylord was a homosexual "the knowledge thereof would and did impair his efficiency as a teacher with resulting injury to the school had he not been discharged." (Finding of fact No. 9.)

The court further found:

> A teacher's efficiency is determined by his relationship with students, their parents, fellow teachers and school administrators. In all of these areas the continued employment of appellant after he became known as a homosexual would result, had he not been discharged, in confusion, suspicion, fear, expressed parental concern and pressure upon the administration from students, parents and fellow teachers, all of which would impair appellant's efficiency as a teacher and injure the school. (Finding of fact No. 10.)

Gaylord assigns error to findings of fact numbers 9 and 10, contending there is no substantial evidence to support either. We do not agree.

First, he argues his homosexuality became known at the school only after the school made it known and that he should not be responsible therefor so as to justify his discharge as a homosexual. The difficulty with this argument is twofold. First, by seeking out homosexual company he took the risk his homosexuality would be discovered. It was he who granted an interview to the boy who talked to him about his homosexual problems. The boy had been referred to Gaylord for that purpose by the homosexual friend to whom Gaylord had responded favorably in answering his advertisement in the paper of the Dorian Society. As a result of that interview the boy came away with the impression plaintiff was a homosexual and later told the assistant high school principal about the matter. The latter in turn conferred with plaintiff for the purpose of verifying the charge that had been made. It was the vice-principal's duty to report the information to his superiors because it involved the performance capabilities of Gaylord. The school cannot be charged with making plaintiff's condition known so as to defeat the school board's duty to protect the school and the students against the impairment of the learning process in all aspects involved.

Second, there is evidence that at least one student expressly objected to Gaylord teaching at the high school because of his homosexuality. Three fellow teachers testified against Gaylord remaining on the teaching staff, testifying it was objectionable to them both as teachers and parents. The vice-principal and the principal, as well as the retired superintendent of instruction, testified his presence on the faculty would create problems. There is conflicting evidence on the issue of impairment but the court had the power to accept the testimony it did on which to base complained of findings. . . . The testimony of the school teachers and administrative personnel constituted substantial evidence sufficient to support the findings as to the impairment of the teacher's efficiency.

It is important to remember that Gaylord's homosexual conduct must be considered in the context of his position of teaching high school students. Such students could treat the retention of the high school teacher by the school board as indicating adult approval of his homosexuality. It would be unreasonable to assume as a matter of law a teacher's ability to perform as a teacher required to teach principles of morality (RCW 28A.67.110) is not impaired and creates no danger of encouraging expression of approval and imitation. Likewise to say that school directors must wait for prior specific overt expression of homosexual conduct before they act to prevent harm from one who chooses to remain "erotically attracted to a notable degree towards persons of his own sex and is psychologically, if not actually, disposed to engage

in sexual activity prompted by this attraction" is to ask the school directors to take an unacceptable risk in discharging their fiduciary responsibility of managing the affairs of the school district.

We do not deal here with homosexuality which does not impair or cannot reasonably be said to impair his ability to perform the duties of an occupation in which the homosexual engages and which does not impair the effectiveness of the institution which employs him. However, even the federal civil service regulations on which Gaylord relies to show a change in attitude towards homosexuals provides:

> [W]hile a person may not be found unsuitable based on unsubstantiated conclusions concerning possible embarrassment to the Federal service, a person may be dismissed or found unsuitable for Federal employment where the evidence establishes that such person's sexual conduct affects job fitness. 2 CCH Employment Practice's Guide; pg. 5339 (1975).

It must be shown that "the conduct of the individual may reasonably be expected to interfere with the ability of the person's fitness in the job or against the ability to discharge its responsibility." These principles are similar to those applicable here. The challenged findings and conclusions are supported by substantial evidence.

Affirmed.

CASE NOTE

Sex Change. A sex change by a teacher may be held to affect fitness to teach. The dismissal of a teacher who underwent a change of sex has been held to constitute incapacity. In a case where a tenured teacher changed his external anatomy to that of a female and was subsequently dismissed by the board, the board reasoned that the situation would cause emotional harm to students. The board did not question the teacher's proficiency in the classroom and did not attempt to establish such a nexus. The court said that a teacher's fitness to teach is not based entirely upon academic proficiency but depends on a broad range of factors. One of those factors, the court said, was the "teacher's impact and effect upon his or her students," and the impact in this case would be harmful to the children. *In re Grossman*, 127 N.J.Super. 13, 316 A.2d 39 (1974).

■ CAUSE OR GOOD CAUSE

Both common law and statute usually provide for dismissal of teachers for "cause" or "good cause." Where tenure statutes specify the causes for dismissal, a teacher cannot be dismissed for causes beyond those specified.[46] If, however, no causes are specified and the statute merely provides for dismissal for cause, then that which constitutes cause is subject to broader interpretation.[47]

The substance of "just cause" may be found in other aspects of inappropriate activity of a teacher. A Pennsylvania court has found that lying and/or making false statements is immorality constituting just cause for dismissal.[48] A teacher's misrepresentations regarding his or her unexcused absences may be within the context of persistent and willful misconduct and may, thereby, be the substantive grounds for dismissal for good or just cause.[49]

Cause may, at times, be rather nebulous, vesting the school board with substantial and broad authority. A Kansas court interpreted that state's tenure law to permit termination or non-renewal of a tenured teacher for good cause, including "any ground which is put forward by the school board in good faith and which is not arbitrary, irrational, unreasonable, or irrelevant to the school board's task of building up and maintaining an efficient school system."[50]

Just cause may emanate from factors other than those of the teacher's making. For example, financial problems of a school district may constitute "just cause" for dismissal. In an Iowa case, just cause was given as the justification for release of a tenured teacher with seventeen years of experience. The reasons given for just cause were budgetary considerations, declining enrollments, and the need to make more efficient use of staff. The district had 757 pupils in 1975, 506 in 1985, and 440 to 461 projected by 1989. The decline in enrollment had caused a loss of state revenues. Evidence, too, was submitted to the court showing that the district was overstaffed. The poor financial condition therefore led the court to uphold the dismissal based on just cause.[51]

"Good cause" must be determined based on the facts of each case.[52] For example, "good cause" has been established to support dismissal where a tenured teacher (1) cohabitated with a teacher of the opposite sex, (2) used a human fetus in the classroom when discussing abortion, (3) talked about abortion, and (4) spoke to classes about personal living arrangements.[53]

Violation of school policy may constitute cause. Dismissal of a tenured teacher was upheld for violating a school policy that stated that "the board of education does not encourage corporal punishment." Over a four-year period, the teacher had kicked a student, struck another in the face, knocked a person to the floor, and committed other similar acts.[54] Needless to say, the court upheld the dismissal for cause.

Failure to abide by school rules may be either "good cause" or insubordination. In a case where a tenured teacher was warned numerous times to stop religious activities such as writing "God is truth and truth is God" on the blackboard, the board dismissed him for cause. The teacher did not deny the allegations and said he would not stop because "he was a Christian and that part of his mission was a sense of evangelism." His actions and refusal to abide by the board's order constituted good grounds for dismissal.[55]

Cause for dismissal may also be supported for violation of a policy prohibiting corporal punishment. In a case where a teacher grabbed a child and kneed him in the back, causing him to cry, and shoved another child to the floor, the court found sufficient cause.[56]

Thus, cause, good cause, or just cause may encompass a host of teacher misbehaviors that could probably be otherwise justified as incompetency, insubordination, neglect of duty, or some other more specific charge. As noted above, however, such other specifications may not be necessary if the school board is vested by the tenure law with the more general catchall term of "cause."[57]

❖ — ❖ — ❖

Teacher's Dismissal for Just Cause Is Appropriate Where Shoplifting Was Determined to Harm Her Effectiveness and Competence

Board of Directors of Lawton-Bronson v. Davies

Supreme Court of Iowa, 1992.
489 N.W.2d 19.

SNELL, Justice.

This is a school teacher termination case under section 279.27 of the Iowa Code (1989). The appellant, Lawton-Bronson Community School District, made findings of just cause to discharge appellee, Kathleen Davies, during the contract year. . . .

Kathleen Davies was employed by the Lawton-Bronson Community School District as an elementary teacher. On November 17, 1989, Davies was arrested for shoplifting at a Younker's Department Store in Sioux City, Iowa. A formal charge of third-degree theft was filed against her on December 20, 1989.

On January 22, 1990, the district's superintendent of schools issued to Davies a notice and recommendation to terminate her employment contract pursuant to Iowa Code section 279.27 (1989). . . .

Davies claims that her compulsion to engage in shoplifting activity is the result of a mental illness/disability and, therefore, such conduct does not rise to the level of just cause for termination of her employment. The board of directors of the school district maintains that the acts of shoplifting and other incidents at the school are undisputed and have detrimentally affected her ability to be a role model to the students. . . .

The school superintendent also provided testimony by several teachers and one parent as to other incidences of Davies' behavior as a teacher. These incidences were: (a) statements to her fifth grade class that she carries a handgun, (b) statements to a student that she understood his pain related to headaches and would like to

fly out of a window, (c) students dictating the substance of classes, (d) laying her head on her desk due to headaches on several occasions, (e) taking several pills in front of students, and (f) making an improper reference to "Jesus Christ" during class. . . .

Several parents expressed concern to the superintendent and other teachers about her ability to be an effective teacher. Five of Davies' colleagues, two of her principals, and the superintendent all testified that the shoplifting incident adversely impacted upon her ability to be an effective role model for fourth and fifth graders and would prevent her from being an effective teacher in the future.

On the issue of Davies being an appropriate role model, the board found that Davies was not a good role model prior to November 17 and, therefore, the knowledge by the district's patrons and students that she was involved in several cases of theft caused an irreversible situation whereby Davies could no longer be an effective teacher or role model. The board further found that fifth grade students would be negatively impacted by the knowledge of the thefts regardless of Davies' ability to be acquitted as a result of any diminished responsibility defense. . . .

. . . In our review, we give weight to the findings of fact made by the board of directors of the school district but are not bound by them. Iowa Code §279.18. We examine the evidence to determine if the decision of the board of directors of the school district has support in a preponderance of the evidence in the record as a whole. . . .

The statute under which this case proceeded provides: "a teacher may be discharged at any time during the contract year for just cause." Iowa Code §279.27 (1991). The term "just cause" includes legitimate reasons relating to teacher fault. In *Briggs v. Board of Directors*, 282 N.W.2d 740, 743 (Iowa 1979), we stated:

> Probably no inflexible "just cause" definition we could devise would be adequate to measure the myriad of situations which may surface in future litigation. It is sufficient here to hold that in the context of teacher fault a "just cause" is one which directly or indirectly significantly and adversely affects what must be the ultimate goal of every

school system: high quality education for the district's students. It relates to job performance including leadership and role model effectiveness.

In applying the "just cause" criteria to this case, the adjudicator and the district court determined that our case of *Smith*, 293 N.W.2d at 221, required that the board be reversed. We thus have an issue both of interpretation and application of our case law, primarily as formulated by the *Smith* case.

In *Smith*, we reviewed the termination of a teacher employed as a counselor who was having difficulties fulfilling his official duties due to a preoccupation with personal problems. Smith was given an extended leave of absence and sought professional psychiatric help. After diagnosis and treatment for a paranoid condition, Smith's doctor testified he no longer suffered from the condition. The doctor further stated that he could not determine when Smith would be fully capable of returning to work but did say that he could try returning to his duties.

We recognized in *Smith* that just cause for termination of a teaching contract may be found as a result of mental or physical disability. . . . Among the appropriate factors to be considered are "the nature and the extent of the duties required by the contract, the character and duration of the illness, the needs of the employer and the extent to which the duties can be performed by another." . . .

Davies argues, on the law, that *Smith* makes no distinction among a teacher's effectiveness, competence, and role modeling and therefore applies to this case. Role modeling comprises a part of a teacher's effectiveness and competence. . . .

It is extremely difficult in this case to compartmentalize those characteristics of Davies that may properly be considered in judging her role as a teacher. To consider the shoplifting incident as the crux of the matter and look for an explanation to Davies' adverse reaction to medication is an oversimplification of the problem facing the school board. Such an approach virtually ignores Davies' prior history of inappropriate conduct in the classroom, which bears not on her teaching skills but on the perception of her by students as someone to emulate.

There is much precedent for requiring a teacher to be a good role model. The United States Supreme Court in *Ambach v. Norwick*, 441 U.S. 68, 78–79, 99 S.Ct. 1589, 1595, 60 L.Ed.2d 49, 57–58 (1978), stated:

> Within the public school system, teachers play a critical part in developing students' attitude toward government and understanding of the role of citizens in our society. . . . Further, a teacher serves as a role model for his students exerting a subtle but important influence over their perception and values. . . .

. . . The particular issue of shoplifting has arisen in other jurisdictions. In *Leslie v. Oxford Area School District*, 54 Pa.Cmwlth. 120, 420 A.2d 764 (1980), the teacher asserted that her act of shoplifting was a result of temporary mental instability brought on by physical and emotional stresses. The Pennsylvania court found that the act of shoplifting is immoral and affects the teacher's ability to provide effective instruction. Regarding the teacher's claim of temporary mental instability, the court said: "The circumstances described are mitigating but they cannot 'eradicate the result or change the complexion of her acts.'" . . .

In its review of Davies' record as a teacher, the board specifically found that she was not a good role model for the students even prior to the shoplifting incident of November 17. It referred to her startling comments and bizarre conduct in the classroom, referenced in this opinion. This finding was followed by a finding that the knowledge by the district's patrons and students of her several cases of theft caused an irreversible situation whereby she could no longer be an effective teacher or role model. . . .

The need for a teacher to be a good example to the students is not denied by Davies in her argument. Rather, she views role modeling as part of a teacher's effectiveness and competence. On this, the board agrees and so do we. As it is artificial to separate these components of a teacher's abilities in making a factual determination of "just cause," so it is strained to interpret the legal requirements in that manner. . . .

. . . The findings by the board are extremely detailed. They lead to a conclusion that Davies' status as a role model was permanently impaired in her employment at the school with no hope of reconstruction due to the small size of the school district and the widespread knowledge of her status. Although not specifically mentioned, we find that the matters required by *Smith* to be considered were substantially included by the board in its determination. Davies was given a fair hearing by the board that met the legal requirements for the protection of her rights.

Our review convinces us that there is substantial evidence to support the board's conclusion. The board has established "just cause" for termination of Davies' employment under section 279.27 by a preponderance of the competent evidence. . . .

REVERSED AND REMANDED.

CASE NOTES

1. *Cause.* Good and just cause includes "any cause bearing a reasonable relationship to a teacher's fitness to discharge [his or her] duties" or "conduct which materially and substantially affects performance." *Fredrickson v. Denver Public School District No. 1*, 819 P.2d 1068 (Colo.1991).

In a rather bizarre case where a teacher shouldered his way into a fourth-grade child's life and then pursued a battle against the child's parent to wrest legal custody from her, the court upheld the teacher's dismissal for good and just cause. *Kerin v. Board of Education, Lamar School District*, 860 P.2d 574 (Colo.App.1993).

2. *Unfitness.* In *Weissman v. Board of Education*, 190 Colo. 414, 547 P.2d 1267 (1976), the court held that in determining whether a teacher's conduct indicates unfitness to teach, certain matters may properly be considered, including the age and maturity of the teacher's students, the likelihood that his or her conduct may have adversely affected students and other teachers, the degree of such adversity, the proximity or remoteness in time of the conduct, the extenuating or aggravating circumstances surrounding the conduct, the likelihood that the conduct may be repeated, the motives underlying it, and the extent to which discipline may have a chilling effect upon the rights of either the teacher involved or other teachers.

3. *Unprofessional Conduct.* Some tenure laws provide for dismissal of teachers for unprofessional conduct. *Black's Law Dictionary* contains the following definition:

> UNPROFESSIONAL CONDUCT. That which is by general opinion considered to be grossly unprofessional, immoral or dishonorable; *State Board of Dental Examiners v. Savell,* 90 Colo. 177, 8 P.2d 693, 697, that which violates ethical code of profession or such conduct which is unbecoming member of profession in good standing. *People v. Gorman,* 346 Ill. 432, 178 N.E. 880, 885. It involves breach of duty which professional ethics enjoin. *People v. Johnson,* 344 Ill. 132, 176 N.E. 278, 282.

See also the authorities annotated under the title "Unprofessional Conduct." 43A Words and Phrases 83. In 68 Am.Jur.2d Schools §161 is found the following:

> Unprofessional Conduct Definition: "Unprofessional Conduct" refers to conduct that violates the rules or the ethical code of a profession in good standing, or which indicates a teacher's unfitness to teach. So construed, a statutory provision authorizing dismissal of a permanent employee for unprofessional conduct is not rendered void for vagueness.

The phrase "unprofessional conduct" is to be construed according to its common and approved usage, having regard to the context in which it is used. *Board of Education of City of Los Angeles v. Swan,* 41 Cal.2d. 546, 261 (1953).

Unprofessional conduct means conduct indicating an unfitness to teach. *Morrison v. State Board of Education,* 1 Cal.3rd 214, 82 Cal.Rptr. 175, 461 P.2d 375 (1969).

In a case where a male teacher admitted to homosexual intimacy with a student, the court upheld the teacher's dismissal for unprofessional conduct. In what could be classified as an Olympian understatement, the court said: "A teacher who invites or permits a student or students to sleep with him and engage in intimate activity compromises his ability to teach." Such activity by definition would, of course, have a detrimental effect on the school and classroom. *Morris v. Clarksville-Montgomery County Consolidated Board of Education,* 867 S.W.2d 324 (Tenn.App.1993).

■ REDUCTION IN FORCE

Some school districts have been faced with declining student enrollments, and as a result, there has been a necessary, corresponding reduction in the number of professional employees. Reductions in force may be brought about through enrollment declines, financial exigencies, reorganization, or the elimination of programs. Therefore, even a tenured teacher may be removed from the workforce if justification is substantiated.

Local school boards may, within their discretion, establish a reduction in force policy, absent contractual obligations created by statutory or collective bargaining agreements. Such a policy should consider (1) the necessity of a reduction in force, (2) the positions eliminated, (3) the bad-faith actions of school boards, and (4) seniority.[58]

Reduction in Force Must Be in Good Faith and for Constitutional Reasons

Zoll v. Eastern Allamakee Community School District

United States Court of Appeals,
Eighth Circuit, 1978.
588 F.2d 246.

Action was brought by former school teacher for reinstatement and back pay following nonrenewal of her contract. The United States District Court for the Northern District of Iowa . . . entered judgment in favor of teacher against superintendent and elementary principal, and superintendent and principal appealed and teacher cross-appealed. The Court of Appeals . . . held that: (1) there was sufficient evidence of illicit motive for nonrenewal of teacher's contract to support jury verdict of liability; (2) no reversible error was committed in charging jury on elements of teacher's case, but (3) district court failed to comply with requisite guidelines for attorney fee awards and decided back pay claims against school district without benefit of

the Supreme Court's recent *Monell* decision, which foreclosed absolute immunity for local governing bodies.

Mrs. Zoll holds a Master's Degree in Elementary Administration and is certified by the State of Iowa as both a teacher and an administrator. Prior to the nonrenewal of her contract, she had been employed as a first-grade teacher in Allamakee County for twenty-nine years. The last fifteen years of her teaching career were with the Eastern Allamakee Community School District which was organized after she began teaching. She was promoted to elementary school principal in the Eastern Allamakee Community School District but resigned after two years to devote her full time to teaching.

In September 1973, Mr. Harold Pronga succeeded Mrs. Zoll as the elementary school principal. In June and July 1974, Mrs. Zoll wrote two letters to the editor of a local newspaper sharply criticizing Mr. Pronga, School Superintendent Duane Fuhrman, and school board members Lawrence Protsman, Hugh Conway, James Mettille and Roy Renk for a decline in administrative concern with academic excellence.

Mrs. Zoll complained that athletics were stressed over academics in the high school and that the quality of the elementary school was also in jeopardy. Her fears were based in part upon Mr. Pronga's refusal to authorize her requisition for work books and his suggestion that Mrs. Zoll teach her students to play "Fish" and "Concentration."

In August, 1974, on her second day at school following the summer vacation, Mrs. Zoll was summoned to Mr. Pronga's office to discuss the letters. Mr. Pronga had informed Superintendent Fuhrman of the planned meeting. At the outset of their discussion, Mr. Pronga read to Mrs. Zoll from his prepared notes: "I am very concerned and equally puzzled by your letters to the editor." Mr. Pronga accused Mrs. Zoll of misrepresenting facts and chastised her for failing to express her feelings through proper channels.

In December 1974, the school board followed the suggestion of the Iowa Department of Public Instruction in adopting a contingency plan for staff reduction in the event of a decline in enrollment. The plan included rules for determining the pool of teachers from which layoffs would be made. Selection from the pool would be by a 100-point system. A maximum of 40 points could be awarded for experience and training. The principal, superintendent and school board could award up to 20 points each, based on their subjective evaluations.

At the February 1975 school board meeting, the board was informed of a projected enrollment decline of first-grade students for the 1975–76 school year which would warrant a staff reduction. The board treated as a pool from which a lay-off would be made the three first-grade teachers: Mrs. Zoll, Mrs. Rebecca Okerlund and Mrs. Jane Meyer. The official decision of which teacher to terminate was postponed until the March board meeting. Mrs. Zoll was advised by a colleague of the school board president that the decision to terminate her was actually made at the closed executive session of the February board meeting.

Out of the potential 100 points, Mrs. Zoll received 57, Mrs. Okerlund 62 1/2, and Mrs. Meyer 72. Mrs. Zoll was erroneously awarded 17 points for experience, although she was entitled to 20 points under the objective scale. Thus, she was actually awarded 54 points, although entitled to 57 points. Mrs. Zoll received the highest point totals on the objective evaluation of experience and training. Out of a possible 40 points, Mrs. Zoll received 40, Mrs. Okerlund 4 1/2 and Mrs. Meyer 16. Mrs. Zoll received the lowest point totals on the subjective evaluations by Mr. Pronga, Mr. Fuhrman and the school board. Out of a possible 60 points, Mrs. Zoll received 17, Mrs. Okerlund 58, and Mrs. Meyer 56.

On April 8, 1975, the school board notified Mrs. Zoll that her contract would not be renewed for the 1975–76 school year. A public hearing was convened by the school board at Mrs. Zoll's request on June 9, 1975, pursuant to Iowa Code §279.13 (1975). At the conclusion of the hearing, the board voted four to one not to renew her contract.

On December 15, 1975, Mrs. Zoll filed suit against Mr. Pronga, Mr. Fuhrman, and the four board members who voted not to renew her contract, alleging that they had refused to renew her teaching contract in retaliation for her exercise of First Amendment rights, in violation of 42 U.S.C. §1983 (1970). . . .

There is sufficient evidence of a retaliatory motive for the nonrenewal of Mrs. Zoll's contract to support the jury verdict. Mrs. Zoll's letters to the editor criticizing the school administration were published in the summer of 1974. On the second day of the 1974–75 school year, Mr. Pronga called Mrs. Zoll to his office to express his displeasure with the letters. Mr. Fuhrman had foreknowledge of the meeting. There was testimony that the decision to terminate Mrs. Zoll was made before the statistical evaluation. Mrs. Zoll's expert witness testified to inconsistencies between the points assigned Mrs. Zoll and the notes and testimony of Mr. Pronga and Mr. Fuhrman.

Under the staff reduction policy which the board had adopted in December 1974, teachers laid off pursuant to the policy were granted certain "recall rights" for a three-year period: "Any staff member laid off due to reduction of staff policy may be recalled if a vacancy exists within three years." Three vacancies arose during the year following Mrs. Zoll's termination. The vacancies were at the first grade, sixth grade and seventh-eighth grade levels. Mrs. Zoll applied for but was not offered any of these positions. Instead, two new teachers were hired and one teacher was transferred to fill the vacancies. The jury could reasonably have believed that the subjective rating of Mrs. Zoll by Mr. Pronga and Mr. Fuhrman was a pretext for discharging her for exercising her First Amendment rights. See *Mt. Healthy City Board of Education v. Doyle,* 429 U.S. 274, 97 S.Ct. 568, 50 L.Ed.2d 471 (1977). . . .

Accordingly, we affirm the entry of judgment of liability on the jury verdict, vacate the attorney's fee award and remand to the district court for reconsideration of the post-trial back pay issue and the attorney's fee award and for further proceedings consistent with this opinion.

Affirmed in part, vacated and remanded in part.

CASE NOTES

1. In abiding by the intent of tenure laws, school boards must follow a protocol that gives priority to tenured teachers in retaining employment. An Oklahoma court has explained: "When declining enrollment requires a reduction-in-force, a school board must balance a district's needs against available resources and take

appropriate action to curtain personnel. While a school board may exercise wide latitude and autonomy in choosing a method for reducing the teaching force, its RIF policy must nonetheless conform to the commands of tenure law. Tenured faculty have a claim to preferential status over nontenured faculty in implementation of a reduction-in-force plan. To hold otherwise would emasculate the statutory tenure policy and let school boards do indirectly what they cannot do directly. Tenure rights must be protected and school boards afforded the necessary discretion to so shape quality education programs as to make them meet the available financial resources. In sum, a school board is always free to adjust its teachers' roll to meet economic necessity, but it cannot invoke unsanctioned grounds to subvert the statutorily mandated security-from-termination protection for tenured teachers." *Babb v. Independent School District No. I-5 of Rogers County, Oklahoma,* 829 P.2d 973 (Okla.1992); see also *Barton v. Independent School District No. I-99,* Custer County, Oklahoma, 914 P.2d 1041 (Okla.1996).

2. A tenured teacher may have "bumping" rights in time of fiscal stress. A Montana court has held that a high school principal with tenure had the right to bump an untenured teacher in a subject matter area in which he was certified to teach. *Holmes v. Board of Trustees of School District Nos. 4, 47 and 2,* 243 Mont. 263, 792 P.2d 10 (1990).

■ CONSTITUTIONAL PROTECTION OF CONTRACTS

Both state[59] and federal[60] constitutions contain protections against the unilateral alteration of contracts by the state to disadvantage individuals in their relationships with the government. Basically, these provisions ensure the citizens that the state will not modify or abolish a contract to which it is a party.

An inherent conflict, however, exists between the guaranteed sanctity of contracts and the police power of the state in subsequent legislatures to make and change laws in the interest of the common good. A legislature cannot be completely bound and restricted by agreements made by earlier legislatures. Thus, the constraints placed on legislatures by the contract

provisions of the state and federal constitutions must necessarily be hedged to allow the government to function freely. The U.S. Supreme Court has declared that

> it is settled that neither the "contract" clause nor the "due process" clause has the effect of overriding the power of the State to establish all regulations that are reasonably necessary to secure the health, safety, good order, comfort, or general welfare of the community; that this power can neither be abdicated nor bargained away, and is inalienable even by express grant; and all contract and property rights are held subject to its fair exercise.[61]

Whether the individual's right to a contract prevails over the state's interest in modifying the agreement is dependent on at least three conditions. First, an agreement between an individual and the state must be clearly a "contract" before it invokes the obligation of contract protection. It cannot be simply a privilege bestowed by the state, or some other relationship defined as something other than a contract. Second, the rights under a contract are determined by the laws existing at the time that the contract was made.[62] Third, where, on balance, the interests of the state in modifying or abrogating the contract are sufficiently weighty and compelling, the interest of the individual must give way to the common and general interest of all the people.

The burden of proof is on the individual to show that a particular relationship with the state is, in fact, a contract. The Supreme Court of the United States in *Dodge v. Board of Education*[63] defined the conditions necessary for a statute to be regarded as a contract:

> In determining whether a law tenders a contract to a citizen it is of first importance to examine the language of the statute. If it provides for the execution of a written contract on behalf of the state the case for an obligation binding upon the state is clear. . . . On the other hand, an act merely fixing salaries of officers creates no contract in their favor and the compensation named may be altered at will by the legislature. This is true also of an act fixing the term or tenure of a public officer or an employee of a state agency. The presumption is that such a law is not intended to create private contractual or vested rights but merely declares a policy to be pursued until the legislature shall ordain otherwise. He who asserts the creation of a contract with the state in such a case has the burden of overcoming the presumption.

The most important precedent rendered by the Supreme Court defining the extent of governmental prerogative with regard to contracts was the famous *Dartmouth College* case,[64] which gave form and substance to Article I, §10, the obligation of contracts provision of the U.S. Constitution. That article states: "No State Shall . . . pass any law . . . impairing the Obligation of Contracts. . . ."

In *Dartmouth College*, the English crown had granted a charter to the college, which had been established in the colony of New Hampshire as a private institution.[65] The college was governed by a self-perpetuating board of twelve members. A conflict that had political ramifications developed between the college president and the board members. Reacting to this controversy, the legislature of New Hampshire, in 1816, enacted legislation that materially altered the charter, making the college a state institution. The college trustees brought an action and claimed, in part, that the act of the legislature was unconstitutional and impaired the obligation of their contract, the original charter. The opinion of the Court, delivered by Justice Marshall, stated:

> The points for consideration are: 1. Is this contract protected by the Constitution of the United States? 2. Is it impaired by the acts under which the defendant holds?
>
> 1. On the first point, it has been argued, that the word "contract" in its broadest sense would comprehend the political relations between the government and its citizens, would extend to offices held within a state, for state purposes, and to many of those laws concerning civil institutions, which must change with circumstances, and be modified by ordinary legislation; which deeply concern the public, and which, to preserve good government, the public judgment must control. . . .
>
> This [charter] is plainly a contract to which the donors, the trustees and the crown (to whose rights and obligation New Hampshire succeeds) were the original parties. It is a contract made on a valuable consideration. It is a contract for the security and disposition of property. It is a contract, on the faith of which, real and personal estate has been conveyed to the corporation. It is, then, a contract within the letter of the Constitution, and within its spirit also unless the fact that the property is invested by the donors in trustees, for the promotion of religion and education, for the benefit of persons who are perpetually changing,

> though the objects remain the same, shall create a particular exception, taking this case out of the prohibition contained in the Constitution. . . .
>
> The opinion of the court, after mature deliberation, is, that this is a contract, the obligation of which cannot be impaired, without violating the Constitution of the United States. This opinion appears to us to be equally supported by reason, and by the former decisions of this court.
>
> 2. We next proceed to the inquiry, whether its obligation has been impaired by those acts of the legislature of New Hampshire, to which the special verdict refers?
>
> From the review of this charter, which has been taken, it appears that the whole power of governing the college, of appointing and removing tutors, of fixing salaries, of directing the course of study to be pursued by the students, and of filling up vacancies created in their own body, was vested in the trustees. On the part of the crown it was expressly stipulated, that this corporation, thus constituted, should continue forever, and that the number of trustees should forever consist of twelve, and no more. By this contract the crown was bound, and could have made no violent alteration in its essential terms, without impairing its obligation.
>
> By the Revolution the duties, as well as the powers, of government devolved on the people of New Hampshire. It is admitted, that among the latter was comprehended the transcendent power of parliament, as well as that of the executive department. It is too clear, to require the support of argument, that all contracts and rights respecting property, remained unchanged by the Revolution. The obligations, then, which were created by the charter to Dartmouth College, were the same in the new, that they had been in the old government. . . . But the Constitution of the United States has imposed this additional limitation, that the legislature of a state shall pass no act "impairing the obligation of contracts." . . .
>
> It results from this opinion, that the acts of the legislature of New Hampshire, which are stated in the special verdict found in this cause, are repugnant to the Constitution of the United States; and that the judgment on this special verdict ought to have been for the plaintiffs. The judgment of the state court must, therefore, be reversed.

Later, in an Indiana case, *State of Indiana ex rel. Anderson v. Brand*, Article I, §10, of the Constitution of the United States was directly applied as a limitation on state legislative actions pertaining to public education. The Indiana legislature passed an act that repealed a 1927 law granting tenure to teachers, and a teacher thereafter sought a *writ of mandamus* to compel her continued employment. She claimed the original act had granted her a continuing contract that could not be impaired nor breached by subsequent legislation. The original act provided:

> It is further agreed by the contracting parties that all of the Teachers' Tenure Law, approved March 8, 1927, shall be in full force and effect in this contract.

The Supreme Court of Indiana ruled in favor of the defendant board of education, and the teacher appealed. The Supreme Court of the United States reversed the Indiana court.[66]

Both of these decisions illustrate the constitutional requirements within which a state legislature must operate when dealing with contracts. Particular application may be noted where legislation such as tenure and retirement statutes may create a contract between the state and an individual.

There is a fine line between the constitutional rights of one individual and the rights of the people as exercised through the elected authority of the legislature to provide for the welfare of the state. This is demonstrated by the dissent of Justice Black in the *Anderson v. Brand* case, when he said that the Supreme Court should not interfere with the determination of educational policy by the Indiana legislature because the legislature of a state cannot make and be held to a contract "with a few citizens, that would take from all the citizens, the continuing power to alter the educational policy for the best interests of Indiana school children. . . . "

❖ — ❖ — ❖

Constitutional Prohibition against Impairment of Contracts Is Not Violated by Additional Test Requirement for Retention of Teaching Certificate

State v. Project Principle, Inc.

Supreme Court of Texas, 1987.
724 S.W.2d 387.

CAMPBELL, Justice. This is a direct appeal from a temporary injunction prohibiting enforcement of Tex.Educ.Code §13.047 (Vernon Supp.1987) on the ground that the statute is unconstitutional. Section 13.047 provides that public school educators, to retain their teaching certificates, must successfully complete an examination known as the Texas Examination for Current Administrators and Teachers, or TECAT. We hold the statute is constitutional and we reverse the judgment of the trial court and dissolve that court's injunction. . . .

On July 3, 1984, the state legislature passed into law House Bill 72. The bill contained numerous educational reforms, including additional school funding, school finance reform, teacher salary increases, and teacher competency testing. . . .

Section 13.047 provides for a testing program by the State Board of Education for continued certification of all educators who have not taken the test required by section 13.032(e) of the Code. However, the section 13.032(e) test was first administered on May 24, 1986; thus, all previously certified teachers, including all members of Project Principle, were required to take the TECAT. . . .

The state argues that the trial court's injunction is in error because section 13.047 impairs no contract rights. Project Principle contends that teaching certificates are contracts with which the legislature may not interfere. We hold that a teaching certificate is not a contract within the meaning of article I, section 16. Rather, the certificate is a license, and like all licenses, is subject to such future restrictions as the state may reasonably impose.

The United States Supreme Court spoke to the impairment of contracts argument more than forty years ago in *Dodge v. Board of Education*, 302 U.S. 74, 79, 58 S.Ct. 98, 100, 82 L.Ed. 57 (1937). In *Dodge*, retired teachers challenged an act of the Illinois legislature which decreased the amounts of annuity payments to retired teachers of Chicago public schools. The teachers claimed that the Act impaired the obligation of contracts in contravention of article I, §10 of the United States Constitution. The Supreme Court of Illinois held that in passing the statute providing for the annuities the state legislature evinced no intent to create a binding contract with teachers. The United States Supreme Court affirmed, stating "the presumption is that [a tenure] law is not intended to create private contractual or vested rights but merely declares a policy to be pursued until the legislature shall ordain otherwise."

As early as 1925 it was recognized in Texas that a teaching certificate is a license. In *Marrs v. Matthews*, 270 S.W. 586 (Tex.Civ.App.—Texarkana 1925, writ ref'd), a teacher claimed that the state superintendent could not cancel his "permanent teacher's certificate" because the language used in describing the offenses for which a certificate may be cancelled was void for vagueness. The teacher also claimed that the statute giving the superintendent the authority to cancel the certificate of any "unworthy" teacher was an attempt to confer judicial powers upon an executive department of the state government. In dissolving the trial court writ enjoining cancellation of the teaching certificate, the court stated that a teaching certificate "is merely a license granted by the state, and is revocable by the state." The court noted that the teacher had "voluntarily sought and secured a statutory privilege to be enjoyed subject to statutory conditions."

Because we hold a teaching certificate is not a contract, the constitutional prohibition against impairment of contracts is not violated when the legislature imposes new conditions for the retention of the certificate. Further, because the certificate is a license and confers no vested rights, the constitutional prohibition against retroactive laws is not violated. It is only when vested rights are impaired that a retroactive law is invalid. . . .

The state contends the trial court's injunction is in error because section 13.047 does not violate due process guarantees. Project Principle contends the statute violates federal and state guarantees of due process. . . . Project Principle argues that after the enactment of section 13.047, educators' certificates are subject to cancellation without a hearing or avenue for appeal upon failure to take the TECAT or to perform satisfactorily on the TECAT.

First, it must be noted that decertification is not automatic upon failure of the examination. Section 13.047 provides that "each teacher must be given more than one opportunity to perform satisfactorily" on the TECAT.

Second, provisions for appeal of "proceedings concerning the suspension, revocation, or cancellation of a [teaching] certificate" are contained in 19 Tex.Admin.Code §157.1(b)(4) (1985). . . . This review provides procedural due process to any teacher who fails to perform satisfactorily on a competency examination. . . .

. . . Project Principle argues that the classification of teachers into a class composed of those who pass the test and a class composed of those who fail the test is subject to strict scrutiny under equal protection analysis. Strict scrutiny is applicable, Project Principle argues, because the classification impinges upon a fundamental right, the right to practice a profession.

. . . Likewise, we hold a person's interest in teaching is not a fundamental right.

The right to teach not being fundamental, a classification which impinges on that right is not subject to strict scrutiny. . . . Rather, the TECAT must be judged by a rational basis standard. We hold that competency testing bears a rational relation to the legitimate state objective of maintaining competent teachers in the public schools. . . .

We reverse the judgment of the trial court and dissolve that court's injunction.

Case Note

The elimination of tenure for principals in Chicago did not violate the federal Constitution. Tenure was found not to be a contract; therefore, Article I, §10, the obligation of contracts provision of the U.S. Constitution, was not violated. *Pittman v. Chicago Board of Education*, 860 F.Supp. 495 (E.D.Ill.1994).

■ ENDNOTES

1. 78 Corpus Juris Secundum §154.

2. Ellwood P. Cubberley, *Public Education in the United States* (Boston: Houghton Mifflin, 1934), p. 371.

3. Ibid., p. 381.

4. R. Freeman Butts and Lawrence A. Cremin, *A History of Education in American Culture* (New York: Henry Holt, 1953), p. 399.

5. Ibid.

6. Ibid.

7. John Swett, "The Examination of Teachers," *National Education Association Proceedings* (1872), pp. 71–82, in Butts and Cremin, *History of Education*, p. 399.

8. Richard J. Coley and Margaret E. Goertz, *Educational Standards in the 50 States: 1990* (Princeton, N.J.: Educational Testing Service, August 1990), pp. 10–15.

9. Harrah Independent School District v. Martin, 440 U.S. 194, 99 S.Ct. 1062 (1979).

10. Wardwell v. Board of Education, 529 F.2d 625 (6th Cir.1976). See McCarthy v. Philadelphia Civil Service Commission, 424 U.S. 645, 96 S.Ct. 1154 (1976).

11. *Black's Law Dictionary*, 7th ed. (St. Paul, Minn.: West, 1999).

12. School District No. 8, Pinal County v. Superior Court of Pinal County, 102 Ariz. 478, 433 P.2d 28 (1967).

13. *Webster's New International Dictionary*, quoted in Beilan v. Board of Public Education, School District of Philadelphia, 357 U.S. 399, 78 S.Ct. 1317 (1958).

14. Board of Directors of Sioux City v. Mroz, 295 N.W. 2d 447 (Iowa 1980).

15. Blunt v. Marion County School Board, 515 F.2d 951 (5th Cir. 1975).

16. Kinsella v. Board of Education, 64 A.D.2d 738, 407 N.Y.S.2d 78 (1978).

17. Board of Education of the School District of Philadelphia v. Kushner, 109 Pa. Cmwlth. 120, 530 A.2d 541 (Pa. 1987).

18. Blunt v. Marion County School Board, op cit.

19. Trustees, Missoula County School District No. 1 v. Anderson, 232 Mont. 501, 757 P.2d 1315 (1988).

20. Gilliland v. Board of Education of Pleasant View Consolidated School District No. 622, 67 Ill.2d 143, 8 Ill.Dec. 84, 365 N.E.2d 322 (1977).

21. *Webster's Third New International Dictionary* (Springfield, Mass.: 1961).

22. *Black's Law Dictionary*, op. cit.

23. School District No. 8, Pinal County v. Superior Court, op. cit.

24. 78 A.L.R.3d 83, 87 (1977).

25. Sims v. Board of Trustees, Holly Springs, 414 So.2d 431 (Miss.1982).

26. Stiver v. State, 221 Ind. 370, 7 N.E.2d 181 (1937); see also 78 A.L.R.3d 83 (1977).

27. Crump v. Board of Education, 79 N.C.App. 372, 339 S.E.2d 483 (1986), review denied, 317 N.C. 333, 346 S.E.2d 137 (1986).

28. Stephens v. Alabama State Tenure Commission, 634 So.2d 549 (Ala.Civ.App.1993).

29. Thompson v. Wake County Board of Education, 31 N.C.App. 401, 230 S.E.2d 164 (1976); see Thompson v. Wake County Board of Education; 292 N.C. 406, 233 S.E.2d 538 (1977).

30. Harris v. Mechanicville Central School District, 45 N.Y.2d 279, 408 N.Y.S.2d 384, 380 N.E.2d 213 (1978).

31. 78 A.L.R.3d 83 (1977).

32. Ibid.

33. Vogulkin v. State Board of Education, 194 Cal.App.2d 424, 15 Cal.Rptr. 335 (1961).

34. Horton v. Jefferson Cty.–DuBois Area Vocational Technical School, 157 Pa.Cmwlth. 424, 630 A.2d 481 (1993); Dohanic v. Department of Education, 111 Pa.Cmwlth. 192, 533 A.2d 812 (1987).

35. Kilpatrick v. Wright, 437 F.Supp. 397 (M.D.Ala.1977).

36. Dupree v. School Committee of Boston, 15 Mass.App. Ct. 535, 446 N.E.2d 1099 (1983).

37. Weissman v. Board of Education of Jefferson County School District No. R-1, 190 Colo. 414, 547 P.2d 1267 (1976).

38. Pettit v. State Board of Education, 10 Cal.3d 29, 109 Cal.Rptr. 665, 513 P.2d 889 (1973).

39. Morrison v. State Board of Education, 1 Cal.3d 214, 82 Cal.Rptr. 175, 461 P.2d 375 (1969).

40. National Gay Task Force v. Board of Education of Oklahoma City, 729 F.2d 1270 (10th Cir. 1984).

41. Ibid.

42. 478 U.S. 186, 106 S.Ct. 2841 (1986), rehearing denied, 478 U.S. 1039, 107 S.Ct. 29 (1986).

43. John E. Nowak, Ronald D. Rotunda, and J. Nelson Young, *Constitutional Law*, 3d ed. (St. Paul, Minn.: West, 1986; 1988 pocket supplement, p. 65; Solem v. Helm, 463 U.S. 277, 103 S.Ct. 3001 (1983).

44. See Hainline v. Bond, 250 Kan. 217, 824 P.2d 959 (1992).

45. Covert v. Bensalem Township School District, 104 Pa.Cmwlth. 441, 522 A.2d 129 (1987).

46. People v. Maxwell, 177 N.Y. 494, 69 N.E. 1092 (1904); School City of Elwood v. State ex rel. Griffin, 203 Ind. 626, 180 N.E. 471 (1932).

47. See Newton Edwards, *The Courts and the Public Schools* (Chicago: University of Chicago Press, 1955), p.481.

48. Board of Education of the School District of Philadelphia, Pennsylvania v. Philadelphia Federation of Teachers AFL-CIO, 464 Pa. 92, 346 A.2d 35 (1975); see Balog v. McKeesport Area School District, 86 Pa.Cmwlth. 132, 484 A.2d 198 (1984).

49. Bethel Park School District v. Krall, 67 Pa.Cmwlth. 143, 445 A.2d 1377 (1982), cert. denied, 464 U.S. 851, 104 S.Ct. 162 (1983).

50. Unified School District No. 434, Osage County v. Hubbard, 19 Kan.App.2d 323, 868 P.2d 1240 (1994); see also Gillett v. Unified School District No. 276, 227 Kan. 71, 605 P.2d 105 (1980).

51. Pocahontas Community School District v. Levene, 409 N.W.2d 698 (Iowa App.1987).

52. Stansberry v. Argenbright, 227 Mont. 123, 738 P.2d 478 (1987).

53. Yanzick v. School District No. 23, Lake County, Montana, 196 Mont. 375, 641 P.2d 431 (1982).

54. Tomczik v. State Tenure Commission, 175 Mich.App. 495, 438 N.W.2d 642 (1989).

55. Rhodes v. Laurel Highlands School District, 118 Pa.Cmwlth. 119, 544 A.2d 562 (1988).

56. Ortbals v. Special School District, 762 S.W.2d 437 (Mo.App.1988).

57. Barcheski v. Board of Education of Grand Rapids Public Schools, 162 Mich.App. 388, 412 N.W.2d 296 (1987).

58. Robert Phay, *Reduction in Force: Legal Issues and Recommended Policy* (Topeka, Kansas: National Organization on Legal Problems of Education, 1980).

59. See Virginia Constitution, art. I, §11.

60. U.S. Constitution, art. I, §10.

61. Atlantic Coast Line R.R. Co. v. City of Goldsboro, 232 U.S. 548, 558, 34 S.Ct. 364, 368 (1914). See also Manigault v. Springs, 199 U.S. 473, 26 S.Ct. 127 (1905); Stone v. Mississippi, 101 U.S. 814 (1880).

62. Ogden v. Saunders, 25 U.S. (12 Wheat.) 213 (1827); Citizens Mutual Building Association v. Edwards, 167 Va. 399, 189 S.E. 453 (1937). For a definitive explanation, see A. E. Dick Howard, *Commentaries on the Constitution of Virginia,* vol. I (Charlottesville: University Press of Virginia, 1974), pp. 206–7.

63. 302 U.S. 74, 58 S.Ct. 98 (1936).

64. Trustees of the Dartmouth College v. Woodward, 17 U.S. (4 Wheat.) 518 (1819).

65. Ibid.

66. State ex rel. Anderson v. Brand, 303 U.S. 95, 58 S.Ct. 443 (1938).

CHAPTER 15

TEACHER RIGHTS AND FREEDOMS

The one certain and fixed point in the entire discussion is this: that freedom of
expression is guaranteed to the citizens of a liberal democracy not for the pleasure
of the citizens but for the health of the state.

—Archibald MacLeish

CHAPTER OUTLINE

- THE SOURCE OF RIGHTS
- ACADEMIC FREEDOM
- FIRST AMENDMENT: PRIMARY REPOSITORY
- PRIVACY
- PRIVACY AND DRUG TESTING OF TEACHERS
- FREEDOM OF RELIGION
- PRIVILEGE AGAINST SELF-INCRIMINATION

THE LEGAL RELATIONSHIP between the teacher and the school board is dependent on essentially three sources of the law: (1) constitutional rights and freedoms of the teacher as a citizen, (2) statutory relationships that govern the conduct of the public schools, and (3) contractual conditions of employment that may be created and agreed to by both the teacher and the employer. These sources are not wholly independent of each other; in fact, they have substantial interdependence. As we have seen in earlier chapters, overlap may come from sev-

eral perspectives. For example, the presence of a statutory tenure contract relationship creates a substantive due process interest as well as a constitutionally protected contract right on behalf of the teacher. Statutes, contracts, and agreements may generally create extenuating circumstances that vest the teacher with additional implicit rights beyond those emanating directly from the state or federal constitution. As we also observed in other chapters, substantive due process interests evolve from the rights and expectations created by the state through statute, regulation, or implication; they do not emanate directly from the federal Constitution itself. The rights and freedoms referred to in the present chapter are different in that they are explicitly and directly derived from the federal Constitution.

These natural rights are of such importance to human existence that they are protected by explicit wording of the Constitution. These rights, according to Justice Black, are set out as a "remarkable collection of 'thou shalt nots,'"[1] or prohibitions against governmental intrusion. The essence of constitutional preservation of these inviolate natural rights is found in the first five words of the First Amendment: "Congress shall make no law."

■ THE SOURCE OF RIGHTS

Under the U.S. Constitution, the source of individual rights and freedoms is found in the Bill of Rights, the first ten amendments. These amendments are prohibitions against governmental intrusion upon fundamental and inalienable human rights that all persons must retain in their relationship to government. The body of the Constitution itself delegated specified powers to the central government and did not state what rights and freedoms were left to the people. This omission greatly concerned Jefferson, who criticized the new Constitution as promulgated in Philadelphia in 1787 because it contained no specific provisions guaranteeing individual rights and freedoms. Jefferson wrote Madison from Paris (where Jefferson was ambassador) praising the new Constitution, but he ended his letter with a denunciation of the Constitutional Convention for not including a bill of rights. He said: "Let me add that a bill of rights is what the people are entitled to against every government on earth, general or particular, and what no just government should refuse, or rest on inference."[2] Jefferson's concern was reflected by others as well, and the ratification of the Constitution by the states was made contingent on the passage of an attendant bill of rights. Madison wrote the proposed bill of rights and presented it to Congress on September 25, 1789, in order to "kill the opposition" to the new Constitution.[3] With the additional assurance protecting the individual from governmental overbear-

ance, the requisite number of state legislatures ratified the Bill of Rights by December 15, 1791.

Among the specifications of "thou shalt nots" contained in the Bill of Rights, the most basic are freedom of religion, speech, press, and assembly and guarantee of due process as well as freedom from warrantless searches and forced self-incrimination. It was not until much later, after the Civil War, that the Fourteenth Amendment's due process and equal protection provisions were added to form the formidable and complete array of specified individual rights that are enjoyed by Americans today.

Yet it was not until well into the twentieth century that the original ten amendments were first applied to encroachments by state governments on individual rights and freedoms.[4] Until that time, the protections were read literally by the courts to mean only that "Congress shall make no law."

In addition to the U.S. Bill of Rights, state constitutions have provided additional protections against encroachments of the state governments on rights of individuals. Most state constitutions have their own bill of rights or provisions that are tantamount to such. Unfortunately, in many instances state courts historically have not been as dedicated to enforcement of individual rights as have the federal courts. More recently, though, state courts have shown new vigor and have greatly enhanced the importance of state constitutional provisions as restraints on unwarranted governmental action.

■ ACADEMIC FREEDOM

The idea of academic freedom apparently traversed the Atlantic Ocean from German universities, where the terms *lernfreiheit*, meaning freedom to learn, and *lehrfreiheit*, meaning freedom to teach, constituted the forerunners of the concept of academic freedom that is held so dear by the great American universities of today. In Germany, the university was viewed as a special place, separate and distinct from society at large, a place where professors could speak without "fear or favor" but in an "atmosphere of consent" that surrounded the whole learning environment of the institution.[5]

The idea of academic freedom in the United States is an important attribute to education regardless of the type of institution where learning takes place, but the necessity of academic freedom to stand against encroachments upon the freedom to learn and teach is of less importance in America than in Germany because of the more pervasive individual protections of our Bill of Rights in the U.S. Constitution. Under the Bill of Rights, all aspects of academic freedom are found in the speech, expression, privacy, and religion provisions of the First Amendment. The Supreme Court has observed the essential nature and desirability of academic freedom and the fact that its essence is contained in the First Amendment. In *Keyishian v. Board of Regents of the University of the State of New York*,[6] the Supreme Court placed the imprimatur of the U.S. Constitution behind the concept when it said: "Our nation is deeply committed to safeguarding academic freedom, which is of transcendent value to all of us and not merely to teachers concerned. That freedom is, therefore, a specific concern of the First Amendment, which does not tolerate laws that cast a pall of orthodoxy over the classroom."[7] In other cases, including *Bakke*[8] and *Sweezy*,[9] the Court has recognized a kind of institutional right encompassed in academic freedom,[10] and at least one lower court has asserted an individual right to academic freedom under the limited circumstances of the university setting.[11] Yet, in each of these cases, it is clear that protection to learn and teach does not emanate directly from any abstract concept of academic freedom but rather is founded in the substantive constitutional protections of free speech and expression embodied in the First Amendment. The student and the teacher are guaranteed *lernfreiheit* and *lehrfreiheit* by virtue of the First Amendment's direct proscription of the state or other entity casting a "pall of orthodoxy over the classroom." Thus, academic freedom is not, in and of itself, a separate constitutional protection, but instead it is the desirable end to be achieved by the enforcement of the individual rights and freedoms in the classroom as guaranteed by the Bill of Rights.[12]

Therefore, while the issue is a bit clouded by several references to academic freedom in constitutional law involving universities, there is no case law to support the proposition that an elementary or secondary school teacher has a constitutional right to academic freedom *per se*. In the public secondary schools, the teacher does not have "unlimited liberty" to determine the structure and content of the courses.[13] Thus, a teacher cannot simply plead denial of academic freedom without buttressing the claim with the substantive grounds of the First Amendment or other provisions of the Bill of Rights.

An allegation of denial of academic freedom standing alone will not prevail unless the teacher can show that as a result of school policy a "pall of orthodoxy" has been cast over the classroom and that the denial offends a specified right under the U.S. Constitution.

■ FIRST AMENDMENT: PRIMARY REPOSITORY

The First Amendment is the basic repository of the primary and essential rights and freedoms. At an earlier point in our nation's constitutional development, public employment was viewed as a privilege and not a right.[14] The basis for this logic, that public employees could not fully retain their political freedoms and hold public employment concurrently, was founded in Justice Holmes's often-quoted assertion, in an 1892 case, that "[t]he petitioner may have a constitutional right to talk politics, but he has no constitutional right to be a policeman."[15]

Some earlier cases involving public school teachers followed this philosophy, holding that the contract provisions between the board and the teacher could prohibit the exercise of various rights and freedoms by teachers; if the teacher violated the provisions of the contract, even though they were repressive of the teacher's rights, dismissal could be upheld.[16] Under such rationale, some courts allowed dismissal of teachers for marriage,[17] absence from school for childbirth,[18] and political discussion in the classroom.[19]

Although the courts were generally split and clearly uncertain as to the political rights and personal freedoms of teachers, the privilege/right dichotomy continued to exist. Where teachers did prevail, the courts based their conclusions on common law reasonableness and not on constitutional rights or freedoms. The common law standard maintained simply that school boards held an implicit common law power, even in absence of statute, to dismiss teachers for valid reasons.[20] The validity of the reasons was many times spurious and bore little relationship to ability to teach. Where statutes did govern dismissals, the teachers' rights could be no less in jeopardy. Some statutes simply invested boards with the power to dismiss teachers at the pleasure of the board.[21] Thus, the teacher employment relationship with the school board was defined by common law reasonableness, contract law, and statutory and regulatory provisions of the state. It did not clearly reach to constitutional rights and freedoms until 1968.

The watershed case in the application of constitutional standards to teacher employment was decided in 1968, *Pickering v. Board of Education*.[22] The U.S. Supreme Court held that freedom of speech, while not absolute in all circumstances, is nevertheless sufficiently strong to require that the state show a "compelling state interest" in order to overcome a teacher's right to speak out on issues of public importance. In so doing, the Court equated teachers' right of free speech with that of other members of the general public to criticize and comment on public policies and issues. Any lingering doubt about the legal dichotomy of privileges versus rights was extinguished by this case, and the dictum of Justice Holmes was repudiated.

After *Pickering*, in search of a new standard, the courts have developed a flexible rule that provides for balancing the public's interest against the private interest of the employee in each circumstance. This balancing, however, does not remove all state restraint on teacher activities; on the contrary, the courts have reflected a strong belief that because of their sensitive position in the classroom, teachers must be held accountable for certain activities both internal and external to the school.[23] The interest of the public is to a great extent dependent on teachers' status, appearance, and stature in the community. The school board must preserve the integrity of the learning processes of the school. Yet, because a teacher enters the school setting with constitutional freedoms of speech and association, the school must have a compelling

reason to overcome the teacher's interest. This means simply that the teacher's rights are not absolute and can be overcome if the public necessity is great enough. The valid rationales used by boards of education in dismissing teachers have ranged from in-school issues, such as insubordination and incompetency, to out-of-school activities that tend to reflect on the welfare of the school, such as sexual misconduct and gambling.

SPEECH RIGHTS OF PUBLIC EMPLOYEES

What a teacher may do or say is governed by the Supreme Court precedents covering the constitutional conditions of public employment. The Supreme Court has more narrowly circumscribed the freedom of speech of public employees than that of the public at large. In a series of cases, the Court has attempted to establish a rationale that answers a basic question: What is it about the government's role as employer that gives it a freer hand in regulating the speech of its employees than it has in regulating the speech of the public at large?[24] In answer to this question, the Court has concluded that practical reality requires that government at certain times, and under certain conditions, be able to restrict employees' speech in order to fulfill its responsibilities to operate effectively and efficiently.[25]

The fundamental maxim of free speech is that government must tolerate and cannot restrain the exercise of free speech in open debate by the public regardless of whether it is offensive, tumultuous, or discordant.[26] The First Amendment reflects the "profound material commitment of the principle that debate on public issues should be uninhibited, robust and wide-open."[27] Yet the Court has never expressed doubt that the government as employer may bar its employees from issuing forth with offensive utterances to either the public or other employees with whom they work.[28] Even though a private person is completely free to uninhibitedly criticize a governor's or a legislator's position on a subject, the Court has never suggested that the governor or legislator (or school superintendent) could not fire a subordinate administrator or government official for similar criticism.[29] Public officials are not constitutionally required to allow public dissent by their subordinates.[30] Different principles of free speech apply to government as employer as opposed to government as sovereign.[31] If speech by employees interferes with governmental operation, it can be curtailed, but speech by nonemployees cannot be inhibited under the same standards.

The Court has said that the extra power accruing to government in regulating the speech of employees comes from the nature of the government's mission as employer. Governmental agencies (or school districts) are charged by law with the responsibility for conducting governmental business. State agencies employ workers to perform assigned tasks as effectively and efficiently as possible. The precedent is well established that when an employee is paid a salary to work and contributes to an agency's effective operation and thereafter begins to do or say things that detract from the agency's effective operation, the government employer must have the power to prevent or restrain the employee from such acts or utterances.

The Supreme Court in a 1994 decision, *Waters v. Churchill*,[32] defined what it called the key decisions to constitutional analysis of government employment decisions. The Court said:

> The key to First Amendment analysis of government employment decisions, then, is this: The government's interest in achieving its goals as effectively and efficiently as possible is elevated from a relatively subordinate interest when it acts as sovereign to a significant one when it acts as employer. The government cannot restrict the speech of the public at large just in the name of efficiency. But where the government is employing someone for the very purpose of effectively achieving its goals, such restrictions may well be appropriate.[33]

The public school teacher or other school employee employed by the school district therefore may be restrained in the exercise of speech to the extent described by the Supreme Court in *Waters*. Under this precedent, the ultimate constitutional analysis requires that the Court weigh the employee's interest against the state's in determining the validity of the restraint. In refining this task, the Court has separated employee speech into that which is a matter of "public concern" and that which is a matter of

"personal interest." The specifics of this standard are set out and clarified by the Supreme Court in *Connick v. Myers*.[34]

SPEECH AND THE *CONNICK* RULE

Connick explains that First Amendment free speech is protected when the employee speaks out on "matters of public concern." These words from *Pickering*[35] mean the court must weigh the employee's interest in speaking on matters of public concern against the state's interest in providing efficient public services. Speech or expression exercised by a public employee concerning matters of private or personal interest and not as a citizen upon matters of public concern is not protected by the First Amendment.

Connick and *Pickering* combined then form a free speech test that is a two-step process. First, the initial inquiry is whether the speech is a matter of public concern; in this regard, *Connick* states:

> When employee expression cannot be fairly considered as relating to any matter of political, social, or other concern to the community, government officials should enjoy wide latitude in managing their offices, without intrusive oversight by the judiciary in the name of the First Amendment.[36]

Second, if the speech is found to be a matter of public concern, the court then must apply the *Pickering* balancing test. The interest of the public employee as a citizen in commenting on matters of public concern must be weighed against the interest of the state as an employer to promote effective and efficient public service.[37]

In *Connick*, a public employee (Assistant District Attorney Myers), when informed that she would be transferred to prosecute cases in a different area of criminal law, opposed her transfer. In response, Myers passed out a questionnaire to fellow assistant district attorneys, soliciting information about office morale and pressure to work in political campaigns. Myers was told the questionnaire constituted insubordination, and her employment was terminated. The Supreme Court upheld Myers's dismissal, finding that the matter was basically of a personal nature and not a matter of public concern of any particular weight or magnitude. Though a question posed did fall under the rubric of "public concern," Myers's First Amendment interest was outweighed by the disruptive nature of the other questions. The beliefs by the state that Myers's actions would disrupt the office, undermine authority, and destroy the close working relationships within the office were reasonably taken in view of the evidence. The fact that Myers issued the questionnaire immediately after the transfer dispute and suggested conflict involving confidence in the conduct of the office lent additional weight in balancing the scales on behalf of the state. In so holding, the Court rejected Myers's contention that the state must bear the burden of clearly demonstrating that the discharge was necessary because the speech "substantially interfered" with the operation of the office. The "substantial interference" standard originally placed on the state in *Tinker*, the armband case, was not applicable here because the extent of a public employee's interest in the exercise of speech was not of "public concern," whereas in *Tinker* a protest of the war in Vietnam was clearly a matter of great political significance.

The speech test of the public employee can be summarized as follows: (1) Public speech is a fundamental constitutional right, and allegations regarding teacher dismissal for exercise of freedom of speech place the burden of proof on the state (or school board); (2) speech can be denied if the interests of the state outweigh the interests of the employee in the exercise of that right; (3) public speech involving matters of public concern imposes an extensive burden on the part of the state to justify denial, in which case the state must "clearly demonstrate" that denial was necessary in order to prevent "substantial interference"; (4) public speech involving private concerns involves a relatively low standard of proof by the state to justify dismissal, one that a school board can easily sustain by showing minimally, as was shown in *Connick*, that the exercise of speech can be reasonably believed to undermine authority, disrupt decorum, or harm working relationships.

Of course, as discussed later in this text, if a teacher does not have tenure and is not dismissed during the term of contract, the school board does not need to give reasons for nonretention unless the nontenured teacher establishes the denial of a fundamental right such as speech. In that event, the *Connick* test of public versus private concern is invoked.

❖ — ❖ — ❖

Teachers Have a Constitutional Right to Speak Out Freely on Matters of Public Concern

Pickering v. Board of Education

Supreme Court of the United States, 1968.
391 U.S. 563, 88 S.Ct. 1731.

Mr. Justice MARSHALL delivered the opinion of the Court. Appellant Marvin L. Pickering, a teacher in Township High School District 205, Will County, Illinois, was dismissed from his position by the appellee Board of Education for sending a letter to a local newspaper in connection with a recently proposed tax increase that was critical of the way in which the Board and the district superintendent of schools had handled past proposals to raise new revenue for the schools. Appellant's dismissal resulted from a determination by the Board, after a full hearing, that the publication of the letter was "detrimental to the efficient operation and administration of the schools of the district" and hence, under the relevant Illinois statute, Ill.Rev.Stat., c. 122, §10-22.4 (1963), that "interests of the schools require[d] [his dismissal]." . . .

The letter constituted, basically, an attack on the School Board's handling of the 1961 bond issue proposals and its subsequent allocation of financial resources between the schools' educational and athletic programs. It also charged the superintendent of schools with attempting to prevent teachers in the district from opposing or criticizing the proposed bond issue.

The Board dismissed Pickering for writing and publishing the letter. Pursuant to Illinois law, the Board was then required to hold a hearing on the dismissal. At the hearing the Board charged that numerous statements in the letter were false and that the publication of the statements unjustifiably impugned the "motives, honesty, integrity, truthfulness, responsibility and competence" of both the Board and the school administration. The Board also charged that the false statements damaged the professional reputations of its members and of the school administrators, would be disruptive of faculty discipline, and would tend to foment "controversy, conflict and dissension" among teachers, administrators, the Board of Education, and the residents of the district. Testimony was introduced from a variety of witnesses on the truth or falsity of the particular statements in the letter with which the Board took issue. The Board found the statements to be false as charged. No evidence was introduced at any point in the proceedings as to the effect of the publication of the letter on the community as a whole or on the administration of the school system in particular, and no specific findings along these lines were made.

. . . It is not altogether clear whether the Illinois Supreme Court held that the First Amendment had no applicability to appellant's dismissal for writing the letter in question or whether it determined that the particular statements made in the letter were not entitled to First Amendment protection. In any event, it clearly rejected Pickering's claim that, on the facts of this case, he could not constitutionally be dismissed from his teaching position.

To the extent that the Illinois Supreme Court's opinion may be read to suggest that teachers may constitutionally be compelled to relinquish the First Amendment rights they would otherwise enjoy as citizens to comment on matters of public interest in connection with the operation of the public schools in which they work, it proceeds on a premise that has been unequivocally rejected in numerous prior decisions of this Court. . . . "[T]he theory that public employment which may be denied altogether may be subjected to any conditions, regardless of how unreasonable, has been uniformly rejected." *Keyishian v. Board of Regents,* supra, 385 U.S. at 605–606, 87 S.Ct. at 685. At the same time it cannot be gainsaid that the State has interests as an employer in regulating the speech of its employees that differ significantly from those it possesses in connection with regulation of the speech of the citizenry in general. The problem in any case is to arrive at a balance between the interests of the teacher, as a citizen, in commenting upon matters of public concern and the interest of the State, as an employer, in promoting the efficiency of the public services it performs through its employees.

The Board contends that "the teacher by virtue of his public employment has a duty of loyalty to support his superiors in attaining the generally accepted goals of education and that, if he must speak out publicly, he should do so factually and accurately, commensurate with his education and experience." Appellant, on the other hand, argues that the test applicable to defamatory statements directed against public officials by persons having no occupational relationship with them, namely, that statements to be legally actionable must be made "with knowledge that [they were] . . . false or with reckless disregard of whether [they were] . . . false or not" . . . should also be applied to public statements made by teachers. . . .

An examination of the statements in appellant's letter objected to by the Board reveals that they, like the letter as a whole, consist essentially of criticism of the Board's allocation of school funds between educational and athletic programs, and of both the Board's and the superintendent's methods of informing, or preventing the informing of, the district's taxpayers of the real reasons why additional tax revenues were being sought for the schools. The statements are in no way directed towards any person with whom appellant would normally be in contact in the course of his daily work as a teacher. Thus no question of maintaining either discipline by immediate superiors or harmony among coworkers is presented here. Appellant's employment relationships with the Board and, to a somewhat lesser extent, with the superintendent are not the kind of close working relationships for which it can persuasively be claimed that personal loyalty and confidence are necessary to their proper functioning. Accordingly, to the extent that the Board's position here can be taken to suggest that even comments on matters of public concern that are substantially correct . . . may furnish grounds for dismissal if they are sufficiently critical in tone, we unequivocally reject it.

We next consider the statements in appellant's letter which we agree to be false. The Board's original charges included allegations that the publication of the letter damaged the professional reputations of the Board and the superintendent and would foment controversy and conflict among the Board, teachers, administrators, and the residents of the district. However, no evidence to support these allegations was introduced at the hearing. So far as the record reveals, Pickering's letter was greeted by everyone but its main target, the Board, with massive apathy and total disbelief. . . .

In addition, the fact that particular illustrations of the Board's claimed undesirable emphasis on athletic programs are false would not normally have any necessary impact on the actual operation of the schools, beyond its tendency to anger the Board. For example, Pickering's letter was written after the defeat at the polls of the second proposed tax increase. It could, therefore, have had no effect on the ability of the school district to raise necessary revenue, since there was no showing that there was any proposal to increase taxes pending when the letter was written.

More importantly, the question whether a school system requires additional funds is a matter of legitimate public concern on which the judgment of the school administration, including the School Board, cannot, in a society that leaves such questions to popular vote, be taken as conclusive. On such a question free and open debate is vital to informed decision-making by the electorate. Teachers are, as a class, the members of a community most likely to have informed and definite opinions as to how funds allotted to the operation of the schools should be spent. Accordingly, it is essential that they be able to speak out freely on such questions without fear of retaliatory dismissal. . . .

What we do have before us is a case in which a teacher has made erroneous public statements upon issues then currently the subject of public attention, which are critical of his ultimate employer but which are neither shown nor can be presumed to have in any way either impeded the teacher's proper performance of his daily duties in the classroom or to have interfered with the regular operation of the schools generally. In these circumstances we conclude that the interest of the school administration in limiting teachers' opportunities to contribute to public debate is not significantly greater than its interest in limiting a similar contribution by any member of the general public.

The public interest in having free and unhindered debate on matters of public importance—

the core value of the Free Speech Clause of the First Amendment—is so great that it has been held that a State cannot authorize the recovery of damages by a public official for defamatory statements directed at him except when such statements are shown to have been made either with knowledge of their falsity or with reckless disregard for their truth or falsity. . . . It is therefore perfectly clear that, were appellant a member of the general public, the State's power to afford the appellee Board of Education or its members any legal right to sue him for writing the letter at issue here would be limited by the requirement that the letter be judged by the standard laid down in *New York Times*. . . .

In sum, we hold that, in a case such as this, absent proof of false statements knowingly or recklessly made by him, a teacher's exercise of his right to speak on issues of public importance may not furnish the basis for his dismissal from public employment. Since no such showing has been made in this case regarding appellant's letter, his dismissal for writing it cannot be upheld and the judgment of the Illinois Supreme Court must, accordingly, be reversed and the case remanded for further proceedings not inconsistent with this opinion. It is so ordered.

Judgment reversed and case remanded with directions.

Case Notes

1. If an employee is dismissed under the *Connick* test, the employer's decision must be made upon a reasonable ascertainment of the facts that led to the dismissal. The Supreme Court said in *Waters v. Churchill* that "we do not believe that the court must apply the *Connick* test only to the facts as the employer thought them to be, without considering the reasonableness of the employer's conclusions. . . . [W]e think employer decision making will not be unduly burdened by having courts look to the facts as the employer reasonably found them to be." 511 U.S. 661, 114 S.Ct. 1878 (1994).

2. A school superintendent who becomes actively involved in a school board election, supporting one candidate over another, and then loses must suffer the consequences. The U.S. Court of Appeals, Fifth Circuit, has held that the nature of the working relationship between

school board and superintendent is by necessity a close and essential one. The superintendent has the power to "make or break" board policies, and, thus, the efficiency of the governance of the school district is dependent on the effectiveness and accord between the superintendent and the board. When the superintendent publicly breaks this bond, he abandons "any shelter otherwise provided him by the First Amendment." This conclusion was reached by reliance on *Pickering. Kinsey v. Salado Independent School District*, 950 F.2d 988 (5th Cir.1992).

3. Speech exercised by the secretary of a school district superintendent in opposing a bond issue was entitled to First Amendment protection absent a showing that the speech interfered with the efficient functioning of the office of the superintendent or impeded the secretary's performance or the performance of those with whom she worked. The court found that there was no evidence that the secretary's speech had either effect. The court in explaining its reasoning elaborated on *Pickering* and *Connick*, saying:

> Under the *Pickering* test, an employee's First Amendment rights are protected "'unless the employer shows that some restriction is necessary to prevent the disruption of official functions or to insure effective performance by the employee.'" The employer's burden to justify its restriction on speech increases in proportion to the value of that speech in the public debate. In focusing on the effective functioning of the employer's enterprise, a court should consider "whether the statement impairs discipline by superiors or harmony among co-workers, has a detrimental impact on close working relationships for which personal loyalty and confidence are necessary, or impedes the performance of the speaker's duties or interferes with the regular operation of the enterprise."

Ware v. Unified School District No. 492, Butler County, State of Kansas, 881 F.2d 906 (10th Cir.1989); *Rankin v. McPherson*, 483 U.S. 378, 107 S.Ct. 2891, 2899, 97 L.Ed.2d 315 (1987).

4. In *Piver*, the court interpreted *Pickering*, saying:

> *Pickering* teaches that a public employee's speech is not constitutionally protected, even if it addresses an issue of public concern, unless the employee's and the audience's interests in the speech

at issue outweigh the harm caused by the speech to the defendant's interests in running the governmental office efficiently.

The court further observed that the interests of a teacher, in speaking out at a board meeting regarding the tenure of another teacher and the discussion of the issue with students in a class, were of public concern protected by the First Amendment. The school board's alleged interest in overcoming the threat of "turmoil" in school was not sufficient to counterbalance the teacher's rights. *Piver v. Pender County Board of Education*, 835 F.2d 1076 (4th Cir.1987).

5. A teacher filing a grievance against the school principal involved topics of "public concern." *Wren v. Spurlock*, 798 F.2d 1313, 1317 (10th Cir.1986), cert. denied, 479 U.S. 1085, 107 S.Ct. 1287 (1987).

6. A school principal's speech to the school board involving a proposed transfer of his wife, an English teacher, was a matter of "public concern." *Lewis v. Harrison School District No. 1*, 805 F.2d 310 (8th Cir.1986), cert. denied, 482 U.S. 905, 107 S.Ct. 2481 (1987).

7. A letter of complaint written by teachers to the Arkansas Department of Education concerning the schools' delay in implementing federally mandated programs for students with disabilities constituted a matter of "public concern." *Southside Public Schools v. Hill*, 827 F.2d 270 (8th Cir.1987).

8. Matters involving a high school's use of collegiate registration, a procedure in which students were permitted to choose their own subjects and teachers, were not of "public concern" and were therefore not protected by the First Amendment. *Ferrara v. Mills*, 781 F.2d 1508 (11th Cir.1986).

9. It is well settled that a teacher, as a citizen, can run for political office, but there is a difference between the right to run for public office and the right to continued public employment after being elected. Common law provides that a teacher or other public employee cannot hold positions simultaneously that are incompatible and therefore present a conflict of interest. Whether a teacher may hold political office and serve as a teacher is dependent upon the statutes of the particular state. Some states have statutes that provide that the teacher cannot serve as a

state legislator and teacher at the same time. But if a state does not have a statute prohibiting serving, then the courts generally have allowed them to serve. A board can reasonably request the teacher to take an unpaid leave of absence while serving in a public position.

10. Some states have passed legislation modeled after the federal Hatch Act, which prohibits participation in partisan politics. The U.S. Supreme Court in *Broadrick v. Oklahoma*, 413 U.S. 601, 93 S.Ct. 2908 (1973), upheld an Oklahoma statute prohibiting public employees from participating in partisan politics. These statutes usually limit activities such as directly raising funds for candidates, becoming a candidate, starting a political party, or actively managing a campaign. See *United States Civil Service Commission v. National Association of Letter Carriers*, 413 U.S. 548, 93 S.Ct. 2880 (1973).

11. A ninth-grade government class is not a public forum, and a teacher could be disciplined for comments made during class regarding lack of discipline at the school. The court in a Colorado case, in applying both *Pickering* and *Hazelwood* precedents, concluded that the teacher could not logically maintain that a regular government class was a public forum that bestowed upon him expansive First Amendment speech protections. The court said, "If the creation and operation of a school newspaper as part of a journalism class can be devoid of an intent to open a classroom for public discourse (as in *Hazelwood*), then an ordinary classroom... is not a public forum." *Miles v. Denver Public Schools*, 944 F.2d 773 (10th Cir.1991).

❖ — ❖ — ❖

Evidence Must Show That Teacher's Exercise of Constitutional Right Was the Motivating Factor Not to Rehire before Judicial Action Is Justified

Mt. Healthy City School District Board of Education v. Doyle

Supreme Court of the United States, 1977.
429 U.S. 274, 97 S.Ct. 568.

Mr. Justice REHNQUIST delivered the opinion of the Court. Respondent Doyle sued petitioner Mt. Healthy Board of Education in the United States District Court for the Southern District of Ohio. Doyle claimed that the Board's refusal to renew his contract in 1971 violated his rights under the First and Fourteenth Amendments to the United States Constitution. After a bench trial the District Court held that Doyle was entitled to reinstatement with back pay. The Court of Appeals for the Sixth Circuit affirmed the judgment. . . .

Doyle was first employed by the Board in 1966. He worked under one-year contracts for the first three years, and under a two-year contract from 1969 to 1971. In 1969 he was elected president of the Teachers' Association, in which position he worked to expand the subjects of direct negotiation between the Association and the Board of Education. During Doyle's one-year term as president of the Association, and during the succeeding year when he served on its executive committee, there was apparently some tension in relations between the Board and the Association.

Beginning early in 1970, Doyle was involved in several incidents not directly connected with his role in the Teachers' Association. In one instance, he engaged in an argument with another teacher which culminated in the other teacher's slapping him. Doyle subsequently refused to accept an apology and insisted upon some punishment for the other teacher. His persistence in the matter resulted in the suspension of both teachers for one day, which was followed by a walkout by a number of other teachers, which in turn resulted in the lifting of the suspensions.

On other occasions, Doyle got into an argument with employees of the school cafeteria over the amount of spaghetti which had been served him; referred to students, in connection with a disciplinary complaint, as "sons of bitches"; and made an obscene gesture to two girls in connection with their failure to obey commands made in his capacity as cafeteria supervisor. Chronologically the last in the series of incidents which respondent was involved in during his employment by the Board was a telephone call by him to a local radio station. It was the Board's consideration of this incident which the court below found to be a violation of the First and Fourteenth Amendments.

In February of 1971, the principal circulated to various teachers a memorandum relating to teacher dress and appearance, which was apparently prompted by the view of some in the administration that there was a relationship between teacher appearance and public support for bond issues. Doyle's response to the receipt of the memorandum—on a subject which he apparently understood was to be settled by joint teacher-administration action—was to convey the substance of the memorandum to a disc jockey at WSAI, a Cincinnati radio station, who promptly announced the adoption of the dress code as a news item. Doyle subsequently apologized to the principal, conceding that he should have made some prior communication of his criticism to the school administration.

Approximately one month later the superintendent made his customary annual recommendations to the Board as to the rehiring of nontenured teachers. He recommended that Doyle not be rehired. The same recommendation was made with respect to nine other teachers in the district, and in all instances, including Doyle's, the recommendation was adopted by the Board. Shortly after being notified of this decision, respondent requested a statement of reasons for the Board's actions. He received a statement citing "a notable lack of tact in handling professional matters which leaves much doubt as to your sincerity in establishing good school relationships." That general statement was followed by references to the radio station incident and to the obscene gesture incident.

The District Court found that all of these incidents had in fact occurred. It concluded that respondent Doyle's telephone call to the radio station was "clearly protected by the First Amendment," and that because it had played a "substantial part" in the decision of the Board not to renew Doyle's employment, he was entitled to reinstatement with backpay. The District Court did not expressly state what test it was applying in determining that the incident in question involved conduct protected by the First Amendment, but simply held that the communication to the radio station was such conduct. The Court of Appeals affirmed in a brief *per curiam* opinion.

Doyle's claims under the First and Fourteenth Amendments are not defeated by the fact that he did not have tenure. Even though he could have been discharged for no reason whatever, and had no constitutional right to a hearing prior to the decision not to rehire him, *Board of Regents v. Roth*, 408 U.S. 564, 92 S.Ct. 2701, 33 L.Ed.2d 548 (1972), he may nonetheless establish a claim to reinstatement if the decision not to rehire him was made by reason of his exercise of constitutionally protected First Amendment freedoms. *Perry v. Sindermann.*

That question of whether speech of a government employee is constitutionally protected expression necessarily entails striking "a balance between the interests of the teacher, as a citizen, in commenting upon matters of public concern and the interest of the State as an employer, in promoting the efficiency of the public services it performs through its employees." *Pickering v. Board of Education.* There is no suggestion by the Board that Doyle violated any established policy, or that its reaction to his communication to the radio station was anything more than an ad hoc response to Doyle's action in making the memorandum public. We therefore accept the District Court's finding that the communication was protected by the First and Fourteenth Amendments. We are not, however, entirely in agreement with that court's manner of reasoning from this finding to the conclusion that Doyle is entitled to reinstatement with backpay.

The District Court made the following "conclusions" on this aspect of the case:

1. If a non-permissible reason, e.g., exercise of First Amendment rights, played a substantial part in the decision not to renew—even in the face of other permissible grounds—the decision may not stand (citations omitted).
2. A non-permissible reason did play a substantial part. That is clear from the letter of the Superintendent immediately following the Board's decision, which stated two reasons—the one, the conversation with the radio station clearly protected by the First Amendment. A court may not engage in any limitation of First Amendment rights based on "tact"—that is not to say that "tactfulness" is irrelevant to other issues in this case.

At the same time, though, it stated that

in fact, as this Court sees it and finds, both the Board and the Superintendent were faced with a situation in which there did exist in fact reason . . . independent of any First Amendment rights or exercise thereof, to not extend tenure.

Since respondent Doyle had no tenure, and there was therefore not even a state law requirement of "cause" or "reason" before a decision could be made not to renew his employment, it is not clear what the District Court meant by this latter statement. Clearly the Board legally *could* have dismissed respondent had the radio station incident never come to its attention. One plausible meaning of the court's statement is that the Board and the Superintendent not only could, but in fact *would* have reached that decision had not the constitutionally protected incident of the telephone call to the radio station occurred. We are thus brought to the issue whether, even if that were the case, the fact that the protected conduct played a "substantial part" in the actual decision not to renew would necessarily amount to a constitutional violation justifying remedial action. We think that it would not.

A rule of causation which focuses solely on whether protected conduct played a part, "substantial" or otherwise, in a decision not to rehire, could place an employee in a better position as a result of the exercise of constitutionally protected conduct than he would have occupied had he done nothing. The difficulty with the rule enunciated by the District Court is that it would require reinstatement in cases where a dramatic and perhaps abrasive incident is inevitably on the minds of those responsible for the decision to rehire, and does indeed play a part in that decision—even if the same decision would have been reached had the incident not occurred. The constitutional principle at stake is sufficiently vindicated if such an employee is placed in no worse a position than if he had not engaged in the conduct. A borderline or marginal candidate should not have the employment question resolved against him because of constitutionally protected conduct. But that same candidate ought not to be able, by engaging in such conduct, to prevent his employer from assessing his performance record and reaching a decision not to rehire on the basis of that record, simply because the protected conduct makes the employer more certain of the correctness of its decision.

This is especially true where, as the District Court observed was the case here, the current decision to rehire will accord "tenure." The long term consequences of an award of tenure are of great moment both to the employee and to the employer. They are too significant for us to hold that the Board in this case would be precluded, because it considered constitutionally protected conduct in deciding not to rehire Doyle, from attempting to prove to a trier of fact that quite apart from such conduct Doyle's record was such that he would not have been rehired in any event. . . .

Initially, in this case, the burden was properly placed upon respondent to show that his conduct was constitutionally protected, and that this conduct was a "substantial factor"—or to put it in other words, that it was a "motivating factor" in the Board's decision not to rehire him. Respondent having carried that burden, however, the District Court should have gone on to determine whether the Board had shown by a preponderance of the evidence that it would have reached the same decision as to respondent's reemployment even in the absence of the protected conduct.

We cannot tell from the District Court opinion and conclusions, nor from the opinion of the Court of Appeals affirming the judgment of the District Court, what conclusion those courts would have reached had they applied this test. The judgment of the Court of Appeals is therefore vacated, and the case remanded for further proceedings consistent with this opinion.

Case Notes

1. The combined meaning of *Pickering, Mt. Healthy,* and *Connick* is interpreted by the Eighth Circuit Court of Appeals in *Roberts v. Van Buren Public Schools,* 773 F.2d 949 (8th Cir.1985):

> *Pickering v. Board of Education,* 391 U.S. 563, 88 S.Ct. 1731, 20 L.Ed.2d 811 (1968), held that "[p]ublic employee[s do] not relinquish First Amendment rights to comment on matters of public interest by virtue of government employment." *Connick v. Myers,* 461 U.S. 138, 140, 103 S.Ct. 1684, 1686, 75 L.Ed.2d 708 (1983). Consideration of such claims involves a three-step analysis. First, plaintiffs must

demonstrate that their conduct was protected; second, plaintiffs must demonstrate that such protected conduct was a substantial or motivating factor in the adverse employment decision; and third, the employer may show that the employment action would have been taken even in the absence of the protected conduct. *Mt. Healthy City School District Board of Education v. Doyle*, 429 U.S. 274, 287, 97 S.Ct. 568, 576, 50 L.Ed.2d 471 (1977).

Since *Connick,* identification of protected activity is a two-step process in itself. As a threshold matter, the speech must have addressed a "matter of public concern," then, the interest of the employee in so speaking must be balanced against "the interest of the State, as an employer, in promoting the efficiency of the public services it performs through its employees." *Pickering,* 391 U.S. at 568, 88 S.Ct. at 1735. This *"Pickering* balance," as it has come to be known, looks to the following factors: (1) the need for harmony in the office or work place; (2) whether the government's responsibilities require a close working relationship to exist between the plaintiff and co-workers when the speech in question has caused or could cause the relationship to deteriorate; (3) the time, manner, and place of the speech; (4) the context in which the dispute arose; (5) the degree of public interest in the speech; and (6) whether the speech impeded the employee's ability to perform his or her duties.

2. Another explanation, combining *Pickering, Mt. Healthy,* and *Connick,* comes from the U.S. Court of Appeals, Fourth Circuit, in *Daniels v. Quinn,* 801 F.2d 687 (4th Cir.1986), which explains the First Amendment free speech rights of a public employee in terms of the three-part inquiry:

The first step is to ask whether the speech was about a matter of legitimate public concern. This question is one of law, not of fact.

If the speech was about a matter of public concern, the question becomes whether the employee would have been discharged "but for" the speech. The defendant-employer will not be liable if the discharge would have occurred for other reasons, such as the plaintiff's own incompetence. This classic motivational question is one of fact. The employee bears the burden of demonstrating that protected speech was a motivating factor in the discharge. The burden then shifts to the employer to show that it would have reached the same decision even in the absence of the protected conduct. *Mt. Healthy v. Doyle,* 429 U.S. at 287, 97 S.Ct. at 576.

If protected speech was the "but for" cause of the discharge, courts must still inquire whether the

degree of public interest in the employee's statement was nonetheless outweighed by the employer's responsibility to manage its internal affairs and provide "effective and efficient" service to the public. If so, then the employer will not be liable. This question is ultimately one of law. *Daniels v. Quinn,* 801 F.2d 687 (4th Cir.1986).

3. A school board's transfer of a teacher to traveling teacher status was upheld as a consideration of public interest outweighing the teacher's individual interests. Memorandums by the teacher, commenting on grading policies, only one of which could be adjudged of public concern, were personal in scope and sarcastic in tone, and the relationship between the teacher and the school had deteriorated to the point of being "filled with animosity." With regard to the *Mt. Healthy* test, the court found that the exercise of speech was not a "substantial and motivating factor in the adverse job action." *Hesse v. Board of Education of Township High School District No. 211, Cook County, Illinois,* 848 F.2d 748 (7th Cir.1988).

4. The questionnaire distributed by Sheila Myers in *Connick v. Myers,* discussed in the text above, queried other employees:

Please take the few minutes it will require to fill this out. You can freely express your opinion WITH ANONYMITY GUARANTEED.

1. How long have you been in the office?
2. Were you moved as a result of the recent transfers?
3. Were the transfers as they effected [sic] you discussed with you by any superior prior to the notice of them being posted?
4. Do you think as a matter of policy, they should have been?
5. From your experience, do you feel office procedure regarding transfers has been fair?
6. Do you believe there is a rumor mill active in the office?
7. If so, how do you think it effects [sic] overall working performance of A.D.A. personnel?
8. If so, how do you think it effects [sic] office morale?
9. Do you generally first learn of office changes and developments through rumor?
10. Do you have confidence in and would you rely on the word of:

Bridget Bane
Fred Harper

Lindsay Larson
Joe Meyer
Dennis Waldron

11. Do you ever feel pressured to work in political campaigns on behalf of office supported candidates?
12. Do you feel a grievance committee would be a worthwhile addition to the office structure?
13. How would you rate office morale?
14. Please feel free to express any comments or feelings you have.

Thank you for your cooperation in this survey.

The court in *Connick* determined the only question that was a matter of "public concern," and therefore constitutionally protected, was Question 11, referring to pressure on employees to work in political campaigns. Since one question was a matter of a public concern, the *Mt. Healthy* test was invoked.

Would Myers have been dismissed if the protected question were not considered? The employer must show that the employment action would have been taken even in the absence of the protected conduct:

> When a public employee speaks not as a citizen upon matters of public concern, but instead as an employee upon matters only of personal interest, absent the most unusual circumstances, a federal court is not the appropriate forum in which to review the wisdom of a personnel decision taken by a public agency allegedly in reaction to the employee's behavior. *Connick v. Myers*, 461 U.S. 138, 103 S.Ct. 1684, 75 L.Ed.2d 708 (1983).

5. The superintendent in *Mt. Healthy* sent a statement to teacher Doyle citing a "lack of tact in handling professional matters" and gave two specific incidents: (1) the radio station incident and (2) the obscene gesture. Since Doyle was untenured, would it have been more prudent for the superintendent not to mention the radio incident in his letter, since it was protected speech? Did mentioning the radio incident shift the burden of proof to the school board?

6. The burden of proof is on the teacher to show that he or she was not rehired because of constitutionally protected conduct. The teacher must also prove that this conduct was the "motivating factor" in the school board's decision not to rehire. From this point, the burden shifts to the defendant school board, which must show by a preponderance of evidence that it would have reached the same decision regardless of whether the teacher had engaged in the constitutionally protected conduct. *McGee v. South Pemiscot School District R-V*, 712 F.2d 339 (8th Cir.1983).

7. Retaliation against a teacher for exercise of a First Amendment right is prohibited by the courts. The reprimand and transfer of teachers as retaliation for their exercise of freedom of speech may subject a school district to Section 1983 liability. In order for a school district to be liable, however, the plaintiff must satisfy four elements in order to sustain a retaliation claim. First, the plaintiff must suffer an adverse employment decision. A valid claim by plaintiff of an adverse employment decision cannot be based on trivial issues such as teaching assignments, room assignments, administrative duties, classroom equipment, teacher recognition, or a host of other relatively inconsequential matters. The courts may, however, hold that reprimands and demotions are of sufficient magnitude to constitute adverse employment decisions. Second, the plaintiff's speech must be of public concern in the context of the U.S. Supreme Court's rationale in *Connick*. To rise to a level of public concern, the plaintiff's speech must be made in his or her role as citizen rather than merely that of an employee expressing matters of personal concern. Third, the plaintiff's interest in commenting on matters of public concern must outweigh the defendant school district's interest in promoting efficiency. This element of the test is called the *Pickering* balance, wherein the court must decide whether the interest of the state, as an employer, is sufficient to outweigh the individual interest of the employee. Of concern to the courts is whether in striking the balance the speech was likely to generate controversy and disruption so as to impede the general performance, operation, and working relationships of the school. Fourth, in order for a complaint of retaliation to be successfully maintained, the plaintiff must show that the exercise of free speech was the motivating reason for the adverse employment decision by the school administration. The U.S. Court of Appeals, Fifth Circuit, held that all four of these elements were present where a school administration instituted an adverse employment

decision moving the teachers to different school campuses of the school district; the action according to the court was in retaliation for the teachers' exercise of free speech. *Harris v. Victoria Independent School District*, 168 F.3d 216 (5th Cir.1999).

8. The balancing of the teacher's free speech interest against the school district's interest may involve a variety of teacher and school relationships. The school district has an overriding pedagogical interest in the curriculum of the school. "The makeup of the curriculum . . . is by definition a legitimate pedagogical concern" of the school district. Where a teacher defied a school official's prescription of a particular school play and, as a result, was transferred to another school, she claimed that her First Amendment freedom of speech rights had been violated. In challenging the board action, she claimed retaliation for the exercise of her academic freedom in the selection and production of school plays. The court ruled against the teacher and pointed out that since she had no constitutionally protected right to select school plays, a claim by her of retaliation could not be sustained. *Boring v. Buncombe County Board of Education*, 136 F.3d 364 (4th Cir.1998).

Freedom of Speech Is Guaranteed to Teacher in Private Communication with Employer

Givhan v. Western Line Consolidated School District

Supreme Court of the United States, 1979.
439 U.S. 410, 99 S.Ct. 693.

Mr. Justice REHNQUIST delivered the opinion of the Court. Petitioner Bessie Givhan was dismissed from her employment as a junior high English teacher at the end of the 1970–1971 school year. At the time of petitioner's termination, respondent Western Line Consolidated School District was the subject of a desegrega-

tion order entered by the United States District Court for the Northern District of Mississippi. Petitioner filed a complaint . . . seeking reinstatement on the ground that nonrenewal of her contract . . . infringed her right of free speech secured by the First and Fourteenth Amendments of the United States Constitution. In an effort to show that its decision was justified, respondent school district introduced evidence of, among other things, a series of private encounters between petitioner and the school principal in which petitioner allegedly made "petty and unreasonable demands" in a manner variously described by the principal as "insulting," "hostile," "loud," and "arrogant." After a two-day bench trial, the District Court held that petitioner's termination had violated the First Amendment. Finding that petitioner had made "demands" on but two occasions and that those demands "were neither 'petty' nor 'unreasonable,' insomuch as all of the complaints in question involved employment policies and practices at [the] school which [petitioner] conceived to be racially discriminatory in purpose or effect," the District Court concluded that "the primary reason for the school district's failure to renew [petitioner's] contract was her criticism of the policies and practices of the school district, especially the school to which she was assigned to teach." . . .

The Court of Appeals for the Fifth Circuit reversed. Although it found the District Court's findings not clearly erroneous, the Court of Appeals concluded that because petitioner had privately expressed her complaints and opinions to the principal, her expression was not protected under the First Amendment. . . .

This Court's decisions in *Pickering, Perry,* and *Mt. Healthy* do not support the conclusion that a public employee forfeits his protection against governmental abridgment of freedom of speech if he decides to express his views privately rather than publicly. While those cases each arose in the context of a public employee's public expression, the rule to be derived from them is not dependent on that largely coincidental fact.

In *Pickering* a teacher was discharged for publicly criticizing, in a letter published in a local newspaper, the school board's handling of prior bond issue proposals and its subsequent allocation of financial resources between the schools' educational and athletic programs. Noting that the free speech rights of public employees are not absolute, the Court held that in determining whether a government employee's speech is constitutionally protected, "the interests of the [employee], as a citizen, in commenting upon matters of public concern" must be balanced against "the interest of the State, as an employer, in promoting the efficiency of the public services it performs through its employees." . . . The Court concluded that under the circumstances of that case "the interest of the school administration in limiting teachers' opportunities to contribute to public debate [was] not significantly greater than its interest in limiting a similar contribution by any member of the general public." Here the opinion of the Court of Appeals may be read to turn in part on its view that the working relationship between principal and teacher is significantly different from the relationship between the parties in *Pickering*. . . . But we do not feel confident that the Court of Appeals' decision would have been placed on that ground notwithstanding its view that the First Amendment does not require the same sort of *Pickering* balancing for the private expression of a public employee as it does for public expression.

Perry and *Mt. Healthy* arose out of similar disputes between teachers and their public employers. As we have noted, however, the fact that each of these cases involved public expression by the employee was not critical to the decision. Nor is the Court of Appeals' view supported by the "captive audience" rationale. Having opened his office door to petitioner, the principal was hardly in a position to argue that he was the *"unwilling* recipient" of her views.

The First Amendment forbids abridgment of the "freedom of speech." Neither the Amendment itself nor our decisions indicate that this freedom is lost to the public employee who arranges to communicate privately with his employer rather than to spread his views before the public. We decline to adopt such a view of the First Amendment.

While this case was pending on appeal to the Court of Appeals, *Mt. Healthy City Board of Education v. Doyle* was decided. In that case this Court rejected the view that a public employee

must be reinstated whenever constitutionally protected conduct plays a "substantial" part in the employer's decision to terminate. Such a rule would require reinstatement of employees that the public employer would have dismissed even if the constitutionally protected conduct had not occurred and, consequently "could place an employee in a better position as a result of the exercise of constitutionally protected conduct than he would have occupied had he done nothing." Thus, the Court held that once the employee has shown that his constitutionally protected conduct played a "substantial" role in the employer's decision not to rehire him, the employer is entitled to show "by a preponderance of the evidence that it would have reached the same decision as to [the employee's] reemployment even in the absence of the protected conduct." Id., at 287, 97 S.Ct., at 576.

The Court of Appeals in the instant case rejected respondents' *Mt. Healthy* claim that the decision to terminate petitioner would have been made even if her encounters with the principal had never occurred:

> The [trial] court did not make an express finding as to whether the same decision would have been made, but on this record the [respondents] do not, and seriously cannot, argue that the same decision would have been made without regard to the "demands." Appellants seem to argue that the preponderance of the evidence shows that the same decision would have been justified, but that is not the same as proving that the same decision would have been made. . . . Therefore [respondents] failed to make a successful "same decision anyway" defense.

Since this case was tried before *Mt. Healthy* was decided, it is not surprising that respondents did not attempt to prove in the District Court that the decision not to rehire petitioner would have been made even absent consideration of her "demands." Thus, the case came to the Court of Appeals in very much the same posture as *Mt. Healthy* was presented in this Court. And while the District Court found that petitioner's "criticism" was the "primary" reason for the school district's failure to rehire her, it did not find that she would have been rehired *but for* her criticism. Respondents' *Mt. Healthy* claim called for a factual determination which could not, on this record, be resolved by the Court of Appeals.

Accordingly, the judgment of the Court of Appeals is vacated and the case remanded for further proceedings consistent with this opinion.

So ordered.

CASE NOTES

1. "*Connick* did not hold that speech relating to employment grievances is always a personal matter; such a view would conflict with the Court's commitment to a case-by-case balancing" and would run counter to *Givhan*. *Piver v. Pender County Board of Education*, 835 F.2d 1076 (4th Cir.1987).

2. "Criticism in private of a public employer's allegedly racially discriminatory policies can be of 'public concern.'" *Piver v. Pender County Board of Education*, supra.

Free Speech Is Not Offended by Teacher Dismissal for Letter to Other Teachers Encouraging Sick-Out

Stroman v. Colleton County School District

United States Court of Appeals, Fourth Circuit, 1993. 981 F.2d 152.

NIEMEYER, Circuit Judge:

John W. Stroman was discharged from his employment as a public school teacher in Colleton County, South Carolina, on May 29, 1987, after he wrote and circulated a letter to fellow teachers, complaining about a change that had been made in the method for paying teachers, criticizing the school district for budgetary mismanagement, and encouraging his fellow teachers to engage in a "sick-out" during the week of final examinations. Following his dismissal, Stroman filed suit under 42 U.S.C. §1983 against the Colleton County School District and its officials, alleging that his dismissal was impermissibly based on his exercise of free speech and

therefore violated the First Amendment. The district court granted defendants' motion for summary judgment, concluding that any protected speech in the letter was not a substantial or motivating factor for Stroman's discharge and that the portion of the letter proposing a "sick-out" did not constitute speech protected by the First Amendment. Although we disagree with some of the district court's reasoning, we nevertheless affirm for the reasons given hereafter.

Because of an impending budgetary crisis, the Colleton County School District announced in the spring of 1987 that, in lieu of paying teachers a lump sum for the summer months, as had been the custom, the School District would pay teachers biweekly.

John Stroman, a teacher for some ten years in Colleton County, responded to the new policy by writing and circulating a letter to fellow teachers in which he expressed his objection to any delay in receiving pay caused by the new policy, criticized the School District's management of the budget, and encouraged a "sick-out" during exam week to "show the administration that we are together as teachers" and "to take a stand." The letter read in relevant part:

Ha! Da! Ha! Ha! Ha!

Last year we got paid in all sorts of manners. This year is worse because we might have to wait for two pay periods before getting paid. Do you know that after the payroll on the 30th all of the money is supposed to be gone? Yes, Mr. Smoak and his convoy were not able to borrow the money on their most recent trip to New York. Everyone knows when you spend money for the coming year to pay off this year's salaries and don't ask to get more to replace it, the deficiency will grow and soon there will be no money. None. If in someway we are paid in June and the rest of the summer, next school year will be worse.

It seems as though the personnel downtown should be able to balance a budget. Do they really know just what's going on? God knows there are enough of them. Funny, Gene Odom was not on that convoy to the city. Just stop and look around: at one school, I know they have seven administrators. Down at Central Office they have several positions filled that one person can do. Have we really grown that much? Funny how new posicions are created for some administrators that were relieved [sic] from another. These are positions we don't need or could be filled by someone with lower salaries. Make a *position* to full [sic] the *person*. People, we are *top-heavy* and can do nothing but sink. And we will be the ones to suffer.

. . . . . .

Some of us may not need all of our money, but some of us do. We must help one another because the next time you may need help. Just think of it. It is time the teachers in this County show the administration that we are together as teachers.

. . . . . .

Some of us will like to have a sick-out exam week if we can get about 10–25% to do so. If you are willing to take a stand with us, please let me (John Stroman) know by Wednesday, May 27, 1987.

. . . . . .

P.S. If you feel as strongly as I do, please discuss it and gather support.

On receiving a copy of the letter, the superintendent of the School District, A.L. Smoak, Jr., became concerned, in particular about the paragraph that proposed a "sick-out," which he marked with a red pencil. He promptly called a meeting with Stroman for the next day to which he also invited Stroman's school principal, Franklin L. Smalls. At the meeting, Stroman admitted that he had drafted and circulated the letter. He also complained to the superintendent that "he was being mistreated as far as his pay was concerned." During the course of the meeting, Smoak handed Stroman a letter of dismissal dated that day, May 29, 1987, which stated in pertinent part:

> This letter is to inform you that you are dismissed and suspended from your duties as a teacher for the Colleton County School District effective immediately. . . . The grounds for dismissal are that you have shown evident unfitness for teaching by proposing to abandon your duties during the week of June 1, 1987, and by inciting and encouraging other teachers to leave their employment during the same week.

No other action was taken to avert the "sick-out," and nearly all of the faculty attended school during the examination period. . . .

The applicable principles are not disputed. A state may not dismiss a public school teacher because of the teacher's exercise of speech protected by the First Amendment. . . . Personal grievances, complaints about conditions of employment, or expressions about other matters of personal interest do not constitute speech about matters of public concern that are protected by the First Amendment, but are matters more immediately concerned with the self-interest of the speaker as employee. *Connick v. Myers*, 461 U.S. 138, 147, 103 S.Ct. 1684, 1690, 75 L.Ed.2d 708 (1983).

. . . [I]n determining whether the teacher's discharge from employment was based on an exercise of conduct protected by the First Amendment, the teacher has the burden of proving that protected speech played a "substantial" role in the termination decision or was "a motivating factor." The employer may nevertheless rebut the showing by proof that it would have discharged the plaintiff "even in the absence of the protected conduct." *Mount Healthy City Bd. of Education v. Doyle*, 429 U.S. 274, 287, 97 S.Ct. 568, 576, 50 L.Ed.2d 471 (1977). The test thus becomes one of whether the teacher would have been retained or rehired "but for" his exercise of speech protected by the First Amendment. *Givhan v. Western Line Consol. Sch. Dist.*, 439 U.S. 410, 417, 99 S.Ct. 693, 697, 58 L.Ed.2d 619 (1979).

. . . We will therefore view the Stroman letter as a whole for purposes of a First Amendment analysis.

The School District urges us nevertheless to find that the letter taken as a whole amounts to no more than a personal grievance, thereby obviating the need for any further constitutional analysis. We agree that a personal grievance prompted the letter, which was written in response to a change in the practice of paying teachers in a lump sum for summer work. The substance of the letter, in large part, seems to be limited to this grievance. . . . Were this the entire evidence, we would readily agree that the speech amounted to no more than an employee grievance not protected by the First Amendment.

Some doubt, however, is raised by the complaints in the letter regarding school officials' alleged mismanagement of the budget. In addition to complaints about publicly funded out-of-town trips by School District personnel, the letter observes that the administration cannot balance a budget and cannot cut unnecessary personnel. It states, "People, we are *top-*

heavy and can do nothing but sink. And we will be the ones to suffer." While these types of comments could be construed as another part of the complaint of an employee unhappy with a change in a pay practice, they might also reflect the complaint of a citizen concerned about budget mismanagement, particularly if taken as a separate statement. . . .

When speech arguably relates to a matter of public concern, we prefer to apply the approach taken in *Connick* and weigh whatever public interest commentary may be contained in the letter against the state's dual interest as a provider of public service and employer of persons hired to provide that service. . . .

In its letter of dismissal to Stroman, the Colleton County School District focused on Stroman's proposal to call a "sick-out" during the week for which final examinations were scheduled. . . . Stroman contends that there was no evidence to suggest that there was a danger that the sick-out would in fact occur and that his letter was only a proposal to engage in one. We think that this contention misses the point. The State's interest is not limited to preventing actual disruption. To have called for a sick-out when teachers were not sick was an appeal for dishonest conduct, conduct that was in violation of School District policy and the teachers' contracts, and conduct that could legitimately have been questioned on professional grounds. The School Board was prompted to fire Stroman not because a sick-out was likely to occur but rather because he exercised such flawed judgment in urging one. Stroman's letter revealed his willingness to abandon his post and to urge others to do likewise. . . .

We therefore hold that any First Amendment interest inherent in the letter that Stroman circulated is outweighed by the *public interest* in having public education provided by teachers loyal to that service and, in particular, in having final examinations proctored and completed in a timely fashion, and the School District's *employer interest* in having its employees abide by reasonable policies adopted to control sick leave and maintain morale and effective operation of the schools. We recognize that Stroman's comments about the School District's purported mismanagement may involve matters of public concern. Nevertheless, we view the essential thrust of the

letter as expressing an employee grievance about changes in the method of pay. Thus we believe that the Supreme Court's conclusion in *Connick* is equally applicable here:

> Myers' questionnaire touched upon matters of public concern in only a most limited sense; her survey, in our view, is most accurately characterized as an employee grievance concerning internal office policy. The limited First Amendment interest involved here does not require that *Connick* tolerate action which he reasonably believed would disrupt the office, undermine his authority, and destroy close working relationships. Myers' discharge therefore did not offend the First Amendment.

461 U.S. at 154, 103 S.Ct. at 1693.

The judgment of the district court is, for the reasons that we have given, affirmed.

AFFIRMED.

❖ — ❖ — ❖

Teacher Dress Policy Is Constitutional

East Hartford Education Association v. Board of Education

United States Court of Appeals,
Second Circuit, 1977.
562 F.2d 838.

MESKILL, Circuit Judge. Although this case may at first appear too trivial to command the attention of a busy court, it raises important issues concerning the proper scope of judicial oversight of local affairs. The appellant here, Richard Brimley, is a public school teacher reprimanded for failing to wear a necktie while teaching his English class. Joined by the teachers union, he sued the East Hartford Board of Education, claiming that the reprimand for violating the dress code deprived him of his rights of free speech and privacy. . . .

In the vast majority of communities, the control of public schools is vested in locally elected bodies. This commitment to local political bodies requires significant public control over what is said and done in school. It is not the federal courts, but local democratic processes, that are primarily responsible for the many routine decisions that are made in public school systems. Accordingly, it is settled that "[c]ourts do not and cannot intervene in the resolution of conflicts which arise in the daily operation of school systems and which do not directly and sharply implicate basic constitutional values." *Epperson v. Arkansas*, 393 U.S. 97, 104, 89 S.Ct. 266, 270, 21 L.Ed.2d 228 (1968).

Federal courts must refrain, in most instances, from interfering with the decisions of school authorities. Even though decisions may appear foolish or unwise, a federal court may not overturn them unless the standard set forth in *Epperson* is met. . . .

Mr. Brimley claims that by refusing to wear a necktie he makes a statement on current affairs which assists him in his teaching. In his brief, he argues that the following benefits flow from his tielessness:

a. He wishes to present himself to his students as a person who is not tied to "establishment conformity."
b. He wishes to symbolically indicate to his students his association with the ideas of the generation to which those students belong, including the rejection of many of the customs and values, and of the social outlook, of the older generation.
c. He feels that dress of this type enables him to achieve closer rapport with his students, and thus enhances his ability to teach.

Appellant's claim, therefore, is that his refusal to wear a tie is "symbolic speech," and, as such, is protected against governmental interference by the First Amendment.

We are required here to balance the alleged interest in free expression against the goals of the school board in requiring its teachers to dress somewhat more formally than they might like. When this test is applied, the school board's position must prevail.

Obviously, a great range of conduct has the symbolic, "speech-like" aspect claimed by Mr. Brimley. To state that activity is "symbolic" is only the beginning, and not the end, of constitutional inquiry. . . .

. . . [T]he claims of symbolic speech made here are vague and unfocused. Through the simple refusal to wear a tie, Mr. Brimley claims that he communicates a comprehensive view of life and society. It may well be, in an age increasingly conscious of fashion, that a significant portion of the population seeks to make a statement of some kind through its clothes. However, Mr. Brimley's message is sufficiently vague to place it close to the "conduct" end of the "speech-conduct" continuum. . . . While the regulation of the school board must still pass constitutional muster, the showing required to uphold it is significantly less than if Mr. Brimley had been punished, for example, for publicly speaking out on an issue concerning school administration.

At the outset, Mr. Brimley had other, more effective means of communicating his social views to his students. He could, for example, simply have told them his views on contemporary America; if he had done this in a temperate way, without interfering with his teaching duties, we would be confronted with a very different First Amendment case. The existence of alternative, effective means of communication, while not conclusive, is a factor to be considered in assessing the validity of a regulation of expressive conduct.

Balanced against appellant's claim of free expression is the school board's interest in promoting respect for authority and traditional values, as well as discipline in the classroom, by requiring teachers to dress in a professional manner. A dress code is a rational means of promoting these goals. As to the legitimacy of the goals themselves, there can be no doubt. In *James v. Board of Education*, Chief Judge Kaufman stated:

> The interest of the state in promoting the efficient operation of its schools extends beyond merely securing an orderly classroom. Although the pros and cons of progressive education are debated heatedly, a principal function of all elementary and secondary education is indoctrinative—whether it be to teach the ABCs or multiplication tables or to transmit the basic values of the community. 461 F.2d 566 (2d Cir.), cert. denied, 409 U.S. 1042, 93 S.Ct. 529 (1972).

This balancing test is primarily a matter for the school board. Were we local officials, and not appellate judges, we might find Mr. Brimley's arguments persuasive. However, our role is not to choose the better educational policy. We may intervene in the decisions of school authorities only when it has been shown that they have strayed outside the area committed to their discretion. If Mr. Brimley's argument were to prevail, this policy would be completely eroded. Because teaching is by definition an expressive activity, virtually every decision made by school authorities would raise First Amendment issues calling for federal court intervention. . . .

Mr. Brimley also claims that the "liberty" interest grounded in the due process clause of the Fourteenth Amendment protects his choice of attire. . . .

If Mr. Brimley has any protected interest in his neckwear, it does not weigh very heavily on the constitutional scales. As with most legislative choices, the board's dress code is presumptively constitutional. It is justified by the same concerns for respect, discipline and traditional values described in our discussion of the First Amendment claim. . . .

Each claim of substantive liberty must be judged in the light of that case's special circumstances. In view of the uniquely influential role of the public school teacher in the classroom, the board is justified in imposing this regulation. As public servants in a special position of trust, teachers may properly be subjected to many restrictions in their professional lives which would be invalid if generally applied. We join the sound views of the First and Seventh Circuits, and follow *Kelley* by holding that a school board may, if it wishes, impose reasonable regulations governing the appearance of the teachers it employs. . . . There being no material factual issue to be decided, the grant of summary judgment is affirmed.

CASE NOTE

A Louisiana school board expanded its student dress code to prohibit employees from wearing beards. The Fifth Circuit Court of Appeals recognized the liberty interest of the individual in choosing how to wear one's hair, but it ruled the school board had made a rational determination in establishing the rule as "a reasonable means of furthering the school board's

undeniable interest in teaching hygiene, instilling discipline, asserting authority, and compelling uniformity." *Domico v. Rapides Parish School Board*, 675 F.2d 100 (5th Cir.1982).

❖ — ❖ — ❖

Teacher's Letter to School Newspaper Responding to Allegations of Sexual Discrimination Addressed a Public Concern

Seemuller v. Fairfax County School Board

United States Court of Appeals,
Fourth Circuit, 1989.
878 F.2d 1578.

BUTZNER, Senior Circuit Judge. The sole issue in this appeal is whether a public school teacher's letter addressed a matter of public concern. Donald Seemuller, a physical education teacher at Lake Braddock High School in Fairfax County, Virginia, appeals the district court's order directing a verdict in favor of the Fairfax County School Board and George Stepp, the principal of Lake Braddock, in this §1983 action alleging violation of Seemuller's first amendment right to freedom of speech. Seemuller contends that the district court erred in ruling that his speech, a letter to the editor published in the school's newspaper, was not on a matter of public concern but was simply a personal response to criticism. Because we find that Seemuller's speech commented on a matter of public concern, we vacate the district court's order and remand for further proceedings.

In December 1986, Lake Braddock's school newspaper, *The Bear Facts*, published an anonymous letter to the editor written by students and captioned "Angered Girls Fight P.E. Discrimination." The letter complained about "a few male chauvinistic P.E. teachers" and gave several supporting examples. . . .

Seemuller responded to the complaint by submitting a letter to the newspaper. Before publication, the paper's faculty advisor and the principal read the letter. They did not object to its publication or ask Seemuller to withdraw it. The principal did not warn Seemuller that publication would lead to disciplinary action. He did not speak to Seemuller about the letter until after it was published.

The paper published the letter under the caption "P.E. Teacher Defends." The letter read as follows:

> Dear Editor,
>
> As a male physical education teacher at Lake Braddock, I was somewhat taken aback by the recent letter accusing some members of our staff of chauvinism. I cannot speak for every member of the staff, but as for myself, I like girls, and the many things they can accomplish. My two females at home are a sixteen year old whom I permit to chauffer my son to and from his many activities, and my wife who is an adequate cook and housekeeper. My wife also does light yard work enabling me to play golf, and pursue many other masculine activities.
>
> Hopefully this letter will convince those girls in physical education at Lake Braddock that we have the utmost respect for their feminine talents.
>
> Sincerely,
> Don Seemuller

In addition to being distributed to students at Lake Braddock, the school's newspaper is mailed to approximately 3,600 families in the school's community. The newspaper's policy is to publish letters to the editor from students, teachers, and parents.

Following publication of Seemuller's letter, the principal told Seemuller that he had received complaints from the community, faculty members, and the Lake Braddock Human Relations Committee. He also said that Seemuller might receive a "needs improvement" rating in "Professional Responsibility" in his final evaluation in April and suggested that Seemuller meet with the Human Relations Committee and write a letter of apology to the newspaper.

Seemuller met with the committee and submitted a letter of apology to the newspaper in May 1987 which appeared under the heading, "Seemuller Apologizes for Satirical Response." . . .

EDITOR'S NOTE

The editorial board respects Mr. Seemuller for discussing and confronting the sexual bias problem that some students see in the physical education department. However, this letter should have been unnecessary. Mr. Seemuller's original statement was facetious and not meant to be offensive. . . .

In his final evaluation in April 1987, as a result of the publication of his letter, Seemuller was rated as "Needs Improvement" in "Professional Responsibility." Seemuller alleges that because of this evaluation he did not receive his step increment in pay for the 1987–1988 school year.

Seemuller filed a grievance in accordance with school board regulations and state law. The deputy superintendent of schools who was designated by the superintendent to consider Seemuller's grievance acknowledged that his letter "was published in the context of school and community concerns about the treatment of females in school programs." The deputy superintendent concluded that Seemuller was able to exercise his "freedom of speech because [his] letter was published." Without further explanation, the school board denied the grievance after reviewing the documents and recommendation of the superintendent. Seemuller then brought this action.

The Supreme Court has explained in a series of cases during the last two decades the principles governing our inquiry. The initial question in deciding a public employee's entitlement to the protection of the first amendment is whether his speech addresses a matter of public concern. . . . In the absence of unusual circumstances, a public employee's speech "upon matters only of personal interest" is not afforded constitutional protection. *Connick v. Myers*, 461 U.S. 138, 147, 103 S.Ct. 1684, 1690, 75 L.Ed.2d 708 (1983). In contrast, a government employee's speech is protected from disciplinary action by his employer if "the interests of the [employee], as a citizen, in commenting upon matters of public concern" outweigh "the interests of the State, as an employer, in promoting the efficiency of the public services it performs through its employees." *Pickering v. Board of Education*, 391 U.S. 563, 568, 88 S.Ct. 1731, 1734, 20 L.Ed.2d 811 (1968). In this case, because the district court found that Seemuller's letter did not comment on a matter of public concern, it did not reach the *Pickering* balancing test. Consequently, the only issue on appeal is whether Seemuller's letter may be "fairly characterized as constituting speech on a matter of public concern." *Connick,* 461 U.S. at 146, 103 S.Ct. at 1689.

Connick also explains that "[w]hether an employee's speech addresses a matter of public concern must be determined by the content, form, and context of a given statement, as revealed by the whole record." . . . In conducting this examination, an appellate court is obligated to make "an independent constitutional judgment on the facts of the case." . . .

Connick dealt with the complaint of an employee who was discharged after she circulated a questionnaire that primarily sought responses about employment conditions in the office where she worked. In ruling that the employee's questionnaire did not involve a matter of public concern, the Court said:

> When employee expression cannot be fairly considered as relating to any matter of political, social, or other concern to the community, government officials should enjoy wide latitude in managing their offices, without intrusive oversight by the judiciary in the name of the First Amendment.
>
> We hold only that when a public employee speaks not as a citizen upon matters of public concern, but instead as an employee upon matters only of personal interest, absent the most unusual circumstances, a federal court is not the appropriate forum in which to review the wisdom of a personnel decision taken by a public agency allegedly in reaction to the employee's behavior. Our responsibility is to ensure that citizens are not deprived of fundamental rights by virtue of working for the government; this does not require a grant of immunity for employee grievances not afforded by the First Amendment to those who do not work for the State.

Connick, 461 U.S. at 146–47, 103 S.Ct. at 1689–90 (citation omitted). . . .

In applying the foregoing principles to the facts of this case, the starting point is the anonymous letters written by students about the physical education department. The paper's editor recognized its content by captioning it "Angered Girls Fight P.E. Discrimination." The letter protested that teachers practice discrimination based on sex. The letter addressed an issue that is no less a matter of public interest than a charge that a school system engages in discrimination based on race. . . .

Seemuller's letter, submitted for publication several weeks later, was a response to the anonymous letter. It starts out by stating that "I was somewhat taken aback by the recent letter accusing some members of our staff of chauvinism." The editor recognized Seemuller's letter as a defense of the department, for it was published with the caption: "P.E. Teacher Defends." Seemuller's letter was intended to address and did address the complaint of discrimination based on sex—a matter of public concern. This is apparent from the letter itself and from Seemuller's testimony at trial: "I was poking fun or making light or telling them to lighten up a little bit, that maybe what they had heard wasn't what really was going on." Asked to describe the letter, he testified: "My letter is, it is a humorous attempt at satire to point out that misperceptions can occur."

In his letter of apology, Seemuller explicitly stated that in his first letter he addressed "male chauvinism in the physical education department" and that the "intent of the letter was satirical in nature." The editor understood that Seemuller's first letter was a "Satirical Response" to the anonymous letter protesting discrimination based on sex. The editor appended a note saying the letter of apology was unnecessary and expressing the hope that Seemuller's treatment will not "scare others from contributing." The editor was aware of the danger of chilling speech protected by the first amendment.

The deputy superintendent of schools who presided over the grievance hearing recognized that Seemuller's letter dealt with a matter of public concern. In her decision she found as a fact that Seemuller's "letter was published in the context of school and community concern about the treatment of females in school programs." The grievance decision acknowledges that Seemuller was exercising his freedom of speech.

The record discloses that even before the anonymous letter was published in December 1986 some girls had complained that they were treated as second class citizens in the school. The exchange of correspondence between the anonymous letter writer and Seemuller sparked much livelier discussion about discrimination based on sex. The day after Seemuller's letter was published the principal met with 32 girls regarding discrimination and assured them he would not tolerate it. Later the school human relations committee met, deplored discrimination based on sex, and urged the principal to take steps to prevent it. Some people, taking Seemuller's letter literally, were offended by it and criticized it as demeaning women. Nevertheless, the fact that some persons considered the letter to be inappropriate or controversial "is irrelevant to the question whether it deals with a matter of public concern." . . . "[T]he public expression of ideas may not be prohibited merely because the ideas are themselves offensive to some of their hearers." . . .

Seemuller's use of satire to comment on a matter of public concern did not deprive him of the protection afforded by the first amendment. From Greek and Roman antiquity until the present time, commentators on public affairs have colored their writing with satire—sometimes humorous, sometimes gentle, sometimes caustic. . . . A teacher's letter criticizing the board of education was spiced with satire, but he was not deprived of the first amendment's protection. . . . Writing in a different context, the Supreme Court has observed that the first amendment protects satirists. . . .

In sum, we conclude that a complaint published in a school newspaper that a public school discriminates on the basis of sex raises a question of public concern. Seemuller's published response to the complaint also commented on a matter of public concern.

The judgment of the district court is vacated, and the case is remanded for further proceedings consistent with this opinion. Seemuller shall recover his costs.

■ PRIVACY

The word "privacy" is not mentioned in the Constitution or the Bill of Rights, yet the right of privacy is so basic and fundamental to individual freedom that it is assumed to emanate implicitly from several sources in the Bill of Rights.

Justice Douglas in *Griswold v. Connecticut*[38] stated that there is a broad right of privacy that may be inferred from several provisions of the Bill of Rights. Justice Stewart dissented in *Gris-*

wold on the grounds that he could find no general rights of privacy in the Bill of Rights or any other section of the Constitution. The Court noted that previous Courts had never held that the Bill of Rights and/or other amendments protected only those rights specifically mentioned by name. The Court said that the various guarantees of the Constitution "create zones of privacy":

> The right of association contained in the penumbra of the First Amendment is one. . . . The Third Amendment in its prohibition against the quartering of soldiers "in any house" in time of peace without the consent of the owner is another facet of that privacy. The Fourth Amendment explicitly affirms the "right of the people to be secure in their persons, houses, papers, and effects, against unreasonable searches and seizures." The Fifth Amendment in its Self-Incrimination Clause enables the citizen to create a zone of privacy which government may not force him to surrender to his detriment. The Ninth Amendment provides: "The enumeration in the Constitution, of certain rights, shall not be construed to deny or disparage others retained by the people."[39]

The Ninth Amendment, though rarely relied upon, is possibly the most inclusive of all because it guarantees natural rights and freedoms to individuals that are not enumerated elsewhere in the Constitution. This amendment was thought necessary by Madison, its author, because he feared that the enumeration of other rights in the first eight amendments would imply to later generations that this list was exhaustive and that no other rights were intended. The simple expedient that he used to combat this assumption was to include a "catchall" amendment to protect all other "great rights of mankind" against governmental intrusion.[40]

The right of privacy also finds basis in the substance of liberty of the due process clause of the Fourteenth Amendment. This was the basis for the Supreme Court's decision in *Roe v. Wade*.[41] The connection between personal privacy and liberty is reinforced by the earlier precedents of *Pierce v. Society of Sisters*[42] and *Meyer v. Nebraska*.[43]

It is the confluence and implication of these specified constitutional rights and freedoms that create the penumbras of privacy that Justice Douglas spoke of in *Griswold*. Because privacy is a fundamental right, governmental restraint can be justified only by a showing of a "compelling state interest."[44]

The essence of the privacy right, because of its breadth, is relatively difficult to circumscribe. Killian, though, explains it best:

> Privacy as a concept appears to encompass at least two different but related aspects. First, it relates to the right or the ability of individuals to determine how much and what information about themselves is to be revealed to others. Second, it relates to the idea of autonomy, the freedom of individuals to perform or not perform certain acts or subject themselves to certain experiences.[45]

SEARCH OF TEACHER WORKPLACES

Few cases have been litigated that would clearly define the teacher's right to privacy against searches of their workplaces at school. "Workplaces" is a term that has been used by the U.S. Supreme Court in describing the places where employees may not have an expectation of privacy.[46] According to the Supreme Court, the "workplace includes those areas and items that are related to work and are generally within the employer's control."[47] Specifically, the Court mentions "hallways, cafeteria, offices, desks, and file cabinets, among other areas," as being part of the public employee's workplace.[48]

Everything that is in the confines of the public school or business is not, however, considered to be within the definition of the workplace; closed luggage, briefcases, and handbags are singled out as examples of items that would not normally be considered in the same context as a teacher's desk or locker.[49]

The designation of workplace is essential to such cases because a public employee does not have an expectation of privacy against the employer's search of a public workplace. The public employee, though, does have a reasonable expectation of privacy against the search of private items, places, or things. Yet, while a public employee does not have an expectation of privacy against the public employer, the public employee does have a reasonable expectation of privacy, in both the workplace and other private places, against intrusions by the police.[50] The Supreme Court has said:

> Individuals do not lose Fourth Amendment rights merely because they work for the government in-

stead of a private employer. The operational realities of the workplace, however, may make some employees' expectations of privacy unreasonable when an intrusion is by a supervisor rather than a law enforcement officer.[51]

With regard to all searches, whether of teachers, students, or other employees, the rule of law to which school authorities must adhere is governed by the standard of reasonableness, as defined in *New Jersey v. T. L. O.*:

> The fundamental command of the Fourth Amendment is that searches and seizures be reasonable, and although both the concept of probable cause and the requirement of a warrant bear on the reasonableness of a search, . . . in certain limited circumstances neither is required.[52]

That which is "reasonable" depends on "balanc[ing] the nature and quality of the intrusion on the individual's Fourth Amendment interests against the importance of the governmental interests alleged to justify the intrusion."[53]

Thus, public employers may search employees' workplaces without probable cause and without a search warrant, but police must obtain and establish probable cause and obtain a search warrant to conduct a legally valid search.

The balancing of the individual's rights against the government's interest may not therefore require that the school district show probable cause for a search. This is, of course, the Court's view, as expounded in *New Jersey v. T. L. O.*[54] regarding student searches, and this standard, as noted above, is applicable with regard to teachers and other public employees. An appropriate school district interest in a search of a teacher's workplace would not require a warrant if the search is for a noninvestigatory work-related reason or for an investigatory search for evidence of suspected work-related employee misfeasance.[55] The government's interest in justifying work-related intrusions by the school district is predicated upon the public's expectation that the school district maintain an "efficient and proper operation of the workplace." The Supreme Court has explained the government's interest in this way:

> Public employers have an interest in ensuring that their agencies operate in an effective and efficient manner, and the work of these agencies inevitably

suffers from the inefficiency, incompetence, mismanagement, or other work-related misfeasance of its employees.[56]

According to the Supreme Court, to require the public employer to justify searches with a showing of probable cause and to obtain warrants for an administratively necessary intrusion would "impose intolerable" burdens on public employers.[57]

In summary, the public school district can conduct warrantless searches of the workplaces of teachers or other employees so long as the intrusions are undertaken with some reasonable basis to further the efficient and competent management of the school district. Searches of personal effects, such as pocketbooks, purses, briefcases, and other items not normally considered a part of the workplace and usually thought of as guarded by a reasonable expectation of privacy, cannot be searched by school officials without a warrant. Searches instigated by the police to obtain evidence to be used in criminal prosecutions require the justification of probable cause, and warrants must be obtained before the search can be undertaken.

TEACHERS' MENTAL AND PHYSICAL EXAMINATIONS

Teachers serve as role models for pupils, and school boards expect high moral standards consistent with that important status. The courts have generally upheld school boards in regulating the personal conduct of teachers, within reasonable limits. Litigation, though, may result when teachers allege school rules invade their privacy.

Most of the litigation concerning a teacher's right of privacy involves issues of morality or fitness to teach, and it has included such issues as homosexual activities, heterosexual improprieties, and use of marijuana and other drugs. The courts attempt to determine a rational nexus between the conduct in question and the professional duties being performed. To sustain its case against a teacher, the school board must establish that the outside activity has a detrimental impact on the teacher's ability to teach. "No person can be denied government employment because of factors unconnected with the responsibilities of that employment."[58]

Teachers' use of the right of privacy has become more frequent in recent years, as schools have sought to test and examine teachers for various reasons. In one such case, a federal district judge rejected the privacy claim of a female teacher who refused to submit to a physical examination by a male physician employed by the school district. The court, in holding against the teacher, said that there was no right of privacy at stake but rather a personal predilection against male physicians.[59]

In another case, a school principal's privacy claim was found to give way to the public interest where the school superintendent had reason to believe that the principal needed psychiatric attention.[60]

———————— ❖ — ❖ — ❖ ————————

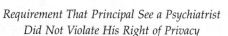

Requirement That Principal See a Psychiatrist Did Not Violate His Right of Privacy

Daury v. Smith

United States Court of Appeals,
First Circuit, 1988.
842 F.2d 9.

BOWNES, Circuit Judge. Plaintiff-appellant Jeffrey Daury appeals the grant of summary judgment in favor of defendants-appellees in his action for deprivation of constitutional rights under 42 U.S.C. §1983. Daury, a "grade leader" in the Pittsfield, Massachusetts school system, alleged in three counts of his complaint that the defendants, by requiring him to consult a psychiatrist as a condition of continued employment, deprived him of his right to privacy as guaranteed by the ninth and fourteenth amendments and his right to liberty as guaranteed by the fourteenth amendment. Daury claimed that as a result of defendants' action he suffered emotional distress, mental anguish, and damage to his health and well-being. Daury further claims that the decision to require him to see a psychiatrist was made in retaliation for his "union activities and free speech" and constituted intentional infliction of emotional distress. . . .

Jeffrey Daury began work for the Pittsfield school system in 1970 as a school principal. Two general aspects of his tenure are relevant to this appeal. First, Daury's favorable work evaluations began to decline in 1979 because defendants received an above average number of complaints concerning Daury from parents. Daury admits that some complaints did issue, but denies the foundation for many of them. Second, from 1979 until some time in 1983, Daury was a member of the negotiating team for the Pittsfield Teacher's Association. Daury asserts that he was very vocal in this role, but concedes that nothing unusual—neither strikes nor picketing—occurred during any period of contract negotiations.

In May 1983, the school committee decided to close one of the schools in the district because of budgetary constraints. It, therefore, became necessary to demote one principal; the committee decided upon Daury, and he was demoted to his present position of grade leader. Daury initiated a grievance procedure, but subsequently abandoned it. The committee has averred that its decision was in strict accordance with the requirement under the collective bargaining agreement that it consider both seniority *and* performance in deciding upon the demotion of a school principal.

Defendants point to three incidents, as well as other matters, leading to their decision to require that Daury see a psychiatrist. The first incident took place in October 1982. During a meeting about school funds between Daury and Theodore Herberg, director of research for the Pittsfield schools, Daury brought up a personal matter. The conversation turned into a near physical altercation; Daury received a written reprimand from Superintendent Davis. Daury filed a grievance and an arbitrator upheld the reprimand.

The second incident occurred in November 1982. Daury discovered documents in his personnel file that he had not signed. This was contrary to the collective bargaining agreement, which required that any document placed in a teacher's personnel file must be first signed by the teacher. Later that same day, Daury encountered Davis and another school administrator in the school parking lot. An argument concerning the unsigned documents ensued, as a result of

which Davis suspended Daury for three days without pay. Again Daury filed a grievance. The arbitrator reduced the suspension to one day, and ordered the documents removed from Daury's file.

The final incident which prompted the school committee to require that Daury see a psychiatrist took place on June 3, 1983. Daury was supervising students crossing the street when a boy (not, as it developed, a student at Daury's school) began to cross in an unsafe manner. Daury told the boy to stop, and the boy swore at him. Daury took hold of him. According to Daury, he held the boy's arm. Defendants were told that Daury grabbed the boy by the neck. A police officer intervened and the boy was released. The boy's parents initiated a criminal complaint against Daury for assault and battery. Two witnesses, including the police officer, testified at trial that Daury put a "stranglehold" on the boy. One of these witnesses, a woman who allegedly viewed the entire incident, had telephoned Davis reporting the incident soon after it happened. Daury was found not guilty and the presiding judge praised his behavior as responsible.

Prior to the criminal trial, Daury and his attorney met in Davis' office with a representative of the Massachusetts Teachers Association (MTA), Assistant Superintendent Bordeau, and Superintendent Davis. Both Bordeau and Davis assert that Daury stated at the meeting that he was under a great deal of pressure and that he thought he needed some tranquilizers. It was tentatively agreed that Daury would be put on a leave of absence with pay until the end of the school year—that is, until the end of June 1983.

The school committee formally approved the paid leave at a meeting held that same evening. In addition, the committee decided that Daury be required to see a psychiatrist before returning to work. . . .

On August 7, 1984, Daury filed suit against the defendants.

Daury alleges that the school committee's order that he see a psychiatrist violated his constitutional right to privacy. More specifically, he maintains that compelling him to submit to a psychiatric examination as a condition to his continued employment forced him to reveal information about his marriage, family history, and other personal relationships, and that this constituted an invasion of privacy regardless of the promise given by the school committee to keep the report confidential.

That a person has a constitutional right to privacy is now well established. . . . Such right includes "the individual interest in avoiding disclosure of personal matters. . . . " . . . The privacy right, however, must often give way to considerations of public interest. . . .

In *Lyons v. Sullivan*, 601 F.2d 7 (1st Cir.), *cert. denied*, 444 U.S. 876, 100 S.Ct. 159, 62 L.Ed.2d 104 (1979), we held that a matter of public concern overrode the right to privacy. Lyons, a public school teacher, filed an unusual complaint in a medical malpractice action, which led the school superintendent to question his mental stability. . . . We found that the superintendent had a reasonable basis for questioning Lyons' mental condition, and that there was no constitutional infirmity in the course of conduct pursued.

As *Lyons* implicitly recognizes, there is a legitimate public interest in providing a safe and healthy educational environment. A school committee, therefore, may justifiably compel a teacher or administrator to submit to a psychiatric examination as a condition of continued employment if the committee has reason to believe that the teacher or administrator may be jeopardizing the welfare of students under his or her supervision.

Viewing the evidence in the light most favorable to Daury, we find no violation of his constitutional rights in the school committee's requiring that Daury see a psychiatrist. The committee simply sought a professional opinion to insure that Daury would not, if he returned to work, jeopardize the school system's interest in providing a safe and healthy educational environment. . . . And Daury offered no specific evidence contradicting the committee's position that it had a reasonable basis for concern.

Daury argues that the June 3, 1983, incident could not have been a real basis for concern because he was eventually acquitted of the criminal charge filed against him. . . . Even if we assume, as Daury contends, that he grabbed the boy by the arm and not around the neck, the fact that the boy's parents filed a criminal complaint suggests that Daury's reaction to the boy's conduct was severe enough to question

his ability to handle the supervision of children, some of whom may be disruptive at times.

In light of all of the information the school committee had—the June 3 incident, Daury's statement that he was under pressure and needed tranquilizers, the two incidents in which he precipitated physical confrontations, and the complaints by parents—we think it was eminently reasonable for the school committee to require that Daury submit to a psychiatric examination. . . .

We think that on this record the school committee acted prudently in requiring that Daury see a psychiatrist. . . .

Plaintiff's complaint does not contain any count stating that defendants, in requiring him to submit to a psychiatric examination, did so in retaliation for plaintiff's union activities and exercise of his right to free speech. None of the counts use the words "retaliation," "union activities," "first amendment," or "free speech." The district court noted this omission but addressed the issue, apparently because plaintiff had argued it in a memorandum to the court. Plaintiff's brief to this court suggests that the allegation was included in Count II of his complaint. His brief states: "The complaint included claims pursuant to 42 U.S.C. 1983 for deprivation of the plaintiff's liberty interest by the defendants' intentional infliction of emotional distress in retaliation for the plaintiff's union activities and free speech." . . .

We will not rewrite plaintiff's complaint to contain a count that was not included in it. . . .

Affirmed.

■ PRIVACY AND DRUG TESTING OF TEACHERS

That the Fourth Amendment safeguards against arbitrary and unwarranted governmental intrusions into the privacy of individuals is a well-established cornerstone of constitutional law. Yet, as seen in the discussion above, the Fourth Amendment does not proscribe all searches and seizures but rather only those that are unreasonable. The reasonableness of the search depends upon all the circumstances surrounding the situation and the nature of the search and seizure itself.[61] What constitutes reasonableness is, of course, the critical question.

As explained above, while the police are required to have probable cause and to obtain a search warrant on the basis of that probable cause before a search can take place, the public school has a special governmental interest that allows warrantless searches based on reasonable suspicion. Yet of late, as the use of drugs has become more prevalent in our society, the courts have been called upon to define privacy rights in a context that does not neatly fit into or follow the normal probable cause or reasonable suspicion precedents. The result has been that the courts have formulated a new category of reasonable searches called "suspicionless searches." In these cases, testing for drugs and alcohol has been permitted without a showing of individualized suspicion.

The precedents for suspicionless searches emanate primarily from four recent U.S. Supreme Court cases where employees were engaged in "safety-sensitive" positions in which the use of drugs or alcohol could cause serious harm to others. In the leading case, *Skinner v. Railway Labor Executives' Association*,[62] the Supreme Court upheld a federal regulation that mandated post-accident toxicological testing of all employees involved in the accident. The Court in *Skinner* pointed out that the government's interest in testing was compelling because "employees subject to the tests discharge duties fraught with risks of injury to others that even a momentary lapse of attention can have disastrous consequences."[63] Thus, testing for drugs and alcohol may be reasonable and justified without particularized suspicion if this deterrent effect is to be realized. This Court concluded that even though the collection and testing of urine samples of employees, in fact, intrudes upon an expectation of privacy protected by the Fourth Amendment, the expectation of privacy can be overcome by a compelling interest of government in seeing that persons in safety-sensitive positions are deterred from using drugs and alcohol.

On the same day that *Skinner* was handed down, the Supreme Court also rendered a further elaboration of the suspicionless search reasoning in *National Treasury Employees Union v. Von Raab*,[64] in which it was established that there are times when Fourth Amendment intrusion serves a special governmental need. When these special needs are present, then the privacy expectations of the individual must be balanced against the government's interest to whether it is impractical to require a search warrant or have a particularized individual suspicion. *Von Raab* concerned the testing of Customs Service employees who carried firearms, enforced drug law, and had access to classified information, among other duties. The Court in *Von Raab* found the need compelling that first-line drug enforcement officials be drug-free and therefore they were subject to drug testing. As a result, drug tests may be allowed if compelling and special governmental reasons are articulated and the balancing analysis set forth in *Von Raab* is utilized. Of course, we are aware of the previously discussed precedent (Chapter 8) in *Vernonia School District 47 J v. Acton*,[65] wherein the U.S. Supreme Court upheld a school district policy of random drug testing of students who participated in school athletic programs. The policy had been prompted by a rampant increase in drug use among students, exacerbated by the use of drugs by student athletes who were by virtue of their sports participation considered to be leaders among the students in the school. The Supreme Court in balancing the interests held that student athletes have a lesser expectation of privacy than the population generally and that this lesser interest could be reasonably limited in stemming the use of drugs. These cases make it clear that even though drug testing by urine analysis is intrusive on the right of privacy, that right can be overcome by the government's interests in a "special needs" exception. Thus, particularized individual suspicion is not necessarily required where "special needs" or "safety-sensitive" conditions supersede the individual privacy interest.

In yet a more recent case, the U.S. Supreme Court struck down a Georgia statute requiring candidates for high political office in Georgia to submit to and pass a drug test within thirty days prior to qualifying for nomination for certain state offices. In holding the law unconstitutional, the Court pointed out that a special need did not exist because there was a lack of evidence demonstrating that a drug problem existed among state officeholders. Importantly, the Supreme Court admonished in *Chandler* that the main rule is that particularized suspicion is required before government can intrude on an individual's right of privacy and that "suspicionless" searches will be permitted only where "special needs" exist. The Court said that when such "special needs" are alleged in justification of Fourth Amendment intrusion, courts must undertake a "context-specific"[66] inquiry, examining closely the competing private and public interests advanced by the parties. In this regard, the Court in *Skinner* had emphasized that suspicionless searches are the exception and not the rule: "In limited circumstances, where the privacy interests implicated by the search are minimal, and where an important governmental interest furthered by the intrusion would be placed in jeopardy by a requirement of individualized suspicion, a search may be reasonable despite the absence of such suspicion."[67]

Taking these Supreme Court precedents into account, the United States Court of Appeals, Fifth Circuit, held in 1998 that two school boards in Louisiana violated the Fourth Amendment privacy interests of teachers by requiring urine analysis of employees without regard to the circumstances.[68] The school boards justified such tests on the rationale of *Skinner*, where the Supreme Court had upheld drug testing of all employees involved in railroad accidents. The Fifth Circuit rejected the *Skinner* railroad application to school employees, pointing out that the "special needs" for railroad safety were quite different from those for deterring drug use in schools. The court said that "special needs are just that, special, an exception to the command of the Fourth Amendment. . . . As destructive as drugs are and as precious are the charges of our teachers, special needs must rest on demonstrated realities."[69] The court concluded that the urine analysis requirements of an employee injured on the job had insufficient nexus between the injury and drug use to justify waiving the individualized suspicion that is required to overcome the privacy interests protected by the Fourth Amendment. On the other hand, the U.S. Court of Appeals, Sixth Circuit, in the *Knox County* case[70] has rendered an opinion upholding suspicionless drug testing of teachers relying for precedents on the U.S. Supreme Court's reasoning in *Skinner*,[71] *Von Raab*,[72] *Chandler*,[73] and *Vernonia*.[74] The Sixth Circuit based its decision on its conclusion that teachers occupy

"safety sensitive" positions, and even though the record of the trial did not indicate that there was a pronounced drug problem in the school system, and thus no "special needs," the suspicionless testing regime was justified because of the unique role that teachers play in the lives of school children. The court observed that in the school setting, where teachers acted *in loco parentis*, the public interest in drug testing outweighed the privacy interests of the teachers in not being tested. The court further pointed out that the teaching profession is by nature and of necessity a heavily regulated profession and that the urine-testing regime was fairly circumscribed and relatively unintrusive, thus reducing the expectation of privacy of the teachers. The *Knox County* case is set out in detail below.

*Suspicionless Drug Testing of
Teachers Is Constitutional*

Knox County Education Association v. Knox County Board of Education

United States Court of Appeals,
Sixth Circuit, 1998.
158 F.3d 361.

ROSEN, District Judge.

This appeal raises challenging and far-reaching constitutional questions concerning drug testing of teachers and other personnel in our nation's schools. Not only are a number of the issues presented here of first-impression for our Circuit, but these issues call upon us to consider and reconcile important constitutional and societal values concerning the environment in which our children are educated. Because the law in this area is unsettled and the issues of significant import to our schools and communities, the Court examines these important questions in some detail and at some length.

Plaintiff Knox County Education Association ("KCEA"), which represents professional employees in the Knox County School System, initiated this action to challenge drug and alcohol testing procedures adopted by Defendant Knox County Board of Education ("Board"), which is the body responsible for the administration, management, and control of the Knox County School System. . . . The policy establishes, inter alia, two different levels of testing: (1) suspicionless drug testing for all individuals who apply for, transfer to, or are promoted to, "safety sensitive" positions within the Knox County School System, including teaching positions; and (2) "reasonable suspicion" drug and/or alcohol testing of all school employees. KCEA challenged both testing programs as violative of the Fourth Amendment's prohibition against unreasonable searches and seizures.

In response, the Board twice moved for summary judgment on the basis that certain positions in the Knox County School System had already been ruled to be "safety sensitive" as a matter of law in a previous decision rendered in litigation challenging an earlier version of the Policy. . . .

The Knox County School System is comprised of eighty-eight schools, fifty-three of which are elementary schools and thirty-five of which are middle or high schools. Fifty-three thousand students attend the Knox County Schools, roughly half of whom are elementary school students and half are middle or high school students.

Thirty-two hundred teachers are employed in the Knox County Schools. . . .

The Security Department reports all incidents, whether criminal or not, that implicate the safety and security of students or staff. The incident reports for 1995–96 school year did not report any unlawful or violent conduct in the fifty-three elementary schools. The records reflect thirty-four assaults on students at the thirty-five middle and high schools, and fourteen assaults on teachers or principals (with no incidents occurring at all in twenty schools). There is no evidence that a pronounced drug/alcohol abuse problem exists among the Knox County teachers, nor is there evidence that the inattentiveness or negligence of a teacher has ever contributed to, or was related in any way, to these assaults or to any security incident.

With respect to non-violent but unlawful conduct, the Board's records indicate that during the 1995–96 school year, thirty-five students were charged with the possession of a weapon and seventy-four were charged with the possession or use of alcohol or drugs. Again, there is no record evidence that a teacher has ever failed to report a student for the use or possession of drugs, alcohol, or weapons. . . .

The Policy divides the tested employees into two distinct groups: (1) those who may be the subject of suspicionless testing (those who may be tested pre-employment for "safety sensitive" positions, pre-transfer for "safety sensitive" positions, and upon return to duty after undergoing rehabilitation); and (2) those who may be tested for reasonable suspicion of drug or alcohol impairment while at work (all employees).

The substance abuse policy prohibits any Board of Education employee from being under the influence of an illegal drug or alcohol while on duty, on Knox County Board of Education property, or in attendance at a System-approved or school-related function. . . .

The Policy allows suspicionless testing for people applying for positions that are "safety sensitive." The Policy defines "safety sensitive" positions as those positions "where a single mistake by such employee can create an immediate threat of serious harm to students and fellow employees." According to the Policy, . . . this category includes principals, assistant principals, teachers, traveling teachers, teacher aides, substitute teachers, school secretaries and school bus drivers.

Applicants for these positions are tested after they are offered a job but before their employment has commenced (i.e., post-offer, pre-employment). They are to be given a copy of the Policy in advance of the physical and are to sign an acknowledgment prior to substance screening, permitting the summary result to be transmitted to the Medical Review Officer ("MRO") and Director of Personnel. An applicant refusing to complete any part of the drug testing procedure will not be considered a valid candidate for employment with the school system, and such refusal will be considered as a withdrawal of the individual's application for employment. If substance screening shows a confirmed positive result for which there is no current physician's prescription, a second confirming test may be requested by the MRO. If the first or any requested second confirming test is positive, any job offer will be revoked. . . .

Section .05 of the Policy provides for drug and/or alcohol screening based upon reasonable suspicion as follows:

> Whenever the Knox County Board of Education, through its Director of Personnel or the person authorized to act as the Director in the Director's absence, and/or the Medical Review Officer, reasonably suspects that an employee's work performance or on-the-job behavior may have been affected in any way by illegal drugs or alcohol, or that an employee has otherwise violated the Knox County Board of Education Drug-Free Workplace Substance Abuse Policy, the employee may be required to submit a breath and/or urine sample for drug and alcohol testing. When a supervisor observes or is notified of behavior or events that lead the supervisor to believe that the employee is in violation of the Drug-Free Workplace Substance Abuse Policy, the Supervisor should notify the Director of Personnel.

An employee who is required to submit to drug/alcohol testing based upon such reasonable suspicion and refuses will be charged with insubordination and [subject to the disciplinary sanctions, including possible termination]. . . .

The ultimate question presented in this case is the reasonableness of a Fourth Amendment search, which is a question of law that we review de novo. . . .

The Fourth Amendment safeguards the privacy of individuals against arbitrary and unwarranted governmental intrusions by providing that "[t]he right of the people to be secure in their persons, houses, papers, and effects against unreasonable searches and seizures, shall not be violated". However, "the Fourth Amendment does not proscribe all searches and seizures, but only those that are unreasonable." . . . The reasonableness of a search "depends upon all of the circumstances surrounding the search or seizure and the nature of the search or seizure itself." . . .

It is now well-settled that drug testing which utilizes urinalysis is a "search" that falls within the ambit of the Fourth Amendment. . . .

As a general rule, in order to be reasonable, a search must be undertaken pursuant to a war-

rant issued upon a showing of probable cause. . . . That is, a valid search must ordinarily be based on an "individualized suspicion of wrongdoing." . . .

However, in *Chandler* [*v. Miller*] the [U.S. Supreme] Court clarified how suspicionless testing—presumably inherently suspect because by definition it is not accompanied by individualized suspicion—can comport with the Fourth Amendment:

> But particularized exceptions to the main rule are sometimes warranted based on "special needs, beyond the normal need for law enforcement." . . . When such "special needs"—concerns other than crime detection—are alleged in justification of a Fourth Amendment intrusion, courts must undertake a context-specific inquiry, examining closely the competing private and public interests advanced by the parties. . . . As Skinner stated: "In limited circumstances, where the privacy interests implicated by the search are minimal, and where an important governmental interest furthered by the intrusion would be placed in jeopardy by a requirement of individualized suspicion, a search may be reasonable despite the absence of such suspicion." . . .

Thus, where a Fourth Amendment intrusion serves special needs, "it is necessary to balance the individual's privacy expectations against the Government's interests to determine whether it is impractical to require a warrant or some level of individualized suspicion in the particular context." . . . Quite simply, then, in evaluating the constitutionality of the Board's drug testing Policy here, we must balance the government's (or public's) interest in testing against the individual's privacy interest.

With regard to the government's interest in testing, the Supreme Court has traditionally focused its analysis on two central factors: (1) whether the group of people targeted for testing exhibits a pronounced drug problem; and, if not, whether the group occupies a unique position such that the existence of a pronounced drug problem is unnecessary to justify suspicionless testing; and (2) the magnitude of the harm that could result from the use of illicit drugs on the job.

The existence of a pronounced drug problem within the group of employees targeted for testing typically tips the equities in favor of upholding suspicionless testing. Thus, as would be expected when using a balancing test, in cases in which a pronounced drug problem exists within the target group, a drug testing regime has a higher likelihood of being deemed constitutional because the more pernicious the drug problem is, the greater the public's interest is in abridging it.

In this case, there is little, if any, evidence of a pronounced drug or alcohol abuse problem among Knox County's teachers or other professional employees. Specifically, there is no empirical or historical evidence of an ongoing abuse problem . . . or evidence of a newly blossoming epidemic of abuse. . . . In fact, since the Policy was implemented in 1989, only one prospective hire has failed the suspicionless drug test.

However, the existence of a pronounced drug problem is not a sine qua non for a constitutional suspicionless drug testing program. The Board argues that there is no indication that teachers are unaffected by the drug use affliction that affects our country as a whole, and that proof of a pronounced drug problem is unnecessary. . . .

We can imagine few governmental interests more important to a community than that of insuring the safety and security of its children while they are entrusted to the care of teachers and administrators. Concomitant with this governmental interest is the community's interest in reasonably insuring that those who are entrusted with the care of our children will not be inclined to influence children—either directly or by example—in the direction of illegal and dangerous activities which undermine values which parents attempt to instill in children in the home. Indeed, teachers occupy a singularly critical and unique role in our society in that for a great portion of a child's life, they occupy a position of immense direct influence on a child, with the potential for both good and bad. Teachers and administrators are not simply role models for children (although we would certainly hope they would be that). Through their own conduct and daily direct interaction with children, they influence and mold the perceptions, and thoughts and values of children. Teachers and administrators are not some distant societal role models, . . . ; rather, on a daily basis, there is a direct nexus between the jobs of teachers and

administrators and the influence they exert upon the children who are in their charge. Indeed, directly influencing children is their job. . . .

In short, although the record evidence does not reflect that the Knox County District school teachers and other such officials have a track record of a pronounced drug problem, the suspicionless testing regime is justified by the unique role they play in the lives of school children and in loco parentis obligations imposed upon them.

The second factor we must consider in the balancing test analysis focuses on the magnitude of harm that could result from the use of illicit drugs in any given set of circumstances. In this case, the public interest proffered by the Board is that teachers, principals, and other such school personnel hold safety-sensitive positions and that the school district has a legitimate and strong interest in safeguarding the health and welfare of its students by ensuring that people in safety-sensitive positions are not under the influence of drugs or alcohol at school. The validity of this argument hinges in large part upon whether or not teachers, principals, and other school officials covered by the testing actually occupy "safety-sensitive" positions. . . .

Although the position of school teacher may not fit neatly into the prototypical "safety-sensitive" position, we do not read the definition of "safety-sensitive" so narrowly as to preclude application to a group of professionals to whom we entrust young children for a prolonged period of time on a daily basis. Simple common sense and experience with life tells us "that even a momentary lapse of attention can have disastrous consequences," . . . particularly if that inattention or lapse were to come at an inopportune moment. . . . For example, young children could cause harm to themselves or others while playing at recess, eating lunch in the cafeteria (if for example, they began choking), or simply while horsing around with each other. Children, especially younger children, are active, unpredictable, and in need of constant attention and supervision. Even momentary inattention or delay in dealing with a potentially dangerous or emergency situation could have grievous consequences.

This is equally true of teaching at the high school level. Not only must teachers observe and report drug use, but they are also charged, by law, with reporting assaults as well. . . . Fifty such incidents occurred in Knox County schools in the 1995–96 school year, and 77 in the 1994–95 school year.

The Court believes that a local school district has a strong and abiding interest in requiring that teachers and other school officials be drug-free so that they can satisfy their statutory obligation to insure the safety and welfare of the children. The fact that the Board has not been able to cite any one specific example in which a teacher or other employee responsible for children has allowed any harm to the children by being in an impaired condition while on the job is certainly not dispositive of the question of whether teachers and administrators hold "safety-sensitive" positions. We do not believe that the Board must wait passively for a disaster to occur before taking preemptive action to minimize the risks of such an occurrence. Indeed, we have no doubt that if a tragedy were to befall one or more of the school children of Knox County that in some manner implicated a teacher or administrator being under the influence of an illegal substance, the members of that community would rightly question why the Board had not taken all efforts possible in advance to prevent such an occurrence.

Finally, we would be remiss if we did not point out that the safety sensitive nature of a teacher's or administrator's job is not limited to the necessity to act at the immediate time of a dangerous event. Rather, school personnel perform an essential monitoring role in preventing incidents from occurring in the first place. Teachers and administrators are in a unique position to observe children and learn if they are involved in activities which can lead to harm or injury to themselves or others. Clearly, if school personnel are themselves under the influence of, or involved in, drugs, their ability to perform this critical function is not only reduced, but they themselves are open to being compromised and undermined. Clearly, a school board has a very strong interest in preventing this as part of its responsibility to insure the safety and security of school children. . . .

Having ruled that the public interest in suspicionless testing is very strong, an analysis of the employee's privacy rights is necessary to determine which of the competing values should prevail in this case. As will become evident in the course of this analysis, because teachers' legitimate expectation of privacy is diminished by their participation in the heavily regulated industry and by the nature of their job, the public interest in suspicionless testing outweighs that private interest. Again, we read the Supreme Court precedents assessing the privacy interests of employees as focusing on two central factors: (1) the intrusiveness of the drug testing scheme; and (2) the degree to which the industry in question is regulated.

We begin by noting that drug testing does implicate the privacy interests of employees on several levels. As the Supreme Court noted in *Skinner,* urination is an intensely private and personal act. . . . The "physical intrusion infringes an expectation of privacy that society is prepared to recognize as reasonable . . . [and] [t]he ensuing chemical analysis of the sample to obtain physiological data is a further invasion of the tested employee's privacy interests." . . . In fact, the testing is deemed a search precisely because it implicates concerns about bodily integrity. . . . Furthermore, "the limitation on an individual's freedom of movement that is necessary to obtain blood, urine, or breath samples" also amounts to a Fourth Amendment violation, if unreasonable. . . .

Although the drug testing regime presented in this case is, in certain respects, somewhat more intrusive than other regimes, judged as a whole it is fairly circumscribed and unintrusive. It does not include a random testing component, and only tests those people who are candidates for, and attempting to transfer to, a select group of positions. There is no ongoing testing once an applicant has received the job and passed the initial test. All specimens identified as positive are re-tested and confirmed using an advanced testing procedure. . . .

All personnel records and information regarding referral, evaluation, substance screen results, and treatment are to be maintained in a confidential manner and no entries concerning such will be placed in the employee's personnel file. . . .

With respect to the procedures for insuring the individual privacy during the actual taking of the urine sample itself, the Policy provides that the urine sample may be given by the individual in private without any monitoring, except in those cases in which there is reason to believe that the individual will adulterate the sample. Although this may be more invasive than some policies, it is not unreasonable. For all of these reasons, we find that the drug testing requirement here is only minimally intrusive and is only so broad as to achieve the legitimate objectives of the Policy.

With respect to the expectation of privacy of school personnel, we must first inquire into the degree with which the teaching and school administration is regulated by the state. The Board contends that the employees subjected to the drug testing participate in a heavily regulated profession and, accordingly, have a diminished expectation of privacy. In support of this contention, the Board cites a panoply of Tennessee regulations that apply to schools in general, and specifically to students, school boards, and teachers. The District Court ruled that teachers do not have a diminished expectation of privacy because those regulations do not, for the most part, apply to teachers regarding safety. We find the District Court erred in its ruling that to be heavily regulated, the regulations in question had to relate exclusively to safety, as this view is simply not supported by the relevant authority. . . .

Thus, the Court believes that when people enter the education profession they do so with the understanding that the profession is heavily regulated as to the conduct expected of people in that field, as well as the responsibilities that they undertake toward students and colleagues in the schools. It does not matter, as the District Court seemed to emphasize, that most of the regulations do not deal with safety per se, although, as noted, a number of the regulations are, in fact, related to safety. As *Vernonia* and *Skinner* make clear, our general focus is not whether teachers are heavily regulated, but if they participate in a heavily regulated profession or industry. In this case, the "industry"—public schools—is heavily regulated, and much of that regulation focuses on the conduct of teachers and principals. . . . [C]ertain portions of Tennessee law specifically require teachers and principals to report activity endangering "life,

health, or safety," and other regulations relate to drug use in the schools. Given this level of regulation, the Court finds that teachers should not be surprised if their own use of drugs is subject to regulation and testing and, as such, their expectation of privacy, at least with respect to drugs and drug usage, might be diminished. . . .

For all of the reasons stated here, we believe that the privacy interest for the employees not to be tested is significantly diminished by the level of regulation of their jobs and by the nature of the work itself. The ultimate inquiry before the Court is whether the search at issue here—the one-time, suspicionless testing of people hired to serve in teaching and administrative positions—is reasonable. On balance, the public interest in attempting to ensure that school teachers perform their jobs unimpaired is evident, considering their unique in loco parentis obligations and their immense influence over students. These public interests clearly outweigh the privacy interests of the teacher not to be tested because the drug-testing regime adopted by Knox County is circumscribed, narrowly-tailored, and not overly intrusive, either in its monitoring procedures or in its disclosure requirements. This is particularly so because it is a one-time test, with advance notice and with no random testing component, and because the school system in which the employees work is heavily regulated, particularly as to drug usage.

Therefore, we REVERSE the District Court's finding this portion of the statute unconstitutional.

The Court now turns to the suspicion-based testing, and finds that this portion of the Policy is also constitutional under the Fourth Amendment. . . .

The Policy provides for testing of an employee if the Director of Personnel "reasonably suspects" that an employee's work performance or on-the-job behavior may have been affected by illegal drugs or alcohol.

These requirements of "reasonable cause" sufficiently limit the discretion of the officials administering the rule and, because the testing is clearly based upon a finding of individualized suspicion, this portion of the Policy comports with the reasonableness requirement of the Fourth Amendment. Thus, for these reasons and those identified by the District Court, we AF-FIRM the District Court's ruling on this aspect of the suspicion-based testing program. . . .

CASE NOTE

The use of dogs to sniff a person's luggage is only minimally intrusive and does not require a search warrant. *United States v. Place*, 462 U.S. 696, 103 S.Ct. 2637 (1983). A search of the exterior of a car by police dogs does not constitute a search requiring a warrant. *Merrett v. Moore*, 58 F.3d 1547 (11th Cir. 1995). See also *United States v. Seals*, 987 F.2d 1102 (5th Cir. 1993). The U.S. Court of Appeals, Eleventh Circuit, held that a teacher's termination was valid when she refused to take a drug test after reasonable suspicion was established by a dog sniffing of her auto. *Hearn v. Board of Education*, 191 F.3d 1329 (11th Cir. 1999).

■ FREEDOM OF RELIGION

All persons in this country have the right of religious freedom as guaranteed by the First Amendment. However, religious freedom, as with other freedoms, is not without certain limits. For example, in *Palmer v. Board of Education of the City of Chicago*, a teacher refused to carry out certain aspects of the approved curriculum because of religious beliefs. The court acknowledged the teacher's right to freedom of belief but also recognized a compelling state interest in the proper education of all its children. The court stated that education "cannot be left to individual teachers to teach the way they please." Teachers have "no constitutional right to require others to submit to [their] views and to forego a portion of their education they would otherwise be entitled to enjoy."[75]

A teacher's religious freedom may extend into several aspects of the educational program. For example, if the tenets of a teacher's religion are violated by the Pledge of Allegiance to the American flag, the teacher cannot be compelled to recite the pledge, but the teacher, in accordance with school board rules, must hold the pledge ceremony for student participation.[76] Religious freedom of teachers is sustained by the courts so long as the exercise of the freedom does not en-croach on the rights of students or is not deleterious to the good conduct of the school.

TITLE VII

The right of religious freedom, where employment is concerned, has been expanded by the 1972 amendments to Title VII of the Civil Rights Act of 1964. The original act prohibited an employer from discriminating against an employee because of race, color, or sex, but it did not specify religion. The 1972 amendments incorporated religion, stating:

> It shall be an unlawful employment practice for an employment agency to fail or refuse for employment, or otherwise to discriminate against, any individual because of his race, color, religion, sex, or national origin, or to classify or refer for employment any individual on the basis of his race, color, religion, sex, or national origin.

The act further states that "[t]he term religion includes all aspects of religious observances and practice, as well as belief, unless an employer demonstrates that he is unable to reasonably accommodate an employee's or prospective employee's religious observance or practice without undue hardship on the conduct of the employer's business."[77]

The burden of proof is on the teacher to initially show that the school board's decision was religiously motivated or involved the denial of religious freedom. If the teacher is able to sustain this burden, then the burden of proof shifts over to the school board to show that a good-faith effort was made to accommodate the teacher's religious beliefs. If this effort is unsuccessful, then the board must show that it could not address the teacher's religious concerns without undue hardship to the school district.

In a case where a teacher who was a member of the World Wide Church of God requested seven days off from school, without pay, to attend a religious festival, the board refused the request and discharged the teacher when the teacher left school and attended anyway.[78] Before leaving, however, the teacher prepared lesson plans and consulted with the school counselor, who served as the substitute teacher. The court determined that the classes had run smoothly and the school district had suffered no undue hardship. The court concluded that the dismissal was unwarranted and violated the teacher's Title VII rights.

In a similar case, a Jewish teacher claimed that he needed more than two days' leave to celebrate religious holidays.[79] He noted that Christian teachers had the benefit of more days that coincided with the regular school calendar. Effectively, the denial of religious holidays compelled the Jewish teacher to choose between employment and religious observances. The court, in holding for the teacher, said that Title VII is violated if "[a]n employer . . . punishes an employee by placing the latter in a position in which he or she must ignore a tenet of faith in order to retain employment."[80]

One of the primary questions raised here is, What does an employer have to do to reasonably accommodate the religious beliefs of an employee? In *Trans World Airlines, Inc. v. Hardison*,[81] the Supreme Court addressed this issue. Title VII did not require TWA "to carve out special exemptions" to permit a special religious observance on Saturday instead of the Sunday. TWA had claimed that special accommodation for an employee on other than regular Christian holidays forced it to incur extraordinary costs for scheduling and replacement personnel. "To require TWA to bear more than a *de minimis* cost, in order to give the employee Saturdays off, is an undue hardship."

In *Ansonia Board of Education v. Philbrook* (discussed further in Chapter 17), the employee and employer each proposed a reasonable accommodation. The court of appeals ruled the employer was required to accept the employee's proposal unless it caused any undue hardship on the employer's business. The Supreme Court reversed the court of appeals and stated:

> An employer has met its obligation under §701(j) when it demonstrates that it has offered a reasonable accommodation to the employee. The employer need not further show that each of the employee's alternative accommodations would result in undue hardship. The extent of undue hardship on the employer's business is at issue only where the employer claims that it is unable to offer any reasonable accommodation without such hardship.[82]

NEITHER INHIBIT NOR PROMOTE RELIGION

The religious provisions of the First Amendment, of course, apply to teachers in their employment capacity. A school board action must meet all conditions of the tripartite test of *Lemon v. Kurtzman* in order not to violate the establishment clause of the First Amendment. As discussed earlier in this text, these conditions specify that the action must (1) have secular purpose, (2) neither inhibit nor promote religion, and (3) not cause excessive entanglement.[83] It is uncertain what affect the recent U.S. Supreme Court decisions in *Agostini* and *Helms* (see Chapter 5) will ultimately have on employment relationships.

Following the First Amendment rule, a New Jersey court held that a teacher-negotiated agreement that allowed for paid leaves of absence for religious believers but made no allowance for nonbelievers violated the First Amendment. The court cited the earlier Supreme Court case of *Torcaso v. Watkins*, which held that it was unconstitutional to "impose requirements which aid all religions as against non-believers."[84]

RELIGIOUS GARB

Whether public school teachers can wear religious garb of any particular religious order or society has been litigated on several occasions. While there is no precise definition of what constitutes religious garments, some states have sought prohibition of any apparel that showed that the person belonged to a particular sect, denomination, or order.[85]

In 1894, the Supreme Court of Pennsylvania held that the wearing by nuns of garb and insignia of the Sisterhood of St. Joseph while teaching in the public schools did not constitute sectarian teaching.[86] The court reasoned that to deny the wearing of such apparel would violate the teachers' religious liberty. Later, the legislature of Pennsylvania prohibited the wearing of garb by public school teachers while in performance of their duties. This statute was subsequently upheld by the Pennsylvania Supreme Court. This time the court maintained that the act was a reasonable exercise of state power in regulating the educational system to prevent sectarian control. The court found that the legislation "is directed against acts, not beliefs, and only against acts of the teacher while engaged in the performance of his or her duties as such teacher."[87]

Litigation over the years in other states has been split on the issue. A New York court in 1906 held that "the influence of such apparel is distinctly sectarian."[88] Similarly, the Nebraska Supreme Court refused to mandate that the state superintendent distribute state school trust funds to a school because of the school's religious emblems; the teachers wore distinctive garb, including the rosary, indicative of the Catholic sisterhood.[89]

On the other hand, the wearing of religious garb has been upheld by at least three state supreme courts. In a North Dakota case, the court held that there was no evidence that nuns imparted religious instruction even though they were dressed in religious garb of the Sisterhood of St. Benedict.[90]

Most recently, in a definitive analysis of the issue, the Supreme Court of Oregon held that a teacher's certification could be revoked for wearing religious garb.[91] In so holding, the court observed that the legislature had a legitimate objective in maintaining the neutrality of the public schools. While the denial of the wearing of religious garb could be interpreted by some as an impingement on the teacher's personal religious freedom, it could just as logically be maintained that the state's condoning of such garb favors that particular religion and, in fact, places the imprimatur of the state behind that particular religious sect. The Oregon court said "that the teacher's appearance in religious garb may leave a conscious or unconscious impression among young people and their parents that the school endorses the particular religious commitment of the person [teacher]."[92]

Any lack of consensus by the courts is due to their legitimate hesitancy to invade the religious rights of either teachers or students. The issue boils down to one of a weighing of interests in view of the particular facts of the case. As the Connecticut Supreme Court has said:

> The decisions in these cases, however, are, as is to be expected, based upon a wide diversity of facts. The only definite conclusion that may be drawn from them is that whether sectarian influence con-

nected with a school is such as to affect its public character is ordinarily a question of fact for the trial court.[93]

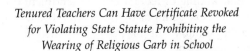

Tenured Teachers Can Have Certificate Revoked for Violating State Statute Prohibiting the Wearing of Religious Garb in School

Cooper v. Eugene School District No. 4J

Supreme Court of Oregon, 1986.
301 Or. 358, 723 P.2d 298.

LINDE, Justice. When Janet Cooper, a special education teacher in the Eugene public schools, became a Sikh, she donned white clothes and a white turban and wore them while teaching her sixth and eighth grade classes. In a letter to the staff of the school where she taught, she wrote that she would wear the turban and often wear white clothing as part of her religious practice, and that she had explained this and other changes in her life to her students.* She continued to wear her white garb after being warned that she faced suspension if she violated a law against wearing religious dress at her work. The law provides, in ORS 342.650:

> No teacher in any public school shall wear any religious dress while engaged in the performance of duties as a teacher.

And, in ORS 342.655:

> Any teacher violating the provisions of ORS 342.650 shall be suspended from employment by the district school board. The board shall report its action to the Superintendent of Public Instruction who shall revoke the teacher's teaching certificate.

Pursuant to these statutes, the school superintendent, acting for the school board, suspended Cooper from teaching and reported this action

---

*Cooper also had married and had changed her name to Karta Kaur Khalsa.

to the Superintendent of Public Instruction, who, after a hearing, revoked Cooper's teaching certificate. This order was challenged on constitutional grounds in the Court of Appeals, which set aside the revocation of the teaching certificate as an excessive sanction under the court's understanding of federal First Amendment doctrine. . . . On petitions by the school district and the Superintendent of Public Instruction, we allowed review. . . .

Cooper's case is not one of declining to comply with an otherwise valid law on grounds of personal religious belief. . . . ORS 342.650 is not neutral toward religion. On the contrary, the religious significance of the teacher's dress is the specific target of this law. The law singles out a teacher's religious dress because it is religious and to the extent that its religious significance is apparent when the wearer is engaged in teaching. The issue therefore is whether the law infringes the right guaranteed to "all men" by Article I, section 2, of the Oregon Constitution "to worship Almighty God according to the dictates of their own consciences," or "control[s] the free exercise, and enjoyment of religious opinions, or interfere[s] with the rights of conscience" contrary to Article I, section 3. . . .

The guarantees of religious freedom in Article I provide:

> Section 2. All men shall be secure in the Natural right, to worship Almighty God according to the dictates of their own consciences.
>
> Section 3. No law shall in any case whatever control the free exercise, and enjoyment of religeous [sic] opinions or interfere with the rights of conscience.
>
> Section 4. No religious test shall be required as a qualification for any office of trust or profit.
>
> Section 5. No money shall be drawn from the Treasury for the benefit of any religeous (sic), or theological institution, nor shall any money be appropriated for the payment of any religeous (sic) services in either house of the Legislative Assembly.
>
> Section 6. No person shall be rendered incompetent as a witness, or juror in consequence of his opinions on matters of religeon (sic); nor be questioned in any Court of Justice touching his religeous (sic) belief to affect the weight of his testimony.
>
> Section 7. The mode of administering an oath, or affirmation shall be such as may be most consistent with, and binding upon the conscience of

the person to whom such oath or affirmation may be administered.

This court in fact has interpreted the meaning of these guarantees independently, sometimes with results contrary to those reached by the United States Supreme Court. . . .

The religion clauses of Oregon's Bill of Rights, Article I, sections 2, 3, 4, 5, 6 and 7, are more than a code. They are specifications of a larger vision of freedom for a diversity of religious beliefs and modes of worship and freedom from state-supported official faiths or modes of worship. The cumulation of guarantees, more numerous and more concrete than the opening clause of the First Amendment, reinforces the significance of the separate guarantees. . . .

. . . If such a law is to be valid, it must be justified by a determination that religious dress necessarily contravenes the wearer's role or function at the time and place beyond any realistic means of accommodation.

The compatibility of religious dress with the role of public school teachers is an old issue under state laws and constitutions. Generally it involved teaching by nuns while wearing the habits of their orders. It is, of course, a different question whether a constitution itself is claimed to forbid the display of the teacher's religious commitment in the public school or whether a ban on religious dress adopted by law or properly delegated rule contravenes the teacher's religious freedom. . . .

The courts' tolerance of overt religious symbolism in public schools has differed over time and perhaps with the religious composition of different communities. Looking beyond the specific facts of the cases, however, the decisions generally have been that more than a teacher's religious dress is needed to show a forbidden sectarian influence in the classroom, but that a rule against such religious dress is permissible to avoid the appearance of sectarian influence, favoritism, or official approval in the public school. The policy choice must be made in the first instance by those with lawmaking or delegated authority to make rules for the schools. The courts' role is to see whether the rule stays within that authority and within the constitution and, if necessary, to give the rule a constitutional interpretation.

Here the policy choice was made by the legislature. There is no reason to believe that when the Legislative Assembly enacted ORS 342.650 in its present form in 1965, it had any aim other than to maintain the religious neutrality of the public schools, to avoid giving children or their parents the impression that the school, through its teacher, approves and shares the religious commitment of one group and perhaps finds that of others less worthy. . . .

We conclude that ORS 342.650 does not impose an impermissible requirement for teaching in the public schools if it is properly limited to actual incompatibility with the teaching function.

. . . The statute, of course, does not forbid the wearing of religious dress outright, but it does forbid doing so while teaching. The law could be described either as denying a teacher's right to practice her religion or as denying a person demonstratively committed to a religious vocation the opportunity to teach in the public schools. . . .

. . . The religious influence on children while in the public school that laws like ORS 342.650, in their concern with the employment of nuns wearing their special garb as public school teachers, legitimately seek to prevent is not the mere knowledge that a teacher is an adherent of a particular religion. Their concern is that the teacher's appearance in religious garb may leave a conscious or unconscious impression among young people and their parents that the school endorses the particular religious commitment of the person whom it has assigned the public role of teacher. This is what makes the otherwise privileged display of a teacher's religious commitment by her dress incompatible with the atmosphere of religious neutrality that ORS 342.650 aims to preserve, or so the school authorities may decide. The statute therefore would not be violated whenever a teacher makes an occasional appearance in religious dress, for instance on her way to or from a seasonal ceremony. . . . Only wearing religious dress as a regular or frequently repeated practice while teaching is grounds for disqualification.

We conclude that, when correctly interpreted and applied, ORS 342.650 survives challenge under Oregon's guarantees of religious freedom. As interpreted in this opinion, we believe it also does not violate the federal First Amendment.

The Court of Appeals thought that revocation of a teaching certificate was an excessive "sanction" discouraging even privileged exercise of First Amendment rights more than is necessary to achieve the law's purpose of maintaining religious freedom and neutrality in the public schools. We do not disagree with the court's general proposition that First Amendment decisions have required limitations on the exercise of First Amendment rights to be no more restrictive than necessary, although we note, as the district argues, that the decisions deal with the coverage of such limitations rather than with the consequence of violating a valid rule.

ORS 342.650 might indeed restrict a teacher's First Amendment rights to the "free exercise" of religion more than necessary if it were applied literally, but where ORS 342.650 can validly be applied, the revocation of a teaching certificate under ORS 342.655 is not a penalty. It is not a withdrawal of a privilege by reason of hostility to a religious or political belief, as when some states disqualified Communists from driving or practicing pharmacy or from living in public housing. . . . It is a disqualification from teaching in public schools based on one's doing so in a manner incompatible with that function. We doubt that the First Amendment draws a line between a law that disqualifies a public school teacher by compelling her discharge and another law that disqualifies her by revoking her certificate to teach in the public schools. ORS 342.655 does not forbid requalifying for a certificate.

Insofar as the decision of the Court of Appeals strikes down ORS 342.655 on that premise, it must be reversed. . . . Because ORS 342.650 and 342.655 can be interpreted to remain within constitutional limits and can be constitutionally administered, the Superintendent's order pursuant to ORS 342.655 is not unlawful for being based on an invalid statute. . . .

The decision of the Court of Appeals is reversed.

CASE NOTES

1. A teacher who was a member of the original African Hebrew Israelites of Ethiopia wore a headwrap to school and was dismissed and denied unemployment benefits. The court held

for the teacher, stating that schools may have reasonable dress codes provided they do not infringe on constitutional rights. *Mississippi Employment Security Commission v. McGlothin,* 556 So.2d 324 (Miss.1990).

2. In another religious garb case, the administrators in a Philadelphia school, acting under authority of statute, requested that a Muslim teacher not wear her religious garb to school and the teacher challenged the statute as a violation of Title VII of the Civil Rights Act of 1964. The court concluded that it would impose an undue hardship on the school board to accommodate the teacher and stated:

> Where the statute bans *all* religious attire and is being enforced by the Commonwealth in a non-discriminatory manner with respect to the Muslim teachers as well as Catholics, we conclude that it is irrelevant whether a portion of those who voted for the statute in 1895 were motivated by a desire to bar Catholic habit from the classroom. We therefore accept that the Commonwealth regards the wearing of religious attire by teachers while teaching as a significant threat to the maintenance of religious neutrality in the public school system, and accordingly conclude that it would impose an undue hardship to require the Commonwealth to accommodate Ms. Reardon and others similarly situated.

United States v. Board of Education of School District of Philadelphia, 911 F.2d 882 (3d Cir.1990).

3. A substitute teacher's interjection of his own religious beliefs into the classroom by reading the Bible aloud and professing his belief in the Biblical version of creation in a fifth grade science class was valid grounds for removing him from the list of teachers eligible for substitute teacher positions. The court rejected the teacher's Title VII claims in holding for the school district. *Helland v. South Bend Community School Corporation,* 93 F.3d 327 (7th Cir.1996), cert. denied, 117 S.Ct. 769 (1997).

■ PRIVILEGE AGAINST SELF-INCRIMINATION

The Fifth Amendment self-incrimination clause, which provides that a person shall not "be compelled in any criminal case to be a witness against himself," was absorbed into the due process clause of the Fourteenth Amendment and made applicable to the states in 1964. The right that no man is bound to accuse himself, *nemo tenetur seipsum prodere,* is extended by the Fifth Amendment to teachers, as it is to all individuals. The right itself, though, does not allow avoidance of questions regarding professional competency or fitness to teach. The self-incrimination clause was intended to protect a person against inquisitional extraction of incriminating evidence in criminal proceedings or in governmental hearings that may result in criminal prosecution. This right extends only to protecting one's self, not another person. If a teacher validly invokes the Fifth Amendment, there can be no presumption of guilt.

In *Slochower v. Board of Public Education,*[94] the Supreme Court held that the dismissal of a Brooklyn College professor for invoking the Fifth Amendment before a congressional committee was unconstitutional. This case cannot, however, be too broadly interpreted, for only a short time later the Supreme Court held in *Beilan v. Board of Education*[95] that a teacher could be dismissed for refusing to answer questions posed by the school superintendent about alleged past subversive activities. The Court found that the dismissal was predicated not on an impermissible inference of criminal guilt drawn from refusal to answer but instead on a finding of insubordination emanating from the fact that the teacher refused to answer.[96] *Slochower* was distinguished from *Beilan* in that the refusal to answer in *Beilan* was directed toward questions posed by a superior in specific regard to fitness to teach and incompetency was specifically cited as the reason for dismissal.

The rationale of *Beilan,* though, comes under a shadow because the Court has ruled subsequently that disbarment of a lawyer for refusing to produce evidence in an ethical practices proceeding was unconstitutional.[97] Also, the dismissal of a policeman for invoking the Fifth Amendment privilege in refusing to answer questions regarding his fitness and concerning conduct that could open him to criminal prosecution was held to be unconstitutional.[98] Although these cases can be distinguished in that the former involved disbarment and denial of future employment and the latter related to criminal evidence, the strength of the *Beilan* decision is substantially diminished if the fitness of a teacher is viewed in the broader constitutional context of subsequent First Amendment and due process cases affecting teachers.

――――――――― ❖ — ❖ — ❖ ―――――――――

Failure of Teacher to Answer Questions Posed by Superintendent Concerning Loyalty May Be Incompetency

Beilan v. Board of Public Education, School District of Philadelphia

Supreme Court of the United States, 1958.
357 U.S. 399, 78 S.Ct. 1317.

Mr. Justice BURTON delivered the opinion of the Court. The question before us is whether the Board of Public Education for the School District of Philadelphia, Pennsylvania, violated the Due Process Clause of the Fourteenth Amendment to the Constitution of the United States when the Board, purporting to act under the Pennsylvania Public School Code, discharged a public school teacher on the ground of "incompetency," evidenced by the teacher's refusal of his Superintendent's request to confirm or refute information as to the teacher's loyalty and his activities in certain allegedly subversive organizations. For the reasons hereafter stated, we hold that it did not.

On June 25, 1952, Herman A. Beilan, the petitioner, who had been a teacher for about twenty-two years in the Philadelphia Public School System, presented himself at his Superintendent's office in response to the latter's request. The Superintendent said he had information which reflected adversely on petitioner's loyalty and he wanted to determine its truth or falsity. In response to petitioner's suggestion

that the Superintendent do the questioning, the latter said he would ask one question and petitioner could then determine whether he would answer it and others of that type. The Superintendent, accordingly, asked petitioner whether or not he had been the Press Director of the Professional Section of the Communist Political Association in 1944. Petitioner asked permission to consult counsel before answering and the Superintendent granted his request.

On October 14, 1952, in response to a similar request, petitioner again presented himself at the Superintendent's office. Petitioner stated that he had consulted counsel and that he declined to answer the question as to his activities in 1944. He announced he would also decline to answer any other "questions similar to it," "questions of this type," or "questions about political and religious beliefs. . . . " The Superintendent warned petitioner that this "was a very serious and a very important matter and that failure to answer the questions might lead to his dismissal." The Superintendent made it clear that he was investigating "a real question of fitness for [petitioner] to be a teacher or to continue in the teaching work." These interviews were given no publicity and were attended only by petitioner, his Superintendent and the Assistant Solicitor of the Board. . . . The only question before us is whether the federal Constitution prohibits petitioner's discharge for statutory "incompetency" based on his refusal to answer the Superintendent's questions.

By engaging in teaching in the public schools, petitioner did not give up his right to freedom of belief, speech or association. He did, however, undertake obligations of frankness, candor and cooperation in answering inquiries made of him by his employing Board examining his fitness to serve it as a public school teacher.

> A teacher works in a sensitive area in a schoolroom. There he shapes the attitude of young minds towards the society in which they live. In this, the state has a vital concern. It must preserve the integrity of the schools. That the school authorities have the right and the duty to screen the officials, teachers, and employees as to their fitness to maintain the integrity of the schools as a part of ordered society, cannot be doubted. *Adler v. Board of Education,* 342 U.S. 485, 493, 72 S.Ct. 380, 385.

As this Court stated in *Garner v. Board of Public Works*, 341 U.S. 716, 720, 71 S.Ct. 909, 912, "We think that a municipal employer is not disabled because it is an agency of the State from inquiring of its employees as to matters that may prove relevant to their fitness and suitability for the public service."

The question asked of petitioner by his Superintendent was relevant to the issue of petitioner's fitness and suitability to serve as a teacher. Petitioner is not in a position to challenge his dismissal merely because of the remoteness in time of the 1944 activities. It was apparent from the circumstances of the two interviews that the Superintendent had other questions to ask. Petitioner's refusal to answer was not based on the remoteness of his 1944 activities. He made it clear that he would not answer any question of the same type as the one asked. Petitioner blocked from the beginning any inquiry into his Communist activities, however relevant to his present loyalty. The Board based its dismissal upon petitioner's refusal to answer any inquiry about his relevant activities—not upon those activities themselves. It took care to charge petitioner with incompetency, and not with disloyalty. It found him insubordinate and lacking in frankness and candor—it made no finding as to his loyalty.

We find no requirement in the federal Constitution that a teacher's classroom conduct be the sole basis for determining his fitness. Fitness for teaching depends on a broad range of factors. The Pennsylvania tenure provision specifies several disqualifying grounds, including immorality, intemperance, cruelty, mental derangement and persistent and willful violation of the school laws, as well as "incompetency." However, the Pennsylvania statute, unlike those of many other States, contains no catchall phrase, such as "conduct unbecoming a teacher," to cover disqualifying conduct not included within the more specific provisions. Consequently, the Pennsylvania courts have given "incompetency" a broad interpretation. . . .

The term "incompetency" has a "common and approved usage." The context does not limit the meaning of the word to lack of substantive knowledge of the subjects to be taught. Common and approved usage give a much wider meaning. For example, in 31 C.J., with reference to a number of supporting decisions, it is defined: "A relative term without technical meaning. It may be employed as meaning disqualification; inability; incapacity; lack of ability, legal qualifications, or fitness to discharge the required duty." . . .

In the instant case, the Pennsylvania Supreme Court has held that "incompetency" includes petitioner's "deliberate and insubordinate refusal to answer the questions of his administrative superior in a vitally important matter pertaining to his fitness." 386 Pa. at page 91, 125 A.2d at page 331. This interpretation is not inconsistent with the federal Constitution.

Petitioner complains that he was denied due process because he was not sufficiently warned of the consequences of his refusal to answer his Superintendent. The record, however, shows that the Superintendent, in his second interview, specifically warned petitioner that his refusal to answer "was a very serious and a very important matter and that failure to answer the questions might lead to his dismissal." That was sufficient warning to petitioner that his refusal to answer might jeopardize his employment. Furthermore, at petitioner's request, his Superintendent gave him ample opportunity to consult counsel. There was no element of surprise.

Our recent decisions in *Slochower v. Board of Higher Education,* 350 U.S. 551, 76 S.Ct. 637, 100 L.Ed. 692, and *Konigsberg v. State Bar of California,* 353 U.S. 252, 77 S.Ct. 722, 1 L.Ed.2d 810, are distinguishable. In each we envisioned and distinguished the situation now before us. In the *Slochower* case, 350 U.S. at page 558, 76 S.Ct. at page 641, the Court said:

It is one thing for the city authorities themselves to inquire into Slochower's fitness, but quite another for his discharge to be based entirely on events occurring before a federal committee whose inquiry was announced as not directed at "the property, affairs, or government of the city, or . . . official conduct of city employees." In this respect the present case differs materially from *Garner* [*Garner v. Board of Public Works,* 341 U.S. 716, 71 S.Ct. 909, 95 L.Ed. 1317], where the city was attempting to elicit information necessary to determine the qualifications of its employees. Here, the Board had possessed the pertinent information for twelve years, and the questions which Professor Slochower refused to answer were admittedly asked for a purpose wholly unrelated to his college functions. On such a record the Board cannot claim that its action was part of a bona fide attempt to gain needed and relevant information.

. . . In the instant case, no inferences at all were drawn from petitioner's refusal to answer. The Pennsylvania Supreme Court merely equated refusal to answer the employing Board's relevant questions with statutory "incompetency."

Inasmuch as petitioner's dismissal did not violate the federal Constitution, the judgment of the Supreme Court of Pennsylvania is affirmed.

CASE NOTES

1. In a sequel to *Beilan* in 1960, the Supreme Court of Pennsylvania held that the plea of a public school teacher of a constitutional privilege against criminal prosecution cannot be presumed to be relevant evidence of incompetency. This court said:

> Just as remaining mute, upon the plea of the Fifth Amendment, carries no implication of guilt of the matter inquired about in the unanswered questions . . . , so also does the plea not carry an implication of the pleader's *incompetency.*

Pleas of the Fifth Amendment before a tribunal empowered to impose criminal liability cannot support a presumption of incompetency as a teacher. *Board of Education of Philadelphia v. Intille,* 401 Pa. 1, 163 A.2d. 420 (1960).

2. The Fifth Amendment privilege to refuse to incriminate oneself is available not just in a criminal court, but also may be invoked before a congressional committee. *Quinn v. United States,* 349 U.S. 155, 75 S.Ct. 668 (1955). The privilege is a personal one to be utilized to defend one's self and cannot be claimed on behalf of another person or a corporation. *McPhaul v. United States,* 364 U.S. 372, 81 S.Ct. 138 (1960), rehearing denied, 364 U.S. 925, 81 S.Ct. 282 (1960). The privilege against self-incrimination cannot be used by the witness as a subterfuge to avoid questions that cannot be used in a criminal proceeding against him or her personally. *Hoffman v. United States,* 341 U.S. 479, 71 S.Ct. 814 (1951). See also John E. Nowack, Ronald D. Rotunda, and J. Nelson Young, *Constitutional Law,* 3d ed. (St. Paul, Minn.: West, 1986), p. 236.

The privilege afforded by the Fifth Amendment is not available to a defendant in a civil proceeding.

■ ENDNOTES

1. Reid v. Covert, 354 U.S. 1, 77 S.Ct. 1222 (1957).

2. Leonard W. Levy, *Constitutional Opinions, Aspects of the Bill of Rights* (New York: Oxford University Press, 1986), p. 113.

3. Ibid., p. 105.

4. Gitlow v. New York, 268 U.S. 652, 45 S.Ct. 625 (1925); Fiske v. Kansas, 274 U.S. 380, 47 S.Ct. 655 (1927); Cantwell v. Connecticut, 310 U.S. 296, 60 S.Ct. 900 (1940); Near v. State of Minnesota, 283 U.S. 697, 51 S.Ct. 625 (1931); De Jonge v. Oregon, 299 U.S. 353, 57 S.Ct. 255 (1937).

5. Richard Hofstadter and Walter P. Metzger, *The Development of Academic Freedom in the United States* (New York: Columbia University Press, 1955), p. 275.

6. 385 U.S. 589, 87 S.Ct. 675 (1967).

7. Ibid.

8. Regents of the University of California v. Bakke, 438 U.S. 265, 98 S.Ct. 2733 (1978).

9. Sweezy v. New Hampshire, 354 U.S. 234, 77 S.Ct. 1203 (1957).

10. Miles v. Denver Public Schools, 944 F.2d 773 (10th Cir.1991).

11. Parate v. Isibor, 868 F.2d 821 (6th Cir.1989).

12. See Board of Education, Island Trees Union Free School District v. Pico, 457 U.S. 853, 102 S.Ct. 2799 (1982).

13. Adams v. Campbell County School District, 511 F.2d 1242 (10th Cir.1975).

14. Justice Holmes's opinion in McAuliffe v. Mayor of New Bedford, 155 Mass. 216, 29 N.E. 517 (1892), indicates that public employment is a privilege. Justice Holmes's often-quoted statement is thought to be the first reference to this idea: "The petitioner may have a constitutional right to talk politics, but he has no constitutional right to be a policeman."

15. Ibid.

16. Backie v. Cromwell Consolidated School District No. 13, 186 Minn. 38, 242 N.W. 389 (1932); Sheldon v. School Committee of Hopedale, 276 Mass. 230, 177 N.E. 94 (1931).

17. Guilford School Township v. Roberts, 28 Ind.App. 355, 62 N.E. 711 (1902); Ansorge v. City of Green Bay, 198 Wis. 320, 224 N.W. 119 (1929).

18. People v. Board of Education, 212 N.Y. 463, 106 N.E. 307 (1914); Auran v. Mentor School District No. 1, 60 N.D. 223, 233 N.W. 644 (1930).

19. Goldsmith v. Board of Education, 66 Cal.App. 157, 225 P. 783 (1924).

20. Crawfordsville v. Hays, 42 Ind. 200 (1873).

21. Gillan v. Board of Regents, 88 Wis. 7, 58 N.W. 1042, 24 A.L.R. 336 (1894).

22. 391 U.S. 563, 88 S.Ct. 1731 (1968).

23. See "Developments in the Law—Academic Freedom," *Harvard Law Review* 81 (1968): pp. 1045–1159.

24. Waters v. Churchill, 511 U.S. 661, 114 S.Ct. 1878 (1994).

25. Ibid.
26. Cohen v. California, 403 U.S. 15, 91 S.Ct. 1780 (1971).
27. New York Times Co. v. Sullivan, 376 U.S. 254, 84 S.Ct. 710 (1964).
28. Waters v. Churchill, 511 U.S. at 697.
29. Branit v. Finkel, 445 U.S. 507, 100 S.Ct. 1287 (1980).
30. Waters v. Churchill, 511 U.S. at 698.
31. Ibid. at 699.
32. Ibid.
33. Ibid.
34. 461 U.S. 138, 103 S.Ct. 1684 (1983).
35. Pickering v. Board of Education, op. cit.
36. Connick v. Myers, op. cit.
37. See Knapp v. Whitaker, 757 F.2d 827 (7th Cir.1985).
38. 381 U.S. 479, 85 S.Ct. 1678 (1965).
39. Ibid., 85 S.Ct. at 1681.
40. Leonard W. Levy, *Original Intent and the Framers' Constitution* (New York: Macmillan, 1988), p. 272.
41. 410 U.S. 113, 93 S.Ct. 705 (1973).
42. 268 U.S. 510, 45 S.Ct. 571 (1925).
43. 262 U.S. 390, 43 S.Ct. 625 (1923).
44. Roe v. Wade, op. cit.
45. Johnny H. Killian, ed., *The Constitution of the United States of America*, 1978 supp. (Washington, D.C.: U.S. Government Printing Office, 1979), p. 5191.
46. O'Connor v. Ortega, 480 U.S. 709, 107 S.Ct. 1492 (1987).
47. Ibid.
48. Ibid.
49. Ibid.
50. Mancusi v. DeForte, 392 U.S. 364, 88 S.Ct. 2120 (1968).
51. O'Connor v. Ortega, op. cit.
52. New Jersey v. T. L. O., 469 U.S. 325, 340, 105 S.Ct. 733, 742 (1985).
53. United States v. Place, 462 U.S. 696, 103 S.Ct. 2637 (1983).
54. New Jersey v. T. L. O., op. cit.
55. O'Connor v. Ortega, op. cit.
56. Ibid.
57. Ibid.
58. Morrison v. State Board of Education, 1 Cal.3d 214, 82 Cal.Rptr. 175, 191, 461 P.2d 375, 391 (1969).
59. Gargiul v. Tompkins, 525 F.Supp. 795 (N.D.N.Y.1981). See also Hoffman v. Jannarone, 401 F.Supp. 1095 (D.N.J.1975).
60. Daury v. Smith, 842 F.2d 9 (1st Cir.1988).
61. United States v. Montoya de Hernandez, 473 U.S. 531, 105 S.Ct. 3304 (1985); see also New Jersey v. T. L. O., 469 U.S. 325, 105 S.Ct. 733 (1985).
62. Skinner v. Railway Labor Executives' Association, 489 U.S. 602, 109 S.Ct. 1402 (1989).
63. Ibid. at 628, 109 S.Ct. 1402.
64. National Treasury Employees Union v. Von Raab, 489 U.S. 656, 109 S.Ct. 1384 (1989).
65. Vernonia School District 47J v. Acton, 515 U.S. 646, 115 S.Ct. 2386 (1995).
66. *Ibid.* at 665–66, 109 S.Ct. at 1390–91.
67. Skinner, 489 U.S. at 624, 109 S.Ct. at 1417.

68. United Teachers of New Orleans v. Orleans Parish School Board, 142 F.3d 853 (5th Cir. 1998).
69. Ibid.
70. Knox County Education Association v. Knox County Board of Education, 158 F.3d 361 (6th Cir.1998).
71. Skinner v. Railway Labor Executives' Association, op. cit.
72. National Treasury Employees Union v. Von Raab, op. cit.
73. Chandler v. Miller, 520 U.S. 305, 117 S.Ct. 1295 (1997).
74. Vernonia School District 47J v. Acton, op. cit.
75. 603 F.2d 1271, 1274 (7th Cir.1979), cert. denied, 444 U.S. 1026, 100 S.Ct. 689 (1980).
76. Russo v. Central School District No. 1, 469 F.2d 623 (2d Cir.1972), cert. denied, 411 U.S. 932, 93 S.Ct. 1899 (1973).
77. Civil Rights Act of 1964, Title VII, as amended 1972 (42 U.S.C.A. §2000e et seq.).
78. Wangsness v. Watertown School District No. 14-4, 541 F.Supp. 332 (D.S.D.1982).
79. Pinsker v. Joint District No. 28J, 554 F.Supp. 1049 (D.Colo.1983).
80. Ibid.
81. 432 U.S. 63, 97 S.Ct. 2264 (1977).
82. Ansonia Board of Education, 479 U.S. 60, 61, 107 S.Ct. 367, 368 (1986).
83. 403 U.S. 602, 91 S.Ct. 2105 (1971).
84. 367 U.S. 488, 81 S.Ct. 1680 (1961); see Hunterdon Central High School Board of Education v. Hunterdon Central High School Teachers' Association, 416 A.2d 980 (1980), aff'd, 429 A.2d 354 (1981).
85. See Donald E. Boles, *The Two Swords* (Ames, Iowa: Iowa State University Press, 1967), p. 222.
86. Hysong v. School District of Gallitzin Borough, 164 Pa. 629, 30 A. 482 (1894).
87. Commonwealth v. Herr, 229 Pa. 132, 78 A. 68 (1910).
88. O'Connor v. Hendrick, 184 N.Y. 421, 77 N.E. 612 (1906).
89. State ex rel. Public School District No. 6 v. Taylor, 122 Neb. 454, 240 N.W. 573 (1932); see also Zellers v. Huff, 55 N.M. 501, 236 P.2d 949 (1951).
90. Gerhardt v. Heid, 66 N.D. 444, 267 N.W. 127 (1936). See also City of New Haven v. Town of Torrington, 132 Conn. 194, 43 A.2d 455 (1945); Rawlings v. Butler, 290 S.W.2d 801 (Ky.1956).
91. Cooper v. Eugene School District No. 4J, 301 Or. 358, 723 P.2d 298 (1986).
92. Ibid., 723 P.2d at 313.
93. City of New Haven v. Town of Torrington, 132 Conn. 194, 43 A.2d 455 (1945).
94. 350 U.S. 551, 76 S.Ct. 637 (1956).
95. 357 U.S. 399, 78 S.Ct. 1317 (1958).
96. "Developments in the Law—Academic Freedom," p. 1076.
97. Spevack v. Klein, 385 U.S. 511, 87 S.Ct. 625 (1967).
98. Garrity v. New Jersey, 385 U.S. 493, 87 S.Ct. 616 (1967).

CHAPTER 16

DUE PROCESS RIGHTS
OF TEACHERS

Where a person's good name, reputation, honor, or integrity is at stake because of what the government is doing to him, notice and an opportunity to be heard are essential.

—William O. Douglas

CHAPTER OUTLINE

- FOUR ASPECTS OF DUE PROCESS
- SUBSTANTIVE DUE PROCESS
- PROCEDURAL DUE PROCESS
- THE VAGUENESS TEST
- LOYALTY OATHS
- THE IRRATIONALITY AND PRESUMPTIONS TEST

NO CONCEPT of fundamental law is more basic to individual rights and freedoms than due process. Both the Fifth and Fourteenth Amendments ensure that no person shall be deprived of "life, liberty, or property, without due process of law." The due process clause was repeated in the post–Civil War Fourteenth Amendment to make certain that the right extended to state governments.[1]

The purpose of the due process is to extend justice and fairness to the individual in relationship to government. Due process provides a bulwark against the encroachment of the state on individual rights and interests. The importance of due process is to establish a fundamental balance between the rights of individuals and the exercise of the police power of the state.

Due process is founded in the Magna Carta, signed by King John at Runnymede in 1215. The most famous passage is clause 39, the grandparent of due process provisions of Anglo-American law, which states: "No free man shall be taken, imprisoned, disseised, outlawed, banished, or in any way destroyed, nor will we proceed against or prosecute him, except by the lawful judgment of his peers and by the law of the land." The "law of the land" of this passage has become known down through the centuries as due process of law.[2]

■ FOUR ASPECTS OF DUE PROCESS

Due process of law in the federal Constitution has four aspects, and each one has been called into play by the courts in litigation involving teachers: (1) substantive due process, (2) procedural due process, (3) the vagueness test, and (4) the irrationality and presumptions test.[3] Each aspect has special meaning in balancing the individual's interest against the state's. Substantive due process is the essence of life, liberty, and property, both explicit and implicit—the nature and substance of the individual's interest. Procedural due process establishes the mechanics of ascertaining the truth about a particular situation. The vagueness test protects the individual against arbitrary and capricious governmental action. The irrationality and presumptions test requires that there be legal logic to the state's action in taking or restricting individual rights or interests.

■ SUBSTANTIVE DUE PROCESS

Substantive due process is explained more fully in the context of student rights in Chapter 8 of this book. While students have a substantive due process interest in their education, teachers likewise have a substantive interest in their employment. A right to be employed in one's chosen occupation is a most important aspect of due process. The U.S. Supreme Court ruled in *Board of Regents v. Roth*[4] that to deny employment as a teacher may implicate both liberty and property interests under the due process clause.

The substance of due process emanates from the words "life, liberty, and property," their implicit as well as explicit meanings. These terms establish the boundaries beyond which government cannot go in expanding its reach into the personal affairs of the individual. Governmental incursion into the hallowed presence of an individual's "life, liberty, and property" is permitted only after justification is established by procedural due process. The state cannot deny a substantive right without a fair hearing.

In determining the substance of due process, the courts have held that the words "liberty" and "property" have extensive meaning beyond the mere right to own and hold real property or to be free from incarceration. The Court in *Roth* stated, "Liberty and property are broad and majestic terms. They are among the great constitutional concepts . . . purposely left to gather meaning from experience. . . . They relate to the whole domain of social and economic fact, and the statesmen who founded this nation knew too well that only a stagnant society remains unchanged."[5]

The Supreme Court emphasized in *Roth*[6] and its companion case *Perry v. Sindermann*[7] the three primary features of substantive due process. First, liberty and property interests are not created by the Constitution itself but rather arise from an independent source such as employment contracts or state tenure laws. A due process interest is therefore different from an equal protection right, which emanates directly from the Constitution. Continued employment gains substantive due process status only if the state creates some formal condition vesting the employee with an expectancy of reemployment. Second, if a liberty or property interest in employment is not created by the state, there exists no requirement of procedural due process should employment status be terminated. Third, if a teacher possesses a liberty or property interest in employment, then procedural due process is required.[8]

A substantive interest may be implicated if a teacher has tenure or is serving during the term of an annual or multiyear contract when the dismissal proceeding is instituted. Simple nonrenewal at the expiration of a specified contract term does not involve a substantive interest, and, therefore, procedural due process is not necessary.[9] But if a teacher is not rehired at the end of a contract period and the nonrenewal is based on reasons that affect substantive rights emanating from due process or other basic rights or freedoms, then initiation of procedural due process is required.

LIBERTY INTERESTS
The concepts of both "liberty" and "property" were given great breadth and scope as contemplated by the framers of the U.S. Constitution. Madison maintained that liberty is the counter-

balance that holds an overbearing government in check. As adherents of Rousseau, most of the framers of the Constitution agreed that liberty is "the noblest faculty of man";[10] it is an essential gift of nature that every person is entitled to enjoy, and it cannot be unilaterally taken away by government except by proper processes of law.

The intent of the word "liberty," as it applies to a teacher's employment, can be simply stated as guaranteeing the right to live and work at whatever job he or she desires. A most complete definition of liberty is given by the Supreme Court of Virginia in a 1903 case:

> The word "liberty" as used in the Constitution of the United States and the several States, has frequently been construed, and means more than mere freedom from restraint. It means not merely the right to go where one chooses, but to do such acts as he may judge best for his interest, not inconsistent with the equal rights of others; that is, to follow such pursuits as may be best adapted to his facilities, and which will give him the highest enjoyment. The liberty mentioned is deemed to embrace the right of the citizen to be free in the enjoyment of all his faculties; to be free to use them in all lawful ways; to live and work where he will; to earn his livelihood by any lawful calling, and for that purpose to enter into all contracts which may be proper, necessary, and essential to his carrying out to a successful conclusion the purpose above mentioned. These are individual rights, formulated as such under the phrase "pursuit of happiness" in the Declaration of Independence, which begins with the fundamental proposition that all men are created equal; that they are endowed by their Creator with certain inalienable rights; that among these are life, liberty, and the pursuit of happiness.[11]

The U.S. Supreme Court applied liberty directly to the employment circumstance of a teacher in *Board of Regents v. Roth*[12] and quoted *Meyer v. Nebraska*,[13] saying: "Without doubt, it denotes not merely freedom from bodily restraint, but also the right of the individual to contract, to engage in any of the common occupations of life."

Any action by the state that stigmatizes a teacher to the degree that future employability is adversely affected is sufficient to implicate due process. As mentioned, a liberty interest is involved if a person is stigmatized with terms such as "dishonesty" and "immorality." The

courts have ruled that the stigmatizing terms must carry over into the employee's private life; mere criticism does not stigmatize.

An employee was charged with insubordination, incompetence, hostility toward authority, and aggressive behavior. The court stated that

> [n]early any reason assigned for dismissal is likely to be to some extent a negative reflection on an individual's ability, temperament, or character. But not every dismissal assumes a constitutional magnitude. The concern is only with the type of stigma that seriously damages an individual's ability to take advantage of other employment opportunities. . . . These allegations certainly are not complimentary and suggest that [the teacher] may have problems in relating to some people, but they do not import serious character defects such as dishonesty or immorality . . . as contemplated by *Roth*.[14]

PROPERTY INTERESTS

According to the Supreme Court in *Roth*, property interests "may take many forms."[15] A person may have a property interest in employment. Such an interest, though, is not absolute, and a person, in order to maintain a property interest in employment, "must have more than an abstract need or desire for it." Rather, he or she must have a "legitimate claim of entitlement to it."[16] If a teacher has a continuing and unlimited employment status extending for an indefinite period of time or holds statutory tenure, then a property interest in the employment is presumed.

The fact that employment as a teacher comes within the scope of a "property" interest was encompassed in the original intent of the Bill of Rights. Madison discussed the question extensively, maintaining that not only does a man have "a right to his property," but also he has "a property in his rights."[17] Madison further asserted that the right of property guaranteed the citizens "free use of their faculties and free choice of their occupations."[18] Madison saw individual rights of property as being so broad as to include "everything to which a man may attach a value and have a right."[19] Such broad interpretation extended far beyond the more simplistic and restricted sense of what constituted property and included the more comprehensive phraseology of "pursuit of happiness." In this broader sense, beyond land, merchandise, or money, Madison stated that a man has property in his opinions and the free communication of them:

> He has a property of peculiar value in his religious opinions, and in the profession and practices dictated by them. He has property very dear to him in the safety and liberty of his person. He has an equal property in the free use of his faculties and free choice of the objects on which to employ them. In a word, as a man is said to have a right to his property, he may be equally said to have a property in his rights.[20]

Thus, property has pervasive substantive meaning, and the implications for teacher dismissal or nonrenewal are very broad indeed.

A substantive property interest in a teaching position may arise when a teacher possesses tenure, holds a permanent or continuing contract, or has a legitimate claim or entitlement to continued employment created by state law or policy of the school board. Too, a continuing long-term, undefined relationship, which may lead a teacher to an objective expectancy of reemployment, may be sufficient to vest the teacher with a substantive property interest. While mere subjective expectancy does not suffice, it is possible for a school to create conditions of employment that suggest entitlement to a legitimate claim to a job, in which case the teacher cannot be terminated without procedural due process.[21]

In welfare cases, the Supreme Court has held that whether and to what extent procedural due process is afforded the individual are influenced by (1) the extent to which he or she may be "condemned to suffer grievous loss" and (2) "whether the recipient's interest in avoiding that loss outweighs the governmental interest," which involves a determination of the private interest that has been affected by governmental action.[22]

The U.S. Court of Appeals, Fifth Circuit, found that a teacher's "expectancy of reemployment" could be of sufficient import to cause the court to invoke due process requirements:[23]

> [A] college can create an obligation as between itself and an instructor where none might otherwise exist under the legal standards for the interpretation of contract relationships regularly applied to transactions in the market place if it adopts regulations and standards of practice governing nontenured employees which create an expectation of reemployment.[24]

Whether there is an entitlement rests on a balancing of the public school's interest against the teacher's individual interest.[25] The school's interest is the desirability of selecting and retaining an effective and competent teaching staff, while the teacher's interest is his or her future employability, professional reputation, and other career interests.[26]

In 1972, the Supreme Court of the United States helped to clarify the property interest issue when it held that nontenured teachers are afforded no "property" interest in the teaching position. This is true so long as dismissal does not permanently impair their future employment opportunities.[27]

On the other hand, in *Sindermann*,[28] the Court said that although subjective "expectancy" of tenure is not protected by the due process clause, it is possible for a college (or school) to have a *de facto* tenure policy that entitles a teacher to a legitimate claim of job tenure that can be terminated only through a hearing process. Although upholding its denial of the validity of "expectancy of reemployment" in *Roth*, the Supreme Court in *Sindermann* found an unusual situation in which the college had created an implied tenure arrangement. In *Sindermann*, the faculty guide prepared by the college itself stated that "the College wishes the faculty member to feel that he has permanent tenure as long as his teaching services are satisfactory."[29] The Court concluded that such a provision may, with other conditions, constitute "an unwritten 'common law,'[30] in a particular university, that certain employees shall have the equivalent of tenure."[31]

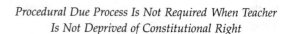

Procedural Due Process Is Not Required When Teacher Is Not Deprived of Constitutional Right

Board of Regents of State Colleges v. Roth

Supreme Court of the United States, 1972.
408 U.S. 564, 92 S.Ct. 2701.

Mr. Justice STEWART delivered the opinion of the Court. In 1968 the respondent, David Roth, was hired for his first teaching job as assistant professor of political science at Wisconsin State University–Oshkosh. He was hired for a fixed term of one academic year. The notice of his faculty appointment specified that his employment would begin on September 1, 1968, and would end on June 30, 1969. The respondent completed that term. But he was informed that he would not be rehired for the next academic year.

The respondent had no tenure rights to continued employment. Under Wisconsin statutory law a state university teacher can acquire tenure as a "permanent" employee only after four years of year-to-year employment. Having acquired tenure, a teacher is entitled to continued employment "during efficiency and good behavior." A relatively new teacher without tenure, however, is under Wisconsin law entitled to nothing beyond his one-year appointment. There are no statutory or administrative standards defining eligibility for reemployment. State law thus clearly leaves the decision whether to rehire a nontenured teacher for another year to the unfettered discretion of university officials.

The procedural protection afforded a Wisconsin State University teacher before he is separated from the University corresponds to his job security. As a matter of statutory law, a tenured teacher cannot be "discharged except for cause upon written charges" and pursuant to certain procedures. A nontenured teacher, similarly, is protected to some extent *during* his one-year term. Rules promulgated by the Board of Regents provide that a nontenured teacher "dismissed" before the end of the year may have some opportunity for review of the "dismissal." But the Rules provide no real protection for a nontenured teacher who simply is not reemployed for the next year. He must be informed by February 1 "concerning retention or nonretention for the ensuing year." But "no reason for nonretention need be given. No review or appeal is provided in such case."

In conformance with these Rules, the President of Wisconsin State University–Oshkosh informed the respondent before February 1, 1969, that he would not be rehired for the 1969–1970 academic year. He gave the respondent no reason for the decision and no opportunity to challenge it at any sort of hearing.

The respondent then brought this action in Federal District Court alleging that the decision not to rehire him for the next year infringed his Fourteenth Amendment rights. (He attacked the decision both in substance and procedure. First, he alleged that the true reason for the decision was to punish him for certain statements critical of the University administration, and that it therefore violated his right to freedom of speech. Second, he alleged that the failure of University officials to give him notice of any reason for nonretention and an opportunity for a hearing violated his right to procedural due process of law.)

The District Court granted summary judgment for the respondent on the procedural issue, ordering the University officials to provide him with reasons and a hearing. 310 F.Supp. 972. The Court of Appeals, with one judge dissenting, affirmed this partial summary judgment. 446 F.2d 806. We granted certiorari. 404 U.S. 909, 92 S.Ct. 227, 30 L.Ed.2d 181. The only question presented to us at this stage in the case is whether the respondent had a constitutional right to a statement of reasons and a hearing on the University's decision not to rehire him for another year. We hold that he did not.

The requirements of procedural due process apply only to the deprivation of interests encompassed by the Fourteenth Amendment's protection of liberty and property. When protected interests are implicated, the right to some kind of prior hearing is paramount. But the range of interests protected by procedural due process is not infinite.

The District Court decided that procedural due process guarantees apply in this case by assessing and balancing the weights of the particular interests involved. . . . But, to determine whether due process requirements apply in the first place, we must look not to the "weight" but to the *nature* of the interest at stake. . . . We must look to see if the interest is within the Fourteenth Amendment's protection of liberty and property.

"Liberty" and "property" are broad and majestic terms. They are among the "[g]reat [constitutional] concepts . . . purposely left to gather meaning from experience. . . . [T]hey relate to the whole domain of social and economic fact, and the statesmen who founded this Nation knew too well that only a stagnant society remains unchanged." *National Mutual Ins. Co. v. Tidewater Transfer Co.,* 337 U.S. 582, 646, 69 S.Ct. 1173, 1195, 93 L.Ed. 1556 (Frankfurter, J., dissenting). For that reason, the Court has fully and finally rejected the wooden distinction between "rights" and "privileges" that once seemed to govern the applicability of procedural due process rights. The Court has also made clear that the property interests protected by procedural due process extend well beyond actual ownership of real estate, chattels, or money. By the same token, the Court has required due process protection for deprivations of liberty beyond the sort of formal constraints imposed by the criminal process.

Yet, while the Court has eschewed rigid or formalistic limitations on the protection of procedural due process, it has at the same time observed certain boundaries. For the words "liberty" and "property" in the Due Process Clause of the Fourteenth Amendment must be given some meaning.

> While this court has not attempted to define with exactness the liberty . . . guaranteed [by the Fourteenth Amendment], the term has received much consideration and some of the included things have been definitely stated. Without doubt, it denotes not merely freedom from bodily restraint but also the right of the individual to contract, to engage in any of the common occupations of life, to acquire useful knowledge, to marry, establish a home and bring up children, to worship God according to the dictates of his own conscience, and generally to enjoy those privileges long recognized . . . as essential to the orderly pursuit of happiness by free men. *Meyer v. Nebraska,* 262 U.S. 390, 399, 43 S.Ct. 625, 626, 67 L.Ed. 1042.

In a Constitution for a free people, there can be no doubt that the meaning of "liberty" must be broad indeed. See e.g., *Bolling v. Sharpe,* 347 U.S. 497, 499–500, 74 S.Ct. 693, 694, 98 L.Ed. 884; *Stanley v. Illinois,* 405 U.S. 645, 92 S.Ct. 1208, 31 L.Ed.2d 551.

There might be cases in which a State refused to reemploy a person under such circumstances that interests in liberty would be implicated. But this is not such a case.

The State, in declining to rehire the respondent, did not make any charge against him that might seriously damage his standing and associations in his community. It did not base the

nonrenewal of his contract on a charge, for example, that he had been guilty of dishonesty, or immorality. Had it done so, this would be a different case. For "[w]here a person's good name, reputation, honor, or integrity is at stake because of what the government is doing to him, notice and an opportunity to be heard are essential." . . . In such a case, due process would accord an opportunity to refute the charge before University officials. In the present case, however, there is no suggestion whatever that the respondent's "good name, reputation, honor, or integrity" is at stake.

Similarly, there is no suggestion that the State, in declining to reemploy the respondent, imposed on him a stigma or other disability that foreclosed his freedom to take advantage of other employment opportunities. The State, for example, did not invoke any regulations to bar the respondent from all other public employment in state universities. Had it done so, this, again, would be a different case. For "[t]o be deprived not only of present government employment but of future opportunity for it certainly is no small injury. . . ."

To be sure, the respondent has alleged that the nonrenewal of his contract was based on his exercise of his right to freedom of speech. But this allegation is not now before us. The District Court stayed proceedings on this issue, and the respondent has yet to prove that the decision not to rehire him was in fact based on his free speech activities.

Hence, on the record before us, all that clearly appears is that the respondent was not rehired for one year at one university. It stretches the concept too far to suggest that a person is deprived of "liberty" when he simply is not rehired in one job but remains as free as before to seek another. . . .

The Fourteenth Amendment's procedural protection of property is a safeguard of the security of interests that a person has already acquired in specific benefits. These interests—property interests—may take many forms.

. . . To have a property interest in a benefit, a person clearly must have more than an abstract need or desire for it. He must have more than a unilateral expectation of it. He must, instead, have a legitimate claim of entitlement to it. It is a purpose of the ancient institution of property to protect those claims upon which people rely in their daily lives, reliance that must not be arbitrarily undermined. It is a purpose of the constitutional right to a hearing to provide an opportunity for a person to vindicate those claims.

Property interests, of course, are not created by the Constitution. Rather they are created and their dimensions are defined by existing rules or understandings that stem from an independent source such as state law—rules or understandings that secure certain benefits and that support claims of entitlement to those benefits. Thus, the welfare recipients in *Goldberg v. Kelly*, *supra*, had a claim of entitlement to welfare payments that was grounded in the statute defining eligibility for them. The recipients had not yet shown that they were, in fact, within the statutory terms of eligibility. But we held that they had a right to a hearing at which they might attempt to do so.

Just as the welfare recipients' "property" interest in welfare payments was created and defined by statutory terms, so the respondent's "property" interest in employment at Wisconsin State University-Oshkosh was created and defined by the terms of his appointment. Those terms secured his interest in employment up to June 30, 1969. But the important fact in this case is that they specifically provided that the respondent's employment was to terminate on June 30. They did not provide for contract renewal absent "sufficient cause." Indeed, they made no provision for renewal whatsoever.

Thus, the terms of the respondent's appointment secured absolutely no interest in reemployment for the next year. They supported absolutely no possible claim of entitlement to reemployment. Nor, significantly, was there any state statute or University rule or policy that secured his interest in reemployment or that created any legitimate claim to it. In these circumstances, the respondent surely had an abstract concern in being rehired, but he did not have a *property* interest sufficient to require the University authorities to give him a hearing when they declined to renew his contract of employment.

Our analysis of the respondent's constitutional rights in this case in no way indicates a view that an opportunity for a hearing or a statement of reasons for nonretention would, or

would not, be appropriate or wise in public colleges and universities. For it is a written Constitution that we apply. Our role is confined to interpretation of that Constitution.

We must conclude that the summary judgment for the respondent should not have been granted, since the respondent has not shown that he was deprived of liberty or property protected by the Fourteenth Amendment. The judgment of the Court of Appeals, accordingly, is reversed and the case is remanded for further proceedings consistent with this opinion. It is so ordered.

— ❖ — ❖ — ❖ —

Teacher with De Facto *Tenure Is Entitled to a Hearing before Termination of Employment*

Perry v. Sindermann

Supreme Court of the United States, 1972.
408 U.S. 593, 92 S.Ct. 2694.

Mr. Justice STEWART delivered the opinion of the Court. From 1959 to 1969 the respondent, Robert Sindermann, was a teacher in the state college system of the State of Texas. After teaching for two years at the University of Texas and four years at San Antonio Junior College, he became a professor of Government and Social Science at Odessa Junior College in 1965. He was employed at the college for four successive years, under a series of one-year contracts. He was successful enough to be appointed, for a time, the cochairman of his department.

During the 1968–1969 academic year, however, controversy arose between the respondent and the college administration. The respondent was elected president of the Texas Junior College Teachers Association. In this capacity, he left his teaching duties on several occasions to testify before committees of the Texas Legislature, and he became involved in public disagreements with the policies of the college's Board of Regents. In particular, he aligned himself with a group advocating the elevation of the college to four-year status—a change opposed by the Regents. And, on one occasion, a newspaper advertisement appeared over his name that was highly critical of the Regents.

Finally, in May 1969, the respondent's one-year employment contract terminated and the Board of Regents voted not to offer him a new contract for the next academic year. The Regents issued a press release setting forth allegations of the respondent's insubordination. But they provided him no official statement of the reasons for the nonrenewal of his contract. And they allowed him no opportunity for a hearing to challenge the basis of the nonrenewal.

The respondent then brought this action in Federal District Court. He alleged primarily that the Regents' decision not to rehire him was based on his public criticism of the policies of the college administration and thus infringed his right to freedom of speech. He also alleged that their failure to provide him an opportunity for a hearing violated the Fourteenth Amendment's guarantee of procedural due process. The petitioners—members of the Board of Regents and the president of the college—denied that their decision was made in retaliation for the respondent's public criticism and argued that they had no obligation to provide a hearing. On the basis of these bare pleadings and three brief affidavits filed by the respondent, the District Court granted summary judgment for the petitioners. It concluded that the respondent had "no cause of action against the [petitioners] since his contract of employment terminated May 31, 1969, and Odessa Junior College has not adopted the tenure system."

The Court of Appeals reversed the judgment of the District Court. 430 F.2d 939. First, it held that, despite the respondent's lack of tenure, the nonrenewal of his contract would violate the Fourteenth Amendment if it in fact was based on his protected free speech. Since the actual reason for the Regents' decision was "in total dispute" in the pleadings, the court remanded the case for a full hearing on this contested issue of fact. Second, the Court of Appeals held that, despite the respondent's lack of tenure, the failure to allow him an opportunity for a hearing would violate the constitutional guarantee of procedural due process if the respondent could show that he had an "expectancy" of reemployment. It, therefore, ordered that this issue of fact

also be aired upon remand. We granted a writ of certiorari, 403 U.S. 917, 91 S.Ct. 2226, 29 L.Ed.2d 694, and we have considered this case along with *Board of Regents v. Roth*, 408 U.S. 564, 92 S.Ct. 2701, 33 L.Ed.2d 548.

The first question presented is whether the respondent's lack of a contractual or tenure right to reemployment, taken alone, defeats his claim that the nonrenewal of his contract violated the First and Fourteenth Amendments. We hold that it does not.

For at least a quarter-century, this Court has made clear that even though a person has no "right" to a valuable governmental benefit and even though the government may deny him the benefit for any number of reasons, there are some reasons upon which the government may not rely. It may not deny a benefit to a person on a basis that infringes his constitutionally protected interests—especially his interest in freedom of speech. For if the government could deny a benefit to a person because of his constitutionally protected speech or associations, his exercise of those freedoms would in effect be penalized and inhibited. This would allow the government to "produce a result which [it] could not command directly." *Speiser v. Randall*, 357 U.S. 513, 526, " S.Ct. 1332, 1342, 2 L.Ed.2d 1460. Such interference with constitutional rights is impermissible. . . .

Thus, the respondent's lack of a contractual or tenure "right" to reemployment for the 1969–1970 academic year is immaterial to his free speech claim. Indeed, twice before, this Court has specifically held that the nonrenewal of a nontenured public school teacher's one-year contract may not be predicated on his exercise of First and Fourteenth Amendment rights. . . . We reaffirm those holdings here.

In this case, of course, the respondent has yet to show that the decision not to renew his contract was, in fact, made in retaliation for his exercise of the constitutional right of free speech. The District Court foreclosed any opportunity to make this showing when it granted summary judgment. Hence, we cannot now hold that the Board of Regents' action was invalid.

But we agree with the Court of Appeals that there is a genuine dispute as to "whether the college refused to renew the teaching contract on an impermissible basis—as a reprisal for the exercise of constitutionally protected rights." 430 F.2d, at 943. The respondent has alleged that his nonretention was based on his testimony before legislative committees and his other public statements critical of the Regents' policies. And he has alleged that this public criticism was within the First and Fourteenth Amendments' protection of freedom of speech. Plainly, these allegations present a bona fide constitutional claim. For this Court has held that a teacher's public criticism of his superiors on matters of public concern may be constitutionally protected and may, therefore, be an impermissible basis for termination of his employment. *Pickering v. Board of Education.*

For this reason we hold that the grant of summary judgment against the respondent, without full exploration of this issue, was improper.

The respondent's lack of formal contractual or tenure security in continued employment at Odessa Junior College, though irrelevant to his free speech claim, is highly relevant to his procedural due process claim. But it may not be entirely dispositive.

We have held today in *Board of Regents v. Roth,* 408 U.S. 564, 92 S.Ct. 2701, that the Constitution does not require opportunity for a hearing before the nonrenewal of a nontenured teacher's contract, unless he can show that the decision not to rehire him somehow deprived him of an interest in "liberty" or that he had a "property" interest in continued employment, despite the lack of tenure or a formal contract. In *Roth* the teacher had not made a showing on either point to justify summary judgment in his favor.

Similarly, the respondent here has yet to show that he has been deprived of an interest that could invoke procedural due process protection. As in *Roth,* the mere showing that he was not rehired in one particular job, without more, did not amount to a showing of a loss of liberty. Nor did it amount to a showing of a loss of property.

But the respondent's allegations—which we must construe most favorably to the respondent at this stage of the litigation—do raise a genuine issue as to his interest in continued employment at Odessa Junior College. He alleged that this interest, though not secured by a formal contractual tenure provision, was secured by a no less binding understanding fostered by the college administration. In particular, the respondent alleged that the college had a *de facto* tenure program, and that he had tenure under that program. He claimed that he and others legitimately relied upon an unusual provision that had been in the college's official Faculty Guide for many years:

> *Teacher Tenure:* Odessa College has no tenure system. The Administration of the College wishes the faculty member to feel that he has permanent tenure as long as his teaching services are satisfactory and as long as he displays a cooperative attitude toward his co-workers and his superiors, and as long as he is happy in his work.

Moreover, the respondent claimed legitimate reliance upon guidelines promulgated by the Coordinating Board of the Texas College and University System that provided that a person, like himself, who had been employed as a teacher in the state college and university system for seven years or more has some form of job tenure. Thus, the respondent offered to prove that a teacher with his long period of service at this particular State College had no less a "property" interest in continued employment than a formally tenured teacher at other colleges, and had no less a procedural due process right to a statement of reasons and a hearing before college officials upon their decision not to retain him.

We have made clear in *Roth* . . . that "property" interests subject to procedural due process protection are not limited by a few rigid, technical forms. Rather, "property" denotes a broad range of interests that are secured by "existing rules or understandings." . . . A person's interest in a benefit is a "property" interest for due process purposes if there are such rules or mutually explicit understandings that support his claim of entitlement to the benefit and that he may invoke at a hearing.

A written contract with an explicit tenure provision clearly is evidence of a formal understanding that supports a teacher's claim of entitlement to continued employment unless sufficient "cause" is shown. Yet absence of such an explicit contractual provision may not always foreclose the possibility that a teacher has a "property" interest in reemployment. For example, the law of contracts in most, if not all, jurisdictions long has employed a process by which agreements, though not formalized in writing, may be "implied." 3 A. Corbin on Contracts §§561–572A. Explicit contractual provisions may be supplemented by other agreements implied from "the promisor's words and conduct in the light of the surrounding circumstances." Id., at §562. And, "[t]he meaning of [the promisor's] words and acts is found by relating them to the usage of the past."

A teacher, like the respondent, who has held his position for a number of years, might be able to show from the circumstances of this service—and from other relevant facts—that he has a legitimate claim of entitlement to job tenure. Just as this Court has found there to be a "common law of a particular industry or of a particular plant" that may supplement a collective-bargaining agreement, *United Steelworkers v. Warrior & Gulf Nav. Co.*, 363 U.S. 574, 579 . . . so there may be an unwritten "common law" in a particular university that certain employees shall have the equivalent of tenure. This is particularly likely in a college or university, like Odessa Junior College, that has no explicit tenure system even for senior members of its faculty, but that nonetheless may have created such a system in practice. . . .

In this case, the respondent has alleged the existence of rules and understandings, promulgated and fostered by state officials, that may justify his legitimate claim of entitlement to continued employment absent "sufficient cause." We disagree with the Court of Appeals insofar as it held that a mere subjective "expectancy" is protected by procedural due process, but we agree that the respondent must be given an opportunity to prove the legitimacy of his claim of such entitlement in light of "the policies and practices of the institution." 430 F.2d, at 943. Proof of such a property interest would not, of course, entitle him to reinstatement. But such proof would obligate college officials to grant a hearing at his request, where he could be informed of the grounds for his nonretention and challenge their sufficiency.

Therefore, while we do not wholly agree with the opinion of the Court of Appeals, its judgment remanding this case to the District Court is affirmed.

Affirmed.

Mr. Justice POWELL took no part in the decision of this case.

CASE NOTES

1. Nonreemployment without a hearing of a nontenured teacher because of general ineffectiveness as a teacher does not violate the First and Fourteenth Amendments. *Robinson v. Jefferson County Board of Education*, 485 F.2d 1381 (5th Cir.1973), rehearing denied, 488 F.2d 1055 (5th Cir.1974).

2. When a nontenured teacher had taught for ten years in a state with no tenure law and was not rehired, the court held that no substantive due process rights existed on behalf of the teacher that would invoke a cause of action under the Civil Rights Act, Section 1983, even though the only rationale used by the school board for dismissal was that the students of the teacher scored below expected levels on achievement tests. *Scheelhaase v. Woodbury Central Community School District*, 488 F.2d 237 (8th Cir.1973).

3. A nontenured teacher's claim of entitlement to a position was, under the Illinois Tenure Act, insufficient to constitute a property interest within the Fourteenth Amendment. Appellant was unable to show that the tenure law limited in any way the authority of the school board to terminate employment prior to acquiring tenure status. *Miller v. School District Number 167, Cook County, Illinois*, 500 F.2d 711 (7th Cir.1974).

4. A probationary teacher had no expectancy of reemployment vesting him with a property interest. *McCullough v. Lohn*, 483 F.2d 34 (5th Cir.1973).

5. When a nontenured teacher was indicted for alleged sexual misconduct with students, the court held that, should he be convicted, the school board was not obligated to provide him with a hearing; however, in the event that he was exonerated by the court, the school board must provide a hearing in order for him to clear his name. The court found, in referring to *Roth*, though, that when a teacher is indicted, it is not the obligation of the school board to hold a hearing prior to his or her trial in order to determine his or her guilt or innocence. To do so,

according to the court, would have placed the board in the untenable position of dispensing findings that "in one direction would have injured the interests of the state, and in another direction would have damaged those of the teacher." *Moore v. Knowles,* 482 F.2d 1069 (5th Cir.1973).

6. When nontenured elementary teachers distributed a poem to students imploring them to throw off the dull discipline of the moral environment of their home life and enter into a new world of love and freedom—freedom to use acid and grass, freedom to engage in sexual activities, and freedom to use vulgarities—the court denied the teachers recovery under the Civil Rights Act. In so doing, the court commented:

> We do not believe that however much the reach of the First Amendment has been extended and however eager today's courts have been to protect the many varieties of claims to civil rights, the appellee school board had to put up with the described conduct of appellants.

Brubaker v. Board of Education, School District 149, Cook County, Illinois, 502 F.2d 973 (7th Cir.1974).

7. A U.S. district court in Minnesota listed five occasions when *Roth* and *Sindermann* dictate a hearing on nonrenewal:

1. When the contract nonrenewal is related to the teacher's exercise of freedom of speech under the First Amendment.

2. When the teacher is confronted with a charge that might seriously damage his or her standing and associations in the community.

3. When the failure to reemploy the teacher imposes a stigma or other disability on him or her that forecloses future freedom to take advantage of other employment opportunities.

4. When the teacher, by virtue of existing state policies, the contract terms, or similar understandings, has a reasonable expectancy of reemployment.

5. When the adverse reports on which action is taken are prepared by the school's superiors or plaintiffs' compatriots and are fabricated, without any foundation or basis in fact whatsoever,

or are maliciously designed so as to use the freedom of the probationary period for reasons of personal calumny, hatred, vindication, or dislike, thus using the probationary period as a sword rather than a shield.

Ferris v. Special School District No. 1, 367 F.Supp. 459 (D.Minn.1973).

8. When there was evidence that teachers' contracts had not been renewed in retaliation for their public comments regarding teachers' salaries and affiliation with a teachers' association, the court held that the nonrenewal of their contracts violated their First Amendment rights of freedom of speech and association. *Greminger v. Seaborne,* 584 F.2d 275 (8th Cir.1978).

9. An allegation by a teacher that nonrenewal of his contract was due to the failure to shave his beard was held by the court to be unfounded and wholly insubstantial. *Ball v. Board of Trustees of Kerrville Independent School District,* 584 F.2d 684 (5th Cir.1978). See also *Carmichael v. Chambers County Board of Education,* 581 F.2d 95 (5th Cir.1978); *Cain v. McQueen,* 580 F.2d 1001 (9th Cir.1978); *Graves v. Duganne,* 581 F.2d 222 (9th Cir.1978).

10. *Stigmatizing Reasons.* The Supreme Court established in *Sindermann* and in *Roth* that a nontenured teacher has a liberty interest not to be stigmatized or to have anything be said that damages his or her good name or reputation. Although the Court established this as a standard, it did not define specifically what "stigmatizing" means. Case law has defined these liberty interests as presented below:

1. Allegations of incompetence, inadequacy, and insubordination have not been found to be stigmatizing. "These allegations certainly are not complimentary and suggest that [the teacher] may have problems . . . but do not import serious character defects . . . as contemplated by *Roth.*" *Gray v. Union County Intermediate Education District,* 520 F.2d 803 (9th Cir.1975).

2. Notice of nonrenewal of a nontenured teacher that is not posted or published does not create a "stigma" upon the teacher's good name, reputation, hono or integrity sufficient to deprive her him of "liberty" under the Fourt

Amendment. *Shirck v. Thomas*, 486 F.2d 691 (7th Cir.1973).

3. Charges of racism have been determined to be a deprivation of a liberty interest, reflecting on a professor's reputation and good name, and therefore require due process to be afforded to prove the charges. *Wellner v. Minnesota State Junior College Board*, 487 F.2d 153 (8th Cir.1973).

4. A school board's charges of "apparent emotional instability" stigmatize a teacher because they go beyond job-related comments. *Bomhoff v. White*, 526 F.Supp. 488 (D.Ariz.1981).

5. The censure by a school board of a guest lecturer for his poor judgment in presenting film clips of bare-chested women to a tenth-grade class did not constitute a violation of due process. *Silano v. Sag Harbor Union Free School District Board of Education*, 42 F.3d 719 (2d Cir.1994), cert. denied, 515 U.S. 1160, 115 S.Ct. 2612 (1995).

■ PROCEDURAL DUE PROCESS

When action is taken against a teacher that may result in the loss of a substantive constitutional interest, the teacher is entitled to procedural due process. Courts require procedural due process when a teacher can show that her or his termination emanates from an exercise of one of her or his fundamental freedoms, such as free speech, expression, and press, or substantive due process interests. The state must show a compelling interest in order to suspend a fundamental right. "Simply because teachers are on the public payroll does not make them second-class citizens in regard to their constitutional rights."[32] Courts will invalidate denial of reemployment when the denial rests on an unconstitutional ⁀striction of a fundamental interest. In *Pred*, the ⁀aid the determination must rest on facts whether the denial of a continuing con- "(a) a reprisal for these actions in of ideas, thoughts, or associations ⁀ermissible nondiscriminatory pro- ⁀ations, and, if so, (b) whether ⁀cumstances in relation to the

reasonable demands of a system of organized responsible learning these actions were protected."[33]

Most essential to due process is the requirement of "fair play."[34] Procedural due process embodies the legal and moral concept of natural justice, which has two main parts: (1) that no person should be condemned without a hearing and (2) that every judge must be free from bias.[35] The fairness of a full hearing sufficient to reveal the relevant facts to a tribunal is required by due process. Procedural due process requires that a person be given "notice and an opportunity to be heard before a final decision is made which would deprive him of life, liberty, or property."[36]

The necessity of procedural due process was well explained by the Virginia Supreme Court over a century ago:

> The authorities on this point are overwhelming, and the decision of all the tribunals of every country where an enlightened jurisprudence prevails, are all one way. It lies at the very foundation of justice, that every person who is to be affected by an adjudication should have the opportunity of being heard in defense, both in repelling the allegations of fact, and upon the matter of law.[37]

HEARING

As discussed earlier in this text in the chapter on student rights, the requirements of procedural due process have been extended from courts of law to administrative tribunals, such as state and local school boards and municipalities. The process due a student where loss of education is in balance requires two essentials. In *Dixon v. Alabama State Board of Education*,[38] the court said:

1. Notice should be given of the hearing "containing a statement of the specific charges and grounds," and

2. A hearing should be held providing the opportunity for both sides to present their stories in considerable detail.[39]

These basic elements of fair play apply to the teacher when his or her substantive interest in a teaching position is jeopardized. The courts require that the formality and intensity of the process due a teacher be dependent on the severity of the impending loss to be suffered.

Due process of law is not a concrete prescription; it is dependent on circumstances. The U.S. Supreme Court has said that due process requires "that the proceedings shall be fair, but fairness is relative, not an absolute concept. . . . What is fair in one set of circumstances may be an act of tyranny in others."[40]

The requirement that all the facts be revealed to objective evaluation is the goal of due process. An English court commenting on due process as the essence of natural justice has concisely summarized the issue, saying that to "act in good faith and fairly listen to both sides . . . is a duty lying upon everyone who decides anything." It is a question of "being required to act fairly."

Because facts and conditions pertaining to specific deprivations differ with each case, and the relative intensity of process varies accordingly, the Supreme Court uses a balancing test to determine what procedures are required. In *Mathews v. Eldridge*, it set out three factors that the courts must consider in determining whether the process is adequate in view of the constitutional deprivation. The factors are as follows:

> First, the private interest that will be affected by the official action; second, the risk of an erroneous deprivation of such interest through the procedures used, and the probable value, if any, of additional or substitute procedural safeguards; and finally, the Government's interest, including the function involved and the fiscal and administrative burdens that the additional or substitute procedural requisites would entail.[41]

All courts now follow the *Mathews* requirements in deciding what process is due. Therefore, according to *Mathews*, the courts must consider two factors on the side of the individual. "1) the importance of the individual liberty or property interest at stake and 2) the extent to which the requested procedure may reduce the possibility of erroneous decision-making."[42] On the other end of the "balance," the court must consider the government's interest involved in the specific deprivation.

In considering the extent of process, the court may need to apply the *Mathews* "balancing test" at any one of three levels. First, the test may be employed to determine if the individual is entitled to a hearing before (rather than after) governmental action has been taken. For example, a school district, in certain circumstances (such as to safeguard the students or the conduct of the school), may deprive a person of property or liberty without a prior hearing, so long as the postdeprivation process procedures are sufficient to protect the individual against arbitrary school district actions.[43]

Second, the application of the balancing test must come into play whether a predeprivation or a postdeprivation hearing is required.[44] In either case, the balancing test may cover the procedural spectrum, ranging from an informal hearing to a full-blown adversarial process.[45]

Third, the standard and extent of proof are also to be considered in balancing the interests. For example, an important deprivation of a liberty or property interest imposed upon a teacher, such as loss of certification and future employability, will necessarily require a relatively high standard of evidence.[46]

In applying the balancing test, the courts have concluded that a teacher or other school employee who has a property or liberty interest in his or her employment is entitled to a pretermination hearing. An employee who does not have either a property or a liberty interest in the employment is not entitled to a hearing. In other words, "when no life, liberty or property interest is at stake, a state is free to deny privileges to individuals without any hearing and, therefore, on an arbitrary basis."[47] Nowak et al. observe that "so long as the government does not violate one of a few express or implied 'fundamental rights,' the Court will not protect the interests of individuals against the state."[48] Yet, where a constitutional right or interest is involved, the public employee is entitled to the safeguards provided by procedural due process.

As indicated above in discussing the *Roth* and *Sindermann* cases, if a constitutional right or interest does exist, the Supreme Court has been "fairly restrictive in its view of what procedures are necessary to safeguard the interest of government employment."[49] Yet the Supreme Court in "balancing the interests" may require lesser procedural intensity for employment termination than for deprivation of some more essential benefit, such as termination of subsistence welfare benefits.[50]

Roth and *Sindermann*, however, while explaining the substantive interests under due process, did not expand definitively upon the procedural process that is due in termination of public employees who have property or liberty interests. Later, the Supreme Court in *Cleveland Board of Education v. Loudermill*[51] held that a government employee who has an entitlement to her or his job, by virtue of her or his property interest, cannot be terminated without pretermination procedural review. The Supreme Court in *Loudermill*, following the balancing rationale in *Mathews v. Eldridge*,[52] found that the state's interest in avoiding the costs and delays of a pretermination process was not of sufficient importance to outweigh the employee's significant interest in continued employment in the school district. Justice White, in writing for the majority in *Loudermill*, indicated that the due process clause requires that the individual receive "notice and a hearing" before she or he is deprived of a constitutionally protected property or liberty interest.[53] Justice White pointed out that while a pretermination hearing is required, it need not be elaborate; the state must give the employee only the opportunity to respond to charges made against her or him. According to Justice White, this could be "something less than a full evidentiary hearing." However, in the case of a teacher with a property interest in continued employment, per *Roth* and *Sindermann*, the pretermination process must be in keeping with the balancing test of *Mathews*, which suggests that a relatively more rigorous and intense process is due.

IMPARTIALITY

Fairness requires that the judge or hearing tribunal be free of bias. The old dictum that "justice should both be done and be manifestly seen to be done"[54] is essential in meeting the strictures of due process. Ultimately, the strength of due process rests not only on whether justice is done, but also on whether the public perceives that justice has been served.

In this regard, the courts have generally held that an administrative agency such as a state or local school board constitutes an unbiased tribunal, even though its own rules may have been broken or it is a party to the action. The leading case on this point is *Hortonville*, in which the U.S. Supreme Court held that a school board, as an administrative agency, must of necessity possess quasi-judicial powers and is presumed, by its nature, to be unbiased unless proven otherwise.[55]

———— ❖ — ❖ — ❖ ————

Public Employee with a Property Interest Is Entitled to a Pretermination Hearing

Cleveland Board of Education v. Loudermill

Supreme Court of the United States, 1985.
470 U.S. 532, 105 S.Ct. 1487.

Justice WHITE delivered the opinion of the Court.

In these cases we consider what pretermination process must be accorded a public employee who can be discharged only for cause.

In 1979 the Cleveland Board of Education . . . hired respondent James Loudermill as a security guard. On his job application, Loudermill stated that he had never been convicted of a felony. Eleven months later, as part of a routine examination of his employment records, the Board discovered that in fact Loudermill had been convicted of grand larceny in 1968. By letter dated November 3, 1980, the Board's Business Manager informed Loudermill that he had been dismissed because of his dishonesty in filling out the employment application. Loudermill was not afforded an opportunity to respond to the charge of dishonesty or to challenge his dismissal. On November 13, the Board adopted a resolution officially approving the discharge.

Under Ohio law, Loudermill was a "classified civil servant." Ohio Rev.Code Ann. §124.11 (1984). Such employees can be terminated only for cause, and may obtain administrative review if discharged. §124.34. Pursuant to this provision, Loudermill filed an appeal with the Cleveland Civil Service Commission on November 12. The Commission appointed a referee, who held a hearing on January 29, 1981. Loudermill argued that he had thought that his 1968 larceny conviction was for a misdemeanor rather than a felony. The referee recommended reinstatement. On July 20, 1981, the full Commission heard argument and orally announced that it would uphold the dismissal. . . .

Although the Commission's decision was subject to judicial review in the state courts, Loudermill instead brought the present suit in the Federal District Court for the Northern District of Ohio. The complaint alleged that §124.34 was unconstitutional on its face because it did not provide the employee an opportunity to respond to the charges against him prior to removal. As a result, discharged employees were deprived of liberty and property without due process. . . .

The other case before us arises on similar facts and followed a similar course. Respondent Richard Donnelly was a bus mechanic for the Parma Board of Education. In August 1977, Donnelly was fired because he had failed an eye examination. He was offered a chance to retake the examination but did not do so. Like Loudermill, Donnelly appealed to the Civil Service Commission. After a year of wrangling about the timeliness of his appeal, the Commission heard the case. It ordered Donnelly reinstated, though without backpay. In a complaint essentially identical to Loudermill's, Donnelly challenged the constitutionality of the dismissal procedures. The District Court dismissed for failure to state a claim, relying on its opinion in *Loudermill*. . . .

Respondents' federal constitutional claim depends on their having had a property right in continued employment. . . . If they did, the State could not deprive them of this property without due process. . . .

Property interests are not created by the Constitution, "they are created and their dimensions are defined by existing rules or understandings that stem from an independent source such as state law. . . ." . . . The Ohio statute plainly creates such an interest. Respondents were "classified civil service employees," Ohio Rev.Code Ann §124.11 (1984), entitled to retain their positions "during good behavior and efficient service," who could not be dismissed "except . . . for . . . misfeasance, malfeasance, or nonfeasance in office," §124.34. The statute plainly supports the conclusion, reached by both lower courts, that respondents possessed property rights in continued employment. Indeed, this question does not seem to have been disputed below.

The Parma Board argues, however, that the property right is defined by, and conditioned on, the legislature's choice of procedures for its deprivation. . . . The Board stresses that in addition to specifying the grounds for termination, the statute sets out procedures by which termination may take place. The procedures were adhered to in these cases. According to petitioner, "[t]o require additional procedures would in effect expand the scope of the property interest itself." . . .

. . . More recently, however, the Court has clearly rejected it. In *Vitek v. Jones*, 445 U.S. 480, 491, 63 L.Ed.2d 552, 100 S.Ct. 1254 (1980), we pointed out that "minimum [procedural] requirements [are] a matter of federal law, they are not diminished by the fact that the State may have specified its own procedures that it may deem adequate for determining the preconditions to adverse official action." . . .

In light of these holdings, it is settled that the "bitter with the sweet" approach misconceives the constitutional guarantee. If a clearer holding is needed, we provide it today. The point is straightforward: the Due Process Clause provides that certain substantive rights—life, liberty, and property—cannot be deprived except pursuant to constitutionally adequate procedures. The categories of substance and procedure are distinct. Were the rule otherwise, the Clause would be reduced to a mere tautology. "Property" cannot be defined by the procedures provided for its deprivation any more than can life or liberty. The right to due process "is conferred, not by legislative grace, but by constitutional guarantee. While the legislature may elect not to confer a property interest in [public] employment, it may not constitutionally authorize the deprivation of such an interest, once conferred, without appropriate procedural safeguards." . . .

In short, once it is determined that the Due Process Clause applies, "the question remains what process is due." . . . The answer to that question is not to be found in the Ohio statute.

An essential principle of due process is that a deprivation of life, liberty, or property "be preceded by notice and opportunity for hearing appropriate to the nature of the case." . . . We have described "the root requirement" of the Due Process Clause as being "that an individual be given an opportunity for a hearing *before* he is deprived of any significant property interest." . . . This principle requires "some kind of a hearing" prior to the discharge of an employee who has a constitutionally protected property interest in his employment. . . . As we pointed out last Term, this rule has been settled for some time now. . . . Even decisions finding no constitutional violation in termination procedures have relied on the existence of some pretermination opportunity to respond. . . .

The need for some form of pretermination hearing, recognized in these cases, is evident from a balancing of the competing interests at stake. These are the private interest in retaining employment, the governmental interest in the expeditious removal of unsatisfactory employees and the avoidance of administrative burdens, and the risk of an erroneous termination. . . .

First, the significance of the private interest in retaining employment cannot be gainsaid. We have frequently recognized the severity of depriving a person of the means of livelihood. . . . While a fired worker may find employment elsewhere, doing so will take some time and is likely to be burdened by the questionable circumstances under which he left his previous job. . . .

Second, some opportunity for the employee to present his side of the case is recurringly of obvious value in reaching an accurate decision. Dismissals for cause will often involve factual disputes. . . . Even where the facts are clear, the appropriateness or necessity of the discharge may not be; in such cases, the only meaningful opportunity to invoke the discretion of the decisionmaker is likely to be before the termination takes effect. . . .

The cases before us illustrate these considerations. Both respondents had plausible arguments to make that might have prevented their discharge. The fact that the Commission saw fit to reinstate Donnelly suggests that an error might have been avoided had he been provided an opportunity to make his case to the Board. As for Loudermill, given the Commission's ruling we cannot say that the discharge was mistaken. Nonetheless, in light of the referee's recommendation, neither can we say that a fully informed decisionmaker might not have exercised its discretion and decided not to dismiss him, notwithstanding its authority to do so. In any event, the termination involved arguable is-

sues, and the right to a hearing does not depend on a demonstration of certain success. . . .

The governmental interest in immediate termination does not outweigh these interests. As we shall explain, affording the employee an opportunity to respond prior to termination would impose neither a significant administrative burden nor intolerable delays. Furthermore, the employer shares the employee's interest in avoiding disruption and erroneous decisions; and until the matter is settled, the employer would continue to receive the benefit of the employee's labors. It is preferable to keep a qualified employee on than to train a new one. A governmental employer also has an interest in keeping citizens usefully employed rather than taking the possibly erroneous and counterproductive step of forcing its employees onto the welfare rolls. Finally, in those situations where the employer perceives a significant hazard in keeping the employee on the job, it can avoid the problem by suspending with pay.

The foregoing considerations indicate that the pretermination "hearing," though necessary, need not be elaborate. We have pointed out that "[t]he formality and procedural requisites for the hearing can vary, depending upon the importance of the interests involved and the nature of the subsequent proceedings." . . . In general, "something less" than a full evidentiary hearing is sufficient prior to adverse administrative action. . . . Under state law, respondents were later entitled to a full administrative hearing and judicial review. The only question is what steps were required before the termination took effect. . . .

The essential requirements of due process, and all that respondents seek or the Court of Appeals required, are notice and an opportunity to respond. The opportunity to present reasons, either in person or in writing, why proposed action should not be taken is a fundamental due process requirement. . . . The tenured public employee is entitled to oral or written notice of the charges against him, an explanation of the employer's evidence, and an opportunity to present his side of the story. . . . To require more than this prior to termination would intrude to an unwarranted extent on the government's interest in quickly removing an unsatisfactory employee. . . .

We conclude that all the process that is due is provided by a pretermination opportunity to respond, coupled with post-termination administrative procedures as provided by the Ohio statute. Because respondents allege in their complaints that they had no chance to respond, the District Court erred in dismissing for failure to state a claim. The judgment of the Court of Appeals is affirmed, and the case is remanded for further proceedings consistent with this opinion.

So ordered.

CASE NOTES

1. *Pretermination Hearing.* For a pretermination hearing to be valid, the employer must give sufficient notice to inform the employee that his or her employment is in jeopardy and must also convey the rationale or evidence supporting the impending dismissal action. The employee must be advised that the meeting is a termination hearing and not merely a meeting to discuss employment conditions or contract modifications. *Calhoun v. Gaines,* 982 F.2d 1470 (10th Cir.1992).

2. *Cross-Examination.* The Ohio Supreme Court has held the pretermination hearing for a public school employee may be constituted of "informal preliminary procedures" if there is a post-termination hearing before an administrative law judge wherein the employee has the opportunity for complete cross-examination of opposing witnesses. *Ohio Association of Public School Employees, AFSCME v. Lakewood City School District Board of Education,* 68 Ohio St.3d 175, 624 N.E.2d 1043 (1994). See also *Brock v. Roadway Express, Inc.,* 481 U.S. 252, 107 S.Ct. 1740 (1987).

3. *Hearsay.* Testimony that is hearsay may be properly admitted at a school board hearing to terminate a tenured teacher's contract. Strict rules of evidence do not apply in such circumstances, and the inclusion of hearsay does not violate principles of due process. In commenting on the use of hearsay testimony, the Supreme Court of Nebraska has said: "Not only may hearsay testimony be admitted at such a hearing, but it also may be given some weight, albeit little, if any." *Johanson v. Board of Education of Lincoln County School District No. 1,* 589 N.W.2d 815 (Neb.1999).

4. When the state confers a license to engage in a profession, trade, or occupation, such a license becomes a valuable right. *Leakey v. Geor-* *gia Real Estate Commission,* 80 Ga.App. 272, 55 S.E.2d 818 (1949). Thus, a license to engage in the teaching profession, once it has been issued, becomes a property right. When a license is issued, its continued possession may become essential to a person's livelihood. To suspend an issued license involves state action that brings into play important issues of due process. *Bell v. Burson,* 402 U.S. 535, 91 S.Ct. 1586 (1971).

The U.S. Supreme Court has said with regard to lawyers' bar membership that "[a] state cannot exclude a person from the practice of . . . any . . . occupation in a manner or for reasons that contravene the Due Process or Equal Protection Clause of the Fourteenth Amendment." *Schware v. Board of Bar Examiners of New Mexico,* 353 U.S. 232, 77 S.Ct. 752 (1957). Yet an individual does not have a constitutional right to practice a profession, since state governments have a prior responsibility to regulate professions.

Because property interests are not created by the Constitution, but rather are created and their dimensions defined by existing state laws or regulations, persons who do not meet the requirements to enter the profession have no vested property interest. Thus, where teachers who have been granted only nonrenewable teaching certificates were denied new certificates, the court ruled that no property right had been denied: The plaintiff teachers "had no property interest in the nonrenewable teaching certificates, absent their compliance with the regulatory requirements for securing such certificates." *State Board of Education v. Drury,* 263 Ga. 429, 437 S.E.2d 290 (1993).

 ❖ — ❖ — ❖

School Board Is an Impartial and Unbiased Tribunal Even Though It Is Both a Party to and a Decision Maker in a Controversy with Teachers

Hortonville Joint School District No. 1 v. Hortonville Education Association

Supreme Court of the United States, 1976.
426 U.S. 482, 96 S.Ct. 2308.

Mr. Chief Justice BURGER delivered the opinion of the Court. We granted certiorari in this case to determine whether School Board members, vested by state law with the power to employ and dismiss teachers, could, consistent with the Due Process Clause of the Fourteenth Amendment, dismiss teachers engaged in a strike prohibited by state law.

The petitioners are a Wisconsin school district, the seven members of its School Board, and three administrative employees of the district. Respondents are teachers suing on behalf of all teachers in the district and the Hortonville Education Association (HEA), the collective-bargaining agent for the district's teachers. . . .

The sole issue in this case is whether the Due Process Clause of the Fourteenth Amendment prohibits this School Board from making the decision to dismiss teachers admittedly engaged in a strike and persistently refusing to return to their duties. The Wisconsin Supreme Court held that state law prohibited the strike and that termination of the striking teachers' employment was within the Board's statutory authority. . . .

Respondents' argument rests in part on doctrines that have no application to this case. They seem to argue that the Board members had some personal or official stake in the decision whether the teachers should be dismissed, . . . and that the Board has manifested some personal bitterness toward the teachers, aroused by teacher criticism of the Board during the strike. . . . [T]he teachers did not show, and the Wisconsin courts did not find, that the Board members had the kind of personal or financial stake in the decision that might create a conflict of interest, and there is nothing in the record to support charges of personal animosity. The Wisconsin Supreme Court was careful "not to suggest . . . that the board members were anything but dedicated public servants, trying to provide the district with quality education . . . within its limited budget." That court's analysis would seem to be confirmed by the Board's repeated invitations for striking teachers to return to work, the final invitation being contained in the letter that notified them of their discharge.

The only other factor suggested to support the claim of bias is that the School Board was involved in the negotiations that preceded and precipitated the striking teachers' discharge. Participation in those negotiations was a statutory duty of the Board. The Wisconsin Supreme Court held that this involvement, without more, disqualified the Board from deciding whether the teachers should be dismissed:

> The board was the collective bargaining agent for the school district and thus was engaged in the collective bargaining process with the teachers' representative, the HEA. It is not difficult to imagine the frustration on the part of the board members when negotiations broke down, agreement could not be reached and the employees resorted to concerted activity. . . . They were . . . not uninvolved in the events which precipitated decisions they were required to make.

Mere familiarity with the facts of a case gained by an agency in the performance of its statutory role does not, however, disqualify a decisionmaker. . . . Nor is a decisionmaker disqualified simply because he has taken a position, even in public, on a policy issue related to the dispute, in the absence of a showing that he is not "capable of judging a particular controversy fairly on the basis of its own circumstances." . . .

Respondents' claim and the Wisconsin Supreme Court's holding reduce to the argument that the Board was biased because it negotiated with the teachers on behalf of the school district without reaching agreement and learned about the reasons for the strike in the course of negotiating. From those premises the Wisconsin court concluded that the Board lost its statutory power to determine that the strike and persistent refusal to terminate it amounted to conduct serious enough to warrant discharge of the strikers. Wisconsin statutes vest in the Board the power to discharge its employees, a power of every employer, whether it has negotiated with the employees before discharge or not. The Fourteenth Amendment permits a court to strip the Board of the otherwise unremarkable power the Wisconsin Legislature has given it only if the Board's prior involvement in negotiating with the teachers means that it cannot act consistently with due process.

Due process, as this Court has repeatedly held, is a term that "negates any concept of inflexible procedures universally applicable to every imaginable situation." . . . Determining what process is due in a given setting requires the Court to take into account the individual's stake in the decision at issue as well as the State's interest in a particular procedure for making it. . . . Our assessment of the interests of the parties in this case leads to the conclusion that . . . the Board's prior role as negotiator does not disqualify it to decide that the public interest in maintaining uninterrupted classroom work required that teachers striking in violation of state law be discharged.

The teachers' interest in these proceedings is, of course, self-evident. They wished to avoid termination of their employment, obviously an important interest, but one that must be examined in light of several factors. Since the teachers admitted that they were engaged in a work stoppage, there was no possibility of an erroneous factual determination on this critical threshold issue. Moreover, what the teachers claim as a property right was the expectation that the jobs they had left to go and remain on strike in violation of law would remain open to them. . . .

State law vests the governmental, or policy-making, function exclusively in the School Board and the State has two interests in keeping it there. First, the Board is the body with overall responsibility for the governance of the school district; it must cope with the myriad day-to-day problems of a modern public school system including the severe consequences of a teachers' strike; by virtue of electing them the constituents have declared the Board members qualified to deal with these problems, and they are accountable to the voters for the manner in which they perform. Second, the state legislature has given to the Board the power to employ and dismiss teachers, as a part of the balance it has struck in the area of municipal labor relations; altering those statutory powers as a matter of federal due process clearly changes that balance. Permitting the Board to make the decision at issue here preserves its control over school district affairs, leaves the balance of power in labor relations where the state legislature struck it, and assures that the decision whether to dismiss the teachers will be made by the body responsible for that decision under state law.

Respondents have failed to demonstrate that the decision to terminate their employment was infected by the sort of bias that we have held to disqualify other decisionmakers as a matter of federal due process. A showing that the Board was "involved" in the events preceding this decision, in light of the important interest in leaving with the Board the power given by the state legislature, is not enough to overcome the presumption of honesty and integrity in policymakers with decisionmaking power. . . . Accordingly, we hold that the Due Process Clause of the Fourteenth Amendment did not guarantee respondents that the decision to terminate their employment would be made or reviewed by a body other than the School Board.

The judgment of the Wisconsin Supreme Court is reversed, and the case is remanded for further proceedings not inconsistent with this opinion.

Reversed and remanded.

CASE NOTES

1. *Impartial Tribunal.* The U.S. Supreme Court has said that the requirement of an impartial tribunal is at the core of due process. See *Tumey v. Ohio*, 273 U.S. 510, 47 S.Ct. 437 (1927). "Due process demands . . . the existence of impartiality on the part of those who function in judicial or quasi-judicial capacity." *Petrowski v. Norwich Free Academy*, 199 Conn. 231, 235, 506 A.2d 139 (1986); see *Marshall v. Jerrico, Inc.*, 446 U.S. 238, 242–43, 100 S.Ct. 1610, 1613–14 (1980).

2. The courts have set a more rigorous standard for judges in courts of law than for persons sitting on administrative tribunals, such as school boards. A federal court has said that "the mere appearance of bias that might disqualify a judge will not disqualify an arbitrator." *Florasynth, Inc. v. Pickholz*, 750 F.2d 171, 173–74 (2d Cir.1984).

3. In administrative hearings, there is a presumption of impartiality, and the burden of disqualification for bias rests upon the one seeking the disqualification. *Withrow v. Larkin*, 421 U.S. 35, 47, 95 S.Ct. 1456, 1464 (1975).

4. To sustain the disqualification of an administrative hearing officer for bias, the plaintiff must demonstrate actual bias rather than mere potential bias. See *Rado v. Board of Education of the Borough of Naugatuck*, 216 Conn. 541, 583 A.2d 102 (1990).

5. Due process is frustrated by the bias of a single member of a school board. The Supreme

Court of North Carolina has held that the bias of one school board member "taints the entire board's decision-making process." The court said:

> A critical component of any quasi-judicial hearing and decision-making by a deliberative body is the give and take which occurs when group members share their observations and opinions. There is a fundamental notion that each member will enter the hearing with an open mind, listen to and view the evidence, share his or her observations, analyses and opinions with the other board members, listen to the other members' comments, and only then finally commit to a vote. One biased member can skew the entire process by what he or she does, or does not do, during the hearing and deliberations.

This same court further commented on the difficulty of erasing all vestiges of bias because of the nature of local school boards as being a part of the fabric of the local community and the attendant possibilities of bias to sway their opinions. The court said:

> Board members will sometimes have discussed certain issues that later became the subject of board deliberations; such knowledge and discussions are inevitable aspects of their multifaceted roles as administrators, investigators and adjudicators. However, when performing their quasi-judicial function during a board hearing and any resulting deliberations, members must be able to set aside their prior knowledge and preconceptions concerning the matter at issue, and base their considerations solely upon the evidence adduced at the hearing.

Crump v. Board of Education of Hickory Administrative School Unit, 326 N.C. 603, 392 S.E.2d 579 (1990).

6. The susceptibility of local school boards to bias and the importance of this recognition to fairness were observed in an opinion by Anthony Kennedy (now U.S. Supreme Court Justice) of the U.S. Court of Appeals for the Ninth Circuit. Kennedy wrote:

> The key component of due process, when a decisionmaker is acquainted with the facts, is the assurance of a central fairness at the hearing . . .
>
> . . . Members of a school board in smaller communities may well have some knowledge of the facts and individuals involved in incidents which they must evaluate. Their obligation is to act impartially and in a fair manner.

Vanelli v. Reynolds School District No. 7, 667 F.2d 773, 779–80 (9th Cir.1982).

7. The fact that a teacher had harassed board members prior to a hearing did not establish bias on the part of the board as to preclude the employee from receiving due process in a dismissal proceeding. *Covert v. Bensalem Township School District,* 104 Pa.Cmwlth. 441, 522 A.2d 129 (1987).

8. *Prejudice.* The values of fairness that underlie the due process clause may be offended if prejudice against the defendant can be shown. The definition of prejudice, however, may be nebulous. Generally, however, it has to do with impediments to "fundamental conceptions of justice which lie at the base of our civil and political institutions." *Mooney v. Holohan,* 294 U.S. 103, 55 S.Ct. 340 (1935). Denial of due process can be alleged if "the community's sense of fair play and decency" is offended. *Rochin v. California,* 342 U.S. 165, 72 S.Ct. 205 (1952).

A question of prejudice as a denial of due process arose in a New York case in which a school board brought a dismissal proceeding against a teacher for sexual intercourse and sexual contact with two female students twenty-four years earlier. The teacher argued that holding a hearing based on misconduct charges after so many years amounted to prejudice and implicated due process. He maintained that values of fairness envisaged by due process were offended because after such a lengthy time he could not launch an effective defense because the time lapse and faded memories effectively prevented him from proving that on the dates of the alleged offenses he was elsewhere; thus, he said the case was prejudiced against him. The court rejected this argument and ruled against his invoking the due process clause, saying that the mere assertion of "dimming of memories as a result of delay does not constitute actual prejudice." He could not establish that there was actual prejudice against him beyond the mere assertion of dimming of memories. According to the court, a different determination could have resulted only if the teacher had been able to show actual prejudice, such as the loss of key documentary evidence or the disappearance or death of a material witness. *DeMichele v. Greenburgh Central High School District No. 7,* 167 F.3d 14 (2d Cir.1999).

■ THE VAGUENESS TEST

A basic principle of due process is that a regulation of a government agency is void for vagueness if its prohibitions are not clearly defined.[56] A school district regulation is not unconstitutional simply because it is poorly written or overly general, for the law does not require scientific and mathematical certainty.[57] A regulation is unconstitutional only if it "is vague, not in the sense that it requires a person to conform his conduct to an imprecise but comprehensive normative standard, but rather in the sense that no standard of conduct is specified at all."[58]

Laws or regulations are overly vague if persons of common intelligence are required to guess as to their actual meaning.[59] Overly vague laws or regulations offend the Constitution because in their lack of certainty of meaning they fail to give fair notice of the conduct that is prohibited and, moreover, they invite arbitrary and discriminatory enforcement.[60] The degree of vagueness tolerated by the Constitution is dependent on the nature of the regulation and its consequences.[61] For example, when a government regulation involves economic regulation or lesser civil penalties, a less stringent vagueness test is required. On the other hand, a much stricter test will be utilized by the courts when a law or regulation threatens to impinge on the exercise of a constitutionally protected right. Thus, if a school board rule appears to interfere directly with a teacher's exercise of a First Amendment right, then the courts will permit less latitude for vagueness. In applying these judicial rules regarding vagueness, the Supreme Court of Colorado found that a school regulation requiring that the teacher inform the principal at least twenty days before the use of a "controversial learning resource" in a classroom was clear enough that the teacher should not have shown a film that showed various scenes of sexual activity and was laced with profanity.[62] The court concluded that this school regulation did not inappropriately burden the teacher's rights of free speech because the policy "reasonably related to a legitimate pedagogical concern" of the school and was not impermissibly vague as it applied specifically to the plaintiff teacher. The court found that such a rule was specific enough in view of the fact that

the school had legitimate control over the curriculum of the school that extended to the use of any controversial matter in the classrooms by the teachers. The teacher had previously viewed the film and should have known that its contents, including excessive nudity, oral sex, masturbation, profanity, cocaine abuse, and graphic violence, could be controversial. Hence, the court in holding that the policy was not vague observed that the terminology provided a comprehensive standard for the teacher to follow and that plaintiff teacher could not legitimately maintain that "no standard of conduct is specified at all."[63]

Thus, where policies of a school are sufficiently clear to be understood by a normal person, the courts will not sustain a plaintiff's "straining to inject doubt as to the meaning of words where no doubt would be felt by the normal reader."[64]

■ LOYALTY OATHS

The vagueness test has been commonly offended by state statutes that extract loyalty oaths as a condition of employment. Such statutes implicitly accuse a person of an offense, and the oath must be taken to gain absolution in the eyes of the state. If the oath is so vague as to be uncertain of meaning, then the oath taker stands accused of an indefinite offense or may be guilty of perjury if he or she did not understand the offense for which the forswearing was required.

During the Red scare after World War I, several states enacted laws requiring special oaths as a condition of teaching in public schools. An increased fear of the spread of communism in the 1930s and a responding upsurge of radicalism led to the enactment of loyalty oaths in twenty-one states by 1936. Even today, legislatures, in fits of patriotism, periodically enact loyalty oaths. Traditionally, such oaths have been quite vague, making it most difficult to determine exactly to what one is swearing.[65]

In *Cramp v. Board of Public Instruction*,[66] the Supreme Court invalidated an oath requiring teachers to swear that they had never lent their "aid, support, advice, counsel, or influence to the Communist Party" because the oath was not sufficiently definitive and was lacking in "terms susceptible of objective measurement." Vagueness, as violative of due process, was also the bane of a 1955 Washington statute that sought to define a "subversive person." The definition was dissected and exposed as to its infirmities by the U.S. Supreme Court in the case of *Baggett v. Bullitt.*[67] The Court observed that teachers are particularly vulnerable when required to swear that they have not aided, abetted, taught, or assisted in a subversive organization. The *Baggett* oath was stricken because the Court found that teaching, by its nature, could influence opinions and even indirectly support a subversive view without the teacher's knowledge or intent to overthrow or do violence to the nation. The Court ruled that statutory language of an oath that requires the "forswearing of an undefined variety of 'guiltless knowing behavior'" is violative of due process.[68]

Too, the uncertain meaning of oaths has the effect of offending the First and Fourteenth Amendments because it hangs as a threat over the freedom of discussion in the classroom. In *Cramp*, the Court said that "[t]he vice of unconstitutional vagueness is further aggravated where . . . the statute in question operates to inhibit the exercise of individual freedoms affirmatively protected by the Constitution."[69] In the classroom, in particular, the vagueness of loyalty oaths forces the teacher to steer far wider of the unlawful zone "in the exercise of free speech than if the boundaries of the forbidden areas were clearly marked."[70]

Though loyalty oaths have been consistently invalidated by decisions of the U.S. Supreme Court, the Court has not said that a properly constituted oath is unconstitutional. Kalven has noted that "[l]oyalty oaths are not *per se* invalid, but the Court will not lift a finger on their behalf."[71]

For the court to uphold an oath and subject a false forswearer to criminal liability requires that the oath taker have (1) knowledge, (2) active membership in a subversive organization, and (3) specific intent to overthrow the government. Kalven observes that the combination of all these requirements is the "functional equivalent of participation in a literal conspiracy."[72]

Two cases indicate the permissible conditions under which oaths may be held valid: *Connell v.*

Higginbotham,[73] a 1971 Florida case, and *Cole v. Richardson,*[74] a 1970 Massachusetts case. The *Connell* case illustrates the disenchantment that the Court has with the negative test oath. Here the Court invalidated a negative forswearing but let stand an affirmative oath of allegiance. In so ruling, the Court presumably concluded that an affirmative oath is permissible because it is merely an inoffensive ceremony. On the other hand, a negative test oath subjects the taker to criminal perjury sanctions and is intended as a device to either disqualify the taker from a public position or to convict him or her in a criminal proceeding.

In *Cole*, the Supreme Court upheld a Massachusetts oath with two clauses. The first clause, an affirmative swearing, said, "I do solemnly swear (or affirm) that I will uphold and defend the Constitution." This part was routine and valid, but the second clause involved the negative, stating that "I will oppose the overthrow of the government . . . by force, violence, or any other illegal or unconstitutional means." The plaintiff had maintained that the second clause tainted and invalidated the first clause. In a four-to-three decision, with Chief Justice Burger writing for the majority, the Court held that the whole oath itself was simply an amenity and that nothing objectionable was intended by the "oppose" clause. Justice Harlan in *Cole*, when vacating the lower court's decision, reflected a growing judicial weariness with the oath cases:

> I am, however, content to acquiesce in the Court's action because of the manifest triviality of the impact of the oath under challenge . . . Almost any word or phrase may be rendered vague and ambiguous by dissection with a semantic scalpel. I do not, however, consider it a provident use of the time of this Court to coach what amounts to little more than verbal calisthenics. This kind of semantic inquiry, however interesting, should not occupy the time of federal courts unless fundamental rights turn on the outcome.[75]

In concluding that the oath in *Cole* was not unconstitutional, the Supreme Court held as follows:

■ The "oath provisions . . . are not inconsistent with the First Amendment."

- The district court properly held that the "up-hold and defend" clause, a paraphrase of the constitutional oath, is permissible.
- The "oppose the overthrow" clause was not designed to require specific action to be taken in some hypothetical or actual situation but was to ensure that those in positions of public trust were willing to commit themselves to live by the constitutional processes of our government.
- The oath is not void for vagueness. Perjury, the sole punishment, requires a knowing and willful falsehood, which removes the danger of punishment without fair notice; there is no problem of punishment inflicted by mere prosecution, as there has been no prosecution under the statute since its enactment, nor has any been planned.
- There is no constitutionally protected right to overthrow a government by force, violence, or illegal or unconstitutional means, and, therefore, there is no requirement that one who refuses to take the Massachusetts oath be granted a hearing for the determination of some other fact before being discharged.

Cole, then, represented a somewhat more tolerant view of oaths than was evidenced in earlier opinions. In the future, the Supreme Court may gives states slightly more latitude in the wording and requirements of oaths. Kalven, in analyzing the intricacies of the oath cases, has drawn four generalizations about the rule of law:[76]

- "It is safe to conclude that the Court will not openly hold that the oath format is itself unconstitutional; and this is true for negative oaths, as well as for oaths of affirmation." Parenthetically, though, one may conclude that negative oaths are more objectionable and will be subject to more intense judicial scrutiny."
- "The oath, however, is a *disfavored device*. It will be construed with the eye of conscience, and, thus held to the most exacting standards of unambiguous drafting; and held also to the most explicit limitations to those of *scienter* (knowing participation). Hence, while the oath format *per se* is not unconstitutional, it

will be difficult in actuality to draft an oath that will pass muster."
- "The legality of an oath will depend not simply on clarity of its wording, but, ultimately on the content of its disqualification."
- "The Court will, to some extent, distinguish between oaths of affirmation and negative loyalty oaths. In theory, only the latter are objectionable; the former are routine, conventional amenities of daily life. *Baggett*, however, indicates that even oaths of affirmation, if they depart from traditional formulae, might be invalid. It is only this last conclusion that the Court's gratuitous performance in *Cole v. Richardson* can, as a matter of logic, be said to unsettle."

Vagueness of Oath Offends Due Process

Wieman v. Updegraff

Supreme Court of the United States, 1952.
344 U.S. 183, 73 S.Ct. 215.

MR. JUSTICE CLARK delivered the opinion of the Court. This is an appeal from a decision of the Supreme Court of Oklahoma upholding the validity of a loyalty oath prescribed by Oklahoma statute for all state officers and employees. . . . Appellants, employed by the State as members of the faculty and staff of Oklahoma Agricultural and Mechanical College, failed, within the thirty days permitted, to take the oath required by the Act. Appellee Updegraff, as a citizen and taxpayer, thereupon brought this suit in the District Court of Oklahoma County to enjoin the necessary state officials from paying further compensation to employees who had not subscribed to the oath. . . . [The appellants] sought a mandatory injunction directing the state officers to pay their salaries regardless of their failure to take the oath. Their objections centered largely on the following clauses of the oath:

That I am not affiliated directly or indirectly . . . with any foreign political agency, party, organization or Government, or with any agency, party, organization, association, or group whatever which has been officially determined by the United States Attorney General or other authorized agency of the United States to be a communist front or subversive organization; . . . that I will take up arms in the defense of the United States in time of War, or National Emergency, if necessary; that within the five (5) years immediately preceding the taking of this oath (or affirmation) I have not been a member of . . . any agency, party, organization, association, or group whatever which has been officially determined by the United States Attorney General or other authorized public agency of the United States to be a communist front or subversive organization.

. . . The purpose of the Act, we are told, "was to make loyalty a qualification to hold public office or be employed by the State." . . . During periods of international stress, the extent of legislation with such objectives accentuates our traditional concern about the relation of government to the individual in a free society. The perennial problem of defining that relationship becomes acute when disloyalty is screened by ideological patterns and techniques of disguise that make it difficult to identify. Democratic government is not powerless to meet this threat, but it must do so without infringing the freedoms that are the ultimate values of all democratic living. In the adoption of such means as it believes effective, the legislature is therefore confronted with the problem of balancing its interest in national security with the often conflicting constitutional rights of the individual. . . . We are thus brought to the question touched on in *Garner, Adler, and Gerende:* whether the Due Process Clause permits a state, in attempting to bar disloyal individuals from its employ, to exclude persons solely on the basis of organizational membership, regardless of their knowledge concerning the organizations to which they had belonged. For, under the statute before us, the fact of membership alone disqualifies. If the rule be expressed as a presumption of disloyalty, it is a conclusive one.

But membership may be innocent. A state servant may have joined a proscribed organization unaware of its activities and purposes. In recent years, many completely loyal persons have severed organizational ties after learning for the first time of the character of groups to which they had belonged. "They had joined, [but] did not know what it was, they were good, fine young men and women, loyal Americans, but they had been trapped into it— because one of the great weaknesses of all Americans, whether adult or youth, is to join something." At the time of affiliation, a group itself may be innocent, only later coming under the influence of those who would turn it toward illegitimate ends. Conversely, an organization formerly subversive and therefore designated as such may have subsequently freed itself from the influences which originally led to its listing.

There can be no dispute about the consequences visited upon a person excluded from public employment on disloyalty grounds. In the view of the community, the stain is a deep one; indeed, it has become a badge of infamy. Especially is this so in time of cold war and hot emotions when "each man begins to eye his neighbor as a possible enemy." Yet under the Oklahoma Act, the fact of association alone determines disloyalty and disqualification; it matters not whether association existed innocently or knowingly. To thus inhibit individual freedom of movement is to stifle the flow of democratic expression and controversy at one of its chief sources. We hold that the distinction observed between the case at bar and *Garner, Adler and Gerende* is decisive. Indiscriminate classification of innocent with knowing activity must fall as an assertion of arbitrary power. The oath offends due process. . . . We need not pause to consider whether an abstract right to public employment exists. It is sufficient to say that constitutional protection does extend to the public servant whose exclusion pursuant to a statute is patently arbitrary or discriminatory. . . .

Reversed.

CASE NOTE

Following *Wieman v. Updegraff,* the U.S. Supreme Court in *Keyishian v. Board of Regents of the University of the State of New York* invalidated a state university oath that required teachers to swear that they had not violated the law by treasonable or seditious utterances or acts. 385 U.S. 589, 87 S.Ct. 675 (1967).

❖ — ❖ — ❖

*Disclaimer Provisions of Loyalty
Oath Are Unconstitutional*

Connell v. Higginbotham

Supreme Court of the United States, 1971.
403 U.S. 207, 91 S.Ct. 1772.

PER CURIAM. This is an appeal from an action commenced in the United States District Court for the Middle District of Florida challenging the constitutionality of §§876.05–876.10 of Fla.Stat. (1965), and the various loyalty oaths upon which appellant's employment as a school teacher was conditioned. The three-judge U.S. District Court declared three of the five clauses contained in the oaths to be unconstitutional, and enjoined the State from conditioning employment on the taking of an oath including the language declared unconstitutional. The appeal is from that portion of the District Court decision, 305 F.Supp. 445, which upheld the remaining two clauses in the oath: I do hereby solemnly swear or affirm (1) "that I will support the Constitution of the United States and of the State of Florida"; and (2) "that I do not believe in the overthrow of the Government of the United States or of the State of Florida by force or violence." [The clauses declared unconstitutional by the Court required the employee to swear (1) "that I am not a member of the Communist Party"; (2) "that I have not and will not lend my aid, support, advice, counsel or influence to the Communist Party"; and (3) "that I am not a member of any organization or party which believes in or teaches, directly or indirectly, the overthrow of the Government of the United States or of Florida by force or violence."]

On January 16, 1969, appellant made application for a teaching position with the Orange County school system. She was interviewed by the principal of Callahan Elementary School, and on January 27, 1969, appellant was employed as a substitute classroom teacher in the fourth grade of that school. Appellant was dismissed from her teaching position on March 18, 1969, for refusing to sign the loyalty oath required of all Florida public employees, Fla.Stat. §876.05.

The first section of the oath upheld by the District Court, requiring all applicants to pledge to support the Constitution of the United States and of the State of Florida, demands no more of Florida public employees than is required of all state and federal officers. U.S. Const., Art. VI, cl. 3. The validity of this section of the oath would appear settled. . . .

The second portion of the oath, approved by the District Court, falls within the ambit of decisions of this Court proscribing summary dismissal from public employment without hearing or inquiry required by due process. . . . That portion of the oath, therefore, cannot stand.

Affirmed in part, and reversed in part.

■ THE IRRATIONALITY AND PRESUMPTIONS TEST

The fourth test imposed by due process on the validity of state actions is the requirement of rationality. The Supreme Court requires that there be a rational connection between the fact proved and the ultimate end presumed.[77] The Court has said that "if the inference of the one from proof of the other is arbitrary because of lack of connection between the two in common experience,"[78] then due process is violated. Moreover, the individual cannot be effectively denied the opportunity to rebut an irrational presumption. Accordingly, the Court has found that irrebuttable presumptions deny due process.[79]

RESIDENT STATUS

An irrebuttable presumption that denies a fundamental interest or right violates due process. In *Vlandis v. Kline*,[80] a college student challenged the constitutional validity of a state law classifying students as nonresidents permanently, conclusive and unchangeable, simply because the students were not in residence at the time that their application to college was submitted. A student challenged this nonresident rule and pointed out that he was denied due process because he could not henceforth be classified as having resident status even though he moved to the state and intended to maintain permanent residence there. The question before the Supreme Court was whether the student had a constitutional right to controvert the presumption of nonresidence by presenting evidence of bona fide residence. The Court concluded that an "irrebuttable presumption . . . is violative of the Due Process Clause, because it provides no opportunity"[81] to rebut the state's presumption by fact or reason. Thus, when the state devises statutes or regulations that classify persons in such a way that they cannot overcome or extricate themselves from the class, then a due process violation may have occurred.

PREGNANCY

Similarly, the Supreme Court has held in *Cleveland Board of Education v. LaFleur*[82] that due process is violated by school board rules that create a conclusive presumption that every pregnant teacher who reaches a particular point of pregnancy becomes physically incapable of continuing to teach. The Court's objection to irrebuttable presumptions is best explained by Corwin:

> Legislative fiat may not take the place of fact, however, in the determination of issues involving life, liberty, or property, and a statute creating a presumption which is entirely arbitrary and which operates to deny a fair opportunity to repel it or to present facts pertinent to one's defense is void.[83]

Even though *LaFleur* was later followed in another pregnancy case voiding a statute that made pregnant women ineligible for unemployment compensation for a period during pregnancy and after childbirth,[84] the Supreme Court, of late, has tended to avoid this aspect of due process. Instead, the Court, under the leadership of both Chief Justices Burger and Rehnquist, has maintained that the protections afforded under the rationale of due process are more logically extended under the equal protection clause of the Fourteenth Amendment. This was the essence of the dissent enunciated in *Vlandis v. Kline*,[85] and it was reinforced by the majority in *Weinberger v. Salfi*. Here the Court imposed the traditional equal protection analysis of strict scrutiny to encompass due process challenges of statutory classifications that create irrebuttable presumptions. Therefore, the Court does not appear to be prone to extend this part of due process to overlap the rights and guaran-

tees already found in equal protection. In the future, the Court will probably "limit the doctrine to those areas which involve fundamental rights or suspect classifications that would, in equal protection analysis, rise to strict, and perhaps intermediate, scrutiny."[86] The technical effect is simply that plaintiffs in the future will avoid this aspect of due process in favor of equal protection whenever state statutes or school board rules are thought to be irrational or unreasonable.

Mandatory Leave Rules and Arbitrary Cutoff Dates for Pregnant Teachers Violate Due Process

Cleveland Board of Education v. LaFleur

Supreme Court of the United States, 1974.
414 U.S. 632, 94 S.Ct. 791.

Mr. Justice STEWART delivered the opinion of the Court. The respondents in No. 72-777 and the petitioner in No. 72-1129 are female public school teachers. During the 1970–1971 school year, each informed her local school board that she was pregnant; each was compelled by the mandatory maternity leave rule to quit her job without pay several months before the expected birth of her child. These cases call upon us to decide the constitutionality of the school boards' rules.

Jo Carol LaFleur and Ann Elizabeth Nelson, the respondents in No. 72-777, are junior high school teachers employed by the Board of Education of Cleveland, Ohio. Pursuant to a rule first adopted in 1952, the school board requires every pregnant school teacher to take maternity leave without pay, beginning five months before the expected birth of her child. Application for such leave must be made no later than two weeks prior to the date of departure. A teacher on maternity leave is not allowed to return to work until the beginning of the next regular school semester which follows the date when her child attains the age of three months. A doctor's certificate attesting to the health of the teacher is a prerequisite to return; an additional physical examination may be required. The teacher on maternity leave is not promised reemployment after the birth of the child; she is merely given priority in reassignment to a position for which she is qualified. Failure to comply with the mandatory maternity leave provisions is ground for dismissal. . . .

The petitioner in No. 72-1129, Susan Cohen, was employed by the School Board of Chesterfield County, Virginia. That school board's maternity leave regulation requires that a pregnant teacher leave work at least four months prior to the expected birth of her child. Notice in writing must be given to the school board at least six months prior to the expected birth date. A teacher on maternity leave is declared reeligible for employment when she submits written notice from a physician that she is physically fit for reemployment, and when she can give assurance that care of the child will cause only minimal interference with her job responsibilities. . . .

This Court has long recognized that freedom of personal choice in matters of marriage and family life is one of the liberties protected by the Due Process Clause of the Fourteenth Amendment. . . . There is a right "to be free from unwarranted governmental intrusion into matters so fundamentally affecting a person as the decision whether to bear or beget a child."

By acting to penalize the pregnant teacher for deciding to bear a child, overly restrictive maternity leave regulations can constitute a heavy burden on the exercise of these protected freedoms. Because public school maternity leave rules directly affect "one of the basic civil rights of man," *Skinner v. Oklahoma*, supra, 316 U.S., at 541, 62 S.Ct., at 1113, the Due Process Clause of the Fourteenth Amendment requires that such rules must not needlessly, arbitrarily, or capriciously impinge upon this vital area of a teacher's constitutional liberty. The question before us in these cases is whether the interests advanced in support of the rules of the Cleveland and Chesterfield County School Boards can justify the particular procedures they have adopted.

The school boards in these cases have offered two essentially overlapping explanations for their mandatory maternity leave rules. First, they contend that the firm cutoff dates are nec-essary to maintain continuity of classroom instruction, since advance knowledge of when a pregnant teacher must leave facilitates the finding and hiring of a qualified substitute. Secondly, the school boards seek to justify their maternity rules by arguing that at least some teachers become physically incapable of adequately performing certain of their duties during the latter part of pregnancy. By keeping the pregnant teacher out of the classroom during these final months, the maternity leave rules are said to protect the health of the teacher and her unborn child, while at the same time assuring that students have a physically capable instructor in the classroom at all times.

It cannot be denied that continuity of instruction is a significant and legitimate educational goal. Regulations requiring pregnant teachers to provide early notice of their condition to school authorities undoubtedly facilitate administrative planning toward the important objective of continuity. . . .

. . . [W]hile the advance-notice provisions in the Cleveland and Chesterfield County rules are wholly rational and may well be necessary to serve the objective of continuity of instruction, the absolute requirements of termination at the end of the fourth or fifth month of pregnancy are not. Were continuity the only goal, cutoff dates much later during pregnancy would serve as well as or better than the challenged rules, providing that ample advance notice requirements were retained. Indeed, continuity would seem just as well attained if the teacher herself were allowed to choose the date upon which to commence her leave, at least so long as the decision were required to be made and notice given of it well in advance of the date selected. . . .

We thus conclude that the arbitrary cutoff dates embodied in the mandatory leave rules before us have no rational relationship to the valid state interest of preserving continuity of instruction. As long as the teachers are required to give substantial advance notice of their condition, the choice of firm dates later in pregnancy would serve the boards' objectives just as well, while imposing a far lesser burden on the women's exercise of constitutionally protected freedom.

The question remains as to whether the cutoff dates at the beginning of the fifth and sixth months can be justified on the other ground advanced by the school boards—the necessity of keeping physically unfit teachers out of the classroom. There can be no doubt that such an objective is perfectly legitimate, both on educational and safety grounds. And, despite the plethora of conflicting medical testimony in these cases, we can assume, *arguendo,* that at least some teachers become physically disabled from effectively performing their duties during the latter stages of pregnancy.

The mandatory termination provisions of the Cleveland and Chesterfield County rules surely operate to insulate the classroom from the presence of potentially incapacitated pregnant teachers. But the question is whether the rules sweep too broadly. . . .

That question must be answered in the affirmative, for the provisions amount to a conclusive presumption that every pregnant teacher who reaches the fifth or sixth month of pregnancy is physically incapable of continuing. There is no individualized determination by the teacher's doctor—or the school board's—as to any particular teacher's ability to continue at her job. The rules contain an irrebuttable presumption of physical incompetency, and that presumption applies even when the medical evidence as to an individual woman's physical status might be wholly to the contrary. . . .

. . . While the regulations no doubt represent a good-faith attempt to achieve a laudable goal, they cannot pass muster under the Due Process Clause of the Fourteenth Amendment, because they employ irrebuttable presumptions that unduly penalize a female teacher for deciding to bear a child.

In addition to the mandatory termination provisions, both the Cleveland and Chesterfield County rules contain limitations upon a teacher's eligibility to return to work after giving birth. Again, the school boards offer two justifications for the return rules—continuity of instruction and the desire to be certain that the teacher is physically competent when she returns to work. As is the case with the leave provisions, the question is not whether the school board's goals are legitimate, but rather whether the particular means chosen to achieve those objectives unduly infringe upon the teacher's constitutional liberty.

. . . [W]e conclude that the Cleveland return rule, insofar as it embodies the three-month age provision, is wholly arbitrary and irrational, and hence violates the Due Process Clause of the Fourteenth Amendment. The age limitation serves no legitimate state interest, and unnecessarily penalizes the female teacher for asserting her right to bear children.

We perceive no such constitutional infirmities in the Chesterfield County rule. In that school system, the teacher becomes eligible for reemployment upon submission of a medical certificate from her physician; return to work is guaranteed no later than the beginning of the next school year following the eligibility determination. The medical certificate is both a reasonable and narrow method of protecting the school board's interest in teacher fitness, while the possible deferring of return until the next school year serves the goal of preserving continuity of instruction. In short, the Chesterfield County rule manages to serve the legitimate state interests here without employing unnecessary presumptions that broadly burden the exercise of protected constitutional liberty.

For the reasons stated, we hold that the mandatory termination provisions of the Cleveland and Chesterfield County maternity regulations violate the Due Process Clause of the Fourteenth Amendment, because of their use of unwarranted conclusive presumptions that seriously burden the exercise of protected constitutional liberty. For similar reasons, we hold the three-month provision of the Cleveland return rule unconstitutional.

■ ENDNOTES

1. U.S. Const. amend. XIV, due process clause.
2. A. E. Dick Howard, *Commentaries on the Constitution of Virginia,* vol. I (Charlottesville: University Press of Virginia, 1974), p. 189.
3. Ibid., pp. 190–201.
4. 408 U.S. 564, 92 S.Ct. 2701 (1972).
5. Ibid.
6. Ibid.
7. Perry v. Sindermann, 408 U.S. 593, 92 S.Ct. 2694 (1972).
8. See *1990 Deskbook Encyclopedia of American School Law* (Rosemount, Minn.: Data Research, Inc., 1990), p. 298.
9. Board of Regents of State Colleges v. Roth, op. cit.
10. Jean-Jacques Rousseau, *The Social Contract and Discourses,* trans. G.D.H. Cole (London: J.M. Dent & Sons Ltd., reprinted, 1988), p. 104.

11. Young v. Commonwealth, 101 Va. 853, 45 S.E. 327 (1903).
12. Board of Regents of State Colleges v. Roth, op. cit.
13. 262 U.S. 390, 43 S.Ct. 625 (1923).
14. Gray v. Union County Intermediate Education District, 520 F.2d 803 (9th Cir.1975).
15. Board of Regents of State Colleges v. Roth, op. cit.
16. Ibid.
17. Leonard W. Levy, *Original Intent and the Framers' Constitution* (New York: Macmillan, 1988), pp. 276–77.
18. Ibid.
19. Ibid.
20. Ibid.
21. Board of Regents of State Colleges v. Roth, op. cit.
22. Goldberg v. Kelly, 397 U.S. 254, 90 S.Ct. 1011 (1970).
23. Ferguson v. Thomas, 430 F.2d 852 (5th Cir.1970).
24. Ibid.
25. Board of Regents of State Colleges v. Roth, op. cit.
26. Ibid.
27. Ibid.
28. Perry v. Sindermann, op.cit.
29. Ibid.
30. Ibid.
31. Ibid.
32. Pred v. Board of Public Instruction of Dade County, 415 F.2d 851 (5th Cir.1969).
33. Ibid.
34. Paul Jackson, *Natural Justice* (London: Sweet & Maxwell, 1973), p. 1.
35. Ibid.
36. Dixon v. Alabama State Board of Education, 294 F.2d 150 (5th Cir.1961), cert. denied, 368 U.S. 930, 82 S.Ct. 368 (1961).
37. Underwood v. McVeigh, 64 Va. (232 Gratt.) 409, 418 (1873).
38. Dixon v. Alabama State Board of Education, op. cit.
39. Ibid.
40. Snyder v. Massachusetts, 291 U.S. 97, 116–17, 54 S.Ct. 330, 336–37 (1934).
41. 424 U.S. 319, 335, 96 S.Ct. 893, 903 (1976).
42. John E. Nowak, Ronald D. Rotunda, and J. Nelson Young, *Constitutional Law*, 3d ed. (St. Paul, Minn.: West, 1986), p. 490.
43. Ibid., p. 491.
44. Ibid.
45. Ibid.
46. See Addington v. Texas, 441 U.S. 418, 99 S.Ct. 1804 (1979); Parham v. J. R., 442 U.S. 584, 99 S.Ct. 2493 (1979).
47. Nowak et al., *Constitutional Law*, p. 455.
48. Ibid., p. 457.
49. Ibid., p. 510.
50. Goldberg v. Kelly, 397 U.S. 254, 90 S.Ct. 1011 (1970).
51. 470 U.S. 532, 105 S.Ct. 1487 (1985).
52. 424 U.S. 319, 96 S.Ct. 893 (1976).
53. Cleveland Board of Education v. Loudermill, op. cit.
54. Jackson, *Natural Justice*, p. 29.
55. Hortonville Joint School District No. 1 v. Hortonville Education Association, 426 U.S. 482, 96 S.Ct. 2308 (1976).
56. Grayned v. City of Rockport, 408 U.S. 104, 92 S.Ct. 2294 (1972).
57. United States v. Powell, 423 U.S. 87, 96 S.Ct. 316 (1975).
58. Coates v. City of Cincinnati, 402 U.S. 611, 91 S.Ct. 1686 (1971).
59. See Connally v. General Construction Company, 269 U.S. 385, 46 S.Ct. 126 (1926).
60. See Grayned v. City of Rockport, op. cit.
61. Village of Hoffman Estates v. Flipside, 455 U.S. 489, 102 S.Ct. 1186 (1982).
62. Board of Education of Jefferson County School District R-1 v. Wilder, 960 P.2d 695 (Colo.1998).
63. Ibid. See Coates v. City of Cincinnati, op. cit.
64. Board of Education of Jefferson County v. Wilder, op. cit. (citing United States v. Powell, 423 U.S. 87, 96 S.Ct. 316 (1975)).
65. Ellen W. Schrecker, *No Ivory Tower, McCarthyism and the Universities* (New York: Oxford University Press, 1986), p. 68.
66. 368 U.S. 278, 82 S.Ct. 275 (1961).
67. 377 U.S. 360, 84 S.Ct. 1316 (1964).
68. Ibid.
69. Cramp v. Board of Public Instruction of Orange County, Fla. 368 U.S. 278, 287, 82 S.Ct. 275, 281 (1961).
70. Speiser v. Randall, 357 U.S. 513, 526, 78 S.Ct. 1332, 1342 (1958).
71. Harry Kalven Jr., *A Worthy Tradition, Freedom of Speech in America*, ed. Jamie Kalven (New York: Harper & Row, 1988), p. 353.
72. Ibid., p. 359.
73. 403 U.S. 207, 91 S.Ct. 1772 (1971).
74. 405 U.S. 676, 92 S.Ct. 1332 (1972). Cole v. Richardson, 397 U.S. 238, 240, 90 S.Ct. 1099, 1100 (1970).
75. Ibid.
76. Kalven, *A Worthy Tradition*, pp. 366–67.
77. Howard, *Commentaries on the Constitution*, p. 201.
78. Tot v. United States, 319 U.S. 463, 63 S.Ct. 1241 (1943).
79. Vlandis v. Kline, 412 U.S. 441, 93 S.Ct. 2230 (1973).
80. 412 U.S. 441, 93 S.Ct. 2230 (1973).
81. Ibid.
82. 414 U.S. 632, 94 S.Ct. 791 (1974).
83. Edward S. Corwin, ed., *The Constitution of the United States of America* (Washington, D.C.: U.S. Government Printing Office, 1952), p. 1212.
84. Turner v. Department of Employment Security, 423 U.S. 44, 96 S.Ct. 249 (1975).
85. 412 U.S. at 459, 463.
86. Johnny H. Killian, ed., *The Constitution of the United States of America*, 1978 Supp. (Washington, D.C.: U.S. Government Printing Office, 1979), p. S209.

CHAPTER 17

DISCRIMINATION IN EMPLOYMENT

All persons without distinction of age or sex, birth or color, origin or condition,
are equal before the law. . . . [T]he rights of all, as they are settled and regulated
by law, are equally entitled to the paternal consideration and protection of the law.

—Lemuel Shaw, *Roberts v. City of Boston*,
59 Mass. (5. Cush.) 198, 206 (1849)

CHAPTER OUTLINE

- RACE DISCRIMINATION
- SEX DISCRIMINATION
- TITLE IX
- SEXUAL HARASSMENT
- RELIGIOUS DISCRIMINATION

- EQUAL PAY ACT
- AGE DISCRIMINATION
- DISCRIMINATION AGAINST PERSONS WITH DISABILITIES
- FAMILY AND MEDICAL LEAVE ACT OF 1993

AMONG THE MOST RELIABLE indications of the economic and social condition of a state or nation are the rate and level of employment of the people. Low rates of unemployment characterize economic success, while high rates of unemployment or underemployment are earmarks of societies that are functioning poorly. If high unemployment or underemployment continues unabated, it may produce strife that can potentially affect the stability of the government. A state or nation that functions effectively is held together by a bond among its people, a sense of community, that requires the fulfillment of duties to others and reciprocal moral obligations that are manifested in some reasonable de-

gree of equality of opportunity for all to obtain a desirable standard of living. Discord in society is generally the result of decisions by a prevailing segment of the society to pursue a course of narrow economic self-interest to the detriment of others. It has been justly maintained that societal interests are best served not by individuals exclusively pursuing their own self-interest but rather by all people cooperatively pursuing the interests of the whole.[1]

The cooperation necessary for a society to function effectively requires that social advantages be distributed with an underlying concern for fairness and justice. Fair opportunity for education and employment is critical—indeed, essential—to the well-being of both the individual and the state.[2] At the very least, there exists a moral obligation to prevent discrimination against certain individuals or groups for reasons unrelated to their capabilities or merits in the marketplace. Factors that condemn certain individuals or groups to lower levels of employment or create employment classes, beyond which elevation is difficult, are obviously harmful to the social fabric. Even though the United States is a large and economically powerful nation, it nevertheless suffers, as do many other nations, from discrimination in the workplace. Employment discrimination in the United States has been particularly acute because of the racial segregation that emanated from early conditions of servitude and slavery, and this unfortunate history has continued to plague the nation ever since.

The people of the United States have sought by both constitutional provision and statutory enactments to rid the nation of the prejudice and bias that emanate from a racially segregated past. The equal protection clause of the Fourteenth Amendment stands as the foremost guarantee against discrimination that may result from policies of state governments. The Congress, in reflecting the more humanitarian impulses of the American people, has supplemented the equal protection clause with several antidiscrimination statutes designed to create a more unified and just society. The centerpiece of these statutory protections is Title VII of the Civil Rights Act of 1964, which is a broad-based legislative prohibition specifically designed to eliminate discrimination in employment due to race, color, religion, sex, and national origin. Title VII seeks to ensure equal opportunity in employment in both the public and the private sectors. This act was promulgated under the authority vested in Congress by the commerce clause of the U.S. Constitution, which empowers Congress to "regulate purely private decision making"[3] that would tend to impede personal mobility or diminish interstate commerce. In interpreting the meaning of Title VII, the courts have given effect to Congress's desire to totally eliminate racial discrimination in public and private employment. The burden of proof borne by the plaintiff in an employment discrimination case is less difficult to carry under Title VII than under the equal protection clause. In claiming a violation of Title VII, the minority plaintiff employee need show only that the employer's policies caused a disproportionate impact on the minority. An action brought under the equal protection clause requires the plaintiff to prove that the employer intended to discriminate.[4]

Other statutes—the Equal Pay Act and the Age Discrimination in Employment Act—prohibit practices that classify persons according to sex or age. (See Appendix B.) Discrimination against persons with disabilities is prohibited in the Rehabilitation Act of 1973 and in the Americans with Disabilities Act of 1990.

This chapter discusses judicial precedents bearing on race, sex, age, and disability discrimination emanating from statutes, court decisions, and regulations that have influenced employment practices in public education.

■ RACE DISCRIMINATION

Since *Brown v. Board of Education* formally confronted racism in America providing the rationale and justification to redress all aspects of a segregated society, numerous employment practices have been litigated regarding discrimination in the public sector. Many cases have challenged hiring and testing practices, reductions of staff resulting in nonretention of minority employees, and reverse discrimination. Most of these cases have been brought under the equal protection clause of the Fourteenth Amendment and Title VII of the Civil Rights Act of 1964.

EQUAL PROTECTION

The equal protection clause of the Fourteenth Amendment prohibits actions by state governments that "draw lines" favoring or disfavoring a particular class of persons based on impermissible criteria. This clause has undoubtedly had greater impact on the social and economic condition in the United States than any other part of the U.S. Constitution and has had a particular influence on equality of employment opportunity. In noting the vital nature of the equal protection clause, *Nowak et al.*[5] have observed that "[i]n recent years the equal protection guarantee has become the single most important concept in the Constitution for the protection of individual rights."[6]

Enacted in 1868, in the aftermath of the Civil War, as a specific prohibition against state discrimination based on race or color, the clause today has evolved, and its applications have broadened to encompass protections against more subtle forms of discrimination. As noted in Chapter 10, the equal protection clause refers only to state governments: "No state shall . . . deny . . . equal protection of the laws." Today, however, through the evolution of judicial precedent, the equality protections guaranteed by the equal protection clause apply with the same force to the federal government through the due process clause of the Fifth Amendment.[7] Thus, neither states nor the federal government can deny equal protection.

Equal protection is premised on the theory of justice that each person has the right to the same advantages as any other person similarly situated.[8] The presumption is that all persons are to be treated equally in their employment, livelihood, and pursuit of happiness unless there exists some legitimate reason for treating them differently. Rakowski succinctly states the moral philosophy and justification that undergird equal protection in this way: "The basic rationale for adopting this principle is simple. People come into the world equally undeserving. Because no one has a greater claim to the earth or what lies on or beneath it than anyone else, all are entitled to equal shares."[9] Dworkin, a preeminent modern legal philosopher, has stated the corollary principle in this way: "People have a right not to suffer disadvantage in the distribution of social good and opportunities, including disadvantage in the liberties due to them . . . , just on the ground of the opinions and the way that the majority or public officials may view the circumstance."[10] Thus, persons equally situated must be treated equally in their employment. Human beings should in every respect be treated uniformly and impartially by government unless there is a good and sufficient reason to do otherwise.[11] There exists the moral presumption that "equality needs no reasons, only inequality does so."[12]

The Supreme Court, in interpreting equal protection's applications to governmental acts with regard to education and employment, has examined the nature of the classification of persons, the value of the advantages or disadvantages distributed, and the particular rationale by which departure from equality is justified. In this regard, the Supreme Court has developed certain tests for review of governmental actions. As discussed in some depth in other chapters of this text, the Court employs three standards of review for equal protection questions: (1) the rational relationship test, (2) the strict scrutiny test, and (3) the intermediate test. The first test is the most deferential to the legislature, presuming validity and placing the burden of proof on the plaintiff to show that the legislative act is unreasonable or irrational. Using this test, the Court will seek to determine whether the government's laws or regulations bear a rational relationship to a legitimate government end. The second type of review, generally referred to as "strict scrutiny," means that the justices will not defer to the government and will shift the burden of proof to the government to defend and to show that the classification and detriment imposed are of a compelling interest to the state. Strict scrutiny is invoked where a fundamental right is affected by a governmental action. The third test, the intermediate test, does not employ either the "rational relationship" or the "strict scrutiny" test but constitutes a middle-level analysis, sometimes described as a balancing test. This third standard tends to be applied in a somewhat *ad hoc* manner, in that the Court does not require a fundamental right to be denied before invoking the test. The Court requires only that there exist a "substantial relationship to an important interest." A good example of the application of this third test is *Plyler v. Doe*,[13] where the Court said that alien children had an important constitutional interest in education even though such an interest could not be construed to be at the higher level of a constitutional right that would qualify to invoke the strict scrutiny test. (See Chapter 6 for a discussion bearing on this point in *Plyler* and Chapter 19 for a corresponding discussion of *Rodriguez*.)[14]

Under equal protection, a question of racial discrimination requires the application of the strict scrutiny test, the most rigorous of the three tests. This is, of course, because discrimination based on race is most odious in view of our country's trials and tribulations in dealing with racial segregation. Thus, the purpose of the equal protection clause "is to prevent the states from purposefully discriminating between individuals on the basis of race."[15] It attempts to remove biased decisions from government. Therefore, discrimination based on race is suspect, and the Court will apply the most rigorous strict scrutiny test to the situation. The Supreme Court has stated that "[d]istinctions between citizens solely because of their ancestry are by their very nature odious to a free people whose institutions are founded upon the doctrine of equality," and "racial discriminations are . . . prohibited."[16] As a result, "preferring members of any one group for no reason other than race or ethnic origin is discrimination for its own sake. This the Constitution forbids."[17] In *Adarand Constructors, Inc. v. Pena*, the Supreme Court reinforced that these rigorous equal protection standards apply to all race classifications.[18]

Thus, if a governmental action distinguishes between individuals on the basis of race, then the courts will employ the strict scrutiny standard. This standard will apply to such actions whether they are "benign" or "remedial." In *City of Richmond v. J. A. Croson Co.*,[19] the Court stated:

> Absent searching judicial inquiry into the justifications for such race-based measures, there is simply no way of determining what classifications are "benign" or "remedial" and what classifications are in fact motivated by illegitimate notions of racial inferiority or simply racial politics. Indeed, the purpose of strict scrutiny is to "smoke out" illegitimate uses of race by assuring that the legislative body is pursuing a goal important enough to warrant use of a highly suspect tool. The test also ensures that the means chosen "fit" this compelling goal so closely that there is little or no possibility that the motive for the classification was illegitimate racial prejudice or stereotype.[20]

When addressing racial discrimination in employment using the strict scrutiny analysis, two questions are posed: (1) Does the racial classification serve a compelling government interest? (2) Is it narrowly tailored to achieve that goal?[21] By using strict scrutiny, the courts "will consistently give racial classifications . . . detailed examination both as to ends and as to means."[22]

TITLE VI

Title VI was passed in accordance with the constitutional authority vested in Congress in Section 5 of the Fourteenth Amendment, which provides that Congress may pass legislation to enforce the Fourteenth Amendment. Although Title VI and Title VII have the same prohibitory scope, they were enacted under different constitutional powers of Congress: Title VI under Section 5 of the Fourteenth Amendment and Title VII under the commerce clause. Title VI of the Civil Rights Act prohibits discrimination based on race, color, or national origin in federally assisted programs. Section 601 of Title VI of the Civil Rights Act reads as follows:

> No person in the United States shall, on the ground of race, color, or national origin, be excluded from participation in, be denied benefits of, or be subjected to discrimination under any program or activity receiving Federal financial assistance.

With Title VI, Congress provided a statutory remedy against discrimination apart from and beyond equal protection. The ultimate enforcement weapon given the federal agencies under this law is the denial of federal funds. It was under Title VI that *Adams v. Richardson*[23] originated, maintaining that the U.S. Department of Health, Education, and Welfare (HEW) had been derelict in its enforcement responsibilities and that federal funds could be withheld from institutions of higher education that discriminated based on race. In that case, a federal court assumed the responsibility for monitoring enforcement of federal regulations promulgated by HEW pursuant to Title VI. The Title VI regulation requires desegregation of faculty, administration, and other personnel positions in public schools and universities.

The Supreme Court has exhibited some uncertainty as to the application of Title VI. The problem lies in whether officials are required to redress *de jure* segregation only or whether they have a corresponding statutory obligation to correct racial imbalance caused by *de facto* segregation as well. In the *Bakke* case, Justice Powell, writing for a splintered majority, said that Title VI requirements were coterminous with those of the equal protection clause and that neither required school officials to correct unintended racial imbalances.[24] It is important to note that the Supreme Court in *Bakke* ruled only that Title VI was violated by discriminatory admissions policies. It did not hold that the admission policy violated Title VI and not the equal protection clause or Title VII of the Civil Rights Act. Justice Powell pointed out that the precedents under equal protection from the school desegregation cases were not relevant to *Bakke* because they involved remedies designed to redress specific constitutional violations pertaining to race. Title VII of the Civil Rights Act did not apply because that title applies to employment discrimination, and precedents pertaining to the employment of racial minorities in business and industry are not applicable to institutional admissions policies. Thus, equal protection, Title VI, and Title VII apply in different ways to protect against discriminatory educational and employment practices. On the other hand, four justices, while agreeing with Powell's general disposition of the case, disagreed with his interpretation of Title VI, maintaining that the congressional aim was to prohibit discrimination, regardless of intent. Writing for these four justices, Justice Stevens said that "the meaning of the Title VI ban on exclusion is crystal clear. Race cannot be the basis of excluding anyone from participation in a federally funded program." He further maintained that it was not necessary to liken Title VI to the equal protection clause, since Title VI emanated from its own legislative intent and history. But the Court in *Bakke* did clearly decide that a higher education institution's admissions policy that uses strict racial preferences violates Title VI, but an admissions program that allows admissions officers to consider race as an affirmative factor without using quotas or clear racial preferences is not violative of either Title VI or the equal protection clause.

Some clarification of the intent questions under Title VI did come forth in 1983 in the case of *Guardians Association v. Civil Service Commission of New York*.[25] In this case, the Court held that a private person may be compensated for a state agency's violation of his or her Title VI rights, but only if the person is able to show intent to discriminate. In other words, as now written, intent must be shown to exist before Title VI is violated and federal funds can be withheld.

TITLE VII

When first enacted in 1964,[26] Title VII did not extend to discriminatory employment practices in educational institutions, but in 1972, the law was amended, eliminating this exemption.[27] As a result, it is Title VII that has been used most often to challenge discrimination in teacher and administrator employment.

An area of major concern in applying Title VII has been employee testing for purposes of hiring and promotion. The Supreme Court has attempted to clarify Title VII by creating a distinction between "disparate impact" and "disparate treatment" cases, and it has applied different judicial standards to those two concepts. One of the first and most important disparate impact cases was *Griggs v. Duke Power Company*,[28] where in 1971 the Supreme Court enunciated the standards regarding employee testing. In this case, the Court found that Title VII of the Civil Rights Act prevented an employer from rejecting black job applicants on the basis of the lack of completion of high school or the results of a general intelligence test. Duke Power Company was unable to show that the general standards it had established were related to job performance. The Court said:

> The facts of this case demonstrate the inadequacy of broad and general testing devices as well as the infirmity of using diplomas or degrees as fixed measures of capability. Nothing in the Act precludes the use of testing or measuring procedures; obviously they are useful. What Congress has forbidden is giving these devices and mechanisms controlling force unless they are demonstrably a reasonable measure of job performance.[29]

After *Griggs*, several lower courts invalidated the use of the Graduate Record Examination and the National Teachers Examination as violative of due process and equal protection because the examinations were not job related. School districts, in these instances, were unable to shoulder the burden of showing job relatedness in the face of the high percentage of black teachers who were disqualified.[30]

According to *Griggs*, after the plaintiff successfully shows a disparate impact for a particular employment practice, the burden of going forward then shifts to the defendant to justify the practice by showing that the imbalance is related to job performance. The Supreme Court has attempted to further clarify the distinction between "disparate treatment" and "disparate impact" cases and has explained the two terms in this way:

> "Disparate treatment" . . . is the most easily understood type of discrimination. The employer simply

treats some people less favorably than others because of their race, color, religion, sex, or national origin. Proof of discriminatory motive is critical, although it can in some situations be inferred from the mere fact of differences in treatment. . . . Undoubtedly disparate treatment was the most obvious and Congress had it in mind when it enacted Title VII. . . . Claims of disparate treatment may be distinguished from claims that stress "disparate impact." The latter involves employment practices that are facially neutral in their treatment of different groups but in fact fall more heavily on one group than another and cannot be justified by business necessity. . . . Proof of discriminatory motive, we have held, is not required under a disparate impact theory.[31]

Disparate treatment cases generally involve a single plaintiff who challenges a particular practice that is detrimental to him or her personally. For example, a faculty member's claim that her promotion in a particular academic department was denied because of bias must be brought as a disparate treatment issue. The facts do not lend themselves to a showing of impact. On the other hand, disparate impact may be more easily shown in cases involving a number of persons who are affected by a particular employment practice, such as a requirement that all employees pass a test.

When a plaintiff presents evidence to substantiate a claim of disparate impact, the employer must then bear the burden of presenting evidence that the particular employment practice was justified as a "business necessity" or that it was "related to job performance." For example, a written examination indicating one's level of verbal skill has been held a valid device to select recruits for a police department.[32] Similarly, the National Teachers Examination has been found to be a valid "job-related" instrument to determine teacher qualifications for employment and pay.[33]

In 1991, the U.S. Congress passed the Civil Rights Act of 1991.[34] The act was passed in response to the perceived weakening of the scope and effectiveness of civil rights protections by the Supreme Court in *Wards Cove Packing Co. v. Atonio.*[35] This act overturned the *Wards Cove* decision, which had placed a greater burden on the plaintiff to prove disparate impact. Congress stated that the purposes of the act are "(1) to provide appropriate remedies for intentional discrimination and unlawful harassment in the workplace; (2) to codify the concept of 'business necessity' and 'job related' enunciated by the Supreme Court in *Griggs* . . . and in the other Supreme Court decisions prior to *Wards Cove*. . . ; (3) to confirm statutory authority and provide statutory guidelines for adjudication of disparate impact suits under Title VII . . . ; and (4) to respond to recent decisions of the Supreme Court by expanding the scope of relevant civil rights statutes in order to provide adequate protection to victims of discrimination."[36]

Also, the 1991 act allowed the plaintiff to recover compensatory and punitive damages under Title VII. The act had as its basic purpose to "strengthen and improve federal civil rights laws, to provide damages in cases of intentional employment discrimination, [and] to clarify provisions regarding disparate impact actions." The act includes the rights of victims of sex discrimination to sue for damages ranging from $50,000 for companies with 100 or fewer workers to $300,000 for employers with more than 500 workers. These damages are recoverable when "unlawful intentional discrimination 'occurred,' not [when] a practice is unlawful because of disparate impact."[37]

Thus, the Supreme Court has enunciated two routes by which plaintiffs can pursue discrimination under Title VII: disparate treatment and disparate impact. Under the former, the initial burden of proof is difficult to bear because the plaintiff must show a discriminatory motive. Under the latter, the initial burden of the plaintiff is less difficult to sustain, but this is offset because the courts have allowed substantial leeway to defendants in showing "business necessity" or "job relatedness."

❖ — ❖ — ❖

Employment Standards and Tests That Are Not Significantly Related to Job Performance Violate Title VII of the Civil Rights Act of 1964

Griggs v. Duke Power Co.

Supreme Court of the United States, 1971.
401 U.S. 424, 91 S.Ct. 849.

Mr. Chief Justice BURGER delivered the opinion of the Court. We granted the writ in this case to resolve the question whether an employer is prohibited by the Civil Rights Act of 1964, Title VII, from requiring a high school education or passing of a standardized general intelligence test as a condition of employment in or transfer to jobs when (a) neither standard is shown to be significantly related to successful job performance, (b) both requirements operate to disqualify Negroes at a substantially higher rate than white applicants, and (c) the jobs in question formerly had been filled only by white employees as part of a longstanding practice of giving preference to whites. . . .

The objective of Congress in the enactment of Title VII is plain from the language of the statute. It was to achieve equality of employment opportunities and remove barriers that have operated in the past to favor an identifiable group of white employees over other employees. Under the Act, practices, procedures, or tests neutral on their face, and even neutral in terms of intent, cannot be maintained if they operate to "freeze" the status quo of prior discriminatory employment practices.

The Court of Appeals' opinion, and the partial dissent, agreed that, on the record in the present case, "whites register far better on the Company's alternative requirements" than Negroes. . . . Because they are Negroes, petitioners have long received inferior education in segregated schools and this court expressly recognized these differences in *Gaston County v. United States*, 395 U.S. 285, 89 S.Ct. 1720 (1969). . . . Congress did not intend by Title VII, however, to guarantee a job to every person regardless of qualifications. In short, the Act does not command that any person be hired simply because he was formerly the subject of discrimination, or because he is a member of a minority group. Discriminatory preference for any group, minority or majority, is precisely and only what Congress has proscribed. What is required by Congress is the removal of artificial, arbitrary, and unnecessary barriers to employment when the barriers operate invidiously to discriminate on the basis of racial or other impermissible classification.

. . . The Act proscribes not only overt discrimination but also practices that are fair in form, but discriminatory in operation. The touchstone is business necessity. If an employment practice that operates to exclude Negroes cannot be shown to be related to job performance, the practice is prohibited.

On the record before us, neither the high school completion requirement nor the general intelligence test is shown to bear a demonstrable relationship to successful performance of the jobs for which it was used. Both were adopted, as the Court of Appeals noted, without meaningful study of their relationship to job-performance ability. . . .

The evidence, however, shows that employees who have not completed high school or taken the tests have continued to perform satisfactorily and make progress in departments for which the high school and test criteria are not used. The promotion record of present employees who would not be able to meet the new criteria thus suggests the possibility that the requirements may not be needed even for the limited purpose of preserving the avowed policy of advancement within the Company. . . .

The Court of Appeals held that the Company had adopted the diploma and test requirements without any "intention to discriminate against Negro employees." . . . But Congress directed the thrust of the Act to the *consequences* of employment practices, not simply the motivation. More than that, Congress has placed on the employer the burden of showing that any given requirement must have a manifest relationship to the employment in question.

The facts of this case demonstrate the inadequacy of broad and general testing devices as well as the infirmity of using diplomas or degrees as fixed measures of capability. . . .

Nothing in the Act precludes the use of testing or measuring procedures; obviously they are useful. What Congress has forbidden is giving these devices and mechanisms controlling force unless they are demonstrably a reasonable measure of job performance. Congress has not commanded that the less qualified be preferred over the better qualified simply because of minority origins. Far from disparaging job qualifications as such, Congress has made such qualifications the controlling factor, so that race, religion, nationality, and sex become irrelevant. What Congress has commanded is that any tests used must measure the person for the job and not the person in the abstract.

❖ — ❖ — ❖

State Use of Test Scores Both for Certification Purposes and as a Salary Factor Does Not Violate Equal Protection Clause or Title VII of Civil Rights Act

United States v. South Carolina

United States District Court,
District of South Carolina, 1977.
445 F.Supp. 1094, affirmed, 434 U.S. 1026,
98 S.Ct. 756 (1978).

Before HAYNSWORTH and RUSSELL, Circuit Judges and SIMONS, District Judge. . . . The defendants are charged with violations of the Fourteenth Amendment to the Constitution of the United States and Title VII of the Civil Rights Act of 1964, as amended, 42 U.S.C. §2000e, et seq., (1970), through the use of minimum score requirements on the National Teacher Examinations (hereinafter "NTE") to certify and determine the pay levels of teachers within the State. . . .

For over thirty years the State of South Carolina and its agencies have used scores on the NTE to make decisions with respect to the certification of teachers and the amount of state aid payable to local school districts. Local school boards within the State use scores on the NTE for selection and compensation of teachers. From 1969 to 1976, a minimum score of 975 was required by the State for its certification and state aid decisions. In June, 1976, after an exhaustive validation study by Educational Testing Service (ETS), and after a critical review and evaluation of this study by the Board of Education's Committee on Teacher Recruitment, Training and Compensation and the Department Staff, the State established new certification requirements involving different minimum scores in various areas of teaching specialization that range from 940 to 1198. . . .

Plaintiffs challenge each of the uses of the NTE. They contend that more blacks than whites historically have failed to achieve the required minimum score, and that this result creates a racial classification in violation of the constitutional and statutory provisions cited in their complaints. . . .

We first consider whether the use by the State and its Board of Education of a minimum score requirement on the NTE violates the equal protection clause of the Fourteenth Amendment. . . .

In disposing of the remaining constitutional claims, separate consideration must be given to the State's use of the test scores to certify teachers and to determine the amount of state aid for local school districts. Plaintiffs allege that the disparate racial impact of defendants' certification and compensation systems creates a racial classification in violation of the Fourteenth Amendment. In order to sustain that allegation, the Supreme Court's decision in *Washington v. Davis*, 426 U.S. 229, 96 S.Ct. 2040, 48 L.Ed. 2d 597 (1976), requires plaintiffs to prove that the State intended to create and use a racial classification. If plaintiffs fail to prove intent (or defendants adequately rebut that proof), then we must evaluate this classification under the rational relationship standard required by the Fourteenth Amendment as to all such classifications.

Because of its paramount importance under *Washington v. Davis*, we look first at whether the plaintiffs have proved that any of the challenged decisions of defendants were motivated by an intent to discriminate. The purpose or intent that we must assess is the purpose or intent that underlies the particular act or acts under review. . . .

South Carolina requires persons who teach in the public schools to hold a certificate issued by the State Board of Education. S.C. Code §21-354. From 1945 to the present the State has had four certification systems, each requiring prospective teachers to take the NTE. Candidates are able to take the NTE an unlimited number of times. (The tests are given by the State three or four times each year).

The record before us indicates that during this period, the racial composition of the South Carolina teacher force has closely paralleled the racial composition of the State's population. . . .

From 1945 through 1968, the State issued four grades of certificates: A, B, C and D. From

1945 through 1956, candidates were awarded certificates based on their relative standing with respect to test scores of all candidates in the State for the year. . . .

In 1957, a new system of absolute, rather than relative, requirements was instituted. Under this system, a score of 500 or more on the Common Examinations portion of the NTE was required for an *A* certificate; a score of 425 to 499 for a *B* certificate; a score of 375 to 424 for a *C* certificate; and a score of 332 to 374 for a *D* certificate. . . .

In 1969, the certification system was further revised by replacing the four-tiered system with two types of certificates: the professional certificate and the warrant. . . . Those who attained scores below 400 were not licensed. In the academic year 1969–70, the maximum score requirement of 400 on the Common Examinations eliminated approximately 41 percent of the graduates of predominantly black colleges and less than 1 percent of the graduates of predominantly white colleges. Similar results were obtained in succeeding years, despite the fact that a score of 400 is usually below the 11th percentile nationally, and almost 90 percent of the candidates who take these tests get a higher score.

In 1976, the certification system was again revised, the two-tiered system being replaced with a single certificate with separate minimum score requirements in each of the eighteen fields of teaching specialty replacing the single minimum score requirement. These combined scores on both common Examinations and Area Examinations ranged from 940 in Agriculture to 1178 in Library and Media Specialties. . . . There are no statistics in the record indicating the impact of the new score requirements because they will be applied first to the class of 1977; however, plaintiffs predict that, under these requirements the disparate impact may be even greater. . . .

With respect to the constitutional challenge to South Carolina's use of the NTE for certification purposes, we conclude that the plaintiffs have not demonstrated the required discriminatory intent with respect to any of the specific decisions setting certification standards based on NTE scores. This is especially true in connection with the State's 1976 change in requirements where there is no indication whatsoever that the State and its officers were motivated by

anything more than a desire to use an accepted and racially neutral standardized test to evaluate the teacher applicants competing for relatively few jobs in South Carolina.

The NTE are developed and administered by ETS, an independent nonprofit organization of recognized professional reputation. ETS recommends that minimum score requirements not be used as a sole determinant of certification decisions where other appropriate information or criteria are available.

In this case, the plaintiffs have come forth with no other reasonably appropriate criteria upon which certification may be properly based.

Neither have plaintiffs been able to establish any defect in the NTE indicating that the examinations themselves discriminate on the basis of race. The choices as to subject matter and question format are reasonable and well-documented on the record, and although other subject matters or other examination forms might be possible or even preferable, there is no proof of any inherent discrimination. The inference that plaintiffs would have us draw from the statistics which indicate that blacks as a group have lower average scores than whites is rebutted by the evidence with respect to the construction of the tests and their content validity. Since we find that the NTE create classifications only on permissible bases (presence or absence of knowledge or skill and ability in applying knowledge), and that they are not used pursuant to any intent to discriminate, their use in making certification decisions by the State is proper and legal.

Plaintiffs raise a separate constitutional challenge to South Carolina's use of the NTE as a partial determinant of the salaries paid to public school teachers. The use of the NTE for salary purposes is distinct from, and, in significant ways, unrelated to the use of the NTE for certification purposes. Accordingly, we must again examine plaintiffs' proof with respect to intent. . . .

We are unable to find a discriminatory intent from these facts, even though the historical background of a dual pay system and a delay in implementing a unitary system after the Fourth Circuit struck down a similar system in another state provide some support for such an inference. Such inference is adequately rebutted by the evidence with respect to what the Legislature actually did. The unitary pay system was based in part on the amount of educational training and years of teaching experience possessed by each teacher. Plaintiffs make no claim that the use of either of these factors was motivated by discriminatory intent, and it is evident that the monetary rewards available through these avenues alone, without regard to the grade of certificate, were significant. The link between the new unitary pay system and the new certification system is not without a reasoned basis. It was important to the State to use its limited resources to improve the quality of the teacher force and to put whatever monetary incentives were available in the salary schedule to that task. As before stated, we have found that no discriminatory intent has been established with respect to the decision in 1945 to adopt a certification system based in part on NTE scores; and, therefore, without independent proof, there is no associated discriminatory intent in linking the certification and salary systems. . . .

In the absence of discriminatory intent, the classifications of teachers for both certification and pay purposes may be assessed under the "rational relationship" standard required by the Fourteenth Amendment of all classifications. . . .

We conclude that the State's use of the NTE for both certification and pay purposes meets the "rational relationship" standard of *McGowan v. Maryland,* supra, and consequently does not violate the equal protection clause of the Fourteenth Amendment. . . .

. . . [W]e find that the defendants have offered a legitimate and important governmental objective for their use of the NTE. The State has the right to adopt academic requirements and to use written achievement tests designed and validated to disclose the minimum amount of knowledge necessary to effective teaching. . . . We conclude that these are entirely legitimate and clearly important governmental objectives.

In considering whether defendants' use of the NTE bears a fair and substantial relationship to these governmental objectives, we conclude that it does.

The record supports the conclusion that the NTE are professionally and carefully prepared to measure the critical mass of knowledge in academic subject matter. The NTE do not measure teaching skills, but do measure the content of the academic preparation of prospective teachers. . . . [T]he NTE program "is neutral on its face and rationally may be said to serve a purpose the Government is constitutionally empowered to pursue." . . . Plaintiffs have not contended nor proved that the NTE are racially biased or otherwise deficient when measured against the applicable professional and legal standards.

Furthermore, there is ample evidence in the record of the content validity of the NTE. The NTE have been demonstrated to provide a useful measure of the extent to which prospective teachers have mastered the content of their teacher training programs. In a similar challenge to a bar examination the Fourth Circuit has held that proof of such content validity is persuasive evidence that the equal protection clause has not been violated. *Richardson v. McFadden*, 540 F.2d 744 (4th Cir.1976). The Supreme Court has held that a substantial relationship between a test and a training program—such as is found here—is sufficient to withstand challenge on constitutional grounds. *Washington v. Davis*, 426 U.S. at 248–52, 96 S.Ct. 2040. State officials surely have the right to require graduation from approved teacher training programs as a prerequisite to being certified to teach in South Carolina. Plaintiffs have acknowledged the substantial relationship between the academic training program and the job of teaching by advocating that a requirement of graduation from an approved program alone is sufficient to protect the public interest. . . .

We also conclude that defendants' use of the NTE for salary purposes bears the necessary relationship to South Carolina's objectives with respect to its public school teaching force. Although the NTE were not designed to evaluate experienced teachers, the State could reasonably conclude that the NTE provided a reliable and economical means for measuring one element of effective teaching—the degree of knowledge possessed by the teacher. . . .

We turn now to the question whether defendants' uses of the NTE violate Title VII, 42 U.S.C.A. §2000e, et seq. . . .

The remaining claims under Title VII must be tested under statutory standards. In *Washington v. Davis*, 426 U.S. 229, 96 S.Ct. 2040, 48 L.Ed.2d 597 (1976), the Supreme Court summarized the order of proof:

Under Title VII, Congress provided that when hiring and promotion practices disqualifying substantially disproportionate numbers of blacks are challenged, discriminatory purpose need not be proved, and that it is an insufficient response to demonstrate some rational basis for the challenged practices. It is necessary, in addition, that they be "validated" in terms of job performance in any one of several ways, perhaps by ascertaining the minimum skill, ability or potential necessary for the position at issue and determining whether the qualifying tests are appropriate for the selection of qualified applicants for the job in question. (Id. at 246, 96 S.Ct. at 2051).

Thus, it was held not sufficient for the governmental entity to prove that the classification resulting from the test scores had a rational basis, that is, that it differentiated between persons who did and did not have some minimum verbal and communication skill. It was necessary, in addition, for the governmental entity to demonstrate that the minimum verbal and communication skill, in turn, had some rational relationship to the legitimate employment objectives of the employer . . . , that the employment practice must be a "business necessity." Id. at 431, 91 S.Ct. 849.

Plaintiffs have proved that the use of NTE scores by the State in its certification decisions disqualifies substantially disproportionate numbers of blacks. The burden of proof was thereby shifted to the defendants, and in an effort to meet this burden the State commissioned an extensive validity study by ETS. The design of this study is novel, but consistent with the basic requirements enunciated by the Supreme Court, and we accordingly hold such study sufficient to meet the burden placed on defendants under Title VII.

The study seeks to demonstrate content validity by measuring the degree to which the content of the tests matches the content of the teacher training programs in South Carolina. It also seeks to establish a minimum score requirement by estimating the amount of knowledge (measured by the ability to answer correctly test questions that have been content-validated) that a minimally qualified teacher candidate in South Carolina would have. . . .

We find that the results of the validity study are sufficiently trustworthy to sustain defen-

dants' burden under Title VII. . . . Plaintiffs misconceive their burden once defendants have made a reasonable showing that the study was executed in a responsible, professional manner designed to produce trustworthy results. In order to rebut the presumption that trustworthy results were indeed produced, plaintiffs must not only show that the study was not executed as intended, but also that the results were adversely affected. . . .

There remains, however, the question whether the State has satisfied the "business necessity" requirement set out in *Griggs v. Duke Power Co.,* 401 U.S. 424, 91 S.Ct. 849, 28 L.Ed.2d 158 (1971). This "business necessity" doctrine appears neither in the explicit language nor the legislative history of Title VII. The Court in *Griggs* and subsequent Title VII cases did not establish judicial standards for determining whether a particular practice is a business necessity. The EEOC Guidelines are of little assistance because they were published before *Griggs* and have not been updated since that time.

We think that *Griggs* did not import into Title VII law the concept of "compelling interest" developed as a part of the "strict scrutiny" standard for assessing certain classifications under the Fourteenth Amendment. Under this concept, the Court would balance the disparate impact on blacks against the business purpose of the employer and uphold the business practice only if it were sufficiently "compelling" to overcome the disparate impact. It is our view that the Supreme Court intended an examination of the alternatives available with respect to the legitimate employment objective identified by the employer to determine whether there is available to the employer an alternative practice that would achieve his business purpose equally well but with a lesser disparate impact by race. In examining alternatives, the risk and cost to the employer are relevant.

Here, plaintiffs have suggested only one alternative to the use of the NTE for certification purposes. Plaintiffs contend that mere graduation from an approved program should be sufficient and would have a lesser disparate impact on blacks. We cannot find that this alternative will achieve the State's purpose in certifying minimally competent persons equally well as the use of a content-validated standardized test.

The record amply demonstrates that there are variations in admissions requirements, academic standards and grading practices at the various teacher training institutions within the State. The approval that the State gives to the teacher training program is to general subject matter areas covered by the program, not to the actual course content of the program, and not to the means used within the program to measure whether individual students have actually mastered the course content to which they have been exposed. The standardized test scores do reflect individual achievement with respect to specific subject matter content, which is directly relevant to (although not sufficient in itself to assure) competence to teach, and thus the use of these scores for certification purposes survives the business necessity test under Title VII.

There remains, finally, the question whether the uses of the NTE for salary purposes are a violation of Title VII. . . .

We believe that a distinction for pay purposes between those who are qualified as well as between those who are not qualified survives the business necessity test. There appears to be no alternative available to the State, within reasonable limits of risk and cost, for providing the incentive necessary to motivate thousands of persons to acquire, generally on their own time and at their own expense, the necessary additional academic training so that they will be minimally competent teachers. Having made the investment of four years in an undergraduate education, it seems reasonable to try to upgrade the talent of unqualified teachers where possible, rather than rejecting them altogether.

In accordance with the foregoing findings and conclusions, we conclude that plaintiff and plaintiff-intervenors have failed to establish their right to any of the relief sought in their respective complaints. It is, therefore,

Ordered that judgment be entered in favor of the defendants.

Case Notes

1. Because of the difficulties of proving intent, most litigation under Title VII has been concerned with disparate impact. A disparate treatment plaintiff, in establishing a *prima facie* case, must show that four basic factors are true:

"(i) that he belongs to a racial minority; (ii) that he applied and was qualified for a job for which the employer was seeking applicants; (iii) that, despite his qualifications, he was rejected; and (iv) that after his rejection, the position remained open and the employer continued to seek applicants from persons of complainant's qualifications." *McDonnell Douglas Corp. v. Green*, 411 U.S. 792, 93 S.Ct. 1817 (1973).

The *McDonnell Douglas* standards for establishing a *prima facie* case are flexible. Facts will vary from case to case, and specifications for *prima facie* proof will not necessarily be the same in every aspect. "A *prima facie* case under *McDonnell Douglas* raises an inference of discrimination only because [the courts] presume these acts, if otherwise unexplained, are more likely than not based on the consideration of impermissible factors." *Furnco Construction Corp. v. Waters*, 438 U.S. 567, 98 S.Ct. 2943 (1978).

Therefore, to dispel the adverse inference from a *prima facie* showing, all the employer needs to do is "articulate some legitimate, nondiscriminatory reason for the employee's rejection." *McDonnell Douglas Corp. v. Green*, 411 U.S. 792, 93 S.Ct. 1817 (1978). After the employer has articulated some legitimate reason, the plaintiff must be afforded the opportunity to present evidence that this is no more than a pretext for discrimination.

2. In *Board of Trustees of Keene State College v. Sweeney*, 439 U.S. 24, 99 S.Ct. 295 (1978), the appeals court had required the defendant university "to prove [the] absence of [a] discriminatory motive." The Supreme Court reaffirmed *Furnco* and distinguished among "articulate," "show," and "prove." "[W]e think that there is a significant distinction between merely 'articulating some legitimate, nondiscriminatory reason' and 'proving absence of discriminatory motive.'" The case was remanded to the lower court to allow the university to articulate a legitimate reason as established and defined by the Supreme Court.

3. Perhaps the best explanation of the evidentiary requirements of Title VII is set forth by Supreme Court Justice Sandra Day O'Connor in *Watson v. Fort Worth Bank and Trust*, 487 U.S. 977, 108 S.Ct. 2777 (1988). In *Watson*, Justice O'Connor clarifies the complexities of the Supreme Court precedents with regard to the proof requirements

for both plaintiffs and defendants under disparate treatment and disparate impact analysis. In the *Watson* case, the Supreme Court vacated a U.S. court of appeals decision and remanded the case, ruling that "a Title VII challenge to a discretionary or subjective promotion system can only be analyzed under the disparate treatment model." In so overruling the lower court, the Supreme Court concluded that "disparate impact analysis is in principle no less applicable to subjective employment criteria than to objective or standardized tests." *Ibid.* at 978, 108 S.Ct. at 2779. The following material is quoted from Justice O'Connor's opinion in *Watson* (the side-heads have been added for emphasis):

DISPARATE TREATMENT. Several of our decisions have dealt with the evidentiary standards that apply when an individual alleges that an employer has treated that particular person less favorably than others because of the plaintiff's race, color, religion, sex, or national origin. In such "disparate treatment" cases, which involve "the most easily understood type of discrimination," . . . the plaintiff is required to prove that the defendant had a discriminatory intent or motive.

BURDEN OF PROOF. In order to facilitate the orderly consideration of relevant evidence, we have devised a series of shifting evidentiary burdens that are "intended progressively to sharpen the inquiry into the elusive factual question of intentional discrimination." . . . Under that scheme, a prima facie case is ordinarily established by proof that the employer, after having rejected the plaintiff's application for a job or promotion, continued to seek applicants with qualifications similar to the plaintiff's. . . . The burden of proving a prima facie case is "not onerous," . . . and the employer in turn may rebut it simply by producing some evidence that it had legitimate, nondiscriminatory reasons for the decision. If the defendant carries this burden of production, the plaintiff must prove by a preponderance of all the evidence in the case that the legitimate reasons offered by the defendant were a pretext for discrimination.

PLAINTIFF BEARS ULTIMATE BURDEN. We have cautioned that these shifting burdens are meant only to aid courts and litigants in arranging the presentation of evidence: "The ultimate burden of persuading the trier of fact that the defendant intentionally discriminated against the plaintiff remains at all times with the plaintiff."

DISPARATE IMPACT. In *Griggs v. Duke Power Co.*, 401 U.S. 424, 91 S.Ct. 849, 28 L.Ed.2d 158 (1971), this Court held that a plaintiff need not necessarily prove intentional discrimination in order to establish that an employer has violated §703. In certain cases, facially neutral employment practices that have significant adverse effects on protected *groups* have been held to violate the Act without proof that the employer adopted those practices with a discriminatory intent. The factual issues and the character of the evidence are inevitably somewhat different when the plaintiff is exempted from the need to prove intentional discrimination. . . . The evidence in these "disparate impact" cases usually focuses on statistical disparities, rather than specific incidents, and on competing explanations for those disparities.

FEATURES OF DISPARATE IMPACT. The distinguishing features of the factual issues that typically dominate in disparate impact cases do not imply that the ultimate legal issue is different than in cases where disparate treatment analysis is used. . . . Nor do we think it is appropriate to hold a defendant liable for unintentional discrimination on the basis of less evidence than is required to prove intentional discrimination. Rather, the necessary premise of the disparate impact approach is that some employment practices, adopted without a deliberately discriminatory motive, may in operation be functionally equivalent to intentional discrimination.

Perhaps the most obvious examples of such functional equivalence have been found where facially neutral job requirements necessarily operated to perpetuate the effects of intentional discrimination that occurred before Title VII was enacted. In *Griggs* itself, for example, the employer had a history of overt racial discrimination that predated the enactment of the Civil Rights Act of 1964. . . . Such conduct had apparently ceased thereafter, but the employer continued to follow employment policies that had "a markedly disproportionate" adverse effect on blacks. . . . The *Griggs* Court found that these policies, which involved the use of general aptitude tests and a high school diploma requirement, were not demonstrably related to the jobs for which they were used. . . .

FACIAL NEUTRALITY. Believing that diplomas and tests could become "masters of reality," which would perpetuate the effects of pre-Act discrimination, the Court concluded that such practices could not be defended simply on the basis of their facial neutrality or on the basis of the employer's lack of discriminatory intent.

This Court has repeatedly reaffirmed the principle that some facially neutral employment practices may violate Title VII even in the absence of a demonstrated discriminatory intent. We have not limited this principle to cases in which the challenged practice served to perpetuate the effects of pre-Act intentional discrimination.

SUBJECTIVE CRITERIA. Each of our subsequent decisions, however, like *Griggs* itself, involved standardized employment tests or criteria. . . . In contrast, we have consistently used conventional disparate-treatment theory, in which proof of intent to discriminate is required, to review hiring and promotion decisions that were based on the exercise of personal judgment or the application of inherently subjective criteria. . . .

Our decisions have not addressed the question whether disparate impact analysis may be applied to cases in which subjective criteria are used to make employment decisions. As noted above, the Courts of Appeals are in conflict on the issue. In order to resolve this conflict, we must determine whether the reasons that support the use of disparate impact analysis apply to subjective employment practices, and whether such analysis can be applied in this new context under workable evidentiary standards. . . .

We are persuaded that our decisions in *Griggs* and succeeding cases could largely be nullified if disparate impact analysis were applied only to standardized selection practices.

SUBJECTIVE VERSUS OBJECTIVE CRITERIA. However one might distinguish "subjective" from "objective" criteria, it is apparent that selection systems that combine both types would generally have to be considered subjective in nature. Thus, for example, if the employer in *Griggs* had consistently preferred applicants who had a high school diploma and who passed the company's general aptitude test, its selection system could nonetheless have been considered "subjective" if it also included brief interviews with the candidates. So long as an employer refrained from making standardized criteria absolutely determinative, it would remain free to give such tests almost as much weight as it chose without risking a disparate impact challenge. If we announced a rule that allowed employers so easily to insulate themselves from liability under *Griggs*, disparate impact analysis might effectively be abolished.

We are also persuaded that disparate impact analysis is in principle no less applicable to subjective employment criteria than to objective or standardized tests. In either case, a facially neutral practice, adopted without discriminatory intent, may have effects that are indistinguishable from intentionally discriminatory practices. It is true, to be sure, that an employer's policy of leaving promotion decisions to the unchecked discretion of lower level supervisors should itself raise no inference of discriminatory conduct. Especially in relatively small businesses like respondent's it may be customary and quite reasonable simply to delegate employment decisions to those employees who are most familiar with the jobs to be filled and with the candidates for those jobs. It does not follow, however, that the particular supervisors to whom this discretion is delegated always act without discriminatory intent. Furthermore, even if one assumed that any such discrimination can be adequately policed through disparate treatment analysis, the problem of subconscious stereotypes and prejudices would remain. . . . If an employer's undisciplined system of subjective decisionmaking has precisely the same effects as a system pervaded by impermissible intentional discrimination, it is difficult to see why Title VII's proscription against discriminatory actions should not apply. In both circumstances, the employer's practices may be said to "adversely affect [an individual's] status as an employee, because of such individual's race, color, religion, sex, or national origin." 42 U.S.C. §2000e-2(a)(2). We conclude, accordingly, that subjective or discretionary employment practices may be analyzed under the disparate impact approach in appropriate cases. . . .

It is completely unrealistic to assume that unlawful discrimination is the sole cause of people failing to gravitate to jobs and employers in accord with the laws of chance. . . . It would be equally unrealistic to suppose that employers can eliminate, or discover and explain, the myriad of innocent causes that may lead to statistical imbalances in the composition of their work forces.

CONGRESSIONAL INTENT. Congress has specifically provided that employers are not required to avoid "disparate impact" as such:

> Nothing contained in [Title VII] shall be interpreted to require any employer . . . to grant preferential treatment to any individual or to any group because of the race, color, religion, sex, or national origin of such individual or group on account of an imbalance which may exist with respect to the total number or percentage of persons of any race, color, religion, sex, or national origin employed by any employer . . . in comparison with the total number or percentage of persons of such race, color, religion, sex, or national origin in any community, State, section, or other area, or in the available work force in any community, State, section, or other area. 42 U.S.C. §2000e-2(j).

EMPLOYER RESPONSE. Preferential treatment and the use of quotas by public employers subject to

Title VII can violate the Constitution; see, *e.g.,* *Wygant v. Jackson Bd. of Education,* 476 U.S. 267, 106 S.Ct. 1842, 90 L.Ed.2d 260 (1986), and it has long been recognized that legal rules leaving any class of employers with "little choice" but to adopt such measures would be "far from the intent of Title VII." . . . [E]xtending disparate impact analysis to subjective employment practices has the potential to create a Hobson's choice for employers and thus to lead in practice to perverse results. If quotas and preferential treatment become the only cost-effective means of avoiding expensive litigation and potentially catastrophic liability, such measures will be widely adopted. The prudent employer will be careful to ensure that its programs are discussed in euphemistic terms, but will be equally careful to ensure that the quotas are met. Allowing the evolution of disparate impact analysis to lead to this result would be contrary to Congress' clearly expressed intent, and it should not be the effect of our decision today.

We do not believe that disparate impact theory need have any chilling effect on legitimate business practices. We recognize, however, that today's extension of that theory into the context of subjective selection practices could increase the risk that employers will be given incentives to adopt quotas or to engage in preferential treatment. Because Congress has so clearly and emphatically expressed its intent that Title VII not lead to this result, 42 U.S.C. §2000e-2(j), we think it imperative to explain in some detail why the evidentiary standards that apply in these cases should serve as adequate safeguards against the danger that Congress recognized. Our previous decisions offer guidance, but today's extension of disparate impact analysis calls for a fresh and somewhat closer examination of the constraints that operate to keep that analysis within its proper bounds.

Plaintiff's Burden. First, we note that the plaintiff's burden in establishing a prima facie case goes beyond the need to show that there are statistical disparities in the employer's work force. The plaintiff must begin by identifying the specific employment practice that is challenged. Although this has been relatively easy to do in challenges to standardized tests, it may sometimes be more difficult when subjective selection criteria are at issue. Especially in cases where an employer combines subjective criteria with the use of more rigid standardized rules or tests, the plaintiff is in our view responsible for isolating and identifying the specific employment practices that are allegedly responsible for any observed statistical disparities. . . .

Causation. Once the employment practice at issue has been identified, causation must be provided;

that is, the plaintiff must offer statistical evidence of a kind and degree sufficient to show that the practice in question has caused the exclusion of applicants for jobs or promotions because of their membership in a protected group. Our formulas, which have never been framed in terms of any rigid mathematical formula, have consistently stressed that statistical disparities must be sufficiently substantial that they raise such an inference of causation. . . .

Statistical Evidence. Nor are courts or defendants obliged to assume that plaintiffs' statistical evidence is reliable. . . . ("If the defendants in a Title VII suit believe there to be any reason to discredit plaintiffs' statistics that does not appear on their face, the opportunity to challenge them is available to the defendants just as in any other lawsuit. They may endeavor to impeach the reliability of the statistical evidence, they may offer rebutting evidence, or they may disparage in arguments or in briefs the probative weight which the plaintiffs' evidence should be accorded . . .").

Business Necessity or Job Relatedness. A second constraint on the application of disparate impact theory lies in the nature of the "business necessity" or "job relatedness" defense. Although we have said that an employer has "the burden of showing that any given requirement must have a manifest relationship to the employment in question," *Griggs,* 401 U.S., at 432, 19 S.Ct., at 854, such a formulation should not be interpreted as implying that the ultimate burden of proof can be shifted to the defendant. On the contrary, the ultimate burden of proving that discrimination against a protected group has been caused by a specific employment practice remains with the plaintiff at all times. Thus, when a plaintiff has made out a prima facie case of disparate impact, and when the defendant has met its burden of producing evidence that its employment practices are based on legitimate business reasons, the plaintiff must "show that other tests or selection devices, without a similarly undesirable racial effect, would also serve the employer's legitimate interest in efficient and trustworthy workmanship." . . . Factors such as the cost or other burdens of proposed alternative selection devices are relevant in determining whether they would be equally as effective as the challenged practice in serving the employer's legitimate business goals. The same factors would also be relevant in determining whether the challenged practice has operated as the functional equivalent of a pretext for discriminatory treatment.

Employer's Evidence. Our cases make it clear that employers are not required, even when defending standardized or objective tests, to introduce formal "validation studies" showing that particular criteria predict actual on-the-job performance. . . .

In the context of subjective or discretionary employment decisions, the employer will often find it easier than in the case of standardized tests to produce evidence of a "manifest relationship to the employment in question." It is self-evident that many jobs, for example those involving managerial responsibilities, require personal qualities that have never been considered amenable to standardized testing. In evaluating claims that discretionary employment practices are insufficiently related to legitimate business purposes, it must be borne in mind that "[c]ourts are generally less competent than employers to restructure business practices, and unless mandated to do so by Congress they should not attempt it." . . . ("[The] criteria [used by a university to award tenure], however difficult to apply and however much disagreement they generate in particular cases, are job related. . . . It would be a most radical interpretation of Title VII for a court to enjoin use of an historically settled process and plainly relevant criteria largely because they lead to decisions which are difficult for a court to review"). In sum, the high standards of proof in disparate impact cases are sufficient in our view to avoid giving employers incentives to modify any normal and legitimate practices by introducing quotas or preferential treatment.

❖ — ❖ — ❖

Percentage of Black Teachers in the School District Compared to Percentage of Blacks in the School Teacher Population in the Relevant Labor Market Is a Statistical Criterion of Discrimination

Hazelwood School District v. United States

Supreme Court of the United States, 1977.
433 U.S. 299, 97 S.Ct. 2736.

Mr. Justice STEWART delivered the opinion of the Court. The petitioner Hazelwood School District covers seventy-eight square miles in the northern part of St. Louis County, Mo. In 1973 the Attorney General brought this lawsuit against Hazelwood and various of its officials, alleging that they were engaged in a "pattern or practice" of employment discrimination in violation of Title VII of the Civil Rights Act of 1964, as amended, 42 U.S.C.A. §2000e et seq. The complaint asked for an injunction requiring Hazelwood to cease its discriminatory practices, to take affirmative steps to obtain qualified Negro faculty members, and to offer employment and give backpay to victims of past illegal discrimination.

Hazelwood was formed from thirteen rural school districts between 1949 and 1951 by a process of annexation. By the 1967–1968 school year, 17,550 students were enrolled in the district, of whom only 59 were Negro; the number of Negro pupils increased to 576 of 25,166 in 1972–1973, a total of just over 2 percent.

From the beginning, Hazelwood followed relatively unstructured procedures in hiring its teachers. . . . Generally, those who had most recently submitted applications were most likely to be chosen for interviews.

Interviews were conducted by a department chairman, program coordinator, or the principal at the school where the teaching vacancy existed. Although those conducting the interviews did fill out forms rating the applicants in a number of respects, it is undisputed that each school principal possessed virtually unlimited discretion in hiring teachers for his school. The only general guidance given to the principals was to hire the "most competent" person available, and such intangibles as "personality, disposition, appearance, poise, voice, articulation, and ability to deal with people" counted heavily. The principal's choice was routinely honored by Hazelwood's superintendent and Board of Education.

. . . As a buyer's market began to develop for public school teachers, Hazelwood curtailed its recruiting efforts. For the 1971–1972 school year, 3,127 persons applied for only 234 teaching vacancies; for the 1972–1973 school year, there were 2,373 applications for 282 vacancies. A number of the applicants who were not hired were Negroes.

Hazelwood hired its first Negro teacher in 1969. The number of Negro faculty members gradually increased in successive years: six of 957 in the 1970 school year; 16 of 1,107 by the end of the 1972 school year; 22 of 1,231 in the 1973 school year. By comparison, according to 1970 census figures, of more than 19,000 teachers employed in that year in the St. Louis area,

15.4 percent were Negro. That percentage figure included the St. Louis City School District, which in recent years has followed a policy of attempting to maintain a 50 percent Negro teaching staff. Apart from that school district, 5.7 percent of the teachers in the county were Negro in 1970.

Drawing upon these historic facts the Government mounted its "pattern or practice" attack in the District Court upon four different fronts. It adduced evidence of (1) a history of alleged racially discriminatory practices, (2) statistical disparities in hiring, (3) the standardless and largely subjective hiring procedures, and (4) specific instances of alleged discrimination against fifty-five unsuccessful Negro applicants for teaching jobs. Hazelwood offered virtually no additional evidence in response, relying instead on evidence introduced by the Government, perceived deficiencies in the Government's case, and its own officially promulgated policy "to hire all teachers on the basis of training, preparation and recommendations, regardless of race, color or creed."

The District Court ruled that the Government had failed to establish a pattern or practice of discrimination. The court was unpersuaded by the alleged history of discrimination, noting that no dual school system had ever existed in Hazelwood. . . .

The Court of Appeals for the Eighth Circuit reversed. After suggesting that the District Court had assigned inadequate weight to evidence of discriminatory conduct on the part of Hazelwood before the effective date of Title VII, the Court of Appeals rejected the trial court's analysis of the statistical data as resting on an irrelevant comparison of Negro teachers to Negro pupils in Hazelwood. The proper comparison, in the appellate court's view, was one between Negro teachers in Hazelwood and Negro teachers in the relevant labor market area. Selecting St. Louis County and St. Louis City as the relevant area the Court of Appeals compared the 1970 census figures, showing that 15.4 percent of teachers in that area were Negro, to the racial composition of Hazelwood's teaching staff. In the 1972–1973 and 1973–1974 school years, only 1.4 percent and 1.8 percent, respectively, of Hazelwood's teachers were Negroes. This statistical disparity, particularly when viewed against

the background of the teacher hiring procedures that Hazelwood had followed, was held to constitute a prima facie case of a pattern or practice of racial discrimination.

. . . Applying that standard, the appellate court found sixteen cases of individual discrimination, which "buttressed" the statistical proof. Because Hazelwood had not rebutted the Government's prima facie case of a pattern or practice of racial discrimination, the Court of Appeals directed judgment for the Government and prescribed the remedial order to be entered. . . .

This Court's recent consideration, in *International Brotherhood of Teamsters v. United States,* of the role of statistics in pattern or practice suits under Title VII provides substantial guidance in evaluating the arguments advanced by the petitioners. In that case we stated that it is the Government's burden to "establish by a preponderance of the evidence that racial discrimination was the [employer's] standard operating procedure—the regular rather than the unusual practice." We also noted that statistics can be an important source of proof in employment discrimination cases. . . . Where gross statistical disparities can be shown, they alone may in a proper case constitute *prima facie* proof of a pattern or practice of discrimination.

There can be no doubt, in light of the *Teamsters* case, that the District Court's comparison of Hazelwood's teacher work force to its student population fundamentally misconceived the role of statistics in employment discrimination cases. The Court of Appeals was correct in the view that a proper comparison was between the racial composition of Hazelwood's teaching staff and the racial composition of the qualified public school teacher population in the relevant labor market. The percentage of Negroes on Hazelwood's teaching staff in 1972–1973 was 1.4 percent and in 1973–1974 it was 1.8 percent. By contrast, the percentage of qualified Negro teachers in the area was, according to the 1970 census, at least 5.7 percent. Although these differences were on their face substantial, the Court of Appeals erred in substituting its judgment for that of the District Court and holding that the Government had conclusively proved its "pattern or practice" lawsuit.

The Court of Appeals totally disregarded the possibility that this prima facie statistical proof in the record might at the trial court level be rebutted by statistics dealing with Hazelwood's hiring after it became subject to Title VII. Racial discrimination by public employers was not made illegal under Title VII until March 24, 1972. A public employer who from that date forward made all its employment decisions in a wholly nondiscriminatory way would not violate Title VII even if it had formerly maintained an all-white work force by purposefully excluding Negroes. For this reason, the Court cautioned in the *Teamsters* opinion that once a prima facie case has been established by statistical work force disparities, the employer must be given an opportunity to show "that the claimed discriminatory pattern is a product of pre-Act hiring rather than unlawful post-Act discrimination."

The record in this case showed that for the 1972–1973 school year, Hazelwood hired 282 new teachers, ten of whom (3.5%) were Negroes; for the following school year it hired 123 new teachers, five of whom (4.1%) were Negroes. Over the two-year period, Negroes constituted a total of fifteen of the 405 new teachers hired (3.7%). Although the Court of Appeals briefly mentioned these data in reciting the facts, it wholly ignored them in discussing whether the Government had shown a pattern or practice of discrimination. And it gave no consideration at all to the possibility that post-Act data as to the number of Negroes hired compared to the total number of Negro applicants might tell a totally different story.

What the hiring figures prove obviously depends upon the figures to which they are compared. The Court of Appeals accepted the Government's argument that the relevant comparison was to the labor market area of St. Louis County and St. Louis City, in which, according to the 1970 census, 15.4 percent of all teachers were Negro. The propriety of that comparison was vigorously disputed by the petitioners, who urged that because the City of St. Louis has made special attempts to maintain a 50 percent Negro teaching staff, inclusion of that school district in the relevant market area distorts the comparison. Were that argument accepted, the percentage of Negro teachers in the relevant labor market area (St. Louis County alone) as shown in the 1970 census would be 5.7 percent rather than 15.4 percent.

The difference between these figures may well be important; the disparity between 3.7 percent (the percentage of Negro teachers hired by Hazelwood in 1972–1973 and 1973–1974) and 5.7 percent may be sufficiently small to weaken the Government's other proof, while the disparity between 3.7 percent and 15.4 percent may be sufficiently large to reinforce it. In determining which of the two figures—or very possibly, what intermediate figure—provides the most accurate basis for comparison to the hiring figures at Hazelwood, it will be necessary to evaluate such considerations as (i) whether the racially based hiring policies of the St. Louis City School District were in effect as far back as 1970, the year in which the census figures were taken; (ii) to what extent those policies have changed the racial composition of that district's teaching staff from what it would otherwise have been; (iii) to what extent St. Louis' recruitment policies have diverted to the city teachers who might otherwise have applied to Hazelwood; (iv) to what extent Negro teachers employed by the city would prefer employment in other districts such as Hazelwood; and (v) what the experience in other school districts in St. Louis County indicates about the validity of excluding the City School District from the relevant labor market.

It is thus clear that a determination of the appropriate comparative figures in this case will depend upon further evaluation by the trial court. As this Court admonished in *Teamsters*, "statistics . . . come in infinite variety. . . . [T]heir usefulness depends on all of the surrounding facts and circumstances." Only the trial court is in a position to make the appropriate determination after further findings. And only after such a determination is made can a foundation be established for deciding whether or not Hazelwood engaged in a pattern or practice of racial discrimination in its employment practices in violation of the law.

We hold, therefore, that the Court of Appeals erred in disregarding the post-Act hiring statistics in the record, and that it should have remanded the case to the District Court for further findings as to the relevant labor market area and for an ultimate determination of whether Hazelwood engaged in a pattern or practice of employment discrimination after March 24, 1972.

Accordingly, the judgment is vacated, and the case is remanded to the District Court for further proceedings consistent with this opinion.

It is so ordered.

CASE NOTES

1. Section 703 of the Civil Rights Act of 1964, 42 U.S.C.A. §2000e-2, provides:

(a) It shall be an unlawful employment practice for an employer—

1. to fail or refuse to hire or to discharge any individual, or otherwise to discriminate against any individual with respect to his compensation, terms, conditions, or privileges of employment, because of such individual's race, color, religion, sex, or national origin; or

2. to limit, segregate, or classify his employees or applicants for employment in any way which would deprive or tend to deprive any individual of employment opportunities or otherwise adversely affect his status as an employee, because of such individual's race, color, religion, sex, or national origin. . . .

(h) Notwithstanding any other provision of this subchapter, it shall not be an unlawful employment practice for an employer . . . to give and to act upon the results of any professionally developed ability test provided that such test, its administration or action upon the results is not designed, intended or used to discriminate because of race, color, religion, sex, or national origin.

2. *BFOQ Defense.* If being of a particular sex, religion, or national origin is a necessary part of a job, then discrimination is justified. Title VII provides a statutory exemption for a bona fide occupational qualification (BFOQ), a trait necessary for the proper conduct of a job. The Montana Supreme Court has upheld a BFOQ requiring that a high school counselor be a woman. The school sought to maintain a staff of two counselors, one male and one female. Upon seeking to fill a vacancy for the position of a female counselor, a male applicant filed a complaint. Evidence presented by the school indicated that female students were uncomfortable discussing intimate personal matters with a male counselor. The school had concluded that it needed a counselor of each sex. The court agreed that in this case gender was a BFOQ.

Stone v. Belgrade School District No. 44, 217 Mont. 309, 703 P.2d 136 (1984).

3. An employment test must have a manifest relationship to the employment in question to be sustained in a Title VII disparate impact action; however, the employment test is not required to test every skill required to perform the job. Widely disparate passing rates among whites, Latinos, and African-Americans indicate adverse impact and support a *prima facie* case of race discrimination. In such circumstance, the state must then carry the burden of presenting evidence that there is a manifest relationship between the skills tested and those required for the job. Too, the test must have content validity, construct validity, or criterion-related validity; courts will require the showing of one type of test validity on one but not all. Thus, a federal court in California upheld the use of employment certification tests for teachers and school administrators that were content valid for the basic job-related skills of reading, writing, and mathematics. *Association of Mexican-American Educators v. California,* 937 F.Supp. 1397 (N.D.Cal.1996).

AFFIRMATIVE ACTION

Affirmative action in employment is a voluntary plan adopted by a school district in an effort to remediate past discrimination. Such a plan is looked upon favorably by the courts so long as it is not too broadly fashioned as to either its remedy or its justification. The Supreme Court has said that we must be mindful of "this Court's and Congress' consistent emphasis on 'the value of voluntary efforts to further the objectives of the law.'"[38] Yet affirmative action in employment plans, if not justified, may result in unlawful reverse discrimination. The lawfulness of such plans has been tested under Title VII, Title VI, and the equal protection clause.

Title VII "does not impose a duty to adopt a hiring procedure that maximizes hiring of minority employees";[39] on the contrary, the act attempts to make employment practices neutral, prohibiting discrimination against an employee. Title VII states specifically that "[n]othing contained in [Title VII] shall be interpreted to require any employer . . . to grant preferential treatment to any individual or any group because of the race, color, religion, sex or national origin of such individual or group."[40] Under Title VII, affirmative action is voluntary. In *McDonald*,[41] the Supreme Court stated: "Title VII, whose terms are not limited to discrimination against members of any particular race, prohibits racial discrimination in private employment against white persons upon the same standards as racial discrimination against nonwhites."[42]

In 1979, in the case of *United Steelworkers v. Weber*[43] employees of a steel company claimed reverse discrimination, citing Title VII. The United Steelworkers and Kaiser Aluminum had negotiated an agreement that included a provision for the elimination of racial imbalance at the Kaiser Aluminum plant. The agreement provided that craft-training positions would be reserved for minorities until the percentage of blacks in the craft workforce equaled the percentage of blacks in the local labor market. In the first year of the agreement, thirteen individuals were selected for craft training, seven blacks and six whites. The most senior black of the group had less seniority than a number of white workers who were not selected. The white workers who were not selected filed suit. The Supreme Court ruled that the mutually agreed upon contract did not violate Title VII because not all private, voluntary, race-conscious affirmative action plans instituted by companies are prohibited.

In 1987, the Supreme Court decided a second Title VII affirmative action case.[44] The Santa Clara County Transit District Board of Supervisors implemented an affirmative action plan. The plan stated that "mere prohibition of discriminatory practices [was] not enough to remedy the effects of past discriminatory practices and to permit attainment of an equitable representation of minorities, women and handicapped persons."[45] Since women were underrepresented in a number of work areas, the plan authorized gender as a "plus" factor to be considered if the candidate was qualified. The plan had no quotas but was an attempt to make the workforce reflect the proportion of women in the area labor market. A vacancy for a road dispatcher occurred where out of 238 positions, none was held by a female. A qualified female was promoted over a qualified man. The Supreme Court cited *Weber* and said that the affirmative action plan was justified because of the "manifest imbalance" reflected in the under-

representation of women in traditionally segregated jobs. Also, it was important that the plan did not unnecessarily trammel the rights of male employees. Johnson, the plaintiff, did not lose his job; he was refused a promotion, but his rights were not trammeled. The plan was intended not to be permanent but to balance the workforce. Therefore, the plan met a remedial need and did not trammel the rights of others, which are the two tests established in *Weber*.[46]

The U.S. Supreme Court has provided guidance as to the boundaries between affirmative action and reverse discrimination under the equal protection clause. In *Wygant*, the Supreme Court invalidated a school board's "affirmative retention" policy, which discriminated against nonminority teachers.[47] Following *Wygant*, the U.S. Court of Appeals, Seventh Circuit, held that a "no minority layoff" clause in a collective bargaining agreement violated both equal protection and Title VII.[48] The court found that the plan, which laid off forty-eight white teachers with greater seniority than black teachers who were retained on the job, constituted an absolute racial preference and was not "narrowly tailored" to serve any remedial affirmative action purpose.

Affirmative action plans will be found to be discriminatory if they are justified on the excessively broad grounds of rectifying social discrimination alone and/or are too broadly fashioned to serve the remedial purposes of removing the vestiges of past discrimination in the schools. To have a valid plan to remediate past discrimination, there must be convincing evidence of prior discrimination by the particular governmental unit, and "[s]ocietal discrimination alone is insufficient to justify a racial classification."[49]

Six different opinions were filed in *Wygant* by the Supreme Court justices, who in the end failed to agree on a standard of review for affirmative action programs in public employment. The Court did, though, reject race-based layoffs, the necessity for which was defended on the rationale that teachers are "role models" and, as such, minority teachers should be employed in the same percentage to all teachers as the minority student population is to all students. The Court was of the opinion that while hiring goals and promotion policies favorable to minorities are acceptable, the actual laying off of teachers from existing jobs is so intrusive and harmful to the individual nonminority teacher that equal protection is violated.

With the recent societal turmoil about race-based programs, the Supreme Court has once again addressed the issue. In 1995,[50] the Supreme Court ruled that all governmental action—whether federal, state, or local—based on race must be analyzed under strict scrutiny and will be held constitutional only if narrowly tailored to further a compelling state interest. This case involved an incentive for prime highway contractors to give subcontracts to companies owned by women or members of minority groups, such as African-Americans, Hispanics, Asian-Americans, and Native Americans. The lowest bid was made by a nonminority firm, but the firm was not chosen because the prime contractor could receive a federal financial subsidy only if the subcontract was given to a company that was owned by a member of a minority. The prime contractor testified that the financial incentive was the only reason he did not give the contract to the lowest bidder, whose owner was a white male.

The Court said that the use of strict scrutiny was the best means to ensure "that courts will consistently give racial classifications a detailed examination, as to both ends and means."[51] The Court further stated: "It is not true that strict scrutiny is strict in theory, but fatal in fact."[52] "Government is not disqualified from acting in response to the unhappy persistence of both the practice and the lingering effects of racial discrimination against minority groups in this country. When race-based action is necessary to further a compelling interest, such action is within constitutional constraints, if it satisfies the narrow tailoring test set out in this Court's previous cases."[53] The Supreme Court remanded the case for further consideration to determine if the use of the subcontractor compensation clause would meet the "compelling reasons" standard. Also, the Court remanded the decision "[b]ecause this decision alters the playing field in some respects . . . , and the precise nature of affirmative duty in employment remains somewhat cloudy."[54] It is yet unclear as to what the impact of this case will be on remedying discrimination in all segments of society, although the Court implied that government does have a

role in this task. Will the strict scrutiny test be lowered to an intermediate level, as suggested by one of the dissenters, to accommodate these societal requirements?

❖ — ❖ — ❖

Affirmative Retention Policy Resulting in Layoffs of Nonminority Teachers with More Seniority Violates Equal Protection

Wygant v. Jackson Board of Education

Supreme Court of the United States, 1986.
476 U.S. 267, 106 S.Ct. 1842.

Justice POWELL announced the judgment of the Court and delivered an opinion in which THE CHIEF JUSTICE and Justice REHNQUIST joined, and which Justice O'CONNOR joined in parts I, II, III-A, III-B, and V.

This case presents the question whether a school board, consistent with the Equal Protection Clause, may extend preferential protection against layoffs to some of its employees because of their race or national origin.

In 1972, the Jackson Board of Education, because of racial tension in the community that extended to its schools, considered adding a layoff provision to the Collective Bargaining Agreement (CBA) between the Board and the Jackson Education Association (the Union) that would protect employees who were members of certain minority groups against layoffs. The Board and the Union eventually approved a new provision, Article XII of the CBA, covering layoffs. It stated:

> In the event that it becomes necessary to reduce the number of teachers through layoff from employment by the Board, teachers with the most seniority in the district shall be retained, except that at no time will there be a greater percentage of minority personnel laid off than the current percentage of minority personnel employed at the time of the layoff. In no event will the number given notice of possible layoff be greater than the number of positions to be eliminated. Each teacher

so affected will be called back in reverse order for positions for which he is certificated maintaining the above minority balance.

When layoffs became necessary in 1974, it was evident that adherence to the CBA would result in the layoff of tenured nonminority teachers while minority teachers on probationary status were retained. Rather than complying with Article XII, the Board retained the tenured teachers and laid off probationary minority teachers, thus failing to maintain the percentage of minority personnel that existed at the time of the layoff. The Union, together with two minority teachers who had been laid off, brought suit in federal court, . . . (*Jackson Education Assn. v. Board of Education,* (*Jackson 1*) (mem. op.)), claiming that the Board's failure to adhere to the layoff provision violated the Equal Protection Clause of the Fourteenth Amendment and Title VII of the Civil Rights Act of 1964.

Petitioners' central claim is that they were laid off because of their race in violation of the Equal Protection Clause of the Fourteenth Amendment. Decisions by faculties and administrators of public schools based on race or ethnic origin are reviewable under the Fourteenth Amendment. This Court has "consistently repudiated '[d]istinctions between citizens solely because of their ancestry' as being 'odious to a free people whose institutions are founded upon the doctrine of equality.'" . . . "Racial and ethnic distinctions of any sort are inherently suspect and thus call for the most exacting judicial examination." *Regents of University of California v. Bakke,* 438 U.S. 265, 291, 98 S.Ct. 2733, 2748, 57 L.Ed.2d 750 (1978). . . .

The Court has recognized that the level of scrutiny does not change merely because the challenged classification operates against a group that historically has not been subject to governmental discrimination. . . . In this case, Article XII of the CBA operates against whites and in favor of certain minorities, and therefore constitutes a classification based on race. "Any preference based on racial or ethnic criteria must necessarily receive a most searching examination to make sure that it does not conflict with constitutional guarantees." *Fullilove v. Klutznick,* 448 U.S. 448, 491, 100 S.Ct. 2758, 2781, 65 L.Ed.2d 902 (1980). . . . There are two prongs

to this examination. First, any racial classification "must be justified by a compelling governmental interest." . . . Second, the means chosen by the State to effectuate its purpose must be "narrowly tailored to the achievement of that goal." . . . We must decide whether the layoff provision is supported by a compelling state purpose and whether the means chosen to accomplish that purpose are narrowly tailored.

The Court of Appeals, relying on the reasoning and language of the District Court's opinion, held that the Board's interest in providing minority role models for its minority students, as an attempt to alleviate the effects of societal discrimination, was sufficiently important to justify the racial classification embodied in the layoff provision. . . . The court discerned a need for more minority faculty role models by finding that the percentage of minority teachers was less than the percentage of minority students.

This Court never has held that societal discrimination alone is sufficient to justify a racial classification. Rather, the Court has insisted upon some showing of prior discrimination by the governmental unit involved before allowing limited use of racial classifications in order to remedy such discrimination.

Unlike the analysis in *Hazelwood,* the role model theory employed by the District Court has no logical stopping point. The role model theory allows the Board to engage in discriminatory hiring and layoff practices long past the point required by any legitimate remedial purpose. Indeed, by tying the required percentage of minority teachers to the percentage of minority students, it requires just the sort of year-to-year calibration the Court stated was unnecessary in *Swann,* 402 U.S., at 31–32, 91 S.Ct., at 1283–1284. . . .

Moreover, because the role model theory does not necessarily bear a relationship to the harm caused by prior discriminatory hiring practices, it actually could be used to escape the obligation to remedy such practices by justifying the small percentage of black teachers by reference to the small percentage of black students. . . . Carried to its logical extreme, the idea that black students are better off with black teachers could lead to the very system the Court rejected in *Brown v. Board of Education,* 347 U.S. 483, 74 S.Ct. 686, 98 L.Ed. 873 (1954) (*Brown I*).

Societal discrimination, without more, is too amorphous a basis for imposing a racially classified remedy. The role model theory announced by the District Court and the resultant holding typify this indefiniteness. . . . No one doubts that there has been serious racial discrimination in this country. But as the basis for imposing discriminatory *legal* remedies that work against innocent people, societal discrimination is insufficient and over-expansive. In the absence of particularized findings, a court could uphold remedies that are ageless in their reach into the past, and timeless in their ability to affect the future.

Respondents also now argue that their purpose in adopting the layoff provision was to remedy prior discrimination against minorities by the Jackson School District in hiring teachers. Public schools, like other public employers, operate under two interrelated constitutional duties. They are under a clear command from this Court, starting with *Brown v. Board of Education*, 349 U.S. 294, 75 S.Ct. 753, 99 L.Ed. 1083 (1955), to eliminate every vestige of racial segregation and discrimination in the schools. Pursuant to that goal, race-conscious remedial action may be necessary. . . . On the other hand, public employers, including public schools, also must act in accordance with a "core purpose of the Fourteenth Amendment" which is to "do away with all governmentally imposed distinctions based on race." . . . These related constitutional duties are not always harmonious; reconciling them requires public employers to act with extraordinary care. In particular, a public employer like the Board must ensure that, before it embarks on an affirmative action program, it has convincing evidence that remedial action is warranted. That is, it must have sufficient evidence to justify the conclusion that there has been prior discrimination.

Evidentiary support for the conclusion that remedial action is warranted becomes crucial when the remedial program is challenged in court by nonminority employees. . . . The ultimate burden remains with the employees to demonstrate the unconstitutionality of an affirmative action program. But unless such a determination is made, an appellate court reviewing a challenge to remedial action by nonminority employees cannot determine whether the race-based action is justified as a remedy for prior discrimination.

Despite the fact that Article XII has spawned years of litigation and three separate lawsuits, no such determination ever has been made. . . .

. . . Here, . . . the means chosen to achieve the Board's asserted purposes is that of laying off nonminority teachers with greater seniority in order to retain minority teachers with less seniority. We have previously expressed concern over the burden that a preferential layoffs scheme imposes on innocent parties. . . . In cases involving valid *hiring* goals, the burden to be borne by innocent individuals is diffused to a considerable extent among society generally. Though hiring goals may burden some innocent individuals, they simply do not impose the same kind of injury that layoffs impose. Denial of a future employment opportunity is not as intrusive as loss of an existing job.

Many of our cases involve union seniority plans with employees who are typically heavily dependent on wages for their day-to-day living. Even a temporary layoff may have adverse financial as well as psychological effects. A worker may invest many productive years in one job and one city with the expectation of earning the stability and security of seniority. "At that point, the rights and expectations surrounding seniority make up what is probably the most valuable capital asset that the worker 'owns,' worth even more than the current equity in his home." . . . Layoffs disrupt these settled expectations in a way that general hiring goals do not.

While hiring goals impose a diffuse burden, often foreclosing only one of several opportunities, layoffs impose the entire burden of achieving racial equality on particular individuals, often resulting in serious disruption of their lives. That burden is too intrusive. We therefore hold that, as a means of accomplishing purposes that otherwise may be legitimate, the Board's layoff plan is not sufficiently narrowly tailored. Other, less intrusive means of accomplishing similar purposes—such as the adoption of hiring goals—are available. For these reasons, the Board's selection of layoffs as the means to accomplish even a valid purpose cannot satisfy the demands of the Equal Protection Clause.

We accordingly reverse the judgment of the Court of Appeals for the Sixth Circuit.

It is so ordered.

———————— ❖ — ❖ — ❖ ————————

Nonremedial Affirmative Action
Plan Violates Title VII

Taxman v. Board of Education of the Township of Piscataway

United States Court of Appeals,
Third Circuit, 1996.
91 F.3d 1547.

Mansmann, Circuit Judge.

In this Title VII matter, we must determine whether the Board of Education of the Township of Piscataway violated that statute when it made race a factor in selecting which of two equally qualified employees to lay off. Specifically, we must decide whether Title VII permits an employer with a racially balanced work force to grant a non-remedial racial preference in order to promote "racial diversity."

It is clear that the language of Title VII is violated when an employer makes an employment decision based upon an employee's race. The Supreme Court determined in *United Steelworkers v. Weber,* however, that Title VII's prohibition against racial discrimination is not violated by affirmative action plans which first . . . "have purposes that mirror those of the statute" and second, do not "unnecessarily trammel the interests of the [nonminority] employees." . . . We hold that Piscataway's affirmative action policy is unlawful because it fails to satisfy either prong of *Weber.* Given the clear antidiscrimination mandate of Title VII, the non-remedial affirmative action plan, even one with a laudable purpose, cannot pass muster. We will affirm the district court's grant of summary judgment to Sharon Taxman. . . .

In 1975, the Board of Education of the Township of Piscataway, New Jersey, developed an affirmative action policy applicable to employment decisions. The Board's Affirmative Action Program . . . was originally adopted in response to a regulation promulgated by the New Jersey Board of Education. That regulation directed local school boards to adopt "affirmative action programs" . . . to address employment as well as school and classroom practices and to ensure equal opportunity to all persons regardless of race, color, creed, religion, sex or national origin. . . .

The Board's affirmative action policy did not have "any remedial purpose"; it was not adopted "with the intention of remedying the results of any prior discrimination or identified underrepresentation of minorities within the Piscataway Public School System." At all relevant times, Black teachers were neither "underrepresented" nor "underutilized" in the Piscataway School District work force. . . .

In May, 1989, the Board accepted a recommendation from the Superintendent of Schools to reduce the teaching staff in the Business Department at Piscataway High School by one. At that time, two of the teachers in the department were of equal seniority, both having begun their employment with the Board on the same day nine years earlier. One of those teachers was intervenor plaintiff Sharon Taxman, who is White, and the other was Debra Williams, who is Black. Williams was the only minority teacher among the faculty of the Business Department.

Decisions regarding layoffs by New Jersey school boards are highly circumscribed by state law; nontenured faculty must be laid off first, and layoffs among tenured teachers in the affected subject area or grade level must proceed in reverse order of seniority. . . . Seniority for this purpose is calculated according to specific guidelines set by state law. . . . Thus, local boards lack discretion to choose between employees for layoff, except in the rare instance of a tie in seniority between the two or more employees eligible to fill the last remaining position.

The Board determined that it was facing just such a rare circumstance in deciding between Taxman and Williams. In prior decisions involving the layoff of employees with equal seniority, the Board had broken the tie through "a random process which included drawing numbers out of a container, drawing lots or having a lottery." In none of those instances, however, had the employees involved been of different races.

In light of the unique posture of the layoffs decision, [the] Superintendent of Schools . . . recommended to the Board that the affirmative action plan be invoked in order to determine which teacher to retain. [The] Superintendent... made this recommendation "because he believed Ms. Williams and Ms. Taxman were tied in seniority, were equally qualified, and because Ms. Williams was the only Black teacher in the Business Education Department."

While the Board recognized that it was not bound to apply the affirmative action policy, it made a discretionary decision to invoke the policy to break the tie between Williams and Taxman. As a result, the Board "voted to terminate the employment of Sharon Taxman, effective June 30, 1988." . . .

At his deposition . . . , the Board's President explained his vote to apply the affirmative action policy as follows: . . .

Asked to articulate the "educational objective" served by retaining Williams rather than Taxman, Kruse stated:

> A. In my own personal perspective I believe by retaining Mrs. Williams it was sending a very clear message that we feel that our staff should be culturally diverse, our student population is culturally diverse and there is a distinct advantage to students, to all students, to be made—come into contact with people of different cultures, different background, so that they are more aware, more tolerant, more accepting, more understanding of people of all background.

> Q. What do you mean by the phrase you used, culturally diverse?

> A. Someone other than—different than yourself. And we have, our student population and our community has people of all different background, ethnic background, religious background, cultural background, and it's important that our school district encourage awareness and acceptance and tolerance and, therefore, I personally think it's important that our staff reflect that too.

In relevant part, Title VII makes it unlawful for an employer "to discriminate against any individual with respect to his competencies, terms, conditions, or privileges of employment" or "to limit, segregate, or classify his employees . . . in any way which would deprive or tend to deprive any individual of employment opportunities or otherwise affect his status as an employee" on the basis of "race, color, religion, sex, or national origin." For a time, the Supreme Court construed this language as absolutely prohibiting discrimination in employment, neither requiring nor permitting any preference for any group. . . .

In 1979, however, the Court interpreted the statute's "antidiscriminatory strategy" in a "fundamentally different way," holding in the seminal case of *United Steelworkers v. Weber* . . . that Title VII's prohibition against racial discrimination does not condemn all voluntary race-conscious affirmative action plans. . . .

. . . The Court upheld the . . . plan because its purpose "mirror[ed] those of the statute" and it did not "unnecessarily trammel the interests of the [nonminority] employees." . . .

The purposes of the plan mirror those of the statute. Both were designed to break down old patterns of racial segregation and hierarchy. Both were structured to "open employment opportunities for Negroes in occupations which have been traditionally closed to them." . . .

At the same time, the plan does not unnecessarily trammel the interests of the white employees. The plan does not require the discharge of white workers and their replacement with new black hires. Nor does the plan create an absolute bar to the advancement of white employees; half of those trained in the program will be white. . . .

In 1987, the Supreme Court decided a second Title VII affirmative action case, *Johnson v. Transportation Agency, Santa Clara County.* There, the Santa Clara County Transit District Board of Supervisors implemented an affirmative action plan stating that "'mere prohibition of discriminatory practices [was] not enough to remedy the effects of past discriminatory practices and to permit attainment of an equitable representation of minorities, women and handicapped persons.'" . . . The plan did not set quotas, but had as its long-term goal the attainment of a work force whose composition reflected the proportion of women in the area labor force. . . .

On December 12, 1979, the Agency announced a vacancy for the promotional position of road dispatcher. At the time, none of the 238 positions in the applicable job category was occupied by a woman. The Agency Director, authorized to choose any of seven applicants who had been deemed eligible, promoted Diane Joyce, a qualified woman, over . . . , a qualified man. . . .

Reviewing Agency statistics which showed that women were concentrated in traditionally female jobs and represented a lower percentage in other jobs than would be expected if traditional segregation had not occurred, the Court concluded that the decision to promote . . . was made pursuant to a plan designed to eliminate work force imbalances in traditionally segregated job categories and thus satisfied *Weber*'s first prong. Moving to *Weber*'s second prong, whether the plan unnecessarily trammeled the rights of male employees, the Court concluded that the plan passed muster because it authorized merely that consideration be given to affirmative action concerns when evaluating applicants; gender was a "plus" factor, only one of several criteria that the Agency Director considered in making his decision. . . .

Having reviewed the analytical framework for assessing the validity of an affirmative action plan as established in *United Steelworkers v. Weber* . . . and refined in *Johnson*, . . . we turn to the facts of this case in order to determine whether the racial diversity purpose of the Board's policy mirrors the purposes of the statute. We look for the purposes of Title VII in the plain meaning of the Act's provisions and in its legislative history and historical context. . . .

Title VII was enacted to further two primary goals: to end discrimination on the basis of race, color, religion, sex or national origin, thereby guaranteeing equal opportunity in the workplace, and to remedy the segregation and underrepresentation of minorities that discrimination has caused in our Nation's work force.

Title VII's first purpose is set forth in section 2000e-2's several prohibitions, which expressly denounce the discrimination which Congress sought to end. . . . This antidiscriminatory purpose is also reflected in the Act's legislative history. . . .

. . . [Title VII] expressly protects the employer's right to insist that any prospective applicant, Negro or white, must meet the applicable job qualifications. Indeed the very purpose of Title VII is to promote hiring on the basis of job qualifications, rather than on the basis of race or color. . . .

Title VII's second purpose, ending the segregative effects of discrimination, is revealed in the congressional debate surrounding the statute's enactment. In *Weber*, the Court carefully catalogued the comments made by the proponents of Title VII which demonstrate the Act's remedial concerns. . . .

The significance of this second corrective purpose cannot be overstated. It is only because Title VII was written to eradicate not only discrimination per se but the consequences of prior discrimination as well, that racial preferences in the form of affirmative action can co-exist with the Act's antidiscrimination mandate.

Thus, based on our analysis of Title VII's two goals, we are convinced that unless an affirmative action plan has a remedial purpose, it cannot be said to mirror the purposes of the statute, and, therefore, cannot satisfy the first prong of the *Weber* test.

We see this case as one involving straightforward statutory interpretation controlled by the text and legislative history of Title VII as interpreted in *Weber* and *Johnson*. . . . The affirmative action plans at issue in *Weber* and *Johnson* were sustained only because the Supreme Court, examining those plans in light of congressional intent, found a secondary congressional objective in Title VII that had to be accommodated— i.e., the elimination of the effects of past discrimination in the workplace. Here, there is no congressional recognition of diversity as a Title VII objective requiring accommodation.

Accordingly, it is beyond cavil that the Board, by invoking its affirmative action policy to lay off Sharon Taxman, violated the terms of Title VII. While the Court in *Weber* and *Johnson* permitted some deviation from the antidiscrimination mandate of the statute in order to erase the effects of past discrimination, these rulings do not open the door to additional non-remedial deviations. Here, as in *Weber* and *Johnson*, the Board must justify its deviation from the statutory mandate based on positive legislative history, not on its idea of what is appropriate. . . .

The Board recognized that there is no positive legislative history supporting its goal of promoting racial diversity "for education's sake," and concedes that there is no caselaw approving such a purpose to support an affirmative action plan under Title VII. . . .

. . . Our analysis of the statute and the caselaw convinces us that a non-remedial affirmative action plan cannot form the basis for deviating from the antidiscrimination mandate of Title VII.

The Board admits that it did not act to remedy the effects of past employment discrimination. . . . Nor does the Board contend that its action here was directed at remedying any de jure or de facto segregation. . . . Even though the Board's race-conscious action was taken to avoid what could have been an all-White faculty within the Business Department, the Board concedes that Blacks are not underrepresented in its teaching work force as a whole or even in the Piscataway High School.

Rather, the Board's sole purpose in applying its affirmative action policy in this case was to obtain an educational benefit which it believed would result from a racially diverse faculty. While the benefits flowing from diversity in the educational context are significant indeed, we are constrained to hold, as did the district court, that inasmuch as "the Board does not even attempt to show that its affirmative action plan was adopted to remedy past discrimination or as the result of a manifest imbalance in the employment of minorities," . . . the Board has failed to satisfy the first prong of the *Weber* test. . . .

We turn next to the second prong of the *Weber* analysis. This second prong requires that we determine whether the Board's policy "unnecessarily trammel[s] . . . [nonminority] interests." Under this requirement, too, the Board's policy is deficient.

We begin by noting the policy's utter lack of definition and structure. While it is not for us to decide how much diversity in a high school facility is "enough," the Board cannot abdicate its responsibility to define "racial diversity" and to determine what degree of racial diversity in the Piscataway School is sufficient. . . .

[T]he Board's policy, devoid of goals and standards, is governed entirely by the Board's whim, leaving the Board free, if it so chooses, to grant racial preferences that do not promote even the policy's claimed purpose. Indeed, under the terms of this policy, the Board, in pursuit of a "racially diverse" work force, could use affirmative action to discriminate against those whom Title VII was enacted to protect. Such a policy unnecessarily trammels the interests of nonminority employees. . . .

Accordingly, we conclude that under the second prong of the *Weber* test, the Board's affirmative action policy violates Title VII. In addition to containing an impermissible purpose, the policy "unnecessarily trammel[s] the interests of the [nonminority] employees." . . .

. . . Our disposition of this matter, . . . rests squarely on the foundation of Title VII. Although we applaud the goal of racial diversity, we cannot agree that Title VII permits an employer to advance that goal through non-remedial discriminatory measures.

Having found that the district court properly concluded that the affirmative action plan applied by the Board to lay off Taxman is invalid under Title VII, . . . we will affirm the judgment of the district court.

CASE NOTES

1. The court in *Wygant* distinguished *Hazelwood*, saying:

> The Court in *Hazelwood* held that the proper comparison for determining the existence of actual discrimination by the school board was "between the racial composition of [the school's] teaching staff and the racial composition of the qualified public school teacher population in the relevant labor market," 433 U.S. at 308, 97 S.Ct. at 2742 (1977).

In contrast, in *Wygant*, the lower court had justified the minority retention policy on a broader societal scale by basing the percentage of minority teachers on the percentage of minority students.

2. Following *Wygant*, the U.S. Court of Appeals, Seventh Circuit, held that the equal protection clause was violated by a collective bargaining agreement provision that provided that no black teachers would be laid off until every white teacher was laid off. The rationale for the agreement was that in the event of economic downturns or shrinkages in student population, a reduction in teaching positions would result in a teaching force with greater percentages of black teachers. The court rejected the measure because it was not narrowly tailored to

the goal of remedying previous discrimination, but created an absolute preference for black teachers. *Britton v. South Bend Community School Corporation*, 819 F.2d 766 (7th Cir.1987).

3. An allegation that a white principal's removal by the school council constituted reverse discrimination in violation of Title VII was not supported by the evidence. *Pilditch v. Board of Education*, 3 F.3d 1113 (7th Cir.1993).

4. Prior to the 1991 amendments, a Title VII plaintiff had no right to seek relief in the form of money damages. Further, prior to those amendments, the Supreme Court had never recognized a Title VII plaintiff's right to a jury trial. See, e.g., *Landgraf v. USI Film Products*, 511 U.S. 244, 114 S.Ct. 1483 (1994). The 1991 Amendments grant a plaintiff the right to seek damages for intentionally discriminatory treatment in employment in violation of Title VII, see, e.g., 42 U.S.C. §1981a(a), and further provide that "if a complaining party seeks . . . damages under this section . . . any party may demand a trial by jury," ibid. §1981a(c).

The 1991 amendments became effective on November 21, 1991, and the Supreme Court has ruled that the provisions of §1981 allowing a plaintiff to recover money damages do not apply to cases arising before their enactment and do not apply "to conduct occurring before November 21, 1991." *Landgraf v. USI Film Products*, 511 U.S. at 282, 114 S.Ct. 1483 (1994); *Joseph v. New York City Board of Education*, 171 F.3d 87 (2d Cir.1999).

■ SEX DISCRIMINATION

Sex-based discrimination in working conditions, compensation, prerequisites for employment, and work-related benefits came under criticism during the early 1960s, and Congress responded by passing legislation to prohibit such discrimination. In recent years, lawsuits have been filed under the equal protection clause of the Fourteenth Amendment, the Equal Pay Act of 1963, Title VII of the Civil Rights Act of 1964, and Title IX of the Education Amendments of 1972,[55] challenging discriminatory practices based on sex.

TITLE VII

Employment discrimination based on gender is prohibited by Title VII.[56] In part, the act provides that it is unlawful for an employer "to fail or refuse to hire or to discharge an individual or otherwise to discriminate against any individual . . . because of such individual's race, color, religion, *sex* or national origin" (italics added). As with racial discrimination (discussed earlier), the plaintiff is required to show (1) that he or she is a member of a class protected by Title VII; (2) that he or she applied and was qualified for the position; (3) that despite such qualifications, he or she was rejected; and (4) that after his or her rejection, the position remained open, and the employer continued to seek similarly qualified applicants.[57] If the plaintiff sustains this *prima facie* case of sex discrimination, then the burden falls on the defendant to present evidence that the employment decision was based on a legitimate nondiscriminatory reason.

The application of this test is as valid for public school districts and universities as for the private sector.[58] If the needs of the school district evolve and become such that the qualifications for a position change, it may be possible for a school board to justify hiring a person of a particular sex.[59] On the other hand, to pass over a female with better qualifications than a male applicant for promotion to an administrative position violates Title VII.[60]

If a teacher establishes a *prima facie* case of discrimination, the school board must present evidence that its rationale for the employment decision was based on nondiscriminatory reasons. Where a school board defended its decision not to promote a black female teacher on the subjective factors of her "lack of interpersonal and management skills" and her "abrasive" personality, the court found that these reasons "articulated legitimate nondiscriminatory reasons" for the board's decision.[61]

If the plaintiff establishes by direct evidence that an employer acted with discriminatory intent, the defense will fail unless the employer can present evidence "that the same decision would have been reached absent illegal motive."[62] Where a female plaintiff presented direct evidence of discrimination, the board's evidence that "she would not have been promoted if she were a man" provided the defendants with a complete defense to the plaintiff's charges.[63] In other words, the employment decision must be gender neutral, or gender must be irrelevant to the determination.[64]

The court must determine, based on proof, what the considerations were that led to the employer's decision. Was the decision based on considerations that were legitimate, illegitimate, or a mixture of the two? The Supreme Court in considering the dilemma of a mixture of the two has held that the language of Title VII that states, in part, "*because* of such individual's sex"[65] (italics added) means that if the evidence is insufficient to discern the causal significance between legitimate and illegitimate considerations, then the court must conclude that the employment decision was made "because of" sex. According to the Court, plaintiffs should be spared the extremely difficult burden of precisely distinguishing causality as to the employer's motives. Therefore, if gender is a discernible aspect of an array of reasons for a decision, the Court will assume that neutrality has not been maintained. In this way, Title VII "forbids employers to make gender an indirect stumbling block to employment opportunity."[66] The Supreme Court has concluded with regard to the plaintiff's burden of proof that

> [i]t is difficult for us to imagine that, in the simple words "because of" Congress meant to obligate plaintiff to identify the precise causal role played by legitimate and illegitimate motivations in the employment decision she challenges. We conclude, instead, that Congress meant to obligate her to prove that the employer relied upon sex-based considerations in coming to its decision.[67]

PREGNANCY

Employers are prohibited by the Pregnancy Discrimination Act of 1978 (PDA),[68] an amendment to Title VII, from discriminating on the basis of pregnancy. The courts have interpreted the act to require that employers treat pregnancy the same as any other disabling illness for purposes of health benefits and other related programs.[69] Leave provisions extended to employees for disabling illnesses must be extended to pregnant employees as well. The rules of proof in establishing discrimination apply to pregnancy allegations in the same manner as to other aspects of Title VII. The plaintiff must establish a *prima facie* case of disparate treatment, and, if successful, the institution must articulate legitimate nondiscriminatory reasons for the employment decision against the woman.[70]

In an oft-litigated case that returned to the U.S. Court of Appeals, Fourth Circuit, three times, the circuit court held that the school district must present evidence of "business necessity" to counter a *prima facie* case of pregnancy discrimination.[71] In this instance, the defendant school district's policy requiring pregnant teachers to report their pregnancies to school officials immediately upon discovery was challenged as a violation of Title VII. The plaintiff, as a result of such disclosure, was not given a contract renewal for the succeeding school year. The fourth circuit held that the plaintiff had established a *prima facie* violation of federal law in that the school's requirement imposed the burden imposed of reporting pregnancies solely on women teachers. The circuit court remanded the case back to the federal district court to decide if the school's interest in continuity of instruction was sufficient to establish a viable defense of "business necessity." Upon rehearing at the lower court level, the school district conceded this point, and the plaintiff prevailed.[72]

BENEFITS

Insurance companies and others use actuarial tables in calculating payments and benefits for insurance and other types of benefit plans. The actuarial tables indicate, on average, that females live longer than males; therefore, females have been charged more at the initial pay-in stage or receive smaller monthly payments at the pay-out stage. These types of programs have been challenged as a form of sex discrimination under Title VII.

The Supreme Court held in the *Manhart* case in 1978 that a pension plan that required female employees to make larger contributions than males for equivalent benefits violated Title VII because the difference in treatment was based strictly on sex.[73]

The state of Arizona[74] developed a different approach, with the differential at the pay-out as opposed to the pay-in stage. Employees were offered a deferred annuity plan and could select from three options: (1) a single lump-sum payment upon retirement, (2) payments at a specified amount for a fixed period of time, or (3) monthly annuity payments for the remainder of their life. The first two options treated males and females equally and were not in dispute. But option three, the monthly annuity plan, was set up in accordance with sex-based mortality tables. If males and females retired at the same age, with the same contributions, males received a greater payment per month. Sex was thus the only factor used to classify the individuals. Citing *Manhart,* the court ruled that the system violated Title VII.

■ TITLE IX

Title IX of the Education Amendments of 1972 was enacted to protect the rights of individuals and to prohibit discrimination based on gender in educational programs or activities receiving federal funds. Title IX is closely patterned after Title VI of the Civil Rights Act of 1964.

Because Title IX is patterned after Title VI and covers students in educational institutions, some courts earlier ruled that Title IX does not cover employees. But the Supreme Court in *North Haven Board of Education v. Bell* stated, "[W]hile section 901(a) does not expressly include or exclude employees within its scope, its broad directive that no person may be discriminated against on the basis of gender includes employees as well as students."[75]

The Civil Rights Restoration Act of 1988 amended Title IX to make it clear that gender-based discrimination involving any program or activity of an institution jeopardizes federal financial assistance for the entire institution. Thus, discrimination against an employee in any school or department of a public school district is presumed to be an offense by the entire school district, and the district's federal funding may be withheld if the situation is not remedied.

Moreover, under the *Franklin v. Gwinnett County Public Schools* decision rendered by the U.S. Supreme Court in 1992 (see Chapter 8), an employee suffering sex discrimination may be entitled to compensatory and punitive damages against the school district. As observed in Chapter 8, litigation has abounded under Title IX since *Gwinnett* and will likely continue.

❖ — ❖ — ❖

Title IX of the Education Amendments of 1972 Protects Employees against Gender Discrimination in Educational Institutions

North Haven Board of Education v. Bell

Supreme Court of the United States, 1982.
456 U.S. 512, 102 S.Ct. 1912.

Justice BLACKMUN delivered the opinion of the Court. At issue here is the validity of regulations promulgated by the Department of Education pursuant to Title IX of the Education Amendments of 1972, Pub.L. 92-318, 86 Stat. 373, 20 U.S.C. §1681 et seq. These regulations prohibit federally funded education programs from discriminating on the basis of gender with respect to employment.

Title IX proscribes gender discrimination in education programs or activities receiving federal financial assistance. Patterned after Title VI of the Civil Rights Act of 1964, Pub.L. 88-352, 78 Stat. 252, 42 U.S.C. §2000d et seq., Title IX, as amended, contains two core provisions. The first is a "program-specific" prohibition of gender discrimination:

"No person in the United States shall, on the basis of sex, be excluded from participation in, be denied the benefits of, or be subjected to discrimination under any education program or activity receiving Federal financial assistance. . . ." §901(a).

Nine statutory exceptions to §901(a)'s coverage follow. See §§901(a)(1)–(9).

The second core provision relates to enforcement. Section 902 authorizes each agency awarding federal financial assistance to any education program to promulgate regulations ensuring that aid recipients adhere to §901(a)'s mandate. The ultimate sanction for noncompliance is termination of federal funds or denial of future grants.

In 1975, the Department of Health, Education, and Welfare (HEW) invoked its §902 authority to issue regulations governing the operation of federally funded education programs. These regulations extend, for example, to policies involving admissions, textbooks, and athletics. Interpreting the term "person" in §901(a) to encompass employees as well as students, HEW included among the regulations a series entitled "Subpart E," which deals with employment practices, ranging from job classifications to pregnancy leave. . . .

Petitioners are two Connecticut public school boards that brought separate suits challenging HEW's authority to issue the Subpart E regulations. Petitioners contend that Title IX was not meant to reach the employment practices of educational institutions.

The North Haven Board of Education (North Haven) receives federal funds for its education programs and activities and is therefore subject to Title IX's prohibition of gender discrimination. Since the 1975–1976 school year, North Haven has devoted between 46.8 percent and 66.9 percent of its federal assistance to the salaries of its employees; this practice is expected to continue.

In January 1978, Elaine Dove, a tenured teacher in the North Haven public school system, filed a complaint with HEW, alleging that North Haven had violated Title IX by refusing to rehire her after a one-year maternity leave. In response to this complaint, HEW began to investigate the school board's employment practices and sought from petitioner information concerning its policies on hiring, leaves of absence, seniority, and tenure. Asserting that HEW lacked authority to regulate employment practices under Title IX, North Haven refused to comply with the request. . . .

The Trumbull Board of Education (Trumbull) likewise receives financial support from the federal government and must therefore adhere to the requirements of Title IX and appropriate implementing regulations. In October 1977, HEW began investigating a complaint filed by respondent Linda Potz, a former guidance counselor in the Trumbull school district. Potz alleged that Trumbull had discriminated against her on the basis of gender with respect to job assignments, working conditions, and the failure to renew her contract. In September 1978, HEW notified Trumbull that it had violated Title IX and warned that corrective action, including respondent's reinstatement, must be taken.

Trumbull then filed suit in the United States District Court for the District of Connecticut, contending that HEW's Title IX employment regulations were invalid. . . .

Our starting point in determining the scope of Title IX is, of course, the statutory language. Section 901(a)'s broad directive that "no person" may be discriminated against on the basis of gender appears, on its face, to include employees as well as students. Under that provision, employees, like other "persons," may not be "excluded from participation in," "denied the benefits of," or "subjected to discrimination under" education programs receiving federal financial support.

Employees who directly participate in federal programs or who directly benefit from federal grants, loans, or contracts clearly fall within the first two protective categories described in §901(a). In addition, a female employee who works in a federally funded education program is "subjected to discrimination under" that program if she is paid a lower salary for like work, given less opportunity for promotion, or forced to work under more adverse conditions than are her male colleagues.

There is no doubt that "if we are to give [Title IX] the scope that its origins dictate, we must accord it a sweep as broad as its language." Because §901(a) neither expressly nor impliedly excludes employees from its reach, we should interpret the provision as covering and protecting these "persons" unless other considerations counsel to the contrary. After all, Congress easily could have substituted "student" or "beneficiary" for the word "person" if it had wished to restrict the scope of §901(a).

Petitioners, however, point to the nine exceptions to §901(a)'s coverage set forth in §§901(a)(1)–(9). . . . The exceptions, the school boards argue, are directed only at students, and thus indicate that §901(a) similarly applies only to students. But the exceptions are not concerned solely with students and student activities: two of them exempt an entire class of institutions—religious and military schools—and are not limited to student-related activities at such schools. See §§901(a)(3), (4). Moreover, petitioners' argument rests on an inference that is by no means compelled; in fact, the absence of a specific exclusion for employment among the list of exceptions tends to support the Court of Appeals' conclusion that Title IX's broad protection of "person[s]" does extend to employees of educational institutions.

Although the statutory language thus seems to favor inclusion of employees, nevertheless, because Title IX does not expressly include or exclude employees from its scope, we turn to the Act's legislative history for evidence as to whether Congress meant somehow to limit the expansive language of §901. . . .

In our view, the legislative history thus corroborates our reading of the statutory language and verifies the Court of Appeals' conclusion that employment discrimination comes within the prohibition of Title IX. . . .

Whether termination of petitioners' federal funds is permissible under Title IX is a question that must be answered by the District Court in the first instance. Similarly, we do not undertake to define "program" in this opinion. Neither of the cases before us advanced beyond a motion for summary judgment, and the record therefore does not reflect whether petitioners' employment practices actually discriminated on the basis of gender or whether any such discrimination comes within the prohibition of Title IX. Neither school board opposed HEW's investigation into its employment practices on the grounds that the complaining employees' salaries were not funded by federal money, that the employees did not work in an education program that received federal assistance, or that the discrimination they allegedly suffered did not affect a federally funded program. Instead, petitioners disputed the Department's authority to regulate any employment practices whatsoever, and the District Court adopted that view, which we find to be error. Accordingly, we affirm the judgment of the Court of Appeals but remand the case for further proceedings consistent with this opinion.

It is so ordered.

■ SEXUAL HARASSMENT

Sexual harassment in employment may be defined as "a demand that a subordinate, usually a woman, grant sexual favors in order to obtain or retain a job benefit."[76]

As discussed in Chapter 8 of this text, sexual harassment may range from verbal innuendo to an overt act, encompassing a substantial diversity of behavior.[77] Employees are protected from sexual harassment in the workplace by Title VII of the Civil Rights Act of 1964 and by Title IX of the Education Amendments of 1972. Court cases in the 1970s began recognizing sexual harassment as an aspect of sex discrimination, but it was not until 1980 that the Equal Employment Opportunity Commission (EEOC) promulgated regulations prohibiting sexual harassment. These regulations state:

> Harassment on the basis of sex is a violation of Sec. 703 of Title VII. Unwelcome sexual advances, requests for sexual favors, and other verbal or physical conduct of a sexual nature constitute harassment when (1) submission to such conduct is made explicitly or implicitly a term or condition of an individual's employment, (2) submission to or rejection of such conduct by an individual is used as a basis for employment decisions affecting such individual, (3) such conduct has the purpose or effect of unreasonably interfering with an individual's work performance or creating an intimidating, hostile, or offensive working environment.[78]

Sexual harassment under Title VII is based on two legal theories: *"quid pro quo"* and "hostile environment."[79]

QUID PRO QUO

This type of sexual harassment occurs when an agent of an employer, usually a man, uses his supervisory status and power to induce a subordinate employee, usually a woman, but not necessarily, to grant sexual favors in exchange for job benefits.[80] The something for something,[81] a favor for a favor, suggests the name *quid pro quo*. Under this theory of sexual harassment, a subordinate employee has been forced to choose between giving sexual favors and suffering an economic detriment.[82] One federal circuit has termed this the "put out or get out" bargain, which makes employment benefits, pay, and/or advancement dependent on being sexually cooperative.[83] The U.S. Supreme Court in *Meritor Savings Bank, FSB v. Vinson*,[84] the leading case on sexual harassment, provides definition:

> . . . [T]he guidelines provide that sexual conduct constitutes prohibited "sexual harassment," whether or not it is directly linked to the grant or denial of

an economic *quid pro quo,* where "such conduct has the purpose or effect of unreasonably interfering with an individual's work performance or creating an intimidating, hostile, or offensive working environment [*non quid pro quo*]."[85]

HOSTILE ENVIRONMENT

The second theory of sexual harassment liability that violates Title VII is unwelcome conduct by a superior, and perhaps by co-workers, that creates an unpleasant workplace; this is called "hostile environment" harassment. Such conduct usually involves a series of incidents and not a single episode.[86] A sexually hostile environment does not necessarily occur because of a sexual advance or an invitation to sexual activity, but rather the hostile conduct occurs because of the victim's gender, such as conduct caused by resentment of women in the workplace and gender prejudice.

In condemning such sexual harassment and justifying its legal prohibition, the Eleventh Circuit Court of Appeals in *Henson v. Dunde*[87] has observed:

> Sexual harassment which creates a hostile or offensive environment for members of one sex is every bit the arbitrary barrier to sexual equality at the workplace that racial harassment is to racial equality. Surely, a requirement that a man or woman run a gauntlet for the privilege of being allowed to work and make a living can be as demeaning and disconcerting as the harshest of racial epithets.

A sexually hostile environment can be so unpleasant that a person is driven off the job; this is called constructive discharge and is prohibited by Title VII.[88] Remedies for constructive discharge include back pay and reinstatement, or front pay in lieu of reinstatement.[89]

In 1993, the Supreme Court in *Harris v. Forklift Systems,* a sexual harassment case, found that a hostile or abusive environment is determined by examining a number of factors and the frequency with which they have occurred. These include the severity of the conduct, whether it was physically threatening or humiliating, and whether it interfered with the employee's work performance. The Court also said, "To be actionable under Title VII as 'abusive work environment' harassment, conduct need not seriously affect the employee's psychological well-being or lead the employee to suffer injury, so long as

the environment would reasonably be perceived, and is perceived, as hostile or abusive." Title VII does not require the employee to prove actual harm, psychological or physical.[90]

RETALIATION

A claim of retaliation may be made by individuals who have previously made known to the employer their opposition to an employment practice that they reasonably believe to be unlawful under Title VII. Section 704(b) protects employees who have filed a charge, testified, assisted, or participated in any manner in an investigation, proceeding, or hearing under Title VII.[91] Allegations of retaliation frequently follow a complaint regarding sexual harassment. The plaintiff need not show that retaliation was the sole motivating factor in order to prevail. Whether the retaliatory motive plays a part in or is the sole cause of the "employer's retaliatory animus," the plaintiff's action will succeed.[92] The current law, enacted in 1991, reversed a holding by the Supreme Court in 1989 that an employer is not liable for intentional discrimination in "mixed motive" cases where it can be shown that it would have made the same decision without the discrimination.[93] For an allegation of retaliation to prevail, the plaintiff must show that a causal connection existed between the plaintiff's claim of sexual harassment and retaliation. Intervening acts may break the causal links in retaliation cases;[94] for example, lapses of time of three months,[95] four months,[96] and six months[97] have been held by the courts to evidence a severing of the causal link.

Whether, and under what circumstances, the employer may be liable for an employee's sexual harassment of another employee continues to be a subject of considerable debate among the federal courts. This is because the U.S. Supreme Court has been unable to lay down a precise standard that would be reasonably applicable in most circumstances. The Supreme Court said in 1998 that since the *Meritor* case, the federal courts of appeals "have struggled to derive manageable standards to govern employer liability for hostile environment harassment perpetrated by supervisory employees."[98] In seeking to provide better guidance with regard to the vicarious liability of the employer, the Supreme Court ruled in *Faragher v. City of Boca Raton,*[99] a case involving a supervisor's sexual harassment of a female lifeguard, that an employer may be liable for the acts of its employees under Title VII; however, the employer can raise an affirmative defense that looks to the reasonableness of the employer's conduct in seeking to prevent and correct the harassing conduct and to the reasonableness of the employee's own responsibility and conduct in seeking to avoid being victimized by a supervisor.[100] In this particular case, the Supreme Court held that the city of Boca Raton was subject to vicarious liability to the female lifeguard because the city had failed to exercise reasonable care to prevent the harassing behavior. The Court found that even though the city had adopted a sexual harassment policy, which it stated in a memorandum that may have been circulated to some employees, it "completely failed to disseminate its policies"[101] among employees in the lifeguard section of the city government. Thus, the city could not show that it had made reasonable attempts to educate and warn employees of the policy against sexual harassment.

Thus, the Court holds that while as a general rule a master (the employer) is liable for the acts of its servants (employees) in the scope of employment, the employer is not liable for acts that go beyond the employment that the servant is hired to perform. It goes without saying that normally a "[h]ostile environment rarely, if ever, is among the official duties of a supervisor."[102]

Yet the employer cannot completely escape the potential for liability by merely asserting that sexual harassment is beyond the scope of employment, that it falls within what common law called "frolic and detour" for which the employer had no vicarious liability. In this regard, the Supreme Court in the *Boca Raton* case said that rather than to conclude that employers were absolutely immune from liability or, on the other hand, to conclude that they were always liable for the acts of their employees, a middle approach is preferred. Under the alternative reasoning, the Court ruled that an employer would be allowed to present an "affirmative defense to liability" showing that it had "exercised reasonable care to avoid harassment and to eliminate it when it might occur."[103] Importantly, this defense can show that the complaining employee failed to act with "reasonable care to take ad-

vantage of the employer's safeguards" and prevent the harm that could have been avoided.[104]

In further elaboration on the requirements of an employer to effectively defend against a supervisory employee's harassment of another employee, in a case styled *Burlington Industries, Inc. v. Ellerth*, decided the same day as the *Boca Raton* lifeguard case, the Supreme Court said that a defense comprises two necessary elements: "(a) that the employer exercised reasonable care to prevent and correct promptly any sexually harassing behavior, and (b) that the plaintiff employee unreasonably failed to take advantage of any preventive or corrective opportunities provided by the employer or to avoid harm otherwise."[105]

❖ — ❖ — ❖

*School Board Was Not Vicariously Liable
for Sexual Harassment of Female Teacher
by Male School Principal*

Masson v. School Board of Dade County, Florida

United States District Court, Second District,
Miami Division, Florida, 1999.
36 F.Supp.2d 1354.

K. MICHAEL MOORE, District Judge. . . .

Plaintiff Carmen Masson ("Masson") filed a two-count amended complaint alleging hostile work environment (count I) and failure to promote (and demoting) (count II), both in violation of Title VII of the Civil Rights Act of 1964, as amended. Defendant Dade County School Board (the "School Board") has answered the complaint and now files this motion for partial summary judgment as to Masson's claim for hostile work environment. . . .

The undisputed facts as taken from Masson's amended complaint and the record are as follows: Masson was hired by the School Board in 1983 as a culinary arts teacher at Lindsey Hopkins Technical Education Center and served there until July 1997. Since 1992, Masson alleges she was subjected to a hostile work environment based upon the actions and explicit sexual remarks of John Leyva ("Leyva"), the school principal since 1991 and Masson's supervisor. The following are allegations made by Masson and undisputed by the School Board concerning Leyva's conduct:

(1) She was offended when she heard Leyva say she was good-looking in addition to being the most competent employee in the kitchen;

(2) At a grievance hearing, Leyva stated "he wouldn't kiss [Masson's] face but would kiss [Masson's] ass for all the work she had done at Lindsey Hopkins to put it on the map;"

(3) Leyva and two female staff members engaged in an inappropriate conversation in Leyva's office concerning sexual portraits, lingerie and sex toys. Masson excused herself from the conversation and left the office;

(4) Leyva was always making remarks about Masson's hair and clothing. In one incident, Leyva said "Your hair looks great. You look like a lion" and he started to approach Masson but stopped and said "I forgot you're married;"

(5) Masson saw Leyva kissing a secretary at school;

(6) In a meeting, after Masson was able to help Leyva obtain additional seating at a school event, Leyva leaned over and kissed Masson on the cheek or jaw; and

(7) An assistant principal said that he would be administering the cafeteria like "ladilla" which Masson took to mean he would be all over the place, like crabs.

Masson also alleges Leyva has a pattern and practice of sexually harassing his other subordinate female employees. . . .

Hostile work environment sexual harassment occurs when "an employer's conduct has the purpose or effect of unreasonably interfering with an individual's work performance or creating an intimidating, hostile or offensive environment." To establish a prima facie case for hostile work environment sexual harassment, Masson must show the following: (1) she belonged to a protected group; (2) she was subjected to unwelcome sexual harassment; (3) the harassment complained of was based upon sex; (4) the harassment complained of affected a term, condi-

tion or privilege of employment; and (5) the School Board knew or should have known of the harassment and failed to take prompt remedial action. . . . The Supreme Court has instructed that for such an allegation to be actionable, "a sexually objectionable environment must be both objectively and subjectively offensive, one that a reasonable person would find hostile or abusive, and one that the victim in fact did perceive to be so." *Faragher v. City of Boca Raton*, 524 U.S. 775, 118 S.Ct. 2275, 2283, 141 L.Ed.2d 662 (1998). Thus, a court should determine whether an environment is sufficiently hostile or abusive by looking at all the circumstances, including the frequency of the conduct, its severity and whether it unreasonably interferes with an employee's work performance or is mere offensive utterance. . . . This inquiry prevents Title VII from becoming a "general civility code" and filters out "the ordinary tribulations of the workplace, such as the sporadic use of abusive language, gender-related jokes, and occasional teasing." . . .

Not surprisingly, the School Board dismisses Masson's allegations as nonactionable, mere offensive speech. This Court certainly has addressed allegations far more outrageous and demeaning than those alleged by Masson. And while Masson's allegations are, in the Court's view, borderline, the Court believes they were severe and pervasive enough to constitute sexual harassment. There is no question Masson subjectively felt the comments were sexually objectionable and the Court believes a reasonable person would see them that way. Accordingly, the Court finds Masson has established a prima facie case of hostile work environment sexual harassment.

The Supreme Court in *Faragher* recently addressed the issue of an employer's liability for a hostile work environment created by an employee's supervisor. The Court stated that "an employer is subject to vicarious liability to a victimized employee for an actionable hostile work environment created by a supervisor with immediate (or successively higher) authority over the employee." *Faragher*, 118 S.Ct at 2292–93; . . . The Court, however, created an affirmative defense for employers where, as here, no tangible employment action was taken against the employee. To take advantage of the defense, the School Board must show (1) "that [the School Board] exercised reasonable care to prevent and correct promptly any sexually harassing behavior," and (2) "that [Masson] unreasonably failed to take advantage of any preventive opportunities provided by the employer or to avoid harm otherwise." . . . The School Board argues it has met its burden under both prongs of the *Faragher* defense in that the School Board exercised reasonable care to prevent harassment and Masson never took advantage of the School Board's antiharassment policy.

With respect to the first prong of the defense, the Supreme Court has stated the following:

> While proof that an employer had promulgated an antiharassment policy with complaint procedure is not necessary in every instance as a matter of law, the need for a stated policy suitable to the employment circumstances may appropriately be addressed in any case when litigating the first element of the defense.

. . . Here, it is undisputed the School Board has an officially promulgated, nondiscrimination/harassment policy and complaint procedure. In support of its argument, the School Board submits the affidavit of Rafael Urrutia, the Director for the School Board's Office of Equal Educational and Employment Opportunity. In his affidavit, Urrutia states that he conducts workshops and training sessions for supervisors concerning compliance with federal and state statutes and School Board rules that prohibit sexual harassment. Urrutia further states the School Board's policy is widely disseminated to employees and that the policy provides a comprehensive procedure for processing harassment complaints. In response, Masson argues the School Board has "failed to develop a comprehensive anti-harassment policy" and in fact did not provide harassment training to supervisors. Masson, however, does not provide factual support for her argument and essentially rests on conclusory allegations about the deficiencies in the School Board's policy. Thus, because Masson does not provide factual evidence to counter Urrutia's statements concerning the School Board's policy, Urrutia's affidavit is essentially undisputed. . . . Thus, the Court finds the School Board has satisfied the first prong of the *Faragher* defense by showing it has exercised reasonable care to prevent sexual harassment by creating and implementing an antiharassment policy and complaint procedure.

With respect to the second prong of the defense, the Supreme Court has stated:

> And while proof that an employee failed to fulfill the corresponding obligation of reasonable care to avoid harm is not limited to showing an unreasonable failure to use any complaint procedure provided by the employer, a demonstration of such failure will normally suffice to satisfy the employer's burden under the second element of the defense.

. . . The School Board argues Masson failed to reasonably avail herself of the avenues created by the School Board's policy to put the School Board on notice of the ongoing harassment. Masson states she complained to Roger Cuevas, the Assistant Superintendent, about being replaced by Tom Saslgiver (a male chef) and that Cuevas "understood my claim to be gender discrimination." Masson further states she complained about the same incident (being replaced) to David Schleiden, the Vocational Supervisor, and also filed six grievances with her union. Finally, Masson claims she faxed a memorandum of understanding to Nelson Diaz, the Superintendent of Management and Labor Relations.

It appears the focus of Masson's communication with these individuals concerned her job reassignment rather than Mr. Leyva's alleged inappropriate conduct. That Masson believes Cuevas understood her claim to be gender discrimination cannot, by itself, support Masson's argument that she complained to others about Leyva's alleged sexual harassment. More importantly, it is undisputed that Masson never took advantage of the School Board policy and never filed a complaint with Urrutia. Masson never argues she was unaware of the policy and does not assert any reason why she chose not to follow its procedures.

While recognizing the "enormous difficulties" involved in lodging complaints about sexual harassment in the workplace, the Eleventh Circuit recently noted:

> Federal law has now attempted to correct the problem of workplace discrimination, but it cannot be done without the cooperation of the victims, notwithstanding that it may be difficult for them to make such efforts. When an employer has taken steps, such as promulgating a considered sexual harassment policy, to prevent sexual harassment in the workplace, an employee must provide

adequate notice that the employer's directives have been breached so that the employer has the opportunity to correct the problem.

. . . Thus, while the School Board's hands may not be clean, the Court cannot in every instance hold it liable for actions about which it is unaware—especially when the complainant does not follow the procedures provided for in the School Board's policies. . . . Accordingly, the Court finds the School Board has met its burden under the second prong of the *Faragher* defense by showing that Masson unreasonably failed to take advantage of any preventive or corrective opportunities provided by the School Board.

Because the School Board has satisfied its burden under *Faragher,* the Court finds there is no genuine issue of material fact that exists to support a finding either (1) that the School Board did not exercise reasonable care in preventing the harassment or (2) that Masson herself acted reasonably to put the School Board on notice of a problem. As a result, summary judgment in favor of the School Board as to count I of the amended complaint is appropriate. . . .

Case Notes

1. *Preventive Action.* Lindemann and Kadue in their seminal book *Sexual Harassment in Employment Law* published by the Bureau of National Affairs, Inc., Washington, D.C. (1992) *Cumulative Supplement,* 1999, indicate preventive actions by employers that would be helpful in defending against liability.

(1) The school district's sexual harassment policy law should be made known to each employee. See *Shrout v. Black Clawson Co.,* 689 F.Supp. 774 (S.D. Ohio 1988).

(2) Information should be conveyed to each employee, independently, through distribution of materials or an employee handbook. Posting the sexual harassment policy on a bulletin board is an effective device. See *Robinson v. Jacksonville Shipyards,* 760 F.Supp. 1486 (M.D.Fla.1991).

(3) Employees should be sensitized to harassment concerns. Many harassers are ignorant to the fact that they are sexually harassing others. Training programs are effective means of demonstrating the employer's commitment to eradicating sexual harassment. See 29 C.F.R. §1604.11(a).

(4) Complaints of harassment should be promptly and thoroughly investigated. The sexual harassment policy of a school district should call for prompt corrective action if the situation is validated. The U.S. Court of Appeals, Eighth Circuit, concluded that the investigation of claims of unlawful harassment within four days of the complaint, which concluded with reprimand of the alleged harassers, was evidence that the employer acted reasonably and was not vicariously liable. *Barrett v. Omaha National Bank,* 726 F.2d 424 (8th Cir.1984). If at all possible, complaints should be reduced to writing and should embody all the relevant details. Such written complaints may require that the employer assist the complainant in recording the allegations.

(5) A well-publicized antifraternization policy is evidence that the employer's intent is not to tolerate sexual harassment. See *Sears v. Ryder Truck Rental,* 596 F.Supp. 1001 (E.D.Mich.1984).

A federal district court in New York has described elements of an effective antiharassment program:

- Issuing a written harassment policy;
- Instructing managers to communicate the company's refusal to tolerate harassment;
- Establishing complaint procedures;
- Insulating complainants from retaliation;
- Vowing to impose appropriate discipline for policy violations;
- Conducting seminars on harassment for employees; and
- Taking effective remedial action in response to complaints.

Additional measures could include

- A sign-off mechanism whereby employees affirm that they have received, read, and understood the employer's policy and the complaint procedure;
- A mechanism for complaining both inside and outside the aggrieved employee's chain of command;
- A process that includes as much confidentiality as practicable;
- A prompt and thorough investigation; and

- Periodic training sessions for employees in recognizing and reporting harassment and for supervisory personnel in deterring harassment and responding to complaints.

The employer who has promulgated an effective antiharassment policy, disseminated the information and procedures contained in the policy to all employees, and demonstrated a commitment to adhering to its policy has fulfilled its obligation. *Trotta v. Mobil Oil Corp.*, 788 F.Supp. 1336, 1351, 62 FEP Cases 695, 707 (S.D.N.Y.1992) (ruling for defendant after bench trial). See also Barbara T. Lindemann and David D. Kadue, *Sexual Harassment in Employment Law, 1999 Cumulative Supplement* (Washington, D.C.: Bureau of National Affairs, Inc., 1999), p. 176.

2. The Supreme Court's decisions in the *Burlington Industries* and *Boca Raton* cases will undoubtedly lead to increased scrutiny of employers' policies by complainants, agencies, and courts. An employer's written policy should

- State that harassment because of membership in any protected group is prohibited;
- Define harassment in plain language and give examples of it so that employees and supervisors understand what types of behavior are prohibited;
- Set up a system so that employees need not approach their supervisor if the supervisor is the alleged harasser;
- Reserve the right to impose discipline for inappropriate conduct discovered during the investigation of a harassment complaint, without regard to whether the discovered conduct is unlawful harassment;
- Provide for a prompt investigation of all reports;
- Provide that any violation of company policy will result in appropriate corrective action, including discipline up to and including the immediate termination of employment;
- State that the employer forbids retaliation for reporting harassment or for cooperating with an investigation of alleged harassment;
- State that the employer will preserve the confidentiality of complainants and witnesses to the extent that the needs of the investigation permit; and
- Document the distribution of the policy to each employee.

See *Burlington Industries Inc. v. Ellerth*, 524 U.S. 742, 118 S.Ct. 2257 (1998); *Faragher v. City of Boca Raton*, 524 U.S. 775, 118 S.Ct. 2275 (1998). See also Barbara T. Lindemann and David D. Kadue, *Sexual Harassment in Employment Law, 1999 Cumulative Supplement* (Washington, D.C.: Bureau of National Affairs, Inc., 1999), pp. 176–177.

The EEOC guidelines further provide that an employer is held responsible

> [f]or its acts and those of its agents and supervisory employees with respect to sexual harassment regardless of whether the specific acts complained of were authorized or even forbidden by the employer and regardless of whether the employer knew or should have known of their occurrence.[106]

Also, an employer is held responsible for acts of sexual harassment between fellow employees where the employer "knows or should have known of the conduct, unless it can show that it took immediate and appropriate corrective actions."[107]

❖ — ❖ — ❖

Principal's Sexual Relationship with Teacher Was Consensual and Did Not Constitute Sexual Harassment under Title VII or Equal Protection

Trautvetter v. Quick

United States Court of Appeals,
Seventh Circuit, 1990.
916 F.2d 1140.

KANNE, Circuit Judge. Plaintiff-appellant, Patsy L. Trautvetter, brought an action in the district court in which she alleged that the defendants had engaged in sexual discrimination in violation of Title VII of the Civil Rights Act of 1964, 78 Stat. 253, as amended 42 U.S.C. §§2000e *et seq.*, and 42 U.S.C. §§1983 and 1985(3). . . .

In the fall of 1975, Patsy Trautvetter began her first year of teaching in the Northeast School Corporation in Sullivan County, Indiana. In 1982, after six years of full-time teaching and one year of maternity leave, she was assigned to teach first grade at Hymera Elementary School. Beginning in the fall of 1985, Ms. Trautvetter returned to Hymera Elementary after a second maternity leave to teach second grade. She has since been teaching at Hymera Elementary continuously. Defendant, John Quick, began his term as the principal of Hymera Elementary in 1981 and, as such, was at all times relevant to these proceedings Trautvetter's immediate supervisor.

Beginning late in the 1985–86 school year and continuing into the 1986–87 school year, Quick made a number of romantic overtures towards Ms. Trautvetter. Initially, she put off these advances by either politely saying "no" or simply "laughing them off." Eventually, however, she began to respond to Quick's romantic suggestions. Indeed, the record reveals that Trautvetter became involved in a sexual relationship with Quick in which both parties participated actively. The "courtship" proceeded as follows.

Quick's first romantic overture towards Ms. Trautvetter occurred on the final day of the 1985–86 school year. A group of teachers, including Ms. Trautvetter and Mr. Quick, had gone out for the evening and eventually ended up at a local bar. Trautvetter left the bar early. After she had arrived home, however, she called the bar and asked that Quick be paged so she could explain to him, for the benefit of another teacher, a joke which had been played on the latter. During the course of that conversation, Quick asked Trautvetter whether her family was home. She responded that they were not. Quick thereafter asked her if she would like to "play house." She replied "no." . . .

In April of 1987, the two agreed to meet on at least two occasions at an abandoned school building in Colemont, Indiana; an out-of-the-way place about which Quick had told her. According to Trautvetter, she and Quick would drive around the surrounding countryside, kissing and petting along the way. On one of these occasions, Quick asked Trautvetter if he could fondle her breasts. She let him do so. Again, at no time either prior to or during this encounter did Ms. Trautvetter tell Quick that she thought his conduct was inappropriate. . . .

On May 8, 1987, Ms. Trautvetter and Mr. Quick drove in Ms. Trautvetter's car to a Regal 8 Motel where they had sexual intercourse. This rendezvous had been planned for a week. Trautvetter testified that she was nervous on this occasion. Trautvetter also testified that she felt no affection for Quick on this occasion, but engaged in intercourse with him only because she "felt she had to be there." The record reveals, however, that Trautvetter was not physically forced to show up at the motel, nor was she forced to engage in the sexual act. Moreover, the record reveals that shortly after that date, Trautvetter sent Quick a note which read, "I'll remember that night [May 8] and hope we will be friends forever." . . .

. . . A few days later, Quick telephoned Trautvetter and told her that his wife was out of town and asked if she could get a babysitter and come over to his house. She told him she could not do that. The following evening, Trautvetter told her husband what had been going on between herself and Quick. . . .

On June 4, 1987, Ms. Trautvetter and her husband (Calvin Trautvetter) went to visit Mr. Quick to discuss the problem. According to Ms. Trautvetter, Mr. Trautvetter informed Mr. Quick that he should stay away from his wife. He also advised Mr. Quick that he should inform his own wife of the situation. . . .

On June 9, 1987, the Trautvetters met with Richard Walters, the superintendent of the Northeast School Corporation. . . . Mr. Walters asked them to "keep it quiet." At this point, however, it is undisputed that Mr. Walters was not aware of Ms. Trautvetter's allegations of sexual harassment; she had not told him. Indeed, Ms. Trautvetter testified that she had not even told her husband of her allegations of sexual harassment at this juncture.

Early in the morning of June 8, 1987, Mr. Walters met with John Quick and his wife. At this meeting, Quick told Mr. Walters of his relationship with Ms. Trautvetter. . . .

On June 23, 1987, Ms. Trautvetter called Mr. Walters to express her concern about her job status for the upcoming school year. She also told Mr. Walters that there was more to her side of the story that she needed to tell him. She did not, however, reveal her side of the story to Mr. Walters on that date.

On June 26, 1987, Ms. Trautvetter met with Mr. Walters and George Baker, a representative of the Indiana State Teacher's Association. During this meeting, Mr. Walters was informed for the first time of Trautvetter's allegations that Quick had pressured her into entering into the sexual relationship. . . .

On July 14, 1987, Mr. Walters and the school corporation's legal counsel, Mr. Springer, met to begin the investigation into Ms. Trautvetter's allegations. . . . All of the persons interviewed (if they were aware of the relationship which existed between Trautvetter and Quick) indicated to Mr. Walters that they thought that relationship was consensual. Moreover, there was no indication from any of those persons that Quick had harassed Trautvetter sexually or otherwise. . . .

Mr. Walters subsequently concluded his investigation. He found that the relationship which existed between Ms. Trautvetter and Mr. Quick was consensual in nature and, as such, that it did not result from any sexual harassment on the part of Mr. Quick. . . . A letter was sent to both parties on July 22, 1987, informing them of that decision. That same letter advised both Ms. Trautvetter and Mr. Quick that a transfer would be considered by the board if either of them felt that their past relationship would interfere with their work relationship. Neither party made such a request for transfer. Although this letter did not constitute an official action of the board in that it had not been put to a "formal vote," it is undisputed that the board was presented with the letter and did not present any objections to its being mailed.

This appeal requires us to examine the often-blurred line which exists between human interaction in the workplace which is purely a private matter and human interaction in the workplace which gives rise to sexual harassment claims actionable under either Title VII or the equal protection clause of the fourteenth amendment. . . .

. . . Ms. Trautvetter argues that the defendants' actions, in both their individual and official capacities, violated her constitutional rights. Her specific allegations refer to: (1) John Quick's sexual advances; and (2) the remaining defendants' alleged failure to take appropriate action which she argues served to condone and perpetuate Quick's acts of sexual harassment. . . .

. . . [W]e must examine whether the alleged sexual advances were "unwelcome." . . . ("The gravamen of any sexual harassment claim is that the alleged sexual advances were 'unwelcome.'")

Although this determination is one that is traditionally left to the trier of fact, . . . the district court concluded for Title VII purposes, based on an examination of the entire record, that Ms. Trautvetter had not raised any genuine issues of material fact as to whether Mr. Quick's sexual advances were "unwelcome." . . . Beyond the fact that Ms. Trautvetter initially declined Mr. Quick's offers for drinks, etc., the record is void of any evidence showing that she declared those advances to be unwelcome. Much to the contrary, the course of conduct, when reviewed in its entirety, appears to substantiate the district court's findings that Ms. Trautvetter grew to "welcome" Mr. Quick's advances and even participated in an active way so as to encourage them. The district court need not have addressed this issue of fact, however, and we will not address it further, in light of our conclusion that Ms. Trautvetter has failed to demonstrate that Mr. Quick's advances constitute the type of *intentional discrimination* based upon an individual's membership in a particular class which has traditionally been viewed as actionable under the equal protection clause of the fourteenth amendment.

Like any other equal protection claim, a claim of sexual harassment under the fourteenth amendment must show that the discrimination was intentional. . . .

In light of this "intent" requirement, the issue which we are presented with in this context . . . is whether Mr. Quick's sexual advances towards Ms. Trautvetter were "because of" her status as a woman or, in the alternative, whether those advances were inspired by characteristics, albeit some sexual, which were personal to Ms. Trautvetter. . . .

. . . Thus, while it is clear that an individual plaintiff may pursue a sexual discrimination claim under the fourteenth amendment based solely upon acts of discrimination directed towards her, it is also clear that such a claim must show an intent to discriminate *because of* her status as a female and not because of characteristics of her gender which are personal to her. Without question, this line becomes indistinct when those factors which are personal to an individual include attributes of sexual attraction. In such a case, a careful analysis of the conduct which is alleged to be harassment is necessary to determine whether it is indeed "harassment" as that term is understood in the Title VII context—the first prong of our analysis. If this distinction—subtle as it is—is not maintained, any consensual workplace romance involving a state supervisor and employee which soured for one reason or another could give rise to equal protection claims if the employee simply alleges that his or her supervisor's conduct during the term of the romance constituted "sexual harassment." Such a scenario constitutes precisely the type of claim which the equal protection clause's "intent to discriminate" requirement was meant to discourage. . . .

. . . [W]e conclude that she has not raised a genuine issue of material fact as to whether Mr. Quick's sexual advances were *because of* her status as a woman. Certainly, the underlying fact is that Ms. Trautvetter is a woman. But, as we have noted, her status as a woman does not itself support an allegation of sexual harassment under the equal protection clause; she must demonstrate in a colorable manner that Mr. Quick's advances were because of her status as a woman as opposed to characteristics, albeit some no doubt sexual, which were personal to her. This she has failed to do. Indeed, there is nothing in the record to indicate that Mr. Quick's feelings were based on anything but a personal attraction to Ms. Trautvetter. Ms. Trautvetter's own testimony leads us to this conclusion; in reference to the March 13, 1987 phone call, Ms. Trautvetter testified that Mr. Quick told her that he "had feelings for her" and he thought they should get together and talk about it.

Significantly, the same cannot be said for our decisions in which sexual harassment has been remedied under the equal protection clause of the fourteenth amendment. . . . Because there is nothing in this record to indicate that Mr. Quick's sexual advances were anything but personal in nature—that is, because there is no showing that Mr. Quick intended to "harass" Ms. Trautvetter simply because she was a woman—we conclude that Ms. Trautvetter has

not raised a genuine issue of material fact as to Mr. Quick's intent and accordingly, affirm the grant of summary judgment on that ground.

For all of the foregoing reasons, we affirm the decision of the district court.

CASE NOTE

Equal Protection. The Seventh Circuit Court of Appeals in *Bohen v. City of East Chicago* was the first federal court to recognize a sexual harassment claim under the equal protection clause of the Fourteenth Amendment (as discussed in *Trautvetter v. Quick*). This action opens another legal approach for public employees. To be successful, the plaintiff must show that the discrimination was intentional. This discrimination may be shown by a single event, but it is unlikely that one event will constitute denial of equal protection. In *Bohen,* the court said, "Forcing women and not men to work in an environment of sexual harassment is no different than forcing women to work in a dirtier or more hazardous environment than men simply because they were women." 799 F.2d 1180 (7th Cir.1986). M. David Alexander and Mary F. Hughes, "Sexual Harassment in the Workplace," in *Principal's Handbook: Issues in School Law,* ed. William E. Camp, Julie K. Underwood, and Mary Jane Connelly (Topeka, Kans.: National Organization on Legal Problems of Education, 1989).

■ RELIGIOUS DISCRIMINATION

Employees' religious rights and freedoms (also see Chapter 15) are protected by both the First Amendment of the U.S. Constitution and Title VII of the Civil Rights Act of 1964, as amended in 1972.

The Civil Rights Act of 1964, Title VII, prohibits any employer from discriminating against an individual because of religion. The 1972 amendment states: "The term religion includes all aspects of religious observance and practice, as well as belief, unless an employer demonstrates that he is unable to reasonably accommodate an employee's or prospective employee's religious observance or practice without undue hardship on the conduct of the employer's business." A primary question emerges as to what the employer must do to reasonably accommodate the religious beliefs of an employee.

In *Trans-World Airlines, Inc. v. Hardison*,[108] the Supreme Court addressed this issue. Hardison, the plaintiff employee, challenged a company rule, claiming violation of Title VII, which prevented him from observing Saturday as a religious holiday. The Court held for the defendant and said that Title VII did not require the company "to carve out special exemptions" to accommodate one's religious beliefs. To require the company—in this case, Trans-World Airlines—"to bear more than a *de minimis* cost" in order to give Hardison Saturdays off is an undue hardship.

As with other aspects of Title VII, the burden of proof to show religious discrimination is borne by the plaintiff, who must show that the employer's decision was religiously related. If the plaintiff sustains this burden, then the employer must in turn present evidence that the encroachment on the employee's religious beliefs could not be reasonably accommodated without undue hardship to the employer.

Employees' work schedules have come into conflict with religious worship in other cases. In one such case, a teacher was dismissed because of absence from the job, without permission, to attend a religious festival.[109] The teacher had arranged for a substitute teacher, instructed the substitute on lesson plans, and so on; the classes had, in fact, run very smoothly. The court determined that to accommodate the teacher resulted in no undue hardship to the school and rendered judgment for the teacher.

In a similar case, the court held that it is a violation of one's freedom of religion to compel an employee to choose between employment and religion. The court said: "[A]n employer who punishes an employee by placing the latter in a position in which he or she must ignore a tenet of faith in order to retain employment violates" Title VII.[110]

The free exercise of religion is also, and more broadly, protected by the First Amendment. As noted in Chapter 5 of this text, the school district, as an arm of the state, cannot defend policies that do not meet the tripartite test of *Lemon v. Kurtzman*.[111] Thus, a provision in a negotiated bargaining agreement between a school district and a teachers union may fail because it cannot be shown to have a secular purpose.[112]

❖ — ❖ — ❖

School Board Has Met Its Obligation under Title VII When It Has Offered Reasonable Accommodation of Teacher's Religion

Ansonia Board of Education v. Philbrook

Supreme Court of the United States, 1986.
479 U.S. 60, 107 S.Ct. 367.

Chief Justice REHNQUIST delivered the opinion of the Court. Petitioner Ansonia Board of Education has employed respondent Ronald Philbrook since 1962 to teach high school business and typing classes in Ansonia, Connecticut. In 1968, Philbrook was baptized into the Worldwide Church of God. The tenets of the church require members to refrain from secular employment during designated holy days, a practice that has caused respondent to miss approximately six school days each year. We are asked to determine whether the employer's efforts to adjust respondent's work schedule in light of his beliefs fulfills its obligation under §701(j) of the Civil Rights Act of 1964, 42 U.S.C. §2000e(j), to "reasonably accommodate to an employee's . . . religious observance or practice without undue hardship on the conduct of the employer's business."

Since the 1967–1968 school year, the school board's collective-bargaining agreements with the Ansonia Federation of Teachers have granted to each teacher 18 days of leave per year for illness, cumulative to 150 and later to 180 days. Accumulated leave may be used for purposes other than illness as specified in the agreement. A teacher may accordingly use five days' leave for a death in the immediate family, one day for attendance at a wedding, three days per year for attendance as an official delegate to a national veterans organization, and the like.... With the exception of the agreement covering the 1967–1968 school year, each contract has specifically provided three days' annual leave for observance of mandatory religious holidays, as defined in the contract. Unlike other categories for which leave is permitted, absences for religious holidays are not charged against the teacher's annual or accumulated leave.

The school board has also agreed that teachers may use up to three days of accumulated leave each school year for "necessary personal business." Recent contracts limited permissible personal leave to those uses not otherwise specified in the contract. This limitation dictated, for example, that an employee who wanted more than three leave days to attend the convention of a national veterans organization could not use personal leave to gain extra days for that purpose. Likewise, an employee already absent three days for mandatory religious observances could not later use personal leave for "[a]ny religious activity," . . . or "[a]ny religious observance." . . . Since the 1978–1979 school year, teachers have been allowed to take one of the three personal days without prior approval; use of the remaining two days requires advance approval by the school principal.

The limitations on the use of personal business leave spawned this litigation. Until the 1976–1977 year, Philbrook observed mandatory holy days by using the three days granted in the contract and then taking unauthorized leave. His pay was reduced accordingly. In 1976, however, respondent stopped taking unauthorized leave for religious reasons, and began scheduling required hospital visits on church holy days. He also worked on several holy days. Dissatisfied with this arrangement, Philbrook repeatedly asked the school board to adopt one of two alternatives. His preferred alternative would allow use of personal business leave for religious observance, effectively giving him three additional days of paid leave for that purpose. Short of this arrangement, respondent suggested that he pay the cost of a substitute and receive full pay for additional days off for religious observances. Petitioner has consistently rejected both proposals. . . .

We find no basis in either the statute or its legislative history for requiring an employer to choose any particular reasonable accommodation. By its very terms the statute directs that any reasonable accommodation by the employer is sufficient to meet its accommodation obligation. The employer violates the statute unless it "demonstrates that [it] is unable to reasonably accommodate . . . an employee's . . . religious observance or practice without undue hardship on the conduct of the employer's business." Thus, where the employer has already reasonably accommodated the employee's religious needs, the statutory inquiry is at an end. The employer need not further show that each of the employee's alternative accommodations would result in undue hardship. . . .

. . . We accordingly hold that an employer has met its obligation under §701(j) when it demonstrates that it has offered a reasonable accommodation to the employee.

The remaining issue in the case is whether the school board's leave policy constitutes a reasonable accommodation of Philbrook's religious beliefs. . . . We think that the school board policy in this case, requiring respondent to take unpaid leave for holy day observance that exceeded the amount allowed by the collective-bargaining agreement, would generally be a reasonable one. In enacting §701(j), Congress was understandably motivated by a desire to assure the individual additional opportunity to observe religious practices, but it did not impose a duty on the employer to accommodate at all costs. . . . The provision of unpaid leave eliminates the conflict between employment requirements and religious practices by allowing the individual to observe fully religious holy days and requires him only to give up compensation for a day that he did not in fact work. Generally speaking, "[t]he direct effect of [unpaid leave] is merely a loss of income for the period the employee is not at work; such an exclusion has no direct effect upon either employment opportunities or job status." . . .

But unpaid leave is not a reasonable accommodation when paid leave is provided for all purposes *except* religious ones. A provision for paid leave "that is part and parcel of the employment relationship may not be doled out in a discriminatory fashion, even if the employer would be free . . . not to provide the benefit at all." . . . Such an arrangement would display a discrimination against religious practices that is the antithesis of reasonableness. Whether the policy here violates this teaching turns on factual inquiry into past and present administration of the personal business leave provisions of the collective-bargaining agreement. The school board contends that the necessary personal business category in the agreement, like other leave provisions, defines a limited purpose leave. Philbrook, on the other hand, asserts that the necessary personal leave category is not so limited, operating as an open-ended leave provision that may be used for a wide range of secular purposes in addition to those specifically provided for in the contract, but not for similar religious purposes. We do not think that the record is sufficiently clear on this point for us to make the necessary factual findings, and we therefore affirm the judgment of the Court of Appeals remanding the case to the District Court. The latter court on remand should make the necessary findings as to past and existing practice in the administration of the collective-bargaining agreement.

It is so ordered.

❖ — ❖ — ❖

Teacher's Contract Nonrenewal Linked to Her Magic Rock Letter Constituted Title VII Religious Discrimination

Cowan v. Strafford R-VI School District

United States Court of Appeals, Eighth Circuit, 1998. 140 F.3d 1153.

PIERSOL, DISTRICT JUDGE.

Strafford R-VI School District appeals from a jury verdict in favor of Leslie Cowan, a former school teacher, in her lawsuit under Title VII of the Civil Rights Act of 1964, 42 U.S.C. §1983, for violation of her First Amendment rights. Cowan has filed a cross-appeal. She appeals from the district court's decision to deny reinstatement as a remedy in this case. We affirm. . . .

Leslie Cowan was hired by the Strafford R-VI School District as a second grade teacher on a probationary basis in the fall of 1990. As a pro-

bationary teacher, her contract was subject to renewal by the School Board on an annual basis. Customarily, the decision of whether or not to renew an elementary school teacher's contract was made by the School Board with the advice of the school principal, Lucille Cogdill, and in general, the school board followed Cogdill's recommendations.

For the first two years of Cowan's tenure, the School Board renewed Cowan's contract. After her third year, however, the School Board voted unanimously not to renew Cowan's contract in accordance with Cogdill's advice. Cowan believes that this action was a result of a "magic rock letter" that she sent home with her second graders on the last day of school. The letter read as follows:

> Dear Second Grader:
> You have completed second grade. Because you have worked so hard, you deserve something special and unique; just like you! That something special is your very own magic rock.
> The magic rock you have will always let you know that you can do anything that you set your mind to. To make your rock work, close your eyes, rub it and say to yourself three times, "I am a special and terrific person, with talents of my own!" Before you put your rock away, think of three good things about yourself. After you have put your rock away, you will know that the magic has worked.
>
> HAVE FUN IN THIRD GRADE!!!!

Cowan attached a rock to this letter and sent one home with each student in May of 1992.

In August of 1992, Cogdill informed Cowan that she had received complaints from parents regarding the "magic rock letter." In particular, Cogdill indicated that two families had decided to move their children to private Christian schools as a direct result of the use of the letter. Cogdill followed up this discussion with an admonition to Cowan to avoid magical ideas in her teaching. After Cogdill spoke with Cowan regarding the letter, she informed the School District Superintendent that the magic rock letter was a cause for concern among community parents. This information was also passed on to the School Board. Also in August of 1992, Cogdill issued "job targets" to Cowan. Job targets are devices used by the School District to indicate areas of needed improvement in a teacher's performance. The job targets issued to Cowan indicated two areas she needed to improve: interpersonal relationships with parents and instructional process.

At the beginning of the 1992–93 school year, Cogdill held a staff meeting in which she informed the teachers that she was concerned about the perception of the school in the community with regard to teaching New Ageism, and she instructed teachers to avoid magical notions in their teaching. In conjunction with this discussion, she announced a seminar coordinated by a local pastor, the Reverend Stark, that was devoted to the issue of New Ageism and the infiltration of New Age thinking in the public schools.

Cogdill had been informed about the seminar by the Reverend Stark personally. He visited Cogdill after he had seen a copy of the magic rock letter brought home by his granddaughter. The Reverend communicated to Cogdill that he considered the letter to be contrary to his religious beliefs. Other members of the Strafford religious community were concerned about the magic rock letter as well. The Reverend Vawter, another local pastor, indicated to his congregants that they needed to be concerned about New Age infiltration of the schools because a teacher in the school system was teaching New Ageism to students through the use of magic rocks.

Over the course of the 1992–93 school year Cogdill showed only lukewarm support for Cowan in her efforts to improve her teaching. Then, in March of 1993, on the eve of the School Board's vote on Cowan's contract renewal, Cogdill suggested to Cowan that she resign because she was not going to be renewed. Cowan did not resign, and shortly thereafter, the School Board voted unanimously not to renew Cowan's contract.

As a consequence of her nonrenewal, Cowan filed suit against the School District alleging that she was not renewed because she had offended the religious sensibilities of the Strafford community. Cowan claimed that the School District acted in violation of her rights under Title VII and the First Amendment. . . .

The School District argues that Cowan did not produce any evidence linking the District's employment decision to the magic rock letter as

required under Title VII. . . . A plaintiff is entitled to have her case analyzed under the mixed motives standard if she presents "'evidence of conduct or statements by persons involved in the decision making process that may be viewed as directly reflecting the alleged discriminatory attitude. . . .'"

. . . [T]here was sufficient evidence presented at trial for a reasonable jury to conclude that persons involved in the decision making process were motivated by religious concerns regarding the teaching of New Ageism. Principal Cogdill received complaints from parents who believed the magic rock letter violated their religious beliefs, and during the 1992–93 school year, there was concern among Strafford's religious community regarding the dissemination of New Age beliefs. Cogdill felt compelled to respond to these concerns. She attended a program on New Ageism sponsored by the local religious community where she was called upon to defend the school against attacks that it was practicing anti-Christian, New Age modes of teaching. In this anti-New Age atmosphere, Cogdill instructed her staff members to limit their use of magical notions. Cogdill singled out Cowan in particular and told her to avoid magical ideas in her teaching. While we question whether Cowan properly pled a prima facie case of religious discrimination, since this issue is not properly before the Court, we conclude that Cogdill's conduct in response to the community apprehensions regarding New Ageism coupled with her generally unsupportive behavior toward Cowan, provided sufficient evidence for the jury to conclude that Cogdill was motivated by religious concerns. . . .

Further, although Cogdill was not a voting member of the School Board, there was substantial evidence to indicate that she was intimately involved in the decision making process that led to Cowan's nonrenewal. Cogdill was present and participated in the closed executive School Board meetings in which all contract decisions were made, she presented her recommendation regarding Cowan's contract, and according to the School Board members who testified at trial, Cogdill's judgment was given great weight. Many of the School Board members conceded that in general, Cogdill's recommendation was the most significant factor in the decision whether to renew a teacher's contract. Under these circumstances Cogdill can clearly be regarded as someone who was part of the decision making process, and a reasonable jury could conclude that her animus toward Cowan infected that process. Therefore, the trial court correctly denied the motion for judgment as a matter of law or new trial. . . .

One of the major factual issues in the case was the timing of the School Board's discussion of Cowan's "job targets" which were issued in August of 1992. School Board member Roger Lile testified at trial that he could remember with certainty that the Board had discussed issuing job targets to Cowan in March of 1992 because it was around the same time that Cowan experienced a miscarriage. In response to this testimony, Cowan took the stand and told the jury that she had suffered a miscarriage in the spring of 1993, not in 1992. If the job targets were not discussed at the March 1992 School Board meeting, the implication was that the job targets were issued in August as a consequence of the magic rock letter.

After the conclusion of the trial, the School District examined Cowan's medical records and found evidence that Cowan had an abortion as a result of an ectopic pregnancy at about the same time Lile believed that she had had a miscarriage. Based upon this evidence, the School District filed its . . . motion arguing that Cowan had lied regarding her pregnancies.

The district court soundly rejected the School District's argument. The medical evidence presented to the court indicates that Cowan had an ectopic or tubal pregnancy that was surgically terminated in the spring of 1992 and suffered a miscarriage in the spring of 1993. This Court agrees with the district court that Cowan did not lie regarding the pregnancy in the spring of 1992. Instead, the School District did not ask Cowan questions that would have elicited the information now complained about regarding that pregnancy. . . .

Finally, the Court must consider whether the trial court erred in granting Cowan equitable relief in the form of two years front pay. The trial court's decision to grant Cowan front pay is reviewed for abuse of discretion. . . . We believe the district court correctly concluded

that the teacher-principal relationship between Cowan and Cogdill was so badly damaged that none could be reestablished. Without such a working relationship the school would not be able to function properly. Thus, where reinstatement presents so extreme a burden this remedy becomes impossible.

Further, we conclude that the trial court correctly determined that two years front pay was the appropriate award in this case. After a finding of discrimination, the court has an obligation to fulfill the make-whole purposes of Title VII. An award of front pay, however, requires the court to consider a number of complicated factors. Here, Cowan was a probationary teacher with a one-year contract, and there was no guarantee that she would continue with the School District because she might move to a different job or because her contract might not be renewed for legitimate reasons. Under such circumstances, the district court did not abuse its discretion in awarding two years front pay. . . .

We affirm the district court's entry of judgment on the jury verdict in this case as there was sufficient evidence presented at trial from which a reasonable jury could find in favor of Cowan. . . . Finally, the district court did not abuse its discretion in refusing to order reinstatement. The facts of this case demonstrate that reinstatement would be impracticable, if not impossible, given the nature of school operations. . . .

■ EQUAL PAY ACT

In 1963, the Fair Labor Standards Act of 1938 was amended to include what is commonly referred to as the Equal Pay Act. The Equal Pay Act is designed to eliminate pay or wage discrimination based on sex where equal work, equal skills, and equal effort are performed under the same working conditions.[113] The act specifies that differential pay may be appropriate if the decision is based on (1) a seniority system, (2) a merit system, (3) a situation in which the quantity and quality of production is a factor, and (4) a situation in which pay differences are based on any factor other than sex.

The Equal Pay Act was incorporated into Title VII of the Civil Rights Act of 1964. Title VII and the Equal Pay Act have almost identical language except that Title VII covers not only sex, but also race, color, religion, and national origin. Title VII states that the employer may provide different compensation "or different terms, conditions, or privileges of employment pursuant to a bona fide seniority or merit system, or a system which measures earnings by quantity or quality of production or to employees who work in different locations, provided that such differences are not the result of an intention to discriminate because of race, color, religion, sex, or national origin."[114]

The reasons for differential pay are the same under both the Equal Pay Act and Title VII; likewise, the standard used to determine unequal pay for equal work is basically the same for both acts: "To establish a claim of unequal pay for equal work a plaintiff has the burden of proof that the employer pays different wages to employees of opposite sexes for equal work on jobs the performance of which requires equal skill, effort, and responsibility, and which are performed under similar working conditions."[115] Congress did not intend pay to be exactly equal but intended to require substantial equality for commensurate skills, effort, responsibility, and working conditions. Cases must be reviewed on a case-by-case basis to see if the remedial provisions of the Equal Pay Act or Title VII can be invoked. Once the employee has established that the pay is unequal for the same work, the burden shifts to the employer to present evidence that the differential pay scale is justified under one of the act's four exceptions listed earlier.

A school district that paid women coaches of girls' teams less than men coaches of boys' teams was held to violate the Equal Pay Act.[116] The U.S. Seventh Circuit Court of Appeals concluded that the "employer cannot divide equal work into two job classifications that carry unequal pay, forbid women to compete for one of the classifications, and defend the resulting inequity in pay by reference to a factor other than the sex of the employees."[117]

The Equal Pay Act reaches into private schools through the coverage of the Fair Labor Standards Act.[118] A federal district court in Ohio held that the compelling interests of the Equal Pay Act substantially outweighed the minimal impact of religious beliefs in discriminating against women by giving men a head-of-household pay supplement.

School District Did Not Violate Title VII Prohibition against Disparate Treatment in Not Hiring Female for School Principalship

Danzl v. North St. Paul–Maplewood–Oakdale Independent School District No. 622

United States Court of Appeals,
Eighth Circuit, 1983.
706 F.2d 813.

FAGG, Circuit Judge. Once again we are asked to determine whether the North St. Paul–Maplewood–Oakdale Independent School District discriminated on the basis of sex, in violation of Title VII of the Civil Rights Act of 1964, when it did not hire Agnes Danzl to fill a one-year high school principal position. The district court found that the school district's articulated nondiscriminatory reasons for not hiring Danzl were pretextual, and held that the school district intentionally discriminated against Danzl solely on the basis of her sex. Because we believe the district court's findings of pretext and intentional discrimination are clearly erroneous, we reverse.

In late July 1979, a vacancy arose for a high school principalship in the school district for the 1979–80 school year. Twelve individuals—ten male and two female—applied for the position. Director of Secondary Education Richard St. Germain selected four finalists—two male and two female—based upon his review of the papers submitted, phone conversations with the applicants and reference checks. Several male applicants with prior principal experience were eliminated by this investigatory process. Between August 15 and August 20, St. Germain interviewed the four finalists.

On August 21, a committee of male and female teachers from the high school interviewed the candidates. Following the interviews, the teachers discussed and rated the candidates, and then met with St. Germain. The teachers agreed that Agnes Danzl, a female, and Jack Edling, a male, were the two leading candidates, but favored Danzl slightly based on the interviews. St. Germain told the teachers committee that he favored Edling; he had contacted various persons regarding Edling, including both administrators and teachers, and the references were very positive. His two reference checks on Danzl, he said, were not as positive. St. Germain had contacted an administrator who knew both candidates and he stated that he would hire Edling over Danzl. Also, one of Danzl's supervisors had stated that he would hesitate to hire Danzl for a high school as large as Burnsville, where she was currently teaching. The teachers, concerned that only administrators had been contacted for Danzl, while both administrators and teachers had been contacted for Edling, asked for time to conduct their own investigation of Danzl. St. Germain was amenable to this procedure.

Three male and female committee members, independent of St. Germain and of one another, contacted three teachers at Burnsville. Each of the references were considered, on balance, unfavorable to Danzl and were similar in content. The references indicated that Danzl was inflexible, had certain staff relations problems, and was insensitive to student needs. After the teachers informed the other committee members of the reference checks, St. Germain polled each member of the committee by phone. Their unanimous choice for the interim principal position was Edling. St. Germain cross-checked the references from the teachers with a Burnsville administrator, who did not disagree, in general, with the unfavorable comments about Danzl. Edling was recommended to the school board which in turn appointed him to the principal position. . . .

There is a three-step allocation of burdens and order of presentation of proof in a Title VII disparate treatment case. The initial burden is on the plaintiff to establish a *prima facie* case of discrimination. If the plaintiff succeeds, the bur-

den then shifts to the defendant to rebut the inference of discrimination by producing evidence that the plaintiff was rejected, or someone else was preferred, for some legitimate nondiscriminatory reason. The defendant's evidence is sufficient if it raises a genuine issue of fact as to whether it discriminated against the plaintiff. In addition, the reasons given must be legally sufficient to justify a judgment for the defendant. Finally, should the defendant carry this burden of production, the plaintiff must demonstrate by a preponderance of the evidence that the proffered reasons were not the true reason for the challenged employment decision. The plaintiff may prove this either by means of affirmative evidence that a discriminatory reason played an impermissible role in the decision or by showing that the proffered nondiscriminatory reasons are unworthy of credence. At all times the ultimate burden of persuasion that the defendant committed intentional discrimination remains with the plaintiff. In discharging this burden, Danzl need not prove that her sex was the sole reason for the challenged employment decision, but need only prove that sex was a factor in the decision.

There is no dispute that plaintiff has established a *prima facie* case of disparate treatment. Similarly, there is no dispute that the school district has met its burden of articulating reasons for not hiring Danzl that are legitimate and nondiscriminatory: (1) the candidate who was hired, Jack Edling, was better qualified because he had experience as a high school principal; and (2) Agnes Danzl had received unfavorable reference checks. Thus, the sole issue before this court concerns the district court's finding that the school district's articulated reasons for not hiring Danzl were a pretext for intentional sexual discrimination. We may not set aside the district court's findings of fact unless they are clearly erroneous. A finding is clearly erroneous if it is not supported by substantial evidence, if it evolves from an erroneous conception of the applicable law, or if the reviewing court on the entire record is left with the definite and firm conviction that a mistake has been made. Moreover, it is now the law that we may reverse a finding of intentional discrimination only if the finding is clearly erroneous.

The first reason the school district proffered for not hiring Danzl was that Edling was better qualified, due to his experience as a high school principal. Rejecting this explanation, the district court first found that Danzl and Edling were equally qualified for the position. This finding is clearly erroneous. We have no doubt that both candidates were qualified for the position. Nevertheless, an employer could distinguish between Edling, who had seven years' experience as a principal and one year's experience as a school superintendent, and Danzl, who had only five years' experience as an associate principal. The district court implied that Danzl made up for any lack of experience with her superior educational qualifications. Danzl had a Ph.D. awarded by an unaccredited school for certain courses and papers, including a dissertation, conducted by correspondence. Edling had a master's degree. Unlike principal experience, an advanced degree was not listed as a qualification for the position. The district court cannot substitute its judgment for the employer's by saying that Danzl's advanced degree compensates for Edling's superior experience. . . .

The district court's alternative rationale for its finding of pretext was that several of the original twelve applicants had experience as a high school principal, but of the final four applicants only Edling possessed such experience. Hence, the district court concluded that if past experience as a secondary school principal was so important, then "Dr. St. Germain had already decided to hire Mr. Edling as of the date the finalists were chosen, and all subsequent selection activities were mere window dressing designed to obscure the true intent of the defendant to hire a male."

This finding is simply without support in the record. When St. Germain selected the four finalists, an extensive and real selection process remained, involving interviews, reference checks, and numerous meetings with administrators, teachers and school district members. It just does not follow that by considering experience as a factor, the school district had therefore preselected Edling among the four finalists. The school district has never contended that experience was an absolute requirement for the job; the vacancy notice stated only that it was a desirable qualification to be considered. Although

the issue is not before us, the district court conceded that principal experience could have been a legitimate requirement for the job of interim principal under the disparate impact test of *Griggs v. Duke Power Co.*, 401 U.S. 424, 91 S.Ct. 849, 28 L.Ed.2d 158 (1971).

Because we find no evidence in the record to contradict the school district's first legitimate nondiscriminatory reason for not hiring Danzl, her lack of principal experience, we conclude that the district court's finding of pretext was clearly erroneous.

The school district's second articulated reason for not hiring Danzl was that it had received several negative references concerning Danzl. The references for Edling, in contrast, were very positive. The district court found this reason pretextual because the references "were not received by the defendants until after the decision to hire Mr. Edling had already been made." There is nothing in the record to support this finding. . . .

We have thoroughly searched the record in this case and have found nothing that supports the district court's finding of intentional discrimination. Both Danzl and Edling, as well as several others, were qualified candidates. Unremarkably, the school district hired the candidate with superior experience and superior references. Although this may not comport with the district court's view of how hiring practices should compensate for years of underrepresentation of women in educational administration, it does not violate Title VII. The employer is free to choose the best candidate for the position without regard to sex. Nothing more than that occurred in this case.

The judgment of the district court is reversed.

■ AGE DISCRIMINATION

In 1967, the federal government passed the Age Discrimination in Employment Act (ADEA),[119] which prohibited discrimination against individuals who are at least forty, but less than seventy, years of age. This act was amended in 1986, striking out the language "but less than seventy years of age." The effect of the amendment is to remove the maximum age limitation applicable to employees who are protected under the act. The act applies equally to all governmental employees, with the exception of fire-fighters and law enforcement officers, who, by virtue of the rigors of their job requirements, are considered separately.[120] The act prohibits discrimination with respect to hiring, discharging, compensation, terms and conditions, privileges, retirement, and demotion. The act is intended not to increase the number of elderly in the workforce, but only to prevent discrimination against them. The act is also intended to supplement the protections provided under the equal protection clause.

As pointed out in Chapter 3 of this book, the ADEA was held by the U.S. Supreme Court in *Kimel v. Florida Board of Regents*[121] to be unconstitutional as violative of state sovereign immunity under the Eleventh Amendment. Yet it was further noted in Chapter 3 that the Eleventh Amendment applied to state government only and may not bestow such immunity on local school districts. In a subsequent interpretation of the meaning of *Kimel,* the U.S. Court of Appeals, Third Circuit, observed that the Supreme Court held "in the ADEA, Congress did not validly abrogate the States' sovereign immunity to suits by private individuals" and it did not determine that the reach of the Eleventh Amendment immunity extended to local school districts. This circuit court ruled that a local school district in Pennsylvania "is not a state or an arm of the state for Eleventh Amendment purposes and therefore is not entitled to sovereign immunity."[122]

Other federal courts have also rendered decisions in several states holding that local school districts in those states are not arms of the state for Eleventh Amendment purposes and are therefore not entitled to Eleventh Amendment immunity. Included in these states are Alabama,[123] Kentucky,[124] Louisiana,[125] Missouri,[126] New York,[127] South Carolina,[128] and Utah.[129] On the other hand, at least one federal court has held that the Eleventh Amendment does apply to give local school districts immunity. This court, ruling in a Maryland case, held that a local school board and its members were state entities for Eleventh Amendment purposes and that they, thereby, could not be held liable for alleged racial discrimination against a child who claimed unlawful racial preference in magnet school admission policies.[130] We should empha-

size, however, that these rulings are careful to consider the state versus local status of school districts only for Eleventh Amendment purposes. To extend generalizations beyond the narrow consideration of Eleventh Amendment immunity would contradict the vastly prevalent legal and historical view of state and federal courts that have ruled that the public schools are state entities. Thus, the prevailing view is that the language of the ADEA imposing liability on state government for violation of the act is unconstitutional, where the ADEA application to local school districts remains valid.

Concerning the substance of the ADEA legislation itself, two cases decided by the Supreme Court are important in understanding mandatory retirement statutes and age discrimination. In the first case, the Court upheld a Massachusetts statute requiring uniformed state police to retire at age fifty.[131] The Court held that government employment is not a fundamental constitutional right, nor age a suspect classification. Therefore, the Court required that the government show a rational interest to support its policy, but it did not require the government to bear the burden of showing a compelling interest in creating the policy. Because the purpose of the Massachusetts statute was to ensure physical preparedness by having younger troopers patrolling the highways, the policy was held to be constitutional. The rationale that younger officers are more physically capable and can provide better protection to all of society was held to be a proper and reasonable societal objective.

In another case, again using the rational interest test, the Supreme Court upheld a statute requiring Foreign Service employees to retire at age sixty. The Court said: "Congress . . . was legitimately intent on stimulating the highest performance in the Foreign Service by assuring that opportunities for promotion would be available despite [the] limits on [the] number of personnel in the Service, and plainly intended to create [a] relatively small, homogeneous and particularly able corps of foreign service officers."[132] This the Court found to be an acceptable objective.

Whether a bona fide occupational qualification (BFOQ) exemption is allowed under the ADEA depends on how narrowly the employer fashions the exemption. In *Western Air Lines, Inc. v. Criswell,*[133] the U.S. Supreme Court established a two-part test for evaluating an employer's exemption. First, the job qualifications must be reasonably necessary to the essence of the business; second, the employer must be "compelled to rely on age as a proxy for a safety-related" job qualification by showing that there exists a factual basis for believing that all persons over a specified age are incapable of performing the duties in a safe and efficient manner or that it is "impossible or highly impractical" to deal with older employees on an individual basis. Thus, the reasonableness of an exemption can be largely determined by the practicality of application and efficacy of implementation.

The ADEA is modeled after Title VII of the 1964 Civil Rights Act. Therefore, the courts have held that the allegations of the party claiming age discrimination will be evaluated under the same factors as established in Title VII. If the action is a private, nonclass action,

> the complainant has the burden of establishing a *prima facie* case, which he can satisfy by showing that (i) he belongs to a special minority; (ii) he applied and was qualified for a job the employer was trying to fill; (iii) though qualified, he was rejected; and (iv) therefore, the employer continued to seek applicants with complainant's qualifications.[134]

After the plaintiff establishes a *prima facie* case, the burden of presenting evidence shifts to the employer, who must articulate legitimate, nondiscriminatory reasons for not employing the individual or individuals.

The Supreme Court in *Hazen Paper Company v. Biggins*[135] used the disparate treatment test from Title VII cases to analyze whether a company had violated the ADEA. In this case, the company dismissed a sixty-two-year-old employee to prevent him from vesting for pension benefit purposes. The Court ruled this did not violate the ADEA because there is no disparate treatment under the ADEA when the motivating factor—in this case, vesting in the retirement system—is based on something other than age. The Court in *Hazen Paper*, when addressing this issue, stated, "Age and years of service are analytically distinct, so that [the] employer could take account of one while ignoring the other, and [a] decision based on years of service is thus not necessarily age-based; firing [an] employee in order to prevent pension benefits from vesting does not . . . violate ADEA."[136]

The principal issue regarding proof in ADEA cases hinges to a substantial degree on whether a court adopts the "disparate treatment" theory or the "disparate impact" theory. As explained above in this chapter, under the discussion of racial discrimination, with disparate treatment the employer treats some people less favorably than others because of race, color, religion or some other protected characteristic, such as age. In disparate treatment cases it is critical that the plaintiff show that the motive of the employer was to discriminate based on age.[137]

In contrast "disparate impact" involves employment practices that are facially neutral, but in fact fall more harshly on one group than on another.[138] "*Hazen Paper* was, by its own terms, a disparate treatment case only." The Supreme Court has not ventured beyond the disparate treatment theory in ADEA cases. Under the disparate treatment test the burden of proof is more difficult for the plaintiff to bear because evidence must show that the employer's intent and motivation was to discriminate based on age.

Early precedents under ADEA held that plaintiffs could establish liability if an employer took personnel actions that had an unjustified adverse impact on the protected age class. As observed above, in these cases the courts applied impact analysis as developed under Title VII. Although the Supreme Court in *Hazen Paper* did not expressly reject disparate impact, it did suggest that impact analysis might not be appropriate under ADEA.[139] Following *Hazen Paper*, lower courts have been divided on whether the employer is liable for unjustified adverse impact that results from a neutral personnel action.[140]

In applying the disparate treatment standard the plaintiff must prove employer's motivation to discriminate, a rather difficult requirement of proof. The plaintiff must create an inference of an age-motivated decision. In determining motivation the courts will determine whether an age reference by the employer is "descriptive" or "valuative." Descriptive references, such as simply observing the ages of employees, does not constitute an inference of illegal age motivation.[141] On the other hand, valuative comments by the employer suggesting an age preference constitutes direct evidence of age-motivation. Thus, for a school administrator to say that "this school district is looking for a younger person" is valuative, and thereby establishes motive to discriminate.

If, however, there are present "reasonable factors other than age" for which personnel decisions are made then there is no discrimination.[142] For example, economic considerations may be legitimate even though older employees suffer more dire consequences. For example, paying more to new hires (as opposed to paying more to younger employees) than is paid to incumbents, for the purpose of attracting better qualified employees, is a "reasonable factor other than age."[143] Similarly, laying off more expensive (rather than older) employees for the purpose of saving money and operating more efficiently . . . even though it impacts adversely on older workers nevertheless has been justified as a "reasonable factor other than age."[144] Thus, when an employer's decision is wholly motivated by factors other than age, the problem of age as a stigmatizing stereotype disappears.[145] ADEA simply requires that employers are to evaluate and treat older employees as to their merits in the workplace and not as to their age.[146]

❖ — ❖ — ❖

Unsuccessful Job Applicant Asserting Disparate Impact under ADEA Must Identify Specific Employment Practice and Offer Statistical Evidence Showing the Practice Caused Exclusion of Job Applicant

Wooden v. Board of Education of Jefferson County, Kentucky

United States Court of Appeals,
Sixth Circuit, 1991.
931 F.2d 376.

RYAN, Circuit Judge.

Plaintiff, Larry Wooden appeals the summary judgment for defendant, Board of Education of Jefferson County, Kentucky, in this action under the Age Discrimination in Employment Act ("ADEA"), 29 U.S.C. §621, *et seq.* Wooden argues that there is sufficient evidence to support his claim for age discrimination and that the Board's salary policy which gives credit for prior teaching experience has a disparate impact on those over forty. For the following reasons we shall affirm the district court's grant of summary judgment in favor of the Board.

Between 1982 and 1984, Wooden, who was fifty-four-years-old at the time this suit was filed, aggressively pursued a full-time teaching position with the Board in either English or Library Science. Wooden had previously taught English and physical education, and served as an audiovisual librarian . . . between 1959–1972. He was out of teaching and pursued private business interests from 1972–1982. In 1983, Wooden had an "initial interview": a step which generally precedes any hiring selection. . . . Between 1982–1987, Wooden worked as a substitute teacher for the Board, and was interviewed five times by principals who were seeking to fill English and Library Science teaching positions. However, Wooden was not recommended by any of the principals, and the jobs were offered to others. In 1987, the Board hired Wooden as a "permanent, part-time employee." All of the positions at the high school where Wooden teaches are designated as permanent, but part-time positions.

Wooden filed this suit in August 1988, alleging that the Board discriminated against him because of his age, in violation of the ADEA, by hiring those younger and less experienced. Additionally, Wooden claimed that the Board's salary policy which limits the credit a teacher receives for experience that is more than ten years old violates the ADEA because it adversely impacts those over forty years old. . . .

Wooden claims that the Board violated the ADEA by hiring younger teachers and those with less experience. It is well settled that in an age discrimination case under the ADEA, the ultimate issue is whether age was a determining factor in the employment decision which adversely affected the claimant. . . . A plaintiff establishes a *prima facie* case of intentional age discrimination when he shows: (1) that he was in the protected age group, between forty and seventy years old; (2) that he "applied and was qualified for a job for which the employer was seeking applicants; (3) that, despite his qualifications, he was rejected; and (4) that after his rejection, the position remained open and the employer continued to seek applicants from persons of complainant's qualifications." . . .

Wooden produced evidence that he is a member of the protected class; that he applied and was qualified for the teaching positions; that he was rejected; and that the Board hired other applicants with similar qualifications. Therefore, Wooden has established a *prima facie* case of age discrimination. Because Wooden has established a *prima facie* case, the burden of production of evidence shifts to the Board to articulate some legitimate nondiscriminatory reason for its decision not to hire him for a full-time teaching position. . . . Once the Board articulates a legitimate nondiscriminatory reason for not hiring Wooden, the burden shifts back to Wooden to show that the Board's reasons were pretextual. Although the burden of production shifts, the burden of persuasion remains at all times with Wooden.

The Board's reason for not hiring Wooden is that it hired better qualified candidates. Board witnesses stated that for each of the positions for which Wooden interviewed, there were over 2000 job applicants. The Board explained that because there was such a large pool to choose from, it hired better qualified teachers and those who made a more favorable impression during the interview. Moreover, the Board demonstrated that thirty-six out of eighty-six, or forty-one percent, of the jobs about which Wooden complains were filled with teachers over the age of forty.

The evidence in the record supports the Board's asserted reason for not hiring Wooden. According to the affidavits of the five individuals who were serving as principals in the schools where Wooden said he had interviews, only one principal, Dr. Birkhead, can specifically remember interviewing Wooden. . . . Even though the remaining principals do not remember interviewing Wooden, all of them said that they relied on qualifications, not age, in making their selection of teachers.

Wooden's personnel file provides another indication that although Wooden was qualified to interview for permanent, full-time teaching positions, other applicants had superior qualifications. His file shows that although Wooden's recent evaluations as a substitute teacher are good to excellent, evaluations completed by principals for whom Wooden worked when he was last employed as a permanent, full-time teacher are only average. . . . Also Wooden's academic record reflects only average grades.

We find the above evidence sufficient to support the Board's contention that Wooden was not hired because the Board hired better qualified persons than Wooden. Thus, the burden shifts back to Wooden to prove that the Board's proffered reason for not hiring him is pretextual.

Wooden argues that the evidence supporting the Board's reason, that he was less qualified than the applicants hired, is so weak that there is a genuine issue as to the Board's motive. . . . In this case, Wooden has produced no such evidence. Although some of the evidence in Wooden's file is dated, he has offered no evidence that would permit a jury to conclude that age was a determining factor in any of the Board's hiring decisions.

In contrast, the Board has submitted evidence relating to all of the hiring decisions about which Wooden complains: 1) Forty-one percent of the jobs were filled with persons older than forty; 2) Wooden had some unfavorable evaluations in his file; 3) Wooden's interviews with principals were unimpressive; and 4) for each job opening there was a pool of over 2000 applicants. Based upon this evidence, the Board was free to exercise its business judgment and hire those that it felt had better qualifications. . . .

Because Wooden has produced no evidence, statistical or otherwise, that the Board's policy violates the ADEA, there is no genuine issue of material fact. Therefore, the district court properly granted the Board's motion for summary judgment.

For all of the foregoing reasons, we AFFIRM the decision of the district court.

CASE NOTES

1. Violation of the ADEA can be demonstrated by plaintiff's showing of either disparate treatment or disparate impact. *Lowe v. Commack*

Union Free School District, 886 F.2d 1364 (2d Cir.1989).

2. The case-supporting claim of disparate treatment can be established if plaintiff can show that age was a "significant contributing factor." Age Discrimination in Employment Act of 1967, §4(a)(1), 29 U.S.C.A. §623(a)(1). See *Lowe v. Commack Union Free School District*, 886 F.2d 1364 (2d Cir.1989).

■ DISCRIMINATION AGAINST PERSONS WITH DISABILITIES

Aware that more than 43 million Americans have one or more physical or mental disabilities and are without general recourse for discrimination based on these disabilities, Congress enacted the Americans with Disabilities Act of 1990 (ADA). In contrast to the Rehabilitation Act of 1973, Section 504, which was conditioned on the receipt of federal funds, the ADA covers all employees in the public and private sectors who work for companies with fifteen or more employees.

The ADA is modeled after the Education for All Handicapped Children Act (EAHCA) in that it is both comprehensive and extensively prescriptive. The ADA covers virtually all aspects of society, including transportation, public accommodations, telecommunications, and other areas. For purposes of liability, the act specifically waives state immunity under the Eleventh Amendment. The act categorically excludes coverage of illegal drug users and defines "disability" as excluding

(1) transvestism, transsexualism, pedophilia, exhibitionism, voyeurism, gender identity disorders not resulting from physical impairment, or other sexual behavior disorders; (2) compulsive gambling, kleptomania, or pyromania; or (3) psychoactive substance use disorders resulting from current illegal use of drugs.[147]

Because of the recency of the legislation, litigation has not yet emerged as to various interpretations of the statute. One can be assured, however, that comprehensive legislation of this nature will produce a plethora of legal actions in the near future.

To the present, though, the focal point of litigation for employees with disabilities has re-mained the Rehabilitation Act of 1973, Section 504. Section 504 is violated if a person with a disability is denied a position "solely by reason of his handicap":

The standards for determining the merits of a case under Section 504 are contained in the statute. First, the statute provides that the individual in question must be an "otherwise qualified handicapped individual"; second, the statute provides that a qualified handicapped individual may not be denied admission to any program or activity or denied the benefits of any program or activity . . . solely on the basis of handicap."[148]

If an individual is not otherwise qualified, he or she cannot be said to have been rejected solely because of disability.

The leading case is *School Board of Nassau County v. Arline*,[149] where a teacher with tuberculosis had been hospitalized with resulting respiratory impairment and sought to return to the classroom. The Court held that tuberculosis was a physiological disorder covered by Section 504. Questions then arose as to whether she was "otherwise qualified" and whether she could be "reasonably accommodated." The Court remanded the case to the district court to determine, based on the development of facts, whether Arline was otherwise qualified. The Court provided guidance, saying that "[a]n otherwise qualified person is one who is able to meet all of the program's requirements in spite of his handicap."

In 1969, a blind English teacher who held a professional certificate from the Pennsylvania Department of Education was refused the opportunity to take the Philadelphia Teacher's Examination. The school district classified her as having a "chronic or acute physical defect" that included blindness. With persistence and legal assistance, the teacher in 1974 was allowed to take the test, which she passed. Because the school district refused to afford her seniority as of the time she properly should have been admitted to take the examination, she filed suit. The court held for the teacher, awarding her retroactive seniority.[150] Significantly, the court held that a disability could not be considered a suspect classification for equal protection purposes. Thus, the issue of disability, as an equal protection issue, must be decided under the rational relationship test, not the more rigorous compelling interest standard. The fact that persons with disabilities do not form a suspect class has important bearing on the necessity for separate statutory protection as provided in Section 504 and the ADA.

In another equal protection case bearing on the issue of suspect class, a blind teacher sued because school policy prevented him from obtaining an administrative position.[151] The policy required that an oral and written examination be completed by each prospective administrator. The plaintiff completed the written section of the test, with the aid of a reader, and performed very poorly. A committee also rated the plaintiff very low on the oral part of the examination. The court held that because physical handicaps are not to be treated as a suspect classification, the school district needed to show only a rational relationship between its policy and its reasonably stated objective. Using this test, the court determined that the plaintiff did not possess the skills and qualifications to be an administrator. The school had a legitimate, rational purpose in seeking competent individuals, and the oral and written test was a reasonable device to ensure such competence.

In a case[152] that helps define the extent of the protections of Section 504, two school van drivers who were insulin-dependent diabetics were demoted to aide positions at a lower rate of pay because of their illness. It was determined that they were not "otherwise qualified" under Section 504 because of safety concerns. The court stated,

> Section 504 of the Rehabilitation Act provides that "no otherwise qualified individual with a disability . . . shall . . . be excluded from the participation in, be denied the benefits of, or be subjected to discrimination under any program or activity receiving Federal financial assistance" solely by reason of her or his disability. An otherwise qualified individual is one who, with reasonable accommodation, can perform the essential functions of the position in question without endangering the health and safety of the individual or others. In determining what kinds of accommodations are reasonable, courts are permitted to take into account the reasonableness of the cost of any necessary workplace accommodation, the availability of alternatives therefor, or other appropriate relief in order to achieve an equitable and appropriate

remedy. An unreasonable accommodation is one which would impose undue hardship on the operation of the program in question."[153]

❖ — ❖ — ❖

Teacher Afflicted with Tuberculosis Was "Handicapped Individual" within the Meaning of Rehabilitation Act of 1973

School Board of Nassau County, Florida v. Arline

Supreme Court of the United States, 1987.
480 U.S. 273, 107 S.Ct. 1123.

Justice BRENNAN delivered the opinion of the Court. Section 504 of the Rehabilitation Act of 1973, 87 Stat. 394, as amended, 29 U.S.C. §794 (Act), prohibits a federally funded state program from discriminating against a handicapped individual solely by reason of his or her handicap. This case presents the questions whether a person afflicted with tuberculosis, a contagious disease, may be considered a "handicapped individual" within the meaning of §504 of the Act, and, if so, whether such an individual is "otherwise qualified" to teach elementary school.

From 1966 until 1979, respondent Gene Arline taught elementary school in Nassau County, Florida. She was discharged in 1979 after suffering a third relapse of tuberculosis within two years. After she was denied relief in state administrative proceedings, she brought suit in federal court, alleging that the School Board's decision to dismiss her because of her tuberculosis violated §504 of the Act.

A trial was held in the District Court, at which the principal medical evidence was provided by Marianne McEuen, M.D., an assistant director of the Community Tuberculosis Control Service of the Florida Department of Health and Rehabilitative Services. According to the medical records reviewed by Dr. McEuen, Arline was hospitalized for tuberculosis in 1957. . . . For the next twenty years, Arline's disease was in remission. . . . Then, in 1977, a culture revealed that tuberculosis was again active in her system; cultures taken in March 1978 and in November 1978 were also positive. . . .

The superintendent of schools for Nassau County, Craig Marsh, then testified as to the School Board's response to Arline's medical reports. After both her second relapse, in the Spring of 1978, and her third relapse in November 1978, the School Board suspended Arline with pay for the remainder of the school year. . . . At the end of the 1978–1979 school year, the School Board held a hearing, after which it discharged Arline "not because she had done anything wrong," but because of the "continued reoccurrence [sic] of tuberculosis." . . .

In her trial memorandum, Arline argued that it was "not disputed that the [School Board dismissed her] solely on the basis of her illness. Since the illness in this case qualifies the Plaintiff as a 'handicapped person' it is clear that she was dismissed solely as a result of her handicap in violation of Section 504." . . . The District Court held, however, that although there was "[n]o question that she suffers a handicap," Arline was nevertheless not "a handicapped person under the terms of that statute." . . .

The Court of Appeals reversed, holding that "persons with contagious diseases are within the coverage of section 504," and that Arline's condition "falls . . . neatly within the statutory and regulatory framework" of the Act. . . .

In enacting and amending the Act, Congress enlisted all programs receiving federal funds in an effort "to share with handicapped Americans the opportunities for an education, transportation, housing, health care, and jobs that other Americans take for granted." 123 Cong.Rec. 13515 (1977) (statement of Sen. Humphrey). To that end, Congress not only increased federal support for vocational rehabilitation, but also addressed the broader problem of discrimination against the handicapped by including §504, an antidiscrimination provision patterned after Title VI of the Civil Rights of 1964. Section 504 of the Rehabilitation Act reads in pertinent part:

> No otherwise qualified handicapped individual in the United States, as defined in section 706(7) of this title, shall, solely by reason of his handicap, be excluded from participation in, be denied the benefits of, or be subjected to discrimination under any program or activity receiving Federal financial assistance. . . . 29 U.S.C. §794.

In 1974 Congress expanded the definition of "handicapped individual" for use in §504 to read as follows:

> [A]ny person who (i) has a physical or mental impairment which substantially limits one or more of such person's major life activities, (ii) has a record of such an impairment, or (iii) is regarded as having such an impairment. 29 U.S.C. §706(7)(B).

The amended definition reflected Congress' concern with protecting the handicapped against discrimination stemming not only from simple prejudice, but from "archaic attitudes and laws" and from "the fact that the American people are simply unfamiliar with and insensitive to the difficulties confront[ing] individuals with handicaps." . . . To combat the effects of erroneous but nevertheless prevalent perceptions about the handicapped, Congress expanded the definition of "handicapped individual" so as to preclude discrimination against "[a] person who has a record of, or is regarded as having, an impairment [but who] may at present have no actual incapacity at all." . . .

In determining whether a particular individual is handicapped as defined by the Act, the regulations promulgated by the Department of Health and Human Services are of significant assistance. As we have previously recognized, these regulations were drafted with the oversight and approval of Congress, . . . [and] they provide "an important source of guidance on the meaning of §504." . . . The regulations are particularly significant here because they define two critical terms used in the statutory definition of handicapped individual. "Physical impairment" is defined as follows:

> [A]ny physiological disorder or condition, cosmetic disfigurement, or anatomical loss affecting one or more of the following body systems: neurological; musculoskeletal; special sense organs; respiratory, including speech organs; cardiovascular; reproductive, digestive, genito-urinary; hemic and lymphatic; skin; and endocrine. . . .

In addition, the regulations define "major life activities" as

> functions such as caring for one's self, performing manual tasks, walking, seeing, hearing, speaking, breathing, learning, and working. . . .

Within this statutory and regulatory framework, then, we must consider whether Arline can be considered a handicapped individual. According to the testimony of Dr. McEuen, Arline suffered tuberculosis "in an acute form in such a degree that it affected her respiratory system," and was hospitalized for this condition. . . . Arline thus had a physical impairment as that term is defined by the regulations, since she had a "physiological disorder or condition . . . affecting [her] . . . respiratory [system]." . . . This impairment was serious enough to require hospitalization, a fact more than sufficient to establish that one or more of her major life activities were substantially limited by her impairment. Thus, Arline's hospitalization for tuberculosis in 1957 suffices to establish that she has a "record of . . . impairment" within the meaning of 29 U.S.C. §706(7)(B)(ii), and is therefore a handicapped individual.

Petitioners concede that a contagious disease may constitute a handicapping condition to the extent that it leaves a person with "diminished physical or mental capabilities," . . . and concede that Arline's hospitalization for tuberculosis in 1957 demonstrates that she has a record of a physical impairment. . . . Petitioners maintain, however, Arline's record of impairment is irrelevant in this case, since the School Board dismissed Arline not because of her diminished physical capabilities, but because of the threat that her relapses of tuberculosis posed to the health of others.

We do not agree with petitioners that, in defining a handicapped individual under §504, the contagious effects of a disease can be meaningfully distinguished from the disease's physical effects on a claimant in a case such as this. Arline's contagiousness and her physical impairment each resulted from the same underlying condition, tuberculosis. It would be unfair to allow an employer to seize upon the distinction between the effects of a disease on others and the effect of a disease on a patient and use that distinction to justify discriminatory treatment. . . .

Allowing discrimination based on the contagious effects of a physical impairment would be inconsistent with the basic purpose of §504, which is to ensure that handicapped individuals are not denied jobs or other benefits because of the prejudiced attitudes or the ignorance of others. By amending the definition of "handicapped individual" to include not only those who are actually physically impaired, but also those who are regarded as impaired and who, as a result, are substantially limited in a major life activity, Congress acknowledged that society's accumulated myths and fears about disability and disease are as handicapping as are the physical limitations that flow from actual impairment. . . . The Act is carefully structured to replace such reflexive reactions to actual or perceived handicaps with actions based on reasoned and medically sound judgments: the definition of "handicapped individual" is broad, but only those individuals who are both handicapped *and* otherwise qualified are eligible for relief. The fact that *some* persons who have contagious diseases may pose a serious health threat to others under certain circumstances does not justify excluding from the coverage of the Act *all* persons with actual or perceived contagious diseases. Such exclusion would mean that those accused of being contagious would never have the opportunity to have their condition evaluated in light of medical evidence and a determination made as to whether they were "otherwise qualified." Rather, they would be vulnerable to discrimination on the basis of mythology—precisely the type of injury Congress sought to prevent. We conclude that the fact that a person with a record of a physical impairment is also contagious does not suffice to remove that person from coverage under §504.

The remaining question is whether Arline is otherwise qualified for the job of elementary school teacher. To answer this question in most cases, the District Court will need to conduct an individualized inquiry and make appropriate findings of fact. . . .

Because of the paucity of factual findings by the District Court, we, like the Court of Appeals, are unable at this stage of the proceedings to resolve whether Arline is "otherwise qualified" for her job. The District Court made no findings as to the duration and severity of Arline's condition, nor as to the probability that she would transmit the disease. Nor did the court determine whether Arline was contagious at the time she was discharged, or whether the School Board could have reasonably accommodated her. Accordingly, the resolution of whether

Arline was otherwise qualified requires further findings of fact.

We hold that a person suffering from the contagious disease of tuberculosis can be a handicapped person within the meaning of the §504 of the Rehabilitation Act of 1973, and that respondent Arline is such a person. We remand the case to the District Court to determine whether Arline is otherwise qualified for her position. The judgment of the Court of Appeals is Affirmed.

CASE NOTES

1. The Supreme Court in footnotes to *Arline* clarified the meanings of "otherwise qualified" and "reasonable accommodation" as follows:

Otherwise Qualified. "An otherwise qualified person is one who is able to meet all of a program's requirements in spite of his handicap." . . . In the employment context, an otherwise qualified person is one who can perform "the essential functions" of the job in question.

Reasonable Accommodation. When a handicapped person is not able to perform the essential functions of the job, the court must also consider whether any "reasonable accommodation" by the employer would enable the handicapped person to perform those functions. Accommodation is not reasonable if it either imposes "undue financial and administrative burdens" on a grantee, or requires "a fundamental alteration in the nature of [the] program" . . . ("where reasonable accommodation does not overcome the effects of a person's handicap, or where reasonable accommodation causes undue hardship to the employer, failure to hire or promote the handicapped person will not be considered discrimination"). . . .

Employers have an affirmative obligation to make a reasonable accommodation for a handicapped employee. Although they are not required to find another job for an employee who is not qualified for the job he or she was doing, they cannot deny an employee alternative employment opportunities reasonably available under the employer's existing policies. . . .

2. The *Arline* court further commented on the undesirability of placing a teacher with an infectious disease in the classroom. The Court said:

A person who poses a significant risk of communicating an infectious disease to others in the workplace will not be otherwise qualified for his or her job if reasonable accommodation will not eliminate that risk. The Act would not require a school board to place a teacher with active, contagious tuberculosis in a classroom with elementary school children. Respondent conceded as much at oral argument.

3. The claim of a disabling condition cannot be made as an afterthought as a defense for incompetence. In a case illustrating this point, a teacher whose primary certification was elementary education was reassigned to teach sixth grade reading, spelling, mathematics, and social studies after seventeen years of exclusively teaching mathematics. The teacher was evaluated and given extensive recommendations for improvement. After failure to improve, the teacher was dismissed for incompetency. The teacher's documentation included numerous spelling, punctuation, and grammatical errors by the teacher, including the misspelling of the names of twenty-five of her students and even the misspelling of her own name. The teacher claimed that she was disabled, and a clinical psychologist diagnosed her as having a learning disability that affected her spelling, punctuation, and grammar. The court upheld the dismissal. Her incompetency in being able to instruct her students, standing alone, was sufficient grounds for termination. *Beck v. James*, 793 S.W.2d 416 (Mo.App.1990).

4. The ADA defines "disability" as "a physical or mental impairment that substantially limits one or more . . . major life activities." 42 U.S.C. §12102(2)(A). In a case involving severely myopic job applicants who brought a disability action against an airline, challenging the airline's minimum vision requirement for global pilots, the U.S. Supreme Court held that the applicants could not be classified as disabled under the ADA, and thereby could not state valid claims under the ADA, because the applicants could fully correct their visual impairment with corrective lenses. According to the Court, Congress did not intend to bring under the ADA's protection all those persons whose uncorrected conditions amount to disabilities. If this were the case, the persons with disabilities in America would number a whopping 160 million people. The Court, thereby, rejected the plaintiffs' allegations that the airline sight standards violated the ADA. The Court further noted that to come under the definition of being

"substantially" limited in a major life activity due to a disability, the person must be precluded from more than one type of job, specialized job, or particular choice of job, and in this case, the airline had many other jobs, other than a global pilot, available that could utilize the plaintiffs' skills and capabilities. *Sutton v. United Airlines, Inc.*, 527 U.S. 471, 119 S.Ct. 2139 (1999).

5. The question of whether a disease prevents an employee from actually performing the duties of the job is often at the heart of conflict between a school district and an employee. In one such case, when a school bus driver was diagnosed as having multiple sclerosis, the school district's physician found her to be medically unqualified to drive a bus. The driver filed a complaint with the New York State Division of Human Rights, charging discrimination. An expert in neurology testified on behalf of the driver, saying she was capable of driving a bus. The court ruled "that the determination that the complainant was unlawfully discriminated against is supported by substantial evidence." The disease did not prevent her from doing her job in a reasonable manner. *Bayport–Blue Point School District v. State Division of Human Rights*, 131 A.D.2d 849, 517 N.Y.S.2d 209 (2 Dept.1987).

--------- ❖ — ❖ — ❖ ---------

Teacher with AIDS Cannot Be Prevented from Returning to the Classroom Solely Because of Fear and Apprehension of Parents

Chalk v. United States District Court Central District of California and Orange County Superintendent of Schools

United States Court of Appeals,
Ninth Circuit, 1988.
840 F.2d 701.

POOLE, Circuit Judge. Petitioner Vincent L. Chalk is a certified teacher of hearing-impaired students in the Orange County Department of Education. In February of 1987, Chalk was diagnosed as having Acquired Immune Deficiency Syndrome (AIDS). Subsequently, the Department reassigned Chalk to an administrative position and barred him from teaching in the classroom. Chalk then filed this action in the district court, claiming that the Department's action violated §504 of the Rehabilitation Act of 1973, 29 U.S.C.A. §794 (West Supp.1987), as amended, which proscribes recipients of federal funds from discriminating against otherwise qualified handicapped persons.

Chalk's motion for a preliminary injunction ordering his reinstatement was denied by the district court, and Chalk brought this appeal. After hearing oral argument, we issued an order reversing the district court and directing it to issue the preliminary injunction. . . . In this opinion, we now set forth in full the reasons underlying our reversal. . . .

As the district court recognized, the Supreme Court recently held that section 504 is fully applicable to individuals who suffer from contagious diseases. *School Bd. of Nassau County v. Arline*, [408] U.S. [273], 107 S.Ct. 1123, 94 L.Ed.2d 307 (1987). . . .

In its opinion, the Court addressed the question which is of central importance to this case: under what circumstances may a person handicapped with a contagious disease be "otherwise qualified" within the meaning of section 504? . . .

. . . [T]he Court recognized the difficult circumstances which confront a handicapped person, an employer, and the public in dealing with the possibility of contagion in the workplace. The problem is in reconciling the needs for protection of other persons, continuation of the work mission, and reasonable accommodation—if possible—of the afflicted individual. The Court effected this reconciliation by formulating a standard for determining when a contagious disease would prevent an individual from being "otherwise qualified":

> A person who poses a significant risk of communicating an infectious disease to others in the workplace will not be otherwise qualified for his or her job if reasonable accommodation will not eliminate that risk. The Act would not require a school board to place a teacher with active, contagious tuberculosis in a classroom with elementary school children. . . .

The application of this standard requires, in most cases, an individualized inquiry and appropriate findings of fact, so that "§504 [may] achieve its goal of protecting handicapped individuals from deprivations based on prejudice, stereotypes, or unfounded fear, while giving appropriate weight to such legitimate concerns of grantees as avoiding exposing others to significant health and safety risks." . . . Specifically, *Arline* requires a trial court to make findings regarding four factors: "(a) the nature of the risk (how the disease is transmitted), (b) the duration of the risk (how long is the carrier infectious), (c) the severity of the risk (what is the potential harm to third parties) and (d) the probabilities the disease will be transmitted and will cause varying degrees of harm." . . . Findings regarding these factors should be based "on reasonable medical judgments given the state of medical knowledge," and courts should give particular deference to the judgments of public health officials.

Chalk submitted in evidence to the district court, and that court accepted, more than 100 articles from prestigious medical journals and the declarations of five experts on AIDS, including two public health officials of Los Angeles County. Those submissions reveal an overwhelming evidentiary consensus of medical and scientific opinion regarding the nature and transmission of AIDS. . . .

Transmission of HIV is known to occur in three ways: (1) through intimate sexual contact with an infected person; (2) through invasive exposure to contaminated blood or certain other bodily fluids; or (3) through perinatal exposure (i.e., from mother to infant). Although HIV has been isolated in several body fluids, epidemiologic evidence has implicated only blood, semen, vaginal secretions, and possibly breast milk in transmission. Extensive and numerous studies have consistently found no apparent risk of HIV infection to individuals exposed through close, non-sexual contact with AIDS patients. . . .

. . . Little in science can be proved with complete certainty, and section 504 does not require such a test. As authoritatively construed by the Supreme Court, section 504 allows the exclusion of an employee only if there is "a *significant* risk of communicating an infectious disease to others." . . . In addition, *Arline* admonishes courts

that they "should defer to the reasonable medical judgments of public health officials." . . . The district judge ignored these admonitions. Instead, he rejected the overwhelming consensus of medical opinion and improperly relied on speculation for which there was no credible support in the record. . . .

Viewing Chalk's submissions in light of these cases, it is clear that he has amply demonstrated a strong probability of success on the merits. We hold that it was error to require that every theoretical possibility of harm be disproved. . . .

We conclude that petitioner met all of the requirements necessary to receive a preliminary injunction. We therefore reverse the district court's order and remand this action with direction to enter a preliminary injunction ordering defendants forthwith to restore petitioner to his former duties as a teacher of hearing-impaired children in the Orange County Department of Education. This panel will retain jurisdiction over any subsequent appeal.

Reversed and remanded.

CASE NOTES

1. The Supreme Court, in *Arline*, specifically delimited its decision to exclude consideration of AIDS as a physical impairment. In a footnote to the case, the Court said:

> The United States argues that it is possible for a person to be simply a carrier of a disease, that is, to be capable of spreading a disease without having a "physical impairment" or suffering from any other symptoms associated with the disease. The United States contends that this is true in the case of some carriers of the Acquired Immune Deficiency Syndrome (AIDS) virus. From this premise the United States concludes that discrimination solely on the basis of contagiousness is never discrimination on the basis of a handicap. The argument is misplaced in this case, because the handicap here, tuberculosis, gave rise both to a physical impairment *and* to contagiousness. This case does not present, and we therefore do not reach, the questions whether a carrier of a contagious disease such as AIDS could be considered to have a physical impairment, or whether such a person could be considered, solely on the basis of contagiousness, a handicapped person as defined by the Act.

2. In order to determine whether a transfer of a teacher with HIV to another job is an adverse employment action, the court must use the objective standard of a reasonable person, to wit: whether a reasonable person in the same or similar circumstances would consider the transfer adverse. *Doe v. DeKalb County School District,* 145 F.3d 1441 (11th Cir.1998).

3. The human immunodeficiency virus (HIV) is a "physical impairment" within the meaning of the ADA from the moment of infection and throughout every stage of the disease. *Bragdon v. Abbott,* 524 U.S. 624, 118 S.Ct. 2196 (1998).

4. The rationale provided by the Supreme Court in *Arline* to determine whether a particular risk of infection to others is significant depends on "(a) the nature of the risk (how the disease is transmitted), (b) the duration of the risk (how long is the carrier infectious), (c) the severity of the risk (what is the potential harm to third parties) and (d) the probabilities the disease will be transmitted and will cause varying degrees of harm." Using this reasoning, the Supreme Court in *Bragdon v. Abbott* found that evidence concerning the possible spread of HIV to a dentist who refused to treat a patient with HIV was sufficiently inconclusive at the time of the incident to conclude that the dentist had violated the ADA. The Court held that the issue was a triable issue of fact and must be determined at the lower court level through presentation of relevant evidence. *Bragdon v. Abbott,* 524 U.S. 624, 118 S. Ct. 2196 (1988).

5. Citing *Franklin v. Gwinnett County Public Schools,* 503 U.S. 60, 112 S.Ct. 1028 (1992), the Eighth Circuit Court of Appeals ruled that Section 504 of the Rehabilitation Act of 1973, 29 U.S.C. §792, provides a full spectrum of remedies, including money damages. *Rodgers v. Magnet Cove Public Schools,* 34 F.3d 642 (8th Cir. 1994). See also *W. B. v. Matula,* 67 F.3d 484 (3d Cir.1995).

6. "The inability to perform a particular job for a particular employer is not sufficient to establish handicap within Rehabilitation Act." The disability must limit employment generally, and the inquiry must be individualized on a case-by-case determination. *Byrne v. Board of Education, School of West Allis–West Milwaukee,* 979 F.2d 560 (7th Cir.1992).

■ FAMILY AND MEDICAL LEAVE ACT OF 1993

In 1993, the U.S. Congress passed the Family and Medical Leave Act (FMLA).[154] The purpose of the act is "to balance the demands of the workplace with the needs of families; and to promote national interest in preserving family integrity." Also, the act is designed to "entitle employees to take reasonable leave for medical reasons, for the birth or adoption of a child, and for the care of a child, or parent, who has a serious health condition."

The FMLA applies to both public and private sector employees. Private employers must have fifty or more eligible employees at any one site to be included under the act. There is a special section for schools, stating that eligible employees of any "local educational agency" and "any private elementary or secondary school" are covered. To be eligible, an employee (or a part-time employee) must have worked for at least one year, providing that at least 1,250 hours of service were completed during the year immediately preceding the start of leave.

The employee may request leave for the birth or adoption of a child (this provision expires one year after the birth or adoption) or for the care of a seriously ill child, parent, or spouse. The term "child" includes biological, adopted, and foster children, stepchildren, and legal wards, with a focus on the actual provider of care. The employee is entitled to up to twelve weeks of unpaid leave within any twelve-month period. The leave may be taken intermittently, as an occasional day leave, or as a reduced workweek. Leave generally requires agreement and coordination with the employer unless it is a "medical necessity."

The FMLA has a section that addresses employees who are "principally in an instructional capacity," which impacts schools. This provision applies where an employee requests leave that is "foreseeable based on planned medical treatment" and where the employee would be on leave for more than 20 percent of the total working days during the instructional period. If this is the case, the employer may require either that the leave be taken for a particular duration, not to exceed the planned medical treatment, or that the employee transfer to a temporary alternative position. This provision is based on the need for instructional continuity. There are also rules for leave falling near the end of the academic term; these rules are designed so as not to jeopardize the instructional integrity of the school.

Litigation involving the FMLA has included the Eleventh Amendment immunity issue discussed earlier in this book that pertains to all federal legislation affecting state governments. The U.S. Court of Appeals, Second Circuit, in *Hale v. Mann*[155] held that FMLA provisions making state governments liable for violation of the act are unconstitutional as violative of the Eleventh Amendment. The court pointed out that the law, as written, is not "congruent" and "proportional" to the goal of allowing family leave, while "minimiz[ing] the potential for employment discrimination on the basis of sex." According to the court, Congress had failed to specifically find that women are disproportionately affected by "serious health conditions,"[156] without which liability under the FMLA cannot be justified as implementing the requirements of the Fourteenth Amendment. (See Chapter 3 of this book for further explanation of the required nexus between federal legislation and Section 5 of the Fourteenth Amendment.) The court pointed out that this "gender-neutral grant of leave is overbroad."[157] The court further explained its reasoning in rejecting the idea that state agencies could be liable to individuals under the FMLA, saying: "There is no evidence that this conferment of federally protected leave is tailored to remedy sex-based employment discrimination. Instead, it seems grossly incongruent and disproportionate to try to remedy intentional sex discrimination with a statute that . . . 'creates substantive rights' and 'statutory entitlements' that do not permit an employer to 'defend by saying that it treated all employees identically.'"[158] The court concluded that Congress, in attempting to make a "substantive change" in state employees' rights, had exceeded its power to remedy or prevent unconstitutional actions. The law is deficient because it inappropriately tries to use the enforcement power of Section 5 of the Fourteenth Amendment, designed to remedy discrimination, to

provide new substantive rights in the absence of Congress's presenting evidence to support the legislation that discrimination had previously existed for a discrete and protected class of persons.[159] This decision, following the U.S. Supreme Court's decision in *Kimel v. Florida Board of Regents*,[160] invalidates the FMLA for Eleventh Amendment immunity purposes only. It does not invalidate the law as it may apply to local school districts in those states where the courts have held that local school districts are not state agencies or arms of the state for Eleventh Amendment purposes.

■ ENDNOTES

1. Francis Fukuyama, *Trust: The Social Virtues and the Creation of Prosperity* (New York: Free Press, 1995), p. 9.
2. John Finnis, *Natural Law and Natural Rights* (Oxford, England: Clarendon Press, 1989), pp. 161–64.
3. 42 U.S.C.A. §2000e-2(a).
4. Griggs v. Duke Power Company, 401 U.S. 424, 91 S.Ct. 849 (1971).
5. John E. Nowak, Ronald D. Rotunda, and J. Nelson Young, *Constitutional Law*, 3d ed. (St. Paul, Minn.: West, 1986), p. 524.
6. Ibid.
7. Bolling v. Sharpe, 347 U.S. 497, 74 S.Ct. 693 (1954).
8. Eric Rakowski, *Equal Justice* (Oxford, England: Clarendon Press, 1993), p. 53.
9. Ibid, p. 74.
10. Ronald Dworkin, "Is There a Right to Pornography?" *Oxford Journal of Legal Studies* 1 (1981).
11. Isaiah Berlin, *Concepts and Categories: Philosophical Essays* (New York: Viking Press, 1978), p. 82.
12. Ibid., p. 84.
13. 457 U.S. 202, 102 S.Ct. 2382 (1982).
14. San Antonio Independent School District v. Rodriguez, 411 U.S. 1, 93 S.Ct. 1278, rehearing denied, 411 U.S. 959, 93 S.Ct. 1919 (1973).
15. Ibid.
16. Johnson v. Transportation Agency, Santa Clara County, California, 480 U.S. 616, 627, 107 S.Ct. 1442, 1449 (1987).
17. Washington v. Davis, 426 U.S. 229, 239, 96 S.Ct. 2040, 2047 (1976).
18. 63 U.S. 4523, 115 S.Ct. at 2111 (1995).
19. 488 U.S. 469, 109 S.Ct. 706 (1989).
20. Ibid.
21. Ibid. at 492, 115 S.Ct. at 2111.
22. Ibid.
23. 480 F.2d 1159 (D.C.Cir.1973).
24. Regents of the University of California v. Bakke, 438 U.S. 265, 98 S.Ct. 2733 (1978).
25. 463 U.S. 582, 103 S.Ct. 3221 (1983).
26. 42 U.S.C.A. §2000e-1.

27. Equal Employment Opportunities Act of 1972, Public Law 92-261.

28. 401 U.S. 424, 91 S.Ct. 849 (1971).

29. Ibid.

30. Armstead v. Starkville Municipal Separate School District, 325 F.Supp. 560 (N.D.Miss.1971), affirmed in part and reversed in part, 461 F.2d 276 (5th Cir.1972); Chance v. Board of Examiners, 458 F.2d 1167 (2d Cir.1972); Baker v. Columbus Municipal Separate School District, 462 F.2d 1112 (5th Cir.1972); United States v. Chesterfield County School District, 484 F.2d 70 (4th Cir.1973); United States v. North Carolina, 400 F.Supp. 343 (E.D.N.C.1975), vacated, 425 F.Supp. 789 (E.D.N.C. 1977).

31. International Brotherhood of Teamsters v. United States, 431 U.S. 324, 97 S.Ct. 1843 (1977).

32. Washington v. Davis, 426 U.S. 229, 96 S.Ct. 2040 (1976).

33. United States v. South Carolina, 445 F.Supp. 1094 (D.S.C. 1977), affirmed, 434 U.S. 1026, 98 S.Ct. 756 (1978).

34. Civil Rights Act of 1991, 42 U.S.C.A. 1981.

35. 490 U.S. 642, 109 S.Ct. 2115 (1989).

36. Ibid. Also see 42 U.S.C.A. 1981(a).

37. Ibid.

38. Johnson v. Transportation Agency, Santa Clara County, California, 480 U.S. 616, 639–42, 107 S.Ct. 1442, 1456–57 (1987), citing Regents of the University of California v. Bakke, 438 U.S. 265, 98 S.Ct. 2733 (1978).

39. Furnco Construction Corp. v. Waters, 438 U.S. 567, 577, 98 S.Ct. 2943, 2950 (1978).

40. Title VII, 42 U.S.C. §2000e-2(j).

41. McDonald v. Santa Fe Trail Transportation Co., 427 U.S. 273, 96 S.Ct. 2574 (1976).

42. Ibid. at 273, 96 S.Ct. at 2575.

43. 443 U.S. 193, 99 S.Ct. 2721 (1979).

44. Johnson v. Transportation Agency, Santa Clara County, California, 480 U.S. 616 n.21, 107 S.Ct. 1442 n.21 (1987).

45. Ibid. at 620, 107 S.Ct. at 1446.

46. Ibid. at 617, 107 S.Ct. at 1444.

47. Wygant v. Jackson Board of Education, 476 U.S. 267, 106 S.Ct. 1842 (1986).

48. Britton v. South Bend Community School Corporation, 819 F.2d 766 (7th Cir.1987), cert. denied, 484 U.S. 925, 108 S.Ct. 288 (1987).

49. Wygant v. Jackson Board of Education, 476 U.S. 267, 106 S.Ct. 1842, 1844 (1986).

50. Adarand Construtcors, Inc. v. Pena, 63 U.S. 4523, 115 S.Ct. 2097 (1995).

51. Ibid., 115 S.Ct. at 2100.

52. Ibid., 115 S.Ct. at 2101.

53. Ibid., 115 S.Ct. at 2118.

54. Ibid.

55. Kern Alexander and M. David Alexander, *The Law of Schools, Students, and Teachers* (St. Paul, Minn.: West, 1984).

56. 42 U.S.C.A. §§2000e to 2000e-17.

57. McDonnell Douglas Corp. v. Green, 411 U.S. 792, 802, 93 S.Ct. 1817, 1924 (1973).

58. Carlile v. South Routt School District RE-3J, 739 F.2d 1496, 1500 (10th Cir.1984).

59. Ibid.

60. Spears v. Board of Education of Pike County, Kentucky, 843 F.2d 882 (6th Cir.1988).

61. Patterson v. Masem, 774 F.2d 251 (8th Cir.1985). See also Wardwell v. School Board, 786 F.2d 1554 (11th Cir.1986).

62. Conner v. Fort Gordon Bus Co., 761 F.2d 1495, 1489 (11th Cir.1985). See also McCarthney v. Griffin-Spalding County Board of Education, 791 F.2d 1549 (11th Cir.1986).

63. McCarthney v. Griffin-Spalding County Board of Education, op. cit.

64. Price Waterhouse v. Hopkins, 490 U.S. 228, 109 S.Ct. 1775 (1989).

65. 42 U.S.C.A. §2000e-2(a)(1), (2).

66. Price Waterhouse v. Hopkins, 490 U.S. at 241–42, 109 S.Ct. at 1786.

67. Ibid.

68. Public Law 95-555, 42 U.S.C.A. §2000e(k).

69. *Deskbook Encyclopedia of American School Law* (Burnsville, Minn.: Oakstone Legal & Publishing, Inc., 2000), pp. 245–46.

70. Sanderson v. St. Louis University, 586 F.Supp. 954 (E.D.Mo.1984).

71. Mitchell v. Board of Trustees of Pickens County School District A, 599 F.2d 582 (4th Cir.1979).

72. Ibid.

73. City of Los Angeles, Department of Water and Power v. Manhart, 435 U.S. 702, 98 S.Ct. 1370 (1978).

74. Arizona Governing Committee v. Norris, 463 U.S. 1073, 103 S.Ct. 3492 (1983).

75. 456 U.S. 512, 102 S.Ct. 1912, 1914 (1982).

76. Barbara Lindemann and David D. Kadue, *Sexual Harassment in Employment Law* (Washington, D.C.: Bureau of National Affairs, Inc., 1992), pp. 3–4.

77. M. David Alexander and Mary F. Hughes, "Sexual Harassment in the Workplace," in *Principal's Handbook: Current Issues in School Law*, ed. William E. Camp, Julie K. Underwood, and Mary Jane Connelly (Topeka, Kans.: National Organization on Legal Problems of Education, 1989).

78. 29 C.F.R. §1604.11(a).

79. See Lindemann and Kadue, *Sexual Harassment in Employment Law*, p. 7.

80. Ibid., p. 7.

81. *Black's Law Dictionary* (St. Paul, Minn.: West, 7th Edition, 1999).

82. Lindemann and Kadue, *Sexual Harassment in Employment Law*, p. 8.

83. Barnes v. Costle, 561 F.2d 983 (D.C. Cir.1977). See also Lindemann and Kadue, *Sexual Harassment in Employment Law*, p. 8.

84. 477 U.S. 57, 106 S.Ct. 2399 (1986).

85. Ibid. at 65, 106 S.Ct. at 2404.

86. See Lindemann and Kadue, *Sexual Harassment in Employment Law*, p. 8.

87. 682 F.2d 897, 902 (11th Cir.1982).

88. Lindemann and Kadue, *Sexual Harassment in Employment Law*, p. 253.

89. Ibid.

90. Harris v. Forklift Systems, Inc., 510 U.S. 17, 114 S.Ct. 367 (1993).

91. Coffman v. Tracker, 141 F.3d 1241 (8th Cir.1998). See Lindemann and Kadue, *Sexual Harassment in Employment Law*, p. 91.

92. Reed v. A.W. Lawrence & Co., 95 F.3d 1170 (2d Cir.1993).

93. See Lindemann and Kadue, *Sexual Harassment in Employment Law,* p. 99, note 63; Price Waterhouse v. Hopkins, 490 U.S. 228, 109 S.Ct. 1775 (1989).

94. Long v. Eastfield College, 88 F. 3d 300 (5th Cir.1996).

95. Cram v. Lamson & Sessions Co., 49 F.3d 466 (8th Cir.1995).

96. Connor v. Schnuck Markets, Inc., 121 F.3d 1390 (10th Cir.1997).

97. Davidson v. Middlefort Clinic, Inc., 133 F.3d 499 (7th Cir.1998).

98. Faragher v. City of Boca Raton, 524 U.S. 775, 118 S.Ct. 2275 (1998).

99. Ibid.

100. Ibid.

101. Ibid.

102. Ibid. See also Lindemann and Kadue, *Sexual Harassment in Employment Law.*

103. Faragher v. City of Boca Raton, op. cit.

104. Ibid.

105. 524 U.S. 742, 118 S.Ct. 2257 (1998).

106. 29 C.F.R. §1604.11(c).

107. Ibid.

108. 432 U.S. 63, 97 S.Ct. 2264 (1977).

109. Wangsness v. Watertown School District No. 14-4, 541 F.Supp. 332 (D.S.D.1982).

110. Pinsker v. Joint District No. 28J, 554 F.Supp. 1049 (D.Colo.1983), judgment affirmed, 735 F.2d 388 (10th Cir.1984).

111. 403 U.S. 602, 91 S.Ct. 2105 (1971).

112. 29 U.S.C.A. §206(d)(1).

113. 42 U.S.C.A. §2000e-2.

114. 42 U.S.C.A. §2000e-1; see Odomes v. Nucare, Inc., 653 F.2d 246, 250 (6th Cir.1981) and Corning Glass Works v. Brennan, 417 U.S. 188, 94 S.Ct. 2223 (1974).

115. 42 U.S.C.A. §2000e-1 ibid. See also Corning Glass Works v. Brennan, 417 U.S. 188, 94 S.Ct. 2223 (1974).

116. EEOC v. Madison Community Unit School District No. 12, 818 F.2d 577 (7th Cir.1987).

117. Ibid.

118. Equal Employment Opportunity Commission v. Tree of Life Christian Schools, 751 F.Supp. 700 (S.D.Ohio 1990).

119. 29 U.S.C.A. §621, as amended in 1986, Age Discrimination in Employment Act.

120. Public Law 99-592, 29 U.S.C.A. §§621–23.

121. 528 U.S. 62, 120 S.Ct. 631 (2000).

122. Narin v. Lower Merion School District, 206 F.3d 323 (3d Cir.2000).

123. Kendrick v. Jefferson County Board of Education, 19 Fed.R.Serv. 1303 (11th Cir.1991).

124. Doe v. Knox County Board of Education, 918 F.Supp. 181 (E.D.Ky.1996).

125. United States v. Orleans Parish School Board, 46 F.Supp. 2d 546 (E.D.La.1999).

126. Equal Employment Opportunity Commission v. Hickman Mills Consolidated School District No. 1, 99 F.Supp. 2d 1070 (W.D. Mo., 2000).

127. Montauk Bus Company, Inc. v. Utica City School District, 30 F.Supp.2d 313 (N.D.N.Y.1998).

128. Green v. Clarendon County School District Three, 923 F.Supp. 829 (D.S.C.1996).

129. Ambus v. Ganite Board of Education, 995 F.2d 992 (10th Cir.1993).

130. Rosenfeld v. Montgomery County Public Schools, 41 F.Supp. 2d 581 (D.Md.1999).

131. Massachusetts Board of Retirement v. Murgia, 427 U.S. 307, 96 S.Ct. 2562 (1976).

132. Vance v. Bradley, 440 U.S. 93, 101, 99 S.Ct. 939, 944 (1979).

133. 472 U.S. 400, 105 S.Ct. 2743 (1985).

134. McDonnell Douglas Corp. v. Green, 411 U.S. 792, 801, 93 S.Ct. 1817, 1824 (1973).

135. 507 U.S. 604, 113 S.Ct. 1701 (1993).

136. Ibid.

137. Hazen Paper Company v. Biggins, 507 U.S. 604, 113 S.Ct. 1701 (1993).

138. Ibid.

139. *Federal Law of Employment Discrimination in a Nutshell,* Mack A. Player, 4th Edition, p. 258, West Group, St. Paul, Minn. 1999.

140. Ibid.

141. Ibid., p. 256.

142. 29 U.S.C.A. 623 (f) (1).

143. *Federal Law of Employment Discrimination in a Nutshell,* Mack A. Player, 4th Edition, p. 260, West Group, St. Paul, Minn. 1999.

144. Book (David) also Davidson v. Board of Governors, State Colleges and Universities, 920 F.2d 441 (7th Cir.1990).

145. Hazen Paper Company v. Biggins, op cit.

146. Western Air Lines, Inc. v. Criswell, 472 U.S. 400, 105 S.Ct. 2743 (1985).

147. 42 U.S.C.A. §12114.

148. Pushkin v. Regents of the University of Colorado, 658 F.2d 1372, 1384 (10th Cir.1981).

149. 480 U.S. 273, 107 S.Ct. 1123 (1987).

150. Gurmankin v. Costanzo, 556 F.2d 184 (3d Cir.1977). See also Gurmankin v. Costanzo, 626 F.2d 1115 (3d Cir.1980).

151. Upshur v. Love, 474 F.Supp. 332 (N.D.Cal.1979).

152. Wood v. Omaha School District, 25 F.3d 667 (8th Cir.1994).

153. Pushkin v. Regents of the University of Colorado, 658 F.2d 1372, 1384 (10th Cir.1981).

154. 29 U.S.C.A. §2601. See Kern Alexander and M. David Alexander, *The Law of Schools, Students, and Teachers in a Nutshell* (St. Paul, Minn.: West, 1995).

155. Hale v. Mann, 219 F.3d 61 (2d Cir. 2000).

156. Ibid.

157. Ibid.

158. Ibid.

159. Ibid.

160. Kimel v. Florida Board of Regents, 528 U.S. 62, 120 S.Ct. 631 (2000).

CHAPTER 18

COLLECTIVE BARGAINING

Refusal to confer and negotiate has been one of the most prolific causes of strife. This is such an outstanding fact in the history of labor disturbances that it is a proper subject of judicial notice.

—Charles Evans Hughes

CHAPTER OUTLINE

- PRIVATE VERSUS PUBLIC SECTOR
- THE RIGHT TO BARGAIN COLLECTIVELY
- SCOPE OF BARGAINING
- COLLECTIVE AND INDIVIDUAL RIGHTS
- CONSTITUTIONAL RIGHTS OF INDIVIDUALS

LABOR LAW in public education encompasses collective bargaining, strikes, wages, hours, and working conditions. With such broad import for the operation of the schools, it is little wonder that the movement toward unionism has had such a profound effect on school administration. This has manifested itself at all levels, from statutory provisions down to the day-to-day contract administration by the school principal. The result has been that the administrative role has, to a great extent, shifted from discretionary activities to duties that are ministerial in nature. Public school labor relations is the story of this legal transition.

Developments in public school labor relations closely track the precedents of the private sector of the 1930s. Differences that cannot be ignored do exist, however, between the public and private sectors, thus preventing direct transference of private sector legal precedents into public practice. Both common law and statutory law that govern public school labor relations are, effectively, modifications of the well-established private sector view of labor relations.

❖ — ❖ — ❖

Historical Development

Charles M. Rehmus, "Labor Relations in the Public Sector," paper prepared for the 3d World Congress, International Industrial Relations Association, London, England (September 3–7, 1973).

BACKGROUND OF PUBLIC EMPLOYEE LABOR RELATIONS

Workers in the industrial private sector in the United States were given the statutory right to organize and bargain collectively in the 1930s. By 1960, approximately 30 percent of all non-agricultural private sector employees were represented by unions. Yet by this same date, there was practically no unionization in the public sector other than in the traditionally organized postal service and in a few other isolated situations.

The reasons for the delay in union organization of employees in the public sector in the United States are complex. In part, they stem from certain philosophical ideas long prevalent in the nation. Traditional concepts of sovereignty asserted that government is and should be supreme, hence immune from contravening forces and pressures such as that of collective bargaining. Related to this concept was that of the illegality of delegation of sovereign power. This assertion was that public decision-making could be done only by elected or appointed public officials, whose unilateral and complete discretion was therefore unchallengeable.

More practical considerations also delayed the advent of public employee unionism in the United States. The private sector unions and their international federations were fully occupied in trying to increase the extent of organization in the private sector. They had neither the money nor energy to turn to the public sector until the 1960s. Equally or more importantly, public employees were not generally dissatisfied with their terms and conditions of employment and, therefore, except in isolated cases, did not press for collective bargaining rights. Though the wages and salaries of public employees in the United States had traditionally lagged slightly behind comparable private sector salaries, the greater fringe benefits and job security associated with public employment were traditionally thought to be adequate compensation.

By the late 1950s and early 1960s, several of these practical considerations that had delayed public employee unionism had disappeared. Moreover, new factors came into play that are difficult to assess as to sequence or relative importance, but in total added to a new militancy. Change increasingly became endemic in American society as more and more groups, including public employees, found it commonplace to challenge the established order. Some public employees were made less secure by organizational and technological changes as government came under pressure to reduce tax increases and, therefore, turned to devices to increase efficiency and lower unit labor costs. Public employee wages and salaries began to lag further behind those in the unionized private sector as the post-war inflationary spiral continued. The private sector international unions saw the large and growing employment in the nonunion public sector as a fertile alternative that might substitute for their failure after 1956 to increase membership steadily in the private sector. Finally, many observers of public employment, both in and out of government, began strongly and publicly to question the logic behind governmentally protected collective bargaining in the private sector and government's complete failure to grant similar privileges and protections in the public sector.

By the 1960s, these practical challenges to the traditional arguments of sovereignty and illegal delegation of powers came to be seen as overriding in a number of government jurisdictions. The City of New York, the school board of that same city, and the State of Wisconsin gave modified collective bargaining rights to their public employees. Most importantly, in 1962 President Kennedy by executive order gave federal employees a limited version of the rights that private employees had received thirty years before. These seminal breakthroughs in granting some form of bargaining right to public employees led increasingly to similar kinds of state legislation, particularly in the more industrialized states. . . . President Nixon in two subsequent executive orders expanded and clarified the bargaining rights of federal employees.

■ PRIVATE VERSUS PUBLIC SECTOR

Before 1932, labor relations in the United States were a product of common law. In our laissez faire economic system, the courts tended to favor industrial management, since the damage done by work stoppages was both social and economic. In the period extending from about

1870 to 1930, business interests held hegemony in labor relations, and the courts backed it up by liberal use of the injunction to suppress strikes, picketing, and boycotts. Further, neither the courts nor the legislatures fashioned remedies for employees to prevent employers from discriminating against union members. Consequently, by 1930, labor unions were quite weak and had relatively little influence on the American economic system.[1]

Aware of the one-sidedness of the legal precedents and the suppressive nature of the injunction and its overuse by the courts, Congress enacted the Norris-LaGuardia Act in 1932, which had as its primary purpose preventing federal courts from issuing injunctions against union activities occurring as a result of labor disputes. Several states followed suit, and within a few years, the scales were tipped in favor of unions, making the use of the injunction almost impossible. Anti-injunction legislation was the seed that allowed labor to develop strength. Modern labor statutes have largely carried forth the anti-injunction theory, allowing injunctions only if union activities violate the law or place the national health and safety in peril.[2]

Following the anti-injunction statute of 1932, the first broad labor relations act was the National Labor Relations Act of 1935 (the Wagner Act). Its purpose was to encourage collective bargaining as a means of promoting industrial peace. The act established the National Labor Relations Board as a regulatory body to prosecute and remedy unfair labor practice. Additionally, the law created procedures for determining employee representation and placed a duty on both parties to bargain in good faith.

The National Labor Relations Act was amended by the Labor Management Relations Act of 1947, more popularly known as the Taft-Hartley Act. With this law, more limitations were placed on union activities through more definitive regulation of unfair labor practices by the union. Later, in 1959, the Taft-Hartley Act itself was amended by the Labor Management Reporting and Disclosure Act. This act was necessitated by widespread union mismanagement and corruption. A Senate investigating committee had found that unions in many cases had misused funds, had been infiltrated by gangsters, and had failed to conduct union business in a democratic manner. Designed to curb

these abuses, the 1959 act specifically delineated employee rights as protection against union abuse, prescribed union election procedures, and established criminal penalties for misappropriation of union funds.[3]

The experience of private sector labor relations laid the groundwork for present statutory and judicial regulation of union activity. State statutes governing public employee collective bargaining reflect this in many ways; for example, scope of bargaining, representation procedures, and impasse redress all have earmarks of the private experience.

The private and public sectors are, however, substantially different, and the application of private labor relations to the public schools has proceeded slowly. Some contend, as did Franklin D. Roosevelt in 1937, that "[t]he process of collective bargaining as usually understood cannot be transplanted into the public service."[4] This view maintains that decision making in education is a sovereign prerogative that cannot be shared. Those who are elected and speak with the voice of the citizenry as a whole must exercise their discretion in such matters, and the decision process that reflects this public will cannot be impaired or delegated. Public employees reject this rationale, arguing that the sovereign, legislature, or public agency is merely another employer with the power to delegate labor-management issues to the decision-making process of the bargaining table.

Most commentators admit, however, that the theoretical differences between the private and public sectors are probably of less practical importance than the more pragmatic distinctions relating to the strike, the process of governmental decision making, existing civil service systems, and the different economic forces and motivations that bear on government as opposed to industry.[5]

At the heart of collective bargaining is the right to strike. From the viewpoint of the employee, if employees cannot strike, negotiations may be a hollow exercise. Labor's position is simply that "[o]ne cannot negotiate without ability to reject the proffered terms. The only way in which employees can reject an employer's offer is to stop work. Consequently, collective bargaining can hardly exist without preserving the right to strike."[6] With few exceptions, though, the people through their state legislatures have rejected the right of public school teachers to strike. Where collective bargaining is permitted by statute, legislation usually falls short of allowing strikes and, in most instances, provides express prohibition. No such restraint, of course, exists in the private sector.

Another essential difference is that in the public sector, especially where school teachers are concerned, statutory budget deadlines and taxing restrictions make the bargaining process dependent on direct legislative action. In states in which local school district taxing leeway is limited, much of the new money for education is derived each year from state tax revenues. In such a situation, the bargaining agreement for increased wages is usually subject to legislative appropriation, regardless of the bargaining agreement.

A further very practical difference between the private and public sectors is that private employees have fewer inherent protections than public employees enjoy. In our system of government, as reviewed in other sections of this book, public school teachers have constitutional rights of equal protection and due process against arbitrary state action, a benefit not enjoyed by employees in the private sector. These constitutional protections coupled with state salary schedules, teacher retirement systems, sick leave, vacation leave, statutory prohibitions of discrimination, and so forth are examples of a public response to public employee needs that would probably not be found in the private sector in the absence of collective bargaining.

Finally, the normal market pressures of the private sector do not exist in the public schools. Public schools cannot lock out employees, go out of business, or raise prices. Beyond this, when the legislature of a state becomes involved, laws can be enacted that quickly change the rules of the game, possibly entirely redefining the criteria for certification for the teacher workforce or unilaterally altering the nature of the public service in its entirety.

These distinctions, though, are held by many union leaders to be more apparent than real, and it is certainly true that a substantial erosion of the differences between private and public bargaining has transpired. To a large extent, some of the traditional points of departure have become irrelevant, but throughout any discussion of this issue, one cannot help observing

that essential differences remain. The employee in the public sector, as a citizen, taxpayer, and human being, has greater potential influence over his or her employment destiny than can be found in the private sector.

As Werne points out,

> The employee in the private sector, except for the very devious method of shareholder voting, has no control over his management, unless by union contract. In the public sector, the employee can remove his employer from office and in not a few cases has effected such removal. In short, the strict dichotomy between employer and employee in the private sector has no exact counterpart in the public sector.[7]

Thus, the law pertaining to labor relations in the public schools may, to a great extent, be characterized as an adaptation of the private sector experience to the differing circumstances of the public schools.

■ THE RIGHT TO BARGAIN COLLECTIVELY

The right of public employees to engage in collective bargaining entails important legal aspects, such as the employees' right to organize, the authority of the school board to bargain, the right to strike, and the authority of the school board to submit to compulsory arbitration. Employees have a right to organize and join labor unions. A North Carolina law forbidding public employees from joining unions was held unconstitutional on its face as violative of the First and Fourteenth Amendments.[8] In *AFSCME v. Woodward*,[9] the court held that employees not only have a right to join labor unions, but also may file suit for damages and injunctive relief under the Civil Rights Act of 1871 if this freedom is denied. In *Woodward*, the court stated:

> The First Amendment protects the right of one citizen to associate with other citizens for any lawful purpose free from government interference. The guarantee of the "right of assembly" protects more than the "right to attend a meeting; it includes the right to express one's attitudes or philosophies by membership in a group or by affiliation with it or by other lawful means. . . ." *Griswold v. Connecticut*, 381 U.S. 479, 85 S.Ct. 1678, 14 L.Ed. 2d 510 (1965); *N.A.A.C.P. v. Alabama ex rel. Patterson*, 357 U.S. 449, 78 S.Ct. 1163, 2 L.Ed. 2d 1488 (1958).[10]

In the absence of statute, authority to bargain may[11] be within the discretion of the local board,[12] but there is no constitutional duty to bargain collectively with an exclusive bargaining agent:

> The refusal of [the School Board] to bargain in good faith does not equal a constitutional violation of plaintiffs-appellees' positive rights of association, free speech, petition, equal protection, or due process. Nor does the fact that the agreement to collectively bargain may be enforceable against a state elevate a contractual right to a constitutional right.[13]

Statutes prohibiting public employees' right to strike do not violate the state or federal constitutional mandates of equal protection. This issue was settled in a New York case contesting the Taylor Law's prohibition against strikes. The New York Court of Appeals held:

> In view of the strong policy considerations which led to the enactment of the Taylor Law, it is our conclusion that the statutory prohibition against strikes by public employees is reasonably designed to effectuate a valid state policy in an area where it has authority to act.[14]

Similarly, the highest court in Indiana has ruled that public school teachers have no inherent right to strike,[15] and these judgments have been reinforced at the federal level where, following a strike by the postal workers in 1970, a three-judge panel held that government employees do not have a right to strike. The federal district court held that neither public nor private employees have an absolute right to strike without statutory authorization. The opinion stated:

> Given the fact that there is no constitutional right to strike, it is not irrational or arbitrary for the Government to condition employment on a promise not to withhold labor collectively, and to prohibit strikes by those in public employment, whether because of the prerogative of the sovereign, some sense of higher obligation associated with public service, to assure the continuing functioning of the Government without interruption, to protect public health and safety or for other reasons.[16]

The public attitude against public employee strikes has become more moderate in recent years, and even the courts, albeit usually in dissents, are tending to view the strike situation more liberally. In a dissent in an Indiana case involving teachers in the city of Anderson, Justice DeBruler summarized arguments in favor of public employee strikes:

- State sovereignty is not necessarily infringed upon if collective bargaining and a limited right to strike are extended to public sector employees.
- The difference between public and private sector employees is in many instances negligible.
- The impact of a private sector strike might be more crippling than a strike by public employees.
- Public employees are guaranteed the same irrevocable rights by the Constitution as employees working in the private sector.
- Public employees must have some means to assert their rights, especially when such rights are not ensured through legislation.[17]

Compulsory interest arbitration has been used in the private sector as an alternative to the strike and may become more common in public education. Impasse resolution in this manner provides that either party may request arbitration of the dispute and that the decision of the arbitrator is binding on both parties. Compulsory arbitration has been extended to firefighters in Wyoming, Rhode Island, Massachusetts, and New York. A statute in Oregon requires binding arbitration in the field of public education, and Minnesota law provides for the director of mediation to resolve impasses by sending the dispute to arbitration.[18]

Without authorization from a statute, however, school boards cannot generally submit to binding arbitration. The Virginia Supreme Court has held that binding rights arbitration imposed by state board regulation constitutes an unlawful denial of local school board power and an unwarranted delegation of authority, and as such, it violates the Virginia Constitution, which makes management of the teaching staff an essential function of the local school board.[19]

In Michigan, however, a court has upheld a state statute that provides for compulsory arbitration. The city of Dearborn had maintained that the act violates the prerogative of city government as delineated in the Michigan Constitution. The court held that validity of the statute should be upheld "unless the contrary clearly appears."[20] Although this case was later reversed on other grounds, it clearly enunciated that a state statute imposing arbitration on local government will be presumed to be valid unless in direct conflict with the state constitution. In the absence of such statute, however, local agencies are not required to delegate their authority to an arbitrator.

------------------- ❖ — ❖ — ❖ -------------------

*Teachers May Organize and Bargain
Collectively but Cannot Strike*

Norwalk Teachers Association v. Board of Education of City of Norwalk

Supreme Court of Errors of Connecticut, 1951.
138 Conn. 269, 83 A.2d 482.

JENNINGS, Justice. This is a suit between the Norwalk Teachers' Association as plaintiff and the Norwalk board of education as defendant for a declaratory judgment. . . . The plaintiff is a voluntary association and an independent labor union to which all but two of the teaching personnel of approximately 300 in the Norwalk school system belong. In April, 1946, there was a dispute between the parties over salary rates. The board of estimate and taxation was also involved. After long negotiations, 230 members of the association rejected the individual contracts of employment tendered them and refused to return to their teaching duties. . . .

The contracts, subject to conditions precedent therein set forth, recognized the plaintiff as the bargaining agent for all of its members, defined working conditions and set up a grievance procedure and salary schedule. Similar contracts were entered into for the succeeding school years, including 1950–1951. From September, 1946, to the present and particularly with reference to the contract for 1950–1951, much doubt and uncertainty have arisen concerning the rights and duties of the respective parties, the interpretation of the contract and the construction of the state statutes relating to schools, education and boards of education. "In addition," the complaint states, "there has been the possibility of strikes, work stoppage or collective refusals to return to work by the teachers through their organization and the possibility of discharges or suspensions by the defendant by reason of difficult personnel relations, all of which tends to disharmony in the operation of the school system and to the ever present possibility that either, or both, of the parties may be unwittingly violating statutes by reason of mistaken or erroneous interpretation thereon." The parties agreed that the contract for the school year 1949–1950 would govern their relations for the school year 1950–1951, that they would join in this action, and "that whatever contractual obligations exist will be forthwith modified so soon as they shall have received from the Court judgments and orders declaring their respective rights, privileges, duties and immunities." The specific points of dispute are stated in the questions reserved, printed in the footnote.* . . .

Few cases involving the right of unions of government employees to strike to enforce their

---

*The plaintiff claimed a declaratory judgment answering and adjudicating the following questions:

"(a) Is it permitted to the plaintiff under our laws to organize itself as a labor union for the purpose of demanding and receiving recognition and collective bargaining?

"(b) Is it permitted to the plaintiff organized as a labor union to demand recognition as such and collective bargaining?

"(c) Is it permissible under Connecticut law for the defendant to recognize the plaintiff for the purpose of collective bargaining?

"(d) Is collective bargaining to establish salaries and working conditions permissible between the plaintiff and the defendant?

"(e) May the plaintiff engage in concerted action such as strike, work stoppage, or collective refusal to enter upon duties?

"(f) Is arbitration a permissible method under Connecticut law to settle or adjust disputes between the plaintiff and the defendant?

"(g) Is mediation a permissible method under the Connecticut law to settle or adjust disputes between the plaintiff and the defendant?

"(h) If the answer to the previous questions is yes, are the State's established administrative facilities, such as the State Board of Mediation and Arbitration and the State Labor Relations Board, available, as they are available in industrial disputes, to the plaintiff and the defendant?

"(i) Does the continuing contract law, so-called, create a status of employment within which the plaintiff may claim employment subject to the right to bargain salaries and working conditions?

"(j) Has the plaintiff the right to establish rules, working conditions and grievance resolution by collective bargaining?"

demands have reached courts of last resort. That right has usually been tested by an application for an injunction forbidding the strike. The right of the governmental body to this relief has been uniformly upheld. It has been put on various grounds: public policy; interference with governmental function; illegal discrimination against the right of any citizen to apply for government employment (where the union sought a closed shop). . . .

The plaintiff, recognizing the unreasonableness of its claims in the case of such employees as the militia and the judiciary, seeks to place teachers in a class with employees employed by the municipality in its proprietary capacity. No authority is cited in support of this proposition. "A town board of education is an agency of the state in charge of education in the town. . . ." . . . In fulfilling its duties as such an agency, it is acting in a governmental, not a proprietary, capacity. . . .

In the American system, sovereignty is inherent in the people. They can delegate it to a government which they create and operate by law. They can give to that government the power and authority to perform certain duties and furnish certain services. The government so created and empowered must employ people to carry on its task. Those people are agents of the government. They exercise some part of the sovereignty entrusted to it. They occupy a status entirely different from those who carry on a private enterprise. They serve the public welfare and not a private purpose. To say that they can strike is the equivalent of saying that they can deny the authority of government and contravene the public welfare. The answer to question (e) is "No."

Questions (a) and (b) relate to the right of the plaintiff to organize itself as a labor union and to demand recognition and collective bargaining. The right to organize is sometimes accorded by statute or ordinance. . . . The right to organize has also been forbidden by statute or regulation. In Connecticut the statutes are silent on the subject. Union organization in industry is now the rule rather than the exception. In the absence of prohibitory statute or regulation, no good reason appears why public employees should not organize as a labor union. *Springfield v. Clouse*, 356 Mo. 1239, 1246, 206 S.W.2d 539. It is the second part of the question (a) that causes

difficulty. The question reads: "Is it permitted to the plaintiff under our laws to organize itself as a labor union for the purpose of demanding and receiving recognition and collective bargaining?" The question is phrased in a very preemptory form. The common method of enforcing recognition and collective bargaining is the strike. It appears that this method has already been used by the plaintiff and that the threat of its use again is one of the reasons for the present suit. As has been said, the strike is not a permissible method of enforcing the plaintiff's demands. The answer to questions (a) and (b) is a qualified "Yes." There is no objection to the organization of the plaintiff as a labor union, but if its organization is for the purpose of "demanding" recognition and collective bargaining, the demands must be kept within legal bounds. What we have said does not mean that the plaintiff has the right to organize for all of the purposes for which employees in private enterprise may unite, as those are defined in §7391 of the General Statutes. Nor does it mean that, having organized, it is necessarily protected against unfair labor practices as specified in §7392 or that it shall be the exclusive bargaining agent for all employees of the unit, as provided in §7393. It means nothing more than that the plaintiff may organize and bargain collectively for the pay and working conditions which it may be in the power of the board of education to grant.

Questions (c) and (d) in effect ask whether collective bargaining between the plaintiff and the defendant is permissible. The statutes and private acts give broad powers to the defendant with reference to educational matters and school management in Norwalk. If it chooses to negotiate with the plaintiff with regard to the employment, salaries, grievance procedure and working conditions of its members, there is no statute, public or private, which forbids such negotiations. It is a matter of common knowledge that this is the method pursued in most school systems large enough to support a teachers' association in some form. It would seem to make no difference theoretically whether the negotiations are with a committee of the whole association or with individuals or small related groups, so long as any agreement made with the committee is confined to members of the association. If the strike threat is absent and the defendant prefers to handle the matter through negotiation with the plaintiff, no reason exists why it should not do so. The claim of the defendant that this would be an illegal delegation of authority is without merit. The authority is and remains in the board. This statement is not to be construed as approval of the existing contracts attached to the complaint. Their validity is not in issue.

As in the case of questions (a) and (b), (c) and (d) are in too general a form to permit a categorical answer. The qualified "Yes" which we give to them should not be construed as authority to negotiate a contract which involves the surrender of the board's legal discretion, is contrary to law or is otherwise ultra vires. For example, an agreement by the board to hire only union members would clearly be an illegal discrimination. *Mugford v. Baltimore*, 185 Md. 266, 270, 44 A.2d 745; Rhyne, *Labor Unions & Municipal Employee Law*, pp. 34, 137, 157. Any salary schedule must be subject to the powers of the board of estimate and taxation. "The salaries of all persons appointed by the board of education . . . shall be as fixed by said board, but the aggregate amount of such salaries . . . shall not exceed the amount determined by the board of estimate and taxation. . . . " 21 Spec. Laws, p. 285, No. 315, §3; *Board of Education of Stamford v. Board of Finance*, 127 Conn. 345, 349, 16 A.2d 601. One of the allegations of the complaint is that the solution of the parties' difficulties by the posing of specific issues is not satisfactory. Whether or not this is so, that course will be necessary if this discussion of general principles is an insufficient guide.

Question (f) reads, "Is arbitration a permissible method under Connecticut law to settle or adjust disputes between the plaintiff and the defendant?" The power of a town to enter into an agreement of arbitration was originally denied on the ground that it was an unlawful delegation of authority. *Griswold v. North Stonington*, 5 Conn. 367, 371. It was later held that not only the amount of damages but liability could be submitted to arbitration. *Hine v. Stephens*, 33 Conn. 497, 504; *Mallory v. Huntington*, 64 Conn. 88, 96, 29 A. 245. The principle applies to the parties to the case at bar. If it is borne in mind that arbitration is the result of mutual agreement, there is no reason to deny the power of the defendant to enter voluntarily into a con-

tract to arbitrate a specific dispute. On a proposal for a submission, the defendant would have the opportunity of deciding whether it would arbitrate as to any question within its power. Its power to submit to arbitration would not extend to questions of policy but might extend to questions of liability. Arbitration as a method of settling disputes is growing in importance and, in a proper case, "deserves the enthusiastic support of the courts." *International Brotherhood of Teamsters v. Shapiro*, 138 Conn. 57, 69, 82 A.2d 345. Agreements to submit all disputes to arbitration, commonly found in ordinary union contracts, are in a different category. If the defendant entered into a general agreement of that kind, it might find itself committed to surrender the broad discretion and responsibility reposed in it by law. For example, it could not commit to an arbitrator the decision of a proceeding to discharge a teacher for cause. So, the matter of certification of teachers is committed to the state board of education. General Statutes, §§1432, 1433, 1435. The best answer we can give to question (f) is, "Yes, arbitration may be a permissible method as to certain specific, arbitrable disputes."

From what has been said, it is obvious that, within the same limitations, mediation to settle or adjust disputes is not only permissible but desirable. The answer to question (g) is "Yes." The state board of mediation and arbitration and the state labor relations board, however, are set up to handle disputes in private industry and are not available to the plaintiff and defendant for reasons given in the opinion of the attorney general dated July 6, 1948. 25 Conn. Atty.Gen.Rep. 270. This was confirmed as to Norwalk teachers by an opinion dated June 12, 1950, not yet published. See also *United States v. United Mine Workers*, 330 U.S. 258, 269, 67 S.Ct. 677, 91 L.Ed. 884. The answer to question (h) is "No."

General Statutes, Sup.1949, §160a, provides in part: "The contract of employment of a teacher shall be renewed for the following school year unless such teacher has been notified in writing prior to March first of that year that such contract will not be renewed." Question (i) asks whether this law creates "a status of employment within which the plaintiff may claim employment subject to the right to bargain salaries and working conditions?" The meaning of this is not clear and the briefs do not clarify it. It is the type of question that should be related to a specific state of facts. It cannot be answered in vacuo.

As to question (j), the plaintiff has no right to establish rules. As stated above, the right is and remains in the board.

Question (g) is answered, "Yes, but not under chapter 369 of the General Statutes as amended." Questions (e), (h) and (j) are answered "No." Question (i) is not answered. No purpose would be served by answering the other questions categorically. Questions (a) and (b) are answered, "Yes, with relation to the plaintiff's own members, provided its demands are kept within legal bounds." Questions (c) and (d) are answered, "Yes, with relation to the plaintiff's own members, provided that this answer shall not be construed as approval of any specific contract which has been or may be entered into between the parties." Question (f) is answered, "Yes, arbitration may be a permissible method as to certain specific, arbitrable disputes." In answering some of these questions we have gone beyond the requirements of the specific questions asked in order to render such assistance as we properly may in helping to solve the difficulties of the parties.

No costs will be taxed in this court to either party.

In this opinion the other judges concurred.

Public Employees Must Have Express Legislative Permission to Strike

Anderson Federation of Teachers, Local 519 v. School City of Anderson

Supreme Court of Indiana, 1969.
252 Ind. 558, 251 N.E.2d 15 (1969), rehearing denied,
252 Ind. 558, 254 N.E.2d 329, cert. denied, 399
U.S. 928, 90 S.Ct. 2243 (1970).

GIVEN, Judge. On May 6, 1968, the Superior Court of Madison County found the appellant, Anderson Federation of Teachers, Local 519, in contempt of court for the violation of a restraining order which had been issued without notice on the 2nd day of May, 1968, directing the appellant, teachers' union, and its members to refrain from picketing and striking against the appellee school corporation. It is from this judgment of contempt that this appeal is taken.

The appellant is an organization of public school teachers employed by the appellee.

The appellee is a municipal corporation organized under the statutes of this state for the purpose of operating the public schools within the boundaries of the School City of Anderson, Indiana.

In the spring of 1968 the appellant and the appellees entered into negotiations concerning salary schedules for the following year. These negotiations apparently were not satisfactory to the appellant for on May 1, 1968, the appellant instituted a strike against the school corporation and established picket lines at the various schools operated by appellee. Evidence discloses that school children were unloaded in the public streets because of the presence of the picket lines. It was this action of picketing by the appellant which precipitated the temporary restraining order issued on May 2, 1968, and it was the continuation of this activity without regard for the restraining order upon which the trial court based its judgment after a hearing on May 6, 1968, that the appellant was in contempt of court for violating the restraining order.

The trial court was in all things correct in its finding and judgment of contempt of court.

It is the contention of the appellant that Indiana's "Little Norris-LaGuardia Act," also known as the anti-injunction statute, the same being Burns' Ind.Stat.Ann. §40-501 et seq., is applicable in this case. This act prohibits the issuance of restraining orders and injunctions in matters involving labor disputes between unions and private employers. We do not agree with the appellant that this act is applicable to disputes concerning public employees. The overwhelming weight of authority in the United States is that government employees may not engage in a strike for any purpose.

The Supreme Court of the United States clearly enunciated the proposition that public employees did not have a right to strike and that the injunctive processes might properly be used to prevent or halt such strikes in the case of *United States v. United Mine Workers (1947)*, 330 U.S. 258, 67 S.Ct. 677, 91 L.Ed. 884. This case has never been overruled or modified. . . .

This same proposition has been followed generally in most of the other state jurisdictions where it has been repeatedly held that strikes by public employees are or should be prohibited and that injunctions should be granted to halt or prevent them. . . .

We find only one case where an injunction to prevent a pending strike of public employees was denied. That case was *Board of Education of City of Minneapolis v. Public School Employees Union (1951)*, 233 Minn. 141, 45 N.W.2d 797, 29 A.L.R.2d 424. That case, however, was overruled in 1966 by the Supreme Court of Minnesota in *Minneapolis Federation of Teachers Local 59, AFL-CIO v. Obermeyer, supra*. . . .

We thus see that both the federal and state jurisdictions and men both liberal and conservative in their political philosophies have uniformly recognized that to allow a strike by public employees is not merely a matter of choice of political philosophies, but is a thing which cannot and must not be permitted if the orderly function of our society is to be preserved. This is not a matter for debate in the political arena for it appears fundamental, as stated by Governor Dewey, public strikes would lead to anarchy, and, as stated by President Roosevelt, the public strike "is unthinkable and intolerable."

The Madison Superior Court, is, therefore, in all things affirmed.

Teachers' Sanctions against Board Are Concerted Action toward Illegal End

Board of Education v. New Jersey Education Association

Supreme Court of New Jersey, 1968.
53 N.J. 29, 247 A.2d 867.

WEINTRAUB, C.J. . . . In February 1967 a dispute arose between the secretary of the Board and defendant Haller, president of UBTA. Haller was a teacher in plaintiff's system but had not yet acquired tenure. On March 14, 1967, the Board met to consider teacher contracts for the following school year and decided not to offer one to Haller and two other nontenure teachers who were active in UBTA. Haller was so notified on March 29. UBTA held a special meeting of its membership on March 31 at which a lengthy resolution was adopted listing seventeen grievances. . . .

Meanwhile, on April 12 UBTA resolved that "sanctions be imposed" against the Board and requested NJEA to follow suit. On April 21 the NJEA resolved to "impose sanctions" on the Board, and gave wide circulation to its resolution. . . .

NJEA proclaimed through the local press that it would be "a violation of the professional code of ethics for any teacher to accept employment in Union Beach or for any administrator to offer employment in Union Beach as long as the sanctions which had been invoked were in effect."

It has long been the rule in our State that public employees may not strike. . . .

Defendants deny there was a "strike." They seek to distinguish the usual concerted refusal to work from what transpired here. As to the teachers employed by the Board, defendants say they merely resigned as of a future date, and with respect to the interference with the Board's recruitment of replacements, defendants, as we understand them, say a refusal to accept employment is inherently different from a quit. But the subject is the public service, and the distinctions defendants advance are irrelevant to it, however arguable they may be in the context of private employment. Unlike the private employer, a public agency may not retire. The public demand for services which makes illegal a strike against government inveighs against any other concerted action designed to deny government the necessary manpower, whether by terminating existing employments in any mode or by obstructing access to the labor market. Government may not be brought to a halt. So our criminal statute, N.J.S. 2A:98-1, N.J.S.A., provides in simple but pervasive terms that any two or more persons who conspire "to commit any act" for the "obstruction of . . . the due administration of the laws" are guilty of a misdemeanor.

Hence, although the right of an individual to resign or to refuse public employment is undeniable, yet two or more may not agree to follow a common course to the end that an agency of government shall be unable to function. Here there was such collective action by agreement both as to the quitting and as to new employment. As to the mass resignations, an agreement to that end must be inferred from the very adoption by the members through their teachers union of the program of sanctions which, despite some verbal obscurity in this regard, quite plainly imports an understanding to withdraw services when the union officialdom "imposes sanctions" upon a school district. The use of "unethical" in condemning new employment because of working conditions must mean it is also "unethical" to continue an existing employment under the same conditions. The full understanding must be that upon the imposition of sanctions, all services will be withdrawn. We have no doubt that the agreement to strike was not articulated because of the established illegality of that course. In any event, if it should be thought the plan did not include the obligation to quit in connection with the imposition of sanctions, we think it clear that the teachers entered into an agreement to quit when they voted in favor of mass resignations and then executed thirty-six of them. Although the Board accepted the resignations and hence does not ask that work stoppage be ended, we are satisfied the stoppage was concerted action to an illegal end.

And with respect to blacklisting of the school district and the scheme of "sanctions" upon teachers who offer or take employment with a "sanctioned" school board, it can escape no one that the purpose is to back up a refusal of others to continue to work. At a minimum the object is to withhold additional services a school district may need to discharge its public duty, which, as we have said, is no less illegal. Such an illegal agreement may come into being at the time of the strike or may antedate it. If individuals enter into a union or association on terms that upon the occurrence of some stipulated event or signal they will impede government in its recruitment of services, that very arrangement constitutes an agreement the law denounces. An agreement not to seek, accept, or solicit em-

ployment in government whenever the upper echelon of the union makes a prescribed pronouncement is, no less than an accomplished shutdown, a thrust at the vitality of government, and comes within the same policy which denounces a concerted strike or quit or slowdown or other obstruction of the performance of official duties.

. . . That the conventional terminology of a "strike" nowhere appears is of no moment. The substance of a situation and not its shape must control. A doctrine designed to protect the public interest is equal to any demand upon it. It does not yield to guise or ingenuity.

. . . The trial court expressly added that "There is no intention, however, of restraining defendants from exercising the right of free speech concerning what they think the conditions are in the Union Beach school system."

What reappears in defendants' argument is a protest that "sanctions" are no more than an expression of disapproval of conditions in the school district and of the conduct of the Board. It is difficult, even in the abstract, to take that view of the terms used. Far from importing a mere denunciation of men and their work, the "imposition of sanctions" imports the imposition of a penalty. . . .

The imposition of "sanctions" was the stipulated signal for unlawful activity. The right to utter even a pleasantry may be lost if it is the agreed call for lawlessness. It need hardly be said that freedom of speech does not include the right to use speech as an instrument to an unlawful end. . . .

The judgment is affirmed (for Board).

CASE NOTES

1. The equitable powers of a state court are sufficient to permit the court to require court-monitored collective bargaining as an element of injunctive relief. *Carroll v. Ringgold Education Association*, 655 A.2d 613 (1996). See also *Armstrong School District v. Armstrong Education Association*, 528 Pa. 170, 595 A.2d 1139 (1991).

2. Refusal to perform extracurricular duties constitutes a strike. "Extracurricular activities are a fundamental part of a child's education,

making the supervision of such activities an integral part of a teacher's duty toward his or her students." *Board of Education of City of Asbury Park v. Asbury Park Education Association,* 145 N.J.Super. 495, 368 A.2d 396 (1976).

3. It is not an unfair labor practice to suspend bargaining during the pendency of an illegal strike in Michigan. The Michigan Employment Relations Commission overruled a prior decision holding that it was an unfair labor practice to cease bargaining during an illegal strike. *Melvindale–Northern Allen Park Federation of Teachers, Local 1051 v. Melvindale–Northern Allen Park Public Schools,* 216 Mich.App. 31, 549 N.W.2d 6 (1996).

4. The state may reduce state aid to a school district for the days on which it is not in session due to a strike. In Michigan, a school district brought action against the Department of Education, challenging a reduction in state aid for the period of a fourteen-day teacher strike. The court allowed the reduction of state aid. *Pontiac School District v. Department of Education,* 204 Mich.App. 525, 516 N.W.2d 516 (1994).

5. The failure of employees to abide by a court-issued injunction may result in related costs being assessed against the teachers union. In a case where negotiations broke down and teachers and supporting personnel went on strike and failed to return when the court issued an injunction requiring the employees to immediately return to work, an appellate court awarded the school board counsel fees and other nonattorney strike-related costs, such as wages for substitute personnel hired to replace striking employees. *Franklin Township Board of Education v. Quakertown Education Association,* 274 N.J.Super. 47, 643 A.2d 34 (App.Div.1994).

6. A teachers' union may be fined by the court for instigating an illegal strike. In an Indiana case where contract negotiations broke down between the school corporation and the National Education Association–South Bend (NEA-SB) and the teachers went out on strike, in violation of an Indiana law and in further violation of a temporary restraining order, the court fine of the NEA–SB was upheld by an appellate court. *National Education Association v. South Bend Community School Corporation,* 655 N.E.2d 516 (Ind.App.1995).

❖ — ❖ — ❖

Public School Employees Do Not Have a First Amendment Right to Select the Bargaining Representative of Their Choice

Indiana State Teachers Association v. Board of School Commissioners of the City of Indianapolis

United States District Court,
District of Indiana, 1996.
918 F.Supp. 266.

BARKER, Chief Judge.

This matter is before the Court on Defendant Board of School Commissioners' ("IPS") Rule 12(b)(6) Motion to Dismiss for failure to state a claim upon which relief can be granted. For the reasons discussed below, IPS' motion is granted. . . .

Plaintiff Indiana State Teachers Association ("ISTA") is a not-for-profit professional association organized to improve the professional status of educational employees in Indiana. Numerous members of ISTA are employed by IPS as non-certificated employees.

In January, 1979, IPS adopted Resolution 7110 ("R. 7110"), which established a nonproliferation policy with regard to collective bargaining. R. 7110 declared that only two bargaining units were appropriate for the purposes of collective bargaining with IPS: a "Teacher Bargaining Unit," and a unit consisting of certain specified "non-certificated Operations employees." . . . Before and since the adoption of R. 7110, IPS has recognized a Local of the American Federation of State, County and Municipal Employees, AFL–CIO ("AFSCME") as the exclusive bargaining representative of the non-certificated bargaining unit. IPS has negotiated, executed and adopted collective bargaining agreements with AFSCME, including an agreement which is presently in effect. . . .

On May 5, 1995, ISTA requested an election to determine the exclusive bargaining representative of the non-certificated unit defined in R. 7110. . . . ISTA informed IPS that it had "acquired an appropriate number of signatures" authorizing ISTA to represent the non-certificated employees, in order to request an election. . . . In July, 1995 IPS adopted Resolution 7371 ("R. 7371"), denying ISTA's request and acknowledging continued support of AFSCME as the exclusive bargaining representative for non-certificated employees.

ISTA brought this §1983 action, alleging that IPS' denial of its election request, and its failure to provide rules under which election requests and other challenges to incumbent exclusive bargaining agents can be made, violates ISTA's Fourteenth Amendment right to equal protection and its members' First Amendment rights of free speech and association. IPS moves to dismiss, asserting that ISTA has failed to allege any set of facts to show that IPS' actions violated either the First or the Fourteenth Amendment.

We find that this is a case whose "doom is foretold" by the absence of any Constitutional violation in the factual scenario provided by ISTA. Taking all of the factual allegations in the complaint as true, we find that ISTA can state no claim under either the First Amendment or the Equal Protection clause of Fourteenth Amendment, and thus has no basis for its §1983 claim.

"The First Amendment protects the right of an individual to speak freely, to advocate ideas, to associate with others, and to petition his government for redress of grievances. And it protects the right of associations to engage in advocacy on behalf of its members." . . . While the First Amendment protects the right of employees to associate and speak freely and petition openly, and protects them from retaliation for doing so, both the Seventh Circuit and the Supreme Court have held that it "does not impose any affirmative obligation on the government to listen, to respond or . . . to recognize the association and bargain with it." . . .

ISTA contends that IPS employees have a First Amendment right to select the bargaining representative of their choice. In order to support this contention, they attempt to elevate the protections of various federal and state labor laws into Constitutional rights. If the National Labor Relations Act ("NLRA") applied to public employees, we do not doubt that IPS employees would have the *statutory* right to engage in collective bargaining and to select the representative of their choice. But the question here is whether they have this right under the First Amendment of the Constitution. ISTA cites *Texas & N.O.R. Co. v. Brotherhood of Railway & Steamship Clerks . . . [and] National Labor Relations Board v. Jones & Laughlin Steel Corp. . . .*

It is telling that in both these cases, the source of the right to collective bargaining and selection of bargaining representatives was statutory, not Constitutional; for the Supreme Court has more recently noted that federal labor relations laws do not apply in the public employment context, and that the First Amendment is not a substitute for these statutory protections. . . . Congress made a decision not to apply the NLRA to public employers and we will not subvert that decision by bootstrapping statutory rights which clearly do not apply in the public employment context into Constitutional ones.

In addition, ISTA cites several state court cases which held that refusal to bargain with public employee organizations and interference in public employees' selection of a bargaining representative were violations of the First Amendment. However, in so holding, these cases relied upon either the NLRA, municipal or state law in recognizing a right of public employees to collective bargaining. Not only are these state court decisions not binding on this court; they fly in the face of binding Seventh Circuit and Supreme Court precedent which clearly establishes that the NLRA does not apply in this context, and that the First Amendment goes no further than to establish the right to organize and speak without retaliation. . . .

For the reasons discussed above, we find that the First Amendment of the Constitution provides no right to collective bargaining, nor do federal or state statutory protections give that right to the non-certificated public school employees involved here. As a result, they also have no right to select collective bargaining representatives of their choice, or to have procedures in place for doing so. Accordingly, because the facts presented by ISTA can state no First Amendment claim, IPS' Motion to Dismiss is granted with regard to ISTA's First Amendment claim.

ISTA's argument "fares no better in equal protection garb." . . . ISTA's Equal Protection claim rests upon its assertion that IPS Resolutions 7110 and 7371, by recognizing AFSCME as the exclusive representative of non-certificated employees and denying ISTA the opportunity to challenge AFSCME in a representative election, create an arbitrary classification between ISTA and AFSCME.

The U.S. Supreme Court recently summarized the standards applicable in equal protection cases:

> Unless a classification warrants some form of heightened review because it jeopardizes exercise of a fundamental right or categorizes on the basis of an inherently suspect characteristic, the equal protection clause requires only that the classification rationally furthers a legitimate state interest.

. . . As demonstrated above, no fundamental right is implicated in this case, nor is a suspect class involved. Therefore, we must accord the classification a "strong presumption of validity," and apply the rational basis test as described above. . . .

In this case, we find that a rational basis exists for IPS' denial of ISTA's request for an election. As stated by this court in a previous case involving an equal protection challenge to IPS' collective bargaining policies:

> . . . the favored position of AFSCME stems from a rational accommodation to the long-standing relationship existing between the Board and AFSCME prior to the declaration of a non-proliferation policy in Resolution 7110.

> . . . In addition, IPS has an existing labor contract with AFSCME and is understandably unwilling to "end unilaterally and abruptly the rights and benefits obtained over the years by AFSCME and its members as contained in the AFSCME labor contract. . . . "

IPS also cites "labor peace" as a basis for their decision. Labor peace has unquestionably been held to be even a "compelling interest" in the context of public education. . . . However, labor peace has traditionally been upheld as a compelling interest or rational basis when a school board seeks to prevent the proliferation of bargaining units, . . . or "inter-union strife." . . . In this case, it is less clear that the interest of "labor peace" is served by denying a rival union's re-

quest for a representative election to determine representation of an existing bargaining unit. In any event, the rational basis standard is not a demanding one, and IPS' preference for continuity in collective bargaining, paired with its long-standing relationship and satisfaction with AFSCME, satisfies the standard. . . .

We recognize that IPS' distinction between AFSCME and ISTA may effectively prevent ISTA from ever challenging AFSCME's tenure as exclusive bargaining representative for the non-certificated employee bargaining unit. Be that as it may, it is not a violation of either the First or the Fourteenth Amendment. The factual allegations in ISTA's complaint, while they describe what might be considered an "unfair" preference for AFSCME over ISTA (and what would presumably be an "unfair labor practice" under the NLRA) cannot state a §1983 claim based upon violations of the First or Fourteenth Amendments. Accordingly, IPS' motion to dismiss is granted with respect to all of ISTA's claims.

It is so ORDERED.

CASE NOTES

1. An elemental point of law is that collective bargaining agreements cannot supersede or conflict with state statute. In a case where a teachers association and the school district entered into a collective bargaining agreement setting the procedures for the dismissal or reelection of probationary teachers, a teacher was not renewed, whereupon she filed a grievance alleging the school district had violated the procedures for nonrenewal of teaching contracts. An arbitrator found the district had violated the agreement and ordered compliance with the negotiated procedures. On appeal, the court vacated the arbitrator's decision because the collective bargaining agreement was directly contrary to the procedures for reemployment of probationary employees as set out in the state's education code. Therefore, the collective bargaining provision violated the state statute, which provided that "collective bargaining agreements in public schools do not supersede provisions of the Education Code." *Board of Education v. Round Valley Teachers Association*, 13 Cal.4th 269, 52 Cal.Rptr. 2d 115, 914 P.2d 193 (1996).

2. The Wisconsin Court of Appeals has held that a state circuit court has the authority to enjoin the school district from proceeding with its bargaining unit clarification petition to the Wisconsin Employment Relations Commission until the parties complete their negotiations. *Madison Teachers, Inc. v. Madison Metropolitan School District*, 197 Wis.2d 731, 541 N.W.2d 786 (Ct.App. 1995).

3. The Supreme Court of Michigan has held that teachers who strike may be discharged without a prior hearing. The court reasoned:

> When public employees strike, the public employer must, like a private employer, be able to hire substitute employees so that the public business is not interrupted. In order to hire competent replacements, it may be necessary for the public employer to offer permanent employment and, thus, displace strikers. Where essential services have been suspended, the hiring of replacements often cannot await time-consuming adjudicatory processes.
>
> The predominant interest secured by predisciplinary hearings . . . is protection against removal of the wrong person and, assuming ultimate employee vindication, protection against interim financial deprivation.
>
> The possibility of removal of a nonstriker is minimized when, as here, the school board gives each striking teacher personal notice of the opportunity to return to the classroom before disciplinary action is taken. While on strike, a teacher receives no compensation; striking teachers do not suffer additional interim financial deprivation when disciplined.

Rockwell v. Board of Education of School District of Crestwood, 393 Mich. 616, 227 N.W.2d 736 (1975), appeal dismissed, 427 U.S. 901, 96 S.Ct. 3184 (1976).

4. An injunction against a teacher work stoppage was upheld where the teachers refused to work unless the school board reinstated certain provisions in a previously expired contract. The board refused to extend the terms of the old contract and, during the period when no contract was in existence, imposed interim operating regulations that eliminated protections of the old contract. The court said that the work stoppage was an illegal strike within the meaning of the state statute prohibiting such stoppages for the purpose of inducing a "change in the conditions" of employment. *Warren Education Association v. Adams*, 57 Mich.App. 496, 226 N.W.2d 536 (1975).

5. Where an illegal teachers' strike caused the students to miss several school days, the school board was justified in shortening the school year and reducing teachers' salaries accordingly. *Ash v. Board of Education*, 699 F.2d 822 (6th Cir.1983).

6. No civil action in tort can lie against a teachers union for striking when an employee relations act provides other remedies. The court reasoned that "public policy considerations interdict the creation of a new cause of action, which would unsettle an already precarious labor-management balance in the public labor relations sector." *Lamphere Schools v. Lamphere Federation of Teachers*, 400 Mich. 104, 252 N.W.2d 818 (1977).

❖ — ❖ — ❖

Binding Arbitration Is an Unlawful Delegation of Power, Violating State Constitution

School Board of the City of Richmond v. Parham

Supreme Court of Virginia, 1978.
218 Va. 950, 243 S.E.2d 468.

CARRICO, Justice. This is an appeal from the final order of the trial court awarding Margaret W. Parham (hereinafter, Parham), a Richmond public schoolteacher, a writ of mandamus against the School Board of the City of Richmond (hereinafter, the School Board). The order compelled the School Board to submit to arbitration a grievance Parham had brought pursuant to the "Procedure for Adjusting Grievances," adopted by the State Board of Education (hereinafter, the State Board). The same order awarded the State Board, an intervenor in the proceeding, a declaratory judgment upholding the constitutionality of a provision of the Procedure which requires binding arbitration of certain disputes between local school boards and their nonsupervisory employees. The sole question for decision is whether the provision for binding arbitration is constitutionally valid.

Adopted in 1973 and subsequently amended, the Procedure prescribes the method for settling employee grievances. . . .

In the present case, Parham unsuccessfully processed her grievance through the several administrative levels prescribed by the Procedure and ultimately presented the dispute to the School Board, where she received an adverse decision. When she called for arbitration, the School Board refused to arbitrate, stating that it questioned the constitutionality of the Procedure "insofar as it compels arbitration binding on school boards in Virginia." Parham then filed her petition for a writ of mandamus to compel the School Board to submit the matter to arbitration.

At the heart of the present controversy are the provisions of Article VIII of the Virginia Constitution, which article relates to education. In pertinent part, the article reads:

§2. *Standards of quality; State and local support of public schools.*—Standards of quality for the several school divisions shall be determined and prescribed from time to time by the Board of Education, subject to revision only by the General Assembly. . . .

§4. *Board of Education.*—The general supervision of the public school system shall be vested in a Board of Education. . . .

§5. *Powers and duties of the Board of Education.*— The powers and duties of the Board of Education shall be as follows. . . .

(e) Subject to the ultimate authority of the General Assembly, the Board shall have primary responsibility and authority for effectuating the educational policy set forth in this Article, and it shall have such other powers and duties as may be prescribed by law. . . .

§7. *School boards.*—The supervision of schools in each school division shall be vested in a school board. . . .

The School Board recognizes that §4 of Article VIII places "general supervision" of the public school system in the hands of the State Board. The School Board notes, however, that, under §7 of Article VIII, the "supervision" of schools is vested in local school boards and that, implementing this constitutional mandate, the General Assembly has conferred upon such local boards extensive authority to execute their supervisory duties. . . .

The School Board argues, however, that "management of a school board's teaching staff and other employees is . . . an essential function of supervision" and that neither the General Assembly nor the State Board can divest local

school boards of this function and place it "in an authority other than the local boards." Yet, the School Board asserts, the effect of the binding arbitration provision of the Procedure is to permit "an outside agency, in the form of an arbitration panel . . . to divest the local board of its essential function by the substitution of [the panel's] judgment for that of the board." As a result of the panel's action, the School Board maintains, a local school board's policies, rules, and regulations relating to the work activity of employees could be altered or rendered meaningless. This, the School Board concludes, is constitutionally impermissible under §7 of Article VIII. . . .

In analyzing the arguments of Parham and the State Board, it is interesting to note that neither of these parties specifically defends the binding arbitration provision of the Procedure; the arguments merely assert the validity of the Procedure in general. The closest approach to a defense of the provision is a statement that "the arbitration panel has no authority whatsoever to make or enforce any decisions as to how the local school is to be operated." This merely evades, rather than answers, the School Board's contention that the arbitration provision permits "an outside agency in the form of an arbitration panel . . . to divest the local board of its essential function [of managing its teaching staff] by the substitution of [the panel's] judgment for that of the board."

This contention of the School Board presents the real question in the case, viz., whether the binding arbitration provision of the Procedure produces an unlawful delegation of power. . . .

There can be no doubt that a delegation of power is involved in the binding arbitration provision. Indeed, the very section of the Procedure which provides that an arbitration panel shall have authority to make a final and binding decision also states that the local school board "hereby delegates such authority to the Panel."

Whether, however, the arbitration provision results in an *unlawful* delegation of authority is a more difficult question. . . .

Although not involving binding arbitration provisions, *Howard v. School Board of Alleghany County,* 203 Va. 55, 122 S.E.2d 891 (1961), is pertinent to resolution of the present case. There, a state statute required the sale of school property if such disposition was favored by a majority of voters in a referendum. Ruling the statute invalid, we said that it was an "essential function" of a local school board's power of supervision, granted by what is now §7 of Article VIII of the Constitution, "to determine whether a particular property is needed for school purposes and the manner in which it shall be used." The effect of the disputed statute, we stated, was "to divest the board of the exercise of that function and lodge it in the electorate," thus stripping the board "of any or all authority to exercise its judgment in the matter." 203 Va. at 58, 122 S.E.2d at 894. This is but another way of saying that the statute produced an unlawful delegation of power.

We believe the binding arbitration provision involved in the present case has the same effect as the offending statute in *Howard*, viz., to remove from a local school board and transfer to others a function essential and indispensable to the exercise of the power of supervision vested by §7 of Article VIII. . . .

Equally clear, the function of *applying* local policies, rules, and regulations, adopted for the management of a teaching staff, is a function essential and indispensable to exercise of the power of supervision vested by §7 of Article VIII. This power of supervision would be an empty one, indeed, if a local school board, once having adopted a valid policy, rule, or regulation, found itself powerless to enforce what it had promulgated. . . .

We conclude, therefore, that the binding arbitration provision of the Procedure produces an unlawful delegation of power, violative of §7 of Article VIII of the Constitution. . . .

Reversed and final judgment.

Lesson Plan and Evaluation of English as Second Language Program Is Management Prerogative and Not Arbitrable

Pawtucket School Committee v. Pawtucket Teachers Alliance

Supreme Court of Rhode Island, 1995.
652 A.2d 970.

PER CURIAM. . . .

In this case plaintiff school committee petitioned for a declaratory judgment in the Superior Court based on the following events. In February 1993, the associate director of the Pawtucket Bilingual/English as a Second Language Program (ESL) issued a directive requiring all teachers in the Limited English Proficiency Program to submit to her, once a month, a copy of their lesson plans for the following week. In that memorandum to the teachers, the director explained that, "[the] purpose of this new procedure is to provide me with a greater knowledge of what is being taught in your classes." The school committee denied the grievance filed by the teachers' alliance and the union sought arbitration under its collective bargaining agreement. The school committee then petitioned the Superior Court for a declaratory judgment and sought to enjoin arbitration.

The plaintiff school committee took the position that the new directive was a management prerogative and therefore not arbitrable. . . . The union argued that the new procedure was a unilateral change in working conditions and therefore constituted a violation of the collective bargaining agreement.

On January 18, 1994, the trial justice found that the lesson plan directive was a management prerogative that is not arbitrable. Judgment was entered for plaintiffs and defendant filed a timely appeal.

. . . The issues before us concern the ESL programs in Pawtucket schools, a duty which is expressly delegated to the school committee through §16-2-9(a)(3) and more specifically by chapter 54 of title 16, of the General Laws entitled "Education of Limited–English Proficient Students." . . .

It was asserted to the court, without contradiction, that in every city or town individuals within the school administration such as the associate director in Pawtucket, act for the school committee in overseeing and evaluating day to day operations in the ESL programs. In this way the school committees succeed in maintaining the necessary management of the schools and the various programs mandated by state and federal law.

We have stated clearly that while the school committee can negotiate many items with the professional and nonprofessional employees of the system, it cannot bargain away statutory powers and responsibilities. . . . In our opinion, evaluating ESL programs and determining whether they conform with state law and the rules and regulations promulgated by the Board of Regents for Elementary and Secondary Education are requirements of state law and cannot be submitted to arbitration. . . .

For these reasons the defendants' appeal is denied and dismissed, the judgment appealed from is affirmed, and the papers of the case are remanded to the Superior Court.

❖ — ❖ — ❖

*Binding Arbitration Is Not an Illegal
Delegation of School Board Power*

City of Biddeford v. Biddeford Teachers Association

Supreme Judicial Court of Maine, 1973.
304 A.2d 387.

WEATHERBEE, Justice. These two complaints necessitate our first examination of the provisions of the Municipal Employees Labor Relations Law, 26 M.R.S.A. Chap. 9-A, which was enacted by the Maine Legislature in 1969. The complaints direct our attention only to the application of the statute to teachers in the public schools.

In the fall of 1970 the Board of Education of the City of Biddeford and the representatives of the Biddeford Teachers Association entered into negotiations in an attempt to effect a contract for the professional services of teachers in the Biddeford public schools for the school year 1971–1972. When the Board and the Association were unable to reach an agreement, the fact-finding procedures provided in section 965(3) were called into play but they proved unsuccessful. Finally, in August of 1971 the parties resorted to the arbitration process found in section 965(4). . . .

The purpose of the Municipal Public Employees Labor Relations Law is stated by 26 M.R.S.A. §961 as follows:

It is declared to be the public policy of this State and it is the purpose of this chapter to promote the improvement of the relationship between public employers and their employees by providing a uniform basis for recognizing the right of public employees to join labor organizations of their own choosing and to be represented by such organizations in collective bargaining for terms and conditions of employment.

. . . The Act makes it the obligation of the public employer and the bargaining agent to meet and bargain collectively and provides a four-step procedure consisting of negotiation, mediation (when jointly requested), fact finding and arbitration. The parties are first obligated to negotiate in good faith concerning "wages, hours, working conditions and contract grievance arbitration"—with the exception—

that public employers of teachers shall meet and consult but not negotiate with respect to educational policies. . . .

Secondly, if the parties are unable to agree after negotiation they may jointly agree upon mediation procedures. Thirdly, if mediation procedures are omitted or are unsuccessful, either one or both may request fact-finding and the parties are then obligated to present their contending positions to the fact-finding board which will, after hearing, submit its findings to the parties. . . .

In brief, this procedure requires each party to choose an arbitrator and the two so chosen shall name a "neutral" arbitrator. The three arbitrators shall then proceed to hear the matter. If the subject of the controversy has been salaries, pensions or insurance, the arbitrator shall *recommend* terms of settlement which are advisory only and may make findings of fact. As to other matters in dispute the arbitrators shall make determinations which are binding upon the parties and "the parties will enter into an agreement or take whatever other action that may be appropriate to carry out and effectuate such binding determinations." The determinations are subject to review in accordance with M.R.C.P., Rule 80B but, in the absence of fraud, the arbitrators' decisions upon questions of fact are final. . . .

While the present actions present many issues concerning various areas of the arbitrators' award, we must first consider the constitutionality of the Act in so far as it requires local school boards, at the request of the teaching employees, to submit to binding arbitration disputes arising both out of the making of the labor contract and out of later employment under the contract. Can the superintending school committees constitutionally delegate this authority to arbitrators? In requiring them to do so, can the Legislature constitutionally take away the authority which local officials had traditionally exercised and repose it in persons who compose ad hoc boards of arbitration? If so, has there been such a valid delegation of authority here? . . .

We find that our Constitution gave the Legislature full responsibility over the subject matter of public schools and education and empowered it to make all reasonable laws in reference to schools and education for the "benefit of the people of this state." Opinions of the Justices, 68 Me. 582 (1876). Except for the areas where the Legislature has from time to time seen fit to impose its own requirements and except for the authority later given to the Commissioner of Education, the responsibilities for operating the public schools have remained in the local school boards.

The Legislature has now decided to take from the school boards the ultimate authority they have exercised in certain areas of school management—that is, as to "hours, and working conditions" and contract grievance arbitration— and to give it to ad hoc boards of arbitration.

It is settled beyond question that the Legislature may properly conclude that the purposes of its legislation may best be carried out through agents and that it may delegate to the agents a portion of its power to facilitate the functioning of the legislative program.

There can be no doubt but that the Legislature, which is the source of all municipal authority, *Squires v. Inhabitants of City of Augusta*, 155 Me. 151, 153 A.2d 80 (1959), has also the power to take back from municipal officers portions of the authority it has earlier given them. . . .

. . . [T]hat experience has taught that certain aspects of this dynamic and complicated municipal employer-employee relationship no longer need remain subject to arbitrary decision by the employer and that in the area of working conditions and hours and of contract grievances the interests of the employees must in fairness be examined by impartial persons. The Legislature appears to believe that this much can be done

without serious disruption of the balancing of operating costs against municipal appropriations.

We realize that in providing that the contract-making process itself (as it affects working conditions and hours) is subject to binding arbitration, our Legislature has moved into an area forbidden by many courts. The Legislature must have concluded that the benefits which are sought by the statute can never be achieved if an impasse occurs at the very beginning of the relationship. This conclusion is not unreasonable.

True, the statute does not contemplate the delegation of authority to public administrative boards or agencies but instead gives it to ad hoc panels whose memberships are not to be controlled by governmental action. Here we are of the opinion that the Legislature, mindful of the denial to municipal employees of such economic weapons as strikes and work stoppages which are available to employees in private employment, has sought to avoid the disruptive feelings of resentment and bitterness which may result if the governmental employee may look only to the government for redress of his grievances.

Where the ultimate arbiter of the dispute is a representative of one side of the dispute, adverse decisions will be hard to accept and the tendency toward alienation will be strong.

We consider that there is a rational reason for the Legislature's decision that its purposes would be best effectuated if the parties are left to choose their own arbitrators in the limited non-policy areas which are subject to arbitration.

CASE NOTES

1. A union's standing to file grievances as well as substantive issues may be subject to reasonable debate and therefore may be submitted to an arbitrator for resolution. *Mora Federation of Teachers, Local 1802 v. Independent School District No. 332*, 352 N.W.2d 489 (Minn.App.1984).

2. A collective bargaining agreement providing that preference in filling a vacancy would be given to the employee with the greatest seniority, when qualifications of applicants were otherwise equal, is binding on a public school board. *Mahoning County Board of Mental Retardation and Developmental Disabilities v. Mahoning*

County TMR Education Association, 22 Ohio St.3d 80, 488 N.E.2d 872 (1986).

3. The Supreme Court of Rhode Island upheld a lower court's contempt of court order issued against teachers for failure to cease and desist from continuing a strike when the court had ordered the teachers to report to classes. *Warwick School Committee v. Warwick Teachers' Union,* 637 A.2d 777 (R.I.1994).

■ SCOPE OF BARGAINING

Collective bargaining in the public sector encompasses three general categories: "(1) mandatory subjects of bargaining, (2) permissive subjects of bargaining, and (3) unlawful subjects of bargaining."[21] In states where collective bargaining is required, school boards must bargain in good faith to the point of impasse.[22] In states where statutes do not require school boards to bargain and the matter is one of discretion or where a "meet and confer" statute governs, the employer is under no duty to bargain at all.[23]

Mandatory bargaining subjects are by and large determined by experience gained in the private sector under the Taft-Hartley Act, which requires bargaining over "wages, hours, and other terms and conditions of employment."[24] Whether a subject is mandatory is at times unclear and often becomes a matter of litigation. Wages and hours may include considerations of salary schedules, overtime, cost-of-living increases, fringe benefits, vacations, holidays, sick leave, retirement benefits, and so on. A Connecticut court has held that teacher loads—defined as number of classes, preparation periods per week, and class sizes—are mandatory subjects of bargaining.[25]

The Supreme Court of Connecticut has held that a statute that provides for teacher evaluations to be "established by the state board of education and such additional performance criteria as the local or regional board of education may, by mutual agreement, establish" implies sufficient flexibility to make teacher evaluations a permissive rather than a mandatory subject of bargaining. A school board may therefore refuse to negotiate with teachers regarding evaluations.[26]

The Supreme Court of Michigan has ruled that early retirement benefits are not wages or salaries; rather, they are working conditions within the meaning of the Michigan school code. A local school board therefore has the authority to include retirement benefits in the collective bargaining agreement.[27]

Other issues that are not clearly mandatory or permissive, but are negotiable, include elimination of a teacher work period and replacement of that period with an additional classroom period;[28] a change in the number of class hours per day;[29] length of the workday, performance of nonteaching duties (such as cleaning venetian blinds and washing windows), workloads, and teacher hours;[30] moving expenses;[31] tuition-free schooling for children of staff members who reside outside the school district;[32] tuition reimbursement for teachers attending approved graduate courses;[33] annual salary adjustments;[34] pay for unused sick leave;[35] a sick leave bank providing for teachers' sharing of sick leave;[36] and in-service education, association rights, and disciplinary actions against employees.[37]

The rights of management have been broadly interpreted in some jurisdictions so as to limit the scope of negotiable items. Management retains the general right to organize and maintain an efficient workforce.[38] "The rule that seems to emerge from reported cases is that the unilateral action of the employer in creating new jobs or in merging jobs already in existence is appropriate . . . [if such action is not done] . . . in an arbitrary or capricious manner."[39] Nonnegotiable management rights have been interpreted to include the "right to make changes in job duties, to create new job classifications, to eliminate jobs, and to combine jobs," so long as the action is taken to improve efficiency of operation and is in good faith.[40]

Nonnegotiable items, in some jurisdictions, have been held to include academic and personal freedom, assignment and transfer, extracurricular compensation (with certain exceptions), recall and reduction of personnel, dismissal procedures, binding arbitration of grievances, procedure for contract nonrenewal, frequency of grade cards, sabbatical leave, number of contract days, supplemental contracts, class size, recall of teachers,[41] imposition of a no-smoking ban,[42] and assignment of special duties during emergency situations.[43]

Courts in other jurisdictions where bargaining is undertaken voluntarily by school boards have held that teachers have a right to engage in "meaningful negotiations, and not be foreclosed from considerations touching on school policy as to class size, time allocations, and other factors influencing the quality of the schools."[44] "Meaningful negotiation" includes the right to execute a written agreement incorporating the terms and conditions agreed upon by both parties and the right to press grievances.

Finally, however, it should be emphasized that the conditions of public school collective bargaining are fully dependent on the state statutory language. For example, in *Kenai*, the Supreme Court of Alaska clearly explains that the extent of management rights and what is negotiable, is dependent on wording of the statute and observes that courts are reticent to expand meanings and to stray too far in drawing implications.[45] In the final analysis the scope of collective bargaining in public schools is dependent on rather strict interpretation of the state statutory requirements.

❖ — ❖ — ❖

Scope of Negotiations Is Essentially a Question for Legislative Guidance

Kenai Peninsula Borough School District v. Kenai Peninsula Education Association

Supreme Court of State of Alaska, 1977.
572 P.2d 416.

CONNOR, Justice. These cases present important questions of labor law and constitutional law concerning the collective bargaining requirements for teachers in the public schools....

... The school boards contend that the submission of educational policies to a good faith collective bargaining requirement would remove the final decisions on such matters from the boards, contrary to the intent of the legislature expressed in AS 14.20.610....

The unions argue that such delegation is perfectly proper, and that there is no delegation of decision-making power inherent in a labor negotiations requirement. They further argue that they represent professional employees, and that their participation in good faith collective bargaining labor negotiations is an attempt by the legislature to provide professional advice to school boards on the management of the schools. . . .

If we were to look to the law concerning bargaining between labor unions and private employers, we would conclude that the scope of negotiable issues is broad. . . .

When we turn to employment in the public sector, and particularly in education, the question of what is properly bargainable is thrown into more doubt. If teachers' unions are permitted to bargain on matters of educational policy, it is conceivable that through successive contracts the autonomy of the school boards could be severely eroded, and the effective control of educational policy shifted from the school boards to the teachers' unions. Such a result could threaten the ability of elective government officials and appointive officers subject to their authority, in this case the school boards and administrators, to perform their functions in the broad public interest. . . .

Furthermore, the statute merely requires the school board to negotiate with the union. It does not require the board to accept any particular proposal the union might offer. It does not require, and probably does not permit, the board to delegate to the union the sole power to make any decision. . . . A statue defining the scope of collective bargaining as broadly as the union would have us do, might well present a more troubling constitutional question. But we find no constitutional infirmity in AS 14.20.550 and .610. The delegation of power problem still bears upon our task of statutory interpretation, however, for in interpreting the relevant statutes we will not readily assume that the legislature intended to divest the school boards of their power to determine matters of educational policy and school system management. . . .

We will now consider the Alaska situation in more detail. At the outset it appears to us that questions concerning salaries, the number of hours to be worked, and amount of leave time are all so closely connected with the economic well-being of the individual teacher that they must be held negotiable under our statutes. The troubling question is what other items are bargainable.

The various trial courts in these cases considered such items as (1) relief from nonprofessional chores, (2) elementary planning time, (3) para-professional tutors, (4) teacher specialist, (5) teacher's aides, (6) class size, (7) pupil-teacher ratio, (8) a teacher ombudsman, (9) teacher evaluation of administrators, (10) school calendar, (11) selection of instructional materials, (12) the use of secondary department heads, (13) secondary teacher preparation and planning time, and (14) teacher representation on school board advisory committees.

The testimony adduced in the trial courts does not provide us with much enlightenment as to why any of these items should fall on one side of the line or another. Realistically the two areas, i.e., (1) educational policy and (2) matters pertaining to employment and professional duties, merge into and blend with each other at many points. Logically and semantically it is nearly impossible to assign specific items to one category and not the other. . . . We are confronted, then, with a situation in which the legislature has not spoken with clarity and concerning which we possess no expertise. We can only conclude that salaries, fringe benefits, the number of hours worked, and the amount of leave time are negotiable . . . we conclude that the other specific items . . . are, under the existing statutory language, non-negotiable.

It would be helpful if the legislature, through future enactments, provided more specific guidance on a number of the items which the unions seek to negotiate. Lacking that guidance, however, we cannot confidently say that the legislature intended any of these items to be bargainable. We cannot, therefore, read the statutes expansively as to the scope of what is negotiable.

As to matters which affect educational policy and are, therefore, not negotiable, we believe that there is nevertheless implicit in our statutes the intention that the school boards meet and confer with the unions. It is desirable that the boards consider teacher proposals on such questions. This will encourage teachers to give the

boards the benefit of their expertise, and to make their positions known for the board's use in establishing educational policy. . . .

Affirmed in part, reversed in part.

CASE NOTES

1. *Scope of Bargaining.* The scope of bargaining for public school teachers has been extensively litigated, generally circumscribing those matters that are bargainable.

Those issues that are usually held by the courts to be outside the scope of mandatory bargaining include the following:

- Curriculum. *Colonial School Board v. Colonial Affiliate, NCCEA/DSEA/NEA,* 449 A.2d 243 (Del.1982).
- Student-faculty ratio. *Rutgers Council of American Association of University Professors v. New Jersey Board of Higher Education,* 126 N.J. Super. 53, 312 A.2d 677 (App.Div.1973).
- Policies on academic freedom and professional ethics. *Kansas Board of Regents v. Pittsburgh State University Chapter of Kansas–National Education Association,* 233 Kan. 801, 808, 667 P.2d 306, 312 (1983).
- Decisions to hire, promote, award tenure, and retrench. *Charles City Education Association v. Public Employment Relations Board,* 291 N.W.2d 663 (Iowa 1980).

Issues that are normally held to be mandatory are working conditions (such as salary), supplementary employment, and rules governing employee travel. *Kansas Board of Regents,* 233 Kan. at 826–28, 667 P.2d at 324–25.

Because of differences in state statutes and court interpretations of those statutes, some subjects of bargaining may have been held to be permissive in certain states but mandatory in others. See *Beloit Education Association v. Wisconsin Employment Relations Commission,* 73 Wis.2d 43, 60–61, 242 N.W.2d 231, 239 (1976) (student discipline); *Burlington County Faculty Association v. Burlington County College,* 64 N.J. 10, 13, 311 A.2d 733, 735 (1973) (calendar); *Beloit Education Association v. Wisconsin Employment Relations Commission,* 73 Wis.2d 43, 62–63, 242 N.W.2d 231, 240 (in-service training); and *Tri-County Educators' Association v. Tri-County Special Education Cooperative,* 225 Kan. 781, 784–85, 594

P.2d 207, 210 (1979) (standards and procedures for teacher evaluation).

2. *Meet and Confer.* Rabban has expressed the general view of public-sector collective bargaining advocates with regard to "meet and confer" statutes. He says:

> Unlike collective bargaining negotiations, "meet and confer" sessions are not expected to lead to legally enforceable agreements. At least in theory, professional employees can give their expert advice, which may benefit the employer and the general public, without jeopardizing the employer's managerial prerogatives or citizens' interests in meaningful participation regarding matters of public concern.
>
> Unfortunately, these well-intentioned "meet and confer" provisions do not seem to have accomplished their purposes. They are often either ineffective or indistinguishable from collective bargaining. "Meet and confer" provisions can relegate unions to the role of impotent discussant rather than the equal negotiator contemplated by true collective bargaining.

Without the requirement of reaching enforceable agreements in good faith, these advisory sessions often amount to no more than "collective begging," easily ignored by the employer. Eventually, the very "meet and confer" process may atrophy. On the other hand, the theoretical differences between "meet and confer" sessions and collective bargaining negotiations often evaporate in practice. The scope of bargaining frequently expands with the duration of the relationship between the union and the employer. Issues originally addressed in "meet and confer" sessions eventually become part of collective bargaining negotiations. David M. Rabban, "Can American Labor Law Accommodate Collective Bargaining by Professional Employees?" *Yale Law Review* 99, no. 4 (January 1990): pp. 710–712.

3. *Statutory Confusion and Scope of Bargaining.* Statutes may tend to be contradictory in delineating what is subject to mandatory bargaining and what is subject to "meet and confer." A Minnesota statute created just such confusion by explicitly excluding "educational policies" from the scope of mandatory bargaining, while requiring the public employer to "meet and confer with professional employees" about the same educational policies and other nonmanda-

tory subjects. Moreover, the statute required that the public employer bargain with only one exclusive bargaining unit and precluded participation by any other professional employees, individually or in groups. Based on this statute, the Minnesota community college faculty senates were denied the ability to influence policy and could not "meet and confer" except through the one elected bargaining unit. The U.S. Supreme Court upheld this denial of alleged faculty rights to participate in university governance through the "meet and confer" process. The Court found that there was no denial of the right of free speech or laudable traditions of faculty senate involvement of such weight as to convince the Court that other professors outside the bargaining unit should be able to "meet and confer" about university academic matters. The Court said: "Faculty involvement in academic governance . . . has much to recommend it as a matter of academic policy, but it finds no basis in the Constitution." *Minnesota State Board for Community Colleges v. Knight*, 465 U.S. 271, 104 S.Ct. 1058 (1984).

4. Agreement by a school board to confine itself in hiring to those applicants within the system is beyond the scope of bargaining and is therefore unenforceable. *Board of Education of North Bergen Township v. North Bergen Federation of Teachers*, 141 N.J.Super. 97, 357 A.2d 302 (App.Div.1976).

5. Early retirement benefits are not salaries; rather, they are "working conditions" within the meaning of the school code. Thus, a board of education has the authority to provide for such benefits in its collective bargaining agreement with the teachers association. In this case, the attorney general had ruled that a school district could not agree in a collective bargaining agreement to provide supplemental retirement benefits beyond those established by statute for the public school retirement system. In disagreeing with the attorney general, the court pointed out that the collective bargaining statute had authorized inclusion of early retirement benefits by providing for "working conditions" and "other related benefits of an economic nature." The court said that the statutory "expression of 'other related benefits of an economic nature' refutes appellant's claim that 'working conditions' is a narrowly defined term meaning only

physical conditions of the workplace. Physical conditions of the workplace are not 'benefits of an economic nature,' and we, therefore, conclude that 'other working conditions' was intended to be more liberally interpreted than the noneconomic physical conditions of the workplace." *Jurva v. Attorney General of State of Michigan*, 419 Mich. 209, 351 N.W.2d 813 (1984).

■ COLLECTIVE AND INDIVIDUAL RIGHTS

Public employee collective bargaining, while authorized and governed by statute, is, to a large degree, a creature of precedents arising from the common law of the courts and quasi-judicial tribunals. Too, the respective rights and powers in public collective bargaining are circumscribed by constitutional constraints at both the state and the federal levels. Because statutes cannot prescribe each and every element and contingency created by the complexities of the bargaining process, judicial and administrative law judgments are required to maintain a smoothly functioning mechanism. The rights of the parties to the bargaining process are founded, more or less, in a utilitarian attitude of pragmatic understandings among management, union, and employee. Such understandings have produced what are considered to be established, acceptable boundaries of bargaining rights.

BARGAINING RIGHTS

Rights of the bargaining process delineate the extent of management, union, and employee powers, the acceptable retention of management power; the necessary reach of union prerogative; and the residual and pervasive power of the individual.

Management Rights

Management has the general right to manage school operations as empowered by statute but is restricted by applicable law that divests certain of these rights in favor of the union or the employee. Even though the school board's rights are not expressly limited by statute, it is nevertheless bound by common law to bargain reasonably, in good faith, without arbitrariness or capriciousness, and without discriminatory intent and motive.[46]

Yet, because school board rights are primarily predicated on applicable state statutes, management rights vary widely from state to state. In the absence of statutorily defined management rights, it is assumed that public sector boards have certain inherent rights that are also found in the private sector as recognized by arbitration decisions.[47]

Union Rights

Union rights, as separate from employee rights, include the rights to represent employees, bargain at the table, enforce the contract, grieve, arbitrate, and, importantly, ensure union security.[48]

Employee Rights

Employees have rights to organize freely,[49] engage in meaningful negotiations, press grievances, and execute written agreements. The boundaries of employees' rights are not precisely coterminus with union rights and may be more extensive. Employees, as individuals, have the rights and freedoms guaranteed by the state and federal constitutions.

■ CONSTITUTIONAL RIGHTS OF INDIVIDUALS

Public school employees do not have a right to bargain collectively in all states, but, as individuals, they have a right to join unions.[50] A state law forbidding public employees from joining unions violates the First and Fourteenth Amendments of the U.S. Constitution. Discrimination against public employees because of union activity may also violate the Civil Rights Act of 1871 as well as the First and Fourteenth Amendments.[51] As mentioned earlier in this chapter, the U.S. Court of Appeals, Eighth Circuit, has said:

> The guarantee of the "right of assembly" protects more than the "right to attend a meeting; it includes the right to express one's attitudes or philosophies by membership in a group or by affiliation with it or by other lawful means."

Bargaining agreements of public agencies have the potential of overreaching the legitimate scope of negotiations and encroaching on the constitutional rights of individuals.

The act of filing a grievance by a teacher does not elevate private speech[52] to the constitutionally protected level of public opinion, as defined by *Connick v. Myers*.[53] The filing of a grievance against a school board does not invoke a First Amendment right to petition government for redress of grievances. A grievance is not a speech activity in the sense that it is of political or "public concern."[54]

The requirement of due process for a discharged employee is satisfied by the offer of arbitration by a school board. The U.S. Court of Appeals, Third Circuit, has held that to provide the employee with the alternative of arbitration fulfills notice and the opportunity for a hearing as envisaged under due process.[55] If a labor dispute results in an illegal strike and the board of education responds by reducing teacher pay for the days they missed while on strike, no substantive property interest is implicated.[56] Where teachers claimed that a pay reduction violated their employment contract, the court concluded that an amended school calendar with a corresponding reduction in teachers' salaries was not violative of due process because the teachers had participated in an unlawful work stoppage.[57]

In a case where a school district dismissed a nontenured teacher and gave as reasons generally poor performance and personality conflicts, the court found that the board action was linked to the teacher's union activities.[58] The evidence indicated that the teacher was given low evaluations by the school principal because of union issues, not teaching performance. The court found that because the dismissal was based on union activities the teacher's First Amendment rights were violated.[59]

At times, the constitutional rights of the individual employee may come in conflict with the bargaining rights of the union. Such conflict has occurred where unions have sought the security of the agency shop.[60] The agency shop is a provision in the contract between the school board and the union that permits the union to charge a fee to all employees, regardless of whether they are union members. Such compulsory payment has been challenged by nonunion employees as a violation of First Amendment rights of free speech and association. In the leading case on the issue, the U.S. Supreme Court has held that employees can be charged dues or assessments only for union expenditures incurred in activities that are not politically or ideologically

objectionable to the employee.[61] The Supreme Court reasoned that single representation promotes peaceful labor relations through strengthening exclusive union representation. It theorized that the stability gained by having one strong bargaining agent for employees enhances labor by reducing the potential of internal turmoil and assists management by having some assurance of continuity in labor's representation.[62] The Supreme Court's position has been that agency shop and union shop agreements are justified because of the government's interest in industrial peace.[63] Yet the Supreme Court will not go so far as to require an employee to join a union or contribute to a union if the dues paid to the union will be used for political or ideological purposes that are objectionable to the employee. Here the constitutional rights of the individual—freedom of expression, association, belief, and conscience—supersede the interest of the government in advancing harmony with the labor unions.[64]

The Supreme Court has observed that a forced exaction of fees for union activities, if used to "subsidize the propagation of political or ideological views" to which the employee objects, violates the basic principles of freedom of belief defended by Madison in his *Memorial and Remonstrance,* where he speaks of "the tyrannical character of forcing an individual to contribute even 'three pence' for the 'propagation of opinions which he disbelieves.'"[65]

Agency Shop Does Not Violate Nonunion Employees' Constitutional Rights unless Fees Are Used to Support Objectionable Political and Ideological Views

Abood v. Detroit Board of Education

Supreme Court of the United States, 1977.
431 U.S. 209, 97 S.Ct. 1782.

Mr. Justice STEWART delivered the opinion of the Court. The State of Michigan has enacted legislation authorizing a system for union representation of local governmental employees. A union and a local government employer are specifically permitted to agree to an "agency shop" arrangement, whereby every employee represented by a union—even though not a union member—must pay to the union, as a condition of employment, a service fee equal in amount to union dues. The issue before us is whether this arrangement violates the constitutional rights of government employees who object to public sector unions as such or to various union activities financed by the compulsory service fees. . . .

Consideration of the question whether an agency shop provision in a collective-bargaining agreement covering governmental employees is, as such, constitutionally valid must begin with two cases in this Court that on their face go far towards resolving the issue. The cases are *Railway Employes' Department v. Hanson* . . . and *International Association of Machinists v. Street*, 367 U.S. 740, 81 S.Ct. 1784, 6 L.Ed.2d 1141.

In the *Hanson* case a group of railroad employees brought an action in a Nebraska court to enjoin enforcement of a union-shop agreement. The challenged clause was authorized, and indeed shielded from any attempt by a State to prohibit it, by the Railway Labor Act, 45 U.S.C.A. §152, Eleventh. . . .

The record in *Hanson* contained no evidence that union dues were used to force ideological conformity or otherwise to impair the free expression of employees, and the Court noted that "[i]f 'assessments' are in fact imposed for purposes not germane to collective bargaining, a different problem would be presented." Id., at 235, 76 S.Ct., at 720 (footnote omitted). But the Court squarely held that "the requirement for financial support of the collective-bargaining agency by all who receive the benefits of its work . . . does not violate . . . the First Amendment." Id., at 238, 76 S.Ct., at 721.

The Court faced a similar question several years later in the *Street* case, which also involved a challenge to the constitutionality of a union shop authorized by the Railway Labor Act. In *Street*, however, the record contained findings that the union treasury to which all employees were required to contribute had been used "to finance the campaigns of candidates for federal and state offices whom [the plaintiffs] opposed, and to promote the propagation of political and economic doctrines, concepts and ideologies with which [they] disagreed." 367 U.S., at 744, 81 S.Ct., at 1787. . . .

The Court ruled that the use of compulsory union dues for political purposes violated the Act itself. Nonetheless, it found that an injunction against enforcement of the union-shop agreement as such was impermissible under *Hanson*, and remanded the case to the Supreme Court of Georgia so that a more limited remedy could be devised.

. . . A union-shop arrangement has been thought to distribute fairly the cost of these activities among those who benefit, and it counteracts the incentive that employees might otherwise have to become "free riders"—to refuse to contribute to the union while obtaining benefits of union representation that necessarily accrue to all employees. . . .

To compel employees financially to support their collective bargaining representative has an impact upon their First Amendment interests. An employee may very well have ideological objections to a wide variety of activities undertaken by the union in its role as exclusive representative. His moral or religious views about the desirability of abortion may not square with the union's policy in negotiating a medical benefits plan. . . . The examples could be multiplied. To be required to help finance the union as a collective-bargaining agent might well be thought, therefore, to interfere in some way with an employee's freedom to associate for the advancement of ideas, or to refrain from doing so, as he sees fit. But the judgment clearly made in *Hanson* and *Street* is that such interference as exists is constitutionally justified by the legislative assessment of the important contribution of the union shop to the system of labor relations established by Congress. "The furtherance of the common cause leaves some leeway for the leadership of the group. As long as they act to promote the cause which justified bringing the group together, the individual cannot withdraw his financial support merely because he disagrees with the group's strategy. If that were allowed, we would be reversing the *Hanson* case, *sub silentio*." . . .

The governmental interests advanced by the agency shop provision in the Michigan statute are much the same as those promoted by similar provisions in federal labor law. The confusion and conflict that could arise if rival teachers' unions, holding quite different views as to the proper class hours, class sizes, holidays, tenure provisions, and grievance procedures, each sought to obtain the employer's agreement are no different in kind from the evils that the exclusivity rule in the Railway Labor Act was designed to avoid. . . . The desirability of labor peace is no less important in the public sector, nor is the risk of "free riders" any smaller. . . .

The distinctive nature of public-sector bargaining has led to widespread discussion about the extent to which the law governing labor relations in the private sector provides an appropriate model. To take but one example, there has been considerable debate about the desirability of prohibiting public employee unions from striking, a step that the State of Michigan itself has taken, Mich.Comp.Laws §423.202. But although Michigan has not adopted the federal model of labor relations in every respect, it has determined that labor stability will be served by a system of exclusive representation and the permissive use of an agency shop in public employment. As already stated, there can be no principled basis for according that decision less weight in the constitutional balance than was given in *Hanson* to the congressional judgment reflected in the Railway Labor Act. The only remaining constitutional inquiry evoked by the appellants' argument, therefore, is whether a public employee has a weightier First Amendment interest than a private employee in not being compelled to contribute to the costs of exclusive union representation. We think he does not.

Public employees are not basically different from private employees; on the whole, they have the same sort of skills, the same needs, and seek the same advantages. "The uniqueness of public employment is *not in the employees* nor in the work performed; the uniqueness is in the special character of the employer." . . . The very real differences between exclusive agent collective bargaining in the public and private sectors are not such as to work any greater infringement upon the First Amendment interests of public employees. A public employee who believes that a union representing him is urging a course that is unwise as a matter of public policy is not barred from expressing his viewpoint. Besides voting in accordance with his convictions, every public employee is largely free to express his views, in public or private, orally or in writing. With some exceptions not pertinent here, public employees are free to participate in the full range of political activities open to other citizens. . . .

There can be no quarrel with the truism that because public employee unions attempt to influence governmental policy-making, their activities—and the views of members who disagree with them—may be properly termed political. But that characterization does not raise the ideas and beliefs of public employees onto a higher plane than the ideas and beliefs of private employees. It is no doubt true that a central purpose of the First Amendment "was to protect the free discussion of governmental affairs." . . . But our cases have never suggested that expression about philosophical, social, artistic, economic, literary, or ethical matters—to take a nonexhaustive list of labels—is not entitled to full First Amendment protection. Union members in both the public and private sector may find that a variety of union activities conflict with their beliefs. . . . Nothing in the First Amendment or our cases discussing its meaning makes the question whether the adjective "political" can properly be attached to those beliefs the critical constitutional inquiry. . . .

. . . We conclude that the Michigan Court of Appeals was correct in viewing this Court's decisions in *Hanson* and *Street* as controlling in the present case insofar as the service charges are applied to collective bargaining, contract administration, and grievance adjustment purposes.

. . . Our decisions establish with unmistakable clarity that the freedom of an individual to associate for the purpose of advancing beliefs and ideas is protected by the First and Fourteenth Amendments. . . . Equally clear is the proposition that a government may not require an individual to relinquish rights guaranteed him by the First Amendment as a condition of public employment. . . . The appellants . . . argue that they may constitutionally prevent the Union's spending a part of their required service fees to contribute to political candidates and to express political views unrelated to its duties as exclusive bargaining representative. We have concluded that this argument is a meritorious one.

One of the principles underlying the Court's decision in *Buckley v. Valeo*, 424 U.S. 1, 96 S.Ct. 612, 46 L.Ed.2d 659, was that contributing to an organization for the purpose of spreading a political message is protected by the First Amendment. Because "[m]aking a contribution . . . enables like-minded persons to pool their resources in furtherance of common political goals," Id., at 22, 96 S.Ct. at 636, the Court reasoned that limitations upon the freedom to contribute "implicate fundamental First Amendment interests," Id., at 23, 96 S.Ct. at 636.

The fact that the appellants are compelled to make, rather than prohibited from making, contributions for political purposes works no less an infringement of their constitutional rights. For at the heart of the First Amendment is the notion that an individual should be free to believe as he will, and that in a free society one's beliefs should be shaped by his mind and his conscience rather than coerced by the State. . . . They are no less applicable to the case at bar, and they thus prohibit the appellees from requiring any of the appellants to contribute to the support of an ideological cause he may oppose as a condition of holding a job as a public school teacher.

We do not hold that a union cannot constitutionally spend funds for the expression of political views, on behalf of political candidates, or towards the advancement of other ideological causes not germane to its duties as collective bargaining representative. Rather, the Constitution requires only that such expenditures be financed from charges, dues, or assessments paid by employees who do not object to advancing those ideas and who are not coerced into doing so against their will by the threat of loss of governmental employment.

There will, of course, be difficult problems in drawing lines between collective bargaining activities, for which contributions may be compelled, and ideological activities unrelated to collective bargaining, for which such compulsion is prohibited. . . . All that we decide is that the general allegations in the complaint, if proven, establish a cause of action under the First and Fourteenth Amendments. . . .

The judgment is vacated, and the case is remanded for further proceedings not inconsistent with this opinion.

It is so ordered.

CASE NOTE

In further elaboration of issues presented in *Abood*, the U.S. Supreme Court has held that procedural safeguards are necessary to prevent an agency shop agreement from resulting in a compulsory subsidization of ideological activities by nonunion employees who object thereto. The fact that nonunion employees' rights are protected by the First Amendment requires that procedures be carefully tailored to minimize the agency shop's infringement on those constitutional rights. The fact that a rebate procedure was in place did not sufficiently protect the nonunion dissenter because such a rebate did not avoid the risk that the dissenter's funds might be used temporarily for an improper purpose. *Chicago Teachers Union, Local No. 1 v. Hudson*, 475 U.S. 292, 106 S.Ct. 1066 (1986).

❖ — ❖ — ❖

Deducting Full Union Fees from Paychecks of Nonmember Teachers and Then Refunding Amount Not Actually Expended for Collective Bargaining Does Not Violate First Amendment

Grunwald v. San Bernardino City Unified School District

United States Court of Appeals,
Ninth Circuit, 1993.
994 F.2d 1370.

KOZINSKI, Circuit Judge:

In this dispute between an employee union and nonmember agency fee payers, we resolve the tension between the First Amendment's guarantee of free speech and the idiomatic truth that there's no such thing as a free lunch.

Plaintiffs are nonunion teachers employed by the San Bernardino Unified School District (the District). Even though they are not members of the San Bernardino Teachers Association (the SBTA or the union), plaintiffs must contribute to it. California law requires these payments because the SBTA and the District have an agency shop agreement under which the SBTA is the teachers' exclusive collective bargaining agent. . . . As beneficiaries of collective bargaining, plaintiffs must help pay for it. . . .

However, the union carries out some activities unrelated to collective bargaining, such as contributing to political candidates. . . . Therefore, agency fee payers* may not be charged the same amount as union members; they must only be charged a lesser amount reflecting a pro rata portion of the union's expenditures on collective bargaining activities. In an effort to satisfy this requirement, the District puts the amounts deducted from the paychecks of agency fee payers in an escrow account. Agency fee payers can get a refund of a portion of these amounts under a procedure set up by agreement between the District and the union. Plaintiffs challenge the constitutionality of this "deduction-escrow-refund" procedure.

The mechanics of the collection procedure are simple: One tenth of the annual union dues is deducted from every teacher's paycheck on the 30th of each month that school is in session—September through June. The union gets the deduction from the paychecks of the union members, but all of the agency fee payers' deductions are put into an independently managed interest-bearing escrow account. The fees stay in escrow until the refund procedure concludes.

The refund process is set in motion no later than October 15th. By that date, the SBTA sends notice to all nonmember contributors telling them how to obtain a rebate of funds not used for collective bargaining. Accompanying this notice is a calculation of the amount the SBTA deems chargeable to representational activities.

To obtain a refund, nonmembers must submit, no later than November 15, a letter objecting to the union's discretionary use of their fees. After they object, teachers may choose one of two routes to get their refund. They can accept the SBTA's calculation of the chargeable percentage, in which case the SBTA gives them a rebate

for the entire year by December 7. Or they can dispute the union's allocation and request that the percentage be determined by arbitration. If they choose arbitration, an arbitrator chosen by the American Arbitration Association decides what portion of the total payment is chargeable to collective bargaining. The challenging fee payers and the SBTA may present evidence, orally or by affidavit, at a hearing to be held no later than December 15—a month after objections are made. The arbitrator must issue his award within 30 days of the close of the hearing, and the SBTA must pay the rebate within 20 days of the arbitrator's decision. Assuming a hearing of roughly a week, the payment date falls sometime in mid-February.

Plaintiffs challenge these SBTA procedures under 42 U.S.C. §1983. They claim the District may not, even temporarily, deduct from their paychecks more than what the union is entitled to receive for collective bargaining activities. Plaintiffs argue that even the temporary retention of funds not allocable to collective bargaining violates their First Amendment right against compelled speech.

Plaintiffs base their argument on the now well-established principle that requiring nonmember employees to contribute to the union's ideological activities runs afoul of the First Amendment. . . .

Two basic principles emerge from the cases reviewing agency shop agreements: First, nonmembers have an absolute right not to support speech they disagree with, so the union must not, under any circumstances, be able to use their money for ideological purposes. . . . Second, nonmembers have a further First Amendment right to a fair, prompt and effective procedure, both for identifying what sums they are required to pay and, if more than that is collected, for obtaining a refund of the excess. . . . For convenience, we will refer to the first of these as the substantive First Amendment right and to the second as the procedural First Amendment right.

The Supreme Court in *Ellis* announced a few of the basic rules for safeguarding nonmembers' substantive First Amendment right. An absolute baseline is that nonmembers may never be charged more than is needed to cover "expenditures [which] are necessarily or reasonably

---

*Nonunion teachers are called agency fee payers because they pay fees under the terms of the District's agency shop agreement. In contrast, the union teachers pay membership dues.

incurred" in collective bargaining. . . . Moreover, money collected from nonmembers may not be used, even temporarily, for ideological purposes, lest they be forced to make "an involuntary loan" which the union can use to promote its political ends. . . . In a passage highly relevant to our case, *Ellis* observed that, to avoid forced subsidies forbidden by the First Amendment, unions must adopt procedures "such as advance reduction of dues and/or interest-bearing escrow accounts." . . . Taking our lead from *Ellis,* we conclude that the District's escrow scheme poses no risk that plaintiffs' substantive free speech rights will be violated. . . .

Plaintiffs nevertheless argue that they suffer a substantive First Amendment injury because they are denied use of their money temporarily, so they can't use it to promote First Amendment causes *they* support. We seriously doubt that this states a First Amendment injury at all, particularly where plaintiffs are either given an advance rebate or paid interest on their money to make up for lost use. Any other conclusion would turn every tax refund suit—indeed every monetary claim against an entity acting under color of law—into a First Amendment case.

In any event, to the extent plaintiffs have suffered an injury it is of a much different character than that contemplated by *Abood, Ellis* and *Hudson*. Those cases categorically prohibit only one type of First Amendment harm: use of nonmembers' money to promote causes they do not believe in. The Supreme Court has recognized in those cases and others that this type of injury is particularly grave: To be forced to promote a cause or express sentiments that run contrary to one's conscience is painful in addition to being unjust. This sort of compelled contribution is forbidden under a broad First Amendment protection which the Court has called the "individual freedom of mind." . . . The agency shop agreement we test here does not inflict this type of First Amendment harm. As to other types of injury plaintiffs may suffer, *Abood, Ellis* and *Hudson* require only a reasonable accommodation. We consider next whether the procedure adopted by the District provides such a reasonable accommodation of plaintiffs' remaining interests.

Even if nonmembers' money can't be used by the union for nonrepresentational purposes, their rights may still be infringed by a deduction-escrow-refund procedure, unless the procedure serves a legitimate purpose and is administered in a fair and impartial fashion. Requiring agency fee payers to go through the inconvenience, embarrassment and delay of recovering even a small sum—practically a sum so small it's hardly worth the hassle—is a burden they cannot be required to bear, unless there's a compelling reason for requiring it and the procedure itself is reasonable.

Hudson provides significant guidance in judging the adequacy of the procedure adopted here. Though *Hudson* noted with approval that the union had created an escrow account to hold 100% of the funds collected from dissenters, the Court commented that an "agency shop agreement itself impinges on the nonunion employees' First Amendment interests, . . . because[, for example,] the nonunion employee has the burden of objection." . . . In the end the *Hudson* court struck down the escrow arrangement offered as a remedy because it remained "flawed in two respects. It [did] not provide an adequate explanation for the advance reduction of dues, and it [did] not provide a reasonably prompt decision by an impartial decisionmaker." . . .

We interpret this language in *Hudson* as expressing a strong preference for identifying nonunion members early enough so that the deduction-escrow-refund procedure can be avoided altogether. To employ the more cumbersome and intrusive deduction-escrow-refund procedure, the union must provide an "adequate explanation," which we interpret to mean that the union must show that the preferred method of doing things is impossible, or, at any rate, far more costly or cumbersome. Moreover, where a deduction-escrow-refund procedure is employed, the refund procedure must be reasonably prompt; the employee must be given sufficient information from which to judge the adequacy of the refund; and, if the challenging employee so chooses, the amount of the refund must ultimately be decided by an impartial decisionmaker.

As to the first inquiry, the union has provided what we consider to be an adequate explanation for resorting to the deduction-escrow-refund procedure: Public school teachers are employed on a school year by school year basis. Virtually all new employees begin work at the same time—around September 1, when the academic year starts. During September, the District and the union first learn two pieces of information necessary to the administration of the agency shop agreement: the home addresses of all new teachers and, most importantly, the names of the teachers who choose to be agency fee payers that year. Thus, the end of September is the earliest point at which the SBTA can identify all agency fee payers and notify them of their right to a refund. The union, in fact, sends out a notice to agency fee payers advising them of their rights no later than October 15.

Under the circumstances it would be highly impractical for the union to separate members from nonmembers and determine the affiliations and addresses of the new teachers before the first monthly paycheck, which comes at the end of September. . . . Because the procedure is reasonable in light of the annual and fluctuating nature of elementary school employment and the burden on agency fee payers is relatively slight, we hold that this is the type of "appropriately justified advance reduction" approved by the Court in *Hudson*. . . .

The scheme scrutinized here also satisfies the twin requirements that nonmembers be provided with a "reasonably prompt decision by an impartial decisionmaker." . . . The scheme adopted here was foreshadowed in *Hudson*:

> [A] full-dress administrative hearing, with evidentiary safeguards, [need not be] part of the "constitutional minimum." Indeed, we think that an expeditious arbitration might satisfy the requirement of a reasonably prompt decision by an impartial decisionmaker, so long as the arbitrator's selection did not represent the Union's unrestricted choice. . . . [S]election of an arbitrator frequently does not represent one party's unrestricted choice from a list of state-approved arbitrators.

. . . Regarding the "impartial decisionmaker," providing for selection of an arbitrator by the AAA does not rise to the level of "unrestricted union choice" forbidden by *Hudson*. Other Circuits agree. . . . Though some have argued that the AAA's origins reveal a pro-union undercurrent, . . . plaintiffs raise no such contention here.

The refund also appears to be reasonably prompt. If the employee does not object to the union's apportionment, his account is settled by December 7. If he does object, arbitration must begin no later than December 15, a month after the end of the objection period. The arbitrator must issue his decision within a month of the close of the proceedings. Within twenty days from the date of the decision, the union must pay back any rebatable portion of the objectors' dues. The only variable in the schedule is the length of the hearing itself. Since the issues are relatively narrow and the union bears the cost of the arbitrator as well as its own representation expenses, we have no reason to believe that the proceeding will be anything but prompt. Because the arbitration timetable is appropriately speedy, and plaintiffs do not claim that the deadlines aren't being met, we hold that the objection process does not impermissibly impinge on plaintiffs' First Amendment rights.

Though individually plaintiffs have very little money at stake in this litigation, they obviously find themselves in an uncomfortable position: They are represented by a union they do not support and to which they are, nevertheless, forced to contribute a portion of their income. It adds insult to injury for them to be deprived, even temporarily, of additional funds to which they are rightfully entitled. This concern is legitimate. But the union has legitimate interests as well. Under applicable law, the union is the bargaining unit's lawful representative, and it is entitled—indeed required—to collect from everyone in the unit a pro rata portion of the funds it expends on representational activities.

Ideally, of course, the union would collect from nonmembers only that amount used for representational purposes. But that is not so easy to accomplish in practice. Here, the union has advanced a legitimate reason for the procedure it has adopted: Its ranks and the ranks of the agency fee payers change from year to year. Mindful of this fact, the union has come up with a procedure that strikes a proper balance between the union's right to charge fees for collective bargaining activities and the plaintiffs' First Amendment right to be free from forced contribution to causes with which they disagree. Tyranny of the majority this is not.

AFFIRMED.

CASE NOTES

1. Nonunion employees of a public school must pay the union's agency fee but are entitled to notice of the fair share fee that they are required to pay. Notice of such fair share fees is adequate without categorization so long as the specification is sufficient to prevent the union's subsidizing ideological views that are contrary to those of the nonunion members. *Jibson v. Michigan Education Association*, 30 F.3d 723 (6th Cir.1994).

2. In an action challenging the union's calculation of agency fees charged to nonmembers, the Sixth Circuit Court of Appeals ruled that nonmembers were entitled to discover the identification of the people who calculated the fees and the documents used for the calculations. Also, the court ruled that extra-unit litigation costs could be charged to the nonmembers, while defensive organizing costs are not chargeable to nonmembers. Defensive organizing costs are those incurred to protect and strengthen the status of the union. The court said that "[t]he rubric includes, among other things, membership retention efforts, resistance to decertification proceedings, and defense against challenges from other unions." *Bromley v. Michigan Education Association—National Education Association*, 82 F.3d 686 (6th Cir.1996).

3. An agency shop fee or a "fair share fee" provided for in a statute does not deny an individual teacher due process. In a case decided by the Minnesota Supreme Court, the primary question was whether the fair share statute was constitutional, since it did not provide for a hearing for individual nonunion teachers before imposition of the fair share fee. The court concluded that the governmental interest in securing the financial stability of the exclusive union representation was sufficiently strong to override the individual's interest in obtaining a prior determination of the fee's validity. *Robbinsdale Education Association v. Robbinsdale Federation of Teachers Local 872*, 307 Minn. 96, 239 N.W.2d 437, vacated and remanded, 429 U.S. 880, 97 S.Ct. 225 (1976), original decision reinstated, 316 N.W.2d 551 (Minn.1982).

4. An agency shop provision in a contract was held invalid in the face of a statute that granted public employees the right to voluntarily join, form, and participate in organizations of their own choosing. The court found that the statute assured the "right not to join" and the forced payment of dues or their equivalent "is tantamount to coercion or, at the very least, toward participation" in the labor organization as expressly forbidden by statute. *Churchill v. S.A.D. No. 49 Teachers Association*, 380 A.2d 186 (Me.1977).

5. The U.S. Supreme Court has upheld a collective bargaining agreement between a board of education and a teachers union giving the union exclusive access to the interschool mail system and teacher mailboxes of the school system. The plaintiffs, a competing union and two of its members, had claimed that the preferential access to the internal mail system violated the First Amendment and the equal protection clause of the Fourteenth Amendment. With regard to the First Amendment, the Court pointed out that equivalent access to all parts of a school building is not guaranteed. "Nowhere [have we] suggested that students, teachers, or anyone else has an absolute constitutional right to use all parts of a school building or its immediate environs for . . . unlimited expressive purposes." See *Grayned v. City of Rockford*, 408 U.S. 104, 92 S.Ct. 2294 (1972). According to the Court, persons do not have the right of access to all types of public property; access depends on the character of the property at issue. The Court delineated three types of public property: (1) streets and parks, which are types of public property that have "[i]mmemorially been held in trust for public use for communication and assembly"; (2) facilities and meeting places where open forums have traditionally existed, as on a university campus, *Widmar v. Vincent*, 454 U.S. 263, 102 S.Ct. 269 (1981); and (3) public property that has not traditionally been an open forum for public communication. Public school mail facilities fall into this third category. School officials may decide what type of selective access will be given to such facilities. The fact that school mail facilities had been opened to such groups as the Girl Scouts and Boys Clubs does not make them an open forum; instead, the Court said that such facilities remain a "limited" public forum that can be regulated by the school board. Thus, the incumbent union may be allowed access, while another union is denied.

Perry Education Association v. Perry Local Educators' Association, 460 U.S. 37, 103 S.Ct. 948 (1983).

6. When teachers voluntarily surrender their individual academic freedom in exchange for the protection of collective action and a group contract, they cannot later avoid their contractual commitments by recalling their constitutional freedoms. Where teachers maintained that school board policy unduly restricted use of certain books, thus violating their First and Fourteenth Amendment rights, the court found that they had no redress, since they had submitted themselves to an employer-employee contractual model that gave the school board the authority to control communication through the assignment of reading material. *Cary v. Board of Education of Adams-Arapahoe School District 28-J,* 427 F.Supp. 945 (D.Colo.1977).

❖ — ❖ — ❖

Freedom of Nonunion Teacher to Speak at Open Meeting Cannot Be Curtailed

City of Madison v. Wisconsin Employment Relations Commission

Supreme Court of the United States, 1976.
429 U.S. 167, 97 S.Ct. 421.

Mr. Chief Justice BURGER delivered the opinion of the Court. The question presented on this appeal from the Supreme Court of Wisconsin is whether a State may constitutionally require that an elected Board of Education prohibit teachers, other than union representatives, to speak at open meetings, at which public participation is permitted, if such speech is addressed to the subject of pending collective-bargaining negotiations.

The Madison Board of Education and Madison Teachers, Inc. (MTI), a labor union, were parties to a collective-bargaining agreement during the calendar year of 1971. In January 1971 negotiations commenced for renewal of the agreement and MTI submitted a number of pro-

posals. One among them called for the inclusion of a so-called "fair-share" clause, which would require all teachers, whether members of MTI or not, to pay union dues to defray the costs of collective bargaining. . . .

During the same month, two teachers, Holmquist and Reed, who were members of the bargaining unit, but not members of the union, mailed a letter to all teachers in the district expressing opposition to the "fair share" proposal. Two hundred teachers replied, most commenting favorably on Holmquist and Reed's position. Thereupon a petition was drafted calling for a one-year delay in the implementation of "fair share" while the proposal was more closely analyzed by an impartial committee. The petition was circulated to all teachers in the district on December 6, 1971. Holmquist and Reed intended to present the results of their petition effort to the school board and to MTI at the school board's public meeting that same evening.

. . . During a portion of the meeting devoted to expression of opinion by the public, the president of MTI took the floor and spoke on the subject of the ongoing negotiations. He concluded his remarks by presenting to the board a petition signed by 1,300–1,400 teachers calling for the expeditious resolution of the negotiations. Holmquist was next given the floor, after John Matthews, the business representative of MTI, unsuccessfully attempted to dissuade him from speaking. Matthews had also spoken to a member of the school board before the meeting and requested that the board refuse to permit Holmquist to speak. Holmquist stated that he represented "an informal committee of seventy-two teachers in forty-nine schools" and that he desired to inform the Board of Education, as he had already informed the union, of the results of an informal survey concerning the "fair share" clause. He then read the petition which had been circulated to the teachers in the district that morning and stated that in the thirty-one schools from which reports had been received 53 percent of the teachers had already signed the petition.

Holmquist stated that neither side had adequately addressed the issue of "fair share" and that teachers were confused about the meaning of the proposal. He concluded by saying: "Due to this confusion, we wish to take no stand on the proposal itself, but ask only that all alternatives be presented clearly to all teachers and more importantly to the general public to whom we are all responsible. We ask simply for communication, not confrontation." The sole response from the school board was a question by the president inquiring whether Holmquist intended to present the board with the petition. Holmquist answered that he would. Holmquist's presentation had lasted approximately two and one-half minutes.

Later that evening, the board met in executive session and voted a proposal acceding to all the union's demands with the exception of "fair share." During a negotiating session the following morning, MTI accepted the proposal and a contract was signed on December 14, 1976.

In January 1972 MTI filed a complaint with the Wisconsin Employment Relations Commission (WERC) claiming that the board had committed a prohibited labor practice by permitting Holmquist to speak at the December 6 meeting. . . .

The Wisconsin court perceived "clear and present danger" based upon its conclusion that Holmquist's speech before the school board constituted "negotiation" with the board. Permitting such "negotiation," the court reasoned, would undermine the bargaining exclusivity guaranteed the majority union under Wis.Stat. §111.70(3)(a)4. From that premise it concluded that teachers' First Amendment rights could be limited. Assuming, *arguendo*, that such a "danger" might in some circumstances justify some limitation of First Amendment rights, we are unable to read this record as presenting such danger as would justify curtailing speech.

The Wisconsin Supreme Court's conclusion that Holmquist's terse statement during the public meeting constituted negotiation with the board was based upon its adoption of the lower court's determination that, "[e]ven though Holmquist's statement superficially appears to be merely a 'position statement,' the court deems from the total circumstances that it constituted 'negotiating.'" This cryptic conclusion seems to ignore the ancient wisdom that calling a thing by a name does not make it so. Holmquist did not seek to bargain or offer to enter into any bargain with the board, nor does it appear that he was authorized by any other

teachers to enter into any agreement on their behalf. Although his views were not consistent with those of MTI, communicating such views to the employer could not change the fact that MTI alone was authorized to negotiate and to enter into a contract with the board.

Moreover, the school board meeting at which Holmquist was permitted to speak was open to the public. He addressed the school board not merely as one of its employees but also as a concerned citizen, seeking to express his views on an important decision of his government. We have held that teachers may not be "compelled to relinquish the First Amendment rights they would otherwise enjoy as citizens to comment on matters of public interest in connection with the operation of the public school in which they work." . . . Where the State has opened a forum for direct citizen involvement, it is difficult to find justification for excluding teachers who make up the overwhelming proportion of school employees and are most vitally concerned with the proceedings. It is conceded that any citizen could have presented precisely the same points and provided the board with the same information as did Holmquist. . . .

The Employment Relations Commission's order was not limited to a determination that a prohibited labor practice had taken place in the past; it also restrains future conduct. By prohibiting the school board from "permitting employees to appear and speak at meetings of the Board of Education," the order constitutes an indirect, but effective, prohibition on persons such as Holmquist from communicating with their government. The order would have a substantial impact upon virtually all communication between teachers and the school board. The order prohibits speech by teachers "on matters subject to collective bargaining." As the dissenting opinion below noted, however, there is virtually no subject concerning the operation of the school system that could not also be characterized as a potential subject of collective bargaining. Teachers not only constitute the overwhelming bulk of employees of the school system, but they are the very core of that system; restraining teachers' expressions to the board on matters involving the operation of the schools would seriously impair the board's ability to govern the district. . . . The challenged portion of the order is designed to govern speech and conduct in the future, not to punish past conduct and as such it is the essence of prior restraint.

The judgment of the Wisconsin Supreme Court is reversed and the case is remanded to that court for further proceedings not inconsistent with this opinion.

Reversed and remanded.

■ ENDNOTES

1. *1975 Guidebook to Labor Relations* (Chicago: Commerce Clearing House, Inc., 1975), pp. 8–9.
2. Ibid.
3. Ibid., p. 11.
4. See Benjamin Werne, *Public Employment Labor Relations* (Charlottesville, Va.: Michie, 1974), p. 5.
5. Ibid., p. 6.
6. Speech by Jerry Wurf, International President of American Federation of State, County, and Municipal Employees, AFL–CIO, United States Conference of Mayors, Honolulu, Hawaii, 1967.
7. Werne, *Public Employment,* p. 11.
8. Atkins v. City of Charlotte, 296 F.Supp. 1068 (W.D.N.C.1969).
9. 406 F.2d 137 (8th Cir.1969).
10. Ibid.
11. This rule can vary among jurisdictions. For example, the Virginia Supreme Court has held that school boards do not have either statutory or constitutional authority to enter into collective bargaining agreements. *Commonwealth v. County Board of Arlington County,* 217 Va. 558, 232 S.E.2d 30 (1977).
12. Chief of Police v. Town of Dracut, 357 Mass. 492, 258 N.E.2d 531 (1970).
13. 48 Am.Jur.2d, §§1027–43.
14. City of New York v. DeLury, 23 N.Y.2d 175, 295 N.Y.S.2d 901, 243 N.E.2d 128, remittur amended, 23 N.Y.2d 766, 296 N.Y.S.2d 958, 244 N.E.2d 472 (1968), appeal dismissed, 394 U.S. 455, 89 S.Ct. 1223 (1969).
15. Anderson Federation of Teachers v. School City of Anderson, 252 Ind. 558, 251 N.E.2d 15 (1969), cert. denied, 399 U.S. 928, 90 S.Ct. 2243 (1970).
16. United Federation of Postal Clerks v. Blount, 325 F.Supp. 879 (D.D.C.), affirmed, 404 U.S. 802, 92 S.Ct. 80 (1971).
17. Anderson Federation of Teachers v. School City of Anderson, op. cit.
18. Hugh D. Jascourt, "Can Compulsory Arbitration Work in Education Collective Bargaining: An Introduction," *Journal of Law and Education* 4, no. 4 (October 1975).
19. School Board of the City of Richmond v. Parham, 218 Va. 950, 243 S.E.2d 468 (1978).
20. Dearborn Fire Fighters Union Local No. 412 v. City of Dearborn, 42 Mich.App. 51, 201 N.W.2d 650 (1972).
21. Werne, *Public Employment,* p. 247.
22. Ibid.
23. Ibid.
24. Labor Management Relations Act, §9(a), 29 U.S.C.A. §159(a).
25. West Hartford Education Association v. Dayson DeCourcy, 162 Conn. 566, 295 A.2d 526 (1972).
26. Wethersfield Board of Education v. Connecticut State Board of Labor Relations, 201 Conn. 685, 519 A.2d 41 (1986).
27. Jurva v. Attorney General, 419 Mich. 209, 351 N.W.2d 813 (1984).
28. NEA v. Unified School District No. 259, 234 Kan. 512, 674 P.2d 478 (1983).
29. Dodge City NEA v. Unified School District No. 443, 6 Kan.App. 2d 810, 635 P.2d 1263 (1981).
30. Byram Township Board of Education v. Byram Township Education Association, 152 N.J.Super. 12, 377 A.2d 745 (App.Div.1977).
31. Kolcum v. Board of Education, 335 A.2d 618 (Del.Super.1975).
32. Board of Education v. New Paltz United Teachers, 57 A.D.2d 583, 393 N.Y.S.2d 588 (2d Dept.1977).
33. Barnett v. Durant Community School, 249 N.W.2d 626 (Iowa 1977).
34. Los Angeles City & County Employees Union v. Los Angeles City Board of Education, 12 Cal.3d 851, 117 Cal.Rptr. 537, 528 P.2d 353 (1974).
35. Chee-Craw Teachers Association v. Unified School District No. 247, 225 Kan. 561, 593 P.2d 406 (1979).
36. Allen v. Town of Sterling, 367 Mass. 844, 329 N.E.2d 756 (1975).
37. Tri-County Educators' Association v. Tri-County Special Education Co-op No. 607, 225 Kan. 781, 594 P.2d 207 (1979).
38. Libby, McNeill, & Libby v. Longshoremen Local 142, 37 LA 466, 467 (1961), cited in Werne, *Public Employment,* p. 153. Benjamin Werne, *The Law and Practice of Public Employment* (Charlottesville, Va: Michie, 1974), p. 153.
39. Ibid.
40. Monsanto Chemical Co. v. Chemical Workers Local 12, 32 LA 260, 263 (1959), cited in Werne, *Public Employment,* p. 153.
41. Chee-Craw Teachers Association v. Unified School District, op. cit.
42. Chambersburg Area School District v. Commonwealth, 60 Pa.Cmwlth. 29, 430 A.2d 740 (1981).
43. Byram Township Board of Education v. Byram Township Education Association, op. cit.
44. Werne, *Public Employment,* p. 124.
45. Kenai Peninsula Borough School District v. Kenai Peninsula Education Association, 572 P.2d 416 (1977).
46. Werne, *Public Employment,* p. 150.
47. Ibid., p. 152.
48. Ibid.
49. AFSCME v. Woodward, 406 F.2d 137 (8th Cir.1969).
50. Atkins v. City of Charlotte, 296 F.Supp. 1068 (W.D.N.C.1969).
51. AFSCME v. Woodward, op. cit.; see also Griswold v. Connecticut, 381 U.S. 479, 85 S.Ct. 1678 (1965); NAACP v. Alabama, 357 U.S. 449, 78 S.Ct. 1163 (1958), reversed and remanded on other grounds, 360 U.S. 240, 79 S.Ct. 1001 (1959).

52. Day v. South Park Independent School District, 768 F.2d (5th Cir.1985).

53. 461 U.S. 138, 103 S.Ct. 1684 (1983).

54. Day v. South Park Independent School District, op. cit.

55. Pederson v. South Williamsport Area School District, 677 F.2d 312 (3d Cir.1982).

56. Ash v. Board of Education, 699 F.2d 822 (6th Cir.1983).

57. Ibid.

58. Hickman v. Valley Local School District, 619 F.2d 606 (6th Cir.1980).

59. Ibid.

60. Bauch v. City of New York, 54 Misc.2d 343, 282 N.Y.S.2d 816 (1967); Board of School Directors of the City of Milwaukee v. Wisconsin Employment Relations Commission, 42 Wis.2d 637, 168 N.W.2d 92 (1969).

61. Abood v. Detroit Board of Education, 431 U.S. 209, 97 S.Ct. 1781 (1977).

62. Ellis v. Brotherhood of Railway, Airline and S.S. Clerks, 466 U.S. 435, 104 S.Ct. 1883 (1984).

63. Ibid.

64. Elrod v. Burns, 427 U.S. 347, 96 S.Ct. 2673 (1976); Kusper v. Pontikes, 414 U.S. 51, 94 S.Ct. 303 (1973); Abood v. Detroit Board of Education, 431 U.S. 209, 97 S.Ct. 1782 (1977).

65. Chicago Teachers Union, Local No. 1 v. Hudson, 475 U.S. 292, 106 S.Ct. 1066 (1986).

CHAPTER 19

FINANCE

[I]f a man be trusted to judge between man and man, it is a precept of the Law of Nature, that he deals Equally between them.

—Thomas Hobbes

CHAPTER OUTLINE

- TAXATION FOR EDUCATION
- DISTRIBUTION OF STATE SCHOOL FUNDS
- LITIGATION UNDER STATE CONSTITUTIONS
- BUDGETING AND ACCOUNTING FOR SCHOOL FUNDS
- PUBLIC SCHOOL INDEBTEDNESS

STATE CONSTITUTIONAL PROVISIONS empowering the legislature to provide for a system of public schools confer on the legislature the authority to tax and distribute funds for public schools. Where litigation does arise, it usually involves the methods used by the legislature to regulate and control revenues and expenditures in the exercise of this authority. A substantial amount of litigation is devoted to the legal requirements for taxation and taxpayers' remedies for payment of illegal taxes as well as legal requirements for budgeting and accounting for school funds. Many cases question the legal authority of school districts to issue bonds, hold bond elections, and impose certain fees and charges on children and parents. Although the volume of cases is relatively small compared to other fiscal matters, the issue of constitutional rights of students and the resulting impact on

state school finance has probably been the most widely publicized area of school finance litigation.

Litigation challenging the constitutionality of state school aid formulas under specific state constitutional provisions represents an evolutionary step in judicial expansion of constitutional protections. These cases in state courts have extended students' rights by placing new limitations on the police power of the state to regulate and control education. Courts once obliquely maintained that education was a privilege bestowed upon the individual by the good will of the state and that it could be altered or even taken away at the state's discretion. This has changed, and education is now being adjudged a fundamental right as guaranteed by the state constitution.

School finance cases therefore represent an important step in legal precedents, not only because they involve limitations on the police power of the state to regulate and control education, but also because they restrict a legislature's power to devise and implement its own system of taxation. Each of these issues has traditionally formed separate precedents.

■ TAXATION FOR EDUCATION

The power of taxation is inherent in the state, limited only by the federal Constitution and the constitution of the state. A state cannot impose an arbitrary or discriminatory tax burden upon a segment of the population, but a state can impose a heavier tax on nonresidents than on residents. Reasonable classifications for tax purposes are permissible, but those that invidiously discriminate violate the equal protection clause of the Fourteenth Amendment.

The courts have held that school districts have no inherent power to levy taxes. This power must be expressly conferred upon the school district by the legislature. In the levy and collection of taxes, school districts must adhere strictly to the language of the statutory authority; the courts are hesitant to extend powers of taxation by statutory implication. The power of a local school district to tax for education funds is not implied by a general statute to establish and operate a local school system. In the absence of contrary constitutional provisions, the legislature may choose to finance education entirely from a tax levied at the state level and redistributed to the school districts.

Some states do, though, have constitutional provisions that expressly vest school districts with taxing power without legislative authorization.[1] These "local constitutional taxing provisions" are relatively few. If such authority is not found in the constitution, then it does not exist without appropriate enabling legislation.[2] Where a constitutional provision appears to send a mixed message, the courts will come down on the side of restraint, limiting local taxing power in the absence of legislative permission.[3]

Of course, legislative acts themselves may be unconstitutional if they conflict with tax provisions in state constitutions. The Texas Supreme Court held unconstitutional legislation enacted in response to the requirements of *Edgewood Independent School District v. Kirby*,[4] which cre-

ated a new state education finance law that established a state-mandated tax, set rates, and prescribed the distribution of the proceeds. The law violated a state constitutional provision that forbade the state to levy an *ad valorem* tax.[5] The constitution clearly stated that "[n]o state *ad valorem* taxes shall be levied upon any property within this State."[6] Thus, this case illustrates how the state legislature itself may be constrained by various constitutional provisions reflecting the desires of the people to govern the important prerogative of taxation.

Yet, where the constitution is silent on the subject of taxation, the general empowerment of the legislature with the responsibility to provide for the general welfare of the people through the exercise of its sovereign police powers constitutes implicit power for the legislature to establish and control the state's tax system.

Where taxing authority is given by statute to local school districts, the statute must be strictly construed to abide by the intent of the legislature. If a school tax levy is illegal because of failure to follow the prescribed procedure, the courts will make a determination depending on whether the statutory provision is mandatory or directory. If the provision is mandatory, the tax is invalid. However, the courts have established no clear guidelines for determining if a provision is mandatory or directory. In these situations, courts are generally faced with the perplexing problems that ensue from finding a tax levy invalid and thereby harming the education program. Because of this, the courts are usually very liberal in this regard and are hesitant to call a tax invalid. If a procedural error is relatively minor and does not deprive the taxpayers of a substantial or fundamental right, the courts will allow the tax to stand.

❖ — ❖ — ❖

The Development of the American State and Local Tax System

With permission of Jerome R. Hellerstein, 3d ed. (St. Paul, Minn.: West Publishing Company, 1969), pp. 1–2, 70–72.

COLONIAL TAXATION

The colonial governments in their early days subsisted on voluntary payments, subsidies and allowances abroad, quit-rents, and occasional fees and fines of early justice. When compulsory levies developed, the tax systems followed the pattern of the local economies. In the democratic New England communities almost everyone owned land; and the distribution of property was fairly equal. Consequently, in New England, in addition to the poll tax, the colonies levied a tax on the gross produce of land, either actual or computed, according to the extent and quality of the land held. Gradually, this levy grew into a real property tax, which was soon expanded into a general property tax. The town artisans and other townsmen who subsisted on the fruit of their labor, instead of property, were not adequately taxed by the property levy. The "faculty tax" was added to reach these persons. The faculty tax was not an income tax, but instead a levy in a fixed amount, imposed rather arbitrarily, according to occupations and callings.

An entirely different development took place in the Southern colonies, dominated by an aristocratic landed gentry with large holdings. There, the land tax played an insignificant role. After slavery was introduced, it became difficult to retain even the poll tax, which became in a sense a property tax on slaves. Consequently, the Southern colonies turned to excise taxes, particularly on imports and exports, which bore heavily on poorer consumers.

The middle colonies, particularly the New Netherlands, reflected the dominance of the moneyed interests and trading classes, who brought with them a Dutch tradition. Here, there was neither the more or less equal distribution of wealth characteristic of New England, nor the preponderance of the landed interests typified by Virginia. Instead of a system of poll and property levies or of excises primarily on imports and exports, the fundamental characteristic of the tax structure was an excise system of taxation of trade, borrowed from Holland.

> Each section, therefore, had a fiscal system more or less in harmony with its economic conditions. It was not until these conditions changed during the eighteenth century that the fiscal systems began somewhat to approach each other; and it was not until much later that we find throughout the country a general property tax based not on the produce, but on the market value of property.

The outstanding development in State and local taxation during the nineteenth century was the rise of the property tax. As stated by Professor Ely, during the period from 1796 to the Civil War "the distinguishing feature of the system of state and local taxation in America may be described in one sentence. It is the taxation of all property, movable or immovable, visible or invisible, or real or personal . . . at one uniform rate."

Nevertheless, the divergence of economic systems was reflected in the development of the State fiscal systems. In the Southern States, with imports and exports as a source of revenue cut off by the federal Constitution, land had to bear a large part of the tax burden. As increased revenues were needed, these States, dominated by landed proprietors at least until the Civil War, turned primarily to license and privilege taxes on peddlers, auctioneers, saloon keepers, traders in slaves and horses, keepers of ferries, toll bridges and turnpikes, and indeed virtually all occupations carried on outside the farms.

In the Northern States, where business interests were dominant, the license or privilege tax system did not take hold. To supplement property tax yields, banks, insurance companies, canals, railroads, and other businesses were taxed; and as corporations came to play a more important role in the economy, general corporate franchise taxes were enacted. These levies were the precursors of the present day corporate taxes on or measured by net income. The newer States adopted the current tax philosophy of the older States, making the property tax the cornerstone of their tax structures. . . .

Early property taxation. Although property taxes were regarded as an extraordinary source of revenue in early history, they, nevertheless, have ancient origins. In Athens, the land tax was originally levied on gross produce, but it gradually developed into a property tax imposed not only on land and houses but also on slaves, cattle, furniture and money. Rome taxed many forms of personalty as well as realty. In Europe, the early property taxes were levied on land but were gradually extended to buildings and cattle, until they became general property taxes. As new types of movable and intangible property developed, evasion became prevalent and assessment difficult. The principle of the general property tax broke down and personal property taxes were gradually abandoned. By 1800, the base of European property taxes had largely dwindled down to land alone or land and buildings.

The development of the general property tax in the United States. . . . [T]he general property tax became formally established in this country for the States and localities during the nineteenth century.

At first the property tax was really a tax on land at a fixed sum per acre of different types of land—cleared and uncleared, cultivated and cleared, and so forth. It soon was expanded to include livestock, buildings, and personal property. Each item of taxable property was listed and taxed at a fixed sum for each cow, each barn, and so on. The increasing complexity of this taxable list led finally to (1) the general property tax—general taxation of all properties, instead of the growing lists of taxable specified properties; (2) appraisal of property—the tax rates were imposed as percentages or per millages of the property valuation, rather than as a fixed sum of money per unit of property; (3) the adoption of the principle of uniformity—whereas earlier laws provided for varying rates for different classes of property, the uniformity concept adopted by State constitutions required real and personal property to be taxed at a uniform proportion of value.

❖ — ❖ — ❖

School Districts Do Not Have Authority to Levy Taxes in Absence of Specific Enabling Legislation

Florida Department of Education v. Glasser

Supreme Court of Florida, 1993.
622 So.2d 944.

SHAW, Justice. . . .

Appellees, individually and as members of the School Board of Sarasota County (school board) filed an action for declaratory judgment against the Sarasota County tax collector. The trial court . . . directed the tax collector to collect and remit to the school board taxes assessed against the nonvoted discretionary millage as set by the school board. The issue presented here is whether a school district has constitutional authority to levy such taxes in the absence of enabling legislation. We answer this query in the negative for the reasons hereinafter expressed.

Statutes are presumed to be constitutional and courts must construe them in harmony with the constitution if it is reasonable to do so. . . . We find that in this instance the constitution and relevant statutes can coact. Our analysis begins with the Florida Constitution. Article VII, in relevant part, provides:

> Section 9. Local taxes.—
> (a) Counties, school districts, and municipalities *shall,* and special districts may, *be authorized by law* to levy ad valorem taxes . . . for their respective purposes. . . .

(Emphasis added.)

We attribute to the words "shall . . . be authorized by law" their plain meaning: legislative authorization is required to trigger this provision; it is not self-executing. *See* 1 *The Oxford English Dictionary* 798–99 (2d ed. 1989) (authorize: "To give legal force to; to make legally valid. To endow with authority"). Had the framers of the 1968 Florida Constitution intended a self-executing grant of power, they could have chosen self-executing language. Our present constitution contains numerous examples of such phrases: "The seat of government shall be the City of Tallahassee, in Leon County. . . ." Art. II, §2, Fla. Const. "The supreme executive power shall be vested in a governor." Art. IV, §1(a), Fla. Const. "The judicial power shall be vested in a supreme court, district courts of appeal, circuit courts and county courts." Art. V, §1, Fla. Const. Had the framers intended to authorize school districts to levy ad valorem taxes, they could have said simply: "School districts are authorized to levy ad valorem taxes."

Our conclusion that the constitutional provision at issue requires legislative enactment is strengthened by the commentary to the 1968 constitutional revision: "The language [of section 9(a)], mandatory in tone, does contemplate a legislative act for they 'shall be authorized by law' to levy ad valorem taxes." 26A Fla.Stat. Ann. 143 (1970) (commentary by Talbot "Sandy" D'Alemberte). The school board nevertheless argues that the word "shall" gives the school district full authorization to levy taxes without the necessity of an enactment. This argument fails to give meaning to the accompanying words "be authorized by law," and for this reason is rejected.

The right to education is basic in a democracy. Without it, neither the student nor the state has a future. Our legislature annually implements a complicated formula to fund this basic right. We find that the legislation at issue here, which is part of the overall funding formula, is in harmony with the Florida Constitution. Accordingly, we reverse the district court and remand for proceedings consistent with this opinion.

It is so ordered.

❖ — ❖ — ❖

Authority to Levy Taxes Must Be Found in Express Legislative Provision

Marion & McPherson Railway Co. v. Alexander

Supreme Court of Kansas, 1901.
63 Kan. 72, 64 P. 978.

CUNNINGHAM, J. The plaintiff in error in this action seeks to enjoin the collection of all taxes levied for school purposes in school district No. 79, Marion county, Kan., in excess of 2 percent on the taxable property owned by it in said district. A graded school district, No. 79, had been organized, identical in boundaries and inhabitants with school district No. 79; such organization being authorized by article 7, c. 92, of the General Statutes of 1889. That article generally provided for the organization of union or graded schools, its principal sections being as follows: Section 107 provides for the selection of a board of directors by the graded school district, and that such board shall consist of a director, clerk, and treasurer. Section 108 directs that such board of directors shall, in all matters relating to the graded schools, possess all the powers and discharge all the like duties of

boards of directors in other districts. Section 109 provides that the union districts thus formed shall be entitled to an equitable share of the school funds, to be drawn from the treasurer of each district so uniting, in proportion to the number of children attending the said graded school for each district. Section 110: "The said union district may levy taxes for the purpose of purchasing a building or furnishing proper buildings, for the accommodation of the school or for the purpose of defraying necessary expenses and paying teachers, but shall be governed in all respects by the law herein provided for levying and collecting district taxes." Section 111 provides certain duties for the clerk of the union district in relation to reports, and that the district treasurer shall apportion the amount of school moneys due the union district, and pay the same over to the treasurer of the union district on order of the clerk and director thereof. Section 112, that the clerk of the union district shall make report to the county superintendent, and discharge all the duties of clerk in like manner as the clerk of the district. Section 113, that the treasurer of the district shall perform all the duties of treasurer as prescribed in the act in like manner as the district treasurer. Section 115, that any single district shall possess power to establish graded schools in like manner and subject to the same provisions as two or more districts united. Section 28 of the same chapter (being the section which gives the general power for levying district taxes) provides: "The inhabitants qualified to vote at a school meeting, lawfully assembled, shall have power: . . . To vote a tax annually not exceeding 2 percent on the taxable property in the district, as the meeting shall deem sufficient for the various school purposes, and distribute the amount as the meeting shall deem proper in the payment of teachers' wages, and to purchase or lease a site."

These are all the sections which afford light for the solution of the question involved. From these, it is contended by plaintiff in error that while the inhabitants of one or more school districts may form a union or graded district, and create the machinery to run the same and to maintain any and all schools therein, the total levy "for the various school purposes" cannot exceed 2 percent on the taxable property in any one district annually. It is contended by the defendants in error that the various sections quoted, conferring as they do upon the various members of the graded school district board all the powers of like officers of ordinary district boards, and erecting a separate entity for the purpose of managing a separate school, and conferring upon that entity the power to levy taxes as found in section 110, give the power to such graded school district to make within its bounds an additional levy not to exceed 2 percent; that is, that it may levy as much as the original school district may, and this in addition to what the original district levies, and not that the total of both levies must be the limit fixed in section 28. The court below took this view of the question. In this we do not agree. We think that by section 28 the entire levy may not exceed 2 percent; and we are strengthened in this conclusion by the language of section 109, which says that a union district shall be entitled to "an equitable share of the school funds," and also by that in section 111—"the district treasurer shall apportion the amount of school money due the union district and pay the same over to the union district." The law fixes the time for holding the annual meetings of the union or graded districts in June, while the annual meetings of school districts occur in July. All these provisions, taken together, indicate that it was the purpose of the legislature that, while the first meeting—that of the graded district—could suggest the levy desired for graded school purposes, the last one only possessed the power to vote the tax which for "the various school purposes" could not in any one year exceed 2 percent. Or, at least, there must be such harmony in the action of both bodies that the aggregate levy may not exceed the limit found in section 28. We may say that the question is not one entirely free from doubt, but can hardly believe that the legislature would have left it in that condition, had its purpose been to confer the right to so largely increase the burden of taxation. The authority to levy taxes is an extraordinary one. It is never left to implication, unless it is a necessary implication. Its warrant must be clearly found in the act of the legislature. Any other rule might lead to great wrong and oppression, and when there is a reasonable doubt as to its existence the right must be denied. Therefore to say that the right is in doubt is to deny its existence. . . .

The levies sought to be enjoined are those for the years 1894 and 1895, and our conclusion is that the judgment of the district court must be reversed, and it be directed to make the injunction perpetual, enjoining all of the defendants from collecting all of said school taxes in excess of 2 percent. All the justices concurring.

CASE NOTES

1. "Neither municipalities nor school districts are sovereigns, and they have no original or fundamental power of legislation or taxation, but have only the right and power to enact those legislative and tax ordinances or resolutions which are authorized by act of the legislature." *Appeal of School District of City of Allentown*, 370 Pa. 161, 87 A.2d 480 (1952).

2. Taxes levied and collected for school purposes are state taxes whether they are collected by the school district or a municipality. In an Alabama case, the court said: "If the Constitution raises the fund and directs its use in furthering a state function, it continues to be such a state fund regardless of the sort of agency designated to administer it." *City Board of Education of Athens v. Williams*, 231 Ala. 137, 163 So. 802 (1935).

3. In relating legislative provisions for taxation to constitutional requirements, the courts have held that revenue statutes must be given a reasonable construction and no statute can circumvent positively stated constitutional provisions. *Mathews v. Board of Education of City of Chicago*, 342 Ill. 120, 174 N.E. 35 (1930).

4. "The power of the board of education of a non–high school district to levy taxes is statutory. The language granting the power is to be strictly construed and will not be extended beyond the plain import of the words used." *People ex rel. Smith, Co. Collector v. Wabash Railway Co.*, 374 Ill. 165, 28 N.E.2d 119 (1940).

5. The intent of the legislature in enacting taxation statutes is often difficult to interpret. A Pennsylvania court in determining that a statute prescribing taxation for "amusements" included admissions to "fairgrounds" had this to say about statutory interpretation:

> The language of a statute must be read in a sense which harmonizes with the subject matter and its general purpose and object. The general design and purpose of the law is to be kept in view. . . .

School District of Cambria Township v. Cambria Co. Legion Recreation Association, 201 Pa.Super. 163, 192 A.2d 149 (1963).

6. Courts will not interfere with the exercise of sound business judgment on the part of taxing authorities but will intervene only to prevent a clear abuse by such officers of their discretionary powers. *People v. Baltimore & Ohio Southwestern Railway Co.*, 353 Ill. 492, 187 N.E. 463 (1933).

7. Where a wrongful tax is collected, the taxpayer may recover only on such remedies as are authorized by law, such as an appeal to set aside or cancel a tax deed and a tax protest. *Wall v. M. & R. Sheep Co.*, 33 Cal.2d 768, 205 P.2d 14 (1949).

8. A person who pays tax voluntarily and not under duress cannot recover the tax. *Harding v. Wiley*, 219 Ill.App. 1 (1920). A mere protest by a taxpayer is not sufficient to constitute payment under compulsion or duress.

9. A person may not question the legality of school funds unless he has a requisite interest in such funds. *Chalupnik v. Savall*, 219 Wis. 442, 263 N.W. 352 (1935).

10. Some states have statutory provisions for a taxpayer protest before a court or board of tax review. The findings of fact or judgment by the court or board will not be disturbed unless clearly arbitrary or against the weight of evidence.

11. Taxpayers may not sit idly by and allow illegal systems of taxation to be installed without protesting and then take advantage of the illegality of the system by collaterally attacking the system when they are sued. In such a case, the Court of Civil Appeals of Texas held that although a scheme of taxation is illegal, the burden is on the taxpayers to show that they have suffered substantial financial loss as a result of the failure of the city and school district to assess property legally. *City of Houston v. McCarthy*, 371 S.W.2d 587 (Tex.Civ.App.1963).

12. Tangible personal property that is located in a state other than that in which the owner is domiciled may be taxed at the place of its location. *Fennell v. Pauley*, 112 Iowa 94, 83 N.W. 799 (1900). The "domicile" of a person is the place where he or she has his or her principal, true, fixed, permanent home and to which he or she has, whenever he or she is absent, the intention of returning; it also means the habitation, fixed in any place, from which a person does not have

any present intention of removing. *State v. Benny*, 20 N.J. 238, 119 A.2d 155 (1955).

13. Intangible personal property is generally taxable at the domicile of the owner. *Scripps v. Board of Review of Fulton Co.*, 183 Ill. 278, 55 N.E. 700 (1899). However, courts have upheld cases in which the state legislature provides that intangible personal property shall be taxed when located other than where the owner is domiciled. In arriving at this conclusion, a Minnesota court stated:

> For many purposes the domicile of the owner is deemed the situs of his personal property. This, however, is only a fiction, from motives of convenience, and is not of universal application, but yields to the actual situs of the property when justice requires that it should. It is not allowed to be controlling in matters of taxation. Thus, corporeal personal property is conceded to be taxable at the place where it is actually situated. A credit which cannot be regarded as situated in a place merely because the debtor resides there, must usually be considered as having its situs where it is owned, at the domicile of the creditor. The creditor, however, may give it a business situs elsewhere; as where he places it in the hands of an agent for collection or renewal, with a view to reloaning the money and keeping it invested as a permanent business. . . . The allegation to pay taxes on property for the support of the government arises from the fact that it is under the protection of the government.

In re Washington County v. Estate of Jefferson, 35 Minn. 215, 28 N.W. 256 (1886).

■ DISTRIBUTION OF STATE SCHOOL FUNDS

> Where constitutionality of a statute is questioned, all reasonable doubt will be resolved in favor of the questioned authority and the act will be declared constitutional unless it can be clearly demonstrated that the legislature did not have the power or authority exercised or that its authority was exercised arbitrarily and capriciously, for instance, as to classification or delegation of authority, to the prejudice of the rights of some of the citizens. Particularly, is this true where the act in question is . . . of great public concern involving the performance of an absolute duty imposed on the legislature by the basic law of the state.[7]

This statement describes the traditional position of the courts on the judicial regulation of such important legislative functions as taxation for public education. Nonintervention has been the watchword for decades when courts have been asked to examine the constitutionality of legislatively prescribed methods of taxation for financing education.

The courts have steadfastly adhered to the philosophy that an act of the legislature will not be rendered invalid unless the act obviously violates certain prescribed constitutional standards. With regard to the constitutionality of state school finance programs, the courts have traditionally been asked to determine only whether such programs created unconstitutional classifications or violated equality and uniformity of taxation requirements. The equal protection clause of the Fourteenth Amendment encompasses, but is not limited to, the same protections as the equality and uniformity of taxation provisions of most state constitutions.

TAXATION AND EQUAL PROTECTION

The equal protection clause was first described as a limitation on state revenue legislation by the Supreme Court of the United States in 1890. The "test" devised by the Supreme Court to determine constitutionality of state taxation has been restated by Justice Jackson:

> Equal protection does not require identity of treatment. It only requires that classification rest on real and not feigned differences, that the distinction have some relevance to the purpose for which the classification is made, and the different treatment be not so disparate, relative to the difference in classification, as to be wholly arbitrary.[8]

The equal protection clause establishes a minimum standard of uniformity to which state tax legislation must conform in addition to, and beyond, similar limitations imposed by state constitutional requirements.[9]

Practically all state constitutions have the equivalent of an "equal protection" provision—that is, some constitutional restriction against "unreasonable classifications." While the U.S. Supreme Court has the ultimate interpretative power regarding "reasonableness" under the federal equal protection clause, state courts have the last word as to the meaning of reasonableness under their respective state constitutions.[10] The primary problem is, of course, the definition of reasonableness or unreasonableness of a classification.

Courts have been hesitant to invalidate legislative acts on the basis of unconstitutional classification because the source of taxation is often tightly interwoven with the government's plan for distribution of funds to local districts. The essence of an illegal constitutional classification is to arbitrarily classify local districts or persons with no regard for their actual conditions or needs. The U.S. Ninth Circuit Court of Appeals speaks of this as fitting tax programs to needs:

> Traditionally classification has been a device for fitting tax programs to local needs and usages in order to achieve an equitable distribution of the tax burden. It has, because of this, been pointed out that in taxation, even more than in other fields, legislatures possess the greatest freedom in classification. Since the members of a legislature necessarily enjoy a familiarity with local conditions which this court cannot have, the presumption of constitutionality can be overcome only by the most explicit demonstration that a classification is a hostile and oppressive discrimination against particular persons and classes. The burden is on the one attacking the legislative arrangement to negate every conceivable basis which might support it.[11]

DISTRIBUTION FORMULAS AND THE EQUAL PROTECTION CLAUSE

Even though the ninth circuit denied that the equality and uniformity of taxation requirements of both state and federal constitutions apply to the distribution of funds, it proceeded nevertheless to lay down "guiding principles" that govern a legislature's distribution of tax funds. Quoting *Corpus Juris Secundum*, the court said:

> In the absence of constitutional regulation the method of apportioning and distributing a school fund, accruing from taxes or other revenue, rests in the wise discretion of the state legislature, which method, in the absence of abuse of discretion or violation of some constitutional provision, cannot be interfered with by the courts. . . . [T]he fact that the fund is distributed unequally among the different districts or political subdivisions does not render it invalid.[12]

In other words, the needs of the various types of school districts and the resulting impact of methods of taxation are a matter that is to be determined by the legislature.

In 1965, however, the theory was advanced that education funding was a constitutionally protected right and must be provided to all on equal terms. Thus, a state that gives fewer dollars for the child in a poorer school district may be held as denying equal protection rights.[13] It was argued that the state has no reasonable equal protection basis on which to justify making a child's education dependent on the wealth of the school district. The U.S. Supreme Court had laid the groundwork for this conclusion by previously holding that to classify persons either on the basis of poverty[14] or according to their location, homesite, or occupation is unreasonable.[15] Therefore, it was concluded, the quality of a child's education could not be contingent upon a state and local taxing and fund distribution system that is based on the property wealth of the local school district.

LITIGATION UNDER FEDERAL EQUAL PROTECTION

By 1968, several suits had been filed, each seeking to have state school finance programs rendered unconstitutional through the application of this logic.

Educators for some time had recognized that all children cannot be educated equally with equal resources. Some children with special learning deficiencies caused by cultural deprivation or mental or physical incapacities need extra funds, but dollar differences due to wealth are unjustified.

In *McInnis v. Shapiro*,[16] the plaintiffs claimed that the Illinois finance system created large variations in expenditures per student from district to district, thereby providing some students with a good education and depriving others who have equal or greater educational need. The court concluded that equal educational expenditures are not required by the Fourteenth Amendment and that variations created by taxation of property in the school districts do not discriminate:

> Unequal educational expenditures per student, based upon the variable property values and tax rates of local school districts, do not amount to an invidious discrimination. Moreover, the statutes which permit these unequal expenditures on a district to district basis are neither arbitrary nor unreasonable.[17]

The *McInnis* court declined to establish judicial standards for determining legislative allocations based on educational needs. Since *McInnis* was summarily affirmed by the U.S. Supreme

Court,[18] this statement represented precedent and had substantial impact on legal thought at that time.

The position in *McInnis* was summed by saying that there were no "discoverable and manageable standards by which a court can determine when the Constitution is satisfied and when it is violated."[19]

McInnis was closely followed by a second case in Virginia, *Burruss v. Wilkerson*.[20] Specifically, plaintiffs claimed the state formula created and perpetuated substantial disparities in educational opportunities throughout the state of Virginia and failed to relate to any of the variety of educational needs present in the several counties and cities of Virginia. In following the hands-off course of *McInnis*, the federal district court in Virginia said:

> . . . [T]he courts have neither the knowledge, nor the means, nor the power to tailor the public moneys to fit the varying needs of these students throughout the state. We can only see to it that the outlays on one group are not invidiously greater or less than that of another. No such arbitrariness is manifest here.[21]

Accordingly, *Burruss* denied relief to plaintiffs under both the "efficiency" provision of the Virginia Constitution and the equal protection clause of the Fourteenth Amendment. The U.S. Supreme Court summarily affirmed this decision.

Only a short time elapsed between *McInnis* and the now-famous decision by the California Supreme Court in *Serrano v. Priest*.[22] In *Serrano*, the court handed down a well-reasoned decision that strongly documented the establishment of a new equal protection application to school finance.

In critically analyzing the California school finance system, the court pointed out that although the basic state aid program in California tended to equalize among school districts, the total system, including state and local funds combined, created great disparities in school revenues; the system as a whole generated school revenue proportional to the wealth of the individual school. After concluding that education is a "fundamental interest" and property wealth is a "suspect classification," the court applied the "strict scrutiny" standard and found the system of finance unconstitutional.

THE *RODRIGUEZ* CASE

In a significant decision that followed *Serrano*, a federal three-judge court in Texas[23] reached the same conclusion. There it was held that plaintiffs had been denied equal protection of the law by the Texas system of financing public schools. Plaintiffs contended that the educational finance system of the state makes education a function of the local property tax base. The court observed that the school finance system of Texas erroneously assumes that the value of property in the various districts will be sufficiently equal to maintain comparable expenditures among districts. This inequality is not corrected to any substantial degree by state funds because when all state and local funds were combined to correct this unconstitutional inequality, there were still great disparities. *Rodriguez* required a standard of "fiscal neutrality," which in essence means that the quality of a child's education should not be a function of the district where the child resides but should be determined by the wealth of the state as a whole. As was the case in *Serrano*, the court maintained that fiscal neutrality required not that all educational expenditures be equal for each child but that they be wealth neutral.

The rationale and precedents of the lower courts in *Serrano* and *Rodriguez*—that a child's education could not be contingent on the wealth of the local school district—were to no avail, however; in 1973, the Supreme Court of the United States handed down a reversal of *Rodriguez*,[24] effectively terminating such state supreme court finance litigation under the equal protection clause. On rehearing *Serrano*, the California Supreme Court was forced to abandon the Fourteenth Amendment as the constitutional basis for overturning the state school aid formula and thereafter relied solely on an equal protection provision in the California Constitution.

Justice Powell, in upholding the constitutionality of the Texas method of financing its schools, maintained that education was not a "fundamental" constitutional right under the equal protection clause, as had been presumed from reading *Brown*; thus, education could not be viewed in special favor by the Court, justifying strict judicial scrutiny. In so holding, the Court reverted to the traditional judicial position of leaving such matters to the wisdom of the legislature. In this regard, Justice Powell concluded:

> Education, perhaps even more than welfare assistance, presents a myriad of "intractable economic, social and even philosophical problems." The very complexity of the problems of financing and managing a statewide public school system suggests that "there will be more than one constitutionally permissible method of solving them," and that, within the limits of rationality, "the legislature's efforts to tackle the problems" should be entitled to respect.[25]

Immediately after this decision, most, if not all, such litigation in the federal courts ceased. It was clear that any future actions, if they were to be successful in attacking methods of state school financing, would have to be pursued in reliance on state constitutional grounds rather than on the Fourteenth Amendment. Subsequent to and in accordance with the Supreme Court's decision in *Rodriguez*, the supreme courts of Michigan[26] and Arizona[27] reversed precedent and upheld the constitutionality of their own state school finance programs. The Michigan Supreme Court had previously held that the Michigan school finance system violated the equal protection provision of the state constitution,[28] but on rehearing, it found no violation of either the state or the federal equal protection clause. Similarly, the Supreme Court of Arizona, in upholding that state's method of financing schools, followed *Rodriguez* in finding that education was not a fundamental right deserving of strict judicial scrutiny.

❖ — ❖ — ❖

State School Finance System That Results in Revenue Disparities Based on Fiscal Ability of School Districts Does Not Violate the Equal Protection Clause of the Fourteenth Amendment

San Antonio Independent School District v. Rodriguez

Supreme Court of the United States, 1973.
411 U.S. 1, 93 S.Ct. 1278, rehearing denied,
411 U.S. 959, 93 S.Ct. 1919 (1973).

Mr. Justice POWELL delivered the opinion of the Court. This suit attacking the Texas system of financing public education was initiated by Mexican-American parents whose children attend the elementary and secondary schools in the Edgewood Independent School District, an urban school district in San Antonio, Texas. They brought a class action on behalf of schoolchildren throughout the State who are members of minority groups or who are poor and reside in school districts having a low property tax base. . . . The complaint was filed in the summer of 1968 and a three-judge court was impaneled in January 1969. In December 1971 the panel rendered its judgment in a *per curiam* opinion holding the Texas school finance system unconstitutional under the Equal Protection Clause of the Fourteenth Amendment. The State appealed, and we noted probable jurisdiction to consider the far-reaching constitutional questions presented. . . . For the reasons stated in this opinion, we reverse the decision of the District Court. . . .

The school district in which appellees reside, the Edgewood Independent School District, has been compared throughout this litigation with the Alamo Heights Independent School District. This comparison between the least and most affluent districts in the San Antonio area serves to illustrate the manner in which the dual system of finance operates and to indicate the extent to which substantial disparities exist despite the State's impressive progress in recent years. Edgewood is one of seven public school districts in the metropolitan area. Approximately 22,000 students are enrolled in its twenty-five elementary and secondary schools. The district is situated in the core-city sector of San Antonio in a residential neighborhood that has little commercial or industrial property. The residents are predominantly of Mexican-American descent: approximately 90 percent of the student population is Mexican-American and over 6 percent is Negro. The average assessed property value per pupil is $5,960—the lowest in the metropolitan area—and the median family income ($4,686) is also the lowest. At an equalized tax rate of $1.05 per $100 of assessed property—the highest in the metropolitan area—the district contributed $26 to the education of each child for the 1967–1968 school year above its Local Fund Assignment for the Minimum Foun-

dation Program. The Foundation Program contributed $222 per pupil for a state-local total of $248. Federal funds added another $108 for a total of $356 per pupil.

Alamo Heights is the most affluent school district in San Antonio. Its six schools, housing approximately 5,000 students, are situated in a residential community quite unlike the Edgewood District. The school population is predominantly "Anglo," having only 18 percent Mexican-Americans and less than 1 percent Negroes. The assessed property value per pupil exceeds $49,000, and the median family income is $8,001. In 1967–1968 the local tax rate of $.85 per $100 of valuation yielded $333 per pupil over and above its contribution to the Foundation Program. Coupled with the $225 provided from that Program, the district was able to supply $558 per student. Supplemented by a $36 per-pupil grant from federal sources, Alamo Heights spent $594 per pupil. . . .

Despite recent increases, substantial interdistrict disparities in school expenditures found by the District Court to prevail in San Antonio and in varying degrees throughout the State still exist. . . .

Texas virtually concedes that its historically rooted dual system of financing education could not withstand the strict judicial scrutiny that this Court has found appropriate in reviewing legislative judgments that interfere with fundamental constitutional rights or that involve suspect classifications. If, as previous decisions have indicated, strict scrutiny means that the State's system is not entitled to the usual presumption of validity, that the State rather than the complainants must carry a "heavy burden of justification," that the State must demonstrate that its educational system has been structured with "precision," and is "tailored" narrowly to serve legitimate objectives and that it has selected the "less drastic means" for effectuating its objectives, the Texas financing system and its counterpart in virtually every other State will not pass muster. The State candidly admits that "[n]o one familiar with the Texas system would contend that it has yet achieved perfection." Apart from its concession that educational financing in Texas has "defects" and "imperfections," the State defends the system's rationality with vigor and disputes the District Court's finding that it lacks a "reasonable basis."

This, then, establishes the framework for our analysis. We must decide, first, whether the Texas system of financing public education operates to the disadvantage of some suspect class or impinges upon a fundamental right explicitly or implicitly protected by the Constitution, thereby requiring strict judicial scrutiny. If so, the judgment of the District Court should be affirmed. If not, the Texas scheme must still be examined to determine whether it rationally furthers some legitimate, articulated state purpose and therefore does not constitute an invidious discrimination in violation of the Equal Protection Clause of the Fourteenth Amendment. . . .

The wealth discrimination discovered by the District Court in this case, and by several other courts that have recently struck down school-financing laws in other States, is quite unlike any of the forms of wealth discrimination heretofore reviewed by this Court. . . .

The case comes to us with no definitive description of the classifying facts or delineation of the disfavored class. Examination of the District Court's opinion and of appellees' complaint, briefs, and contentions at oral argument suggests, however, at least three ways in which the discrimination claimed here might be described. The Texas system of school financing might be regarded as discriminating (1) against "poor" persons whose incomes fall below some identifiable level of poverty or who might be characterized as functionally "indigent," or (2) against those who are relatively poorer than others, or (3) against all those who, irrespective of their personal incomes, happen to reside in relatively poorer school districts. Our task must be to ascertain whether, in fact, the Texas system has been shown to discriminate on any of these possible bases and, if so, whether the resulting classification may be regarded as suspect.

The precedents of this Court provide the proper starting point. The individuals, or groups of individuals, who constituted the class discriminated against in our prior cases shared two distinguishing characteristics: because of their impecunity they were completely unable to pay for some desired benefit, and as a consequence, they sustained an absolute deprivation of a meaningful opportunity to enjoy that benefit. . . .

Only appellees' first possible basis for describing the class disadvantaged by the Texas school-financing system—discrimination against a class of definably "poor" persons—might arguably meet the criteria established in . . . prior cases. Even a cursory examination, however, demonstrates that neither of the two distinguishing characteristics of wealth classifications can be found here. First, in support of their charge that the system discriminates against the "poor," appellees have made no effort to demonstrate that it operates to the peculiar disadvantage of any class fairly definable as indigent, or as composed of persons whose incomes are beneath any designated poverty level. Indeed, there is reason to believe that the poorest families are not necessarily clustered in the poorest property districts. A recent and exhaustive study of school districts in Connecticut concluded that "[i]t is clearly incorrect . . . to contend that the 'poor' live in 'poor' districts. . . . Thus, the major factual assumption of *Serrano*—that the educational financing system discriminates against the 'poor'—is simply false in Connecticut." Defining "poor" families as those below the Bureau of the Census "poverty level," the Connecticut study found, not surprisingly, that the poor were clustered around commercial and industrial areas—those same areas that provide the most attractive sources of property tax income for school districts. Whether a similar pattern would be discovered in Texas is not known, but there is no basis on the record in this case for assuming that the poorest people—defined by reference to any level of absolute impecunity—are concentrated in the poorest districts.

Second, neither appellees nor the District Court addressed the fact that, unlike each of the foregoing cases, lack of personal resources has not occasioned an absolute deprivation of the desired benefit. The argument here is not that the children in districts having relatively low assessable property values are receiving no public education; rather, it is that they are receiving a poorer quality education than that available to children in districts having more assessable wealth. Apart from the unsettled and disputed question whether the quality of education may be determined by the amount of money expended for it, a sufficient answer to appellees' argument is that, at least where wealth is involved, the Equal Protection Clause does not require absolute equality or precisely equal advantages. Nor indeed, in view of the infinite variables affecting the educational process, can any system assure equal quality of education except in the most relative sense. . . .

For these two reasons—the absence of any evidence that the financing system discriminates against any definable category of "poor" people or that it results in the absolute deprivation of education—the disadvantaged class is not susceptible of identification in traditional terms.

As suggested above, appellees and the District Court may have embraced a second or third approach, the second of which might be characterized as a theory of relative or comparative discrimination based on family income. Appellees sought to prove that a direct correlation exists between the wealth of families within each district and the expenditures therein for education. That is, along a continuum, the poorer the family the lower the dollar amount of education received by the family's children. . . . These questions need not be addressed in this case, however, since appellees' proof fails to support their allegations or the District Court's conclusions. . . .

This brings us, then, to the third way in which the classification scheme might be defined—*district* wealth discrimination. Since the only correlation indicated by the evidence is between district property wealth and expenditures, it may be argued that discrimination might be found without regard to the individual income characteristics of district residents. . . . Alternatively, as suggested in Mr. Justice MARSHALL's dissenting opinion, the class might be defined more restrictively to include children in districts with assessable property which falls below the statewide average, or median, or below some other artificially defined level.

However described, it is clear that appellees' suit asks this Court to extended its most exacting scrutiny to review a system that allegedly discriminates against a large, diverse, and amorphous class, unified only by the common factor of residence in districts that happen to have less taxable wealth than other districts. The system of alleged discrimination and the class it defines have none of the traditional indicia of suspectness: the class is not saddled with such disabilities, or subjected to such a history of purposeful unequal treatment, or relegated to such a position of political powerlessness as to command extraordinary protection from the majoritarian political process.

We thus conclude that the Texas system does not operate to the peculiar disadvantage of any suspect class. But in recognition of the fact that this Court has never heretofore held that wealth discrimination alone provides an adequate basis for invoking strict scrutiny, appellees have not relied solely on this contention. They also assert that the State's system impermissibly interferes with the exercise of a "fundamental" right and that accordingly the prior decisions of this Court require the application of the strict standard of judicial review. . . . It is this question—whether education is a fundamental right, in the sense that it is among the rights and liberties protected by the Constitution—which has so consumed the attention of courts and commentators in recent years. . . .

Nothing this Court holds today in any way detracts from our historical dedication to public education. We are in complete agreement with the conclusion of the three-judge panel below that "the grave significance of education both to the individual and to our society" cannot be doubted. But the importance of a service performed by the State does not determine whether it must be regarded as fundamental for purposes of examination under the Equal Protection Clause. . . . It is not the province of this Court to create substantive constitutional rights in the name of guaranteeing equal protection of the laws. Thus, the key to discovering whether education is "fundamental" is not to be found in comparisons of the relative societal significance of education as opposed to subsistence or housing. Nor is it to be found by weighing whether education is as important as the right to travel. Rather, the answer lies in assessing whether there is a right to education explicitly or implicitly guaranteed by the Constitution. . . .

Education, of course, is not among the rights afforded explicit protection under our federal Constitution. Nor do we find any basis for saying it is implicitly so protected. As we have said, the undisputed importance of education will not alone cause this Court to depart from the usual standard for reviewing a State's social and economic legislation. It is appellees' contention, however, that education is distinguishable from other services and benefits provided by the State because it bears a peculiarly close relationship to other rights and liberties accorded protection under the Constitution. Specifically, they insist that education is itself a fundamental personal right because it is essential to the effective exercise of First Amendment freedoms and to intelligent utilization of the right to vote. . . .

. . . We need not dispute any of these propositions. The Court has long afforded zealous protection against unjustifiable governmental interference with the individual's rights to speak and to vote. Yet we have never presumed to possess either the ability or the authority to guarantee to the citizenry the most *effective* speech or the most *informed* electoral choice. That these may be desirable goals of a system of freedom of expression and of a representative form of government is not to be doubted. These are indeed goals to be pursued by a people whose thoughts and beliefs are freed from governmental interference. But they are not values to be implemented by judicial intrusion into otherwise legitimate state activities.

Even if it were conceded that some identifiable quantum of education is a constitutionally protected prerequisite to the meaningful exercise of either right, we have no indication that the present levels of educational expenditures in Texas provide an education that falls short. Whatever merit appellees' argument might have if a State's financing system occasioned an absolute denial of educational opportunities to any of its children, that argument provides no basis for finding an interference with fundamental rights where only relative differences in spending levels are involved and where—as is true in the present case—no charge fairly could be made that the system fails to provide each child with an opportunity to acquire the basic minimal skills necessary for the enjoyment of the rights of speech and of full participation in the political process. . . .

It should be clear, for the reasons stated above and in accord with the prior decisions of this Court, that this is not a case in which the challenged state action must be subjected to the searching judicial scrutiny reserved for laws that create suspect classifications or impinge upon constitutionally protected rights.

We need not rest our decision, however, solely on the inappropriateness of the strict-scrutiny test. A century of Supreme Court adjudication under the Equal Protection Clause affirmatively supports the application of the traditional standard of review, which requires only that the State's system be shown to bear some rational relationship to legitimate state purposes. This case represents far more than a challenge to the manner in which Texas provides for the education of its children. We have here nothing less than a direct attack on the way in which Texas has chosen to raise and disburse state and local tax revenues. We are asked to condemn the State's judgment in conferring on political subdivisions the power to tax local property to supply revenues for local interests. In so doing, appellees would have the Court intrude in an area in which it has traditionally deferred to state legislatures. . . .

In addition to matters of fiscal policy, this case also involves the most persistent and difficult questions of educational policy, another area in which this Court's lack of specialized knowledge and experience counsels against premature interference with the informed judgments made at the state and local levels. Education, perhaps even more than welfare assistance, presents a myriad of "intractable economic, social, and even philosophical problems." . . . The very complexity of the problems of financing and managing a statewide public school system suggests that "there will be more than one constitutionally permissible method of solving them," and that, within the limits of rationality, "the legislature's efforts to tackle the problems" should be entitled to respect. . . . On even the most basic questions in this area the scholars and educational experts are divided. Indeed, one of the major sources of controversy concerns the extent to which there is a demonstrable correlation between educational expenditures and the quality of education—an assumed correlation underlying virtually every legal conclusion drawn by the District Court in this case. Related to the questioned relationship between cost and quality is the equally unsettled controversy as to the proper goals of a system of public education. And the question regarding the most effective relationship between state boards of education and local school boards, in terms of their respective responsibilities and degrees of control, is now undergoing searching reexamination. The ultimate wisdom as to these and related problems of education is not likely to be divined for all time even by the scholars who now so earnestly debate the issues. In such circumstances, the judiciary is well advised to refrain from imposing on the States inflexible constitutional restraints that could circumscribe or handicap the continued research and experimentation so vital to finding even partial solutions to educational problems and to keeping abreast of ever-changing conditions. . . .

The foregoing considerations buttress our conclusion that Texas' system of public school finance is an inappropriate candidate for strict judicial scrutiny. . . .

. . . While it is no doubt true that reliance on local property taxation for school revenues provides less freedom of choice with respect to expenditures for some districts than for others, the existence of "some inequality" in the manner in which the State's rationale is achieved is not alone a sufficient basis for striking down the entire system. . . . It may not be condemned simply because it imperfectly effectuates the State's goals. . . . Nor must the financing system fail because, as appellees suggest, other methods of satisfying the State's interest, which occasion "less drastic" disparities in expenditures, might be conceived. Only where state action impinges on the exercise of fundamental constitutional rights or liberties must it be found to have chosen the least restrictive alternative. . . . The people of Texas may be justified in believing that other systems of school financing, which place more of the financial responsibility in the hands of the State, will result in a comparable lessening of desired local autonomy. . . .

Appellees further urge that the Texas system is unconstitutionally arbitrary because it allows the availability of local taxable resources to turn on "happenstance." . . . But any scheme of local taxation—indeed the very existence of identifiable local governmental units—requires the establishment of jurisdictional boundaries that are inevitably arbitrary. It is equally inevitable that some localities are going to be blessed with more taxable assets than others. . . .

In sum, to the extent that the Texas system of school financing results in unequal expenditures between children who happen to reside in different districts, we cannot say that such disparities are the product of a system that is so irrational as to be invidiously discriminatory. . . . In its essential characteristics, the Texas plan for financing public education reflects what many educators for a half century have thought was an enlightened approach to a problem for which there is no perfect solution. . . . We hold that the Texas plan abundantly satisfies this standard.

. . . The consideration and initiation of fundamental reforms with respect to state taxation and education are matters reserved for the legislative processes of the various States, and we do no violence to the values of federalism and separation of powers by staying our hand. We hardly need add that this Court's action today is not to be viewed as placing its judicial imprimatur on the status quo. The need is apparent for reform in tax systems which may well have relied too long and too heavily on the local property tax. And certainly innovative thinking as to public education, its methods, and its funding is necessary to assure both a higher level of quality and greater uniformity of opportunity. These matters merit the continued attention of the scholars who already have contributed much by their challenges. But the ultimate solutions must come from the lawmakers and from the democratic pressures of those who elect them.

Reversed.

———————————————❖———————————————

PAPASON AND FUNDAMENTALITY

Rodriguez may not, however, be the final word by the U.S. Supreme Court on public school finance. Even though the Court's basic position has not changed, two cases rendered after *Rodriguez*, *Plyler v. Doe*[29] and *Papason v. Allain*[30] (see Chapter 6 of this text), suggest that *Rodriguez* is not a complete foreclosure of further federal litigation regarding the fundamentality of education and equity in state funding of education. In *Plyler*,[31] the Court expands on the requirements of the equal protection clause, pointing out that "all persons similarly circumstanced shall be treated alike," but it goes further to say that the state legislatures "must have substantial latitude to establish classifications that roughly approximate the nature of the problem perceived."[32] The Court in *Plyler*, applying these principles, held that the state of Texas could not deny state school funding for the education of undocumented alien children who enter Texas from Mexico. According to the Court, Texas had violated the equal protection clause by classifying alien children differently for funding purposes. In *Plyler*, the Court adhered to its *Rodriguez* precedent in reaffirming that education is not a "fundamental right" under the equal protection clause, but interestingly, and possibly significantly, it further noted that "education has a *fundamental* role in maintaining the fabric of our society."[33] A question, of course, arises as to the context and meaning of the Court's use of the term "fundamental." The Court elaborated, saying: "Public education is not a 'right' granted to individuals by the Constitution. But neither is it merely some governmental 'benefit' indistinguishable from some other forms of social welfare."[34] Such language would appear to represent a possible thoughtful retreat from the stark position taken by the Court in *Rodriguez*.

The Supreme Court's position in *Rodriguez* is further refined in *Papason v. Allain*, wherein the Court held unconstitutional a Mississippi school aid formula that distributed a relatively small amount of categorical funds in an unequal manner. In *Papason*, the Court distinguished *Rodriguez* on the narrow ground that the Mississippi fund distribution involved only state funds, where *Rodriguez* encompassed local property tax funds and it was these local funds that caused unequalized educational opportunity throughout the state. This narrow distinction would appear to be questionable in light of the plethora of federal and state case law that has clearly held that funds for education obtained from local taxation are, in fact, state funds. Virtually all precedents tell us that it matters not where the taxes are levied, collected, and deposited— their nature as a state tax remains.

Moreover, the Supreme Court in *Papason* appears to invite further discussion of the "fundamentality" question when it states that "this

Court has not yet definitively settled the questions whether a minimally adequate education is a fundamental right and whether a statute alleged to discriminatorily infringe that right should be accorded heightened equal protection review."[35] Thus, the Supreme Court's statements in both *Plyler* and *Papason* would appear to reduce the certainty and apparent adamancy of the Supreme Court's *Rodriguez* position on the fundamentality of education.

THE EMERGENCE OF THE INTERMEDIATE TEST

A further and relevant issue that could be a precursor of a possible lifting of the weight of the *Rodriguez* precedent is the fact that since *Rodriguez* in 1973, the U.S. Supreme Court has added another test in determining constitutionality under the equal protection clause. This so-called intermediate test falls somewhere between the rigid dichotomy between the rational relationship and strict scrutiny tests. This development suggests that lower federal courts may have considerably more latitude in examining state school finance litigation in the future, and, consequently, plaintiff children's complaints could possibly revive the equal protection clause as a source of constitutional challenge.

Nowak et al. explained the status of the three tests that are now applicable to interpretations of the equal protection clause. See the following for a summary of these tests.

The Rational Relationship Test. The first standard of review is the rational relationship test . . . developed for use in both equal protection and substantive due process issues in the post-1937 decisions in Court. The court will not grant any significant review of legislative decisions to classify persons in terms of general economic legislation. In this area the justices have determined that they have no unique function to perform; they have no institutional capability to assess the scope of legitimate governmental ends in these areas or the reasonableness of classifications that is in any way superior to that of the legislature. Thus, if a classification is of this type the Court will ask only whether it is conceivable that the classification bears a rational relationship to an end of government which is not prohibited by the Constitution. So long as it is arguable that the other branch of government had such a basis for creating the classification a court should not invalidate the law.

The Strict Scrutiny Test. The second type of review under the equal protection guarantee is generally referred to as "strict scrutiny." This test means that the justices will not defer to the decision of the other branches of government but will instead independently determine the degree of relationship which the classification bears to a constitutionally compelling end. . . . The Court will not accept every permissible government purpose as sufficient to support a classification under this test, but will instead require the government to show that it is pursuing a "compelling" or "overriding" end—one whose value is so great that it justifies the limitation of fundamental constitutional values.

Even if the government can demonstrate such an end, the Court will not uphold the classification unless the justices have independently reached the conclusion that the classification is necessary to promote that compelling interest. . . .

The Intermediate Test. [I]n more recent years there have appeared a number of cases in which the Court has given very little deference to legislative judgments when reviewing legislation classifications but in which the Court has not employed either the traditional rational basis or compelling interest standard. This form of independent, but not technically "strict scrutiny," review has appeared in a variety of modern cases. . . .

The standard of review of these cases eliminates the strong presumption of constitutionality that exists under the rational basis standard of review but it allows the government to employ a . . . classification so long as it is a reasonable means of achieving substantial government ends and not merely the arbitrary classifying of people. . . .

The most recent decisions demonstrate that the Court will review classifications based on illegitimacy in a meaningful way: the Court now requires that the use of such classifications be substantially related to a legitimate governmental interest. While the precise nature of this test is unclear, what is clear is that a majority of the justices now require some demonstration that the classification is not an arbitrary burden on illegitimates or their parents due to moral approbation of stereotypes. . . .

Source: Reprinted from John E. Nowak, Ronald D. Rotunda, and J. Nelson Young, *Constitutional Law* (St. Paul, Minn.: West Publishing Company, 1986), pp. 530–52, with permission of the West Publishing Corporation.

❖ — ❖ — ❖

Disparities in State Distribution of a Particular Fund May Violate Equal Protection

Papason v. Allain

Supreme Court of the United States, 1986.
478 U.S. 265, 106 S.Ct. 2932.

Justice WHITE delivered the opinion of the Court.

In this case, we consider the claims of school officials and schoolchildren in 23 northern Mississippi counties that they are being unlawfully denied the economic benefits of public school lands granted by the United States to the State of Mississippi well over 100 years ago. Specifically, we must determine to what extent these claims are barred by the Eleventh Amendment and, with respect to those claims that are not barred, if any, whether the complaint is sufficient to withstand a motion to dismiss for failure to state a claim.

The history of public school lands in the United States stretches back over 200 years. Even before the ratification of the Constitution, the Congress of the Confederation initiated a practice with regard to the Northwest Territory which was followed with most other public lands that eventually became States and were admitted to the Union. In particular, the Land Ordinance of 1785, which provided for the survey and sale of the Northwest Territory, "reserved the lot No. 16, of every township, for the maintenance of public schools within the said township. . . . " 1 *Laws of the United States* 565 (1815). . . .

In 1798, Congress created the Mississippi Territory, which included what is now about the southern third of the States of Mississippi and Alabama. . . . In 1803, Congress provided for the sale and survey of all Mississippi Territory lands to which Indian title had been extinguished but excepted "the section number sixteen, which shall be reserved in each township for the support of schools within the same." . . . In 1804, the Mississippi Territory was extended northward to the southern boundary of Tennessee. . . . Two years later, Congress authorized the selection of lands in lieu of unavailable Sixteenth Sections in the Territory. 2 Stat. 401 (1806). Eventually, in 1817, Mississippi was admitted as a State, and a further Land Sales Act provided for the survey and sale of those lands in the northern part of the new State that had not been covered by the 1803 Act. The 1817 Act provided that these lands were to be "surveyed and divided in the manner provided by law for the surveying of the other public lands of the United States in the Mississippi territory"; thus, the Act required that "the section No. 16 in each township . . . shall be reserved for the support of schools therein." . . . The Sixteenth Section lands and lands selected in lieu thereof were granted to the State of Mississippi. . . .

By their own terms, however, these Acts did not apply to the lands in northern Mississippi that were held by the Chickasaw Indian Nation, an area essentially comprising what came to be the northern 23 counties in the State. This land was held by the Chickasaws until 1832, when it was ceded to the United States by the Treaty of Pontitoc Creek. . . . Although that Treaty provided that the land would be surveyed and sold "in the same manner and on the same terms and conditions as the other public lands," . . . no Sixteenth Section lands were reserved from sale. . . . In 1836, Congress attempted to remedy this oversight by providing for the reservation of lands in lieu of the Sixteenth Section lands and for the vesting of the title to these lands "in the State of Mississippi, for the use of schools within [the Chickasaw Cession] in said State." . . . These Chickasaw Cession Lieu Lands, some 174,555 acres, . . . were selected and given to the State. In 1856, however, with authority expressly given by Congress, 10 Stat. 6 (1852), the state legislature sold these lands and invested the proceeds, approximately $1,047,300, . . . in 8% loans to the State's railroads. 1856 Miss. Laws, ch 56. These railroads and the State's investment in them, unfortunately, were subsequently destroyed during the Civil War and never replaced. . . .

Thus, the State has delegated the management of this property to local school boards throughout the State: Where Sixteenth Section lands lie within a school district or where Lieu Lands were originally appropriated for a township that lies within a school district, the board of education of that district has "control and jurisdiction of said school trust lands and of all funds arising from any disposition thereof heretofore and hereafter made." . . . In this respect, the board of education is "under the general supervision of the state land commissioner." Further, the State has, by statute, set forth certain prescriptions for the management of these lands. . . . Most important for purposes of this case is Miss. Code Ann. §29-3-109 (Supp. 1985), which provides:

> All expendable funds derived from sixteenth section or lieu lands shall be credited to the school districts of the township in which such sixteenth section lands may be located, or to which any sixteenth sections lieu lands may belong. Such funds shall not be expended except for the purpose of education of the educable children of the school district to which they belong, or as otherwise may be provided by law.

Consequently, all proceeds from Sixteenth Section and Lieu Lands are allocated directly to the specific township in which these lands are located or to which those lands apply. With respect to the Chickasaw Cession counties, to which no lands now belong, the state legislature has for over 100 years paid "interest" on the lost principal acquired from the sale of those lands in the form of annual appropriations to the Chickasaw Cession schools. Originally, the rate was 8%, but since 1890 the rate has been 6%. See Miss. Const., Art. 8, §212. The annual amount until 1985 was $62,191. . . .

The result of this dual treatment has for many years been a disparity in the level of school funds from Sixteenth Section lands that are available to the Chickasaw Cession schools as compared to the schools in the remainder of the State. In 1984, for example, the legislative appropriation for the Chickasaw Cession resulted in an estimated average per pupil income relative to the Sixteenth Section substitute appropriation of $0.63 per pupil. The average Sixteenth Section income in the rest of the State, in comparison, was estimated to be $75.34 per pupil. . . . It is this disparity which gave rise to the present action.

In 1981, the petitioners, local school officials and schoolchildren from the Chickasaw Cession, filed suit in the United States District Court for the Northern District of Mississippi against the respondents, an assortment of state officials, challenging the disparity in Sixteenth Section funds. . . .

Based on these allegations, the petitioners sought various forms of relief for breach of the trust regarding the Chickasaw Cession Sixteenth Section lands and for denial of equal protection. . . .

In *Rodriguez*, the Court upheld against an equal protection challenge Texas' system of financing its public schools, under which funds for the public schools were derived from two main sources. Approximately half of the funds came from the Texas Minimum Foundation School Program, a state program aimed at guaranteeing a certain level of minimum education for all children in the State. . . . Most of the remainder of the funds came from local sources—in particular local property taxes. . . . As a result of this dual funding system, most specifically as a result of differences in amounts collected from local property taxes, "substantial interdistrict disparities in school expenditures [were] found . . . in varying degrees throughout the State." . . .

In examining the equal protection status of these disparities, the Court declined to apply any heightened scrutiny based either on wealth as a suspect classification or on education as a fundamental right. As to the latter, the Court recognized the importance of public education but noted that education "is not among the rights afforded explicit protection under our Federal Constitution." . . . The Court did not, however, foreclose the possibility "that some identifiable quantum of education is a constitutionally protected prerequisite to the meaningful exercise of either [the right to speak or the right to vote]." . . . Given the absence of such radical denial of educational opportunity, it was concluded that the State's school financing scheme would be constitutional if it bore "some rational relationship to a legitimate state purpose." . . .

Almost 10 years later, the Court again considered the equal protection status of the administration of the Texas public schools—this time in relation to the State's decision not to expend any state funds on the education of children who were not "legally admitted" to the United States. *Plyler v. Doe*, 457 U.S. 202, 72

L.Ed.2d 786, 102 S.Ct. 2382 (1982). The Court did not, however, measurably change the approach articulated in *Rodriguez*. It reiterated that education is not a fundamental right and concluded that undocumented aliens were not a suspect class. . . . Nevertheless, it concluded that the justifications for the discrimination offered by the State were "wholly insubstantial in light of the costs involved to these children, the State, and the Nation." . . .

The complaint in this case asserted not simply that the petitioners had been denied their right to a minimally adequate education but also that such a right was fundamental and that because that right had been infringed the State's action here should be reviewed under strict scrutiny. . . . As *Rodriguez* and *Plyler* indicate, this Court has not yet definitively settled the questions whether a minimally adequate education is a fundamental right and whether a statute alleged to discriminatorily infringe that right should be accorded heightened equal protection review. . . .

The petitioners do not allege that schoolchildren in the Chickasaw Counties are not taught to read or write; they do not allege that they receive no instruction on even the educational basics; they allege no actual facts in support of their assertion that they have been deprived of a minimally adequate education. As we see it, we are not bound to credit and may disregard the allegation that the petitioners have been denied a minimally adequate education.

Concentrating instead on the disparities in terms of Sixteenth Section Lands benefits that the complaint in fact alleged and that are documented in the public record, we are persuaded that the Court of Appeals properly determined that *Rodriguez* dictates the applicable standard of review. The differential treatment alleged here constitutes an equal protection violation only if it is not rationally related to a legitimate state interest. . . .

. . . As we read their complaint, the petitioners do not challenge the overall organization of the Mississippi public school financing program. Instead, their challenge is restricted to one aspect of that program: The Sixteenth Section and Lieu Lands funding. All of the allegations in the complaint center around disparities in the distribution of these particular benefits, and no allegations concerning disparities in other public school funding programs are included.

Consequently, this is a very different claim than the claim made in *Rodriguez*. In *Rodriguez*, the contention was that the State's overall system of funding was unconstitutionally discriminatory. There, the Court examined the basic structure of that system and concluded that it was rationally related to a legitimate state purpose. In reaching that conclusion, the Court necessarily found that funding disparities resulting from differences in local taxes were acceptable because related to the state goal of allowing a measure of effective local control over school funding levels. *Rodriguez* did not, however, purport to validate all funding variations that might result from a State's public school funding decisions. It held merely that the variations that resulted from allowing local control over local property tax funding of the public schools were constitutionally permissible in that case.

Here, the petitioners' claim goes neither to the overall funding system nor to the local ad valorem component of that system. Instead, it goes solely to the Sixteenth Section and Lieu Lands portion of the State's public school funding. And, as to this claim, we are unpersuaded that *Rodriguez* resolves the equal protection question in favor of the State. The allegations of the complaint are that the State is distributing the income from Sixteenth Section lands or from lieu lands or funds unequally among the school districts, to the detriment of the Chickasaw Cession schools and their students. The Sixteenth Section and Lieu Lands in Mississippi were granted to and held by the State itself. Under state law, these lands "constitute property held in trust for the benefit of the public schools and must be treated as such," . . . but in carrying out the trust, the State has vested the management of these lands in the local school boards throughout the State, under the supervision of the Secretary of State, and has credited the income from these lands to the "school districts of the township in which such sixteenth section lands may be located, or to which any sixteenth section lieu lands may belong," such income to be used for the purpose of educating the children of the school district or as otherwise may be provided by law. . . . This case is therefore very different from *Rodriguez*, where the differential financing available to school districts was traceable to school district funds available from local real estate taxation, not to a state decision to divide state resources unequally among school districts. The rationality of the disparity in *Rodriguez*, therefore, which rested on the fact that funding disparities based on differing local wealth were a necessary adjunct of allowing meaningful local control over school funding, does not settle the constitutionality of disparities alleged in this case, and we differ with the Court of Appeals in this respect.

. . . Neither the Court of Appeals nor the parties have addressed the equal protection issue as we think it is posed by this case: Given that the State has title to assets granted to it by the Federal Government for the use of the State's schools, does the Equal Protection Clause permit it to distribute the benefit of these assets unequally among the school districts as it now does?

A crucial consideration in resolving this issue is whether the federal law requires the State to allocate the economic benefits of school lands to schools in the townships in which those lands are located. If, as a matter of federal law, the State has no choice in the matter, whether the complaint states an equal protection claim depends on whether the federal policy is itself violative of the Clause. If it is, the State may properly be enjoined from implementing such policy. Contrariwise, if the federal law is valid and the State is bound by it, then it provides a rational reason for the funding disparity. Neither the courts below nor the parties have addressed the equal protection issue in these terms. Another possible consideration in resolving the equal protection issue is that school lands require management and that the State has assigned this task to the individual districts in which the lands are located, subject to supervision by the State. The significance, if any, in equal protection terms of this allocation of duties in justifying assigning the income exclusively to those who perform the management function and none of it to those districts that have no lands to manage is a matter that is best addressed by the lower courts in the first instance.

Accordingly, the judgment of the Court of Appeals is affirmed insofar as it affirmed the dismissal of petitioners' breach of trust and related claims. With respect to the affirmance of the District Court's dismissal of the equal protection claim, the judgment of the Court of Appeals is vacated, and the case is remanded to that court for further proceedings consistent with this opinion.

So ordered.

■ LITIGATION UNDER STATE CONSTITUTIONS

Litigation in the realm of state school aid distribution has returned to state courts, and since *Rodriguez,* the actions now test state formulas in light of only state constitutional provisions. Bases for such litigation may be found in equal protection, uniformity, equality, thorough and efficient, or other provisions of state constitutions. *Rodriguez* continues, though, to have substantial influence in shaping state courts' views of their own constitutions. In a Louisiana case,[36] the U.S. Court of Appeals, Fifth Circuit held that the method of school financing in that state did not differ significantly from that of Texas (litigated in *Rodriguez*) and that, as such, it was not unconstitutionally discriminatory against the poor people in poor school districts. The Supreme Court of Idaho held, in a three-to-two decision, that the education finance law of that state did not violate the "uniform system" requirement of that state's constitution.[37] In so doing, the court refused to recognize education as a "fundamental interest" under the Idaho Constitution and, in the same vein, turned back the plaintiff's equal protection claim. Decisions in Illinois,[38] Kansas,[39] Montana,[40] Oregon,[41] New York,[42] and Georgia[43] have likewise denied relief to plaintiffs where challenges to the school finance law were predicated on state constitutional provisions. The Oregon Supreme Court observed that it could interpret the equal protection clause of the Oregon Constitution more broadly than the Supreme Court interpreted the federal Constitution in *Rodriguez,* but it declined to do so. The court refused to acknowledge that education was a fundamental right, and the fact that education was mentioned in the Oregon Constitution was not sufficient to establish its fundamentality. Further, the court found that the word "uniform" in the constitution required

the legislature merely to provide a minimum program of educational opportunity throughout the state. Complete uniformity, the court decided, would infringe on the state's reasonable objective to maintain local control of education.

In an important case that departed from the influence of *Rodriguez,* the New Jersey Supreme Court in *Robinson v. Cahill* relied on the state's "thorough and efficient" clause to invalidate the state school aid formula.[44] This court made it clear that the state had an obligation to correct the fiscal imbalances created by local school district organization and fiscal ability variations. It further found that the "thorough and efficient" standard required equal educational opportunity and that if local government failed to so provide, then the state must act either to compel local districts to meet the constitutional mandate or to meet the obligation itself. In broadly defining the "thorough and efficient" standard, the court said:

> The Constitution's guarantee must be understood to embrace that educational opportunity which is needed in the contemporary setting to equip a child for his role as a citizen and as a competitor in the labor market.[45]

Because of the variation in the education provisions of state constitutions and the diversity in state school finance formulas, one can expect little consistency in state court views on school finance equalization. While several courts have declined to intervene in school finance issues, others, as in *Robinson,* have held that methods of financing the schools are unconstitutional.

In Connecticut, the court held the equal protection provision of the state constitution was violated by the state educational finance formula, which allocated money to local school districts on a flat grant basis, not taking into consideration the fiscal ability of local school districts.[46] The court reasoned that, under the Connecticut Constitution, education was a fundamental right because it was explicitly recognized in Article VIII, §I and the history and tradition of the state demonstrated a commitment to the education of children. In holding the system unconstitutional and mandating that the legislature redress the faults, the court observed that absolute equality was not required and cost differences due to variations in educational needs and economic conditions may be taken into account.

In 1983, the Supreme Court of Arkansas held that state's system of financing public schools unconstitutional. The court noted that minimal education programs are not enough to satisfy the equal opportunity demanded by equal protection. It said that "bare and minimal sufficiency does not translate into equal educational opportunity."[47] Today, the state cases are about evenly split in finding against the plaintiff children[48] and the defendant states.[49] Franklin and Hickrod[50] observe that the split in the views of the state courts is primarily due to whether the courts believe education is a fundamental right for equal protection purposes and apparently does not depend on the wording of the education clauses. Where the courts are influenced by *Rodriguez* in the interpretation of the equal protection clause, the defendant state will most likely prevail. Where the state courts go beyond the *Rodriguez* equal protection interpretation and rule that state equal protection is broader and more encompassing than the federal version, plaintiff poor school districts are most likely to prevail. This latter approach was followed in *Serrano I*,[51] wherein the California Supreme Court refused to restrict the meaning of the equal protection clause of the California Constitution to the more narrow definition imposed by *Rodriguez*.

FUTURE DIRECTIONS OF STATE LITIGATION

In states where plaintiffs have prevailed and state school finance programs have been held unconstitutional, the courts have put slightly different twists on their reasoning, suggesting directions of future litigation. First, the *Serrano II*[52] type of rationale may be employed by the court, holding that education is a fundamental right and that malapportionment of school funds violates the state equal protection clause. Second, alternatively, the state school finance program may be held invalid under the *Robinson v. Cahill* type of reasoning, which relies solely on the education provision of the state constitution without invoking equal protection.[53] In this regard, the Supreme Court of Ohio in *DeRolph v. State*[54] found it unnecessary to address the fundamentality issue of equal protection in holding

the state's method of funding the public schools of Ohio unconstitutional. As in *Robinson*, the Ohio court found that the education provision of the Ohio Constitution requiring a "thorough and efficient" system of education was sufficient constitutional basis to invalidate an inadequate and inequitable state funding formula. Third, a state court may hold, as did the court in *Pauley v. Kelly*, that the education provision of the state constitution is sufficient to establish fundamentality of education and that the two provisions (the education clause and the equal protection clause) work in concert to require strict judicial scrutiny of state school finance legislation.[55] In *Pauley*, the court viewed the state equal protection clause and the education provision as being "harmonious" with and complementary to one another. Fourth, the state court may hold that the education provision alone—whether the wording is "equal," "uniform," "efficient," or "thorough and efficient"—by its inclusion in the state constitution establishes the fundamentality of education and thereby implicitly justifies more intensive judicial oversight of legislative discretion.[56]

Regardless of the rationale, though, a trend has developed for state courts to be less deferential to the state legislatures in matters pertaining to education. In particular, the school finance cases in Kentucky,[57] New Jersey,[58] and Texas[59] suggest a much more active role to be played by the state courts in interpreting the intent of education provisions of state constitutions.[60]

FUNDAMENTALITY AND STATE CONSTITUTIONS

Government could not function effectively if it were not permitted to classify persons for various reasons to alleviate problems, bestow benefits, or, in some cases, impose detriments. Government, however, cannot classify and create distinctions for illegitimate or discriminatory purposes. Some distinctions may be unimportant, while others may strike at the basic fabric of society and offend individuals and the common good of the state. Governmental discrimination is not in and of itself violative of equal protection unless the distinctions drawn affect "fundamental interests" and "suspect" classifications of people. Equal protection forbids only unreasonable discrimination or harmful and invidious discrimination.

One court explained the matter of equal protection in this way:

> There are a number of reasons why the Equal Protection Clause has not historically been thought to require that all legislation be applied equally to all citizens. First, government must be able to draw reasonable distinctions among its citizens in awarding benefits and imposing burdens. Second, there is the traditional deference of courts to the Legislature's expression of the will of the people. Third, any strictly egalitarian view of the Equal Protection Clause could not be justified historically in terms of the intention of those who drafted and ratified it. Fourth, "equality" is itself such an ephemeral concept that judicial review on an abstract "equality" standard is bound to be unmanageable.[61]

If disparate allocation of governmental benefits can be justified on a basis of reasonable classification or if the interests involved are not fundamental, then statutes will be regarded as constitutional. On the other hand, if a statute divides persons into suspect classes and if the benefits and detriments affect a fundamental interest, then the statute may be unconstitutional. On the other hand, if no fundamental interest is at stake, the effects of the disparity are by definition constitutionally inconsequential, and equal protection is not implicated.

In *Rodriguez*,[62] discussed above, the U.S. Supreme Court held that education is not a fundamental right and disparate allocation of resources among school districts does not discriminate against any particular "suspect classification" of children. The court in *Rodriguez* basically ruled that a state legislature can heap benefits on some wealthy school districts and deprive others of fiscal resources and not offend the federal equal protection clause.

Contrarily, the California Supreme Court has held that the equal protection clause of a state's constitution cannot be confined to the scope of federal equal protection but can exceed it in breadth in application to state legislation.[63] In this regard, the *Serrano* court said:

> . . . [O]ur state equal protection provisions, while substantially equivalent of the guarantees contained in the Fourteenth Amendment to the United States Constitution, are possessed of an independent vitality which, in a given case, may de-

mand an analysis different from that which would obtain if only the federal standard were applicable.

Based on this "independent vitality," the California Supreme Court found that wealth differentials among school districts involve a suspect classification; it further found that the benefits and detriments bestowed on these suspect classes are highly significant because they affect a fundamental interest, education. Accordingly, the court elevated the judicial test from "rational relationship" to "strict scrutiny" and found the California state system of school finance to be constitutionally deficient.[64]

Even though the Supreme Court of Connecticut found an "independent vitality" in its own constitution as well, the court determined that sole reliance on equal protection was not necessary because that state's education provision (Article VIII, §1) establishes education as a "fundamental right."[65]

The reasoning of the Connecticut court was basically similar to that of the West Virginia Supreme Court in *Pauley*, where the state equal protection clause and the education provision were adjudged to be complementary and harmonious, requiring a strict scrutiny analysis of state school finance statutes.[66]

Several other state supreme courts, however, have not extended their own state equal protection clauses beyond the rationale of *Rodriguez*. For example, the Supreme Court of Georgia has found that education is not a fundamental right in that state, concluding, "[W]e hold that education, per se, is not a 'fundamental right' and that the Georgia public school system must stand if it satisfies the 'rational relationship' test."[67] Accordingly, this court found that the Georgia school finance system was not unconstitutional.

State court precedent is divided as to whether education is a fundamental right for equal protection purposes.[68] More recently though, the supreme courts of Kentucky[69] and Texas[70] have found it unnecessary to examine the "vitality" of their state equal protection clauses in order to declare that education is a fundamental interest. These state courts have refused to be drawn into the technicalities of the federal judicial review tests of equal protection in interpreting their own constitutions. Rather, they have concluded that the inherent importance of education to the republican form of government and the historical antecedents to the education provisions of their respective state constitutions provide ample evidence of the fundamentality of education. Both the Kentucky and Texas courts have seemed to imply that education is fundamental because it could arguably be defended as a natural right[71] or as an aspect of natural justice, in the same context as liberty and property.[72] In this regard, the Kentucky court cited constitutional debates where it was strongly maintained that "public schools . . . are a part and parcel of our free institutions, woven into the very web and woof of popular government,"[73] and the Texas court quoted favorably from its own constitutional convention record, which declared that "[education] must be classed among the abstract rights, based on apparent natural justice."[74]

The Supreme Court of Montana also found it unnecessary to deal with the equal protection issue because it had already found that education is a fundamental right, as evidenced by its inclusion in the education provision (Article X, §1) of the Montana Constitution.[75]

There thus appears to be a trend for the state courts to evaluate the constitutionality of state school finance programs in light of the state constitution's education provisions rather than on the basis of the equal protection clauses. Their presumption is that where a state constitution specifically requires the state legislature to provide for education, there is good reason to assume that the framers of the state constitution viewed education as a fundamental right.

———————— ❖ — ❖ — ❖ ————————

State Financing System That Causes Wide Disparities in Revenue among Local School Districts Violates "Efficient" Provision of Education Clause of Texas Constitution

Edgewood Independent School District v. Kirby

Supreme Court of Texas, 1989.
777 S.W.2d. 391.

MAUZY, Justice. At issue is the constitutionality of the Texas system for financing the education of public school children. Edgewood Independent School District, sixty-seven other school districts, and numerous individual school children and parents filed suit seeking a declaration that the Texas school financing system violates the Texas Constitution. . . .

The basic facts of this cause are not in dispute. The only question is whether those facts describe a public school financing system that meets the requirements of the Constitution. As summarized and excerpted, the facts are as follows.

There are approximately three million public school children in Texas. The legislature finances the education of these children through a combination of revenues supplied by the state itself and revenues supplied by local school districts which are governmental subdivisions of the state. Of total education costs, the state provides about forty-two percent, school districts provide about fifty percent, and the remainder comes from various other sources including federal funds. School districts derive revenues from local ad valorem property taxes, and the state raises funds from a variety of sources including the sales tax and various severance and excise taxes.

There are glaring disparities in the abilities of the various school districts to raise revenues from property taxes because taxable property wealth varies greatly from district to district. The wealthiest district has over $14,000,000 of property wealth per student, while the poorest has approximately $20,000; this disparity reflects a 700 to 1 ratio. The 300,000 students in the lowest-wealth schools have less than 3% of the state's property wealth to support their education while the 300,000 students in the highest-wealth schools have over 25% of the state's property wealth; thus the 300,000 students in the wealthiest districts have more than eight times the property value to support their education as the 300,000 students in the poorest districts. The average property wealth in the 100 wealthiest districts is more than twenty times greater than the average property wealth in the 100 poorest districts. Edgewood I.S.D. has $38,854 in property wealth per student; Alamo Heights I.S.D., in the same county, has $570,109 in property wealth per student.

The state has tried for many years to lessen the disparities through various efforts to supplement the poorer districts. Through the Foundation School Program, the state currently attempts to ensure that each district has sufficient funds to provide its students with at least a basic education. . . . Under this program, state aid is distributed to the various districts according to a complex formula such that property-poor districts receive more state aid than do property-rich districts. However, the Foundation School Program does not cover even the cost of meeting the state-mandated minimum requirements. Most importantly, there are no Foundation School Program allotments for school facilities or for debt service. The basic allotment and the transportation allotment understate actual costs, and the career ladder salary supplement for teachers is underfunded. For these reasons and more, almost all school districts spend additional local funds. Low-wealth districts use a significantly greater proportion of their local funds to pay the debt service on construction bonds while high-wealth districts are able to use their funds to pay for a wide array of enrichment programs.

Because of the disparities in district property wealth, spending per student varies widely, ranging from $2,112 to $19,333. Under the existing system, an average of $2,000 more per year is spent on each of the 150,000 students in the wealthiest districts than is spent on the 150,000 students in the poorest districts.

The lower expenditures in the property-poor districts are not the result of lack of tax effort. Generally, the property-rich districts can tax low and spend high while the property-poor districts must tax high merely to spend low. . . .

Property-poor districts are trapped in a cycle of poverty from which there is no opportunity to free themselves. Because of their inadequate tax base, they must tax at significantly higher rates in order to meet minimum requirements for accreditation; yet their educational programs are typically inferior. The location of new industry and development is strongly influenced by tax rates and the quality of local schools. Thus, the property-poor districts with their high tax rates and inferior schools are unable to attract new industry or development and so have little opportunity to improve their tax base.

The amount of money spent on a student's education has a real and meaningful impact on the educational opportunity offered that student. High-wealth districts are able to provide for their students broader educational experiences including more extensive curricula, more up-to-date technological equipment, better libraries and library personnel, teacher aides, counseling services, lower student-teacher ratios, better facilities, parental involvement programs, and drop-out prevention programs. They are also better able to attract and retain experienced teachers and administrators.

The differences in the quality of educational programs offered are dramatic. For example, San Elizario I.S.D. offers no foreign language, no pre-kindergarten program, no chemistry, no physics, no calculus, and no college preparatory or honors program. It also offers virtually no extracurricular activities such as band, debate, or football. At the time of trial, one-third of Texas school districts did not even meet the state-mandated standards for maximum class size. The great majority of these are low-wealth districts. In many instances, wealthy and poor districts are found contiguous to one another within the same county.

Based on these facts, the trial court concluded that the school financing system violates the Texas Constitution's equal rights guarantee of article I, section 3, the due course of law guarantee of article I, section 19, and the "efficiency" mandate of article VII, section 1. The court of appeals reversed. We reverse the judgment of the court of appeals and, with modification, affirm the judgment of the trial court.

Article VII, section 1 of the Texas Constitution provides:

> A general diffusion of knowledge being essential to the preservation of the liberties and rights of the people, it shall be the duty of the Legislature of the State to establish and make suitable provision for the support and maintenance of an efficient system of public free schools.

The court of appeals declined to address petitioners' challenge under this provision and concluded instead that its interpretation was a "political question." Said the court:

> That provision does, of course, require that the school system be "efficient," but the provision pro-

vides no guidance as to how this or any other court may arrive at a determination of what is efficient or inefficient. Given the enormous complexity of a school system educating three million children, this Court concludes that which is, or is not, "efficient" is essentially a political question not suitable for judicial review.

We disagree. This is not an area in which the Constitution vests exclusive discretion in the legislature; rather the language of article VII, section 1 imposes on the legislature an affirmative duty to establish and provide for the public free schools. This duty is not committed unconditionally to the legislature's discretion, but instead is accompanied by standards. By express constitutional mandate, the legislature must make "suitable" provision for an "efficient" system for the "essential" purpose of a "general diffusion of knowledge." While these are admittedly not precise terms, they do provide a standard by which this court must, when called upon to do so, measure the constitutionality of the legislature's actions. . . . We do not undertake this responsibility lightly and we begin with a presumption of constitutionality. . . . If the system is not "efficient" or not "suitable," the legislature has not discharged its constitutional duty and it is *our* duty to say so.

The Texas Constitution derives its force from the people of Texas. This is the fundamental law under which the people of this state have consented to be governed. In construing the language of article VII, section 1, we consider "the intent of the people who adopted it." . . .

The State argues that, as used in article VII, section 1, the word "efficient" was intended to suggest a simple and inexpensive system. Under the Reconstruction Constitution of 1869, the people had been subjected to a militaristic school system with the state exercising absolute authority over the training of children. . . . Thus, the State contends that delegates to the 1875 Constitutional Convention deliberately inserted into this provision the word "efficient" in order to prevent the establishment of another Reconstruction-style, highly centralized school system.

While there is some evidence that many delegates wanted an economical school system, there is no persuasive evidence that the delegates used the term "efficient" to achieve that end. . . . It must be recognized that the Constitution requires an "efficient," not an "economical," "inexpensive," or "cheap" system. The language of the Constitution must be presumed to have been carefully selected. . . . The framers used the term "economical" elsewhere and could have done so here had they so intended.

There is no reason to think that "efficient" meant anything different in 1875 from what it now means. "Efficient" conveys the meaning of effective or productive of results and connotes the use of resources so as to produce results with little waste; this meaning does not appear to have changed over time. . . . One dictionary used by the framers defined efficient as follows:

> Causing effects; producing results; actively operative; not inactive, slack or incapable; characterized by energetic and useful activity. . . .

N. Webster, *An American Dictionary of the English Language* 430 (1864). In 1890, this court described "efficient" machinery as being "such as is capable of well producing the effect intended to be secured by the use of it for the purpose for which it was made." . . .

Considering "the general spirit of the times and the prevailing sentiments of the people," it is apparent from the historical record that those who drafted and ratified article VII, section 1 never contemplated the possibility that such gross inequalities could exist within an "efficient" system. . . .

We conclude that, in mandating "efficiency," the constitutional framers and ratifiers did not intend a system with such vast disparities as now exist. Instead, they stated clearly that the purpose of an efficient system was to provide for a "*general* diffusion of knowledge." (Emphasis added.) The present system, by contrast, provides not for a diffusion that is general, but for one that is limited and unbalanced. The resultant inequalities are thus directly contrary to the constitutional vision of efficiency. . . .

By statutory directives, the legislature has attempted through the years to reduce disparities and improve the system. There have been good faith efforts on the part of many public officials, and some progress has been made. However, as the undisputed facts of this case make painfully clear, the reality is that the constitutional mandate has not been met.

The legislature's recent efforts have focused primarily on increasing the state's contributions. More money allocated under the present system would reduce some of the existing disparities between districts but would at best only postpone the reform that is necessary to make the system efficient. A band-aid will not suffice; the system itself must be changed.

We hold that the state's school financing system is neither financially efficient nor efficient in the sense of providing for a "general diffusion of knowledge" statewide, and therefore that it violates article VII, section 1 of the Texas Constitution. Efficiency does not require a per capita distribution, but it also does not allow concentrations of resources in property-rich school districts that are taxing low when property-poor districts that are taxing high cannot generate sufficient revenues to meet even minimum standards. There must be a direct and close correlation between a district's tax effort and the educational resources available to it; in other words, districts must have substantially equal access to similar revenues per pupil at similar levels of tax effort. Children who live in poor districts and children who live in rich districts must be afforded a substantially equal opportunity to have access to educational funds. Certainly, this much is required if the state is to educate its populace efficiently and provide for a general diffusion of knowledge statewide.

Under article VII, section 1, the obligation is the legislature's to provide for an efficient system. In setting appropriations, the legislature must establish priorities according to constitutional mandate; equalizing educational opportunity cannot be relegated to an "if funds are left over" basis. We recognize that there are and always will be strong public interests competing for available state funds. However, the legislature's responsibility to support public education is different because it is constitutionally imposed. Whether the legislature acts directly or enlists local government to help meet its obligation, the end product must still be what the constitution commands—i.e., an efficient system of public free schools throughout the state. . . . This

does not mean that the state may not recognize differences in area costs or in costs associated with providing an equalized educational opportunity to atypical students or disadvantaged students. Nor does it mean that local communities would be precluded from supplementing an efficient system established by the legislature; however, any local enrichment must derive solely from local tax effort.

Some have argued that reform in school finance will eliminate local control, but this argument has no merit. An efficient system does not preclude the ability of communities to exercise local control over the education of their children. It requires only that the funds available for education be distributed equitably and evenly. An efficient system will actually allow for more local control, not less. It will provide property-poor districts with economic alternatives that are not now available to them. Only if alternatives are indeed available can a community exercise the control of making choices.

Our decision today is not without precedent. Courts in nine other states with similar school financing systems have ruled those systems to be unconstitutional for varying reasons. . . .

Although we have ruled the school financing system to be unconstitutional, we do not now instruct the legislature as to the specifics of the legislation it should enact; nor do we order it to raise taxes. The legislature has primary responsibility to decide how best to achieve an efficient system. We decide only the nature of the constitutional mandate and whether that mandate has been met. Because we hold that the mandate of efficiency has not been met, we reverse the judgment of the court of appeals. The legislature is duty-bound to provide for an efficient system of education, and only if the legislature fulfills that duty can we launch this great state into a strong economic future with educational opportunity for all.

Because of the enormity of the task now facing the legislature and because we want to avoid any sudden disruption in the educational processes, we modify the trial court's judgment so as to stay the effect of its injunction until May 1, 1990. However, let there be no misunderstanding. A remedy is long overdue. The legislature must take immediate action. We reverse the judgment of the court of appeals and affirm the trial court's judgment as modified.

CASE NOTES

1. In subsequent legal action in Texas following *Edgewood Independent School District v. Kirby*, the Supreme Court of Texas in *Edgewood Independent School District v. Meno*, 917 S.W.2d 717 (Tex.1995), held that the term "efficiency" in the Texas Constitution is not synonymous with equity at all levels of funding, meaning that unequalized supplementation of revenues from local tax sources is not constitutionally prohibited. The court concluded that a systemic gap of $600 per weighted student at a given tax rate between poorer and more affluent school districts did not render the school financing legislation inefficient in violation of the Texas Constitution.

2. *The Perpetual New Jersey School Finance Litigation.* New Jersey has experienced the longest-running production in the theatre of school finance litigation, dating back to 1970. The first round of this generational struggle commenced in 1970, when students in poor urban school districts brought suit to enforce the New Jersey Constitution's educational guarantee. *Robinson v. Cahill*, 118 N.J.Super. 223, 287 A.2d 187 (Law Div.1972). In successive decisions, this court found that the system of public school funding then in place was unconstitutional. See *Robinson v. Cahill*, 62 N.J. 473, 303 A.2d 273 (1973); *Robinson v. Cahill*, 63 N.J. 196, 306 A.2d 65, cert. denied, 414 U.S. 976, 94 S.Ct. 292 (1973); *Robinson v. Cahill*, 67 N.J. 35, 335 A.2d 6 (1975); *Robinson v. Cahill*, 69 N.J. 133, 351 A.2d 713, cert. denied, 423 U.S. 913, 96 S.Ct. 217 (1975). The legislature responded by enacting the Public School Education Act of 1975 (c. 212, L. 1975, N.J.S.A. 18A:7A-1 et. seq.), which the New Jersey Supreme Court found to be facially constitutional. *Robinson v. Cahill*, 69 N.J. 449, 355 A.2d 129 (1976); *Robinson v. Cahill*, 70 N.J. 155, 358 A.2d 457 (1976); *Robinson v. Cahill*, 70 N.J. 464, 360 A.2d 400 (1976).

The second round of the struggle commenced in 1981, when public school students from Camden, East Orange, Irvington, and Jersey City challenged the constitutionality of the 1975 act as applied. In *Abbott v. Burke*, 119 N.J. 287, 575 A.2d 359 (1990) (*Abbott II*), as a remedial measure the court ordered that the 1975 act be amended or new legislation be passed to ensure substantial equality in funding between the special needs districts (SNDs) and the property-rich districts. The court required that the level of funding "be adequate to provide for the special needs of these poorer urban districts" and "address their extreme disadvantages." The court also determined that special programs and services were required in the SNDs.

The legislature then enacted the Quality Education Act of 1990. The court, in 1994, found that statute unconstitutional as applied to the SNDs because it failed to ensure parity of educational spending. *Abbott v. Burke*, 136 N.J. 444, 451, 643 A.2d 575 (1994) (*Abbott III*). The court reiterated its conclusion from *Abbott II* that achievement of educational success in the SNDs would not occur until such supplemental programs and services were identified and implemented.

In response to *Abbott III*, the legislature, in 1996, passed the Comprehensive Educational Improvement and Financing Act (CEIFA). Plaintiffs challenged the new legislation. The court found CEIFA to be facially constitutional in its adoption of substantive standards, referred to as "Core Curriculum Content Standards" (CCCS), that served to define a thorough and efficient education. *Abbott v. Burke* IV, 149 N.J. 145 at 168, 693 A.2d 417 at 428 (*Abbott IV*). However, the Court found CEIFA to be unconstitutional as applied to the SNDs because the statute failed to guarantee sufficient funds to enable students in those districts to achieve the requisite academic standards. Too, the Demonstrably Effective Program Aid (DEPA) and Early Childhood Program Aid (ECPA) were not based on a study of the students' actual needs or the costs of meeting those needs; and because the statute failed to address the facilities problems of the SNDs, this part of the law was unconstitutional.

In the latest scene, *Abbott V*, the Supreme Court of New Jersey found the funding system to be constitutional on its face, but again unconstitutional as it applied to SNDs. The court then mandated a series of measures to address the funding needs of these SNDs. See *Abbott v. Burke*, 153 N.J. 480, 710 A.2d 450 (1998) (*Abbott V*).

———— ❖ — ❖ — ❖ ————

*Education Not a Fundamental Right and
Disparities in Funding Are Rationally
Related to Legitimate State Goal*

Committee for Educational Rights v. Edgar

Supreme Court of Illinois, 1996.
174 Ill.2d 1, 672 N.E.2d 1178.

Justice NICKELS delivered the opinion of the court:

This appeal draws us into the sensitive and controversial area of public school finance. The plaintiffs in this action are the Committee for Educational Rights (which consists of more than 60 school districts associated pursuant to an intergovernmental agreement), the boards of education of 37 school districts named individually, and a number of students and their parents. The defendants are Governor Jim Edgar, the State Board of Education and State Superintendent of Education Joseph A. Spagnolo. . . .

In their five-count complaint, plaintiffs allege that under the present financing scheme, vast differences in educational resources and opportunities exist among the State's school districts as a result of differences in local taxable property wealth. During the 1989–90 school year, the average tax base in the wealthiest 10% of elementary schools was over 13 times the average tax base in the poorest 10%. For high school and unit school districts, the ratios of the average tax bases in the wealthiest and poorest districts were 8.1 to 1 and 7 to 1, respectively, during the 1989–90 school year.

Plaintiffs allege in their complaint that the general state aid formula does not effectively equalize funding among wealthy and poor districts. While the general state aid formula ensures minimum funding at the foundation level, the wealthiest districts are able to raise funds through property taxes considerably in excess of the foundation level. Moreover, the provision of a minimum grant—equal to 7% of the foundation level—to even the wealthiest school districts is counter-equalizing.

Plaintiffs allege that disparities among wealthy and poor districts are reflected in various measures of educational funding; in several "key indicators" of educational quality (such as the percentage of teachers with master's degrees, teacher experience, teacher salaries, administrator salaries and pupil/administrator ratios); and in a comparison of the facilities, resources and course offerings in two neighboring school districts with dramatically disparate tax bases. According to the complaint, these disparities are attributable to variations in property wealth rather than tax effort; on average, the poorest school districts tax at higher rates than the wealthiest. . . .

We first consider the dismissal of plaintiffs' claims that the statutory system for financing public schools violates the education article of our state constitution. Section 1 of article X of the Illinois Constitution of 1970 provides:

> "A fundamental goal of the People of the State is the educational development of all persons to the limits of their capacities.
>
> *The State shall provide for an efficient system of high quality public educational institutions and services.* Education in public schools through the secondary level shall be free. There may be such other free education as the General Assembly provides by law.
>
> The state has the primary responsibility for financing the system of public education." (Emphasis added.) Ill. Const.1970, art. X, §1.

Plaintiffs' challenge to the statutory system for financing public schools is based on the emphasized language above. First, plaintiffs contend that because the system produces vast disparities in the level of funding and educational resources available to various school districts based on differences in local taxable property wealth, it is not "efficient" within the meaning of the constitution. Second, plaintiffs argue that school districts with low property tax bases are unable to provide a "high quality" education to their students due to inadequate funding. Third, plaintiffs contend that under the financing scheme, funding is insufficient to provide a "high quality" education to at risk children.

We first consider plaintiffs' argument that the present school funding system is not "efficient" within the meaning of the constitution because it produces disparities in educational resources and services based on differences in local taxable property wealth. In plaintiffs' view, the efficiency requirement guarantees some measure of equality in educational funding and opportunity. Plaintiffs deny that they seek absolute uniformity in educational offerings or precisely equal spending for each pupil in the state. Plaintiffs would apparently approve variations in educational spending from district to district based on criteria such as local differences in the costs of resources and special educational needs in particular districts. However, plaintiffs maintain that a school district's property wealth is "educationally irrelevant" and is not a proper factor upon which to set the level of resources available to the district. . . .

As this case turns upon the meaning of constitutional language, a brief summary of the general principles of constitutional interpretation may be helpful. . . .

"Efficient" has been defined as follows:

> "1: serving as or characteristic of an efficient cause: causally productive: OPERANT . . . 2: marked by ability to choose and use the most effective and least wasteful means of doing a task or accomplishing a purpose. . . ." Webster's Third New International Dictionary 725 (1981).

This definition does not inherently compel the conclusion that an "efficient system" of public schools necessarily involves statewide parity of educational opportunity and resources. However, we do not believe that the precise meaning of the word "efficient" as used in section 1 of the education article is entirely clear and free from doubt, or that "efficient" could not conceivably be interpreted in the manner that plaintiffs claim. . . .

The education article of the 1970 Constitution originated as a proposal submitted by the education committee of the Sixth Illinois Constitutional Convention. . . .

The constitutional requirement that the State provide for an efficient system of high quality educational institutions and services corresponds to section 1 of article VIII of the 1870 Constitution, which stated, "The general assembly shall provide a thorough and efficient system of free schools, whereby all children of this state may receive a good common school education." Ill. Const.1870, art. VIII, §1. Under the

1870 Constitution, this court consistently held that the question of the efficiency and thoroughness of the school system was one solely for the legislature to answer, and that the courts lacked the power to intrude. . . .

However, under a limited exception to this principle it was held that pursuant to the "thorough and efficient" requirement school district boundaries must be established so that the districts are compact and contiguous. . . .

The framers of the 1970 Constitution embraced this limited construction that the constitutional efficiency requirement authorized judicial review of school district boundaries, but they did not intend to otherwise limit legislative discretion. . . .

Disparity in educational funding was a highly charged and controversial subject during the constitutional convention, but it was not touched upon to any significant degree in connection with section 1's efficiency requirement. Instead, the debate over unequal opportunities and resources ultimately led to the incorporation of section 1's final sentence, which provides that "[t]he State has the primary responsibility for financing the system of public education." Ill. Const.1970, art. X, §1. . . .

In our view, . . . the framers of the 1970 Constitution viewed educational equality and "efficiency" to be separate and distinct subjects. The framers of the 1970 Constitution grappled with the issue of unequal educational funding and opportunity, and chose to address the problem with a purely hortatory statement of principle. To ignore this careful and deliberate choice by interpreting the efficiency requirement as an enforceable guarantee of equality would do violence to the framers' understanding of the education article. . . .

In view of all the foregoing considerations, we agree with the courts below that disparities in educational funding resulting from differences in local property wealth do not offend section 1's efficiency requirement. . . .

The remaining question under section 1 of the education article pertains to its guarantee of a system of "high quality" educational institutions and services. There is no dispute as to the nature of this guarantee in the abstract. Instead, the central issue is whether the quality of education is capable of or properly subject to measurement by the courts. Plaintiffs maintain that it is the courts' duty to construe the constitution and determine whether school funding legislation conforms with its requirements and cite a number of decisions from other jurisdictions in which courts have concluded that similar constitutional challenges are capable of judicial resolution. As explained below, however, we conclude that questions relating to the quality of education are solely for the legislative branch to answer. . . .

Our constitutional jurisprudence in the field of public education has been guided by considerations of separation of powers. In federal courts, the principles of separation of powers find expression in the so-called "political question" doctrine. . . .

. . . What constitutes a "high quality" education, and how it may best be provided, cannot be ascertained by any judicially discoverable or manageable standards. The constitution provides no principled basis for a judicial definition of high quality. It would be a transparent conceit to suggest that whatever standards of quality courts might develop would actually be derived from the constitution in any meaningful sense. Nor is education a subject within the judiciary's field of expertise, such that a judicial role in giving content to the education guarantee might be warranted. Rather, the question of educational quality is inherently one of policy involving philosophical and practical considerations that call for the exercise of legislative and administrative discretion.

To hold that the question of educational quality is subject to judicial determination would largely deprive the members of the general public of a voice in a matter which is close to the hearts of all individuals in Illinois. . . .

We conclude that the question of whether the educational institutions and services in Illinois are "high quality" is outside the sphere of the judicial function. To the extent plaintiffs' claim that the system for financing public schools is unconstitutional rests on perceived deficiencies in the quality of education in public schools, the claim was properly dismissed. For the foregoing reasons, we affirm the dismissal of plaintiffs' claims under the education article of our state constitution. . . .

We next consider whether the alleged disparities in educational funding and opportunity due to variations in local property wealth give rise to a cause of action under the equal protection clause of our state constitution (Ill. Const.1970, art. I, §2). . . .

While plaintiffs and *amici* perceptively characterize the relationship between education and certain basic aspects of citizenship, we disagree with their conclusion that this relationship justifies treating education as *itself* a fundamental right for equal protection purposes. . . . In this regard it is significant that while the framers of the 1970 Constitution recognized the importance of "the educational development of all persons to the limits of their capacities," they stopped short of declaring such educational development to be a "right," choosing instead to identify it as a "fundamental *goal*." . . .

While education is certainly a vitally important governmental function . . . , it is not a fundamental individual right for equal protection purposes, and thus the appropriate standard of review is the rational basis test. Under the rational basis test, judicial review of a legislative classification is limited and generally deferential. . . .

The general structure of the state's system of funding public schools through state and local resources—and the particular amounts allocated for distribution as general state aid—represent legislative efforts to strike a balance between the competing considerations of educational equality and local control. Certainly reasonable people might differ as to which consideration should be dominant. However, the highly deferential rational basis test does not permit us to substitute our judgment in this regard for that of the General Assembly, and we have no basis to conclude that the manner in which the General Assembly has struck the balance between equality and local control is so irrational as to offend the guarantee of equal protection. . . .

. . . In accordance with *Rodriguez* and the majority of state court decisions, and for all the reasons set forth above, we conclude that the State's system of funding public education is rationally related to the legitimate State goal of promoting local control. . . .

. . . Plaintiffs' complaint was properly dismissed, and we therefore affirm the judgment of the appellate court.

Affirmed.

CASE NOTE

Committee for Educational Rights v. Edgar, above, was followed by *Lewis v. Spagnolo,* 186 Ill.2d 198, 710 N.E.2d 798 (1999), in which the Supreme Court of Illinois reaffirmed its decision in *Edgar.* The court again made it quite clear that education is not a fundamental right in Illinois and that the quality of education is therefore solely a legislative matter and is not justiciable in the courts.

❖ — ❖ — ❖

State System of School Funding Violates the "Thorough and Efficient" Provision of the Education Clause of the Ohio Constitution

DeRolph v. State

Supreme Court of Ohio, 1997.
78 Ohio St.3d 193, 677 N.E.2d 733.

FRANCIS E. SWEENEY, Sr., Justice.

In 1802, when our forefathers convened to write our state Constitution, they carried within them a deep-seated belief that liberty and individual opportunity could be preserved only by educating Ohio's citizens. These ideals, which spurred the War of Independence, were so important that education was made part of our first Bill of Rights. Section 3, Article VIII of the Ohio Constitution of 1802. Beginning in 1851, our Constitution has required the General Assembly to provide enough funding to secure a "thorough and efficient system of common schools throughout the State."

Over the last two centuries, the education of our citizenry has been deemed vital to our democratic society and to our progress as a state. Education is essential to preparing our youth to be productive members of our society, with the skills and knowledge necessary to compete in the modern world. In fact, the mission statement of defendant, State Board of Education, echoes these concerns:

The mission of education is to prepare students of all ages to meet, to the best of their abilities, the ac-

ademic, social, civic, and employment needs of the twenty-first century, by providing high-quality programs that emphasize the lifelong skills necessary to continue learning, communicate clearly, solve problems, use information and technology effectively, and enjoy productive employment.

State Board of Education, Preparing Ohio Schools for the 21st Century, Sept. 1990, ii.

Today, Ohio stands at a crossroads. We must decide whether the promise of providing to our youth a free, public elementary and secondary education in a "thorough and efficient system" has been fulfilled. The importance of this case cannot be overestimated. It involves a wholesale constitutional attack on Ohio's system of funding public elementary and secondary education. Practically every Ohioan will be affected by our decision: the 1.8 million children in public schools and every taxpayer in the state. For the 1.8 million children involved, this case is about the opportunity to compete and succeed.

Upon a full consideration of the record and in analyzing the pertinent constitutional provision, we can reach but one conclusion: the current legislation fails to provide for a thorough and efficient system of common schools, in violation of Section 2, Article VI of the Ohio Constitution. . . .

Ohio's statutory scheme for financing public education is complex. At the heart of the present controversy is the School Foundation Program (R.C. Chapter 3317) for allocation of state basic aid and the manner in which the allocation formula and other school funding factors have caused or permitted to continue vast wealth-based disparities among Ohio's schools, depriving many of Ohio's public school students of high quality educational opportunities.

According to statute, the revenue available to a school district comes from two primary sources: state revenue, most of which is provided through the School Foundation Program, and local revenue, which consists primarily of locally voted school district property tax levies. Federal funds play a minor role in the financing scheme. Ohio relies more on local revenue than state revenue, contrary to the national trend.

In urging this court to strike the statutory provisions relating to Ohio's school financing system, appellants argue that the state has failed in its constitutional responsibility to provide a thorough and efficient system of public schools. We agree.

Section 2, Article VI of the Ohio Constitution requires the state to provide and fund a system of public education and includes an explicit directive to the General Assembly:

> The general assembly shall make such provisions, by taxation, or otherwise, as, with the income arising from the school trust fund, will secure a thorough and efficient system of common schools throughout the State. . . .

The delegates to the 1850–1851 Constitutional Convention recognized that it was the state's duty to both present and future generations of Ohioans to establish a framework for a "full, complete and efficient system of public education." II Report of the Debates and Proceedings of the Convention for the Revision of the Constitution of the State of Ohio, 1850–51 (1851) ("Debates"). Thus, throughout their discussions, the delegates stressed the importance of education and reaffirmed the policy that education shall be afforded to every child in the state regardless of race or economic standing. Debates at 11, 13. Furthermore, the delegates were concerned that the education to be provided to our youth not be mediocre but be as perfect as could humanly be devised. Debates at 698–699. These debates reveal the delegates' strong belief that it is the state's obligation, through the General Assembly, to provide for the full education of all children within the state.

Dr. Samuel Kern Alexander, a leading professor in the area of school law and school finance, testified that, in the context of the historical development of the phrase "thorough and efficient," it is the state's duty to provide a system which allows its citizens to fully develop their human potential. In such a system, rich and poor people alike are given the opportunity to become educated so that they may flourish and our society may progress. It was believed by the leading statesmen of the time that only in this way could there be an efficient educational system throughout the state.

This court has construed the words "thorough and efficient" in light of the constitutional debates and history surrounding them. In *Miller v. Korns* (1923), 107 Ohio St. 287, 297–298, 140 N.E. 773, 776, this court defined what is meant

by a "thorough and efficient" system of common schools throughout the state:

> This declaration is made by the people of the state. It calls for the upbuilding of a system of schools throughout the state, and the attainment of efficiency and thoroughness in that system is thus expressly made a purpose, not local, not municipal, but state-wide.
>
> With this very purpose in view, regarding the problem as a state-wide problem, the sovereign people made it mandatory upon the General Assembly to secure not merely a system of common schools, but a system thorough and efficient throughout the state.
>
> A thorough system could not mean one in which part or any number of the school districts of the state were starved for funds. An efficient system could not mean one in which part or any number of the school districts of the state lacked teachers, buildings, or equipment.

Cincinnati School Dist. Bd. of Edn. v. Walter (1979), 58 Ohio St.2d 368, 387, 12 O.O.3d 327, 338, 390 N.E.2d 813, 825, cited *Miller* with approval. Additionally, *Walter* recognized that while the General Assembly has wide discretion in meeting the mandate of Section 2, Article VI, this discretion is not without limits. *Id.* *Walter* found that a school system would not be thorough and efficient if "a school district was receiving so little local and state revenue that the students were effectively being deprived of educational opportunity." *Id.*

Other states, in declaring their state funding systems unconstitutional, have also addressed the issue of what constitutes a "thorough and efficient" or a "general or uniform" system of public schools. We recognize that some of these decisions were decided on different grounds or involved different education provisions. Despite these differences, we still are persuaded by the basic principles underlying these decisions.

For instance, in *Edgewood Indep. School Dist. v. Kirby*, supra, 777 S.W.2d 391, the Texas Supreme Court invalidated its state funding structure, in which annual per-student expenditures varied from $2,112 in the poorest districts to $19,333 in the wealthiest districts. The court noted:

> Property-poor districts are trapped in a cycle of poverty from which there is no opportunity to free themselves. Because of their inadequate tax base, they must tax at significantly higher rates in order

to meet minimum requirements for accreditation; yet their educational programs are typically inferior. The location of new industry and development is strongly influenced by tax rates and the quality of local schools. Thus, the property-poor districts with their high tax rates and inferior schools are unable to attract new industry or development and so have little opportunity to improve their tax base. . . .

In 1989, the General Assembly directed the Superintendent of Public Instruction to conduct a survey of Ohio's public school buildings. The purpose of this survey was to determine the cost of bringing all facilities into compliance with state building codes and asbestos removal requirements, as well as all other state and local provisions related to health and safety. *Id.*

The results of this study were published in the 1990 Ohio Public School Facility Survey. The survey identified a need for $10.2 billion in facility repair and construction.

Among its findings, the survey determined that one-half of Ohio's school buildings were fifty years old or older, and fifteen percent were seventy years old or older. A little over half of these buildings contained satisfactory electrical systems: however, only seventeen percent of the heating systems and thirty-one percent of the roofs were deemed to be satisfactory. Nineteen percent of the windows and twenty-five percent of the plumbing and fixtures were found to be adequate. Only twenty percent of the buildings had satisfactory handicapped access. A scant thirty percent of the school facilities had adequate fire alarm systems and exterior doors.

Over three years after the 1990 survey was published, the current Superintendent of Public Instruction, John Theodore Sanders, averred that his visits to Ohio school buildings demonstrated that some students were "making do in a decayed carcass from an era long passed," and others were educated in "dirty, depressing places." . . .

In addition to deteriorating buildings and related conditions, it is clear from the record that many of the school districts throughout the state cannot provide the basic resources necessary to educate our youth. For instance, many of the appellant school districts have insufficient funds to purchase textbooks and must rely on old, outdated books. For some classes, there were no textbooks at all. For example, at Southern Local during the 1992–1993 school year, none of the students in a Spanish I class had a textbook at the beginning of the year. Later, there was a lottery for books. Students who picked the lucky numbers received a book.

The accessibility of everyday supplies is also a problem, forcing schools to ration such necessities as paper, chalk, art supplies, paper clips, and even toilet paper. A system without basic instructional materials and supplies can hardly constitute a thorough and efficient system of common schools throughout the state as mandated by our Constitution.

Additionally, many districts lack sufficient funds to comply with the state law requiring a district-wide average of no more than twenty-five students for each classroom teacher. Indeed, some schools have more than thirty students per classroom teacher, with one school having as many as thirty-nine students in one sixth grade class. As the testimony of educators established, it is virtually impossible for students to receive an adequate education with a student-teacher ratio of this magnitude.

The curricula in the appellant school districts are severely limited compared to other school districts and compared to what might be expected of a system designed to educate Ohio's youth and to prepare them for a bright and prosperous future. . . .

None of the appellant school districts is financially able to keep up with the technological training needs of the students in the districts. The districts lack sufficient computers, computer labs, hands-on computer training, software, and related supplies to properly serve the students' needs. In this regard, it does not appear likely that the children in the appellant school districts will be able to compete in the job market against those students with sufficient technological training.

Lack of sufficient funding can also lead to poor academic performance. . . .

All the facts documented in the record lead to one inescapable conclusion—Ohio's elementary and secondary public schools are neither thorough nor efficient. The operation of the appellant school districts conflicts with the historical notion that the education of our youth is of utmost concern and that Ohio children should be educated adequately so that they are able to participate fully in society. Our state Constitution was drafted with the importance of education in mind. In contrast, education under the legislation being reviewed ranks miserably low in the state's priorities. In fact, the formula amount is established after the legislature determines the total dollars to be allocated to primary and secondary education in each biennial budget. Consequently, the present school financing system contravenes the clear wording of our Constitution and the framers' intent.

Furthermore, rather than following the constitutional dictate that it is the state's obligation to fund education (as this opinion has repeatedly underscored), the legislature has thrust the majority of responsibility upon local school districts. This, too, is contrary to the clear wording of our Constitution. The responsibility for maintaining a thorough and efficient school system falls upon the state. When a district falls short of the constitutional requirement that the system be thorough and efficient, it is the state's obligation to rectify it. . . .

Clearly, the current school financing scheme is a far cry from thorough and efficient. Instead, the system has failed to educate our youth to their fullest potential.

In so finding, we reject appellees' contention that *Walter* is controlling. The equal yield formula challenged in *Walter* was repealed shortly after the case was decided. . . . Moreover, *Walter* involved a challenge to only one aspect of school funding. In contrast, the case at bar involves a wholesale constitutional attack on the entire system. Additionally, in creating the funding system at issue in *Walter*, the General Assembly had relied on a determination of a legislative committee that the statutorily guaranteed amount actually was sufficient to provide a high quality education. . . . Here, however, the evidence clearly indicates that the funding level set by today's School Foundation Program has absolutely no connection with what is necessary to provide each district enough money to ensure an adequate educational program. The system in place today differs dramatically from that in place nearly twenty years ago; thus, our holding in *Walter* does not control the outcome in this case.

We also reject the notion that the wide disparities in educational opportunity are caused by the poorer school districts' failure to pass levies. The evidence reveals that the wide disparities are caused by the funding system's overreliance on the tax base of individual school districts. What this means is that the poor districts simply cannot raise as much money even with identical tax effort. . . .

We recognize that disparities between school districts will always exist. By our decision today, we are not stating that a new financing system must provide equal educational opportunities for all. In a Utopian society, this lofty goal would be realized. We, however, appreciate the limitations imposed upon us. Nor do we advocate a "Robin Hood" approach to school financing reform. We are not suggesting that funds be diverted from wealthy districts and given to the less fortunate. There is no "leveling down" component in our decision today.

Moreover, in no way should our decision be construed as imposing spending ceilings on more affluent school districts. School districts are still free to augment their programs if they choose to do so. However, it is futile to lay the entire blame for the inadequacies of the present system on the taxpayers and the local boards of education. Although some districts have the luxury of deciding where to allocate extra dollars, many others have the burden of deciding which educational programs to cut or what financial institution to contact to obtain yet another emergency loan. Our state Constitution makes the state responsible for educating our youth. Thus, the state should not shirk its obligation by espousing cliches about "local control."

We recognize that money alone is not the panacea that will transform Ohio's school system into a model of excellence. Although a student's success depends upon numerous factors besides money, we must ensure that there is enough money that students have the chance to succeed because of the educational opportunity provided, not in spite of it. Such an opportunity requires, at the very least, that all of Ohio's children attend schools which are safe and conducive to learning. At the present, Ohio does not provide many of its students with even the most basic of educational needs. . . .

School funding has been, and continues to be, a Herculean task. As thirty-seven lawmakers concede in their *amicus curiae* brief, despite their recent efforts, the General Assembly has not funded our public schools properly. They assert that unless this court rules in favor of the appellants, the urgency of resolving public school funding will quickly fade. We find that this brief eloquently expresses the helplessness felt even by many of our state legislators.

We know that few issues have the potential to stir such passion as school financing. In many districts in this great state of ours, students and teachers must fight a demoralizing uphill battle to make the system work. All parties concede that the current system needs to be reformed.

By our decision today, we send a clear message to lawmakers: the time has come to fix the system. Let there be no misunderstanding. Ohio's public school financing scheme must undergo a complete systematic overhaul. . . . The funding laws reviewed today are inherently incapable of achieving their constitutional purpose.

We therefore hold that Ohio's elementary and secondary public school financing system violates Section 2, Article VI of the Ohio Constitution, which mandates a thorough and efficient system of common schools throughout the state. . . .

Although we have found the school financing system to be unconstitutional, we do not instruct the General Assembly as to the specifics of the legislation it should enact. However, we admonish the General Assembly that it must create an entirely new school financing system. In establishing such a system, the General Assembly shall recognize that there is but one system of public education in Ohio: It is a statewide system, expressly created by the state's highest governing document, the Constitution. Thus, the establishment, organization, and maintenance of public education are the state's responsibility. Because of its importance, education should be placed high in the state's budgetary priorities. A thorough and efficient system of common schools includes facilities in good repair and the supplies, materials, and funds necessary to maintain these facilities in a safe manner, in compliance with all local, state, and federal mandates.

We recognize that a new funding system will require time for adequate study, drafting of the appropriate legislation, and transition from the present scheme of financing to one in conform-

ity with this decision. Therefore, we stay the effect of this decision for twelve months.

Appellants are entitled to recover against the state their attorney fees and costs as found by the trial court. . . .

The court of appeals' judgment is reversed. We remand this cause to the trial court with directions to enter judgment consistent with this opinion. The trial court is to retain jurisdiction until the legislation is enacted and in effect, taking such action as may be necessary to ensure conformity with this opinion.

Judgment reversed and cause remanded.

CASE NOTES

1. In *DeRolph I*, above, a majority of the Ohio Supreme Court concluded that Ohio's system of elementary and secondary public schools, in place at that time, fell well short of the mandate of Article VI, Section 2 of the Constitution. *DeRolph I* recognized that, despite the earnest efforts of the general assembly, it was simply impossible to characterize the existing system as "thorough and efficient." Accordingly, the court declared the system unconstitutional and stated that the general assembly must devise and implement a "thorough and efficient" system.

In *DeRolph II*, the court again considered the same basic constitutional question as in *DeRolph I*: Can the revised system be characterized as thorough and efficient pursuant to Article VI, Section 2 of the Ohio Constitution? Although the key inquiry was the same, the specifics changed commensurately with the state's attempts to institute the necessary reforms. In considering the remedy enacted in response to *DeRolph I*, the court found that the legislature had failed to create "an entirely new public school financing system and perform a systemic overhaul of the funding of primary and secondary schools" as the court had mandated. The court therefore maintained jurisdiction and allowed the legislature additional time to comply with the constitutional requirement of a "thorough and efficient" system, Article VI, Section 2, Ohio Constitution, to be effected by June 15, 2001. *DeRolph v. State*, 89 Ohio St.3d 1, 728 N.E.2d 993 (2000) (*DeRolph II*).

2. As observed in the preceding text, inequities in the distribution of funds for public

schools have been challenged under (1) state equal protection clauses and/or (2) state education provisions. The state equal protection clauses are general constitutional provisions prohibiting government from invidiously discriminating against any particular class of persons by denial of fundamental rights. Equal protection is a prohibition, a "thou shalt not," that protects individuals against the state. On the other hand, the education provisions are affirmative mandates requiring that state legislatures provide for the education of the people. Plaintiffs have used both types of provisions in efforts to strike down state school finance programs that combine state and local revenues in a manner that greatly favors children in affluent school districts. The state courts have responded to these challenges in several basic ways. First, they have held that education is not a fundamental right and that disparity of resources is not irrational and is not violative of equal protection. Second, they have held that education is a fundamental right and that under a strict scrutiny analysis the state cannot succeed in showing that it has a compelling interest in distributing funds in a disproportionate manner. Third, they have held that education is a fundamental right and that the state's disparate allocation of school funds is defensible under strict scrutiny analysis. Fourth, they have found a declaration of fundamentality unnecessary and have held that the distribution of funds is not rational. Fifth, they have held that education is not fundamental for equal protection purposes and have found the funding method unconstitutional under the education provision of the state constitution. Sixth, they have held that education is fundamental, have found that widely unequal revenues per pupil violate the education provision of the state constitution, and have determined it unnecessary to rule on the application of equal protection.

The notes that follow summarize and consolidate these court decisions into five categories: (a) education is not fundamental, (b) education is fundamental, (c) a finding of fundamentality is not necessary to hold a state school finance program unconstitutional, (d) education is fundamental but not equal, and (e) local control is not an adequate defense.

a. *Education Is Not a Fundamental Right.* Education is not a fundamental right in Rhode Island. The Supreme Court of Rhode Island in overruling a lower court said that the education clause (Rhode Island Constitution, Article XII) does not confer a fundamental right to an education on the children of Rhode Island, "nor does it guarantee 'equal, adequate, and meaningful education.'" According to the Rhode Island high court, to assume fundamentality drew a conclusion that was clearly wrong based on the historical record of the Rhode Island Constitution. *City of Pawtucket v. Sundlin,* 662 A.2d 40 (R.I.1995).

Education is not a fundamental right under the Maryland Declaration of Rights, Maryland Constitution, Article XXIV. "The right to adequate education in Maryland is no more fundamental than the right to personal security, to fire protection, to welfare subsidies, to health care or like vital governmental services." The Maryland Supreme Court further held that Article VIII of the Maryland Constitution, which requires the general assembly to establish and maintain a thorough and efficient system of free public schools throughout the state, "is not alone sufficient to elevate education to fundamental status." *Hornbeck v. Somerset County Board of Education,* 295 Md. 597, 458 A.2d 758, 786 (1983).

The Supreme Court of Colorado has said that the "heartfelt recognition and endorsement of the importance of education does not elevate public education to the fundamental interest warranting strict scrutiny." This court saw the property-poor school districts' plea for fiscal equity as ultimately an attack on local control. The Colorado court, in denying fundamental status to education, followed the reasoning of *Rodriguez* and held that the plaintiff children did not constitute the suspect class necessary to justify the invoking of the strict scrutiny test of equal protection. Moreover, it held that the wide disparity in revenues per pupil among Colorado school districts could be justified as rational because it furthered the objective of local control. *Lujan v. Colorado State Board of Education,* 649 P.2d 1005 (Colo.1982).

The fact that education is provided for in the state constitution does not make it a fundamental right for purposes of equal protection. The Oklahoma Supreme Court has held that provisions of the state constitution requiring establishment and maintenance of a public school system merely mandated establishment and maintenance of a system and did not guarantee equality of educational opportunity in the sense that expenditures should be equalized. *Fair School Finance Council of Oklahoma, Inc. v. State,* 746 P.2d 1135 (Okl.1987).

The Georgia Supreme Court has held that education is "vital" but not fundamental. This court adopted the *Rodriguez* position that education is no more fundamental than food, lodging, police, fire protection, water, and health services, all of which are governed locally with wide differences in expenditures. The Georgia court, however, failed to reconcile the fact that education is the only one of these services set out and specified by the state constitution as a direct responsibility of the state legislature. *McDaniel v. Thomas,* 248 Ga. 632, 285 S.E.2d 156 (1981).

The Court of Appeals of New York has also denied that education is a fundamental constitutional right. This court observed in the *Levittown* case that education is "unquestionably high on the list of priorities of governmental concern and responsibility ..., enlisting most active attention of the citizenry and the legislature," but this "does not automatically entitle public education" to be classified as a fundamental right. *Board of Education, Levittown Union Free School District v. Nyquist,* 57 N.Y.2d 27, 453 N.Y.S.2d 643, 439 N.E.2d 359 (1982).

The Supreme Court of Idaho perceived a connection between the fundamentality of education and the destruction of local control of education. This court said: "[W]e refuse to classify the right to education as a fundamental right which compels the State, for the purposes of financing, to wipe out local entities and finance on the basis of revenues raised by some sort of statewide system." *Thompson v. Engelking,* 96 Idaho 793, 537 P.2d 635 (1975).

Florida voters included a new education clause in that state's constitutional amendments of 1998. The precedent set earlier in *Coalition for Adequacy and Fairness in School Funding, Inc. v. Chiles,* 680 So.2d 400 (1996), in which plaintiffs, in bearing the burden of proof, were unable to show that the method of funding provided "inadequate" support for the public schools, will of necessity be reevaluated in light of the new wording in the constitution. Under the old constitutional provision, education was not a fundamental right; whether it will be under the new language remains to be determined.

In Oregon, the court assumed that equity of funding and local control were incompatible. In choosing between the two, the court apparently felt local control was more important than equity. In this case, the court did not explicitly reject the fundamentality of education and the strict scrutiny standard but created its own balancing test whereby it weighed the detriment of unequal revenues against the "ostensible justification" of local control. *Olsen v. State,* 276 Or. 9, 554 P.2d 139 (1976).

In *East Jackson Public Schools v. State,* 133 Mich.App. 132, 348 N.W.2d 303, 305 (1984), the court maintained that the Michigan constitutional provision mandating that the legislature "maintain and support a system of free public elementary and secondary schools" grants only a right to an adequate education. In *Richland County v. Campbell,* 294 S.C. 346, 364 S.E.2d 470, 472 (1988), the court said that the South Carolina constitutional requirement that the legislature maintain and support public schools guarantees equal standards and equal opportunity only under the method of funding chosen by the legislature.

Other cases finding that education is not a fundamental right, and thus that there is no justification for the courts' application of strict scrutiny to school finance legislation, include *Milliken v. Green,*

390 Mich. 389, 212 N.W.2d 711 (1973); *Danson v. Casey*, 484 Pa. 415, 399 A.2d 360 (1979); *Bensalem Township School District v. Commonwealth*, 105 Pa.Cmwlth. 388, 524 A.2d 1027 (1987), remanded, 518 Pa. 581, 544 A.2d 1318 (1988); *Board of Education of the City School District of Cincinnati v. Walter*, 58 Ohio St.3d 368, 390 N.E.2d 813 (1979), cert. denied, 444 U.S. 1015, 100 S.Ct. 665 (1980), but see *DeRolph v. State*, 78 Ohio St.3d 193, 677 N.E.2d 733 (1997); *Britt v. North Carolina State Board of Education*, 86 N.C.App. 282, 357 S.E.2d 432 (1987); *School Board of the Parish of Livingston v. Louisiana State Board of Elementary and Secondary Education*, 830 F.2d 563 (5th Cir.1987), cert. denied, 487 U.S. 1223, 108 S.Ct. 2884 (1988); and *Richland County v. Campbell*, 294 S.C. 346, 364 S.E.2d 470 (1988).

The Supreme Court of Pennsylvania has ruled that the state's constitutional mandate that the general assembly provide for a "thorough and efficient" system does not confer an individual right upon each student to any particular level or quality of education. The provision does impose upon the legislature a constitutional duty to provide for the maintenance of a thorough and efficient system of public schools; however, the plaintiff in order to prevail must prove that the legislature is unreasonable, arbitrary, or capricious in the distribution of state and local funds. In *Marrero*, the plaintiff school district was unable to bear this burden of proof in order to show that the legislature did not provide adequate funding to support the unique educational needs of students in an urban environment; thus, the defendant state prevailed. *Marrero v. Commonwealth*, 709 A.2d 956 (1998).

Twenty years after its *Shofstall* decision, the Arizona Supreme Court in *Roosevelt Elementary School District v. Bishop*, 179 Ariz. 233, 877 P.2d 806 (1994), held that the state's education financing system, taken as a whole, did not comply with Article XI, Section 1 of the Arizona Constitution because it directly caused substantial capital facility disparities. The system was "a combination of heavy reliance on local property taxation, arbitrary school district boundaries, and only partial attempts at equalization." The court said that the state's financing scheme could do nothing but produce disparities. The case was remanded to the trial court to retain jurisdiction to enforce the court's mandate.

In 1996, the legislature amended the financing system but preserved intact the overall scheme. The trial court and the supreme court concluded that the amendments were insufficient to comply with the latter court's mandate. In 1997, the legislature amended the system again with the Assistance to Build Classrooms Fund (ABC legislation), 1997 Ariz. Sess. Laws Ch. 4. In April 1997, the governor filed a motion in the superior court seeking a declaration that the latest amendments complied with the supreme court's mandate. After an evidentiary hearing, the trial court concluded that the amendments were insufficient.

In response, the Arizona Supreme Court, *en banc*, rejected the legislative remedy, saying that the new school funding program as written into law was incapable of curing the unconstitutional inequities, improperly delegated to the local school districts the responsibility to fund capital facilities, and overall did not satisfy the state constitutional requirements to provide for a general and uniform system of education. The court then mandated that the legislature act to fashion a funding system that would comport with the state constitution. *Hull v. Albrecht*, 190 Ariz. 520, 950 P.2d 1141 (1997).

b. *Education Is a Fundamental Right.* In declaring that education is a fundamental right in New Hampshire, the supreme court of that state explained that it is of persuasive force that "educational adequacy recognizes the role of education in preparing citizens to participate in the exercise of voting and first amendment rights. The latter being recognized as fundamental, it is illogical to place the means to exercise those rights on less substantial constitutional footing than the rights themselves. We hold that in this State a constitutionally adequate public education is a fundamental right." *Claremont School District v. Governor*, 703 A.2d 1353 (N.H.1997). The requirements of the state of Washington's constitution that the "legislature shall provide for a general and uniform system of public schools" (Article IX, §2) and that the legislature has a "paramount duty" to "make ample provision for education of all children" (Article IX, §1) make it clear that the children of Washington have a constitutionally "guaranteed education," in which the first priority is to provide "fully sufficient funds." Consequently, all children residing within Washington's borders "have a 'right' to be amply provided with an education." That "right" is constitutionally paramount and must be achieved through a "general and uniform system of public schools" (Article IX, §2). Further, the education that is provided must be "without distinction or preference on account of race, color, caste, or sex." West's Wash. Rev. Code Ann., Const. Art. 9, §1. *Seattle School District No. 1 of King County v. State*, 90 Wash.2d 476, 585 P.2d 71 (1978).

In *Pauley v. Kelly*, the Supreme Court of West Virginia held that the requirements of the state constitution mandating that the legislature provide for a "thorough and efficient system of free schools" make education a "fundamental, constitutional right in West Virginia" (Article XII, §1). 162 W.Va. 672, 255 S.E.2d 859 (1979).

The Supreme Court of Kentucky held that education is a fundamental right for children in Kentucky and based its opinion on the "animus" of Section 183 of the Kentucky Constitution, which requires that the general assembly "provide an efficient system of common schools throughout the state." The term "animus" is defined as the "intention, design, disposition or mind." *Black's Law Dictionary* (St. Paul, Minn.: West, 7th Edition, 1999), p. 114. Thus, fundamentality of education derives from the intention and design of the

framers of the affirmative constitutional mandate that the legislature provide for education. The Kentucky court, having found that education is fundamental and that the system of financing the public schools was not "efficient" under Section 183, concluded that an equal protection analysis was unnecessary. *Rose v. Council for Better Education, Inc.*, 790 S.W.2d 186 (Ky.1989).

The system of state school funding in Alabama has been held unconstitutional under that state's constitution. The Circuit Court of Montgomery County, Alabama, has ruled that education is a fundamental right in Alabama and that the inadequate and unequal distribution of state and local funds among school districts violated the education clause of the Alabama Constitution, which requires "the Legislature to establish, organize and maintain a liberal system of public schools." This lower court further held that the method of distribution of school funds violated the state's equal protection clause, saying: "[T]his Court holds that the Alabama system of public schools fails to provide plaintiffs the equal protection of the laws under *any* standard of equal protection review. . . ." This court concluded that even under the *"least* searching tier of equal protection analysis," the rational relationship standard, the Alabama system could not "pass constitutional muster." Finally, this lower court also concluded that the state financing scheme created such inadequacies and disparities in funding as to violate due process of law as assured by the Alabama Constitution.

The finding by a state court that education is a fundamental right does not mean that the burden of proof shifts to the state to prove that its funding scheme is compelling; for example, the North Carolina Supreme Court, after ruling that education is a fundamental right in that state, still imposed the burden of proof on the plaintiff poor school districts to show that the state legislature's school financing formula was irrational. In North Carolina, the plaintiffs were unable to sustain this burden. *Leandro v. State,* 346 N.C. 336, 488 S.E. 249 (1997).

In Alabama, however, in response to the lower circuit court's decision for the plaintiff poor school districts, the state senate appealed to the Alabama Supreme Court, inquiring as to whether a circuit court could issue a declaratory judgment mandating that the legislature correct the constitutional deficiencies. The Supreme Court of Alabama responded in the affirmative, ruling that "the circuit court has the power, and indeed the duty, . . . to interpret the constitution, and its interpretation, unless changed by a competent court having the power to overturn it, must be accepted and followed. . . ." See *Opinion of the Justices,* 624 So.2d 107 (Ala.1993); *Pinto v. Alabama Coalition for Equity,* 662 So.2d 894 (Ala. 1995).

In *Committee for Educational Equality v. State,* 878 S.W.2d 446 (Mo.1994), the Missouri Supreme Court refused to stay a lower court decision that ruled that education in Missouri is a constitutional right.

Other court decisions declaring that education is fundamental include *Knowles v. State Board of Education,* 219 Kan. 271, 547 P.2d 699 (1976); *Buse v. Smith,* 74 Wis.2d 550, 247 N.W.2d 141 (1976); *Kukor v. Grover,* 148 Wis.2d 469, 436 N.W.2d 568 (1989); *Serrano v. Priest,* 5 Cal.3d 584, 96 Cal.Rptr. 601, 487 P.2d 1241 (1971); *Serrano v. Priest,* 18 Cal.3d 728, 135 Cal.Rptr. 345, 557 P.2d 929 (1976), cert. denied, 432 U.S. 907, 97 S.Ct. 2951 (1977); *Serrano v. Priest,* 226 Cal.Rptr. 584 (1986); *Horton v. Meskill,* 172 Conn. 615, 376 A.2d 359 (1977); *State ex rel. Board of Education for the County of Grant v. Manchin,* 179 W.Va. 235, 366 S.E.2d 743 (1988); *Washakie County School District No. 1 v. Herschler,* 606 P.2d 310 (Wyo.1980), cert. denied sub nom. *Hot Springs County School District Number 1 v. Washakie County School District Number 1,* 449 U.S. 824, 101 S.Ct. 86 (1980); and *Edgewood Independent School District v. Kirby,* 777 S.W.2d 391 (Tex.1989).

c. *Finding of Fundamentality Is Unnecessary to Invalidate Funding Scheme.* In 1997, the Supreme Court of Ohio saw no need to deal with the equal protection fundamentality issue in holding the funding scheme of that state unconstitutional under the "thorough and efficient" provision of the education clause. *DeRolph v. State,* 78 Ohio St.3d. 193, 677 N.E.2d 733 (1997). The Supreme Court of Arkansas found it unnecessary to address the fundamentality question to justify strict scrutiny because from the evidence presented, the court was able to conclude that the system of school financing did not even meet the lesser test of rationality. In so holding, the court said that "we find no constitutional basis for the present system, as it has no rational bearing on the educational needs of the districts." *DuPree v. Alma School District No. 30 of Crawford County,* 279 Ark. 340, 651 S.W.2d 90 (1983).

Without commenting on the fundamentality of education, the Supreme Court of South Carolina held that plaintiff school districts that alleged inadequacy of funding had stated a justiciable claim, and the case was remanded to a lower court for hearing. In interpreting the education clause of the state constitution (Article XI, §3), the court said that the words "The General Assembly shall provide for the maintenance and support of a system of free public schools" placed a duty on the legislature to provide for a "minimally adequate education." This means the legislature must provide for safe facilities; the ability to read, write, and speak the English language; and programs of study to provide for a knowledge of mathematics, physical science, economics, history, government, and social and political systems. *Abbeville County School District v. State,* 335 S.C. 58, 515 S.E.2d 535 (1999).

Likewise, the Montana Supreme Court held it did not need to consider the fundamentality question under the equal protection provision of that state's constitution because the school funding scheme directly violated the education provision of the state constitution. Thus, recourse to the equal protection clause was obviated. *Helena Elementary School District No. 1 v.*

State, 236 Mont. 44, 769 P.2d 684 (1989), opinion amended by 236 Mont. 44, 784 P.2d 412 (1990).

The New Jersey Supreme Court in *Robinson v. Cahill* set the initial precedent in holding a system of school financing unconstitutional without invoking fundamentality and the state's equal protection clause. The New Jersey court foresaw unusual and unnecessary complications in attempting to address the educational equity issue in terms of equal protection. Instead, the court based its opinion of unconstitutionality of the New Jersey finance program on the "thorough and efficient" clause of the education provision of the New Jersey Constitution (Article VIII, §4, Part 1).

The viability and conclusiveness of the New Jersey court's 1973 decision relying on the "thorough and efficient" requirement of the education provision were later reinforced by the same court in *Abbott v. Burke,* 119 N.J. 287, 575 A.2d 359 (1990), wherein the method of distributing funds among the school districts of New Jersey was again held to be unconstitutional.

In 1994, the Supreme Court of New Jersey again intervened, this time holding that the Quality Education Act, enacted by the legislature in a compromise attempt to meet constitutional requirements, failed to ensure substantial equivalence between special needs districts and richer districts in expenditures per pupil for regular education. Abbott v. Burke, 136 N.J. 444, 643 A.2d 575 (1994).

d. *Education Is Fundamental But Not Equal.* The Supreme Court of Virginia, a court not famous for its propensities toward equality, held in a bit of perverse logic that even though the Virginia Constitution clearly establishes education as a fundamental right, "nowhere does the Constitution require equal, or substantially equal, funding or programs among" school divisions. *Scott v. Commonwealth,* 247 Va. 379, 443 S.E.2d 138 (1994).

e. *Local Control Is Not an Adequate Defense.* In 1993, the Supreme Court of Tennessee upheld a lower court decision that found that inequities and inadequacies of funding among Tennessee school districts were of such magnitude as to support a finding of unconstitutionality under the equal protection provision of that state's constitution. The court rejected the state's contention that the need for local control justified expenditure disparities. The court said:

> Those jurisdictions finding no equal protection violation in a system based on district wealth generally uphold the system of funding by finding a legitimate state purpose in maintaining local control. We find however, two fallacies in this reasoning. First, to alter the state financing system to provide greater equalization among districts does not in any way dictate that local control must be reduced. Second, as pointed out in *Serrano* [*v. Priest,* 18 Cal.3d 728, 761, 135 Cal.Rptr. 345, 364, 557 P.2d 929, 948 (1976)], "The notion of local control was a 'cruel illusion' for the poor districts due to limitations placed upon them by the system itself. . . . [So long as the assessed valuation within a district's boundaries is a major determinant of how much it can spend for its schools, only a district with a large tax base will truly be able to decide how much it really cares about education. The poor district cannot freely choose to tax itself into an excellence which its tax rolls cannot provide.] Far from being necessary to promote local fiscal choice, the present system actually deprives the less wealthy districts of the option." Consequently, even without deciding whether the right to a public education is fundamental, we can find no constitutional basis for the present system, as it has no rational bearing on the educational needs of the districts.

Tennessee Small School Systems v. McWherter, 851 S.W.2d 139 (Tenn.1993).

■ BUDGETING AND ACCOUNTING FOR SCHOOL FUNDS

For a school district to effectively plan for educational activities and account for the expenditure of tax funds, provisions must be made for budgetary and accounting procedures. School boards are generally given wide latitude in the determination of how educational funds will be expended. The attitude of the courts has been that a school district, being charged with the responsibility for operating the schools, should have as much freedom as possible to determine how and where the funds will be spent. This broad budgetary authority, of course, extends to teachers' salaries, subject only to legislative or constitutional restraints against arbitrary, discriminatory, or unreasonable classifications.

The exception to this rule is where the legislature has prescribed that school boards be fiscally dependent on city government. In such a case, the board must submit its budget for review and approval by the city government. However, where a city council has the authority to fix the amount of the school budget, it may not direct the itemized expenditure of the gross amount authorized; the board may spend the money for any purpose permitted by law. In instances where the law requires only the submission of the budget and does not specify control or approval authority, the courts have held that the reviewing agency cannot reduce the budget.

A school district must expend monies for the purpose for which they are collected. If a statute requires fund accounting for special tax money, the school board must establish and deposit the money in such a fund. In such a case, a taxpayer may not require an accounting for the school funds beyond seeing that they are used for the purpose for which they were levied and collected.

Funds Collected and Allocated for a Particular Public Purpose Cannot Be Lawfully Diverted to Another Purpose

San Benito Independent School District v. Farmers' State Bank

Court of Civil Appeals, Texas, 1935.
78 S.W.2d 741.

SMITH, Justice. On May 16, 1932, Farmers' State Bank & Trust Company of San Benito was closed and its affairs were taken over by the state banking commissioner for administration, as provided by law. Up to that time San Benito Independent School District maintained four separate checking accounts in the bank, which was the district treasury, as follows:

First, an "interest and sinking fund account," from taxes assessed, collected, and deposited in said account for the purpose of paying interest and principal upon the district's bonded debt, in which account there was a balance, at the time the bank failed, of $12,942.68;

Second, a "local maintenance fund account," in which were deposited taxes assessed and collected for the specific purpose of local maintenance, exclusive of teachers' salaries, in which there was a balance of $318.25;

Third, an "interest and penalty refunding account," in which had been deposited interest and penalties unlawfully collected from the taxpayers, which under the law were required to be refunded to those paying them. In this account there was a balance, at the time the bank failed, of $124.16. The balances in the three foregoing accounts aggregated $13,385.09;

Fourth, a "state available warrant fund account," in which were deposited, as received, funds received from the state for the specific purpose of paying teachers' salaries. In this account, however, there was no balance on hand at the time the bank failed. Moreover, at that time the bank held unpaid district warrants drawn against that account in the aggregate amount of $3,409.18, which the bank carried, not as an overdraft, but as assets.

In this situation the district brought this action against the bank and banking commissioner to recover $13,385.09, being the amount of the balance of funds on deposit in the first three accounts mentioned, and prayed that the amount of the unpaid warrants held by the bank against the exhausted fourth, or "state available warrant fund account," be offset against the district's claim, leaving a balance of $9,975.91, for which net amount the district prayed judgment.

The bank and banking commissioner answered, setting up their claims of $3,409.18, represented by the unpaid district warrants held by them against the exhausted "state available warrant fund account," and, asserting that that claim against that fund could not lawfully be applied as an offset against the district's claim upon deposits in the other three specific fund accounts, prayed for direct judgment upon said warrants.

The trial court rendered judgment in favor of the district for the amount of its deposits in the bank, and in favor of the banking commissioner for the amount of the unpaid warrants held by him, but denied the district's prayer that the latter recovery be applied as an offset. The district has appealed. . . .

It is too well settled to require citation, or any extended discussion, that a public fund collected and allocated for a particular public purpose cannot be lawfully diverted to the use of another particular public purpose. Under that wise rule, when applied here, when the taxpayer pays a certain tax for the specific purpose of liquidating a particular public bonded indebtedness of his school district, the funds derived therefrom cannot lawfully be used for the purpose of paying teachers' salaries, chargeable under the law to a different public fund; when lawful interest and penalties have been collected from the taxpayers and segregated into a particular fund, and is required by law to be refunded to the taxpayer, as is the case here, that fund may not lawfully be diverted to the payment of teachers' salaries chargeable to another specific fund, as is sought to be done by appellant; when a specific tax has been levied and assessed by a school district and paid by the taxpayers, for the particular purpose of "local maintenance" (exclusive of teachers' salaries), and the fund so collected has been segregated and allocated to that purpose, as was done here, the district may not divert that fund to another for the purpose of paying teachers' salaries, as is sought to be done by the district in this case.

So when the bank acquired the warrants against the district's "state available fund" account, which was exhausted, at least for the time being, it could not lawfully collect them by charging the amounts thereof to the accounts of the interest and sinking fund, or the local maintenance fund, or the interest and penalty refunding fund; it could only hold the warrants until the account against which they were drawn was replenished, and it was so holding them, as among its assets, when it ceased to do business.

The corporate school district, as are all municipal corporations, is but a trustee or guardian of the public funds coming into its possession under the law, and may disburse those funds only in the manner and for the purposes prescribed by law. As the funds in question were gathered in, the district, in obedience to law, allocated them to the several purposes for which they were paid in, and deposited them with the bank in appropriate separate accounts kept for each specific fund. When so segregated into separate accounts, the district had no power or authority to transfer any part of the funds from either account and apply it to the purposes of any other account, any more than a trustee of several persons or estates could divert the funds of one cestui que trust to the use of another. Nor could the bank, in this case, lawfully pay the warrants drawn on one particular account out of the funds of another particular account, any more than it could charge the draft of one individual depositor to the account of another. The rights, capacities and interests of the respective parties are thus fixed by settled principles of law, and there being no mutuality of rights, interests and capacities between the district as trustee of the "available state" fund and account, and the same entity as trustee of the other three specific funds and accounts, it could not appropriate the one to the uses of the others.

The inevitable conclusion is, then, that in balancing the accounts between the district and the bank, the claim of the latter against the "state available fund" of the former could not be applied as an offset against the obligations of the bank to the other three separate fund accounts. The bank could not enforce such offset in an action thereon, nor may the district enforce it in this action.

The judgment is affirmed.

CASE NOTES

1. The extent of budget itemization necessary to meet statutory requirements has been described in an Arizona case. The Arizona statute requiring budgetary information divided the school budget into major general categories and then subdivided these categories into subitems. The operating expense category was broken down into two broad sections, administration

and instruction. Each of these sections was divided into forty-one subitems. A controversy arose as to whether the forty-one subitems were merely explanatory of the major categories or whether the expenditures of the board of education were restricted to the amounts in the subitems, making transfer of funds among subitems illegal. The statute governing this question stated:

> No expenditure shall be made for a purpose not particularly itemized and included in such budget, and no expenditure shall be made, and no debt, obligation or liability shall be incurred or created in any year for any purpose itemized in such budget in excess of the amount specified for such item.

The court in interpreting this statute defined the word "purpose" in light of the judicial principle that where the language of a statute may be subject to more than one interpretation, the court will adopt the one that is reasonable in view of the particular situation being litigated. The court said:

> Since the word "purpose" as used in [the statute] is susceptible of more than one interpretation, we are bound to declare as the intention of the legislature the alternative which is reasonable and convenient. It appears to us that to bind either the school district or the superintendent to a forty-one line operating expense budget, as advocated by the [treasurer], would be impractical, unduly restrictive, and lead to absurd results.

Isley v. School District No. 2 of Maricopa County, 81 Ariz. 280, 305 P.2d 432 (1956).

2. An Oklahoma court upheld a state board of education directive requiring school districts to treat as current expenses certain items that taxpayers insisted should have been recorded as capital outlay expenditures. The state board of education had acted under a statute providing that the state board shall prescribe a list of appropriation accounts by which funds of school districts shall be budgeted. *St. Louis–San Francisco Railway Co. v. McCurtain County, Oklahoma Excise Board,* 352 P.2d 896 (Okl.1960).

3. Where a school tax levy raises revenues in excess of the requested budgetary amount, the school board is entitled to the surplus. In Montgomery County, Maryland, where the county levies the tax rate requested by the school district, the county tax collector on many occasions received more from the school tax levy than was requested by the school board. The surplus remained in the county treasury and amounted to more than $1 million. The school board brought suit against Montgomery County to obtain the funds. The court held that when the levy was actually and unconditionally made by the county, the statutes were explicit in declaring that no part of the sum levied for the use of the public schools could be used for any other purpose and that the amount so levied each year must be paid by the county treasurer to the school board. *Board of Education of Montgomery County v. Montgomery County,* 237 Md. 191, 205 A.2d 202 (1964).

4. In the case of a fiscally dependent school district, a Connecticut court held that where a school budget is submitted to a municipal reviewing agency and the expenditures are for purposes described by statute to be within the board of education's authority to effectuate, the finance board has no power to refuse to include an appropriation for such expenditure in its budget. This statement is qualified by the fact that the reviewing agency may refuse appropriation if the financial condition of the town does not permit such expenditures. This is, of course, an extremely important limitation, since in Connecticut it is within the review board's authority to pronounce that the town is not in a financial position to support such expenditures for education and it can thereby cut the school budget. *Board of Education of Town of Stamford v. Board of Finance of Town of Stamford,* 127 Conn. 345, 16 A.2d 601 (1940).

5. In another case involving the authority of the town board of finance to control educational expenditures in a Connecticut school district, the court held that placement of certain funds to be used for school purposes in the general government budget contravened a statute permitting the board of education to transfer the unexpended or uncontracted-for portion of appropriations for school purposes to any other item and this constituted an illegal restriction on the appropriation. *Board of Education of Town of Ellington v. Town of Ellington,* 151 Conn. 1, 193 A.2d 466 (1963).

6. A school district may not, in the absence of any statute expressly permitting it, accumulate

surpluses beyond those required to operate for the ensuing year. The theory is that a school district levying taxes sufficient to maintain a large surplus should reduce its tax levy. One court held that a tax levy that created a surplus of over 50 percent of the entire school district budget exceeded the amount reasonably contemplated for a contingency. The court went on to say:

> A tax levy is required to be a reasonable approximation of the amount required. It has not been the policy of the law to permit the creation of funds by taxation in large amounts for future use, except where statutory authorization exists as in the case of building funds, sinking funds, and the like.

Kissinger v. School District No. 49 of Clay County, 163 Neb. 33, 77 N.W.2d 767 (1956).

❖ — ❖ — ❖

Money or Property Derived under the Auspices of the Public School Is Accountable in the Same Manner as Other Tax Funds

Petition of Auditors of Hatfield Township School District

Superior Court of Pennsylvania, 1947.
161 Pa.Super. 388, 54 A.2d 833.

ARNOLD, Judge. This appeal is from an order of the court below directing the officers, directors and supervising principal of the Hatfield Joint Consolidated School District to comply with a duces tecum subpoena issued by the official auditors calling for the production of various books, vouchers and papers.

The Hatfield Joint Consolidated School District was formed by the school districts of the borough of Hatfield and the township of Hatfield. Its bank account is carried by its treasurer in the Hatfield National Bank under the name "Hatfield Joint Consolidated School District," hereafter called the "official account." The warrants or vouchers thereon are executed by the proper officers of the district.

In the same bank is an account called "Hatfield Joint School Accounts," and the sole right to withdraw funds therefrom is possessed by Elmer B. Laudenslager, the supervising principal. This we will refer to as the "activities account." The appellants challenge the right of the statutory auditors to examine this account. . . .

Appellants have asked us to determine whether the activities account is subject to official audit even though no tax moneys were in it, and state: "This question is a matter of interest to every district in the Commonwealth. The decision in this case will affect every school district . . . [and] . . . will decide once and for all the status of such funds . . . even as the legislature established the status of the cafeteria funds. Section 8 of Act of 1931, P.L. 243, and Act of 1945, P.L. 688, 24 P.S. §331." Indeed the evidence in this case disclosed four other nearby communities operating a similar system, and in fact the system is widespread. It is fraught with great danger. High school football and other athletics have achieved great popularity, and this means that almost any school district, depending in a degree upon the skill of the athletes, has athletic events the admission fees of which aggregate a large sum of money, probably in excess of $10,000. It would be a great blow to the public school system if by embezzlement or lack of care such funds should be lost. Not only has the school board a moral duty to perform but there is also a legislative imperative. The public school system of this commonwealth is entirely statutory. Within the constitutional limitations the legislature is supreme and there reposes in the courts no power to permit deviation from its commands; and neither the local school districts nor the State Department of Education may bypass the duties enjoined.

In the so-called activity accounts various situations obtain. Of course if pupils of a class give money to a supervising principal to purchase for them class jewelry or similar things the school district has no official duty (although it may have a moral duty), for the supervising principal acts as agent of the pupils. This is the smaller end of the problem. At the other pole, a school district, acting under the express provisions of §405 of the Code, 24 P.S. §339, has athletic events. These activities produce large sums of money from paid admissions. Under the instant system these sums of money are not disbursed through the treasurer, nor through a resolution of the board, but are solely at the command of one individual, who has no statutory standing or duty. It is possible that some school districts may neither *directly* nor *indirectly* furnish any money for the playing field or stadium; or for the coaching of the athletes, or for their uniforms or playing togs, or for the apparatus with which the sport is connected, or for the lighting of the field; although it is very doubtful whether such case exists. But it is certainly true that, if a school district operates and expends tax money for the acquisition, maintenance or lighting of the playing field, or for the payment of services of a coach, the admissions charged result from the use of public property and from the expenditure of tax moneys and are the property of the school district, must go into the official account of the treasurer thereof, and are subject to audit.

The moneys derived from the sale of admissions to witness the event in question come into being because of (1) the use and wear of the school building and grounds; (2) the use and wear of personal property owned by the district; (3) the payment to employees such as coaches for their services; (4) the payment by the district for light, heat and various maintenance charges, including janitor service. By reason of the use of these public funds the event takes place, and from it are reaped the admission fees paid to witness the performance. The pupils are not expected to and do not furnish any of the money. The admission fees could not belong to them, and indeed if taken they would be professionals instead of amateurs. The spectators are not to get their money back. No one has any investment except the school district. The money raised by admissions therefore belongs to the district, which by its property and funds made the admission fees possible.

Of lesser importance, but in the same category, are the admission fees charged for dramatic and musical enterprises held in the buildings of the district. These belong to the district for the same reasons and with the same results. For instance, the school districts usually and properly provide musical instruments, just as they provide equipment and uniforms for athletics. In the instant case admission fees were expended through the activities account for such instruments, but it was frankly admitted that when bought the instruments belonged to the district. So do the admission fees themselves.

We have not attempted to discuss each situation that may present itself, but where moneys or property are derived directly or indirectly through the use of school buildings, or from the expenditure of public funds of the district, the moneys thus derived are public property, must be handled exactly as tax moneys and be paid to the district treasurer. . . .

Order affirmed.

■ PUBLIC SCHOOL INDEBTEDNESS

The authority of school districts to issue bonds must be clearly and expressly conferred by statute. The failure of a school board to comply with the statutory conditions for school bond issuance will render the bonds illegal.

Bonds issued for a specific purpose must be used for that purpose and no other. It has been held that bonds approved by the voters for "erecting and constructing a new roof" for a school building were illegal when the statute provided for bonds to be issued for the purpose of "erecting and equipping, or purchasing and equipping" school houses.[76] In another case, a court held a statute authorizing a bond election for the "erection and enlargement" of school buildings could not be construed to include the issuance of bonds for the purpose of equipping school buildings.[77]

While earlier cases generally held that statutory procedures for school bond elections were to be strictly followed and failure to do so would make the bonds illegal, more recent cases tend to allow some flexibility so long as irregularities do not affect the results of the election. It has been held that where the voters in a bond election authorize bonds for a greater amount than is consistent with the law, the voter authorization is not illegal, and the school board may issue bonds for the amount prescribed by law.

Generally, the courts have held that a bondholder cannot recover on an illegal bond even if he or she is an innocent purchaser. This rule, however, has been modified in some states, where it has been held that where illegal bonds have been sold and the funds applied to the improvement of the district, the bondholder may recover under *quantum meruit*. Also, the courts will permit the holder of an illegal bond to recover if the money is identifiable and has not been commingled with other funds of the district. The courts, in some cases, have allowed the holder to recover property purchased with illegal bond proceeds if no other money of the district was used in payment for the property.

The constitutions of most states make provision for debt limitations, the maximum percentage of which a local school district may not exceed. Courts have held that the percentage of indebtedness is to be computed using the amount of bonds that actually has been issued and not the amount that was projected at the time of a bond election. While a state legislature must conform to prescribed constitutional requirements regarding indebtedness, some state legislatures have sought to avoid stringent constitutional debt restrictions that severely limit educational facility construction. One such device resorted to by a few states is the "holding company" or the "local school building authority." This method of financing school construction effectively increases the debt capacity of a local school district and has been upheld by the courts.[78]

————— ❖ — ❖ — ❖ —————

*Legislature Has Power to Direct Local
Authorities to Create Debt for
Public School Building*

Revell v. Mayor of City of Annapolis

Court of Appeals of Maryland, 1895.
81 Md. 1, 31 A. 695.

ROBINSON, C. J. The act of 1894, c. 620, provides for the erection of a public school building in the city of Annapolis, and to pay for the same, it authorizes and directs the school commissioners of Anne Arundel county to borrow money, not exceeding the sum of $20,000, on

bonds to be indorsed by the county commissioners; and for the same purpose it directs that the city of Annapolis shall issue bonds to the amount of $10,000, and that said bonds shall be issued without submitting the question of their issue to the voters of said city. The city of Annapolis has refused to issue the bonds as thus directed by the act, and the question is whether the legislature has the power to direct that the city authorities shall issue bonds to raise money to be applied to the erection of a public school building in said city. This power is denied, on the broad ground that it is not competent for the legislature to compel a municipal corporation to create a debt or levy a tax for a local purpose, in which the state has no concern, or to assume a debt not within the corporate powers of a municipal government. If the correctness of this general proposition be conceded for the purposes of this case, we do not see how it affects in any manner the validity of the act now in question. We cannot agree that the erection of buildings necessary for the public schools is a matter of merely local concern, in which the state has no interest. In this country the people are not only in theory, but in practice, the source of all governmental power, and the stability of free institutions mainly rests upon an enlightened public opinion. Fully recognizing this, the constitution declares that it shall be the duty of the legislature "to establish throughout the state a thorough and efficient system of free public schools, and to provide by taxation or otherwise" for their maintenance and support. . . . And the legislature has accordingly established a public school system, and has provided for its support by state and local taxation. It cannot be said, therefore, that the erection of buildings for public school purposes is a matter in which the state has no concern; nor can we agree that the creation of a debt for such purposes is not within the ordinary functions of municipal government. What is a municipal corporation? It is but a subordinate part of the state government, incorporated for public purposes, and clothed with special and limited powers of legislation in regard to its own local affairs. It has no inherent legislative power, and can exercise such powers only as have been expressly or by fair implication delegated to it by the legislature. The control of highways and bridges within the corporate limits; the power to provide for an efficient police force; to pass all necessary laws and ordinances for the preservation of the health, safety, and welfare of its people; and the power to provide for the support of its public schools by local taxation,—are all among the ordinary powers delegated to municipal corporations. And the public schools in Baltimore city are not only under the control and supervision of the city authorities, but are mainly supported by municipal taxation. It is no answer to say that the public schools in Annapolis are under the control of the school commissioners of Anne Arundel county, and that under its charter it has no power to create a debt or levy taxes for their support. The legislature may, at its pleasure, alter, amend, and enlarge its powers. It may authorize the city authorities to establish public schools within the corporate limits, and direct that bonds shall be issued to raise money for their support, payable at intervals during a series of years. There is no difference in principle between issuing bonds and the levying of a tax in one year sufficient to meet the necessary expenditure. . . .

If the legislature has the power to direct the city authorities to create a debt for a public school building, the exercise of this power in no manner depends upon their consent or upon the consent of the qualified voters of the city. We recognize the force of the argument that the question whether a municipal debt is to be created ought to be left to the discretion and judgment of the people who are to bear the burden. We recognize the fact that the exercise of this power by the legislature may be liable to abuse. But this abuse of a power is no argument against its exercise. The remedy, however, in such cases, is with the people to whom the members of the legislature are responsible for the discharge of the trust committed to them. It is a matter over which the courts have no control. If the debt to be created was for a private purpose, that would present quite a different question, for it is a fundamental principle, inherent in the nature of taxation itself, that all burdens and taxes shall be levied for public, and not for private, purposes. Be that as it may, it is well settled in this state that the legislature has the power to compel a municipal corpora-

tion to levy a tax or incur a debt for a public purpose, and one within the ordinary functions of a municipal government. . . .

In closing his argument, the counsel for the appellees suggested that the act was invalid because it was in conflict with the Fourteenth Amendment of the federal Constitution which forbids the taking of "property without due process of law." . . . It is a sufficient answer to this objection to say that the act in question, which requires the city authorities to issue bonds to raise money to pay the cost of a public school building, is a lawful exercise of legislature power, and, this being so, taxes levied to pay such bonds are not open to the objection of taking property without due process of law. Nor can we agree that the act is in conflict with section 33, art. 3, of the constitution, which declares that the general assembly shall pass no special law for any case for which provision has been made by an existing general law. The general law provides, it is true, that the school commissioners of Anne Arundel county shall have the control and supervision of the public schools in said county, with power to build, repair, and furnish schoolhouses. But it does not authorize the commissioners to borrow money upon bonds to be indorsed by the county commissioners for such purposes, nor does it provide for the apportionment of the cost of a public school building to be erected in the city of Annapolis between the county and the city. This could only be done by special act, and, this being so, the special act is not in conflict with the constitution, which forbids the passing of a special act for any purpose for which provision has been made by an existing general law. It follows from what we have said that the judgment sustaining the demurrer in this case must be overruled.

———————— ❖ — ❖ — ❖ ————————

Issuance of Municipal Bonds without
Statutory Authorization Is Ultra Vires

Hewitt v. Board of Education

Supreme Court of Illinois, 1880.
94 Ill. 528.

Mr. Chief Justice WALKER delivered the opinion of the Court. This was an action of assumpsit, brought by Hewitt in the circuit court of McLean county, against the "Board of Education of Normal School District," on a bond for $500, and two coupons of $25 each. The bond was dated the 1st of September, 1873, payable five years after its date, with ten percent interest, and it was payable to John Gregory or order. It was indorsed by him in blank, and he negotiated it to the Home Bank, of which appellant purchased, taking no further indorsement. . . .

The evidence tended to show that the bond was not issued to pay for a school house site, or to erect a building thereon. It also tended to prove that Gregory was, at the time the bond was issued to him, a member of the board, and that appellant was aware of the fact when he purchased the bond. As these were controverted facts, and were found by the circuit court against appellant, and as the Appellate Court has affirmed the judgment of the circuit court, we must take the affirmance as a finding of the facts as they were found by the circuit court, and we are precluded from reviewing these controverted facts, but are bound by the finding of the Appellate Court.

The fact, then, that the bond was not issued for an authorized purpose, undeniably rendered it void. Municipal corporations are not usually endowed with power to enter into traffic or general business, and are only created as auxiliaries to the government in carrying into effect some special governmental policy, or to aid in preserving the order and in promoting the well-being of the locality over which their authority extends. Where a corporation is created for business purposes, all persons may presume such bodies, when issuing their paper, are acting within the scope of their power. Not so with municipalities. Being created for governmental purposes, the borrowing of money, the purchase of property on time, and the giving of commercial paper, are not inherent, or even powers usually conferred; and unless endowed with such power in their charters, they have no authority to make and place on the market such paper, and persons dealing in it must see that the power exists. This has long been the rule of this court. . . . We might refer to other cases where it has been held that bonds issued without author-

ity are void, even in the hands of purchasers before maturity and without actual notice.

A person taking bonds of a municipal corporation has access to the records of the body, and it is his duty to see that such instruments are issued in pursuance of authority, and when without power, they must be held void in whosesoever hands they are found. If, therefore, this bond was not issued to purchase a school house site, or for erecting a school building, as the Appellate Court seems to have found, the bond is void, as it was issued without power, and this, too, in the hands of a person taking without actual notice.

Again, this bond was issued without authority, and was void. . . .

The judgment of the Appellate Court is affirmed.

CASE NOTES

1. The legislature may prescribe the conditions by which school bonds shall be issued. Failure to follow prescribed conditions will render the bonds illegal. *Dupont v. Mills*, 39 Del. 42, 196 A. 168 (1937).

2. In an 1893 case, the U.S. Circuit Court for the District of Nebraska held that a statute providing that "any school district shall have power and authority to borrow money to pay for the sites of schoolhouses" does not confer authority on the school district to issue negotiable securities. Such securities issued by school districts are void even in the hands of an innocent purchaser. *Ashuelot National Bank v. School District No. 7*, 56 Fed. 197 (C.C.A.Neb.1893).

3. Statutes relating to school bond elections frequently state that the notice of election or resolution shall relate to a single purpose only. The notice or resolution must state specifically the issues in order that the voter can make a clear choice. Such a statutory provision in Ohio provides for the notice of a bond election for "one purpose" but defines "one purpose" quite broadly as being,

in the case of a school district, any number of school buildings; and in any case, all expenditures, including the acquisition of a site and purchase of equipment, for any one utility building, or other structure, or group of buildings or structures for the same general purpose . . . included in the same resolution.

Pursuant to this statute, an action was brought contesting a bond election for which the resolution had provided for (1) the acquisition of real estate, construction of fireproof school buildings, and the provision of furniture and furnishing therefor; and (2) improvement of nonfireproof school buildings and the provision of furniture and furnishings therefor. The court held that this resolution violated the statutory mandate for "one purpose," and it stated:

> The purpose of the statute is to prevent the union in one act of diverse, incongruous and disconnected matters, having no relation to or connection with each other . . . ; to give electors a choice to secure what they desire without the necessity of accepting something which they do not want . . . ; and to prevent double propositions being placed before a voter having but a single expression to answer all propositions, thus making logrolling impossible. . . . In applying the rule, the courts invoke a test as to the existence of a natural relationship between the various structures or objects united in one proposition so that they form "but one rounded whole."

State ex rel. Board of Education v. Thompson, 167 Ohio St. 23, 145 N.E.2d 668 (1957).

4. One court has held that a statute authorizing the school district to issue bonds "for the purpose of raising funds to pay the cost of the equipping, enlarging, remodeling, repairing, and improving" of the schoolhouse and "the purchase, repairing, and installation of equipment thereof" did not authorize a rural high school district to issue bonds for the purpose of raising funds to pay the cost of removing a schoolhouse from one site to another. *Byer v. Rural High School District No. 4 of Brown County,* 169 Kan. 351, 219 P.2d 382 (1950).

5. Courts have held that school district indebtedness, subject to legal limitations, extends only to voluntary indebtedness. A judgment against a school district for a sum of money is not considered the creation of a debt within the meaning of constitutional debt limitations. Such debt is not subject to collateral attack by a taxpayers' suit to avoid taxation. *Edmundson v. Independent School District,* 98 Iowa 639, 67 N.W. 671 (1896).

6. It has generally been held that a school district whose boundaries overlap or are coterminous with a civil government has a separate computation in determining indebtedness. *Vallelly v. Board of Park Commissioners,* 16 N.D. 25, 111 N.W. 615, 171 A.L.R. 732 (1907).

7. In determining whether an indebtedness limit has been exceeded, the amount of indebtedness is determined at the time the bonds are issued and not at the time the bonds are voted. *Hebel v. School District R-1, Jefferson County,* 131 Colo. 105, 279 P.2d 673 (1955).

8. Refunding bonds do not increase the indebtedness of a school district. *Prohm v. Non-High School District No. 216,* 7 Ill.2d 421, 130 N.E.2d 917 (1955).

9. The constitutions in Indiana and Kentucky limit the indebtedness of school districts and other political subdivisions to a mere 2 percent of the value of the taxable property in the district. These constitutional debt limitations are the lowest of any of the states in the nation. To bypass or avoid these uncommonly strict limitations, both states have enacted statutes that allow for the use of school building corporations in financing school construction. Such a procedure permits the formation of a holding company that is authorized to construct a school building and incur the indebtedness. The school building corporation contracts with the school district to lease the building to the district for a number of years, and when the rental payments have paid off the bonded indebtedness, the building becomes the property of the school district. This type of purchase on an installment arrangement does not increase the indebtedness of the school district. The Supreme Court of Indiana had this to say about the constitutionality of the procedure:

> The fact that the building company was willing to give the school building to the [school district] when the building company had been paid an amount equal to its investment . . . does not change the lease-contract into a contract to purchase. It is true that the [school district], through the device of a long term lease providing for annual rental payments, may become the owner of the school building which [under the constitutional limitation] it could not have acquired . . . by issuing bonds. But it does not follow that either the arrangement or the result constitutes an evasion of

the limitations of the [Constitution]. The lease-contract is not in contravention of [the Constitution] unless it necessarily created a legally enforceable debt obligation for an amount in excess of the amount permitted by [the Constitution].

Jefferson School Township v. Jefferson Township School Building Co., 212 Ind. 542, 10 N.E.2d 608 (1937); *Kees v. Smith*, 235 Ind. 687, 137 N.E.2d 541 (1956).

■ ENDNOTES

1. See 68 Am.Jur.2d §46.
2. Schutes v. Eberly, 82 Ala. 242, 2 So. 345 (1887); Grainger County v. State, 111 Tenn. 234, 80 S.W. 750 (1904).
3. Florida Department of Education v. Glasser, 622 So.2d 944 (Fla.1993).
4. 777 S.W.2d 391 (Tex.1984) (*Edgewood I*); Edgewood Independent School District v. Kirby, 804 S.W.2d 491 (Tex.1991) (*Edgewood II*).
5. Texas Const., Art. VIII, §1-e.
6. Ibid.
7. This discussion is adapted from a chapter by Kern Alexander and K. Forbis Jordan in *Financing Education: Fiscal and Legal Alternatives*, ed. R. L. Johns, Kern Alexander, and K. Forbis Jordan (Columbus, Ohio: Charles Merrill Company, 1972, pp. 470–508). See also School District No. 25 of Woods County v. Hodge, 199 Okl. 81, 183 P.2d 575 (1947).
8. Bell's Gap Railroad Co. v. Pennsylvania, 134 U.S. 232, 10 S.Ct. 533 (1890).
9. Wade J. Newhouse, *Constitutional Uniformity and Equality in State Taxation* (Ann Arbor: University of Michigan Law School, 1959), p. 602.
10. Ibid., p. 608.
11. Hess v. Mullaney, 213 F.2d 635 (9th Cir.1954), cert. denied, Hess v. Dewey, 348 U.S. 836, 75 S.Ct. 50 (1954).
12. 79 C.J.S. §411.
13. "Is Denial of Equal Educational Opportunity Constitutional?" *Administrator's Notebook* 13, no. 6 (February 1965). See also Arthur E. Wise, *Rich Schools Poor Schools* (Chicago: University of Chicago Press, 1968).
14. Griffin v. Illinois, 351 U.S. 12, 76 S.Ct. 585 (1956).
15. Baker v. Carr, 369 U.S. 186, 82 S.Ct. 691 (1962).
16. 293 F.Supp. 327 (N.D.Ill.1968), affirmed sub nom. McInnis v. Ogilvie, 394 U.S. 322, 89 S.Ct. 1197 (1969).
17. McInnis v. Ogilvie, 394 U.S. at p. 336.
18. McInnis v. Ogilvie, 394 U.S. 322, 89 S.Ct. 1197 (1969).
19. McInnis v. Shapiro, op. cit.
20. 310 F.Supp. 572 (W.D.Va.1969), affirmed, 397 U.S. 44, 90 S.Ct. 812 (1970).
21. Ibid.
22. 5 Cal.3d 584, 96 Cal.Rptr. 601, 487 P.2d 1241 (1971), appeal after remand, 18 Cal.3d 728, 135 Cal.Rptr. 345, 557 P.2d 929 (1976), cert. denied, 432 U.S. 907, 97 S.Ct. 2951 (1977).
23. San Antonio Independent School District v. Rodriguez, 411 U.S. 1, 93 S.Ct. 1278 (1973);

24. San Antonio Independent School District v. Rodriguez, 411 U.S. 1, 93 S.Ct. 1278 (1973); Serrano v. Priest, 5 Cal.3d 584, 96 Cal.Rptr. 601, 487 P.2d 1241 (1971), appeal after remand, 18 Cal.3d 728, 135 Cal.Rptr. 345, 557 P.2d 929 (1976), cert. denied, 432 U.S. 907, 97 S.Ct. 2951 (1977); Serrano v. Priest, 226 Cal.Rptr. 584 (1986).
25. San Antonio Independent School District v. Rodriguez, 411 U.S. 1, 93 S.Ct. 1278 (1973).
26. Milliken v. Green, 389 Mich. 1, 203 N.W.2d 457 (1972), vacated, 390 Mich. 389, 212 N.W.2d 711 (1973).
27. Shofstall v. Hollins, 110 Ariz. 88, 515 P.2d 590 (1973).
28. Milliken v. Green, 389 Mich. 1, 203 N.W.2d 457 (1972), vacated, 390 Mich. 389, 212 N.W.2d 711 (1973).
29. 457 U.S. 202, 102 S.Ct. 2382 (1982).
30. 478 U.S. 265, 106 S.Ct. 2932 (1986).
31. Plyler v. Doe, op. cit.
32. Ibid.
33. Ibid.
34. Ibid.
35. Papason v. Allain, op. cit.
36. School Board of Parish of Livingston v. Louisiana State Board of Elementary & Secondary Education, 830 F.2d 563 (5th Cir.1987).
37. Thompson v. Engelking, 96 Idaho 793, 537 P.2d 635 (1975).
38. Blase v. Illinois, 55 Ill.2d 94, 302 N.E.2d 46 (1973).
39. Knowles v. State Board of Education, 219 Kan. 271, 547 P.2d 699 (1976).
40. Helena Elementary School District No. 1 v. State, 236 Mont. 44, 769 P.2d 684 (1989), opinion amended by 784 P.2d 412 (1990).
41. Olsen v. State, 276 Or. 9, 554 P.2d 139 (1976).
42. Board of Education v. Nyquist, 94 Misc.2d 466, 408 N.Y.S.2d 606 (1978), affirmed, 83 A.D.2d 217, 443 N.Y.S.2d 843 (1981), reversed, 57 N.Y.2d 27, 453 N.Y.S.2d 643, 439 N.E.2d 359 (1982), appeal dismissed, 459 U.S. 1139, 103 S.Ct. 775 (1983).
43. McDaniel v. Thomas, 248 Ga. 632, 285 S.E.2d 156 (1981).
44. 62 N.J. 473, 303 A.2d 273, on reargument, 63 N.J. 196, 306 A.2d 65 (1973), 69 N.J. 449, 355 A.2d 129, opinion supplemented, 70 N.J. 155, 358 A.2d 457, injunction dissolved, 70 N.J. 464, 360 A.2d 400 (1976).
45. Robinson v. Cahill, 303 A.2d at 295.
46. Horton v. Meskill, 172 Conn. 615, 376 A.2d 359 (1977), 187 Conn. 187, 445 A.2d 579 (1982), 195 Conn. 24, 486 A.2d 1099 (1985).
47. DuPree v. Alma School District No. 30, 279 Ark. 340, 651 S.W.2d 90 (1983).
48. Shofstall v. Hollins, 110 Ariz. 88, 515 P.2d 590 (1973); Milliken v. Green, 390 Mich. 389, 212 N.W.2d 711 (1973); Thompson v. Engelking, 96 Idaho 793, 537 P.2d 635 (1975); Olsen v. State, 276 Or. 9, 554 P.2d 139 (1976); Danson v. Casey, 484 Pa. 415, 399 A.2d 360 (1979); Bensalem Township School District v. Commonwealth, 105 Pa.Cmwlth. 388, 524 A.2d 1027 (1987), remanded, 518 Pa. 581, 544 A.2d 1318 (1988); Board of Education of City School District of City of Cincinnati v. Walter, 58 Ohio St.2d 368, 390 N.E.2d 813 (1979), cert. denied, 444 U.S. 1015, 100 S.Ct. 665 (1980); McDaniel v. Thomas, 248 Ga. 632, 285 S.E.2d 156 (1981); Lujan v. Colorado State Board

of Education, 649 P.2d 1005 (Colo.1982); Board of Education, Levittown Union Free School District v. Nyquist, 94 Misc.2d 466, 408 N.Y.S.2d 606 (1978), judgment modified, 83 A.D.2d 217, 443 N.Y.S.2d 843 (1981), order modified, 57 N.Y.2d 27, 453 N.Y.S.2d 643, 439 N.E.2d 359 (1982), appeal dismissed, 459 U.S. 1138, 103 S.Ct. 775 (1983); Dumain v. Carey, 133 A.D.2d 206, 519 N.Y.S.2d 17 (1987); Hornbeck v. Somerset County Board of Education, 295 Md. 597, 458 A.2d 758 (1983); Fair School Finance Council of Oklahoma, Inc. v. State of Oklahoma, 746 P.2d 1135 (Okl.1987); Britt v. North Carolina State Board of Education, 86 N.C.App. 282, 357 S.E.2d 432 (1987); School Board of the Parish of Livingston v. Louisiana State Board of Elementary and Secondary Education, 830 F.2d 563 (5th Cir.1987), cert. denied, 487 U.S. 1223, 108 S.Ct. 2884 (1988); Richland County v. Campbell, 294 S.C. 346, 364 S.E.2d 470 (1988).

49. Robinson v. Cahill, 62 N.J. 473, 303 A.2d 273, cert. denied, 414 U.S. 976, 94 S.Ct. 292 (1973); Knowles v. State Board of Education, 219 Kan. 271, 547 P.2d 699 (1976); Buse v. Smith, 74 Wis.2d 550, 247 N.W.2d 141 (1976); Kukor v. Grover, 148 Wis.2d 469, 436 N.W.2d 568 (1989); Serrano v. Priest, 5 Cal.3d 584, 96 Cal.Rptr. 601, 487 P.2d 1241 (1971); Serrano v. Priest, 18 Cal.3d 728, 135 Cal.Rptr. 345, 557 P.2d 929 (1976), cert. denied, 432 U.S. 907, 97 S.Ct. 2951 (1977); Serrano v. Priest, 226 Cal.Rptr. 584 (1986); Horton v. Meskill, 172 Conn. 615, 376 A.2d 359 (1977); Seattle School District No. 1 v. State, 90 Wash.2d 476, 585 P.2d 71 (1978); Pauley v. Kelly, 162 W.Va. 672, 255 S.E.2d 859 (1979); State ex rel. Board of Education for Grant County v. Manchin, 179 W.Va. 235, 366 S.E.2d 743 (1988); Washakie County School District No. 1 v. Herschler, 606 P.2d 310 (Wyo.1980), cert. denied sub nom. Hot Springs County School District No. 1 v. Washakie County School District No. 1, 449 U.S. 824, 101 S.Ct. 86 (1980); DuPree v. Alma School District No. 30, 279 Ark. 340, 651 S.W.2d 90 (1983); Helena Elementary School District No. 1 v. State, 236 Mont. 44, 769 P.2d 684 (1989), opinion amended, 236 Mont. 44, 784 P.2d 412 (1990); Rose v. Council for Better Education, Inc., 790 S.W.2d 186 (Ky.1989); Edgewood Independent School District v. Kirby, 777 S.W.2d 391 (Tex.1989).

50. David L. Franklin and G. Alan Hickrod, "School Finance Equity: The Courts Intervene," *Policy Briefs* nos. 6 and 7 (1990): pp. 1–2.

51. Serrano v. Priest (1976), op. cit.

52. Ibid.

53. Robinson v. Cahill, op. cit.

54. 78 Ohio St.3d 193, 677 N.E.2d 733 (1997).

55. 162 W.Va. 672, 255 S.E.2d 859 (1979); Pauley v. Bailey, 174 W.Va. 167, 324 S.E.2d 128 (1984).

56. See Kern Alexander, "The Common School Ideal and the Limits of Legislative Authority: The Kentucky Case," *Harvard Journal on Legislation* 28, no. 2 (Summer 1991): pp. 341–366.

57. Rose v. Council for Better Education, Inc., 790 S.W.2d 186 (Ky.1989).

58. Robinson v. Cahill, op. cit.

59. Edgewood Independent School District v. Kirby, 777 S.W.2d 391 (Tex.1989). See also Edgewood Independent School District v. Kirby, 804 S.W.2d 491 (Tex.1991).

60. Alexander, "The Common School Ideal."

61. Milliken v. Green, 390 Mich. 389, 212 N.W.2d 711 (1973).

62. San Antonio Independent School District v. Rodriguez, op. cit.

63. Serrano v. Priest (1976), op. cit.

64. Ibid.

65. Horton v. Meskill, op. cit.

66. Pauley v. Kelly, op. cit.

67. McDaniel v. Thomas, op. cit.

68. Franklin and Hickrod, "School Finance Equity."

69. Rose v. Council for Better Education, Inc., op. cit.

70. Edgewood Independent School District v. Kirby, op. cit.

71. Alexander, "The Common School Ideal."

72. Edgewood Independent School District v. Kirby, op. cit.

73. Rose v. Council for Better Education, Inc., op. cit., 206.

74. Edgewood Independent School District v. Kirby, op. cit., citing S. McKay, *Austin, Texas: Debates in the Texas Constitutional Convention of 1875* (1930), p. 198.

75. Helena Elementary School District No. 1 v. State, 769 P.2d at 691.

76. School District No. 6 in Chase County v. Robb, 150 Kan. 402, 93 P.2d 905 (1939).

77. Jewett v. School District No. 25 in Fremont County, 49 Wyo. 277, 54 P.2d 546 (1936).

78. Kees v. Smith, 235 Ind. 687, 137 N.E.2d 541 (1956); Waller v. Georgetown Board of Education, 209 Ky. 726, 273 S.W. 498 (1925).

CHAPTER 20

PROPERTY

All property in this country is held under the implied obligation that the owner's use of it shall not be injurious to the community.

—John M. Harlan

CHAPTER OUTLINE

- PURCHASE OF PROPERTY FOR SPECIAL PURPOSE
- SCHOOL BUILDINGS
- SCHOOL SITE SELECTION

- EMINENT DOMAIN
- ADVERSE POSSESSION
- REVERSION OF SCHOOL PROPERTY

SCHOOL PROPERTY is state property held in trust for public school purposes.[1] By vesting a local school district with the power to acquire and hold property, the legislature does not relinquish its control. School property remains the property of the state, and the power of the local district may be expanded or abolished at the will of the legislature. For example, it is conceivable that a state legislature may decide to vest the control of school property in a local agency other than a school district. In such a case, the school district would, abiding by the statute, relinquish control over the property in favor of the other agency.

The same reasoning prevails when the legislature decides to reorganize many small school districts into larger, more comprehensive district units. The property now owned by the smaller districts becomes, by statute, the property of the new, larger consolidated district. The state legislature in this case has merely changed the trustee in which control of school property is vested.

School Property Is Public Property and Newly Created Public School District Is Not Required to Compensate Old School Board for Property Taken from It

City of Baker School Board v. East Baton Rouge Parish School Board

Court of Appeals of Louisiana,
First Circuit, 2000.
754 So.2d 291.

LeBLANC, J.

This controversy concerns the title to and questions whether compensation is due for the public school facilities located in the newly-created City of Baker School District.

Before 1995, the whole of East Baton Rouge Parish was included in the East Baton Rouge Parish School District. However, by statewide election in 1995, a new school system within the incorporated limits of the City of Baker was created. Pursuant to the statutory scheme set out in La.R.S. 17:72, members of the City of Baker School Board (the "Baker Board") were elected and by this litigation seek to clarify matters of ownership of public school facilities, land, property and ten buses (the "school property") located within its limits. The Baker Board filed for a declaratory judgment, naming the East Baton Rouge Parish School Board (the "Parish Board") as defendant. By joint stipulation, the parties acknowledged the Parish Board holds title to the property in question, but the Baker Board asserts it should be declared the owner of the property, without compensation due to the Parish Board. . . .

Public education is a function of the sovereign. La. Const. art. 8, §1. . . . School boards perform the function of the sovereign in implementing the constitutional mandate to provide public schools and to administer public education. . . . School boards are agencies of the state. . . . The task of educating the children of Louisiana rests with the individual school boards throughout the state. . . . The ownership, management and control of property within a school board's district is vested in the district, in the manner of a statutory trustee, for the accomplishment of its duty. . . . The general rule of ownership of property of school districts was stated in 68 Am.Jur.2d *Schools* §74 (1993), as follows:

> The ownership of school property is generally in the local district or school board as trustee for the public at large. School property is thus considered public property and is not to be regarded as the private property of the school district by which it is held or in which it is located [footnotes omitted].

The Baker Board, as successor to the Parish Board for the accomplishment of the duty to educate, became the successor of the property through which the duty is to be accomplished.

While actual ownership remains with the public at large, title follows the agency obligated to carry out the responsibility. Title to the school property at issue transfers to the Baker Board.

Concerning the issue of compensation, we find none due the Parish Board. There has been no taking. The transfer of legal title from the Parish Board to the Baker Board is merely the transfer from one trustee to another. As stated above, the public owns the school property. Moreover, while the Parish Board is no longer the title owner of the property, it also is no longer mandated to educate the children living within the boundaries of the Baker Board. The release of the obligation follows the transfer of legal title to the property.

For the foregoing reasons, the judgment of the trial court is affirmed. . . .

AFFIRMED.

Absent Legislation to the Contrary, a School District, as a State Agency, Is Not Subject to Local Municipal Zoning Ordinance

City of Bloomfield v. Davis County Community School District

Supreme Court of Iowa, 1963.
254 Iowa 900, 119 N.W.2d 909.

GARFIELD, Chief Justice. This is an action in equity by the City of Bloomfield to enjoin defendants, Davis County Community School District, and its contractor, Boatman, from installing in a restricted residence district in plaintiff city a bulk storage tank for gasoline and a pump to supply its school buses therewith. . . .

On September 19, 1933, the council of plaintiff city passed ordinance 84 designating and establishing a restricted residence district in the city. Section 2 of the ordinance provides: "That no buildings or other structures, except residences, school houses, churches, and other similar structures shall hereafter be erected, reconstructed, altered, repaired or occupied within said district without first securing from the city council permit therefor. . . ."

Section 3 of the ordinance provides: "Any building or structure erected, altered, repaired or used in violation of any of the provisions of this ordinance, is hereby declared to be a nuisance. . . ."

The only contention of defendants we find it necessary to consider is that ordinance 84 should not be held applicable to them to prevent installation on this school-owned site of this gasoline facility for servicing its school buses because the school district is an arm of the state and proposes to use its property for a governmental purpose. . . .

The law seems quite well settled that a municipal zoning ordinance is not applicable to the state or any of its agencies in the use of its property for a governmental purpose unless the legislature has clearly manifested a contrary intent. . . .

C.J.S. Zoning, §135 says, "Ordinarily, a governmental body is not subject to zoning restrictions in its use of property for governmental purposes."

The underlying logic of some of these authorities is, in substance, that the legislature could not have intended, in the absence of clear expression to the contrary, to give municipalities authority to thwart the state, or any of its agencies in performing a duty imposed upon it by statute.

There can be no doubt the school district is an arm or agency of the state and that the maintenance of public schools, including providing transportation to the pupils entitled to it as required by statute, is a governmental function. Certainly it is not a proprietary one. . . .

Code section 297.1, I.C.A. states, "The board of each school corporation may fix the site for each schoolhouse. . . ." Section 297.3 says, "Any school corporation . . . may take and hold an area equal to two blocks . . . for a schoolhouse site, and not exceeding thirty acres for school playground, stadium, or field house, *or other purposes for each such site."* (Emphasis added.)

Section 285.10, which requires local school boards to provide transportation for each pupil legally entitled thereto, states, in subsection 2, that local school boards "Establish, maintain

and operate bus routes for the transportation of pupils so as to provide for the economical and efficient operation thereof. . . ." Section 285.10 also provides, in subsection 5, that local boards "Exercise any and all powers and duties relating to transportation of pupils enjoined upon them by law."

Section 285.11 provides that in the operation of bus routes and contracting for transportation, "The boards shall take advantage of all tax exemptions on fuel, equipment, *and of such other economies as are available."* (Emphasis added.)

We think furnishing economical transportation to pupils entitled to it is as much a school matter, over which the district has exclusive jurisdiction, as maintenance of the school buildings or location of the high school football field. (Plaintiff concedes a football stadium is generally held to come within the meaning of a schoolhouse. See also *Livingston v. Davis*, 243 Iowa 21, 27, 50 N.W.2d 592, 596, 27 A.L.R.2d 1237.) . . .

No statute has come to our attention which indicates a clear legislative intent that the state or such of its agencies as defendant district, in the use of its property for a governmental purpose, must comply with a municipal zoning ordinance. Unless our decision is to be contrary to the uniform current of authority on the subject, we must hold defendant district, in the location of this tank and pump to supply fuel to its buses, is not subject to ordinance 84. . . .

We think this opinion does not conflict with our decision in *Cedar Rapids Community School Dist. v. City of Cedar Rapids*, supra, 252 Iowa 205, 106 N.W.2d 655, that the school district was subject to certain building ordinances of the city in renovating and constructing school buildings. No zoning ordinance or question as to the district's right to make use of its property in performing a duty enjoined on it by law—such as transportation of pupils—was there involved. The two cases are further to be distinguished on the ground that here the state appears to have taken over the field of legislation pertaining to transportation of pupils and therefore municipalities may not interfere in that field. See C.J.S. Zoning §10.

Defendants are entitled to an injunction to restrain plaintiff from interfering with their installation of the gasoline tank and pump on the ground owned by the school district north of the high school football field. For decree accordingly the cause is—reversed and remanded.

All Justices concur.

School District Is Obliged to Adhere to Minimum Building Code Standards

Edmonds School District No. 15 v. City of Mountlake Terrace

Supreme Court of Washington, 1970.
77 Wash.2d 609, 465 P.2d 177.

HALE, Judge. A kind of sibling rivalry in governmental affairs brings the Edmonds School District and the City of Mountlake Terrace here on a declaratory judgment suit. The school district's claim of sovereign immunity from the city's building code is met by the city's equally vehement claim of sovereign authority to enforce the code. Failing to obtain in the superior court a declaratory judgment that it need not comply with the building code, the district now appeals from a judgment favoring its intergovernmental rival. . . .

The school district brings this suit for a declaratory judgment asking that ordinance No. 391, the building code of the City of Mountlake Terrace, be held inapplicable to and not binding upon the school district in the construction of its high school addition. From a summary judgment denying this relief and dismissing the complaint with prejudice, the district appeals.

Each party claims superior rights over the other deriving from their common source of governmental power, the sovereign state. They present two main questions: Has the state designated which of the two agencies should exercise its sovereign authority with respect to building permits and minimum setback requirements? Is there an irreconcilable dichotomy between the delegation to the school district of the sovereign's constitutional duty to educate the chil-

dren of the state and the city's exercise of the police power in adopting and enforcing a building code?

Are the two sets of delegated powers in conflict? The school district says that the city, in forcing compliance with its building code, is transgressing and trespassing upon its powers and duties as an agency of the sovereign state, to build, operate and maintain public high schools. The district's function of providing the land, materials and designs for school buildings cannot, it contends, be lawfully preempted nor frustrated in any way by a municipality any more than a city could enforce its standards upon the sovereign state against its will.

Education is one of the paramount duties of the state. The duty and power to educate the people are not only inherent qualities of sovereignty but are expressly made an attribute of sovereignty in the State of Washington by the state constitution. Const. art. 9, §§1, 2. The state exercises its sovereign powers and fulfills its duties of providing education largely by means of a public school system under the direction and administration of the State Superintendent of Public Instruction, State Board of Education, school districts and county school boards.

School districts are, in law, municipal corporations with direct authority to establish, maintain and operate public schools and to erect and maintain buildings for that and allied purposes. RCW 28.58. In essence, a school district is a corporate arm of the state established as a means of carrying out the state's constitutional duties (RCW 28.57.135) and exercising the sovereign's powers in providing education. The state has thus made the local school district its corporate agency for the administration of a constitutionally required system of free public education. . . . The state now requires school districts to have the plans and specifications, including those features pertaining to heating, lighting, ventilating and safety, approved by the county superintendent of schools before entering into any school building construction contracts. RCW 28.58.301.

But in other spheres of governmental activity, the statute has allocated some of its sovereign powers and responsibilities to cities, too. Under Const. art. 11, §11, a city may make and enforce all police and sanitary regulations within its limits which do not conflict with general laws. By statute, cities are charged with the sovereign exercise of the police power to maintain peace and good government and to provide for the general welfare of their inhabitants through law not inconsistent with the constitution and statutes of the state. RCW 35.24.290(18). A city and other kinds of municipal corporations, too, are agencies of the state to accomplish these ends. Among these police powers, of course, is the capability of adopting and enforcing building codes. Just as the state has vested in the state superintendent, state board, and the school districts many of its attributes of sovereignty pertaining to education, it has done the same to incorporated cities with respect to the general police powers, among which are zoning and building regulations.

The City of Mountlake Terrace cannot, under existing statutes, supersede, set aside, invalidate or impair the educational processes of or limit the standard prescribed by the state for the operation of the public schools, for that would be an infringement upon state sovereignty. But the state, in delegating to school districts power to build, maintain and operate public schools, has not prescribed minimum standards for street offsets, nor directed that building permits be waived in the construction of public school buildings or additions. It has left its subordinate municipalities free to regulate each other in those activities which traditionally are thought to lie within their particular competence and are more proximate to their respective functions. Fixing minimum offsets for streets, alleys, front, side and back yards would, unless the state has said otherwise, fit more relevantly into a city building code than into the general rules for the operation and maintenance of a high school. . . .

There is little doubt that the State of Washington . . . has the constitutional power to prescribe standards for and regulate school construction, and may, as an attribute of its sovereignty, deprive municipalities of any voice in these matters. But the state has not thus far exercised this power nor prohibited cities from exacting a building permit fee, nor relieved school districts within the corporate limits of a city from paying such fee or complying with the setback provisions of the municipal building code. Unless the state has, so to speak, preempted the field of building standards or specifically ousted the municipality of jurisdiction over school construction, we think the school district is obliged to comply with the minimum standards set forth in the city's building code.

Arguments of the district and amicus curiae convey a concern that, if the court holds a school district amenable to a municipal building code, the ruling will ultimately operate to permit cities—and counties—to interfere with or impinge upon the operation, management and control of the public schools. These fears, we think, are illusory. In the matter of education, a school district is deemed to be an arm of the state for the administration of the school system. . . . It follows that the school district exercises the paramount power of the state in providing education and carries out the will of the sovereign state as to all matters involved in the educational processes and in the conduct, operation and management of the schools. We find nothing in the constitution or existing law which would enable a city legislative body to trespass or impinge upon or interfere with the conduct and operation of the public schools. We do not apprehend that requiring the Edmonds School District to pay for a building permit and set back its new addition from the street or property lines in accordance with the city building code empowers the city to assume any responsibilities or control over the way the educational process is conducted. Such matters as curriculum, textbooks, teaching methods, grading, school hours and holidays, extracurricular school activities or those concerning the selection, tenure and compensation of school personnel—indeed, the thousand and one activities and facilities by which the school districts of the State of Washington afford an education to the children of the state, and adults, too—remain outside of the authority and control of the cities.

Affirmed.

CASE NOTES

1. "A community unit school district, like any other school district established under enabling legislation, is entirely subject to the will of the legislature thereafter. With or without the consent of the inhabitants of a school district, over their protests, even without notice or hearing,

the state may take the school facilities in the district, without giving compensation therefore, and vest them in other districts or agencies. The state may hold or manage the facilities directly or indirectly. The area of the district may be contracted or expanded, it may be divided, united in whole or in part with another district, and the district may be abolished. The 'property of the school district' is a phrase which is misleading. The district owns no property, all school facilities, such as grounds, buildings, equipment, etc., being in fact and law the property of the state and subject to the legislative will." *People v. Deatherage*, 401 Ill. 25, 81 N.E.2d 581 (1948).

An Indiana court held: "Under the constitution and laws of this state, school property is held in trust for school purposes by the persons or corporations authorized for the time being by statute to control the same. It is in the power of the legislature, at any time, to change the trustee." *Carson v. State*, 27 Ind. 465 (1867).

2. The courts have consistently held that school property may be taken from one school district and vested in other agencies. In a school district organization case that has implications for the school district's control over property, an Illinois court held: "The state may, with or without the consent of the inhabitants or against their protest, and with or without notice or hearing, take their property [property of the district] without compensation and vest it in other agencies, or hold it itself, expand or contract the territorial area, divide it, unite a whole or part of it with another municipality, apportion the common property and the common burdens in accordance with the legislative will, and it may abolish the municipality [or school district] altogether." *People ex rel. Taylor v. Camargo Community Consolidated School District No. 158*, 313 Ill. 321, 145 N.E. 154 (1924).

■ PURCHASE OF PROPERTY FOR SPECIAL PURPOSES

Taxpayers have, on many occasions, questioned a board of education's use of tax money for the purchase of property that does not fall strictly within the generally accepted definitions of a school or classroom instructional purpose. The purchase of property for such things as athletic fields, playgrounds, recreational centers, and camps has been litigated.

The weight of authority indicates that the courts tend to interpret the authority of a board of education in this area broadly and, especially in recent years, have expanded their interpretation of the purposes and objectives of public education. However, there are boundaries beyond which it may be questionable for a board of education to tread. For example, a "liberal-minded" Florida court held it permissible for a board of education to purchase property in another county for a camp and recreational grounds.[2] On the other hand, a more cautious Kentucky court has held that there was no authorization for a board of education to purchase a recreation center in another county.[3]

———————— ❖ — ❖ — ❖ ————————

School Board Has the Implied Authority to Purchase Land Outside Geographical Boundaries of School District

In re Board of Public Instruction of Alachua County

Supreme Court of Florida, 1948.
160 Fla. 490, 35 So.2d 579.

TERRELL, Justice. . . . The question for determination is whether or not the Board of Public Instruction of Alachua County is authorized to purchase and take title to lands outside the geographical limits of the county for the purpose of administering its public school program.

Appellants contend that this question should be answered in the negative. To support this contention they rely on certain provisions of Chapter 230, Florida Statutes 1941, F.S.A., particularly sections 230.22 and 230.23, defining the powers and duties of Boards of Public Instruction. . . . They contend that said statutes and decisions restrict the power of the Board of Public Instruction in the exercise of its school program to the county over which it exercises jurisdiction and that it is without authority to enter another county or to purchase lands beyond its borders for any purpose. . . .

An adequate public school program is no longer limited to exploiting the three R's and acquiring such facilities as are necessary to do so. It contemplates the development of mental, manual and other skills that may not derive from academic training. It is predicated on the premise that a personality quotient is just as important as an intelligence quotient and that training the character and the emotions is just as important as training the mind if the product is to be a well balanced citizen.

. . . Section 230.23, among other things, authorizes the County Board of Public Instruction to assume such responsibilities as may be vested in it by law, or as may be required by the State Board of Education or as in the opinion of the County Board of Public Instruction are necessary to provide for the more efficient operation of the County school system in carrying out the purposes of the School Code. As to property ownership, the latter section provides that the County Board of Public Instruction shall retain possession of all property to which title is not held by the County Board and to attain possession of and accept and hold under proper title all property which may at any time be acquired by the County Board for educational purposes in the County.

. . . It is not at all clear that the legislature intended the words "in the county" to limit land purchase to lands in the county. It would be just as reasonable to conclude that the intent was to authorize the purchase of lands anywhere they might aid the county's school program.

The reason for purchasing the lands in question was to provide a camp and a recreational ground to aid the educational program of Alachua County. It was situated on a lake across the county line in Clay County but within easy reach of the schools of Alachua County. It is shown to be well adapted for that purpose and was being offered at a nominal price. Competitive sports are now a recognized part of the public school program. Eminent psychologists proclaim the doctrine that competitive sports contribute more to one's personality quotient and ability to work with people than any other

school activity. Athletic coaches and physical directors tell us that the Olympic Games and other forms of physical competition have done more to put an end to class hatreds and promote international harmony than the United Nations Assembly, the reason being that they are conducted by a strict moral code that insures just treatment to all who participate in them.

This is a mere incident to the manner in which the public school program has been bounced out of its traditional groove and invaded by new experiments in education. An adequate school program is now as diversified as an experimental farm program and the very purpose of the School Code was to give sanction to such a program. The progenitors of the three R's would doubtless have "thrown a fit" if the School Board had talked about purchasing lands for a recreational center. The barn yard and the woodpile filled the need of a recreational center for them. It met the challenge of the time but its exponents, the three R's and the little red school house that symbolized it now repose in the museum of modern education. What we are concerned with is a system to cope with this machine age that we are in danger of becoming victims of if we do not become its masters.

We have learned that the public school program has a definite relation to the economy of our people, that the great majority of them must make their living with their hands and that those who do so must acquire different skills and trades from those who pursue the learned professions, various businesses and specialized activities. We have also learned that, while skill in the three R's was adequate for a rural democracy when the nearest neighbor was three miles away and it was sometimes three hundred yards from the front door to the front gate, it is entirely inadequate for an urban democracy where you speak to your neighbor through the window and sometimes live with a flock of them under the same roof. A democracy in which we cultivate our farms with machines, travel by automobile, send our mail by airplane and flip a gadget to warm the house, start breakfast and relieve much of the day's drudgery. Such is the social era that the public school program must prepare the citizen for, and the School Code was designed to provide the wherewith for such a program. County lines may be treated as a fiction rather than a barrier to such a program.

It follows that the question confronting us impels an affirmative answer. To construe the School Code otherwise would render it impossible to bring about the public school program adequate for the needs contemplated by the legislature. So the fact that the lands in question were without the geographical limits of Alachua County is not material if they are essential to carry out its public school program.

Affirmed.

CASE NOTES

1. In a ruling similar to the *Alachua County* case, the Kentucky Court of Appeals upheld a cooperative arrangement by which the Jefferson County Board of Education jointly with the Jefferson County Fiscal Court created a Jefferson County Board of Recreation. The activities of the recreation board were financed jointly by the cooperating agencies upon submission and approval of a budget by each agency. The primary legal question was, Does a statute that provides that any school district may join with a city or county in "providing and conducting public playgrounds and recreational centers" extend sufficient authority for the school district to budget funds and purchase property for the establishment of playgrounds, parks, and recreation centers? The court said it did and reasoned: "We think the statute is plain in extending the authority; it is subject to no other construction. It is true that there is no explicit provision for the expenditure by the board of such sum or sums as may appear to it in the exercise of reasonable discretion to further the intended purpose. The force of the argument is that while the school district may join in 'providing and conducting' the enterprise, the county must bear all incident expenses. The power and authority granted by a statute is not always limited to that which is specifically conferred, but includes that which is necessarily implied as incident to the accomplishment of those things which are expressly authorized."

Dodge v. Jefferson County Board of Education, 298 Ky. 1, 181 S.W.2d 406 (1944).

2. The authority of a school district to purchase or construct teachers' homes has been upheld by the courts. One court had this to say: "An adequate public school system program now contemplates the development of skills that flow from the head, the hand, the heart. . . . Expenditures for facilities that aid these purposes may be lawfully made from the public school funds." *Taylor v. Board of Public Instruction of Lafayette County, Florida*, 157 Fla. 422, 26 So.2d 180 (1946). Evidently, the reasoning of this court was that homes for teachers would enhance the educational process to a sufficient degree to pay dividends through increased educational attainment of the pupils.

Conversely, it has been held that public school funds may not be used to provide a house for the school superintendent. *Fulk v. School District No. 8 of Lancaster County*, 155 Neb. 630, 53 N.W.2d 56 (1952). However, this view seems to be in the minority.

■ SCHOOL BUILDINGS

Since much of the educational dollar goes for capital outlay and by far the greatest portion of this money comes from local taxation, it is inevitable that people in the community will, from time to time, question the propriety of the expenditure of such money for certain capital construction purposes. In settling these disputes, the courts have found it necessary to define just what the legislature meant when it provided for local school boards to construct "school buildings" and "schoolhouses." Such an interpretation naturally reverts to a discussion of the parameters of educational purposes and the means by which to accomplish such purposes.

For example, in discussing educational purposes the courts have held both for and against the construction of football stadiums; however, the precedent seems to support the conclusion that stadiums do serve a school purpose and thereby constitute a schoolhouse within the meaning of statute. The rule seems to be that a schoolhouse is a place where instruction and training are given in any branch or branches of the educational endeavor regardless of whether such exercises are mental or physical.

———————— ❖ — ❖ — ❖ ————————

Term "Schoolhouse" Is Broad Enough to Imply Authority to Build a Stadium

Alexander v. Phillips

Supreme Court of Arizona, 1927.
31 Ariz. 503, 254 P. 1056.

LOCKWOOD, J. Plaintiff brought this action for the purpose of restraining the issue of some $80,000 in bonds of the Phoenix union high school district of Maricopa County, Ariz. . . . The second question is the vital point in the case. In substance it is: May a high school district in Arizona issue bonds to build a "stadium"? The purpose for which school bonds may be issued is governed by the provisions of paragraph 2736, R.S.A.1913, Civil Code, as amended by chapter 24, Session Laws of 1925, which reads, so far as material to this feature of the case, as follows:

> 2736. The board of trustees of any school district may, whenever in their judgment it is advisable, and must, upon petition of fifteen per cent of the school electors, as shown by the poll list at the last preceding annual school election, residing in the district, call an election for the following purposes: . . .

> (3) To decide whether the bonds of the district shall be issued and sold for the purpose of raising money for purchasing or leasing school lots, *for building schoolhouses,* and supplying same with furniture and apparatus, and improving grounds, or for the purpose of liquidating any indebtedness already incurred for such purposes. (Italics ours.)

The matter then for our determination is whether a stadium is a "schoolhouse" within the provision of paragraph 2736. The word "stadium" comes from the Greek, and was originally a measure of distance. From this, by easy transition, the term was applied first to a foot race of that distance, and then to the place

where the race was run, usually an open area some 600 feet long, and flanked by terraced elevations providing seats for the spectators of the race. The modern definition follows the old one, but is somewhat broader in its scope and is technically given as:

> A similar modern structure with its enclosure used for athletic games. . . . Webster's New International Dictionary (1925 Ed.).

This is also the popular definition, and we may therefore assume that when the question was submitted to the electors of the district, it was understood by them that the proceeds of the bonds would be used to erect a structure where various forms of athletic games could be given by the students of the high school and spectators could be properly accommodated while watching them.

Is such a structure a "schoolhouse"? The terms "schoolhouse" and "school" are properly defined as follows:

> Schoolhouse—a building which is appropriated for the use of a school or schools, or as a place in which to give instruction.
> School—a place for instruction in any branch or branches of knowledge. Webster's New International Dictionary (1925 Ed.).

Was the stadium for which the bonds of the district were to be issued a "building which is appropriated for the use of a school or schools"? . . . No one would maintain that it was within the unfettered discretion of the pupils, the teachers, or any independent set of men or women to determine what should be taught in our public schools. Only the people, speaking through the proper authorities, can determine this question, and the law therefore provides in what branches of human knowledge instruction may be given. We therefore hold that the proper definition of a "schoolhouse" within the meaning of paragraph 2736, supra, is: Any building which is appropriated for a use prescribed or permitted by the law to public schools.

. . . The founders of our first public schools believed all that was necessary, or at least then advisable, was the most elementary mental training, and therefore for many years public school education was confined principally to the teaching of the "three R's." But as the world progressed, it was recognized more and more fully that man, using the language of the motto of one of our great philanthropic institutions, is composed of "body, mind, and spirit," and that the complete citizen must be trained in all three fields. . . . For this reason the new generation of educators has added to the mental education, which was all that was given by the public schools of the past, the proper training of the body, and a gymnasium is now accepted to be as properly a schoolhouse as is the chemical laboratory or the study hall. Not only is this true, but the public is realizing that, even on the mental side, the field is broadening, and, whereas fifty years ago such a thing as an auditorium with a stage was practically unheard of in connection with the public school, now even the rural school of three or four rooms is not considered to be properly equipped without such a structure, either separate or in combination with the ordinary lecture room.

We thus see that the branches of human knowledge taught in the public schools have been vastly expanded in the last few generations. Has this expansion been sufficient to bring within its scope a structure of the class in question? It is a well-known fact, of which this court properly takes judicial notice, that the large majority of the higher institutions of learning in the country are erecting stadiums differing from that proposed for the Phoenix union high school only in size, and it is commonly accepted that they are not only a proper but almost a necessary part of the modern college. This is true both of our privately endowed and our publicly maintained universities. That athletic games under proper supervision tend to the proper development of the body is a self-evident fact. It is not always realized, however, that they have a most powerful and beneficial effect upon the development of character and morale. To use the one game of football as an illustration, the boy who makes a successful football player must necessarily learn self-control under the most trying circumstances, courage, both physical and moral, in the face of strong opposition, sacrifice of individual ease for a community purpose, teamwork to the exclusion of individual glorification, and above all that "die in the last ditch" spirit which leads a man to do for a cause everything that is reasonably possible, and, when that

is done, to achieve the impossible by sheer willpower. The same is true to a greater or lesser degree of practically every athletic sport which is exhibited in a stadium.

It seems to us that, to hold things of this kind are less fitted for the ultimate purpose of our public schools, to wit, the making of good citizens, physically, mentally, and morally, than the study of algebra and Latin, is an absurdity. Competitive athletic games therefore, from every standpoint, may properly be included in a public school curriculum. The question then is, Does the law of Arizona so include them?

The Eighth Legislature has specifically directed that all public school pupils not physically disabled must take, as part of the regular school work, a course in physical education, which is declared to include "athletic games and contests." So far as the instant case is concerned, this of course is merely illustrative of the present trend of thought along the lines of physical education. At the time the election referred to was held, paragraph 2733, R.S.A.1913, Civil Code, provided among other things, as follows:

> Under such conditions as are provided for by law, boards of trustees may employee such special teachers in drawing, music, domestic science, manual training, kindergarten, commercial work, agriculture and other special subjects as they shall deem advisable.

We think "other special subjects" reasonably includes physical education, and indeed, by virtue of this provision, not only practically all high schools in the state of Arizona, but many of the grammar schools, have for years employed physical and athletic directors, both men and women, and physical education for both boys and girls is a subject required in the courses of study adopted by a large majority of our high schools and approved by the state board of education in pursuance of paragraph 2778, R.S.A.1913; the Phoenix union high school being among this number.

If physical education be one of the special subjects permitted by law, it is a matter for the reasonable discretion of our school authorities as to how such subject should be taught and no parent who has ever had a child participate in any form of the athletic games and contests recognized and given by the various schools of this state, and who has noted the increased interest shown and effort put forth by the participants when such games and sports are open to the view of their schoolmates, friends, and parents, both in intra and inter mural competition, but will realize the educational value both of the games and of a suitable place for giving them.

For the foregoing reasons, we are of the opinion (1) that physical education is one of the branches of knowledge legally imparted in the Phoenix union high school; (2) that competitive athletic games and sports in both intra and inter mural games are legal and laudable methods of imparting such knowledge; and (3) that a structure whose chief purpose is to provide for the better giving of such competitive athletic games and sports as aforesaid is reasonably a schoolhouse within the true spirit and meaning of paragraph 2736, supra.

In view of the foregoing conclusions, it is not necessary to consider the other legal questions raised by plaintiff.

The judgment of the superior court of Maricopa county is affirmed.

CASE NOTES

1. The Kentucky Court of Appeals has held that an auditorium-gymnasium is a "school building" within the meaning of statutes. *Rainer v. Board of Education of Prestonsburg Independent School District*, 273 S.W.2d 577 (Ky.1954). The court in this case distinguished its reasoning from an earlier case in which it held that a football stadium did not constitute a "school building." *Board of Education of Louisville v. Williams*, 256 S.W.2d 29 (Ky.1953). The court reasoned that in the *Rainer* case the use of the auditorium-gymnasium constituted a useful educational purpose, where use of the stadium did not.

In the 1953 *Louisville* case, the court disagreed with the ruling in the case of *Alexander v. Phillips*, the principal case just presented, and said: "The case of *Alexander v. Phillips*, apparently the leading case in point, differs in that the voters in that case specifically voted for construction of the stadium, where the Louisville voters only authorized an eight million dollar bond issue for 'school buildings.'" The Kentucky court further commented on the Arizona

case, saying: "The court apparently reasoned that, since a school house was a place for instruction, and since some athletic instruction took place in a stadium, a stadium was therefore a school house. This dubious logic was supported by a eulogy on the spiritual values of interscholastic athletic contests, of which the court took judicial notice. We think *Alexander v. Phillips* is not persuasive as to the intent of the Kentucky legislature in authorizing special taxes and special bond issues for 'school buildings.'"

2. The Supreme Court of Oregon has ruled that a swimming pool falls within the statutory meaning of the term "school building." The court reasoned: "We believe that it was the legislative purpose to empower the issuance of bonds by school districts for the erection on school lands of any structure which the district was authorized to construct and which it deemed necessary or desirable in carrying out its educational program." In rejecting the criterion as to whether the pool was enclosed, the court further stated: "The statute reflects the intent to make the function of the structure rather than its architectural design the criterion in determining whether the bonds may be issued." *Petition of School Board of School District No. U2-20 Jt., Multnomah County*, 232 Or. 593, 377 P.2d 4 (1962).

3. Courts in other jurisdictions have upheld the authority of the school district to construct a gymnasium, *Burlington ex rel. Board of School Commissioners v. Mayor of Burlington*, 98 Vt. 388, 127 A. 892 (1925); a building for dramatics and athletics, *Woodson v. School District No. 28*, 127 Kan. 651, 274 P. 728 (1929); a recreation field, *Wilkinsburg v. School District*, 298 Pa. 193, 148 A. 77 (1929); and a building for a gymnasium, home economics, and vocational training, *Young v. Linwood School District No. 17*, 193 Ark. 82, 97 S.W.2d 627 (1936).

4. In a case questioning whether a constitutional provision of taxes for "school purposes" included school buildings, the court held that

> the unfettered term "school purpose" has an all-inclusive meaning including the erection of school buildings. In this case the court it seems used reverse implication in reasoning that: "If the General Assembly [in redrafting the applicable constitutional amendment] had intended to limit the application of amendment to the usual and ordi-

nary expenses of maintaining and operating schools or 'school district purposes excluding the erection of buildings,' it could have easily clarified the situation by the use of some such expression."

Rathjen v. Reorganized School District R-11 of Shelby County, 365 Mo. 518, 284 S.W.2d 516 (1955).

■ SCHOOL SITE SELECTION

A major responsibility of a school board is the location and selection of an appropriate property for the furtherance of the educational purposes of the school district. Many cases have arisen contesting the board's authority to select sites and the appropriateness of the selection. Usually, such cases evolve from the efforts of a board to consolidate small schools into larger, more centralized schools that provide not only more efficient operation, but also greater educational opportunities for the children.

The courts have uniformly held that it is within the discretion of a board of education to determine what school site will best meet the educational needs of the children and the mere fact that others do not agree is not grounds for interfering with the board's decision.

Courts Will Not Intervene unless Board's Decision Is Tainted with Fraud or Abuse of Discretion

Mullins v. Board of Education of Etowah County

Supreme Court of Alabama, 1947.
249 Ala. 44, 29 So.2d 339.

STAKELY, Justice. This is an appeal from a decree of the equity court sustaining the demurrer to the bill of complaint. . . . The purpose of the bill is to enjoin the respondents from constructing a proposed school building in a particular community in Etowah County or in the alternative to declare legal rights of the Board of

Education and Superintendent of Education of Etowah County.

The allegations of the bill in substance show the following. The respondents have requested and received bids for the proposed construction of a school building to consist of eighteen rooms or more, to be located in the Southside Community in Etowah County, Alabama. The building is to "consist of grammar school and high school grades, a vocational school and an agricultural school." . . .

The community now served by the John S. Jones Junior High School is more thickly populated and has more children of school age than the Southside Community. More students from the community served by the John S. Jones Junior High School would attend the proposed school than students of the Southside Community. The proposed plan would necessitate the transportation of a greater number of children for much greater distances and would remove the Junior High School grades from the John S. Jones Junior High School. . . .

The plan, if put into effect, will result in the construction in the Southside Community of a school building larger than needed by that community to care for the school children residing therein and a portion of the building so constructed would remain empty and unused. The respondents further propose to remove from neighboring communities, including the John S. Jones community, sufficient students to fill the proposed building, which will leave portions of the school facilities now being used in the John S. Jones community empty and unused. In either event the result will be a waste of funds and facilities held by respondents to the detriment of the taxpayers in the county and will prevent construction of much needed school buildings in other communities in Etowah County. The construction of a smaller and less expensive building for Southside High School will be adequate and sufficient to serve the needs of school children living in Southside Community.

It is further alleged that "the proposed action of the defendants . . . is a gross abuse of the discretion vested in them by the laws of the State of Alabama."

This court is committed to the view that the courts of this state will not ordinarily seek to control the exercise of the broad discretion given by the statutes to the county board of education since the powers vested in it are quasi-judicial as well as administrative. This principle prevails even though in the exercise of discretion there may have been error or bad judgment. The courts will act, however, if the acts of county boards of education are tainted with fraud or bad faith or gross abuse of discretion. . . .

It is conceded by appellants that there is nothing to show either fraud or bad faith in the present bill.

It is insisted, however, that the allegations of the bill present a case showing gross abuse of discretion. So far as we are aware this court has not attempted to define precisely "gross abuse of discretion," perhaps for the reason that it is best to allow the facts and circumstances peculiar to each case to determine its presence or absence. In a general way, however, we say that it means such an arbitrary and unreasonable act or conclusion as to shock the sense of justice and indicate lack of fair and careful consideration. . . .

The broad powers conferred on the county board of education to which we have referred include the power to consolidate schools and to arrange for transportation of pupils to and from such consolidated school (§76, Title 52, Code of 1940), the power to determine the "kind, grade and location of schools" (§113, Title 52, Code of 1940) and the power to adopt "a building program adequate to the present and future needs of the schools in the county" (§116, Title 52, Code of 1940). Do the allegations of the bill remove the case from within the discretion of the board to an arbitrary, unreasonable and unjustifiable misuse of power? Do the allegations of the bill overcome the presumption which is in favor of the reasonableness and propriety of the action of the board? It does not appear so to us.

The proposed school is to replace a school destroyed by fire in a community now without a school. Construing the bill against the pleader, it does not appear with sufficient certainty how much money is to be used to consummate the plan or how much empty or waste space will be created in the new school or be left in the John S. Jones Junior High School. There is nothing to show the dimensions, area or topography of the proposed site. There is nothing to show to what extent the proposed site is or is not a suitable school center or in a central location from the standpoint of other communities, not just the community in which one school, the John S. Jones Junior High School, is located. There is nothing to show a bad location from the standpoint of roads or the condition thereof.

Beyond all this there is nothing to show that the plan is out of step with the future needs of the schools of the county so far as they may be reasonably foreseen. §116, Title 52, Code of 1940, supra. In the absence of a contrary showing it must be assumed that the authorities gave careful and due consideration to the growing and expanding needs of education in the county. The statutes as well as the high purposes of education contemplate that a plan should be adopted that has vision and foresight. A sparsely settled community today may well be a populous community tomorrow. Matters which may create irritations today because of inconvenience, etc., may be relatively unimportant in comparison with a long range plan.

The allegations of the bill will not be aided by the general allegation that "the proposed action of the defendants is a gross abuse of discretion" because this is "merely to apply an epithet without defining the act." . . . The court acted correctly in sustaining the demurrer to the bill.

Affirmed.

CASE NOTES

1. In a later Alabama case contesting the school board's selection of a school site for a high school, it was alleged that (1) the population of the proposed site area was not sufficient to support a high school and (2) the geographical conditions were not suitable for a high school. The court cited the principal case just presented, *Mullins v. Board of Education of Etowah County*, 249 Ala. 44, 29 So.2d 339 (1947), and said that it would not interfere unless the board's action constituted "gross abuse of discretion" and that in this case the selection of this particular school site did not demonstrate such gross abuse. The court further said that the complainants must show the board's action was a "gross abuse of discretion" and "such an arbitrary and unreasonable act or conclusion as to shock the sense of justice and indicate lack of

fair and careful consideration." The court ruled the complainants had failed to do this. *Board of Education of Blount County v. Phillips*, 264 Ala. 603, 89 So.2d 96 (1956).

2. In an Indiana case, a taxpayer sought a *writ of mandamus* to compel the school trustee to build a school building at a specified site. The court denied the writ and held that *mandamus* does not lie to compel a school township trustee to provide for the construction of a school building—especially where it does not clearly appear that it is the trustee's duty to construct the building and that he or she has the means to do so. *Good v. Howard*, 174 Ind. 358, 92 N.E. 115 (1910). Of course, the authority of the old township trustee is of little relevance today, except that the axiom holds true that a taxpayer cannot substitute his or her discretion for that of a school board or a trustee and compel the construction of a school building.

3. When a board of education selected a site for a school building and a large group of taxpayers objected, signed a petition, and brought an action to prevent purchase of the site, the court found that the evidence concerning the adequacy of the site was conflicting and said: "We do not deem it necessary to go into a detailed analysis of the proof. It is not the court's duty to select a site; it is only to determine whether the board of education abused a sound discretion in performing that duty. The weight of proof is largely with the board of education; and, if we had any doubt upon the question, it must be resolved in favor of the board of education. . . . Not only does the good faith of the board of education stand unimpeached; but, under the rule by which we will not set aside a finding of fact by the [board of education] where the proof is contradictory we will not disturb [its] judgment in the case." *Spaulding v. Campbell County Board of Education*, 239 Ky. 277, 39 S.W.2d 490 (1931).

■ EMINENT DOMAIN

Eminent domain is the power of the government to take private property for public use. Through the right of eminent domain, the state can reassert, for reason of public exigency and for the public good, its dominion over any portion of the property of a state. Therefore, when a statute

so provides, a public board of education can condemn and take for public use property needed for public school purposes; without legislative authorization, however, the right of eminent domain lies dormant and cannot be exercised.

Also, the power of eminent domain as exercised by local school boards must satisfy both state and federal constitutional provisions. Federal constitutional provisions that must be carefully observed are the Fifth Amendment, which prohibits depriving any person of life, liberty, or property without due process of law and taking private property for public use without just compensation, and the Fourteenth Amendment, which prohibits any state from depriving any person of life, liberty, or property without due process of law and from denying any person within its jurisdiction the equal protection of the laws. Comparable clauses are included in state constitutions. Such constitutional provisions make it necessary that owners be justly compensated for their property. The question of what just compensation is has been the impetus for much litigation. Generally, however, the fair market value or the value of the property between a willing buyer and a willing seller is the measure of compensation to be awarded the owner.

In taking private property for public use, the public agency must show a necessity for the land and therefore cannot condemn more property than the public necessity dictates.

It is a general rule that a school board cannot take land that is already being used by another public agency; however, it has been held, in some cases, that where two public agencies need land, the agency with the more pressing need will prevail.

❖ — ❖ — ❖

Eminent Domain Can Be Exercised to Condemn Property for "Public Use"

Oxford County Agricultural Society v. School District No. 17

Supreme Judicial Court of Maine, 1965.
161 Me. 334, 211 A.2d 893.

WEBBER, Justice. On appeal. The defendant School Administrative District No. 17, a quasi-municipal corporation charged with the responsibility of providing public school education, seeks to take property of the plaintiff Oxford County Agricultural Society by eminent domain. The District requires the property for the location of a new high school. It has general statutory authority to take by eminent domain for its lawful purposes but it has never been given specific legislative authority to take the property of this plaintiff.

The . . . issue is whether or not the Society's property is devoted to public uses to such an extent and in such a manner as to provide it with an exemption from condemnation. The plaintiff conducts an annual fair on the property in question which has all the usual attributes of an agricultural fair with which Maine people have long been familiar. . . . The plaintiff is a private voluntary corporation chartered by the Legislature. It is not a political subdivision of the state nor is it invested with any political or governmental function. It was not created to assist in the conduct of government nor was it created by the sovereign will of the Legislature without the consent of the persons who constitute it. These persons may decline or refuse to execute powers granted by legislative charter. They may at any time dissolve and abandon it and are under no legal obligation to conduct an annual fair or to carry on or continue any of the activities which are said to benefit the public. The principles governing exemption from condemnation were well stated in *Tuomey Hospital v. City of Sumter* (1964), 134 S.E.2d (S.C.) 744, 747:

> We recognize that it is difficult to give an accurate and comprehensive definition of the term "public use." The distinction between public and private use lies in the character of the use and must to a large extent depend upon the facts of each case. There are, however, certain essential characteristics which must be present if the use is to be deemed public and not private within the meaning of the law of eminent domain. . . .
>
> The general rule, to which we adhere, was thus stated in the case of the *President and Fellows of Middlebury College v. Central Power Corporation of Vermont*, 101 Vt. 325, 143 A. 384, 388: "It is essential to a public use, as the term is used in proceedings involving the law of condemnation or eminent domain, that the public must, to some extent, be enti-

tled to use or enjoy the property, not by favor, but as a matter of right. . . . The test whether a use is public or not is whether a public trust is imposed upon the property; whether the public has a legal right to the use, which cannot be gainsaid or denied, or withdrawn at the pleasure of the owner."

We are satisfied that the statement set forth in 18 Am.Jur. 720, Sec. 94, accurately summarizes the requirements for exemption:

> To exempt property from condemnation under a general grant of the power of eminent domain, it is not enough that it has been voluntarily devoted by its owner to a public or semipublic use. If the use by the public is permissive and may be abandoned at any time, the property is not so held as to be exempt. The test of whether or not property has been devoted to public use is what the owner must do, not what he may choose to do. It is immaterial how the property was acquired; if its owner has devoted it to a public use which he is under a legal obligation to maintain, it comes within the protection of the rule exempting it from condemnation.

We conclude, as did the justice below, that the property of the Society is not immune from condemnation by the District. . . .

Appeal denied.

❖ — ❖ — ❖

"Proper School Purpose" Provision in Eminent Domain Statute Allows School District to Condemn Property for Parking Facilities and School Administration Building

In re School District of Pittsburgh

Supreme Court of Pennsylvania, 1968.
430 Pa. 566, 244 A.2d 42.

EAGEN, Justice. . . . The precise issue presented here is whether the lower court correctly determined that the acquisition of land for parking facilities for employees and visitors to the School Administration Building is not a "proper school purpose" within the meaning of the Act of March 10, 1949. . . .

On June 21, 1966, the Board of Public Education of the School District of Pittsburgh [hereinafter Board] passed a resolution authorizing the filing of declarations of taking for the involved properties [primarily to provide parking facilities at the School Administration Building]. . . . The lower court sustained the preliminary objections solely because it concluded that the Board's condemnation power does not extend to the acquisition of land for parking facilities for administrative employees.

The Board's condemnation power flows from the Act of March 10, 1949, P.L. 30, Art. VII, 24 P.S. §7-701 et seq. Section 703, 24 P.S. §7-703 provides:

> In order to comply with the provisions of this act, and subject to the conditions thereof, the board of school directors of each district is hereby vested with the necessary power and authority to acquire, in the name of the district, by purchase, lease, gift, devise, agreement, condemnation, or otherwise, any and all such real estate . . . as the board of school directors may deem necessary to furnish suitable sites for proper school purposes for said district. . . .

In interpreting the statute we must, of course, bear in mind that provisions conferring the power of eminent domain must be strictly construed. Act of May 28, 1937, P.L. 1019, Art. IV, §58, 46 P.S. §558. Strict construction does not require, however, that a statute be construed as narrowly as possible, or that it be construed so literally and without common sense that its obvious intent is frustrated. . . .

A close examination of Section 703 of March 10, 1949, supra, indicates that the power and authority of the Board to acquire real estate is limited to acquisition "for proper school purposes" not only when the acquisition is by condemnation, but also when it is by "purchase, lease, gift, devise, agreement . . . or otherwise." Thus, if the Board cannot condemn real estate for the purpose of using it as a parking lot, it apparently cannot lease, purchase or otherwise acquire real estate for parking purposes. To deny the Board this power is serious not only because off street parking usually is desirable for buildings located in congested urban areas, but also because this Court has held that a school board may be compelled to comply with a zoning ordinance requiring provision for off street parking in the erection of a new building. . . .

In approaching the question of whether or not the legislature intended to deny the Board this power, it is significant that the phrase "proper school purposes" in Section 703 of the Act of March 10, 1949, supra, replaced the phrase "school buildings and playgrounds" in Section 602 of the Act of May 18, 1911, P.L. 309. This substitution, fairly read, not only left the Board's power less precisely defined, but also broadened it somewhat. Thus the acquisition of a building to be used solely for administration undoubtedly is for a proper school purpose although an administration building may not be unquestionably within the term "schoolbuilding," which could be read to imply a school house where classes are held.

We think that the acquisition of land for off street parking for school district facilities, including an administration building, is for a "proper school purpose." With particular reference to an administration building, there are two obvious reasons why numerous automobiles are incident to its operation. First, superintendents and supervisors that have central offices in an administration building must have occasion when duty requires their presence in scattered parts of the school district. The availability and effectiveness of these professionals no doubt is greatly enhanced by their use of automobile transportation. Second, teachers, principals and other staff scattered throughout the school system must have occasion when they are required to attend meetings together in the central administration building. To do so without an excessive investment in time, they frequently will have to use automobile transportation. With reference to any school district facility, automobiles will be incident to its operation for other reasons. For instance, professionals, as well as secretarial, clerical and maintenance staff, may not accept employment unless they can commute to and from work by automobile. This might be common in areas where public transportation does not serve either the employee's home or the school district's facility. Even where public transportation is available, we must recognize that today a great part of the public is unwilling to use it because they are almost addicted to the convenience and independence provided by the automobile. Since automobiles are a necessary incident to the operation of school district facilities, off street parking is a practical necessity. The streets simply are not adequate and sometimes are not available for parking. Consequently, the acquisition of land for off street parking, which is a practical necessity to the effective and efficient operation of a school system, is certainly a "proper school purpose." To interpret the statute any more narrowly would be to frustrate its obvious intent to delegate to the Board authority to discharge the legislature's constitutional obligation to provide for an efficient public school system. . . .

Reversed.

❖ — ❖ — ❖

Courts Are Bound to Abide by School Board's Exercise of Power of Eminent Domain unless Decision Is Arbitrary Abuse of Discretion

Dare County Board of Education v. Sakaria

Court of Appeals of North Carolina, 1995.
118 N.C.App. 609, 456 S.E.2d 842.

GREENE, Judge.

Elpis Sakaria, Raj Alexander Trust, Elpis J.G.B. Sakaria, Trustee, Jera Associates, and Jack and Lillian Hillman appeal from a 27 April 1994 final judgment and 25 May 1994 corrected judgment entered in Dare County Superior Court, decreeing that the Dare County Board of Education (plaintiff) has the authority to condemn lands for construction and use of proposed school facilities. . . .

Plaintiff is responsible for the operation of the Cape Hatteras School (the School) in Buxton, North Carolina, which is located on the Pamlico Sound side of Hatteras Island, part of the Outer Banks. Beginning in 1985 and again in 1988, plaintiff recognized that the School needed additional athletic facilities in order to meet state and southern accreditation requirements and began efforts to expand the School's athletic facilities in 1985. Plaintiff owns a 12.5 acre tract

of land which is located west of the School's campus, which includes all land from the highway to the Pamlico Sound east of defendants' lots. Therefore, defendants' lots are surrounded by plaintiff's property on three sides, and the Pamlico Sound on the fourth side. Because portions of plaintiff's land and defendants' lands are wetlands, they are within the jurisdictional bounds of the United States Army Corps of Engineers (the Corps) under Section 404 of the Clean Water Act, 33 U.S.C. §1344 and Section 10 of the Rivers and Harbors Act of 1899, 33 U.S.C. §403 and of the North Carolina Department of Environment, Health and Natural Resources, Division of Coastal Management (Coastal Management) and subject to numerous state and federal regulations.

Plaintiff planned to use its 12.5 acre lot, which contains 3.1 acres of wetlands, to expand the School's athletic facilities. In June 1988, Coastal Management denied plaintiff's requests for a dredge and fill permit and water quality certification to make the 12.5 acre tract suitable for building athletic fields because plaintiff's proposal would result in an unacceptable loss of wetlands. A second permit application by plaintiff in 1992 was denied by both Coastal Management and the Division of Environmental Management after the coastal wetlands were realigned. On 9 February 1993, plaintiff adopted a resolution approving condemnation of defendant's six lots, lot 5 belonging to the Hillmans and lot 6 belonging to Sakaria, and submitted a proposal involving defendants' lots to the Corps on 15 February 1993. Under this proposal, defendants' lots 5 and 6 would be used only as a source of fill and for wetlands mitigation. This proposal received a conditional permit from the Corps. On 19 February 1993, plaintiff filed four separate actions in Dare County Superior Court to condemn the six lots. . . .

At trial, Allen Burrus (Mr. Burrus), a member of plaintiff, testified that after Coastal Management denied a permit to use plaintiff's 12.5 acres for additional facilities, plaintiff "formed an ad hoc committee" which looked for available and suitable properties that were within "five miles of the facility," consisted of "eight or ten acres" and "had to be accessible by road, hard road." Mr. Burrus testified that the properties considered by the ad hoc committee were unavailable because they either did not meet the criteria necessary for school facilities, were deemed an Area of Environmental Concern, consisted of federal property belonging to the National Park Service, or were rejected by the various federal and state agencies having jurisdiction over the wetlands.

Mr. Burrus testified that in order to get a permit from the Corps, plaintiff had to mitigate damages to wetlands, and defendants' property was being offered to satisfy that mitigation "[n]ot completely but at least partly." . . . Mr. Burrus stated that plaintiff's ad hoc committee had "looked for complete sites" and, therefore, had not searched "for alternatives to find a half acre that can be offered for mitigation." Mr. Burrus agreed that there are numerous parcels within Dare County that would contain a half acre of property that could be used to satisfy the mitigation requirement, but because the agencies presented to plaintiff "in verbal exchanges more than once" that on-site mitigation would increase its chances of obtaining a permit, plaintiff looked for "on-site, on-kind mitigation." Mr. Burrus agreed, however, that the Corps permitted off-site mitigation. . . .

The issues presented are (I) whether N.C. Gen.Stat. §115C-517 permits a local board of education to condemn land solely used as wetlands mitigation and a source of fill; and (II) if so, whether plaintiff's action of condemning lots 5 and 6 as necessary to build athletic facilities was an arbitrary abuse of discretion. . . .

Defendants first argue that taking lots 5 and 6 only "for mitigation and as a source of fill is neither authorized by the limited grant of authority contained in N.C.G.S. §115C-517 nor clearly implied by that grant" because such uses are not "to construct any 'school facility.'" We reject this argument.

Eminent domain is the "power of the State or some agency authorized by it to take or damage private property for a public purpose upon payment of just compensation," and the manner in which eminent domain may be exercised is prescribed by our General Assembly. . . . Because the exercise of the power of eminent domain is in derogation of property rights, all laws conferring this power must be strictly construed; therefore, statutory grants of the power of eminent domain are "limited to the express terms or clear implication of the act or acts in which the grant of the power of eminent domain is contained." . . .

Local boards of education possess the power of eminent domain and have broad discretion to condemn under Chapter 40A of the General Statutes a "suitable site or right-of-way" for "a school, school building, school bus garage or for a parking area or access road suitable for school buses or for other school facilities" whenever the board is unable to acquire or enlarge the suitable site or right-of-way by gift or purchase. N.C.G.S. §115C-517 (1994). "[T]he determination of the local board of education of the land necessary for such purposes shall be conclusive" provided that no more than a total of fifty acres for one site is condemned. . . . Plaintiff, therefore, has the discretion under Section 115C-517 to determine what land constitutes a "suitable site" to construct its athletic facilities and what land is "necessary" to construct its athletic facilities, which may, depending on the circumstances of a particular case, encompass more than the actual land on which the athletic facility sits. Plaintiff, therefore, had the discretion under Section 115C-517 to determine that lots 5 and 6 are "necessary" to construct its proposed athletic facilities. . . .

Under Section 115C-517, the courts are bound by the discretionary decision of a local board of education in selecting and determining the land necessary to construct a school, school building, school bus garage, a parking area, an access road suitable for school buses or "other school facilities" unless that decision is an "arbitrary abuse of discretion or disregard of law." . . . A discretionary act is an arbitrary abuse of discretion when it is "not done according to reason or judgment, but depending upon the will alone" and "done without reason." . . .

Defendant argues that plaintiff's decision to use lots 5 and 6 only for wetlands mitigation and as a source of fill is arbitrary and capricious because "there were alternate sources available to meet [plaintiff]'s mitigation needs," and plaintiff did not explore available off-site mitigation alternatives. We disagree.

The evidence in this record shows that because the area on Hatteras Island on which plaintiff is proposing to build an athletic facility is an ecologically sensitive area containing a significant portion of wetlands which are under the jurisdiction of the Corps and Coastal Management and subject to other federal and state agencies, plaintiff cannot construct its proposed athletic facility without having additional land for wetlands mitigation and as a source for fill. For mitigation purposes, plaintiff has to create wetlands to replace the acre of wetlands which was to be filled under its proposal. . . . Although there is evidence that alternate sites were available which plaintiff did not consider, we cannot say on this record that plaintiff's decision to condemn lots 5 and 6 was "not done according to reason or judgment, but depending upon the will alone" and "done without reason." Therefore, plaintiff's decision that lots 5 and 6 are necessary for construction of its athletic facilities was not an arbitrary abuse of discretion.

. . . For these reasons, the decision of the trial court is

Affirmed.

Case Notes

1. A local school district is not defined as a "government agency" within the state environmental statute and is therefore not bound to abide by the strictures of the state environmental act. *Thornton v. Clarke County School District,* 270 Ga. 633, 514 S.E. 2d 11 (1999).

2. A Florida statute illustrates a typical right of eminent domain conferred upon a school district: "There is conferred upon the county board in each of the several counties in the state the authority and right to take private property for any public school purpose or use when, in the opinion of the county board, such property is needed in the operation of any or all of the public schools within the county, including property needed for any school purpose or use in any school district or districts within the county. The absolute fee simple title to all property so taken and acquired shall vest in the county board of such county unless the county board seeks to appropriate a particular right or estate in such property." West's Fla.Stat.Ann. §235.05.

3. Where a school district takes property by condemnation and the statutes do not require title to be taken in fee simple, the courts have held that a school district obtains only an easement or a qualified fee. The court in a Pennsyl-

vania case held that, under a condemnation proceeding, "whatever kind of right, estate, or easement, the school district acquired, terminated when it ceased to use it for the purpose for which the land was appropriated, and the title reverted to the original owner or those who hold under him." *Lazarus v. Morris,* 212 Pa. 128, 61 A. 815 (1905).

4. To condemn property, boards of education must show that the property will be used for a public school use. An Alabama court has held that an administrative building for the school superintendent and his or her staff constitutes a public use and falls within statutory provisions that provide for condemnation for "other public school purposes." *Smith v. City Board of Education of Birmingham,* 272 Ala. 227, 130 So.2d 29 (1961).

5. The prevailing view is that one public agency may condemn property belonging to another public agency if a "more necessary need" exists. In a case illustrating this view, the Supreme Court of North Dakota held that "the convenience to the public arising out of the use of certain property as a school site and grounds exceeded the convenience to the public arising from the use as a park." *Board of Education of Minot v. Park District of Minot, N.D.,* 70 N.W.2d 899 (N.D.1955). A Massachusetts court held that school property could be taken for use as a public road. The court weighed the need for the road against the harm incurred and ruled that the road was the "more necessary need." The court said in part: "[T]here is much greater freedom of choice as to where a schoolhouse shall be put than where roads shall run. . . . " *Easthampton v. County Commissioners of Hampshire,* 154 Mass. 424, 28 N.E. 298 (1891).

6. In a case illustrating the use of fair market value as the measure of damages, a school board in Louisiana contested a court's valuation of a condemned tract of land. The jury had assessed a value of $1,200 for a school site of 5.9 acres. On appeal, the board showed that similar land in the neighborhood was selling between $5 and $25 per acre. Based on this evidence, the total award was reduced to $300. *Ouachita Parish School Board v. Clark,* 197 La. 131, 1 So.2d 54 (1941).

7. Under condemnation procedures, the usual redress open to a landowner is an action to recover compensation and damages for the loss of property. The award to the owner is usu-

ally based on the appraised fair market value of property. However, some courts have used other measures, such as the "substitute facility approach," in the condemnation of special-purpose property. For example, where a highway intersects a school campus, cutting growth potential or isolating a building, the courts may apply this alternative standard. *Commonwealth, Department of Highways v. City of Winchester,* 431 S.W.2d 707 (Ky.1968). The U.S. Supreme Court has said: "[W]e are not to make a fetish of market value 'since it may not be the best measure of value in some cases.' Where the highest and best use of the property is for municipal or governmental purposes, as to which no market value properly exists, some other method of arriving at just compensation must be adopted, and the cost of providing property in substitution for the property taken may reasonably be the basis of the award." *United States v. Cors,* 337 U.S. 325, 69 S.Ct. 1086 (1949).

■ ADVERSE POSSESSION

Adverse possession is a means of acquiring property; it is of occasional concern to school district authorities. All states have statutes that limit the times during which certain actions may be brought. These are called statutes of limitations and apply not only to matters concerning property, but also to other areas of law, such as actions for contracts under seal, actions for wrongful death, and actions for liability for torts. Statutes of limitations for recovery of property have particular significance because the running of the statutes has not only procedural, but also proprietary significance. In other words, if the statute of limitations for recovery of possession of property is twenty years and the owner of the land does not initiate an action within this time against someone in actual open possession of the property, the owner loses his or her title to the land, his or her right of action is dead, and the person in possession of the property acquires title. However, in order to gain title to property by adverse possession, the occupant must exercise dominion over the property in a manner that is actual, uninterrupted, open, notorious, hostile, and exclusive, with a claim of ownership such as will notify parties seeking information that the property is not held in subordination to any claim by others but held against all titles and claims.[4]

Party Seeking to Acquire Property by Adverse Possession Must Establish an Open, Notorious, and Hostile Claim

Lovejoy v. School District No. 46, Sedgwick County

Supreme Court of Colorado, 1954.
129 Colo. 306, 269 P.2d 1067.

HOLLAND, Justice. . . . The sole question here involved is whether or not the district, by being in possession and holding school on the premises for a long period of time more than the statutory period of eighteen years, was entitled to possession and to have title quieted in it by adverse possession.

The fact that the district had established a school on the land involved about the year 1886, and that there had been continuously conducted a school thereon until the year 1947, is not disputed. The proof offered by the School District lacks any showing of a clear, positive and unequivocal act on the part of the district during any of the time involved that would disclose its claim or right to the land by adverse possession. Mere occupancy alone seems to be relied upon until after the spring of 1947, when a question arose between Phyllis Lovejoy, the fee owner of the quarter section, and District No. 68 as to the ownership of the building. Since the building was a permanent fixture, she authorized her attorney, on April 30, 1951, to write the president of School District No. 68, requesting the Board to remove the school building. This incident was notice to the District that she claimed ownership of the land, and there appears no denial of her claim at that time. If the District then claimed ownership of the land, there then was an open opportunity for it to assert such claim of ownership; however, it consulted an attorney and then decided to claim ownership by adverse possession. By such action, a strong presumption follows that the School District, in effect, admitted that its claim was not open, hostile and notorious, as is necessary in reliance upon adverse possession.

Numerous witnesses, of the community, were called by plaintiff, some of whom had resided there for many years, and one in particular who attended the second term of school in 1887. None of the witnesses could recall any incident whereby it was known that the District claimed ownership to the land, but all were of the same positive impression that the District owned the building. . . .

The very essence of adverse possession is that the possession must be hostile, not only against the true owner, but against the world as well. An adverse claim must be hostile at its inception, because, if the original entry is not openly hostile or adverse, it does not become so, and the statute does not begin to run as against a rightful owner until the adverse claimant disavows the idea of holding for, or in subservience to another, it actually sets up an exclusive right in himself by some clear, positive and unequivocal act. The character of the possession must become hostile in order that it may be deemed to be adverse. And this hostility must continue for the full statutory period. 1 Am.Jur., p. 871, §137. The statute begins to run at the time the possession of the claimant becomes adverse to that of the owner, and this occurs when the claimant sets up title in himself, by some clear, positive and unequivocal act.

No one representing School District No. 68 ever asserted that the District owned the land until immediately before the commencement of this action. The District, without color of title to possession, had to be in possession under an open and notorious claim of ownership. Under the circumstances here, mere occupancy was not sufficient to put any of the true owners on notice that the District claimed the land, and the burden of proof, as to open, notorious and hostile claim, is upon the District when it claims title by adverse possession without color of title. Every reasonable presumption is made in favor of the true owner as against adverse possession. *Evans v. Welch*, 29 Colo. 355, 68 P. 776.

In support of the general trend of the testimony that it was never known that the District claimed the land, only the building, it is to be noted that the District first claimed that it had a full acre after that time a right of way ditch cut across the corner of the section, which left an area of more than two acres, and the school land up to the ditch as a playground, and the fences along the ditch were not shown to have been placed there by the School District. Had the District been making a claim to the ground, it follows that there would have been no uncertainty as to the extent and boundaries thereof. The school board knew almost two years before this suit was commenced that Phyllis Lovejoy claimed ownership of the land when she asked them to remove the building. If originally this was a case of permission to use the ground, it would be in subordination to the title and here the burden was upon the District to prove that such notice was given, which it failed to meet.

There is no reason to discuss the question of the judgment for damages, since our determination of the rights of the parties involved necessitates a reversal of the judgment, and that the complaint be dismissed.

The judgment is reversed and the cause remanded with direction to the trial court to dismiss the complaint.

CASE NOTES

1. Adverse possession must be open, visible, continuous, and exclusive, with a claim of ownership such as will notify parties seeking information upon the subject that the premises are held not in subordination to any claim of others but against all titles and claimants.

The placing of a permanent school building and other necessary appendages on the land of another, and conducting school thereon, is evidence of adverse and hostile possession under which title may be claimed after fifteen years. *Liles v. Smith*, 206 Okl. 458, 244 P.2d 582 (1952).

2. A claim of adverse possession cannot lie against the state. Because school districts are agents of the state, school property cannot be taken by adverse possession regardless of its use over time. The Supreme Court of Pennsylvania has said that "it is well established that the local school districts are merely agents of the Commonwealth to which the legislature has delegated authority in order to fulfill the state's responsibility to provide public education." *Pennsylvania Federation of Teachers v. School Dis-*

trict of Philadelphia, 506 Pa. 196, 484 A.2d 751 (1984). Similarly, another Pennsylvania court said: "Clearly, school districts are agents of the Commonwealth. Because a claim of adverse possession cannot lie against the Commonwealth, it cannot lie against the School District." *Lysicki v. Montour School District,* 701 A.2d 630 (1997).

■ REVERSION OF SCHOOL PROPERTY

Land may be conveyed to school districts under the same rules of future interests as for similar transactions between private persons. Under common law, the only way a fee-simple estate could be created was by the use of the words "and his heirs" or "and their heirs." However, under modern statutes these words of inheritance are not necessary to create a fee-simple estate. The name of the grantee only is sufficient to take a fee-simple estate unless a lesser estate is described.[5]

When a school district acquires property and the words used in the conveyance are "to X school district" or "to X school district and his heirs" and the grantor does not indicate a lesser estate, the school district obtains title in fee-simple absolute. A fee-simple absolute estate is the largest, exclusive, and most extensive interest that can be enjoyed in land. It is an estate when lands are given to a person or, in our case, a school district, and to his or her heirs absolutely without limit or end.[6]

However, many times grantors who convey property to school districts for school purposes desire that the land will sooner or later revert to them when it is no longer used for school purposes. In such cases, deeds making the conveyances of land must be unmistakably clear as to their intent; without sufficient clarity, the courts will not permit a reversion. A New Jersey court had this to say about the interpretation of such deeds: "Conditions, when they tend to destroy estates, are stricti juris and to be construed strictly. . . . Conditions subsequent, especially when relied upon to work a forfeiture, must be created by express terms or clear implication, and are strictly construed. . . ."[7]

The condition subsequent of which the court speaks is a determinable fee, the limitations of which are usually identified by the words "so

long as," "until," "while," or "during." An example of such a condition is as follows: A, the fee-simple owner, conveys Blackacre to a school district for so long as said property is used for school purposes. In this case, the school district has a determinable fee simple, and A has a possibility of reverter.

In a case in which land was conveyed to a school district "for school purposes only," it was contended that the property should revert to the grantor when it was no longer used for school purposes. The court held that the words "for school purposes only" were neither preceded nor followed by words of condition, such as those listed above. The court said: "The words upon which the appellant relies as debasing the fee are merely superfluous and not expressive of any intention of the parties to the conveyance as to the effect to be given to it."[8] In this case, the clause merely duplicated a limitation that was already imposed on school property anyway.

The following case discusses the relationship between the grantor and the school district when subsequent conditions exist or are alleged to exist.

Reversionary Interest Does Not Come into Play as Long as Property Is Used for School Purposes

Williams v. McKenzie

Court of Appeals of Kentucky, 1924.
203 Ky. 376, 262 S.W. 598.

TURNER, C. On the 29th of August, 1895, appellee, W.H. McKenzie, and one Melvin Fyffe conveyed to the trustees of common school district No. 8 of Johnson county a tract of land of less than one acre, about one-half of which was from the property of appellee, and the other half from that of Fyffe. The conveyance was made "in consideration of their respect for the system of common schools of Johnson county," and was absolute on its face except as hereinafter pointed out. The habendum clause is:

> To have and to hold the same, with all the appurtenances thereon, to the second party and their

heirs and assigns forever, with covenants of general warranty.

However, after the description of the property there is appended the following:

> It is expressly understood that the aforesaid property is to belong to the aforesaid school district so long as it is used for common school purposes, but whenever the same is no longer so used it is to revert back to the parties of the first part, and the party of the second part is to have the right to remove the school building and fixtures on said premises.

As indicated in the face of the instrument, the property conveyed had been probably for some years before the conveyance used for school purposes; at any rate, a schoolhouse was erected on it, and it has been continuously used for school purposes at all times since that day, and is yet so used.

Thereafter by operation of law the title so held by the common school district became vested in the county board of education, and in November, 1920, the board of education, in consideration of $50 and the customary royalty, leased the same for oil and gas development to the appellant Junior Oil Company. Thereafter the latter under the lease drilled a well on that part of the school lot formerly belonging to appellee, McKenzie, and brought in thereon a producing oil well, whereupon, in December, 1921, McKenzie instituted this equitable action seeking to cancel the deed of August, 1895, and the lease so made by the board and to have it adjudged the title thereto was in him, and to enjoin the oil company from entering upon the same, or using or claiming the same, and asking for an accounting for the oil taken therefrom.

The original petition alleges, in substance, that the board of education had no right or authority to make the lease to the oil company for oil and gas development, and that the oil company had moved onto the property for the purpose of developing the same for such purposes, and asserting the right so to do, whereby a cloud was cast upon plaintiff's title. It is further alleged that the board of education had title to such lot only for the purpose of conducting thereon a common school for educational purposes, and that the conversion of same by it to commercial purposes was equivalent to an abandonment by it of the original purpose for which the grant was made, and by such acts it abandoned the property for the original purpose, whereby the title to same reverted to plaintiff. . . .

It will be observed that by the deed of August 1895, appellee parted with his whole interest in the property. He made no reservation or exception, nor was there a condition or restriction of any nature upon the present title conveyed. He only provided that the title so conveyed should revert to him in the uncertain event that the property should ever cease to be used for common school purposes. He provided only for a mere possible reverter to himself if the property should ever cease to be used for such purposes. The questions, therefore, which it seems necessary to determine, are:

1. What estate did the grantees take in the deed of 1895, and what are their rights in the property while the same is still being used for common school purposes?
2. What estate, if any, remains in the grantor under that deed while the same continues to be used for common school purposes, and has he such a right or interest during that time as authorizes him to maintain an action for waste?
3. Have school authorities owning property in use for school purposes the right or power to lease the same for mineral development purposes, the funds, if any, derived therefrom to be used for schools?

Questions 1 and 2 are in effect one and the same, for, if the grantees in the deed took such estate as entitles them to the unrestricted use of the property before the reversion provided for takes place, then it is clear there is no such right or estate left in the grantor as entitles him to maintain an action for waste.

The grantor clearly parted with his whole present interest, and after parting with it engrafts upon the estate conveyed a possible reversionary interest in himself if the property should ever cease to be used for common school purposes, which is manifestly a thing which may or may never happen. The thing which will operate as a reversion in the grantor is and can be only the action of the grantees themselves or their successors in title.

A qualified or determinable fee is defined in 10 R.C.L. 652, as follows:

A qualified or determinable fee is an estate limited to a person and his heirs, with a qualification annexed to it by which it is provided that it must determine whenever that qualification is at an end. Because the estate may last forever it is a fee; and because it may end on the happening of the event it is called a determinable or qualified fee.

Such an estate is defined in 21 C.J. 922, in the following way:

Although distinctions have been made or discussed by some authorities, the terms "base fee," "qualified fee" and "determinable fee" are generally used interchangeably to denote a fee which has a qualification subjoined thereto, and which must be determined whenever the qualification annexed to it is at an end. This estate is a fee, because by possibility it may endure forever in a man and his heirs; yet as that duration depends upon the concurrence of collateral circumstances which qualify and debase the purity of the donation it is therefore a qualified or base fee.

Manifestly the estate passing under the deed in question is embraced by these definitions. The grantor parted with all present interest in the property, and conveyed it to the grantees without limitation or restriction of title, with the lone qualification that, if it should ever cease to be used for common school purposes, the title should revert to him. In conveying such a title, with no other limitation or restriction, the grantor not only divests himself of all present title, but places the unlimited and unrestricted use and occupation of the property in his grantee until such time, if ever, the event happens which will determine the estate conveyed. Such an estate, being one which may last forever, is from necessity such as carries with it the unlimited right to use and control the property at all times before the happening of the event which will end the estate. . . .

In 21 C.J. 923, in discussing the incidents of such an estate, it is said:

Until its determination such an estate has all the incidents of a fee simple; and, while this estate continues, and until the qualification upon which it is limited is at an end, the grantee or proprietor had the same rights and privileges over his estate as if it was a fee simple. He has an absolute right to the exclusive possession, use, and enjoyment of the land, and has complete dominion over it all for purposes as though he held it in fee simple.

. . . [T]he holder of a determinable fee before its determination has all the rights of a fee simple title holder, and . . . the holder of a mere possible estate in reversion has not sufficient right or interest in the property to authorize him to maintain an action for waste. . . .

The property in this case has been used for school purposes now for thirty years or more, and there is nothing in the pleadings or evidence to suggest any purpose upon the part of the school authorities to abandon its use for such purpose, and consequently there is nothing to indicate that the title conveyed to the school trustees will at any time in the near future be determined by the cessation of the use of the property for such purposes.

Appellee, however, relies upon a certain class of cases holding that, where property has been conveyed for school purposes and a reversionary clause is inserted, its use for school purposes works a forfeiture of the original grant, and the reversion takes place. But that class of cases has no application here whatsoever, for the very plain and sufficient reason that the property here is not being used for other than school purposes, or in any such way as to interfere with the efficient and orderly administration of the school. There is no allegation that the oil development has or will so interfere with the school; and, even if there was, appellee, who is not now a resident of the school district, is not in position to make that question.

But it is earnestly argued that, the county board of education being the creature of the statute for a specific purpose, its only duty and authority lies in the administration of educational affairs; that it is not authorized to go into the field of speculation and engage in hazardous industrial affairs, even though such activities might result profitably, and for that reason alone the oil lease given by the school board was invalid and properly cancelled. In the first place, the mere leasing of its property to others for development purposes is not engaging in a commercial venture, but is, properly speaking, only an effort to get from its property the real values therefrom, to the end that there may be a more efficient administration of school affairs.

In support of this argument reliance is had upon the case of *Herald v. Board of Education*, 65 W.Va. 765, 65 S.E. 102, 31 L.R.A. (N.S.) 588. In that case it was held by a majority of the Supreme Court of West Virginia that a school board under the statutes of that state had no power to lease a schoolhouse lot for oil and gas purposes, even though the school authorities had the absolute fee simple title thereto.

Under the provisions of section 4437, Ky.Stats., 1915 Ed., which was in effect at the time the deed was made from appellee to the school board, such school trustees were authorized to "take, hold and dispose of real and personal estate for the maintenance, use and benefit of the common school of their district." . . .

Oil and gas are fugitive minerals; they are connected by underground streams or crevices by which they may be drained from one property onto another, and there brought to the surface. There can be no sound or practical reason given that will deprive school authorities who own property under which there are valuable minerals from entering into contracts for its development, and particularly would this seem to be true when the character of the mineral is such that adjoining landowners may profit at the expense of the school property by the failure of the school authorities to enter into such contracts. It is shown in this record that there are on adjoining lands other producing oil wells very near to the property lines of the school lot, and it is perfectly apparent that if the well on the school lot had not been drilled the oil on the school lot would soon have been drained from it by such wells, and the school authorities would have thereby been deprived of the chief wealth on the property to which they had title for the benefit of the school. There was, however, in the West Virginia case referred to, a strong dissenting opinion, in which we fully concur. That opinion, after discussing the West Virginia statute, said:

> I think the statute not only expressly but impliedly gives this board ample power to lease this property. This ought especially to be so where the product, as in this case, is oil and gas, fugitive in nature and which will be drained and carried away by operations on adjoining lands.

We are of the opinion, therefore, that under the statute in existence at the time the title was conveyed to the school authorities the board of education had the right to execute the lease in question, and, having the right to do so, it was its duty to do so to prevent the valuable mineral product on the school property from being appropriated by others.

The views which we have here expressed make it unnecessary to discuss the other questions presented.

The judgment is reversed, with directions to set aside the judgment entered, to dismiss the plaintiff's petition, and on the counter-claim and cross-petition to quiet the present title of the school board and to enjoin appellee from further claiming any present right or interest in the school lot.

Whole court sitting.

CASE NOTES

1. *Fee-Simple Absolute.* "The terms 'fee,' 'fee simple,' and 'fee-simple absolute' are equivalent." *Boon v. Boon*, 348 Ill. 120, 180 N.E. 792, 794 (1932). "A fee-simple absolute is an estate limited absolutely to a man and his heirs and assigns forever without limitation or condition." *Rathbun v. State*, 284 Mich. 521, 280 N.W. 35, 40 (1938). "The word 'fee,' used alone, is sufficient designation of this species of estate, and hence 'simple' is not a necessary part of the title, but it is added as a means of clearly distinguishing this estate from a fee-tail or from a variety of conditional estates." *Black's Law Dictionary* (St. Paul, Minn.: West, 7th Edition, 1999). "Fee tail is a freehold estate in which there is a fixed line of inheritable succession limited to the issue of the body of the grantee or devisee, and in which regular or general succession of heirs is cut off." *Coleman v. Shoemaker*, 147 Kan. 689, 78 P.2d 905, 907 (1938). "Fee" derives from feudal times when it constituted "a freehold estate in lands, held of a superior lord, as a reward for services, and on condition of rendering some service in return for it. The true meaning of the word 'fee' is the same as that of 'feud' or 'fief'. . . ." See *Black's Law Dictionary*, 7th Edition, 1999, pp. 741–42.

2. Whether a board of education by conveyance obtains a fee-simple title or some type

of defeasible fee is explained by the Kentucky Court of Appeals:

> When a limitation merely states the purpose for which the land is conveyed, such limitation usually does not indicate an intent to create an estate in fee simple which is to expire automatically upon the cessation of use for the purpose named. Additional facts, however, can cause such an intent to be found. Among the facts sufficient to have this result are clauses in other parts of the same instrument, the relation between the consideration paid for the conveyance and the market value of the land in question, and the situation under which the conveyance was obtained.

Scott County Board of Education v. Pepper, 311 S.W.2d 189 (Ky.1958).

3. Property obtained by a school district with a fee-simple determinable provision in the deed—providing that if the land is abandoned and "not used for school purposes," then property reverts—was held sufficient to take the property from the school district when the property was no longer in use. *School District No. 6 in Weld County v. Russell*, 156 Colo. 75, 396 P.2d 929 (1964).

■ ENDNOTES

1. Carson v. State, 27 Ind. 465 (1867).
2. In re Board of Public Instruction of Alachua County, 160 Fla. 490, 35 So.2d 579 (1948).
3. Wilson v. Graves County Board of Education, 307 Ky. 203, 210 S.W.2d 350 (1948).
4. Liles v. Smith, 206 Okl. 458, 244 P.2d 582 (1952).
5. Chester H. Smith, *Survey of the Law of Real Property* (St. Paul, Minn.: West, 1956), p. 85.
6. *Black's Law Dictionary*, revised 4th ed. (St. Paul, Minn.: West, 7th Edition, 1999), p. 742.
7. Board of Education of Borough of West Paterson v. Brophy, 90 N.J.Eq. 57, 106 A. 32 (1919).
8. T.W. Phillips Gas and Oil Co. v. Lingenfelter, 262 Pa. 500, 105 A. 888 (1919).

APPENDIX A

SELECTED CONSTITUTIONAL PROVISIONS

■ CONSTITUTION OF THE UNITED STATES

We the People of the United States, in Order to form a more perfect Union, establish Justice, insure domestic Tranquillity, provide for the common defence, promote the general Welfare, and secure the Blessings of Liberty to ourselves and our Posterity, do ordain and establish this Constitution for the United States of America.

ARTICLE. I.

Section. 1. All legislative Powers herein granted shall be vested in a Congress of the United States, which shall consist of a Senate and House of Representatives.

Section. 2. The House of Representatives shall be composed of Members chosen every second Year by the People of the several States, and the Electors in each State shall have the Qualifications requisite for Electors of the most numerous Branch of the State Legislature.

. . .

Section. 7. All Bills for raising Revenue shall originate in the House of Representatives; but the Senate may propose or concur with amendments as on other Bills.

Every Bill which shall have passed the House of Representatives and the Senate, shall, before it become a Law, be presented to the President of the United States; If he approves he shall sign it, but if not he shall return it, with his Objections to that House in which it shall have originated, who shall enter the Objections at large on their Journal, and

proceed to reconsider it. If after such Reconsideration two thirds of that House shall agree to pass the Bill, it shall be sent, together with the Objections, to the other House, by which it shall likewise be reconsidered, and if approved by two thirds of that House, it shall become a Law. But in all such Cases the Votes of both Houses shall be determined by yeas and Nays, and the Names of the Persons voting for and against the Bill shall be entered on the Journal of each House respectively. If any Bill shall not be returned by the President within ten Days (Sunday excepted) after it shall have been presented to him, the Same shall be a Law, in like Manner as if he had signed it, unless the Congress by their Adjournment prevents its Return, in which Case it shall not be a Law.

. . .

Section. 8. The Congress shall have Power To lay and collect Taxes, Duties, Imposts and Excises, to pay the Debts and provide for the common Defence and general Welfare of the United States; but all Duties, Imposts and Excises shall be uniform throughout the United States;

To borrow Money on the credit of the United States;

To regulate Commerce with foreign Nations, and among the several States, and with the Indian Tribes;

. . .

To promote the Progress of Science and useful Arts, by securing for limited Times to Authors and Inventors the exclusive Right to their respective Writings and Discoveries;

. . .

Section. 9. The Privilege of the Writ of Habeas Corpus shall not be suspended, unless when in Cases of Rebellion or Invasion the public Safety may require it.

No Bill of Attainder or ex post facto Law shall be passed.

. . .

Section. 10. No State shall enter into any Treaty, Alliance, or Confederation; grant Letters of Marque and Reprisal; coin Money; emit Bills of Credit; make any Thing but gold and silver Coin a Tender in Payment of Debts; pass any Bill of Attainder, ex post facto Law, or Law impairing the Obligation of Contracts, or grant any Title of Nobility.

. . .

ARTICLE. II.

Section. 1. The executive Power shall be vested in a President of the United States of America. . . .

Section. 2. The President shall be Commander in Chief of the Army and Navy of the United States, and of the Militia of the several States. . . .

He shall have Power, by and with the Advice and Consent of the Senate, to make Treaties, provided two thirds of the Senators present concur; and he shall nominate, and by and with the Advice and Consent of the Senate, shall appoint Ambassadors, other public Ministers and Consuls, Judges of the supreme Court, and all other Officers of the United States, whose Appointments are not herein otherwise provided for, and which shall be established by Law: but the Congress may by Law vest the Appointment of such inferior Officers, as they think proper, in the President alone, in the Courts of Law, or in the Heads of Departments. . . .

Section. 4. The United States shall guarantee to every State in this Union a Republican Form of Government, and shall protect each of them against Invasion; and on Application of the Legislature, or of the Executive (when the Legislature cannot be convened) against domestic Violence.

ARTICLE. III.

Section. 1. The judicial Power of the United States, shall be vested in one supreme Court, and in such inferior Courts as the Congress may from time to time ordain and establish. The Judges, both of the supreme and inferior Courts, shall hold their Offices during good Behaviour, and shall, at stated Times, receive for their Services, a Compensation, which shall not be diminished during their Continuance in Office.

Section. 2. The judicial Power shall extend to all Cases, in Law and Equity, arising under this Constitution, the Laws of the United States, and

Treaties made, or which shall be made, under their Authority;—to all Cases affecting Ambassadors, other public Ministers and Consuls;—to all Cases of admiralty and maritime Jurisdiction;—to Controversies to which the United States shall be a Party;—to Controversies between two or more States;—between a State and Citizens of another State;—between Citizens of different States;—between Citizens of the same State claiming Lands under Grants of different States, and between a State, or the Citizens thereof, and foreign States, Citizens or Subjects.

. . .

The Trial of all Crimes, except in Cases of Impeachment, shall be by Jury; and such Trial shall be held in the State where the said Crimes shall have been committed; but when not committed within any State, the Trial shall be at such Place or Places as the Congress may by Law have directed.

. . .

ARTICLE. IV.

Section. 1. Full Faith and Credit shall be given in each State to the public Acts, Records, and judicial Proceedings of every other State. And the Congress may by general Laws prescribe the Manner in which such Acts, Records and Proceedings shall be proved, and the Effect thereof.

Section. 2. The Citizens of each State shall be entitled to all Privileges and Immunities of Citizens in the several States.

. . .

Section. 3. New States may be admitted by the Congress into this Union; but no new State shall be formed or erected within the Jurisdiction of any other State; nor any State be formed by the Junction of two or more States, or Parts of States, without the Consent of the Legislatures of the States concerned as well as of the Congress.

. . .

ARTICLE. V.

The Congress, whenever two thirds of both Houses shall deem it necessary, shall propose Amendments to this Constitution, or, on the Application of the Legislatures of two thirds of the several States, shall call a Convention for proposing Amendments, which, in either Case, shall be valid to all Intents and Purposes, as Part of this Constitution, when ratified by the Legislatures of three fourths of the several States, or by Conventions in three fourths thereof, as the one or the other Mode of Ratification may be proposed by the Congress; Provided that no Amendment which may be made prior to the Year One thousand eight hundred and eight shall in any Manner affect the first and fourth Clauses in the Ninth Section of the first Article; and that no State, without its Consent, shall be deprived of its equal Suffrage in the Senate.

ARTICLE. VI.

. . .

This Constitution, and the Laws of the United States which shall be made in Pursuance thereof; and all Treaties made, or which shall be made, under the Authority of the United States, shall be the supreme Law of the Land; and the Judges in every State shall be bound thereby, any Thing in the Constitution or Laws of any State to the Contrary notwithstanding.

The Senators and Representatives before mentioned, and the Members of the several State Legislatures, and all executive and judicial Officers, both of the United States and of the several States, shall be bound by Oath or Affirmation, to support this Constitution; but no religious Test shall ever be required as a Qualification to any Office or public Trust under the United States.

ARTICLE. VII.

The Ratification of the Conventions of nine States, shall be sufficient for the Establishment of this Constitution between the States so ratifying the Same.

. . .

■ AMENDMENTS TO THE CONSTITUTION OF THE UNITED STATES OF AMERICA

Articles in Addition to, and Amendment of, the Constitution of the United States of America, Proposed by Congress, and Ratified by the Several States, Pursuant to the Fifth Article of the Original Constitution

AMENDMENT [I.] [1791]

Congress shall make no law respecting an establishment of religion, or prohibiting the free exercise thereof; or abridging the freedom of speech, or of the press; or the right of the people peaceably to assemble, and to petition the Government for a redress of grievances.

AMENDMENT II. [1791]

A well regulated Militia, being necessary to the security of a free State, the right of the people to keep and bear Arms, shall not be infringed.

AMENDMENT III. [1791]

No Soldier shall, in time of peace be quartered in any house, without the consent of the Owner, nor in time of war, but in a manner to be prescribed by law.

AMENDMENT IV. [1791]

The right of the people to be secure in their persons, houses, papers, and effects, against unreasonable searches and seizures, shall not be violated, and no Warrants shall issue, but upon probable cause, supported by Oath or affirmation, and particularly describing the place to be searched, and the persons or things to be seized.

AMENDMENT V. [1791]

No person shall be held to answer for a capital, or otherwise infamous crime, unless on a presentment or indictment of a Grand Jury, except in cases arising in the land or naval forces, or in the Militia, when in actual service in time of War or public danger; nor shall any person be subject for the same offence to be twice put in jeopardy of life or limb; nor shall be compelled in any criminal case to be a witness against himself, nor be deprived of life, liberty, or property, without due process of law; nor shall private property be taken for public use, without just compensation.

AMENDMENT VI. [1791]

In all criminal prosecutions, the accused shall enjoy the right to a speedy and public trial, by an impartial jury of the State and district wherein the crime shall have been committed, which district shall have been previously ascertained by law, and to be informed of the nature and cause of the accusation; to be confronted with the witnesses against him; to have compulsory process for obtaining witnesses in his favor, and to have the Assistance of Counsel for his defence.

AMENDMENT VII. [1791]

In Suits at common law, where the value in controversy shall exceed twenty dollars, the right of trial by jury shall be preserved, and no fact tried by a jury, shall be otherwise reexamined in any Court of the United States, than according to the rules of the common law.

AMENDMENT VIII. [1791]

Excessive bail shall not be required, nor excessive fines imposed, nor cruel and unusual punishments inflicted.

AMENDMENT IX. [1791]

The enumeration in the Constitution, of certain rights, shall not be construed to deny or disparage others retained by the people.

AMENDMENT X. [1791]

The powers not delegated to the United States by the Constitution, nor prohibited by it to the States, are reserved to the States respectively, or to the people.

AMENDMENT XI. [1798]

The Judicial power of the United States shall not be construed to extend to any suit in law or equity, commenced or prosecuted against one of the United States by Citizens of another State, or by Citizens or Subjects of any Foreign State.

. . .

AMENDMENT XIII. [1865]

Section 1. Neither slavery nor involuntary servitude, except as a punishment for crime whereof the party shall have been duly convicted, shall exist within the United States, or any place subject to their jurisdiction.

Section 2. Congress shall have power to enforce this article by appropriate legislation.

AMENDMENT XIV. [1868]

Section 1. All persons born or naturalized in the United States and subject to the jurisdiction thereof, are citizens of the United States and of the State wherein they reside. No State shall make or enforce any law which shall abridge the privileges or immunities of citizens of the United States; nor shall any State deprive any person of life, liberty, or property, without due process of law; nor deny to any person within its jurisdiction the equal protection of the laws.

. . .

Section 5. The Congress shall have power to enforce, by appropriate legislation, the provisions of this article.

AMENDMENT XV. [1870]

Section 1. The right of citizens of the United States to vote shall not be denied or abridged by the United States or by any State on account of race, color, or previous condition of servitude.

Section 2. The Congress shall have power to enforce this article by appropriate legislation.

. . .

AMENDMENT XIX. [1920]

The right of citizens of the United States to vote shall not be denied or abridged by the United States or by any State on account of sex.

Congress shall have power to enforce this article by appropriate legislation.

. . .

AMENDMENT XXVI [1971]

Section 1. The right of citizens of the United States, who are eighteen years of age or older, to vote shall not be denied or abridged by the United States or by any State on account of age.

Section 2. The Congress shall have power to enforce this article by appropriate legislation.

APPENDIX B

SELECTED FEDERAL STATUTES

■ CIVIL RIGHTS ACTS OF 1866 AND 1870, 42 U.S.C. §1981

[Section 1981 provides:]

All persons within the jurisdiction of the United States shall have the same right . . . to make and enforce contracts, to sue, be parties, give evidence, and to the full and equal benefit of all laws and proceedings for the security of persons and property as is enjoyed by white citizens, and shall be subject to like punishments, pains, penalties, taxes, licenses, and exactions of every kind, and to no other.

■ THE CIVIL RIGHTS ACT OF 1871, 42 U.S.C. §1983

[Section 1983 provides:]

Every person who, under color of any statute, ordinance, regulation, custom or usage, of any State or Territory, subjects, or causes to be subjected, any citizen of the United States or other person within the jurisdiction thereof to the deprivation of any rights, privileges or immunities secured by the Constitution and laws, shall be liable to the party injured in an action at law, suit in equity, or other proper proceeding for redress.

■ THE CIVIL RIGHTS ACT OF 1871, 42 U.S.C. §§1985 AND 1986

[Section 1985(3) provides:]

If two or more persons in any State or Territory conspire or go in disguise on the highway or on the premises of another, for the purpose of depriving, either directly or indirectly, any person or class of persons of the equal protection of the laws, or of equal privileges and immunities under the laws: or for the purpose of preventing or hindering the constituted authorities of any State or Territory from giving or securing to all persons within such State or Territory the equal protection of the laws . . . : in any case of conspiracy set forth in this section, if one or more persons engaged therein do, or cause to be done, any act in furtherance of the object of such conspiracy, whereby another is injured in his person or property, or deprived of having and exercising any right or privilege of a citizen of the United States, the party so injured or deprived may have an action for the recovery of damages, occasioned by such injury or deprivation, against any one or more of the conspirators.

[Section 1986 provides:]

Every person who, having knowledge that any of the wrongs conspired to be done, and mentioned in Section 1985 of this title, are about to be committed, and having the power to prevent or aid in preventing the commission of the same, neglects or refuses so to do, if such wrongful act be committed, shall be liable to the party injured, or his legal representatives, for all damages caused by such wrongful act, which such person by reasonable diligence could have prevented; and such damages may be recovered in an action on the case; and any number of persons guilty of such wrongful neglect or refusal may be joined as defendants in the action. . . .

■ CIVIL RIGHTS ACTS OF 1866 AND 1870, 42 U.S.C. §1988

[As amended 1976, Section 1988 provides:]

Proceedings in vindication of civil rights. The jurisdiction in civil and criminal matters conferred on the district courts by the provisions of this chapter and Title 18, for the protection of all persons in the United States in their civil rights, and for their vindication, shall be exercised and enforced in conformity with the laws of the United States, so far as such laws are suitable to carry the same into effect; but in all cases where they are not adapted to the object, or are deficient in the provisions necessary to furnish suitable remedies and punish offenses against law, the common law, as modified and changed by the constitution and statutes of the State wherein the court having jurisdiction of such civil or criminal cause is held, so far as the same is not inconsistent with the Constitution and laws of the United States, shall be extended to and govern the said courts in the trial and disposition of the cause, and, if it is of a criminal nature, in the infliction of punishment on the party found guilty. In any action or proceeding to enforce a provision of sections 1981, 1982, 1983, 1985, and 1986 of this title, title IX of Public Law 92-318, or in any civil action or proceeding, by or on behalf of the United States of America, to enforce, or charging a violation of, a provision of the United States Internal Revenue Code, or title VI of the Civil Rights Act of 1964, the court, in its discretion, may allow the prevailing party, other than the United States, a reasonable attorney's fee as part of the costs.

As amended Pub.L. 94-559, §2, Oct. 19, 1976, 90 Stat. 2641.

■ CIVIL RIGHTS ACT OF 1964, TITLE VI (SELECTED PARTS), 42 U.S.C.A. §§2000D–D-1

FEDERALLY ASSISTED PROGRAMS

§2000d. Prohibition against exclusion from participation in, denial of benefits of, and discrimination under Federally assisted programs on ground of race, color, or national origin

No person in the United States shall, on the ground of race, color, or national origin, be excluded from participation in, be denied the benefits of, or be subjected to discrimination under any program or activity receiving Federal financial assistance.

Pub.L. 88-352, Title VI, §601, July 2, 1964, 78 Stat. 252.

§2000d-1. Federal authority and financial assistance to programs or activities by way of grant, loan, or contract other than contract of insurance or guaranty; rules and regulations; approval by President; compliance with requirements; reports to Congressional committees; effective date of administrative action

Each Federal department and agency which is empowered to extend Federal financial assistance to any program or activity, by way of grant, loan, or contract other than a contract of insurance or guaranty, is authorized and directed to effectuate the provisions of section 2000d of this title with respect to such program or activity by issuing rules, regulations, or orders of general applicability which shall be consistent with achievement of the objectives of the statute authorizing the financial assistance in connection with which the action is taken. No such rule, regulation, or order shall become effective unless and until approved by the President. Compliance with any requirement adopted pursuant to this section may be effected (1) by the termination of or refusal to grant or to continue assistance under such program or activity to any recipient as to whom there has been an express finding on the record, after opportunity for hearing, of a failure to comply with such requirement, but such termination or refusal shall be limited to the particular political entity, or part thereof, or other recipient as to whom such a finding has been made and, shall be limited in its effect to the particular program, or part thereof, in which such noncompliance has been so found, or (2) by any other means authorized by law: *Provided, however,* That no such action shall be taken until the department or agency concerned has advised the appropriate person or persons of the failure to comply with the requirement and has determined that compliance cannot be secured by voluntary means. In the case of any action terminating, or refusing to grant or continue, assistance because of failure to comply with a requirement imposed pursuant to this section, the head of the Federal department or agency shall file with the committees of the House and Senate having legislative jurisdiction over the program or activity involved a full written report of the circumstances and the grounds for such action. No such action shall become effective until thirty days have elapsed after the filing of such report.

Pub.L. 88-352, Title VI, §602, July 2, 1964, 78 Stat. 252.

■ CIVIL RIGHTS ACT OF 1964, TITLE VII (SELECTED PARTS), 42 U.S.C.A. §2000E-2

EQUAL EMPLOYMENT OPPORTUNITIES

§2000e-2. Unlawful employment practices

Employer practices

(a) It shall be an unlawful employment practice for an employer—

(1) to fail or refuse to hire or to discharge any individual, or otherwise to discriminate against any individual with respect to his compensation, terms, conditions, or privileges of employment, because of such individual's race, color, religion, sex, or national origin; or

(2) to limit, segregate, or classify his employees or applicants for employment in any way which would deprive or tend to deprive any individual of employment opportunities or otherwise adversely affect his status as an employee, because of such individual's race, color, religion, sex, or national origin.

Employment agency practices

(b) It shall be an unlawful employment practice for an employment agency to fail or refuse to refer for employment, or otherwise to discriminate against, any individual because of his race, color, religion, sex, or national origin, or to classify or refer for employment any individual on the basis of his race, color, religion, sex, or national origin. . . .

Training programs

(d) It shall be an unlawful employment practice for any employer, labor organization, or joint labor-management committee controlling apprenticeship or other training or retraining, including on-the-job training programs to discriminate against any individual because of his race, color, religion, sex, or national origin in admission to, or employment in, any program established to provide apprenticeship or other training.

Business or enterprises with personnel qualified on basis of religion, sex, or national origin; educational institutions with personnel of particular religion

(e) Notwithstanding any other provision of this subchapter, (1) it shall not be an unlawful employ-ment practice for an employer to hire and employ employees, for an employment agency to classify, or refer for employment any individual, for a labor organization to classify its membership or to classify or refer for employment any individual, or for an employer, labor organization, or joint labor-management committee controlling apprenticeship or other training or retraining programs to admit or employ any individual in any such program, on the basis of his religion, sex, or national origin in those certain instances where religion, sex, or national origin is a bona fide occupational qualification reasonably necessary to the normal operation of that particular business or enterprise, and (2) it shall not be an unlawful employment practice for a school, college, university, or other educational institution or institution of learning to hire and employ employees of a particular religion if such school, college, university, or other educational institution or institution of learning is, in whole or in substantial part, owned, supported, controlled, or managed by a particular religion or by a particular religious corporation, association, or society, or if the curriculum of such school, college, university, or other educational institution or institution of learning is directed toward the propagation of a particular religion. . . .

Seniority or merit system; quantity or quality of production; ability tests; compensation based on sex and authorized by minimum wage provisions

(h) Notwithstanding any other provision of this subchapter, it shall not be an unlawful employment practice for an employer to apply different standards of compensation, or different terms, conditions, or privileges of employment pursuant to a bona fide seniority or merit system, or a system which measures earnings by quantity or quality of production or to employees who work in different locations, provided that such differences are not the result of an intention to discriminate because of race, color, religion, sex, or national origin, nor shall it be an unlawful employment practice for an employer to give and to act upon the results of any professionally developed ability test provided that such test, its administration or action upon the results is not designed, intended, or used to discriminate because of race, color, religion, sex, or national origin. It shall not be an unlawful employment practice under this subchapter for any employer to differentiate upon the basis of sex in determining the amount of the wages or compensation paid or to be paid to employees of such employer if such differentiation is authorized by the provisions of section 206(d) of Title 29. . . .

Preferential treatment not to be granted on account of existing number or percentage imbalance

(j) Nothing contained in this subchapter shall be interpreted to require any employer, employment agency, labor organization, or joint labor-management committee subject to this subchapter to grant preferential treatment to any individual or to any group because of the race, color, religion, sex, or national origin of such individual or group on account of an imbalance which may exist with respect to the total number or percentage of persons of any race, color, religion, sex, or national origin employed by any employer, referred or classified for employment by any employment agency or labor organization, admitted to membership or classified by any labor organization, or admitted to, or employed in, any apprenticeship or other training program, in comparison with the total number or percentage of persons of such race, color, religion, sex, or national origin in any community, State, section, or other area, or in the available work force in any community, State, section, or other area.

Pub.L. 88-352, Title VII, §703, July 2, 1964, 78 Stat. 255; Pub.L. 92-261, §8(a), (b), Mar. 24, 1972, 86 Stat. 109.

■ CIVIL RIGHTS ACT OF 1991, P.L. 102–166

An Act to amend the Civil Rights Act of 1964 to strengthen and improve Federal civil rights laws, to provide for damages in cases of intentional employment discrimination, to clarify provisions regarding disparate impact actions, and for other purposes.

. . .

SECTION 2. FINDINGS

The Congress finds that—

(1) additional remedies under Federal law are needed to deter unlawful harassment and intentional discrimination in the workplace;

(2) the decision of the Supreme Court in Wards Cove Packing Co. v. Antonio, 490 U.S. 642 (1989) has weakened the scope and effectiveness of Federal civil rights protections; and

(3) legislation is necessary to provide additional protections against unlawful discrimination in employment.

SECTION 3. PURPOSES

The purposes of this Act are—

(1) to provide appropriate remedies for intentional discrimination and unlawful harassment in the workplace;

(2) to codify the concepts of "business necessity" and "job related" enunciated by the Supreme

Court in Griggs v. Duke Power Co., 401 U.S. 424 (1971), and in the other Supreme Court decisions prior to Wards Cove Packing Co. v. Antonio, 490 U.S. 642 (1989);

(3) to confirm statutory authority and provide statutory guidelines for the adjudication of disparate impact suits under title VII of the Civil Rights Act of 1964 (42 U.S.C. 2000e et seq.); and

(4) to respond to recent decisions of the Supreme Court by expanding the scope of relevant civil rights statutes in order to provide adequate protection to victims of discrimination.

■ DISCRIMINATION BASED ON SEX, TITLE IX (SELECTED PARTS), 20 U.S.C.A. §1681

§1681. SEX

Prohibition against discrimination; exceptions

(a) No person in the United States shall, on the basis of sex, be excluded from participation in, be denied the benefits of, or be subjected to discrimination under any education program or activity receiving Federal financial assistance, except that:

Classes of educational institutions subject to prohibition

(1) in regard to admissions to educational institutions, this section shall apply only to institutions of vocational education, professional education, and graduate higher education, and to public institutions of undergraduate higher education;

Educational institutions commencing planned change in admissions

(2) in regard to admissions to educational institutions, this section shall not apply (A) for one year from June 23, 1972, nor for six years after June 23, 1972, in the case of an educational institution which has begun the process of changing from being an institution which admits only students of one sex to being an institution which admits students of both sexes, but only if it is carrying out a plan for such a change which is approved by the Commissioner of Education or (B) for seven years from the date an educational institution begins the process of changing from being an institution which admits only students of only one sex to being an institution which admits students of both sexes, but only if it is carrying out a plan for such a change which is approved by the Commissioner of Education, whichever is the later;

Educational institutions of religious organizations with contrary religious tenets

(3) this section shall not apply to an educational institution which is controlled by a religious organization if the application of this subsection would not be consistent with the religious tenets of such organization;

Educational institutions training individuals for military services or merchant marine

(4) this section shall not apply to an educational institution whose primary purpose is the training of individuals for the military services of the United States, or the merchant marine;

Public educational institutions with traditional and continuing admissions policy

(5) in regard to admissions this section shall not apply to any public institution of undergraduate higher education which is an institution that traditionally and continually from its establishment has had a policy of admitting only students of one sex;

Social fraternities or sororities; voluntary youth service organizations

(6) this section shall not apply to membership practices—

(A) of a social fraternity or social sorority which is exempt from taxation under section 501(a) of Title 26, the active membership of which consists primarily of students in attendance at an institution of higher education, or

(B) of the Young Men's Christian Association, Young Women's Christian Association, Girl Scouts, Boy Scouts, Camp Fire Girls, and voluntary youth service organizations which are so exempt, the membership of which has traditionally been limited to persons of one sex and principally to persons of less than nineteen years of age;

Boy or girl conferences

(7) this section shall not apply to—

(A) any program or activity of the American Legion undertaken in connection with the organization or operation of any Boys State conference, Boys Nation conference, Girls State conference, or Girls Nation conference; or

(B) any program or activity of any secondary school or educational institution specifically for—

(i) the promotion of any Boys State conference, Boys Nations conference, Girls State conference, or Girls Nations conference; or

(ii) the selection of students to attend any such conference;

Father-son or mother-daughter activities at educational institutions

(8) this section shall not preclude father-son or mother-daughter activities at an educational institution, but if such activities are provided for students of one sex, opportunities for reasonably comparable activities shall be provided for students of the other sex; and

Institution of higher education scholarship awards in "beauty" pageants

(9) this section shall not apply with respect to any scholarship or other financial assistance awarded by an institution of higher education to any individual because such individual has received such award in any pageant in which the attainment of such award is based upon a combination of factors related to the personal appearance, poise, and talent of such individual and in which participation is limited to individuals of one sex only, so long as such pageant is in compliance with other non-discrimination provisions of Federal law.

Preferential or disparate treatment because of imbalance in participation or receipt of Federal benefits; statistical evidence of imbalance

(b) Nothing contained in subsection (a) of this section shall be interpreted to require any educational institution to grant preferential or disparate treatment to the members of one sex on account of an imbalance which may exist with respect to the total number or percentage of persons of that sex participating in or receiving the benefits of any federally supported program or activity, in comparison with the total number or percentage of persons of that sex in any community, State, section, or other area: Provided, That this subsection shall not be construed to prevent the consideration in any hearing or proceeding under this chapter of statistical evidence tending to show that such an imbalance exists with respect to the participation in, or receipt of the benefits of, any such program or activity by the members of one sex.

Educational institution defined

(c) For purposes of this chapter an educational institution means any public or private preschool, elementary, or secondary school, or any institution of vocational, professional, or higher education, except that in the case of an educational institution composed of more than one school, college, or department which are administratively separate units, such term means each such school, college, or department.

■ EQUAL PAY ACT (SELECTED PARTS), 29 U.S.C.A. §206

§206. MINIMUM WAGE

. . .

Prohibition of sex discrimination

(d)(1) No employer having employees subject to any provisions of this section shall discriminate, within any establishment in which such employees are employed, between employees on the basis of sex by paying wages to employees in such establishment at a rate less than the rate at which he pays wages to employees of the opposite sex in such establishment for equal work on jobs the performance of which requires equal skill, effort, and responsibility, and which are performed under similar working conditions, except where such payment is made pursuant to (i) a seniority system; (ii) a merit system; (iii) a system which measures earnings by quantity or quality of production; or (iv) a differential based on any other factor other than sex: *Provided,* That an employer who is paying a wage rate differential in violation of this subsection shall not, in order to comply with the provisions of this subsection, reduce the wage rate of any employee.

(2) No labor organization, or its agents, representing employees of an employer having employees subject to any provisions of this section shall cause or attempt to cause such an employer to discriminate against an employee in violation of paragraph (1) of this subsection.

(3) For purposes of administration and enforcement, any amounts owing to any employee which have been withheld in violation of this subsection shall be deemed to be unpaid minimum wages or unpaid overtime compensation under this chapter.

(4) As used in this subsection, the term "labor organization" means any organization of any kind, or any agency or employee representation committee or plan, in which employees participate and which exists for the purpose, in whole or in part, of dealing with employers concerning grievances, labor disputes, wages, rates of pay, hours of employment, or conditions of work.

■ FAMILY RIGHTS AND PRIVACY ACT (BUCKLEY AMENDMENT) (SELECTED PARTS), 20 U.S.C.A. §1232G

§1232G. FAMILY EDUCATIONAL AND PRIVACY RIGHTS

Conditions for availability of funds to educational agencies or institutions; inspection and review of education records; specific information to be made available; procedure for access to education records; reasonableness of time for such access; hearings; written explanations by parents; definitions

(a)(1)(A) No funds shall be made available under any applicable program to any educational agency or institution which has a policy of denying, or which effectively prevents, the parents of students who are or have been in attendance at a school of such agency or at such institution, as the case may be, the right to inspect and review the education records of their children. If any material or document in the education record of a student includes information on more than one student, the parents of one of such students shall have the right to inspect and review only such part of such material or document as relates to such student or to be informed of the specific information contained in such part of such material. Each educational agency or institution shall establish appropriate procedures for the granting of a request by parents for access to the education records of their children within a reasonable period of time, but in no case more than forty-five days after the request has been made. . . .

(2) No funds shall be made available under any applicable program to any educational agency or institution unless the parents of students who are or have been in attendance at a school of such agency or at such institution are provided an opportunity for a hearing by such agency or institution, in accordance with regulations of the Secretary, to challenge the content of such student's education records, in order to insure that the records are not inaccurate, misleading, or otherwise in violation of the privacy or other rights of students, and to provide an opportunity for the correction or deletion of any such inaccurate, misleading, or otherwise inappropriate data contained therein and to insert into such records a written explanation of the parents respecting the content of such records. . . .

Release of education records; parental consent requirement; exceptions; compliance with judicial orders and subpoenas; audit and evaluation of Federally-supported education programs; record-keeping

(b)(1) No funds shall be made available under any applicable program to any educational agency or institution which has a policy or practice of permitting the release of education records (or personally identifiable information contained therein other than directory information, as defined in paragraph (5) of subsection (a) of this section) of students without the written consent of their parents to any individual, agency, or organization, other than to the following—

(A) other school officials, including teachers within the educational institution or local educational agency who have been determined by such agency or institution to have legitimate educational interests;

(B) officials of other schools or school systems in which the student seeks or intends to enroll, upon condition that the student's parents be notified of the transfer, receive a copy of the record if desired, and have an opportunity for a hearing to challenge the content of the record;

(C) authorized representatives of (i) the Comptroller General of the United States, (ii) the Secretary, (iii) an administrative head of an education agency (as defined in section 1221e-3(c) of this title), or (iv) State educational authorities, under the conditions set forth in paragraph (3) of this subsection;

(D) in connection with a student's application for, or receipt of, financial aid;

(E) State and local officials or authorities to whom such information is specifically required to be reported or disclosed pursuant to State statute adopted prior to November 19, 1974;

(F) organizations conducting studies for, or on behalf of, educational agencies or institutions for the purpose of developing, validating, or administering predictive tests, administering student aid programs, and improving instruction, if such studies are conducted in such a manner as will not permit the personal identification of students and their parents by persons other than representatives of such organizations and such information will be destroyed when no longer needed for the purpose for which it is conducted;

(G) accrediting organizations in order to carry out their accrediting functions;

(H) parents of a dependent student of such parents, as defined in section 152 of Title 26; and

(I) subject to regulations of the Secretary, in connection with an emergency, appropriate persons if the knowledge of such information is necessary to protect the health or safety of the student or other persons.

Nothing in clause (E) of this paragraph shall prevent a State from further limiting the number or type of State or local officials who will continue to have access thereunder.

(2) No funds shall be made available under any applicable program to any educational agency or institution which has a policy or practice of releasing, or providing access to, any personally identifiable information in education records other than directory information, or as is permitted under paragraph (1) of this subsection unless—

(A) there is written consent from the student's parents specifying records to be released, the reasons for such release, and to whom, and with a copy of the records to be released to the student's parents and the student if desired by the parents, or

(B) such information is furnished in compliance with judicial order, or pursuant to any lawfully issued subpoena, upon condition that parents and the students are notified of all such orders or subpoenas in advance of the compliance therewith by the educational institution or agency. . . .

Students' rather than parents' permission or consent

(d) For the purposes of this section, whenever a student has attained eighteen years of age, or is attending an institution of postsecondary education the permission or consent required of and the rights accorded to the parents of the student shall thereafter only be required of and accorded to the student. . . .

Pub.L. 90-247, Title IV, §438, as added Pub.L. 93-380, Title V, §513(a), Aug. 21, 1974, 88 Stat. 571, and amended Pub.L. 93-568 §2(a), Dec. 31, 1974, 88 Stat. 1858.

■ FAMILY RIGHTS AND PRIVACY ACT, PART 4: RECORDS, PRIVACY, 20 U.S.C.A. §1232H

§1232H. PROTECTION OF PUPIL RIGHTS

(a) Inspection of instructional materials by parents or guardians.

All instructional materials, including teacher's manuals, films, tapes, or other supplementary material which will be used in connection with any survey, analysis, or evaluation as part of any applicable program shall be available for inspection by the parents or guardians of the children.

(b) Limits on survey, analysis, or evaluations

No student shall be required, as part of any applicable program, to submit to a survey, analysis, or evaluation that reveals information concerning—

(1) political affiliations;

(2) mental and psychological problems potentially embarrassing to the student or his family;

(3) sex behavior and attitudes;

(4) illegal, anti-social, self-incriminating and demeaning behavior;

(5) critical appraisals of other individuals with whom respondents have close family relationships;

(6) legally recognized privileged or analogous relationships, such as those of lawyers, physicians, and ministers; or

(7) income (other than that required by law to determine eligibility for participation in a program or for receiving financial assistance under such program), without the prior consent of the student (if the student is an adult or emancipated minor), or in the case of an unemancipated minor, without the prior written consent of the parent.

(c) Notice

Educational agencies and institutions shall give parents and students effective notice of their rights under this section.

■ INDIVIDUALS WITH DISABILITIES EDUCATION ACT AMENDMENTS OF 1997 (SELECTED PARTS), 20 U.S.C. §§1400–1485.

SEC. 602. DEFINITIONS

. . .

(3) CHILD WITH A DISABILITY—

(A) IN GENERAL—The term "child with a disability" means a child—

(i) with mental retardation, hearing impairments (including deafness), speech or language impairments, visual impairments (including blindness), serious emotional disturbance (hereinafter referred to as "emotional disturbance"), orthopedic impairments, autism, traumatic brain injury, other health impairments, or specific learning disabilities; and

(ii) who, by reason thereof, needs special education and related services.

(B) CHILD AGED 3 THROUGH 9—The term "child with a disability" for a child aged 3 through 9 may, at the discretion of the State and the local educational agency, include a child—

(i) experiencing developmental delays, as defined by the State and as measured by appropriate diagnostic instruments and procedures, in one or more of the following areas: physical development, cognitive development, communication development, social or emotional development, or adaptive development; and

(ii) who, by reason thereof, needs special education and related services.

. . .

(8) FREE APPROPRIATE PUBLIC EDUCATION—The term "free appropriate public education" means special education and related services that—

(A) have been provided at public expense, under public supervision and direction, and without charge;

(B) meet the standards of the State educational agency;

(C) include an appropriate preschool, elementary, or secondary school education in the State involved; and

(D) are provided in conformity with the individualized education program required.

. . .

(11) INDIVIDUALIZED EDUCATION PROGRAM—The term "individualized education program" or "IEP" means a written statement for each child with a disability that is developed, reviewed, and revised in accordance with section 614(d).

. . .

(22) RELATED SERVICES—The term "related services" means transportation, and such developmental, corrective, and other supportive services (including speech-language pathology and audiology services, psychological services, physical and occupational therapy, recreation, including therapeutic recreation, social work services, counseling services, including rehabilitation counseling, orientation and mobility services, and medical services, except that such medical services shall be for diagnostic and evaluation purposes only) as may be required to assist a child with a disability to benefit from special education, and includes the early identification and assessment of disabling conditions in children.

. . .

(25) SPECIAL EDUCATION—The term "special education" means specially designed instruction, at no cost to parents, to meet the unique needs of a child with a disability, including—

(A) instruction conducted in the classroom, in the home, in hospitals and institutions, and in other settings; and

(B) instruction in physical education.

(26) SPECIFIC LEARNING DISABILITY—

(A) IN GENERAL—The term "specific learning disability" means a disorder in one or more of the basic psychological processes involved in understanding or in using language, spoken or written, which disorder may manifest itself in imperfect ability to listen, think, speak, read, write, spell, or do mathematical calculations.

(B) DISORDERS INCLUDED—Such term includes such conditions as perceptual disabilities, brain injury, minimal brain dysfunction, dyslexia, and developmental aphasia.

(C) DISORDERS NOT INCLUDED—Such term does not include a learning problem that is primarily the result of visual, hearing, or motor disabilities, of mental retardation, of emotional disturbance, or of environmental, cultural, or economic disadvantage.

. . .

SEC. 604. ABROGATION OF STATE SOVEREIGN IMMUNITY

(a) IN GENERAL—A State shall not be immune under the eleventh amendment to the Constitution of the United States from suit in Federal court for a violation of this Act.

(b) REMEDIES—In a suit against a State for a violation of this Act, remedies (including remedies both at law and in equity) are available for such a violation to the same extent as those remedies are available for such a violation in the suit against any public entity other than a State.

. . .

SEC. 612. STATE ELIGIBILITY

(a) IN GENERAL—A State is eligible for assistance under this part for a fiscal year if the State demonstrates to the satisfaction of the Secretary that the State has in effect policies and procedures to ensure that it meets each of the following conditions:

(1) FREE APPROPRIATE PUBLIC EDUCATION—

(A) IN GENERAL—A free appropriate public education is available to all children with disabilities residing in the State between the ages of 3 and 21, inclusive, including children with disabilities who have been suspended or expelled from school.

(B) LIMITATION—The obligation to make a free appropriate public education available to all children with disabilities does not apply with respect to children:

(i) aged 3 through 5 and 18 through 21 in a State to the extent that its application to those children would be inconsistent with State law or practice, or the order of any court, respecting the provision of public education to children in those age ranges; and

(ii) aged 18 through 21 to the extent that State law does not require that special education and related services under this part be provided to children with disabilities who, in the educational placement prior to their incarceration in an adult correctional facility:

(I) were not actually identified as being a child with a disability . . . or

(II) did not have an individualized education program under this part.

. . .

(5) LEAST RESTRICTIVE ENVIRONMENT—

(A) IN GENERAL—To the maximum extent appropriate, children with disabilities, including children in public or private institutions or other care facilities, are educated with children who are not disabled, and special classes, separate schooling, or other removal of children with disabilities from the regular educational environment occurs only when the nature or severity of the disability of a child is such that education in regular classes with the use of supplementary aids and services cannot be achieved satisfactorily.

. . .

(10) CHILDREN IN PRIVATE SCHOOLS—

(A) CHILDREN ENROLLED IN PRIVATE SCHOOLS BY THEIR PARENTS—

(i) IN GENERAL—To the extent consistent with the number and location of children with disabilities in the State who are enrolled by their parents in private elementary and secondary schools, provision is made for the participation of those children in the program assisted or carried out under this part by providing for such children special education and related services in accordance with the following requirements, unless the Secretary has arranged for services to those children under subsection (f):

(I) Amounts expended for the provision of those services by a local educational agency shall be equal to a proportionate amount of Federal funds made available under this part.

(II) Such services may be provided to children with disabilities on the premises of private, including parochial, schools, to the extent consistent with law.

(ii) CHILD-FIND REQUIREMENT—The requirements of paragraph (3) of this subsection (relating to child find) shall apply with respect to children with disabilities in the State who are enrolled in private, including parochial, elementary and secondary schools.

(B) CHILDREN PLACED IN, OR REFERRED TO, PRIVATE SCHOOLS BY PUBLIC AGENCIES—

(i) IN GENERAL—Children with disabilities in private schools and facilities are provided special education and related services, in accordance with an individualized education program, at no cost to their parents, if such children are placed in, or referred to, such schools or facilities by the State or appropriate local educational agency as the means of carrying out the requirements of this part or any other applicable law requiring the provision of special education and related services to all children with disabilities within such State.

(ii) STANDARDS—In all cases described in clause (i), the State educational agency shall determine whether such schools and facilities meet standards that apply to State and local educational agencies and that children so served have all the rights they would have if served by such agencies.

(C) Payment for education of children enrolled in private schools without consent of or referral by the public agency—

(i) In general—Subject to subparagraph (A), this part does not require a local educational agency to pay for the cost of education, including special education and related services, of a child with a disability at a private school or facility if that agency made a free appropriate public education available to the child and the parents elected to place the child in such private school or facility.

(ii) Reimbursement for private school placement—If the parents of a child with a disability, who previously received special education and related services under the authority of a public agency, enroll the child in a private elementary or secondary school without the consent of or referral by the public agency, a court or a hearing officer may require the agency to reimburse the parents for the cost of that enrollment if the court or hearing officer finds that the agency had not made a free appropriate public education available to the child in a timely manner prior to that enrollment.

(iii) Limitation on reimbursement—The cost of reimbursement described in clause (ii) may be reduced or denied—

(I) if—

(aa) at the most recent IEP meeting that the parents attended prior to removal of the child from the public school, the parents did not inform the IEP Team that they were rejecting the placement proposed by the public agency to provide a free appropriate public education to their child, including stating their concerns and their intent to enroll their child in a private school at public expense; or

(bb) 10 business days (including any holidays that occur on a business day) prior to the removal of the child from the public school, the parents did not give written notice to the public agency of the information described in division (aa);

(II) if, prior to the parents' removal of the child from the public school, the public agency informed the parents, through the notice requirements described in section 615(b)(7), of its intent to evaluate the child (including a statement of the purpose of the evaluation that was appropriate and reasonable), but the parents did not make the child available for such evaluation; or

(III) upon a judicial finding of unreasonableness with respect to actions taken by the parents.

. . .

SEC. 614. EVALUATIONS, ELIGIBILITY DETERMINATIONS, INDIVIDUALIZED EDUCATION PROGRAMS, AND EDUCATIONAL PLACEMENTS

(a) Evaluations and reevaluations—

. . .

(2) Conduct of evaluation—In conducting the evaluation, the local educational agency shall—

(A) use a variety of assessment tools and strategies to gather relevant functional and developmental information, including information provided by the parent, that may assist in determining whether the child is a child with a disability and the content of the child's individualized education program, including information related to enabling the child to be involved in and progress in the general curriculum or, for preschool children, to participate in appropriate activities;

(B) not use any single procedure as the sole criterion for determining whether a child is a child with a disability or determining an appropriate educational program for the child; and

(C) use technically sound instruments that may assess the relative contribution of cognitive and behavioral factors, in addition to physical or developmental factors.

. . .

(d) Individualized education programs—

(1) Definitions—As used in this title:

(A) Individualized education program— The term "individualized education program" or "IEP" means a written statement for each child with a disability that is developed, reviewed, and revised in accordance with this section and that includes—

(i) a statement of the child's present levels of educational performance, including—

(I) how the child's disability affects the child's involvement and progress in the general curriculum; or

(II) for preschool children, as appropriate, how the disability affects the child's participation in appropriate activities;

(ii) a statement of measurable annual goals, including benchmarks or short-term objectives, related to—

(I) meeting the child's needs that result from the child's disability to enable the child to be involved in and progress in the general curriculum; and

(II) meeting each of the child's other educational needs that result from the child's disability;

(iii) a statement of the special education and related services and supplementary aids and services to be provided to the child, or on behalf of the child, and a statement of the program modifications or supports for school personnel that will be provided for the child—

(I) to advance appropriately toward attaining the annual goals;

(II) to be involved and progress in the general curriculum in accordance with clause (i) and to participate in extracurricular and other nonacademic activities; and

(III) to be educated and participate with other children with disabilities and nondisabled children in the activities described in this paragraph;

. . .

SEC. 615. PROCEDURAL SAFEGUARDS

(a) Establishment of procedures—Any State educational agency, State agency, or local educational agency that receives assistance under this part shall establish and maintain procedures in accordance with this section to ensure that children with disabilities and their parents are guaranteed procedural safeguards with respect to the provision of free appropriate public education by such agencies.

(b) Types of procedures—The procedures required by this section shall include—

(1) an opportunity for the parents of a child with a disability to examine all records relating to such child and to participate in meetings with respect to the identification, evaluation, and educational placement of the child, and the provision of a free appropriate public education to such child, and to obtain an independent educational evaluation of the child;

(2) procedures to protect the rights of the child whenever the parents of the child are not known, the agency cannot, after reasonable efforts, locate the parents, or the child is a ward of the State, including the assignment of an individual (who shall not be an employee of the State educational agency, the local educational agency, or any other agency that is involved in the education or care of the child) to act as a surrogate for the parents;

. . .

■ AGE DISCRIMINATION ACT, 29 U.S.C. §621 (§623)

(a) It shall be unlawful for an employer—

(1) to fail or refuse to hire or to discharge any individual or otherwise discriminate against any individual with respect to his compensation, terms, conditions, or privileges of employment, because of such individual's age. . . .

(c) It shall be unlawful for a labor organization—

(1) to exclude or to expel from its membership, or otherwise to discriminate against, any individual because of his age. . . .

(3) to cause or attempt to cause an employer to discriminate against an individual in violation of this section. . . .

(f) It shall not be unlawful for an employer, employment agency, or labor organization—

(1) to take any action otherwise prohibited under subsections (a), (b), (c), or (e) of this section where age is a bona fide occupational qualification reasonably necessary to the normal operation of the particular business, or where the differentiation is based on reasonable factors other than age. . . .

(3) to discharge or otherwise discipline an individual for good cause. . . .

■ EQUAL EDUCATION OPPORTUNITIES ACT, 20 U.S.C. §1703

[Section 1703 provides:]

No State shall deny equal educational opportunity to an individual on account of his or her race, color, sex, or national origin, by—

(a) the deliberate segregation by an educational agency of students on the basis of race, color, or national origin among or within schools. . . .

(c) the assignment by an educational agency of a student to a school, other than the one closest to his or her place of residence within the school district in which he or she resides, if the assignment results in a greater degree of segregation of students on the basis of race, color, sex, or national origin. . . .

(d) discrimination by an educational agency on the basis of race, color, or national origin in the employment, employment conditions, or assignment to schools of its faculty or staff, except to fulfill the purposes of subsection (f) below. . . .

(e) the transfer by an educational agency, whether voluntary or otherwise, of a student from one school to another if the purpose and effect of such transfer is to increase segregation of students on the basis of race, color, or national origin among the schools of such agency; or

(f) the failure by an educational agency to take appropriate action to overcome language barriers that impede equal participation by its students in its instructional programs.

■ REHABILITATION ACT OF 1973, 29 U.S.C. §794 (§504)

[The act provides in part:]

No otherwise qualified handicapped individual . . . shall, solely by reason of his handicap, be excluded from the participation in, be denied the benefits of, or be subjected to discrimination under any program or activity receiving Federal financial assistance.

■ EQUAL ACCESS ACT, 20 U.S.C. §§4071 AND 4072

§4071. DENIAL OF EQUAL ACCESS PROHIBITED

(a) Restriction of limited open forum on basis of religious, political, philosophical, or other speech content prohibited

It shall be unlawful for any public secondary school which receives Federal financial assistance and which has a limited open forum to deny equal access or a fair opportunity to, or discriminate against, any students who wish to conduct a meeting within that limited open forum on the basis of the religious, political, philosophical, or other content of the speech at such meetings.

(b) "Limited open forum" defined

A public secondary school has a limited open forum whenever such school grants an offering to or opportunity for one or more noncurriculum related student groups to meet on school premises during noninstructional time.

(c) Fair opportunity criteria

Schools shall be deemed to offer a fair opportunity to students who wish to conduct a meeting within its limited open forum if such school uniformly provides that—

(1) the meeting is voluntary and student-initiated;

(2) there is no sponsorship of the meeting by the school, the government, or its agents or employees;

(3) employees or agents of the school or government are present at religious meetings only in a nonparticipatory capacity;

(4) the meeting does not materially and substantially interfere with the orderly conduct of educational activities within the school; and

(5) nonschool persons may not direct, conduct, control, or regularly attend activities of student groups.

(d) Construction of subchapter with respect to certain rights

Nothing in this subchapter shall be construed to authorize the United States or any State or political subdivision thereof—

(1) to influence the form or content of any prayer or other religious activity;

(2) to require any person to participate in prayer or other religious activity;

(3) to expend public funds beyond the incidental cost of providing the space for student-initiated meetings;

(4) to compel any school agent or employee to attend a school meeting if the content of the speech at the meeting is contrary to the beliefs of the agent or employee;

(5) to sanction meetings that are otherwise unlawful;

(6) to limit the rights of groups of students which are not of a specified numerical size; or

(7) to abridge the constitutional rights of any person.

(e) Federal financial assistance to schools unaffected

Notwithstanding the availability of any other remedy under the Constitution or the laws of the United States, nothing in this subchapter shall be construed to authorize the United States to deny or withhold Federal financial assistance to any school.

(f) Authority of schools with respect to order, discipline, well-being, and attendance concerns

Nothing in this subchapter shall be construed to limit the authority of the school, its agents or employees, to maintain order and discipline on school premises, to protect the well-being of students and faculty, and to assure that attendance of students at meetings is voluntary.

§4072. DEFINITIONS

As used in this subchapter—

(1) The term "secondary school" means a public school which provides secondary education as determined by State law.

(2) The term "sponsorship" includes the act of promoting, leading, or participating in a meeting. The assignment of a teacher, administrator, or other school employee to a meeting for custodial purposes does not constitute sponsorship of the meeting.

(3) The term "meeting" includes those activities of student groups which are permitted under a school's limited open forum and are not directly related to the school curriculum.

(4) The term "noninstructional time" means time set aside by the school before actual classroom instruction begins or after actual classroom instruction ends.

■ FAMILY AND MEDICAL LEAVE ACT, 29 U.S.C. §§2601, 2611, AND 2612

§2601. FINDINGS AND PURPOSES

(a) Findings

Congress finds that—

(1) the number of single-parent households and two-parent households in which the single parent or both parents work is increasing significantly;

(2) it is important for the development of children and the family unit that fathers and mothers be able to participate in early child-rearing and the care of family members who have serious health conditions;

(3) the lack of employment policies to accommodate working parents can force individuals to choose between job security and parenting;

(4) there is inadequate job security for employees who have serious health conditions that prevent them from working for temporary periods;

(5) due to the nature of the roles of men and women in our society, the primary responsibility for family caretaking often falls on women, and such responsibility affects the working lives of women more than it affects the working lives of men; and

(6) employment standards that apply to one gender only have serious potential for encouraging employers to discriminate against employees and applicants for employment who are of that gender.

(b) Purposes

It is the purpose of this Act—

(1) to balance the demands of the workplace with the needs of families, to promote the stability and economic security of families, and to promote national interests in preserving family integrity;

(2) to entitle employees to take reasonable leave for medical reasons, for the birth or adoption of a child, and for the care of a child, spouse, or parent who has a serious health condition;

(3) to accomplish the purposes described in paragraphs (1) and (2) in a manner that accommodates the legitimate interests of employers;

(4) to accomplish the purposes described in paragraphs (1) and (2) in a manner that, consistent with the Equal Protection Clause of the Fourteenth Amendment, minimizes the potential for employment discrimination on the basis of sex by ensuring generally that leave is available for eligible medical reasons (including maternity-related disability) and for compelling family reasons, on a gender-neutral basis; and

(5) to promote the goal of equal employment opportunity for women and men, pursuant to such clause.

§2611. DEFINITIONS

As used in this subchapter:

. . .

(2) Eligible employee

(A) In general

The term "eligible employee" means an employee who has been employed—

(i) for at least 12 months by the employer with respect to whom leave is requested under section 2612 of this title; and

(ii) for at least 1,250 hours of service with such employer during the previous 12-month period.

(B) Exclusions

The term "eligible employee" does not include—

(i) any Federal officer or employee covered under subchapter V of chapter 63 of Title 5; or

(ii) any employee of an employer who is employed at a worksite at which such employer employs less than 50 employees if the total number of employees employed by that employer within 75 miles of that worksite is less than 50.

. . .

(5) Employment benefits

The term "employment benefits" means all benefits provided or made available to employees by an employer, including group life insurance, health insurance, disability insurance, sick leave, annual leave, educational benefits, and pensions, regardless of whether such benefits are provided by a practice or written policy of an employer or through an "employee benefit plan."

§2612. LEAVE REQUIREMENT

(a) In general

(1) Entitlement to leave

Subject to section 2613 of this title, an eligible employee shall be entitled to a total of 12 workweeks of leave during any 12-month period for one or more of the following:

(A) Because of the birth of a son or daughter of the employee and in order to care for such son or daughter.

(B) Because of the placement of a son or daughter with the employee for adoption or foster care.

(C) In order to care for the spouse, or a son, daughter, or parent, of the employee, if such spouse, son, daughter, or parent has a serious health condition.

(D) Because of a serious health condition that makes the employee unable to perform the functions of the position of such employee.

(2) Expiration of entitlement

The entitlement to leave under subparagraphs (A) and (B) of paragraph (1) for a birth or placement of a son or daughter shall expire at the end of the 12-month period beginning on the date of such birth or placement.

(b) Leave taken intermittently or on reduced leave schedule

(1) In general

Leave under subparagraph (A) or (B) of subsection (a)(1) of this section shall not be taken by an employee intermittently or on a reduced leave schedule unless the employee and the employer of the employee agree otherwise. Subject to paragraph (2), subsection (e)(2) of this section, and section 2613(b)(5) of this title, leave under subparagraph (C) or (D) of subsection (a)(1) of this section may be taken intermittently or on a reduced leave schedule when medically necessary. The taking of leave intermittently or on a reduced leave schedule pursuant to this paragraph shall not result in a reduction in the total amount of leave to which the employee is entitled under subsection (a) of this section beyond the amount of leave actually taken.

(2) Alternative position

If an employee requests intermittent leave, or leave on a reduced leave schedule, under subparagraph (C) or (D) of subsection (a)(1) of this section, that is foreseeable based on planned medical treatment, the employer may require such employee to transfer temporarily to an available alternative position offered by the employer for which the employee is qualified and that—

(A) has equivalent pay and benefits; and

(B) better accommodates recurring periods of leave than the regular employment position of the employee.

(c) Unpaid leave permitted

Except as provided in subsection (d) of this section, leave granted under subsection (a) of this section may consist of unpaid leave. Where an employee is otherwise exempt under regulations issued by the Secretary pursuant to section 213(a)(1) of this title, the compliance of an employer with this subchapter by providing unpaid leave shall not affect the exempt status of the employee under such section.

(d) Relationship to paid leave

(1) Unpaid leave

If an employer provides paid leave for fewer than 12 workweeks, the additional weeks of leave necessary to attain the 12 workweeks of leave required under this subchapter may be provided without compensation.

(2) Substitution of paid leave

(A) In general

An eligible employee may elect, or an employer may require the employee, to substitute any of the accrued paid vacation leave, personal leave, or family leave of the employee for leave provided under subparagraph (A), (B), or (C) of subsection (a)(1) of this section for any part of the 12-week period of such leave under such subsection.

(B) Serious health condition

An eligible employee may elect, or an employer may require the employee, to substitute any of the accrued paid vacation leave, personal leave, or medical or sick leave of the employee for leave provided under subparagraph (C) or (D) of subsection (a)(1) of this section for any part of the 12-week period of such leave under such subsection, except that nothing in this subchapter shall require an employer to provide paid sick leave or paid medical leave in any situation in which such employer would not normally provide any such paid leave.

(e) Foreseeable leave

(1) Requirement of notice

In any case in which the necessity for leave under subparagraph (A) or (B) of subsection (a)(1) of this section is foreseeable based on an expected birth or placement, the employee shall provide the employer with not less than 30 days' notice, before the date the leave is to begin, of the employee's intention to take leave under such subparagraph, except that if the date of the birth or placement requires leave to begin in less than 30 days, the employee shall provide such notice as is practicable.

(2) Duties of employee

In any case in which the necessity for leave under subparagraph (C) or (D) of subsection (a)(1) of this section is foreseeable based on planned medical treatment, the employee—

(A) shall make a reasonable effort to schedule the treatment so as not to disrupt unduly the operations of the employer, subject to the approval of the health care provider of the employee or the health care provider of the son, daughter, spouse, or parent of the employee, as appropriate; and

(B) shall provide the employer with not less than 30 days' notice, before the date the leave is to begin, of the employee's intention to take leave under such subparagraph, except that if the date of the treatment requires leave to begin in less than 30 days, the employee shall provide such notice as is practicable.

(f) Spouses employed by same employer

In any case in which a husband and wife entitled to leave under subsection (a) of this section are employed by the same employer, the aggregate number of workweeks of leave to which both may be entitled may be limited to 12 workweeks during any 12-month period, if such leave is taken—

(1) under subparagraph (A) or (B) of subsection (a)(1) of this section; or

(2) to care for a sick parent under subparagraph (c) of such subsection.

APPENDIX C

PUBLIC SCHOOLS PROVISIONS IN STATE CONSTITUTIONS

ALABAMA

The legislature shall establish, organize, and maintain a liberal system of public schools throughout the state for the benefit of the children thereof between the ages of seven and twenty-one years. *Constitution of Alabama of 1901, Article XIV. Education. Sec. 256.*

ALASKA

The legislature shall by general law establish and maintain a system of public schools open to all children of the State, and may provide for other public educational institutions. *Constitution of Alaska 1956, Article VII. Section 1 Public Education.*

ARIZONA

The Legislature shall provide for a system of common schools by which a free school shall be established and maintained in every school district for at least six months in each year, which school shall be open to all pupils between the ages of six and twenty-one years. *Constitution of the State of Arizona, Article XI. Education, Section 1.*

ARKANSAS

Intelligence and virtue being the safeguards of liberty and the bulwark of free and good government, the State shall ever maintain a general, suitable efficient system of free public schools and shall adopt all suitable means to secure to the people the advantages and opportunities of education.

Constitution of Arkansas 1874, Article 14. Education section 1 Free school system.

CALIFORNIA

A general diffusion of knowledge and intelligence being essential to the preservation of the rights and liberties of the people, the Legislature shall encourage by all suitable means the promotion of intellectual, scientific, moral, and agricultural improvement. *Constitution of the State of California 1879, Article IX. Education, Section 1.*

COLORADO

The general assembly shall, as soon as practicable, provide for the establishment and maintenance of a thorough and uniform system of free public schools throughout the state, wherein all residents of the state, between the ages of six and twenty-one years, may be educated gratuitously. *Constitution of the State of Colorado [1876], Article IX, Education, Section 2.*

CONNECTICUT

There shall always be free public elementary and secondary schools in the state. The general assembly shall implement this principle by appropriate legislation. *Constitution of the State of Connecticut 1965, Article Eighth, of Education, Section 1.*

DELAWARE

The General Assembly shall provide for the establishment and maintenance of a general and efficient system of free public schools, and may require by law that every child, not physically or mentally disabled, shall attend the public school, unless educated by other means. *Constitution of Delaware 1897, Article X, Education, Section 1.*

FLORIDA
The education of children is a fundamental value of the people of the State of Florida. It is, therefore, a paramount duty of the state to make adequate provision for the education of all children residing within its borders. Adequate provision shall be made by law for a uniform, efficient, safe, secure and high quality system of free public schools that allows students to obtain high quality education and for the establishment, maintenance, and operation of institutions of higher learning and other public education programs that the needs of the people may require. *Florida Constitution 1968, Article IX, Education, Section 1.*

GEORGIA
The provision of an adequate public education for the citizens shall be a primary obligation of the State of Georgia. Public education for the citizens prior to the college or postsecondary level shall be free and shall be provided for by taxation. *Constitution of the State of Georgia 1976, Article VIII, Education, Section I, Public Education.*

HAWAII
The State shall provide for the establishment, support and control of a statewide system of public schools free from sectarian control, a state university, public libraries and such other educational institutions as may deemed desirable, including physical facilities therefor. *The Constitution of the State of Hawaii 1959, Article X, Education, Section 1.*

IDAHO
The stability of a republican form of government depending mainly upon the intelligence of the people, it shall be the duty of the legislature of Idaho to establish and maintain a general, **uniform** and thorough system of public, free common schools. *Constitution of Idaho 1890, Article IX. Education, Section 1.*

ILLINOIS
A fundamental goal of the People of the State is the educational development of all persons to the limits of their capacities. The State shall provide for an efficient system of high quality public educational institutions and services. Education in public schools through secondary level shall be free. There may be such other free education as the General Assembly provides by law. The State has the primary responsibility for financing the system of public education. *Constitution of the State of Illinois 1970, Article X. Education, Section 1.*

INDIANA
Knowledge and learning, generally diffused throughout a community being essential to the preservation of a free government; it shall be the duty of the General Assembly to encourage, by all suitable means, moral, intellectual, scientific, and agricultural improvement; and to provide, by law, for a general and uniform system of Common Schools, wherein tuition shall by without charge, and equally open to all. *Constitution of the State of Indiana 1851, Article 8. Education, Section 1.*

IOWA
The common schools provisions, apparently superceded or obsolete, have been omitted from the Constitution. The Constitution of Iowa of 1846 provided education clauses. These clauses were later abolished and statutory provisions were enacted relating to the same subject matter; these can be found in Chapters 256 and 262 of Iowa code.

KANSAS
The legislature shall provide for intellectual, educational, vocational and scientific improvement by establishing and maintaining public schools, educational institutions and related activities which may be organized and changed in such manner as may be provided by law. *Constitution of the State of Kansas 1859, Article 6.—Education, Section 1.*

KENTUCKY
The General Assembly shall, by appropriate legislation, provide for an efficient system of common schools throughout the State. *Constitution of Kentucky 1891, Education, Section 183.*

LOUISIANA
The legislature shall provide for the education of the people of the state and shall establish and maintain a public educational system. *Constitution of the State of Louisiana of 1974, Article VIII. Education, Section 1.*

MAINE
A general diffusion of the advantages of education being essential to the preservation of the rights and liberties of the people; to promote the important object, the Legislature are authorized, and it shall be their duty to require, the several towns to make suitable provision, at their own expense, for

the support and maintenance of public schools; . . . *Constitution of the State of Maine 1983, Article VIII. [Education], Section 1.*

MARYLAND

The General Assembly, at its First Session after the adoption of this Constitution, shall by Law establish throughout the State a thorough and efficient System of Free Public Schools; and shall provide by taxation, or otherwise, for their maintenance. *Constitution of Maryland 1864, Article VIII. Education, Section 1.*

MASSACHUSETTS

Wisdom, and knowledge, as well as virtue, diffused generally among the body of the people, being necessary for the preservation of their rights and liberties; and as these depend on spreading the opportunities and advantages. *Constitution or Form of Government for the Commonwealth of Massachusetts 1854, Part the Second Frame of Government, Chapter V. The University at Cambridge, and Encouragement of Literature, Etc. Section II, The Encouragement of Literature, Etc.*

MICHIGAN

Religion, morality and knowledge being necessary to good government and the happiness of mankind, schools and the means of education shall forever be encouraged. *Constitution of the State of Michigan 1963 Article VIII. Education, Section 1.*

MINNESOTA

The stability of a republican form of government depending mainly upon the intelligence of the people, it is the duty of the legislature to establish a general and uniform system of public schools. The legislature shall make such provisions by taxation or otherwise as will secure a thorough and efficient system of public schools throughout the state. *Constitution of the State of Minnesota 1974, Article XIII. Section 1.*

MISSISSIPPI

The Legislature shall, by general law, provide for the establishment, maintenance and support of free public schools upon such conditions and limitations as the Legislature may prescribe. *The Constitution of the State of Mississippi 1890, Article 8. Education, Section 201.*

MISSOURI

A general diffusion of knowledge and intelligence being essential to the preservation of the rights and liberties of the people, the general assembly shall establish and maintain free public schools for the gratuitous instruction of all persons in this state within ages not in excess of twenty-one years as prescribed by law. *Constitution of 1945 of the State of Missouri, Article IX. Education, Section 1(a).*

MONTANA

(1) It is the goal of the people to establish a system of education which will develop the full educational potential of each person. Equality of educational opportunity is guaranteed to each person of the state.

(2) . . .

(3) The legislature shall provide a basic system of free quality public elementary and secondary schools. . . .

The Constitution of the State of Montana 1972, Article X. Education, Section 1.

NEBRASKA

The Legislature shall provide for the free instruction in the common schools of this state of all persons between the ages of five and twenty-one years. Legislature may provide for the education of other persons in educational institutions owned and controlled by the state or a political subdivision thereof. *Constitution of Nebraska 1972, Article VII. Education, Section 1.*

NEVADA

The legislature shall provide for a uniform system of common schools, by which a school shall be established and maintained in each school district at least six months in every year, and any school district which shall allow instruction of a sectarian character therein may be deprived of its proportion of the interest of the public school fund during such neglect or infraction, and the legislature may pass such laws as will tend to secure a general attendance of the children in each school district upon said public schools. *Nevada Constitution 1938, Article II. Education, Section 2.*

NEW HAMPSHIRE

Knowledge and learning, generally diffused through a community, being essential to the preservation of a free government; and spreading the opportunities and advantages of education through the various parts of the country, being highly conducive to promote this end; it shall be the duty of the legislators and magistrates, in all future periods of this government, to cherish the interest of literature and the sciences, and all seminaries and public schools, to encourage private and public institutions, rewards, and immunities for the promotion of agriculture, arts, sciences, commerce, trade manufactures, and natural history of the country; to countenance and inculcate the principles of humanity and general benevolence. . . . *Constitution of the State of New Hampshire 1903, Article 83.*

NEW JERSEY

The Legislature shall provide for the maintenance and support of a thorough and efficient system of free public schools for the instruction of all the children in the State between the ages of five and eighteen years. *Constitution of New Jersey 1947, Article VIII. Section IV.*

NEW MEXICO

A uniform system of free public schools sufficient for the education of, and open to, all the children of school age in the state shall be established and maintained. *New Mexico Statutes Constitution 1911, Article XII. Education. Section 1.*

NEW YORK

The legislature shall provide for the maintenance and support of a system of free common schools, wherein all the children of this state may be educated. *Constitution of the State of New York 1938, Article XI—Education, Section 1.*

NORTH CAROLINA

The General Assembly shall provide by taxation and otherwise for a general and uniform system of free public schools which shall be maintained at least nine months in every year, and wherein equal opportunities shall be provided for all students. *Constitution of North Carolina 1971, Article 9. Education, Section 2.*

NORTH DAKOTA

A high degree of intelligence, patriotism, integrity and morality on the part of every voter in a government by the people being necessary in order to insure the continuance of that government and the prosperity and happiness of the people, the legislative assembly shall make provision for the establishment and maintenance of a system of public schools which shall be open to all children of the state of North Dakota and free from sectarian control. *Constitution of North Dakota 1972, Article VIII. Education, Section 1.*

OHIO

The general assembly shall make such provisions, by taxation, or otherwise, as, with the income arising from the school trust fund, will secure a thorough and efficient system of common schools throughout the State; but, no religion or other sect, or sects, shall ever have any exclusive right to, or control any part of the school funds of this state. *Constitution of the State of Ohio 1851, Article VI, Education, O Const VI Section 2.*

OKLAHOMA

The Legislature shall establish and maintain a system of free public schools wherein all the children of the State may be educated. Article XIII, Section 1. Provisions shall be made for the establishment and maintenance of a system of public schools, which shall be open to all the children of the state and free from sectarian control; and said schools shall always be conducted in English; Provided, that nothing herein shall preclude the teaching of other languages in said public schools. *Constitution of the State of Oklahoma 1907, Article XIII.—Education, Section 1 And Article I Section 5.*

OREGON

The Legislative Assembly shall provide by law for the establishment of a uniform, and general system of common schools. *Constitution of Oregon 1859, Article VIII. Education and School Lands, Section 3.*

PENNSYLVANIA

The General Assembly shall provide for the maintenance and support of a thorough and efficient system of public education to serve the needs of the Commonwealth. *Constitution of the Commonwealth of Pennsylvania 1873, Article III. B. Education, Section 14.*

RHODE ISLAND

The diffusion of knowledge, as well as of virtue among the people, being essential to the preservation of their rights and liberties, it shall be the duty of the general assembly to promote public schools and public libraries, and to adopt all means which it may deem necessary and proper to secure to the people the advantages and opportunities of education and public library services. *Constitution of the State of Rhode Island and Providence Plantations 1965, Article XII of Education, Section 1.*

SOUTH CAROLINA

The General Assembly shall provide for the maintenance and support of a system of free public schools open to all children in the State and shall establish, organize and support such other public institutions of learning, as may be desirable. *The Constitution of the State of South Carolina 1895, Article XI. Public Education, Section 3.*

SOUTH DAKOTA

The stability of a republican form of government depending on the morality and intelligence of the people, it shall be the duty of the Legislature to establish and maintain a general and uniform system of public schools wherein tuition shall be without charge, and equally open to all; and to adopt all suitable means to secure to the people the advantages and opportunities of education. *Constitution of South Dakota 1889, Article VIII. Education and School Lands, Section 1.*

TENNESSEE

The State of Tennessee recognizes the inherent value of education and encourages its support. The General Assembly shall provide for the maintenance, support and eligibility standards of a system of free public schools. . . . *Tennessee Constitution 1978, Article XI. Section 12.*

TEXAS

A general diffusion of knowledge being essential to the preservation of the liberties and rights of the people, it shall be the duty of the Legislature of the State to establish and make suitable provision for the support and maintenance of an efficient system of public free schools. *Constitution of the State of Texas 1876, Article VII. Education, Section 1.*

UTAH

The Legislature shall provide for the establishment and maintenance of the state's education systems including: (a) a public education system, which shall be open to all children of the state; and (b) a higher education system. Both systems shall be free from sectarian control. *Constitution of Utah 1896, Article X. Education, Section 1.*

VERMONT

Laws for the encouragement of virtue and prevention of vice and immorality ought to be constantly kept in force, and duly executed; and a competent number of schools ought to be maintained in each town unless the general assembly permits other provisions for the convenient instruction of youth. . . . *Constitution of the State of Vermont Chapter II 1793, Section 68.*

VIRGINIA

The General Assembly shall provide for a system of free public elementary and secondary schools for all children of school age throughout the Commonwealth and shall seek to ensure that an educational program of high quality is established and continually maintained. *Virginia Constitution of 1971, Article VIII. Education, Section 1.*

WASHINGTON

The legislature shall provide for a general and uniform system of public schools. The public school system shall include common schools, and such high schools, normal schools, and technical schools as may hereafter be established. But the entire revenue derived from the common school fund and the state tax for common schools shall be exclusively applied to the support of the common schools. *Constitution of the State of Washington, 1889, Article IX. Education, Section 2.*

WEST VIRGINIA

The legislature shall provide, by general law, for a thorough and efficient system of free schools. *Constitution of West Virginia, 1877, Article XII, Section 1.*

WISCONSIN

The legislature shall provide by law for the establishment of district schools, which shall be as nearly uniform as practicable; and such schools shall be free and without charge for tuition to all children between the ages of 4 and 20 years; and no sectarian instruction shall be allowed therein; but the legislature by law may, for the purpose of religious instruction outside the district schools, authorize the release of students during regular school hours. *Constitution of the State of Wisconsin 1972, Article X. Education, Section 3.*

WYOMING

The legislature shall provide for the establishment and maintenance of a complete and uniform system of public instruction, embracing free elementary schools of every needed kind and grade, a university with such technical and professional departments as the public good may require and the means of the state allow, and such other institutions as may be necessary. *Wyoming Constitution, 1890, Article 7. Education, Section 1.*

APPENDIX D

GLOSSARY OF TERMS*

Ab initio: From the beginning.

Ad libitum: At the pleasure of the court.

Ad litem: For the purposes of the suit or while the suit is pending.

Ad valorem: According to the value, e.g., a duty or tax.

Adverse possession: A method of acquisition of title by possession for a statutory period under certain conditions.

Allegation: A statement of fact made in a legal proceeding.

Annotation: A remark, note, or commentary on some passage of a book, intended to illustrate its meaning.

Appeal: An application by an appellant to a higher court to rectify the order of the court below.

Appellant: One who appeals from a judicial decision.

Appellate court: A higher court which hears a case from a lower court on appeal.

Appellee: The person against whom an appeal is taken; the respondent to an appeal.

Arbitrary: Means in an "arbitrary" manner, as fixed or done capriciously or at pleasure, without adequate determining principle; not founded in the nature of things; nonrational; not done or acting according to reason or judgment; depending on the will alone; absolutely in power; capricious; tyrannical; despotic.

Assault: Threatening to strike or harm.

Assumpsit: An early form of action in English law, later used in America, under which plaintiff seeks to recover damages for non-performance of a parol or simple contract.

Battery: Beating and wounding, including every touching or laying hold, however trifling, of another's person or clothes in an angry, insolent, or hostile manner.

Bill: A formal declaration, complaint, or statement of particular things in writing. As a legal term, this word has many meanings and applications, the more important of which are enumerated in *Black's Law Dictionary*.

Bona fide: With good faith, honestly, openly.

Breach: A breaking; either the invasion of a right, or the violation of a duty.

Certiorari: (To be more fully informed) An original writ or action whereby a cause is removed from an inferior to a superior court for trial. The record of proceedings is then transmitted to the superior court. The term is most commonly used when requesting the U.S. Supreme Court to hear a case from a lower court.

Citation: A writ issued out of a court of competent jurisdiction, commanding a person therein named to appear on a day named and do something therein mentioned, or show cause why he should not.

Civil action: An action which has for its object the recovery of private or civil rights, or compensation for their infraction.

Class bill or suit: One in which one or more members of a class sue either for themselves or for themselves and other members of a class.

Code: A compilation of statutes, scientifically analyzed into chapters, subheadings, and sections with a table of contents and an index. A collection or system of laws.

Collateral: By the side of; indirect. Not directly concerned with the issue.

*These definitions were selected from *Black's Law Dictionary* by Henry Campbell Black, West Publishing Company, St. Paul, Minn.

Collateral attack: An attempt to avoid, defeat, or evade a judicial proceeding, or deny its force and effect, in some incidental proceeding not provided by law for the express purpose of attacking it.

Comity: That body of rules or agreements that states or nations observe toward each other from courtesy or mutual convenience. Voluntary consent.

Common law: Legal principles derived from usage and custom, or from court decisions affirming such usage and custom, or from the acts of Parliament in force at the time of the American Revolution, as distinguished from law created by enactment of American legislatures.

Concurring opinion: An opinion, separate from that which embodies the views and decision of the majority of the court, prepared and filed by a judge who agrees in the general result of the decision, and which either reinforces the majority opinion by the expression of the particular judge's own views or reasoning, or (more commonly) voices his or her disapproval of the grounds of the decision or the arguments on which it was based, though approving the final result.

Consideration in contracts: The inducement to a contract. The cause, motive, price, or impelling influence that induces a contracting party to enter into a contract.

Contract: A promissory agreement between two or more persons that creates, modifies, or destroys a legal relation.

Contributory negligence: Negligence of the plaintiff which, combined with the negligence of the defendant, was the proximate cause of the injury complained of.

Court of record: A court that keeps a permanent record of its proceedings. Frequently, appellate courts are called courts of record because their proceedings are published.

Curia: A court.

Damages: A pecuniary compensation or indemnity, which may be recovered in the courts by any person who has suffered loss, detriment, or injury, whether to his or her person, property, or rights through the unlawful act or omission or negligence of another.

Declaratory relief: The opinion of a court on a question of law that, without ordering anything to be done, simply declares the rights of the parties.

Decree: The judgment of a court of equity or admiralty, answering for most purposes to the judgment of a court of common law.

De facto: (In fact) A *de facto* officer is in actual possession of an office without lawful title. A *de facto* corporation may be reorganized as legally effective even though defective in some particular.

Defamation: Scandalous words written or spoken concerning another, tending to the injury of his or her reputation, for which an action on the case for damages would lie.

Defendant: One required to make answer in a suit—the one against whom the suit is brought.

Defendant in error: The distinctive term appropriate to the party against whom a writ of error is sued out.

De jure: (By right) A *de jure* officer has just claim and rightful title to an office, though not necessarily in actual possession thereof; a legal or true corporation or officer as opposed to one that is *de facto*.

De minimus: A matter that is insignificant or not worthy of judicial attention.

Demurrer: A plea by one of the parties to an action, who, while admitting for the sake of argument all the material facts properly pleaded by the opposing party, contends the existence of the facts does not constitute grounds for action.

Devise: A testamentary disposition of land or realty; a gift of real property by the last will and testament of the donor.

Dicta: Opinions, remarks, or statements by a judge that are not necessary for the resolution of the case.

Dictum: The expression by a judge of an opinion on a point of law not necessary to the decision on the case; not binding on other judges.

Directory: A provision in a statute, rule of procedure, or the like, which is a mere direction or instruction of no obligatory force, and involves no invalidating consequence for its disregard, as opposed to an imperative or mandatory provision, which must be followed.

Discretionary power: Involves the exercise of judgment in reaching a decision; deciding whether to do something.

Dissenting opinion: An opinion disagreeing with that of the majority, handed down by one or more members of the court.

Due process: Law in the regular course of administration through courts of justice, according to those rules and forms that have been established for the protection of private rights.

Ejusdem generis: Of the same kind or nature.

Eminent domain: The power to take private property for public use.

En banc: In the bench, all judges sitting.

Enjoin: To require, command, positively direct. To require a person, by writ of injunction from a court of equity, to perform, or to abstain or desist from, some act.

Equity: A system of law that affords a remedy where there is no complete or adequate remedy at law. A court of law assesses damages; a court of equity renders a decision in mandamus, injunction, or specific performance.

Error case: Appeal on questions of law or a reference to a "writ of error" requesting reversal for a mistaken or incorrect judgment.

Estop: To stop, bar, or impede; to prevent, to preclude.

Estoppel: A person's own act or acceptance stops or closes his or her mouth to allege or plead the truth.

Et al.: And others.

Ex cathedra: To speak with authority.

Exculpatory: Excusing, clearing from alleged fault or guilt.

Executory: That which is yet to be performed or accomplished.

Ex officio: By virtue of his or her office.

Ex parte: By or for one party.

Ex post facto: (After the fact) Act passed after another act that retroactively changes the legal consequences of that act. Federal Constitution prohibits passage of *ex post facto* criminal law.

Ex rel.: At the instance of; on behalf of; on relation of information.

Fee simple: A fee simple absolute is an estate limited absolutely to a person and his or her heirs and assigns forever without limitation or condition.

Governmental function: One imposed or required of a municipal corporation for the protection of the general public; a function relating to the corporation's purpose for existing.

Habeas corpus: Latin for "you have the body." A writ of habeas corpus commands that the accused party be brought before the court, to produce "the body of the prisoner," to bring the person detained before a judge.

Hearsay evidence: Evidence not proceeding from the personal knowledge of the witness, but from the mere repetition of what he or she has heard others say.

Injunction: A prohibitive writ issued by a court of equity forbidding the defendant to do some act he or she is threatening, or forbidding him or her to continue doing some act that is injurious to the plaintiff and cannot be adequately redressed by an action at law.

In loco parentis: In place of the parent; charged with some of the parent's rights, duties, and responsibilities.

In re: In the affair; in the matter of; concerning. This is the usual method of entitling a judicial proceeding in which there are no adversary parties.

Ipso facto: By the very act itself, i.e., as the necessary consequence of the act.

Ipso jure: By the mere operation of the law.

Laches: Negligence, or unreasonable delay in pursuing a legal remedy, whereby a person forfeits his or her right.

Legacy: A disposition of personalty by will.

Liability: The word is a broad legal term and has been referred to as of the most comprehensive significance, including almost every character of hazard or responsibility, absolute, contingent, or likely.

Libel: Defamation by printed or written communication.

Liquidated: Fixed, ascertained, e.g., damages, the exact amount of which must be paid, or may be collected, upon a default or breach of contract.

Liquidated damages: The term is applicable when the amount of the damages has been ascertained by the judgment in the action, or when a specific sum of money has been expressly stipulated by the parties to a bond or other contract as the amount of damages to be recovered by either party for a breach of the agreement by the other.

Mala in se (Malum in se): Acts wrong in themselves, whether prohibited by human law or not.

Mala prohibita (Malum prohibitum): Acts prohibited by human laws, but not necessarily wrong in themselves.

Malfeasance: The commission of an unlawful act.

Malice: Hatred, ill will; a formed design of doing an unlawful act.

Mandamus: A writ of mandamus is a command from a court of law directed to an inferior court, officer, corporate body, or person regarding him, her, or them to do some particular thing.

Ministerial: Belonging to a minister or subordinate who is bound to follow instructions; opposed to judicial or discretionary.

Misfeasance: A wrongful act, negligence, or the improper performance of some lawful act.

Municipal corporation: A body politic created by the incorporation of the inhabitants as an agency of the state to regulate and administer the local affairs thereof; a voluntary corporation; a city, village, or borough. The term is sometimes used in a broader sense and includes all types of local governmental bodies, including school districts.

Negligence: Want of care.

Nolens volens: Whether willing or unwilling; consenting or not.

Nominal damages: A trifling sum awarded to a plaintiff when no substantial loss or injury has occurred.

Nuisance: Anything that unlawfully results in harm, inconvenience, or damage.

Obiter dicta: The words generally mean "a remark by the way," an aside statement or remark by a judge, a *gratis* observation, that is not binding on the parties.

Original jurisdiction: The jurisdiction of a court to entertain a case in its inception, as contrasted with the appellate jurisdiction.

Parol: By word of mouth.

Per curiam: By the court, opinion written by the whole court as opposed to an opinion written by any one judge.

Per se: By itself, alone.

Petition: Written application or prayer to the court for the redress of a wrong or the grant of a privilege or license.

Plaintiff: Person who brings an action, the one who sues by filing a complaint.

Plenary: Full; conclusive.

Plurality decision: A plurality is the greatest number of judges agreeing with one particular opinion or reason of a decision. A case may be decided before an appellate court by a vote of a plurality and not a majority of judges.

Police power: Inherent or plenary legislative power to enact laws for the comfort, health, and prosperity of the state. The right to modify for the common good. In short, the right of the sovereign to govern.

Prayer: The request contained in a bill in equity that the court will grant the process, aid, or relief that the complainant desires.

Precedent: A decision considered as furnishing an example or authority for an identical or similar case afterward arising on a similar question of law.

Prima facie: At first view; on the first aspect. *Prima facie* evidence, presumptions, etc., are such as will prevail, if not rebutted or disproved.

Privies of parties: Persons connected with mutual interest in the same action.

Proprietary functions: Those functions exercised by a municipality for the improvement of the territory within the corporate limits, or the doing of such things as inure to the benefit, pecuniarily or otherwise, of the municipality. Things not normally required by law or things not governmental in nature. Operation of an athletic contest where a fee is charged may be an example in some states.

Punitive damages: An award to punish.

Quantum meruit: (As much as he or she has earned) Action brought by a party to a contract against the other, not founded on the contract itself, but on an implied promise to pay for so much as the party suing has done, or as much as reasonably deserved for work or labor.

Quasi: As if; almost.

Quasi-municipal corporation (or quasi corporation): A political or civil subdivision of the state, created by law, to assist the state in administering the state's affairs—an involuntary corporation. Example: a school district.

Quid pro quo: "Something for something"; a consideration.

Quo warranto: (By what authority) A writ, or proceeding, by which the government inquires into the right of a person, or corporation, to hold an office, or exercise a franchise, which was never lawfully held, or which has been forfeited by neglect or abuse.

Ratification: In a broad sense, the confirmation of a previous act done either by the party himself or herself or by another; confirmation of a voidable act.

Ratio decidendi: The key point in a case that is the basis for the court's decision.

Remand a case: An action by an appellate court to send the case back to the court from which it came for further proceedings there.

Res judicata: A matter judicially decided.

Respondeat superior: The responsibility of a master for the acts of his or her servants.

Respondent: The one making an answer—the defendant.

Restrain: To prohibit from action; to enjoin.

Restraining order: An injunction.

Reversion: The residue of an estate left by operation of law in the grantor or his or her heirs, or in the heirs, or in the heirs of a testator, commencing in possession on the determination of a particular estate granted or devised.

Slander: Defamation by spoken word.

Specific performance: A requirement by a court of equity that both parties go through with a contract.

Star Chamber: A court in English law established to provide equitable relief for aggrieved parties who could find no relief at common law. Abuse of power by this court eventually led to its abolition.

Stare decisis: Adherence to precedent. When the court has made a declaration of legal principle, it is the law until changed by a competent authority.

Statute: Law enacted by the legislative power of a country or state.

Subpoena duces tecum: A process by which a court commands a witness to produce some document or paper that is pertinent to the controversy being litigated.

Substantive law: The positive law of rights and duties.

Tenure: Right to perform duties and receive emoluments thereof.

Title to property: Title is the means whereby the owner of lands has the just possession of his or her property.

Tort: Legal injury or wrong committed upon the person or property of another independent of contract.

Trespass: The unauthorized entry upon, taking, or interfering with the property of another. Also, common law form of action brought to obtain damages for unlawful injury.

Ultra vires: An *ultra vires* contract is one beyond the powers of the corporation to make. In other words, it is one the corporation had no authority to make.

Void: Null; ineffectual; nugatory; having no legal force or binding effect; unable, in law, to support the purpose for which it was intended.

Voidable: That may be avoided, or declared void; not absolutely void, or void in itself.

Writ of Certiorari: (See Certiorari)

INDEX